CHILDREN AND THE LAW

CHILDREN AND THE LAW

An Interdisciplinary Approach with Cases, Materials, and Comments

Katherine Hunt Federle

OXFORD
UNIVERSITY PRESS

Oxford University Press is a department of the University of Oxford. It furthers the University's objective of excellence in research, scholarship, and education by publishing worldwide.

Oxford New York
Auckland Cape Town Dar es Salaam Hong Kong Karachi Kuala Lumpur Madrid Melbourne Mexico City Nairobi New Delhi Shanghai Taipei Toronto

With offices in
Argentina Austria Brazil Chile Czech Republic France Greece Guatemala Hungary Italy Japan Poland Portugal Singapore South Korea Switzerland Thailand Turkey Ukraine Vietnam

Published in the United States of America by
Oxford University Press
198 Madison Avenue, New York, NY 10016

Library of Congress Cataloging-in-Publication Data
Federle, Katherine Hunt.
Children and the law : an interdisciplinary approach with cases, materials and comments / Katherine Hunt Federle.
p. cm.
Includes bibliographical references and index.
ISBN 978-0-19-538799-5 ((hardback) : alk. paper)
1. Children—Legal status, laws, etc.—United States. I. Title.
KF479.F43 2012
344.7303'27—dc23 2012009581

9 8 7 6 5 4 3 2 1

Printed in the United States of America on acid-free paper

Note to Readers

This publication is designed to provide accurate and authoritative information in regard to the subject matter covered. It is based upon sources believed to be accurate and reliable and is intended to be current as of the time it was written. It is sold with the understanding that the publisher is not engaged in rendering legal, accounting, or other professional services. If legal advice or other expert assistance is required, the services of a competent professional person should be sought. Also, to confirm that the information has not been affected or changed by recent developments, traditional legal research techniques should be used, including checking primary sources where appropriate.

(Based on the Declaration of Principles jointly adopted by a Committee of the American Bar Association and a Committee of Publishers and Associations.)

Contents

V. Children and Decision Making

Preface

It is axiomatic that the best lawyers integrate theory with practice. In the child-law field, a rich understanding of legal theory may be especially critical because so much of the underlying theory about the rights of children remains undeveloped. Moreover, to practice in the field requires more than just legal knowledge; an understanding of child psychology, child development, neuroscience, history, and social work is critical to serving as an effective advocate for the child client. Therefore, the best child advocates have a familiarity with and understanding of the value that other disciplines provide. This approach to treating the whole child (a "holistic" model) is widely viewed as a best-practices model.

This coursebook is designed to integrate theory and practice while placing child law in a larger multidisciplinary context. While gaining a critical perspective on how other disciplines may or may not inform legal and social policy choices, students will develop a deeper understanding of the law. Not only is this essential to an appreciation of the law's complexity, but it is also critical to a more nuanced approach to practice in a field that is inherently interdisciplinary. Thus, by examining articles, studies, and research from other disciplines in addition to legal cases and statutes within the context of a best-practices model, this coursebook seeks to bridge the artificial division between legal theory and the practice of law.

Section I of the coursebook is designed to provide students with an overview of four different perspectives on the juvenile court and juvenile law. These four—from history, philosophy, international and comparative law, and social science—form the basis for subsequent investigations of the underlying political, legal, and legislative policy choices undergirding juvenile law. The instructor may choose to teach these materials together or integrate them into the other sections of the coursebook.

Because of its practice orientation, this book is organized around issues that frequently arise in juvenile court. The text is divided into four main sections: II, Children and Crime; III, Children and Protection; IV, Children and Restraints on Liberty; and V, Children and Decision Making. Section II focuses broadly on the criminal capability, culpability, and accountability of children. Section III examines the laws and policies relating to the protection of children in their families. In section IV, students will explore status offenses and other restrictions on liberties. Section V considers issues related to children in schools, medical decision making,

First Amendment freedoms, and emancipation. Each section contains cases, selected statutes, and excerpts from legal writings designed to provide students with a grounding in the law. There also are extensive excerpts from writings in other disciplines.

Because courses in juvenile law are diverse, this coursebook is designed flexibly, to allow instructors to tailor the materials to their needs. For those wishing to teach a survey course in children and the law, the entire coursebook may be assigned. Its shorter length permits broad coverage of the materials. If the book is assigned for a course in juvenile justice, sections I, II, and IV offer material that is sufficiently rich to allow more in-depth coverage. For a course in child protection, sections I and III and portions of section V provide materials for a detailed semester course. Instructors also may wish to integrate subsections of section V into the material in section II. Alternatively, section V may be omitted if time is short.

I extend my thanks to my students in my Children and the Law classes over the years who have shared their enthusiasm for and commitment to juvenile law. I am indebted to the many student research assistants who have worked on various parts of this coursebook and whose hours in the library perusing arcane materials and state codes enabled me to go beyond the anecdotal to offer the reader some hard data. Thanks also are due to the librarians at the Ohio State University Moritz College of Law and especially Katherine Hall and Stephanie Zimmer, who always were willing to help me find an elusive text or a misplaced source. I would be remiss if I failed to thank Dean Alan Michaels and the Moritz College of Law for the support that made this book possible.

Most important, I wish to thank my husband, Paul Skendelas, for his love, help, support, and enthusiasm for this project, without which I would still be writing. And to my children, from whom I continue to learn so much, I remain deeply grateful for your love and understanding.

For the Student

If you are reading this introduction, you probably are enrolled in a course on children and the law. You may be wondering what "children and the law" is, about the scope of the course, and why child law is an area worthy of study. The law treats children as a distinct and special group, worthy of protection but also warranting constraint and punishment. The law recognizes the culpability of children while simultaneously acknowledging that their incapacities subject them to parental control and custody. Moreover, because children have a special status, certain substantive areas of law may develop special rules for children.

This coursebook is intended to help you not only to explore what the law governing children is but also to understand how and why it has evolved as it has. Moreover, the coursebook will help you critically examine the laws and policies affecting children and their families. Especially important to your study are the information and insights that other disciplines offer. The materials in the coursebook, then, include not only cases, statutes, and legal text but also research, studies, articles, and statistical information from social scientists, doctors, philosophers, and historians. In addition, international and comparative perspectives are offered to give you an additional context from which to evaluate the laws affecting children.

This coursebook also is designed to integrate theoretical understandings within a practical context. Because "children and the law" is a broad subject, this coursebook focuses primarily on the legal issues that arise in juvenile court. Judges and lawyers have the most direct contact with children and their legal problems in the juvenile-court setting. In 2008, for example, juvenile courts in the United States handled more than 1.5 million delinquency cases and more than 156,000 status offense cases. Because juvenile-court practice is multidisciplinary—requiring lawyers and judges to work with social workers, doctors, psychologists, psychiatrists, and other professionals to craft solutions to the problems faced by children—this coursebook will facilitate your understanding of how these other approaches may differ from, or even be antithetical to, the legal perspective.

The coursebook is divided into five main sections. Sections II, III, IVA, and V share a similar structure. Each of these sections begins by exploring the constitutional framework within which the law is situated. In sections II, III, IVA, VB, and VC, the procedural framework for resolving legal issues is considered. Finally, the ways in which the state responds to the child's behavior or problems are considered in the dispositional framework.

Section I of the coursebook is designed to provide an overview of four different perspectives on the juvenile court and juvenile law. These perspectives form the basis for subsequent discussions about the underlying political, legal, and legislative policy choices undergirding juvenile law. The first subsection provides a brief overview of the development of the juvenile court from a historical perspective. In the next subsection, you will examine the justifications for state involvement in the lives of children and explore the jurisprudential bases for according children rights. The third subsection introduces you to the United Nations Convention on the Rights of the Child, a document signed by every country in the world except the United States and Somalia. In its final part, section I provides an overview of social-science methodologies and explores the limits the law has placed on these methodologies.

Section II, Children and Crime, focuses broadly on the criminal capability, culpability, and accountability of children. The materials cover the constitutional framework for treating juveniles as delinquents, the procedural framework in which a delinquency case is processed, and the various dispositional options available once a juvenile is found to be delinquent. Specialized dispositions, such as those for juveniles found to be sexual offenders, are examined. The materials also explore hybrid legal approaches such as blended sentencing, in which a juvenile receives a suspended adult sentence in addition to a traditional juvenile disposition. The dispositional materials end with a discussion of the various mechanisms for trying a juvenile as an adult. Throughout the section, students will examine the underlying legal policy assumptions by exploring relevant findings from other disciplines, such as sociology, psychology, and neuroscience.

Section III, Children and Protection, explores the laws and policies relating to the protection of children in their families. The materials cover the constitutional and legal bases for removing children from their families, the legal grounds for finding that a child is abused or neglected, and the dispositional alternatives available once a parent is found to be abusive or neglectful. This includes an examination of foster care and the reasons state intervention may be terminated. Last, the materials analyze the legal and constitutional grounds for terminating parental rights. Source materials from law, medicine, psychology, sociology, and social work are excerpted to provide a greater understanding of the constitutional and legal frameworks.

In section IV, Children and Restraints on Liberty, you will explore the constitutional and procedural frameworks for status offenses. In addition, you will examine the welter of state and federal laws that restrict children's liberty. These include alcohol, tobacco, and firearms regulations; restrictions on driving and voting; and labor laws. Within the legal context, you will consider the state's authority to constrain liberty and whether such constraints violate the rights of children and their families. As with the preceding sections, the materials will introduce research and findings from other disciplines. These fields include medicine, criminology, sociology, child development, political science, and women's studies.

Finally, section V, Children and Decision Making, will examine issues related to children in schools, medical decision making, First Amendment freedoms, and emancipation. The coursebook includes materials on relevant United States Supreme Court cases on free speech, religion, and abortion, plus other legal materials on these subjects. Selected cases and statutes on medical decision making are included, along with materials examining the use of corporal punishment, school discipline, and emancipation. You also will explore the perspectives of other disciplines and consider the policy choices the law has made.

I believe I have compiled materials that will inform you of the many deeply theoretical and substantive issues in juvenile law. But these are not simply the musings of an "ivory tower" academic. Because my own experience is that of a lawyer for children and a law professor, I know that these complexities are faced by the many juvenile-court judges and practitioners who struggle on a daily basis to find workable solutions for the problems faced by children. Despite these challenges, many juvenile-court judges and practitioners are dedicated, hard-working professionals who derive considerable satisfaction from helping children and their families. It is my hope that you will come away from this course not only better informed but also inspired to do the same.

I

INTRODUCTION

A. Historical Perspectives

Holly Brewer, *The Transformation of Domestic Law, in* The Cambridge History of Law in America 288, 288–289, 302, 303–304, 311 (Michael Grossberg & Christopher Tomlin, eds., 2008).

Relationships, particularly the status of "dependent" groups, usually thought of as static throughout the colonial and early national periods of American history, and in early modern Britain too, were recreated over the course of the eighteenth century through common law justifications of a particular domestic order. These acts of creation occurred during a period of dramatic struggle over the basis of authority, not only over abstract political authority but over the rules that should govern the household and indeed over the very definitions of household and domestic. The results diminished the legal powers of lords and masters and increased those of fathers and husbands. These changes were accomplished with a legal sleight-of-hand that made the powers of husbands and fathers seem eternal within the common law and obscured the frequent conflicts between the authority of masters and those of fathers and husbands.... Consequently, the struggle over domestic space and authority was central to a larger struggle over rights and political authority....

Parents' custodial authority was weak in early-modern Anglo-America, far weaker than it would be by the late eighteenth century....

As a concept, custody in its modern sense of parental authority and responsibility simply did not exist, partly because the idea was not needed in a world where children could enter their own binding contracts and possessed a legal identity no different from that of adults. Children... could be punished for many different crimes—especially once older than age 8—and could form many kinds of contracts....

Childhood per se entailed few legal restrictions. Teenagers could be elected to Parliament in England or to the House of Burgesses in Virginia during the seventeenth century. Legally a male could hold most appointed offices at age eleven.... In England and Virginia one qualified to sit on a jury at age fourteen (higher in New England). At least in the early seventeenth century, one could testify at any age. In this part of the legal landscape, as elsewhere, status trumped everything else. All criminal records, for example, stated the status of the accused: virtually none stated the age. Those who held positions of political and legal authority while still teenagers—John Randolph, for example, who was appointed king's attorney for several Virginia counties at age eighteen—came from the most powerful families. Those bound into apprenticeships by the churchwardens though both parents might be alive came from the least powerful, the families of the poor.

As consent became more important to the law over the course of the early modern period (growing out of broad religious and political debates), childhood would emerge as a much clearer category of law and experience. Children lost their independent legal and political identity, and parents gained the power to make decisions for them. These changes challenged old elite practices that allocated authority by birth status irrespective of age. They also reflected changing norms about the meaning of consent that grew out of broad economic and political changes....

By the end of the eighteenth century and the beginning of the nineteenth, Anglo-American domestic law had begun to take coherent form.... Blackstone was key to this transition

William Blackstone, 1 Commentaries on the Laws of England 332, 368, 372–373 (1765).

The three great relations in private life are, 1. That of *master and servant*.... 2. That of *husband and wife*.... 3. That of *parent and child,* which is consequential to that of marriage, being its principal end and design; and it is by virtue of this relation that infants are protected, maintained, and educated....

[T]he duties of parents... principally consist in three particulars; their maintenance, their protection, and their education....

The *power* of parents over their children is derived from... their duty... partly to enable the parent more effectually to perform his duty, and partly at a recompense for his care and trouble.... The legal power of a father—for a mother, as such, is entitled to no power, but only to reverence and respect... over the persons of his children ceases as the age of twenty-one: for they are then enfranchised by arriving at years of discretion, or that point which the law has established, as some must necessarily be established, when the empire of the father, or other guardian, gives place to the empire of reason. Yet till that age arrives, this empire of the father continues....

The *duties* of children to their parents arise from a principle of natural justice and retribution. For to those who gave us existence we naturally owe subjection and obedience during our minority, and honour and reverence ever after.

Holly Brewer, By Birth or Consent: Children, Law, and the Anglo-American Revolution in Authority 174, 338–343, 347 (2005).

Coke, Hale, and Blackstone were the most important of the common law reformers, not only because they tried more to shape the law but because their authority was so great that they largely succeeded. Each openly acknowledged that he sought to make the law conform to "reason"; each ignored precedents that did not fit with his revision and reduction of the common law. While they sometimes justified reform on a theoretical level, they rarely acknowledged their alterations as new, always camouflaging them as precedent....

When he encountered Blackstone's admission that "some of our common lawyers have held that an infant of any age (even four years old) might make a testament," the eminent legal scholar William Holdsworth wrote, "This is clearly a misprint for fourteen." Those who have stumbled across evidence of age limits of fourteen for jurors or of no age limits on voters before the late seventeenth century have usually hidden that information in statements to the effect that "there were always age limits" or assumed that de facto age limits existed even if not written into law. To see the mark of a young child on a labor contract or to run across evidence that a child of four or nine married makes us think that something must be wrong with the evidence....

The common law itself is partly responsible for this inability to recognize how children's status has changed. With its reliance on custom, it has been seen by lawyers and judges themselves as having stable central concepts, especially the concept of meaningful consent. Yet, as Blackstone and Coke said so clearly, anything that is not reasonable is not precedent, an axiom that leaves open flexibility to new norms that ignore old practices when those no longer seem "reasonable."...

Another explanation for why these differences in children's status and competence have been so easily dismissed is our strong assumptions about children's abilities and fathers' authority historically. It seems ridiculous to us that a four-year-old could make a will, or even that a fourteen-year-old sit on a jury. Likewise, historians have tended to naturalize fatherly power, often equating it simply with "patriarchal power" and claiming it has always been the norm, that fathers have always governed their children....

If there is anything ancient about patriarchal power in England, it concerned the privileges of the lord, not the father....

By the late eighteenth century, however, fathers' legal authority over their own children was in most cases stronger than lords' or masters'. Blackstone's treatise fits much better with our preconceptions about what the common law of custody was—because he framed that law....

...[S]tatus, especially in terms of the power of the lords, was embedded into the law. While their youth made it more likely that children had lower status, rank outweighed age in allocating power....The struggle over the legal status of children thus was more than a struggle over simple custody. It was a struggle over the basis of power itself and whether that power should belong to lords or to fathers: to an aristocracy or to all men....

...The American Revolution applied an ax to ideas of inherited authority and the rights of blood and lineage. At the same time it helped to consolidate newer justifications of parental authority, which gave fathers, in particular, much more legal authority over children under twenty-one. Children became subjects incapable of consent, because they did not have reason. But the emphasis on their informed consent provided an excuse to deny equality and consent to others on the same grounds. Comparing women, blacks, and other groups to children in their reasoning abilities would become common in the wake of the Revolution for those who sought to legitimate elements of the older order....

...The new principle that consent must be "informed" and reasonable, which led to the exclusion of children, was part of what made democratic political ideology viable, acceptable, and, above all, legitimate. The principle that responsibility was necessary for both criminal matters and voting became established as consent became more important to the law, at the same time as birth and perpetual status became less important....

At the same time and in response to the same Revolutionary ideologies, children as a group gained legal provisions and protections with respect to their education and nurture. Indeed, the period after the American Revolution marked the origins of public education as a system for broad learning available to most children. This connected to Revolutionary ideals in two respects: as citizens they needed education to help them qualify for their future political roles and to fulfill the promises of equality of opportunity. Likewise, in response to the emphasis on paternal custody, protecting the nuclear family became more of a goal of social policy so that families were more likely to be permitted to stay together. All children could potentially gain equality when they acquired reason....

More than a generation of scholars have debated whether "the discovery of childhood"...occurred during the seventeenth and eighteenth centuries. But rather than a "discovery" of the innate nature of childhood...definitions of what it means to be a child and an adult were changing in response to fundamental religious and political debates.

QUESTIONS

1. Brewer states that "without a meaningful definition of consent, we would have no democracy." Do you agree? Why is consent central to democracy? Does it necessarily follow that children had to be excluded from those who could give consent?

2. Was the "discovery of childhood" an enlightened advancement? Have the lives of children been improved as a consequence?

3. Children had more rights in colonial and early America. Do you think children were better off having these rights? Should children have rights at all?

Michael Grossberg, *Changing Conceptions of Child Welfare in the United States, 1820–1935, in* A Century of Juvenile Justice 7–8, 9, 15–16, 18–19, 20–21 (Margaret K. Rosenheim et al., eds., 2002).

[S]ignificant changes began to occur in the early decades of the nineteenth century. New conceptions of childhood and new concerns about the disorderly and dependent young helped spur a reexamination of child welfare. As family historians have described in detail, new family beliefs and practices treated children more than ever before as distinct individuals with special needs and began to separate childhood out as a distinct phase of life....In particular, the rise of a new set of ideas that have come to be called romanticism gave Americans an entirely new image of children's inner natures....Americans came to regard children as innately good rather than depraved....

As a result of these new views of children and their place in society, policymakers struggled to find a way to talk about children as somehow distinct individuals and yet not adults in a system that tied power to individual autonomy. The result was to emphasize needs....

New ideas about children...were intertwined with the emergence of a massive humanitarian reform movement in the 1820s and 1830s that became a major source of child welfare innovation. Reformers tended to see social problems as dire threats to the larger society. They acted as well on the new belief that individual failings caused social ills and shared a new, optimistic faith in the possibilities of individual reformation. Unlike most colonials, who had assumed poverty and other human ills were natural and unchanging parts of human existence, antebellum Americans and particularly humanitarian reformers believed that individuals were largely responsible for their own fate. That idea encouraged the conviction that poverty and other human miseries were the results of individual failings that could be cured and thus spurred a greater sense of responsibility for the fate of strangers....

The House of Refuge was created specifically for the children of failed families.... These public institutions were the product of growing concerns about the plight of disorderly and dependent youths and about the consequences of consigning such children along with other paupers to almshouses where they were often mistreated and given little schooling. And they sprang as well from growing dissatisfaction with the tradition of outdoor relief and other established methods of support, such as auctioning off paupers. Though omnibus institutions like almshouses and workhouses had long been used to care for the needy, and orphanages flourished in the era as the primary institutional alternative to families, the House of Refuge illustrates the tenor of the era and the growing links between child welfare and juvenile justice. Antebellum institutional reformers argued that the new, specialized institutions would not be dumping grounds but rather reformatories that would provide the proper environment for individual reformation impossible in the traditional poor-law system. The new institutions also represented an expanding sense of civic responsibility toward the young as well as the now entrenched conviction that disorderly and dependent children needed specialized care and treatment....

New York City established the first juvenile reformatory in 1824. Others soon followed. Believing that a structured environment could remold youthful characters, the founders of refuges stressed rigorous discipline, education, and work as the principal means of reformation.... [T]he New York House of Refuge offered its inmates "such employment as will tend to encourage industry," basic education in "reading, writing, and arithmetic," and instruction in "the nature of their moral and religious obligations." Equally important, the institutions were granted broad jurisdiction over criminal, vagrant, neglected, or even unruly children to achieve their goals and thus lumped all disorderly and dependent children together and offered them basically the same treatment. Splitting disorderly and dependent children from adults and lumping them together as objects of similar policies would become a characteristic feature of American policies that increasingly combined child welfare and juvenile justice into a single set of practices and institutions....

By the 1850s and 1860s, however, uncertain and limited support, overcrowding, and mismanagement had undermined the therapeutic goals of the Houses of Refuge. And little evidence emerged to demonstrate that their regimented routines had fulfilled the promised goal of individual reformation. Nevertheless, the institutional movement spread across the republic. The transfer of children from poorhouses to specialized institutions continued in various states for the rest of the century. Institutionalization had acquired its own appeal; if nothing else, it took children off the streets and out of failed families. The reformatories became a fundamental way of dealing with disorderly and other dependent youths.... Following similar logic and with similar faith in the curative powers of managed environments, religious denominations, ethnic groups, and fraternal and benevolent societies established orphanages so that children of deceased or disabled members could be raised in the faith and according to the traditions and values of their parents. Indeed, sectarian orphanages became the most prevalent form of specialized institution for the young. Many of these also elicited public support and served as way stations for impoverished or troubled families temporarily unable to care for children. Though they never dominated the assistance given disorderly and dependent children, institutions became permanent fixtures of American child welfare and were its most visible symbols until the advent of the juvenile court....

...In 1853 the Reverend Charles Loring Brace founded the New York Children's Aid Society. Brace was driven to act out of fear of children, not simply fear for children: "There are no dangers to the value of property or the permanency of our institutions, so great as those from the existence of...a class of vagabond, ignorant, or ungoverned children." He coined the phrase "the dangerous classes" to describe the "outcasts, vicious, reckless multitude of New York boys, swarming...in every foul alley and low street." If these boys were neglected by society as they had been by their parents, Brace foresaw the possibility of "an explosion from this class which might leave the city in ashes and blood." Alarmed over increasing juvenile delinquency and crime among the city's youths, and fearful of what might happen to property, morality, and political life if nothing were done to relieve New York of its homeless, vagrant, and delinquent children, he founded the Children's Aid Society to save the city....

...Brace became a staunch opponent of institutionalization and championed placing urban children in rural families. The controversial policy sprang from his belief in the moral efficacy of family life, supplemented by public schools, and in the discipline inculcated in the young by doing farm work and home chores. He fervently believed that this environment would reclaim children from the vicious education of the streets; in some ways this was a resurrected version of the discarded apprentice ideal. Brace implemented his plan by sending children to farm families in the West beginning in 1854. Over the next twenty-five years orphan trains removed more than fifty thousand children from New York City.

Brace's placement policy stirred intense opposition. Child reformers complained that the Children's Aid Society did little to ensure that girls and boys were placed well and treated well. They claimed that too often children were overworked, poorly fed and clothed, and rarely sent to school. Opposition also came from the poor, many of whom did not want their children sent so far from home. Even some western states opposed the policy, protesting that it turned them into dumping grounds for disorderly and delinquent urban youth, some of whom ran away from their new families. A few states banned the practice altogether, and others required the Children's Aid Society to post a bond for each child in the event that he or she became a public burden. Finally, the Catholic Church charged that the western placements represented yet another Protestant strategy to convert the Catholic children of the city. Thus Brace's program was a further incentive for the church to construct its own institutions for disorderly and needy Catholic children and helped spur the creation of a separate Catholic child welfare system.

Though the western placement policy remained controversial and little copied, more and more urban Americans founded Children's Aid Societies in the middle of the nineteenth century. The proliferation of the societies represented the growing conclusion that other policies had failed to resolve the problems of disorderly and dependent youth, particularly the specialized asylums, and a growing distrust (if not fear) of working-class families and their children. Their diffusion also demonstrated the increasing tendency of American social welfare policies to treat the young as distinct individuals with their own needs and interests separate from those of their families and thus in need of their own welfare programs. Finally, the Children's Aid Society movement represented the growing appeal of family care, indeed the advent of supervised foster families, rather than institutional treatment of the disorderly and dependent young. It thus initiated what would be a recurrent debate over the virtues and problems of institutionalization versus deinstitutionalization that would also be a permanent component of American child welfare.

NOTES AND QUESTIONS

1. The Houses of Refuge were grim places. Children rose at dawn and followed a highly regimented schedule that included morning school, breakfast, hard labor, a one-hour break for dinner, hard labor again until 5:00 p.m., a half-hour break for a meal, then more schooling until 8:00 p.m., at which time children were sent to bed. Corporal punishment, solitary confinement, and whippings were common. Most children worked in large workshops making shoes or nails, doing laundry, or spinning cotton. Upon reaching the age of majority, children were apprenticed but rarely in a skilled trade. 1 CHILDREN AND YOUTH IN AMERICA: A DOCUMENTARY HISTORY 1600–1865 (Robert H. Bremner et al., eds., 1970).

2. Do you think children received better treatment at the hands of these reformers? At the time the first House of Refuge was established, America was experiencing severe economic downturns while trying to deal with large numbers of predominantly Irish Catholic immigrants. Many of the reformers feared social unrest and generally viewed the Irish as unsuitable and unfit parents. How much of the reformist impulse actually masked concerns about these immigrant families?

3. The Children's Aid Society sent its last orphan train to Texas in 1929. Approximately 250,000 children were relocated through the program. Because record keeping was poor, we do not know what happened to all of the children who were placed out, although it seems clear that the experiences of these children were mixed. Some had happy childhoods and grew up to be successful adults; in fact, two became governors of their respective states, and one became a Supreme Court justice (although whether he became a United States Supreme Court Justice or a state supreme court justice and his identity remain unknown and unverified). However, others grew up to be thieves and—at least in one case—a murderer. In many instances, children were simply lost and never heard from again. STEPHEN O'CONNOR, ORPHAN TRAINS: THE STORY OF CHARLES LORING BRACE AND THE CHILDREN HE SAVED AND FAILED (2001).

4. Did children and their families have rights? Were the rights of children and their parents violated by these practices? When reading the following three cases, consider whether the changes wrought by Blackstone and others authorize greater state intrusion into the lives of children and their families.

EX PARTE CROUSE
Supreme Court of Pennsylvania
4 Whart. 9 (1839)

This was a *habeas corpus* directed to the keeper and managers of the "House of Refuge," in the county of Philadelphia, requiring them to produce before the Court one Mary Ann Crouse, an infant, detained in that institution. The petition for the *habeas corpus* was in the name of her father.

By the return to the writ it appeared, that the girl had been committed to the custody of the managers by virtue of a warrant under the hand and seal of Morton M'Michael, Esq., a justice of the peace of the county of Philadelphia, which recited that complaint and due proof had been made before him by Mary Crouse, the mother of the said Mary Ann Crouse, "that the said infant by reason of vicious conduct, has rendered her control beyond the power of the said complainant, and made it manifestly requisite that from regard to the moral and future welfare of the said infant she should be placed under the guardianship of the managers of the House of Refuge"; and the said alderman certified that in his opinion the said infant was "a proper subject for the said House of Refuge."...

The House of Refuge is not a prison, but a school. Where reformation, and not punishment, is the end, it may indeed be used as a prison for juvenile convicts who would else be committed to a common gaol; and in respect to these, the constitutionality of the act which incorporated it, stands clear of controversy.... The object of the charity is reformation, by training its inmates to industry; by imbuing their minds with principles of morality and religion; by furnishing them with means to earn a living; and, above all, by separating them from the corrupting influence of improper associates. To this end, may not the natural parents, when unequal to the task of education, or unworthy of it, be superseded by the *parens patriae*, or common guardian of the community? It is to be remembered that the public has a paramount interest in the virtue and knowledge of its members, and that, of strict right, the business of education belongs to it. That parents are ordinarily entrusted with it, is because it can seldom be put into better hands; but where they are incompetent or corrupt, what is there to prevent the public from withdrawing their faculties, held, as they obviously are, at its sufferance? The right of parental control is a natural, but not an unalienable one.... As to abridgment of indefeasible rights by confinement of the person, it is no more than what is borne, to a greater or less extent, in every school; and we know of no natural right to exemption from restraints which conduce to an infant's welfare.... The infant has been snatched from a course which must have ended in confirmed depravity; and, not only is the restraint of her person lawful, but it would be an act of extreme cruelty to release her from it.

QUESTIONS

1. Does the court state that parents have custodial rights? Why, then, may the parents be stripped of those rights in this case? The mother of Mary Ann filed the complaint against her daughter. Should that make any difference? What evidence is there that the child will end in "confirmed depravity"?

2. The court calls the House of Refuge "a school." Given what you know about the Houses of Refuge, do you think this is an accurate characterization?

PEOPLE EX REL. O'CONNELL V. TURNER
Supreme Court of Illinois
55 Ill. 280 (1870)

Mr. Justice Thornton delivered the opinion of the Court....

The petition of Michael O'Connell represents, that he is the father of Daniel, a boy between fourteen and fifteen years of age, and that he is restrained of his liberty contrary to the law, without conviction of crime....

The only question for determination, is the power of the legislature to pass the laws, under which this boy was arrested and confined....

...[T]he act of 1867 provides, that "whenever any police magistrate, or justice of the peace, shall have brought before him any boy or girl, within the ages of six or sixteen years, who he has reason to believe is a vagrant, or is destitute of proper parental care, or is growing up in mendicancy, ignorance, idleness or vice," he shall cause such boy or girl to be arrested.... The judge is empowered to issue a summons, to the child's father, mother, guardian, or whosoever may have the care of the child...and upon return of due service of the summons, an investigation shall be had. The section then directs "if, upon such examination, such judge shall be of opinion that said boy or girl is a proper subject for commitment to the reform school, and that his or her moral welfare, and the good of society, require that he or she should be sent to said school for employment, instruction and reformation, he shall so decide, and direct the clerk of the court of which he is judge, to make out a warrant of commitment to said reform school; and such child shall thereupon be committed."...

The contingencies enumerated, upon the happening of either of which the power may be exercised, are vagrancy, destitution of proper parental care, mendicancy, ignorance, idleness or vice. Upon proof of any one, the child is deprived of home, and parents, and friends, and confined for more than half of an ordinary life. It is claimed, that the law is administered for the moral welfare and intellectual improvement of the minor, and the good of society. From the record before us, we know nothing of the management. We are only informed that a father desires the custody of his child; and that he is restrained of his liberty. Therefore, we can only look at the language of the law, and the power granted.

What is proper parental care? The best and kindest parents would differ, in the attempt to solve the question. No two scarcely agree; and when we consider the watchful supervision, which is so unremitting over the domestic affairs of others, the conclusion is forced upon us, that there is not a child in the land who could not be proved, by two or more witnesses, to be in this sad condition. Ignorance, idleness, vice, are relative terms. Ignorance is always preferable to error, but, at most, is only venial. It may be general or it may be limited. Though it is sometimes said, that "idleness is the parent of vice," yet the former may exist without the latter. It is strictly an abstinence from labor or employment. If the child perform all its duties to parents and to society, the State has no right to compel it to labor. Vice is a very comprehensive term. Acts, wholly innocent in the estimation of many good men, would, according to the code of ethics of others, show fearful depravity. What is the standard to be? What extent of enlightenment, what amount of industry, what degree of virtue, will save from the threatened imprisonment? In our solicitude to form youth for the duties of civil life, we should not forget the rights which inhere both in parents and children. The principle of the absorption of the child in, and its complete subjection to the despotism of, the State, is wholly inadmissible in the modern civilized world.

The parent has the right to the care, custody and assistance of his child. The duty to maintain and protect it, is a principle of natural law. He may even justify an assault and battery, in the defense of his children, and uphold them in their law suits. Thus the law recognizes the power of parental affection, and excuses acts which, in the absence of such a relation, would be punished. Another branch of parental duty, strongly inculcated by writers on natural law, is the education of children. To aid in the performance of these duties, and enforce obedience, parents have authority over them. The municipal law should not disturb this relation, except for the strongest reasons. The ease with which it may be disrupted under the laws in question; the slight evidence required, and the informal mode of procedure, make them conflict with the natural right of the parent. Before any abridgment of the right, gross misconduct or almost total unfitness on the part of the parent, should be clearly proved....

But even the power of the parent must be exercised with moderation. He may use correction and restraint, but in a reasonable manner. He has the right to enforce only such discipline, as may be necessary to the discharge of his sacred trust; only moderate correction and temporary confinement. We are not governed by the twelve tables, which formed the Roman law. The fourth table gave fathers the power of life and death, and of sale, over their children. In this age and country, such provisions would be atrocious. If a father confined or imprisoned his child for one year, the majesty of the law would frown upon the unnatural act, and every tender mother and kind father would rise up in arms against such monstrous inhumanity. Can the State, as *parens patriae,* exceed the power of the natural parent, except in punishing crime?

These laws provide for the "safe keeping" of the child; they direct his "commitment," and only a "ticket of leave," or the uncontrolled discretion of a board of guardians, will permit the imprisoned boy to breathe the pure air of heaven outside his prison walls, and to feel the instincts of manhood by contact with the busy world.... The confinement may be from one to fifteen years, according to the age of the child. Executive clemency can not open the prison doors, for no offense has been committed. The writ of *habeas corpus*...can afford no relief, for the sovereign power of the State, as *parens patriae,* has determined the imprisonment beyond recall. Such a restraint upon natural liberty is tyranny and oppression. If, without crime, without the conviction of any offense, the children of the State are to be thus confined for the "good of society," then society had better be reduced to its original elements, and free government acknowledged a failure....

...If improperly or illegally restrained, it is our duty...to liberate. The welfare and rights of the child are also to be considered. The disability of minors does not make slaves or criminals of them. They are entitled to legal rights, and are under legal liabilities. An implied contract for necessaries is binding on them. The only act which they are under a legal incapacity to perform, is the appointment of an attorney. All their other acts are merely voidable or confirmable. They are liable for torts, and punishable for crime.... Every child over ten years of age may be found guilty of crime. For robbery, burglary or arson, any minor may be sent to the penitentiary. Minors are bound to pay taxes for the support of the government, and constitute a part of the militia, and are compelled to endure the hardship and privation of a soldier's life, in defense of the constitution and the laws; and yet it is assumed, that to them, liberty is a mere chimera....

Can we hold children responsible for crime; liable for their torts; impose onerous burdens upon them, and yet deprive them of the enjoyment of liberty, without charge or conviction of crime? The bill of rights declares, that "all men are, by nature, free and independent, and have certain inherent and inalienable rights—among these are life, liberty, and the pursuit of happiness."... Shall we say to the children of the State, you shall not enjoy this right—a right independent of all human laws and regulations? It is declared in the constitution; is higher than constitution and law, and should be held forever sacred.

Even criminals can not be convicted and imprisoned without due process of law—without a regular trial, according to the course of the common law. Why should minors be imprisoned for misfortune? Destitution of proper parental care, ignorance, idleness and vice, are misfortunes, not crimes. In all criminal prosecutions against minors, for grave and heinous offenses, they have the right to demand the nature and cause of the accusation, and a speedy public trial by an impartial jury. All this must precede the final commitment to prison. Why should children, only guilty of misfortune, be deprived of liberty without "due process of law"?

It can not be said, that in this case, there is no imprisonment. This boy is deprived of a father's care; bereft of home influences; has no freedom of action; is committed for an uncertain time; is branded a prisoner; made subject to the will of others.... Other means of a milder character; other influences of a more kindly nature; other laws less in restraint of liberty, would better accomplish the reformation of the depraved, and infringe less upon inalienable rights.

It is a grave responsibility to pronounce upon the acts of the legislative department. It is, however, the solemn duty of the courts to adjudge the law, and guard, when assailed, the liberty of the citizen. The constitution is the highest law; it commands and protects all. Its declaration of rights is an express limitation of legislative power, and as the laws under which the detention is had, are in conflict with its provisions, we must so declare.

It is therefore ordered, that Daniel O'Connell be discharged from custody.

QUESTIONS

1. Besides the fact that this case was decided by the Illinois Supreme Court while *Ex parte Crouse* was decided by the Pennsylvania Supreme Court, are there any other significant differences between the two cases that may explain the dissimilar outcomes?
2. Is the court unpersuaded that the child lacks proper parental care? Or is the court simply saying that the evidence failed to establish that the parent was unfit?
3. Does the court find that the institutionalization of Daniel violated his rights? His father's rights? Does the state ever have the power to remove the child from his home? Why?
4. Why would a child be capable of entering into a contract but incapable of "the appointment of an attorney"?

IN RE FERRIER
Supreme Court of Illinois
103 Ill. 367 (1882)

...The petition set forth that Winifred Breen, the appellant, was a girl nine years old; had repeatedly been picked up by the police and others while wandering about the streets at night; was a truant from school, and had not proper parental care, and was in imminent danger of ruin and harm, etc.

Three witnesses testified as to the character and habits of the girl, Winifred Breen, stating that she was without proper parental care; that she wandered upon the streets of Chicago at all hours of the day and night; that she had been frequently picked up by the policemen of the city, late at night and miles away from her usual place of abode, and had been confined all night in police stations; that she kept bad company, and was in great danger of being ruined; that the mother of the child is weak-minded, and at times insane, having on one occasion attempted to hang Winifred; that she was unfit to have the control of the child, and incapable of managing her; that the step-father is poor and an invalid, earning only a small salary, and is compelled to be absent from his home the entire day, and he found it impossible to control the girl, and that she had been guilty of thefts and falsehood. The fourth witness, Mrs. Beveridge, stated that she was president of the Industrial School for Girls; that the school is situated in Evanston, in Cook county, on a five-acre tract of beautiful rolling ground, over which the inmates have free range as a play-ground; that there is no more restraint upon their liberty than that imposed upon children in an ordinary family or institution of learning; that they are taught ordinary household duties, sewing, and the ordinary branches of English education; that parents are permitted to visit their children when they desire, and that children are given places in private families whenever suitable places can be procured, but not without their and their parents' consent. The girl herself testified that she sometimes ran away; that her mother tried to hang witness, and then tried to hang herself; that she was afraid of her mother; that she knew about this industrial school and wanted to go there. The father of the child, if still living, appears to have been a worthless character,—a professional thief,—who when last heard from, three years ago, was at the Bridewell, and the mother was divorced from him.

The jury returned a verdict that Winifred Breen was a dependent girl, and that the facts set forth in the petition were true, and thereupon the county judge entered an order that said Winifred should be committed to said Industrial School for Girls, and appointed Mrs. Ellen Woodward, one of the vice-presidents of the school, guardian of the child, in accordance with a provision of the act. The county attorney, whom the court had appointed counsel for the girl, and who appeared for her, took an appeal to this court

Section 3 of the act under which this proceeding was taken, is as follows: "Any responsible person... may petition the county court... to inquire into the alleged dependency of any female infant... and every female infant who comes within the following descriptions shall be considered a dependent girl, viz: Every female infant who begs or receives alms while actually selling or pretending to sell any article in public, or who frequents any street, alley or other place for the purpose of begging or receiving alms, or who, having no permanent place of abode, proper parental care or guardianship, or sufficient means of subsistence, or who for other cause is a wanderer through streets and alleys, and in other public places, or who lives with or frequents the company of, or consorts with, reputed thieves or other vicious persons, or who is found in a house of ill-fame, or in a poor house." The petition is to be verified by oath, and notice is to be given to the parents and guardian. The female infant is brought before the court, and if without counsel, it is made the duty of the court to assign counsel for her, and a trial is had before a jury of six. Section 2 declares: "The object of industrial schools for girls shall be to provide a home and proper training school for such girls committed to their charge."...

It is insisted that the law under which the proceeding was had is unconstitutional—first, as being in violation of the Bill of Rights as to personal liberty, in respect of the provision that no person shall be deprived of life, liberty or property without due process of law, and People v. Turner, 55 Ill. 280, is relied upon as being a decisive authority in favor of appellant in this respect.... That school was established under a statute different and much less careful in its provisions, and nearer in its approach to a criminal enactment, than the one in question. The judge was the only one to decide in the matter. Criminals between six and sixteen years of age, convicted of crime punishable by fine or imprisonment, were confined there. That institution was regarded in that case as a place of confinement, and for punishment, and the commitment to it was regarded as imprisonment.

In the statute now under consideration, anxious provision is made for the due protection of all just rights. To begin, there must be the petition of a responsible person, verified by oath, setting forth the facts, and if there be a parent or a guardian, it must also show that the parent or guardian is not a fit person to have the custody of the infant, there must be notice to the parents, the child must be brought before the court, there is a trial as to the facts by six jurymen, defence by counsel is provided, proof is made before a court of record of the facts alleged, there is the verdict of a jury of six men, and if, by the 4th section, after the verdict of the jury the judge is of the opinion that the girl should be sent to the industrial school, then he may order that she be committed there.... This institution is not a prison, but it is a school, and the sending of a young female child there to be taken care of, who is uncared for, and with no one to care for her, we do not regard imprisonment. We perceive hardly any more restraint of liberty than is found in any well regulated school. Such a degree of restraint is essential in the proper education of a child, and it is in no just sense an infringement of the inherent and inalienable right to personal liberty so much dwelt upon in the argument.

The power conferred under the act in question upon the county court is but of the same character of the jurisdiction exercised by the court of chancery over the persons and property of infants, having foundation in the prerogative of the Crown, flowing from its general power and duty, as *parens patriae,* to protect those who have no other lawful protector. That jurisdiction extends to the care and person of the infant, so far as is necessary for his protection and education, and upon this ground that court interferes with the ordinary rights of parents in regard to the custody and care of their children, for although, in general, parents are intrusted with the custody of the persons and the education of their children, yet this is done upon the natural presumption that the children will be properly taken care of, and will be brought up with a due education. But whenever this presumption is removed, and the parent is grossly unfit and fails in this respect, the court of chancery will interfere, and deprive him of the custody of his children, and appoint a suitable person to act as guardian, and to take care of them, and to superintend their education.... The right to liberty which is guaranteed is not that of entire unrestrainedness of action. Civil government in itself implies an abridgment of natural liberty.... It is not natural but civil liberty of which a person may not be deprived without due process of law. There are restrictions imposed upon personal liberty which spring from the helpless or dependent condition of individuals in the various relations of life, among them being those of parent and child....

We find here no more than such proper restraint which the child's welfare and the good of the community manifestly require, and which rightly pertains to the relations above named, and find no such invasion of the right to personal liberty as requires us to pronounce this statute to be unconstitutional. The decision in [People ex rel. O'Connor v. Turner] as to the reform school, we do not think should be applied to this industrial school. The courts in other states have sustained similar laws. *Ex parte Crouse*, 4 Whart. 11; *Roth & Boyle v. House of Refuge*, 31 Md. 329; *Prescott v. The State*, 19 Ohio St. 184; *Milwaukee Industrial School v. Supervisors of Milwaukee Co.*, 40 Wis. 328.

It is objected that there was not reasonable notice given. The statute provides merely that notice to the parents shall be given. There was here written notice served upon the mother, with a copy of the petition, on the day before the trial. The step-father appeared. We think there was notice in compliance with the statute. There was opportunity to be present, and to apply for further time if not ready for the investigation.

A jury of twelve men was demanded and denied, and it is insisted there was error in this denial. The statute provides for a jury of only six. The constitutional provision that "the right of trial by jury, as heretofore enjoyed, shall remain inviolate," does not apply. This is not a proceeding according to the course of the common law, in which the right of a trial by jury is guaranteed, but the proceeding is a statutory one, and the statute, too, enacted since the adoption of the constitution. There was not, at the time of such adoption, the enjoyment of a jury trial in such a case.

QUESTIONS

1. Is *Ferrier* inconsistent with *O'Connell*? If not, how is it consistent?

2. Does the statute provide sufficient procedural protections? Would it violate constitutional law principles if the statute did not accord children these rights?

3. Look at Section 3 of the act. Does the state have a legitimate basis for removing girls who are found begging or wandering in the streets or who consort with "vicious persons"? Consider these questions as you read the next excerpt.

David S. Tanenhaus, *The Evolution of Juvenile Courts in the Early Twentieth Century: Beyond the Myth of Immaculate Construction*, in A CENTURY OF JUVENILE JUSTICE 42–43, 52, 53–55, 59–60, 61–62, 63, 64, 66 (Margaret K. Rosenheim et al., eds., 2002).

The world's first juvenile court law was enacted during a tense centennial moment. The Illinois General Assembly had waited until April 14, 1899, the last day of the last legislative session of the nineteenth century, to approve "An Act for the Treatment and Control of Dependent, Neglected and Delinquent Children." The law, when it went into effect on July 1, 1899, established the Cook County Juvenile Court (more generally known as the Chicago Juvenile Court). Led by the visionary philanthropist Lucy Flower and her friend Julia Lathrop, a child-welfare expert who later became the first Chief of the United States Children's Bureau in 1912, the moral crusaders for juvenile justice could now breathe a temporary sigh of relief. After a decade of concerted work, they had finally succeeded in writing their ideals about childhood innocence and public responsibility into law. In Chicago, the nation's second largest and fastest growing city, the cases of dependent and neglected children as well as ones accused of committing crimes could now be heard in a separate children's court. A sympathetic judge could now use his discretion to apply individualized treatments to rehabilitate children, instead of punishing them. Yet, as Flower and Lathrop understood perfectly well, especially after the long struggle to pass the legislation, their efforts to secure justice for the child had only begun.

Illinois's pioneering juvenile court act read like a rough blueprint. Most of the features that later became the hallmarks of progressive juvenile justice—private hearings, confidential records, the complaint system, detention homes, and probation officers—were either omitted entirely from the initial law or were included without any provisions for public funding. As a result, the world's first juvenile court opened on July 3, 1899, with an open hearing, a public record, no means to control its calendar (i.e., no complaint system), and without public funds to pay either the salaries of probation officers or to maintain a detention home for children. It would, in fact, take more than eight years before the completion of the city's first juvenile court building....

A publicly funded detention home did eventually become part of the Chicago Juvenile Court and was located in the Juvenile Court Building that opened in August 1907....The use of detention homes had become at least a fairly standard practice in urban courts by the Roaring Twenties....

Probation officers were the "right arm of the court" because they investigated homes; interviewed neighbors, teachers, and employers; made recommendations to the judge about what should be done with children; represented them during hearings; and supervised those on probation....

Scholars have described this entry by probation officers into the home as the beginning of a "therapeutic state," in which public officials work to "normalize" the social behavior of "deviants." The child who got into trouble with the law, according to this interpretation, not only brought the state into his or her life, but also opened up the family home to state intervention and extended supervision. Thus, the entire family, not only the child, became the subject for extended case work, which could involve demands to change jobs, find a new residence, become a better housekeeper, prepare different meals, give up alcohol, and abstain from sex....

[However] in Chicago heavy caseloads that averaged between 50 to 150 children per officer made it unrealistic to expect a probation officer "to exercise much more than the somewhat humorously designated 'official parenthood' over most members of such a brood." In fact, due to heavy caseloads, some officers in Chicago and other large cities even met groups of children at settlement houses or libraries instead of visiting them in their homes....

Although the limited number of probation officers certainly diluted the ability of the juvenile court to police the home, the authority to investigate homes did exist, and the progressives wanted to expand the probation department to take full advantage of this power. Lathrop, for example, proposed two solutions to the problem of inadequate probation. First, she called for Cook County to fund the officers. Second, to ensure that these positions did not become subject to patronage, she declared that the Civil Service Commission should administer a merit examination to all applicants.

The [Juvenile Court Committee (JCC), a separate organization established by the Chicago Women's Club,] drafted a bill to amend the Juvenile Court Act to allow for such a system to be put into place. In... 1905... the JCC's bill... was unanimously passed by both houses of the General Assembly and signed into law by [the] Governor.... According to the new law, the circuit court judges would inform the County Board of County Commissioners how many officers, including a chief probation officer, the juvenile court would require for the coming year. The commissioners would then determine whether the number was appropriate and what their salaries should be.

Probation had certainly become a distinguishing feature of juvenile justice by the mid-1920s, but the majority of probation officers were generally underpaid and extremely overworked.

In addition to the problems associated with probation officers handling far too many cases, judges…were also overwhelmed by their unwieldy calendars.…

The problem was that under the Juvenile Court Act the judge was required to hear *all* cases in which a petition had been filed.…

[The judge] devised an ingenious remedy: the complaint system.…[C]oncerned individuals should make an informal complaint to the court's probation department instead of filing a formal petition against a child. This procedural change would allow the probation staff to investigate cases to determine whether they merited judicial attention.

This policy gave the probation officers the discretion to determine which children should be brought to court. It also allowed these officers to use the threat of future legal action as a means to encourage cooperation with their commands.…

Other courts also adopted variations on the complaint system in the early twentieth century.…Thus, by the mid-1920s, the complaint system, like detention and probation, had become a distinguishing feature of progressive juvenile justice.

Private hearings, the final distinguishing feature of progressive juvenile justice…involved removing the general public from juvenile court hearings. The sponsors of the 1899 Illinois juvenile court legislation had wanted juvenile court hearings to be closed to spectators in order to protect the privacy of children and their families. The sponsors of the legislation believed that closed hearings would shield children from stigmatizing publicity and contribute to the court's mission of rehabilitation. Accordingly, the second provision of the juvenile court bill of 1899 had stated that "when a case is being heard, all persons not officers of the court or witnesses, and those having a direct interest in the case being heard, shall be excluded from the court room."

Critics of the city's private charity organizations, however, objected to the idea of closed hearings because they would envelop state action in secrecy. On the eve of the house hearings on the bill, the *Chicago Daily Inter-Ocean* ran a sensational front-page story with the lead "Child Slaves," which explained these concerns about secrecy. The article quoted anonymous sources, including "a prominent Representative," who declared that closed hearings in the juvenile court would only contribute to the enslaving of poor children by allowing charity organizations to remove them from their families and sell them as cheap laborers. The proposed juvenile court would allow charity associations to bring these poor children before the court, have them declared "dependent" by the court, and then sell the child to a downstate, out-of-state, or—worst of all—Canadian farmer.…

The argument that private charity organizations stole poor children drew upon a reservoir of mistrust about private charity organizations dating to the mid-nineteenth century, which then was directed at the juvenile court. In New York, for example, similar accusations had been leveled at Charles Loring Brace's Children's Aid Society and its placing-out program of collecting street urchins and sending them to live in the Midwest. At the turn of the twentieth century, the charges of child slavery, or "traffic in children," reflected a new version of this older concern about separating children from their parents.

As a result of this campaign against closed hearings, the controversial provision was removed from the Illinois bill to secure its passage. Thus, juvenile court hearings in the Cook

County Juvenile Court were open to the public. The local papers did, in fact, cover the new court's early cases and published stories about the children, including their names, addresses, and alleged offenses. Spectators also came to the court to see the most sensational cases....

Yet progressive supporters of the court, including the presiding judges, adapted to the public nature of these early cases by using the free publicity to explain the rehabilitative mission of the court and helped to make the case for its benefits to the public. These efforts to educate the public about the court were critical to establishing the legitimacy of the new institution....

Although the progressive child savers learned how to use publicity to help legitimate the juvenile court, they still wanted to limit public access to juvenile court and give judges as much control of the courtroom as possible....

Private hearings had, however, become fairly standard practice by the time that many of the most influential studies of juvenile justice were published in the 1920s. Later in the twentieth century, scholars relied upon these important studies from the 1920s, many of which were reprinted in the 1970s, to make generalizations about "the progressive juvenile court," including the assumption that private hearings had always been one of the distinguishing features of juvenile justice.

The last major addition to the juvenile court in the early twentieth century was the installation of psychiatric clinics. Although the use of clinics in the juvenile justice system was extremely rare before the First World War, psychological and psychiatric approaches to the prevention of juvenile delinquency, including shifting the focus from adolescents to very young children, were the wave of the future.

QUESTIONS

1. Was the first juvenile court a radical departure from other courts? What were the juvenile court's distinguishing features? Did subsequent changes improve the way the legal system responded to children?

2. The National Council of Juvenile and Family Court Judges (NCJFCJ) noted that the juvenile court historically closed its proceedings, records, and documents to avoid stigmatizing the juvenile. However, because many juvenile court judges say that juveniles no longer feel stigmatized by a delinquency adjudication and that the behavior is "well-known to those in the juvenile's life," there is less reason to keep juvenile proceedings confidential. The NCJFCJ thus recommends that juvenile court proceedings should be presumptively open to the general public "unless sufficient evidence supports a finding that an open hearing will harm the juvenile and that the juvenile's interests outweigh the public's interest." NAT'L COUNCIL JUV. & FAM. CT. JUDGES, OFF. JUV. JUST. & DELINQ. PREVENTION, JUVENILE DELINQUENCY GUIDELINES: IMPROVING COURT PRACTICE IN JUVENILE DELINQUENCY CASES 40 (2005). The NCJFCJ also suggests that while "general investigative information" about the facts of the case, witness testimony, and documentary evidence be made available to the public, "personal information" about the child's social history and background should be kept confidential. *Id.* at 41–42. Is this position supported by the historical evidence? Do you agree that public access and openness are preferable? What are the arguments for and against such a position?

3. Kristen Henning argues that the erosion of confidentiality in juvenile courts and the concomitant access to the records by schools and public housing authorities may make the public less safe over time by inhibiting juvenile rehabilitation. She nevertheless argues that while public housing authorities should be denied access to these records under all circumstances, school authorities should continue to have access to juvenile records in certain cases in order to enhance the safety of the school environment and to assist in children's rehabilitation. Kristin Henning, *Eroding Confidentiality in Delinquency Proceedings: Should Schools and Public Housing Authorities Be Notified?* 79 N.Y.U. L. Rev. 520, 524 (2004). Do you agree?

B. Philosophical Perspectives

The notion of capacity as a prerequisite to having rights has both historical and analytical relevance to the American legal tradition of individualism. Seventeenth- and eighteenth-century social compact theorists constructed a rights theory premised on a competence to contract that excluded children from the class of rights holders. Our nation's founders were deeply influenced by social compact theory and, as we have seen in the preceding section, constructed a new social order in which children were redefined as dependent and incompetent.

In thinking about children's rights today, it is useful to think about how we account for rights generally. One could argue, for example, that there are two broad accounts of rights: will theory and interest theory. Under will theory, a right, in its most basic form, is the exercise of choice. In other words, the rights holder may choose to compel performance of some duty owed to the rights holder by another or may decide to waive the obligation entirely. Significantly, it is the rights holder who has the power to decide whether the duty bearer must fulfill his or her obligations to the rights holder. Consequently, performance of the duty is conditional, for without the preexisting right and its demand, there is no obligation. Moreover, will theory suggests that the rights holder must have the capacity to make and exercise his or her choice regarding the performance of that duty.

If, however, having a right is not dependent on the ability to demand performance of a corresponding obligation, then the extent of the rights holder's capacities to exercise his or her rights would be irrelevant. By rejecting the claim that rights are correlative to duties, interest theory purports to resolve the problem of having a right without having the present ability to exercise it. Under this view, a right is an interest that has been identified as being worthy of protection by the imposition of some obligation. Consequently, the right exists irrespective of the rights holder's decision (or capacity) to exercise the right, the identity of the obligor, and the nature of the duties imposed by the right. Furthermore, not all interests will generate rights, and the questions of which interests do and whether they may be waived are answered by a specific substantive account of those rights.

Children's rights proponents and opponents thus tend to define rights as either choice (will theory) or protective (interest theory) rights. For example, some will theorists simply presume that the child does have sufficient capacity to exercise choice and thus should have the same political and legal rights held by adults. Others suggest that children have variable capacities that render a blanket presumption of incompetence illegitimate, immoral, or unwise. Some proponents argue that because of culturally constructed notions about what it means to be a child, or paternalistic practices, we underestimate the child's abilities. Still others contend that incompetent children should not be denied rights simply because they are unable to exercise them and construct systems of agents or proxies who will exercise children's rights for them.

On the other hand, will theorists who oppose children's rights argue that children lack the ability for choice essential to the exercise of a right. Some opponents note that the psychological and sociological research does not support the contention that children are competent. Others argue, quite correctly, that the law has long assumed the necessity of competency. Asserting that children need a protective environment in which to develop their capacities, they contend that according children rights prematurely will damage individual liberty because children are incapable of making meaningful and rational choices. Some opponents also note that childhood is a time of dependency and incompetency, requiring extensive parental authority. Consequently, according children rights prematurely is detrimental to their welfare because they lack the capacity to make meaningful and rational choices.

Under interest theory, children's incompetencies create legally enforceable rights. The premise here is that children have a moral right to be cared for, loved, and nurtured because they are incapable of caring for themselves. We can account for that right, the interest theorists contend, only if we characterize children's rights as a set of goods or needs, in which no one good (such as liberty) takes precedence and any need may be overridden by another if they conflict. In the case of children, we may order these interests: the more important the need, the greater the right. We protect this set of goods by imposing moral or legal constraints on others with respect to those interests; the duty imposed, therefore, does not preexist the right, and performance of the obligation is not contingent upon the request or waiver of the interest holder. Children thus have certain limited legal rights because they have needs and wants that some adult (usually a parent) must satisfy to ensure their survival. From this perspective, one could argue that a rights theory that rejects children's dependencies is definitionally inconceivable.

Other theorists, however, argue that the child's right to self-determination limits the scope of paternalistic action taken on behalf of the child. Although children need nurturing and protection because of their incompetencies, the decisions made by adults must take into account the fact that children will themselves mature and become responsible adults. For that reason, adults must recognize that the actions they take should not unduly limit the opportunities available to children as they mature. Parents, therefore, must preserve the rights children are not capable of exercising by limiting their parental power. The child's incapacities thus mandate respect for the child's potentialities and create a right to an open future.

Feminist theory, in contrast, has deemphasized the significance of competency in rights talk by focusing on the relationships between individuals. Within feminist thought, concepts of autonomy and individuality are fundamentally hierarchical and patriarchal because they disadvantage certain groups, most notably women and people of color. Moreover, notions of individuality and autonomy minimalize the essential interconnectedness of human beings and serve to isolate us from one another. But feminist theorists argue that we should reconceive rights by considering the interconnectedness and mutual dependencies of people. Thus, feminist theorists reconstruct rights talk by emphasizing the relationships between individuals and by rejecting traditional rights discourse in which autonomy is a central value.

Feminist theory is particularly appealing to children's rights theorists because it apparently redresses the problem of the competent rights holder. From a feminist perspective, traditional rights rhetoric unnecessarily excludes interpersonal relationships and emphasizes individual autonomy, thereby making it difficult to account for children as rights holders. Decisions about children's competencies, therefore, are not based on scientific evidence but are merely political choices that reflect certain beliefs about what children may need. But the notion of the autonomous rights holder is itself a fiction, for it ignores the many ways in which adults are dependent on one another. Feminist rights talk, moreover, encompasses notions of mutual connection and need irrespective of notions of capacity and individual responsibility.

When reading the excerpts in this section, consider how notions of rights may structure our understandings about children and their role in society.

Bruce C. Hafen, *Children's Liberation and the New Egalitarianism: Some Reservations about Abandoning Youth to Their "Rights,"* 1976 B.Y.U. L. Rev. 605, 613, 644, 647–648, 650, 656.

The law has long assumed the necessity of capacity. The assumption is reflected in the freedom of children to vote, hold office, marry, drive automobiles, shoot firearms, gamble, enter into contracts, consent to sexual acts, and to make many other binding decisions about their own lives. The presumption of minors' incapacity has been so strong that the growth of democratic ideals in American society, rather than encouraging the "liberation" of children from limitations upon their liberty, has encouraged even greater discrimination on the basis of age—to protect children from the excesses of their immature faculties and to promote the development of their ability ultimately to assume responsibility. The juvenile court movement and the expansion of compulsory public education are obvious examples of the way American democratization has reflected the views of Locke and Mill about protecting and developing the capacities of the young....

When children are involved, a significant distinction can be drawn between legal rights that protect one from undue interference by the state or from the harmful acts of others and legal rights that permit persons to make affirmative choices of binding consequence, such as voting, marrying, exercising religious preferences, and choosing whether to seek education. For purposes of this discussion, the first category will be referred to as rights of protection; the second, rights of choice....

The serious question about the capacity limitation is where to draw the age line above which a given right or activity may be permitted. Children develop from incapacity toward capacity. That incontrovertible natural pattern is consistent with the presumption that capacity does not exist for children as a class until the general weight of evidence shows that a given level of capacity does in fact exist....

The development of the capacity to function as a mature, independent member of society is essential to the meaningful exercise of the full range of choice rights characteristic of the individual tradition. Precisely because of their lack of capacity, minors should enjoy legally protected rights to special treatment (including some protection against their own immaturity) that will optimize their opportunities for the development of mature capabilities that are in their best interest. Children will outgrow their restricted state, but the more important question is whether they will outgrow it with maximized capacities. An assumption that rational and moral capacity exists, when in fact it does not exist, may lead to an abandonment of the protections, processes, and opportunities that can develop these very capacities.... For these reasons, some distinction between rights of protection and rights of choice must be preserved.

The individual tradition is at the heart of American culture. Yet the fulfillment of individualism's promise of personal liberty depends, paradoxically, upon the maintenance of a set of corollary traditions that require what may seem to be the opposite of personal liberty: submission to authority, acceptance of responsibility, and the discharge of duty. The family tradition is among the most essential corollaries to the individual tradition, because it is in families that both children and parents experience the need for and the value of authority, responsibility, and duty in their most pristine forms. When individualism breaks loose from its corollaries, however, its tendency to destroy personal fulfillment and human relationships is exposed.

NOTES AND QUESTIONS

1. Is Hafen correct when he says that "the law has long presumed the necessity of capacity"? Would historian Holly Brewer agree? To what extent should the law acknowledge its historical antecedents?

2. The 1970s saw the rise of the children's liberation movement in the United States (often referred to derogatorily as "kiddie's lib"). Two of its leading proponents, Richard Farson and John Holt, argue that because children are discriminated against and oppressed by society, granting them rights will "restore their childhoods." Thus, children should and must have the same political and legal rights held by adults. Do you agree? Is there historical support for their position?

3. Onora O'Neill rejects the claim that children are an oppressed group in society. According to O'Neill, the dependence of children is unlike the unnatural and forced dependence of oppression experienced by others, such as women and African-Americans, because children may escape their dependency by growing up. Onora O'Neill, *Children's Rights and Children's Lives*, 98 Ethics 445 (1988). Do you find this persuasive?

4. Hillary Rodham argues that a presumption of incompetency should be set aside in favor of a more discriminating set of assumptions about the capacity of children, tied to age and individual ability. She instead proposes that we presume capacity. Hillary Rodham, *Children under the Law*, 43 Harv. Educ. Rev. 487, 508 (1973). After graduating from Yale Law School in 1973, Rodham worked briefly as a staff attorney for the Children's Defense Fund (CDF) before marrying the future president Bill Clinton in 1975. She subsequently served as chair of the board of directors of the CDF from 1986 to 1992.

5. Should one's status as a rights holder be tied to age and individual ability? What about those individuals who reach adulthood but never attain or, because of advancing age, lose that ability?

Michael Freeman, The Rights and the Wrongs of Children 54–55, 57–58 (1983).

The general justification of children's rights lies within an over-arching theory of human rights. A theory of human rights requires the treatment of persons as equals. It expresses a normative attitude of respect for individual autonomy. It is not dependent on actual autonomy, rather on the capacity for it.... To deny a person rights is to fail to recognize his capacity for autonomy.

Of all moral theories...it is Rawls's notion of equality at the stage of a hypothetical social contract which comes closest to expressing the ideas of treating persons as equals with respect to their capacity for autonomy. The principles of justice which Rawls believes we would choose in the "original position" behind a "veil of ignorance" are equal liberty and opportunity and an arrangement of social and economic inequalities so that they are both to the greatest benefit of the least advantaged and attached to offices and positions open to all under conditions of fair equality of opportunity.... The legal system has a part to play in ensuring fair equality of opportunity (through race relations and equal opportunities legislation, for example). Other institutions also play a part: schools, media and family can all help to promote capacities to assist young people to shape their lives according to rational goals.

...The principles of justice delineated in the previous paragraph confine paternalism, without totally eliminating it. Parties to the hypothetical social contract would know that some human beings are less capable than others: they would know about variations in intelligence and strength and they would know of the very limited capacities of small children and rather fuller, if not complete, capacities of older children and adolescents. These are matters that they would take into account in constructing principles to govern institutions in society. They would bear in mind in particular how the actions of those with limited capacities now might thwart their autonomy in time to come when their incapacities are no longer.

These considerations would lead to an acceptance of intervention in people's lives to protect them against irrational actions....

To bring children to a capacity where they are able to take full responsibility as free, rational agents...children must be accorded two types of right. The right to equal opportunity demands that their needs as children be met: good parenting, good teaching, particularly directed towards self-critical awareness, etc. Though the ingredients of this right are much the most important, it is not necessary to spell them out in this context. The right to liberal paternalism is more controversial and must be described.

It has been indicated already that intervention in another's conduct is justified if he lacks rational capacities and the irrational conduct is likely to lead to a severe and permanent weakening of his capacity to achieve his own ends. What notion of irrationality can we apply to a child, particularly a young child who lacks the capacity for "reflective self-evaluation"...? We could use a standard selected by parents. We could use a notion employed by the state, like the "best interests" of the child. There are dangers in selecting standards of rationality in either of these ways. What we are looking for is something more value-free and independent of the participants....

The question we should ask ourselves is: what sorts of action or conduct would we wish, as children, to be shielded against on the assumption that we would want to mature to a rationally autonomous adulthood and be capable of deciding on our own system of ends as free and rational beings? We would choose principles that would enable children to mature to independent adulthood. Our definition of irrationality would be such as to preclude action and conduct which would frustrate such a goal; within the constraints of such a definition we would defend a version of paternalism. It is not paternalism in its classical sense. Furthermore, it is a two-edged sword in that since the goal is rational independence those who exercise constraints must do so in such a way as to enable children to develop their capacities.

NOTES AND QUESTIONS

1. John Rawls argues that justice is the governing principle of any political society, without which its laws and institutions may be reformed or abolished. Given the primacy of justice, Rawls contends that it and its principles, rather than participation in a given society or the formation of a particular form of government, are the objects of the social contract. Rawls thus imagines the formation of the social contract as the collective effort of a group of rational and disinterested men and women who, unable to know of their future positions in society or of their conceptions of the good, create a state in which no one is advantaged or disadvantaged by the choices made during the contract's formation. The rights and obligations of the citizen and the state naturally flow from this just conception of the political society: once the veil of ignorance is lifted, no party to the original contract should desire its rescission.

Rawls states that "the capacity for moral personality is a sufficient condition for being entitled to equal justice." Thus, children have the potential to acquire moral personhood, but because they actually lack the capacity for reason, they must be protected from the "weakness and infirmities of their reason and will in society." Rawls thus would authorize guardians to act on behalf of children in a manner most likely to secure their approval when they become rational persons. Rawls nevertheless would require that the guardian account for the individual child's preferences and interests to the extent that they are rational and limits the guardian's authority to the pursuit of the child's expressed conception of good, if the child is capable of having a conception of the good, has formed a conception, and has expressed it. He also contends that moral considerations limit paternalism in ways that preserve future individual freedom. John Rawls, A Theory of Justice (1971).

2. Do you think Rawls's conception of rights advantages children? If we adopted his approach, would there be any actual differences in the way we treat children?

3. Is Freeman correct when he says that the justification for children's rights lies in human rights? What does he mean?

4. Laurence Houlgate argues that Rawls's conception of rights unfairly discriminates against children simply because of their age. Rawls's paternalism provides a sufficient justification to intervene but only in the lives of the incompetent, a distinction, Houlgate insists, that discriminates not between children and adults but between the competent and the incompetent. Laurence D. Houlgate, The Child and the State: A Normative Theory of Juvenile Rights 87–90 (1980). Thus, Houlgate contends that it is unjust to deny children rights in the absence of empirical evidence that they lack capacity. *Id.* at 102–103. Do we have evidence that children lack capacity?

Martha Minow, *Rights for the Next Generation: A Feminist Approach to Children's Rights*, 9 Harv. Women's L.J. 1, 18, 23–24 (1986).

To the extent that the dominant conception of rights presumes both autonomy and a direct relationship between the individual and the state, rights for children are even more problematic than rights for adults. Conceptually and practically, children in our society are not autonomous persons but instead dependents who are linked legally and daily to adults entrusted with their care. Children are doubly dependent. Their dependency is constructed by legal rules and also is in their lives as lived. This double dependency situates children outside the sphere of rights-bearing persons in a system that makes independence a premise for the grant of rights. Children's dependencies specifically situate them within the sphere of the private family, where parents stand between children and the state....

...The critical need for the juvenile court, and other institutions addressing children's rights, is to focus on the preconditions for relationships. Treating children as though they already had working relationships with parents or other adults, and as though enforcing rights and duties alone would the problems brought to the court, could miss what those problems are truly about. What legal rules governing child custody, education, and child support would promote settings where children thrive? Similarly, what rules would promote adults' abilities to create these settings? To pose such questions and provide working answers to them, the juvenile court should be authorized to commandeer resources such as public support benefits, homemaker assistance, day-care volunteers, and job-training for both youths and their care-takers. Although it would be difficult theoretically, practically, and politically to empower the juvenile court to promote the preconditions for relationships in these ways, I suggest that pursuing this line of inquiry holds promise of breaking out of patterns of disillusionment. Reforms in the past at first treated children differently from adults, then treated them like adults, and in each instance, built bureaucratic institutions and a public sense of futility. The goal for the future is to devise reforms that help people help themselves—reforms that acknowledge the public as well as private influences on and preconditions for human relationships....

Children lack the autonomy presumed under one version of what rights mean. But so do adults. Children need environments where they can learn what is just, learn what it means to have their needs met, and learn what it means to have and fulfill obligations and to meet the needs of others. Adults need this too—from other adults, and from children as well. Debating whether children should be treated like adults for one purpose but not for another misses these points. So does debating whether children are entitled to liberty or custody, although both of these norms contain hints of an important line of inquiry. That inquiry addresses the interrelationships and tensions between rights for children that constrain abuses of power by their parents and by the state, and rights for children that promote their abilities to form relationships of trust, meaning, and affection with people in their daily lives and their broader communities.

NOTE

1. Consider the following:

[Minow's] emphasis on relationships presupposes a connection between adults and children that merely underscores children's dependencies rather than rendering them irrelevant....The interconnectedness of adults and children is different in origin; children have no real choice in the creation or continuation of the relationship precisely because they are

> thought to "need" these relationships, and they need these relationships because they are immature and incompetent....
>
> Second, if we speak of children's rights in relationships, we are inevitably caught in that spiral of capacity that diverts us from our task of honestly assessing the power we have over our children. Minow's theory really is little more than a sophisticated version of the argument that children should have rights because of their incompetencies.

Katherine Hunt Federle, *On the Road to Reconceiving Rights for Children: A Postfeminist Analysis of the Capacity Principle*, 42 De Paul L. Rev. 983, 1019–1020 (1993). Do you agree? Why or why not?

Barbara Bennett Woodhouse, *Hatching the Egg: A Child-Centered Perspective on Parents' Rights*, 14 Cardozo L. Rev. 1747, 1814–1815, 1816–1817, 1818 (1993).

I propose a new perspective on generational justice that recognizes that meeting the needs of children is the primary concern of family law, and justice towards the next generation its motivating force. Justice across generations, or generism, calls for a metaphor of dynamic stewardship, in which power over children is conferred by the community, with children's interests and their emerging capacities the foremost consideration. Stewardship must be earned through actual care giving, and lost if not exercised with responsibility. Generism would place children, not adults, firmly at the center and take as its central values not adult individualism, possession, and autonomy, as embodied in parental rights, nor even the dyadic intimacy of parent/child relationships. It would value most highly concrete service to the needs of the next generation, in public and private spheres, and encourage adult partnership and mutuality in the work of family, as well as collective community responsibility for the well-being of children....

Realism compels a consciously child-centered evaluation of power over children as a necessary antidote to children's own powerlessness. In an ideal world, generational relations might perhaps begin from a firm base of adult concern for children that warranted a reciprocal concern for adults. We are too far from that ideal to make fairness to adults and adults' interests a co-equal point of reference with concern for children....

Fairness also compels a child-centered perspective. Adults enter into relationships of power with children at a time when children have no say in the matter. In order to be legitimate and not constitute a form of bondage, adult power over children should not be predicated on "right," but rather it should be earned through demonstrated responsibility. This conclusion flows from the recognition that children are humans deserving of respect and are not to be objectified—a principle that has a long history in descriptions of just relations between people and generations.

Finally, generism brings intangible as well as tangible rewards to its practitioners. The fact that generism requires the current generation to give generously to the next should not obscure the personal dividends to adults, in the form of intangible generativity, as well as tangible financial security, that such an investment strategy provides.

Laura Purdy, *Why Children Shouldn't Have Equal Rights,* 2 Internat'l J. Children's Rts. 223, 226–227, 228, 230, 240 (1994).

Proponents of CL [children's liberation] generally assume that the instrumental rationality is the morally relevant feature that could justify different treatment for children and adults. But, they maintain, there is no neat dividing line between the two classes with respect to this trait. However, I believe that there are sufficiently large differences in instrumental reasoning between most children and most adults to justify different treatment. Furthermore, instrumental reasoning is not the only morally relevant criterion here: at least as important are prudential and moral action.

Instrumental reason is the ability to judge what steps are necessary to attain a particular goal. It is not an all-or-nothing proposition, and people—even adults—have it in varying degrees, and it is plausible to believe that this capacity is a major component of any worthwhile notion of intelligence....

...As proponents of CL point out, some children are remarkably good at instrumental reasoning. This gift tends to bring its own rewards, since such children are better at getting what they want. However, it is not sufficient for granting children equal rights; in addition, it must be linked with prudence and morality....

Prudence and morality depend upon a number of basic traits, such as rationality, the willingness to work hard, and the desire to do a good job. I call these traits "enabling virtues," and they depend in turn on self-control. In addition, prudence requires a willingness to evaluate and order one's life goals; morality requires genuine care and concern for others, and a willingness to put the interests of others before one's own....

...[C]hildren are not necessarily oppressed by protections and limits that would be inappropriate for adults, ones that increase the probability of their developing prudence and morality. Deciding what limits make sense needs an issue-by-issue investigation. The evidence so far suggests that an optimum environment includes relatively high limits and demands on young children, followed by a carefully graduated expansion of both freedom and responsibility as they grow older. They also need education, and perhaps work, in limited amounts. This approach increases the burden of proof on limits to liberty as children grow older, but also the degree to which children would be held accountable for their behavior. It recommends that majority be attained by steps, as children mature; that approach would to some extent reduce the arbitrariness of an all-or-nothing legal marker of adulthood. We already take that approach with driving, and expanding it would make the system fairer at the same time as it underlines the link between freedom and responsibility.

The place to start working out the details of any new system is probably with a thorough scrutiny of existing protectionist laws pertaining to children. Only those which clearly promote the kind of development recommended here are defensible, and solid evidence is required, not the mere speculation that so often passes for evidence. I suspect, for example, that children, or at least teenagers, should probably have most, if not all, the same civil rights as adults. I also believe that there are overriding reasons for granting them the right to seek medical care, including abortion services, without parental consent.

However, there may be freedoms children now enjoy that are indefensible. For example, the law may now be in some cases inconsistent, granting them freedom without corresponding responsibility; in some such cases, adding responsibility would make sense, in others limiting freedom. Another trouble spot is behavior that causes serious and irreversible harm. In those cases, new legal limits might be justifiable; where they would be ineffective, imaginative new approaches are needed. A case in point might be mandated counseling for pregnant girls to guarantee that they learn what responsibilities are involved in bringing another life into this world.

NOTES AND QUESTIONS

1. Would putting children first as Woodhouse suggests mean that parental rights should be subordinated to the interests of children? Melinda A. Roberts, a professor of philosophy at the College of New Jersey, suggests that allowing children's needs and interests to trump is not always fair. Moreover, acknowledging that both parents and children have needs that must be protected may be enough to "remedy the wrongs imposed" by our legal system. Melinda A. Roberts, *Parent and Child in Conflict: Between Liberty and Responsibility*, 10 NOTRE DAME J.L. ETHICS & PUB. POL'Y 485, 503–504 (1996).

2. Do you agree with Purdy that rights must be "linked with prudence and morality"? Would this suggest that some adults, too, should be denied rights? Anne McGillivray contends that Purdy creates a straw argument, "rights equals liberationism equals autonomy which means nobody can tell you what to do," that fails to acknowledge the relational and situational constraints placed on all autonomous actors and actions. For McGillivray, rights convey "notional equality, equal moral worth"; thus, children, as human beings, have rights from birth, and any limitations placed on the exercise of those rights must be justified. Anne McGillivray, *Why Children Do Have Equal Rights: In Reply to Laura Purdy*, 2 INTERNAT'L J. CHILDREN'S RTS. 243, 244–245 (1994). Do you agree?

Katherine Hunt Federle, *Looking Ahead: An Empowerment Perspective on the Rights Of Children*, 68 TEMPLE L. REV. 1585, 1594–1596, 1597–1598 (1995).

[P]ower must be an essential part of our rights rhetoric if our theory of rights is to have any coherence. Because power pervades our personal and institutional interactions, a coherent theory of rights must acknowledge the reality and experience of being powerless.... Importantly, grounding notions of rights in a conception of power permits us to focus on a particular interaction within its social, political, or legal context and to consider the ways in which personal and institutional constructs may intersect to disempower individuals....

... [T]he intrinsic worth of rights lies in their potential to remedy powerlessness.... Having power commands the respect of others in our society and demands that one be taken seriously; it permits claims to be made and heard while recognizing the claimant's independent value as a human being. But having power suggests that someone else is powerless; thus, power's exclusionary effects may reinforce existing hierarchies and perpetuate inequality. A coherent account of rights, therefore, must recognize this connection between power, respect, and inequality by insuring that the most powerless have rights and may make rights claims.

This approach explicitly rejects claims that rights isolate children from their communities. Some commentators worry that our rights talk promotes an image of a rights holder as an insular and autonomous being unconnected to her larger community. From this perspective, children's rights claims are particularly problematic because the needs of children seem inconsistent with the demands of radical liberalism. These claims, however, stem from impoverished notions of rights, in which autonomy and capacity are central values and children are excluded from the class of rights holders because of their incompetencies. Such accounts invariably emphasize the vulnerability and helplessness of children and find that the needs of children seem to demand their dependence upon others within the larger community.

Rights talk, however, does have a place in the lives of children. Rights play an important role within our social, legal, and political institutions and it is difficult to see why we should exclude children from our rights rhetoric if we reconceive our notions of rights. Rights also offer the possibility of improving children's experiences by recognizing and remedying their powerlessness. Moreover, a rights-based approach provides greater protections for those who lack power than one in which the good will or good faith of others is offered as an alternative to rights. The latter approach actually disadvantages children; certainly, there is evidence to suggest that when we try to act on behalf of children, our efforts seldom have neutral consequences and, in fact, cause greater harm....

How, then, may we account for power yet still value rights? From an empowerment perspective, rights themselves are a form of power; they are a means of empowering the powerless. Empowerment rights are concerned exclusively with the dynamics of power in personal and institutional interactions and with equalizing power within those relationships. Furthermore, empowerment rights recapture our rights rhetoric from powerful elites who have used rights talk as a way to maintain and perpetuate hierarchy and exclusion. Consequently, empowerment rights flow, somewhat paradoxically, to the least powerful. Thus, while having a right accords the rights holder power, obtaining the right suggests the disempowerment of the claimant. In other words, rights are valuable because they provide the powerless with access to political and legal hierarchies and with a means of challenging their oppression and subordination.

Moreover, empowerment rights are fundamental for they provide a context in which to assess all other rights claims. By rejecting the capacity of the rights holder as a prerequisite to having and exercising rights, empowerment rights allow us to reconsider the status of children as rights holders and to see how other accounts of rights fail to accommodate the powerlessness of children. Empowerment rights reveal why our rights talk is incoherent by illuminating the ways in which rights rhetoric masks the exercise of power. Furthermore, empowerment rights reject the exclusionary and hierarchical consequences of rights theories that rest on notions of capacity. In this sense, empowerment rights are primary and lie beneath other kinds of rights for they enable the powerless to make rights claims in the first instance.

Empowerment rights also permit us to reassess the validity of our stated reasons for intervening in the lives of children. For example, parentalistic practices perpetuate the powerlessness of children by reaffirming their vulnerability and helplessness. Parentalistic justifications do not enable children to protect themselves, but empower adults to act on behalf of children;

thus, when we intervene to protect children from others, we implicitly acknowledge their powerlessness. From an empowerment rights perspective, however, such justifications are unacceptable because they disempower children; moreover, good intentions often mask the negative consequences of parentalism. Empowerment rights, therefore, challenge those who wish to protect children by acting in their best interests to promote the empowerment of children.

NOTES AND QUESTIONS

1. Are rights power? Would empowering children improve their lives?

2. Emily Buss argues that "because many children lack the capacity to appreciate their influence over their lawyers or the court, lawyers often will do children a considerable disservice if they premise their representation on the empowerment ideal.... While [the legal profession is] heady with empowerment talk, we may be particularly ill-suited to bring this power to children." Emily Buss, *Confronting Developmental Barriers to the Empowerment of Children*, 84 CORNELL L. REV. 895, 898 (1999). Buss contends that because the child's sociocognitive development is less sophisticated, the child may have difficulty comprehending and negotiating the attorney-client relationship, the legal context, and the "emotional content" of the proceedings. Consequently, lawyers should "approach their representation as a teaching opportunity—an opportunity to begin to expose a child to what it means to engage in the decision-making process and take some control." *Id.* at 956. Do you think lawyers should "teach" their clients? Is this any different from what lawyers already do?

MARTIN GUGGENHEIM, WHAT'S WRONG WITH CHILDREN'S RIGHTS xii–xiii (2005).

"Children's rights" is both deeper and more shallow than is often recognized. It has less substantive content and is less coherent than many would suppose. It has provided very little by way of a useful analytic tool for resolving knotty social problems. One of its shibboleths, for example, is its call for "child-centeredness." But this attractive phrase tells us nothing about how to use it or what are its sensible limits. It surely calls for too much to examine matters affecting children exclusively from the child's perspective....

Nor could child-centeredness be a manifesto to do things children themselves want at the time. Our society is premised on the opposite concept. Adults decide what the rules are for children based on what adults believe is good for them. When this manifesto dictates only that we should do what is good for them, the problem becomes, of course, gaining consensus.

But there is also much more to children's rights than is apparent. It has staying power because it serves adults too. Adults gain in a number of important ways by presenting themselves as caring about children. Across a very wide range of areas, including disputes between adoptive parents and unwed fathers, between biological parents and others who act as parents but lack legally enforceable rights, between grandparent and parents, between divorcing parents, between child welfare agencies and parents, and between parents and state officials over details of childrearing, the rhetoric of children's rights works well for adults on a number of levels.

Sometimes, it serves as a useful subterfuge for the adult's actual motives. It can be an effective diverter of attention, shifting the focus to a more sympathetic party than the adult. Other times, it is used to assuage guilt for the adult's bad behavior or intentions. Children's rights can be useful for masking selfishness by invoking a language of altruism. It can also provide a legal basis to achieve a result that would be difficult to achieve otherwise. Time and again we will see the frequency with which the concept of children's rights is used by adults to try to gain some advantage in their struggles with other adults....

"Children's rights" has become a mantra invoked by adults to help them in their own fights with other adults in all sorts of contexts. This happens at a national level every four years when we have a presidential campaign. Both the Republicans and Democrats fight furiously with each other, trying to win the mantle of being more child-friendly and child-focused than the other side. But winning that battle only occasionally (and incidentally) proves to be any kind of victory for children.

Katherine Hunt Federle, *Rights, Not Wrongs*, 17 Internat'l J. Children's Rts. 321, 328–329 (2009).

Ultimately, Guggenheim appears to be claiming that because adults manipulate the concept of children's rights for their own purposes, whether motivated by self-interest or a misplaced sense of doing good, children should not have rights. To say that a right is contingent on others respecting the right is to suggest that more powerful elites may prevent those less powerful from making rights claims by simply using others' rights for their own purposes. The real problem here is not that adults may use children's rights claims to their own advantage but that the rights claims made on behalf of children are incoherent. When we speak about the best interests of children, we are not speaking about rights in any meaningful sense because we invariably define best interests in light of our own adult biases and norms. Coupling rights with capacity also creates confusion about the roles and responsibilities of the child advocate, thus increasing the likelihood that what is done on behalf of children may run counter to a strong notion of rights....

Guggenheim nevertheless rejects...children's rights theories, arguing that children's rights claims should be recast "from rights to what is fair and just for children." It is not clear how this reformulation would rectify the problems Guggenheim recounts, since in many ways this sounds very much like a best interests test. It could simply be that Guggenheim does not think rights have any value at all, although his passionate defence of parental rights belies that notion (leaving one with the slightly uncomfortable feeling that this is a strategic position undertaken to benefit the parents he represents). In all fairness, however, the crux of his thesis seems to be that there is no value to providing children with rights. In my view, that is an extraordinary position for a lawyer to take.

Rights do have a place in the lives of children. Rights have a transformative aspect because they have the potential to reduce victimization and dependence by changing the rights holder into a powerful individual who commands the respect of those in the legal system. We cannot trample on the rights of others without expecting some consequence; simply because we have failed to respect rights, or that we have manipulated rights holders for our own purposes (nefarious or otherwise), it does not follow that those rights holders no longer have any rights. The point is that rights create mutual zones of respect, challenging those who want to act in the best interests of children to promote the empowerment of children instead. In practice, this would mean that we would respect the relationships the child has with both parents, we would view with dismay attempts to sever those relationships, and stand against unnecessary or unthinking state interventions. Is this not what we would want for our children and our society?

NOTES AND QUESTIONS

1. Do adults use children? Should children be denied rights because others may manipulate those rights for their own purposes and ends? Does it make sense for children to have rights at all?

2. Joel Feinberg proposes that children should have a right to an "open future." From this perspective, the child has a right to keep future options open until he or she reaches adulthood, when he or she then is capable of making his or her own choices. These "rights-in-trust" can be violated by adults to the extent that the adult may prevent the child from exercising a choice that would foreclose a future option. Joel Feinberg, *The Child's Right to an Open Future*, in 1 CHILDREN' RIGHTS 213, 214–216 (Michael D. Freeman, ed., 2004). What sorts of choices could a child make that would violate his future options? Would refusing to practice an instrument qualify?

3. Consider the case of Rifqa Bary. A seventeen-year-old cheerleader and excellent student living with her parents in New Albany, Ohio, she ran away from home, claiming her father threatened to kill her for converting to Christianity from Islam. After managing to get to Florida and being taken in by pastors of the Evangelical Global Revolution Church, whom she had met through Facebook, Rifqa alleged that her parents had threatened to commit an honor killing against her. May her parents insist that she follow their religious beliefs, or may Rifqa adopt her own religious beliefs? Would either violate her right to an open future? How would this claim be resolved under the various rights theories articulated in the preceding excerpts?

C. International and Comparative Perspectives

League of Nations, Geneva Declaration of the Rights of the Child (1929).

By the present Declaration of the Rights of the Child, commonly known as "Declaration of Geneva," men and women of all nations, recognizing that mankind owes to the Child the best that it has to give, declare and accept it as their duty that, beyond and above all considerations of race, nationality or creed:

1. The child must be given the means requisite for its normal development, both materially and spiritually;
2. The child that is hungry must be fed; the child that is sick must be nursed; the child that is backward must be helped; the delinquent child must be reclaimed; and the orphan and the waif must be sheltered and succored;
3. The child must be the first to receive relief in times of distress;
4. The child must be put in a position to earn a livelihood, and must be protected against every form of exploitation;
5. The child must be brought up in the consciousness that its talents must be devoted to the service of fellow men.

NOTES AND QUESTIONS

1. Ellen Key (1849–1926), a Swedish feminist and author, was among the first to articulate a modern account of children's rights. In Century of the Child, originally published in Swedish in 1900, Key envisioned advancements in law that would prohibit corporal punishment, abolish illegitimacy, and promote greater child-centeredness in education. She believed so strongly in the importance of motherhood and child rearing that she argued that the state should support women and their children. This idea formed the basis for subsequent social legislation in several countries.

2. Janusz Korczak was the pen name of Henryk Goldszmit (1878–1942), a Polish-Jewish pediatrician and children's author. Through his writings, most notably HOW TO LOVE A CHILD (1920) and THE RIGHT OF THE CHILD TO RESPECT (1929), he argued for the right to respect the failure and tears of children, rights to privacy and property, and the "right to an answer to his questions." He was critical of the Geneva Declaration of the Rights of the Child, claiming that it merely set out duties to, not rights for, children. Philip E. Veerman, *Janusz Korczak and the Rights of the Child*, 62 CONCERN: JOURNAL OF NAT'L CHILDREN'S BUREAU 7, 7–8 (1987). Do you agree?

Korczak is perhaps best known for his remarkable bravery and commitment to the children in his care. Director of an orphanage for Jewish children before World War II, he remained with the children when the orphanage was forced to relocate to the Warsaw Ghetto by the Nazis in 1940. On August 5, 1942, German soldiers arrived to take the children to Treblinka, the Nazi death camp. Refusing to leave his wards, Korczak boarded the train bound for Treblinka and was never heard from again.

> The evacuation of the Jewish orphanage run by Janusz Korczak had been ordered for that morning. The children were to have been taken away alone. He had the chance to save himself, and it was only with difficulty that he persuaded the Germans to take him too. He had spent long years of his life with children and now, on this last journey he would not leave them alone. He wanted to ease things for them. He told the orphans they were going out into the country, so they ought to be cheerful. At last they would be able to exchange the horrible suffocating city walls for meadows of flowers, streams where they could bathe, woods full of berries and mushrooms. He told them to wear their best clothes, and so they came out into the yard, two by two, nicely dressed and in a happy mood. The little column was led by an SS man who loved children, as Germans do, even those he was about to see on their way into the next world. He took a special liking to a boy of twelve, a violinist who had his instrument under his arm. The SS man told him to go to the head of the procession of children and play—and so they set off.
>
> When I met them in Gesia Street the smiling children were singing in chorus, the little violinist was playing for them and Korczak was carrying two of the smallest infants, who were beaming too, and telling them some amusing story.
>
> I am sure that even in the gas chamber, as the Cyclon B gas was stifling childish throats and striking terror instead of hope into the orphans' hearts, the Old Doctor must have whispered with one last effort, 'It's all right, children, it will be all right,' so that at least he could spare his little charges the fear of passing from life to death.

WLADYSLAW SZPILMAN, THE PIANIST: THE EXTRAORDINARY TRUE STORY OF ONE MAN'S SURVIVAL IN WARSAW, 1939–1945, 95–96 (Anthea Bell, trans., 1999).

3. In 1919, the Covenant of the League of Nations, establishing the League of Nations, was signed by forty-four countries. Despite the involvement of and strong support for the League from President Woodrow Wilson, the United States refused to ratify the covenant. The League was liquidated on April 26, 1946, having proved ineffectual in preventing the aggression of Hitler and World War II.

4. The Geneva Declaration was based on the Declaration of the Rights of the Child, drafted and approved by the Save the Children International Union (SCIU) in 1923. The SCIU was established by Eglantyne Webb, who was instrumental in creating the international movement for children's rights. The SCIU declaration was adopted by the League of Nations the following year. The SCIU subsequently merged with the International Association for the Promotion of Child

Welfare after World War II to become the International Union for Child Welfare (IUCW). The IUCW urged the United Nations to embrace the principles articulated in the Geneva Declaration. Cynthia Price Cohen, *The Human Rights of Children*, 12 Cap. U.L. Rev. 369, 371–372 (1983). On November 20, 1959, the United Nations adopted the Declaration of the Rights of the Child.

United Nations Declaration of the Rights of the Child (1959).

Whereas mankind owes to the child the best it has to give,

Now therefore,

The General Assembly

Proclaims this Declaration of the Rights of the Child to the end that he may have a happy childhood and enjoy for his own good and for the good of society the rights and freedoms herein set forth…

Principle 1

The child shall enjoy all the rights set forth in this Declaration. Every child, without any exception whatsoever, shall be entitled to these rights, without distinction or discrimination on account of race, colour, sex, language, religion, political or other opinion, national or social origin, property, birth or other status, whether of himself or of his family.

Principle 2

The child shall enjoy special protection, and shall be given opportunities and facilities, by law and by other means, to enable him to develop physically, mentally, morally, spiritually and socially in a healthy and normal manner and in conditions of freedom and dignity. In the enactment of laws for this purpose, the best interests of the child shall be the paramount consideration.

Principle 3

The child shall be entitled from his birth to a name and a nationality.

Principle 4

The child shall enjoy the benefits of social security. He shall be entitled to grow and develop in health; to this end, special care and protection shall be provided both to him and to his mother, including adequate pre-natal and post-natal care. The child shall have the right to adequate nutrition, housing, recreation and medical services.

Principle 5

The child who is physically, mentally or socially handicapped shall be given the special treatment, education and care required by his particular condition.

Principle 6

The child, for the full and harmonious development of his personality, needs love and understanding. He shall, wherever possible, grow up in the care and under the responsibility of his parents, and, in any case, in an atmosphere of affection and of moral and material security; a child of tender years shall not, save in exceptional circumstances, be separated from his mother. Society and the public authorities shall have the duty to extend particular care to children without a family and to those without adequate means of support. Payment of State and other assistance towards the maintenance of children of large families is desirable.

Principle 7

The child is entitled to receive education, which shall be free and compulsory, at least in the elementary stages. He shall be given an education which will promote his general culture and enable him, on a basis of equal opportunity, to develop his abilities, his individual judgment, and his sense of moral and social responsibility, and to become a useful member of society.

The best interests of the child shall be the guiding principle of those responsible for his education and guidance; that responsibility lies in the first place with his parents.

The child shall have full opportunity for play and recreation, which should be directed to the same purposes as education; society and the public authorities shall endeavour to promote the enjoyment of this right.

Principle 8

The child shall in all circumstances be among the first to receive protection and relief.

Principle 9

The child shall be protected against all forms of neglect, cruelty and exploitation. He shall not be the subject of traffic, in any form.

The child shall not be admitted to employment before an appropriate minimum age; he shall in no case be caused or permitted to engage in any occupation or employment which would prejudice his health or education, or interfere with his physical, mental or moral development.

Principle 10

The child shall be protected from practices which may foster racial, religious and any other form of discrimination. He shall be brought up in a spirit of understanding, tolerance, friendship among peoples, peace and universal brotherhood, and in full consciousness that his energy and talents should be devoted to the service of his fellow men.

NOTES AND QUESTIONS

1. The foundation for the United Nations was laid in 1944 at a meeting among representatives from China, the United Kingdom, the United States, and the Union of Soviet Socialist

Republics at Dumbarton Oaks in Washington, D.C. The final text of an agreement was worked out between April and June 1945, and on June 26, 1945, fifty countries signed the Charter of the United Nations in San Francisco. (Poland, the fifty-first country, was not able to send a representative to the San Francisco conference but is considered an original member.) The United Nations officially came into existence on October 24, 1945.

The UN has the authority to take action on a wide range of issues, including peacekeeping, conflict prevention, promoting social progress and human rights, and providing humanitarian assistance. Today there are 192 member states, each with a single vote in the General Assembly, the chief representative and policy-making body. The General Assembly may make only non-binding recommendations to the member states.

2. A declaration is not legally binding on the assenting member states but carries with it some moral authority because it represents a statement of the international community. Why, then, should the UN ever bother to adopt declarations?

3. In what ways does the UN Declaration differ from the Geneva Declaration? Is the concern raised by Janusz Korczak about the Geneva Convention adequately addressed in the UN Declaration? Does the UN Declaration acknowledge that children have rights? If so, what are they?

United Nations Convention on the Rights of the Child, adopted Nov. 20, 1989, 1577 U.N.T.S. 3 (entered into force Sept. 2, 1990).

... **Article 3**

1. In all actions concerning children, whether undertaken by public or private social welfare institutions, courts of law, administrative authorities or legislative bodies, the best interests of the child shall be a primary consideration.
2. States Parties undertake to ensure the child such protection and care as is necessary for his or her well-being, taking into account the rights and duties of his or her parents, legal guardians, or other individuals legally responsible for him or her, and, to this end, shall take all appropriate legislative and administrative measures.
3. States Parties shall ensure that the institutions, services and facilities responsible for the care or protection of children shall conform with the standards established by competent authorities, particularly in the areas of safety, health, in the number and suitability of their staff, as well as competent supervision....

Article 5

States Parties shall respect the responsibilities, rights and duties of parents or, where applicable, the members of the extended family or community as provided for by local custom, legal guardians or other persons legally responsible for the child, to provide, in a manner consistent with the evolving capacities of the child, appropriate direction and guidance in the exercise by the child of the rights recognized in the present Convention.

Article 6

1. States Parties recognize that every child has the inherent right to life.
2. States Parties shall ensure to the maximum extent possible the survival and development of the child.

Article 7

1. The child shall be registered immediately after birth and shall have the right from birth to a name, the right to acquire a nationality and, as far as possible, the right to know and be cared for by his or her parents.
2. States Parties shall ensure the implementation of these rights in accordance with their national law and their obligations under the relevant international instruments in this field, in particular where the child would otherwise be stateless.

Article 8

1. States Parties undertake to respect the right of the child to preserve his or her identity, including nationality, name and family relations as recognized by law without unlawful interference.
2. Where a child is illegally deprived of some or all of the elements of his or her identity, States Parties shall provide appropriate assistance and protection, with a view to re-establishing speedily his or her identity.

Article 9

1. States Parties shall ensure that a child shall not be separated from his or her parents against their will, except when competent authorities subject to judicial review determine, in accordance with applicable law and procedures, that such separation is necessary for the best interests of the child. Such determination may be necessary in a particular case such as one involving abuse or neglect of the child by the parents, or one where the parents are living separately and a decision must be made as to the child's place of residence.
2. In any proceedings pursuant to paragraph 1 of the present article, all interested parties shall be given an opportunity to participate in the proceedings and make their views known.
3. States Parties shall respect the right of the child who is separated from one or both parents to maintain personal relations and direct contact with both parents on a regular basis, except if it is contrary to the child's best interests.
4. Where such separation results from any action initiated by a State Party, such as the detention, imprisonment, exile, deportation or death (including death arising from any cause while the person is in the custody of the State) of one or both parents or of the child, that State Party shall, upon request, provide the parents, the child or, if appropriate, another member of the family with the essential information concerning the whereabouts of the absent member(s) of the family unless the provision of the information would be detrimental to the well-being of the child. States Parties shall further ensure that the submission of such a request shall of itself entail no adverse consequences for the person(s) concerned.

Article 10...

2. A child whose parents reside in different States shall have the right to maintain on a regular basis, save in exceptional circumstances personal relations and direct contacts with both parents....

Article 12

1. States Parties shall assure to the child who is capable of forming his or her own views the right to express those views freely in all matters affecting the child, the views of the child being given due weight in accordance with the age and maturity of the child.
2. For this purpose, the child shall in particular be provided the opportunity to be heard in any judicial and administrative proceedings affecting the child, either directly, or through a representative or an appropriate body, in a manner consistent with the procedural rules of national law.

Article 13

1. The child shall have the right to freedom of expression; this right shall include freedom to seek, receive and impart information and ideas of all kinds, regardless of frontiers, either orally, in writing or in print, in the form of art, or through any other media of the child's choice....

Article 14

1. States Parties shall respect the right of the child to freedom of thought, conscience, and religion.
2. States Parties shall respect the rights and duties of the parents and, when applicable, legal guardians, to provide direction to the child in the exercise of his or her right in a manner consistent with the evolving capacities of the child.
3. Freedom to manifest one's religion or beliefs may be subject only to such limitations as are prescribed by law and are necessary to protect public safety, order, health or morals, or the fundamental rights and freedoms of others.

Article 15

1. States Parties recognize the rights of the child to freedom of association and to freedom of peaceful assembly....

Article 16

1. No child shall be subjected to arbitrary or unlawful interference with his or her privacy, family, home or correspondence, nor to unlawful attacks on his or her honour and reputation.
2. The child has the right to the protection of the law against such interference or attacks....

Article 18...

3. States Parties shall take all appropriate measures to ensure that children of working parents have the right to benefit from child-care services and facilities for which they are eligible.

Article 19

1. States Parties shall take all appropriate legislative, administrative, social and educational measures to protect the child from all forms of physical or mental violence, injury or abuse, neglect or negligent treatment, maltreatment or exploitation, including sexual abuse, while in the care of parent(s), legal guardian(s) or any other person who has the care of the child....

Article 23...

2. States Parties recognize the right of the disabled child to special care and shall encourage and ensure the extension, subject to available resources, to the eligible child and those responsible for his or her care, of assistance for which application is made and which is appropriate to the child's condition and to the circumstances of the parents or others caring for the child.
3. Recognizing the special needs of a disabled child, assistance extended in accordance with paragraph 2 of the present article shall be provided free of charge, whenever possible, taking into account the financial resources of the parents or others caring for the child and shall be designed to ensure that the disabled child has effective access to and receives education, training, health care services, rehabilitation services, preparation for employment and recreation opportunities in a manner conducive to the child's achieving the fullest possible social integration and individual development, including his or her cultural and spiritual development....

Article 24

1. States Parties recognize the right of the child to the enjoyment of the highest attainable standard of health and to facilities for the treatment of illness and rehabilitation of health....

Article 25

States Parties recognize the right of a child who has been placed by the competent authorities for the purposes of care, protection or treatment of his or her physical or mental health, to a periodic review of the treatment provided to the child and all other circumstances relevant to his or her placement.

Article 26

1. States Parties shall recognize for every child the right to benefit from social security, including social insurance, and shall take the necessary measures to achieve the full realization of this right in accordance with their national law....

Article 27

1. States Parties recognize the right of every child to a standard of living adequate for the child's physical, mental, spiritual, moral and social development....

Article 28

1. States Parties recognize the right of the child to education....

Article 30

In those States in which ethnic, religious or linguistic minorities or persons of indigenous origin exist, a child belonging to such a minority or who is indigenous shall not be denied the right, in community with other members of his or her group, to enjoy his or her own culture, to profess and practise his or her own religion, or to use his or her own language.

Article 31

1. States Parties recognize the right of the child to rest and leisure, to engage in play and recreational activities appropriate to the age of the child and to participate freely in cultural life and the arts.
2. States Parties shall respect and promote the right of the child to participate fully in cultural and artistic life and shall encourage the provision of appropriate and equal opportunities for cultural, artistic, recreational and leisure activity.

Article 32

1. States Parties recognize the right of the child to be protected from economic exploitation and from performing any work that is likely to be hazardous or to interfere with the child's education, or to be harmful to the child's health or physical, mental, spiritual, moral or social development....

Article 40

1. States Parties recognize the right of every child alleged as, accused of, or recognized as having infringed the penal law to be treated in a manner consistent with the promotion of the child's sense of dignity and worth, which reinforces the child's respect for the human rights and fundamental freedoms of others and which takes into account the child's age and the desirability of promoting the child's reintegration and the child's assuming a constructive role in society....
2. To this end, and having regard to the relevant provisions of international instruments, States Parties shall, in particular, ensure that...
   (b) Every child alleged as or accused of having infringed the penal law has at least the following guarantees:
      (i) To be presumed innocent until proven guilty according to law;
      (ii) To be informed promptly and directly of the charges against him or her, and, if appropriate, through his or her parents or legal guardians, and to have legal or other appropriate assistance in the preparation and presentation of his or her defence;

(iii) To have the matter determined without delay by a competent, independent and impartial authority or judicial body in a fair hearing according to law, in the presence of legal or other appropriate assistance and, unless it is considered not to be in the best interest of the child, in particular, taking into account his or her age or situation, his or her parents or legal guardians;

(iv) Not to be compelled to give testimony or to confess guilt; to examine or have examined adverse witnesses and to obtain the participation and examination of witnesses on his or her behalf under conditions of equality;

(v) If considered to have infringed the penal law, to have this decision and any measures imposed in consequence thereof reviewed by a higher competent, independent and impartial authority or judicial body according to law;

(vi) To have the free assistance of an interpreter if the child cannot understand or speak the language used;

(vii) To have his or her privacy fully respected at all stages of the proceedings.

3. States Parties shall seek to promote the establishment of laws, procedures, authorities and institutions specifically applicable to children alleged as, accused of, or recognized as having infringed the penal law, and, in particular:

(a) The establishment of a minimum age below which children shall be presumed not to have the capacity to infringe the penal law;

(b) Whenever appropriate and desirable, measures for dealing with such children without resorting to judicial proceedings, providing that human rights and legal safeguards are fully respected....

Article 43

1. For the purpose of examining the progress made by States Parties in achieving the realization of the obligations undertaken in the present Convention, there shall be established a Committee on the Rights of the Child, which shall carry out the functions hereinafter provided.

NOTES AND QUESTIONS

1. The text of the Convention was adopted by the General Assembly on November 29, 1989. Unlike a declaration, a convention is a legally binding treaty. Twenty states must ratify the Convention on the Rights of the Child for it to be enforceable against states parties. To date, the Convention on the Rights of the Child has been ratified by 193 countries. Only two, Somalia (which has no formal government) and the United States, have yet to ratify. The U.S. Delegate to the UN under President Bill Clinton, Madeleine Albright, signed the Convention in 1995, but it has never been forwarded to the Senate for its consent to ratification.

By its own terms, states that have ratified the Convention must submit a report to the UN Committee on the Rights of the Child regarding their implementation of the Convention. The committee is made up of a group of experts elected by the UN General Assembly that meets in Geneva three times a year. After the report's submission, a state's governmental delegation meets with the committee to review its laws and practices. The committee then issues recommendations. Subsequent reports must be submitted every five years.

2. The failure of the United States to ratify stems from numerous legal, political, and religious objections to the Convention. Under U.S. law, two-thirds of the Senate must consent before the president may ratify a treaty. Traditionally, the United States has been reluctant to submit to international legal obligations, so it is unsurprising that there is some resistance to ratifying the Convention. Moreover, because the Convention, if ratified, would be federal law, it would usurp a traditional state role in regulating children and families.

Political conservative organizations (and particularly religious groups) have vigorously opposed the Convention, arguing that it usurps state and federal authority, undermines parents, and will destroy families. These groups, including Focus on the Family, the John Birch Society, the Family Research Council, and the Christian Coalition, have lobbied members of the Senate to oppose ratification. In June 1995, for example, Senator Jesse Helms, who then was chair of the Senate Foreign Relations Committee, introduced a resolution opposing the Convention because it "undermined the rights of the family." Do you think this is a valid concern? What articles support this contention? What articles undermine this claim?

3. Consider the rights articulated in Articles 24, 26, and 27, and compare them with the rights in Articles 13, 14, 15, and 16. Are they the same or different? Do they differ appreciably from rights already accorded under the U.S. Constitution? Is there historical and/or philosophical support for the extension of these rights to children? To what extent does federal law provide for many of the rights articulated in the Convention?

4. On May 25, 2000, the UN adopted two optional protocols to the Convention. (A protocol is essentially an amendment to an existing treaty.) The first, the Optional Protocol to the Convention on the Rights of the Child on the Involvement of Children in Armed Conflicts, G.A. Res. 54/263, Annex I, U.N. Docs. A/RES/54/263 (May 25, 2000), states that anyone under the age of eighteen may not be conscripted into the armed forces (although volunteers are permissible) and should not take a direct part in hostilities. The second, the Optional Protocol to the Convention on the Rights of the Child on the Sale of Children, Child Prostitution and Child Pornography, G.A. Res. 54/263, Annex II, U.N. Doc. A/RES/54/263 (May 25, 2000), prohibits the sale of children, child prostitution, and child pornography. The United States ratified both protocols on December 23, 2002, but with a number of reservations, including the understanding that the United States does not become a party to the Convention on the Rights of the Child. (A reservation purports to exclude or modify the legal effect of a treaty with respect to the state making the reservation.) The United States submits regular reports to the Committee on the Rights of the Child regarding its compliance with the optional protocols. Why would the United States ratify the protocols but not the Convention?

5. How should the Convention accommodate cultural differences? Michael Freeman states that the Convention adopts a universalist response, in that rights may be determined by reference to certain overriding values that would displace cultural norms or practices. Michael D. A. Freeman, *Introduction*, in 1 Children's Rights xi, xxv–xxvi (Michael D. A. Freeman, ed., 2004). Philip Alston, who served as UNICEF's legal adviser throughout the period of the drafting of the Convention, explains that the universality of the Convention is possible largely because of the demise of the Cold War. He contends that the ideological divide over the primacy of civil and political rights (Western) versus economic, social, and cultural rights (Eastern) largely suppressed debate about the degree to which cultural norms should be accounted for in

human rights formulations. The end of the Cold War, however, largely freed the drafting process from the East-West political debate, resulting in a document embracing universal human rights norms. Philip Alston, *The Best Interests Principle: Towards a Reconciliation of Culture and Human Rights*, in THE BEST INTERESTS OF THE CHILD 1, 5–7 (Philip Alston, ed., 1994). Is this the correct approach? To what extent should cultural norms trump rights norms? Alston argues that while culture is a factor to be considered, it must "not be accorded the status of a metanorm which trumps rights." *Id.* at 20. Others concur, warning that cultural relativism is used to mask repressive state practices resulting in violations of human rights norms. Adamantia Pollis, *Cultural Relativism Revisited: Through a State Prism*, 18 HUM. RTS. Q. 316, 322 (1996); Jack Donnelly, *Cultural Relativism and Universal Human Rights*, in HUMAN RIGHTS IN THEORY AND PRACTICE 109, 118–121 (Jack Donnelly, ed., 1989). Do you agree?

To what extent do states parties to the Convention raise cultural values, norms, or traditions when submitting periodic reports to the Committee on the Rights of the Child? In one study of the reports to the committee, states parties appear to embrace the Convention and its universality but describe a struggle between an "enlightened state" and a populace resistant to cultural change. Although such contentions may mask governmental inaction or delay, deflect attention from governmental policies that have negative impact on the child, or exaggerate cultural difference, the author found little evidence of state manipulation or misrepresentation. Rather, the challenge is whether the universal human rights norms articulated by the Convention will have any real force in the absence of broad acceptance at the grassroots level. Sonia Harris-Short, *International Human Rights Law: Imperialist, Inept and Ineffective? Cultural Relativism and the UN Convention on the Rights of the Child*, 25 HUM. RTS. Q. 130, 164–167, 173 (2003). Should each society embrace and implement the principles articulated by the Convention? Or is this merely an attempt to impose "Western" values on others?

D. Social Science Perspectives

In 1908, the U. S. Supreme Court agreed to hear the appeal of a laundry owner challenging the constitutionality of an Oregon law that limited the workday of any woman or girl who worked in a laundry or factory to ten hours. Two briefs were filed on behalf of the state, one written by an Oregon district attorney, the other by Boston lawyer (and subsequent Supreme Court justice) Louis Brandeis. The mere fact that two briefs were filed was remarkable enough, but the 113-page brief submitted by Brandeis (and coauthored by Josephine C. Goldmark of the National Consumers' League, who received no formal recognition, presumably because she was a nonlawyer) cited data and expert opinions on the social, economic, and physical consequences of an overworked female labor force. The U.S. Supreme Court, noting that the social science data provided in the "Brandeis Brief" (as it came to be known) would receive "judicial cognizance," even though it was not legal authority, unanimously upheld the Oregon law. *Muller v. Oregon*, 208 U.S. 412 (1908). For a brief history of the events surrounding the filing of the Brandeis Brief, see Ronald K. L. Collins & Jennifer Friesen, *Looking Back on Muller v. Oregon*, 69 A.B.A. J. 294 (1983).

Since the Brandeis Brief was filed, judges, lawyers, and legislators have relied on social science to inform policy making and resolve disputes. But what exactly is social science? Typically, when we speak of social science, we mean those fields of study that explore certain aspects of human society and interaction. They may include sociology, criminology, history, psychology, political science, and economics. Social scientists may use multiple methodologies when examining their subjects, some of which may be empirical and thus more "scientific," while others may be more interpretive.

John Monahan and Laurens Walker at the University of Virginia School of Law contend that social science typically is used as a legal analytical tool in four different ways. First, social science may be used to determine the particular facts in a specific case (the "adjudicative facts"). Thus, in a trademark-infringement action, for example, social science research may be used to establish consumer confusion. Social science also may be used to shape legal doctrine ("legislative facts"). In school-desegregation cases, for example, social science was used to highlight the effects of desegregation on African-American children. Third, social science may be used to provide a framework for deciding the facts of the present case by relying on more generalized research findings (for example, research demonstrating the characteristics of battered-child syndrome as evidence that the child in question has been battered). Last, social science may be used to develop litigation strategies (using social science to select the "best" jury in a criminal case, for example). John Monahan & Laurens Walker, Social Science in Law: Cases and Materials (2006).

1. THE LEGAL APPROACH

DAUBERT V. MERRELL DOW PHARMACEUTICALS
Supreme Court of the United States
509 U.S. 579 (1993)

Justice Blackmun delivered the opinion of the Court.

In this case we are called upon to determine the standard for admitting expert scientific testimony in a federal trial.

Petitioners Jason Daubert and Eric Schuller are minor children born with serious birth defects. They and their parents sued respondent in California state court, alleging that the birth defects had been caused by the mothers' ingestion of Bendectin, a prescription antinausea drug marketed by respondent. Respondent removed the suits to federal court on diversity grounds.

After extensive discovery, respondent moved for summary judgment, contending that Bendectin does not cause birth defects in humans and that petitioners would be unable to come forward with any admissible evidence that it does. In support of its motion, respondent submitted an affidavit of Steven H. Lamm, physician and epidemiologist, who is a well-credentialed expert on the risks from exposure to various chemical substances. Doctor Lamm stated that he had reviewed all the literature on Bendectin and human birth defects—more than 30 published studies involving over 130,000 patients. No study had found Bendectin to be a human teratogen (*i.e.*, a substance capable of causing malformations in fetuses)....

Petitioners...responded to respondent's motion with the testimony of eight experts of their own, each of whom also possessed impressive credentials. These experts had concluded that Bendectin can cause birth defects. Their conclusions were based upon "in vitro" (test tube) and "in vivo" (live) animal studies that found a link between Bendectin and malformations; pharmacological studies of the chemical structure of Bendectin that purported to show similarities between the structure of the drug and that of other substances known to cause birth defects; and the "reanalysis" of previously published epidemiological (human statistical) studies.

The District Court granted respondent's motion for summary judgment. The court stated that scientific evidence is admissible only if the principle upon which it is based is "'sufficiently established to have general acceptance in the field to which it belongs.'" 727 F.Supp. 570, 572 (S.D. Cal. 1989) quoting *United States v. Kilgus*, 571 F.2d 508, 510 (CA 9 1978). The court concluded that petitioners' evidence did not meet this standard. Given the vast body of epidemiological data concerning Bendectin, the court held, expert opinion which is not based on epidemiological evidence is not admissible to establish causation. 727 F.Supp., at 575. Thus, the animal-cell studies, live-animal studies, and chemical-structure analyses on which petitioners had relied could not raise by themselves a reasonably disputable jury issue regarding causation. *Ibid.* Petitioners' epidemiological analyses, based as they were on recalculations of data in previously published studies that had found no causal link between the drug and birth defects, were ruled to be inadmissible because they had not been published or subjected to peer review. *Ibid.*

The United States Court of Appeals for the Ninth Circuit affirmed. 951 F.2d 1128 (1991). Citing *Frye v. United States,* 54 App.D.C. 46, 47, 293 F. 1013, 1014 (1923), the court stated that expert opinion based on a scientific technique is inadmissible unless the technique is "generally accepted" as reliable in the relevant scientific community. 951 F.2d, at 1129–1130. . . .

In the 70 years since its formulation in the *Frye* case, the "general acceptance" test has been the dominant standard for determining the admissibility of novel scientific evidence at trial. Although under increasing attack of late, the rule continues to be followed by a majority of courts. . . .

The *Frye* test has its origin in a short and citation-free 1923 decision concerning the admissibility of evidence derived from a systolic blood pressure deception test, a crude precursor to the polygraph machine. In what has become a famous (perhaps infamous) passage, the Court of Appeals for the District of Columbia described the device and its operation and declared:

> "Just when a scientific principle or discovery crosses the line between the experimental and demonstrable stages is difficult to define. Somewhere in this twilight zone the evidential force of the principle must be recognized, and while courts will go a long way in admitting expert testimony deduced from a well-recognized scientific principle or discovery, *the thing from which the deduction is made must be sufficiently established to have gained general acceptance in the particular field in which it belongs.*" 54 App.D.C., at 47, 293 F., at 1014 (emphasis added). . . .

The merits of the *Frye* test have been much debated, and scholarship on its proper scope and application is legion. Petitioners' primary attack, however, is not on the content but on the continuing authority of the rule. They contend that the *Frye* test was superseded by the adoption of the Federal Rules of Evidence. We agree. . . .

Rule 702, governing expert testimony, provides:

> "If scientific, technical, or other specialized knowledge will assist the trier of fact to understand the evidence or to determine a fact in issue, a witness qualified as an expert by knowledge, skill, experience, training, or education, may testify thereto in the form of an opinion or otherwise."

Nothing in the text of this Rule establishes "general acceptance" as an absolute prerequisite to admissibility. Nor does respondent present any clear indication that Rule 702 or the Rules as a whole were intended to incorporate a "general acceptance" standard. The drafting history makes no mention of *Frye*, and a rigid "general acceptance" requirement would be at odds with the "liberal thrust" of the Federal Rules and their "general approach of relaxing the traditional barriers to 'opinion' testimony." *Beech Aircraft Corp. v. Rainey,* 488 U.S., at 169 (citing Rules 701 to 705). . . . Given the Rules' permissive backdrop and their inclusion of a specific rule on expert testimony that does not mention "'general acceptance,'" the assertion that the Rules somehow assimilated *Frye* is unconvincing. *Frye* made "general acceptance" the exclusive test for admitting expert scientific testimony. That austere standard, absent from, and incompatible with, the Federal Rules of Evidence, should not be applied in federal trials.

That the *Frye* test was displaced by the Rules of Evidence does not mean, however, that the Rules themselves place no limits on the admissibility of purportedly scientific evidence. Nor is the trial judge disabled from screening such evidence. To the contrary, under the Rules the trial judge must ensure that any and all scientific testimony or evidence admitted is not only relevant, but reliable.

The primary locus of this obligation is Rule 702, which clearly contemplates some degree of regulation of the subjects and theories about which an expert may testify. "*If scientific,* technical, or other specialized *knowledge will assist the trier of fact* to understand the evidence or to determine a fact in issue" an expert "may testify *thereto.*" The subject of an expert's testimony must be "scientific... knowledge." The adjective "scientific" implies a grounding in the methods and procedures of science. Similarly, the word "knowledge" connotes more than subjective belief or unsupported speculation. The term "applies to any body of known facts or to any body of ideas inferred from such facts or accepted as truths on good grounds." Webster's Third New International Dictionary 1252 (1986). Of course, it would be unreasonable to conclude that the subject of scientific testimony must be "known" to a certainty; arguably, there are no certainties in science.... But, in order to qualify as "scientific knowledge," an inference or assertion must be derived by the scientific method. Proposed testimony must be supported by appropriate validation—*i.e.*, "good grounds," based on what is known. In short, the requirement that an expert's testimony pertain to "scientific knowledge" establishes a standard of evidentiary reliability.

Rule 702 further requires that the evidence or testimony "assist the trier of fact to understand the evidence or to determine a fact in issue." This condition goes primarily to relevance. "Expert testimony which does not relate to any issue in the case is not relevant and, ergo, non-helpful." ... Rule 702's "helpfulness" standard requires a valid scientific connection to the pertinent inquiry as a precondition to admissibility....

Faced with a proffer of expert scientific testimony, then, the trial judge must determine at the outset, pursuant to Rule 104(a), whether the expert is proposing to testify to (1) scientific knowledge that (2) will assist the trier of fact to understand or determine a fact in issue. This entails a preliminary assessment of whether the reasoning or methodology underlying the testimony is scientifically valid and of whether that reasoning or methodology properly can be applied to the facts in issue. We are confident that federal judges possess the capacity to undertake this review. Many factors will bear on the inquiry, and we do not presume to set out a definitive checklist or test. But some general observations are appropriate.

Ordinarily, a key question to be answered in determining whether a theory or technique is scientific knowledge that will assist the trier of fact will be whether it can be (and has been) tested. "Scientific methodology today is based on generating hypotheses and testing them to see if they can be falsified; indeed, this methodology is what distinguishes science from other fields of human inquiry." ...

Another pertinent consideration is whether the theory or technique has been subjected to peer review and publication. Publication (which is but one element of peer review) is not a *sine qua non* of admissibility; it does not necessarily correlate with reliability, and in some instances well-grounded but innovative theories will not have been published. Some propositions, moreover, are too particular, too new, or of too limited interest to be published. But submission to the scrutiny of the scientific community is a component of "good science," in part because it increases the likelihood that substantive flaws in methodology will be detected. The fact of publication (or lack thereof) in a peer reviewed journal thus will be a relevant, though not dispositive, consideration in assessing the scientific validity of a particular technique or methodology on which an opinion is premised.

Additionally, in the case of a particular scientific technique, the court ordinarily should consider the known or potential rate of error, ... and the existence and maintenance of standards controlling the technique's operation.

Finally, "general acceptance" can yet have a bearing on the inquiry. A "reliability assessment does not require, although it does permit, explicit identification of a relevant scientific community and an express determination of a particular degree of acceptance within that community." *United States v. Downing,* 753 F.2d, at 1238.... Widespread acceptance can be an important factor in ruling particular evidence admissible, and "a known technique which has been able to attract only minimal support within the community," *Downing,* 753 F.2d, at 1238, may properly be viewed with skepticism.

The inquiry envisioned by Rule 702 is, we emphasize, a flexible one. Its overarching subject is the scientific validity—and thus the evidentiary relevance and reliability—of the principles that underlie a proposed submission. The focus, of course, must be solely on principles and methodology, not on the conclusions that they generate....

To summarize: "General acceptance" is not a necessary precondition to the admissibility of scientific evidence under the Federal Rules of Evidence, but the Rules of Evidence—especially Rule 702—do assign to the trial judge the task of ensuring that an expert's testimony both rests on a reliable foundation and is relevant to the task at hand. Pertinent evidence based on scientifically valid principles will satisfy those demands.

The inquiries of the District Court and the Court of Appeals focused almost exclusively on "general acceptance," as gauged by publication and the decisions of other courts. Accordingly, the judgment of the Court of Appeals is vacated, and the case is remanded for further proceedings consistent with this opinion....

Chief Justice Rehnquist, with whom Justice Stevens joins, concurring in part and dissenting in part.

...The Court concludes, correctly in my view, that the *Frye* rule did not survive the enactment of the Federal Rules of Evidence, and I therefore join Parts I and II-A of its opinion. The second question presented in the petition for certiorari necessarily is mooted by this holding, but the Court nonetheless proceeds to construe Rules 702 and 703 very much in the abstract, and then offers some "general observations."...

The Court speaks of its confidence that federal judges can make a "preliminary assessment of whether the reasoning or methodology underlying the testimony is scientifically valid and of whether that reasoning or methodology properly can be applied to the facts in issue." The Court then states that a "key question" to be answered in deciding whether something is "scientific knowledge" "will be whether it can be (and has been) tested." Following this sentence are three quotations from treatises, which not only speak of empirical testing, but one of which states that the "'criterion of the scientific status of a theory is its falsifiability, or refutability, or testability.'"

I defer to no one in my confidence in federal judges; but I am at a loss to know what is meant when it is said that the scientific status of a theory depends on its "falsifiability," and I suspect some of them will be, too.

I do not doubt that Rule 702 confides to the judge some gatekeeping responsibility in deciding questions of the admissibility of proffered expert testimony. But I do not think it imposes on them either the obligation or the authority to become amateur scientists in order to perform that role. I think the Court would be far better advised in this case to decide only the questions presented, and to leave the further development of this important area of the law to future cases.

DAUBERT V. MERRELL DOW PHARMACEUTICALS
United States Court of Appeals, Ninth Circuit
43 F.3d 1311 (1995)

[On remand from the United States Supreme Court, the Ninth Circuit Court of Appeals determined the admissibility of the plaintiffs' expert testimony rather than remand the case to the district court in the first instance in "the interests of justice and judicial economy" and to offer "guidance on the application of the Daubert standard."]

KOZINSKI, Circuit Judge....

Federal judges ruling on the admissibility of expert scientific testimony face a far more complex and daunting task in a post-*Daubert* world than before.... Under *Daubert,* we must engage in a difficult, two-part analysis. First, we must determine nothing less than whether the experts' testimony reflects "scientific knowledge," whether their findings are "derived by the scientific method," and whether their work product amounts to "good science." 509 U.S. at 589, 593, 113 S.Ct. at 2795, 2797. Second, we must ensure that the proposed expert testimony is "relevant to the task at hand," *id.* at 593, 113 S.Ct. at 2797, i.e., that it logically advances a material aspect of the proposing party's case. The Supreme Court referred to this second prong of the analysis as the "fit" requirement. *Id.* at 591, 113 S.Ct. at 2796.

The first prong of *Daubert* puts federal judges in an uncomfortable position. The question of admissibility only arises if it is first established that the individuals whose testimony is being proffered are experts in a particular scientific field; here, for example, the Supreme Court waxed eloquent on the impressive qualifications of plaintiffs' experts. *Id.* at 580 n. 2, 113 S.Ct. at 2791 n. 2. Yet something doesn't become "scientific knowledge" just because it's uttered by a scientist; nor can an expert's self-serving assertion that his conclusions were "derived by the scientific method" be deemed conclusive, else the Supreme Court's opinion could have ended with footnote two. As we read the Supreme Court's teaching in *Daubert,* therefore, though we are largely untrained in science and certainly no match for any of the witnesses whose testimony we are reviewing, it is our responsibility to determine whether those experts' proposed testimony amounts to "scientific knowledge," constitutes "good science," and was "derived by the scientific method."

The task before us is more daunting still when the dispute concerns matters at the very cutting edge of scientific research, where fact meets theory and certainty dissolves into probability. As the record in this case illustrates, scientists often have vigorous and sincere disagreements as to what research methodology is proper, what should be accepted as sufficient proof for the existence of a "fact," and whether information derived by a particular method can tell us anything useful about the subject under study.

Our responsibility, then, unless we badly misread the Supreme Court's opinion, is to resolve disputes among respected, well-credentialed scientists about matters squarely within their expertise, in areas where there is no scientific consensus as to what is and what is not "good science," and occasionally to reject such expert testimony because it was not "derived by the scientific method." Mindful of our position in the hierarchy of the federal judiciary, we take a deep breath and proceed with this heady task....

The Supreme Court's opinion in *Daubert* focuses closely on the language of Fed.R.Evid. 702, which permits opinion testimony by experts as to matters amounting to "scientific... knowledge." The Court recognized, however, that knowledge in this context does not mean absolute certainty. 509 U.S. at 589, 113 S.Ct. at 2795. Rather, the Court said, "in order to qualify as 'scientific knowledge,' an inference or assertion must be derived by the scientific method." *Id.* Elsewhere in its opinion, the Court noted that Rule 702 is satisfied where the proffered testimony is "based on scientifically valid principles." *Id.* at 597, 113 S.Ct. at 2799. Our task, then, is to analyze not what the experts say, but what basis they have for saying it.

Which raises the question: How do we figure out whether scientists have derived their findings through the scientific method or whether their testimony is based on scientifically valid principles? Each expert proffered by the plaintiffs assures us that he has "utiliz[ed] the type of data that is generally and reasonably relied upon by scientists" in the relevant field, *see, e.g.*, Newman Aff. at 5, and that he has "utilized the methods and methodology that would generally and reasonably be accepted" by people who deal in these matters, *see, e.g.*, Gross Aff. at 5. The Court held, however, that federal judges perform a "gatekeeping role," *Daubert*, 509 U.S. at 595, 113 S.Ct. at 2798; to do so they must satisfy themselves that scientific evidence meets a certain standard of reliability before it is admitted. This means that the expert's bald assurance of validity is not enough. Rather, the party presenting the expert must show that the expert's findings are based on sound science, and this will require some objective, independent validation of the expert's methodology.

While declining to set forth a "definitive checklist or test," *id.* at 591, 113 S.Ct. at 2796, the Court did list several factors federal judges can consider in determining whether to admit expert scientific testimony under Fed.R.Evid. 702: whether the theory or technique employed by the expert is generally accepted in the scientific community; whether it's been subjected to peer review and publication; whether it can be and has been tested; and whether the known or potential rate of error is acceptable. *Id.* at 591–593, 113 S.Ct. at 2796–97. We read these factors as illustrative rather than exhaustive; similarly, we do not deem each of them to be equally applicable (or applicable at all) in every case. Rather, we read the Supreme Court as instructing us to determine whether the analysis undergirding the experts' testimony falls within the range of accepted standards governing how scientists conduct their research and reach their conclusions.

One very significant fact to be considered is whether the experts are proposing to testify about matters growing naturally and directly out of research they have conducted independent of the litigation, or whether they have developed their opinions expressly for purposes of testifying. That an expert testifies for money does not necessarily cast doubt on the reliability of his testimony, as few experts appear in court merely as an eleemosynary gesture. But in determining whether proposed expert testimony amounts to good science, we may not ignore the fact that a scientist's normal workplace is the lab or the field, not the courtroom or the lawyer's office.

That an expert testifies based on research he has conducted independent of the litigation provides important, objective proof that the research comports with the dictates of good science. *See* Peter W. Huber, Galileo's Revenge: Junk Science in the Courtroom 206–09 (1991) (describing how the prevalent practice of expert-shopping leads to bad science). For one thing, experts whose findings flow from existing research are less likely to have been biased toward a particular conclusion by the promise of remuneration; when an expert prepares reports and findings before being hired as a witness, that record will limit the degree to which he can tailor his testimony to serve a party's interests. Then, too, independent research carries its own indicia of reliability, as it is conducted, so to speak, in the usual course of business and must normally satisfy a variety of standards to attract funding and institutional support. Finally, there is usually a limited number of scientists actively conducting research on the very subject that is germane to a particular case, which provides a natural constraint on parties' ability to shop for experts who will come to the desired conclusion. That the testimony proffered by an expert is based directly on legitimate, preexisting research unrelated to the litigation provides the most persuasive basis for concluding that the opinions he expresses were "derived by the scientific method."

We have examined carefully the affidavits proffered by plaintiffs' experts, as well as the testimony from prior trials that plaintiffs have introduced in support of that testimony, and find that none of the experts based his testimony on preexisting or independent research. While plaintiffs' scientists are all experts in their respective fields, none claims to have studied the effect of Bendectin on limb reduction defects before being hired to testify in this or related cases.

If the proffered expert testimony is not based on independent research, the party proffering it must come forward with other objective, verifiable evidence that the testimony is based on "scientifically valid principles." One means of showing this is by proof that the research and analysis supporting the proffered conclusions have been subjected to normal scientific scrutiny through peer review and publication. Huber, Galileo's Revenge at 209 (suggesting that "[t]he ultimate test of [a scientific expert's] integrity is her readiness to publish and be damned").

Peer review and publication do not, of course, guarantee that the conclusions reached are correct; much published scientific research is greeted with intense skepticism and is not borne out by further research. But the test under *Daubert* is not the correctness of the expert's conclusions but the soundness of his methodology. That the research is accepted for publication in a reputable scientific journal after being subjected to the usual rigors of peer review is a significant indication that it is taken seriously by other scientists, i.e., that it meets at least the minimal criteria of good science. *Daubert,* 509 U.S. at 593, 113 S.Ct. at 2797 ("[S]crutiny of the scientific community is a component of 'good science'"). If nothing else, peer review and publication "increase the likelihood that substantive flaws in methodology will be detected." *Daubert,* 509 U.S. at 593, 113 S.Ct. at 2797.

Bendectin litigation has been pending in the courts for over a decade, yet the only review the plaintiffs' experts' work has received has been by judges and juries, and the only place their theories and studies have been published is in the pages of federal and state reporters. None of the plaintiffs' experts has published his work on Bendectin in a scientific journal or solicited formal review by his colleagues. Despite the many years the controversy has been brewing, no one in the scientific community—except defendant's experts—has deemed these studies worthy of verification, refutation or even comment. It's as if there were a tacit understanding within the scientific community that what's going on here is not science at all, but litigation.

Establishing that an expert's proffered testimony grows out of pre-litigation research or that the expert's research has been subjected to peer review are the two principal ways the proponent of expert testimony can show that the evidence satisfies the first prong of Rule 702. Where such evidence is unavailable, the proponent of expert scientific testimony may attempt to satisfy its burden through the testimony of its own experts. For such a showing to be sufficient, the experts must explain precisely how they went about reaching their conclusions and point to some objective source—a learned treatise, the policy statement of a professional association, a published article in a reputable scientific journal or the like—to show that they have followed the scientific method, as it is practiced by (at least) a recognized minority of scientists in their field. *See United States v. Rincon,* 28 F.3d 921, 924 (9th Cir. 1994) (research must be described "in sufficient detail that the district court [can] determine if the research was scientifically valid").

Plaintiffs have made no such showing. As noted above, plaintiffs rely entirely on the experts' unadorned assertions that the methodology they employed comports with standard scientific procedures. In support of these assertions, plaintiffs offer only the trial and deposition testimony of these experts in other cases. While these materials indicate that plaintiffs' experts have relied on animal studies, chemical structure analyses and epidemiological data, they neither explain the methodology the experts followed to reach their conclusions nor point to any external source to validate that methodology. We've been presented with only the experts' qualifications, their conclusions and their assurances of reliability. Under *Daubert,* that's not enough....

In elucidating the second requirement of Rule 702, *Daubert* stressed the importance of the "fit" between the testimony and an issue in the case: "Rule 702's 'helpfulness' standard requires a valid scientific connection to the pertinent inquiry as a precondition to admissibility." 509 U.S. at 591, 113 S.Ct. at 2796. Here, the pertinent inquiry is causation. In assessing whether the proffered expert testimony "will assist the trier of fact" in resolving this issue, we must look to the governing substantive standard, which in this case is supplied by California tort law....

California tort law requires plaintiffs to show not merely that Bendectin increased the likelihood of injury, but that it more likely than not caused *their* injuries....

As the district court properly found below, "the strongest inference to be drawn for plaintiffs based on the epidemiological evidence is that Bendectin could *possibly* have caused plaintiffs' injuries." 727 F.Supp. at 576. The same is true of the other testimony derived from animal studies and chemical structure analyses-these experts "testify to a possibility rather than a probability." Plaintiffs do not quantify this possibility, or otherwise indicate how their conclusions about causation should be weighted, even though the substantive legal standard has always required proof of causation by a preponderance of the evidence....

The district court's grant of summary judgment is **AFFIRMED.**

NOTES AND QUESTIONS

1. Do you think the Ninth Circuit correctly applied the *Daubert* test? Does it differ in any appreciable way from the *Frye* test? If you were the district court judge, what else would you like to know before ruling on the admissibility of the expert testimony?

2. In *General Electric Company v. Joiner,* 522 U.S. 136 (1997), the U.S. Supreme Court held that an appellate court should apply an abuse of discretion standard when reviewing the decision of a trial court to accept or admit expert testimony. Two years later, the Court made it clear that *Daubert* applied to all expert testimony, not just to scientific expert testimony. *Kumho Tire Company v. Carmichael,* 526 U.S. 137 (1999). Rule 702 of the Federal Rules of Evidence was amended in 2000 to reflect the Court's decisions in *Daubert* and *Kumho.*

3. The Federal Judicial Center, headed by Judge William Schwarzer, anticipated the Supreme Court's decision in *Daubert* and published the first edition of the *Reference Manual on Scientific Evidence* shortly after the opinion was released. David L. Faigman, *The Tipping Point in the Law's Use of Science: The Epidemic of Scientific Sophistication That Begins with DNA Profiling*

and Toxic Torts, 67 BROOKLYN L. REV. 111, 122 (2001). The Federal Judicial Center now maintains an online publication, the 1,038-page *Reference Manual on Scientific Evidence* (2d ed., 2000), http://www.fjc.gov/public/pdf.nsf/lookup/SciMan3D01.pdf/$file/SciMan3D01.pdf, that is freely accessible. Do you agree with the *Daubert* Court that judges are capable of making an assessment about the scientific validity of proffered expert testimony? Does the need for a 1,038-page reference manual support or undermine your confidence in the ability of judges to review scientific evidence critically?

4. Justice Blackmun, who authored the opinion in *Daubert*, was actively interested in science. Before joining the Supreme Court, Blackmun served as general counsel to the Mayo Clinic, where he returned the summer before writing *Roe v. Wade*, 410 U.S. 113 (1973), to research medical issues related to pregnancy. His opinion in *Ballew v. Georgia*, 435 U.S. 223 (1978), also relied on empirical research. Faigman, *The Tipping Point*, 120–121.

5. Twenty-five states have adopted the *Daubert* test, fifteen states and the District of Columbia continue to apply the *Frye* test, six states apply *Daubert* factors but have not specifically rejected the *Frye* test, and four states have developed their own tests. See Alice B. Lustre, *Annotation, Post-Daubert Standards for Admissibility of Scientific and Other Expert Evidence in State Courts*, 90 A.L.R. 5th 453 (Supp. 2010).

6. Despite a general scientific consensus by the mid-1980s that Bendectin was not a teratogen (a substance causing malformation in an embryo), litigation continued for at least another decade. Merrell Dow withdrew Bendectin from the U.S. market, largely in response to the litigation. The U.S. Food and Drug Administration concluded that Bendectin was safe, as did officials in a number of other countries where the drug was sold, including Canada, Switzerland, West Germany, Australia, and the United Kingdom. (The drug, available under the brand name Diclectin, is available through prescription in Canada.) Some criticized the litigation as evidence that the tort system had gone awry. For in-depth analyses of the Bendectin litigation, see JOSEPH SANDERS, BENDECTIN ON TRIAL: A STUDY OF MASS TORT LITIGATION (1998); MICHAEL D. GREEN, BENDECTIN AND BIRTH DEFECTS: THE CHALLENGES OF MASS TOXIC SUBSTANCES LITIGATION (1996).

2. SOCIAL SCIENCE METHODOLOGIES

Robert F. Kelly & Sarah H. Ramsey, *Assessing and Communicating Social Science Information in Family and Child Judicial Settings: Standards for Judges and Allied Professionals*, 45 FAM. CT. REV. 22, 23–34 (2007).

It is useful to think of the scientific method and its emphasis on process and standards as a large, funnel-shaped filter.... There are three major levels of filtration and each is associated with certain fundamental elements of the scientific method. They are: (1) a system of logic based on empirical testing by which scientific inferences are made; (2) a system of standards by which research designs and analyses may be judged; and (3) a system of social practices through which the scientific community socializes it[s] members, judges new knowledge, and communicates and integrates this knowledge. Claims that have fared well through most or all of these three levels of filtration constitute the current state of scientific knowledge. Scientific knowledge evolves over time and is never a definitively settled matter....

Conceptually, it is also important to distinguish between two types of social science claims that family courts may consider, *direct research claims* and *science-based practice claims*. In a direct research claim, an expert witness, brief, book, article, or speaker makes direct reference to findings from a particular study or body of social science literature....The second type of social science claim, science-based practice claim, is less direct in that an expert, who may not be a social scientist, proffers information to the court, usually about a specific party in the case, that is formed from the expert's use of an assessment or clinical strategy that is based in scientific literature....

FILTRATION LEVEL 1...THE LOGIC OF SCIENTIFIC INFERENCE, FALSIFIABLE CLAIMS, AND TESTING

The logical system that science uses to produce knowledge begins with causal claims about how a certain system operates; in the social sciences these claims concern social systems such as the family, education, the economy, or government. The claims normally are stated as hypotheses, in which there is a suspected cause (an independent variable) and suspected effect (a dependent variable)....

A fundamental element of any hypothesis is that it must be stated in a manner that is falsifiable....A second fundamental element of the logic of science requires that hypotheses be rigorously tested against empirical reality to determine if they are supported or falsified. It is through this continuous process of stating hypotheses in falsifiable terms and testing them that theories are developed and scientific progress is made. If there is no empirical testing, which can prove hypotheses false, there is no science. Importantly, these fundamental elements in the logic of science are contained in *Daubert*: Can the scientific claim be empirically tested and has it been empirically tested?...

...[A]ll scientific hypotheses, even if repeatedly supported, must remain subject to future testing and falsification. This means that, when any form of scientific information, including social science information, is presented in judicial settings, the court should seek to determine whether it is the best information available at that time—not the true information for all time....

FILTRATION LEVEL 2...FOUR TYPES OF METHODOLOGICAL VALIDITY

For the empirical testing of falsifiable hypotheses required by the logic of scientific inference to be meaningful, a rigorous methodology must be employed to conduct the testing....The requirement for methodological rigor aligns with the second *Daubert* standard, namely that there should be an acceptable error rate in the methods or techniques used to test the claim. In the social sciences, methodological rigor may be assessed in terms of four types of validity related to data collection, design, and analysis. [They are measurement validity, internal validity and causal inference, external validity, and analytic validity.]

1. Measurement Validity

...Measurement validity is the ability of a given research protocol to measure what it intends to measure....

The underlying logic for assessing measurement validity typically involves two determinations. First, the degree to which the measure gives consistent results when applied to the same or similar subjects under the same conditions must be determined—this is called reliability. Second, it must be determined whether the measure makes sense in the real world and is related in a predictable manner to other independently derived measures of the same concept or theoretically related concepts. When a measure repeatedly passes tests of its validity, it is said to be well-validated....

2. Internal Validity and Causal Inference

Internal validity is an assessment of the rigor with which a design can test a hypothesis such as X causes Y....

Achieving high internal validity requires a design that meets two conditions. First, the design needs a group of participants who were exposed to the independent variable (the experimental group) that can be compared to a group that was not exposed (the control group) on the dependent variable.... Second, these comparison groups must be constructed in a manner that reasonably neutralizes confounding influences. Achieving these two conditions requires some type of control group or the use of techniques that simulate a control group. A control group is not exposed to the independent variable treatment of interest, but is as similar as possible in other relevant ways to the group that did receive the treatment.

In the social sciences a variety of research designs are used to meet these conditions and these designs vary in their degree of internal validity. The most rigorous and therefore the most ideal of these designs is the *classic randomized experiment* in which random assignment is used to create experimental and control groups. The least rigorous of these designs is the one-group pretest/posttest design in which there is no control group. Between these poles of rigor in internal validity is a class of designs referred to as *quasi-experimental designs* in which a control group of some type exists, but the control group has not been produced by random assignment. For ethical, political, and other reasons, it is not always possible to use randomized field experiments and, as a result, quasi-experimental designs are commonly used in the social sciences....

...If...the study has neither a control group nor a reasonable approximation to one, the findings should be treated with substantial skepticism because the study has not addressed the problem of plausible alternative explanations....

3. External Validity: Sampling, Generalizing, and Fit between Research and Legal Applications

A third fundamental methodological standard is external validity, which refers to the appropriate generalization and use of research findings [and] may be defined as the degree to which a study's results may be generalized to populations and conditions beyond the actual subjects and conditions of the study....

When considering external validity, a key initial concern is whether the participants in the study are representative of the population the study wishes to represent. Samples may be selected in many ways, but it is well understood that the optimal way to select a sample is with a random function, which results in random or probability samples....

Even when samples are randomly selected, the representativeness of the resulting sample may be subverted by a low response rate, that is, the people who decide not to participate in the study may differ systematically from those who do participate, thereby creating a biased sample. Similar problems, referred to generically as *selection bias*, also occur due to nonparticipation in censuses of entire populations. Attrition, a loss of participants over time in longitudinal sample or population studies, also creates selection bias concerns....

...[T]here is another external validity issue related to the use of social science research in judicial proceedings, namely the nature and degree of fit between the research and its intended legal application [that is, its] relevance...to the legal issue.... First, it is essential to consider the extent to which the research is related to the legal question the court is addressing, because often there is little or no directly related social science research available....

Second, in determining the degree of relevance of research findings to a specific case, it is important to be mindful that it is problematic to make direct inferences from research based on population or sample characteristics to individuals in specific cases. Doing so runs the risk of *statistical discrimination*, which refers to the problem of inference in treating an individual in a sample or population as if he or she possessed the average tendencies or characteristics of the sample or population....

4. Analytic Validity

...The fourth methodological standard, analytic validity, may be defined as (a) the appropriate match between the data to be analyzed and the technique(s) used in the analysis, (b) the appropriate application of the analytic techniques to data, and (c) the appropriate interpretation of the results of the analysis.

...When testing for a relationship between two or more variables in a sample-based data set, such as the relationship between joint physical custody and postsettlement litigation, researchers typically report the level of statistical significance of the relationship.... In basic terms, statistical significance refers to a measure of the likelihood that the relationship between two or more variables in a sample has occurred by chance (due to the use of the random function to select the sample), rather than the fact that the relationship actually exists in the population.

Two problems related to statistical significance commonly arise. First, performing significance tests presupposes that the data for the analysis come from a randomly selected sample.... Similarly, when the intended randomness of the sample is seriously compromised by response and attrition rate problems, the sample may be so nonrandom that the use of significance tests is questionable....

Second, although statistical significance is related, it is not the same thing as *practical* or *substantive significance*, which refers to the degree to which the size of a relationship among variables is sufficient to meaningfully influence a real decision. For example, because statistical significance is strongly influenced by the size of the sample used in analyses, large samples may yield statistically significant findings that are inconsequential in terms of the size of the effect of one variable on another. Independent of the statistical significance of a relationship, it would still be necessary to decide whether the statistically significant effect was large enough to justify a change in law or procedure. Ultimately, in a legal or policy context value judgments must be made about any statistically significant finding....

FILTRATION LEVEL 3...COMMUNITY REVIEW, COMMUNICATION, AND INTEGRATION

Beyond the logic for developing and testing hypotheses...and the standards for the collection and analysis of empirical data...there is a third fundamental system of the scientific method, namely the established practices and norms through which scientific research findings are reviewed and communicated by the scientific community and then integrated into the existing body of scientific knowledge. These processes bear directly on the...*Daubert* inquiries—whether the scientific claim has been published in a peer-reviewed publication and whether the claim has gained general acceptance by the scientific community....

1. Peer Review and Communication

A fundamental method the scientific community uses to ensure the quality of scientific knowledge is the filter of prepublication peer review....After a research report is submitted to a single social scientific journal, the authors' identities and affiliations are removed and copies are sent to reviewers who have expertise in the areas covered by the paper. Blind peer review typically involves multiple reviewers who assess the scientific merit of the report. Specifically, they assess the research in terms of the logical and methodological standards of the scientific method discussed in previous sections paying close attention to design, data collection, analyses, interpretations, and the relationship of the study's findings to existing research and theory. In the social sciences, most papers are either rejected or given "revise and resubmit" decisions. Publication rates vary among social science disciplines and journals, but for lead journals published by professional associations, the annual acceptance rate likely is in the range of 10 to 15 percent....

...Once a paper passes peer review, it is communicated to the scientific community through publication. This communication is crucial because it allows the entire community to work with the new findings and it sets the stage for more widespread community review and the finding's eventual integration into the collective, current scientific knowledge base.

2. Integration

With publication, an important and dynamic process begins that bears directly on...determining if a scientific claim has achieved general acceptance in the scientific community....

- *Postpublication Critical Review*: Members of the scientific community may conduct their own evaluations of the new findings by assessing their logical integrity and methodological rigor, comparing them to related published research findings, and commenting on them in print or at conferences. To the degree that postpublication critical commentary does not identify serious problems and does find support for the findings in related research, it will gain greater acceptance.
- *Replication*: Members of the scientific community may access the data set upon which the published findings are based and attempt to independently replicate them. To the degree that they can be replicated, the finding will gain greater acceptance.
- *Confirmation by New Research*: The publication of the new research findings may encourage others to undertake new and related research in order to confirm, modify,

or refute the findings. To the degree that the findings are confirmed, they will gain wider acceptance.

Published results of this integrative process may be found in *scientific literature reviews*, which appear in a variety of forms.... In qualitative literature reviews, the writer carefully gathers relevant studies, summarizes them, and produces an integrative statement based on the researcher's judgment. In quantitative literature reviews, the writer uses a set of techniques known as meta-analysis to quantitatively summarize research results on topics for which large numbers of studies exist.

NOTES AND QUESTIONS

1. Given the prevalence of social science in law, should there be limits on its use? How can we decide what is "good" social science and what is "junk" science?

2. As the preceding excerpt makes clear, empirical research is about testing and retesting hypotheses to determine if they are falsifiable. But why do scientists start with the presumption that their hypotheses are not true? Philosopher of science Karl Popper argued that we cannot generalize from individual observations; thus, we cannot conclude that all flowers are red simply because we have observed only red flowers. Instead, scientists establish a null hypothesis, so rather than trying to establish that all flowers are red, the null hypothesis would seek to establish that all flowers are not red. If some sufficient quantum of evidence is found to establish that the null hypothesis is not true, then the null hypothesis has been falsified. If, however, the evidence is inconclusive, then scientists say they have failed to reject the null hypothesis.

3. Once a researcher has indentified a question or problem, he or she must decide on the purpose of the study. For example, the research may be descriptive (to describe some aspect of the world around us) or causal (to investigate the relationships among different variables). Moreover, the researcher may want to consider the data at a single point in time (known as cross-sectional research) or over time (longitudinal research). The latter may involve trend analysis (looking at the results of surveys administered over a number of years, such as uniform crime reports), panel data (surveys conducted of the same groups over time), or cohort studies (for example, a study of all people born in the year 1988 conducted over time).

The researcher also must consider validity and reliability when choosing a research design. Validity is the degree to which an empirical study generates accurate data and conclusions. If the research design permits valid inferences to be drawn about the relationships among variables and has considered and accounted for alternative explanations, then the design has internal validity. In other words, the design itself is structured to prevent threats to the accuracy of the study's conclusion. For example, researchers try to ensure that the effects they are seeing are not the result of subjects dropping out of a treatment program prematurely (mortality), of preexisting differences between groups that are not the subject of study (selection), of a change in the measuring instrument across the true period of the study (instrumentation), of placement in experimental groups on the basis of some criterion such as a pretest score rather than through randomization (statistical regression), or of a historical event that occurs between the pretest and the posttest when the event is not the subject of the research (history).

External validity is the degree to which research findings from a particular study may be generalized to different situations, people, or times. Consider, for example, the number of studies conducted on college campuses involving college students as test subjects (perhaps you participated in one or two studies yourself). Would the findings from a study of the sleeping patterns of college students generalize to the larger adult population? To high school students?

Analytic validity simply means that the study measures what it is saying it measures. Researchers thus must find ways to define variables so that they are quantifiable. While some variables are readily quantifiable (the number of children who leave school before graduating), others may be more challenging (the political ideologies of high school students). Thus, researchers must define their variables so that they may be measured and the data interpreted. Moreover, this allows other researchers to conduct their own studies to see if the findings may be replicated. Last, the measure must be reliable, meaning that it produces the same or a similar result when measuring the same condition.

Researchers collect data in a number of different ways. They may conduct surveys or interviews, use existing data, study a sample of a population, or conduct an experiment. There are certain techniques associated with each methodology, advantages and limitations to each, and more optimal approaches depending on the research question. For example, when a researcher conducts an experiment, he or she will randomly assign the items to be studied to two (or more) groups, called an experimental group and a control group. The groups will receive the same treatment with the exception of one event or stimulus, called the independent variable. The researcher then will look for differences in outcomes (dependant variables) between the groups and determine if those differences are attributable to the independent variable.

Researchers then must organize, analyze, and evaluate the data. Because the data must be quantifiable, researchers record the data in some systematic or standardized form known as coding. In its most basic form, coding simply involves assigning numbers to variables. Some variables are by their nature quantifiable—such as age or height or weight. Other variables, called categorical variables, involve some characteristic that is being studied, such as gender or religions affiliation. These variables are assigned different numbers, but the numbers do not have any mathematical relationship to each other. (Assigning 0 to male and 1 to female does not mean that the quality of femaleness is worth more than the quality of maleness, at least in mathematical terms.) Ordinal variables also involve a nonnumerical quality of an observation, but the order of the scale matters because the ranking of the observation has some meaning, such as completion of schooling (elementary school, high school, college, graduate school).

After coding, researchers evaluate the data. There are a number of different ways the data may be analyzed, and more than one method may be used to evaluate a data set. For example, researchers may use statistics to describe the data. This could include information about the frequency of a response; the mean, median, mode, and range of the data; and the shape of the distribution of the data.

To test their working hypotheses, researchers rely on concepts of statistical significance. Statistical significance, by convention, simply means that if a result has a 5 percent or less chance of occurring but it nevertheless does occur, then the result is considered statistically important. There are a number of tests researchers may use to determine statistical significance. The chi-square statistic, for example, enables researchers to calculate the probability of a particular event. The t-test permits researchers to compare the means between two groups to determine the probability that the differences between the groups are significant, while the analysis of variance (known as ANOVA) measures how different the means are across more than two groups and how each observation differs from the overall mean.

Researchers also may want to measure the relationships among variables. Correlation captures the relationship between two variables. Regression analysis explores the relationships among more than two variables and, specifically, will reveal a relationships between the independent variable and the dependant variables. Although these methods will not explain the reason for the relationships among two or more variables, they will reveal statistically significant correlations.

4. Mark Klock argues that lawyers and judges should have a certain level of "statistical literacy." To that end, he proposes that law schools should teach a basic statistics course or that statistics should be a prerequisite to law school admission. Mark Klock, *Finding Random Coincidences While Searching for the Holy Writ of Truth: Specification Searches in Law and Public Policy or Cum Hoc Ergo Propter Hoc*, 2001 Wis. L. Rev. 1007, 1063. Do you agree?

5. *Problem.* As a result of a series of ear infections, eighteen-month-old Sara fell behind on her vaccination schedule. At one doctor's visit, when she was nineteen months old, Sara received five inoculations, for measles, mumps, rubella, polio, varicella, diphtheria, pertussis, tetanus, and Haemophilus influenzae. At the time Sara received her vaccinations, thimerosol, a mercury-based preservative, was used routinely in vaccinations (it was eliminated from childhood vaccines manufactured after 2001). Shortly after receiving her shots, Sara fell ill. She lost words she had known how to speak, stopped making eye contact, and began to exhibit repetitive behaviors and social withdrawal typical of autism. She also began to suffer from seizures. Prior to the vaccinations, Sara had been developing normally. Since she became ill, doctors have discovered that Sara has a rare mitochondrial disorder that could increase her susceptibility to infection.

Sara's parents would like to receive compensation for the injuries their daughter has suffered. When Congress enacted the National Childhood Vaccine Injury Act of 1986, Pub. L. No. 99-660, 100 Stat. 3743 (1986), it created the National Vaccine Injury Compensation Program, a no-fault system to provide compensation to people injured by certain vaccines. All such claims are handled by a special federal vaccine court within the U.S. Court of Federal Claims. How would you determine if Sara's parents have a legitimate claim? What studies would you use? How would you determine their scientific validity?

II

CHILDREN AND CRIME

A. Introduction

1. PHILOSOPHICAL ORIGINS

Julian W. Mack, *The Juvenile Court*, 23 Harvard Law Review 104, 107, 109, 116–117, 119–120 (1909).

Why is it not just and proper to treat these juvenile offenders, as we deal with the neglected children, as a wise and merciful father handles his own child whose errors are not discovered by the authorities? Why is it not the duty of the state, instead of asking merely whether a boy or a girl has committed a specific offense, to find out what he is, physically, mentally, morally, and then if it learns that he is treading the path that leads to criminality, to take him in charge, not so much to punish as to reform, not to degrade but to uplift, not to crush but to develop, not to make him a criminal but a worthy citizen.

And it is this thought—the thought that the child who has begun to go wrong, who is incorrigible, who has broken a law or an ordinance, is to be taken in hand by the state, not as an enemy but as a protector, as the ultimate guardian, because either the unwillingness or inability of the natural parents to guide it toward good citizenship has compelled the intervention of the public authorities; it is this principle, which, to some extent theretofore applied in Australia and a few American states, was first fully and clearly declared, in the Act under which the Juvenile Court of Cook County, Illinois, was opened in Chicago, on July 1, 1899....

To get away from the notion that the child is to be dealt with as a criminal; to save it from the brand of criminality, the brand that sticks to it for life; to take it in hand and instead of first stigmatizing and then reforming it, to protect it from the stigma,—this is the work which is now being accomplished by dealing even with most of the delinquent children through the court that represents the *parens patriae* power of the state, the court of chancery. Proceedings are brought to have a guardian or representative of the state appointed to look after the child, to have the state intervene between the natural parent and the child because the child needs it, as evidenced by some of its acts, and because the parent is either unwilling or unable to train the child properly....

Most of the children who come before the court are, naturally, the children of the poor. In many cases the parents are foreigners, frequently unable to speak English, and without an understanding of American methods and views. What they need, more than anything else, is kindly assistance....

... [The judge] must be a student of and deeply interested in the problems of philanthropy and child life, as well as a lover of children. He must be able to understand the boys' point of view and ideas of justice; he must be willing and patient enough to search out the underlying causes of the trouble and to formulate the plan by which, through the coöperation, ofttimes, of many agencies, the cure may be effected....

The problem for determination by the judge is not, Has this boy or girl committed a specific wrong, but What is he, how has he become what he is, and what had best be done in his interest and in the interest of the state to save him from a downward career....

The child who must be brought into court should, of course, be made to know that he is face to face with the power of the state, but he should at the same time, and more emphatically, be made to feel that he is the object of its care and solicitude. The ordinary trappings of the court-room are out of place in such hearings. The judge on a bench, looking down upon the boy standing at the bar, can never evoke a proper sympathetic spirit. Seated at a desk, with the child at his side, where he can on occasion put his arm around his shoulder and draw the lad to him, the judge, while losing none of his judicial dignity, will gain immensely in the effectiveness of his work.

Anthony Platt, The Child Savers: The Invention of Delinquency 137–138, 139, 142–143 (1969).

The juvenile court was a special tribunal created by statute to determine the legal status of "troublesome" children. Underlying the juvenile court act was the concept of *parens patriae* by which the courts were authorized to use wide discretion in resolving the problems of "its least fortunate junior citizens." The administration of juvenile justice differed in many important respects from the criminal court process. A child was not accused of a crime but offered assistance and guidance; intervention in his life was not supposed to carry the stigma of a criminal record; judicial records were not generally available to the press or public, and hearings were conducted in relative privacy; proceedings were informal and due process safeguards were not applicable due to the court's civil jurisdiction.

The original juvenile court statutes enabled the courts to investigate a wide variety of youthful needs and misbehavior.... "[T]he critical philosophical position of the reform movement was that no formal, legal distinctions should be made between the delinquent and the dependent or neglected." Statutory definitions of "delinquency" included (1) acts that would be criminal if committed by adults, (2) acts that violated county, town or municipal ordinances, and (3) violations of vaguely defined catchalls—such as "vicious or immoral behavior," "incorrigibility," "truancy," "profane or indecent language," "growing up in idleness," "living with any vicious or disreputable person," etc.—which indicated, if unchecked, the possibility of more serious misconduct in the future....

The juvenile court movement went far beyond a humanitarian concern for the special treatment of adolescents. It brought within the ambit of governmental control a set of youthful activities that had been previously ignored or handled informally. It was not by accident that the behavior selected for penalizing by the child savers—drinking, begging, roaming the streets, frequenting dance-halls and movies, fighting, sexuality, staying out late at night, and incorrigibility—was primarily attributable to the children of lower-class migrant and immigrant families....

The role model for juvenile court judges was doctor-counselor rather than lawyer. "Judicial therapists" were expected to establish a one-to-one relationship with "delinquents" in the same way that a country doctor might give his time and attention to a favorite patient. The courtroom was arranged like a clinic and the vocabulary of the participants was largely composed of medical metaphors. "We can not know the child without a thorough examination," wrote Judge Julian Mack. "We must reach into the soul-life of the child."

NOTES AND QUESTIONS

1. Judge Julian W. Mack served as the second presiding judge of the Cook County Juvenile Court, after Judge Richard Tuthill. An impressive legal scholar, Mack went to Harvard Law School immediately after graduating from high school, where he was one of the founders of the *Harvard Law Review.* He became a member of the Northwestern University law faculty and was a founding member of the University of Chicago Law School, whose faculty he subsequently joined. Mack served as a federal judge on the Sixth and Second Circuits until he retired in 1940. He was active in the Zionist movement and helped to establish the World Jewish Congress. Mack's article, which is excerpted above, is one of the ten most-cited law review articles of the past century.

2. Platt contends that the child savers "should in no sense be considered libertarians or humanists." Do you agree? Is the view espoused by Mack simply antiquated? Consider this statute:

As used in this chapter, "unruly child" includes any of the following:

(A) Any child who does not submit to the reasonable control of the child's parents, teachers, guardian, or custodian, by reason of being wayward or habitually disobedient;

(B) Any child who is an habitual truant from school and who previously has not been adjudicated an unruly child for being an habitual truant;

(C) Any child who behaves in a manner as to injure or endanger the child's own health or morals or the health or morals of others.

Ohio Rev. Code Ann. § 2151.022 (West 2009).

2. SOCIAL SCIENCE ORIGINS

Herbert Lou, Juvenile Courts in the United States 2 (1927).

The juvenile court is conspicuously a response to the modern spirit of social justice. It is perhaps the first legal tribunal where law and science, especially the science of medicine and those sciences which deal with human behavior, such as biology, sociology, and psychology, work side by side. It recognizes the fact that the law unaided is incompetent to decide what is adequate treatment of delinquency and crime. It undertakes to define and readjust social situations without the sentiment of prejudice. Its approach to the problem which the child presents is scientific, objective, and dispassionate. The methods which it uses are those of social case work, in which every child is studied and treated as an individual.

These principles upon which the juvenile court acts are radically different from those of the criminal courts. In place of judicial tribunals, restrained by antiquated procedure saturated in an atmosphere of hostility, trying cases for determining guilt and inflicting punishment according to inflexible rules of law, we have now juvenile courts, in which the relations of the child to his parents or other adults and to the state or society are defined and are adjusted summarily according to the scientific findings about the child and his environments. In place of magistrates, limited by the outgrown custom and compelled to walk in the paths fixed by the law of the realm, we have now socially-minded judges, who hear and adjust cases according not to rigid rules of law but to what the interests of society and the interests of the child or good conscience demand. In place of juries, prosecutors, and lawyers, trained in the old conception of law and staging dramatically, but often amusingly, legal battles, as the necessary paraphernalia of a criminal court, we have now probation officers, physicians, psychologists, and psychiatrists, who search for the social, physiological, psychological, and mental backgrounds of the child in order to arrive at reasonable just solutions of individual cases. In other words, in this new court we tear down primitive prejudice, hatred, and hostility toward the lawbreaker in that most hide-bound of all human institutions, the court of law, and we attempt, as far as possible, to administer justice in the name of truth, love and understanding.

Victoria Getis, The Juvenile Court and the Progressives 153–157 (2000).

The juvenile court movement was built upon the reformers' faith in science and the abilities of the state to address social problems....

Reformers combined their faith in science with a faith in the ameliorative power of the state. While they agreed that the state should act to solve social problems, they disagreed on why the state was empowered to act, and they disagreed on the proper relationship between the family and the government. The opinions that reformers expressed about the government accorded with a national trend toward giving the state more authority over families. They also reflected the wide range of opinion on the proper role of the state. The juvenile court law was a direct result of reformers' expansive view of the state and their optimism about its possibilities....

After the court began operations, the reformers who had created it continued their involvement in the cause of eradicating juvenile delinquency. Reformers commissioned studies of the court from University of Chicago sociologists, and they made data available to the sociologists. In the years before 1918, Chicago sociologists adopted and reinforced reformers' theories about delinquency and society and proposed their own solutions to solving delinquency. In the 1920s the sociologists gained a more sophisticated understanding of the city and began to favor—but not necessarily to practice—detachment in the use of their science....

Psychology, unlike sociology, had long incorporated treatment of individuals into its scientific methods. Chicago's clinical psychologists did not debate the field's relationship to reform. Psychologists working at the Juvenile Psychopathic Institute did not disdain the work of the reformers; psychology's association with the court was strongly influenced by members of the reform coalition. By focusing intensively on the individual delinquent, Chicago psychologists reasoned, they could discover the mental basis for deviance. The study of the individual...created a model of studying delinquency that influenced sociologists in the postwar years, during which psychologists and sociologists treated delinquency as an area suitable for both cooperation and rivalry....

The reformers' faith in science also created two different strands of social work in the city. The reformers urged functionary social workers to take up positions in social agencies and they created the schools and networks that launched policy social workers into national prominence....Functionary social workers adopted a psychological outlook that focused on individual adjustment to the environment. They came to dominate the support services of the court and other institutions dealing with delinquents. At the same time, policy social workers worked for social change based on scientific research in regional and national programs pertaining to delinquency.

Functionary social workers held a series of assumptions about delinquency and the children with whom they came into contact in the court....To the court functionaries, deviance could be traced to recent immigrants—largely Catholic and Eastern European—and this assumption meant that they did not search further for important facts concerning delinquency. The court was not a social laboratory for the men and women who staffed it....

Policy social workers...used the court and its data in much the same way as did the sociologists. Their imperative to research and reform, however, had little impact on the functionary social workers and hence on the juvenile court in Chicago.

Charles Richmond Henderson, *The Prevention of Crime, Not Merely Its Punishment,* 1 J. Am. Inst. Crim. L. & Criminology 175, 11, 12 (1910).

[W]e have found that most children, if well nourished and brought up, have a fair chance to make reliable citizens. As the medical profession has cut down the list of inherited diseases, and as crime is seen to have no special microbe for ancestor, the meliorist concentrates energy on infant welfare, instruction of mothers, pure milk, open windows, higher wages, improved dwellings, prohibition of crowding in sleeping rooms, ventilation of workplaces, industrial insurance. Misery drives to drink and crime; and therefore all agencies of economic betterment erect barriers to anti-social conduct. The temptation...in commerce is to heartless exploitation of the public; hence pure food laws and governmental control of monopolistic corporations.

The State itself is becoming more conscious of its obligations as employer and as lawgiver; it begins to see that slow, costly and uncertain administration of criminal law irritates and exasperates. By developing a program of constructive social legislation it diminishes the friction of life and appears before the workmen not merely in repressive and hateful attitude, but as father and friend....

...While the administration of justice holds the adult offender by the throat, the ministers of culture and progress take care that the children and youth are kept afar from contact with the police, the courts and the prison, all of which are at best but a pathetic confession of social neglect, a costly apparatus, whose product is an army of cripples, whose position is always unstable, whose return to vicious ways bitter experience has led most men to expect under too great stress.

Charles Richmond Henderson, *Prevention of Delinquency,* 4 J. AM. INST. CRIM. L. & CRIMINOLOGY 798, 800 (1914).

If a city has multitudes of unclean, immoral, lazy and frivolous youth, a burden and a menace, it is because the systems of poor relief and of education are neglected by those who are responsible. Owing to the close relation of poor relief to education in depressed homes, there should be a close co-operation of visitors with the agent of compulsory attendance; for the school alone cannot deal with the economic misery which is so generally associated with parental failure. The most attractive industrial schools and the most vigorous agents of compulsory attendance will back down in the presence of an incurable deficit in the household budget.

William Healy, *The Individual Study of the Young Criminal,* 1 J. AM. INST. CRIM. L. & CRIMINOLOGY 50, 50, 62 (1910).

The anti-social acts which we call criminal are just as much the outcome of physical and mental capabilities, of emotions, desires, obstinacies, weaknesses of character, imitation, submission to psychological influences of the crowd and other definite reactions to environment as are the more socially desirable aspects of conduct....

...[I]t seems to us that we get, by a fairly intensive investigation of the individual, his antecedents and his environment; familial, educational and otherwise, a quite unexpected degree of enlightenment upon the causative factors of his career.... It rather seems to me that crime is like some physically abnormal action of the individual, such as a peculiar gait, which might arise from a variety of causes, internal or external, weakness, intoxication, lesion of the nervous system, visual defect, local pain, an uneven sidewalk. The case consequently must require careful, individual diagnosis before the rational treatment can be instituted which is really adapted to its needs....

In the above study we have taken a small group of delinquents and found them to have immensely varying needs, capabilities and adaptabilities.... We know by court records that old methods are largely a flat failure as a deterrent to crime. In place, then, of any policy of repression or effort at reformation in large groups, what are the more constructive methods that offer greater chances of success? The amount of alterability in the whole situation is, plainly enough, the sum total of the alterabilities of the individuals concerned. Then it follows that if, as we have seen, the needs and possibilities of these individuals are extremely various, greatly varying methods of meeting those needs and developing those possibilities must be inaugurated, if the full amount of modification of the situation is to be realized. Just how much alleviation the entire crime situation can be subjected to is, of course, altogether unknown, and it certainly will remain unknown until the most rational procedures of treatment follow the most rational methods of diagnosis—especially until the importance of the young criminal as a factor is realized, his importance as an individual at the age when the twig is bent, needing individualistic study and individualistic treatment.

NOTES AND QUESTIONS

1. Charles Richmond Henderson was appointed as the second faculty member to the newly created Department of Sociology at the University of Chicago in 1892, a position he held until his death in 1915. He was a former Baptist minister, and his teaching and writings had a religious tone that some found offensive. Henderson did not believe that crime was hereditary; rather, he looked to social, psychological, and environmental causes for an explanation. He was deeply committed to reform efforts and charitable causes; he helped establish the Chicago Bureau of Charities and in 1912 became the president of United Charities.

2. Dr. William Healy was the director of the Juvenile Psychopathic Institute in Chicago. The JPI was founded in 1909 and funded by Ethel Sturges Dummer, a member of the Juvenile Protection League and from one of Chicago's founding (and wealthy) families. Healy was extremely influential; judges, reformers, and academics visited the JPI, and new clinics were established in other cities. In Chicago itself, other courts and institutions created their own clinics modeled after the JPI.

Healy rejected the idea that there was a single cause of delinquency. (In fact, he acknowledged that the JPI was misnamed because very little evidence was found that the children referred to the juvenile court were psychopathic.) In *The Individual Study of the Young Criminal*, excerpted above, Healy listed a number of observations about each of the children identified in his case study. The list was extraordinarily broad and included such facts as poverty; "mental subnormality"; "cheap plays and nickel shows"; poor education; poor health; parental ignorance, neglect, or alcoholism; epilepsy; feeble-mindedness; lack of supervision; "high mental capacity, out of all proportion to his environment"; and "bad companions." William Healy, *The Individual Study of the Young Criminal*, J. AM. INST. CRIM. L. & CRIMINOLOGY 50, 61 (1910).

3. Do we have a better understanding of the causes of delinquency today? Do you think delinquent activity has its roots in individual behavior? In environmental factors? In both?

3. LEGAL ORIGINS

HERBERT LOU, JUVENILE COURTS IN THE UNITED STATES 5, 6–7 (1927).

The English court of chancery, it should be noted, dealt entirely with children whom we designate variously and sometimes interchangeably as "neglected," "dependent," or "destitute." The doctrine of the state as *parens patriae* was recognized as applying to this class of children for many years in many of the states in this country. When juvenile court laws were enacted by the various states, the same doctrine was extended to delinquent children....

From the standpoint of the delinquency jurisdiction of the juvenile court, it has often been held that the court is founded on the theory of the common-law age of criminal responsibility. It is a fundamental maxim of the common law that no person can be guilty of a crime unless he did the act complained of with a *mens rea,* a guilty mind. A child under seven years of age has been treated as being *doli incapax,* that is, incapable of felonious intent. The existence of a guilty mind, so as to render a child between seven and fourteen years of age criminally responsible, may be established by evidence that the youthful offender is of such intelligence as to understand the nature and consequences of his misconduct and to appreciate that it was wrong. Legal guilt itself thus depends upon a psychological condition; and this, in turn depends partly upon age. The age limit below which there was no criminal responsibility has been modified and extended by statutes from time to time both in this country and in England. For this reason, it has sometimes been held by some authorities that by extending the jurisdictional age the legislation creating the juvenile court has merely carried this idea forward and widened the application of the common-law rule.

The theory of the juvenile court, which stresses the moving forward of the common-law age of criminal responsibility, cannot be pushed to its logical conclusion. No one can doubt for a moment that an adolescent of eighteen or even twenty-one years of age is responsible, at least to a limited degree, for his acts, if all human conduct is not taken as something caused. Both crime and delinquency are based upon intent, for the juvenile court has retained that element at least in the distinction between delinquency and dependency or neglect. The only difference seems to lie in the question whether or not the state, as a policy, desires to stigmatize those who offend against the law as being criminal and to prescribe different methods of treatment in order to achieve the end in view. Moreover, whereas in the common law no provision was made for those below the age of responsibility, provision was made in the juvenile-court law for all of these under the less opprobrious name "delinquents." Responsibility does not necessarily go with punishment, for the juvenile-court law recognizes responsibility, but the weapons which it uses are reformation, protection, and education rather than punishment.

If we believe the theory that all human institutions can be traced to their origins, its delinquency jurisdiction arose mainly on the side of the criminal law. There may be some historical reason for ascribing the basis of delinquency jurisdiction to the legal fiction of the age of criminal responsibility, yet its logical justification seems to lie in the recognition of the failure of the older criminal courts to prevent crime and in the experimentation in judicial methods and procedure. It is an attempt to relieve juvenile offenders under certain circumstances from the rigidity of the law prevailing in courts of more general jurisdiction.

QUESTIONS

1. What is the difference between a court of chancery and a criminal court? Why would it matter if the juvenile court's origins were in chancery? In criminal law? Is the distinction a meaningful one today?

4. PERSPECTIVES ON ADOLESCENT DEVELOPMENT

Donna M. Bishop & Hillary B. Farber, *Joining the Legal Significance of Adolescent Development with the Legal Rights Provided by Gault*, 60 RUTGERS L. REV. 125, 149–159 (2007).

The teen years are a period of rapid and pervasive change in children's cognitive, emotional, and social capacities. Although in most states youth between the ages of ten and seventeen fall within the purview of the juvenile law, are subject to the same rules, and are presumed to have the same capacities, research indicates a broad spectrum of competencies within this age range. There is "good reason to believe that individuals at the point of entry into adolescence are very different than are individuals who are making the transition out of adolescence."

A. Cognitive Development

There are significant differences in the cognitive capacities of preteens and early teens, compared to older teens and adults. Developmental theory and research indicate that the capacity to utilize logical reasoning skills in decision making—that is, to envision alternative behavioral choices, identify the consequences associated with each, assess the likelihood of these consequences, and weigh the alternatives and their consequences in terms of one's values and preferences—emerges in early adolescence. Although there is much individual variability in the age at which these abilities emerge, there is general agreement that few acquire them before age twelve, while most have them by age fourteen or fifteen.

A considerable amount of experimental research conducted in laboratory settings indicates that, by mid-adolescence, most youths have capacities for reasoning and understanding that are roughly equivalent to those of adults.... But the laboratory setting is artificial. In the laboratory, cognitive capacities are typically assessed by presenting subjects with hypothetical scenarios to which they are asked to respond by making and explaining decisions....

In the real world, people base decisions and judgments on the information they possess. Unlike the laboratory, where all subjects have the same information, people in the real world have acquired, through education and experience, different amounts of information about what options are available to them, the nature of those options, and their consequences. Decision making is generally better if we have the benefit of previous experience in making decisions, particularly if the kind of decision we are called on to make is one that we have made before. Decision making is a skill that, like most skills, is learned, and we cannot learn to do well without practice. Thus, despite the fact that their capacities for understanding and reasoning may be equal to adults, the decision making of even mid- to late-adolescents is likely to be impaired. Simply by virtue of their relative lack of education and experience, teens are less likely than adults to be cognizant of all of their options, to recognize or appreciate all of the ramifications of behavioral alternatives, and to weigh the alternatives in a way that does not produce outcomes that may be unfavorable or even injurious to them.

Psychosocial factors play an important role in decision making. They are often referred to as "judgment" factors because they refer to things like risk perceptions, self-perceptions, emotions, motivations, time perspective, and responsiveness to others, which influence our preferences and, ultimately, the judgments that we make. Researchers have identified multiple psychosocial factors that are especially salient during the teen years, and which contribute to the adolescent characteristics of immaturity, impetuosity, and vulnerability.... Psychosocial development lags behind cognitive development—it continues to develop throughout adolescence and into the early adult years—and it appears to have a biological base....

B. Neuropsychological Research

Advances in neuroscience have produced a new body of knowledge showing that fundamental differences in the psychosocial maturity of adolescents and adults are rooted in biochemical changes in the structures and processes of the brain. Research has focused especially on two areas of the brain. The first involves the limbic and paralimbic regions. These are sensation- and reward-seeking areas of the brain, which are activated by external stimuli, including social and emotional stimuli. They are responsible for the almost spontaneous gut reactions and impulses that we have when we are exposed to things provocative. The other region of the brain that is especially important to judgment and decision making involves the prefrontal and parietal cortices. The region where these are located is often described as the "executive" or "cognitive control" center, because this is the thinking portion of the brain responsible for foresight, planning, strategic thinking, and self-regulation. Importantly, the frontal regions regulate the expression of impulses emanating from the limbic region.

The executive center of the brain develops gradually, and its development is generally not complete until people reach their early twenties. Therefore, although they may have developed adult-like capacities for understanding and reasoning by mid-adolescence, youth do not acquire adult-like capacities for behavioral self-regulation until much later.

For reasons that are not entirely clear, with the onset of puberty the limbic regions become more sensitive (i.e., more easily aroused) and more active. Both the intensity and lability of mood that we associate with adolescence are presumably manifestations of this change in the functioning of the limbic system. While the limbic system of adolescents is often bursting with emotions and impulses, the frontal lobes do not keep pace, but continue to develop at a much slower rate. Consequently, during the period between the onset of puberty and the maturation of the frontal cortices some eight to ten years later, individuals may have considerable difficulty modulating their emotions. When a teen is emotionally aroused (e.g., in the company of friends, out on dates, in situations of stress or excitement or danger), the executive center of his or her brain is not able to effectively rein in inclinations emanating from the limbic regions. This may account for teens' greater tendency to drive after drinking, engage in unprotected sex, ride motorcycles without a helmet, jump out of airplanes, and engage in other risky behaviors. Teens may understand the risks; however, as neuroscientist Deborah Yurgelun-Todd explains, "[g]ood judgment is learned,... [and] you can't learn it if you don't have the necessary hardware."... Adolescent brains are not equipped to respond to emotional situations in the same ways as adult brains. "At-risk" adolescents see fewer options, their time perspective is shortened, and their ability to foresee more distal consequences is constrained. At other times, when they are not in a state of emotional arousal or stress—conditions more akin to the experimental laboratory setting—the reasoning and planning capacities of the brain can work more effectively. It is only in the early twenties, when the frontal lobe matures, that individuals reach psychological adulthood and are better able to check emotions and impulses. It is at this time that individuals become less likely to act without thinking or to engage in risky and thrill-seeking behaviors, and more capable of exercising foresight (delaying gratification), resisting external pressures (developing autonomy), and channeling negative emotions in constructive ways.

C. Psychosocial Factors Affecting Adolescent Judgment

Several psychosocial factors have been identified as essential to an understanding of the distinctive character of adolescent decision making. Although different scholars assign somewhat different labels, the following four categories capture the factors fairly well: (1) susceptibility to external influence; (2) orientation toward risk; (3) temporal orientation; and (4) capacity for self-regulation....

1. Susceptibility to External Influence

Scientific research confirms popular wisdom that adolescents are very much influenced by their peers, and less capable than adults of making autonomous decisions. Adolescence is a life period in which youth become increasingly less dependent on parents and increasingly more oriented toward peers. Most spend a great deal of time in the company of peers, and much of their behavior is group behavior. Adolescence is also a time of identity formation, and peer groups often provide the context in which teens experiment with new identities outside of their families....Teens frequently compare themselves to their peers and model their behavior (e.g., speech, clothing, hairstyles, and demeanor) after them, both as a sign of belonging or "fitting in" and to gain acceptance and approval. Peers also influence one another more directly, often pressing each other to engage in risky behaviors. In the company of peers, the probability of engaging in risky behaviors is amplified; adolescents' desire for peer approval and fear of ridicule and rejection cause them to engage in acts that they would not otherwise commit.

The presence of peers greatly increases the probability of risk taking among teens. Most juvenile crime—but not most adult crime—is committed in groups; in the context of the peer group, dares and challenges often precipitate the commission of illegal acts. Participation in group behaviors that may even be at odds with one's personal value system can carry important social benefits and avoid painful social costs. It demonstrates loyalty to the group, solidifies friendships, and serves as a means of acquiring status. Failure to participate, on the other hand, brings the prospect of ridicule and fear of rejection by the group on whom one has come to depend, or to which one hopes to belong....

While mid-adolescents are more responsive than either younger children or adults to behavioral cues from peers, there is some suggestion that younger juveniles—children and preteens—may be especially vulnerable to behavioral cues from adult authority figures, including police and judges. We all know how easily children can be enticed—even after good parental training about the dangers involved—to speak to strangers and to respond to the ruses of child molesters. When placed in situations, especially stressful ones that are new to them, young people look to adults—as they look to their parents—to help them to navigate unfamiliar terrain. Children are dependent on adults and look to them for assistance and approval. Yet, they overestimate adults' power, and therefore may be especially deferential and compliant with requests, commands, and suggestions from teachers, clergy, police, judges, and other authority figures....

2. Orientation toward Risk

Perhaps in part because of the hyperactivity of their limbic systems, adolescents are more likely than adults to engage in risky behaviors (e.g., criminal behavior, unprotected sex, smoking, drinking), and, as we have seen, the probability of engaging in risky behaviors is magnified when young people are in the company of peers.... A considerable body of research supports the view that, when considering the consequences of their actions, adolescents more than adults differentially attend and give greater weight to anticipated benefits or gains and less to potential losses or risks....

3. Temporal Orientation

Faced with a situation in which a decision regarding some behavioral alternative must be made, adolescents tend to give more consideration to short-term consequences, and less to long-term ones. Compared with adults, they have limited time perspective. Furthermore, in the analysis of costs and benefits, they tend to discount whatever long-term consequences they do see. As a result, they tend, more than adults, to opt for immediate gratification—postponing their homework to hang out with friends, or spending their money now on things that they will forget about in a week instead of saving for something they really want. As most every parent who has weathered the teen years knows, adolescents tend to need things "this minute" and with urgency—"I've simply got to have it."

The foreshortened time perspective of youth, compared to adults, also relates to their involvement in crime. Before committing crime, delinquent youths seldom consider the prospect of being caught and incarcerated, or the length of time they might be incarcerated. When they are sentenced to a term of years, it is difficult for them to project what incarceration will mean in terms of life opportunities and life experiences forgone. The perceived difference between a sentence of five years and ten years is a lot less meaningful to a teen than to an adult. Temporal perspective, then, may have important implications for juvenile decision making with respect to the exercise of trial rights and their participation in plea negotiations.

The teen's inability to project consequences into the distant future and to accord them much weight is also linked to social class. Poor urban children and adolescents tend to be more present-oriented than their middle-class suburban counterparts. This may be a function of high rates of violence in poor inner-city neighborhoods: when people are dying at an early age, one doesn't think about life far into the future.

4. Capacity for Self-Regulation

Compared to adults, young people have lesser ability to restrain their impulses—what psychologists call "response inhibition." For reasons undoubtedly related in part to limbic system arousal, they experience emotional urges more intensely, and the underdevelopment of the frontal lobes means that they have lesser capacity to hold these urges in check, or channel them into more appropriate outlets. There are additional psychosocial reasons for youths' impetuosity. They lack experience that would help them to think before acting, they are subject to pressures to act from peers, and their identities are still forming and are fragile. Consider, for example, that for young boys, adolescence is the stage when there is a major focus on masculine identity. It should not be surprising that challenges to that identity—insults, slurs on a boy's reputation for toughness—are often the triggers for episodes of impulsive violence. When situations are stressful and emotions are high ("hot cognitions"), adolescent judgment is severely impaired relative to the situation of "cold cognitions," where emotions are calm and consequences are more readily apparent and considered. In situations of "hot cognitions," adolescents are less sensitive to contextual cues that might temper their decisions. Compared to adults, they have lesser capacity for self-regulation of both impulses and emotions.

NOTES AND QUESTIONS

1. In light of the scientific evidence, should juveniles be held accountable for their criminal conduct? Is the juvenile court a reasonable alternative to criminal accountability?

2. Consider the *mens rea* scheme developed by the Model Penal Code and adopted by a majority of American jurisdictions in some form. The Model Penal Code defines culpability in this way:

(2) Kinds of Culpability Defined.

- (a) Purposely. A person acts purposely with respect to a material element of an offense when:
  - (i) if the element involves the nature of his conduct or a result thereof, it is his conscious object to engage in conduct of that nature or to cause such a result; and
  - (ii) if the element involves the attendant circumstances, he is aware of the existence of such circumstances or he believes or hopes that they exist.
- (b) Knowingly. A person acts knowingly with respect to a material element of an offense when:
  - (i) if the element involves the nature of his conduct or the attendant circumstances, he is aware that his conduct is of that nature or that such circumstances exist; and
  - (ii) if the element involves a result of his conduct, he is aware that it is practically certain that his conduct will cause such a result.
- (c) Recklessly. A person acts recklessly with respect to a material element of an offense when he consciously disregards a substantial and unjustifiable risk that the material element exists or will result from his conduct. The risk must be of such a nature and degree that, considering the nature and purpose of the actor's conduct and the circumstances known to him, its disregard involves a gross deviation from the standard of conduct that a law-abiding person would observe in the actor's situation.
- (d) Negligently. A person acts negligently with respect to a material element of an offense when he should be aware of a substantial and unjustifiable risk that the material element exists or will result from his conduct. The risk must be of such a nature and degree that the actor's failure to perceive it, considering the nature and purpose of his conduct and the circumstances known to him, involves a gross deviation from the standard of care that a reasonable person would observe in the actor's situation.

Model Penal Code, § 2.02(2) (1962). In light of what you have read about adolescent development, do you think a juvenile is capable of acting with purpose as it is defined by the Model Penal Code? With knowledge?

3. As you may recall from your criminal law class, we usually justify punishment on retributive or utilitarian grounds (or some combination of the two). In light of the scientific evidence about development, do you believe we can justify the punishment of juveniles on the grounds that they are morally culpable? On the other hand, if we wish to justify the punishment of juveniles on utilitarian grounds, is deterrence likely to be effective? Does the juvenile court, because its jurisdiction typically is limited by the age of majority, provide a reasoned policy response to this problem?

4. PBS's *Frontline* has examined cognitive development in a comprehensive and engaging report entitled "Inside the Teenage Brain." The video is available through PBS.

5. INFANCY

IN RE WILLIAM A.
Court of Appeals of Maryland
548 A.2d 130 (1988)

ELDRIDGE, Judge.

This case presents the question of whether the common law infancy defense is applicable in juvenile delinquency proceedings.

On July 6, 1984, the defendant, William A., accompanied his father and uncle to a food warehouse in Baltimore City. There, his father and uncle cut and removed copper piping from the premises. William assisted by carrying various materials from the storage facility. When the police arrived, they observed William's father and uncle carrying copper piping from the premises and William carrying a box of paper for a copying machine.

A second incident occurred on September 25, 1984. On that date, William A. accompanied his uncle to the premises of a car wash. When police arrived at the scene, they found that the car wash had been broken into, and they found William in a van nearby. His uncle had apparently fled the scene. When the police questioned William, he explained that he was "junking" with his uncle "as he always did." He also stated that he had been paid to accompany his uncle. At the time of both incidents, William was 13 years old.

On October 4, 1984, the State filed two petitions alleging that William A. had committed acts which, if committed by an adult, would be crimes, and that, therefore, William was delinquent....

On February 27, 1985, William was found delinquent by a juvenile master. William filed exceptions to the Master's recommended findings and conclusions, and a hearing was held in the Circuit Court for Baltimore City. At the hearing, the defendant argued, *inter alia,* that, because juvenile delinquency adjudications are based upon acts constituting crimes if committed by adults, the infancy defense should be available to children in delinquency proceedings. The defendant argued that children between ages 7 and 14 were entitled to a presumption of incapacity in juvenile delinquency proceedings and that the State in the instant cases had failed to rebut the presumption.

The circuit court overruled the defendant's exceptions, concluding that the infancy defense was inapplicable in juvenile delinquency proceedings. At a later disposition hearing, William was committed to the Juvenile Services Administration.

William appealed to the Court of Special Appeals. In an unreported opinion, the appellate court affirmed the circuit court's judgment. The court held that the infancy defense does not apply in delinquency proceedings, relying on an earlier Court of Special Appeals decision to the same effect, *In re Davis,* 17 Md.App. 98, 299 A.2d 856 (1973). Thereafter, we granted William's petition for a writ of certiorari.

The common law defense of infancy, or *doli incapax* as it was otherwise known, was explained by the Court of Special Appeals in *Adams v. State,* 8 Md.App. 684, 687–689, 262 A.2d 69, *cert. denied,* 258 Md. 725, *cert. denied,* 400 U.S. 928, 91 S.Ct. 193, 27 L.Ed.2d 188 (1970), as follows (footnotes omitted):

> Since the Code of Hammurabi (*circa* 2250 B.C.) and down through the ages, society, under the law, has viewed and treated offenders of tender years in a light differently and more favorably than that accorded adults accused of breaching the law. Over the centuries and during the evolution of the common law of England, there emerged a rule of law governing "the responsibility of infants" under which an individual below the age of seven years cannot be found guilty of committing a crime; an individual above fourteen years charged with a crime is to be adjudged as an adult; and between the ages of seven and fourteen there is a rebuttable presumption that such individual is incapable of committing a crime. In the absence of any pertinent legislative enactment in this State, the common law principles, as stated above, would appear to govern in Maryland and we so hold.
>
> In the case at bar, the appellant was shown to be thirteen years, ten and a half months of age at the time the crime was committed. It was, therefore, incumbent upon the State to produce sufficient evidence to overcome the presumption that the appellant was *doli incapax,* an expression ordinarily employed by the text writers. The proof necessary to meet this burden has been variously phrased: It must be shown that the individual "had discretion to judge between good and evil"; "knew right from wrong"; had "a guilty knowledge of wrong-doing"; was "competent to know the nature and consequences of his conduct and to appreciate that it was wrong." Perhaps the most modern definition of the test is simply that the surrounding circumstances must demonstrate, beyond a reasonable doubt, that the individual knew what he was doing and that it was wrong.
>
> It is generally held that the presumption of *doli incapax* is "extremely strong at the age of seven and diminishes gradually until it disappears entirely at the age of fourteen * * *." Since the strength of the presumption of incapacity decreases with the increase in the years of the accused, the quantum of proof necessary to overcome the presumption would diminish in substantially the same ratio.

With the advent of juvenile delinquency proceedings in lieu of criminal prosecutions, the issue arose in a number of jurisdictions as to whether, absent express statutory language, the infancy defense remained applicable in the delinquency proceedings. Some courts, like the Court of Special Appeals in *In re Davis, supra,* took the position that the defense was inapplicable. *See,* e.g., *Jennings v. State,* 384 So.2d 104 (Ala.1980); *Gammons v. Berlat,* 144 Ariz. 148, 696 P.2d 700 (1985); *State v. D.H.,* 340 So.2d 1163 (Fla. 1976); *In Interest of Dow,* 75 Ill.App.3d 1002, 31 Ill.Dec. 39, 393 N.E.2d 1346 (1979); *In the Matter of Skinner,* 272 S.C. 135, 249 S.E.2d 746 (1978). The rationale of these cases is essentially the same, and was expressed by the Court of Special Appeals in *Davis* as follows (17 Md.App. at 104, 299 A.2d at 860):

> Under the [juvenile] statute, by its purpose and the very principles it advances, the child under the jurisdiction of a juvenile court is conclusively presumed *doli incapax.* The child is delinquent, not because he committed a crime, but because he committed an *act* which would be a crime

> if committed by a person who is not a child, and because he requires supervision, treatment or rehabilitation. He must be *doli capax* to commit a crime, but not to commit a delinquent act. The *raison d'etre* of the Juvenile Causes Act is that a child does not commit a crime when he commits a delinquent act and therefore is not a criminal. He is not to be punished but afforded supervision and treatment to be made aware of what is right and what is wrong so as to be amenable to the criminal laws.

Or, as another writer expressed it (Walkover, *The Infancy Defense in the New Juvenile Court,* 31 UCLA L.Rev. 503, 516-517 (1984)),

> [b]ecause *parens patriae* theory depends on the notion that the child is being helped and thus is not being tried for a crime and punished as a criminal, there was no need to determine whether the child had the capacity to act in a culpable fashion. Indeed, assertion of the defense could be viewed as wrongfully precluding treatment for those very children most susceptible to the benefits of intervention, children who had committed wrongs without a clear sense of the wrongfulness of their acts.

In the instant case the State, essentially reflecting the above view, argues that the mental state of the defendant is irrelevant in a juvenile delinquency adjudicatory proceeding and that, therefore, the infancy defense has no place. The State asserts (brief, p. 4):

> In effect, a juvenile proceeding is an acknowledgment that the person before the court is *doli incapax* and therefore subject to treatment, not punishment. As a result, the question of mental state is irrelevant to the question of whether a "delinquent act" has been committed. The mental awareness of wrongdoing is relevant only to the question of whether a child needs guidance, treatment, or rehabilitation and, if so, the nature of the remedy.

Other courts, however, have reached the contrary conclusion, holding that the defense of infancy is fully applicable in juvenile delinquency proceedings. *See,* e.g., *In re R,* 1 Cal.3d 855, 464 P.2d 127, 83 Cal.Rptr. 671 (1970); *Matter of Andrew M,* 91 Misc.2d 813, 398 N.Y.S.2d 824 (1977); *Com. v. Durham,* 255 Pa.Super. 539, 389 A.2d 108 (1978); *State v. Q.D.,* 102 Wash.2d 19, 685 P.2d 557 (1984). *See also* Walkover, *supra,* 31 UCLA L.Rev. at 562.

A principal reason supporting the applicability of the defense is that juvenile statutes typically require, for a delinquency adjudication, that the child commit an act which constitutes a crime if committed by an adult, and if the child lacks capacity to have the requisite mens rea for a particular crime, he has not committed an act amounting to a crime. Another reason often given is that the pertinent statutes do not expressly render inapplicable the infancy defense, and that, to presume a repeal by implication, would largely eradicate the defense....

An additional reason given by the cases upholding the applicability of the infancy defense in juvenile delinquency proceedings, relates to the evolving nature of those proceedings. As explained by the Supreme Court of Washington in *State v. Q.D., supra,* 102 Wash.2d at 23, 685 P.2d at 560:

> The juvenile justice system in recent years has evolved from parens patriae scheme to one more akin to adult criminal proceedings. The United States Supreme Court has been critical of the parens patriae scheme as failing to provide safeguards due an adult criminal defendant, while

> subjecting the juvenile defendant to similar stigma, and possible loss of liberty. *See In re Gault,* 387 U.S. 1, 87 S.Ct. 1428, 18 L.Ed.2d 527 (1966); and *In re Winship,* 397 U.S. 358, 90 S.Ct. 1068, 25 L.Ed.2d 368 (1977)....Being a criminal defense, [the infancy defense] should be available to juvenile proceedings that are criminal in nature.

One commentator, in urging that the infancy defense remain applicable in juvenile delinquency proceedings, has stated (Walkover, *supra,* 31 UCLA L.Rev. at 562):

> Careful review of the recent history of the juvenile court reveals that the juvenile justice system has turned from rehabilitation to principles of accountability in dealing with youthful offenders. In light of this, continued reliance on the rehabilitative ideal to undercut key protections against sanctioning the innocent in the justice process, such as the infancy defense, is intellectually and institutionally problematic....
>
> Non-culpable children faced with the criminal process must be protected, not by the state, but from the state. There is nothing unique in the juvenile process, including the concept of lesser culpability, that excludes it from this conclusion. This, in sum, is the received wisdom of the last twenty-five years of juvenile sociological and jurisprudential study.

We agree with those courts which have held that the infancy defense applies in juvenile delinquency adjudicatory hearings....

As previously discussed, Maryland law defines a "delinquent act" as "an act which would be a crime if committed by an adult." § 3-801(k) of the Courts and Judicial Proceedings Article. Most crimes require some mens rea characteristics; they are elements of the crimes. If, when one commits an act, the requisite mens rea for a crime does not exist, the act does not constitute a crime. The defense of infancy relates to the presence or absence of the mens rea required for an act to constitute a crime....Consequently, the infancy defense relates to whether the act committed by a juvenile "would be a crime if committed by an adult," as prescribed in § 3-801(k) of the juvenile causes subtitle of the Courts and Judicial Proceedings Article....

We cannot accept the State's position that, under the juvenile causes subtitle, "mental state is irrelevant to the question of whether a 'delinquent act' has been committed." Such a holding would render a great deal of nonculpable conduct subject to delinquency proceedings.

NOTES AND QUESTIONS

1. What exactly was the infancy defense at the common law? Does it seem like a better approach?

2. It appears that most courts ruling on the issue have held that the infancy defense no longer applies in juvenile court. Andrew M. Carter, *Age Matters: The Case for a Constitutionalized Infancy Defense,* 54 U. Kan. L. Rev. 687, 721 (2006) ("decisions have almost uniformly resolved against recognition of the infancy defense in juvenile proceedings"); Lara Bazelon, *Exploding the Superpredator Myth: Why Infancy Is the Preadolescent's Best Defense in Juvenile Court,* 75 N.Y.U. L. Rev. 159, 161 & n. 7 (2000) (stating that only four states—California, Maryland, New Jersey, and Washington—apply

the infancy defense in juvenile proceedings). Nevertheless, should the infancy defense still be available in juvenile court proceedings? Should special defenses be available in juvenile court?

3. The majority of states does not establish a minimum age for culpability in juvenile court. However, several states establish an age below which a juvenile may not be charged with a delinquent act. Most of these jurisdictions establish a minimum age of ten; see, e.g., Ark. Code Ann., § 9-27-303(15)(A) (West 2010) (age ten for noncapital crimes); Colo. Rev. Stat. Ann., § 19-2-104(1)(a) (West 2010); Kan. Stat. Ann., § 38-23-2(i) (2009); La. Children's Code art. 730(6) (2010); Minn. Stat. Ann., § 260C.007(6)(12) (West 2010); Miss. Code Ann., § 43-21-105(i) (2010); 42 Pa. Cons. Stat. Ann., § 6302 (West 2010); S.D. Codified Laws, § 26-8C-2 (Michie 2010); Tex. Fam. Code Ann., § 51.02(2) (Vernon 2010); Vt. Stat. Ann. tit. 33, § 5102(2)(C) (2010); Wis. Stat. Ann., § 938.02(3m) (West 2010). However, a few extend delinquency jurisdiction to seven-year-olds, Ariz. Rev. Stat., § 8-201(13)(a)(v) (2010); Mass. Gen. Laws Ann. ch. 119, § 52 (West 2010); N.Y. Fam. Ct. Act, § 301.2 (1) (McKinney 2010); and one state holds six-year-olds liable for their delinquent acts, N.C. Gen. Stat., § 7B-1501(7) (2010). Do those jurisdictions establishing a minimum age for delinquency jurisdiction comport with the common-law rule? Should they?

In light of the material you have read on adolescent development, do you think there should be a minimum age at which a minor could be charged with a delinquent act? What age would that be? Do any of the age limitations in these statutes correspond to our understanding of adolescent development?

4. Reconsider the court's decision in *William A.* If there is a rebuttable presumption of incapacity, who has the burden of establishing the minor's incapacity or capacity? What is that burden? Is the decision in *William A.* constitutionally sound? The California Supreme Court, on the other hand, requires "clear proof" that a "child under the age of fourteen at the time of committing the act appreciated its wrongfulness." *In re Gladys R.*, 464 P.2d 127, 132–133 (Cal. 1970). In making that determination, "the juvenile court must therefore consider the child's age, experience, and understanding in determining whether he would be capable of committing [delinquent] conduct. Id. at 134. In New Jersey, the standard of proof is preponderance of the evidence. *In the interest of C.P.*, 514 A.2d 850, 854 (N.J. Super. Ct. Ch. Div. 1986). Washington requires the state to rebut the presumption of incapacity by clear and convincing proof. *State v. Q.D.*, 685 P.2d 557, 559 (Wash. 1984).

5. Article 40(3)(a) of the United Nations Convention on the Rights of the Child requires states parties to establish a "minimum age below which children shall be presumed not to have the capacity to infringe penal law." Convention on the Rights of the Child, art. 40(3)(a), Nov. 20, 1989, 1577 U.N.T.S. 3. In the United Kingdom, a state party, the minimum age of criminal responsibility ranges from eight years old (Scotland) to ten years old (England and Wales). Despite the absence of a specific age requirement, the UN Committee on the Rights of the Child has expressed concern that the age of criminal responsibility is too low and has recommended that the United Kingdom consider raising the age. UN Committee on the Rights of the Child, Report of the Committee on the Rights of the Child: Sixth to Eleventh Session, UN New York 1996, pp. 73, 76. More recently, the Committee on the Rights of the Child recommended that states parties set the age of criminal responsibility at "an internationally acceptable level," finding that ten years of age is "still too low." UN Committee on the Rights of the Child, Concluding Observations: Australia, U.N. Doc. CRC/C/15/Add. 268 (2005), at paras. 73–74. Is there an internationally acceptable age for criminal responsibility? If so, what is it?

B. Constitutional Framework

KENT V. UNITED STATES
Supreme Court of the United States
383 U.S. 541 (1966)

MR. JUSTICE FORTAS delivered the opinion of the Court....

Morris A. Kent, Jr., first came under the authority of the Juvenile Court of the District of Columbia in 1959. He was then aged 14. He was apprehended as a result of several house-breakings and an attempted purse snatching. He was placed on probation, in the custody of his mother who had been separated from her husband since Kent was two years old. Juvenile Court officials interviewed Kent from time to time during the probation period and accumulated a "Social Service" file.

On September 2, 1961, an intruder entered the apartment of a woman in the District of Columbia. He took her wallet. He raped her. The police found in the apartment latent fingerprints. They were developed and processed. They matched the fingerprints of Morris Kent, taken when he was 14 years old and under the jurisdiction of the Juvenile Court. At about 3 p.m. on September 5, 1961, Kent was taken into custody by the police. Kent was then 16 and therefore subject to the "exclusive jurisdiction" of the Juvenile Court. He was still on probation to that court as a result of the 1959 proceedings.

Upon being apprehended, Kent was taken to police headquarters where he was interrogated by police officers. It appears that he admitted his involvement in the offense which led to his apprehension and volunteered information as to similar offenses involving housebreaking, robbery, and rape. His interrogation proceeded from about 3 p.m. to 10 p.m. the same evening.

Some time after 10 p.m. petitioner was taken to the Receiving Home for Children. The next morning he was released to the police for further interrogation at police headquarters, which lasted until 5 p.m.

The record does not show when his mother became aware that the boy was in custody but shortly after 2 p.m. on September 6, 1961, the day following petitioner's apprehension, she retained counsel.

Counsel, together with petitioner's mother, promptly conferred with the Social Service Director of the Juvenile Court. In a brief interview, they discussed the possibility that the Juvenile Court might waive jurisdiction...and remit Kent to trial by the District Court. Counsel made known his intention to oppose waiver.

Petitioner was detained at the Receiving Home for almost a week. There was no arraignment during this time, no determination by a judicial officer of probable cause for petitioner's apprehension.

During this period of detention and interrogation, petitioner's counsel arranged for examination of petitioner by two psychiatrists and a psychologist. He thereafter filed with the Juvenile Court a motion for a hearing on the question of waiver of Juvenile Court jurisdiction, together with an affidavit of a psychiatrist certifying that petitioner "is a victim of severe psychopathology" and recommending hospitalization for psychiatric observation. Petitioner's counsel, in support of his motion to the effect that the Juvenile Court should retain jurisdiction of petitioner, offered to prove that if petitioner were given adequate treatment in a hospital under the aegis of the Juvenile Court, he would be a suitable subject for rehabilitation.

At the same time, petitioner's counsel moved that the Juvenile Court should give him access to the Social Service file relating to petitioner which had been accumulated by the staff of the Juvenile Court during petitioner's probation period, and which would be available to the Juvenile Court judge in considering the question whether it should retain or waive jurisdiction. Petitioner's counsel represented that access to this file was essential to his providing petitioner with effective assistance of counsel.

The Juvenile Court judge did not rule on these motions. He held no hearing. He did not confer with petitioner or petitioner's parents or petitioner's counsel. He entered an order reciting that after "full investigation, I do hereby waive" jurisdiction of petitioner and directing that he be "held for trial for (the alleged) offenses under the regular procedure of the U.S. District Court for the District of Columbia." He made no findings. He did not recite any reason for the waiver. He made no reference to the motions filed by petitioner's counsel. We must assume that he denied, sub silentio, the motions for a hearing, the recommendation for hospitalization for psychiatric observation, the request for access to the Social Service file, and the offer to prove that petitioner was a fit subject for rehabilitation under the Juvenile Court's jurisdiction.

Presumably, prior to entry of his order, the Juvenile Court judge received and considered recommendations of the Juvenile Court staff, the Social Service file relating to petitioner, and a report dated September 8, 1961 (three days following petitioner's apprehension), submitted to him by the Juvenile Probation Section. The Social Service file and the September 8 report were later sent to the District Court and it appears that both of them referred to petitioner's mental condition. The September 8 report spoke of "a rapid deterioration of (petitioner's) personality structure and the possibility of mental illness." As stated, neither this report nor the Social Service file was made available to petitioner's counsel.

The provision of the Juvenile Court Act governing waiver expressly provides only for "full investigation." It states the circumstances in which jurisdiction may be waived and the child held for trial under adult procedures, but it does not state standards to govern the Juvenile Court's decision as to waiver....

Petitioner appealed from the Juvenile Court's waiver order to the Municipal Court of Appeals, which affirmed, and also applied to the United States District Court for a writ of habeas corpus, which was denied. On appeal from these judgments, the United States Court of Appeals held on January 22, 1963, that neither appeal to the Municipal Court of Appeals nor habeas corpus was available. In the Court of Appeals' view, the exclusive method of reviewing the Juvenile Court's waiver order was a motion to dismiss the indictment in the District Court.

Meanwhile, on September 25, 1961, shortly after the Juvenile Court order waiving its jurisdiction, petitioner was indicted by a grand jury of the United States District Court for the District of Columbia. The indictment contained eight counts alleging two instances of housebreaking, robbery, and rape, and one of housebreaking and robbery. On November 16, 1961, petitioner moved the District Court to dismiss the indictment on the grounds that the waiver was invalid. He also moved the District Court to constitute itself a Juvenile Court as authorized by [the D.C. Code]. After substantial delay occasioned by petitioner's appeal and habeas corpus proceedings, the District Court addressed itself to the motion to dismiss on February 8, 1963.

The District Court denied the motion to dismiss the indictment. The District Court ruled that it would not "go behind" the Juvenile Court judge's recital that his order was entered "after full investigation."...

On March 7, 1963, the District Court held a hearing on petitioner's motion to determine his competency to stand trial. The court determined that petitioner was competent.

At trial, petitioner's defense was wholly directed toward proving that he was not criminally responsible because "his unlawful act was the product of mental disease or mental defect."...Extensive evidence, including expert testimony, was presented to support this defense. The jury found as to the counts alleging rape that petitioner was "not guilty by reason of insanity." Under District of Columbia law, this made it mandatory that petitioner be transferred to St. Elizabeth's Hospital, a mental institution, until his sanity is restored. On the six counts of housebreaking and robbery, the jury found that petitioner was guilty.

Kent was sentenced to serve five to 15 years on each count as to which he was found guilty, or a total of 30 to 90 years in prison. The District Court ordered that the time to be spent at St. Elizabeth's on the mandatory commitment after the insanity acquittal be counted as part of the 30- to 90-year sentence. Petitioner appealed to the United States Court of Appeals for the District of Columbia Circuit. That court affirmed.

Before the Court of Appeals and in this Court, petitioner's counsel has urged a number of grounds for reversal. He argues that petitioner's detention and interrogation, described above, were unlawful. He contends that the police failed to follow the procedure prescribed by the Juvenile Court Act in that they failed to notify the parents of the child and the Juvenile Court itself...; that petitioner was deprived of his liberty for about a week without a determination of probable cause which would have been required in the case of an adult...; that he was interrogated by the police in the absence of counsel or a parent...without warning of his right to remain silent or advice as to his right to counsel...; and that petitioner was fingerprinted in violation of the asserted intent of the Juvenile Court Act and while unlawfully detained and that the fingerprints were unlawfully used in the District Court proceeding.

These contentions...suggest basic issues as to the justifiability of affording a juvenile less protection than is accorded to adults suspected of criminal offenses, particularly where, as here, there is an absence of any indication that the denial of rights available to adults was offset, mitigated or explained by action of the Government, as parens patriae, evidencing the special solicitude for juveniles commanded by the Juvenile Court Act. However, because we remand the case on account of the procedural error with respect to waiver of jurisdiction, we do not pass upon these questions....

...Petitioner attacks the waiver of jurisdiction on a number of statutory and constitutional grounds. He contends that the waiver is defective because no hearing was held; because no findings were made by the Juvenile Court; because the Juvenile Court stated no reasons for waiver; and because counsel was denied access to the Social Service file which presumably was considered by the Juvenile Court in determining to waive jurisdiction.

We agree that the order of the Juvenile Court waiving its jurisdiction and transferring petitioner for trial in the United States District Court for the District of Columbia was invalid. There is no question that the order is reviewable on motion to dismiss the indictment in the District Court, as specified by the Court of Appeals in this case....

We agree with the Court of Appeals that the statute contemplates that the Juvenile Court should have considerable latitude within which to determine whether it should retain jurisdiction over a child or—subject to the statutory delimitation—should waive jurisdiction. But this latitude is not complete. At the outset, it assumes procedural regularity sufficient in the particular circumstances to satisfy the basic requirements of due process and fairness, as well as compliance with the statutory requirement of a "full investigation." The statute gives the Juvenile Court a substantial degree of discretion as to the factual considerations to be evaluated, the weight to be given them and the conclusion to be reached. It does not confer upon the Juvenile Court a license for arbitrary procedure. The statute does not permit the Juvenile Court to determine in isolation and without the participation or any representation of the child the "critically important" question whether a child will be deprived of the special protections and provisions of the Juvenile Court Act. It does not authorize the Juvenile Court, in total disregard of a motion for hearing filed by counsel, and without any hearing or statement or reasons, to decide—as in this case—that the child will be taken from the Receiving Home for Children and transferred to jail along with adults, and that he will be exposed to the possibility of a death sentence instead of treatment for a maximum, in Kent's case, of five years, until he is 21.

We do not consider whether, on the merits, Kent should have been transferred; but there is no place in our system of law for reaching a result of such tremendous consequences without ceremony—without hearing, without effective assistance of counsel, without a statement of reasons. It is inconceivable that a court of justice dealing with adults, with respect to a similar issue, would proceed in this manner. It would be extraordinary if society's special concern for children, as reflected in the District of Columbia's Juvenile Court Act, permitted this procedure. We hold that it does not.

1. The theory of the District's Juvenile Court Act, like that of other jurisdictions, is rooted in social welfare philosophy rather than in the corpus juris. Its proceedings are designated as civil rather than criminal. The Juvenile Court is theoretically engaged in determining the needs of the child and of society rather than adjudicating criminal conduct. The objectives are to provide measures of guidance and rehabilitation for the child and protection for society, not to fix criminal responsibility, guilt and punishment. The State is *parens patriae* rather than prosecuting attorney and judge. But the admonition to function in a "parental" relationship is not an invitation to procedural arbitrariness.

2. Because the State is supposed to proceed in respect of the child as *parens patriae* and not as adversary, courts have relied on the premise that the proceedings are "civil" in nature and not criminal, and have asserted that the child cannot complain of the deprivation of important rights available in criminal cases. It has been asserted that he can claim only the fundamental due process right to fair treatment. For example, it has been held that he is not entitled to bail; to indictment by grand jury; to a speedy and public trial; to trial by jury; to immunity against self-incrimination; to confrontation of his accusers; and in some jurisdictions (but not in the District of Columbia...), that he is not entitled to counsel.

While there can be no doubt of the original laudable purpose of juvenile courts, studies and critiques in recent years raise serious questions as to whether actual performance measures well enough against theoretical purpose to make tolerable the immunity of the process from the reach of constitutional guaranties applicable to adults. There is much evidence that some juvenile courts, including that of the District of Columbia, lack the personnel, facilities and techniques to perform adequately as representatives of the State in a *parens patriae* capacity, at least with respect to children charged with law violation. There is evidence, in fact, that there may be grounds for concern that the child receives the worst of both worlds: that he gets neither the protections accorded to adults nor the solicitous care and regenerative treatment postulated for children.

This concern, however, does not induce us in this case to accept the invitation to rule that constitutional guaranties which would be applicable to adults charged with the serious offenses for which Kent was tried must be applied in juvenile court proceedings concerned with allegations of law violation....

3. It is clear beyond dispute that the waiver of jurisdiction is a "critically important" action determining vitally important statutory rights of the juvenile.... The Juvenile Court is vested with "original and exclusive jurisdiction" of the child. This jurisdiction confers special rights and immunities. He is, as specified by the statute, shielded from publicity. He may be confined, but with rare exceptions he may not be jailed along with adults. He may be detained, but only until he is 21 years of age. The court is admonished by the statute to give preference to retaining the child in the custody of his parents "unless his welfare and the safety and protection of the public can not be adequately safeguarded without... removal." The child is protected against consequences of adult conviction such as the loss of civil rights, the use of adjudication against him in subsequent proceedings, and disqualification for public employment.

The net, therefore, is that petitioner—then a boy of 16—was by statute entitled to certain procedures and benefits as a consequence of his statutory right to the "exclusive" jurisdiction of the Juvenile Court. In these circumstances, considering particularly that decision as to waiver of jurisdiction and transfer of the matter to the District Court was potentially as important to petitioner as the difference between five years' confinement and a death sentence, we conclude that, as a condition to a valid waiver order, petitioner was entitled to a hearing, including access by his counsel to the social records and probation or similar reports which presumably are considered by the court, and to a statement of reasons for the Juvenile Court's decision. We believe that this result is required by the statute read in the context of constitutional principles relating to due process and the assistance of counsel....

... [T]he Court of Appeals... did note... that the determination of whether to transfer a child from the statutory structure of the Juvenile Court to the criminal processes of the District Court is "critically important." We hold that it is, indeed, a "critically important" proceeding. The Juvenile Court Act confers upon the child a right to avail himself of that court's "exclusive" jurisdiction....

Meaningful review requires that the reviewing court should review. It should not be remitted to assumptions. It must have before it a statement of the reasons motivating the waiver including, of course, a statement of the relevant facts. It may not "assume" that there are adequate reasons, nor may it merely assume that "full investigation" has been made. Accordingly, we hold that it is incumbent upon the Juvenile Court to accompany its waiver order with a statement of the reasons or considerations therefor. We do not read the statute as requiring that this statement must be formal or that it should necessarily include conventional findings of fact. But the statement should be sufficient to demonstrate that the statutory requirement of "full investigation" has been met; and that the question has received the careful consideration of the Juvenile Court; and it must set forth the basis for the order with sufficient specificity to permit meaningful review.

Correspondingly, we conclude that an opportunity for a hearing which may be informal, must be given the child prior to entry of a waiver order.... [Under District of Columbia law] the child is entitled to counsel in connection with a waiver proceeding, and... counsel is entitled to see the child's social records. These rights are meaningless—an illusion, a mockery—unless counsel is given an opportunity to function.

The right to representation by counsel is not a formality. It is not a grudging gesture to a ritualistic requirement. It is of the essence of justice. Appointment of counsel without affording an opportunity for hearing on a "critically important" decision is tantamount to denial of counsel. There is no justification for the failure of the Juvenile Court to rule on the motion for hearing filed by petitioner's counsel, and it was error to fail to grant a hearing.

We do not mean by this to indicate that the hearing to be held must conform with all of the requirements of a criminal trial or even of the usual administrative hearing; but we do hold that the hearing must measure up to the essentials of due process and fair treatment.

With respect to access by the child's counsel to the social records of the child, we deem it obvious that since these are to be considered by the Juvenile Court in making its decision to waive, they must be made available to the child's counsel.... The statute expressly provides that the record shall be withheld from "indiscriminate" public inspection, "except that such records or parts thereof shall be made available by rule of court or special order of court to such persons as have a legitimate interest in the protection... of the child...." Counsel, therefore, have a "legitimate interest" in the protection of the child, and must be afforded access to these records.

We do not agree... that counsel's role is limited to presenting "to the court anything on behalf of the child which might help the court in arriving at a decision; it is not to denigrate the staff's submissions and recommendations." On the contrary, if the staff's submissions include materials which are susceptible to challenge or impeachment, it is precisely the role of counsel to "denigrate" such matter. There is no irrebuttable presumption of accuracy attached to staff reports. If a decision on waiver is "critically important" it is equally of "critical importance" that the material submitted to the judge—which is protected by the statute only against "indiscriminate" inspection—be subjected, within reasonable limits... to examination, criticism and refutation. While the Juvenile Court judge may, of course, receive *ex parte* analyses and recommendations from his staff, he may not, for purposes of a decision on waiver, receive and rely upon secret information, whether emanating from his staff or otherwise....

Ordinarily we would reverse the Court of Appeals and direct the District Court to remand the case to the Juvenile Court for a new determination of waiver.... However, petitioner has now passed the age of 21 and the Juvenile Court can no longer exercise jurisdiction over him.... Accordingly, we vacate the order of the Court of Appeals and the judgment of the District Court and remand the case to the District Court for a hearing *de novo* on waiver, consistent with this opinion. If that court finds that waiver was inappropriate, petitioner's conviction must be vacated. If, however, it finds that the waiver order was proper when originally made, the District Court may proceed, after consideration of such motions as counsel may make and such further proceedings, if any, as may be warranted, to enter an appropriate judgment.

Reversed and remanded.

MR. JUSTICE STEWART, with whom MR. JUSTICE BLACK, MR. JUSTICE HARLAN and MR. JUSTICE WHITE join, dissenting.

This case involves the construction of a statute applicable only to the District of Columbia. Our general practice is to leave undisturbed decisions of the Court of Appeals for the District of Columbia Circuit concerning the import of legislation governing the affairs of the District. It appears, however, that two cases decided by the Court of Appeals subsequent to its decision in the present case may have considerably modified the court's construction of the statute. Therefore, I would vacate this judgment and remand the case to the Court of Appeals for reconsideration in the light of its subsequent decisions.

NOTES AND QUESTIONS

1. On remand to the district court, the waiver was again found to be valid "because…the defendant's…civil commitment…was an inappropriate alternative to waiver." On appeal, the Court of Appeals reversed, holding that the lower court finding "turns civil commitment law on its head." *Kent v. United States*, 401 F.2d 408, 409–410 (D.C. Cir. 1968). The Court of Appeals also found that waiver was "inappropriate" in light of the lower court's finding that Kent was suffering from a serious mental illness.

It is true that the juvenile court has "a substantial degree of discretion" in determining whether to retain jurisdiction over a child. *Kent v. United States,* 383 U.S. 541 at 554, 86 S. Ct. 1045, 1054, 16 L. Ed. 2d 84. But this discretion must be exercised in accordance with the spirit of the Juvenile Court Act.…

Parens patriae requires that the juvenile court do what is best for the child's care and rehabilitation so long as this disposition provides adequate protection for society. In the instant case, no concern was shown for Kent's care and rehabilitation, and mechanisms by which society could be protected were ignored.

The juvenile authorities who waived Kent knew that he was seriously ill and in need of treatment. The Government argues, however, that their decision to waive does not indicate a lack of concern for Kent's care and rehabilitation.…The argument is, at best, disingenuous. It overlooks the fundamental point that waiver is a judgment that an adult criminal prosecution should be instituted against the juvenile. The purpose of this exercise is to obtain a conviction for which the juvenile may be penalized as an adult. The exercise succeeded when the jury convicted Kent on several counts even though it recognized full well that he was suffering from a serious mental illness.

Treatment of a sick juvenile is not a concern of an adult criminal proceeding. Kent's case bears this out. Before trial the district court sent him to District of Columbia General Hospital and then to Saint Elizabeth's Hospital for mental examinations, not treatment. Upon completion of these examinations on April 9, 1962, he spent eleven months in a prison prior to trial without any psychiatric attention.…

> It seems clear that the chief reason for waiver was that the juvenile court could retain jurisdiction over Kent for only five years and that he was unlikely to recover within this period. The paradoxical result is that the sicker a juvenile is, the less care he receives from the juvenile court.

401 F.2d at 411–412. The Court of Appeals ordered the conviction vacated but stayed the decision for thirty days to give the state time to institute civil commitment proceedings. *Id.*

What does Catherine Ross mean when she states that Judge Bazelon recognized that "[r]ehabilitation—a gift of the state—was possible only after meeting the security needs of society." Catherine J. Ross, *Disposition in a Discretionary Regime: Punishment and Rehabilitation in the Juvenile Justice System*, 36 B.C. L. REV. 1037, 1050–1051 (1995). Do you agree?

2. The author of the appellate court decision on remand was Judge David L. Bazelon. Appointed to the Court of Appeals for the District of Columbia in 1949 by President Harry S. Truman, Bazelon served as chief judge from 1962 to 1978. He also served as a member of the National Institutes of Health Advisory Commission and was a lecturer in law and psychiatry at Johns Hopkins University, the University of Pennsylvania, and the Menninger Clinic. In addition, Bazelon was president of the American Orthopsychiatric Association from 1967 to 1970. The Bazelon Center for Mental Health was named in his honor in 1993.

3. The sole dissenter from the appellate court decision was Judge Warren Burger. Arguing that the lower court's determination may be overturned only if found clearly erroneous, the dissent contends that the appellate court reconstituted itself "as the Juvenile Court...to reach a factual determination contrary to that already worked out in the District Court sitting as a juvenile court." 401 F.2d at 415 (Burger, J., dissenting).

Burger joined the District of Columbia Court of Appeals in 1956 and in 1969 was named by President Richard Nixon to serve as chief justice of the United States Supreme Court. He and Bazelon had a long and bitter feud over the meaning and scope of criminal responsibility. LINDA GREENHOUSE, BECOMING JUSTICE BLACKMUN.

4. The Supreme Court in *Kent* appended a copy of a 1959 policy memorandum from the D.C. Juvenile Court listing the factors that a juvenile judge should consider in deciding whether the juvenile court's jurisdiction will be waived.

> An offense falling within the statutory limitations (set forth above) will be waived if it has prosecutive merit and if it is heinous or of an aggravated character, or—even though less serious—if it represents a pattern of repeated offenses which indicate that the juvenile may be beyond rehabilitation under Juvenile Court procedures, or if the public needs the protection afforded by such action.
>
> The determinative factors which will be considered by the Judge are the following:
>
> 1. The seriousness of the alleged offense to the community and whether the protection of the community requires waiver.
> 2. Whether the alleged offense was committed in an aggressive, violent, premeditated or willful manner.
> 3. Whether the alleged offense was against persons or against property, greater weight being given to offenses against persons especially if personal injury resulted.
> 4. The prosecutive merit of the complaint, i.e., whether there is evidence upon which a Grand Jury may be expected to return an indictment (to be determined by consultation with the United States Attorney).
> 5. The desirability of trial and disposition of the entire offense in one court when the juvenile's associates in the alleged offense are adults who will be charged with a crime in the U.S. District Court for the District of Columbia.

6. The sophistication and maturity of the juvenile as determined by consideration of his home, environmental situation, emotional attitude and pattern of living.
7. The record and previous history of the juvenile, including previous contacts with the Youth Aid Division, other law enforcement agencies, juvenile courts and other jurisdictions, prior periods of probation to this Court, or prior commitments to juvenile institutions.
8. The prospects for adequate protection of the public and the likelihood of reasonable rehabilitation of the juvenile (if he is found to have committed the alleged offense) by the use of procedures, services and facilities currently available to the Juvenile Court.

Kent, 383 U.S. at 566–567. In light of the rehabilitative purposes of the juvenile court, do you think the criteria are consistent with those goals?

IN RE GAULT
Supreme Court of the United States
387 U.S. 1 (1967)

MR. JUSTICE FORTAS delivered the opinion of the Court....

I

On Monday, June 8, 1964, at about 10 a.m., Gerald Francis Gault and a friend, Ronald Lewis, were taken into custody by the Sheriff of Gila County. Gerald was then still subject to a six months' probation order which had been entered on February 25, 1964, as a result of his having been in the company of another boy who had stolen a wallet from a lady's purse. The police action on June 8 was taken as the result of a verbal complaint by a neighbor of the boys, Mrs. Cook, about a telephone call made to her in which the caller or callers made lewd or indecent remarks. It will suffice for purposes of this opinion to say that the remarks or questions put to her were of the irritatingly offensive, adolescent, sex variety.

At the time Gerald was picked up, his mother and father were both at work. No notice that Gerald was being taken into custody was left at the home. No other steps were taken to advise them that their son had, in effect, been arrested. Gerald was taken to the Children's Detention Home. When his mother arrived home at about 6 o'clock, Gerald was not there. Gerald's older brother was sent to look for him at the trailer home of the Lewis family. He apparently learned then that Gerald was in custody. He so informed his mother. The two of them went to the Detention Home. The deputy probation officer, Flagg, who was also superintendent of the Detention Home, told Mrs. Gault "why Jerry was there" and said that a hearing would be held in Juvenile Court at 3 o'clock the following day, June 9.

Officer Flagg filed a petition with the court on the hearing day, June 9, 1964. It was not served on the Gaults. Indeed, none of them saw this petition until the habeas corpus hearing on August 17, 1964. The petition was entirely formal. It made no reference to any factual basis for the judicial action which it initiated. It recited only that "said minor is under the age of eighteen years, and is in need of the protection of this Honorable Court; (and that) said minor is a delinquent minor." It prayed for a hearing and an order regarding "the care and custody of said minor." Officer Flagg executed a formal affidavit in support of the petition.

On June 9, Gerald, his mother, his older brother, and Probation Officers Flagg and Henderson appeared before the Juvenile Judge in chambers. Gerald's father was not there. He was at work out of the city. Mrs. Cook, the complainant, was not there. No one was sworn at this hearing. No transcript or recording was made. No memorandum or record of the substance of the proceedings was prepared. Our information about the proceedings and the subsequent hearing on June 15, derives entirely from the testimony of the Juvenile Court Judge, Mr. and Mrs. Gault and Officer Flagg at the habeas corpus proceeding conducted two months later. From this, it appears that at the June 9 hearing Gerald was questioned by the judge about the telephone call. There was conflict as to what he said. His mother recalled that Gerald said he only dialed Mrs. Cook's number and handed the telephone to his friend, Ronald. Officer Flagg recalled that Gerald had admitted making the lewd remarks. Judge McGhee testified that Gerald "admitted making one of these (lewd) statements." At the conclusion of the hearing, the judge said he would "think about it." Gerald was taken back to the Detention Home. He was not sent to his own home with his parents. On June 11 or 12, after having been detained since June 8, Gerald was released and driven home. There is no explanation in the record as to why he was kept in the Detention Home or why he was released. At 5 p.m. on the day of Gerald's release, Mrs. Gault received a note signed by Officer Flagg. It was on plain paper, not letterhead. Its entire text was as follows:

> "Mrs. Gault:
> Judge McGHEE has set Monday June 15, 1964 at 11:00 A.M. as the date and time for further Hearings on Gerald's delinquency
> /s/ Flagg"

At the appointed time on Monday, June 15, Gerald, his father and mother, Ronald Lewis and his father, and Officers Flagg and Henderson were present before Judge McGhee. Witnesses at the habeas corpus proceeding differed in their recollections of Gerald's testimony at the June 15 hearing. Mr. and Mrs. Gault recalled that Gerald again testified that he had only dialed the number and that the other boy had made the remarks. Officer Flagg agreed that at this hearing Gerald did not admit making the lewd remarks. But Judge McGhee recalled that "there was some admission again of some of the lewd statements. He–he didn't admit any of the more serious lewd statements." Again, the complainant, Mrs. Cook, was not present. Mrs. Gault asked that Mrs. Cook be present "so she could see which boy that done the talking, the dirty talking over the phone." The Juvenile Judge said "she didn't have to be present at that hearing." The judge did not speak to Mrs. Cook or communicate with her at any time. Probation Officer Flagg had talked to her once—over the telephone on June 9.

At this June 15 hearing a "referral report" made by the probation officers was filed with the court, although not disclosed to Gerald or his parents. This listed the charge as "Lewd Phone Calls." At the conclusion of the hearing, the judge committed Gerald as a juvenile delinquent to the State Industrial School "for the period of his minority (that is, until 21), unless sooner discharged by due process of law." An order to that effect was entered. It recites that "after a full hearing and due deliberation the Court finds that said minor is a delinquent child, and that said minor is of the age of 15 years."

No appeal is permitted by Arizona law in juvenile cases. On August 3, 1964, a petition for a writ of habeas corpus was filed with the Supreme Court of Arizona and referred by it to the Superior Court for hearing.

At the habeas corpus hearing on August 17, Judge McGhee was vigorously cross-examined as to the basis for his actions. He testified that he had taken into account the fact that Gerald was on probation. He was asked "under what section of... the code you found the boy delinquent?"

His answer is set forth in the margin.[1] In substance, he concluded that Gerald came within ARS § 8-201, subsec. 6(a), which specifies that a "delinquent child" includes one "who has violated a law of the state or an ordinance or regulation of a political subdivision thereof." The law which Gerald was found to have violated is ARS § 13-377. This section of the Arizona Criminal Code provides that a person who "in the presence or hearing of any woman or child... uses vulgar, abusive or obscene language, is guilty of a misdemeanor...." The penalty specified in the Criminal Code, which would apply to an adult, is $5 to $50, or imprisonment for not more than two months. The judge also testified that he acted under ARS § 8-201, subsec. 6(d) which includes in the definition of a "delinquent child" one who, as the judge phrased it, is "habitually involved in immoral matters."[6]

Asked about the basis for his conclusion that Gerald was "habitually involved in immoral matters," the judge testified, somewhat vaguely, that two years earlier, on July 2, 1962, a "referral" was made concerning Gerald, "where the boy had stolen a baseball glove from another boy and lied to the Police Department about it." The judge said there was "no hearing," and "no accusation" relating to this incident, "because of lack of material foundation." But it seems to have remained in his mind as a relevant factor. The judge also testified that Gerald had admitted making other nuisance phone calls in the past which, as the judge recalled the boy's testimony, were "silly calls, or funny calls, or something like that."...

... In their jurisdictional statement and brief in this Court, appellants... urge that we hold the Juvenile Code of Arizona invalid on its face or as applied in this case because, contrary to the Due Process Clause of the Fourteenth Amendment, the juvenile is taken from the custody of his parents and committed to a state institution pursuant to proceedings in which the Juvenile Court has virtually unlimited discretion, and in which the following basic rights are denied:

1. Notice of the charges;
2. Right to counsel;

1. "Q. All right. Now, Judge, would you tell me under what section of the law or tell me under what section of—of the code you found the boy delinquent?
"A. Well, there is a—I think it amounts to disturbing the peace. I can't give you the section, but I can tell you the law, that when one person uses lewd language in the presence of another person, that it can amount to—and I consider that when a person makes it over the phone, that it is considered in the presence, I might be wrong, that is one section. The other section upon which I consider the boy delinquent is Section 8-201, Subsection (d), habitually involved in immoral matters."

6. ARS § 8-201, subsec. 6, the section of the Arizona Juvenile Code which defines a delinquent child, reads: "Delinquent child" includes:
"(a) A child who has violated a law of the state or an ordinance or regulation of a political subdivision thereof.
"(b) A child who, by reason of being incorrigible, wayward or habitually disobedient, is uncontrolled by his parent, guardian or custodian.
"(c) A child who is habitually truant from school or home.
"(d) A child who habitually so deports himself as to injure or endanger the morals or health of himself or others."

3. Right to confrontation and cross-examination;
4. Privilege against self-incrimination;
5. Right to a transcript of the proceedings; and
6. Right to appellate review....

II

The Supreme Court of Arizona held that due process of law is requisite to the constitutional validity of proceedings in which a court reaches the conclusion that a juvenile has been at fault, has engaged in conduct prohibited by law, or has otherwise misbehaved with the consequence that he is committed to an institution in which his freedom is curtailed....

This Court has not heretofore decided the precise question. In *Kent v. United States*, 383 U.S. 541 (1966), we considered the requirements for a valid waiver of the "exclusive" jurisdiction of the Juvenile Court of the District of Columbia so that a juvenile could be tried in the adult criminal court of the District. Although our decision turned upon the language of the statute, we emphasized the necessity that "the basic requirements of due process and fairness" be satisfied in such proceedings....Accordingly...neither the Fourteenth Amendment nor the Bill of Rights is for adults alone.

We do not in this opinion consider the impact of these constitutional provisions upon the totality of the relationship of the juvenile and the state. We do not even consider the entire process relating to juvenile "delinquents." For example, we are not here concerned with the procedures or constitutional rights applicable to the pre-judicial stages of the juvenile process, nor do we direct our attention to the post-adjudicative or dispositional process. We consider only the problems presented to us by this case. These relate to the proceedings by which a determination is made as to whether a juvenile is a "delinquent" as a result of alleged misconduct on his part, with the consequence that he may be committed to a state institution. As to these proceedings, there appears to be little current dissent from the proposition that the Due Process Clause has a role to play. The problem is to ascertain the precise impact of the due process requirement upon such proceedings.

From the inception of the juvenile court system, wide differences have been tolerated—indeed insisted upon—between the procedural rights accorded to adults and those of juveniles. In practically all jurisdictions, there are rights granted to adults which are withheld from juveniles....

The history and theory underlying this development are well-known, but a recapitulation is necessary for purposes of this opinion. The Juvenile Court movement began in this country at the end of the last century. From the juvenile court statute adopted in Illinois in 1899, the system has spread to every State in the Union, the District of Columbia, and Puerto Rico. The constitutionality of juvenile court laws has been sustained in over 40 jurisdictions against a variety of attacks.

The early reformers were appalled by adult procedures and penalties, and by the fact that children could be given long prison sentences and mixed in jails with hardened criminals. They were profoundly convinced that society's duty to the child could not be confined by the concept of justice alone. They believed that society's role was not to ascertain whether the child was "guilty" or "innocent," but "What is he, how has he become what he is, and what had best be done in his interest and in the interest of the state to save him from a downward career."[16] The child—essentially good, as they saw it—was to be made "to feel that he is the object of (the state's) care and solicitude,"[17] not that he was under arrest or on trial. The rules of criminal procedure were therefore altogether inapplicable. The apparent rigidities, technicalities, and harshness which they observed in both substantive and procedural criminal law were therefore to be discarded. The idea of crime and punishment was to be abandoned. The child was to be "treated" and "rehabilitated" and the procedures, from apprehension through institutionalization, were to be "clinical" rather than punitive.

These results were to be achieved, without coming to conceptual and constitutional grief, by insisting that the proceedings were not adversary, but that the state was proceeding as *parens patriae*. The Latin phrase proved to be a great help to those who sought to rationalize the exclusion of juveniles from the constitutional scheme; but its meaning is murky and its historic credentials are of dubious relevance. The phrase was taken from chancery practice, where, however, it was used to describe the power of the state to act *in loco parentis* for the purpose of protecting the property interests and the person of the child. But there is no trace of the doctrine in the history of criminal jurisprudence. At common law, children under seven were considered incapable of possessing criminal intent. Beyond that age, they were subjected to arrest, trial, and in theory to punishment like adult offenders. In these old days, the state was not deemed to have authority to accord them fewer procedural rights than adults.

The right of the state, as *parens patriae*, to deny to the child procedural rights available to his elders was elaborated by the assertion that a child, unlike an adult, has a right "not to liberty but to custody." He can be made to attorn to his parents, to go to school, etc. If his parents default in effectively performing their custodial functions—that is, if the child is "delinquent"—the state may intervene. In doing so, it does not deprive the child of any rights, because he has none. It merely provides the "custody" to which the child is entitled. On this basis, proceedings involving juveniles were described as "civil" not "criminal" and therefore not subject to the requirements which restrict the state when it seeks to deprive a person of his liberty.

Accordingly, the highest motives and most enlightened impulses led to a peculiar system for juveniles, unknown to our law in any comparable context. The constitutional and theoretical basis for this peculiar system is—to say the least—debatable. And in practice, as we remarked in the Kent case, supra, the results have not been entirely satisfactory. Juvenile Court history has again demonstrated that unbridled discretion, however benevolently motivated, is frequently a poor substitute for principle and procedure. In 1937, Dean Pound wrote: "The powers of the Star Chamber were a trifle in comparison with those of our juvenile courts. . . ." The absence of substantive standards has not necessarily meant that children receive careful, compassionate, individualized treatment. The absence of procedural rules based upon constitutional principle has not always produced fair, efficient, and effective procedures. Departures from established principles of due process have frequently resulted not in enlightened procedure, but in arbitrariness. . . .

Failure to observe the fundamental requirements of due process has resulted in instances, which might have been avoided, of unfairness to individuals and inadequate or inaccurate findings of fact and unfortunate prescriptions of remedy. Due process of law is the primary

16. Julian Mack, The Juvenile Court, 23 Harv.L.Rev. 104, 119–120 (1909).

17. *Id.*, at 20.

and indispensable foundation of individual freedom. It is the basic and essential term in the social compact which defines the rights of the individual and delimits the powers which the state may exercise. As Mr. Justice Frankfurter has said: "The history of American freedom is, in no small measure, the history of procedure." But, in addition, the procedural rules which have been fashioned from the generality of due process are our best instruments for the distillation and evaluation of essential facts from the conflicting welter of data that life and our adversary methods present. It is these instruments of due process which enhance the possibility that truth will emerge from the confrontation of opposing versions and conflicting data. "Procedure is to law what 'scientific method' is to science."

It is claimed that juveniles obtain benefits from the special procedures applicable to them which more than offset the disadvantages of denial of the substance of normal due process. As we shall discuss, the observance of due process standards, intelligently and not ruthlessly administered, will not compel the States to abandon or displace any of the substantive benefits of the juvenile process. But it is important, we think, that the claimed benefits of the juvenile process should be candidly appraised. Neither sentiment nor folklore should cause us to shut our eyes, for example, to such startling findings as that reported in an exceptionally reliable study of repeaters or recidivism conducted by the Stanford Research Institute for the President's Commission on Crime in the District of Columbia. This Commission's Report states:

> "In fiscal 1966 approximately 66 percent of the 16- and 17-year-old juveniles referred to the court by the Youth Aid Division had been before the court previously. In 1965, 56 percent of those in the Receiving Home were repeaters. The SRI study revealed that 61 percent of the sample Juvenile Court referrals in 1965 had been previously referred at least once and that 42 percent had been referred at least twice before." *Id.*, at 773.

Certainly, these figures . . . could not lead us to conclude that the absence of constitutional protections reduces crime, or that the juvenile system, functioning free of constitutional inhibitions as it has largely done, is effective to reduce crime or rehabilitate offenders. We do not mean by this to denigrate the juvenile court process or to suggest that there are not aspects of the juvenile system relating to offenders which are valuable. But the features of the juvenile system which its proponents have asserted are of unique benefit will not be impaired by constitutional domestication. For example, the commendable principles relating to the processing and treatment of juveniles separately from adults are in no way involved or affected by the procedural issues under discussion. Further, we are told that one of the important benefits of the special juvenile court procedures is that they avoid classifying the juvenile as a "criminal." The juvenile offender is now classed as a "delinquent." There is, of course, no reason why this should not continue. It is disconcerting, however, that this term has come to involve only slightly less stigma than the term "criminal" applied to adults. It is also emphasized that in practically all jurisdictions, statutes provide that an adjudication of the child as a delinquent shall not operate as a civil disability or disqualify him for civil service appointment. There is no reason why the application of due process requirements should interfere with such provisions.

Beyond this, it is frequently said that juveniles are protected by the process from disclosure of their deviational behavior. As the Supreme Court of Arizona phrased it in the present case, the summary procedures of Juvenile Courts are sometimes defended by a statement that it is the law's policy "to hide youthful errors from the full gaze of the public and bury them in the graveyard of the forgotten past." This claim of secrecy, however, is more rhetoric than reality. Disclosure of court records is discretionary with the judge in most jurisdictions. Statutory restrictions almost invariably apply only to the court records, and even as to those the evidence is that many courts routinely furnish information to the FBI and the military, and on request to government agencies and even to private employers. Of more importance are police records. In most States the police keep a complete file of juvenile "police contacts" and have complete discretion as to disclosure of juvenile records. Police departments receive requests for information from the FBI and other law-enforcement agencies, the Armed Forces, and social service agencies, and most of them generally comply. Private employers word their application forms to produce information concerning juvenile arrests and court proceedings, and in some jurisdictions information concerning juvenile police contacts is furnished private employers as well as government agencies.

In any event, there is no reason why, consistently with due process, a State cannot continue if it deems it appropriate, to provide and to improve provision for the confidentiality of records of police contacts and court action relating to juveniles. It is interesting to note, however, that the Arizona Supreme Court used the confidentiality argument as a justification for the type of notice which is here attacked as inadequate for due process purposes. The parents were given merely general notice that their child was charged with "delinquency." No facts were specified. The Arizona court held, however, as we shall discuss, that in addition to this general "notice," the child and his parents must be advised "of the facts involved in the case" no later than the initial hearing by the judge. Obviously, this does not "bury" the word about the child's transgressions. It merely defers the time of disclosure to a point when it is of limited use to the child or his parents in preparing his defense or explanation.

Further, it is urged that the juvenile benefits from informal proceedings in the court. The early conception of the Juvenile Court proceeding was one in which a fatherly judge touched the heart and conscience of the erring youth by talking over his problems, by paternal advice and admonition, and in which, in extreme situations, benevolent and wise institutions of the State provided guidance and help "to save him from downward career."[36] Then, as now, goodwill and compassion were admirably prevalent. But recent studies have, with surprising unanimity, entered sharp dissent as to the validity of this gentle conception. They suggest that the appearance as well as the actuality of fairness, impartiality and orderliness—in short, the essentials of due process—may be a more impressive and more therapeutic attitude so far as the juvenile is concerned. For example, in a recent study, the sociologists Wheeler and Cottrell observe that when the procedural laxness of the "*parens patriae*" attitude is followed by stern disciplining, the contrast may have an adverse effect upon the child, who feels that he has been deceived or enticed. They conclude as follows: "Unless appropriate due process of law is followed, even the juvenile who has violated the law may not feel that he is being fairly treated and may therefore resist the rehabilitative efforts of court personnel." Of course, it is not suggested that juvenile court judges should fail appropriately to take account, in their demeanor and conduct, of the emotional and psychological attitude of the juveniles with whom they are confronted. While due process requirements will, in some instances, introduce a degree of order and regularity to Juvenile Court proceedings to determine delinquency, and in contested cases will introduce some elements of the adversary system, nothing will require that

36. Mack, The Juvenile Court, 23 Harv.L.Rev. 104, 120 (1909).

the conception of the kindly juvenile judge be replaced by its opposite, nor do we here rule upon the question whether ordinary due process requirements must be observed with respect to hearings to determine the disposition of the delinquent child.

Ultimately, however, we confront the reality of that portion of the Juvenile Court process with which we deal in this case. A boy is charged with misconduct. The boy is committed to an institution where he may be restrained of liberty for years. It is of no constitutional consequence—and of limited practical meaning—that the institution to which he is committed is called an Industrial School. The fact of the matter is that, however euphemistic the title, a "receiving home" or an "industrial school" for juveniles is an institution of confinement in which the child is incarcerated for a greater or lesser time. His world becomes "a building with whitewashed walls, regimented routine and institutional hours. . . ." Instead of mother and father and sisters and brothers and friends and classmates, his world is peopled by guards, custodians, state employees, and "delinquents" confined with him for anything from waywardness to rape and homicide.

In view of this, it would be extraordinary if our Constitution did not require the procedural regularity and the exercise of care implied in the phrase "due process." Under our Constitution, the condition of being a boy does not justify a kangaroo court. The traditional ideas of Juvenile Court procedure, indeed, contemplated that time would be available and care would be used to establish precisely what the juvenile did and why he did it—was it a prank of adolescence or a brutal act threatening serious consequences to himself or society unless corrected? Under traditional notions, one would assume that in a case like that of Gerald Gault, where the juvenile appears to have a home, a working mother and father, and an older brother, the Juvenile Judge would have made a careful inquiry and judgment as to the possibility that the boy could be disciplined and dealt with at home, despite his previous transgressions. Indeed, so far as appears in the record before us, except for some conversation with Gerald about his school work and his "wanting to go to . . . Grand Canyon with his father," the points to which the judge directed his attention were little different from those that would be involved in determining any charge of violation of a penal statute. The essential difference between Gerald's case and a normal criminal case is that safeguards available to adults were discarded in Gerald's case. The summary procedure as well as the long commitment was possible because Gerald was 15 years of age instead of over 18.

If Gerald had been over 18, he would not have been subject to Juvenile Court proceedings. For the particular offense immediately involved, the maximum punishment would have been a fine of $5 to $50, or imprisonment in jail for not more than two months. Instead, he was committed to custody for a maximum of six years. If he had been over 18 and had committed an offense to which such a sentence might apply, he would have been entitled to substantial rights under the Constitution of the United States as well as under Arizona's laws and constitution. The United States Constitution would guarantee him rights and protections with respect to arrest, search, and seizure, and pretrial interrogation. It would assure him of specific notice of the charges and adequate time to decide his course of action and to prepare his defense. He would be entitled to clear advice that he could be represented by counsel, and, at least if a felony were involved, the State would be required to provide counsel if his parents were unable to afford it. If the court acted on the basis of his confession, careful procedures would be required to assure its voluntariness. If the case went to trial, confrontation and opportunity for cross-examination would be guaranteed. So wide a gulf between the State's treatment of the adult and of the child requires a bridge sturdier than mere verbiage, and reasons more persuasive than cliche can provide. As Wheeler and Cottrell have put it, "The rhetoric of the juvenile court movement has developed without any necessarily close correspondence to the realities of court and institutional routines."

In *Kent v. United States*, *supra*, we stated that the Juvenile Court Judge's exercise of the power of the state as *parens patriae* was not unlimited. We said that "the admonition to function in a 'parental' relationship is not an invitation to procedural arbitrariness." With respect to the waiver by the Juvenile Court to the adult court of jurisdiction over an offense committed by a youth, we said that "there is no place in our system of law for reaching a result of such tremendous consequences without ceremony—without hearing, without effective assistance of counsel, without a statement of reasons." We announced with respect to such waiver proceedings that while "We do not mean... to indicate that the hearing to be held must conform with all of the requirements of a criminal trial or even of the usual administrative hearing; but we do hold that the hearing must measure up to the essentials of due process and fair treatment." We reiterate this view, here in connection with a juvenile court adjudication of "delinquency," as a requirement which is part of the Due Process Clause of the Fourteenth Amendment of our Constitution....

III

Notice of Charges

Appellants allege that the Arizona Juvenile Code is unconstitutional or alternatively that the proceedings before the Juvenile Court were constitutionally defective because of failure to provide adequate notice of the hearings. No notice was given to Gerald's parents when he was taken into custody on Monday, June 8. On that night, when Mrs. Gault went to the Detention Home, she was orally informed that there would be a hearing the next afternoon and was told the reason why Gerald was in custody. The only written notice Gerald's parents received at any time was a note on plain paper from Officer Flagg delivered on Thursday or Friday, June 11 or 12, to the effect that the judge had set Monday, June 15, "for further Hearings on Gerald's delinquency."

A "petition" was filed with the court on June 9 by Officer Flagg, reciting only that he was informed and believed that "said minor is a delinquent minor and that it is necessary that some order be made by the Honorable Court for said minor's welfare." The applicable Arizona statute provides for a petition to be filed in Juvenile Court, alleging in general terms that the child is "neglected, dependent or delinquent." The statute explicitly states that such a general allegation is sufficient, "without alleging the facts." There is no requirement that the petition be served and it was not served upon, given to, or shown to Gerald or his parents....

...Notice, to comply with due process requirements, must be given sufficiently in advance of scheduled court proceedings so that reasonable opportunity to prepare will be afforded, and it must "set forth the alleged misconduct with particularity." It is obvious, as we have discussed above, that no purpose of shielding the child from the public stigma of knowledge of his having been taken into custody and scheduled for hearing is served by the procedure approved by the court below. The "initial hearing" in the present case was a hearing on the merits. Notice at that time is not timely; and even if there were a conceivable purpose served by the deferral proposed by the court below, it would have to yield to the requirements that the child and his parents or guardian be notified, in writing, of the specific charge or factual allegations to be considered at the hearing, and that such written notice be given at the earliest practicable time, and in any event sufficiently in advance of the hearing to permit preparation. Due process of law requires notice of the sort we have described—that is, notice which would be deemed constitutionally adequate in a civil or criminal proceeding. It does not allow a hearing to be held in which a youth's freedom and his parents' right to his custody are at stake without giving them timely notice, in advance of the hearing, of the specific issues that they must meet. Nor, in the circumstances of this case, can it reasonably be said that the requirement of notice was waived.

IV

Right to Counsel

Appellants charge that the Juvenile Court proceedings were fatally defective because the court did not advise Gerald or his parents of their right to counsel, and proceeded with the hearing, the adjudication of delinquency and the order of commitment in the absence of counsel for the child and his parents or an express waiver of the right thereto. The Supreme Court of Arizona pointed out that "(t)here is disagreement (among the various jurisdictions) as to whether the court must advise the infant that he has a right to counsel." . . . The court argued that "The parent and the probation officer may be relied upon to protect the infant's interests." Accordingly it rejected the proposition that "due process requires that an infant have a right to counsel." It said that juvenile courts have the discretion, but not the duty, to allow such representation; it referred specifically to the situation in which the Juvenile Court discerns conflict between the child and his parents as an instance in which this discretion might be exercised. We do not agree. Probation officers, in the Arizona scheme, are also arresting officers. They initiate proceedings and file petitions which they verify, as here, alleging the delinquency of the child; and they testify, as here, against the child. And here the probation officer was also superintendent of the Detention Home. The probation officer cannot act as counsel for the child. His role in the adjudicatory hearing, by statute and in fact, is as arresting officer and witness against the child. Nor can the judge represent the child. There is no material difference in this respect between adult and juvenile proceedings of the sort here involved. . . . A proceeding where the issue is whether the child will be found to be "delinquent" and subjected to the loss of his liberty for years is comparable in seriousness to a felony prosecution. The juvenile needs the assistance of counsel to cope with problems of law, to make skilled inquiry into the facts, to insist upon regularity of the proceedings, and to ascertain whether he has a defense and to prepare and submit it. The child "requires the guiding hand of counsel at every step in the proceedings against him." Just as in *Kent v. United States*, *supra*, 383 U.S., at 561–562, we indicated our agreement with the United States Court of Appeals for the District of Columbia Circuit that the assistance of counsel is essential for purposes of waiver proceedings, so we hold now that it is equally essential for the determination of delinquency, carrying with it the awesome prospect of incarceration in a state institution until the juvenile reaches the age of 21. . . .

. . . In at least one-third of the States, statutes now provide for the right of representation by retained counsel in juvenile delinquency proceedings, notice of the right, or assignment of counsel, or a combination of these. In other States, court rules have similar provisions.

The President's Crime Commission has recently recommended that in order to assure "procedural justice for the child," it is necessary that "Counsel . . . be appointed as a matter of course wherever coercive action is a possibility, without requiring any affirmative choice by child or parent." As stated by the authoritative "Standards for Juvenile and Family Courts," published by the Children's Bureau of the United States Department of Health, Education, and Welfare:

> "As a component part of a fair hearing required by due process guaranteed under the 14th amendment, notice of the right to counsel should be required at all hearings and counsel provided upon request when the family is financially unable to employ counsel." Standards, p. 57.

This statement was "reviewed" by the National Council of Juvenile Court Judges at its 1965 Convention and they "found no fault" with it. . . .

We conclude that the Due Process Clause of the Fourteenth Amendment requires that in respect of proceedings to determine delinquency which may result in commitment to an institution in which the juvenile's freedom is curtailed, the child and his parents must be notified of the child's right to be represented by counsel retained by them, or if they are unable to afford counsel, that counsel will be appointed to represent the child.

At the habeas corpus proceeding, Mrs. Gault testified that she knew that she could have appeared with counsel at the juvenile hearing. This knowledge is not a waiver of the right to counsel which she and her juvenile son had, as we have defined it. They had a right expressly to be advised that they might retain counsel and to be confronted with the need for specific consideration of whether they did or did not choose to waive the right. If they were unable to afford to employ counsel, they were entitled in view of the seriousness of the charge and the potential commitment, to appointed counsel, unless they chose waiver. Mrs. Gault's knowledge that she could employ counsel was not an "intentional relinquishment or abandonment" of a fully known right.

V

Confrontation, Self-Incrimination, Cross-Examination

Appellants urge that the writ of habeas corpus should have been granted because of the denial of the rights of confrontation and cross-examination in the Juvenile Court hearings, and because the privilege against self-incrimination was not observed. The Juvenile Court Judge testified at the habeas corpus hearing that he had proceeded on the basis of Gerald's admissions at the two hearings. Appellants attack this on the ground that the admissions were obtained in disregard of the privilege against self-incrimination. If the confession is disregarded, appellants argue that the delinquency conclusion, since it was fundamentally based on a finding that Gerald had made lewd remarks during the phone call to Mrs. Cook, is fatally defective for failure to accord the rights of confrontation and cross-examination which the Due Process Clause of the Fourteenth Amendment of the Federal Constitution guarantees in state proceedings generally.

Our first question, then, is whether Gerald's admission was improperly obtained and relied on as the basis of decision, in conflict with the Federal Constitution. For this purpose, it is necessary briefly to recall the relevant facts.

Mrs. Cook, the complainant, and the recipient of the alleged telephone call, was not called as a witness. Gerald's mother asked the Juvenile Court Judge why Mrs. Cook was not present and the judge replied that "she didn't have to be present." So far as appears, Mrs. Cook was spoken to only once, by Officer Flagg, and this was by telephone. The judge did not speak with her on any occasion. Gerald had been questioned by the probation officer after having been taken into custody. The exact circumstances of this questioning do not appear but any admissions Gerald may have made at this time do not appear in the record. Gerald was also questioned by the Juvenile Court Judge at each of the two hearings. The judge testified in the habeas corpus proceeding that Gerald admitted making "some of the lewd statements…(but not) any of the more serious lewd statements." There was conflict and uncertainty among the witnesses at the habeas corpus proceeding—the Juvenile Court Judge, Mr. and Mrs. Gault, and the probation officer—as to what Gerald did or did not admit.

We shall assume that Gerald made admissions of the sort described by the Juvenile Court Judge, as quoted above. Neither Gerald nor his parents were advised that he did not have to testify or make a statement, or that an incriminating statement might result in his commitment as a "delinquent."

The Arizona Supreme Court rejected appellants' contention that Gerald had a right to be advised that he need not incriminate himself. It said: "We think the necessary flexibility for individualized treatment will be enhanced by a rule which does not require the judge to advise the infant of a privilege against self-incrimination."

In reviewing this conclusion of Arizona's Supreme Court, we emphasize again that we are here concerned only with a proceeding to determine whether a minor is a "delinquent" and which may result in commitment to a state institution. Specifically, the question is whether, in such a proceeding, an admission by the juvenile may be used against him in the absence of clear and unequivocal evidence that the admission was made with knowledge that he was not obliged to speak and would not be penalized for remaining silent. In light of *Miranda v. Arizona*, 384 U.S. 436 (1966), we must also consider whether, if the privilege against self-incrimination is available, it can effectively be waived unless counsel is present or the right to counsel has been waived.

It has long been recognized that the eliciting and use of confessions or admissions require careful scrutiny….

This Court has emphasized that admissions and confessions of juveniles require special caution. In *Haley v. Ohio*, 332 U.S. 596 [1948], where this Court reversed the conviction of a 15-year-old boy for murder, MR. JUSTICE DOUGLAS said:

> "What transpired would make us pause for careful inquiry if a mature man were involved. And when, as here, a mere child—an easy victim of the law—is before us, special care in scrutinizing the record must be used. Age 15 is a tender and difficult age for a boy of any race. He cannot be judged by the more exacting standards of maturity. That which would leave a man cold and unimpressed can overawe and overwhelm a lad in his early teens. This is the period of great instability which the crisis of adolescence produces. A 15-year-old lad, questioned through the dead of night by relays of police, is a ready victim of the inquisition. Mature men possibly might stand the ordeal from midnight to 5 a.m. But we cannot believe that a lad of tender years is a match for the police in such a contest. He needs counsel and support if he is not to become the victim first of fear, then of panic. He needs someone on whom to lean lest the overpowering presence of the law, as he knows it, crush him. No friend stood at the side of this 15-year-old boy as the police, working in relays, questioned him hour after hour, from midnight until dawn. No lawyer stood guard to make sure that the police went so far and no farther, to see to it that they stopped short of the point where he became the victim of coercion. No counsel or friend was called during the critical hours of questioning."

In *Haley*, as we have discussed, the boy was convicted in an adult court, and not a juvenile court. In notable decisions, the New York Court of Appeals and the Supreme Court of New Jersey have recently considered decisions of Juvenile Courts in which boys have been adjudged "delinquent" on the basis of confessions obtained in circumstances comparable to those in *Haley*. In both instances, the State contended before its highest tribunal that constitutional requirements governing inculpatory statements applicable in adult courts do not apply to juvenile proceedings. In each case, the State's contention was rejected, and the juvenile court's determination of delinquency was set aside on the grounds of inadmissibility of the confession. *In Matters of Gregory W. and Gerald S.*, 19 N.Y.2d 55, 277 N.Y.S.2d 675, 224 N.E.2d 102 (1966) (opinion by Keating, J.), and *In Interests of Carlo and Stasilowicz*, 48 N.J. 224, 225 A.2d 110 (1966) (opinion by Proctor, J.).

The privilege against self-incrimination is, of course, related to the question of the safeguards necessary to assure that admissions or confessions are reasonably trustworthy, that they are not the mere fruits of fear or coercion, but are reliable expressions of the truth. The roots of the privilege are, however, far deeper. They tap the basic stream of religious and political principle because the privilege reflects the limits of the individual's attornment to the state and—in a philosophical sense—insists upon the equality of the individual and the state. In other words, the privilege has a broader and deeper thrust than the rule which prevents the use of confessions which are the product of coercion because coercion is thought to carry with it the danger of unreliability. One of its purposes is to prevent the state, whether by force or by psychological domination, from overcoming the mind and will of the person under investigation and depriving him of the freedom to decide whether to assist the state in securing his conviction.

It would indeed be surprising if the privilege against self-incrimination were available to hardened criminals but not to children. The language of the Fifth Amendment, applicable to the States by operation of the Fourteenth Amendment, is unequivocal and without exception. And the scope of the privilege is comprehensive....

With respect to juveniles, both common observation and expert opinion emphasize that the "distrust of confessions made in certain situations"... is imperative in the case of children from an early age through adolescence....

The authoritative "Standards for Juvenile and Family Courts" concludes that, "Whether or not transfer to the criminal court is a possibility, certain procedures should always be followed. Before being interviewed (by the police), the child and his parents should be informed of his right to have legal counsel present and to refuse to answer questions or be fingerprinted if he should so decide."

Against the application to juveniles of the right to silence, it is argued that juvenile proceedings are "civil" and not "criminal," and therefore the privilege should not apply. It is true that the statement of the privilege in the Fifth Amendment, which is applicable to the States by reason of the Fourteenth Amendment, is that no person "shall be compelled in any criminal case to be a witness against himself." However, it is also clear that the availability of the privilege does not turn upon the type of proceeding in which its protection is invoked, but upon the nature of the statement or admission and the exposure which it invites. The privilege may, for example, be claimed in a civil or administrative proceeding, if the statement is or may be inculpatory.

It would be entirely unrealistic to carve out of the Fifth Amendment all statements by juveniles on the ground that these cannot lead to "criminal" involvement. In the first place, juvenile proceedings to determine "delinquency," which may lead to commitment to a state institution, must be regarded as "criminal" for purposes of the privilege against self-incrimination. To hold otherwise would be to disregard substance because of the feeble enticement of the "civil" label-of-convenience which has been attached to juvenile proceedings. Indeed, in over half of the States, there is not even assurance that the juvenile will be kept in separate institutions, apart from adult "criminals." In those States juveniles may be placed in or transferred to adult penal institutions after having been found "delinquent" by a juvenile court. For this purpose, at least, commitment is a deprivation of liberty. It is incarceration against one's will, whether it is called "criminal" or "civil." And our Constitution guarantees that no person shall be "compelled" to be a witness against himself when he is threatened with deprivation of his liberty—a command which this Court has broadly applied and generously implemented in accordance with the teaching of the history of the privilege and its great office in mankind's battle for freedom.

In addition, apart from the equivalence for this purpose of exposure to commitment as a juvenile delinquent and exposure to imprisonment as an adult offender, the fact of the matter is that there is little or no assurance in Arizona, as in most if not all of the States, that a juvenile apprehended and interrogated by the police or even by the Juvenile Court itself will remain outside of the reach of adult courts as a consequence of the offense for which he has been taken into custody. In Arizona, as in other States, provision is made for Juvenile Courts to relinquish or waive jurisdiction to the ordinary criminal courts. In the present case, when Gerald Gault was interrogated concerning violation of a section of the Arizona Criminal Code, it could not be certain that the Juvenile Court Judge would decide to "suspend" criminal prosecution in court for adults by proceeding to an adjudication in Juvenile Court.

It is also urged, as the Supreme Court of Arizona here asserted, that the juvenile and presumably his parents should not be advised of the juvenile's right to silence because confession is good for the child as the commencement of the assumed therapy of the juvenile court process, and he should be encouraged to assume an attitude of trust and confidence toward the officials of the juvenile process. This proposition has been subjected to widespread challenge on the basis of current reappraisals of the rhetoric and realities of the handling of juvenile offenders.

In fact, evidence is accumulating that confessions by juveniles do not aid in "individualized treatment," as the court below put it, and that compelling the child to answer questions, without warning or advice as to his right to remain silent, does not serve this or any other good purpose. In light of the observations of Wheeler and Cottrell, and others, it seems probable that where children are induced to confess by "paternal" urgings on the part of officials and the confession is then followed by disciplinary action, the child's reaction is likely to be hostile and adverse—the child may well feel that he has been led or tricked into confession and that despite his confession, he is being punished.

Further, authoritative opinion has cast formidable doubt upon the reliability and trustworthiness of "confessions" by children.... The recent decision of the New York Court of Appeals referred to above, *In Matters of Gregory W. and Gerald S.* deals with a dramatic and, it is to be hoped, extreme example. Two 12-year-old Negro boys were taken into custody for the brutal assault and rape of two aged domestics, one of whom died as the result of the attack. One of the boys was schizophrenic and had been locked in the security ward of a mental institution at the time of the attacks. By a process that may best be described as bizarre, his confession was obtained by the police. A psychiatrist testified that the boy would admit "whatever he thought was expected so that he could get out of the immediate situation." The other 12-year-old also "confessed." Both confessions were in specific detail, albeit they contained various inconsistencies. The Court of Appeals, in an opinion by Keating, J., concluded that the confessions were products of the will of the police instead of the boys. The confessions were therefore held involuntary and the order of the Appellate Division affirming the order of the Family Court adjudging the defendants to be juvenile delinquents was reversed....

We conclude that the constitutional privilege against self-incrimination is applicable in the case of juveniles as it is with respect to adults. We appreciate that special problems may arise with respect to waiver of the privilege by or on behalf of children, and that there may well be some differences in technique—but not in principle—depending upon the age of the child and the presence and competence of parents. The participation of counsel will, of course, assist the police, Juvenile Courts and appellate tribunals in administering the privilege. If counsel was not present for some permissible reason when an admission was obtained, the greatest care must be taken to assure that the admission was voluntary, in the sense not only that it was not coerced or suggested, but also that it was not the product of ignorance of rights or of adolescent fantasy, fright or despair.

The "confession" of Gerald Gault was first obtained by Officer Flagg, out of the presence of Gerald's parents, without counsel and without advising him of his right to silence, as far as appears. The judgment of the Juvenile Court was stated by the judge to be based on Gerald's admissions in court. Neither "admission" was reduced to writing, and, to say the least, the process by which the "admissions," were obtained and received must be characterized as lacking the certainty and order which are required of proceedings of such formidable consequences. Apart from the "admission," there was nothing upon which a judgment or finding might be based. There was no sworn testimony. Mrs. Cook, the complainant, was not present....No reason is suggested or appears for a different rule in respect of sworn testimony in juvenile courts than in adult tribunals. Absent a valid confession adequate to support the determination of the Juvenile Court, confrontation and sworn testimony by witnesses available for cross-examination were essential for a finding of "delinquency" and an order committing Gerald to a state institution for a maximum of six years.

As we said in *Kent v. United States*, 383 U.S. 541 (1966), with respect to waiver proceedings, "there is no place in our system of law of reaching a result of such tremendous consequences without ceremony...." We now hold that, absent a valid confession, a determination of delinquency and an order of commitment to a state institution cannot be sustained in the absence of sworn testimony subjected to the opportunity for cross-examination in accordance with our law and constitutional requirements.

VI

Appellate Review and Transcript of Proceedings

Appellants urge that the Arizona statute is unconstitutional under the Due Process Clause because, as construed by its Supreme Court, "'there is no right of appeal from a juvenile court order...." The court held that there is no right to a transcript because there is no right to appeal and because the proceedings are confidential and any record must be destroyed after a prescribed period of time. Whether a transcript or other recording is made, it held, is a matter for the discretion of the juvenile court.

This Court has not held that a State is required by the Federal Constitution "to provide appellate courts or a right to appellate review at all." In view of the fact that we must reverse the Supreme Court of Arizona's affirmance of the dismissal of the writ of habeas corpus for other reasons, we need not rule on this question in the present case or upon the failure to provide a transcript or recording of the hearings—or, indeed, the failure of the Juvenile Judge to state the grounds for his conclusion. Cf. *Kent v. United States*, *supra*, 383 U.S., at 561, where we said, in the context of a decision of the juvenile court waiving jurisdiction to the adult court, which by local law, was permissible: "...it is incumbent upon the Juvenile Court to accompany its waiver order with a statement of the reasons or considerations therefor." As the present case illustrates, the consequences of failure to provide an appeal, to record the proceedings, or to make findings or state the grounds for the juvenile court's conclusion may be to throw a burden upon the machinery for habeas corpus, to saddle the reviewing process with the burden of attempting to reconstruct a record, and to impose upon the Juvenile Judge the unseemly duty of testifying under cross-examination as to the events that transpired in the hearings before him.

For the reasons stated, the judgment of the Supreme Court of Arizona is reversed and the cause remanded for further proceedings not inconsistent with this opinion....

MR. JUSTICE BLACK, concurring.

The juvenile court laws of Arizona and other States, as the Court points out, are the result of plans promoted by humane and forward-looking people to provide a system of courts, procedures, and sanctions deemed to be less harmful and more lenient to children than to adults. For this reason such state laws generally provide less formal and less public methods for the trial of children. In line with this policy, both courts and legislators have shrunk back from labeling these laws as "criminal" and have preferred to call them "civil." This, in part, was to prevent the full application to juvenile court cases of the Bill of Rights safeguards, including notice as provided in the Sixth Amendment, the right to counsel guaranteed by the Sixth, the right against self-incrimination guaranteed by the Fifth, and the right to confrontation guaranteed by the Sixth. The Court here holds, however, that these four Bill of Rights safeguards apply to protect a juvenile accused in a juvenile court on a charge under which he can be imprisoned for a term of years. This holding strikes a well-nigh fatal blow to much that is unique about the juvenile courts in the Nation....

The juvenile court planners envisaged a system that would practically immunize juveniles from "punishment" for "crimes" in an effort to save them from youthful indiscretions and stigmas due to criminal charges or convictions. I agree with the Court, however, that this exalted ideal has failed of achievement since the beginning of the system. Indeed, the state laws from the first one on contained provisions, written in emphatic terms, for arresting and charging juveniles with violations of state criminal laws, as well as for taking juveniles by force of law away from their parents and turning them over to different individuals or groups or for confinement within some state school or institution for a number of years....

Where a person, infant or adult, can be seized by the State, charged, and convicted for violating a state criminal law, and then ordered by the State to be confined for six years, I think the Constitution requires that he be tried in accordance with the guarantees of all the provisions of the Bill of Rights made applicable to the States by the Fourteenth Amendment. Undoubtedly this would be true of an adult defendant, and it would be a plain denial of equal protection of the laws—an invidious discrimination—to hold that others subject to heavier punishments could, because they are children, be denied these same constitutional safeguards. I consequently agree with the Court that the Arizona law as applied here denied to the parents and their son the right of notice, right to counsel, right against self-incrimination, and right to confront the witnesses against young Gault. Appellants are entitled to these rights, not because "fairness, impartiality and orderliness—in short, the essentials of due process"—require them and not because they are "the procedural rules which have been fashioned from the generality of due process," but because they are specifically and unequivocally granted by provisions of the Fifth and Sixth Amendments which the Fourteenth Amendment makes applicable to the States.

A few words should be added because of the opinion of my Brother Harlan who rests his concurrence and dissent on the Due Process Clause alone. He reads that clause alone as allowing this Court "to determine what forms of procedural protection are necessary to guarantee the fundamental fairness of juvenile proceedings" "in a fashion consistent with the 'traditions and conscience of our people.'"...

I cannot subscribe to any such interpretation of the Due Process Clause. Nothing in its words or its history permits it, and "fair distillations of relevant judicial history" are no substitute for the words and history of the clause itself. The phrase "due process of law" has through the years evolved as the successor in purpose and meaning to the words "law of the land" in Magna Charta which more plainly intended to call for a trial according to the existing law of the land in effect at the time an alleged offense had been committed. That provision in Magna Charta was designed to prevent defendants from being tried according to criminal laws or proclamations specifically promulgated to fit particular cases or to attach new consequences to old conduct. Nothing done since Magna Charta can be pointed to as intimating that the Due Process Clause gives courts power to fashion laws in order to meet new conditions, to fit the "decencies" of changed conditions, or to keep their consciences from being shocked by legislation, state or federal.

And, of course, the existence of such awesome judicial power cannot be buttressed or created by relying on the word "procedural." Whether labeled as "procedural" or "substantive," the Bill of Rights safeguards, far from being mere "tools with which" other unspecified "rights could be fully vindicated," are the very vitals of a sound constitutional legal system designed to protect and safeguard the most cherished liberties of a free people. These safeguards were written into our Constitution not by judges but by Constitution makers. Freedom in this Nation will be far less secure the very moment that it is decided that judges can determine which of these safeguards "should" or "should not be imposed" according to their notions of what constitutional provisions are consistent with the "traditions and conscience of our people." Judges with such power, even though they profess to "proceed with restraint," will be above the Constitution, with power to write it, not merely to interpret it, which I believe to be the only power constitutionally committed to judges.

There is one ominous sentence, if not more, in my Brother Harlan's opinion which bodes ill, in my judgment, both for legislative programs and constitutional commands. Speaking of procedural safeguards in the Bill of Rights, he says:

> "These factors in combination suggest that legislatures may properly expect only a cautious deference for their procedural judgments, but that, conversely, courts must exercise their special responsibility for procedural guarantees with care to permit ample scope for achieving the purposes of legislative programs.... (T)he court should necessarily proceed with restraint."

It is to be noted here that this case concerns Bill of Rights Amendments; that the "procedure" power my Brother HARLAN claims for the Court here relates solely to Bill of Rights safeguards; and that he is here claiming for the Court a supreme power to fashion new Bill of Rights safeguards according to the Court's notions of what fits tradition and conscience. I do not believe that the Constitution vests any such power in judges, either in the Due Process Clause or anywhere else. Consequently, I do not vote to invalidate this Arizona law on the ground that it is "unfair" but solely on the ground that it violates the Fifth and Sixth Amendments made obligatory on the States by the Fourteenth Amendment. It is enough for me that the Arizona law as here applied collides head-on with the Fifth and Sixth Amendments in the four respects mentioned. The only relevance to me of the Due Process Clause is that it would, of course, violate due process or the "law of the land" to enforce a law that collides with the Bill of Rights.

MR. JUSTICE WHITE, concurring.

I join the Court's opinion except for Part V. I also agree that the privilege against compelled self-incrimination applies at the adjudicatory stage of juvenile court proceedings. I do not, however, find an adequate basis in the record for determination whether that privilege was violated in this case. The Fifth Amendment protects a person from being "compelled" in any criminal proceeding to be a witness against himself. Compulsion is essential to a violation. It may be that when a judge, armed with the authority he has or which people think he has, asks questions of a party or a witness in an adjudicatory hearing, that person, especially if a minor, would feel compelled to answer, absent a warning to the contrary or similar information from some other source. The difficulty is that the record made at the habeas corpus hearing, which is the only information we have concerning the proceedings in the juvenile court, does not directly inform us whether Gerald Gault or his parents were told of Gerald's right to remain silent; nor does it reveal whether the parties were aware of the privilege from some other source, just as they were already aware that they had the right to have the help of counsel and to have witnesses on their behalf. The petition for habeas corpus did not raise the Fifth Amendment issue nor did any of the witnesses focus on it....

...I would not reach the Fifth Amendment issue here. I think the Court is clearly ill-advised to review this case on the basis of *Miranda v. Arizona*, since the adjudication of delinquency took place in 1964, long before the Miranda decision.... Under these circumstances, this case is a poor vehicle for resolving a difficult problem. Moreover, no prejudice to appellants is at stake in this regard. The judgment below must be reversed on other grounds and in the event further proceedings are to be had, Gerald Gault will have counsel available to advise him.

For somewhat similar reasons, I would not reach the questions of confrontation and cross-examination which are also dealt with in Part V of the opinion.

MR. JUSTICE HARLAN, concurring in part and dissenting in part.

Each of the 50 States has created a system of juvenile or family courts, in which distinctive rules are employed and special consequences imposed. The jurisdiction of these courts commonly extends both to cases which the States have withdrawn from the ordinary processes of criminal justice, and to cases which involve acts that, if performed by an adult, would not be penalized as criminal. Such courts are denominated civil, not criminal, and are characteristically said not to administer criminal penalties. One consequence of these systems, at least as Arizona construes its own, is that certain of the rights guaranteed to criminal defendants by the Constitution are withheld from juveniles. This case brings before this Court for the first time the question of what limitations the Constitution places upon the operation of such tribunals. For reasons which follow, I have concluded that the Court has gone too far in some respects, and fallen short in others, in assessing the procedural requirements demanded by the Fourteenth Amendment.

I

I must first acknowledge that I am unable to determine with any certainty by what standards the Court decides that Arizona's juvenile courts do not satisfy the obligations of due process. The Court's premise, itself the product of reasoning which is not described, is that the "constitutional and theoretical basis" of state systems of juvenile and family courts is "debatable"; it buttresses these doubts by marshaling a body of opinion which suggests that the accomplishments of these courts have often fallen short of expectations. The Court does not indicate at what points or for what purposes such views, held either by it or by other observers, might be pertinent to the present issues. Its failure to provide any discernible standard for the measurement of due process in relation to juvenile proceedings unfortunately might be understood to mean that the Court is concerned principally with the wisdom of having such courts at all.

If this is the source of the Court's dissatisfaction, I cannot share it. I should have supposed that the constitutionality of juvenile courts was beyond proper question under the standards now employed to assess the substantive validity of state legislation under the Due Process Clause of the Fourteenth Amendment. It can scarcely be doubted that it is within the State's competence to adopt measures reasonably calculated to meet more effectively the persistent problems of juvenile delinquency; as the opinion for the Court makes abundantly plain, these are among the most vexing and ominous of the concerns which now face communities throughout the country.

The proper issue here is, however, not whether the State may constitutionally treat juvenile offenders through a system of specialized courts, but whether the proceedings in Arizona's juvenile courts include procedural guarantees which satisfy the requirements of the Fourteenth Amendment....

The central issue here, and the principal one upon which I am divided from the Court, is the method by which the procedural requirements of due process should be measured....

The... three criteria by which the procedural requirements of due process should be measured [are] first, no more restrictions should be imposed than are imperative to assure the proceedings' fundamental fairness; second, the restrictions which are imposed should be those which preserve, so far as possible, the essential elements of the State's purpose; and finally, restrictions should be chosen which will later permit the orderly selection of any additional protections which may ultimately prove necessary. In this way, the Court may guarantee the fundamental fairness of the proceeding, and yet permit the State to continue development of an effective response to the problems of juvenile crime.

II

Measured by these criteria, only three procedural requirements should, in my opinion, now be deemed required of state juvenile courts by the Due Process Clause of the Fourteenth Amendment: first, timely notice must be provided to parents and children of the nature and terms of any juvenile court proceeding in which a determination affecting their rights or interests may be made; second, unequivocal and timely notice must be given that counsel may appear in any such proceeding in behalf of the child and its parents, and that in cases in which the child may be confined in an institution, counsel may, in circumstances of indigency, be appointed for them; and third, the court must maintain a written record, or its equivalent, adequate to permit effective review on appeal or in collateral proceedings. These requirements would guarantee to juveniles the tools with which their rights could be fully vindicated, and yet permit the States to pursue without unnecessary hindrance the purposes which they believe imperative in this field. Further, their imposition now would later permit more intelligent assessment of the necessity under the Fourteenth Amendment of additional requirements, by creating suitable records from which the character and deficiencies of juvenile proceedings could be accurately judged. I turn to consider each of these three requirements.

The Court has consistently made plain that adequate and timely notice is the fulcrum of due process, whatever the purposes of the proceeding.... Notice is ordinarily the prerequisite to effective assertion of any constitutional or other rights; without it, vindication of those rights must be essentially fortuitous. So fundamental a protection can neither be spared here nor left to the "favor or grace" of state authorities....

Provision of counsel and of a record, like adequate notice, would permit the juvenile to assert very much more effectively his rights and defenses, both in the juvenile proceedings and upon direct or collateral review. The Court has frequently emphasized their importance in proceedings in which an individual may be deprived of his liberty; this reasoning must include with special force those who are commonly inexperienced and immature. The facts of this case illustrate poignantly the difficulties of review without either an adequate record or the participation of counsel in the proceeding's initial stages. At the same time, these requirements should not cause any substantial modification in the character of juvenile court proceedings: counsel, although now present in only a small percentage of juvenile cases, have apparently already appeared without incident in virtually all juvenile courts; and the maintenance of a record should not appreciably alter the conduct of these proceedings.

The question remains whether certain additional requirements, among them the privilege against self-incrimination, confrontation, and cross-examination, must now, as the Court holds, also be imposed....

In my view, the Court should approach this question in terms of the criteria, described above, which emerge from the history of due process adjudication. Measured by them, there are compelling reasons at least to defer imposition of these additional requirements. First, quite unlike notice, counsel, and a record, these requirements might radically alter the character of juvenile court proceedings. The evidence from which the Court reasons that they would not is inconclusive, and other available evidence suggests that they very likely would. At the least, it is plain that these additional requirements would contribute materially to the creation in these proceedings of the atmosphere of an ordinary criminal trial, and would, even if they do no more, thereby largely frustrate a central purpose of these specialized courts. Further, these are restrictions intended to conform to the demands of an intensely adversary system of criminal justice; the broad purposes which they represent might be served in juvenile courts with equal effectiveness by procedural devices more consistent with the premises of proceedings in those courts. As the Court apparently acknowledges, the hazards of self-accusation, for example, might be avoided in juvenile proceedings without the imposition of all the requirements and limitations which surround the privilege against self-incrimination. The guarantee of adequate notice, counsel, and a record would create conditions in which suitable alternative procedures could be devised; but, unfortunately, the Court's haste to impose restrictions taken intact from criminal procedure may well seriously hamper the development of such alternatives. Surely this illustrates that prudence and the principles of the Fourteenth Amendment alike require that the Court should now impose no more procedural restrictions than are imperative to assure fundamental fairness, and that the States should instead be permitted additional opportunities to develop without unnecessary hindrance their systems of juvenile courts.

I find confirmation for these views in two ancillary considerations. First, it is clear that an uncertain, but very substantial number of the cases brought to juvenile courts involve children who are not in any sense guilty of criminal misconduct. Many of these children have simply the misfortune to be in some manner distressed; others have engaged in conduct, such as truancy, which is plainly not criminal. Efforts are now being made to develop effective, and entirely noncriminal, methods of treatment for these children. In such cases, the state authorities are in the most literal sense acting *in loco parentis*; they are, by any standard, concerned with the child's protection, and not with his punishment. I do not question that the methods employed in such cases must be consistent with the constitutional obligation to act in accordance with due process, but certainly the Fourteenth Amendment does not demand that they be constricted by the procedural guarantees devised for ordinary criminal prosecutions. It must be remembered that the various classifications of juvenile court proceedings are, as the vagaries of the available statistics illustrate, often arbitrary or ambiguous; it would therefore be imprudent, at the least, to build upon these classifications rigid systems of procedural requirements which would be applicable, or not, in accordance with the descriptive label given to the particular proceeding. It is better, it seems to me, to begin by now requiring the essential elements of fundamental fairness in juvenile courts, whatever the label given by the State to the proceedings; in this way the Court could avoid imposing unnecessarily rigid restrictions, and yet escape dependence upon classifications which may often prove to be illusory. Further, the provision of notice, counsel, and a record would permit orderly efforts to determine later whether more satisfactory classifications can be devised, and if they can, whether additional procedural requirements are necessary for them under the Fourteenth Amendment.

Second, it should not be forgotten that juvenile crime and juvenile courts are both now under earnest study throughout the country. I very much fear that this Court, by imposing these rigid procedural requirements, may inadvertently have served to discourage these efforts to find more satisfactory solutions for the problems of juvenile crime, and may thus now hamper enlightened development of the systems of juvenile courts....

III

Finally, I turn to assess the validity of this juvenile court proceeding under the criteria discussed in this opinion. Measured by them, the judgment below must, in my opinion, fall. Gerald Gault and his parents were not provided adequate notice of the terms and purposes of the proceedings in which he was adjudged delinquent; they were not advised of their rights to be represented by counsel; and no record in any form was maintained of the proceedings. It follows, for the reasons given in this opinion, that Gerald Gault was deprived of his liberty without due process of law, and I therefore concur in the judgment of the Court.

MR. JUSTICE STEWART, dissenting.

The Court today uses an obscure Arizona case as a vehicle to impose upon thousands of juvenile courts throughout the Nation restrictions that the Constitution made applicable to adversary criminal trials. I believe the Court's decision is wholly unsound as a matter of constitutional law, and sadly unwise as a matter of judicial policy.

Juvenile proceedings are not criminal trials. They are not civil trials. They are simply not adversary proceedings. Whether treating with a delinquent child, a neglected child, a defective child, or a dependent child, a juvenile proceeding's whole purpose and mission is the very opposite of the mission and purpose of a prosecution in a criminal court. The object of the one is correction of a condition. The object of the other is conviction and punishment for a criminal act.

In the last 70 years many dedicated men and women have devoted their professional lives to the enlightened task of bringing us out of the dark world of Charles Dickens in meeting our responsibilities to the child in our society. The result has been the creation in this century of a system of juvenile and family courts in each of the 50 States. There can be no denying that in many areas the performance of these agencies has fallen disappointingly short of the hopes and dreams of the courageous pioneers who first conceived them. For a variety of reasons, the reality has sometimes not even approached the ideal, and much remains to be accomplished in the administration of public juvenile and family agencies—in personnel, in planning, in financing, perhaps in the formulation of wholly new approaches.

I possess neither the specialized experience nor the expert knowledge to predict with any certainty where may lie the brightest hope for progress in dealing with the serious problems of juvenile delinquency. But I am certain that the answer does not lie in the Court's opinion in this case, which serves to convert a juvenile proceeding into a criminal prosecution.

The inflexible restrictions that the Constitution so wisely made applicable to adversary criminal trials have no inevitable place in the proceedings of those public social agencies known as juvenile or family courts. And to impose the Court's long catalog of requirements upon juvenile proceedings in every area of the country is to invite a long step backwards into the nineteenth century. In that era there were no juvenile proceedings, and a child was tried in a conventional criminal court will all the trappings of a conventional criminal trial. So it was that a 12-year-old boy named James Guild was tried in New Jersey for killing Catharine Beakes. A jury found him guilty of murder, and he was sentenced to death by hanging. The sentence was executed. It was all very constitutional.

A State in all its dealings must, of course, accord every person due process of law. And due process may require that some of the same restrictions which the Constitution has placed upon criminal trials must be imposed upon juvenile proceedings. For example, I suppose that all would agree that a brutally coerced confession could not constitutionally be considered in a juvenile court hearing. But it surely does not follow that the testimonial privilege against self-incrimination is applicable in all juvenile proceedings. Similarly, due process clearly requires timely notice of the purpose and scope of any proceedings affecting the relationship of parent and child.... But it certainly does not follow that notice of a juvenile hearing must be framed with all the technical niceties of a criminal indictment.

In any event, there is no reason to deal with issues such as these in the present case. The Supreme Court of Arizona found that the parents of Gerald Gault "knew of their right to counsel, to subpoena and cross examine witnesses, of the right to confront the witnesses against Gerald and the possible consequences of a finding of delinquency." 99 Ariz. 181, 185, 407 P.2d 760, 763. It further found that "Mrs. Gault knew the exact nature of the charge against Gerald from the day he was taken to the detention home." 99 Ariz., at 193, 407 P.2d, at

768. And, as MR. JUSTICE WHITE correctly points out, . . . no issue of compulsory self-incrimination is presented by this case.

I would dismiss the appeal.

QUESTIONS

1. According to the Court, what constitutional rights do juveniles in delinquency proceedings have? What is the source of those rights?

2. Why does Justice Black concur? Why does he disagree with Justice Harlan?

3. Why does Justice White concur? Do you think his interpretation of the record below is correct?

4. Why does Harlan concur in part and dissent in part? Would he extend the same constitutional protections to juveniles as Justice Fortas? How would they differ? What is the constitutional basis for this difference?

5. Fortas provides a historical overview of the juvenile court's development. Do you think his historical analysis is correct?

6. The Court also discusses social science. How did that help the Court reach its legal conclusions?

7. *Gault* was decided long before the Convention on the Rights of the Child was ratified. To what extent do you think the CRC is consistent with *Gault*?

IN RE WINSHIP
Supreme Court of the United States
397 U.S. 358 (1970)

MR. JUSTICE BRENNAN delivered the opinion of the Court.

Constitutional questions decided by this Court concerning the juvenile process have centered on the adjudicatory stage at "which a determination is made as to whether a juvenile is a 'delinquent' as a result of alleged misconduct on his part, with the consequence that he may be committed to a state institution." *In re Gault*, 387 U.S. 1, 13 (1967). *Gault* decided that, although the Fourteenth Amendment does not require that the hearing at this stage conform with all the requirements of a criminal trial or even of the usual administrative proceeding, the Due Process Clause does require application during the adjudicatory hearing of "'the essentials of due process and fair treatment.'" *Id.*, at 30. This case presents the single, narrow question whether proof beyond a reasonable doubt is among the "essentials of due process and fair treatment" required during the adjudicatory stage when a juvenile is charged with an act which would constitute a crime if committed by an adult.[1]

1. Thus, we do not see how it can be said in dissent that this opinion "rests entirely on the assumption that all juvenile proceedings are 'criminal prosecutions,' hence subject to constitutional limitations."

Section 712 of the New York Family Court Act defines a juvenile delinquent as "a person over seven and less than sixteen years of age who does any act which, if done by an adult, would constitute a crime." During a 1967 adjudicatory hearing, conducted pursuant to § 742 of the Act, a judge in New York Family Court found that appellant, then a 12-year-old boy, had entered a locker and stolen $112 from a woman's pocketbook. The petition which charged appellant with delinquency alleged that his act, "if done by an adult, would constitute the crime or crimes of Larceny." The judge acknowledged that the proof might not establish guilt beyond a reasonable doubt, but rejected appellant's contention that such proof was required by the Fourteenth Amendment. The judge relied instead on § 744(b) of the New York Family Court Act which provides that "(a)ny determination at the conclusion of (an adjudicatory) hearing that a (juvenile) did an act or acts must be based on a preponderance of the evidence." During a subsequent dispositional hearing, appellant was ordered placed in a training school for an initial period of 18 months, subject to annual extensions of his commitment until his 18th birthday—six years in appellant's case.

I

The requirement that guilt of a criminal charge be established by proof beyond a reasonable doubt dates at least from our early years as a Nation.... Although virtually unanimous adherence to the reasonable-doubt standard in common-law jurisdictions may not conclusively establish it as a requirement of due process, such adherence does "reflect a profound judgment about the way in which law should be enforced and justice administered."

Expressions in many opinions of this Court indicate that it has long been assumed that proof of a criminal charge beyond a reasonable doubt is constitutionally required....

The reasonable-doubt standard plays a vital role in the American scheme of criminal procedure. It is a prime instrument for reducing the risk of convictions resting on factual error. The standard provides concrete substance for the presumption of innocence—that bedrock "axiomatic and elementary" principle whose "enforcement lies at the foundation of the administration of our criminal law."...

The requirement of proof beyond a reasonable doubt has this vital role in our criminal procedure for cogent reasons. The accused during a criminal prosecution has at stake interest of immense importance, both because of the possibility that he may lose his liberty upon conviction and because of the certainty that he would be stigmatized by the conviction. Accordingly, a society that values the good name and freedom of every individual should not condemn a man for commission of a crime when there is reasonable doubt about his guilt....

Moreover, use of the reasonable-doubt standard is indispensable to command the respect and confidence of the community in applications of the criminal law. It is critical that the moral force of the criminal law not be diluted by a standard of proof that leaves people in doubt whether innocent men are being condemned. It is also important in our free society that every individual going about his ordinary affairs have confidence that his government cannot adjudge him guilty of a criminal offense without convincing a proper factfinder of his guilt with utmost certainty.

Lest there remain any doubt about the constitutional stature of the reasonable-doubt standard, we explicitly hold that the Due Process Clause protects the accused against conviction except upon proof beyond a reasonable doubt of every fact necessary to constitute the crime with which he is charged.

II

We turn to the question whether juveniles, like adults, are constitutionally entitled to proof beyond a reasonable doubt when they are charged with violation of a criminal law. The same considerations that demand extreme caution in factfinding to protect the innocent adult apply as well to the innocent child. We do not find convincing the contrary arguments of the New York Court of Appeals. *Gault* rendered untenable much of the reasoning relied upon by that court to sustain the constitutionality of § 744(b).... In effect the Court of Appeals distinguished the proceedings in question here from a criminal prosecution by use of what *Gault* called the "civil label-of-convenience which has been attached to juvenile proceedings." 387 U.S., at 50. But *Gault* expressly rejected that distinction as a reason for holding the Due Process Clause inapplicable to a juvenile proceeding. 387 U.S., at 50–51.... We made clear in that decision that civil labels and good intentions do not themselves obviate the need for criminal due process safeguards in juvenile courts, for "(a) proceeding where the issue is whether the child will be found to be 'delinquent' and subjected to the loss of his liberty for years is comparable in seriousness to a felony prosecution." *Id.*, at 36.

Nor do we perceive any merit in the argument that to afford juveniles the protection of proof beyond a reasonable doubt would risk destruction of beneficial aspects of the juvenile process. Use of the reasonable-doubt standard during the adjudicatory hearing will not disturb New York's policies that a finding that a child has violated a criminal law does not constitute a criminal conviction, that such a finding does not deprive the child of his civil rights, and that juvenile proceedings are confidential. Nor will there be any effect on the informality, flexibility, or speed of the hearing at which the factfinding takes place. And the opportunity during the post-adjudicatory or dispositional hearing for a wide-ranging review of the child's social history and for his individualized treatment will remain unimpaired. Similarly, there will be no effect on the procedures distinctive to juvenile proceedings that are employed prior to the adjudicatory hearing....

We conclude, as we concluded regarding the essential due process safeguards applied in *Gault*, that the observance of the standard of proof beyond a reasonable doubt "will not compel the States to abandon or displace any of the substantive benefits of the juvenile process." *Gault*, *supra*, at 21.

Finally, we reject the Court of Appeals' suggestion that there is, in any event, only a "tenuous difference" between the reasonable-doubt and preponderance standards.... In this very case, the trial judge's ability to distinguish between the two standards enabled him to make a finding of guilt that he conceded he might not have made under the standard of proof beyond a reasonable doubt....

III

In sum, the constitutional safeguard of proof beyond a reasonable doubt is as much required during the adjudicatory stage of a delinquency proceeding as are those constitutional safeguards applied in *Gault*—notice of charges, right to counsel, the rights of confrontation and examination, and the privilege against self-incrimination. We therefore hold, in agreement with Chief Judge Fuld in dissent in the Court of Appeals, "that, where a 12-year-old child is charged with an act of stealing which renders him liable to confinement for as long as six years, then, as a matter of due process the case against him must be proved beyond a reasonable doubt." 24 N.Y.2d, at 207, 299 N.Y.S.2d, at 423, 247 N.E.2d, at 260.

Reversed.

Mr. Justice Harlan, concurring.

...While I am in full agreement that this statutory provision offends the requirement of fundamental fairness embodied in the Due Process Clause of the Fourteenth Amendment, I am constrained to add something to what my Brother Brennan has written for the Court, lest the true nature of the constitutional problem presented become obscured or the impact on state juvenile court systems of what the Court holds today be exaggerated....

I

...First, in a judicial proceeding in which there is a dispute about the facts of some earlier event, the factfinder cannot acquire unassailably accurate knowledge of what happened. Instead, all the factfinder can acquire is a belief of what *probably* happened. The intensity of this belief—the degree to which a factfinder is convinced that a given act actually occurred—can, of course, vary. In this regard, a standard of proof represents an attempt to instruct the fact-finder concerning the degree of confidence our society thinks he should have in the correctness of factual conclusions for a particular type of adjudication. Although the phrases "preponderance of the evidence" and "proof beyond a reasonable doubt" are quantitatively imprecise, they do communicate to the finder of fact different notions concerning the degree of confidence he is expected to have in the correctness of his factual conclusions.

A second proposition, which is really nothing more than a corollary of the first, is that the trier of fact will sometimes, despite his best efforts, be wrong in his factual conclusions. In a lawsuit between two parties, a factual error can make a difference in one of two ways. First, it can result in a judgment in favor of the plaintiff when the true facts warrant a judgment for the defendant. The analogue in a criminal case would be the conviction of an innocent man. On the other hand, an erroneous factual determination can result in a judgment for the defendant when the true facts justify a judgment in plaintiff's favor. The criminal analogue would be the acquittal of a guilty man.

The standard of proof influences the relative frequency of these two types of erroneous outcomes. If, for example, the standard of proof for a criminal trial were a preponderance of the evidence rather than proof beyond a reasonable doubt, there would be a smaller risk of factual errors that result in freeing guilty persons, but a far greater risk of factual errors that result in convicting the innocent. Because the standard of proof affects the comparative frequency of these two types of erroneous outcomes, the choice of the standard to be applied in a particular kind of litigation should, in a rational world, reflect an assessment of the comparative social disutility of each.

When one makes such an assessment, the reason for different standards of proof in civil as opposed to criminal litigation becomes apparent. In a civil suit between two private parties for money damages, for example, we view it as no more serious in general for there to be an erroneous verdict in the defendant's favor than for there to be an erroneous verdict in the plaintiff's favor....

In a criminal case, on the other hand, we do not view the social disutility of convicting an innocent man as equivalent to the disutility of acquitting someone who is guilty....

In this context, I view the requirement of proof beyond a reasonable doubt in a criminal case as bottomed on a fundamental value determination of our society that it is far worse to convict an innocent man than to let a guilty man go free. It is only because of the nearly complete and long-standing acceptance of the reasonable-doubt standard by the States in criminal trials that the Court has not before today had to hold explicitly that due process, as an expression of fundamental procedural fairness, requires a more stringent standard for criminal trials than for ordinary civil litigation.

II

When one assesses the consequences of an erroneous factual determination in a juvenile delinquency proceeding in which a youth is accused of a crime, I think it must be concluded that, while the consequences are not identical to those in a criminal case, the differences will not support a distinction in the standard of proof. First, and of paramount importance, a factual error here, as in a criminal case, exposes the accused to a complete loss of his personal liberty through a state-imposed confinement away from his home, family, and friends. And, second, a delinquency determination, to some extent at least, stigmatizes a youth in that it is by definition bottomed on a finding that the accused committed a crime.... I think here, as in a criminal case, it is far worse to declare an innocent youth a delinquent. I therefore agree that a juvenile court judge should be no less convinced of the factual conclusion that the accused committed the criminal act with which he is charged than would be required in a criminal trial.

III

I wish to emphasize, as I did in my separate opinion in *Gault*, 387 U.S. 1, 65, that there is no automatic congruence between the procedural requirements imposed by due process in a criminal case, and those imposed by due process in juvenile cases.... In this regard, I think it worth emphasizing that the requirement of proof beyond a reasonable doubt that a juvenile committed a criminal act before he is found to be a delinquent does not (1) interfere with the worthy goal of rehabilitating the juvenile, (2) make any significant difference in the extent to which a youth is stigmatized as a "criminal" because he has been found to be a delinquent, or (3) burden the juvenile courts with a procedural requirement that will make juvenile adjudications significantly more time consuming, or rigid.

MR. CHIEF JUSTICE BURGER, with whom MR. JUSTICE STEWART joins, dissenting.

The Court's opinion today rests entirely on the assumption that all juvenile proceedings are "criminal prosecutions," hence subject to constitutional limitations. This derives from earlier holdings, which, like today's holding, were steps eroding the differences between juvenile courts and traditional criminal courts. The original concept of the juvenile court system was to provide a benevolent and less formal means than criminal courts could provide for dealing with the special and often sensitive problems of youthful offenders. Since I see no constitutional requirement of due process sufficient to overcome the legislative judgment of the States in this area, I dissent from further straitjacketing of an already overly restricted system....

Much of the judicial attitude manifested by the Court's opinion today and earlier holdings in this field is really a protest against inadequate juvenile court staffs and facilities; we "burn down the stable to get rid of the mice." The lack of support and the distressing growth of juvenile crime have combined to make for a literal breakdown in many if not most juvenile courts. Constitutional problems were not seen while those courts functioned in an atmosphere where juvenile judges were not crushed with an avalanche of cases.

My hope is that today's decision will not spell the end of a generously conceived program of compassionate treatment intended to mitigate the rigors and trauma of exposing youthful offenders to a traditional criminal court....

Mr. Justice Black, dissenting....

...The Court has never clearly held...that proof beyond a reasonable doubt is either expressly or impliedly commanded by any provision of the Constitution. The Bill of Rights, which in my view is made fully applicable to the States by the Fourteenth Amendment does by express language provide for, among other things, a right to counsel in criminal trials, a right to indictment, and the right of a defendant to be informed of the nature of the charges against him. And in two places the Constitution provides for trial by jury, but nowhere in that document is there any statement that conviction of crime requires proof of guilt beyond a reasonable doubt....I believe the Court has no power to add to or subtract from the procedures set forth by the Founders. I realize that it is far easier to substitute individual judges' ideas of "fairness" for the fairness prescribed by the Constitution, but I shall not at any time surrender my belief that that document itself should be our guide, not our own concept of what is fair, decent, and right....

I admit a strong, persuasive argument can be made for a standard of proof beyond a reasonable doubt in criminal cases—and the majority has made that argument well—but it is not for me as a judge to say for that reason that Congress or the States are without constitutional power to establish another standard that the Constitution does not otherwise forbid. It is quite true that proof beyond a reasonable doubt has long been required in federal criminal trials. It is also true that this requirement is almost universally found in the governing laws of the States. And as long as a particular jurisdiction requires proof beyond a reasonable doubt, then the Due Process Clause commands that every trial in that jurisdiction must adhere to that standard. But when, as here, a State through its duly constituted legislative branch decides to apply a different standard, then that standard, unless it is otherwise unconstitutional, must be applied to insure that persons are treated according to the "law of the land." The State of New York has made such a decision, and in my view nothing in the Due Process Clause invalidates it.

NOTES AND QUESTIONS

1. To what extent do you think the result in *Winship* was determined by *Gault*?

2. Why does Justice Harlan concur? How does his interpretation of the Due Process Clause differ?

3. Justice Black concurred in *Gault*. Are you surprised by his dissent in *Winship*? To what extent does the Court use juvenile cases to establish broad constitutional principles with subsequent import for adult rights claims? Is that what happened in *Winship*? For a discussion of how the Court uses juvenile cases to establish the parameters of constitutional rights, see Katherine Hunt Federle, *The Second Amendment Rights of Children*, 89 Iowa L. Rev. 609 (2004).

4. Both Justice Stewart and Chief Justice Burger dissent. What is the basis for their disagreement?

MCKEIVER V. PENNSYLVANIA
Supreme Court of the United States
403 U.S. 528 (1971)

Mr. Justice Blackmun announced the judgments of the Court and an opinion in which The Chief Justice, Mr. Justice Stewart, and Mr. Justice White join.

These cases present the narrow but precise issue whether the Due Process Clause of the Fourteenth Amendment assures the right to trial by jury in the adjudicative phase of a state juvenile court delinquency proceeding.

I...

...[I]t is apparent that:

1. Some of the constitutional requirements attendant upon the state criminal trial have equal application to that part of the state juvenile proceeding that is adjudicative in nature. Among these are the rights to appropriate notice, to counsel, to confrontation and to cross-examination, and the privilege against self-incrimination. Included, also, is the standard of proof beyond a reasonable doubt.
2. The Court, however, has not yet said that all rights constitutionally assured to an adult accused of crime also are to be enforced or made available to the juvenile in his delinquency proceeding. Indeed, the Court specifically has refrained from going that far....
3. The Court, although recognizing the high hopes and aspirations of Judge Julian Mack, the leaders of the Jane Addams School and the other supporters of the juvenile court concept, has also noted the disappointments of the system's performance and experience and the resulting widespread disaffection. There have been, at one and the same time, both an appreciation for the juvenile court judge who is devoted, sympathetic, and conscientious, and a disturbed concern about the judge who is untrained and less than fully imbued with an understanding approach to the complex problems of childhood and adolescence. There has been praise for the system and its purposes, and there has been alarm over its defects.
4. The Court has insisted that these successive decisions do not spell the doom of the juvenile court system or even deprive it of its "informality, flexibility, or speed." On the other hand, a concern precisely to the opposite effect was expressed by the two dissenters in *Winship*. *Id.* at 375–376.

II

With this substantial background already developed, we turn to the facts of the present cases:

No. 322. Joseph McKeiver, then age 16, in May 1968 was charged with robbery, larceny, and receiving stolen goods (felonies under Pennsylvania law...) as acts of juvenile delinquency. At the time of the adjudication hearing he was represented by counsel.[2] His request for a jury trial

2. At McKeiver's hearing his counsel advised the court that he had never seen McKeiver before and "was just in the middle of interviewing" him. The court allowed him five minutes for the interview. Counsel's office, Community Legal Services, however, had been appointed to represent McKeiver five months earlier.

was denied and his case was heard by Judge Theodore S. Gutowicz of the Court of Common Pleas, Family Division, Juvenile Branch, of Philadelphia County, Pennsylvania. McKeiver was adjudged a delinquent upon findings that he had violated a law of the Commonwealth.... On appeal, the Superior Court affirmed without opinion.

Edward Terry, then age 15, in January 1969 was charged with assault and battery on a police officer and conspiracy (misdemeanors under Pennsylvania law...), as acts of juvenile delinquency. His counsel's request for a jury trial was denied and his case was heard by Judge Joseph C. Bruno of the same Juvenile Branch of the Court of Common Pleas of Philadelphia County. Terry was adjudged a delinquent on the charges. This followed an adjudication and commitment in the preceding week for an assault on a teacher. He was committed, as he had been on the earlier charge, to the Youth Development Center at Cornwells Heights. On appeal, the Superior Court affirmed without opinion.

The Supreme Court of Pennsylvania granted leave to appeal in both cases and consolidated them. The single question considered, as phrased by the court, was "whether there is a constitutional right to a jury trial in juvenile court." The answer, one justice dissenting, was in the negative....

...It suffices to say that McKeiver's offense was his participating with 20 or 30 youths who pursued three young teenagers and took 25 cents from them; that McKeiver never before had been arrested and had a record of gainful employment; that the testimony of two of the victims was described by the court as somewhat inconsistent and as "weak"; and that Terry's offense consisted of hitting a police officer with his fists and with a stick when the officer broke up a boys' fight Terry and others were watching.

No. 128. Barbara Burrus and approximately 45 other black children, ranging in age from 11 to 15 years, were the subjects of juvenile court summonses issued in Hyde County, North Carolina, in January 1969.

The charges arose out of a series of demonstrations in the county in late 1968 by black adults and children protesting school assignments and a school consolidation plan. Petitions were filed by North Carolina state highway patrolmen. Except for one relating to James Lambert Howard, the petitions charged the respective juveniles with wilfully impeding traffic. The charge against Howard was that he wilfully made riotous noise and was disorderly in the O. A. Peay School in Swan Quarter; interrupted and disturbed the school during its regular sessions; and defaced school furniture. The acts so charged are misdemeanors under North Carolina law.

The several cases were consolidated into groups for hearing before District Judge Hallett S. Ward, sitting as a juvenile court. The same lawyer appeared for all the juveniles. Over counsel's objection, made in all except two of the cases, the general public was excluded. A request for a jury trial in each case was denied.

The evidence as to the juveniles other than Howard consisted solely of testimony of highway patrolmen. No juvenile took the stand or offered any witness. The testimony was to the effect that on various occasions the juveniles and adults were observed walking along Highway 64 singing, shouting, clapping, and playing basketball. As a result, there was interference with traffic. The marchers were asked to leave the paved portion of the highway and they were warned that they were committing a statutory offense. They either refused or left the roadway and immediately returned. The juveniles and participating adults were taken into custody. Juvenile petitions were then filed with respect to those under the age of 16.

The evidence as to Howard was that on the morning of December 5, he was in the office of the principal of the O. A. Peay School with 15 other persons while school was in session and was moving furniture around; that the office was in disarray; that as a result the school closed before noon; and that neither he nor any of the others was a student at the school or authorized to enter the principal's office.

In each case the court found that the juvenile had committed "an act for which an adult may be punished by law." A custody order was entered declaring the juvenile a delinquent "in need of more suitable guardianship" and committing him to the custody of the County Department of Public Welfare for placement in a suitable institution "until such time as the Board of Juvenile Correction or the Superintendent of said institution may determine, not inconsistent with the laws of this State." The court, however, suspended these commitments and placed each juvenile on probation for either one or two years conditioned upon his violating none of the State's laws, upon his reporting monthly to the County Department of Welfare, upon his being home by 11 p.m. each evening, and upon his attending a school approved by the Welfare Director. None of the juveniles has been confined on these charges....

...The North Carolina Court of Appeals affirmed. In its turn the Supreme Court of North Carolina deleted that portion of the order in each case relating to commitment, but otherwise affirmed....

III

It is instructive to review, as an illustration, the substance of Justice Roberts' opinion for the Pennsylvania court. He observes, that "(f)or over sixty-five years the Supreme Court gave no consideration at all to the constitutional problems involved in the juvenile court area"; that *Gault* "is somewhat of a paradox, being both broad and narrow at the same time"; that it "is broad in that it evidences a fundamental and far-reaching disillusionment with the anticipated benefits of the juvenile court system"; that it is narrow because the court enumerated four due process rights which it held applicable in juvenile proceedings, but declined to rule on two other claimed rights; that as a consequence the Pennsylvania court was "confronted with a sweeping rationale and a carefully tailored holding," that the procedural safeguards "*Gault* specifically made applicable to juvenile courts have already caused a significant 'constitutional domestication' of juvenile court proceedings," that those safeguards and other rights, including the reasonable-doubt standard established by *Winship*, "insure that the juvenile court will operate in an atmosphere which is orderly enough to impress the juvenile with the gravity of the situation and the impartiality of the tribunal and at the same time informal enough to permit the benefits of the juvenile system to operate" (footnote omitted), that the "proper inquiry, then, is whether the right to a trial by jury is 'fundamental' within the meaning of *Duncan*, in the context of a juvenile court which operates with all of the above constitutional safeguards," and that his court's inquiry turned "upon whether there are elements in the juvenile process which render the right to a trial by jury less essential to the protection of an accused's rights in the juvenile system than in the normal criminal process."

Justice Roberts then concluded that such factors do inhere in the Pennsylvania juvenile system:...Although realizing that "faith in the quality of the juvenile bench is not an entirely satisfactory substitute for due process," the judges in the juvenile courts "do take a different view of their role than that taken by their counterparts in the criminal courts." While one regrets its inadequacies, "the juvenile system has available and utilizes much more fully various diagnostic and rehabilitative services" that are "far superior to those available in the regular criminal process." Although conceding that the post-adjudication process "has in many respects fallen far short of its goals, and its reality is far harsher than its theory," the end result of a declaration of delinquency "is significantly different from and less onerous than a finding of criminal guilt" and "we are not yet convinced that the current practices do not contain the seeds from which a truly appropriate system can be brought forth."... Finally, "of all the possible due process rights which could be applied in the juvenile courts, the right to trial by jury is the one which would most likely be disruptive of the unique nature of the juvenile process." It is the jury trial that "would probably require substantial alteration of the traditional practices." The other procedural rights held applicable to the juvenile process "will give the juveniles sufficient protection" and the addition of the trial by jury "might well destroy the traditional character of juvenile proceedings."

The court concluded, that it was confident "that a properly structured and fairly administered juvenile court system can serve our present societal needs without infringing on individual freedoms."

IV

The right to an impartial jury "(i)n all criminal prosecutions" under federal law is guaranteed by the Sixth Amendment. Through the Fourteenth Amendment that requirement has now been imposed upon the States "in all criminal cases which—were they to be tried in a federal court—would come within the Sixth Amendment's guarantee." This is because the Court has said it believes "that trial by jury in criminal cases is fundamental to the American scheme of justice."

This, of course, does not automatically provide the answer to the present jury trial issue, if for no other reason than that the juvenile court proceeding has not yet been held to be a "criminal prosecution," within the meaning and reach of the Sixth Amendment, and also has not yet been regarded as devoid of criminal aspects merely because it usually has been given the civil label.

Little, indeed, is to be gained by any attempt simplistically to call the juvenile court proceeding either "civil" or "criminal." The Court carefully has avoided this wooden approach....

Thus, accepting "the proposition that the Due Process Clause has a role to play," our task here with respect to trial by jury, as it was in *Gault* with respect to other claimed rights, "is to ascertain the precise impact of the due process requirement."

V

The Pennsylvania juveniles' basic argument is that they were tried in proceedings "substantially similar to a criminal trial." They say that a delinquency proceeding in their State is initiated by a petition charging a penal code violation in the conclusory language of an indictment; that a juvenile detained prior to trial is held in a building substantially similar to an adult prison; that in Philadelphia juveniles over 16 are, in fact, held in the cells of a prison; that counsel and the prosecution engage in plea bargaining; that motions to suppress are routinely heard and decided; that the usual rules of evidence are applied; that the customary common-law defenses are available; that the press is generally admitted in the Philadelphia juvenile courtrooms; that members of the public enter the room; that arrest and prior record may be reported by the press (from police sources, however, rather than from the juvenile court records); that, once adjudged delinquent, a juvenile may be confined until his majority in what amounts to a prison...; and that the stigma attached upon delinquency adjudication approximates that resulting from conviction in an adult criminal proceeding.

The North Carolina juveniles particularly urge that the requirement of a jury trial would not operate to deny the supposed benefits of the juvenile court system; that the system's primary benefits are its discretionary intake procedure permitting disposition short of adjudication, and its flexible sentencing permitting emphasis on rehabilitation; that realization of these benefits does not depend upon dispensing with the jury; that adjudication of factual issues on the one hand and disposition of the case on the other are very different matters with very different purposes; that the purpose of the former is indistinguishable from that of the criminal trial; that the jury trial provides an independent protective factor; that experience has shown that jury trials in juvenile courts are manageable; that no reason exists why protection traditionally accorded in criminal proceedings should be denied young people subject to involuntary incarceration for lengthy periods; and that the juvenile courts deserve healthy public scrutiny.

VI

All the litigants here agree that the applicable due process standard in juvenile proceedings, as developed by *Gault* and *Winship*, is fundamental fairness. As that standard was applied in those two cases, we have an emphasis on factfinding procedures. The requirements of notice, counsel, confrontation, cross-examination, and standard of proof naturally flowed from this emphasis. But one cannot say that in our legal system the jury is a necessary component of accurate factfinding. There is much to be said for it, to be sure, but we have been content to pursue other ways for determining facts. Juries are not required, and have not been, for example, in equity cases, in workmen's compensation, in probate, or in deportation cases. Neither have they been generally used in military trials. In *Duncan* the Court stated, "We would not assert, however, that every criminal trial—or any particular trial—held before a judge alone is unfair or that a defendant may never be as fairly treated by a judge as he would be by a jury." 391 U.S., at 158. In *DeStefano*, for this reason and others, the Court refrained from retrospective application of *Duncan*, an action it surely would have not taken had it felt that the integrity of the result was seriously at issue. And in *Williams v. Florida*, 399 U.S. 78 (1970), the Court saw no particular magic in a 12-man jury for a criminal case, thus revealing that even jury concepts themselves are not inflexible.

We must recognize, as the Court has recognized before, that the fond and idealistic hopes of the juvenile court proponents and early reformers of three generations ago have not been realized. The devastating commentary upon the system's failures as a whole, contained in the President's Commission on Law Enforcement and Administration of Justice, Task Force Report: Juvenile Delinquency and Youth Crime 7–9 (1967), reveals the depth of disappointment in what has been accomplished. Too often the juvenile court judge falls far short of that stalwart, protective, and communicating figure the system envisaged.[4] The community's unwillingness to provide people and facilities and to be concerned, the insufficiency of time

4. "A recent study of juvenile court judges...revealed that half had not received undergraduate degrees; a fifth had received no college education at all; a fifth were not members of the bar." Task Force Report 7.

devoted, the scarcity of professional help, the inadequacy of dispositional alternatives, and our general lack of knowledge all contribute to dissatisfaction with the experiment.[5]

The Task Force Report, however, also said, *id.*, at 7, "To say that juvenile courts have failed to achieve their goals is to say no more than what is true of criminal courts in the United States. But failure is most striking when hopes are highest."

Despite all these disappointments, all these failures, and all these shortcomings, we conclude that trial by jury in the juvenile court's adjudicative stage is not a constitutional requirement. We so conclude for a number of reasons:

1. The Court has refrained, in the cases heretofore decided, from taking the easy way with a flat holding that all rights constitutionally assured for the adult accused are to be imposed upon the state juvenile proceeding....
2. There is a possibility, at least, that the jury trial, if required as a matter of constitutional precept, will remake the juvenile proceeding into a fully adversary process and will put an effective end to what has been the idealistic prospect of an intimate, informal protective proceeding.
3. The Task Force Report, although concededly pre-Gault, is notable for its not making any recommendation that the jury trial be imposed upon the juvenile court system. This is so despite its vivid description of the system's deficiencies and disappointments. Had the Commission deemed this vital to the integrity of the juvenile process, or to the handling of juveniles, surely a recommendation or suggestion to this effect would have appeared. The intimations, instead, are quite the other way. Task Force Report 38. Further, it expressly recommends against abandonment of the system and against the return of the juvenile to the criminal courts.
4. The Court specifically has recognized by dictum that a jury is not a necessary part even of every criminal process that is fair and equitable. *Duncan v. Louisiana*, 391 U.S., at 149–150, n. 14.
5. The imposition of the jury trial on the juvenile court system would not strengthen greatly, if at all, the fact-finding function, and would, contrarily, provide an attrition of the juvenile court's assumed ability to function in a unique manner. It would not remedy the defects of the system. Meager as has been the hoped-for advance in the juvenile field, the alternative would be

5. "What emerges, then, is this: In theory the juvenile court was to be helpful and rehabilitative rather than punitive. In fact the distinction often disappears, not only because of the absence of facilities and personnel but also because of the limits of knowledge and technique. In theory the court's action was to affix no stigmatizing label. In fact a delinquent is generally viewed by employers, schools, the armed services—by society generally—as a criminal. In theory the court was to treat children guilty of criminal acts in noncriminal ways. In fact it labels truants and runaways as junior criminals.

In theory the court's operations could justifiably be informal, its findings and decisions made without observing ordinary procedural safeguards, because it would act only in the best interest of the child. In fact it frequently does nothing more nor less than deprive a child of liberty without due process of law—knowing not what else to do and needing, whether admittedly or not, to act in the community's interest even more imperatively than the child's. In theory it was to exercise its protective powers to bring an errant child back into the fold. In fact there is increasing reason to believe that its intervention reinforces the juvenile's unlawful impulses. In theory it was to concentrate on each case the best of current social science learning. In fact it has often become a vested interest in its turn, loathe to cooperate with innovative programs or avail itself of forward-looking methods." Task Force Report 9.

regressive, would lose what has been gained, and would tend once again to place the juvenile squarely in the routine of the criminal process.

6. The juvenile concept held high promise. We are reluctant to say that, despite disappointments of grave dimensions, it still does not hold promise, and we are particularly reluctant to say, as do the Pennsylvania appellants here, that the system cannot accomplish its rehabilitative goals. So much depends on the availability of resources, on the interest and commitment of the public, on willingness to learn, and on understanding as to cause and effect and cure. In this field, as in so many others, one perhaps learns best by doing. We are reluctant to disallow the States to experiment further and to seek in new and different ways the elusive answers to the problems of the young, and we feel that we would be impeding that experimentation by imposing the jury trial. The States, indeed, must go forward. If, in its wisdom, any State feels the jury trial is desirable in all cases, or in certain kinds, there appears to be no impediment to its installing a system embracing that feature. That, however, is the State's privilege and not its obligation.
7. Of course there have been abuses. The Task Force Report has noted them. We refrain from saying at this point that those abuses are of constitutional dimension. They relate to the lack of resources and of dedication rather than to inherent unfairness.
8. There is, of course, nothing to prevent a juvenile court judge, in a particular case where he feels the need, or when the need is demonstrated, from using an advisory jury.
9. "The fact that a practice is followed by a large number of states is not conclusive in a decision as to whether that practice accords with due process, but it is plainly worth considering in determining whether the practice 'offends some principle of justice so rooted in the traditions and conscience of our people as to be ranked as fundamental.'" It therefore is of more than passing interest that at least 28 States and the District of Columbia by statute deny the juvenile a right to a jury trial in cases such as these. The same result is achieved in other States by judicial decision. In 10 States statutes provide for a jury trial under certain circumstances.
10. Since Gault and since Duncan the great majority of States, in addition to Pennsylvania and North Carolina, that have faced the issue have concluded that the considerations that led to the result in those two cases do not compel trial by jury in the juvenile court....
11. Stopping short of proposing the jury trial for juvenile proceedings are the Uniform Juvenile Court Act, § 24(a), approved in July 1968 by the National Conference of Commissioners on Uniform State Laws; the Standard Juvenile Court Act, Art. V, § 19, proposed by the National Council on Crime and Delinquency...and the Legislative Guide for Drafting Family and Juvenile Court Acts § 29(a) (Dept. of H.E.W., Children's Bureau Pub. No. 472-1969).
12. If the jury trial were to be injected into the juvenile court system as a matter of right, it would bring with it into that system the traditional delay, the formality, and the clamor of the adversary system and, possibly, the public trial. It is of interest that these very factors were stressed by the District Committee of the Senate when, through Senator Tydings, it recommended, and Congress then approved, as a provision in the District of Columbia Crime Bill, the abolition of the jury trial in the juvenile court.
13. Finally, the arguments advanced by the juveniles here are, of course, the identical arguments that underlie the demand for the jury trial for criminal proceedings. The arguments necessarily equate the juvenile proceeding—or at least the adjudicative phase of it—with the criminal trial. Whether they should be so equated is our issue. Concern

> about the inapplicability of exclusionary and other rules of evidence, about the juvenile court judge's possible awareness of the juvenile's prior record and of the contents of the social file; about repeated appearances of the same familiar witnesses in the persons of juvenile and probation officers and social workers—all to the effect that this will create the likelihood of pre-judgment—chooses to ignore it seems to us, every aspect of fairness, of concern, of sympathy, and of paternal attention that the juvenile court system contemplates.

If the formalities of the criminal adjudicative process are to be superimposed upon the juvenile court system, there is little need for its separate existence. Perhaps that ultimate disillusionment will come one day, but for the moment we are disinclined to give impetus to it.

Affirmed.

MR. JUSTICE WHITE, concurring.

Although the function of the jury is to find facts, that body is not necessarily or even probably better at the job than the conscientious judge. Nevertheless, the consequences of criminal guilt are so severe that the Constitution mandates a jury to prevent abuses of official power by insuring, where demanded, community participation in imposing serious deprivations of liberty and to provide a hedge against corrupt, biased, or political justice. We have not, however, considered the juvenile case a criminal proceeding within the meaning of the Sixth Amendment and hence automatically subject to all of the restrictions normally applicable in criminal cases. The question here is one of due process of law and I join the plurality opinion concluding that the States are not required by that clause to afford jury trials in juvenile courts where juveniles are charged with improper acts.

The criminal law proceeds on the theory that defendants have a will and are responsible for their actions. A finding of guilt establishes that they have chosen to engage in conduct so reprehensible and injurious to others that they must be punished to deter them and others from crime. Guilty defendants are considered blameworthy; they are branded and treated as such, however much the State also pursues rehabilitative ends in the criminal justice system.

For the most part, the juvenile justice system rests on more deterministic assumptions. Reprehensible acts by juveniles are not deemed the consequence of mature and malevolent choice but of environmental pressures (or lack of them) or of other forces beyond their control. Hence the state legislative judgment not to stigmatize the juvenile delinquent by branding him a criminal; his conduct is not deemed so blameworthy that punishment is required to deter him or others. Coercive measures, where employed, are considered neither retribution nor punishment. Supervision or confinement is aimed at rehabilitation, not at convincing the juvenile of his error simply by imposing pains and penalties. Nor is the purpose to make the juvenile delinquent an object lesson for others, whatever his own merits or demerits may be. A typical disposition in the juvenile court where delinquency is established may authorize confinement until age 21, but it will last no longer and within that period will last only so long as his behavior demonstrates that he remains an unacceptable risk if returned to his family. Nor is the authorization for custody until 21 any measure of the seriousness of the particular act that the juvenile has performed....

...To the extent that the jury is a buffer to the corrupt or overzealous prosecutor in the criminal law system, the distinctive intake policies and procedures of the juvenile court system to a great extent obviate this important function of the jury. As for the necessity to guard against judicial bias, a system eschewing blameworthiness and punishment for evil choice is itself an operative force against prejudice and short-tempered justice. Nor where juveniles are involved is there the same opportunity for corruption to the juvenile's detriment or the same temptation to use the courts for political ends.

Not only are those risks that mandate juries in criminal cases of lesser magnitude in juvenile court adjudications, but the consequences of adjudication are less severe than those flowing from verdicts of criminal guilt. This is plainly so in theory, and in practice there remains a substantial gulf between criminal guilt and delinquency, whatever the failings of the juvenile court in practice may be. Moreover, to the extent that current unhappiness with juvenile court performance rests on dissatisfaction with the vague and overbroad grounds for delinquency adjudications, with faulty judicial choice as to disposition after adjudication, or with the record of rehabilitative custody, whether institutional or probationary, these shortcomings are in no way mitigated by providing a jury at the adjudicative stage....

...Of course, there are strong arguments that juries are desirable when dealing with the young, and States are free to use juries if they choose. They are also free if they extend criminal court safeguards to juvenile court adjudications, frankly to embrace condemnation, punishment, and deterrence as permissible and desirable attributes of the juvenile justice system. But the Due Process Clause neither compels nor invites them to do so.

MR. JUSTICE BRENNAN, concurring in the judgment in No. 322 and dissenting in No. 128.

...For me...the question in these cases is whether jury trial is among the "essentials of due process and fair treatment." *In re Gault*, 387 U.S. 1, 30 (1967), required during the adjudication of a charge of delinquency based upon acts that would constitute a crime if engaged in by an adult. See *In re Winship*, 397 U.S. 358, 359 and n.1 (1970). This does not, however, mean that the interests protected by the Sixth Amendment's guarantee of jury trial in all "criminal prosecutions" are of no importance in the context of these cases. The Sixth Amendment, where applicable, commands, not a particular procedure, protected by a particular procedure, that is, trial by jury. The Due Process Clause commands not a particular procedure, but only a result: in my Brother BLACKMUN's words, "fundamental fairness...(in) factfinding." In the context of these and similar juvenile delinquency proceedings, what this means is that the States are not bound to provide jury trials on demand so long as some other aspect of the process adequately protects the interests that Sixth Amendment jury trials are intended to serve.

In my view, therefore, the due process question cannot be decided upon the basis of general characteristics of juvenile proceedings, but only in terms of the adequacy of a particular state procedure to "protect the (juvenile) from oppression by the Government," and to protect him against "the compliant, biased, or eccentric judge."

Examined in this light, I find no defect in the Pennsylvania cases before us. The availability of trial by jury allows an accused to protect himself against possible oppression by what is in essence an appeal to the community conscience, as embodied in the jury that hears his case. To some extent, however, a similar protection may be obtained when an accused may in essence appeal to the community at large, by focusing public attention upon the facts of his trial, exposing improper judicial behavior to public view, and obtaining, if necessary, executive redress through the medium of public indignation. Of course, the Constitution, in the context of adult criminal trials, has rejected the notion that public trial is an adequate substitution for trial by jury in serious cases. But in the context of juvenile delinquency proceedings, I cannot say that it is beyond the competence of a State to conclude that juveniles who fear that delinquency proceedings will mask judicial oppression may obtain adequate protection by focusing community attention upon the trial of their cases. For, however much the juvenile system may have failed in practice, its very existence as an ostensibly beneficent and noncriminal process for the care and guidance of young persons demonstrates the existence of the community's sympathy and concern for the young. Juveniles able to bring the community's attention to bear upon their trials may therefore draw upon a reservoir of public concern unavailable to the adult criminal defendant. In the Pennsylvania cases before us, there appears to be no statutory ban upon admission of the public to juvenile trials. Appellants themselves, without contradiction, assert that "the press is generally admitted" to juvenile delinquency proceedings in Philadelphia. Most important, the record in these cases is bare of any indication that any person whom appellants sought to have admitted to the courtroom was excluded. In these circumstances, I agree that the judgment in No. 322 must be affirmed.

The North Carolina cases, however, present a different situation. North Carolina law either permits or requires exclusion of the general public from juvenile trials. In the cases before us, the trial judge "ordered the general public excluded from the hearing room and stated that only officers of the court, the juveniles, their parents or guardians, their attorney and witnesses would be present for the hearing," notwithstanding petitioners' repeated demand for a public hearing. The cases themselves, which arise out of a series of demonstrations by black adults and juveniles who believed that the Hyde County, North Carolina, school system unlawfully discriminated against black schoolchildren, present a paradigm of the circumstances in which there may be a substantial "temptation to use the courts for political ends." And finally, neither the opinions supporting the judgment nor the respondent in No. 128 has pointed to any feature of North Carolina's juvenile proceedings that could substitute for public or jury trial in protecting the petitioners against misuse of the judicial process. Accordingly, I would reverse the judgment in No. 128.

MR. JUSTICE HARLAN, concurring in the judgments.

If I felt myself constrained to follow *Duncan v. Louisiana*, 391 U.S. 145 (1968), which extended the Sixth Amendment right of jury trial to the States, I would have great difficulty, upon the premise seemingly accepted in my Brother BLACKMUN's opinion, in holding that the jury trial right does not extend to state juvenile proceedings. That premise is that juvenile delinquency proceedings have in practice actually become in many, if not all, respects criminal trials.... If that premise be correct, then I do not see why, given *Duncan*, juveniles as well as adults would not be constitutionally entitled to jury trials, so long as juvenile delinquency systems are not restructured to fit their original purpose. When that time comes I would have no difficulty in agreeing with my Brother BLACKMUN, and indeed with my Brother WHITE, the author of *Duncan*, that juvenile delinquency proceedings are beyond the pale of *Duncan*.

I concur in the judgments in these cases, however, on the ground that criminal jury trials are not constitutionally required of the States, either as a matter of Sixth Amendment law or due process....

MR. JUSTICE DOUGLAS, with whom MR. JUSTICE BLACK and MR. JUSTICE MARSHALL concur, dissenting.

...I believe the guarantees of the Bill of Rights, made applicable to the States by the Fourteenth Amendment, require a jury trial.

In the Pennsylvania cases one of the appellants was charged with robbery, larceny, and receiving stolen goods as acts of juvenile delinquency. He was found a delinquent and placed on probation. The other appellant was charged with assault and battery on a police officer and conspiracy as acts of juvenile delinquency. On a finding of delinquency he was committed to a youth center. Despite the fact that the two appellants, aged 15 and 16, would face potential incarceration until their majority, they were denied a jury trial.

In the North Carolina cases petitioners are students, from 11 to 15 years of age, who were charged under one of three criminal statutes: (1) "disorderly conduct" in a public building, (2) "willful" interruption or disturbance of a public or private school, or (3) obstructing the flow of traffic on a highway or street.

Conviction of each of these crimes would subject a person, whether juvenile or adult, to imprisonment in a state institution. In the case of these students the possible term was six to 10 years; it would be computed for the period until an individual reached the age of 21. Each asked for a jury trial which was denied. The trial judge stated that the hearings were juvenile hearings, not criminal trials. But the issue in each case was whether they had violated a state criminal law. The trial judge found in each case that the juvenile had committed "an act for which an adult may be punished by law" and held in each case that the acts of the juvenile violated one of the criminal statutes cited above. The trial judge thereupon ordered each juvenile to be committed to the state institution for the care of delinquents and then placed each on probation for terms from 12 to 24 months.

We held in *In re Gault*, 387 U.S. 1, 13, that "neither the Fourteenth Amendment nor the Bill of Rights is for adults alone." As we noted in that case, the Juvenile Court movement was designed to avoid procedures to ascertain whether the child was "guilty" or "innocent" but to bring to bear on these problems a "clinical" approach. It is, of course, not our task to determine as a matter of policy whether a "clinical" or "punitive" approach to these problems should be taken by the States. But where a State uses its juvenile court proceedings to prosecute a juvenile for a criminal act and to order "confinement" until the child reaches 21 years of age or where the child at the threshold of the proceedings faces that prospect, then he is entitled to the same procedural protection as an adult....

Just as courts have sometimes confused delinquency with crime, so have law enforcement officials treated juveniles not as delinquents but as criminals. As noted in the President's Crime Commission Report:

> "In 1965, over 100,000 juveniles were confined in adult institutions. Presumably most of them were there because no separate juvenile detention facilities existed. Nonetheless, it is clearly undesirable that juveniles be confined with adults." President's Commission on Law Enforcement and Administration of Justice, Challenge of Crime in a Free Society 179 (1967).

Even when juveniles are not incarcerated with adults the situation may be no better. One Pennsylvania correctional institution for juveniles is a brick building with barred windows, locked steel doors, a cyclone fence topped with barbed wire, and guard towers. A former juvenile judge described it as "a maximum security prison for adjudged delinquents."

In the present cases imprisonment or confinement up to 10 years was possible for one child and each faced at least a possible five-year incarceration. No adult could be denied a jury trial in those circumstances. The Fourteenth Amendment, which makes trial by jury provided in the Sixth Amendment applicable to the States, speaks of denial of rights to "any person," not denial of rights to "any adult person"; and we have held indeed that where a juvenile is charged with an act that would constitute a crime if committed by an adult, he is entitled to be tried under a standard of proof beyond a reasonable doubt. *In re Winship*, 397 U.S. 358....

Practical aspects... are urged against allowing a jury trial in these cases. They have been answered by Judge De Ciantis of the Family Court of Providence, Rhode Island, in a case entitled *In the Matter of McCloud*, decided January 15, 1971. A juvenile was charged with the rape of a 17-year-old female and Judge De Ciantis granted a motion for a jury trial in an opinion, a part of which I have attached as an appendix to this dissent. He there concludes that "the real traumatic" experience of incarceration without due process is "the feeling of being deprived of basic rights." He adds:...

> "The child who feels that he has been dealt with fairly and not merely expediently or as speedily as possible will be a better prospect for rehabilitation. Many of the children who come before the court come from broken homes, from the ghettos; they often suffer from low self-esteem; and their behavior is frequently a symptom of their own feelings of inadequacy. Traumatic experiences of denial of basic rights only accentuate the past deprivation and contribute to the problem. Thus, a general societal attitude of acceptance of the juvenile as a person entitled to the same protection as an adult may be the true beginning of the rehabilitative process."

Judge De Ciantis goes on to say that "(t)rial by jury will provide the child with a safeguard against being prejudged" by a judge who may well be prejudiced by reports already submitted to him by the police or caseworkers in the case. Indeed the child, the same as the adult, is in the category of those described in the Magna Carta:

> "No freeman may be... imprisoned... except by the lawful judgment of his peers, or by the law of the land."

These cases should be remanded for trial by jury on the criminal charges filed against these youngsters.

APPENDIX TO OPINION OF DOUGLAS, J., DISSENTING [Excerpt of Opinion by Judge De Ciantis In *In The Matter Of Mccloud*]

TRAUMA

The fact is that the procedures which are now followed in juvenile cases are far more traumatic than the potential experience of a jury trial. Who can say that a boy who is arrested and handcuffed, placed in a lineup, transported in vehicles designed to convey dangerous criminals, placed in the same kind of a cell as an adult, deprived of his freedom by lodging him in an institution where he is subject to be transferred to the state's prison and in the "hole" has not undergone a traumatic experience?

The experience of a trial with or without a jury is meant to be impressive and meaningful. The fact that a juvenile realizes that his case will be decided by twelve objective citizens would allow the court to retain its meaningfulness without causing any more trauma than a trial before a judge who perhaps has heard other cases involving the same juvenile in the past and may be influenced by those prior contacts. To agree that a jury trial would expose a juvenile to a traumatic experience is to lose sight of the real traumatic experience of incarceration without due process....

BACKLOG

An argument has been made that to allow jury trials would cause a great backlog of cases and, ultimately, would impair the functioning of the juvenile court. The fact however is that there is no meaningful evidence that granting the right to jury trials will impair the function of the court. Some states permit jury trials in all juvenile court cases; few juries have been demanded, and there is no suggestion from these courts that jury trials have impeded the system of juvenile justice.

In Colorado, where jury trials have been permitted by statute, Judge Theodore Rubin of the Denver Juvenile Court has indicated that jury trials are an important safeguard and that they have not impaired the functioning of the Denver Juvenile Courts. For example, during the first seven months of 1970, the two divisions of the Denver Juvenile Court have had fewer than two dozen jury trials, in both delinquency and dependency-neglect cases. In Michigan, where juveniles are also entitled to a jury trial, Judge Lincoln of the Detroit Juvenile Court indicates that his court has had less than five jury trials in the year 1969 to 1970....

In fact the very argument of expediency, suggesting "supermarket" or "assembly line" justiceis one of the most forceful arguments in favor of granting jury trials. By granting the juvenile the right to a jury trial, we would, in fact, be protecting the accused from the judge who is under pressure to move the cases, the judge with too many cases and not enough time. It will provide a safeguard against the judge who may be prejudiced against a minority group or who may be prejudiced against the juvenile brought before him because of some past occurrence which was heard by the same judge.

There have been criticisms that juvenile court judges, because of their hearing caseload, do not carefully weigh the evidence in the adjudicatory phase of the proceedings. It is during this phase that the judge must determine whether in fact the evidence has been established beyond a reasonable doubt that the accused committed the acts alleged in the petition. Regardless of the merit of these criticisms, they have impaired the belief of the juveniles of the bar and of the public as to the opportunity for justice in the juvenile court. Granting the juvenile the right to demand that the facts be determined by a jury will strengthen the faith of all concerned parties in the juvenile system.

It is important to note, at this time, a definite side benefit of granting jury trials, i.e., an aid to rehabilitation. The child who feels that he has been dealt with fairly and not merely expediently or as speedily as possible will be a better prospect for rehabilitation. Many of the children who come before the court come from broken homes, from the ghettos; they often suffer from low self-esteem; and their behavior is frequently a symptom of their own feelings of inadequacy. Traumatic experiences of denial of basic rights only accentuate the past deprivation and contribute to the problem. Thus, a general societal attitude of acceptance of the juvenile as a person entitled to the same protection as an adult may be the true beginning of the rehabilitative process.

Public Trial

Public trial in the judgment of this Court does not affect the juvenile court philosophy. . . .

In fact, the juvenile proceedings as presently conducted are far from secret. Witnesses for the prosecution and for the defense, social workers, court reporters, students, police trainees, probation counselors, and sheriffs are present in the courtroom. Police, the Armed Forces, the Federal Bureau of Investigation obtain information and have access to the police files. There seems no more reason to believe that a jury trial would destroy confidentiality than would witnesses summoned to testify. . . .

Judge's Expertise

The Court is also aware of the argument that the juvenile court was created to develop judges who were experts in sifting out the real problems behind a juvenile's breaking the law; therefore, to place the child's fate in the hands of a jury would defeat that purpose. This will, however, continue to leave the final decision of disposition solely with the judge. The role of the jury will be only to ascertain whether the facts, which give the court jurisdiction, have been established beyond a reasonable doubt. The jury will not be concerned with social and psychological factors. These factors, along with prior record, family and educational background, will be considered by the judge during the dispositional phase.

Taking into consideration the social background and other facts, the judge, during the dispositional phase, will determine what disposition is in the best interests of the child and society. It is at this stage that a judge's expertise is most important, and the granting of a jury trial will not prevent the judge from carrying out the basic philosophy of the juvenile court.

Trial by jury will provide the child with a safeguard against being prejudged. The jury clearly will have no business in learning of the social report or any of the other extraneous matter unless properly introduced under the rules of evidence. Due process demands that the trier of facts should not be acquainted with any of the facts of the case or have knowledge of any of the circumstances, whether through officials in his own department or records in his possession. . . .

Waiver of Jury Trial

Counsel also questions whether a child can waive his right to a jury trial or, in fact, whether a parent or counsel may waive.

When the waiver comes up for hearing, the Court could, at its discretion, either grant or refuse the juvenile's waiver of a jury trial, and/or appoint a guardian or legal counsel to advise the child.

My experience has shown that the greatest percentage of juveniles who appear before the court in felony cases have lived appalling lives due to parental neglect and brutality, lack of normal living conditions, and poverty. This has produced in them a maturity which is normally acquired much later in life. They are generally well aware of their rights in a court of law. However, in those cases where a child clearly needs guidance, the court-appointed guardian or attorney could explain to him the implications of a waiver. . . .

Counsel is placed with the responsibility of explaining to the juvenile the significance of guilty and nolo contendere pleas, of instructing the juvenile on the prerogative to take the witness stand, and is expected to advise his client in the same manner as he would an adult about to stand trial. And now counsel suggests to the Court that counsel is not capable of explaining and waiving the right to a jury trial. The Court fails to see the distinction between this waiver and the absolute waiver, to wit, a guilty plea. Counsel should act in the best interest of his client, even if this may be in conflict with the parents....

The Court could easily require that a waiver of a jury trial be made in person by the juvenile in writing, in open court, with the consent and approval of the Court and the attorney representing both the juvenile and the state. The judge could ascertain as to whether the juvenile can intelligently waive his right and, if necessary, appoint counsel to advise the youth as to the implications connected with the waiver. This could be accomplished without any difficulty through means presently available to the Court.

Jury of Peers

One of the most interesting questions raised is that concerning the right of a juvenile to a trial by his peers. Counsel has suggested that a jury of a juvenile's peers would be composed of other juveniles, that is, a "teenage jury." The word "peers" means nothing more than citizens. The phrase "judgment of his peers" means at common law, a trial by a jury of twelve men. "Judgment of his peers" is a term expressly borrowed from the Magna Charta, and it means a trial by jury. Are we now to say that a juvenile is a second-class citizen, not equal to an adult? The Constitution has never been construed to say women must be tried by their peers, to wit, by all-female juries, or Negroes by all-Negro juries.

The only restriction on the makeup of the jury is that there can be no systematic exclusion of those who meet local and federal requirements, in particular, voting qualifications.

The Court notes that presently in some states 18-year-olds can vote. Presumably, if they can vote, they may also serve on juries....

Criminal Proceeding

The argument that the adjudication of delinquency is not the equivalent of criminal process is spurious. This Court has discussed the futility of making distinctions on the basis of labels in prior decisions. Because the legislature dictates that a child who commits a felony shall be called a delinquent does not change the nature of the crime....

It is noteworthy that in our statute there is not an express statutory provision indicating that the proceedings are civil. Trial by jury in Rhode Island is guaranteed to *all* persons, whether in criminal cases or in civil cases. That right existed prior to the adoption of the Constitution; and certainly whether one is involved in a civil or criminal proceeding of the Family Court in which his "liberty" is to be "taken" "imprisoned" "outlawed" and "banished" he is entitled to a trial by jury.

This Court believes that although the juvenile court was initially created as a social experiment, it has not ceased to be part of the judicial system. In view of the potential loss of liberty at stake in the proceeding, this Court is compelled to accord due process to all the litigants who come before it; and, therefore, all of the provisions of the Bill of Rights, including trial by jury, must prevail.

QUESTIONS

1. A criminal defendant has a Sixth Amendment right to a jury trial under certain circumstances. Why doesn't a juvenile charged with a delinquent act have the same right?

2. Consider the reasons the plurality gives for concluding that juveniles do not have a right to a jury trial in delinquency proceedings. Are those reasons persuasive? Are they still valid today?

3. Does the case leave open the possibility that jury trials may be constitutionally mandated under certain circumstances? Under what circumstances would a denial of a jury trial in a delinquency proceeding violate due process?

4. Justice Brennan, generally considered a "liberal" justice, agreed with the plurality that Pennsylvania could properly deny juveniles a jury trial. Nevertheless, he concluded that the North Carolina procedures violated due process. Why?

5. Should a juvenile have a right to a jury trial? What reasons support the argument that juveniles should have such a right? How would you argue that juveniles in delinquency proceedings do not—and should not—have such a right? Do you find the appendix to the dissenting opinion persuasive?

BREED V. JONES
Supreme Court of the United States
421 U.S. 519 (1975)

MR. CHIEF JUSTICE BURGER delivered the opinion of the Court.

We granted certiorari to decide whether the prosecution of respondent as an adult, after Juvenile Court proceedings which resulted in a finding that respondent had violated a criminal statute and a subsequent finding that he was unfit for treatment as a juvenile, violated the Fifth and Fourteenth Amendments to the United States Constitution.

On February 9, 1971, a petition was filed in the Superior Court of California, County of Los Angeles, Juvenile Court, alleging that respondent, then 17 years of age, was a person described by Cal.Welf. & Inst'ns Code § 602 (1966), in that, on or about February 8, while armed with a deadly weapon, he had committed acts which, if committed by an adult, would constitute the crime of robbery in violation of Cal. Penal Code § 211 (1970). The following day, a detention hearing was held, at the conclusion of which respondent was ordered detained pending a hearing on the petition.

The jurisdictional or adjudicatory hearing was conducted on March 1, pursuant to Cal.Welf. & Inst'ns Code § 701 (1966). After taking testimony from two prosecution witnesses and respondent, the Juvenile Court found that the allegations in the petition were true and that respondent was a person described by § 602, and it sustained the petition. The proceedings were continued for a dispositional hearing, pending which the court ordered that respondent remain detained.

At a hearing conducted on March 15, the Juvenile Court indicated its intention to find respondent "not...amenable to the care, treatment and training program available through the facilities of the juvenile court" under Cal.Welf. & Inst'ns Code § 707 (Supp. 1967).

Respondent's counsel orally moved "to continue the matter on the ground of surprise," contending that respondent "was not informed that it was going to be a fitness hearing." The court continued the matter for one week, at which time, having considered the report of the probation officer assigned to the case and having heard her testimony, it declared respondent "unfit for treatment as a juvenile," and ordered that he be prosecuted as an adult.

Thereafter, respondent filed a petition for a writ of habeas corpus in Juvenile Court, raising the same double jeopardy claim now presented. Upon the denial of that petition, respondent sought habeas corpus relief in the California Court of Appeal, Second Appellate District. Although it initially stayed the criminal prosecution pending against respondent, that court denied the petition....

After a preliminary hearing respondent was ordered held for trial in Superior Court, where an information was subsequently filed accusing him of having committed robbery, in violation of Cal. Penal Code § 211 (1970), while armed with a deadly weapon, on or about February 8, 1971. Respondent entered a plea of not guilty, and he also pleaded that he had "already been placed once in jeopardy and convicted of the offense charged, by the judgment of the Superior Court of the County of Los Angeles, Juvenile Court, rendered... on the 1st day of March, 1971." App. 47. By stipulation, the case was submitted to the court on the transcript of the preliminary hearing. The court found respondent guilty of robbery in the first degree under Cal. Penal Code § 211a (1970) and ordered that he be committed to the California Youth Authority. No appeal was taken from the judgment of conviction.

On December 10, 1971, respondent, through his mother as guardian ad litem, filed the instant petition for a writ of habeas corpus in the United States District Court for the Central District of California. In his petition he alleged that his transfer to adult court pursuant to Cal. Welf. & Inst'ns Code § 707 and subsequent trial there "placed him in double jeopardy." The District Court denied the petition, rejecting respondent's contention that jeopardy attached at his adjudicatory hearing. It concluded that the "distinctions between the preliminary procedures and hearings provided by California law for juveniles and a criminal trial are many and apparent and the effort of (respondent) to relate them is unconvincing," and that "even assuming jeopardy attached during the preliminary juvenile proceedings... it is clear that no new jeopardy arose by the juvenile proceeding sending the case to the criminal court."

The Court of Appeals reversed, concluding that applying double jeopardy protection to juvenile proceedings would not "impede the juvenile courts in carrying out their basic goal of rehabilitating the erring youth," and that the contrary result might "do irreparable harm to or destroy their confidence in our judicial system." The court therefore held that the Double Jeopardy Clause "is fully applicable to juvenile court proceedings."...

I

The parties agree that, following his transfer from Juvenile Court, and as a defendant to a felony information, respondent was entitled to the full protection of the Double Jeopardy Clause of the Fifth Amendment, as applied to the States through the Fourteenth Amendment. In addition, they agree that respondent was put in jeopardy by the proceedings on that information, which resulted in an adjudication that he was guilty of robbery in the first degree and in a sentence of commitment. Finally, there is no dispute that the petition filed in Juvenile Court and the information filed in Superior Court related to the "same offence" within the meaning of the constitutional prohibition. The point of disagreement between the parties, and the question for our decision, is whether, by reason of the proceedings in Juvenile Court, respondent was "twice put in jeopardy."

II

Jeopardy denotes risk. In the constitutional sense, jeopardy describes the risk that is traditionally associated with a criminal prosecution. Although the constitutional language, "jeopardy of life or limb," suggests proceedings in which only the most serious penalties can be imposed, the Clause has long been construed to mean something far broader than its literal language. At the same time, however, we have held that the risk to which the Clause refers is not present in proceedings that are not "essentially criminal."

Although the juvenile-court system had its genesis in the desire to provide a distinctive procedure and setting to deal with the problems of youth, including those manifested by antisocial conduct, our decisions in recent years have recognized that there is a gap between the originally benign conception of the system and its realities. With the exception of *McKeiver v. Pennsylvania*, 403 U.S. 528 (1971), the Court's response to that perception has been to make applicable in juvenile proceedings constitutional guarantees associated with traditional criminal prosecutions. *In re Gault*, 387 U.S. 1 (1967); *In re Winship*, 397 U.S. 358 (1970). In so doing the Court has evinced awareness of the threat which such a process represents to the efforts of the juvenile court system, functioning in a unique manner, to ameliorate the harshness of criminal justice when applied to youthful offenders. That the system has fallen short of the high expectations of its sponsors in no way detracts from the broad social benefits sought or from those benefits that can survive constitutional scrutiny.

We believe it is simply too late in the day to conclude, as did the District Court in this case, that a juvenile is not put in jeopardy at a proceeding whose object is to determine whether he has committed acts that violate a criminal law and whose potential consequences include both the stigma inherent in such a determination and the deprivation of liberty for many years. For it is clear under our cases that determining the relevance of constitutional policies, like determining the applicability of constitutional rights, in juvenile proceedings, requires that courts eschew "the 'civil' label-of-convenience which has been attached to juvenile proceedings," *In re Gault*, *supra*, at 50, and that "the juvenile process... be candidly appraised." 387 U.S., at 21. See *In re Winship*, *supra*, 397 U.S., at 365–366.

As we have observed, the risk to which the term jeopardy refers is that traditionally associated with "actions intended to authorize criminal punishment to vindicate public justice." Because of its purpose and potential consequences, and the nature and resources of the State, such a proceeding imposes heavy pressures and burdens—psychological, physical, and financial—on a person charged. The purpose of the Double Jeopardy Clause is to require that he be subject to the experience only once "for the same offence."

In *In re Gault*, *supra*, at 36, this Court concluded that, for purposes of the right to counsel, a "proceeding where the issue is whether the child will be found to be 'delinquent' and subjected to the loss of his liberty for years is comparable in seriousness to a felony prosecution." See *In re Winship*, *supra*, at 366. The Court stated that the term "delinquent" had "come to involve only slightly less stigma than the term 'criminal' applied to adults," *In re Gault*, *supra*, at 24; see *In re Winship*, *supra*, at 367, and that, for purposes of the privilege against self-incrimination, "commitment is a deprivation of liberty. It is incarceration against one's will, whether it is called 'criminal' or 'civil.'" *In re Gault, supra*, at 50. See 387 U.S., at 27; *In re Winship, supra*, at 367.

Thus, in terms of potential consequences, there is little to distinguish an adjudicatory hearing such as was held in this case from a traditional criminal prosecution. For that reason, it engenders elements of anxiety and insecurity in a juvenile, and imposes a "heavy personal strain." And we can expect that, since our decisions implementing fundamental fairness in the juvenile court system, hearings have been prolonged, and some of the burdens incident to a juvenile's defense increased, as the system has assimilated the process thereby imposed.

We deal here, not with "the formalities of the criminal adjudicative process," *McKeiver v. Pennsylvania*, 403 U.S., at 551 (opinion of Blackmun, J.), but with an analysis of an aspect of the juvenile-court system in terms of the kind of risk to which jeopardy refers. Under our decisions we can find no persuasive distinction in that regard between the proceeding conducted in this case pursuant to Cal.Welf. & Inst'ns Code § 701 (1966) and a criminal prosecution, each of which is designed "to vindicate (the) very vital interest in enforcement of criminal laws." We therefore conclude that respondent was put in jeopardy at the adjudicatory hearing. Jeopardy attached when respondent was "put to trial before the trier of the facts" that is, when the Juvenile Court, as the trier of the facts, began to hear evidence.

III

Petitioner argues that, even assuming jeopardy attached at respondent's adjudicatory hearing, the procedures by which he was transferred from Juvenile Court and tried on a felony information in Superior Court did not violate the Double Jeopardy Clause.... First, petitioner reasons that the procedure violated none of the policies of the Double Jeopardy Clause or that, alternatively, it should be upheld by analogy to those cases which permit retrial of an accused who has obtained reversal of a conviction on appeal. Second, pointing to this Court's concern for "the juvenile court's assumed ability to function in a unique manner," *McKeiver v. Pennsylvania, supra*, at 547, petitioner urges that, should we conclude traditional principles "would otherwise bar a transfer to adult court after a delinquency adjudication," we should avoid that result here because it "would diminish the flexibility and informality of juvenile court proceedings without conferring any additional due process benefits upon juveniles charged with delinquent acts."

A

We cannot agree with petitioner that the trial of respondent in Superior Court on an information charging the same offense as that for which he had been tried in Juvenile Court violated none of the policies of the Double Jeopardy Clause. For, even accepting petitioner's premise that respondent "never faced the risk of more than one punishment," we have pointed out that "the Double Jeopardy Clause...is written in terms of potential or risk of trial and conviction, not punishment."...

Respondent was subjected to the burden of two trials for the same offense; he was twice put to the task of marshaling his resources against those of the State, twice subjected to the "heavy personal strain" which such an experience represents. We turn, therefore, to inquire whether either traditional principles or "the juvenile court's assumed ability to function in a unique manner," *McKeiver v. Pennsylvania, supra*, at 547, supports an exception to the "constitutional policy of finality" to which respondent would otherwise be entitled....

B...

..."[C]ontinuing jeopardy"...has occasionally been used to explain why an accused who has secured the reversal of a conviction on appeal may be retried for the same offense. Probably a more satisfactory explanation lies in analysis of the respective interests involved. Similarly, the fact that the proceedings against respondent had not "run their full course," within the contemplation of the California Welfare and Institutions Code, at the time of transfer, does not satisfactorily explain why respondent should be deprived of the constitutional protection against a second trial.

The possibility of transfer from juvenile court to a court of general criminal jurisdiction is a matter of great significance to the juvenile. See *Kent v. United States*, 383 U.S. 541 (1966). At the same time, there appears to be widely shared agreement that not all juveniles can benefit from the special features and programs of the juvenile-court system and that a procedure for transfer to an adult court should be available. This general agreement is reflected in the fact that an overwhelming majority of jurisdictions permits transfer in certain circumstances. As might be expected, the statutory provisions differ in numerous details. Whatever their differences, however, such transfer provisions represent an attempt to impart to the juvenile-court system the flexibility needed to deal with youthful offenders who cannot benefit from the specialized guidance and treatment contemplated by the system.

We do not agree with petitioner that giving respondent the constitutional protection against multiple trials in this context will diminish flexibility and informality to the extent that those qualities relate uniquely to the goals of the juvenile-court system. We agree that such a holding will require, in most cases that the transfer decision be made prior to an adjudicatory hearing. To the extent that evidence concerning the alleged offense is considered relevant, it may be that, in those cases where transfer is considered and rejected, some added burden will be imposed on the juvenile courts by reason of duplicative proceedings. Finally, the nature of the evidence considered at a transfer hearing may in some States require that, if transfer is rejected, a different judge preside at the adjudicatory hearing.

We recognize that juvenile courts, perhaps even more than most courts, suffer from the problems created by spiraling caseloads unaccompanied by enlarged resources and manpower. And courts should be reluctant to impose on the juvenile-court system any additional requirements which could so strain its resources as to endanger its unique functions. However, the burdens that petitioner envisions appear to us neither qualitatively nor quantitatively sufficient to justify a departure in this context from the fundamental prohibition against double jeopardy.

A requirement that transfer hearings be held prior to adjudicatory hearings affects not at all the nature of the latter proceedings. More significantly, such a requirement need not affect the quality of decision making at transfer hearings themselves.... [T]he Court has never attempted to prescribe criteria for, or the nature and quantum of evidence that must support a decision to transfer a juvenile for trial in adult court. We require only that, whatever the relevant criteria, and whatever the evidence demanded, a State determine whether it wants to treat a juvenile within the juvenile-court system before entering upon a proceeding that may result in an adjudication that he has violated a criminal law and in a substantial deprivation of liberty, rather than subject him to the expense, delay, strain, and embarrassment of two such proceedings.

Moreover, we are not persuaded that the burdens petitioner envisions would pose a significant problem for the administration of the juvenile-court system. The large number of jurisdictions that presently require that the transfer decision be made prior to an adjudicatory hearing, and the absence of any indication that the juvenile courts in those jurisdictions have not been able to perform their task within that framework, suggest the contrary. The likelihood that in many cases the lack of need or basis for a transfer hearing can be recognized promptly reduces the number of cases in which a commitment of resources is necessary. In addition, we have no reason to believe that the resources available to those who recommend transfer or participate in the process leading to transfer decisions are inadequate to enable them to gather the information relevant to informed decision prior to an adjudicatory hearing.

To the extent that transfer hearings held prior to adjudication result in some duplication of evidence if transfer is rejected, the burden on juvenile courts will tend to be offset somewhat by the cases in which, because of transfer, no further proceedings in juvenile court are required. Moreover, when transfer has previously been rejected, juveniles may well be more likely to admit the commission of the offense charged, thereby obviating the need for adjudicatory hearings, than if transfer remains a possibility. Finally, we note that those States which presently require a different judge to preside at an adjudicatory hearing if transfer is rejected also permit waiver of that requirement. Where the requirement is not waived, it is difficult to see a substantial strain on judicial resources....

...[W]e are persuaded that transfer hearings prior to adjudication will aid the objectives of that system. What concerns us here is the dilemma that the possibility of transfer after an adjudicatory hearing presents for a juvenile, a dilemma to which the Court of Appeals alluded. Because of that possibility, a juvenile, thought to be the beneficiary of special consideration, may in fact suffer substantial disadvantages. If he appears uncooperative, he runs the risk of an adverse adjudication, as well as of an unfavorable dispositional recommendation. If, on the other hand, he is cooperative, he runs the risk of prejudicing his chances in adult court if transfer is ordered. We regard a procedure that results in such a dilemma as at odds with the goal that, to the extent fundamental fairness permits, adjudicatory hearings be informal and nonadversary. See *In re Gault*, 387 U.S., at 25–27; *In re Winship*, 397 U.S., at 366–367; *McKeiver v. Pennsylvania*, 403 U.S., at 534. Knowledge of the risk of transfer after an adjudicatory hearing can only undermine the potential for informality and cooperation which was intended to be the hallmark of the juvenile-court system. Rather than concerning themselves with the matter at hand, establishing innocence or seeking a disposition best suited to individual correctional needs, the juvenile and his attorney are pressed into a posture of adversary wariness that is conducive to neither....

IV

We hold that the prosecution of respondent in Superior Court, after an adjudicatory proceeding in Juvenile Court, violated the Double Jeopardy Clause of the Fifth Amendment, as applied to the States through the Fourteenth Amendment. The mandate of the Court of Appeals, which was stayed by that court pending our decision, directs the District Court "to issue a writ of habeas corpus directing the state court, within 60 days, to vacate the adult conviction of Jones and either set him free or remand him to the juvenile court for disposition." Since respondent is no longer subject to the jurisdiction of the California Juvenile Court, we vacate the judgment and remand the case to the Court of Appeals for such further proceedings consistent with this opinion as may be appropriate in the circumstances.

SWISHER V. BRADY
Supreme Court of the United States
438 U.S. 204 (1978)

MR. CHIEF JUSTICE BURGER delivered the opinion of the Court.

This is an appeal from a three-judge District Court for the District of Maryland. Nine minors, appellees here, brought an action under 42 U.S.C. § 1983, seeking a declaratory judgment and injunctive relief to prevent the State from filing exceptions with the Juvenile Court to proposed findings and recommendations made by masters of that court. The minors' claim was based on an alleged violation of the Double Jeopardy Clause of the Fifth Amendment, as applied to the States through the Fourteenth Amendment. The District Court's jurisdiction was invoked under 28 U.S.C. §§ 1343, 2281, and 2284 (as then written); this Court's jurisdiction, under 28 U.S.C. § 1253....

Prior to July 1975, the use of masters in Maryland juvenile proceedings was governed by Rule 908(e), Maryland Rules of Procedure. It provided that a master "shall hear such cases as may be assigned to him by the court." The Rule further directed that, at the conclusion of the hearing, the master transmit the case file and his "findings and recommendations" to the Juvenile Court. If no party filed exceptions to these findings and recommendations, they were to be "promptly...confirmed, modified or remanded by the judge." If, however, a party filed exceptions—and in delinquency hearings, only the State had the authority to do so—then, after notice, the Juvenile Court judge would "hear the entire matter or such specific matters as set forth in the exceptions *de novo*."

In the city of Baltimore, after the State filed a petition alleging that a minor had committed a delinquent act, the clerk of the Juvenile Court generally would assign the case to one of seven masters. In the ensuing unrecorded hearing, the State would call its witnesses and present its evidence in accordance with the rules of evidence applicable in criminal cases. The minor could offer evidence in defense. At the conclusion of the presentation of evidence, the master usually would announce his findings and contemplated recommendations. In a minority of those cases where the recommendations favored the minor's position, the State would file exceptions, whereupon the Juvenile Court judge would try the case *de novo*.

In 1972, a Baltimore City Master concluded, after a hearing, that the State had failed to show beyond a reasonable doubt that a minor, William Anderson, had assaulted and robbed a woman. His recommendation to the Juvenile Court judge reflected that conclusion. The State filed exceptions. Anderson responded with a motion to dismiss the notice of exceptions, contending that Rule 908(e), with its provision for a de novo hearing, violated the Double Jeopardy Clause. The Juvenile Court judge ruled that juvenile proceedings as such were not outside the scope of the Double Jeopardy Clause. He then held that the proceeding before him on the State's exceptions would violate Anderson's right not to be twice put in jeopardy and, on that basis, granted the motion to dismiss. The judge granted the same relief to similarly situated minors, including several who later initiated the present litigation.

The State appealed and the Court of Special Appeals reversed. *In re Anderson*, 20 Md.App. 31, 315 A.2d 540 (1974). That court assumed, for purposes of its decision, that jeopardy attached at the commencement of the initial hearing before the master. It held, however:

> "[T]here is *no adjudication* by reason of the master's findings and recommendations. The proceedings before the master and his findings and recommendations are simply the first phase of the hearing which continues with the consideration by the juvenile judge. Whether the juvenile judge, in the absence of exceptions, accepts the master's findings or recommendations, modifies them or remands them, or whether, when exceptions are filed, he hears the matter himself de novo, there is merely a continuance of the hearing and the initial jeopardy. In other words, *the hearing*, and the jeopardy thereto attaching, terminate only upon a valid adjudication *by the juvenile judge*, not upon the findings and recommendations of the master."...

On appeal by the minors, the Court of Appeals affirmed, although on a rationale different from that of the intermediate appellate court. *In re Anderson*, 272 Md. 85, 321 A.2d 516 (1974). It held that "a hearing before a master is not such a hearing as places a juvenile in jeopardy." Central to this holding was the court's conclusion that masters in Maryland serve only as ministerial assistants to judges; although authorized to hear evidence, report findings, and make recommendations to the judge, masters are entrusted with none of the judicial power of the State, including the *sine qua non* of judicial office—the power to enter a binding judgment.

In November 1974, five months after the Court of Appeals' decision, nine juveniles sought federal habeas corpus relief, contending that by taking exceptions to masters' recommendations favorable to them the State was violating their rights under the Double Jeopardy Clause. These same nine minors also initiated a class action under 42 U.S.C. § 1983 in which they sought a declaratory judgment and injunctive relief against the future operation of Rule 908(e). The sole constitutional basis for their complaint was, again, the Double Jeopardy Clause. A three-judge court was convened to hear this matter, and it is the judgment of that court we now review.

Before either the three-judge District Court or the single judge reviewing the habeas corpus petitions could act, the Maryland Legislature enacted legislation which, for the first time, provided a statutory basis for the use of masters in juvenile court proceedings. In doing so, it modified slightly the scheme previously operative under Rule 908(e). The new legislation required that hearings before a master be recorded and that, at their conclusion, the master submit to the Juvenile Court judge written findings of fact, conclusions of law, and recommendations. Either party was authorized to file exceptions and could elect a hearing on the record or a *de novo* hearing before the judge. The legislature specified that the master's "proposals and recommendations...for juvenile causes do not constitute orders or final action of the court." Accordingly, the judge could, even in the absence of exceptions, reject a master's recommendations and conduct a *de novo* hearing or, if the parties agreed, a hearing on the record.

In June 1975, within two months of the enactment of § 3-813 and before its July 1, 1975, effective date, the single-judge United States District Court held that the Rule 908(e) provision for a *de novo* hearing on the State's exceptions violated the Double Jeopardy Clause. In that court's view, a juvenile was placed in jeopardy as soon as the State offered evidence in the hearing before a master. The court also concluded that to subject a juvenile to a *de novo* hearing before the Juvenile Court judge was to place him in jeopardy a second time. Accordingly, it granted habeas corpus relief to the six petitioners already subjected by the State to a *de novo* hearing. The petitions of the remaining three, who had not yet been brought before the Juvenile Court judge, were dismissed without prejudice as being premature.

In response to both the enactment of § 3-813 and the decision in [the United States District Court], the Maryland Court of Appeals, in the exercise of its rulemaking power, promulgated a new rule, and the one currently in force, Rule 911, to govern the use of masters in juvenile proceedings. Rule 911 differs from the statute in significant aspects. First, in order to emphasize the nonfinal nature of a master's conclusions, it stresses that all of his "findings, conclusions, recommendations or . . . orders" are only proposed. Second, the State no longer has power to secure a *de novo* hearing before the Juvenile Court judge after unfavorable proposals by the master. The State still may file exceptions, but the judge can act on them only on the basis of the record made before the master and "such additional [relevant] evidence . . . to which the parties raise no objection." The judge retains his power to accept, reject, or modify the master's proposals, to remand to the master for further hearings, and to supplement the record for his own review with additional evidence to which the parties do not object.

Thus, Rule 911 is a direct product of the desire of the State to continue using masters to meet the heavy burden of juvenile court caseloads while at the same time assuring that their use not violate the constitutional guarantee against double jeopardy. To this end, the Rule permits the presentation and recording of evidence in the absence of the only officer authorized by the state constitution, and by statute, to serve as factfinder and judge.

After the effective date of Rule 911, July 1, 1975, the plaintiffs in the § 1983 action amended their complaint to bring Rule 911 within its scope. They continued to challenge the state procedure, however, only on the basis of the Double Jeopardy Clause. Other juveniles intervened as the ongoing work of the juvenile court brought them within the definition of the proposed class. Their complaints in intervention likewise rested only on the Double Jeopardy Clause.

The three-judge District Court certified the proposed class under Fed.Rule Civ.Proc. 23(b)(2) to consist of all juveniles involved in proceedings where the State had filed exceptions to a master's proposed findings of nondelinquency. That court then held that a juvenile subjected to a hearing before a master is placed in jeopardy, even though the master has no power to enter a final order. It also held that the Juvenile Court judge's review of the record constitutes a "second proceeding at which [the juvenile] must once again marshal whatever resources he can against the State's and at which the State is given a second opportunity to obtain a conviction." Accordingly, the three-judge District Court enjoined the defendant state officials from taking exceptions to either a master's proposed finding of nondelinquency or his proposed disposition. . . .

> "A State may not put a defendant in jeopardy twice for the same offense. *Benton v. Maryland*, 395 U.S. 784. The constitutional protection against double jeopardy unequivocally prohibits a second trial following an acquittal. The public interest in the finality of criminal judgments is so strong that an acquitted defendant may not be retried even though 'the acquittal was based upon an egregiously erroneous foundation.' . . . If the innocence of the accused has been

> confirmed by a final judgment, the Constitution conclusively presumes that a second trial would be unfair.
>
> "Because jeopardy attaches before the judgment becomes final, the constitutional protection also embraces the defendant's 'valued right to have his trial completed by a particular tribunal.'...Consequently, as a general rule, the prosecutor is entitled to one, and only one, opportunity to require an accused to stand trial."

In the application of these general principles, the narrow question here is whether the State in filing exceptions to a master's proposals, pursuant to Rule 911, thereby "require[s] an accused to stand trial" a second time. We hold that it does not. Maryland has created a system with Rule 911 in which an accused juvenile is subjected to a single proceeding which begins with a master's hearing and culminates with an adjudication by a judge.

Importantly, a Rule 911 proceeding does not impinge on the purposes of the Double Jeopardy Clause. A central purpose "of the prohibition against successive trials" is to bar "the prosecution [from] another opportunity to supply evidence which it failed to muster in the first proceeding." A Rule 911 proceeding does not provide the prosecution that forbidden "second crack." The State presents its evidence once before the master. The record is then closed, and additional evidence can be received by the Juvenile Court judge only with the consent of the minor.

The Double Jeopardy Clause also precludes the prosecutor from "enhanc[ing] the risk that an innocent defendant may be convicted," by taking the question of guilt to a series of persons or groups empowered to make binding determinations. Appellees contend that in its operation Rule 911 gives the State the chance to persuade two such factfinders: first the master, then the Juvenile Court judge. In support of this contention they point to evidence that juveniles and their parents sometimes consider the master "the judge" and his recommendations "the verdict." Within the limits of jury trial rights, see, *McKeiver v. Pennsylvania*, 403 U.S. 528 (1971), and other constitutional constraints, it is for the State, not the parties, to designate and empower the factfinder and adjudicator. And here Maryland has conferred those roles only on the Juvenile Court judge....

Finally, there is nothing in the record to indicate that the procedure authorized under Rule 911 unfairly subjects the defendant to the embarrassment, expense, and ordeal of a second trial....Indeed, there is nothing to indicate that the juvenile is even brought before the judge while he conducts the "hearing on the record," or that the juvenile's attorney appears at the "hearing" and presents oral argument or written briefs. But even if there were such participation or appearance, the burdens are more akin to those resulting from a judge's permissible request for post-trial briefing or argument following a bench trial than to the "expense" of a full-blown second trial....

In their effort to characterize a Rule 911 proceeding as two trials for double jeopardy purposes, appellees rely on two decisions of this Court, *Breed v. Jones*, 421 U.S. 519 (1975), and *United States v. Jenkins*, 420 U.S. 358 (1975).

In *Breed*, we held that a juvenile was placed twice in jeopardy when, after an adjudicatory hearing in Juvenile Court on a charge of delinquent conduct, he was transferred to adult criminal court, tried, and convicted for the same conduct. All parties conceded that jeopardy attached at the second proceeding in criminal court. The State contended, however, that jeopardy did not attach in the Juvenile Court proceeding, although that proceeding could have culminated in a deprivation of the juvenile's liberty. We rejected this contention and also the contention that somehow jeopardy "continued" from the first to the second trial. *Breed* is therefore inapplicable to the Maryland scheme, where juveniles are subjected to only one proceeding, or "trial."

Appellees also stress this language from *Jenkins*:

> "[I]t is enough for purposes of the Double Jeopardy Clause... that further proceedings of some sort, devoted to the resolution of factual issues, going to the elements of the offense charged, would have been required upon reversal and remand. *Even if the District Court were to receive no additional evidence, it would still be necessary for it to make supplemental findings....* [To do so] would violate the Double Jeopardy Clause." 420 U.S., at 370 (emphasis added).

Although we doubt that the Court's decision in a case can be correctly identified by reference to three isolated sentences, any language in *Jenkins* must now be read in light of our subsequent decision in *United States v. Scott*, 437 U.S. 82 (1978). In *Scott* we held that it is not all proceedings requiring the making of supplemental findings that are barred by the Double Jeopardy Clause, but only those that follow a previous trial ending in an acquittal; in a conviction either not reversed on appeal or reversed because of insufficient evidence, see *Burks v. United States, supra*, or in a mistrial ruling not prompted by "manifest necessity," see *Arizona v. Washington*, 434 U.S. 497 (1978). A Juvenile Court judge's decision terminating a Rule 911 proceeding follows none of those occurrences. Furthermore, *Jenkins* involved appellate review of the final judgment of a trial court fully empowered to enter that judgment. Nothing comparable occurs in a Rule 911 proceeding.

To the extent the Juvenile Court judge makes supplemental findings in a manner permitted by Rule 911—either *sua sponte*, in response to the State's exceptions, or in response to the juvenile's exceptions, and either on the record or on a record supplemented by evidence to which the parties raise no objection—he does so without violating the constraints of the Double Jeopardy Clause.

Accordingly, we reverse and remand for further proceedings consistent with this opinion....

MR. JUSTICE MARSHALL, with whom MR. JUSTICE BRENNAN and MR. JUSTICE POWELL join, dissenting.

... [T]he Court reaches a result that it would not countenance were this a criminal prosecution against an adult, for the juvenile defendants here are placed twice in jeopardy just as surely as if an adult defendant, after acquittal in a trial court, were convicted on appeal.... Maryland's scheme raises serious due process questions because the judge making the final adjudication of guilt has not heard the evidence and may reverse the master's findings of nondelinquency based on the judge's review of a cold record. For these reasons, I dissent.

...I agree with the Court that jeopardy does attach at the master's hearing.... In *Breed v. Jones, supra,* we held that jeopardy attaches "at a proceeding whose object is to determine whether [a juvenile] has committed acts that violate a criminal law." 421 U.S., at 529. The master's hearing clearly has this as an object. Under Maryland law, the master is empowered to conduct a full "adjudicatory hearing," in order "to determine whether the allegations in the petition... are true." And it is at this hearing that the State introduces the evidence on which it seeks to have the determination of guilt or innocence rest.

My disagreement with the Court lies in its misapplication of well-settled double jeopardy rules applicable once jeopardy has attached. As the Court itself recognizes...the

Double Jeopardy Clause "unequivocally prohibits a second trial following an acquittal." Just as unequivocally, it prevents the prosecution from seeking review or reversal of a judgment of acquittal on appeal. And even where the first trial does not end in a final judgment, the "defendant's valued right to have his trial completed by a particular tribunal," absent a "'manifest necessity'" for terminating the first proceedings, is protected by this Clause.

These rules are designed to serve the underlying purposes of the Double Jeopardy Clause, the most fundamental of which is to protect an accused from the governmental harassment and oppression that can so easily arise from the massed power of the State in confrontation with an individual. As the Court recognizes, the Double Jeopardy Clause serves to preclude the State from having "'another opportunity to supply evidence which it failed to muster in the first proceeding'"; to avoid the risk that a defendant, though in fact innocent, may be convicted by a successive decisionmaker; and to prevent the State from unfairly subjecting a defendant "to the embarrassment, expense, and ordeal of a second trial."

... [T]he Court reaches its result primarily by ignoring the undisputed fact that state law commits to the master a factfinding function. Admittedly, the Maryland proceedings are somewhat difficult to classify into the customary pigeonholes of double jeopardy analysis, but that is precisely because the State has engaged in a novel redefinition of trial and appellate functions in a quasi-criminal proceeding, intentionally designed to avoid the constraints of the Double Jeopardy Clause.... [O]ur Constitution is not so fragile an instrument that its substantive prohibitions may be evaded by formal designations that fail to correspond with the actual functions performed.

Viewing the master and judge in terms of their relative functions, I think the appropriate analogy is between a trial judge and an appellate court with unusually broad powers of review. In the cases before us, the masters had made unequivocal findings, on the facts, that the State had not proved its case, and the State sought to have the judge overturn these findings. By ignoring these functional considerations, the Court permits the State to circumvent the protections of the Double Jeopardy Clause by a mere change in the formal definitions of finality....

... It is inaccurate, however, to say that only the judge is "authorized" under Maryland law to act as a factfinder. The master does not simply act as a referee at the hearing, deciding evidentiary questions and creating a record placed before the judge. Rather, Rule 911 directs that, at the end of the disposition hearing (which follows the adjudicatory hearing), the master "transmit to the judge the entire file in the case, together with a written report of his proposed findings of fact, conclusions of law, recommendations and proposed orders with respect to adjudication and disposition." Rule 911(b).

That Maryland contemplates an actual factfinding function for the master is emphasized by the fact that neither the Rule nor the statute requires the "judge" to read the entire record, listen to the tape recording of the adjudicatory hearing, or otherwise expose himself to the full factual record as it was presented to the master....

Even if the master's findings are not regarded as an acquittal, the Double Jeopardy Clause does more than simply protect acquittals from review on direct appeal. It also protects the defendant's right to go to judgment before a "particular tribunal" once jeopardy has attached, absent a "'manifest necessity'" justifying termination of the first proceeding. This rule is designed in part to ensure that the government not be able to bolster its case by additional evidence or arguments, once it believes that its evidence has not persuaded the first tribunal. But the Maryland system is structured so as to give the State precisely this type of proscribed opportunity, where it disagrees with the favorable rulings of the first trier of fact.

As recognized by the Court, jeopardy attaches at the master's hearing. This hearing is a formal, adjudicatory proceeding at which the State's witnesses testify and are cross-examined; the juvenile may present evidence in his own defense; and the juvenile is entitled to counsel and to remain silent. Presentation of evidence at that proceeding is keyed to the reactions and attitudes of the presiding master, who acts, for purposes of the adjudicatory hearing, as the "particular tribunal." A juvenile who has had such a hearing may justifiably expect that, when the master who has heard all this evidence announces a finding in his favor, it will be final. But a juvenile tried before a master in Maryland is never, as a matter of law, entitled to have his trial "completed" before the master, since his recommendations must be confirmed by the judge and may be ignored by him.

Thus, endemic to the Maryland system is a kind of interrupted proceeding which ensures that the defendant cannot get the benefit of the first trier of fact's reaction to the evidence. The system thereby poses a substantial risk that innocent defendants may be found guilty, since it allows the State a second opportunity to persuade a decisionmaker of the juvenile's guilt, after the first trier of fact has concluded that the State has not proved its case....

...It is argued by *amicus*, however, that the Maryland system, even if it were found to avoid double jeopardy problems, violates the Due Process Clause by permitting ultimate factfinding by a judge who did not actually conduct the trial. The Court does not reach this issue, apparently believing that it is not properly presented here. It is thus important to emphasize that the Maryland system and ones like it have not been held constitutional today; the Court's only holding is that such systems are not unconstitutional under the Double Jeopardy Clause. It is entirely open to this Court, and lower courts, to find in another case that a system like that in Maryland violates the Due Process Clause....

Over 30 years ago...we recognized the importance to a reliable factfinding process of hearing live witnesses. The issue there was whether, on a federal habeas corpus petition, a District Judge could utilize a United States Commissioner to hold the evidentiary hearing and make recommended findings of fact and conclusions of law. Although our holding that the prisoner had a right to testify and present his evidence before a judge was a statutory one, our reasoning went to the fundamental nature of the kind of factfinding on which many judicial determinations must rest:

> "One of the essential elements of the determination of the crucial facts is the weighing and appraising of the testimony....We cannot say that an appraisal of the truth of the prisoner's oral testimony by a master or commissioner is, in the light of the purpose and object of the proceeding, the equivalent of the judge's own exercise of the function of the trier of the facts." *Id.*, at 352, 61 S.Ct., at 1018....

...[T]he master's function at the hearing is, in large part, to assess the credibility of the witnesses. That function simply cannot be replicated by the "judge," acting in his essentially appellate capacity reviewing the record; as *amicus* cogently notes, "[t]rials-by-transcript can never be more than trials by substantial evidence." It would thus appear that the Maryland system of splitting the hearing of evidence from the final adjudication violates the Due Process Clause.

It is no answer to this problem that the juvenile defendant may elect to submit additional material to the judge when the State takes an exception to the master's finding. In the first place, the State apparently must agree to the supplementation of the record, and can thus stymie a defendant's efforts to persuade the judge that he is not guilty. See Rule 911(c). But more importantly, when a juvenile seeks to reopen the proceeding before the judge—in order to avoid having a case decided against him on the basis of a cold record in violation of the Due Process Clause—he is being subjected to a second trial of the sort clearly prohibited by the Double Jeopardy Clause....

That the current Maryland scheme cannot pass constitutional muster does not necessarily mean that the idea of using masters, or some other class of specially trained or selected personnel for juvenile court adjudications, is either unconstitutional or unwise. Using masters to adjudicate the more common charges may save scarce judicial resources for the more difficult cases. It may also aid the ultimate goals of a juvenile justice system by ensuring that the decisionmakers have some familiarity with the special problems of juvenile dispositions. But the State must find a way of implementing this concept without jeopardizing the constitutional rights of juveniles. Whether it does so by endowing masters with the power to make final adjudications or by some other means, matters not. What does matter is that, absent compelling circumstances not present here, the system of juvenile justice in this country must not be permitted to fall below the minimum constitutional standards set for adult criminal proceedings.

Accordingly, I dissent.

QUESTIONS

1. In *Breed*, how does the procedure violate the Double Jeopardy Clause? Why is there no constitutional violation in *Swisher*? Do you think the two cases may be reconciled? How?

2. If a delinquency case is not a criminal proceeding, then why is double jeopardy violated in *Breed*? What if the state is unable to prove that a juvenile committed a delinquent act? Could the state then file a petition alleging that the juvenile is a status offender based on exactly the same conduct without running afoul of double jeopardy? Why?

SCHALL V. MARTIN
United States Supreme Court
467 U.S. 253 (1984)

Justice Rehnquist delivered the opinion of the Court.

Section 320.5(3)(b) of the New York Family Court Act authorizes pretrial detention of an accused juvenile delinquent based on a finding that there is a "serious risk" that the child "may before the return date commit an act which if committed by an adult would constitute a crime." Appellees brought suit on behalf of a class of all juveniles detained pursuant to that provision. The District Court struck down § 320.5(3)(b) as permitting detention without due process of law and ordered the immediate release of all class members. *United States ex rel. Martin v. Strasburg*, 513 F.Supp. 691 (SDNY 1981). The Court of Appeals for the Second Circuit affirmed, holding the provision "unconstitutional as to all juveniles" because the statute is administered in such a way that "the detention period serves as punishment imposed without proof of guilt established according to the requisite constitutional standard." *Martin v. Strasburg*, 689 F.2d 365, 373-374 (1982). We noted probable jurisdiction, and now reverse. We conclude that preventive detention under the FCA serves a legitimate state objective, and that the procedural protections afforded pretrial detainees by the New York statute satisfy the requirements of the Due Process Clause of the Fourteenth Amendment to the United States Constitution.

I

Appellee Gregory Martin was arrested on December 13, 1977, and charged with first-degree robbery, second-degree assault, and criminal possession of a weapon based on an incident in which he, with two others, allegedly hit a youth on the head with a loaded gun and stole his jacket and sneakers. See petitioners' Exhibit 1b. Martin had possession of the gun when he was arrested. He was 14 years old at the time and, therefore, came within the jurisdiction of New York's Family Court. The incident occurred at 11:30 at night, and Martin lied to the police about where and with whom he lived. He was consequently detained overnight.

A petition of delinquency was filed, and Martin made his "initial appearance" in Family Court on December 14th, accompanied by his grandmother. The Family Court Judge, citing the possession of the loaded weapon, the false address given to the police, and the lateness of the hour, as evidencing a lack of supervision, ordered Martin detained under § 320.5(3)(b). A probable-cause hearing was held five days later, on December 19th, and probable cause was found to exist for all the crimes charged. At the fact finding hearing held December 27–29, Martin was found guilty on the robbery and criminal possession charges. He was adjudicated a delinquent and placed on two years' probation. He had been detained pursuant to § 320.5(3)(b), between the initial appearance and the completion of the fact finding hearing, for a total of 15 days.

Appellees Luis Rosario and Kenneth Morgan, both age 14, were also ordered detained pending their fact finding hearings. Rosario was charged with attempted first-degree robbery and second-degree assault for an incident in which he, with four others, allegedly tried to rob two men, putting a gun to the head of one of them and beating both about the head with sticks. At the time of his initial appearance, on March 15, 1978, Rosario had another delinquency petition pending for knifing a student, and two prior petitions had been adjusted. Probable cause was found on March 21. On April 11, Rosario was released to his father, and the case was terminated without adjustment on September 25, 1978.

Kenneth Morgan was charged with attempted robbery and attempted grand larceny for an incident in which he and another boy allegedly tried to steal money from a 14-year-old girl and her brother by threatening to blow their heads off and grabbing them to search their pockets.... Morgan, like Rosario, was on release status on another petition (for robbery and criminal possession of stolen property) at the time of his initial appearance on March 27, 1978. He had been arrested four previous times, and his mother refused to come to court because he had been in trouble so often she did not want him home. A probable-cause hearing was set for March 30, but was continued until April 4, when it was combined with a fact finding hearing. Morgan was found guilty of harassment and petit larceny and was ordered placed with the Department of Social Services for 18 months. He was detained a total of eight days between his initial appearance and the fact finding hearing.

On December 21, 1977, while still in preventive detention pending his fact finding hearing, Gregory Martin instituted a habeas corpus class action on behalf of "those persons who are, or during the pendency of this action will be, preventively detained pursuant to" § 320.5(3)(b) of the FCA. Rosario and Morgan were subsequently added as additional named plaintiffs. These three class representatives sought a declaratory judgment that § 320.5(3)(b) violates the Due Process and Equal Protection Clauses of the Fourteenth Amendment....

At trial, appellees offered in evidence the case histories of 34 members of the class, including the three named petitioners. Both parties presented some general statistics on the relation between pretrial detention and ultimate disposition. In addition, there was testimony concerning juvenile proceedings from a number of witnesses, including a legal aid attorney specializing in juvenile cases, a probation supervisor, a child psychologist, and a Family Court Judge. On the basis of this evidence, the District Court rejected the equal protection challenge as "insubstantial," but agreed with appellees that pretrial detention under the FCA violates due process. The court ordered that "all class members in custody pursuant to Family Court Act Section [320.5(3)(b)] shall be released forthwith."

The Court of Appeals affirmed. After reviewing the trial record, the court opined that "the vast majority of juveniles detained either have their petitions dismissed before an adjudication of delinquency or are released after adjudication." The court concluded from that fact that § 320.5(3)(b) "is utilized principally, not for preventive purposes, but to impose punishment for unadjudicated criminal acts."...

II

There is no doubt that the Due Process Clause is applicable in juvenile proceedings. "The problem," we have stressed, "is to ascertain the precise impact of the due process requirement upon such proceedings." *In re Gault*, 387 U.S. 1, 13–14 (1967). We have held that certain basic constitutional protections enjoyed by adults accused of crimes also apply to juveniles. But the Constitution does not mandate elimination of all differences in the treatment of juveniles. See, *e.g., McKeiver v. Pennsylvania*, 403 U.S. 528 (1971) (no right to jury trial). The State has "a *parens patriae* interest in preserving and promoting the welfare of the child," *Santosky v. Kramer*, 455 U.S. 745, 766 (1982), which makes a juvenile proceeding fundamentally different from an adult criminal trial. We have tried, therefore, to strike a balance—to respect the "informality" and "flexibility" that characterize juvenile proceedings, *In re Winship, supra*, at 366, and yet to ensure that such proceedings comport with the "fundamental fairness" demanded by the Due Process Clause. *Breed v. Jones, supra*, at 531; *McKeiver, supra*, at 543 (plurality opinion).

The statutory provision at issue in these cases, § 320.5(3)(b), permits a brief pretrial detention based on a finding of a "serious risk" that an arrested juvenile may commit a crime before his return date. The question before us is whether preventive detention of juveniles pursuant to § 320.5(3)(b) is compatible with the "fundamental fairness" required by due process. Two separate inquiries are necessary to answer this question. First, does preventive detention under the New York statute serve a legitimate state objective? And, second, are the procedural safeguards contained in the FCA adequate to authorize the pretrial detention of at least some juveniles charged with crimes?

A

Preventive detention under the FCA is purportedly designed to protect the child and society from the potential consequences of his criminal acts. When making any detention decision, the Family Court judge is specifically directed to consider the needs and best interests of the juvenile as well as the need for the protection of the community. As an initial matter, therefore, we must decide whether, in the context of the juvenile system, the combined interest in protecting both the community and the juvenile himself from the consequences of future criminal conduct is sufficient to justify such detention.

The "legitimate and compelling state interest" in protecting the community from crime cannot be doubted. We have stressed before that crime prevention is "a weighty social objective," and this interest persists undiluted in the juvenile context. See *In re Gault*, *supra*, at 20 n.26. The harm suffered by the victim of a crime is not dependent upon the age of the perpetrator. And the harm to society generally may even be greater in this context given the high rate of recidivism among juveniles. *In re Gault*, *supra*, at 22.

The juvenile's countervailing interest in freedom from institutional restraints, even for the brief time involved here, is undoubtedly substantial as well. But that interest must be qualified by the recognition that juveniles, unlike adults, are always in some form of custody. *Lehman v. Lycoming County Children's Services*, 458 U.S. 502, 510–511 (1982); *In re Gault*, *supra*, at 17. Children, by definition, are not assumed to have the capacity to take care of themselves. They are assumed to be subject to the control of their parents, and if parental control falters, the State must play its part as *parens patriae*. In this respect, the juvenile's liberty interest may, in appropriate circumstances, be subordinated to the State's "*parens patriae* interest in preserving and promoting the welfare of the child." *Santosky v. Kramer*, *supra*, at 766.

The New York Court of Appeals, in upholding the statute at issue here, stressed at some length "the desirability of protecting the juvenile from his own folly." Society has a legitimate interest in protecting a juvenile from the consequences of his criminal activity—both from potential physical injury which may be suffered when a victim fights back or a policeman attempts to make an arrest and from the downward spiral of criminal activity into which peer pressure may lead the child....

The substantiality and legitimacy of the state interests underlying this statute are confirmed by the widespread use and judicial acceptance of preventive detention for juveniles. Every State, as well as the United States in the District of Columbia, permits preventive detention of juveniles accused of crime. A number of model juvenile justice Acts also contain provisions permitting preventive detention. And the courts of eight States, including the New York Court of Appeals, have upheld their statutes with specific reference to protecting the juvenile and the community from harmful pretrial conduct, including pretrial crime.

"The fact that a practice is followed by a large number of states is not conclusive in a decision as to whether that practice accords with due process, but it is plainly worth considering in determining whether the practice 'offends some principle of justice so rooted in the traditions and conscience of our people as to be ranked as fundamental.'" In light of the uniform legislative judgment that pretrial detention of juveniles properly promotes the interests both of society and the juvenile, we conclude that the practice serves a legitimate regulatory purpose compatible with the "fundamental fairness" demanded by the Due Process Clause in juvenile proceedings. *Cf. McKeiver v. Pennsylvania*, 403 U.S., at 548 (plurality opinion).

Of course, the mere invocation of a legitimate purpose will not justify particular restrictions and conditions of confinement amounting to punishment. It is axiomatic that "[d]ue process requires that a pretrial detainee not be punished." *Bell v. Wolfish*, 441 U.S., at 535, n. 16. Even given, therefore, that pretrial detention may serve legitimate regulatory purposes, it is still necessary to determine whether the terms and conditions of confinement under § 320.5(3)(b) are in fact compatible with those purposes. "A court must decide whether the disability is imposed for the purpose of punishment or whether it is but an incident of some other legitimate governmental purpose." *Bell v. Wolfish*, *supra*, 441 U.S., at 538. Absent a showing of an express intent to punish on the part of the State, that determination generally will turn on "whether an alternative purpose to which [the restriction] may rationally be connected is assignable for it, and whether it appears excessive in relation to the alternative purpose assigned [to it]."

There is no indication in the statute itself that preventive detention is used or intended as a punishment. First of all, the detention is strictly limited in time. If a juvenile is detained at his initial appearance and has denied the charges against him, he is entitled to a probable-cause hearing to be held not more than three days after the conclusion of the initial appearance or four days after the filing of the petition, whichever is sooner.... If the Family Court judge finds probable cause, he must also determine whether continued detention is necessary....

Detained juveniles are also entitled to an expedited fact finding hearing. If the juvenile is charged with one of a limited number of designated felonies, the fact finding hearing must be scheduled to commence not more than 14 days after the conclusion of the initial appearance. If the juvenile is charged with a lesser offense, then the fact finding hearing must be held not more than three days after the initial appearance. In the latter case, since the times for the probable-cause hearing and the fact finding hearing coincide, the two hearings are merged.

Thus, the maximum possible detention [under the statute] of a youth accused of a serious crime, assuming a 3-day extension of the fact finding hearing for good cause shown, is 17 days. The maximum detention for less serious crimes, again assuming a 3-day extension for good cause shown, is six days. These time frames seem suited to the limited purpose of providing the youth with a controlled environment and separating him from improper influences pending the speedy disposition of his case....

...When a juvenile is remanded after his initial appearance, he cannot, absent exceptional circumstances, be sent to a prison or lockup where he would be exposed to adult criminals. Instead, the child is screened by an "assessment unit" of the Department of Juvenile Justice. The assessment unit places the child in either nonsecure or secure detention. Nonsecure detention involves an open facility in the community, a sort of "halfway house," without locks, bars, or security officers where the child receives schooling and counseling and has access to recreational facilities.

Secure detention is more restrictive, but it is still consistent with the regulatory and *parens patriae* objectives relied upon by the State. Children are assigned to separate dorms based on age, size, and behavior. They wear street clothes provided by the institution and partake in educational and recreational programs and counseling sessions run by trained social workers. Misbehavior is punished by confinement to one's room. We cannot conclude from this record that the controlled environment briefly imposed by the State on juveniles in secure pretrial detention "is imposed for the purpose of punishment" rather than as "an incident of some other legitimate governmental purpose." *Bell v. Wolfish*, 441 U.S., at 538.

The Court of Appeals, of course, did conclude that the underlying purpose of § 320.5(3)(b) is punitive rather than regulatory. But the court did not dispute that preventive detention might serve legitimate regulatory purposes or that the terms and conditions of pretrial confinement in New York are compatible with those purposes. Rather, the court invalidated a significant aspect of New York's juvenile justice system based solely on some case histories and a statistical study which appeared to show that "the vast majority of juveniles detained under [§ 320.5(3)(b)] either have their petitions dismissed before an adjudication of delinquency or are released after adjudication."...

...But even assuming it to be the case that "by far the greater number of juveniles incarcerated under [§ 320.5(3)(b)] will never be confined as a consequence of a disposition imposed after an adjudication of delinquency," we find that to be an insufficient ground for upsetting the widely shared legislative judgment that preventive detention serves an important and legitimate function in the juvenile justice system....

Pretrial detention need not be considered punitive merely because a juvenile is subsequently discharged subject to conditions or put on probation. In fact, such actions reinforce the original finding that close supervision of the juvenile is required. Lenient but supervised disposition is in keeping with the Act's purpose to promote the welfare and development of the child....

Even when a case is terminated prior to fact finding, it does not follow that the decision to detain the juvenile amounted to a due process violation. A delinquency petition may be dismissed for any number of reasons collateral to its merits, such as the failure of a witness to testify. The Family Court judge cannot be expected to anticipate such developments at the initial hearing. He makes his decision based on the information available to him at that time, and the propriety of the decision must be judged in that light....

It may be, of course, that in some circumstances detention of a juvenile would not pass constitutional muster. But the validity of those detentions must be determined on a case-by-case basis. Section 320.5(3)(b) is not invalid "on its face" by reason of the ambiguous statistics and case histories relied upon by the court below....Preventive detention under the FCA serves the legitimate state objective, held in common with every State in the country, of protecting both the juvenile and society from the hazards of pretrial crime.

B

Given the legitimacy of the State's interest in preventive detention, and the nonpunitive nature of that detention, the remaining question is whether the procedures afforded juveniles detained prior to fact-finding provide sufficient protection against erroneous and unnecessary deprivations of liberty. See *Mathews v. Eldridge*, 424 U.S., at 335. In *Gerstein v. Pugh*, 420 U.S., at 114, we held that a judicial determination of probable cause is a prerequisite to any extended restraint on the liberty of an adult accused of crime. We did not, however, mandate a specific time-table. Nor did we require the "full panoply of adversary safeguards—counsel, confrontation, cross-examination, and compulsory process for witnesses." *Id.*, at 119. Instead, we recognized "the desirability of flexibility and experimentation by the States." *Id.*, at 123. *Gerstein* arose under the Fourth Amendment, but the same concern with "flexibility" and "informality," while yet ensuring adequate predetention procedures, is present in this context. *In re Winship*, 397 U.S., at 366; *Kent v. United States*, 383 U.S. 541, 554 (1966).

In many respects, the FCA provides far more predetention protection for juveniles than we found to be constitutionally required for a probable-cause determination for adults in *Gerstein*. The initial appearance is informal, but the accused juvenile is given full notice of the charges against him and a complete stenographic record is kept of the hearing. The juvenile appears accompanied by his parent or guardian. He is first informed of his rights, including the right to remain silent and the right to be represented by counsel chosen by him or by a law guardian assigned by the court. The initial appearance may be adjourned for no longer than 72 hours or until the next court day, whichever is sooner, to enable an appointed law guardian or other counsel to appear before the court. When his counsel is present, the juvenile is informed of the charges against him and furnished with a copy of the delinquency petition. A representative from the presentment agency appears in support of the petition.

The nonhearsay allegations in the delinquency petition and supporting depositions must establish probable cause to believe the juvenile committed the offense. Although the Family Court judge is not required to make a finding of probable cause at the initial appearance, the youth may challenge the sufficiency of the petition on that ground.... Thus, the juvenile may oppose any recommended detention by arguing that there is not probable cause to believe he committed the offense or offenses with which he is charged. If the petition is not dismissed, the juvenile is given an opportunity to admit or deny the charges.

At the conclusion of the initial appearance, the presentment agency makes a recommendation regarding detention. A probation officer reports on the juvenile's record, including other prior and current Family Court and probation contacts, as well as relevant information concerning home life, school attendance, and any special medical or developmental problems. He concludes by offering his agency's recommendation on detention. Opposing counsel, the juvenile's parents, and the juvenile himself may all speak on his behalf and challenge any information or recommendation. If the judge does decide to detain the juvenile under § 320.5(3)(b), he must state on the record the facts and reasons for the detention.[27]

As noted, a detained juvenile is entitled to a formal, adversarial probable-cause hearing within three days of his initial appearance, with one 3-day extension possible for good cause shown. The burden at this hearing is on the presentment agency to call witnesses and offer evidence in support of the charges. Testimony is under oath and subject to cross-examination. The accused juvenile may call witnesses and offer evidence in his own behalf. If the court finds probable cause, the court must again decide whether continued detention is necessary. Again, the facts and reasons for the detention must be stated on the record.

27. Given that under *Gerstein*, 420 U.S., at 119–123, a probable-cause hearing may be informal and nonadversarial, a Family Court judge could make a finding of probable cause at the initial appearance. That he is not required to do so does not, under the circumstances, amount to a deprivation of due process. Appellees fail to point to a single example where probable cause was not found after a decision was made to detain the child.

In sum, notice, a hearing, and a statement of facts and reasons are given prior to any detention. A formal probable-cause hearing is then held within a short while thereafter, if the fact finding hearing is not itself scheduled within three days. These flexible procedures have been found constitutionally adequate under the Fourth Amendment, see *Gerstein v. Pugh*, and under the Due Process Clause, see *Kent v. United States*, *supra*, at 557. Appellees have failed to note any additional procedures that would significantly improve the accuracy of the determination without unduly impinging on the achievement of legitimate state purposes.

Appellees argue, however, that the risk of erroneous and unnecessary detentions is too high despite these procedures because the standard for detention is fatally vague. Detention under § 320.5(3)(b) is based on a finding that there is a "serious risk" that the juvenile, if released, would commit a crime prior to his next court appearance.... But appellees claim, and the District Court agreed, that it is virtually impossible to predict future criminal conduct with any degree of accuracy. Moreover, they say, the statutory standard fails to channel the discretion of the Family Court judge by specifying the factors on which he should rely in making that prediction....

Our cases indicate, however, that from a legal point of view there is nothing inherently unattainable about a prediction of future criminal conduct. Such a judgment forms an important element in many decisions, and we have specifically rejected the contention, based on the same sort of sociological data relied upon by appellees and the District Court, "that it is impossible to predict future behavior and that the question is so vague as to be meaningless."

We have also recognized that a prediction of future criminal conduct is "an experienced prediction based on a host of variables" which cannot be readily codified. Judge Quinones of the Family Court testified at trial that he and his colleagues make a determination under § 320.5(3)(b) based on numerous factors including the nature and seriousness of the charges; whether the charges are likely to be proved at trial; the juvenile's prior record; the adequacy and effectiveness of his home supervision; his school situation, if known; the time of day of the alleged crime as evidence of its seriousness and a possible lack of parental control; and any special circumstances that might be brought to his attention by the probation officer, the child's attorney, or any parents, relatives, or other responsible persons accompanying the child. The decision is based on as much information as can reasonably be obtained at the initial appearance.

Given the right to a hearing, to counsel, and to a statement of reasons, there is no reason that the specific factors upon which the Family Court judge might rely must be specified in the statute. As the New York Court of Appeals concluded, *People ex rel. Wayburn v. Schupf*, 39 N.Y.2d, at 690, "to a very real extent Family Court must exercise a substitute parental control for which there can be no particularized criteria." There is also no reason, we should add, for a federal court to assume that a state court judge will not strive to apply state law as conscientiously as possible.

It is worth adding that the Court of Appeals for the Second Circuit was mistaken in its conclusion that "[i]ndividual litigation... is a practical impossibility because the periods of detention are so short that the litigation is mooted before the merits are determined." In fact, one of the juveniles in the very case histories upon which the court relied was released from pretrial detention on a writ of habeas corpus issued by the State Supreme Court. New York courts also have adopted a liberal view of the doctrine of "capable of repetition, yet evading review" precisely in order to ensure that pretrial detention orders are not unreviewable....

The required statement of facts and reasons justifying the detention and the stenographic record of the initial appearance will provide a basis for the review of individual cases. Pretrial detention orders in New York may be reviewed by writ of habeas corpus brought in State Supreme Court. And the judgment of that court is appealable as of right and may be taken directly to the Court of Appeals if a constitutional question is presented. Permissive appeal from a Family Court order may also be had to the Appellate Division. Or a motion for reconsideration may be directed to the Family Court judge. These post detention procedures provide a sufficient mechanism for correcting on a case-by-case basis any erroneous detentions....

III

The dissent would apparently have us strike down New York's preventive detention statute on two grounds: first, because the preventive detention of juveniles constitutes poor public policy, with the balance of harms outweighing any positive benefits either to society or to the juveniles themselves, and, second, because the statute could have been better drafted to improve the quality of the decision making process. But it is worth recalling that we are neither a legislature charged with formulating public policy nor an American Bar Association committee charged with drafting a model statute. The question before us today is solely whether the preventive detention system chosen by the State of New York and applied by the New York Family Court comports with constitutional standards. Given the regulatory purpose for the detention and the procedural protections that precede its imposition, we conclude that § 320.5(3)(b) of the New York FCA is not invalid under the Due Process Clause of the Fourteenth Amendment.

The judgment of the Court of Appeals is

Reversed.

Justice Marshall, with whom Justice Brennan and Justice Stevens join, dissenting.

The New York Family Court Act governs the treatment of persons between 7 and 16 years of age who are alleged to have committed acts that, if committed by adults, would constitute crimes. The Act contains two provisions that authorize the detention of juveniles arrested for offenses covered by the Act for up to 17 days pending adjudication of their guilt. Section 320.5(3)(a) empowers a judge of the New York Family Court to order detention of a juvenile if he finds "there is a substantial probability that [the juvenile] will not appear in court on the return date." Section 320.5(3)(b), the provision at issue in these cases, authorizes detention if the judge finds "there is a serious risk [the juvenile] may before the return date commit an act which if committed by an adult would constitute a crime."

There are few limitations on § 320.5(3)(b). Detention need not be predicated on a finding that there is probable cause to believe the child committed the offense for which he was arrested. The provision applies to all juveniles, regardless of their prior records or the severity of the offenses of which they are accused. The provision is not limited to the prevention of dangerous crimes; a prediction that a juvenile if released may commit a minor misdemeanor is sufficient to justify his detention....

The Court today holds that preventive detention of a juvenile pursuant to § 320.5(3)(b) does not violate the Due Process Clause. Two rulings are essential to the Court's decision:

that the provision promotes legitimate government objectives important enough to justify the abridgment of the detained juveniles' liberty interests; and that the provision incorporates procedural safeguards sufficient to prevent unnecessary or arbitrary impairment of constitutionally protected rights....

I

The District Court made detailed findings, which the Court of Appeals left undisturbed, regarding the manner in which § 320.5(3)(b) is applied in practice. Unless clearly erroneous, those findings are binding upon us, see Fed.Rule Civ.Proc. 52(a), and must guide our analysis of the constitutional questions presented by these cases.

The first step in the process that leads to detention under § 320.5(3)(b) is known as "probation intake." A juvenile may arrive at intake by one of three routes: he may be brought there directly by an arresting officer; he may be detained for a brief period after his arrest and then taken to intake; he may be released upon arrest and directed to appear at a designated time. The heart of the intake procedure is a 10-to-40-minute interview of the juvenile, the arresting officer, and sometimes the juvenile's parent or guardian. The objectives of the probation officer conducting the interview are to determine the nature of the offense the child may have committed and to obtain some background information on him.

On the basis of the information derived from the interview and from an examination of the juvenile's record, the probation officer decides whether the case should be disposed of informally ("adjusted") or whether it should be referred to the Family Court. If the latter, the officer makes an additional recommendation regarding whether the juvenile should be detained. "There do not appear to be any governing criteria which must be followed by the probation officer in choosing between proposing detention and parole.... "

The actual decision whether to detain a juvenile under [the statute] is made by a Family Court judge at what is called an "initial appearance"—a brief hearing resembling an arraignment. The information on which the judge makes his determination is very limited. He has before him a "petition for delinquency" prepared by a state agency, charging the juvenile with an offense, accompanied with one or more affidavits attesting to the juvenile's involvement. Ordinarily the judge has in addition the written report and recommendation of the probation officer. However, the probation officer who prepared the report rarely attends the hearing. Nor is the complainant likely to appear. Consequently, "[o]ften there is no one present with personal knowledge of what happened."

In the typical case, the judge appoints counsel for the juvenile at the time his case is called. Thus, the lawyer has no opportunity to make an independent inquiry into the juvenile's background or character, and has only a few minutes to prepare arguments on the child's behalf. The judge ordinarily does not interview the juvenile, makes no inquiry into the truth of allegations in the petition, and does not determine whether there is probable cause to believe the juvenile committed the offense. The typical hearing lasts between 5 and 15 minutes, and the judge renders his decision immediately afterward.

Neither the statute nor any other body of rules guides the efforts of the judge to determine whether a given juvenile is likely to commit a crime before his trial. In making detention decisions, "each judge must rely on his own subjective judgment, based on the limited information available to him at court intake and whatever personal standards he himself has developed in exercising his discretionary authority under the statute." Family Court judges are not provided information regarding the behavior of juveniles over whose cases they have presided, so a judge has no way of refining the standards he employs in making detention decisions.

After examining a study of a sample of 34 cases in which juveniles were detained[7] along with various statistical studies of pretrial detention of juveniles in New York[8] the District Court made findings regarding the circumstances in which the provision habitually is invoked. Three of those findings are especially germane to appellees' challenge to the statute. First, a substantial number of "first offenders" are detained pursuant to [the statute]. For example, at least 5 of the 34 juveniles in the sample had no prior contact with the Family Court before being detained and at least 16 had no prior adjudications of delinquency. Second, many juveniles are released—for periods ranging from five days to several weeks—after their arrests and are then detained despite the absence of any evidence of misconduct during the time between their arrests and "initial appearances." Sixteen of the thirty-four cases in the sample fit this pattern.... Third, "the overwhelming majority" of the juveniles detained under § 320.5(3)(b) are released either before or immediately after their trials, either unconditionally or on parole. At least 23 of the juveniles in the sample fell into this category.

Finally, the District Court made a few significant findings concerning the conditions associated with "secure detention" pursuant to § 320.5(3)(b). In a "secure facility," "[t]he juveniles are subjected to strip-searches, wear institutional clothing and follow institutional regimen. At Spofford [Juvenile Detention Center], which is a secure facility, some juveniles who have had dispositional determinations and were awaiting placement (long term care) commingle with those in pretrial detention (short term care)."...

II

A

As the majority concedes, the fact that § 320.5(3)(b) applies only to juveniles does not insulate the provision from review under the Due Process Clause. "[N]either the Fourteenth Amendment nor the Bill of Rights is for adults alone." *In re Gault*, 387 U.S. 1, 13 (1967). Examination of the provision must of course be informed by a recognition that juveniles have

7. The majority refuses to consider the circumstances of these 34 cases, dismissing them as unrepresentative, and focuses instead on the lurid facts associated with the cases of the three named appellees. I cannot agree that the sample is entitled to so little weight. There was uncontested testimony at trial to the effect that the 34 cases were typical.... At no point in this litigation have appellants offered an alternative selection of instances in which § 320.5(3)(b) has been invoked. And most importantly, despite the fact that the District Court relied heavily on the sample when assessing the manner in which the statute is applied, appellants did not dispute before the Court of Appeals the representativeness of the 34 cases. When the defendants in a plaintiff class action challenge on appeal neither the certification of the class nor the plaintiffs' depiction of the character of the class, we ought to analyze the case as it comes to us and not try to construct a new version of the facts on the basis of an independent and selective review of the record.

8. As the Court of Appeals acknowledged, there are defects in all of the available statistical studies. Most importantly, none of the studies distinguishes persons detained under § 320.5(3)(a) from persons detained under § 320.5(3)(b). However, these flaws did not disable the courts below from making meaningful—albeit rough—generalizations regarding the incidence of detention under the latter provision. Especially when conjoined with the sample of 34 cases submitted by appellees, the studies are sufficient to support the three findings enumerated in the text....

different needs and capacities than adults, see *McKeiver v. Pennsylvania*, 403 U.S. 528, 550 (1971), but the provision still "must measure up to the essentials of due process and fair treatment," *Kent v. United States*, 383 U.S. 541, 562 (1966).

To comport with "fundamental fairness," § 320.5(3)(b) must satisfy two requirements. First, it must advance goals commensurate with the burdens it imposes on constitutionally protected interests. Second, it must not punish the juveniles to whom it applies....

...It is manifest that § 320.5(3)(b) impinges upon fundamental rights. If the "liberty" protected by the Due Process Clause means anything, it means freedom from physical restraint. Only a very important government interest can justify deprivation of liberty in this basic sense.

The majority seeks to evade the force of this principle by discounting the impact on a child of incarceration pursuant to § 320.5(3)(b). The curtailment of liberty consequent upon detention of a juvenile, the majority contends, is mitigated by the fact that "juveniles, unlike adults, are always in some form of custody." In any event, the majority argues, the conditions of confinement associated with "secure detention" under § 320.5(3)(b) are not unduly burdensome.

The majority's arguments do not survive scrutiny. Its characterization of preventive detention as merely a transfer of custody from a parent or guardian to the State is difficult to take seriously. Surely there is a qualitative difference between imprisonment and the condition of being subject to the supervision and control of an adult who has one's best interests at heart. And the majority's depiction of the nature of confinement under § 320.5(3)(b) is insupportable on this record.... For example, Judge Quinones, a Family Court Judge with eight years of experience, described the conditions of detention as follows:

> "...Juvenile Center, as much as we might try, is not the most pleasant place in the world. If you put them in detention, you are liable to be exposing these youngsters to all sorts of things. They are liable to be exposed to assault, they are liable to be exposed to sexual assaults. You are taking the risk of putting them together with a youngster that might be much worse than they, possibly might be, and it might have a bad effect in that respect."

Many other observers of the circumstances of juvenile detention in New York have come to similar conclusions.[13]

In short, fairly viewed, pretrial detention of a juvenile pursuant to § 320.5(3)(b) gives rise to injuries comparable to those associated with imprisonment of an adult. In both situations, the detainee suffers stigmatization and severe limitation of his freedom of movement. Indeed, the impressionability of juveniles may make the experience of incarceration more injurious to them than to adults; all too quickly juveniles subjected to preventive detention come to see society at large as hostile and oppressive and to regard themselves as irremediably "delinquent." Such serious injuries to presumptively innocent persons—encompassing the curtailment of their constitutional rights to liberty—can be justified only by a weighty public interest that is substantially advanced by the statute....

13. All of the 34 juveniles in the sample were detained in Spofford Juvenile Center, the detention facility for New York City. Numerous studies of that facility have attested to its unsavory characteristics. Conditions in Spofford have been successfully challenged on constitutional grounds, but nevertheless remain grim. Not surprisingly, a former New York City Deputy Mayor for Criminal Justice has averred that "Spofford is, in many ways, indistinguishable from a prison."

B

Appellants and the majority contend that § 320.5(3)(b) advances a pair of intertwined government objectives: "protecting the community from crime," and "protecting a juvenile from the consequences of his criminal activity."...

Appellees and some amici argue that public purposes of this sort can never justify incarceration of a person who has not been adjudicated guilty of a crime, at least in the absence of a determination that there exists probable cause to believe he committed a criminal offense. We need not reach that [categorical] argument in these cases because, even if the purposes identified by the majority are conceded to be compelling, they are not sufficiently promoted by detention pursuant to § 320.5(3)(b) to justify the concomitant impairment of the juveniles' liberty interests.... [T]wo circumstances in combination render § 320.5(3)(b) invalid *in toto*: in the large majority of cases in which the provision is invoked, its asserted objectives are either not advanced at all or are only minimally promoted; and, as the provision is written and administered by the state courts, the cases in which its asserted ends are significantly advanced cannot practicably be distinguished from the cases in which they are not.

1

Both of the courts below concluded that only occasionally and accidentally does pretrial detention of a juvenile under § 320.5(3)(b) prevent the commission of a crime.... First, Family Court judges are incapable of determining which of the juveniles who appear before them would commit offenses before their trials if left at large and which would not. In part, this incapacity derives from the limitations of current knowledge concerning the dynamics of human behavior. On the basis of evidence adduced at trial, supplemented by a thorough review of the secondary literature, the District Court found that "no diagnostic tools have as yet been devised which enable even the most highly trained criminologists to predict reliably which juveniles will engage in violent crime." The evidence supportive of this finding is overwhelming.[19] An independent impediment to identification of the defendants who would misbehave if released is the paucity of data available at an initial appearance....

Second, § 320.5(3)(b) is not limited to classes of juveniles whose past conduct suggests that they are substantially more likely than average juveniles to misbehave in the immediate future. The provision authorizes the detention of persons arrested for trivial offenses[21] and persons without any prior contacts with juvenile court. Even a finding that there is probable cause to believe a juvenile committed the offense with which he was charged is not a prerequisite to his detention.

19. See, e.g., American Psychiatric Association, Clinical Aspects of the Violent Individual 27-28 (1974); Cocozza & Steadman, The Failure of Psychiatric Predictions of Dangerousness: Clear and Convincing Evidence, 29 Rutgers L.Rev. 1084, 1094–1101 (1976); Diamond, The Psychiatric Prediction of Dangerousness, 123 U.Pa.L.Rev. 439 (1974); Ennis & Litwack, Psychiatry and the Presumption of Expertise: Flipping Coins In the Courtroom, 62 Calif.L.Rev. 693 (1974); Schlesinger, The Prediction of Dangerousness in Juveniles: A Replication, 24 Crime & Delinquency 40, 47 (1978); Steadman & Cocozza, Psychiatry, Dangerousness and the Repetitively Violent Offender, 69 J.Crim.L. & C. 226, 229–231 (1978); Wenk, Robison, & Smith, Can Violence Be Predicted?, 18 Crime & Delinquency 393, 401 (1972); Preventive Detention: An Empirical Analysis, 6 Harv.Civ.Rights-Civ.Lib.L.Rev. 289 (1971).

21. For example, Tyrone Parson, aged 15, one of the members of the sample, was arrested for enticing others to play three-card monte. After being detained for five days under § 320.5(3)(b), the petition against him was dismissed on the ground that "the offense alleged did not come within the provisions of the penal law."

Third, the courts below concluded that circumstances surrounding most of the cases in which § 320.5(3)(b) has been invoked strongly suggest that the detainee would not have committed a crime during the period before his trial if he had been released. In a significant proportion of the cases, the juvenile had been released after his arrest and had not committed any reported crimes while at large; it is not apparent why a juvenile would be more likely to misbehave between his initial appearance and his trial than between his arrest and initial appearance. Even more telling is the fact that "the vast majority" of persons detained under § 320.5(3)(b) are released either before or immediately after their trials. The inference is powerful that most detainees, when examined more carefully than at their initial appearances, are deemed insufficiently dangerous to warrant further incarceration.

The rarity with which invocation of § 320.5(3)(b) results in detention of a juvenile who otherwise would have committed a crime fatally undercuts the two public purposes assigned to the statute by the State and the majority. The argument that § 320.5(3)(b) serves "the State's '*parens patriae* interest in preserving and promoting the welfare of the child,'" now appears particularly hollow. Most juveniles detained pursuant to the provision are not benefited thereby, because they would not have committed crimes if left to their own devices (and thus would not have been exposed to the risk of physical injury or the perils of the cycle of recidivism). On the contrary, these juveniles suffer several serious harms: deprivation of liberty and stigmatization as "delinquent" or "dangerous," as well as impairment of their ability to prepare their legal defenses. The benefits even to those few juveniles who would have committed crimes if released are not unalloyed; the gains to them are partially offset by the aforementioned injuries....

The argument that § 320.5(3)(b) protects the welfare of the community fares little better. Certainly the public reaps no benefit from incarceration of the majority of the detainees who would not have committed any crimes had they been released. Prevention of the minor offenses that would have been committed by a small proportion of the persons detained confers only a slight benefit on the community. Only in occasional cases does incarceration of a juvenile pending his trial serve to prevent a crime of violence and thereby significantly promote the public interest. Such an infrequent and haphazard gain is insufficient to justify curtailment of the liberty interests of all the presumptively innocent juveniles who would have obeyed the law pending their trials had they been given the chance....

2...

...It is possible, the majority acknowledges, that "in some circumstances detention of a juvenile [pursuant to § 320.5(3)(b)] would not pass constitutional muster. But the validity of those detentions must be determined on a case-by-case basis."

There are some obvious practical impediments to adoption of the majority's proposal. Because a juvenile may not be incarcerated under § 320.5(3)(b) for more than 17 days, it would be impracticable for a particular detainee to secure his freedom by challenging the constitutional basis of his detention; by the time the suit could be considered, it would have been rendered moot by the juvenile's release or long-term detention pursuant to a delinquency adjudication. Nor could an individual detainee avoid the problem of mootness by filing a suit for damages or for injunctive relief. This Court's declaration that § 320.5(3)(b) is not unconstitutional on its face would almost certainly preclude a finding that detention of a juvenile pursuant to the statute violated any clearly established constitutional rights; in the absence of such a finding all state officials would be immune from liability in damages. And, under current doctrine pertaining to the standing of an individual victim of allegedly unconstitutional conduct to obtain an injunction against repetition of that behavior, it is far from clear that an individual detainee would be able to obtain an equitable remedy.

But even if these practical difficulties could be surmounted, the majority's proposal would be inadequate. Precisely because of the unreliability of any determination whether a particular juvenile is likely to commit a crime between his arrest and trial, no individual detainee would be able to demonstrate that he would have abided by the law had he been released. In other words, no configuration of circumstances would enable a juvenile to establish that he fell into the category of persons unconstitutionally detained rather than the category constitutionally detained....

C

The findings reviewed in the preceding section lend credence to the conclusion reached by the courts below: § 320.5(3)(b) "is utilized principally, not for preventive purposes, but to impose punishment for unadjudicated criminal acts."

The majority contends that, of the many factors we have considered in trying to determine whether a particular sanction constitutes "punishment," the most useful are "whether an alternative purpose to which [the sanction] may rationally be connected is assignable for it, and whether it appears excessive in relation to the alternative purpose assigned." The alternative purpose assigned by the State to § 320.5(3)(b) is the prevention of crime by the detained juveniles. But, as has been shown, that objective is advanced at best sporadically by the provision. Moreover, § 320.5(3)(b) frequently is invoked under circumstances in which it is extremely unlikely that the juvenile in question would commit a crime while awaiting trial. The most striking of these cases involve juveniles who have been at large without mishap for a substantial period of time prior to their initial appearances, and detainees who are adjudged delinquent and are nevertheless released into the community....

The inference that § 320.5(3)(b) is punitive in nature is supported by additional materials in the record. For example, Judge Quinones and even appellants' counsel acknowledged that one of the reasons juveniles detained pursuant to § 320.5(3)(b) usually are released after the determination of their guilt is that the judge decides that their pretrial detention constitutes sufficient punishment....

In summary, application of the litmus test the Court recently has used to identify punitive sanctions supports the finding of the lower courts that preventive detention under § 320.5(3)(b) constitutes punishment....

III

If the record did not establish the impossibility, on the basis of the evidence available to a Family Court judge at a § 320.5(3)(b) hearing, of reliably predicting whether a given juvenile would commit a crime before his trial, and if the purposes relied upon by the State were promoted sufficiently to justify the deprivations of liberty effected by the provision, I would nevertheless still strike down § 320.5(3)(b) because of the absence of procedural safeguards in the provision....

Appellees point out that § 320.5(3)(b) lacks two crucial procedural constraints. First, a New York Family Court judge is given no guidance regarding what kinds of evidence he should consider or what weight he should accord different sorts of material in deciding whether to detain a juvenile.... Second, § 320.5(3)(b) does not specify how likely it must be that a juvenile will commit a crime before his trial to warrant his detention. The provision indicates only that there must be a "serious risk" that he will commit an offense and does not prescribe the standard of proof that should govern the judge's determination of that issue.

Not surprisingly, ... different judges have adopted different ways of estimating the chances whether a juvenile will misbehave in the near future.... This discretion exercised by Family Court judges in making detention decisions gives rise to two related constitutional problems. First, it creates an excessive risk that juveniles will be detained "erroneously"—i.e., under circumstances in which no public interest would be served by their incarceration. Second, it fosters arbitrariness and inequality in a decision making process that impinges upon fundamental rights.

A

One of the purposes of imposing procedural constraints on decisions affecting life, liberty, or property is to reduce the incidence of error. In *Mathews v. Eldridge*, 424 U.S. 319 (1976), the Court identified a complex of considerations that has proved helpful in determining what protections are constitutionally required in particular contexts to achieve that end:

> "[I]dentification of the specific dictates of due process generally requires consideration of three distinct factors: First, the private interest that will be affected by the official action; second, the risk of an erroneous deprivation of such interest through the procedures used, and the probable value, if any, of additional or substitute procedural safeguards; and finally, the Government's interest, including the function involved and the fiscal and administrative burdens that the additional or substitute procedural requirement would entail. *Id.*, at 335."

As Judge Newman recognized, a review of these three factors in the context of New York's preventive-detention scheme compels the conclusion that the Due Process Clause is violated by § 320.5(3)(b) in its present form. First, the private interest affected by a decision to detain a juvenile is personal liberty....

Second, there can be no dispute that there is a serious risk under the present statute that a juvenile will be detained erroneously—i.e., despite the fact that he would not commit a crime if released.... [T]he vast majority of detentions pursuant to § 320.5(3)(b) advance no state interest; only rarely does the statute operate to prevent crime.... Opportunities for improvement in the extant regime are apparent even to a casual observer. Most obviously, some measure of guidance to Family Court judges regarding the evidence they should consider and the standard of proof they should use in making their determinations would surely contribute to the quality of their detention determinations.

The majority purports to see no value in such additional safeguards, contending that activity of estimating the likelihood that a given juvenile will commit a crime in the near future involves subtle assessment of a host of variables, the precise weight of which cannot be determined in advance. A review of the hearings that resulted in the detention of the juveniles included in the sample of 34 cases reveals the majority's depiction of the decision making process to be hopelessly idealized. For example, the operative portion of the initial appearance of Tyrone Parson, the three-card monte player, consisted of the following:

> "**COURT OFFICER:** Will you identify yourself.
> "**TYRONE PARSON:** Tyrone Parson, Age 15.

> "**THE COURT:** Miss Brown, how many times has Tyrone been known to the Court?
> "**MISS BROWN:** Seven times.
> "**THE COURT:** Remand the respondent." Petitioners' Exhibit 18a.[35]

This kind of parody of reasoned decision making would be less likely to occur if judges were given more specific and mandatory instructions regarding the information they should consider and the manner in which they should assess it.

Third and finally, the imposition of such constraints on the deliberations of the Family Court judges would have no adverse effect on the State's interest in detaining dangerous juveniles and would give rise to insubstantial administrative burdens. For example, a simple directive to Family Court judges to state on the record the significance they give to the seriousness of the offense of which a juvenile is accused and to the nature of the juvenile's background would contribute materially to the quality of the decision making process without significantly increasing the duration of initial appearances.

In summary, the three factors enumerated in *Mathews* in combination incline overwhelmingly in favor of imposition of more stringent constraints on detention determinations....

B

A principle underlying many of our prior decisions in various doctrinal settings is that government officials may not be accorded unfettered discretion in making decisions that impinge upon fundamental rights. Two concerns underlie this principle: excessive discretion fosters inequality in the distribution of entitlements and harms, inequality which is especially troublesome when those benefits and burdens are great; and discretion can mask the use by officials of illegitimate criteria in allocating important goods and rights.

So, in striking down on vagueness grounds a vagrancy ordinance, we emphasized the "unfettered discretion it places in the hands of the...police." *Papachristou v. City of Jacksonville*, 405 U.S. 156, 168 (1972)....

The concerns that powered these decisions are strongly implicated by New York's preventive-detention scheme. The effect of the lack of procedural safeguards constraining detention decisions under § 320.5(3)(b) is that the liberty of a juvenile arrested even for a petty crime is dependent upon the "caprice" of a Family Court judge. The absence of meaningful guidelines creates opportunities for judges to use illegitimate criteria when deciding whether juveniles should be incarcerated pending their trials—for example, to detain children for the express purpose of punishing them. Even the judges who strive conscientiously to apply the law have little choice but to assess juveniles' dangerousness on the basis of whatever standards they deem appropriate. The resultant variation in detention decisions gives rise to a level of inequality in the deprivation of a fundamental right too great to be countenanced under the Constitution.

IV

The majority acknowledges—indeed, founds much of its argument upon—the principle that a State has both the power and the responsibility to protect the interests of the children within

35. Parson's case is not unique. The hearings accorded Juan Santiago and Daniel Nelson, for example, though somewhat longer in duration, were nearly as cavalier and undiscriminating.

its jurisdiction.... Yet the majority today upholds a statute whose net impact on the juveniles who come within its purview is overwhelmingly detrimental. Most persons detained under the provision reap no benefit and suffer serious injuries thereby. The welfare of only a minority of the detainees is even arguably enhanced. The inequity of this regime, combined with the arbitrariness with which it is administered, is bound to disillusion its victims regarding the virtues of our system of criminal justice. I can see—and the majority has pointed to—no public purpose advanced by the statute sufficient to justify the harm it works.

I respectfully dissent.

QUESTIONS

1. What test does the Court use to determine whether the procedures used satisfy due process? How does the Court apply that test to the facts of this case?

2. The Court cites *Gault* for the proposition that children are always in some form of custody. Is this an accurate reading of *Gault* or a constitutional sleight-of-hand?

3. In *Gerstein v. Pugh*, 420 U.S. 103 (1975), the Supreme Court held that an individual arrested without a warrant must be presented "promptly" to a neutral magistrate who then makes a probable cause determination. But what does "promptly" mean? In *County of Riverside v. McLaughlin*, 500 U.S. 44, 56 (1991), decided after *Schall*, the Court held that presentment must occur within forty-eight hours after a warrantless arrest. In *Schall*, how long must a juvenile wait before a magistrate determines probable cause? Does that comport with *McLaughlin*?

4. When the Court decided *Schall*, it had not yet considered the constitutionality of the pretrial detention of adults. In 1987, the Court upheld a statute authorizing pretrial detention of arrestees charged with certain serious felonies in *United States v. Salerno*, 481 U.S. 739 (1987). Implicitly acknowledging that preventive detention had been upheld in *Schall* in part because of the decidedly different nature of the liberty interest involved, the *Salerno* Court made clear that "even competent adults may face substantial liberty restrictions" where the state's interest is sufficiently compelling. *Id.* at 749–750. The Court, quoting directly from *Schall*, also reiterated that "'there is nothing inherently unattainable about a prediction of future criminal conduct,'" and found the procedural protections sufficient to prevent erroneous deprivations of liberty. *Id.* at 751–752. Is *Schall* another example of the Court's use of juvenile cases to explore the boundaries of individual rights?

5. The dissent argues that the due-process rights of juveniles were violated. Does the dissent apply a different test in reaching this conclusion? If not, what is the dissent arguing?

C. Procedural Framework

1. INITIAL CONTACT WITH GOVERNMENTAL OFFICIALS

T.L.O. V. NEW JERSEY
Supreme Court of the United States
469 U.S. 325 (1985)

JUSTICE WHITE delivered the opinion of the Court....

I

On March 7, 1980, a teacher at Piscataway High School in Middlesex County, N.J., discovered two girls smoking in a lavatory. One of the two girls was the respondent T.L.O., who at that time was a 14-year-old high school freshman. Because smoking in the lavatory was a violation of a school rule, the teacher took the two girls to the Principal's office, where they met with Assistant Vice Principal Theodore Choplick. In response to questioning by Mr. Choplick, T.L.O.'s companion admitted that she had violated the rule. T.L.O., however, denied that she had been smoking in the lavatory and claimed that she did not smoke at all.

Mr. Choplick asked T.L.O. to come into his private office and demanded to see her purse. Opening the purse, he found a pack of cigarettes, which he removed from the purse and held before T.L.O. as he accused her of having lied to him. As he reached into the purse for the cigarettes, Mr. Choplick also noticed a package of cigarette rolling papers. In his experience, possession of rolling papers by high school students was closely associated with the use of marihuana. Suspecting that a closer examination of the purse might yield further evidence of drug use, Mr. Choplick proceeded to search the purse thoroughly. The search revealed a small amount of marihuana, a pipe, a number of empty plastic bags, a substantial quantity of money in one-dollar bills, an index card that appeared to be a list of students who owed T.L.O. money, and two letters that implicated T.L.O. in marihuana dealing.

Mr. Choplick notified T.L.O.'s mother and the police, and turned the evidence of drug dealing over to the police. At the request of the police, T.L.O.'s mother took her daughter to police headquarters, where T.L.O. confessed that she had been selling marihuana at the high school. On the basis of the confession and the evidence seized by Mr. Choplick, the State brought delinquency charges against T.L.O. in the Juvenile and Domestic Relations Court of

Middlesex County. Contending that Mr. Choplick's search of her purse violated the Fourth Amendment, T.L.O. moved to suppress the evidence found in her purse as well as her confession, which, she argued, was tainted by the allegedly unlawful search. The Juvenile Court denied the motion to suppress. *State ex rel. T.L.O.*, 178 N.J.Super. 329, 428 A.2d 1327 (1980). Although the court concluded that the Fourth Amendment did apply to searches carried out by school officials, it held that

> "a school official may properly conduct a search of a student's person if the official has a reasonable suspicion that a crime has been or is in the process of being committed, *or* reasonable cause to believe that the search is necessary to maintain school discipline or enforce school policies." *Id.*, 178 N.J.Super., at 341, 428 A.2d, at 1333 (emphasis in original).

Applying this standard, the court concluded that the search conducted by Mr. Choplick was a reasonable one. The initial decision to open the purse was justified by Mr. Choplick's well-founded suspicion that T.L.O. had violated the rule forbidding smoking in the lavatory. Once the purse was open, evidence of marihuana violations was in plain view, and Mr. Choplick was entitled to conduct a thorough search to determine the nature and extent of T.L.O.'s drug-related activities. *Id.*, 178 N.J.Super., at 343, 428 A.2d, at 1334. Having denied the motion to suppress, the court on March 23, 1981, found T.L.O. to be a delinquent and on January 8, 1982, sentenced her to a year's probation.

On appeal from the final judgment of the Juvenile Court, a divided Appellate Division affirmed the trial court's finding that there had been no Fourth Amendment violation.... T.L.O. appealed the Fourth Amendment ruling, and the Supreme Court of New Jersey reversed the judgment of the Appellate Division and ordered the suppression of the evidence found in T.L.O.'s purse. *State ex rel. T.L.O.*, 94 N.J. 331, 463 A.2d 934 (1983).

The New Jersey Supreme Court agreed with the lower courts that the Fourth Amendment applies to searches conducted by school officials. The court also rejected the State of New Jersey's argument that the exclusionary rule should not be employed to prevent the use in juvenile proceedings of evidence unlawfully seized by school officials. Declining to consider whether applying the rule to the fruits of searches by school officials would have any deterrent value, the court held simply that the precedents of this Court establish that "if an official search violates constitutional rights, the evidence is not admissible in criminal proceedings." *Id.*, 94 N.J., at 341, 463 A.2d, at 939 (footnote omitted)....

We granted the State of New Jersey's petition for certiorari. 464 U.S. 991 (1983). Although the State had argued in the Supreme Court of New Jersey that the search of T.L.O.'s purse did not violate the Fourth Amendment, the petition for certiorari raised only the question whether the exclusionary rule should operate to bar consideration in juvenile delinquency proceedings of evidence unlawfully seized by a school official without the involvement of law enforcement officers. When this case was first argued last Term, the State conceded for the purpose of argument that the standard devised by the New Jersey Supreme Court for determining the legality of school searches was appropriate and that the court had correctly applied that standard; the State contended only that the remedial purposes of the exclusionary rule were not well served by applying it to searches conducted by public authorities not primarily engaged in law enforcement.

Although we originally granted certiorari to decide the issue of the appropriate remedy in juvenile court proceedings for unlawful school searches, our doubts regarding the wisdom of deciding that question in isolation from the broader question of what limits, if any, the Fourth Amendment places on the activities of school authorities prompted us to order reargument on that question. Having heard argument on the legality of the search of T.L.O.'s purse, we are satisfied that the search did not violate the Fourth Amendment.[3]

II

In determining whether the search at issue in this case violated the Fourth Amendment, we are faced initially with the question whether that Amendment's prohibition on unreasonable searches and seizures applies to searches conducted by public school officials. We hold that it does.

It is now beyond dispute that "the Federal Constitution, by virtue of the [Fourth] Amendment, prohibits unreasonable searches and seizures by state officers." Equally indisputable is the proposition that the Fourteenth Amendment protects the rights of students against encroachment by public school officials....

These two propositions—that the Fourth Amendment applies to the States through the Fourteenth Amendment, and that the actions of public school officials are subject to the limits placed on state action by the Fourteenth Amendment—might appear sufficient to answer the suggestion that the Fourth Amendment does not proscribe unreasonable searches by school officials. On reargument, however, the State of New Jersey has argued that the history of the Fourth Amendment indicates that the Amendment was intended to regulate only searches and seizures carried out by law enforcement officers; accordingly, although public school officials are concededly state agents for purposes of the Fourteenth Amendment, the Fourth Amendment creates no rights enforceable against them.

It may well be true that the evil toward which the Fourth Amendment was primarily directed was the resurrection of the pre-Revolutionary practice of using general warrants or "writs of assistance" to authorize searches for contraband by officers of the Crown. But this Court has never limited the Amendment's prohibition on unreasonable searches and seizures to operations conducted by the police. Rather, the Court has long spoken of the Fourth Amendment's strictures as restraints imposed upon "governmental action"—that is, "upon the activities of sovereign authority."...

Notwithstanding the general applicability of the Fourth Amendment to the activities of civil authorities, a few courts have concluded that school officials are exempt from the dictates of the Fourth Amendment by virtue of the special nature of their authority over schoolchildren. Teachers and school administrators, it is said, act *in loco parentis* in their dealings with students: their authority is that of the parent, not the State, and is therefore not subject to the limits of the Fourth Amendment.

3. In holding that the search of T.L.O.'s purse did not violate the Fourth Amendment, we do not implicitly determine that the exclusionary rule applies to the fruits of unlawful searches conducted by school authorities. The question whether evidence should be excluded from a criminal proceeding involves two discrete inquiries: whether the evidence was seized in violation of the Fourth Amendment, and whether the exclusionary rule is the appropriate remedy for the violation. Neither question is logically antecedent to the other, for a negative answer to either question is sufficient to dispose of the case. Thus, our determination that the search at issue in this case did not violate the Fourth Amendment implies no particular resolution of the question of the applicability of the exclusionary rule.

Such reasoning is in tension with contemporary reality and the teachings of this Court. We have held school officials subject to the commands of the First Amendment, see *Tinker v. Des Moines Independent Community School District*, 393 U.S. 503 (1969), and the Due Process Clause of the Fourteenth Amendment, see *Goss v. Lopez*, 419 U.S. 565 (1975). If school authorities are state actors for purposes of the constitutional guarantees of freedom of expression and due process, it is difficult to understand why they should be deemed to be exercising parental rather than public authority when conducting searches of their students. More generally, the Court has recognized that "the concept of parental delegation" as a source of school authority is not entirely "consonant with compulsory education laws." *Ingraham v. Wright*, 430 U.S. 651, 662 (1977). Today's public school officials do not merely exercise authority voluntarily conferred on them by individual parents; rather, they act in furtherance of publicly mandated educational and disciplinary policies. In carrying out searches and other disciplinary functions pursuant to such policies, school officials act as representatives of the State, not merely as surrogates for the parents, and they cannot claim the parents' immunity from the strictures of the Fourth Amendment.

III

To hold that the Fourth Amendment applies to searches conducted by school authorities is only to begin the inquiry into the standards governing such searches. Although the underlying command of the Fourth Amendment is always that searches and seizures be reasonable, what is reasonable depends on the context within which a search takes place. The determination of the standard of reasonableness governing any specific class of searches requires "balancing the need to search against the invasion which the search entails." *Camara v. Municipal Court*, *supra*, at 536-537. On one side of the balance are arrayed the individual's legitimate expectations of privacy and personal security; on the other, the government's need for effective methods to deal with breaches of public order....

...A search of a child's person or of a closed purse or other bag carried on her person,[5] no less than a similar search carried out on an adult, is undoubtedly a severe violation of subjective expectations of privacy....

Of course, the Fourth Amendment does not protect subjective expectations of privacy that are unreasonable or otherwise "illegitimate." See, e.g., *Hudson v. Palmer*, 468 U.S. 517 (1984).... To receive the protection of the Fourth Amendment, an expectation of privacy must be one that society is "prepared to recognize as legitimate." *Hudson v. Palmer*, *supra*, at 526. The State of New Jersey has argued that because of the pervasive supervision to which children in the schools are necessarily subject, a child has virtually no legitimate expectation of privacy in articles of personal property "unnecessarily" carried into a school. This argument has two factual premises: (1) the fundamental incompatibility of expectations of privacy with the maintenance of a sound educational environment; and (2) the minimal interest of the child in bringing any items of personal property into the school. Both premises are severely flawed.

5. We do not address the question, not presented by this case, whether a schoolchild has a legitimate expectation of privacy in lockers, desks, or other school property provided for the storage of school supplies. Nor do we express any opinion on the standards (if any) governing searches of such areas by school officials or by other public authorities acting at the request of school officials.

Although this Court may take notice of the difficulty of maintaining discipline in the public schools today, the situation is not so dire that students in the schools may claim no legitimate expectations of privacy. We have recently recognized that the need to maintain order in a prison is such that prisoners retain no legitimate expectations of privacy in their cells, but it goes almost without saying that "[t]he prisoner and the schoolchild stand in wholly different circumstances, separated by the harsh facts of criminal conviction and incarceration." *Ingraham v. Wright*, *supra*, at 669. We are not yet ready to hold that the schools and the prisons need be equated for purposes of the Fourth Amendment.

Nor does the State's suggestion that children have no legitimate need to bring personal property into the schools seem well anchored in reality. Students at a minimum must bring to school not only the supplies needed for their studies, but also keys, money, and the necessaries of personal hygiene and grooming. In addition, students may carry on their persons or in purses or wallets such nondisruptive yet highly personal items as photographs, letters, and diaries. Finally, students may have perfectly legitimate reasons to carry with them articles of property needed in connection with extracurricular or recreational activities. In short, schoolchildren may find it necessary to carry with them a variety of legitimate, noncontraband items, and there is no reason to conclude that they have necessarily waived all rights to privacy in such items merely by bringing them onto school grounds.

Against the child's interest in privacy must be set the substantial interest of teachers and administrators in maintaining discipline in the classroom and on school grounds. Maintaining order in the classroom has never been easy, but in recent years, school disorder has often taken particularly ugly forms: drug use and violent crime in the schools have become major social problems. See generally 1 NIE, U.S. Dept. of Health, Education and Welfare, Violent Schools—Safe Schools: The Safe School Study Report to the Congress (1978). Even in schools that have been spared the most severe disciplinary problems, the preservation of order and a proper educational environment requires close supervision of schoolchildren, as well as the enforcement of rules against conduct that would be perfectly permissible if undertaken by an adult.... Accordingly, we have recognized that maintaining security and order in the schools requires a certain degree of flexibility in school disciplinary procedures, and we have respected the value of preserving the informality of the student-teacher relationship....

...It is evident that the school setting requires some easing of the restrictions to which searches by public authorities are ordinarily subject. The warrant requirement, in particular, is unsuited to the school environment: requiring a teacher to obtain a warrant before searching a child suspected of an infraction of school rules (or of the criminal law) would unduly interfere with the maintenance of the swift and informal disciplinary procedures needed in the schools. Just as we have in other cases dispensed with the warrant requirement when "the burden of obtaining a warrant is likely to frustrate the governmental purpose behind the search," we hold today that school officials need not obtain a warrant before searching a student who is under their authority.

The school setting also requires some modification of the level of suspicion of illicit activity needed to justify a search. Ordinarily, a search—even one that may permissibly be carried out without a warrant—must be based upon "probable cause" to believe that a violation of the law has occurred. However, "probable cause" is not an irreducible requirement of a valid search. The fundamental command of the Fourth Amendment is that searches and seizures be reasonable, and although "both the concept of probable cause and the requirement of a warrant bear on the reasonableness of a search,...in certain limited circumstances neither is required." Thus, we have in a number of cases recognized the legality of searches and seizures based on suspicions that, although "reasonable," do not rise to the level of probable cause. Where a careful balancing of governmental and private interests suggests that the public interest is best served by a Fourth Amendment standard of reasonableness that stops short of probable cause, we have not hesitated to adopt such a standard.

We join the majority of courts that have examined this issue in concluding that the accommodation of the privacy interests of schoolchildren with the substantial need of teachers and administrators for freedom to maintain order in the schools does not require strict adherence to the requirement that searches be based on probable cause to believe that the subject of the search has violated or is violating the law. Rather, the legality of a search of a student should depend simply on the reasonableness, under all the circumstances, of the search. Determining the reasonableness of any search involves a twofold inquiry: first, one must consider "whether the...action was justified at its inception," *Terry v. Ohio*, 392 U.S. [1], 20 [(1967)]; second, one must determine whether the search as actually conducted "was reasonably related in scope to the circumstances which justified the interference in the first place," ibid. Under ordinary circumstances, a search of a student by a teacher or other school official[7] will be "justified at its inception" when there are reasonable grounds for suspecting that the search will turn up evidence that the student has violated or is violating either the law or the rules of the school.[8] Such a search will be permissible in its scope when the measures adopted are reasonably related to the objectives of the search and not excessively intrusive in light of the age and sex of the student and the nature of the infraction.

This standard will, we trust, neither unduly burden the efforts of school authorities to maintain order in their schools nor authorize unrestrained intrusions upon the privacy of schoolchildren. By focusing attention on the question of reasonableness, the standard will spare teachers and school administrators the necessity of schooling themselves in the niceties of probable cause and permit them to regulate their conduct according to the dictates of reason and common sense. At the same time, the reasonableness standard should ensure that the interests of students will be invaded no more than is necessary to achieve the legitimate end of preserving order in the schools.

7. We here consider only searches carried out by school authorities acting alone and on their own authority. This case does not present the question of the appropriate standard for assessing the legality of searches conducted by school officials in conjunction with or at the behest of law enforcement agencies, and we express no opinion on that question. Cf. *Picha v. Wielgos*, 410 F.Supp. 1214, 1219–1221 (ND Ill.1976) (holding probable-cause standard applicable to searches involving the police).

8. We do not decide whether individualized suspicion is an essential element of the reasonableness standard we adopt for searches by school authorities. In other contexts, however, we have held that although "some quantum of individualized suspicion is usually a prerequisite to a constitutional search or seizure[,]...the Fourth Amendment imposes no irreducible requirement of such suspicion." Exceptions to the requirement of individualized suspicion are generally appropriate only where the privacy interests implicated by a search are minimal and where "other safeguards" are available "to assure that the individual's reasonable expectation of privacy is not 'subject to the discretion of the official in the field.'" Because the search of T.L.O.'s purse was based upon an individualized suspicion that she had violated school rules, we need not consider the circumstances that might justify school authorities in conducting searches unsupported by individualized suspicion.

IV

There remains the question of the legality of the search in this case.... Our review of the facts surrounding the search leads us to conclude that the search was in no sense unreasonable for Fourth Amendment purposes.

The incident that gave rise to this case actually involved two separate searches, with the first—the search for cigarettes—providing the suspicion that gave rise to the second—the search for marihuana. Although it is the fruits of the second search that are at issue here, the validity of the search for marihuana must depend on the reasonableness of the initial search for cigarettes, as there would have been no reason to suspect that T.L.O. possessed marihuana had the first search not taken place....

...T.L.O. had been accused of smoking, and had denied the accusation in the strongest possible terms when she stated that she did not smoke at all. Surely it cannot be said that under these circumstances, T.L.O.'s possession of cigarettes would be irrelevant to the charges against her or to her response to those charges. T.L.O.'s possession of cigarettes, once it was discovered, would both corroborate the report that she had been smoking and undermine the credibility of her defense to the charge of smoking. To be sure, the discovery of the cigarettes would not prove that T.L.O. had been smoking in the lavatory; nor would it, strictly speaking, necessarily be inconsistent with her claim that she did not smoke at all. But it is universally recognized that evidence, to be relevant to an inquiry, need not conclusively prove the ultimate fact in issue, but only have "any tendency to make the existence of any fact that is of consequence to the determination of the action more probable or less probable than it would be without the evidence." The relevance of T.L.O.'s possession of cigarettes to the question whether she had been smoking and to the credibility of her denial that she smoked supplied the necessary "nexus" between the item searched for and the infraction under investigation. Thus, if Mr. Choplick in fact had a reasonable suspicion that T.L.O. had cigarettes in her purse, the search was justified despite the fact that the cigarettes, if found, would constitute "mere evidence" of a violation....

...Mr. Choplick's suspicion that there were cigarettes in the purse was not an "inchoate and unparticularized suspicion or 'hunch,'" *Terry v. Ohio*, 392 U.S., at 27; rather, it was the sort of "common-sense conclusio[n] about human behavior" upon which "practical people"—including government officials—are entitled to rely. Of course, even if the teacher's report were true, T.L.O. *might* not have had a pack of cigarettes with her; she might have borrowed a cigarette from someone else or have been sharing a cigarette with another student. But the requirement of reasonable suspicion is not a requirement of absolute certainty: "sufficient probability, not certainty, is the touchstone of reasonableness under the Fourth Amendment." Because the hypothesis that T.L.O. was carrying cigarettes in her purse was itself not unreasonable, it is irrelevant that other hypotheses were also consistent with the teacher's accusation. Accordingly, it cannot be said that Mr. Choplick acted unreasonably when he examined T.L.O.'s purse to see if it contained cigarettes.[12]

12. T.L.O. contends that even if it was reasonable for Mr. Choplick to open her purse to look for cigarettes, it was not reasonable for him to reach in and take the cigarettes out of her purse once he found them. T.L.O.'s argument is based on the fact that the cigarettes were not "contraband," as no school rule forbade her to have them. Thus, according to T.L.O., the cigarettes were not subject to seizure or confiscation by school authorities, and Mr. Choplick was not entitled to take them out of T.L.O.'s purse regardless of whether he was entitled to peer into the purse to see if they were there. Such hairsplitting argumentation has no place in an

Our conclusion that Mr. Choplick's decision to open T.L.O.'s purse was reasonable brings us to the question of the further search for marihuana once the pack of cigarettes was located. The suspicion upon which the search for marihuana was founded was provided when Mr. Choplick observed a package of rolling papers in the purse as he removed the pack of cigarettes. Although T.L.O. does not dispute the reasonableness of Mr. Choplick's belief that the rolling papers indicated the presence of marihuana, she does contend that the scope of the search Mr. Choplick conducted exceeded permissible bounds when he seized and read certain letters that implicated T.L.O. in drug dealing.... The discovery of the rolling papers concededly gave rise to a reasonable suspicion that T.L.O. was carrying marihuana as well as cigarettes in her purse. This suspicion justified further exploration of T.L.O.'s purse, which turned up more evidence of drug-related activities: a pipe, a number of plastic bags of the type commonly used to store marihuana, a small quantity of marihuana, and a fairly substantial amount of money. Under these circumstances, it was not unreasonable to extend the search to a separate zippered compartment of the purse; and when a search of that compartment revealed an index card containing a list of "people who owe me money" as well as two letters, the inference that T.L.O. was involved in marihuana trafficking was substantial enough to justify Mr. Choplick in examining the letters to determine whether they contained any further evidence....

Because the search resulting in the discovery of the evidence of marihuana dealing by T.L.O. was reasonable, the New Jersey Supreme Court's decision to exclude that evidence from T.L.O.'s juvenile delinquency proceedings on Fourth Amendment grounds was erroneous. Accordingly, the judgment of the Supreme Court of New Jersey is

Reversed.

Justice Powell, with whom Justice O'Connor joins, concurring....

...I would place greater emphasis...on the special characteristics of elementary and secondary schools that make it unnecessary to afford students the same constitutional protections granted adults and juveniles in a nonschool setting.

In any realistic sense, students within the school environment have a lesser expectation of privacy than members of the population generally.... It is simply unrealistic to think that students have the same subjective expectation of privacy as the population generally. But for purposes of deciding this case, I can assume that children in school—no less than adults—have privacy interests that society is prepared to recognize as legitimate.

However one may characterize their privacy expectations, students properly are afforded some constitutional protections. In an often quoted statement, the Court said that students do not "shed their constitutional rights...at the schoolhouse gate." *Tinker v. Des Moines Independent Community School District*, 393 U.S. 503, 506 (1969). The Court also has "emphasized the need for affirming the comprehensive authority of the states and of school officials...to prescribe and control conduct in the schools." *Id.*, at 507. The Court has balanced the interests of the student against the school officials' need to maintain discipline by recognizing qualitative differences between the constitutional remedies to which students and adults are entitled....

...In *Ingraham v. Wright*, 430 U.S. 651 (1977), we declined to extend the Eighth Amendment to prohibit the use of corporal punishment of school children as authorized by Florida law. We

inquiry addressed to the issue of reasonableness. We find that neither in opening the purse nor in reaching into it to remove the cigarettes did Mr. Choplick violate the Fourth Amendment....

emphasized in that opinion that familiar constraints in the school, and also in the community, provide substantial protection against the violation of constitutional rights by school authorities. "[A]t the end of the school day, the child is invariably free to return home. Even while at school, the child brings with him the support of family and friends and is rarely apart from teachers and other pupils who may witness and protest any instances of mistreatment." *Id.*, at 670....

The special relationship between teacher and student also distinguishes the setting within which schoolchildren operate. Law enforcement officers function as adversaries of criminal suspects. These officers have the responsibility to investigate criminal activity, to locate and arrest those who violate our laws, and to facilitate the charging and bringing of such persons to trial. Rarely does this type of adversarial relationship exist between school authorities and pupils.... The attitude of the typical teacher is one of personal responsibility for the student's welfare as well as for his education.

The primary duty of school officials and teachers, as the Court states, is the education and training of young people. A State has a compelling interest in assuring that the schools meet this responsibility. Without first establishing discipline and maintaining order, teachers cannot begin to educate their students. And apart from education, the school has the obligation to protect pupils from mistreatment by other children, and also to protect teachers themselves from violence by the few students whose conduct in recent years has prompted national concern. For me, it would be unreasonable and at odds with history to argue that the full panoply of constitutional rules applies with the same force and effect in the schoolhouse as it does in the enforcement of criminal laws.

JUSTICE BLACKMUN, concurring in the judgment....

...I write separately, because I believe the Court omits a crucial step in its analysis of whether a school search must be based upon probable cause. The Court correctly states that we have recognized limited exceptions to the probable-cause requirement "[w]here a careful balancing of governmental and private interests suggests that the public interest is best served" by a lesser standard. I believe that we have used such a balancing test, rather than strictly applying the Fourth Amendment's Warrant and Probable-Cause Clause, only when we were confronted with "a special law enforcement need for greater flexibility."...

The Court's implication that the balancing test is the rule rather than the exception is troubling for me because it is unnecessary in this case. The elementary and secondary school setting presents a special need for flexibility justifying a departure from the balance struck by the Framers.... Maintaining order in the classroom can be a difficult task. A single teacher often must watch over a large number of students, and, as any parent knows, children at certain ages are inclined to test the outer boundaries of acceptable conduct and to imitate the misbehavior of a peer if that misbehavior is not dealt with quickly.... Every adult remembers from his own schooldays the havoc a water pistol or peashooter can wreak until it is taken away.... Indeed, because drug use and possession of weapons have become increasingly common among young people, an immediate response frequently is required not just to maintain an environment conducive to learning, but to protect the very safety of students and school personnel.

Such immediate action obviously would not be possible if a teacher were required to secure a warrant before searching a student. Nor would it be possible if a teacher could not conduct a necessary search until the teacher thought there was probable cause for the search. A teacher has neither the training nor the day-to-day experience in the complexities of probable cause that a law enforcement officer possesses, and is ill-equipped to make a quick judgment about the existence of probable cause. The time required for a teacher to ask the questions or make the observations that are necessary to turn reasonable grounds into probable cause is time during which the teacher, and other students, are diverted from the essential task of education. A teacher's focus is, and should be, on teaching and helping students, rather than on developing evidence against a particular troublemaker....

...The special need for an immediate response to behavior that threatens either the safety of schoolchildren and teachers or the educational process itself justifies the Court in excepting school searches from the warrant and probable-cause requirement, and in applying a standard determined by balancing the relevant interests. I agree with the standard the Court has announced, and with its application of the standard to the facts of this case....

JUSTICE BRENNAN, with whom JUSTICE MARSHALL joins, concurring in part and dissenting in part.

I fully agree with Part II of the Court's opinion. Teachers, like all other government officials, must conform their conduct to the Fourth Amendment's protections of personal privacy and personal security....It would be incongruous and futile to charge teachers with the task of embuing their students with an understanding of our system of constitutional democracy, while at the same time immunizing those same teachers from the need to respect constitutional protections.

I do not, however, otherwise join the Court's opinion. Today's decision sanctions school officials to conduct full-scale searches on a "reasonableness" standard whose only definite content is that it is *not* the same test as the "probable cause" standard found in the text of the Fourth Amendment. In adopting this unclear, unprecedented, and unnecessary departure from generally applicable Fourth Amendment standards, the Court carves out a broad exception to standards that this Court has developed over years of considering Fourth Amendment problems....

I

Three basic principles underlie this Court's Fourth Amendment jurisprudence. First, warrantless searches are per se unreasonable, subject only to a few specifically delineated and well-recognized exceptions. Second, full-scale searches—whether conducted in accordance with the warrant requirement or pursuant to one of its exceptions—are "reasonable" in Fourth Amendment terms only on a showing of probable cause to believe that a crime has been committed and that evidence of the crime will be found in the place to be searched. Third, categories of intrusions that are substantially less intrusive than full-scale searches or seizures may be justifiable in accordance with a balancing test even absent a warrant or probable cause, provided that the balancing test used gives sufficient weight to the privacy interests that will be infringed.

Assistant Vice Principal Choplick's thorough excavation of T.L.O.'s purse was undoubtedly a serious intrusion on her privacy. The search at issue here encompassed a detailed and minute examination of respondent's pocketbook, in which the contents of private papers and letters were thoroughly scrutinized....

A

I agree that schoolteachers or principals, when not acting as agents of law enforcement authorities, generally may conduct a search of their students' belongings without first obtaining a warrant.... The Warrant Clause is something more than an exhortation to this Court to maximize social welfare as *we* see fit. It requires that the authorities must obtain a warrant before conducting a full-scale search. The undifferentiated governmental interest in law enforcement is insufficient to justify an exception to the warrant requirement. Rather, some *special* governmental interest beyond the need merely to apprehend lawbreakers is necessary to justify a categorical exception to the warrant requirement. For the most part, special governmental needs sufficient to override the warrant requirement flow from "exigency"—that is, from the press of time that makes obtaining a warrant either impossible or hopelessly infeasible. Only after finding an extraordinary governmental interest of this kind do we—or ought we—engage in a balancing test to determine if a warrant should nonetheless be required.

To require a showing of some extraordinary governmental interest before dispensing with the warrant requirement is not to undervalue society's need to apprehend violators of the criminal law. To be sure, forcing law enforcement personnel to obtain a warrant before engaging in a search will predictably deter the police from conducting some searches that they would otherwise like to conduct. But this is not an unintended *result* of the Fourth Amendment's protection of privacy; rather, it is the very *purpose* for which the Amendment was thought necessary....

In this case, such extraordinary governmental interests do exist and are sufficient to justify an exception to the warrant requirement. Students are necessarily confined for most of the school day in close proximity to each other and to the school staff. I agree with the Court that we can take judicial notice of the serious problems of drugs and violence that plague our schools. As JUSTICE BLACKMUN notes, teachers must not merely "maintain an environment conducive to learning" among children who "are inclined to test the outer boundaries of acceptable conduct," but must also "protect the very safety of students and school personnel." A teacher or principal could neither carry out essential teaching functions nor adequately protect students' safety if required to wait for a warrant before conducting a necessary search.

B

I emphatically disagree with the Court's decision to cast aside the constitutional probable-cause standard when assessing the constitutional validity of a schoolhouse search. The Court's decision jettisons the probable-cause standard—the only standard that finds support in the text of the Fourth Amendment—on the basis of its Rorschach-like "balancing test." Use of such a "balancing test" to determine the standard for evaluating the validity of a full-scale search represents a sizable innovation in Fourth Amendment analysis. This innovation finds support neither in precedent nor policy and portends a dangerous weakening of the purpose of the Fourth Amendment to protect the privacy and security of our citizens....

II

Applying the constitutional probable-cause standard to the facts of this case, I would find that Mr. Choplick's search violated T.L.O.'s Fourth Amendment rights. After escorting T.L.O. into his private office, Mr. Choplick demanded to see her purse. He then opened the purse to find evidence of whether she had been smoking in the bathroom. When he opened the purse, he discovered the pack of cigarettes. At this point, his search for evidence of the smoking violation was complete.

Mr. Choplick then noticed, below the cigarettes, a pack of cigarette rolling papers. Believing that such papers were "associated," with the use of marihuana, he proceeded to conduct a detailed examination of the contents of her purse, in which he found some marihuana, a pipe, some money, an index card, and some private letters indicating that T.L.O. had sold marihuana to other students....

On my view of the case, we need not decide whether the initial search conducted by Mr. Choplick—the search for evidence of the smoking violation that was completed when Mr. Choplick found the pack of cigarettes—was valid. For Mr. Choplick at that point did not have probable cause to continue to rummage through T.L.O.'s purse. Mr. Choplick's suspicion of marihuana possession at this time was based *solely* on the presence of the package of cigarette papers. The mere presence without more of such a staple item of commerce is insufficient to warrant a person of reasonable caution in inferring both that T.L.O. had violated the law by possessing marihuana and that evidence of that violation would be found in her purse. Just as a police officer could not obtain a warrant to search a home based solely on his claim that he had seen a package of cigarette papers in that home, Mr. Choplick was not entitled to search possibly the most private possessions of T.L.O. based on the mere presence of a package of cigarette papers. Therefore, the fruits of the illegal search must be excluded and the judgment of the New Jersey Supreme Court affirmed.

III...

On my view, the presence of the word "unreasonable" in the text of the Fourth Amendment does not grant a shifting majority of this Court the authority to answer *all* Fourth Amendment questions by consulting its momentary vision of the social good. Full-scale searches unaccompanied by probable cause violate the Fourth Amendment. I do not pretend that our traditional Fourth Amendment doctrine automatically answers all of the difficult legal questions that occasionally arise. I do contend, however, that this Court has an obligation to provide some coherent framework to resolve such questions on the basis of more than a conclusory recitation of the results of a "balancing test." The Fourth Amendment itself supplies that framework and, because the Court today fails to heed its message, I must respectfully dissent.

Justice Stevens, with whom Justice Marshall joins, and with whom Justice Brennan joins as to Part I, concurring in part and dissenting in part....

...Because T.L.O.'s suspected misconduct was not illegal and did not pose a serious threat to school discipline, the New Jersey Supreme Court held that Choplick's search of her purse was an unreasonable invasion of her privacy and that the evidence which he seized could not be used against her in criminal proceedings. The New Jersey court's holding was a careful response to the case it was required to decide.

The State of New Jersey sought review in this Court, first arguing that the exclusionary rule is wholly inapplicable to searches conducted by school officials, and then contending that the Fourth Amendment itself provides no protection at all to the student's privacy. The Court has accepted neither of these frontal assaults on the Fourth Amendment. It has, however, seized upon this "no smoking" case to announce "the proper standard" that should govern searches by school officials who are confronted with disciplinary problems far more severe than smoking in the restroom. Although I join Part II of the Court's opinion, I continue to believe that the Court has unnecessarily and inappropriately reached out to decide a constitutional question. More importantly, I fear that the concerns that motivated the Court's activism have produced a holding that will permit school administrators to search students suspected of violating only the most trivial school regulations and guidelines for behavior.

I

The question the Court decides today—whether Mr. Choplick's search of T.L.O.'s purse violated the Fourth Amendment—was not raised by the State's petition for writ of certiorari. That petition only raised one question: "Whether the Fourth Amendment's exclusionary rule applies to searches made by public school officials and teachers in school." The State quite properly declined to submit the former question because "[it] did not wish to present what might appear to be solely a factual dispute to this Court." Since this Court has twice had the threshold question argued, I believe that it should expressly consider the merits of the New Jersey Supreme Court's ruling that the exclusionary rule applies.

The New Jersey Supreme Court's holding on this question is plainly correct. As the state court noted, this case does not involve the use of evidence in a school disciplinary proceeding; the juvenile proceedings brought against T.L.O. involved a charge that would have been a criminal offense if committed by an adult. Accordingly, the exclusionary rule issue decided by that court and later presented to this Court concerned only the use in a criminal proceeding of evidence obtained in a search conducted by a public school administrator.

Having confined the issue to the law enforcement context, the New Jersey court then reasoned that this Court's cases have made it quite clear that the exclusionary rule is equally applicable "whether the public official who illegally obtained the evidence was a municipal inspector, or a school administrator or law enforcement official." It correctly concluded "that if an official search violates constitutional rights, the evidence is not admissible in criminal proceedings."

When a defendant in a criminal proceeding alleges that she was the victim of an illegal search by a school administrator, the application of the exclusionary rule is a simple corollary of the principle that "all evidence obtained by searches and seizures in violation of the Constitution is, by that same authority, inadmissible in a state court."...

Schools are places where we inculcate the values essential to the meaningful exercise of rights and responsibilities by a self-governing citizenry. If the Nation's students can be convicted through the use of arbitrary methods destructive of personal liberty, they cannot help but feel that they have been dealt with unfairly. The application of the exclusionary rule in criminal proceedings arising from illegal school searches makes an important statement to young people that "our society attaches serious consequences to a violation of constitutional rights," and that this is a principle of "liberty and justice for all."

Thus, the simple and correct answer to the question presented by the State's petition for certiorari would have required affirmance of a state court's judgment suppressing evidence. That result would have been dramatically out of character for a Court that not only grants prosecutors relief from suppression orders with distressing regularity, but also is prone to rely on grounds not advanced by the parties in order to protect evidence from exclusion. In characteristic disregard of the doctrine of judicial restraint, the Court avoided that result in this case by ordering reargument and directing the parties to address a constitutional question that the parties, with good reason, had not asked the Court to decide. Because judicial activism undermines the Court's power to perform its central mission in a legitimate way, I dissented from the reargument order. I have not modified the views expressed in that dissent, but since the majority has brought the question before us, I shall explain why I believe the Court has misapplied the standard of reasonableness embodied in the Fourth Amendment.

II

The search of a young woman's purse by a school administrator is a serious invasion of her legitimate expectations of privacy. A purse "is a common repository for one's personal effects and therefore is inevitably associated with the expectation of privacy." Although such expectations must sometimes yield to the legitimate requirements of government, in assessing the constitutionality of a warrantless search, our decision must be guided by the language of the Fourth Amendment.... In order to evaluate the reasonableness of such searches, "it is necessary 'first to focus upon the governmental interest which allegedly justifies official intrusion upon the constitutionally protected interests of the private citizen,' for there is 'no ready test for determining reasonableness other than by balancing the need to search [or seize] against the invasion which the search [or seizure] entails.'"

The "limited search for weapons" in *Terry* was justified by the "immediate interest of the police officer in taking steps to assure himself that the person with whom he is dealing is not armed with a weapon that could unexpectedly and fatally be used against him." 392 U.S., at 23, 25, 88 S.Ct., at 1881, 1882. When viewed from the institutional perspective, "the substantial need of teachers and administrators for freedom to maintain order in the schools," is no less acute. Violent, unlawful, or seriously disruptive conduct is fundamentally inconsistent with the principal function of teaching institutions which is to educate young people and prepare them for citizenship. When such conduct occurs amidst a sizable group of impressionable young people, it creates an explosive atmosphere that requires a prompt and effective response.

Thus, warrantless searches of students by school administrators are reasonable when undertaken for those purposes. But the majority's statement of the standard for evaluating the reasonableness of such searches is not suitably adapted to that end. The majority holds that "a search of a student by a teacher or other school official will be 'justified at its inception' when there are reasonable grounds for suspecting that the search will turn up evidence *that the student has violated or is violating* either the law or *the rules of the school.*" This standard will permit teachers and school administrators to search students when they suspect that the search will reveal evidence of even the most trivial school regulation or precatory guideline for student behavior. The Court's standard for deciding whether a search is justified "at its inception" treats all violations of the rules of the school as though they were fungible. For the Court, a search for curlers and sunglasses in order to enforce the school dress code is apparently just as important as a search for evidence of heroin addiction or violent gang activity.

... In arguing that teachers and school administrators need the power to search students based on a lessened standard, the United States as *amicus curiae* relies heavily on empirical evidence of a contemporary crisis of violence and unlawful behavior that is seriously undermining the process of education in American schools. A standard better attuned to this concern would permit teachers and school administrators to search a student when they have reason to believe that the search will uncover *evidence that the student is violating the law or engaging in conduct that is seriously disruptive of school order, or the educational process....*

The logic of distinguishing between minor and serious offenses in evaluating the reasonableness of school searches is almost too clear for argument. In order to justify the serious intrusion on the persons and privacy of young people that New Jersey asks this Court to approve, the State must identify "some real immediate and serious consequences." While school administrators have entirely legitimate reasons for adopting school regulations and guidelines for student behavior, the authorization of searches to enforce them "displays a shocking lack of all sense of proportion."...

...The Court's standard for evaluating the "scope" of reasonable school searches is obviously designed to prohibit physically intrusive searches of students by persons of the opposite sex for relatively minor offenses. The Court's effort to establish a standard that is, at once, clear enough to allow searches to be upheld in nearly every case, and flexible enough to prohibit obviously unreasonable intrusions of young adults' privacy only creates uncertainty in the extent of its resolve to prohibit the latter. Moreover, the majority's application of its standard in this case—to permit a male administrator to rummage through the purse of a female high school student in order to obtain evidence that she was smoking in a bathroom—raises grave doubts in my mind whether its effort will be effective. Unlike the Court, I believe the nature of the suspected infraction is a matter of first importance in deciding whether *any* invasion of privacy is permissible.

III...

...Like the New Jersey Supreme Court, I would view this case differently if the Assistant Vice Principal had reason to believe T.L.O.'s purse contained evidence of criminal activity, or of an activity that would seriously disrupt school discipline. There was, however, absolutely no basis for any such assumption—not even a "hunch."

In this case, Mr. Choplick overreacted to what appeared to be nothing more than a minor infraction—a rule prohibiting smoking in the bathroom of the freshmen's and sophomores' building. It is, of course, true that he actually found evidence of serious wrongdoing by T.L.O., but no one claims that the prior search may be justified by his unexpected discovery. As far as the smoking infraction is concerned, the search for cigarettes merely tended to corroborate a teacher's eyewitness account of T.L.O.'s violation of a minor regulation designed to channel student smoking behavior into designated locations. Because this conduct was neither unlawful nor significantly disruptive of school order or the educational process, the invasion of privacy associated with the forcible opening of T.L.O.'s purse was entirely unjustified at its inception....

...The rule the Court adopts today is so open-ended that it may make the Fourth Amendment virtually meaningless in the school context. Although I agree that school administrators must have broad latitude to maintain order and discipline in our classrooms, that authority is not unlimited.

IV

The schoolroom is the first opportunity most citizens have to experience the power of government. Through it passes every citizen and public official, from schoolteachers to policemen and prison guards. The values they learn there, they take with them in life. One of our most cherished ideals is the one contained in the Fourth Amendment: that the government may not intrude on the personal privacy of its citizens without a warrant or compelling circumstance. The Court's decision today is a curious moral for the Nation's youth. Although the search of T.L.O.'s purse does not trouble today's majority, I submit that we are not dealing with "matters relatively trivial to the welfare of the Nation. There are village tyrants as well as village Hampdens, but none who acts under color of law is beyond reach of the Constitution."

I respectfully dissent.

NOTES AND QUESTIONS

1. The Court first articulated what has come to be called the special-needs doctrine in *T.L.O.* Generally speaking, the police or other governmental agents must have probable cause and a warrant to engage in searches and seizures. Nevertheless, there are instances in which the police need not obtain a warrant or even have probable cause prior to conducting a search or a seizure. The special needs exception to the warrant and probable-cause requirements applies when special needs beyond the normal need for law enforcement make the warrant and/or probable-cause requirements impracticable. What are the special needs articulated by the *T.L.O.* Court that justified the search? When does the rule apply?

2. Why do Justices Powell and O'Connor concur? Is their view of the relationship between teacher and pupil correct? Why or why not?

3. What is the basis for Justice Brennan's dissent? Is he correct? Does the Court create a new Fourth Amendment doctrine?

4. Justice Stevens articulates an alternative standard for resolving these cases. What is it? How would it work in practice? Is it more likely to protect the Fourth Amendment rights of schoolchildren?

5. Is Justice Blackmun correct when he says that the "Court omits a crucial step in its analysis of whether a school search must be based upon probable cause"? What is that crucial step? Consider Justice Blackmun's concurrence when reading the following excerpt.

BOARD OF EDUCATION OF INDEPENDENT SCHOOL DISTRICT NO. 92 V. EARLS
Supreme Court of the United States
536 U.S. 822 (2002)

Justice Thomas delivered the opinion of the Court....

I

The city of Tecumseh, Oklahoma, is a rural community located approximately 40 miles southeast of Oklahoma City. The School District administers all Tecumseh public schools. In the fall of 1998, the School District adopted the Student Activities Drug Testing Policy (Policy), which requires all middle and high school students to consent to drug testing in order to participate in any extracurricular activity. In practice, the Policy has been applied only to competitive extracurricular activities sanctioned by the Oklahoma Secondary Schools Activities Association, such as the Academic Team, Future Farmers of America, Future Homemakers of America, band, choir, pom-pom, cheerleading, and athletics. Under the Policy, students are required to take a drug test before participating in an extracurricular activity, must submit to random drug testing while participating in that activity, and must agree to be tested at any time upon reasonable suspicion. The urinalysis tests are designed to detect only the use of illegal drugs, including amphetamines, marijuana, cocaine, opiates, and [barbiturates], not medical conditions or the presence of authorized prescription medications.

At the time of their suit, both respondents attended Tecumseh High School. Respondent Lindsay Earls was a member of the show choir, the marching band, the Academic Team, and the National Honor Society. Respondent Daniel James sought to participate in the Academic Team. Together with their parents, Earls and James brought a...42 U.S.C. § 1983, action against the School District, challenging the Policy both on its face and as applied to their participation in extracurricular activities. They alleged that the Policy violates the Fourth Amendment as incorporated by the Fourteenth Amendment and requested injunctive and declarative relief. They also argued that the School District failed to identify a special need for testing students who participate in extracurricular activities, and that the "Drug Testing Policy neither addresses a proven problem nor promises to bring any benefit to students or the school."

Applying the principles articulated in *Vernonia School Dist. 47J v. Acton,* 515 U.S. 646 (1995), in which we upheld the suspicionless drug testing of school athletes, the United States District Court for the Western District of Oklahoma rejected respondents' claim that the Policy was unconstitutional and granted summary judgment to the School District. The court noted that "special needs" exist in the public school context and that, although the School District did "not show a drug problem of epidemic proportions," there was a history of drug abuse starting in 1970 that presented "legitimate cause for concern." 115 F.Supp.2d 1281, 1287 (2000). The District Court also held that the Policy was effective because "[i]t can scarcely be disputed that the drug problem among the student body is effectively addressed by making sure that the large number of students participating in competitive, extracurricular activities do not use drugs." *Id.*, at 1295.

The United States Court of Appeals for the Tenth Circuit reversed, holding that the Policy violated the Fourth Amendment. The Court of Appeals agreed with the District Court that the Policy must be evaluated in the "unique environment of the school setting," but reached a different conclusion as to the Policy's constitutionality. 242 F.3d 1264, 1270 (2001). Before imposing a suspicionless drug testing program, the Court of Appeals concluded that a school "must demonstrate that there is some identifiable drug abuse problem among a sufficient number of those subject to the testing, such that testing that group of students will actually redress its drug problem." *Id.*, at 1278. The Court of Appeals then held that because the School District failed to demonstrate such a problem existed among Tecumseh students participating in competitive extracurricular activities, the Policy was unconstitutional. We granted certiorari, 534 U.S. 1015, 122 S.Ct. 509, 151 L.Ed.2d 418 (2001), and now reverse....

II...

Given that the School District's Policy is not in any way related to the conduct of criminal investigations,...respondents do not contend that the School District requires probable cause before testing students for drug use. Respondents instead argue that drug testing must be based at least on some level of individualized suspicion. It is true that we generally determine the reasonableness of a search by balancing the nature of the intrusion on the individual's privacy against the promotion of legitimate governmental interests. But we have long held that "the Fourth Amendment imposes no irreducible requirement of [individualized] suspicion." "[I]n certain limited circumstances, the Government's need to discover such latent or hidden conditions, or to prevent their development, is sufficiently compelling to justify the intrusion on privacy entailed by conducting such searches without any measure of individualized suspicion." Therefore, in the context of safety and administrative regulations, a search unsupported by probable cause may be reasonable "when 'special needs, beyond the normal need for law enforcement, make the warrant and probable-cause requirement impracticable.'"

Significantly, this Court has previously held that "special needs" inhere in the public school context. See *Vernonia*, *supra*, at 653; *T.L.O.*, *supra*, at 339–340. While schoolchildren do not shed their constitutional rights when they enter the schoolhouse, see *Tinker v. Des Moines Independent Community School Dist.*, 393 U.S. 503, 506 (1969), "Fourth Amendment rights...are different in public schools than elsewhere; the 'reasonableness' inquiry cannot disregard the schools' custodial and tutelary responsibility for children." *Vernonia*, 515 U.S., at 656. In particular, a finding of individualized suspicion may not be necessary when a school conducts drug testing.

In *Vernonia*, this Court held that the suspicionless drug testing of athletes was constitutional. The Court, however, did not simply authorize all school drug testing, but rather conducted a fact-specific balancing of the intrusion on the children's Fourth Amendment rights against the promotion of legitimate governmental interests. See *id.*, at 652–653. Applying the principles of *Vernonia* to the somewhat different facts of this case, we conclude that Tecumseh's Policy is also constitutional.

A

We first consider the nature of the privacy interest allegedly compromised by the drug testing....

Respondents argue that because children participating in nonathletic extracurricular activities are not subject to regular physicals and communal undress, they have a stronger expectation of privacy than the athletes tested in *Vernonia*. This distinction, however, was not essential to our decision in *Vernonia*, which depended primarily upon the school's custodial responsibility and authority.

In any event, students who participate in competitive extracurricular activities voluntarily subject themselves to many of the same intrusions on their privacy as do athletes. Some of these clubs and activities require occasional off-campus travel and communal undress. All of them have their own rules and requirements for participating students that do not apply to the student body as a whole. For example, each of the competitive extracurricular activities governed by the Policy must abide by the rules of the Oklahoma Secondary Schools Activities Association, and a faculty sponsor monitors the students for compliance with the various rules dictated by the clubs and activities....This regulation of extracurricular activities further diminishes the expectation of privacy among schoolchildren....We therefore conclude that the students affected by this Policy have a limited expectation of privacy.

B

Next, we consider the character of the intrusion imposed by the Policy. See *Vernonia*, *supra*, at 658. Urination is "an excretory function traditionally shielded by great privacy." [*Skinner v. Railway Executives' Assn.*, 489 U.S. 602, 626 (1989)]. But the "degree of intrusion" on one's privacy caused by collecting a urine sample "depends upon the manner in which production of the urine sample is monitored."

Under the Policy, a faculty monitor waits outside the closed restroom stall for the student to produce a sample and must "listen for the normal sounds of urination in order to guard against tampered specimens and to insure an accurate chain of custody." The monitor then pours the sample into two bottles that are sealed and placed into a mailing pouch along with a consent form signed by the student. This procedure is virtually identical to that reviewed in *Vernonia*, except that it additionally protects privacy by allowing male students to produce their samples behind a closed stall. Given that we considered the method of collection in *Vernonia* a "negligible" intrusion, 515 U.S., at 658, the method here is even less problematic.

In addition, the Policy clearly requires that the test results be kept in confidential files separate from a student's other educational records and released to school personnel only on a "need to know" basis. Respondents nonetheless contend that the intrusion on students' privacy is significant because the Policy fails to protect effectively against the disclosure of confidential information and, specifically, that the school "has been careless in protecting that information: for example, the Choir teacher looked at students' prescription drug lists and left them where other students could see them." Brief for Respondents 24. But the choir teacher is someone with a "need to know," because during off-campus trips she needs to know what medications are taken by her students. Even before the Policy was enacted the choir teacher had access to this information. In any event, there is no allegation that any other student did see such information. This one example of alleged carelessness hardly increases the character of the intrusion.

Moreover, the test results are not turned over to any law enforcement authority. Nor do the test results here lead to the imposition of discipline or have any academic consequences. *Cf. Vernonia*, *supra*, at 658, and n. 2. Rather, the only consequence of a failed drug test is to limit the student's privilege of participating in extracurricular activities. Indeed, a student may test positive for drugs twice and still be allowed to participate in extracurricular activities. After the first positive test, the school contacts the student's parent or guardian for a meeting. The student may continue to participate in the activity if within five days of the meeting the student shows proof of receiving drug counseling and submits to a second drug test in two weeks. For the second positive test, the student is suspended from participation in all extracurricular activities for 14 days, must complete four hours of substance abuse counseling, and must submit to monthly drug tests. Only after a third positive test will the student be suspended from participating in any extracurricular activity for the remainder of the school year, or 88 school days, whichever is longer.

Given the minimally intrusive nature of the sample collection and the limited uses to which the test results are put, we conclude that the invasion of students' privacy is not significant.

C

Finally, this Court must consider the nature and immediacy of the government's concerns and the efficacy of the Policy in meeting them. See *Vernonia*, 515 U.S., at 660. This Court has already articulated in detail the importance of the governmental concern in preventing drug use by schoolchildren. See, *id.*, at 661–662. The drug abuse problem among our Nation's youth has hardly abated since *Vernonia* was decided in 1995. In fact, evidence suggests that it has only grown worse. As in *Vernonia*, "the necessity for the state to act is magnified by the fact that this evil is being visited not just upon individuals at large, but upon children for whom it has undertaken a special responsibility of care and direction." *Id.*, at 662. The health and safety risks identified in *Vernonia* apply with equal force to Tecumseh's children. Indeed, the nationwide drug epidemic makes the war against drugs a pressing concern in every school.

Additionally, the School District in this case has presented specific evidence of drug use at Tecumseh schools. Teachers testified that they had seen students who appeared to be under the influence of drugs and that they had heard students speaking openly about using drugs. A drug dog found marijuana cigarettes near the school parking lot. Police officers once found drugs or drug paraphernalia in a car driven by a Future Farmers of America member. And the school board president reported that people in the community were calling the board to discuss the "drug situation."...

...We have recognized...that "[a] demonstrated problem of drug abuse... [is] not in all cases necessary to the validity of a testing regime," but that some showing does "shore up an assertion of special need for a suspicionless general search program." The School District has provided sufficient evidence to shore up the need for its drug testing program.

Furthermore, this Court has not required a particularized or pervasive drug problem before allowing the government to conduct suspicionless drug testing. For instance, in [*Treasury Employees v. Von Raab*, 489 U.S. 656 (1989)], the Court upheld the drug testing of customs officials on a purely preventive basis, without any documented history of drug use by such officials. In response to the lack of evidence relating to drug use, the Court noted generally that "drug abuse is one of the most serious problems confronting our society today," and that programs to prevent and detect drug use among customs officials could not be deemed unreasonable. *Id.* at 674....

Given the nationwide epidemic of drug use, and the evidence of increased drug use in Tecumseh schools, it was entirely reasonable for the School District to enact this particular drug testing policy....

We also reject respondents' argument that drug testing must presumptively be based upon an individualized reasonable suspicion of wrongdoing because such a testing regime would be less intrusive. In this context, the Fourth Amendment does not require a finding of individualized suspicion, and we decline to impose such a requirement on schools attempting to prevent and detect drug use by students....

Finally, we find that testing students who participate in extracurricular activities is a reasonably effective means of addressing the School District's legitimate concerns in preventing, deterring, and detecting drug use. While in *Vernonia* there might have been a closer fit between the testing of athletes and the trial court's finding that the drug problem was "fueled by the 'role model' effect of athletes' drug use," such a finding was not essential to the holding. 515 U.S., at 663. *Vernoni*a did not require the school to test the group of students most likely to use drugs, but rather considered the constitutionality of the program in the context of the public school's custodial responsibilities....

III

Within the limits of the Fourth Amendment, local school boards must assess the desirability of drug testing schoolchildren. In upholding the constitutionality of the Policy, we express no opinion as to its wisdom. Rather, we hold only that Tecumseh's Policy is a reasonable means of furthering the School District's important interest in preventing and deterring drug use among its schoolchildren. Accordingly, we reverse the judgment of the Court of Appeals.

Justice Breyer, concurring.

I agree with the Court that *Vernonia School Dist. 47J v. Acton*, 515 U.S. 646 (1995), governs this case and requires reversal of the Tenth Circuit's decision....I reach this conclusion primarily for the reasons given by the Court, but I would emphasize several underlying considerations, which I understand to be consistent with the Court's opinion.

I...

...First, the drug problem in our Nation's schools is serious in terms of size, the kinds of drugs being used, and the consequences of that use both for our children and the rest of us....

Second, the government's emphasis upon supply side interdiction apparently has not reduced teenage use in recent years....

Third, public school systems must find effective ways to deal with this problem. Today's public expects its schools not simply to teach the fundamentals, but "to shoulder the burden of feeding students breakfast and lunch, offering before and after school child care services, and providing medical and psychological services," all in a school environment that is safe and encourages learning....

Fourth, the program at issue here seeks to discourage demand for drugs by changing the school's environment in order to combat the single most important factor leading schoolchildren to take drugs, namely, peer pressure. It offers the adolescent a nonthreatening reason to decline his friend's drug-use invitations, namely, that he intends to play baseball, participate in debate, join the band, or engage in any one of half a dozen useful, interesting, and important activities.

II

In respect to the privacy-related burden that the drug testing program imposes upon students, I would emphasize the following: First, not everyone would agree with this Court's characterization of the privacy-related significance of urine sampling as "'negligible.'"...I believe it important that the school board provided an opportunity for the airing of these differences at public meetings designed to give the entire community "the opportunity to be able to participate" in developing the drug policy....

Second, the testing program avoids subjecting the entire school to testing....

Third, a contrary reading of the Constitution, as requiring "individualized suspicion" in this public school context, could well lead schools to push the boundaries of "individualized suspicion" to its outer limits, using subjective criteria that may "unfairly target members of unpopular groups," or leave those whose behavior is slightly abnormal stigmatized in the minds of others....

I cannot know whether the school's drug testing program will work. But, in my view, the Constitution does not prohibit the effort. Emphasizing the considerations I have mentioned, along with others to which the Court refers, I conclude that the school's drug testing program, constitutionally speaking, is not "unreasonable."...

Justice O'Connnor, with whom Justice Souter joins, dissenting.

I dissented in *Vernonia*,...and continue to believe that case was wrongly decided. Because *Vernonia* is now this Court's precedent, and because I agree that petitioners' program fails even under the balancing approach adopted in that case, I join Justice Ginsburg's dissent.

Justice Ginsburg, with whom Justice Stevens, Justice O'Connor, and Justice Souter join, dissenting.

Seven years ago, in *Vernonia School Dist. 47J v. Acton*, 515 U.S. 646 (1995), this Court determined that a school district's policy of randomly testing the urine of its student athletes for illicit drugs did not violate the Fourth Amendment. In so ruling, the Court emphasized that drug use "increase[d] the risk of sports-related injury" and that Vernonia's athletes were the "leaders" of an aggressive local "drug culture" that had reached "'epidemic proportions.'" *Id.*, at 649. Today, the Court relies upon *Vernonia* to permit a school district with a drug problem its superintendent repeatedly described as "not…major" to test the urine of an academic team member solely by reason of her participation in a nonathletic, competitive extracurricular activity—participation associated with neither special dangers from, nor particular predilections for, drug use.…

I

A

A search unsupported by probable cause nevertheless may be consistent with the Fourth Amendment "when special needs, beyond the normal need for law enforcement, make the warrant and probable-cause requirement impracticable." In *Vernonia*, this Court made clear that "such 'special needs'…exist in the public school context." 515 U.S., at 653.…The *Vernonia* Court concluded that a public school district facing a disruptive and explosive drug abuse problem sparked by members of its athletic teams had "special needs" that justified suspicionless testing of district athletes as a condition of their athletic participation.

This case presents circumstances dispositively different from those of *Vernonia*. True, as the Court stresses, Tecumseh students participating in competitive extracurricular activities other than athletics share two relevant characteristics with the athletes of *Vernonia*. First, both groups attend public schools.…Concern for student health and safety is basic to the school's caretaking.…

Those risks, however, are present for *all* schoolchildren. *Vernonia* cannot be read to endorse invasive and suspicionless drug testing of all students upon any evidence of drug use, solely because drugs jeopardize the life and health of those who use them.…

The second commonality to which the Court points is the voluntary character of both interscholastic athletics and other competitive extracurricular activities.

The comparison is enlightening. While extracurricular activities are "voluntary" in the sense that they are not required for graduation, they are part of the school's educational program; for that reason, the petitioner is justified in expending public resources to make them available. Participation in such activities is a key component of school life, essential in reality for students applying to college, and, for all participants, a significant contributor to the breadth and quality of the educational experience. Students "volunteer" for extracurricular pursuits in the same way they might volunteer for honors classes: They subject themselves to additional requirements, but they do so in order to take full advantage of the education offered them.

Voluntary participation in athletics has a distinctly different dimension: Schools regulate student athletes discretely because competitive school sports by their nature require communal undress and, more important, expose students to physical risks that schools have a duty to mitigate. For the very reason that schools cannot offer a program of competitive athletics without intimately affecting the privacy of students, *Vernonia* reasonably analogized school athletes to "adults who choose to participate in a closely regulated industry."…

In short, *Vernonia* applied, it did not repudiate, the principle that "the legality of a search of a student should depend simply on the reasonableness, *under all the circumstances*, of the search." *T.L.O.*, 469 U.S., at 341 (emphasis added). Enrollment in a public school, and election to participate in school activities beyond the bare minimum that the curriculum requires, are indeed factors relevant to reasonableness, but they do not on their own justify intrusive, suspicionless searches. *Vernonia*, accordingly, did not rest upon these factors; instead, the Court performed what today's majority aptly describes as a "fact-specific balancing."... Balancing of that order, applied to the facts now before the Court, should yield a result other than the one the Court announces today.

B

In this case... Lindsay Earls and her parents allege that the School District handled personal information collected under the policy carelessly, with little regard for its confidentiality. Information about students' prescription drug use, they assert, was routinely viewed by Lindsay's choir teacher, who left files containing the information unlocked and unsealed, where others, including students, could see them; and test results were given out to all activity sponsors whether or not they had a clear "need to know."...

... [T]he "nature and immediacy of the governmental concern," *Vernonia*, 515 U.S., at 660, faced by the Vernonia School District dwarfed that confronting Tecumseh administrators. Vernonia initiated its drug testing policy in response to an alarming situation: "[A] large segment of the student body, particularly those involved in interscholastic athletics, was in a state of rebellion...." *Id.*, at 649. Tecumseh, by contrast, repeatedly reported to the Federal Government during the period leading up to the adoption of the policy that "types of drugs [other than alcohol and tobacco] including controlled dangerous substances, are present [in the schools] but have not identified themselves as major problems at this time." As the Tenth Circuit observed, "without a demonstrated drug abuse problem among the group being tested, the efficacy of the District's solution to its perceived problem is... greatly diminished." 242 F.3d, at 1277.

Not only did the Vernonia and Tecumseh districts confront drug problems of distinctly different magnitudes, they also chose different solutions: Vernonia limited its policy to athletes; Tecumseh indiscriminately subjected to testing all participants in competitive extracurricular activities. Urging that "the safety interest furthered by drug testing is undoubtedly substantial for all children, athletes and nonathletes alike,"... the Court cuts out an element essential to the *Vernonia* judgment. Citing medical literature on the effects of combining illicit drug use with physical exertion, the *Vernonia* Court emphasized that "the particular drugs screened by [Vernonia's] Policy have been demonstrated to pose substantial physical risks to athletes." 515 U.S., at 662.

At the margins, of course, no policy of *random* drug testing is perfectly tailored to the harms it seeks to address. The School District cites the dangers faced by members of the band, who must "perform extremely precise routines with heavy equipment and instruments in close proximity to other students," and by Future Farmers of America, who "are required to individually control and restrain animals as large as 1500 pounds." For its part, the United States acknowledges that "the linebacker faces a greater risk of serious injury if he takes the field under the influence of drugs than the drummer in the halftime band," but parries that "the risk of injury to a student who is under the influence of drugs while playing golf, cross country, or volleyball (sports covered by the policy in *Vernonia*) is scarcely any greater than the risk of injury to a student...handling a 1500-pound steer...or working with cutlery or other sharp instruments." One can demur to the Government's view of the risks drug use poses to golfers, for golfers were surely as marginal among the linebackers, sprinters, and basketball players targeted for testing in *Vernonia* as steer-handlers are among the choristers, musicians, and academic-team members subject to urinalysis in Tecumseh. Notwithstanding nightmarish images of out-of-control flatware, livestock run amok, and colliding tubas disturbing the peace and quiet of Tecumseh, the great majority of students the School District seeks to test in truth are engaged in activities that are not safety sensitive to an unusual degree. There is a difference between imperfect tailoring and no tailoring at all.

The Vernonia district, in sum, had two good reasons for testing athletes: Sports team members faced special health risks and they "were the leaders of the drug culture." *Vernonia*, 515 U.S., at 649. No similar reason, and no other tenable justification, explains Tecumseh's decision to target for testing all participants in every competitive extracurricular activity.

Nationwide, students who participate in extracurricular activities are significantly less likely to develop substance abuse problems than are their less-involved peers. See, e.g., N. Zill, C. Nord, & L. Loomis, Adolescent Time Use, Risky Behavior, and Outcomes 52 (1995) (tenth graders "who reported spending no time in school-sponsored activities were...49 percent more likely to have used drugs" than those who spent 1–4 hours per week in such activities). Even if students might be deterred from drug use in order to preserve their extracurricular eligibility, it is at least as likely that other students might forgo their extracurricular involvement in order to avoid detection of their drug use. Tecumseh's policy thus falls short doubly if deterrence is its aim: It invades the privacy of students who need deterrence least, and risks steering students at greatest risk for substance abuse away from extracurricular involvement that potentially may palliate drug problems.

To summarize, this case resembles *Vernonia* only in that the School Districts in both cases conditioned engagement in activities outside the obligatory curriculum on random subjection to urinalysis. The defining characteristics of the two programs, however, are entirely dissimilar. The Vernonia district sought to test a subpopulation of students distinguished by their reduced expectation of privacy, their special susceptibility to drug-related injury, and their heavy involvement with drug use. The Tecumseh district seeks to test a much larger population associated with none of these factors. It does so, moreover, without carefully safeguarding student confidentiality and without regard to the program's untoward effects. A program so sweeping is not sheltered by *Vernonia*; its unreasonable reach renders it impermissible under the Fourth Amendment.

II...

It is a sad irony that the petitioning School District seeks to justify its edict here by trumpeting "the schools' custodial and tutelary responsibility for children." *Vernonia*, 515 U.S., at 656. In regulating an athletic program or endeavoring to combat an exploding drug epidemic, a school's custodial obligations may permit searches that would otherwise unacceptably abridge students' rights. When custodial duties are not ascendant, however, schools' tutelary obligations to their students require them to "teach by example" by avoiding symbolic measures that diminish constitutional protections. "That [schools] are educating the young for citizenship is reason for scrupulous protection of Constitutional freedoms of the individual, if we are not to strangle the free mind at its source and teach youth to discount important principles of our government as mere platitudes." *West Virginia Bd. of Ed. v. Barnette*, 319 U.S. 624, 637 (1943).

For the reasons stated, I would affirm the judgment of the Tenth Circuit declaring the testing policy at issue unconstitutional.

NOTES AND QUESTIONS

1. After the Court's decision in *Earls*, are there any limits placed on searches and seizures conducted by school officials? If so, what are they?

2. Is Justice Thomas correct when he says that the distinction between athletes' and nonathletes' privacy decision in *Vernonia* was not essential to the Court's decision, "which depended primarily upon the school's custodial responsibility and authority"? Do you also agree that the invasion of privacy is "negligible"?

3. Justice Ginsburg concurred in *Acton* but dissented in *Earls*. Can these two decisions be reconciled? Ginsburg also cites a study that finds that students who engage in extracurricular activities are less likely to use drugs. Is this persuasive? What else would you like to know about the study?

4. Does *Earls* effectively overrule *T.L.O.*? Why or why not?

5. *Locker searches.* May schools search student lockers? If so, does the search violate the students' legitimate expectations of privacy? Consider the following excerpt from *State v. Jones*, 666 N.W.2d 142, 147–148 (Iowa 2003):

> Some courts have concluded that there is no expectation of privacy in a student locker, particularly in situations in which there exists a school or state regulation specifically disclaiming any privacy right. *See In re Patrick Y.*, 358 Md. 50, 746 A.2d 405, 414 (2000); *Shoemaker v. State*, 971 S.W.2d 178, 182 (Tex.App. 1998); *In re Isiah B.*, 176 Wis.2d 639, 500 N.W.2d 637, 641 (1993); *see also Zamora v. Pomeroy*, 639 F.2d 662, 670–71 (10th Cir. 1981); *State v. Stein*, 203 Kan. 638, 456 P.2d 1, 3 (1969); *People v. Overton*, 24 N.Y.2d 522, 301 N.Y.S.2d 479, 249 N.E.2d 366, 368 (1969). Other courts have concluded that a student does have a legitimate expectation of privacy in the contents of a school locker, even if a school or state regulation exists. *See In re Interest of S.C.*, 583 So.2d 188, 191-92 (Miss. 1991); *In re Adam*, 120 Ohio App.3d 364, 697 N.E.2d 1100, 1106–07 (1997); *In re Dumas*, 357 Pa.Super. 294, 515 A.2d 984, 985-86 (1986); *see also Commonwealth v. Snyder*, 413 Mass. 521, 597 N.E.2d 1363, 1366 (1992); *State v. Joseph T.*, 175 W.Va. 598, 336 S.E.2d 728, 736 (1985); *In re Isiah B.*, 500 N.W.2d at 648 (Bablitch, J., concurring) ("Negating a constitutional 'expectation' of privacy based upon whether or not a person was notified of the impending search sets a dangerous precedent for intrusions upon Fourth Amendment rights").

Which view is the better one? What are the implications if students have no legitimate expectations of privacy in their lockers?

If there is a legitimate expectation of privacy, does the standard articulated in *T.L.O.* or in *Acton* and *Earls* apply? In *In re Juvenile 2006-406*, 931 A.2d 1229 (2007), an assistant principal, acting on information received from students and passed on to him by a teacher that the juvenile had a "large pot pipe," searched the juvenile's locker and discovered the pipe, marijuana, a lighter, and thirty-two dollars in cash. Despite the fact that mere possession of drug paraphernalia is not unlawful, the New Hampshire Supreme Court upheld the search. Noting that the standard articulated in *T.L.O.* governs searches by public school officials, the court found that the search was justified at its inception because the assistant principal had "reasonable grounds for suspecting that a search of places where a large pot pipe might be located would also turn up marijuana.... Moreover, given the age of the student (fifteen years old), and the moderate degree of intrusiveness of the search and its primary objective (the detection of marijuana in association with a large pot pipe)," the scope of the search was permissible.

On the other hand, in *State v. Jones, supra*, a local high school conducted an annual "pre-winter break cleanout" of lockers. Three to four days before the cleanout, students were asked to report to their lockers at an assigned time so that the locker contents could be surveyed by a faculty member. About 300 of the 1,700 students failed to report at the assigned time, so the following day, school aides opened the remaining lockers. In the locker belonging to Marzel Jones, aides found only a blue jacket. Feeling the contents of the pocket, the aides felt what proved to be a bag of marijuana. Jones subsequently was charged with possession of a controlled substance. The Iowa Supreme Court found that while students had a legitimate expectation of privacy in their lockers, despite the existence of a school district policy and state law authorizing locker searches, a random search conducted without individualized suspicion was reasonable under the standard enunciated in *Earls*.

Does it really matter which standard is applied? Why?

6. *Metal detectors, magnetometers, and wands.* May a school require students to pass through a metal detector every time they enter the school building? In *People v. Pruitt*, 662 N.E.2d 540 (Ill. App. 1996), the court said:

> Magnetometers, or metal detectors, have become standard equipment in airports and public buildings. They are used to detect concealed weapons. When conducted by public officers, a metal detector walk-through is a search for Fourth Amendment purposes. *McMorris v. Alioto* (9th Cir. 1978), 567 F.2d 897 (persons entering a state courthouse required to walk through metal detectors); *United States v. Epperson* (4th Cir.1972), 454 F.2d 769 (airport passengers required to walk through metal detectors to reach airplanes).
>
> Performing a search is "the very purpose and function of a magnetometer: to search for metal and disclose its presence in areas where there is a normal expectation of privacy." *Epperson*, 454 F.2d at 770.
>
> Airport and courthouse metal detector searches are regularly upheld when challenged. Courts take judicial notice that threats of violence have been directed to these public buildings. See *United States v. Cyzewski* (5th Cir. 1973), 484 F.2d 509. These threats are balanced against the minimally intrusive nature of a metal detector search. The conclusion, invariably, is that the search, administrative in nature, satisfied the Fourth Amendment's basic concern of reasonableness.

Pruitt, 662 N.E.2d at 545.

Does it matter if the state has a compulsory attendance law requiring students to attend school? Again, consider *Pruitt*:

> Defendant contends the airport and courthouse cases do not apply here because those cases are based on consent. That is, the individuals facing a metal detector walk-through in an airport or courthouse can choose to turn around. Pruitt was required by law to attend school. He was given no notice that the metal detectors were inside the schools. He had no choice.
>
> Whether airline passengers and lawyers and litigants who are due to appear in courtrooms have any real choice is a serious question we need not answer. We note, however, that

> the lawyers who argued this case were required to walk through metal detectors in order to reach the courtroom.
>
> We do not believe the absence of consent has any real impact on the balancing test we are required to conduct in this school search case. The *T.L.O.* decision tells us to strike a balance between the schoolchild's legitimate expectation of privacy and the schools' equally legitimate need to maintain a safe learning environment. *T.L.O.*, 469 U.S. at 340, 105 S.Ct. at 742, 83 L.Ed.2d at 733. Consent or lack of it is not part of the equation.
>
> Eleven years ago, in *T.L.O.*, the Supreme Court observed that "...drug use and violent crime in the schools have become major social problems." *T.L.O.*, 469 U.S. at 339, 105 S.Ct. at 741, 83 L.Ed.2d at 733.
>
> We long for the time when children did not have to pass through metal detectors on their way to class, when hall monitors were other children, not armed guards, when students dressed for school without worrying about gang colors. Those were the days when sharp words, crumpled balls of paper, and, at worst, the bully's fists were the weapons of choice.

Pruitt, 662 N.E.2d at 545. Do you agree? If a student does not walk through the metal detector, does that give school officials grounds to search the student? If the student was required to attend an after-school program and the student arrived late, so that the hand-held wand was no longer available, would school officials have grounds to search the student? See *Commonwealth v. Smith*, 889 N.E.2d 439 (Mass. App. 2008); *D.I.R. v. State*, 683 N.E.2d 251 (Ind. App. 1997).

7. *Canine sniffs.* In *Doran v. Contoocook Valley School District*, 616 F.Supp.2d 184 (D.N.H. 2009), school officials, believing that there was a drug problem at the local high school, arranged for local police to conduct a sweep of the school using drug-sniffing dogs. At the designated time, teachers told students to exit the building, leave their personal belongings behind, and proceed to the football field. Students were not told the reason for the drill, nor were they free to leave the field for the duration of the search. In the meantime, New Hampshire State Police arrived with two police dogs and conducted the sweep. The dogs alerted eight times, and school officials decided whether or not they would search the identified belongings. No illegal substances were uncovered (apparently to the surprise of the local police chief). In a subsequent action challenging the constitutionality of the search on Fourth Amendment grounds, the court stated:

> The first issue is whether a search implicating the Fourth Amendment occurred when the defendants used drug dogs to sniff the school grounds and personal property of students at ConVal High....
>
> Courts across this country have taken up the issue of drug detection dog sniffs in a variety of circumstances. The existing precedents, those binding on this court and those merely persuasive, leave little doubt that the mere use of trained drug dogs on school grounds to sniff students' personal items does not qualify as a search within the meaning of the Fourth Amendment. When confronted with cases involving dog sniffs for illegal drugs in other contexts, the United States Supreme Court has repeatedly concluded that the Fourth Amendment is not implicated by such searches. *See, e.g., Illinois v. Caballes*, 543 U.S. 405, 409, 125 S.Ct. 834, 160 L.Ed.2d 842 (2005) ("[T]he use of a well-trained narcotics-detection canine—one that 'does not expose noncontraband items that otherwise would remain hidden from public view,' during a lawful traffic stop, generally does not implicate legitimate privacy interests....Any intrusion on respondent's privacy expectations does not rise to the level of a constitutionally cognizable infringement" [internal citations omitted]); *City of Indianapolis v. Edmond*, 531 U.S. 32, 40, 121 S.Ct. 447, 148 L.Ed.2d 333 (2000) ("It is well established that a vehicle stop at a highway checkpoint effectuates a seizure within the meaning of the Fourth

Amendment…a sniff by a dog that simply walks around a car is 'much less intrusive than a typical search'"); *United States v. Place*, 462 U.S. 696, 707, 103 S.Ct. 2637, 77 L.Ed.2d 110 ("[W]e conclude that the particular course of investigation that the agents intended to pursue here—exposure of respondent's luggage, which was located in a public place, to a trained canine—did not constitute a 'search' within the meaning of the Fourth Amendment").

Similarly, in *United States v. Esquilin*, the U.S. Court of Appeals for the First Circuit held that a canine sniff of a hotel room—wherein the canine sniffed furniture and a retail clothing bag—was not a search. 208 F.3d 315, 318 (1st Cir. 2000). In applying the holding of *United States v. Place*, the First Circuit noted that the essential factor in the analysis is whether "the observing person or the sniffing canine are legally present at their vantage when their respective senses are aroused by obviously incriminating evidence." *Id.* (quoting *United States v. Reed*, 141 F.3d 644, 649 [6th Cir.1998]). Other courts of appeals have followed suit. *See, e.g., United States v. Hayes*, 551 F.3d 138, 145 (2d Cir. 2008) ("[D]efendant has no legitimate expectation of privacy in the front yard of his home insofar as the presence of the scent of narcotics in the air was capable of being sniffed by the police canine"); *Reed*, 141 F.3d at 649 ("[T]he limiting and discriminating nature of a sniff does 'not constitute a search within the meaning of the Fourth Amendment'"); *Jennings v. Joshua Indep. Sch. Dist.*, 877 F.2d 313, 316 (5th Cir. 1989) ("The use of trained canines to sniff automobiles parked on public parking lots does not constitute a search within the meaning of the fourth amendment"); *Horton*, 690 F.2d at 477 (dog sniff of school lockers not a search under the Fourth Amendment).

The same principles guiding the courts' decisions that canine sniffs of school lockers, cars, and luggage are not searches within the meaning of the Fourth Amendment apply to the sniffs of students' personal belongings as well. A canine sniff of personal belongings "does not expose noncontraband items that otherwise would remain hidden from public view." *Place*, 462 U.S. at 707, 103 S.Ct. 2637; *see Horton* [*v. Goose Creek Independent School District*,] 690 F.2d [470,] at 477 [(5th Cir. 1982)]. It is less intrusive than the typical search because it does not require an officer to rummage through one's bags. *See Doe v. Little Rock Sch. Dist.*, 380 F.3d 349, 355 (8th Cir. 2004) ("Full-scale searches that involve people rummaging through personal belongings concealed within a container are manifestly more intrusive than searches effected by using metal detectors or dogs"). Moreover, a canine sniff only identifies the presence or absence of narcotics, and this limited disclosure ensures "that the owner of the property is not subjected to the embarrassment and inconvenience entailed in less discriminate and more intrusive investigative methods." *Place*, 462 U.S. at 707, 103 S.Ct. 2637. Of course, sniffs of one's person raise an entirely distinct—and more problematic—set of issues. *See B.C. v. Plumas Unified Sch. Dist.*, 192 F.3d 1260, 1267 (9th Cir. 1999) (noting that because "the body and its odors are highly personal," canine sniffs of one's person are "highly intrusive"). The facts at issue here, however, do not require the court to wade into these troubled waters, because canine sniffs of property implicate none of those concerns. Plaintiff's students were not illegally searched in violation of their Fourth Amendment rights.

Id. at 191–193. What does the court mean when it says that sniffs of a person raise "more problematic" issues? If a drug-sniffing dog alerts, does that provide reasonable suspicion warranting a search of the student's person? See *Horton v. Goose Creek Independent School Dist.*, 690 F.2d 470 (5th Cir. 1982).

8. *Parked cars.* If a student drives to school, does that mean that the student has a diminished expectation of privacy in that vehicle? Generally, courts have applied the two-pronged test of *T.L.O.* requiring reasonable suspicion in deciding whether to uphold the search of student vehicles

at school. See *State v. Best*, 2010 WL 363502 (N.J. 2010) (upholding search of vehicle based on reasonable suspicion that juvenile had provided another student with prescription drug); *Butler v. Rio Rancho Pub. Sch. Bd. of Educ.*, 245 F.Supp.2d 1188, 1200 (D.N.M. 2002), rev'd and remanded on other grounds, 341 F.3d 1197 (10th Cir. 2003) (search of vehicle driven to school by juvenile but belonging to juvenile's brother, in which weapons were found, based on reasonable suspicion); *Anders v. Fort Wayne Cmty. Schs.*, 124 F.Supp.2d 618, 622–623 (N.D.Ind. 2000) (search of vehicle in school lot supported by reasonable suspicion where school resource officer thought juvenile had violated school rules by going outside without a pass and skipping class); *Shamberg v. State*, 762 P.2d 488, 492 (Alaska Ct.App. 1988) (reasonable suspicion to search vehicle where safety officer believed juvenile was intoxicated and had come to school in his car in that condition); *In re P.E.A.*, 754 P.2d 382, 388 (Colo. 1988) (search of juvenile's vehicle supported by reasonable suspicion where student reported that two other minors were selling marijuana in school, searches of persons and lockers turned up no evidence of drugs, but one of them had ridden in juvenile's vehicle that morning); *State v. Williams*, 791 N.E.2d 608, 611–612 (2003) (search of juvenile's vehicle based on reasonable suspicion where another student informed school that juvenile had handgun used in a burglary in juvenile's vehicle); *Covington County v. G.W.*, 767 So.2d 187, 192–194 (Miss. 2000) (based on tip from student that juvenile had been drinking beer in school parking lot, school officials had reasonable suspicion to search juvenile's vehicle); *In re Michael R.*, 11 Neb.App. 903, 662 N.W.2d 632, 637 (2003) (school official hearing juvenile tell another student he had "big bags" gave official reasonable suspicion to believe that juvenile was selling marijuana, thus search of person, which uncovered no contraband, and subsequent search of vehicle based on reasonable suspicion constitutionally permissible); *F.S.E. v. State*, 993 P.2d 771, 772 (Okla.Crim.App. 1999) (school official who smelled marijuana on juvenile had reasonable suspicion to search juvenile's vehicle for evidence of drugs); and *State v. Slattery*, 56 Wash.App. 787 P.2d 932, 933–934 (1990) (school officials had reasonable suspicion to search juvenile's vehicle where student had informed them that juvenile was selling marijuana in school parking lot).

Problem. The high school secretary informed the assistant vice principal that a student was leaving school early to attend a funeral. The assistant principal was suspicious of the student's motives for leaving because of an earlier conversation in which the student had indicated that he did not sell drugs—on campus. The assistant vice principal contacted the juvenile's relatives and learned that he was not attending a funeral. Believing that the student was trying to skip school, he searched the student's person, his locker, and eventually his vehicle, and these searches did not turn up any evidence of contraband. Later, although the minor did not consent to the search of his car, in order to obtain a parking permit to park his vehicle in the school parking lot, he had to consent to a search of its contents. The search of the juvenile's car produced marijuana, and the minor was charged with possession of a controlled substance. The minor filed a motion to suppress the drugs. If you were the trial judge, would you grant or deny the motion? Why?

9. *Who is a school official? T.L.O.*, *Acton*, and *Earls* all apply to searches conducted by school officials. But who are school officials? Consider this excerpt from *R.D.S. v. State*, 245 S.W.3d 356, 367–368 (Tenn. 2008):

> Since *T.L.O.* was decided, there has been an increasing presence of law enforcement officers in public schools through a variety of programs and arrangements aimed at combating crime and providing students with a safe and secure learning environment. Michael Pinard, *From the Classroom to the Courtroom: Reassessing Fourth Amendment Standards in Public School Searches Involving Law Enforcement Authorities*, 45 Ariz. L.Rev. 1067, 1067–68

(2003) ("Pinard"); *see generally* Jacqueline A. Stefkovich & Judith A. Miller, *Law Enforcement Officers in Public Schools: Student Citizens in Safe Havens?* 1999 BYU Educ. & L.J. 25, 31–32 (1999). Many local governments have elected to blend the traditional duties of school officials and law enforcement officers in an effort to protect students and teachers. One such program is the national School Resource Officer program, which places law enforcement officers in schools to perform traditional law enforcement duties in addition to teaching law enforcement-related classes and counseling students "based on the expertise of a law enforcement officer." Other programs place law enforcement officers in schools "through liaison programs between public schools and local police departments," or "outside of physically placing officers in schools, some…school districts have forged interdependent relationships between school officials and local police departments." Pinard, 45 Ariz. L. Rev. at 1068.

Increasingly, SROs and other law enforcement officers are becoming more involved in searches on school premises. The majority of jurisdictions which have faced the issue of what standard to apply to SROs or law enforcement officers assigned to schools have applied the reasonable suspicion standard. *See, e.g., People v. Dilworth*, 169 Ill.2d 195, 214 Ill.Dec. 456, 661 N.E.2d 310, 317 (1996) (holding that reasonable suspicion applies to liaison officer searching on own initiative); *Commonwealth v. J.B.*, 719 A.2d 1058, 1062 (Pa.Super.Ct. 1998) (holding that searches of public school students conducted by school police officers are subject to reasonable suspicion standard); *Russell v. State*, 74 S.W.3d 887, 891 (Tex.App. 2002) (applying reasonableness standard to officer assigned to school); *In re Angelia D.B.*, 211 Wis.2d 140, 564 N.W.2d 682, 690 (1997) (holding that the reasonable grounds standard applied to search conducted by officer at request of and in conjunction with school officials). *But see A.J.M. v. State*, 617 So.2d 1137, 1138 (Fla.Dist.Ct.App. 1993) (holding that a school resource officer employed by sheriff's office must have probable cause to search); *Patman v. State*, 244 Ga.App. 833, 537 S.E.2d 118, 120 (2000) (holding that a police officer working special duty at a high school must have probable cause).

These courts have considered such facts as whether the law enforcement officer was in uniform, had an office on the school's campus, and how long each day the officer remained at the school. *See T.S. v. State*, 863 N.E.2d 362, 369 (Ind.App. 2007); *In re William V.*, 111 Cal.App.4th 1464, 4 Cal.Rptr.3d 695, 697 (2003). The Indiana Supreme Court in *Dilworth* relied in part upon a school handbook that delineated the duties of the school liaison officer. 214 Ill.Dec. 456, 661 N.E.2d at 320. Additionally, the Florida District Court of Appeals cited a Florida statute outlining the duties of law enforcement officers assigned to the schools. *See State v. N.G.B.*, 806 So.2d 567, 568 (Fla.Dist.Ct.App. 2002) (citing Fla. Stat. § 1006.12 [2001] replaced by Fla. Stat. § 1006.12 [2003]). Another important consideration is whether the law enforcement officer is employed by the school system or an independent law enforcement agency. *See T.S.*, 863 N.E.2d at 369 (noting that the school liaison officer was employed by the Indianapolis Public School Police); *State v. D.S.*, 685 So.2d 41, 43 (Fla.Dist.Ct.App. 1996) (noting that the law enforcement officer conducting the challenged search was employed by the local school system and not by an independent municipal or county law enforcement agency).

In contrast, where law enforcement officers, not associated with the school system, initiate a search, or where school officials act at the behest of law enforcement agencies, the probable cause standard is generally applied. *See, e.g., F.P. v. State*, 528 So.2d 1253, 1254 (Fla.Dist.Ct.App. 1988) (holding that the "school official exception" to the probable cause requirement does not apply when search is carried out at direction of police); *State v. Tywayne H.*, 123 N.M. 42, 933 P.2d 251, 254 (Ct.App. 1997) (holding that probable cause was required when a search was conducted completely at the discretion of the police officers); *In re Thomas B.D.*, 326 S.C. 614, 486

S.E.2d 498, 499–500 (Ct.App. 1997) (holding that probable cause was required when police conducted a search in furtherance of law enforcement objective, rather than on behalf of school).

School officials and law enforcement officers play fundamentally different roles in our society. A school official's basic task is to educate students in a safe environment, whereas a law enforcement officer's primary duty is to detect and deter crime. Law enforcement officers must generally satisfy the higher probable cause standard in order to conduct a search, because they stand in an adversarial role to citizens and the punishment for violating a criminal statute is more severe than the consequences of violating a school regulation.

10. *Consent to search.* In *Schneckloth v. Bustamonte*, 412 U.S. 218 (1973), the United States Supreme Court held that voluntary consent to a search is an exception to the warrant requirement. A court faced with an alleged consent search must examine the facts of the event to determine if the consent was voluntary under the totality of the circumstances and not the result of police coercion. *Id.* at 227, 229. The state has the burden of proving that consent was voluntarily given, although the state need not prove that the defendant knew that he had the right to refuse consent as a prerequisite to demonstrating that consent was voluntary. *Id.* at 232–233. Nor must the police warn of the right to refuse consent. *Id.* at 231–232. Although no one factor is determinative, the court may consider the defendant's age, intelligence, and lack of education, along with the circumstances surrounding the securing of the consent. *Id.* at 226–227.

Given a minor's age and vulnerability, may a minor consent to a search by law enforcement? Typically, courts have applied the totality of the circumstances test, acknowledging that age is but one factor for the court to consider. See, e.g., *In Interest of R.A.*, 937 P.2d 731 (Colo. 1997) (in considering validity of consent, age and presence of parents are factors but not to be given any greater weight than any other factor when considering totality of circumstances); *In re Trader*, 1993 WL 265173, at *3 (Del. Fam. Ct. Mar. 29, 1993) (holding that sixteen-year-old boy voluntarily consented to search; while offender's young age was relevant, police officer did not act in "intimidating, overbearing or coercive fashion" and juvenile's actions during stop and search did "not fit the personality profile of an individual whose will was being overborne" by police officer); *State v. C.S.*, 632 So. 2d 675, 675 (Fla. Dist. Ct. App. 1994) (considering totality of circumstances, juvenile's consent to police officer's search of his automobile was voluntary because facts that defendant was a minor, officer had youth's license and registration, and youth responded quickly to officer's request were outweighed by facts that initial stop was lawful, officer was nonthreatening, and officer advised juvenile that he could refuse consent); *In re Clinton G.*, 669 N.W.2d 467 (Neb. App. 2003) (consent to search juvenile's person voluntary where no evidence of duress, coercion, threat, or promise made by law enforcement); *City of Fargo v. Ellison*, 635 N.W.2d 151 (N.D. 2001) (consent involuntary where minor twice attempted to end conversation with police at her door, once by attempting to close door and once by retreating from open door and withdrawing within her apartment, and that she consented to police entry and search only after she was threatened with both arrest and handcuffing); *In Interest of Jermaine*, 582 A.2d 1058 (Pa. Super. 1990) (age of juvenile [sixteen and a half] at time approached by police officer in Penn Station does not alone render consent involuntary); *In re L.C.*, 2003 WL 21241582 (Tex. App. 2003) (consent to search juvenile's person voluntary despite officer's persistent attempts to determine consent). But see *In re J.M.*, 619 A.2d 497 (D.C. 1992) (remanding to trial court judge to make explicit findings regarding significance of age on minor's ability to consent); *State v. Allen*, 612 P.2d 199 (Mont. 1980) (finding minor lacked capacity to consent to search where police failed to inform juvenile of her rights under

Montana Youth Court Act, which required police to inform minor of her rights and to obtain waiver of rights on agreement of minor and her parents or on advice of counsel).

May third parties consent to a search? A third party with common authority over the item to be searched may provide valid consent, through either actual or apparent authority. *United States v. Matlock*, 415 U.S. 164, 171 (1974). Common authority is based on mutual use of property by persons generally having joint access or control. Third-party consent derives its legitimacy from the concept of assumption of risk: "Common authority is, of course, not to be implied from the mere property interest a third party has in the property. The authority which justifies the third-party consent does not rest upon the law of property…but rests rather on mutual use of the property by persons generally having joint access or control for most purposes, so that it is reasonable to recognize that any of the co-inhabitants has the right to permit the inspection in his own right and that the others have assumed the risk that one of their number might permit the common area to be searched." *Id.* at 171, n. 7. It is also possible for the police to rely on the apparent authority of a third party to justify a warrantless search. When the police are mistaken about the actual authority of a third party to grant consent, the entry will not be constitutionally unreasonable if the officers' belief in the legal capacity of the third party to give consent is reasonable. *Illinois v. Rodriguez*, 497 U.S. 177, 186 (1990). A parent-child relationship raises a presumption of shared authority to consent; thus, courts have upheld the authority of a minor child to consent to a search when the minor has common authority and mutual use of the property or item to be searched. See George Blum, Annotation, *Admissibility of Evidence Discovered in Search of Adult Defendant's Property or Residence Authorized by Defendant's Minor Child—State Cases*, 51 A.L.R. 5th 425 (1997). Generally, "there is no *per se* rule that all minors lack the authority to consent to a search." *Abdella v. O'Toole*, 343 F.Supp.2d 129, 135 (D. Conn. 2004). Youth is simply one factor to be considered when assessing the validity of the child's consent. See *State v. Tomlinson*, 648 N.W.2d 367, 376 (Wis. 2002) ("[w]hether the child possesses such authority will depend on a number of factors, and courts must look at the totality of the circumstances to make such a determination"); *State v. Butzke*, 584 N.W.2d 449, 458 (Neb. App. 1998) (the court must analyze voluntariness and common authority over the premises, or whether law enforcement reasonably believed the child had apparent authority); *State v. Kriegh*, 937 P.2d 453, 457 (Kan. App. 1997) ("[a]lthough age is a factor to consider in ascertaining whether consent was given willingly, minority status alone does not prevent one from giving consent"); *State v. Will*, 885 P.2d 715, 720 (Or. App. 1994) ("age is *merely one factor* to be considered in determining the scope of the minor's authority to consent and whether the minor's consent was knowing and voluntary" [citation omitted]); *Saavedra v. State*, 622 So.2d 952, 956 (Fla. 1993) ("the State must show by clear and convincing evidence from the totality of the circumstances that the minor gave free and voluntary consent"); *Davis v. State*, 262 Ga. 578, 422 S.E.2d 546, 549 (Ga. 1992) (a court must "examine a child's mental maturity and his ability to understand the circumstances in which he is placed, and the consequences of his actions"); and *People v. Jacobs*, 729 P.2d 757, 764 (Cal. 1987) ("[a]s a child advances in age she acquires greater discretion to admit visitors on her own authority"). On the other hand, at least one court has found that age is never a factor in determining the voluntariness of consent. *Lenz v. Winburn*, 51 F.3d 1540, 1543 (11th Cir. 1995). But see *State v. Schwarz*, 136 P.3d 989 (Mont. 2006) (child under the age of 16 lacks capacity or authority to consent to search of parents' home).

Parents, too, have the authority to consent to a search of their child's property. Often the justification for the search of a minor's belongings is grounded in the notion that the parent is still exercising parental control and authority, that the parent has access to the child's bedroom, or that the area to be searched is in common usage. A parent's right to consent may even prevail over the objections of the minor. Wayne R. LaFave, Jerold H. Israel, Nancy J. King, Orin S. Kerr, 2 Criminal Procedure § 3.10(e) (2009). But see *In re S.L.M.*, 206 P.3d 283 (Or. App. 2009) (mother acted as agent of police when police "encouraged" her to dump contents of child's purse on back seat of police car although child had refused to consent to search of purse).

Is a child deemed to have consented to a search of her locker, belongings, and vehicle simply by bringing them onto school grounds? Some school districts have an official school policy that grants school officials an implied consent to search a student's property or a student's belongings while the student is at school. Does this comport with the Fourth Amendment?

Do school officials have authority to consent to a search by law enforcement of a student or a student's belongings? Consider the facts in *Lopera v. Town of Coventry*, 652 F.Supp.2d 203, 209–210 (D. R.I. 2009):

> On September 28, 2006, the Central Falls High School boys soccer team played an away game against Coventry High School. The Central Falls team arrived by bus. Before the game began, five or six Central Falls players used the bathrooms located inside the Coventry boys locker room. While inside, one of the Central Falls players noticed a security guard keeping an eye on them.
>
> The game was played and resulted in a tie. After the game, Coach Marchand (the Central Falls coach) sent his team to the bus and followed behind them. Before Coach Marchand reached the bus, approximately twenty players from the Coventry football team stopped him, and in profanity-laced terms accused the Central Falls players of stealing electronic devices (iPods and cell phones) from the Coventry locker room.
>
> Coach Marchand told the football players that he would get to the bottom of the allegation and had them follow him to the team bus. The Central Falls players already were on the bus waiting to leave. Coach Marchand entered the bus and told his players: "everybody needs to put their game bag, varsity bag and their book bags...on their laps." The coach and his assistant coach then searched each bag for the alleged stolen items. If one of his players had an iPod or cell phone, Coach Marchand asked for proof of ownership. In his deposition, he characterized the search as a good one—"I think we did a Columbo search, you know, CSI." The entire search took twenty to twenty-five minutes and none of the missing items were found.
>
> When Coach Marchand exited the bus, the original group of twenty football players had grown to about fifty or sixty students and adults. The Coventry Athletic Director was also waiting. According to Coach Marchand, at this point the crowd was extremely vocal, shouting derogatory and racist remarks at his team and threatening not to disperse until the missing items were found.
>
> As Coach Marchand began to discuss the situation with the Coventry Athletic Director, the four Defendant police officers arrived on scene. The officers entered the parking lot with sirens wailing and "boxed-in" the bus with their police cruisers. Coach Marchand and the Athletic Director then brought the officers up to speed on the situation. Coach Marchand informed the officers that the crowd suspected his team of stealing (or in the coach's own words: that his players were the "prime suspects"). A discussion ensued and at some point, after a "pregnant pause" in the conversation, the topic of whether the officers could do their own search came up. The parties agree it was at this point Coach Marchand consented to another search of his players. (In his deposition, however, Coach Marchand explained that he only consented because he felt compelled to do so under the circumstances.)

> After obtaining Coach Marchand's consent, the officers ordered the Central Falls players to exit the bus with their belongings and stand with their backs against the bus. Up to this point, the police officers made little to no effort to quell or disperse the crowd, even as the crowd verbally assailed the players shouting racist epithets and accusations of theft.[2]
>
> The search of the players began with the officers ordering each player to step forward one at a time with his bag. The officers then sorted through the contents of each bag on the hood of a police cruiser. If one of the officers discovered an iPod or cell phone, he held it up for the crowd to see—purportedly to allow the "victims" a chance to identify the stolen property. Some of the boys were asked to stretch their waist band and lift their shirt so the officers could make sure they were not hiding anything, and a few of the boys were subjected to pat down searches. The entire search by the police, all of which took place in front of the angry mob, lasted approximately one hour and none of the missing items were found.
>
> Undeterred, the mob persisted in its boorish behavior, even after the search ended. Concerned that the mob would take matters into its own hands, the officers in classic too little, too late fashion decided for safety reasons to escort the bus out of town.

On what basis, if any, could the consent to search be justified?

11. *Strip searches.*

SAFFORD UNIFIED SCHOOL DISTRICT #1 V. REDDING
Supreme Court of the United States
129 S.Ct. 2633 (2009)

JUSTICE SOUTER delivered the opinion of the Court.

The issue here is whether a 13-year-old student's Fourth Amendment right was violated when she was subjected to a search of her bra and underpants by school officials acting on reasonable suspicion that she had brought forbidden prescription and over-the-counter drugs to school. Because there were no reasons to suspect the drugs presented a danger or were concealed in her underwear, we hold that the search did violate the Constitution, but because there is reason to question the clarity with which the right was established, the official who ordered the unconstitutional search is entitled to qualified immunity from liability.

I

The events immediately prior to the search in question began in 13-year-old Savana Redding's math class at Safford Middle School one October day in 2003. The assistant principal of the school, Kerry Wilson, came into the room and asked Savana to go to his office. There, he showed her a day planner, unzipped and open flat on his desk, in which there were several knives, lighters, a permanent marker, and a cigarette. Wilson asked Savana whether the planner

2. For example, one player heard a woman in the crowd call the boys "spics." Coach Marchand testified that people in the crowd used phrases like "those people," "they're good at hiding things," "they're sneaky, you know it," and made reference to the boys being from "the ghetto."

was hers; she said it was, but that a few days before she had lent it to her friend, Marissa Glines. Savana stated that none of the items in the planner belonged to her.

Wilson then showed Savana four white prescription-strength ibuprofen 400-mg pills, and one over-the-counter blue naproxen 200-mg pill, all used for pain and inflammation but banned under school rules without advance permission. He asked Savana if she knew anything about the pills. Savana answered that she did not. Wilson then told Savana that he had received a report that she was giving these pills to fellow students; Savana denied it and agreed to let Wilson search her belongings. Helen Romero, an administrative assistant, came into the office, and together with Wilson they searched Savana's backpack, finding nothing.

At that point, Wilson instructed Romero to take Savana to the school nurse's office to search her clothes for pills. Romero and the nurse, Peggy Schwallier, asked Savana to remove her jacket, socks, and shoes, leaving her in stretch pants and a T-shirt (both without pockets), which she was then asked to remove. Finally, Savana was told to pull her bra out and to the side and shake it, and to pull out the elastic on her underpants, thus exposing her breasts and pelvic area to some degree. No pills were found.

Savana's mother filed suit against Safford Unified School District #1, Wilson, Romero, and Schwallier for conducting a strip search in violation of Savana's Fourth Amendment rights. The individuals (hereinafter petitioners) moved for summary judgment, raising a defense of qualified immunity. The District Court for the District of Arizona granted the motion on the ground that there was no Fourth Amendment violation, and a panel of the Ninth Circuit affirmed. 504 F.3d 828 (2007)....

...[T]he Ninth Circuit held that the strip search was unjustified under the Fourth Amendment test for searches of children by school officials set out in *New Jersey v. T.L.O.*, 469 U.S. 325 (1985). The Circuit then applied the test for qualified immunity, and found that Savana's right was clearly established at the time of the search: "'[t]hese notions of personal privacy are "clearly established" in that they inhere in all of us, particularly middle school teenagers, and are inherent in the privacy component of the Fourth Amendment's proscription against unreasonable searches.'" *Id.*, at 1088–1089 (quoting *Brannum v. Overton Cty. School Bd.*, 516 F.3d 489, 499 [C.A.6 2008])....

II...

III

A

In this case, the school's policies strictly prohibit the nonmedical use, possession, or sale of any drug on school grounds, including "'[a]ny prescription or over-the-counter drug, except those for which permission to use in school has been granted pursuant to Board policy.'" A week before Savana was searched, another student, Jordan Romero (no relation of the school's administrative assistant), told the principal and Assistant Principal Wilson that "certain students were bringing drugs and weapons on campus," and that he had been sick after taking some pills that "he got from a classmate." On the morning of October 8, the same boy handed Wilson a white pill that he said Marissa Glines had given him. He told Wilson that students were planning to take the pills at lunch.

Wilson learned from Peggy Schwallier, the school nurse, that the pill was Ibuprofen 400 mg, available only by prescription. Wilson then called Marissa out of class. Outside the classroom, Marissa's teacher handed Wilson the day planner, found within Marissa's reach, containing various contraband items. Wilson escorted Marissa back to his office.

In the presence of Helen Romero, Wilson requested Marissa to turn out her pockets and open her wallet. Marissa produced a blue pill, several white ones, and a razor blade. Wilson asked where the blue pill came from, and Marissa answered, "'I guess it slipped in when *she* gave me the IBU 400s.'" *Id.*, at 13a. When Wilson asked whom she meant, Marissa replied, "'Savana Redding.'" Ibid. Wilson then enquired about the day planner and its contents; Marissa denied knowing anything about them. Wilson did not ask Marissa any followup questions to determine whether there was any likelihood that Savana presently had pills: neither asking when Marissa received the pills from Savana nor where Savana might be hiding them.

Schwallier did not immediately recognize the blue pill, but information provided through a poison control hotline indicated that the pill was a 200-mg dose of an anti-inflammatory drug, generically called naproxen, available over the counter. At Wilson's direction, Marissa was then subjected to a search of her bra and underpants by Romero and Schwallier, as Savana was later on. The search revealed no additional pills.

It was at this juncture that Wilson called Savana into his office and showed her the day planner. Their conversation established that Savana and Marissa were on friendly terms: while she denied knowledge of the contraband, Savana admitted that the day planner was hers and that she had lent it to Marissa. Wilson had other reports of their friendship from staff members, who had identified Savana and Marissa as part of an unusually rowdy group at the school's opening dance in August, during which alcohol and cigarettes were found in the girls' bathroom. Wilson had reason to connect the girls with this contraband, for Wilson knew that Jordan Romero had told the principal that before the dance, he had been at a party at Savana's house where alcohol was served. Marissa's statement that the pills came from Savana was thus sufficiently plausible to warrant suspicion that Savana was involved in pill distribution.

This suspicion of Wilson's was enough to justify a search of Savana's backpack and outer clothing.[3] If a student is reasonably suspected of giving out contraband pills, she is reasonably suspected of carrying them on her person and in the carryall that has become an item of student uniform in most places today. If Wilson's reasonable suspicion of pill distribution were not understood to support searches of outer clothes and backpack, it would not justify any search worth making. And the look into Savana's bag, in her presence and in the relative privacy of Wilson's office, was not excessively intrusive, any more than Romero's subsequent search of her outer clothing.

B

Here it is that the parties part company, with Savana's claim that extending the search at Wilson's behest to the point of making her pull out her underwear was constitutionally unreasonable. The exact label for this final step in the intrusion is not important, though strip search is a fair way to speak of it.... Although Romero and Schwallier stated that they did not see anything when Savana followed their instructions, we would not define strip search and its Fourth Amendment consequences in a way that would guarantee litigation about who was looking and

3. There is no question here that justification for the school officials' search was required in accordance with the *T.L.O.* standard of reasonable suspicion, for it is common ground that Savana had a reasonable expectation of privacy covering the personal things she chose to carry in her backpack, cf. 469 U.S., at 339, and that Wilson's decision to look through it was a "search" within the meaning of the Fourth Amendment.

how much was seen. The very fact of Savana's pulling her underwear away from her body in the presence of the two officials who were able to see her necessarily exposed her breasts and pelvic area to some degree, and both subjective and reasonable societal expectations of personal privacy support the treatment of such a search as categorically distinct, requiring distinct elements of justification on the part of school authorities for going beyond a search of outer clothing and belongings.

Savana's subjective expectation of privacy against such a search is inherent in her account of it as embarrassing, frightening, and humiliating. The reasonableness of her expectation (required by the Fourth Amendment standard) is indicated by the consistent experiences of other young people similarly searched, whose adolescent vulnerability intensifies the patent intrusiveness of the exposure. See Brief for National Association of Social Workers et al. as *Amici Curiae* 6–14; Hyman & Perone, The Other Side of School Violence: Educator Policies and Practices That May Contribute to Student Misbehavior, 36 J. School Psychology 7, 13 (1998) (strip search can "result in serious emotional damage"). The common reaction of these adolescents simply registers the obviously different meaning of a search exposing the body from the experience of nakedness or near undress in other school circumstances. Changing for gym is getting ready for play; exposing for a search is responding to an accusation reserved for suspected wrongdoers and fairly understood as so degrading that a number of communities have decided that strip searches in schools are never reasonable and have banned them no matter what the facts may be, see, e.g., New York City Dept. of Education, Reg. No. A-432, p. 2 (2005), online at http://docs.nycenet.edu/docushare/dsweb/Get/Document-21/A-432.pdf ("Under no circumstances shall a strip-search of a student be conducted").

The indignity of the search does not, of course, outlaw it, but it does implicate the rule of reasonableness as stated in *T.L.O.*, that "the search as actually conducted [be] reasonably related in scope to the circumstances which justified the interference in the first place." 469 U.S., at 341 (internal quotation marks omitted). The scope will be permissible, that is, when it is "not excessively intrusive in light of the age and sex of the student and the nature of the infraction." *Id.*, at 342.

Here, the content of the suspicion failed to match the degree of intrusion. Wilson knew beforehand that the pills were prescription-strength ibuprofen and over-the-counter naproxen, common pain relievers equivalent to two Advil, or one Aleve. He must have been aware of the nature and limited threat of the specific drugs he was searching for, and while just about anything can be taken in quantities that will do real harm, Wilson had no reason to suspect that large amounts of the drugs were being passed around, or that individual students were receiving great numbers of pills.

Nor could Wilson have suspected that Savana was hiding common painkillers in her underwear. Petitioners suggest, as a truth universally acknowledged, that "students... hid[e] contraband in or under their clothing," ... and cite a smattering of cases of students with contraband in their underwear. But when the categorically extreme intrusiveness of a search down to the body of an adolescent requires some justification in suspected facts, general background possibilities fall short; a reasonable search that extensive calls for suspicion that it will pay off. But nondangerous school contraband does not raise the specter of stashes in intimate places, and there is no evidence in the record of any general practice among Safford Middle School students of hiding that sort of thing in underwear; neither Jordan nor Marissa suggested to Wilson that Savana was doing that, and the preceding search of Marissa that Wilson ordered yielded nothing. Wilson never even determined when Marissa had received the pills from Savana; if it had been a few days before, that would weigh heavily against any reasonable conclusion that Savana presently had the pills on her person, much less in her underwear.

In sum, what was missing from the suspected facts that pointed to Savana was any indication of danger to the students from the power of the drugs or their quantity, and any reason to suppose that Savana was carrying pills in her underwear. We think that the combination of these deficiencies was fatal to finding the search reasonable....

We do mean, though, to make it clear that the *T.L.O.* concern to limit a school search to reasonable scope requires the support of reasonable suspicion of danger or of resort to underwear for hiding evidence of wrongdoing before a search can reasonably make the quantum leap from outer clothes and backpacks to exposure of intimate parts. The meaning of such a search, and the degradation its subject may reasonably feel, place a search that intrusive in a category of its own demanding its own specific suspicions.

IV

A school official searching a student is "entitled to qualified immunity where clearly established law does not show that the search violated the Fourth Amendment."...To be established clearly, however, there is no need that "the very action in question [have] previously been held unlawful."...The unconstitutionality of outrageous conduct obviously will be unconstitutional, this being the reason, as Judge Posner has said, that "[t]he easiest cases don't even arise."...But even as to action less than an outrage, "officials can still be on notice that their conduct violates established law...in novel factual circumstances." *Hope v. Pelzer,* 536 U.S. 730, 741 (2002).

T.L.O. directed school officials to limit the intrusiveness of a search, "in light of the age and sex of the student and the nature of the infraction," 469 U.S., at 342, and as we have just said at some length, the intrusiveness of the strip search here cannot be seen as justifiably related to the circumstances. But we realize that the lower courts have reached divergent conclusions regarding how the *T.L.O.* standard applies to such searches.

A number of judges have read *T.L.O.* as the en banc minority of the Ninth Circuit did here. The Sixth Circuit upheld a strip search of a high school student for a drug, without any suspicion that drugs were hidden next to her body. *Williams v. Ellington*, 936 F.2d 881, 882–883, 887 (1991). And other courts considering qualified immunity for strip searches have read *T.L.O.* as "a series of abstractions, on the one hand, and a declaration of seeming deference to the judgments of school officials, on the other," *Jenkins v. Talladega City Bd. of Ed.*, 115 F.3d 821, 828 (C.A.11 1997) (en banc), which made it impossible "to establish clearly the contours of a Fourth Amendment right...[in] the wide variety of possible school settings different from those involved in *T.L.O.*" itself. Ibid. See also *Thomas v. Roberts*, 323 F.3d 950 (C.A.11 2003) (granting qualified immunity to a teacher and police officer who conducted a group strip search of a fifth grade class when looking for a missing $26).

We think these differences of opinion from our own are substantial enough to require immunity for the school officials in this case. We would not suggest that entitlement to qualified immunity is the guaranteed product of disuniform views of the law in the other federal, or state, courts, and the fact that a single judge, or even a group of judges, disagrees about the contours of a right does not automatically render the law unclear if we have been clear. That said, however, the cases viewing school strip searches differently from the way we see them are numerous enough, with well-reasoned majority and dissenting opinions, to counsel doubt that we were sufficiently clear in the prior statement of law. We conclude that qualified immunity is warranted.

V

The strip search of Savana Redding was unreasonable and a violation of the Fourth Amendment, but petitioners Wilson, Romero, and Schwallier are nevertheless protected from liability through qualified immunity. Our conclusions here do not resolve, however, the question of the liability of petitioner Safford Unified School District #1 under *Monell v. New York City Dept. of Social Servs.*, 436 U.S. 658, 694, 98 S.Ct. 2018, 56 L.Ed.2d 611 (1978), a claim the Ninth Circuit did not address. The judgment of the Ninth Circuit is therefore affirmed in part and reversed in part, and this case is remanded for consideration of the *Monell* claim....

Justice Stevens, with whom Justice Ginsburg joins, concurring in part and dissenting in part.

In *New Jersey v. T.L.O.*, 469 U.S. 325 (1985), the Court established a two-step inquiry for determining the reasonableness of a school official's decision to search a student. First, the Court explained, the search must be "'justified at its inception'" by the presence of "reasonable grounds for suspecting that the search will turn up evidence that the student has violated or is violating either the law or the rules of the school." *Id.*, at 342. Second, the search must be "permissible in its scope," which is achieved "when the measures adopted are reasonably related to the objectives of the search and *not excessively intrusive in light of the age and sex of the student and the nature of the infraction.*" *Ibid.* (emphasis added).

Nothing the Court decides today alters this basic framework. It simply applies *T.L.O.* to declare unconstitutional a strip search of a 13-year-old honors student that was based on a groundless suspicion that she might be hiding medicine in her underwear. This is, in essence, a case in which clearly established law meets clearly outrageous conduct. I have long believed that "'[i]t does not require a constitutional scholar to conclude that a nude search of a 13-year-old child is an invasion of constitutional rights of some magnitude.'" *Id.*, at 382, n. 25 (Stevens, J., concurring in part and dissenting in part) (quoting *Doe v. Renfrow*, 631 F.2d 91, 92–93 (C.A.7 1980)). The strip search of Savana Redding in this case was both more intrusive and less justified than the search of the student's purse in *T.L.O.* Therefore, while I join Parts I–III of the Court's opinion, I disagree with its decision to extend qualified immunity to the school official who authorized this unconstitutional search....

The Court of Appeals properly rejected the school official's qualified immunity defense, and I would affirm that court's judgment in its entirety.

Justice Ginsburg, concurring in part and dissenting in part.

I agree with the Court that Assistant Principal Wilson's subjection of 13-year-old Savana Redding to a humiliating stripdown search violated the Fourth Amendment. But I also agree with Justice Stevens...that our opinion in *New Jersey v. T.L.O.*, 469 U.S. 325 (1985), "clearly established" the law governing this case....

In contrast to *T.L.O.*, where a teacher discovered a student smoking in the lavatory, and where the search was confined to the student's purse, the search of Redding involved her body and rested on the bare accusation of another student whose reliability the Assistant Principal had no reason to trust. The Court's opinion in *T.L.O.* plainly stated the controlling Fourth Amendment law: A search ordered by a school official, even if "justified at its inception," crosses the constitutional boundary if it becomes "excessively intrusive in light of the age and sex of the student and the nature of the infraction." 469 U.S., at 342 (internal quotation marks omitted).

Here, "the nature of the [supposed] infraction," the slim basis for suspecting Savana Redding, and her "age and sex," *ibid.*, establish beyond doubt that Assistant Principal Wilson's order cannot be reconciled with this Court's opinion in *T.L.O.* Wilson's treatment of Redding was abusive and it was not reasonable for him to believe that the law permitted it....

Justice THOMAS, concurring in the judgment in part and dissenting in part.

I agree with the Court that the judgment against the school officials with respect to qualified immunity should be reversed. Unlike the majority, however, I would hold that the search of Savana Redding did not violate the Fourth Amendment. The majority imposes a vague and amorphous standard on school administrators. It also grants judges sweeping authority to second-guess the measures that these officials take to maintain discipline in their schools and ensure the health and safety of the students in their charge. This deep intrusion into the administration of public schools exemplifies why the Court should return to the common-law doctrine of *in loco parentis* under which "the judiciary was reluctant to interfere in the routine business of school administration, allowing schools and teachers to set and enforce rules and to maintain order." *Morse v. Frederick*, 551 U.S. 393, 414 (2007). But even under the prevailing Fourth Amendment test established by *New Jersey v. T.L.O.*, 469 U.S. 325 (1985), all petitioners, including the school district, are entitled to judgment as a matter of law in their favor.

I

"Although the underlying command of the Fourth Amendment is always that searches and seizures be reasonable, what is reasonable depends on the context within which a search takes place." *Id.*, at 337. Thus, although public school students retain Fourth Amendment rights under this Court's precedent, see *id.*, at 333–337, those rights "are different... than elsewhere; the 'reasonableness' inquiry cannot disregard the schools' custodial and tutelary responsibility for children," *Vernonia School Dist. 47J v. Acton*, 515 U.S. 646, 656 (1995); *see also T.L.O.*, 469 U.S., at 339.... For nearly 25 years this Court has understood that "[m]aintaining order in the classroom has never been easy, but in more recent years, school disorder has often taken particularly ugly forms: drug use and violent crime in the schools have become major social problems." Ibid....

For this reason, school officials retain broad authority to protect students and preserve "order and a proper educational environment" under the Fourth Amendment. *Id.*, at 339. This authority requires that school officials be able to engage in the "close supervision of schoolchildren, as well as... enforc[e] rules against conduct that would be perfectly permissible if undertaken by an adult." *Ibid.*... [T]he Court in *T.L.O.* held that a school search is "reasonable" if it is "'justified at its inception'" and "'reasonably related in scope to the circumstances which justified the interference in the first place.'" *Id.*, at 341–342....

A

Here, petitioners had reasonable grounds to suspect that Redding was in possession of prescription and nonprescription drugs in violation of the school's prohibition of the "non-medical use, possession, or sale of a drug" on school property or at school events. 531 F.3d 1071, 1076 (C.A.9 2008) (en banc); see also *id.*, at 1107 (Hawkins, J., dissenting).... As an initial matter, school officials were aware that a few years earlier, a student had become "seriously ill" and "spent several days in intensive care" after ingesting prescription medication obtained from a classmate. Fourth Amendment searches do not occur in a vacuum; rather, context must inform the judicial inquiry. In this instance, the suspicion of drug possession arose at a middle school that had "a history of problems with students using and distributing prohibited and illegal substances on campus." …

B

The remaining question is whether the search was reasonable in scope. Under *T.L.O.*, "a search will be permissible in its scope when the measures adopted are reasonably related to the objectives of the search and not excessively intrusive in light of the age and sex of the student and the nature of the infraction." 469 U.S., at 342. The majority concludes that the school officials' search of Redding's underwear was not "'reasonably related in scope to the circumstances which justified the interference in the first place,'" … notwithstanding the officials' reasonable suspicion that Redding "was involved in pill distribution." According to the majority, to be reasonable, this school search required a showing of "danger to the students from the power of the drugs or their quantity" or a "reason to suppose that [Redding] was carrying pills in her underwear." Each of these additional requirements is an unjustifiable departure from bedrock Fourth Amendment law in the school setting, where this Court has heretofore read the Fourth Amendment to grant considerable leeway to school officials. Because the school officials searched in a location where the pills could have been hidden, the search was reasonable in scope under *T.L.O.*…

… [T]he "nature of the infraction" referenced in *T.L.O.* delineates the proper scope of a search of students in a way that is identical to that permitted for searches outside the school—*i.e.*, the search must be limited to the areas where the object of that infraction could be concealed.… A search of a student therefore is permissible in scope under *T.L.O.* so long as it is objectively reasonable to believe that the area searched could conceal the contraband. The dissenting opinion below correctly captured this Fourth Amendment standard, noting that "if a student brought a baseball bat on campus in violation of school policy, a search of that student's shirt pocket would be patently unjustified." 532 F.3d, at 1104 (opinion of Hawkins, J.)….

Redding would not have been the first person to conceal pills in her undergarments. Nor will she be the last after today's decision, which announces the safest place to secrete contraband in school.…

II

By declaring the search unreasonable in this case, the majority has "'surrender[ed] control of the American public school system to public school students'" by invalidating school policies that treat all drugs equally and by second-guessing swift disciplinary decisions made by school officials. See *Morse*, 551 U.S., at 421, 127 S.Ct. 2618 (Thomas, J., concurring)….

"[I]n the early years of public schooling," courts applied the doctrine of *in loco parentis* to transfer to teachers the authority of a parent to "'command obedience, to control stubbornness, to quicken diligence, and to reform bad habits.'" *Morse*, *supra*, at 413–14 (Thomas, J., concurring)…. So empowered, schoolteachers and administrators had almost complete discretion to establish and enforce the rules they believed were necessary to maintain control over their classrooms.… The perils of judicial policymaking inherent in applying Fourth Amendment protections to public schools counsel in favor of a return to the understanding that existed in this Nation's first public schools, which gave teachers discretion to craft the rules needed to carry out the disciplinary responsibilities delegated to them by parents.

If the common-law view that parents delegate to teachers their authority to discipline and maintain order were to be applied in this case, the search of Redding would stand. There can be no doubt that a parent would have had the authority to conduct the search at issue in this case. Parents have "immunity from the strictures of the Fourth Amendment" when it comes to searches of a child or that child's belongings. *T.L.O.*, 469 U.S., at 337; see also *id.*, at 336, (A parent's authority is "not subject to the limits of the Fourth Amendment"); *Griffin v. Wisconsin*, 483 U.S. 868, 876, 107 S.Ct. 3164, 97 L.Ed.2d 709 (1987) ("[P]arental custodial authority" does not require "judicial approval for [a] search of a minor child's room").

As acknowledged by this Court, this principle is based on the "societal understanding of superior and inferior" with respect to the "parent and child" relationship. In light of this relationship, the Court has indicated that a parent can authorize a third-party search of a child by consenting to such a search, even if the child denies his consent.... [S]ee also 4 W. LaFave, Search and Seizure § 8.3(d), p. 160 (4th ed. 2004) ("[A] father, as the head of the household with the responsibility and the authority for the discipline, training and control of his children, has a superior interest in the family residence to that of his minor son, so that the father's consent to search would be effective notwithstanding the son's contemporaneous on-the-scene objection" (internal quotation marks omitted)). Certainly, a search by the parent himself is no different, regardless of whether or not a child would prefer to be left alone. See *id.*, § 8.4(b), at 202 ("[E]ven [if] a minor child... may think of a room as 'his,' the overall dominance will be in his parents" (internal quotation marks omitted)).

Restoring the common-law doctrine of *in loco parentis* would not, however, leave public schools entirely free to impose any rule they choose. "If parents do not like the rules imposed by those schools, they can seek redress in school boards or legislatures; they can send their children to private schools or home school them; or they can simply move." See *Morse*, 551 U.S., at 419 (Thomas, J., concurring). Indeed, parents and local government officials have proved themselves quite capable of challenging overly harsh school rules or the enforcement of sensible rules in insensible ways....

In the end, the task of implementing and amending public school policies is beyond this Court's function. Parents, teachers, school administrators, local politicians, and state officials are all better suited than judges to determine the appropriate limits on searches conducted by school officials. Preservation of order, discipline, and safety in public schools is simply not the domain of the Constitution. And, common sense is not a judicial monopoly or a Constitutional imperative.

III

"[T]he nationwide drug epidemic makes the war against drugs a pressing concern in every school." *Board of Ed. of Independent School Dist. No. 92 of Pottawatomie Cty. v. Earls*, 536 U.S. 822, 834 (2002). And yet the Court has limited the authority of school officials to conduct searches for the drugs that the officials believe pose a serious safety risk to their students. By doing so, the majority has confirmed that a return to the doctrine of *in loco parentis* is required to keep the judiciary from essentially seizing control of public schools. Only then will teachers again be able to "'govern the[ir] pupils, quicken the slothful, spur the indolent, restrain the impetuous, and control the stubborn'" by making "'rules, giv[ing] commands, and punish[ing] disobedience'" without interference from judges. See *Morse*, *supra*, at 414.... I cannot join this regrettable decision. I, therefore, respectfully dissent from the Court's determination that this search violated the Fourth Amendment.

11a. Under what circumstances would a strip search of a student by school officials be justified? Could school officials require a student to remove her pants and her underwear while searching for an iPod stolen in class? *Foster v. Raspberry*, 652 F.Supp.2d 1342 (M.D. Ga. 2009). Is a strip search of a group of students constitutionally permissible when an allegation has been made that certain unidentified students have been bringing marijuana cigarettes to school? *Pendleton v. Fassett*, 2009 WL 2849542 (W.D. Ky. 2009).

11b. *Effects of strip searches on children and adolescents.* While strip searches are obviously intrusive, they may have more lasting effects on children and adolescents. "With the onset of puberty, most young people begin to make a thorough assessment of themselves.... This critical self-appraisal is accompanied by self-conscious behavior that makes adolescents vulnerable to embarrassment." F. Philip Rice & Kim Gale Dolgin, The Adolescent: Development, Relationships, and Culture 168 (11th ed., 2005). Strip searching adolescents may "result in serious emotional damage, including the development of, or increase in, oppositional behavior." Irwin A. Hyman & Donna C. Perone, *The Other Side of School Violence: Educator Policies and Practices That May Contribute to Student Misbehavior,* 36 J. Sch. Psychol. 7, 13 (1998); and has a negative impact on self-esteem. Kristin D. Eisenbraun, *Violence in Schools: Prevalence, Prediction, and Prevention,* 12 Aggression & Violent Behav. 459, 465 (2007). Students who have been strip searched "often cannot concentrate in school, and, in many cases, transfer or even drop out." Laura L. Finley, *Examining School Searches as Systemic Violence,* 14 Critical Criminology 117, 126 (2006). "Psychological experts have also testified that victims often suffered post-search symptoms including 'sleep disturbance, recurrent and intrusive recollections of the event, inability to concentrate, anxiety, depression and development of phobic reactions,' and that some victims have been moved to attempt suicide." Steven F. Shatz et al., *The Strip Search of Children and the Fourth Amendment,* 26 U.S.F.L. Rev. 1, 12 (1991).

In one study of seven students who had been strip-searched by school officials, a psychological evaluation indicated that all seven evidenced symptoms of stress, and two were diagnosed with posttraumatic stress disorder. Responses included "refusal to go back to school, ruminations about revenge, undesired thoughts about the incident, loss of faith in school staff whom they once trusted, increased tendency toward either avoidance and withdrawal or aggression, and increased anger and defiance at home. These symptoms lasted long enough in the older students to result in attempts to withdraw from school and alleged delinquent behavior." Hyman & Perone, *supra,* at 14. Thus strip searches may increase student mistrust and alienation, Hyman & Perone, *supra,* at 15; and may lead to more, rather than less, school misconduct. Eisenbraun, *supra,* at 465.

Some jurisdictions prohibit or limit the use of strip searches in schools. See Wis. Stat. § 948.50(3); Cal. Educ. Code § 49050 (no body cavity search or inspection of "underclothing, breast, buttocks, or genitalia"); Iowa Code § 808A.2(4)(a) and (b) (no body-cavity or strip search); Okla. Stat. tit. 70, § 24-102 (no strip search); N.J. Stat. Ann. § 18A:37-6.1 (no body-cavity or strip search); S.C. Code Ann. § 59-63-1140 (no strip search); Wash. Rev. Code § 28A.600.230(3) (no body-cavity or strip search). Similarly, some school districts also prohibit strip searches. See, e.g., New York City Dept. of Education, Regulation A-432 (2005), at http://docs.nycenet.edu/docushare/dsweb/Get/Document-21/A-432.pdf; School Board of the City of Virginia Beach Regulation 5-65.1 (2001), at http://www.vbschools.com/policies/5-65_1r.asp (strip searches not permitted, but school official may conduct search of student's person or clothing if student poses an immediate danger to himself or others by possessing item). Other school districts limit the circumstances under which a strip search may be conducted. See, e.g., Pitt County Board of Education, Policy 10.201 (2008), at http://www.pitt.k12.nc.us/boe/files/10/10.201-P_Search_and_Seizure_

Procedures.doc ("A strip search involves such a severe intrusion into personal privacy that it should be conducted only on the basis of probable cause and by law enforcement officials. School personnel should not be present in the event a strip search takes place. In addition, parents should be notified, if possible, and asked to be present during the strip search").

11c. In his dissent, Justice Thomas argues that school officials have every reason to punish the unauthorized possession of prescription drugs as severely as the possession of street drugs:

> As one study noted, "more young people ages 12–17 abuse prescription drugs than any illicit drug except marijuana—more than cocaine, heroin, and methamphetamine combined." Executive Office of the President, Office of National Drug Control Policy (ONDCP), Prescription for Danger 1 (Jan. 2008) (hereinafter Prescription for Danger). And according to a 2005 survey of teens, "nearly one in five (19 percent or 4.5 million) admit abusing prescription drugs in their lifetime." Columbia University, The National Center on Addiction and Substance Abuse (CASA), "You've Got Drugs!" V: Prescription Drug Pushers on the Internet 2 (July 2008); see also Dept. of Health and Human Services, National Institute on Drug Abuse, High School and Youth Trends 2 (Dec. 2008) ("In 2008, 15.4 percent of 12th-graders reported using a prescription drug nonmedically within the past year")....
>
> ...In a 2008 survey, "44 percent of teens sa[id] drugs are used, kept or sold on the grounds of their schools." CASA, National Survey of American Attitudes on Substance Abuse XIII: Teens and Parents 19 (Aug. 2008) (hereinafter National Survey). The risks posed by the abuse of these drugs are every bit as serious as the dangers of using a typical street drug.
>
> Teenagers are nevertheless apt to "believe the myth that these drugs provide a medically safe high." ONDCP, Teens and Prescription Drugs: An Analysis of Recent Trends on the Emerging Drug Threat 3 (Feb. 2007) But since 1999, there has "been a dramatic increase in the number of poisonings and even deaths associated with the abuse of prescription drugs." Prescription for Danger 4; see also Dept. of Health and Human Services, The NSDUH Report: Trends in Nonmedical Use of Prescription Pain Relievers: 2002 to 2007, p. 1 (Feb. 5, 2009) ("[A]pproximately 324,000 emergency department visits in 2006 involved the nonmedical use of pain relievers"); CASA, Under the Counter: The Diversion and Abuse of Controlled Prescription Drugs in the U.S., p. 25 (July 2005) ("In 2002, abuse of controlled prescription drugs was implicated in at least 23 percent of drug-related emergency department admissions and 20.4 percent of all single drug-related emergency department deaths").

Is his use of social science persuasive? What additional information would you like to know?

12. *Videotaping.* May schools videotape students? Consider this:

> In an effort to improve security at LMS, the Overton County School Board approved the installation of video surveillance equipment throughout the school building. The school board engaged the education technology firm, Edutech, Inc., to install cameras and monitoring equipment. The board ordered the Director of Schools, William Needham, to oversee the project. Needham delegated his authority for the installation of the monitoring equipment to the LMS Principal, Melinda Beatty, who delegated her authority to the Assistant Principal, Robert Jolley. None of the defendants promulgated any guidelines, written or otherwise, determining the number, location, or operation of the surveillance cameras.
>
> After several meetings, Assistant Principal Jolley and an Edutech representative decided to install the cameras throughout the school in areas facing the exterior doors, in hallways leading to exterior doors, and in the boys' and girls' locker rooms. The cameras were installed and were operational by July 2002.

> The images captured by the cameras were transmitted to a computer terminal in Jolley's office where they were displayed and were stored on the computer's hard drive. Jolley testified that, in September 2002, he discovered that the locker room cameras were videotaping areas in which students routinely dressed for athletic activities. He said that he immediately notified Principal Beatty of the situation and suggested that the placement of the cameras be changed. But, the cameras were not removed nor were their locations changed for the remainder of the fall semester.
>
> In addition to Jolley receiving the images on his computer, they were also accessible via remote internet connection. Any person with access to the software username, password, and Internet Protocol (IP) address could access the stored images. Neither Jolley nor anyone else had ever changed the system password or username from its default setting. The record indicates that the system was accessed ninety-eight different times between July 12, 2002, and January 10, 2003, including through internet service providers located in Rock Hill, South Carolina; Clarksville, Tennessee; and Gainsboro, Tennessee.
>
> During a girls' basketball game at LMS on January 9, 2003, visiting team members from Allons Elementary School noticed the camera in the girls' locker room and brought this to the attention of their coach, Kathy Carr. Carr questioned Principal Beatty, who assured Carr that the camera was not activated. In fact, the camera was activated and had recorded images of the Allons team members in their undergarments when they changed their clothes. After the game, Carr reported the camera incident to the Allons school principal, who contacted Defendant Needham later that evening. Needham immediately accessed the security system from his home and viewed the recorded images. The following morning, January 10, Needham, Beatty, and two other officials viewed the images in Needham's office by remote access. Needham later stated that in his opinion, the videotapes of the 10 to 14 year old girls contained "nothing more than images of a few bras and panties." School employees removed the locker room cameras later that day.
>
> From July 2002 to January 2003, when the cameras were operational, a number of children from Overton County Schools and schools from the surrounding counties used the LMS locker rooms for athletic events and were videotape recorded while changing their clothes.

Brannum v. Overton County School Board, 516 F.3d 489, 492–493 (6th Cir. 2008). Thirty-four students filed suit, alleging that the videotaping violated the Fourth and Fourteenth Amendments. Do you agree? Why or why not?

13. *Zero-tolerance policies.*

> The increased interdependency between schools officials and law enforcement authorities has led to more expansive definitions and interpretations of criminal behavior among school children. As a result, students are now brought into the "myriad recesses of the criminal justice system" for certain behaviors that would have once resulted in less severe consequences.
>
> This increased use of the criminal justice system is exacerbated by the proliferation of zero tolerance policies. These policies, which have blossomed over the past decade, have been described as "administrative rules intended to address specific problems associated with school safety and discipline." The infusion of both these zero tolerance policies and the increased law enforcement presence in public schools has criminalized a wide range of student behavior, some of which had previously been monitored through school disciplinary processes.
>
> Nationally, zero tolerance policies in public schools are widely considered to have found their origins in the Gun Free Schools Act of 1994 [20 U.S.C. § 8921 (repealed 2002)]. This act was implemented in response to heightened awareness and fear of school violence involving

weapons. The Act requires each state receiving federal funding pursuant to the Elementary and Secondary Education Act to have a law "requiring local educational agencies to expel from school for a period of not less than 1 year a student who is determined to have brought a firearm to a school, or to have possessed a firearm at a school." The Act also requires the local education agency to enact a policy mandating the referral of any student found to have a firearm in any of its schools to the juvenile justice or criminal justice system.

[In 1994, Congress enacted the Federal Gun Free Schools Act, which conditioned federal funding on compliance with a mandatory one-year expulsion for possession of a firearm.] The Gun Free Schools Act focused on firearms. However, several states and schools have adopted more expansive definitions of weapons. These expansive definitions allow students to be severely disciplined—through suspension, expulsion, arrest and/or prosecution—for possessing items, or "weapons," that once would have either resulted in less severe punishment or even no punishment at all.

In addition to expanding the types of weapons that could lead to disciplinary action against students, zero tolerance policies ushered in expanded categories of conduct not contemplated by the Gun Free Schools Act. A vast literature chronicles the wide range of behaviors that have brought punitive sanctions upon students, including introduction to the criminal justice system. Critics assert that while zero tolerance policies were originally aimed to rid schools of dangerous weapons, they have reached past their intended purpose to criminalize student behavior which poses no threat to physical well-being or safety. As a result, many incidents that were not previously considered to be crimes, such as schoolyard fights and perceived threats can now be and, in fact, often are....

Several studies illustrate that students of color, particularly African-Americans, are disproportionately punished in public schools throughout the country. Moreover, these students are disproportionately subjected to the most punitive sanctions such as suspensions and expulsions, including the mandatory sanctions that are wedded to zero tolerance policies. While several theories have been posited to explain these discrepancies, one consistent theory is that cultural gulfs separate students of color from many school teachers and administrators, which result in varying behavioral interpretations based on difference, as well as categorization and stereotype....

In addition to cultural differences, another explanation for these punishment discrepancies is simply that zero tolerance policies are more likely to exist in schools with considerable percentages of students of color. Statistics gathered by the United States Department of Education's National Center for Education Statistics illustrate that in the 1996–97 school year, the vast majority of public schools reported having zero tolerance policies for various student offenses—including violence, weapons possession, alcohol, drugs and tobacco. However, the highest percentages of schools implementing these polices were those with a minority enrollment of fifty percent or higher.

Accordingly, students of color are disproportionately affected and punished by zero tolerance policies. Because of the increased law enforcement presence in public schools, particularly schools with considerable percentages of students of color, these policies and protocols have converged to disproportionately track students of color into the juvenile justice and criminal justice systems....

...[T]he *T.L.O.* reasonable suspicion standard should be replaced by the probable cause standard when school officials conduct searches [to uncover evidence of criminal activity] in the presence of officers employed by law enforcement agencies. In addition, reasonable

> suspicion should be replaced by probable cause when school officials conduct these searches outside the physical presence of law enforcement officers, but act pursuant to policies that limit, if not eviscerate, their discretion and attach reporting requirements to law enforcement authorities for behavior that could lead to the student's arrest. Both of these search scenarios portray an overarching law enforcement purpose. Conversely, the reasonable suspicion standard should be applicable in those situations where school officials perform searches with no law enforcement involvement and where the purpose of the search is to uncover evidence of a school rule violation that does not impose independent criminal liability.

Michael Pinard, *From the Classroom to the Courtroom: Assessing Fourth Amendment Standards in Public School Searches Involving Law Enforcement Authorities*, 45 ARIZ. L. REV. 1067, 1108–1111, 1113–1115, 1116, 1120 (2003). Do you believe that the standards proposed by Pinard would divert the school-to-prison pipeline?

14. *Cell phones, texting, and "sexting."* May school officials access the contents of a student's cell phone? If so, under what circumstances? Assume that a high school has a policy permitting students to bring cell phones to school but prohibiting them from using or displaying them during school hours. A student brings his cell phone to school, and during school hours, it falls out of his pocket and lands on the floor. A teacher, seeing the phone, confiscates it and takes it to the assistant principal. The assistant principal proceeds to call numbers in the student's cell phone, sends texts, accesses voice mail, and conducts a conversation using instant messaging, in an attempt to ascertain if the student and others are violating the school's policy. Does this constitute a violation of the student's Fourth Amendment rights? *Klump v. Nazareth Area School District*, 425 F.Supp.2d 622 (E.D. Pa. 2006).

Sexting is the act of sending sexually explicit messages or photographs electronically, usually between cell phones. Although sexting may have been around as long as the technology has been available, it recently has drawn the attention of authorities, parents, and scholars because of its apparent popularity with teenagers—and its unintended consequences. In Ohio, for example, a teenage girl committed suicide after her ex-boyfriend distributed nude photos she had sent of herself. See Mike Celizic, "Her Teen Committed Suicide over 'Sexting,'" *Today Show*, http://today.msnbc.msn.com/id/29546030. Teens may be prosecuted for sending or receiving sexually suggestive photos under various criminal laws; some of these provisions may trigger juvenile sex-offender registration statutes, which require convicted teens to register their names and addresses with law enforcement for a term of years, often extending well into adulthood. Sex-offender registrants also may be prohibited from living in certain neighborhoods or obtaining employment in certain fields. Some states have been considering the enactment of new laws aimed at criminalizing sexting between teens.

The prevalence of sexting among teens is unclear. In an online survey conducted by Cox Communications, the National Center for Missing and Exploited Children, and Harris Interactive in March 2009, 9 percent of teens ages thirteen to eighteen had sent a sexually suggestive text message or e-mail with nude or nearly nude photos, 3 percent had forwarded one, and 17 percent had received a sexually suggestive text message or e-mail with nude or nearly nude photos. Cox Communications Teen Online & Wireless Safety Survey, in Partnership with the National Center for Missing & Exploited Children (NCMEC) and John Walsh, May 2009, http://www.cox.com/takecharge/safe_teens_2009/media/2009_teen_survey_internet_and_wireless_safety.pdf. MTV and the Associated Press also conducted a poll in September 2009 and found that one in ten young adults between the ages of fourteen and twenty-four have shared a naked image of themselves with someone else, and 15 percent have had someone send them naked pictures or videos of themselves. Another 8 percent have received nude images of someone else they knew personally. MTV-AP Digital Abuse Study, Executive Summary, AThinLine.org, http://www.athinline.org/MTV-AP_Digital_Abuse_Study_Executive_Summary.pdf.

The Pew Research Center's Internet & American Life Project conducted a nationally representative telephone sample of cell-phone-owning youths between the ages of twelve and seventeen, occurring between June and September 2009. Eight hundred teens were surveyed, and of those, 4 percent said they had sent nude or nearly nude images of themselves, while 15 percent had received nude or nearly nude images of someone they knew. Older teens were more likely to have engaged in sexting; 8 percent of seventeen-year-olds said they had sent nude or nearly nude images of themselves, and 30 percent said they had received such images. Of teens who paid for all of their cell-phone costs, 17 percent engaged in sexting, compared with only 3 percent of teens who did not pay or paid only a portion of the costs of operating a cell phone. In separate focus-group surveys, researchers found that sexually suggestive texts were sent between romantic partners, between romantic partners and shared outside the relationship, or between two people at least one of whom wished to become a romantic partner. Amanda Lenhart, "Teens and Sexting: How and Why Minor Teens Are Sending Sexually Suggestive Nude or Nearly Nude Images via Text Messaging," http://pewresearch.org/assets/pdf/teens-and-sexting.pdf.

May school officials constitutionally seize student cell phones and search for evidence of sexting? Assume that school officials confiscated several student cell phones and found photos of "scantily clad," nude, and partially nude girls. School officials turned the phones over to the local district attorney, who stated publicly that the students who possessed these images could be prosecuted for possessing or distributing child pornography and, if found guilty, could be subject to sex-offender registration laws. The district attorney threatened to prosecute the students whose cell phones contained the photos, along with the girls pictured in the photos, unless they agreed to probation, paying a $100 program fee, and participating in a six-to-nine-month program focused on education and counseling. Some of the parents of the minors involved have come to you seeking legal advice. What would you tell them? See *Miller v. Skumanick*, 598 F.3d 139 (3d Cir. 2010).

15. The School Survey on Crime and Safety is completed annually by public school principals or the persons with the most knowledge about crime, discipline, and safety issues at the school. According to the most recent survey, schools most commonly require visitors to sign in or check in (99 percent), prohibit tobacco use on school grounds (91 percent), and control access to school buildings during school hours (90 percent). The least common security measures include daily metal-detector checks (1 percent), drug testing of students involved in extracurricular activities other than athletics (4 percent), random metal-detector checks (5 percent), drug testing of student athletes (6 percent), requiring students to wear identification badges (8 percent), and random sweeps for contraband, excluding canine sniffs (11 percent). Of those surveyed, 22 percent indicated that they used random dog sniffs to search for drugs. Rachel Dinkes et al., "Indicators of School Crime and Safety: 2009," National Center for Education Statistics, Institute of Education Sciences, U.S. Department of Education, and Bureau of Justice Statistics, http://nces.ed.gov/pubsearch/pubsinfo.asp?pubid=2010012. What do the data suggest to you about searches of children in schools?

2. INTERROGATIONS: THE DUE PROCESS FRAMEWORK

HALEY V. OHIO
Supreme Court of the United States
332 U.S. 596 (1948)

MR. JUSTICE DOUGLAS announced the judgment of the Court and an opinion in which MR. JUSTICE BLACK, MR. JUSTICE MURPHY, and MR. JUSTICE RUTLEDGE join.

Petitioner was convicted in an Ohio court of murder in the first degree and sentenced to life imprisonment. The Court of Appeals of Ohio sustained the judgment of conviction over the objection that the admission of petitioner's confession at the trial violated the Fourteenth Amendment of the Constitution. The Ohio Supreme Court, being of the view that no debatable constitutional question was presented, dismissed the appeal. The case is here on a petition for a writ of certiorari which we granted because we had doubts whether the ruling of the court below could be squared with Chambers v. Florida, 309 U.S. 227; Malinski v. New York, 324 U.S. 401 and like cases in this Court.

A confectionery store was robbed near midnight on October 14, 1945, and William Karam, its owner, was shot. It was the prosecutor's theory, supported by some evidence which it is unnecessary for us to relate, that petitioner, a Negro boy age 15, and two others, Willie Lowder, age 16, and Al Parks, age 17, committed the crime, petitioner acting as a lookout. Five days later—around midnight October 19, 1945—petitioner was arrested at his home and taken to police headquarters.

There is some contrariety in the testimony as to what then transpired. There is evidence that he was beaten. He took the stand and so testified. His mother testified that the clothes he wore when arrested, which were exchanged two days later for clean ones she brought to the jail, were torn and blood-stained. She also testified that when she first saw him five days after his arrest he was bruised and skinned. The police testified to the contrary on this entire line of testimony. So we put to one side the controverted evidence. Taking only the undisputed testimony... we have the following sequence of events. Beginning shortly after midnight this 15-year-old lad was questioned by the police for about five hours. Five or six of the police questioned him in relays of one or two each. During this time no friend or counsel of the boy was present. Around 5 a.m.—after being shown alleged confessions of Lowder and Parks—the boy confessed. A confession was typed in question and answer form by the police. At no time was this boy advised of his right to counsel; but the written confession started off with the following statement:

> "we want to inform you of your constitutional rights, the law gives you the right to make this statement or not as you see fit. It is made with the understanding that it may be used at a trial in court either for or against you or anyone else involved in this crime with you, of your

own free will and accord, you are under no force or duress or compulsion and no promises are being made to you at this time whatsoever.

"Do you still desire to make this statement and tell the truth after having had the above clause read to you?

A. Yes."

He was put in jail about 6 or 6:30 a.m. on Saturday, the 20th, shortly after the confession was signed. Between then and Tuesday, the 23d, he was held incommunicado. A lawyer retained by his mother tried to see him twice but was refused admission by the police. His mother was not allowed to see him until Thursday, the 25th. But a newspaper photographer was allowed to see him and take his picture in the early morning hours of the 20th, right after he had confessed. He was not taken before a magistrate and formally charged with a crime until the 23d—three days after the confession was signed.

The trial court, after a preliminary hearing on the voluntary character of the confession, allowed it to be admitted in evidence over petitioner's objection that it violated his rights under the Fourteenth Amendment. The court instructed the jury to disregard the confession if it found that he did not make the confession voluntarily and of his free will.

But the ruling of the trial court and the finding of the jury on the voluntary character of the confession do not foreclose the independent examination which it is our duty to make here. If the undisputed evidence suggests that force or coercion was used to exact the confession, we will not permit the judgment of conviction to stand even though without the confession there might have been sufficient evidence for submission to the jury.

We do not think the methods used in obtaining this confession can be squared with that due process of law which the Fourteenth Amendment commands.

What transpired would make us pause for careful inquiry if a mature man were involved. And when, as here, a mere child—an easy victim of the law—is before us, special care in scrutinizing the record must be used. Age 15 is a tender and difficult age for a boy of any race. He cannot be judged by the more exacting standards of maturity. That which would leave a man cold and unimpressed can overawe and overwhelm a lad in his early teens. This is the period of great instability which the crisis of adolescence produces. A 15-year-old lad, questioned through the dead of night by relays of police, is a ready victim of the inquisition. Mature men possibly might stand the ordeal from midnight to 5 a.m. But we cannot believe that a lad of tender years is a match for the police in such a contest. He needs counsel and support if he is not to become the victim first of fear, then of panic. He needs someone on whom to lean lest the overpowering presence of the law, as he knows it, may not crush him. No friend stood at the side of this 15-year-old boy as the police, working in relays, questioned him hour after hour, from midnight until dawn. No lawyer stood guard to make sure that the police went so far and no farther, to see to it that they stopped short of the point where he became the victim of coercion. No counsel or friend was called during the critical hours of questioning. A photographer was admitted once this lad broke and confessed. But not even a gesture towards getting a lawyer for him was ever made.

This disregard of the standards of decency is underlined by the fact that he was kept incommunicado for over three days during which the lawyer retained to represent him twice tried to see him and twice was refused admission. A photographer was admitted at once; but his closest friend—his mother—was not allowed to see him for over five days after his arrest. It is said that these events are not germane to the present problem because they happened after the confession was made. But they show such a callous attitude of the police towards the safeguards which respect for ordinary standards of human relationships compels that we take with a grain of salt their present apologia that the five-hour grilling of this boy was conducted in a fair and dispassionate manner. When the police are so unmindful of these basic standards of conduct in their public dealings, their secret treatment of a 15-year-old boy behind closed doors in the dead of night becomes darkly suspicious.

The age of petitioner, the hours when he was grilled, the duration of his quizzing, the fact that he had no friend or counsel to advise him, the callous attitude of the police towards his rights combine to convince us that this was a confession wrung from a child by means which the law should not sanction....

But we are told that this boy was advised of his constitutional rights before he signed the confession and that, knowing them, he nevertheless confessed. That assumes, however, that a boy of fifteen, without aid of counsel, would have a full appreciation of that advice and that on the facts of this record he had a freedom of choice. We cannot indulge those assumptions.... Formulas of respect for constitutional safeguards cannot prevail over the facts of life which contradict them....

... The Fourteenth Amendment prohibits the police from using the private, secret custody of either man or child as a device for wringing confessions from them.

Reversed.

Mr. Justice Frankfurter, joining in reversal of judgment....

It would disregard standards that we cherish as part of our faith in the strength and well-being of a rational, civilized society to hold that a confession is "voluntary" simply because the confession is the product of a sentient choice....

... Of course, the police meant to exercise pressures upon Haley to make him talk. That was the very purpose of their procedure. In concluding that a statement is not voluntary which results from pressures such as were exerted in this case to make a lad of fifteen talk when the Constitution gave him the right to keep silent and when the situation was so contrived that appreciation of his rights and thereby the means of asserting them were effectively withheld from him by the police, I do not believe I express a merely personal bias against such a procedure. Such a finding, I believe, reflects those fundamental notions of fairness and justice in the determination of guilt or innocence which lie embedded in the feelings of the American people and are enshrined in the Due Process Clause of the Fourteenth Amendment. To remove the inducement to resort to such methods this Court has repeatedly denied use of the fruits of illicit methods.

Mr. Justice Burton, with whom The Chief Justice, Mr. Justice Reed and Mr. Justice Jackson concur, dissenting....

The question in this case is the simple one—was the confession in fact voluntary? As in many other cases it is difficult, because of conflicting testimony, to determine this controlling fact. It may not be possible to become absolutely certain of it. Self-serving perjury, however, must not be the passkey to a mandatory exclusion of the confession from use as evidence. It is for the trial judge and the jury, under the safeguards of constitutional due process of criminal law, to apply even-handed justice to the determination of the factual issues....

This Court properly reserves to itself an opportunity to consider the record in a case like this independently from the consideration given to that record by the lower courts. However, when credibility plays as large a part in the record as it does in this case, this Court rarely can justify a reversal of the judgment of the trial court and the verdict of the jury. This is increasingly true where the judgment of the trial court has been affirmed, as here, by two State courts of review. In the preliminary examination as to the admissibility of the confession in this case, the trial court may have believed the police and disbelieved the accused. On that basis, there is more than ample evidence to support the trial court's conclusion in refusing to exclude the confession. A similar statement may be made as to the presentation of evidence to the jury....

In testing due process this Court must first make sure of its facts. Until a better way is found for testing credibility than by the examination of witnesses in open court, we must give trial courts and juries that wide discretion in this field to which a living record, as distinguished from a printed record, logically entitles them. In this living record there are many guideposts to the truth which are not in the printed record. Without seeing them ourselves, we will do well to give heed to those who have seen them.

GALLEGOS V. COLORADO
Supreme Court of the United States
370 U.S. 49 (1962)

Mr. Justice Douglas delivered the opinion of the Court.

Petitioner, a child of 14, and another juvenile followed an elderly man to a hotel, got into his room on a ruse, assaulted him, overpowered him, stole $13 from his pockets, and fled. All this happened on December 20, 1958. Petitioner was picked up by the police on January 1, 1959, and immediately admitted the assault and robbery. At that time, however, the victim of the robbery was still alive, though hospitalized. He died on January 26, 1959, and forthwith an information charging first degree murder was returned against petitioner. A jury found him guilty, the crucial evidence introduced at the trial being a formal confession which he signed on January 7, 1959, after he had been held for five days during which time he saw no lawyer, parent or other friendly adult....

After petitioner's arrest on January 1, the following events took place. His mother tried to see him on Friday, January 2, but permission was denied, the reason given being that visiting hours were from 7 p.m. to 8 p.m. on Monday and Thursday. From January 1 through January 7, petitioner was in Juvenile Hall, where he was kept in security, though he was allowed to eat with the other inmates. He was examined by the police in Juvenile Hall January 2, and made a confession which an officer recorded in longhand. On January 3, 1959, a complaint was filed against him in the Juvenile Court by the investigating detectives.

The State in its brief calls this preliminary procedure in Juvenile Hall being "booked in." As noted, petitioner signed a full and formal confession on January 7. The trial in the Juvenile Court took place January 16 on a petition dated January 13 containing a charge of "assault to injure." He was committed to the State Industrial School for an indeterminate period. Thereafter, as noted above, the victim of the robbery died and the murder trial was held.

Confessions obtained by "secret inquisitorial processes" are suspect, since such procedures are conducive to the use of physical and psychological pressures. The reason that due process, as used in the Fourteenth Amendment, condemns the obtaining of confessions in that manner is a compound of two influences. First is the procedural requirement [of due process and s]econd is the element of compulsion which is condemned by the Fifth Amendment....

The application of these principles involves close scrutiny of the facts of individual cases. The length of the questioning, the use of fear to break a suspect, the youth of the accused are illustrative of the circumstances on which cases of this kind turn. The youth of the suspect was the crucial factor in *Haley v. Ohio*....

There is no guide to the decision of cases such as this, except the totality of circumstances that bear on the two factors we have mentioned. The youth of the petitioner, the long detention, the failure to send for his parents, the failure immediately to bring him before the judge of the Juvenile Court, the failure to see to it that he had the advice of a lawyer or a friend—all these combine to make us conclude that the formal confession on which this conviction may have rested was obtained in violation of due process.

MR. JUSTICE FRANKFURTER and MR. JUSTICE WHITE took no part in the consideration or decision of this case.

MR. JUSTICE CLARK, with whom MR. JUSTICE HARLAN and MR. JUSTICE STEWART join, dissenting....

The Court sets aside the conviction here on due process grounds, finding that the formal confession made by petitioner on January 7 was obtained by "secret inquisitorial processes" and other forms of compulsion. In so doing it turns its back on the spontaneous oral admissions made by petitioner at the time of arrest on January 1, as well as a detailed confession made the next day, all long before the formal confession was given five days later. Moreover, I find nothing in the record that suggests any "secret inquisitorial processes" were used or any compulsion was exerted upon petitioner even during that longer period. With due deference I cannot see how the Court concludes from the record that petitioner was "cut off from contact with any lawyer or adult advisor" and "made accessible only to the police," that there was a failure to bring him before the juvenile judge in the manner required in juvenile delinquency cases, or that Gallegos' case is in anywise on the same footing with Haley v. Ohio, 332 U.S. 596, 68 S.Ct. 302, 92 L.Ed. 224 (1948), or other cases cited by the majority....

...In regard to these confessions, the test of voluntariness as evidenced by the "totality of circumstances" leads the Court not to question them. Here there were no "secret inquisitorial processes" or compulsion of any kind as the Court envisions in relation to the confession of January 7. The Court's only criticism is that petitioner "would have no way of knowing what the consequences of his confession were without advice as to his rights...." The truth of the matter is that the singular circumstance pointed out by the Court has never been thought to render a confession inadmissible.

The Court is overturning petitioner's conviction because it flows in part from the formal confession of January 7. I cannot draw from this record a conclusion that this confession was involuntary. Petitioner freely admitted in testimony before the trial judge that he was not threatened or physically coerced in any way and that he was not intensively questioned. Moreover, prior to the formal confession he was told that he did not have to make a statement and warned of the possibility of a murder charge, as well as informed that he could have an attorney and his parents present....

Petitioner was never placed in solitary confinement, as might be implied from the Court's opinion, but was merely kept out of the organized activities until the unit supervisor could determine whether his full-time participation would have an adverse effect on others. And even under this schedule he had all his meals with the other boys and conversed freely with them.

Nor was petitioner "cut off" from contact with lawyers or adults and "made accessible only to the police." His mother made no effort to obtain an attorney although informed of the right to do so.[4] And she was not prevented from seeing him but was merely asked to comply with reasonable visiting regulations. She was informed on two occasions that she could see him Monday, January 5, two days before the formal confession which the Court finds invalid, but she did not attempt to do so. And petitioner himself passed up the offer to confer with his parents and an attorney before making this confession.

As I have noted, in light of these facts I cannot conclude that this confession was involuntary....

NOTES AND QUESTIONS

1. Prior to 1964, the United States Supreme Court relied on the due process clause to determine the voluntariness of confessions. The Court applied a "totality of the circumstances" test in determining whether the confession was voluntary. What were the factors used by the Court in *Haley* and *Gallegos* to determine voluntariness?

2. In *Massiah v. United States*, 377 U.S. 201 (1964), the Supreme Court held that when government agents "deliberately elicit" incriminating statements from an indicted defendant in the absence of counsel, those agents have violated the defendant's Sixth Amendment right to counsel. *Massiah* and its progeny, however, make it clear that the rule is limited to confessions obtained after the initiation of criminal proceedings. Because the Court has never held that the Sixth Amendment applies to juvenile delinquency proceedings, would the *Massiah* rule apply?

3. Two years later, the Court decided *Miranda v. Arizona*, 384 U.S. 436 (1966). The Court held that the state may not use inculpatory or exculpatory statements obtained during custodial interrogation unless procedural safeguards are used to ensure the privilege against self-incrimination and the state obtains a knowing, intelligent, and voluntary waiver of rights. Although it is fair to say that most courts apply *Miranda* when assessing the admissibility of a confession, there still may be reason to assess the voluntariness of a confession under the Due Process Clause. By its own terms, *Miranda* applies only to custodial interrogation; thus, if the person is not in custody or is not interrogated, *Miranda* does not apply. See, e.g., *Arizona v. Fulminante*, 499 U.S. 279 (1991). A confession obtained in violation of *Miranda* may be admissible to impeach the defendant, *Harris v. New York*, 401 U.S. 222 (1971); however, a confession obtained in violation of the Due Process Clause is inadmissible at trial in the prosecution's case-in-chief and for impeachment purposes. *Mincey v. Arizona*, 437 U.S. 385 (1978). Additionally, the rights protected by *Miranda* may be waived, but the court may still examine the voluntariness of the waiver. See, e.g., *Colorado v. Connelly*, 479 U.S. 157 (1986).Under what circumstances would a confession be voluntary for *Miranda* purposes but involuntary under the Due Process Clause? Since the voluntariness of a confession and the validity of a waiver of rights under *Miranda* are both analyzed under a totality-of-the-circumstances test, is there any real difference?

4. Indeed, no attorney was obtained for petitioner's trial in the juvenile court.

4. *Gault*, citing *Miranda*, made clear that the Fifth Amendment privilege against self-incrimination applies to juveniles in addition to adults. What reasons did the Court articulate for extending the right to minors? What concerns did the Court address?

5. Does *Miranda* apply to juveniles? Consider the Court's decision in the following case when framing your answer.

THE FIFTH AMENDMENT FRAMEWORK

FARE V. MICHAEL C.
Supreme Court of the United States
442 U.S. 707 (1979)

MR. JUSTICE BLACKMUN delivered the opinion of the Court.

In *Miranda v. Arizona*, 384 U.S. 436 (1966), this Court established certain procedural safeguards designed to protect the rights of an accused, under the Fifth and Fourteenth Amendments, to be free from compelled self-incrimination during custodial interrogation. The Court specified, among other things, that if the accused indicates in any manner that he wishes to remain silent or to consult an attorney, interrogation must cease, and any statement obtained from him during interrogation thereafter may not be admitted against him at his trial. *Id.*, at 444–445, 473–474.

In this case, the State of California, in the person of its acting chief probation officer, attacks the conclusion of the Supreme Court of California that a juvenile's request, made while undergoing custodial interrogation, to see his *probation officer* is per se an invocation of the juvenile's Fifth Amendment rights as pronounced in *Miranda*.

I

Respondent Michael C. was implicated in the murder of Robert Yeager. The murder occurred during a robbery of the victim's home on January 19, 1976. A small truck registered in the name of respondent's mother was identified as having been near the Yeager home at the time of the killing, and a young man answering respondent's description was seen by witnesses near the truck and near the home shortly before Yeager was murdered.

On the basis of this information, Van Nuys, Cal., police took respondent into custody at approximately 6:30 p.m. on February 4. Respondent then was $16^1/_2$ years old and on probation to the Juvenile Court. He had been on probation since the age of 12. Approximately one year earlier he had served a term in a youth corrections camp under the supervision of the Juvenile Court. He had a record of several previous offenses, including burglary of guns and purse snatching, stretching back over several years.

Upon respondent's arrival at the Van Nuys station house two police officers began to interrogate him. The officers and respondent were the only persons in the room during the interrogation. The conversation was tape-recorded. One of the officers initiated the interview by informing respondent that he had been brought in for questioning in relation to a murder. The officer fully advised respondent of his *Miranda* rights. The following exchange then occurred, as set out in the opinion of the California Supreme Court:

"Q.... Do you understand all of these rights as I have explained them to you?
"A. Yeah.
"Q. Okay, do you wish to give up your right to remain silent and talk to us about this murder?
"A. What murder? I don't know about no murder.
"Q. I'll explain to you which one it is if you want to talk to us about it.
"A. Yeah, I might talk to you.
Q. Do you want to give up your right to have an attorney present here while we talk about it?
"A. *Can I have my probation officer here?*
"Q. Well I can't get a hold of your probation officer right now. You have the right to an attorney.
"A. How I know you guys won't pull no police officer in and tell me he's an attorney?
"Q. Huh?
"A. [How I know you guys won't pull no police officer in and tell me he's an attorney?]
"Q. Your probation officer is Mr. Christiansen.
"A. Yeah.
"Q. Well I'm not going to call Mr. Christiansen tonight. There's a good chance we can talk to him later, but I'm not going to call him right now. If you want to talk to us without an attorney present, you can. If you don't want to, you don't have to. But if you want to say something, you can, and if you don't want to say something you don't have to. That's your right. You understand that right?
"A. Yeah.
"Q. Okay, will you talk to us without an attorney present?
"A. Yeah I want to talk to you."

Respondent thereupon proceeded to answer questions put to him by the officers. He made statements and drew sketches that incriminated him in the Yeager murder.

Largely on the basis of respondent's incriminating statements, probation authorities filed a petition in Juvenile Court alleging that respondent had murdered Robert Yeager, and that respondent therefore should be adjudged a ward of the Juvenile Court. Respondent thereupon moved to suppress the statements and sketches he gave the police during the interrogation. He alleged that the statements had been obtained in violation of *Miranda* in that his request to see his probation officer at the outset of the questioning constituted an invocation of his Fifth Amendment right to remain silent, just as if he had requested the assistance of an attorney. Accordingly, respondent argued that since the interrogation did not cease until he had a chance to confer with his probation officer, the statements and sketches could not be admitted against him in the Juvenile Court proceedings. In so arguing, respondent relied by analogy on the decision in *People v. Burton*, 6 Cal.3d 375, 491 P.2d 793 (1971), where the Supreme Court of California had held that a minor's request, made during custodial interrogation, to see his parents constituted an invocation of the minor's Fifth Amendment rights.

In support of his suppression motion, respondent called his probation officer, Charles P. Christiansen, as a witness. Christiansen testified that he had instructed respondent that if at any time he had "a concern with his family," or ever had "a police contact," App. 27, he should get in touch with his probation officer immediately. The witness stated that, on a previous occasion, when respondent had had a police contact and had failed to communicate with Christiansen, the probation officer had reprimanded him. *Id.*, at 28. This testimony, respondent argued, indicated that when he asked for his probation officer, he was in fact asserting his right to remain silent in the face of further questioning.

In a ruling from the bench, the court denied the motion to suppress....

On appeal, the Supreme Court of California took the case by transfer from the California Court of Appeal and, by a divided vote, reversed....

II

...This Court...has not heretofore extended the *per se* aspects of the *Miranda* safeguards beyond the scope of the holding in the *Miranda* case itself.[4] We therefore must examine the California court's decision to determine whether that court's conclusion so to extend *Miranda* is in harmony with *Miranda*'s underlying principles. For it is clear that "a State may not impose...greater restrictions as a matter of *federal constitutional law* when this Court specifically refrains from imposing them." *Oregon v. Hass*, 420 U.S. 714, 719 (1975) (emphasis in original)....

The rule the Court established in *Miranda* is clear. In order to be able to use statements obtained during custodial interrogation of the accused, the State must warn the accused prior to such questioning of his right to remain silent and of his right to have counsel, retained or appointed, present during interrogation. 384 U.S., at 473. "Once the warnings have been given, the subsequent procedure is clear." *Ibid.*

> If the individual indicates in any manner, at any time prior to or during questioning, that he wishes to remain silent, the interrogation must cease. At this point he has shown that he intends to exercise his Fifth Amendment privilege; any statement taken after the person invokes his privilege cannot be other than the product of compulsion, subtle or otherwise....If the individual states that he wants an attorney, the interrogation must cease until an attorney is present. At that time, the individual must have an opportunity to confer with the attorney and to have him present during any subsequent questioning. If the individual cannot obtain an attorney and he indicates that he wants one before speaking to police, they must respect his decision to remain silent. *Id.*, at 473–474 (footnote omitted).

Any statements obtained during custodial interrogation conducted in violation of these rules may not be admitted against the accused, at least during the State's case in chief. *Id.*, at 479....

...*Miranda*'s holding has the virtue of informing police and prosecutors with specificity as to what they may do in conducting custodial interrogation, and of informing courts under what circumstances statements obtained during such interrogation are not admissible. This gain in specificity, which benefits the accused and the State alike, has been thought to outweigh

4. Indeed, this Court has not yet held that *Miranda* applies with full force to exclude evidence obtained in violation of its proscriptions from consideration in juvenile proceedings, which for certain purposes have been distinguished from formal criminal prosecutions. See *McKeiver v. Pennsylvania*, 403 U.S. 528, 540–541 (1971) (plurality opinion). We do not decide that issue today. In view of our disposition of this case, we assume without deciding that the *Miranda* principles were fully applicable to the present proceedings.

the burdens that the decision in *Miranda* imposes on law enforcement agencies and the courts by requiring the suppression of trustworthy and highly probative evidence even though the confession might be voluntary under traditional Fifth Amendment analysis.

The California court in this case, however, significantly has extended this rule by providing that a request by a juvenile for his probation officer has the same effect as a request for an attorney....

The rule in *Miranda*, however, was based on this Court's perception that the lawyer occupies a critical position in our legal system because of his unique ability to protect the Fifth Amendment rights of a client undergoing custodial interrogation. Because of this special ability of the lawyer to help the client preserve his Fifth Amendment rights once the client becomes enmeshed in the adversary process, the Court found that "the right to have counsel present at the interrogation is indispensable to the protection of the Fifth Amendment privilege under the system" established by the Court. *Id.*, at 469. Moreover, the lawyer's presence helps guard against overreaching by the police and ensures that any statements actually obtained are accurately transcribed for presentation into evidence. *Id.*, at 470.

The *per se* aspect of *Miranda* was thus based on the unique role the lawyer plays in the adversary system of criminal justice in this country. Whether it is a minor or an adult who stands accused, the lawyer is the one person to whom society as a whole looks as the protector of the legal rights of that person in his dealings with the police and the courts. For this reason, the Court fashioned in *Miranda* the rigid rule that an accused's request for an attorney is per se an invocation of his Fifth Amendment rights, requiring that all interrogation cease.

A probation officer is not in the same posture with regard to either the accused or the system of justice as a whole. Often he is not trained in the law, and so is not in a position to advise the accused as to his legal rights. Neither is he a trained advocate, skilled in the representation of the interests of his client before both police and courts. He does not assume the power to act on behalf of his client by virtue of his status as adviser, nor are the communications of the accused to the probation officer shielded by the lawyer-client privilege.

Moreover, the probation officer is the employee of the State which seeks to prosecute the alleged offender. He is a peace officer, and as such is allied, to a greater or lesser extent, with his fellow peace officers. He owes an obligation to the State, notwithstanding the obligation he may also owe the juvenile under his supervision. In most cases, the probation officer is duty bound to report wrongdoing by the juvenile when it comes to his attention, even if by communication from the juvenile himself. Indeed, when this case arose, the probation officer had the responsibility for filing the petition alleging wrongdoing by the juvenile and seeking to have him taken into the custody of the Juvenile Court. It was respondent's probation officer who filed the petition against him, and it is the acting chief of probation for the State of California, a probation officer, who is petitioner in this Court today.[5]

5. When this case arose, a California statute provided that a proceeding in juvenile court to declare a minor a ward of the court was to be commenced by the filing of a petition by a probation officer. This provision since has been amended to provide that most such petitions are to be filed by the prosecuting attorney. Respondent argues that, whatever the status of the probation officer as a peace officer at the time this case arose, the amendment of [the statute] indicates that in the future a probation officer is not to be viewed as a legal adversary of the accused juvenile.

In these circumstances, it cannot be said that the probation officer is able to offer the type of independent advice that an accused would expect from a lawyer retained or assigned to assist him during questioning. Indeed, the probation officer's duty to his employer in many, if not most, cases would conflict sharply with the interests of the juvenile. For where an attorney might well advise his client to remain silent in the face of interrogation by the police, and in doing so would be "exercising [his] good professional judgment...to protect to the extent of his ability the rights of his client," *Miranda v. Arizona*, 384 U.S., at 480–481, a probation officer would be bound to advise his charge to cooperate with the police....

By the same token, a lawyer is able to protect his client's rights by learning the extent, if any, of the client's involvement in the crime under investigation, and advising his client accordingly. To facilitate this, the law rightly protects the communications between client and attorney from discovery. We doubt, however, that similar protections will be afforded the communications between the probation officer and the minor. Indeed, we doubt that a probation officer, consistent with his responsibilities to the public and his profession, could withhold from the police or the courts facts made known to him by the juvenile implicating the juvenile in the crime under investigation.

We thus believe it clear that the probation officer is not in a position to offer the type of legal assistance necessary to protect the Fifth Amendment rights of an accused undergoing custodial interrogation that a lawyer can offer. The Court in *Miranda* recognized that "the attorney plays a vital role in the administration of criminal justice under our Constitution." 384 U.S., at 481. It is this pivotal role of legal counsel that justifies the *per se* rule established in *Miranda*, and that distinguishes the request for counsel from the request for a probation officer, a clergyman, or a close friend. A probation officer simply is not necessary, in the way an attorney is, for the protection of the legal rights of the accused, juvenile or adult. He is significantly handicapped by the position he occupies in the juvenile system from serving as an effective protector of the rights of a juvenile suspected of a crime....

Nor do we believe that a request by a juvenile to speak with his probation officer constitutes a *per se* request to remain silent. As indicated, since a probation officer does not fulfill the important role in protecting the rights of the accused juvenile that an attorney plays, we decline to find that the request for the probation officer is tantamount to the request for an attorney. And there is nothing inherent in the request for a probation officer that requires us to find that a juvenile's request to see one necessarily constitutes an expression of the juvenile's right to remain silent. As discussed below, courts may take into account such a request in evaluating whether a juvenile in fact had waived his Fifth Amendment rights before confessing. But in other circumstances such a request might well be consistent with a desire to speak with the police. In the absence of further evidence that the minor intended in the circumstances to invoke his Fifth Amendment rights by such a request, we decline to attach such overwhelming significance to this request.

We hold, therefore, that it was error to find that the request by respondent to speak with his probation officer *per se* constituted an invocation of respondent's Fifth Amendment right to be free from compelled self-incrimination. It therefore was also error to hold that because

We disagree. The fact that a California probation officer in 1976 was responsible for initiating a complaint is only one factor in our analysis. The fact remains that a probation officer does not fulfill the role in our system of criminal justice that an attorney does, regardless of whether he acts merely as a counselor or has significant law enforcement duties....

the police did not then cease interrogating respondent the statements he made during interrogation should have been suppressed.

III

Miranda further recognized that after the required warnings are given the accused, "[i]f the interrogation continues without the presence of an attorney and a statement is taken, a heavy burden rests on the government to demonstrate that the defendant knowingly and intelligently waived his privilege against self-incrimination and his right to retained or appointed counsel." 384 U.S., at 475. We noted in *North Carolina v. Butler*, 441 U.S., at 373, that the question whether the accused waived his rights "is not one of form, but rather whether the defendant in fact knowingly and voluntarily waived the rights delineated in the *Miranda* case." Thus, the determination whether statements obtained during custodial interrogation are admissible against the accused is to be made upon an inquiry into the totality of the circumstances surrounding the interrogation, to ascertain whether the accused in fact knowingly and voluntarily decided to forgo his rights to remain silent and to have the assistance of counsel. *Miranda v. Arizona*, 384 U.S., at 475–477.

This totality-of-the-circumstances approach is adequate to determine whether there has been a waiver even where interrogation of juveniles is involved. We discern no persuasive reasons why any other approach is required where the question is whether a juvenile has waived his rights, as opposed to whether an adult has done so. The totality approach permits—indeed, it mandates—inquiry into all the circumstances surrounding the interrogation. This includes evaluation of the juvenile's age, experience, education, background, and intelligence, and into whether he has the capacity to understand the warnings given him, the nature of his Fifth Amendment rights, and the consequences of waiving those rights.

Courts repeatedly must deal with these issues of waiver with regard to a broad variety of constitutional rights. There is no reason to assume that such courts—especially juvenile courts, with their special expertise in this area—will be unable to apply the totality-of-the-circumstances analysis so as to take into account those special concerns that are present when young persons, often with limited experience and education and with immature judgment, are involved. Where the age and experience of a juvenile indicate that his request for his probation officer or his parents is, in fact, an invocation of his right to remain silent, the totality approach will allow the court the necessary flexibility to take this into account in making a waiver determination....

We feel that the conclusion of the Juvenile Court was correct. The transcript of the interrogation reveals that the police officers conducting the interrogation took care to ensure that respondent understood his rights. They fully explained to respondent that he was being questioned in connection with a murder. They then informed him of all the rights delineated in *Miranda*, and ascertained that respondent understood those rights. There is no indication in the record that respondent failed to understand what the officers told him. Moreover, after his request to see his probation officer had been denied, and after the police officer once more had explained his rights to him, respondent clearly expressed his willingness to waive his rights and continue the interrogation.

Further, no special factors indicate that respondent was unable to understand the nature of his actions. He was a $16^{1}/_{2}$-year-old juvenile with considerable experience with the police. He had a record of several arrests. He had served time in a youth camp, and he had been on probation for several years. He was under the full-time supervision of probation authorities. There is no indication that he was of insufficient intelligence to understand the rights he was waiving, or what the consequences of that waiver would be. He was not worn down by improper interrogation tactics or lengthy questioning or by trickery or deceit.

On these facts, we think it clear that respondent voluntarily and knowingly waived his Fifth Amendment rights. Respondent argues, however, that any statements he made during interrogation were coerced. Specifically, respondent alleges that the police made threats and promises during the interrogation to pressure him into cooperating in the hope of obtaining leniency for his cooperative attitude. He notes also that he repeatedly told the officers during his interrogation that he wished to stop answering their questions, but that the officers ignored his pleas. He argues further that the record reveals that he was afraid that the police would coerce him, and that this fear caused him to cooperate. He points out that at one point the transcript revealed that he wept during the interrogation.

Review of the entire transcript reveals that respondent's claims of coercion are without merit. As noted, the police took care to inform respondent of his rights and to ensure that he understood them. The officers did not intimidate or threaten respondent in any way. Their questioning was restrained and free from the abuses that so concerned the Court in *Miranda*. See 384 U.S., at 445–455. The police did indeed indicate that a cooperative attitude would be to respondent's benefit, but their remarks in this regard were far from threatening or coercive. And respondent's allegation that he repeatedly asked that the interrogation cease goes too far: at some points he did state that he did not know the answer to a question put to him or that he could not, or would not, answer the question, but these statements were not assertions of his right to remain silent.

IV

...We conclude...that whether the statements obtained during subsequent interrogation of a juvenile who has asked to see his probation officer, but who has not asked to consult an attorney or expressly asserted his right to remain silent, are admissible on the basis of waiver remains a question to be resolved on the totality of the circumstances surrounding the interrogation. On the basis of the record in this case, we hold that the Juvenile Court's findings that respondent voluntarily and knowingly waived his rights and consented to continued interrogation, and that the statements obtained from him were voluntary, were proper, and that the admission of those statements in the proceeding against respondent in Juvenile Court was correct.

Mr. Justice Marshall, with whom Mr. Justice Brennan and Mr. Justice Stevens join, dissenting.

In *Miranda v. Arizona*, 384 U.S. 436 (1966), this Court sought to ensure that the inherently coercive pressures of custodial interrogation would not vitiate a suspect's privilege against self-incrimination....

As this Court has consistently recognized, the coerciveness of the custodial setting is of heightened concern where, as here, a juvenile is under investigation. In *Haley v. Ohio*, 332 U.S. 596 (1948), the plurality reasoned that because a $15^1/_2$-year-old minor was particularly susceptible to overbearing interrogation tactics, the voluntariness of his confession could not "be judged by the more exacting standards of maturity." *Id.*, at 599. The Court reiterated this point in *Gallegos v. Colorado*, 370 U.S. 49, 54 (1962), observing that a 14-year-old suspect could not "be compared with an adult in full possession of his senses and knowledgeable of the consequences of his admissions." The juvenile defendant, in the Court's view, required

> "the aid of more mature judgment as to the steps he should take in the predicament in which he found himself. A lawyer or an adult relative or friend could have given the petitioner the protection which his own immaturity could not." *Ibid.*

And, in *In re Gault*, 387 U.S. 1, 55 (1967), the Court admonished that "the greatest care must be taken to assure that [a minor's] admission was voluntary."

It is therefore critical in the present context that we construe *Miranda*'s prophylactic requirements broadly to accomplish their intended purpose—"dispel[ling] the compulsion inherent in custodial surroundings." 384 U.S., at 458. To effectuate this purpose, the Court must ensure that the "protective device" of legal counsel, *id.*, at 465–466, 469, be readily available, and that any intimation of a desire to preclude questioning be scrupulously honored. Thus, I believe *Miranda* requires that interrogation cease whenever a juvenile requests an adult who is obligated to represent his interests. Such a request, in my judgment, constitutes both an attempt to obtain advice and a general invocation of the right to silence.... Requiring a strict verbal formula to invoke the protections of *Miranda* would "protect the knowledgeable accused from stationhouse coercion while abandoning the young person who knows no more than to ask for the... person he trusts."

On my reading of *Miranda*, a California juvenile's request for his probation officer should be treated as a *per se* assertion of Fifth Amendment rights. The California Supreme Court determined that probation officers have a statutory duty to represent minors' interests and, indeed, are "trusted guardian figure[s]" to whom a juvenile would likely turn for assistance. 21 Cal.3d, at 476, 579 P.2d, at 10. In addition, the court found, probation officers are particularly well suited to assist a juvenile "on such matters as to whether or not he should obtain an attorney" and "how to conduct himself with police." *Id.*, at 476, 477, 579 P.2d, at 10. Hence, a juvenile's request for a probation officer may frequently be an attempt to secure protection from the coercive aspects of custodial questioning.

This Court concludes, however, that because a probation officer has law enforcement duties, juveniles generally would not call upon him to represent their interests, and if they did, would not be well served. But that conclusion ignores the California Supreme Court's express determination that the officer's responsibility to initiate juvenile proceedings did not negate his function as personal adviser to his wards.... Further, although the majority here speculates that probation officers have a duty to advise cooperation with the police,... respondent's probation officer instructed all his charges "not to go and admit openly to an offense, [but rather] to get some type of advice from... parents or a lawyer." Absent an explicit statutory provision or judicial holding, the officer's assessment of the obligations imposed by state law is entitled to deference by this Court.

Thus, given the role of probation officers under California law, a juvenile's request to see his officer may reflect a desire for precisely the kind of assistance *Miranda* guarantees an accused before he waives his Fifth Amendment rights. At the very least, such a request signals a desire to remain silent until contact with the officer is made....

Mr. Justice Powell, dissenting.

Although I agree with the Court that the Supreme Court of California misconstrued *Miranda v. Arizona*, 384 U.S. 436 (1966), I would not reverse the California court's judgment.

This Court repeatedly has recognized that "the greatest care" must be taken to assure that an alleged confession of a juvenile was voluntary. See, *e.g.*, *In re Gault*, 387 U.S. 1, 55 (1967); *Gallegos v. Colorado*, 370 U.S. 49, 54 (1962); *Haley v. Ohio*, 332 U.S. 596, 599–600 (1948) (plurality opinion). Respondent was a young person, 16 years old at the time of his arrest and the subsequent prolonged interrogation at the stationhouse. Although respondent had had prior brushes with the law, and was under supervision by a probation officer, the taped transcript of his interrogation—as well as his testimony at the suppression hearing—demonstrates that he was immature, emotional,[2] and uneducated, and therefore was likely to be vulnerable to the skillful, two-on-one, repetitive style of interrogation to which he was subjected.

When given *Miranda* warnings and asked whether he desired an attorney, respondent requested permission to "have my probation officer here," a request that was refused. That officer testified later that he had communicated frequently with respondent, that respondent had serious and "extensive" family problems, and that the officer had instructed respondent to call him immediately "at any time he has a police contact, even if they stop him and talk to him on the street." The reasons given by the probation officer for having so instructed his charge were substantially the same reasons that prompt this Court to examine with special care the circumstances under which a minor's alleged confession was obtained. After stating that respondent had been "going through problems," the officer observed that "many times the kids don't understand what is going on, and what they are supposed to do relative to police. . . ." This view of the limited understanding of the average 16-year-old was borne out by respondent's question when, during interrogation, he was advised of his right to an attorney: "How I know you guys won't pull no police officer in and tell me he's an attorney?" . . .

The police then proceeded, despite respondent's repeated denial of any connection to the murder under investigation, . . . persistently to press interrogation until they extracted a confession. . . . It is clear that the interrogating police did not exercise "the greatest care" to assure that respondent's "admission was voluntary."[4] In the absence of counsel, and having refused to call the probation officer, they nevertheless engaged in protracted interrogation.

Although I view the case as close, I am not satisfied that this particular 16-year-old boy, in this particular situation, was subjected to a fair interrogation free from inherently coercive circumstances. For these reasons, I would affirm the judgment of the Supreme Court of California.

NOTES AND QUESTIONS

1. Does *Miranda* apply when considering the admissibility of statements in delinquency proceedings?

2. The Juvenile Court Judge observed that he had "heard the tapes" of the interrogation, and was "aware of the fact that Michael [respondent] was crying at the time he talked to the police officers."

4. Minors who become embroiled with the law range from the very young up to those on the brink of majority. Some of the older minors become fully "street-wise," hardened criminals, deserving no greater consideration than that properly accorded all persons suspected of crime. Other minors are more of a child than an adult. As the Court indicated in *In re Gault*, 387 U.S. 1 (1967), the facts relevant to the care to be exercised in a particular case vary widely. They include the minor's age, actual maturity, family environment, education, emotional and mental stability, and, of course, any prior record he might have.

2. Is a request to speak to a probation officer an invocation of the right to counsel? Would the *Gault* court consider such a request to be an invocation of the right to counsel?

3. Is asking to speak to a probation officer the same as asserting one's right to remain silent? Should it be?

4. As noted above, *Miranda* only applies to custodial interrogations. In *Miranda*, the Supreme Court defined custody as taking a person into custody or otherwise depriving him of his freedom of action in any significant way. In determining whether a person is in custody for *Miranda* purposes, a court must consider all of the circumstances surrounding the interrogation and whether a reasonable person would have felt he was not free to terminate the interrogation and leave. The determination is an objective one and does not depend on the subjective views of the police or the suspects being questioned. *Stansbury v. California*, 511 U.S. 318 (1994). What are the characteristics of the reasonable person? Are the juvenile's age and immaturity factors in determining whether the youth is in custody for the purposes of *Miranda*? Consider the following case excerpt when formulating your answer.

YARBOROUGH V. ALVARADO
Supreme Court of the United States
541 U.S. 652 (2004)

[Police investigating a murder asked the parents of seventeen-year-old Michael Alvarado to bring him to the police station to be interviewed. Upon arrival around lunchtime, the investigating officer escorted Alvarado to an interview room while his parents waited in the lobby, although they had asked to accompany him. The interview lasted about two hours and was recorded without the minor's knowledge. The questions focused on another youth, appeals were made for Alvarado to tell the truth, he was twice offered the opportunity to take a break, and at the end of the interview, he was returned to his parents in the lobby. Alvarado subsequently was convicted of murder and sentenced to fifteen years to life. After he challenged the admissibility of his confession on appeal, the state appellate court confirmed, and the state supreme court denied discretionary review. Alvarado then filed a petition for writ of *habeas corpus* in the U.S. District Court for the Central District of California. The district court found that Alvarado was not in custody for *Miranda* purposes. The Ninth Circuit reversed, holding that the state court erred in failing to take into account Alvarado's age and inexperience in assessing whether a reasonable person in his position would have felt free to leave.]

Justice Kennedy delivered the opinion of the Court....

Our more recent cases instruct that custody must be determined based on how a reasonable person in the suspect's situation would perceive his circumstances....

...[I]n *Thompson v. Keohane*, 516 U.S. 99 (1995), the Court offered the following description of the *Miranda* custody test:

> "Two discrete inquiries are essential to the determination: first, what were the circumstances surrounding the interrogation; and second, given those circumstances, would a reasonable person have felt he or she was not at liberty to terminate the interrogation and leave. Once the scene is set and the players' lines and actions are reconstructed, the court must apply an objective test to resolve the

> ultimate inquiry: was there a formal arrest or restraint on freedom of movement of the degree associated with a formal arrest." 516 U.S., at 112 (internal quotation marks and footnote omitted)....

Based on these principles, we conclude that the state court's application of our clearly established law was reasonable....On one hand, certain facts weigh against a finding that Alvarado was in custody. The police did not transport Alvarado to the station or require him to appear at a particular time. Cf. *Oregon v. Mathiason*, 429 U.S. [492], 495 [(1977)]. They did not threaten him or suggest he would be placed under arrest. *Ibid.* Alvarado's parents remained in the lobby during the interview, suggesting that the interview would be brief. See *Berkemer v. McCarty*, 468 U.S. [420], 441–442 [(1984)]. In fact, according to trial counsel for Alvarado, he and his parents were told that the interview was "'not going to be long.'" During the interview, Comstock [the investigating officer] focused on [the codefendant's] crimes rather than Alvarado's. Instead of pressuring Alvarado with the threat of arrest and prosecution, she appealed to his interest in telling the truth and being helpful to a police officer. Cf. *Mathiason*, *supra*, at 495. In addition, Comstock twice asked Alvarado if he wanted to take a break. At the end of the interview, Alvarado went home. All of these objective facts are consistent with an interrogation environment in which a reasonable person would have felt free to terminate the interview and leave. Indeed, a number of the facts echo those of *Mathiason*, a *per curiam* summary reversal in which we found it "clear from these facts" that the suspect was not in custody. 429 U.S., at 495.

Other facts point in the opposite direction. Comstock interviewed Alvarado at the police station. The interview lasted two hours, four times longer than the 30-minute interview in *Mathiason*. Unlike the officer in *Mathiason*, Comstock did not tell Alvarado that he was free to leave. Alvarado was brought to the police station by his legal guardians rather than arriving on his own accord, making the extent of his control over his presence unclear. Counsel for Alvarado alleges that Alvarado's parents asked to be present at the interview but were rebuffed, a fact that—if known to Alvarado—might reasonably have led someone in Alvarado's position to feel more restricted than otherwise. These facts weigh in favor of the view that Alvarado was in custody.

These differing indications lead us to hold that the state court's application of our custody standard was reasonable. The Court of Appeals was nowhere close to the mark when it concluded otherwise. Although the question of what an "unreasonable application" of law might be is difficult in some cases, it is not difficult here. The custody test is general, and the state court's application of our law fits within the matrix of our prior decisions....

The Court of Appeals reached the opposite result by placing considerable reliance on Alvarado's age and inexperience with law enforcement. Our Court has not stated that a suspect's age or experience is relevant to the *Miranda* custody analysis, and counsel for Alvarado did not press the importance of either factor on direct appeal or in habeas proceedings. According to the Court of Appeals, however, our Court's emphasis on juvenile status in other contexts demanded consideration of Alvarado's age and inexperience here. The Court of Appeals viewed the state court's failure to "'extend a clearly established legal principle [of the relevance of juvenile status] to a new context'" as objectively unreasonable in this case, requiring issuance of the writ....

...Our opinions applying the *Miranda* custody test have not mentioned the suspect's age, much less mandated its consideration. The only indications in the Court's opinions relevant to a suspect's experience with law enforcement have rejected reliance on such factors.

There is an important conceptual difference between the *Miranda* custody test and the line of cases from other contexts considering age and experience. The *Miranda* custody inquiry is an objective test. As we stated in *Keohane*, "[o]nce the scene is set and the players' lines and actions are reconstructed, the court must apply an objective test to resolve the ultimate inquiry." 516 U.S, at 112 (internal quotation marks omitted). The objective test furthers "the clarity of [*Miranda*'s] rule," ensuring that the police do not need "to make guesses as to [the circumstances] at issue before deciding how they may interrogate the suspect." To be sure, the line between permissible objective facts and impermissible subjective experiences can be indistinct in some cases. It is possible to subsume a subjective factor into an objective test by making the latter more specific in its formulation. Thus the Court of Appeals styled its inquiry as an objective test by considering what a "reasonable 17-year-old, with no prior history of arrest or police interviews," would perceive.

At the same time, the objective *Miranda* custody inquiry could reasonably be viewed as different from doctrinal tests that depend on the actual mindset of a particular suspect, where we do consider a suspect's age and experience. For example, the voluntariness of a statement is often said to depend on whether "the defendant's will was overborne," *Lynumn v. Illinois*, 372 U.S. 528, 534 (1963), a question that logically can depend on "the characteristics of the accused," *Schneckloth v. Bustamonte*, 412 U.S. 218, 226 (1973). The characteristics of the accused can include the suspect's age, education, and intelligence, see *ibid.*, as well as a suspect's prior experience with law enforcement, see *Lynumn*, *supra*, at 534. In concluding that there was "no principled reason" why such factors should not also apply to the *Miranda* custody inquiry, the Court of Appeals ignored the argument that the custody inquiry states an objective rule designed to give clear guidance to the police, while consideration of a suspect's individual characteristic—including his age—could be viewed as creating a subjective inquiry. For these reasons, the state court's failure to consider Alvarado's age does not provide a proper basis for finding that the state court's decision was an unreasonable application of clearly established law....

The state court considered the proper factors and reached a reasonable conclusion. The judgment of the Court of Appeals is

Reversed.

JUSTICE O'CONNOR, concurring.

I join the opinion of the Court, but write separately to express an additional reason for reversal. There may be cases in which a suspect's age will be relevant to the "custody" inquiry under *Miranda v. Arizona*, 384 U.S. 436 (1966). In this case, however, Alvarado was almost 18 years old at the time of his interview. It is difficult to expect police to recognize that a suspect is a juvenile when he is so close to the age of majority. Even when police do know a suspect's age, it may be difficult for them to ascertain what bearing it has on the likelihood that the suspect would feel free to leave. That is especially true here; $17^1/_2$-year-olds vary widely in their reactions to police questioning, and many can be expected to behave as adults. Given these difficulties, I agree that the state court's decision in this case cannot be called an unreasonable application of federal law simply because it failed explicitly to mention Alvarado's age.

JUSTICE BREYER, with whom JUSTICE STEVENS, JUSTICE SOUTER, and JUSTICE GINSBURG join, dissenting.

In my view, Michael Alvarado clearly was "in custody" when the police questioned him (without *Miranda* warnings) about the murder.... Would a "reasonable person" in Alvarado's "position" have felt he was "at liberty to terminate the interrogation and leave"? A court must answer this question in light of "all of the circumstances surrounding the interrogation." And the obvious answer here is "no."...

What reasonable person in the circumstances—brought to a police station by his parents at police request, put in a small interrogation room, questioned for a solid two hours, and confronted with claims that there is strong evidence that he participated in a serious crime, could have thought to himself, "Well, anytime I want to leave I can just get up and walk out"? If the person harbored any doubts, would he still think he might be free to leave once he recalls that the police officer has just refused to let his parents remain with him during questioning? Would he still think that he, rather than the officer, controls the situation?...

The facts to which the majority points make clear what the police did *not* do, for example, come to Alvarado's house, tell him he was under arrest, handcuff him, place him in a locked cell, threaten him, or tell him explicitly that he was not free to leave. But what is important here is what the police *did* do—namely, have Alvarado's parents bring him to the station, put him with a single officer in a small room, keep his parents out, let him know that he was a suspect, and question him for two hours. These latter facts compel a single conclusion: A reasonable person in Alvarado's circumstances would not have felt free to terminate the interrogation and leave.

What about Alvarado's youth? The fact that Alvarado was 17 helps to show that he was unlikely to have felt free to ignore his parents' request to come to the station. And a 17-year-old is more likely than, say, a 35-year-old, to take a police officer's assertion of authority to keep parents outside the room as an assertion of authority to keep their child inside as well....

...Our cases do instruct lower courts to apply a "reasonable person" standard. But the "reasonable person" standard does not require a court to pretend that Alvarado was a 35-year-old with aging parents whose middle-aged children do what their parents ask only out of respect. Nor does it say that a court should pretend that Alvarado was the statistically determined "average person"—a working, married, 35-year-old white female with a high school degree. See U.S. Dept. of Commerce, Bureau of Census, Statistical Abstract of the United States: 2003 (123d ed.).

Rather, the precise legal definition of "reasonable person" may, depending on legal context, appropriately account for certain personal characteristics. In negligence suits, for example, the question is what would a "reasonable person" do "'under the same or similar circumstances.'" In answering that question, courts enjoy "latitude" and may make "allowance not only for external facts, but sometimes for certain characteristics of the actor himself," including physical disability, youth, or advanced age. This allowance makes sense in light of the tort standard's recognized purpose: deterrence. Given that purpose, why pretend that a child is an adult or that a blind man can see?

In the present context, that of *Miranda*'s "in custody" inquiry, the law has introduced the concept of a "reasonable person" to avoid judicial inquiry into subjective states of mind, and to focus the inquiry instead upon objective circumstances that are known to both the officer and the suspect and that are likely relevant to the way a person would understand his situation....

In this case, Alvarado's youth is an objective circumstance that was known to the police. It is not a special quality, but rather a widely shared characteristic that generates commonsense conclusions about behavior and perception. To focus on the circumstance of age in a case like this does not complicate the "in custody" inquiry. And to say that courts should ignore widely shared, objective characteristics, like age, on the ground that only a (large) minority of the population possesses them would produce absurd results, the present instance being a case in point....

Our cases also make clear that to determine how a suspect would have "gaug[ed]" his "freedom of movement," a court must carefully examine "all of the circumstances surrounding the interrogation," including, for example, how long the interrogation lasted (brief and routine or protracted?), how the suspect came to be questioned (voluntarily or against his will?), where the questioning took place (at a police station or in public?), and what the officer communicated to the individual during the interrogation (that he was a suspect? that he was under arrest? that he was free to leave at will?). In the present case, every one of these factors argues—and argues strongly—that Alvarado was in custody for *Miranda* purposes when the police questioned him.

Common sense, and an understanding of the law's basic purpose in this area, are enough to make clear that Alvarado's age—an objective, widely shared characteristic about which the police plainly knew—is also relevant to the inquiry. Unless one is prepared to pretend that Alvarado is someone he is not, a middle-aged gentleman, well versed in police practices, it seems to me clear that the California courts made a serious mistake. I agree with the Ninth Circuit's similar conclusions. Consequently, I dissent.

5. When is a minor in custody for purposes of *Miranda*? Is a 17-year-old juvenile in custody when he is kept at home by his parents in order to be interviewed by a police officer, the interview occurs in the minor's home, and his parents are asked to leave the room after the minor denies the allegations? *Lee v. State*, 988 So.2d 52 (Fla. App. 1st Dist. 2008). Is a 15-year-old boy who is placed in a residential treatment facility for sexually abusive boys pursuant to the state's abuse and neglect jurisdiction in custody when he makes statements to the treatment staff that implicate him in criminal activity? *State v. Miller*, 2005-Ohio-4032 (Ohio App. 2d Dist.). What if the minor had been adjudicated delinquent, was committed to a sex-offender treatment facility, and, during that commitment, made incriminating statements to the staff? *Welch v. Commonwealth*, 149 S.W.3d 407 (Ky. 2004). If a juvenile absconds from a secure juvenile facility and subsequently turns himself in, is he in custody when he is questioned by intake staff about his whereabouts and activities during the time he was gone? *State v. Swink*, 11 P.3d 299 (Utah App. 2000). Is an 11-year-old boy in custody when he voluntarily goes to the police station, is questioned until 2:00 a.m., but police officers testify that they never intended to elicit incriminating statements from the boy? *People v. T.C.*, 898 P.2d 20 (Colo. 1995).

6. Is a minor in custody for *Miranda* purposes when he is at school? Consider *In re C.H.*, 763 N.W.2d 708 (Neb. 2009) (minor in custody for *Miranda* purposes, when minor was interviewed in principal's office by police officers investigating serious offense, was not advised that he was free to leave or not under arrest or that he did not have to talk to police or answer any questions, and he was placed in custody at the conclusion of the interrogation); *In re D.A.R.*, 73 S.W.3d 505, 512 (Tx.Ct.App. 2002) (holding that child was in custody when he had initially been questioned by the school's assistant principal, had returned to class, and was then summoned back to the school office to speak with investigating officer); *In re Doe*, 130 Idaho 811, 948 P.2d 166, 174 (Idaho Ct.App. 1997) (holding that *Miranda* warnings were required when child suspect was removed from class to speak with two police officers in closed room adjoining the principal's office); *In re G.S.P.*, 610 N.W.2d 651, 659 (Minn.Ct.App. 2000) (holding that student was in custody when questioned by principal and police officer in principal's office and not informed that he was not under arrest and did not have to answer any questions); *In re L.M.*, 993 S.W.2d 276,

290 (Tx.Ct.App. 1999) (holding that child suspect was in custody when interviewed by investigating officers in a separate room in the offices of the juvenile shelter where she was placed after being arrested for offense at issue); *In re T.J.C.*, 662 N.W.2d 175, 181 (Minn.Ct.App. 2003) (holding that fifteen-year-old suspect was in custody when summoned from his classroom to principal's office for police interview), *rev'd on other grounds*, 667 N.W.2d 108 (Minn. 2003); *State v. D.R.*, 84 Wash.App. 832, 930 P.2d 350, 353 (1997) (holding that juvenile suspect was in custody when summoned to assistant principal's office and interviewed by plainclothes officer, because "a reasonable 14-year-old in D.R.'s position would have reasonably supposed his freedom of action was curtailed"); *In re Killitz*, 59 Or.App. 720, 651 P.2d 1382 (1982) (holding that juvenile suspect who was summoned to principal's office during school hours, where he was questioned by a police officer, was in custody). But see *Doe v. Bagan*, 41 F.3d 571, 575 n. 3 (10th Cir. 1994) (holding that even though nine-year-old suspect may not have felt free to leave, he was not in *Miranda* custody when interviewed by two social services workers in principal's office at school); *State v. Budke*, 372 N.W.2d 799, 801 (Minn.Ct.App. 1985) (finding no custody where eighteen-year-old suspect was informed by interrogating officer that he was free to leave the principal's office at any time); *In re Loredo*, 125 Or.App. 390, 865 P.2d 1312, 1314–1315 (1993) (distinguishing *Killitz* and holding that student was not in custody because officer informed child he was not under arrest, could leave at any time, and did not have to answer any questions).

In light of the aforementioned cases, how would a court resolve the following? A high school student was given a hall pass and told to report to the assistant principal's office to speak to a police detective. In the office were the detective and two assistant principals. The door was closed but unlocked. The minor sat in a chair near the door, one of the vice principals sat behind his desk, the other stood by a filing cabinet, and the detective sat in a chair in the corner. The detective did not read the student *Miranda* warnings and proceeded to question the student. The detective did not raise his voice during the interview, did not tell the student that he was free to leave or not free to leave, and did not arrest the student after questioning ended. Was the minor's Fifth Amendment privilege against self-incrimination violated? *In re A.A.*, 2009-Ohio-4094 (Ohio App. 9th Dist. 2009)

7. Do school officials need to give *Miranda* warnings before questioning students? Generally, school officials are not law-enforcement agents and thus need not give *Miranda* warnings when questioning students. However, when school officials act as agents or instruments of the police, then *Miranda* warnings must be given prior to custodial interrogation. In *State v. Tinkham*, 719 A.2d 580 (N.H. 1998), Deborah Brooks, the school principal, recovered a bag of marijuana from a student and learned that the student had purchased the drugs from Frederick Tinkham at school. The principal took the marijuana to the police station and told police that she planned to question the minor the next day about the drugs. No evidence was introduced indicating that the police suggested this particular course of action or participated in the questioning. The New Hampshire Supreme Court stated:

> Although school principals are "responsible for administration and discipline within the school," *Navajo Co. Juv. Act. No. JV91000058*, 183 Ariz. 204, 901 P.2d 1247, 1249 (Ariz.Ct.App. 1995), and "must regularly conduct inquiries concerning both violations of school rules and violations of law," [*State v.*] *Biancamano*, 666 A.2d [199,] 203 [overruled on other grounds, *State v. Dalziel*, 867 A.2d 1167 (2005)] they are not law enforcement agents. They are "neither trained nor equipped to conduct police investigations," *Biancamano*, 666 A.2d at 203, and, unlike law enforcement agents, enforcing the law is not their primary mission. *Navajo Co. Juv. Act. No. JV91000058*, 901 P.2d at 1249.... Our conclusion that Brooks is not a law enforcement officer is in accordance with the reasoning of the many jurisdictions that have

refused to require public school officials to administer *Miranda* warnings. *See, e.g., Navajo Co. Juv. Act. No. JV91000058*, 901 P.2d at 1249....

We next address whether Brooks acted as an agent of the police, because a school official acting as an instrument or agent of the police may be required to administer *Miranda* warnings.... Here, there was no affirmative act by any police officer inducing Brooks to question the defendant. In fact, it was Brooks who approached the Wolfeboro police and told them of her conversation with the student who implicated the defendant, and that she planned on questioning the defendant when she returned to school. The record does not reflect that the Wolfeboro police made any suggestions to Brooks or directed her course of action. Moreover, "[t]he fact that the school administrators had every intention of turning the marihuana over to the police does not make them agents or instrumentalities of the police in questioning [the defendant]."

We therefore conclude that because Brooks was neither a law enforcement officer nor an agent of the police, *Miranda* warnings were not required. The need to question students about possible misconduct is necessary to maintain a safe school environment and demands that school officials receive some latitude in their questioning. *See T.L.O.*, 469 U.S. at 339–40, 105 S.Ct. 733....

Id. at 583-584.

Are school resource officers law-enforcement agents or school officials for *Miranda* purposes? Under a state statue, a court may appoint school police officers to serve in the school districts within their jurisdiction and may grant them the same powers as are extended to municipal police officers. The school police officers then are considered employees of the school district. Under these circumstances, would a school police officer have to give *Miranda* warnings before engaging in custodial interrogation? See *In re R.H.*, 791 A.2d 331 (Pa. 2002). What if school officials and the school resource officer have "an understanding" that school officials will investigate certain offenses because school officials can "play by different rules"? See *In re T.A.G.*, 663 S.E.2d 392 (Ga. App. 2008); *State v. Heirtzler*, 789 A.2d 634 (N.H. 2001).

8. According to the School Survey on Crime and Safety, in 2007–08, 85 percent of all schools recorded at least one criminal incident at school and reported 62 percent of those incidents to police. Also, 45.1 percent of city schools, 43.2 percent of schools with a minority enrollment of 50 percent or more, and 47.1 percent of schools providing free lunches to more than 75 percent of the student body reported incidents of violent crime to the police. City schools, compared with schools with different urbanicities, had the highest rates of violent and serious violent crime per 1,000 students (35.8/1,000 and 1.9/1,000, respectively). These schools also had a higher rate of reporting violent and serious violent crimes to the police (9/1,000 for violent crimes and 1/1,000 for serious violent crimes). Schools with minority enrollments of 50 percent or more had even higher incidence rates of violent and serious violent crimes (36.6/1,000 and 2.0/1,000, respectively), a lower rate of reporting for violent crimes (8.3/1,000), and the same rate of reporting for serious violent crimes (1/1,000) as did city schools. Schools with the highest percentage of students receiving free lunches had the highest rates of violent crime (45.0/1,000) and serious violent crime (2.8/1,000). These schools had similar rates of reporting violent (8.3/1,000) and serious violent crimes (1.1/1,000). Rachel Dinkes, et al., *References, Indicators of School Crime and Safety: 2009*, National Center for Education Statistics, Institute of Education Sciences, U.S. Department of Education, and Bureau of Justice Statistics, http://nces.ed.gov/pubsearch/pubsinfo.asp?pubid=2010012. Do the data indicate that schools and law enforcement collaborate frequently, thus implying an agency relationship?

9. *Interrogation.* Interrogation encompasses not only express questioning but also "its functional equivalent," that is, "any words or actions on the part of the police... that the police should know are reasonably likely to elicit an incriminating response." *Rhode Island v. Innis*, 446 U.S. 291,

301 (1980). Do the police need to take particular care when the suspect in police custody is a juvenile? Did a police officer interrogate a juvenile suspect when, after executing an arrest warrant for the minor for theft of a firearm, the officer said, "I told him that my interest is in returning this firearm, and if he would somehow—he can help himself if he would give this firearm back to me or know who has it, we'd go from there, and hopefully it would benefit him down the road, and I would stand up for him and let everybody know in the criminal justice system what a good deed he did by returning this firearm"? See *In re D.H.*, 863 A.2d 562 (Pa. Super. 2004). Did the police interrogate a juvenile when, after executing an arrest warrant, the officer said, "You said you were going to turn yourself in yesterday when I spoke to you, you said you were going to turn yourself in at 8:00 in the morning"? *Commonwealth v. Clark C.*, 797 N.E.2d 5 (Mass. App. 2005).

10. *Warnings.* In *Miranda,* the Supreme Court held that the police must provide warnings to a suspect in custody prior to commencing interrogation. These warnings include the right to remain silent, an explanation that "anything said can and will be used against the individual in court," "the right to consult with a lawyer and to have the lawyer with him during interrogation," and that a lawyer will be appointed if the individual is indigent. *Miranda*, 384 U.S. at 468–471. Nevertheless, the Supreme Court has held that no "talismanic incantation" of the warnings is required, provided the warnings actually given are the "fully effective equivalent" of the *Miranda* warnings. *California v. Prysock*, 453 U.S. 355, 359–360 (1981). Thus, a statement that the police "have no way of giving you a lawyer, but one will be appointed for you, if you wish, when you go to court" did not render the warnings defective. *Duckworth v. Eagan*, 492 U.S. 195, 203 (1989).

11. *Specialized warnings.* Must the police tell a minor he may be subject to criminal prosecution before questioning him? *State v. Fardan*, 773 N.W.2d 303 (Minn. 2009) (police should warn minor that statement may be used against him in criminal prosecution before proceeding with interrogation, but warnings may still be adequate if knowledge of potential criminal prosecution could be imputed to minor by considering circumstances surrounding the interrogation); *Elvik v. State*, 965 P.2d 281 (Nev. 1998) (juvenile should be informed of possibility of adult trial, but "where the nature of the charges and the identity of the interrogator reflect the existence of an unquestionably adversary police atmosphere and the suspect is reasonably mature and sophisticated with regard to the nature of the process, resulting statements will be admissible in a criminal trial provided that the record otherwise supports a finding of voluntariness"); *State v. Benoit*, 490 A.2d 295 (N.H. 1985) ("when a confession is to be admitted against a child in adult *criminal* court, we are persuaded that for a judge to conclude that the statements were made knowingly and intelligently, the child, when facing a charge that would be a felony if committed by an adult, must have been advised of the possibility of his being tried as an adult and of his being subject to adult criminal sanctions"); *State v. Perez*, 591 A.2d 119 (Conn. 1991) (rejecting rule that requires police to inform minor of possibility of criminal trial and reaffirming reliance on totality-of-circumstances test).

Should juveniles receive a simplified version of *Miranda*? Some commentators have said yes. IJA-ABA Standards Relating to Interim Status: The Release, Control, and Detention of Accused Juvenile Offenders between Arrest and Disposition, § 5-3 (1980) (officer should explain in clearly understandable language the warnings required by the constitution); National Advisory Committee for Juvenile Justice and Delinquency Prevention, *Standards for the Administration of Juvenile Justice* § 2.247 (1980) (warnings "explained in language understandable by the juvenile"). In *State v. Benoit*, 490 A.2d 295 (N.H. 1985), the New Hampshire Supreme Court offered this:

> Before I am allowed to ask you any questions, you must understand that you have certain rights, or protections, that have been given to you by law. These rights make sure that you

will be treated fairly. You will not be punished for deciding to use these rights. I will read your rights and explain them to you. You may ask questions as we go along so that you can fully understand what your rights are. Do you understand me so far? Yes—No—.

1. You have the right to remain silent. This means that you do not have to say or write anything. You do not have to talk to anyone or answer any questions we ask you. You will not be punished for deciding not to talk to us. Do you understand this right? Yes—No—.

2. Anything you say can and will be used against you in a court. This means that if you do say or write anything, what you say or write will be used in a court to prove that you may have broken the law. Do you understand this? Yes—No—.

3. You have the right to talk to a lawyer before any questioning. You have the right to have the lawyer with you while you are being questioned. The lawyer will help you decide what you should do or say. The things you say to the lawyer cannot be used in court to prove that you may have broken the law. If you decide you want a lawyer, we will not question you until you have been allowed to talk to the lawyer. Do you understand this right? Yes—No—.

4. If you want to talk to a lawyer and you cannot afford one, we will get you a lawyer at no cost to you before any questioning begins. This means that if you want a lawyer and you cannot pay for one, you still may have one. Do you understand this right? Yes—No—.

5. You can refuse to answer any or all questions at any time. You also can ask to have a lawyer with you at any time. This means that if you decide, at any time during questioning, that you do not want to talk, you may tell us to stop and you cannot be asked any more questions. Also, if you decide you would like to talk to a lawyer at any time during questioning, you will not be asked any more questions until a lawyer is with you. Do you understand this right? Yes—No—.

6. (In felony cases only) There is a possibility that you may not be brought to juvenile court but instead will be treated as an adult in criminal court. There you could go to a county jail or the State prison. If you are treated as an adult you will have to go through the adult criminal system, just as if you were 18 years old. If that happens, you will not receive the protections of the juvenile justice system. Do you understand this? Yes—No—.

7. Do you have any questions so far? Yes—No—.

(This portion is now to be read by the child.)

I can read and understand English. Yes—No—.

I have been read and I have read my rights as listed above. I fully understand what my rights are. I do not want to answer any questions at this time and I would like to have a lawyer.

Signature of child _______________ Date ________ Time

Waiver of Rights

(This portion is to be read by the child.)

I can read and understand English. Yes—No—.

I have been read and I have read my rights as listed above. I fully understand what my rights are. I have been asked if I have any questions and I do not have any. I am willing to give up my right to silence and answer questions. I give up my right to have a lawyer present. I do not wish to speak to a lawyer before I answer any questions. No promises or threats or offers of deals have been made to me to make me give up my rights. I understand that I may change my mind at any time and say that I want my rights if I choose. However, if I change my mind, it will not affect what I have already done or said.

Signature of child _______________ Date ________ Time

Signature of witness _______________ Date ________ Time

Id. at 306–307. Do you think juveniles will understand their rights more readily with this form?

Some jurisdictions require specialized warnings pursuant to a statute or court rule. Does a failure to comply with these additional requirements render the minor's confession inadmissible? *Taylor v. Commonwealth*, 276 S.W.3d 800 (Ky. 2009) (technical noncompliance with statute requiring police to notify parent of child's arrest, the specific charges, and the reason for taking child into custody does not render voluntary confession inadmissible); *Ford v. State*, 138 P.3d 500 (Nev. 2006) (statute requiring police to notify parent that child is in custody is not a condition precedent to obtaining a confession); *Shackleford v. Commonwealth*, 547 S.E.2d 899 (Va. 2001) (failure to inform minor of purported right to speak to embassy official did not violate Vienna Convention or constitutional rights); *State v. Perry*, 954 S.W.2d 554 (Mo. App. S.D. 1997) (totality of circumstances indicates that police substantially complied with court rule requiring that juvenile be informed that statements may be used in adult court proceeding). If law-enforcement authorities in one state obtain a statement from the minor, who then is tried in another state, should the prosecuting state suppress the confession if investigating authorities failed to comply with the procedures of the prosecuting state governing juvenile confessions? *Vega v. State*, 255 S.W.3d 87 (Tex. App. Corpus Christi 2007); *United States v. Doe*, 170 F.3d 1162 (9th Cir. 1999) (failure to comply with federal statute requiring officer to notify parents of juvenile's custody and *Miranda* rights harmless error under totality of circumstances).

12. *Waiver.* In *Miranda*, the Supreme Court held that a suspect could waive his rights but that such waiver must be made knowingly, intelligently, and voluntarily. Such waiver may not be implied from the silence of the accused. In *North Carolina v. Butler*, 441 U.S. 369 (1979), however, the Court held that while the state must prove that a waiver has occurred, the waiver itself could be "inferred from the actions and words of the person interrogated." *Id.* at 375–376. In determining whether the waiver is voluntary, the Court has stated that it must be "the product of a free and deliberate choice rather than intimidation, coercion, or deception." *Moran v. Burbine*, 475 U.S. 412, 421 (1986). The voluntariness determination under *Miranda*, however, does not require more than that required under the Fourteenth Amendment. *Colorado v. Connelly*, 479 U.S. 153, 169–170 (1986). To determine if the waiver is knowing and intelligent, the Court has held that it "must have been made with a full awareness of both the nature of the right being abandoned and the consequences of the decision to abandon it." *Moran*, 475 U.S. at 421.

Fare made clear that the Court would apply a totality-of-the-circumstances test when assessing the validity of waivers made by juveniles. Because the test is broad, judges exercise considerable discretion when determining the validity of a waiver. Barry Feld argues that judges admit most confessions and exclude only the most egregious ones; but even those are excluded in a "haphazard" fashion. Barry Feld, *Criminalizing Juvenile Justice: Rules of Procedure for the Juvenile Court*, 69 MINN. L. REV. 141, 176 n. 2 (1984). Thus, judges may uphold waivers simply on the basis of police statements that "they read the *Miranda* warnings and the child agreed to talk." Wallace J. Mlyniec, *A Judge's Ethical Dilemma: Assessing a Child's Capacity to Choose*, 64 FORDHAM L. REV. 1873, 1902 (1996). Even the confessions of juveniles who may be mentally disabled, illiterate, or with low IQs may be admitted. Regrettably, these juveniles also are more likely to waive their rights and provide false confessions. Kevin P. Weis, *Confessions of Mentally Retarded Juveniles and the Validity of Miranda Rights Waiver*, 37 BRANDEIS L.J. 117, 126 (1998). There also is some evidence that juveniles who confess receive harsher sentences than those who deny wrongdoing. R. Barry Ruback & Paula J. Vardaman, *Decision Making in Delinquency Cases: The Role of Race and Juveniles' Admission/Denial of Crime*, 21 LAW & HUMAN BEHAVIOR 47 (1997).

13. *Capacity of minors to waive* Miranda *rights.* Do minors have the capacity to knowingly, intelligently, and voluntarily waive their *Miranda* rights? Saul Kassin, Steven Drizin, Thomas Grisso, Gisli Gudjonsson, Richard Leo, and Allison Redlich, respected researchers in the area of confessions, note that the studies overwhelmingly support the conclusion that minors are less likely to understand *Miranda* warnings, more suggestible, and at higher risk for providing involuntary or false confessions:

> Some studies have shown that many defendants, especially adolescents, who seem to have an adequate factual understanding of *Miranda* warnings, do not grasp their relevance to the situation they are in.... For example, one may factually understand that "I can have an attorney before and during questioning" yet not know what an attorney is or what role an attorney would play. Others may understand the attorney's role but disbelieve that it would apply in their own situation—as when youth cannot imagine that an adult would take their side against other adults, or when a person with paranoid tendencies believes that any attorney, even his own, would oppose him.
>
> The ability to grasp the relevance of the warnings beyond having a mere factual understanding of what they say is sometimes referred to as having a "rational understanding" or "appreciation" of the warnings. Many states, however, require only a factual understanding of *Miranda* rights for a "knowing and intelligent" waiver.... In those states that apply a strict factual understanding standard, youth who technically understand the warnings (e.g., "I can have an attorney to talk to" or "I can stay silent") but harbor faulty beliefs that may distort the significance of these warnings ("An attorney will tell the court whatever I say" or "You have to tell the truth in court, so eventually I'll have to talk if they want me to") are considered capable of having made a valid waiver, even if they have no recognition of the meanings of the words or a distorted view of their implications....
>
> There is strong evidence that juveniles are at risk for involuntary and false confessions in the interrogation.... Juveniles are over represented in the pool of identified false confession cases: 35% of the proven false confessors in the Drizin and Leo (2004) sample were younger than age 18, and within this sample of juveniles, 55% were aged 15 or younger. Comparatively, of all persons arrested for murder and rape, only 8 and 16%, respectively, are juveniles.... Numerous high-profile cases, such as the Central Park Jogger case,... have demonstrated the risks of combining young age, and the attributes that are associated with it (e.g., suggestibility, heightened obedience to authority, and immature decision-making abilities), and the psychologically oriented interrogation tactics described earlier. Hence, Inbau et al. (2001) concede that minors are at special risk for false confession and advise caution when interrogating a juvenile. Referring to the presentation of fictitious evidence, for example, they note: "This technique should be avoided when interrogating a youthful suspect with low social maturity" (p. 429).
>
> The field of developmental psychology was born over a century ago in the influential writings of James Baldwin, Charles Darwin, G. Stanley Hall, and William Stern.... Since that time, basic research has shown that children and adolescents are cognitively and psychosocially less mature than adults—and that this immaturity manifests in impulsive decision making, decreased ability to consider long-term consequences, engagement in risky behaviors, and increased susceptibility to negative influences. Specifically, this body of research indicates that early adolescence marks the onset of puberty, heightening emotional arousability, sensation seeking, and reward orientation; that mid-adolescence is a period of increased vulnerability to risk-taking and problems in affect and behavior; and that late adolescence is a period in which the frontal lobes continue to mature, facilitating regulatory competence and executive functioning.... Recent neurological research on brain development dovetails with findings from

behavioral studies. Specifically, these studies have shown continued maturation during adolescence in the limbic system (emotion regulation) and in the prefrontal cortex (planning and self-control), with gray matter thinning and white matter increasing....

The developmental capabilities and limitations of adolescents are highly relevant to behavior in the interrogation room. In *Roper v. Simmons* (2005), Justice Kennedy cited three general differences between juveniles and adults in support of the Court's reasoning for abolishing the death penalty for juveniles. First, he addressed the lessened maturity and responsibility of juveniles compared to adults with specific mention to the 18-year bright-line requirements for marriage without parental consent, jury duty, and voting. Second, Justice Kennedy noted that "juveniles are more vulnerable or susceptible to negative influences and outside pressures, including peer pressure" (p. 15). Consistent with this portrait, Drizin and Leo (2004) found in their sample of false confessions that several involved two or more juveniles (out of 38 multiple false confession cases, half involved juveniles). In recommending that police "play one [suspect] against the other," Inbau et al. (2001) note that this tactic may be especially effective on young, first-time offenders (pp. 292–293). Third, Justice Kennedy recognized that juveniles' personality or "character" is not as well developed as adults'. In light of the volatility of adolescence, it is interesting that Inbau et al. (2001) also suggest "themes" for confession that exploit a juvenile's restless energy, boredom, low resistance to temptation, and lack of supervision.

Drawing on basic principles of developmental psychology, there is now a wealth of forensically oriented research indicating that juveniles—suspects, defendants, and witnesses—have age-related limitations of relevance to the legal system in comparison to adults. For example, individuals younger than 16 years generally have impairments in adjudicative competence (e.g., the ability to help in one's own defense) and comprehension of legal terms.... In a subset of studies particularly germane to interrogations, several researchers employing a range of methodologies have shown that the risk of false confession is heightened during childhood and adolescence relative to adulthood. Of particular note, as described earlier, juveniles are more likely than adults to exhibit deficits in their understanding and appreciation of the *Miranda* rights that were explicitly put into place to protect people subject to "inherently coercive" interrogations....

In the first set of studies, laboratory-based experiments have examined juveniles' responses in mock crimes and interrogations. Using the Kassin and Kiechel (1996) computer crash paradigm, Redlich and Goodman (2003) found that juveniles aged 12- and 13-years-old, and 15- and 16-years-old, were more likely to confess than young adults (aged 18–26 years), especially when confronted with false evidence of their culpability. In fact, a majority of the younger participants, in contrast to adults, complied with the request to sign a false confession without uttering a word. In another laboratory experiment, researchers examined the effect of positive and negative reinforcement on children aged 5 through 8 years.... Reinforcement strongly affected children's likelihood of making false statements: Of those in the reinforcement condition, 52% made false admissions of guilty knowledge and 30% made false admissions of having witnessed the crime (within a span of 3.5 minutes!). In contrast, of children in the control condition, only 36 and 10% made false guilty knowledge and admissions, respectively. These findings mirror the vast majority of studies on the interview-relevant abilities of child-victim/witnesses....

In a second set of studies, youths have made decisions in response to hypothetical scenarios. Goldstein et al. (2003) investigated male juvenile offenders' self-reported likelihood of providing false confessions across different interrogation situations and found that younger age significantly predicted false confessions (25% surmised that they would definitely confess despite innocence to at least one of the situations). Similarly, Grisso et al. (2003) examined juveniles' and young adults' responses to a hypothetical mock-interrogation situation—specifically, whether they would confess to police, remain silent, or deny the offense. Compared to individuals aged 16 and older, those between 11 and 15 were significantly more likely to report that they would confess.

In a third set of studies, juveniles have been asked to self-report on actual interrogation experiences. In a sample of 114 justice-involved juveniles, Viljoen, Klaver, and Roesch (2005) found that suspects who were 15-years old and younger, compared to those who were 16- and 17-years old, were significantly more likely to waive their right to counsel and to confess. Overall, only 11 (less than 10%) said they had asked for an attorney during police questioning…and 9 (6%) said they had at some point falsely confessed. A survey of over 10,000 Icelandic students aged 16–24 years similarly revealed that of those with interrogation experiences, 7% claimed to have falsely confessed, with the rates being higher among those with more than one interrogation experience….In a massive and more recent effort, more than 23,000 juveniles from grades 8, 9, and 10 (average age of 15.5 years) were surveyed from seven countries—Iceland, Norway, Finland, Latvia, Lithuania, Russia, and Bulgaria. Overall, 11.5% (2,726) reported having been interrogated by police. Within this group, 14% reported having given a false confession….

Saul M. Kassin et al., *Police-Induced Confessions: Risk Factors and Recommendations,* 34 LAW & HUM. BEHAV. 3, 8, 19–20 (2010).

14. *Additional procedural safeguards.* Should courts require additional procedural safeguards to ensure that waivers are made knowingly, intelligently, and voluntarily? Some states require police to record or videotape custodial interrogations. See, e.g., *In re Jerrell C.J.*, 699 N.W.2d 110 (Wis. 2005) (requiring that all custodial interrogations of juveniles be recorded); *State v. Scales*, 518 N.W.2d 587 (Minn. 1994) (officers must record all questioning that occurs in a place of detention); *Stephan v. State*, 711 P.2d 1156 (Alaska 1985) (unexcused failure to record suspect's confession in a place of detention violates defendant's right to due process); Tex. Code Ann. Crim. Proc. Art. 38.22 § 3 (2010) (no oral statement obtained during custodial interrogation may be used unless it is recorded). Others, such as Illinois, Maine, New Mexico, New Jersey, North Carolina, and the District of Columbia, require confessions to be recorded under certain circumstances. Moreover, many police departments voluntarily and routinely record custodial interrogations, indicating that the practice is widespread. Saul M. Kassin, et al., *Police-Induced Confessions: Risk Factors and Recommendations,* 34 LAW & HUM. BEHAV. 3, 26 (2010). How the interrogation is recorded may be just as crucial as the fact of recording. Some studies have found that it is important not only to record the entire session but also to place the camera to show both the suspect and the interrogators. These studies suggest that when only the suspect is visible, observers (including experienced trial judges) tend to assess the situation as less coercive than when the interrogator is visible. *Id.* at 27. In light of the empirical evidence about juvenile confessions, however, would such procedures make any difference?

15. *Parental presence as an additional procedural safeguard.* Should a minor's statement made in the absence of a parent be inadmissible? *Murray v. State*, 578 S.E.2d 853 (Ga. 2003) (minor's statement not rendered inadmissible because made in absence of parent); *State v. Fernandez*, 712 So.2d 485 (La. 1998) (absence of parent during custodial interrogation only one factor to consider in totality of circumstances); *Ingram v. State*, 729 So.2d 883 (Ala. Crim. App. 1996) (although minor was not advised that he had right to have parent present during questioning pursuant to court rule, rule does not apply when counsel is present). Should the court admit

a confession when the police deliberately excluded the parent from the interrogation? *State v. Presha*, 748 A.2d 1108 (N.J. 2000).

Would the presence of a parent help the child? What if the parent was the complaining witness? What if the parent coerced the child into confessing? What if the parent waived the child's *Miranda* rights? The empirical evidence suggests otherwise.

> [M]any states require the presence of a parent or other interested adult when youth make decisions about their *Miranda* rights.... These rules are intended to offer youth assistance in thinking through the decision while recognizing that caretakers cannot themselves waive their children's rights in delinquency or criminal investigations. Studies have shown, however, that the presence of parents at *Miranda* waiver events typically does not result in any advice at all or, when it does, provides added pressure for the youth to waive rights and make a statement.... The presence of parents may be advisable, but it does not offer a remedy for the difficulties youth face in comprehending or responding to requests for a waiver of their rights.

Kassin et al., *Police-Induced Confessions*, *supra*, at 9.

16. *Younger children.* Are different procedural protections appropriate for younger juveniles? Consider *In the Matter of B.M.B.*, 955 P.2d 1302 (Kansas 1998), where the police obtained a confession from B.M.B., who was ten years old at the time. Should the child's confession be admissible? Are there any procedural protections that would ensure that the confession was made intelligently, knowingly, and voluntarily? The empirical evidence indicates that children younger than fifteen have a much poorer understanding of *Miranda* warnings:

> In one comprehensive study, 55% of 430 youth of ages 10–16 misunderstood one or more of the *Miranda* warnings (for example, "That means I can't talk until they tell me to"). Across these studies, the understanding of adolescents ages 15–17 with near-average levels of verbal intelligence tends not to have been inferior to that of adults. But youth of that age with IQ scores below 85, and average youth below age 14, performed much poorer, often misunderstanding two or more of the warnings.
>
> Studies of adolescents indicate that youth under age 15 on average perform differently from older adolescents and adults. They are more likely to believe that they should waive their rights and tell what they have done, partly because they are still young enough to believe that they should never disobey authority. Studies have also shown that they are more likely to decide about waiver on the basis of the potential for immediate negative consequences—for example, whether they will be permitted to go home if they waive their rights—rather than considering the longer-range consequences associated with penalties for a delinquency adjudication.... Young adolescents presented with hypothetical waiver decisions are less likely than older adolescents to engage in reasoning that involves adjustment of their decisions based on the amount of evidence against them or the seriousness of the allegations.... These results regarding the likelihood of immature decision-making processes are consistent with research on the development of psychosocial abilities of young adolescents in everyday circumstances... and other legal contexts....

Kassin et al., *Police-Induced Confessions*, *supra*, at 8.

17. *Presence of an attorney.* Kassin et al. argue that an attorney (or a trained advocate) must be present before a child may be interrogated. Some states also require that the minor be represented by counsel at an interrogation. See *In the Interest of J.D.Z.*, 431 N.W.2d 272 (N.D. 1988); Iowa Stat. § 232.11. Nevertheless, some studies have found that juveniles may be punished more severely when they appear with counsel. Barry C. Feld, *The Right to Counsel in Juvenile Court: An Empirical Study of When Lawyers Appear and the Difference They Make*, 79 J. Crim. L. & Criminology 1185

(1989); Barry C. Feld, Justice for Children: The Right to Counsel and Juvenile Courts (1993). As a policy matter, would you favor such a requirement? Why or why not?

18. *Assertion of* Miranda *rights. Fare* made clear that the request to speak to a probation officer was neither an invocation of the right to counsel nor an assertion of the right to remain silent. Nevertheless, the distinction between the rights being asserted is an important one. The Supreme Court has held that the police must "scrupulously honor" the suspect's assertion of his right to remain silent. *Michigan v. Moseley*, 423 U.S. 96 (1975). On the other hand, when a suspect asserts his right to counsel, the police may not resume questioning unless the suspect initiates further communication with the police. *Edwards v. Arizona*, 451 U.S. 477 (1981). The assertion of the right to counsel, however, must be unambiguous. *Davis v. United States*, 512 U.S. 452 (1994). Would a request to speak to a parent constitute an invocation of the right to silence? The right to counsel? What if the request were ambiguous? See, *Ex parte Hall*, 863 So.2d 1079 (Ala. 2003).

19. *Problem.* Police, investigating a multiple homicide, arrested four men and obtained their confessions after interrogation. Further investigation led to the recovery of the murder weapon, a .22-caliber rifle, from its owner, who denied any involvement in the murders. However, he did indicate that he had lent the rifle to two juveniles, who, he claimed, had borrowed the rifle shortly before the murders. Police approached one of the juveniles at a high school football game where the minor was participating in a flag ceremony as a member of his high school ROTC. The minor voluntarily accompanied the police to the police station. Questioning began at 9:25 p.m. and concluded the next day at 10:00 a.m. The police read the minor his *Miranda* rights, telling him that the warnings were "just formalities" and that he would not need a lawyer unless he was involved in a crime, while assuring him that he was not suspected of any wrongdoing. Three detectives took turns during the night to question the minor, who, sitting all night in a straight-backed chair, was at times "nonresponsive." The minor subsequently confessed to the homicides. If you were the trial judge hearing this case, would you grant the minor's request to suppress his confession? Why or why not?

J.D.B. V. NORTH CAROLINA
Supreme Court of the United States
131 S.Ct. 2394 (2011)

Justice Sotomayor delivered the opinion of the Court.

This case presents the question whether the age of a child subjected to police questioning is relevant to the custody analysis of *Miranda v. Arizona*, 384 U.S. 436 (1966). It is beyond dispute that children will often feel bound to submit to police questioning when an adult in the same circumstances would feel free to leave. Seeing no reason for police officers or courts to blind themselves to that commonsense reality, we hold that a child's age properly informs the *Miranda* custody analysis.

I

A

Petitioner J.D.B. was a 13-year-old, seventh-grade student attending class at Smith Middle School in Chapel Hill, North Carolina when he was removed from his classroom by a uniformed police officer, escorted to a closed-door conference room, and questioned by police for at least half an hour.

This was the second time that police questioned J.D.B. in the span of a week. Five days earlier, two home break-ins occurred, and various items were stolen. Police stopped and questioned J.D.B. after he was seen behind a residence in the neighborhood where the crimes occurred. That same day, police also spoke to J.D.B.'s grandmother—his legal guardian—as well as his aunt.

Police later learned that a digital camera matching the description of one of the stolen items had been found at J.D.B.'s middle school and seen in J.D.B.'s possession. Investigator DiCostanzo, the juvenile investigator with the local police force who had been assigned to the case, went to the school to question J.D.B. Upon arrival, DiCostanzo informed the uniformed police officer on detail to the school (a so-called school resource officer), the assistant principal, and an administrative intern that he was there to question J.D.B. about the break-ins. Although DiCostanzo asked the school administrators to verify J.D.B.'s date of birth, address, and parent contact information from school records, neither the police officers nor the school administrators contacted J.D.B.'s grandmother.

The uniformed officer interrupted J.D.B.'s afternoon social studies class, removed J.D.B. from the classroom, and escorted him to a school conference room. There, J.D.B. was met by DiCostanzo, the assistant principal, and the administrative intern. The door to the conference room was closed. With the two police officers and the two administrators present, J.D.B. was questioned for the next 30 to 45 minutes. Prior to the commencement of questioning, J.D.B. was given neither *Miranda* warnings nor the opportunity to speak to his grandmother. Nor was he informed that he was free to leave the room.

Questioning began with small talk—discussion of sports and J.D.B.'s family life. DiCostanzo asked, and J.D.B. agreed, to discuss the events of the prior weekend. Denying any wrongdoing, J.D.B. explained that he had been in the neighborhood where the crimes occurred because he was seeking work mowing lawns. DiCostanzo pressed J.D.B. for additional detail about his efforts to obtain work; asked J.D.B. to explain a prior incident, when one of the victims returned home to find J.D.B. behind her house; and confronted J.D.B. with the stolen camera. The assistant principal urged J.D.B. to "do the right thing," warning J.D.B. that "the truth always comes out in the end."

Eventually, J.D.B. asked whether he would "still be in trouble" if he returned the "stuff." In response, DiCostanzo explained that return of the stolen items would be helpful, but "this thing is going to court" regardless.... ("[W]hat's done is done[;] now you need to help yourself by making it right"). DiCostanzo then warned that he may need to seek a secure custody order if he believed that J.D.B. would continue to break into other homes. When J.D.B. asked what a secure custody order was, DiCostanzo explained that "it's where you get sent to juvenile detention before court."

After learning of the prospect of juvenile detention, J.D.B. confessed that he and a friend were responsible for the break-ins. DiCostanzo only then informed J.D.B. that he could refuse to answer the investigator's questions and that he was free to leave.[2] Asked whether

2. The North Carolina Supreme Court noted that the trial court's factual findings were "uncontested and therefore ... binding" on it. *In re J.D.B.*, 363 N.C. 664, 668, 686 S.E.2d 135, 137 (2009). The court described the sequence of events set forth in the text. See *id.*, at 670–671, 686 S.E.2d, at 139. ("Immediately following J.D.B.'s initial confession, Investigator DiCostanzo informed J.D.B. that he did not have to speak with him and that

he understood, J.D.B. nodded and provided further detail, including information about the location of the stolen items. Eventually J.D.B. wrote a statement, at DiCostanzo's request. When the bell rang indicating the end of the schoolday, J.D.B. was allowed to leave to catch the bus home.

B

Two juvenile petitions were filed against J.D.B., each alleging one count of breaking and entering and one count of larceny. J.D.B.'s public defender moved to suppress his statements and the evidence derived therefrom, arguing that suppression was necessary because J.D.B. had been "interrogated by police in a custodial setting without being afforded *Miranda* warning[s]," and because his statements were involuntary under the totality of the circumstances test,...; see *Schneckloth v. Bustamonte*, 412 U.S. 218, 226 (1973) (due process precludes admission of a confession where "a defendant's will was overborne" by the circumstances of the interrogation). After a suppression hearing at which DiCostanzo and J.D.B. testified, the trial court denied the motion, deciding that J.D.B. was not in custody at the time of the schoolhouse interrogation and that his statements were voluntary. As a result, J.D.B. entered a transcript of admission to all four counts, renewing his objection to the denial of his motion to suppress, and the court adjudicated J.D.B. delinquent.

A divided panel of the North Carolina Court of Appeals affirmed. *In re J.D.B.*, 196 N.C.App. 234, 674 S.E.2d 795 (2009). The North Carolina Supreme Court held, over two dissents, that J.D.B. was not in custody when he confessed, "declin[ing] to extend the test for custody to include consideration of the age...of an individual subjected to questioning by police." *In re J.D.B.*, 363 N.C. 664, 672, 686 S.E.2d 135, 140 (2009).[3]

We granted certiorari to determine whether the *Miranda* custody analysis includes consideration of a juvenile suspect's age. 562 U.S. ___, (2010).

II

A

Any police interview of an individual suspected of a crime has "coercive aspects to it." *Oregon v. Mathiason*, 429 U.S. 492, 495 (1977) (*per curiam*). Only those interrogations that occur while a suspect is in police custody, however, "heighte[n] the risk" that statements obtained are not the product of the suspect's free choice. *Dickerson v. United States*, 530 U.S. 428, 435 (2000).

By its very nature, custodial police interrogation entails "inherently compelling pressures." *Miranda*, 384 U.S., at 467. Even for an adult, the physical and psychological isolation of custodial interrogation can "undermine the individual's will to resist and...compel him

he was free to leave" (internal quotation marks and alterations omitted)). Though less than perfectly explicit, the trial court's order indicates a finding that J.D.B. initially confessed prior to DiCostanzo's warnings. Nonetheless, both parties' submissions to this Court suggest that the warnings came after DiCostanzo raised the possibility of a secure custody order but before J.D.B. confessed for the first time. Because we remand for a determination whether J.D.B. was in custody under the proper analysis, the state courts remain free to revisit whether the trial court made a conclusive finding of fact in this respect.

3. J.D.B.'s challenge in the North Carolina Supreme Court focused on the lower courts' conclusion that he was not in custody for purposes of *Miranda v. Arizona*, 384 U.S. 436 (1966). The North Carolina Supreme Court did not address the trial court's holding that the statements were voluntary, and that question is not before us.

to speak where he would not otherwise do so freely." *Ibid.* Indeed, the pressure of custodial interrogation is so immense that it "can induce a frighteningly high percentage of people to confess to crimes they never committed." *Corley v. United States*, 556 U.S. 303, ___ (2009) (slip op. at 16) (citing Drizin & Leo, The Problem of False Confessions in the Post–DNA World, 82 N. C. L. Rev. 891, 906–907 (2004)); see also *Miranda*, 384 U.S., at 455. That risk is all the more troubling—and recent studies suggest, all the more acute—when the subject of custodial interrogation is a juvenile. See Brief for Center on Wrongful Convictions of Youth et al. as *Amici Curiae* 21–22 (collecting empirical studies that "illustrate the heightened risk of false confessions from youth").

Recognizing that the inherently coercive nature of custodial interrogation "blurs the line between voluntary and involuntary statements," *Dickerson*, 530 U.S., at 435; this Court in *Miranda* adopted a set of prophylactic measures designed to safeguard the constitutional guarantee against self-incrimination. Prior to questioning, a suspect "must be warned that he has a right to remain silent, that any statement he does make may be used as evidence against him, and that he has a right to the presence of an attorney, either retained or appointed." 384 U.S., at 444; see also *Florida v. Powell*, 559 U.S. ___, ___, (2010) ("The four warnings *Miranda* requires are invariable, but this Court has not dictated the words in which the essential information must be conveyed"). And, if a suspect makes a statement during custodial interrogation, the burden is on the Government to show, as a "prerequisit[e]" to the statement's admissibility as evidence in the Government's case in chief, that the defendant "voluntarily, knowingly and intelligently" waived his rights.[4] *Miranda*, 384 U.S., at 444, 475–476; *Dickerson*, 530 U.S., at 443–444.

Because these measures protect the individual against the coercive nature of custodial interrogation, they are required "'only where there has been such a restriction on a person's freedom as to render him 'in custody.''" *Stansbury v. California*, 511 U.S. 318, 322 (1994) (*per curiam*) (quoting *Oregon v. Mathiason*, 429 U.S. 492, 495 (1977) (*per curiam*)). As we have repeatedly emphasized, whether a suspect is "in custody" is an objective inquiry.

> "Two discrete inquiries are essential to the determination: first, what were the circumstances surrounding the interrogation; and second, given those circumstances, would a reasonable person have felt he or she was at liberty to terminate the interrogation and leave. Once the scene is set and the players' lines and actions are reconstructed, the court must apply an objective test to resolve the ultimate inquiry: was there a formal arrest or restraint on freedom of movement of the degree associated with formal arrest." *Thompson v. Keohane*, 516 U.S. 99, 112 (1995) (internal quotation marks, alteration, and footnote omitted).

See also *Yarborough v. Alvarado*, 541 U.S. 652, 662–663 (2004); *Stansbury*, 511 U.S., at 323; *Berkemer v. McCarty*, 468 U.S. 420, 442, and n. 35 (1984). Rather than demarcate a limited set of relevant circumstances, we have required police officers and courts to "examine all of the circumstances surrounding the interrogation," *Stansbury*, 511 U.S., at 322, including any circumstance that "would have affected how a reasonable person" in the suspect's position

4. *Amici* on behalf of J.D.B. question whether children of all ages can comprehend *Miranda* warnings and suggest that additional procedural safeguards may be necessary to protect their *Miranda* rights. Brief for Juvenile Law Center et al. as *Amici Curiae* 13–14, n. 7. Whatever the merit of that contention, it has no relevance here, where no *Miranda* warnings were administered at all.

"would perceive his or her freedom to leave," *id.*, at 325. On the other hand, the "subjective views harbored by either the interrogating officers or the person being questioned" are irrelevant. *Id.*, at 323. The test, in other words, involves no consideration of the "actual mindset" of the particular suspect subjected to police questioning. *Alvarado*, 541 U.S., at 667; see also *California v. Beheler*, 463 U.S. 1121, 1125, n. 3 (1983) (*per curiam*).

The benefit of the objective custody analysis is that it is "designed to give clear guidance to the police." *Alvarado*, 541 U.S., at 668. But see *Berkemer*, 468 U.S., at 441 (recognizing the "occasiona[l]... difficulty" that police and courts nonetheless have in "deciding exactly when a suspect has been taken into custody"). Police must make in-the-moment judgments as to when to administer *Miranda* warnings. By limiting analysis to the objective circumstances of the interrogation, and asking how a reasonable person in the suspect's position would understand his freedom to terminate questioning and leave, the objective test avoids burdening police with the task of anticipating the idiosyncrasies of every individual suspect and divining how those particular traits affect each person's subjective state of mind. See *id.*, at 430–431 (officers are not required to "make guesses" as to circumstances "unknowable" to them at the time); *Alvarado*, 541 U.S., at 668 (officers are under no duty "to consider... contingent psychological factors when deciding when suspects should be advised of their *Miranda* rights").

B

The State and its *amici* contend that a child's age has no place in the custody analysis, no matter how young the child subjected to police questioning. We cannot agree. In some circumstances, a child's age "would have affected how a reasonable person" in the suspect's position "would perceive his or her freedom to leave." *Stansbury*, 511 U.S., at 325. That is, a reasonable child subjected to police questioning will sometimes feel pressured to submit when a reasonable adult would feel free to go. We think it clear that courts can account for that reality without doing any damage to the objective nature of the custody analysis.

A child's age is far "more than a chronological fact." *Eddings v. Oklahoma*, 455 U.S. 104, 115 (1982); accord, *Gall v. United States*, 552 U.S. 38, 58 (2007); *Roper v. Simmons*, 543 U.S. 551, 569 (2005); *Johnson v. Texas*, 509 U.S. 350, 367 (1993). It is a fact that "generates commonsense conclusions about behavior and perception." *Alvarado*, 541 U.S., at 674 (Breyer, J., dissenting). Such conclusions apply broadly to children as a class. And, they are self-evident to anyone who was a child once himself, including any police officer or judge.

Time and again, this Court has drawn these commonsense conclusions for itself. We have observed that children "generally are less mature and responsible than adults," *Eddings*, 455 U.S., at 115–116; that they "often lack the experience, perspective, and judgment to recognize and avoid choices that could be detrimental to them," *Bellotti v. Baird*, 443 U.S. 622, 635 (1979) (plurality opinion); that they "are more vulnerable or susceptible to... outside pressures" than adults, *Roper*, 543 U.S., at 569; and so on. See *Graham v. Florida*, 560 U.S. ___, ___, (2010) (slip op. at 17) (finding no reason to "reconsider" these observations about the common "nature of juveniles"). Addressing the specific context of police interrogation, we have observed that events that "would leave a man cold and unimpressed can overawe and overwhelm a lad in his early teens." *Haley v. Ohio*, 332 U.S. 596, 599 (1948) (plurality opinion); see also *Gallegos v. Colorado*, 370 U.S. 49, 54 (1962) ("[N]o matter how sophisticated," a juvenile subject of police interrogation "cannot be compared" to an adult subject). Describing no one child in particular, these observations restate what "any parent knows"—indeed, what any person knows—about children generally. *Roper*, 543 U.S., at 569.[5]

Our various statements to this effect are far from unique. The law has historically reflected the same assumption that children characteristically lack the capacity to exercise mature judgment and possess only an incomplete ability to understand the world around them. See, e.g., 1 W. Blackstone, Commentaries on the Laws of England *464–*465 (hereinafter Blackstone) (explaining that limits on children's legal capacity under the common law "secure them from hurting themselves by their own improvident acts"). Like this Court's own generalizations, the legal disqualifications placed on children as a class—e.g., limitations on their ability to alienate property, enter a binding contract enforceable against them, and marry without parental consent—exhibit the settled understanding that the differentiating characteristics of youth are universal.[6]

Indeed, even where a "reasonable person" standard otherwise applies, the common law has reflected the reality that children are not adults. In negligence suits, for instance, where liability turns on what an objectively reasonable person would do in the circumstances, "[a]ll American jurisdictions accept the idea that a person's childhood is a relevant circumstance" to be considered. Restatement (Third) of Torts § 10, Comment *b*, p. 117 (2005); see also *id.*, Reporters' Note, pp. 121–122 (collecting cases); Restatement (Second) of Torts § 283A, Comment *b*, p. 15 (1963–1964) ("[T]here is a wide basis of community experience upon which it is possible, as a practical matter, to determine what is to be expected of [children]").

As this discussion establishes, "[o]ur history is replete with laws and judicial recognition" that children cannot be viewed simply as miniature adults. *Eddings*, 455 U.S., at 115–116. We see no justification for taking a different course here. So long as the child's age was known to the officer at the time of the interview, or would have been objectively apparent to any reasonable officer, including age as part of the custody analysis requires officers neither to consider circumstances "unknowable" to them, *Berkemer*, 468 U.S., at 430, nor to "anticipat[e] the frailties or idiosyncrasies" of the particular suspect whom they question, *Alvarado*, 541 U.S., at 662 (internal quotation marks omitted). The same "wide basis of community experience" that makes it possible, as an objective matter, "to determine what is to be expected" of

5. Although citation to social science and cognitive science authorities is unnecessary to establish these commonsense propositions, the literature confirms what experience bears out. See, e.g., *Graham v. Florida*, 560 U.S. ___, ___ (2010) (slip op. at 17) ("[D]evelopments in psychology and brain science continue to show fundamental differences between juvenile and adult minds").

6. See, e.g., 1 E. Farnsworth, Contracts § 4.4, p. 379, and n. 1 (1990) ("Common law courts early announced the prevailing view that a minor's contract is 'voidable' at the instance of the minor" (citing 8 W. Holdsworth, History of English Law 51 (1926))); 1 D. Kramer, Legal Rights of Children § 8.1, p. 663 (rev. 2d ed. 2005) ("[W]hile minor children have the right to acquire and own property, they are considered incapable of property management" (footnote omitted)); 2 J. Kent, Commentaries on American Law *78–*79, *90 (G. Comstock ed., 11th ed. 1867); see generally *id.*, at *233 (explaining that, under the common law, "[t]he necessity of guardians results from the inability of infants to take care of themselves... and this inability continues, in contemplation of law, until the infant has attained the age of [21]"); 1 Blackstone *465 ("It is generally true, that an infant can neither aliene his lands, nor do any legal act, nor make a deed, nor indeed any manner of contract, that will bind him"); *Roper v. Simmons*, 543 U.S. 551, 569 (2005) ("In recognition of the comparative immaturity and irresponsibility of juveniles, almost every State prohibits those under 18 years of age from voting, serving on juries, or marrying without parental consent").

children in other contexts,...likewise makes it possible to know what to expect of children subjected to police questioning.

In other words, a child's age differs from other personal characteristics that, even when known to police, have no objectively discernible relationship to a reasonable person's understanding of his freedom of action. *Alvarado* holds, for instance, that a suspect's prior interrogation history with law enforcement has no role to play in the custody analysis because such experience could just as easily lead a reasonable person to feel free to walk away as to feel compelled to stay in place. 541 U.S., at 668. Because the effect in any given case would be "contingent [on the] psycholog[y]" of the individual suspect, the Court explained, such experience cannot be considered without compromising the objective nature of the custody analysis. *Ibid.* A child's age, however, is different. Precisely because childhood yields objective conclusions like those we have drawn ourselves—among others, that children are "most susceptible to influence," *Eddings*, 455 U.S., at 115, and "outside pressures," *Roper*, 543 U.S., at 569—considering age in the custody analysis in no way involves a determination of how youth "subjectively affect[s] the mindset" of any particular child, Brief for Respondent 14.[7]

In fact, in many cases involving juvenile suspects, the custody analysis would be nonsensical absent some consideration of the suspect's age. This case is a prime example. Were the court precluded from taking J.D.B.'s youth into account, it would be forced to evaluate the circumstances present here through the eyes of a reasonable person of average years. In other words, how would a reasonable adult understand his situation, after being removed from a seventh-grade social studies class by a uniformed school resource officer; being encouraged by his assistant principal to "do the right thing"; and being warned by a police investigator of the prospect of juvenile detention and separation from his guardian and primary caretaker? To describe such an inquiry is to demonstrate its absurdity. Neither officers nor courts can reasonably evaluate the effect of objective circumstances that, by their nature, are specific to children without accounting for the age of the child subjected to those circumstances.

Indeed, although the dissent suggests that concerns "regarding the application of the *Miranda* custody rule to minors can be accommodated by considering the unique circumstances present when minors are questioned in school," the effect of the schoolhouse setting cannot be disentangled from the identity of the person questioned. A student—whose presence at school is compulsory and whose disobedience at school is cause for disciplinary action—is in a far different position than, say, a parent volunteer on school grounds to chaperone an event, or an adult from the community on school grounds to attend a basketball game. Without asking whether the person "questioned in school" is a "minor," the coercive effect of the schoolhouse setting is unknowable.

Our prior decision in *Alvarado* in no way undermines these conclusions. In that case, we held that a state-court decision that failed to mention a 17-year-old's age as part of the *Miranda* custody analysis was not objectively unreasonable under the deferential standard of review set forth by the Antiterrorism and Effective Death Penalty Act of 1996 (AEDPA), 110 Stat. 1214. Like the North Carolina Supreme Court here, see 363 N.C., at 672, 686 S.E.2d, at 140, we observed that accounting for a juvenile's age in the *Miranda* custody analysis "could be viewed as creating a subjective inquiry," 541 U.S., at 668. We said nothing, however, of

7. Thus, contrary to the dissent's protestations, today's holding neither invites consideration of whether a particular suspect is "unusually meek or compliant," nor "expan[ds]" the *Miranda* custody analysis into a test that requires officers to anticipate and account for a suspect's every personal characteristic.

whether such a view would be correct under the law. Cf. *Renico v. Lett*, 559 U.S. ___, ___, n. 3 (2010) (slip op., at 11, n. 3) ("[W]hether the [state court] was right or wrong is not the pertinent question under AEDPA"). To the contrary, Justice O'Connor's concurring opinion explained that a suspect's age may indeed "be relevant to the 'custody' inquiry." *Alvarado*, 541 U.S., at 669.

Reviewing the question *de novo* today, we hold that so long as the child's age was known to the officer at the time of police questioning, or would have been objectively apparent to a reasonable officer, its inclusion in the custody analysis is consistent with the objective nature of that test.[8] This is not to say that a child's age will be a determinative, or even a significant, factor in every case. Cf. *ibid.* (O'CONNOR, J., concurring) (explaining that a state-court decision omitting any mention of the defendant's age was not unreasonable under AEDPA's deferential standard of review where the defendant "was almost 18 years old at the time of his interview" [and] suggesting that "teenagers nearing the age of majority" are likely to react to an interrogation as would a "typical 18-year-old in similar circumstances"). It is, however, a reality that courts cannot simply ignore.

III

The State and its *amici* offer numerous reasons that courts must blind themselves to a juvenile defendant's age. None is persuasive.

To start, the State contends that a child's age must be excluded from the custody inquiry because age is a personal characteristic specific to the suspect himself rather than an "external" circumstance of the interrogation. Brief for Respondent 21; see also *id.*, at 18–19 (distinguishing "personal characteristics" from "objective facts related to the interrogation itself" such as the location and duration of the interrogation). Despite the supposed significance of this distinction, however, at oral argument counsel for the State suggested without hesitation that at least some undeniably personal characteristics—for instance, whether the individual being questioned is blind—are circumstances relevant to the custody analysis. See Tr. of Oral Arg. 41. Thus, the State's quarrel cannot be that age is a personal characteristic, without more.[9]

The State further argues that age is irrelevant to the custody analysis because it "go[es] to how a suspect may internalize and perceive the circumstances of an interrogation." Brief for Respondent 12; see also Brief for United States as *Amicus Curiae* 21 (hereinafter U.S. Brief) (arguing that a child's age has no place in the custody analysis because it goes to whether a suspect is "particularly susceptible" to the external circumstances of the interrogation (some

8. This approach does not undermine the basic principle that an interrogating officer's unarticulated, internal thoughts are never—in and of themselves—objective circumstances of an interrogation. See... *Stansbury v. California*, 511 U.S. 318, 323 (1994) (*per curiam*). Unlike a child's youth, an officer's purely internal thoughts have no conceivable effect on how a reasonable person in the suspect's position would understand his freedom of action. See *id.*, at 323–325; *Berkemer v. McCarty*, 468 U.S. 420, 442 (1984). Rather than "overtur[n]" that settled principle, the limitation that a child's age may inform the custody analysis only when known or knowable simply reflects our unwillingness to require officers to "make guesses" as to circumstances "unknowable" to them in deciding when to give *Miranda* warnings, *Berkemer*, 468 U.S., at 430–431.

9. The State's purported distinction between blindness and age—that taking account of a suspect's youth requires a court "to get into the mind" of the child, whereas taking account of a suspect's blindness does not, Tr. of Oral Arg. 41–42—is mistaken. In either case, the question becomes how a reasonable person would understand the circumstances, either from the perspective of a blind person or, as here, a 13-year-old child.

internal quotation marks omitted)). But the same can be said of every objective circumstance that the State agrees is relevant to the custody analysis: Each circumstance goes to how a reasonable person would "internalize and perceive" every other. See, *e.g.*, *Stansbury*, 511 U.S., at 325. Indeed, this is the very reason that we ask whether the objective circumstances "add up to custody," *Keohane*, 516 U.S., at 113, instead of evaluating the circumstances one by one.

In the same vein, the State and its *amici* protest that the "effect of... age on [the] perception of custody is internal," Brief for Respondent 20, or "psychological," U.S. Brief 21. But the whole point of the custody analysis is to determine whether, given the circumstances, "a reasonable person [would] have felt he or she was... at liberty to terminate the interrogation and leave." *Keohane*, 516 U.S., at 112. Because the *Miranda* custody inquiry turns on the mindset of a reasonable person in the suspect's position, it cannot be the case that a circumstance is subjective simply because it has an "internal" or "psychological" impact on perception. Were that so, there would be no objective circumstances to consider at all.

Relying on our statements that the objective custody test is "designed to give clear guidance to the police," *Alvarado*, 541 U.S., at 668, the State next argues that a child's age must be excluded from the analysis in order to preserve clarity. Similarly, the dissent insists that the clarity of the custody analysis will be destroyed unless a "one-size-fits-all reasonable-person test" applies. In reality, however, ignoring a juvenile defendant's age will often make the inquiry more artificial, and thus only add confusion. And in any event, a child's age, when known or apparent, is hardly an obscure factor to assess. Though the State and the dissent worry about gradations among children of different ages, that concern cannot justify ignoring a child's age altogether. Just as police officers are competent to account for other objective circumstances that are a matter of degree such as the length of questioning or the number of officers present, so too are they competent to evaluate the effect of relative age. Indeed, they are competent to do so even though an interrogation room lacks the "reflective atmosphere of a [jury] deliberation room."... The same is true of judges, including those whose childhoods have long since passed. In short, officers and judges need no imaginative powers, knowledge of developmental psychology, training in cognitive science, or expertise in social and cultural anthropology to account for a child's age. They simply need the common sense to know that a 7-year-old is not a 13-year-old and neither is an adult.

There is, however, an even more fundamental flaw with the State's plea for clarity and the dissent's singular focus on simplifying the analysis: Not once have we excluded from the custody analysis a circumstance that we determined was relevant and objective, simply to make the fault line between custodial and noncustodial "brighter." Indeed, were the guiding concern clarity and nothing else, the custody test would presumably ask only whether the suspect had been placed under formal arrest. *Berkemer*, 468 U.S., at 441; see ibid. (acknowledging the "occasiona[l]... difficulty" police officers confront in determining when a suspect has been taken into custody). But we have rejected that "more easily administered line," recognizing that it would simply "enable the police to circumvent the constraints on custodial interrogations established by *Miranda*." Ibid.; see also *ibid.*, n. 33.[10]

10. Contrary to the dissent's intimation, *Miranda* does not answer the question whether a child's age is an objective circumstance relevant to the custody analysis. *Miranda* simply holds that warnings must be given once a suspect is in custody, without "paus[ing] to inquire in individual cases whether the defendant was aware of his rights without a warning being given." 384 U.S., at 468; see also *id.*, at 468–469 ("Assessments of the knowledge the defendant possessed, based on information as to age, education, intelligence, or prior

Finally, the State and the dissent suggest that excluding age from the custody analysis comes at no cost to juveniles' constitutional rights because the due process voluntariness test independently accounts for a child's youth. To be sure, that test permits consideration of a child's age, and it erects its own barrier to admission of a defendant's inculpatory statements at trial. See *Gallegos*, 370 U.S., at 53–55; *Haley*, 332 U.S., at 599–601;... ("[C]ourts should be instructed to take particular care to ensure that [young children's] incriminating statements were not obtained involuntarily"). But *Miranda*'s procedural safeguards exist precisely because the voluntariness test is an inadequate barrier when custodial interrogation is at stake. See 384 U.S., at 458 ("Unless adequate protective devices are employed to dispel the compulsion inherent in custodial surroundings, no statement obtained from the defendant can truly be the product of his free choice"); *Dickerson*, 530 U.S., at 442 ("[R]eliance on the traditional totality-of-the-circumstances test raise[s] a risk of overlooking an involuntary custodial confession"); see also *supra*, at 2400–2401. To hold, as the State requests, that a child's age is never relevant to whether a suspect has been taken into custody—and thus to ignore the very real differences between children and adults—would be to deny children the full scope of the procedural safeguards that *Miranda* guarantees to adults.

The question remains whether J.D.B. was in custody when police interrogated him. We remand for the state courts to address that question, this time taking account of all of the relevant circumstances of the interrogation, including J.D.B.'s age at the time. The judgment of the North Carolina Supreme Court is reversed, and the case is remanded for proceedings not inconsistent with this opinion.

JUSTICE ALITO, with whom THE CHIEF JUSTICE, JUSTICE SCALIA, and JUSTICE THOMAS join, dissenting.

The Court's decision in this case may seem on first consideration to be modest and sensible, but in truth it is neither. It is fundamentally inconsistent with one of the main justifications for the *Miranda* rule: the perceived need for a clear rule that can be easily applied in all cases. And today's holding is not needed to protect the constitutional rights of minors who are questioned by the police.

Miranda's prophylactic regime places a high value on clarity and certainty. Dissatisfied with the highly fact-specific constitutional rule against the admission of involuntary confessions, the *Miranda* Court set down rigid standards that often require courts to ignore personal characteristics that may be highly relevant to a particular suspect's actual susceptibility to police pressure. This rigidity, however, has brought with it one of *Miranda*'s principal strengths—"the ease and clarity of its application" by law enforcement officials and courts. See *Moran v. Burbine*, 475 U.S. 412, 425–426 (1986). A key contributor to this clarity, at least up until now, has been *Miranda*'s objective reasonable-person test for determining custody.

Miranda's custody requirement is based on the proposition that the risk of unconstitutional coercion is heightened when a suspect is placed under formal arrest or is subjected to some functionally equivalent limitation on freedom of movement. When this custodial threshold is reached, *Miranda* warnings must precede police questioning. But in the interest

contact with authorities, can never be more than speculation; a warning is a clearcut fact" (footnote omitted)). That conclusion says nothing about whether age properly informs whether a child is in custody in the first place.

of simplicity, the custody analysis considers only whether, under the circumstances, a hypothetical reasonable person would consider himself to be confined.

Many suspects, of course, will differ from this hypothetical reasonable person. Some, including those who have been hardened by past interrogations, may have no need for *Miranda* warnings at all. And for other suspects—those who are unusually sensitive to the pressures of police questioning—*Miranda* warnings may come too late to be of any use. That is a necessary consequence of *Miranda*'s rigid standards, but it does not mean that the constitutional rights of these especially sensitive suspects are left unprotected. A vulnerable defendant can still turn to the constitutional rule against actual coercion and contend that that his confession was extracted against his will.

Today's decision shifts the *Miranda* custody determination from a one-size-fits-all reasonable-person test into an inquiry that must account for at least one individualized characteristic—age—that is thought to correlate with susceptibility to coercive pressures. Age, however, is in no way the only personal characteristic that may correlate with pliability, and in future cases the Court will be forced to choose between two unpalatable alternatives. It may choose to limit today's decision by arbitrarily distinguishing a suspect's age from other personal characteristics—such as intelligence, education, occupation, or prior experience with law enforcement—that may also correlate with susceptibility to coercive pressures. Or, if the Court is unwilling to draw these arbitrary lines, it will be forced to effect a fundamental transformation of the *Miranda* custody test—from a clear, easily applied prophylactic rule into a highly fact-intensive standard resembling the voluntariness test that the *Miranda* Court found to be unsatisfactory.

For at least three reasons, there is no need to go down this road. First, many minors subjected to police interrogation are near the age of majority, and for these suspects the one-size-fits-all *Miranda* custody rule may not be a bad fit. Second, many of the difficulties in applying the *Miranda* custody rule to minors arise because of the unique circumstances present when the police conduct interrogations at school. The *Miranda* custody rule has always taken into account the setting in which questioning occurs, and accounting for the school setting in such cases will address many of these problems. Third, in cases like the one now before us, where the suspect is especially young, courts applying the constitutional voluntariness standard can take special care to ensure that incriminating statements were not obtained through coercion.

Safeguarding the constitutional rights of minors does not require the extreme makeover of *Miranda* that today's decision may portend.

I

In the days before *Miranda*, this Court's sole metric for evaluating the admissibility of confessions was a voluntariness standard rooted in both the Fifth Amendment's Self-Incrimination Clause and the Due Process Clause of the Fourteenth Amendment. See *Bram v. United States*, 168 U.S. 532, 542 (1897) (Self-Incrimination Clause); *Brown v. Mississippi*, 297 U.S. 278 (1936) (due process). The question in these voluntariness cases was whether the particular "defendant's will" had been "overborne." *Lynumn v. Illinois*, 372 U.S. 528, 534 (1963). Courts took into account both "the details of the interrogation" *and* "the characteristics of the accused," *Schneckloth v. Bustamonte*, 412 U.S. 218, 226 (1973), and then "weigh[ed] . . . the circumstances of pressure against the power of resistance of the person confessing." *Stein v. New York*, 346 U.S. 156, 185 (1953).

All manner of individualized, personal characteristics were relevant in this voluntariness inquiry. Among the most frequently mentioned factors were the defendant's education, physical condition, intelligence, and mental health. *Withrow v. Williams*, 507 U.S. 680, 693 (1993); see *Clewis v. Texas*, 386 U.S. 707, 712 (1967) ("only a fifth-grade education"); *Greenwald v. Wisconsin*, 390 U.S. 519, 520–521 (1968) (*per curiam*) (had not taken blood-pressure medication); *Payne v. Arkansas*, 356 U.S. 560, 562, n. 4 (1958) ("mentally dull" and "'slow to learn'"); *Fikes v. Alabama*, 352 U.S. 191, 193, 196, 198 (1957) ("low mentality, if not mentally ill"). The suspect's age also received prominent attention in several cases, e.g., *Gallegos v. Colorado*, 370 U.S. 49, 54 (1962), especially when the suspect was a "mere child." *Haley v. Ohio*, 332 U.S. 596, 599 (1948) (plurality opinion). The weight assigned to any one consideration varied from case to case. But all of these factors, along with anything else that might have affected the "individual's . . . capacity for effective choice," were relevant in determining whether the confession was coerced or compelled. See *Miranda v. Arizona*, 384 U.S. 436, 506–507 (1966) (Harlan, J., dissenting).

The all-encompassing nature of the voluntariness inquiry had its benefits. It allowed courts to accommodate a "complex of values," *Schneckloth*, *supra*, at 223, 224, and to make a careful, highly individualized determination as to whether the police had wrung "a confession out of [the] accused against his will." *Blackburn v. Alabama*, 361 U.S. 199, 206–207 (1960). But with this flexibility came a decrease in both certainty and predictability, and the voluntariness standard proved difficult "for law enforcement officers to conform to, and for courts to apply in a consistent manner." *Dickerson v. United States*, 530 U.S. 428, 444 (2000).

In *Miranda*, the Court supplemented the voluntariness inquiry with a "set of prophylactic measures" designed to ward off the "'inherently compelling pressures' of custodial interrogation." See *Maryland v. Shatzer*, 559 U.S. ___, ___, (2010) (slip op., at 4) (quoting *Miranda*, 384 U.S., at 467). *Miranda* greatly simplified matters by requiring police to give suspects standard warnings before commencing any custodial interrogation. See *id.*, at 479. Its requirements are no doubt "rigid," see *Fare v. Michael C.*, 439 U.S. 1310, 1314 (1978) (Rehnquist, J., in chambers), and they often require courts to suppress "trustworthy and highly probative" statements that may be perfectly "voluntary under [a] traditional Fifth Amendment analysis." *Fare v. Michael C.*, 442 U.S. 707, 718 (1979). But with this rigidity comes increased clarity. *Miranda* provides "a workable rule to guide police officers," *New York v. Quarles*, 467 U.S. 649, 658 (1984) (internal quotation marks omitted), and an administrable standard for the courts. As has often been recognized, this gain in clarity and administrability is one of *Miranda*'s "principal advantages." *Berkemer v. McCarty*, 468 U.S. 420, 430 (1984); see also *Missouri v. Seibert*, 542 U.S. 600, 622 (2004) (Kennedy, J., concurring in judgment).

No less than other facets of *Miranda*, the threshold requirement that the suspect be in "custody" is "designed to give clear guidance to the police." *Yarborough v. Alvarado*, 541 U.S. 652, 668, 669 (2004). Custody under *Miranda* attaches where there is a "formal arrest" or a "restraint on freedom of movement" akin to formal arrest. *California v. Beheler*, 463 U.S. 1121, 1125 (1983) (*per curiam*) (internal quotation marks omitted). This standard is "objective" and turns on how a hypothetical "reasonable person in the position of the individual being questioned would gauge the breadth of his or her freedom of action." *Stansbury v. California*, 511 U.S. 318, 322–323, 325 (1994) (*per curiam*) (internal quotation marks omitted).

Until today, the Court's cases applying this test have focused solely on the "objective circumstances of the interrogation," *id.*, at 323, not the personal characteristics of the interrogated. *E.g.*, *Berkemer*, *supra*, at 442, and n. 35; but cf. *Schneckloth*, 412 U.S., at 226 (voluntariness inquiry requires consideration of "the details of the interrogation" *and* "the characteristics of the accused"). Relevant factors have included such things as where the questioning occurred, how long it lasted, what was said, any physical restraints placed on the suspect's movement, and whether the suspect was allowed to leave when the questioning was through. The totality of *these* circumstances—the external circumstances, that is, of the interrogation itself—is what has mattered in this Court's cases. Personal characteristics of suspects have consistently been rejected or ignored as irrelevant under a one-size-fits-all reasonable-person standard. *Stansbury, supra*, at 323 ("[C]ustody depends on the objective circumstances of the interrogation, not on the subjective views harbored by either the interrogating officers or the person being questioned").

For example, in *Berkemer v. McCarty, supra*, police officers conducting a traffic stop questioned a man who had been drinking and smoking marijuana before he was pulled over. *Id.*, at 423. Although the suspect's inebriation was readily apparent to the officers at the scene, *ibid.*, the Court's analysis did not advert to this or any other individualized consideration. Instead, the Court focused only on the external circumstances of the interrogation itself. The opinion concluded that a typical "traffic stop" is akin to a "*Terry* stop" and does not qualify as the equivalent of "formal arrest." *Id.*, at 439.

California v. Beheler, supra, is another useful example. There, the circumstances of the interrogation were "remarkably similar" to the facts of the Court's earlier decision in *Oregon v. Mathiason*, 429 U.S. 492 (1977) (*per curiam*)—the suspect was "not placed under arrest," he "voluntarily [came] to the police station," and he was "allowed to leave unhindered by police after a brief interview." 463 U.S., at 1123, 1121. A California court in *Beheler* had nonetheless distinguished *Mathiason* because the police knew that Beheler "had been drinking earlier in the day" and was "emotionally distraught." 463 U.S., at 1124–1125. In a summary reversal, this Court explained that the fact "[t]hat the police knew more" personal information about Beheler than they did about Mathiason was "irrelevant." *Id.*, at 1125. Neither one of them was in custody under the objective reasonable-person standard. *Ibid.*; see also *Alvarado, supra*, at 668, 669 (experience with law enforcement irrelevant to *Miranda* custody analysis "as a *de novo* matter").[8]

The glaring absence of reliance on personal characteristics in these and other custody cases should come as no surprise. To account for such individualized considerations would be to contradict *Miranda*'s central premise. The *Miranda* Court's decision to adopt its inflexible prophylactic requirements was expressly based on the notion that "[a]ssessments of the knowledge the defendant possessed, based on information as to his age, education, intelligence, or prior contact with authorities, can never be more than speculation." 384 U.S., at 468–469.

II

In light of this established practice, there is no denying that, by incorporating age into its analysis, the Court is embarking on a new expansion of the established custody standard.

8. The Court claims that "[n]ot once" have any of our cases "excluded from the custody analysis a circumstance that we determined was relevant and objective, simply to make the fault line between custodial and noncustodial 'brighter.'" Surely this is incorrect. The very act of adopting a reasonable-person test necessarily excludes all sorts of "relevant and objective" circumstances—for example, all the objective circumstances of a suspect's life history—that might otherwise bear on a custody determination.

And since *Miranda* is this Court's rule, "not a constitutional command," it is up to the Court "to justify its expansion." Cf. *Arizona v. Roberson*, 486 U.S. 675, 688 (1988) (KENNEDY, J., dissenting). This the Court fails to do.

In its present form, *Miranda*'s prophylactic regime already imposes "high cost[s]" by requiring suppression of confessions that are often "highly probative" and "voluntary" by any traditional standard. *Oregon v. Elstad*, 470 U.S. 298, 312 (1985); see *Dickerson*, 530 U.S., at 444 (under *Miranda* "statements which may be by no means involuntary, made by a defendant who is aware of his 'rights,' may nonetheless be excluded and a guilty defendant go free as a result"). Nonetheless, a "core virtue" of *Miranda* has been the clarity and precision of its guidance to "police and courts." *Withrow v. Williams*, 507 U.S. 680, 694 (1993) (internal quotation marks omitted); see *Moran*, 475 U.S., at 425 ("[O]ne of the principal advantages of *Miranda* is the ease and clarity of its application" (internal quotation marks omitted)). This increased clarity "has been thought to outweigh the burdens" that *Miranda* imposes. *Fare*, 442 U.S., at 718. The Court has, however, repeatedly cautioned against upsetting the careful "balance" that *Miranda* struck, *Moran*, *supra*, at 424, and it has "refused to sanction attempts to expand [the] *Miranda* holding" in ways that would reduce its "clarity." See *Quarles*, 467 U.S., at 658 (citing cases). Given this practice, there should be a "strong presumption" against the Court's new departure from the established custody test. See *United States v. Patane*, 542 U.S. 630, 640 (2004) (plurality opinion). In my judgment, that presumption cannot be overcome here.

A

The Court's rationale for importing age into the custody standard is that minors tend to lack adults' "capacity to exercise mature judgment" and that failing to account for that "reality" will leave some minors unprotected under *Miranda* in situations where they perceive themselves to be confined. I do not dispute that many suspects who are under 18 will be more susceptible to police pressure than the average adult. As the Court notes, our pre-*Miranda* cases were particularly attuned to this "reality" in applying the constitutional requirement of voluntariness in fact. It is no less a "reality," however, that many persons *over* the age of 18 are also more susceptible to police pressure than the hypothetical reasonable person. See *Payne*, 356 U.S., at 567 (fact that defendant was a "mentally dull 19-year-old youth" relevant in voluntariness inquiry). Yet the *Miranda* custody standard has never accounted for the personal characteristics of these or any other individual defendants.

Indeed, it has always been the case under *Miranda* that the unusually meek or compliant are subject to the same fixed rules, including the same custody requirement, as those who are unusually resistant to police pressure. *Berkemer*, 468 U.S., at 442, and n. 35 ("[O]nly relevant inquiry is how a reasonable man in the suspect's position would have understood his situation"). *Miranda*'s rigid standards are both overinclusive and underinclusive. They are overinclusive to the extent that they provide a windfall to the most hardened and savvy of suspects, who often have no need for *Miranda*'s protections. Compare *Miranda*, *supra*, at 471–472 ("[N]o amount of circumstantial evidence that the person may have been aware of" his rights can overcome *Miranda*'s requirements), with *Orozco v. Texas*, 394 U.S. 324, 329 (1969) (WHITE, J., dissenting) ("Where the defendant himself [w]as a lawyer, policeman, professional criminal, or otherwise has become aware of what his right to silence is, it is sheer fancy to assert that his answer to every question asked him is compelled unless he is advised of those rights with which he is already intimately familiar"). And *Miranda*'s requirements are underinclusive to the extent that they fail to account for "frailties," "idiosyncrasies," and other individualized considerations that might cause a person to bend more easily during a confrontation with the police. See *Alvarado*, 541 U.S., at 662 (internal quotation marks omitted). Members of this Court have seen this rigidity as a major weakness in *Miranda*'s "code of rules for confessions." See 384 U.S., at 504 (HARLAN, J., dissenting); *Fare*, 439 U.S., at 1314 (REHNQUIST, J., in chambers) ("[T]he rigidity of [*Miranda*'s] prophylactic rules was a principal weakness in the view of dissenters and critics outside the Court"). But if it is, then the weakness is an inescapable consequence of the *Miranda* Court's decision to supplement the more holistic voluntariness requirement with a one-size-fits-all prophylactic rule.

That is undoubtedly why this Court's *Miranda* cases have never before mentioned "the suspect's age" or any other individualized consideration in applying the custody standard. See *Alvarado, supra*, at 666. And unless the *Miranda* custody rule is now to be radically transformed into one that takes into account the wide range of individual characteristics that are relevant in determining whether a confession is voluntary, the Court must shoulder the burden of explaining why age is different from these other personal characteristics.

Why, for example, is age different from intelligence? Suppose that an officer, upon going to a school to question a student, is told by the principal that the student has an I.Q. of 75 and is in a special-education class. Cf. *In re J.D.B.*, 363 N.C. 664, 666, 686 S.E.2d 135, 136–137 (2009). Are those facts more or less important than the student's age in determining whether he or she "felt…at liberty to terminate the interrogation and leave"? See *Thompson v. Keohane*, 516 U.S. 99, 112 (1995). An I.Q. score, like age, is more than just a number. And an individual's intelligence can also yield "conclusions" similar to those "we have drawn ourselves" in cases far afield of *Miranda*….

How about the suspect's cultural background? Suppose the police learn (or should have learned…) that a suspect they wish to question is a recent immigrant from a country in which dire consequences often befall any person who dares to attempt to cut short any meeting with the police.[9] Is this really less relevant than the fact that a suspect is a month or so away from his 18th birthday?

The defendant's education is another personal characteristic that may generate "conclusions about behavior and perception." Under today's decision, why should police officers and courts "blind themselves," to the fact that a suspect has "only a fifth-grade education"? See *Clewis*, 386 U.S., at 712 (voluntariness case). Alternatively, what if the police know or should know that the suspect is "a college-educated man with law school training"? See *Crooker v. California*, 357 U.S. 433, 440 (1958), overruled by *Miranda, supra*, at 479, and n. 48. How are these individual considerations meaningfully different from age in their "relationship to a reasonable person's understanding of his freedom of action"? The Court proclaims that "[a] child's age…is different," but the basis for this *ipse dixit* is dubious.

I have little doubt that today's decision will soon be cited by defendants—and perhaps by prosecutors as well—for the proposition that all manner of other individual characteristics should be treated like age and taken into account in the *Miranda* custody calculus. Indeed, there are already lower court decisions that take this approach. See *United States v. Beraun-Panez*, 812 F.2d 578, 581, modified 830 F.2d 127 (C.A.9 1987) ("reasonable person who was an

9. Cf. *United States v. Chalan*, 812 F.2d 1302, 1307 (C.A.10 1987) (rejecting claim that Native American suspect was "in custody" for *Miranda* purposes because, by custom, obedience to tribal authorities was "expected of all tribal members").

alien"); *In re Jorge D.*, 202 Ariz. 277, 280, 43 P.3d 605, 608 (App. 2002) (age, maturity, and experience); *State v. Doe*, 130 Idaho 811, 818, 948 P.2d 166, 173 (1997) (same); *In re Joshua David C.*, 116 Md.App. 580, 594, 698 A.2d 1155, 1162 (1997) ("education, age, and intelligence").

In time, the Court will have to confront these issues, and it will be faced with a difficult choice. It may choose to distinguish today's decision and adhere to the arbitrary proclamation that "age... is different." Or it may choose to extend today's holding and, in doing so, further undermine the very rationale for the *Miranda* regimH4

B

If the Court chooses the latter course, then a core virtue of *Miranda*—the "ease and clarity of its application"—will be lost. *Moran*, 475 U.S., at 425; see *Fare*, 442 U.S., at 718 (noting that the clarity of *Miranda*'s requirements "has been thought to outweigh the burdens that the decision... imposes"). However, even today's more limited departure from *Miranda*'s one-size-fits-all reasonable-person test will produce the very consequences that prompted the *Miranda* Court to abandon exclusive reliance on the voluntariness test in the first place: The Court's test will be hard for the police to follow, and it will be hard for judges to apply. See *Dickerson v. United States*, 530 U.S. 428, 444 (2000).

The Court holds that age must be taken into account when it "was known to the officer at the time of the interview," or when it "would have been objectively apparent" to a reasonable officer. The first half of this test overturns the rule that the "initial determination of custody" does not depend on the "subjective views harbored by... interrogating officers." *Stansbury*, 511 U.S., at 323. The second half will generate time-consuming satellite litigation over a reasonable officer's perceptions. When, as here, the interrogation takes place in school, the inquiry may be relatively simple. But not all police questioning of minors takes place in schools. In many cases, courts will presumably have to make findings as to whether a particular suspect had a sufficiently youthful look to alert a reasonable officer to the possibility that the suspect was under 18, or whether a reasonable officer would have recognized that a suspect's I.D. was a fake. The inquiry will be both "time-consuming and disruptive" for the police and the courts. See *Berkemer*, 468 U.S., at 432 (refusing to modify the custody test based on similar considerations). It will also be made all the more complicated by the fact that a suspect's dress and manner will often be different when the issue is litigated in court than it was at the time of the interrogation.

Even after courts clear this initial hurdle, further problems will likely emerge as judges attempt to put themselves in the shoes of the average 16-year-old, or 15-year-old, or 13-year-old, as the case may be. Consider, for example, a 60-year-old judge attempting to make a custody determination through the eyes of a hypothetical, average 15-year-old. Forty-five years of personal experience and societal change separate this judge from the days when he or she was 15 years old. And this judge may or may not have been an average 15-year-old. The Court's answer to these difficulties is to state that "no imaginative powers, knowledge of developmental psychology, [or] training in cognitive science" will be necessary. Judges "simply need the common sense," the Court assures, "to know that a 7-year-old is not a 13-year-old and neither is an adult." It is obvious, however, that application of the Court's new rule demands much more than this.

Take a fairly typical case in which today's holding may make a difference. A 16½-year-old moves to suppress incriminating statements made prior to the administration of *Miranda* warnings. The circumstances are such that, if the defendant were at least 18, the court would not find that he or she was in custody, but the defendant argues that a reasonable 16½ -year-old would view the situation differently. The judge will not have the luxury of merely saying: "It is common sense that a 16½ -year-old is not an 18-year-old. Motion granted." Rather, the judge will be required to determine whether the differences between a typical 16½ -year-old and a typical 18-year-old with respect to susceptibility to the pressures of interrogation are sufficient to change the outcome of the custody determination. Today's opinion contains not a word of actual guidance as to how judges are supposed to go about making that determination.

C

Petitioner and the Court attempt to show that this task is not unmanageable by pointing out that age is taken into account in other legal contexts. In particular, the Court relies on the fact that the age of a defendant is a relevant factor under the reasonable-person standard applicable in negligence suits. But negligence is generally a question for the jury, the members of which can draw on their varied experiences with persons of different ages. It also involves a *post hoc* determination, in the reflective atmosphere of a deliberation room, about whether the defendant conformed to a standard of care. The *Miranda* custody determination, by contrast, must be made in the first instance by police officers in the course of an investigation that may require quick decisionmaking. See *Quarles*, 467 U.S., at 658 (noting "the importance" under *Miranda* of providing "a workable rule 'to guide police officers, who have only limited time and expertise to reflect on and balance the social and individual interests involved in the specific circumstances they confront'"); *Alvarado*, 541 U.S., at 668, 669 ("[T]he custody inquiry states an objective rule designed to give clear guidance to the police").

Equally inapposite are the Eighth Amendment cases the Court cites in support of its new rule. Those decisions involve the "judicial exercise of independent judgment" about the constitutionality of certain punishments. Like the negligence standard, they do not require on-the-spot judgments by the police.

Nor do state laws affording extra protection for juveniles during custodial interrogation provide any support for petitioner's arguments. States are free to enact additional restrictions on the police over and above those demanded by the Constitution or *Miranda*. In addition, these state statutes generally create clear, workable rules to guide police conduct. See Brief for Petitioner 16–17 (citing statutes that require or permit parents to be present during custodial interrogation of a minor, that require minors to be advised of a statutory right to communicate with a parent or guardian, and that require parental consent to custodial interrogation). Today's decision, by contrast, injects a new, complicating factor into what had been a clear, easily applied prophylactic rule. See *Alvarado, supra*, at 668–669.[10]

10. The Court also relies on North Carolina's concession at oral argument that a court could take into account a suspect's blindness as a factor relevant to the *Miranda* custody determination. This is a far-fetched hypothetical, and neither the parties nor their *amici* cite any case in which such a problem has actually arisen. Presumably such a case would involve a situation in which a blind defendant was given "a typed document advising him that he [was] free to leave." See Brief for Juvenile Law Center as *Amicus Curiae* 23. In such a case, furnishing this advice in a form calculated to be unintelligible to the suspect would be tantamount to failing to provide the advice at all. And advice by the police that a suspect is or is not free to leave at will has

III

The Court's decision greatly diminishes the clarity and administrability that have long been recognized as "principal advantages" of *Miranda*'s prophylactic requirements. See, e.g., *Moran*, 475 U.S., at 425. But what is worse, the Court takes this step unnecessarily, as there are other, less disruptive tools available to ensure that minors are not coerced into confessing.

As an initial matter, the difficulties that the Court's standard introduces will likely yield little added protection for most juvenile defendants. Most juveniles who are subjected to police interrogation are teenagers nearing the age of majority.[11] These defendants' reactions to police pressure are unlikely to be much different from the reaction of a typical 18-year-old in similar circumstances. A one-size-fits-all *Miranda* custody rule thus provides a roughly reasonable fit for these defendants.

In addition, many of the concerns that petitioner raises regarding the application of the *Miranda* custody rule to minors can be accommodated by considering the unique circumstances present when minors are questioned in school. See Brief for Petitioner 10–11 (reciting at length the factors petitioner believes to be relevant to the custody determination here, including the fact that petitioner was removed from class by a police officer, that the interview took place in a school conference room, and that a uniformed officer and a vice principal were present). The *Miranda* custody rule has always taken into account the setting in which questioning occurs, restrictions on a suspect's freedom of movement, and the presence of police officers or other authority figures. See *Alvarado, supra*, at 665; *Maryland v. Shatzer*, 559 U.S. ___, ___, (2010) (slip op., at 14). It can do so here as well.[12]

Finally, in cases like the one now before us, where the suspect is much younger than the typical juvenile defendant, courts should be instructed to take particular care to ensure that incriminating statements were not obtained involuntarily. The voluntariness inquiry is flexible and accommodating by nature, see *Schneckloth*, 412 U.S., at 224, and the Court's precedents already make clear that "special care" must be exercised in applying the voluntariness test where the confession of a "mere child" is at issue. *Haley*, 332 U.S., at 599 (plurality opinion). If *Miranda*'s rigid, one-size-fits-all standards fail to account for the unique needs of juveniles, the response should be to rigorously apply the constitutional rule against coercion to ensure that the rights of minors are protected. There is no need to run *Miranda* off the rails.

The Court rests its decision to inject personal characteristics into the *Miranda* custody inquiry on the principle that judges applying *Miranda* cannot "blind themselves to . . . commonsense reality." But the Court's shift is fundamentally at odds with the clear prophylactic rules that *Miranda* has long enforced. *Miranda* frequently requires judges to blind themselves to the reality that many un-Mirandized custodial confessions are "by no means involuntary" or

always been regarded as a circumstance regarding the conditions of the interrogation that must be taken into account in making the *Miranda* custody determination.

11. See Dept of Justice, Federal Bureau of Investigation, 2008 Crime in the United States (Sept. 2009), online at http://www2.fbi.gov/ucr/cius2008/data/table_38.html (all Internet materials as visited June 8, 2011, and available in Clerk of Court's case file) (indicating that less than 30% of juvenile arrests in the United States are of suspects who are under 15).

12. The Court thinks it would be "absur[d]" to consider the school setting without accounting for age, but the real absurdity is for the Court to require police officers to get inside the head of a reasonable minor while making the quick, on-the-spot determinations that *Miranda* demands.

coerced. *Dickerson*, 530 U.S., at 444. It also requires police to provide a rote recitation of *Miranda* warnings that many suspects already know and could likely recite from memory.[13] Under today's new, "reality"-based approach to the doctrine, perhaps these and other principles of our *Miranda* jurisprudence will, like the custody standard, now be ripe for modification. Then, bit by bit, *Miranda* will lose the clarity and ease of application that has long been viewed as one of its chief justifications.

I respectfully dissent.

QUESTIONS

1. Does the Court overrule *Yarborough*? If not, how does the Court reconcile the two cases?

2. Why shouldn't we take age into account when determining whether someone is in custody? Does that render the *Miranda* inquiry unduly subjective? What is wrong with subjectivity? Or is age subjective?

3. The dissent seems to think that this case will cause serious inroads into *Miranda* as a prophylactic rule. Do you agree?

4. Do you think police may now question children without triggering *Miranda* as long as the children are told that they are free to leave? Does this change the way interrogations occur in the school setting? What about if a parent is present?

13. Surveys have shown that "[l]arge majorities" of the public are aware that "individuals arrested for a crime" have a right to "remai[n] silent (81%)," a right to "a lawyer (95%)," and a right to have a lawyer "appointed" if the arrestee "cannot afford one (88%)." See Belden, Russonello & Stewart, Developing a National Message for Indigent Defense: Analysis of National Survey 4 (Oct. 2001), online at http://www.nlada.org/DMS/Documents/1211996548.53/Pollingresultsreport.pdf.

3. IDENTIFICATION PROCEDURES AND CONFIDENTIALITY: LINEUPS, SHOW-UPS, PHOTO ARRAYS, AND FINGERPRINTS

A criminal suspect's Sixth Amendment rights are not violated when the police require him to participate in a preindictment lineup, *Kirby v. Illinois*, 406 U.S. 682 (1972); or show photographs of the suspect to a witness after adversarial judicial proceedings have been initiated, because a noncorporeal display is not a critical stage of the prosecution, *United States v. Ash*, 413 U.S. 300 (1973). Nevertheless, a pretrial identification procedure may violate the Due Process Clause of the Fourteenth Amendment when it is unnecessarily suggestive and is conducive to mistaken identification. *Stovall v. Denno*, 388 U.S. 293 (1967). The question, ultimately, is the reliability of the identification; thus, an out-of-court identification will be excluded only if it is the result of an unnecessarily suggestive identification process. Are there special considerations when police show photographs of juveniles? Consider the next two cases when formulating your answer.

STATE EX REL. A.M.
Court of Appeal of Louisiana, Fourth Circuit
983 So.2d 176 (2008)

ROLAND L. BELSOME, Judge.

Defendant-Appellant appeals his conviction by the Orleans Parish Juvenile Court for one count of carjacking....

Cheryl Green testified that at approximately 7:55 p.m. on January 29, 2007, as she was walking to her vehicle at a filling station, she was approached by a young man who asked her for a ride. Ms. Green stated that she opened the door and allowed the boy to enter her vehicle. As she was driving, when she asked the boy where he wanted to go, he told her to get out of the car. In response, Ms. Green stated that she refused, pushing him, indicating she would not get out because this was her car. Ms. Green testified that after pushing her back, the boy punched her in the mouth, knocking out one tooth and shattering some of her other teeth, and drove away in her vehicle. Ms. Green further testified that after she exited the vehicle, she walked to a nearby house, knocked on the door, and one of the occupants called the police. When the police arrived to take her statement, Ms. Green stated that she described the offender as a black male child wearing an orange hooded jacket, but denied providing an approximate age of the offender.

Detective Gregory Powell of the New Orleans Police Department investigated the carjacking incident. Detective Powell testified that as part of his investigation, he canvassed the area surrounding the filling station and questioned individuals in the area, where he obtained the first name A___. Based on the information that he received from this investigation, Detective Powell stated that he went to Sarah T. Reed High School, where he spoke with the assistant principal to determine whether an African-American student was enrolled by the name of

A___ who was approximately five feet, four inches tall. Detective Powell testified that he was then given a book with a listing of all the students, and he went through the book and wrote down information for all of the students with the first name A___. The detective stated that he subsequently spoke with a few teachers to determine which student by the name of A___ fit the physical description that he had obtained from his investigation. Although Detective Powell was unable to obtain a photograph from the school, he testified that he did ultimately obtain a photograph of A.M., which he included in the photographic lineup that he showed to Ms. Green.

Ms. Green testified that in late February 2007, she received a telephone call from Detective Powell, and that he requested to meet with her so that she could review a photo lineup. Ms. Green subsequently met with Detective Powell in his police vehicle to view the lineup of six photographs and identified the defendant from the lineup as the offender. Ms. Green testified that after she selected the defendant's photograph, Detective Powell instructed Ms. Green to put her signature on the back of the photograph that she selected. Ms. Green also identified the defendant in open court as the person who carjacked her on January 29, 2007....

Prior to the commencement of trial on May 11, 2007, the court heard an oral motion to suppress the identification of A.M., at which time the State presented testimony from Ms. Green and Detective Powell, both of whom were cross-examined by counsel for defendant. Additionally, the State offered the photographic lineup and the court admitted same, ultimately denying the motion to suppress, but noting the defendant's objection. At the conclusion of proceedings, the court adjudicated A.M. delinquent of carjacking....

In the first assignment of error, the defendant asserts that the trial court erred in failing to suppress the identification of A.M. because the picture lineup was suggestive and thus created a substantial likelihood of misidentification. The defendant argues that the photo of A.M. was not taken at A.M.'s age as of the alleged crime and that one of the photographs in the lineup appeared to be a female.

To suppress an identification, a defendant must first establish that the identification procedure was suggestive. An identification procedure is unduly suggestive if a witness' attention is focused on the defendant. Strict identity of physical characteristics of the individuals in the photographs is unnecessary; all that is needed is a "sufficient resemblance to reasonably test identification." A defendant who attempts to suppress an identification must prove not only that the identification itself was suggestive, but also that a likelihood of misidentification existed as a result of the identification procedure.

Even if an identification is considered suggestive, however, an out-of-court identification will be admissible if it is reliable under the totality of the circumstances....

In this case, Detective Powell testified that he assembled the photographic lineup by entering A.M.'s information into a computer. The computer then printed out approximately twenty photographs at random that matched the age, complexion, and gender of the suspect. Detective Powell testified that he entered in the age of thirteen for A.M., and that of the twenty photographs that the computer produced, he chose five others to include in the lineup with A.M.'s photograph. Detective Powell further stated that he tried to vary the background colors in the photographs so that one background was not different than the others.

Upon a careful review of the record, we find that the identification was suggestive. Although Detective Powell used the photographs in the lineup that were randomly selected by the computer, A.M.'s photograph is nonetheless distinguishable from the others. In the lineup, A.M.'s face fills the entire frame, while the others' faces do not. Accordingly, this Court must look to several factors to determine, under the totality of the circumstances, whether the suggestive lineup presented a substantial likelihood of misidentification at trial. The United States Supreme Court has established a five-part test for determining whether a suggestive identification is reliable under the totality of the circumstances:

> These [factors] include the opportunity of the witness to view the criminal at the time of the crime, the witness' degree of attention, the accuracy of his prior description of the criminal, the level of certainty demonstrated at the confrontation, and the time between the crime and the confrontation. Against these factors is to be weighed the corrupting effect of the suggestive identification itself.

Manson v. Brathwaite, 432 U.S. 98, 114, 97 S.Ct. 2243, 2253, 53 L.Ed.2d 140 (1977).

Applying the first factor to the instant case, we find that, according to Ms. Green's testimony, she had a sufficient opportunity to closely view the defendant on the date of the incident, both when the defendant approached her at the filling station and while the two conversed in Ms. Green's vehicle before the carjacking occurred. Likewise, we find that the second factor, the witness's degree of attention, weighs in favor of admissibility. Ms. Green did not testify that her view of the defendant's face was obstructed in any way when...he approached her and asked her for a ride. Although Ms. Green testified that she was watching the road while driving, she had an adequate opportunity to view the defendant at close range when speaking with him in her vehicle and during the shoving match that preceded the carjacking. We find that Ms. Green's attention during her encounter in the vehicle was sufficiently focused on the defendant. The accuracy of Ms. Green's prior description of her attacker, the third factor, is neutral in this case. Ms. Green testified that on the date of the incident, she described the person who carjacked her to Detective Powell as a black male child who wore an orange hooded jacket, but that she did not recall any of the officers asking her to estimate a particular age range of the carjacker.

Conversely, we find that the fourth factor in the *Manson v. Brathwaite* analysis, the witness' level of certainty at the confrontation, weighs heavily in favor of admissibility in this case. Ms. Green testified that in February 2007, Detective Powell showed her the photo array and asked her whether she recognized her attacker, and that, upon reviewing each of the photographs, she recognized A.M. as the boy who carjacked her. Ms. Green further stated that she was not coerced into selecting the defendant's photograph and that the detective did not in any way point to any of the photographs in the lineup. Ms. Green was again presented with the lineup during her testimony on May 11, 2007, and when she was asked how she knew the defendant's photograph was the same one that she had chosen in February, she stated that she remembered the defendant's nose, because "he had a cute nose." Ms. Green then identified the defendant as the person who carjacked her in open court.

Finally, the fifth factor, the length of time between the crime and the confrontation, likewise weighs in favor of reliability and admissibility. In this case, just under a month had elapsed between the carjacking incident and Ms. Green's review of the photo array with Detective Powell....

Pursuant to the guidelines in *Manson v. Brathwaite*, we now turn to the issue of whether the suggestive lineup had any corrupting effect. We find that it did not. In this case, as noted above, Ms. Green had sufficient opportunity to view her carjacker face-to-face and was presented with a photo array soon after her attack. Nothing in the record indicates any intention by the State to guide Ms. Green's attention to the defendant. Accordingly, upon a careful review of the record, we find that Ms. Green would have properly identified the defendant as the person who carjacked her even if the lineup had not been unduly suggestive.

Therefore, because Ms. Green's identification of the defendant was reliable under the totality of the circumstances, the identification of the defendant was properly admitted by the trial court.

J.Y. V. STATE
Court of Appeals of Indiana
816 N.E.2d 909 (2004)

NAJAM, Judge.

J.Y. appeals from his adjudication as a delinquent child for committing Attempted Child Molesting, as a Class B felony, and Child Molesting, as a Class C felony, when committed by an adult....

On April 22, 2003, in the early evening, then eight-year-old A.B., an African-American girl, was riding her bike in the alley behind her house in South Bend when she encountered two Caucasian, teenaged boys who are brothers. One or both of the boys forced A.B. into a van parked off of the alley, shoving or dragging her through a large, broken-out window. Inside the van, the rear seat cushions were folded flat, creating a large, mattress-like area. The younger brother removed A.B.'s clothes, began to rub his penis on the outside of A.B.'s vagina, and ejaculated onto her abdomen and the van's seat cushion. During that time, the older brother was standing right outside the van. Then the younger brother exited the van, and the older brother entered the van and began rubbing his penis on the outside of A.B.'s vagina. A.B. shouted out "No!" and the boy stopped without ejaculating. A.B. then exited the van and went home.

A.B. did not tell her grandmother, her legal guardian, about the incident. But the next day at school, A.B. told her teacher what had happened. Accordingly, A.B.'s teacher took her to the principal's office, and the principal telephoned A.B.'s grandmother, Freddie Blake. A social worker assigned to the school drove A.B. home and then accompanied A.B. and Blake to the hospital for a physical examination. The physician who examined A.B. did not find any signs of sexual assault.

On April 25, 2003, A.B. underwent a videotaped interview with Angie Scott, a social worker with the CASIE Center. During that interview, A.B. reluctantly described the encounter and stated that the assailants were two Caucasian, teenaged brothers, one of whom is named Michael. A.B. did not provide either Scott or police with any additional physical characteristics to describe the boys.

Detective Cynthia Eastman of the South Bend Police Department began her investigation into the alleged sexual assault and learned that the van was owned by Tom Fairres, a Caucasian man living in a house across the alley from A.B.'s house and whose three Caucasian, teenaged sons were living with him. Detective Eastman obtained photographs of Fairres' sons T.Y., J.Y., and C.Y. to include in a photo array for A.B.'s consideration. In addition to those three photos, which had been copied from the boys' school identification cards, Detective Eastman chose three additional photos of boys who were roughly the same ages as the suspects and who shared some of the same basic physical characteristics. In the photo array, Fairres' three sons are wearing white t-shirts, and the other three boys are wearing collared shirts and ties. Two of the other boys are also wearing blazers.

Detective Eastman showed the photo array to A.B. in the principal's office at her school. Also present were Blake and A.B.'s teacher. Detective Eastman advised A.B. that her assailants' photographs might not be in the array. After looking at the array for less than one minute, A.B. began shaking and pointed at the photographs numbered 2 and 5. Those photographs depicted J.Y. and C.Y., respectively....

...When A.B. testified, she could not identify either J.Y. or his brother, who were both sitting in the courtroom. A.B. referred to the older assailant as "Plain Old Boy," but there was no evidence showing that that was J.Y.'s nickname. A.B. used J.Y.'s first name to identify the older assailant, but did not indicate when or where she had heard his name. And, instead of pointing to J.Y. in making the identification, she pointed to someone else sitting in the back row of the gallery in the courtroom. J.Y. was sitting toward the front of the courtroom at his counsel's table. A.B. subsequently testified that neither of the assailants was present in the courtroom. At the conclusion of the hearing, the juvenile court adjudicated J.Y. a delinquent child. This appeal ensued....

J.Y. first contends that the juvenile court abused its discretion when it admitted into evidence Detective Eastman's testimony regarding A.B.'s out-of-court identification of him after looking at a photo array. Specifically, J.Y. maintains that the photo array was impermissibly suggestive and, as such, that the identification violated his right to due process. We must agree.

Due process of law under the Fourteenth Amendment to the United States Constitution requires suppression of testimony about a pre-trial identification when the procedure employed is unnecessarily suggestive.... Otherwise, the defendant is subjected to the unacceptable risk that the identification process was conducted in such a way that it created a substantial likelihood of irreparable misidentification. Whether the procedure employed was unnecessarily suggestive in a particular case is to be determined under the totality of the circumstances....

Factors to be considered in evaluating the likelihood of a misidentification include: (1) the opportunity of the witness to view the criminal at the time of the crime; (2) the witness's degree of attention; (3) the accuracy of the witness's prior description of the criminal; and (4) the level of certainty demonstrated by the witness.... Among other factors the court may consider are: (1) the manner and form in which the police asked the witness to identify the suspect and the witness's interpretation of their directives; and (2) whether the police focused on the defendant as the prime suspect, either by their attitude or the makeup of the photo array.

In this case, the photo array consists of black-and-white copies of six photographs. T.Y. and J.Y. are depicted in the photographs numbered one and two, respectively. Each of them is wearing a white t-shirt, and each has dark, short hair. The photographs are candid shots; the boys are not posed, the lighting is such that the boys' faces are mostly in shadow, and the darkness of their faces is exacerbated by the use of all-white backgrounds. Neither boy is smiling in the photographs. The photographs of T.Y. and J.Y. are almost indistinguishable, although they are not twins.

The boys depicted in photographs numbered three, four, and six are in the same age group as J.Y. and C.Y. But those photos are school portraits; the boys are posed, and the lighting is such that the boy's face in number three is almost completely illuminated, and the boys' faces in numbers four and six are mostly illuminated. The backgrounds in each of the photos are dark. Those boys are wearing collared shirts with ties, and two of them are wearing blazers. All three boys have dark, short hair, although one of the boys has blonde highlights. Also, all of the boys are smiling.

Finally, in his photograph, C.Y. is wearing a white t-shirt, but, unlike the photographs of T.Y. and J.Y., the photograph appears to be a school portrait. The background consists of light and dark contours. While the lighting on his face is better than that in his brothers' photographs, it is not as good as the lighting on the other boys' faces. The quality of the copy is poor, which gives C.Y.'s face a dark, grainy appearance. C.Y. displays what might be considered a smile; while his teeth are showing, the ends of his mouth are not drawn upward.

Our review of relevant Indiana case law reveals no reported case where our courts have held that a photo array was impermissibly suggestive....

...[T]here are essentially two sets of photographs in the array. One set consists of J.Y. and his two brothers, each wearing a white t-shirt, with T.Y. and J.Y. looking exactly alike, not smiling, with faces in shadow, and with white backgrounds. The other set of photographs consists of the other three boys, who are all posed, smiling, and wearing dress clothes. A.B. never described what the perpetrators were wearing at the time of the attack. Given her young age, A.B. might well be inclined to believe that the boys wearing dress clothes and smiling were not her attackers. As a whole, the remarkable differences in appearance between J.Y. and his brothers and the other three boys, including their clothing and demeanor, and the difference in the quality and composition of the two sets of photographs, render the photo array impermissibly suggestive....

...[W]e think that the photo array is impermissibly suggestive in that the defendant and his two brothers are all suspects and their physical characteristics, dress, and demeanor stand out so strikingly when compared with those of the three other individuals in the array. In other words, while J.Y. does not stand out virtually alone when compared with his two brothers, J.Y. and his brothers stand out "strikingly" in their characteristics when compared with the other three boys. Thus, the array creates... "a substantial likelihood of irreparable misidentification."

In addition to the content of the photo array, the totality of the circumstances indicates a reasonable likelihood of misidentification in this case. There is scant evidence of how dark or light it was both inside and outside the van at the time of the attack. During her videotaped interview, A.B. stated only that it was "getting dark" outside. A photograph taken of the inside of the van shows what appear to be curtains capable of covering some of the van's windows. More importantly, A.B.'s inability to describe her assailants' height, weight, attire, hair color, or facial features following the assault supports a reasonable inference that either they were not discernible or that she was not paying close attention to the perpetrators' identities. A.B. was able to state only that her assailants were two "white boys" who were brothers and that one of them was named Michael.

Detective Eastman testified during voir dire that A.B. studied the photo array "intently" and that A.B. "visibly started shaking" and pointed to the photographs numbered two and five, one right after the other, in "less than a minute." Detective Eastman also testified that, prior to showing A.B. the photo array, she admonished A.B. that the suspects might not be included in the array. She further instructed A.B. to disregard the subjects' clothing and to be aware that hairstyles can change. Finally, Detective Eastman told A.B., "don't feel bad if you don't recognize the person that did this, because he might not be here." In short, there is no evidence that anyone influenced A.B. in picking out J.Y. from the photo array. But J.Y. maintains that when A.B. looked at the photo array, she was likely "eager to please the authority figures present, her [grand]mother, teacher and police officer."

Regardless, under the totality of the circumstances, we conclude that J.Y. was denied his right to due process. The photo array was impermissibly suggestive; A.B. was unable to describe her assailants with any specificity; A.B. used the wrong name to identify C.Y.; A.B. could not identify J.Y. during the final hearing; and A.B. testified that neither assailant was in the courtroom. Thus, the only evidence implicating J.Y. is A.B.'s identification based upon the photo array. There is no corroborating, substantial evidence of probative value regarding identity. The juvenile court abused its discretion when it permitted A.B.'s out-of-court identification of J.Y. into evidence.

NOTES AND QUESTIONS

1. Do these cases apply the law regarding the admissibility of eyewitness identifications properly? Why or why not?

2. Do you think the police must take additional precautions when juvenile suspects are involved? What would those be?

3. *Fingerprints and photographs.* All states permit law-enforcement agencies to fingerprint and photograph juveniles, although some states limit fingerprinting and photographing to those juveniles of a certain age or those who have been arrested for a felony. Other states may require the police to obtain court permission prior to fingerprinting or photographing the juvenile. In forty-four states, fingerprints and photographs may be placed in a statewide information bank, although some states may maintain a separate data bank for juveniles. Howard N. Snyder & Melissa Sickmund, U.S. Dep't of Justice, Juvenile Offenders & Victims: 2006 National Report 109 (2006). Should the police be able to fingerprint and photograph juveniles? Does this undermine one of the important aspects of a separate juvenile court, namely confidentiality?

4. Under what circumstances could fingerprinting and photographing a juvenile violate the Due Process Clause? Could fingerprinting and photographing a minor also violate the Fourth Amendment? Under what circumstances? Assume that a state statute requires the destruction of a juvenile's fingerprints when no juvenile petition is filed against the minor. If the state failed to destroy the fingerprints and they subsequently were used to tie the juvenile (now an adult) to a burglary, would the evidence be admissible? Have the suspect's rights been violated? *In the Matter of Quadon H.*, 866 N.Y.S.2d 693 (N.Y. App. Div. 2008). If the police lack probable cause, may they nevertheless obtain a court order authorizing the fingerprinting of a juvenile? *In re Order Requiring Fingerprinting of a Juvenile*, 537 N.E.2d 1286 (Ohio 1989).

a. DNA TESTING

The Justice for All Act of 2004, Pub. L. No. 108-405, § 203(a)(1) (2004), amending the DNA Identification Act of 1994, 42 U.S.C. § 14132, authorized the inclusion of juvenile DNA in the federal DNA database. To date, thirty states authorize the inclusion of DNA obtained from juveniles, although twenty states specifically prohibit its inclusion. Of those states authorizing the inclusion of juvenile DNA, eleven permit the inclusion of DNA obtained from juveniles who have only been arrested or charged. See American Society of Law, Medicine, and Ethics, Special Report: Survey of DNA Database Statutes, in "Inclusion Criteria" Workbook (2006), http://www.aslme.org/dna_04/grid/statute_grid.html (last visited April 10, 2010).

Are the collection and storage of DNA from juvenile suspects constitutional? What constitutional rights are violated by taking a sample without the consent of the minor?

IN RE ROBERT K.
Appellate Court of Illinois, Second District
785 N.E.2d 562 (2003)

Presiding Justice HUTCHINSON delivered the opinion of the court....

> "Section 5-4-3(a) provides, in relevant part, as follows:
>
> Any person convicted of, found guilty under the Juvenile Court Act of 1987 for, or who received a disposition of court supervision for, a qualifying offense or attempt of a qualifying offense * * * shall, regardless of the sentence or disposition imposed, be required to submit specimens of blood to the Illinois Department of State Police in accordance with the provisions of this Section, provided such person is:
>
> * * *
>
> (1.5) found guilty or given supervision under the Juvenile Court Act of 1987 for a qualifying offense or attempt of a qualifying offense on or after the effective date of this amendatory Act of 1996[.]"

Qualifying offenses under the statute include aggravated criminal sexual assault and criminal sexual abuse. All blood samples collected pursuant to this section must be forwarded to the Division of Forensic Services of the Illinois Department of State Police for analysis and categorizing into DNA profiles and placed into a database. The DNA profiles of all individuals who are required to submit blood samples pursuant to this statute are confidential and are maintained by the Division of Forensic Services. The information may be released only to peace officers of the United States and of other states and territories. This database may be uploaded into a national database and may not be subject to expungement....

This court has previously upheld section 5-4-3(a) of the Code against a fourth amendment challenge.... In determining whether the suspicionless search and seizure required by section 5-4-3(a) ran afoul of the fourth amendment, we balanced the State's interest in obtaining DNA profiles, the degree to which the DNA profiles actually advanced that interest, and the gravity of intrusion upon personal privacy....

We also found that the physical intrusion imposed by the testing mandated by section 5-4-3(a) was relatively slight and posed no threat to the health or safety of the individual tested. Finally, we explained that a convicted sex offender has only a minimal privacy interest in his or her identity and that such an identification becomes a matter of legitimate state interest to solve other past and future crimes. Finding that the blood sampling required by section 5-4-3(a) was functionally equivalent to fingerprinting, we held that DNA profiling of convicted sex offenders did not violate the fourth amendment prohibition against unreasonable searches and seizures.

Courts in other jurisdictions have uniformly upheld the constitutionality of similar statutes requiring blood samples to be taken from sex offenders for DNA profiling....

Although respondent acknowledges this weight of authority, he asserts that these cases are distinguishable because he is a minor and was only adjudicated delinquent under the Juvenile Court Act as opposed to being tried and convicted as an adult. Respondent asserts that his privacy interests were heightened due to his status as a juvenile offender. Respondent notes that the Juvenile Court Act limits access to juvenile court and law enforcement records. The Juvenile Court Act also provides for the expungement or sealing of juvenile records at age 17 or upon the termination of all juvenile court proceedings, whichever event occurs later. Respondent argues that the placement of his blood profile identification in the DNA database created by section 5-4-3(a) will deprive him of the privacy protections afforded under the Juvenile Court Act.

We agree with respondent that one of the goals of the Juvenile Court Act is to protect the privacy of juveniles; however, respondent's status as a minor does not provide him with a greater constitutional right to privacy than offenders who have already attained the age of majority. The juvenile court system is a purely statutory creation and the legislature has the authority to define its limits. As such, any privacy rights accorded by the Juvenile Court Act are not of a constitutional dimension. Therefore, for purposes of fourth amendment analysis, a juvenile offender has no greater privacy interest in his or her identity than an adult offender....

...Any slight intrusion upon respondent's privacy in providing a blood sample is significantly outweighed by the State's compelling interest in solving other past and future crimes. As such, we hold that the warrantless and suspicionless blood sampling mandated by section 5-4-3(a) of the Code does not violate the fourth amendment guarantee against unreasonable searches and seizures.

The respondent's second contention on appeal is that section 5-4-3(a) of the Code is invalid because it is irreconcilably inconsistent with the purpose and policy of the Juvenile Court Act. Respondent argues that the purpose of the Juvenile Court Act is to rehabilitate juveniles and provide juveniles with a second chance....

...[S]ection 5-4-3(a) of the Code is not ambiguous in its application to juveniles. As detailed above, the statute plainly requires that any person found guilty under the Juvenile Court Act for committing a qualifying offense shall "be required to submit specimens of blood to the Illinois Department of State Police." In his appellate brief, respondent acknowledges that the statute clearly requires all minors adjudicated delinquent of certain qualifying offenses to provide blood samples for DNA profiling. As the language of section 5-4- 3(a) plainly indicates the legislature's intent, we need not consider the primary purpose of the Juvenile Court Act or resort to other tools of statutory construction to construe the statute's meaning.

Lacking a statutory ambiguity, respondent is left to argue that section 5-4-3(a) cannot be enforced because it is inconsistent with the philosophy and the purpose of the Juvenile Court Act. However, this is not a sufficient legal basis to overturn a statute. All statutes are presumed valid. Simply because section 5-4-3(a) conflicts with the philosophy or purpose of another statute does not necessarily render it invalid. Aside from his fourth amendment argument, respondent fails to raise any other constitutional or legal basis that would support his assertions that the statute is invalid. Although respondent argued at trial that the statute constituted cruel and unusual punishment, violated the separation of powers, and improperly required trial courts to exercise their contempt powers, he does not raise these issues for our consideration on appeal and we do not consider them here....

...The requirements of section 5-4-3(a) do not prevent a trial court from conducting juvenile proceedings as required by the provisions of the Juvenile Court Act. More specifically, the blood draw requirement does not prevent the trial court from effectuating the confidentiality and dispositional provisions of the Juvenile Court Act. For example, the trial court may still limit the general public's access to the proceedings, prevent any party present in court from disclosing the juvenile's name, and restrict the disclosure of the juvenile's court and law enforcement records. Additionally, although section 5-4-3(a) mandates the trial court to require a juvenile found guilty of committing a qualifying offense to submit a blood sample, it does not preclude the trial court from exercising its discretion under the Juvenile Court Act to fashion an appropriate disposition for each individual case. Finally, we note that the permanent record created by section 5-4-3(a) of the Code is of respondent's DNA profile, not specific information about his juvenile offense. The provisions of section 5-4-3(f) require that this information be kept confidential and be made available only to peace officers.

IN RE WELFARE OF C.T.L.
Court of Appeals of Minnesota
722 N.W.2d 484 (2006)

PETERSON, Judge...

Respondent C.T.L., a juvenile, was charged with one count each of fifth-degree assault, in violation of Minn.Stat. § 609.224, subd. 1(1)(2) (2004), and aiding and abetting first-degree aggravated robbery, in violation of Minn.Stat. § 609.245, subd. 1 (2004). Appellant State of Minnesota moved for an order requiring C.T.L. to report to the sheriff's office immediately after his initial appearance in district court to provide a biological specimen for the purpose of DNA analysis pursuant to Minn.Stat. § 299C.105 (Supp. 2005). Respondent then moved for an order finding that the provisions of Minn.Stat. § 299C.105 that require law-enforcement personnel to obtain biological samples from certain defendants before any finding of guilt violate the Fourth Amendment to the United States Constitution and Article I, Section 10, of the Minnesota Constitution. Respondent also moved for an order certifying the issue of the statute's constitutionality to this court as an important or doubtful question....

The state does not dispute that taking and analyzing biological specimens as required under the statute is a search under the Fourth Amendment....

In *Schmerber v. California*, 384 U.S. 757, 86 S.Ct. 1826, 16 L.Ed.2d 908 (1966), the United States Supreme Court explained the role of the Fourth Amendment when the state directs that a biological specimen be taken from a person and analyzed. *Schmerber* involved a defendant who was arrested at a hospital while receiving treatment for injuries that he had suffered when the automobile that he apparently had been driving was involved in an accident. *Id.* at 758, 86 S.Ct. at 1829. A police officer directed that a blood sample be drawn from the defendant by a physician at the hospital, and a chemical analysis of the sample indicated intoxication....

In considering whether administering the blood test violated the Fourth Amendment, the Supreme Court explained that

> the Fourth Amendment's proper function is to constrain, not against all intrusions as such, but against intrusions which are not justified in the circumstances, or which are made in an improper manner. In other words, the questions we must decide in this case are whether the police were justified in requiring [the defendant] to submit to the blood test, and whether the means and procedures employed in taking his blood respected relevant Fourth Amendment standards of reasonableness.

Id. at 768, 86 S.Ct. at 1834.

The Supreme Court acknowledged that there was plainly probable cause for the officer to arrest the defendant and charge him with driving an automobile under the influence of alcohol. *Id.* But the court determined that the considerations that ordinarily permit a search of a defendant incident to an arrest

> have little applicability with respect to searches involving intrusions beyond the body's surface....
>
> Although the facts which established probable cause to arrest in this case also suggested the required relevance and likely success of a test of [the defendant's] blood for alcohol, the question remains whether the arresting officer was permitted to draw these inferences himself, or was required instead to procure a warrant before proceeding with the test. Search warrants are ordinarily required for searches of dwellings, and absent an emergency, no less could be required where intrusions into the human body are concerned. The requirement that a warrant be obtained is a requirement that inferences to support the search "be drawn by a neutral and detached magistrate instead of being judged by the officer engaged in the often competitive enterprise of ferreting out crime." The importance of informed, detached and deliberate determinations of the issue whether or not to invade another's body in search of evidence of guilt is indisputable and great.

Id. at 769–70, 86 S.Ct. at 1835....

The Supreme Court then recognized that the officer who directed the physician to draw the defendant's blood might reasonably have believed that the delay necessary to obtain a warrant threatened the destruction of the evidence because the amount of alcohol in the blood begins to diminish shortly after drinking stops. *Id.* at 770, 86 S.Ct. at 1835. Given the fact that the evidence could disappear during the time that it would take to seek out a magistrate and obtain a search warrant, the Supreme Court held that the officer's attempt to secure evidence of blood-alcohol content was an appropriate incident to the defendant's arrest. *Id.* at 771, 86 S.Ct. at 1836.

The significant principle to be drawn from *Schmerber* with respect to Minn.Stat. § 299C.105, subd. 1(a), is that establishing probable cause to arrest a person is not, by itself, sufficient to permit a biological specimen to be taken from the person without first obtaining a search warrant. In *Schmerber*, the facts that established probable cause to arrest the defendant were the smell of liquor on his breath, and the blood-shot, watery, and glassy appearance of his eyes. *Id.* at 769, 86 S.Ct. at 1835. These symptoms of drunkenness also suggested that there was alcohol in the defendant's blood. But, by itself, the strong inference that there was alcohol in the defendant's blood was not enough to permit the police officer to direct the physician to draw the defendant's blood. It was only because evidence of alcohol in the defendant's blood could disappear during the time it would take to obtain a search warrant that the Supreme Court permitted the search without a warrant....

...[J]ust as in *Schmerber*, where the existence of probable cause to arrest the defendant was not sufficient to permit an intrusion into his body without a warrant, a determination of probable cause to support a criminal charge, even if it is made by a judge, is not sufficient to permit a biological specimen to be taken from the person charged without a warrant. The fact that a judge has determined that the evidence in a case brings a charge against the defendant within reasonable probability does not mean that the judge has also determined that there is a fair probability that contraband or evidence of a crime will be found in a biological specimen taken from the defendant.

By directing that biological specimens be taken from individuals who have been charged with certain offenses solely because there has been a judicial determination of probable cause to support a criminal charge, Minn.Stat. § 299C.105, subd. 1(a)(1) and (3), dispense with the requirement under the Fourth Amendment that before conducting a search, law-enforcement personnel must obtain a warrant based on a neutral and detached magistrate's determination that there is a fair probability that the search will produce contraband or evidence of a crime. Under the statute, it is not necessary for anyone to even consider whether the biological specimen to be taken is related in any way to the charged crime or to any other criminal activity.

Citing federal court opinions that conclude that requiring a defendant to submit to DNA sampling does not violate the defendant's Fourth Amendment right against unreasonable searches and seizures, the state argues that this court should examine the reasonableness of Minn.Stat. § 299C.105 under a general balancing test that weighs a defendant's right to privacy against the state's interest in collecting and storing DNA samples. But all of the opinions that the state cites involve statutes that require specimens for DNA testing to be taken only from individuals who have been convicted of a criminal offense, and when weighing the individual's right to privacy against the state's interest in DNA testing, the opinions recognize that an individual who has been convicted of an offense has a reduced expectation of privacy and conclude that this reduced expectation of privacy does not outweigh the state's interest in DNA testing.

The question certified by the district court involves only biological specimens to be taken from individuals who have been charged with a criminal offense but who have not been convicted. Therefore, the reduced expectation of privacy that was present in the cases the state cites is not present here.

Furthermore, Minn.Stat. § 299C.105, subd. 3, requires the BCA to destroy a biological specimen and remove information about the specimen from the combined DNA index system when the person from whom the specimen was taken is found not guilty or the charge against the person is dismissed. This requirement suggests that the legislature has determined that the state's interest in collecting and storing DNA samples is outweighed by the privacy interest of a person who has not been convicted. Consequently, unless the privacy expectation of a person who has been charged and is awaiting the disposition of the charge is different from the privacy expectation of a person who was charged but the charge was dismissed or the person was found not guilty, we see no basis for concluding that the state's interest in taking a biological specimen from a person solely because the person has been charged outweighs the person's right to privacy. And because a person who has been charged is presumed innocent until proved guilty, we see no basis for concluding that before being convicted, a charged person's privacy expectation is different from the privacy expectation of a person who was charged but the charge was dismissed or the person was found not guilty. Therefore, we conclude that the privacy interest of a person who has been charged but has not been convicted is not outweighed by the state's interest in collecting and analyzing a DNA sample.

b. COURT RECORDS AND COURT PROCEEDINGS

SMITH V. DAILY MAIL PUBLISHING CO.
Supreme Court of the United States
443 U.S. 97 (1979)

MR. CHIEF JUSTICE BURGER delivered the opinion of the Court.

We granted certiorari to consider whether a West Virginia statute violates the First and Fourteenth Amendments of the United States Constitution by making it a crime for a newspaper to publish, without the written approval of the juvenile court, the name of any youth charged as a juvenile offender.

(1)

The challenged West Virginia statute provides:

> "[N]or shall the name of any child, in connection with any proceedings under this chapter, be published in any newspaper without a written order of the court...." W.Va.Code § 49-7-3 (1976)....

On February 9, 1978, a 15-year-old student was shot and killed at Hayes Junior High School in St. Albans, W. Va., a small community located about 13 miles outside of Charleston, W. Va. The alleged assailant, a 14-year-old classmate, was identified by seven different eyewitnesses and was arrested by police soon after the incident.

The Charleston Daily Mail and the Charleston Gazette, respondents here, learned of the shooting by monitoring routinely the police band radio frequency; they immediately dispatched reporters and photographers to the junior high school. The reporters for both papers obtained the name of the alleged assailant simply by asking various witnesses, the police, and an assistant prosecuting attorney who were at the school.

The staffs of both newspapers prepared articles for publication about the incident. The Daily Mail's first article appeared in its February 9 afternoon edition. The article did not mention the alleged attacker's name. The editorial decision to omit the name was made because of the statutory prohibition against publication without prior court approval.

The Gazette made a contrary editorial decision and published the juvenile's name and picture in an article about the shooting that appeared in the February 10 morning edition of the paper. In addition, the name of the alleged juvenile attacker was broadcast over at least three different radio stations on February 9 and 10. Since the information had become public knowledge, the Daily Mail decided to include the juvenile's name in an article in its afternoon paper on February 10.

On March 1, an indictment against the respondents was returned by a grand jury. The indictment alleged that each knowingly published the name of a youth involved in a juvenile proceeding in violation of W.Va.Code § 49-7-3 (1976). Respondents then filed an original-jurisdiction petition with the West Virginia Supreme Court of Appeals, seeking a writ of prohibition against the prosecuting attorney and the Circuit Court Judges of Kanawha County, petitioners here. Respondents alleged that the indictment was based on a statute that violated the First and Fourteenth Amendments of the United States Constitution and several provisions of the State's Constitution and requested an order prohibiting the county officials from taking any action on the indictment.

The West Virginia Supreme Court of Appeals issued the writ of prohibition. Relying on holdings of this Court, it held that the statute abridged the freedom of the press. The court reasoned that the statute operated as a prior restraint on speech and that the State's interest in protecting the identity of the juvenile offender did not overcome the heavy presumption against the constitutionality of such prior restraints.

We granted certiorari.

(2)

Respondents urge this Court to hold that because § 49-7-3 requires court approval prior to publication of the juvenile's name it operates as a "prior restraint" on speech. [R]espondents...argue, the statute bears "a 'heavy presumption' against its constitutional validity." They claim that the State's interest in the anonymity of a juvenile offender is not sufficient to overcome that presumption.

Petitioners do not dispute that the statute amounts to a prior restraint on speech. Rather, they take the view that even if it is a prior restraint the statute is constitutional because of the significance of the State's interest in protecting the identity of juveniles.

(3)...

Whether we view the statute as a prior restraint or as a penal sanction for publishing lawfully obtained, truthful information is not dispositive because even the latter action requires the highest form of state interest to sustain its validity. Prior restraints have been accorded the most exacting scrutiny in previous cases. However, even when a state attempts to punish publication after the event it must nevertheless demonstrate that its punitive action was necessary to further the state interests asserted....

One case that involved a classic prior restraint is particularly relevant to our inquiry. In *Oklahoma Publishing Co. v. District Court*, 430 U.S. 308 (1977), we struck down a state-court injunction prohibiting the news media from publishing the name or photograph of an 11-year-old boy who was being tried before a juvenile court. The juvenile court judge had permitted reporters and other members of the public to attend a hearing in the case, notwithstanding a state statute closing such trials to the public. The court then attempted to halt publication of the information obtained from that hearing. We held that once the truthful information was "publicly revealed" or "in the public domain" the court could not constitutionally restrain its dissemination....

...[I]f a newspaper lawfully obtains truthful information about a matter of public significance then state officials may not constitutionally punish publication of the information, absent a need to further a state interest of the highest order....Here respondents relied upon routine newspaper reporting techniques to ascertain the identity of the alleged assailant. A free press cannot be made to rely solely upon the sufferance of government to supply it with information. If the information is lawfully obtained, as it was here, the state may not punish its publication except when necessary to further an interest more substantial than is present here.

(4)

The sole interest advanced by the State to justify its criminal statute is to protect the anonymity of the juvenile offender. It is asserted that confidentiality will further his rehabilitation because publication of the name may encourage further antisocial conduct and also may cause the juvenile to lose future employment or suffer other consequences for this single offense. In *Davis v. Alaska*, 415 U.S. 308 (1974), similar arguments were advanced by the State to justify not permitting a criminal defendant to impeach a prosecution witness on the basis of his juvenile record. We said there that "[w]e do not and need not challenge the State's interest as a matter of its own policy in the administration of criminal justice to seek to preserve the anonymity of a juvenile offender." *Id.*, at 319. However, we concluded that the State's policy must be subordinated to the defendant's Sixth Amendment right of confrontation. *Ibid.* The important rights created by the First Amendment must be considered along with the rights of defendants guaranteed by the Sixth Amendment. Therefore, the reasoning of *Davis* that the constitutional right must prevail over the state's interest in protecting juveniles applies with equal force here.

The magnitude of the State's interest in this statute is not sufficient to justify application of a criminal penalty to respondents. Moreover, the statute's approach does not satisfy constitutional requirements. The statute does not restrict the electronic media or any form of publication, except "newspapers," from printing the names of youths charged in a juvenile proceeding. In this very case, three radio stations announced the alleged assailant's name before the Daily Mail decided to publish it. Thus, even assuming the statute served a state interest of the highest order, it does not accomplish its stated purpose.

In addition, there is no evidence to demonstrate that the imposition of criminal penalties is necessary to protect the confidentiality of juvenile proceedings....[A]ll 50 states have statutes that provide in some way for confidentiality, but only 5, including West Virginia, impose criminal penalties on nonparties for publication of the identity of the juvenile. Although every state has asserted a similar interest, all but a handful have found other ways of accomplishing the objective.

(5)

Our holding in this case is narrow. There is no issue before us of unlawful press access to confidential judicial proceedings, there is no issue here of privacy or prejudicial pretrial publicity. At issue is simply the power of a state to punish the truthful publication of an alleged juvenile delinquent's name lawfully obtained by a newspaper. The asserted state interest cannot justify the statute's imposition of criminal sanctions on this type of publication. Accordingly, the judgment of the West Virginia Supreme Court of Appeals is

Affirmed....

MR. JUSTICE REHNQUIST, concurring in the judgment.

...The Court...concludes that the asserted state interest is not sufficient to justify punishment of publication of truthful, lawfully obtained information about a matter of public significance. So valued is the liberty of speech and of the press that there is a tendency in cases such as this to accept virtually any contention supported by a claim of interference with speech or the press. I would resist that temptation. In my view, a State's interest in preserving the anonymity of its juvenile offenders—an interest that I consider to be, in the words of the Court, of the "highest order"—far outweighs any minimal interference with freedom of the press that a ban on publication of the youths' names entails.

It is a hallmark of our juvenile justice system in the United States that virtually from its inception at the end of the last century its proceedings have been conducted outside of the public's full gaze and the youths brought before our juvenile courts have been shielded from publicity. This insistence on confidentiality is born of a tender concern for the welfare of the child, to hide his youthful errors and "'bury them in the graveyard of the forgotten past.'" *In re Gault*, 387 U.S. 1, 24-25 (1967). The prohibition of publication of a juvenile's name is designed to protect the young person from the stigma of his misconduct and is rooted in the principle that a court concerned with juvenile affairs serves as a rehabilitative and protective agency of the State. Publication of the names of juvenile offenders may seriously impair the rehabilitative goals of the juvenile justice system and handicap the youths' prospects for adjustment in society and acceptance by the public. This exposure brings undue embarrassment to the families of youthful offenders and may cause the juvenile to lose employment opportunities or provide the hardcore delinquent the kind of attention he seeks, thereby encouraging him to commit further antisocial acts. Such publicity also renders nugatory States' expungement laws, for a potential employer or any other person can retrieve the information the States seek to "bury" simply by visiting the morgue of the local newspaper. The resultant widespread dissemination of a juvenile offender's name, therefore, may defeat the beneficent and rehabilitative purposes of a State's juvenile court system.[1]

By contrast, a prohibition against publication of the names of youthful offenders represents only a minimal interference with freedom of the press. West Virginia's statute, like similar laws in other States, prohibits publication only of the name of the young person. The press is free to describe the details of the offense and inform the community of the proceedings against the juvenile. It is difficult to understand how publication of the youth's name is in any way necessary to performance of the press' "watchdog" role. In those rare instances

1. That publicity may have a harmful impact on the rehabilitation of a juvenile offender is not mere hypothesis. Recently, two clinical psychologists conducted an investigation into the effects of publicity on a juvenile. They concluded that publicity "placed additional stress on [the juvenile] during a difficult period of adjustment in the community, and it interfered with his adjustment at various points when he was otherwise proceeding adequately." Howard, Grisso, & Neems, Publicity and Juvenile Court Proceedings, 11 Clearinghouse Rev. 203, 210 (1977). Publication of the youth's name and picture also led to confrontations between the juvenile and his peers while he was in detention. Ibid. While this study obviously is not controlling, it does indicate that the concerns that prompted enactment of state laws prohibiting publication of the names of juvenile offenders are not without empirical support.

where the press believes it is necessary to publish the juvenile's name, the West Virginia law, like the statutes of other States, permits the juvenile court judge to allow publication. The juvenile court judge, unlike the press, is capable of determining whether publishing the name of the particular young person will have a deleterious effect on his chances for rehabilitation and adjustment to society's norms....

Although I disagree with the Court that a state statute punishing publication of the identity of a juvenile offender can never serve an interest of the "highest order" and thus pass muster under the First Amendment, I agree with the Court that West Virginia's statute "does not accomplish its stated purpose." The West Virginia statute prohibits only newspapers from printing the names of youths charged in juvenile proceedings. Electronic media and other forms of publication can announce the young person's name with impunity.... This statute thus largely fails to achieve its purpose. It is difficult to take very seriously West Virginia's asserted need to preserve the anonymity of its youthful offenders when it permits other, equally, if not more, effective means of mass communication to distribute this information without fear of punishment. I, therefore, join in the Court's judgment striking down the West Virginia law. But for the reasons previously stated, I think that a generally effective ban on publication that applied to all forms of mass communication, electronic and print media alike, would be constitutional.

NOTES

1. All but two states permit the media to access the identity of the juvenile offender in a delinquency proceeding. In thirty states, access is limited to certain types of cases or by offender characteristics, such as age. In another fourteen states, delinquency proceedings are open, and the media may obtain the identity of the juvenile offender by attending the hearings. If the information regarding the offender's identity is obtained independently or if the court grants access, the media may discover the identity of the offender in four states. Howard N. Snyder & Melissa Sickmund, U.S. Dep't of Justice, Juvenile Offenders & Victims: 2006 National Report 109 (2006).

HOWARD N. SNYDER & MELISSA SICKMUND, U.S. DEP'T OF JUSTICE, JUVENILE OFFENDERS & VICTIMS: 2006 NATIONAL REPORT 108–109 (2006).

The legislation that created the first juvenile court in Illinois stated that the hearings should be open to the public. Thus, the public could monitor the activities of the court to ensure that the court handled cases in line with community standards.

In 1920, all but 7 of the 45 states that established separate juvenile courts permitted publication of information about juvenile court proceedings. The Standard Juvenile Court Act (1925) did not ban the publication of juveniles' names. By 1952, however, many states that adopted the Act had statutes that excluded the general public from juvenile court proceedings.

The commentary to the 1959 version of the Act referred to the hearings as "private, not secret." It added that reporters should be permitted to attend hearings, with the understanding that they not disclose the identity of the juvenile. The rationale for this confidentiality was "to prevent the humiliation and demoralizing effect of publicity." It was also thought that publicity might propel youth into further delinquent acts to gain more recognition.

As juvenile courts became more formalized and concerns about rising juvenile crime increased, the pendulum began to swing back toward more openness. By 1988, statutes in 15 states permitted the public to attend certain delinquency hearings....

As of the end of the 2004 legislative session, statutes or court rules in 14 states open delinquency hearings to the general public. Such statutes typically state that all hearings must be open to the public except on special order of the court. The court may close hearings to the public when it is in the best interests of the child and the public. In 7 of the 14 states, the state constitution has broad open court provisions. Ohio has a similar open court provision; however, in 2000, the Ohio Supreme Court ruled that juvenile proceedings are not presumed to be open or closed to the public. The Ohio court held that the traditional interests of confidentiality and rehabilitation prevent the public from having a constitutional right of access to juvenile delinquency proceedings....

In addition to the 14 states with open delinquency hearings, 21 states have statutes that open delinquency hearings for some types of cases. The openness restrictions typically involve age and/or offense criteria. For example, a statute might allow open hearings if the youth is charged with a felony and was at least 16 years old at the time of the crime. Some statutes also limit open hearings to those involving youth with a particular criminal history. For example, hearings might be open only if the youth met age and offense criteria and had at least one prior felony conviction (criminal court) or felony adjudication (juvenile court)....

Although legal and social records maintained by law enforcement agencies and juvenile courts have traditionally been confidential, legislatures have made significant changes over the past decade in how the justice system treats information about juvenile offenders. In most states, the juvenile code specifies which individuals or agencies are allowed access to such records.

Formerly confidential records are now being made available to a wide variety of individuals. Many states open records to schools and youth serving agencies as well as individuals and agencies within the justice system. However, access is not necessarily unlimited or automatic. It may be restricted to certain parts of the record and may require a court order.

As of the end of the 2004 legislative session, juvenile codes in all states allow information contained in juvenile court records to be specifically released to one or more of the following parties: the prosecutor, law enforcement, social services agencies, schools, the victim, or the public.

In all states, laws allow those with a "legitimate interest" to have at least partial access to juvenile court or law enforcement records. Interested parties generally must obtain the court's permission to gain access. Many states allow access by the juvenile who is the subject of the proceedings (35 states), the juvenile's parents or guardian (40 states), or the juvenile's attorney (40 states)....

As of the end of the 2004 legislative session, 44 states have school notification laws. Under these laws, schools are notified when students are involved with law enforcement or courts for committing delinquent acts. Some statutes limit notification to youth charged with or convicted of serious or violent crimes.

4. INTAKE AND DIVERSION

Howard N. Snyder & Melissa Sickmund, U.S. Dep't of Justice, Juvenile Offenders and Victims: 2006 National Report 104–106 (2006).

From state to state, case processing of juvenile law violators varies. Even within states, case processing may vary from community to community, reflecting local practice and tradition. Any description of juvenile justice processing in the U.S. must, therefore, be general, outlining a common series of decision points....

At arrest, a decision is made either to send the matter further into the justice system or to divert the case out of the system, often into alternative programs. Generally, law enforcement makes this decision after talking to the victim, the juvenile, and the parents and after reviewing the juvenile's prior contacts with the juvenile justice system. In 2003, 20 percent of all juvenile arrests were handled within the police department and resulted in release of the youth; in 7 of 10 arrests, the cases were referred to juvenile court. The remaining arrests were referred for criminal prosecution or to other agencies.

Federal regulations discourage holding juveniles in adult jails and lock-ups. If law enforcement must detain a juvenile in secure custody for a brief period to contact a parent or guardian or to arrange transportation to a juvenile detention facility, federal regulations require that the juvenile be securely detained for no longer than 6 hours and in an area that is not within sight or sound of adult inmates....

Law enforcement accounted for 84 percent of all delinquency cases referred to juvenile court in 2000. The remaining referrals were made by others such as parents, victims, school personnel, and probation officers....

The court intake function is generally the responsibility of the juvenile probation department and/or the prosecutor's office. Intake decides whether to dismiss the case, to handle the matter informally, or to request formal intervention by the juvenile court.

To make this decision, an intake officer or prosecutor first reviews the facts of the case to determine whether there is sufficient evidence to prove the allegation. If not, the case is dismissed. If there is sufficient evidence, intake then determines whether formal intervention is necessary.

Nearly half of all cases referred to juvenile court intake are handled informally. Many informally processed cases are dismissed. In the other informally processed cases, the juvenile voluntarily agrees to specific conditions for a specific time period. These conditions often are outlined in a written agreement, generally called a "consent decree." Conditions may include such things as victim restitution, school attendance, drug counseling, or a curfew.

In most jurisdictions, a juvenile may be offered an informal disposition only if he or she admits to committing the act. The juvenile's compliance with the informal agreement often is monitored by a probation officer. Thus, this process is sometimes labeled "informal probation."

If the juvenile successfully complies with the informal disposition, the case is dismissed. If, however, the juvenile fails to meet the conditions, the case is referred for formal processing and proceeds as it would have if the initial decision had been to refer the case for an adjudicatory hearing.

If the case is to be handled formally in juvenile court, intake files one of two types of petitions: a delinquency petition requesting an adjudicatory hearing or a petition requesting a waiver hearing to transfer the case to criminal court.

A delinquency petition states the allegations and requests that the juvenile court adjudicate (or judge) the youth a delinquent, making the juvenile a ward of the court. This language differs from that used in the criminal court system, where an offender is convicted and sentenced.

In response to the delinquency petition, an adjudicatory hearing is scheduled. At the adjudicatory hearing (trial), witnesses are called and the facts of the case are presented. In nearly all adjudicatory hearings, the determination that the juvenile was responsible for the offense(s) is made by a judge; however, in some states, the juvenile has the right to a jury trial. . . .

Juvenile courts may hold delinquents in a secure juvenile detention facility if this is determined to be in the best interest of the community and/or the child.

After arrest, law enforcement may bring the youth to the local juvenile detention facility. A juvenile probation officer or detention worker reviews the case to decide whether the youth should be detained pending a hearing before a judge. In all states, a detention hearing must be held within a time period defined by statute, generally within 24 hours.

At the detention hearing, a judge reviews the case and determines whether continued detention is warranted. In 2000, juveniles were detained in 20 percent of delinquency cases processed by juvenile courts.

Detention may extend beyond the adjudicatory and dispositional hearings. If residential placement is ordered, but no placement beds are available, detention may continue until a bed becomes available. . . .

A waiver petition is filed when the prosecutor or intake officer believes that a case under jurisdiction of the juvenile court would be handled more appropriately in criminal court. The court decision in these matters follows a review of the facts of the case and a determination that there is probable cause to believe that the juvenile committed the act. With this established, the court then decides whether juvenile court jurisdiction over the matter should be waived and the case transferred to criminal court.

The judge's decision in such cases generally centers on the issue of the juvenile's amenability to treatment in the juvenile justice system. The prosecution may argue that the juvenile has been adjudicated several times previously and that interventions ordered by the juvenile court have not kept the juvenile from committing subsequent criminal acts. The prosecutor may also argue that the crime is so serious that the juvenile court is unlikely to be able to intervene for the time period necessary to rehabilitate the youth.

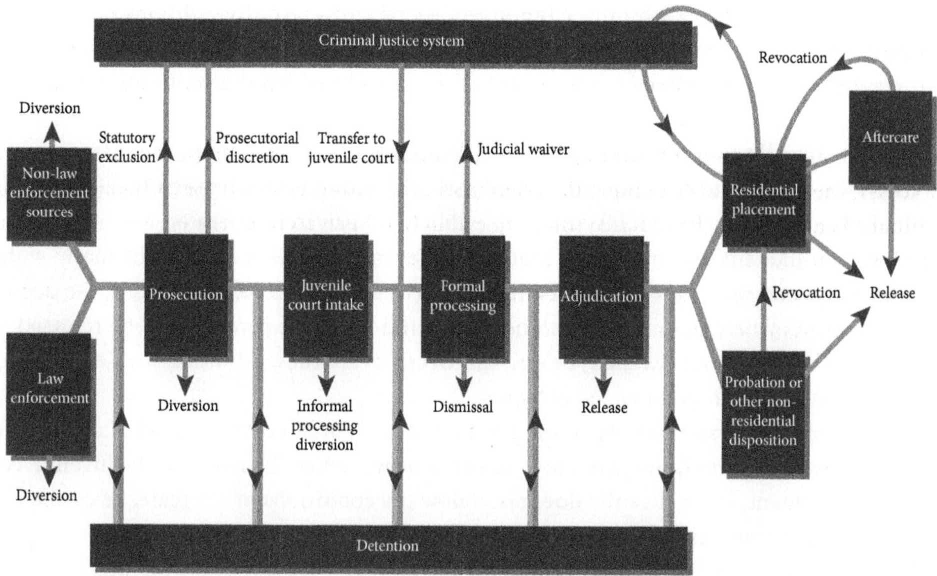

What are the stages of delinquency case processing in the juvenile justice system?

Note: This chart gives a simplified view of case flow through the juvenile justice system. Procedures vary among jurisdictions.

If the judge decides that the case should be transferred to criminal court, juvenile court jurisdiction is waived and the case is filed in criminal court. In 2000, juvenile courts waived fewer than 1 percent of all formally processed delinquency cases. If the judge does not approve the waiver request, generally an adjudicatory hearing is scheduled in juvenile court....

In more than half of the states, legislatures have decided that in certain cases (generally those involving serious offenses), juveniles should be tried as criminal offenders. The law excludes such cases from juvenile court; prosecutors must file them in criminal court. In a smaller number of states, legislatures have given both the juvenile and adult courts original jurisdiction in certain cases. Thus, prosecutors have discretion to file such cases in either criminal court or juvenile court....

Once the juvenile is adjudicated delinquent in juvenile court, probation staff develop a disposition plan. To prepare this plan, probation staff assess the youth, available support systems, and programs. The court may also order psychological evaluations, diagnostic tests, or a period of confinement in a diagnostic facility.

At the disposition hearing, probation staff present dispositional recommendations to the judge. The prosecutor and the youth may also present dispositional recommendations. After considering the recommendations, the judge orders a disposition in the case....

Most juvenile dispositions are multifaceted and involve some sort of supervised probation. A probation order often includes additional requirements such as drug counseling, weekend confinement in the local detention center, or restitution to the community or victim. The term of probation may be for a specified period of time or it may be open ended.

Review hearings are held to monitor the juvenile's progress. After conditions of probation have been successfully met, the judge terminates the case. In 2000, formal probation was the most severe disposition ordered in 63 percent of the cases in which the youth was adjudicated delinquent....

In 2000, juvenile courts ordered residential placement in 24 percent of the cases in which the youth was adjudicated delinquent. Residential commitment may be for a specific or indeterminate time period. The facility may be publicly or privately operated and may have a secure, prison-like environment or a more open (even home-like) setting. In many states, when the judge commits a juvenile to the state department of juvenile corrections, the department determines where the juvenile will be placed and when the juvenile will be released. In other states, the judge controls the type and length of stay; in these situations, review hearings are held to assess the progress of the juvenile....

Upon release from an institution, the juvenile is often ordered to a period of aftercare or parole. During this period, the juvenile is under supervision of the court or the juvenile corrections department. If the juvenile does not follow the conditions of aftercare, he or she may be recommitted to the same facility or may be committed to another facility.

NOTES AND QUESTIONS

1. In 1999, about one in four Americans, or 70.5 million, were younger than eighteen. The juvenile population is projected to rise only 8 percent through 2015, the smallest increase for any segment of the population. However, if race and ethnicity are considered, the expected increases in juvenile populations are significantly higher; thus, while the increase in the white juvenile population will be only 3 percent, for African-American children it is expected to increase 19 percent, for Hispanic juveniles 59 percent, and for Asian/Pacific Islander youths 74 percent. *OJJDP Statistical Briefing Book*, http://ojjdp.ncjrs.gov/ojstatbb/population/qa01101.asp?qaDate+19990930, released Sept. 30, 1999.

2. More than 2 million juveniles were arrested in 2008. Nevertheless, the number of juvenile arrests has declined 16 percent since 1999. The number of arrests for violent index crimes (murder, nonnegligent manslaughter, forcible rape, robbery, and aggravated assault) declined 9 percent in this same period, while arrests for property index crimes (burglary, larceny theft, motor-vehicle theft, and arson) declined 20 percent. The number of arrests for index crimes declined steeply for many index offenses (50 percent for motor-vehicle theft, 27 percent for forcible rape) but increased for only one index offense (25 percent for robbery). If, however, one considers the peak year for arrests of certain index crimes, the number of arrests has declined dramatically. Thus, the violent-crime index arrest rates for juveniles fell 40 percent between 1994 and 2008. Charles Puzzanchera, *U.S. Dep't of Justice, Juvenile Justice Bulletin: Juvenile Arrests 2008* (December 2009).

The arrest rates for black youths are disproportionate when compared with the racial composition of the age cohort. In 2008, 78 percent of children between the ages of ten and seventeen were white, 16 percent were black, 5 percent were Asian, and 1 percent were Native American. However, black youths made up 52 percent of all arrests for violent crimes, compared with 47 percent for white youths. Similarly, 33 percent of arrests for property crimes were of black youths, while 66 percent were of white youths. Moreover, the arrest rates for black youths historically have been disproportionately higher than arrest rates for white youths. For example, in the 1980s, the arrest rate of black youths for violent crimes was between six and seven times higher than the rate for arrests of white youths. Although the ratio declined in the 1990s, the rate of arrests has increased again since 2004; thus, the arrest rate of black youths for violent crimes is five times higher than that of white youths. Even with declining arrest rates for property crimes, the black youth arrest rate is double that of the white rate. *Id.* at 9.

Arrests between 1999 and 2008 also indicate that while the overall arrest rates for juveniles have been declining, the arrest rates for females have decreased less than the rates for boys and in some instances have increased, while the rates for boys have decreased or increased at slower rates. For example, the female arrest rate for robbery increased by 38 percent, while the male arrest rate increased by 24 percent; on the other hand, the female arrest rate for aggravated assault decreased by 17 percent, but the male arrest rate decreased by 22 percent. For property-crime index offenses, the female arrest rate increased by 1 percent, while the male arrest rate decreased by 29 percent. Nevertheless, the female arrest rate for violent-crime index offenses decreased by 10 percent, and the male arrest rate decreased by 8 percent. *Id.* at 8.

3. The state of Ohio permits any person to file a sworn complaint in juvenile court alleging that a child is delinquent. Ohio Rev. Code § 2152.021 (2010). Is there any role at intake for a prosecutor or a probation officer under such a statute? Is such an approach problematic? Does it matter who makes the intake decision? Former juvenile court judge H. Ted Rubin traces the role that prosecutors have come to play in the juvenile court intake process:

> Discretionary intake was consistent with a parens patriae juvenile court and its extensive informality, broadly defined jurisdiction, and largely unchecked authority. The awesome powers of the court did not need to be exercised with each child; informal probation officer advice or supervision, and the apparent acceptance of this counsel, was seen as a satisfactory end point. Formal petitions and formal hearing with the judge could be used later if the child did not respond to informal approaches. In earlier and simpler times, the court could engineer a working relationship with police agencies to accept the probation department's screening-out practices, at least with lesser offenders....
>
> Historically, intake has been a review of legal and social factors, with the emphasis placed frequently on the latter dimensions. The legal facts, in addition to age, county of residence, and place of offense, encompass the correlation between the offense facts and the required elements of the offense, the seriousness of the offense and the harm or damage done, the offense record and prior dispositions, and any present legal status (e.g ., formal probation). The absence of legal training on the part of intake officers has placed them at a disadvantage in this respect; not infrequently they place the law in limbo in conducting the evaluation. This failure to conduct careful legal screening has often led to unrepresented youngsters' accepting terms of informal probation or later admitting to the offense before the judge without anyone's having scrutinized the legal sufficiency of the case. Competent evaluation of the legal correctness of police interrogation or search and seizure practices should not be expected of intake officers but

should be accomplished before the imposition of coerced informal services and before the decision to file a case. The contention has grown that the legal evaluation role is one for the prosecutor....

The prosecutor entry into juvenile court trials heightened prosecutor interest in influencing or controlling the front end of the juvenile justice system. Prosecutors began to object when a judge gave them a contested case to prosecute and the petition was improperly prepared, probable cause was absent, evidence had been gathered contrary to constitutional requirements, witnesses had not been interviewed, or the case was de minimus and did not merit prosecution. The adult processing model, with its increased use of prosecutor screening of police reports and criminal charges, enhanced prosecutor interest in developing a parallel approach for juvenile justice....

Law enforcement agency criticism of probation intake decision making has also influenced the trend toward prosecutor involvement. Police agency and prosecution office views on crime control are more similar than police agency and probation office perspectives. Although specialized juvenile police officers and probation intake officers may adhere to a common philosophical approach, the police juvenile specialist works within an overall organization whose orientation is a stricter law enforcement view. Police tend to be more critical of a probation decision that rejects filing because a youth has become contrite or cooperative than of a prosecutor's rejection because of a faulty police report. Prosecutors also began applying their considerable legislative influence to secure changes in the juvenile intake process. When prosecutors urge a stronger juvenile court role for themselves as an adjunct to increasing public protection, legislatures tend to respond....

...Defense attorneys have not been hostile to the emerging prosecutor role....The defense attorney wants legally insufficient and de minimus cases thrown out, and prosecutors do that better than intake officers....Defense concerns with the irregularity of intake decision making are better answered by the prosecutor's offense criteria. Child advocacy groups share many defense counsel concerns, although they are nervous that a stronger prosecutor role will result in harsher juvenile processing decisions. In some communities, the advent of prosecutor control of intake has resulted in significantly more formal petitions....

...The prosecutor's authority in the juvenile intake process is likely to develop into a controlling one, stimulated by the prosecutor's public protection image, the increased interest in handling juveniles according to offense and prior record, and diminished confidence in the ideal of rehabilitation.

H. Ted Rubin, *The Emerging Prosecutor Dominance of the Juvenile Court Intake Process*, 26 CRIME & DELINQ. 299, 304, 311, 312, 318 (1980). The National Council of Juvenile and Family Court Judges also recommends the use of prosecutors to screen complaints and make initial determinations about the legal sufficiency of any allegation before it is referred for further processing. NATIONAL COUNCIL OF JUVENILE & FAMILY COURT JUDGES, JUVENILE DELINQUENCY GUIDELINES 66–67 (2005). Do you agree? Is such an approach consistent with the juvenile court's philosophy?

4. *Diversion.*

Diversion covers a wide range of interventions that are alternatives to initial or continued formal processing in the system (Kammer et al., 1997). The idea behind diversion is that processing through the juvenile justice system may do more harm than good for some offenders (Lundman, 1993). First offenders or minor offenders may be diverted to an intervention at intake processing or prior to formal adjudication. Juveniles may be diverted from detention while awaiting adjudication and disposition. After adjudication, minors may be diverted from incarceration by being placed on probation or given some other sanction or intervention.

One concern that is often raised about diversion programs is that they may result in net widening which is "a phenomenon whereby a program is set up to divert youth away from an institutional placement or some other type of juvenile court disposition, but, instead, merely brings more youth into the juvenile justice system who previously would never have entered." A true diversion program takes only juveniles who would ordinarily be involved in the juvenile justice system and places them in an alternative program.

The array of interventions covered under the term *diversion* makes it difficult to generalize about them or their effects. Some researchers have found significantly lower recidivism rates among diverted juveniles than among controls who received normal juvenile justice system processing. Other research has found no difference in recidivism rates between juveniles diverted from the juvenile justice system and those who remained in it or more recidivism among diverted juveniles. The variety in findings may be due to the types of juveniles involved and the types of treatment and services provided.

For a diversion program to be successful, it may have to provide intensive and comprehensive services, services that include the juveniles' families and take into account community, school, and peer interactions, and use experienced caseworkers. [Researchers] found that whether intervention occurred in the juvenile justice system or in another program, juveniles experienced increases in their perception of being labeled as delinquent and increases in self-reported delinquency. It is even possible that some diversion programs are more intrusive than traditional juvenile justice processing....

Victim-offender mediation is one increasingly popular form of diversion. A national survey discovered 94 victim-offender programs dealing with juveniles in 1996, 46 of which were dedicated exclusively to them. The programs ranged from having 1 to 900 case referrals, with a mean of 136 cases. Referrals to victim-offender mediation are typically for vandalism, minor assaults, theft, and burglary. The vast majority of mediation cases are first-time offenders. Typically, mediation occurs prior to adjudication. Some pressure appears to be mounting to include more serious cases in mediation programs. Whether more serious or complicated cases can be handled through mediation remains to be seen....

On balance, the research on diversion and intensive probation...suggests that some community-based interventions can serve the needs of many juvenile offenders without added danger to the community. There also may be advantages to keeping juveniles in a less restrictive setting. Well-structured and well-run programs with appropriate services have the potential for improving the lives of diverted juveniles and their families and maintaining community safety.

JUVENILE CRIME, JUVENILE JUSTICE, 167, 169, 174, 175, 176 (National Academy of Sciences, Joan McCord, Cathy Spatz Widom, & Nancy Crowell, eds., 2001). Who should make the diversion decision? Should diversion be available only to those minors who admit to their wrongdoing?

5. In 2007, approximately 56 percent of all delinquency cases were handled formally, while 44 percent were handled informally. Of the cases that were handled informally, 42 percent were dismissed. In the remaining 56 percent of the cases that were handled informally, the minors voluntarily agreed to informal sanctions, which included informal probation, fines, restitution, or referrals to social service agencies. CHARLES PUZZANCHERA, BENJAMIN ADAMS, & MELISSA SICKMUND, NATIONAL CENTER FOR JUVENILE JUSTICE, JUVENILE COURT STATISTICS 2006–2007, 58 (2010).

5. BAIL AND PREVENTIVE DETENTION

SCHALL V. MARTIN
United States Supreme Court
467 U.S. 253 (1984)
(See Section II.B. above, p. 149)

NOTES AND QUESTIONS

1. Most states have statutes or court rules that list criteria for determining whether a juvenile should be detained prior to trial. The National Council of Juvenile and Family Court Judges The Juvenile Justice Standards do not provide for preventive detention; rather, they favor release or placement in the least restrictive alternative. JUVENILE JUSTICE STANDARDS RELATING TO INTERIM STATUS: THE RELEASE, CONTROL, AND DETENTION OF ACCUSED JUVENILE OFFENDERS BETWEEN ARREST AND DISPOSITION, 3.1–3.5, 4.2, 5.1, 5.6, 9.2 (1980).

2. Between 1985 and 2005, detention increased by 48 percent in juvenile delinquency cases. The proportion of detained cases during that time ranged from 17 percent to 22 percent. OJJDP Statistical Briefing Book, http://ojjdp.ncjrs.gov/ojstatbb/court/qa06301.asp?qaDate=2005, released Sept. 12, 2005. The increase in detention varied across types of cases. For person offenses, the number of cases involving detention increased by 144 percent, drug cases by 110 percent, and public order offenses by 108 percent. The number of property-offense cases involving detention, however, declined by 22 percent. *Id.* The number of detained cases also varied by race. Between 1985 and 2005, the number of African-American youths detained increased by 97 percent, Asian youths by 137 percent, and white youths by 24 percent. *Id.*

3. Does a minor have a right to a probable-cause determination? In *Gerstein v. Pugh*, 420 U.S. 103 (1975), the Supreme Court held that pursuant to the Fourth Amendment, when police arrest without a warrant, a neutral and detached magistrate must make a prompt determination that the arrest was based on probable cause. That hearing, however, may be held outside the presence of the arrestee, and the determination may be based on hearsay testimony. In *County of Riverside v. McLaughlin*, 500 U.S. 44 (1991), the Supreme Court held that a probable-cause determination is prompt if it is held within forty-eight hours of the arrest, although reasonable delay may postpone the hearing beyond the time period. Is a juvenile entitled to a probable-cause hearing? See, e.g., *In re D.E.R.*, 225 P.3d 1187 (Kan. 2010); *R.W.T. v. Dalton*, 712 F.2d 1225 (8th Cir. 1983); *Bell v. Superior Court*, 574 P.2d 39 (Ariz. Ct. App. 1977). How long may the juvenile be held before the probable-cause determination is made? Is a statute that provides for a determination of probable cause within

seventy-two hours constitutional? See *Alfredo A. v. Superior Court*, 865 P.2d 56, cert. denied, 513 U.S. 822 (1994).

4. Does a minor have a right to counsel at the detention hearing? Some states provide the minor with counsel at the detention hearing. See, e.g., Ohio Rev. Code § 2151.352 (2010). In criminal prosecutions, the accused has a right to counsel under the Sixth Amendment at the time judicial proceedings are initiated. *Brewer v. Williams*, 430 U.S. 387 (1977); *United States v. Gouveia*, 467 U.S. 180 (1984). But if the state statutes are silent on the issue, does the minor have a constitutional right to counsel? Consider *In re C.J.*, 764 N.E.2d 1153, 1162 (Ill. App. Ct. 2002):

> [T]he minor's constitutional challenge is inapplicable because the sixth amendment does not govern juvenile cases. That amendment grants assistance of counsel "[i]n all criminal prosecutions" at those critical stages that greatly impact an accused's liberty. U.S. Const., amend. VI; see generally *Coleman v. Alabama*, 399 U.S. 1, 90 S.Ct. 1999, 26 L.Ed.2d 387 (1970). Our Supreme Court has addressed whether juvenile proceedings may be classified as "criminal prosecutions" for purposes of a potential sixth amendment analysis, and has, time and again, specifically found that that they may not. See *Middendorf* [*v. Henry*], 425 U.S. [25,] 38, 96 S.Ct. [1281,] 1289, 47 L.Ed.2d [556,] 566 [(1976)] (juvenile proceeding, even though it "may result in deprivation of liberty[,] is nonetheless not a 'criminal proceeding' within the meaning of the Sixth Amendment"); *McKeiver*, 403 U.S. at 541, 91 S.Ct. at 1984, 29 L.Ed.2d at 658 (juvenile court proceedings have "not yet been held to be a 'criminal prosecution,' within the meaning and reach of the sixth amendment"). In addition, the Supreme Court has found that even adult probable cause proceedings do not amount to a "critical stage" that would employ Sixth Amendment examination. See *Gerstein v. Pugh*, 420 U.S. 103, 122, 95 S.Ct. 854, 867, 43 L.Ed.2d 54, 70 (1975).

Do you think the court in *C.J.* is correct? Is there another constitutional basis on which the minor could rest a claim that he is entitled to counsel at the detention hearing?

5. The Eighth Amendment to the United States Constitution states that "excessive bail shall not be required." Does a minor have a constitutional right to bail in a delinquency case?

STATE V. M.L.C.
Supreme Court of Utah
933 P.2d 380 (1997)

RUSSON, Justice:

M.L.C., a minor, appeals from an order of the third district juvenile court denying him bail from the time he was charged with aggravated robbery by criminal information in juvenile court until he was bound over to district court to be tried as an adult pursuant to the Serious Youth Offender Act. We affirm.

Background

In October 1995, when he was sixteen years of age, M.L.C. was charged by criminal information in the third district juvenile court with aggravated robbery, a first degree felony in violation of section 76-6-302 of the Utah Code, and a firearm sentencing enhancement pursuant to section 76-3-203 of the Utah Code. This information was filed in accordance with the Serious Youth Offender Act, Utah Code Ann. § 78-3a-25.1 (Supp. 1995), which required a determination by the juvenile court as to whether M.L.C. should be bound over to district court to be tried as an adult pursuant to the criminal information or whether he should remain in juvenile court and the criminal information be treated as though it were a juvenile petition.

Prior to the determination hearing, M.L.C. moved the juvenile court to set bail. The juvenile court denied the motion on the basis of sections 78-3a-30(10) and 78-3a-25.1 of the Utah Code. Section 78-3a-30(10) provides that provisions of the law relating to bail are generally not applicable to children under eighteen years of age. Section 78-3a-25.1 provides that juveniles charged in juvenile court with certain aggravated offenses may be bound over to the district court to be tried and sentenced as adults and that, once bound over, such juveniles have the same right to bail as do adult defendants.

Subsequently, the juvenile court conducted the determination hearing. This hearing was required to determine whether there was probable cause to believe that M.L.C. had committed the alleged aggravated robbery and, if so, whether certain conditions existed that would nevertheless require the matter to remain in juvenile court as provided by section 78-3a-25.1(3) of the Utah Code. The juvenile court determined that M.L.C., indeed, should be bound over to district court to be tried as an adult and set bail at $20,000. Thereafter, M.L.C. appealed the juvenile court's initial order denying bail pending the bindover determination.

M.L.C. argues on appeal that he was entitled to bail immediately upon the filing of a criminal information in juvenile court under the serious youth offender statute, even though the juvenile court had not yet determined, pursuant to the statute, whether he would be bound over to district court to be tried as an adult or remain in juvenile court and have the information treated as a juvenile petition. He argues that at the time of the filing of the criminal information in juvenile court, he was a "person charged with a crime" and, thus, entitled to the right to bail guaranteed by article I, section 8 of the Utah Constitution, which provides, with certain enumerated exceptions, "All persons charged with a crime shall be bailable. . . . " M.L.C. also argues that the denial of bail prior to a determination of his status violates the unnecessary rigor clause of article I, section 9 of the Utah Constitution, as well as the Excessive Bail Clause of the Eighth Amendment of the United States Constitution. In addition, M.L.C. argues that the denial of bail violates the Equal Protection Clause of the Fourteenth Amendment of the United States Constitution and the uniform operation of laws clause of article I, section 24 of the Utah Constitution inasmuch as juveniles and adults charged with the same crimes are treated disparately.

The State responds that serious youth offenders are not entitled to bail unless and until the juvenile court determines that bindover to adult district court is appropriate. Until bindover, the State argues, the juvenile does not have the status of a criminal defendant and, thus, does not have a federal or state constitutional right to bail. Additionally, the State argues that denying bail to charged serious youth offenders prior to bindover does not implicate the uniform operation of laws clause of the Utah Constitution or the Fourteenth Amendment to the United States Constitution inasmuch as there is no basis for treating adult and juvenile offenders as similarly situated groups and, moreover, all juveniles, including serious youth offenders, are denied preadjudication bail eligibility.

Standard of Review

Whether sections 78-3a-25.1(5) and 78-3a-30(10) violate the bail provisions of the Eighth Amendment of the United States Constitution and article I, sections 8 and 9 of the Utah Constitution are questions of law, which this court reviews for correctness. *State v. Mohi*, 901 P.2d 991, 995 (Utah 1995). Likewise, whether such statutory provisions violate the Equal Protection Clause of the Fourteenth Amendment of the United States Constitution and the uniform operation of laws clause of article I, section 24 of the Utah Constitution are questions of law, which we review for correctness. *Id.* Doubts regarding the constitutionality of a statute should be resolved in favor of its constitutionality. *Id.*

Analysis

M.L.C.'s appeal became technically moot once he was bound over to the district court and immediately became eligible for bail. While we typically refrain from adjudicating moot questions, we recognize an exception to this rule where the "alleged wrong is 'capable of repetition yet evading review.'" *In re Giles*, 657 P.2d 285, 286 (1982) (quoting *Southern Pac. Terminal Co. v. Interstate Commerce Comm'n*, 219 U.S. 498, 515, 31 S.Ct. 279, 283, 55 L.Ed. 310 [1911]). Section 78-3a-25.1 provides that persons charged under the statute will either be bound over to district court where the statute explicitly states that they will be eligible for bail, Utah Code Ann. § 78-3a-25.1(5), or be retained in juvenile court as if charged by petition. Utah Code Ann. § 78-3a-25.1(3)(d), (4). A challenge to the denial of bail prior to bindover, as in the instant case, is likely to be mooted by either of these statutory procedures. Thus, the issues presented by this appeal are likely to evade review in the future. Accordingly, we proceed to address the issues presented.

Article I, section 8 of the Utah Constitution provides that "[a]ll persons charged with a crime shall be bailable," with certain enumerated exceptions not at issue here. However, juveniles appearing in juvenile court proceedings have been treated differently from adults appearing in adult court with respect to bail issues. In particular, section 78-3a-30(10) of the Utah Code provides, "Provisions of law regarding bail are not applicable to children detained or taken into custody. . . ." And section 78-3a-44 provides, "Proceedings in children's cases shall be regarded as civil proceedings, with the court exercising equitable powers."

In *R. v. Whitmer*, 30 Utah 2d 206, 208, 515 P.2d 617, 619-20 (1973), this court held that the excessive bail provision of article I, section 9 did not apply to juvenile court proceedings because "[t]he section of our Constitution proscribing excessive bail has application to criminal cases, where a presumption of innocence prevails, and does not apply to the proceedings in Juvenile Courts."

Moreover, most courts considering whether the excessive bail provision of the Eighth Amendment of the United States Constitution confers a right to bail upon juveniles have held that juveniles do not have a constitutional right to bail. *See, e.g., D.B. v. Tewksbury*, 545 F.Supp. 896, 906 (D.Or. 1982) ("[C]hildren are not entitled to a jury trial, to indictment by Grand Jury, or to bail"); *L.O.W. v. District Court*, 623 P.2d 1253, 1258–59 (Colo. 1981) (en banc) (holding that juveniles do not have right to bail under United States or Colorado constitution); *Aubry v. Gadbois*, 50 Cal.App.3d 470, 123 Cal.Rptr. 365, 367 (1975) ("The Eighth Amendment . . . confers a right to bail on no one, whether adult or juvenile"); *see also* Joseph T. Bockrath, Annotation, *Right of Bail in Proceedings in Juvenile Courts*, 53 A.L.R.3d 848, 851 (1973).

In 1995, the Utah Legislature passed the Serious Youth Offender Act, whereby a criminal information could be filed against a juvenile between the ages of sixteen and eighteen in juvenile court as to certain enumerated felonies but requiring the juvenile court to determine whether the juvenile should be bound over to district court or remain in juvenile court. Utah Code Ann. § 78-3a-25.1. M.L.C. argues that a juvenile charged under the serious youth offender statute is, in fact, a person "charged with a crime" within the meaning of article I, section 8 of the Utah Constitution and, thus, is entitled to bail. We disagree.

While a "criminal information" may be filed in juvenile court, it has no legal effect as such until the juvenile court so determines. A hearing must be held in juvenile court to determine whether the minor will remain in juvenile court and have the criminal information treated as though it were a juvenile petition or whether the juvenile should be bound over to district court to be tried as an adult on the criminal information. At such hearing, the State has the burden to establish probable cause that the minor committed one of the nine felonies enumerated in the statute before the juvenile court judge can bind him over to trial in district court. Utah Code Ann. § 78-3a-25.1(3). However, even if the State establishes probable cause, the juvenile is given the opportunity, pursuant to the statute, to prove the existence of certain factors which would require that the juvenile remain in juvenile court. *Id.* If such factors were established, the juvenile court judge would be compelled to treat the information as a juvenile petition and the juvenile would be held for trial as a juvenile. Utah Code Ann. § 78-3a-25.1(3)(d). In such a case, the matter would continue as a civil matter, pursuant to section 78-3a-44 of the Utah Code, and the juvenile would not be entitled to bail. *See Whitmer*, 30 Utah 2d at 208, 515 P.2d at 619–20. On the other hand, if probable cause were established and the juvenile did not prove the existence of the retention factors, the juvenile court would be compelled to order the juvenile bound over to district court to be tried as an adult on the criminal information. At that time, the juvenile would immediately be entitled to the same rights to bail applicable to all persons charged in district court. *See* Utah Code Ann. § 78-3a-25.1(5). Accordingly, while the juvenile is before the juvenile court for such determination and until the juvenile is bound over to district court on the criminal information, he or she is not a person actually "charged with a crime" within the meaning of article I, section 8 of the Utah Constitution, and thus, denial of bail prior to bindover does not violate this provision.

M.L.C. also contends that denying bail to juveniles charged under the serious youth offender statute pending a bindover determination violates the unnecessary rigor provision of article I, section 9 of the Utah Constitution, which provides, "Persons arrested or imprisoned shall not be treated with unnecessary rigor." We find this argument to be without merit....

M.L.C. also argues that denying bail to juveniles charged under the serious youth offender statute violates the Eighth Amendment to the United States Constitution. The Eighth Amendment provides, "Excessive bail shall not be required, nor excessive fines imposed, nor cruel and unusual punishments inflicted." U.S. Const. amend. VIII. M.L.C. concedes that the Eighth Amendment "says nothing about whether bail shall be available at all." *United States v. Salerno*, 481 U.S. 739, 752, 107 S.Ct. 2095, 2104, 95 L.Ed.2d 697 (1987). In fact, the United States Supreme Court has observed that the Eighth Amendment "fails to say all arrests must be bailable." *Carlson v. Landon*, 342 U.S. 524, 546, 72 S.Ct. 525, 537, 96 L.Ed. 547 (1952). Furthermore, the United States Supreme Court has not addressed whether juveniles have a constitutional right to bail under the Eighth Amendment. *See In re Whittington*, 391 U.S. 341, 88 S.Ct. 1507, 20 L.Ed.2d 625 (1968).

For essentially the same reasons that led us to determine in *Whitmer* that the excessive bail provisions of the Utah Constitution do not apply to juveniles, we hold that the denial of bail to a juvenile prior to bindover under section 78-3a-25.1 does not violate the excessive bail provisions of the Eighth Amendment. Until bindover, the juvenile is still subject to the jurisdiction of the juvenile court and the juvenile court may retain jurisdiction. Moreover,

> juveniles seeking release pending adjudication are not situated like adults applying for bail pending trial. A child does not have the unqualified right of individual liberty that an adult has because a child is subject to parental control. Therefore, the full basis for bail does not exist with regard to children, for a child released on bail would not gain individual freedom from custody but would simply be restored to parental control.

Morris v. D'Amario, 416 A.2d 137, 140 (R.I.1980); *see also Pauley v. Gross*, 1 Kan.App.2d 736, 574 P.2d 234, 240 (1977) (denying bail to child is different from denying bail to adult because children are already subject to parental or other control). Accordingly, denying bail to charged serious youth offenders prior to bindover does not violate the Excessive Bail Clause of the Eighth Amendment to the United States Constitution.

M.L.C. also contends that denying bail to juveniles charged under the serious youth offender statute violates the uniform operation of laws clause of article I, section 24 of the Utah Constitution and the Fourteenth Amendment to the United States Constitution inasmuch as the statute's provisions deny bail to juveniles charged with certain enumerated crimes until bindover, while adults charged with the same offenses are eligible for bail.

Article I, section 24 of the Utah Constitution provides, "All laws of a general nature shall have uniform operation." M.L.C. argues that because both adults and juveniles may be charged with the aggravated offenses enumerated in section 78-3a-25.1(1), juveniles and adults are appropriately grouped together for purposes of an article I, section 24 analysis. M.L.C. also argues that section 78-3a-25.1 divides this class of persons into two groups, adults who are taken before a magistrate and routinely allowed bail and juveniles who are denied bail until bindover. Because the crimes charged are identical and the potential punishments are identical, M.L.C. argues that the different treatment afforded juveniles and adults violates article I, section 24.

In analyzing claims under article I, section 24,

> we must first determine what classifications, if any, are created by the statute. Second, we must determine whether different classes or subclasses are treated disparately. Finally, if any disparate treatment exists between classes or subclasses, we must determine whether the legislature had any reasonable objective that warrants the disparity.

Mohi, 901 P.2d at 997; *see also Malan v. Lewis*, 693 P.2d 661, 670 (Utah 1984).

This court has already held that the different treatment afforded juveniles and adults with respect to bail is not unconstitutional. *Whitmer*, 30 Utah 2d at 208, 515 P.2d at 619. Furthermore, as we have already determined, a juvenile charged under the serious youth offender statute is to be considered a juvenile in juvenile court unless and until the juvenile court makes a determination that such juvenile should be bound over to district court to stand trial on the criminal information.

Treating a juvenile—including a juvenile charged under the serious youth offender statute prior to bindover—differently from an adult with respect to bail is not arbitrary but is reasonably related to the purposes of the Juvenile Courts Act, including section 78-3a-25.1, which M.L.C. does not challenge. In part, the purposes of the Juvenile Courts Act are to

> (a) promote public safety and individual accountability by the imposition of appropriate sanctions on persons who have committed acts in violation of law;
> (b) order appropriate measures to promote guidance and control, preferably in the child's own home, as an aid in the prevention of future unlawful conduct and the development of responsible citizenship;
> (c) where appropriate, order rehabilitation, reeducation, and treatment for persons who have committed acts bringing them within the court's jurisdiction;...
> (g) consistent with the ends of justice, strive to act in the best interests of the children in all cases and attempt to preserve and strengthen family ties where possible.

Utah Code Ann. § 78-3a-102(5) (1996). The protective and rehabilitative purposes of the Juvenile Courts Act are reasonably related to denying bail to juveniles, including a juvenile charged under the serious youth offender statute prior to a determination that he or she will be bound over to district court. Accordingly, denying a charged serious youth offender bail until bindover to district court does not violate article I, section 24 of the Utah Constitution.

Likewise, because prior to bindover, juveniles and adults are not in the same class, we need not address M.L.C.'s contention that the denial of prebindover bail violates equal protection under the Fourteenth Amendment of the United States Constitution. *See State v. Taylor*, 541 P.2d 1124, 1125 (Utah 1975) ("All that is required, under the Fourteenth Amendment, is equality among members of each class."); *Malan*, 693 P.2d at 669.

Conclusion

On the basis of the foregoing, we hold that the juvenile court did not err in denying bail to M.L.C. prior to the time he was bound over to district court to be tried as an adult. We therefore affirm.

NOTES AND QUESTIONS

1. In *In re Whittington*, 391 U.S. 341 (1968), the Supreme Court, in a *per curiam* opinion, vacated and remanded the case of a fourteen-year-old Ohio boy who was adjudicated delinquent on the basis of a trial judge's finding that probable cause existed to believe that he had committed second-degree murder. The adjudication occurred two months before the Court's decision in *In re Gault*. Does *Gault* resolve the question of a minor's right to bail?

2. Some states expressly deny the minor a right to bail. See, e.g., Haw. Rev. Stat. § 571-32(h) (2010); N.J. Stat. § 2A:4A-40 (2010); Or. Rev. Stat. § 419C.179 (2010). Other states expressly allow bail. Conn. Gen. Stat. § 46b-133(b) (2010); Mass. Gen. Laws ch. 119, § 67 (2010); Okla. Stat. Ann. Tit. 10A, § 2-2-403(B) (2010).

3. If children are not entitled to many of the same procedural protections as adults, must the state afford them special treatment?

D.B. V. TEWKSBURY
United States District Court for the District of Oregon
545 F.Supp. 896 (1982)

FRYE, District Judge:

This is a civil rights action brought pursuant to 42 U.S.C. § 1983. Plaintiffs and members of plaintiffs' class are all children who are presently confined, or who are subject to confinement in the Columbia County Correctional Facility (CCCF), an adult jail, in St. Helens, Oregon. Plaintiffs challenge the constitutionality of defendants' actions in confining plaintiffs and members of their class in CCCF. Plaintiffs seek declaratory and injunctive relief....

The named plaintiffs are children, all of whom have been detained in CCCF....

Defendant Graham Tewksbury is the Director of the Columbia County Juvenile Department. Defendants A. J. Ahlborn, Robert M. Hunt, and Marion Sahagian are commissioners of the Columbia County Board of Commissioners. Defendant Tom Tennant is the Sheriff of Columbia County....

Children detained in CCCF are usually placed in quarters consisting of multiple-occupancy cells with a common day space. They may be placed in isolation cells, however. Each multiple-occupancy cell contains steel bed frames, a toilet-sink installation, one overhead light, and a steel-barred wall with a sliding door. Children are locked inside the cells from 10 p. m. to 6 a. m.

The day room area, i.e., the common room, contains a metal picnic table, fluorescent lighting fixtures, and a single shower unit. There is no natural light in the cells occupied by children. Illumination is sufficient for overall visibility. All walls, floors, and ceilings are solid concrete or concrete block materials. The walls are painted blue.

Doors entering into these areas are either steel bars or solid metal. Each door contains a small viewing window and a food service slot. Children are detained in cells geared for as many as three children. Sometimes children ranging in age from 12 to 17 years are placed in the same cell.

Children held in CCCF are not issued sheets, mattress covers, or pillows. They sleep on mattresses covered with urethane and they are given a wool blanket. Occasionally children are not given mattresses. Those children placed in isolation cells sleep on cement floors.

Female children are not advised by matrons that sanitary napkins or tampons are available. If requested, however, they are made available. Matrons are not stationed within the secure detention area of CCCF. In order to obtain a sanitary napkin or tampon, female children must strike their cell doors or yell to attract the attention of a male corrections officer, who in turn contacts a matron. There are no full-time matrons available during night shifts, but if a female child is detained during the night, a part-time matron is called and is available....

...The intake process at CCCF is essentially an *admissions* process rather than a *screening* process. Part of the reason that children are detained at CCCF rather than being placed elsewhere is that there are no written criteria upon which to make decisions regarding who should be detained in CCCF. There is no policy as to who makes a decision when a child is to be lodged in jail. There is a phone list for jail staff to use to try to reach juvenile counselors, but counselors are sometimes unavailable....

All clothing of children detained in CCCF is confiscated. Children are issued jail clothes which consist of jeans, a shirt, and socks for boys, and slacks, a blouse, and socks for girls. No child lodged in CCCF may have underwear.

Toilet facilities at CCCF are not screened from view and children using these toilet facilities are visible to other children and to corrections officers. The day room area has a shower which can be used at all times when the children are not locked in their cells. On occasion showers in CCCF are not equipped with shower curtains. Children showering are visible to other children and to corrections officers. Female children using the toilet or shower are visible to male corrections officers. Male children using the toilet or shower are visible to matrons.

Children in CCCF are sometimes placed in either of two isolation cells. These are 8' × 8' windowless concrete block rooms, barren of all furniture and furnishings. Sometimes it is very cold in the isolation cells. Near the center of the isolation cell there is a sewer hole which is the only facility for urination and defecation.

Lighting and the mechanism for flushing the sewer hole for each isolation cell are controlled outside the cell by the corrections staff. Lights in the isolation cells are sometimes left on or off for long periods of time. Sometimes the sewer hole is not flushed for long periods. When the mechanism for the sewer hole is flushed by a corrections staff officer, water and sewage gushes onto the cell floor....

For a child to be placed in isolation, that child must be moved down a corridor immediately outside the adult male dormitory cell. The child can see the adult male prisoners, and the adult male prisoners can see him or her. When the isolation cell door is closed, children in isolation and the adults in the dormitory cell can and do communicate by talking in loud voices....

There are no written standards for placement of children in isolation....

Meals served to children are planned, prepared, and served by corrections officers. Corrections officers must prepare meals in addition to performing their other duties. Corrections officers are not trained in nutrition or food preparation. They are not supervised by a nutritionist or a dietitian. There are no written menus. Meals are prepared from foods available in storage. Food served to children is the same as that served to adult prisoners and to the corrections personnel themselves, except that children at CCCF are not allowed to buy food through the commissary, while adult prisoners are. Special dietary needs of children, or special dietary needs of a child such as a diabetic child are not considered.

No medical screening procedure is used for children admitted to CCCF other than a visual inspection by an untrained corrections officer....

K. K. was... detained at CCCF while intoxicated. Because of belligerent behavior, he was placed in a juvenile section in handcuffs. He received no medical screening, monitoring, or assistance, and was later found on his cell floor in a pool of vomit and urine. He was then taken to Columbia District Hospital where he was admitted for observation.

There is no daily sick call for children at CCCF....

There are no special rules or procedures for the treatment of emotionally disturbed children who panic in a jail setting. There is no emergency medical health service. There are no psychiatrists, psychologists, or counselors on call.

There are no educational programs for children at CCCF. Children are not allowed to have books or magazines or pencils and paper. This policy is not the jail's policy, but the policy of the Juvenile Department....

There are no recreational programs, materials, or activities for children at CCCF....

There are no facilities or equipment for exercise....

Children are treated considerably differently from adults. Adults have access to books, television, radio, cards, and other recreational materials; children do not. Adults are allowed to have underwear brought to them at CCCF; children are not. Adults have regular visitation and may visit with friends as well as families; children have no regularly scheduled visitation. Adults are allowed to send and receive mail; children are not allowed to send or receive mail. Adults are provided paper, writing material, envelopes, and stamps. Children are not allowed to have paper, writing material, envelopes, or stamps. Adults are allowed to make one phone call upon admission; children are not allowed to make a phone call upon admission. Adults are allowed to make phone calls during their period of incarceration. Children at CCCF, prior to the court entering its preliminary injunction dated June 10, 1981, were prohibited from making phone calls without Juvenile Department permission. When an attorney comes to CCCF to see an adult inmate, this visitation is allowed. If an attorney comes to CCCF to see a child, the attorney must go through the Juvenile Department to gain access to the child. An inmate manual governs the conduct of adults held in CCCF. Children are not advised what behavior will result in disciplinary action or sanctions. There are no grievance procedures for children.

Parents are not allowed to visit children confined in CCCF without permission of the Juvenile Department. Visitation with children in CCCF is controlled by the Juvenile Department and not the jail....

There are no formal written policies and procedures pertaining to the care and treatment of juveniles at CCCF....

There are no written rules governing the conduct of children held in CCCF....

All full-time corrections officers at CCCF are men....

Corrections officers at CCCF are basically jail staff....

Although there is no evidence to indicate physical abuse such as beatings, there is evidence that corrections personnel have made verbal threats toward detained children and have refused to tell them the time of day when requested. Since there is no natural light in the children's cells and since there are no clocks, children often become disoriented as to time....

Oregon statutory law allows a child to be detained in local correctional facilities such as CCCF so long as the portion of the facility holding the child is screened from the sight and sound of adult prisoners. ORS 419.575, ORS 169.079 (1979) (amended 1981; renumbered ORS 169.740). Under Oregon law, then, plaintiffs may legitimately be incarcerated in CCCF prior to an adjudication of their status or guilt. It is the scope of their federal constitutional rights during this period of confinement before a hearing that is the focus of this case.

The Due Process Clause of the Fourteenth Amendment to the United States Constitution requires that a pretrial detainee not be punished. *Bell v. Wolfish*, 441 U.S. 520, 99 S.Ct. 1861, 60 L.Ed.2d 447 (1979). A state does not acquire the power to punish a person—adult or child (assuming a child is convicted of committing a crime)—until after it has secured a formal adjudication of guilt in accordance with due process of law. Not every disability imposed in preadjudication detention amounts to "punishment," however. The very fact of detention implies a measure of restriction of movement, choice, privacy, and comfort.

This court must determine whether the conditions imposed upon plaintiffs are imposed for the purpose of punishment or whether they are incidents of some other legitimate governmental purpose. In this case the determination is simple. Defendant Tewksbury has stated publicly and expressly that he intends to punish children detained in CCCF. It is the express intent of defendants that plaintiffs' confinements in CCCF be punishments. The intent to punish is carried out in the extraordinary conditions of confinement imposed on plaintiffs while confined in CCCF. Confinement of child pretrial detainees in CCCF as it now exists is punishment prior to an adjudication of guilt.

Defendants have violated plaintiffs' due process rights under the Fourteenth Amendment to be free from pretrial punishments by confining plaintiffs in CCCF. Those extraordinary conditions which alone and in combination constitute punishment are:

1. Failure to provide any form of work, exercise, education, recreation, or recreational materials.
2. Failure to provide minimal privacy when showering, using toilets, or maintaining feminine hygiene.
3. Placement of intoxicated or drugged children in isolation cells without supervision or medical attention.
4. Placement of younger children in isolation cells as a means of protecting them from older children.
5. Failure to provide adequate staff supervision to protect children from harming themselves and/or other children.
6. Failure to allow contact between children and their families.
7. Failure to provide an adequate diet.
8. Failure to train staff to be able to meet the psychological needs of confined children.
9. Failure to provide written institutional rules, sanctions for violation of those rules, and a grievance procedure.
10. Failure to provide adequate medical care....

The court must now turn to the issue of whether it is constitutionally permissible to lodge children who have been accused of committing crimes in adult jails pending adjudication of the charges against them.... Would it be constitutionally permissible to lodge children accused of committing crimes in these jails?

In deciding this issue, the court declines to rule on the "punishment" aspect of the due process clause of the 14th Amendment. Instead the court will rely on the "fundamental fairness" doctrine enunciated in *In Re Gault*, 387 U.S. 1, 87 S.Ct. 1428, 18 L.Ed.2d 527 (1967) and juvenile cases decided after the *Gault* decision.

Due process—or fundamental fairness—does not guarantee to children all the rights in the adjudication process which are constitutionally assured to adults accused of committing crimes. For example, children are not entitled to a jury trial, to indictment by Grand Jury, or to bail. In lieu of these constitutional rights, children are not to be treated or considered as criminals. An adjudication of a child as guilty does not have the effect of a conviction nor is such child deemed a criminal. Even upon a finding of "guilt" as to the criminal charges, the child may not be imprisoned in adult jails as punishment for his acts. ORS 419.507, 419.509.

Juvenile proceedings, in the State of Oregon as elsewhere, are in the nature of a guardianship imposed by the state as *parens patriae* to provide the care and guidance that under normal circumstances would be furnished by the natural parents. It is, then, fundamentally fair—constitutional—to deny children charged with crimes rights available to adults charged with crimes if that denial is offset by a special solicitude designed for children.

But when the denial of constitutional rights for children is not offset by a "special solicitude" but by lodging them in adult jails, it is fundamentally unfair. When children who are found guilty of committing criminal acts cannot be placed in adult jails, it is fundamentally unfair to lodge children accused of committing criminal acts in adult jails.

In 1966 the United States Supreme Court envisioned the problem confronting this court:

> "... There is evidence, in fact, that there may be grounds for concern that the child receives the worst of both worlds: that he gets neither the protections accorded to adults nor the solicitous care and regenerative treatment postulated for children."

Kent v. United States, 383 U.S. 541, 556, 86 S.Ct. 1045, 1054, 16 L.Ed.2d 84 (1966).

The supervisors at jails are guards—not guardians. Jails hold convicted criminals and adults charged with crimes. Jails are prisons, with social stigmas. Children identify with their surroundings. They may readily perceive themselves as criminals, for who goes to jail except for criminals? A jail is not a place where a truly concerned natural parent would lodge his or her child for care and guidance. A jail is not a place where the state can constitutionally lodge its children under the guise of *parens patriae*.

To lodge a child in an adult jail pending adjudication of criminal charges against that child is a violation of that child's due process rights under the Fourteenth Amendment to the United States Constitution.

NOTES AND QUESTIONS

1. *The Deinstitutionalization Mandate.* In 1974, Congress enacted the Juvenile Justice and Delinquency Prevention Act (JJDPA). Under the JJDPA, youths may not be detained in adult jails and lockups except for limited times before or after a court hearing (six hours), in rural areas (twenty-four hours plus weekends and holidays), or in unsafe travel conditions. 42 U.S.C. § 5633(a)(13). This provision does not apply to children who are tried or convicted in adult criminal court. This provision is designed to protect children from psychological abuse, physical assault, and isolation. Children housed in adult jails and lockups have been found to be eight times more likely to commit suicide, two times more likely to be assaulted by staff, and 50 percent more likely to be attacked with a weapon than children housed in juvenile facilities.

When children are placed in an adult jail or lockup, as noted in the exceptions listed above, "sight and sound" contact with adults is prohibited under the JJDPA. This provision seeks to prevent children from threats, intimidation, or other forms of psychological abuse and physical assault. Under "sight and sound," children cannot be housed next to adult cells; share dining halls, recreation areas, or any other common spaces with adults; or be placed in any circumstance that could expose them to threats or abuse from adult offenders.

In 1992, the JJDPA was amended to require states to assess and address the disproportionate contact of youths of color at key contact points in the juvenile justice system—from arrest to detention to confinement. Studies indicate that youths of color receive tougher sentences and are more likely to be incarcerated than white youths for the same offenses. With youths of color making up one-third of the youth population but two-thirds of youths in contact with the juvenile justice system, this provision requires states and local jurisdictions to address the reasons for such disproportionate minority contact.

2. Despite the mandates of the JJDPA, juveniles are still placed in adult facilities. The Campaign for Youth Justice, in a 2007 report, identifies many of the problems faced by youths incarcerated in adult facilities:

> Every day in America, an average of 7,500 youth are incarcerated in adult jails. The annual number of youth who are placed in adult jails is even higher—ten or twenty times the daily average according to some researchers—to account for the "turnover rate" of youth entering and exiting adult jails....
>
> It is extremely difficult to keep youth safe in adult jails. When youth are placed with adults in jails, youth are at greater risk of physical and sexual assaults. For example, according to the U.S. Department of Justice Bureau of Justice Statistics (BJS) in 2005 and 2006, 21% and 13% respectively, of the victims of inmate-on-inmate sexual violence in jails were youth under the age of 18—a surprisingly high percentage of victims considering that only 1% of jail inmates are juveniles.
>
> Recognizing the risks to youth in jails, some jailers separate youth from adult inmates. However, this is not an adequate solution either. Separating youth from adults in jail can reduce the physical or emotional harm that may result from contact with adult offenders, but unfortunately these youths are then often placed in isolation, a dangerous setting for youth. Youth in isolation are frequently locked down 23 hours a day in small cells with no natural light. Even limited exposure to such an environment can cause anxiety, paranoia, exacerbate existing mental disorders, and increase risk of suicide. In fact, youth have the highest suicide rate of all inmates in jails. Youth are 19 times more likely to commit suicide in jail than youth in the general population and 36 times more likely to commit suicide in an adult jail than in a juvenile detention facility. Jail staff is simply not equipped to protect youth from the dangers of adult jails.
>
> Jails do not have the capacity to provide the necessary education and other programs crucial for the healthy development of adolescents. Even though legally required to, few jails provide appropriate education to youth. A BJS survey found that 40% of jails provided no educational services at all, only 11% of jails provided special education services, and only 7% provided vocational training. As many as one-half of all youth transferred to the adult system do not receive adult convictions, and are returned to the juvenile justice system or are not convicted at all. Many of these youths will have spent *at least one month* in an adult jail and one in five of these youths will have spent *over six months* in an adult jail. Without adequate education and other services, jails take youth off course....
>
> ...Adult jails are designed to house adults, whereas juvenile detention facilities are designed for youth. The result is that juvenile and adult detention facilities provide radically different services for the people in their facilities. From intake processes to meals to health

care, adolescents have specific needs that jails are often ill-equipped to handle. For example, youth have different nutritional requirements because they are growing rapidly.... If youth do not receive appropriate physical and mental health care, their development can be compromised forever.

One main reason why juvenile detention facilities are better suited for adolescents is staffing. Jail staff who supervise youth are often put in awkward and dangerous positions because the "right way" to handle 99% of the inmates in their facilities (the adults) is usually the "wrong way" for the remaining 1% (developing youth who happen to be inmates). Juvenile detention facilities generally operate with higher levels of staffing (one staff person to eight youth) compared to jails (ratios can be as high as one staff person to 64 inmates).... Additional staffing is critical for engaging youth in exercise, education, and pro-social activities necessary for proper development. Juvenile detention facilities also find it easier to offer these activities because they usually have access to dayrooms, classroom spaces, or gyms, and are not as constrained by the physical limitations of many jails. Many jails are unable to offer these programs because youth need to be kept safe from the other adult inmates, and as a result are kept within cells or sections of jails.

The lack of education programs in jails has particularly serious consequences for youth who can be detained for several months pre-trial. Because of their age, most youth in jails have not completed their high school education and need classes to graduate or obtain a GED, or to acquire vocational skills to get a job. Without adequate schooling, too many youth are at risk of falling further and further behind academically even though they are legally entitled to an education. Most states have mandatory attendance laws requiring that children attend school unless they have obtained a diploma or a GED. The federal special education law, Individuals with Disabilities Education Act (IDEA), also requires jails to provide special education services for qualifying youth; however, jails frequently have difficulty meeting their legal obligations.... While juvenile detention centers often have full-time education staff, adult jails have weak educational programs and it is rare for jails to have classrooms for education....

Another danger caused by housing youth within adult jails is that jails expose youth to "role models." By exposing juveniles to a criminal culture where inmates commit crimes against each other, adult institutions may socialize juveniles into become chronic offenders when they otherwise would not have....

According to the Surgeon General of the United States, youth suicide is a major public health problem: suicide is the third leading cause of death among 15-to 24-year-olds.... The best estimates reported by the CDC are from a 1978 study, which found that youth in adult jails were 36 times more likely to commit suicide in an adult jail than in a juvenile detention facility.

More recent estimates of youth suicide rates are available from the U.S. Department of Justice's Bureau of Justice Statistics. The findings are just as grim—jail inmates under 18 had the highest suicide rate of all inmates (101 per 100,000 during 2000–2002). By comparison, the suicide rate for 14-to-17-year-olds not in jail during the same time period was just 5.32 per 100,000. Youth in adult jails are 19 times more likely to commit suicide than are their counterparts in the general population....

Youth held in jails for short periods of time are at great risk of suicide too. The Bureau of Justice Statistics found that suicides in jails were heavily concentrated in the first week spent in custody (48%), with almost a quarter of suicides taking place on the day of admission to jail (14%) or on the following day (9%). It appears that youth held in all jails, large and small, are at risk. Rates of inmate suicide were closely related to jail size, with the smallest facilities recording the highest suicide rates.

There are several reasons why suicide rates for incarcerated juveniles are so high. Experts have identified mental disorders, substance abuse, impulsive aggression, parental depression and substance abuse, family discord and abuse, and poor family support as risk factors for adolescent suicide in the general population. Many of these same risk factors are prevalent for youth held in jails. Experts surmise that juveniles in the adult system experience, similar, if not greater, rates of mental disorder and related problems compared with youth in the juvenile justice system. . . .

Tragically, many adult jails are not equipped to identify and respond to the mental health needs of youth. Many jails lack appropriate screening and assessment tools to identify mental health problems in youth. . . .

Almost every jail and prison across America experiences problems with sexual violence. . . .

. . . [A]vailable data are likely to underestimate the true level of sexual violence currently occurring in adult jails.

The data do confirm that youth are at high risk of being sexually assaulted in jails. In 2005 and 2006, 21% and 13%, respectively, of all victims of substantiated incidents of inmate-on-inmate sexual violence in jails were juveniles under the age of 18—an extremely high proportion of victims given their relatively low numbers in jail populations (typically only 1% of all inmates are juveniles).

Even for youth not directly assaulted, the psychological effects of being in constant and legitimate fear of sexual assault, or of witnessing the sexual assault of others, can be devastating. . . . [M]any youth become disciplinary problems as a self-protective mechanism.

Federal law requires states to keep youth who are under the jurisdiction of the juvenile court out of adult jail, but there is a loophole: the law does not apply to youth charged as adults. Most states permit the pre-trial detention of youth in jails, and only 20 states require that youth must be segregated from adult inmates. Regardless of the specific legal requirements, jail officials face a Catch-22: separating youth from adult inmates is beneficial in that it minimizes contact with people who can pose grave physical and emotional threats to youth, but when a youth is separated, he or she is often placed in isolation, which can exacerbate mental health issues and suicidal impulses.

When youth are segregated in jails, they often are placed in conditions that mimic the isolation or solitary confinement conditions in "supermax" facilities reserved for the most hardened adult offenders. Youth can be locked down 23 or 24 hours a day in small cells that may measure 48 to 80 square feet with no natural light, no control over the electric light in their cell, and no view outside of their cell. They have no contact with other prisoners, even verbal contact, and no meaningful contact with staff. . . . Research shows that these periods of segregation are harmful to individuals and makes it more difficult to treat them successfully. . . . [T]he effects of isolation are profound and disabling because people lose their ability to test social reality.

CAMPAIGN FOR YOUTH JUSTICE, JAILING JUVENILES: THE DANGERS OF INCARCERATING YOUTH IN ADULT JAILS IN AMERICA, 4, 6–7, 10, 13, 14 (2007).

3. The Annie E. Casey Foundation implemented a Juvenile Detention Alternatives Initiative in 1992 to reduce reliance on the secure detention of juveniles. The purpose of the Juvenile Detention Alternatives Initiative is to demonstrate that jurisdictions can safely reduce reliance on secure detention. Their objectives are to eliminate the inappropriate or unnecessary use of secure detention, minimize rearrest and failure-to-appear rates pending adjudication, ensure appropriate conditions of confinement in secure facilities, redirect public finances to sustain successful reforms, and reduce racial and ethnic disparities. At the cooperating sites, the JDAI has lowered detention populations, reduced juvenile crime substantially, and reduced racial disparities. RICHARD MENDEL, ANNIE E. CASEY FOUNDATION, TWO DECADES OF JDAI: FROM DEMONSTRATION PROJECT TO NATIONAL STANDARD (2009). Does this suggest that juvenile detention actually increases juvenile offending?

6. TRIAL RIGHTS

a. RIGHT TO COUNSEL

IN RE GAULT
Supreme Court of the United States
387 U.S. 1 (1967)

MR. JUSTICE FORTAS delivered the opinion of the Court....

Appellants charge that the Juvenile Court proceedings were fatally defective because the court did not advise Gerald or his parents of their right to counsel, and proceeded with the hearing, the adjudication of delinquency and the order of commitment in the absence of counsel for the child and his parents or an express waiver of the right thereto. The Supreme Court of Arizona pointed out that "(t)here is disagreement (among the various jurisdictions) as to whether the court must advise the infant that he has a right to counsel." ... The court argued that "The parent and the probation officer may be relied upon to protect the infant's interests." Accordingly it rejected the proposition that "due process requires that an infant have a right to counsel." It said that juvenile courts have the discretion, but not the duty, to allow such representation; it referred specifically to the situation in which the Juvenile Court discerns conflict between the child and his parents as an instance in which this discretion might be exercised. We do not agree. Probation officers, in the Arizona scheme, are also arresting officers. They initiate proceedings and file petitions which they verify, as here, alleging the delinquency of the child; and they testify, as here, against the child. And here the probation officer was also superintendent of the Detention Home. The probation officer cannot act as counsel for the child. His role in the adjudicatory hearing, by statute and in fact, is as arresting officer and witness against the child. Nor can the judge represent the child. There is no material difference in this respect between adult and juvenile proceedings of the sort here involved.... A proceeding where the issue is whether the child will be found to be "delinquent" and subjected to the loss of his liberty for years is comparable in seriousness to a felony prosecution. The juvenile needs the assistance of counsel to cope with problems of law, to make skilled inquiry into the facts, to insist upon regularity of the proceedings, and to ascertain whether he has a defense and to prepare and submit it. The child "requires the guiding hand of counsel at every step in the proceedings against him." Just as in *Kent v. United States*, *supra*, [383 U.S.,] at 561–562, we indicated our agreement with the United States Court of Appeals for the District of Columbia Circuit that the assistance of counsel is essential for purposes of waiver proceedings, so we hold now that it is equally essential for the determination of delinquency, carrying with it the awesome prospect of incarceration in a state institution until the juvenile reaches the age of 21....

...In at least one-third of the States, statutes now provide for the right of representation by retained counsel in juvenile delinquency proceedings, notice of the right, or assignment of counsel, or a combination of these. In other States, court rules have similar provisions.

The President's Crime Commission has recently recommended that in order to assure "procedural justice for the child," it is necessary that "Counsel... be appointed as a matter of course wherever coercive action is a possibility, without requiring any affirmative choice by child or parent." As stated by the authoritative "Standards for Juvenile and Family Courts," published by the Children's Bureau of the United States Department of Health, Education, and Welfare:

> "As a component part of a fair hearing required by due process guaranteed under the 14th amendment, notice of the right to counsel should be required at all hearings and counsel provided upon request when the family is financially unable to employ counsel." Standards, p. 57.

This statement was "reviewed" by the National Council of Juvenile Court Judges at its 1965 Convention and they "found no fault" with it....

We conclude that the Due Process Clause of the Fourteenth Amendment requires that in respect of proceedings to determine delinquency which may result in commitment to an institution in which the juvenile's freedom is curtailed, the child and his parents must be notified of the child's right to be represented by counsel retained by them, or if they are unable to afford counsel, that counsel will be appointed to represent the child.

At the habeas corpus proceeding, Mrs. Gault testified that she knew that she could have appeared with counsel at the juvenile hearing. This knowledge is not a waiver of the right to counsel which she and her juvenile son had, as we have defined it. They had a right expressly to be advised that they might retain counsel and to be confronted with the need for specific consideration of whether they did or did not choose to waive the right. If they were unable to afford to employ counsel, they were entitled in view of the seriousness of the charge and the potential commitment, to appointed counsel, unless they chose waiver. Mrs. Gault's knowledge that she could employ counsel was not an "intentional relinquishment or abandonment" of a fully known right.

NOTES AND QUESTIONS

1. What is the basis for the right to counsel in a delinquency proceeding? What is the scope of the right? Is it identical to a criminal defendant's right to counsel? If not, how does it differ?

2. *Gault* spawned a vigorous scholarly debate about the role and responsibilities of counsel for the child in a delinquency proceeding. See, e.g., Norman Lefstein, *In re Gault, Juvenile Courts and Lawyers*, 53 A.B.A. J. 811 (1967); Monrad G. Paulsen, *The Constitutional Domestication of the Juvenile Court*, 1967 Sup. Ct. Rev. 233; Elizabeth D. Dyson & Richard B. Dyson, *Family Courts in the United States*, 9 J. Fam. L. 1, 58 (1969); Theodore McMillian & Dorothy L. McMurtry, *The Role of the Defense Lawyer in the Juvenile Court—Advocate or Social Worker?* 14 St. Louis U. L.J. 561, 598 (1970). Current academic and professional thinking, however, clearly supports the view that the attorney for the child in a delinquency proceeding is a zealous advocate who represents the child's express preferences. Kristin Henning, *Loyalty, Paternalism, and Rights: Client Counseling Theory and the Role of Child's Counsel in Delinquency Cases*, 81 Notre Dame L. Rev. 245, 256 (2005). Accord American Bar Association—Institute of Judicial Administration, Juvenile Justice Standards Relating to Counsel for Private Parties, Standard

3.1(a)(1980) ("However engaged, the lawyer's principal duty is the representation of the client's legitimate interests"); Nat'l Juv. Defender Ctr., Role of Juvenile Defense Counsel in Delinquency Court 7 (2009) (juvenile defense counsel "advocate[es] for the client's expressed interests, not the client's 'best interest' as determined by counsel"). Nevertheless, in practice, it is clear that many lawyers advocate for their clients' best interests, in part because of the juvenile court's paternalistic history; systemic pressures to act as a best-interests advocate; unclear statutes, case law, and ethical rules; and perceptions that children are incompetent decision makers. Henning, *supra*, at 260–280.

3. Every state, along with the District of Columbia, has a statute providing the minor with counsel in a delinquency proceeding. Nevertheless, some states extend the right to counsel only to those children who face a risk of confinement or a sufficiently severe penalty. See *C.M. v. State*, 855 So.2d 582 (Ala. Crim. App. 2002) (because trial court had determined that juvenile would not be committed to youth detention facility, minor not entitled to court-appointed counsel pursuant to Ala. Code § 12-15-63[a] requiring the appointment of counsel "in a proceeding in which there is a reasonable likelihood such may result in a commitment to an institution in which the freedom of the child is curtailed"); Ariz. Rev. Stat. § 8-221 (2010) ("In all proceedings involving offenses, dependency or termination of parental rights that are conducted pursuant to this title and that may result in detention, a juvenile has the right to be represented by counsel"); Minn. Stat. § 260B.163(4)(a)(2012) (child not entitled to counsel if charged with a petty offense); N.J. Stat. Ann. § 2A: 4A-39(a) (West 2010) ("A juvenile shall have the right, as provided by the Rules of Court, to be represented by counsel at every critical stage in the proceeding which, in the opinion of the court may result in the institutional commitment of the juvenile"); S.C. Code Ann. § 63-19-1030 (Law. Co-op 2010) (in delinquency proceedings that may result in commitment to an institution in which the child's freedom is curtailed, child and child's parents must be informed of right to counsel). Are these limitations on the right to counsel constitutional in light of *Gault*?

4. In 2001, the National Juvenile Defender Center (NJDC) began conducting assessments of individual states to determine how state courts were implementing the *Gault* mandate. Between 2001 and 2007, NJDC conducted assessments in sixteen states and found that juvenile indigent defense was a patchwork of chaotic and underfunded delivery systems. See, e.g., Nat'l Juv. Just. Center et al., An Assessment of Access to Couns. and Quality of Representation in Delinq. Proc. in Ind. (2006); Nat'l Juv. Just. Center et al., An Assessment of Access to Couns. and Quality of Representation in Delinq. Proc. in Fla. (2006); Nat'l Juv. Just. Center et al., An Assessment of Access to Couns. and Quality of Representation in Delinq. Proc. in Md. (2003); Nat'l Juv. Just. Center et al., An Assessment of Access to Couns. and Quality of Representation in Delinq. Proc. in Pa. (2003); Nat'l Juv. Just. Center et al., An Assessment of Access to Couns. and Quality of Representation in Delinq. Proc. in Me. (2003); Nat'l Juv. Just. Center et al., An Assessment of Access to Couns. and Quality of Representation in Delinq. Proc. in N.C. (2003); Nat'l Juv. Just. Center et al., An Assessment of Access to Couns. and Quality of Representation in Delinq. Proc. in Mont. (2003); Nat'l Juv. Just. Center et al., An Assessment of Access to Couns. and Quality of Representation in Delinq. Proc. in Ohio (2003); Nat'l Juv. Just. Center et al., An Assessment of Access to Couns. and Quality of Representation in Delinq. Proc. in Wash. (2003); Nat'l Juv. Just. Center et al., An Assessment of Access to Couns. and Quality of Representation in Delinq. Proc. in Ky. (2002); Nat'l Juv. Just. Center et al., An Assessment of Access to Couns. and Quality of

Representation in Delinq. Proc. in Va. (2002); Nat'l Juv. Just. Center et al., An Assessment of Access to Couns. and Quality of Representation in Delinq. Proc. in Ga. (2001); Nat'l Juv. Just. Center et al., An Assessment of Access to Couns. and Quality of Representation in Delinq. Proc. in La. (2001); Nat'l Juv. Just. Center et al., An Assessment of Access to Couns. and Quality of Representation in Delinq. Proc. in Tex. (2000); Nat'l Juv. Just. Center et al., An Assessment of Access to Couns. and Quality of Representation in Youth Ct. Proc. in Miss. (2007); Children and Family Just. Center et al., An Assessment of Access to Couns. and Quality of Representation in Delinq. Proc. in Ill. (2007).

Between the fall of 2009 and the spring of 2010, NJDC released assessments of three additional states: Nebraska, South Carolina, and West Virginia. Nat'l Juv. Defender Center, Juvenile Legal Defense: A Report on Access to Couns. and Quality of Representation for Children in Nebraska (2009); Nat'l Juv. Defender Center, Juvenile Indigent Defense: A Report on Access to Couns. and Quality of Representation in Delinq. Proc. (2010); Nat'l Juv. Defender Center, West Virginia: An Assessment of Access to Couns. and Quality of Representation in Juv. Delinq. Ct. (2010). As in previous reports, NJDC found limited resources and experience, poor funding, high caseloads, insufficient access to investigators, inadequate courthouse facilities, and a paucity of training.

Drawing on the findings of NJDC, Katherine Hunt Federle contends that despite *Gault*'s clear mandate,

> [c]hildren routinely are unrepresented in delinquency proceedings: many waive their right to counsel, based on a lack of understanding about the significance of the charges and the consequences of proceeding without legal assistance, or as a result of pressure, subtle or otherwise, from the judge, court personnel, or their parents. When children do assert their right to counsel, they nevertheless may be ineligible to receive free legal assistance because of extremely narrow definitions of indigency that exclude many families who fall well below the poverty line. This may leave parents in the untenable position of having to choose between retaining legal counsel and providing basic necessities; but even once the decision is made to secure legal assistance, the process of obtaining court-appointed counsel may be so confusing and time-consuming that children still appear in court without representation. On the other hand, many parents regardless of their socioeconomic status may simply be unwilling to hire private lawyers because they are angry, confused about the need for counsel, or do not understand the consequences of a juvenile delinquency adjudication.
>
> Securing appointed counsel, however, does not ensure highly skilled, competent, and zealous representation. Perhaps in part because *Gault* extended the right to counsel only to the adjudicatory phase of a delinquency proceeding, lawyers are seldom appointed to represent children at initial proceedings or detention hearings. Moreover, there is considerable evidence that attorneys for children fail to investigate or file pretrial motions and provide little or no assistance during or after the dispositional hearings. Systemic problems, like crippling caseloads, little to no training, resource constraints, and poor pay, further depress the quality of representation. Additionally, court culture may create a set of expectations and norms that pressure lawyers into acting as best interests advisors rather than as the zealous advocates for their clients' express preferences. Lawyers and judges themselves devalue the work done in juvenile court, seeing it as a mere stepping stone to "better"—and higher-paying—positions.

Katherine Hunt Federle, *Lawyering in Juvenile Court: Lessons from a Civil* Gideon *Experiment*, 37 FORDHAM URB. L.J. 93, 106–107 (2010). See also Wallace J. Mlyniec, *In re Gault at 40: The Right to Counsel in Juvenile Court—A Promise Unfulfilled*, 44 CRIM. L. BULL. 371, 383 (2008).

5. *Appointment of counsel for the indigent. Gault* states that "the Due Process Clause of the Fourteenth Amendment requires that in respect of proceedings to determine delinquency which may result in commitment to an institution in which the juvenile's freedom is curtailed, the child and his parents must be notified of the child's right to be represented by counsel retained by them, or if they are unable to afford counsel, that counsel will be appointed to represent the child." 387 U.S. at 41. Similarly, a criminal defendant has a Sixth Amendment right to appointed counsel in all felony cases or where a loss of liberty is involved. *Gideon v. Wainwright*, 372 U.S. 335 (1963) (Sixth Amendment requires states to appoint counsel for indigent defendants in all felony cases); *Scott v. Illinois*, 440 U.S. 367 (1979) (no indigent criminal defendant may be sentenced to term of imprisonment unless state has afforded him right to assistance of appointed counsel). But how should a court determine if a child is unable to afford counsel? North Carolina has established a statutory presumption that all juveniles are indigent, N.C. Gen. Stat. § 7B-2000(b) (2010); but the overwhelming majority of the states considers the financial status of the juvenile's parents or legal guardians in determining indigency. Thus, Wis. Stat. § 938.23(4) requires the appointment of counsel for any juvenile who has a right to or, in the discretion of the court, has been afforded counsel, although the court has the authority to seek reimbursement "in any manner suitable to the court regardless of the person's ability to pay." Under New Hampshire law, the court shall appoint counsel to a minor if the court determines that the minor is "financially unable to independently obtain counsel." Nevertheless, the court shall order any person "liable for support [and] financially able to pay" to reimburse the state for the cost (in whole or in part) of the minor's court-appointed counsel. N.H. Rev. Stat. Ann. §§ 169-B:12(I), (III).

Should parents be required to hire private counsel? What if the parents are able to pay but refuse to retain a lawyer? Ellen Marrus suggests that some parents, even though they do not qualify for indigent assistance, may be forced to choose between paying the rent or buying food and retaining counsel for their child. Other parents may feel that the child should be taught a lesson and that providing the child with counsel may allow the child to escape some well-deserved punishment. Additionally, some parents simply may not understand the legal system or the consequences of a delinquency adjudication and feel that because the child is guilty, there is no reason to hire a lawyer. On the other hand, parents may believe, naively, that the system will exonerate their child from wrongdoing. Ellen Marrus, *Best Interests Equals Zealous Advocacy: A Not So Radical View of Holistic Representation of Children Accused of Crime*, 62 MD. L. REV. 288, 315 (2003).

Under these circumstances, many states authorize the court to appoint independent counsel for the child and seek reimbursement for the costs. See, e.g., Del. Fam. Ct. R. Crim. Pro. R. 44(a) (2010) (court may appoint counsel at custodian's expense where custodian has financial ability but has refused to obtain counsel for child); Fla. Stat. Ann. § 985.033(4) (West 2011) (nonindigent parents may be held in civil contempt for refusal to obtain private counsel and ordered to pay costs); N.M. Stat. Ann. § 32A-2-14(B) (Michie 2010) (if parent is financially able to pay but unwilling to do so, court shall order parent to reimburse public defender for cost of representation); Wash. Rev. Code § 13.40.140(2) (2010) (juvenile may not be deprived of counsel because parent, guardian, or custodian refuses to pay); Wyo. Stat. Ann. § 14-6-222(b) (2010) (if person responsible for child's support able but unwilling to obtain counsel for child, court shall appoint and may order reimbursement of counsel fees). If the child and the parent have conflicting interests (for example, the parent is the complainant), some courts also have the authority to appoint counsel for the child. See La. Child. Code Ann. Art. 809(D) (West 2010) (if court finds the interests of the child and his parent conflict, court shall appoint counsel for the child); Mich. Comp. Laws § 712A.17c(2)(b) (2010) (court shall appoint counsel for the child when parent is the complainant or victim).

Marrus argues that requiring parents to reimburse the state for the costs of the child's counsel "may exacerbate existing family tensions and result in further acting-out by the child." Marrus, *supra*, at 316. Do you agree? Should the state assume the costs of appointing counsel for children in delinquency cases?

6. *Effective assistance of counsel.* A criminal defendant has a Sixth Amendment right not only to counsel but also to the effective assistance of counsel. In *Strickland v. Washington*, 466 U.S. 668 (1984), the United States Supreme Court held that to establish constitutionally ineffective representation, the defendant must show that his lawyer was incompetent (counsel's acts or omissions were "outside the range of professionally competent assistance") and that the defendant was prejudiced by counsel's incompetence ("there is a reasonable probability that, but for counsel's unprofessional errors, the result of the proceeding would have been different"). But what is the standard for assessing the effectiveness of counsel in juvenile delinquency proceedings? State courts that have considered the issue seem to apply the *Strickland* test. But very few juveniles claim ineffective assistance of counsel. According to Barbara Fedders, of the 6 million juveniles adjudicated delinquent between 1995 and 2005, only 290 filed ineffective-assistance claims that resulted in opinions published by Westlaw or Lexis/Nexis. Only 41 of the 290 resulted in any appellate relief. Barbara Fedders, *Losing Hold of the Guiding Hand: Ineffective Assistance of Counsel in Juvenile Delinquency Representation*, 14 Lewis & Clark L. Rev. 771, 806 (2010).

Why are so few claims of ineffective assistance of counsel filed? Fedders suggests that the *Strickland* standard discourages such claims from being made because it is so difficult to prove. Additionally, public defender offices that handle their own appeals may be loath to find that one of their own attorneys was ineffective, necessitating withdrawal. Even when such claims are made on appeal, much of the evidence of ineffectiveness may fall outside the record, precluding a claim on direct appeal. Of course, there also is the possibility that appellate counsel may truly be ineffective and never raise the claim, assuming that the child even gets an appointed lawyer for his appeal in the first instance. *Id.* at 809–812.

Are lawyers appointed to represent juveniles on appeal? In a study of all appeals of juvenile and criminal cases in Pennsylvania in 1990, the adult appeal rate was eleven times greater than the juvenile appeal rate, controlling for the same type of offense and taking into account the greater number of possible claims of procedural errors that could be raised in criminal cases. The study's author then conducted interviews with juvenile court judges, public defenders, and private attorneys who received court appointments.

> The defenders' interview responses quickly revealed an important aspect of the values and perspectives of the juvenile court community. While a few defenders view their roles as advocates whose sole job is to protect the child's legal rights, many see their roles in multidimensional terms. Concern with the long-term developmental needs of the child and with legal advocacy prompts some attorneys to see appeals as an obstacle to getting the child back on track. They fear that the taking of an appeal merely encourages the child to hold a cynical view....

Defenders observe that children don't always understand the consequences of court actions. In commitment cases, the child has often cycled through the court system before, perhaps several times, and some parents don't want the child to return to the home, especially if the placement involves a good school or drug and alcohol program. In consequence, many defenders view the attorney's role as a combination of advocate and guardian, with a goal of salvaging the children.... Since children are far less aware of their rights than adults and far less assertive in securing them, many defenders feel they must perform balancing acts in helping them get along with their lives while at the same time representing their legal interests....

... Almost all of the defenders, in describing the decision not to take an appeal, omit any reference to the child or the parents or guardian as participants in the process. More typical is the total absence of any decision-making process at all. This is especially true in busy court systems where defenders have so little time between cases that the thought of an appeal often never even arises. Follow-up questions reveal, with only a few exceptions, that neither the juvenile nor the parents or guardians are advised of the right to appeal.

The defenders proffered several justifications for this practice. Some said that the likelihood of success on appeal is slim because the superior and supreme courts try very hard to affirm the trial judge. Others suggest that appeals are futile because children get short sentences and it takes months to decide an appeal. Several defenders spoke of the chronic underfunding of their offices such that they simply don't have the resources to file juvenile appeals. Most even doubted whether taking appeals is truly in the child's best interests. On this point, one defender said that when taking an appeal, the client must be advised not to discuss the case with anyone, including placement counselors and teachers, during the pendency of the appeal. This means that the child may not be able to participate in available rehabilitation programs, such as group therapy, which are premised on the child's admission of the crime as a critical step toward emotional and psychological health. Taking an appeal could defeat the treatment plan.

Additionally, all of the defenders said that the trial court does not inform the juveniles of their appellate rights, and there is no legal obligation to do so. Under the Pennsylvania Rules of Criminal Procedure, adults must be advised of their post-trial rights on the record. The procedural rules do not apply to juveniles.

The juvenile court judges who were interviewed indicated mixed expectations as to the impact of appeals on minors. Some felt that appeals would undermine the rehabilitation process. Three types of harmful effects were predicted: (1) a child may not fully engage in the treatment program if he or she holds out hope of reversal on appeal; (2) an appeal might foster disrespect for the judicial system and the law (a "beat the system" attitude), especially if the appeal results in a windfall acquittal; and (3) a new adjudicatory or disposition hearing only prolongs the legal saga deflecting the child's attention and energy from more productive pursuits. According to the judges, each effect could increase the rate of juvenile recidivism. On the other hand, some judges thought that appeals might produce a positive result. "If there has been an error, or a miscarriage of justice, an appeal should remedy that. Unfair treatment only engenders contempt for the law."

Donald J. Harris, *Due Process vs. Helping Kids in Trouble: Implementing the Right to Appeal from Adjudications of Delinquency in Pennsylvania*, 98 Dick. L. Rev. 209, 223–225 (1994). What is the role of counsel for the child on appeal? Should it differ from the role of trial counsel?

7. *Waiver of the right to counsel.*

IN RE C.S.
Supreme Court of Ohio
874 N.E.2d 1177 (Ohio 2007)

O'CONNOR, J.

Forty years after the Supreme Court's watershed ruling in *In re Gault* (1967), 387 U.S. 1, 87 S.Ct. 1428, 18 L.Ed.2d 527, we address important questions concerning the scope of a juvenile's right to counsel in a delinquency proceeding and the waiver of that right. We hold that the juvenile's right to counsel is a right that he may waive, subject to certain conditions....

Appellant, C.S., was brought before the Juvenile Division of the Licking County Court of Common Pleas on August 9, 2005. At that time, he was almost 14 years old.

C.S.'s appearance in court was for purposes of two cases. The first...charged C.S. with two counts of grand theft, felonies of the fourth degree if committed by an adult. The second...alleged that C.S. had violated conditions of his probation, which had been imposed in an earlier, unrelated assault case.

The facts of the theft case are largely undisputed; C.S. and one of his friends waived their rights to an attorney and made admissions to the police. Those admissions included statements that they had stolen two cars and had used them to traverse three central Ohio counties while committing various criminal acts from August 3, 2005, through August 7, 2005. Indeed, the magistrate hearing the case initially termed the boys' activities "a regular crime spree." The crime spree allegedly included the theft of the cars and the destruction of one, the repeated burglarizing of a trailer (stealing electronic equipment and a firearm from it), the procurement and use of alcohol and cocaine-laced marijuana, engaging in sexual relations with an adult woman, and cruelty to animals (shooting a cow and a horse multiple times)....

At some point prior to an initial hearing held on August 9, 2005, C.S. and his mother received the common pleas court's notice and order to appear....

Included on the first page of the document is a section captioned "Your Right to an Attorney." That section clearly states, that "[y]ou have the right to be represented by an attorney at all stages of this proceeding" and that an attorney will be appointed if "you cannot afford an attorney and you qualify under State guidelines."

The document further states, "You should contact the Clerk's Office seven (7) days in advance of your scheduled hearing and the Clerk will advise you how to apply for a Court-appointed attorney." Given that C.S. does not appear to have been taken into custody until August 7 or August 8, and that his hearing was held on August 9, he could not have complied with that notice provision.

On the page that follows, after a section that sets forth "Your Rights in Court," the papers contain a section entitled "Waiver of Attorney." That section states, "The undersigned have read the instructions concerning our right to an attorney and the right to a Court-appointed attorney, if applicable. Knowing and understanding these rights, we hereby waive our right to be represented by an attorney or Court-appointed attorney. We further understand that we can be represented by an attorney in the future simply by advising the Court of our intention to do so." Ms. S. and C.S. signed the lines designated for "parent" and "juvenile" in that section.

At the hearing, the magistrate stated in open court that he had "two sets of rights papers"—an apparent reference to the notice to appear and its explanation of rights. The magistrate verified that C.S. had received the papers, read them, and understood the rights set forth on them and that C.S. and his mother had signed the papers.

The magistrate also inquired of C.S. and his mother as follows:

> "THE COURT: Do you understand that you have the right to be represented by an attorney at today's hearing?
> "C.S.: Yes, sir.
> "THE COURT: If you cannot afford an attorney and you qualify under state guidelines, I will appoint an attorney to represent you. Do you understand that?
> "C.S.: Yes, sir.
> "THE COURT: Do you wish to go forward with today's hearing without an attorney?
> "C.S.: Yes, sir.
> "THE COURT: Ms. S., do you agree with C.S.'s decision today to go forward without an attorney?
> "MS. S.: Yes, sir."
> The magistrate then explained the charges against appellant, including the degree of the offenses charged. After each offense was stated, the magistrate asked C.S. whether he understood the charge. Each time, C.S. answered that he did.

After each affirmative response, the magistrate asked whether C.S. admitted or denied the charge. C.S. admitted every charge. The magistrate then continued:

> "THE COURT: If you admit these charges today, C.S., that's basically the same as pleading guilty. Do you understand that?
> "C.S.: Yes, sir.
> "THE COURT: As a result then we would not have an adjudicatory hearing or trial in either of these cases. Do you understand that?
> "C.S.: Yes, sir.
> "THE COURT: Instead we would proceed directly to disposition, that is, for me to decide what punishment or conditions if any that should be imposed upon you. Do you understand that?
> "C.S.: Yes, sir.
> "THE COURT: By entering that plea you will be—well, first of all, that disposition in your case in [the theft case] could include a commitment to the custody of the Ohio Department of Youth Services for a minimum period of six months or twelve months and a maximum period not to exceed age twenty-one. Do you understand that?
> "C.S.: Yes, sir.
> "THE COURT: Do you understand what the Ohio Department of Youth Services is?
> "C.S.: Yes, sir.
> "THE COURT: What is it?
> "C.S.: Juvenile prison, sir.
> "THE COURT: That's correct. By entering that plea of admit you will be waiving or giving up certain Constitutionally guaranteed rights that you would otherwise enjoy. Among the rights that you will be giving up is the right to remain silent. Do you understand that?
> "C.S.: Yes, sir.
> "THE COURT: You will also be giving up the right to call witnesses and to present evidence in your defense. Do you understand that?
> "C.S.: Yes, sir.

"THE COURT: And you'll be giving up the right to question and to cross-examine prosecution witnesses. Do you understand that?
"C.S.: Yes, sir.
"THE COURT: Ordinarily, C.S., the State of Ohio would be required to prove these cases against you beyond a reasonable doubt. If you enter a plea of admit, however, the State of Ohio will not have to prove anything at all. Do you understand that?
"C.S.: Yes, sir.
"THE COURT: Have there been any promises or threats of any sort to cause you to enter these pleas?
"C.S.: No, sir.
"THE COURT: Ms. S., do you agree with C.S.'s decision today to enter pleas of admission to these charges?
"MS. S.: Yes, sir.
"THE COURT: Then, C.S., I'll accept the pleas of admission. Is there any statement about this situation that you wish to make?
"C.S.: No, sir.
"THE COURT: Have you talked with your mother since you got arrested?
"C.S.: No, sir.
"THE COURT: Ms. S., did you have an opportunity to read the police report?
"MS. S.: No, sir.
"THE COURT: I think it's safe to say, Ms. S. and C.S. * * *—it's safe to assume that there will be more * * * felony charges coming. I—I don't know when. It'll—it's going to be in the jurisdiction of Perry County. They'll transfer those cases up here so we'll deal with them, but in terms of the filing the complaints, it'll be the Perry County Prosecutor that has to file those complaints. But we'll cross that bridge when we come to it. I just wanted you to know that because of the burglaries, the firearm thefts, the discharging of the firearm, animal cruelty, underage consumption, drug-felony drug possession charges—what else? What am I missing? That's probably it. Underage alcohol, possession of marijuana, possession of cocaine, burglary, animal cruelty, theft of a firearm. That pretty much covers it, doesn't it?
"C.S.: Yes sir. B and E, sir.
"THE COURT: And the B and E. Well, burglary. It'll be a burglary because it's a home. Did you do—oh, well, the trailer, was it—someone living in that trailer too?
"C.S.: It—it was a camper, sir.
"THE COURT: Okay. So that'd probably be a B and E so you'd get a B and E and a burglary. So all together, once those all get filed, you're probably looking at another three years on top of that once you add all those together. So that—that'll be coming at some time, Ms. S. A regular crime spree. Steals two cars. Basically totals them both. Shoots a cow. Shoots a horse. Steals a gun. Breaks into a house. Smokes dope. Has sex with an adult woman. Alcohol. Cocaine. Hope it was worth it. Ms. S., is there anything that you wish to say?
"MS. S.: No, sir.
"THE COURT: Do you know what I think, C.S., is the biggest injustice in this whole situation? Do you know?
"C.S.: No, sir.
"THE COURT: Well, I'll tell you what I think is the biggest injustice in the whole situation. The biggest injustice * * * is that I can only give you a year in prison. Based on what you've

done over the past week, you ought to stay in prison until you're twenty-one years of age in my opinion, but I can't do that. To me, that's wrong. That's a disservice to every other taxpaying, law-abiding citizen of the state of Ohio that I can't lock you up [until you turn] twenty-one based on what you've been doing for the past week. The biggest injustice in this case is that I can only give you a year in prison. * * * [T]he way this commitment works is I'm going to commit you to [DYS] today for a minimum of a year. Okay. But at the end of that year, however, that doesn't mean you automatically get out. The end of that year means simply that your case goes before the review authority to decide whether or not you should get out on parole. They don't have to let you out. So based on the nature of the offense, based on the opinion of our probation director * * * and based on your conduct in [DYS], it's entirely possible that you will do more than a year. But the only thing that I can guarantee that you'll do is a year. * * * So you're looking at another two and a half years on top of that once those charges are filed by Perry County. C.S., based upon your pleas of admission and the facts contained in the report, I'll adjudicate you a probation violator as alleged in the motion. I'll order that you be released unsuccessfully in that—in that and all other cases. I'll order that you be released from probation unsuccessfully in all cases. Do you understand that?

"C.S.: Yes, sir.

"THE COURT: In [the theft case], based upon your pleas of admission and the facts contained in the report, I'll adjudicate you delinquent on both counts. * * * On both counts, I'll order you committed to the custody of the Ohio Department of Youth Services for a minimum period of six months and a maximum period not to exceed your twenty-first birthday. I'll order that those two counts run consecutive to each other for an initial minimum commitment of twelve months. And * * * the Department of Youth Services is to ensure that [C.S.'s older brother] and C.S. are not in the same facility. I know that was your plan. Your plan was that they be in—you were—you were anxious to be arrested on these felonies so that you could go to [DYS] and be with your brother again. You're going to [DYS] but I'll ensure you're not in the same facility."

C.S. and his mother were informed of their right to object to the magistrate's decision, see Juv.R. 40, and acknowledged receipt of the magistrate's decision. They waived objections and consented to the magistrate's decision.

After the trial court accepted the magistrate's decision, C.S. appealed on various grounds. One of those claims is pertinent here. C.S. argued that the trial court violated his rights to counsel and due process as those rights are conferred by the Fifth, Sixth, and Fourteenth Amendments to the United States Constitution, Sections 10 and 16, Article I of the Ohio Constitution, R.C. 2151.352, and Juv.R. 4 and 29.

After the court of appeals rejected that claim of error, we accepted C.S.'s discretionary appeal...to address two propositions of law. First, we address the meaning and effect of the portion of R.C. 2151.352 that states, "Counsel must be provided for a child not represented by the child's parent, guardian, or custodian," whether the right to counsel conferred on a juvenile can be waived, and, if so, what constitutes a valid waiver. Second, we decided whether strict compliance with Juv.R. 29 is required or whether substantial compliance is sufficient....

In declaring that the juvenile facing commitment to an institution has a right to counsel "'at every step in the proceedings against him,'" *In re Gault*, 387 U.S. at 36, 87 S.Ct. 1428, 18 L.Ed.2d 527, quoting *Powell v. Alabama* (1932), 287 U.S. 45, 69, 53 S.Ct. 55, 77 L.Ed. 158, the Supreme Court reinforced its belief that the appointment of counsel for a juvenile is not a mere formality or "a grudging gesture to a ritualistic requirement"; it is a venerable right at the core of the administration of justice and due process. *Kent*, 383 U.S. at 561, 86 S.Ct. 1045, 16 L.Ed.2d 84.

Indeed, it was the understanding of the right to due process that drove the court's holdings in *Kent*, *Gault*, and *Winship*. Those cases make clear that the right to counsel in a juvenile case flows to the juvenile through the Due Process Clause of the Fourteenth Amendment, not the Sixth Amendment. *Gault*, 387 U.S. at 41, 87 S.Ct. 1428, 18 L.Ed.2d 527. And although modern juvenile proceedings share some indicia of the criminal courts, juvenile proceedings are not considered criminal prosecutions for purposes of Sixth Amendment analyses. *McKeiver*, 403 U.S. at 553, 91 S.Ct. 1976, 29 L.Ed.2d 647.

Because the juvenile's right to counsel is predicated on due process, it is malleable rather than rigid. As the Supreme Court has explained, "For all its consequence, 'due process' has never been, and perhaps can never be, precisely defined.... [T]he phrase expresses the requirement of 'fundamental fairness,' a requirement whose meaning can be as opaque as its importance is lofty. Applying the Due Process Clause is therefore an uncertain enterprise which must discover what 'fundamental fairness' consists of in a particular situation by first considering any relevant precedents and then by assessing the several interests that are at stake." *Lassiter v. Dept. of Social Servs. of Durham Cty., North Carolina* (1981), 452 U.S. 18, 24–25, 101 S.Ct. 2153, 68 L.Ed.2d 640....

The fact that the right to counsel in a juvenile case arises from due process does not diminish its importance. A juvenile typically lacks sufficient maturity and good judgment to make good decisions consistently and sufficiently foresee the consequences of his actions. See, e.g., *Roper v. Simmons* (2005), 543 U.S. 551, 569–570, 125 S.Ct. 1183, 161 L.Ed.2d 1; *Planned Parenthood of Cent. Missouri v. Danforth* (1976), 428 U.S. 52, 102, 96 S.Ct. 2831, 49 L.Ed.2d 788 (Stevens, J., concurring in part and dissenting in part). Thus, "[t]he juvenile needs the assistance of counsel to cope with problems of law, to make skilled inquiry into the facts, to insist upon regularity of the proceedings and to ascertain whether he has a defense and to prepare and submit it." (Footnote omitted.) *Gault*, 387 U.S. at 36, 87 S.Ct. 1428, 18 L.Ed.2d 527.

Given the importance of counsel in juvenile proceedings, the General Assembly codified a juvenile's constitutional right to appointed counsel in the wake of Gault. Indeed, through R.C. 2151.352, the legislature provided a statutory right to appointed counsel that goes beyond constitutional requirements....

R.C. 2151.352...provides, "Counsel must be provided for a child not represented by the child's parent, guardian, or custodian. If the interests of two or more such parties conflict, separate counsel shall be provided for each of them."...

We have also incorporated constitutional safeguards in our rules of procedure. According to Juv.R. 4(A), "[e]very party shall have the right to be represented by counsel and every child * * * the right to appointed counsel if indigent." Similarly, Juv.R. 29(B) mandates that "[a]t the beginning of the hearing," the court inform unrepresented parties of their rights to counsel. Juv.R. 29(B)(3). The rules also recognize that, like an adult, a juvenile may waive his right to counsel. Juv.R. 3; Juv.R. 29(B)(3) and (4). This case directly implicates R.C. 2151.352's requirement that "[c]ounsel must be provided for a child not represented by the child's parent" and those requirements that arise from the application of Juv.R. 29(D) to that right.

C.S. avers that...R.C. 2151.352...—which states that "[c]ounsel must be provided for a child not represented by the child's parent, guardian, or custodian"—offends his constitutional right to counsel. The crux of C.S.'s claim is that the statute implicitly, and improperly, permits a child's parent (or guardian or custodian) to substitute for an attorney in juvenile court proceedings. He argues that the juvenile's right to counsel "as provided by the Sixth Amendment to the United States Constitution and Section Ten, Article One of the Ohio Constitution is fundamental" and cannot be satisfied by any "representation" by the child's parent. He also contends that the statute cannot be construed as creating a nonwaiveable right to counsel and that the fifth sentence must therefore be severed from the statute....

...The first prong of his contention is that the statute requires that counsel *must* be appointed for the juvenile and that the right cannot be waived if the child is not represented by a parent, guardian, or custodian. The second prong of the attack asserts that the statute therefore conflicts with Juv.R. 3, which provides that the "rights of a child * * * may be waived." He argues that this perceived conflict—between a right that cannot be waived per R.C. 2151.352 and a right that can be waived per Juv.R. 3—has led to divergent results in the courts, some of which have found that a parent, custodian, or guardian, rather than an attorney, can represent the juvenile.

In reading the statute, we must consider the definition of "represent," giving effect to the usual, normal, and customary meaning of the word, and being faithful to the language of and legislative intent behind the statute....

Taken alone, the ordinary use of the word "represent" does not necessarily shed light on its intended meaning in this context. At the time the statute was enacted, as now, the word "represent" had myriad meanings: "[t]o act for," "[t]o stand in the place of," Ballantine's Law Dictionary (3d Ed. 1969) 1095, or "to exhibit; to expose before the eyes," or "to stand in his place; to supply his place; to act as his substitute," Black's Law Dictionary (4th Ed. 1968) 1465. We believe, however, that the legislature's use of the word is clearer when taken in its constitutional context.

As C.S. acknowledges in his brief, "the General Assembly's intent in enacting [the language] was to protect the parties' due process rights in juvenile court in accordance with the then-recently issued decision, *In re Gault* [1967], 387 U.S. 1, 87 S.Ct. 1428, 18 L.Ed.2d 527." Clearly, the General Assembly's general intent in enacting R.C. 2151.352 was to ensure the juvenile's constitutional right to representation by an attorney—not representation by a parent, custodian, or guardian.

In enacting this statute, we presume, the General Assembly was mindful of the common law....Because the common law does not permit parents to appear pro se on behalf of their minor children in civil cases,...a fortiori, the common law would not permit parents to act pro se on behalf of their children in a delinquency case.

Moreover, at the time it enacted R.C. 2151.352, the Ohio legislature was well aware that this court has the exclusive authority to regulate, control, and define the practice of law, including prohibitions on lay representation, that we had held that "no one, other than an attorney, may appear in court as a representative of another, whether or not such representative is to receive a fee for his services," and that we had defined the practice of law as including representation before a court, as well as other tasks, including "all advice to clients and all actions taken for them in matters connected with the law...." We did not then, and we do not now, countenance a parent who is not an attorney representing a child in court in the capacity of counsel.

Indeed, "[i]t has long been recognized that the right to counsel is the right to the effective assistance of counsel." *McMann v. Richardson* (1970), 397 U.S. 759, 771, 90 S.Ct. 1441, 25 L.Ed.2d 763, fn. 4. Most parents are not attorneys and will not be able to provide effective counsel because they are not trained in the law. Because even the best-intentioned parents will lack the skill and familiarity with law and procedure to adequately represent their children in delinquency proceedings, they may not do so.

But that conclusion does not mean that we do not recognize the important role that a parent plays in the juvenile court process. In *Gault,* the court quoted a portion of the President's Crime Commission's Report: "'The presence of an independent legal representative of the child, *or of his parent,* is the keystone of the whole structure of guarantees that a minimum system of procedural justice requires.'" (Emphasis added.) 387 U.S. at 39, 87 S.Ct. 1428, 18 L.Ed.2d 527, fn. 65....

We believe that...the statute reflects the General Assembly's understanding that *Gault* held that the juvenile may waive his rights, including his right to counsel, see *Gault,* 387 U.S. at 41–42, 87 S.Ct. 1428, 18 L.Ed.2d 527, and that it codifies that right of waiver but only if the juvenile is advised by a parent in considering waiver. The Second District's assessment of the statute in *In re R.B.,* 166 Ohio App.3d 626, 2006-Ohio-264, 852 N.E.2d 1219, is similar.

There, the court of appeals found that the provision meant that "[i]f a child appears before the court who is not represented by the child's parent, guardian, or custodian, then the trial court 'must' provide counsel. Only if the child has some adult to advise him may the child knowingly and voluntarily waive his right to counsel. That construction of the statute serves an apparent purpose of assuring that a child's waiver of the right to counsel is knowing and voluntary, and it reconciles the quoted provisions, giving meaning to each." The Second District's approach is consistent with the holdings of other states' appellate courts in cases interpreting similar statutory language. *In re D.S.* (N.D. 1978), 263 N.W.2d 114, 120 ("We conclude * * * that [statutory language stating that '(c)ounsel must be provided for a child not represented by his parent, guardian, or custodian'] imposes a mandatory duty to provide counsel for a child at all stages of the proceedings under the Uniform Juvenile Court Act providing the child is not represented by his parent, guardian, or custodian [and that] this right to counsel cannot be waived by a child who is not represented by his parent, guardian, or custodian"); *A.C.G. v. State* (1974), 131 Ga.App. 156, 205 S.E.2d 435 ("The [juvenile's] right to counsel may be waived, however, unless the child is 'not represented by his parent, guardian, or custodian'").

We are also persuaded by the reasoning of the Supreme Court of Connecticut in its rejection of the notion of nonwaiver. As that court noted, "a per se rule of nonwaivability might actually frustrate a principal goal of juvenile law of encouraging children to accept responsibility for their transgressions and take an active role in their rehabilitation. * * * Without minimizing the significance of this inevitable tension [between the juvenile courts' roles of protecting society and nurturing and rehabilitating juveniles], we are persuaded that allowing a child to make an informed and deliberate choice about legal representation, if properly supervised by the trial court, can advance both the goal of control and that of treatment. * * * To mandate the presence of counsel * * * might serve to reduce the child's own sense of involvement and might enhance his perception of his own role as merely that of spectator. * * * [W]e believe that the waiver of counsel decision, *in itself,* can be a significant rehabilitative moment for the child." (Emphasis *sic.*) *In re Manuel R.* (1988), 207 Conn. 725, 734–736, 543 A.2d 719.

We hold that the word "represent" in...R.C. 2151.352 means to counsel or advise the juvenile in a delinquency proceeding. We further hold that in a delinquency proceeding, a juvenile may waive his constitutional right to counsel, subject to certain standards articulated below, if he is counseled and advised by his parent, custodian, or guardian. If the juvenile is not counseled by his parent, guardian, or custodian and has not consulted with an attorney, he may not waive his right to counsel.

In a delinquency case, a judge, acting as parens patriae, has the inherent authority to appoint counsel for the juvenile to determine whether he should waive his rights. We decline, however, to require a judge to do so in each case.[3] ...

... [W]e hold that a judge must appoint counsel for a juvenile if there is a conflict between the juvenile and his parent, custodian, or guardian on the question of whether counsel should be waived. Accord *United States v. M.I.M.* (C.A.1, 1991), 932 F.2d 1016, 1018–1019. In so doing, we recognize that no case in Ohio has held that a parent can waive the constitutional right of a juvenile in a delinquency proceeding, and we make clear that no parent has that authority.

Our holdings here comport with similar decisions in other state courts that have addressed this issue, with Juv.R. 3 (which expressly countenances waiver) and with the precepts of *Gault*, which were concerned with the fundamental fairness of juvenile proceeding for all parties concerned, including the juvenile, his parents, and the state.

In rendering our decision, we reinforce the vital role a parent can play in a delinquency proceeding.

"The law's concept of the family rests on the presumption that parents possess what a child lacks in maturity, experience, and capacity for judgment required for making life's difficult decisions." *Parham v. J.R.* (1979), 442 U.S. 584, 602, 99 S.Ct. 2493, 61 L.Ed.2d 101. *Gault* itself presented such a scenario, with a mother who was engaged fully in securing her child's best interests and whom the court recognized could help her son determine whether to waive his rights. See 387 U.S. at 42, 87 S.Ct. 1428, 18 L.Ed.2d 527. The value of the parent in such decision-making remains today in Ohio's juvenile courts, as juveniles decide whether to waive their right to counsel.

Having determined that the right to counsel may be waived, we must determine the indicia of a valid waiver.

In holding that the constitutional right to counsel may be waived by a juvenile, we apply the definition of waiver used in *State v. Foster*—an "intentional relinquishment or abandonment of a known right." 109 Ohio St.3d 1, 2006-Ohio-856, 845 N.E.2d 470, at ¶ 31. As in cases involving adults, there is a strong presumption against waiver of the constitutional right to counsel. *Johnson v. Zerbst* (1938), 304 U.S. 458, 464, 58 S.Ct. 1019, 82 L.Ed. 1461.

An effective waiver of the right to counsel by a juvenile must be voluntary, knowing, and intelligent. In a juvenile court proceeding in which the judge acts as parens patriae, the judge must scrupulously ensure that the juvenile fully understands, and intentionally and intelligently relinquishes, the right to counsel.... *Von Moltke v. Gillies* (1948), 332 U.S. 708, 722, 68 S.Ct. 316, 92 L.Ed. 309 ("It is the solemn duty of a federal judge before whom a defendant appears without counsel to make a thorough inquiry and to take all steps necessary to insure the fullest protection of this constitutional right at every stage of the proceedings"); *In re*

3. In essence, [the language] of R.C. 2151.352 is an "independent advice/interested adult" standard that we have declined to adopt, absent legislative action, in other circumstances. Though there may be a number of policy reasons to support the legislative imposition of a bright-line rule requiring a juvenile to consult with an attorney before waiving his constitutional rights, see, e.g., Minnesota Juv. Delinquency Proc.R. 3.04, Subdivision 1; *State ex rel. J.M. v. Taylor* (1981), 166 W.Va. 511, 276 S.E.2d 199, we do not believe that it is required by the Due Process Clause of the United States Constitution.

Manuel R., 207 Conn. at 737–738, 543 A.2d 719 ("It is now commonly recognized that courts should take 'special care' in scrutinizing a purported confession or waiver by a child"), citing *Haley*, 332 U.S. at 599, 68 S.Ct. 302, 92 L.Ed. 224.

In the discharge of that duty, the judge is to engage in a meaningful dialogue with the juvenile. Instead of relying solely on a prescribed formula or script for engaging a juvenile during the consideration of the waiver, the inquisitional approach is more consistent with the juvenile courts' goals, and is best suited to address the myriad factual scenarios that a juvenile judge may face in addressing the question of waiver.

We agree with the Supreme Court of Nebraska's recent holding that a totality-of-the-circumstances analysis is the proper test to be used in ascertaining whether there has been a valid waiver of counsel by a juvenile. *In re Dalton S.* (2007), 273 Neb. 504, 514, 730 N.W.2d 816. See, also, *Fare v. Michael C.* (1979), 442 U.S. 707, 725, 99 S.Ct. 2560, 61 L.Ed.2d 197 (applying totality-of-circumstances test to juvenile's waiver of rights). The judge must consider a number of factors and circumstances, including the age, intelligence, and education of the juvenile; the juvenile's background and experience generally and in the court system specifically; the presence or absence of the juvenile's parent, guardian, or custodian; the language used by the court in describing the juvenile's rights; the juvenile's conduct; the juvenile's emotional stability; and the complexity of the proceedings. *In re Dalton S.*, 273 Neb. at 515, 730 N.W.2d 816. Accord *Michael C.*, 442 U.S. at 725, 99 S.Ct. 2560, 61 L.Ed.2d 197.

In cases such as this one, in which a juvenile is charged with a serious offense, the waiver of the right to counsel must be made in open court, recorded, and in writing. If a written waiver has been executed, the juvenile court judge must consider the form used and the juvenile's literacy level to ensure that the juvenile has an intelligent understanding of the document and an appreciation of the gravity of signing it....

Though it is not dispositive, a key factor in the totality of the circumstances is the degree to which the juvenile's parent is capable of assisting and willing to assist the juvenile in the waiver analysis. See *Huff v. K.P.* (N.D.1981), 302 N.W.2d 779, 782. The juvenile court judge must be aware that not all parents may sufficiently counsel and advise, that is, "represent," their child in a delinquency proceeding.[4]

The juvenile court judge must be guided by Juv.R. 29 in the process of considering a waiver of counsel and in accepting an admission. Juv.R. 29(B) mandates that the juvenile court judge must advise a juvenile, at the commencement of the adjudicatory hearing, of certain rights, including the rights to counsel. Juv.R. 29(D) further mandates that before an admission can be accepted, the juvenile court judge must be satisfied that the admission is voluntarily made with the understanding of the nature of the allegations and the consequences of the admission and that by entering the admission, the juvenile is waiving the rights to confront witnesses and challenge evidence, to remain silent, and to introduce his own evidence.

As many Ohio courts of appeals recognize, "An admission in a juvenile proceeding, pursuant to Juv.R. 29, is analogous to a guilty plea made by an adult pursuant to Crim.R. 11

4. In some cases, a parent's failure to advocate for her child may arise from misguided Solomonic wisdom,...while in others, it may be virtually impossible to advocate effectively for the child because of parental responsibilities to the juvenile's victims,...because the parent herself is a victim, or the parent is otherwise in an antagonistic capacity,...or has "her own agenda, or [is] advocating her own best interest, which may or may not also be the child's."...In such circumstances, there is no fundamental fairness in permitting the parent to represent the child, even in the limited capacity of determining whether to waive counsel.

in that both require that a trial court personally address the defendant on the record with respect to the issues set forth in the rules." ...

We hold that in a juvenile delinquency case, the preferred practice is strict compliance with Juv.R. 29(D). We further hold, however, that if the trial court substantially complies with Juv.R. 29(D) in accepting an admission by a juvenile, the plea will be deemed voluntary absent a showing of prejudice by the juvenile or a showing that the totality of the circumstances does not support a finding of a valid waiver. For purposes of juvenile delinquency proceedings, substantial compliance means that in the totality of the circumstances, the juvenile subjectively understood the implications of his plea.

We believe that our holdings here reflect and reinforce the constitutional right to counsel that flows properly to the juvenile in a delinquency case, while being true to the General Assembly's intent in enacting R.C. 2151.352....

Although the magistrate secured representations from C.S. and his mother that they had signed the "rights papers," the record is not clear as to the knowingness of the waiver and the intelligent relinquishment of rights. At the time C.S. waived his rights, with his mother's assent, there were clear portents of additional, significant charges that would have been felony offenses had they been committed by an adult. In fact, after C.S. had waived counsel, the magistrate specifically mentioned the possibility that additional felony charges could be forthcoming.

There is ample evidence in the record to suggest that from the time C.S. first spoke to police until he waived his right to counsel in the courtroom, his focus was on being committed so that he could be close to his older brother, who had previously been committed to the custody of the Department of Youth Services. His rationale for the admission cannot be said to be intelligent, as evidenced by the judge's conclusion that the two youths should not be housed together.

An important aspect of our consideration in this case is our concern that there was not any meaningful advice rendered to C.S. in his decision to waive counsel. We acknowledge that an inference can be drawn that this family, through its past dealings with the juvenile courts, may have had an understanding of the process in which C.S. was engaged. But we are not satisfied that there was a sufficient showing that Ms. S. was in a position to render any meaningful advice to her son in this case.

Ms. S. had not spoken with her son since his arrest, and she had not had an opportunity to read the police report detailing his prodigious criminal activity before agreeing that he should waive his right to legal counsel. The magistrate did not ask about those facts until after he had secured the waiver of counsel and accepted C.S.'s admissions. We would not condone an attorney's failure to meet with a client prior to advising him to waive his rights to counsel or appearing before a judge for a plea hearing, and we are not satisfied that any meaningful advice was offered by Ms. S. in this matter.

Ms. S.'s only inquiry during the hearing related not to the evidence against her son, to the controlling law, or to her son's rights. Rather, like her son, she was focused on whether C.S. could be placed in the same facility in which his brother was housed. Her focus on the place of confinement was not based on the services available to her son in a particular facility but, rather, on a pragmatic concern: her means of transportation were limited, and it would be easier for her to visit her children if they were in the same institution.

In the circumstances before us, we are not persuaded that the waiver of counsel was valid. We thus vacate the court of appeals' judgment to the extent that it held that there was a sufficient showing of a valid waiver of counsel, and we remand the cause to the juvenile court. In so doing, we do not intimate any opinion on the disposition rendered by the magistrate.

We recognize that this case presents one of the difficult ones for a juvenile court. Despite his youth, C.S. has a significant history of alcohol and drug abuse, violence, and other behaviors that are destructive both to himself and to the community. He is on a collision course with tragedy. The magistrate's clear frustration with C.S., and with the limits of the juvenile court system, is understandable, as is a significant period of incarceration. But that frustration, and the judge's broad discretion in imposing disposition, cannot override the need for the careful consideration of the fairness and due process rights that *Gault* demands and the application of those principles in all delinquency cases.

Judgment reversed and cause remanded....

LANZINGER, J., dissenting.

I would affirm the judgment of the Licking County Court of Appeals with respect to its holding that there was a sufficient showing of the valid waiver of counsel in this case.

The record reveals that C.S. acknowledged reading and signing a form that included the statement "You have the right to be represented by an attorney at all stages of this proceeding" and informed him that an attorney will be appointed if "you cannot afford an attorney and you qualify under State guidelines." The waiver of attorney that C.S. and his mother signed stated, "The undersigned have read the instructions concerning our right to an attorney and the right to a Court-appointed attorney, if applicable. Knowing and understanding these rights, we hereby waive our right to be represented by an attorney or Court-appointed attorney. We further understand that we can be represented by an attorney in the future simply by advising the Court of our intention to do so." During a colloquy with the magistrate regarding his rights, C.S. answered "yes" to the question "Do you understand that?" at least nine times. The magistrate in juvenile court determined that a valid waiver of counsel was made in accepting the plea....

The words that the majority focuses on are "Counsel must be provided for a child not represented by the child's parent, guardian, or custodian." R.C. 2151.352 is a statute that relates to all juvenile proceedings, not simply delinquency adjudications. The sentence merely explains that counsel must be available (i.e., be provided) at a juvenile proceeding if a child's parent, guardian, or custodian is not. There is no question that a juvenile is entitled to representation by legal counsel at all stages of juvenile proceedings. As the majority rightly observes, a juvenile's right to counsel is not the same as the right to be "represented" by a parent, guardian, or custodian. Yet by creating a new requirement that a parent offer "meaningful advice" before a child may waive the right to counsel, the majority seems to consider parental and attorney advice to be equal, at least on the issue of waiver.

The juvenile rules allow waiver of counsel in juvenile proceedings with consent of the court. Juv.R. 3. At the beginning of an adjudicatory hearing, the juvenile court shall "[i]nform unrepresented parties of their right to counsel and determine if those parties are waiving their right to counsel"; "[a]ppoint counsel for any unrepresented party under Juv.R. 4(A) who does not waive the right to counsel"; and "[i]nform any unrepresented party who waives the right to counsel of the right: to obtain counsel at any stage of the proceedings, to remain silent, to offer evidence, to cross-examine witnesses, and, upon request, to have a record of all proceedings made, at public expense if indigent." Juv.R. 29(B)(3) through (5).

Before permitting a waiver of counsel, the court has a duty to make an inquiry to determine that the waiver is of "a fully known right" and is voluntarily, knowingly, and intelligently made. *In re Gault* (1967), 387 U.S. 1, 42, 87 S.Ct. 1428, 18 L.Ed.2d 527.... The "right to the assistance of counsel implicitly embodies a 'correlative right to dispense with a lawyer's help.'" *Faretta v. California* (1975), 422 U.S. 806, 814, 95 S.Ct. 2525, 45 L.Ed.2d 562, quoting *Adams v. United States ex rel. McCann* (1942), 317 U.S. 269, 279, 63 S.Ct. 236, 87 L.Ed. 268.

I agree that the totality of circumstances should be considered to ascertain the validity of the waiver but disagree with the majority's emphasis on C.S.'s mother's intent. "Meaningful advice" from a parent was not required for a valid waiver until now, and any assistance that C.S.'s mother offered him would have been considered part of the totality of the circumstances the court would consider in determining whether C.S. validly waived the right to counsel. Nothing in rule or statute requires "a sufficient showing that [the parent is] in a position to render * * * meaningful advice to her son."... Besides being unnecessary, such an ambiguous standard will be difficult to apply.

C.S.'s mother's motivation in having her two children placed in the same facility should not invalidate C.S.'s waiver when, as the record shows, he waived his right to counsel and admitted to the charges against him after a colloquy with the judge that occurred in open court.

I agree with the court of appeals that "[t]he record reflects that appellant's admission to the charges was given knowingly, intelligently, and voluntarily and that the trial court obtained a valid waiver of Appellant's right to counsel." I therefore respectfully dissent.

a. What is the legal basis for the court's holding? Is it statutory or constitutional?

b. Does the dissent disagree with the rule articulated by the majority? If not, what is the basis for the disagreement?

c. *Nonwaivable right to counsel.* Some jurisdictions prohibit waiver of the right to counsel by a juvenile under certain circumstances. See, e.g., Ark. Code Ann. §§ 9-27-317(d)–(f) (2010) (no waiver where parent has filed petition against juvenile or juvenile is likely to be committed to an institution or juvenile is designated an extended juvenile jurisdiction offender); Iowa Code § 232.11(2) (2010) (child cannot waive right to counsel at detention, waiver, adjudicatory, and dispositional hearings); Ky. Rev. Stat. Ann. § 610.060(2)(a) (Baldwin 2010) (court shall not accept plea or conduct adjudicatory hearing in any case for which court intends to impose detention or commitment unless child is represented by counsel); La. Child. Code Ann. Art. 810(D) (West 2010) (child cannot waive right to counsel if charged with felony, in probation or parole revocation proceedings, or in proceedings where it is recommended that child be placed in mental hospital, psychiatric unit, or substance abuse facility); N.J. Stat. Ann. § 2A:4A-39(b)(3) (West 2010) (incompetent juvenile may not waive any right); Tex. Fam. Code § 51.10(b) (Vernon 2010) (child's right to counsel shall not be waived at transfer, adjudicatory, dispositional, commitment, and mental health proceedings); Wis. Stat. § 938.23(1m)(a) (2010) (juvenile younger than fifteen may not waive right to counsel). On the other hand, the court in *C.S.* refused to hold that the child could not waive his right to counsel. Do you find the reasons for permitting waiver of the right persuasive? Why shouldn't a child be able to waive his right to counsel? What kind of right cannot be waived by the rights holder? If the reason for denying waiver of the right is a concern that the child lacks judgment, why should the child have any rights? And why should we hold the child accountable for his misbehavior under these circumstances?

d. *Waivable right to counsel.* Most states permit the child to waive his right to counsel; nevertheless, states limit the circumstances under which a minor may waive the right. For example, a few states require the child to consult with counsel before making the decision to waive.

Alaska Stat. Ann. § 47.12.090(a) (West 2010) (if charged with felony-level offense, child cannot waive right to counsel until child consults with counsel); Fla. R. 8.165 (waiver only after child had meaningful opportunity to confer with counsel about right, consequences of waiver, and any other factors that would assist child in making decision); Md. Code Ann. Cts. & Jud. Proc. § 3-8A-20(b)(3)(i) (2010) (child may not waive right to counsel unless child is in presence of counsel and has consulted with counsel); Mont. Code Ann. § 41-5-331(2)(c) (2010) (when youth younger than sixteen and his parents disagree, youth may waive right to counsel only on advice of counsel); N.J. Stat. Ann. § 2A:4A-39(b)(1) (2010) (child cannot waive any rights except in presence of and after consultation with counsel); Va. Code Ann. § 16.1-266(C)(3) (Michie 2010) (child charged with felony may waive only after child consults with an attorney). Should children be required to consult with counsel before making a decision about waiving the right to counsel? In a review of ninety-nine reported cases challenging a juvenile's waiver of his right to counsel, Mary Berkheiser found that eighty of the waivers were overturned on appeal. In more than 30 percent of the cases, juveniles were not advised of their right to counsel at all; in other cases, the record made no mention of advising youths of their rights or of the waiver proceedings. In some of the cases, courts provided an explanation of rights but never followed up with any colloquy regarding why the juveniles were waiving the right to counsel, engaged in a less than sufficient inquiry about waiver, or even accepted waivers that were obviously involuntary. Mary Berkheiser, *The Fiction of Juvenile Right to Counsel: Waiver in the Juvenile Courts*, 54 Fla. L. Rev. 577, 609–611 (2002). Berkheiser concludes that juveniles in delinquency proceedings should have a nonwaivable right to counsel because of their limited decision-making abilities and the lack of understanding of their legal rights. *Id.* at 627–630, 637–638. Do you agree?

Other states require parental participation or consultation in the waiver decision. Ariz. Rev. Stat. Ann. § 8-221 (West 2010) (right to counsel waived by both parent and child); Ark. Code Ann. § 9-27-317(a)(3) (West 2009) (parent must agree with juvenile's decision to waive right to counsel); Ind. Code Ann. § 31-32-5-1 (West 2010) (parent may waive right if parent has no adverse interest to child, parent has had "meaningful consultation" with child, and child knowingly and voluntarily joins waiver); La. Child. Code Ann. Art. 810(A) (West 2010) (child may waive right to counsel after consultation with attorney or parent subject to certain exceptions); Mich. Comp. Laws Ann. § 712a.17c(3) (West 2010) (child may not waive right to counsel if parent or guardian *ad litem* objects); N.H. Rev. Stat. Ann. § 169-B:12(II) (2010) (court may accept waiver of right to counsel only when minor is represented by nonhostile parent, and both parent and child agree to waive); 42 Pa. Cons. Stat. Ann. § 6337 (West 2010) (parent may waive child's right to counsel if there is no conflict of interest between parent and child); Va. Code Ann. § 16.1-266(C)(3) (2010) (in nonfelony case, child and parent consent in writing to waiver, and waiver is consistent with interests of child); Wash. Rev. Code § 13.40.140(10) (2010) (parent must waive right for juvenile younger than twelve). On the other hand, some states specifically prohibit parental waiver of the child's right to counsel. Ky. Rev. Stat. Ann. § 610.060(1)(e) (Baldwin 2010) (rights of child may not be waived by parent); N.J. Stat. Ann. § 2A:4A-39(b)(1) (West 2010) (parent may not waive rights of competent juvenile); Md. Code Ann. Cts. & Jud. Proc. § 3-8A-20(b)(2) (2010) (parent may not waive child's right to assistance of counsel). Should a parent have the authority to waive the child's right to counsel? What kind of right may be waived by a third party? And is a parent more likely to make a "better" decision?

Are juveniles better off if they do not have lawyers? A number of studies have found that juveniles fare worse when they are represented by counsel, even when controlling for type of offense and prior record. M. A. Bortner, Inside a Juvenile Court: The Tarnished

Ideal of Individualized Justice 139–140 (1982); William Vaughan Stapleton & Lee E. Teitelbaum, In Defense of Youth: A Study of the Role of Counsel in American Juvenile Courts 64–65 (1972); Stevens H. Clarke & Gary G. Koch, *Juvenile Court: Therapy or Crime Control and Do Lawyers Make a Difference?* 14 Law & Soc'y Rev. 263, 304–306 (1980); David Duffee & Larry Siegel, *The Organization Man: Legal Counsel in the Juvenile Court*, 7 Crim. L. Bull. 544, 548–549 (1971); Barry C. Feld, *In re Gault Revisited: A Cross-State Comparison of the Right to Counsel in Juvenile Court*, 34 Crime & Delinq. 393, 393 (1988); David W. Hayeslip, Jr., *The Impact of Defense Attorney Presence on Juvenile Court Dispositions*, 30 Juv. & Fam. Ct. J. 9, 12 (1979). Even using a detailed regression analysis and controlling for disparities in seriousness of offense, prior criminal history, and detention status, researchers still found that representation by counsel had an independent—and negative—effect on case outcomes. Barry C. Feld, *The Right to Counsel in Juvenile Court: An Empirical Study of When Lawyers Appear and the Difference They Make*, 79 J. Crim. L. & Criminology 1185, 1239, 1259, 1260, 1306–1312 (1989). Feld suggests a number of different reasons for the effect, including incompetent juvenile defense lawyers, court-appointed counsel who feel they cannot upset judges for fear of losing future appointments, juvenile judges who may treat represented juveniles more formally and severely, and attorneys who may view the role of counsel for the child as nonadversarial. *Id.* at 1330–1334.

Janet Ainsworth notes that inadequate and incompetent lawyering may be systemic. Many public defenders assign their newest lawyers to juvenile court, who then must cope with heavy caseloads, inadequate supervision, and the temptation to cut corners in order to expedite case processing, a temptation encouraged by the judges themselves. Janet E. Ainsworth, *Re-Imagining Childhood and Reconstructing the Legal Order: The Case for Abolishing the Juvenile Court*, 69 N.C. L. Rev. 1083, 1127–1128 (1991). In fact, judges may be antagonistic to a juvenile court model that envisions zealous advocacy on behalf of children and may direct that hostility to both lawyer and client. *Id.* at 1127. Attorneys for children also may feel tremendous pressure to cooperate with the court, rather than zealously defending their clients; when coupled with ambiguous feelings about the appropriate role of defense counsel in juvenile court, lawyers for kids may consciously seek harsher penalties, believing them to be in the clients' best interests. *Id.* at 1127–1129. If these studies are correct, then isn't a decision to waive the right to counsel a rational one?

e. *Validity of waiver.* A criminal defendant may waive his Sixth Amendment right to counsel but only if it is made knowingly and intelligently. *Johnson v. Zerbst*, 304 U.S. 458 (1938). Nevertheless, there is a presumption against waiver, which "imposes the serious and weighty responsibility upon the trial judge of determining whether there is an intelligent and competent waiver by the accused" on the record. *Id.* at 465. Although a criminal defendant has a Sixth Amendment right to counsel, he also has a constitutional right to represent himself. In *Faretta v. Californ*ia, 422 U.S. 806 (1975), the United States Supreme Court held that a criminal defendant may voluntarily and knowingly waive his right to counsel and represent himself. *Id.* at 835. The trial court must ensure that the defendant is "made aware of the dangers and disadvantages of self-representation, so that the record will establish that 'he knows what he is doing and his choice is made with eyes wide open.'" *Id.*

How should a juvenile court determine the validity of a minor's waiver of the right to counsel? One possibility is the application of a juvenile totality-of-the-circumstances rule that requires special scrutiny of juvenile waivers. Lucy S. McGough & Lauren Cangelosi, *Lost Causes*, 65 La. L. Rev. 1125, 1133 (2005). It appears, however, that the majority of states apply the "adult rule" and consider the totality of the circumstances in assessing whether the waiver of the right to counsel was knowing and voluntary. *Id.* See also Robert E. Shepherd, Jr., *Juvenile's Waiver of the Right to Counsel*, 13 CRIM. JUST. 38, 39 (1998). The court in *C.S.* applied a totality-of-the-circumstances test to determine if the waiver of the right to counsel was knowing, intelligent, and voluntary. Among the factors to be considered are "the age, intelligence, and education of the juvenile; the juvenile's background and experience generally and in the court system specifically; the presence or absence of the juvenile's parent, guardian, or custodian; the language used by the court in describing the juvenile's rights; the juvenile's conduct; the juvenile's emotional stability; and the complexity of the proceedings." *In re C.S.*, 874 N.E.2d at 1193. Is this the adult rule or a juvenile rule? Of the many factors the court could consider, which seemed dispositive?

Is there socioscientific evidence to support the claims that children do not understand their rights and have limited decision-making ability in the context of waiver of the right to counsel? Consider this excerpt:

> Several studies have found that prior experience with the legal system is unrelated to level of understanding of Fifth and Sixth Amendment rights. Juveniles who have been referred to court on multiple occasions do not demonstrate significantly better comprehension than those who are in court for the first time. This is an especially important finding in light of the fact that, in assessing the validity of a waiver in terms of the totality of the circumstances test, courts routinely consider youths' prior experience with the legal system as a factor, and typically assume that understanding is enhanced by prior experience in the system....
>
> ...[O]f the four statements in the *Miranda* warnings, juveniles most often misunderstand the right to counsel. Young people frequently have mistaken beliefs about who counsel is or what she does. They tend to believe that defense attorneys—especially public defenders—work for the court. They also frequently believe that the attorney's job is to defend only the innocent, and that the attorney should turn in a client if he learns that the client is guilty. This is consistent with the finding that, in response to hypothetical vignettes, younger adolescents were significantly less likely to assert the right to counsel when the story character was guilty than when the character was innocent. Among adults, the opposite was true: they were more likely to invoke the right to counsel when the character was guilty than when she was innocent. Of great interest, Ferguson and Douglas, who interviewed ninety delinquent subjects, reported that many explained that they had not retained counsel because they were guilty.
>
> Another study reported that most younger adolescents, and a substantial proportion of fifteen-year olds, believed that attorneys are authorized to tell judges and police what was discussed in their confidential conversations. In yet another study, juvenile offenders were asked why they must be truthful with their attorneys. Nearly one-third reported that it was so the lawyer could decide whether to advocate for them, report their guilt to the court, or decide whether to release them or send them up....
>
> Using vignettes, recent research has also inquired specifically about the connection between psychosocial characteristics and young people's legal decision making. Grisso and his colleagues found, for example, that juveniles fifteen and under were significantly more compliant with authority (i.e., they confessed to police, provided full disclosure to counsel, and accepted a plea agreement) than youths aged sixteen to seventeen, or adults. Younger juveniles were much less able than older ones to recognize risks associated with waiving their rights or to think in terms of long-term consequences, and they significantly underestimated how unpleasant the negative consequences would be. Moreover, compared

to adults, all subjects under eighteen significantly underestimated the likelihood of negative consequences flowing from their legal decisions. Finally, on measures of resistance to peer influence, young juveniles who said they would remain silent at interrogation were much more likely than older youths to change their minds and confess when they were told that a peer had recommended that they confess. Among those who initially confessed, however, young juveniles were more likely to stick with that choice than older youths when told that a peer had recommended that they remain silent. In other words, among young adolescents, there was a bias toward compliance with adult authority that was reinforced by peers.

The high rates of impairment in juveniles' understanding of, appreciation of, and ability to exercise their right to counsel in either the interrogation setting or the courtroom [indicate] to us that special protections are required to insure that these constitutionally guaranteed rights are accessible to kids. The research literature tells us that juveniles under fifteen are significantly impaired in their cognitive functioning. While most research indicates that adolescents aged fifteen and older have cognitive understanding that is closer to that of an adult, the judgment of older youths is nonetheless impaired because they tend to discount risks, fail to appreciate the negative consequences of alternatives, fail to consider long-term consequences, and are susceptible to external pressures to make decisions that may not be in their best interests. Moreover, the research reported here has almost certainly underestimated juveniles' impairments, as research has not been carried out under real-world conditions of stress. In light of all these considerations, we believe that fairness requires that juveniles have the benefit of a nonwaivable right to counsel at every step in delinquency proceedings in order to fulfill the promise of Gault.

Donna M. Bishop and Hillary B. Farber, *The Promise of In re Gault: Promoting and Protecting the Right to Counsel in Juvenile Court*, 60 Rutgers L. Rev. 125, 164, 165–167 (2007). Do you agree with the authors' contention that juveniles are too impaired to knowingly, intelligently, and voluntarily waive the right to trial counsel?

8. Article 40(2)(b)(ii) of the United Nations Convention on the Rights of the Child provides that every child accused of infringing the penal law has a guarantee "to have legal or other appropriate assistance in the preparation and presentation of his or her defense." Convention on the Rights of the Child art. 40(2)(b)(ii), Nov. 20, 1989, 1577 U.N.T.S. 3. In its interpretation of the Convention, the UN Committee on the Rights of the Child also considers other United Nations rules and guidelines. Thus, Rule 15(1) of the United Nations Standard Minimum Rules for the Administration of Juvenile Justice (the "Beijing Rules"), adopted by the General Assembly on November 25, 1985, states that "the juvenile shall have the right to be represented by a legal adviser or to apply for free legal aid where there is no provision for such aid in the country." United Nations Standard Minimum Rules for the Administration of Justice ("The Beijing Rules"), G.A. Res. 40/33, U.N. GAOR, 40th Sess., Annex, Supp. No. 53, at 207 U.N. Doc. A/40/53 (1985). Similarly, Rule 18(a) of the United Nations Rules for the Protection of Juveniles Deprived of Their Liberty states that juveniles who are detained "should have the right to legal counsel and be enabled to apply for free legal aid, where such aid is available, and to communicate regularly with their legal advisers." United Nations Rules for the Protection of Juveniles Deprived of Their Liberty, G.A. Res. 45/113, U.N. GAOR, 45th Sess., Annex, Supp. No. 49A, at 205 U.N. Doc. A/45/113 (1990). The Committee on the Rights of the Child has expressed concern when a state party has failed to provide legal representation. For example, after reviewing Nigeria's Second Report, the Committee "urge[d] the State party to, in particular... guarantee

that all persons below 18 have the right to appropriate legal assistance and defence." Nigeria CRC/C/15/Add. 257 (2005), at para. 81(b). Do you think if the United States were a state party, it would be in compliance with the Convention's mandate?

b. RIGHT TO A JURY TRIAL

MCKEIVER V. PENNSYLVANIA
Supreme Court of the United States
403 U.S. 528 (1971)
(See Section II.B. above, p. 121)

NOTES AND QUESTIONS

1. Currently, twenty-eight states and the District of Columbia deny juveniles the right to a jury trial in delinquency proceedings. Although claims have been made that the juvenile system has become more punitive and thus virtually indistinguishable from the criminal system, courts in these jurisdictions routinely have rejected constitutional challenges on the ground that the juvenile system is still protective and rehabilitative in nature. See, e.g., *David G. v. Pollard ex rel. County of Pima*, 86 P.3d 364 (Ariz. 2004) (forcing juvenile to be tried by a jury does not promote the informality and flexibility that juvenile courts strive to achieve and stigmatizes juvenile); *In the Interest of D.J.*, 817 So.2d 26 (La. 2002) (noting disparity in penalties and limits posed by statute on punishing offenders younger than fourteen, "we are 'not yet ready to spell the doom of the juvenile court system by requiring jury trials in juvenile adjudications'"); *In the Interest of J.F.*, 714 A.2d 467 (Pa. Super. Ct. 1998) ("concern for the juvenile remains a cornerstone of our system of juvenile justice"); *State v. Chavez*, 180 P.3d 1250 (2008) (juvenile justice system is not so altered that juveniles charged with violent and serious violent offenses are entitled to jury trial because these juveniles still remain eligible for rehabilitative programs while incarcerated).

Nevertheless, at least twelve states recognize a general right to a jury trial in delinquency proceedings. Alaska Stat. § 47.12.110 (2010); Mass. Ann. Laws ch. 119, §§ 55A, 56 (Law. Co-op. 2010); Mich. Comp. Laws Ann. § 712A.17(2) (2010); Mont. Code Ann. § 41-5-1502 (2010) (on demand); N.M. Stat. Ann. § 32A-2-16 (2010) (to same extent as if an adult); Okla. Stat. tit. 10A, § 2-2-401 (2010); Tex. Fam. Code Ann. § 54.03 (2010); Va. Code Ann. § 16.1-272 (2010) (in any case in which juvenile is indicted); W. Va. Code § 49-5-6 (2010) (for any act which if committed by adult would expose adult to incarceration); Wyo. Stat. § 14-6-223 (2010) (on demand); Wis. Stat. § 48.31 (2010); *In re L.M.*, 186 P.3d 164 (Kan. 2008). In 2008, the Kansas Supreme Court in *In re L.M.* reconsidered its prior holding denying juveniles the right to a jury trial in delinquency proceedings. The Court stated:

> [T]he Kansas Legislature has significantly changed the language of the Kansas Juvenile Offender Code (KJOC) since the [Kansas Supreme Court] decided this issue 24 years ago. The juvenile code is now called the Revised Kansas Juvenile Justice Code [KJJC]....

In 1982, the KJOC was focused on rehabilitation and the State's parental role in providing guidance, control, and discipline. However, under the KJJC, the focus has shifted to protecting the public, holding juveniles accountable for their behavior and choices, and making juveniles more productive and responsible members of society. These purposes are more aligned with the legislative intent for the adult sentencing statutes, which include protecting the public by incarcerating dangerous offenders for a long period of time, holding offenders accountable by prescribing appropriate consequences for their actions, and encouraging offenders to be more productive members of society by considering their individual characteristics, circumstances, needs, and potentialities in determining their sentences.

In addition to being more aligned with the purpose of the criminal sentencing statutes, the KJJC also incorporates language similar to that found in the Kansas Criminal Code, and the Kansas Code of Criminal Procedure. Under the KJJC, a juvenile is required to plead guilty, not guilty, or nolo contendere like adults charged with a crime.... [A] "dispositional proceeding" under the KJOC is now referred to as a "sentencing proceeding" in the KJJC. The "State youth center" referred to in the KJOC, is now called a "Juvenile correctional facility." Moreover, the KJJC emulates the language of the Kansas Criminal Code when it refers to the term of commitment to a juvenile correctional facility as a "term of incarceration."...

The legislature also emulated the structure of the Kansas Sentencing Guidelines when it established a sentencing matrix for juveniles based on the level of the offense committed and, in some cases, the juvenile's history of juvenile adjudications....

The KJJC is also similar to the adult sentencing guidelines in imposing a term of aftercare on any juvenile sentenced in accordance with the juvenile placement matrix. Another similarity between the KJJC and the adult sentencing guidelines is the juvenile offender's opportunity to earn good time credits to reduce his or her term of incarceration.

In addition to reflecting the provisions of the sentencing guidelines, the KJJC also establishes sentencing options that are similar to those available for adult offenders. Both adults and juveniles may be sentenced to probation; a community-based program; house arrest; a short-term behavior-modification program like a sanctions house or conservation camp; placement in an out-of-home facility; or incarceration in a correctional facility. The district court also has authority to order both adults and juveniles to attend counseling; drug and alcohol evaluations; mediation; or educational programs. In addition, the district court may require both adults and juveniles to perform charitable or community service; pay restitution; or pay a fine....

... [T]he legislature has removed some of the protective provisions that made the juvenile system more child-cognizant and confidential, a key consideration in the *McKeiver* plurality decision....

... [U]nder the KJJC, the official file must be open to the public unless a judge orders it to be closed for juveniles under the age of 14 based on finding that it is in the best interests of the juvenile. Similarly, law enforcement records and municipal court records for any juvenile age 14 and over are subject to the same disclosure restrictions as the records for adults. Only juveniles under the age of 14 may have their law enforcement and municipal records kept confidential. The legislature has also eliminated the presumption of confidentiality for hearings, opening all hearings to the public unless the juvenile is under the age of 16 and the judge concludes that a public hearing would not be in the juvenile's best interests.

These changes to the juvenile justice system have eroded the benevolent parens patriae character that distinguished it from the adult criminal system. The United States Supreme

> Court relied on the juvenile justice system's characteristics of fairness, concern, sympathy, and paternal attention in concluding that juveniles were not entitled to a jury trial. *McKeiver,* 403 U.S. at 550, 91 S.Ct. 1976. Likewise, this court relied on that parens patriae character in reaching its decision [twenty-four years ago]. However, because the juvenile justice system is now patterned after the adult criminal system, we conclude that the changes have superseded the *McKeiver* and [our] Courts' reasoning and those decisions are no longer binding precedent for us to follow. Based on our conclusion that the Kansas juvenile justice system has become more akin to an adult criminal prosecution, we hold that juveniles have a constitutional right to a jury trial under the Sixth and Fourteenth Amendments....
>
> ...Because the KJJC has lost the parens patriae character of the former KJOC and has transformed into a system for prosecuting juveniles charged with committing crimes, we conclude that the proceedings under the KJJC fit within the meaning of the phrase "all prosecutions" as set forth in § 10 [of the Kansas Constitution], and juveniles have a right to a jury trial under the Kansas Constitution.

Id. at 168–170, 172. Are you persuaded by the Kansas Supreme Court's view that the juvenile justice system is punitive? If so, is the Supreme Court's reasoning in *McKeiver* still valid?

2. Is there a point at which a jury trial in a juvenile proceeding is constitutionally mandated? Some states, for example, extend the right to a jury trial to those proceedings in which the juvenile may receive a criminal sentence in addition to or in lieu of a traditional juvenile disposition. Known as blended sentences, these statutory schemes typically permit juvenile court judges, after adjudication, to impose a criminal sentence of imprisonment but suspend imposition of that sentence pending the successful completion of some juvenile disposition. On the other hand, seventeen states have criminal blended-sentencing laws. In these jurisdictions, juveniles who have been tried in criminal courts may receive juvenile dispositions, in lieu of or in addition to an adult criminal sentence.

Under what circumstances would a state's failure to provide jury trials to juveniles who receive blended sentences violate the Sixth Amendment? The Due Process Clause of the Fourteenth Amendment?

3. In *Blakely v. Washington*, 542 U.S. 296 (2004), the United States Supreme Court held that no sentence imposed in a criminal case after a jury trial may be enhanced beyond the statutory maximum for that offense unless the aggravating fact is found by the jury. A year later, the United States Supreme Court reiterated its position in *United States v. Booker*, 543 U.S. 220 (2005), that the maximum sentence a judge may impose must rest "solely on the basis of the facts reflected in the jury verdict or admitted by the defendant." In other words, any factor required to impose a greater term must be decided by the jury and not the judge. The Supreme Court made clear that to impose a sentence greater than the statutory maximum, without the necessary factual findings from the jury that would warrant an enhanced sentence, violates the defendant's right to a jury trial under the Sixth Amendment to the United States Constitution. Consider again blended-sentencing schemes. If a juvenile receives a jury trial because he is eligible to receive a blended sentence and is adjudicated delinquent, must the jury make the necessary factual findings to warrant the imposition of an adult criminal sentence? See *State v. D.H.*, 901 N.E.2d 209 (Ohio 2009), cert. denied, 129 S.Ct. 2775 (2009); Barry C. Feld, *The Constitutional Tension between Apprendi and McKeiver: Sentence Enhancements Based on Delinquency Convictions and the Quality of Justice in Juvenile Courts*, 38 WAKE FOREST L. REV. 1111 (2003); Andrea Knox, Note, *Blakely*

and Blended Sentencing: A Constitutional Challenge to Sentencing Child "Criminals," 70 OHIO ST. L.J. 1261 (2009).

4. *Right to a speedy trial.* The Sixth Amendment provides, in part, that "[i]n all criminal prosecutions, the accused shall enjoy the right to a speedy...trial." In *Barker v. Wingo*, 407 U.S. 514 (1972), the United States Supreme Court established a four-factor balancing test in determining whether a criminal defendant's right to a speedy trial has been violated. The first factor, the length of the delay, is the "triggering mechanism" for an initial finding that the delay is "presumptively prejudicial"; without such a finding, a court need not consider the other factors. Second, the court must consider the reason for the delay: whether it is attributable to the state or the defendant, whether the state has acted in bad faith, or whether there is some neutral reason, such as docket congestion, that resulted in postponement of trial. Third, the court must determine whether the defendant asserted his right to a speedy trial. Finally, the court must assess the degree of prejudice to the defendant resulting from the delay, taking into account the defendant's ability to defend himself after a long delay, the length of the defendant's pretrial incarceration, and the anxiety that arises from a pending criminal case.

Are juveniles entitled to a speedy trial in juvenile court proceedings? The United States Supreme Court has never held that juveniles have a federal constitutional right to a speedy trial; consequently, states vary greatly in their approach to juvenile speedy-trial rights. Some states have held that juveniles do have constitutional speedy-trial rights. See, e.g., *R.D.S.M. v. Intake Officer*, 565 P.2d 855 (Alaska 1977) (juveniles have a right to a speedy trial under both federal and state constitution); *In re Thomas J.*, 811 A.2d 310 (Md. 2002) (juveniles have a right to speedy trial under Due Process Clause of Fourteenth Amendment and Article 21 of Maryland Declaration of Rights); *In re Benjamin L.*, 708 N.E.2d 156 (N.Y. 1999) (right to speedy trial guaranteed by state Due Process Clause extends to juveniles in delinquency proceedings, applying a five-factor test); *In re Eric A. L.*, 153 P.3d 32 (Nev. 2007) (juveniles have right to speedy trial under Due Process Clause, applying five-factor test articulated by New York Court of Appeals in *In re Benjamin L.*); *State v. Hoffman*, 78 P.3d 1289 (Wash. 2003) (juvenile speedy-trial rule designed to protect constitutional right to a speedy trial). On the other hand, twenty-seven states provide a time limit for juvenile adjudications through state statutes or court rules. See Jeffrey A. Butts and Joseph B. Sanborn Jr., *Is Juvenile Justice Just Too Slow?* 83 JUDICATURE 16, 20 (1999). In other jurisdictions, local court rules may require the adjudicatory hearing to be held within a certain time. *Id.* However, almost all states (forty-three) provide a time limit for juveniles being detained prior to adjudication. *Id.* at 22. Jeffrey A. Butts, Office of Juvenile Justice and Delinquency Prevention, Delays in Juvenile Court Processing of Delinquency Cases Fact Sheet 60 (March 1997). Juveniles tried in federal court who have been detained pending trial have a right to an adjudication within thirty days of detention under the Federal Juvenile Delinquency Act, 18 U.S.C. § 5036 (2010).

The Institute of Judicial Administration and the American Bar Association (IJA-ABA) recommend adjudication within thirty days of the complaint and disposition within sixty days of the complaint for youths who have been released. Juvenile Justice Standards Relating to Interim Status § 7.10 (Institute of Judicial Administration and the American Bar Association, 1996). For youths who have been detained, the IJA-ABA standards recommend fifteen days to adjudication and thirty days to disposition. *Id.*

The Convention on the Rights of the Child also mandates that every child charged with a violation of the penal law has a guarantee "to have the matter determined without delay by a competent, independent and impartial authority or judicial body in a fair hearing according to law." Convention on the Rights of the Child art. 40(2)(b)(iii), Nov. 20, 1989, 1577 U.N.T.S. 3. The Committee on the Rights of the Child has stated:

> Internationally there is a consensus that for children in conflict with the law the time between the commission of the offence and the final response to this act should be as short as possible. The longer this period, the more likely it is that the response loses its desired positive, pedagogical impact, and the more the child will be stigmatized....
>
> The Committee recommends the States Parties to set and implement time limits for the period between the commission of the offence and the completion of the police investigation, the decision of the prosecutor (or other competent body) to bring charges against the child, and the final adjudication and disposition by the court or other competent judicial body. These time limits should be much shorter than the ones for adults. But at the same time, decisions without delay should be the result of a process in which the human rights of the child and legal safeguards are fully respected.

United Nations Committee on the Rights of the Child, General Comment No. 10 (2007), Children's Rights in Juvenile Justice, U.N. Doc. CRC/C/GC/10, at para. 23.

Is the Committee on the Rights of the Child correct when it states that a lengthy delay between arrest and disposition minimizes the efficacy of punishment? Researchers argue that because adolescence is characterized by a period of cognitive, emotional, and physical changes, the juvenile may be less able to cope with delay. Moreover, postponing adjudication and disposition may impede the juvenile's ability to learn from his mistakes, thereby having an impact on the efficacy of punishment. Additionally, because adolescence is a period of rapid change, the reason for the offending behavior or the selection of a treatment modality may no longer be valid in light of the child's current developmental orientation. Thus, case-processing time is a particularly critical issue in juvenile court. JEFFREY A. BUTTS & GREGORY J. HALEMBA, WAITING FOR JUSTICE 5–6 (1996); Anne Rankin Mahoney, *Time and Process in Juvenile Court*, 10 JUSTICE SYSTEM J. 37, 39 (1985); Robert E. Shepherd, Jr., *Speedy Trials for Juveniles*, 14 CRIM. JUST. 53, 53 (Winter 2000).

5. *Right to a public trial.* The Sixth Amendment also guarantees a right to a public trial in criminal prosecutions. Although the Supreme Court has never explicitly held that juveniles in delinquency proceedings have a right to a public trial, Justice Brennan noted that the denial of a public trial under certain circumstances may give rise to a "misuse of the judicial process," particularly when there is no right to a jury trial. *McKeiver v. Pennsylvania*, 403 U.S. 528, 556 (1970) (Brennan, J., concurring). Is Brennan correct? Should juveniles have a right to a public trial? The Louisiana Supreme Court has held that public trials are essential to due process and are required under the Louisiana constitution. See *In re Dino*, 359 So.2d 586, 597 (La. 1978), cert. denied, 439 U.S. 1047 (1978). Some states have created a statutory right for juveniles or their guardians to request public access. See, e.g., Cal. Welf. & Inst. Code § 676 (West 2010). The IJA-ABA standards recommend presumptive access to juvenile proceedings. See Juvenile Justice Standards Relating to Adjudication § 6.1 (Institute of Judicial Administration and the American Bar Association, 1996). Unlike a statutory or constitutional right, the presumption permits, but does not mandate, a public trial; the decision to open the proceedings is left to the court's discretion.

Currently, only three states mandate closed juvenile proceedings. Neb. Rev. Stat. § 43-277.01 (2010); N.H. Rev. Stat. Ann. § 169-B:34(I)(a) (2010); Or. Unif. Trial Ct. R. 3.180(2)(c). Sixteen states have presumptively open proceedings but allow the court to close the proceedings under certain circumstances. Ariz. Juv. Ct. R. 19(B); Ark. Code Ann. § 9-27-325(i)(2) (2010); Colo. Rev. Stat. § 19-1-106(2) (2010); Fla. Stat. § 985.035(1) (2010); Iowa Code § 232.39 (2010);

Kan. Stat. Ann. § 38-2353(a) (2010) (limiting court's discretion to close proceedings to those juveniles younger than sixteen); Md. R. Juv. Causes § 11-110; Mich. Comp. Laws § 712A.17(7) (2002); Mont. Code Ann. § 41-5-1502(7) (2009); Nev. Rev. Stat. 62D.010(2) (2009); N.M. Stat. Ann. § 32A-2-16(B) (Conway Green 2010); N.C. Gen. Stat. § 7B-2402 (2010); Ohio Rev. Code Ann. § 2151.35(A)(1) (West 2010); Tenn. R. Juv. P. 27; Tex. Fam. Code Ann. § 54.08 (West 2009); Wash. Rev. Code § 13.40.140(6) (2010). Another thirty-two states and the District of Columbia close (or presumptively close) the proceedings but may authorize the court to open the proceedings under certain circumstances. Ala. Code § 12-15-129 (2010); Alaska Stat. § 47.10.070(c) (2010); D.C. Code § 16-2316(e) (2010); Cal. Welf. & Inst. Code § 676(a) (West 2009); Conn. Gen,. Stat. Ann. § 46b-122 (2010); Del. Code Ann. tit. 10, § 1063(a) (2010); Ga. Code Ann. § 15-11-78 (2010); Haw. Rev. Stat. §§ 571-41(b) (2010); Idaho Code Ann. § 20-525(1) (2010); 705 Ill. Comp. Stat. Ann. 405/1-5(6) (2010); Ind. Code §§ 31-32-6-2–31-32-6-3 (2010); Ky. Rev. Stat. Ann. § 610.070(3) (West 2010); La. Child. Code Ann. art. 879 (2010); Me. Rev. Stat. tit. 15, § 3307(2) (2009); Mass. Gen. Laws ch. 119, § 65 (2010); Minn. Stat. § 260B.163(c) (2010); Miss. Code Ann. § 43-21-203(6) (2010); Mo. Rev. Stat. § 211.171(6) (2010); N.J. Ct. R. 5:19-2(a)(1)–(a)(2); N.Y. Fam. Ct. Act § 341.1 (McKinney 2010); N.D. Cent. Code § 27-20-24(5) (2009); Okla. Stat. tit. 10A § 2-2-402 (2010) (specifying presumptively closed proceedings for first-time offenders but mandating public proceedings for subsequent adjudications); 42 Pa. Cons. Stat. § 6336(e) (2010); R.I. Gen. Laws § 14-1-30 (2010); S.C. Code Ann. § 20-7-755 (2009); S.D. Codified Laws § 26-7A-36 (2010); Utah Code Ann. § 78A-6-114 (West 2010); Vt. Stat. Ann. tit. 33, § 5110(b) (2010); Va. Code Ann. § 16.1-302(C) (2010); W. Va. Code § 49-5-2(i) (2010); Wis. Stat. § 48.299(1)(a) (2009); Wyo. Stat. Ann. § 14-6-224(b) (2010).

In an earlier reading from Section I.A, you may recall that juvenile court proceedings originally were open to the public. Are those reasons for requiring open proceedings still valid today? Why or why not?

6. Look again at Article 40 of the Convention on the Rights of the Child, *supra*, Section I.C. Do juvenile proceedings in the United States comport with Article 40? In what way are they similar? How are they different?

c. COMPETENCE TO STAND TRIAL

In *Dusky v. United States*, 362 U.S. 402 (1960), the United States Supreme Court held that the Due Process Clause is violated when an incompetent criminal defendant is made to stand trial. In determining whether a criminal defendant is incompetent to proceed, the court must ascertain whether the defendant has the "sufficient present ability to consult with his lawyer with a reasonable degree of rational understanding [and] a rational as well as factual understanding of the proceedings against him." *Id.* at 402. Whenever "sufficient doubt exists as to the accused's present competence," the court must hold a hearing to determine the defendant's competence to proceed. *Pate v. Robinson*, 383 U.S. 375 (1966). Questions about the defendant's competence may be raised at any time prior to or during a proceeding, and the issue may be raised by any party or by the court itself. Once a court finds an accused incompetent to proceed, the court may order the defendant's hospitalization in an attempt to restore competency, but the Constitution places some outside limits on the length of time an individual may be held while attempting to restore competency. In *Jackson v. Indiana*, 406 U.S. 715 (1972), the Supreme Court held that the Due Process Clause requires that the "nature and duration of the commitment bear some reasonable relation to the purpose for which the individual is committed." Thus, a court either must release the unrestorable incompetent or civilly commit him.

Should a juvenile in a delinquency proceeding be able to raise a claim that he is incompetent to proceed? If so, should the *Dusky* standard or some other standard apply?

IN RE CAREY
Court of Appeals of Michigan
615 N.W.2d 742 (2000)

BANDSTRA, C.J.

In this appeal we consider whether a court must determine the competency of a juvenile accused of an offense when a claim is raised that the juvenile is incompetent to stand trial in the adjudicative phase of a delinquency proceeding. We hold that the Due Process Clause requires this determination. We further hold that, in making this determination, the provisions of the Mental Health Code applicable to determinations of adult competency for criminal trials should be employed. We reverse and remand for further proceedings....

Although this state has not addressed the issue of competency determinations in juvenile proceedings, a number of other jurisdictions have concluded that competency, if properly raised, must be determined by the court. In *James H. v. Superior Court of Riverside Co.*, 77 Cal.App.3d 169, 174, 143 Cal.Rptr. 398 (1978), the California Court of Appeals held that juveniles had a due process right to be afforded a hearing when a question arose with respect to competency. The court reasoned that an incompetent juvenile would be unable to cooperate with counsel, thus denying the juvenile the effective assistance of counsel. *Id.* The court also held that the trial court had the inherent power to conduct a competency hearing; thus, it reasoned, the lack of statutory procedures did not preclude holding a hearing. *Id.* at 175, 143 Cal.Rptr. 398. The Supreme Court of Louisiana concluded that the right of an incompetent juvenile not to be subjected to juvenile proceedings was "fundamental" and "essential," and analogized this right to the right not to be tried in absentia. *In re Causey,* 363 So.2d 472, 476 (La., 1978). In *In re Two Minor Children,* 95 Nev. 225, 230–231, 592 P.2d 166 (1979), the Nevada Supreme Court similarly found a due process right to a competency hearing. Its holding was based on Justice Black's concurring opinion in *Gault, supra* at 61, 87 S.Ct. 1428, as well as *James H., supra.* The Minnesota Supreme Court held, as the Louisiana Supreme Court had earlier, that the right of an incompetent juvenile not to be subjected to juvenile proceedings was fundamental. *In re Welfare of SWT,* 277 N.W.2d 507, 511 (Minn., 1979). In *State ex rel. Dandoy v. Superior Ct.*, 127 Ariz. 184, 187, 619 P.2d 12 (1980), the Arizona Supreme Court reached a similar conclusion, relying again on the right to effective counsel as the basis for concluding that a juvenile must be able to confer with counsel. The District of Columbia Court of Appeals found that the juvenile system under review did not adequately protect the right of an incompetent juvenile not to be tried. *In re WAF,* 573 A.2d 1264, 1266 (D.C.App., 1990). The Georgia Court of Appeals found that "a want of competence renders [the rights recognized in *Gault* and its progeny] meaningless." *In re S.H.*, 220 Ga.App. 569, 571, 469 S.E.2d 810 (1996). The Washington Court of Appeals, in addressing the procedure to be followed for competency proceedings involving juveniles, recognized without discussion the right of juveniles to a competency determination. *State v. EC,* 83 Wash.App. 523, 527–528, 922 P.2d 152 (1996). The Ohio Court of Appeals found that the right not to be tried while incompetent is "as fundamental in juvenile proceedings as it is in criminal trials of adults." *In re Williams,* 116 Ohio App.3d 237, 241, 687 N.E.2d 507 (1997). It appears that all courts that have spoken on this issue have recognized the right of juveniles to a competency determination.

We find the reasoning presented in these cases to be persuasive. The purpose of the trial phase of a juvenile proceeding is to determine whether the juvenile comes within the jurisdiction of the court. The trial court's basis for jurisdiction is provided by statute. The court may take jurisdiction only if the juvenile has violated a law. The trial phase of a delinquency proceeding, then, is nothing more than a fact-finding mission to determine whether the juvenile has in fact violated any law, thus authorizing the court to exercise jurisdiction over the juvenile. Even though, as previously mentioned, juvenile proceedings are not considered adversarial, they have many of the trappings of criminal proceedings; the petition is filed by the prosecutor, notice is required, there must be a preliminary hearing, which resembles an arraignment in criminal proceedings, and the functions of the prosecutor and court are the equivalent to their functions in a criminal proceeding.... [D]ue process requires that a juvenile must be afforded the right to counsel during these proceedings. *Gault, supra* at 41, 87 S.Ct. 1428. This right to counsel means little if the juvenile is unaware of the proceedings or unable to communicate with counsel because of a psychological or developmental disability. Cf. *Cooper v. Oklahoma,* 517 U.S. 348, 368, 116 S.Ct. 1373, 134 L.Ed.2d 498 (1996); *Dusky v. United States,* 362 U.S. 402, 402, 80 S.Ct. 788, 4 L.Ed.2d 824 (1960) (common-law standard for determining competency is whether defendant has sufficient present ability to consult with lawyer with a reasonable degree of rational understanding and whether defendant has a rational as well as factual understanding of the proceedings against him). We conclude, as have many other jurisdictions, that the right not to be tried while incompetent is as fundamental in juvenile proceedings as it is in the criminal context.

There is no rule or statute of procedure that expressly controls the procedure for making a competency determination in juvenile cases....

Nonetheless... there is a due process right not to be subjected to the adjudicative phase of a delinquency proceeding while not competent. It is thus incumbent on us to provide some direction to the trial courts in making this important determination....

We believe that the Mental Health Code provisions for competency determinations can provide a useful guide[3] for the trial courts in this context. As summarized above, they provide

3. Even though we conclude that the Mental Health Code should be used as a guide for the conduct of juvenile competency determinations, the express language of the code may limit the specific procedures to be used. For instance, the code directs the trial court to order a defendant alleged to be incompetent to undergo an examination by personnel of the Institute for Forensic Psychiatry or another facility certified by the Department of Mental Health to perform examinations relating to the issue of incompetence to stand trial. However, the institute has limited statutory powers, which do not appear to include the examination of juveniles who have not been charged as an adult with a crime. Nonetheless, the provisions call for examination by a facility certified by the Department of Mental Health to conduct competency examinations. Any such facilities could be used, providing that they are found to be qualified to determine the competency of juveniles involved in delinquency proceedings. The trial courts should apply the Mental Health Code in making juvenile competency determinations to the extent possible, recognizing that its provisions may sometimes need to be liberally construed or modified for application in this context.

a standard of competency and a process by which questions of competency can be raised and determined. We hold that, in the absence of other applicable rules or statutes, these provisions should be used to assure that the due process rights of a juvenile are protected.

In reaching this conclusion, however, we further note that it is possible that a juvenile, merely because of youthfulness, would be unable to understand the proceedings with the same degree of comprehension an adult would. *Causey, supra* at 476. See Grisso, The Competence of Adolescents as Trial Defendants, 3 Psych., Pub. Pol'y & L. 3, 14 (1997). Accordingly, we further hold that, in juvenile competency hearings, competency evaluations should be made in light of juvenile, rather than adult, norms. *Williams, supra* at 242, 687 N.E.2d 507. A juvenile need not be found incompetent just because, under adult standards, the juvenile would be found incompetent to stand trial in a criminal proceeding.[4]

We reverse and remand for proceedings consistent with this opinion.

NOTES AND QUESTIONS

1. What does the court mean when it says that a "juvenile need not be found incompetent just because, under adult standards, the juvenile would be found incompetent to stand trial in a criminal proceeding"? Does this mean that a juvenile found incompetent under *Dusky* may nevertheless be found competent to proceed in a delinquency proceeding? Why is this constitutional?

2. Thirteen states apply a criminal competency provision to juveniles in delinquency proceedings. See, e.g., Ark. Code Ann. § 9-27-502(a)(1) (2010); Me. Rev. Stat. Ann. tit. 15, § 3318 (2010); N.C. Gen. Stat. § 7B-2401 (2010); S.C. Code Ann. § 44-23-410(A) (2009); W. Va. Code Ann. § 27-6A-9 (West 2010); *Smith v. State*, 918 A.2d 1144 (Del. 2007); *In re T.D.W.*, 441 N.E.2d 155, 156–157 (Ill. App. Ct. 1982), overruled on other grounds by *People v. Gentry*, 815 N.E.2d 27, 32 (Ill. App. Ct. 2004); *In re K.G.*, 808 N.E.2d 631, 637–638 (Ind. 2004); *In re A.B.*, 715 N.W.2d 767 (Iowa Ct. App. 2006); *In re Carey, supra*; *In re Two Minor Children*, 592 P.2d 166, 169 (Nev. 1979); *In re Johnson*, 1983 WL 2516, at *5 (Ohio Ct. App. 2d Dist. Oct. 25, 1983); *State v. E.C.*, 922 P.2d 152, 155–156 (Wash. Ct. App. 1996). Eighteen jurisdictions have enacted rules or statutes governing juvenile competency standards. See Ariz. Rev. Stat. § 8-291.02 (2010); Cal. Fam. & Juv. R. 5.645; Colo. Rev. Stat. § 19-2-1301 (2008); Conn. Super. Ct. R. 31a-14; D.C. Code Ann. § 16-2315 (2010); Fla. Stat. Ann. § 985.19 (West 2010); Ga. Code Ann. § 15-11-152 (West 2010); Kan. Stat. Ann. § 38-2348 (2010); La. Child. Code Ann. art. 832 (2010); Md. Code Ann., Cts. & Jud. Proc. § 3-8A-17.1 (West 2010); Minn. R. Juv. Delinq. Proc. 20.01; N.M. Stat. § 32A-2-17 (2010); N.Y. Jud. Ct. Acts Law § 322.1 (McKinney 2010); Tex. Fam. Code Ann. § 55.31 (Vernon 2010); Vt. R. Fam. Proc. 1(i); Va. Code Ann. § 16.1-356 (2010); Wis. Stat. Ann. § 938.295 (West 2010); Wyo. Stat. Ann. § 14-6-219 (2010). However, in twenty states, there is no clearly defined rule governing juveniles' competence to proceed in delinquency cases. For a survey of

4. By outlining the procedure to be followed, we do not intend to usurp the authority of our Supreme Court or the Michigan Legislature. We have discussed the procedure for conducting competency hearings for juveniles only because of the lack of any court rule or statute to guide the trial courts. We invite our Supreme Court to promulgate rules of procedure for juvenile competency determinations, and our Legislature to enact any statutory provisions it deems necessary.

the law pertaining to juvenile competency in delinquency proceedings, see Joseph B. Sanborn, Jr., *Juveniles' Competency to Stand Trial: Wading through the Rhetoric and the Evidence*, 99 J. Crim. L. & Criminology 135, 140–142 & tbl. 1 (2009).

3. Should a juvenile's immaturity be taken into account when assessing his competence to proceed? In *In re A.B.*, 2006 WL 469945, a juvenile court judge dismissed a delinquency petition alleging that fourteen-year-old A.B. had sexually abused another minor on the ground that A.B. was incompetent to proceed. Neither expert who examined A.B. found that he suffered from a mental illness, although one expert testified that A.B. had a borderline IQ and an extremely limited understanding of the court proceedings and their consequences. The Iowa Court of Appeals held that "[l]imiting incompetency in delinquency proceedings to cases in which the child is incompetent by reason of a 'mental disorder' would fail to recognize that a juvenile's inability to appreciate the charge, understand the proceedings, or assist effectively in the defense may be the result of immaturity, lack of intellectual capacity, or both. We conclude that limiting determinations of incompetency in juvenile cases to those cases in which the inability to appreciate, understand, and assist is based on a 'mental disorder' would offend rights to due process." *Id.* at *3. Why would this violate due process? By this approach, would most juveniles be deemed incompetent?

4. In 1996, the John D. and Catherine T. MacArthur Foundation established the Research Network on Adolescent Development and Juvenile Justice to study, among other things, adolescents' capacities as trial defendants. In a large-scale study conducted by the network's researchers, 1,400 youths ages eleven to twenty-four were interviewed in Philadelphia, Los Angeles, northern Florida, and Virginia. Assessing competence to proceed based on the *Dusky* legal standard, researchers found that 30 percent of children ages eleven to thirteen, 19 percent of children ages fourteen to fifteen, 12 percent of sixteen- and seventeen-year-olds, and 12 percent of those ages eighteen to twenty-four had impairments in reasoning and ability that might lead a court to conclude that these individuals were incompetent to proceed. Additionally, researchers assessed the participants' emotional maturity. Using an assessment tool specifically designed for the study, participants were asked to provide the best and worst choices in three hypothetical situations (speaking with the police during interrogation when one is guilty of a crime, revealing information during an attorney-client consultation, and responding to a plea offer in which the individual would agree to testify against other defendants after pleading guilty). Again, the study found that younger children displayed less maturity in decision making than did older children and young adults (for example, younger children may be more likely to confess rather than remain silent or accept a plea offer), with few statistically significant differences among those participants older than fifteen. Those participants with lower IQs performed more poorly on all items, a finding that is particularly significant given that two-thirds of those younger than fifteen in the sample who had IQs lower than 89 were in juvenile detention. Thomas Grisso et al., *Juveniles' Competence to Stand Trial: A Comparison of Adolescents' and Adults' Capacities as Trial Defendants*, 27 Law & Hum. Behav. 333 (2003).

If juveniles, particularly younger juveniles, are more incompetent and less mature, could they ever stand trial? Would such a proceeding comport with due process? Should there be a lower standard in juvenile delinquency proceedings? Consider this proposal by Elizabeth Scott and Thomas Grisso:

> ...[T]he research on adolescent development and adjudicative competence challenges courts to consider incompetence claims based on immaturity along with those caused by

mental illness and disability. We will argue, however, that the features that distinguish incompetence based on immaturity from the more familiar variations make this simple doctrinal response inadequate. The incorporation of a developmental competence requirement into youth crime regulation necessitates more extensive institutional and doctrinal adjustments, if substantial disruption of criminal and juvenile proceedings is to be avoided. Most importantly, the adoption of dual standards of competence is necessary if juvenile delinquency proceedings are to serve as default dispositions for youths found incompetent in criminal courts; generally, this is the key to avoiding an institutional crisis under which large numbers of incompetent youths cannot be adjudicated in either court. We argue that youths who are incompetent under the Dusky standard can be subject to a relaxed competence standard in juvenile court without violating constitutional norms so long as the dispositions to which they are subject are different in purpose and punitiveness from criminal sentences....

The unique features of developmental incompetence create a dilemma for courts unless appropriate mechanisms are available for responding to youths who are incompetent to proceed under the conventional legal standard. To be sure, some youths may be found incompetent simply because they lack adequate understanding about the purposes and operation of a criminal trial. They may respond to focused "competence training" programs designed to provide instruction that will enable them to function in their assigned role with at least minimal effectiveness. The question is how to respond to youths whose developmental incapacity is not correctable with short-term remedial instruction.

It is critically important to find a satisfactory answer to this question. Consider the dilemma faced by a criminal court judge deliberating about the competence of a thirteen-year-old charged with aggravated assault and armed robbery. The charges arose from an incident in which the youth and his friends allegedly ran off with an elderly woman's purse after attacking her brutally with a tire iron, causing her to suffer serious injuries. The youth, because of his extreme immaturity and low IQ, fails to comprehend the seriousness of the charges or the consequences of conviction. He can provide little assistance to his attorney, and it seems highly unlikely that these deficits can be remedied in the near future. If the court decides, as it should, that the youth is incompetent, neither dismissal of the charges nor long-term indefinite confinement ("waiting for maturity") will be acceptable dispositions; the former sacrifices public safety and accountability, and the latter violates constitutional norms.

In our view, the disposition that is appropriate for this youth and for most developmentally incompetent youths is adjudication in a juvenile delinquency proceeding. If a juvenile court adjudicates the charges against the youth, it can determine whether he committed the crime and, if so, it can structure a disposition based on remediation, accountability, and public safety. This outcome is possible only if criminal and juvenile courts apply dual standards of competence, such that a youth who is found incompetent in a criminal proceeding can be adjudicated under more relaxed criteria in juvenile court. Such a regime largely resolves the dispositional quandary faced by courts dealing with immature youths charged with serious crimes. On the other hand, if a uniform standard is applied in both judicial contexts, the youth excluded from criminal court on grounds of incompetence would also be unable to participate in delinquency proceedings.

The application of dual competence standards in criminal and delinquency proceedings is important for another reason; it is the means to avoid profound disruption of juvenile delinquency proceedings. Although few thirteen-year-olds are subject to criminal charges, many face adjudication in juvenile court. The research evidence suggests that evenhanded application of adult competence criteria may well result in the disqualification of a substantial percentage of youngsters from adjudication in any court. This outcome is jarring in light of uncontroversial premises of juvenile court jurisdiction; few would challenge the appropriateness of delinquency proceedings for younger teens. Thus, as a policy matter, a strong case can be made for a relaxed juvenile court competence standard under which immature youths could be tried in delinquency proceedings, even though they are incompetent to stand trial under adult criteria.

The critical question then becomes whether less demanding competence criteria in juvenile court satisfy the mandates of due process....

The principle of fundamental fairness is the broad constitutional standard under which courts evaluate procedural challenges in both criminal and delinquency proceedings. The Supreme Court has made clear, however, that due process does not require that the constitutional protections afforded youths in juvenile court replicate those offered defendants in criminal trials. Emphasizing the unique features of juvenile proceedings, the Court has found that some important safeguards, such as the rights to a jury trial and to bail, would undermine the purposes of the juvenile justice system and are not essential to fair process in this setting....

...The Supreme Court has emphasized that the Constitution does not require the wholesale incorporation of adult procedural rights into delinquency proceedings, but has offered no test to guide the determination of whether a contested procedural protection is required by fundamental fairness. However, several themes that can be extracted from the Court's examination of due process claims in this context inform our analysis. First, the Court has emphasized that a procedural safeguard that is likely to be "disruptive of the unique nature of the juvenile process" and to dilute its beneficial aspects may not be required in juvenile court. For reasons that we have discussed, this consideration is highly salient in evaluating the impact of a uniform competence standard. However, this deference rests on the assumption that a juvenile delinquency proceeding is different from a criminal trial in ways that serve the interests of youths facing charges in juvenile court. This qualifying condition is important to our analysis, leading us to conclude that, regardless of its disruptive impact, a relaxed juvenile court competence standard is constitutionally sufficient only if delinquency proceedings promote the welfare of youths who do not meet the adult standard. Finally, the Court has focused on whether a contested procedural safeguard is important for accurate fact-finding in the adjudication of criminal charges. We extend this concern to examine whether a relaxed juvenile court competence standard adequately satisfies the purposes of the competence requirement as applied in this setting.

As to the first consideration about the disruptiveness of the proposed procedure, the earlier discussion makes clear that serious disruption of delinquency proceedings is likely to follow if a uniform competence standard is applied in criminal and juvenile courts and that this can be avoided by adopting a relaxed standard. First, juvenile courts that apply the adult standard are likely to be burdened with a flood of petitions for competence evaluations and hearings, resulting in a major diversion of financial and human resources to a process that most would agree should have limited importance in this legal setting. Also, if many younger defendants are found incompetent under the adult standard, government efforts to protect the public from youth crime, to hold young offenders accountable, and to provide them with rehabilitative services will be undermined. As we have argued, a doctrinal regime under which many younger teens—particularly those charged with serious crimes—might be immune from prosecution probably would be rejected as unacceptable, and ultimately, would undermine the legitimacy of the juvenile court. Under a tailored juvenile court standard, this procedural safeguard can function to exclude only those youths whose extreme immaturity makes even juvenile court adjudication inappropriate.

Although the potentially disruptive impact of a uniform competence standard seems clear, the constitutional adequacy of a dual-standards regime also depends on whether delinquency proceedings differ substantially from criminal proceedings, such that the more protective adult standard is not mandated in this setting. The interest of adult defendants facing criminal punishment justifies the existing competence requirement and serves as a baseline for evaluating the interests of juveniles in delinquency proceedings. In other cases dealing with procedures resulting in deprivations of liberty, the Court has made clear that the state's purposes in restricting liberty and the impact on affected individuals are key to evaluating the mandates of due process. For example, where the state's purpose in confining an individual is to provide treatment for mental illness, the procedural requirements of criminal proceedings can be relaxed.

A relaxed competence standard will meet this second condition of "distinctiveness" if delinquency proceedings are different from criminal trials in two important dimensions. The first concerns the severity of punishment and its impact on the future lives of young offenders. Juvenile court sanctions, especially for serious crimes, must be of shorter duration than those imposed on adult criminals. Moreover, dispositions should be completed within a self-contained juvenile correctional system, such that they do not extend into adulthood or affect adult status or opportunities. The traditional juvenile justice system was characterized by dispositions more lenient than the adult system, and contemporary regimes can be evaluated along this dimension as well. If the dispositional differences are insufficient in this regard, the adult standard must be applied.

The distinctiveness condition also requires that the purposes of delinquency proceedings must be broader than those of criminal proceedings and must include consideration of the welfare of young offenders. Today, to be sure, criminal and delinquency proceedings both aim to punish offenders, deter crime and protect public safety through the incapacitation of dangerous persons. However, the juvenile system, traditionally at least, also has been committed to treatment and to offering dispositions that enhance the likelihood that delinquent youths will become productive adults. This distinction from the adult justice system is important in the justification of a relaxed competence standard in delinquency proceedings.

The upshot of our analysis is that whether a juvenile court adjudication is sufficiently different from a criminal trial to justify relaxing the constitutionally required competence standard depends in part on institutional features defining the juvenile justice system and its purposes. If youths facing adjudication in juvenile court are subject to dispositions that are more lenient than criminal punishment and that are aimed (in part) at promoting youth welfare, then the stakes they face are lower than (and different from) those facing criminal defendants and the need for adult procedural safeguards to protect their interests is less compelling. Under these conditions, a relaxed standard in delinquency proceedings may be justified, given the disruptive impact on delinquency proceedings of applying a uniform standard. On the other hand, if juvenile proceedings and criminal trials are alike in their consequences and purposes, then accused youths should receive the same protections as criminal defendants.

Assuming the institutional preconditions are met (for now), a relaxed standard will meet the mandate of fundamental fairness only if it also satisfies the underlying purposes of the criminal competence requirement—the promotion of dignity, accuracy, and defendant participation. Under the competence criteria that we endorse, a youth facing a delinquency proceeding must have a basic understanding of the charges and proceeding and of her position as defendant in that proceeding, and the capacity to communicate with her attorney. This standard accommodates the developmental incapacities that might leave many youths incompetent to be tried as adults, while at the same time requiring basic comprehension of the delinquency proceeding, its meaning, and consequences.

To elaborate a bit on the operation of a relaxed standard, a youth faced with a serious delinquency charge must understand why he faces a deprivation of liberty and the possible extent of that confinement. But, because the consequences are less far-reaching than those of a criminal proceeding, a lesser ability to foresee remote consequences would be sufficient. The youth must also understand that his attorney's role is to advocate for him, that the prosecutor aims to convict and punish him, and that the judge will decide whether he committed the crime based on the evidence. But he need not understand how advocacy is translated into practice in a way that would be required of an adult. He must also have the capacity to provide his attorney with an account of relevant events and to answer questions so that the attorney can plan and execute a defense. But he need not have the ability to weigh the value of defense strategies, or to advise counsel accordingly. In delinquency proceedings, attorneys will often have an additional burden of explanation and solicitation of assent in planning a defense. It seems likely, however, that in practice, attorneys already play this role with younger clients, whose questionable competence heretofore has not been expressly acknowledged....

In a regime of dual standards, very few youths will be in the category of defendants who cannot be adjudicated in juvenile proceedings due to their incompetence. Of this small group, some may attain competence in a reasonable period through training, and most of the rest will be subject to dispositions that assure that they receive adequate supervision and useful remedial services. Thus, dealing with this group creates little threat of systemic crisis, in sharp contrast to the potential disruption of both juvenile and criminal proceedings that is likely to occur under a uniform standard.

Elizabeth S. Scott & Thomas Grisso, *Developmental Incompetence, Due Process, and Juvenile Justice Policy*, 83 N.C. L. Rev. 793, 827–828, 831–833, 834–838, 840 (2005).

d. THE INSANITY DEFENSE

Unlike competence to proceed, the insanity defense raises a claim about the defendant's mental state at the time he or she committed the offense. The dominant test employed by state and federal courts is the *M'Naghten* rule: "it must be clearly proved that at the time of the committing of the act, the party accused was laboring under such a defect of reason, from disease of the mind, as not to know the nature and quality of the act he was doing; or, if he did know it, that he did not know he was doing what was wrong." *M'Naghten's Case*, 10 Cl. & Fin. 200, 210, 8 Eng. Rep. 718, 722 (1843). Because the Supreme Court has not recognized *M'Naghten* as a fundamental principle, states have been free to define the contours of the insanity test and to assign the burden of proof and persuasion. Thus, a state may presume the sanity of a criminal defendant and place the burden of persuasion on a defendant who wishes to raise the insanity defense. *Patterson v. New York*, 432 U.S. 197, 205 (1977). Similarly, a state may choose to limit the insanity defense to the first prong of the *M'Naghten* test without running afoul of the Due Process Clause. *Clark v. Arizona*, 548 U.S. 735, 752–756 (2006).

Does the defense apply to juvenile delinquency proceedings? A few states have provided juveniles with a right to raise the defense of insanity by statute or court rule. See, e.g., Fla. R. Juv. P. Rule 8.095 (2010); Me. Rev. Stat. Ann. §§ 3310, 3318 (2010); N.J. Stat. Ann. § 2A:4A-40 (2010) (all defenses available to adult charged with crime, violation, or offense available to juvenile charged with committing a delinquent act); Or. Rev. Stat. Ann. § 419C.411(2) (2010); Vernon's Tex. Fam. Code §55.51 (2010); Wis. Stat. Ann. § 938.40(4)(c) (West 2010). Other state courts have held that the state's criminal statute providing an insanity defense applies to juveniles charged with delinquent acts. *In re Natalie Z.*, 153 P.3d 1081 (Ariz. 2007) (state criminal statute applicable to delinquency proceedings, but evidence did not warrant finding of insanity under state statute); *In re J.T.S.*, 2006 WL 1751279 (Iowa App.) (juvenile did not present sufficient evidence under state criminal statute to warrant finding of insanity); *In re Ricks*, 421 N.W.2d 667 (Mich. App. 1988) (assuming without deciding that insanity defense applies to juvenile proceedings, but see *In re Smith*, 2007 WL 293508 (Mich. App.) (not clear that insanity defense applies to delinquency proceedings)). Additionally, a few states have found that a juvenile has a constitutional right to raise the insanity defense in delinquency proceedings. *In re Causey*, 363 So.2d 472 (La. 1978) (constitutional right to raise insanity defense under state and federal Due Process Clauses, although no statutory right exists); *In re Stapelkemper*, 562 P.2d 815 (Mont. 1977) (due process mandates right to raise insanity defense during adjudicatory phase of delinquency proceeding, but because a transfer hearing is not an adjudicatory proceeding, no right to raise insanity defense during transfer hearings); *In re Two Minor Children*, 592 P.2d 166 (Nev. 1979) (due process requires that juveniles be permitted to plead, and have tried, insanity defense). On the other hand, a few states deny juveniles the right to an insanity defense on either statutory or constitutional grounds or both. *Golden v. State*, 21 S.W.3d 801 (Ark. 2000) (juvenile does not have due process right to raise defense of insanity where no statute authorizes the assertion of defense and not a violation of equal protection since juveniles and adults not similarly situated); *In re C.W.M.*, 407 A.2d 617 (D.C. 1979) (failure to provide juvenile with insanity defense violates neither Due Process nor Equal Protection Clauses, but his mental condition is relevant to disposition); *In re Chambers*, 688 N.E.2d 25 (Ohio App. 3d Dist. 1996), appeal not allowed, 678 N.E.2d 221 (Ohio 1997) (insanity plea a feature of criminal cases, and juvenile delinquency proceedings are not criminal cases; moreover, no provision in juvenile rules for plea of insanity); *Commonwealth v. Chatman*, 538 S.E.2d 304 (Va. 2000) (juvenile has neither constitutional nor statutory right to assert insanity defense during adjudicatory phase of a delinquency proceeding); D.C. Stat. § 16-235(d) (2010) (results of mental examination inadmissible for purposes of establishing an insanity defense). Nevertheless, the issue remains unresolved in a significant number of jurisdictions.

Problem. Should juveniles have a constitutional right to plead not guilty by reason of insanity? Assume that you are counsel for a state's senate majority leader. She has asked you to draft a memo identifying the legal, psychological, fiscal, and political ramifications of a decision to extend the insanity defense to juveniles in light of the underlying policy, practices, and goals of the juvenile justice system. What would you tell her?

D. Dispositional Framework

1. OVERVIEW

Crystal Knoll & Melissa Sickmund, U.S. Dep't of Justice, Delinquency Cases in Juvenile Court, 2007, 3–4 (June 2010), www.ncjrs.gov/pdffiles/ojjdp/230168.pdf.

In 2007, juveniles were adjudicated delinquent in 63 percent (586,200) of petitioned cases, a 74 percent increase from 1985. The court holds disposition hearings to decide what sanctions should be imposed on a juvenile who has been adjudicated delinquent and whether the juvenile should be placed under court supervision. Many cases result in multifaceted dispositions, and most involve some type of probation supervision. A probation order often includes additional requirements, such as drug counseling, restitution to the victim, or community service. In 2007, formal probation was the most severe disposition ordered in 56 percent of cases in which the juvenile was adjudicated delinquent, and 25 percent of cases were ordered to residential placement as the most severe disposition. A smaller proportion of cases received some other sanction as their most severe disposition. The proportion of adjudicated cases ordered to probation has fluctuated within a relatively narrow range over the years (55 percent–60 percent during the 1985–2007 time period). In comparison, the proportion of cases resulting in residential placement dropped from 31 percent in 1985 to 25 percent in 2007 and the proportion receiving other sanctions increased from 11 percent to 19 percent during that time.

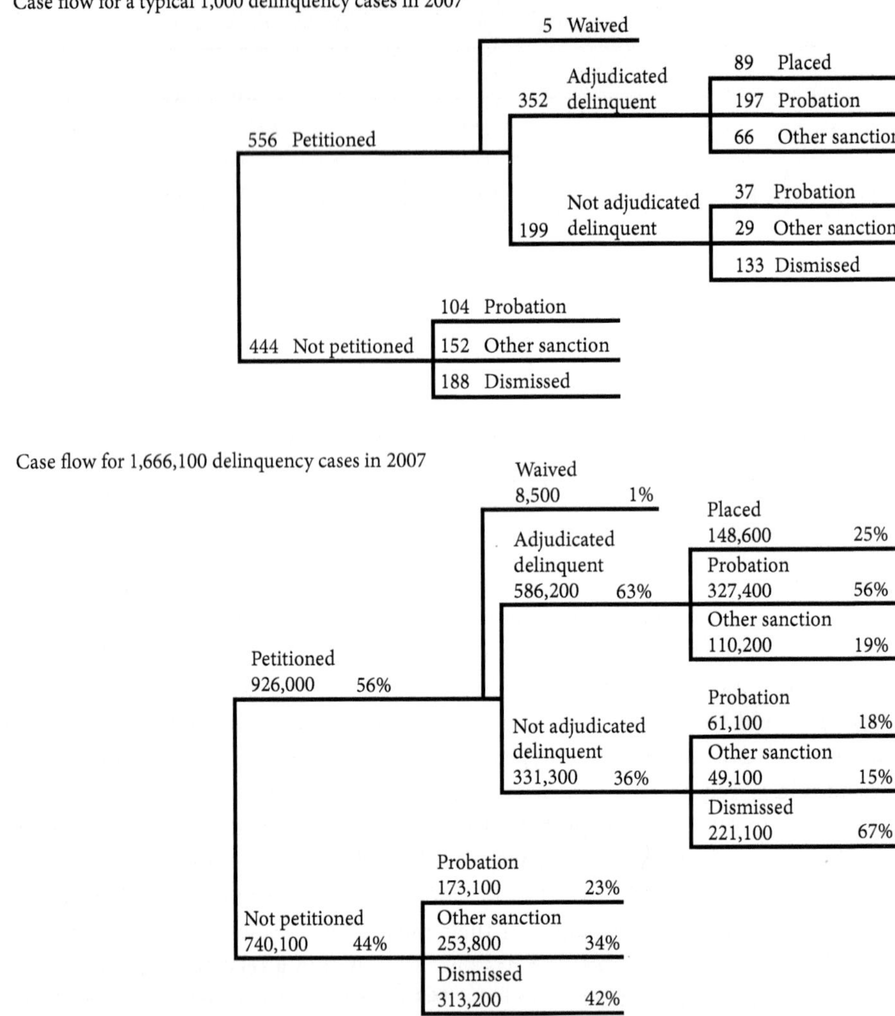

Notes: Cases are categorized by their most severe or restrictive sanction. Detail may not add to totals because of roundting. Annual case processing flow diagrams for 1985 through 2007 are available at www.ojjdp.ncjrs.gov/ojstatbb/court/faqs.asp.

NOTES AND QUESTIONS

1. By offense category, probation remained the most severe disposition likely to be imposed after adjudication. In person- and property-offense cases, 58 percent of those adjudicated received probation as the most severe sanction. In drug-offense cases, 61 percent received probation as the most restrictive sanction. Curiously, in public order cases, which involve adjudications for offenses such as obstruction of justice, disorderly conduct, liquor-law violations, weapons offenses, and nonviolent sex offenses, probation was imposed in 49 percent of the

cases. Out-of-home placements were ordered most often in person cases (29 percent), followed by property and public-order offenses (25 percent). Out-of-home placements were ordered less often in adjudicated drug-offense cases (21 percent). Charles Puzzanchera, Benjamin Adams, & Melissa Sickmund, National Center for Juvenile Justice, Juvenile Court Statistics 2006–2007, 60–61 (2010).

Of the more than 1.6 million delinquency cases handled by the juvenile courts in 2007, 54 percent involved children younger than sixteen. 61 percent of person-offense cases and 56 percent of property-offense cases involved children younger than sixteen. *Id.* at 9 tbl. Nevertheless, juvenile courts imposed probation as the most severe sanction in 59 percent of all cases involving children younger than sixteen compared with 53 percent of all cases involving children sixteen or older. Of children whose cases were ordered by the court to be placed out of the home, 24 percent were younger than sixteen, while 27 percent of children sixteen or older received a similar disposition. *Id.* at 62.

Of these cases, 27 percent involved girls. *Id.* at 9 tbl. These cases were less likely to be adjudicated, but once they were, courts were more likely to impose probation as the most serious sanction (58 percent for girls compared with 55 percent for boys). Courts also were less likely to place girls out of the home (19 percent of all adjudicated cases) compared with boys (27 percent of all adjudicated cases). Nevertheless, girls were more likely to receive other sanctions (including fines, restitution, community service, and referrals involving little or no court involvement) than boys (23 percent for girls compared with 18 percent for boys). *Id.* at 62.

Of all delinquency cases in 2007, 64 percent involved white youths. Although cases involving white youths were less likely to be petitioned than cases involving black, Native American, or Asian youths, once petitioned, cases with white youths were more likely to be adjudicated (65 percent) than cases with black (60 percent) or Asian (64 percent) youths. However, these cases were less likely to be adjudicated than those involving Native American youths (71 percent). White and Asian youths were most likely to receive probation (59 percent of adjudicated cases), followed by Native American youths (55 percent), while black youths were least likely to receive probation as the most severe sanction (50 percent). Black and Native American youths were more likely to be placed out of the home (29 percent of adjudicated cases) compared with Asian (24 percent) and white (23 percent) youths. Other sanctions were imposed in 17 percent of the cases involving Native American and Asian youths, in 18 percent of cases with white youths, and in 20 percent of those involving black youths.

2. *Trends in disposition.* Historically, probation has been the most common disposition imposed in juvenile court. In 1985, courts imposed probation as the most severe sanction in 58 percent of the cases compared with 56 percent in 2007. *Id.* at 55. However, the number of cases involving probation doubled between 1985 and 1997, before declining by 17 percent in 2007. *Id.* at 54. Since 1991, children younger than sixteen were more likely to be placed on probation than older youths, while the use of probation for both girls and boys declined equally. *Id.* at 56. The use of probation increased for Native American and white youths between 1985 and 2007, while it decreased for black and Asian youths. *Id.* at 57.

The number of cases involving of out-of-home placements increased by 42 percent between 1985 and 2007, although the use of out-of-home placements has been declining since 1997. The use of out-of-home placements, however, varies by offense type. Since 1985, out-of-home placements increased by 28 percent in person offenses, 5 percent in drug cases, and 8 percent in public-order offenses. But out-of-home placements declined by 22 percent in property cases. Nevertheless, since 1997, the number of cases involving out-of-home placements decreased by 2 percent for person offenses, 34 percent for property offenses, and 18 percent for drug cases. For public-order cases, however, out-of-home placements increased by 4 percent during this time. *Id.* at 50. Between 1985 and 2007, the use of out-of-home placements declined more for children younger than sixteen than for children sixteen and older, although both groups experienced declines. Boys were more likely to be placed out of the home than girls for the same offense, *id.* at 52; while blacks and Native Americans were more likely than whites to be placed out of the home for person and property offenses, *id.* at 53.

3. *Restorative justice.* What are the underlying justifications for punishing the juvenile offender? Do they comport with the juvenile court's historical underpinnings? How does the juvenile court balance the therapeutic approach against the need for retribution? Advocates of restorative justice argue that both the rehabilitative and the punitive approaches place the offender in a "passive role, as the object of services on one hand, and punishment and surveillance on the other," without requiring positive and constructive actions on the offender's part. The restorative-justice approach, however, focuses on repairing the harm done to individual victims and the community by the individual offender by rebuilding these relationships through negotiation, mediation, reparations, and victim empowerment. Thus, restorative justice emphasizes balance among three system goals: community protection, competency development, and accountability. Accountability requires juvenile offenders to "make amends" for the harm done by restoring or repaying the loss to the victim and the community. Competency development is rehabilitative: the juvenile who leaves the system should be more capable of being a productive and responsible member of society. Community safety must be secured but through the least restrictive measures possible and by utilizing a series of varied and graduated sanctions designed to respond to the varying levels of risk that individual offenders may pose. This approach also envisions the active participation of victims and communities through victim restoration and the participation of communities in shaming and reintegrating offenders. Gordon Bazemore & Mark Umbreit, U.S. Dep't of Justice, Balanced and Restorative Justice for Juveniles: A Framework for Juvenile Justice in the 21st Century (1997), https://www.ncjrs.gov/pdffiles/framwork.pdf.

Is there empirical evidence that restorative justice works? Although there is evidence that restorative justice has positive outcomes for participants and may work well in granting closure or restoring dignity (see, e.g., JOHN BRAITHWAITE, RESTORATIVE JUSTICE AND RESPONSE REGULATION (2001)), the evidence regarding a reduction in recidivism is mixed. Nevertheless, there are more recent studies suggesting that restorative justice has a positive effect on reducing recidivism. Issues relating to the effect of extralegal factors on restorative-justice outcomes are just beginning to be explored systematically, although there are some indications that extralegal factors, such as poverty, gender, and parental neglect, may affect recidivism. For an overview of the empirical literature on restorative justice, see Nancy Rodriguez, *Restorative Justice at Work: Examining the Impact of Restorative Justice Resolutions on Juvenile Recidivism*, 53 CRIME & DELINQ. 355 (2007).

2. TRADITIONAL JUVENILE DISPOSITIONS

a. DETERMINATE VS. INDETERMINATE SENTENCING

Barry C. Feld, *Juvenile and Criminal Justice Systems' Responses to Youth Violence*, 24 CRIME & JUST. 189, 223–24 (1998).

Most states' juvenile codes authorized courts to impose indeterminate sentences because penal therapists cannot predict in advance the course or duration of treatment necessary to attain success.... Traditionally, juvenile court judges exercised virtually unrestricted discretion to dismiss, place on probation, remove from home, or institutionalize a youth....

...Indeterminate sentencing statutes typically provide for an unspecified period of confinement and a wide range between the minimum and maximum terms available. Corrections officials base their release decisions, in part, on youths' behavior during confinement and progress toward rehabilitative goals rather than on formal standards or the committing offense.

By contrast, when judges sentence juveniles under a determinate or presumptive sentencing framework, they typically impose proportional sanctions within a relatively narrow dispositional range based on the seriousness of the offense, offense history, and age. In several states, courts impose mandatory minimum sentences based on the offense for which they convicted the youth. In other states, correctional administrators determine youths' presumptive length of institutional stay or eligibility for parole shortly after their commitment based on formal standards that prescribe terms proportional to the seriousness of the offense or prior record.

NOTES AND QUESTIONS

1. Feld indicates that almost half the states use a determinate sentencing scheme. *Id.* at 224. But how do indeterminate and determinate sentencing provisions work? In the state of Washington (which was the first state to enact a determinate sentencing scheme for juveniles), juvenile judges sentence juveniles according to a sentencing grid, based on the seriousness of the offense and the juvenile's prior record. The grid provides a range of sanctions; in some instances, juveniles might receive dispositions that are harsher than those that could be imposed on adult offenders. Nevertheless, under certain statutorily specified circumstances, courts may opt to suspend the imposition of disposition, impose mental-health or chemical-dependency dispositions, or impose a sentence outside the standard range if to do otherwise would be a "manifest injustice." Wash. Rev. Code Ann. § 13.40.0357 (West 2011). On the other hand, juvenile judges in Iowa must impose the "least restrictive alternative" in light of the seriousness of the offense, prior record, age, and "culpability" of the child. The court has a range of dispositional options that it may enter, and the statute provides the court with broad discretion to fashion an appropriate disposition. Iowa Code § 232.52 (Supp. 2009).

What are the advantages and disadvantages of each approach? Do you think the outcomes for juveniles will vary dramatically under one scheme or the other? In what ways? If probation is the most common disposition, is the distinction between determinate and indeterminate sentencing really significant?

b. DISPOSITIONAL CONDITIONS

Ohio Rev. Code Ann. § 2152.19 (West 2010)

(A) If a child is adjudicated a delinquent child, the court may make any of the following orders of disposition, in addition to any other disposition authorized or required by this chapter:

(1) Any order that is authorized... for the care and protection of an abused, neglected, or dependent child;

(2) Commit the child to the temporary custody of any school, camp, institution, or other facility operated for the care of delinquent children...;

(3) Place the child in a detention facility... for up to ninety days;

(4) Place the child on community control under any sanctions, services, and conditions that the court prescribes. As a condition of community control in every case and in addition to any other condition that it imposes upon the child, the court shall require the child to abide by the law during the period of community control. As referred to in this division, community control includes, but is not limited to, the following sanctions and conditions:

(a) A period of basic probation supervision in which the child is required to maintain contact with a person appointed to supervise the child in accordance with sanctions imposed by the court;

(b) A period of intensive probation supervision in which the child is required to maintain frequent contact with a person appointed by the court to supervise the child while the child is seeking or maintaining employment and participating in training, education, and treatment programs as the order of disposition;

(c) A period of day reporting in which the child is required each day to report to and leave a center or another approved reporting location at specified times in order to participate in work, education or training, treatment, and other approved programs at the center or outside the center;

(d) A period of community service of up to five hundred hours for an act that would be a felony or a misdemeanor of the first degree if committed by an adult, up to two hundred hours for an act that would be a misdemeanor of the second, third, or fourth degree if committed by an adult, or up to thirty hours for an act that would be a minor misdemeanor if committed by an adult;

(e) A requirement that the child obtain a high school diploma, a certificate of high school equivalence, vocational training, or employment;

(f) A period of drug and alcohol use monitoring;

(g) A requirement of alcohol or drug assessment or counseling, or a period in an alcohol or drug treatment program with a level of security for the child as determined necessary by the court;

(h) A period in which the court orders the child to observe a curfew that may involve daytime or evening hours;

(i) A requirement that the child serve monitored time;

(j) A period of house arrest without electronic monitoring or continuous alcohol monitoring;

(k) A period of electronic monitoring or continuous alcohol monitoring without house arrest, or house arrest with electronic monitoring or continuous alcohol monitoring or both electronic monitoring and continuous alcohol monitoring, that does not exceed the maximum sentence of imprisonment that could be imposed upon an adult who commits the same act.

A period of house arrest with electronic monitoring or continuous alcohol monitoring or both electronic monitoring and continuous alcohol monitoring, imposed under this division shall not extend beyond the child's twenty-first birthday...;

(l) A suspension of the driver's license, probationary driver's license, or temporary instruction permit issued to the child for a period of time prescribed by the court, or a suspension of the registration of all motor vehicles registered in the name of the child for a period of time prescribed by the court...;

(5) Commit the child to the custody of the court;

(6) Require the child to not be absent without legitimate excuse from the public school the child is supposed to attend for five or more consecutive days, seven or more school days in one school month, or twelve or more school days in a school year...;

(8) Make any further disposition that the court finds proper, except that the child shall not be placed in any of the following:

(a) A state correctional institution, a county, multicounty, or municipal jail or workhouse, or another place in which an adult convicted of a crime, under arrest, or charged with a crime is held....

(C) The court may establish a victim-offender mediation program in which victims and their offenders meet to discuss the offense and suggest possible restitution. If the court obtains the assent of the victim of the delinquent act committed by the child, the court may require the child to participate in the program.

(D) (1) If a child is adjudicated a delinquent child for committing an act that would be a felony if committed by an adult and if the child caused, attempted to cause, threatened to cause, or created a risk of physical harm to the victim of the act, the court, prior to issuing an order of disposition under this section, shall order the preparation of a victim impact statement....The court shall consider the victim impact statement in determining the order of disposition to issue for the child....

(F) (1) During the period of a delinquent child's community control granted under this section, authorized probation officers who are engaged within the scope of their supervisory duties or responsibilities may search, with or without a warrant, the person of the delinquent child, the place of residence of the delinquent child, and a motor vehicle, another item of tangible or intangible personal property, or other real property in which the delinquent child has a right, title, or interest or for which the delinquent child has the express or implied permission of a person with a right, title, or interest to use, occupy, or possess if the probation officers have reasonable grounds to believe that the delinquent child is not abiding by the law or otherwise is not complying with the conditions of the delinquent child's community control. The court that places a delinquent child on community control under this section shall provide the delinquent child with a written notice that informs the delinquent child that authorized probation officers who are engaged within the scope of their supervisory duties or responsibilities may conduct those types of searches during the period of community control if they have reasonable grounds to believe that the delinquent child is not abiding by the law or otherwise is not complying with the conditions of the delinquent child's community control....

(2) The court that places a child on community control under this section shall provide the child's parent, guardian, or other custodian with a written notice that informs them that authorized probation officers may conduct searches.... The notice shall specifically state that a permissible search might extend to a motor vehicle, another item of tangible or intangible personal property, or a place of residence or other real property in which a notified parent, guardian, or custodian has a right, title, or interest and that the parent, guardian, or custodian expressly or impliedly permits the child to use, occupy, or possess.

NOTES

1. Dispositional statutes, such as the one above, are quite broad and are designed to provide courts with considerable flexibility in crafting an appropriate disposition. Nevertheless, probation remains the most common disposition. Typically, a juvenile placed on probation is supervised by a juvenile probation officer who works for the juvenile court (not the prosecutor) and may make recommendations that run counter to those made by the state. Conditions of probation vary widely and may include mandatory meetings with the probation officer, mandatory school attendance, and a requirement that the juvenile remain law-abiding. The juvenile court also may order the juvenile to write an apology letter, perform community service, pay a fine, or provide restitution to the victim.

2. Electronic monitoring (EM) is another common option that courts may use pre- or post-adjudication. An electronic monitoring device (EMD), typically attached to a juvenile's ankle or wrist, tracks the juvenile's location using GPS technology and alerts the monitor if the juvenile leaves a designated area. EM is commonly used as an alternative to detention or institutionalization, and the American Bar Association has endorsed its use. American Bar Association, Resolution in Favor of Electronic Monitoring of Juveniles, http://new.abanet.org/sections/criminaljustice/PublicDocuments/policy%20jj%20prisons.pdf.

3. As with a criminal case, the juvenile court may order an adjudicated delinquent to pay a fine, court costs, or restitution or to perform community service either as an additional condition or as a way to make restitution or work off a fine. The amount of the fine often is determined by reference to the relevant criminal statute, and there may be statutes governing court costs, restitution, and the number of community-service hours that may be imposed. Revocation of a driver's license or learner's permit also may be ordered in connection with certain types of offenses. Juveniles may be ordered into substance-abuse counseling or treatment and to submit to drug screening to monitor ongoing abuse. There is some empirical evidence that certain treatment modalities may be particularly effective at reducing substance abuse among juveniles, including multidimensional family therapy and cognitive-behavioral group treatment. For a meta-analysis of various studies examining the effectiveness of different treatment protocols for substance-abusing youth, see

Michael G. Vaughn and Matthew O. Howard, *Adolescent Substance Abuse Treatment: A Synthesis of Controlled Evaluations*, 14 Research on Social Work Practice 325 (2004).

c. RIGHT TO TREATMENT AND CONDITIONS OF CONFINEMENT

In 1974, the Seventh Circuit Court of Appeals held that juveniles have a right to treatment under the Due Process Clause of the Fourteenth Amendment. *Nelson v. Heyne*, 491 F.2d 352 (1974). The rationale behind the right was simple: "effective treatment must be the quid pro quo for society's right to exercise its parens patriae controls." *Id.* at 360 (citing *Martarella v. Kelley*, 349 F.Supp. 575, 600 [S.D.N.Y. 1972]). If youths were being subjected to the benevolent protection of the state, those youths had the right to receive some therapeutic benefit from that protection. *Id.* In support of this position, the Seventh Circuit noted that the United States Supreme Court in *Kent v. United States*, 383 U.S. 541 (1996), and *In re Gault*, 387 U.S. 1 (1967), assumed that a state must provide rehabilitative treatment in order for juvenile courts to be valid. The *Nelson* court went on to hold that the institutional system of classification then in use (the Quay System of Behavior Classification, which classified inmates into four personality types and set improvement goals based on those determinations but offered an unclear amount of individualized counseling) did not fulfill the juvenile's right to treatment. *Nelson*, 491 F.2d at 360.

Throughout the 1970s, several district courts held that juveniles have a right to treatment as a *quid pro quo*, under the substantive Due Process Clause, or the Eighth Amendment prohibition against cruel and unusual punishment. See, e.g., *Inmates of the Boys' Training Schools v. Affleck*, 346 F. Supp. 1354 (D.R.I. 1972); *Martarella v. Kelley*, 349 F.Supp. 575, 585 (S.D.N.Y. 1972); *Morgan v. Sproat*, 432 F. Supp. 1130 (S.D. Miss. 1977). However, the courts moved away from a strong right to treatment in the 1980s and 1990s, spurred by a shift in legislation emphasizing the need to protect the community from juvenile offenders, dwindling judicial support for an expansive right to training, and rehabilitation. Paul Holland & Wallace J. Mlyniec, *Whatever Happened to the Right to Treatment? The Modern Quest for a Historical Promise*, 68 Temp. L. Rev. 1791 (1995). Holland and Mlyniec nevertheless argue that juveniles have a right to rehabilitative care and treatment embedded in state juvenile codes, many of which still retain rehabilitative goals. *Id.* at 1816–1822.

Douglas E. Abrams, *Reforming Juvenile Delinquency Treatment to Enhance Rehabilitation, Personal Accountability, and Public Safety*, 84 Or. L. Rev. 1001, 1002–1004, 1010–1011 (2005).

"Juvenile justice facilities across the nation," *U.S. News & World Report* found in July of 2004, "are in a dangerously advanced state of disarray, with violence an almost everyday occurrence and rehabilitation the exception rather than the rule. Abuse of juvenile inmates by staff is routine." In 2005, the U.S. Justice Department found that sexual violence is reported in juvenile prisons at rates ten times higher than in adult lockups. Neither finding surprised juvenile justice professionals who have watched the nation's juvenile corrections facilities spiral downward for decades. "Conditions in many American juvenile detention centers are awful," one commentator wrote in 1998, "and they have been for years."

The Justice Department has assumed a central role in efforts to reform state systems that confine delinquents: youths who have committed acts that would be crimes if committed by an adult. Primary authority comes from the Civil Rights of Institutionalized Persons Act (CRIPA) [42 U.S.C. § 1997–1997j (2011)], enacted in 1980 after Congress found nationwide conditions of juvenile confinement "barbaric."

CRIPA authorizes the Justice Department to sue state and local governments to remedy "egregious or flagrant" conditions that deny constitutional or federal statutory rights to persons residing or confined in public institutions, including juvenile correctional facilities. The federal courts may order remedies that "insure the minimum corrective measures necessary to insure the full enjoyment" of these rights. The Department may also sue under the Violent Crime Control and Law Enforcement Act of 1994, which prohibits a "pattern or practice" of civil rights abuses by law enforcement officers.

After learning of alleged constitutional or statutory violations from any source, Justice Department personnel inspect a juvenile facility with expert consultants in a variety of fields, including juvenile justice administration, mental health care, medicine, psychology, and education. The Department's report detailing constitutional and statutory violations opens negotiations with the state for corrective action, with the prospect of a federal enforcement lawsuit for violations left unremedied.

Beginning in the 1980s, the Justice Department has inspected more than 100 juvenile correctional facilities nationwide, leading to CRIPA agreements or consent decrees covering more than thirty facilities where conditions had fallen below minimum constitutional standards. Under Democratic and Republican administrations alike, the Department has quickened the pace since 1994.

... More than a century after the creation of the nation's first juvenile court grounded in rehabilitative impulses, many states still maintain inhumane, thoroughly ineffective juvenile prisons that neither rehabilitate children nor protect public safety. States lock up status offenders and nonviolent youths who could be treated more effectively in less expensive community-based alternative settings. Mentally ill and otherwise fragile children are beaten by guards, physically and sexually assaulted by more vicious youths while guards turn their backs, and left in fear for their lives. Children are denied needed mental health and medical treatment, and deprived of education guaranteed to them by state and federal law. Overcrowded prison cells are often little more than roach-infested cages reeking of sewage and urine. Recidivism rates frequently exceed fifty percent, compromising public safety because most repeat juvenile offenders do not turn to white collar crime. Instead they commit new violent crimes against innocent victims whom a lower rate would spare....

Private lawsuits continue, but the Justice Department's CRIPA inspections have assumed center stage in the past decade. The Department's reports concerning inspected juvenile prisons are in the nature of allegations before trial or settlement, but the Department's findings have usually recited conditions that the media and children's advocates had widely reported, and that authorities had knowingly ignored, for years. In some states, federal courts had ordered corrective action as much as a quarter century earlier, only to have the governor and legislature turn deaf ears. Most of the inspected states have acknowledged the accuracy of the Department's findings.

The Justice Department's CRIPA inspections doubtlessly focus on states the Agency deems most troubling, but the sheer volume of states inspected so recently in such a short period suggests that the Department has only scratched the surface.

NOTES AND QUESTIONS

1. To date, the Justice Department has conducted inspections in Georgia, Mississippi, Louisiana, Indiana, Arizona, Nevada, Ohio, Hawaii, Michigan, Oklahoma, Texas, Puerto Rico, Arkansas, Maryland, South Dakota, New York, and Los Angeles, and a number of lawsuits have been filed. The problems uncovered by the Justice Department are nothing short of horrific. They include filthy, vermin-infested living conditions, sewage seeping into cells, inadequate toilet facilities, physical abuse and neglect of youth by correctional officials, failure to provide mental-health and medical treatment, shackling, excessive use of isolation, sexual assault, failure to provide educational services, overcrowding, beatings, peeling paint, exposed wiring, suicides, and violence perpetrated by other youths. For information about the Justice Department's litigation on behalf of institutionalized youths, see http://www.justice.gov/crt/about/spl/juveniles.php.

2. Missouri has developed a juvenile correctional system that some have called a model for reform. A report by the Annie E. Casey Foundation has found that Missouri's approach has resulted in low recidivism rates, a strong safety record, high rates of educational success, and positive transitions back into the community, all at a cost that is equal to or lower than most other correctional systems. Missouri has done so by creating a four-level continuum of programs, ranging from community care to secure care. However, all programs are small and regionally based, and each youth is provided with extensive and individualized treatment and attention. The facilities themselves are designed to be warm and comfortable; youths sleep in carpeted dorm rooms decorated with handmade posters and artwork, and they are permitted to wear their own clothes. Staff members do not carry mace or weapons. Missouri does not permit the use of pepper spray, hog-ties, or face-down restraints, and handcuffs and shackles are permitted only in rare emergencies. Youths also are provided with small classroom settings in which to learn and are offered work experience and community-service experience while institutionalized. Annie E. Casey Found., The Missouri Model: Reinventing the Practice of Rehabilitating Youthful Offenders (2010), http://www.aecf.org/~/media/Pubs/Initiatives/Juvenile%20Detention%20Alternatives%20Initiative/MOModel/MO_Fullreport_webfinal.pdf.

In light of the Missouri experience, why do states still rely on harsh institutionalization practices?

d. SPECIAL POPULATIONS

Juveniles with special needs often are overlooked in the juvenile correctional system. For example, studies have found that LGBTQ youths are not protected from physical, sexual, and psychological abuse while institutionalized; they may be placed in isolation or unduly restrictive settings in order to "protect" them from other youths; and they do not receive specialized services. Moreover, there is evidence that correctional staff members interpret benign behaviors as sexualized and punish them. Staff also may feel uncomfortable with the expression of gender identity and may forbid, punish, harass, or ridicule that expression. Housing decisions also may be made without respect for gender identity, and these youths also may be denied specialized medical services, such as hormone treatments. See, e.g., Katayoon Majd, Jody Marksamer, & Carolyn Reyes, The Equity Project, Hidden Injustice: Lesbian, Gay, Bisexual, and Transgender Youth in Juvenile Courts 101–112 (2009), http://www.equityproject.org/pdfs/hidden_injustice.pdf. See also *R.G. v. Koller*, 415 F.Supp.2d 1129 (D. Haw. 2006) (due process rights of LGBTQ wards violated by use of isolation to "protect" them, and prison officials deliberately indifferent to verbal, physical, and sexual abuse of wards in violation of due process).

Juveniles who are institutionalized also can have serious substance-abuse or mental-health disorders that largely go unrecognized and untreated. Although it is unclear precisely how many juveniles suffer from mental-health disorders, some estimates place the number of juveniles with serious emotional disturbance at about 20 percent, compared with 9 percent to 13 percent of juveniles in the general population. "In addition to this sizable group of juveniles 'who critically need access to mental health services,' it is clear that 'most youth in the juvenile justice system have a diagnosable mental illness and could benefit from some services.'" Thomas L. Hafemeister, *Parameters and Implementation of a Right to Mental Health Treatment for Juvenile Offenders*, 12 VA. J. SOC. POL'Y & L. 61, 66–67 (2004). Some smaller-scale studies have found that as many as two-thirds to three-quarters of institutionalized juveniles met the criteria for a mental or psychiatric disorder. *Id.* at 67–68. Nevertheless, when programs are available, they are "'woefully inadequate, uncoordinated, and fragmented'" and may even be counterproductive. *Id.* at 71. See, e.g., Joseph J. Cocozza & Kathleen R. Skowyra, *Youth with Mental Health Disorders: Issues and Emerging Responses*, 7 JUVENILE JUSTICE 3 (2001); Cynthia Conward, *The Juvenile Justice System: Not Necessarily in the Best Interests of Children*, 33 NEW ENG. L. REV. 39 (1998); John S. Lyons et al., *Mental Health Service Needs of Juvenile Offenders: A Comparison of Detention, Incarceration, and Treatment Settings*, 4 CHILDREN'S SERVICES: SOCIAL POLICY, RESEARCH, AND PRACTICE 69 (2001). See also *A.M. v. Luzerne County Juvenile Det. Ctr.*, 372 F.3d 572 (3d Cir. 2004) (care must be provided when mental-health and behavioral problems of minor in custody of youth detention center constituted a "serious mental health need").

Minority youths, overrepresented in the juvenile correctional system, also may have a set of special needs that are overlooked. Brent Pattison argues that these youths need "culturally appropriate treatment" adapted to their "unique needs." Brent Pattison, *Minority Youth in Juvenile Correctional Facilities: Cultural Differences and the Right to Treatment*, 16 LAW & INEQUALITY 573, 577 (1998):

> Mental health professionals have noted the importance of the culturally unique treatment needs of minority youths. For example, language differences may be a barrier to effective treatment for some minority youths. In addition, when juvenile justice professionals do not understand the youth's cultural background, the youth's "cultural traits, behaviors or beliefs will likely be misinterpreted as dysfunctions to be overcome." Finally, there is evidence that the characteristics of a particular mental illness may be different for minority youths. For example, many Black juvenile delinquents suffer from depression and mental illnesses that are more severe than those of their White counterparts. Given these differences, culturally appropriate treatment is more likely to be successful.
>
> Ethnic minorities are also exposed disproportionately to certain aggravating factors that contribute to delinquent behavior, such as racial discrimination, neighborhood crime and

> poverty. Current treatment programs may provide discipline and structure for a youth in the short term, but may not deal with environmental influences on the youth's delinquent behavior. Any effort to provide treatment for minority offenders should take into account the effect of the socioeconomic position of minority youths.

Id. at 581–582.

Girls, too, may not receive the services they need. Although far more boys than girls enter the delinquency system, the number of girls charged with delinquent acts has been increasing. Although Congress specifically recognized the increasing arrest rate among girls, gender-responsive programming has been slow to develop. Effective gender-competent programming emphasizes "the need for building girls' confidence, which can, in turn, lead to resilience from delinquency. Relationships also play a crucial role in girls' development. School success, spiritual connections, and a supportive family environment can mitigate the loss of self-esteem and ease the struggle through adolescence." Christy Sharp & Jessica Simon, Child Welfare League of America, Girls in the Juvenile Justice System: The Need for More Gender-Responsive Services 8 (2004). To accomplish this, girls need a "safe" space, removed from adolescent males, time to talk, opportunities to develop positive relationships with female friends and relatives, and opportunities to express their individuality and life experiences within their cultural contexts. Gender-competent programming also must focus on health and sex education, implement changes to school curricula to emphasize the unique contributions of women, and be adequately funded to ensure that girls reap the benefits of the programming. *Id.* at 21–22.

Researchers have identified a few successful gender-competent programs for girls. PACE (Practical, Academic, and Cultural Education) Center for Girls is a gender-competent, non-profit, nonresidential, community-based program providing education, training, counseling, and advocacy for girls ages twelve to seventeen. PACE offers educational services, life-management classes, counseling, career-preparation services, and volunteer opportunities. Based in Florida, PACE staffs seventeen centers and serves approximately 2,000 girls annually. Girls Incorporated is a national network of nonprofit organizations serving 150,000 girls at more than 1,400 sites every year. All sites encourage girls to be "strong, smart, and bold," by offering educational and career guidance and opportunities, emotional support, sex and health education, drug-abuse prevention, media literacy, and sports participation. Children of the Night, a private nonprofit organization, assists children living on the streets and forced into prostitution. The organization operates a twenty-four-hour hotline, offers shelter, assists with the prosecution of pimps, and facilitates community services, treatment services, and foster-home placement.

For an excellent and comprehensive discussion of the gendered approach to female delinquency, see MEDA CHESNEY-LIND & RANDALL G. SHELDEN, GIRLS, DELINQUENCY, AND JUVENILE JUSTICE (3d ed., 2004).

e. COLLATERAL CONSEQUENCES

Although a juvenile may complete the terms of his juvenile disposition successfully, there may nevertheless be additional consequences associated with that adjudication that deny a youth future opportunities. For example, delinquent acts not committed on school grounds may result in suspension, expulsion, or exclusion from extracurricular activities. Adjudications may be used against the juvenile in subsequent juvenile or adult proceedings and may lead to transfer for adult prosecution or enhanced sentencing upon conviction. Delinquency adjudications also may result in loss of a driver's license for nontraffic offenses such as drug crimes and loss of the right to possess or carry firearms. Juveniles must report delinquency adjudications to military recruiters even though their records have been expunged or sealed. Although delinquency adjudications are not considered convictions for immigration purposes, they may prevent a finding of "good moral character" in naturalization cases. Additionally, applicants for professional licenses also may have to report prior juvenile adjudications. For an in-depth, state-by-state analysis of the collateral consequences of delinquency adjudications, see http://www.abanet.org/crimjust/juvjus/cjmcollconseq2.html. The American Bar Association also has adopted a resolution urging federal, state, and local governments to limit the collateral consequences of a juvenile adjudication. http://www.campaignforyouthjustice.org/documents/ABA%20-%20102A%20-%20Collateral%20Consequences%20for%20JuvenilesRev.pdf. In light of the extensive collateral consequences for juvenile adjudications, what justification is there for denying juveniles the full panoply of constitutional rights?

3. SPECIAL JUVENILE DISPOSITIONS

a. BLENDED SENTENCES

Even those juveniles who remain in the juvenile justice system may be subject to criminal penalties. These laws, known as blended sentences, are authorized in fourteen states and permit juvenile courts to impose adult sanctions on certain qualifying juvenile offenders. Typically, these laws authorize a juvenile judge to impose a criminal sentence, usually in addition to the juvenile disposition, that the court then suspends on condition that the juvenile successfully completes his juvenile term. In some models, however, the court may directly impose an adult sentence in lieu of a juvenile disposition. In others, the court has the authority to impose a term of incarceration that may extend years beyond the age limits of the court's jurisdiction without reference to the minor's adjustment or rehabilitation.

Juvenile blended-sentencing provisions may be more expansive than transfer laws. In some states, for example, the age at which a juvenile may be transferred to criminal court for trial is higher than the age for blended-sentencing eligibility. Thus, children who because of age would otherwise not be eligible for transfer nevertheless may be subject to criminal sanctions. Even juveniles in those states with expansive waiver provisions may be at higher risk for actual imposition of adult sanctions through the blended-sentencing laws. Waiver to criminal court typically is an irrevocable and final decision. In jurisdictions where courts retain discretion to transfer, judges may be reluctant to waive younger children or youths with less serious offense histories. The decision to pursue a blended sentence thus may be a way to reach juveniles who might not be transferred or who otherwise would not warrant transfer. For a discussion of blended sentences, see, e.g., Nat'l Ctr. for Juvenile Justice, Different from Adults: An Updated Analysis of Juvenile

Transfer and Blended Sentencing Laws, with Recommendations for Reform (2008), www.modelsforchange.net/publications/181; Richard E. Redding & James C. Howell, *Blended Sentencing in American Juvenile Courts*, in THE CHANGING BORDERS OF JUVENILE JUSTICE: TRANSFER OF ADOLESCENTS TO THE CRIMINAL COURT (Jeffrey Fagan & Franklin E. Zimring eds., 2000); Marcy R. Podkopacz & Barry C. Feld, *The Back-Door to Prison: Waiver Reform, Blended Sentencing, and the Law of Unintended Consequences*, 91 J. CRIM. L. & CRIMINOLOGY 997 (2001).

b. SEX-OFFENDER REGISTRATION LAWS

Juveniles who commit sex offenses, often against other minors, face the likelihood of severe sanctions and the long-term consequences of sex-offender registration laws comparable to those faced by adults. The length of reporting and registration obligations may last well beyond the maximum age of the juvenile court's jurisdiction and, in limited circumstances, can continue for life. Two federal measures, commonly called Megan's Law and the Adam Walsh Act, were passed after the sexual assaults and murders of the children for whom they are named. They are based, in large part, on a philosophy that sex offenders cannot be cured and that they will pose a risk to society throughout their lives. Consequently, these measures establish a national sex-offender registry, create community-notification provisions, mandate conformity among the states, and establish a tiered classification system for sexual offenders that determines the length of time the offender will remain in the registry and be subject to reporting and notification requirements. The Adam Walsh Act, 42 U.S.C. § 16901 et seq. (2006), also extended many of these requirements to juveniles adjudicated delinquent for certain specified sexual offenses. Most states, however, are not in compliance with the Adam Walsh Act and cite the juvenile registration and reporting requirements as a primary factor for noncompliance. Nat'l Consortium for Justice Information & Statistics, SEARCH Survey on State Compliance with the Sex Offender Registration and Notification Act (SORNA) (April 2009), http://www.search.org/mes/pdf/SORNA-StateComplianceSurvey2009Rev071609.pdf.

Generally, sex-offender registration laws require the offender to provide identifying information, and sometimes even a photograph, to the designated authority within a specified time period. The offender also is required to update that registration information periodically on threat of further prosecution. Local authorities may be required to notify the members of the community in which he lives of his status as a sexual offender. In some states, a period of incarceration may be followed by indefinite civil commitment for those individuals who are found to be sexually violent. Moreover, the registration requirements in some states may require all juveniles to register regardless of age or type of offense, even when the sexual activity is arguably consensual. Nor are juvenile registrants necessarily exempt from community-notification requirements that result in the publication of the names of juvenile sex offenders, raising issues about the confidentiality of juvenile court records.

Are juvenile sex-offender registration laws necessary? Consider the following excerpt when formulating your answer.

David Finkelhor, Richard Ormrod, & Mark Chaffin, U.S. Dep't of Justice, Juveniles Who Commit Sex Offenses against Minors 2–3 (December 2009), https://www.ncjrs.gov/pdffiles1/ojjdp/227763.pdf.

Early thinking about juvenile sex offenders was based on what was known about adult child molesters, particularly adult pedophiles, given findings that a significant portion of them began their offending during adolescence. However, current clinical typologies and models emphasize that this retrospective logic has obscured important motivational, behavioral, and prognostic differences between juvenile sex offenders and adult sex offenders and has overestimated the role of deviant sexual preferences in juvenile sex crimes. More recent models emphasize the diversity of juvenile sex offenders, their favorable prognosis suggested by low sex-offense recidivism rates, and the commonalities between juvenile sex offending and other juvenile delinquency.

Clinical studies also underscore a diversity of behaviors, characteristics, and future risk. For example, the sexual behaviors that bring youth into clinical settings can include events as diverse as sharing pornography with younger children, fondling a child over the clothes, grabbing peers in a sexual way at school, date rape, gang rape, or performing oral, vaginal, or anal sex on a much younger child. Offenses can involve a single event, a few isolated events, or a large number of events with multiple victims. Juvenile sex offenders come from a variety of social and family backgrounds and can either be well functioning or have multiple problems. A number have experienced a high accumulated burden of adversity, including maltreatment or exposure to violence; others have not. In some cases, a history of childhood sexual abuse appears to contribute to later juvenile sex offending, but most sexual abuse victims do not become sex offenders in adolescence or adulthood. Among preteen children with sexual behavior problems, a history of sexual abuse is particularly prevalent.

In addition to a diversity of backgrounds, diversity in motivation is evident. Some juvenile sex offenders appear primarily motivated by sexual curiosity. Others have longstanding patterns of violating the rights of others. Some offenses occur in conjunction with serious mental health problems. Some of the offending behavior is compulsive, but it more often appears impulsive or reflects poor judgment.

Similarly, clinical data point to variability in risk for future sex offending as an adult. Multiple short- and long-term clinical followup studies of juvenile sex offenders consistently demonstrate that a large majority (about 85–95 percent) of sex-offending youth have no arrests or reports for future sex crimes. When previously sex-offending youth do have future arrests, they are far more likely to be for nonsexual crimes such as property or drug offenses than for sex crimes. These empirical findings contrast with popular thought and widely publicized anecdotal cases that disproportionately portray incidences of sex crime recidivism. Nevertheless, a small number of sex-offending youth are at elevated risk to progress to adult sex offenses. To identify those who are more likely to progress to future offending, researchers have developed actuarial risk assessment tools that have demonstrated some predictive validity; efforts to refine these tools are underway.

NOTES AND QUESTIONS

1. To what extent do sex-offender registration laws comport with the underlying purposes of the juvenile court? Are they constitutional? In *United States v. Juvenile Male*, 590 F.3d 924 (9th Cir. 2010), fifteen-year-old S.E. admitted to aggravated sexual abuse (in a federal district court in Montana exercising its juvenile delinquency jurisdiction pursuant to 18 U.S.C. § 5031 et seq.) one year prior to the passage of the Adam Walsh Act and the registration and notification provisions known as SORNA. In 2007, S.E. was ordered to register as a sex offender under SORNA. He challenged the order, arguing that the retroactive application of SORNA violated the Ex Post Facto Clause of the United States Constitution. Although S.E. conceded that Congress's intent in enacting SORNA was not punitive, he nevertheless argued that the act was punitive in its effects. A unanimous court agreed:

> Historically, our country has had two separate systems of justice, one for adults and the other for juveniles. The criminal justice system that applies to adults is fundamentally a public one. We view its public nature as an essential protection for the rights of both the defendant and society at large....
>
> Juvenile adjudications, by contrast, by and large take place outside the public domain. We have historically made the decision to shield juvenile offenders from the public eye—both from the protections that public scrutiny provides against government oppression, and from the burdens that public scrutiny imposes through the stigmatization of those convicted of crimes. As Chief Justice, then Justice, Rehnquist explained, "[i]t is a hallmark of our juvenile justice system in the United States that virtually from its inception at the end of the [nineteenth] century its proceedings have been conducted outside of the public's full gaze and the youths brought before our juvenile courts have been shielded from publicity." *Smith v. Daily Mail Pub. Co.*, 443 U.S. 97, 107, 99 S.Ct. 2667, 61 L.Ed.2d 399 (1979) (Rehnquist, J., concurring). Juveniles are denied certain procedural rights afforded to adult criminal defendants, including a public trial by jury, but they are, in turn, beneficiaries of an adjudicatory system designed, though not always successfully, to rehabilitate rather than punish—a system ill-suited to public exposure.... Our punitive system is public; our rehabilitative system for juveniles, quite deliberately, is not.
>
> In light of these two different systems of justice—one public and punitive, the other largely confidential and rehabilitative—the impact of sex offender registration and reporting upon former juvenile offenders and upon convicted adults differs in ways that we cannot ignore.... We are... compelled to conclude, for what it's worth, that it would be a breach of faith to those young persons, some of whom are now elderly, who voluntarily accepted status as a juvenile delinquent believing that their juvenile offense would not later be made known to the world at large....
>
> [W]e conclude that the retroactive application of SORNA's juvenile registration provision imposes a disability that is neither "minor" nor "indirect," but rather severely damaging to former juvenile offenders' economic, social, psychological, and physical well-being.... In fact, given the degree of damage former juvenile offenders may suffer in their adult lives by the retroactive application of the statutory requirement, we conclude that this factor is by far the most compelling in our analysis....
>
> Confidentiality in juvenile proceedings is not absolute, but it is generally carefully protected: The norm in juvenile delinquency adjudications is closed proceedings and sealed records. Such

confidentiality has historically been one of the most significant factors differentiating juvenile adjudications, which are designed to be rehabilitative, from adult criminal proceedings, which are designed to be punitive. District judges do have discretion to open juvenile proceedings and unseal portions of the record of juvenile adjudications.... However, judges may not expose all juvenile proceedings to public scrutiny as a general practice.... It is clear that a large-scale release of juvenile records of the magnitude authorized by SORNA, and the ensuing public display of those records on the internet, was prohibited under federal law as it existed prior to the passage of SORNA, and will have a significant and adverse life-long impact upon the individuals affected.

SORNA's juvenile registration provision, therefore, does not merely provide for further public access to information already available; it makes public information about sex offenders that would otherwise permanently remain confidential and exposes persons who were adjudicated delinquent years before to public humiliation and ignominy for the first time. It also seriously jeopardizes the ability of such individuals to obtain employment, housing, and education. The registration and notification system here cannot be compared to a visit to a criminal archive, as such a visit would yield no information about juvenile adjudications. The disadvantages that flow to former juvenile offenders on account of having a public record as sex offenders must be attributed to SORNA alone.

Under SORNA, moreover, individuals who *twenty or thirty years ago* pled true to acts of juvenile delinquency—and who did so with the expectation that their adjudication would remain confidential—may, decades later, be required to publicly expose that information to friends, family, colleagues, and neighbors. Indeed, most of those affected by the retroactive application of SORNA's juvenile registration provision are not juveniles but adults. Many of these individuals have for many years led entirely law-abiding and productive lives that may be dramatically disrupted by the registration requirements. Some, had they known that they would years later be subject to registration requirements, might not have pled true to the charges at all.

Beyond these societal consequences of public registration as a sex offender, SORNA imposes additional administrative burdens in the form of "periodic in person verification." 42 U.S.C. § 16916 ("[A] sex offender shall appear in person, allow the jurisdiction to take a current photograph, and verify the information in each registry in which that offender is required to be registered").... Every former juvenile offender subject to SORNA ... must register in person four times a year for at least 25 years. This requirement for appearances every three months before law enforcement officials is neither "minor" nor "indirect." ...

Because SORNA's juvenile registration provision, retroactively applied to former juvenile offenders, imposes a serious disability by making public otherwise confidential delinquency records relating to sexual offenses, and because the in-person registration requirement is substantially burdensome, SORNA's juvenile registration provision imposes an onerous "affirmative disability or restraint" on former juvenile offenders. As we have already stated, this factor weighs heavily in support of a finding that SORNA's juvenile registration requirement has a punitive effect. Given the severity of its burdens, it would be difficult to reach any other conclusion....

... SORNA was enacted "[i]n order to protect the public from sex offenders and offenders against children, and *in response to the vicious attacks by violent predators against the victims listed below....*" 42 U.S.C. § 16901 (emphasis added). The statute subsequently lists seventeen individual victims and details the crimes that were committed against them, strongly suggesting that the motivation behind SORNA's passage was not only to protect public safety in the future but also to "revisit past crimes." Senator Grassley's floor statement similarly reflects a retributive sentiment that colored the legislative proceedings: "Child sex offenders are the most heinous of all criminals. I can honestly tell you that I would just as soon lock up all the child molesters and child pornography makers and murderers in this country and throw away the key." 152 Cong. Rec. S8012, S8021 (daily ed. July 20, 2006) (statement of Sen. Grassley).

The purpose of the Ex Post Facto Clause is to prevent the passage of "potentially vindictive legislation." SORNA's legislative text and history contain substantial warning signs that its aim, while principally regulatory, to be sure, is also in some measure punitive.

We next consider whether SORNA's juvenile registration provision has a non-punitive purpose and, if it does, whether the requirement is excessive in relation to that goal. We must determine "whether the disability is imposed for the purpose of punishment or whether it is but an incident of some other legitimate governmental purpose." *Bell v. Wolfish*, 441 U.S. 520, 538, 99 S.Ct. 1861, 60 L.Ed.2d 447 (1979). If the statute is reasonably related to a non-punitive purpose then the statute is not usually considered punitive. *Id.* at 539, 99 S.Ct. 1861....

On the one hand, Congress has extended SORNA's juvenile registration requirement to only a portion of those who were adjudicated delinquents: those who were "14 years of age or older at the time of the offense and the offense adjudicated was comparable to or more severe than aggravated sexual abuse...." 42 U.S.C. § 16911(8)....

On the other hand... [g]iven the low risk that former juvenile sex offenders pose to public safety and the lifetime confidentiality that most former juveniles would otherwise enjoy, retroactively applying SORNA's juvenile registration provision is an exceptionally severe means of achieving the statute's nonpunitive goal....

...Studies cited in the legislative history of this bill indicate that the recidivism rates for juvenile offenders are significantly lower than for adult offenders. *See* 152 Cong. Rec. S8012-02, S8023 (daily ed. July 20, 2006) (statement of Sen. Kennedy) ("For juveniles, the public notification provision in this bill is harsh given their low rate of recidivism, which is less than 8 percent according to the most recent studies"); Coalition for Juvenile Justice, Comments in Opposition to Interim Rule RIN 1.105-AB22, 3 (2007) (citing study showing 5 to 14% recidivism rate for juveniles, as compared to 40% rate of recidivism for adults); Human Rights Watch, supra, at 69–70 (listing studies finding low recidivism rates among juvenile sex offenders). Research suggests, moreover, that only a small portion of adult sex offenders previously committed sex offenses as juveniles. *See* Human Rights Watch at 70.

These statistics are not surprising. Juveniles are as a general matter less mature, more impulsive, and more confused about sexually appropriate behavior than adults. They do not understand their sexual drives as well or know how to deal with them. We do not, of course, excuse such conduct as mere juvenile exuberance. We simply recognize that the predictive value of an individual's conduct, especially sexual conduct, at the age of fourteen or fifteen is, under most circumstances, limited. For that reason, requiring former juvenile sex offenders to register as such many decades thereafter will often not only be unnecessary to secure the safety of the community but may even be counterproductive.

It is worth noting that, in practice, those who are primarily affected by SORNA's retroactive application to former juvenile offenders are not the most likely to recidivate—they are, rather, those adults who are forced to register solely because they committed an offense as a juvenile, but who have lived the rest of their adult lives without committing another such crime. Adults who re-offended in the past after their initial juvenile offense are required to register in any event by SORNA's retroactive application to adult sex offenders, and adults who re-offend in the future are required to register by SORNA's basic provisions.

In addition to the personal toll on those who are labeled as sex offenders, registration of former juvenile offenders undermines the rehabilitative goals of our juvenile justice system as a whole, and derails the historical effort to avoid permanently or publicly stigmatizing juveniles as criminals. It may also seriously affect the lives of the spouses and children of these former juvenile sexual offenders. Sacrificing confidentiality and lessening the chance of rehabilitation for former juvenile sex offenders who have not re-offended are severe measures to aid in achieving public safety, in light of the importance of the contravening interests and the relatively low risk that such offenders pose to the community. Indeed, the severity of the measures may well increase the risk of recidivism within a population that otherwise has the greatest potential for rehabilitation....

The retroactive application of SORNA's provision requiring registration and reporting by former juvenile offenders imposes immense burdens, not only through onerous in-person registration and reporting requirements, but, more important, through the publication and dissemination of highly prejudicial juvenile adjudication records of individuals who have committed no offenses since their adolescence—records that would otherwise remain sealed. The juvenile registration requirement, for the first time under federal law, exposes thousands of former juvenile offenders to public notoriety and subjects them to lifetime condemnation and ostracism by their community. The effects of this exposure are wide-ranging, and likely include serious housing, employment, and educational disadvantages.... The publicity that once juvenile offenders, now law abiding adults, face is, moreover, something that has traditionally attached to juvenile offenders only if they are transferred to an adult—and punitive—system. Historically, public exposure constitutes an integral part of a punitive and not a juvenile or rehabilitative regime. Additionally, while it is indisputable that SORNA was enacted as a regulatory measure in order to promote public safety, there is evidence that this non-punitive aim was mixed to some degree with a less evident desire for retribution as well. Finally, imposing the burdens of registration upon former juvenile offenders is a harsh measure in view of the low rate of recidivism for juvenile offenders and the importance of the countervailing goal of rehabilitation; it is a close question, however, whether it is excessive in light of Congress's non-punitive objectives. All this, of course, is in addition to the onerous requirement that these former juvenile offenders report in person every three months to law enforcement authorities for a large portion of their adult lives.

...[T]he effect of the Attorney General's regulation that retroactively imposes SORNA's juvenile registration and reporting requirement upon former juvenile offenders who were found delinquent prior to the passage of the statute, is punitive. Of this, we are fully persuaded. The requirement serves to convert a rehabilitative judicial proceeding, sheltered from the public eye, into a punitive one, exposed for all to see, and with long-lasting substantially adverse and harsh effects. In some instances, the retroactive implementation of SORNA's provisions will most certainly wreak havoc upon the lives of those whose conduct as juveniles offended the fundamental values of our society but who, we hope, have been rehabilitated. For these reasons, we conclude that the retroactive application of SORNA's juvenile registration and reporting requirement violates the Ex Post Facto Clause of the United States Constitution.

Id. at 931–933, 934–936, 938–939, 940-942. Without reaching the constitutional issue, the United States Supreme Court vacated the Ninth Circuit's decision on the grounds that the issue was moot. *United States v. Juvenile Male*, 131 S.Ct. 2860 (2011). Nevertheless, do you think the Ninth Circuit was correct? Do you think the court's reasoning might also apply to juveniles who are adjudicated delinquent after the effective date of the act?

4. TRANSFER TO CRIMINAL COURT

KENT V. UNITED STATES
Supreme Court of the United States
383 U.S. 541 (1966)
(See Section II.B. above, p. 85)

Patrick Griffin et al., U.S. Dep't of Justice, Trying Juveniles as Adults: An Analysis of State Transfer Laws and Reporting 2, 4–6 (September 2011), www.ncjrs.gov/pdffiles1/ojjdp/232434.pdf.

...[A]ll states have transfer laws that allow or require criminal prosecution of some young offenders, even though they fall on the juvenile side of the jurisdictional age limit.

Transfer laws are not new, but legislative changes in recent decades have greatly expanded their scope. As a result, the transfer "exception" has become a far more prominent feature of the nation's response to youthful offending....

Transfer laws vary considerably from state to state, particularly in terms of flexibility and breadth of coverage, but all fall into three basic categories:

- Judicial waiver laws allow juvenile courts to waive jurisdiction on a case-by-case basis, opening the way for criminal prosecution. A case that is subject to waiver is filed originally in juvenile court but may be transferred with a judge's approval, based on articulated standards, following a formal hearing. Even though all states set minimum thresholds and prescribe standards for waiver, the waiver decision is usually at the discretion of the judge. However, some states make waiver presumptive in certain classes of cases, and some even specify circumstances under which waiver is mandatory.
- Prosecutorial discretion or concurrent jurisdiction laws define a class of cases that may be brought in either juvenile or criminal court. No hearing is held to determine which court is appropriate, and there may be no formal standards for deciding between them. The decision is entrusted entirely to the prosecutor.
- Statutory exclusion laws grant criminal courts exclusive jurisdiction over certain classes of cases involving juvenile-age offenders. If a case falls within a statutory exclusion category, it must be filed originally in criminal court.

All states have at least one of the above kinds of transfer laws. In addition, many have one or more of the following:

- "Once adult/always adult" laws are a special form of exclusion requiring criminal prosecution of any juvenile who has been criminally prosecuted in the past—usually without regard to the seriousness of the current offense.
- Reverse waiver laws allow juveniles whose cases are in criminal court to petition to have them transferred to juvenile court.

- Blended sentencing laws may either provide juvenile courts with criminal sentencing options (juvenile blended sentencing) or allow criminal courts to impose juvenile dispositions (criminal blended sentencing)....

A total of 45 states have laws designating some category of cases in which waiver of jurisdiction may be considered, generally on the prosecutor's motion, and granted on a discretionary basis. This is the oldest and still the most common form of transfer, although most states have other, less traditional forms as well.

Discretionary waiver statutes prescribe broad standards to be applied, factors to be considered, and procedures to be followed in waiver decisionmaking and require that prosecutors bear the burden of proving that waiver is appropriate. Although waiver standards and evidentiary factors vary from state to state, most take into account both the nature of the alleged crime and the individual youth's age, maturity, history, and rehabilitative prospects.

In addition, most states set a minimum threshold for waiver eligibility: generally a minimum age and a specified type or level of offense, and sometimes a sufficiently serious record of previous delinquency. Waiver thresholds are often quite low.... [H]owever... waivers are likely to be relatively rare. Nationally, the proportion of juvenile cases in which prosecutors seek waiver is not known, but waiver is granted in less than 1 percent of petitioned delinquency cases....

In 15 states, presumptive waiver laws define a category of cases in which waiver from juvenile court to criminal court is presumed appropriate. Statutes in these states leave the decision in the hands of a judge but weight it in favor of transfer. A juvenile who meets age, offense, or other statutory thresholds for presumptive waiver must present evidence rebutting the presumption, or the court will grant waiver and the case will be tried in criminal court....

Fifteen states require juvenile courts to waive jurisdiction over cases that meet specified age/offense or prior record criteria. Cases subject to mandatory waiver are initiated in juvenile court, but the court has no other role than to confirm that the statutory requirements for mandatory waiver are met....

Only fifteen states now rely solely on traditional hearing-based, judicially controlled forms of transfer.... In these states, all cases against juvenile-age offenders (except those who have already been criminally prosecuted once) begin in juvenile court and must be literally transferred by individual court order, to courts with criminal jurisdiction.

In all other states, cases against some accused juveniles are filed directly in criminal court....

Laws in 15 states designate some category of cases in which both juvenile and criminal courts have jurisdiction, so prosecutors may choose to file in either one court or the other. The choice is considered to be within the prosecutor's executive discretion, comparable with the charging decision.

In fact, prosecutorial discretion laws are usually silent regarding standards, protocols, or appropriate considerations for decisionmaking. Even in those few states where statutes provide some general guidance to prosecutors, or at least require them to develop their own decisionmaking guidelines, there is no hearing, no evidentiary record, and no opportunity for defendants to test (or even to know) the basis for a prosecutor's decisions to proceed in criminal court. As a result, it is possible that prosecutorial discretion laws in some places operate like statutory exclusions, sweeping whole categories into criminal court with little or no individualized consideration....

A total of 29 states have statutes that simply exclude some juvenile-age offenders from the jurisdiction of their juvenile courts, generally by defining the term "child" for delinquency purposes to leave out youth who meet certain age/offense or prior record criteria. Because such youth cannot by definition be "delinquent children," their cases are handled entirely in criminal court....

Murder is the offense most commonly singled out by statutory exclusion laws....

Some states exclude less serious offenses, especially where older juveniles or those with serious delinquency histories are involved....

NOTES AND QUESTIONS

1. The report notes that only about 1 percent of all juvenile cases are transferred to criminal court for trial. Nevertheless, as many as 175,000 juveniles may be tried in criminal court each year because of statutory exclusion laws. *Id.* at 21. However, it is not clear exactly how many juveniles actually are tried in criminal courts as a result of statutory exclusion or prosecutorial discretion, because there is no national data set tracking these cases. Moreover, most states fail to track all of their juvenile transfer cases. A 1998 study of juvenile transfer in forty large urban jurisdictions found that only 23.7 percent of transferred juveniles were judicially waived to criminal court; most were waived by prosecutors filing directly in criminal court (34.7 percent) or transferred through statutory exclusion (41.6 percent). Of the youth waived, 96 percent were male and 62 percent were black. The most serious charge filed at the time of arrest was either robbery (31 percent) or assault (21 percent). *Id.* at 12.

2. What happens after transfer? Forty-eight states permit juveniles to be held in adult jails pending their criminal trials; in fourteen of these states, jailing is mandatory. *Id.* at 22. Once transferred, juveniles charged with violent offenses were more likely to be convicted than adults charged with similar crimes. *Id.* at 13. Across all felony offenses, transferred juveniles were more likely to be sentenced to prison, and for longer terms, than adult defendants. *Id.* at 24. Transferred juveniles also were more likely to receive longer probationary terms. *Id.* Once convicted, some juveniles may serve a portion of their prison terms in juvenile facilities, others in specially designated facilities or in adult prisons. *Id.* at 25.

3. Does transfer deter crime? The research does not support the claim that transfer laws deter crime. While some research suggests that transfer laws might have a deterrent effect among youths if sufficiently publicized, most studies are unable to establish a causal link between transfer laws and a reduction in crime. In fact, some research suggests that transfer laws may have a counter-deterrent effect by increasing subsequent offending. These studies found that transferred juveniles had a higher recidivism rate than juveniles who were not transferred; moreover, they engaged in reoffending sooner and with more frequency, perhaps because of the unavailability of rehabilitative services or the association with more hardened adult offenders. On the other hand, there is some evidence that transfer may have a deterrent effect for certain types of offenders. *Id.* at 26.

4. *Criminal blended sentencing.* In eighteen states, criminal court judges may sentence convicted transferred juveniles to juvenile dispositions under certain specified circumstances. Under these laws, transferred juveniles are returned to the juvenile correctional system, although the statutes may mandate the imposition of a suspended criminal sentence in

addition to a juvenile disposition. *Id.* at 7. While criminal blended sentencing restores some individualization to the process of transfer, it nevertheless applies only to a small group of transferred juveniles.

5. Is statutory exclusion constitutional? Why doesn't a statute that permits a prosecutor to decide whether to try a juvenile as an adult violate due process? See, e.g., *United States v. Bland*, 472 F.2d 1329 (1972), cert. denied, 412 U.S. 909 (1973).

6. Is the juvenile court judge's decision to transfer a juvenile to criminal court for trial a final appealable order? What are some of the advantages to permitting a juvenile to appeal the decision to transfer immediately? What are the disadvantages? Compare *In re Becker*, 314 N.E.2d 158 (Ohio 1974) (not a final appealable order) with *In re J.G.*, 627 A.2d 362 (Vt. 1993) (appeal from collateral order to transfer is discretionary) and *In re A.M.*, 34 F.3d 153 (3d Cir. 1994) (juvenile transfer order is considered a final appealable order).

7. When a juvenile is transferred to criminal court for trial, are there any limits on the sentence he or she may receive if found guilty? The next case examines that issue.

MILLER V. ALABAMA
Supreme Court of the United States
No. 10-9646, argued March 20, 2012, decided June 25, 2012

JUSTICE KAGAN delivered the opinion of the Court.

The two 14-year-old offenders in these cases were convicted of murder and sentenced to life imprisonment without the possibility of parole. In neither case did the sentencing authority have any discretion to impose a different punishment. State law mandated that each juvenile die in prison even if a judge or jury would have thought that his youth and its attendant characteristics, along with the nature of his crime, made a lesser sentence (for example, life *with* the possibility of parole) more appropriate. Such a scheme prevents those meting out punishment from considering a juvenile's "lessened culpability" and greater "capacity for change," *Graham v. Florida*, 560 U.S. _______ (2010) (slip op., at 17, 23), and runs afoul of our cases' requirement of individualized sentencing for defendants facing the most serious penalties. We therefore hold that mandatory life without parole for those under the age of 18 at the time of their crimes violates the Eighth Amendment's prohibition on "cruel and unusual punishments."

I

A

In November 1999, petitioner Kuntrell Jackson, then 14 years old, and two other boys decided to rob a video store. En route to the store, Jackson learned that one of the boys, Derrick Shields, was carrying a sawed-off shotgun in his coat sleeve. Jackson decided to stay outside when the two other boys entered the store. Inside, Shields pointed the gun at the store clerk, Laurie Troup, and demanded that she "give up the money." *Jackson v. State*, 359 Ark. 87, 89, 194 S.W.3d 757, 759 (2004) (internal quotation marks omitted). Troup refused. A few moments later, Jackson went into the store to find Shields continuing to demand money. At trial, the parties disputed whether Jackson warned Troup that "[w]e ain't playin'," or instead told his friends, "I thought you all was playin'." *Id.*, at 91, 194 S.W.3d, at 760 (internal quotation marks omitted). When Troup threatened to call the police, Shields shot and killed her. The three boys fled empty-handed. See *id.*, at 89–92, 194 S.W.3d, at 758–760.

Arkansas law gives prosecutors discretion to charge 14-year-olds as adults when they are alleged to have committed certain serious offenses. See Ark. Code Ann. § 9-27-318(c)(2) (1998). The prosecutor here exercised that authority by charging Jackson with capital felony murder and aggravated robbery. Jackson moved to transfer the case to juvenile court, but after considering the alleged facts of the crime, a psychiatrist's examination, and Jackson's juvenile arrest history (shoplifting and several incidents of car theft), the trial court denied the motion, and an appellate court affirmed. See *Jackson v. State*, No. 02-535, 2003 WL 193412, *1 (Ark. App., Jan. 29, 2003); §§ 9-27-318(d), (e). A jury later convicted Jackson of both crimes. Noting that "in view of [the] verdict, there's only one possible punishment," the judge sentenced Jackson to life without parole. App. in No. 10-9647, p. 55 (hereinafter Jackson App.); see Ark. Code Ann. § 5-4-=104(b) (1997) ("A defendant convicted of capital murder or treason shall be sentenced to death or life imprisonment without parole").[1] Jackson did not challenge the sentence on appeal, and the Arkansas Supreme Court affirmed the convictions. See 359 Ark. 87, 194 S.W.3d 757.

Following *Roper v. Simmons*, 543 U.S. 551 (2005), in which this Court invalidated the death penalty for all juvenile offenders under the age of 18, Jackson filed a state petition for habeas corpus. He argued, based on *Roper*'s reasoning, that a mandatory sentence of life without parole for a 14-year-old also violates the Eighth Amendment. The circuit court rejected that argument and granted the State's motion to dismiss. See Jackson App. 72–76. While that ruling was on appeal, this Court held in *Graham v. Florida* that life without parole violates the Eighth Amendment when imposed on juvenile nonhomicide offenders. After the parties filed briefs addressing that decision, the Arkansas Supreme Court affirmed the dismissal of Jackson's petition. See *Jackson v. Norris*, 2011 Ark. 49, _______ S.W.3d _______. The majority found that *Roper* and *Graham* were "narrowly tailored" to their contexts: "death-penalty cases involving a juvenile and life-imprisonment-without-parole cases for nonhomicide offenses involving a juvenile." *Id.*, at 5, _______ S.W.3d, at _______. Two justices dissented. They noted that Jackson was not the shooter and that "any evidence of intent to kill was severely lacking." *Id.*, at 10, _______ S.W.3d, at _______ (Danielson, J., dissenting). And they argued that Jackson's mandatory sentence ran afoul of *Graham*'s admonition that "'[a]n offender's age is relevant to the Eighth Amendment, and criminal procedure laws that fail to take defendants' youthfulness into account at all would be flawed.'" *Id.*, at 10–11, _______ S.W.3d, at _______ (quoting *Graham*, 560 U.S., at _______, (slip op., at 25)).[2]

1. Jackson was ineligible for the death penalty under *Thompson v. Oklahoma*, 487 U.S. 815 (1988) (plurality opinion), which held that capital punishment of offenders under the age of 16 violates the Eighth Amendment.

2. For the first time in this Court, Arkansas contends that Jackson's sentence was not mandatory. On its view, state law then in effect allowed the trial judge to suspend the life-without-parole sentence and commit Jackson to the Department of Human Services for a "training-school program," at the end of which he could be placed on probation. Brief for Respondent in No. 10-9647, pp. 36–37 (hereinafter Arkansas Brief) (citing Ark. Code Ann. § 12-28-403(b)(2) (1999)). But Arkansas never raised that objection in the state courts, and they treated Jackson's sentence as mandatory. We abide by that interpretation of state law. See, *e.g.*, *Mullaney v. Wilbur*, 421 U.S. 684, 690–691(1975).

B

Like Jackson, petitioner Evan Miller was 14 years old at the time of his crime. Miller had by then been in and out of foster care because his mother suffered from alcoholism and drug addiction and his stepfather abused him. Miller, too, regularly used drugs and alcohol; and he had attempted suicide four times, the first when he was six years old. See *E.J.M. v. State*, 928 So.2d 1077, 1081 (Ala. Crim. App. 2004) (Cobb, J., concurring in result); App. in No. 10-9646, pp. 26–28 (hereinafter Miller App.).

One night in 2003, Miller was at home with a friend, Colby Smith, when a neighbor, Cole Cannon, came to make a drug deal with Miller's mother. See 6 Record in No. 10-9646, p. 1004. The two boys followed Cannon back to his trailer, where all three smoked marijuana and played drinking games. When Cannon passed out, Miller stole his wallet, splitting about $300 with Smith. Miller then tried to put the wallet back in Cannon's pocket, but Cannon awoke and grabbed Miller by the throat. Smith hit Cannon with a nearby baseball bat, and once released, Miller grabbed the bat and repeatedly struck Cannon with it. Miller placed a sheet over Cannon's head, told him "'I am God, I've come to take your life,'" and delivered one more blow. *Miller v. State*, 63 So.3d 676, 689 (Ala. Crim. App. 2010). The boys then retreated to Miller's trailer, but soon decided to return to Cannon's to cover up evidence of their crime. Once there, they lit two fires. Cannon eventually died from his injuries and smoke inhalation. See *id.*, at 683–685, 689.

Alabama law required that Miller initially be charged as a juvenile, but allowed the District Attorney to seek removal of the case to adult court. See Ala. Code § 12-15-34 (1977). The D.A. did so, and the juvenile court agreed to the transfer after a hearing. Citing the nature of the crime, Miller's "mental maturity," and his prior juvenile offenses (truancy and "criminal mischief"), the Alabama Court of Criminal Appeals affirmed. *E.J.M. v. State*, No. CR-03-0915, pp. 5–7 (Aug. 27, 2004) (unpublished memorandum).[3] The State accordingly charged Miller as an adult with murder in the course of arson. That crime (like capital murder in Arkansas) carries a mandatory minimum punishment of life without parole. See Ala. Code §§ 13A-5-40(9), 13A-6-2(c) (1982).

Relying in significant part on testimony from Smith, who had pleaded to a lesser offense, a jury found Miller guilty. He was therefore sentenced to life without the possibility of parole. The Alabama Court of Criminal Appeals affirmed, ruling that life without parole was "not overly harsh when compared to the crime" and that the mandatory nature of the sentencing scheme was permissible under the Eighth Amendment. 63 So.3d, at 690; see *id.*, at 686–691. The Alabama Supreme Court denied review.

We granted certiorari in both cases, see 565 U.S. _______ (2011) (No. 10-9646); 565 U.S. _______ (2011) (No. 10-9647), and now reverse.

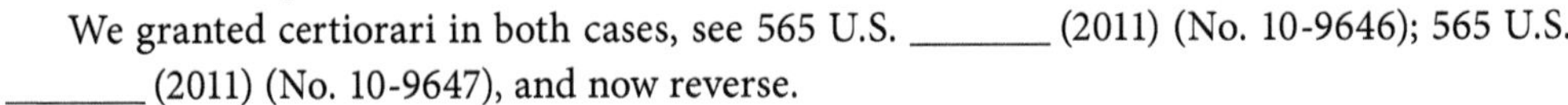

3. The Court of Criminal Appeals also affirmed the juvenile court's denial of Miller's request for funds to hire his own mental expert for the transfer hearing. The court pointed out that under governing Alabama Supreme Court precedent, "the procedural requirements of a trial do not ordinarily apply" to those hearings. *E.J.M. v. State*, 928 So.2d 1077 (Ala. Crim. App. 2004) (Cobb, J., concurring in result) (internal quotation marks omitted). In a separate opinion, Judge Cobb agreed on the reigning precedent, but urged the State Supreme Court to revisit the question in light of transfer hearings' importance. See *id.*, at 1081 ("[A]lthough later mental evaluation as an adult affords some semblance of procedural due process, it is, in effect, too little, too late").

II

The Eighth Amendment's prohibition of cruel and unusual punishment "guarantees individuals the right not to be subjected to excessive sanctions." *Roper*, 543 U.S., at 560. That right, we have explained, "flows from the basic 'precept of justice that punishment for crime should be graduated and proportioned'" to both the offender and the offense. *Ibid.* (quoting *Weems v. United States*, 217 U.S. 349, 367, (1910)). As we noted the last time we considered life-without-parole sentences imposed on juveniles, "[t]he concept of proportionality is central to the Eighth Amendment." *Graham*, 560 U.S., at _______ (slip op., at 8). And we view that concept less through a historical prism than according to "'the evolving standards of decency that mark the progress of a maturing society.'" *Estelle v. Gamble*, 429 U.S. 97, 102 (1976) (quoting *Trop v. Dulles*, 356 U.S. 86, 101 (1958) (plurality opinion)).

The cases before us implicate two strands of precedent reflecting our concern with proportionate punishment. The first has adopted categorical bans on sentencing practices based on mismatches between the culpability of a class of offenders and the severity of a penalty. See *Graham*, 560 U.S., at _______ (slip op., at 9–10) (listing cases). So, for example, we have held that imposing the death penalty for nonhomicide crimes against individuals, or imposing it on mentally retarded defendants, violates the Eighth Amendment. See *Kennedy v. Louisiana*, 554 U.S. 407 (2008); *Atkins v. Virginia*, 536 U.S. 304 (2002). Several of the cases in this group have specially focused on juvenile offenders, because of their lesser culpability. Thus, *Roper* held that the Eighth Amendment bars capital punishment for children, and *Graham* concluded that the Amendment also prohibits a sentence of life without the possibility of parole for a child who committed a nonhomicide offense. *Graham* further likened life without parole for juveniles to the death penalty itself, thereby evoking a second line of our precedents. In those cases, we have prohibited mandatory imposition of capital punishment, requiring that sentencing authorities consider the characteristics of a defendant and the details of his offense before sentencing him to death. See *Woodson v. North Carolina*, 428 U.S. 280 (1976) (plurality opinion); *Lockett v. Ohio*, 438 U.S. 586 (1978). Here, the confluence of these two lines of precedent leads to the conclusion that mandatory life-without-parole sentences for juveniles violate the Eighth Amendment.[4]

To start with the first set of cases: *Roper* and *Graham* establish that children are constitutionally different from adults for purposes of sentencing. Because juveniles have diminished culpability and greater prospects for reform, we explained, "they are less deserving of the most severe punishments." *Graham*, 560 U.S., at _______ (slip op., at 17). Those cases relied on three significant gaps between juveniles and adults. First, children have a "'lack of maturity and an underdeveloped sense of responsibility,'" leading to recklessness, impulsivity, and heedless risk-taking. *Roper*, 543 U.S., at 569. Second, children "are more vulnerable...to negative influences and outside pressures," including from their family and peers; they have limited "contro[l] over their own environment" and lack the ability to extricate themselves from horrific, crime-producing settings. *Ibid.* And third, a child's character is not as "well

4. The three dissenting opinions here each take issue with some or all of those precedents. That is not surprising: their authors (and joiner) each dissented from some or all of those precedents. While the dissents seek to relitigate old Eighth Amendment battles, repeating many arguments this Court has previously (and often) rejected, we apply the logic of *Roper*, *Graham*, and our individualized sentencing decisions to these two cases.

formed" as an adult's; his traits are "less fixed" and his actions less likely to be "evidence of irretrievabl[e] deprav[ity]." *Id.*, at 570.

Our decisions rested not only on common sense—on what "any parent knows"—but on science and social science as well. *Id.*, at 569. In *Roper*, we cited studies showing that "'[o]nly a relatively small proportion of adolescents'" who engage in illegal activity "'develop entrenched patterns of problem behavior.'" *Id.*, at 570 (quoting Steinberg & Scott, Less Guilty by Reason of Adolescence: Developmental Immaturity, Diminished Responsibility, and the Juvenile Death Penalty, 58 Am. Psychologist 1009, 1014 (2003)). And in *Graham*, we noted that "developments in psychology and brain science continue to show fundamental differences between juvenile and adult minds"—for example, in "parts of the brain involved in behavior control." 560 U.S., at _______ (slip op., at 17).[5] We reasoned that those findings—of transient rashness, proclivity for risk, and inability to assess consequences—both lessened a child's "moral culpability" and enhanced the prospect that, as the years go by and neurological development occurs, his "'deficiencies will be reformed.'" *Id.*, at _______ (slip op., at 18) (quoting *Roper*, 543 U.S., at 570).

Roper and *Graham* emphasized that the distinctive attributes of youth diminish the penological justifications for imposing the harshest sentences on juvenile offenders, even when they commit terrible crimes. Because "'[t]he heart of the retribution rationale'" relates to an offender's blameworthiness, "'the case for retribution is not as strong with a minor as with an adult.'" *Graham*, 560 U.S., at _______ (slip op., at 20–21) (quoting *Tison v. Arizona*, 481 U.S. 137, 149 (1987); *Roper*, 543 U.S., at 571). Nor can deterrence do the work in this context, because "'the same characteristics that render juveniles less culpable than adults'"—their immaturity, recklessness, and impetuosity—make them less likely to consider potential punishment. *Graham*, 560 U.S., at _______ (slip op., at 21) (quoting *Roper*, 543 U.S., at 571). Similarly, incapacitation could not support the life-without-parole sentence in *Graham*: Deciding that a "juvenile offender forever will be a danger to society" would require "mak[ing] a judgment that [he] is incorrigible"—but "'incorrigibility is inconsistent with youth.'" 560 U.S., at _______ (slip op., at 22) (quoting *Workman v. Commonwealth*, 429 S.W.2d 374, 378 (Ky.App. 1968)). And for the same reason, rehabilitation could not justify that sentence. Life without parole "forswears altogether the rehabilitative ideal." *Graham*, 560 U.S., at _______ (slip op., at 23). It reflects "an irrevocable judgment about [an offender's] value and place in society," at odds with a child's capacity for change. *Ibid.*

Graham concluded from this analysis that life-without-parole sentences, like capital punishment, may violate the Eighth Amendment when imposed on children. To be sure, *Graham*'s flat ban on life without parole applied only to nonhomicide crimes, and the Court took care to distinguish those offenses from murder, based on both moral culpability and consequential harm. See *id.*, at _______ (slip op., at 18). But none of what it said about children—about

5. The evidence presented to us in these cases indicates that the science and social science supporting *Roper*'s and *Graham*'s conclusions have become even stronger. See, *e.g.*, Brief for American Psychological Association et al. as *Amici Curiae* 3 ("[A]n ever-growing body of research in developmental psychology and neuroscience continues to confirm and strengthen the Court's conclusions"); *id.*, at 4 ("It is increasingly clear that adolescent brains are not yet fully mature in regions and systems related to higher-order executive functions such as impulse control, planning ahead, and risk avoidance"); Brief for J. Lawrence Aber et al. as *Amici Curiae* 12–28 (discussing post-*Graham* studies); *id.*, at 26–27 ("Numerous studies post-*Graham* indicate that exposure to deviant peers leads to increased deviant behavior and is a consistent predictor of adolescent delinquency" (footnote omitted)).

their distinctive (and transitory) mental traits and environmental vulnerabilities—is crime-specific. Those features are evident in the same way, and to the same degree, when (as in both cases here) a botched robbery turns into a killing. So *Graham*'s reasoning implicates any life-without-parole sentence imposed on a juvenile, even as its categorical bar relates only to nonhomicide offenses.

Most fundamentally, *Graham* insists that youth matters in determining the appropriateness of a lifetime of incarceration without the possibility of parole. In the circumstances there, juvenile status precluded a life-without-parole sentence, even though an adult could receive it for a similar crime. And in other contexts as well, the characteristics of youth, and the way they weaken rationales for punishment, can render a life-without-parole sentence disproportionate. Cf. *id.*, at _______ (slip op., at 20–23) (generally doubting the penological justifications for imposing life without parole on juveniles). "An offender's age," we made clear in *Graham*, "is relevant to the Eighth Amendment," and so "criminal procedure laws that fail to take defendants' youthfulness into account at all would be flawed." *Id.*, at _______ (slip op., at 25). THE CHIEF JUSTICE, concurring in the judgment, made a similar point. Although rejecting a categorical bar on life-without-parole sentences for juveniles, he acknowledged "*Roper*'s conclusion that juveniles are typically less culpable than adults," and accordingly wrote that "an offender's juvenile status can play a central role" in considering a sentence's proportionality. *Id.*, at _______ (slip op., at 5–6); see *id.*, at _______ (slip op., at 12) (Graham's "youth is one factor, among others, that should be considered in deciding whether his punishment was unconstitutionally excessive").[6]

But the mandatory penalty schemes at issue here prevent the sentencer from taking account of these central considerations. By removing youth from the balance—by subjecting a juvenile to the same life-without-parole sentence applicable to an adult—these laws prohibit a sentencing authority from assessing whether the law's harshest term of imprisonment proportionately punishes a juvenile offender. That contravenes *Graham*'s (and also *Roper*'s) foundational principle: that imposition of a State's most severe penalties on juvenile offenders cannot proceed as though they were not children.

And *Graham* makes plain these mandatory schemes' defects in another way: by likening life-without-parole sentences imposed on juveniles to the death penalty itself. Life-without-parole terms, the Court wrote, "share some characteristics with death sentences that are shared by no other sentences." 560 U.S., at _______ (slip op., at 19). Imprisoning an offender until he dies alters the remainder of his life "by a forfeiture that is irrevocable." *Ibid.* (citing *Solem v. Helm*, 463 U.S. 277, 300–301 (1983)). And this lengthiest possible incarceration is an "especially harsh punishment for a juvenile," because he will almost inevitably serve "more years and a greater percentage of his life in prison than an adult offender." *Graham*, 560 U.S., at _______ (slip op., at 19–20). The penalty when imposed on a teenager, as compared with an older person, is therefore "the same ... in name only." *Id.*, at _______ (slip op., at 20). All of that suggested a distinctive set of legal rules: In part because we viewed this ultimate penalty for juveniles as akin to the death penalty, we treated it similarly to that most severe punishment.

6. In discussing *Graham*, the dissents essentially ignore all of this reasoning. Indeed, THE CHIEF JUSTICE ignores the points made in his own concurring opinion. The only part of *Graham* that the dissents see fit to note is the distinction it drew between homicide and nonhomicide offenses. But contrary to the dissents' charge, our decision today retains that distinction: *Graham* established one rule (a flat ban) for nonhomicide offenses, while we set out a different one (individualized sentencing) for homicide offenses.

We imposed a categorical ban on the sentence's use, in a way unprecedented for a term of imprisonment. See *id.*, at ______ (slip op., at 9); *id.*, at ______ (THOMAS, J., dissenting) (slip op., at 7) ("For the first time in its history, the Court declares an entire class of offenders immune from a noncapital sentence using the categorical approach it previously reserved for death penalty cases alone"). And the bar we adopted mirrored a proscription first established in the death penalty context—that the punishment cannot be imposed for any nonhomicide crimes against individuals. See *Kennedy*, 554 U.S. 407; *Coker v. Georgia*, 433 U.S. 584 (1977).

That correspondence—*Graham*'s "[t]reat[ment] [of] juvenile life sentences as analogous to capital punishment," 560 U.S., at ______ (ROBERTS, C.J., concurring in judgment) (slip op., at 5)—makes relevant here a second line of our precedents, demanding individualized sentencing when imposing the death penalty. In *Woodson*, 428 U.S. 280, we held that a statute mandating a death sentence for first-degree murder violated the Eighth Amendment. We thought the mandatory scheme flawed because it gave no significance to "the character and record of the individual offender or the circumstances" of the offense, and "exclud[ed] from consideration... the possibility of compassionate or mitigating factors." *Id.*, at 304. Subsequent decisions have elaborated on the requirement that capital defendants have an opportunity to advance, and the judge or jury a chance to assess, any mitigating factors, so that the death penalty is reserved only for the most culpable defendants committing the most serious offenses. See, *e.g.*, *Sumner v. Shuman*, 483 U.S. 66, 74–76 (1987); *Eddings v. Oklahoma*, 455 U.S. 104, 110–112 (1982); *Lockett*, 438 U.S., at 597–609 (plurality opinion).

Of special pertinence here, we insisted in these rulings that a sentencer have the ability to consider the "mitigating qualities of youth." *Johnson v. Texas*, 509 U.S. 350, 367 (1993). Everything we said in *Roper* and *Graham* about that stage of life also appears in these decisions. As we observed, "youth is more than a chronological fact." *Eddings*, 455 U.S., at 115. It is a time of immaturity, irresponsibility, "impetuousness[,] and recklessness." *Johnson*, 509 U.S., at 368. It is a moment and "condition of life when a person may be most susceptible to influence and to psychological damage." *Eddings*, 455 U.S., at 115. And its "signature qualities" are all "transient." *Johnson*, 509 U.S., at 368. *Eddings* is especially on point. There, a 16-year-old shot a police officer point-blank and killed him. We invalidated his death sentence because the judge did not consider evidence of his neglectful and violent family background (including his mother's drug abuse and his father's physical abuse) and his emotional disturbance. We found that evidence "particularly relevant"—more so than it would have been in the case of an adult offender. 455 U.S., at 115. We held: "[J]ust as the chronological age of a minor is itself a relevant mitigating factor of great weight, so must the background and mental and emotional development of a youthful defendant be duly considered" in assessing his culpability. *Id.*, at 116.

In light of *Graham*'s reasoning, these decisions too show the flaws of imposing mandatory life-without-parole sentences on juvenile homicide offenders. Such mandatory penalties, by their nature, preclude a sentencer from taking account of an offender's age and the wealth of characteristics and circumstances attendant to it. Under these schemes, every juvenile will receive the same sentence as every other—the 17-year-old and the 14-year-old, the shooter and the accomplice, the child from a stable household and the child from a chaotic and abusive one. And still worse, each juvenile (including these two 14-year-olds) will receive the same sentence as the vast majority of adults committing similar homicide offenses—but really, as *Graham* noted, a *greater* sentence than those adults will serve.[7] In meting out the death penalty, the elision of all these differences would be strictly forbidden. And once again, *Graham* indicates that a similar rule should apply when a juvenile confronts a sentence of life (and death) in prison.

So *Graham* and *Roper* and our individualized sentencing cases alike teach that in imposing a State's harshest penalties, a sentencer misses too much if he treats every child as an adult. To recap: Mandatory life without parole for a juvenile precludes consideration of his chronological age and its hallmark features—among them, immaturity, impetuosity, and failure to appreciate risks and consequences. It prevents taking into account the family and home environment that surrounds him—and from which he cannot usually extricate himself—no matter how brutal or dysfunctional. It neglects the circumstances of the homicide offense, including the extent of his participation in the conduct and the way familial and peer pressures may have affected him. Indeed, it ignores that he might have been charged and convicted of a lesser offense if not for incompetencies associated with youth—for example, his inability to deal with police officers or prosecutors (including on a plea agreement) or his incapacity to assist his own attorneys. See, *e.g., Graham*, 560 U.S., at ______ (slip op., at 27) ("[T]he features that distinguish juveniles from adults also put them at a significant disadvantage in criminal proceedings"); *J.D.B. v. North Carolina*, 564 U.S. _______, _______ (2011) (slip op., at 5–6) (discussing children's responses to interrogation). And finally, this mandatory punishment disregards the possibility of rehabilitation even when the circumstances most suggest it.

Both cases before us illustrate the problem. Take Jackson's first. As noted earlier, Jackson did not fire the bullet that killed Laurie Troup; nor did the State argue that he intended her death. Jackson's conviction was instead based on an aiding-and-abetting theory; and the appellate court affirmed the verdict only because the jury could have believed that when Jackson entered the store, he warned Troup that "[w]e ain't playin'," rather than told his friends that "I thought you all was playin'." See 359 Ark., at 90–92, 194 S.W.3d, at 759–760; *supra*, at 2. To be sure, Jackson learned on the way to the video store that his friend Shields was carrying a gun, but his age could well have affected his calculation of the risk that posed, as well as his willingness to walk away at that point. All these circumstances go to Jackson's culpability for the offense. See *Graham*, 560 U.S., at _______ (slip op., at 18) ("[W]hen compared to an adult murderer, a juvenile offender who did not kill or intend to kill has a twice diminished moral culpability"). And so too does Jackson's family background and immersion in violence: Both his mother and his grandmother had previously shot other individuals. See Record in No. 10-9647, pp. 80–82. At the least, a sentencer should look at such facts before depriving a 14-year-old of any prospect of release from prison.

That is true also in Miller's case. No one can doubt that he and Smith committed a vicious murder. But they did it when high on drugs and alcohol consumed with the adult victim. And if ever a pathological background might have contributed to a 14-year-old's commission of a crime, it is here. Miller's stepfather physically abused him; his alcoholic and drug-addicted

7. Although adults are subject as well to the death penalty in many jurisdictions, very few offenders actually receive that sentence. See, *e.g.*, Dept. of Justice, Bureau of Justice Statistics, S. Rosenmerkel, M. Durose, & D. Farole, Felony Sentences in State Courts 2006—Statistical Tables, p. 28 (Table 4.4) (rev. Nov. 22, 2010). So in practice, the sentencing schemes at issue here result in juvenile homicide offenders receiving the same nominal punishment as almost all adults, even though the two classes differ significantly in moral culpability and capacity for change.

mother neglected him; he had been in and out of foster care as a result; and he had tried to kill himself four times, the first when he should have been in kindergarten. See 928 So.2d, at 1081 (Cobb, J., concurring in result); Miller App. 26–28; *supra*, at 4. Nonetheless, Miller's past criminal history was limited—two instances of truancy and one of "second-degree criminal mischief." No. CR-03-0915, at 6 (unpublished memorandum). That Miller deserved severe punishment for killing Cole Cannon is beyond question. But once again, a sentencer needed to examine all these circumstances before concluding that life without any possibility of parole was the appropriate penalty.

We therefore hold that the Eighth Amendment forbids a sentencing scheme that mandates life in prison without possibility of parole for juvenile offenders. Cf. *Graham*, 560 U.S., at _______ (slip op., at 24) ("A State is not required to guarantee eventual freedom," but must provide "some meaningful opportunity to obtain release based on demonstrated maturity and rehabilitation"). By making youth (and all that accompanies it) irrelevant to imposition of that harshest prison sentence, such a scheme poses too great a risk of disproportionate punishment. Because that holding is sufficient to decide these cases, we do not consider Jackson's and Miller's alternative argument that the Eighth Amendment requires a categorical bar on life without parole for juveniles, or at least for those 14 and younger. But given all we have said in *Roper*, *Graham*, and this decision about children's diminished culpability and heightened capacity for change, we think appropriate occasions for sentencing juveniles to this harshest possible penalty will be uncommon. That is especially so because of the great difficulty we noted in *Roper* and *Graham* of distinguishing at this early age between "the juvenile offender whose crime reflects unfortunate yet transient immaturity, and the rare juvenile offender whose crime reflects irreparable corruption." *Roper*, 543 U.S., at 573; *Graham*, 560 U.S., at _______ (slip op., at 17). Although we do not foreclose a sentencer's ability to make that judgment in homicide cases, we require it to take into account how children are different, and how those differences counsel against irrevocably sentencing them to a lifetime in prison.[8]

III

Alabama and Arkansas offer two kinds of arguments against requiring individualized consideration before sentencing a juvenile to life imprisonment without possibility of parole. The States (along with the dissents) first contend that the rule we adopt conflicts with aspects of our Eighth Amendment caselaw. And they next assert that the rule is unnecessary because individualized circumstances come into play in deciding whether to try a juvenile offender as an adult. We think the States are wrong on both counts.

A

The States (along with Justice Thomas) first claim that *Harmelin v. Michigan*, 501 U.S. 957 (1991), precludes our holding. The defendant in *Harmelin* was sentenced to a mandatory life-without-parole term for possessing more than 650 grams of cocaine. The Court upheld

8. Given our holding, and the dissents' competing position, we see a certain irony in their repeated references to 17-year-olds who have committed the "most heinous" offenses, and their comparison of those defendants to the 14-year-olds here.... Our holding requires factfinders to attend to exactly such circumstances—to take into account the differences among defendants and crimes. By contrast, the sentencing schemes that the dissents find permissible altogether preclude considering these factors.

that penalty, reasoning that "a sentence which is not otherwise cruel and unusual" does not "becom[e] so simply because it is 'mandatory.'" *Id.*, at 995. We recognized that a different rule, requiring individualized sentencing, applied in the death penalty context. But we refused to extend that command to noncapital cases "because of the qualitative difference between death and all other penalties." *Ibid.*; see *id.*, at 1006 (Kennedy, J., concurring in part and concurring in judgment). According to Alabama, invalidating the mandatory imposition of life-without-parole terms on juveniles "would effectively overrule *Harmelin*." Brief for Respondent in No. 10-9646, p. 59 (hereinafter Alabama Brief); see Arkansas Brief 39.

We think that argument myopic. *Harmelin* had nothing to do with children and did not purport to apply its holding to the sentencing of juvenile offenders. We have by now held on multiple occasions that a sentencing rule permissible for adults may not be so for children. Capital punishment, our decisions hold, generally comports with the Eighth Amendment—except it cannot be imposed on children. See *Roper*, 543 U.S. 551; *Thompson*, 487 U.S. 815. So too, life without parole is permissible for nonhomicide offenses—except, once again, for children. See *Graham*, 560 U.S., at ______ (post op., 24). Nor are these sentencing decisions an oddity in the law. To the contrary, "'[o]ur history is replete with laws and judicial recognition' that children cannot be viewed simply as miniature adults." *J.D.B.*, 564 U.S., at ______ (post op., 10–11) (quoting *Eddings*, 455 U.S., at 115–116, citing examples from criminal, property, contract, and tort law). So if (as *Harmelin* recognized) "death is different," children are different too. Indeed, it is the odd legal rule that does *not* have some form of exception for children. In that context, it is no surprise that the law relating to society's harshest punishments recognizes such a distinction. Cf. *Graham*, 560 U.S., at ______ (Roberts, C.J., concurring in judgment) (post op., 7) ("*Graham*'s age places him in a significantly different category from the defendan[t] in... *Harmelin*"). Our ruling thus neither overrules nor undermines nor conflicts with *Harmelin*.

Alabama and Arkansas (along with The Chief Justice and Justice Alito) next contend that because many States impose mandatory life-without-parole sentences on juveniles, we may not hold the practice unconstitutional. In considering categorical bars to the death penalty and life without parole, we ask as part of the analysis whether "'objective indicia of society's standards, as expressed in legislative enactments and state practice,'" show a "national consensus" against a sentence for a particular class of offenders. *Graham*, 560 U.S., at ______ (post op., 10) (quoting *Roper*, 543 U.S., at 563). By our count, 29 jurisdictions (28 States and the Federal Government) make a life-without-parole term mandatory for some juveniles convicted of murder in adult court.[9] The States argue that this number precludes our holding.

9. The States note that 26 States and the Federal Government make life without parole the mandatory (or mandatory minimum) punishment for some form of murder, and would apply the relevant provision to 14-year-olds (with many applying it to even younger defendants). See Alabama Brief 17–18. In addition, life without parole is mandatory for older juveniles in Louisiana (age 15 and up) and Texas (age 17). See La. Child. Code Ann., Arts. 857(A), (B) (West Supp. 2012); La.Rev.Stat. Ann. §§ 14:30(C), 14:30.1(B) (West Supp. 2012); Tex. Family Code Ann. §§ 51.02(2)(A), 54.02(a)(2)(A) (West Supp. 2011); Tex. Penal Code Ann. § 12.31(a) (West 2011). In many of these jurisdictions, life without parole is the mandatory punishment only for aggravated forms of murder. That distinction makes no difference to our analysis. We have consistently held that limiting a mandatory death penalty law to particular kinds of murder cannot cure the law's "constitutional vice" of disregarding the "circumstances of the particular offense and the character and propensities of the offender." *Roberts v. Louisiana*, 428 U.S. 325, 333 (1976) (plurality opinion); see *Sumner v. Shuman*, 483 U.S. 66 (1987). The same analysis applies here, for the same reasons.

We do not agree; indeed, we think the States' argument on this score *weaker* than the one we rejected in *Graham*. For starters, the cases here are different from the typical one in which we have tallied legislative enactments. Our decision does not categorically bar a penalty for a class of offenders or type of crime—as, for example, we did in *Roper* or *Graham*. Instead, it mandates only that a sentencer follow a certain process—considering an offender's youth and attendant characteristics—before imposing a particular penalty. And in so requiring, our decision flows straightforwardly from our precedents: specifically, the principle of *Roper*, *Graham*, and our individualized sentencing cases that youth matters for purposes of meting out the law's most serious punishments. When both of those circumstances have obtained in the past, we have not scrutinized or relied in the same way on legislative enactments. See, *e.g.*, *Sumner v. Shuman*, 483 U.S. 66 (relying on *Woodson*'s logic to prohibit the mandatory death penalty for murderers already serving life without parole); *Lockett*, 438 U.S., at 602–608 (plurality opinion) (applying *Woodson* to require that judges and juries consider all mitigating evidence); *Eddings*, 455 U.S., at 110–117 (similar). We see no difference here.

In any event, the "objective indicia" that the States offer do not distinguish these cases from others holding that a sentencing practice violates the Eighth Amendment. In *Graham*, we prohibited life-without-parole terms for juveniles committing nonhomicide offenses even though 39 jurisdictions permitted that sentence. See 560 U.S., at _______ (slip op., 11). That is 10 *more* than impose life without parole on juveniles on a mandatory basis.[10] And in *Atkins*, *Roper*, and *Thompson*, we similarly banned the death penalty in circumstances in which "less than half" of the "States that permit[ted] capital punishment (for whom the issue exist[ed])"

10. In assessing indicia of societal standards, *Graham* discussed "actual sentencing practices" in addition to legislative enactments, noting how infrequently sentencers imposed the statutorily available penalty. 560 U.S., at ——— (slip op., 11). Here, we consider the constitutionality of mandatory sentencing schemes—which by definition remove a judge's or jury's discretion—so no comparable gap between legislation and practice can exist. Rather than showing whether sentencers consider life without parole for juvenile homicide offenders appropriate, the number of juveniles serving this sentence... merely reflects the number who have committed homicide in mandatory-sentencing jurisdictions. For the same reason, The Chief Justice's comparison of ratios in this case and *Graham* carries little weight. He contrasts the number of mandatory life-without-parole sentences for juvenile murderers, relative to the number of juveniles arrested for murder, with "the corresponding number" of sentences in *Graham* (*i.e.*, the number of life-without-parole sentences for juveniles who committed serious nonhomicide crimes, as compared to arrests for those crimes). But because the mandatory nature of the sentences here necessarily makes them more common, The Chief Justice's figures do not "correspon[d]" at all. The higher ratio is mostly a function of removing the sentencer's discretion.

Where mandatory sentencing does not itself account for the number of juveniles serving life-without-parole terms, the evidence we have of practice supports our holding. Fifteen jurisdictions make life without parole discretionary for juveniles. See Alabama Brief 25 (listing 12 States); Cal. Penal Code Ann. § 190.5(b) (West 2008); Ind. Code § 35-50-2-3(b) (2011); N.M. Stat. §§ 3 1-18-13(B), 31-18-14, 31-18-15.2 (2010). According to available data, only about 15% of all juvenile life-without-parole sentences come from those 15 jurisdictions, while 85% come from the 29 mandatory ones. See Tr. of Oral Arg. in No. 10-9646, p. 19; Human Rights Watch, State Distribution of Youth Offenders Serving Juvenile Life without Parole (JLWOP), Oct. 2, 2009, online at http:// www.hrw.org/news/2009/10/02/state-distribution-juvenile-offenders-serving-juvenile-life-without-parole (as visited June 21, 2012, and available in Clerk of Court's case file). That figure indicates that when given the choice, sentencers impose life without parole on children relatively rarely. And contrary to The Chief Justice's argument, we have held that when judges and juries do not often choose to impose a sentence, it at least should not be mandatory. See *Woodson v. North Carolina*, 428 U.S. 280, 295–296 (1976) (plurality opinion) (relying on the infrequency with which juries imposed the death penalty when given discretion to hold that its mandatory imposition violates the Eighth Amendment).

had previously chosen to do so. *Atkins*, 536 U.S., at 342 (Scalia, J., dissenting) (emphasis deleted); see *id.*, at 313–315 (majority opinion); *Roper*, 543 U.S., at 564–565; *Thompson*, 487 U.S., at 826–827, 108 S.Ct. 2687 (plurality opinion). So we are breaking no new ground in these cases.[11]

Graham and *Thompson* provide special guidance, because they considered the same kind of statutes we do and explained why simply counting them would present a distorted view. Most jurisdictions authorized the death penalty or life without parole for juveniles only through the combination of two independent statutory provisions. One allowed the transfer of certain juvenile offenders to adult court, while another (often in a far-removed part of the code) set out the penalties for any and all individuals tried there. We reasoned that in those circumstances, it was impossible to say whether a legislature had endorsed a given penalty for children (or would do so if presented with the choice). In *Thompson*, we found that the statutes "t[old] us that the States consider 15-year-olds to be old enough to be tried in criminal court for serious crimes (or too old to be dealt with effectively in juvenile court), but t[old] us nothing about the judgment these States have made regarding the appropriate punishment for such youthful offenders." 487 U.S., at 826, n. 24 (plurality opinion) (emphasis deleted); see also *id.*, at 850 (O'Connor, J., concurring in judgment); *Roper*, 543 U.S., at 596, n. (O'Connor, J., dissenting). And *Graham* echoed that reasoning: Although the confluence of state laws "ma[de] life without parole possible for some juvenile nonhomicide offenders," it did not "justify a judgment" that many States actually "intended to subject such offenders" to those sentences. 560 U.S., at _______ (slip op., 16).[12]

All that is just as true here. Almost all jurisdictions allow some juveniles to be tried in adult court for some kinds of homicide. See Dept. of Justice, H. Snyder & M. Sickmund, Juvenile Offenders and Victims: 2006 National Report 110–114 (hereinafter 2006 National Report). But most States do not have separate penalty provisions for those juvenile offenders. Of the 29 jurisdictions mandating life without parole for children, more than half do so by virtue of generally applicable penalty provisions, imposing the sentence without regard to age.[13] And indeed, some of those States set no minimum age for who may be transferred to

11. In response, The Chief Justice complains: "To say that a sentence may be considered unusual because so many legislatures approve it stands precedent on its head." To be clear: That description in no way resembles our opinion. We hold that the sentence violates the Eighth Amendment because, as we have exhaustively shown, it conflicts with the fundamental principles of *Roper*, *Graham*, and our individualized sentencing cases. We then show why the number of States imposing this punishment does not preclude our holding, and note how its mandatory nature (in however many States adopt it) makes use of actual sentencing numbers unilluminating.

12. The Chief Justice attempts to distinguish *Graham* on this point, arguing that there "the extreme rarity with which the sentence in question was imposed could suggest that legislatures did not really intend the inevitable result of the laws they passed." But neither *Graham* nor *Thompson* suggested such reasoning, presumably because the time frame makes it difficult to comprehend. Those cases considered what legislators intended when they enacted, at different moments, separate juvenile-transfer and life-without-parole provisions—by definition, before they knew or could know how many juvenile life-without-parole sentences would result.

13. See Ala. Code §§ 13A-5-45(f), 13A-6-2(c) (2005 and Cum. Supp. 2011); Ariz. Rev. Stat. Ann. § 13-752 (West 2010), § 41-1604.09(I) (West 2011); Conn. Gen. Stat. § 53a-35a(1) (2011); Del. Code Ann., Tit. 11, § 4209(a) (2007); Fla. Stat. § 775.082(1) (2010); Haw. Rev. Stat. § 706-656(1) (1993); Idaho Code § 18-4004 (Lexis 2004); Mich. Comp. Laws Ann. § 791.234(6)(a) (West Cum. Supp. 2012); Minn. Stat. Ann. §§ 609.106, subd. 2 (West 2009); Neb. Rev. Stat. § 29-2522 (2008); N.H. Rev. Stat. Ann. § 630:1-a (West 2007); 18 Pa. Cons. Stat.

adult court in the first instance, thus applying life-without-parole mandates to children of any age—be it 17 or 14 or 10 or 6.[14] As in *Graham*, we think that "underscores that the statutory eligibility of a juvenile offender for life without parole does not indicate that the penalty has been endorsed through deliberate, express, and full legislative consideration." 560 U.S., at _______ (slip op., at 16). That Alabama and Arkansas can count to 29 by including these possibly (or probably) inadvertent legislative outcomes does not preclude our determination that mandatory life without parole for juveniles violates the Eighth Amendment.

B

Nor does the presence of discretion in some jurisdictions' transfer statutes aid the States here. Alabama and Arkansas initially ignore that many States use mandatory transfer systems: A juvenile of a certain age who has committed a specified offense will be tried in adult court, regardless of any individualized circumstances. Of the 29 relevant jurisdictions, about half place at least some juvenile homicide offenders in adult court automatically, with no apparent opportunity to seek transfer to juvenile court.[15] Moreover, several States at times lodge this decision exclusively in the hands of prosecutors, again with no statutory mechanism for judicial reevaluation.[16] And those "prosecutorial discretion laws are usually silent regarding standards, protocols, or appropriate considerations for decisionmaking." Dept. of Justice, Office of Juvenile Justice and Delinquency Prevention, P. Griffin, S. Addie, B. Adams, & K. Firestine, Trying Juveniles as Adults: An Analysis of State Transfer Laws and Reporting 5 (2011).

Even when States give transfer-stage discretion to judges, it has limited utility. First, the decisionmaker typically will have only partial information at this early, pretrial stage about either the child or the circumstances of his offense. Miller's case provides an example. As noted earlier, see n. 3, *supra*, the juvenile court denied Miller's request for his own mental-health expert at the transfer hearing, and the appeals court affirmed on the ground that Miller was not then entitled to the protections and services he would receive at trial. See No. CR-03-0915, at 3–4 (unpublished memorandum). But by then, of course, the expert's testimony could

§§ 1102(a), (b), 61 Pa. Cons. Stat. § 6137(a)(1) (Supp. 2012); S.D. Codified Laws § 22-6-1(1) (2006), § 24-15-4 (2004); Vt. Stat. Ann., Tit. 13, § 2311(c) (2009); Wash. Rev. Code § 10.95.030(1) (2010).

14. See Del. Code Ann., Tit. 10, § 1010 (1999 and Cum. Supp. 2010), Tit. 11, § 4209(a) (2007); Fla. Stat. § 985.56 (2010), 775.082(1); Haw. Rev. Stat. § 571-22(d) (1993), § 706-656(1); Idaho Code §§ 20-508, 20-509 (Lexis Cum. Supp. 2012), § 18-4004; Mich. Comp. Laws Ann. § 712A.2d (West 2009), § 791.234(6)(a); Neb. Rev. Stat. §§ 43-247, 29-2522 (2008); 42 Pa. Cons. Stat. § 6355(e) (2000), 18 Pa. Cons. Stat. § 1102. Other States set ages between 8 and 10 as the minimum for transfer, thus exposing those young children to mandatory life without parole. See S.D. Codified Laws §§ 26-8C-2, 26-11-4 (2004), § 22-6-1 (age 10); Vt. Stat. Ann., Tit. 33, § 5204 (2011 Cum. Supp.), Tit. 13, § 2311(a) (2009) (age 10); Wash. Rev. Code §§ 9A.04.050, 13.40.110 (2010), § 10.95.030 (age 8).

15. See Ala. Code § 12-15-204(a) (Cum. Supp. 2011); Ariz. Rev. Stat. Ann. § 13-501(A) (West Cum. Supp. 2011); Conn. Gen. Stat. § 46b-127 (2011); Ill. Comp. Stat. ch. 705, §§ 405/5-130(1)(a), (4)(a) (West 2010); La. Child. Code Ann., Art. 305(A) (West Cum. Supp. 2012); Mass. Gen. Laws, ch. 119, § 74 (West 2010); Mich. Comp. Laws Ann. § 712A.2(a) (West 2002); Minn. Stat. Ann. § 260B.007, subd. 6(b) (West Cum. Supp. 2011), § 260B.101, subd. 2 (West 2007); Mo. Rev. Stat. §§ 211.021(1), (2) (2011); N.C. Gen. Stat. Ann. §§ 7B-1501(7), 7B-1601(a), 7B-2200 (Lexis 2011); N.H. Rev. Stat. Ann. § 169-B:2(IV) (West Cum. Supp. 2011), § 169-B:3 (West 2010); Ohio Rev. Code Ann. § 2152.12(A)(1)(a) (Lexis 2011); Tex. Family Code Ann. § 51.02(2); Va. Code Ann. §§ 16.1-241(A), 16.1–269.1(B), (D) (Lexis 2010).

16. Fla. Stat. Ann. § 985.557(1) (West Supp. 2012); Mich. Comp. Laws Ann. § 712A.2(a)(1); Va. Code Ann. §§ 16.1-241(A), 16.1-269.1(C), (D).

not change the sentence; whatever she said in mitigation, the mandatory life-without-parole prison term would kick in. The key moment for the exercise of discretion is the transfer— and as Miller's case shows, the judge often does not know then what she will learn, about the offender or the offense, over the course of the proceedings.

Second and still more important, the question at transfer hearings may differ dramatically from the issue at a post-trial sentencing. Because many juvenile systems require that the offender be released at a particular age or after a certain number of years, transfer decisions often present a choice between extremes: light punishment as a child or standard sentencing as an adult (here, life without parole). In many States, for example, a child convicted in juvenile court must be released from custody by the age of 21. See, *e.g.*, Ala. Code § 12-15-117(a) (Cum. Supp. 2011); see generally 2006 National Report 103 (noting limitations on the length of juvenile court sanctions). Discretionary sentencing in adult court would provide different options: There, a judge or jury could choose, rather than a life-without-parole sentence, a lifetime prison term *with* the possibility of parole or a lengthy term of years. It is easy to imagine a judge deciding that a minor deserves a (much) harsher sentence than he would receive in juvenile court, while still not thinking life-without-parole appropriate. For that reason, the discretion available to a judge at the transfer stage cannot substitute for discretion at post-trial sentencing in adult court—and so cannot satisfy the Eighth Amendment.

IV

Graham, *Roper*, and our individualized sentencing decisions make clear that a judge or jury must have the opportunity to consider mitigating circumstances before imposing the harshest possible penalty for juveniles. By requiring that all children convicted of homicide receive lifetime incarceration without possibility of parole, regardless of their age and age-related characteristics and the nature of their crimes, the mandatory sentencing schemes before us violate this principle of proportionality, and so the Eighth Amendment's ban on cruel and unusual punishment. We accordingly reverse the judgments of the Arkansas Supreme Court and Alabama Court of Criminal Appeals and remand the cases for further proceedings not inconsistent with this opinion.

It is so ordered.

Justice Breyer, with whom Justice Sotomayor joins, concurring.

I join the Court's opinion in full. I add that, if the State continues to seek a sentence of life without the possibility of parole for Kuntrell Jackson, there will have to be a determination whether Jackson "kill[ed] or intend[ed] to kill" the robbery victim. *Graham v. Florida*, 560 U.S. _______ (2010) (slip op., at 18). In my view, without such a finding, the Eighth Amendment as interpreted in *Graham* forbids sentencing Jackson to such a sentence, regardless of whether its application is mandatory or discretionary under state law.

In *Graham* we said that "when compared to an adult murderer, a juvenile offender *who did not kill or intend to kill* has a twice diminished moral culpability." *Ibid.* (emphasis added). For one thing, "compared to adults, juveniles have a lack of maturity and an underdeveloped sense of responsibility; they are more vulnerable or susceptible to negative influences and outside pressures, including peer pressure; and their characters are not as well formed." *Id.*, at _______ (slip op., at 17) (internal quotation marks omitted). See also *ibid.* ("[P]sychology and brain science continue to show fundamental differences between juvenile and adult minds" making their actions "less likely to be evidence of 'irretrievably depraved character' than are the actions of adults" (quoting *Roper v. Simmons*, 543 U.S. 551, 570 (2005))). For another thing, *Graham* recognized that lack of intent normally diminishes the "moral culpability" that attaches to the crime in question, making those that do not intend to kill "categorically less deserving of the most serious forms of punishment than are murderers." 560 U.S., at _______ (slip op., at 18) (citing *Kennedy v. Louisiana*, 554 U.S. 407, 434–435 (2008); *Enmund v. Florida*, 458 U.S. 782 (1982); *Tison v. Arizona*, 481 U.S. 137 (1987)). And we concluded that, because of this "twice diminished moral culpability," the Eighth Amendment forbids the imposition upon juveniles of a sentence of life without parole for nonhomicide cases. *Graham*, *supra*, at _______, _______ (slip op., at 18, 32).

Given *Graham*'s reasoning, the kinds of homicide that can subject a juvenile offender to life without parole must exclude instances where the juvenile himself neither kills nor intends to kill the victim. Quite simply, if the juvenile either kills or intends to kill the victim, he lacks "twice diminished" responsibility. But where the juvenile neither kills nor intends to kill, both features emphasized in *Graham* as extenuating apply. The dissent itself here would permit life without parole for "juveniles who commit the worst types of murder," but that phrase does not readily fit the culpability of one who did not himself kill or intend to kill.

I recognize that in the context of felony-murder cases, the question of intent is a complicated one. The felony-murder doctrine traditionally attributes death caused in the course of a felony to all participants who intended to commit the felony, regardless of whether they killed or intended to kill. See 2 W. LaFave, Substantive Criminal Law §§ 14.5(a) and (c) (2d ed. 2003). This rule has been based on the idea of "transferred intent"; the defendant's intent to commit the felony satisfies the intent to kill required for murder. See S. Kadish, S. Schulhofer, & C. Streiker, Criminal Law and Its Processes 439 (8th ed. 2007); 2 C. Torcia, Wharton's Criminal Law § 147 (15th ed. 1994).

But in my opinion, this type of "transferred intent" is not sufficient to satisfy the intent to murder that could subject a juvenile to a sentence of life without parole. As an initial matter, this Court has made clear that this artificially constructed kind of intent does not count as intent for purposes of the Eighth Amendment. We do not rely on transferred intent in determining if an adult may receive the death penalty. Thus, the Constitution forbids imposing capital punishment upon an aider and abettor in a robbery, where that individual did not intend to kill and simply was "in the car by the side of the road . . . , waiting to help the robbers escape." *Enmund*, *supra*, at 788. Cf. *Tison*, *supra*, at 157–158 (capital punishment permissible for aider and abettor where kidnaping led to death because he was "actively involved" in every aspect of the kidnaping and his behavior showed "a reckless disregard for human life"). Given *Graham*, this holding applies to juvenile sentences of life without parole *a fortiori*. Indeed, even juveniles who meet the *Tison* standard of "reckless disregard" may not be eligible for life without parole. Rather, *Graham* dictates a clear rule: The only juveniles who may constitutionally be sentenced to life without parole are those convicted of homicide offenses who "kill or intend to kill." 560 U.S., at _______ (slip op., at 18).

Moreover, regardless of our law with respect to adults, there is no basis for imposing a sentence of life without parole upon a juvenile who did not himself kill or intend to kill. At base, the theory of transferring a defendant's intent is premised on the idea that one engaged in a dangerous felony should understand the risk that the victim of the felony could be killed, even by a confederate. See 2 LaFave, *supra*, § 14.5(c). Yet the ability to consider the full consequences of a course of action and to adjust one's conduct accordingly is precisely what we know juveniles lack capacity to do effectively. Justice Frankfurter cautioned, "Legal theories and their phrasing in other cases readily lead to fallacious reasoning if uncritically transferred to a determination of a State's duty toward children." *May v. Anderson*, 345 U.S. 528, 536 (1953) (concurring opinion). To apply the doctrine of transferred intent here, where the juvenile did not kill, to sentence a juvenile to life without parole would involve such "fallacious reasoning." *Ibid.*

This is, as far as I can tell, precisely the situation present in Kuntrell Jackson's case. Jackson simply went along with older boys to rob a video store. On the way, he became aware that a confederate had a gun. He initially stayed outside the store, and went in briefly, saying something like "We ain't playin'" or "I thought you all was playin'," before an older confederate shot and killed the store clerk. *Jackson v. State*, 359 Ark. 87, 91, 194 S.W.3d 757, 760 (2004). Crucially, the jury found him guilty of first-degree murder under a statute that permitted them to convict if, Jackson "attempted to commit or committed an aggravated robbery, and, in the course of that offense, he, or an accomplice, caused [the clerk's] death under circumstance manifesting extreme indifference to the value of human life." *Ibid.* See Ark. Code Ann. § 5-10-101(a)(1) (1997). Thus, to be found guilty, Jackson did not need to kill the clerk (it is conceded he did not), nor did he need to have intent to kill or even "extreme indifference." As long as one of the teenage accomplices in the robbery acted with extreme indifference to the value of human life, Jackson could be convicted of capital murder. *Ibid.*

The upshot is that Jackson, who did not kill the clerk, might not have intended to do so either. See *Jackson v. Norris*, 2011 Ark. 49, at 10, _______ S.W.3d (Danielson, J., dissenting) ("[A]ny evidence of [Jackson's] intent to kill was severely lacking"). In that case, the Eighth Amendment simply forbids imposition of a life term without the possibility of parole. If, on remand, however, there is a finding that Jackson did intend to cause the clerk's death, the question remains open whether the Eighth Amendment prohibits the imposition of life without parole upon a juvenile in those circumstances as well.

CHIEF JUSTICE ROBERTS, with whom JUSTICE SCALIA, JUSTICE THOMAS, and JUSTICE ALITO join, dissenting.

Determining the appropriate sentence for a teenager convicted of murder presents grave and challenging questions of morality and social policy. Our role, however, is to apply the law, not to answer such questions. The pertinent law here is the Eighth Amendment to the Constitution, which prohibits "cruel and unusual punishments." Today, the Court invokes that Amendment to ban a punishment that the Court does not itself characterize as unusual, and that could not plausibly be described as such. I therefore dissent.

The parties agree that nearly 2,500 prisoners are presently serving life sentences without the possibility of parole for murders they committed before the age of 18. Brief for Petitioner in No. 10-9647, p. 62, n. 80 (Jackson Brief); Brief for Respondent in No. 10-9646, p. 30 (Alabama Brief). The Court accepts that over 2,000 of those prisoners received that sentence because it was mandated by a legislature. And it recognizes that the Federal Government and most States impose such mandatory sentences. Put simply, if a 17-year-old is convicted of deliberately murdering an innocent victim, it is not "unusual" for the murderer to receive a mandatory sentence of life without parole. That reality should preclude finding that mandatory life imprisonment for juvenile killers violates the Eighth Amendment.

Our precedent supports this conclusion. When determining whether a punishment is cruel and unusual, this Court typically begins with "'objective indicia of society's standards, as expressed in legislative enactments and state practice.'" *Graham v. Florida*, 560 U.S. ______, ______ (2010) (slip op., at 10); see also, *e.g.*, *Kennedy v. Louisiana*, 554 U.S. 407, 422 (2008); *Roper v. Simmons*, 543 U.S. 551, 564 (2005). We look to these "objective indicia" to ensure that we are not simply following our own subjective values or beliefs. *Gregg v. Georgia*, 428 U.S. 153, 173 (1976) (joint opinion of STEWART, POWELL, and STEVENS, JJ.). Such tangible evidence of societal standards enables us to determine whether there is a "consensus against" a given sentencing practice. *Graham*, *supra*, at ______ (slip op., at 10). If there is, the punishment may be regarded as "unusual." But when, as here, most States formally require and frequently impose the punishment in question, there is no objective basis for that conclusion.

Our Eighth Amendment cases have also said that we should take guidance from "evolving standards of decency that mark the progress of a maturing society." *Ante*... (quoting *Estelle v. Gamble*, 429 U.S. 97, 102 (1976); internal quotation marks omitted). Mercy toward the guilty can be a form of decency, and a maturing society may abandon harsh punishments that it comes to view as unnecessary or unjust. But decency is not the same as leniency. A decent society protects the innocent from violence. A mature society may determine that this requires removing those guilty of the most heinous murders from its midst, both as protection for its other members and as a concrete expression of its standards of decency. As judges we have no basis for deciding that progress toward greater decency can move only in the direction of easing sanctions on the guilty.

In this case, there is little doubt about the direction of society's evolution: For most of the 20th century, American sentencing practices emphasized rehabilitation of the offender and the availability of parole. But by the 1980's, outcry against repeat offenders, broad disaffection with the rehabilitative model, and other factors led many legislatures to reduce or eliminate the possibility of parole, imposing longer sentences in order to punish criminals and prevent them from committing more crimes. See, *e.g.*, Alschuler, The Changing Purposes of Criminal Punishment, 70 U. Chi. L.Rev. 1, 1–13 (2003); see generally Crime and Public Policy (J. Wilson & J. Petersilia eds. 2011). Statutes establishing life without parole sentences in particular became more common in the past quarter century. See *Baze v. Rees*, 553 U.S. 35, 78, and n. 10 (2008) (STEVENS, J., concurring in judgment). And the parties agree that most States have changed their laws relatively recently to expose teenage murderers to mandatory life without parole. Jackson Brief 54–55; Alabama Brief 4–5.

The Court attempts to avoid the import of the fact that so many jurisdictions have embraced the sentencing practice at issue by comparing this case to the Court's prior Eighth Amendment cases. The Court notes that *Graham* found a punishment authorized in 39 jurisdictions unconstitutional, whereas the punishment it bans today is mandated in 10 fewer. *Ante*, at 21. But *Graham* went to considerable lengths to show that although theoretically allowed in many States, the sentence at issue in that case was "exceedingly rare" in practice. 560 U.S., at ______ (slip op., at 16). The Court explained that only 123 prisoners in the entire Nation were serving life without parole for nonhomicide crimes committed as juveniles, with more than half in a single State. It contrasted that with statistics showing nearly 400,000 juveniles were arrested for serious nonhomicide offenses in a single year. Based on the sentence's rarity despite the many opportunities to impose it, *Graham* concluded that there was a national consensus against life without parole for juvenile nonhomicide crimes. *Id.*, at ______ (slip op., at 13–16).

Here the number of mandatory life without parole sentences for juvenile murderers, relative to the number of juveniles arrested for murder, is over 5,000 times higher than the corresponding number in *Graham*. There is thus nothing in this case like the evidence of national consensus in *Graham*.[1]

The Court disregards these numbers, claiming that the prevalence of the sentence in question results from the number of statutes requiring its imposition. True enough. The sentence at issue is statutorily mandated life without parole. Such a sentence can only result from statutes requiring its imposition. In *Graham* the Court relied on the low number of actual sentences to explain why the high number of statutes allowing such sentences was not dispositive. Here, the Court excuses the high number of actual sentences by citing the high number of statutes imposing it. To say that a sentence may be considered unusual *because* so many legislatures approve it stands precedent on its head.[2]

The Court also advances another reason for discounting the laws enacted by Congress and most state legislatures. Some of the jurisdictions that impose mandatory life without parole on juvenile murderers do so as a result of two statutes: one providing that juveniles charged with serious crimes may be tried as adults, and another generally mandating that those convicted of murder be imprisoned for life. According to the Court, our cases suggest that where the sentence results from the interaction of two such statutes, the legislature can be considered to have imposed the resulting sentences "inadvertent[ly]." The Court relies on *Graham* and *Thompson v. Oklahoma*, 487 U.S. 815, 826, n. 24 (1988) (plurality opinion), for the proposition that these laws are therefore not valid evidence of society's views on the punishment at issue.

It is a fair question whether this Court should ever assume a legislature is so ignorant of its own laws that it does not understand that two of them interact with each other, especially on an issue of such importance as the one before us. But in *Graham* and *Thompson* it was at least plausible as a practical matter. In *Graham*, the extreme rarity with which the sentence in question was imposed could suggest that legislatures did not really intend the inevitable result of the laws they passed. See 560 U.S., at ______ (slip op., at 15–16). In *Thompson*, the sentencing practice was even rarer—only 20 defendants had received it in the last century. 487 U.S., at 832 (plurality opinion). Perhaps under those facts it could be argued that the legislature was not fully aware that a teenager could receive the particular sentence in question. But here the

1. *Graham* stated that 123 prisoners were serving life without parole for nonhomicide offenses committed as juveniles, while in 2007 alone 380,480 juveniles were arrested for serious nonhomicide crimes. 560 U.S., at ______ (slip op., at 13–14). I use 2,000 as the number of prisoners serving mandatory life without parole sentences for murders committed as juveniles, because all seem to accept that the number is at least that high. And the same source *Graham* used reports that 1,170 juveniles were arrested for murder and nonnegligent homicide in 2009. Dept. of Justice, Office of Juvenile Justice and Delinquency Prevention, C. Puzzanchera & B. Adams, Juvenile Arrests 2009, p. 4 (Dec. 2011).

2. The Court's reference to discretionary sentencing practices is a distraction. The premise of the Court's decision is that mandatory sentences are categorically different from discretionary ones. So under the Court's own logic, whether discretionary sentences are common or uncommon has nothing to do with whether mandatory sentences are unusual. In any event, if analysis of discretionary sentences were relevant, it would not provide objective support for today's decision. The Court states that "about 15% of all juvenile life-without-parole sentences"—meaning nearly 400 sentences—were imposed at the discretion of a judge or jury. Thus the number of discretionary life without parole sentences for juvenile murderers, relative to the number of juveniles arrested for murder, is about 1,000 times higher than the corresponding number in *Graham*.

widespread and recent imposition of the sentence makes it implausible to characterize this sentencing practice as a collateral consequence of legislative ignorance.[3]

Nor do we display our usual respect for elected officials by asserting that legislators have *accidentally* required 2,000 teenagers to spend the rest of their lives in jail. This is particularly true given that our well-publicized decision in *Graham* alerted legislatures to the possibility that teenagers were subject to life with parole only because of legislative inadvertence. I am aware of no effort in the wake of *Graham* to correct any supposed legislative oversight. Indeed, in amending its laws in response to *Graham* one legislature made especially clear that it *does* intend juveniles who commit first-degree murder to receive mandatory life without parole. See Iowa Code Ann. § 902.1 (West Cum. Supp. 2012).

In the end, the Court does not actually conclude that mandatory life sentences for juvenile murderers are unusual. It instead claims that precedent "leads to" today's decision, primarily relying on *Graham* and *Roper*. Petitioners argue that the reasoning of those cases "compels" finding in their favor. Jackson Brief 34. The Court is apparently unwilling to go so far, asserting only that precedent points in that direction. But today's decision invalidates the laws of dozens of legislatures and Congress. This Court is not easily led to such a result. See, *e.g.*, *United States v. Harris*, 106 U.S. 629, 635 (1883) (courts must presume an Act of Congress is constitutional "unless the lack of constitutional authority... is clearly demonstrated"). Because the Court does not rely on the Eighth Amendment's text or objective evidence of society's standards, its analysis of precedent alone must bear the "heavy burden [that] rests on those who would attack the judgment of the representatives of the people." *Gregg*, 428 U.S., at 175. If the Court is unwilling to say that precedent compels today's decision, perhaps it should reconsider that decision.

In any event, the Court's holding does not follow from *Roper* and *Graham*. Those cases undoubtedly stand for the proposition that teenagers are less mature, less responsible, and less fixed in their ways than adults—not that a Supreme Court case was needed to establish that. What they do not stand for, and do not even suggest, is that legislators—who also know that teenagers are different from adults—may not require life without parole for juveniles who commit the worst types of murder.

That *Graham* does not imply today's result could not be clearer. In barring life without parole for juvenile nonhomicide offenders, *Graham* stated that "[t]here is a line 'between homicide and other serious violent offenses against the individual.'" 560 U.S., at _______ (slip op., at 18) (quoting *Kennedy*, 554 U.S., at _______ (slip op., at 27). The whole point of drawing a line between one issue and another is to say that they are different and should be treated differently. In other words, the two are in different categories. Which *Graham* also said: "defendants who do not kill, intend to kill, or foresee that life will be taken are *categorically* less deserving of the most serious forms of punishment than are murderers." 560 U.S., at _______ (slip op., at 18) (emphasis added). Of course, to be especially clear that what is said about one issue does not apply to another, one could say that the two issues cannot be compared. *Graham* said that too: "Serious nonhomicide crimes... cannot be compared to murder." *Ibid.* (internal quotation marks omitted). A case that expressly puts an issue in a different category

3. The Court claims that I "take issue with some or all of these precedents" and "seek to relitigate" them. Not so: applying this Court's cases exactly as they stand, I do not believe they support the Court's decision in this case.

from its own subject, draws a line between the two, and states that the two should not be compared, cannot fairly be said to control that issue.

Roper provides even less support for the Court's holding. In that case, the Court held that the death penalty could not be imposed for offenses committed by juveniles, no matter how serious their crimes. In doing so, *Roper* also set itself in a different category than this case, by expressly invoking "special" Eighth Amendment analysis for death penalty cases. 543 U.S., at 568–569. But more importantly, *Roper* reasoned that the death penalty was not needed to deter juvenile murderers in part because "life imprisonment without the possibility of parole" was available. *Id.*, at 572. In a classic bait and switch, the Court now tells state legislatures that— *Roper*'s promise notwithstanding—they do not have power to guarantee that once someone commits a heinous murder, he will never do so again. It would be enough if today's decision proved JUSTICE SCALIA's prescience in writing that *Roper*'s "reassurance . . . gives little comfort." *Id.*, at 623 (dissenting opinion). To claim that *Roper* actually "leads to" revoking its own reassurance surely goes too far.

Today's decision does not offer *Roper* and *Graham*'s false promises of restraint. Indeed, the Court's opinion suggests that it is merely a way station on the path to further judicial displacement of the legislative role in prescribing appropriate punishment for crime. The Court's analysis focuses on the mandatory nature of the sentences in this case. But then—although doing so is entirely unnecessary to the rule it announces—the Court states that even when a life without parole sentence is not mandatory, "we think appropriate occasions for sentencing juveniles to this harshest possible penalty will be uncommon." Today's holding may be limited to mandatory sentences, but the Court has already announced that discretionary life without parole for juveniles should be "uncommon"—or, to use a common synonym, "unusual."

Indeed, the Court's gratuitous prediction appears to be nothing other than an invitation to overturn life without parole sentences imposed by juries and trial judges. If that invitation is widely accepted and such sentences for juvenile offenders do in fact become "uncommon," the Court will have bootstrapped its way to declaring that the Eighth Amendment absolutely prohibits them.

This process has no discernible end point—or at least none consistent with our Nation's legal traditions. *Roper* and *Graham* attempted to limit their reasoning to the circumstances they addressed—*Roper* to the death penalty, and *Graham* to nonhomicide crimes. Having cast aside those limits, the Court cannot now offer a credible substitute, and does not even try. After all, the Court tells us, "none of what [*Graham*] said about children . . . is crime-specific." The principle behind today's decision seems to be only that because juveniles are different from adults, they must be sentenced differently. There is no clear reason that principle would not bar all mandatory sentences for juveniles, or any juvenile sentence as harsh as what a similarly situated adult would receive. Unless confined, the only stopping point for the Court's analysis would be never permitting juvenile offenders to be tried as adults. Learning that an Amendment that bars only "unusual" punishments requires the abolition of this uniformly established practice would be startling indeed.

It is a great tragedy when a juvenile commits murder—most of all for the innocent victims. But also for the murderer, whose life has gone so wrong so early. And for society as well, which has lost one or more of its members to deliberate violence, and must harshly punish another. In recent years, our society has moved toward requiring that the murderer, his age notwithstanding, be imprisoned for the remainder of his life. Members of this Court may disagree with that choice. Perhaps science and policy suggest society should show greater mercy to young killers, giving them a greater chance to reform themselves at the risk that they will kill again. But that is not our decision to make. Neither the text of the Constitution nor our precedent prohibits legislatures from requiring that juvenile murderers be sentenced to life without parole. I respectfully dissent.

JUSTICE THOMAS, with whom JUSTICE SCALIA joins, dissenting.

Today, the Court holds that "mandatory life without parole for those under the age of 18 at the time of their crimes violates the Eighth Amendment's prohibition on 'cruel and unusual punishments.'" To reach that result, the Court relies on two lines of precedent. The first involves the categorical prohibition of certain punishments for specified classes of offenders. The second requires individualized sentencing in the capital punishment context. Neither line is consistent with the original understanding of the Cruel and Unusual Punishments Clause. The Court compounds its errors by combining these lines of precedent and extending them to reach a result that is even less legitimate than the foundation on which it is built. Because the Court upsets the legislatively enacted sentencing regimes of 29 jurisdictions without constitutional warrant, I respectfully dissent.[1]

I...

The Eighth Amendment, made applicable to the States by the Fourteenth Amendment, provides that: "Excessive bail shall not be required, nor excessive fines imposed, nor cruel and unusual punishments inflicted." As I have previously explained, "the Cruel and Unusual Punishments Clause was originally understood as prohibiting torturous *methods* of punishment—specifically methods akin to those that had been considered cruel and unusual at the time the Bill of Rights was adopted." *Graham, supra*, at _______ (dissenting opinion) (slip op., at 3) (internal quotation marks and citations omitted).[2] The clause does not contain a "proportionality principle." *Ewing v. California*, 538 U.S. 11, 32 (2003) (THOMAS, J., concurring in judgment); see generally *Harmelin v. Michigan*, 501 U.S. 957, 975–985 (1991) (opinion of SCALIA, J.). In short, it does not authorize courts to invalidate any punishment they deem disproportionate to the severity of the crime or to a particular class of offenders. Instead, the clause "leaves the unavoidably moral question of who 'deserves' a particular nonprohibited method of punishment to the judgment of the legislatures that authorize the penalty." *Graham, supra*, at _______ (THOMAS, J., dissenting).

The legislatures of Arkansas and Alabama, like those of 27 other jurisdictions, have determined that all offenders convicted of specified homicide offenses, whether juveniles or

1. I join THE CHIEF JUSTICE's opinion because it accurately explains that, even accepting the Court's precedents, the Court's holding in today's cases is unsupportable.

2. Neither the Court nor petitioners argue that petitioners' sentences would have been among "the 'modes or acts of punishment that had been considered cruel and unusual at the time that the Bill of Rights was adopted.'" *Graham*, 560 U.S., at _______ (THOMAS, J., dissenting) (slip op., at 10, n. 3) (quoting *Ford v. Wainwright*, 477 U.S. 399, 405, (1986)). Nor could they. Petitioners were 14 years old at the time they committed their crimes. When the Bill of Rights was ratified, 14-year-olds were subject to trial and punishment as adult offenders. See *Roper v. Simmons*, 543 U.S. 551, 609, n. 1, (2005) (SCALIA, J., dissenting). Further, mandatory death sentences were common at that time. See *Harmelin v. Michigan*, 501 U.S. 957, 994–995 (1991). It is therefore implausible that a 14-year-old's mandatory prison sentence—of any length, with or without parole—would have been viewed as cruel and unusual.

not, deserve a sentence of life in prison without the possibility of parole. Nothing in our Constitution authorizes this Court to supplant that choice.

II

To invalidate mandatory life-without-parole sentences for juveniles, the Court also relies on its cases "prohibit[ing] mandatory imposition of capital punishment." The Court reasons that, because *Graham* compared juvenile life-without-parole sentences to the death penalty, the "distinctive set of legal rules" that this Court has imposed in the capital punishment context, including the requirement of individualized sentencing, is "relevant" here. But even accepting an analogy between capital and juvenile life-without-parole sentences, this Court's cases prohibiting mandatory capital sentencing schemes have no basis in the original understanding of the Eighth Amendment, and, thus, cannot justify a prohibition of sentencing schemes that mandate life-without-parole sentences for juveniles.

A

In a line of cases following *Furman v. Georgia*, 408 U.S. 238 (1972) (*per curiam*), this Court prohibited the mandatory imposition of the death penalty. See *Woodson v. North Carolina*, 428 U.S. 280 (1976) (plurality opinion); *Roberts v. Louisiana*, 428 U.S. 325 (1976) (same); *Sumner v. Shuman* (1987). *Furman* first announced the principle that States may not permit sentencers to exercise unguided discretion in imposing the death penalty. See generally 408 U.S. 238. In response to *Furman*, many States passed new laws that made the death penalty mandatory following conviction of specified crimes, thereby eliminating the offending discretion. See *Gregg v. Georgia*, 428 U.S. 153, 180–181 (1976) (joint opinion of Stewart, Powell, and Stevens, JJ.). The Court invalidated those statutes in *Woodson*, *Roberts*, and *Sumner*. The Court reasoned that mandatory capital sentencing schemes were problematic, because they failed "to allow the particularized consideration" of "relevant facets of the character and record of the individual offender or the circumstances of the particular offense." *Woodson*, *supra*, at 303–304 (plurality opinion).[3]

In my view, *Woodson* and its progeny were wrongly decided. As discussed above, the Cruel and Unusual Punishments Clause, as originally understood, prohibits "torturous *methods* of punishment." See *Graham*, 560 U.S., at _______ (Thomas, J., dissenting) (slip op., at 3) (internal quotation marks omitted). It is not concerned with whether a particular lawful method of punishment—whether capital or noncapital—is imposed pursuant to a mandatory or discretionary sentencing regime. See *Gardner v. Florida*, 430 U.S. 349, 371 (1977) (Rehnquist, J., dissenting) ("The prohibition of the Eighth Amendment relates to the character of the punishment, and not to the process by which it is imposed"). In fact, "[i]n the early days of the Republic," each crime generally had a defined punishment "prescribed with specificity by the

3. The Court later extended *Woodson*, requiring that capital defendants be permitted to present, and sentencers in capital cases be permitted to consider, any relevant mitigating evidence, including the age of the defendant. See, *e.g.*, *Lockett v. Ohio*, 438 U.S. 586, 597–608 (1978) (plurality opinion); *Eddings v. Oklahoma*, 455 U.S. 104, 110–112 (1982); *Skipper v. South Carolina*, 476 U.S. 1, 4–5 (1986); *Johnson v. Texas*, 509 U.S. 350, 361–368 (1993). Whatever the validity of the requirement that sentencers be permitted to consider all mitigating evidence when deciding whether to impose a *nonmandatory* capital sentence, the Court certainly was wrong to prohibit *mandatory* capital sentences. See *Graham v. Collins*, 506 U.S. 461, 488–500 (1993) (Thomas, J., concurring).

legislature." *United States v. Grayson*, 438 U.S. 41, 45 (1978). Capital sentences, to which the Court analogizes, were treated no differently. "[M]andatory death sentences abounded in our first Penal Code" and were "common in the several States—both at the time of the founding and throughout the 19th century." *Harmelin*, 501 U.S., at 994–995; see also *Woodson*, *supra*, at 289 (plurality opinion) ("At the time the Eighth Amendment was adopted in 1791, the States uniformly followed the common-law practice of making death the exclusive and mandatory sentence for certain specified offenses"). Accordingly, the idea that the mandatory imposition of an otherwise-constitutional sentence renders that sentence cruel and unusual finds "no support in the text and history of the Eighth Amendment." *Harmelin*, *supra*, at 994.

Moreover, mandatory death penalty schemes were "a perfectly reasonable legislative response to the concerns expressed in *Furman*" regarding unguided sentencing discretion, in that they "eliminat[ed] explicit jury discretion and treat[ed] all defendants equally." *Graham v. Collins*, 506 U.S. 461, 487 (1993) (THOMAS, J., concurring). And, as Justice White explained more than 30 years ago, "a State is not constitutionally forbidden to provide that the commission of certain crimes conclusively establishes that a criminal's character is such that he deserves death." *Roberts*, *supra*, at 358 (dissenting opinion). Thus, there is no basis for concluding that a mandatory capital sentencing scheme is unconstitutional. Because the Court's cases requiring individualized sentencing in the capital context are wrongly decided, they cannot serve as a valid foundation for the novel rule regarding mandatory life-without-parole sentences for juveniles that the Court announces today.

B

In any event, this Court has already declined to extend its individualized-sentencing rule beyond the death penalty context. In *Harmelin*, the defendant was convicted of possessing a large quantity of drugs. 501 U.S., at 961 (opinion of SCALIA, J.). In accordance with Michigan law, he was sentenced to a mandatory term of life in prison without the possibility of parole. *Ibid.* Citing the same line of death penalty precedents on which the Court relies today, the defendant argued that his sentence, due to its mandatory nature, violated the Cruel and Unusual Punishments Clause. *Id.*, at 994–995 (opinion of the Court).

The Court rejected that argument, explaining that "[t]here can be no serious contention ... that a sentence which is not otherwise cruel and unusual becomes so simply because it is 'mandatory.'" *Id.*, at 995. In so doing, the Court refused to analogize to its death penalty cases. The Court noted that those cases had "repeatedly suggested that there is no comparable [individualized-sentencing] requirement outside the capital context, because of the qualitative difference between death and all other penalties." *Ibid.* The Court observed that, "even where the difference" between a sentence of life without parole and other sentences of imprisonment "is the greatest," such a sentence "cannot be compared with death." *Id.*, at 996. Therefore, the Court concluded that the line of cases requiring individualized sentencing had been drawn at capital cases, and that there was "no basis for extending it further." *Ibid.*

Harmelin's reasoning logically extends to these cases. Obviously, the younger the defendant, "the great[er]" the difference between a sentence of life without parole and other terms of imprisonment. *Ibid.* But under *Harmelin*'s rationale, the defendant's age is immaterial to the Eighth Amendment analysis. Thus, the result in today's cases should be the same as that in *Harmelin*. Petitioners, like the defendant in *Harmelin*, were not sentenced to death.

Accordingly, this Court's cases "creating and clarifying the individualized capital sentencing doctrine" do not apply. *Id.*, at 995 (internal quotation marks omitted).

Nothing about our Constitution, or about the qualitative difference between any term of imprisonment and death, has changed since *Harmelin* was decided 21 years ago. What *has* changed (or, better yet, "evolved") is this Court's ever-expanding line of categorical proportionality cases. The Court now uses *Roper* and *Graham* to jettison *Harmelin*'s clear distinction between capital and noncapital cases and to apply the former to noncapital juvenile offenders.[4] The Court's decision to do so is even less supportable than the precedents used to reach it.... JUSTICE ALITO, with whom JUSTICE SCALIA joins, dissenting.

The Court now holds that Congress and the legislatures of the 50 States are prohibited by the Constitution from identifying any category of murderers under the age of 18 who must be sentenced to life imprisonment without parole. Even a $17^1/_2$-year-old who sets off a bomb in a crowded mall or guns down a dozen students and teachers is a "child" and must be given a chance to persuade a judge to permit his release into society. Nothing in the Constitution supports this arrogation of legislative authority.

The Court long ago abandoned the original meaning of the Eighth Amendment, holding instead that the prohibition of "cruel and unusual punishment" embodies the "evolving standards of decency that mark the progress of a maturing society." *Trop v. Dulles*, 356 U.S. 86, 101 (1958) (plurality opinion); see also *Graham v. Florida*, 560 U.S. _______, _______ (2010) (slip op., at 7); *Kennedy v. Louisiana*, 554 U.S. 407, 419 (2008); *Roper v. Simmons*, 543 U.S. 551, 560–561 (2005); *Atkins v. Virginia*, 536 U.S. 304, 311–312 (2002); *Hudson v. McMillian*, 503 U.S. 1, 8 (1992); *Ford v. Wainwright*, 477 U.S. 399, 406 (1986); *Rhodes v. Chapman*, 452 U.S. 337, 346 (1981); *Estelle v. Gamble*, 429 U.S. 97, 102 (1976). Both the provenance and philosophical basis for this standard were problematic from the start. (Is it true that our society is inexorably evolving in the direction of greater and greater decency? Who says so, and how did this particular philosophy of history find its way into our fundamental law? And in any event, aren't elected representatives more likely than unaccountable judges to reflect changing societal standards?) But at least at the start, the Court insisted that these "evolving standards" represented something other than the personal views of five Justices. See *Rummel v. Estelle*, 445 U.S. 263, 275 (1980) (explaining that "the Court's Eighth Amendment judgments should neither be nor appear to be merely the subjective views of individual Justices"). Instead, the Court looked for objective indicia of our society's moral standards and the trajectory of our moral "evolution." See *id.*, at 274–275 (emphasizing that "'judgment should be informed by objective factors to the maximum possible extent'" (quoting *Coker v. Georgia*, 433 U.S. 584, 592 (1977) (plurality opinion))).

In this search for objective indicia, the Court toyed with the use of public opinion polls, see *Atkins*, *supra*, at 316, n. 21, and occasionally relied on foreign law, see *Roper v. Simmons*, *supra*, at 575; *Enmund v. Florida*, 458 U.S. 782, 796, n. 22 (1982); *Thompson v. Oklahoma*, 487 U.S. 815, 830–831; *Coker*, 433 U.S., at 596, n. 10 (plurality opinion).

4. In support of its decision not to apply *Harmelin* to juvenile offenders, the Court also observes that "'[o]ur history is replete with laws and judicial recognition that children cannot be viewed simply as miniature adults.'" *Ante*... (quoting *J.D.B. v. North Carolina*, 564 U.S. ______ (2011) (slip op., at 10–11) (some internal quotation marks omitted)). That is no doubt true as a general matter, but it does not justify usurping authority that rightfully belongs to the people by imposing a constitutional rule where none exists.

In the main, however, the staple of this inquiry was the tallying of the positions taken by state legislatures. Thus, in *Coker*, which held that the Eighth Amendment prohibits the imposition of the death penalty for the rape of an adult woman, the Court noted that only one State permitted that practice. *Id.*, at 595–596. In *Enmund*, where the Court held that the Eighth Amendment forbids capital punishment for ordinary felony murder, both federal law and the law of 28 of the 36 States that authorized the death penalty at the time rejected that punishment. 458 U.S., at 789.

While the tally in these early cases may be characterized as evidence of a national consensus, the evidence became weaker and weaker in later cases. In *Atkins*, which held that low-IQ defendants may not be sentenced to death, the Court found an anti-death-penalty consensus even though more than half of the States that allowed capital punishment permitted the practice. See 536 U.S., at 342 (Scalia, J., dissenting) (observing that less than half of the 38 States that permit capital punishment have enacted legislation barring execution of the mentally retarded). The Court attempted to get around this problem by noting that there was a pronounced trend against this punishment. See *id.*, at 313–315 (listing 18 States that had amended their laws since 1986 to prohibit the execution of mentally retarded persons).

The importance of trend evidence, however, was not long lived. In *Roper*, which outlawed capital punishment for defendants between the ages of 16 and 18, the lineup of the States was the same as in *Atkins*, but the trend in favor of abolition—five States during the past 15 years—was less impressive. *Roper*, 543 U.S., at 564–565. Nevertheless, the Court held that the absence of a strong trend in support of abolition did not matter. See *id.*, at 566 ("Any difference between this case and *Atkins* with respect to the pace of abolition is thus counterbalanced by the consistent direction of the change").

In *Kennedy v. Louisiana*, the Court went further. Holding that the Eighth Amendment prohibits capital punishment for the brutal rape of a 12-year-old girl, the Court disregarded a nascent legislative trend *in favor of permitting capital punishment* for this narrowly defined and heinous crime. See 554 U.S., at 433 (explaining that, although "the total number of States to have made child rape a capital offense…is six," "[t]his is not an indication of a trend or change in direction comparable to the one supported by data in *Roper*"). The Court felt no need to see whether this trend developed further—perhaps because true moral evolution can lead in only one direction. And despite the argument that the rape of a young child may involve greater depravity than some murders, the Court proclaimed that homicide is categorically different from all (or maybe almost all) other offenses. See *id.*, at 438 (stating that nonhomicide crimes, including child rape, "may be devastating in their harm…but in terms of moral depravity and of the injury to the person and to the public, they cannot be compared to murder in their severity and irrevocability" (internal quotation marks and citation omitted)). As the Court had previously put it, "death is different." *Ford*, *supra*, at 411 (plurality opinion).

Two years after *Kennedy*, in *Graham v. Florida*, any pretense of heeding a legislative consensus was discarded. In *Graham*, federal law and the law of 37 States and the District of Columbia permitted a minor to be sentenced to life imprisonment without parole for nonhomicide crimes, but despite this unmistakable evidence of a national consensus, the Court held that the practice violates the Eighth Amendment. See 560 U.S., at _______ (Thomas, J., dissenting). The Court, however, drew a distinction between minors who murder and minors who commit other heinous offenses, so at least in that sense the principle that death is different lived on.

Today, that principle is entirely put to rest, for here we are concerned with the imposition of a term of imprisonment on offenders who kill. The two (carefully selected) cases before us concern very young defendants, and despite the brutality and evident depravity exhibited by at least one of the petitioners, it is hard not to feel sympathy for a 14-year-old sentenced to life without the possibility of release. But no one should be confused by the particulars of the two cases before us. The category of murderers that the Court delicately calls "children" (murderers under the age of 18) consists overwhelmingly of young men who are fast approaching the legal age of adulthood. Evan Miller and Kuntrell Jackson are anomalies; much more typical are murderers like Donald Roper, who committed a brutal thrill-killing just nine months shy of his 18th birthday. *Roper*, 543 U.S., at 556.

Seventeen-year-olds commit a significant number of murders every year,[1] and some of these crimes are incredibly brutal. Many of these murderers are at least as mature as the average 18-year-old. See *Thompson*, 487 U.S., at 854 (O'CONNOR, J., concurring in judgment) (noting that maturity may "vary widely among different individuals of the same age"). Congress and the legislatures of 43 States have concluded that at least some of these murderers should be sentenced to prison without parole, and 28 States and the Federal Government have decided that for some of these offenders life without parole should be mandatory. The majority of this Court now overrules these legislative judgments.[2]

It is true that, at least for now, the Court apparently permits a trial judge to make an individualized decision that a particular minor convicted of murder should be sentenced to life without parole, but do not expect this possibility to last very long. The majority goes out of its way to express the view that the imposition of a sentence of life without parole on a "child" (*i.e.*, a murderer under the age of 18) should be uncommon. Having held in *Graham* that a trial judge with discretionary sentencing authority may not impose a sentence of life without parole on a minor who has committed a nonhomicide offense, the Justices in the majority may soon extend that holding to minors who commit murder. We will see.

What today's decision shows is that our Eighth Amendment cases are no longer tied to any objective indicia of society's standards. Our Eighth Amendment case law is now entirely inward looking. After entirely disregarding objective indicia of our society's standards in *Graham*, the Court now extrapolates from *Graham*. Future cases may extrapolate from today's holding, and this process may continue until the majority brings sentencing practices into line with whatever the majority views as truly evolved standards of decency.

1. Between 2002 and 2010, 17-year-olds committed an average combined total of 424 murders and nonnegligent homicides per year. See Dept. of Justice, Bureau of Justice Statistics, § 4, Arrests, Age of Persons Arrested (Table 4.7).

2. As the Court noted in *Mistretta v. United States*, 488 U.S. 361, 366 (1989), Congress passed the Sentencing Reform Act of 1984 to eliminate discretionary sentencing and parole because it concluded that these practices had led to gross abuses. The Senate Report for the 1984 bill rejected what it called the "outmoded rehabilitation model" for federal criminal sentencing. S.Rep. No. 98-225, p. 38 (1983). According to the Report, "almost everyone involved in the criminal justice system now doubts that rehabilitation can be induced reliably in a prison setting, and it is now quite certain that no one can really detect whether or when a prisoner is rehabilitated." *Ibid.* The Report also "observed that the indeterminate-sentencing system had two 'unjustifi[ed]' and 'shameful' consequences. The first was the great variation among sentences imposed by different judges upon similarly situated offenders. The second was uncertainty as to the time the offender would spend in prison. Each was a serious impediment to an evenhanded and effective operation of the criminal justice system." *Mistretta*, *supra*, at 366 (quoting S. Rep. No. 98-225, at 38, 65 (citation omitted)).

The Eighth Amendment imposes certain limits on the sentences that may be imposed in criminal cases, but for the most part it leaves questions of sentencing policy to be determined by Congress and the state legislatures—and with good reason. Determining the length of imprisonment that is appropriate for a particular offense and a particular offender inevitably involves a balancing of interests. If imprisonment does nothing else, it removes the criminal from the general population and prevents him from committing additional crimes in the outside world. When a legislature prescribes that a category of killers must be sentenced to life imprisonment, the legislature, which presumably reflects the views of the electorate, is taking the position that the risk that these offenders will kill again outweighs any countervailing consideration, including reduced culpability due to immaturity or the possibility of rehabilitation. When the majority of this Court countermands that democratic decision, what the majority is saying is that members of society must be exposed to the risk that these convicted murderers, if released from custody, will murder again.

Unless our cases change course, we will continue to march toward some vision of evolutionary culmination that the Court has not yet disclosed. The Constitution does not authorize us to take the country on this journey.

QUESTIONS

1. After *Miller*, may a state impose a sentence of life without the possibility of parole on a juvenile criminal offender? Under what circumstances?

2. In Eighth Amendment analysis, the Court will consider whether a national consensus exists against a particular sentence. Is there a national consensus disfavoring life without the possibility of parole for juveniles? How does the Court treat this issue? Do you think Justice Alito has the better argument?

3. What is Chief Justice Roberts arguing? Do you think he is correct?

4. What impact did the socioscientific evidence on child development have on the outcome? If the human brain does not fully mature until after the age of twenty-one, does that mean that young adult defendants are also less culpable?

5. Why does Justice Breyer argue that the state must make a determination about Kuntrell Jackson's intent to kill before imposing a life sentence? Why doesn't that same concern extend to Evan Miller?

6. Of the five opinions in *Miller*, which would you characterize as the least consistent with the Court's precedents? Why?

III

CHILDREN AND PROTECTION

A. Historical Origins

John E. B. Myers, Child Protection in America 27–31, 33, 34, 35–36, 37, 38, 39 (2006).

The New York Society for the Prevention of Cruelty to Children resulted from the rescue of a little girl named Mary Ellen Wilson.... Mary Ellen's mother, Francis Connor, arrived in New York City from London in 1858. Francis married Thomas Wilson, who died fighting in the Civil War. Now a poor pregnant widow, Francis struggled to survive. After Mary Ellen's birth in 1863, Francis found work as a hotel maid, and she boarded Mary Ellen with a woman named Score, paying Score eight dollars a month for Mary Ellen's care.

In 1864, Mary Ellen's mother disappeared, and the money for the baby's care dried up. Score took Mary Ellen to the Department of Charities, where the child lived until 1866 when, at eighteen months of age, she was indentured to Thomas McCormack and his wife Mary. Soon thereafter, Mr. McCormack died, and Mary took a new husband, Francis Connolly.

Mary Ellen spent eight long years with Mary and Francis Connolly, years filled with neglect and cruelty. Mary Ellen was not permitted to play with other children. Nor was she allowed outside, except occasionally at night. She was beaten routinely. When the Connollys went out, Mary Ellen was locked in. She had only one item of clothing, a threadbare dress over an undergarment. She slept on a piece of carpet on the floor.

In late 1873, a religious missionary to the poor named Etta Angell Wheeler was visiting a woman in the tenements of Hell's Kitchen, one of New York's worst slums. The woman told Wheeler that a little girl who used to live nearby "was often cruelly whipped and very frequently left alone the entire day with the windows darkened." Wheeler investigated.... [She] cajoled her way into the apartment, where, in Wheeler's own words, she "saw a pale, thin child, barefooted, in a thin, scanty dress, so tattered that I could see she wore but one garment besides. It was December and the weather was bitterly cold. She was a tiny mite, the size of five years, though as afterward appeared, she was then nine. Across the table lay a brutal whip of twisted leather strands and the child's meager arms and legs bore many marks of its use. But the saddest part of her story was written on her face, in its look of suppression and misery, the face of a child unloved, of a child that had seen only the fearsome side of life."

Etta Wheeler was determined to rescue Mary Ellen. She went to the police, but they said there was nothing they could do without more evidence of assault. Wheeler visited several child-helping charities, but they declined because they lacked authority to intervene in the family. In April 1874, after four months of futile efforts, Wheeler was running out of ideas. She had thought several times of asking for help from Henry Bergh, the influential founder of the American Society for the Prevention of Cruelty to Animals.... Wheeler plucked up the courage and went to Bergh's office, where he listened courteously. The next day, Wheeler . . . encountered an investigator sent by Henry Bergh.

Bergh contacted the lawyer for the animal protection society, Elbridge Gerry, and asked Gerry to find a legal means to rescue Mary Ellen. . . . Gerry located a little-used law that fit the bill. The law was a variant on the ancient writ of habeas corpus. Gerry drew up the necessary papers and asked Judge Abraham Lawrence to issue a warrant authorizing the police to take Mary Ellen into custody. The judge obliged, and on April 9, 1874, New York City police officer Christian McDougal, assisted by Alanzo Evans from the animal protection society, went to the Connollys' apartment and whisked Mary Ellen to safety. . . . The child was taken to police headquarters where the matron took a scrub brush to her. Mary Ellen was filthy; her hair matted and filled with vermin. It took several tubs of hot water to remove the dirt caked on her body.

Later that morning, Officer McDougal carried Mary Ellen into Judge Lawrence's courtroom. . . . [T]he judge was shocked at the sight of the little girl. . . .

Elbridge Gerry informed the judge of the case while Henry Bergh and Etta Wheeler listened. In the judge's chambers, Mary Ellen . . . said she could not remember ever "having been kissed by any one—have never been kissed by mamma. I do not want to go back to live with mamma, because she beats me so."

The next day, everyone was back in court, and by this time, Mary Ellen's story was front-page news. Etta Wheeler's husband was a newspaper man. . . . After several days of testimony from various witnesses, Judge Lawrence removed Mary Ellen from the Connollys' custody.

Later in 1874, Mrs. Connolly was prosecuted before a different judge for assaulting Mary Ellen with scissors. . . . Mrs. Connolly was convicted and sent to prison for a year. . . .

. . . Judge Lawrence placed [Mary Ellen] in the Sheltering Arms, an institution for homeless children. Etta Wheeler did not believe an institution was the place for Mary Ellen, so Wheeler asked the judge if Mary Ellen could live with Wheeler's own mother on a farm. . . . Judge Lawrence approved. . . . Etta Wheeler's mother died shortly thereafter, but Etta's sister stepped in and raise Mary Ellen as a daughter. . . .

With Mary Ellen safe, Elbridge Gerry and Henry Bergh discussed the need for an organization to protect children. Laws were on the books to begin the work, but no government agency or private organization had specific responsibility for child protection. Charles Loring Brace's Children's Aid Society and other charities helped many abused and neglected children, but they did not view themselves as child protection agencies. The police often stepped in, but child protection was not the focus of police work. . . .

As Gerry and Bergh discussed the problem, they drew on their experience protecting animals. Bergh had founded the American Society for the Prevention of Cruelty to Animals (ASPCA) in 1866, and Gerry was the society's lawyer. . . . Although ASPCA agents were not police officers . . . they had limited police power delegated by the City. ASPCA agents received reports of animal cruelty, conducted investigations, wore badges, made arrests, and prosecuted abusers in court. Gerry and Bergh incorporated the law enforcement-prosecution model into child protection.

Gerry took the lead in planning a child protection society. . . . [O]n December 15, 1874 . . . the New York Society for the Prevention of Cruelty to Children (NYSPCC) [was launched]. . . .

Elbridge Gerry viewed the [NYSPCC] as a law enforcement agency, not a social service agency. . . . Agents of the NYSPCC, like their counterparts in animal protection, received complaints of child abuse and neglect, investigated, and brought prosecutions in court. NYSPCC employees worked closely with police and sometimes wore badges. . . .

Although agents of the NYSPCC viewed their primary mission as enforcing criminal laws against cruelty, the society did more than prosecute. Often, prosecution was unnecessary, and agents helped families connect with social and financial resources. Agents used the threat of prosecution to coerce better parenting. The society pioneered the provision of temporary shelter care and emergency medical care for children removed from their parents and for children suspected of crime who would otherwise be sent to jail....

News of the New York SPCC spread, and reformers in other cities created nongovernmental child protection agencies.... [By] 1922, the number exceeded 300. Although 300 is impressive, many cities and nearly all rural areas had little or no access to a SPCC....

The law enforcement approach to child protection, exemplified by the New York SPCC, was popular. Before long, however, a competing perspective emerged that was based as much on social work as on prosecution....

...The American Human Association eventually embraced the social work function of protective work.

Lela B. Costin et al., The Politics of Child Abuse in America 46, 99, 107, 109–110 (1996).

The "discovery" of child abuse in the urban industrial world and organized attention to it occurred more than a century ago with the founding in 1874 of the New York Society for the Prevention of Cruelty to Children (SPCC), the first organization of its kind anywhere. The movement spread rapidly throughout American cities and into countries of Europe.... By 1921, however, formal efforts to "rescue" children from "cruelty" at the hands of their parents or other caretakers had lost momentum....

[A] constellation of forces...came together and created a disappearance of child abuse from the national agenda...the decline of feminism; blurred definitions of categories of children; disenchantment with the juvenile court; artificial distinctions between child welfare and family welfare agencies; the impact of psychoanalytical knowledge; an avoidance of the use of authority; and the impact of the economic and social conditions after 1930. Other conditions also served to reinforce the growing rejection of uninvited intervention into homes where the abuse of children was suspected. Most significant, the conflicting goals of family privacy and child protection precluded consideration of a mandate to report alleged child abuse....

Even as child abuse receded as a public concern, several institutional developments after the 1920s served to set the stage for its revival. Prominent among these were the major expansions of the American welfare state during the New Deal....

...Title IV [of the Social Security Act of 1935] introduced what was later to become the Aid to Families with Dependent Children (AFDC) program, which provided public relief to needy children through cash grants to their families. Title V reestablished Maternal and Child Welfare Services..."for the protection and care of homeless, dependent, and neglected children, and children in danger of becoming delinquent."...As a result of the Social Security Act of 1935, leadership for child welfare shifted largely from the private, voluntary sector to the public, governmental sector....

As an open-ended entitlement, AFDC expanded in relation to the number of eligible beneficiaries.... [I]ncreases in the number of AFDC families resulted in a corresponding increase in the number of social workers.... It soon became apparent that those states that had hired professionally trained social workers had, in so doing, brought upon themselves a degree of critical inspection of public welfare for which they were unprepared....

Much to the chagrin of elected officials, the critique of public welfare coming from the professional social workers swelled in proportion to rising caseloads.... The Nixon administration eventually addressed the problem of the rise in the number of social workers that occurred concomitant with increases in the number of AFDC cases by separating "income maintenance" from "social services," then limiting federal appropriations for social services under the Title XX program.... The income maintenance function of AFDC would remain an open-ended entitlement.... The social services function, however, was transformed into a capped entitlement....

... The concession social work made to get out from the onus of petty welfare accounting... proved to be a Faustian bargain.... [T]he value of Title XX appropriations declined steadily, until by the early 1990s they had half the value originally established in 1974.

NOTES AND QUESTIONS

1. Mary Ellen Wilson lived happily ever after. She married Lewis Schutt when she was twenty-four and in 1897, gave birth to her first child, whom she named Etta. She had a second child, Florence, four years later. Both of Mary Ellen's daughters attended college and became teachers. Mary Ellen died on October 30, 1956, at the age of ninety-two. JOHN E. B. MYERS, CHILD PROTECTION IN AMERICA 33 (2006).

2. To what extent is child protection informed by dominant notions of poverty, class, and ethnicity? Are such considerations relevant?

3. To what extent do you think the child-protection system in the United States remains punitive in its orientation? Do you think the system is protective of children?

4. Why does the state have the authority to remove children from their homes?

B. The Medical and Psychological Consequences of Abuse and Neglect

Child Welfare Information Gateway, Long Term Consequences of Abuse and Neglect, 1–6 (2008), http://www.childwelfare.gov/pubs/factsheets/long_term_consequences.pdf.

An estimated 905,000 children were victims of child abuse or neglect in 2006. While physical injuries may or may not be immediately visible, abuse and neglect can have consequences for children, families, and society that last lifetimes, if not generations.

The impact of child abuse and neglect is often discussed in terms of physical, psychological, behavioral, and societal consequences. In reality, however, it is impossible to separate them completely. Physical consequences, such as damage to a child's growing brain, can have psychological implications such as cognitive delays or emotional difficulties. Psychological problems often manifest as high-risk behaviors. Depression and anxiety, for example, may make a person more likely to smoke, abuse alcohol or illicit drugs, or overeat. High-risk behaviors, in turn, can lead to long-term physical health problems such as sexually transmitted diseases, cancer, and obesity.

This factsheet provides an overview of some of the most common physical, psychological, behavioral, and societal consequences of child abuse and neglect, while acknowledging that much crossover among categories exists.

Factors Affecting the Consequences of Child Abuse and Neglect

Not all abused and neglected children will experience long-term consequences. Outcomes of individual cases vary widely and are affected by a combination of factors, including:

- The child's age and developmental status when the abuse or neglect occurred
- The type of abuse (physical abuse, neglect, sexual abuse, etc.)
- The frequency, duration, and severity of abuse
- The relationship between the victim and his or her abuser

Researchers also have begun to explore why, given similar conditions, some children experience long-term consequences of abuse and neglect while others emerge relatively unscathed. The ability to cope, and even thrive, following a negative experience is sometimes referred to as “resilience.” A number of protective and promotive factors may contribute to an abused or neglected child’s resilience. These include individual characteristics, such as optimism, self-esteem, intelligence, creativity, humor, and independence, as well as the acceptance of peers and positive individual influences such as teachers, mentors, and role models. Other factors can include the child’s social environment and the family’s access to social supports. Community well-being, including neighborhood stability and access to safe schools and adequate health care, are other protective and promotive factors.

Physical Health Consequences

The immediate physical effects of abuse or neglect can be relatively minor (bruises or cuts) or severe (broken bones, hemorrhage, or even death). In some cases the physical effects are temporary; however, the pain and suffering they cause a child should not be discounted. Meanwhile, the long-term impact of child abuse and neglect on physical health is just beginning to be explored. According to the National Survey of Child and Adolescent Well-Being (NSCAW), more than one-quarter of children who had been in foster care for longer than 12 months had some lasting or recurring health problem. Below are some outcomes researchers have identified:

Shaken baby syndrome. Shaking a baby is a common form of child abuse. The injuries caused by shaking a baby may not be immediately noticeable and may include bleeding in the eye or brain, damage to the spinal cord and neck, and rib or bone fractures.

Impaired brain development. Child abuse and neglect have been shown, in some cases, to cause important regions of the brain to fail to form or grow properly, resulting in impaired development. These alterations in brain maturation have long-term consequences for cognitive, language, and academic abilities. NSCAW found more than three-quarters of foster children between 1 and 2 years of age to be at medium to high risk for problems with brain development, as opposed to less than half of children in a control sample.

Poor physical health. Several studies have shown a relationship between various forms of household dysfunction (including childhood abuse) and poor health. Adults who experienced abuse or neglect during childhood are more likely to suffer from physical ailments such as allergies, arthritis, asthma, bronchitis, high blood pressure, and ulcers.

Psychological Consequences

The immediate emotional effects of abuse and neglect—isolation, fear, and an inability to trust—can translate into lifelong consequences, including low self-esteem, depression, and relationship difficulties. Researchers have identified links between child abuse and neglect and the following:

Difficulties during infancy. Depression and withdrawal symptoms were common among children as young as 3 who experienced emotional, physical, or environmental neglect.

Poor mental and emotional health. In one long-term study, as many as 80 percent of young adults who had been abused met the diagnostic criteria for at least one psychiatric disorder at age 21. These young adults exhibited many problems, including depression, anxiety, eating disorders, and suicide attempts. Other psychological and emotional conditions associated with abuse and neglect include panic disorder, dissociative disorders, attention-deficit/

hyperactivity disorder, depression, anger, posttraumatic stress disorder, and reactive attachment disorder.

Cognitive difficulties. NSCAW found that children placed in out-of-home care due to abuse or neglect tended to score lower than the general population on measures of cognitive capacity, language development, and academic achievement. A 1999 LONGSCAN study also found a relationship between substantiated child maltreatment and poor academic performance and classroom functioning for school-age children.

Social difficulties. Children who experience rejection or neglect are more likely to develop antisocial traits as they grow up. Parental neglect is also associated with borderline personality disorders and violent behavior.

Behavioral Consequences

Not all victims of child abuse and neglect will experience behavioral consequences. However, behavioral problems appear to be more likely among this group, even at a young age. An NSCAW survey of children ages 3 to 5 in foster care found these children displayed clinical or borderline levels of behavioral problems at a rate more than twice that of the general population. Later in life, child abuse and neglect appear to make the following more likely:

Difficulties during adolescence. Studies have found abused and neglected children to be at least 25 percent more likely to experience problems such as delinquency, teen pregnancy, low academic achievement, drug use, and mental health problems. Other studies suggest that abused or neglected children are more likely to engage in sexual risk-taking as they reach adolescence, thereby increasing their chances of contracting a sexually transmitted disease.

Juvenile delinquency and adult criminality. According to a National Institute of Justice study, abused and neglected children were 11 times more likely to be arrested for criminal behavior as a juvenile, 2.7 times more likely to be arrested for violent and criminal behavior as an adult, and 3.1 times more likely to be arrested for one of many forms of violent crime (juvenile or adult).

Alcohol and other drug abuse. Research consistently reflects an increased likelihood that abused and neglected children will smoke cigarettes, abuse alcohol, or take illicit drugs during their lifetime. According to a report from the National Institute on Drug Abuse, as many as two-thirds of people in drug treatment programs reported being abused as children.

Abusive behavior. Abusive parents often have experienced abuse during their own childhoods. It is estimated approximately one-third of abused and neglected children will eventually victimize their own children.

Societal Consequences

While child abuse and neglect almost always occur within the family, the impact does not end there. Society as a whole pays a price for child abuse and neglect, in terms of both direct and indirect costs.

Direct costs. Direct costs include those associated with maintaining a child welfare system to investigate and respond to allegations of child abuse and neglect, as well as expenditures by the judicial, law enforcement, health, and mental health systems. A 2001 report by Prevent Child Abuse America estimates these costs at $24 billion per year.

Indirect costs. Indirect costs represent the long-term economic consequences of child abuse and neglect. These include costs associated with juvenile and adult criminal activity, mental illness, substance abuse, and domestic violence. They can also include loss of productivity due to unemployment and underemployment, the cost of special education services, and increased use of the health care system. Prevent Child Abuse America estimated these costs at more than $69 billion per year.

C. The Constitutional Framework in Abuse and Neglect Cases

MEYER V. NEBRASKA
Supreme Court of the United States
262 U.S. 390 (1923)

MR. JUSTICE MCREYNOLDS delivered the opinion of the Court.

Plaintiff in error was tried and convicted in the district court for Hamilton county, Nebraska, under an information which charged that on May 25, 1920, while an instructor in Zion Parochial School he unlawfully taught the subject of reading in the German language to Raymond Parpart, a child of 10 years, who had not attained and successfully passed the eighth grade. The information is based upon "An act relating to the teaching of foreign languages in the state of Nebraska," approved April 9, 1919 (Laws 1919, c. 249), which follows:

> "Section 1. No person, individually or as a teacher, shall, in any private, denominational, parochial or public school, teach any subject to any person in any language than the English language.
>
> "Sec. 2. Languages, other than the English language, may be taught as languages only after a pupil shall have attained and successfully passed the eighth grade as evidenced by a certificate of graduation issued by the county superintendent of the county in which the child resides.
>
> "Sec. 3. Any person who violates any of the provisions of this act shall be deemed guilty of a misdemeanor and upon conviction, shall be subject to a fine of not less than twenty-five dollars ($25), nor more than one hundred dollars ($100), or be confined in the county jail for any period not exceeding thirty days for each offense.
>
> "Sec. 4. Whereas, an emergency exists, this act shall be in force from and after its passage and approval."

The Supreme Court of the state affirmed the judgment of conviction. It declared the offense charged and established was "the direct and intentional teaching of the German language as a distinct subject to a child who had not passed the eighth grade," in the parochial school maintained by Zion Evangelical Lutheran Congregation, a collection of Biblical stories being used therefore. And it held that the statute forbidding this did not conflict with the

Fourteenth Amendment, but was a valid exercise of the police power. The following excerpts from the opinion sufficiently indicate the reasons advanced to support the conclusion.

"The salutary purpose of the statute is clear. The Legislature had seen the baneful effects of permitting foreigners, who had taken residence in this country, to rear and educate their children in the language of their native land. The result of that condition was found to be inimical to our own safety. To allow the children of foreigners, who had emigrated here, to be taught from early childhood the language of the country of their parents was to rear them with that language as their mother tongue. It was to educate them so that they must always think in that language, and, as a consequence, naturally inculcate in them the ideas and sentiments foreign to the best interests of this country. The statute, therefore, was intended not only to require that the education of all children be conducted in the English language, but that, until they had grown into that language and until it had become a part of them, they should not in the schools be taught any other language. The obvious purpose of this statute was that the English language should be and become the mother tongue of all children reared in this state. The enactment of such a statute comes reasonably within the police power of the state.

"It is suggested that the law is an unwarranted restriction, in that it applies to all citizens of the state and arbitrarily interferes with the rights of citizens who are not of foreign ancestry, and prevents them, without reason, from having their children taught foreign languages in school. That argument is not well taken, for it assumes that every citizen finds himself restrained by the statute. The hours which a child is able to devote to study in the confinement of school are limited. It must have ample time for exercise or play. Its daily capacity for learning is comparatively small. A selection of subjects for its education, therefore, from among the many that might be taught, is obviously necessary. The Legislature no doubt had in mind the practical operation of the law. The law affects few citizens, except those of foreign lineage. Other citizens, in their selection of studies, except perhaps in rare instances, have never deemed it of importance to teach their children foreign languages before such children have reached the eighth grade. In the legislative mind, the salutary effect of the statute no doubt outweighed the restriction upon the citizens generally, which, it appears, was a restriction of no real consequence."

The problem for our determination is whether the statute as construed and applied unreasonably infringes the liberty guaranteed to the plaintiff in error by the Fourteenth Amendment. "No state...shall deprive any person of life, liberty or property without due process of law." While this court has not attempted to define with exactness the liberty thus guaranteed, the term has received much consideration and some of the included things have been definitely stated. Without doubt, it denotes not merely freedom from bodily restraint but also the right of the individual to contract, to engage in any of the common occupations of life, to acquire useful knowledge, to marry, establish a home and bring up children, to worship God according to the dictates of his own conscience, and generally to enjoy those privileges long recognized at common law as essential to the orderly pursuit of happiness by free men. The established doctrine is that this liberty may not be interfered with, under the guise of protecting the public interest, by legislative action which is arbitrary or without reasonable relation to some purpose within the competency of the state to effect. Determination by the Legislature of what constitutes proper exercise of police power is not final or conclusive but is subject to supervision by the courts.

The American people have always regarded education and acquisition of knowledge as matters of supreme importance which should be diligently promoted.... Corresponding to the right of control, it is the natural duty of the parent to give his children education suitable to their station in life; and nearly all the states, including Nebraska, enforce this obligation by compulsory laws.

Practically, education of the young is only possible in schools conducted by especially qualified persons who devote themselves thereto. The calling always has been regarded as useful and honorable, essential, indeed, to the public welfare. Mere knowledge of the German language cannot reasonably be regarded as harmful. Heretofore it has been commonly looked upon as helpful and desirable. Plaintiff in error taught this language in school as part of his occupation. His right thus to teach and the right of parents to engage him so to instruct their children, we think, are within the liberty of the amendment.

The challenged statute forbids the teaching in school of any subject except in English; also the teaching of any other language until the pupil has attained and successfully passed the eighth grade, which is not usually accomplished before the age of twelve. The Supreme Court of the state has held that "the so-called ancient or dead languages" are not "within the spirit or the purpose of the act." Latin, Greek, Hebrew are not proscribed; but German, French, Spanish, Italian, and every other alien speech are within the ban. Evidently the Legislature has attempted materially to interfere with the calling of modern language teachers, with the opportunities of pupils to acquire knowledge, and with the power of parents to control the education of their own.

It is said the purpose of the legislation was to promote civic development by inhibiting training and education of the immature in foreign tongues and ideals before they could learn English and acquire American ideals, and "that the English language should be and become the mother tongue of all children reared in this state." It is also affirmed that the foreign born population is very large, that certain communities commonly use foreign words, follow foreign leaders, move in a foreign atmosphere, and that the children are thereby hindered from becoming citizens of the most useful type and the public safety is imperiled.

That the state may do much, go very far, indeed, in order to improve the quality of its citizens, physically, mentally and morally, is clear; but the individual has certain fundamental rights which must be respected. The protection of the Constitution extends to all, to those who speak other languages as well as to those born with English on the tongue. Perhaps it would be highly advantageous if all had ready understanding of our ordinary speech, but this cannot be coerced by methods which conflict with the Constitution—a desirable end cannot be promoted by prohibited means.

For the welfare of his Ideal Commonwealth, Plato suggested a law which should provide: "That the wives of our guardians are to be common, and their children are to be common, and no parent is to know his own child, nor any child his parent.... The proper officers will take the offspring of the good parents to the pen or fold, and there they will deposit them with certain nurses who dwell in a separate quarter; but the offspring of the inferior, or of the better when they chance to be deformed, will be put away in some mysterious, unknown place, as they should be." In order to submerge the individual and develop ideal citizens, Sparta assembled the males at seven into barracks and intrusted their subsequent education and training to official guardians. Although such measures have been deliberately approved by men of great genius their ideas touching the relation between individual and state were wholly different from those upon which our institutions rest; and it hardly will be affirmed that any Legislature could impose such restrictions upon the people of a state without doing violence to both letter and spirit of the Constitution.

The desire of the Legislature to foster a homogeneous people with American ideals prepared readily to understand current discussions of civic matters is easy to appreciate. Unfortunate experiences during the late war and aversion toward every character of truculent adversaries were certainly enough to quicken that aspiration. But the means adopted, we think, exceed the limitations upon the power of the state and conflict with rights assured to plaintiff in error. The interference is plain enough and no adequate reason therefor in time of peace and domestic tranquility has been shown.

The power of the state to compel attendance at some school and to make reasonable regulations for all schools, including a requirement that they shall give instructions in English, is not questioned. Nor has challenge been made of the state's power to prescribe a curriculum for institutions which it supports. Those matters are not within the present controversy. Our concern is with the prohibition approved by the Supreme Court. *Adams v. Tanner*, [244 U.S. 590,] 594 [1916], pointed out that mere abuse incident to an occupation ordinarily useful is not enough to justify its abolition, although regulation may be entirely proper. No emergency has arisen which renders knowledge by a child of some language other than English so clearly harmful as to justify its inhibition with the consequent infringement of rights long freely enjoyed. We are constrained to conclude that the statute as applied is arbitrary and without reasonable relation to any end within the competency of the state.

As the statute undertakes to interfere only with teaching which involves a modern language, leaving complete freedom as to other matters, there seems no adequate foundation for the suggestion that the purpose was to protect the child's health by limiting his mental activities. It is well known that proficiency in a foreign language seldom comes to one not instructed at an early age, and experience shows that this is not injurious to the health, morals or understanding of the ordinary child.

The judgment of the court below must be reversed and the cause remanded for further proceedings not inconsistent with this opinion.

[Justices Holmes and Sutherland dissented.]

NOTES AND QUESTIONS

1. What is the constitutional problem with the Nebraska statute? Whose constitutional rights did it violate?

2. According to the Court, what authority does the state have to regulate schools? Why does the state have this power? What was the state's justification for enacting the statute?

3. Why would the state of Nebraska enact such a law? To what extent do you think World War I played a role? Barbara Bennett Woodhouse offers this explanation:

> The law at issue in *Meyer*, known as the "Siman law" after its sponsor, Nebraska State Senator Harry Siman, passed the legislature of Nebraska in 1919. It prohibited the teaching of foreign languages in the primary grades of all schools, public or private. The Siman law was not an aberration. Sixteen states enacted similar laws in 1919 alone. By 1923, thirty-one states had laws mandating English as the sole language of instruction either in public or in all schools. These language laws sprang, in some measure, from anti-German bias of the war

years. They were rooted, however, in a more enduring conflict—the struggle between cultural pluralism and the felt need to articulate a national identity, evident in the long-standing tensions between English-speaking settlers of the Midwest and the large German, Polish, and Scandinavian communities in these states. These immigrant groups often formed isolated cultural enclaves with clubs, parochial schools, ethnic parishes, banks, stores, and insurance companies in which all business was conducted in the language of the home country. To their American-born neighbors, coming from a tradition that mixed the meliorative, unifying strains of populism and progressivism with a nativist distrust for anything foreign, this failure to assimilate seemed at once a threat and a challenge for progressive reform.

The growth of private religious schools, importing teachers from the Old Country who taught in German, Polish, Italian, or Czech, posed a particular threat to a cherished agent of social equality and acculturation—the common school movement....

Contemporary historians of American education have hotly debated both the aims and effects of the common school movement. Until recently, historians depicted the story of American education as a steady march, led by benevolent and disinterested reformers, from the darkness of ignorance to the light of equal opportunity through free public education. Beginning in the 1960's, however, revisionist historians sought to debunk this view as myth. Their studies of class conflict portray the common school movement and "progressive" school reformers as agents of a ruling business elite that effectively subjugated working-class and especially immigrant children through a form of cultural imperialism.

Other modern historians have suggested that pluralist politics kept the public schools from becoming the captive of any one group and that issues of schooling as it affected class, ethnicity, status, and economics were mediated through many subtle and changing political alliances. Regardless of which account one now finds persuasive, Americans in the half-century before *Meyer*...generally viewed the mission of the common school as threefold: to train citizens to exercise their rights in a democracy; to imbue immigrants and the poor with "American" ideals and culture; and to equalize opportunity for advancement in an egalitarian society. "Americans understood that mass education and egalitarian citizenship were inextricably linked." The common schools would function not as vehicles for private advancement but as servants of the community, dedicated to socialization of children to life in a modern America. English, as the language of instruction, would be the primary agent of acculturation.

Into this idealized setting came the immigrant parents, who by-passed public education and turned to church schools to meet their need to reaffirm cherished traditions. In the reformers' eyes, the vision of common schools in which all of the children of a community might meet and learn from each other could never be realized as long as the common schools must compete with schools that were "agents of churches and immigrant communities and dedicated to their service." School boards tried a variety of strategies to promote universal common schooling, from frankly pluralist policies, such as offering classes in foreign language and culture to attract immigrant students, to restrictive rules that sought to force assimilation by suppressing foreign languages....

...In 1913, only five years before the Nebraska legislature passed the Siman law, the German-American Alliance in Nebraska had gained sufficient power to pass the Mockett laws requiring that the public elementary school teach a modern language if fifty parents in the district so requested. The "language issue" caused dissension not only between immigrants and nativists but also within immigrant communities. Attitudes toward language preservation divided Progressives from traditionalists and the young from the older generation. Although the conservative Lutheran synods fought to preserve their power through

> separate parochial schools, "modern" German-Americans such as Senator Gratz Brown of Missouri saw common education as the key for immigrants of every tongue to attain "a common destiny" and a "single nationality." ...
>
> Thus, the clash of immigrant cultural identity with the ideal of assimilation through the mandatory teaching of English was nothing new in 1918. The law at issue in *Meyer* was not solely a response to wartime panic but reflected preexisting tensions—political, educational, generational, and cultural—which the war had exacerbated but did not create. The Siman law reached an extreme, however, in extending beyond English as the basic school language to prohibit any foreign language instruction in formal elementary school settings, public or private.

Barbara Bennett Woodhouse, *"Who Owns the Child?" Meyer and Pierce and the Child as Property*, 33 WM. & MARY L. REV. 995, 1003–1007, 1008, 1009 (1992). How, then, would you characterize the Supreme Court's ruling?

PIERCE V. SOCIETY OF THE SISTERS OF THE HOLY NAMES OF JESUS AND MARY

Supreme Court of the United States

268 U.S. 510 (1925)

MR. JUSTICE MCREYNOLDS delivered the opinion of the Court.

These appeals are from decrees, based upon undenied allegations, which granted preliminary orders restraining appellants from threatening or attempting to enforce the Compulsory Education Act adopted November 7, 1922, under the initiative provision of her Constitution by the voters of Oregon. They present the same points of law; there are no controverted questions of fact. Rights said to be guaranteed by the federal Constitution were specially set up, and appropriate prayers asked for their protection.

The challenged act, effective September 1, 1926, requires every parent, guardian, or other person having control or charge or custody of a child between 8 and 16 years to send him "to a public school for the period of time a public school shall be held during the current year" in the district where the child resides; and failure so to do is declared a misdemeanor. There are exemptions—not specially important here—for children who are not normal, or who have completed the eighth grade, or whose parents or private teachers reside at considerable distances from any public school, or who hold special permits from the county superintendent. The manifest purpose is to compel general attendance at public schools by normal children, between 8 and 16, who have not completed the eighth grade. And without doubt enforcement of the statute would seriously impair, perhaps destroy, the profitable features of appellees' business and greatly diminish the value of their property.

Appellee the Society of Sisters is an Oregon corporation, organized in 1880, with power to care for orphans, educate and instruct the youth, establish and maintain academies or schools, and acquire necessary real and personal property. It has long devoted its property and effort to the secular and religious education and care of children, and has acquired the valuable good will of many parents and guardians. It conducts interdependent primary and high schools and junior colleges, and maintains orphanages for the custody and control of children between 8 and 16. In its primary schools many children between those ages are taught the subjects usually pursued in Oregon public schools during the first eight years. Systematic religious instruction and moral training according to the tenets of the Roman Catholic Church are also regularly provided. All courses of study, both temporal and religious, contemplate continuity of training under appellee's charge; the primary schools are essential to the system and the most profitable. It owns valuable buildings, especially constructed and equipped for school purposes. The business is remunerative—the annual income from primary schools exceeds $30,000—and the successful conduct of this requires long time contracts with teachers and parents. The Compulsory Education Act of 1922 has already caused the withdrawal from its schools of children who would otherwise continue, and their income has steadily declined. The appellants, public officers, have proclaimed their purpose strictly to enforce the statute.

After setting out the above facts, the Society's bill alleges that the enactment conflicts with the right of parents to choose schools where their children will receive appropriate mental and religious training, the right of the child to influence the parents' choice of a school, the right of schools and teachers therein to engage in a useful business or profession, and is accordingly repugnant to the Constitution and void. And, further, that unless enforcement of the measure is enjoined the corporation's business and property will suffer irreparable injury.

Appellee Hill Military Academy is a private corporation organized in 1908 under the laws of Oregon, engaged in owning, operating, and conducting for profit an elementary, college preparatory, and military training school for boys between the ages of 5 and 21 years. The average attendance is 100, and the annual fees received for each student amount to some $800. The elementary department is divided into eight grades, as in the public schools; the college preparatory department has four grades, similar to those of the public high schools; the courses of study conform to the requirements of the state board of education. Military instruction and training are also given, under the supervision of an army officer. It owns considerable real and personal property, some useful only for school purposes. The business and incident good will are very valuable. In order to conduct its affairs, long time contracts must be made for supplies, equipment, teachers, and pupils. Appellants, law officers of the state and county, have publicly announced that the Act of November 7, 1922, is valid and have declared their intention to enforce it. By reason of the statute and threat of enforcement appellee's business is being destroyed and its property depreciated; parents and guardians are refusing to make contracts for the future instruction of their sons, and some are being withdrawn.

The Academy's bill states the foregoing facts and then alleges that the challenged act contravenes the corporation's rights guaranteed by the Fourteenth Amendment and that unless appellants are restrained from proclaiming its validity and threatening to enforce it irreparable injury will result. The prayer is for an appropriate injunction.

No answer was interposed in either cause, and after proper notices they were heard by three judges on motions for preliminary injunctions upon the specifically alleged facts. The court ruled that the Fourteenth Amendment guaranteed appellees against the deprivation of their property without due process of law consequent upon the unlawful interference by appellants with the free choice of patrons, present and prospective. It declared the right to conduct schools was property and that parents and guardians, as a part of their liberty, might direct the education of children by selecting reputable teachers and places. Also, that these schools were not unfit or harmful to the public, and that enforcement of the challenged statute would unlawfully deprive them of patronage and thereby destroy appellees' business and property. Finally, that the threats to enforce the act would continue to cause irreparable injury; and the suits were not premature.

No question is raised concerning the power of the state reasonably to regulate all schools, to inspect, supervise and examine them, their teachers and pupils; to require that all children of proper age attend some school, that teachers shall be of good moral character and patriotic disposition, that certain studies plainly essential to good citizenship must be taught, and that nothing be taught which is manifestly inimical to the public welfare.

The inevitable practical result of enforcing the act under consideration would be destruction of appellees' primary schools, and perhaps all other private primary schools for normal children within the state of Oregon. These parties are engaged in a kind of undertaking not inherently harmful, but long regarded as useful and meritorious. Certainly there is nothing in the present records to indicate that they have failed to discharge their obligations to patrons, students, or the state. And there are no peculiar circumstances or present emergencies which demand extraordinary measures relative to primary education.

Under the doctrine of *Meyer v. Nebraska*, 262 U.S. 390, we think it entirely plain that the Act of 1922 unreasonably interferes with the liberty of parents and guardians to direct the upbringing and education of children under their control. As often heretofore pointed out, rights guaranteed by the Constitution may not be abridged by legislation which has no reasonable relation to some purpose within the competency of the state. The fundamental theory of liberty upon which all governments in this Union repose excludes any general power of the state to standardize its children by forcing them to accept instruction from public teachers only. The child is not the mere creature of the state; those who nurture him and direct his destiny have the right, coupled with the high duty, to recognize and prepare him for additional obligations.

Appellees are corporations, and therefore, it is said, they cannot claim for themselves the liberty which the Fourteenth Amendment guarantees. Accepted in the proper sense, this is true. But they have business and property for which they claim protection. These are threatened with destruction through the unwarranted compulsion which appellants are exercising over present and prospective patrons of their schools. And this court has gone very far to protect against loss threatened by such action....

Generally, it is entirely true, as urged by counsel, that no person in any business has such an interest in possible customers as to enable him to restrain exercise of proper power of the state upon the ground that he will be deprived of patronage. But the injunctions here sought are not against the exercise of any proper power. Plaintiffs asked protection against arbitrary, unreasonable, and unlawful interference with their patrons and the consequent destruction of their business and property. Their interest is clear and immediate....

The suits were not premature. The injury to appellees was present and very real, not a mere possibility in the remote future. If no relief had been possible prior to the effective date of the act, the injury would have become irreparable. Prevention of impending injury by unlawful action is a well-recognized function of courts of equity.

The decrees below are

Affirmed.

NOTES AND QUESTIONS

1. Who challenged the Oregon statute? What was the legal basis for the challenge? Whose constitutional rights were at stake?

2. Why would a state mandate attendance at public schools? Woodhouse argues that "[t]he guiding sentiment behind the Oregon law... seems to have been an odd commingling of patriotic fervor, blind faith in the cure-all powers of common schooling, anti-Catholic and anti-foreign prejudice, and the conviction that private and parochial schools were breeding grounds of Bolshevism." Woodhouse, *"Who Owns the Child?" supra*, at 1017–1018. Noting that the law drew support from a variety of organizations, including the Scottish Rite Masons, the American Legion, and the Ku Klux Klan, Woodhouse also contends that the law was aimed at "class leveling." *Id.* at 1018.

3. How would you characterize the *Meyer* and *Pierce* decisions? Justice McReynolds, who authored both opinions, was one of the "Four Horsemen" who opposed New Deal legislation. Woodhouse argues that *Meyer* and *Pierce* constitutionalize a "patriarchal notion of parental rights," in which children are "mere chattel." Do you agree?

PRINCE V. MASSACHUSETTS
Supreme Court of the United States
321 U.S. 158 (1944)

Mr. Justice Rutledge delivered the opinion of the Court.

The case brings for review another episode in the conflict between Jehovah's Witnesses and state authority. This time Sarah Prince appeals from convictions for violating Massachusetts' child labor laws, by acts said to be a rightful exercise of her religious convictions.

When the offenses were committed she was the aunt and custodian of Betty M. Simmons, a girl nine years of age. Originally there were three separate complaints. They were, shortly, for (1) refusal to disclose Betty's identity and age to a public officer whose duty was to enforce the statutes; (2) furnishing her with magazines, knowing she was to sell them unlawfully, that is, on the street; and (3) as Betty's custodian, permitting her to work contrary to law. The complaints were made, respectively, pursuant to §§ 79, 80 and 81 of Chapter 149, Gen. Laws of Mass. The Supreme Judicial Court reversed the conviction under the first complaint on state grounds; but sustained the judgments founded on the other two. They present the only questions for our decision. These are whether §§ 80 and 81, as applied, contravene the Fourteenth Amendment by denying or abridging appellant's freedom of religion and by denying to her the equal protection of the laws.

Sections 80 and 81 form parts of Massachusetts' comprehensive child labor law. They provide methods for enforcing the prohibitions of § 69, which is as follows:

"No boy under twelve and no girl under eighteen shall sell, expose or offer for sale any newspapers, magazines, periodicals or any other articles of merchandise of any description, or exercise the trade of bootblack or scavenger, or any other trade, in any street or public place."

Sections 80 and 81, so far as pertinent, read:

"Whoever furnishes or sells to any minor any article of any description with the knowledge that the minor intends to sell such article in violation of any provision of sections sixty-nine to seventy-three, inclusive, or after having received written notice to this effect from any officer charged with the enforcement thereof, or knowingly procures or encourages any minor to violate any provisions of said sections, shall be punished by a fine of not less than ten nor more than two hundred dollars or by imprisonment for not more than two months, or both." § 80.

"Any parent, guardian or custodian having a minor under his control who compels or permits such minor to work in violation of any provision of sections sixty to seventy-four, inclusive, . . . shall for a first offence be punished by a fine of not less than two nor more than ten dollars or by imprisonment for not more than five days, or both. . . ." § 81.

The story told by the evidence has become familiar. It hardly needs repeating, except to give setting to the variations introduced through the part played by a child of tender years. Mrs. Prince, living in Brockton, is the mother of two young sons. She also has legal custody of Betty Simmons who lives with them. The children too are Jehovah's Witnesses and both Mrs. Prince and Betty testified they were ordained ministers. The former was accustomed to go each week on the streets of Brockton to distribute "Watchtower" and "Consolation," according to the usual plan. She had permitted the children to engage in this activity previously, and had been warned against doing so by the school attendance officer, Mr. Perkins. But, until December 18, 1941, she generally did not take them with her at night.

That evening, as Mrs. Prince was preparing to leave her home, the children asked to go. She at first refused. Childlike, they resorted to tears and, motherlike, she yielded. Arriving downtown, Mrs. Prince permitted the children "to engage in the preaching work with her upon the sidewalks." That is, with specific reference to Betty, she and Mrs. Prince took positions about twenty feet apart near a street intersection. Betty held up in her hand, for passersby to see, copies of "Watch Tower" and "Consolation." From her shoulder hung the usual canvas magazine bag, on which was printed "Watchtower and Consolation 5¢ per copy." No one accepted a copy from Betty that evening and she received no money. Nor did her aunt. But on other occasions, Betty had received funds and given out copies.

Mrs. Prince and Betty remained until 8:45 p.m. A few minutes before this Mr. Perkins approached Mrs. Prince. A discussion ensued. He inquired and she refused to give Betty's name. However, she stated the child attended the Shaw School. Mr. Perkins referred to his previous warnings and said he would allow five minutes for them to get off the street. Mrs. Prince admitted she supplied Betty with the magazines and said, "(N)either you nor anybody else can stop me. . . . This child is exercising her God-given right and her constitutional right to preach the gospel, and no creature has a right to interfere with God's commands." However, Mrs. Prince and Betty departed. She remarked as she went, "I'm not going through this any more. We've been through it time and time again. I'm going home and put the little girl to bed." It may be added that testimony, by Betty, her aunt and others, was offered at the trials, and was excluded, to show that Betty believed it was her religious duty to perform this work and failure would bring condemnation "to everlasting destruction at Armageddon."

As the case reaches us, the questions are no longer open whether what the child did was a "sale" or an "offer to sell" within § 69 or was "work" within § 81. The state court's decision has foreclosed them adversely to appellant as a matter of state law. The only question remaining therefore is whether, as construed and applied, the statute is valid. Upon this the court said: "We think that freedom of the press and of religion is subject to incidental regulation to the slight degree involved in the prohibition of the selling of religious literature in streets and public places by boys under twelve and girls under eighteen and in the further statutory provisions herein considered, which have been adopted as a means of enforcing that prohibition."

Appellant does not stand on freedom of the press. Regarding it as secular, she concedes it may be restricted as Massachusetts has done. Hence, she rests squarely on freedom of religion under the First Amendment, applied by the Fourteenth to the states. She buttresses this foundation, however, with a claim of parental right as secured by the due process clause of the latter Amendment. Cf. *Meyer v. Nebraska*, 262 U.S. 390. These guaranties, she thinks, guard alike herself and the child in what they have done. Thus, two claimed liberties are at stake. One is the parent's, to bring up the child in the way he should go, which for appellant means to teach him the tenets and the practices of their faith. The other freedom is the child's, to observe these; and among them is "to preach the gospel...by public distribution" of "Watchtower" and "Consolation," in conformity with the scripture: "A little child shall lead them."

If by this position appellant seeks for freedom of conscience a broader protection than for freedom of the mind, it may be doubted that any of the great liberties insured by the First Article can be given higher place than the others. All have preferred position in our basic scheme. All are interwoven there together. Differences there are, in them and in the modes appropriate for their exercise. But they have unity in the charter's prime place because they have unity in their human sources and functionings. Heart and mind are not identical. Intuitive faith and reasoned judgment are not the same. Spirit is not always thought. But in the everyday business of living, secular or otherwise, these variant aspects of personality find inseparable expression in a thousand ways. They cannot be altogether parted in law more than in life.

To make accommodation between these freedoms and an exercise of state authority always is delicate. It hardly could be more so than in such a clash as this case presents. On one side is the obviously earnest claim for freedom of conscience and religious practice. With it is allied the parent's claim to authority in her own household and in the rearing of her children. The parent's conflict with the state over control of the child and his training is serious enough when only secular matters are concerned. It becomes the more so when an element of religious conviction enters. Against these sacred private interests, basic in a democracy, stand the interests of society to protect the welfare of children, and the state's assertion of authority to that end, made here in a manner conceded valid if only secular things were involved. The last is no mere corporate concern of official authority. It is the interest of youth itself, and of the whole community, that children be both safeguarded from abuses and given opportunities for growth into free and independent well-developed men and citizens. Between contrary pulls of such weight, the safest and most objective recourse is to the lines already marked out, not precisely but for guides, in narrowing the no man's land where this battle has gone on.

The rights of children to exercise their religion, and of parents to give them religious training and to encourage them in the practice of religious belief, as against preponderant sentiment and assertion of state power voicing it, have had recognition here, most recently in *West Virginia State Board of Education v. Barnette*, 319 U.S. 624. Previously in *Pierce v. Society of Sisters*, 268 U.S. 510, 45 S.Ct. 571, this Court had sustained the parent's authority to provide religious with secular schooling, and the child's right to receive it, as against the state's requirement of attendance at public schools. And in *Meyer v. Nebraska*, 262 U.S. 390, 43 S.Ct. 625, children's rights to receive teaching in languages other than the nation's common tongue were guarded against the state's encroachment. It is cardinal with us that the custody, care and nurture of the child reside first in the parents, whose primary function and freedom include preparation for obligations the state can neither supply nor hinder. *Pierce v. Society of Sisters, supra*. And it is in recognition of this that these decisions have respected the private realm of family life which the state cannot enter.

But the family itself is not beyond regulation in the public interest, as against a claim of religious liberty. *Reynolds v. United States*, 98 U.S. 145; *Davis v. Beason*, 133 U.S. 333. And neither rights of religion nor rights of parenthood are beyond limitation. Acting to guard the general interest in youth's well being, the state as parens patriae may restrict the parent's control by requiring school attendance, regulating or prohibiting the child's labor, and in many other ways. Its authority is not nullified merely because the parent grounds his claim to control the child's course of conduct on religion or conscience. Thus, he cannot claim freedom from compulsory vaccination for the child more than for himself on religious grounds. The right to practice religion freely does not include liberty to expose the community or the child to communicable disease or the latter to ill health or death. The catalogue need not be lengthened. It is sufficient to show what indeed appellant hardly disputes, that the state has a wide range of power for limiting parental freedom and authority in things affecting the child's welfare; and that this includes, to some extent, matters of conscience and religious conviction.

But it is said the state cannot do so here. This, first, because when state action impinges upon a claimed religious freedom, it must fall unless shown to be necessary for or conducive to the child's protection against some clear and present danger, and, it is added, there was no such showing here. The child's presence on the street, with her guardian, distributing or offering to distribute the magazines, it is urged, was in no way harmful to her, nor in any event more so than the presence of many other children at the same time and place, engaged in shopping and other activities not prohibited. Accordingly, in view of the preferred position the freedoms of the First Article occupy, the statute in its present application must fall. It cannot be sustained by any presumption of validity. And, finally, it is said, the statute is, as to children, an absolute prohibition, not merely a reasonable regulation, of the denounced activity.

Concededly a statute or ordinance identical in terms with § 69, except that it is applicable to adults or all persons generally, would be invalid. But the mere fact a state could not wholly prohibit this form of adult activity, whether characterized locally as a "sale" or otherwise, does not mean it cannot do so for children. Such a conclusion granted would mean that a state could impose no greater limitation upon child labor than upon adult labor. Or, if an adult were free to enter dance halls, saloons, and disreputable places generally, in order to discharge his conceived religious duty to admonish or dissuade persons from frequenting such places, so would be a child with similar convictions and objectives, if not alone then in the parent's company, against the state's command.

The state's authority over children's activities is broader than over like actions of adults. This is peculiarly true of public activities and in matters of employment. A democratic society rests, for its continuance, upon the healthy, well-rounded growth of young people into full maturity as citizens, with all that implies. It may secure this against impeding restraints and dangers, within a broad range of selection. Among evils most appropriate for such action are the crippling effects of child employment, more especially in public places, and the possible harms arising from other activities subject to all the diverse influences of the street. It is too late now to doubt that legislation appropriately designed to reach such evils is within the state's police power, whether against the parent's claim to control of the child or one that religious scruples dictate contrary action.

It is true children have rights, in common with older people, in the primary use of highways. But even in such use streets afford dangers for them not affecting adults. And in other uses, whether in work or in other things, this difference may be magnified. This is so not only when children are unaccompanied but certainly to some extent when they are with their parents. What may be wholly permissible for adults therefore may not be so for children, either with or without their parents' presence.

Street preaching, whether oral or by handing out literature, is not the primary use of the highway, even for adults. While for them it cannot be wholly prohibited, it can be regulated within reasonable limits in accommodation to the primary and other incidental uses. But, for obvious reasons, notwithstanding appellant's contrary view, the validity of such a prohibition applied to children not accompanied by an older person hardly would seem open to question. The case reduces itself therefore to the question whether the presence of the child's guardian puts a limit to the state's power. That fact may lessen the likelihood that some evils the legislation seeks to avert will occur. But it cannot forestall all of them. The zealous though lawful exercise of the right to engage in propagandizing the community, whether in religious, political or other matters, may and at times does create situations difficult enough for adults to cope with and wholly inappropriate for children, especially of tender years, to face. Other harmful possibilities could be stated, of emotional excitement and psychological or physical injury. Parents may be free to become martyrs themselves. But it does not follow they are free, in identical circumstances, to make martyrs of their children before they have reached the age of full and legal discretion when they can make that choice for themselves. Massachusetts has determined that an absolute prohibition, though one limited to streets and public places and to the incidental uses proscribed, is necessary to accomplish its legitimate objectives. Its power to attain them is broad enough to reach these peripheral instances in which the parent's supervision may reduce but cannot eliminate entirely the ill effects of the prohibited conduct. We think that with reference to the public proclaiming of religion, upon the streets and in other similar public places, the power of the state to control the conduct of children reaches beyond the scope of its authority over adults, as is true in the case of other freedoms, and the rightful boundary of its power has not been crossed in this case.

In so ruling we dispose also of appellant's argument founded upon denial of equal protection. It falls with that based on denial of religious freedom, since in this instance the one is but another phrasing of the other. Shortly, the contention is that the street, for Jehovah's Witnesses and their children, is their church, since their conviction makes it so; and to deny them access to it for religious purposes as was done here has the same effect as excluding altar boys, youthful choristers, and other children from the edifices in which they practice their religious beliefs and worship. The argument hardly needs more than statement, after what has been said, to refute it. However Jehovah's Witnesses may conceive them, the public highways have not become their religious property merely by their assertion. And there is no denial of equal protection in excluding their children from doing there what no other children may do.

Our ruling does not extend beyond the facts the case presents. We neither lay the foundation "for any (that is, every) state intervention in the indoctrination and participation of children in religion" which may be done "in the name of their health and welfare" nor give warrant for "every limitation on their religious training and activities." The religious training and indoctrination of children may be accomplished in many ways, some of which, as we have noted, have received constitutional protection through decisions of this Court. These and all others except the public proclaiming of religion on the streets, if this may be taken as either training or indoctrination of the proclaimer, remain unaffected by the decision.

The judgment is

Affirmed.

Mr. Justice Murphy, dissenting:

This attempt by the state of Massachusetts to prohibit a child from exercising her constitutional right to practice her religion on the public streets cannot, in my opinion, be sustained.

The record makes clear the basic fact that Betty Simmons, the nine-year old child in question, was engaged in a genuine religious, rather than commercial, activity. She was a member of Jehovah's Witnesses and had been taught the tenets of that sect by her guardian, the appellant. Such tenets included the duty of publicly distributing religious tracts on the street and from door to door. Pursuant to this religious duty and in the company of the appellant, Betty Simmons on the night of December 18, 1941, was standing on a public street corner and offering to distribute Jehovah's Witness literature to passersby. There was no expectation of pecuniary profit to herself or to appellant. It is undisputed, furthermore, that she did this of her own desire and with appellant's consent. She testified that she was motivated by her love of the Lord and that He commanded her to distribute this literature; this was, she declared, her way of worshipping God. She was occupied, in other words, in "an age-old form of missionary evangelism" with a purpose "as evangelical as the revival meeting." *Murdock v. Pennsylvania*, 319 U.S. 105, 108, 109.

Religious training and activity, whether performed by adult or child, are protected by the Fourteenth Amendment against interference by state action, except insofar as they violate reasonable regulations adopted for the protection of the public health, morals and welfare. Our problem here is whether a state, under the guise of enforcing its child labor laws, can lawfully prohibit girls under the age of eighteen and boys under the age of twelve from practicing their religious faith insofar as it involves the distribution or sale of religious tracts on the public streets. No question of freedom of speech or freedom of press is present and we are not called upon to determine the permissible restraints on those rights. Nor are any truancy or curfew restrictions in issue. The statutes in question prohibit all children within the specified age limits from selling or offering to sell "any newspapers, magazines, periodicals or any other articles of merchandise of any description... in any street or public place." Criminal sanctions are imposed on the parents and guardians who compel or permit minors in their control to engage in the prohibited transactions. The state court has construed these statutes to cover the activities here involved,... thereby imposing an indirect restraint through the parents and guardians on the free exercise by minors of their religious beliefs. This indirect restraint is no less effective than a direct one. A square conflict between the constitutional guarantee of religious freedom and the state's legitimate interest in protecting the welfare of its children is thus presented.

As the opinion of the Court demonstrates, the power of the state lawfully to control the religious and other activities of children is greater than its power over similar activities of adults. But that fact is no more decisive of the issue posed by this case than is the obvious fact that the family itself is subject to reasonable regulation in the public interest. We are concerned solely with the reasonableness of this particular prohibition of religious activity by children.

In dealing with the validity of statutes which directly or indirectly infringe religious freedom and the right of parents to encourage their children in the practice of a religious belief, we are not aided by any strong presumption of the constitutionality of such legislation. *United States v. Carolene Products Co.*, 304 U.S. 144, note 4. On the contrary, the human freedoms enumerated in the First Amendment and carried over into the Fourteenth Amendment are to be presumed to be invulnerable and any attempt to sweep away those freedoms is prima facie invalid. It follows that any restriction or prohibition must be justified by those who deny that the freedoms have been unlawfully invaded. The burden was therefore on the state of Massachusetts to prove the reasonableness and necessity of prohibiting children from engaging in religious activity of the type involved in this case.

The burden in this instance, however, is not met by vague references to the reasonableness underlying child labor legislation in general. The great interest of the state in shielding minors from the evil vicissitudes of early life does not warrant every limitation on their religious training and activities. The reasonableness that justifies the prohibition of the ordinary distribution of literature in the public streets by children is not necessarily the reasonableness that justifies such a drastic restriction when the distribution is part of their religious faith. *Murdock v. Pennsylvania, supra*, 319 U.S. 111. If the right of a child to practice its religion in that manner is to be forbidden by constitutional means, there must be convincing proof that such a practice constitutes a grave and immediate danger to the state or to the health, morals or welfare of the child. The vital freedom of religion, which is "of the very essence of a scheme of ordered liberty," cannot be erased by slender references to the state's power to restrict the more secular activities of children.

The state, in my opinion, has completely failed to sustain its burden of proving the existence of any grave or immediate danger to any interest which it may lawfully protect. There is no proof that Betty Simmons' mode of worship constituted a serious menace to the public. It was carried on in an orderly, lawful manner at a public street corner. And "one who is rightfully on a street which the state has left open to the public carries with him there as elsewhere the constitutional right to express his views in an orderly fashion. This right extends to the communication of ideas by handbills and literature as well as the spoken word." *Jamison v. Texas*, 318 U.S. 413, 416. The sidewalk, no less than the cathedral or the evangelist's tent, is a proper place, under the Constitution, for the orderly worship of God. Such use of the streets is as necessary to the Jehovah's Witnesses, the Salvation Army and others who practice religion without benefit of conventional shelters as is the use of the streets for purposes of passage.

It is claimed, however, that such activity was likely to affect adversely the health, morals and welfare of the child. Reference is made in the majority opinion to "the crippling effects of child employment, more especially in public places, and the possible harms arising from other activities subject to all the diverse influences of the street." To the extent that they flow from participation in ordinary commercial activities, these harms are irrelevant to this case. And the bare possibility that such harms might emanate from distribution of religious literature is not, standing alone, sufficient justification for restricting freedom of conscience and religion. Nor can parents or guardians be subjected to criminal liability because of vague possibilities that their religious teachings might cause injury to the child. The evils must be grave, immediate, substantial. Yet there is not the slightest indication in this record, or in sources subject to judicial notice, that children engaged in distributing literature pursuant to their religious beliefs have been or are likely to be subject to any of the harmful "diverse influences of the street." Indeed, if probabilities are to be indulged in, the likelihood is that children engaged in serious religious endeavor are immune from such influences. Gambling, truancy, irregular eating and sleeping habits, and the more serious vices are not consistent with the high moral character ordinarily displayed by children fulfilling religious obligations. Moreover, Jehovah's Witness children invariably make their distributions in groups subject at all times to adult or parental control, as was done in this case. The dangers are thus exceedingly remote, to say the least. And the fact that the zealous exercise of the right to propagandize the community may result in violent or disorderly situations difficult for children to face is no excuse for prohibiting the exercise of that right.

No chapter in human history has been so largely written in terms of persecution and intolerance as the one dealing with religious freedom. From ancient times to the present day, the ingenuity of man has known no limits in its ability to forge weapons of oppression for use against those who dare to express or practice unorthodox religious beliefs. And the Jehovah's Witnesses are living proof of the fact that even in this nation, conceived as it was in the ideals of freedom, the right to practice religion in unconventional ways is still far from secure. Theirs is a militant and unpopular faith, pursued with a fanatical zeal. They have suffered brutal beatings; their property has been destroyed; they have been harassed at every turn by the resurrection and enforcement of little used ordinances and statutes. To them, along with other present-day religious minorities, befalls the burden of testing our devotion to the ideals and constitutional guarantees of religious freedom. We should therefore hesitate before approving the application of a statute that might be used as another instrument of oppression....

Mr. Justice Jackson:

The novel feature of this decision is this: the Court holds that a state may apply child labor laws to restrict or prohibit an activity of which, as recently as last term, it held: "This form of religious activity occupies the same high estate under the First Amendment as do worship in the churches and preaching from the pulpits. It has the same claim to protection as the more orthodox and conventional exercises of religion.... [T]he mere fact that the religious literature is 'sold' by itinerant preachers rather than 'donated' does not transform evangelism into a commercial enterprise. If it did, then the passing of the collection plate in church would make the church service a commercial project. The constitutional rights of those spreading their religious beliefs through the spoken and printed word are not to be gauged by standards governing retailers or wholesalers of books." *Murdock v. Pennsylvania*, 319 U.S. 105, 109, 111.

It is difficult for me to believe that going upon the streets to accost the public is the same thing for application of public law as withdrawing to a private structure for religious worship. But if worship in the churches and the activity of Jehovah's Witnesses on the streets "occupy the same high estate" and have the "same claim to protection" it would seem that child labor laws may be applied to both if to either. If the *Murdock* doctrine stands along with today's decision, a foundation is laid for any state intervention in the indoctrination and participation of children in religion, provided it is done in the name of their health or welfare.

This case brings to the surface the real basis of disagreement among members of this Court in previous Jehovah's Witness cases. *Murdock v. Pennsylvania*, 319 U.S. 105; *Martin v. Struthers*, 319 U.S. 141; *Jones v. Opelika*, 316 U.S. 584; *Douglas v. Jeannette*, 319 U.S. 157. Our basic difference seems to be as to the method of establishing limitations which of necessity bound religious freedom.

My own view may be shortly put: I think the limits begin to operate whenever activities begin to affect or collide with liberties of others or of the public. Religious activities which concern only members of the faith are and ought to be free—as nearly absolutely free as anything can be. But beyond these, many religious denominations or sects engage in collateral and secular activities intended to obtain means from unbelievers to sustain the worshippers and their leaders. They raise money, not merely by passing the plate to those who voluntarily attend services or by contributions by their own people, but by solicitations and drives addressed to the public by holding public dinners and entertainments, by various kinds of sales and Bingo games and lotteries. All such money-raising activities on a public scale are, I think, Caesar's affairs and may be regulated by the state so long as it does not discriminate against one because he is doing them for a religious purpose, and the regulation is not arbitrary and capricious, in violation of other provisions of the Constitution.

The Court in the *Murdock* case rejected this principle of separating immune religious activities from secular ones in declaring the disabilities which the Constitution imposed on local authorities. Instead, the Court now draws a line based on age that cuts across both true exercise of religion and auxiliary secular activities. I think this is not a correct principle for defining the activities immune from regulation on grounds of religion, and *Murdock* overrules the grounds on which I think affirmance should rest. I have no alternative but to dissent from the grounds of affirmance of a judgment which I think was rightly decided, and upon right grounds, by the Supreme Judicial Court of Massachusetts.

Mr. Justice Roberts and Mr. Justice Frankfurter join in this opinion.

NOTES AND QUESTIONS

1. What does the statute prohibit? Whose constitutional rights were allegedly infringed by the statute? Did the Court uphold the statute? On what grounds?

2. Is Justice Jackson concurring or dissenting? What is the distinction he draws? Do you think that is a workable distinction?

3. What is the basis for Justice Murphy's dissent? Do you find his arguments persuasive?

4. Do you think that *Prince* is consistent with *Meyer* and *Pierce*? Why? Where does parental authority end and state control begin?

5. Do any of these cases recognize children's constitutional rights? If so, what are they?

WISCONSIN V. YODER
Supreme Court of the United States
406 U.S. 205 (1972)

Mr. Chief Justice Burger delivered the opinion of the Court.

On petition of the State of Wisconsin, we granted the writ of certiorari in this case to review a decision of the Wisconsin Supreme Court holding that respondents' convictions for violating the State's compulsory school-attendance law were invalid under the Free Exercise Clause of the First Amendment to the United States Constitution made applicable to the States by the Fourteenth Amendment. For the reasons hereafter stated we affirm the judgment of the Supreme Court of Wisconsin.

Respondents Jonas Yoder and Wallace Miller are members of the Old Order Amish religion, and respondent Adin Yutzy is a member of the Conservative Amish Mennonite Church. They and their families are residents of Green County, Wisconsin. Wisconsin's compulsory school-attendance law required them to cause their children to attend public or private school until reaching age 16 but the respondents declined to send their children, ages 14 and 15, to public school after they complete the eighth grade. The children were not enrolled in any private school, or within any recognized exception to the compulsory-attendance law, and they are conceded to be subject to the Wisconsin statute.

On complaint of the school district administrator for the public schools, respondents were charged, tried, and convicted of violating the compulsory-attendance law in Green County Court and were fined the sum of $5 each. Respondents defended on the ground that the application of the compulsory-attendance law violated their rights under the First and Fourteenth Amendments. The trial testimony showed that respondents believed, in accordance with the tenets of Old Order Amish communities generally, that their children's attendance at high school, public or private, was contrary to the Amish religion and way of life. They believed that by sending their children to high school, they would not only expose themselves to the danger of the censure of the church community, but, as found by the county court, also endanger their own salvation and that of their children. The State stipulated that respondents' religious beliefs were sincere.

In support of their position, respondents presented as expert witnesses scholars on religion and education whose testimony is uncontradicted. They expressed their opinions on the relationship of the Amish belief concerning school attendance to the more general tenets of their religion, and described the impact that compulsory high school attendance could have on the continued survival of Amish communities as they exist in the United States today. The history of the Amish sect was given in some detail, beginning with the Swiss Anabaptists of the 16th century who rejected institutionalized churches and sought to return to the early, simple, Christian life deemphasizing material success, rejecting the competitive spirit, and seeking to insulate themselves from the modern world. As a result of their common heritage, Old Order Amish communities today are characterized by a fundamental belief that salvation requires life in a church community separate and apart from the world and worldly influence. This concept of life aloof from the world and its values is central to their faith.

A related feature of Old Order Amish communities is their devotion to a life in harmony with nature and the soil, as exemplified by the simple life of the early Christian era that continued in America during much of our early national life. Amish beliefs require members of the community to make their living by farming or closely related activities. Broadly speaking, the Old Order Amish religion pervades and determines the entire mode of life of its adherents. Their conduct is regulated in great detail by the *Ordnung*, or rules, of the church community. Adult baptism, which occurs in late adolescence, is the time at which Amish young people voluntarily undertake heavy obligations, not unlike the Bar Mitzvah of the Jews, to abide by the rules of the church community.

Amish objection to formal education beyond the eighth grade is firmly grounded in these central religious concepts. They object to the high school, and higher education generally, because the values they teach are in marked variance with Amish values and the Amish way of life; they view secondary school education as an impermissible exposure of their children to a "worldly" influence in conflict with their beliefs. The high school tends to emphasize intellectual and scientific accomplishments, self-distinction, competitiveness, worldly success, and social life with other students. Amish society emphasizes informal learning-through-doing; a life of "goodness," rather than a life of intellect; wisdom, rather than technical knowledge; community welfare, rather than competition; and separation from, rather than integration with, contemporary worldly society.

Formal high school education beyond the eighth grade is contrary to Amish beliefs, not only because it places Amish children in an environment hostile to Amish beliefs with increasing emphasis on competition in class work and sports and with pressure to conform to the styles, manners, and ways of the peer group, but also because it takes them away from their community, physically and emotionally, during the crucial and formative adolescent period of life. During this period, the children must acquire Amish attitudes favoring manual work and self-reliance and the specific skills needed to perform the adult role of an Amish farmer or housewife. They must learn to enjoy physical labor. Once a child has learned basic reading, writing, and elementary mathematics, these traits, skills, and attitudes admittedly fall within the category of those best learned through example and "doing" rather than in a classroom. And, at this time in life, the Amish child must also grow in his faith and his relationship to the Amish community if he is to be prepared to accept the heavy obligations imposed by adult baptism. In short, high school attendance with teachers who are not of the Amish faith—and may even be hostile to it—interposes a serious barrier to the integration of the Amish child into the Amish religious community. Dr. John Hostetler, one of the experts on Amish society, testified that the modern high school is not equipped, in curriculum or social environment, to impart the values promoted by Amish society.

The Amish do not object to elementary education through the first eight grades as a general proposition because they agree that their children must have basic skills in the "three R's" in order to read the Bible, to be good farmers and citizens, and to be able to deal with non-Amish people when necessary in the course of daily affairs. They view such a basic education as acceptable because it does not significantly expose their children to worldly values or interfere with their development in the Amish community during the crucial adolescent period. While Amish accept compulsory elementary education generally, wherever possible they have established their own elementary schools in many respects like the small local schools of the past. In the Amish belief higher learning tends to develop values they reject as influences that alienate man from God.

On the basis of such considerations, Dr. Hostetler testified that compulsory high school attendance could not only result in great psychological harm to Amish children, because of the conflicts it would produce, but would also, in his opinion, ultimately result in the destruction of the Old Order Amish church community as it exists in the United States today. The testimony of Dr. Donald A. Erickson, an expert witness on education, also showed that the Amish succeed in preparing their high school age children to be productive members of the Amish community. He described their system of learning through doing the skills directly relevant to their adult roles in the Amish community as "ideal" and perhaps superior to ordinary high school education. The evidence also showed that the Amish have an excellent record as law-abiding and generally self-sufficient members of society.

Although the trial court in its careful findings determined that the Wisconsin compulsory school-attendance law "does interfere with the freedom of the Defendants to act in accordance with their sincere religious belief" it also concluded that the requirement of high school attendance until age 16 was a "reasonable and constitutional" exercise of governmental power, and therefore denied the motion to dismiss the charges. The Wisconsin Circuit Court affirmed the convictions. The Wisconsin Supreme Court, however, sustained respondents' claim under the Free Exercise Clause of the First Amendment and reversed the convictions. A majority of the court was of the opinion that the State had failed to make an adequate showing that its interest in "establishing and maintaining an educational system overrides the defendants' right to the free exercise of their religion."

I

There is no doubt as to the power of a State, having a high responsibility for education of its citizens, to impose reasonable regulations for the control and duration of basic education. See, *e.g.*, *Pierce v. Society of Sisters*, 268 U.S. 510, 534 (1925). Providing public schools ranks at the very apex of the function of a State. Yet even this paramount responsibility was, in Pierce, made to yield to the right of parents to provide an equivalent education in a privately operated system. There the Court held that Oregon's statute compelling attendance in a public school from age eight to age 16 unreasonably interfered with the interest of parents in directing the rearing of their off-spring, including their education in church-operated schools. As that case suggests, the values of parental direction of the religious upbringing and education of their children in their early and formative years have a high place in our society. Thus a State's interest in universal education, however highly we rank it, is not totally free from a balancing process when it impinges on fundamental rights and interests, such as those specifically protected by the Free Exercise Clause of the First Amendment, and the traditional interest of parents with respect to the religious upbringing of their children so long as they, in the words of *Pierce*, "prepare (them) for additional obligations." 268 U.S., at 535.

It follows that in order for Wisconsin to compel school attendance beyond the eighth grade against a claim that such attendance interferes with the practice of a legitimate religious belief, it must appear either that the State does not deny the free exercise of religious belief by its requirement, or that there is a state interest of sufficient magnitude to override the interest claiming protection under the Free Exercise Clause. Long before there was general acknowledgment of the need for universal formal education, the Religion Clauses had specifically and firmly fixed the right to free exercise of religious beliefs, and buttressing this fundamental right was an equally firm, even if less explicit, prohibition against the establishment of any religion by government. The values underlying these two provisions relating to religion have been zealously protected, sometimes even at the expense of other interests of admittedly high social importance. The invalidation of financial aid to parochial schools by government grants for a salary subsidy for teachers is but one example of the extent to which courts have gone in this regard, notwithstanding that such aid programs were legislatively determined to be in the public interest and the service of sound educational policy by States and by Congress.

The essence of all that has been said and written on the subject is that only those interests of the highest order and those not otherwise served can overbalance legitimate claims to the free exercise of religion. We can accept it as settled, therefore, that, however strong the State's interest in universal compulsory education, it is by no means absolute to the exclusion or subordination of all other interests.

II

We come then to the quality of the claims of the respondents concerning the alleged encroachment of Wisconsin's compulsory school-attendance statute on their rights and the rights of their children to the free exercise of the religious beliefs they and their forebears have adhered to for almost three centuries. In evaluating those claims we must be careful to determine whether the Amish religious faith and their mode of life are, as they claim, inseparable and interdependent. A way of life, however virtuous and admirable, may not be interposed as a barrier to reasonable state regulation of education if it is based on purely secular considerations; to have the protection of the Religion Clauses, the claims must be rooted in religious belief. Although a determination of what is a "religious" belief or practice entitled to constitutional protection may present a most delicate question, the very concept of ordered liberty precludes allowing every person to make his own standards on matters of conduct in which society as a whole has important interests. Thus, if the Amish asserted their claims because of their subjective evaluation and rejection of the contemporary secular values accepted by the majority, much as Thoreau rejected the social values of his time and isolated himself at Walden Pond, their claims would not rest on a religious basis. Thoreau's choice was philosophical and personal rather than religious, and such belief does not rise to the demands of the Religion Clauses.

Giving no weight to such secular consideration, however, we see that the record in this case abundantly supports the claim that the traditional way of life of the Amish is not merely a matter of personal preference, but one of deep religious conviction, shared by an organized group, and intimately related to daily living. That the Old Order Amish daily life and religious practice stem from their faith is shown by the fact that it is in response to their literal interpretation of the Biblical injunction from the Epistle of Paul to the Romans, "be not conformed to this world. . . . " This command is fundamental to the Amish faith. Moreover, for the Old Order Amish, religion is not simply a matter of theocratic belief. As the expert witnesses explained, the Old Order Amish religion pervades and determines virtually their entire way of life, regulating it with the detail of the Talmudic diet through the strictly enforced rules of the church community.

The record shows that the respondents' religious beliefs and attitude toward life, family, and home have remained constant—perhaps some would say static—in a period of unparalleled progress in human knowledge generally and great changes in education. The respondents freely concede, and indeed assert as an article of faith, that their religious beliefs and what we would today call "life style" have not altered in fundamentals for centuries. Their way of life in a church-oriented community, separated from the outside world and "worldly" influences, their attachment to nature and the soil, is a way inherently simple and uncomplicated, albeit difficult to preserve against the pressure to conform. Their rejection of telephones, automobiles, radios, and television, their mode of dress, of speech, their habits of manual work do indeed set them apart from much of contemporary society; these customs are both symbolic and practical.

As the society around the Amish has become more populous, urban, industrialized, and complex, particularly in this century, government regulation of human affairs has correspondingly become more detailed and pervasive. The Amish mode of life has thus come into conflict increasingly with requirements of contemporary society exerting a hydraulic insistence on conformity to majoritarian standards. So long as compulsory education laws were confined to eight grades of elementary basic education imparted in a nearby rural schoolhouse, with a large proportion of students of the Amish faith, the Old Order Amish had little basis to fear that school attendance would expose their children to the worldly influence they reject. But modern compulsory secondary education in rural areas is now largely carried on in a consolidated school, often remote from the student's home and alien to his daily home life. As the record so strongly shows, the values and programs of the modern secondary school are in sharp conflict with the fundamental mode of life mandated by the Amish religion; modern laws requiring compulsory secondary education have accordingly engendered great concern and conflict. The conclusion is inescapable that secondary schooling, by exposing Amish children to worldly influences in terms of attitudes, goals, and values contrary to beliefs, and by substantially interfering with the religious development of the Amish child and his integration into the way of life of the Amish faith community at the crucial adolescent stage of development, contravenes the basic religious tenets and practice of the Amish faith, both as to the parent and the child.

The impact of the compulsory-attendance law on respondents' practice of the Amish religion is not only severe, but inescapable, for the Wisconsin law affirmatively compels them, under threat of criminal sanction, to perform acts undeniably at odds with fundamental tenets of their religious beliefs. Nor is the impact of the compulsory-attendance law confined to grave interference with important Amish religious tenets from a subjective point of view. It carries with it precisely the kind of objective danger to the free exercise of religion that the First Amendment was designed to prevent. As the record shows, compulsory school attendance to age 16 for Amish children carries with it a very real threat of undermining the Amish community and religious practice as they exist today; they must either abandon belief and be assimilated into society at large, or be forced to migrate to some other and more tolerant region.

In sum, the unchallenged testimony of acknowledged experts in education and religious history, almost 300 years of consistent practice, and strong evidence of a sustained faith pervading and regulating respondents' entire mode of life support the claim that enforcement of the State's requirement of compulsory formal education after the eighth grade would gravely endanger if not destroy the free exercise of respondents' religious beliefs.

III

Neither the findings of the trial court nor the Amish claims as to the nature of their faith are challenged in this Court by the State of Wisconsin. Its position is that the State's interest in universal compulsory formal secondary education to age 16 is so great that it is paramount to the undisputed claims of respondents that their mode of preparing their youth for Amish life, after the traditional elementary education, is an essential part of their religious belief and practice. Nor does the State undertake to meet the claim that the Amish mode of life and education is inseparable from and a part of the basic tenets of their religion—indeed, as much a part of their religious belief and practices as baptism, the confessional, or a sabbath may be for others.

Wisconsin concedes that under the Religion Clauses religious beliefs are absolutely free from the State's control, but it argues that "actions," even though religiously grounded, are outside the protection of the First Amendment. But our decisions have rejected the idea that religiously grounded conduct is always outside the protection of the Free Exercise Clause. It is true that activities of individuals, even when religiously based, are often subject to regulation by the States in the exercise of their undoubted power to promote the health, safety, and general welfare, or the Federal Government in the exercise of its delegated powers. But to agree that religiously grounded conduct must often be subject to the broad police power of the State is not to deny that there are areas of conduct protected by the Free Exercise Clause of the First Amendment and thus beyond the power of the State to control, even under regulations of general applicability. This case, therefore, does not become easier because respondents were convicted for their "actions" in refusing to send their children to the public high school; in this context belief and action cannot be neatly confined in logic-tight compartments.

Nor can this case be disposed of on the grounds that Wisconsin's requirement for school attendance to age 16 applies uniformly to all citizens of the State and does not, on its face, discriminate against religions or a particular religion, or that it is motivated by legitimate secular concerns. A regulation neutral on its face may, in its application, nonetheless offend the constitutional requirement for governmental neutrality if it unduly burdens the free exercise of religion. The Court must not ignore the danger that an exception from a general obligation of citizenship on religious grounds may run afoul of the Establishment Clause, but that danger cannot be allowed to prevent any exception no matter how vital it may be to the protection of values promoted by the right of free exercise....

We turn, then, to the State's broader contention that its interest in its system of compulsory education is so compelling that even the established religious practices of the Amish must give way. Where fundamental claims of religious freedom are at stake, however, we cannot accept such a sweeping claim; despite its admitted validity in the generality of cases, we must searchingly examine the interests that the State seeks to promote by its requirement for compulsory education to age 16, and the impediment to those objectives that would flow from recognizing the claimed Amish exemption.

The State advances two primary arguments in support of its system of compulsory education. It notes, as Thomas Jefferson pointed out early in our history, that some degree of education is necessary to prepare citizens to participate effectively and intelligently in our open political system if we are to preserve freedom and independence. Further, education prepares individuals to be self-reliant and self-sufficient participants in society. We accept these propositions.

However, the evidence adduced by the Amish in this case is persuasively to the effect that an additional one or two years of formal high school for Amish children in place of their long-established program of informal vocational education would do little to serve those interests. Respondents' experts testified at trial, without challenge, that the value of all education must be assessed in terms of its capacity to prepare the child for life. It is one thing to say that compulsory education for a year or two beyond the eighth grade may be necessary when its goal is the preparation of the child for life in modern society as the majority live, but it is quite another if the goal of education be viewed as the preparation of the child for life in the separated agrarian community that is the keystone of the Amish faith. See *Meyer v. Nebraska*, 262 U.S., at 400.

The State attacks respondents' position as one fostering "ignorance" from which the child must be protected by the State. No one can question the State's duty to protect children from ignorance but this argument does not square with the facts disclosed in the record. Whatever their idiosyncrasies as seen by the majority, this record strongly shows that the Amish community has been a highly successful social unit within our society, even if apart from the conventional "mainstream." Its members are productive and very law-abiding members of society; they reject public welfare in any of its usual modern forms. The Congress itself recognized their self-sufficiency by authorizing exemption of such groups as the Amish from the obligation to pay social security taxes.

It is neither fair nor correct to suggest that the Amish are opposed to education beyond the eighth grade level. What this record shows is that they are opposed to conventional formal education of the type provided by a certified high school because it comes at the child's crucial adolescent period of religious development. Dr. Donald Erickson, for example, testified that their system of learning-by-doing was an "ideal system" of education in terms of preparing Amish children for life as adults in the Amish community, and that "I would be inclined to say they do a better job in this than most of the rest of us do." As he put it, "These people aren't purporting to be learned people, and it seems to me the self-sufficiency of the community is the best evidence I can point to—whatever is being done seems to function well."

We must not forget that in the Middle Ages important values of the civilization of the Western World were preserved by members of religious orders who isolated themselves from all worldly influences against great obstacles. There can be no assumption that today's majority is "right" and the Amish and others like them are "wrong." A way of life that is odd or even erratic but interferes with no rights or interests of others is not to be condemned because it is different.

The State, however, supports its interest in providing an additional one or two years of compulsory high school education to Amish children because of the possibility that some such children will choose to leave the Amish community, and that if this occurs they will be ill-equipped for life. However, on this record, that argument is highly speculative. There is no specific evidence of the loss of Amish adherents by attrition, nor is there any showing that upon leaving the Amish community Amish children, with their practical agricultural training and habits of industry and self-reliance, would become burdens on society because of educational shortcomings. Indeed, this argument of the State appears to rest primarily on the State's mistaken assumption, already noted, that the Amish do not provide any education for their children beyond the eighth grade, but allow them to grow in "ignorance." To the contrary, not only do the Amish accept the necessity for formal schooling through the eighth grade level, but continue to provide what has been characterized by the undisputed testimony of expert educators as an "ideal" vocational education for their children in the adolescent years.

There is nothing in this record to suggest that the Amish qualities of reliability, self-reliance, and dedication to work would fail to find ready markets in today's society. Absent some contrary evidence supporting the State's position, we are unwilling to assume that persons possessing such valuable vocational skills and habits are doomed to become burdens on society should they determine to leave the Amish faith, nor is there any basis in the record to warrant a finding that an additional one or two years of formal school education beyond the eighth grade would serve to eliminate any such problem that might exist.

Insofar as the State's claim rests on the view that a brief additional period of formal education is imperative to enable the Amish to participate effectively and intelligently in our democratic process, it must fall. The Amish alternative to formal secondary school education has enabled them to function effectively in their day-to-day life under self-imposed limitations on relations with the world, and to survive and prosper in contemporary society as a separate, sharply identifiable and highly self-sufficient community for more than 200 years in this country. In itself this is strong evidence that they are capable of fulfilling the social and political responsibilities of citizenship without compelled attendance beyond the eighth grade at the price of jeopardizing their free exercise of religious belief. When Thomas Jefferson emphasized the need for education as a bulwark of a free people against tyranny, there is nothing to indicate he had in mind compulsory education through any fixed age beyond a basic education. Indeed, the Amish communities singularly parallel and reflect many of the virtues of Jefferson's ideal of the "sturdy yeoman" who would form the basis of what he considered as the ideal of a democratic society. Even their idiosyncratic separateness exemplifies the diversity we profess to admire and encourage.

The requirement for compulsory education beyond the eighth grade is a relatively recent development in our history. Less than 60 years ago, the educational requirements of almost all of the States were satisfied by completion of the elementary grades, at least where the child was regularly and lawfully employed. The independence and successful social functioning of the Amish community for a period approaching almost three centuries and more than 200 years in this country are strong evidence that there is at best a speculative gain, in terms of meeting the duties of citizenship, from an additional one or two years of compulsory formal education. Against this background it would require a more particularized showing from the State on this point to justify the severe interference with religious freedom such additional compulsory attendance would entail.

We should also note that compulsory education and child labor laws find their historical origin in common humanitarian instincts, and that the age limits of both laws have been coordinated to achieve their related objectives. In the context of this case, such considerations, if anything, support rather than detract from respondents' position. The origins of the requirement for school attendance to age 16, an age falling after the completion of elementary school but before completion of high school, are not entirely clear. But to some extent such laws reflected the movement to prohibit most child labor under age 16 that culminated in the provisions of the Federal Fair Labor Standards Act of 1938. It is true, then, that the 16-year child labor age limit may to some degree derive from a contemporary impression that children should be in school until that age. But at the same time, it cannot be denied that, conversely, the 16-year education limit reflects, in substantial measure, the concern that children under that age not be employed under conditions hazardous to their health, or in work that should be performed by adults.

The requirement of compulsory schooling to age 16 must therefore be viewed as aimed not merely at providing educational opportunities for children, but as an alternative to the equally undesirable consequence of unhealthful child labor displacing adult workers, or, on the other hand, forced idleness. The two kinds of statutes—compulsory school attendance and child labor laws—tend to keep children of certain ages off the labor market and in school; this regimen in turn provides opportunity to prepare for a livelihood of a higher order than that which children could pursue without education and protects their health in adolescence.

In these terms, Wisconsin's interest in compelling the school attendance of Amish children to age 16 emerges as somewhat less substantial than requiring such attendance for children generally. For, while agricultural employment is not totally outside the legitimate concerns of the child labor laws, employment of children under parental guidance and on the family farm from age 14 to age 16 is an ancient tradition that lies at the periphery of the objectives of such laws. There is no intimation that the Amish employment of their children on family farms is in any way deleterious to their health or that Amish parents exploit children at tender years. Any such inference would be contrary to the record before us. Moreover, employment of Amish children on the family farm does not present the undesirable economic aspects of eliminating jobs that might otherwise be held by adults.

IV

Finally, the State, on authority of Prince v. Massachusetts, argues that a decision exempting Amish children from the State's requirement fails to recognize the substantive right of the Amish child to a secondary education, and fails to give due regard to the power of the State as parens patriae to extend the benefit of secondary education to children regardless of the wishes of their parents. Taken at its broadest sweep, the Court's language in *Prince*, might be read to give support to the State's position. However, the Court was not confronted in *Prince* with a situation comparable to that of the Amish as revealed in this record; this is shown by the Court's severe characterization of the evils that it thought the legislature could legitimately associate with child labor, even when performed in the company of an adult. 321 U.S., at 169–170. . . .

This case, of course, is not one in which any harm to the physical or mental health of the child or to the public safety, peace, order, or welfare has been demonstrated or may be properly inferred. The record is to the contrary, and any reliance on that theory would find no support in the evidence.

Contrary to the suggestion of the dissenting opinion of Mr. Justice Douglas, our holding today in no degree depends on the assertion of the religious interest of the child as contrasted with that of the parents. It is the parents who are subject to prosecution here for failing to cause their children to attend school, and it is their right of free exercise, not that of their children, that must determine Wisconsin's power to impose criminal penalties on the parent. The dissent argues that a child who expresses a desire to attend public high school in conflict with the wishes of his parents should not be prevented from doing so. There is no reason for the Court to consider that point since it is not an issue in the case. The children are not parties to this litigation. The State has at no point tried this case on the theory that respondents were preventing their children from attending school against their expressed desires, and indeed the record is to the contrary.[21] The State's position from the outset has been that it is empowered to apply its compulsory-attendance law to Amish parents in the same manner as to other parents—that is, without regard to the wishes of the child. That is the claim we reject today.

21. The only relevant testimony in the record is to the effect that the wishes of the one child who testified corresponded with those of her parents. Testimony of Frieda Yoder, Tr. 92–94, to the effect that her personal religious beliefs guided her decision to discontinue school attendance after the eighth grade. The other children were not called by either side.

Our holding in no way determines the proper resolution of possible competing interests of parents, children, and the State in an appropriate state court proceeding in which the power of the State is asserted on the theory that Amish parents are preventing their minor children from attending high school despite their expressed desires to the contrary. Recognition of the claim of the State in such a proceeding would, of course, call into question traditional concepts of parental control over the religious upbringing and education of their minor children recognized in this Court's past decisions. It is clear that such an intrusion by a State into family decisions in the area of religious training would give rise to grave questions of religious freedom comparable to those raised here and those presented in *Pierce v. Society of Sisters*, 268 U.S. 510 (1925). On this record we neither reach nor decide those issues.

The State's argument proceeds without reliance on any actual conflict between the wishes of parents and children. It appears to rest on the potential that exemption of Amish parents from the requirements of the compulsory-education law might allow some parents to act contrary to the best interests of their children by foreclosing their opportunity to make an intelligent choice between the Amish way of life and that of the outside world. The same argument could, of course, be made with respect to all church schools short of college. There is nothing in the record or in the ordinary course of human experience to suggest that non-Amish parents generally consult with children of ages 14-16 if they are placed in a church school of the parents' faith.

Indeed it seems clear that if the State is empowered, as parens patriae, to "save" a child from himself or his Amish parents by requiring an additional two years of compulsory formal high school education, the State will in large measure influence, if not determine, the religious future of the child. Even more markedly than in *Prince*, therefore, this case involves the fundamental interest of parents, as contrasted with that of the State, to guide the religious future and education of their children. The history and culture of Western civilization reflect a strong tradition of parental concern for the nurture and upbringing of their children. This primary role of the parents in the upbringing of their children is now established beyond debate as an enduring American tradition. If not the first, perhaps the most significant statements of the Court in this area are found in *Pierce v. Society of Sisters*, in which the Court observed:

> "Under the doctrine of *Meyer v. Nebraska*, 262 U.S. 390, we think it entirely plain that the Act of 1922 unreasonably interferes with the liberty of parents and guardians to direct the upbringing and education of children under their control. As often heretofore pointed out, rights guaranteed by the Constitution may not be abridged by legislation which has no reasonable relation to some purpose within the competency of the State. The fundamental theory of liberty upon which all governments in this Union repose excludes any general power of the State to standardize its children by forcing them to accept instruction from public teachers only. The child is not the mere creature of the State; those who nurture him and direct his destiny have the right, coupled with the high duty, to recognize and prepare him for additional obligations." 268 U.S., at 534–535.

The duty to prepare the child for "additional obligations," referred to by the Court, must be read to include the inculcation of moral standards, religious beliefs, and elements of good citizenship. *Pierce*, of course, recognized that where nothing more than the general interest of the parent in the nurture and education of his children is involved, it is beyond dispute that the State acts "reasonably" and constitutionally in requiring education to age 16 in some public or private school meeting the standards prescribed by the State.

However read, the Court's holding in *Pierce* stands as a charter of the rights of parents to direct the religious upbringing of their children. And, when the interests of parenthood are combined with a free exercise claim of the nature revealed by this record, more than merely a "reasonable relation to some purpose within the competency of the State" is required to sustain the validity of the State's requirement under the First Amendment. To be sure, the power of the parent, even when linked to a free exercise claim, may be subject to limitation under *Prince* if it appears that parental decisions will jeopardize the health or safety of the child, or have a potential for significant social burdens. But in this case, the Amish have introduced persuasive evidence undermining the arguments the State has advanced to support its claims in terms of the welfare of the child and society as a whole. The record strongly indicates that accommodating the religious objections of the Amish by forgoing one, or at most two, additional years of compulsory education will not impair the physical or mental health of the child, or result in an inability to be self-supporting or to discharge the duties and responsibilities of citizenship, or in any other way materially detract from the welfare of society.

In the face of our consistent emphasis on the central values underlying the Religion Clauses in our constitutional scheme of government, we cannot accept a parens patriae claim of such all-encompassing scope and with such sweeping potential for broad and unforeseeable application as that urged by the State.

V

For the reasons stated we hold, with the Supreme Court of Wisconsin, that the First and Fourteenth Amendments prevent the State from compelling respondents to cause their children to attend formal high school to age 16. Our disposition of this case, however, in no way alters our recognition of the obvious fact that courts are not school boards or legislatures, and are ill-equipped to determine the "necessity" of discrete aspects of a State's program of compulsory education. This should suggest that courts must move with great circumspection in performing the sensitive and delicate task of weighing a State's legitimate social concern when faced with religious claims for exemption from generally applicable education requirements. It cannot be overemphasized that we are not dealing with a way of life and mode of education by a group claiming to have recently discovered some "progressive" or more enlightened process for rearing children for modern life.

Aided by a history of three centuries as an identifiable religious sect and a long history as a successful and self-sufficient segment of American society, the Amish in this case have convincingly demonstrated the sincerity of their religious beliefs, the interrelationship of belief with their mode of life, the vital role that belief and daily conduct play in the continued survival of Old Order Amish communities and their religious organization, and the hazards presented by the State's enforcement of a statute generally valid as to others. Beyond this, they have carried the even more difficult burden of demonstrating the adequacy of their alternative mode of continuing informal vocational education in terms of precisely those overall interests that the State advances in support of its program of compulsory high school education. In light of this convincing showing, one that probably few other religious groups or sects could make, and weighing the minimal difference between what the State would require and what the Amish already accept, it was incumbent on the State to show with more particularity how its admittedly strong interest in compulsory education would be adversely affected by granting an exemption to the Amish.

Nothing we hold is intended to undermine the general applicability of the State's compulsory school-attendance statutes or to limit the power of the State to promulgate reasonable standards that, while not impairing the free exercise of religion, provide for continuing agricultural vocational education under parental and church guidance by the Old Order Amish or others similarly situated. The States have had a long history of amicable and effective relationships with church-sponsored schools, and there is no basis for assuming that, in this related context, reasonable standards cannot be established concerning the content of the continuing vocational education of Amish children under parental guidance, provided always that state regulations are not inconsistent with what we have said in this opinion.

Affirmed.

MR. JUSTICE POWELL and MR. JUSTICE REHNQUIST took no part in the consideration or decision of this case.

MR. JUSTICE STEWART, with whom MR. JUSTICE BRENNAN joins, concurring....

This case in no way involves any questions regarding the right of the children of Amish parents to attend public high schools, or any other institutions of learning, if they wish to do so. As the Court points out, there is no suggestion whatever in the record that the religious beliefs of the children here concerned differ in any way from those of their parents. Only one of the children testified. The last two questions and answers on her cross-examination accurately sum up her testimony:

> "Q. So I take it then, Frieda, the only reason you are not going to school, and did not go to school since last September, is because of *your* religion?
> "A. Yes.
> "Q. That is the only reason?
> "A. Yes." (Emphasis supplied.)

It is clear to me, therefore, that this record simply does not present the interesting and important issue discussed in Part II of the dissenting opinion of MR. JUSTICE DOUGLAS.

MR. JUSTICE WHITE, with whom MR. JUSTICE BRENNAN and MR. JUSTICE STEWART join, concurring.

Cases such as this one inevitably call for a delicate balancing of important but conflicting interests. I join the opinion and judgment of the Court because I cannot say that the State's interest in requiring two more years of compulsory education in the ninth and tenth grades outweighs the importance of the concededly sincere Amish religious practice to the survival of that sect.

This would be a very different case for me if respondents' claim were that their religion forbade their children from attending any school at any time and from complying in any way with the educational standards set by the State....

...As recently as last Term, the Court reemphasized the legitimacy of the State's concern for enforcing minimal educational standards. In the present case, the State is not concerned with the maintenance of an educational system as an end in itself, it is rather attempting to nurture and develop the human potential of its children, whether Amish or non-Amish: to expand their knowledge, broaden their sensibilities, kindle their imagination, foster a spirit of free inquiry, and increase their human understanding and tolerance. It is possible that most Amish children will wish to continue living the rural life of their parents, in which case their training at home will adequately equip them for their future role. Others, however, may wish to become nuclear physicists, ballet dancers, computer programmers, or historians, and for these occupations, formal training will be necessary. There is evidence in the record that many children desert the Amish faith when they come of age.... In the circumstances of this case, although the question is close, I am unable to say that the State has demonstrated that Amish children who leave school in the eighth grade will be intellectually stultified or unable to acquire new academic skills later. The statutory minimum school attendance age set by the State is, after all, only 16.

Decision in cases such as this and the administration of an exemption for Old Order Amish from the State's compulsory school-attendance laws will inevitably involve the kind of close and perhaps repeated scrutiny of religious practices, as is exemplified in today's opinion, which the Court has heretofore been anxious to avoid. But such entanglement does not create a forbidden establishment of religion where it is essential to implement free exercise values threatened by an otherwise neutral program instituted to foster some permissible, nonreligious state objective. I join the Court because the sincerity of the Amish religious policy here is uncontested, because the potentially adverse impact of the state requirement is great, and because the State's valid interest in education has already been largely satisfied by the eight years the children have already spent in school.

MR. JUSTICE DOUGLAS, dissenting in part.

I

I agree with the Court that the religious scruples of the Amish are opposed to the education of their children beyond the grade schools, yet I disagree with the Court's conclusion that the matter is within the dispensation of parents alone. The Court's analysis assumes that the only interests at stake in the case are those of the Amish parents on the one hand, and those of the State on the other. The difficulty with this approach is that, despite the Court's claim, the parents are seeking to vindicate not only their own free exercise claims, but also those of their high-school-age children.

It is argued that the right of the Amish children to religious freedom is not presented by the facts of the case, as the issue before the Court involves only the Amish parents' religious freedom to defy a state criminal statute imposing upon them an affirmative duty to cause their children to attend high school.

First, respondents' motion to dismiss in the trial court expressly asserts, not only the religious liberty of the adults, but also that of the children, as a defense to the prosecutions. It is, of course, beyond question that the parents have standing as defendants in a criminal prosecution to assert the religious interests of their children as a defense. Although the lower courts and a majority of this Court assume an identity of interest between parent and child, it is clear that they have treated the religious interest of the child as a factor in the analysis.

Second, it is essential to reach the question to decide the case, not only because the question was squarely raised in the motion to dismiss, but also because no analysis of religious-liberty claims can take place in a vacuum. If the parents in this case are allowed a religious exemption, the inevitable effect is to impose the parents' notions of religious duty upon their children. Where the child is mature enough to express potentially conflicting desires, it would be an invasion of the child's rights to permit such an imposition without canvassing his views. As in *Prince v. Massachusetts*, 321 U.S. 158, it is an imposition resulting from this very litigation. As the child has no other effective forum, it is in this litigation that his rights should be considered. And, if an Amish child desires to attend high school, and is mature enough to have that desire respected, the State may well be able to override the parents' religiously motivated objections.

Religion is an individual experience. It is not necessary, nor even appropriate, for every Amish child to express his views on the subject in a prosecution of a single adult. Crucial, however, are the views of the child whose parent is the subject of the suit. Frieda Yoder has in fact testified that her own religious views are opposed to high-school education. I therefore join the judgment of the Court as to respondent Jonas Yoder. But Frieda Yoder's views may not be those of Vernon Yutzy or Barbara Miller. I must dissent, therefore, as to respondents Adin Yutzy and Wallace Miller as their motion to dismiss also raised the question of their children's religious liberty.

II

This issue has never been squarely presented before today. Our opinions are full of talk about the power of the parents over the child's education. See *Pierce v. Society of Sisters*, 268 U.S. 510; *Meyer v. Nebraska*, 262 U.S. 390. And we have in the past analyzed similar conflicts between parent and State with little regard for the views of the child. See *Prince v. Massachusetts*, *supra*. Recent cases, however, have clearly held that the children themselves have constitutionally protectible interests. Recent cases, have clearly held that the children themselves have constitutionally protectible interests.

These children are "persons" within the meaning of the Bill of Rights. We have so held over and over again. In *Haley v. Ohio*, 332 U.S. 596, we extended the protection of the Fourteenth Amendment in a state trial of a 15-year-old boy. In *In re Gault*, 387 U.S. 1, 13, we held that "neither the Fourteenth Amendment nor the Bill of Rights is for adults alone." In *In re Winship*, 397 U.S. 358, we held that a 12-year-old boy, when charged with an act which would be a crime if committed by an adult, was entitled to procedural safeguards contained in the Sixth Amendment.

In *Tinker v. Des Moines Independent Community School District*, 393 U.S. 503, we dealt with 13-year-old, 15-year-old, and 16-year-old students who wore armbands to public schools and were disciplined for doing so. We gave them relief, saying that their First Amendment rights had been abridged.

> "Students in school as well as out of school are "persons" under our Constitution. They are possessed of fundamental rights which the State must respect, just as they themselves must respect their obligations to the State." *Id.*, at 511, 89 S.Ct., at 739.

In *Board of Education v. Barnette*, 319 U.S. 624, we held that school-children, whose religious beliefs collided with a school rule requiring them to salute the flag, could not be required to do so. While the sanction included expulsion of the students and prosecution of the parents, *id.*, at 630, the vice of the regime was its interference with the child's free exercise of religion. We said: "Here... we are dealing with a compulsion of students to declare a belief." *Id.*, at 631. In emphasizing the important and delicate task of boards of education we said:

> "That they are educating the young for citizenship is reason for scrupulous protection of Constitutional freedoms of the individual, if we are not to strangle the free mind at its source and teach youth to discount important principles of our government as mere platitudes." *Id.*, at 637.

On this important and vital matter of education, I think the children should be entitled to be heard. While the parents, absent dissent, normally speak for the entire family, the education of the child is a matter on which the child will often have decided views. He may want to be a pianist or an astronaut or an oceanographer. To do so he will have to break from the Amish tradition.

It is the future of the student, not the future of the parents, that is imperiled by today's decision. If a parent keeps his child out of school beyond the grade school, then the child will be forever barred from entry into the new and amazing world of diversity that we have today. The child may decide that that is the preferred course, or he may rebel. It is the student's judgment, not his parents', that is essential if we are to give full meaning to what we have said about the Bill of Rights and of the right of students to be masters of their own destiny. If he is harnessed to the Amish way of life by those in authority over him and if his education is truncated, his entire life may be stunted and deformed. The child, therefore, should be given an opportunity to be heard before the State gives the exemption which we honor today.

The views of the two children in question were not canvassed by the Wisconsin courts. The matter should be explicitly reserved so that new hearings can be held on remand of the case.[4]

III

I think the emphasis of the Court on the "law and order" record of this Amish group of people is quite irrelevant. A religion is a religion irrespective of what the misdemeanor or felony records of its members might be. I am not at all sure how the Catholics, Episcopalians, the Baptists, Jehovah's Witnesses, the Unitarians, and my own Presbyterians would make out if subjected to such a test. It is, of course, true that if a group or society was organized to perpetuate crime and if that is its motive, we would have rather startling problems akin to those that were raised when some years back a particular sect was challenged here as operating on a fraudulent basis. But no such factors are present here, and the Amish, whether with a high or low criminal record, certainly qualify by all historic standards as a religion within the meaning of the First Amendment.

The Court rightly rejects the notion that actions, even though religiously grounded, are always outside the protection of the Free Exercise Clause of the First Amendment. In so

4. Canvassing the views of all school-age Amish children in the State of Wisconsin would not present insurmountable difficulties. A 1968 survey indicated that there were at that time only 256 such children in the entire State. Comment, 1971 Wis. L. Rev. 832, 852 n. 132.

ruling, the Court departs from the teaching of *Reynolds v. United States*, 98 U.S. 145, 164, where it was said concerning the reach of the Free Exercise Clause of the First Amendment, "Congress was deprived of all legislative power over mere opinion, but was left free to reach actions which were in violation of social duties or subversive of good order." In that case it was conceded that polygamy was a part of the religion of the Mormons. Yet the Court said, "It matters not that his belief (in polygamy) was a part of his professed religion: it was still belief and belief only." *Id.*, at 167.

Action, which the Court deemed to be antisocial, could be punished even though it was grounded on deeply held and sincere religious convictions. What we do today, at least in this respect, opens the way to give organized religion a broader base than it has ever enjoyed.

In another way, however, the Court retreats when in reference to Henry Thoreau it says his "choice was philosophical and personal rather than religious, and such belief does not rise to the demands of the Religion Clauses." That is contrary to what we held in *United States v. Seeger*, 380 U.S. 163, where we were concerned with the meaning of the words "religious training and belief" in the Selective Service Act, which were the basis of many conscientious objector claims. We said:

> "Within that phrase would come all sincere religious beliefs which are based upon a power or being, or upon a faith, to which all else is subordinate or upon which all else is ultimately dependent. The test might be stated in these words: A sincere and meaningful belief which occupies in the life of its possessor a place parallel to that filled by the God of those admittedly qualifying for the exemption comes within the statutory definition. This construction avoids imputing to Congress an intent to classify different religious beliefs, exempting some and excluding others, and is in accord with the well-established congressional policy of equal treatment for those whose opposition to service is grounded in their religious tenets." *Id.*, at 176.

Welsh v. United States, 398 U.S. 333, was in the same vein, the Court saying:

> "In this case, Welsh's conscientious objection to war was undeniably based in part on his perception of world politics. In a letter to his local board, he wrote:
>
> "'I can only act according to what I am and what I see. And I see that the military complex wastes both human and material resources, that it fosters disregard for (what I consider a paramount concern) human needs and ends; I see that the means we employ to "defend" our "way of life" profoundly change that way of life. I see that in our failure to recognize the political, social, and economic realities of the world, we, as a nation, fail our responsibility as a nation.'" *Id.*, at 342.

The essence of Welsh's philosophy, on the basis of which we held he was entitled to an exemption, was in these words:

> "'I believe that human life is valuable in and of itself; in its living; therefore I will not injure or kill another human being. This belief (and the corresponding "duty" to abstain from violence toward another person) is not "superior to those arising from any human relation." On the contrary: it *is essential to every human relation*. I cannot, therefore, conscientiously comply

with the Government's insistence that I assume duties which I feel are immoral and totally repugnant.'" *Id.*, at 343.

I adhere to these exalted views of "religion" and see no acceptable alternative to them now that we have become a Nation of many religions and sects, representing all of the diversities of the human race. *United States v. Seeger*, 380 U.S., at 192-193 (concurring opinion).

NOTES AND QUESTIONS

1. Why is the Wisconsin statute at issue in this case constitutionally problematic?

2. According to Chief Justice Burger, whose constitutional rights are violated? How?

3. Do you think Burger correctly characterized *Meyer* and *Pierce*? Did *Yoder* overrule *Prince*? Can *Yoder* and *Prince* be reconciled according to the Court? Consider this statement from the Court's opinion: "[T]he Court was not confronted in *Prince* with a situation comparable to that of the Amish as revealed in this record; this is shown by the Court's severe characterization of the evils that it thought the legislature could legitimately associate with child labor, even when performed in the company of an adult." Do you agree? Why does Justice Douglas say, "I think the emphasis of the Court on the 'law and order' record of this Amish group of people is quite irrelevant"?

Some prominent scholars criticized the Court's opinion in *Yoder*. Laurence Tribe, for example, argued that "[t]he Court's lengthy recital of Amish virtues was consistent with the conclusion that a less praiseworthy sect, or even one with a shorter history, might not be eligible for an exemption." Laurence H. Tribe, American Constitutional Law 1259 (2d ed. 1988). See also David M. Smolin, *The Jurisprudence of Privacy in a Splintered Supreme Court*, 75 Marq. L. Rev. 975, 1023 (1992) ("strong hints that only the Amish have such a right").

4. Why does Justice White concur?

5. What about the constitutional rights of the children in *Yoder*? How does Burger treat their claims? What about Justice Stewart? What does Douglas think? Do you think there may have been support from a majority of the Court for Douglas's views?

6. Do Jehovah's Witnesses make "bad" parents? Do Amish make "good" parents? The Amish have, in many ways, moved beyond the lifestyle that Burger so rhapsodically describes. Today, only about one-third of Amish men work on farms; the other two-thirds work in cottage industries such as woodworking shops, sawmills, and metal manufacturers. Donald B. Kraybill, The Riddle of Amish Culture 240 (rev. ed. 2001). In fact, the practice has become so prevalent that the Amish sought an exemption to the Fair Labor Standards Act that prohibits children from working in these dangerous occupations. In 2004, Congress enacted an exception to the Act's prohibitions on oppressive child labor. The provision permits children between the ages of fourteen and eighteen who are exempt "from compulsory school attendance beyond the eighth grade" to work in a place of business where "machinery is used to process wood products" and are supervised by an adult relative or an "adult member of the same religious sect or division." Children who meet these criteria may not operate or assist in the operation of the machinery, must be protected from flying debris, and must wear safety equipment to protect them from excessive noise and dust. 29 U.S.C.A. § 213(c)(7)(A)-(B) (West 2011). Do you think such an

exemption is justified? Is there now sufficient evidence of harm? In light of these changes, do you think that the *Yoder* decision should stand? Why?

TROXEL V. GRANVILLE
Supreme Court of the United States
530 U.S. 57 (2000)

Justice O'Connor announced the judgment of the Court and delivered an opinion, in which The Chief Justice, Justice Ginsburg, and Justice Breyer join.

Section 26.10.160(3) of the Revised Code of Washington permits "[a]ny person" to petition a superior court for visitation rights "at any time," and authorizes that court to grant such visitation rights whenever "visitation may serve the best interest of the child." Petitioners Jenifer and Gary Troxel petitioned a Washington Superior Court for the right to visit their grandchildren, Isabelle and Natalie Troxel. Respondent Tommie Granville, the mother of Isabelle and Natalie, opposed the petition. The case ultimately reached the Washington Supreme Court, which held that § 26.10.160(3) unconstitutionally interferes with the fundamental right of parents to rear their children.

I

Tommie Granville and Brad Troxel shared a relationship that ended in June 1991. The two never married, but they had two daughters, Isabelle and Natalie. Jenifer and Gary Troxel are Brad's parents, and thus the paternal grandparents of Isabelle and Natalie. After Tommie and Brad separated in 1991, Brad lived with his parents and regularly brought his daughters to his parents' home for weekend visitation. Brad committed suicide in May 1993. Although the Troxels at first continued to see Isabelle and Natalie on a regular basis after their son's death, Tommie Granville informed the Troxels in October 1993 that she wished to limit their visitation with her daughters to one short visit per month.

In December 1993, the Troxels commenced the present action by filing, in the Washington Superior Court for Skagit County, a petition to obtain visitation rights with Isabelle and Natalie. The Troxels filed their petition under two Washington statutes, [of which only one] is at issue in this case. Section 26.10.160(3) provides: "Any person may petition the court for visitation rights at any time including, but not limited to, custody proceedings. The court may order visitation rights for any person when visitation may serve the best interest of the child whether or not there has been any change of circumstances." At trial, the Troxels requested two weekends of overnight visitation per month and two weeks of visitation each summer. Granville did not oppose visitation altogether, but instead asked the court to order one day of visitation per month with no overnight stay. In 1995, the Superior Court issued an oral ruling and entered a visitation decree ordering visitation one weekend per month, one week during the summer, and four hours on both of the petitioning grandparents' birthdays.

Granville appealed, during which time she married Kelly Wynn. Before addressing the merits of Granville's appeal, the Washington Court of Appeals remanded the case to the Superior

Court for entry of written findings of fact and conclusions of law. On remand, the Superior Court found that visitation was in Isabelle's and Natalie's best interests:

> "The Petitioners [the Troxels] are part of a large, central, loving family, all located in this area, and the Petitioners can provide opportunities for the children in the areas of cousins and music.
>
> "... The children would be benefitted from spending quality time with the Petitioners, provided that that time is balanced with time with the childrens' [*sic*] nuclear family. The court finds that the childrens' [*sic*] best interests are served by spending time with their mother and stepfather's other six children."

Approximately nine months after the Superior Court entered its order on remand, Granville's husband formally adopted Isabelle and Natalie.

The Washington Court of Appeals reversed the lower court's visitation order and dismissed the Troxels' petition for visitation, holding that nonparents lack standing to seek visitation under § 26.10.160(3) unless a custody action is pending. In the Court of Appeals' view, that limitation on nonparental visitation actions was "consistent with the constitutional restrictions on state interference with parents' fundamental liberty interest in the care, custody, and management of their children." ...

The Washington Supreme Court granted the Troxels' petition for review and, after consolidating their case with two other visitation cases, affirmed. The court disagreed with the Court of Appeals' decision on the statutory issue and found that the plain language of § 26.10.160(3) gave the Troxels standing to seek visitation, irrespective of whether a custody action was pending. The Washington Supreme Court nevertheless agreed with the Court of Appeals' ultimate conclusion that the Troxels could not obtain visitation of Isabelle and Natalie pursuant to § 26.10.160(3). The court rested its decision on the Federal Constitution, holding that § 26.10.160(3) unconstitutionally infringes on the fundamental right of parents to rear their children. In the court's view, there were at least two problems with the nonparental visitation statute. First, according to the Washington Supreme Court, the Constitution permits a State to interfere with the right of parents to rear their children only to prevent harm or potential harm to a child. Section 26.10.160(3) fails that standard because it requires no threshold showing of harm. Second, by allowing "'any person' to petition for forced visitation of a child at 'any time' with the only requirement being that the visitation serve the best interest of the child," the Washington visitation statute sweeps too broadly.... The Washington Supreme Court held that "[p]arents have a right to limit visitation of their children with third persons," and that between parents and judges, "the parents should be the ones to choose whether to expose their children to certain people or ideas." Four justices dissented from the Washington Supreme Court's holding on the constitutionality of the statute.

We granted certiorari and now affirm the judgment.

II

The demographic changes of the past century make it difficult to speak of an average American family. The composition of families varies greatly from household to household. While many children may have two married parents and grandparents who visit regularly, many other children are raised in single-parent households. In 1996, children living with only one parent accounted for 28 percent of all children under age 18 in the United States. U.S. Dept. of Commerce, Bureau of Census, Current Population Reports, 1997 Population Profile of the United States 27 (1998). Understandably, in these single-parent households, persons outside the nuclear family are called upon with increasing frequency to assist in the everyday tasks of child rearing. In many cases, grandparents play an important role. For example, in 1998, approximately 4 million children—or 5.6 percent of all children under age 18—lived in the household of their grandparents. U.S. Dept. of Commerce, Bureau of Census, Current Population Reports, Marital Status and Living Arrangements: March 1998 (Update), p. i (1998).

The nationwide enactment of nonparental visitation statutes is assuredly due, in some part, to the States' recognition of these changing realities of the American family. Because grandparents and other relatives undertake duties of a parental nature in many households, States have sought to ensure the welfare of the children therein by protecting the relationships those children form with such third parties. The States' nonparental visitation statutes are further supported by a recognition, which varies from State to State, that children should have the opportunity to benefit from relationships with statutorily specified persons—for example, their grandparents. The extension of statutory rights in this area to persons other than a child's parents, however, comes with an obvious cost. For example, the State's recognition of an independent third-party interest in a child can place a substantial burden on the traditional parent-child relationship. Contrary to JUSTICE STEVENS' accusation, our description of state nonparental visitation statutes in these terms, of course, is not meant to suggest that "children are so much chattel." Rather, our terminology is intended to highlight the fact that these statutes can present questions of constitutional import. In this case, we are presented with just such a question.

The Fourteenth Amendment provides that no State shall "deprive any person of life, liberty, or property, without due process of law." We have long recognized that the Amendment's Due Process Clause, like its Fifth Amendment counterpart, "guarantees more than fair process." The Clause also includes a substantive component that "provides heightened protection against government interference with certain fundamental rights and liberty interests."

The liberty interest at issue in this case—the interest of parents in the care, custody, and control of their children—is perhaps the oldest of the fundamental liberty interests recognized by this Court. More than 75 years ago, in *Meyer v. Nebraska*, 262 U.S. 390, 399, 401 (1923), we held that the "liberty" protected by the Due Process Clause includes the right of parents to "establish a home and bring up children" and "to control the education of their own." Two years later, in *Pierce v. Society of Sisters*, 268 U.S. 510, 534–535 (1925), we again held that the "liberty of parents and guardians" includes the right "to direct the upbringing and education of children under their control." We explained in *Pierce* that "[t]he child is not the mere creature of the State; those who nurture him and direct his destiny have the right, coupled with the high duty, to recognize and prepare him for additional obligations." *Id.*, at 535. We returned to the subject in *Prince v. Massachusetts*, 321 U.S. 158 (1944), and again confirmed that there is a constitutional dimension to the right of parents to direct the upbringing of their children. "It is cardinal with us that the custody, care and nurture of the child reside first in the parents, whose primary function and freedom include preparation for obligations the state can neither supply nor hinder." *Id.*, at 166.

In subsequent cases also, we have recognized the fundamental right of parents to make decisions concerning the care, custody, and control of their children. See, *e.g.*, *Stanley v. Illinois*, 405 U.S. 645, 651 (1972) ("It is plain that the interest of a parent in the companionship, care, custody, and management of his or her children 'come[s] to this Court with a momentum for respect lacking when appeal is made to liberties which derive merely from shifting economic arrangements'" [citation omitted]); *Wisconsin v. Yoder*, 406 U.S. 205, 232 (1972) ("The history and culture of Western civilization reflect a strong tradition of parental concern for the nurture and upbringing of their children. This primary role of the parents in the upbringing of their children is now established beyond debate as an enduring American tradition"); *Quilloin v. Walcott*, 434 U.S. 246, 255 (1978) ("We have recognized on numerous occasions that the relationship between parent and child is constitutionally protected"); *Parham v. J. R.*, 442 U.S. 584, 602 (1979) ("Our jurisprudence historically has reflected Western civilization concepts of the family as a unit with broad parental authority over minor children. Our cases have consistently followed that course"); *Santosky v. Kramer*, 455 U.S. 745, 753 (1982) (discussing "[t]he fundamental liberty interest of natural parents in the care, custody, and management of their child").... In light of this extensive precedent, it cannot now be doubted that the Due Process Clause of the Fourteenth Amendment protects the fundamental right of parents to make decisions concerning the care, custody, and control of their children.

Section 26.10.160(3), as applied to Granville and her family in this case, unconstitutionally infringes on that fundamental parental right. The Washington nonparental visitation statute is breathtakingly broad. According to the statute's text, "[*a*]*ny person* may petition the court for visitation rights *at any time*," and the court may grant such visitation rights whenever "visitation may serve *the best interest of the child*." § 26.10.160(3) (emphases added). That language effectively permits any third party seeking visitation to subject any decision by a parent concerning visitation of the parent's children to state-court review. Once the visitation petition has been filed in court and the matter is placed before a judge, a parent's decision that visitation would not be in the child's best interest is accorded no deference. Section 26.10.160(3) contains no requirement that a court accord the parent's decision any presumption of validity or any weight whatsoever. Instead, the Washington statute places the best-interest determination solely in the hands of the judge. Should the judge disagree with the parent's estimation of the child's best interests, the judge's view necessarily prevails. Thus, in practical effect, in the State of Washington a court can disregard and overturn *any* decision by a fit custodial parent concerning visitation whenever a third party affected by the decision files a visitation petition, based solely on the judge's determination of the child's best interests. The Washington Supreme Court had the opportunity to give § 26.10.160(3) a narrower reading, but it declined to do so. See, *e.g.*, 137 Wash.2d, at 5, 969 P.2d, at 23 ("[The statute] allow[s] any person, at any time, to petition for visitation without regard to relationship to the child, without regard to changed circumstances, and without regard to harm"); *id.*, at 20, 969 P.2d, at 30 ("[The statute] allow[s] 'any person' to petition for forced visitation of a child at 'any time' with the only requirement being that the visitation serve the best interest of the child").

Turning to the facts of this case, the record reveals that the Superior Court's order was based on precisely the type of mere disagreement we have just described and nothing more. The Superior Court's order was not founded on any special factors that might justify the State's interference with Granville's fundamental right to make decisions concerning the rearing of her two daughters. To be sure, this case involves a visitation petition filed by grandparents soon after the death of their son—the father of Isabelle and Natalie—but the combination of several factors here compels our conclusion that § 26.10.160(3), as applied, exceeded the bounds of the Due Process Clause.

First, the Troxels did not allege, and no court has found, that Granville was an unfit parent. That aspect of the case is important, for there is a presumption that fit parents act in the best interests of their children.As this Court explained in *Parham*:

> "[O]ur constitutional system long ago rejected any notion that a child is the mere creature of the State and, on the contrary, asserted that parents generally have the right, coupled with the high duty, to recognize and prepare [their children] for additional obligations.... The law's concept of the family rests on a presumption that parents possess what a child lacks in maturity, experience, and capacity for judgment required for making life's difficult decisions. More important, historically it has recognized that natural bonds of affection lead parents to act in the best interests of their children." 442 U.S., at 602 (alteration in original) (internal quotation marks and citations omitted).

Accordingly, so long as a parent adequately cares for his or her children (i.e., is fit), there will normally be no reason for the State to inject itself into the private realm of the family to further question the ability of that parent to make the best decisions concerning the rearing of that parent's children.

The problem here is not that the Washington Superior Court intervened, but that when it did so, it gave no special weight at all to Granville's determination of her daughters' best interests. More importantly, it appears that the Superior Court applied exactly the opposite presumption. In reciting its oral ruling after the conclusion of closing arguments, the Superior Court judge explained:

> "The burden is to show that it is in the best interest of the children to have some visitation and some quality time with their grandparents. I think in most situations a commonsensical approach [is that] it is normally in the best interest of the children to spend quality time with the grandparent, unless the grandparent, [*sic*] there are some issues or problems involved wherein the grandparents, their lifestyles are going to impact adversely upon the children. That certainly isn't the case here from what I can tell." Verbatim Report of Proceedings in *In re Troxel*, No. 93-3-00650-7 (Wash.Super.Ct., Dec. 14, 19, 1994), p. 213 (hereinafter Verbatim Report).

The judge's comments suggest that he presumed the grandparents' request should be granted unless the children would be "impact[ed] adversely." In effect, the judge placed on Granville, the fit custodial parent, the burden of *disproving* that visitation would be in the best interest of her daughters. The judge reiterated moments later: "I think [visitation with the Troxels] would be in the best interest of the children and I haven't been shown it is not in [the] best interest of the children." *Id.*, at 214.

The decisional framework employed by the Superior Court directly contravened the traditional presumption that a fit parent will act in the best interest of his or her child. In that respect, the court's presumption failed to provide any protection for Granville's fundamental constitutional right to make decisions concerning the rearing of her own daughters. In an ideal world, parents might always seek to cultivate the bonds between grandparents and their grandchildren. Needless to say, however, our world is far from perfect, and in it the decision whether such an intergenerational relationship would be beneficial in any specific case is for the parent to make in the first instance. And, if a fit parent's decision of the kind at issue here becomes subject to judicial review, the court must accord at least some special weight to the parent's own determination.

Finally, we note that there is no allegation that Granville ever sought to cut off visitation entirely. Rather, the present dispute originated when Granville informed the Troxels that she would prefer to restrict their visitation with Isabelle and Natalie to one short visit per month and special holidays. In the Superior Court proceedings Granville did not oppose visitation but instead asked that the duration of any visitation order be shorter than that requested by the Troxels. While the Troxels requested two weekends per month and two full weeks in the summer, Granville asked the Superior Court to order only one day of visitation per month (with no overnight stay) and participation in the Granville family's holiday celebrations. See 87 Wash.App., at 133, 940 P.2d, at 699; Verbatim Report 9 ("Right off the bat we'd like to say that our position is that grandparent visitation is in the best interest of the children. It is a matter of how much and how it is going to be structured") (opening statement by Granville's attorney). The Superior Court gave no weight to Granville's having assented to visitation even before the filing of any visitation petition or subsequent court intervention. The court instead rejected Granville's proposal and settled on a middle ground, ordering one weekend of visitation per month, one week in the summer, and time on both of the petitioning grandparents' birthdays. Significantly, many other States expressly provide by statute that courts may not award visitation unless a parent has denied (or unreasonably denied) visitation to the concerned third party.

Considered together with the Superior Court's reasons for awarding visitation to the Troxels, the combination of these factors demonstrates that the visitation order in this case was an unconstitutional infringement on Granville's fundamental right to make decisions concerning the care, custody, and control of her two daughters. The Washington Superior Court failed to accord the determination of Granville, a fit custodial parent, any material weight. In fact, the Superior Court made only two formal findings in support of its visitation order. First, the Troxels "are part of a large, central, loving family, all located in this area, and the [Troxels] can provide opportunities for the children in the areas of cousins and music." App. 70a. Second, "[t]he children would be benefitted from spending quality time with the [Troxels], provided that that time is balanced with time with the childrens' [*sic*] nuclear family." *Ibid.* These slender findings, in combination with the court's announced presumption in favor of grandparent visitation and its failure to accord significant weight to Granville's already having offered meaningful visitation to the Troxels, show that this case involves nothing more than a simple disagreement between the Washington Superior Court and Granville concerning her children's best interests. The Superior Court's announced reason for ordering one week of visitation in the summer demonstrates our conclusion well: "I look back on some personal experiences.... We always spen[t] as kids a week with one set of grandparents and another set of grandparents, [and] it happened to work out in our family that [it] turned out to be an enjoyable experience. Maybe that can, in this family, if that is how it works out." Verbatim Report 220–221. As we have explained, the Due Process Clause does not permit a State to infringe on the fundamental right of parents to make child rearing decisions simply because a state judge believes a "better" decision could be made. Neither the Washington nonparental visitation statute generally—which places no limits on either the persons who may petition for visitation or the circumstances in which such a petition may be granted—nor the Superior Court in this specific case required anything more. Accordingly, we hold that § 26.10.160(3), as applied in this case, is unconstitutional.

Because we rest our decision on the sweeping breadth of § 26.10.160(3) and the application of that broad, unlimited power in this case, we do not consider the primary constitutional question passed on by the Washington Supreme Court—whether the Due Process Clause requires all nonparental visitation statutes to include a showing of harm or potential harm to the child as a condition precedent to granting visitation. We do not, and need not, define today the precise scope of the parental due process right in the visitation context. In this respect, we agree with Justice Kennedy that the constitutionality of any standard for awarding visitation turns on the specific manner in which that standard is applied and that the constitutional protections in this area are best "elaborated with care." Because much state-court adjudication in this context occurs on a case-by-case basis, we would be hesitant to hold that specific nonparental visitation statutes violate the Due Process Clause as a *per se* matter.

Justice Stevens criticizes our reliance on what he characterizes as merely "a guess" about the Washington courts' interpretation of § 26.10.160(3). Justice Kennedy likewise states that "[m]ore specific guidance should await a case in which a State's highest court has considered all of the facts in the course of elaborating the protection afforded to parents by the laws of the State and by the Constitution itself." We respectfully disagree. There is no need to hypothesize about how the Washington courts might apply § 26.10.160(3) because the Washington Superior Court did apply the statute in this very case. Like the Washington Supreme Court, then, we are presented with an actual visitation order and the reasons why the Superior Court believed entry of the order was appropriate in this case. Faced with the Superior Court's application of § 26.10.160(3) to Granville and her family, the Washington Supreme Court chose not to give the statute a narrower construction. Rather, that court gave § 26.10.160(3) a literal and expansive interpretation. As we have explained, that broad construction plainly encompassed the Superior Court's application of the statute.

There is thus no reason to remand the case for further proceedings in the Washington Supreme Court. As Justice Kennedy recognizes, the burden of litigating a domestic relations proceeding can itself be "so disruptive of the parent-child relationship that the constitutional right of a custodial parent to make certain basic determinations for the child's welfare becomes implicated." In this case, the litigation costs incurred by Granville on her trip through the Washington court system and to this Court are without a doubt already substantial. As we have explained, it is apparent that the entry of the visitation order in this case violated the Constitution. We should say so now, without forcing the parties into additional litigation that would further burden Granville's parental right. We therefore hold that the application of § 26.10.160(3) to Granville and her family violated her due process right to make decisions concerning the care, custody, and control of her daughters.

Accordingly, the judgment of the Washington Supreme Court is affirmed.

Justice Souter, concurring in the judgment.

I concur in the judgment affirming the decision of the Supreme Court of Washington, whose facial invalidation of its own state statute is consistent with this Court's prior cases addressing the substantive interests at stake. I would say no more....

The Supreme Court of Washington invalidated its state statute based on the text of the statute alone, not its application to any particular case. Its ruling rested on two independently sufficient grounds: the failure of the statute to require harm to the child to justify a disputed visitation order, and the statute's authorization of "any person" at "any time" to petition for and to receive visitation rights subject only to a free-ranging best-interests-of-the-child standard.

I see no error in the second reason, that because the state statute authorizes any person at any time to request (and a judge to award) visitation rights, subject only to the State's particular best-interests standard, the state statute sweeps too broadly and is unconstitutional on its face. Consequently, there is no need to decide whether harm is required or to consider the precise scope of the parent's right or its necessary protections.

We have long recognized that a parent's interests in the nurture, upbringing, companionship, care, and custody of children are generally protected by the Due Process Clause of the Fourteenth Amendment. See, *e.g.*, *Meyer v. Nebraska*, 262 U.S. 390, 399, 401 (1923); *Pierce v. Society of Sisters*, 268 U.S. 510, 535 (1925); *Stanley v. Illinois*, 405 U.S. 645, 651 (1972); *Wisconsin v. Yoder*, 406 U.S. 205, 232 (1972); *Quilloin v. Walcott*, 434 U.S. 246, 255 (1978); *Parham v. J. R.*, 442 U.S. 584, 602 (1979); *Santosky v. Kramer*, 455 U.S. 745, 753 (1982); *Washington v. Glucksberg*, 521 U.S. 702, 720 (1997). As we first acknowledged in *Meyer*, the right of parents to "bring up children," 262 U.S., at 399, and "to control the education of their own" is protected by the Constitution, *id.*, at 401.

On the basis of this settled principle, the Supreme Court of Washington invalidated its statute because it authorized a contested visitation order at the intrusive behest of any person at any time subject only to a best-interests-of-the-child standard. In construing the statute, the state court explained that the "any person" at "any time" language was to be read literally, 137 Wash.2d, at 10–11, 969 P.2d, at 25–27, and that "[m]ost notably the statut[e] do[es] not require the petitioner to establish that he or she has a substantial relationship with the child," *id.*, at 20–21, 969 P.2d, at 31. Although the statute speaks of granting visitation rights whenever "visitation may serve the best interest of the child," Wash. Rev.Code § 26.10.160(3) (1994), the state court authoritatively read this provision as placing hardly any limit on a court's discretion to award visitation rights. As the court understood it, the specific best-interests provision in the statute would allow a court to award visitation whenever it thought it could make a better decision than a child's parent had done. On that basis in part, the Supreme Court of Washington invalidated the State's own statute....

Our cases, it is true, have not set out exact metes and bounds to the protected interest of a parent in the relationship with his child, but *Meyer*'s repeatedly recognized right of upbringing would be a sham if it failed to encompass the right to be free of judicially compelled visitation by "any party" at "any time" a judge believed he "could make a 'better' decision" than the objecting parent had done. The strength of a parent's interest in controlling a child's associates is as obvious as the influence of personal associations on the development of the child's social and moral character. Whether for good or for ill, adults not only influence but may indoctrinate children, and a choice about a child's social companions is not essentially different from the designation of the adults who will influence the child in school. Even a State's considered judgment about the preferable political and religious character of schoolteachers is not entitled to prevail over a parent's choice of private school. *Pierce*, *supra*, at 535 ("The fundamental theory of liberty upon which all governments in this Union repose excludes any general power of the State to standardize its children by forcing them to accept instruction from public teachers only. The child is not the mere creature of the State; those who nurture him and direct his destiny have the right, coupled with the high duty, to recognize and prepare him for additional obligations"). It would be anomalous, then, to subject a parent to any individual judge's choice of a child's associates from out of the general population merely because the judge might think himself more enlightened than the child's parent. To say the least (and as the Court implied in *Pierce*), parental choice in such matters is not merely a default rule in the absence of either governmental choice or the government's designation of an official with the power to choose for whatever reason and in whatever circumstances.

Since I do not question the power of a State's highest court to construe its domestic statute and to apply a demanding standard when ruling on its facial constitutionality, this for me is the end of the case. I would simply affirm the decision of the Supreme Court of Washington that its statute, authorizing courts to grant visitation rights to any person at any time, is unconstitutional. I therefore respectfully concur in the judgment.

JUSTICE THOMAS, concurring in the judgment.

I write separately to note that neither party has argued that our substantive due process cases were wrongly decided and that the original understanding of the Due Process Clause precludes judicial enforcement of unenumerated rights under that constitutional provision. As a result, I express no view on the merits of this matter, and I understand the plurality as well to leave the resolution of that issue for another day.*

Consequently, I agree with the plurality that this Court's recognition of a fundamental right of parents to direct the upbringing of their children resolves this case. Our decision in *Pierce v. Society of Sisters*, 268 U.S. 510 (1925), holds that parents have a fundamental constitutional right to rear their children, including the right to determine who shall educate and socialize them. The opinions of the plurality, JUSTICE KENNEDY, and JUSTICE SOUTER recognize such a right, but curiously none of them articulates the appropriate standard of review. I would apply strict scrutiny to infringements of fundamental rights. Here, the State of Washington lacks even a legitimate governmental interest—to say nothing of a compelling one—in second-guessing a fit parent's decision regarding visitation with third parties. On this basis, I would affirm the judgment below.

JUSTICE STEVENS, dissenting.

The Court today wisely declines to endorse either the holding or the reasoning of the Supreme Court of Washington. In my opinion, the Court would have been even wiser to deny certiorari. Given the problematic character of the trial court's decision and the uniqueness of the Washington statute, there was no pressing need to review a State Supreme Court decision that merely requires the state legislature to draft a better statute.

Having decided to address the merits, however, the Court should begin by recognizing that the State Supreme Court rendered a federal constitutional judgment holding a state law invalid on its face. In light of that judgment, I believe that we should confront the federal questions presented directly. For the Washington statute is not made facially invalid either because it may be invoked by too many hypothetical plaintiffs, or because it leaves open the possibility that someone may be permitted to sustain a relationship with a child without having to prove that serious harm to the child would otherwise result.

I

In response to Tommie Granville's federal constitutional challenge, the State Supreme Court broadly held that Wash. Rev.Code § 26.10.160(3) (Supp. 1996) was invalid on its face under

*. This case also does not involve a challenge based upon the Privileges and Immunities Clause and thus does not present an opportunity to reevaluate the meaning of that Clause.

the Federal Constitution. Despite the nature of this judgment, Justice O'Connor would hold that the Washington visitation statute violated the Due Process Clause of the Fourteenth Amendment only as applied. I agree with Justice Souter that this approach is untenable.

The task of reviewing a trial court's application of a state statute to the particular facts of a case is one that should be performed in the first instance by the state appellate courts. In this case, because of their views of the Federal Constitution, the Washington state appeals courts have yet to decide whether the trial court's findings were adequate under the statute. Any as-applied critique of the trial court's judgment that this Court might offer could only be based upon a guess about the state courts' application of that State's statute, and an independent assessment of the facts in this case—both judgments that we are ill-suited and ill-advised to make.[3]

While I thus agree with Justice Souter in this respect, I do not agree with his conclusion that the State Supreme Court made a definitive construction of the visitation statute that necessitates the constitutional conclusion he would draw. As I read the State Supreme Court's opinion, its interpretation of the Federal Constitution made it unnecessary to adopt a definitive construction of the statutory text, or, critically, to decide whether the statute had been correctly applied in this case. In particular, the state court gave no content to the phrase, "best interest of the child," content that might well be gleaned from that State's own statutes or decisional law employing the same phrase in different contexts, and from the myriad other state statutes and court decisions at least nominally applying the same standard. Thus, I believe that Justice Souter's conclusion that the statute unconstitutionally imbues state trial court judges with "'too much discretion in every case,'" is premature.

We are thus presented with the unconstrued terms of a state statute and a State Supreme Court opinion that, in my view, significantly misstates the effect of the Federal Constitution upon any construction of that statute. Given that posture, I believe the Court should identify and correct the two flaws in the reasoning of the state court's majority opinion, and remand for further review of the trial court's disposition of this specific case.

II

In my view, the State Supreme Court erred in its federal constitutional analysis because neither the provision granting "any person" the right to petition the court for visitation, nor the absence of a provision requiring a "threshold...finding of harm to the child," provides a sufficient basis for holding that the statute is invalid in all its applications. I believe that a facial challenge should fail whenever a statute has "a 'plainly legitimate sweep.'" Under the Washington statute, there are plainly any number of cases—indeed, one suspects, the most common to arise—in which the "person" among "any" seeking visitation is a once-custodial caregiver, an intimate relation, or even a genetic parent. Even the Court would seem to agree that in many circumstances, it would be constitutionally permissible for a court to award some visitation of a child to a parent or previous caregiver in cases of parental separation or divorce, cases of disputed custody, cases involving temporary foster care or guardianship, and so forth. As the statute plainly sweeps in a great deal of the permissible, the State Supreme Court majority incorrectly concluded that a statute authorizing "any person" to file a petition seeking visitation privileges would invariably run afoul of the Fourteenth Amendment.

3. Unlike Justice O'Connor, I find no suggestion in the trial court's decision in this case that the court was applying any presumptions at all in its analysis, much less one in favor of the grandparents....

The second key aspect of the Washington Supreme Court's holding—that the Federal Constitution requires a showing of actual or potential "harm" to the child before a court may order visitation continued over a parent's objections—finds no support in this Court's case law.... [W]e have never held that the parent's liberty interest in this relationship is so inflexible as to establish a rigid constitutional shield, protecting every arbitrary parental decision from any challenge absent a threshold finding of harm. The presumption that parental decisions generally serve the best interests of their children is sound, and clearly in the normal case the parent's interest is paramount. But even a fit parent is capable of treating a child like a mere possession.

Cases like this do not present a bipolar struggle between the parents and the State over who has final authority to determine what is in a child's best interests. There is at a minimum a third individual, whose interests are implicated in every case to which the statute applies—the child.

It has become standard practice in our substantive due process jurisprudence to begin our analysis with an identification of the "fundamental" liberty interests implicated by the challenged state action. My colleagues are of course correct to recognize that the right of a parent to maintain a relationship with his or her child is among the interests included most often in the constellation of liberties protected through the Fourteenth Amendment. Our cases leave no doubt that parents have a fundamental liberty interest in caring for and guiding their children, and a corresponding privacy interest—absent exceptional circumstances—in doing so without the undue interference of strangers to them and to their child. Moreover, and critical in this case, our cases applying this principle have explained that with this constitutional liberty comes a presumption (albeit a rebuttable one) that "natural bonds of affection lead parents to act in the best interests of their children." *Parham v. J. R.*, 442 U.S. 584, 602 (1979)....

Despite this Court's repeated recognition of these significant parental liberty interests, these interests have never been seen to be without limits. In *Lehr v. Robertson*, 463 U.S. 248 (1983), for example, this Court held that a putative biological father who had never established an actual relationship with his child did not have a constitutional right to notice of his child's adoption by the man who had married the child's mother. As this Court had recognized in an earlier case, a parent's liberty interests "'do not spring full-blown from the biological connection between parent and child. They require relationships more enduring.'" *Id.*, at 260 (quoting *Caban v. Mohammed*, 441 U.S. 380, 397 (1979)).

Conversely, in *Michael H. v. Gerald D.*, 491 U.S. 110 (1989), this Court concluded that despite both biological parenthood and an established relationship with a young child, a father's due process liberty interest in maintaining some connection with that child was not sufficiently powerful to overcome a state statutory presumption that the husband of the child's mother was the child's parent. As a result of the presumption, the biological father could be denied even visitation with the child because, as a matter of state law, he was not a "parent." A plurality of this Court there recognized that the parental liberty interest was a function, not simply of "isolated factors" such as biology and intimate connection, but of the broader and apparently independent interest in family. See, *e.g.*, *id.*, at 123; see also *Lehr*, 463 U.S., at 261; *Smith v. Organization of Foster Families For Equality & Reform*, 431 U.S. 816, 842–847 (1977); *Moore v. East Cleveland*, 431 U.S. 494, 498–504 (1977).

A parent's rights with respect to her child have thus never been regarded as absolute, but rather are limited by the existence of an actual, developed relationship with a child, and are tied to the presence or absence of some embodiment of family. These limitations have arisen, not simply out of the definition of parenthood itself, but because of this Court's assumption that a parent's interests in a child must be balanced against the State's long-recognized interests as *parens patriae,* and, critically, the child's own complementary interest in preserving relationships that serve her welfare and protection.

While this Court has not yet had occasion to elucidate the nature of a child's liberty interests in preserving established familial or family-like bonds, it seems to me extremely likely that, to the extent parents and families have fundamental liberty interests in preserving such intimate relationships, so, too, do children have these interests, and so, too, must their interests be balanced in the equation. At a minimum, our prior cases recognizing that children are, generally speaking, constitutionally protected actors require that this Court reject any suggestion that when it comes to parental rights, children are so much chattel. The constitutional protection against arbitrary state interference with parental rights should not be extended to prevent the States from protecting children against the arbitrary exercise of parental authority that is not in fact motivated by an interest in the welfare of the child.

This is not, of course, to suggest that a child's liberty interest in maintaining contact with a particular individual is to be treated invariably as on a par with that child's parents' contrary interests. Because our substantive due process case law includes a strong presumption that a parent will act in the best interest of her child, it would be necessary, were the state appellate courts actually to confront a challenge to the statute as applied, to consider whether the trial court's assessment of the "best interest of the child" incorporated that presumption.... For the purpose of a facial challenge like this, I think it safe to assume that trial judges usually give great deference to parents' wishes, and I am not persuaded otherwise here.

But presumptions notwithstanding, we should recognize that there may be circumstances in which a child has a stronger interest at stake than mere protection from serious harm caused by the termination of visitation by a "person" other than a parent. The almost infinite variety of family relationships that pervade our ever-changing society strongly counsel against the creation by this Court of a constitutional rule that treats a biological parent's liberty interest in the care and supervision of her child as an isolated right that may be exercised arbitrarily. It is indisputably the business of the States, rather than a federal court employing a national standard, to assess in the first instance the relative importance of the conflicting interests that give rise to disputes such as this. Far from guaranteeing that parents' interests will be trammeled in the sweep of cases arising under the statute, the Washington law merely gives an individual—with whom a child may have an established relationship—the procedural right to ask the State to act as arbiter, through the entirely well-known best-interests standard, between the parent's protected interests and the child's. It seems clear to me that the Due Process Clause of the Fourteenth Amendment leaves room for States to consider the impact on a child of possibly arbitrary parental decisions that neither serve nor are motivated by the best interests of the child.

Accordingly, I respectfully dissent.

Justice Scalia, dissenting.

In my view, a right of parents to direct the upbringing of their children is among the "unalienable Rights" with which the Declaration of Independence proclaims "all men... are endowed by their Creator." And in my view that right is also among the "othe[r] [rights] retained by the people" which the Ninth Amendment says the Constitution's enumeration of rights "shall not be construed to deny or disparage." The Declaration of Independence, however, is not a legal prescription conferring powers upon the courts; and the Constitution's refusal to "deny or disparage" other rights is far removed from affirming any one of them, and even further removed from authorizing judges to identify what they might be, and to enforce the judges' list against laws duly enacted by the people. Consequently, while I would think it entirely compatible with the commitment to representative democracy set forth in the founding documents to argue, in legislative chambers or in electoral campaigns, that the State has *no power* to interfere with parents' authority over the rearing of their children, I do not believe that the power which the Constitution confers upon me *as a judge* entitles me to deny legal effect to laws that (in my view) infringe upon what is (in my view) that unenumerated right.

Only three holdings of this Court rest in whole or in part upon a substantive constitutional right of parents to direct the upbringing of their children—two of them from an era rich in substantive due process holdings that have since been repudiated. See *Meyer v. Nebraska*, 262 U.S. 390, 399, 401 (1923); *Pierce v. Society of Sisters*, 268 U.S. 510, 534–535 (1925); *Wisconsin v. Yoder*, 406 U.S. 205, 232–233 (1972). Cf. *West Coast Hotel Co. v. Parrish*, 300 U.S. 379 (1937) (overruling *Adkins v. Children's Hospital of D.C.*, 261 U.S. 525 (1923)). The sheer diversity of today's opinions persuades me that the theory of unenumerated parental rights underlying these three cases has small claim to *stare decisis* protection.... While I would not now overrule those earlier cases (that has not been urged), neither would I extend the theory upon which they rested to this new context.

Judicial vindication of "parental rights" under a Constitution that does not even mention them requires (as Justice Kennedy's opinion rightly points out) not only a judicially crafted definition of parents, but also—unless, as no one believes, the parental rights are to be absolute—judicially approved assessments of "harm to the child" and judicially defined gradations of other persons (grandparents, extended family, adoptive family in an adoption later found to be invalid, long-term guardians, etc.) who may have some claim against the wishes of the parents. If we embrace this unenumerated right, I think it obvious—whether we affirm or reverse the judgment here, or remand as Justice Stevens or Justice Kennedy would do—that we will be ushering in a new regime of judicially prescribed, and federally prescribed, family law. I have no reason to believe that federal judges will be better at this than state legislatures; and state legislatures have the great advantages of doing harm in a more circumscribed area, of being able to correct their mistakes in a flash, and of being removable by the people.

For these reasons, I would reverse the judgment below.

Justice Kennedy, dissenting.

The Supreme Court of Washington has determined that petitioners Jenifer and Gary Troxel have standing under state law to seek court-ordered visitation with their grandchildren, notwithstanding the objections of the children's parent, respondent, Tommie Granville.... After acknowledging this statutory right to sue for visitation, the State Supreme Court invalidated the statute as violative of the United States Constitution, because it interfered with a parent's right to raise his or her child free from unwarranted interference. Although parts of the court's decision may be open to differing interpretations, it seems to be agreed that the court invalidated the statute on its face, ruling it a nullity.

The first flaw the State Supreme Court found in the statute is that it allows an award of visitation a nonparent without a finding that harm to the child would result if visitation were withheld; and the second is that the statute allows any person to seek visitation at any time. In my view the first theory is too broad to be correct, as it appears to contemplate that the best interests of the child standard may not be applied in any visitation case. I acknowledge the distinct possibility that visitation cases may arise where, considering the absence of other protection for the parent under state laws and procedures, the best interests of the child standard would give insufficient protection to the parent's constitutional right to raise the child without undue intervention by the State; but it is quite a different matter to say, as I understand the Supreme Court of Washington to have said, that a harm to the child standard is required in every instance.

Given the error I see in the State Supreme Court's central conclusion that the best interests of the child standard is never appropriate in third-party visitation cases, that court should have the first opportunity to reconsider this case. I would remand the case to the state court for further proceedings. If it then found the statute has been applied in an unconstitutional manner because the best interests of the child standard gives insufficient protection to a parent under the circumstances of this case, or if it again declared the statute a nullity because the statute seems to allow any person at all to seek visitation at any time, the decision would present other issues which may or may not warrant further review in this Court. These include not only the protection the Constitution gives parents against state-ordered visitation but also the extent to which federal rules for facial challenges to statutes control in state courts. These matters, however, should await some further case. The judgment now under review should be vacated and remanded on the sole ground that the harm ruling that was so central to the Supreme Court of Washington's decision was error, given its broad formulation.

Turning to the question whether harm to the child must be the controlling standard in every visitation proceeding, there is a beginning point that commands general, perhaps unanimous, agreement in our separate opinions: As our case law has developed, the custodial parent has a constitutional right to determine, without undue interference by the state, how best to raise, nurture, and educate the child. The parental right stems from the liberty protected by the Due Process Clause of the Fourteenth Amendment. See, *e.g., Meyer v. Nebraska*, 262 U.S. 390, 399, 401 (1923); *Pierce v. Society of Sisters*, 268 U.S. 510, 534–535 (1925); *Prince v. Massachusetts*, 321 U.S. 158, 166 (1944); *Stanley v. Illinois*, 405 U.S. 645, 651–652 (1971); *Wisconsin v. Yoder*, 406 U.S. 205, 232–233 (1972); *Santosky v. Kramer*, 455 U.S. 755, 753–754 (1982). *Pierce* and *Meyer*, had they been decided in recent times, may well have been grounded upon First Amendment principles protecting freedom of speech, belief, and religion. Their formulation and subsequent interpretation have been quite different, of course; and they long have been interpreted to have found in Fourteenth Amendment concepts of liberty an independent right of the parent in the "custody, care and nurture of the child," free from state intervention. *Prince, supra*, at 166. The principle exists, then, in broad formulation; yet courts must use considerable restraint, including careful adherence to the incremental instruction given by the precise facts of particular cases, as they seek to give further and more precise definition to the right.

The State Supreme Court sought to give content to the parent's right by announcing a categorical rule that third parties who seek visitation must always prove the denial of visitation would harm the child. After reviewing some of the relevant precedents, the Supreme Court of Washington concluded "'[t]he requirement of harm is the sole protection that parents have against pervasive state interference in the parenting process.'" For that reason, "[s]hort of preventing harm to the child," the court considered the best interests of the child to be "insufficient to serve as a compelling state interest overruling a parent's fundamental rights."

While it might be argued as an abstract matter that in some sense the child is always harmed if his or her best interests are not considered, the law of domestic relations, as it has evolved to this point, treats as distinct the two standards, one harm to the child and the other the best interests of the child. The judgment of the Supreme Court of Washington rests on that assumption, and I, too, shall assume that there are real and consequential differences between the two standards.

On the question whether one standard must always take precedence over the other in order to protect the right of the parent or parents, "[o]ur Nation's history, legal traditions, and practices" do not give us clear or definitive answers. The consensus among courts and commentators is that at least through the 19th century there was no legal right of visitation; court-ordered visitation appears to be a 20th-century phenomenon. See, *e.g.*, 1 D. Kramer, Legal Rights of Children 124, 136 (2d ed. 1994); 2 J. Atkinson, Modern Child Custody Practice § 8.10 (1986).... Early 20th-century exceptions did occur, often in cases where a relative had acted in a parental capacity, or where one of a child's parents had died. As a general matter, however, contemporary state-court decisions acknowledge that "[h]istorically, grandparents had no legal right of visitation," and it is safe to assume other third parties would have fared no better in court.

To say that third parties have had no historical right to petition for visitation does not necessarily imply, as the Supreme Court of Washington concluded, that a parent has a constitutional right to prevent visitation in all cases not involving harm. True, this Court has acknowledged that States have the authority to intervene to prevent harm to children, see, *e.g.*, *Prince*, *supra*, at 168–169; *Yoder*, *supra*, at 233–234, but that is not the same as saying that a heightened harm to the child standard must be satisfied in every case in which a third party seeks a visitation order. It is also true that the law's traditional presumption has been "that natural bonds of affection lead parents to act in the best interests of their children," *Parham v. J. R.*, 442 U.S. 584, 602 (1979); and "[s]imply because the decision of a parent is not agreeable to a child or because it involves risks does not automatically transfer the power to make that decision from the parents to some agency or officer of the state," *id.*, at 603. The State Supreme Court's conclusion that the Constitution forbids the application of the best interests of the child standard in any visitation proceeding, however, appears to rest upon assumptions the Constitution does not require.

My principal concern is that the holding seems to proceed from the assumption that the parent or parents who resist visitation have always been the child's primary caregivers and that the third parties who seek visitation have no legitimate and established relationship with the child. That idea, in turn, appears influenced by the concept that the conventional nuclear family ought to establish the visitation standard for every domestic relations case. As we all know, this is simply not the structure or prevailing condition in many households. For many boys and girls a traditional family with two or even one permanent and caring parent is simply not the reality of their childhood. This may be so whether their childhood has been marked by tragedy or filled with considerable happiness and fulfillment.

Cases are sure to arise—perhaps a substantial number of cases—in which a third party, by acting in a caregiving rôle over a significant period of time, has developed a relationship with a child which is not necessarily subject to absolute parental veto. Some pre-existing relationships, then, serve to identify persons who have a strong attachment to the child with the concomitant motivation to act in a responsible way to ensure the child's welfare. As the State Supreme Court was correct to acknowledge, those relationships can be so enduring that "in certain circumstances where a child has enjoyed a substantial relationship with a third person, arbitrarily depriving the child of the relationship could cause severe psychological harm to the child," and harm to the adult may also ensue. In the design and elaboration of their visitation laws, States may be entitled to consider that certain relationships are such that to avoid the risk of harm, a best interests standard can be employed by their domestic relations courts in some circumstances.

Indeed, contemporary practice should give us some pause before rejecting the best interests of the child standard in all third-party visitation cases, as the Washington court has done. The standard has been recognized for many years as a basic tool of domestic relations law in visitation proceedings. Since 1965 all 50 States have enacted a third-party visitation statute of some sort. Each of these statutes, save one, permits a court order to issue in certain cases if visitation is found to be in the best interests of the child. While it is unnecessary for us to consider the constitutionality of any particular provision in the case now before us, it can be noted that the statutes also include a variety of methods for limiting parents' exposure to third-party visitation petitions and for ensuring parental decisions are given respect. Many States limit the identity of permissible petitioners by restricting visitation petitions to grandparents, or by requiring petitioners to show a substantial relationship with a child, or both. The statutes vary in other respects—for instance, some permit visitation petitions when there has been a change in circumstances such as divorce or death of a parent, and some apply a presumption that parental decisions should control. Georgia's is the sole state legislature to have adopted a general harm to the child standard, and it did so only after the Georgia Supreme Court held the State's prior visitation statute invalid under the Federal and Georgia Constitutions.

In light of the inconclusive historical record and case law, as well as the almost universal adoption of the best interests standard for visitation disputes, I would be hard pressed to conclude the right to be free of such review in all cases is itself "'implicit in the concept of ordered liberty.'" In my view, it would be more appropriate to conclude that the constitutionality of the application of the best interests standard depends on more specific factors. In short, a fit parent's right vis-a-vis a complete stranger is one thing; her right vis-a-vis another parent or a *de facto* parent may be another. The protection the Constitution requires, then, must be elaborated with care, using the discipline and instruction of the case law system. We must keep in mind that family courts in the 50 States confront these factual variations each day, and are best situated to consider the unpredictable, yet inevitable, issues that arise.

It must be recognized, of course, that a domestic relations proceeding in and of itself can constitute state intervention that is so disruptive of the parent-child relationship that the constitutional right of a custodial parent to make certain basic determinations for the child's welfare becomes implicated. The best interests of the child standard has at times been criticized as indeterminate, leading to unpredictable results. If a single parent who is struggling to raise a child is faced with visitation demands from a third party, the attorney's fees alone might destroy her hopes and plans for the child's future. Our system must confront more often the reality that litigation can itself be so disruptive that constitutional protection may be required; and I do not discount the possibility that in some instances the best interests of the child standard may provide insufficient protection to the parent-child relationship. We owe it to the Nation's domestic relations legal structure, however, to proceed with caution.

It should suffice in this case to reverse the holding of the State Supreme Court that the application of the best interests of the child standard is always unconstitutional in third-party visitation cases. Whether, under the circumstances of this case, the order requiring visitation over the objection of this fit parent violated the Constitution ought to be reserved for further proceedings. Because of its sweeping ruling requiring the harm to the child standard, the Supreme Court of Washington did not have the occasion to address the specific visitation order the Troxels obtained. More specific guidance should await a case in which a State's highest court has considered all of the facts in the course of elaborating the protection afforded to parents by the laws of the State and by the Constitution itself. Furthermore, in my view, we need not address whether, under the correct constitutional standards, the Washington statute can be invalidated on its face. This question, too, ought to be addressed by the state court in the first instance.

In my view the judgment under review should be vacated and the case remanded for further proceedings.

NOTES AND QUESTIONS

1. How many opinions were written in the case? What conclusions do you draw from this fact?

2. Justice O'Connor wrote the opinion for the Court. How many justices joined her opinion? What did she say was wrong with the Washington statute? Why does Justice Souter concur?

3. Are parental rights fundamental rights? If so, what level of scrutiny will the Court apply when considering the constitutionality of a statute infringing on parental rights? Is this the level of scrutiny applied by O'Connor? Why does Justice Thomas concur?

4. Justices Stevens, Scalia, and Kennedy all dissent. Why do they disagree with the plurality?

5. What similarities, if any, do you see between Stevens's dissent and Douglas's dissent in *Yoder*?

6. A number of scholars have commented on the implications of the Court's approach for the rights of children. For a few of these articles, see, e.g., Alessia Bell, Note, *Public Child and Private Child: Troxel v. Granville and the Constitutional Rights of Family Members*, 36 Harv. C.R.-C.L. L. Rev. 225, 244 (2001) ("*Troxel* thus marks an important step in the Court's family law jurisprudence. At best, *Troxel* promotes intrafamily diversity, preserves parents' liberty interest, and protects children"); Chesa Boudin, *Children of Incarcerated Parents: The Child's Constitutional Right to the Family Relationship*, 101 J. Criminal Law & Criminology 77 (2011) (arguing that *Troxel*'s recognition of due process right of family integrity extends to decision to incarcerate parents); Emily Buss, *Adrift in the Middle: Parental Rights after Troxel v. Granville*, 2000 Sup. Ct. Rev. 279 (arguing children better served by a robust account of fundamental parental rights that *Troxel* undermines); David Meyer, *Lochner Redeemed: Family Privacy after Troxel and Carhart*, 48 U.C.L.A. L. Rev. 1125 (2001) ("the reasonableness test in *Troxel* permits courts to take account of the varied and potentially conflicting interests of parents, children, and extended family in passing judgment on the state's intrusion"); Dana Prescott, *Biological Altruism, Splitting Siblings and the Judicial Process: A Child's Right to Constitutional Protection in Family Dislocation*, 71 U.M.K.C. L. Rev. 623 (2003) (arguing that *Troxel* may signal willingness of Court to accord child standing to raise constitutional right to maintain biological relationship); Kyle C. Velte, *Towards Constitutional Recognition of the Lesbian-Parented Family*,

26 N.Y.U. Rev. L. & Soc. Change 245, 297 (2000–01) (*Troxel* plurality decision, by recognizing various family forms and rejecting strict scrutiny, holds promise for children and nonlegal parents of lesbian-parented families); Barbara Bennett Woodhouse, *Talking about Children's Rights in Judicial Custody and Visitation Decision-Making*, 36 Fam. L.Q. 105 (2002) (arguing that after *Troxel*, "at least six of the justices would weigh children's interest in protection of intimate relationships in the balance of constitutional rights"); Barbara Bennett Woodhouse & Sacha Coupet, *Troxel v. Granville: Implications for at Risk Children and the Amicus Curiae Role of University-Based Interdisciplinary Centers for Children*, 32 Rutgers L.J. 857 (2000) (authors of *amicus* brief urged court to avoid making sweeping statements about parental rights by showing that excessive deference to biological parents might lead to more children in state care).

7. Gary Troxel, Gretchen Christopher, and Barbara Ellis were the founding members of the musical group the Fleetwoods. They had eleven songs make it to *Billboard*'s Top 100, including two number-one hits in 1959: "Come Softly to Me" and "Mr. Blue." Troxel was drafted into the Navy and was replaced by another singer in the early 1960s. In the 1980s, Troxel formed a new Fleetwoods group and continues to perform. He lives in Mount Vernon, Washington, with his wife, Jenifer. They have ten grandchildren and one great-grandchild. Does Troxel's background suggest that he would be a positive influence in his grandchildren's lives? A negative one? Is it relevant that his son committed suicide? What if Tommie and Kelly decide that the children should no longer have any contact with their paternal grandparents? Would your answer differ if Brad were still alive and he and Tommie had decided to cut off contact? Why? Who should decide whether the Troxels may continue to have a relationship with their grandchildren?

D. The Procedural Framework in Abuse and Neglect Cases

1. REPORTING CHILD ABUSE AND NEGLECT

In 1962, C. Henry Kempe and his colleagues published an article entitled "The Battered-Child Syndrome" in the *Journal of the American Medical Association*. C. Henry Kempe et al., *The Battered-Child Syndrome*, 181 J. Am. Med. Ass'n 17 (July 7, 1962). A survey of 71 responding hospitals found 302 suspected cases of battered-child syndrome; in 33 of the cases, the children died; in 85 of the cases, the children suffered permanent brain injury. A survey of 77 district attorneys found 447 similar cases; 45 of these children died, while 29 suffered permanent brain damage. Kempe et al. argued that doctors had a special responsibility to conduct a full evaluation and ensure that the trauma did not recur. After the article was released, the national media picked up the story. By 1967, all fifty states had enacted child-abuse reporting laws. John E. B. Myers, *A Short History of Child Protection in America*, 42 Fam. L.Q. 449, 456 (2008).

In 1974, Congress enacted the Child Abuse Prevention and Treatment Act (CAPTA), Pub. L. No. 93-247, § 1191, 88 Stat. 4 (1974). Among other things, the Act established the National Center for Child Abuse and Neglect, provided a definition of abuse and neglect, mandated reporting, and provided for immunity for good-faith reporting. In 1975, a model statute was released to provide states with a framework for complying with the federal guidelines. Child Abuse & Neglect Project, Education Comm'n of the States, Report No. 71, Child Abuse and Neglect: Model Legislation for the States (1975). In a few years, most state laws had been revised to meet the federal requirements. The structure of reporting child abuse and neglect is remarkably similar across the states because of CAPTA and the model statute; nevertheless, there are differences, as the following materials make clear.

CHILD ABUSE PREVENTION AND TREATMENT ACT (CAPTA) 42 U.S.C. § 5106a (2010)

(a) Development and operation grants

The Secretary shall make grants to the States, from allotments made under subsection (f) for each State that applies for a grant under this section, for purposes of assisting the States in improving the child protective services system of each such State in—

(1) the intake, assessment, screening, and investigation of reports of child abuse or neglect....

(b) Eligibility requirements...

(2) Contents

A State plan...shall contain a description of the activities that the State will carry out using amounts received under the grant to achieve the objectives of this subchapter, including...

(B) an assurance in the form of a certification by the Governor of the State that the State has in effect and is enforcing a State law, or has in effect and is operating a statewide program, relating to child abuse and neglect that includes—

(i) provisions or procedures for an individual to report known and suspected instances of child abuse and neglect, including a State law for mandatory reporting by individuals required to report such instances...

(iv) procedures for the immediate screening, risk and safety assessment, and prompt investigation of such reports...

(vii) provisions for immunity from prosecution under State and local laws and regulations for individuals making good faith reports of suspected or known instances of child abuse or neglect...

(xii) provisions requiring, and procedures in place that facilitate the prompt expungement of any records that are accessible to the general public or are used for purposes of employment or other background checks in cases determined to be unsubstantiated or false, except that nothing in this section shall prevent State child protective services agencies from keeping information on unsubstantiated reports in their casework files to assist in future risk and safety assessment....

N.H. REV. STAT. ANN. § 169-C:29 (2012) PERSONS REQUIRED TO REPORT

Any physician, surgeon, county medical examiner, psychiatrist, resident, intern, dentist, osteopath, optometrist, chiropractor, psychologist, therapist, registered nurse, hospital personnel (engaged in admission, examination, care and treatment of persons), Christian Science practitioner, teacher, school official, school nurse, school counselor, social worker, day care worker, any other child or foster care worker, law enforcement official, priest, minister, or rabbi or any other person having reason to suspect that a child has been abused or neglected shall report the same in accordance with this chapter.

N.H. REV. STAT. ANN. § 169-C:30 (2012) NATURE AND CONTENT OF REPORT

An oral report shall be made immediately by telephone or otherwise, and followed within 48 hours by a report in writing, if so requested, to the department. Such report shall, if known, contain the name and address of the child suspected of being neglected or abused and the person responsible for the child's welfare, the specific information indicating neglect or the nature and extent of the child's injuries (including any evidence of previous injuries), the identity of the person or persons suspected of being responsible for such neglect or abuse, and any other information that might be helpful in establishing neglect or abuse or that may be required by the department.

N.H. REV. STAT. ANN. § 169-C:31 (2012) IMMUNITY FROM LIABILITY

Anyone participating in good faith in the making of a report pursuant to this chapter is immune from any liability, civil or criminal, that might otherwise be incurred or imposed. Any such participant has the same immunity with respect to participation in any investigation by the department or judicial proceeding resulting from such report.

N.H. REV. STAT. ANN. § 169-C:32 (2012) ABROGATION OF PRIVILEGED COMMUNICATION

The privileged quality of communication between husband and wife and any professional person and his patient or client, except that between attorney and client, shall not apply to proceedings instituted pursuant to this chapter and shall not constitute grounds for failure to report as required by this chapter.

N.H. REV. STAT. ANN. § 169-C:39 (2012) PENALTY FOR VIOLATION

Anyone who knowingly violates any provision of this subdivision shall be guilty of a misdemeanor.

NOTES AND QUESTIONS

1. Under the New Hampshire statute, when is the reporting obligation triggered? Most states require reporting when there is reasonable cause to suspect or believe that a child has been abused or neglected. Other states require reporting when a person has reasonable cause to know, see, e.g., Colo. Rev. Stat. § 19-3-304 (2011); in good faith suspects, see. e.g., Del. Code Ann. tit. 16, § 903 (2010); or has cause to believe or suspect that the child is abused or neglected. See, e.g., La. Child. Code Ann. art. 609 (2011). Do you think these standards are clear? Do you favor this approach to reporting? Why?

2. The majority of states require that once the standard is met, the reporter must make the report "immediately." Some states further define "immediately" as within twenty-four hours, see, e.g., Ga. Code Ann., § 19-7-5(e) (2010); Idaho Code Ann. § 16-1605 (2010); or within forty-eight hours, Tex. Fam. Code Ann. § 261.101(b) (West 2009). Other states use terms such as "promptly," see, e.g., Kan. Stat. Ann. § 38-2223(a) (2009); "as soon as practicable," Conn. Gen. Stat. § 17a-101b (2010); or "at the first opportunity," see, e.g., Wash. Rev. Code § 26.44.030 (2010). Seven states do not impose a time requirement. See, e.g., Del. Code Ann. tit.16, § 903 (2011). Under the New Hampshire law, when must a reporter notify authorities that he or she believes the child has been abused or neglected?

3. Under New Hampshire law, whom should the reporter notify? Most states require reporting directly to the agency in charge of child welfare or to either the agency or the police. A few states require employees of schools and hospitals to report to the head of their institution. See, e.g., N.Y. Soc. Serv. Law § 413 (McKinney 2010). Two states, Arkansas and Florida, direct all reporting to a hotline. See Ark. Code Ann. § 12-18-402 (2010); Fla. Stat. § 39.201 (2010). Do you like the hotline approach? Or do you think reporting directly to the agency is better?

4. Of course, anyone may report a suspected case of child abuse or neglect, but some states require certain individuals to report. When these mandatory reporters fail to report, they may face criminal or civil penalties. Most states make failing to report child abuse a misdemeanor for mandatory reporters. Generally, these statutes specify a punishment requiring not more than six months in jail or a fine of five hundred dollars. See, e.g., Ala. Code § 26-14-13 (2010). However, the punishments vary greatly. In West Virginia, the maximum penalty for failing to report is ten days in jail or a one-hundred-dollar fine. W. Va. Code § 49-6A-8 (2010). In Mississippi, however, failure to report could result in a year in jail or a five-thousand-dollar fine. Miss. Code Ann. § 43-21-353. In Delaware, the civil penalty for failing to report could range from ten thousand dollars to fifty thousand dollars. Del. Code Ann. tit.16, § 914. What are the policy justifications for making failure to report a misdemeanor? A felony? Should failure to report be criminalized at all? One commentator suggests that imposing civil liability on mandated reporters will encourage unsubstantiated reporting, thereby increasing the workload for already overworked child-protection agency workers. Steven J. Singley,

Failure to Report Suspected Child Abuse: Civil Liability of Mandated Reporters, 19 J. Juv. L. 236 (1998). But see Marc A. Franklin & Matthew Ploeger, *Of Rescue and Report: Should Tort Law Impose a Duty to Rescue Endangered Persons or Abused Children?* 40 Santa Clara L. Rev. 991 (2000) (arguing that case for civil duty of easy rescue not established but civil duty to report child abuse closer question because need for child abuse reporting more pressing, child victims unable to articulate harm, less infringement on personal freedoms, act of reporting itself unlikely to harm child or reporter, harm occurs slowly so allows legal system chance to measure harm caused by delay).

5. Most states identify certain professionals as mandatory reporters. Doctors, nurses, teachers, law-enforcement officers, social workers, day-care workers, mental-health workers, clergy, domestic-violence advocates, and other professionals in the child-welfare and juvenile-justice systems are most often required to report child abuse. Eighteen states take a broader approach, requiring that all people must report. See, e.g., Ind. Code § 31-33-5-1 (2011). However, in a few of those states, reporters are obligated to report only when they learned of the abuse in their professional capacities. See, e.g., 23 Pa. Cons. Stat. § 6311 (2010). Oklahoma and Texas require all individuals to report and provide no exceptions from the reporting obligation. See, e.g., Okla. Stat. tit. 10A, § 1-2-101 (2010); Tex. Fam. Code Ann. § 261.101 (West 2009).

6. Reporting statutes vary significantly in regard to the abrogation or retention of evidentiary privileges. The most commonly abrogated privileges are the doctor-patient and husband-wife privileges. Child Welfare Information Gateway, Mandatory Reporters of Child Abuse and Neglect: Summary of State Laws 4 (2010), http:// www.childwelfare.gov:80/systemwide/laws_policies/statutes/manda.pdf. States most often preserve the clergy-penitent privilege, although in many jurisdictions, the privilege may be limited to the confessional. Nevertheless, some states (New Hampshire, North Carolina, Oklahoma, Rhode Island, Texas, and West Virginia) abrogate the privilege entirely. *Id.*

At least twenty-one states explicitly reaffirm the attorney-client privilege. Nevertheless, because a number of states mandate that "all persons" must report, it is not always clear if an attorney must report based on receipt of a confidential communication. Arkansas requires attorneys *ad litem* to report. Ark. Code Ann. § 12-18-402 (2010). Additionally, some states may require certain lawyers, such as district attorneys or judges, to report. Moreover, some states abolish the attorney-client privilege altogether for the purposes of reporting. See, e.g., Miss. Code Ann. § 43-21-353 (2010); Ohio Rev. Code Ann. § 2151.421 (LexisNexis 2010) (privilege abolished for client younger than eighteen); Tex. Fam. Code Ann. § 261.101 (West 2009). Several commentators have been highly critical of legislative attempts to include attorneys as mandatory reporters. See, e.g., Adrienne Jennings Lockie, *Salt in the Wounds: Why Attorneys Should Not Be Mandated Reporters of Child Abuse*, 36 N.M. L. Rev. 125 (2006); Ellen Marrus, *Please Keep My Secret: Child Abuse Reporting Statutes, Confidentiality, and Juvenile Delinquency*, 11 Geo. J. Legal Ethics 509 (1998); Robert P. Mosteller, *Child Abuse Reporting and Attorney-Client Confidences: The Reality and the Specter of Lawyer as Informant*, 42 Duke L.J. 203 (1992).

7. Imagine you are in a state that mandates reporting by attorneys. You are about to meet your juvenile client for the first time. She has been charged with an assault for allegedly hitting her mother. Do you want to tell her about the mandatory-reporting statute? What if she reveals that her mother is abusing her but does not want you to tell anyone?

8. Many scholars have argued that lawyers would be more effective if they worked collaboratively with other professionals across disciplines. See, e.g., *Special Issue on Legal Representation of Children: Proceedings of the UNLV Conference on Representing Children in Families: Children's Advocacy and Justice Ten Years after Fordham, Recommendations of the UNLV Conference on Representing Children in Families: Child Advocacy and Justice Ten Years after Fordham*, 6 Nev. L.J.

592, 598 (2006) (recommending interdisciplinary legal services for children); Annie G. Steinberg, *Child-Centered, Vertically Structured, and Interdisciplinary: An Integrative Approach to Children's Policy, Practice, and Research*, 40 Fam. Ct. Rev. 116 (2002) (discussing child-centered interdisciplinary practice); Christina Zawisza & Adela Beckerman, *Two Heads Are Better Than One: The Case-Based Rationale for Dual Disciplinary Teaching in Child Advocacy Clinics*, 7 Fla. Coastal L. Rev. 631 (2006) (recounting insights with interdisciplinary practice in children and family law matters). Would your answer change if you worked in an interdisciplinary collaborative with other professionals, such as social workers or psychiatrists? For a thoughtful discussion of mandatory reporting within an interdisciplinary collaborative, see Alexis Anderson, Lynn Barenberg, & Paul Tremblay, *Professional Ethics in Interdisciplinary Collaboratives: Zeal, Paternalism and Mandated Reporting*, 13 Clinical L. Rev. 659 (2007). See also Jean Koh Peters, *Concrete Strategies for Managing Ethically-Based Conflicts between Children's Lawyers and Consulting Social Workers Who Serve the Same Client*, 1 Ky. Child. Rts. J. 15 (1991).

9. To receive federal grants under CAPTA, states must have provisions governing immunity for good-faith reporting. 42 U.S.C.A. § 5106a(b)(2)(A)(vii) (2010). Almost all states provide immunity from criminal and civil liability for reporters who make their reports in good faith or some variation of that language. California provides immunity for any report by a mandated reporter, Cal. Penal Code § 11172 (West 2010); and New Jersey provides immunity for any report made, N.J. Stat. Ann. § 9:6-8.13 (West 2010).

Douglas J. Besharov, *Child Abuse Realities: Over-Reporting and Poverty*, 8 Va. J. Soc. Pol'y & L. 165, 195–200 (2000).

Confusion about reporting is largely caused by the vagueness of reporting laws—aggravated by the failure of child protective agencies to provide realistic guidance about deciding to report. As far back as 1987, a national group of thirty-eight child protective professionals from nineteen states met for three days at Airlie House, Virginia, under the auspices of the American Bar Association's National Legal Resource Center for Child Advocacy and Protection in association with the American Public Welfare Association and the American Enterprise Institute. The "Airlie House Group," as it has come to be called, developed policy guidelines for reporting and investigation decision making. (This writer was the "rapporteur" for the effort.) One of the group's major conclusions was that there should be better guidelines for public and professional education about what should and should not be reported. This group urged, "[b]etter public and professional materials are needed to obtain more appropriate reporting." The group specifically recommended that educational materials and programs: (1) clarify the legal definitions of child abuse and neglect, (2) give general descriptions of reportable situations (including specific examples), and (3) explain what to expect when a report is made. Brochures and other materials for laypersons, including public service announcements, should give specific information about what to report—and what not to report.

Based on these recommendations, a relatively clear agenda for reform emerges: (1) clarify child abuse reporting laws, (2) provide continuing public education and professional training, (3) screen reports, (4) modify liability laws, (5) give feedback to persons who report, and (6) adopt an agency policy.

1. Clarify child abuse reporting laws:

Existing laws are often vague and overbroad. They should be rewritten to provide real guidance about what conditions should, and should not, be reported. This can be accomplished without making a radical departure from present laws or practices. The key is to describe reportable conditions in terms of specific parental behaviors or conditions that are tied to severe and demonstrable harms (or potential harms) to children.

It would help, for example, to make a distinction between (1) direct evidence, meaning firsthand accounts or observations of seriously harmful parental behavior, and (2) circumstantial evidence, meaning concrete facts, such as the child's physical condition, which suggest that the child has been abused or neglected. (Behavioral indicators, however, should not, by themselves, be considered a sufficient basis for a report.)

Direct evidence includes: eyewitness observations of a parent's abusive or neglectful behavior; the child's description of being abused or neglected, unless there is a specific reason for disbelief; the parent's own description of abusive or neglectful behavior (unless it is long past); accounts of child maltreatment from spouses or other family members; films, photographs or other visual material depicting a minor's sexually explicit activity; newborns denied nutrition, life-sustaining care, or other medically-indicated treatment; children in physically dangerous situations; young children left alone; apparently abandoned children; demonstrated parental disabilities (for example, mental illness or retardation or alcohol or drug abuse) severe enough to make child abuse or child neglect likely; and demonstrated parental inability to care for a newborn baby.

Circumstantial evidence includes: "suspicious" injuries suggesting physical abuse; physical injuries or medical findings suggesting sexual abuse; signs of sexual activity in young children; signs of severe physical deprivation on the child's body; severe dirt and disorder in the home suggesting general child neglect; apparently untreated physical injuries, illnesses, or impairments suggesting medical neglect; "accidental" injuries suggesting gross inattention to the child's need for safety; apparent parental indifference to a child's severe psychological or developmental problems; apparent parental condemnation of or indifference to a child's misbehavior suggesting improper ethical guidance; chronic and unexplained absences from school suggesting parental responsibility for the non-attendance; and newborns showing signs of fetal exposure to drugs or alcohol.

2. Provide continuing public education and professional training:

Few people fail to report because they want children to suffer abuse and neglect. Likewise, few people make deliberately false reports. Most involve an honest desire to protect children coupled with confusion about what conditions are reportable. Thus, educational efforts should emphasize the conditions that do not justify a report, as well as those that do.

3. Screen reports:

No matter how well professionals are trained and no matter how extensive public education efforts are, there will always be a tendency for persons to report cases that should not be investigated. Until recently, most states did not have formal policies and procedures for determining whether to accept a call for investigation. Such policies should be adopted by all states and they should provide explicit guidance about the kinds of cases that should not be assigned for investigation.

Reports should be rejected when the allegations fall outside the agency's definitions of "child abuse" and "child neglect," as established by state law. Often, the family has a coping problem for which they would be more appropriately referred to another social service agency. Prime examples include children beyond the specified age, alleged perpetrators falling outside the legal definition, and family problems not amounting to child maltreatment. Reports should also be rejected when the caller can give no credible reason for suspecting that the child has been abused or neglected. (Although actual proof of the maltreatment is not required, some evidence is.) Reports whose unfounded or malicious nature is established by specific evidence, of course, should also be rejected. Anonymous reports, reports from estranged spouses, and even previous unfounded reports from the same source should not be automatically rejected, but they need to be carefully evaluated. And, finally, reports in which insufficient information is given to identify or locate the child should likewise be screened (although the information may be kept for later use if a subsequent report about the same child is made).

In questionable circumstances, the agency should contact the caller again before deciding to reject a report. When appropriate, rejected reports should be referred to other agencies that can provide services needed by the family.

4. Modify liability laws:

Current laws provide immunity for anyone who makes a report in good faith, but give no protection to those who, in a good faith exercise of professional judgment, decide that a child has not been abused or neglected and, hence, should not be reported. This combination of immunities and penalties encourages the over-reporting of questionable situations.

5. Give feedback to persons who report:

If persons who report are not told what happened, they may conclude that the agency's response was ineffective or even harmful to the child, and the next time they suspect that a child is maltreated, they may decide not to report. In addition, finding out whether their suspicions were valid also refines their diagnostic skills and thus improves the quality and accuracy of their future reports. Reporters also need such information to interpret subsequent events and to monitor the child's condition.

6. Adopt an agency policy:

Appropriate reporting of suspected child maltreatment requires a sophisticated knowledge of many legal, administrative, and diagnostic matters. To help ensure that staffs respond properly, an increasing number of public and private agencies are adopting formal agency policies about reporting. Some state laws mandate them. The primary purpose of these policies, or agency protocols, is to inform staff members of their obligation to report and of the procedures to be followed. Such formal policies serve another important function use: They are an implicit commitment by agency administrators to support front-line staff members who decide to report. Moreover, the very process of drafting a written document can clarify previously ambiguous or ill-conceived agency policies....

In the wake of welfare reform, the ways in which child protective agencies respond to the condition of poverty takes on added importance. As noted, the combination of over-reporting and the overreaction to poverty-related child maltreatment can endanger children who are in real jeopardy. Social agencies fail to protect children who need help the most—the victims of physical brutality—by not removing them from their abusive parents. At the same time, they overreact to cases of social deprivation in poor families. In fact, poor, socially deprived children are more likely to be placed in foster care than are abused children. These disadvantaged children, in no real danger of physical injury, languish for years in foster care. Living in emotionally traumatic conditions, hundreds of thousands of poor children suffer more harm than if they were simply left at home.

To say that poor children are inappropriately included in programs for abused and neglected children is not the same as saying that they do not have pressing needs, nor that they should not be the concern of public and private programs. But the nature of the intervention should be different—and it should be voluntary. Child protective agencies have not been established as society's response to poverty, and for them to assume this role misdirects their resources from their proper mission.

Margaret F. Brinig, *Choosing the Lesser Evil: Comments on Besharov's "Child Abuse Realities,"* 8 Va. J. Soc. Pol'y & L. 205, 205, 212–214, 216–218, (2000).

Determining the degree of state intervention into intra-family decision making requires an unhappy choice between allowing abuse to continue or interfering with some families that would be better left alone.... The difference in our approach lies in the choice we think is the lesser evil of the two, not that we think that either the harms associated with state involvement or the risk of non-intervention is a good thing....

...Most of the time, children who remain with their parents without intervention are in the very best atmosphere for children. However, once parents have abused children, I believe the presumption shifts, and intervention ought to come more frequently. The stark form of the dilemma, as I see it, is the choice between sometimes unnecessarily interfering with parental autonomy (my choice) and sometimes mistakenly allowing repeated abuse (Mr. Besharov's)....

Mr. Besharov says that no one can know which parents will be repeat child abusers—in other words, that the number of mistaken "false positives" is unacceptably high. I believe there are some indicia that can improve the accuracy of judgments (largely made by social workers or law enforcement officers, but sometimes by judges who decide whether or not to return children to their homes). I would therefore favor the use of profiles that might help identify times when the state should intervene or proceed with termination of parental custody. These profiles focus both on past *behavior* of the parent (since in most cases some abuse will already have occurred) as opposed to mere *characteristics*.... Some behaviors are particularly predictive of repeat abuse once an incident of abuse has been identified. For instance, various studies of abused children show that those with parents who abuse substances are likely candidates for repeat abuse.... I would change the burden of proof from a presumption that a mother who abuses illegal drugs during pregnancy is acting in the best interests of the child to one that presumes that the mother is not, and thus, the child should be removed....

Is Mr. Besharov correct that the categories of abuse are overinclusive and thus contribute to excessive state intervention? Perhaps. But...adopting a more restrictive policy of intervention places the risk of error on a child who might be left with abusive parents, who may face prolonged stay in foster care, or who may confront a return to an abusive home. These harms seem more substantial, especially if we can increase the accuracy of intervention approaches....

Both Professor Besharov and I (and, presumably, most of those who have thought about the problem) would have the area occupied by abusers and the occasions of family interventions correspond exactly. The world being what it is, we cannot do so. Curtailing definitions of abuse does not help parents or children. Parents seem infinitely inventive in abusing their children, and abuse often escalates. Thus, even if it is not obvious at the first sign of abuse that the parent will be a repeat offender, steps must be taken to ensure that the child will not be seriously damaged by remaining in an abusive atmosphere.

In conclusion, Mr. Besharov and I present two different aspects of the same picture. The problem stems from society's inability to accurately predict behavior in combination with the conflicting rights and needs of parents and children. Besharov chooses to protect parental autonomy and, in so doing, hopes to benefit the majority. In contrast, I choose to protect child-victims. Rather than limiting the degree of intervention and placing children at risk of further abuse, I offer suggestions for reducing the incidence of error in intervention decisions.

NOTES AND QUESTIONS

1. What point is Besharov making? Do you think Brinig summarizes his argument accurately? What policy choice would you make?

2. In 1988, Congress directed the U.S. Department of Health and Human Services to collect and analyze data about child abuse and neglect in the United States. 42 U.S.C. § 5104 (2010). The states, the District of Columbia, and Puerto Rico voluntarily submit their maltreatment data to the National Child Abuse and Neglect Data System (NCANDS), which analyzes the data and publishes a report. The first report was issued in 1990, the most recent in 2011. The 2011 report is based on data compiled in federal fiscal year 2010. In 2010, approximately 3.3 million referrals for maltreatment involving an estimated 5.9 million children were made to child-protection service agencies in the United States. U.S. Dep't of Health & Human Servs., Admin. for Children & Families, Admin. on Children, Youth, and Families, Children's Bureau, Child Maltreatment 2010 5 (2011). Three-fifths of all referrals came from professionals. *Id.* Teachers (16.4 percent), law enforcement and legal personnel (16.7 percent), social-services staff (11.5 percent), and medical professionals (8.2 percent) accounted for more than half of all reports. *Id.* at 7–8. Neglect remained the most common form of maltreatment, accounting for 78.3 percent of all maltreated children. *Id.* at 24.

2. INVESTIGATING CHILD ABUSE AND NEGLECT

Child Welfare Information Gateway, Making and Screening Reports of Child Abuse and Neglect: Summary of State Laws 3–4 (2009), http://www.childwelfare.gov/systemwide/laws_policies/statutes/repproc.pdf.

The laws and policies in all jurisdictions specify procedures for the initial response required by the agencies receiving the reports. The ultimate purpose of the reporting system is to ensure the child's safety and well-being. In most States, the agency that receives a report of suspected child abuse or neglect will first screen the report to determine whether it meets the criteria for acceptance. For acceptance, the report must concern actions that meet the statutory definition of child abuse or neglect in that State. Typically, this will involve situations of harm or threatened harm to a child committed by a parent, guardian, or other person responsible for the child's care. Reports that do not meet the statutory criteria are screened out.

Reports that meet the criteria are screened in and accepted for investigation, usually by the State CPS agency. All States require CPS to initiate an investigation in a timely manner, generally within 72 hours. In addition, most States require investigations to be initiated immediately, in as little as 2 hours and no longer than 24 hours, when there is reasonable cause to believe that a child is in imminent danger.

The approaches used to screen reports vary from State to State, but nearly all States utilize a type of safety assessment to determine which reports require immediate responses. Approximately 30 States and the District of Columbia categorize reports based on the level of risk of harm to the child and assign different response times. Eleven States use differential response systems in which more serious cases are assigned to be investigated, and less serious cases are assigned to receive family assessments.

Investigations may be conducted by the child protective agency (CPS), a law enforcement agency, or cooperatively by both agencies; family assessments are conducted by CPS. In approximately 15 States and the Virgin Islands, cases that involve physical or sexual abuse or possible criminal conduct may be investigated by a law enforcement agency. In nine States, reports are referred to law enforcement agencies when the alleged perpetrator is a person other than the parent or other caregiver. Most States also require cross-reporting among professional entities. Typically, reports are shared among social services agencies, law enforcement agencies, and prosecutors' offices.

NOTES AND QUESTIONS

1. According to the Children's Bureau, 22. percent of reports were substantiated; 63.5 percent of cases were unsubstantiated. U.S. Dep't of Health & Human Servs., Admin. for Children & Families, Admin. on Children, Youth, and Families, Children's Bureau, Child Maltreatment 2010 7 (2011). Based on this information, do you think Besharov is right? Why?

2. CAPTA provides funding for the development and implementation of procedures relating to the investigation of child-abuse and -neglect cases. Today, every state has procedures for maintaining records of child abuse and neglect. Most states maintain a centralized statewide database of child-abuse and -neglect investigation records. See, e.g., Ala. Code § 26-14-8 (1998), Alaska Stat. § 47.17.040 (1990), Ariz. Rev. Stat. Ann. §§ 8-804 to 8-804.01 (2012), Cal. Penal Code § 11170 (West 2011), Conn. Gen. Stat. § 17a-101k (2005), Del. Code Ann. tit. 16, § 905 (2010), Fla. Stat. § 39.201 (eff. Oct. 2012), Haw. Rev. Stat. § 350-2 (2010), Idaho Code Ann. § 16-1629 (2010), 325 Ill. Comp. Stat. 5/7.7 (2010), Ind. Code § 31-33-26-2 (2007), Iowa Code § 235A.14 (1997), La. Child. Code Ann. arts. 616–616.2 (2004), Md. Code Ann., Fam. Law § 5-714 (West 2007), Mass. Gen. Laws ch. 119, § 51F (2008), Mich. Comp. Laws § 722.627 (2011), Miss. Code. Ann. § 43-21-257 (2003), Mo. Rev. Stat. § 210.145 (2007), Mont. Code Ann. § 41-3-202 (2005), Neb. Rev. Stat. § 28-718 (2012), Nev. Rev. Stat. § 432.100 (2005), N.H. Rev. Stat. Ann. § 169-C:35 (2010), N.J. Rev. Stat. § 9:6-8.11 (2006),

N.Y. Soc. Serv. Law § 422 (McKinney 2011), N.C. Gen. Stat. § 7B-311 (2010), N.D. Cent. Code § 50-25.1-05.5 (1995), Okla. Stat. tit. 10A, § 1-2-108 (2009), Or. Rev. Stat. § 419B.030 (1993), 23 Pa. Cons. Stat. Ann. § 6331 (1995), R.I. Gen. Laws § 42-72-7 (1979), S.C. Code Ann. § 63-7-1920 (2008), S.D. Codified Laws § 26-8A-10 (2011), Tenn. Code Ann. § 37-1-406 (2012), Tex. Fam. Code Ann. § 261.002 (West 2005), Utah Code Ann. § 62A-4a-1003 (West 2009), Vt. Stat. Ann. tit. 33, § 4916 (2010), Va. Code Ann. § 63.2-1514 (2010), Wyo. Stat. Ann. § 14-3-213 (2005). Central registries and the systematic record keeping of child-abuse and -neglect reports serve to assist in the identification and protection of abused and neglected children. State agencies usually use central registries to facilitate investigation, treatment, and prevention of child abuse and to maintain statistical information for staffing and funding purposes. In a majority of states, central registries may be used by employers to screen individuals seeking employment in child care, education, or health care. Foster care or prospective adoptive parents also will be screened. Typically, central registry records include the child's name and address; the name of the mother, father, or guardian; the names of any siblings; the nature of the harm to the child; the name of the alleged perpetrator; and the findings of any investigations. Some jurisdictions maintain all investigation records, while others may keep only those involving substantiated reports. Who has access to the information, how long the record is maintained, and the procedures for expunging the record vary from state to state.

The Adam Walsh Child Protection and Safety Act of 2006 requires the Department of Health and Human Services (HHS) to create a national child-abuse registry and to conduct a feasibility study regarding implementation issues. In 2009, HHS issued an interim report. U.S. Dept. of Health & Human Servs., Interim Report to the Congress on the Feasibility of a National Child Abuse Registry 1, http:// aspe.hhs.gov/hsp/09/ChildAbuseRegistryInterimReport/report.pdf (May 2009). HHS reached the following four conclusions:

> *Conclusion 1: Potential benefits of a national child abuse registry are largely unknown.* There is no data available with which to quantify improvements in child safety that may result from the implementation of a national child abuse registry. In particular, it is unknown how frequently perpetrators are substantiated for child maltreatment in multiple states. This interim report identifies and describes the major components of anticipated costs of implementing a national child abuse registry. Key among these would be the costs of establishing secure electronic systems to protect the data from unauthorized use, and addressing procedural weaknesses in some jurisdictions' CPS systems to assure the accuracy and reliability of information included in a national registry. The gap in information regarding the frequency with which a national child abuse registry could be helpful to child maltreatment investigators will be a primary focus of additional feasibility study activities.
>
> *Conclusion 2: A lack of incentives for participation could result in a database that includes little information and fails to fulfill its intent.* The submission of data to a national child abuse registry would be voluntary, creating the risk that HHS could create a database to which few jurisdictions would provide data, making it of little practical value. Only if a national child abuse registry is constructed in a way that meets the needs of state and local child protection agencies and creates conditions under which they would be willing to provide the necessary data, could a national registry become a useful child protection tool. Additional work to assess states' likelihood of participating in a national child abuse registry as described in the Adam Walsh Act will be conducted as part of our further feasibility activities.
>
> *Conclusion 3: Before implementation could begin, legislative change would be needed to permit the collection of sufficient information to accurately identify perpetrators.* The Adam Walsh

Act limits identifying information in a national child abuse registry to the perpetrator's name. This statutory language must be changed before a national child abuse registry could be implemented. Because many names are common, name cannot be the only field used to determine whether or not there is a match between the individual about whom an inquiry is made and a perpetrator listed in a national child abuse registry. Even with additional identifying fields, however, high false positive and false negative rates must be anticipated.

Conclusion 4: Clarification is required on several key issues that are ambiguous in the authorizing statute; these must be resolved either within HHS or by Congress before implementation could proceed. Key among these is whether a national registry is to be used only for investigative inquiries or also for child abuse history checks related to employment and licensing purposes. Employment/licensing checks are not mentioned explicitly in the Adam Walsh Act, but would be allowed under the existing statutory language regarding access to information in the national child abuse registry. In many states, such employment checks far outnumber investigative uses of their child abuse registries. Basic decisions are also needed regarding how to maintain restricted access and validate the identities of legitimate users.

Id. at 2. One of the central concerns identified in the HHS report is "procedural weakness": the failure of the states to provide accurate information and a process to challenge the information maintained in the central registries. A number of recent challenges to central registries have met with success. The next case discusses the constitutional problems such registries might create.

HUMPHRIES V. LOS ANGELES COUNTY, STATE OF CALIFORNIA

United States Court of Appeals for the Ninth Circuit

554 F.3d 1170 (2009)

BYBEE, Circuit Judge:

Appellants Craig and Wendy Humphries are living every parent's nightmare. Accused of abuse by a rebellious child, they were arrested, and had their other children taken away from them. When a doctor confirmed that the abuse charges could not be true, the state dismissed the criminal case against them. The Humphries then petitioned the criminal court, which found them "factually innocent" of the charges for which they had been arrested, and ordered the arrest records sealed and destroyed. Similarly, the juvenile court dismissed all counts of the dependency petition as "not true."

Notwithstanding the findings of two California courts that the Humphries were "factually innocent" and the charges "not true," the Humphries were identified as "substantiated" child abusers and placed on California's Child Abuse Central Index ("the CACI"), a database of known or suspected child abusers. As the Humphries quickly learned, California offers no procedure to remove their listing on the database as suspected child abusers, and thus no opportunity to clear their names. More importantly, California makes the CACI database available to a broad array of government agencies, employers, and law enforcement entities and even requires some public and private groups to consult the database before making hiring, licensing, and custody decisions.

This case presents the question of whether California's maintenance of the CACI violates the Due Process Clause of the Fourteenth Amendment because identified individuals are not given a fair opportunity to challenge the allegations against them. We hold that it does.

I. FACTS AND PROCEEDINGS

A. The Statutory Scheme...

California maintains a database of "reports of suspected child abuse and severe neglect," known as the Child Abuse Central Index or CACI. Cal. Penal Code § 11170(a)(2). California has collected such information since 1965, see 1965 Cal. Stat. 1171, and since 1988, the maintenance of the CACI has been governed by the Child Abuse and Neglect Reporting Act ("CANRA"), Cal. Penal Code §§ 11164–11174....

There are many different ways a person can find themself [*sic*] listed in the CACI. CANRA mandates that various statutorily enumerated individuals report instances of known or suspected child abuse and neglect either to a law enforcement agency or to a child welfare agency. *Id.* § 11165.9. These agencies, in turn, are required to conduct "an active investigation," *id.* § 11169(a), which involves investigating the allegation and determining whether the incident is "substantiated, inconclusive, or unfounded," Cal. Code Regs. tit. 11, § 901(a) (2008).

In an attempt by the legislature to demonstrate how many negatives it could place in a single provision, CANRA then provides that the agency shall send the California Department of Justice ("CA DOJ") a written report "of every case it investigates of known or suspected child abuse or severe neglect which is determined not to be unfounded," but that the "agency shall not forward a report to the [CA DOJ] unless it has conducted an active investigation and determined that the report is not unfounded." Cal. Penal Code § 11169(a). CANRA defines a report as "unfounded" if it is "determined by the investigator who conducted the investigation [1] to be false, [2] to be inherently improbable, [3] to involve an accidental injury, or [4] not to constitute child abuse or neglect." *Id.* § 11165.12(a). There is no further definition of what it means for a report to be "false" or "inherently improbable," and no discussion of the standard of proof by which that determination is to be made. Presumably, a report is "not unfounded" if the investigator determines that it meets none of these four criteria.

CANRA defines two other categories of reports, those that are "substantiated" and those that are "inconclusive." A "substantiated report" means that "the investigator who conducted the investigation" determined that the report "constitute[d] child abuse or neglect...based upon evidence that makes it more likely than not that child abuse or neglect occurred." *Id.* § 11165.12(b). An "inconclusive report" means that "the investigator who conducted the investigation" found the report "not to be unfounded, but the findings are inconclusive and there is insufficient evidence to determine whether child abuse or neglect...occurred." *Id.* § 11165.12(c). Both inconclusive and substantiated reports are submitted to the CA DOJ for inclusion in the CACI. *See id.* §§ 11169(a), (c), 11170(a)(3).

To summarize, we understand section 11169(a), when read in conjunction with section 11165.12, to require agencies to investigate all reports of child abuse. Each reported incident of child abuse must then be categorized as (1) "substantiated," meaning it is more likely than not that child abuse or neglect occurred; (2) "inconclusive," meaning there is insufficient evidence to determine whether child abuse and/or neglect occurred; or (3) "unfounded," meaning the report is false, inherently improbable, an accidental injury, or does not constitute child abuse or neglect. It appears that "substantiated" and "inconclusive" reports include everything that is "not unfounded." The agency must submit both "substantiated" and "inconclusive" reports for inclusion in the CACI.

Given the high standard of proof required for a report to be dismissed as "unfounded"—false or inherently improbable—and the low standard of proof required for a report to be categorized as "substantiated"—more likely than not—with "inconclusive" presumably encompassing everything in between, we understand the minimum evidence required for CANRA to compel the submission of a report to be something less than a preponderance, but more than a scintilla. CANRA further requires that the CA DOJ "shall maintain an index of all reports of child abuse and severe neglect submitted pursuant to" the process described above. *Id.* § 11170(a)(1). The CACI is maintained by means of a computerized data bank....

CANRA states that the CA DOJ shall make the information in the CACI available to a broad range of third parties for a variety of purposes. For example, the information in the CACI is made available

> to the State Department of Social Services, or to any county licensing agency that has contracted with the state for the performance of licensing duties... concerning any person who is an applicant for licensure or any adult who resides or is employed in the home of an applicant for licensure or who is an applicant for employment in a position having supervisorial or disciplinary power over a child or children, or who will provide 24-hour care for a child or children in a residential home or facility, pursuant to [various statutory sections].

Cal. Penal Code § 11170(b)(4). The information is also provided to persons "making inquiries for purposes of pre-employment background investigations for peace officers, child care licensing or employment, adoption, or child placement." Cal. Code Regs. tit. 11, § 907(b) (2008); *see also* Cal. Penal Code § 11170(b)(8). The "Court Appointed Special Advocate program that is conducting a background investigation of an applicant seeking employment with the program or a volunteer position as a Court Appointed Special Advocate" also has access to CACI information. Cal. Penal Code § 11170(b)(5).

The scope of CANRA is not limited to California institutions. CANRA makes the CACI information available "to an out-of-state agency, for purposes of approving a prospective foster or adoptive parent or relative caregiver for placement of a child" so long as "the out-of-state statute or interstate compact provision that requires that the information received in response to the inquiry shall be disclosed and used for no purpose other than conducting background checks in foster or adoptive cases." *Id.* § 11170(e)(1). Thus, it appears that if another state's agencies require CACI information for foster or adoptive purposes, the CA DOJ is also obligated to make it available.[1]...

Although CANRA itself only requires that the CA DOJ make this information available, other statutory provisions mandate that certain agencies consult the CACI prior to issuing a variety of state-issued licenses or other benefits. For example, California Health and Safety Code § 1522.1 provides that "[p]rior to granting a license to, or otherwise approving, any individual to care for children, the [State Department of Social Services] shall check the [CACI]." Cal. Health & Safety Code § 1522.1(a); *see id.* § 1502(b). Similarly, in order to work as

1. Although the CACI information can apparently be released under these statutes to administrative agencies, private licensing agencies, private employers, or law enforcement entities, we will generally refer to these groups collectively throughout the opinion as "agencies...."

a volunteer in crisis nurseries, California law mandates that "[v]olunteers shall complete a [CACI] check." *Id.* § 1526.8(b)(2). Also, "[p]rior to granting a license to or otherwise approving any individual to care for children in either a family day care home or a day care center, the [State Department of Social Services] shall check the [CACI]." *Id.* § 1596.877(b). California Welfare and Institutions Code § 361.4 similarly requires that

> [w]henever a child may be placed in the home of a relative, or a prospective guardian or other person who is not a licensed or certified foster parent, the county social worker shall cause a check of the [CACI]...to be requested from the [CA DOJ]. The [CACI] check shall be conducted on all persons over 18 years of age living in the home.

CAL. WELF. & INST. CODE § 361.4(c). Finally, California has implemented a pilot program through the State Department of Social Services ("DSS") to create a "child-centered resource family approval process" in lieu of existing processes for "licensing foster family homes, approving relatives and nonrelative extended family members as foster care providers, and approving adoptive families." *Id.* § 16519.5(a). The approval standards under this statute include "utilizing a check of the [CACI]." *Id.* § 16519.5(d)(1)(A)(i). Based on these provisions, it is apparent that the CACI listing plays an integral role in obtaining many rights under California law, including employment, licenses, volunteer opportunities, and even child custody. See also Alisha M. Santana, *A Pointer System That Points to the Nonexistent: Problems with the Child Abuse Central Index (CACI)*, 4 WHITTIER J. CHILD & FAM. ADVOC. 115, 115–16 (2004) (describing the case of a grandmother denied custody of her grandchildren because DSS discovered two hits on the CACI matching her name)....

CANRA requires that at the time the agency forwards the report to the CA DOJ for inclusion in the CACI, "the agency shall also notify in writing the known or suspected child abuser that he or she has been reported to the [CACI]." CAL. PENAL CODE § 11169(b). The identified child abuser may obtain the report of suspected child abuse and information contained within their CACI listing. *Id.* § 11167.5(b)(11). Understandably, notified individuals who believe that they have wrongfully been included in the CACI would want to be removed from the CACI as expeditiously as possible. CANRA provides that an individual who was originally listed in the CACI pursuant to an "inconclusive or unsubstantiated report" will be deleted from the CACI after ten years, as long as no subsequent report containing his or her name is received within that time period. *Id.* § 11170(a)(3). There is no provision for removing an individual who was originally listed in the CACI pursuant to a "substantiated report"; such a person apparently remains listed in the CACI permanently. *See id.* § 11170(a)(1).

CANRA offers no procedure for challenging a listing on the CACI. CANRA does provide that "[i]f a report has previously been filed which subsequently proves to be unfounded, [the CA DOJ] shall be notified in writing of that fact and shall not retain the report." *Id.* § 11169(a). The statute does not describe who must notify the CA DOJ of that fact, or how the determination that a report has "subsequently prove[d] to be unfounded" is to be made. CANRA also provides that the CACI "shall be continually updated by the department and shall not contain any reports that are determined to be unfounded." *Id.* § 11170(a)(1). By using the passive voice, CANRA fails to specify who is supposed to determine that a report is unfounded, or how to make that decision in order to remove unfounded reports from the CACI.

Apparently, only the submitting agency can decide if a report has proved unfounded. CANRA provides that "[t]he submitting agencies are responsible for the accuracy, completeness, and retention of the reports," thus suggesting that the submitting agencies are also responsible for removing reports that are determined to be unfounded. *Id.* § 11170(a)(2). Furthermore, as explained above, CANRA defines an "unfounded report" as "a report that is determined *by the investigator who conducted the investigation* to be false, to be inherently improbable, to involve an accidental injury, or not to constitute child abuse or neglect." *Id.* § 11165.12(a) (emphasis added); see id. § 11165.12(b) (a "substantiated report" means "a report that is *determined by the investigator*...") (emphasis added). Whether this definition solely references the initial determination of listing someone on the CACI, or whether it also constitutes the definition for a continuing obligation to remove someone from the CACI is unclear. These provisions suggest, however, that the investigator and agency that conducted the investigation are responsible for making, and thus correcting, the determination that a report is unfounded.

Although CANRA itself provides no procedure for an individual to challenge a CACI listing, nothing in the statute prevents a submitting agency from enacting some procedure to allow an individual to challenge their listing or seek to have a determination made that a report is "unfounded." *See id.* § 11170(a)(2). CANRA also contemplates that the CA DOJ "may adopt rules governing recordkeeping and reporting," which may allow the CA DOJ to enact some procedure beyond that provided by CANRA. *Id.* § 11170(a)(1). To this point, we are unaware of any regulations that provide additional regulatory procedures for challenging a listing on the CACI or the validity of the underlying report. To the contrary, the CA DOJ explicitly "presumes that the substance of the information provided is accurate and does not conduct a separate investigation to verify the accuracy of the investigation conducted by the submitting agency." Cal. Code Regs. tit. 11, § 904 (2008).

B. The Humphries' Nightmare

The Humphries' nightmarish encounter with the CANRA system began on March 17, 2001, when S.H., Craig's fifteen year-old daughter from a previous marriage, took their car and drove to her biological mother's home in Utah. S.H. had previously lived in Utah with her biological mother and stepfather and their three younger children. In June 2000, S.H.'s biological mother called Craig and said she wanted S.H. to live with the Humphries in Valencia, California, on a trial basis. The night of March 17, S.H. took the Humphries' car without their knowledge, drove to her mother's home in Utah, and reported that the Humphries had been abusing her for several months. An emergency room physician diagnosed "non-accidental trauma, with extremity contusions."...

Based on an investigation from the Utah police, the victim's statement, and emergency room records describing the victim's allegations, on April 11, 2001, Michael L. Wilson, a detective for the Family Crimes Bureau of the Los Angeles County Sheriff's Department ("LASD"), obtained probable cause warrants to arrest the Humphries for cruelty to a child, Cal. Penal Code § 273a(a), and torture, *id.* § 206. On April 16, Detective Wilson, accompanied by fellow detective Charles Ansberry, arrested Craig and Wendy Humphries, and booked them on the single charge of felony torture under California Penal Code § 206. The same day, a Sheriff's deputy, without a warrant, picked up the Humphries' two other children from their schools and placed them in protective custody.[3] Both children denied any fear of abuse

3. The Humphries have asserted a § 1983 claim regarding the warrantless seizure of the children. That claim is not before us on this appeal.

or mistreatment and indicated their desire to return home. Custody of the children was then transferred to the County Department of Children and Family Services, which placed the children in foster care.

On April 17, 2001, the day after the Humphries were arrested, Detective Wilson completed a child abuse investigation report identifying the Humphries' case as a "substantiated report" of child abuse. Pursuant to CANRA, this information was sent to the CA DOJ, which in turn created a CACI listing identifying Craig and Wendy Humphries as child abuse suspects with a "substantiated" report....

On April 18, 2001, Detective Wilson filed a complaint in the Los Angeles County Superior Court, charging the Humphries with corporal injury to a child, Cal. Penal Code § 273d(a), and cruelty to a child by endangering health, *id.* § 273a(b), both misdemeanors.

On August 29, 2001, the Humphries' criminal case was dismissed. The prosecutor had learned that in November 2000, Dr. Isaac Benjamin Paz surgically removed a melanoma on S.H.'s shoulder. S.H. had follow-up visits with Dr. Paz in December 2000 and March 2001, periods that corresponded with S.H.'s claims of abuse. On all these occasions, Dr. Paz examined S.H.'s entire body, and saw no sign of abuse. The prosecutor determined that this information "contradict[ed] the basic part of [S.H.'s] testimony that she was injured during the entire time" and agreed that the Humphries criminal case for the misdemeanor charges should be dismissed in furtherance of justice. The felony torture charges on which the Humphries had originally been booked were also dismissed.

The Humphries then successfully petitioned the criminal court under California Penal Code § 851.8 for orders finding them "factually innocent" of the felony torture charge, and requiring the arrest records pertaining to that charge be sealed and destroyed. A finding of factual innocence means that the court found "that no reasonable cause exists to believe that the arrestee committed the offense for which the arrest was made." CAL. PENAL CODE § 851.8(b)....

On April 17, 2001, in separate, non-criminal proceedings, Detective Wilson requested that Los Angeles County file a juvenile court dependency petition to have the Humphries' two children declared dependent children of the juvenile court based on the fact that their "sibling has been abused or neglected." On April 19, the County filed a dependency petition against the Humphries based on S.H.'s allegations. After a hearing on June 12, the juvenile court ordered that the Humphries retain custody of their children, and dismissed all counts as "not true." ...[8]

As required by CANRA, in May 2001, the Humphries were notified that they were listed in the CACI. The notice informed them that if they believed the report was unfounded, and they desired a review, that they should address their request to Detective Wilson. In May 2002, the Humphries contacted LASD's Family Crimes Bureau through their attorney. They discovered that Detective Wilson no longer worked at the Bureau and there was no available procedure for them to challenge their listing in the CACI. On May 9, 2002, LASD Sergeant Michael Becker advised the Humphries' attorney that after conducting an investigation, the

8. Under the California Rules of Court, the juvenile court is only authorized to find allegations "true" or "not proved." The state and county parties argue that the juvenile court's "not true" finding does not mean that the allegations are affirmatively false. Regardless, there is no dispute that the juvenile court wrote that the allegations were "not true." Any argument regarding whether the judge should or should not have done so should have been made at the time of the juvenile court proceedings....

LASD would not reverse its report labeling the Humphries as "substantiated" child abusers for the purposes of the CACI. Becker indicated that the fact that charges were filed "would indicate to us that some sort of crime did occur" and the fact that the case was dismissed "would not negate the entries" into the CACI.

In October 2003, the CA DOJ asked LASD to complete a confirmation questionnaire regarding the Humphries' CACI listing. The questionnaire was answered by a civilian clerical worker who confirmed that the report was still "substantiated" as of October 31, 2003. Despite the fact that two independent California tribunals had found that the allegations underlying the Humphries' CACI listing were "not true" and that the Humphries are "factually innocent," the CA DOJ continues to list the Humphries in the CACI as substantiated child abusers. Furthermore, because the Humphries were listed pursuant to a "substantiated report," they will remain listed on the CACI indefinitely.

In addition to the harm already dealt to the Humphries' reputation by appearing on a list of actual or suspected child abusers, the Humphries have also alleged that the CACI now places a burden on their ability to pursue some of their normal goals and activities. The Humphries have indicated that they are hesitant to seek these opportunities for fear that the CACI listing will both influence their ability to obtain certain benefits and further injure their already damaged reputation. For example, the Humphries have expressed a desire to work or volunteer at the Florence Crittenton Center in Los Angeles, a community center offering child care and a variety of other services. Bernice Williams, the Human Resources Manager at the center stated, by affidavit, that all adults must undergo a CACI check prior to obtaining clearance to volunteer or teach at the center. Thus, the Humphries will have to submit to a CACI search before even having an opportunity to volunteer or work at the center.

Similarly, Wendy currently works as a special education teacher and resource specialist at a public school in California. She possesses a number of teaching credentials that must be periodically renewed in order to maintain her current employment—a renewal process that requires her to apply to the California Commission on Teacher Credentialing ("CCTC"). The Humphries have introduced evidence indicating that the information available on the CACI might have an impact on her ability to obtain educational credentials.

Wendy has also indicated a desire to pursue a degree in psychology from the University of California at Los Angeles. Two courses of interest within the psychology department, 134 A/D and 134 B/E, place all of the students in a child care program licensed by the state of California. To enroll in these classes, all potential students must pay for and submit to a CACI check....

The Humphries... sought relief pursuant to 42 U.S.C. § 1983. They alleged that three actions by California officials deprived them of various rights under the United States Constitution: the Humphries' arrest and incarceration, the Humphries' initial and continued inclusion in CACI, and the seizure and subsequent placement of the Humphries' children in temporary protective custody....

Appellees, the County of Los Angeles, Sheriff Leroy D. Baca, and Detectives Wilson and Ansberry ("County Appellees") and California Attorney General Bill Lockyer ("State") (collectively "Appellees"), moved for summary judgment on all claims. The district court denied Appellees' motion for summary judgment on the § 1983 claim regarding the warrantless seizure of the children, but granted Appellees' motion for summary judgment on the § 1983 claim arising out of the Humphries' initial and continued inclusion in the CACI, as well as the § 1983 claim arising out of the Humphries' arrest and incarceration. The Humphries appeal the grant of summary judgment with regard to their claims relating to their inclusion in the CACI, arguing that the Appellees' conduct in listing their names on the CACI and making CACI-related information available to third parties violates their right to due process under the Fourteenth Amendment.

II. ANALYSIS

To establish a prima facie case under § 1983, the Humphries must establish that: (1) the conduct complained of was committed by a person acting under color of state law; and (2) the conduct violated a right secured by the Constitution and laws of the United States. *West v. Atkins*, 487 U.S. 42, 48, 108 S.Ct. 2250, 101 L.Ed.2d 40 (1988). Furthermore, the Supreme Court has insisted that even if there is a qualified immunity issue, we must still consider the threshold question of the "existence or nonexistence of a constitutional right as the first inquiry." *Saucier v. Katz*, 533 U.S. 194, 201, 121 S.Ct. 2151, 150 L.Ed.2d 272 (2001). There is no question that the Humphries' listing on the CACI occurs under color of state law. Thus, the issue in this appeal is whether the initial and continued inclusion of the Humphries on the CACI deprives them of any rights secured by the Constitution and laws of the United States. We find that it does. Accordingly, after our discussion of the existence of a constitutional violation we consider whether the individual and institutional Appellees are entitled to immunity for their acts.

A. Procedural Due Process

The Humphries argue that Appellees violated their Fourteenth Amendment right to procedural due process by listing and continuing to list them on the CACI, without any available process to challenge that listing. In procedural due process claims, the deprivation of a constitutionally protected interest "is not itself unconstitutional; what is unconstitutional is the deprivation of such an interest without due process of law." *Zinermon v. Burch*, 494 U.S. 113, 125, 110 S.Ct. 975, 108 L.Ed.2d 100 (1990). Our analysis proceeds in two steps: "the first asks whether there exists a liberty or property interest which has been interfered with by the State; the second examines whether the procedures attendant upon that deprivation were constitutionally sufficient." *Ky. Dep't of Corr. v. Thompson*, 490 U.S. 454, 460, 109 S.Ct. 1904, 104 L.Ed.2d 506 (1989) (internal citations omitted). The district court found that the Humphries' listing on the CACI did not deprive them of any constitutionally protected liberty or property interest. The court did not reach the second step of the due process analysis.

1. Deprivation of a Protected Liberty Interest

The Humphries contend that they have a liberty interest under the "stigma-plus" test of *Paul v. Davis*, 424 U.S. 693, 96 S.Ct. 1155, 47 L.Ed.2d 405 (1976). The Humphries argue that the stigma of being listed in the CACI as substantiated child abusers, plus the various statutory consequences of being listed on the CACI constitutes a liberty interest, of which they may not be deprived without process of law. We agree.[11]

11. The Humphries also argue that they have a protected liberty interest created by the mandatory language in CANRA; a protected liberty interest in informational and familial privacy arising under the California Constitution;...a protected liberty interest in familial privacy and autonomy under the federal constitution;

In *Wisconsin v. Constantineau*, the Supreme Court held that a liberty interest may be implicated "where a person's good name, reputation, honor, or integrity is at stake because of what the government is doing to him." 400 U.S. 433, 437, 91 S.Ct. 507, 27 L.Ed.2d 515 (1971). The following year the Court stated that a government employee's liberty interest would be implicated if he were dismissed based on charges that "imposed on him a stigma or other disability that foreclosed his freedom to take advantage of other employment opportunities." *Board of Regents v. Roth*, 408 U.S. 564, 573, 92 S.Ct. 2701, 33 L.Ed.2d 548 (1972). In *Paul v. Davis*, the Supreme Court clarified that procedural due process protections apply to reputational harm only when a plaintiff suffers stigma from governmental action plus alteration or extinguishment of "a right or status previously recognized by state law." 424 U.S. 693, 711, 96 S.Ct. 1155, 47 L.Ed.2d 405 (1976). This holding has come to be known as the "stigma-plus test." *See Hart v. Parks*, 450 F.3d 1059, 1070 (9th Cir. 2006)....

As the district court found, being labeled a child abuser by being placed on the CACI is "unquestionably stigmatizing." We have observed that there is "[n]o doubt...that being falsely named as a suspected child abuser on an official government index is defamatory." *Miller v. California*, 355 F.3d 1172, 1178 (9th Cir. 2004); see also *Valmonte v. Bane*, 18 F.3d 992, 1000 (2d Cir. 1994) (finding it beyond dispute that inclusion on a child abuse registry damages reputation by "branding" an individual as a child abuser). Indeed, "no conduct so unequivocally violates American ethics as...sexual predation upon the most vulnerable members of our society." *Nicanor-Romero v. Mukasey*, 523 F.3d 992, 999 (9th Cir. 2008) (citation omitted). The horror deepens when such abuse occurs at the hands of the parents, who have an obligation to protect their children. *See id.* at 1013 (Bybee, J., dissenting) ("Our recognition that the victim's vulnerability or intimate relationship with her victimizer can render an act inherently base or vile simply reflects contemporary American mores").

The Court has identified stigma on the basis of lesser accusations. In Constantineau, the chief of police had posted the plaintiff's name on a list that prohibited her from purchasing alcohol pursuant to a state statute forbidding the sale of alcoholic beverages to persons who had become hazardous by reasons of their "excessive drinking." 400 U.S. at 434–35, 91 S.Ct. 507. In *Paul*, the plaintiff's picture appeared on a flyer of individuals who were suspected of shoplifting. 424 U.S. at 695, 96 S.Ct. 1155. In both cases the Court found stigma. *Constantineau*, 400 U.S. at 435-37, 91 S.Ct. 507; *Paul*, 424 U.S. at 697, 701, 96 S.Ct. 1155 (stating that imputing criminal behavior to an individual is generally considered "defamatory per se" and implicitly finding stigma by holding that stigma alone is insufficient). Being labeled a child abuser is indisputably more stigmatizing than being labeled an excessive drinker or a shoplifter. Indeed, to be accused of child abuse may be our generation's contribution to defamation per se, a kind of moral leprosy....

The more difficult issue is whether the Humphries can satisfy the "plus" test. The Humphries must show that, as the result of being listed in the CACI, "a right or status previously recognized by state law was distinctly altered or extinguished." *Paul*, 424 U.S. at 711, 96

and a protected liberty interest created by the sealing orders and California Penal Code § 851.8. Because we hold that the Humphries have been deprived of due process of law, and because it is not evident they would be entitled to any greater process or remedy if they successfully pressed these remaining liberty interests, we will not reach the merits of these arguments. We also decline to reach the Humphries' ill-developed claims to substantive due process based on a right of parents with children to live without unwarranted government interference and the Appellees' conduct relating to the sealing orders....

S.Ct. 1155; *see also Siegert v. Gilley*, 500 U.S. 226, 233, 111 S.Ct. 1789, 114 L.Ed.2d 277 (1991) (reaffirming that an injury to reputation by itself is not a protected liberty interest under the Fourteenth Amendment).

As the Court explained in *Paul*, when the chief of police in Constantineau posted the plaintiff's name on a list forbidding the sale of alcohol to her, it "significantly altered her status as a matter of state law" by depriving her "of a right previously held under state law[—]the right to purchase or obtain liquor in common with the rest of the citizenry." *Paul*, 424 U.S. at 708, 96 S.Ct. 1155. The Court concluded that "it was that alteration of legal status which, combined with the injury resulting from the defamation, justified the invocation of procedural safeguards." *Id.* at 708–09, 96 S.Ct. 1155.

In *Paul* itself, the Louisville Chief of Police placed Davis' name on a flyer distributed to Louisville merchants containing a list of individuals thought to be active in shoplifting. *Id.* at 695, 96 S.Ct. 1155. In contrast to the mandatory nature of the statute in Constantineau, the flyer merely "came to the attention" of Davis' supervisor who warned him not to repeat his actions in the future. *Id.* at 696, 96 S.Ct. 1155. The Court found that this harm to Davis' reputation was not sufficient to create a liberty interest. *Id.* at 712, 96 S.Ct. 1155. Notably, no law had required the Chief of Police to distribute this flyer, nor did any law require employers to check the list. Thus, although any impairment to Davis' employment opportunities "flow[ed] from the flyer in question," his injury only occurred because the flyer happened to have "c[o]me to the attention of [his] supervisor." *Id.* at 696–97, 96 S.Ct. 1155....

The Humphries allege more than mere reputational harm—being listed on the CACI alters their rights in two general ways. First, state statutes mandate that licensing agencies search the CACI and conduct an additional investigation prior to granting a number of rights and benefits. These rights include gaining approval to care for children in a day care center or home, obtaining a license or employment in child care, volunteering in a crisis nursery, receiving placement or custody of a relative's child, or qualifying as a resource family. These benefits are explicitly conditioned on the agency checking the CACI and conducting an additional investigation. Second, information in the CACI is specifically made available to other identified agencies: state contracted licensing agencies overseeing employment positions dealing with children, persons making pre-employment investigations for "peace officers, child care licensing or employment, adoption, or child placement," individuals in the Court Appointed Special Advocate program conducting background investigations for potential Court Appointed Special Advocates, and out-of-state agencies making foster care or adoptive decisions. Although these agencies are not explicitly required by CANRA to consult the CACI, they may, as a practical matter, be required to do so by their own regulations or practices, as discussed below. Thus, inclusion in the CACI alters the Humphries' legal rights or status in a variety of ways that Californians who are not listed on the CACI are not subject to: applying for custody of a relative's child, becoming guardians or adoptive parents (inside or outside of California), obtaining a license for child care, becoming licensed or employed in a position dealing with children, obtaining employment as a peace-officer, and involvement in adoption and child placement. We have mentioned, and the district court found, that the Humphries were directly affected in their eligibility to work or volunteer at a local community center. The Humphries also introduced evidence indicating that Wendy was affected in her ability to renew her teaching credentials.

We recognize that being listed on the CACI may not fully extinguish the Humphries' rights or status. Agencies that obtain information from the CACI are responsible for "drawing independent conclusions regarding the quality of the evidence disclosed." Thus, for example, inclusion on the CACI does not necessarily bar the Humphries from obtaining a license for child care, but it does guarantee that the licensing entity will conduct an investigation anew before issuing or denying the license. However, we need not find that an agency will necessarily deny the Humphries a license to satisfy the "plus" test. Outright denial would mean that a listing on the CACI has extinguished the Humphries' legal right or status. Rather, *Paul* provides that stigma-plus applies when a right or status is "altered *or* extinguished." 424 U.S. at 711, 96 S.Ct. 1155 (emphasis added).

We hold that where a state statute creates both a stigma and a tangible burden on an individual's ability to obtain a right or status recognized by state law, an individual's liberty interest has been violated. A tangible burden exists in this context where a law effectively requires agencies to check a stigmatizing list and investigate any adverse information prior to conferring a legal right or benefit. As outlined above, California created the CACI via CANRA and explicitly requires agencies to consult the CACI and perform an independent investigation before granting a number of licenses and benefits. This requirement places a tangible burden on a legal right that satisfies the "plus" test.

We find that a tangible burden also exists where the plaintiff can show that, as a practical matter, the law creates a framework under which agencies reflexively check the stigmatizing listing—whether by internal regulation or custom—prior to conferring a legal right or benefit. CANRA appears to create such a legal framework. CANRA explicitly provides that a variety of agencies will have access to the CACI, and we cannot turn a blind eye to the actions of these other agencies merely because they are not explicitly required by statute to receive CACI information.

The record before us on this latter point is admittedly sparse. Nevertheless, as a practical matter, it is difficult to imagine that an agency charged with protecting California's children—through granting or denying licenses to work in child care, allowing people to engage in adoption or child-placement services, or considering potential Court Appointed Special Advocates—would fail to consult the CACI. There is possibly no information more relevant to determining whether a person should be permitted to have a license to work or care for children than whether that person has abused an innocent child in the past. As Bernice Williams, the Human Resources Manager at the Florence Crittenton Center in Los Angeles stated in her affidavit, "Before any adult is cleared to teach at our school, to work at our day care center, or to work or volunteer anywhere within our facility, he or she must undergo Livescan screening, including a [CA DOJ CACI] check." We would be surprised to hear anything differently from other agencies or entities responsible for providing for the safety and education of children. Indeed, on top of the need to protect California's youth, hiring or giving a license to someone without checking the CACI could potentially lead to tort liability under California law. Once an agency consults the CACI and finds adverse information, CANRA requires the agency to conduct an investigation and come to its own conclusion. Cal. Penal Code § 11170(b)(9)(A).

Viewing the evidence in the light most favorable to the Humphries, we conclude that California has implemented a system whereby the CACI is reflexively consulted prior to the conferral of legal rights or benefits under California law, even where the statute does not necessarily require agencies to check the list on its face. The CANRA both stigmatizes the Humphries and creates an impediment to the Humphries' ability to obtain legal rights. The Humphries have asserted the existence of a sufficient liberty interest under the stigma-plus test, of which they may not be deprived without due process of law....

In reaching this holding, we find the Second Circuit's reasoning in *Valmonte v. Bane* persuasive. 18 F.3d 992 (2d Cir. 1994). In *Valmonte*, the Second Circuit heard a challenge to the New York Central Register of Child Abuse and Maltreatment. Under the New York scheme, the Department of Social Services determined whether an allegation of child abuse was "indicated" or "unfounded." *Id.* at 995. If there was "some credible evidence" supporting a complaint, the report was deemed "indicated" and went into the Central Register; otherwise, it was deemed "unfounded," expunged from the Central Register, and destroyed. *Id.* As in California, state agencies, private businesses, and licensing agencies were required to check whether potential employees or applicants were on the Central Register. *Id.* The agency or business could hire the person only if the employer maintained a written record explaining why the person was suitable for employment or a license. *Id.* at 996. The court found that because agencies and employers would learn of Valmonte's inclusion on the Central Register "by operation of law... and... likely... will choose not to hire her due to her status" the New York scheme "[did] not simply defame Valmonte, it place[d] a tangible burden on her employment prospects." *Id.* at 999, 1001. The Second Circuit explained that "[t]his is not just the intangible deleterious effect that flows from a bad reputation. Rather, it is a specific deprivation of her opportunity to seek employment caused by a statutory impediment established by the state." *Id.* at 1001. Valmonte stands for the proposition that to satisfy stigma-plus, a child abuse registry does not need to create a per se bar to employment; it is sufficient that a child abuse registry, by operation of law, creates a "statutory impediment" or a "tangible burden" to being hired. *Id.* at 1001–02. *See also Dupuy v. Samuels*, 397 F.3d 493, 503–04, 509–11 (7th Cir. 2005) (finding that where "child care workers effectively are barred from future employment in the child care field once an indicated finding of child abuse or neglect against them is disclosed to, and used by, licensing agencies" a protected liberty interest is "squarely implicate[d]" under *Paul*).

Appellees argue that the CACI differs from the statute in Valmonte, because there is no requirement in California that an agency maintain a written record explaining why the person was suitable for employment or other government right. We disagree. The CACI requires agencies to undergo the same investigation to independently establish eligibility for a government benefit. The mere fact that agencies in California are not required to write anything down does not place any less of a burden on the Humphries' ability to obtain employment, a license, or custody than Valmonte experienced under the New York statute.

We emphasize that an injury that results merely from simple defamation is not a constitutional liberty interest under the "stigma-plus" test. *Siegert v. Gilley*, 500 U.S. 226, 233–34, 111 S.Ct. 1789, 114 L.Ed.2d 277 (1991). Employment, licensing, custody, or other legal rights under California law are not refused merely because of the deleterious effect of a bad reputation. By operation of law, California has effectively required agencies to consult the CACI, agencies will have to conduct an additional investigation to determine if the Humphries should be eligible for a government benefit, and those agencies will therefore be more hesitant to issue that benefit. As in *Valmonte*, the Humphries will not lose these benefits based merely on their reputation, these benefits "will be refused... simply because [their] inclusion on the list results in an added burden on employers who will therefore be reluctant to hire [them]." 18 F.3d at 1001.

We note that the Eleventh Circuit, in *Smith v. Siegelman*, denied a stigma-plus claim where the plaintiff was designated a child sexual abuser and placed on Alabama's Central Registry on Child Abuse and Neglect. 322 F.3d 1290, 1296–98 (11th Cir. 2003). We think

Smith rests on a different footing. It appears that Alabama did not mandate that potential employers consult the Registry; rather, "the information on the Registry is made available to an employer or potential employer where the employment involves care or supervision of children." *Id.* at 1297; *see also* ALA. CODE § 26-14-8(d) (providing that the information in the registry "may be made available" to employers). Accordingly, the Eleventh Circuit held that the Alabama scheme was governed by Paul because the plaintiff "was [not] denied any right or status other than his not being branded a child sexual abuser." *Id.* at 1297. As we have explained, the CACI is more than a registry that an employer "may" consult. By law, licensing agencies must consult the CACI, investigate, and use the CACI information in making their licensing decisions.... The CACI is much closer to the New York Central Register than the Alabama Registry. *See Valmonte*, 18 F.3d at 1002 (explaining that "the injury associated with the [New York] Central Register is not simply that it exists, or that the list is available to potential employers" but rather that "employers must consult the list").

In addition, the Eleventh Circuit either did not have evidence of or did not consider the possibility that as a result of the statutory framework other entities were effectively required to consult the registry as a matter of internal rule or custom. To the extent that the Eleventh Circuit refuses to recognize a liberty interest where the state functionally requires agencies to consult a stigmatizing list prior to conferring a government benefit, we must disagree. A state can alter a legal right or status without using the word "must"—the word "may" in conjunction with a rule or custom of "must" can equally deprive a citizen of a liberty interest giving rise to a procedural due process claim.

Thus, we conclude that the Humphries' legal rights or status have been altered. First, California has explicitly required some agencies to search a stigmatizing listing and conduct an additional investigation before issuing a license or benefit under state law. Second, California has made CACI information available to a variety of other agencies, and the Humphries have introduced evidence that those agencies—especially agencies charged with ensuring the safety and well-being of children—reflexively check the CACI before issuing a government license or benefit. Thus, being listed on the CACI places an added burden on entities wishing to confer legal rights or benefits, makes the chances of receiving a benefit conferred under California law less likely, and practically guarantees that conferral of that benefit will be delayed. Accordingly, we hold that the Humphries have satisfied the first step of the procedural due process analysis: They have a liberty interest in both their good name and using it to obtain a license, secure employment, become guardians, volunteer or work for CASA, or adopt. Listing the Humphries on the CACI places a tangible burden on their ability to exercise this liberty interest. We proceed to consider whether they have been deprived of this interest without due process of law.

2. Adequacy of the Procedural Safeguards

The Humphries must show that the procedural safeguards of their liberty interest established by the state are constitutionally insufficient to protect their rights. *Ky. Dep't of Corr. v. Thompson*, 490 U.S. 454, 460, 109 S.Ct. 1904, 104 L.Ed.2d 506 (1989). California currently provides some minimal safeguards against erroneously listing someone on the CACI. In the first place, a reporting agency must conduct "an active investigation and determine[] that the report is not unfounded." CAL. PENAL CODE § 11169(a). Once the agency creates the report and forwards it to the CA DOJ, if a report "subsequently proves to be unfounded" the CA DOJ has a duty to "not retain the report." *Id.* Although this entire process is spelled out in the passive voice, it appears that the agency has the duty to correct its files and thus to decide if they are unfounded. *See id.* § 11170(a)(2) ("The submitting agencies are responsible for the accuracy, completeness, and retention of the reports"). CANRA also provides that the CACI "shall be continually updated by the [CA DOJ] and shall not contain any reports that are determined to be unfounded." Cal. Penal Code § 11170(a)(1). Once a report has been made to the CA DOJ and an entry made on the CACI, "the agency shall also notify in writing the known or suspected child abuser that he or she has been reported to the [CACI]." *Id.* § 11169(b).

A person who believes he has been wrongfully listed on the CACI has two possible remedies under CANRA. First, a listed person might try to get the agency who originally reported the information to the CACI to correct its reports. As noted above, it appears that California agencies have a general duty to maintain accurate records and to advise CA DOJ of any report that subsequently proves unfounded. Cal. Penal Code §§ 11169(a), 11170(a)(1). CANRA does not identify how an agency is to ensure that it has accurate records or who is responsible for correcting any errors. The CA DOJ's responsibility is limited to ensuring that the CACI "accurately reflects the report it receives from the submitting agency"—it does not appear to have any duty to ensure the accuracy of the report itself. *Id.* § 11170(a)(2); Cal. Code Regs. tit. 11, § 904 (2008) (stating that the CA DOJ "presumes that the substance of the information provided is accurate and does not conduct a separate investigation to verify the accuracy of the investigation conducted by the submitting agency"). At best, CANRA implies that reports are subject to correction "by the investigator who conducted the investigation." *Id.* § 11165.12. However, California provides no formal mechanism for requesting that an investigator review a report or for appealing an investigator's refusal to revisit a prior report. Thus, for this first avenue of obtaining relief, at best an informal process exists in which the person seeking review must contact the agency blindly and hope the investigator is responsive. It is not clear what a person seeking review is to do if the investigator has transferred from the agency, retired, or died.

Second, the person may rely on a licensing or employing agency to conduct its own investigation and to "draw[] independent conclusions regarding the quality of the evidence disclosed, and its sufficiency for making decisions regarding investigation, prosecution, licensing, placement of a child, employment or volunteer positions with a CASA program, or employment as a peace officer." *Id.* § 11170(b)(9)(A). Indeed, no particular process is required prior to the agency "drawing independent conclusions." Unless the agency unilaterally undertakes its own detailed investigation, it may only perpetuate any errors contained in the original report, even as it draws its own "independent conclusions." In addition, even if the agency has the time, funding, and resources to determine that the evidence contained in the CACI is erroneous or unfounded, it does not have power to expunge the listing. Thus, in the best case scenario for an innocent person placed on the CACI, the only remedy under this avenue for relief is that the agency might still confer the government benefit after taking the time to conduct an added background investigation. The CACI listing, however, remains.

We evaluate the process that California provides persons listed on the CACI under the three part test set out in *Mathews v. Eldridge*, 424 U.S. 319, 335, 96 S.Ct. 893, 47 L.Ed.2d 18 (1976). *Mathews* instructs us to balance (1) the private interest affected by the official action; (2) the risk of erroneous deprivation and the probable value of additional procedural safeguards; and (3) the governmental interest, including the fiscal and administrative burdens of additional procedures. *Id.* The procedural due process inquiry is made "case-by-case based on the total circumstances." *California ex rel. Lockyer v. F.E.R.C.*, 329 F.3d 700, 711 (9th Cir. 2003). We will consider the private and governmental interests first, followed by a discussion of the risk of error in the procedures established by the state.

a. Private Interest

The Humphries' argument in support of their private interest at stake is essentially coextensive with their argument in support of their liberty interest....

b. Governmental Interest

There is no doubt that California has a vital interest in preventing child abuse and that the creation or maintenance of a central index, such as the CACI, is an effective and responsible means for California to secure its interest. *See Santosky v. Kramer*, 455 U.S. 745, 766, 102 S.Ct. 1388, 71 L.Ed.2d 599 (1982); *People v. Stockton Pregnancy Control Med. Clinic*, 203 Cal.App.3d 225, 249 Cal.Rptr. 762, 772 (1988) (finding the goals of detecting and preventing child abuse are a "compelling" government interest). Nevertheless, the operative question is not whether California has a significant interest in maintaining CACI—no one doubts that it does—but rather whether California has a significant interest in having a limited process by which an individual can challenge inclusion on the CACI, and to what extent adding additional processes will interfere with the overarching interest in protecting children from abuse.

We do not question, for example, that California has a significant interest in maintaining even "inconclusive" reports, which are reports that are neither "substantiated" nor "unfounded." *See* Cal. Penal Code §§ 11165.12, 11169(a). Such reports that only hint at abuse, when coupled with other information, can reveal patterns that might not otherwise be detected and can be useful to law enforcement. But it is equally apparent that California can have no interest in maintaining a system of records that contains incorrect or even false information. First, the effectiveness of a system listing individuals that pose a danger to children becomes less effective if a larger and larger percentage of the population erroneously becomes listed due to unsubstantiated claims. To clarify our point through an extreme example, it is obvious that if one hundred percent of the population were erroneously included in the CACI, it would provide no benefit to California in identifying dangerous individuals. Thus, the more false information included in a listing index such as the CACI, the less useful it becomes as an effective tool for protecting children from child abuse. In addition, there is a great human cost in California, as elsewhere, to being falsely accused of being a child abuser. These costs are not only borne by the individuals falsely accused, but by their children and extended families, their neighbors and their employers. Indeed, with the same passion that California condemns the child abuser for his atrocious acts, it has an interest in protecting its citizens against such calumny.

California contends that requiring any process beyond what it currently provides will substantially impair the state's ability to protect children because hearings are time-consuming and drain limited resources, resulting in less efficient delivery of primary services such as protecting children. It is true, of course, that giving individuals some additional procedure by which they can challenge their listing on CACI will impose administrative and fiscal burdens on California. However, generally these burdens are precisely the sort of administrative costs that we expect our government to shoulder. The state has not provided any evidence that the process required to sort through claims of an erroneous listing in the CACI is any more burdensome than the process due in any other context.

c. Risk of Erroneous Deprivation

The final, and perhaps most important, *Mathews* factor is the risk of erroneous deprivation and the probable value of additional procedural safeguards. As we evaluate this factor, we ask "considering the current process, what is the chance the state will make a mistake?" In this case, we ask, "after examining the process by which persons are listed on the CACI, what is the risk of someone being erroneously listed?" In light of the Humphries' allegations—and keeping in mind that we are reviewing a grant of summary judgment in favor of the state—the answer is "quite likely."

Appellees argue that the current procedures present little risk of erroneous deprivation because an agency may transmit a child abuse report only after it "has conducted an active investigation and determined that the report is not unfounded." CAL. PENAL CODE § 11169(a). We are not assuaged. A determination that the report is "not unfounded" is a very low threshold. As we explained above, CANRA defines an "unfounded report" as a report that the investigator determines "to be false, to be inherently improbable, to involve an accidental injury, or not to constitute child abuse or neglect." CAL. PENAL CODE § 11165.12(a). Effectively, a determination that a report is "not unfounded" merely means that the investigator could not affirmatively say that the report is "false." This is the reverse of the presumption of innocence in our criminal justice system: the accused is presumed to be a child abuser and listed in CANRA unless the investigator determines that the report is false, improbable, or accidental. Incomplete or inadequate investigations must be reported for listing on the CACI.

We have no evidence in the record that indicates exactly how many "false positives" reporting agencies receive. *See Broam v. Bogan*, 320 F.3d 1023, 1032 (9th Cir. 2003); *see also Kennedy v. Louisiana*, 554 U.S. 407, 128 S.Ct. 2641, 2663, 171 L.Ed.2d 525 (2008) (noting "[t]he problem of unreliable, induced, and even imagined child testimony"). However, given the high stakes in child abuse cases, presumably an agency investigation and child abuse report can be triggered by as little as an anonymous phone call. It is apparent in such a system there is a real danger of prank and spite calls. California should investigate such reports, and it can—and perhaps should—retain records on any reports it cannot determine to be "unfounded." When it retains all reports that are "not unfounded," it assumes a substantial risk that some of its reports are false, even if the investigator cannot prove to his own satisfaction that they are "unfounded." We understand the need for investigators who work off of hunches, disparate patterns, and minute clues to maintain files on unsubstantiated reports of child abuse for their own investigative purposes. But when such reports find their way into the CACI, there is a real risk that people, like the Humphries, will have to explain publicly how their names ended up on the state's child abuse database.

The record is devoid of any systematic study of the error rate in the CACI. We do note that in a 2004 self-study of CANRA, a California task force reported on a pilot program in San Diego County, where "DOJ discovered that approximately 50 percent of CACI listings originating from [one agency] should be purged because the supporting documentation was no longer maintained at the local level." *Child Abuse and Neglect Reporting Act Task Force Report* 24 (2004). The task force found that "[if] this percentage held true for the entire State it is possible that half of the 800,000 records which DOJ presently maintains in CACI should be purged." *Id.* We will not infer too much from this limited study, except to remark that it confirms our own observations about the low threshold for putting names on the CACI and the tendency to overinclude. As an initial matter then, we conclude that there is a substantial risk that California will deprive innocent persons of their "reputation-plus" by maintaining files on them in the CACI.

Any errors introduced at the time information is posted to the CACI arguably can be corrected. As we have noted, once the information is posted, the CA DOJ must notify the known or suspected child abuser that he has been reported to the CACI. CAL. PENAL CODE § 11169(b). At that point, if the person believes he has been reported in error, he has three options. First, he can try to informally persuade the investigator who reported it in the first place. Second, he can wait until an agency or other entity that is required to consult the CACI receives the information and rely on the agency or other entity's "independent conclusions regarding the quality of the evidence disclosed, and its sufficiency for making decisions." *Id.* § 11170(b)(9)(A). Third, once an agency makes an adverse decision, some persons have a right to appeal the decision in court. *See, e.g.*, CAL. HEALTH & SAFETY CODE § 1526 (providing a hearing after the denial of a license); CAL. FAMILY CODE § 8720 (providing for judicial review of an adoption denial).

None of these means for correcting erroneous information in the CACI is well designed to do so. We consider each in turn.

1. *Persuading the investigator.* First, attempting to persuade the investigating officer is not a satisfactory way to correct the records. The Humphries received notice that their names had been referred to the CACI. They were not told what information was there—although, given their recent experience, they had a pretty good idea—and were told, "If you believe the report is unfounded...please address your request to Detective M. Wilson." In other words, the only recourse offered to the Humphries was to try to get the investigator who had made the original determination that their case was "substantiated" to change his mind. Nothing in CANRA instructs Detective Wilson how to deal with the Humphries.[14] He is not required to respond to the Humphries or address their concerns or pleas in any way, he has been given no standard for reevaluating his initial judgment, and no one else other than Detective Wilson is required to respond to the Humphries. If Detective Wilson refuses to reconsider his original evaluation, the Humphries have no statutory recourse elsewhere within the LASD.

The Humphries are in a tough position. They are not the only ones. Under the California scheme, Detective Wilson has been placed in a difficult situation, because he has been asked to revisit his initial judgment. Detective Wilson is, by training and employment, an investigator, not an adjudicator. That is not to say that investigators do not have to make important judgments; they do, but these judgments are subject to review, and Detective Wilson has none of the usual checks and balances to rely on. In the course of a criminal investigation, he may have his work reviewed by a superior within the LASD, or the District Attorney's office may review his judgment to decide whether to file formal charges. However, these reviews are likely to take place before any information is posted to the CACI and would have no effect

14. Detective Wilson had actually left the department before the Humphries could petition him to revisit his decision. We refer to Detective Wilson in our analysis here as a surrogate for the investigating officer under the statutory scheme to show the limitations in the process afforded by CANRA.

on any review Wilson would undertake at the Humphries' request.[15] Effectively, Detective Wilson has been tasked with being investigator, prosecutor, judge, and jury with respect to the Humphries' CACI listing. He alone makes the initial judgment to place the Humphries on the CACI, with all of its legal consequences. Moreover, his judgment is apparently unreviewable except by himself. Since CANRA does not provide for formal review of a CACI listing, it also means that there are no standards for an investigator to review his prior decisions. Under such circumstances—where there is no standard, no superior outlet for review, and thus no danger of being overturned—it is unlikely that an investigator will, in effect, reverse himself. Any errors made in the initial referral to the CACI are, therefore, likely to be perpetuated through an informal appeal.

The California system asks too much of its investigators in this situation. . . .

2. *Reaching an independent agency conclusion.* Appellees also argue that there is little risk of erroneous deprivation because an agency that has consulted the CACI must base its decision regarding the listed person on its own "independent conclusions." CAL. PENAL CODE § 11170(b)(9)(A). Furthermore, California regulations make it "the responsibility of authorized individuals or entities to obtain and review the underlying investigative report and make their own assessment of the merits of the child abuse report." CAL. CODE REGS. tit. 11, § 902 (2008). The decision maker "shall not act solely upon [CACI] information." *Id.*

First, we note that by the time the decision maker has referenced the CACI and become charged with undertaking an additional investigation, the individual liberty interest in avoiding stigma and alteration of a legal right has already occurred. Of course, the Due Process Clause does not always require the state to offer process to a person prior to the deprivation of a liberty interest, but we note for purposes of determining the adequacy of the process offered by Appellees—additional investigation of a CACI listing to determine if a person should receive a government benefit—is the very type of interference with a liberty interest that an innocent person listed on the CACI seeks to avoid.

Second, even if the agency conducts a thorough investigation, nothing the agency decides affects the CACI listing; that is, even if an agency, conducting its own investigation, decides that the claims against a listed person are unfounded, the agency has no power to correct the CACI listing. The person is stuck in CACI-limbo. Thus, the process proffered by Appellees fails to address the stigma of being listed on the CACI and resolve the fact that other agencies will still be forced to consult the CACI to confer other benefits under the law.

Disregarding these limitations temporarily, it is not clear to us that an agency, in reality, can or will regularly engage in the process required to determine that charges against an individual are unfounded. As a practical matter, when a person's name appears on the CACI, the agency must take that fact seriously and presume that the person has committed some kind of child abuse, even if there is no record of conviction. For example, before issuing a license for child care, we cannot imagine that an agency would issue the license to a person listed on the CACI—if it considers doing so at all—without undertaking an investigation to

15. This is demonstrated clearly in the Humphries' case. Although the Humphries had been booked on felony torture, the district attorney rejected the attempt to file a felony action against them, and only allowed the case to be filed for misdemeanor consideration. The district attorney then dismissed the remainder of the Humphries' case after learning of Dr. Paz's examinations of S.H.'s entire body with no sign of abuse. Nevertheless, this district attorney "review" of Detective Wilson's judgment had no effect on the Humphries' CACI listing.

disprove whatever evidence existed that caused the person to be listed in the first place. To restate it in CANRA's own terms, the agency must satisfy itself that information that was "not unfounded" is "unfounded." The agency must be prepared to contradict the investigating agency.

The older the evidence, or the more involved the allegations, the more expensive it will be for the agency to disprove the allegations. We are not unfamiliar with the budgetary and time constraints that hamper government agencies. An agency with a limited budget, presented with the choice of thoroughly investigating allegations of child abuse so that it can issue a license, or simply denying the license after a cursory investigation so that it can spend its resources elsewhere, can reasonably be expected to choose the latter. We do not mean to imply that California agencies will not behave honestly or forthrightly, but we cannot help but observe that such entities bear a substantial burden, embedded in CANRA, to justify issuing a license to a person listed on the CACI. In sum, any agency—and especially agencies that deal with children—are likely to presume the integrity of the information found on the CACI, assume that individuals listed on the CACI actually abused children, and deny the license rather than risk awarding, for example, a child care license to a listed individual.

This case illustrates these problems. The Humphries allege that they have been erroneously placed on the CACI. In order to clear their name from this stigma, they must apply for a legal right or benefit of the state and subject themselves to an additional investigation before that right or benefit will be conferred. If Craig or Wendy Humphries sought a license to care for children, the licensing agency would have to obtain and review the Humphries' 2001 "file prepared by the child protective agency which investigated the child abuse report." CAL. HEALTH & SAFETY CODE § 1522.1(a). That file contains Detective Wilson's conclusion that the Humphries were "substantiated" child abusers. In order to protect the children that the Humphries will deal with, the agency is going to start with the presumption that it must deny the license unless it finds evidence contrary to Detective Wilson's investigation. So far as we can determine, the Humphries' file does not include the result of the dependency proceeding (including the finding of "not true"), or information about the dropped criminal charges (including the finding of "factually innocent"). Faced with the cost and time of investigating seven-year old allegations, there is no reason to assume that any agency would attempt to track down this information on its own. In the Humphries' case, the existence of such court records, if they could get them before the licensing agency, might go a long way to rebutting the presumption. Other applicants, however, may not be so fortunate as to have faced formal proceedings and had the proceedings resolved so clearly in their favor. In the case of a person who is accused of child abuse, but never formally charged, the agency would have to reinvestigate the underlying allegations, possibly requiring the examination of witnesses in order to satisfy itself that the original charges were erroneous. In the end, the agency may do what Sergeant Becker did when asked to review Detective Wilson's file. He simply relied on the fact that charges were filed as evidence "that some sort of crime did occur" and refused to give any weight to the fact that the charges were dismissed in court.

3. *Seeking court review.* Finally, Appellees argue that some persons adversely affected by decisions resulting from their listing on the CACI may seek redress in the legal system on a case-by-case basis. *See, e.g.*, CAL. HEALTH & SAFETY CODE § 1526 (providing a hearing after the denial of a license); CAL. FAMILY CODE § 8720 (providing for judicial review of an adoption denial). The administrative review process offers some check on the system. As we know from our own experience, court review of agency decisions can be a cumbersome process.

What is most troubling about the states' argument, however, is that even court review cannot solve the problem. Even if an individual is ultimately successful and obtains, for example, a child-care license, the court's favorable disposition has no apparent impact on the individual's listing on the CACI. Thus, the judicial review afforded by the statute faces the same problem as the original agency determination: It cannot end the stigma or the tangible burden on government rights that an individual listed on the CACI faces.

Again, the Humphries' experience is instructive. The Humphries have taken advantage of every procedure available to them, including the California courts. They went to the dependency court, which found that the allegations were "not true" and returned their children to them. They went to the prosecutor, who dropped all the charges against them. They went to the criminal court, which declared them "factually innocent" and sealed their arrest records. None of this had any effect on their CACI listing. They will remain on the CACI until the investigating agency submits corrected information to the system. There is no effective procedure for the Humphries to challenge this listing, and no way for them to be removed from the listing. The Humphries have been given no opportunity to be heard on the CACI listing.

In sum, we are not persuaded that California has provided a sufficient process for ensuring that persons like the Humphries do not suffer the stigma of being labeled child abusers plus the loss of significant state benefits, such as child-care licenses or employment. The processes in place in California do not adequately reduce the risk of error. In *Valmonte*, which we previously discussed, the New York Central Register had far more procedural protections than the CACI—including a hotline for addressing erroneous listings, a formal investigation procedure, and two administrative hearings on expungement—yet the Second Circuit found that there was a high risk of erroneous deprivation. 18 F.3d at 995–97, 1003–04. "The crux of the problem with the procedures," according to the Second Circuit, was that New York's "'some credible evidence' standard results in many individuals being placed on the list who do not belong there." *Id.* at 1004. Again, unlike in California, in New York there was a detailed procedure for expungement from the list. *Id.* at 995–97. When the court looked at that procedure, it determined that seventy-five percent of those challenging their inclusion on the list were successful. *Id.* at 1003. This confirmed to the court that the original listing determination was suspect. *Id.* at 1003–04.

Here, we do not have comparable statistical data on the rate of error because California has no expungement procedure. However, California's standard for referring names to the CACI—"not unfounded"—is, if anything, more encompassing than New York's word formula—"some credible evidence." Additionally, as we previously noted, even California has recognized, in its task force report, that it may have a high error rate on the CACI, perhaps as high as fifty percent. *Child Abuse and Neglect Reporting Act Task Force Report* at 24. We acknowledge that this figure is not necessarily statistically significant, and we will not treat it as such; however, it does serve as a general indication that a large percentage of the individuals listed on the CACI might have a legitimate basis for expungement. If we can learn any lesson from New York's experience, it is that California's CACI has the potential to be overinclusive, and perhaps vastly so. We note that as of 2004, there were an estimated 810,000 suspects on the CACI. *Id.* at 7. We echo the Second Circuit's observation: "[I]t [is] difficult to fathom how such a huge percentage of [Californians] could be included on a list... unless there has been a high rate of error in determinations." *Valmonte*, 18 F.3d at 1004. We conclude that there is a substantial risk that individuals will be erroneously listed on the CACI, and that California offers insufficient means for correcting those errors.

d. Balancing

Mathews requires that we consider the risk of error in light of the individuals' interest and the government's interest. *See Hamdi v. Rumsfeld*, 542 U.S. 507, 529, 124 S.Ct. 2633, 159 L.Ed.2d 578 (2004) ("The *Mathews* calculus... contemplates a judicious balancing of these concerns..."). In the end, this is not a difficult case. The lack of any meaningful, guaranteed procedural safeguards before the initial placement on CACI combined with the lack of any effective process for removal from CACI violates the Humphries' due process rights. Undoubtedly, California has a strong interest in protecting its youngest and most vulnerable residents from abuse, but that interest is not harmed by a system which seeks to clear those falsely accused of child abuse from the state's databases. CANRA creates too great a risk of individuals being placed on the CACI list who do not belong there, and then remaining on the index indefinitely.

Beyond declaring that California's procedural protections are constitutionally inadequate, we do not propose to spell out here precisely what kind of procedure California must create. The state has a great deal of flexibility in fashioning its procedures, and it should have the full range of options open to it. We do not hold that California must necessarily create some hearing prior to listing individuals on CACI. At the very least, however, California must promptly notify a suspected child abuser that his name is on the CACI and provide "some kind of hearing" by which he can challenge his inclusion. *See Goss v. Lopez*, 419 U.S. 565, 578, 95 S.Ct. 729, 42 L.Ed.2d 725 (1975); Henry J. Friendly, "*Some Kind of Hearing*," 123 U. Pa. L.Rev. 1267 (1975) (discussing the various forms that a hearing can take). The opportunity to be heard on the allegations ought to be before someone other than the official who initially investigated the allegation and reported the name for inclusion on the CACI, and the standards for retaining a name on the CACI after it has been challenged ought to be carefully spelled out.

Nothing we have said here infringes on the ability of the police, or other agencies, to conduct a full investigation into allegations of child abuse. The need for such investigations—which, we acknowledge, are intrusive and difficult to conduct—is obvious. Nor does anything we have said undermine the ability of appropriate law enforcement agencies to maintain records on such investigations, even if the investigations do not result in formal charges or convictions. Again, we understand the need for law enforcement to rely on hunches and to collect bits and pieces of information to establish a history or pattern that may lead to formal charges in future cases. The mere maintenance of such investigatory files apart from the CACI does not raise concerns under the Due Process Clause. What California has done is not just maintain a central investigatory file, but attach legal consequences to the mere listing in such files. Once California effectively required agencies to consult the CACI before issuing licenses, the CACI ceased to be a mere investigatory tool. The fact of listing on the CACI became, in substance, a judgment against those listed....

III. CONCLUSION

For the reasons described above, CANRA violates the Humphries' procedural due process rights, in violation of 42 U.S.C. § 1983. We therefore reverse the district court's grant of summary judgment to the State and the County and remand for further proceedings consistent with this opinion.

NOTES AND QUESTIONS

1. What constitutional rights were violated? How?

2. What procedural protections were in place? Why were they inadequate? What procedural protections does the Court say need to be provided?

3. What process is constitutionally sufficient? Must an individual be given a hearing before his name is added to the registry? Who has the burden? Must the state establish that its decisions were correct or that the individual abused or neglected a child? Must the individual challenging the statute show that the state was wrong? What is the burden of proof? See *In re W.B.M.*, 690 S.E.2d 41 (N.C. Ct. App. 2010). Is probable cause sufficient? See *Jamison v. Dep't Soc. Servs., Fam. Div.*, 218 S.W.3d 399 (Mo. 2007).

4. How do we balance the state's interest in protecting children against the constitutional rights of individuals accused of abuse or neglect? Where would you draw the line?

5. Do you think a national child-abuse registry is a good idea? Do you agree with HHS that there are too many procedural weaknesses in the state systems to make such a registry meaningful?

6. The Ninth Circuit ordered the defendants in *Humphries* to pay attorney's fees, totaling approximately $600,000, of which Los Angeles County was to pay $60,000. The county appealed to the Supreme Court, alleging that it was not liable. In a prior decision, *Monell v. New York City Dept. of Social Servs.*, the Court had held that under 42 U.S.C. § 1883, a municipal entity could be held liable only if the injury to plaintiffs was the result of a municipal policy or custom. Because *Monell* dealt directly with monetary damages, the case left open the question whether *Monell* applied when the plaintiffs sought prospective relief. In *Los Angeles County v. Humphries*, 131 S.Ct. 447 (2010), the Supreme Court reversed and remanded on the issue of the county's liability, holding that *Monell* did apply even when plaintiffs sought prospective relief. The Court, however, left the Ninth Circuit's ruling on the due-process violations intact. Do you think the Supreme Court's decision undermines the ability of plaintiffs like the Humphries to sue?

7. *Children's Advocacy Centers.* Some states assign the investigation of child abuse and neglect to Children's Advocacy Centers (CACs). The first CAC in the United States was established in Huntsville, Alabama, in 1985. In 1990, Congress enacted the Victims of Child Abuse Act, Pub. L. No. 101-647, §§ 225–231, 104 Stat. 4798, 4798–4809 (1990). Among other things, the Act provided discretionary funds to promote multidisciplinary child-abuse investigation and prosecution programs. 42 U.S.C. § 13002 (2010). Today, there are approximately seven hundred CACs nationwide. The National Children's Alliance (NCA) accredits CACs. The Office of Juvenile Justice and Delinquency Prevention (OJJDP) supports four Regional Children's Advocacy Centers to help in the development and improvement of CACs across the country.

CACs generally conduct interviews of children in child-friendly surroundings and in age-appropriate ways for the purposes of investigating and prosecuting child abuse and neglect. Typically, the allegations involve sexual or serious physical abuse. The NCA has ten accreditation standards; these require, among other things, that CACs provide a child-appropriate and child-friendly facility, typically separated from police stations, child-services agencies, and the court. Investigations must be conducted by a multidisciplinary team, usually made up of law-enforcement officers, social workers or other child-protective-services investigators, prosecutors, and mental-health and medical professionals. The standards require a single developmentally appropriate interview with the child conducted by an experienced team member, although other members of the team may watch through closed-circuit television or one-way mirrors. NCA also recommends subsequent case reviews, to determine appropriate courses of action and the provision of services. In the weeks after the initial interview, the team reviews the case to give professionals further opportunities to refine planning, share new information, engage in team problem solving, and refer a child for additional services. Accredited CACs also refer children for medical examinations as needed and must work with a child's family to secure needed services, such as child psychotherapy and victims' advocacy services. National Children's Alliance, Standards for Accredited Members—Revised 2008, http://www.nationalchildrensalliance.org/index.php?s=76. Do you think CACs are a good idea? What, if any, concerns do you have?

8. *Emergency removal.* Every state and the District of Columbia authorize the pre-judicial removal of children from their parents' custody. In 2010, there were more than three hundred thousand removals in the United States based on reports from forty-six states, although not all were pre-judicial. Child Maltreatment 2010, *supra*, at 98 tbl. (2011). All fifty states and the District of Columbia authorize emergency removals. On what basis may a state remove a child? Generally, most states permit removal when there is imminent danger of abuse or neglect or to the child's health and welfare as a result of the child's surroundings. *See, e.g.*, Ala. Code § 12-15-306 (2008); Alaska Stat. § 47.10.142 (2004); Ariz. Rev. Stat. Ann. § 8-821 (2008); Ark. Code Ann. § 12-18-1001 (2011); Cal. Welf. & Inst. Code § 305 (West 2012); Colo. Rev. Stat. § 19-1-113 (2003); Conn. Gen. Stat. § 17a-101g (2011); Del. Code Ann. tit. 13, § 2512 (2009); D.C. Code § 16-2309 (2007); Fla. Stat. § 39.401 (2012); Ga. Code Ann. § 15-11-15 (2009); Haw. Rev. Stat. § 587A-8 (2010); Idaho Code Ann. § 16-1608 (2005); 325 Ill. Comp. Stat. § 5/5 (1998); Ind. Code § 31-34-2-3 (1997); Iowa Code § 232.79 (2001); Kan. Stat. Ann. § 38-2242 (2010); Ky. Rev. Stat. Ann. § 620.060 (West 1998); La. Child. Code Ann. art. 621 (2006); Md. Code Ann., Fam. Law § 5-709 (West 1989); Mass. Gen. Laws ch. 119, § 51B (2012); Mich. Comp. Laws § 722.628 (2008); Minn. Stat. § 260C.175 (2010); Miss. Code. Ann. § 43-21-303 (1980); Mo. Rev. Stat. § 210.125 (1982); Mont. Code Ann. § 41-3-301(2011); Neb. Rev. Stat. § 43-248 (2010); Nev. Rev. Stat. § 432B.390 (2011); N.H. Rev. Stat. Ann. § 169-C:6 (2004); N.J. Rev. Stat. § 9:6-8.29 (1999); N.M. Stat. Ann. § 32A-4-6 (West 2009); N.Y. Fam. Ct. Act § 1024 (McKinney 2009); N.C. Gen. Stat. § 7B-500 (2001); N.D. Cent. Code § 27-20-13 (2007); Ohio Rev. Code Ann. § 2151.31 (West 2002); Okla. Stat. tit. 10A, § 1-4-201 (2009); Or. Rev. Stat. § 419B.150 (2001); 42 Pa. Cons. Stat. § 6324 (2002); R.I. Gen. Laws § 14-1-22 (1956); S.C. Code Ann. § 63-7-620 (2008); S.D. Codified Laws § 26-7A-12 (1996); Tenn. Code Ann. § 37-1-114 (1999); Tex. Fam. Code Ann. § 262.104 (West 2005); Utah Code Ann. § 62A-4a-202.1 (West 2012); Vt. Stat. Ann. tit. 33, § 5301 (2010); Va. Code Ann. § 16.1-251 (2010); Wash. Rev. Code § 26.44.050 (2012); W. Va. Code § 49-6-9 (2000); Wis. Stat. § 938.19 (2009); Wyo. Stat. Ann. § 14-3-405 (2005). A few jurisdictions authorize emergency removal if there is some evidence that the child's death may be imminent. *See, e.g.*, Ky. Rev. Stat. Ann. § 620.060 (West 1998). In other states, emergency removal is warranted when the parent is under the influence or has possession of illegal drugs, Ariz. Rev. Stat. Ann. § 8-821 (2008); Tex. Fam. Code Ann. § 262.104 (West 2005); the child is suffering from serious physical injury or needs medical treatment immediately, Ariz. Rev. Stat. Ann. § 8-821 (2008); Mo. Rev. Stat. § 210.125 (1982); N.M. Stat. Ann. § 32A-4-6 (West 2009); S.C. Code Ann. § 63-7-620 (2008); W. Va. Code § 49-6-9 (2000); Wyo. Stat. Ann. § 14-3-405 (2005); the child is suffering from a serious mental or emotional injury, Ariz. Rev. Stat. Ann. § 8-821 (2008); the child has been or is at risk of being sexually abused, Alaska Stat. § 47.10.142 (2004); Ark. Code Ann. § 12-18-103 (2011); Cal. Welf. & Inst. Code § 305 (West 2012); Ky. Rev. Stat. Ann. § 620.060 (West 1998);

Tex. Fam. Code Ann. § 262.104 (West 2005); the child's parents or guardians caused the death of another child as a result of abuse or neglect, N.M. Stat. Ann. § 32A-4-6 (West 2009); the child's parents have been abusive or neglectful toward another child, N.M. Stat. Ann. § 32A-4-6 (West 2009); Ohio Rev. Code Ann. § 2151.31 (West 2002); the child has no parent or caregiver able to provide a safe environment, Ala. Code § 12-15-306 (2008); Fla. Stat. § 39.401 (2012); Haw. Rev. Stat. § 587A-8 (2010); Ky. Rev. Stat. Ann. § 620.060 (West 1998); the child has been abandoned, Alaska Stat. § 47.10.142 (2004); Ark. Code Ann. § 12-18-1001 (2011); Fla. Stat. § 39.401 (2012); N.M. Stat. Ann. § 32A-4-6 (West 2009); S.D. Codified Laws § 26-7A-12 (1996); W. Va. Code § 49-6-9 (2000); Wyo. Stat. Ann. § 14-3-405 (2005); or as a result of the parent's illness or injury, the parent cannot provide for the child, Ga. Code Ann. § 15-11-14 (2009).

The length of time for a postremoval hearing varies from state to state, but most states require a hearing within twenty-four hours, see, e.g., Fla. Stat. § 39.401 (2008); N.H. Rev. Stat. Ann. § 169-C:6 (2004); Tex. Fam. Code Ann. § 262.106 (West 1999) (next working day); Wis. Stat. § 938.21 (2011); forty-eight hours, Alaska Stat. § 47.10.142 (2004); Idaho Code Ann. § 16-1608 (2005); N.J. Rev. Stat. § 9:6-8.30 (2006); N.Y. Fam. Ct. Act § 1026 (McKinney) (petition must be filed within twenty-four hours of removal, and hearing must be held twenty-four hours after petition is filed); Okla. Stat. tit. 10A, § 1-4-203 (2009); Wyo. Stat. Ann. § 14-3-409 (2009); or seventy-two hours, Ala. Code § 12-15-308 (2008); Ga. Code Ann. § 15-11-15 (2009); Haw. Stat. § 587A-15 (2010); Kan. Stat. Ann. § 38-2242 (2010); Ky. Rev. Stat. Ann. § 620.060 (West 1998); Mass. Gen. Laws ch. 119, § 24 (2008); Minn. Stat. § 260C.178 (2012); Ohio Rev. Code Ann. § 2151.31 (West 2002); S.C. Code Ann. § 63-7-710 (2008); S.D. Codified Laws § 26-7A-13.1 (1996); Tenn. Code Ann. § 37-1-114 (1999); Vt. Stat. Ann. tit. 33, § 5307 (2010); or at the earliest possible time, Colo. Rev. Stat. § 19-1-113 (2003). In some jurisdictions, however, hearings may be held between four and ten days after the removal. See, e.g., Ariz. Rev. Stat. Ann. § 8-824 (2010) (seven days); Ark. Code Ann. § 9-27-315 (2005) (five days); Ga. Code Ann. § 15-11-14 (West 2009) (seven days on non-abuse-related matters); Iowa Code § 232.95 (2004) (ten days); N.C. Gen. Stat. § 7B-506 (2007) (if a nonsecure custody order has been entered, then a hearing on the merits must be held within seven days); N.D. Cent. Code § 27-20-17 (2007) (four days); N.M. Stat. Ann. § 32A-4-18 (West 2009) (within ten days); 42 Pa. Cons. Stat. § 6335 (1999) (within ten days); Va. Code Ann. § 16.1-251 (2003) (five business days).

Emergency removals nevertheless trigger constitutional concerns. The federal circuits that have addressed the issue generally agree that a child-abuse or -neglect investigation may involve a search or seizure for Fourth Amendment purposes. But if the Fourth Amendment does apply, must the state have probable cause and a warrant prior to removal, or does one of the exceptions to the warrant requirement apply? Doriane Coleman notes:

> The [Supreme] Court has yet to rule on the applicability of the special needs exception to child welfare investigations. The federal appellate courts, however, began their examination of the broader relationship of the Fourth Amendment to these investigations in the mid-1980s.... [E]ight of the twelve circuits have resolved at least some of the questions that arise in this context.
>
> All eight circuits agree that maltreatment investigations constitute Fourth Amendment "searches" and "seizures," and that CPS and the police participating in such investigations are state actors. Moreover, courts that have had occasion to address the issue have held that although certain aspects of parental privacy are protected under the Fourth and Fourteenth Amendments, the child has enforceable Fourth Amendment rights separate

> from her parents. This is consistent with the Supreme Court's approach in cases where children are subject to official searches and seizures.
>
> The circuits disagree about whether child maltreatment investigations trigger the Fourth Amendment's particularized warrant and probable cause requirements, or whether they come within the special needs exception. Only a few circuits have explicitly discussed "special needs." In effect, however, only the First and Fourth Circuits appear to recognize the exception's applicability at least to certain kinds of child welfare investigations. Five other circuits, the Second, Third, Fifth, Ninth, and Tenth, either categorically or probably have rejected its applicability in this setting. The position of the remaining circuit, the Seventh, is equivocal; it has suggested, in different cases, both that the special needs exception and the arrest standard—a warrant or probable cause or exigent circumstances—applies.
>
> Notably, courts that favor the Fourth Amendment's particularized warrant and probable cause requirements reject the argument that state officials need unfettered discretion to conduct this class of investigations simply because they concern children. Instead, they equate child abuse with other violent crimes for which no exception exists to the Fourth Amendment's usual strictures; they find that the exigent circumstances exception is an adequate tool to protect children who the government legitimately perceives to be at risk; and they recognize that in many of the cases in which the government intrudes, not only does it fail to find abuse or neglect, but it often itself causes substantial harm to children and families through its intervention....
>
> Finally, because all of these appellate decisions have been reached on facts that involve either intrusions into the personal residence—in the guise of investigatory home visits—or interviews coupled with examinations of the children who are the subject of maltreatment reports, we know very little about how the courts would rule in cases involving less intrusive searches and seizures. The fact that the decisions often fail to distinguish between their special needs and reasonableness analyses compound this uncertainty. Thus, for example, the cases tell us little about whether a student's brief detention at school by a state official, such as a teacher, an administrator, a social worker, or a police officer, would trigger the Fourth Amendment's particularized warrant and probable cause requirements in jurisdictions that already use that standard in more intrusive contexts.

Doriane Lambelet Coleman, *Storming the Castle to Save the Children: The Ironic Costs of a Child Welfare Exception to the Fourth Amendment*, 47 Wm. & Mary L. Rev. 413, 469–476, 478–479 (2005). The Supreme Court in *Camreta v. Greene*, 131 S.Ct. 2020 (2011), had an opportunity to clarify whether the Fourth Amendment applied to "less intrusive searches and seizures." In *Camreta*, an interview of a student at school by a social worker and a police officer investigating allegations that she had been sexually abused by her father triggered a Fourth Amendment violation. The Court, however, dismissed the case as moot and ordered the Ninth Circuit opinion finding a Fourth Amendment violation withdrawn. *Id.* at 2035–2036.

Emergency-removal procedures also raise substantive and procedural due process issues. While there seems to be little doubt that the Fourteenth Amendment protects a parental liberty interest, what procedures must be afforded parents before that parental liberty interest may be infringed? In the emergency-removal context, one of the questions is whether state officials must obtain judicial approval *before* removing children from parental custody. Although the Supreme Court has not yet reached the issue, the federal courts of appeals have grappled with the question. The majority view is that a state may remove children from parental custody without a warrant when the children are "threatened with imminent harm [and] when it is justified by emergency circumstances."

Doe v. Kearney, 329 F.3d 1286, 1293 (11th Cir. 2003) (citing *Mabe v. San Bernardino County, Dep't of Pub. Soc. Servs.*, 237 F.3d 1101, 1106 (9th Cir. 2001); *Brokaw v. Mercer County*, 235 F.3d 1000, 1020 (7th Cir. 2000); *Tenenbaum v. Williams*, 193 F.3d 581, 593–594 (2d Cir. 1999); *Hollingsworth v. Hill*, 110 F.3d 733, 739 (10th Cir. 1997); *Jordan by Jordan v. Jackson*, 15 F.3d 333, 346 (4th Cir. 1994)). See also *Brown v. Daniels*, 128 Fed. Appx. 910, 915 (3d Cir. 2005). The mere possibility of danger is insufficient, *Roska v. Peterson*, 328 F.3d 1230, 1245 (10th Cir. 2003); and the circumstances must be "extraordinary," *Hollingsworth*, 110 F.3d at 739. Moreover, the Second Circuit has held that "where there is reasonable time consistent with the safety of the child to obtain a judicial order, the 'emergency' removal of a child is unwarranted." *Tenenbaum*, 193 F.3d at 596.

What is the standard for removing a child under emergency circumstances? A majority of the circuits addressing the issue have held that reasonable suspicion is sufficient. See, e.g., *Gomes v. Woods*, 451 F.3d 1122, 1130 (10th Cir. 2006); *Hatch v. Dep't for Children, Youth, & Their Families*, 274 F.3d 12, 21 (1st Cir. 2001); *Brokaw v. Mercer County*, 235 F.3d 1000, 1019 (7th Cir. 2000); *Croft v. Westmoreland County Children & Youth Servs.*, 103 F.3d 1123, 1126 (3d Cir. 1997); *Thomason v. SCAN Volunteer Servs., Inc.*, 85 F.3d 1365, 1373 (8th Cir. 1996); *Gottlieb v. County of Orange*, 84 F.3d 511, 518 (2d Cir. 1996); *Manzano v. S.D. Dep't of Soc. Servs.*, 60 F.3d 505, 511 (8th Cir. 1995). On the other hand, the Ninth Circuit requires "reasonable cause to believe that the child is in imminent danger of serious bodily injury and that the scope of the intrusion is reasonably necessary to avert that specific injury." *Wallis v. Spencer*, 202 F.3d 1126, 1138 (9th Cir. 2000). Similarly, the Eleventh Circuit has held that the "state may not remove a child from parental custody without judicial authorization unless there is probable cause to believe the child is threatened with imminent harm." *Doe v. Kearney*, 329 F.3d 1286, 1295. After a prejudicial removal has been effectuated, due process mandates a prompt postremoval hearing. *K.D. v. County of Crow Wing*, 434 F.3d 1051, 1056 n. 6 (8th Cir. 2006) (state bears burden to initiate prompt judicial proceedings to provide postdeprivation hearing); *Brokaw v. Mercer County*, 235 F.3d 1000, 1020 (7th Cir. 2000) (due process guarantees prompt and fair postdeprivation hearing); *Campbell v. Burt*, 141 F.3d 927, 929 (9th Cir. 1998) (procedural due process guarantees prompt postdeprivation judicial review); *Weller v. Dep't of Soc. Servs. for Baltimore*, 901 F.2d 387, 396 (4th Cir. 1990) (state has the burden to initiate prompt judicial proceedings). For critiques of emergency removal, *see, e.g.*, Mark R. Brown, *Rescuing Children from Abusive Parents: The Constitutional Value of Pre-Deprivation Process*, 65 Ohio St. L.J. 913 (2004); Paul Chill, *Burden of Proof Begone: The Pernicious Effect of Emergency Removal in Child Protective Proceedings*, 41 Fam. Ct. Rev. 457 (2003); Peggy Cooper Davis & Gautam Barua, *Custodial Choices for Children at Risk: Bias, Sequentiality, and the Law*, 2 U. Chi. L. Sch. Roundtable 139, 146 (1995); Theo Liebmann, *What's Missing from Foster Care Reform? The Need for Comprehensive, Realistic, and Compassionate Removal Standards*, 28 Hamline J. Pub. L. & Pol'y 141 (2006); Michael S. Wald, *State Intervention on Behalf of "Neglected" Children: Standards of Removal of Children from Their Homes, Monitoring the Status of Children in Foster Care, and Termination of Parental Rights*, 28 Stan. L. Rev. 623 (1976); Jessica Dixon Weaver, *The Principle of Subsidiarity Applied: Reforming the Legal Framework to Capture the Psychological Abuse of Children*, 18 Va. J. Soc. Pol'y & Law 247 (2011); Alyson Oswald, Comment, *They Took My Child! An Examination of the Circuit Split over Emergency Removal of Children from Parental Custody*, 53 Cath. U. L. Rev. 1161 (2004).

9. Problem. Steven and Debra have a sixteen-year-old daughter, Clarissa. Steven also has six other children with other women, and Debra also has six other children with other men. Steven and Debra do not live together. Clarissa lives with Steven. Clarissa's school counselor called the Child Abuse Hotline to report that Clarissa had drunk nontoxic paint, had expressed

thoughts of suicide, and was behaving aggressively. She also indicated that Clarissa was living somewhere other than with her father and that the environment was "unsuitable." A social worker with Child Protective Services, Adam, contacted Steven and explained that the hotline had been contacted. Steven said that Clarissa was simply trying to get attention and that he had filed several runaway petitions with the court seeking her return. While Steven said that Adam could visit his apartment, Steven indicated that he did not know why such a home visit was necessary. Adam then told Steven that if he did not "cooperate," Adam would seek a court order. After three attempts to gain access to the home, Adam sought an order to obtain entry to Steven's apartment. The order listed Clarissa's name along with the names of Debra's other children who did not live with Steven but for whom there were abuse or neglect case files. The order was issued, and Adam and several New York police officers entered the apartment. According to Adam, the children were dirty, there was no food in the refrigerator, one of the children had a foot injury, and there was inadequate lighting and little bedding. (Steven disputed this account, indicating that the children were bathed regularly and that there was food, adequate lighting, and bedding.) Adam removed the six children and placed them in emergency foster care pending a hearing. A removal hearing was held forty-eight hours after the children were taken from the apartment. Did the state violate the constitutional rights of Steven and his children? Which rights? Would your answer differ if you knew that subsequent to the children being taken into custody, Clarissa said that she had been sexually abused by Steven, and his other children claimed that they were beaten by Steven and his live-in companion?

10. *Fifth Amendment issues.* Does a parent have a Fifth Amendment privilege to remain silent in child-abuse and -neglect proceedings? William Wesley Patton has describer the Fifth Amendment issue at the investigatory stage this way:

> [At] this early investigative stage...the parents' fifth amendment privilege against self-incrimination is first implicated and is perhaps most in jeopardy for several reasons. First, few parents have counsel prior to the detention hearing. Unrepresented parents usually cooperate with social workers investigating the abuse allegations in order to both quickly regain custody of their child and convince the worker to proceed informally rather than in court. Second, in many jurisdictions the county attorney with discretion to prosecute the parents for criminal child abuse is often the same attorney representing the government in the dependency action. Third, in many jurisdictions the prosecutor in the criminal child abuse trial may discover the parents' dependency pretrial statements contained in social worker reports or made during dependency settlement negotiations. Finally, since parents are not normally in custody during the initial child dependency pretrial investigations, police, social workers and prosecuting attorneys need not give parents Miranda admonitions. Prosecutors thus indirectly gain discovery of parents' statements which would be undiscoverable during formal criminal investigations.

William Wesley Patton, *The World Where Parallel Lines Converge: The Privilege against Self-Incrimination in Concurrent Civil and Criminal Child Abuse Proceedings*, 24 Ga. L. Rev. 473, 478–480 (1990). Some state statutes even permit inferences to be drawn from a parent's silence or noncooperation at depositions and may deem the questions admitted. *Id.* at 483-484. The informalism evident in child-welfare cases encourages parents to "cooperate" while "suppress[ing] rights talk and discourag[ing] parties from using those procedural protections that are available to them." Amy Sinden, *"Why Won't Mom Cooperate?": A Critique of Informality in Child Welfare Proceedings*, 11 Yale J. L. & Feminism 339, 350 (1999). The Supreme Court has considered the parent's right to assert the privilege in the following case.

BALTIMORE CITY DEPARTMENT OF SOCIAL SERVICES V. BOUKNIGHT
Supreme Court of the United States
493 U.S. 549 (1990)

Justice O'Connor delivered the opinion of the Court.

In this action, we must decide whether a mother, the custodian of a child pursuant to a court order, may invoke the Fifth Amendment privilege against self-incrimination to resist an order of the juvenile court to produce the child. We hold that she may not.

I

Petitioner Maurice M. is an abused child. When he was three months old, he was hospitalized with a fractured left femur, and examination revealed several partially healed bone fractures and other indications of severe physical abuse. In the hospital, respondent Bouknight, Maurice's mother, was observed shaking Maurice, dropping him in his crib despite his spica cast, and otherwise handling him in a manner inconsistent with his recovery and continued health. Hospital personnel notified the Baltimore City Department of Social Services (BCDSS)... of suspected child abuse. In February 1987, BCDSS secured a court order removing Maurice from Bouknight's control and placing him in shelter care. Several months later, the shelter care order was inexplicably modified to return Maurice to Bouknight's custody temporarily. Following a hearing held shortly thereafter, the juvenile court declared Maurice to be a "child in need of assistance," thus asserting jurisdiction over Maurice and placing him under BCDSS' continuing oversight. BCDSS agreed that Bouknight could continue as custodian of the child, but only pursuant to extensive conditions set forth in a court-approved protective supervision order. The order required Bouknight to "cooperate with BCDSS," "continue in therapy," participate in parental aid and training programs, and "refrain from physically punishing [Maurice]." The order's terms were "all subject to the further Order of the Court." Bouknight's attorney signed the order, and Bouknight in a separate form set forth her agreement to each term.

Eight months later, fearing for Maurice's safety, BCDSS returned to juvenile court. BCDSS caseworkers related that Bouknight would not cooperate with them and had in nearly every respect violated the terms of the protective order. BCDSS stated that Maurice's father had recently died in a shooting incident and that Bouknight, in light of the results of a psychological examination and her history of drug use, could not provide adequate care for the child. On April 20, 1988, the court granted BCDSS' petition to remove Maurice from Bouknight's control for placement in foster care. BCDSS officials also petitioned for judicial relief from Bouknight's failure to produce Maurice or reveal where he could be found. The petition recounted that on two recent visits by BCDSS officials to Bouknight's home, she had refused to reveal the location of the child or had indicated that the child was with an aunt whom she would not identify. The petition further asserted that inquiries of Bouknight's known relatives had revealed that none of them had recently seen Maurice and that BCDSS had prompted the police to issue a missing persons report and referred the case for investigation by the police homicide division. Also on April 20, the juvenile court, upon a hearing on the petition, cited Bouknight for violating the protective custody order and for failing to appear at the hearing. Bouknight had indicated to her attorney that she would appear with the child, but also expressed fear that if she appeared the State would "'snatch the child.'" The court issued an order to show cause why Bouknight should not be held in civil contempt for failure to produce the child. Expressing concern that Maurice was endangered or perhaps dead, the court issued a bench warrant for Bouknight's appearance.

Maurice was not produced at subsequent hearings. At a hearing one week later, Bouknight claimed that Maurice was with a relative in Dallas. Investigation revealed that the relative had not seen Maurice. The next day, following another hearing at which Bouknight again declined to produce Maurice, the juvenile court found Bouknight in contempt for failure to produce the child as ordered. There was and has been no indication that she was unable to comply with the order. The court directed that Bouknight be imprisoned until she "purge[d] herself of contempt by either producing [Maurice] before the court or revealing to the court his exact whereabouts."

The juvenile court rejected Bouknight's subsequent claim that the contempt order violated the Fifth Amendment's guarantee against self-incrimination. The court stated that the production of Maurice would purge the contempt and that "[t]he contempt is issued not because she refuse[d] to testify in any proceeding... [but] because she has failed to abide by the Order of this Court, mainly [for] the production of Maurice M." While that decision was being appealed, Bouknight was convicted of theft and sentenced to 18 months' imprisonment in separate proceedings. The Court of Appeals of Maryland vacated the juvenile court's judgment upholding the contempt order. *In re Maurice M.*, 314 Md. 391, 550 A.2d 1135 (1988). The Court of Appeals found that the contempt order unconstitutionally compelled Bouknight to admit through the act of production "a measure of continuing control and dominion over Maurice's person" in circumstances in which "Bouknight has a reasonable apprehension that she will be prosecuted." *Id.*, at 403–404, 550 A.2d, at 1141. CHIEF JUSTICE REHNQUIST granted BCDSS' application for a stay of the judgment and mandate of the Maryland Court of Appeals, pending disposition of the petition for a writ of certiorari. 488 U.S. 1301 (1988) (in chambers). We granted certiorari, 490 U.S. 1003 (1989), and we now reverse.

II

The Fifth Amendment provides that "No person... shall be compelled in any criminal case to be a witness against himself." The Fifth Amendment's protection "applies only when the accused is compelled to make a testimonial communication that is incriminating." *Fisher v. United States*, 425 U.S. 391, 408 (1976); see *Doe v. United States*, 487 U.S. 201, 207, 209–210, n. 8 (1988) (*Doe II*); *Schmerber v. California*, 384 U.S. 757, 761 (1966) ("[T]he privilege protects an accused only from being compelled to testify against himself, or otherwise provide the State with evidence of a testimonial or communicative nature"). The juvenile court concluded that Bouknight could comply with the order through the unadorned act of producing the child, and we thus address that aspect of the order. When the government demands that an item be produced, "the only thing compelled is the act of producing the [item]." *Fisher, supra*, 425 U.S. at 410, n. 11; see *United States v. Doe*, 465 U.S. 605, 612 (1984) (*Doe I*). The Fifth Amendment's protection may nonetheless be implicated because the act of complying with the government's demand testifies to the existence, possession, or authenticity of the things produced. See *Doe II, supra*, 487 U.S., at 209; *Doe I, supra*, 465 U.S., at 612–614, and n. 13; *Fisher, supra*, 425 U.S., at 410–413. But a person may not claim the Amendment's protections based upon the incrimination that may result from the contents or nature of the thing demanded. *Doe I*, 465 U.S., at 612, and n. 10; *id.*, at 618 (O'Connor, J., concurring); *Fisher, supra*, 425 U.S., at 408–410. Bouknight therefore cannot claim the privilege based upon anything that examination of Maurice might reveal, nor can she assert the privilege upon the theory that compliance would assert that the child produced is in fact Maurice (a fact the State could readily establish, rendering any testimony regarding existence or authenticity insufficiently incriminating, see *Fisher, supra*, at 411). Rather, Bouknight claims the benefit of the privilege because the act of production would amount to testimony regarding her control over, and possession of, Maurice. Although the State could readily introduce evidence of Bouknight's continuing control over the child—e.g., the custody order, testimony of relatives, and Bouknight's own statements to Maryland officials before invoking the privilege—her implicit communication of control over Maurice at the moment of production might aid the State in prosecuting Bouknight.

The possibility that a production order will compel testimonial assertions that may prove incriminating does not, in all contexts, justify invoking the privilege to resist production. Even assuming that this limited testimonial assertion is sufficiently incriminating and "sufficiently testimonial for purposes of the privilege," *Fisher, supra*, at 411, Bouknight may not invoke the privilege to resist the production order because she has assumed custodial duties related to production and because production is required as part of a noncriminal regulatory regime.

The Court has on several occasions recognized that the Fifth Amendment privilege may not be invoked to resist compliance with a regulatory regime constructed to effect the State's public purposes unrelated to the enforcement of its criminal laws. In *Shapiro v. United States*, 335 U.S. 1 (1948), the Court considered an application of the Emergency Price Control Act of 1942 and a regulation issued thereunder which required licensed businesses to maintain records and make them available for inspection by administrators. The Court indicated that no Fifth Amendment protection attached to production of the "required records," which the "'defendant was required to keep, not for his private uses, but for the benefit of the public, and for public inspection.'" *Id.*, at 17–18 (quoting *Wilson v. United States*, 221 U.S. 361, 381 (1911)). The Court's discussion of the constitutional implications of the scheme focused upon the relation between the Government's regulatory objectives and the Government's interest in gaining access to the records in Shapiro's possession:

> "It may be assumed at the outset that there are limits which the Government cannot constitutionally exceed in requiring the keeping of records which may be inspected by an administrative agency and may be used in prosecuting statutory violations committed by the recordkeeper himself. But no serious misgiving that those bounds have been overstepped would appear to be evoked when there is a sufficient relation between the activity sought to be regulated and the public concern so that the Government can constitutionally regulate or forbid the basic activity concerned, and can constitutionally require the keeping of particular records, subject to inspection by the Administrator." 335 U.S., at 32.

See also *In re Harris*, 221 U.S. 274, 279 (1911) (Holmes, J.) (regarding a court order that a bankrupt produce account books, "[t]he question is not of testimony but of surrender—not of compelling the bankrupt to be a witness against himself in a criminal case, past or future, but of compelling him to yield possession of property that he no longer is entitled to keep"). The Court has since refined those limits to the government's authority to gain access to items or information vested with this public character. The Court has noted that "the requirements at issue in Shapiro were imposed in 'an essentially non-criminal and regulatory area of inquiry,'" and that Shapiro's reach is limited where requirements "are directed to a 'selective group inherently suspect of criminal activities.'" *Marchetti v. United States*, 390 U.S. 39, 57 (1968) (quoting *Albertson v. Subversive Activities Control Board*, 382 U.S. 70, 79 (1965)); see *Grosso v. United States*, 390 U.S. 62, 68 (1968) (*Shapiro* inapplicable because "[h]ere, as in *Marchetti*, the statutory obligations are directed almost exclusively to individuals inherently suspect of criminal activities"); *Haynes v. United States*, 390 U.S. 85, 98–99 (1968).

California v. Byers, 402 U.S. 424 (1971), confirms that the ability to invoke the privilege may be greatly diminished when invocation would interfere with the effective operation of a generally applicable, civil regulatory requirement. In *Byers*, the Court upheld enforcement of California's statutory requirement that drivers of cars involved in accidents stop and provide their names and addresses. A plurality found the risk of incrimination too insubstantial to implicate the Fifth Amendment, *id.*, at 427–428, and noted that the statute "was not intended to facilitate criminal convictions but to promote the satisfaction of civil liabilities," *id.*, at 430, was "'directed at the public at large,'" *ibid.* (quoting *Albertson v. Subversive Activities Control Board*, *supra*, 382 U.S., at 79), and required disclosure of no inherently illegal activity. See also *United States v. Sullivan*, 274 U.S. 259 (1927) (rejecting Fifth Amendment objection to requirement to file income tax return). Justice Harlan, the author of *Marchetti*, *Grosso*, and *Haynes*, concurred in the judgment. He distinguished those three cases as considering statutory schemes that "focused almost exclusively on conduct which was criminal," 402 U.S., at 454. While acknowledging that in particular cases the California statute would compel incriminating testimony, he concluded that the noncriminal purpose and the general applicability of the reporting requirement demanded compliance even in such cases. *Id.*, at 458.

When a person assumes control over items that are the legitimate object of the government's noncriminal regulatory powers, the ability to invoke the privilege is reduced. In *Wilson v. United States*, *supra*, the Court surveyed a range of cases involving the custody of public documents and records required by law to be kept because they related to "the appropriate subjects of governmental regulation and the enforcement of restrictions validly established." *Id.*, 221 U.S., at 380. The principle the Court drew from these cases is:

> "[W]here, by virtue of their character and the rules of law applicable to them, the books and papers are held subject to examination by the demanding authority, the custodian has no privilege to refuse production although their contents tend to criminate him. In assuming their custody he has accepted the incident obligation to permit inspection." *Id.*, at 382.

See also *Braswell v. United States*, 487 U.S. 99, 109–113 (1988); *Curcio v. United States*, 354 U.S. 118, 123–124 (1957) ("A custodian, by assuming the duties of his office, undertakes the obligation to produce the books of which he is custodian in response to a rightful exercise of the State's visitorial powers"). In *Shapiro*, the Court interpreted this principle as extending well beyond the corporate context, 335 U.S., at 16–20, and emphasized that Shapiro had assumed and retained control over documents in which the Government had a direct and particular regulatory interest. *Id.*, at 7–8. Indeed, it was in part Shapiro's custody over items having this public nature that allowed the Court in *Marchetti*, *supra*, 390 U.S., at 57, *Grosso*, *supra*, 390 U.S., at 69, and *Haynes*, *supra*, 390 U.S., at 99, to distinguish the measures considered in those cases from the regulatory requirement at issue in *Shapiro*.

These principles readily apply to this case. Once Maurice was adjudicated a child in need of assistance, his care and safety became the particular object of the State's regulatory interests. See 314 Md., at 404, 550 A.2d, at 1141; Md.Cts. & Jud.Proc.Code Ann. §§ 3-801(e), 3-804(a) (Supp. 1989); see also App. 105 ("This court has jurisdiction to require at all times to know the whereabouts of the minor child. We asserted jurisdiction over that child in the spring of 1987..."). Maryland first placed Maurice in shelter care, authorized placement in foster care, and then entrusted responsibility for Maurice's care to Bouknight. By accepting care of Maurice subject to the custodial order's conditions (including requirements that she cooperate with BCDSS, follow a prescribed training regime, and be subject to further court orders), Bouknight submitted to the routine operation of the regulatory system and agreed to hold Maurice in a manner consonant with the State's regulatory interests and subject to inspection by BCDSS. Cf. *Shapiro v. United States, supra*. In assuming the obligations attending custody, Bouknight "has accepted the incident obligation to permit inspection." *Wilson*, 221 U.S., at 382. The State imposes and enforces that obligation as part of a broadly directed, noncriminal regulatory regime governing children cared for pursuant to custodial orders. See Md.Cts. & Jud.Proc.Code Ann. § 3-802(a) (1984) (setting forth child protective purposes of subtitle, including "provid[ing] for the care, protection, and wholesome mental and physical development of children coming within the provisions of this subtitle"); see also Md.Cts. & Jud.Proc. Code Ann. § 3-820(b), (c) (Supp.1989); *In re Jessica M.*, 312 Md. 93, 538 A.2d 305 (1988).

Persons who care for children pursuant to a custody order, and who may be subject to a request for access to the child, are hardly a "'selective group inherently suspect of criminal activities.'" *Marchetti, supra*, 390 U.S., at 57 (quoting *Albertson v. Subversive Activities Control Board*, 382 U.S., at 79). The juvenile court may place a child within its jurisdiction with social service officials or "under supervision in his own home or in the custody or under the guardianship of a relative or other fit person, upon terms the court deems appropriate." Md.Cts. & Jud.Proc.Code Ann. § 3-82(c)(1)(i) (Supp.1989). Children may be placed, for example, in foster care, in homes of relatives, or in the care of state officials. See, *e.g.*, *In re Jessica M., supra*; *In re Arlene G.*, 301 Md. 355, 483 A.2d 39 (1984); *Maryland Dept. of Health and Mental Hygiene v. Prince George's County Dept. of Social Services*, 47 Md.App. 436, 423 A.2d 589 (1980). Even when the court allows a parent to retain control of a child within the court's jurisdiction, that parent is not one singled out for criminal conduct, but rather has been deemed to be, without the State's assistance, simply "unable or unwilling to give proper care and attention to the child and his problems." Md.Cts. & Jud.Proc.Code Ann. § 3-801(e) (Supp. 1989); see *In re Jertrude O.*, 56 Md.App. 83, 466 A.2d 885 (1983), cert. denied, 298 Md. 309, 469 A.2d 863 (1984). The provision that authorized the juvenile court's efforts to gain production of Maurice reflects this broad applicability. See Md.Cts. & Jud.Proc.Code Ann. § 3-81(c) (1984) ("If a parent, guardian, or custodian fails to bring the child before the court when requested, the court may issue a writ of attachment directing that the child be taken into custody and brought before the court. The court may proceed against the parent, guardian, or custodian for contempt"). This provision "fairly may be said to be directed at... parents, guardians, and custodians who accept placement of juveniles in custody." 314 Md., at 418, 550 A.2d, at 1148 (McAuliffe, J., dissenting).

Similarly, BCDSS' efforts to gain access to children, as well as judicial efforts to the same effect, do not "focu[s] almost exclusively on conduct which was criminal." *Byers*, 402 U.S., at 454 (Harlan, J., concurring in judgment). Many orders will arise in circumstances entirely devoid of criminal conduct. Even when criminal conduct may exist, the court may properly request production and return of the child, and enforce that request through exercise of the contempt power, for reasons related entirely to the child's well-being and through measures unrelated to criminal law enforcement or investigation. See Maryland Cts. & Jud.Proc.Code Ann. § 3-81(c) (1984). This case provides an illustration: concern for the child's safety underlay the efforts to gain access to and then compel production of Maurice. Finally, production in the vast majority of cases will embody no incriminating testimony, even if in particular cases the act of production may incriminate the custodian through an assertion of possession or the existence, or the identity, of the child. Cf. *Byers*, 402 U.S., at 430–431; *id.*, at 458 (Harlan, J., concurring in judgment). These orders to produce children cannot be characterized as efforts to gain some testimonial component of the act of production. The government demands production of the very public charge entrusted to a custodian, and makes the demand for compelling reasons unrelated to criminal law enforcement and as part of a broadly applied regulatory regime. In these circumstances, Bouknight cannot invoke the privilege to resist the order to produce Maurice.

We are not called upon to define the precise limitations that may exist upon the State's ability to use the testimonial aspects of Bouknight's act of production in subsequent criminal proceedings. But we note that imposition of such limitations is not foreclosed. The same custodial role that limited the ability to resist the production order may give rise to corresponding limitations upon the direct and indirect use of that testimony. See *Braswell*, 487 U.S., at 118, and n. 11. The State's regulatory requirement in the usual case may neither compel incriminating testimony nor aid a criminal prosecution, but the Fifth Amendment protections are not thereby necessarily unavailable to the person who complies with the regulatory requirement after invoking the privilege and subsequently faces prosecution. See *Marchetti*, 390 U.S., at 58–59 (the "attractive and apparently practical" course of subsequent use restriction is not appropriate where a significant element of the regulatory requirement is to aid law enforcement); see also *Leary v. United States*, 395 U.S. 6, 26–27 (1969); *Haynes*, 390 U.S., at 100; *Grosso*, 390 U.S., at 69; cf. *Doe I*, 465 U.S., at 617, n. 17 (scope of restriction). In a broad range of contexts, the Fifth Amendment limits prosecutors' ability to use testimony that has been compelled. See *Simmons v. United States*, 390 U.S. 377, 391–394 (1968) (no subsequent admission of testimony provided in suppression hearing); *Murphy v. Waterfront Comm'n of New York Harbor*, 378 U.S. 52, 75–76, 79 (1964) (Fifth Amendment bars use, in criminal processes, in other jurisdictions of testimony compelled pursuant to a grant of use immunity in one jurisdiction); *Maness v. Meyers*, 419 U.S. 449, 474–475 (1975) (White, J., concurring in result); *Adams v. Maryland*, 347 U.S. 179, 181 (1954) ("[A] witness does not need any statute to protect him from the use of self-incriminating testimony he is compelled to give over his objection. The Fifth Amendment takes care of that without a statute"); see also *New Jersey v. Portash*, 440 U.S. 450 (1979); *Garrity v. New Jersey*, 385 U.S. 493, 500 (1967). But cf. *Doe I*, *supra*, 465 U.S., at 616–617 (construing federal use immunity statute, 18 U.S.C. §§ 6001–6005); *Pillsbury Co. v. Conboy*, 459 U.S. 248, 261–262 (1983) (declining to supplement previous grant of federal use immunity).

III

The judgment of the Court of Appeals of Maryland is reversed, and the cases are remanded to that court for further proceedings not inconsistent with this opinion....

Justice Marshall, with whom Justice Brennan joins, dissenting.

Although the Court assumes that respondent's act of producing her child would be testimonial and could be incriminating, it nonetheless concludes that she cannot invoke her privilege against self-incrimination and refuse to reveal her son's current location. Neither of the reasons the Court articulates to support its refusal to permit respondent to invoke her constitutional privilege justifies its decision. I therefore dissent.

I

The Court correctly assumes that Bouknight's production of her son to the Maryland court would be testimonial because it would amount to an admission of Bouknight's physical control over her son. See *Fisher v. United States*, 425 U.S. 391, 410 (1976) (acts of production are testimonial if they contain implicit statement of fact). Accord, *United States v. Doe*, 465 U.S. 605, 612–613 (1984). The Court also assumes that Bouknight's act of production would be self-incriminating. I would not hesitate to hold explicitly that Bouknight's admission of possession or control presents a "'real and appreciable'" threat of self-incrimination. *Marchetti v. United States*, 390 U.S. 39, 48 (1968). Bouknight's ability to produce the child would conclusively establish her actual and present physical control over him, and thus might "prove a significant 'link in a chain' of evidence tending to establish [her] guilt." *Ibid.* (footnote omitted).

Indeed, the stakes for Bouknight are much greater than the Court suggests. Not only could she face criminal abuse and neglect charges for her alleged mistreatment of Maurice, but she could also be charged with causing his death. The State acknowledges that it suspects that Maurice is dead, and the police are investigating his case as a possible homicide. In these circumstances, the potentially incriminating aspects to Bouknight's act of production are undoubtedly significant.

II

Notwithstanding the real threat of self-incrimination, the Court holds that "Bouknight may not invoke the privilege to resist the production order because she has assumed custodial duties related to production and because production is required as part of a noncriminal regulatory regime." In characterizing Bouknight as Maurice's "custodian," and in describing the relevant Maryland juvenile statutes as part of a noncriminal regulatory regime, the Court relies on two distinct lines of Fifth Amendment precedent, neither of which applies to this litigation.

A

The Court's first line of reasoning turns on its view that Bouknight has agreed to exercise on behalf of the State certain custodial obligations with respect to her son, obligations that the Court analogizes to those of a custodian of the records of a collective entity. This characterization is baffling, both because it is contrary to the facts of this case and because this Court has never relied on such a characterization to override the privilege against self-incrimination except in the context of a claim of privilege by an agent of a collective entity.[1]

1. The Court claims that the principle espoused in the collective entity cases was "extend[ed] well beyond the corporate context" in *Shapiro v. United States*, 335 U.S. 1 (1948). *Shapiro*, however, did not rest on the existence of an agency relationship between a collective entity and the custodian of its records. Instead, the

Jacqueline Bouknight is Maurice's mother; she is not, and in fact could not be, his "custodian" whose rights and duties are determined solely by the Maryland juvenile protection law. See Md.Cts. & Jud.Proc.Code Ann. § 3-801(j) (Supp. 1989) (defining "custodian" as "person or agency to whom legal custody of a child has been given by order of the court, other than the child's parent or legal guardian"). Although Bouknight surrendered physical custody of her child during the pendency of the proceedings to determine whether Maurice was a "child in need of assistance" (CINA) within the meaning of the Maryland Code, § 3-801(e), Maurice's placement in shelter care was only temporary and did not extinguish her legal right to custody of her son. See § 3-801(r). When the CINA proceedings were settled, Bouknight regained physical custody of Maurice and entered into an agreement with the Baltimore City Department of Social Services (BCDSS). In that agreement, which was approved by the juvenile court, Bouknight promised, among other things, to "cooperate with BCDSS," but she retained legal custody of Maurice.

A finding that a child is in need of assistance does not by itself divest a parent of legal or physical custody, nor does it transform such custody to something conferred by the State. See, *e.g.*, *In re Jertrude O.*, 56 Md.App. 83, 97–98, 466 A.2d 885, 893 (1983) (proving a child is a CINA differs significantly from proving that the parent's rights to legal and physical custody should be terminated). Thus, the parent of a CINA continues to exercise custody because she is the child's parent, not because the State has delegated that responsibility to her. Although the State has obligations "[t]o provide for the care, protection, and wholesome mental and physical development of children" who are in need of assistance, Md.Cts. & Jud.Proc.Code Ann. § 3-802(a)(1) (1984), these duties do not eliminate or override a parent's continuing legal obligations similarly to provide for her child.

In light of the statutory structure governing a parent's relationship to a CINA, Bouknight is not acting as a custodian in the traditional sense of that word because she is not acting on behalf of the State. In reality, she continues to exercise her parental duties, constrained by an agreement between her and the State. That agreement, which includes a stipulation that Maurice was a CINA, allows the State, in certain circumstances, to intercede in Bouknight's relationship with her child. It does not, however, confer custodial rights and obligations on Bouknight in the same way corporate law creates the custodial status of a corporate agent.

Moreover, the rationale for denying a corporate custodian Fifth Amendment protection for acts done in her representative capacity does not apply to this case. The rule for a custodian of corporate records rests on the well-established principle that a collective entity, unlike a natural person, has no Fifth Amendment privilege against self-incrimination. See *Hale v. Henkel*, 201 U.S. 43, 69–70 (1906) (corporation has no privilege); *United States v. White*, 322 U.S. 694, 701 (1944) (labor union has no privilege). Because an artificial entity can act only

petitioner was denied the Fifth Amendment privilege because the records sought were kept as part of a generalized regulatory system that required all businesses, unincorporated as well as incorporated, to retain records of certain transactions. See 335 U.S., at 22–23, 27, 33. *Shapiro* turned on the Court's view "that the privilege which exists as to private papers cannot be maintained in relation to 'records required by law to be kept in order that there may be suitable information of transactions which are the appropriate subjects of governmental regulation and the enforcement of restrictions validly established.'" *Id.*, at 33 (quoting *Davis v. United States*, 328 U.S. 582, 589–590 (1946)). See also *Marchetti v. United States*, 390 U.S. 39, 57 (1968) (describing rationale in *Shapiro*); ante, at 907 (emphasizing that *Shapiro* had custody of "documents in which the Government had a direct and particular regulatory interest" (emphasis added)). Thus, *Shapiro* is properly analyzed with the cases concerning testimony required as a part of a noncriminal regulatory regime, rather than with the cases concerning testimony compelled from custodians of collective entities' records.

through its agents, a custodian of such an entity's documents may not invoke her personal privilege to resist producing documents that may incriminate the entity, even if the documents may also incriminate the custodian. *Wilson v. United States*, 221 U.S. 361, 384–385 (1911). As we explained in *White*:

> "[I]ndividuals, when acting as representatives of a collective group, cannot be said to be exercising their personal rights and duties nor to be entitled to their purely personal privileges. Rather they assume the rights, duties and privileges of the artificial entity or association of which they are agents or officers and they are bound by its obligations.... And the official records and documents of the organization that are held by them *in a representative rather than in a personal capacity* cannot be the subject of the personal privilege against self-incrimination, even though production of the papers might tend to incriminate them personally." 322 U.S., at 699 (citations omitted; emphasis added).

Jacqueline Bouknight is not the agent for an artificial entity that possesses no Fifth Amendment privilege. Her role as Maurice's parent is very different from the role of a corporate custodian who is merely the instrumentality through whom the corporation acts. I am unwilling to extend the collective entity doctrine into a context where it denies individuals, acting in their personal rather than representative capacities, their constitutional privilege against self-incrimination.

B

The Court's decision rests as well on cases holding that "the ability to invoke the privilege may be greatly diminished when invocation would interfere with the effective operation of a generally applicable, civil regulatory requirement." The cases the Court cites have two common features: they concern civil regulatory systems not primarily intended to facilitate criminal investigations, and they target the general public. See *California v. Byers*, 402 U.S. 424, 430–431 (1971) (determining that a "hit and run" statute that required a driver involved in an accident to stop and give certain information was primarily civil). In contrast, regulatory regimes that are directed at a "'selective group inherently suspect of criminal activities,'" *Marchetti*, 390 U.S., at 57 (quoting *Albertson v. Subversive Activities Control Board*, 382 U.S. 70, 79 (1965)), do not result in a similar diminution of the Fifth Amendment privilege.

1

Applying the first feature to this case, the Court describes Maryland's juvenile protection scheme as "a broadly directed, noncriminal regulatory regime governing children cared for pursuant to custodial orders." The Court concludes that Bouknight cannot resist an order necessary for the functioning of that system. The Court's characterization of Maryland's system is dubious and highlights the flaws inherent in the Court's formulation of the appropriate Fifth Amendment inquiry. Virtually any civil regulatory scheme could be characterized as essentially noncriminal by looking narrowly or, as in this case, *solely* to the avowed noncriminal purpose of the regulations. If one focuses instead on the practical effects, the same scheme could be seen as facilitating criminal investigations. The fact that the Court holds Maryland's juvenile statute to be essentially noncriminal, notwithstanding the overlapping purposes underlying that statute and Maryland's criminal child abuse statutes, proves that the Court's test will never be used to find a relationship between the civil scheme and law enforcement goals significant enough to implicate the Fifth Amendment.

The regulations embodied in the juvenile welfare statute are intimately related to the enforcement of state criminal statutes prohibiting child abuse, Md.Ann.Code, Art. 27, § 35A (1987). State criminal decisions suggest that information supporting criminal convictions is often obtained through civil proceedings and the subsequent protective oversight by BCDSS. See, *e.g.*, Lee v. State, 62 Md.App. 341, 489 A.2d 87 (1985). See also 3 Code of Md.Regs. §§ 07.02.07.08(A)(1) and 07.02.07.08(C)(1)(b) (1988) (requiring Social Services Administration to maintain a Child Abuse Central Registry and allowing law enforcement officials access to the Registry). In this respect, Maryland's juvenile protection system resembles the revenue system at issue in *Marchetti*, which required persons engaged in the business of accepting wagers to provide certain information about their activities to the Federal Government. Focusing on the effects of the regulatory scheme, the Court held that this revenue system was not the sort of neutral civil regulatory scheme that could trump the Fifth Amendment privilege. Even though the Government's "principal interest [was] evidently the collection of revenue," 390 U.S., at 57, the information sought would increase the "likelihood that any past or present gambling offenses [would] be discovered and successfully prosecuted," *id.*, at 52.

In contrast to *Marchetti*, the Court here disregards the practical implications of the civil scheme and holds that the juvenile protection system does not "'focu[s] almost exclusively on conduct which was criminal.'" I cannot agree with this approach. The State's goal of protecting children from abusive environments through its juvenile welfare system cannot be separated from criminal provisions that serve the same goal. When the conduct at which a civil statute aims—here, child abuse and neglect—is frequently the same conduct subject to criminal sanction, it strikes me as deeply problematic to dismiss the Fifth Amendment concerns by characterizing the civil scheme as "unrelated to criminal law enforcement or investigation." . . . A civil scheme that *inevitably* intersects with criminal sanctions may not be used to coerce, on pain of contempt, a potential criminal defendant to furnish evidence crucial to the success of her own prosecution.

I would apply a different analysis, one that is more faithful to the concerns underlying the Fifth Amendment. This approach would target respondent's particular claim of privilege, the precise nature of the testimony sought, and the likelihood of self-incrimination caused by this respondent's compliance. "To sustain the privilege, it need only be evident from the implications of the question, in the setting in which it is asked, that a responsive answer to the question or an explanation of why it cannot be answered might be dangerous because injurious disclosure could result." *Hoffman v. United States*, 341 U.S. 479, 486–487 (1951). Accord, *Marchetti*, *supra*, 390 U.S., at 48; *Malloy v. Hogan*, 378 U.S. 1, 11–12 (1964). This analysis unambiguously indicates that Bouknight's Fifth Amendment privilege must be respected to protect her from the serious risk of self-incrimination.

An individualized inquiry is preferable to the Court's analysis because it allows the privilege to turn on the concrete facts of a particular case, rather than on abstract characterizations concerning the nature of a regulatory scheme. Moreover, this particularized analysis would not undermine any appropriate goals of civil regulatory schemes that may intersect with criminal prohibitions. Instead, the ability of a State to provide immunity from criminal prosecution permits it to gather information necessary for civil regulation, while also preserving the integrity of the privilege against self-incrimination. The fact that the State throws a wide net in seeking information does not mean that it can demand from the few persons whose Fifth Amendment rights are implicated that they participate in their own criminal prosecutions. Rather, when the State demands testimony from its citizens, it should do so with an explicit grant of immunity.

2

The Court's approach includes a second element; it holds that a civil regulatory scheme cannot override Fifth Amendment protection unless it is targeted at the general public. Such an analysis would not be necessary under the particularized approach I advocate. Even under the Court's test, however, Bouknight's right against self-incrimination should not be diminished because Maryland's juvenile welfare scheme clearly is not generally applicable. A child is considered in need of assistance because "[h]e is mentally handicapped or is not receiving ordinary and proper care and attention, and... [h]is parents... are unable or unwilling to give proper care and attention to the child and his problems." Md.Cts. & Jud.Proc. Code Ann. § 3-801(e) (Supp. 1989). The juvenile court has jurisdiction only over children who are alleged to be in need of assistance, not over all children in the State. See § 3-804(a). It thus has power to compel testimony only from those parents whose children are alleged to be CINA's. In other words, the regulatory scheme that the Court describes as "broadly directed," is actually narrowly targeted at parents who through abuse or neglect deny their children the minimal reasonable level of care and attention. Not all such abuse or neglect rises to the level of criminal child abuse, but parents of children who have been so seriously neglected or abused as to warrant allegations that the children are in need of state assistance are clearly "a selective group inherently suspect of criminal activities."

III

In the end, neither line of precedents relied on by the Court justifies riding roughshod over Bouknight's constitutional privilege against self-incrimination. The Court cannot accurately characterize her as a "custodian" in the same sense as the Court has used that word in the past. Nor is she the State's "agent," whom the State may require to act on its behalf. Moreover, the regulatory scheme at issue here is closely intertwined with the criminal regime prohibiting child abuse and applies only to parents whose abuse or neglect is serious enough to warrant state intervention.

Although I am disturbed by the Court's willingness to apply inapposite precedent to deny Bouknight her constitutional right against self-incrimination, especially in light of the serious allegations of homicide that accompany this civil proceeding, I take some comfort in the Court's recognition that the State may be prohibited from using any testimony given by Bouknight in subsequent criminal proceedings.[2] Because I am not content to deny Bouknight

2. I note, with both exasperation and skepticism about the bona fide nature of the State's intentions, that the State may be able to grant Bouknight use immunity under a recently enacted immunity statute, even though it has thus far failed to do so. See 1989 Md.Laws, ch. 288 (amending § 9-123). Although the statute applies only to testimony "in a criminal prosecution or a proceeding before a grand jury of the State," Md.Cts. & Jud.Proc.Code Ann. § 9-123(b)(1) (Supp. 1989), the State represented to this Court that "[a]s a matter of law, [granting limited use immunity for the testimonial aspects of Bouknight's compliance with the production order] would now be possible," Tr. of Oral Arg. 10. If such a grant of immunity has been possible since July 1989 and the State has refused to invoke it so that it can litigate Bouknight's claim of privilege, I have difficulty believing that the State is sincere in its protestations of concern for Maurice's well-being.

the constitutional protection required by the Fifth Amendment *now* in the hope that she will not be convicted *later* on the basis of her own testimony, I dissent.

NOTES AND QUESTIONS

1. According to the Court, why were Bouknight's rights not violated? How is she not compelled to incriminate herself? Do you think the analogy to record keeping is a sound one?

2. Do you think the dissent has the better argument? Why?

3. Under the civil contempt doctrine, a court may order the contemnor jailed for refusing to comply with a court order. The imprisonment is not punishment but rather a way for the court to ensure compliance with the court's orders. Once the contemnor agrees to comply with the court's orders, the court will order his or her release. In this sense, the contemnor "holds the keys" to his or her own prison cell. In 1995, after what may be one of the longest contempt terms ever served, Judge David Mitchell ordered Jacqueline Bouknight to be released from jail after seven years. Bouknight has never revealed Maurice's whereabouts, other than to say that he is still alive. See *Mother Ends 7-Year Jail Stay, Still Silent about Missing Child*, New York Times, Nov. 2, 1995, at A18. Her contempt sentence was longer than she would have served had she been convicted of manslaughter. Albert W. Alschuler, *A Peculiar Privilege in Historical Perspective: The Right to Remain Silent*, 94 Mich. L. Rev. 2625, 2636 n. 43 (1996).

4. After *Bouknight* was decided, a number of commentators criticized the decision. See, e.g., William Wesley Patton, *The World Where Parallel Lines Converge: The Privilege against Self-Incrimination in Concurrent Civil and Criminal Child Abuse Proceedings*, 24 Ga. L. Rev. 473 (1990); Irene Merker Rosenberg, *Bouknight: Of Abused Children and the Parental Privilege against Self-Incrimination*, 76 Iowa L. Rev. 535 (1991); Geoffrey J. English, Recent Developments, *Child Abuse and the Fifth Amendment: Baltimore City Department of Social Services v. Bouknight*, 13 Harv. J. L. & Pub. Pol'y 1017 (1990); Peter Marshall Varney, *State v. Adams: When Mommy Talks, You Better Pay Attention. And, If No Indictment Has Been Issued, You Can Use Her Uncounseled Statements Against Her in Court*, 76 N.C. L. Rev. 2388 (1998).

5. In *Ohio v. Reiner*, 532 U.S. 17 (2001), the defendant was prosecuted for the death of his child on the theory that he had shaken the infant, causing massive trauma to the child's brain ("shaken baby syndrome"). At trial, the defense theory was that the twenty-four-year-old nanny had caused the injuries. The nanny asserted her Fifth Amendment privilege while simultaneously declaring her innocence. Granted transactional immunity, the nanny then testified that she had nothing to do with the injuries sustained by the child. The defendant was convicted, given a suspended sentence, and placed on probation for five years. In a *per curiam* decision, the Supreme Court held that the Fifth Amendment privilege applies where a witness's answers "could reasonably 'furnish a link in the chain of evidence' against him." *Id.* at 19. Because she was alone with the child for extended periods of time within the time frame during which the child received his fatal injuries and the defense theory targeted her as the perpetrator, the Court concluded that she had a valid Fifth Amendment privilege against self-incrimination. *Id.* at 21–22. Recall that Bouknight also asserted her innocence. How can we reconcile *Reiner* with *Bouknight*?

3. STATE LIABILITY FOR FAILING TO ACT

DESHANEY V. WINNEBAGO COUNTY DEPARTMENT OF SOCIAL SERVICES
Supreme Court of the United States
489 U.S. 189 (1989)

CHIEF JUSTICE REHNQUIST delivered the opinion of the Court.

Petitioner is a boy who was beaten and permanently injured by his father, with whom he lived. Respondents are social workers and other local officials who received complaints that petitioner was being abused by his father and had reason to believe that this was the case, but nonetheless did not act to remove petitioner from his father's custody. Petitioner sued respondents claiming that their failure to act deprived him of his liberty in violation of the Due Process Clause of the Fourteenth Amendment to the United States Constitution. We hold that it did not.

I

The facts of this case are undeniably tragic. Petitioner Joshua DeShaney was born in 1979. In 1980, a Wyoming court granted his parents a divorce and awarded custody of Joshua to his father, Randy DeShaney. The father shortly thereafter moved to Neenah, a city located in Winnebago County, Wisconsin, taking the infant Joshua with him. There he entered into a second marriage, which also ended in divorce.

The Winnebago County authorities first learned that Joshua DeShaney might be a victim of child abuse in January 1982, when his father's second wife complained to the police, at the time of their divorce, that he had previously "hit the boy causing marks and [was] a prime case for child abuse." App. 152–153. The Winnebago County Department of Social Services (DSS) interviewed the father, but he denied the accusations, and DSS did not pursue them further. In January 1983, Joshua was admitted to a local hospital with multiple bruises and abrasions. The examining physician suspected child abuse and notified DSS, which immediately obtained an order from a Wisconsin juvenile court placing Joshua in the temporary custody of the hospital. Three days later, the county convened an ad hoc "Child Protection Team"—consisting of a pediatrician, a psychologist, a police detective, the county's lawyer, several DSS caseworkers, and various hospital personnel—to consider Joshua's situation. At this meeting, the Team decided that there was insufficient evidence of child abuse to retain Joshua in the custody of the court. The Team did, however, decide to recommend several measures to protect Joshua, including enrolling him in a preschool program, providing his father with certain counselling services, and encouraging his father's girlfriend to move out of the home. Randy DeShaney entered into a voluntary agreement with DSS in which he promised to cooperate with them in accomplishing these goals.

Based on the recommendation of the Child Protection Team, the juvenile court dismissed the child protection case and returned Joshua to the custody of his father. A month later, emergency room personnel called the DSS caseworker handling Joshua's case to report that he had once again been treated for suspicious injuries. The caseworker concluded that there was no basis for action. For the next six months, the caseworker made monthly visits to the DeShaney home, during which she observed a number of suspicious injuries on Joshua's head; she also noticed that he had not been enrolled in school, and that the girlfriend had not moved out. The caseworker dutifully recorded these incidents in her files, along with her continuing suspicions that someone in the DeShaney household was physically abusing Joshua, but she did nothing more. In November 1983, the emergency room notified DSS that Joshua had been treated once again for injuries that they believed to be caused by child abuse. On the caseworker's next two visits to the DeShaney home, she was told that Joshua was too ill to see her. Still DSS took no action.

In March 1984, Randy DeShaney beat 4-year-old Joshua so severely that he fell into a life-threatening coma. Emergency brain surgery revealed a series of hemorrhages caused by traumatic injuries to the head inflicted over a long period of time. Joshua did not die, but he suffered brain damage so severe that he is expected to spend the rest of his life confined to an institution for the profoundly retarded. Randy DeShaney was subsequently tried and convicted of child abuse.

Joshua and his mother brought this action under 42 U.S.C. § 1983 in the United States District Court for the Eastern District of Wisconsin against respondents Winnebago County, DSS, and various individual employees of DSS. The complaint alleged that respondents had deprived Joshua of his liberty without due process of law, in violation of his rights under the Fourteenth Amendment, by failing to intervene to protect him against a risk of violence at his father's hands of which they knew or should have known. The District Court granted summary judgment for respondents.

The Court of Appeals for the Seventh Circuit affirmed, 812 F.2d 298 (1987), holding that petitioners had not made out an actionable § 1983 claim for two alternative reasons. First, the court held that the Due Process Clause of the Fourteenth Amendment does not require a state or local governmental entity to protect its citizens from "private violence, or other mishaps not attributable to the conduct of its employees." *Id.*, at 301. In so holding, the court specifically rejected the position endorsed by a divided panel of the Third Circuit in *Estate of Bailey by Oare v. County of York*, 768 F.2d 503, 510–511 (1985), and by dicta in *Jensen v. Conrad*, 747 F.2d 185, 190–194 (CA4 1984), cert. denied, 470 U.S. 1052 (1985), that once the State learns that a particular child is in danger of abuse from third parties and actually undertakes to protect him from that danger, a "special relationship" arises between it and the child which imposes an affirmative constitutional duty to provide adequate protection. 812 F.2d, at 303–304. Second, the court held, in reliance on our decision in *Martinez v. California*, 444 U.S. 277, 285 (1980), that the causal connection between respondents' conduct and Joshua's injuries was too attenuated to establish a deprivation of constitutional rights actionable under § 1983. 812 F.2d, at 301–303. The court therefore found it unnecessary to reach the question whether respondents' conduct evinced the "state of mind" necessary to make out a due process claim after *Daniels v. Williams*, 474 U.S. 327 (1986), and *Davidson v. Cannon*, 474 U.S. 344 (1986). 812 F.2d, at 302.

Because of the inconsistent approaches taken by the lower courts in determining when, if ever, the failure of a state or local governmental entity or its agents to provide an individual with adequate protective services constitutes a violation of the individual's due process rights, see *Archie v. Racine*, 847 F.2d 1211, 1220–1223, and n. 10 (CA7 1988) (en banc) (collecting cases), cert. pending, No. 88-576, and the importance of the issue to the administration of state and local governments, we granted certiorari. 485 U.S. 958 (1988). We now affirm.

II

The Due Process Clause of the Fourteenth Amendment provides that "[n]o State shall... deprive any person of life, liberty, or property, without due process of law." Petitioners contend that the State deprived Joshua of his liberty interest in "free[dom] from... unjustified intrusions on personal security," see *Ingraham v. Wright*, 430 U.S. 651, 673 (1977), by failing to provide him with adequate protection against his father's violence. The claim is one invoking the substantive rather than the procedural component of the Due Process Clause; petitioners do not claim that the State denied Joshua protection without according him appropriate procedural safeguards, see *Morrissey v. Brewer*, 408 U.S. 471, 481 (1972), but that it was categorically obligated to protect him in these circumstances, see *Youngberg v. Romeo*, 457 U.S. 307, 309 (1982).[2]

But nothing in the language of the Due Process Clause itself requires the State to protect the life, liberty, and property of its citizens against invasion by private actors. The Clause is phrased as a limitation on the State's power to act, not as a guarantee of certain minimal levels of safety and security. It forbids the State itself to deprive individuals of life, liberty, or property without "due process of law," but its language cannot fairly be extended to impose an affirmative obligation on the State to ensure that those interests do not come to harm through other means. Nor does history support such an expansive reading of the constitutional text. Like its counterpart in the Fifth Amendment, the Due Process Clause of the Fourteenth Amendment was intended to prevent government "from abusing [its] power, or employing it as an instrument of oppression," *Davidson v. Cannon*, *supra*, 474 U.S., at 348.... Its purpose was to protect the people from the State, not to ensure that the State protected them from each other. The Framers were content to leave the extent of governmental obligation in the latter area to the democratic political processes.

Consistent with these principles, our cases have recognized that the Due Process Clauses generally confer no affirmative right to governmental aid, even where such aid may be necessary to secure life, liberty, or property interests of which the government itself may not deprive the individual. See, *e.g.*, *Harris v. McRae*, 448 U.S. 297 (1980) (no obligation to fund abortions or other medical services) (discussing Due Process Clause of Fifth Amendment); *Lindsey v. Normet*, 405 U.S. 56, 74 (1972) (no obligation to provide adequate housing) (discussing Due Process Clause of Fourteenth Amendment); see also *Youngberg v. Romeo*, *supra*, 457 U.S., at 317 ("As a general matter, a State is under no constitutional duty to provide substantive services for those within its border"). As we said in *Harris v. McRae*: "Although the liberty protected by the Due Process Clause affords protection against unwarranted *government* interference,... it does not confer an entitlement to such [governmental aid] as may be necessary to realize all the advantages of that freedom." 448 U.S., at 317–318 (emphasis added). If the Due Process Clause does not require the State to provide its citizens with particular protective services, it follows that the State cannot be held liable under the Clause for injuries that could have been averted

2. Petitioners also argue that the Wisconsin child protection statutes gave Joshua an "entitlement" to receive protective services in accordance with the terms of the statute, an entitlement which would enjoy due process protection against state deprivation under our decision in *Board of Regents of State Colleges v. Roth*, 408 U.S. 564 (1972). Brief for Petitioners 24–29. But this argument is made for the first time in petitioners' brief to this Court: it was not pleaded in the complaint, argued to the Court of Appeals as a ground for reversing the District Court, or raised in the petition for certiorari. We therefore decline to consider it here.

had it chosen to provide them.[3] As a general matter, then, we conclude that a State's failure to protect an individual against private violence simply does not constitute a violation of the Due Process Clause.

Petitioners contend, however, that even if the Due Process Clause imposes no affirmative obligation on the State to provide the general public with adequate protective services, such a duty may arise out of certain "special relationships" created or assumed by the State with respect to particular individuals. Petitioners argue that such a "special relationship" existed here because the State knew that Joshua faced a special danger of abuse at his father's hands, and specifically proclaimed, by word and by deed, its intention to protect him against that danger. Having actually undertaken to protect Joshua from this danger—which petitioners concede the State played no part in creating—the State acquired an affirmative "duty," enforceable through the Due Process Clause, to do so in a reasonably competent fashion. Its failure to discharge that duty, so the argument goes, was an abuse of governmental power that so "shocks the conscience," *Rochin v. California*, 342 U.S. 165, 172 (1952), as to constitute a substantive due process violation.

We reject this argument. It is true that in certain limited circumstances the Constitution imposes upon the State affirmative duties of care and protection with respect to particular individuals. In *Estelle v. Gamble*, 429 U.S. 97 (1976), we recognized that the Eighth Amendment's prohibition against cruel and unusual punishment, made applicable to the States through the Fourteenth Amendment's Due Process Clause, *Robinson v. California*, 370 U.S. 660 (1962), requires the State to provide adequate medical care to incarcerated prisoners. 429 U.S., at 103–104. We reasoned that because the prisoner is unable "'by reason of the deprivation of his liberty [to] care for himself,'" it is only "'just'" that the State be required to care for him. *Ibid.*, quoting *Spicer v. Williamson*, 191 N.C. 487, 490, 132 S.E. 291, 293 (1926).

In *Youngberg v. Romeo*, 457 U.S. 307 (1982), we extended this analysis beyond the Eighth Amendment setting, holding that the substantive component of the Fourteenth Amendment's Due Process Clause requires the State to provide involuntarily committed mental patients with such services as are necessary to ensure their "reasonable safety" from themselves and others. *Id.*, at 314–325; see *id.*, at 315, 324 (dicta indicating that the State is also obligated to provide such individuals with "adequate food, shelter, clothing, and medical care"). As we explained: "If it is cruel and unusual punishment to hold convicted criminals in unsafe conditions, it must be unconstitutional [under the Due Process Clause] to confine the involuntarily committed—who may not be punished at all—in unsafe conditions." *Id.*, at 315–316; see also *Revere v. Massachusetts General Hospital*, 463 U.S. 239, 244 (1983) (holding that the Due Process Clause requires the responsible government or governmental agency to provide medical care to suspects in police custody who have been injured while being apprehended by the police).

But these cases afford petitioners no help. Taken together, they stand only for the proposition that when the State takes a person into its custody and holds him there against his will, the Constitution imposes upon it a corresponding duty to assume some responsibility for his safety and general well-being. See *Youngberg v. Romeo*, *supra*, 457 U.S., at 317 ("When a person is institutionalized—and wholly dependent on the State[,] . . . a duty to provide certain

3. The State may not, of course, selectively deny its protective services to certain disfavored minorities without violating the Equal Protection Clause. See *Yick Wo v. Hopkins*, 118 U.S. 356 (1886). But no such argument has been made here.

services and care does exist"). The rationale for this principle is simple enough: when the State by the affirmative exercise of its power so restrains an individual's liberty that it renders him unable to care for himself, and at the same time fails to provide for his basic human needs—*e.g.*, food, clothing, shelter, medical care, and reasonable safety—it transgresses the substantive limits on state action set by the Eighth Amendment and the Due Process Clause. See *Estelle v. Gamble, supra*, 429 U.S., at 103–104; *Youngberg v. Romeo, supra*, 457 U.S., at 315–316. The affirmative duty to protect arises not from the State's knowledge of the individual's predicament or from its expressions of intent to help him, but from the limitation which it has imposed on his freedom to act on his own behalf. See *Estelle v. Gamble, supra*, 429 U.S., at 103 ("An inmate must rely on prison authorities to treat his medical needs; if the authorities fail to do so, those needs will not be met"). In the substantive due process analysis, it is the State's affirmative act of restraining the individual's freedom to act on his own behalf—through incarceration, institutionalization, or other similar restraint of personal liberty—which is the "deprivation of liberty" triggering the protections of the Due Process Clause, not its failure to act to protect his liberty interests against harms inflicted by other means.[8]

The *Estelle–Youngberg* analysis simply has no applicability in the present case. Petitioners concede that the harms Joshua suffered occurred not while he was in the State's custody, but while he was in the custody of his natural father, who was in no sense a state actor.[9] While the State may have been aware of the dangers that Joshua faced in the free world, it played no part in their creation, nor did it do anything to render him any more vulnerable to them. That the State once took temporary custody of Joshua does not alter the analysis, for when it returned him to his father's custody, it placed him in no worse position than that in which he would have been had it not acted at all; the State does not become the permanent guarantor of an individual's safety by having once offered him shelter. Under these circumstances, the State had no constitutional duty to protect Joshua.

It may well be that, by voluntarily undertaking to protect Joshua against a danger it concededly played no part in creating, the State acquired a duty under state tort law to provide him with adequate protection against that danger. See Restatement (Second) of Torts § 323 (1965) (one who undertakes to render services to another may in some circumstances be held

8. Of course, the protections of the Due Process Clause, both substantive and procedural, may be triggered when the State, by the affirmative acts of its agents, subjects an involuntarily confined individual to deprivations of liberty which are not among those generally authorized by his confinement. See, *e.g.*, *Whitley v. Albers, supra*, 475 U.S., at 326–327 (shooting inmate); *Youngberg v. Romeo, supra*, 457 U.S., at 316 (shackling involuntarily committed mental patient); *Hughes v. Rowe*, 449 U.S. 5, 11 (1980) (removing inmate from general prison population and confining him to administrative segregation); *Vitek v. Jones*, 445 U.S. 480, 491–494 (1980) (transferring inmate to mental health facility).

9. Complaint ¶ 16, App. 6 ("At relevant times to and until March 8, 1984, [the date of the final beating,] Joshua DeShaney was in the custody and control of Defendant Randy DeShaney"). Had the State by the affirmative exercise of its power removed Joshua from free society and placed him in a foster home operated by its agents, we might have a situation sufficiently analogous to incarceration or institutionalization to give rise to an affirmative duty to protect. Indeed, several Courts of Appeals have held, by analogy to *Estelle* and *Youngberg*, that the State may be held liable under the Due Process Clause for failing to protect children in foster homes from mistreatment at the hands of their foster parents. See *Doe v. New York City Dept. of Social Services*, 649 F.2d 134, 141–142 (CA2 1981), after remand, 709 F.2d 782, cert. denied *sub nom. Catholic Home Bureau v. Doe*, 464 U.S. 864 (1983); *Taylor ex rel. Walker v. Ledbetter*, 818 F.2d 791, 794–797 (CA11 1987) (en banc), cert. pending *Ledbetter v. Taylor*, No. 87-521. We express no view on the validity of this analogy, however, as it is not before us in the present case.

liable for doing so in a negligent fashion); see generally W. Keeton, D. Dobbs, R. Keeton, & D. Owen, Prosser and Keeton on the Law of Torts § 56 (5th ed. 1984) (discussing "special relationships" which may give rise to affirmative duties to act under the common law of tort). But the claim here is based on the Due Process Clause of the Fourteenth Amendment, which, as we have said many times, does not transform every tort committed by a state actor into a constitutional violation. See *Daniels v. Williams*, 474 U.S., at 335–336; *Parratt v. Taylor*, 451 U.S., at 544; *Martinez v. California*, 444 U.S. 277, 285 (1980); *Baker v. McCollan*, 443 U.S. 137, 146 (1979); *Paul v. Davis*, 424 U.S. 693, 701 (1976). A State may, through its courts and legislatures, impose such affirmative duties of care and protection upon its agents as it wishes. But not "all common-law duties owed by government actors were...constitutionalized by the Fourteenth Amendment." *Daniels v. Williams*, *supra*, 474 U.S., at 335. Because, as explained above, the State had no constitutional duty to protect Joshua against his father's violence, its failure to do so—though calamitous in hindsight—simply does not constitute a violation of the Due Process Clause.[10]

Judges and lawyers, like other humans, are moved by natural sympathy in a case like this to find a way for Joshua and his mother to receive adequate compensation for the grievous harm inflicted upon them. But before yielding to that impulse, it is well to remember once again that the harm was inflicted not by the State of Wisconsin, but by Joshua's father. The most that can be said of the state functionaries in this case is that they stood by and did nothing when suspicious circumstances dictated a more active role for them. In defense of them it must also be said that had they moved too soon to take custody of the son away from the father, they would likely have been met with charges of improperly intruding into the parent-child relationship, charges based on the same Due Process Clause that forms the basis for the present charge of failure to provide adequate protection.

The people of Wisconsin may well prefer a system of liability which would place upon the State and its officials the responsibility for failure to act in situations such as the present one. They may create such a system, if they do not have it already, by changing the tort law of the State in accordance with the regular lawmaking process. But they should not have it thrust upon them by this Court's expansion of the Due Process Clause of the Fourteenth Amendment.

Affirmed.

Justice Brennan, with whom Justice Marshall and Justice Blackmun join, dissenting.

"The most that can be said of the state functionaries in this case," the Court today concludes, "is that they stood by and did nothing when suspicious circumstances dictated a more active role for them." Because I believe that this description of respondents' conduct tells only part of the story and that, accordingly, the Constitution itself "dictated a more active role" for respondents in the circumstances presented here, I cannot agree that respondents had no constitutional duty to help Joshua DeShaney.

10. Because we conclude that the Due Process Clause did not require the State to protect Joshua from his father, we need not address respondents' alternative argument that the individual state actors lacked the requisite "state of mind" to make out a due process violation. See *Daniels v. Williams*, 474 U.S., at 334, n. 3. Similarly, we have no occasion to consider whether the individual respondents might be entitled to a qualified immunity defense, see *Anderson v. Creighton*, 483 U.S. 635 (1987), or whether the allegations in the complaint are sufficient to support a § 1983 claim against the county and DSS under *Monell v. New York City Dept. of Social Services*, 436 U.S. 658 (1978), and its progeny.

It may well be, as the Court decides, that the Due Process Clause as construed by our prior cases creates no general right to basic governmental services. That, however, is not the question presented here; indeed, that question was not raised in the complaint, urged on appeal, presented in the petition for certiorari, or addressed in the briefs on the merits. No one, in short, has asked the Court to proclaim that, as a general matter, the Constitution safeguards positive as well as negative liberties.

This is more than a quibble over dicta; it is a point about perspective, having substantive ramifications. In a constitutional setting that distinguishes sharply between action and inaction, one's characterization of the misconduct alleged under § 1983 may effectively decide the case. Thus, by leading off with a discussion (and rejection) of the idea that the Constitution imposes on the States an affirmative duty to take basic care of their citizens, the Court foreshadows—perhaps even preordains—its conclusion that no duty existed even on the specific facts before us. This initial discussion establishes the baseline from which the Court assesses the DeShaneys' claim that, when a State has—"by word and by deed"—announced an intention to protect a certain class of citizens and has before it facts that would trigger that protection under the applicable state law, the Constitution imposes upon the State an affirmative duty of protection.

The Court's baseline is the absence of positive rights in the Constitution and a concomitant suspicion of any claim that seems to depend on such rights. From this perspective, the DeShaneys' claim is first and foremost about inaction (the failure, here, of respondents to take steps to protect Joshua), and only tangentially about action (the establishment of a state program specifically designed to help children like Joshua). And from this perspective, holding these Wisconsin officials liable—where the only difference between this case and one involving a general claim to protective services is Wisconsin's establishment and operation of a program to protect children—would seem to punish an effort that we should seek to promote.

I would begin from the opposite direction. I would focus first on the action that Wisconsin has taken with respect to Joshua and children like him, rather than on the actions that the State failed to take. Such a method is not new to this Court. Both *Estelle v. Gamble*, 429 U.S. 97 (1976), and *Youngberg v. Romeo*, 457 U.S. 307 (1982), began by emphasizing that the States had confined J. W. Gamble to prison and Nicholas Romeo to a psychiatric hospital. This initial action rendered these people helpless to help themselves or to seek help from persons unconnected to the government. See *Estelle*, *supra*, 429 U.S. at 104 ("[I]t is but just that the public be required to care for the prisoner, who cannot by reason of the deprivation of his liberty, care for himself"); *Youngberg*, *supra*, 457 U.S. at 317 ("When a person is institutionalized—and wholly dependent on the State—it is conceded by petitioners that a duty to provide certain services and care does exist"). Cases from the lower courts also recognize that a State's actions can be decisive in assessing the constitutional significance of subsequent inaction. For these purposes, moreover, actual physical restraint is not the only state action that has been considered relevant. See, *e.g.*, *White v. Rochford*, 592 F.2d 381 (CA7 1979) (police officers violated due process when, after arresting the guardian of three young children, they abandoned the children on a busy stretch of highway at night).

Because of the Court's initial fixation on the general principle that the Constitution does not establish positive rights, it is unable to appreciate our recognition in *Estelle* and *Youngberg* that this principle does not hold true in all circumstances. Thus, in the Court's view, *Youngberg* can be explained (and dismissed) in the following way: "In the substantive due process analysis, it is the State's affirmative act of restraining the individual's freedom to act on his own behalf—through incarceration, institutionalization, or other similar restraint of personal liberty—which is the 'deprivation of liberty' triggering the protections of the Due Process Clause, not its failure to act to protect his liberty interests against harms inflicted by other means." This restatement of *Youngberg*'s holding should come as a surprise when one recalls our explicit observation in that case that Romeo did not challenge his commitment to the hospital, but instead "argue[d] that he ha[d] a constitutionally protected liberty interest in safety, freedom of movement, and training within the institution; and that petitioners infringed these rights *by failing to provide* constitutionally required conditions of confinement." 457 U.S., at 315 (emphasis added). I do not mean to suggest that "the State's affirmative act of restraining the individual's freedom to act on his own behalf," ante, at 1006, was irrelevant in *Youngberg*; rather, I emphasize that this conduct would have led to no injury, and consequently no cause of action under § 1983, unless the State then had failed to take steps to protect Romeo from himself and from others. In addition, the Court's exclusive attention to state-imposed restraints of "the individual's freedom to act on his own behalf," suggests that it was the State that rendered Romeo unable to care for himself, whereas in fact—with an I.Q. of between 8 and 10, and the mental capacity of an 18-month-old child, 457 U.S., at 309—he had been quite incapable of taking care of himself long before the State stepped into his life. Thus, the fact of hospitalization was critical in *Youngberg* not because it rendered Romeo helpless to help himself, but because it separated him from other sources of aid that, we held, the State was obligated to replace. Unlike the Court, therefore, I am unable to see in *Youngberg* a neat and decisive divide between action and inaction.

Moreover, to the Court, the only fact that seems to count as an "affirmative act of restraining the individual's freedom to act on his own behalf" is direct physical control. I would not, however, give *Youngberg* and *Estelle* such a stingy scope. I would recognize, as the Court apparently cannot, that "the State's knowledge of [an] individual's predicament [and] its expressions of intent to help him" can amount to a "limitation…on his freedom to act on his own behalf" or to obtain help from others. Thus, I would read *Youngberg* and *Estelle* to stand for the much more generous proposition that if a State cuts off private sources of aid and then refuses aid itself, it cannot wash its hands of the harm that results from its inaction.

Youngberg and *Estelle* are not alone in sounding this theme. In striking down a filing fee as applied to divorce cases brought by indigents, see *Boddie v. Connecticut*, 401 U.S. 371 (1971), and in deciding that a local government could not entirely foreclose the opportunity to speak in a public forum, see, *e.g.*, *Schneider v. State*, 308 U.S. 147 (1939); *Hague v. Committee for Industrial Organization*, 307 U.S. 496 (1939); *United States v. Grace*, 461 U.S. 171 (1983), we have acknowledged that a State's actions—such as the monopolization of a particular path of relief—may impose upon the State certain positive duties. Similarly, *Shelley v. Kraemer*, 334 U.S. 1 (1948), and *Burton v. Wilmington Parking Authority*, 365 U.S. 715 (1961), suggest that a State may be found complicit in an injury even if it did not create the situation that caused the harm.

Arising as they do from constitutional contexts different from the one involved here, cases like *Boddie* and *Burton* are instructive rather than decisive in the case before us. But they set a tone equally well established in precedent as, and contradictory to, the one the Court sets by situating the DeShaneys' complaint within the class of cases epitomized by the Court's decision in *Harris v. McRae*, 448 U.S. 297 (1980). The cases that I have cited tell us that *Goldberg v. Kelly*, 397 U.S. 254 (1970) (recognizing entitlement to welfare under state law), can stand side by side with *Dandridge v. Williams*, 397 U.S. 471, 484 (1970) (implicitly rejecting idea that welfare is a fundamental right), and that *Goss v. Lopez*, 419 U.S. 565, 573 (1975) (entitlement to public education under state law), is perfectly consistent with *San Antonio Independent School Dist. v. Rodriguez*, 411 U.S. 1, 29–39 (1973) (no fundamental right to education). To put the point more directly, these cases signal that a State's prior actions may be decisive in analyzing the constitutional significance of its inaction. I thus would locate the DeShaneys' claims within the framework of cases like *Youngberg* and *Estelle*, and more generally, *Boddie* and *Schneider*, by considering the actions that Wisconsin took with respect to Joshua.

Wisconsin has established a child-welfare system specifically designed to help children like Joshua. Wisconsin law places upon the local departments of social services such as respondent (DSS or Department) a duty to investigate reported instances of child abuse. See Wis.Stat. § 48.981(3) (1987–1988). While other governmental bodies and private persons are largely responsible for the reporting of possible cases of child abuse, see § 48.981(2), Wisconsin law channels all such reports to the local departments of social services for evaluation and, if necessary, further action. § 48.981(3). Even when it is the sheriff's office or police department that receives a report of suspected child abuse, that report is referred to local social services departments for action, see § 48.981(3)(a); the only exception to this occurs when the reporter fears for the child's *immediate* safety. § 48.981(3)(b). In this way, Wisconsin law invites—indeed, directs—citizens and other governmental entities to depend on local departments of social services such as respondent to protect children from abuse.

The specific facts before us bear out this view of Wisconsin's system of protecting children. Each time someone voiced a suspicion that Joshua was being abused, that information was relayed to the Department for investigation and possible action. When Randy DeShaney's second wife told the police that he had "'hit the boy causing marks and [was] a prime case for child abuse,'" the police referred her complaint to DSS. When, on three separate occasions, emergency room personnel noticed suspicious injuries on Joshua's body, they went to DSS with this information. When neighbors informed the police that they had seen or heard Joshua's father or his father's lover beating or otherwise abusing Joshua, the police brought these reports to the attention of DSS. And when respondent Kemmeter, through these reports and through her own observations in the course of nearly 20 visits to the DeShaney home, compiled growing evidence that Joshua was being abused, that information stayed within the Department—chronicled by the social worker in detail that seems almost eerie in light of her failure to act upon it. (As to the extent of the social worker's involvement in, and knowledge of, Joshua's predicament, her reaction to the news of Joshua's last and most devastating injuries is illuminating: "'I just knew the phone would ring some day and Joshua would be dead.'" 812 F.2d 298, 300 (CA7 1987).)

Even more telling than these examples is the Department's control over the decision whether to take steps to protect a particular child from suspected abuse. While many different people contributed information and advice to this decision, it was up to the people at DSS to make the ultimate decision (subject to the approval of the local government's Corporation Counsel) whether to disturb the family's current arrangements. When Joshua first appeared at a local hospital with injuries signaling physical abuse, for example, it was DSS that made the decision to take him into temporary custody for the purpose of studying his situation—and it was DSS, acting in conjunction with the corporation counsel, that returned him to his father. Unfortunately for Joshua DeShaney, the buck effectively stopped with the Department.

In these circumstances, a private citizen, or even a person working in a government agency other than DSS, would doubtless feel that her job was done as soon as she had reported her suspicions of child abuse to DSS. Through its child-welfare program, in other words, the State of Wisconsin has relieved ordinary citizens and governmental bodies other than the Department of any sense of obligation to do anything more than report their suspicions of child abuse to DSS. If DSS ignores or dismisses these suspicions, no one will step in to fill the gap. Wisconsin's child-protection program thus effectively confined Joshua DeShaney within the walls of Randy DeShaney's violent home until such time as DSS took action to remove him. Conceivably, then, children like Joshua are made worse off by the existence of this program when the persons and entities charged with carrying it out fail to do their jobs.

It simply belies reality, therefore, to contend that the State "stood by and did nothing" with respect to Joshua. Through its child-protection program, the State actively intervened in Joshua's life and, by virtue of this intervention, acquired ever more certain knowledge that Joshua was in grave danger. These circumstances, in my view, plant this case solidly within the tradition of cases like *Youngberg* and *Estelle*.

It will be meager comfort to Joshua and his mother to know that, if the State had "selectively den[ied] its protective services" to them because they were "disfavored minorities," their § 1983 suit might have stood on sturdier ground. Because of the posture of this case, we do not know why respondents did not take steps to protect Joshua; the Court, however, tells us that their reason is irrelevant so long as their inaction was not the product of invidious discrimination. Presumably, then, if respondents decided not to help Joshua because his name began with a "J," or because he was born in the spring, or because they did not care enough about him even to formulate an intent to discriminate against him based on an arbitrary reason, respondents would not be liable to the DeShaneys because they were not the ones who dealt the blows that destroyed Joshua's life.

I do not suggest that such irrationality was at work in this case; I emphasize only that we do not know whether or not it was. I would allow Joshua and his mother the opportunity to show that respondents' failure to help him arose, not out of the sound exercise of professional judgment that we recognized in *Youngberg* as sufficient to preclude liability, see 457 U.S., at 322–323, but from the kind of arbitrariness that we have in the past condemned. See, *e.g.*, *Daniels v. Williams*, 474 U.S. 327, 331 (1986) (purpose of Due Process Clause was "to secure the individual from the arbitrary exercise of the powers of government" (citations omitted)); *West Coast Hotel Co. v. Parrish*, 300 U.S. 379, 399 (1937) (to sustain state action, the Court need only decide that it is not "arbitrary or capricious"); *Euclid v. Ambler Realty Co.*, 272 U.S. 365, 389 (1926) (state action invalid where it "passes the bounds of reason and assumes the character of a merely arbitrary fiat," quoting *Purity Extract & Tonic Co. v. Lynch*, 226 U.S. 192, 204 (1912)).

Youngberg's deference to a decisionmaker's professional judgment ensures that once a caseworker has decided, on the basis of her professional training and experience, that one course of protection is preferable for a given child, or even that no special protection is required, she will not be found liable for the harm that follows. (In this way, *Youngberg*'s vision of substantive due process serves a purpose similar to that served by adherence to procedural norms, namely, requiring that a state actor stop and think before she acts in a way that may lead to a loss of liberty.) Moreover, that the Due Process Clause is not violated by merely negligent conduct, see *Daniels*, *supra*, and *Davidson v. Cannon*, 474 U.S. 344 (1986), means that a social worker who simply makes a mistake of judgment under what are admittedly complex and difficult conditions will not find herself liable in damages under § 1983.

As the Court today reminds us, "the Due Process Clause of the Fourteenth Amendment was intended to prevent government 'from abusing [its] power, or employing it as an instrument of oppression.'" My disagreement with the Court arises from its failure to see that inaction can be every bit as abusive of power as action, that oppression can result when a State undertakes a vital duty and then ignores it. Today's opinion construes the Due Process Clause to permit a State to displace private sources of protection and then, at the critical moment, to shrug its shoulders and turn away from the harm that it has promised to try to prevent. Because I cannot agree that our Constitution is indifferent to such indifference, I respectfully dissent.

JUSTICE BLACKMUN, dissenting.

Today, the Court purports to be the dispassionate oracle of the law, unmoved by "natural sympathy." But, in this pretense, the Court itself retreats into a sterile formalism which prevents it from recognizing either the facts of the case before it or the legal norms that should apply to those facts. As JUSTICE BRENNAN demonstrates, the facts here involve not mere passivity, but active state intervention in the life of Joshua DeShaney—intervention that triggered a fundamental duty to aid the boy once the State learned of the severe danger to which he was exposed.

The Court fails to recognize this duty because it attempts to draw a sharp and rigid line between action and inaction. But such formalistic reasoning has no place in the interpretation of the broad and stirring Clauses of the Fourteenth Amendment. Indeed, I submit that these Clauses were designed, at least in part, to undo the formalistic legal reasoning that infected antebellum jurisprudence, which the late Professor Robert Cover analyzed so effectively in his significant work entitled Justice Accused (1975).

Like the antebellum judges who denied relief to fugitive slaves, see *id.*, at 119–121, the Court today claims that its decision, however harsh, is compelled by existing legal doctrine. On the contrary, the question presented by this case is an open one, and our Fourteenth Amendment precedents may be read more broadly or narrowly depending upon how one chooses to read them. Faced with the choice, I would adopt a "sympathetic" reading, one which comports with dictates of fundamental justice and recognizes that compassion need not be exiled from the province of judging. Cf. A. Stone, Law, Psychiatry, and Morality 262 (1984) ("We will make mistakes if we go forward, but doing nothing can be the worst mistake. What is required of us is moral ambition. Until our composite sketch becomes a true portrait of humanity we must live with our uncertainty; we will grope, we will struggle, and our compassion may be our only guide and comfort").

Poor Joshua! Victim of repeated attacks by an irresponsible, bullying, cowardly, and intemperate father, and abandoned by respondents who placed him in a dangerous predicament and who knew or learned what was going on, and yet did essentially nothing except, as the Court revealingly observes, "dutifully recorded these incidents in [their] files." It is a sad commentary upon American life, and constitutional principles—so full of late of patriotic fervor and proud proclamations about "liberty and justice for all"—that this child, Joshua DeShaney, now is assigned to live out the remainder of his life profoundly retarded. Joshua and his mother, as petitioners here, deserve—but now are denied by this Court—the opportunity to have the facts of their case considered in the light of the constitutional protection that 42 U.S.C. § 1983 is meant to provide.

NOTES AND QUESTIONS

1. According to the majority, what must a plaintiff establish in order to make out a due process violation for the state's failure to act? What did Joshua DeShaney allege? Why was that insufficient as a matter of law? Under what circumstances would the state be liable for the harm caused?

2. Does Justice Brennan disagree with the majority's articulation of the necessary elements of a due process violation? If not, why is Brennan dissenting? Do you agree with his characterization of Wisconsin's child-abuse regulatory scheme?

3. Although Justice Blackmun joins in Brennan's dissenting opinion, he writes a separate dissent. Why?

4. *Bouknight* was decided after *DeShaney*. Do you think the state in *Bouknight* had a special relationship with Maurice? If so, should the state be held liable for its failure to protect the child?

5. Consider again the Convention on the Rights of the Child. How would this case be resolved under the Convention? Is there room for positive rights under the U.S. Constitution?

6. After *DeShaney*, the lower courts generally have considered two broad questions: whether a special relationship exists between the state and the child and, if so, what the plaintiff must prove to establish liability. Some circuit courts have held that when the state places a child in foster care, it has created a special relationship, analogous to that with other institutionalized persons, and the state may be liable under the substantive Due Process Clause for state-created danger that occurs while in that placement. See, e.g., *Doe ex rel. Johnson v. South Carolina Dep't of Soc. Servs.*, 597 F.3d 163 (4th Cir. 2010), cert. denied, 131 S.Ct. 392 (2010); *J.R. v. Gloria*, 593 F.3d 73 (1st Cir. 2010) (assuming *arguendo* that special relationship exists when state places children in foster care); *Nicini v. Morra*, 212 F.3d 798 (3d Cir. 2000); *Lintz v. Skipski*, 25 F.3d 304, 305 (6th Cir. 1994); *Norfleet v. Arkansas Dep't of Human Servs.*, 989 F.2d 289, 293 (8th Cir. 1993); *Lipscomb v. Simmons*, 962 F.2d 1374, 1379 (9th Cir. 1992); *Yvonne L. v. New Mexico Dep't of Human Servs.*, 959 F.2d 883, 891–893 (10th Cir. 1992); *K.H. ex rel. Murphy v. Morgan*, 914 F.2d 846, 848–849 (7th Cir. 1990); *Doe v. New York City Dep't of Soc. Servs.*, 649 F.2d 134 (2d Cir. 1981).

If there is a special relationship, the federal courts have held that the plaintiff must establish that the state acted with deliberate indifference. Negligence is insufficient for due process claims. See *Daniels v. Williams*, 474 U.S. 327 (1986) and *Davidson v. Cannon*, 474 U.S. 344 (1986). The Supreme Court has made clear that in an emergency, the acts of the state must not only be deliberately indifferent; those acts must also "shock the conscience." *County of Sacramento v. Lewis*, 523 U.S. 833 (1998). If there is no emergency, however, the lower courts have applied the deliberate-indifference or -recklessness standard. But what exactly is deliberate indifference? The Ninth Circuit Court of Appeals has offered this explanation:

> This court has only addressed the application of the deliberate indifference standard with respect to foster children in one case. *See Gibson v. Merced County Department of Human Resources*, 799 F.2d 582, 589–90 (9th Cir. 1986). In *Gibson*, we held that state officials were not

deliberately indifferent to a foster child's liberty interest when they removed the child from uncooperative foster parents who were attempting to prevent the child's reunification with her natural mother. *See id.* Although we did not discuss the deliberate indifference standard in *Gibson*, we have addressed that standard at length in resolving cases involving prisoners alleging deliberate indifference. In the prisoner cases we have held that deliberate indifference "requires an objective risk of harm and a subjective awareness of that harm." *Conn v. City of Reno*, 591 F.3d 1081, 1095 (9th Cir. 2010), *as amended* (citation and emphasis omitted); *see also, Simmons v. Navajo County*, 609 F.3d 1011, 1017 (9th Cir. 2010) (concluding that "[a] prison official cannot be liable for deliberate indifference unless he or she knows of and disregards an excessive risk to inmate health or safety; the official must both be aware of facts from which the inference could be drawn that a substantial risk of serious harm exists, and he must also draw the inference") (citation and internal quotation marks omitted); *Clouthier v. County of Contra Costa*, 591 F.3d 1232, 1242 (9th Cir. 2010) (recognizing that the objective component requires a showing of "a substantial risk of serious harm" and the subjective component requires a showing that the official was "aware of facts from which the inference could be drawn that a substantial risk of serious harm exist[ed], and he... also dr[e]w the inference"). These cases inform our analysis and our review of precedent from our sister circuits.

In the specific context of cases involving foster care, the Fifth, Sixth, and Eighth Circuits have held that deliberate indifference is established if an "official [was] both aware of facts from which the inference could be drawn that a substantial risk of serious harm exist[ed] and [the official]... also dr[e]w the inference." *Hernandez ex rel. Hernandez v. Texas Dep't of Protective & Regulatory Servs.*, 380 F.3d 872, 881 (5th Cir. 2004) (citation omitted); *Arledge v. Franklin County, Ohio*, 509 F.3d 258, 261, 263 (6th Cir. 2007) (same); *James ex rel. James v. Friend*, 458 F.3d 726, 730 (8th Cir. 2006) (same). This analysis is identical to the subjective deliberate indifference component that we have articulated in prisoner cases and includes by implication the objective component requiring the existence of a substantial risk of serious harm.

The Second, Third, Fourth, Seventh, Tenth, and Eleventh Circuits have each phrased the deliberate indifference test along the same lines. *See Doe v. New York City Dep't of Social Services*, 649 F.2d 134, 145 (2d Cir. 1981) (explaining that deliberate indifference "cannot exist absent some knowledge triggering an affirmative duty to act..."); *Nicini v. Morra*, 212 F.3d 798, 811–12 (3d Cir. 2000) (defining deliberate indifference as "conduct [that] shocks the conscience" while assuming that the "should have known" standard applies); *White by White v. Chambliss*, 112 F.3d 731, 737 (4th Cir. 1997) (including a requirement that state officials "were plainly placed on notice of a danger and chose to ignore the danger notwithstanding the notice"); *J.H. ex rel. Higgin v. Johnson*, 346 F.3d 788, 792 (7th Cir. 2003) (requiring subjective actual knowledge or suspicion of the risk); *Roska ex rel. Roska v. Peterson*, 328 F.3d 1230, 1246 (10th Cir. 2003) (holding that state actors may be liable for placing children in a foster home "they know or suspect to be dangerous to the children...") (citation omitted); *H.A.L. ex rel. Lewis v. Foltz*, 551 F.3d 1227, 1231–32 (11th Cir. 2008) (assigning liability if the official was "deliberately indifferent to a known and substantial risk to the child of serious harm").

We are persuaded by our precedent and cases from other circuits analyzing the issue, that the deliberate indifference standard, as applied to foster children, requires a showing of an objectively substantial risk of harm and a showing that the officials were subjectively aware of facts from which an inference could be drawn that a substantial risk of serious harm existed and that either the official actually drew that inference or that a reasonable official would have been compelled to draw that inference. *See Clouthier*, 591 F.3d at 1242; *see also Conn*, 591 F.3d at 1095–96;

> *Arledge*, 509 F.3d at 263; *James*, 458 F.3d at 730; *Hernandez*, 380 F.3d at 881. We also conclude that the subjective component may be inferred "from the fact that the risk of harm is obvious." *Hernandez*, 380 F.3d at 881 (citation and emphasis omitted); *Arledge*, 509 F.3d at 263.

Tamas v. Dep't of Soc. & Health Servs., 630 F.3d 833, 844–845 (9th Cir. 2010). Under the standards articulated by the various circuit courts, do you think it likely that a plaintiff will prevail on a claim that the state violated the substantive Due Process Clause? In *J.R. v. Gloria*, *supra*, the state placed twin brothers in a foster home. The foster parents had two male boarders who served as de facto caretakers for the boys, but the child-protective agency never did background checks on the male boarders. During the eighteen months the twins resided in the foster home, there were several reports of behavioral problems and physical injuries to the twins, but the agency concluded that none of these reports substantiated abuse. Finally, a teacher called the abuse hotline and reported bruises on the boys' arms. At that time, they told the investigator that one of the male boarders had hit them with a belt and that he had done so in the past. The boys were removed, and the agency subsequently learned that the boys also had been sexually assaulted. The boys now have a number of severe developmental challenges and require institutional care. Based on the deliberate-indifference standard, do you believe the *Tamas* court would find the state liable for its failure to protect the twins?

7. In *Town of Castle Rock v. Gonzales*, 545 U.S. 748 (2005), Gonzales had obtained a restraining order against her husband that limited the time he could spend with her three daughters. One evening, she discovered that the girls were missing and contacted police. Despite the restraining order and a statutory directive that the police were required to enforce restraining orders, the police did nothing. At one point, Gonzales spoke to her husband on the phone and discovered that he was at an amusement park with their children. Again, she contacted the police, and again, they did nothing. Her husband and three daughters subsequently died that same night after a shootout with police. Despite the clear statutory directive, the Supreme Court held that the state had no duty to protect individuals from private actors, foreclosing any possibility left open by *DeShaney* that plaintiffs may have procedural due process remedies against state inaction. After *Gonzales*, is there any real protection for children placed in foster care?

4. JUDICIAL PROCEDURES

a. INITIAL HEARINGS

National Council of Juvenile and Family Court Judges, Resource Guidelines: Improving Court Practice in Child Abuse & Neglect Cases 30–32, 36, 39–41 (1995), http://www.ncjfcj.org/images/stories/dept/ppcd/pdf/resguide.pdf.

The preliminary protective hearing is the first court hearing in a juvenile abuse or neglect case. A preliminary protective hearing is referred to in some jurisdictions as a "shelter care hearing," "detention hearing," "emergency removal hearing," or "temporary custody hearing." The preliminary protective hearing occurs either immediately before or immediately after a child is removed from home in an emergency. This initial hearing may be preceded by an ex parte order directing placement of the child. In extreme cases, a child may have been removed from home without prior court approval, and the preliminary protective hearing is the first review of the placement by the court....

The main purpose of the preliminary protective hearing is to make a decision concerning whether or not the child can be immediately and safely returned home while the trial is pending. This initial decision is often the most important decision to be made in an abuse and neglect case. Although it is made on an emergency basis, the decision must be based upon a competent assessment of risks and dangers to the child.

The preliminary protective hearing is an emergency matter. The family is often in crisis. Great demands are placed upon the social service agency to stabilize the situation and to provide services to permit the child to safely remain at home or return home. Unfortunately, many social service agencies believe it is safer to remove the child as a preventive measure and return the child to the family only after a full investigation is completed. This perspective ignores the great risk of out-of-home placements, the disruption such placements cause to the child and the family, and the emotional and fiscal costs involved in placing children. It also ignores the reality that safe, in-home caretakers can often be found if adequate investigation is undertaken and services are provided.

To evaluate the likelihood and severity of harm if the child is returned home, the court must take into account not only the facts and circumstances that gave rise to the original removal of the child (i.e., the parents' or guardian's possible abuse or neglect), but also what might be done to safeguard the child in the home. That is, the court should evaluate both the current danger to the child, and what can be done to eliminate the danger. Harmful consequences of removal should also be considered. Removal is always a traumatic experience for a child. Once a child is removed it becomes logistically and practically more difficult to help a family resolve its problems.

A primary goal of the court should be to make the preliminary protective hearing as thorough and meaningful as possible. The court should conduct an in-depth inquiry concerning the circumstances of the case. It should hear from all interested persons present. As part of its inquiry, the court should evaluate whether the need for immediate placement of the child could be eliminated by providing additional services or by implementing court orders concerning the conduct of the child's caretaker. If the court determines that the child needs to be placed, the court must evaluate the appropriateness of the placement proposed by the agency and seek the least disruptive alternative that can meet the needs of the child. For example, the court should explore whether the needs of the child could be met in the home of a relative....

When preliminary protective hearings are thorough and timely, some cases can be resolved with no need for subsequent court hearings and reviews. In other cases, a thorough and early preliminary protective hearing can help simplify and shorten early hearings and can move the case more quickly to the later stages of adjudication, disposition, and review. This not only preserves court resources but reduces the cost and harm of unnecessary, prolonged out-of-home placement of children.

A timely and thorough preliminary protective hearing can shorten the time of foster care and speed the judicial process. By ensuring speedy notice of all parties, the hearing avoids delays due to difficulties with service of process. By ensuring early, active representation of parties, the hearing avoids trial delays due to scheduling conflicts and the late appointment of unprepared advocates. By clearing the trial (adjudication) date at a very early time, the hearing avoids later scheduling conflicts that otherwise would delay trial dates. By thoroughly exploring all issues at the preliminary protective hearing, the court can resolve and dismiss some cases on the spot, move quickly on some pretrial issues (such as discovery or court-ordered examination of parties), encourage early settlement of the case, encourage prompt delivery of appropriate services to the family, and monitor agency casework at a critical stage of the case.

Another purpose of the preliminary protective hearing is for the court to begin setting a problem-solving atmosphere so the child can remain safely at home or be safely returned home as quickly as possible. Parents are often angry and emotionally distraught at this hearing. The agency may have filed for emergency removal because the relationship between the social worker and parents has broken down. The adversarial nature of court proceedings can aggravate tensions between the parties. The court should take active steps to defuse hostilities, to gain the cooperation of the parties, and to assist parties in attacking the problem rather than each other.

Although the judge or judicial officer should not assume the role of caseworker, there are practical steps that a court can take to gain the cooperation of the parties and develop a problem-solving atmosphere. The court should remember that for many parents the preliminary protective hearing will be their first experience in court. The court can explain the hearing process to the parents so they are less confused. The court can explain that it is not an arm of the agency, but that its role is to be an impartial decisionmaker, acting upon information provided by all parties. The court can carefully listen and seek to thoroughly understand the perceptions and concerns of all parties present at the hearing. The court can insist that proper decorum is maintained by each party so that all persons present are treated with dignity and respect. The court can attempt to identify areas of agreement and mediate areas of dispute between parties so that some disputes are resolved by agreement rather than through contested hearings.

At the conclusion of the preliminary protective hearing, the parties should leave with a decision from the court concerning the placement of the child that is based on thorough understanding and careful consideration of the circumstances of the case. The parties should see that the court has taken an active role to move the case forward and to make certain that the agency responds to the needs of the family and child in a timely manner. The parties should leave the hearing with the perception that they were treated fairly by a court that is concerned about their interests and that is striving to build a working relationship between the parties so that the need for court intervention can be ended as quickly as possible.

A complete preliminary protective hearing requires a substantial initial investment of time and resources. Such an investment results in better decisions for children and their families, and preserves the resources of the court and child welfare system. Significant costs are incurred when a child is unnecessarily placed outside of the home. A child can suffer serious emotional and behavioral problems from the disruption and upheaval caused by placement. The parents' feelings of inadequacy and helplessness may be intensified, thereby making efforts to change their behavior even more difficult. The family may lose its income and housing, if the family has been dependent on public assistance. As a result of these and other effects of removing a child, extra efforts must often be made and significant costs incurred to resolve problems as early as possible in each case.

By insisting that adequate services are delivered to safely prevent the need for placement and by making certain that decisions to remove children from their homes are made with great care, courts can avoid costs associated with unnecessary placements. By investing the time to carefully review agency efforts and to suggest or order additional or more appropriate services, the court may find that its own time and resources are saved when cases are resolved in a more timely manner....

To make sure that parents, custodians, and other witnesses are present during preliminary protective hearings, special efforts are required. Understandable explanations of what has happened must be handed to parents, custodians, or caretakers when children are first removed. A written notification in understandable language must state the reason for removal, the time and place of the hearing, the name and number of a person to call to obtain court-appointed counsel, and the need for immediate action.

For parents, custodians, and other caretakers who are not present when children are taken, the agency must make diligent efforts to provide them with this information. At the hearing, the agency caseworker must explain what has been done to notify the parties. Finally, court staff must be available to take calls from parents and to arrange for the appointment of counsel.

Perhaps the most important factor in influencing whether parents and others will actually appear at the preliminary protective hearing is the attitude of the assigned caseworker. Juvenile and family courts should require caseworkers to exert their best efforts to have parents and other necessary witnesses attend the preliminary protective hearing. In some cases, this may even involve arranging appropriate transportation for parties.

Courts can take several approaches to persuade caseworkers both to attend preliminary protective hearings and to encourage parents and others to attend. To ensure that attorneys and other advocates are present during preliminary protective hearings, the court may need to take even stronger steps. Where attorneys are appointed from lists, the court may need to revise procedures for the appointment of counsel so that appointment occurs prior to the preliminary protective hearing. Attorneys and parties may need to be instructed to appear before the hearing begins so that: (a) their eligibility for appointed counsel can be determined in advance; and (b) parties can confer with counsel before the hearing begins.

Where courts enter into contracts with outside organizations to provide legal representation for parents and children, the contracts need to specify that the advocates will be present prior to preliminary protective hearings to meet with their clients and that they will prepare for the hearing to the extent practical given the limited time available....

It is important for petitions to be filed at or before preliminary protective hearings for at least two reasons. First, if the petition is ready at the time of the hearing, it can be given to parents on the spot, avoiding the need for service at parents' homes. Second, service of the petition at the preliminary protective hearing provides the parties with adequate notice of the reasons for the court proceedings. To provide proper notice of the charges, the petition must contain a complete and accurate statement of the reasons for agency intervention....

One of the most important functions of the court during the preliminary protective hearing is to oversee the agency's early efforts to locate and notify missing parties and relatives. During the preliminary protective hearing, the court should inquire about parties who are not present and should require an explanation of agency efforts to locate and notify them of the proceeding. Speedy decisionmaking is critical in child abuse or neglect cases, and timely notice to the parties helps prevent delays....

If the petition and summons have been prepared in advance of the preliminary protective hearing and the parties are present, the preliminary protective hearing provides an excellent opportunity to efficiently complete service of process....

If a party is unrepresented by counsel at the preliminary protective hearing, the court should advise the party of the right to counsel, including the right to court-appointed counsel, where applicable. Even when the parties are represented at the hearing, the court should explain the nature of the hearing and the proceedings that will follow....

Given the short time from removal of the child to the time of the preliminary protective hearing, it is not reasonable to expect lengthy reports and written assessments to be submitted in advance of the hearing. However, agency staff should be expected to submit a brief written description of the circumstances surrounding the removal of the child and the agency's prior efforts, if any, to preserve the family. This report should be provided to the other parties and their attorneys as early as possible in advance of the hearing and no later than one hour in advance. Advance submission of the report is needed to give the parents an opportunity to offer a defense or to propose alternatives to foster placement....

At the conclusion of the hearing, the court's written findings of fact and conclusions of law should be prepared and distributed in person to the parties. This should occur at the conclusion of the hearing while the parties are still present. Handing out an order and findings addressing the issues gives the parties an immediate, written record of what has been decided, what they are expected to do prior to the next hearing, any social services voluntarily accepted, and the date and time of the next hearing....

Along with its legal conclusions, the court should provide a brief explanation of the facts upon which its conclusions are based. The court's entry need not be elaborate, but should document that the court has addressed each of the basic issues presented at a preliminary protective hearing, and that the court's decision is based upon a reasoned analysis of the evidence presented. The entry should also document the court's orders and expectations concerning the parents' and the agency's future conduct.

NOTES AND QUESTIONS

1. The National Council of Juvenile and Family Court Judges (NCJFCJ) developed the Resource Guidelines to establish "the essential elements of properly conducted court hearings." Nat'l Council Juv. & Fam. Ct. Judges, Resource Guidelines: Improving Court Practice in Abuse and Neglect Cases 11 (1995), http://www.ncjfcj.org/images/stories/dept/ppcd/pdf/resguide.pdf. As the Resource Guidelines were being developed, the NCJFCJ also established the Child Victims Act Model Court Project in 1992. Today, there are thirty-six courts in twelve jurisdictions participating as model courts and implementing the Resource Guidelines. According to NCJFCJ, model courts pioneered such practices as dependency drug treatment and mental-health treatment courts, one-family–one-judge calendaring, strict no-continuance policies, and setting the date and time for the next hearing before the end of the current hearing. Nat'l Council Juv. & Fam. Ct. Judges, The Resource Guidelines: Supporting Best Practices and Building Foundations for Innovation in Child Abuse and Neglect Cases, Looking Back and Moving Forward 24 (2009), http://www.ncjfcj.org/images/stories/dept/ppcd/pdf/rg.supporting%20best%20practices%20and%20building%20foundations%20for.pdf. Model courts also have noted reductions in case backlogs, declines in the number of children in foster care, and decreases in the average number of months a case remains open. *Id.* at 25. What do you think of these improvements?

2. The Preliminary Protective Hearings Guidelines also state that the following individuals should be present at the hearings: a judge or judicial officer; parents whose rights have not been terminated, including putative fathers; relatives with legal standing or other custodial adults; the assigned caseworker; the attorney for the state; the attorney for the parents; a legal advocate or guardian *ad litem* for the child; a court reporter (or "suitable technology"); and security personnel. Why is the child not included? The guidelines state:

> Children often should be present at the preliminary protective hearing, but their attendance can depend upon many factors including the age of the child, the physical and emotional condition of the child, and degree that requiring the child to be present might traumatize the child. As an alternative to bringing the child to a hearing, the agency may choose to present the child's hearsay statements and then allow the child's guardian ad litem to have access to the child at an off-site location or by telephone. In all cases, the child should be accessible in the event that the court determines that the child's presence is necessary.

Nat'l Council Juv. & Fam. Ct. Judges, Resource Guidelines: Improving Court Practice in Abuse and Neglect Cases, at 34. Do you agree?

3. What procedural protections should be accorded at a preremoval hearing? The United States District Court for the Eastern District of Kentucky, in finding that Kentucky's procedures for the removal of children from their parents violated due process, stated:

> In analyzing what process, if any, was due the plaintiffs in this case under the fourteenth amendment, the court employed the factors set out in *Mathews v. Eldridge*, 424 U.S. 319, 96 S.Ct. 893, 47 L.Ed.2d 18 (1976). Under the *Mathews* test, the first consideration is the type of private interest being affected. It has been recognized in numerous cases that family integrity is an interest of the very strongest type. *See, e.g., Stanley v. Illinois*, 405 U.S. 645, 92 S.Ct. 1208, 31 L.Ed.2d 551 (1972); *Smith v. Organization of Foster Families for Equity and Reform*, 431 U.S. 816, 97 S.Ct. 2094, 53 L.Ed.2d 14 (1977); *Santosky v. Kramer*, 455 U.S. 745, 102 S.Ct. 1388, 71 L.Ed.2d 599 (1982). These cases derive from the same body of case law as *Meyer v. Nebraska*, 262 U.S. 390, 43 S.Ct. 625, 67 L.Ed. 1042 (1923); *Pierce v. Society of Society of Sisters*, 268 U.S. 510, 45 S.Ct. 571, 69 L.Ed. 1070 (1925); *Griswold v. Connecticut*, 381 U.S. 479, 85 S.Ct. 1678, 14 L.Ed.2d 510 (1965); and *Moore v. City of East Cleveland*, 431 U.S. 494, 97 S.Ct. 1932, 52 L.Ed.2d 531 (1977). Although it sometimes permits the state to intrude into family matters, the Constitution of the United States quite properly recognizes that the right of a person to raise his or her own family is an interest of profound and fundamental importance.
>
> The second factor to be considered under *Mathews* is the value of an individual hearing in the particular situation involved. Common sense indicates that factual disputes will occur frequently concerning the quality of parental care. For example, authorities might discover that a child is not attending school. Upon further investigation, however, it may be revealed that there is some misunderstanding with the teacher and that the parents are not really culpable. Perhaps the parents are facing a financial crisis of a temporary nature, or perhaps the parent and a particular social worker have a personality conflict that is creating a problem. The logic of providing some form of a hearing in such situations, where one may be deprived of an important interest, has been recognized by the United States Supreme Court in *Goss v. Lopez*, 419 U.S. 565, 95 S.Ct. 729, 42 L.Ed.2d 725 (1975), a school expulsion case.
>
> The third factor employed in *Mathews* is the public burden as compared with the private benefit. The requirement of a due process hearing prior to the removal of a child in a non-emergency situation would impose no significant burden on the public. This is not a

case, for example, where millions of dollars in welfare benefits might never be recovered if they are improperly paid. Moreover, the interest to be protected is a weighty one.

Tested by the principles set out in *Mathews*, section 208.430(2) of Kentucky Revised Statutes fails to provide due process of law. The previously cited cases dictate that families be afforded a pre-removal hearing in non-emergency cases and a prompt post-removal hearing following an emergency removal of a child. Thus, to the extent that this statute would permit a removal without such protection, it is violative of the fourteenth amendment.

Similarly, the procedures employed by the defendants, which permit removal of children from the homes of their natural parents without proper findings of fact, are also unconstitutional. This principle was recognized in *Roe v. Conn*, 417 F.Supp. 769, 778 (M.D.Ala. 1976), in which it was asserted that, "before intrusion into the affairs of the family is allowed, the State should have reliable evidence that a child is in need of protective care." *Id.* at 778. The court indicated that "this fact finding process, as a matter of basic fairness, should provide notice to the parents and child of the evidence... and provide them with an opportunity for rebuttal at a hearing before an impartial tribunal." *Id.* This does not mean, however, that a formal hearing before a judge is always required. In some situations, a judicial hearing may not be suitable. What the Constitution requires is a fundamentally fair hearing, which sometimes may be accomplished outside of the judicial context.

The statute and the practices employed by defendants pursuant to section 208.430(2) are further unconstitutional for failing to include standards to govern the removal of children from their homes. Due process requires that there be some limits on social worker discretion in this regard and that the parents be given adequate notice of the circumstances under which their children may be removed.

Siereveld v. Conn, 557 F.Supp. 1178, 1182-83 (E.D. Ky. 1983). Do you think the Resource Guidelines comport with due process principles?

b. ADJUDICATION OF ABUSE AND NEGLECT

Child Welfare Information Gateway, Factsheet: What Is Child Abuse and Neglect? 2–4 (2008), http://www.childwelfare.gov/pubs/factsheets/whatiscan.pdf.

Within the minimum standards set by CAPTA, each State is responsible for providing its own definitions of child abuse and neglect. Most States recognize four major types of maltreatment: physical abuse, neglect, sexual abuse, and emotional abuse. Although any of the forms of child maltreatment may be found separately, they often occur in combination. In many States, abandonment and parental substance abuse are also defined as forms of child abuse or neglect....

Physical abuse is nonaccidental physical injury (ranging from minor bruises to severe fractures or death) as a result of punching, beating, kicking, biting, shaking, throwing, stabbing, choking, hitting (with a hand, stick, strap, or other object), burning, or otherwise harming a child, that is inflicted by a parent, caregiver, or other person who has responsibility for the child. Such injury is considered abuse regardless of whether the caregiver intended to hurt the child. Physical discipline, such as spanking or paddling, is not considered abuse as long as it is reasonable and causes no bodily injury to the child.

Neglect is the failure of a parent, guardian, or other caregiver to provide for a child's basic needs. Neglect may be:

- Physical (e.g., failure to provide necessary food or shelter, or lack of appropriate supervision)
- Medical (e.g., failure to provide necessary medical or mental health treatment)
- Educational (e.g., failure to educate a child or attend to special education needs)
- Emotional (e.g., inattention to a child's emotional needs, failure to provide psychological care, or permitting the child to use alcohol or other drugs)

These situations do not always mean a child is neglected. Sometimes cultural values, the standards of care in the community, and poverty may be contributing factors, indicating the family is in need of information or assistance. When a family fails to use information and resources, and the child's health or safety is at risk, then child welfare intervention may be required. In addition, many States provide an exception to the definition of neglect for parents who choose not to seek medical care for their children due to religious beliefs that may prohibit medical intervention.

Sexual abuse includes activities by a parent or caregiver such as fondling a child's genitals, penetration, incest, rape, sodomy, indecent exposure, and exploitation through prostitution or the production of pornographic materials....

Emotional abuse (or psychological abuse) is a pattern of behavior that impairs a child's emotional development or sense of self-worth. This may include constant criticism, threats, or rejection, as well as withholding love, support, or guidance. Emotional abuse is often difficult to prove and, therefore, child protective services may not be able to intervene without evidence of harm or mental injury to the child. Emotional abuse is almost always present when other forms are identified.

Abandonment is now defined in many States as a form of neglect. In general, a child is considered to be abandoned when the parent's identity or whereabouts are unknown, the child has been left alone in circumstances where the child suffers serious harm, or the parent has failed to maintain contact with the child or provide reasonable support for a specified period of time.

Substance abuse is an element of the definition of child abuse or neglect in many States. Circumstances that are considered abuse or neglect in some States include:

- Prenatal exposure of a child to harm due to the mother's use of an illegal drug or other substance
- Manufacture of methamphetamine in the presence of a child
- Selling, distributing, or giving illegal drugs or alcohol to a child
- Use of a controlled substance by a caregiver that impairs the caregiver's ability to adequately care for the child

States wishing to obtain federal grants are required by 42 U.S.C. § 5106a(b)(2)(B)(ii)(I) (2011) to establish a "definition under Federal law of what constitutes abuse and neglect." CAPTA defines abuse and neglect to mean "at a minimum, any recent act or failure to act on the part of a parent or caretaker, which results in death, serious physical or emotional harm, sexual abuse or exploitation, or an act or failure to act which presents an imminent risk of serious harm." CAPTA Reauthorization Act of 2010, Pub.L. 111-320, title I, § 142(a)(2), Dec. 20, 2010, 124 Stat. 3477, 3483. CAPTA defines sexual abuse as "the employment, use, persuasion, inducement, enticement, or coercion of any child to engage in, or assist any other person to engage in, any sexually explicit conduct or simulation of such conduct for the purpose of producing a visual depiction of such conduct"; or "the rape, and in cases of caretaker or inter-familial relationships, statutory rape, molestation, prostitution, or other form of sexual exploitation of children, or incest with children." 42 U.S.C. § 5106g(4) (2011). Withholding medically indicated treatment under the Act is "the failure to respond to the infant's life-threatening conditions by providing treatment (including appropriate nutrition, hydration, and medication) which, in the treating physician's or physicians' reasonable medical judgment, will be most likely to be effective in ameliorating or correcting all such conditions." 42 U.S.C. § 5106g(5) (2011). Treatment (other than appropriate nutrition, hydration, and medication) is not required when in the treating physician's medical judgment, the infant is irreversibly comatose, treatment would prolong dying, treatment is ineffective in correcting the life-threatening conditions, or it would be futile and treatment itself inhumane. 42 U.S.C. §§ 5106g(5)(A), (B), (C). However, 42 U.S.C. § 5106i states that nothing in the Act should be construed as establishing a federal requirement that a parent or legal guardian must provide medical treatment if such treatment conflicts with the religious beliefs of the parent or legal guardian. States, however, are free to make case-by-case determinations, except when medical treatment is withheld from infants.

Nevertheless, there is considerable variability among state definitions of abuse and neglect. Consider the following statutory excerpts.

ALABAMA CODE § 12-15-301 (2011)

For purposes of this article, the following words and phrases shall have the following meanings:

(1) Abandonment. A voluntary and intentional relinquishment of the custody of a child by a parent, or a withholding from the child, without good cause or excuse, by the parent, of his or her presence, care, love, protection, maintenance, or the opportunity for the display of filial affection, or the failure to claim the rights of a parent, or failure to perform the duties of a parent.

(2) Abuse. Harm or the risk of harm to the emotional, physical health, or welfare of a child. Harm or the risk of harm to the emotional, physical health, or welfare of a child can occur through nonaccidental physical or mental injury, sexual abuse, or attempted sexual abuse or sexual exploitation or attempted sexual exploitation....

(7) Neglect. Negligent treatment or maltreatment of a child, including, but not limited to, the failure to provide adequate food, medical treatment, supervision, education, clothing, or shelter....

(12) Sexual Abuse. Sexual abuse includes the employment, use, persuasion, inducement, enticement, or coercion of any child to engage in, or having a child assist any person to engage in, any sexually explicit conduct or any simulation of the conduct for the purpose of producing any visual depiction of the conduct. Sexual abuse also includes rape, molestation,

prostitution, or other forms of sexual exploitation or abuse of children, or incest with children, as those acts are defined in this article or by Alabama law.

(13) Sexual Exploitation. Sexual exploitation includes allowing, permitting, or encouraging a child to engage in prostitution and allowing, permitting, encouraging, or engaging in the obscene or pornographic photographing, filming, or depicting of a child.

MONTANA CODE ANNOTATED § 41-3-102 (2010)

As used in this chapter, the following definitions apply:

(1)(a) "Abandon," "abandoned," and "abandonment" mean:

- (i) leaving a child under circumstances that make reasonable the belief that the parent does not intend to resume care of the child in the future;
- (ii) willfully surrendering physical custody for a period of 6 months and during that period not manifesting to the child and the person having physical custody of the child a firm intention to resume physical custody or to make permanent legal arrangements for the care of the child;
- (iii) that the parent is unknown and has been unknown for a period of 90 days and that reasonable efforts to identify and locate the parent have failed; or
- (iv) the voluntary surrender...by a parent of a newborn who is no more than 30 days old to an emergency services provider....

(b) The terms do not include the voluntary surrender of a child to the department solely because of parental inability to access publicly funded services....

(4)(a) "Adequate health care" means any medical care or nonmedical remedial health care recognized by an insurer licensed to provide disability insurance under Title 33, including the prevention of the withholding of medically indicated treatment or medically indicated psychological care permitted or authorized under state law.

(b) This chapter may not be construed to require or justify a finding of child abuse or neglect for the sole reason that a parent or legal guardian, because of religious beliefs, does not provide adequate health care for a child. However, this chapter may not be construed to limit the administrative or judicial authority of the state to ensure that medical care is provided to the child when there is imminent substantial risk of serious harm to the child....

(7)(a) "Child abuse or neglect" means:

- (i) actual physical or psychological harm to a child;
- (ii) substantial risk of physical or psychological harm to a child; or
- (iii) abandonment.

(b)(i) The term includes:

- (A) actual physical or psychological harm to a child or substantial risk of physical or psychological harm to a child by the acts or omissions of a person responsible for the child's welfare; or
- (B) exposing a child to the criminal distribution of dangerous drugs,...the criminal production or manufacture of dangerous drugs,...or the operation of an unlawful clandestine laboratory....

(c) In proceedings under this chapter in which the federal Indian Child Welfare Act is applicable, this term has the same meaning as "serious emotional or physical damage to the child" as used in 25 U.S.C. 1912(f).

(d) The term does not include self-defense, defense of others, or action taken to prevent the child from self-harm that does not constitute physical or psychological harm to a child....

(19) "Physical abuse" means an intentional act, an intentional omission, or gross negligence resulting in substantial skin bruising, internal bleeding, substantial injury to skin, subdural hematoma, burns, bone fractures, extreme pain, permanent or temporary disfigurement, impairment of any bodily organ or function, or death.

(20) "Physical neglect" means either failure to provide basic necessities, including but not limited to appropriate and adequate nutrition, protective shelter from the elements, and appropriate clothing related to weather conditions, or failure to provide cleanliness and general supervision, or both, or exposing or allowing the child to be exposed to an unreasonable physical or psychological risk to the child.

(21)(a) "Physical or psychological harm to a child" means the harm that occurs whenever the parent or other person responsible for the child's welfare:

(i) inflicts or allows to be inflicted upon the child physical abuse, physical neglect, or psychological abuse or neglect;

(ii) commits or allows sexual abuse or exploitation of the child;

(iii) induces or attempts to induce a child to give untrue testimony that the child or another child was abused or neglected by a parent or other person responsible for the child's welfare;

(iv) causes malnutrition or a failure to thrive or otherwise fails to supply the child with adequate food or fails to supply clothing, shelter, education, or adequate health care, though financially able to do so or offered financial or other reasonable means to do so;

(v) exposes or allows the child to be exposed to an unreasonable risk to the child's health or welfare by failing to intervene or eliminate the risk; or

(vi) abandons the child.

(b) The term does not include a youth not receiving supervision solely because of parental inability to control the youth's behavior....

(23)(a) "Psychological abuse or neglect" means severe maltreatment through acts or omissions that are injurious to the child's emotional, intellectual, or psychological capacity to function, including the commission of acts of violence against another person residing in the child's home.

(b) The term may not be construed to hold a victim responsible for failing to prevent the crime against the victim....

(27)(a) "Sexual abuse" means the commission of sexual assault, sexual intercourse without consent, indecent exposure, deviate sexual conduct, sexual abuse, ritual abuse, or incest....

(b) Sexual abuse does not include any necessary touching of an infant's or toddler's genital area while attending to the sanitary or health care needs of that infant or toddler by a parent or other person responsible for the child's welfare.

(28) "Sexual exploitation" means allowing, permitting, or encouraging a child to engage in a prostitution offense,...or allowing, permitting, or encouraging sexual abuse of children....

(33)(a) "Withholding of medically indicated treatment" means the failure to respond to an infant's life-threatening conditions by providing treatment, including appropriate nutrition, hydration, and medication, that, in the treating physician's or physicians' reasonable medical judgment, will be most likely to be effective in ameliorating or correcting the conditions.

(b) The term does not include the failure to provide treatment, other than appropriate nutrition, hydration, or medication, to an infant when, in the treating physician's or physicians' reasonable medical judgment:

(i) the infant is chronically and irreversibly comatose;

(ii) the provision of treatment would:

(A) merely prolong dying;

(B) not be effective in ameliorating or correcting all of the infant's life-threatening conditions; or

(C) otherwise be futile in terms of the survival of the infant; or

(iii) the provision of treatment would be virtually futile in terms of the survival of the infant and the treatment itself under the circumstances would be inhumane. For purposes of this subsection (33), "infant" means an infant less than 1 year of age or an infant 1 year of age or older who has been continuously hospitalized since birth, who was born extremely prematurely, or who has a long-term disability. The reference to less than 1 year of age may not be construed to imply that treatment should be changed or discontinued when an infant reaches 1 year of age or to affect or limit any existing protections available under state laws regarding medical neglect of children 1 year of age or older.

RHODE ISLAND GENERAL LAWS § 40-11-2 (2010)

(1) "Abused and/or neglected child" means a child whose physical or mental health or welfare is harmed or threatened with harm when his or her parent or other person responsible for his or her welfare:

(i) Inflicts or allows to be inflicted upon the child physical or mental injury, including excessive corporal punishment; or

(ii) Creates or allows to be created a substantial risk of physical or mental injury to the child, including excessive corporal punishment; or

(iii) Commits or allows to be committed, against the child, an act of sexual abuse; or

(iv) Fails to supply the child with adequate food, clothing, shelter, or medical care, though financially able to do so or offered financial or other reasonable means to do so; or

(v) Fails to provide the child with a minimum degree of care or proper supervision or guardianship because of his or her unwillingness or inability to do so by situations or conditions such as, but not limited to, social problems, mental incompetency, or the use of a drug, drugs, or alcohol to the extent that the parent or other person responsible for the child's welfare loses his or her ability or is unwilling to properly care for the child; or

(vi) Abandons or deserts the child; or

(vii) Sexually exploits the child in that the person allows, permits or encourages the child to engage in prostitution…; or

(viii) Sexually exploits the child in that the person allows, permits, encourages or engages in the obscene or pornographic photographing, filming or depiction of the child in a setting which taken as a whole suggests to the average person that the child is about to engage in or has engaged in, any sexual act, or which depicts any such child under eighteen (18) years of age, performing sodomy, oral copulation, sexual intercourse, masturbation, or bestiality; or

(ix) Commits or allows to be committed any sexual offense against the child...; or

(x) Commits or allows to be committed against any child an act involving sexual penetration or sexual contact if the child is under fifteen (15) years of age; or if the child is fifteen (15) years or older, and (1) force or coercion is used by the perpetrator, or (2) the perpetrator knows or has reason to know that the victim is a severely impaired person..., or physically helpless....

(6) "Institutional child abuse and neglect" means situations of known or suspected child abuse or neglect where the person allegedly responsible for the abuse or neglect is a foster parent or the employee of a public or private residential child care institution or agency; or any staff person providing out-of-home care or situations where the suspected abuse or neglect occurs as a result of the institution's practices, policies, or conditions....

(8) "Mental injury" includes a state of substantially diminished psychological or intellectual functioning in relation to, but not limited to, such factors as: failure to thrive; ability to think or reason; control of aggressive or self-destructive impulses; acting-out or misbehavior, including incorrigibility, ungovernability, or habitual truancy; provided, however, that the injury must be clearly attributable to the unwillingness or inability of the parent or other person responsible for the child's welfare to exercise a minimum degree of care toward the child....

(12) "Shaken baby syndrome" means a form of abusive head trauma, characterized by a constellation of symptoms caused by other than accidental traumatic injury resulting from the violent shaking of and/or impact upon an infant or young child's head.

NOTES AND QUESTIONS

1. How do these statutes define abuse? Neglect? Are the definitions the same? Do you think these statutes provide sufficient guidance to courts, caseworkers, and parents regarding what conduct is prohibited? Should statutes defining abuse and neglect provide more concrete definitions?

2. Recall that more than three-fourths of all maltreatment cases involve neglect. Should we require more specific definitions for neglect? A number of commentators have argued that more specific definitions may disadvantage children. See, e.g., MICHAEL S. WALD ET AL., PROTECTING ABUSED AND NEGLECTED CHILDREN 192 (1988) ("Our data clearly demonstrate that the great majority of the abused and neglected children were at substantial risk in terms of academic and social development even if they were not at risk of serious physical injury"); Howard Dubowitz et al., *A Conceptual Definition of Child Neglect*, 20 CRIM. JUST. & BEHAV. 8, 22 (1993) (arguing the focus should be on basic unmet needs of children rather than behavior of parents); Marsha Garrison, *Child Welfare Decisionmaking: In Search of the Least Drastic Alternative*, 75 GEO. L. J. 1745, 1799 (1987) ("In view of the varied circumstances that can evidence a serious risk to a child's well-being, and the concomitant difficulty of formulating a precise definition of the circumstances in which intervention is appropriate,...a somewhat open-ended definition of neglect, which relies on a broad array of symptoms and measurements is warranted" because children are better served by such an approach). Janet Weinstein and Ricardo Weinstein argue that because the human brain will not develop without appropriate

stimulation, the law should recognize inadequate brain development as a basis for the exercise of the state's neglect jurisdiction. They also propose a new definition of neglect to encompass the failure to provide physical safety, nutrition, medical care, and environmental stimulation and nurturing sufficient to ensure healthy development. Janet Weinstein & Ricardo Weinstein, *Before It's Too Late: Neuropsychological Consequences of Child Neglect and Their Implications for Law and Social Policy*, 33 U. Mich. J. L. Ref. 561, 600–601 (2000). What do you think of this proposed definition?

3. To what extent do poverty and race affect maltreatment? Bruce A. Boyer & Amy E. Halbrook, *Advocating for Children in Care in a Climate of Economic Recession: The Relationship between Poverty and Child Maltreatment*, 6 Nw. J. L. & Soc. Pol'y 300, 301–304 (2011):

> More than thirty years ago, Professor Leroy Pelton wrote about what he termed the "myth of classlessness," positing that many of the problems associated with child maltreatment are better understood as a reflection of the conditions in which many families live. Pelton cautioned that miscasting child abuse and neglect as a medical or psychodynamic problem related to behavior, rather than as a socioeconomic problem, would interfere with society's ability and willingness to develop effective interventions aimed at the roots of child maltreatment. Critics of CAPTA and the underlying philosophy espoused by its chief sponsor continue to echo many of these same themes, raising questions that take on added importance in a time of a deepening economic crisis. If we do not understand how entrenched social problems shape child maltreatment, we cannot possibly hope to forge effective strategies or solutions—on either an individual or a macro level—that actually serve the interests of children at risk of becoming involved in the child protection system.
>
> In the years since Professor Pelton's early work, social scientists have gathered a great deal of information about the relationship between poverty and child maltreatment. To be sure, child welfare professionals do not profess to understand fully the dynamics of how living in poverty aggravates either the occurrence of reports of child maltreatment or actual maltreatment itself. There is no single explanation for why children living in poverty are at a higher risk of reported abuse or neglect. Social scientists continue to debate the extent to which the root causes of this relationship arise from community norms, social isolation, chronic resource deficits, or simply from the increased exposure of poor families to public systems that often lead to protective interventions.
>
> Regardless of what may explain this correlation, its existence is beyond any reasonable dispute. In the past several decades, study after study has documented that children living in poverty are substantially more likely than children of affluence to be defined as abused or neglected and taken into foster care. Studies have documented increased rates of child maltreatment when measured in conjunction with nearly every marker of low socioeconomic status, including teen parenting; single-parent families; large sibling groups; and children whose parents are unemployed, lack a high school education, or receive public assistance.
>
> While the relationship between poverty and all forms of maltreatment is significant, it is especially so with child neglect, which encompasses forms of maltreatment related to environmental deprivations such as inadequate food and shelter or the failure to provide other forms of necessary care. Data collected by the United States Department of Health and Human Services for the 2010 National Incidence Study on Child Abuse and Neglect (NIS-4) indicated that among low socioeconomic status households, rates of reported child maltreatment were five times higher than for all other children and seven times higher in categories labeled as neglect. As the level of family income decreases, reports of neglect

increase at an even faster rate than reports of abuse. One study found that, while all forms of maltreatment increase with lower levels of family income, the relationship between poverty and neglect is especially pronounced: for families living in the highest levels of poverty, neglect accounts for nearly two-thirds of all reports of harm. The underlying message of all of these studies is succinctly described in Andrea Sedlak's *Supplementary Analyses of Race Differences in Child Maltreatment Rates in the NIS-4*: "[I]ncome, or socioeconomic status, is the strongest predictor of maltreatment rates."

It is also important to acknowledge that state interventions aimed at child maltreatment continue to affect racial minorities disproportionately. A policy brief released in 2005 by the Annie E. Casey Foundation noted that while children of color made up 42 percent of the U.S. child population, they made up 57 percent of all children in foster care. Staggeringly, African American children made up 15 percent of the total U.S. child population, yet they made up 33.9 percent of the population of children in foster care. Compared to non-Hispanic white children, African American children were disproportionately represented at a rate of 3.09 to 1. Native American children were disproportionately represented at a rate of 2.95 to 1. Beyond the problem of overrepresentation, research indicates that children of color receive fewer supportive services than their white peers, stay in the system longer, are less likely to be reunited with their families, and take longer to be adopted.

The NIS-4, relying on data gathered in 2005 and 2006, reported, for the first time, race differences in child maltreatment rates, with black children experiencing several types of maltreatment at a higher rate than white children. This statistic correlates closely with the increasing disparity in income distribution by race: according to NIS-4, only 21.8 percent of white children in the study were classified as low socioeconomic status, compared with 61.6 percent of black children. From their analysis of the NIS-4 data, the study authors concluded that the higher incidence of maltreatment of black children most likely arises not because of their race, but because of their lower socioeconomic status. The implications of this disparity, in a society that purports to administer justice without regard to race, are profound.

Do you think that children of affluent parents are less likely to be abused or neglected? Or less likely to be reported? Why? Should poverty be a basis for neglect? Some states make clear that a child may not be removed for neglect solely on the basis of the parents' financial circumstances. See, *e.g.*, La. Children's Code Art. 603 (2011) ("inability of a parent or caretaker to provide for a child due to inadequate financial resources shall not, for that reason alone, be considered neglect"). Is this a sound policy approach? Is it constitutional to remove a child from his or her family when the parents are unable to provide for the child's needs because of their impoverishment? See Daan Braveman & Sarah Ramsey, *When Welfare Ends: Removing Children from the Home for Poverty Alone*, 70 Temp. L. Rev. 447 (1997) (arguing that Fourteenth Amendment would prohibit removal based on poverty alone).

The National Incidence Study (NIS) is a congressionally mandated research protocol to provide estimates of the incidence of child abuse and neglect in the United States. The NIS relies on information collected by state child-protective agencies for children who were investigated along with data about children who were screened out or not investigated by such agencies but who were deemed maltreated by community professionals. To date, four studies have been conducted. For the first time, NIS-4 found statistically significant racial differences in the rates of maltreatment. The authors of the study attribute this finding to better data estimation in NIS-4 and also to the increasing socioeconomic gap between white and African-American children and their families. "Income, or socioeconomic status, is the strongest predictor of maltreatment rates, but since the time of the NIS–3, incomes of Black families have not kept pace with the incomes of White families." Andrea J. Sedlak et al., Supplementary Analyses of Race Differences in Child Maltreatment Rates in the NIS-4, Admin. for Children and Families, Dep't. of Health and Human Services (2010), http://www.acf.hhs.gov/programs/opre/abuse_neglect/natl_incid/reports/supp_analysis/nis4_supp_analysis_race_diff_mar2010.pdf.

The NIS-4 findings on race were a departure from the findings of NIS-2 and NIS-3, which found no racial differences in maltreatment. The authors of NIS-3 concluded that racial differences arise because of differences in the way the child-welfare system responds to African-American children and their families. Nevertheless, NIS-4 confirmed that racial differences in maltreatment rates exist. To what extent do racial prejudices and biases affect child welfare? Based on work presented at the Race and Child Welfare Conference that took place at Harvard Law School in January 2011, conference organizers concluded that higher rates of contact between the child-welfare system and African-American families reflect differences in the underlying incidence of actual maltreatment, "which contradicts the belief that black children are included at high rates…because of racial bias." Elizabeth Bartholet et al., Race and Child Welfare 3–4 (2011), http://www.law.harvard.edu/programs/about/cap/cap-conferences/rd-conference/rd-conference-papers/rd-conference---issue-brief---final.pdf.

Long before the NIS-4 reported its findings on racial disparity, Dorothy Roberts argued that there is racially disparate treatment of African-American children in the child-welfare system. While acknowledging that "poverty is key to explaining why any child gets in the system," Roberts argues that even if one assumes that the racial difference evident in the child-welfare system is attributable to the lower socioeconomic status of African-American children and their families, that difference ultimately results from conceptual flaws in the child-welfare system.

> The child welfare system is designed not as a way for government to assist parents in taking care of their children, but as a means to punish parents for their failures by threatening to take their children away. The child *welfare* system, then, is a misnomer. The primary mission of state agencies is not to promote children's welfare. Rather, their purpose has become child *protection*: they try to protect children from the effects of society's colossal failure to care enough about children's welfare. The system is activated only after children have already experienced harm and puts all the blame on parents for their children's problems. This punitive function falls heaviest on African American parents because they are most likely to suffer from poverty and institutional discrimination, and to be blamed for the effects on their children….
>
> Even if the racial disparity could be explained entirely by higher black poverty rates and not intentional discrimination, this would not negate the racist impact of the system or the racist reasons for its inequities. State disruption of families is one symptom of this institutionalized discrimination. It reflects the persistent gulf between the material welfare of black and white children in America. The racial disparity in the child welfare system—even if related directly to economic inequality—ultimately results from racial injustice.

Dorothy Roberts, *Child Welfare and Civil Rights*, 2003 U. Ill. L. Rev. 171, 176–177. Do you agree? If Roberts is correct, what is the remedy?

i. Abuse

According to the most recent NCANDS report, 17.6 percent of maltreated children are physically abused, 9.2 percent are sexually abused, and 8.1 percent are psychologically maltreated. U.S. Dep't of Health & Human Servs., Admin. for Children & Families, Admin. on Children,

Youth, and Families, Children's Bureau, Child Maltreatment 2010 23 (2011). What constitutes physical abuse? Consider the following case when formulating your answer.

PARKER V. ARKANSAS DEPARTMENT OF HUMAN SERVICES
Court of Appeals of Arkansas
2011 Ark. App. 8

JOSEPHINE LINKER HART, Judge.

This dependency-neglect case involves allegations that a mother subjected her eleven month-old son to Munchausen Syndrome by Proxy. Appellant Kristen Parker challenges the sufficiency of the evidence to support the circuit court's determination that her son, M.P., who was born on November 26, 2008, was dependent-neglected. We affirm.

The child was admitted to Arkansas Children's Hospital (ACH) on November 11, 2009, for fever, vomiting, and reduced oral intake, after being seen in the emergency room on two previous occasions for similar complaints. The staff at ACH alleged that appellant had tampered with M.P.'s intravenous line; reported symptoms that were inconsistent with the child's physical examinations; and requested the physicians to perform an endoscopic procedure on M.P. that they did not believe was needed. DHS filed a petition for emergency custody of M.P. in the Saline County Circuit Court on November 19, 2009, on the basis of the following affidavit:

> b. On November 16, 2009, FSW was notified there were concerns that Munchausen Syndrome by Proxy may have taken place with [M.P.] The mother was observed tampering with the IV three times, it was out the first time, she was then told not to touch the IV again. The second time it was out and clamped in two places, she was told again to not touch the IV. The third time, IV monitoring alarm was silenced and a blue clamp was removed from under the tape and used to clamp off the IV; there was blood in the hub of the IV. The mother was observed reviewing the patient's red folder without aid for interpretation. The mother took the child's temperature rectally and asked was the temperature high enough for medication; she also requested a scope for the patient, because he has been throwing up since birth. She was also observed moving the bed to avoid being monitored. The mother also refused to speak to a social worker, saying that she was a nurse and knew about Munchausen's Syndrome by Proxy, when no one had ever mentioned that to her. On few different occasions, mother seemed to handle patient roughly, trying to force-feed his bottle, when patient was crying and turning his head away. There was contradictory history of feeding disorder and possible pediatric condition falsification, such as having a high fever, which was not to be true. Also the A/O was seen mixing liquid substance into patients' bottle while on restricted feeds. There were also other symptoms reported by mother that was [*sic*] not observed.

The circuit court entered an emergency custody order on November 19, 2009, and held a probable-cause hearing five days later. In the order finding probable cause, the court authorized supervised visitation for appellant.

Appellant attended the adjudication hearing held on February 11, 2009, with her attorney. Persons testifying at the hearing included appellant; Skye Adams, a social worker at

ACH; Dr. Jerry Jones, a pediatrician at ACH who specializes in child-maltreatment evaluations; Dr. Laura Sisterhen, a pediatrician at ACH; Jessica Hamilton, a registered nurse at ACH; Christine Jeffrey, a registered nurse at ACH; Craig Jones, a social worker who has seen appellant at the direction of DHS; Roderick Rhodes, M.P.'s grandfather; Brooke Hobby, an LPN who is a close friend of appellant; and Dr. Chad Rodgers, M.P.'s primary-care physician.

Dr. Jones testified that Dr. Sisterhen asked him to consult with her and the hospital's team for at-risk children about her concerns that appellant was requesting potentially risky inappropriate or unneeded care for M.P. He stated that the concerns expressed at the conference were that appellant appeared highly anxious, making frequent telephone calls to Dr. Rodgers and the hospital's telephone help-line; that appellant appeared so stressed on one occasion that she had to leave the area and take a handful of pills; that appellant had reported that M.P. had not eaten or drunk much for two months, even though the child was at the ninety-fifth percentile for weight and height; that appellant had stated that she did not need a visit by a social worker because she fed her baby and knew about Munchausen by Proxy; that the high fevers that she had described were not present on prior visits; that she had asked for an unnecessary scope to be performed; that on two occasions, the child's IV had been disconnected; that on one occasion, the IV had been clamped closed under a bandage; that appellant had falsified M.P.'s high fever and had wanted the IV fluids to be continued, even though it was not indicated; and that, on the 13th or 14th of November, the nurses reported that appellant had given something in a dropper to M.P. that had not been prescribed. He said that the team decided to conduct a period of close observation.

Dr. Jones stated that, after the conference, he met with appellant, who provided a history of the child's having eaten very well, which contradicted the history that she had given to the other physicians. He explained that this was of particular concern because physicians rely on parents to give an accurate history of the child's symptoms; if the history is not reliable, the physicians could perform procedures that are risky, that result in repeated or prolonged hospitalizations, and that could affect the child's physical and emotional development, especially considering the risk of acquiring an infection in the hospital. Dr. Jones stated that even a relatively routine procedure involves a certain amount of risk and that he considered a parent's clamping or disconnecting an IV to be very serious. He testified that the child did not need a scope and was, in fact, very well-developed and well-nourished. Dr. Jones opined that M.P. was a victim of child-maltreatment syndrome, specifically, pediatric condition falsification, which is a preferred term for Munchausen by Proxy. He also said that he did not believe that it was necessary for appellant to be given a psychological evaluation before he could conclude that this had occurred. He conceded that he had no evidence that appellant had actually made the child ill, but he believed that she had falsified M.P.'s condition. He added that she had also taken the child to Dr. Rodgers when there was nothing wrong with him. Dr. Jones acknowledged, however, that M.P. had suffered from a recent ear infection and may have had a fever; that M.P. had had tubes placed in his ears; that it is not unusual for a mother to be highly stressed and anxious when a young child has medical difficulties; and that appellant had previously lost a child.

Dr. Laura Sisterhen testified that M.P. was admitted to her care on November 11, 2009. She stated that M.P. had been seen in the emergency room on November 9 and 10 for complaints of fever, reduced oral intake, and decreased urine output; on the day of admission to the hospital for dehydration, appellant had stated that he had run a fever as high as 105 degrees. Under her care, she said, he was given intravenous fluids. Because M.P. developed a bloody discharge from one of his ears, and because appellant raised concerns about M.P.'s having choked on food, Dr. Sisterhen sought speech pathology and ear, nose, and throat consultations. Dr. Sisterhen said that appellant asked for a scope to see why M.P. was choking but did not tell her that the child had already been seen by an ear, nose, and throat specialist for ear infections the previous summer.

Dr. Sisterhen said that appellant's description of M.P.'s feeding history varied daily. Even though appellant had concerns about his not being able to eat solid food well or drink from a cup, he was observed at the hospital drinking from a cup and eating solid food without problems. Dr. Sisterhen said that, without a straight-forward history, it was hard to evaluate whether M.P. was at risk for aspiration but because of his lack of overt signs of obstruction or frequent aspiration, she did not believe that it was necessary for M.P.'s airways to be scoped. She testified that, throughout his hospitalization, M.P. looked like a well-child; he was playful, very alert, and active, even on the first day of his hospital stay. She said that when she talked to appellant about her observations, appellant replied that he was not having any urine output or eating or drinking. On the third day of the hospitalization, appellant told her in the morning that he had not had a wet diaper all night, but upon inspection, his diaper was soaking wet. Dr. Sisterhen said that M.P.'s temperature was normal. She said that, although appellant was pleasant, she seemed very anxious about M.P. and his health and would cry at times. She added that she never saw a real maternal bond between appellant and M.P.

Dr. Sisterhen stated that appellant admitted that she had disconnected the IV. She said that, even though the nurses had asked appellant not to do so, she did it again. She said that M.P.'s hospital stay was prolonged—which was risky—by appellant's reporting of his symptoms and tampering with the IV. Dr. Sisterhen said that, after Dr. Jones interviewed appellant, appellant asked her if he was a social worker. When she replied that he was a physician, appellant responded defensively, stating that she knew about Munchausen by Proxy. She conceded that she had no evidence that appellant had caused M.P. to run a fever or vomit but believed that this case was unusual because of appellant's history of appointments, calling after hours, and calling the primary care physician on his cell phone multiple times. Dr. Sisterhen said that none of the symptoms for which he was admitted were documented at the hospital, although appellant took his temperature rectally, indicating a fever, while he was there. She admitted that she had received a report of M.P.'s choking on a chicken nugget at the hospital and that, on November 13th, she had noticed a discharge crusted around M.P.'s ear and on the bed.

Jessica Hamilton testified that, on one occasion, she was called into M.P.'s room by appellant and found the IV tubing hanging on the pole. She said that appellant explained that she had worked in an emergency room and had disconnected the IV because she needed to remove M.P.'s shirt. Ms. Hamilton stated that she informed appellant that if she needed a nurse to disconnect the IV, she should let one of the nurses know, because that was their responsibility. She said that, even though appellant appeared to understand this, the IV was again disconnected and clamped in two different places. She stated that she again explained to appellant that she should not touch the IV equipment. She said that the child's chart indicated that someone had removed the ace wrap with the IV hose and had clamped the tubing near the IV. Ms. Hamilton testified that it is the hospital's practice to check the patient's temperature orally or under the arm, and when she checked M.P.'s temperature and determined he had no fever, appellant personally took M.P.'s temperature rectally. Ms. Hamilton said that, on another occasion, appellant came to the nurses' station, stating that he had been throwing up since he was born and that he needed a scope. According to Ms. Hamilton, M.P. was a normal, active, and smiling eleven-month-old, and she never observed a fever, although he did vomit once during the three days that he was under her care. She also said that she did not believe that appellant's explanation of M.P.'s feeding history was consistent.

Skye Adams, who did the child-abuse assessment, testified that appellant was upset when she learned that the team at ACH was going to report the case to the Child Abuse Hotline. She said that appellant yelled at her but soon after apologized for her behavior. Ms. Adams's assessment was admitted into evidence. This report noted that appellant is bipolar, receives disability, and had lost a child fifteen years ago. Christine Jeffrey testified that, while M.P. was in her care for two days (in a room with a video camera), she saw appellant adding something to M.P.'s bottle to thicken it, contrary to doctor's orders. She also said that appellant moved M.P.'s crib partially out of the video camera's view. She stated that appellant became angry at the social worker, but appellant made no threats and later apologized.

Craig Jones testified that DHS had referred appellant to his care, and that, since December 11, 2009, he had seen her five times. He said that it was too soon to arrive at a psychiatric diagnosis for her, but his provisional diagnosis was that she suffered from an adjustment disorder, unspecified, a recently resolved relational issue with a partner, and, based on her description of services that she had received through the Veterans Administration, borderline personality disorder. He emphasized, however, that he needed more information and was not able to make a firm diagnosis of the neglected child's perpetrator.

Dr. Chad Rodgers testified that he had served as M.P.'s pediatrician all of his life and had seen M.P., who was premature, about eleven times, most recently a month before the hearing, for ear infections, wheezing, reflux, vomiting, diarrhea, runny nose, and cough. He stated that appellant had not called him on his cell phone until the hospitalization and explained that he had previously instructed appellant to add some cereal to M.P.'s bottle to help with his reflux. He admitted that he had become concerned in November 2009 because, even though appellant had reported a lot of vomiting and refusal to drink, M.P. appeared very well and hydrated in his office visits. He said that he trusted Dr. Jones's assessment. He stated that he knew that appellant had lost a child and that M.P. was the only child she would be able to have, and described her personality as a little dramatic and over-concerned. He said that M.P. was happy, growing well, and had a pretty good relationship with appellant, and that, if he had believed that maltreatment had occurred, he would have reported it.

Roderick Rhodes and Brooke Hobby testified that they believed that appellant is a good mother to M.P. Appellant testified that, after working as a certified nursing assistant, she had joined the Navy, from which she was discharged on disability after two years because of back, knee, and shoulder problems. She said that her first child had died shortly after birth and she had miscarried before becoming pregnant with M.P., who was born two months prematurely. She said that she and M.P. had lived with her parents since she separated from her husband. Appellant testified that M.P. had spit up frequently and that the doctor had told her to add rice cereal to his bottle to help with reflux. She said that she had taken him to the Little Rock Pediatric Clinic and hospital after-hours clinics for well-child visits, reflux, ear infections, asthma, allergies, pneumonia, cough, runny nose, and fever; that she had handled many of her questions by calling the nurse at the medical exchange; that an ear, nose, and throat specialist had seen M.P.; and that M.P. had been circumcised at ACH.

Appellant testified that she had taken M.P. to the emergency room on October 29 and November 9 and 10, 2009. She said that, on November 9, he had a fever of 105.9 degrees, was lethargic, and vomiting; he was discharged early the next morning. The next day, she said, she took M.P. to Dr. Rodgers's office because he had stopped taking his bottle; Dr. Rodgers ordered some blood work and told her to see if she could get M.P. to drink any fluid. At home, she said, M.P. drank some Gatorade but threw up some pizza. Appellant said that his temperature went to 103.4 degrees, and she called the medical exchange for Dr. Rodgers; she then took M.P. to the emergency room at ACH, where he was admitted. Appellant said that, when M.P. was first admitted, Dr. Sisterhen told her to feed him whatever he wanted, with no restrictions, and that she was permitted to keep his labeled rice cereal, soy-milk formula, and baby-food fruit in the hospital refrigerator. She explained that she moved his crib in the next room to which he was assigned because the light was shining on his head; she was not aware that there was a camera in the room.

Appellant acknowledged disconnecting M.P.'s IV on the 11th so she could change his shirt, after getting no response to her request for help from his nurse, Jessica Hamilton. She said that she then asked the nurse to reconnect it, and a male nurse came in, cleaned off the tubing, and reconnected it; it was disconnected for only two or three minutes. She also explained her disconnection of the IV tubing on the 12th after M.P. had pulled loose the brown stocking that covered the plastic cap over the site of the IV; this stocking was designed to keep the baby from pulling the IV out. She said that, even though she asked for help with the stocking from the nurses, they did not provide any help, and M.P. pulled the stocking all the way up his arm and grabbed the tubing. Appellant described her two choices at that point:

> I could undo it and hang it back over and stop him from pulling on the tubing, or I could let him continue to do it and risk a chance of him actually pulling the actual tube out and catheter out and have to re-site the IV.... So I called the nurse again, and I had told them what he was doing. I got no response. I sat there, and I was holding him for about 15 minutes waiting....
>
> ...So I unhooked it, and I hung it back over the top. And I sat there, and I was holding him. So what happened was the alarm started going off, and it beeps when it's not connected. So what happened was I silenced it, and I called the nurse.... I said, his monitor's going off. I said, I've asked ya'll would you please come back in here and fix the stocking on his arm and reconnect the tubing. I said because he's going to pull his IV out. It was about ten minutes later, and I'm rocking him, and this curly-headed nurse comes in and she has a gentleman behind her, and I haven't been introduced to her. She wasn't my nurse for that night. They were in the middle of shift change. But it's not documented in her notes. So the nurse comes in, and I sat M.P. down on the bed. And she lifts up the cap, the plastic thing that's over there, and you've got to keep in mind I've already pulled the stocking off. So she lifts up the cap and there's tape over the cap. So she lifts up the cap, and she's messing with it underneath, and she takes the tubing, and she didn't even wipe it off with alcohol swab. She takes the tubing and she sticks it back in there, and she goes, I don't even know, she goes, I don't even know what I'm messing with here.... I don't even know how this goes on. But I assume she reconnected it because she messed with the machine, and she started letting it flow again. And it wasn't showing occluded, and I'm sorry that I'm using these terms. You have to understand I worked in the emergency room, and so I know what—anyway it wasn't showing occluded. It was showing that it was flowing. So I assume that it was running. So I put M.P. back, and we were rocking in the chair. So we're rocking, no problem. I'm still waiting for the stocking to be replaced because it still at this point has not been replaced. So I'm having to hold him. So I noticed that my shirt is wet. And I've got this big wet spot down here. So I pull M.P. away from me, and I look down,... and I feel his diaper, and he's not wet. And then I look down around me. And then his IV tubing is

> sitting down on the floor. And so there's a big puddle of water. So I called the nurse again.... I said his IV tubing is down on the floor, and my shirt is wet. And they said, okay, Ms. Parker. We'll send somebody in. So I'm automatically assuming they're thinking, okay, well, she did this. And so when finally the nurse came in it was my nighttime nurse, the 7:00 p to 7:00 a, and I don't remember her name. She didn't introduce herself.... And I explained to her that the curly-headed nurse with the gentleman behind her had just came in and re-connected the IV. And she asked me why it was disconnected in the first place for her to come in. I said, because I had, he had pulled his stocking off, and he was pulling on his IV. I said, I went to the front desk. I asked for some scissors to replace the stocking, and they said they would order some up. She said, oh, yeah, I got the scissors, but they're not supposed to be on the unit so I took them away. And we were in the middle of shift change. So I told her, I said, I was rocking him. I got this wet spot. I thought he had wet through his diaper. I looked down, the IV tubing's on the floor. And I said, hence why it's hanging up over here again. So I said, there it is disconnected again. So I wasn't aware that anything was clamped off under here or anything because I didn't touch it.

In the adjudication order, the circuit court made the following findings:

> 4. The Court finds that the juvenile, M.P.... is dependent-neglected as a result of parental unfitness, neglect, and abuse. The Court finds that the juvenile has been subjected to Pediatric Condition Falsification, Munchausen syndrome by proxy, also known as factitious illness by proxy, as reported and confirmed by medical personnel or a medical facility....
>
> 13. The Court carefully considered the testimony of... all witnesses, found the testimony of Dr. Jerry Jones and Dr. Laura Sisterhen to be the most credible. Specifically, the Court carefully considered the mother's testimony and found her not to be credible. The Court finds that Kristin Parker gave unsatisfactory explanations for disconnecting or otherwise tampering with the child's IV. Physicians at Arkansas Children's Hospital, Dr. Laura Sisterhen and Dr. Jerry Jones, were unable to observe or confirm the conditions and symptoms reported by the mother, *i.e.*, fever, vomiting, dehydration, diarrhea, lack of urine output, gagging, choking, reflux, difficulty in swallowing, etc. There was no clinical evidence of the mother's reported illnesses. The mother's reported history, at best, included inconsistencies; *i.e.* she reported that the child had not eaten properly for two months; however, the child is in the 96th percentile for his age and weight. The result of this, at best, included unnecessary hospitalization and treatment for M.P., which increased the risk of infection.

The court set reunification as the goal and continued supervised visitation.

On appeal, appellant argues that the evidence did not support the circuit court's finding that the child was dependent-neglected. She points out that she has not been diagnosed with Munchausen Syndrome by Proxy; that M.P. was diagnosed with illnesses on the occasions that he was taken to the emergency room; that there was no evidence that she caused those illnesses; that he did not undergo unnecessary medical procedures; and that he had to see the doctor after he was in foster care. She also asserts that Dr. Jones's conclusion was based on nothing more than speculation and was offered as a rationalization for the hospital's conduct toward her when their relationship became strained. Although appellant admits that she removed M.P.'s IV, she points out that no harm resulted. She contends that there was no basis to conclude that she was abusive for simply being attentive to her child's medical needs.

Adjudication hearings are held to determine whether the allegations in a petition are substantiated by the proof. Dependency-neglect allegations must be proven by a preponderance of the evidence. Ark. Code Ann. § 9-27-325(h)(2)(B) (Repl. 2009). We will not reverse the circuit court's findings unless they are clearly erroneous. *Seago v. Arkansas Dep't of Human Servs.*, 2009 Ark.App. 767, ___ S.W.3d ___. In reviewing a dependency-neglect adjudication, we defer to the circuit court's evaluation of the credibility of the witnesses. *Id.*

Arkansas Code Annotated section 9-27-303(18)(A) (Repl. 2009) defines a "dependent-neglected juvenile" as any juvenile who is at substantial risk of serious harm as a result of abuse, among other acts or omissions. Section 9-27-303(3)(A)(vii)(j) defines "abuse" as "[s]ubjecting a child to Munchausen syndrome by proxy, also known as factitious illness by proxy, when reported and confirmed by medical personnel or a medical facility." The statute does not require that actual physical injury occur. Munchausen syndrome by proxy has been defined as follows:

> Munchausen syndrome by proxy is the name given to factitious disorders in children produced by their parents or caregivers. The American Psychiatric Association defines factitious disorder by proxy as "the deliberate production or feigning of physical or psychological signs or symptoms in another person who is under the individual's care," motivated by the perpetrator's need to assume the sick role by proxy. Munchausen syndrome is distinguished from Munchausen syndrome by proxy in that the medical attention is sought for oneself.

In re Hope L. v. Benjamin L., 278 Neb. 869, 895–96, 775 N.W.2d 384, 402 (2009).

We recognize that the evidence presented at the adjudication hearing by DHS was countered by evidence that, before M.P.'s admission to ACH in November 2009, no medical professional had raised any concerns about appellant's behavior or M.P.'s well-being; that M.P. was born prematurely; that it is not unusual for premature infants to have reflux; that M.P. had suffered from ear infections frequently enough to warrant the surgical placement of tubes in his ears at ACH; and that M.P. was happy, active, well-nourished, and growing well. Nevertheless, we do defer to the trial court's superior position to observe the parties and judge the witnesses' credibility. Given the standard of review that we follow in cases such as this, we cannot say that the circuit court's findings were clearly erroneous.

Affirmed.

NOTES AND QUESTIONS

1. Do you think the state met its burden of proving that the child was abused? If the statute had not included any reference to Münchausen syndrome by proxy, do you think the state could establish abuse? Why?

2. *Münchausen syndrome by proxy.* The American Psychological Association, which publishes the *Diagnostic and Statistical Manual of Mental Disorders* (DSM), lists the recognized mental disorders. The fourth edition, text revision, published in 2000 (DSM-IV-TR), identifies factitious disorders as disorders "characterized by physical or psychological symptoms that are intentionally produced or feigned in order to assume the sick role." A factitious disorder by proxy, often called Münchausen syndrome by proxy is the deliberate production or feigning of physical or psychological signs or symptoms in another person who is under the individual's care.

Typically the victim is a young child and the perpetrator is the child's mother. The motivation for the perpetrator's behavior is presumed to be a psychological need to assume the sick role by proxy. External incentives for the behavior, such as economic gain, are absent. The behavior is not better accounted for by another mental disorder. The perpetrator induces or simulates the illness or disease process in the victim and then presents the victim for medical care while disclaiming any knowledge about the actual etiology of the problem. The most common induced and simulated conditions include persistent vomiting or diarrhea, respiratory arrest, asthma, central nervous system dysfunction (e.g., seizures, uncoordination, loss of consciousness), fever, infection, bleeding, failure to thrive, hypoglycemia, electrolyte disturbances, and rash. The simulation of mental disorders in the victim is much less frequently reported. The type and severity of signs and symptoms are limited only by the medical sophistication and opportunities of the perpetrator. Cases are often characterized by an atypical clinical course in the victim and inconsistent laboratory test results that are at variance with the seeming health of the victim.

The victim is usually a preschool child, although newborns, adolescents, and adults may be used as victims. With older children, consideration should be given to the possibility of collaboration with the perpetrator in the production of signs and symptoms.

AM. PSYCHOL. ASS'N., DIAGNOSTIC AND STATISTICAL MANUAL OF MENTAL DISORDERS 781 (4th ed., text. rev. 2000).

3. The American Professional Society on the Abuse of Children (APSAC) is a national nonprofit organization that offers expert training and education to professionals who serve children and families affected by child maltreatment and violence, including doctors, psychiatrists, psychologists, police, social workers, therapists, and lawyers. APSAC has drawn a distinction between the abuse of the child and the psychiatric disorder in the parent by labeling the abuse as pediatric condition falsification. Catherine C. Ayoub et al., APSAC Taskforce on Munchausen by Proxy, Definitions Working Group, *Position Paper: Definitional Issues in Munchausen by Proxy*, 7 CHILD MALTREATMENT 105, 106 (2002). Nevertheless, it is important to recognize that simply because a parent lies about how the child was injured, that does not indicate Münchausen syndrome by proxy; rather, the parent may be seeking to gain some advantage in a custody dispute, may wish the child to stay home from school to help with parenting responsibilities, may have some other identifiable psychiatric disorder, or may simply be lying to cover an intentional act of child abuse. *Id.* at 108–109.

4. How common is Münchausen by proxy? Because of the nature of the disorder, it is difficult to tell how many cases in the United States go undetected; however, some estimate at least six hundred new cases a year based on suffocation and nonaccidental poisoning alone. *Id.* at 105. Nevertheless, the disorder is rare. John Stirling, Am. Acad. Pediatrics, Comm. on Child Abuse & Neglect, *Beyond Munchausen Syndrome by Proxy: Identification and Treatment of Child Abuse in a Medical Setting*, 119 PEDIATRICS 1026, 1026 (2007) (while questioning how disorder could be identified as syndrome given the wide range of behaviors associated with it, nevertheless noting that child abuse is a medical diagnosis that does not depend on motivations of caregiver). For a critique of the syndrome, see Melinda Cleary, *Mothering under the Microscope: Gender Bias in Law and Medicine and the Problem of Munchausen Syndrome by Proxy*, 7 T.M. COOLEY J. PRAC. & CLINICAL L. 183 (2005); Eric G. Mart, *Problems with the Diagnosis of Factitious Disorder by Proxy in Forensic Settings*, 17 AM. J. FORENSIC PSYCHOL. 69 (1999); Sean A. Spence et al., *"Munchausen's Syndrome by Proxy" or a "Miscarriage of Justice"? An Initial Application of Functional Neuroimaging to the Question of Guilt versus Innocence*, 23 EUROPEAN PSYCHIATRY 309, 309–310 (2007) (fMRI scan conducted on woman consistent with

her claims she did not poison her child despite criminal conviction based on Münchausen by proxy testimony).

5. To prove abuse by alleging that the child's mother, a licensed practical nurse, suffered from Münchausen syndrome by proxy, could the state offer expert testimony "(1) that perpetrators of MSBP typically are the children's mothers; (2) that they often are health care professionals themselves; and (3) that the father in MSBP cases is often emotionally or physically absent"? See *In re Adoption of Keefe*, 733 N.E.2d 1075, 1080 (Mass. App. 2000); *contra In the Matter of Aaron S.*, 163 Misc.2d 967, 977, 625 N.Y.S.2d 786 (N.Y. Fam. Ct. 1993), aff'd *sub nom. In re Suffolk County Dept. of Social Servs.*, 215 A.D.2d 395, 626 N.Y.S.2d 227 (N.Y. App. Div. 1995).

6. NCANDS defines physical abuse as "physical acts that caused or could have caused physical injury to a child." Certain types of injuries in infants and toddlers, such as multiple, unexplained fractures, may be indicative of physical abuse. The American Academy of Pediatrics Committee on Child Abuse and Neglect, however, notes that a number of medical conditions may cause multiple bone fractures in infants and young toddlers. These include osteogenesis imperfecta (a genetic disorder), rickets (a vitamin D deficiency uncommonly seen in some breastfed infants or dark-skinned children with inadequate exposure to sunlight), osteomyelitis (bone inflammation usually caused by an infection), copper deficiency (present in some preterm infants, which can cause bone fractures), and handling paralyzed infants whose bone structure is fragile. Carole Jenny, Am. Acad. Pediatrics, Comm. on Child Abuse & Neglect, *Evaluating Infants and Young Children with Multiple Fractures*, 118 PEDIATRICS 1299, 1299–1301 (2006). The committee nevertheless rejects theories that infants may suffer temporarily from brittle-bone disease. "Temporary brittle-bone disease is neither clinically validated nor generally accepted by expert professionals and should not be invoked to explain multiple fractures in an infant." *Id.* at 1301.

7. *Shaken baby syndrome.* Abusive head trauma (AHT) is another example of physical abuse. It is often called "shaken baby syndrome," but shaking is merely one way of causing neurological injury to a newborn, infant, or child. Physical evidence often cited by courts consists of subdural hematomas and retinal hemorrhages. Blunt impact or shaking and blunt impact also may cause injuries, including mental retardation, cerebral palsy, seizure disorders, learning disabilities, blindness, or even death. The American Academy of Pediatrics, recognizing the educational utility of keeping the term "shaken baby syndrome" in the popular lexicon, nevertheless "recommends adoption of the term 'abusive head trauma' as the diagnosis used in the medical chart to describe the constellation of cerebral, spinal, and cranial injuries that result from inflicted head injury to infants and young children." Cindy W. Christian & Robert M. Block, Am. Acad. Pediatrics, Comm. on Child Abuse & Neglect, *Policy Statement: Abusive Head Trauma in Infants and Children*, 123 PEDIATRICS 1409, 1410 (2009).

ii. Corporal punishment

Parents generally are privileged to use corporal punishment, although that punishment must not be "unreasonable" or "excessive." But when does corporal punishment become abusive? Is it abuse if a parent uses an open hand and leaves a bruise? When a belt or switch is used? If the child experiences pain well after the punishment has ceased? The next case grapples with some of these issues.

WILLIS V. INDIANA
Supreme Court of Indiana
888 N.E.2d 177 (2008)

RUCKER, Justice.

This case requires us to examine the balance that must be struck in determining when a parent's use of physical force as a form of discipline crosses the line into criminal conduct. We conclude the line was not crossed in this instance.

Background and Procedural History

Sophia Willis is a single mother raising her eleven-year-old son, J.J., who has a history of untruthfulness and taking property belonging to others. The events at issue in this case began at an elementary school Friday, February 3, 2006. On that date J.J.'s fifth grade teacher, Ms. McCuen, saw J.J. giving a bag of women's clothing to a classmate. Finding this to be an "odd exchange," Ms. McCuen contacted J.J.'s mother. Willis met with Ms. McCuen and identified the clothing as hers.

Experiencing ongoing disciplinary problems with J.J., Willis sent him to her sister's home over the next two days to ponder her options. When J.J. returned on Sunday Willis had a long conversation with her son and questioned him about his conduct. J.J. denied taking the clothing and instead concocted a story that shifted blame to other students. Willis warned that if he did not tell the truth he would be punished. J.J. again gave the same story. In response Willis instructed J.J. to remove his pants and place his hands on the upper bunk bed. J.J. complied, and Willis proceeded to strike him five to seven times with either a belt or an extension cord.[1] Although trying to swat J.J. on the buttocks, his attempt to avoid the swats resulted in some of them landing on his arm and thigh leaving bruises. J.J. testified that during this exchange his mother was "mad." Willis countered that she was not angry but "disappointed."

The following Monday J.J. returned from gym class and asked to see the school nurse.[2] Showing the nurse the bruises, J.J. told her that he received a "whooping" from his mother "[b]ecause I had took some clothes and I had lied." The nurse contacted child protective services that in turn contacted the Indianapolis Police Department.

Willis was arrested and charged with battery as a Class D felony. After a bench trial she was found guilty as charged. At the sentencing hearing, the trial court acknowledged that Willis was a single mother attempting to raise a sometimes rebellious son. (The trial judge emphasized there were "obviously some disciplinary issues with regard to [J.J.]".) . . . Noting the uncertainty of the law in this area, the trial court also observed, "[T]his is a tough area of the law. . . . Because you know that a person's intent was not to do the wrong thing. . . . I don't have a good answer for you [as to where to draw the line]. . . . I do believe that as the case law

1. The evidence on this point is in conflict. Willis testified she used a belt and introduced it as Defendant's Exhibit C. J.J. testified that his mother used an extension cord. For purposes of determining guilt and imposing sentence, the trial court declared, "I think it wouldn't matter if it was a belt or an extension cord."

2. According to J.J., Ms. McCuen noticed the marks on his arm as he was returning from gym. Only then did he ask to see the nurse. Ms. McCuen testified that her attention was drawn to J.J. upon his return from gym and she sent him to the nurse because "[h]e asked me if being hit with an extension cord was abuse."

is written that the incident that was before [the court] rose to the level of D Felony, Battery on a Child." Exercising its discretion to enter judgment of conviction as a Class A misdemeanor, the trial court sentenced Willis to 365 days in jail with 357 days suspended to probation.

Contending that she had the legal authority to discipline her son, Willis appealed on grounds that the evidence was not sufficient to sustain the conviction. Sympathizing with Willis' argument that she is a single parent doing the best she can and acknowledging that this is a "closer case" than other reported Indiana decisions, the Court of Appeals affirmed the judgment of the trial court. *See Willis v. State*, 866 N.E.2d 374, 376 (Ind.Ct.App.2007). Having previously granted Willis' petition to transfer, we now reverse the judgment of the trial court. Additional facts are set forth below as relevant.

Discussion

A parent has a fundamental liberty interest in maintaining a familial relationship with his or her child. *See Quilloin v. Walcott*, 434 U.S. 246, 255, 98 S.Ct. 549, 54 L.Ed.2d 511 (1978); *Wisconsin v. Yoder*, 406 U.S. 205, 231–32, 92 S.Ct. 1526, 32 L.Ed.2d 15 (1972). This fundamental interest includes the right of parents "to direct the upbringing and education of children," *Pierce v. Soc'y of Sisters*, 268 U.S. 510, 534–35, 45 S.Ct. 571, 69 L.Ed. 1070 (1925); *see also Yoder*, 406 U.S. at 213–14, 92 S.Ct. 1526, including the use of reasonable or moderate physical force to control behavior. See I.C. § 31-34-1-15(1). (Entitled "Circumstances Under Which a Child Is a Child in Need of Services," the statute provides in part, "This chapter does not... [l]imit the right of a parent, guardian, or custodian of a child to use reasonable corporal punishment when disciplining the child.") However, the potential for child abuse cannot be taken lightly. Consequently, the State has a powerful interest in preventing and deterring the mistreatment of children. *See Prince v. Dep't of Child Servs.*, 861 N.E.2d 1223, 1229 (Ind.Ct.App.2007) ("[A] parent's right to her children is balanced against the State's limited authority to interfere for the protection of the children"); *Parker v. Monroe County Dep't of Pub. Welfare*, 533 N.E.2d 177, 179 (Ind.Ct.App.1989) ("Fundamental rights to family integrity protect the relationship between parent and child from state action; however, in the event of parental neglect, abuse, or abandonment, the State has a compelling interest in protecting the welfare of the child"). The difficult task of prosecutors and the courts is to determine when parental use of physical force in disciplining children turns an otherwise law-abiding citizen into a criminal.

A parental privilege to use moderate or reasonable physical force, without criminal liability, was recognized at common law. For example, Blackstone observed, "[B]attery is, in some cases, justifiable or lawful; as where one who hath authority, a parent or master, gives moderate correction to his child, his scholar, or his apprentice." William Blackstone, 3 Blackstone's Commentaries on the Laws of England 120 (Oxford reprint 1992). A similar view has been expressed in this state's jurisprudence. *See e.g., Hinkle v. State*, 127 Ind. 490, 26 N.E. 777, 778 (1891) ("[F]ather has the right to administer proper and reasonable chastisement to his child without being guilty of an assault and battery, but he has no right to administer unreasonable chastisement, or to be guilty of cruel and inhuman treatment of his child...."); *Hornbeck v. State*, 16 Ind.App. 484, 45 N.E. 620, 620 (1896) ("The law is well settled that a parent has the right to administer proper and reasonable chastisement to his child without being guilty of an assault and battery...").

A number of jurisdictions have specifically codified a parental discipline privilege.[5] Although Indiana has not yet done so, our courts have construed Indiana Code section 35-41-3-1—the defense of legal authority—as including reasonable parental discipline that would otherwise constitute battery. *See Cooper v. State*, 831 N.E.2d 1247, 1252 (Ind.Ct.App.2005). Over several decades our courts have addressed parental claims of legal authority. *See e.g., Johnson v. State*, 804 N.E.2d 255, 257 (Ind.Ct.App.2004); *Dyson v. State*, 692 N.E.2d 1374, 1376 (Ind. Ct.App.1998); *Townsend v. State*, 616 N.E.2d 47, 50 (Ind.Ct.App.1993), *rev'd on other grounds*, 632 N.E.2d 727, 730–31 (Ind.1994); *Smith v. State*, 489 N.E.2d 140, 141–42 (Ind.Ct.App.1986). Nonetheless, as the Court of Appeals has observed, there is still "precious little Indiana caselaw providing guidance as to what constitutes proper and reasonable parental discipline of children, and there are no bright-line rules." *Mitchell v. State*, 813 N.E.2d 422, 427 (Ind. Ct.App.2004). We agree. And since adoption of the Criminal Code, this Court has not had the occasion to address the parental discipline privilege.

As a matter of judicial declaration or legislative enactment, several jurisdictions have embraced some, parts, or all of either the Model Penal Code or the Restatement (Second) of Torts to identify permissible parental conduct in the discipline of children. . . .

. . . [T]he Model Penal Code is not a helpful source to inform our decision on the law in this area.

In contrast, the Restatement provides, "A parent is privileged to apply such reasonable force or to impose such reasonable confinement upon his [or her] child as he [or she] reasonably believes to be necessary for its proper control, training, or education." Restatement of the Law (Second) Torts, § 147(1) (1965). We adopt the Restatement view. Not only is it entirely consistent with the law in this jurisdiction, but also it provides guidance on the factors that may be considered in determining the reasonableness of punishment. It reads:

> In determining whether force or confinement is reasonable for the control, training, or education of a child, the following factors are to be considered:
>
> (a) whether the actor is a parent;
>
> (b) the age, sex, and physical and mental condition of the child;
>
> (c) the nature of his offense and his apparent motive;
>
> (d) the influence of his example upon other children of the same family or group;
>
> (e) whether the force or confinement is reasonably necessary and appropriate to compel obedience to a proper command;
>
> (f) whether it is disproportionate to the offense, unnecessarily degrading, or likely to cause serious or permanent harm.

Restatement, *supra*, § 150. We hasten to add that this list is not exhaustive. There may be other factors unique to a particular case that should be taken into consideration. And obviously, not

5. Ala.Code § 13A-3-24(1) (2005); Alaska Stat. § 11.81.430(1)(a) (2006); Ariz.Rev.Stat. Ann. § 13-403(1) (2001); Ark.Code Ann. § 5-2-605(1) (Supp. 2007); Colo.Rev.Stat. Ann. § 18-1-703(1)(a) (2007); Conn. Gen.Stat. Ann. § 53a-18(1) (2007); Del.Code Ann. tit. 11, § 468(1) (2007); Guam Code. Ann. tit. 9, § 7.94 (2007); Haw.Rev.Stat. § 703-309(1) (1993); Mo. Ann. Stat. § 563.061(1) (1999); Mont.Code Ann. § 45-3-107 (2007); Neb.Rev.Stat. § 28-1413 (1995); N.Y. Penal Law § 35.10 (Supp. 2008); N.D. Cent.Code § 12.1-05-05(1) (Supp. 2007); Or.Rev. Stat. § 161.205(1) (2003); 18 Pa. Cons.Stat. Ann. § 509(1) (1998); S.D. Codified Laws § 22-18-5 (1998); Tex. Penal Code Ann. § 9.61(a) (2003).

all of the listed factors may be relevant or applicable in every case. But in either event they should be balanced against each other, giving appropriate weight as the circumstances dictate, in determining whether the force is reasonable.

The defense of parental privilege, like self-defense, is a complete defense. That is to say a valid claim of parental privilege is a legal justification for an otherwise criminal act. I.C. § 35-41-3-1. In order to negate a claim of parental privilege, the State must disprove at least one element of the defense beyond a reasonable doubt. Thus, to sustain a conviction for battery where a claim of parental privilege has been asserted, the State must prove that either: (1) the force the parent used was unreasonable or (2) the parent's belief that such force was necessary to control her child and prevent misconduct was unreasonable. See Restatement, *supra*, § 147....

Several of the factors suggested by the Restatement are helpful in evaluating the facts in this case. Although we know that J.J. is an eleven-year-old male child, there is nothing in the record concerning his physical or mental condition. In any event, "A punishment which would not be too severe for a boy of twelve may be obviously excessive if imposed upon a child of four or five." Restatement, *supra*, § 150 cmt. c. As for the nature of the offense and J.J.'s apparent motive, the record is not clear as to why J.J. took his mother's clothing to school and then lied about it. That aside, most parents would likely consider as serious their eleven-year-old child's behavior in being untruthful and taking property of others. At the very least a parent might consider that such behavior could set the stage for more aberrant behavior later in life. Willis expressed her concerns in this regard, "[H]e's going to do it again.... [H]e's already done it again.... And I hate to say it, but I know my son will end up back in the court system." Comments to the Restatement provide, "[A] more severe punishment may be imposed for a serious offense, or an intentional one, than for a minor offense, or one resulting from a mere error of judgment or careless inattention. The fact that the child has shown a tendency toward certain types of misconduct may justify a punishment which would be clearly excessive if imposed upon a first offender." Restatement, *supra*, § 150 cmt. c. Clearly J.J. was not a first offender.

Concerning whether the force Willis employed against J.J. was reasonably necessary and appropriate to compel obedience to her insistence that he tell the truth, again the Restatement is instructive. "As in all cases in which the question arises as to whether there has been excessive means of carrying out the privilege [to use force], the actor is not privileged to use a means to compel obedience if a less severe method appears to be likely to be equally effective." Restatement, *supra*, § 150 cmt. d. The record shows that Willis has used progressive forms of discipline. Typical punishment was to send J.J. to his room, ground him, or withhold privileges such as television, games, and time spent outdoors. According to Willis, after grounding failed the last time J.J. was caught stealing, she decided harsher punishment—swatting with a belt—would be more effective. As Willis explained, "I thought about it over the entire weekend and I even tried to talk to him again. And he continued to lie.... I didn't know what else to do."

Considering whether the punishment J.J. received was unnecessarily degrading, [disproportionate] to the offense J.J. committed, or likely to cause J.J. serious or permanent harm, we make the following observations. J.J. received five to seven swats on his buttocks, arm, and thigh for what many parents might reasonably consider a serious offense. We find nothing particularly degrading about this manner of punishment. Nor, in context, is it readily apparent that the punishment was disproportionate to the offense. The question is whether the manner of punishment was "likely to cause [J.J.] serious or permanent harm." Restatement, *supra*, § 150(f). The best answer to this question is J.J.'s own testimony which indicated that the swats hurt "[f]or a minute" but did not hurt the next day when he returned to school. To be sure the bruising was still apparent, but there is no indication that the school nurse provided any medical attention or even suggested that medical attention was necessary. In essence it appears from the record that the bruises were neither serious nor permanent. This fact militates against a conclusion that the punishment was unreasonable. *See State v. Wilder*, 748 A.2d 444, 455 (Me.2000) (concluding that to trigger criminal liability the physical harm caused by the parent's use of force as a method of discipline must result in more than transient pain and minor, temporary marks or bruises); *T.G. v. Dep't of Children & Families*, 927 So.2d 104, 106 (Fla.Dist.Ct.App.2006) (Bruises are not necessarily indicative of excessive corporal punishment).

In response to a charge of battery, Willis raised the defense of parental discipline privilege. Considering the totality of the circumstances, we are not persuaded that the State disproved the defense beyond a reasonable doubt. We therefore set aside Willis' conviction.

Conclusion

We reverse the judgment of the trial court.

SHEPARD, C.J. and DICKSON and BOEHM, JJ., concur.

SULLIVAN, J., dissents with separate opinion.

SULLIVAN, Justice, dissenting....

We see on appeal many cases of child abuse in which the parents claim that they were only disciplining their children, that they reasonably believed that the force they used was necessary to control their children or prevent misconduct. By authorizing parents to impose as much force they believe is necessary unless the State proves beyond a reasonable doubt that either (1) the force used was unreasonable; or (2) the parents' belief was unreasonable, the Court increases the quantum of effort that the State will be required to expend in its efforts to protect children from abuse. As such, the Court's opinion constitutes a change in our State's policy toward child abuse. Particularly given the commitment of time and resources that the legislative and executive branches have devoted to this subject for the last two decades and more, I believe that such a policy change should be made by the legislative and executive branches, not the judiciary.

NOTES AND QUESTIONS

1. According to the court, when does corporal punishment constitute abuse? What did the state fail to prove?

2. What exactly were the injuries inflicted on J.J.? How were they inflicted? Do you think the court is correct when it says that it does not matter whether a belt or an extension cord was used?

3. The *Willis* case involves a criminal prosecution. Parental abuse or neglect under certain circumstances may result in criminal charges in addition to or in lieu of child-protection proceedings. Do you think the fact that Willis was being prosecuted made a difference to the outcome? Why?

4. Do parents have a constitutional right to punish their children corporally? In *Hamilton ex rel. Letham v. Letham*, 270 P.3d 1024 (2012), the Hawaii Supreme Court, in a unanimous opinion, said yes.

It is now established that parents may discipline their children as part of the parents' liberty interest in the care, custody, and control of their children. "[T]he interest of parents in the care, custody, and control of their children... is perhaps the oldest of the fundamental liberty interests recognized by [the United States Supreme Court]." *In re Doe*, 99 Hawai'i 522, 532, 57 P.3d 447, 457 (2002) (citing *Troxel v. Granville*, 530 U.S. 57, 65, 120 S.Ct. 2054, 147 L.Ed.2d 49 (2000)). The Court has not been squarely presented with the question whether the right to care for children also includes a right to use corporal punishment to discipline them. *See Sweaney v. Ada County, Idaho*, 119 F.3d 1385, 1391 (9th Cir. 1997) (holding that there is no clearly established federal constitutional right of a parent to inflict corporal punishment on a child). However, the Court has decided a number of cases that suggest it would recognize a parent's right to use corporal punishment. *See Troxel*, 530 U.S. at 65, 120 S.Ct. 2054 (plurality opinion) ("[T]he [constitutional] liberty [interest] of parents and guardians includes the right to direct the upbringing and education of children under their control)" (internal quotation marks and citations omitted); *Parham v. J.R.*, 442 U.S. 584, 602, 99 S.Ct. 2493, 61 L.Ed.2d 101 (1979) ("Our jurisprudence historically has reflected Western civilization concepts of the family as a unit with broad parental authority over minor children"); *Ingraham v. Wright*, 430 U.S. 651, 661, 670, 97 S.Ct. 1401, 51 L.Ed.2d 711 (1977) (suggesting that parents are privileged to use force to discipline their children inasmuch as the Court observed that the prevalent rule in this country today permits teachers to use "such force as [the] teacher... reasonably believes to be necessary for (the child's) proper control, training, or education") (internal quotation marks and citations omitted).

Additionally, "Independent of the federal constitution... parents have a substantive liberty interest in the care, custody, and control of their children protected by the due process clause of article 1, section 5 of the Hawai'i Constitution." *In re Doe*, 99 Hawai'i at 533, 57 P.3d at 458. It is well-established that imposing discipline is part and parcel of caring for children, since a parent may not be able to care properly for, or exercise control over, an unruly child without the ability to impose discipline. *See Ingraham*, 430 U.S. at 661, 97 S.Ct. 1401. Such discipline has included corporal punishment. *See id.* ("Professional and public opinion is sharply divided on the practice [of corporal punishment], and has been for more than a century. Yet we can discern no trend toward its elimination"); *State v. Crouser*, 81 Hawai'i 5, 14, 911 P.2d 725, 734 (1996) (explaining, for purposes of criminal liability, that it is "well-established," in Hawai'i, "that parents have a privilege to subject children to reasonable corporal punishment"). The right to discipline is therefore inherent in the right to care, custody, and control of one's children, as guaranteed by the Hawai'i Constitution....

Reasonableness is the standard that has long been employed by the states in the area of parental discipline. See Doriane Lambelet Coleman, et. al., *Where and How to Draw the Line between Reasonable Corporal Punishment and Abuse*, 73–SPG Law & Contemp. Probs. 107, 137 (2010) [hereinafter, *Where and How to Draw the Line*] ("[S]tates have long provided parents with an exception to tort and criminal-law prohibitions against physical assaults when they can establish a disciplinary motive for the assault and when the assault itself is 'reasonable.' Twentieth-century case law is thus replete with holdings like this one:

'A parent has the right to punish a child within the bounds of moderation and reason, so long as he or she does it for the welfare of the child.'") (citing cases); *see also* Restatement (Second) of Torts § 147 (1965) (based on survey of states, "[a] parent is privileged to apply such reasonable force or to impose such reasonable confinement upon his child as he reasonably believes is necessary for [his child's] proper control, training, or education"); *G.C. v. R.S.*, 71 So.3d 164, 166 (Fla.App.2011) ("The common law recognize[s] a parent's right to discipline his or her child in a reasonable manner") (internal quotation marks and citations omitted); *State v. Bell*, 223 N.W.2d 181, 184 (Iowa 1974) ("Parents have a right to inflict corporal punishment on their child, but that right is restricted by moderation and reasonableness"); *State v. Thorpe*, 429 A.2d 785, 788 (R.I.1981) ("[A] parent has a right to use reasonable and timely [corporal] punishment as may be necessary to correct faults in his/her growing children"); *Diehl v. Commonwealth*, 9 Va.App. 191, 385 S.E.2d 228, 230 (1989) ("It is settled in Virginia that while a parent has the right to discipline his or her child the punishment must be within the bounds of moderation"); *Where and How to Draw the Line*, 73–SPG Law & Contemp. Probs. at 117 n. 37 ("Even in states that lack physical-discipline exceptions within their family or juvenile-court codes, courts have recognized a parent's physical-discipline privilege based on a statutory privilege found in the criminal code or a common-law privilege") (citing *Lovan C. v. Dep't of Children & Families*, 86 Conn.App. 290, 860 A.2d 1283, 1288 (2004); *In re W.G.*, 349 N.W.2d 487, 487 (Iowa 1984))....

The formulations for determining whether a parent's conduct is reasonably related to discipline vary among the states, but they are more similar than not. Based on a survey of authorities, Restatement (Second) of Torts § 150 (1965) provides as follows:

> In determining whether force or confinement is reasonable for the control, training, or education of a child, the following factors are to be considered:
>
> (a) whether the actor is a parent;
>
> (b) the age, sex, and physical and mental condition of the child;
>
> (c) the nature of his offense and his apparent motive;
>
> (d) the influence of his example upon other children of the same family or group;
>
> (e) whether the force or confinement is reasonably necessary and appropriate to compel obedience to a proper command;
>
> (f) whether it is disproportionate to the offense, unnecessarily degrading, or likely to cause serious or permanent harm.

States consider essentially the same factors. For example, in Connecticut, "[i]n a substantiation of abuse hearing...the hearing officer must determine whether the punishment was reasonable and whether the parent believed the punishment was necessary to maintain discipline or promote the child's welfare." *Lovan C.*, 860 A.2d at 1289. "The hearing officer must assess the reasonableness of the punishment in light of the child's misbehavior and the surrounding circumstances, including the parent's motive, the type of punishment administered, the amount of force used and the child's age, size and ability to understand the punishment." *Id.* Several other courts have identified similar circumstances, such as "the age, size, sex, and physical condition of both child and parent, the nature of the child's misconduct, the kind of marks or wounds inflicted on the child's body, the nature of the instrument used for punishment, etc." *State v. Singleton*, 41 Wash.App. 721, 705 P.2d 825, 827 (1985) (citing cases).

The factors considered by other states are coextensive with the test employed by Hawai'i in the context of the criminal parental discipline defense....In applying such a standard, the surrounding circumstances, including factors such as the nature of the

> misbehavior, the child's age and size, and the nature and propriety of the force used, have been universally considered and should also guide the courts in this state.

Id. at 1031–1032, 1037–1038. If parents have a constitutional right to punish their children corporally, where does this leave children?

5. The American Academy of Pediatrics opposes the use of spanking and other forms of corporal punishment by parents. "Corporal punishment is of limited effectiveness and has potentially deleterious side effects." Am. Acad. of Pediatrics, Comm. on Psychosocial Aspects of Child and Family Health, *Guidance for Effective Discipline*, 101 PEDIATRICS 723, 723 (1998). The AAP recommends that parents use forms of discipline other than physical punishment because of the danger to health that corporal punishment creates and the lack of efficacy that corporal punishment has compared with using other strategies, such as time-outs or removal of privileges. *Id.* at 726. Although the American Medical Association has not formally released a policy against corporal punishment by parents, it did endorse a report by Elizabeth T. Gershoff in 2009 that recommended that parents avoid using physical discipline. Elizabeth T. Gershoff, *More Harm Than Good: A Summary of Scientific Research on the Intended and Unintended Effects of Corporal Punishment on Children*, 73 LAW & CONTEMP. PROBS. 31, 55 (Spring 2010), citing Report on Physical Punishment of Children, List of Endorsers, Phoenix Children's Hospital (Oct. 1, 2009), http://www.phoenixchildrens.com/about/community-outreach-education/pdfs/child-abuse-prevention/Report-on-PP-List-of-Endorsers-October-1-2009.pdf, citing Elizabeth T. Gershoff, Report on Physical Punishment in the United States: What Research Tells Us about Its Effects on Children, Cent. for Effective Discipline & Phoenix Children's Hosp. (2008), http://www.phoenixchildrens.com/PDFs/principles_and_practices-of_effective_ discipline.pdf (last visited Dec. 10, 2009). The American Psychological Association and the National Association of Social Workers also contend that there are more constructive ways to discipline children. Corporal Punishment, American Psychological Association Council Policy Manual, http://www.apa.org/about/policy/corporal-punishment.aspx; Abstract, Physical Punishment of Children, Social Work Speaks, 8th ed., NASW Policy Statements (2009), http://www.naswds.org/resources/abstracts/abstracts/physical.asp.

6. Article 19 of the United Nations Convention on the Rights of the Child requires states parties to protect children from "all forms of physical or mental violence" while in the care of parents or others. Noting that "different forms of violence are interlinked" and that "tolerance of violence in one sphere makes it difficult to resist it in another, the Committee on the Rights of the Child has required states parties to protect children from all forms of corporal punishment and has recommended the repeal of any domestic legislation that would permit corporal punishment at home, even when used as a form of discipline. Committee on the Rights of the Child, Recommendations on Violence against Children, within the Family and in Schools, ¶¶ 701–706, September/October 2001, http://www.ohchr.org/EN/HRBodies/CRC/Documents/Recommandations/school.pdf. Thirty countries ban the use of corporal punishment in the home. Sweden, the first country to do so, banned corporal punishment in 1979; South Sudan, the newest African country, did so in 2011. The Global Initiative to End All Corporal Punishment of Children, States with Full Abolition, http://www.endcorporalpunishment.org/pages/progress/prohib_states.html.

7. Does the empirical research support a ban on corporal punishment? Some research has shown that corporal punishment in the home can cause deleterious effects that harm the child not only physically but also mentally. See, e.g., Gershoff, *More Harm Than Good*, *supra*; Jennifer E. Lansford, *The Special Problem of Cultural Differences in Effects of Corporal*

Punishment, 73 LAW & CONTEMP. PROBS. 89, 89 (Spring 2010), citing generally Elizabeth T. Gershoff, *Corporal Punishment by Parents and Associated Child Behaviors and Experiences: A Meta-Analytic and Theoretical Review*, 128 PSYCHOL. BULL. 539 (2002). For example, corporal punishment may increase the risk of physical abuse. A meta-analysis by Gershoff found that "the more parents used nonabusive corporal punishment (for example, spanking and slapping), the more likely they were to engage in abusive behaviors (for example, beating the child up or punching them with a fist)." Gershoff, *More Harm Than Good*, *supra*, at 42. Yet physical abuse is not the only deleterious effect of corporal punishment. "In particular, the more frequently or severely children are spanked or hit, the more likely they are to have symptoms of depression or anxiety." *Id.* at 43–44. Corporal punishment also has been found to have detrimental affects on a child's relationship with his or her parents, increase aggression in the child, decrease the child's cognitive abilities, and increase his or her antisocial behavior (such as lying or stealing). *Id.* at 45–47.

Other studies, however, have shown that the harmful effects of corporal punishment depend on cultural and societal norms. Jennifer E. Lansford et al., *Physical Discipline and Children's Adjustment: Cultural Normativeness as a Moderator*, 76 CHILD DEVEL. 1234, 1244 (2005); Lansford, *The Special Problem of Cultural Differences*, *supra*, at 105; Doriane Lambelet Coleman et al., *Where and How to Draw the Line between Reasonable Corporal Punishment and Abuse*, 73 LAW & CONTEMP. PROBS. 107, 147 (Spr. 2010). In societies where corporal punishment is common, its effects are less detrimental to children than in societies where physical punishment is infrequent. Lansford, *The Special Problem of Cultural Differences*, *supra*, at 105; Coleman et al., *Where and How to Draw the Line*, *supra*, at 147. A meta-analysis by Lansford also contends that the context in which corporal punishment occurs may dictate the extent to which it has deleterious effects. "[When] parents' use of corporal punishment conveys to children that their parents reject them, this perception can increase children's adjustment problems." Lansford, *The Special Problem of Cultural Differences*, *supra*, at 105.

Other researchers argue that studies finding negative associations with corporal punishment draw conclusions about correlation without adequately controlling for other influential factors. Robert E. Larzelere & Diana Baumrind, *Are Spanking Injunctions Scientifically Supported?* 73 LAW & CONTEMP. PROBS. 57, 61 (Spring 2010). Robert Larzelere and Diana Baumrind have noted that "[b]ecause abusive behaviors are not excluded [from the corporal punishment data], the negative effects of severe corporal punishment may cloud the effects of mild corporal punishment such as spanking." *Id.* at 67–68. Larzelere and Baumrind also compared mild corporal punishment with alternative disciplinary methods and found that when "controlling for preexisting differences...all kinds of nonphysical punishment also predicted higher antisocial behavior," behaviors similar to those found when corporal punishment was utilized. *Id.* at 79, citing Robert E. Larzelere et al., *Differences in Causal Estimates from Longitudinal Analyses of Residualized vs. Simple Gain Scores: Contrasting Controls for Selection and Regression Artifacts*, 34 INT'L J. BEHAV. DEV. 180 (2010); Robert E. Larzelere, Ronald B. Cox, Jr., & Gail L. Smith, *Do Nonphysical Punishments Reduce Antisocial Behavior More Than Spanking? A Comparison Using the Strongest Previous Causal Evidence against Spanking*, 10:10 BMC PEDIATRICS 1 (2010). "[T]he strongest causally relevant evidence against customary spanking yields small, apparently detrimental effects that can easily be due to a combination of several substantive and methodological factors that bias the results." *Id.* at 81.

Problem. Should corporal punishment be banned in the United States? In 2007, a bill was introduced in the Massachusetts legislature to criminalize the corporal punishment of children in the home. Kristin Collins Cope, *The Age of Discipline: The Relevance of Age to the Reasonableness of Corporal Punishment*, 73 Law & Contemp. Probs. 167, 167 (Spr. 2010). Although the bill did not become law, do you think it is a good idea to prohibit corporal punishment by parents and family members?

iii. Emotional abuse

Jessica Dixon Weaver, *The Principle of Subsidiarity Applied: Reforming the Legal Framework to Capture the Psychological Abuse of Children*, 18 Va. J. Soc. Pol'y & L. 247, 257, 262, 263, 264, 266, 267 (2011).

In its simplest form, psychological abuse is a repeated pattern of damaging interactions between parent(s) and child that becomes typical of their relationship. Psychological maltreatment is the most common form of child abuse. While often occurring alone, it is also present in physical or sexual abuse. The psychological abuse component of physical and sexual abuse is most damaging to children and leads to long-term harmful consequences....

The NIS-4...however, reveals startling statistics about the increase in the percentage of children experiencing emotional abuse or neglect....Children ages 0 to 2 were at a 259% higher risk at the time of the NIS-4 than at the time of the NIS-3. The increase in incidence rate was nearly as large for children ages 3 to 5, at 214%. The rates of emotional abuse have decreased under the Harm Standard since the NIS-2 and NIS-3. The Third National Incidence Study also showed a decrease in the frequency of emotional abuse under the Endangerment Standard. However, the rate of emotional neglect has doubled under the Endangerment Standard since the NIS-3 and more than quadrupled since the NIS-2....

Domestic violence increases the likelihood that children will experience psychological abuse. The children of fathers who are abusive to their partners are 30–60% more likely to be physically abused. Apart from possible physical abuse, studies show that children who witness abuse are at a higher risk for a wide range of behavioral, emotional, and intellectual problems....

The harm caused by psychological abuse varies. Exposure to any type of abusive condition in childhood disrupts the normal course of development and leads to maladaptive behaviors. Proof of this is clear in studies of the family background of juvenile delinquents, which show that a very high percentage of young offenders were abused. Female juvenile offenders have an even higher correlation, with a startling 92% reporting some form of physical, sexual, or emotional abuse and 25% claiming to have been shot or stabbed at least once....

Psychological maltreatment is often difficult to substantiate in court. Children's behavior can be indicative of abuse but is not evidence of it. Since there are multiple pathways to particular behaviors, assessors are cautioned about inferring causation from behavior. It is also true that some victims of psychological maltreatment show no discernible signs of distress. Dispositional evaluations can reveal the child's perception of events in order to determine the precipitants for incidents of abuse and to assess the nature and strength of the child's relationships with her parents.

NOTES AND QUESTIONS

1. APSAC defines psychological maltreatment as "a repeated pattern of caregiver behavior or extreme incident(s) that convey to children that they are worthless, flawed, unloved, unwanted, endangered, or only of value in meeting another's needs." Stuart N. Hart et al., *Psychological Maltreatment*, in The APSAC Handbook on Child Maltreatment 125, 126 (3d ed. 2011). The APSAC guidelines define six subtypes of psychological maltreatment: spurning, terrorizing, isolating, exploiting/corrupting, denying emotional responsiveness, and mental health, emotional, and educational neglect. *Id.* at 126. The American Academy of Pediatrics defines psychological maltreatment as "a repeated pattern of damaging interactions between parent(s) and child that becomes typical of the relationship. In some situations, the pattern is chronic and pervasive; in others, the pattern occurs only when triggered by alcohol or other potentiating factors. Occasionally, a very painful singular incident, such as an unusually contentious divorce, can initiate psychological maltreatment." Steven W. Kairys & Charles F. Johnson, Am. Acad. Pediatrics, Comm. on Child Abuse & Neglect, *The Psychological Maltreatment of Children—A Technical Report*, 109 Pediatrics e68, e68 (2002) (reaff'd October 2005). In addition to the behaviors noted in the APSAC guidelines, the AAP also indicates that witnessing domestic violence and unreliable or inconsistent parenting leading to contradictory and ambivalent demands may be indicative of psychological abuse. *Id.* From a psychologist's point of view, however, psychological maltreatment is conceptually distinct from emotional abuse, because psychological development is separate from emotional development. Kieran O'Hagan, *Emotional and Psychological Abuse: Problems of Definition*, 19 Child Abuse & Neglect 449 (1995).

Deleterious effects of emotional abuse include childhood depression, anxiety, low self-esteem, aggression, violence, suicidal ideation, impulse-control problems, emotional unresponsiveness, physical self-abuse, substance abuse, eating disorders, posttraumatic stress disorder, and low academic achievement. See, e.g., Kairys & Johnson, *The Psychological Maltreatment of Children, supra*, at e69. Children who have been emotionally abused also may have physical symptoms. Weaver, *The Principle of Subsidiarity Applied*, at 266–267. Of course, it should be apparent that these problems may be attributable to causes other than child abuse. See, e.g., James Garabarino, *Not All Bad Outcomes Are the Result of Child Abuse*, 3 Dev. & Psychopathology 45 (1991).

2. *Problem.* Consider the following facts: On January 18, 2006, C.L.Z. and her grandmother went to the Satilla Square shopping center. At approximately 5:00 p.m., Tina Crews, who worked at the shopping center, saw C.L.Z. and her grandmother as they walked past her office. Crews took note of them because the grandmother was yelling at C.L.Z. When Crews left work at 6:00 p.m., she saw C.L.Z. and her grandmother in the parking lot at their vehicle. C.L.Z., who was crying, had a purple sweater tied over her eyes. The grandmother was "very mad" and was pushing the back of C.L.Z.'s head, trying to make C.L.Z. face the vehicle. As Crews approached the grandmother, another witness, Heather Flowers, told Crews that she had already called the police to report the incident.

Flowers was in the shopping-center parking lot shortly before 6:00 p.m. when she first saw the grandmother and C.L.Z. As they walked across the parking lot, the grandmother would periodically stop, bend down to the child's level, and yell angrily at C.L.Z., "screaming at the top of her lungs." Flowers did not see C.L.Z. misbehave or try to get away from her grandmother. Once C.L.Z. and her grandmother reached their vehicle, the grandmother, who was still "screaming," put her hand on the back of C.L.Z.'s head and "forcefully" pushed her, face first, into the side panel of the vehicle. When C.L.Z. turned her head, the grandmother pushed her face back against the vehicle. The grandmother then blindfolded C.L.Z. with a purple piece of clothing. Flowers called the police.

When Officer Donna Waters arrived at the shopping center, C.L.Z. was sitting inside the vehicle, and the grandmother was leaning inside the vehicle yelling at C.L.Z. Waters stood nearby for several minutes and observed the grandmother "throwing stuff around" in the vehicle, walking around the vehicle, and yelling at C.L.Z., who was "just sitting there."

Do you think that C.L.Z. is an emotionally or psychologically abused child based on the preceding definitions? Why? See *In the Interest of C.L.Z.*, 641 S.E.2d 243 (Ga. App. 2007).

3. What is the burden of proof required to establish child abuse? About nineteen states require proof by clear and convincing evidence at the initial abuse or neglect adjudication. See Ala. Code § 12-15-310 (LexisNexis 2009); Ga. Unif. Juv. Ct. R. 11.2 (2011); Iowa Code § 232.96 (2001); Kan. Stat. Ann. § 38-2250 (2006); Mass. Ann. Laws ch. 119, § 26 (LexisNexis 2008); Minn. Stat. § 260C.163 (2012); Mo. Sup. Ct. R. 124.06 cmt. (2011); N.M. Stat. Ann. § 32A-4-20 (LexisNexis 2009); N.C. Gen. Stat. § 7B-807 (2011); N.D. Cent. Code §27-20-29 (2011); Ohio Rev. Code § 2151.35 (2011); 42 Pa. Cons. Stat. § 6341 (2008); R.I. R. Juv. P. R. 17 (2012); S.D. Codified Laws § 26-7A-82 (1991); Tenn. Code Ann. § 37-1-129 (2012); Utah Code Ann. § 78A-6-311 (2008); W. Va. Code Ann. § 49-6-2 (2012); Wis. Stat. Ann. § 48.31 (2009). However, the clear majority of states only require proof by a preponderance of the evidence. See Alaska Stat. § 47.10.011 (1998); Ariz. Rev. Stat. § 8-844 (LexisNexis 2007); Ark. Code Ann. § 9-27-325 (2011); Cal. Welf. & Inst. Code § 355 (Deering 2003); Colo. Rev. Stat. § 19-3-505 (2006); 1A Conn. Prac., Juv. Law § 35a-3 (2011); Del. Fam. Ct. R. Civ. P. R. 213 (2011); D.C. Code Ann. § 16-2317 (LexisNexis 2007): Fla. Stat. Ann. § 39.507 (LexisNexis 2008); Haw. Rev. Stat. Ann. § 571-41 (LexisNexis 2004); Idaho Code Ann. § 16-1619 (2010); 705 Ill. Comp. Stat. Ann. 405/2-21 (LexisNexis 2003); Ind. Code Ann. § 31-34-12-3 (LexisNexis 1997); Ky. Rev. Stat. Ann. § 620.100 (LexisNexis 2005); La. Child. Code Ann. art. 665 (1991); Me. Rev. Stat. Ann. tit. 22, § 4035 (2007); Md. Code Ann., Cts. & Jud. Proc. § 3-817 (LexisNexis 2005); Mich. Ct. R. 3.972 (2011); Miss. Code Ann. § 43-21-561 (2010); Mont. Code Ann. § 41-3-422 (2007); Neb. Rev. Stat. Ann. § 43-279.01 (LexisNexis 1989); Nev. Rev. Stat. Ann. § 432B.530 (LexisNexis 2003); N.H. Rev. Stat. Ann. §169-C:13 (LexisNexis 1979); N.J. Stat. Ann. § 9:6-8.46 (2005); N.Y. Fam. Ct. Law § 1046 (Consol. 2009); Okla. Stat. Ann. tit. 10A, § 1-4-601 (2009); Or. Rev. Stat. § 419B.310 (2001); S.C. Code Ann. §63-7-1650(D) (2008); S.D. Codified Laws § 26-7A-82 (1991); Tex. Fam. Code Ann. § 105.005 (Vernon 2008); Vt. Stat. Ann. tit. 33, § 5315 (2007); Va. Code Ann. § 16.1-277.02 (2011); Wash. Rev. Code Ann. § 13.34.110 (LexisNexis 2007); Wyo. Stat. Ann. § 14-3-425 (1997). What should the burden of proof be at the initial adjudicatory hearing for abuse or neglect? Are there valid reasons for requiring a lower burden of proof? A higher burden of proof?

iv. Fetal abuse

FERGUSON V. CITY OF CHARLESTON
Supreme Court of the United States
532 U.S. 67 (2001)

Justice Stevens delivered the opinion of the Court.

In this case, we must decide whether a state hospital's performance of a diagnostic test to obtain evidence of a patient's criminal conduct for law enforcement purposes is an unreasonable search if the patient has not consented to the procedure. More narrowly, the question is whether the interest in using the threat of criminal sanctions to deter pregnant women from using cocaine can justify a departure from the general rule that an official nonconsensual search is unconstitutional if not authorized by a valid warrant.

I

In the fall of 1988, staff members at the public hospital operated in the city of Charleston by the Medical University of South Carolina (MUSC) became concerned about an apparent increase in the use of cocaine by patients who were receiving prenatal treatment.[1] In response to this perceived increase, as of April 1989, MUSC began to order drug screens to be performed on urine samples from maternity patients who were suspected of using cocaine. If a patient tested positive, she was then referred by MUSC staff to the county substance abuse commission for counseling and treatment. However, despite the referrals, the incidence of cocaine use among the patients at MUSC did not appear to change.

Some four months later, Nurse Shirley Brown, the case manager for the MUSC obstetrics department, heard a news broadcast reporting that the police in Greenville, South Carolina, were arresting pregnant users of cocaine on the theory that such use harmed the fetus and was therefore child abuse.[2] Nurse Brown discussed the story with MUSC's general counsel, Joseph C. Good, Jr., who then contacted Charleston Solicitor Charles Condon in order to offer MUSC's cooperation in prosecuting mothers whose children tested positive for drugs at birth.

After receiving Good's letter, Solicitor Condon took the first steps in developing the policy at issue in this case. He organized the initial meetings, decided who would participate, and issued the invitations, in which he described his plan to prosecute women who tested positive for cocaine while pregnant. The task force that Condon formed included representatives of MUSC, the police, the County Substance Abuse Commission and the Department of Social Services. Their deliberations led to MUSC's adoption of a 12-page document entitled "POLICY M-7," dealing with the subject of "Management of Drug Abuse During Pregnancy."

The first three pages of Policy M-7 set forth the procedure to be followed by the hospital staff to "identify/assist pregnant patients suspected of drug abuse." The first section, entitled the "Identification of Drug Abusers," provided that a patient should be tested for cocaine through a urine drug screen if she met one or more of nine criteria.[4] It also stated that a

1. As several witnesses testified at trial, the problem of "crack babies" was widely perceived in the late 1980's as a national epidemic, prompting considerable concern both in the medical community and among the general populace.

2. Under South Carolina law, a viable fetus has historically been regarded as a person; in 1995, the South Carolina Supreme Court held that the ingestion of cocaine during the third trimester of pregnancy constitutes criminal child neglect. *Whitner v. South Carolina*, 328 S.C. 1, 492 S.E.2d 777 (1997), cert. denied, 523 U.S. 1145 (1998).

4. Those criteria were as follows:

"1. No prenatal care

"2. Late prenatal care after 24 weeks gestation

"3. Incomplete prenatal care

"4. Abruptio placentae

"5. Intrauterine fetal death

"6. Preterm labor "of no obvious cause"

chain of custody should be followed when obtaining and testing urine samples, presumably to make sure that the results could be used in subsequent criminal proceedings. The policy also provided for education and referral to a substance abuse clinic for patients who tested positive. Most important, it added the threat of law enforcement intervention that "provided the necessary 'leverage' to make the [p]olicy effective." That threat was, as respondents candidly acknowledge, essential to the program's success in getting women into treatment and keeping them there.

The threat of law enforcement involvement was set forth in two protocols, the first dealing with the identification of drug use during pregnancy, and the second with identification of drug use after labor. Under the latter protocol, the police were to be notified without delay and the patient promptly arrested. Under the former, after the initial positive drug test, the police were to be notified (and the patient arrested) only if the patient tested positive for cocaine a second time or if she missed an appointment with a substance abuse counselor.[5] In 1990, however, the policy was modified at the behest of the solicitor's office to give the patient who tested positive during labor, like the patient who tested positive during a prenatal care visit, an opportunity to avoid arrest by consenting to substance abuse treatment.

The last six pages of the policy contained forms for the patients to sign, as well as procedures for the police to follow when a patient was arrested. The policy also prescribed in detail the precise offenses with which a woman could be charged, depending on the stage of her pregnancy. If the pregnancy was 27 weeks or less, the patient was to be charged with simple possession. If it was 28 weeks or more, she was to be charged with possession and distribution to a person under the age of 18—in this case, the fetus. If she delivered "while testing positive for illegal drugs," she was also to be charged with unlawful neglect of a child. Under the policy, the police were instructed to interrogate the arrestee in order "to ascertain the identity of the subject who provided illegal drugs to the suspect." Other than the provisions describing the substance abuse treatment to be offered to women who tested positive, the policy made no mention of any change in the prenatal care of such patients, nor did it prescribe any special treatment for the newborns.

II

Petitioners are 10 women who received obstetrical care at MUSC and who were arrested after testing positive for cocaine. Four of them were arrested during the initial implementation of the policy; they were not offered the opportunity to receive drug treatment as an alternative to arrest. The others were arrested after the policy was modified in 1990; they either failed to comply with the terms of the drug treatment program or tested positive for a second time. Respondents include the city of Charleston, law enforcement officials who helped develop and enforce the policy, and representatives of MUSC.

Petitioners' complaint challenged the validity of the policy under various theories, including the claim that warrantless and nonconsensual drug tests conducted for criminal

"7. IUGR [intrauterine growth retardation] "of no obvious cause"

"8. Previously known drug or alcohol abuse

"9. Unexplained congenital anomalies."

5. Despite the conditional description of the first category, when the policy was in its initial stages, a positive test was immediately reported to the police, who then promptly arrested the patient.

investigatory purposes were unconstitutional searches. Respondents advanced two principal defenses to the constitutional claim: (1) that, as a matter of fact, petitioners had consented to the searches; and (2) that, as a matter of law, the searches were reasonable, even absent consent, because they were justified by special non-law-enforcement purposes. The District Court rejected the second defense because the searches in question "were not done by the medical university for independent purposes. [Instead,] the police came in and there was an agreement reached that the positive screens would be shared with the police." Accordingly, the District Court submitted the factual defense to the jury with instructions that required a verdict in favor of petitioners unless the jury found consent. The jury found for respondents.

Petitioners appealed, arguing that the evidence was not sufficient to support the jury's consent finding. The Court of Appeals for the Fourth Circuit affirmed, but without reaching the question of consent. 186 F.3d 469 (1999). Disagreeing with the District Court, the majority of the appellate panel held that the searches were reasonable as a matter of law under our line of cases recognizing that "special needs" may, in certain exceptional circumstances, justify a search policy designed to serve non-law-enforcement ends.[7] On the understanding "that MUSC personnel conducted the urine drug screens for medical purposes wholly independent of an intent to aid law enforcement efforts," the majority applied the balancing test used in *Treasury Employees v. Von Raab*, 489 U.S. 656 (1989), and *Vernonia School Dist. 47J v. Acton*, 515 U.S. 646 (1995), and concluded that the interest in curtailing the pregnancy complications and medical costs associated with maternal cocaine use outweighed what the majority termed a minimal intrusion on the privacy of the patients. In dissent, Judge Blake concluded that the "special needs" doctrine should not apply and that the evidence of consent was insufficient to sustain the jury's verdict. 186 F.3d, at 487–488.

We granted certiorari, 528 U.S. 1187 (2000), to review the appellate court's holding on the "special needs" issue. Because we do not reach the question of the sufficiency of the evidence with respect to consent, we necessarily assume for purposes of our decision—as did the Court of Appeals—that the searches were conducted without the informed consent of the patients. We conclude that the judgment should be reversed and the case remanded for a decision on the consent issue.

III

Because MUSC is a state hospital, the members of its staff are government actors, subject to the strictures of the Fourth Amendment. *New Jersey v. T.L.O.*, 469 U.S. 325, 335–337 (1985). Moreover, the urine tests conducted by those staff members were indisputably searches within the meaning of the Fourth Amendment. *Skinner v. Railway Labor Executives' Assn.*, 489 U.S.

7. The term "special needs" first appeared in Justice Blackmun's opinion concurring in the judgment in *New Jersey v. T.L.O.*, 469 U.S. 325, 351 (1985). In his concurrence, Justice Blackmun agreed with the Court that there are limited exceptions to the probable-cause requirement, in which reasonableness is determined by "a careful balancing of governmental and private interests," but concluded that such a test should only be applied "in those exceptional circumstances in which special needs, beyond the normal need for law enforcement, make the warrant and probable-cause requirement impracticable...." *Ibid.* This Court subsequently adopted the "special needs" terminology in *O'Connor v. Ortega*, 480 U.S. 709, 720 (1987) (plurality opinion), and *Griffin v. Wisconsin*, 483 U.S. 868, 873 (1987), concluding that, in limited circumstances, a search unsupported by either warrant or probable cause can be constitutional when "special needs" other than the normal need for law enforcement provide sufficient justification. See also *Vernonia School Dist. 47J v. Acton*, 515 U.S. 646, 652–653 (1995).

602, 617 (1989).[9] Neither the District Court nor the Court of Appeals concluded that any of the nine criteria used to identify the women to be searched provided either probable cause to believe that they were using cocaine, or even the basis for a reasonable suspicion of such use. Rather, the District Court and the Court of Appeals viewed the case as one involving MUSC's right to conduct searches without warrants or probable cause. Furthermore, given the posture in which the case comes to us, we must assume for purposes of our decision that the tests were performed without the informed consent of the patients.

Because the hospital seeks to justify its authority to conduct drug tests and to turn the results over to law enforcement agents without the knowledge or consent of the patients, this case differs from the four previous cases in which we have considered whether comparable drug tests "fit within the closely guarded category of constitutionally permissible suspicionless searches." *Chandler v. Miller*, 520 U.S. 305, 309 (1997). In three of those cases, we sustained drug tests for railway employees involved in train accidents, *Skinner v. Railway Labor Executives' Assn.*, 489 U.S. 602 (1989), for United States Customs Service employees seeking promotion to certain sensitive positions, *Treasury Employees v. Von Raab*, 489 U.S. 656 (1989), and for high school students participating in interscholastic sports, *Vernonia School Dist. 47J v. Acton*, 515 U.S. 646 (1995). In the fourth case, we struck down such testing for candidates for designated state offices as unreasonable. *Chandler v. Miller*, 520 U.S. 305 (1997).

In each of those cases, we employed a balancing test that weighed the intrusion on the individual's interest in privacy against the "special needs" that supported the program. As an initial matter, we note that the invasion of privacy in this case is far more substantial than in those cases. In the previous four cases, there was no misunderstanding about the purpose of the test or the potential use of the test results, and there were protections against the dissemination of the results to third parties. The use of an adverse test result to disqualify one from eligibility for a particular benefit, such as a promotion or an opportunity to participate in an extracurricular activity, involves a less serious intrusion on privacy than the unauthorized dissemination of such results to third parties. The reasonable expectation of privacy enjoyed by the typical patient undergoing diagnostic tests in a hospital is that the results of those tests will not be shared with nonmedical personnel without her consent. See Brief for American Medical Association et al. as *Amici Curiae* 11; Brief for American Public Health Association as *Amicus Curiae* 6, 17–19.[13] In none of our prior cases was there any intrusion upon that kind of expectation.

9. In arguing that the urine tests at issue were not searches, the dissent attempts to disaggregate the taking and testing of the urine sample from the reporting of the results to the police. However, in our special needs cases, we have routinely treated urine screens taken by state agents as searches within the meaning of the Fourth Amendment even though the results were not reported to the police, see, *e.g.*, *Chandler v. Miller*, 520 U.S. 305 (1997); *Vernonia School Dist. 47J v. Acton*, 515 U.S. 646 (1995); *Skinner v. Railway Labor Executives' Assn.*, 489 U.S. 602, 617 (1989); *Treasury Employees v. Von Raab*, 489 U.S. 656 (1989), and respondents here do not contend that the tests were not searches. Rather, they argue that the searches were justified by consent and/or by special needs.

13. There are some circumstances in which state hospital employees, like other citizens, may have a duty to provide law enforcement officials with evidence of criminal conduct acquired in the course of routine treatment, see, *e.g.*, S.C.Code Ann. § 20-7-510 (2000) (physicians and nurses required to report to child welfare agency or law enforcement authority "when in the person's professional capacity the person" receives information that a child has been abused or neglected). While the existence of such laws might lead a patient to expect that members of the hospital staff might turn over evidence acquired in the course of treatment to

The critical difference between those four drug-testing cases and this one, however, lies in the nature of the "special need" asserted as justification for the warrantless searches. In each of those earlier cases, the "special need" that was advanced as a justification for the absence of a warrant or individualized suspicion was one divorced from the State's general interest in law enforcement. This point was emphasized both in the majority opinions sustaining the programs in the first three cases, as well as in the dissent in the *Chandler* case. In this case, however, the central and indispensable feature of the policy from its inception was the use of law enforcement to coerce the patients into substance abuse treatment. This fact distinguishes this case from circumstances in which physicians or psychologists, in the course of ordinary medical procedures aimed at helping the patient herself, come across information that under rules of law or ethics is subject to reporting requirements, which no one has challenged here. See, *e.g.*, Council on Ethical and Judicial Affairs, American Medical Association, PolicyFinder, Current Opinions E–5.05 (2000) (requiring reporting where "a patient threatens to inflict serious bodily harm to another person or to him or herself and there is a reasonable probability that the patient may carry out the threat"); Ark.Code Ann. § 12-12-602 (1999) (requiring reporting of intentionally inflicted knife or gunshot wounds); Ariz.Rev.Stat. Ann. § 13-3620 (Supp. 2000) (requiring "any... person having responsibility for the care or treatment of children" to report suspected abuse or neglect to a peace officer or child protection agency).[18]

Respondents argue in essence that their ultimate purpose—namely, protecting the health of both mother and child—is a beneficent one. In Chandler, however, we did not simply accept the State's invocation of a "special need." Instead, we carried out a "close review" of the scheme at issue before concluding that the need in question was not "special," as that term has been defined in our cases. 520 U.S., at 322. In this case, a review of the M-7 policy plainly reveals that the purpose actually served by the MUSC searches "is ultimately indistinguishable from the general interest in crime control." *Indianapolis v. Edmond*, 531 U.S. 32, 44 (2000).

In looking to the programmatic purpose, we consider all the available evidence in order to determine the relevant primary purpose. See, *e.g.*, *id.*, at 45–47. In this case, as Judge Blake put it in her dissent below, "it... is clear from the record that an initial and continuing focus of the policy was on the arrest and prosecution of drug-abusing mothers...." 186 F.3d, at 484. Tellingly, the document codifying the policy incorporates the police's operational guidelines. It devotes its attention to the chain of custody, the range of possible criminal charges, and the logistics of police notification and arrests. Nowhere, however, does the document discuss different courses of medical treatment for either mother or infant, aside from treatment for the mother's addiction.

Moreover, throughout the development and application of the policy, the Charleston prosecutors and police were extensively involved in the day-to-day administration of the policy. Police and prosecutors decided who would receive the reports of positive drug screens and what information would be included with those reports. Law enforcement officials also

which the patient had consented, they surely would not lead a patient to anticipate that hospital staff would intentionally set out to obtain incriminating evidence from their patients for law enforcement purposes.

18. Our emphasis on this distinction should make it clear that, contrary to the hyperbole in the dissent, we do not view these reporting requirements as "clearly bad." Those requirements are simply not in issue here.

helped determine the procedures to be followed when performing the screens.[19] In the course of the policy's administration, they had access to Nurse Brown's medical files on the women who tested positive, routinely attended the substance abuse team's meetings, and regularly received copies of team documents discussing the women's progress. Police took pains to coordinate the timing and circumstances of the arrests with MUSC staff, and, in particular, Nurse Brown.

While the ultimate goal of the program may well have been to get the women in question into substance abuse treatment and off of drugs, the immediate objective of the searches was to generate evidence *for law enforcement purposes* in order to reach that goal. The threat of law enforcement may ultimately have been intended as a means to an end, but the direct and primary purpose of MUSC's policy was to ensure the use of those means. In our opinion, this distinction is critical. Because law enforcement involvement always serves some broader social purpose or objective, under respondents' view, virtually any nonconsensual suspicionless search could be immunized under the special needs doctrine by defining the search solely in terms of its ultimate, rather than immediate, purpose. Such an approach is inconsistent with the Fourth Amendment. Given the primary purpose of the Charleston program, which was to use the threat of arrest and prosecution in order to force women into treatment, and given the extensive involvement of law enforcement officials at every stage of the policy, this case simply does not fit within the closely guarded category of "special needs."[23]

The fact that positive test results were turned over to the police does not merely provide a basis for distinguishing our prior cases applying the "special needs" balancing approach to the determination of drug use. It also provides an affirmative reason for enforcing the strictures of the Fourth Amendment. While state hospital employees, like other citizens, may have a duty to provide the police with evidence of criminal conduct that they inadvertently acquire in the course of routine treatment, when they undertake to obtain such evidence from their patients *for the specific purpose of incriminating those patients*, they have a special obligation to make sure that the patients are fully informed about their constitutional rights, as standards of knowing waiver require. Cf. *Miranda v. Arizona*, 384 U.S. 436 (1966).

As respondents have repeatedly insisted, their motive was benign rather than punitive. Such a motive, however, cannot justify a departure from Fourth Amendment protections, given the pervasive involvement of law enforcement with the development and application of the MUSC policy. The stark and unique fact that characterizes this case is that Policy M-7 was designed to obtain evidence of criminal conduct by the tested patients that would be turned over to the police and that could be admissible in subsequent criminal prosecutions. While respondents are correct that drug abuse both was and is a serious problem, "the gravity of the threat alone cannot be dispositive of questions concerning what means law enforcement officers may employ to pursue a given purpose." *Indianapolis v. Edmond*, 531 U.S., at 42–43.

19. Accordingly, the police organized a meeting with the staff of the police and hospital laboratory staffs, as well as Nurse Brown, in which the police went over the concept of a chain of custody system with the MUSC staff.

23. It is especially difficult to argue that the program here was designed simply to save lives. *Amici* claim a near consensus in the medical community that programs of the sort at issue, by discouraging women who use drugs from seeking prenatal care, harm, rather than advance, the cause of prenatal health. See Brief for American Medical Association as *Amicus Curiae* 6–22; Brief for American Public Health Association et al. as *Amici Curiae* 17–21; Brief for NARAL Foundation et al. as *Amici Curiae* 18–19.

The Fourth Amendment's general prohibition against nonconsensual, warrantless, and suspicionless searches necessarily applies to such a policy. See, *e.g.*, *Chandler*, 520 U.S., at 308; *Skinner*, 489 U.S., at 619.

Accordingly, the judgment of the Court of Appeals is reversed, and the case is remanded for further proceedings consistent with this opinion....

Justice Kennedy, concurring in the judgment.

I agree that the search procedure in issue cannot be sustained under the Fourth Amendment. My reasons for this conclusion differ somewhat from those set forth by the Court, however, leading to this separate opinion.

I

The Court does not dispute that the search policy at some level serves special needs, beyond those of ordinary law enforcement, such as the need to protect the health of mother and child when a pregnant mother uses cocaine. Instead, the majority characterizes these special needs as the "ultimate goal[s]" of the policy, as distinguished from the policy's "immediate purpose," the collection of evidence of drug use, which, the Court reasons, is the appropriate inquiry for the special needs analysis.

The majority views its distinction between the ultimate goal and immediate purpose of the policy as critical to its analysis. The distinction the Court makes, however, lacks foundation in our special needs cases. All of our special needs cases have turned upon what the majority terms the policy's ultimate goal. For example, in *Skinner v. Railway Labor Executives' Assn.*, 489 U.S. 602 (1989), had we employed the majority's distinction, we would have identified as the relevant need the collection of evidence of drug and alcohol use by railway employees. Instead, we identified the relevant need as "[t]he Government's interest in regulating the conduct of railroad employees to ensure [railroad] safety." *Id.*, at 620. In *Treasury Employees v. Von Raab*, 489 U.S. 656 (1989), the majority's distinction should have compelled us to isolate the relevant need as the gathering of evidence of drug abuse by would-be drug interdiction officers. Instead, the special needs the Court identified were the necessities "to deter drug use among those eligible for promotion to sensitive positions within the [United States Customs] Service and to prevent the promotion of drug users to those positions." *Id.*, at 666. In *Vernonia School Dist. 47J v. Acton*, 515 U.S. 646 (1995), the majority's distinction would have required us to identify the immediate purpose of gathering evidence of drug use by student-athletes as the relevant "need" for purposes of the special needs analysis. Instead, we sustained the policy as furthering what today's majority would have termed the policy's ultimate goal: "[d]eterring drug use by our Nation's schoolchildren," and particularly by student-athletes, because "the risk of immediate physical harm to the drug user or those with whom he is playing his sport is particularly high." *Id.*, at 661–662.

It is unsurprising that in our prior cases we have concentrated on what the majority terms a policy's ultimate goal, rather than its proximate purpose. By very definition, in almost every case the immediate purpose of a search policy will be to obtain evidence. The circumstance that a particular search, like all searches, is designed to collect evidence of some sort reveals nothing about the need it serves. Put a different way, although procuring evidence is the immediate result of a successful search, until today that procurement has not been identified as the special need which justifies the search.

II

While the majority's reasoning seems incorrect in the respects just discussed, I agree with the Court that the search policy cannot be sustained. As the majority demonstrates and well explains, there was substantial law enforcement involvement in the policy from its inception. None of our special needs precedents has sanctioned the routine inclusion of law enforcement, both in the design of the policy and in using arrests, either threatened or real, to implement the system designed for the special needs objectives. The special needs cases we have decided do not sustain the active use of law enforcement, including arrest and prosecutions, as an integral part of a program which seeks to achieve legitimate, civil objectives. The traditional warrant and probable-cause requirements are waived in our previous cases on the explicit assumption that the evidence obtained in the search is not intended to be used for law enforcement purposes. Most of those tested for drug use under the policy at issue here were not brought into direct contact with law enforcement. This does not change the fact, however, that, as a systemic matter, law enforcement was a part of the implementation of the search policy in each of its applications. Every individual who tested positive was given a letter explaining the policy not from the hospital but from the solicitor's office. Everyone who tested positive was told a second positive test or failure to undergo substance abuse treatment would result in arrest and prosecution. As the Court holds, the hospital acted, in some respects, as an institutional arm of law enforcement for purposes of the policy. Under these circumstances, while the policy may well have served legitimate needs unrelated to law enforcement, it had as well a penal character with a far greater connection to law enforcement than other searches sustained under our special needs rationale.

In my view, it is necessary and prudent to be explicit in explaining the limitations of today's decision. The beginning point ought to be to acknowledge the legitimacy of the State's interest in fetal life and of the grave risk to the life and health of the fetus, and later the child, caused by cocaine ingestion. Infants whose mothers abuse cocaine during pregnancy are born with a wide variety of physical and neurological abnormalities. See Chiriboga, Brust, Bateman, & Hauser, Dose-Response Effect of Fetal Cocaine Exposure on Newborn Neurologic Function, 103 Pediatrics 79 (1999) (finding that, compared with unexposed infants, cocaine-exposed infants experienced higher rates of intrauterine growth retardation, smaller head circumference, global hypertonia, coarse tremor, and extensor leg posture). Prenatal exposure to cocaine can also result in developmental problems which persist long after birth. See Arendt, Angelopoulos, Salvator, & Singer, Motor Development of Cocaine-exposed Children at Age Two Years, 103 Pediatrics 86 (1999) (concluding that, at two years of age, children who were exposed to cocaine in utero exhibited significantly less fine and gross motor development than those not so exposed); Chasnoff et al., Prenatal Exposure to Cocaine and Other Drugs: Outcome at Four to Six Years, 846 Annals of the New York Academy of Sciences 314, 319–320 (J. Harvey and B. Kosofsky eds. 1998) (finding that 4- to 6-year-olds who were exposed to cocaine in utero exhibit higher instances of depression, anxiety, social, thought, and attention problems, and delinquent and aggressive behaviors than their unexposed counterparts). There can be no doubt that a mother's ingesting this drug can cause tragic injury to a fetus and a child. There should be no doubt that South Carolina can impose punishment upon an expectant mother who has so little regard for her own unborn that she risks causing him or her lifelong damage and suffering. The State, by taking special measures to give rehabilitation and training to expectant mothers with this tragic addiction or weakness, acts well within its powers and its civic obligations.

The holding of the Court, furthermore, does not call into question the validity of mandatory reporting laws such as child abuse laws which require teachers to report evidence of child abuse to the proper authorities, even if arrest and prosecution is the likely result. That in turn highlights the real difficulty. As this case comes to us, and as reputable sources confirm, see K. Farkas, Training Health Care and Human Services Personnel in Perinatal Substance Abuse, in Drug & Alcohol Abuse Reviews, Substance Abuse During Pregnancy and Childhood 13, 27–28 (R. Watson ed. 1995); U.S. Dept. of Health and Human Services, Substance Abuse and Mental Health Services Administration, Pregnant, Substance-Using Women 48 (1993), we must accept the premise that the medical profession can adopt acceptable criteria for testing expectant mothers for cocaine use in order to provide prompt and effective counseling to the mother and to take proper medical steps to protect the child. If prosecuting authorities then adopt legitimate procedures to discover this information and prosecution follows, that ought not to invalidate the testing. One of the ironies of the case, then, may be that the program now under review, which gives the cocaine user a second and third chance, might be replaced by some more rigorous system. We must, however, take the case as it comes to us; and the use of handcuffs, arrests, prosecutions, and police assistance in designing and implementing the testing and rehabilitation policy cannot be sustained under our previous cases concerning mandatory testing.

III

An essential, distinguishing feature of the special needs cases is that the person searched has consented, though the usual voluntariness analysis is altered because adverse consequences (*e.g.*, dismissal from employment or disqualification from playing on a high school sports team) will follow from refusal. The person searched has given consent, as defined to take into account that the consent was not voluntary in the full sense of the word. See *Skinner*, 489 U.S., at 615; *Von Raab*, 489 U.S., at 660–661; *Acton*, 515 U.S., at 650–651. The consent, and the circumstances in which it was given, bear upon the reasonableness of the whole special needs program.

Here, on the other hand, the question of consent, even with the special connotation used in the special needs cases, has yet to be decided. Indeed, the Court finds it necessary to take the unreal step of assuming there was no voluntary consent at all. Thus, we have erected a strange world for deciding the case.

My discussion has endeavored to address the permissibility of a law enforcement purpose in this artificial context. The role played by consent might have affected our assessment of the issues. My concurrence in the judgment, furthermore, should not be interpreted as having considered or resolved the important questions raised by Justice Scalia with reference to whether limits might be imposed on the use of the evidence if in fact it were obtained with the patient's consent and in the context of the special needs program. Had we the prerogative to discuss the role played by consent, the case might have been quite a different one. All are in agreement, of course, that the Court of Appeals will address these issues in further proceedings on remand....

Justice Scalia, with whom The Chief Justice and Justice Thomas join as to Part II, dissenting.

There is always an unappealing aspect to the use of doctors and nurses, ministers of mercy, to obtain incriminating evidence against the supposed objects of their ministration—although here, it is correctly pointed out, the doctors and nurses were ministering not just to the mothers but also to the children whom their cooperation with the police was meant to protect. But whatever may be the correct social judgment concerning the desirability of what occurred here, that is not the issue in the present case. The Constitution does not resolve all difficult social questions, but leaves the vast majority of them to resolution by debate and the democratic process—which would produce a decision by the citizens of Charleston, through their elected representatives, to forbid or permit the police action at issue here. The question before us is a narrower one: whether, whatever the desirability of this police conduct, it violates the Fourth Amendment's prohibition of unreasonable searches and seizures. In my view, it plainly does not.

I

The first step in Fourth Amendment analysis is to identify the search or seizure at issue. What petitioners, the Court, and to a lesser extent the concurrence really object to is not the urine testing, but the hospital's reporting of positive drug-test results to police. But the latter is obviously not a search. At most it may be a "derivative use of the product of a past unlawful search," which, of course, "work[s] no new Fourth Amendment wrong" and "presents a question, not of rights, but of remedies." *United States v. Calandra*, 414 U.S. 338, 354 (1974). There is only one act that could conceivably be regarded as a search of petitioners in the present case: the taking of the urine sample. I suppose the testing of that urine for traces of unlawful drugs could be considered a search of sorts, but the Fourth Amendment protects only against searches of citizens' "persons, houses, papers, and effects"; and it is entirely unrealistic to regard urine as one of the "effects" (*i.e.*, part of the property) of the person who has passed and abandoned it. Cf. *California v. Greenwood*, 486 U.S. 35 (1988) (garbage left at curb is not property protected by the Fourth Amendment). Some would argue, I suppose, that testing of the urine is prohibited by some generalized privacy right "emanating" from the "penumbras" of the Constitution (a question that is not before us); but it is not even arguable that the testing of urine that has been lawfully obtained is a Fourth Amendment search. (I may add that, even if it were, the factors legitimizing the taking of the sample, which I discuss below, would likewise legitimize the testing of it.)

It is rudimentary Fourth Amendment law that a search which has been consented to is not unreasonable. There is no contention in the present case that the urine samples were extracted forcibly. The only conceivable bases for saying that they were obtained without consent are the contentions (1) that the consent was coerced by the patients' need for medical treatment, (2) that the consent was uninformed because the patients were not told that the tests would include testing for drugs, and (3) that the consent was uninformed because the patients were not told that the results of the tests would be provided to the police.[1] (When the court below

1. The Court asserts that it is improper to "disaggregate the taking and testing of the urine sample from the reporting of the results to the police," because "in our special needs cases, we have routinely treated urine screens taken by state agents as searches within the meaning of the Fourth Amendment." But in all of those cases, the urine was obtained involuntarily. See *Chandler v. Miller*, 520 U.S. 305 (1997); *Vernonia School Dist. 47J v. Acton*, 515 U.S. 646 (1995); *Skinner v. Railway Labor Executives' Assn.*, 489 U.S. 602 (1989); *Treasury Employees v. Von Raab*, 489 U.S. 656 (1989). Where the taking of the urine sample is unconsented (and thus

said that it was reserving the factual issue of consent, see 186 F.3d 469, 476 (C.A.4 1999), it was referring at most to these three—and perhaps just to the last two.)

Under our established Fourth Amendment law, the last two contentions would not suffice, even without reference to the special-needs doctrine. The Court's analogizing of this case to *Miranda v. Arizona*, 384 U.S. 436 (1966), and its claim that "standards of knowing waiver" apply, are flatly contradicted by our jurisprudence, which shows that using lawfully (but deceivingly) obtained material for purposes other than those represented, and giving that material or information derived from it to the police, is not unconstitutional. In *Hoffa v. United States*, 385 U.S. 293 (1966), "[t]he argument [was] that [the informant's] failure to disclose his role as a government informant vitiated the consent that the petitioner gave" for the agent's access to evidence of criminal wrongdoing, *id.*, at 300. We rejected that argument, because "the Fourth Amendment [does not protect] a wrongdoer's misplaced belief that a person to whom he voluntarily confides his wrongdoing will not reveal it." *Id.*, at 302. Because the defendant had voluntarily provided access to the evidence, there was no reasonable expectation of privacy to invade. Abuse of trust is surely a sneaky and ungentlemanly thing, and perhaps there should be (as there are) laws against such conduct by the government. See, *e.g.*, 50 U.S.C. § 403-7 (1994 ed., Supp. IV) (prohibiting the "Intelligence Community['s]" use of journalists as agents). That, however, is immaterial for Fourth Amendment purposes, for "*however strongly* a defendant may trust an apparent colleague, his expectations in this respect are not protected by the Fourth Amendment when it turns out that the colleague is a government agent regularly communicating with the authorities." *United States v. White*, 401 U.S. 745, 749 (1971) (emphasis added). The *Hoffa* line of cases, I may note, does not distinguish between operations meant to catch a criminal in the act, and those meant only to gather evidence of prior wrongdoing. See, *e.g.*, *United States v. Miller*, 425 U.S. 435, 440–443 (1976); cf. *Illinois v. Perkins*, 496 U.S. 292, 298 (1990) (relying on *Hoffa* in holding the *Miranda* rule did not require suppression of an inmate confession given an agent posing as a fellow prisoner).

Until today, we have *never* held—or even suggested—that material which a person voluntarily entrusts to someone else cannot be given by that person to the police, and used for whatever evidence it may contain. Without so much as discussing the point, the Court today opens a hole in our Fourth Amendment jurisprudence, the size and shape of which is entirely indeterminate. Today's holding would be remarkable enough if the confidential relationship violated by the police conduct were at least one protected by state law. It would be surprising to learn, for example, that in a State which recognizes a spousal evidentiary privilege the police cannot use evidence obtained from a cooperating husband or wife. But today's holding goes even beyond that, since there does not exist any physician-patient privilege in South Carolina. See, *e.g.*, *Peagler v. Atlantic Coast R.R. Co.*, 232 S.C. 274, 101 S.E.2d 821 (1958). Since the Court declines even to discuss the issue, it leaves law enforcement officials entirely in the dark as to when they can use incriminating evidence obtained from "trusted" sources. Presumably the lines will be drawn in the case-by-case development of a whole new branch of Fourth Amendment jurisprudence, taking yet another social judgment (which confidential relationships ought not be invaded by the police) out of democratic control, and confiding it

a Fourth Amendment search), the subsequent testing and reporting of the results to the police are obviously part of (or infected by) the same search; but where, as here, the taking of the sample was not a Fourth Amendment search, it is necessary to consider separately whether the testing and reporting were.

to the uncontrolled judgment of this Court—uncontrolled because there is no common-law precedent to guide it. I would adhere to our established law, which says that information obtained through violation of a relationship of trust is obtained consensually, and is hence not a search.

There remains to be considered the first possible basis for invalidating this search, which is that the patients were coerced to produce their urine samples by their necessitous circumstances, to wit, their need for medical treatment of their pregnancy. If that was coercion, it was not coercion applied by the government—and if such nongovernmental coercion sufficed, the police would never be permitted to use the ballistic evidence obtained from treatment of a patient with a bullet wound. And the Fourth Amendment would invalidate those many state laws that require physicians to report gunshot wounds, evidence of spousal abuse, and (like the South Carolina law relevant here, see S.C.Code Ann. § 20-7-510 (2000)) evidence of child abuse.

II

I think it clear, therefore, that there is no basis for saying that obtaining of the urine sample was unconstitutional. The special-needs doctrine is thus quite irrelevant, since it operates only to validate searches and seizures that are otherwise unlawful. In the ensuing discussion, however, I shall assume (contrary to legal precedent) that the taking of the urine sample was (either because of the patients' necessitous circumstances, or because of failure to disclose that the urine would be tested for drugs, or because of failure to disclose that the results of the test would be given to the police) coerced. Indeed, I shall even assume (contrary to common sense) that the testing of the urine constituted an unconsented search of the patients' effects. On those assumptions, the special-needs doctrine would become relevant; and, properly applied, would validate what was done here.

The conclusion of the Court that the special-needs doctrine is inapplicable rests upon its contention that respondents "undert[ook] to obtain [drug] evidence from their patients" not for any medical purpose, but "*for the specific purpose of incriminating those patients.*" In other words, the purported medical rationale was merely a pretext; there was no special need. See *Skinner v. Railway Labor Executives' Assn.*, 489 U.S. 602, 621, n. 5 (1989). This contention contradicts the District Court's finding of fact that the goal of the testing policy "was not to arrest patients but to facilitate their treatment and protect both the mother and unborn child." This finding is binding upon us unless clearly erroneous, see Fed. Rule Civ. Proc. 52(a). Not only do I find it supportable; I think any other finding would have to be overturned.

The cocaine tests started in April 1989, *neither at police suggestion nor with police involvement.* Expectant mothers who tested positive were referred by hospital staff for substance-abuse treatment...—an obvious health benefit to both mother and child. And, since "[i]nfants whose mothers abuse cocaine during pregnancy are born with a wide variety of physical and neurological abnormalities," which require medical attention, the tests were of additional medical benefit in predicting needed postnatal treatment for the child. Thus, in their origin—before the police were in any way involved—the tests had an immediate, not merely an "ultimate," purpose of improving maternal and infant health. Several months after the testing had been initiated, a nurse discovered that local police were arresting pregnant users of cocaine for child abuse, the hospital's general counsel wrote the county solicitor to ask "what, if anything, our Medical Center needs to do to assist you in this matter," the police suggested ways to avoid tainting evidence, and the hospital and police in conjunction used the testing program as a means of securing what the Court calls the "ultimate" health benefit of coercing drug-abusing mothers into drug treatment. Why would there be any reason to believe that, once this policy of using the drug tests for their "ultimate" health benefits had been adopted, use of them for their original, *immediate*, benefits somehow disappeared, and testing somehow became in its entirety nothing more than a "pretext" for obtaining grounds for arrest? On the face of it, this is incredible. The only evidence of the exclusively arrest-related purpose of the testing adduced by the Court is that the police-cooperation policy *itself* does not describe how to care for cocaine-exposed infants. But *of course* it does not, since that policy, adopted months after the cocaine testing was initiated, had as its only health object the "ultimate" goal of inducing drug treatment through threat of arrest. Does the Court really believe (or even *hope*) that, once invalidation of the program challenged here has been decreed, drug testing will cease?

In sum, there can be no basis for the Court's purported ability to "distinguis[h] this case from circumstances in which physicians or psychologists, in the course of ordinary medical procedures aimed at helping the patient herself, come across information that . . . is subject to reporting requirements," unless it is this: That the *addition* of a law-enforcement-related purpose to a legitimate medical purpose destroys applicability of the "special-needs" doctrine. But that is quite impossible, since the special-needs doctrine was developed, and is ordinarily employed, precisely to enable searches by law enforcement officials who, of course, ordinarily have a law enforcement objective. Thus, in *Griffin v. Wisconsin*, 483 U.S. 868 (1987), a probation officer received a tip from a detective that petitioner, a felon on probation, possessed a firearm. Accompanied by police, he conducted a warrantless search of petitioner's home. The weapon was found and used as evidence in the probationer's trial for unlawful possession of a firearm. See *id.*, at 870–872. Affirming denial of a motion to suppress, we concluded that the "special need" of assuring compliance with terms of release justified a warrantless search of petitioner's home. Notably, we observed that a probation officer is not

> "the police officer who normally conducts searches against the ordinary citizen. He is an employee of the State Department of Health and Social Services who, while assuredly charged with protecting the public interest, is also supposed to have in mind the welfare of the probationer. . . . In such a setting, we think it reasonable to dispense with the warrant requirement." *Id.*, at 876–877.

Like the probation officer, the doctors here do not "ordinarily conduc[t] searches against the ordinary citizen," and they are "supposed to have in mind the welfare of the [mother and child]." That they have in mind in addition the provision of evidence to the police should make no difference. The Court suggests that if police involvement in this case was in some way incidental and after-the-fact, that would make a difference in the outcome. But in *Griffin*, even more than here, police were involved in the search from the very beginning; indeed, the initial tip about the gun came from a detective. Under the factors relied upon by the Court, the use of evidence approved in *Griffin* would have been permitted only if the parole officer had been untrained in chain-of-custody procedures, had not known of the possibility a gun was present, and had been unaccompanied by police when he simply happened upon the weapon. Why any or all of these is constitutionally significant is baffling.

Petitioners seek to distinguish *Griffin* by observing that probationers enjoy a lesser expectation of privacy than does the general public. That is irrelevant to the point I make here, which is that the presence of a law enforcement purpose does not render the special-needs doctrine inapplicable. In any event, I doubt whether Griffin's reasonable expectation of privacy in his home was any less than petitioners' reasonable expectation of privacy in their urine taken, or in the urine tests performed, in a hospital—especially in a State such as South Carolina, which recognizes no physician-patient testimonial privilege and requires the physician's duty of confidentiality to yield to public policy, see *McCormick v. England*, 328 S.C. 627, 633, 640–642, 494 S.E.2d 431, 434, 438–439 (App. 1997); and which requires medical conditions that indicate a violation of the law to be reported to authorities, see, *e.g.*, S.C.Code Ann. § 20-7-510 (2000) (child abuse). Cf. *Whalen v. Roe*, 429 U.S. 589, 597–598 (1977) (privacy interest does not forbid government to require hospitals to provide, for law enforcement purposes, names of patients receiving prescriptions of frequently abused drugs).

The concurrence makes essentially the same basic error as the Court, though it puts the point somewhat differently: "The special needs cases we have decided," it says, "do not sustain the active use of law enforcement... as an integral part of a program which seeks to achieve legitimate, civil objectives." *Griffin* shows that is not true. Indeed, *Griffin* shows that there is not even any truth in the more limited proposition that our cases do not support application of the special-needs exception where the "legitimate, civil objectives" are sought only through the use of law enforcement means. (Surely the parole officer in *Griffin* was using threat of reincarceration to assure compliance with parole.) But even if this latter proposition were true, it would invalidate what occurred here only if the drug testing sought exclusively the "ultimate" health benefits achieved by coercing the mothers into drug treatment through threat of prosecution. But in fact the drug testing sought, independently of law enforcement involvement, the "immediate" health benefits of identifying drug-impaired mother and child for necessary medical treatment. The concurrence concedes that if the testing is conducted for medical reasons, the fact that "prosecuting authorities *then* adopt legitimate procedures to discover this information and prosecution follows... ought not to invalidate the testing." But here the police involvement in each case did *take place after* the testing was conducted for independent reasons. Surely the concurrence cannot mean that no police-suggested procedures (such as preserving the chain of custody of the urine sample) can be applied until *after* the testing; or that the police-suggested procedures must have been *designed* after the testing. The facts in *Griffin* (and common sense) show that this cannot be so. It seems to me that the only real distinction between what the concurrence must reasonably be thought to be approving, and what we have here, is that here the police took the lesser step of initially *threatening* prosecution rather than bringing it.

As I indicated at the outset, it is not the function of this Court—at least not in Fourth Amendment cases—to weigh petitioners' privacy interest against the State's interest in meeting the crisis of "crack babies" that developed in the late 1980's. I cannot refrain from observing, however, that the outcome of a wise weighing of those interests is by no means clear. The initial goal of the doctors and nurses who conducted cocaine testing in this case was to refer pregnant drug addicts to treatment centers, and to prepare for necessary treatment of their possibly affected children. When the doctors and nurses agreed to the program providing test results to the police, they did so because (in addition to the fact that child abuse was required by law to be reported) they wanted to use the sanction of arrest as a strong incentive for their addicted patients to undertake drug-addiction treatment. And the police themselves used it for that benign purpose, as is shown by the fact that only 30 of 253 women testing positive for cocaine were ever arrested, and only 2 of those prosecuted. It would not be unreasonable to conclude that today's judgment, authorizing the assessment of damages against the county solicitor and individual doctors and nurses who participated in the program, proves once again that no good deed goes unpunished.

But as far as the Fourth Amendment is concerned: There was no unconsented search in this case. And if there was, it would have been validated by the special-needs doctrine. For these reasons, I respectfully dissent.

NOTES AND QUESTIONS

1. Why does the policy violate the Fourth Amendment? Is it the absence of consent that renders the policy unconstitutional? Doesn't the state have a special interest in protecting unborn children? Why is that insufficient? Would Justice Kennedy answer these questions in the same way as the majority?

2. What is the basis of the disagreement between the majority and the dissent? Would the result have been different if, all else being the same, the state had used the drug-test results to initiate civil child-abuse proceedings instead of criminal proceedings?

3. The criminal or civil prosecution of pregnant women has been criticized overwhelmingly by medical and health professionals for a variety of reasons. See, e.g., Am. Acad. Pediatrics, Comm. on Substance Abuse, *Drug Exposed Infants*, 86 PEDIATRICS 639, 641 (1990) ("may discourage mothers and their infants from receiving the very medical care and social support systems that are crucial to their treatment"); Am. C. Obstetricians & Gynecologists, Comm. on Ethics, Comm. Op. 473 *Substance Abuse Reporting and Pregnancy: The Role of the Obstetrician-Gynecologist*, 117 OBSTETRICS & GYNECOLOGY 200 (2011) ("Seeking obstetric-gynecologic care should not expose a woman to criminal or civil penalties, such as incarceration, involuntary commitment, loss of custody of her children, or loss of housing. These approaches treat addiction as a moral failing. Addiction is a chronic, relapsing biological and behavioral disorder with genetic components. The disease of substance addiction is subject to medical and behavioral management in the same fashion as hypertension and diabetes"); Am. Med. Ass'n, Treatment versus Criminalization: Physician Role in Drug Addiction During Pregnancy, Resolution 131 (1990) ("therefore be it…resolved that the AMA oppose legislation which criminalizes maternal drug addiction"); Am. Nurses Ass'n, Position Statement on Opposition to Criminal Prosecution of Women for Use of Drugs While Pregnant and Support for Treatment Services for Alcohol and Drug Dependent Women of Childbearing Age (Apr. 5, 1991) ("The American Nurses Association recognizes alcohol and other drug problems as treatable illnesses. The threat of criminal prosecution is counterproductive in that it prevents many women from seeking prenatal care and treatment for their alcohol and other drug problems"); Am. Psychiatric Ass'n, Care of Pregnant and Newly Delivered Women Addicts, Position Statement, APA Document Reference No. 200101 (March 2001) ("policies of prosecuting pregnant and/or postpartum women who have used either alcohol or illegal substances during pregnancy, on grounds of 'prenatal child abuse' [and their]

subsequent incarceration, either in jails, prisons or in locked psychiatric unit both deprives the mother of her liberty and seriously disrupt the incipient or nascent maternal-infant bond.... Such policies are likely to deter pregnant addicts from seeking either prenatal care or addiction treatment, because of fear of prosecution and/or civil commitment"); Am. Psychol. Ass'n, Resolution on Substance Abuse by Pregnant Women (August 1991) ("alcohol and drug abuse by pregnant women is a public health problem and that laws, regulations and policies that treat chemical dependency primarily as a criminal justice matter requiring punitive sanctions are inappropriate"); Am. Pub. Health Ass'n, *Illicit Drug Use by Pregnant Women, Policy Statement No. 9020*, 8 AM. J. PUB. HEALTH 240 (1990) ("Recognizing that pregnant drug-dependent women have been the object of criminal prosecution in several states, and that women who might want medical care for themselves and their babies may not feel free to seek treatment because of fear of criminal prosecution related to illicit drug use... [the Association] recommends that no punitive measures be taken against pregnant women who are users of illicit drugs when no other illegal acts, including drug-related offenses, have been committed"); Nat'l Ass'n Pub. Child Welfare Administrators, Guiding Principles for Working with Substance-Abusing Families and Drug-Exposed Children: The Child Welfare Response 3 (1991) ("laws, regulations, or policies that respond to addiction in a primarily punitive nature, requiring human service workers and physicians to function as law enforcement agents are inappropriate").

4. Punishing pregnant women has raised a number of additional constitutional concerns. Some commentators have focused on due process concerns such as vagueness, others on substantive due process concerns grounded in liberty and autonomy. Still others argue that there are equal-protection problems and that minority women are disproportionately affected. See, e.g., Dorothy E. Roberts, *Punishing Drug Addicts Who Have Babies: Women of Color, Equality, and the Right of Privacy*, 104 HARV. L. REV. 1419 (1991) (discussing the disparate impact of nationwide prosecutions of poor women of color for prenatal drug abuse as a reproductive-rights issue that serves to perpetuate historical devaluation of black motherhood); Sarah Letitia Kowalski, Comment, *Looking for a Solution: Determining Fetal Status for Prenatal Drug Prosecutions*, 38 SANTA CLARA L. REV. 1255 (1998) (discussing how prosecutions for prenatal drug use violate the constitutional right to privacy, and advocating a "facilitative model" balancing maternal and fetal interests by providing greater prenatal care and substance-abuse treatment); Note, *Maternal Rights and Fetal Wrongs: The Case against the Criminalization of "Fetal Abuse,"* 101 HARV. L. REV. 994 (1988) (discussing prenatal drug-abuse prosecutions as problematic because of constitutional problems along with the deterrent effect they serve for women who might otherwise seek prenatal care, while also advocating an "educative/funding approach" as an alternative); Carol Jean Sovinski, Comment, *The Criminalization of Maternal Substance Abuse: A Quick Fix to a Complex Problem*, 25 PEPP. L. REV. 107 (1997) (discussing constitutional and deterrence problems with prenatal substance-abuse prosecutions and proposing increased treatment options as a more viable alternative); Sue Thomas, Lisa Rickert, & Carol Cannon, *The Meaning, Status, and Future of Reproductive Autonomy: The Case of Alcohol Use During Pregnancy*, 15 UCLA WOMEN'S L. J. 1 (2006). "Despite increased health care costs imposed by their tobacco use, there are no sterilization campaigns for mothers who use tobacco. No pregnant women have been charged with child abuse for tobacco use in pregnancy. Teachers do not dread having a 'tobacco kid' assigned to their class." Frank et al., *Growth, Development, and Behavior*, at 1621.

5. The 2009 National Survey on Drug Use and Health, conducted by the Substance Abuse and Mental Health Services Administration (SAMHSA), found that 4.5 percent of pregnant women

indicated that they had used illegal drugs in the preceding month. Substance Abuse and Mental Health Services Administration, Office of Applied Studies, Results from the 2009 National Survey on Drug Use and Health: Volume I. Summary of National Findings 22 (2010), http://www.oas.samhsa.gov/NSDUH/2k9NSDUH/2k9ResultsP.pdf. Alcohol and tobacco use, however, is higher among pregnant women. Ten percent of pregnant women indicated alcohol use, 4.4 percent said they had engaged in binge drinking while pregnant, and 0.8 percent said they had used alcohol heavily during pregnancy. Binge drinking during the first trimester, however, was 11.9 percent. *Id.* at 31. Past-month cigarette use among pregnant women was 15.3 percent; however, among pregnant women ages fifteen to seventeen, cigarette use was 20.6 percent. *Id.* at 45. What, if anything, should we do to prevent alcohol, tobacco, and drug use during pregnancy?

6. To what extent may the state regulate the behavior of pregnant women? Substance abuse during pregnancy is child abuse in fifteen states. Guttmacher Institute, State Policies in Brief, Substance Abuse During Pregnancy 1, http://www.guttmacher.org/statecenter/spibs/spib_SADP.pdf. Minnesota, Wisconsin, and South Dakota permit the state to confine pregnant women who are abusing alcohol or illegal substances. See, e.g., Minn. Stat. § 253B.02 (2011) (woman during pregnancy who engages in habitual or excessive use of certain illicit drugs or alcohol); S.D. Codified Laws § 34-20A-70 (2004) (authorizing involuntary civil commitment of pregnant woman who is abusing alcohol or drugs); Wis. Stat. Ann. § 48.193 (West 2011) (authorizing court to place pregnant woman in custody). What if the pregnant woman is not complying with a doctor's orders? Some states may intervene when the expectant mother is HIV-positive and refuses to undergo forced azidothymidine (AZT) treatment, the pregnant woman will not undergo a medically indicated cesarean section when her doctor believes the procedure is necessary to save the life of the fetus or the expectant mother, or the woman refuses blood transfusions on religious grounds. See Joanne E. Brosh & Monica K. Miller, *Regulating Pregnancy Behaviors: How the Constitutional Rights of Minority Women Are Disproportionately Compromised*, 16 Am. U. J. Gender, Soc. Pol'y & L. 437, 440–441, 443–444 (2008).

7. The medical profession recognized early the connection between alcohol exposure and birth defects. See Sterling K. Clarren, *Recognition of Fetal Alcohol Syndrome*, 245 J.A.M.A. 2436 (1981) (giving a historical analysis of studies on alcohol exposure and birth defects from 1899 on). Fetal alcohol syndrome (FAS) is a "constellation of physical, behavioral, and cognitive abnormalities" stemming from prenatal exposure to alcohol. Am. Acad. Pediatrics, Comm. on Substance Abuse & Comm. on Child. with Disabilities, *Fetal Alcohol Syndrome and Alcohol-Related Neurodevelopmental Disorders*, 106 Pediatrics 358, 358 (2000). Children who do not meet the full diagnostic criteria for FAS but whose mothers nevertheless drank during pregnancy may be diagnosed with alcohol-related neurodevelopmental disorder (ARND) or alcohol-related birth defects (ARBD). *Id.* Growth abnormalities, mental retardation, facial anomalies, cleft palates, impaired judgment, poor attention skills, impulsivity, impaired abstract reasoning, lying, stealing, and poor coordination are among the many problems experienced by these children. *Id.* Moreover, these problems persist into adulthood, and adults diagnosed with FAS, ARND, or ARBD present secondarily with mental-health issues, chemical dependency, and legal problems. *Id.*

Use of tobacco during pregnancy also has well-documented and clear teratogenic effects. Smoking during pregnancy increases risks of infant mortality, moderate impairment of cognitive functioning, low birth weight, and a range of behavioral problems. Deborah A. Frank et al., *Growth, Development, and Behavior in Early Childhood following Prenatal Cocaine Exposure: A Systematic Review*, 285 J.A.M.A. 1613, 1620–1621 (2001). Tobacco smoking while pregnant and exposing the child to secondhand smoke after birth has "persistent adverse effects on lung function," increases the "likelihood of addiction at a later age," and is causally related to sudden infant death syndrome (SIDS). Am. Acad. Pediatrics, Comm. on Envtl. Health, Comm. on Native Am. Child Health, & Comm. on Adolescence, *Secondhand and Prenatal Tobacco Exposure*, 124 PEDIATRICS e1017, e1018 tbl.1 (2009). There is also clear evidence that nicotine affects the developing fetal brain by restricting blood flow, depriving it of oxygen, and disturbing neurotransmitter networks. Frank et al., *Growth, Development, and Behavior*, at 1620.

Nevertheless, states have focused enforcement efforts primarily on pregnant women who use illegal substances, particularly cocaine and crack, because of concerns that these drugs would have devastating and long-lasting effects on the development of infants and children. A predicted epidemic of "crack babies," however, proved to be nothing more than a myth. See, *e.g.*, Susan Oakie, *The Epidemic That Wasn't*, NEW YORK TIMES, Jan. 27, 2009, D1. A review of studies on prenatal cocaine exposure found no effects on physical growth, developmental scores, behavioral disturbance, or language of children exposed prenatally to cocaine or crack. Frank et al., *Growth, Development, and Behavior*, at 1618–1619. Although acknowledging that much is still unknown about the effects of prenatal cocaine exposure, the authors nevertheless conclude that "among children up to 6 years of age, there is no convincing evidence that prenatal cocaine exposure is associated with any developmental toxicity different in severity, scope, or kind from the sequelae of many other risk factors. Many findings once thought to be specific effects of in utero cocaine exposure can be explained in whole or in part by other factors, including prenatal exposure to tobacco, marijuana, or alcohol and the quality of the child's environment." *Id.* at 1621, 1624. "Paradoxically, the more we understand about the way in which exposure to different conditions or substances affects the fetus, the less confident we can be about which substance or condition caused which problem." Cheryl M. Plambeck, *Divided Loyalties*, 23 J. LEG. MED. 1, 12 (2002).

v. Sexual abuse

42 U.S.C. § 5106h (2010)

(4) The term sexual abuse includes:

(A) the employment, use, persuasion, inducement, enticement, or coercion of any child to engage in, or assist any other person to engage in, any sexually explicit conduct or simulation of such conduct for the purpose of producing a visual depiction of such conduct; or

(B) the rape, and in cases of caretaker or inter-familial relationships, statutory rape, molestation, prostitution, or other form of sexual exploitation of children, or incest with children....

NOTES AND QUESTIONS

1. Where is the line between inappropriate conduct and sexual abuse? If a parent kisses a child on the lips, is that sexual abuse? What if a parent takes a bath with a toddler? Could a parent take a picture of her naked child while in the tub? In FRAMING INNOCENCE: A MOTHER'S PHOTOGRAPHS, A PROSECUTOR'S ZEAL, AND A SMALL TOWN'S RESPONSE, author Lynn Powell tells the story of Cynthia Stewart, who was prosecuted under civil and criminal statutes for sexual

abuse in Ohio, based on photographs she had taken of her eight-year-old daughter, Nora, in the shower. Do you think this behavior is merely inappropriate, or does it amount to sexual abuse?

2. In 1983, psychiatrist Roland Summit identified a syndrome he labeled Child Sexual Abuse Accommodation Syndrome. Roland C. Summit, *The Child Sexual Abuse Accommodation Syndrome*, 7 Child Abuse & Neglect 177 (1983). Summit identified two "preconditions" for the child's victimization: the child is convinced of the need for secrecy and, because of the child's subordinate status, the child is helpless. *Id.* at 181–183. These are followed by what Summit called "sequential contingencies." To cope with the ongoing abuse, the child comes to believe that he or she is responsible for the abuse and seeks love and acceptance from the abuser while maintaining secrecy. *Id.* at 184–185. The child then may reveal the secret, although that revelation may be a "delayed, conflicted, and unconvincing disclosure." *Id.* at 186. Because family members react by denying the abuse and believe that the child is lying, *id.* at 186–187, she will recant, *id.* at 188.

Summit's model was very influential in the psychological field; see R. Kim Oates & Anne Cohn Donnelly, *Influential Papers in Child Abuse*, 21 Child Abuse & Neglect 319 (1997) (noting that 242 professional experts cited Summit's paper as second-most influential work in field of child protection); and it generally has been accepted that recantation is common in child-sex-abuse cases. See, e.g., John E. B. Myers et al., *Expert Testimony in Child Sexual Abuse Litigation*, 68 Neb. L. Rev. 1, 68 (1989) (delay and recantation common in intrafamilial child sexual abuse). The empirical evidence is less clear. Although recantation rates range from 4 percent to 22 percent in various studies, most studies of recantation are methodologically flawed. "It is more accurate to state that we simply do not yet know how often and why children recant their statements about actually having been sexually abused." Erna Olafson & Cindy S. Lederman, *The State of the Debate about Children's Disclosure Patterns in Child Sexual Abuse Cases*, 57 Juv. & Fam. Ct. J. 27, 34 (Winter 2006). However, a more recent study of a random sample of 257 substantiated child-sexual-abuse cases filed in dependency court found children recanted in 58 of the cases, or 23.1 percent. Lindsay C. Malloy, Thomas D. Lyon, & Jodi A. Quas, *Filial Dependency and Recantation of Child Sexual Abuse Allegations*, 46 J. Am. Acad. Child & Adolescent Psychiatry 162, 165 (2007). Although this study found the highest rate of recantation reported, the authors note that the study's findings still fail to support Summit's claims that a majority of children recant. *Id.* at 166. The high rate of recantation also was not positively correlated to the strength or weakness of the evidence of child sexual abuse, although the rate in stronger cases was lower (ranging from 16.7 percent, where the perpetrator admitted, to 20.0 percent, where there was medical evidence). *Id.* The authors suggest that children who recant may be more susceptible to family pressures to deny the abuse. *Id.* at 167.

3. Article 19 of the United Nations Convention on the Rights of the Child states that parties to the Convention "shall take all appropriate legislative, administrative, social and educational measures to protect the child from all forms of physical or mental violence, injury or abuse, neglect or negligent treatment, maltreatment or exploitation, including sexual abuse, while in the care of parent(s), legal guardian(s) or any other person who has the care of the child." Article 34 directs states parties to protect children from all forms of sexual abuse and exploitation. The Council of Europe Convention on the Protection of Children against Sexual Exploitation and Sexual Abuse is the first international treaty to address all forms of sexual violence against children, including within the family, child prostitution, pornography, and sex tourism. Opened for signature Oct. 25, 2007, CETS No. 201 (entered into force Jan. 7, 2010). The United States has not ratified

the Convention on the Rights of the Child, nor has it signed or ratified the Convention on the Protection of Children against Sexual Exploitation and Sexual Abuse.

4. Child sexual abuse is not simply an American problem. The World Health Organization estimates that 150 million girls and 73 million boys have experienced sexual violence, most often perpetrated by family members or other people living in or visiting the home. Paulo Sergio Pinheiro, United Nations, Secretary General's Study on Violence against Children, World Report on Violence against Children 54 (2006). "Over the last two decades...Finland, Germany, Israel, Norway, Sweden, [and] the United Kingdom...like most other western industrialized nations, have witnessed substantial increases in the number of reported incidents of child sexual maltreatment." Michael E. Lamb, *The Investigation of Child Sexual Abuse: An International, Interdisciplinary Consensus Statement*, 28 FAM. L. Q. 151, 152 (1994). While it is hard to compare incidence studies across countries, it appears that child-sexual-abuse rates tend to be around 10 percent in many Western nations. See Table 1: Prevalence Studies of Child Sexual Abuse in Different Countries, National Society for the Prevention of Cruelty to Children, http://www.nspcc.org.uk/Inform/research/briefings/prevalencetable1_wdf49715.pdf. Nevertheless, in some countries, the rates may be substantially higher. See, e.g., Kofi E. Boakye, *Culture and Nondisclosure of Child Sexual Abuse in Ghana: A Theoretical and Empirical Exploration*, 34 LAW & SOC. INQUIRY 951 (2009) (arguing that prevalence of sexual abuse is much higher because of stigma associated with abuse); Jennifer Bays Beinart, Note, *Beyond Trafficking and Sexual Exploitation: Protecting India's Children from Inter- and Intrafamilial Abuse*, 21 IND. INT'L & COMP. L. REV. 47, 48 (2011) (noting that 53 percent of India's children have been sexually abused).

vi. Neglect

Martin Guggenheim, *Book Review, Somebody's Children: Sustaining the Family's Place in Child Welfare Policy*, 113 HARV. L. REV. 1716, 1724–1725, 1736–1737 (2000).

[T]he current foster care population may be grouped into three categories. First, the most serious category, constituting about 10% of current caseloads, includes "serious and criminal cases." The second group encompasses serious cases that do not require criminal justice intervention. The final group of cases are those in which a child is at a relatively lower risk of serious harm, and the parents may be willing to work with an agency to secure needed services. Together, the latter two groups comprise 90% of the caseload. Typically, these cases involve less serious physical abuse (for example, a single, minor injury such as a bruise or a scratch) or less severe neglect (such as parental drug or alcohol abuse with no other apparent protective issues, dirty clothes or a dirty home, lack of supervision of a school-age child, or missed school or medical appointments). Many of these lower-risk neglect cases are poverty-related, resulting from inadequate housing or inappropriate child-care arrangements while a parent works....

In the early 1970s, liberals seeking to improve the lives of poor children realized the importance of developing new strategies to secure bipartisan support for government spending toward that end. Chiefly the work of Senator Walter Mondale, the new strategy found its home in the field of child abuse and protection. Mondale led the legislative effort that resulted in the passage of the Child Abuse Prevention and Treatment Act (CAPTA) in 1974. CAPTA directed a significant amount of federal money to states to fund efforts to protect children from harm. As part of a conscious plan to prevent the proposal from being viewed as a disguised poverty program, Mondale emphasized that child abuse was a "national" problem, not a "poverty problem." Stressing that child abuse affected families of all classes and that federal money would help children who were both rich and poor, Mondale won support for the proposal from politicians across party lines. Ever since, "child abuse and neglect" in the United States have come to be seen and defined as an individual problem caused by individual sets of parents. No longer a social problem, child welfare has come to be viewed as a matter of individual failure. Much of the public debate has ignored or understated the evidence suggesting a correlation between abuse and neglect on the one hand and poverty on the other. Indeed, a remarkable characteristic of the growth of support for child protection in the United States has been the deliberate claim that middle-class and upper-class children need child protective legislation just as much as do poor children.

NOTES AND QUESTIONS

1. Do you agree? What should we do for children whose parents are unable to provide them with adequate food, clothing, and shelter? Would you characterize the inability to provide for a child as an act of commission or omission?

2. *"Dirty home" cases.* Sometimes the state intervenes when the children are living in filthy or unsanitary conditions. Should that be a basis for intervention?

IN RE AISLINN L.
California Court of Appeals
2001 WL 1408492

O'LEARY, J.

Lisa L. and Jason L., Sr., appeal the jurisdictional and dispositional orders adjudging their children dependent pursuant to Welfare and Institutions Code section 300, subdivision (b), primarily due to the filthy and unsanitary condition of their home. The juvenile court removed the children from the parents' custody and ordered family reunification services. They both contend there is insufficient evidence to support the orders and visitation is inadequate. Lisa additionally argues reunification services are inadequate, and Jason, Sr., complains there was no good cause for the juvenile court to order him to undergo an Evidence Code section 730 evaluation. We reject their contentions and affirm the orders.

I

This dependency proceeding involves the seven children of Lisa and Jason, Sr., 12-year-old Aislinn, 10-year-old Courtney, 9-year-old Jason, Jr., 7-year-old Justin, 4-year-old Ryan,

2-year-old Hanna, and Tyler, who was born in January 2001, after the six other children were taken into protective custody.

The six older children were taken into protective custody in November 2000 due to the unsafe and unhealthy condition of their home. The home was filthy—cluttered with trash, food, and dirty clothes. The house was infested with cockroaches; open containers of food lay around with live and dead bugs in them.

There were numerous prior substantiated reports of general neglect involving this family, beginning in 1991, when the children were taken into protective custody due to the unsafe condition of the house. There was trash everywhere, including spoiled food and soiled diapers. Dirty laundry was strewn about the kitchen and dining room. A child's portable toilet, half-filled with urine, was in the living room. Cockroaches and cockroach eggs were everywhere, including in the sink and food. Other dangers abounded. There were fire hazards, extension cords draped across the top of the stove, and knives and prescription drug bottles were out where the children could reach them. The children were returned to the parents once the house was cleaned up, and in January 1992, the juvenile court dismissed the dependency petition.

In July 1997, a report was filed with SSA after Jason, Jr., was found wandering the streets unsupervised. At the time about 100 rats, which Lisa raised to sell, were found in unkempt cages in the house. The family declined services.

In October 1997, more reports of general neglect came in. SSA again found the house returned to a filthy condition. Rats were everywhere, some were dead. Rat droppings were on the floors. The children were unsupervised, unkempt, smelly, and dirty. Family maintenance noncourt services were provided.

In February 1998, the home was again found to be filthy, smelling of animal feces, rat and mice cages were everywhere, and the house was infested with cockroaches. Similar reports were again substantiated in March 1998 and February 2000.

The current petitions were filed after school officials reported that the children consistently arrived at school dirty and smelly. Jason, Jr., had insect bites all over his body. Justin had been diagnosed as autistic.

A police officer and Orange County Social Services Agency (SSA) caseworker went to the home to investigate. They found the front gate leading to the house was padlocked, so the children had to climb over the fence to get in. The house was vile. Trash and dirty laundry were everywhere. The house was infested with cockroaches. There were no sheets or blankets on the children's beds. A pair of pants, filled with feces, lay on the bathroom floor. Used toilet paper was tossed about; the toilet was unflushed for days. A moldy bowl of cereal sat on a dresser. The female police officer found the conditions so bad that she began "dry-heaving" and had to leave the house. Criminal child neglect charges were filed against Lisa and Jason, Sr.

Lisa explained that because she was pregnant, she could not take medication for her depression and diabetes. She instructed the older girls to clean the house, but they preferred to be outside playing. She told the boys to take showers, but they did not. Jason, Jr.'s red bumps were flea bites. Three of the children suffered from allergies, two from asthma, and Justin was mildly autistic. Lisa claimed that she had a pest control service come routinely. She had missed the last appointment. She stated the clothes, although clean, were all around because they were going through them to find things for the new baby.

The children generally denied the home was unlivable, although they knew it was messy and wished it were cleaner. They denied any physical or substance abuse by the parents. They all wanted to go home once the house was clean.

Jason, Sr., denied the home was unhealthful. He knew there was a problem with pests and agreed that while the children were out of the home, he and Lisa would be more aggressive about treating the problem.

Because the problem was long-term and recurring, SSA recommended against Conditional Release to Intensive Supervision Program (CRISP). It did permit the parents to have unmonitored visitation with the children at Orangewood Children's Home.

At the detention hearing on December 5, the juvenile court ordered the children remain in protective custody. At a progress review hearing on December 11, some progress had been made in getting the house cleaned up. Nonetheless, the juvenile court would not return the children to the parents' custody.

In preparing the January 5, 2001, report for the pretrial hearing, the caseworker interviewed several of the children. They reported the older children were assigned chores. Aislinn was responsible for the laundry, except for her father's—Jason, Sr., apparently made sure his own clothes were clean. Courtney was to wash the dishes, and Jason, Jr., and Justin were responsible for trash pickup. Aislinn acknowledged the roach problem but denied anyone became sick from them. Courtney revealed there had been another child, a baby named Brandon, who died at around six months of age from sudden infant death syndrome.

The parents frequently permitted unrelated adult men to stay in the home, but the children denied these men behaved inappropriately. The older children had been placed in an assessment facility; Ryan had not adjusted well. Hanna, who was in a foster home, immediately began calling her foster mother "mommy," a reaction which troubled the caseworker.

When interviewed, Lisa had trouble focussing and concentrating. She admitted she had emotional swings and had been referred to a psychologist after Hanna's birth. Her suggestions as to how to correct problems in the home were largely aimed at what responsibility the children needed to take, not anything she should do. She told the caseworker, "I can help them, I can show them how, I can help them choose, but they need to make the choice themselves." Jason, Sr., claimed the conditions at the home had improved. He too attributed the filthy condition of the house to the children and did not acknowledge any responsibility on his own part for its condition.

The caseworker noted the parents had made progress in cleaning the home. However, she was concerned they could not solve the problems in the long term, given their recurring nature. "Unless the underlying causes of [their] inability to maintain the home... are discovered, they will simply continue to recreate the very environment which they have recently worked hard to clean." She speculated one or both parents might suffer from some sort of mental disorder.

At the end of December, the parents were having unmonitored visits with the children. But criminal charges against the parents were proceeding, and the criminal court had ordered no contact. The caseworker stated that if the no-contact order was lifted, she would consider returning the children, a couple at a time, under CRISP.

In her January 18, 2001, supplemental report, the caseworker advised that the district attorney had agreed to the parents visiting the children. The parents did not appear for the pretrial hearing in the criminal case, so the order was not lifted. Jason, Sr., subsequently went to the district attorney's office and obtained a modification of the no-contact order. Lisa was in the hospital for the birth of Tyler, so her no-contact order was not changed. Justin, who was autistic, had never been evaluated at the Orange County Regional Center. A CRISP supervisor had advised the caseworker CRISP would not be appropriate due to the long-term recurring nature of the family's problems.

Tyler was born on January 16, 2001. A hospital hold was placed on him and a petition filed based on the condition of the home, the presence of unrelated transient men in the home, and Lisa's "mental health issues." He was placed in a medical foster home with unmonitored visitation.

On February 20, the caseworker reported that Lisa had been visiting Tyler. On January 25, Lisa had to have emergency hernia surgery. Afterwards, Tyler's pediatrician authorized Lisa to continue to breastfeed. The foster mother was convinced something in Lisa's breast milk, possibly from medications, was causing severe diaper rash and other health problems. The caseworker, based on advice from a public health nurse, ordered Lisa to stop breastfeeding the baby. Lisa had obtained a referral to a psychologist.

The no-contact order had been modified, and the parents were seeing the older children but made little effort with regard to Hanna. A public health nurse had seen Lisa at the home. She noticed a lot of dirt, grime, and clutter, however, she saw nothing she considered unsafe. Nonetheless, she believed it would not take much for "a neglectful situation to develop if the children were returned." Lisa told the nurse she did not drive because she suffered from panic attacks.

The children, for the first time, began talking to the caseworker about their home life. Up until then, they had been very secretive and protective. Jason, Jr., said his parents fought and that Jason, Sr., frequently slapped Lisa. Jason, Jr., often ran away from home when fights took place, as did his older siblings, and sometimes he would take the younger children with him. Fights were often about one of the "boarders," a man named "Jesse." Jason, Jr., reported that Jesse and Lisa frequently "slept together" on the couch. Jesse routinely hit the boys with a belt when they misbehaved, and the parents not only condoned it, but would often invite him to do so. Once, Jesse was driving Jason, Jr., in a car and tried to talk Jason, Jr., into jumping out of the moving car. The caseworker also learned the parents were talking to the children about the dependency proceedings and the contents of the various reports, despite contrary instructions from the caseworker, and telling them there was a conspiracy to keep them apart.

The foster mother of Aislinn, Jason, Justin, and Ryan observed that often when approached about misbehaving, the children would flinch as if to ward off being hit. She said the children had to be taught how to properly use the toilet and behaved like animals at the dinner table. The foster mother of Courtney and Hanna reported that both girls had head lice. Courtney panicked when told about the problem and said her parents had shaved her head in the past when she had lice. Aislinn confirmed that the children frequently had head lice and that her parents had shaved her head when she was nine.

SSA filed amended petitions as to the six older children alleging they came under section 300, subdivision (b) because the home was unsafe and unhealthy, pending criminal charges against the parents due to the condition of the home, and the parents' inability to maintain a safe and healthy home despite the 1991 detention of three of the children and the numerous contacts with SSA on subsequent occasions. The petitions also contained allegations regarding the parents' history of permitting unrelated transient men to live in the home and allowing one of these men to hit the male children with a belt, the parents' failure to get appropriate services to treat Justin's autism, Lisa's history of mental health problems which impaired her ability to adequately care for the children, and the history of domestic violence between the parents.

An amended petition as to Tyler alleged he came within section 300, subdivision (b) due to the parents' history of permitting unrelated transient men to live in the home, Lisa's history of mental health problems which impaired her ability to adequately care for the children, and the history of domestic violence between the parents. It also alleged Tyler came within section 300, subdivision (j), due to the abuse and neglect of his siblings. The domestic violence allegations were eventually stricken by the juvenile court.

The caseworker testified that since the children's detention, the home had been improved significantly, and she did not see any significant hazards. If there had been no history with this family, she would have recommended the children be returned. However, theirs was a long-term problem, and the caseworker was certain that if the children were returned, the home would rapidly deteriorate. She believed criminal charges would not have been filed if the district attorney did not consider the problem significant.

The parents argued that because the house had been cleaned up, there was no basis for declaring the children dependent or for keeping them out of their custody. The juvenile court disagreed. It found all of the children came within section 300, subdivision (b), and Tyler additionally came within section 300, subdivision (j), and declared them all dependent children. It found by clear and convincing evidence returning the children home would be detrimental, and it vested custody with SSA. It approved and adopted the reunification plan proposed by SSA and ordered monitored visitation and Evidence Code section 730 evaluations of both parents.

II

Lisa and Jason, Sr., contend the evidence is insufficient to support the jurisdictional findings or to support removing the children from their custody. We disagree.

The jurisdictional finding that a minor is a person described in section 300 must be supported by a preponderance of the evidence. (§ 355; *Cynthia D. v. Superior Court* (1993) 5 Cal.4th 242, 248.) In making its dispositional order, the juvenile court may not remove a child from parental custody unless it finds, by clear and convincing evidence, at least one of the matters set out in subdivision (b) of section 361, including that it is not safe to return the child to his or her parents. (§ 361, subd. (b)(1); *Cynthia D., supra*, 5 Cal.4th at p. 248.)

On appeal, we must affirm the jurisdictional and dispositional findings if supported by substantial evidence, contradicted or uncontradicted. (*In re Heather A.* (1996) 52 Cal.App.4th 183, 193.) "In making this determination, we draw all reasonable inferences from the evidence to support the findings and orders of the dependency court; we review the record in the light most favorable to the court's determinations; and we note that issues of fact and credibility are the province of the trial court. [Citation.]" (*Ibid.*) We have reviewed the record and find substantial evidence supports both the jurisdictional and dispositional orders.

Jurisdiction

All of the children were declared dependent under section 300, subdivision (b), which provides for jurisdiction if "[t]he child has suffered, or there is a substantial risk that the child will suffer, serious physical harm or illness, as a result of the failure or inability of his or her parent[s] . . . to adequately supervise or protect the child, . . . or by the willful or negligent failure of the parent[s] ... to provide the child with adequate food, clothing, shelter, or medical treatment, or by the inability of the parent or guardian to provide regular care for the child due to the parent's or guardian's mental illness, developmental disability, or substance abuse." Substantial evidence supports this finding.

The record demonstrates the parents maintained filthy and unsanitary living conditions for these children. When the children were detained in November, they were filthy and smelled, prompting complaints from school officials. Police found the home unlivable. Trash, dirty laundry, and dirty dishes were everywhere, and the house was completely infested with cockroaches. Human waste was found on the bathroom floor, the toilet was unflushed for days, and used toilet paper lay on the floor. There were no sheets or blankets on the children's beds. One of the boys had flea bites all over his body; two of the girls had head lice. Indeed, the situation was so bad that criminal child abuse charges were filed against the parents. Furthermore, the dreadful conditions of the home were nothing new. The police and SSA had been responding to complaints since 1991.

Both parents complain that because they had made progress in cleaning up their house by the time of the combined jurisdictional/dispositional hearing, there was no basis for declaring the children dependent. Both contend the trial court improperly based jurisdiction on the past unsanitary condition of the home, rather than its current cleaned-up state. While it is true that "the question under section 300 is whether circumstances *at the time of the [jurisdictional] hearing* subject the minor to the defined risk of harm" (see *In re Rocco M.* (1991) 1 Cal.App.4th 814, 824, original italics), "evidence of past conduct may be probative of current conditions...." (*Ibid.*; see also *In re Diamond H.* (2000) 82 Cal.App.4th 1127, 1135 ["'in determining whether the child is in present need of the juvenile court's protection, the court may consider past events'"].) The facts are that the children have repeatedly been found living in vile conditions. When SSA intervenes, the parents manage to restore some semblance of order, only to have it slip away the minute they are no longer being scrutinized. These facts are highly relevant in determining the current conditions.

Both parents also complain there was no evidence the children were actually harmed by the unsanitary conditions of the home. To the contrary, there is evidence the children were currently suffering. They were frequently filthy and smelly. Several of them suffered from respiratory illnesses, although the cause was not known, and two had head lice. Furthermore, actual harm is not required. Jurisdiction is appropriate if there is a risk of harm in the future. (§ 300, subd. (b).) The juvenile court could reasonably conclude there was such a risk.

Lisa and Jason, Sr., also argue that even if sufficient evidence supports jurisdiction as to the six older children, the record does not support it as to Tyler. He was born *after* the other children were taken into custody and after the parents had made significant progress in cleaning up their house. Thus, there was no showing the parents had failed to provide an adequate home for him. But Tyler was adjudicated a dependent child not only under section 300, subdivision (b), but under subdivision (j), which provides for declaring jurisdiction due to the circumstances surrounding the abuse or neglect of a sibling.

We disagree with Jason, Sr.'s, characterization of this case as being an example of a simple dirty house case in which an overreaching caseworker has imposed the "cultural mores of Orange County middle class life" upon this family. Both parents rely upon this court's opinion in *In re Paul E.* (1995) 39 Cal.App.4th 996 in support of their argument that jurisdiction is not supported by the record. In that case, jurisdiction was declared over the four-year-old child due to the dirty and unsanitary conditions of his home, although he was not removed from his parents' custody. The parents improved the living conditions. However, the caseworker remained concerned about their ability to function as parents. The house was still messy and dirty, but the unsanitary conditions had been remedied. The caseworker identified three trivial hazards, which the parents immediately fixed. The caseworker nonetheless took the child into custody because the parents failed to "'progress in recognizing the dirty condition of the house demonstrat[ing] that they were limited by their own ability.'" (*Id.* at p. 1000.) We reversed the dispositional order and chided social services agencies that "cast themselves in the role of a super-OSHA for families." (*Id.* at p. 1005, fn. omitted.)

But the facts in *In re Paul E.* are simply not comparable to the facts presented here. *In re Paul E.* truly involved a simple messy house, with a few trivial hazards, kept by parents who otherwise doted on their only child. Here, we have a family of seven children, who for over ten years have lived in squalor. SSA has repeatedly intervened, prodding the parents to briefly improve the home. But in the end, the filthy conditions always returned. Neither parent seemed particularly concerned about the living conditions and both largely attributed them to the children's failures rather than their own. The record amply supports the juvenile court's jurisdictional findings.

Disposition

We also conclude sufficient evidence supports removing the children from the parents' custody. "A removal order is proper if it is based on proof of parental inability to provide proper care for the minor and proof of a potential detriment to the minor if he or she remains with the parent. [Citation.] The parent need not be dangerous and the minor need not have been actually harmed before removal is appropriate. The focus of the statute is on averting harm to the child. [Citations.]" (*In re Diamond H., supra*, 82 Cal.App.4th at p. 1136.)

Whether the conditions in the home presented a risk of harm to the children is a factual issue. The record supports the juvenile court's order. When the children were initially detained, the house was unclean and unsanitary and the children unkempt. We need not repeat the description. The parents had made progress in cleaning the house up by the time of the dispositional hearing. They had removed large quantities of trash, fixed plumbing, and had pest control services treat the cockroach infestation. There was food in the refrigerator, and sheets were on the beds. But a nurse who visited the home reported it was still very dirty and it would take very little for the conditions to quickly return to those found when the children were detained. The caseworker believed that until the root of the problem was discovered, returning the children would result in a recurrence of the conditions. Contrary to the parents' claim, these concerns were far more than mere speculation—the parents' history bears them out. Each time authorities have intervened in this home, conditions improved only to deteriorate once there was no oversight.

The parents argue the children should not have been removed because there were less drastic measures which could have been taken. Specifically, they contend the court should have ordered CRISP. We disagree. CRISP is not a court-ordered alternative, rather it is a contract between SSA and the parents in lieu of filing a dependency petition. (§ 301, subd. (a).) Furthermore, this family has received similar services in the past, to no avail.

III

Lisa challenges the adequacy of the reunification plan approved by the juvenile court. Although county counsel has not responded to her argument, we reject her complaint.

Lisa argues the service plan is too generic and not specifically tailored to her family's needs. She claims the service plan needs a specific "cockroach component" which should include that SSA be ordered to pay for cockroach extermination and an industrial house-cleaning (including furniture, carpet, and drapery cleaning) so the house will be suitable for her children. Furthermore, she argues SSA should provide her with specific instructions on how to keep house, e.g., how to do laundry, vacuum, etc. She also contends the plan must be tailored to address the chaos of a household with seven children, one of whom is autistic. And finally, if the caseworker was concerned that the older girls were being "parentified" by being expected to bear the burden of housekeeping and assume a parental role, the counseling requirement did not address this problem. The family therapist should be ordered to address this specific issue and the problem with the parents' attitude about the need for housecleaning.

Lisa is correct that the reunification service plan must be designed to eliminate the conditions which led to the jurisdictional finding. (§ 362, subd. (c).) The service plan adequately addresses the specific concerns. It requires the parents to complete a parenting class. They must participate in counseling to address: the circumstances which lead to the children's removal; the possible obsessive compulsive or attention deficit disorders; and the family roles and age-appropriate responsibilities. They must provide SSA with proof of legal source of income sufficient to meet the family's needs, demonstrate adequate understanding of, and obtain appropriate services for, Justin's autism. Most importantly, the parents must "maintain stable, *suitable* housing," which necessarily means a home which is not unsanitary and unhealthful. There is no evidence in the record supporting Lisa's claim that as a matter of law the county should bear the expense of cleaning the house.

IV

Both parents complain that visitation is inadequate. Unfortunately, county counsel again does not address the argument. Nonetheless, we find no abuse of discretion.

"Visitation shall be as frequent as possible, consistent with the well-being of the child." (§ 362.1, subd. (a)(1)(A).) Here, the juvenile court approved the SSA's recommendation that visitation be monitored. The parents complain that weekly monitored visitation is inadequate and urge us to direct the juvenile court to order more frequent, unmonitored visits. Preliminarily, we see no indication that the frequency of visitation was limited. Even if it were, the parents have not shown it was inadequate. Furthermore, the juvenile court found there was "ample evidence [the] parents are making inappropriate comments to the minors" during visits and telephone calls. The parents do not dispute this finding. Accordingly, the juvenile court ordered that visits and telephone calls be monitored. Its order was appropriate.

V

Finally, Jason, Sr., contends the juvenile court erred when it ordered him to undergo an Evidence Code section 730 evaluation. Such an examination, he urges may only be ordered upon a showing of "good cause," because it is extremely intrusive. He argues good cause did not exist here as there was no evidence he suffers from any mental disorder.

The "good cause" standard to which Jason, Sr., applies to an application for an order for a mental examination in an ordinary civil action under Code of Civil Procedure section 2032. (See Code Civ. Proc., § 2032, subd. (d) ["the court shall grant a motion for a physical or mental examination only for good cause shown"]; *Board of Trustees v. Superior Court* (1969) 274 Cal.App.2d 377, 380.) Under Evidence Code section 730, the juvenile court may appoint one or more experts to investigate and to testify as an expert as to any pertinent fact or matter. (*In re Marriage of Kim* (1989) 208 Cal.App.3d 364, 372.) The juvenile court's appointment of a psychiatric evaluator pursuant to Evidence Code section 730 is discretionary. (*In re Marriage of Kim*, *supra*, 208 Cal.App.3d at p. 372.)

The juvenile court did not abuse its discretion. There is a 10-year history of these parents permitting their home to be unhealthy and unsanitary. Both parents indicated they were quite comfortable with the condition of their house and felt they bore little responsibility for the problems. The juvenile court was justified in its concern that there was more than sloppy housekeeping at work here and that until the underlying cause of the problem was identified, a long-range solution would not be found. Under the circumstances ordering an Evidence Code section 730 evaluation of *both* parents was not unreasonable. In any event, in his reply brief, Jason, Sr., represents that the psychological evaluation has been performed, making his argument moot.

The orders are affirmed.

We concur: RYLAARSDAM, ACTING P.J. and BEDSWORTH, J.

3. Why did the court in *Aislinn L.* affirm the lower court's finding of dependency? What facts do you think the court found dispositive? How did the court distinguish this case from *Paul E.*? Do you think the children wanted to be removed from their parents' custody?

4. Do you think the social workers involved with the case provided the family with sufficient assistance? Today, social workers try to keep children in the home by helping the mother clean the house. Donna L. Franklin, Ensuring Inequality: The Structural Transformation of the African-American Family (1997) (discussing new social-work practice paradigm where the social worker helps the mother clean the home rather than removing children from the dirty home). Do you think that the parents in *Aislinn L.* received this sort of aid?

There is evidence that the mother suffered from some psychological problems. Mental illness is a not uncommon problem among mothers who find themselves in the child welfare system.

> Perhaps the primary reason mothers of children under age eighteen do not seek needed mental health services is the fear of losing custody of their children. Their fears are justified. Mothers with serious mental illness are many times more likely to lose custody of their children than healthy mothers. Children of mothers with serious mental illness are at a heightened risk of depressed life outcomes, but data showing that these children are at greater risk of maltreatment is elusive.
>
> Avoiding treatment in order to avoid child welfare attention may put a child at risk, but that "hard choice" is not always clearly a bad one. Mothers with mental illness know treatment non-compliance may result in custody loss, but they also know compliance limits their actual parenting ability. For example, lithium, the "treatment of choice for manic-depressive

illness" can have side effects such as reduced memory, drowsiness or nausea, all of which make caring for children more difficult, but medication non-compliance can trigger active illness that might also leave children at risk. A woman may also stop taking medications during pregnancy to protect the child's health to the detriment of her own.

"Being mentally ill" is not all that defines a woman who happens to "be mentally ill," but it does inform and determine other aspects of her life. Most live in poverty, a risk factor closely related to child maltreatment. "Inadequate housing"—a ubiquitous problem of poverty—"appears to be a particularly potent risk factor" for abuse or neglect. Mentally ill mothers also experience family disruptions, single-parent status, social isolation and related stressors that can put children at risk.

In combination, such stressors can have snowballing effects on parenting.... [T]he mother may be unable to clean the house, remember a child's appointments and school activities, or even get out of bed in the morning. Serious child safety concerns cannot be far behind.

Jennifer E. Spreng, *The Private World of Juvenile Court: Mothers, Mental Illness and the Relentless Machinery of the State*, 17 Duke J. Gender L. & Pol'y 189, 192–194 (2010). See also Alisa Busch & Allison Redlich, *Patients' Perception of Possible Child Custody or Visitation Loss for Nonadherence to Psychiatric Treatment*, 58 Psychiatric Services 999, 999 (2007); Lenore M. McWey et al., *Mental Health Issues and the Foster Care System: An Examination of the Impact of the Adoption and Safe Families Act*, 32 J. Marital & Fam. Therapy 195, 201 (depression was most pervasive diagnosis in cohort of termination-of-rights cases in Virginia). Nevertheless, mentally ill mothers are not more likely to abuse or neglect their children, although they are more likely to lose custody. Jung Min Park et al., *Involvement in the Child Welfare System among Mothers with Serious Mental Illness*, 57 Psychiatric Servs. 493, 493–494 (2006). Should the courts take a different approach when the parent is mentally ill?

Just how punitive should the state be when pursuing a parent with a dirty home? Jimmy Alford had a compromised immune system stemming from a chromosomal anomaly and functioned at the level of a three-year-old. Although his mother conscientiously provided Jimmy with personal and medical care, her home was filthy. There were pet droppings, Jimmy slept on a dirty mattress on the floor, and she had been warned many times by the state child-services agency that the living conditions were hazardous. Jimmy suddenly died at age fourteen of septicemia, a blood-borne infection. The state then charged his mother with child neglect causing great bodily harm, a second-degree felony. What result? See *Wesson v. State*, 899 So.2d 382 (Fla. App. 2005).

vii. Failure to thrive

A.B. V. DEPARTMENT OF PUBLIC WELFARE
Commonwealth Court of Pennsylvania
869 A.2d 1129 (2005)

OPINION BY President Judge COLINS.

A.B. (Appellant) petitions for review of an adjudication of the Department of Public Welfare (DPW) denying her request to expunge a report of indicated child abuse filed by a caseworker for Fayette County Children and Youth Services (CYS) pursuant to the Child Protective Services Law (Law).[1]

A.B. is the natural mother of J.B., a male child born prematurely on September 10, 2001, and weighing 4 pounds, 8 and ½ ounces at birth. After his birth, J.B. remained hospitalized for several weeks before being discharged into A.B.'s care. Although A.B. initially attempted to breast feed J.B., she was unsuccessful in doing so, and bottle fed J.B. while the latter was in her care from September 2001 through December 10, 2001. The record indicates that J.B. was a difficult infant to feed and that A.B. failed to properly feed J.B. during the aforementioned time period, resulting in J.B.'s failure to appropriately gain weight. A.B. admitted that J.B. was improperly fed while in her care prior to December 10, 2001.

On December 10, 2001, J.B. was admitted to the hospital following an office visit to his pediatrician, Bchara Janadari, M.D. On five separate visits prior to and including December 10, 2001, Dr. Janadari examined J.B., weighed him, and recorded the changes in J.B.'s weight as follows:

Date	Weight	Change +/-	
October 12, 2001	5 lbs., 6 oz.		N/A
November 16, 2001	5 lbs., 6 oz.		none
November 19, 2001	5 lbs., 12 oz.	+	+6 oz.
November 27, 2001	5 lbs., 11 oz.	-	-1 oz.
December 10, 2001	5 lbs., 4 oz.	-	-7 oz.

According to the record, there was no medical explanation for J.B.'s failure to gain weight while in A.B.'s care, and after December 12, 2001, CYS assumed custody of J.B. After being removed from A.B.'s care, J.B. was hospitalized and diagnosed with mild anemia, but he gained weight. On December 19, 2001, J.B. weighed 6 lbs., 10 ounces. Thereafter, while in foster care, J.B. gained weight appropriately and did not lose weight from one medical appointment to the next. On January 24, 2002, CYS filed an indicated report of child abuse against A.B. with the ChildLine Registry. Subsequently, DPW denied A.B.'s request to expunge her name from the ChildLine Registry, from which decision A.B. appealed on February 19, 2002.

A hearing was conducted on January 16, 2003, during which A.B.'s counsel argued that DPW failed to offer sufficient evidence to support the conclusion that A.B. failed to properly feed the subject child, therefore endangering said child's life or impairing the child's functioning.

Further, A.B.'s counsel contended that even if his client's errors of commission or omission rose to a failure to provide J.B. with the "essentials of life," such behavior was the result of a major depressive disorder from which A.B. was suffering during this time period.

After reviewing the hearing testimony, briefs, and exhibits submitted by the respective parties, the administrative law judge (ALJ) concluded that DPW had established that A.B.'s

1. 23 Pa.C.S. §§ 6301–6385. Section 6341(a)(2) of the Law states, in pertinent part:

Any person named as a perpetrator…in an indicated report of child abuse may, within 45 days of being notified of the status of the report, request the secretary to amend or expunge an indicated report on the grounds that it is inaccurate or it is being maintained in a manner inconsistent with this chapter. 23 Pa.C.S. § 6341(a)(2).

name should properly be kept in the ChildLine Registry as a perpetrator of child abuse (serious physical neglect) and recommended that A.B.'s appeal be denied. On June 9, 2004, the Bureau of Hearings and Appeals adopted the ALJ's recommendation in its entirety. This appeal followed.

On appeal, A.B. argues that the ALJ erred in concluding that A.B.'s mental state was "irrelevant" during the time period in which she failed to provide life essentials to J.B. It is A.B.'s contention that the plain language of 23 Pa.C.S. § 6303(b)(1)(iv) regarding serious physical neglect requires a statutory construction encompassing knowledge, intent, or capacity on the part of the perpetrator, all of which A.B. did not and could not have had because she was suffering from major depression. Therefore, A.B. avers that she cannot be held accountable for serious physical neglect within the meaning of Section 6303(b)(1)(iv). Additionally, A.B. maintains that the ALJ erred in concluding that her failure to adequately feed J.B. endangered J.B.'s life and development because DPW failed to proffer any medical or other evidence in support of this conclusion.

Upon review of the record, this Court notes that even if A.B. suffered from post-partum depression from the time of J.B.'s birth on September 10, 2001 to December 10, 2001, such post-partum depression in and of itself is insufficient to establish serious physical neglect based upon a child's alleged "failure to thrive" so as to constitute child abuse within the meaning of the Law and DPW regulations. In *Commonwealth v. Tharp*, 574 Pa. 202 n. 12, 830 A.2d 519, 526 n. 12 (2003), *cert. denied*, 541 U.S. 1045, 124 S.Ct. 2161, 158 L.Ed.2d 736 (2004), this Court stated:

> Failure to thrive is a serious medical condition in which a child's height, weight, and motor development fall significantly short of the average growth rates of normal children. About 10 percent of failure to thrive cases have an organic cause; the rest result from disturbed parent-child relationships manifested in severe physical and emotional neglect of the child. In the Interest of Patricia S., 326 Pa.Super. 434, 474 A.2d 318, 319 (1984) (citing Interdisciplinary Glossary on Child Abuse and Neglect, LEGAL, MEDICAL, SOCIAL WORK TERMS, DHEW Pub. No. (OHDS) 78-30137, reprinted in CHILD ABUSE AND NEGLECT LITIGATION, DHHS Pub. No. (OHDS) 80-30268 (March 1981)).

Applying the foregoing to the present matter, the weight records kept by Dr. Janadari for J.B.'s five visits indicate that between the first and fifth visit, J.B.'s actual weight loss was only 2 ounces. This cannot be deemed a significant loss, considering that J.B. was born prematurely, weighed only 4 pounds, 8 and ½ ounces at birth, and remained hospitalized for several weeks before being released into A.B.'s custody. During the hearing, Dr. Janadari conceded that many premature babies are "slow feeders" and may be more difficult to feed than non premature babies. He also repeatedly indicated that, except for mild anemia, there were no other medical problems exhibited by J.B. other than being underweight.

Because J.B. was not responding to A.B.'s feeding methods in terms of gaining weight, Dr. Janadari cautiously placed J.B. in the hospital for several days, where J.B. was fed the same formula in approximately the same amount as A.B. stated she had fed the child. Subsequently, A.B. received outside agency assistance in learning how to properly feed J.B. During the follow-up period after being released from the hospital, J.B., according to the record, seems to be eating and maintaining his weight without significant problems. In this regard, the following testimony elicited from A.B. during the January 16, 2003 hearing is relevant:

[Direct Examination of A.B.]

> Q. During that period of time [September to December 10, 2001], did you have a bonding problem with J., that you can remember?
> A. I felt that...he [J.B.] didn't like me. What was wrong with me? That's what I felt...he was more difficult to feed because he cried a lot. My other son did not...I felt like okay....Don't you like me? I'm trying to do everything for you.
> Q....[Y]ou kept your doctor's appointments with Dr. Janadari appropriately?
> A. Yes....
> Q. Okay. That was the appointment on December 10th?
> A. Right.
> Q. When he [Dr. Janadari] had to place the baby in the hospital?
> A. Right....He asked me what was going on with him [J.B.]. And I said at that time I tried to do everything by myself. That's what I was doing and that's what I tried to explain to him...That's what I told him, I said, the baby's crying....At the time, I had no help.
> Q. Did you realize that J. wasn't getting enough to eat?
> A. That's when I realized....He said we got to do something. You need some help....So then they took him [J.B.] to the hospital.

(Hearing Notes of Testimony, 1/16/03/ pp. 97–100.)

In consideration of the foregoing, we conclude that during the defined time period from September 2001 through December 10, 2001, although J.B. was deemed underweight by Dr. Janadari, his two ounce weight loss without other medical problems was not sufficiently significant to be characterized as "failing to thrive" while in A.B.'s custody as a result of being deprived of the "essentials of life." Further, in the matter *sub judice*, considering J.B.'s premature birth, small birth weight, and problematic eating pattern from the outset, we find that DPW failed to establish that A.B.'s feeding of J.B., even given the difficulties she indicated when testifying at the hearing such as J.B.'s spitting up while being fed, rose to the level of serious physical neglect based upon a "failure to thrive," that would warrant her being classified as a perpetrator of child abuse within the meaning of the Law.

Accordingly, we reverse DPW's adjudication.

NOTES AND QUESTIONS

1. What is the failure to thrive? The American Academy of Pediatrics defines failure to thrive as the cessation of appropriate weight gain, although there may be normal height gain. Robert W. Block & Nancy F. Krebs, Am. Acad. of Pediatrics, Comm. on Child Abuse & Neglect, *Failure to Thrive as a Manifestation of Child Neglect*, 116 PEDIATRICS 1234, 1234 (2005). "Poverty is the single greatest risk factor for failure to thrive." *Id.* Although the fundamental cause of failure to thrive is malnutrition, the AAP recognizes that not all cases of nutritional deficiency constitute child neglect. Disease (including cerebral palsy, inborn metabolic disorders, and cystic

fibrosis), breastfeeding difficulties, improper feeding techniques, and lead poisoning may cause failure to thrive. *Id.* Nevertheless, the AAP identifies certain risk factors associated with failure to thrive caused by child neglect. They include maladaptive social behaviors of the parent, the separation of the infant from his or her caregivers because of a prolonged hospitalization resulting from premature birth or low birth weight, substance abuse, previous child abuse, family violence, single parenthood, and, in middle- and upper-class families, a focus on career or other activities away from the home that may indicate emotional immaturity and failure to adhere to medical regimens. *Id.* at 1234–1235. Diagnosis of child neglect requires the exclusion of other organic explanations.

2. Do you think the state established that A.B.'s failure to thrive was caused by child neglect?

viii. Emotional neglect

IN RE RONNIE XX
New York Supreme Court Appellate Division
708 N.Y.S.2d 521 (2000)

LAHTINEN, J.

Appeal from an order of the Family Court of Chemung County (Castellino, J.), entered December 7, 1998, which, *inter alia*, partially granted petitioner's application, in a proceeding pursuant to Family Court Act article 10, and adjudicated one of respondent's three children to be neglected.

On April 12, 1998, respondent's then 14-year-old daughter, Charlotte "XX," allegedly attempted suicide. Respondent was not at home at the time of Charlotte's alleged suicide attempt but upon her return home that evening she was informed of the incident by her son. After attempting to discuss this matter with Charlotte, respondent telephoned the crisis intervention team who came to respondent's home and transported Charlotte to a nearby hospital in the City of Elmira, Chemung County. Respondent testified that a member of the crisis intervention team suggested that she not accompany Charlotte to the hospital.

Shortly after her admission to the hospital it was determined that Charlotte was in need of an immediate psychological evaluation at an appropriate facility. Respondent was called at home and informed that Charlotte needed to be evaluated at a facility in Steuben County, an hour from respondent's home, or at a facility in Erie County, three hours away. Respondent refused to authorize the evaluation at the recommended facilities, claiming that her own medical conditions prevented her from traveling to either location and that such an evaluation was unnecessary since Charlotte had been admitted to the facility in Steuben County on February 20, 1998 for evaluation and discharged the next day because it was determined that she did not need inpatient treatment.

As a result of respondent's apparent unwillingness to authorize the recommended evaluation, a report was filed with the State Central Registry charging respondent with emotional neglect and failing to provide Charlotte with appropriate medical care. A caseworker in petitioner's Child Protective Services Unit received the "hot-line" report and initiated an investigation. The caseworker talked with respondent on April 12, 1998 in an attempt to obtain her authorization for the recommended evaluation. Respondent refused to authorize the evaluation but did sign a consent for temporary placement of Charlotte with petitioner. Charlotte was transported the next day to the facility in Steuben County for the recommended evaluation.

On April 14, 1998, a caseworker informed respondent that Charlotte was to be discharged from the facility because it was determined she did not need to be an inpatient. Respondent expressed no surprise at the news of Charlotte's pending discharge and advised the caseworker that she could not and would not travel to Steuben County to pick up Charlotte. Petitioner then decided to place Charlotte in foster care and file a neglect petition.

On April 24, 1998, respondent filed a petition for custody of Charlotte alleging that she was told to sign over temporary custody of Charlotte so she could receive help in a Steuben County facility. On May 5, 1998, Family Court (O'Shea, J.) found no imminent risk to Charlotte and returned her to respondent's custody on certain conditions to be supervised by petitioner. On the same day, petitioner filed an amended neglect petition, with affidavits from the two caseworkers and a letter signed by two members of the staff at the Steuben County facility, charging respondent and her live-in companion[2] with neglect of her three children.

Following a fact-finding hearing on August 18, 1998, Family Court (Castellino, J.) dismissed the petition with regard to the allegations of derivative neglect (see, Family Ct. Act § 1046[a][i]) of respondent's other two children but found Charlotte to be a neglected child. Family Court concluded in a written decision dated September 24, 1998 that petitioner proved by a preponderance of the evidence that:

> * * * when Charlotte made an apparent suicide attempt, and the treating hospital recommended to the respondent that Charlotte receive further psychiatric evaluation, the respondent's refusal to authorize such treatment, without first having made an affirmative effort to speak with Charlotte's doctor or investigate Charlotte's medical status, constituted an unreasonable risk to Charlotte's health and placed Charlotte's mental or emotional condition in danger of impairment.

Following a dispositional hearing, Charlotte was continued in the custody of respondent under petitioner's supervision for a period of 12 months on certain terms and conditions. Respondent now appeals.[3]

Family Court Act § 1012 defines a "neglected child," in relevant part, as follows:

> (f) "Neglected child" means a child less than eighteen years of age
> (i) whose physical, mental or emotional condition has been impaired or is in imminent danger of becoming impaired as a result of the failure of his parent or other person legally responsible for his care to exercise a minimum degree of care.

The statute requires a showing, by a preponderance of the evidence, of parental misconduct and harm or potential harm to the child as a result of that misconduct (*see*, *Matter of*

2. The portion of the amended petition charging respondent's companion with neglect was deemed dismissed by a Family Court order dated July 15, 1998.

3. Although the order appealed from has expired, an adjudication of neglect may affect a parent's status in future proceedings and an appeal from such a finding is not moot (*see*, *Matter of Jeffrey D. [Darrie D.]*, 233 A.D.2d 668, 669, 650 N.Y.S.2d 340).

Jessica YY. [Pamela YY.], 258 A.D.2d 743, 744, 685 N.Y.S.2d 489; *Matter of Jennifer N. [Janine O.]*, 173 A.D.2d 971, 972, 569 N.Y.S.2d 480; *Matter of William EE. [Donald EE.]*, 157 A.D.2d 974, 976, 550 N.Y.S.2d 455). Since we conclude that petitioner has failed to sustain its burden of proof with regard to either of the required showings, we reverse.

In the first instance, petitioner alleged and Family Court found that respondent's failure to authorize the recommended evaluation for Charlotte constituted parental misconduct. The record indicates that respondent was contacted by the hospital around noon on April 12, 1998 and asked to authorize an evaluation of Charlotte at an appropriate psychiatric center. Although respondent "never authorized the evaluation," she did transfer temporary custody of Charlotte to petitioner on April 12, 1998 so that they could authorize the treatment. It is not alleged and does not appear from the record that Charlotte's evaluation was delayed by any action or failure to act on the part of respondent. Indeed, respondent's April 24, 1998 petition for custody alleged that her consent to temporary placement of Charlotte on April 12, 1998 was authorization for the requested evaluation which was performed at the facility in Steuben County on April 13, 1998. Since we find that respondent did authorize treatment, no parental misconduct occurred.

Second, petitioner failed to produce sufficient evidence concerning Charlotte's mental or emotional condition before, on and after April 12, 1998 to establish that an impairment occurred or that there was an imminent danger of an impairment of Charlotte's emotional or mental health resulting from respondent's action or inaction on April 12, 1998. Neither caseworker interviewed Charlotte's brother or anyone else, other than Charlotte, who was present at the time of the alleged attempted suicide. The only witnesses produced by petitioner at the fact-finding hearing were the two caseworkers who testified at length about respondent's uncooperative behavior in attempting to obtain her authorization for Charlotte's April 12, 1998 psychological evaluation, but knew little about a suicide attempt by Charlotte two months earlier, a resulting one-day referral to the Steuben County facility for evaluation and previous efforts by respondent to obtain counseling services for herself and Charlotte. No medical testimony was offered, no medical records from any health care facility were introduced and Charlotte did not testify. On this record, it is clear that petitioner has failed to demonstrate how respondent's apparent refusal to authorize an immediate psychological evaluation of Charlotte on April 12, 1998 impaired or posed an imminent danger of impairing her mental or emotional condition (*see*, *Matter of Jennifer N. [Janine O.]*, *supra*, at 972–973, 569 N.Y.S.2d 480; *Matter of William EE. [Donald EE.]*, *supra*, at 976, 550 N.Y.S.2d 455).

Lastly, our decision should not be read as an approval of respondent's inappropriate response in dealing with her daughter Charlotte's obvious needs. Rather, this case is decided solely on petitioner's failure to sustain its burden of proof in this neglect proceeding....

NOTES AND QUESTIONS

1. Do you think Charlotte is emotionally neglected? How much responsibility should we assign to parents whose children commit or attempt to commit suicide? When twelve-year-old Daniel Scruggs committed suicide, his mother, Judith, was charged criminally with three counts of risk of injury to a minor and one count of cruelty to persons. Daniel had been bullied repeatedly at school, his clothes were dirty and mismatched, he would go for days without showering, and he was repeatedly

absent from school. When he did attend, he would soil himself in order to be sent home. His mother denied knowledge of the bullying, even though she was a teacher's aide at Daniel's school. She found his body twelve hours after Daniel killed himself while she was at home between jobs. The child-protective-services agency had closed its case on Daniel six days before he committed suicide. Daniel never received any services prior to his death. Vanessa Gardianos, Note, *Adolescent Suicide: A Call for Parental Liability*, 24 St. John's J. Leg. Commentary 201, 206=209 (2009).

2. To what extent should courts rely on the child-welfare system when parents are involved in a custody dispute? In *B.K. v. Dep't Children & Fam. Servs.*, 950 N.E.2d 446 (Mass. App. 2011), the parents were engaged in a contentious custody battle, and the mother alleged that the father had sexually abused his younger daughter. Despite court orders requiring the father to stay away from the children's school and to have no contact with the children, the father dropped a letter off for his younger daughter at school, contacted the children via e-mail, and sent them presents through parents of classmates. The appellate court characterized this behavior as emotionally neglectful, because noncompliance with an order issued in the daughter's best interests demonstrated a failure "to provide the 'minimally adequate' emotional stability and growth necessary for the daughter's well-being."

> The timing and context of the letter also support the finding of emotional neglect. As noted above, the parties were engaged in a contentious custody dispute. The younger daughter was trying to maintain a position of neutrality, and her therapist believed that it was important that she be kept "out of the mill" of the animosity between the parents. The probate judge's order was designed to achieve that end. The hearing officer found that the timing and content of the letter showed that the father was attempting to curry favor with the daughter in order to gain an advantage in the probate proceedings, regardless of the emotional detriment to her. In this context, the hearing officer's finding of neglect by the father when he put his own emotional needs ahead of his daughter's was well-supported, particularly where the father demonstrated a repeated pattern of violating the Probate and Family Court order....
>
> From the timing and contents of the letter, as well as the manner of its delivery, the hearing officer could reasonably infer that the father sought to gain an advantage in the custody proceedings through the goodwill of his daughter, regardless of the consequences of his behavior on her emotional well-being.

Id. at 450. See also *In re Jessica G.*, 573 N.Y.S.2d 251 (N.Y. Fam. Ct. 1991) (mother's repeated false claims of sexual abuse of her daughter resulting in several physical exams, including gynecological exams, and coaching daughter to say she had been touched inappropriately constituted substantial risk of mental and emotional impairment). Would you characterize these behaviors as emotionally neglectful?

ix. Failure to protect

NICHOLSON V. SCOPETTA
Court of Appeals of New York
820 N.E.2d 840 (2004)

KAYE, Chief Judge.

In this federal class action, the United States Court of Appeals for the Second Circuit has certified three questions centered on New York's statutory scheme for child protective proceedings. The action is brought on behalf of mothers and their children who were separated because the mother had suffered domestic violence, to which the children were exposed, and the children were for that reason deemed neglected by her.

In April 2000, Sharwline Nicholson, on behalf of herself and her two children, brought an action pursuant to 42 USC § 1983 against the New York City Administration for Children's Services (ACS). The action was later consolidated with similar complaints by Sharlene Tillet and Ekaete Udoh—the three named plaintiff mothers. Plaintiffs alleged that ACS, as a matter of policy, removed children from mothers who were victims of domestic violence because, as victims, they "engaged in domestic violence" and that defendants removed and detained children without probable cause and without due process of law. That policy, and its implementation—according to plaintiff mothers—constituted, among other wrongs, an unlawful interference with their liberty interest in the care and custody of their children in violation of the United States Constitution.

In August 2001, the United States District Court for the Eastern District of New York certified two subclasses: battered custodial parents (Subclass A) and their children (Subclass B) (*Nicholson v. Williams*, 205 F.R.D. 92, 95, 100 [E.D.N.Y.2001]). For each plaintiff, at least one ground for removal was that the custodial mother had been assaulted by an intimate partner and failed to protect the child or children from exposure to that domestic violence.

In January 2002, the District Court granted a preliminary injunction, concluding that the City "may not penalize a mother, not otherwise unfit, who is battered by her partner, by separating her from her children; nor may children be separated from the mother, in effect visiting upon them the sins of their mother's batterer" (*In re Nicholson*, 181 F.Supp.2d 182, 188 [E.D.N.Y. 2002]; *see also Nicholson v. Williams*, 203 F Supp 2d 153 [E.D.N.Y. 2002] [108-page elaboration of grounds for injunction]).

The court found that ACS unnecessarily, routinely charged mothers with neglect and removed their children where the mothers—who had engaged in no violence themselves—had been the victims of domestic violence; that ACS did so without ensuring that the mother had access to the services she needed, without a court order, and without returning these children promptly after being ordered to do so by the court; that ACS caseworkers and case managers lacked adequate training about domestic violence, and their practice was to separate mother and child when less harmful alternatives were available; that the agency's written policies offered contradictory guidance or no guidance at all on these issues; and that none of the reform plans submitted by ACS could reasonably have been expected to resolve the problems within the next year (203 F.Supp.2d at 228–229).

The District Court concluded that ACS's practices and policies violated both the substantive due process rights of mothers and children not to be separated by the government unless the parent is unfit to care for the child, and their procedural due process rights (181 F.Supp.2d at 185). The injunction, in relevant part, "prohibit[ed] ACS from carrying out *ex parte* removals 'solely because the mother is the victim of domestic violence,' or from filing an Article Ten petition seeking removal on that basis" (*Nicholson v. Scoppetta*, 344 F.3d 154, 164 [2d Cir. 2003] [internal citations omitted]).

On appeal, the Second Circuit held that the District Court had not abused its discretion in concluding that ACS's practice of effecting removals based on a parent's failure to prevent his or her child from witnessing domestic violence against the parent amounted to a policy or custom of ACS, that in some circumstances the removals may raise serious questions of federal constitutional law, and that the alleged constitutional violations, if any, were at least plausibly attributable to the City (344 F.3d at 165-167, 171-176).[4] The court hesitated, however, before reaching the constitutional questions, believing that resolution of uncertain issues of New York statutory law would avoid, or significantly modify, the substantial federal constitutional issues presented (*id.* at 176).

Given the strong preference for avoiding unnecessary constitutional adjudication, the importance of child protection to New York State and the integral part New York courts play in the removal process, the Second Circuit, by three certified questions, chose to put the open state statutory law issues to us for resolution. We accepted certification (1 N.Y.3d 538, 775 N.Y.S.2d 233, 807 N.E.2d 283 [2003]), and now proceed to answer those questions.[5]

Certified Question No. 1: Neglect

> "Does the definition of a 'neglected child' under N.Y. Family Ct. Act § 1012(f), (h) include instances in which the sole allegation of neglect is that the parent or other person legally responsible for the child's care allows the child to witness domestic abuse against the caretaker?" (344 F.3d at 176.)

We understand this question to ask whether a court reviewing a Family Court Act article 10 petition may find a respondent parent responsible for neglect based on evidence of two facts only: that the parent has been the victim of domestic violence, and that the child has been exposed to that violence. That question must be answered in the negative. Plainly, more is required for a showing of neglect under New York law than the fact that a child was exposed to domestic abuse against the caretaker. Answering the question in the affirmative, moreover, would read an unacceptable presumption into the statute, contrary to its plain language.

Family Court Act § 1012(f) is explicit in identifying the elements that must be shown to support a finding of neglect. As relevant here, it defines a "neglected child" to mean:

> "a child less than eighteen years of age
>
> "(i) whose physical, mental or emotional condition has been impaired or is in imminent danger of becoming impaired as a result of the failure of his parent or other person legally responsible for his care to exercise a minimum degree of care...
>
> "(B) in providing the child with proper supervision or guardianship, by unreasonably inflicting or allowing to be inflicted harm, or a substantial risk thereof, including the infliction of excessive corporal punishment; or by misusing a drug or drugs; or by misusing alcoholic beverages to the extent that he loses self-control of his actions; or by any other acts of a similarly serious nature requiring the aid of the court."

4. Chief Judge Walker dissented, concluding that the injunction should be vacated because the evidence did not support the District Court's findings underpinning the injunction. In his view, the District Court's central factual finding that ACS had a policy of regularly separating battered mothers and children unnecessarily was "simply unsustainable" (*id.* at 177).

5. We are not asked to, nor do we, apply our answers to the trial record, though recognizing that in the inordinately complex human dilemma presented by domestic violence involving children, the law may be easier to state than apply.

Thus, a party seeking to establish neglect must show, by a preponderance of the evidence (*see* Family Ct. Act § 1046[b] [i]), first, that a child's physical, mental or emotional condition has been impaired or is in imminent danger of becoming impaired and second, that the actual or threatened harm to the child is a consequence of the failure of the parent or caretaker to exercise a minimum degree of care in providing the child with proper supervision or guardianship. The drafters of article 10 were "deeply concerned" that an imprecise definition of child neglect might result in "unwarranted state intervention into private family life" (Besharov, Practice Commentaries, McKinney's Cons. Laws of N.Y., Book 29A, Family Ct. Act § 1012, at 320 [1999 ed]).

The first statutory element requires proof of actual (or imminent danger of) physical, emotional or mental impairment to the child (*see Matter of Nassau County Dept. of Social Servs. [Dante M.] v. Denise J.*, 87 N.Y.2d 73, 78–79, 637 N.Y.S.2d 666, 661 N.E.2d 138 [1995]). This prerequisite to a finding of neglect ensures that the Family Court, in deciding whether to authorize state intervention, will focus on serious harm or potential harm to the child, not just on what might be deemed undesirable parental behavior. "Imminent danger" reflects the Legislature's judgment that a finding of neglect may be appropriate even when a child has not actually been harmed; "imminent danger of impairment to a child is an independent and separate ground on which a neglect finding may be based" (*Dante M.*, 87 N.Y.2d at 79, 637 N.Y.S.2d 666, 661 N.E.2d 138). Imminent danger, however, must be near or impending, not merely possible.

In each case, additionally, there must be a link or causal connection between the basis for the neglect petition and the circumstances that allegedly produce the child's impairment or imminent danger of impairment. In *Dante M.*, for example, we held that the Family Court erred in concluding that a newborn's positive toxicology for a controlled substance alone was sufficient to support a finding of neglect because the report, in and of itself, did not prove that the child was impaired or in imminent danger of becoming impaired (87 N.Y.2d at 79, 637 N.Y.S.2d 666, 661 N.E.2d 138). We reasoned, "[r]elying solely on a positive toxicology result for a neglect determination fails to make the necessary causative connection to all the surrounding circumstances that may or may not produce impairment or imminent risk of impairment in the newborn child" (*id.*). The positive toxicology report, in conjunction with other evidence—such as the mother's history of inability to care for her children because of her drug use, testimony of relatives that she was high on cocaine during her pregnancy and the mother's failure to testify at the neglect hearing—supported a finding of neglect and established a link between the report and physical impairment.

The cases at bar concern, in particular, alleged threats to the child's emotional, or mental, health. The statute specifically defines "[i]mpairment of emotional health" and "impairment of mental or emotional condition" to include

> "a state of substantially diminished psychological or intellectual functioning in relation to, but not limited to, such factors as failure to thrive, control of aggressive or self-destructive impulses, ability to think and reason, or acting out or misbehavior, including incorrigibility, ungovernability or habitual truancy" (Family Ct. Act § 1012 [h]).

Under New York law, "such impairment must be clearly attributable to the unwillingness or inability of the respondent to exercise a minimum degree of care toward the child" (*id.*). Here, the Legislature recognized that the source of emotional or mental impairment—unlike physical injury—may be murky, and that it is unjust to fault a parent too readily. The Legislature therefore specified that such impairment be "clearly attributable" to the parent's failure to exercise the requisite degree of care.

Assuming that actual or imminent danger to the child has been shown, "neglect" also requires proof of the parent's failure to exercise a minimum degree of care. As the Second Circuit observed, "a fundamental interpretive question is what conduct satisfies the broad, tort-like phrase, 'a *minimum* degree of care.' The Court of Appeals has not yet addressed that question, which would be critical to defining appropriate parental behavior" (344 F.3d at 169).

"[M]inimum degree of care" is a "baseline of proper care for children that all parents, regardless of lifestyle or social or economic position, must meet" (Besharov at 326). Notably, the statutory test is "minimum degree of care"—not maximum, not best, not ideal—and the failure must be actual, not threatened (*see e.g.* Matter of Hofbauer, 47 N.Y.2d 648, 656, 419 N.Y.S.2d 936, 393 N.E.2d 1009 [1979] [recognizing, in the context of medical neglect, the court's role is not as surrogate parent and the inquiry is not posed in absolute terms of whether the parent has made the "right" or "wrong" decision]).

Courts must evaluate parental behavior objectively: would a reasonable and prudent parent have so acted, or failed to act, under the circumstances then and there existing (*see Matter of Jessica YY.*, 258 A.D.2d 743, 744, 685 N.Y.S.2d 489 [3d Dept. 1999]). The standard takes into account the special vulnerabilities of the child, even where general physical health is not implicated (*see Matter of Sayeh R.*, 91 N.Y.2d 306, 315, 317, 670 N.Y.S.2d 377, 693 N.E.2d 724 [1997] [mother's decision to demand immediate return of her traumatized children without regard to their need for counseling and related services "could well be found to represent precisely the kind of failure 'to exercise a minimum degree of care' that our neglect statute contemplates"]). Thus, when the inquiry is whether a mother—and domestic violence victim—failed to exercise a minimum degree of care, the focus must be on whether she has met the standard of the reasonable and prudent person in similar circumstances.

As the Subclass A members point out, for a battered mother—and ultimately for a court—what course of action constitutes a parent's exercise of a "minimum degree of care" may include such considerations as: risks attendant to leaving, if the batterer has threatened to kill her if she does; risks attendant to staying and suffering continued abuse; risks attendant to seeking assistance through government channels, potentially increasing the danger to herself and her children; risks attendant to criminal prosecution against the abuser; and risks attendant to relocation.[6] Whether a particular mother in these circumstances has actually failed to exercise a minimum degree of care is necessarily dependent on facts such as the severity and frequency of the violence, and the resources and options available to her (*see Matter of Melissa U.*, 148 A.D.2d 862, 538 N.Y.S.2d 958 [3d Dept. 1989]; *Matter of James MM. v. June OO.*, 294 A.D.2d 630, 740 N.Y.S.2d 730 [3d Dept. 2002]).

6. The Legislature has recognized this "quandary" that a victim of domestic violence encounters (Senate Mem. in Support, 2002 McKinney's Session Laws of N.Y., at 1861). To avoid punitive responses from child protective services agencies, the Legislature attempted to increase awareness of child protective agencies of the dynamics of domestic violence and its impact on child protection by amending the Social Services Law to mandate comprehensive domestic violence training for child protective services workers (*id.*).

Only when a petitioner demonstrates, by a preponderance of evidence, that both elements of section 1012(f) are satisfied may a child be deemed neglected under the statute. When "the sole allegation" is that the mother has been abused and the child has witnessed the abuse, such a showing has not been made. This does not mean, however, that a child can never be "neglected" when living in a household plagued by domestic violence. Conceivably, neglect might be found where a record establishes that, for example, the mother acknowledged that the children knew of repeated domestic violence by her paramour and had reason to be afraid of him, yet nonetheless allowed him several times to return to her home, and lacked awareness of any impact of the violence on the children, as in *Matter of James MM.*, 294 A.D.2d at 632, 740 N.Y.S.2d 730; or where the children were exposed to regular and continuous extremely violent conduct between their parents, several times requiring official intervention, and where caseworkers testified to the fear and distress the children were experiencing as a result of their long exposure to the violence (*Matter of Theresa CC.*, 178 A.D.2d 687, 576 N.Y.S.2d 937 [3d Dept. 1991]).

In such circumstances, the battered mother is charged with neglect not because she is a victim of domestic violence or because her children witnessed the abuse, but rather because a preponderance of the evidence establishes that the children were actually or imminently harmed by reason of her failure to exercise even minimal care in providing them with proper oversight.

Certified Question No. 2: Removals

Next, we are called upon to focus on removals by ACS, in answering the question:

> "Can the injury or possible injury, if any, that results to a child who has witnessed domestic abuse against a parent or other caretaker constitute 'danger' or 'risk' to the child's 'life or health,' as those terms are defined in the N.Y. Family Ct. Act §§ 1022, 1024, 1026–1028?" (344 F.3d at 176–177.)

The cited Family Court Act sections relate to the removal of a child from home. Thus, in essence, we are asked to decide whether emotional injury from witnessing domestic violence can rise to a level that establishes an "imminent danger" or "risk" to a child's life or health, so that removal is appropriate either in an emergency or by court order.

While we do not reach the constitutional questions, it is helpful in framing the statutory issues to note the Second Circuit's outline of the federal constitutional questions relating to removals. Their questions emerge in large measure from the District Court's findings of an "agency-wide practice of removing children from their mother without evidence of a mother's neglect and without seeking prior judicial approval" (203 F.Supp.2d at 215), and Family Court review of removals that "often fails to provide mothers and children with an effective avenue for timely relief from ACS mistakes" (*id.* at 221).

Specifically, as to ex parte removals, the Circuit Court identified procedural due process and Fourth Amendment questions focused on whether danger to a child could encompass emotional trauma from witnessing domestic violence against a parent, warranting emergency removal. Discussing the procedural due process question, the court remarked that:

> "there is a strong possibility that if New York law does not authorize *ex parte* removals, our opinion in *Tenenbaum* at least arguably could weigh in favor of finding a procedural due

> process violation in certain circumstances. If New York law does authorize such removals, *Tenenbaum* likely does not prohibit us from deferring to that judgment. In either case, the underlying New York procedural rules will also be an important component of our balancing. Thus, the state-law question of statutory interpretation will either render unnecessary, or at least substantially modify, the federal constitutional question" (344 F.3d at 172).[7]

The court also questioned whether "in the context of the seizure of a child by a state protective agency the Fourth Amendment might impose any additional restrictions above and beyond those that apply to ordinary arrests" (*id.* at 173).

As to court-ordered removals, the Second Circuit recognized challenges based on substantive due process, procedural due process—the antecedent of Certified Question No. 3—and the Fourth Amendment. The substantive due process question concerned whether the City had offered a reasonable justification for the removals. The Second Circuit observed that "there is a substantial Fourth Amendment question presented if New York law does not authorize removals in the circumstances alleged" (*id.* at 176).

Finally, in certifying the questions to us, the court explained that:

> "[t]here is...some ambiguity in the statutory language authorizing removals pending a final determination of status. Following an emergency removal, whether ex parte or by court order, the Family Court must return a removed child to the parent's custody absent 'an imminent risk' or 'imminent danger' to 'the child's life or health.' At the same time, the Family Court must consider the 'best interests of the child' in assessing whether continuing removal is necessary to prevent threats to the child's life or health. Additionally, in order to support removal, the Family Court must 'find[] that removal is necessary to avoid imminent risk.' How these provisions should be harmonized seems to us to be the province of the Court of Appeals" (344 F.3d at 169 [internal citations omitted]).

The Circuit Court summarized the policy challenged by plaintiffs and found by the District Court as "the alleged practice of removals based on a theory that allowing one's child to witness ongoing domestic violence is a form of neglect, either simply because such conduct is presumptively neglectful or because in individual circumstances it is shown to threaten the child's physical or emotional health" (*id.* at 166 n. 5).

It is this policy, viewed in light of the District Court's factual findings, that informs our analysis of Certified Question No. 2. In so doing, we acknowledge the Legislature's expressed goal of "placing increased emphasis on preventive services designed to maintain family relationships rather than responding to children and families in trouble only by removing the child from the family" (*see Mark G. v. Sabol*, 93 N.Y.2d 710, 719, 695 N.Y.S.2d 730, 717 N.E.2d

7. In *Tenenbaum v. Williams*, 193 F.3d 581 [2d Cir. 1999], a child's parents brought an action pursuant to 42 USC § 1983 challenging the New York City Child Welfare Administration's removal of their five year old from her kindergarten class—under the emergency removal provision of Family Court Act § 1024—and taking her to the emergency room where a pediatrician and a gynecologist examined her for signs of possible sexual abuse. When they found none, the child was returned to her parents. The Second Circuit reversed the District Court's judgment in pertinent part and held that a jury could have concluded that the emergency removal for the medical examination violated the parents' and child's procedural due process rights, and the child's Fourth Amendment rights.

1067 [1999] [emphasis omitted] [construing Child Welfare Reform Act of 1979 (L. 1979, chs. 610, 611)]). We further acknowledge the legislative findings, made pursuant to the Family Protection and Domestic Violence Intervention Act of 1994, that

> "[t]he corrosive effect of domestic violence is far reaching. The batterer's violence injures children both directly and indirectly. Abuse of a parent is detrimental to children whether or not they are physically abused themselves. Children who witness domestic violence are more likely to experience delayed development, feelings of fear, depression and helplessness and are more likely to become batterers themselves" (L. 1994, ch. 222, § 1; *see also People v. Wood*, 95 N.Y.2d 509, 512, 719 N.Y.S.2d 639, 742 N.E.2d 114 [2000] [though involving a batterer, not a victim]).

These legislative findings represent two fundamental—sometimes conflicting—principles. New York has long embraced a policy of keeping "biological families together" (*Matter of Marino S.*, 100 N.Y.2d 361, 372, 763 N.Y.S.2d 796, 795 N.E.2d 21 [2003]). Yet "when a child's best interests are endangered, such objectives must yield to the State's paramount concern for the health and safety of the child" (*id.*).

As we concluded in response to Certified Question No. 1, exposing a child to domestic violence is *not* presumptively neglectful. Not every child exposed to domestic violence is at risk of impairment. A fortiori, exposure of a child to violence is not presumptively ground for removal, and in many instances removal may do more harm to the child than good. Part 2 of article 10 of the Family Court Act sets forth four ways in which a child may be removed from the home in response to an allegation of neglect (or abuse) related to domestic violence: (1) temporary removal with consent; (2) preliminary orders after a petition is filed; (3) preliminary orders before a petition is filed; and (4) emergency removal without a court order. The issue before us is whether emotional harm suffered by a child exposed to domestic violence, where shown, can warrant the trauma of removal under any of these provisions.

The Practice Commentaries state, and we agree, that the sections of part 2 of article 10 create a "continuum of consent and urgency and mandate a hierarchy of required review" before a child is removed from home (*see* Besharov, Practice Commentaries, McKinney's Cons. Laws of N.Y., Book 29A, Family Ct. Act § 1021, at 5 [1999 ed.]).

Consent Removal

First, section 1021 provides that a child may be removed "from the place where he is residing with the written consent of his parent or other person legally responsible for his care, if the child is an abused or neglected child under this article" (Family Ct. Act § 1021; *see Tenenbaum v. Williams*, 193 F.3d 581, 590 n. 5 [2d Cir. 1999]; *Matter of Jonathan P.*, 283 A.D.2d 675, 724 N.Y.S.2d 213 [3d Dept. 2001]). This section is significant because "many parents are willing and able to understand the need to place the child outside the home and because resort to unnecessary legal coercion can be detrimental to later treatment efforts" (Besharov at 6).

Postpetition Removal

If parental consent cannot be obtained, section 1027, at issue here, provides for preliminary orders after the filing of a neglect (or abuse) petition. Thus, according to the statutory continuum, where the circumstances are not so exigent, the agency should bring a petition and seek a hearing *prior* to removal of the child. In any case involving abuse—or in any case where the child has already been removed without a court order—the Family Court must hold a hearing as soon as practicable after the filing of a petition, to determine whether the child's interests require protection pending a final order of disposition (Family Ct. Act § 1027 [a]). As is relevant here, the section further provides that in any other circumstance (such as a neglect case), after the petition is filed any person originating the proceeding (or the Law Guardian) may apply for—or the court on its own may order—a hearing to determine whether the child's interests require protection, pending a final order of disposition (*id.*).

For example, in *Matter of Adam DD.*, 112 A.D.2d 493, 490 N.Y.S.2d 907 [3d Dept. 1985], after filing a child neglect petition, petitioner Washington County Department of Social Services sought an order under section 1027. At a hearing, evidence demonstrated that respondent mother had told her son on several occasions that she intended to kill herself, and Family Court directed that custody be placed with petitioner on a temporary basis for two months. At the subsequent dispositional hearing, a psychiatrist testified that respondent was suffering from a type of paranoid schizophrenia that endangered the well-being of the child, and recommended the continued placement with petitioner. A second psychiatrist concurred. The Appellate Division concluded that the record afforded a basis for Family Court to find neglect because of possible impairment of the child's emotional health, and continued placement of the child with petitioner.

While not a domestic violence case, *Matter of Adam DD.* is instructive because it concerns steps taken in the circumstance where a child is emotionally harmed by parental behavior. The parent's repeated threats of suicide caused emotional harm that could be akin to the experience of a child who witnesses repeated episodes of domestic violence perpetrated against a parent. In this circumstance, the agency did not immediately remove the child, but proceeded with the filing of a petition and a hearing.

Upon such a hearing, if the court finds that removal is necessary to avoid imminent risk to the child's life or health, it is required to remove or continue the removal and remand the child to a place approved by the agency (Family Ct Act § 1027[b][i]). In undertaking this inquiry, the statute also requires the court to consider and determine whether continuation in the child's home would be contrary to the best interests of the child (*id.*).

The Circuit Court has asked us to harmonize the "best interests" test with the calculus concerning "imminent risk" and "imminent danger" to "life or health" (344 F.3d at 169). In order to justify a finding of imminent risk to life or health, the agency need not prove that the child has suffered actual injury (*see Matter of Kimberly H.*, 242 A.D.2d 35, 38, 673 N.Y.S.2d 96 [1st Dept. 1998]). Rather, the court engages in a fact-intensive inquiry to determine whether the child's emotional health is at risk. Section 1012(h), moreover, sets forth specific factors, evidence of which may demonstrate "substantially diminished psychological or intellectual functioning" (*see also Matter of Sayeh R.*, 91 N.Y.2d 306, 314–316, 670 N.Y.S.2d 377, 693 N.E.2d 724 [1997]; *Matter of Nassau County Dept. of Social Servs. [Dante M.] v. Denise J.*, 87 N.Y.2d 73, 78–79, 637 N.Y.S.2d 666, 661 N.E.2d 138 [1995]). As noted in our discussion of Certified Question No. 1, section 1012(h) contains the caveat that impairment of emotional health must be "clearly attributable to the unwillingness or inability of the respondent to exercise a minimum degree of care toward the child" (*see Matter of Theresa CC.*, 178 A.D.2d 687, 576 N.Y.S.2d 937 [3d Dept. 1991]).

Importantly, in 1988, the Legislature added the "best interests" requirement to the statute, as well as the requirement that reasonable efforts be made "to prevent or eliminate the need for removal of the child from the home" (L. 1988, ch. 478, § 5). These changes were apparently necessary to comport with federal requirements under title IV-E of the Social Security Act (42 USC §§ 670–679b), which mandated that federal "foster care maintenance payments may be made on behalf of otherwise eligible children who were removed from the home of a specified relative pursuant to a voluntary placement agreement, or as the result of a 'judicial determination to the effect that continuation therein would be contrary to the welfare of the child and . . . that reasonable efforts [to prevent the need for removal] have been made'" (Policy Interpretation Question of U.S. Dept. of Health & Human Servs., May 3, 1986, Bill Jacket, L. 1988, ch. 478, at 32–33). The measures "ensure[d] that children involved in the early stages of child protective proceedings and their families receive appropriate services to prevent the children's removal from their homes whenever possible" (Mem. from Cesar A. Perales to Evan A. Davis, Counsel to Governor, July 27, 1988, Bill Jacket, L. 1988, ch. 478, at 14).

> "By contrast, the City at the time took the position that
>
> [t]he mixing of the standards 'best interest of the child' and 'imminent risk' is confusing. It makes no sense for a court to determine as part of an 'imminent risk' decision, what is in the 'best interest of the child.' If the child is in 'imminent risk,' his/her 'best interest' is removal from the home. A 'best interest' determination is more appropriately made after an investigation and a report have been completed and all the facts are available" (Letter from Legis. Rep. James Brennan, City of New York Off. of Mayor, to Governor Mario M. Cuomo, July 27, 1988, Bill Jacket, L. 1988, ch. 478, at 23).

In this litigation, the City posits that the "best interests" determination is part of the Family Court's conclusion that there is imminent risk warranting removal, and concedes that whether a child will be harmed by the removal is a relevant consideration. The City thus recognizes that the questions facing a Family Court judge in the removal context are extraordinarily complex. As the Circuit Court observed, "it could be argued that the exigencies of the moment that threaten the welfare of a child justify removal. On the other hand, a blanket presumption in favor of removal may not fairly capture the nuances of each family situation" (344 F.3d at 174).

The plain language of the section and the legislative history supporting it establish that a blanket presumption favoring removal was never intended. The court *must do* more than identify the existence of a risk of serious harm. Rather, a court must weigh, in the factual setting before it, whether the imminent risk to the child can be mitigated by reasonable efforts to avoid removal. It must balance that risk against the harm removal might bring, and it must determine factually which course is in the child's best interests.

Additionally, the court must specifically consider whether imminent risk to the child might be eliminated by other means, such as issuing a temporary order of protection or providing services to the victim (Family Ct. Act § 1027[b][iii], [iv]). The Committee Bill Memorandum supporting this legislation explains the intent that "[w]here one parent is abusive but the child may safely reside at home with the other parent, the abuser should be removed. This will spare children the trauma of removal and placement in foster care" (Mem. of Children and Families Standing Comm., Bill Jacket, L. 1989, ch. 727, at 7).

These legislative concerns were met, for example, in *Matter of Naomi R.*, 296 A.D.2d 503, 745 N.Y.S.2d 485 [2d Dept. 2002], where, following a hearing pursuant to section 1027, Family Court issued a temporary order of protection against a father, excluding him from the home, on the ground that he allegedly sexually abused one of his four children. Evidence established that the father's return to the home, even under the mother's supervision, would present an imminent risk to the health and safety of all of the children. Thus, pending a full fact-finding hearing, Family Court took the step of maintaining the integrity of the family unit and instead removed the abuser.

Ex Parte Removal by Court Order

If the agency believes that there is insufficient time to file a petition, the next step on the continuum should not be emergency removal, but ex parte removal by court order (*see e.g. Matter of Nassau County Dept. of Social Servs. [Dante M.] v. Denise J.*, 87 N.Y.2d 73, 637 N.Y.S.2d 666, 661 N.E.2d 138 [1995]). Section 1022 of the Family Court Act provides that the court may enter an order directing the temporary removal of a child from home before the filing of a petition if three factors are met.

First, the parent must be absent or, if present, must have been asked and refused to consent to temporary removal of the child and must have been informed of an intent to apply for an order. Second, the child must appear to suffer from abuse or neglect of a parent or other person legally responsible for the child's care to the extent that immediate removal is necessary to avoid imminent danger to the child's life or health. Third, there must be insufficient time to file a petition and hold a preliminary hearing.

Just as in a section 1027 inquiry, the court must consider whether continuation in the child's home would be contrary to the best interests of the child; whether reasonable efforts were made prior to the application to prevent or eliminate the need for removal from the home; and whether imminent risk to the child would be eliminated by the issuance of a temporary order of protection directing the removal of the person from the child's residence. Here, the court must engage in a fact-finding inquiry into whether the child is at risk and appears to suffer from neglect.

The Practice Commentaries suggest that section 1022 may be unfamiliar, or seem unnecessary, to those in practice in New York City, "where it is common to take emergency protective action without prior court review" (Besharov, Practice Commentaries, McKinney's Cons. Laws of N.Y., Book 29A, Family Ct. Act § 1022, at 10 [1999 ed.]). If, as the District Court's findings suggest, this was done in cases where a court order could be obtained, the practice contravenes the statute. Section 1022 ensures that in most urgent situations, there will be judicial oversight in order to prevent well-meaning but misguided removals that may harm the child more than help. As the comment to the predecessor statute stated, "[t]his section... [is] designed to avoid a premature removal of a child from his home by establishing a procedure for an early judicial determination of urgent need" (Committee Comments, McKinney's Cons. Laws of N.Y., Book 29A, Family Ct. Act § 322 [1963 ed.]).

Whether analyzing a removal application under section 1027 or section 1022, or an application for a child's return under section 1028, a court must engage in a balancing test of the imminent risk with the best interests of the child and, where appropriate, the reasonable efforts made to avoid removal or continuing removal. The term "safer course" (*see e.g. Matter of Kimberly H.*, 242 A.D.2d 35, 673 N.Y.S.2d 96 [1st Dept. 1998]; *Matter of Tantalyn TT.*, 115

A.D.2d 799, 495 N.Y.S.2d 740 [3d Dept. 1985]) should not be used to mask a dearth of evidence or as a watered-down, impermissible presumption.

Emergency Removal without Court Order

Finally, section 1024 provides for emergency removals without a court order. The section permits removal without a court order and without consent of the parent if there is reasonable cause to believe that the child is in such urgent circumstance or condition that continuing in the home or care of the parent presents an imminent danger to the child's life or health, and there is not enough time to apply for an order under section 1022 (Family Ct. Act § 1024[a]; *see generally Matter of Joseph DD.*, 300 A.D.2d 760, 760 n. 1, 752 N.Y.S.2d 407 [3d Dept. 2002] [noting that removal under such emergency circumstances requires the filing of an article 10 petition "forthwith" and prompt court review of the nonjudicial decision pursuant to Family Ct. Act § 1026 (c) and § 1028]; *see also Matter of Karla V.*, 278 A.D.2d 159, 717 N.Y.S.2d 598 [1st Dept. 2000]). Thus, emergency removal is appropriate where the danger is so immediate, so urgent that the child's life or safety will be at risk before an ex parte order can be obtained. The standard obviously is a stringent one.

Section 1024 establishes an objective test, whether the child is in such circumstance or condition that remaining in the home presents imminent danger to life or health. In construing "imminent danger" under section 1024, it has been held that whether a child is in "imminent danger" is necessarily a fact-intensive determination. "It is not required that the child be injured in the presence of a caseworker nor is it necessary for the alleged abuser to be present at the time the child is taken from the home. It is sufficient if the officials have persuasive evidence of serious ongoing abuse and, based upon the best investigation reasonably possible under the circumstances, have reason to fear imminent recurrence" (*Gottlieb v. County of Orange*, 871 F.Supp. 625, 628–629 [S.D.N.Y. 1994], citing *Robison v. Via*, 821 F.2d 913, 922 [2d Cir. 1987]). The Gottlieb court added that, "[s]ince this evidence is the basis for removal of a child, it should be as reliable and thoroughly examined as possible to avoid unnecessary harm to the family unit" (871 F.Supp. at 629).

Section 1024 concerns, moreover, only the very grave circumstance of danger to life or health. While we cannot say, for all future time, that the possibility can never exist, in the case of emotional injury—or, even more remotely, the risk of emotional injury—caused by witnessing domestic violence, it must be a rare circumstance in which the time would be so fleeting and the danger so great that emergency removal would be warranted.

Certified Question No. 3: Process

Finally, the Second Circuit asks us:

> "Does the fact that the child witnessed such abuse suffice to demonstrate that 'removal is necessary,' N.Y. Family Ct. Act §§ 1022, 1024, 1027, or that 'removal was in the child's best interests,' N.Y. Family Ct. Act §§ 1028, 1052(b)(i)(A), or must the child protective agency offer additional, particularized evidence to justify removal?" (344 F.3d at 177.)

The Circuit Court has before it the procedural due process question whether, if New York law permits a presumption that removal is appropriate based on the witnessing of domestic violence, that presumption would comport with *Stanley v. Illinois*, 405 U.S. 645, 92 S.Ct. 1208, 31

L.Ed.2d 551 [1972] [recognizing a father's procedural due process interest in an individualized determination of fitness]. All parties maintain, however, and we concur, that under the Family Court Act, there can be no "blanket presumption" favoring removal when a child witnesses domestic violence, and that each case is fact-specific. As demonstrated in our discussion of Certified Question No. 2, when a court orders removal, particularized evidence must exist to justify that determination, including, where appropriate, evidence of efforts made to prevent or eliminate the need for removal and the impact of removal on the child.

The Circuit Court points to two cases in which removals occurred based on domestic violence without corresponding expert testimony on the appropriateness of removal in the particular circumstance (*Matter of Carlos M.*, 293 A.D.2d 617, 741 N.Y.S.2d 82 [2d Dept. 2002]; *Matter of Lonell J.*, 242 A.D.2d 58, 673 N.Y.S.2d 116 [1st Dept. 1998]). Both cases were reviewed on the issue whether there was sufficient evidence to support a finding of neglect. In *Carlos M.*, the evidence showed a 12-year history of domestic violence between the parents which was not only witnessed by the children but also often actually spurred their intervention. In *Lonell J.*, caseworkers testified at a fact-finding hearing about the domestic violence perpetrated by the children's father against their mother, as well as the unsanitary condition of the home and the children's poor health.

We do not read *Carlos M.* or *Lonell J.* as supportive of a presumption that if a child has witnessed domestic violence, the child has been harmed and removal is appropriate. That presumption would be impermissible. In each case, multiple factors formed the basis for intervention and determinations of neglect. As the First Department concluded in *Lonell J.*, moreover, "nothing in section 1012 itself requires expert testimony, as opposed to other convincing evidence of neglect" (242 A.D.2d at 61, 673 N.Y.S.2d 116). Indeed, under section 1046(a) (viii), which sets forth the evidentiary standards for abuse and neglect hearings, competent expert testimony on a child's emotional condition may be heard. The *Lonell J.* court expressed concern that while older children can communicate with a psychological expert about the effects of domestic violence on their emotional state, much younger children often cannot (242 A.D.2d at 62, 673 N.Y.S.2d 116). The court believed that "[t]o require expert testimony of this type in the latter situation would be tantamount to refusing to protect the most vulnerable and impressionable children. While violence between parents adversely affects all children, younger children in particular are most likely to suffer from psychosomatic illnesses and arrested development" (*id.*).

Granted, in some cases, it may be difficult for an agency to show, absent expert testimony, that there is imminent risk to a child's emotional state, and that any impairment of emotional health is "clearly attributable to the unwillingness or inability of the respondent to exercise a minimum degree of care toward the child" (Family Ct Act § 1012[h]). Yet nothing in the plain language of article 10 requires such testimony. The tragic reality is, as the facts of *Lonell J.* show, that emotional injury may be only one of the harms attributable to the chaos of domestic violence.

Accordingly, the certified questions should be answered in accordance with this opinion.

NOTES AND QUESTIONS

1. The plaintiffs and the City of New York subsequently signed a settlement agreement in which the city agreed to comply with the law. The city also agreed that the plaintiffs were

entitled to attorney's fees as the prevailing party. David Lansner, The Nicholson Decisions: New York's Response to 'Failure to Protect' Allegations, 12 A.B.A. Comm'n on Domestic Violence e-newsletter (Fall 2008), http://www.americanbar.org/content/newsletter/publications/cdv_enewsletter_home/vol12_expert1.html. There are indications, however, that the practice of removing children from their abused mothers continues. See Joanne N. Sirotkin with Christine M. Fecko, A Case Study in Post-*Nicholson* Litigation, 12 A.B.A. Comm'n on Domestic Violence e-newsletter (Fall 2008), http://www.americanbar.org/content/newsletter/publications/cdv_enewsletter_home/vol12_expert2.html.

2. Should the victim of domestic violence be held responsible for failing to protect her child from witnessing the abuse? There is considerable evidence that exposure to domestic violence as a child leads to subsequent problems in childhood and into adulthood. See, e.g., Abigail H. Gewirtz & Jeffrey L. Edleson, *Young Children's Exposure to Intimate Partner Violence: Towards a Developmental Risk and Resilience Framework for Research and Intervention*, 22 J. Fam. Violence 151, 155 (2007). Among the effects reported are depression, posttraumatic stress disorder, anxiety, aggressive and destructive behaviors, cognitive delays, and physical abuse. Patricia Van Horn & Betsy McAlister Groves, *Children Exposed to Domestic Violence: Making Trauma-Informed Custody and Visitation Decisions*, 57 Juv. & Fam. Ct. J. 51, 52–53 (Winter 2006). The effects may be even more pronounced for children younger than five. *Id.* at 53. Nevertheless, some studies indicate that not all children are deeply affected by domestic violence. See, e.g., John H. Grych, Ernest N. Jouriles, Paul R. Swank, Renee McDonald, & William D. Norwood, *Patterns of Adjustment among Children of Battered Women*, 68 J. Consulting & Clinical Psychol. 84, 91 (2000); Cris M. Sullivan, Jennifer Juras, Deborah Bybee, Huong Nguyen, & Nicole Allen, *How Children's Adjustment Is Affected by Their Relationships to Their Mothers' Abusers*, 15 J. Interpersonal Violence 587, 589 (2000). When should the victim become the victimizer? What if the victim of abuse covers it up? See *In re Gabriel E.*, 867 N.E.2d 59 (Ill. App. 2007).

x. Medical neglect

NEW JERSEY DIVISION OF YOUTH AND FAMILY SERVICES V. M.A

Superior Court of New Jersey, Appellate Division

No. AHU 08-335 (Feb. 3, 2011)

PER CURIAM.

M.A. appeals from a final determination of the Director of the Department of Children and Families (Director) in the Division of Youth and Family Services (Division), finding that she neglected her infant child K.A. by failing to provide him with necessary medical care. We affirm.

Here, the Division informed M.A. that it had substantiated a finding that she had medically neglected K.A. M.A. requested a dispositional review in order to contest this finding. The Division's finding was affirmed. Thereafter, M.A. requested an administrative hearing, and the Division referred the matter to the Office of Administrative Law for a hearing before an Administrative Law Judge (ALJ).

The evidence presented at the hearing indicated that M.A. had given birth to K.A. on June 27, 2005. L.A. is the child's biological father. The child had tested positive for presumptive medium-chain acyl-CoA dehydrogenase deficiency (MCAD). An individual with MCAD cannot convert fatty acids into "fuel" for the body. A child with this disorder must be fed approximately every two to four hours so the body has sufficient nutrition. In addition to the recommended frequent feedings, carnitine supplements are often suggested. Carnitine assists the fatty acids to oxidize, and facilitates the production of ketones, which can take the place of sugar or carbohydrates in the body.

An individual with MCAD can become hypoglycemic, which may lead to metabolic decompensation that can cause such effects as Attention Deficit Hyperactivity Disorder (ADHD) and certain developmental delays. In addition, a child with MCAD is at substantial risk during times of illness and physical stress. In certain circumstances, MCAD can lead to death if not properly treated.

On July 1, 2005, St. Peter's University Hospital (St. Peter's) confirmed K.A.'s presumptive diagnosis of MCAD. Dr. Debra-Lynn Day-Salvatore (Dr. Day-Salvatore), Director of the Institute for Genetic Medicine (Institute) at St. Peter's, attempted to schedule an appointment for K.A. on July 7, 2005; however, his parents declined that appointment. Dr. Day-Salvatore first saw K.A. on August 19, 2005.

The doctor counseled the family and explained the risks associated with MCAD and the appropriate treatment for the condition, including a feeding schedule, glucose monitoring and possible carnitine supplementation. K.A.'s parents decided not to have DNA tests performed on the child, although such tests had been recommended to further confirm the MCAD diagnosis. On August 24, 2005, Dr. Day-Salvatore wrote to K.A.'s pediatrician, Dr. Vidya Vakil (Dr. Vakil), and advised her concerning the initial consultation.

In addition, on August 25, 2005, Dr. Day-Salvatore wrote to K.A.'s parents and confirmed the diagnosis of MCAD. She again recommended carnitine supplementation to minimize the risk that K.A. would experience a metabolic crisis. The doctor also recommended that M.A. contact her directly so that a treatment plan for K.A. would be established.

On September 1, 2005, M.A. called Dr. Day-Salvatore, but the doctor was not available at that time. M.A. did not leave her phone number and said that she would call again. M.A. did not call St. Peter's again until June 2006.

The record indicates that M.A. failed to bring K.A. for visits with Dr. Vakil that had been scheduled for August 27, 2005, and September 16, 2005. M.A. brought K.A. for an appointment with Dr. Vakil on November 8, 2005. Dr. Vakil noted in her chart that M.A. would not permit K.A. to receive all of his vaccines at the same time, and M.A. had requested that only two vaccines be administered at a time.

Dr. Vakil also noted that M.A. had not started K.A. on carnitine, as had been recommended. Dr. Vakil suggested that the parents follow up at a metabolic treatment center (MTC), and she gave them the number for Children's Hospital of Philadelphia (CHOP).

K.A. was taken to see Dr. Vakil on December 21, 2005. The doctor's chart indicates that, at the time, K.A.'s weight had dropped to the tenth percentile compared to boys of his age. K.A. was not brought for his scheduled appointment with Dr. Vakil on February 17, 2006. However, Dr. Vakil saw the child in March [2006], and she again gave M.A. the number for CHOP so that K.A. could be seen at a MTC.

K.A. was not taken for his May 1, 2006, appointment, although Dr. Vakil saw the child on May 27, 2006, when his father brought him to see the doctor for a rash. Dr. Vakil again advised that the child needed to be seen at a MTC. The doctor said that K.A. should return in a week; however, K.A.'s parents failed to take him to the doctor at that time.

On June 15, 2006, M.A. phoned Dr. Day-Salvatore and advised that K.A. had possibly lost five pounds in a week. The doctor attempted to return the call but there was no answer. Eventually, Dr. Day-Salvatore was able to contact M.A. and offered to see K.A. on June 19, 2006. M.A. said that the following day would be better for her.

On the morning of June 20, 2006, M.A. called St. Peter's and said that she had been on their way to the hospital but had gotten stuck in traffic. Nearly two hours later, M.A. called Dr. Day-Salvatore and said that she had returned home. Dr. Day-Salvatore advised M.A. to take K.A. to the St. Peter's emergency room if he was experiencing acute illness.

On June 21, 2006, M.A. called Dr. Day-Salvatore and said that K.A. had gained back all of his weight and was fine. However, at 11:00 p.m. on June 22, 2006, M.A. brought K.A. to the St. Peter's emergency room. The doctor there found that K.A. was not suffering from any acute illness but his weight was below the fifth percentile on the growth chart.

K.A. was seen by Dr. Vakil on June 29, 2006, in the company of one of the Division's caseworkers. The child then weighed about eighteen pounds, which was still below the fifth percentile on the growth chart. M.A. advised the Division's caseworker that she wanted to have the child evaluated at Cooper University Hospital; however, she did not schedule an appointment there for two weeks. The Division scheduled the appointment for August 11, 2006. The Division also scheduled an appointment for K.A. at the Dorothy B. Hersh Child Protection Center on August 11, 2006.

Dr. Susan Hodgson (Dr. Hodgson) evaluated K.A. on August 11, 2006, and reviewed the child's medical records. Dr. Hodgson found K.A. had "without question" been medically neglected. She wrote that K.A. is a child with a "potentially life-threatening" disorder, who had shown a significant decrease in weight and who had not been given carnitine supplements or metabolic testing between August 19, 2005, and June 26, 2006.

Dr. Rhonda Schnur of Cooper Hospital saw K.A. on August 24, 2006. At that time, K.A.'s growth parameters had fallen below the third percentile on the growth charts. Dr. Schnur concluded that K.A. was "fail[ing] to thrive." M.A. again refused DNA testing, even though Dr. Schnur said that such tests would provided a better understanding of the child's "severe carnitine deficiency and failure to thrive." Dr. Schnur subsequently treated K.A., and noted that he had severe developmental delays, including no head growth, possible ADHD, head-banging, and speech delay.

M.A. testified that, at times, St. Peter's had turned her away from scheduled appointments when she was only five or ten minutes late. M.A. stated that she was concerned about the side effects of carnitine supplements. M.A. claimed that she was not supposed to follow up at St. Peter's until a year had gone by. She explained the reasons why she did not bring K.A. for certain appointments. M.A. insisted that she made up for the missed appointments.

M.A. further testified that she called Dr. Day-Salvatore on June 16, 2006, because she was concerned about K.A.'s weight loss. M.A. claimed that she had been told that Dr. Day-Salvatore would not see her if she was even a minute late. She stated that she ran into heavy traffic on the way to the appointment and returned home. She asserted that she did not believe K.A. was failing to thrive in June 2006.

The ALJ issued an initial decision in which he concluded that the Division had proven that K.A. had been "abused or neglected" as that term is defined in N.J.S.A. 9:6-8.21(c). The ALJ found that, although M.A. was a concerned parent, her testimony about the missed appointments and concerns about the suggested treatments were not credible. The ALJ further found that the evidence established that a significant amount of time had passed before K.A. was seen by a doctor for his condition, and only then when M.A. thought the child was in crisis.

The ALJ made the following additional findings of fact:

> The record presented in this case demonstrates that K.A.'s physical condition was placed in imminent danger of becoming impaired as the result of the failure of [M.A.] to exercise a minimum degree of care in providing the [child] with proper supervision or guardianship, by unreasonably allowing [a] substantial risk of harm [to be inflicted]. . . . In the present matter, M.A. had the benefit of knowing early [on] that K.A. suffered from a chronic condition which could lead to further medical complications. Armed with that information, the record demonstrates that M.A. failed to provide a minimum degree of care in that she frequently missed doctor's appointments and failed to follow up as advised by doctors. While incidents can and do occur, the frequency with which appointments were missed or delayed, or advice not heeded[,] placed K.A.'s physical condition in danger of becoming impaired. While this would be cause for concern in a vacuum, what was known about K.A.'s condition serves to exacerbate this concern. [M.A.'s] statements regarding worries as to side effects of various treatments are unpersuasive, as the documents make clear the rarity of occurrences and the record is devoid of any indication of these concerns being raised at the time treatment was attempted. Rather they appear to be compiled in preparation for the hearing in this matter, an excuse rather than a reason.

Thereafter, M.A. filed exceptions to the ALJ's initial decision with the Director. The Director found, however, that the record supported the ALJ's findings and reaffirmed the Division's determination that M.A. had neglected K.A. by failing to provide the child with the medical care required for his condition.

On appeal, M.A. argues that the Division's finding of neglect should be reversed because it is "unreasonable" and not supported by the evidence in the record. M.A. also argues that the ALJ erred by finding that her testimony was not credible.

"In light of the executive function of administrative agencies, judicial capacity to review administrative actions is severely limited." *George Harms Constr. Co. v. N.J. Tpk. Auth.*, 137 N.J. 8, 27, 644 A.2d 76 (1994) (citing *Gloucester Cnty. Welfare Bd. v. N.J. Civil Serv. Comm'n*, 93 N.J. 384, 390, 461 A.2d 575 (1983)). "Courts can intervene only in those rare circumstances in which an agency action is clearly inconsistent with its statutory mission or with other State policy." *Ibid.*

In determining whether the agency's action is arbitrary or unreasonable, we consider: 1) whether the agency's decision offends either the State or Federal Constitution; 2) whether the action violated express or implied legislative policies; 3) whether there is substantial credible evidence in the record to support the agency's findings; and 4) whether the agency clearly erred in reaching a conclusion unsupported by relevant factors. *Ibid.* (citing *Campbell v. Dep't of Civil Serv.*, 39 N.J. 556, 562, 189 A.2d 712 (1963); *In re Larsen*, 17 N.J.Super. 564, 570, 86 A.2d 430 (App.Div. 1952)).

N.J.S.A. 9:6-8.21(c) provides that a child is considered "abused or neglected" if the parent or guardian of a child less than eighteen years of age:

> (1) inflicts or allows to be inflicted upon such child physical injury by other than accidental means which causes or creates a substantial risk of death, or serious or protracted disfigurement, or protracted impairment of physical or emotional health or protracted loss or impairment of the function of any bodily organ; (2) creates or allows to be created a substantial or ongoing risk of physical injury to such child by other than accidental means which would be likely to cause death or serious or protracted disfigurement, or protracted loss or impairment of the function of any bodily organ;...(4) or a child whose physical, mental, or emotional condition has been impaired or is in imminent danger of becoming impaired as the result of the failure of his parent or guardian, as herein defined, to exercise a minimum degree of care...(b) in providing the child with proper supervision or guardianship, by unreasonably inflicting or allowing to be inflicted harm, or substantial risk thereof[.]

The Supreme Court has explained that, for the purpose of applying this statute, a parent or guardian fails to exercise a "minimum degree of care when he or she is aware of the dangers inherent in a situation and fails adequately to supervise the child or recklessly creates a risk of serious injury to that child." *G.S. v. N.J. Div. of Youth & Family Servs.*, 157 N.J. 161, 181, 723 A.2d 612 (1999). Minimum degree of care refers to conduct that is "grossly or wantonly negligent, but not necessarily intentional[,]" rather than conduct that is simply negligent. *Id.* at 178, 723 A.2d 612.

We are satisfied that there is sufficient credible evidence in the record to support the Division's finding that M.A. medically neglected K.A. and, as a consequence, K.A. was an "abused or neglected" child, as defined in N.J.S.A. 9:6-8.21(c)(4)(b). The record supports the Division's finding that M.A. failed to provide appropriate medical treatment for K.A.'s diagnosed MCAD in the first year of his life, thereby subjecting him to a risk of serious injury.

We find no merit in M.A.'s assertion that the ALJ erred by finding her testimony to be lacking in credibility. Here, the ALJ correctly noted that M.A.'s testimony was contradicted by the documentary evidence presented at the hearing, as well as by Dr. Day-Salvatore's testimony, which the ALJ found credible and persuasive. Our deference to the ALJ's credibility findings is warranted because the ALJ heard the testimony and was better able to assess the credibility of the witnesses than an appellate court.

NOTES AND QUESTIONS

1. Is there sufficient evidence to find that K.A. was medically neglected? Why? To what extent may a parent make medical decisions for a child? What if a parent decides to discontinue her child's medication prescribed by the child's psychologist without first consulting the psychologist because she felt the medication was causing problems for the child? See *In re A.A.*, 807 N.Y.S.2d 181 (N.Y. 2005). Do you think that a parent could refuse to allow her child to be vaccinated?

2. The AAP's Committee on Child Abuse and Neglect identifies several factors necessary for a diagnosis of medical neglect. They include harm or risk of harm to the child because of the lack of health care, the proffered care results in a "significant net benefit" to the child, the benefit is "significantly greater than its morbidity" such that a reasonable caregiver would choose treatment, "access to health care is available and not used," and the "caregiver understands the advice given." Carole Jenny, Am. Acad. Pediatrics, Comm. on Child Abuse and Neglect, *Recognizing and Responding to Medical Neglect*, 120 PEDIATRICS 1385, 1385 (2007). Do you think that K.A. was medically neglected as defined by the AAP?

3. *First Amendment.* Most states provide a religious exemption for parents who fail to provide medical treatment to their children. All but two states exempt vaccinations for children based on parental religious belief. Religious Exemptions from Healthcare for Children, Child, Inc., http://childrenshealthcare.org/?page_id=24. Does this mean that children may be medically neglected if their parents have a religious objection to the proposed course of treatment?

> When children whose parents fail, for religious reasons, to secure or consent to necessary medical care for them *do* come to the attention of state officials, courts have some authority to order medical treatment over the parents' objections. A substantial amount of litigation and commentary has surrounded the question of when a court order is appropriate. Courts have uniformly found it appropriate to order medical treatment for a child, over parents' objection that doing so violates their First Amendment right to the free exercise of religion, when treatment is necessary to prevent the child from dying. Most courts have held that intervention is also appropriate when necessary to prevent "grievous harm" to a child, which one state court defined as "a significant impairment of vital physical or mental functions, protracted disability, permanent disfigurement, or similar defects or infirmities."
>
> A few courts, however, have held that no injury short of death suffices to override the religious objection of parents. Moreover, no court has ordered treatment to prevent harm to a child that is less than "grievous" when parents objected on religious grounds, and some have indicated that they would not do so. Thus, state legislatures and state and federal courts allow certain parents, those with particular religious beliefs, to do something that parents generally are prohibited from doing—to deny their children medical care necessary to prevent significant harm. In a few cases, parents have been deemed entitled to do this even when the harm to their children would be grievous.

James G. Dwyer, *The Children We Abandon: Religious Exemptions to Child Welfare and Education Laws as Denials of Equal Protection to Children of Religious Objectors*, 74 N.C. L. REV. 1321, 1355–1356 (1996) (arguing that religious exemption laws violate equal-protection rights of children). See also James G. Dwyer, *Spiritual Treatment Exemptions to Child Medical Neglect Laws: What We Outsiders Should Think*, 76 NOTRE DAME L. REV. 147 (2000) (state fails to take into account principles that apply to nonautonomous adults when considering right of parents to refuse medical treatment); James G. Dwyer, *Parents' Religion and Children's Welfare: Debunking the Doctrine of Parents' Rights*, 82 CAL. L. REV. 1371 (1994) (dispense with parental rights because in some cases parents are entitled to treat children in ways that are at odds with children's temporal interests).

4. The American Academy of Pediatrics and the American Medical Association, too, are opposed to religious exemptions for the denial of medical treatment to a child. Am. Acad. of Pediatrics, *Religious Objections to Medical Care*, 99 PEDIATRICS 279, 279 (1997); Am. Med. Ass'n, Policy H-515.988, Repeal of Religious Exemptions in Child Abuse and Medical Practice

Statutes, accessible at https://ssl3.ama-assn.org/apps/ecomm/PolicyFinderForm.pl?site=www.ama-assn.org&uri=/ama1/pub/upload/mm/PolicyFinder/policyfiles/HnE/H-515.988.htm.

5. Should parents be exempted from their decision to deny their child medical treatment based on the parents' religious beliefs? For various approaches to the problem, see Henry J. Abraham, *Abraham, Isaac and the State: Faith-Healing and Legal Intervention*, 27 U. Rich. L. Rev. 951, 977 (1993) (repeal of spiritual treatment exemptions "would send the unambiguous message that, in the context of a medical emergency, prayer and faith-healing efforts, however laudable, caring and arguably efficacious they may be, are acceptable to the state only if a child's life or safety is also protected by the provision of any needed medical treatment"); John Dwight Ingram, *State Interference with Religiously Motivated Decisions on Medical Treatment*, 93 Dick. L. Rev. 41, 41 (1988) ("constitutional protections of religious freedom prohibit the state from interfering with religiously motivated decisions regarding the rendering of medical care"); Elizabeth A. Lingle, *Treating Children by Faith: Colliding Constitutional Issues*, 17 J. Legal Med. 301, 330 (1996) (opposing exemptions); Ann MacLean Massie, *The Religion Clauses and Parental Health Care Decisionmaking for Children: Suggestions for a New Approach*, 21 Hastings Const. L. Q. 725, 739 (1994) (spiritual treatment exemptions violate Establishment Clause); Janna C. Merrick, *Christian Science Healing of Minor Children: Spiritual Exemption Statutes, First Amendment Rights, and Fair Notice*, 10 Issues in L. & Med. 321, 341–342 (1994) (arguing for repeal of spiritual treatment exemptions but stating courts should order treatment over the objection of parents "only in cases of very serious illness where reliable and proven therapies can effectively manage the disease"); Paula A. Monopoli, *Allocating the Costs of Parental Free Exercise: Striking a New Balance between Sincere Religious Belief and a Child's Right to Medical Treatment*, 18 Pepp. L. Rev. 319, 322 (1991) (eliminating spiritual treatment exemptions would not violate parents' rights to free exercise of religion); Barry Nobel, *Religious Healing in the Courts: The Liberties and Liabilities of Patients, Parents and Healers*, 16 U. Puget Sound L. Rev. 599, 603 (1993) ("[c]ourts should refrain from interfering with the parent-child relationship absent life-threatening circumstances accompanied by the probability—rather than the possibility—of medical cure"); Rita Swan, *On Statutes Depriving a Class of Children of Rights to Medical Care: Can This Discrimination Be Litigated?* 2 Quinnipiac Health L. J. 73, 92–94 (1998) (spiritual treatment exemptions unconstitutional); Jennifer Trahan, *Constitutional Law: Parental Denial of a Child's Medical Treatment for Religious Reasons*, 1989 Ann. Surv. Am. L. 307, 340 (1990) (proposing model medical-neglect statute that precludes exemption on the grounds of religious belief).

6. Is an obese child neglected? The CDC defines obesity, which is not to be confused with being overweight, as any child who is above the 95th percentile for children of the same age and sex. Obesity contributes to high blood pressure, high cholesterol, breathing problems, and social and psychological problems in children and adolescents. Centers for Disease Control and Prevention, Basics about Childhood Obesity, http://www.cdc.gov/obesity/childhood/basics.html. Some in the medical profession have argued that childhood obesity should be considered child neglect when the family fails to seek medical care, fails to provide the recommended medical care, or fails to control the child's behavior. See Todd Varness, et al., *Childhood Obesity and Medical Neglect*, 123 Pediatrics 399 (2009).

7. Dental neglect, as defined by the American Academy of Pediatric Dentistry, is the "willful failure of parent or guardian to seek and follow through with treatment necessary to ensure a level of oral health essential for adequate function and freedom from pain and infection."

Nancy Kellogg, Am. Acad. Pediatrics, Am. Acad. Pediatric Dentistry, Comm. on Child Abuse & Neglect, *Oral and Dental Aspects of Child Abuse and Neglect*, 116 PEDIATRICS 1565, 1566 (2005). To what extent may dental neglect be driven by poverty?

xi. Educational neglect

IN RE AMURAH B.
Superior Court of Connecticut
49 Conn. L. Rptr. 525 (2010)

N. RUBINOW, J.

This memorandum of decision addresses the issues raised by the oral motions to dismiss submitted by the respondent parents, Angie M. and Jason B. at the close of evidence at a neglect trial pursuant to Practice Book Sec. 15-8. For the following reasons, the court finds that the petitioner has met the assigned burden of presenting evidence sufficient to make out a prima facie case, Accordingly, the department's objections to the motions to dismiss are hereby SUSTAINED, while the respondent parents' motion to dismiss is hereby DENIED.

I.

PROCEDURAL HISTORY

On April 17, 2009, the Commissioner of the Department of Children and Families (DCF or Department) filed petitions alleging that each of the above children was neglected in that she was, in the alternative, "being denied proper care and attention, physically, educationally, emotionally or morally." The respondent parents denied the allegations of the petitions. Trial of the matters was scheduled to commence on January 5, 2010.

Prior to the commencement of evidence, the court ordered bifurcation of the adjudicatory and dispositional issues raised by the petitions, pursuant to Practice Book Sec. 35a-7. In support of the adjudicatory aspect of its petitions, DCF presented its evidence at trial on January 5 and on January 19, 2010, addressing the circumstances affecting the children prior to the adjudicatory date. On the second day of trial, after DCF had rested its evidence on adjudicatory issues, the respondent mother orally moved the court to dismiss the petitions pursuant to Practice Book Sec. 15-8, asserting that the department had failed to present a prima facie case of neglect as to any of the children. The respondent father joined in this motion; the children's attorney took no position at that time.

DCF orally objected to the motion to dismiss, contending that the evidence was sufficient to establish neglect, because during the relevant adjudicatory period each child was denied proper educational care and attention in that she did not attend their school regularly, and thus was deprived of the opportunity to access the educational opportunities scheduled for her. In support of its objection, DCF relied in part upon General Statutes 10-184. The parents responded that the children received adequate educational attention during this period as evidenced by their grades and consistent promotions, so that the department's evidence of non-attendance at school could not be sufficient to support the petitions. . . .

. . . Through counsel, the children filed a brief on February 3, 2010 arguing that because "the state is unable to provide any express provisions in Connecticut statutory or case law providing for a finding of neglect under the circumstances of this case where absenteeism is the primary concern, the attorney for the children has no objection to the respondent parents' motion to dismiss." . . .

II

APPLICABLE LEGAL PRINCIPLES

Pursuant to Practice Book § 32a-3(a), "[t]he standard of proof applied in a neglect, uncared-for or dependency proceeding is a fair preponderance of the evidence." Thus, in this matter, DCF bears the burden of proving the petition's allegations by a fair preponderance of the evidence. The respondents claim that DCF's evidence, as presented in its case in chief, is insufficient to meet the burden assigned by Practice Book § 32a-3(a); the children's attorney has no objection to the granting of this motion to dismiss. DCF objects, arguing that it has met its designated burden by both direct and circumstantial evidence. . . .

Defining neglect for matters arising prior to January 1, 2010, § 46b-120(9) provides, in relevant part, that: "a child or youth may be found 'neglected' who . . . (B) is being denied proper care and attention . . . *educationally*. . . ." (Emphasis added.) As the Department has correctly observed, "[o]ur courts have not specifically addressed what constitutes educational neglect." Department's Memorandum filed February 2, 2010. Therefore, to assess the respondents' motion to dismiss in the context of the department's allegations of neglect, the court turns to the statutory and common law establishing Connecticut's expectations for the education of children of school age. In this state, education has long been recognized as being fundamental to the well-being of a child. "'Connecticut has for centuries recognized it as her right and duty to provide for the proper education of the young.' *State ex rel. Huntington v. Huntington School Committee*, 82 Conn. 563, 566, 74 A. 882. Education is so important that the state has made it compulsory through a requirement of attendance. General Statutes 10-184." *Horton v. Meskill*, 172 Conn. 615, 647, 376 A.2d 359 (1977). As a matter of public policy, General Statutes § 10-184 provides that "All parents and those who have the care of children shall bring them up in some lawful and honest employment and instruct them or cause them to be instructed in reading, writing, spelling, English grammar, geography, arithmetic and United States history and in citizenship, including a study of the town, state and federal governments." To implement this policy, § 10-184 further establishes that "each parent or other person having control of a child five years of age and over and under eighteen years of age *shall cause such child to attend a public school regularly during the hours and terms the public school in the district in which such child resides is in session*, unless such child is a high school graduate or the parent or person having control of such child is able to show that the child is elsewhere receiving equivalent instruction in the studies taught in the public schools." (Emphasis added.) Accordingly, a parent who fails to comply with the legislation implementing the public policy favoring education becomes subject to prosecution for violation of § 10-184 and imposition of the penalty established by General Statutes § 10-185, which provides: "Each day's failure on the part of a person to comply with any provision of section 10-184 shall be a distinct offense, punishable by a fine not exceeding twenty-five dollars."[6] ...

Connecticut's appellate courts have not yet opined as to whether a finding that children did not attend school, inferentially due to parents' failure to cause them to attend school in violation of General Statutes § 10-184, coupled with direct evidence that the children have to "catch up" with the rest of the class when they do attend school, is competent to establish a prima facie case of neglect, even where the children are performing on an average level academically and socially. However, the foregoing principles guide the court's application of General Statute § 46b-120(9), to the facts of this case, and support the conclusion that, if credited and the inferences remain unrebutted, such evidence would be legally sufficient to achieve the department's goal.

The reasoning employed by other Juvenile Courts in Connecticut which have considered the subject of whether a child's nonattendance at school is competent to establish educational neglect, albeit under circumstances different from those here presented, and without attention to the implications of § 10-184, supports this court's present determination....

Similarly, this court's finding that DCF has met its burden of establishing a prima facie case of educational neglect is consistent with rulings from other jurisdictions in which similar facts have been considered, albeit often in the context of differing legislative schemes, with like result. For instance, in *In re Welfare of B.A.B.*, 572 N.W.2d 776, 779 (Minn.App. 1998), the court held that a parent's persistent failure to secure a child's regular attendance at school supported an adjudication that the child was in need of protective services. The court rejected the argument that as a matter of law, it could not conclude that the parent was educationally neglectful because the absences had not met the threshold requirement for a finding of habitual truancy. *Id.* Similarly, in *Matter of J.W.*, 226 Mont. 491, 499, 736 P.2d 960 (1987), the court held that the parent's failure to ensure that the child attended school regularly constituted educational neglect. Although the Montana court made no findings that poor school attendance affected the child's academic performance, it rejected the parent's argument that the child's poor school attendance was a matter for the school authorities, and not for child protection services, and based its determination that the child was subject to educational neglect based on the fact that the mother was responsible for the child's excessive absences. In *In re Dareth O.*, 304 App. Div.2d 667, 668, 758 N.Y.S.2d 372 (2003), the court held that unrebutted evidence of excessive school absences was sufficient to establish the mother's educational neglect in the child protective proceeding, without discussing any adverse impact caused by the child's excessive absences upon her school performance. In *In re Ashley X.*, 50 App. Div.3d 1194, 1195, 854 N.Y.S.2d 794 (2008), however, the court properly identified educationally neglected when the child had multiple absences and the teacher indicated that the child's learning could improve through regular attendance. Addressing the subject of a causal effect upon the child due to nonattendance at school, the Ashley X. court reasoned that in New York, educational neglect "may be premised upon proof that a child has a significant rate of unexcused absences from school which detrimentally affects the child's education, and

6. The court notes that our "[s]tatutes also describe the responsibilities of school children to attend school." *Burns v. Board of Education*, 228 Conn. 640, 649, 638 A.2d 1 (1994). The Department is clearly aware of the availability of support for truant children that is available to Families with Service Needs (FWSN) petitions. The evidence in DCF's case in chief was void, however, of any effort on DCF's behalf to pursue FWSN petitions for some or all of the children relevant to attendance during the 2007–2008 and/or 2008–2009 school years.

that the requisite education was not provided from a source other than the public school...." (Citations omitted.) *Id.* Even the reasoning used by the court *In re D.H.*, 178 Ga.App. 119, 342 S.E.2d 367 (1986), cited by the respondent mother, is consistent with this court's conclusion that because § 10-184 effectively requires school attendance by the children who are the subject of the pending petition, the department may prove neglect through evidence allowing the inference that the respondent parents did not cause Amurah, Kayla, Mylin, Jada and/or Soleil "to attend a public school regularly during the hours and terms the public school in the district in which such child resides is in session."

A finding that the petitioner has presented prima facie evidence of educational neglect does not eliminate the opportunity for a respondent parent to present explanatory or even exculpatory evidence, or to attack the quality and impact of the direct and circumstantial evidence submitted during the case in chief. To the contrary, in this case, DCF's evidence of educational neglect may properly be subject to rebuttal by other evidence of events relating the relevant period preceding April 17, 2009 the adjudicatory date. For instance, in *In re Jamol F.*, 24 Misc.3d 772, 784, 878 N.Y.S.2d 581 (2009), the New York family court held that the parent had rebutted the protective services' prima facie case of educational neglect. In New York, "[p]roof that a minor child is not attending public or parochial school in the district in which the parent resides makes out a prima facie case of educational neglect.... Proof of a prima facie case does not, however, create a conclusive presumption of parental culpability or risk of impairment. It simply creates a permissible inference that the finder-of-fact may choose to draw upon all the evidence in the record. It does not compel a finding in accordance with that inference...." (Citations omitted.) *Id.*, at 781–82, 878 N.Y.S.2d 581. Thus, the court found that the child's excessive unexcused absences from school did not constitute educational neglect because they were not caused by the parent's behavior, but rather that the mother was making reasonable efforts to discipline her son for not attending school, attempting to obtain an appropriate alternate placement, and maintaining contact with school officials. *Id.*, at 785, 878 N.Y.S.2d 581.

The respondent father has argued that "more than a mere per se violation of [§ 10-184] or an arbitrary number of absences must be shown to establish that a child has been neglected. The state must provide evidence of a detrimental effect on a child based upon the conduct alleged to be neglectful to sustain its burden." Father's Memorandum of Law, filed February 2, 2010. In view of the clear and explicit mandate of § 10-184, and in recognition of § 10-185's criminal penalties as contemplated for a parent's violation of the statute requiring that a child be caused to attend school, the court finds that the element of "detrimental effect" is not essential to a finding of neglect at the adjudicatory stage.[9] Even if a finding of detrimental effect is, however, a mandatory element of a finding of educational neglect in this state, as discussed in Part III, the department's evidence thus far, if credited, is competent to establish that each child has in fact been subjected to a negative impact as a result of nonattendance and/or tardiness at school. Accordingly, this aspect of the respondents' argument cannot support the motion to dismiss.

9. In reaching this determination, the court fully credits the aspect of the respondent father's causation argument that would be relevant to the subject of disposition upon a finding of educational neglect; in the dispositional phase, the court would be required to assess, among other things, the effect if any of educational neglect upon his or her status qua commitment, placement, protective disposition or service implementation through the issuance of the specific steps contemplated by § 46b-129(j).

For the foregoing reasons, the court concludes that in Connecticut, a determination [of] educational neglect can be proved by competent direct and/or circumstantial evidence that a child failed to attend a public school regularly during the hours and terms of that public school because a parent failed to cause that child to so attend school. With or without a resultant adverse impact upon the child's educational experience, such a determination would be fully consistent with the edict of § 10-184 and with the fundamental elements of our state's child protection legislation as a whole.[10]

III

RESOLUTION OF THE PARTIES' CLAIMS...

... [T]he following general findings could be made from the evidence adduced in DCF's case in chief, relevant to the motion to dismiss, and/or through reasonable inferences drawn therefrom: that the children have been enrolled in public elementary and middle schools in their city of residence; that there were many days during the 2008–2009 year, prior to the April 2009 adjudicatory date, when children at issue did not attend school and/or were tardy; that as a result of their tardiness or missing school days, the children were impacted as they were not exposed to the information and/or skill development that had been taught in their absence and were obligated to "catch up" with their classmates; that the children did not consistently demonstrate their full academic potential and failed to reach this goal because their tardiness and/or absences interfered with their academic progress; and that the children were consistently promoted to the next grade notwithstanding these factors.

As to Amurah, specific evidence is sufficient to support the further conclusion that she was enrolled in 8th grade during the 2008–2009 school year. During the first three quarters of that year, Amurah missed approximately 19 days of school, representing 12 absences, six days of suspension, and one dismissal by the nurse; in addition, she was tardy on 24 days. During the second quarter of 8th grade, during which Amurah missed at least 7 days of school, her average in Integrated Language Arts fell from a B+ to a C-; her grade in music fell from an A to an F.[14] If credited, then, through the evidence applicable to Amurah's status, DCF has met its burden of proving that because this child did not attend school regularly during the hours and terms the school in which she was enrolled was in session, she was adversely impacted from an educational perspective, and did not receive adequate educational attention.[15] Thus, the evidence is sufficient to support the determination that the petitioner has made out a prima facie case of educational neglect as to Amurah....

10. ... [T]he legislative history of Public Acts 2000, No. 00-157, §§ 1 and 8, which amended § 10-184... reveals a focused discussion upon the importance of ensuring that children in this state obtain a high school diploma. This discussion centered around the serious financial and social impact of a child's failure to obtain a high school diploma, and included reference to the correlation between not obtaining a high school diploma and the potential for a child's future incarceration.

14. The court notes that for the 2008–2009 school year, which includes time extending beyond the adjudicatory period, Amurah was awarded a C+ in Integrated Language Arts. Despite A's awarded in the first, third and fourth quarters of this school year, Amurah's final grade in Music was a D+, demonstrating the marked impact of the F earned in the second quarter.

15. The evidence does not permit the inference that any of the children's grades were lowered as a disciplinary measure in response to her repeated absences.

As to Kayla, specific evidence is sufficient to support the further conclusion that during the 2007–2008 school [year], when she was enrolled in 6th grade, Kayla missed approximately 32 days of school, representing 31 absences and 1 day of suspension. In addition, she was tardy on at least 47 days. Although she received A's in some of her 6th grade classes, and improved her social studies grades over the school year, her absences interfered with her progress in science; Kayla received a C+ for the first quarter of 6th grade science, but received a final grade of D-. Kayla's Integrated Language Arts quarterly grades included 3 Cs and a C+; Kayla was capable of better work, but her attendance needed to improve to achieve the goal of improved performance in school.

Kayla was enrolled in 7th grade during the 2008–2009 school year. During the first three quarters of this school year, she missed approximately 19 days of school, representing 19 absences, and she was tardy on 26 days. During the second quarter, during which Kayla was absent at least 6 days, her average in Integrated Language Arts fell from a B to a C+; her grade in Music fell from an A to an F; and her grade in Science fell from an A to a C-. Despite the laudatory comments concerning Kayla's effort and class participation in 7th grade, if credited, through the totality of the evidence applicable to Kayla's status in a reasonable time period prior to the adjudicatory date, DCF has met its burden of proving that because this child did not attend school regularly during the hours and terms the school in which she was enrolled was in session, she was adversely impacted from an educational perspective, and did not receive adequate educational attention. Thus, the evidence is sufficient to support the determination that the petitioner has made out a prima facie case of educational neglect as to Kayla....

As to Soleil, specific evidence is sufficient to support the further conclusion that during the first three quarters of the 2008–2009 school year, when she was enrolled in 4th grade, this child was absent from school on approximately 22 days; in addition, she was tardy 33 times. In 4th grade, Soleil performed at an average level in her reading group, was accepted by her peers, got along with everyone and was not ostracized, and seemed to be "on target" with regard to expectations for 4th graders at her school. Nonetheless, these absences had an impact upon her performance and grades; without the benefit of contemporaneous classroom instruction, Soleil was required to "catch up" on work the other students had performed and skills they had learned in class while she was not present.[16] Despite the positive comments concerning Soleil's effort and class participation in [4]th grade, if credited, through the totality of the evidence applicable to this child's status in a reasonable time period prior to the adjudicatory date, DCF has met its burden of proving that because this child did not attend school regularly during the hours and terms the school in which she was enrolled was in session, she also was adversely impacted from an educational perspective, and did not receive adequate educational attention. Thus, the evidence is sufficient to support the determination that the petitioner has made out a prima facie case of educational neglect as to Soleil....

As to Jada, specific evidence is sufficient to support the further conclusion that during the first three quarters of the 2008–2009 school year, when she was enrolled in 2nd grade, this child was absent approximately 27 times; in addition, she was tardy on 36 days, and was dismissed by

16. Soleil's 4th grade teacher wrote weekly notes to the respondent parents explaining that the child's tardiness and absences were keeping her from improving. The respondent parents' receipt of the notes was apparent as Soleil returned them to school bearing the respondents' signatures.

the nurse on 5 occasions.[17] During that period, Jada's teacher attempted to reach the respondent parents by phone, and through the school nurse, to discuss the impact these absences and tardy arrivals were having upon the child. As those efforts were unsuccessful, the teacher frequently wrote notes home to Jada's parents during this period instructing the respondents on the importance of getting the child to school regularly, and on time. Because she was tardy and absent so often, Jada missed lessons that had been taught while she was not in class, missed morning sessions in which the students reviewed what they had learned on prior days, missed opportunities to build upon past instruction, and did not reach the academic level she otherwise could have achieved. Although some of her grades did improve during that school year, if credited, through the totality of the evidence applicable to Jada's status in a reasonable time period prior to the adjudicatory date, DCF has met its burden of proving that because this child did not attend school regularly during the hours and terms the school in which she was enrolled was in session, as she was adversely impacted from an educational perspective, she did not receive adequate educational attention. (Ex. N.) Thus, the evidence is sufficient to support the determination that the petitioner has made out a prima facie case of educational neglect as to Jada....

Finally, as to Mylin, specific evidence is sufficient to support the further conclusion that during the first three quarters of the 2008–2009 school year, when she was a kindergartener, this child missed approximately 16 days of the scheduled morning-only classes, and was tardy on 36 occasions. Mylin's tardiness interrupted the structure of the kindergarten curriculum being taught to her; she missed between fifteen to thirty half-hour classes during this period, and did not return most homework. Although she socialized well and was chronologically young for kindergarten placement, Mylin's school performance would have improved if she had better attendance. If credited, then, through the evidence applicable to Mylin's status during a reasonable time prior to the adjudicatory date, DCF has met its burden of proving that because this child did not attend school regularly during the hours and terms the school in which she was enrolled was in session, she was adversely impacted from an educational perspective, and did not receive adequate educational attention. Thus, the evidence is sufficient to support the determination that the petitioner has made out a prima facie case of educational neglect as to Mylin....

IV

CONCLUSION...

...Considering a similar case in which a parent's rights to make decisions about a child's education was placed at issue by the child's non-attendance at school, the Supreme Court in Alaska has stated, "[w]e agree that the right of parents to the care, custody and control of their children is an important and substantial right protected by, although not specifically enumerated in, both the United States and Alaska Constitutions.... While parental rights may be

17. At least two of these dismissals were related to head lice with which Jada was affected. Head lice is a not-uncommon problem affecting elementary school children; its mundane status of this condition is apparent in its status as a line item upon the form used by the school nurse to record interactions with students. The school nurse had first noted that Jada was affected by head lice on September 14, 2006. On several occasions during the 2006–2007, 2007–2008, and 2008–2009 school years, the school nurse had called Jada's parent and provided both instructions and shampoo to address the head lice and/or nits that were affecting the child. Jada was seen by the school due to her scratching or noted presence of head lice or nits on approximately three occasions during the 2007–2008 school year; and on approximately nine occasions during the 2008–2009 school year.

of like importance, there is an additional consideration involved. *The parents' constitutional right to the care and custody of their children must be balanced against the rights of their children to an adequate home and education.*" (Citations omitted; emphasis added.) *In the Matter of S.D., Jr.*, 549 P.2d 1190, 1200–01 (Alaska 1976).

In the present case, neither the respondent parents nor the children have submitted, and the court is unaware of, any pertinent Connecticut authority that either would render the parent's right to make decisions concerning the care and control of his or her children superior to the children's right to education, as established by the legislation discussed above, nor that § 10-184's requirement for parents to cause their children to attend school regularly unreasonably interferes with the aforementioned constitutional rights. Accordingly, as did the Alaskan Supreme Court, this court has balanced the respondent parents' constitutional right to the care and custody of their children, and finds that this right is outweighed, under the circumstances of this case, by the children's right to such educational opportunities as are made available to them through attendance at school regularly during the hours and terms the school in the district in which the children reside is in session....

...Accordingly, despite the respondent parents' protests to the contrary, the court finds that DCF has submitted evidence which, if credited, is sufficient to support its allegation of educational neglect as to each child.

NOTES AND QUESTIONS

1. What does the court say constitutes educational neglect? Do you think the children were harmed by their tardiness and absences? Did the court find that the number of absences and tardies was excessive? Of what relevance was the fact that Jada had head lice?

2. *Homeschooling.* Homeschooling has grown in popularity since the 1980s and now is legal in all fifty states. Approximately 1.5 million students were homeschooled in 2007, or 2.9 percent of the school-age population, a 74-percent increase since 1999. Of homeschooled students, 77 percent were white, and 89 percent lived in two-parent households. Of homeschooling parents, 36 percent identified the need to provide religious or moral schooling as the most important reason for homeschooling their children. Nat'l Ctr. for Educ. Statistics, U.S. Dep't of Educ., Issue Brief No. 2009-030, 1.5 Million Homeschooled Students in the United States in 2007 (2008), http://nces.ed.gov/pubs2009/2009030.pdf. Why has homeschooling become so popular, and should the state be able to regulate it? Consider the next excerpt when formulating your answers.

Kimberly A. Yuracko, *Education off the Grid: Constitutional Constraints on Homeschooling*, 96 Cal. L. Rev. 123, 126–128, 128–129, 130, 155, 180, 182–184 (2008).

By the early 1990's, however, homeschooling had expanded and divided into two distinct movements: one secular and the other conservative Christian. Mitchell Stevens, who has performed the most extensive sociological study of contemporary homeschooling to date, explains: "[H]ome schoolers were divided into two quite different movement worlds. They read different publications, attended different support groups, and heeded different kinds of advice about how to act politically." These two factions were not, however, of equal size and strength. The Christian homeschooling movement came to dominate its secular counterpart in size, profile and political influence. In other words, while homeschoolers themselves continue to be a diverse lot, the homeschooling movement has become defined and driven by its conservative Christian majority.

At the heart of the Christian homeschooling movement is the Home School Legal Defense Association (HSLDA). HSLDA's commitment to ensuring parents' unfettered right to homeschool flows from two core ideological beliefs. The first is a belief in parental control—indeed ownership—of children. "Parental rights are under siege," HSLDA warns. "The basic fundamental freedom of parents to raise their children hangs in the balance. Have we forgotten whose children they are anyway? They are a God-given responsibility to parents," HSLDA proclaims. Indeed, Michael Farris, an HSLDA founder and its former president, argues that "[t]he right of parents to control the education of their children is so fundamental that it deserves the extraordinary level of protection as an absolute right." The second is a belief in the need for Christian families to separate and shield their children from harmful secular social values. Public schools, Farris cautions, have been "promoting values that are questionable or clearly wrong: the acceptability of homosexuality as an alternative lifestyle; the acceptability of premarital sex as long as it is 'safe'; the acceptability of relativistic moral standards." Such indoctrination, he argues, is "probably more dangerous to our ultimate freedom than armed enemies." Fortunately, according to Farris, the moral obligation to protect one's child from such indoctrination is protected by a constitutional right. "[P]arents have the constitutional right to obey the dictates of God concerning education of their children."

Motivated by these beliefs, HSLDA—along with the National Center for Home Education (NCHE), HSLDA's service arm designed to link, inform and organize state homeschool leaders, and the Congressional Action Program (CAP), HSLDA's lobbying organization—has become a powerful political force. For the last two decades HSLDA has opposed virtually all state oversight and regulation of homeschooling. The clout of HSLDA and its grassroots Christian activists is now well-recognized in political circles. Indeed, in 2000 former U.S. Representative Bill Godling from Pennsylvania, the former chair of the House Committee of Education and the Workforce, called homeschoolers "the most effective educational lobby on Capitol Hill." ...

... Over the past 15 years, HSLDA has devoted its resources to challenging teacher certification requirements for homeschool teachers, subject matter requirements for homeschools, testing requirements for homeschooled children, and home inspection visits of homeschools. As a result of HSLDA's work, state laws regulating homeschooling have become increasingly lenient. According to HSLDA, only twenty-five states presently require standardized testing and evaluation of homeschooled students. Moreover, ten states labeled by HSLDA as having the lowest regulation of homeschooling do not even require homeschooling parents to notify the state of their intent to homeschool.... States are not only looking the other way when homeschoolers do not comply with state laws, but actually changing their laws to grant even greater freedom to homeschoolers....

... [S]tates have an obligation, stemming from both state and federal constitutions to provide children with a basic minimum level of education. When homeschooling parents take on the public function of providing education, they become bound by this obligation. States violate their own constitutional obligations when they permit homeschooling families to reject this basic minimum....

...[I]n addition to a basic minimum level of education, some students may have a constitutionally protected right, stemming from the Equal Protection Clause, to an education above the basic minimum. I have argued, more specifically, and in gendered terms, that the Equal Protection Clause prohibits state authorization of extreme inequality in the educations provided to homeschooled girls and boys within the same family....

The extent to which a basic minimum level of education actually infringes on parental autonomy depends to some degree, of course, on how states interpret their own required minima. If states conceive of the basic minimum as requiring only those skills necessary for the barest conception of citizenship—namely the ability to vote—then the minimum probably requires no more than basic literacy. Conceived in this way, the minimum would impose truly negligible limitations on parental autonomy. Parents would be required to teach their children to read, but beyond this they would be free to educate, miseducate and indoctrinate their children as they saw fit.

The more likely scenario, however, is one in which states interpret their education clauses as requiring not only that children learn to read but that they acquire both a set of skills and base of knowledge necessary for effective participation in the market and substantive participation in the democratic process. This scenario is both more interesting and complicated in terms of its implications for illiberal parents. It may be that the basic minimum level of education is not in fact compatible with any and all sorts of fact or value teaching. Some kinds of teaching may not just supplement the basic minimum level of education, but may in a sense depress it. The basic minimum may, for example, simply preclude the teaching of certain counterfactual claims such as the natural superiority and inferiority of the races or the danger of intellectual development to women's health. In addition, the basic minimum may limit the extent to which parents may teach their children idiosyncratic and illiberal beliefs and values without labeling or framing them as such. In other words, the minimum may require that if parents want to teach against the enlightenment they have to label what they are doing as such.

Illiberal homeschoolers may, then, be correct in their contention that even minimal education requirements impair their ability to effectively direct their children's education and socialization. This contention, however, seems to do no more than reveal the lie of liberalism generally. A liberal society cannot in fact be wholly neutral toward competing conceptions of the good. Liberalism does involve at least minimal commitments to rationality and autonomy. It is not surprising then that both federal and state constitutions are themselves not wholly neutral with respect to competing conceptions of the good, particularly when it comes to children.

3. Is homeschooling a bad idea? Should the state regulate homeschooling to the extent that it regulates public schooling? Should the same standards apply? Not all states look the other way when it comes to homeschooling. Under New York law, for example, parents must notify the school superintendent of their intention to homeschool, complete a detailed individualized home-instruction plan that must be approved by the school superintendent, submit quarterly reports, provide instruction in certain required subjects, meet attendance requirements, and perform an annual assessment, among other things. N.Y. Compiled Codes R. & Regs. tit. 8, § 100.10 (2011). In *In re William A.A.*, 807 N.Y.S.2d 181 (App. Div. 2005), the mother removed her special-needs son from public school because she did not agree with his educational placement. While she worked during the day, she left her son at home alone to do his homework, although his ODD diagnosis and reading disability indicated that he needed structure and assistance. Although the mother testified that she taught her son for several hours after she returned home

from work, she had no written records to support her claim, nor did she comply with other mandatory homeschooling requirements, which included maintaining records, filing reports, and performing an annual assessment. She also failed to obtain educational testing to support her view that her son's educational placement was inappropriate. The court found that the state had established a *prima facie* case of educational neglect.

xii. Derivative neglect

IN RE JANIYAH T.
New York Family Court
906 N.Y.S.2d 780 (2010)

EMILY M. OLSHANSKY, J.

Amanda T. (hereinafter "respondent mother") is the mother of the two subject children, Janiyah T., born July 22, 2004 and Kamiyah C., born September 27, 2007. Lateek C. (hereinafter "respondent father") is the father of Kamiyah and a person legally responsible for Janiyah. On January 30, 2007, at approximately 11:30 PM, New York City Children's Services (hereinafter "NYCCS") removed the subject children from the care of the respondents without a court order pursuant to Family Court Act § 1021.

On February 1, 2008, NYCCS filed abuse petitions against both respondents. The petitions allege that, on or about January 30, 2007, respondent father inflicted excessive corporal punishment on Janiyah causing marks, bruises and two black eyes. Further, the petitions allege that in November 2007, respondent father hit Janiyah with a belt in the face causing bruising. In addition, the petitions allege that respondent mother failed to provide adequate care and supervision for Janiyah by allowing respondent father to remain in the home with the children after November 2007 when she learned that he had beaten Janiyah. Finally, the petitions allege that Kamiyah is a derivatively abused and neglected child by virtue of the abuse of Janiyah.

On the day the petitions were filed, this Court granted the request of NYCCS for a remand of the children. Thereafter, respondent mother requested a Family Court Act § 1028 hearing seeking the immediate return of the children. The matter was resolved without a hearing by JHO Staton and the children were paroled to respondent mother on the condition that she comply with Family Preservation Program (FPP) services, complete parenting skills and anger management programs and enforce the temporary order of protection entered against respondent father. The temporary order of protection excluded respondent father from the home, directed that he not commit any family offenses against either child and that he stay away from Janiyah. He was granted supervised visitation with Kamiyah.

LEGAL ANALYSIS…

NYCCS Has Established a Prima Facie Case of Neglect, not Abuse, against Respondent Father/Person Legally Responsible as to Janiyah

A parent or person legally responsible is liable for the abuse of a child pursuant to Family Court Act § 1012(e)(i) or (e)(ii), when either they inflict or allow to be inflicted upon such child, physical injury by other than accidental means which causes or creates a substantial risk of death, or serious or protracted disfigurement, or protracted impairment of physical or emotional health or protracted loss or impairment of the function of any bodily organ, or create or allow to be created a substantial risk of physical injury to such child by other than accidental means which would likely cause death or serious or protracted disfigurement or the protracted impairment of physical or emotional health or the protracted loss or the impairment of the function of any bodily organ.

The Family Court Act defines a neglected child as "one whose physical, mental or emotional condition has been impaired or is in imminent danger of becoming impaired as a result of the failure of (respondent) to exercise a minimum degree of care" (Family Ct Act § 1012(f)(i)). The physical impairment referred to in FCA § 1012(f)(i) involves a lower threshold of resultant harm than the serious physical injury required in abuse cases....

The neglect statute establishes a minimum baseline of proper care for children and under this standard parental behavior is evaluated objectively according to how a reasonable and prudent parent would have acted. A parent must exercise this minimum degree of care so as not to place the child at imminent risk of impairment. In order to establish neglect, NYCCS must show by a preponderance of the credible evidence that the child has been harmed or threatened with harm. In the absence of such proof, the statutory requirement of impairment or imminent danger of impairment will not be satisfied and neglect will not be established.

NYCCS is not required to prove a course of conduct. It is well-settled that a single incident may be sufficient to establish neglect where a parent fails to exercise reasonable care and as a result the child's physical, mental or emotional condition has been impaired or is in imminent danger of becoming impaired.

This is particularly true where the parent was aware or should have been aware of the intrinsic danger of their actions and the situation.

Respondent Father Neglected Janiyah

In the instant case, the credible evidence adduced during fact-finding established that respondent father hit Janiyah on two separate occasions, twice leaving a bruise or other marks on her face. Nevertheless, since the unimpeached expert testimony of Dr. Hosneara Masub, M.D. established that the dark marks around Janiyah's eyes were not the result of inflicted trauma—but instead an allergic reaction—NYCCS has failed to establish that respondent father inflicted injuries which "created a substantial risk of death, or serious or protracted disfigurement, or protracted impairment of physical or emotional health or protracted loss or impairment of the function of any bodily organ." The evidence does, however, establish the lower threshold of harm required to sustain a finding of neglect.

It is undisputed that in November 2007, respondent father hit Janiyah with a belt in the face causing bruising. According to respondent father's testimony, the child, then three years old, was disrespectful and unresponsive to his efforts to speak with her. Nevertheless, he testified that he did not mean to hit her in the face and that he only meant to hit her with the belt on her hand. He stated that he hit her in the face with the belt when she moved. Apparently, he did not expect that she would move.

It is the view of this Court, that these actions were inconsistent with how a reasonable and prudent parent would have acted under the circumstances and that, as a result, the child's physical, mental and emotional condition were impaired or placed at imminent risk of impairment. A reasonably prudent parent under these circumstances would not have struck a three-year-old child with a belt with sufficient force to leave marks. Even if the Court were to accept respondent's assertions that he hit the child with the belt in the face by accident and that he only meant to hit her on the hand, the result would be the same since the force used was excessive and it resulted in marks on the child's face and fear of respondent father. In addition, the risk that a three year old would move when she is threatened with a belt and therefore sustain bruising on some other part of her body is something that respondent knew or should have known was one of the inherent dangers of hitting a small child with a belt.

Janiyah also described a second incident when respondent father again hit her in the face. Janiyah told the NYCCS caseworker that the second incident occurred on January 30, 2008. She said that during the second incident, respondent father hit her in the face, legs and back. The child's out of court statements are adequately corroborated by the caseworker's testimony describing the bruise on the child's nose. The statements are further corroborated by the caseworker's testimony about the child's fearful and distressed reaction when she realized that they were driving near respondent father's home.

Janiyah's statements are also corroborated by the testimony of Dr. Hosneara Masub, M.D. Dr. Masub was [subpoenaed] by NYCCs however, after she appeared in court and was interviewed by counsel, NYCCS decided not to actually call her. Instead, Dr. Masub was called as respondent father's witness and without objection was qualified as an expert in pediatric medicine. She testified that she saw the child on February 12, 2008. She testified that she observed the mark on Janiyah's face as well as the dark circles around her eyes. She testified, however, that in her opinion, within a reasonable degree of medical certainty, the dark marks under the child's eyes were the result of an allergic reaction—not inflicted trauma. According to Dr. Masub, the other mark on the child's face was not the result of an allergic reaction. Her testimony was unrebutted.

Respondent father asserts that Dr. Masub's testimony undermines the child's credibility and supports his claim that the second beating did not occur. The Court rejects this assertion. Although Dr. Masub's testimony establishes that the January 30, 2008 incident did not cause the dark circles under the child's eyes, it did not establish that the incident never occurred. In fact, the doctor's testimony provides additional corroboration for the child's statement that respondent father hit her and caused a mark on her face. In the Court's view, these incidents are sufficient to establish by a preponderance of the evidence that Janiyah's physical, mental or emotional condition were impaired or placed at imminent danger of impairment sufficient to establish neglect based on excessive corporal punishment. Accordingly, the allegations of abuse are dismissed and pursuant to Family Court Act § 1051(b), the Court amends the petitions to conform to the proof and enters a finding of neglect pursuant to Family Court Act § 1012(f)(i)(B).

Respondent Mother Neglected Janiyah

In the instant case, respondent mother was out of the home in November 2007, when respondent father hit three-year-old Janiyah in the face with a belt leaving a mark. Upon her return home, both respondent father and Janiyah told her about what happened. Despite that knowledge, she failed to take any action to protect Janiyah and ensure that respondent father did not strike her again.

Furthermore, when respondent mother was first interviewed by NYCCS, she denied that the 2007 incident had taken place. Likewise, when Janiyah was first interviewed, she was reluctant to reveal what had happened. She told the caseworker that it was "a secret" and that "Mommy told me not to tell the truth." Respondent mother did not testify at the fact-finding hearing. Accordingly, the Court draws the strongest negative inference against her that the evidence will permit, that is, that she realized Janiyah was at risk when she was with respondent father but failed to immediately take the necessary steps to protect her.

Since the allegations of abuse by respondent father have been dismissed, the allegations that respondent mother failed to protect Janiyah from abuse are likewise dismissed. Nevertheless, pursuant to Family Court Act § 1051(b), the Court amends the petitions to conform to the proof and enters a finding of neglect against respondent mother pursuant to Family Court Act § 1012(f)(i)(B) based on her failure to take appropriate steps after the November 2007 incident to protect her daughter from future acts of excessive corporal punishment inflicted by respondent father.

NYCCS Has Established a Prima Facie Case of Derivative Neglect against Respondent Father as to Kamiyah but not against Respondent Mother

Family Court Act § 1046(a)(i) provides that "proof of the abuse or neglect of one child shall be admissible evidence on the issue of the abuse or neglect of any other child of... the respondent." Even in the absence of direct evidence of actual abuse or neglect of a second child, a derivative finding may be made where the evidence as to the directly abused or neglected child demonstrates such an impaired level of parental judgment as to create a substantial risk of harm for any child in their care, thereby making such a child neglected under Family Court Act § 1012(f)(i)(B).

Nevertheless, although the statute requires that evidence as to the neglect of one child be considered on the issue of the neglect of another child in the home, such evidence is not conclusive and does not establish a prima facie case of neglect of another child in the parent's care. In other words, the fact that one child has been neglected, standing alone, is insufficient without more to support a finding that the child's sibling is also neglected.

The determinative factor is whether the nature of the neglect, notably its duration and the circumstances surrounding its commission evidences such a fundamental flaw in respondent's understanding of the duties of parenthood that it can reasonably be concluded that the condition still exists. Unless the underlying finding provides a reliable indicator that the sibling's physical, mental or emotional condition is in imminent danger of becoming impaired a finding of derivative neglect cannot stand. In considering whether to enter a derivative finding, the courts have considered and attempted to balance a number of somewhat overlapping factors. Included among them are the following: [whether the underlying neglect was based on a single incident or a course of conduct; the seriousness of the underlying acts of abuse and neglect and the role played by the parent; whether the underlying conditions leading to the underlying finding have changed; whether the parent has completed all recommended services; whether there is direct evidence that the other children in the home were actually harmed or placed at imminent risk of harm].

The Instant Case

Application of these factors to the case at bar, leads this Court to conclude that respondent father derivatively neglected Kamiyah, although respondent mother did not. In reaching this conclusion, the Court has considered each of the factors outlined above in light of the testimony and documentary evidence introduced.

First, the Court has considered that the underlying neglect is based on acts of commission by respondent father. Second, the Court has considered that the excessive corporal punishment inflicted by respondent father upon the three-year-old subject child was fairly serious and in response to minor infractions. Third, the Court has considered that the punishment inflicted by respondent father was not an isolated incident but a pattern that he believed was justified. During the fact-finding, he testified that he struck the child because "children should not be disrespectful of adults" and "that was how I was brought up." In the Court's view, he failed to take full responsibility for his actions. Instead, he blamed the child and continued to believe that his actions were justified. Fourth, although the underlying finding is based on incidents that occurred in January 2008 and November 2007—24 and 21 months prior to the conclusion of the fact-finding hearing—respondent father introduced no evidence of his rehabilitation. Indeed, despite the passage of time, respondent father still has not addressed—let alone overcome—the problems that led to the filing of the original petition. In fact, at the time that the fact-finding concluded, he had not even started parenting skills or anger management—let alone completed them.

It is the view of this Court that the duration, seriousness and other circumstances surrounding the original neglect evidence a fundamental flaw in respondent father's understanding of the duties of parenthood to the extent that it can reasonably be inferred that the conditions that led to the underlying incident still exist. Accordingly, even without direct evidence of neglect as to Kamiyah, the Court finds that her physical, mental or emotional condition are at risk of impairment while she is in the care of respondent father.

In contrast, NYCCS has failed to introduce sufficient evidence to establish a *prima facie* case of derivative neglect against respondent mother. In reaching this conclusion, the Court has considered that the underlying neglect by respondent mother is not based on her physical or sexual abuse of the child; nor is it based on her inflicting excessive corporal punishment.

In addition, the Court has considered that the underlying neglect finding against respondent mother is not based on a course of conduct. Instead, it is based on a limited incident when she failed protect Janiyah from further acts of corporal punishment despite her knowledge of the November 2007 incident.

Further, the Court has considered that respondent mother's circumstances have changed significantly during the last two years. During that time, respondent mother has separated from respondent father and cooperated with all orders entered by this Court. The children have been home with her since March 12, 2008. Since then, the children have been well cared for and there have been no further incidents. The children have been described as clean and well-dressed. They have had no bruises or other signs of maltreatment. They have reported that their mother takes good care of them.

Moreover, the Court has considered that respondent mother has fully cooperated with services. In fact, by April 2009, she had completed a 12-week parenting skills program and a 12-week anger management program at Community Counseling and Mediation. On October 12, 2009, after respondent father came to her home in violation of the Court's order, respondent mother contacted the police and thereafter sought an order of protection against him. By October 28, 2009, she had fully complied with FPP services.

In other words, the circumstances surrounding the original neglect do not evidence a fundamental flaw in respondent mother's understanding of the duties of parenthood. Although respondent mother's conduct toward her daughter Janiyah fell below a minimum degree of care when she failed to take action to protect her after the November 2007 incident, her conduct on that occasion is not a reliable indicator that any other child in her care is at imminent risk of impairment. Indeed, the evidence adduced is to the contrary and the Law Guardian supports the dismissal of the derivative allegations.

Finally, the Court rejects any suggestion that respondent mother's failure to testify requires a different result. Although her failure to testify warrants the drawing of the strongest negative inference that the evidence will allow, that inference cannot provide a missing element of proof where it otherwise does not exist. In the instant case, the mother's failure to testify is insufficient to establish derivative neglect since the underlying finding does not provide a reliable indicator that Kamiyah's physical, mental or emotional condition is in imminent danger of becoming impaired.

NOTES AND QUESTIONS

1. Why does the court find that the father is neglectful but not abusive? How could the court simply substitute neglect for abuse? Does the court's finding violate due process concepts? In what way? Is it possible that neglect becomes a catchall category when the state is unable to prove abuse? If so, might that explain why neglect cases account for such a significant percentage of maltreatment cases?

2. What is derivative neglect? Was there any evidence that Kamiyah was harmed? Does it seem that the court is speculating that harm may occur in the absence of any real evidence of harm? Is that constitutionally problematic?

C. EVIDENTIARY ISSUES

MARYLAND V. CRAIG
Supreme Court of the United States
497 U.S. 836 (1990)

JUSTICE O'CONNOR delivered the opinion of the Court.

This case requires us to decide whether the Confrontation Clause of the Sixth Amendment categorically prohibits a child witness in a child abuse case from testifying against a defendant at trial, outside the defendant's physical presence, by one-way closed circuit television.

I

In October 1986, a Howard County grand jury charged respondent, Sandra Ann Craig, with child abuse, first and second degree sexual offenses, perverted sexual practice, assault, and battery. The named victim in each count was a 6-year-old girl who, from August 1984 to June 1986, had attended a kindergarten and prekindergarten center owned and operated by Craig.

In March 1987, before the case went to trial, the State sought to invoke a Maryland statutory procedure that permits a judge to receive, by one-way closed circuit television, the testimony of a child witness who is alleged to be a victim of child abuse.[1] To invoke the procedure, the trial judge must first "determin[e] that testimony by the child victim in the courtroom will result in the child suffering serious emotional distress such that the child cannot reasonably communicate." Md.Cts. & Jud.Proc.Code Ann. § 9-102(a)(1)(ii) (1989). Once the procedure is invoked, the child witness, prosecutor, and defense counsel withdraw to a separate room; the judge, jury, and defendant remain in the courtroom. The child witness is then examined and cross-examined in the separate room, while a video monitor records and displays the witness' testimony to those in the courtroom. During this time the witness cannot see the defendant. The defendant remains in electronic communication with defense counsel, and objections may be made and ruled on as if the witness were testifying in the courtroom.

In support of its motion invoking the one-way closed circuit television procedure, the State presented expert testimony that the named victim as well as a number of other children who were alleged to have been sexually abused by Craig, would suffer "serious emotional distress such that [they could not] reasonably communicate," § 9-102(a)(1)(ii), if required to testify in the courtroom. The Maryland Court of Appeals characterized the evidence as follows:

> "The expert testimony in each case suggested that each child would have some or considerable difficulty in testifying in Craig's presence. For example, as to one child, the expert said that what 'would cause him the most anxiety would be to testify in front of Mrs. Craig....' The child

1. Maryland Cts. & Jud.Proc.Code Ann. § 9-102 of the Courts and Judicial Proceedings Article of the Annotated Code of Maryland (1989) provides in full:

"(a)(1) In a case of abuse of a child as defined in § 5-701 of the Family Law Article or Article 27, § 35A of the Code, a court may order that the testimony of a child victim be taken outside the courtroom and shown in the courtroom by means of a closed circuit television if:

(i) The testimony is taken during the proceeding; and

(ii) The judge determines that testimony by the child victim in the courtroom will result in the child suffering serious emotional distress such that the child cannot reasonably communicate.

(2) Only the prosecuting attorney, the attorney for the defendant, and the judge may question the child.

(3) The operators of the closed circuit television shall make every effort to be unobtrusive.

(b)(1) Only the following persons may be in the room with the child when the child testifies by closed circuit television:

(i) The prosecuting attorney;

(ii) The attorney for the defendant;

(iii) The operators of the closed circuit television equipment; and

(iv) Unless the defendant objects, any person whose presence, in the opinion of the court, contributes to the well-being of the child, including a person who has dealt with the child in a therapeutic setting concerning the abuse.

(2) During the child's testimony by closed circuit television, the judge and the defendant shall be in the courtroom.

(3) The judge and the defendant shall be allowed to communicate with the persons in the room where the child is testifying by any appropriate electronic method.

(c) The provisions of this section do not apply if the defendant is an attorney pro se.

(d) This section may not be interpreted to preclude, for purposes of identification of a defendant, the presence of both the victim and the defendant in the courtroom at the same time." ...

'wouldn't be able to communicate effectively.' As to another, an expert said she 'would probably stop talking and she would withdraw and curl up.' With respect to two others, the testimony was that one would 'become highly agitated, that he may refuse to talk or if he did talk, that he would choose his subject regardless of the questions' while the other would 'become extremely timid and unwilling to talk.'" 316 Md. 551, 568–569, 560 A.2d 1120, 1128–1129 (1989).

Craig objected to the use of the procedure on Confrontation Clause grounds, but the trial court rejected that contention, concluding that although the statute "take[s] away the right of the defendant to be face to face with his or her accuser," the defendant retains the "essence of the right of confrontation," including the right to observe, cross-examine, and have the jury view the demeanor of the witness. The trial court further found that, "based upon the evidence presented... the testimony of each of these children in a courtroom will result in each child suffering serious emotional distress... such that each of these children cannot reasonably communicate." The trial court then found the named victim and three other children competent to testify and accordingly permitted them to testify against Craig via the one-way closed circuit television procedure. The jury convicted Craig on all counts, and the Maryland Court of Special Appeals affirmed the convictions, 76 Md.App. 250, 544 A.2d 784 (1988).

The Court of Appeals of Maryland reversed and remanded for a new trial. 316 Md. 551, 560 A.2d 1120 (1989). The Court of Appeals rejected Craig's argument that the Confrontation Clause requires in all cases a face-to-face courtroom encounter between the accused and his accusers, *id.*, at 556–562, 560 A.2d, at 1122–1125, but concluded:

"[U]nder § 9-102(a)(1)(ii), the operative 'serious emotional distress' which renders a child victim unable to 'reasonably communicate' must be determined to arise, at least primarily, from face-to-face confrontation with the defendant. Thus, we construe the phrase 'in the courtroom' as meaning, for sixth amendment and [state constitution] confrontation purposes, 'in the courtroom in the presence of the defendant.' Unless prevention of 'eyeball-to-eyeball' confrontation is necessary to obtain the trial testimony of the child, the defendant cannot be denied that right." *Id.*, at 566, 560 A.2d, at 1127.

Reviewing the trial court's finding and the evidence presented in support of the § 9-102 procedure, the Court of Appeals held that, "as [it] read *Coy* [*v. Iowa*, 487 U.S. 1012 (1988)], the showing made by the State was insufficient to reach the high threshold required by that case before § 9-102 may be invoked." *Id.* 316 Md., at 554–555, 560 A.2d, at 1121 (footnote omitted).

We granted certiorari to resolve the important Confrontation Clause issues raised by this case. 493 U.S. 1041 (1990).

II

The Confrontation Clause of the Sixth Amendment, made applicable to the States through the Fourteenth Amendment, provides: "In all criminal prosecutions, the accused shall enjoy the right... to be confronted with the witnesses against him."

We observed in *Coy v. Iowa* that "the Confrontation Clause guarantees the defendant a face-to-face meeting with witnesses appearing before the trier of fact." 487 U.S., at 1016 (citing *Kentucky v. Stincer*, 482 U.S. 730, 748 (1987) (MARSHALL, J., dissenting)); see also

Pennsylvania v. Ritchie, 480 U.S. 39, 51 (1987) (plurality opinion); *California v. Green*, 399 U.S. 149, 157 (1970); *Snyder v. Massachusetts*, 291 U.S. 97, 106 (1934); *Dowdell v. United States*, 221 U.S. 325, 330 (1911); *Kirby v. United States*, 174 U.S. 47, 55 (1899); *Mattox v. United States*, 156 U.S. 237, 244 (1895). This interpretation derives not only from the literal text of the Clause, but also from our understanding of its historical roots. See *Coy, supra*, 487 U.S., at 1015–1016; *Mattox, supra*, 156 U.S., at 242 (Confrontation Clause intended to prevent conviction by affidavit); *Green, supra*, 399 U.S., at 156 (same); cf. 3 J. Story, Commentaries on the Constitution § 1785, p. 662 (1833).

We have never held, however, that the Confrontation Clause guarantees criminal defendants the absolute right to a face-to-face meeting with witnesses against them at trial. Indeed, in *Coy v. Iowa*, we expressly "le[ft] for another day...the question whether any exceptions exist" to the "irreducible literal meaning of the Clause: 'a right to meet face to face all those who appear and give evidence at trial.'" 487 U.S., at 1021 (quoting *Green, supra*, 399 U.S., at 175 (Harlan, J., concurring)). The procedure challenged in *Coy* involved the placement of a screen that prevented two child witnesses in a child abuse case from seeing the defendant as they testified against him at trial. See 487 U.S., at 1014–1015. In holding that the use of this procedure violated the defendant's right to confront witnesses against him, we suggested that any exception to the right "would surely be allowed only when necessary to further an important public policy"—*i.e.*, only upon a showing of something more than the generalized, "legislatively imposed presumption of trauma" underlying the statute at issue in that case. *Id.*, at 1021; see also *id.*, at 1025 (O'Connor, J., concurring). We concluded that "[s]ince there ha[d] been no individualized findings that these particular witnesses needed special protection, the judgment [in the case before us] could not be sustained by any conceivable exception." *Id.*, at 1021. Because the trial court in this case made individualized findings that each of the child witnesses needed special protection, this case requires us to decide the question reserved in *Coy*.

The central concern of the Confrontation Clause is to ensure the reliability of the evidence against a criminal defendant by subjecting it to rigorous testing in the context of an adversary proceeding before the trier of fact. The word "confront," after all, also means a clashing of forces or ideas, thus carrying with it the notion of adversariness. As we noted in our earliest case interpreting the Clause:

> "The primary object of the constitutional provision in question was to prevent depositions or ex parte affidavits, such as were sometimes admitted in civil cases, being used against the prisoner in lieu of a personal examination and cross-examination of the witness in which the accused has an opportunity, not only of testing the recollection and sifting the conscience of the witness, but of compelling him to stand face to face with the jury in order that they may look at him, and judge by his demeanor upon the stand and the manner in which he gives his testimony whether he is worthy of belief." *Mattox, supra*, 156 U.S., at 242–243.

As this description indicates, the right guaranteed by the Confrontation Clause includes not only a "personal examination," 156 U.S., at 242, but also "(1) insures that the witness will give his statements under oath—thus impressing him with the seriousness of the matter and guarding against the lie by the possibility of a penalty for perjury; (2) forces the witness to submit to cross-examination, the 'greatest legal engine ever invented for the discovery of truth'; [and] (3) permits the jury that is to decide the defendant's fate to observe the demeanor of the witness in making his statement, thus aiding the jury in assessing his credibility." *Green*, *supra*, 399 U.S., at 158 (footnote omitted).

The combined effect of these elements of confrontation—physical presence, oath, cross-examination, and observation of demeanor by the trier of fact—serves the purposes of the Confrontation Clause by ensuring that evidence admitted against an accused is reliable and subject to the rigorous adversarial testing that is the norm of Anglo-American criminal proceedings. See *Stincer, supra*, 482 U.S., at 739 ("[T]he right to confrontation is a functional one for the purpose of promoting reliability in a criminal trial"); *Dutton v. Evans*, 400 U.S. 74, 89 (1970) (plurality opinion) ("[T]he mission of the Confrontation Clause is to advance a practical concern for the accuracy of the truth-determining process in criminal trials by assuring that 'the trier of fact [has] a satisfactory basis for evaluating the truth of the [testimony]'"); *Lee v. Illinois*, 476 U.S. 530, 540 (1986) (confrontation guarantee serves "symbolic goals" and "promotes reliability"); see also *Faretta v. California*, 422 U.S. 806, 818 (1975) (Sixth Amendment "constitutionalizes the right in an adversary criminal trial to make a defense as we know it"); *Strickland v. Washington*, 466 U.S. 668, 684–685 (1984).

We have recognized, for example, that face-to-face confrontation enhances the accuracy of factfinding by reducing the risk that a witness will wrongfully implicate an innocent person. See *Coy, supra*, 487 U.S., at 1019–1020 ("It is always more difficult to tell a lie about a person 'to his face' than 'behind his back.'... That face-to-face presence may, unfortunately, upset the truthful rape victim or abused child; but by the same token it may confound and undo the false accuser, or reveal the child coached by a malevolent adult"); *Ohio v. Roberts*, 448 U.S. 56, 63, n. 6 (1980); see also 3 W. Blackstone, Commentaries *373–*374. We have also noted the strong symbolic purpose served by requiring adverse witnesses at trial to testify in the accused's presence. See *Coy*, 487 U.S., at 1017, 108 S.Ct., at 2801 ("[T]here is something deep in human nature that regards face-to-face confrontation between accused and accuser as 'essential to a fair trial in a criminal prosecution'") (quoting *Pointer v. Texas*, 380 U.S. 400, 404 (1965)).

Although face-to-face confrontation forms "the core of the values furthered by the Confrontation Clause," *Green*, 399 U.S., at 157, we have nevertheless recognized that it is not the sine qua non of the confrontation right. See *Delaware v. Fensterer*, 474 U.S. 15, 22 (1985) (per curiam) ("[T]he Confrontation Clause is generally satisfied when the defense is given a full and fair opportunity to probe and expose [testimonial] infirmities [such as forgetfulness, confusion, or evasion] through cross-examination, thereby calling to the attention of the factfinder the reasons for giving scant weight to the witness' testimony"); *Roberts, supra*, 448 U.S., at 69 (oath, cross-examination, and demeanor provide "all that the Sixth Amendment demands: 'substantial compliance with the purposes behind the confrontation requirement'") (quoting *Green, supra*, 399 U.S., at 166); see also *Stincer*, 482 U.S. at 739–744 (confrontation right not violated by exclusion of defendant from competency hearing of child witnesses, where defendant had opportunity for full and effective cross-examination at trial); *Davis v. Alaska*, 415 U.S. 308, 315–316 (1974); *Douglas v. Alabama*, 380 U.S. 415, 418 (1965); *Pointer, supra*, 380 U.S., at 406–407; 5 J. Wigmore, Evidence § 1395, p. 150 (J. Chadbourn rev. 1974).

For this reason, we have never insisted on an actual face-to-face encounter at trial in every instance in which testimony is admitted against a defendant. Instead, we have repeatedly held that the Clause permits, where necessary, the admission of certain hearsay statements against a defendant despite the defendant's inability to confront the declarant at trial. See, *e.g.*, *Mattox*, 156 U.S., at 243 ("[T]here could be nothing more directly contrary to the letter of the provision in question than the admission of dying declarations"); *Pointer, supra*, 380 U.S., at 407 (noting exceptions to the confrontation right for dying declarations and "other analogous situations"). In *Mattox*, for example, we held that the testimony of a Government witness at a former trial against the defendant, where the witness was fully cross-examined but had died after the first trial, was admissible in evidence against the defendant at his second trial. See 156 U.S., at 240–244. We explained:

> "There is doubtless reason for saying that…if notes of [the witness'] testimony are permitted to be read, [the defendant] is deprived of the advantage of that personal presence of the witness before the jury which the law has designed for his protection. But general rules of law of this kind, however beneficent in their operation and valuable to the accused, must occasionally give way to considerations of public policy and the necessities of the case. To say that a criminal, after having once been convicted by the testimony of a certain witness, should go scot free simply because death has closed the mouth of that witness, would be carrying his constitutional protection to an unwarrantable extent. The law in its wisdom declares that the rights of the public shall not be wholly sacrificed in order that an incidental benefit may be preserved to the accused." *Id.*, at 243.

We have accordingly stated that a literal reading of the Confrontation Clause would "abrogate virtually every hearsay exception, a result long rejected as unintended and too extreme." *Roberts*, 448 U.S., at 63. Thus, in certain narrow circumstances, "competing interests, if 'closely examined,' may warrant dispensing with confrontation at trial." *Id.*, at 64 (quoting *Chambers v. Mississippi*, 410 U.S. 284, 295 (1973), and citing *Mattox, supra*). We have recently held, for example, that hearsay statements of nontestifying co-conspirators may be admitted against a defendant despite the lack of any face-to-face encounter with the accused. See *Bourjaily v. United States*, 483 U.S. 171 (1987); *United States v. Inadi*, 475 U.S. 387 (1986). Given our hearsay cases, the word "confronted," as used in the Confrontation Clause, cannot simply mean face-to-face confrontation, for the Clause would then, contrary to our cases, prohibit the admission of any accusatory hearsay statement made by an absent declarant—a declarant who is undoubtedly as much a "witness against" a defendant as one who actually testifies at trial.

In sum, our precedents establish that "the Confrontation Clause reflects a *preference* for face-to-face confrontation at trial," *Roberts, supra*, 448 U.S., at 63, 100 S.Ct., at 2537 (emphasis added; footnote omitted), a preference that "must occasionally give way to considerations of public policy and the necessities of the case," *Mattox, supra*, 156 U.S., at 243. "[W]e have attempted to harmonize the goal of the Clause—placing limits on the kind of evidence that may be received against a defendant—with a societal interest in accurate factfinding, which may require consideration of out-of-court statements." *Bourjaily, supra*, 483 U.S., at 182. We have accordingly interpreted the Confrontation Clause in a manner sensitive to its purposes and sensitive to the necessities of trial and the adversary process. See, *e.g.*, *Kirby*, 174 U.S., at 61 ("It is scarcely necessary to say that to the rule that an accused is entitled to be confronted with witnesses against him the admission of dying declarations is an exception which arises from the necessity of the case"); *Chambers, supra*, 410 U.S., at 295 ("Of course, the right to confront and to cross-examine is not absolute and may, in appropriate cases, bow to accommodate other legitimate interests in the criminal trial process"). Thus, though we reaffirm the importance of face-to-face confrontation with witnesses appearing at trial, we cannot say that such confrontation is an indispensable element of the Sixth Amendment's guarantee of the right to confront one's accusers. Indeed, one commentator has noted that "[i]t is all but universally assumed that there are circumstances that excuse compliance with the right of confrontation." Graham, The Right of Confrontation and the Hearsay Rule: Sir Walter Raleigh Loses Another One, 8 Crim.L.Bull. 99, 107–108 (1972).

This interpretation of the Confrontation Clause is consistent with our cases holding that other Sixth Amendment rights must also be interpreted in the context of the necessities of trial and the adversary process. See, *e.g.*, *Illinois v. Allen*, 397 U.S. 337, 342–343 (1970) (right to be present at trial not violated where trial judge removed defendant for disruptive behavior); *Ritchie*, 480 U.S., at 51–54 (plurality opinion) (right to cross-examination not violated where State denied defendant access to investigative files); *Taylor v. Illinois*, 484 U.S. 400, 410–416 (1988) (right to compulsory process not violated where trial judge precluded testimony of a surprise defense witness); *Perry v. Leeke*, 488 U.S. 272, 280–285 (1989) (right to effective assistance of counsel not violated where trial judge prevented testifying defendant from conferring with counsel during a short break in testimony). We see no reason to treat the face-to-face component of the confrontation right any differently, and indeed we think it would be anomalous to do so.

That the face-to-face confrontation requirement is not absolute does not, of course, mean that it may easily be dispensed with. As we suggested in *Coy*, our precedents confirm that a defendant's right to confront accusatory witnesses may be satisfied absent a physical, face-to-face confrontation at trial only where denial of such confrontation is necessary to further an important public policy and only where the reliability of the testimony is otherwise assured. See 487 U.S., at 1021 (citing *Roberts*, *supra*, 448 U.S. at 64; *Chambers*, *supra*, 410 U.S. at 295); *Coy*, *supra*, 487 U.S., at 1025 (O'Connor, J., concurring).

III

Maryland's statutory procedure, when invoked, prevents a child witness from seeing the defendant as he or she testifies against the defendant at trial. We find it significant, however, that Maryland's procedure preserves all of the other elements of the confrontation right: The child witness must be competent to testify and must testify under oath; the defendant retains full opportunity for contemporaneous cross-examination; and the judge, jury, and defendant are able to view (albeit by video monitor) the demeanor (and body) of the witness as he or she testifies. Although we are mindful of the many subtle effects face-to-face confrontation may have on an adversary criminal proceeding, the presence of these other elements of confrontation—oath, cross-examination, and observation of the witness' demeanor—adequately ensures that the testimony is both reliable and subject to rigorous adversarial testing in a manner functionally equivalent to that accorded live, in-person testimony. These safeguards of reliability and adversariness render the use of such a procedure a far cry from the undisputed prohibition of the Confrontation Clause: trial by ex parte affidavit or inquisition, see *Mattox*, 156 U.S., at 242; see also *Green*, 399 U.S., at 179 (Harlan, J., concurring) ("[T]he Confrontation Clause was meant to constitutionalize a barrier against flagrant abuses, trials by anonymous accusers, and absentee witnesses"). Rather, we think these elements of effective confrontation not only permit a defendant to "confound and undo the false accuser, or reveal the child coached by a malevolent adult,"

Coy, *supra*, 487 U.S., at 1020, but may well aid a defendant in eliciting favorable testimony from the child witness. Indeed, to the extent the child witness' testimony may be said to be technically given out of court (though we do not so hold), these assurances of reliability and adversariness are far greater than those required for admission of hearsay testimony under the Confrontation Clause. See *Roberts*, 448 U.S., at 66. We are therefore confident that use of the one-way closed circuit television procedure, where necessary to further an important state interest, does not impinge upon the truth-seeking or symbolic purposes of the Confrontation Clause.

The critical inquiry in this case, therefore, is whether use of the procedure is necessary to further an important state interest. The State contends that it has a substantial interest in protecting children who are allegedly victims of child abuse from the trauma of testifying against the alleged perpetrator and that its statutory procedure for receiving testimony from such witnesses is necessary to further that interest.

We have of course recognized that a State's interest in "the protection of minor victims of sex crimes from further trauma and embarrassment" is a "compelling" one. *Globe Newspaper Co. v. Superior Court of Norfolk County*, 457 U.S. 596, 607 (1982); see also *New York v. Ferber*, 458 U.S. 747, 756–757 (1982); *FCC v. Pacifica Foundation*, 438 U.S. 726, 749–750 (1978); *Ginsberg v. New York*, 390 U.S. 629, 640 (1968); *Prince v. Massachusetts*, 321 U.S. 158, 168 (1944). "[W]e have sustained legislation aimed at protecting the physical and emotional well-being of youth even when the laws have operated in the sensitive area of constitutionally protected rights." *Ferber*, *supra*, 458 U.S., at 757. In *Globe Newspaper*, for example, we held that a State's interest in the physical and psychological well-being of a minor victim was sufficiently weighty to justify depriving the press and public of their constitutional right to attend criminal trials, where the trial court makes a case-specific finding that closure of the trial is necessary to protect the welfare of the minor. See 457 U.S., at 608–609. This Term, in *Osborne v. Ohio*, 495 U.S. 103 (1990), we upheld a state statute that proscribed the possession and viewing of child pornography, reaffirming that "'[i]t is evident beyond the need for elaboration that a State's interest in 'safeguarding the physical and psychological well-being of a minor' is 'compelling.''" *Id.*, at 109 (quoting *Ferber*, *supra*, 458 U.S., at 756–757).

We likewise conclude today that a State's interest in the physical and psychological well-being of child abuse victims may be sufficiently important to outweigh, at least in some cases, a defendant's right to face his or her accusers in court. That a significant majority of States have enacted statutes to protect child witnesses from the trauma of giving testimony in child abuse cases attests to the widespread belief in the importance of such a public policy. See *Coy*, 487 U.S., at 1022–1023 (O'Connor, J., concurring) ("Many States have determined that a child victim may suffer trauma from exposure to the harsh atmosphere of the typical courtroom and have undertaken to shield the child through a variety of ameliorative measures"). Thirty-seven States, for example, permit the use of videotaped testimony of sexually abused children; 24 States have authorized the use of one-way closed circuit television testimony in child abuse cases; and 8 States authorize the use of a two-way system in which the child witness is permitted to see the courtroom and the defendant on a video monitor and in which the jury and judge are permitted to view the child during the testimony.

The statute at issue in this case, for example, was specifically intended "to safeguard the physical and psychological well-being of child victims by avoiding, or at least minimizing, the emotional trauma produced by testifying." *Wildermuth v. State*, 310 Md. 496, 518, 530 A.2d 275, 286 (1987). The *Wildermuth* court noted:

> "In Maryland, the Governor's Task Force on Child Abuse in its *Interim Report* (Nov. 1984) documented the existence of the [child abuse] problem in our State. *Interim Report* at 1. It brought the picture up to date in its Final Report (Dec. 1985). In the first six months of 1985, investigations of child abuse were 12 percent more numerous than during the same period of 1984. In 1979, 4,615 cases of child abuse were investigated; in 1984, 8,321. *Final Report* at iii. In its *Interim Report* at 2, the Commission proposed legislation that, with some changes, became § 9-102. The proposal was 'aimed at alleviating the trauma to a child victim in the courtroom atmosphere by allowing the child's testimony to be obtained outside of the courtroom.' *Id.*, at 2. This would both protect the child and enhance the public interest by encouraging effective prosecution of the alleged abuser." *Id.*, at 517, 530 A.2d, at 285.

Given the State's traditional and "'transcendent interest in protecting the welfare of children,'" *Ginsberg*, 390 U.S., at 640 (citation omitted), and buttressed by the growing body of academic literature documenting the psychological trauma suffered by child abuse victims who must testify in court, see Brief for American Psychological Association as *Amicus Curiae* 7–13; G. Goodman et al., Emotional Effects of Criminal Court Testimony on Child Sexual Assault Victims, Final Report to the National Institute of Justice (presented as conference paper at annual convention of American Psychological Assn., Aug. 1989), we will not second-guess the considered judgment of the Maryland Legislature regarding the importance of its interest in protecting child abuse victims from the emotional trauma of testifying. Accordingly, we hold that, if the State makes an adequate showing of necessity, the state interest in protecting child witnesses from the trauma of testifying in a child abuse case is sufficiently important to justify the use of a special procedure that permits a child witness in such cases to testify at trial against a defendant in the absence of face-to-face confrontation with the defendant.

The requisite finding of necessity must of course be a case-specific one: The trial court must hear evidence and determine whether use of the one-way closed circuit television procedure is necessary to protect the welfare of the particular child witness who seeks to testify. See *Globe Newspaper Co.*, 457 U.S., at 608–609 (compelling interest in protecting child victims does not justify a mandatory trial closure rule); *Coy*, 487 U.S., at 1021; *id.*, at 1025 (O'Connor, J., concurring); see also *Hochheiser v. Superior Court*, 161 Cal.App.3d 777, 793, 208 Cal.Rptr. 273, 283 (1984). The trial court must also find that the child witness would be traumatized, not by the courtroom generally, but by the presence of the defendant. See, *e.g.*, *State v. Wilhite*, 160 Ariz. 228, 772 P.2d 582 (1989); *State v. Bonello*, 210 Conn. 51, 554 A.2d 277 (1989); *State v. Davidson*, 764 S.W.2d 731 (Mo.App. 1989); *Commonwealth v. Ludwig*, 366 Pa.Super. 361, 531 A.2d 459 (1987). Denial of face-to-face confrontation is not needed to further the state interest in protecting the child witness from trauma unless it is the presence of the defendant that causes the trauma. In other words, if the state interest were merely the interest in protecting child witnesses from courtroom trauma generally, denial of face-to-face confrontation would be unnecessary because the child could be permitted to testify in less intimidating surroundings, albeit with the defendant present. Finally, the trial court must find that the emotional distress suffered by the child witness in the presence of the defendant is more than *de minimis*, *i.e.*, more than "mere nervousness or excitement or some reluctance to testify," *Wildermuth*, *supra*, 310 Md., at 524, 530 A.2d, at 289; see also *State v. Mannion*, 19

Utah 505, 511–512, 57 P. 542, 543–544 (1899). We need not decide the minimum showing of emotional trauma required for use of the special procedure, however, because the Maryland statute, which requires a determination that the child witness will suffer "serious emotional distress such that the child cannot reasonably communicate," § 9-102(a)(1)(ii), clearly suffices to meet constitutional standards.

To be sure, face-to-face confrontation may be said to cause trauma for the very purpose of eliciting truth, cf. *Coy, supra*, 487 U.S., at 1019–1020, but we think that the use of Maryland's special procedure, where necessary to further the important state interest in preventing trauma to child witnesses in child abuse cases, adequately ensures the accuracy of the testimony and preserves the adversary nature of the trial. See *supra*, at 3166–3167. Indeed, where face-to-face confrontation causes significant emotional distress in a child witness, there is evidence that such confrontation would in fact *disserve* the Confrontation Clause's truth-seeking goal. See, *e.g., Coy, supra*, 487 U.S., at 1032 (BLACKMUN, J., dissenting) (face-to-face confrontation "may so overwhelm the child as to prevent the possibility of effective testimony, thereby undermining the truth-finding function of the trial itself"); Brief for American Psychological Association as *Amicus Curiae* 18–24; *State v. Sheppard*, 197 N.J.Super. 411, 416, 484 A.2d 1330, 1332 (1984); Goodman & Helgeson, Child Sexual Assault: Children's Memory and the Law, 40 U. Miami L. Rev. 181, 203–204 (1985); Note, Videotaping Children's Testimony: An Empirical View, 85 Mich. L. Rev. 809, 813-820 (1987).

In sum, we conclude that where necessary to protect a child witness from trauma that would be caused by testifying in the physical presence of the defendant, at least where such trauma would impair the child's ability to communicate, the Confrontation Clause does not prohibit use of a procedure that, despite the absence of face-to-face confrontation, ensures the reliability of the evidence by subjecting it to rigorous adversarial testing and thereby preserves the essence of effective confrontation. Because there is no dispute that the child witnesses in this case testified under oath, were subject to full cross-examination, and were able to be observed by the judge, jury, and defendant as they testified, we conclude that, to the extent that a proper finding of necessity has been made, the admission of such testimony would be consonant with the Confrontation Clause.

IV

The Maryland Court of Appeals held, as we do today, that although face-to-face confrontation is not an absolute constitutional requirement, it may be abridged only where there is a "'case-specific finding of necessity.'" 316 Md., at 564, 560 A.2d, at 1126 (quoting *Coy, supra*, 487 U.S., at 1025 (O'CONNOR, J., concurring)). Given this latter requirement, the Court of Appeals reasoned that "[t]he question of whether a child is unavailable to testify... should not be asked in terms of inability to testify in the ordinary courtroom setting, but in the much narrower terms of the witness's inability to testify in the presence of the accused." 316 Md., at 564, 560 A.2d, at 1126 (footnote omitted). "[T]he determinative inquiry required to preclude face-to-face confrontation is the effect of the presence of the defendant on the witness or the witness's testimony." *Id.*, at 565, 560 A.2d, at 1127. The Court of Appeals accordingly concluded that, as a prerequisite to use of the § 9-102 procedure, the Confrontation Clause requires the trial court to make a specific finding that testimony by the child in the courtroom *in the presence of the defendant* would result in the child suffering serious emotional distress such that the child could not reasonably communicate. *Id.*, at 566, 560 A.2d, at 1127. This conclusion, of course, is consistent with our holding today.

In addition, however, the Court of Appeals interpreted our decision in *Coy* to impose two subsidiary requirements. First, the court held that "§ 9-102 ordinarily cannot be invoked unless the child witness initially is questioned (either in or outside the courtroom) in the defendant's presence." *Id.*, at 566, 560 A.2d, at 1127; see also *Wildermuth*, 310 Md., at 523–524, 530 A.2d, at 289 (personal observation by the judge should be the rule rather than the exception). Second, the court asserted that, before using the one-way television procedure, a trial judge must determine whether a child would suffer "severe emotional distress" if he or she were to testify by two-way closed circuit television. 316 Md., at 567, 560 A.2d, at 1128.

Reviewing the evidence presented to the trial court in support of the finding required under § 9-102(a)(1)(ii), the Court of Appeals determined that "the finding of necessity required to limit the defendant's right of confrontation through invocation of § 9-102...was not made here." *Id.*, at 570–571, 560 A.2d, at 1129. The Court of Appeals noted that the trial judge "had the benefit only of expert testimony on the ability of the children to communicate; he did not question any of the children himself, nor did he observe any child's behavior on the witness stand before making his ruling. He did not explore any alternatives to the use of one-way closed-circuit television." *Id.*, at 568, 560 A.2d, at 1128 (footnote omitted). The Court of Appeals also observed that "the testimony in this case was not sharply focused on the effect of the defendant's presence on the child witnesses." *Id.*, at 569, 560 A.2d, at 1129. Thus, the Court of Appeals concluded:

> "Unable to supplement the expert testimony by responses to questions put by him, or by his own observations of the children's behavior in Craig's presence, the judge made his § 9-102 finding in terms of what the experts had said. He ruled that 'the testimony of each of these children *in a courtroom* will [result] in each child suffering serious emotional distress...such that each of these children cannot reasonably communicate.' He failed to find—indeed, on the evidence before him, *could not have found*—that this result would be the product of testimony in a courtroom in the defendant's presence or outside the courtroom but in the defendant's televised presence. That, however, is the finding of necessity required to limit the defendant's right of confrontation through invocation of § 9-102. Since that finding was not made here, and since the procedures we deem requisite to the valid use of § 9-102 were not followed, the judgment of the Court of Special Appeals must be reversed and the case remanded for a new trial." *Id.*, at 570–571, 560 A.2d, at 1129 (emphasis added).

The Court of Appeals appears to have rested its conclusion at least in part on the trial court's failure to observe the children's behavior in the defendant's presence and its failure to explore less restrictive alternatives to the use of the one-way closed circuit television procedure. See *id.*, at 568–571, 560 A.2d, at 1128–1129. Although we think such evidentiary requirements could strengthen the grounds for use of protective measures, we decline to establish, as a matter of federal constitutional law, any such categorical evidentiary prerequisites for the use of the one-way television procedure. The trial court in this case, for example, could well have found, on the basis of the expert testimony before it, that testimony by the child witnesses in the courtroom in the defendant's presence "will result in [each] child suffering serious emotional distress such that the child cannot reasonably communicate," § 9-102(a)(1)(ii). See *id.*, at 568–569, 560 A.2d, at 1128–1129.... So long as a trial court makes such a case-specific finding of necessity, the Confrontation Clause does not prohibit a State from using a one-way closed circuit television procedure for the receipt of testimony by a child witness in a child abuse case. Because the Court of Appeals held that the trial court had not made the requisite finding of necessity under its interpretation of "the high threshold required by [*Coy*] before § 9-102 may be invoked," 316 Md., at 554–555, 560 A.2d, at 1121 (footnote omitted), we cannot be certain whether the Court of Appeals would reach the same conclusion in light of the legal standard we establish today. We therefore vacate the judgment of the Court of Appeals of Maryland and remand the case for further proceedings not inconsistent with this opinion....

Justice Scalia, with whom Justice Brennan, Justice Marshall, and Justice Stevens join, dissenting.

Seldom has this Court failed so conspicuously to sustain a categorical guarantee of the Constitution against the tide of prevailing current opinion. The Sixth Amendment provides, with unmistakable clarity, that "[i]n all criminal prosecutions, the accused shall enjoy the right... to be confronted with the witnesses against him." The purpose of enshrining this protection in the Constitution was to assure that none of the many policy interests from time to time pursued by statutory law could overcome a defendant's right to face his or her accusers in court. The Court, however, says:

> "We... conclude today that a State's interest in the physical and psychological well-being of child abuse victims may be sufficiently important to outweigh, at least in some cases, a defendant's right to face his or her accusers in court. That a significant majority of States have enacted statutes to protect child witnesses from the trauma of giving testimony in child abuse cases attests to the widespread belief in the importance of such a public policy."

Because of this subordination of explicit constitutional text to currently favored public policy, the following scene can be played out in an American courtroom for the first time in two centuries: A father whose young daughter has been given over to the exclusive custody of his estranged wife, or a mother whose young son has been taken into custody by the State's child welfare department, is sentenced to prison for sexual abuse on the basis of testimony by a child the parent has not seen or spoken to for many months; and the guilty verdict is rendered without giving the parent so much as the opportunity to sit in the presence of the child, and to ask, personally or through counsel, "it is really not true, is it, that I—your father (or mother) whom you see before you—did these terrible things?" Perhaps that is a procedure today's society desires; perhaps (though I doubt it) it is even a fair procedure; but it is assuredly not a procedure permitted by the Constitution.

Because the text of the Sixth Amendment is clear, and because the Constitution is meant to protect against, rather than conform to, current "widespread belief," I respectfully dissent.

I

According to the Court, "we cannot say that [face-to-face] confrontation [with witnesses appearing at trial] is an indispensable element of the Sixth Amendment's guarantee of the right to confront one's accusers." That is rather like saying "we cannot say that being tried before a jury is an indispensable element of the Sixth Amendment's guarantee of the right to jury trial." The Court makes the impossible plausible by recharacterizing the Confrontation Clause, so that confrontation (redesignated "face-to-face confrontation") becomes only one of many "elements of confrontation." The reasoning is as follows: The Confrontation Clause guarantees not only what it explicitly provides for—"face-to-face" confrontation—but also implied and collateral rights such as cross-examination, oath, and observation of demeanor (TRUE); the purpose of this entire cluster of rights is to ensure the reliability of evidence (TRUE); the Maryland procedure preserves the implied and collateral rights (TRUE), which adequately ensure the reliability of evidence (perhaps TRUE); therefore the Confrontation Clause is not violated by denying what it explicitly provides for—"face-to-face" confrontation (unquestionably FALSE). This reasoning abstracts from the right to its purposes, and then eliminates the right. It is wrong because the Confrontation Clause does not guarantee reliable evidence; it guarantees specific trial procedures that were thought to assure reliable evidence, undeniably among which was "face-to-face" confrontation. Whatever else it may mean in addition, the defendant's constitutional right "to be confronted with the witnesses against him" means, always and everywhere, at least what it explicitly says: the "'right to meet face to face all those who appear and give evidence at trial.'" *Coy v. Iowa*, 487 U.S. 1012, 1016 (1988), quoting *California v. Green*, 399 U.S. 149, 175 (1970) (Harlan, J., concurring).

The Court supports its antitextual conclusion by cobbling together scraps of dicta from various cases that have no bearing here. It will suffice to discuss one of them, since they are all of a kind: Quoting *Ohio v. Roberts*, 448 U.S. 56, 63 (1980), the Court says that "[i]n sum, our precedents establish that 'the Confrontation Clause reflects a *preference* for face-to-face confrontation at trial.'"... But *Roberts*, and all the other "precedents" the Court enlists to prove the implausible, dealt with the *implications* of the Confrontation Clause, and not its literal, unavoidable text. When *Roberts* said that the Clause merely "reflects a preference for face-to-face confrontation at trial," what it had in mind as the nonpreferred alternative was not (as the Court implies) the appearance of a witness at trial without confronting the defendant. That has been, until today, not merely "nonpreferred" but utterly unheard-of. What *Roberts* had in mind was the receipt of *other-than-first-hand testimony* from witnesses at trial—that is, witnesses' recounting of hearsay statements by absent parties who, *since they did not appear at trial*, did not have to endure face-to-face confrontation. Rejecting that, I agree, was merely giving effect to an evident constitutional preference; there are, after all, many exceptions to the Confrontation Clause's hearsay rule. But that the defendant should be confronted by the witnesses who appear at trial is not a preference "reflected" by the Confrontation Clause; it is a constitutional right unqualifiedly guaranteed.

The Court claims that its interpretation of the Confrontation Clause "is consistent with our cases holding that other Sixth Amendment rights must also be interpreted in the context of the necessities of trial and the adversary process." I disagree. It is true enough that the "necessities of trial and the adversary process" limit the *manner* in which Sixth Amendment rights may be exercised, and limit the *scope* of Sixth Amendment guarantees to the extent that scope is textually indeterminate. Thus (to describe the cases the Court cites): The right to confront is not the right to confront in a manner that disrupts the trial. *Illinois v. Allen*, 397 U.S. 337 (1970). The right "to have compulsory process for obtaining witnesses" is not the right to call witnesses in a manner that violates fair and orderly procedures. *Taylor v. Illinois*, 484 U.S. 400 (1988). The scope of the right "to have the assistance of counsel" does not include consultation with counsel at all times during the trial. *Perry v. Leeke*, 488 U.S. 272 (1989). The scope of the right to cross-examine does not include access to the State's investigative files. *Pennsylvania v. Ritchie*, 480 U.S. 39 (1987). But we are not talking here about denying expansive scope to a Sixth Amendment provision whose scope for the purpose at issue is textually unclear; "to confront" plainly means to encounter face-to-face, whatever else it may mean in addition. And we are not talking about the manner of arranging that face-to-face encounter, but about whether it shall occur at all. The "necessities of trial and the adversary process" are irrelevant here, since they cannot alter the constitutional text.

II

Much of the Court's opinion consists of applying to this case the mode of analysis we have used in the admission of hearsay evidence. The Sixth Amendment does not literally contain a prohibition upon such evidence, since it guarantees the defendant only the right to confront "the witnesses against him." As applied in the Sixth Amendment's context of a prosecution, the noun "witness"—in 1791 as today—could mean either (a) one "who knows or sees any thing; one personally present" or (b) "one who gives testimony" or who "testifies," *i.e.*, "[i]n *judicial proceedings*, [one who] make[s] a solemn declaration under oath, for the purpose of establishing or making proof of some fact to a court." 2 N. Webster, An American Dictionary of the English Language (1828) (emphasis added). See also J. Buchanan, Linguae Britannicae Vera Pronunciatio (1757). The former meaning (one "who knows or sees") would cover hearsay evidence, but is excluded in the Sixth Amendment by the words following the noun: "witnesses *against him*." The phrase obviously refers to those who give testimony against the defendant at trial. We have nonetheless found implicit in the Confrontation Clause some limitation upon hearsay evidence, since otherwise the government could subvert the confrontation right by putting on witnesses who know nothing except what an absent declarant said. And in determining the scope of that implicit limitation, we have focused upon whether the reliability of the hearsay statements (which are not *expressly* excluded by the Confrontation Clause) "is otherwise assured." The same test cannot be applied, however, to permit what is explicitly forbidden by the constitutional text; there is simply no room for interpretation with regard to "the irreducible literal meaning of the Clause." *Coy, supra*, 487 U.S., at 1020–1021.

Some of the Court's analysis seems to suggest that the children's testimony here was itself hearsay of the sort permissible under our Confrontation Clause cases. That cannot be. Our Confrontation Clause conditions for the admission of hearsay have long included a "general requirement of unavailability" of the declarant. *Idaho v. Wright*, 497 U.S. 805, 815. "In the usual case…, the prosecution must either produce, or demonstrate the unavailability of, the declarant whose statement it wishes to use against the defendant." *Ohio v. Roberts*, 448 U.S., at 65. We have permitted a few exceptions to this general rule—*e.g.*, for co-conspirators' statements, whose effect cannot be replicated by live testimony because they "derive [their] significance from the circumstances in which [they were] made," *United States v. Inadi*, 475 U.S. 387, 395 (1986). "Live" closed-circuit television testimony, however—if it can be called hearsay at all—is surely an example of hearsay as "a weaker substitute for live testimony," *id.*, at 394, which can be employed only when the genuine article is unavailable. "When two versions of the same evidence are available, longstanding principles of the law of hearsay, applicable as well to Confrontation Clause analysis, favor the better evidence." *Ibid.* See also *Roberts, supra* (requiring unavailability as precondition for admission of prior testimony); *Barber v. Page*, 390 U.S. 719 (1968) (same).

The Court's test today requires unavailability only in the sense that the child is unable to testify in the presence of the defendant.[1] That cannot possibly be the relevant sense. If unconfronted testimony is admissible hearsay when the witness is unable to confront the defendant, then presumably there are other categories of admissible hearsay consisting of unsworn testimony when the witness is unable to risk perjury, un-cross-examined testimony when the witness is unable to undergo hostile questioning, etc. *California v. Green*, 399 U.S. 149 (1970), is not precedent for such a silly system. That case held that the Confrontation Clause does not bar admission of prior testimony when the declarant is sworn as a witness but refuses to answer. But in *Green*, as in most cases of refusal, we could not know why the declarant refused to testify. Here, by contrast, we know that it is precisely because the child is unwilling to testify in the presence of the defendant. That unwillingness cannot be a valid excuse under the Confrontation Clause, whose very object is to place the witness under the sometimes hostile glare of the defendant. "That face-to-face presence may, unfortunately, upset the truthful rape victim or abused child; but by the same token it may confound and undo the false accuser, or reveal the child coached by a malevolent adult." *Coy*, 487 U.S., at 1020. To say that a defendant loses his right to confront a witness when that would cause the witness not to testify is rather like saying that the defendant loses his right to counsel when counsel would save him, or his right to subpoena witnesses when they would exculpate him, or his right not to give testimony against himself when that would prove him guilty.

III

The Court characterizes the State's interest which "outweigh[s]" the explicit text of the Constitution as an "interest in the physical and psychological well-being of child abuse victims," an "interest in protecting" such victims "from the emotional trauma of testifying." That is not so. A child who meets the Maryland statute's requirement of suffering such "serious emotional distress" from confrontation that he "cannot reasonably communicate" would seem entirely safe. Why would a prosecutor want to call a witness who cannot reasonably communicate? And if he did, it would be the State's own fault. Protection of the child's interest—as far as the Confrontation Clause is concerned[2] —is entirely within Maryland's control. The State's interest here is in fact no more and no less than what the State's interest always is when it seeks to get a class of evidence admitted in criminal proceedings: more convictions of guilty defendants. That is not an unworthy interest, but it should not be dressed up as a humanitarian one.

And the interest on the other side is also what it usually is when the State seeks to get a new class of evidence admitted: fewer convictions of innocent defendants—specifically, in the present context, innocent defendants accused of particularly heinous crimes. The

1. I presume that when the Court says "trauma would impair the child's ability to communicate," it means that trauma would make it impossible for the child to communicate. That is the requirement of the Maryland law at issue here: "serious emotional distress such that the child cannot reasonably communicate." Md.Cts. & Jud.Proc.Code Ann. § 9-102(a)(1)(ii) (1989). Any implication beyond that would in any event be dictum.

2. A different situation would be presented if the defendant sought to call the child. In that event, the State's refusal to compel the child to appear, or its insistence upon a procedure such as that set forth in the Maryland statute as a condition of its compelling him to do so, would call into question—initially, at least, and perhaps exclusively—the scope of the defendant's Sixth Amendment right "to have compulsory process for obtaining witnesses in his favor."

"special" reasons that exist for suspending one of the usual guarantees of reliability in the case of children's testimony are perhaps matched by "special" reasons for being particularly insistent upon it in the case of children's testimony. Some studies show that children are substantially more vulnerable to suggestion than adults, and often unable to separate recollected fantasy (or suggestion) from reality. See Lindsay & Johnson, Reality Monitoring and Suggestibility: Children's Ability to Discriminate among Memories from Different Sources, in Children's Eyewitness Memory 92 (S. Ceci, M. Toglia, & D. Ross eds. 1987); Feher, The Alleged Molestation Victim, the Rules of Evidence, and the Constitution: Should Children Really Be Seen and Not Heard? 14 Am.J.Crim.L. 227, 230–233 (1987); Christiansen, The Testimony of Child Witnesses: Fact, Fantasy, and the Influence of Pretrial Interviews, 62 Wash.L.Rev. 705, 708–711 (1987). The injustice their erroneous testimony can produce is evidenced by the tragic Scott County investigations of 1983–1984, which disrupted the lives of many (as far as we know) innocent people in the small town of Jordan, Minnesota. At one stage those investigations were pursuing allegations by at least eight children of multiple murders, but the prosecutions actually initiated charged only sexual abuse. Specifically, 24 adults were charged with molesting 37 children. In the course of the investigations, 25 children were placed in foster homes. Of the 24 indicted defendants, one pleaded guilty, two were acquitted at trial, and the charges against the remaining 21 were voluntarily dismissed. See Feher, *supra*, at 239–240. There is no doubt that some sexual abuse took place in Jordan; but there is no reason to believe it was as widespread as charged. A report by the Minnesota attorney general's office, based on inquiries conducted by the Minnesota Bureau of Criminal Apprehension and the Federal Bureau of Investigation, concluded that there was an "absence of credible testimony and [a] lack of significant corroboration" to support reinstitution of sex-abuse charges, and "no credible evidence of murders." H. Humphrey, Report on Scott County Investigation 8, 7 (1985). The report describes an investigation full of well-intentioned techniques employed by the prosecution team, police, child protection workers, and foster parents, that distorted and in some cases even coerced the children's recollection. Children were interrogated repeatedly, in some cases as many as 50 times, *id.*, at 9; answers were suggested by telling the children what other witnesses had said, *id.*, at 11; and children (even some who did not at first complain of abuse) were separated from their parents for months, *id.*, at 9. The report describes the consequences as follows:

> "As children continued to be interviewed the list of accused citizens grew. In a number of cases, it was only after weeks or months of questioning that children would "admit" their parents abused them....
>
> In some instances, over a period of time, the allegations of sexual abuse turned to stories of mutilations, and eventually homicide." *Id.*, at 10–11.

The value of the confrontation right in guarding against a child's distorted or coerced recollections is dramatically evident with respect to one of the misguided investigative techniques the report cited: some children were told by their foster parents that reunion with their real parents would be hastened by "admission" of their parents' abuse. *Id.*, at 9. Is it difficult to imagine how unconvincing such a testimonial admission might be to a jury that witnessed the child's delight at seeing his parents in the courtroom? Or how devastating it might be if, pursuant to a psychiatric evaluation that "trauma would impair the child's ability to communicate" in front of his parents, the child were permitted to tell his story to the jury on closed-circuit television?

In the last analysis, however, this debate is not an appropriate one. I have no need to defend the value of confrontation, because the Court has no authority to question it. It is not within our charge to speculate that, "where face-to-face confrontation causes significant emotional distress in a child witness," confrontation might "in fact *disserve* the Confrontation Clause's truth-seeking goal." If so, that is a defect in the Constitution—which should be amended by the procedures provided for such an eventuality, but cannot be corrected by judicial pronouncement that it is archaic, contrary to "widespread belief," and thus null and void. For good or bad, the Sixth Amendment requires confrontation, and we are not at liberty to ignore it. To quote the document one last time (for it plainly says all that need be said): "In *all* criminal prosecutions, the accused shall enjoy the right...to be confronted with the witnesses against him" (emphasis added).

The Court today has applied "interest-balancing" analysis where the text of the Constitution simply does not permit it. We are not free to conduct a cost-benefit analysis of clear and explicit constitutional guarantees, and then to adjust their meaning to comport with our findings. The Court has convincingly proved that the Maryland procedure serves a valid interest, and gives the defendant virtually everything the Confrontation Clause guarantees (everything, that is, except confrontation). I am persuaded, therefore, that the Maryland procedure is virtually constitutional. Since it is not, however, actually constitutional I would affirm the judgment of the Maryland Court of Appeals reversing the judgment of conviction.

NOTES AND QUESTIONS

1. What is the difference between a statement that violates the hearsay rule and one that violates the Confrontation Clause? What is the problem with the Maryland procedure? According to the majority, does it violate either the hearsay rule or the Confrontation Clause? Why?

2. What is the issue according to the dissent? What exactly is constitutionally problematic about the Maryland procedure?

3. Were you surprised to see that Justice Scalia wrote the dissenting opinion? Scalia authored the Court's opinion in *Coy v. Iowa*, cited above. In *Coy*, the Court held that the use of a screen placed between the defendant and the child witness during the defendant's criminal trial violated the Confrontation Clause because it denied the defendant the opportunity for a face-to-face encounter with his accuser. Scalia stated that "the Confrontation Clause guarantees the defendant a face-to-face meeting with witnesses appearing before the trier of fact." 487 U.S. 1012, 1016 (1988). Do you think Scalia is correct?

4. Forty-six states permit the use of closed-circuit television (CCTV) for a child to testify without appearing in court. Twenty-four states explicitly permit the use of CCTV in criminal proceedings. Margaret Brancatelli, Facilitating Children's Testimony: Closed Circuit Television, Update, Nat'l Dist. Att'ys Ass'n/Nat'l Ctr. for Prosecution of Child Abuse, Alexandria, Va., 2009, at 1, http:// www.ndaa.org/publications/newsletters/update_vol_21_no_11.pdf. Children's out-of-court statements also may be admitted through a variety of traditional hearsay exceptions. Courts

typically rely on such exceptions as excited utterances, statements made for the purposes of medical diagnosis or treatment, or a "residual" hearsay exception. Some states, however, have created exceptions specifically for out-of-court statements made by abused children. At least twenty-four states have such exceptions, which apply specifically to admit the out-of-court statements in criminal, family, and juvenile proceedings when the statements have been made to an investigative interviewer. See, e.g., Ark. R. Evid. 803(25), codified at Ark. Code Ann. § 16-41-101 (1999); Cal. Evid. Code §§ 1253, 1360 (West Supp. 2010); Del. Code Ann. tit. 11, § 3513 (West 2006 & Supp. 2009); Fla. Stat. Ann. § 90.803(23) (West 1999); Ga. Code Ann. § 24-3-16 (1995); 725 Ill. Comp. Stat. Ann. 5/115-10 (2012); 735 Ill. Comp. Stat. Ann. 5/8-2601 (2012); 750 Ill. Comp. Stat. Ann. 5/606 (West 2009); Md. Code Ann., Crim. Proc. § 11-304 (2011); Mass. Gen. Laws Ann. ch. 233, §§ 81–83 (West 2000); Mich. Ct. R. § 3.972(C)(2) (2011); Minn. Stat. Ann. § 595.02 (West 2000); Minn. Stat. Ann. § 260C.165 (West 2000); Miss. Code Ann. § 13-1-403 (2009); Miss. R. Evid. 803(25) (2009); Mo. Rev. Stat. § 491.075 (2008); Nev. Rev. Stat. § 51.385 (2007); N.J. R. Evid. 803(c)(27) (2009); N.Y. Fam. Ct. Act § 1046(vi) (McKinney 2010); Ohio Evid. R. 807 (2007); Or. Rev. Stat. § 40.460 (2012); 42 Pa. Cons. Stat. Ann. §§ 5985.1, 5986 (West 2004); S.C. Code Ann. § 17-23-175 (West Supp. 2009); S.C. Code Ann. § 19-1-180 (West Supp. 2009); S.D. Codified Laws § 19-16-39 (2011); Tenn. Code Ann. § 24-7-120 (2009); Tenn. R. Evid. 803(25) (2009); Tex. Code Crim. Proc. Ann. art. 38.071–.072 (Vernon 2011); Va. Code Ann. § 63.2-1522 (2002); Va. R. Evid. 804 (2009); Wash. Rev. Code § 9A.44.120 (LexisNexis 2009).

5. In *Crawford v. Washington*, 541 U.S. 36 (2004), Scalia, writing for seven members of the Court, overruled *Ohio v. Roberts*, 448 U.S. 56 (1980), cited by the Court in *Craig*. In *Roberts*, the Court held that the Confrontation Clause does not bar admission of an unavailable witness's statement against a criminal defendant if the statement bears "adequate 'indicia of reliability.'" *Id.* at 42. In *Crawford*, however, the Court held that the Confrontation Clause barred the "admission of testimonial statements of a witness who did not appear at trial unless he was unavailable to testify, and the defendant had had a prior opportunity for cross-examination." *Id.* at 53–54. The Court, however, declined the opportunity to define "testimonial." "We leave for another day any effort to spell out a comprehensive definition of 'testimonial.' Whatever else the term covers, it applies at a minimum to prior testimony at a preliminary hearing, before a grand jury, or at a former trial; and to police interrogations." *Id.* at 68.

> Is *Craig* good law after *Crawford*? Myrna Raeder, a leading scholar on this issue, argues that *Craig*'s balancing test rejects the "absolute" nature of the right to face-to-face confrontation, and instead relies on the *Mattox v. United States* view that personal presence "must occasionally give way to considerations of public policy and the necessities of the case." Undoubtedly, *Craig* is at odds with *Crawford*'s observation that "[b]y replacing categorical constitutional guarantees with open-ended balancing tests, we do violence to their design." Yet, to date challenges to *Craig* have failed. This result is supported by *Crawford*'s concern with out-of-court hearsay, not in-court testimony, as well as by the fact that *Crawford* specifically called into question the holding of only one case, *White v. Illinois*, thereby implicitly approving *Craig*. However, *Craig*'s continued viability is ultimately dependent upon whether Justice Scalia's concept of confrontation continues to prevail. To date, he has written all of the Supreme Court's opinions embracing "testimonialism." In contrast, he dissented in *Craig*, decrying its cost-benefit analysis as "virtually" but not "actually" constitutional. Moreover, Justice Scalia's decision in *Coy v. Iowa*, which was limited by *Craig*, has never been overruled.

Myrna S. Raeder, *Distrusting Young Children Who Allege Sexual Abuse: Why Stereotypes Don't Die and Ways to Facilitate Child Testimony*, 16 Widener L. Rev. 239, 263–264 (2010). Do *Craig* and *Crawford* mean that such testimonial statements also are inadmissible in delinquency proceedings when a minor is accused of committing a criminal act?

6. Raeder argues that in civil abuse and neglect cases, however, a more flexible due-process standard applies. *Id.* at 270–272. Consequently, statements by a child declarant that might violate the Confrontation Clause if the proceeding were criminal nevertheless would be admissible in a civil case. Given what is at stake for parents in these proceedings, do you think that approach makes sense?

7. Are special procedures even necessary? John E. B. Myers has suggested that "despite the difficulty, most children are able to testify in the traditional manner, especially when they are prepared and supported through the process." JOHN E. B. MYERS, MYERS ON EVIDENCE IN CHILD, DOMESTIC AND ELDER ABUSE CASES § 3.01 (2007).

d. RIGHT TO COUNSEL

The United States Supreme Court has never held that a parent is constitutionally entitled to appointed counsel at the adjudicatory stage of an abuse or neglect proceeding. Nevertheless, most states require the appointment of counsel for indigent parents at the initial adjudication for abuse or neglect of a child. See Ala. Code § 12-15-305 (2008); Alaska Stat. Child in Need of Aid Rule 12 (2005); Ark. Code Ann. § 9-27-316 (2005); Cal. Welf. & Inst. Code § 317 (2011); Colo. Rev. Stat. § 19-3-202 (2003); Conn. Gen. Stat. § 46b-136 (2011); D.C. Code § 16-2304 (2000); Fla. Stat. § 39.013 (2012); Ga. Code Ann. § 15-11-6 (West 2000); Idaho Code Ann. § 16-1613 (2005); 705 Ill. Comp. Stat. § 405/1-5 (2006); Iowa Code § 232.89 (2002); Kan. Stat. Ann. § 38-2205 (2006); Ky. Rev. Stat. Ann. § 620.100 (West 2005); La. Child. Code Ann. art. 608 (2007); Me. Rev. Stat. tit. 22, § 4005 (2009); Md. Code Ann., Cts. & Jud. Proc. § 3-813 (West 2001); Mass. Gen. Laws ch. 119, § 29 (2011); Mont. Code Ann. § 41-3-425 (2011); N.H. Rev. Stat. Ann. § 169-C:10 (2011); N.J. Stat. Ann. § 9:6-8.43 (West 2006); N.Y. Fam. Ct. Act § 262 (McKinney 2012); N.C. Gen. Stat. § 7B-602 (2011); Ohio Rev. Code Ann. § 2151.352 (West 2005); Pa. Juv. Ct. Rule 1151 (2011); R.I. Gen. Laws § 40-11-7.1 (1996); S.C. Code Ann. § 63-7-1620 (2010); Tenn. Code Ann. § 37-1-126 (2010); Utah Code Ann. § 78A-6-317 (West 2010); Va. Code Ann. § 16.1-266 (2005); Wash. Rev. Code § 13.34.090 (2000); W. Va. Code § 49-6-2 (2012). A few states authorize but do not mandate the appointment of counsel for parents. Haw. Rev. Stat. § 587A-17 (2010); Ind. Code § 31-32-4-3 (1997); Minn. Stat. § 260C.163 (2012); Nev. Rev. Stat. § 432B.420 (2003); Wyo. Stat. Ann. § 14-3-211 (1978).

Does a child have the right to counsel in abuse or neglect proceedings? CAPTA requires the appointment of a guardian *ad litem* for states interested in receiving funding "in every case involving a victim of child abuse or neglect which results in a judicial proceeding." 42 U.S.C. § 5106a(b)(2)(B)(xiii) (2011). The guardian *ad litem*, who may be an attorney or court-appointed special advocate (CASA), must have "appropriate" training, "including training in early childhood, child, and adolescent development." The guardian *ad litem* must "obtain first-hand, a clear understanding of the situation and needs of the child; and... make recommendations to the court concerning the best interests of the child." 42 U.S.C. §§ 5106a(b)(2)(B)(xiii)(I)–(II). Nevertheless, a number of jurisdictions provide counsel to the child in an abuse or neglect proceeding. All of these states have been found to be in compliance with CAPTA, and the federal guidelines suggest that the appointment of counsel serves the child's best interests. Andrea Khoury, *Why a Lawyer? The Importance of Client-Directed Legal Representation for Youth*, 48 FAM. CT. REV. 277, 281 (2010) (arguing that client-directed representation for children in abuse and neglect proceedings is consistent with federal law).

Exactly how many states authorize the appointment of client-directed lawyers for children? See, e.g., U.S. State by State Chart, compiled by the Yale Representing Children Worldwide Project, http://www.law.yale.edu/rcw/rcw/summary.htm (twenty-one states require the appointment of an attorney or an attorney and a GAL). See also Alaska Stat. § 47.10.050 (1998) (may appoint counsel for the child); Alaska Child in Need of Aid R. 12 (2005) (appoint counsel when in the interest of justice); Del. Code Ann. tit. 13, § 2504 (West 2009) (may appoint counsel to represent child's wishes); Ga. Code Ann. § 15-11-6 (West 2000) (counsel must be provided for child not represented by parent); Iowa Code § 232.89 (2002) (appoint counsel and GAL for child); Ky. Rev. Stat. Ann. § 620.100 (West 2005) (child has right to counsel); La. Child. Code Ann. art. 607 (2007) (court shall appoint qualified, independent counsel); Md. Code Ann., Cts. & Jud. Proc. § 3-813 (West 2001) (child shall be represented by counsel); Mass. Gen. Laws ch. 119, § 29 (2011) (child has right to counsel); Minn. Stat. § 260C.163 (2010) (counsel for child ten years of age or older); Mont. Code Ann. § 41-3-425 (2005) (child has right to counsel); N.H. Rev. Stat. Ann. § 169-C:10 (2011) (court may appoint attorney for child when child's express preferences differ from assessment of best interests); Ohio Rev. Code Ann. § 2151.352 (West 2005) (child has right to counsel); Okla. Stat. tit. 10A, § 1-4-306 (2011) (attorney for child to represent child's express wishes); Or. Rev. Stat. § 419B.195 (2003) (court may appoint counsel for child); S.C. Code Ann. § 63-7-1620 (2010) (court may appoint counsel for child); Vt. Stat. Ann. tit. 33, § 5112 (2009) (court shall appoint attorney and GAL for child); W. Va. Code § 49-6-2 (2012) (child has right to counsel); Wis. Stat. § 48.23 (2009) (child may be represented by counsel at discretion of court); Wyo. Stat. Ann. § 14-3-211 (1978) (court shall appoint counsel for child).

Does the child have a constitutional right to counsel? The next case addresses that issue.

KENNY A. V. PERDUE
United States District Court for the Northern District of Georgia
356 F.Supp.2d 1353 (2005)

SHOOB, Senior District Judge.

This action is before the Court on motions for summary judgment filed by defendants Fulton County and DeKalb County. For the following reasons, the Court denies both motions.

Background

This is a class action brought on behalf of foster children in Fulton and DeKalb Counties. In addition to plaintiffs' claims against the state agencies and state officials responsible for operating Georgia's foster care system, plaintiffs also assert a claim against Fulton County and DeKalb County (County Defendants) for their alleged failure to provide foster children with adequate and effective legal representation in deprivation[1] and termination-of-parental-rights (TPR) proceedings.

Specifically, plaintiffs allege that the inadequate number of child advocate attorney positions funded by County Defendants results in extremely high caseloads for the attorneys, making effective representation of the class of plaintiff foster children structurally impossible in all proceedings before the juvenile courts where deprivation is alleged. In Count XIII of their First Amended Complaint, plaintiffs allege that this failure to provide adequate and effective legal representation violates plaintiffs' due process rights under the Georgia Constitution and, with respect to TPR proceedings, their statutory rights under O.C.G.A. § 15-11-98(a).[2] To correct these alleged deficiencies, plaintiffs pray for class-wide prospective injunctive and declaratory relief.

Deprivation cases consist of a series of hearings and review proceedings that take place over the course of a child's stay in the Georgia foster care system. These include (1) the initial 72-hour detention hearing, where the judge must determine whether there are reasonable grounds to believe that the child is deprived and whether the child should be returned to his or her parents or retained in the custody of the Division of Family and Children Services (DFCS) until the adjudicatory hearing occurs; (2) the adjudicatory hearing, where the juvenile court hears evidence and makes a determination on the merits of whether a child is deprived; (3) the dispositional hearing, where the juvenile court must determine what is to be done with the deprived child, including where and with whom the child is to be placed at that time; and (4) periodic review proceedings conducted either by the court or a citizen review panel. *See* O.C.G.A. §§ 15-11-39, 15-11-54 through 15-11-56, and 15-11-58(k). In addition, some deprivation cases also include TPR proceedings. *See* O.C.G.A. §§ 15-11-94 through 15-11-106.

In both Fulton and DeKalb Counties, child advocate attorneys are responsible for representing allegedly deprived children in all of these proceedings. Fulton County employs four child advocate attorneys, while DeKalb County employs five.[3] As of March 2004, there were 1,757 plaintiff foster children in custody in Fulton County and 914 in DeKalb County. This equates to a caseload of 439.2 child clients per attorney in Fulton County, and 182.8 child clients per attorney in DeKalb County. The American Bar Association, the United States Department of Health and Human Services, and the National Association of Counsel for Children (NACC) have each established standards of practice for lawyers who represent children in abuse and neglect cases. In light of the minimum requirements for effective advocacy set forth in these standards, the NACC recommends that no child advocate attorney should maintain a caseload of over 100 individual child clients at a time.

1. Under Georgia law, a "deprived child" is one who:
   (A) Is without proper parental care or control, subsistence, education as required by law, or other care or control necessary for the child's physical, mental, or emotional health or morals;
   (B) Has been placed for care or adoption in violation of law;
   (C) Has been abandoned by his or her parents or other legal custodian; or
   (D) Is without a parent, guardian, or custodian.

O.C.G.A. § 15-11-2(8).

2. In response to County Defendants' motions for summary judgment, plaintiffs also allege violation of a statutory right to counsel in deprivation proceedings under O.C.G.A. § 15-11-6(b).

3. When this suit was filed, DeKalb County employed only two child advocate attorneys.

Summary Judgment Standard

Under Rule 56(c) of the Federal Rules of Civil Procedure, summary judgment is appropriate when there is "no genuine issue as to any material fact...and the moving party is entitled to judgment as a matter of law." In *Celotex Corp. v. Catrett*, 477 U.S. 317, 106 S.Ct. 2548, 91 L.Ed.2d 265 (1986), the Supreme Court held that this burden could be met if the moving party demonstrates that there is "an absence of evidence to support the non-moving party's case." *Id.* at 325, 106 S.Ct. 2548. At that point, the burden shifts to the non-moving party to go beyond the pleadings and present specific evidence giving rise to a triable issue. *Id.* at 324, 106 S.Ct. 2548.

The Court, however, must construe the evidence and all inferences drawn from the evidence in the light most favorable to the non-moving party. *WSB-TV v. Lee*, 842 F.2d 1266, 1270 (11th Cir. 1988). Moreover, because the summary judgment standard mirrors that required for a judgment as a matter of law, summary judgment is not appropriate unless "under the governing law, there can be but one reasonable conclusion as to the verdict." *Anderson v. Liberty Lobby, Inc.*, 477 U.S. 242, 250, 106 S.Ct. 2505, 91 L.Ed.2d 202 (1986) (citation omitted).

Discussion

I. Summary of the Parties' Contentions and the Court's Conclusions

Notwithstanding the large caseloads carried by child advocate attorneys, County Defendants contend that they are entitled to summary judgment on plaintiffs' claim that they fail to provide adequate and effective legal representation to plaintiff foster children. First, County Defendants argue that, although they voluntarily provide representation to children in all deprivation proceedings, Georgia law requires provision of counsel to children only in TPR proceedings, and that plaintiff foster children therefore have no right to effective legal representation in general deprivation proceedings. Second, County Defendants contend that plaintiffs are not entitled to injunctive relief because (1) they have failed to show any irreparable injury arising from the Counties' alleged failure to provide effective assistance of counsel, and (2) they have an adequate legal remedy for any ineffective assistance in the form of either State Bar disciplinary proceedings or private actions for damages against the child advocate attorneys. Third, County Defendants argue that declaratory relief is inappropriate because state law clearly affords plaintiff foster children a right to counsel only in TPR proceedings, so there is no uncertainty as to their legal rights. Finally, County Defendants argue that the appropriate level of funding for child advocate attorneys is a legislative function that should not be interfered with by the Court.

In response, plaintiffs argue that they have both a statutory and a constitutional right to counsel in all deprivation cases, not just TPR proceedings, and that this right includes the right to effective assistance of counsel. Plaintiffs also contend that they have satisfied the irreparable harm requirement for injunctive relief because there is sufficient evidence in the record to create a genuine issue of fact as to whether they are receiving, or face a substantial risk of receiving, ineffective assistance of counsel. Specifically, plaintiffs cite evidence that child advocate attorneys' caseloads in both Fulton and DeKalb Counties are substantially above the 100 individual clients at a time recommended by the NACC, and that these excessive caseloads prevent them from carrying out their basic professional responsibilities. Plaintiffs also cite testimonial and documentary evidence, including child advocate attorney files for the named plaintiffs, showing that child advocates are providing ineffective assistance of counsel. Plaintiffs also argue that, contrary to County Defendants' argument, the filing of a Bar complaint is not an adequate legal remedy because the Georgia Bar Association has no authority to award class-wide injunctive or declaratory relief aimed at structural reform. Moreover, plaintiffs argue, it is not the incompetence of individual attorneys that is the problem, but rather systemic problems in the Fulton and DeKalb systems, specifically underfunding and the resultant excessive caseloads. Finally, plaintiffs contend that they have established the need for declaratory relief in order to clarify whether they have the statutory and constitutional rights to effective assistance of counsel that they claim.

The Court concludes that plaintiff foster children have both a statutory and a constitutional right to counsel in all deprivation proceedings, including but not limited to TPR proceedings. The Court further concludes that plaintiffs have presented sufficient evidence to create a genuine issue for trial as to whether they are threatened with irreparable harm because they are receiving, or face a substantial risk of receiving, ineffective assistance of counsel in such proceedings. The Court rejects County Defendants' argument that plaintiffs have an adequate legal remedy in the form of State Bar complaints or lawsuits filed against individual child advocate attorneys because such actions cannot remedy the systemic deficiencies cited by plaintiffs. The Court concludes that the parties' sharp dispute over whether plaintiffs have a right to counsel in deprivation proceedings, and whether that right is being violated, clearly presents a live controversy for which declaratory relief is appropriate. Finally, the Court rejects County Defendants' argument that only the legislature has the authority to correct this problem. If plaintiffs prove their case at trial, then this Court has not only the authority but the obligation to grant appropriate injunctive relief.

II. Statutory Right to Counsel

The parties agree that plaintiff foster children have a statutory right to counsel in TPR proceedings, as set out in O.C.G.A. § 15-11-98(a). The parties, however, dispute whether there is a statutory right to counsel in general deprivation proceedings. Plaintiffs contend that such a right arises under O.C.G.A. § 15-11-6(b). The Court agrees.

Georgia Code section 15-11-6(b) provides in pertinent part as follows:

> *Right to Legal Representation.* Except as otherwise provided under this article, a party is entitled to representation by legal counsel at all stages of any proceedings alleging delinquency, unruliness, incorrigibility, or deprivation and if, as an indigent person, a party is unable to employ counsel, he or she is entitled to have the court provide counsel for him or her.... Counsel must be provided for a child not represented by the child's parent, guardian, or custodian. If the interests of two or more parties conflict, separate counsel shall be provided for each of them.

O.C.G.A. § 15-11-6(b). This statute makes clear, at the very least, that a child in a deprivation proceeding is entitled to counsel if his or her parent, guardian, or custodian does not attend. In addition, because a child in a deprivation proceeding is a "party" to the proceeding, the final sentence of the statute means that, even if the child's parent, guardian, or custodian does attend the proceeding, if there is a conflict between the child and the parent, guardian, or custodian, then the child is entitled to separate counsel.

The only question, then, is under what circumstances such a conflict exists. In answering this question, the Court is guided by the Georgia Code's direction that statutory provisions governing juvenile proceedings "shall be liberally construed to the end... [t]hat children whose well-being is threatened shall be assisted and protected...." O.C.G.A. § 15-11-1(1). Applying this principle, the Attorney General of Georgia has found that there is an "inherent conflict of interests" between a child and his parent or caretaker in a deprivation proceeding.

1976 Op. Att'y Gen. No. 76-131 at 237. Given the fact that it is the parent or caretaker who is alleged to have abused or neglected the child, the Court finds the Attorney General's opinion persuasive. *See Campbell v. Poythress*, 216 Ga.App. 834, 836, 456 S.E.2d 110 (1995) (recognizing Georgia Attorney General opinion as persuasive authority). Accordingly, the Court concludes that in a deprivation proceeding there is an inherent conflict of interests between the child and his or her parent, guardian, or custodian, which requires appointment of separate counsel for the child pursuant to O.C.G.A. § 15-11-6(b).[6]

County Defendants' argument that this interpretation of O.C.G.A. § 15-11-6(b) conflicts with O.C.G.A. § 15-11-9(b) is without merit. The latter statute provides in part that the juvenile court "shall appoint a guardian ad litem for a child who is a party to the [deprivation] proceeding if the child has no parent, guardian, or custodian appearing on the child's behalf or if the interests of the parent, guardian, or custodian appearing on the child's behalf conflict with the child's interests or in any other case in which the interests of the child require a guardian." O.C.G.A. § 15-11-9(b). There is no conflict, however, in requiring the appointment of both an attorney and a guardian ad litem for the child. Indeed, the two Code sections expressly *require* the appointment of *both* an attorney and a guardian ad litem in cases where the child is not represented by his or her parent, guardian, or custodian. Compare O.C.G.A. § 15-11-6(b) ("Counsel *must* be provided for a child not represented by the child's parent, guardian, or custodian") (emphasis added); and O.C.G.A. § 15-11-9(b) ("The court... *shall* appoint a guardian ad litem for a child who is a party to the proceeding if the child has no parent, guardian, or custodian appearing on the child's behalf....") (emphasis added).

Clearly, therefore, the legislature did not intend the appointment of a guardian ad litem as a substitute for the appointment of counsel. *See also* O.C.G.A. § 15-11-98(a) (providing for appointment of both an attorney and a guardian ad litem for child in TPR proceeding). Thus, there is no conflict created by construing Section 15-11-6(b) to require the appointment of separate counsel for the child in conflict of interest situations simply because Section 15-11-9(b) requires appointment of a guardian ad litem in the same situations.

III. Constitutional Right to Counsel

Even if there were not a statutory right to counsel for children in deprivation cases and TPR proceedings, the Court concludes that such a right is guaranteed under the Due Process Clause of the Georgia Constitution, Art. I, § 1, ¶ 1. It is well settled that children are afforded protection under the Due Process Clauses of both the United States and Georgia Constitutions and are entitled to constitutionally adequate procedural due process when their liberty or property rights are at stake. *See, e.g., Goss v. Lopez*, 419 U.S. 565, 95 S.Ct. 729, 42 L.Ed.2d 725 (1975) (lack of adequate procedures used by school in suspending students violated due process); *In re Gault*, 387 U.S. 1, 87 S.Ct. 1428, 18 L.Ed.2d 527 (1967) (holding that minors have due process right to counsel in delinquency proceedings); *K.E.S. v. Georgia*, 134 Ga.App. 843, 847, 216 S.E.2d 670

6. Even after the Division of Family and Children Services (DFCS) has assumed custody of the child, there continues to be a conflict of interests between the child and DFCS, which precludes the attorneys who represent DFCS from also representing the child. This is true because the institutional concerns of DFCS may conflict with the needs of the deprived child. For example, there is evidence that a shortage of family foster homes in Fulton and DeKalb Counties has led DFCS to place children in inappropriate and overcrowded homes, to shuffle children from one placement to another, and to overuse institutional placements. Because such conflicts between the broad programmatic needs of DFCS and the specific needs of the individual child may arise in every case, children are entitled to representation by separate counsel throughout the course of the deprivation proceedings.

(1975) (recognizing minors' right to counsel established in *In re Gault*). The question, therefore, is whether plaintiff foster children have liberty or property interests at stake in deprivation and TPR proceedings, and, if so, what process is due when those interests are threatened.

The Court finds that children have fundamental liberty interests at stake in deprivation and TPR proceedings. These include a child's interest in his or her own safety, health, and well-being, as well as an interest in maintaining the integrity of the family unit and in having a relationship with his or her biological parents. On the one hand, an erroneous decision that a child is not deprived or that parental rights should not be terminated can have a devastating effect on a child, leading to chronic abuse or even death. On the other hand, an erroneous decision that a child is deprived or that parental rights should be terminated can lead to the unnecessary destruction of the child's most important family relationships.

Furthermore, a child's liberty interests continue to be at stake even after the child is placed in state custody. At that point, a "special relationship" is created that gives rise to rights to reasonably safe living conditions and services necessary to ensure protection from physical, psychological, and emotional harm. *See Taylor v. Ledbetter*, 818 F.2d 791, 795 (11th Cir. 1987); *LaShawn A. v. Dixon*, 762 F.Supp. 959, 993 (D.D.C. 1991). Thus, a child's fundamental liberty interests are at stake not only in the initial deprivation hearing but also in the series of hearings and review proceedings that occur as part of a deprivation case once a child comes into state custody.

Given the liberty interests at stake, the question becomes what process is constitutionally required to safeguard those interests. To determine what process is due under the Due Process Clause of the Georgia Constitution, Georgia courts apply the three-part federal test enunciated in *Mathews v. Eldridge*, 424 U.S. 319, 334–35, 96 S.Ct. 893, 47 L.Ed.2d 18 (1976):

> [O]ur prior decisions indicate that identification of the specific dictates of due process generally requires consideration of three distinct factors: First, the private interest that will be affected by the official action; second, the risk of an erroneous deprivation of such interest through the procedures used, and the probable value, if any, of additional or substitute procedural safeguards; and finally, the Government's interest, including the function involved and the fiscal and administrative burdens that the additional or substitute procedural requirement would entail.

See Hood v. Carsten, 267 Ga. 579, 580–81, 481 S.E.2d 525 (1997). Applying the *Mathews* test to this case, the Court concludes that plaintiff foster children have a right to counsel in deprivation and TPR proceedings under the Due Process Clause of the Georgia Constitution.

First, the Court rejects County Defendants' contention that in deprivation and TPR proceedings, "a child's liberty interest is not at stake because no matter the result, they are not at risk of losing any liberty." This argument completely ignores the child's fundamental liberty interests in health, safety, and family integrity which, as discussed above, are clearly at stake in such proceedings. The Court also rejects County Defendants' argument that deprivation and TPR proceedings present no threat to children's physical liberty. To the contrary, the evidence shows that foster children in state custody are subject to placement in a wide array of different types of foster care placements, including institutional facilities where their physical liberty is greatly restricted. Indeed, plaintiffs have pointed to evidence that foster children are often forced to live in such institutional settings because suitable family foster homes are not available. The Court concludes that the private liberty interests at stake support a due process right to counsel in deprivation and TPR proceedings.

Second, the Court finds that there is a significant risk that erroneous decisions will be made during the course of deprivation and TPR proceedings. As an initial matter, the standards employed by juvenile courts in deprivation and TPR proceedings allow wide room for judicial discretion and thus for subjective determinations. *See In the Interest of Z.B.*, 252 Ga.App. 335, 339, 556 S.E.2d 234 (2001) ("In determining how the interest of the child is best served, the juvenile court is vested with a broad discretion which will not be controlled in the absence of manifest abuse"). Such "imprecise substantive standards that leave determinations unusually open to the subjective values of the judge" serve "to magnify the risk of erroneous factfinding." *Santosky v. Kramer*, 455 U.S. 745, 762, 102 S.Ct. 1388, 71 L.Ed.2d 599 (1982). In addition, plaintiffs have pointed to strong empirical evidence that DFCS makes erroneous decisions on a routine basis that affect the safety and welfare of foster children.

Contrary to County Defendants' argument, juvenile court judges, court appointed special advocates (CASAs), and citizen review panels do not adequately mitigate the risk of such errors. Judges, unlike child advocate attorneys, cannot conduct their own investigations and are entirely dependent on others to provide them information about the child's circumstances. Similarly, citizen review panels must rely on facts presented to them by state and county personnel, including local DFCS offices. As a result, their reviews are only as good as the information provided to them by DFCS and other state and local agencies. CASAs are also volunteers who do not provide legal representation to a child. Moreover, CASAs are appointed in only a small number of cases. The Court concludes that only the appointment of counsel can effectively mitigate the risk of significant errors in deprivation and TPR proceedings.

Finally, the Court must consider the government's interest, including the function involved and the fiscal and administrative burdens that a right to counsel would entail. In this case, the function involved is that of the state as *parens patriae*, which refers to "the state in its capacity as provider of protection to those unable to care for themselves." Black's Law Dictionary 1144 (8th ed. 2004); *see Blackburn v. Blackburn*, 249 Ga. 689, 692 n. 5, 292 S.E.2d 821 (1982) (The basis of this doctrine [of *parens patriae*] is that the state has a legitimate interest in protecting those individuals unable to protect themselves). As parens patriae, the government's overriding interest is to ensure that a child's safety and well-being are protected. *See Williams v. Crosby*, 118 Ga. 296, 298, 45 S.E. 282 (1903) ("[T]he *parens patriae* must protect the helpless and the innocent"). As discussed above, such protection can be adequately ensured only if the child is represented by legal counsel throughout the course of deprivation and TPR proceedings. Therefore, it is in the state's interest, as well as the child's, to require the appointment of a child advocate attorney. This fundamental interest far outweighs any fiscal or administrative burden that a right to appointed counsel may entail.

IV. Injunctive Relief

The right to counsel, of course, means the right to effective counsel. *See Evitts v. Lucey*, 469 U.S. 387, 395, 105 S.Ct. 830, 83 L.Ed.2d 821 (1985) (quoting *McMann v. Richardson*, 397 U.S. 759, 771 n. 14, 90 S.Ct. 1441, 25 L.Ed.2d 763 (1970)) ("It has long been recognized that the right to counsel is the right to the effective assistance of counsel"); *Nicholson v. Williams*, 203 F.Supp.2d 153, 239 (E.D.N.Y. 2002) ("The right to appointed counsel when necessary for due process is a right to effective counsel"). County Defendants argue that plaintiffs have failed to present sufficient evidence of ineffective assistance of counsel to support issuance of an injunction. The Court disagrees.

First, it is important to note that in a class action like this one, which seeks only prospective injunctive and declaratory relief to redress institutional deficiencies in the provision of counsel, class members need not "establish that ineffective assistance was inevitable for each of the class members." *Luckey v. Harris*, 860 F.2d 1012, 1017 (11th Cir. 1988). Instead, class members need only meet the traditional standard for the application of equitable relief, namely, a "likelihood of substantial and immediate irreparable injury" if relief is not granted, and "the inadequacy of remedies at law." *Id.* Evidence of "systemic" deficiencies, such as inadequate resources for appointed counsel, is sufficient to meet this standard. *Id.* at 1018; *see also Nicholson*, 203 F.Supp.2d at 240 ("[W]here the state imposes systemic barriers to effective representation, prospective injunctive relief without individualized proof of injury is necessary and appropriate"). In this case, plaintiffs have presented evidence that meets the *Luckey* standard, thus creating a genuine issue of material fact as to whether they are receiving, or face a substantial risk of receiving, ineffective assistance of counsel.

Plaintiffs cite deposition testimony and documentary evidence showing that effective assistance of counsel by a child advocate attorney requires that he or she carry out certain minimum legal tasks as part of the representation. These tasks include meeting with the child prior to court hearings and when apprised of emergencies or significant events impacting the child; conducting investigations and discovery, including interviewing individuals involved with the child, such as caseworkers and foster parents, and reviewing all judicial, medical, social services, educational, and other records pertaining to the child; evaluating the child's need for particular services; monitoring the implementation of all court orders; participating in all hearings; and filing all relevant motions and appeals.

Plaintiffs also cite the NACC recommendation that, in order to perform these essential tasks, a child advocate attorney should represent no more than 100 individual clients at a time. The evidence shows that this recommendation is based on the assumption that a child advocate attorney will spend an average of 20 hours representing each child and will work 2000 hours in a year. The recommended caseload limit is meant to apply regardless of how many support staff an attorney might have and assumes that child advocate attorneys are not required to perform non-legal, administrative tasks. Based on his extensive experience in the child welfare area and his participation in the development of the NACC caseload limit, NACC Executive Director Marvin Ventrell testified that a child advocate attorney could not possibly provide effective representation if the attorney had a number of clients significantly above 100, and certainly not if the attorney had a caseload of 200 clients. The evidence shows that each of the four child advocate attorneys in Fulton County represent almost 450 clients, while the five child advocate attorneys in DeKalb County each represent approximately 200 clients.

In addition, plaintiffs have presented testimonial and documentary evidence showing that Fulton and DeKalb Counties' child advocate attorneys are overwhelmed by their caseloads and cannot provide effective representation to their child clients. Mary Hermann, a Fulton County child advocate attorney, testified that the only thing she does in every case is read the initial deprivation petition, that she does not meet with all of her clients, that meeting with a child client is purely "aspirational," and that she does not know how many children she currently represents or how many children her office currently represents. Dorothy Murphy, a DeKalb County child advocate attorney, testified that DeKalb's child advocates office has been providing inadequate representation since "the year it was formed" and admitted that she provided inadequate assistance to the plaintiffs in this case. She further testified that she had "failed to personally meet or speak with 90 percent of [her] own clients," and that there are cases where no one ever reviewed the medical, social service, education, or other records for a child, met with the foster care provider, or even met with the child. She also testified that because of her caseload, she often does not have time to investigate whether her child client is receiving appropriate medical or social services or to monitor whether her child client is in a safe foster care placement. In fact, she admitted, "I don't know where a lot of the children that I represent are."

Plaintiffs also point to evidence from the named plaintiffs' own child advocate attorney files. This evidence shows that the child advocate attorneys often failed to meet with their clients, failed to monitor compliance with court orders, and failed to ensure that their clients' foster care placements were safe and appropriate. All of this evidence is more than sufficient to create a genuine issue for trial as to whether plaintiff foster children, including the named plaintiffs, are receiving, or face a substantial risk of receiving, ineffective assistance of counsel.

Plaintiffs have also shown that they have no adequate remedy at law. Contrary to County Defendants' argument, filing a complaint with the State Bar is not an adequate legal remedy. The State Bar has authority only to discipline individual attorneys, not to award the type of class-wide relief that plaintiffs seek. Given the evidence showing that the ineffective assistance problem arises not from personal deficiencies in individual attorneys but from systemic problems in the Fulton and DeKalb County child welfare systems, such a limited remedy is totally inadequate. For the same reason, malpractice lawsuits filed against individual attorneys also provide an inadequate remedy for the harm alleged.

V. Declaratory Relief

Contrary to County Defendants' contention, the Court concludes that declaratory relief is clearly appropriate in this case because there is an "actual controversy" regarding plaintiffs' right to legal counsel in deprivation cases. *See* 28 U.S.C. § 2201 ("In a case of actual controversy within its jurisdiction, . . . any court of the United States, upon the filing of an appropriate pleading, may declare the rights and other legal relations of any interested party seeking such declaration, whether or not further relief is or could be sought"). Although both sides agree that there is a statutory right to counsel in TPR proceedings, County Defendants deny that there is any right to counsel in general deprivation cases, while plaintiffs insist that they have both statutory and constitutional rights to counsel in such cases. Furthermore, County Defendants and plaintiffs vigorously dispute whether plaintiffs have been denied effective assistance of counsel in either general deprivation cases or TPR proceedings. Clearly, therefore, there is a controversy between the parties regarding plaintiffs' rights that is sufficient to invoke the Court's jurisdiction to render declaratory relief.

VI. Public Policy

County Defendants argue that public policy considerations mandate that plaintiffs not be allowed to circumvent the Georgia legislature, which has sole authority to determine the appropriate amount of funding for child advocate attorneys. This argument is without merit. If this Court finds that plaintiff foster children's right to counsel is being violated, then it is the obligation of the Court to order an appropriate remedy even if such an order requires the state to appropriate additional funds to hire more child advocate attorneys. County Defendants cite no authority to the contrary.

Summary

For the foregoing reasons, the Court DENIES defendant Fulton County's motion for summary judgment and DENIES defendant DeKalb County's motion for summary judgment.

NOTES AND QUESTIONS

1. The District Court subsequently sent the case to mediation, and the parties entered into a consent decree. The one issue on which they could not agree was attorney's fees. Pursuant to 42 U.S.C. § 1988, the court, in its discretion, may allow attorney's fees to the prevailing party in an action brought pursuant to 42 U.S.C. § 1982. The district court subsequently awarded the children's lawyers $10.5 million and an additional $4.5 million as an enhancement, noting, among other things, that the attorneys had exhibited "a higher degree of skill, commitment, dedication, and professionalism...than the Court has seen displayed by the attorneys in any other case during its 27 years on the bench." *Kenny A. ex rel. Winn v. Perdue*, 454 F.Supp.2d 1260, 1289 (N.D. Ga. 2006). The Eleventh Circuit affirmed the award. *Kenny A. ex rel. Winn v. Perdue*, 532 F.3d 1209 (11th Cir. 2008). The United States Supreme Court granted *certiorari* and held that while attorney's fees may be enhanced under certain circumstances, the district court failed to provide proper justification for its award. *Perdue v. Kenny A. ex rel. Winn*, 130 S.Ct. 1662 (2010).

2. On what basis did the district court conclude that children have a right to counsel in abuse and neglect proceedings? What tests did the court apply?

3. Should children have a lawyer in abuse and neglect proceedings? Why? What is the lawyer's role under these circumstances? Why doesn't the appointment of a lawyer for the parents adequately protect the child's interests? What if a lawyer's client is very young? Is a guardian *ad litem* sufficient? These issues are hotly debated among scholars and advocates. The dominant view among scholars and commentators is that children are entitled to be represented by lawyers who advocate for their express preferences. See, e.g., Linda D. Elrod, *Client-Directed Lawyers for Children: It Is the "Right" Thing to Do*, 27 Pace L. Rev. 869 (2007); Katherine Hunt Federle, *Children's Rights and the Need for Protection*, 34 Fam. L. Q. 421 (2000); Andrea Khoury, *Why a Lawyer? The Importance of Client-Directed Legal Representation for Youth*, 48 Fam. Ct. Rev. 277 (2010); Erik Pitchal, *Children's Constitutional Right to Counsel in Dependency Cases*, 15 Temp. Pol. & Civ. Rts. L. Rev. 663, 684 (2006); Catherine Ross, *From Vulnerability to Voice: Appointing Counsel for Children in Civil Litigation*, 64 Fordham L. Rev. 1571 (1996); Jacob Ethan Smiles, *A Child's Due Process Right to Legal Counsel in Abuse and Neglect Dependency Proceedings*, 37 Fam. L. Q. 485 (Fall 2003); Merril Sobie, *The Child Client: Representing Children in Child Protective Proceedings*, 22 Touro L. Rev. 745 (2006); LaShanda Taylor, *A Lawyer for Every Child: Client-Directed Representation in Dependency Cases*, 47 Fam. Ct. Rev. 605 (2009) (explaining commitment to client-directed representation in proposed ABA Model Act Governing the Representation of Children in Abuse, Neglect, and Dependency Proceedings); Shannan L. Wilber, *Independent Counsel for Children*, 27 Fam. L. Q. 349, 354–357 (1993). See also Am. Bar Ass'n, Standards of Practice for Lawyers Who Represent Children in Abuse and Neglect Cases (1996), http:// www.abanet.org/child/repstandwhole.pdf (setting forth professional standards for children's lawyers, emphasizing the importance of protecting children's legal rights in abuse and neglect cases); Am. Bar Ass'n, Juvenile Justice Standards Annotated: A Balanced Approach (Robert E. Shepherd, Jr., ed., 1996) (offering guidelines for representation and adjudication in the juvenile-justice context); *Recommendations of the UNLV Conference on Representing Children in Families: Child Advocacy and Justice Ten Years after Fordham*, 6 Nev. L. J. 592 (2006); *Recommendations of the Conference on Ethical Issues in the Legal Representation of Children*, 64 Fordham L. Rev. 1301 (1996), reprinted in 6 Nev. L. J. 1408 (2006).

On the other hand, a number of scholars have argued that children do not need or should not have lawyers acting as lawyers and may be better served by best-interest advocacy. See, e.g., DONALD DUQUETTE, ADVOCATING FOR THE CHILD IN PROTECTION PROCEEDINGS: A HANDBOOK FOR LAWYERS AND COURT APPOINTED SPECIAL ADVOCATES (1990); MARTIN GUGGENHEIM, WHAT'S WRONG WITH CHILDREN'S RIGHTS (2005); Barbara Ann Atwood, *The Uniform Representation of Children in Abuse, Neglect, and Custody Proceedings Act: Bridging the Divide between Pragmatism and Idealism*, 42 FAM. L. Q. 63 (2008); Donald N. Duquette, *Legal Representation for Children in Protection Proceedings: Two Distinct Lawyer Roles Are Required*, 34 FAM. L. Q. 441 (2000); Brian G. Fraser, *Independent Representation for the Abused and Neglected Child: The Guardian ad Litem*, 13 CAL. W. L. REV. 16 (1976); Martin Guggenheim, *How Children's Lawyers Serve State Interests*, 6 NEV. L. J. 805 (2006) (arguing against providing young children with lawyers in most legal proceedings); Martin Guggenheim, *Reconsidering the Need for Counsel for Children in Custody, Visitation, and Child Protection Proceedings*, 29 LOY. U. CHI. L. J. 299 (1998); Tara Lea Muhlhauser, *From "Best" to "Better": The Interests of Children and the Role of a Guardian ad Litem*, 66 N.D. L. REV. 633 (1990); Michael S. Piraino, *Lay Representation of Abused and Neglected Children: Variations on Court Appointed Special Advocate Programs and Their Relationship to Quality Advocacy*, 1 J. CTR. FOR CHILD. & CTS. 63 (1999). See also Unif. Representation of Children in Abuse, Neglect, and Custody Proceedings Act (amended 2007), 9C U.L.A. 26 (Supp. 2010).

A review of literature on child-abuse and -neglect detection and prevention suggests ways in which states can more effectively deal with the harms that adult caregivers inflict upon children. See, e.g., JOHN MYERS, CHILD PROTECTION IN AMERICA 134–227 (2006) (analyzing the causes of child abuse and how the child-protection system can be improved to reduce abuse and neglect); Duncan Lindsey & Aron Shlonsky, *Closing Reflections: Future Research Directions and a New Paradigm*, in CHILD WELFARE RESEARCH 375–378 (Duncan Lindsay & Aron Shlonsky eds., 2008) (concluding that the child-welfare system must shift its focus and work on efforts to prevent child maltreatment); JENNIFER A. REICH, FIXING FAMILIES: PARENTS, POWER, AND THE CHILD WELFARE SYSTEM 7 (2005) (reviewing CPS's effectiveness as an agency); DOROTHY ROBERTS, SHATTERED BONDS: THE COLOR OF CHILD WELFARE 267–276 (2002) (noting that the child-protection system is disproportionately failing black children and needs to change the purpose of its services and the way they are administered); JOAN SHIREMAN, CRITICAL ISSUES IN CHILD WELFARE 390–396 (2003) (noting that the most important movements in the child-welfare field are toward professionalizing the field and providing greater support to parents); U.S. ADVISORY BD. ON CHILD ABUSE AND NEGLECT (ABCAN), U.S. DEP'T OF HEALTH & HUMAN SERVS., NEIGHBORS HELPING NEIGHBORS: A NEW NATIONAL STRATEGY FOR THE PROTECTION OF CHILDREN 27–30 (1993) (discussing possible responses to the foster-care crisis); ELIZABETH BARTHOLET, NOBODY'S CHILDREN: ABUSE AND NEGLECT, FOSTER DRIFT, AND THE ADOPTION ALTERNATIVE 163–203 (1999) (emphasizing that supporting the family is the best solution, but if it is not viable to do so, then the system needs to act quickly to protect abused children, i.e., via removal or parental termination); JANE WALDFOGEL, THE FUTURE OF CHILD PROTECTION 208–234 (1998) (discussing proposed CPS reformations from narrowing reporting laws to involving more community partners in the child-welfare system); RICHARD WEISSBOURD, THE VULNERABLE CHILD 223–237 (1996) (analyzing the impact of socioeconomic and family dynamics on children and offering suggestions on how cities can help children); JOHN M. HAGEDORN, FORSAKING OUR CHILDREN: BUREAUCRACY AND REFORM IN THE CHILD PROTECTION SYSTEM 139–157 (1995) (emphasizing that reforms should be analyzed carefully in order to make sure that they are having a positive impact on the child-welfare system).

E. Permanency Hearings

1. STATUTORY FRAMEWORK

Dispositional hearings, known as permanency hearings, are held after the court determines that a child is abused or neglected. Federal law requires states seeking federal funds to comply with certain procedural requirements. For example, state agencies must complete a detailed "case plan" outlining the agency's plan for finding permanency for the abused or neglected child. 42 U.S.C. § 675 (2011). Under the law, permanency may mean reunification with the child's parents, permanent custody, or adoption with a relative or someone else. 42 U.S.C. § 675 (2011). Permanency hearings must be held within twelve months of the child's "entry into foster care" and every year thereafter, defined as the earlier of the date of a judicial finding that the child was abused or neglected or sixty days after the child was removed from the child's parent or other caregiver. 42 U.S.C. § 675(5) (2011). At the permanency-plan hearing, the court determines the child's permanency plan. 42 U.S.C. § 675(5) (2011).

Federal law requires the state to make "reasonable efforts" to effectuate the permanency plan selected by the court, by reunifying children with their families or moving the child toward another permanent placement in a "timely manner." 42 U.S.C. §§ 671(a)(15)(B)–(C) (2011). Federal funding is contingent on a judicial finding that the agency has made reasonable efforts; if the requisite finding is not made, the state cannot obtain federal funds for that child. 45 C.F.R. §§ 1356.21(b)(2)(i)–(ii) (2011). In addition to the timelines and reasonable-efforts requirements, federal law requires the application of "procedural safeguards" to hearings pertaining to the child's removal from home, visitation rights of the parents, and any change in the child's placement. 42 U.S.C. § 675(5)(C)(ii) (2011). Children must be consulted in "an age-appropriate manner" about their permanency plans. 42 U.S.C. § 675(5)(C)(iii) (2011).

After the court has determined the permanency plan, the child's status must be reviewed at least once every six months by the court or by administrative review. 42 U.S.C. § 675(5)(B) (2011). Administrative review "means a review open to the participation of the parents of the child, conducted by a panel of appropriate persons at least one of whom is not responsible for the case management of, or the delivery of services to, either the child or the parents who are the subject of the review." 42 U.S.C. § 675(6) (2011). The court or administrative agency must review "the continuing necessity for and appropriateness of the placement, the extent of compliance with the case plan, and the extent of progress which has been made toward alleviating or mitigating the causes necessitating placement in foster care, and to project a likely date by which the child may be returned to and safely maintained in the home or placed for adoption or legal guardianship." 42 U.S.C. § 675(5)(b) (2011).

What exactly should happen at a permanency hearing? The National Council of Juvenile and Family Court Judges has issued guidelines to assist courts in making the necessary findings at a permanency hearing. Nat'l Council of Juvenile & Family Court Judges, Adoption & Permanency Guidelines: Improving Court Practice in Child Abuse & Neglect Cases (2000). The guidelines require judges to make specific findings of fact and conclusions of law, including the reasonable-efforts finding, and a determination about the permanency plan. *Id.* at 22. The guidelines mandate the presence of parents and their attorneys, the caseworker, the state's attorney, the child, the child's guardian *ad litem*, the child's attorney if applicable, foster parents, and relatives. *Id.* at 20. The guidelines also urge the written submission of permanency-plan proposals and objections in advance of the hearing. *Id.* at 19.

Is there a procedural gap between the adjudicatory hearing in an abuse or neglect case and the final hearing to determine permanency? Some states mandate certain procedural protections at the permanency hearing. These jurisdictions, for example, may provide parties with the right to introduce evidence, cross-examine witnesses, and present evidence but may nevertheless allow the introduction of hearsay. Other state statutes may be silent on these matters. Josh Gupta-Kagan, *Filling the Due Process Donut Hole: Abuse and Neglect Cases between Disposition and Permanency*, 10 Conn. Pub. Int. L.J. 13, 24–27 (2010). The states also vary widely in their approach to permitting appeals from permanency findings. *Id.* at 29. What process should be due parents who have been found to be abusive or neglectful?

2. REASONABLE EFFORTS

In 1980, Congress passed the Adoption Assistance and Child Welfare Act (AACWA), Pub. L. No. 96-272, § 94 Stat. 500, in response to concerns that too many children had been removed unnecessarily from their homes and were languishing in foster care. The AACWA required child-welfare agencies to make reasonable efforts to "[prevent] the unnecessary separation of children from their families by identifying family problems, assisting families in resolving their problems, and preventing breakup of the family where the prevention of child removal is desirable and possible." *Id.* Reasonable efforts were not defined. The AACWA also required the juvenile court judge to determine if the agency had made reasonable efforts.

What if a state fails to make reasonable efforts when required to do so? The next case addresses this problem.

SUTER V. ARTIST M.
Supreme Court of the United States
503 U.S. 347 (1992)

Chief Justice Rehnquist delivered the opinion of the Court.

This case raises the question whether private individuals have the right to enforce by suit a provision of the Adoption Assistance and Child Welfare Act of 1980 (Adoption Act or Act), 94 Stat. 500, 42 U.S.C. §§ 620–628, 670–679a, either under the Act itself or through an action under 42 U.S.C. § 1983.[1] The Court of Appeals for the Seventh Circuit held that 42 U.S.C. § 671(a)(15) contained an implied right of action, and that respondents could enforce this section of the Act through an action brought under § 1983 as well. We hold that the Act does not create an enforceable right on behalf of respondents.

The Adoption Act establishes a federal reimbursement program for certain expenses incurred by the States in administering foster care and adoption services. The Act provides that States will be reimbursed for a percentage of foster care and adoption assistance payments when the State satisfies the requirements of the Act. 42 U.S.C. §§ 672–674, 675(4)(A) (1988 ed. and Supp. I).

To participate in the program, States must submit a plan to the Secretary of Health and Human Services for approval by the Secretary. §§ 670, 671. Section 671 lists 16 qualifications which state plans must contain in order to gain the Secretary's approval. As relevant here, the Act provides:

> "(a) Requisite features of State plan
>
> "In order for a State to be eligible for payments under this part, it shall have a plan approved by the Secretary which—...
>
> "(3) provides that the plan shall be in effect in all political subdivisions of the State, and, if administered by them, be mandatory upon them;...
>
> "(15) effective October 1, 1983, provides that, in each case, reasonable efforts will be made (A) prior to the placement of a child in foster care, to prevent or eliminate the need for removal of the child from his home, and (B) to make it possible for the child to return to his home...." §§ 671(a)(3), (15).

Petitioners in this action are Sue Suter and Gary T. Morgan, the Director and the Guardianship Administrator, respectively, of the Illinois Department of Children and Family Services (DCFS). DCFS is the state agency responsible for, among other things, investigating charges of child abuse and neglect and providing services to abused and neglected children and their families. DCFS is authorized under Illinois law, see Ill.Rev.Stat., ch. 37, ¶ 802-1 *et seq.* (1989), to gain temporary custody of an abused or neglected child after a hearing and order by the Juvenile Court. Alternatively, the court may order that a child remain in his home under a protective supervisory order entered against his parents. See *Artist M. v. Johnson*, 917 F.2d 980, 982–983 (CA7 1990). Once DCFS has jurisdiction over a child either in its temporary custody, or in the child's home under a protective order, all services are provided to the child and his family by means of an individual caseworker at DCFS to whom the child's case is assigned. App. 35–39.

Respondents filed this class-action suit seeking declaratory and injunctive relief under the Adoption Act. They alleged that petitioners, in contravention of 42 U.S.C. § 671(a)(15), failed to make reasonable efforts to prevent removal of children from their homes and to facilitate reunification of families where removal had occurred. This failure occurred, as alleged by respondents, because DCFS failed promptly to assign caseworkers to children placed in

1. Section 1983 provides, in relevant part: "Every person who, under color of any statute, ordinance, regulation, custom, or usage, of any State or Territory or the District of Columbia, subjects or causes to be subjected, any citizen of the United States or other person within the jurisdiction thereof to the deprivation of any rights, privileges, or immunities, secured by the Constitution and laws shall be liable to the party injured in an action at law, suit in equity, or other proper proceeding for redress."

DCFS custody and promptly to reassign cases when caseworkers were on leave from DCFS. App. 6–8. The District Court, without objection from petitioners, certified two separate classes seeking relief, including all children who are or will be wards of DCFS and are placed in foster care or remain in their homes under a judicial protective order. *Artist M. v. Johnson*, 726 F.Supp. 690, 691 (ND Ill. 1989). The District Court denied a motion to dismiss filed by petitioners, holding, as relevant here, that the Adoption Act contained an implied cause of action and that suit could also be brought to enforce the Act under 42 U.S.C. § 1983. 726 F.Supp., at 696, 697.

The District Court then entered an injunction requiring petitioners to assign a caseworker to each child placed in DCFS custody within three working days of the time the case is first heard in Juvenile Court, and to reassign a caseworker within three working days of the date any caseworker relinquishes responsibility for a particular case. App. to Pet. for Cert. 56a. The 3-working-day deadline was found by the District Court to "realistically reflec[t] the institutional capabilities of DCFS," *id.*, at 55a, based in part on petitioners' assertion that assigning caseworkers within that time frame "would not be overly burdensome." *Id.*, at 54a. The District Court, on partial remand from the Court of Appeals, made additional factual findings regarding the nature of the delays in assigning caseworkers and the progress of DCFS reforms at the time the preliminary injunction was entered. App. 28–50.

The Court of Appeals affirmed. 917 F.2d 980 (CA7 1990). Relying heavily on this Court's decision in *Wilder v. Virginia Hospital Assn.*, 496 U.S. 498 (1990), the Court of Appeals held that the "reasonable efforts" clause of the Adoption Act could be enforced through an action under § 1983. 917 F.2d, at 987–989. That court, applying the standard established in *Cort v. Ash*, 422 U.S. 66, 45 L.Ed.2d 26 (1975), also found that the Adoption Act created an implied right of action such that private individuals could bring suit directly under the Act to enforce the provisions relied upon by respondents. 917 F.2d, at 989–991. We granted certiorari, 500 U.S. 915 (1991), and now reverse.[6]

6. Subsequent to oral argument, respondents notified the Court of the entry of a consent decree in the case of *B.H. v. Suter*, No. 88-C 5599 (ND Ill.), which they suggest may affect our decision on the merits, or indeed may make the instant action moot. We find no merit to respondents' contentions, and conclude that the *B.H.* consent decree has no bearing on the issue the Court decides today. Sue Suter, petitioner in this case, is the defendant in the *B.H.* suit, which alleges statewide deficiencies in the operations of DCFS. See *B.H. v. Johnson, supra*. The class approved in *B.H.* contains "all persons who are or will be in the custody of [DCFS] and who have been or will be placed somewhere other than with their parents." 715 F.Supp., at 1389.

Respondents suggest that because petitioner has agreed in the *B.H.* consent decree to provide "reasonable efforts" to maintain and reunify families, she is somehow precluded from arguing in this case that § 671(a)(15) does not grant a right for individual plaintiffs to enforce that section by suit. As we have recognized previously this Term, however, parties may agree to provisions in a consent decree which exceed the requirements of federal law. *Rufo v. Inmates of Suffolk County Jail*, 502 U.S. 367, 389 (1992). Paragraph two of the *B.H.* decree itself provides that the decree is not an admission of any factual or legal issue. In addition, the *B.H.* consent decree does not require "reasonable efforts" with no further definition, but rather defines the standard against which those efforts are to be measured. See *B.H.* Consent Decree ¶¶ 8, 16(a), pp. 12, 20. Thus, the agreement embodied in the consent decree is not inconsistent with the position petitioner asserts here, namely, that § 671(a)(15) requiring "reasonable efforts," without further definition, does not create an enforceable right on behalf of respondents to enforce the clause by suit.

Respondents next contend that the *B.H.* decree "may also render much of this case moot." Supp. Brief for Respondents 8. Although petitioner here is the defendant in *B.H.*, the class certified in *B.H.* does not include children living at home under a protective order, and therefore is more narrow than the class certified in the instant suit. In addition, while DCFS agrees in the *B.H.* consent decree to certain obligations, for example, a

In *Maine v. Thiboutot*, 448 U.S. 1 (1980), we first established that § 1983 is available as a remedy for violations of federal statutes as well as for constitutional violations. We have subsequently recognized that § 1983 is not available to enforce a violation of a federal statute "where Congress has foreclosed such enforcement of the statute in the enactment itself and where the statute did not create enforceable rights, privileges, or immunities within the meaning of § 1983." *Wright v. Roanoke Redevelopment and Housing Authority*, 479 U.S. 418, 423 (1987).

In *Pennhurst State School and Hospital v. Halderman*, 451 U.S. 1 (1981), we held that § 111 of the Developmentally Disabled Assistance and Bill of Rights Act of 1975, 42 U.S.C. § 6010 (1976 ed. and Supp. III), did not confer an implied cause of action. That statute, as well as the statute before us today, was enacted by Congress pursuant to its spending power. In *Pennhurst*, we noted that it was well established that Congress has the power to fix the terms under which it disburses federal money to the States. 451 U.S., at 17, citing *Oklahoma v. United States Civil Service Comm'n*, 330 U.S. 127 (1947); *Rosado v. Wyman*, 397 U.S. 397 (1970). As stated in *Pennhurst*:

> "The legitimacy of Congress' power to legislate under the spending power thus rests on whether the State voluntarily and knowingly accepts the terms of the 'contract.' There can, of course, be no knowing acceptance if a State is unaware of the conditions or is unable to ascertain what is expected of it. Accordingly, if Congress intends to impose a condition on the grant of federal moneys, it must do so unambiguously." 451 U.S., at 17 (citations and footnote omitted).

We concluded that the statutory section sought to be enforced by the *Pennhurst* respondents did not provide such unambiguous notice to the States because it spoke in terms "intended to be hortatory, not mandatory." *Id.*, at 24.

In *Wright*, the Brooke Amendment to existing housing legislation imposed a ceiling on the rent which might be charged low-income tenants living in public housing projects. The regulations issued by the Department of Housing and Urban Development in turn defined rent to include "'a reasonable amount for [use of] utilities,'" and further defined how that term would be measured. *Wright, supra*, 479 U.S., at 420–421, n. 3. We held that tenants had an enforceable right to sue the Housing Authority for utility charges claimed to be in violation of these provisions. In *Wilder*, 496 U.S., at 503, the Boren Amendment to the Medicaid Act required that Medicaid providers be reimbursed according to rates that the "'State finds, and makes

ceiling on the number of cases handled by each caseworker, none of these obligations subsumes the injunction entered by the District Court and affirmed by the Court of Appeals below, requiring petitioners to provide a caseworker within three days of when a child is first removed from his home. Cf. *Johnson v. Board of Ed. of Chicago*, 457 U.S. 52 (1982) (*per curiam*).

In short, the situation in this case is quite different from that in the cases cited by respondents in which this Court remanded for further proceedings after events subsequent to the filing of the petition for certiorari or the grant of certiorari affected the case before the Court. Unlike the parties in *J. Aron & Co. v. Mississippi Shipping Co.*, 361 U.S. 115 (1959) (*per curiam*), the parties in the case before the Court have not entered a consent decree. Unlike *Kremens v. Bartley*, 431 U.S. 119 (1977), the *B.H.* decree does nothing to change the class at issue or the claims of the named class members. And unlike *American Foreign Service Assn. v. Garfinkel*, 490 U.S. 153 (1989) (*per curiam*), where we noted that "[e]vents occurring since the District Court issued its ruling place this case in a light far different from the one in which that court considered it," *id.*, at 158, the issue whether the reasonable efforts clause creates an enforceable right on behalf of respondents is the same now as it was when decided by the District Court below.

assurances satisfactory to the Secretary,'" are "'reasonable and adequate'" to meet the costs of "'efficiently and economically operated facilities.'" Again, we held that this language created an enforceable right, on the part of providers seeking reimbursement, to challenge the rates set by the State as failing to meet the standards specified in the Boren Amendment.

In both *Wright* and *Wilder* the word "reasonable" occupied a prominent place in the critical language of the statute or regulation, and the word "reasonable" is similarly involved here. But this, obviously, is not the end of the matter. The opinions in both *Wright* and *Wilder* took pains to analyze the statutory provisions in detail, in light of the entire legislative enactment, to determine whether the language in question created "enforceable rights, privileges, or immunities within the meaning of § 1983." *Wright, supra*, 479 U.S. at 423. And in *Wilder*, we caution that "'[s]ection 1983 speaks in terms of "*rights*, privileges, or immunities," not violations of federal law.'" *Wilder, supra*, 496 U.S., at 509, quoting *Golden State Transit Corp. v. Los Angeles*, 493 U.S. 103, 106 (1989).

Did Congress, in enacting the Adoption Act, unambiguously confer upon the child beneficiaries of the Act a right to enforce the requirement that the State make "reasonable efforts" to prevent a child from being removed from his home, and once removed to reunify the child with his family? We turn now to that inquiry.

As quoted above, 42 U.S.C. § 671(a)(15) requires that to obtain federal reimbursement, a State have a plan which "provides that, in each case, reasonable efforts will be made...to prevent or eliminate the need for removal of the child from his home, and...to make it possible for the child to return to his home...." As recognized by petitioners, respondents, and the courts below, the Act is mandatory in its terms. However, in the light shed by *Pennhurst*, we must examine exactly what is required of States by the Act. Here, the terms of § 671(a) are clear: "In order for a State to be eligible for payments under this part, it shall have a plan approved by the Secretary." Therefore the Act does place a requirement on the States, but that requirement only goes so far as to ensure that the State have a plan approved by the Secretary which contains the 16 listed features.

Respondents do not dispute that Illinois in fact has a plan approved by the Secretary which provides that reasonable efforts at prevention and reunification will be made. Tr. of Oral Arg. 29–30. Respondents argue, however, that § 1983 allows them to sue in federal court to obtain enforcement of this particular provision of the state plan. This argument is based, at least in part, on the assertion that 42 U.S.C. § 671(a)(3) requires that the State have a plan which is "in effect." This section states that the state plan shall "provid[e] that the plan shall be in effect in all political subdivisions of the State, and, if administered by them, be mandatory upon them." But we think that "in effect" is directed to the requirement that the plan apply to all political subdivisions of the State, and is not intended to otherwise modify the word "plan."[10]

10. Respondents also based their claim for relief on 42 U.S.C. § 671(a)(9) which states that the state plan shall "provid[e] that where any agency of the State has reason to believe that the home or institution in which a child resides whose care is being paid for in whole or in part with funds provided under this part or part B of this subchapter is unsuitable for the child because of the neglect, abuse, or exploitation of such child, it shall bring such condition to the attention of the appropriate court or law enforcement agency...."

As this subsection is merely another feature which the state plan must include to be approved by the Secretary, it does not afford a cause of action to the respondents anymore than does the "reasonable efforts" clause of § 671(a)(15).

In *Wilder*, the underlying Medicaid legislation similarly required participating States to submit to the Secretary of Health and Human Services a plan for medical assistance describing the State's Medicaid program. But in that case we held that the Boren Amendment actually required the States to adopt reasonable and adequate rates, and that this obligation was enforceable by the providers. We relied in part on the fact that the statute and regulations set forth in some detail the factors to be considered in determining the methods for calculating rates. *Wilder*, 496 U.S., at 519, n. 17.

In the present case, however, the term "reasonable efforts" to maintain an abused or neglected child in his home, or return the child to his home from foster care, appears in quite a different context. No further statutory guidance is found as to how "reasonable efforts" are to be measured. This directive is not the only one which Congress has given to the States, and it is a directive whose meaning will obviously vary with the circumstances of each individual case. How the State was to comply with this directive, and with the other provisions of the Act, was, within broad limits, left up to the State.

Other sections of the Act provide enforcement mechanisms for the "reasonable efforts" clause of 42 U.S.C. § 671(a)(15). The Secretary has the authority to reduce or eliminate payments to a State on finding that the State's plan no longer complies with § 671(a) or that "there is a substantial failure" in the administration of a plan such that the State is not complying with its own plan. § 671(b). The Act also requires that in order to secure federal reimbursement for foster care payments made with respect to a child involuntarily removed from his home the removal must be "the result of a judicial determination to the effect that continuation [in the child's home] would be contrary to the welfare of such child and (effective October 1, 1983) that reasonable efforts of the type described in section 671(a)(15) of this title have been made." § 672(a)(1). While these statutory provisions may not provide a comprehensive enforcement mechanism so as to manifest Congress' intent to foreclose remedies under § 1983,[11] they do show that the absence of a remedy to private plaintiffs under § 1983 does not make the "reasonable efforts" clause a dead letter.[12]

The regulations promulgated by the Secretary to enforce the Adoption Act do not evidence a view that § 671(a) places any requirement for state receipt of federal funds other than the requirement that the State submit a plan to be approved by the Secretary. The regulations provide that to meet the requirements of § 671(a)(15) the case plan for each child must "include a description of the services offered and the services provided to prevent removal of the child from the home and to reunify the family." 45 CFR § 1356.21(d)(4)(1991). Another regulation, entitled "requirements and submittal," provides that a state plan must specify "which preplacement preventive and reunification services are available to children and families in

11. We have found an intent by Congress to foreclose remedies under § 1983 where the statute itself provides a comprehensive remedial scheme which leaves no room for additional private remedies under § 1983. *Smith v. Robinson*, 468 U.S. 992 (1984); *Middlesex County Sewerage Authority v. National Sea Clammers Assn.*, 453 U.S. 1 (1981). We need not consider this question today due to our conclusion that the Adoption Act does not create the federally enforceable right asserted by respondents.

12. The language of other sections of the Act also shows that Congress knew how to impose precise requirements on the States aside from the submission of a plan to be approved by the Secretary when it intended to. For example, 42 U.S.C. § 672(e) provides that "[n]o Federal payment may be made under this part" for a child voluntarily placed in foster care for more than 180 days unless within that period there is a judicial determination that the placement is in the best interest of the child. That the "reasonable efforts" clause is not similarly worded buttresses a conclusion that Congress had a different intent with respect to it.

need." § 1357.15(e)(1).[14] What is significant is that the regulations are not specific and do not provide notice to the States that failure to do anything other than submit a plan with the requisite features, to be approved by the Secretary, is a further condition on the receipt of funds from the Federal Government. Respondents contend that "[n]either [petitioners] nor amici supporting them present any legislative history to refute the evidence that Congress intended 42 U.S.C. § 671(a)(15) to be enforceable." Brief for Respondents 33. To the extent such history may be relevant, our examination of it leads us to conclude that Congress was concerned that the required reasonable efforts be made by the States, but also indicated that the Act left a great deal of discretion to them.[15]

Careful examination of the language relied upon by respondents, in the context of the entire Act, leads us to conclude that the "reasonable efforts" language does not unambiguously confer an enforceable right upon the Act's beneficiaries. The term "reasonable efforts" in this context is at least as plausibly read to impose only a rather generalized duty on the State, to be enforced not by private individuals, but by the Secretary in the manner previously discussed.

Having concluded that § 671(a)(15) does not create a federally enforceable right to "reasonable efforts" under § 1983, the conclusion of the Court of Appeals that the Adoption Act contains an

14. The regulation, 45 CFR § 1357.15(e)(2) (1991), goes on to provide a list of which services may be included in the State's proposal: "Twenty-four hour emergency caretaker, and homemaker services; day care; crisis counseling; individual and family counseling; emergency shelters; procedures and arrangements for access to available emergency financial assistance; arrangements for the provision of temporary child care to provide respite to the family for a brief period, as part of a plan for preventing children's removal from home; other services which the agency identifies as necessary and appropriate such as home-based family services, self-help groups, services to unmarried parents, provision of, or arrangements for, mental health, drug and alcohol abuse counseling, vocational counseling or vocational rehabilitation; and post adoption services."

15. The Report of the Senate Committee on Finance describes how under the system before the Adoption Act States only received reimbursement for payments made with respect to children who were removed from their homes, and how the Act contains a number of provisions in order to "deemphasize the use of foster care," including reimbursing States for developing and administering adoption assistance programs and programs for "tracking" children in foster care, placing a cap on the amount of federal reimbursements a State may receive for foster care maintenance payments, and "specifically permitting expenditures for State... services to reunite families." S.Rep. No. 96-336, p. 12 (1979). This Senate Report shows that Congress had confidence in the ability and competency of state courts to discharge their duties under what is now § 672(a) of the Act. *Id.*, at 16 ("The committee is aware of allegations that the judicial determination requirement can become a mere *pro forma* exercise in paper shuffling to obtain Federal funding. While this could occur in some instances, the committee is unwilling to accept as a general proposition that the judiciaries of the States would so lightly treat a responsibility placed upon them by Federal statute for the protection of children").

The House Ways and Means Committee Report on the Adoption Act similarly recognizes that "the entire array of possible preventive services are not appropriate in all situations. The decision as to the appropriateness of specific services in specific situations will have to be made by the administering agency having immediate responsibility for the care of the child." H.R.Rep. No. 96-136, p. 47 (1979).

Remarks on the floor of both the House and the Senate further support these general intentions. See, *e.g.*, 125 Cong.Rec. 22113 (1979) (remarks of Rep. Brodhead) ("What the bill attempts to do is to get the States to enact a series of reforms of their foster care laws, because in the past there has been too much of a tendency to use the foster care program. The reason there has been that tendency is because... it becomes a little more expensive for the State to use the protective services than foster care. Through this bill, we want to free up a little bit of money... so you will have an incentive to keep a family together"); *id.*, at 29939 (remarks of Sen. Cranston, sponsor of the Adoption Act) ("This requirement in the State plan under [§ 671(a)(15)] would be reinforced by the new requirement under [§ 672] that each State with a plan approved... may make foster care maintenance payments only for a child who has been removed from a home as a result of an explicit judicial determination that reasonable efforts to prevent the removal have been made, in addition to the judicial determination required by existing law that continuation in the home would be contrary to the welfare of the child").

implied right of action for private enforcement, 917 F.2d, at 989, may be disposed of quickly. Under the familiar test of *Cort v. Ash*, 422 U.S. 66 (1975), the burden is on respondents to demonstrate that Congress intended to make a private remedy available to enforce the "reasonable efforts" clause of the Adoption Act.[16] The most important inquiry here as well is whether Congress intended to create the private remedy sought by the plaintiffs. *Transamerica Mortgage Advisors, Inc. v. Lewis*, 444 U.S. 11, 15–16 (1979) ("[W]hat must ultimately be determined is whether Congress intended to create the private remedy asserted"). As discussed above, we think that Congress did not intend to create a private remedy for enforcement of the "reasonable efforts" clause.

We conclude that 42 U.S.C. § 671(a)(15) neither confers an enforceable private right on its beneficiaries nor creates an implied cause of action on their behalf.

The judgment of the Court of Appeals is therefore

Reversed.

Justice Blackmun, with whom Justice Stevens joins, dissenting.

The Adoption Assistance and Child Welfare Act of 1980 (Adoption Act or Act) conditions federal funding for state child welfare, foster care, and adoption programs upon, *inter alia*, the State's express commitment to make, "in each case, reasonable efforts" to prevent the need for removing children from their homes and "reasonable efforts," where removal has occurred, to reunify the family. 42 U.S.C. § 671(a)(15). The Court holds today that the plaintiff children in this case may not enforce the State's commitment in federal court either under 42 U.S.C. § 1983 or under the Act itself.

In my view, the Court's conclusion is plainly inconsistent with this Court's decision just two Terms ago in *Wilder v. Virginia Hospital Assn.*, 496 U.S. 498 (1990), in which we found enforceable under § 1983 a functionally identical provision of the Medicaid Act requiring "reasonable" reimbursements to health-care providers. More troubling still, the Court reaches its conclusion without even stating, much less applying, the principles our precedents have used to determine whether a statute has created a right enforceable under § 1983. I cannot acquiesce in this unexplained disregard for established law. Accordingly, I dissent.

I

A

Section 1983 provides a cause of action for the "deprivation of any rights, privileges, or immunities, secured by the Constitution and laws" of the United States. We recognized in *Maine v. Thiboutot*, 448 U.S. 1 (1980), that § 1983 provides a cause of action for violations of federal statutes, not just the Constitution. Since *Thiboutot*, we have recognized two general exceptions to this rule. First, no cause of action will lie where the statute in question does not "'create enforceable rights, privileges, or immunities within the meaning of § 1983.'" *Wilder*, 496 U.S., at 508 (quoting *Wright v. Roanoke Redevelopment and Housing Authority*, 479 U.S. 418,

16. As established in *Cort v. Ash*, 422 U.S. 66 (1975), these factors are:

"First, is the plaintiff one of the class for whose *especial* benefit the statute was enacted, that is, does the statute create a federal right in favor of the plaintiff? Second, is there any indication of legislative intent, explicit or implicit, either to create such a remedy or to deny one? Third, is it consistent with the underlying purposes of the legislative scheme to imply such a remedy for the plaintiff? And finally, is the cause of action one traditionally relegated to state law, in an area basically the concern of the States, so that it would be inappropriate to infer a cause of action based solely on federal law?" *Id.*, at 78 (internal quotation marks omitted; emphasis in original).

423 (1987)). Second, § 1983 is unavailable where "Congress has foreclosed such enforcement of the statute in the enactment itself." 496 U.S., at 508.

In determining the scope of the first exception—whether a federal statute creates an "enforceable right"—the Court has developed and repeatedly applied a three-part test. We have asked (1) whether the statutory provision at issue "'was intend[ed] to benefit the putative plaintiff.'" *Id.*, at 509 (quoting *Golden State Transit Corp. v. Los Angeles*, 493 U.S. 103, 106 (1989)). If so, then the provision creates an enforceable right unless (2) the provision "reflects merely a 'congressional preference' for a certain kind of conduct rather than a binding obligation on the governmental unit," 496 U.S., at 509 (quoting *Pennhurst State School and Hospital v. Halderman*, 451 U.S. 1, 19 (1981)), or unless (3) the plaintiff's interest is so "'vague and amorphous'" as to be "'beyond the competence of the judiciary to enforce.'" 496 U.S., at 509 (quoting *Golden State*, 493 U.S., at 106, in turn quoting *Wright*, 479 U.S., at 431–432). See also *Dennis v. Higgins*, 498 U.S. 439, 448–449 (1991) (quoting and applying the three-part test as stated in *Golden State*). The Court today has little difficulty concluding that the plaintiff children in this case have no enforceable rights, because it does not mention—much less apply—this firmly established analytic framework.

B

In *Wilder*, we held that under the above three-part test, the Boren Amendment to the Medicaid Act creates an enforceable right. As does the Adoption Act, the Medicaid Act provides federal funding for state programs that meet certain federal standards and requires participating States to file a plan with the Secretary of Health and Human Services. Most relevant here, the Medicaid Act, like the Adoption Act, requires that the State undertake a "reasonableness" commitment in its plan. With respect to the rate at which providers are to be reimbursed, the Boren Amendment requires:

> "A State plan for medical assistance must—...
>
> "provide...for payment...[of services] provided under the plan through the use of rates (determined in accordance with methods and standards developed by the State...) which the State finds, and makes assurances satisfactory to the Secretary, are *reasonable and adequate* to meet the costs which must be incurred by efficiently and economically operated facilities in order to provide care and services in conformity with applicable State and Federal laws, regulations, and quality and safety standards and to assure that individuals eligible for medical assistance have *reasonable* access...to inpatient hospital services of *adequate* quality." 42 U.S.C. § 1396a(a)(13)(A) (emphasis supplied).

In *Wilder*, we had no difficulty concluding that the reimbursement provision of the Boren Amendment "was intend[ed] to benefit" the plaintiff providers of Medicaid services. 496 U.S., at 509. We also concluded that the second part of the test was satisfied. The amendment, we held, does not simply express a "congressional preference" for reasonable and adequate reimbursement rates; rather, it imposes a "binding obligation" on the State to establish and maintain such rates. *Id.*, at 512. In so concluding, we emphasized two features of the Medicaid reimbursement scheme. First, we observed that the language of the provision is "cast in mandatory rather than precatory terms," stating that the plan "*must*" provide for reasonable and adequate reimbursement. *Ibid.* Second, we noted that the text of the statute expressly conditions federal funding on state compliance with the amendment and requires the Secretary to withhold funds from noncomplying States. *Ibid.* In light of these features of the Medicaid Act, we rejected the argument, advanced by the defendant state officials and by the United States as *amicus curiae,* that the only enforceable state obligation is the obligation to file a plan with the Secretary, to find that its rates are reasonable and adequate, and to make assurances to that effect in the plan. *Id.*, at 512–515. Rather, we concluded, participating States are required actually to provide reasonable and adequate rates, not just profess to the Secretary that they have done so. *Ibid.*

Finally, we rejected the State's argument that Medicaid providers' right to "reasonable and adequate" reimbursement is "too vague and amorphous" for judicial enforcement. We acknowledged that the State has "substantial discretion" in choosing among various methods of calculating reimbursement rates. *Id.*, at 519; see also *id.*, at 505–508. A State's discretion in determining how to calculate what rates are "reasonable and adequate," we concluded, "may affect the standard under which a court reviews" the State's reimbursement plan, but it does not make the right to reasonable reimbursement judicially unenforceable. *Id.*, at 519.

C

These principles, as we applied them in *Wilder*, require the conclusion that the Adoption Act's "reasonable efforts" clause[1] establishes a right enforceable under § 1983. Each of the three elements of our three-part test is satisfied. First, and most obvious, the plaintiff children in this case are clearly the intended beneficiaries of the requirement that the State make "reasonable efforts" to prevent unnecessary removal and to reunify temporarily removed children with their families.

Second, the "reasonable efforts" clause imposes a binding obligation on the State because it is "cast in mandatory rather than precatory terms," providing that a participating State "*shall* have a plan approved by the Secretary which...*shall be in effect* in all political subdivisions of the State, and, if administered by them, be *mandatory* upon them." Further, the statute requires the plan to "provid[e] that, in each case, reasonable efforts *will be made.*" Moreover, as in *Wilder*, the statutory text expressly conditions federal funding on state compliance with the plan requirement and requires the Secretary to reduce payments to a State if "in the administration of [the State's] plan there is a substantial failure to comply with the provisions of the plan." 42 U.S.C. § 671(b). Under our holding in *Wilder*, these provisions of the Adoption Act impose a binding obligation on the State. Indeed, neither the petitioner state officials nor *amicus* United States dispute this point. Brief for Petitioners 17; Reply Brief for Petitioners 3, n. 2; Brief for United States as *Amicus Curiae* 13–14.

What petitioners and *amicus* United States do dispute is whether the third element of the *Golden State-Wilder-Dennis* test has been satisfied: They argue that the "reasonable efforts" clause of the Adoption Act is too "vague and amorphous" to be judicially enforced. Aware

1. "In order for a State to be eligible for payments under this part, it shall have a plan approved by the Secretary which—...(3) provides that the plan shall be in effect in all political subdivisions of the State, and, if administered by them, be mandatory upon them; [and]...(15)...provides that, in each case, reasonable efforts will be made (A) prior to the placement of a child in foster care, to prevent or eliminate the need for removal of the child from his home, and (B) to make it possible for the child to return to his home." 42 U.S.C. § 671(a).

that *Wilder* enforced an apparently similar "reasonableness" clause, they argue that *this* clause is categorically different.

According to petitioners, the Court would not have found the Boren Amendment's reasonableness clause enforceable had the statute not provided an "objective benchmark" against which "reasonable and adequate" reimbursement rates could be measured. Reasonable and adequate rates, the Boren Amendment provides, are those that meet the costs that would be incurred by "an 'efficiently and economically operated facilit[y]' providing care in compliance with federal and state standards while at the same time ensuring 'reasonable access' to eligible participants." *Wilder*, 496 U.S., at 519 (quoting 42 U.S.C. § 1396a(a)(13)(A)). Petitioners claim that, given this benchmark, "reasonable and adequate" rates can be ascertained by "*monetary* calculations easily determined based on prevailing rates in the market." Brief for Petitioners 21. By contrast, they observe, there is "no market for 'reasonable efforts' to keep or return a child home, and such 'reasonable efforts' cannot be calculated or quantified." *Ibid.*

Petitioners misunderstand the sense in which the "benchmark" in *Wilder* is "objective." The Boren Amendment does not simply define "reasonable and adequate" rates as market rates. Rather, it defines a "reasonable and adequate" rate by referring to what *would* be provided by a *hypothetical* facility—one that operates "efficiently and economically," "compli[es] with federal and state standards," and "ensur[es] 'reasonable access' to eligible participants." Whether particular existing facilities meet those criteria is not a purely empirical judgment that requires only simple "monetary calculations." Indeed, the Boren Amendment's specification of the words "reasonable and adequate" ultimately refers us to a *second* reasonableness clause: The "benchmark" facility, we are told, is one that "ensure[s] '*reasonable access*' to eligible participants." This second reasonableness clause is left undefined. Contrary to petitioners' suggestions, then, the "reasonable and adequate" rates provision of the Boren Amendment is not "objective" in the sense of being mechanically measurable. The fact that this Court found the provision judicially enforceable demonstrates that an asserted right is not "vague and amorphous" simply because it cannot be easily "calculated or quantified."

Petitioners also argue that the right to "reasonable efforts" is "vague and amorphous" because of substantial disagreement in the child-welfare community concerning appropriate strategies. Furthermore, they contend, because the choice of a particular strategy in a particular case necessarily will depend upon the facts of that case, a court-enforced right to reasonable efforts either will homogenize very different situations or else will fragment into a plurality of "rights" that vary from State to State. For both of these reasons, petitioners contend, Congress left the question of what efforts are "reasonable" to state juvenile courts, the recognized experts in such matters.

Here again, comparison with *Wilder* is instructive. The Court noted the lack of consensus concerning which of various possible methods of calculating reimbursable costs would best promote efficient operation of health-care facilities. See *Wilder*, 496 U.S., at 506–507. The Court further noted that Congress chose a standard that leaves the States considerable autonomy in selecting the methods they will use to determine which reimbursement rates are "reasonable and adequate." *Id.*, at 506–508, 515. The result, of course, is that the "content" of the federal right to reasonable and adequate rates—the method of calculating reimbursement and the chosen rate—varies from State to State. And although federal judges are hardly expert either in selecting methods of Medicaid cost reimbursement or in determining whether particular rates are "reasonable and adequate," neither the majority nor the dissent found that the right to reasonable and adequate reimbursement was so vague and amorphous as to be "beyond the competence of the judiciary to enforce." See *id.*, at 519–520; *id.*, at 524. (REHNQUIST, C.J., dissenting). State flexibility in determining what is "reasonable," we held,

> "may affect the standard under which a court reviews whether the rates comply with the amendment, but it does not render the amendment unenforceable by a court. While there may be a range of reasonable rates, there certainly are *some* rates outside that range that no State could ever find to be reasonable and adequate under the Act." *Id.*, at 519–520.

The same principles apply here. There may be a "range" of "efforts" to prevent unnecessary removals or secure beneficial reunifications that are "reasonable." *Id.*, at 520. It may also be that a court, in reviewing a State's strategies of compliance with the "reasonable efforts" clause, would owe substantial deference to the State's choice of strategies. That does not mean, however, that *no* State's efforts could *ever* be deemed "unreasonable." As in *Wilder*, the asserted right in this case is simply not inherently "beyond the competence of the judiciary to enforce." *Ibid.*

Petitioners' argument that the "reasonable efforts" clause of the Adoption Act is so vague and amorphous as to be unenforceable assumes that in *Wright* and *Wilder* the Court was working at the outer limits of what is judicially cognizable: Any deviation from *Wright* or *Wilder*, petitioners imply, would go beyond the bounds of judicial competence. There is absolutely nothing to indicate that this is so. See *Wilder*, 496 U.S., at 520 (inquiry into reasonableness of reimbursement rates is "*well within* the competence of the Judiciary") (emphasis supplied). Federal courts, in innumerable cases, have routinely enforced reasonableness clauses in federal statutes. See, *e.g.*, *Virginian R. Co. v. Railway Employees*, 300 U.S. 515, 518, 550 (1937) (enforcing "every reasonable effort" provision of the Railway Labor Act and noting that "whether action taken or omitted is . . . reasonable [is an] everyday subjec[t] of inquiry by courts in framing and enforcing their decrees"). Petitioners have not shown that the Adoption Act's reasonableness clause is exceptional in this respect.

II

The Court does not explain why the settled three-part test for determining the enforceability of an asserted right is not applied in this case. Moreover, the reasons the Court does offer to support its conclusion—that the Adoption Act's "reasonable efforts" clause creates no enforceable right—were raised and rejected in *Wilder*.

The Court acknowledges that the Adoption Act is "mandatory in its terms." It adopts, however, a narrow understanding of what is "mandatory." It reasons that the language of § 671(a), which provides that "[i]n order for a State to be eligible for payments under this part, it shall have a plan approved by the Secretary," requires participating States only to submit and receive approval for a plan that contains the features listed in §§ 671(a)(1) to (16). According to the Court, the beneficiaries of the Act enjoy at most a procedural right under § 671(a)—the right to require a participating State to prepare and file a plan—not a substantive right to require the State to live up to the commitments stated in that plan, such as the commitment to make "reasonable efforts" to prevent unnecessary removals and secure beneficial reunifications of families. Since the State of Illinois has filed a plan that the Secretary has approved, the Court reasons, the State has violated no right enforceable in federal court.

The Court's reasoning should sound familiar: The state officials in *Wilder* made exactly the same argument, and this Court rejected it. In *Wilder*, we noted that the Medicaid Act expressly conditions federal funding on state compliance with the provisions of an approved plan, and that the Secretary is required to withhold payments from noncomplying States. See *Wilder*, 496 U.S., at 512 (citing 42 U.S.C. § 1396c).[2] In substantially identical language, the Adoption Act, too, requires States to live up to the commitments stated in their plans.[3] To be sure, the Court's reasoning is consistent with the *dissent* in *Wilder*. See *id.*, at 524, 527–528 (REHNQUIST, C.J., dissenting). But it flatly contradicts what the Court *held* in that case.

The Court attempts to fend off this conclusion in two ways, neither of them persuasive. First, the Court seeks to distinguish *Wilder*, asserting that our conclusion—that the Boren Amendment gave the health-care providers a substantive right to reasonable and adequate reimbursement—"relied in part on the fact that the statute and regulations set forth in some detail the factors to be considered in determining the methods for calculating rates." (citing *Wilder*, 496 U.S., at 519, n. 17). By contrast, the Court continues, neither the provisions of the Adoption Act nor the implementing regulations offer any guidance as to how the term "reasonable efforts" should be interpreted.

Even assuming that it is accurate to call the statute and regulations involved in that case "detailed,"[4] the Court has misread *Wilder*. The Court there referred to the relative specificity of the statute and regulations not to demonstrate that the health-care providers enjoyed a substantive right to reasonable and adequate rates—we had already concluded that the State was under a binding obligation to adopt such rates, see *Wilder*, 496 U.S., at 514–515—but only to reinforce our conclusion that the providers' interest was not so "vague and amorphous" as to be "beyond the competence of judicial enforcement." See 496 U.S., at 519, n. 17. Under our three-part test, the Court would not have inquired whether that interest was "vague and amorphous" unless it had *already* concluded that the State was required to do more than simply file a paper plan that lists the appropriate factors.

Second, the Court emphasizes: "Other sections of the [Adoption] Act provide enforcement mechanisms for the reasonable efforts clause of 42 U.S.C. § 671(a)(15)." Such "mechanisms" include the Secretary's power to cut off or reduce funds for noncompliance with the state plan,

2. "If the Secretary... finds... that in the administration of the plan there is a failure to comply substantially with any... provision [required to be included in the plan,] the Secretary shall notify [the] State agency that further payments will not be made...." 42 U.S.C. § 1396c.

3. "[I]n any case in which the Secretary finds... there is a substantial failure to comply with the provisions of [an approved] plan, the Secretary shall notify the State that further payments will not be made..., or that such payments will be made to the State but reduced by an amount which the Secretary determines appropriate...." 42 U.S.C. § 671(b).

4. Petitioners suggest a sharp contrast between the implementing regulations considered in *Wilder* and the implementing regulation for the Adoption Act "reasonable efforts" provision: The former, they say, require the State to consider certain factors, but the latter merely provides "a laundry list of services the States *may* provide." Brief for Petitioners 34 (citing 45 CFR § 1357.15(e) (1991)). Further, petitioners emphasize HHS's remark during rulemaking that States must retain flexibility in administering the Adoption Act's "reasonable efforts" requirement. Brief for Petitioners 34–35.

Neither of these factors marks a significant difference between *Wilder* and the present case. The difference between *requiring* States to *consider* certain factors, as in *Wilder*, and *permitting* States to *provide* certain listed services, as in the present case, is hardly dramatic. As for the second asserted difference, *Wilder* itself emphasized that States must retain substantial discretion in calculating "reasonable and adequate" reimbursement rates.

and the requirement of a state judicial finding that "reasonable efforts" have been made before federal funds may be used to reimburse foster care payments for a child involuntarily removed.

The Court has apparently forgotten that ever since *Rosado v. Wyman*, 397 U.S. 397 (1970), the power of the Secretary to enforce congressional spending conditions by cutting off funds has not prevented the federal courts from enforcing those same conditions. See *id.*, at 420, 422–423. Indeed, we reasoned in *Wilder* that a similar "cutoff" provision *supports* the conclusion that the Medicaid Act creates an enforceable right, because it puts the State "on notice" that it may not simply adopt the reimbursement rates of its choosing. See 496 U.S., at 514. As for the Court's contention that § 671(a)(15) should be enforced through individual removal determinations in state juvenile court, the availability of a state judicial forum can hardly deprive a § 1983 plaintiff of a federal forum. *Monroe v. Pape*, 365 U.S. 167, 183 (1961). The Court's reliance on enforcement mechanisms other than § 1983, therefore, does not support its conclusion that the "reasonable efforts" clause of the Adoption Act creates no enforceable right.

The Court, without acknowledgment, has departed from our precedents in yet another way. In our prior cases, the existence of other enforcement mechanisms has been relevant not to the question whether the statute at issue creates an enforceable right, but to whether the second exception to § 1983 enforcement applies—whether, that is, "'Congress has foreclosed such enforcement of the statute in the enactment itself.'" *Wilder*, 496 U.S., at 508 (quoting *Wright v. Roanoke Redevelopment and Housing Authority*, 479 U.S., at 423). In determining whether this second exception to § 1983 enforcement applies, we have required the defendant not merely to point to the existence of alternative means of enforcement, but to demonstrate "by express provision or other specific evidence from the statute itself that Congress intended to foreclose [§ 1983] enforcement." 496 U.S., at 520–521. We have said repeatedly that we will not "lightly" conclude that Congress has so intended. *Id.*, at 520 (quoting *Wright*, 479 U.S., at 423–424, in turn quoting *Smith v. Robinson*, 468 U.S. 992, 1012 (1984)). In only two instances, where we concluded that "the statute itself provides a comprehensive remedial scheme which leaves no room for additional private remedies under § 1983," have we held that Congress has intended to foreclose § 1983 enforcement. See *Smith v. Robinson*, 468 U.S. 992 (1984) ("carefully tailored" mixed system of enforcement beginning with local administrative review and culminating in a right to judicial review); *Middlesex County Sewerage Authority v. National Sea Clammers Assn.*, 453 U.S. 1 (1981) (enforcement scheme authorizing Environmental Protection Agency to bring civil suits, providing for criminal penalties, and including two citizen-suit provisions).

The Court does not find these demanding criteria satisfied here. Instead, it simply circumvents them altogether: The Court holds that even if the funding cutoff provision in the Adoption Act is not an "express provision" that "provides a comprehensive remedial scheme" leaving "no room for additional private remedies under § 1983," *Wilder*, 496 U.S., at 520, that provision nevertheless precludes § 1983 enforcement. In so holding, the Court has inverted the established presumption that a private remedy is available under § 1983 unless "Congress has affirmatively withdrawn the remedy." 496 U.S., at 509, n. 9 (citing *Golden State Transit Corp. v. Los Angeles*, 493 U.S., at 106–107, and *Wright*, 479 U.S., at 423–424).

III

In sum, the Court has failed, without explanation, to apply the framework our precedents have consistently deemed applicable; it has sought to support its conclusion by resurrecting arguments decisively rejected less than two years ago in *Wilder*; and it has contravened 22 years of precedent by suggesting that the existence of other "enforcement mechanisms" precludes § 1983 enforcement. At least for this case, it has changed the rules of the game without offering even minimal justification, and it has failed even to acknowledge that it is doing anything more extraordinary than "interpret[ing]" the Adoption Act "by its own terms." Readers of the Court's opinion will not be misled by this hollow assurance. And, after all, we are dealing here with children. I would affirm the judgment of the Court of Appeals.[5] I dissent.

NOTES AND QUESTIONS

1. Under what circumstances does a federal law create a private right enforceable under 42 U.S.C. § 1983? Did the AACWA create such a right? Why? What is the dissent's view?

2. Congress responded to *Suter* by amending federal law.

> In an action brought to enforce a provision of this chapter, such provision is not to be deemed unenforceable because of its inclusion in a section of this chapter requiring a State plan or specifying the required contents of a State plan. This section is not intended to limit or expand the grounds for determining the availability of private actions to enforce State plan requirements other than by overturning any such grounds applied in Suter v. Artist M., 112 S.Ct. 1360 (1992), but not applied in prior Supreme Court decisions respecting such enforceability; provided, however, that this section is not intended to alter the holding in Suter v. Artist M. that section 671(a)(15) of this title is not enforceable in a private right of action.

42 U.S.C. § 1320a-2 (1994). What exactly does this mean?

3. The Adoption and Safe Families Act (ASFA) was enacted in 1997. Because of congressional concerns about children still languishing in foster care and state interpretations of AACWA mandates that children must be reunified even when to do so would be dangerous, ASFA carved out a number of exceptions to the reasonable-efforts requirement to reunify children and their families. ASFA also allows states to create their own exceptions to reasonable efforts. Nevertheless, ASFA kept the reasonable-efforts requirement found in AACWA.

4. Several courts have found that the AACWA and ASFA create privately enforceable rights for children in care. See, e.g., *Kenny A. ex rel. Winn v. Purdue*, 356 F.Supp.2d 1353 (N.D. Ga. 2005); *Jeanine B. v. McCallum*, No. 93-C-0547, 2001 WL 748062 (E.D. Wis. June 19, 2001); *Brian A. v. Sundquist*, 149 F. Supp. 2d 941 (M.D. Tenn. 2000) (finding an enforceable right to "timely written case plans, containing specific mandated elements, which are reviewed and updated at specific intervals" and to an adequate statewide information system); *Ocean v. Kearney*, 123 F. Supp. 2d 618 (S.D. Fla. 2000); *Marisol A. v. Giuliani*, 929 F. Supp. 662, 682–683 (S.D. N.Y. 1996); *Jeanine B. v. Thompson*, 877 F. Supp. 1269, 1283 (E.D. Wis. 1995). Other courts, however, have reached the opposite conclusion. See, e.g., *31 Foster Children v. Bush*, 329 F.3d 1255 (11th Cir. 2003); *Daniel H. ex rel. Hardaway v. City of New York*, 115 F. Supp. 2d 423 (S.D. N.Y. 2000);

5. Since I conclude that respondents have a cause of action under § 1983, I need not reach the question, decided in the affirmative by the Court of Appeals, whether petitioners may pursue a private action arising directly under the Adoption Act.

Charlie H. v. Whitman, 83 F. Supp. 2d 476 (D. N.J. 2000); *Mark G. v. Sabol*, 247 A.D.2d 15 (N.Y. App. Div. 1998), aff'd as modified, 93 N.Y.2d 710 (1999).

5. Do children in care have other remedies? For example, may children sue state agents in tort when they are harmed by actions of their foster parents? See, e.g., *Miller v. Martin*, 838 So.2d 761 (La. 2003) (department vicariously liable for foster parents' negligent acts); *Simmons v. Robinson*, 409 S.E.2d 381 (S.C. 1991) (foster mother a licensee and not an employee or independent contractor, which precludes vicarious liability and insurance coverage); *Commerce Bank v. Youth Servs. of Mid-Ill., Inc.*, 775 N.E.2d 297 (Ill. 2002) (whether agency relationship existed between foster parent and agency, thus creating liability based on doctrine of *respondeat superior*, a question of fact); *I.H. ex rel. Litz v. County of Lehigh*, 610 F.3d 797 (3d Cir. 2010) (no master-servant relationship existed between foster parent and foster-care agency, so agency not vicariously liable for foster parent's ordinary negligence).

6. Are foster parents liable in tort for their negligent acts? If the state in which the suit had been brought had a parental-immunity doctrine, should it extend to foster parents? What if the state had abolished the parental-immunity doctrine? Are foster parents employees of the state? Independent contractors? See, e.g., *Hunte v. Blumenthal*, 680 A.2d 1231 (Conn. 1996) (foster parents are state employees); *Nichol v. Stass*, 735 N.E.2d 582 (Ill. 2000) (foster parents are independent contractors, and limited form of parental immunity is available to them); *Mitzner v. State*, 891 P.2d 435 (Kan. 1995) (foster parents are independent contractors); *McCabe v. Dutchess County*, 72 A.D.3d 145, 895 N.Y.S.2d 446 (N.Y. App. Div. 2010) (child has no cognizable claim against foster parent for negligent supervision); *Rourk v. State*, 821 P.2d 273 (Ariz. App. 1991) (parental-immunity doctrine does not apply to foster parent); Mich. Comp. Laws § 722.163 (2002) (foster child may maintain negligence action against foster parent unless alleged negligent act involved exercise of reasonable parental authority).

7. What does it mean to make "reasonable efforts"? Most state statutes define reasonable efforts broadly, but they generally include the provision of services that will help families create a safe and stable home for their children. Family therapy, parenting classes, drug- and alcohol-abuse treatment, respite care, parent support groups, and home-visiting programs are typical services that an agency may provide. The social worker plays an important role in abuse and neglect cases, by working with children and their families, to provide services, monitor the case, and supply evidence to the court. The social-work perspective, however, may not mesh well with the lawyer's perspective. Social workers approach abuse and neglect as a systems problem with the family and may have difficulty understanding the lawyer's allegiance to a single family member. Mary Kay Kisthardt, *Working in the Best Interest of Children: Facilitating the Collaboration of Lawyers and Social Workers in Abuse and Neglect Cases*, 30 Rutgers L. Rec. 1 (2006). Moreover, social work has "not produced a systematic body of knowledge"; rather, much of social-work knowledge stems from a number of sources, including practice, governmental policy, and the social sciences. Karen M. Staller, *Knowledge Utilization in Social Work and Legal Practice*, 25 J. Soc. & Soc. Welfare 91, 102 (1998). How should lawyers and social workers talk across their disciplines?

3. REUNIFICATION

Half of the children who exited foster care in 2010 were reunified with a parent or primary caretaker. U.S. Department of Health and Human Services, Administration for Children and

Families, Children's Bureau, The AFCARS Report: Preliminary FY 2010 Estimates as of June 2011 (2010), www.acf.hhs.gov/programs/cb/stats_research/afcars/tar/report18.htm. The empirical research suggests that certain agency-level strategies, such as utilization of caseworkers with greater experience, social-work education, appropriate training, and specialized competencies, are better able to facilitate permanency. See, e.g., E. Albers et al., *Children in Foster Care: Possible Factors Affecting Permanency Planning*, 10 Child & Adolescent Soc. Work J. 329 (1993); National Center for Youth Law, Improving the Child Welfare Workforce: Lessons Learned from Class Action Litigation (2007), www.youthlaw.org/publications/yln/2007/january_march_2007/improving_the_child_welfare_workforce; Barbara A. Pine, Robin Spath, & Stephanie Gosteli, *Defining and Achieving Family Reunification*, in Child Welfare for the Twenty First Century: A Handbook of Practices, Policies, and Programs 378 (G. P. Mallon & P. Hess eds., 2005). Flexible funding that allows agencies to provide better community-based services to families also may lead to greater rates of reunification. See, e.g., Fred Wulczyn, *Family Reunification*, 14 The Future of Children 94 (2004).

At the individual-caseworker level, engagement of families and cognitive-behavioral, multisystemic, and skills-focused services also have been found to be most effective in reunifying children with their families. Geraldine M. MacDonald, Effective Interventions for Child Abuse and Neglect: An Evidence-Based Approach to Planning and Evaluating Interventions (2001); Jacqueline Corcoran, *Family Interventions with Child Physical Abuse and Neglect: A Critical Review*, 22 Child. & Youth Servs. Rev. 563 (2000); Kari Dawson & Marianne Berry, *Engaging Families in Child Welfare Services: An Evidence-Based Approach to Best Practice*, 81 Child Welfare 293 (2002); Susan P. Kemp et al., *Engaging Parents in Child Welfare Services: Bridging Family Needs and Child Welfare Mandates*, 88 Child Welfare 101 (2009). Providing families with concrete services such as food, transportation, and housing assistance, in addition to teaching families how to access community-based resources, also facilitates reunification. Tyrone C. Cheng, *Factors Associated with Reunification: A Longitudinal Analysis of Long-Term Foster Care*, 32 Child. & Youth Servs. Rev. 1311 (2010); Sam Choi & Joseph P. Ryan, *Co-occurring Problems for Substance Abusing Mothers in Child Welfare: Matching Services to Improve Family Reunification*, 29 Child. & Youth Servs. Rev. 1395 (2007); Tina L. Rzepnicki, John R. Schuerman, & Penny Johnson, *Facing Uncertainty: Reuniting High-Risk Families*, in Child Welfare Research Review, Vol. 2, 229 (Jill D. Berrick, Richard P. Barth, & Neil Gilbert eds., 1997).

Delay, however, is a significant problem. Martin Guggenheim, *Parental Rights in Child Welfare Cases in New York City Family Courts*, 40 Colum. J. L. & Soc. Probs. 507, 508–509 (2007). He also argues that lawyers for parents must "penetrate the administrative world of agency practice in order to ensure excellent child welfare practice." *Id.* at 521. By spending time out of court engaged in advocacy for the client at administrative reviews and staying "connected" with the client, lawyers for parents should be able to move the case plan forward in a timely fashion. *Id.* at 521–522. Given that half of the children were reunified, do you think the child-welfare system should devote more of its resources to providing preventive and preremoval services?

Concurrent planning. ASFA authorizes but does not mandate states to engage in concurrent planning. 42 U.S.C. § 671(a)(15)(F). Concurrent planning is a process that allows caseworkers to pursue multiple permanency options simultaneously. For example, in certain cases, caseworkers may provide both reunification and adoption services at the same time to eliminate the delays in achieving permanency that would likely occur if the options were pursued sequentially. The Chafee Foster Care Independence Act also envisions the use of concurrent planning for teenagers in order to ensure that they have emotional supports in place if no adoptive home can be found by the time they turn eighteen. About forty-two states and the District of Columbia authorize the use of concurrent planning. Most states authorize but do not require permanency planning, but a few states mandate its use under certain circumstances. Kentucky, for example, requires permanency planning only when a newborn has been abandoned Ky. Rev. Stat. Ann. § 620.350(2)(b) (2011); in Mississippi and Oklahoma, however, agencies must engage in concurrent planning when the child first enters care. Miss. Code Ann. § 43-15-13(2)(f), (8) (2009); Okla. Stat. Ann. tit. 10A, § 1-4-706(B) (2009).

How effective is reunification likely to be given that caseworkers may engage in concurrent planning? William Wesley Patton and Amy Pellman argue that concurrent planning is deeply problematic. It requires a greater resource commitment than current funding permits, burdens already overworked caseworkers who now must do more without a subsequent reduction in caseload, necessitates an expeditious handling of cases that is not possible because of overcrowded court dockets, envisions competent counsel when attorney caseloads are overwhelming, and fails to account for strong sibling relationships that may be severed by an emphasis on speed. William Wesley Patton & Amy M. Pellman, *The Reality of Concurrent Planning: Juggling Multiple Family Plans Expeditiously without Sufficient Resources*, 9 U.C. Davis J. Juv. L. & Pol'y 171 (2005). There is empirical evidence that caseworkers, judges, and attorneys share the concern that concurrent planning may undermine efforts to reunify children with their families. See, e.g., Amy D'Andrade, Laura Frame, & Jill Duer Berrick, *Concurrent Planning in Public Child Welfare Agencies: Oxymoron or Work in Progress?* 28 Child. & Youth Servs. Rev. 78, 88 (2006). There also is evidence that concurrent planning simply is not used to the extent the law permits. *Id.*

4. KINSHIP CARE

If a child cannot remain home at any time during the pendency of the proceedings, the court may place the child elsewhere. Federal law requires states to give "preference to an adult relative over a non-related caregiver when determining placement for a child, provided that the relative caregiver meets all relevant State child protection standards." 42 U.S.C. § 671(a)(19) (2011). The Fostering Connections to Success and Increasing Adoptions Act of 2008, Pub. L. No. 110-351, § 103, 122 Stat. 3956, 3956, also requires states to identify the child's relatives when a child is removed from parental custody and to inform the relatives about foster parenting and the availability of support services. As of 2010, approximately 26 percent of all children placed outside the home were placed with a relative. Children's Bureau, U.S. Dep't of Health & Human Servs., The AFCARS Report—Preliminary FY 2010 Estimates as of June 2011 (18) (2011), http:// www.acf.hhs.gov/programs/cb/stats_research/afcars/tar/report18.htm.

Are kinship placements better than other out-of-home placements? While kinship placement appears to be more stable, the empirical evidence that child functioning is better in kinship care is inconclusive. David J. Herring et al., *Evolutionary Theory and Kinship Care: An Initial Test of Two Hypotheses*, 38 Cap. U. L. Rev. 291, 295–296 (2009). There is some evidence that children who were placed in kinship care sooner have fewer behavioral problems than children who were placed in kinship care later or were placed elsewhere. *Id.* at 297. The nature and degree of relatedness between the child and the kinship caregiver also may affect the quality of the child's placement. *Id.* at 298. Nevertheless, a study of children placed in kinship care with a variety of different relatives found no significant differences in the percentage of children who received services or experienced juvenile detention or jail or on the stability of the placement. *Id.* at 315.

Despite a stated preference for kinship care, kinship caregivers receive less training and support and fewer services and have fewer economic and physical resources than nonkin caregivers. *Id.* at 295. Dorothy Roberts argues that funding schemes force kinship caregivers to assent to greater state oversight and supervision. She notes that many kinship caregivers are poor and need financial assistance if they are to support relative children. Because states are given the freedom to structure funding for kinship placements, welfare and foster-care payments are more generous. Consequently, kinship caregivers must submit to various state regulations in order to receive funding. Moreover, such financial incentives may discourage informal placements with relatives because of financial disincentives. Dorothy E. Roberts, *Kinship Care and the Price of State Support for Children*, 76 CHI-KENT L. REV. 1619 (2001).

The Fostering Connections to Success and Increasing Adoptions Act of 2008, Pub. L. No. 110-351, made numerous amendments to promote the safety, permanency, and well-being of children and youths in foster care. Among the changes made by the law were several intended to strengthen family connections for children and youths and to support greater use of kinship care when it is a safe and appropriate option. Among other provisions, states must now "exercise due diligence" in identifying and notifying all of the child's adult relatives within thirty days that the child has been or is being removed from the parent's custody; the relative's options for participating in caring for the child and the consequence of failing to respond to the notice; requirements for becoming a foster parent and services and support that are available to foster parents; and instructions on how the relative may qualify for kinship-guardianship-assistance payments if such payments are available in that state. 42 U.S.C. § 671(a)(29) (2010). States are required to use search technology to locate adult relatives and to explore the family member's willingness to accept permanent custody of the child. 42 U.S.C.A. §§ 627(a)(2) (2010). States also may create kinship-navigator programs to assist a caregiver in identifying, locating, and using programs and services for the child and the caregiver. 42 U.S.C. § 627(a)(1) (2010). The Act also allows child-welfare agencies to waive nonsafety-related licensing standards for relative foster-family homes on a case-by-case basis. 42 U.S.C. § 671(a)(10) (2010). Nevertheless, states are not granting waivers for a variety of reasons, including family preferences and state laws prohibiting the practice. Children's Bureau Administration on Children, Youth and Families Administration for Children and Families U.S. Department of Health and Human Services, Report to Congress on States' Use of Waivers of Non-Safety Licensing Standards for Relative Foster Family Homes (2011), http://www.acf.hhs.gov/programs/cb/pubs/statesuse/statesuse.pdf.

5. FOSTER CARE

In the United States, "foster care" refers to the temporary placement of a child with individuals who are not the child's parents, custodians, or legal guardians. The placement may be voluntary—that is, made with the child's parents' permission—or involuntary. Moreover, the type of placement will vary depending on the child's needs, age, and availability but includes placement in private homes and in group homes and institutional settings. Foster care is thus a component of the state's overall system for dealing with abused, neglected, and dependent children and needs to be considered within that context. Because children experience the state's protective system through foster care, the costs are exceedingly high, and the outcomes for children are often poor, considerable time and effort have been expended to remedy foster care's ills.

a. THE HISTORY OF FOSTER CARE

Tim Hacsi, *From Indenture to Family Foster Care: A Brief History of Child Placing*, in A History of Child Welfare 155 (Eve Smith & Lisa Merkel-Holguin eds., 1996).

Throughout American history, some children from impoverished families have always been reared in the homes of other people, but the *ways* that they were cared for have changed. In colonial America, children from all classes were sometimes indentured to families where they were to live, work, and learn a trade; this was an especially common way of caring for orphans and other dependent children, but it was seen as appropriate for children from other classes as well....

In the eighteenth century, local government officials known as the overseers of the poor were charged with distributing poor relief. These officials had the authority to indenture children from poor families in lieu of providing relief, and they did so regularly. In the colonial era, the duties of masters under indenture were spelled out in practical terms: children were to be fed, clothed, housed, and taught skills. Some children were taught to read and write, but education was not a universal component. The indenture relationship was primarily economic rather than emotional or psychological in nature....

Although used as a placement for children from low-income families, indenture in colonial America was by no means limited to children of the poor. It was commonplace for children from families that were not poor to be sent to other people's homes at the age of 13 or 14. Sometimes a formal contract of indenture was drawn up; in other cases the arrangement was informal....

In the first few decades of the nineteenth century, an urban middle class emerged with a new conception of childhood as a distinct phase of human development. Children's characters were to be shaped not by breaking their wills as in the colonial era, but by leading them to internalize beliefs about behavior and morality....

By the early nineteenth century, indenture was no longer used by all classes; only children from low-income families were indentured. Public officials continued to indenture orphans, half-orphans, and other dependent children whose parents were unable to provide for them or were for some reason deemed unfit. Masters had to meet somewhat higher expectations about what to provide apprentices.... Although still widely used, indenture was clearly on the wane by the middle of the nineteenth century.

In a reaction to the cholera epidemic of 1832 and poverty in the nation's rapidly growing urban centers, numerous religious and charitable organizations founded orphan asylums.... Many orphan asylum superintendents placed small children with families where they would receive more individual attention than was possible in an asylum. Asylums also indentured older children in the hope that they would learn a trade, although by the late nineteenth century asylums were increasingly likely to provide some form of manual training within the institution itself [citations omitted].

Nevertheless, between 1830 and 1860 orphan asylums became the nation's predominant method of caring for dependent children. By the 1880s, however, orphan asylums were facing heavy criticism, usually accompanied by arguments favoring placing children with families. It was no coincidence that Charles Loring Brace, the most famous critic of asylums, was also the nation's most influential advocate of placing-out....

In 1853, the idea of placing children in homes rather than institutions gained new life when Brace founded the New York Children's Aid Society (CAS). CAS's fundamental assumption was that children should be placed in rural homes rather than in institutions. Brace was anti-urban, anti-immigrant, and anti-Catholic.... As a result, CAS's child-placing approach combined anti-institutional thought with anti-urban fears by trying to place children from urban slums in the country, usually with Protestant farmers [citations omitted].

Children came to CAS in a variety of ways. Agents swept the streets looking for street children and vagrants who did not have homes. Orphan asylums and infant asylums brought children to CAS, as did public officials. Most child-placing agencies that came into existence later found homes for their children within a day's travel of their original homes, but CAS wanted to move children as far from the city as possible. The CAS "orphan trains" became famous. Aside from the distance children traveled, these placements were similar to those made by asylums.... CAS avoided using indenture contracts because it considered them too binding, but older children were placed largely in response to the needs of rural western states for more farm labor. In this respect, placing-out was quite like informal indenture.

A 14- or 15-year-old child working for a living was commonplace in the late nineteenth century. Middle-class children might still be in school at that age, but working-class and impoverished children were almost always employed to help their families....

... CAS's placing-out system was designed to "protect" children from the urban environment and from their own parents, who were presumed to be unworthy individuals incapable of rearing children properly. All ties between children and their biological parents were to be ended....

... [U]nlike orphan asylums, however, the placing organizations were almost always Protestant....

Although some Catholic groups did place children in families, they usually favored institutional care, partly because of the difficulty in finding rural Catholic homes for placement. But the few Catholic agencies that regularly placed children in families used placing-out as a complement to Catholic orphan asylums; unlike CAS, they were not opposed to institutional care.

The desire to remove children from supposedly unworthy, perhaps even dangerous, parents created a sense of urgency among placing-out advocates....

Placing agencies usually found homes by advertising for them, but rarely bothered to screen the respondents. After children were placed, agencies maintained little or no contact with them. Even when agencies wanted to check up on placement homes, insufficient funds often kept them from doing so [citation omitted].Those agencies that did check on children often found that placements were not working, and that the children had to be moved. Children under the care of Pennsylvania's Children's Aid Society for more than a year, for example, often experienced four or more placements....

...[A]sylum supporters criticized placing-out agencies because they did not carefully examine the new homes they found for their children. In particular, Catholics attacked CAS for placing Catholic children in Protestant homes....Not surprisingly, the more careful the examination of prospective placement homes, the lower the rate of acceptance.

Children under the age of five who were placed were the most likely to be adopted (whether legally or de facto) by their new parents....Unfortunately, most placements seem to have involved older children. Of the more than 22,000 children placed in "permanent" homes by CAS between 1854 and 1900, over 17,400 (78 percent) were older than 10. Since most placement homes wanted children who could work to earn their keep, a disparity existed between the best age for children to be placed and the requests from potential parents [citations omitted].

A disparity also existed between what placement agencies wanted and what the parents of the children wanted. In the late nineteenth century, placing-out (like institutional care) was often used by families to help them weather difficult times brought on by a death, serious illness, or long period of unemployment. The majority of children who entered the care of placement agencies were brought by parents or other relatives, many of whom tried to reclaim their children when the family was back on its feet. Despite the hopes of most placing-out advocates, many children returned to their families within a few years of being placed elsewhere [citations omitted].

In the last quarter of the nineteenth century, child abuse and parental neglect began to be recognized as important problems. During the 1870s, Societies for the Prevention of Cruelty to Children (SPCC) began to appear in eastern cities. SPCCs often removed children from abusive or neglectful homes and placed them in other homes or orphan asylums; courts granted these societies what amounted to police powers to remove children when they saw fit....The main problem of dependent children was their family's poverty, but neglected children were "the offspring of parents who *can*, but *do not*, provide suitably for them, and whose vicious lives render them unfit to have the care of them." [Citation omitted.] In practice, once children were in the child welfare system, "dependent" and "neglected" children were treated the same. The line distinguishing dependent children from neglected children was elusive. Though some of these parents undoubtedly were "bad" parents, most were simply impoverished....

...Older children placed in "free" homes, like indentured children, were expected to work to earn their keep. Younger children were not expected to work; they were to be taken in for love. Ironically, placement agencies began making payments to foster families in an effort to ensure that children would not be valued exclusively for their labor....

...Changing to boarding-out led placing agencies to look more closely at the situation within the placement home. After all, agencies did not want to pay people to rear children unless they were doing a good job....

Between 1880 and 1920, the question of whether to pay adults who took in other people's children complicated the debate on home placement versus institutional care....Supporters of free placements feared that if money were paid to some foster parents, the pool of free homes would dry up. Supporters of board payment hoped to ensure that young children were not worked to earn their keep. Gradually, boarding-out won the battle, but it took more than half a century. In the South, where child welfare developments lagged, placing-out remained far more common than boarding-out in the late 1920s....

The growing popularity of boarding-out, sometimes known as foster care, was intimately tied to the growth of the juvenile court system in the three decades after 1900....The creation of a court system specifically for minors greatly increased the number of children who became state wards....In many states, mothers' pensions, the successor to outdoor relief and the predecessor of Aid to Families with Dependent Children, were awarded on the basis of an investigation by an officer of the juvenile court. If the officer found the mother to be unworthy of aid, as often happened, the result might be worse for the family than if the family had not sought help. In such cases, the court might remove the child to a foster home [citation omitted].

The growing involvement of government in child welfare, first at the state and later at the federal level, was a central reason for the expansion of foster care in the twentieth century. The rise of the juvenile court, which now plays a crucial role in the out-of-home care system, is the most obvious example, but not the only one. State Boards of Charity, which proliferated in the late nineteenth century and gained increased powers during the Progressive Era, strongly favored home placement over asylums....

When a state government became involved in placing or boarding children in homes, some manner of state regulation usually followed. As in many other aspects of child welfare, California acted well before most other states. By 1915, California was licensing and regulating, if only loosely, agencies that found placement homes for children [citation omitted]. By 1920, California was making payments to boarding homes, including those arranged by private agencies, so long as the children had been "committed by the juvenile courts of the state as needy." [Citation omitted.]

By the 1920s, placing-out had been replaced by boarding-out in a number of cities....In the 1920s, even CAS stopped its orphan train shipments of children to the rural West [citation omitted].

By the 1930s, it was becoming clear that boarding-out was out-pacing both institutional care and free placing-out. The decline of the latter methods became certain with the creation of Aid to Dependent Children (ADC, later AFDC) as Title IV of the Social Security Act in 1935. Under ADC, available federal funds that could be used to keep impoverished families together rose dramatically. As a result, many families that previously would have turned to an orphan asylum or child placement agency were able to keep their children at home. At the same time, the increasing financial involvement of state governments in the child welfare system meant that when children were removed from their homes, they were more likely to be boarded in a family than placed in an asylum. By 1950, more children were in foster homes than in institutions; by 1960, almost twice as many children were in foster care as were in institutions; and, in 1968, more than three times as many children were in foster care as in institutions [citation omitted].

In the 1940s and 1950s, as foster care expanded and the use of asylums declined, the total number of dependent children being cared for outside of their own homes stayed relatively stable, between 3.5 and 4.5 per thousand children under the age of 18 [citation omitted]. During the 1960s and 1970s, however, the foster care population exploded, reaching a peak in the late 1970s [citation omitted]. The most important factor driving skyrocketing foster care populations during this period was the rediscovery of child abuse.

Research during the 1950s led some physicians to conclude that large numbers of parents were abusing their children. In 1962, an article entitled "The Battered-Child Syndrome" was published in an important medical journal; in short order, the popular press was running feature articles on child abuse [citation omitted]. In fact, more children enter foster care due to neglect than abuse, although the lines between the two are often blurry, just as the distinction between neglect and simple poverty has never been absolutely clear.

Federal funding was an additional reason for the dramatic rise in foster care populations between 1960 and 1977. . . . At that time, rules regarding AFDC payments were changed to allow payments for children in foster care whose biological families were eligible. Later amendments to the Social Security Act, Titles IV-B and XX, also made federal money available for foster care [citation omitted]. In 1961, Title IV-A of the Social Security Act made federal matching payments available to states *only* for children placed in foster care by a court decision, whose families also met other AFDC requirements. The availability of federal AFDC money for foster care clearly helped spur the growth of foster care caseloads. By 1976, the number of children in AFDC foster care was well over 100,000 [citation omitted].

The most important federal legislation of recent years regarding foster care is the Adoption Assistance and Child Welfare Act of 1980. This act targets money toward preventive services and efforts aimed at reuniting families, thus attempting to shift policy away from family breakup and toward family maintenance.

Although AFDC and foster care are separate systems (aside from the federal funding sometimes available for foster care), the availability and generosity of AFDC clearly affects the number of families that come under the jurisdiction of foster care. The purchasing power of AFDC grants has dropped dramatically since 1970. In 1990 inflation-adjusted dollars, the median monthly AFDC grant for a family of three with no other income fell from $601 in 1970 to just $364 in 1990 [citation omitted].

Under these conditions, it should be no surprise that, after dropping in the late 1970s and early 1980s, the number of children in foster care has risen rapidly over the last decade. This recent urban surge in the foster care population has other important aspects: the number of infants under one year of age in foster care has risen; in some cities, many children are born addicted to drugs, including crack. Not only are more children entering foster care but, on the average, they are staying longer. . . .

An important additional reason for the increase in foster care caseloads has been the growing popularity of foster placement with relatives, that is, kinship care. By 1990, formal kinship foster care had become an important part of foster care services. Informal care by relatives, however, has always been used for large numbers of children without viable parents, and remains far more common. Between 1980 and 1992, the number of children being reared by their grandparents rose from two to three million, a number that dwarfs the foster care population [citation omitted].

Today, the foster care system serves a population whose central problem is poverty, as it always has been. Tragically however, the children now coming into foster care are poorer, younger, and far more troubled than those in the past, and they are staying in care for longer periods of time. . . .

One of the most dramatic differences between placing-out and today's foster care system is that foster care is usually intended to provide temporary care for children, with the hope that they can someday be returned to their parents. . . .

In fact, the question of whether families should be kept together or children should be permanently removed from their parents remains.

QUESTIONS

1. How would you characterize the history of foster care? Do you think a better understanding of its history explains the current state of foster care?

b. THE CURRENT STATE OF FOSTER CARE

Children's Bureau, Admin. for Child. & Fam., U.S. Dep't Health & Hum. Services, Trends in Foster Care and Adoption—FY 2002–FY 2010, Based on Data Submitted by States as of June, 2011, http://www.acf.hhs.gov/programs/cb/stats_research/afcars/trends_june2011.pdf.

Technical Discussion

Even though the number of children served is calculated by summing the children in care on the first day of the year plus the entries into foster during the year, another way of counting the number of children served is by adding the number of children in foster care on the last day of the year to the number of exits from foster care during the FFY [federal fiscal year]. We compared the numbers derived from both approaches, and they are equal in FFY 2006, FFY 2008 and FFY 2010, but there is less than a one percent discrepancy in the other years. Most of these differences can be attributed to rounding.

Because the number of entries exceeds the number of exits from FFY 2002 to FFY 2006, we would expect that the number of children/youth in care as of September 30th would have increased during this period. This, however, did not occur, as the number of children in care actually declined. The primary contributing factor to this phenomenon is that, in the AFCARS database, each child is counted only once and the information included on the child in the database is from their most recent foster care episode. However, there are some children who were in foster care on the first day of the year but exited and re-entered during the year one or more times prior to entering their most recent foster care episode. In addition, they remained in foster care through the last day of the fiscal year (September 30) in their most recent foster care episode. In these circumstances, the exit associated with their "in care" status on the first day of the year is not counted, even though it occurred during the fiscal year. We estimate the number of these uncounted exits to be approximately 6,000 per year.

There is also a data quality issue that has had an impact on the number of exits. AFCARS data are submitted every six months and cover a six-month period. Sometimes a child who is reported during one six-month period does not appear in the next period, and there is no record that the child exited. Reviews of these cases have shown that the majority are situations in which the child actually exited, but the exit was not reported to AFCARS. However, because the actual number of these "dropped" exits cannot be calculated, they have not been accounted for in the exit count. As this issue has been brought to the attention of States, the quality of the data has improved dramatically and the number of dropped cases has decreased. For instance, the number of these dropped cases has declined from around 8,000 in FY 2006 to about 3,000 in FY 2007 and FY 2008, and about 4,000 in FY 2009. Therefore, these dropped cases constitute less than 2 percent of the reported discharges in the three most recent years. Please note that dropped cases are not counted in any of these counts.

Data Discussion

Children in Foster Care on September 30: The data show a substantial decline in the number of children in foster care on the last day of each federal fiscal year (September 30) between FY 2002 and FY 2010, with a small exception in FY 2005. A similar pattern is seen in the total number of children served during these years. The number of children served declined from 800,000 in FY 2002 to 662,000 in FY 2010.

Entries to Foster Care: In FY 2005, the number of entries into foster care reached its highest point to date with 307,000 entries reported that year. Since that time, however, the number of entries has declined to 254,000 in FY 2010, the lowest number since AFCARS data have been reported. The number of exits, which increased between FY 2002 (278,000) and FY 2006 (295,000), declined to 254,000 in FY 2010, excluding children who exited but re-entered during the same year and children whose discharge dates were missing from the file (see technical discussion above). Between FY 2007 and FY 2009, the number of exits were greater than the number of entries into foster care, and in FY 2010 the numbers entering and exiting care were almost the same.

NOTES AND QUESTIONS

1. The Children's Bureau was created in 1912 by President Taft and has primary responsibility for administering federal child-welfare programs. As part of its mission, the Bureau administers state and federal reporting and data-collection systems, including the Adoption and Foster Care Analysis Reporting System (AFCARS), the National Child Abuse and Neglect Data System (NCANDS), the National Youth in Transition Database (NYTD), and the State Automated Child Welfare Information System (SACWIS).

2. AFCARS was created pursuant to 42 U.S.C. § 679, and a series of regulations implementing the statute were enacted in 1994. Through AFCARS, the Children's Bureau collects information on all children in foster care for whom state child-welfare agencies have responsibility for placement, care, or supervision and on children who are adopted through the state's public child-welfare agency. AFCARS also includes information on foster and adoptive parents. States are required to submit AFCARS data semiannually.

3. Federal law provides foster-care subsidies to the states. Because these are uncapped entitlements, states have an incentive to seek as much reimbursement as possible for each child placed in foster care. However, to be eligible for these subsidies, states must establish in the first

instance that the child would be AFDC-eligible. 42 U.S.C. § 672(a)(3) (2011). Aid to Families with Dependent Children, known as AFDC or welfare, was replaced by TANF—Temporary Assistance to Needy Families—in 1996 (popularly referred to as welfare reform). States are required to find that a child is AFDC-eligible in order to request reimbursement for foster-care costs. This requires an assessment of the child's AFDC eligibility as it existed in the former state-welfare plan on July 16, 1996. Cynthia Andrews Scarcella et al., The Urban Inst., The Cost of Protecting Vulnerable Children V: Understanding State Variation in Child Welfare Financing 1–2 (2006), http://www.urban.org/publications/310586.html. If the child is not AFDC-eligible, then the state and local governments would absorb the entire cost of the foster-care placement.

Susan Mangold argues that these funding incentives drive state agencies to maximize reimbursement at the expense of children and their families. Susan Vivian Mangold, *Poor Enough to Be Eligible? Child Abuse, Neglect, and the Poverty Requirement*, 81 St. John's L. Rev. 575 (2007). Because foster-care subsidies are tied to welfare eligibility, states try to qualify as many children as possible. However, the process for determining AFDC eligibility is cumbersome and time-consuming, so states increasingly have hired outside contractors to make the income and compliance determinations. States then are eligible to seek reimbursement for the maintenance payments (the cost to feed, shelter, and clothe a foster child) and also the administrative expenses associated with the foster-care placement. The net result is that states spend more on administration than on service-delivery maintenance payments. Mangold argues that eliminating the income-eligibility-determination requirements would make more money available for service delivery.

How would you change federal incentives, if at all? What would be your objectives?

C. THE FOSTER CHILD'S RIGHT TO A FAMILY

SMITH V. ORGANIZATION OF FOSTER FAMILIES FOR EQUALITY AND REFORM (O.F.F.E.R.)
Supreme Court of the United States
431 U.S. 816 (1977)

Mr. Justice Brennan delivered the opinion of the Court.

Appellees, individual foster parents[1] and an organization of foster parents, brought this civil rights class action pursuant to 42 U.S.C. § 1983 in the United States District Court for

1. Appellee Madeleine Smith is the foster parent with whom Eric and Danielle Gandy have been placed since 1970. The Gandy children, who are now 12 and 9 years old respectively, were voluntarily placed in foster care by their natural mother in 1968, and have had no contact with her at least since being placed with Mrs. Smith. The foster-care agency has sought to remove the children from Mrs. Smith's care because her arthritis, in the agency's judgment makes it difficult for her to continue to provide adequate care. A foster-care review proceeding under N.Y.Soc.Serv. Law § 392 (McKinney 1976), resulted in an order, subsequent to the decision of the District Court, directing that foster care be continued and apparently contemplating, though not specifically ordering, that the children will remain in Mrs. Smith's care. *In re Gandy*, Nos. K-26 63/74 S, K-26 64/74 S (Fam.Ct.N.Y.Cty., Nov. 22, 1976). Appellees Ralph and Christiane Goldberg were the foster

the Southern District of New York, on their own behalf and on behalf of children for whom they have provided homes for a year or more. They sought declaratory and injunctive relief against New York State and New York City officials,[2] alleging that the procedures governing the removal of foster children from foster homes provided in N.Y.Soc.Serv. Law §§ 383(2) and 400 (McKinney 1976), and in 18 N.Y.C.R.R. § 450.14 (1974) violated the Due Process and Equal Protection Clauses of the Fourteenth Amendment. The District Court appointed independent counsel for the foster children to forestall any possibility of conflict between their interests and the interests asserted by the foster parents. A group of natural mothers of children in foster care[5] were granted leave to intervene on behalf of themselves and others similarly situated.

A divided three-judge District Court concluded that "the pre-removal procedures presently employed by the State are constitutionally defective," holding that "before a foster child can be peremptorily transferred from the foster home in which he has been living, be it to another foster home or to the natural parents who initially placed him in foster care, he is entitled to a hearing at which all concerned parties may present any relevant information to the administrative decisionmaker charged with determining the future placement of the child," *Organization of Foster Families v. Dumpson*, 418 F.Supp. 277, 282 (1976). Four appeals to this Court were taken from the ensuing judgment declaring the challenged statutes unconstitutional and permanently enjoining their enforcement. The New York City officials are appellants in No. 76-180. The New York State officials are appellants in No. 76-183. Independent counsel appointed for the foster children appeals on their behalf in No. 76-5200. The intervening natural mothers are appellants in No. 76-5193. We noted probable jurisdiction of the four appeals. 429 U.S. 883 (1976). We reverse.

parents of Rafael Serrano, now 14. His parents placed him in foster care voluntarily in 1969 after an abuse complaint was filed against them. It is alleged that the agency supervising the placement had informally indicated to Mr. and Mrs. Goldberg that it intended to transfer Rafael to the home of his aunt in contemplation of permanent placement. This effort has apparently failed. A petition for foster-care review under Soc.Serv. Law s 392 filed by the agency alleges that the Goldbergs are now separated, Mrs. Goldberg having moved out of the house, taking her own child but leaving Rafael. The child is now in a residential treatment center, where Mr. Goldberg continues to visit him. App. to Reply Brief for Appellants in No. 76-180.

Appellees Walter and Dorothy Lhotan were foster parents of the four Wallace sisters, who were voluntarily placed in foster care by their mother in 1970. The two older girls were placed with the Lhotans in that year, their two younger sisters in 1972. In June 1974, the Lhotans were informed that the agency had decided to return the two younger girls to their mother and transfer the two older girls to another foster home. The agency apparently felt that the Lhotans were too emotionally involved with the girls and were damaging the agency's efforts to prepare them to return to their mother. The state courts have ordered that all the Wallace children be returned to their mother, *State ex rel. Wallace v. Lhotan*, 51 A.D.2d 252, 380 N.Y.S.2d 250, appeal dismissed and leave to appeal denied, 39 N.Y.2d 705, 384 N.Y.S.2d 1027, 349 N.E.2d 882 (1976). We are told that the children have been returned and are adjusting successfully. Reply Brief for Appellants in No. 76-5200, pp. 1a–10a.

2. Defendants in the District Court included various New York State and New York City child welfare officials, and officials of a voluntary child-care agency and the Nassau County Department of Social Services. The latter two defendants have not appealed.

5. Intervenor Naomi Rodriguez, who is blind, placed her newborn son Edwin in foster care in 1973 because of marital difficulties. When Mrs. Rodriguez separated from her husband three months later, she sought return of her child. Her efforts over the next nine months to obtain return of the child were resisted by the agency, apparently because it felt her handicap prevented her from providing adequate care. Eventually, she sought return of her child in the state courts, and finally prevailed, three years after she first sought return of the child. *Rodriguez v. Dumpson*, 52 A.D.2d 299, 383 N.Y.S.2d 883 (1976). The other named intervenors describe similar instances of voluntary placements during family emergencies followed by lengthy and frustrating attempts to get their children back.

I

A detailed outline of the New York statutory system regulating foster care is a necessary preface to a discussion of the constitutional questions presented.

A

The expressed central policy of the New York system is that "it is generally desirable for the child to remain with or be returned to the natural parent because the child's need for a normal family life will usually best be met in the natural home, and... parents are entitled to bring up their own children unless the best interests of the child would be thereby endangered," Soc. Serv. Law § 384-b(1)(a)(ii) (McKinney Supp. 1976–1977). But the State has opted for foster care as one response to those situations where the natural parents are unable to provide the "positive, nurturing family relationships" and "normal family life in a permanent home" that offer "the best opportunity for children to develop and thrive." §§ 384-b(1)(b), (1)(a)(i).

Foster care has been defined as "(a) child welfare service which provides substitute family care for a planned period for a child when his own family cannot care for him for a temporary or extended period, and when adoption is neither desirable nor possible." Child Welfare League of America, Standards for Foster Family Care Service, 5 (1959).[8] Thus, the distinctive features of foster care are, first, "that it is care in a *family*, it is noninstitutional substitute care," and, second, "that it is for a *planned* period either temporary or extended. This is unlike adoptive placement, which implies a permanent substitution of one home for another." Kadushin 355.

Under the New York scheme children may be placed in foster care either by voluntary placement or by court order. Most foster care placements are voluntary.[9] They occur when physical or mental illness, economic problems, or other family crises make it impossible for natural parents, particularly single parents, to provide a stable home life for their children for some limited period.[10] Resort to such placements is almost compelled when it is not possible

8. The term "foster care" is often used more generally to apply to any type of care that substitutes others for the natural parent in the parental role, including group homes, adoptive homes, and institutions, as well as foster family homes. A. Kadushin, Child Welfare Services 355 (1967) (hereafter Kadushin). Cf. Mnookin, Foster Care in Whose Best Interests? 43 Harv.Educ.Rev. 599, 600 (1973) (hereafter Mnookin I). Since this case is only concerned with children in foster family homes, the term will generally be used here in the more restricted sense defined in the text.

9. The record indicates that as many as 80 percent of the children in foster care in New York City are voluntarily placed. Deposition of Prof. David Fanshel, App. 178a. But cf. Child Welfare Information Services, Characteristics of Children in Foster Care, New York City Reports, Table No. 11 (Dec. 31, 1976). Other studies from New York and elsewhere variously estimate the percentage of voluntary placements between 50 percent and 90 percent. See, *e.g.*, Mnookin I 601; Areen, Intervention between Parent and Child: A Reappraisal of the State's Role in Child Neglect and Abuse Cases, 63 Geo.L.J. 887, 921–922, and n. 185 (1975); Levine, Caveat Parens: A Demystification of the Child Protection System, 35 U.Pitt.L.Rev. 1, 29 (1973).

10. Experienced commentators have suggested that typical parents in this situation might be "(a) divorced parent in a financial bind, an unwed adolescent mother still too immature to rear a child, or a welfare mother confronted with hospitalization and therefore temporarily incapable of caring for her child." Weiss & Chase, The Case for Repeal of Section 383 of the New York Social Services Law, 4 Colum. Human Rights L.Rev. 325, 326 (1972). A leading text on child-care services suggests that "(f)amily disruption, marginal economic circumstances, and poor health" are principal factors leading to placement of children in foster care. Kadushin 366. Other studies suggest, however, that neglect, abuse, abandonment and exploitation of children, which

in such circumstance to place the child with a relative or friend, or to pay for the services of a homemaker or boarding school.

Voluntary placement requires the signing of a written agreement by the natural parent or guardian, transferring the care and custody of the child to an authorized child welfare agency.[11] N.Y.Soc.Serv. Law § 384-a(1) (McKinney Supp. 1976–1977). Although by statute the terms of such agreements are open to negotiation, § 384-a(2)(a), it is contended that agencies require execution of standardized forms. Brief for Appellants in No. 76-5193, p. 25 n. 17. See App. 63a–64a, 65a–67a. The agreement may provide for return of the child to the natural parent at a specified date or upon occurrence of a particular event, and if it does not, the child must be returned by the agency, in the absence of a court order, within 20 days of notice from the parent. § 384-a(2)(a).

The agency may maintain the child in an institutional setting, §§ 374-b, 374-c, 374-d (McKinney 1976), but more commonly acts under its authority to "place out and board out" children in foster homes. § 374(1).[13] Foster parents, who are licensed by the State or an authorized foster-care agency, §§ 376, 377, provide care under a contractual arrangement with the agency, and are compensated for their services. See 18 N.Y.C.R.R. §§ 606.2, 606.6 (1977); App. 76a, 81a. The typical contract expressly reserves the right of the agency to remove the child on request. 418 F.Supp., at 281; App. 76a, 79a. See N.Y.Soc.Serv. Law s 383(2) (McKinney 1976).[14] Conversely, the foster parent may cancel the agreement at will.[15]

The New York system divides parental functions among agency, foster parents, and natural parents, and the definitions of the respective roles are often complex and often unclear. The law transfers "care and custody" to the agency, § 384-a; see also § 383(2), but day-to-day supervision of the child and his activities, and most of the functions ordinarily associated with legal custody, are the responsibility of the foster parent.[17] Nevertheless, agency supervision of

presumably account for most of the children who enter foster care by court order, see *infra*, at 2101–2102, are also involved in many cases of voluntary placement. See *infra*, at 2104–2105; Kadushin 366.

11. "Authorized agency" is defined in N.Y.Soc.Serv. Law § 371(10) (McKinney 1976) and "includes any local public welfare children's bureau, such as the defendants New York City Bureau of Child Welfare and Nassau County Children's Bureau, and any voluntary child-care agency under the supervision of the New York State Board of Social Welfare, such as the defendant Catholic Guardian Society of New York." 418 F.Supp., at 278 n. 5.

An amicus curiae brief states that in New York City, 85 percent of the children in foster care are placed with voluntary child-care agencies licensed by the State, while most children in foster care outside New York City are placed directly with the local Department of Social Services. Brief for Legal Aid Society of City of New York, Juvenile Rights Division, as Amicus Curiae 14 n. 22.

13. The record indicates that at the end of 1973, of 48,812 children in foster care under the supervision of the New York State Board of Social Welfare and the New York State Department of Social Services, 35,287 (about 72 percent) were placed in foster family homes, and the rest in institutions or other facilities. App. 117a.

14. Such contractual provisions are apparently also characteristic of foster-care arrangements in other States. See, *e.g.*, Mnookin I 610.

15. See, *e.g.*, the case of appellees Ralph and Christiane Goldberg, n. 1, *supra*. Evidence in the record indicates that as many as one-third of all transfers within the foster-care system are at the request of the foster parents. Affidavit of Carol J. Parry, App. 90a.

17. "Legal custody is concerned with the rights and duties of the person (usually the parent) having custody to provide for the child's daily needs to feed him, clothe him, provide shelter, put him to bed, send him to school, see that he washes his face and brushes his teeth." Kadushin 354–355. Obviously, performance of these functions directly by a state agency is impractical.

the performance of the foster parents takes forms indicating that the foster parent does not have the full authority of a legal custodian.[18] Moreover, the natural parent's placement of the child with the agency does not surrender legal guardianship;[19] the parent retains authority to act with respect to the child in certain circumstances.[20] The natural parent has not only the right but the obligation to visit the foster child and plan for his future; failure of a parent with capacity to fulfill the obligation for more than a year can result in a court order terminating the parent's rights on the ground of neglect. §§ 384-b(4), (7). See also § 384-b(5); N.Y.Dom. Rel. Law s 111 (McKinney Supp. 1976–1977); N.Y. Family Court Acts 611 (McKinney Supp. 1976–1977).[21]

Children may also enter foster care by court order. The Family Court may order that a child be placed in the custody of an authorized child-care agency after a full adversary judicial hearing under Art. 10 of the New York Family Court Act, if it is found that the child has been abused or neglected by his natural parents. §§ 1052, 1055. In addition, a minor adjudicated a juvenile delinquent, or "person in need of supervision" may be placed by the court with an agency. §§ 753, 754, 756. The consequences of foster-care placement by court order do not differ substantially from those for children voluntarily placed, except that the parent is not entitled to return of the child on demand pursuant to Soc.Serv.Law § 384-a(2)(a); termination of foster care must then be consented to by the court. § 383(1).[22]

B

The provisions of the scheme specifically at issue in this litigation come into play when the agency having legal custody determines to remove the foster child from the foster home, either because it has determined that it would be in the child's best interests to transfer him to some other foster home, or to return the child to his natural parents in accordance with

18. "The agency sets limits and advances directives as to how the foster parents are to behave toward the child a situation not normally encountered by natural parents. The shared control and responsibility for the child is clearly set forth in the instruction pamphlets issued to foster parents." *Id.*, at 394. Agencies frequently prohibit corporal punishment; require that children over a certain age be given an allowance; forbid changes in the child's sleeping arrangements or vacations out of State without agency approval; require the foster parent to discuss the child's behavioral problems with the agency. *Id.*, at 394–395. Furthermore, since the cost of supporting the child is borne by the agency, the responsibility, as well as the authority, of the foster parent is shared with the agency. *Ibid.*

19. Voluntary placement in foster care is entirely distinct from the "surrender" of both "the guardianship of the person and the custody" of a child under Soc.Serv. Law § 384, which frees the child for adoption. § 384(2). "Adoption is the legal proceeding whereby a person takes another person into the legal relation of child and thereby acquires the rights and incurs the responsibilities of parent in respect of such other person." N.Y.Dom.Rel. Law § 110 (McKinney 1964). A child may also be freed for adoption by abandonment or consent. § 111 (McKinney Supp. 1976–1977); Soc.Serv. Law § 384-b.

20. "(A)lthough the agency usually obtains legal custody in foster family care, the child still legally 'belongs' to the parent and the parent retains guardianship. This means that, for some crucial aspects of the child's life, the agency has no authority to act. Only the parent can consent to surgery for the child, or consent to his marriage, or permit his enlistment in the armed forces, or represent him at law." Kadushin 355. But see Soc.Serv. Law § 383-b.

21. The agreement transferring custody to the agency must inform the parent of these obligations. §§ 384-a(2)(c)(iii), (iv).

22. The Family Court is also empowered permanently to sever the ties of parent and child if the parent fails to maintain contact with the child while in foster care. § 384-b(4)-(7).

the statute or placement agreement. Most children are removed in order to be transferred to another foster home.[23] The procedures by which foster parents may challenge a removal made for that purpose differ somewhat from those where the removal is made to return the child to his natural parent.

Section 383(2)...provides that the "authorized agency placing out or boarding (a foster) child...may in its discretion remove such child from the home where placed or boarded." Administrative regulations implement this provision. The agency is required, except in emergencies, to notify the foster parents in writing 10 days in advance of any removal. 18 N.Y.C.R.R. § 450.10(a) (1976). The notice advises the foster parents that if they object to the child's removal they may request a "conference" with the Social Services Department. *Ibid.* The department schedules requested conferences within 10 days of the receipt of the request. § 450.10(b). The foster parent may appear with counsel at the conference, where he will "be advised of the reasons (for the removal of the child), and be afforded an opportunity to submit reasons why the child should not be removed." § 450.10(a).[25] The official must render a decision in writing within five days after the close of the conference, and send notice of his decision to the foster parents and the agency. § 450.10(c). The proposed removal is stayed pending the outcome of the conference. § 450.10(d).

If the child is removed after the conference, the foster parent may appeal to the Department of Social Services for a "fair hearing," that is, a full adversary administrative hearing, under Soc.Serv.Law § 400, the determination of which is subject to judicial review under N.Y.Civ. Prac.Law § 7801 et seq. (McKinney 1963); Art. 78; however, the removal is not automatically stayed pending the hearing and judicial review.

This statutory and regulatory scheme applies statewide.[28] In addition, regulations promulgated by the New York City Human Resources Administration, Department of Social Services

23. The record shows that in 1973–1974 approximately 80 percent of the children removed from foster homes in New York State after living in the foster home for one year or more were transferred to another foster placement. Thirteen percent were returned to the biological parents, and 7 percent were adopted. Tr. of Oral Arg. 34; Brief for Appellees 20.

25. The State argues that while § 450.10 provides minimum requirements for notice to the foster family of the agency's intention to remove the child and the reasons for that decision, the close contact between the agency and the foster parent insures that in most circumstances the foster parent is informed well in advance of any projected removal. In fact, 18 N.Y.C.R.R. § 606.16 (1976) requires the agency in some circumstances to begin for the discharge of the children from foster care, in cooperation with all parties involved, as early as six months in advance. Brief for Appellants in No. 76-183, pp. 21–23.

28. There is some dispute whether the procedures set out in 18 N.Y.C.R.R. § 450.10 and Soc.Serv.Law § 400 apply in the case of a foster child being removed from his foster home to be returned to his natural parents. Application of these procedures to children who have been placed voluntarily, for example, arguably conflicts with the requirement of § 384-a(2)(a) that children in that situation be returned to the natural parent as provided in the placement agreement or within 20 days of demand. Similarly, if the child has been ordered returned by a court, it is unclear what purpose could be served by an administrative conference or hearing on the correctness of the decision to remove the child from the foster home. Moreover, since the § 400 hearing takes place after removal of the child from the foster home, the hearing would have no purpose if the child has been returned to its parents, since the agency apparently has no authority to take the child back from its parents against their will without court intervention.

Nevertheless, nothing in either the statute or the regulations limits the availability of these procedures to transfers within the foster-care system. Each refers to the decision to *remove* a child from the foster family home, and thus on its face each would seem to cover removal for the purpose of returning the child to its parents. Furthermore, it is undisputed on this record that the actual administrative practice in New York is

Special Services for Children (SSC) provide even greater procedural safeguards there. Under SSC Procedure No. 5 (Aug. 5, 1974), in place of or in addition to the conference provided by the state regulations, the foster parents may request a full trial-type hearing *before* the child is removed from their home. This procedure applies, however, only if the child is being transferred to another foster home, and not if the child is being returned to his natural parents.

One further preremoval procedural safeguard is available. Under Soc.Serv.Law § 392, the Family Court has jurisdiction to review, on petition of the foster parent or the agency, the status of any child who has been in foster care for 18 months or longer.[30] The foster parents, the natural parents, and all interested agencies are made parties to the proceeding. § 392(4). After hearing, the court may order that foster care be continued, or that the child be returned to his natural parents, or that the agency take steps to free the child for adoption.[31] § 392(7). Moreover, § 392(8) authorizes the court to issue an "order of protection" which "may set forth reasonable conditions of behavior to be observed for a specified time by a person or agency who is before the court." Thus, the court may order not only that foster care be continued, but additionally, "in assistance or as a condition of" that order that the agency leave the child with the present foster parent. In other words, § 392 provides a mechanism whereby a foster parent may obtain preremoval judicial review of an agency's decision to remove a child who has been in foster care for 18 months or more.

C

Foster care of children is a sensitive and emotion-laden subject, and foster-care programs consequently stir strong controversy. The New York regulatory scheme is no exception. New York would have us view the scheme as described in its brief:

> "Today New York premises its foster care system on the accepted principle that the placement of a child into foster care is solely a temporary, transitional action intended to lead to the future reunion of the child with his natural parent or parents, or if such a reunion is not possible, to legal adoption and the establishment of a new permanent home for the child." Brief for Appellants in No. 76-183, p. 3.

Some of the parties and *amici* argue that this is a misleadingly idealized picture. They contend that a very different perspective is revealed by the empirical criticism of the system presented in the record of this case and confirmed by published studies of foster care.

to provide the conference and hearing in all cases where they are requested, regardless of the destination of the child. In the absence of authoritative state-court interpretation to the contrary, we therefore assume that these procedures are available whenever a child is removed from a foster family home.

30. The agency is required to initiate such a review when a child has remained in foster care for 18 months, § 392(2)(a), and if the child remains in foster care, the court "shall rehear the matter whenever it deems necessary or desirable, or upon petition by any party entitled to notice in proceedings under this section, but at least every twenty-four months." § 392(10).

31. If the agency already has guardianship as well as custody of the foster child, as in the case of a surrender or previous court order terminating the guardianship of the natural parent for neglect, the court may simply order that the child be placed for adoption, s 392(7)(d); if the agency does not have guardianship, as in the case of children placed in foster care temporarily either by court order or by voluntary placement, the court may direct the agency to initiate a proceeding to free the child for adoption under §§ 384-b, 392(7)(c).

From the standpoint of natural parents, such as the appellant intervenors here, foster care has been condemned as a class-based intrusion into the family life of the poor. See, *e.g.*, Jenkins, Child Welfare as a Class System, in Children and Decent People 3 (A. Schorr ed. 1974). And see generally ten Broek, California's Dual System of Family Law: Its Origins, Development and Present Status (pt. I), 16 Stan.L.Rev. 257 (1964); (pt. II), 16 Stan.L.Rev. 900 (1964); (pt. III), 17 Stan.L.Rev. 614 (1965). It is certainly true that the poor resort to foster care more often than other citizens. For example, over 50 percent of all children in foster care in New York City are from female-headed families receiving Aid to Families with Dependent Children. Foundation for Child Development, State of the Child: New York City 61 (1976). Minority families are also more likely to turn to foster care; 52.3 percent of the children in foster care in New York City are black and 25.5 percent are Puerto Rican. Child Welfare Information Services, Characteristics of Children in Foster Care, New York City Reports, Table No. 2 (Dec. 31, 1976). This disproportionate resort to foster care by the poor and victims of discrimination doubtless reflects in part the greater likelihood of disruption of poverty-stricken families. Commentators have also noted, however, that middle- and upper-income families who need temporary care services for their children have the resources to purchase private care. See, *e.g.*, Rein, Nutt, & Weiss 24, 25. The poor have little choice but to submit to state-supervised child care when family crises strike. *Id.*, at 34.

The extent to which supposedly "voluntary" placements are in fact voluntary has been questioned on other grounds as well. For example, it has been said that many "voluntary" placements are in fact coerced by threat of neglect proceedings[34] and are not in fact voluntary in the sense of the product of an informed consent. Mnookin I 599, 601. Studies also suggest that social workers of middle-class backgrounds, perhaps unconsciously, incline to favor continued placement in foster care with a generally higher-status family rather than return the child to his natural family, thus reflecting a bias that treats the natural parents' poverty and lifestyle as prejudicial to the best interests of the child. Rein, Nutt, & Weiss 42–44; Levine, Caveat Parents: A Demystification of the Child Protection System, 35 U. Pitt. L. Rev. 1, 29 (1973). This accounts,[35] it has been said, for the hostility of agencies to the efforts of natural parents to obtain the return of their children.[36]

34. See, *e.g.*, the case of Rafael Serrano, the foster child of appellees Ralph and Christiane Goldberg, n. 1, supra.

35. Other factors alleged to bias agencies in favor of retention in foster care are the lack of sufficient staff to provide social work services needed by the natural parent to resolve their problems and prepare for return of the child; policies of many agencies to discourage involvement of the natural parent in the care of the child while in foster care; and systems of foster-care funding that encourage agencies to keep the child in foster care. Wald 677–679. See also E. Sherman, R. Neuman, & A. Shyne, Children Adrift in Foster Care: A Study of Alternative Approaches 4–5 (1973).

36. For an example of this problem, see the case of intervenor Naomi Rodriguez, n. 5, supra. Recent legislative reforms in New York that decrease agencies' discretion to retain a child in foster care are apparently designed to meet these objections. For example, Soc.Serv.Law § 384-a(2)(a) gives parents of children in voluntary foster placement greater rights to the return of their children. Since the statute permits placement agreements of varied terms, however, and since many children in foster care are not voluntarily placed, there may still be situations in which the agency has considerable discretion in deciding whether or not to return the child to the natural parent. The periodic court review provided by § 392 is also intended in part to meet these objections, but critics of foster care have argued that given the heavy caseloads, such review may often be perfunctory. Mnookin, Child-Custody Adjudication: Judicial Functions in the Face of Indeterminacy, 39(3) Law & Contemp. Probs. 226, 274–275 (1975) (hereafter Mnookin II). Moreover, judges too may find it

Appellee foster parents as well as natural parents question the accuracy of the idealized picture portrayed by New York. They note that children often stay in "temporary" foster care for much longer than contemplated by the theory of the system. See, *e.g.*, Kadushin 411–412; Mnookin I 610–613; Wald 662–663; Rein, Nutt, & Weiss 37–39.[37] The District Court found as a fact that the median time spent in foster care in New York was over four years. 418 F.Supp., at 281. Indeed, many children apparently remain in this "limbo" indefinitely. Mnookin II 226, 273. The District Court also found that the longer a child remains in foster care, the more likely it is that he will never leave: "(T)he probability of a foster child being returned to his biological parents declined markedly after the first year in foster care." 418 F.Supp., at 279 n. 6. See also E. Sherman, R. Neuman, & A. Shyne, Children Adrift in Foster Care: A Study of Alternative Approaches 3 (1973); Fanshel, The Exit of Children from Foster Care: An Interim Research Report, 50 Child Welfare 65, 67 (1971). It is not surprising then that many children, particularly those that enter foster care at a very early age[38] and have little or no contact with their natural parents during extended stays in foster care,[39] often develop deep emotional ties with their foster parents.[40]

Yet such ties do not seem to be regarded as obstacles to transfer of the child from one foster placement to another. The record in this case indicates that nearly 60 percent of the children

difficult, in utilizing vague standards like "the best interests of the child," to avoid decisions resting on subjective values.

37. The New York Legislature has recognized the merit of this criticism. Social Serv.Law § 384-b(1)(b), adopted in 1976, states:

> "The legislature further finds that many children who have been placed in foster care experience unnecessarily protracted stays in such care without being adopted or returned to their parents or other custodians. Such unnecessary stays may deprive these children of positive, nurturing family relationships and have deleterious effects on their development into responsible, productive citizens."

38. In New York City, 23.1 percent of foster children enter foster care when under one year of age, and 43 percent at age three or under. Child Welfare Information Services, *supra*, n. 9, Table No. 5. Cf. E. Sherman, R. Neuman, & A. Shyne, *supra*, at 24 (18 percent of foster-care children in Rhode Island study were under one year of age when they entered foster care, and 43 percent were under the age of three).

39. One study of parental contacts in New York City found that 57.4 percent of all foster children had had no contact with their natural parents for the previous six months. Child Welfare Information Services, Parental Visiting Information, New York City Reports, Table No. 1 (Dec. 31, 1976).

40. The development of such ties points up an intrinsic ambiguity of foster care that is central to this case. The warmer and more homelike environment of foster care is intended to be its main advantage over institutional child care, yet because in theory foster care is intended to be only temporary, foster parents are urged not to become too attached to the children in their care. Mnookin I 613. Indeed, the New York courts have upheld removal from a foster home for the very reason that the foster parents had become too emotionally involved with the child. *In re Jewish Child Care Assn. (Sanders)*, 5 N.Y.2d 222, 183 N.Y.S.2d 65, 156 N.E.2d 700 (1959). See also the case of the Lhotans, named appellees in this case, n. 1, *supra*.

On the other hand, too warm a relation between foster parent and foster child is not the only possible problem in foster care. Qualified foster parents are hard to find, Kadushin 367–372, 415–417, and very little training is provided to equip them to handle the often complicated demands of their role, Rein, Nutt, & Weiss 44–45; it is thus sometimes possible that foster homes may provide inadequate care. Indeed, situations in which foster children were mistreated or abused have been reported. Wald 645. And the social work services that are supposed to be delivered to both the natural and foster families are often limited, due to the heavy caseloads of the agencies. Kadushin 413; Mnookin II 274. Given these problems, and given that the very fact of removal from even an inadequate natural family is often traumatic for the child, Wald 644–645, it is not surprising that one commentator has found "rather persuasive, if still incomplete, evidence that throughout the United States, children in foster care are experiencing high rates of psychiatric disturbance." Eisenberg, The Sins of the Fathers: Urban Decay and Social Pathology, 32 Am.J. of Orthopsychiatry 5, 14 (1962).

in foster care in New York City have experienced more than one placement, and about 28 percent have experienced three or more. App. 189a. See also Wald 645–646; Mnookin I 625–626. The intended stability of the foster-home management is further damaged by the rapid turnover among social work professionals who supervise the foster-care arrangements on behalf of the State. *Id.*, at 625; Rein, Nutt, & Weiss 41; Kadushin 420. Moreover, even when it is clear that a foster child will not be returned to his natural parents, it is rare that he achieves a stable home life through final termination of parental ties and adoption into a new permanent family. Fanshel, Status Changes of Children in Foster Care: Final Results of the Columbia University Longitudinal Study, 55 Child Welfare 143, 145, 157 (1976); Mnookin II 275–277; Mnookin I 612–613.

The parties and *amici* devote much of their discussion to these criticisms of foster care, and we present this summary in the view that some understanding of those criticisms is necessary for a full appreciation of the complex and controversial system with which this lawsuit is concerned.[41] But the issue presented by the case is a narrow one. Arguments asserting the need for reform of New York's statutory scheme are properly addressed to the New York Legislature. The relief sought in this case is entirely procedural. Our task is only to determine whether the District Court correctly held that the present procedures preceding the removal from a foster home of children resident there a year or more are constitutionally inadequate. To that task we now turn.

II

A

Our first inquiry is whether appellees have asserted interests within the Fourteenth Amendment's protection of "liberty" and "property." *Board of Regents v. Roth*, 408 U.S. 564, 571(1972).

The appellees have not renewed in this Court their contention, rejected by the District Court, 418 F.Supp., at 280–281, that the realities of the foster-care system in New York gave them a justified expectation amounting to a "property" interest that their status as foster parents would be continued. Our inquiry is therefore narrowed to the question whether their asserted interests are within the "liberty" protected by the Fourteenth Amendment.

The appellees' basic contention is that when a child has lived in a foster home for a year or more, a psychological tie is created between the child and the foster parents which constitutes the foster family the true "psychological family" of the child. See J. Goldstein, A. Freud, & A. Solnit, Beyond the Best Interests of the Child (1973). That family, they argue, has a "liberty

41. It must be noted, however, that both appellee foster parents and intervening natural parents present incomplete pictures of the foster-care system. Although seeking relief applicable to all removal situations, the foster parents focus on intra-foster-care transfers, portraying a foster-care system in which children neglected by their parents and condemned to a permanent limbo of foster care are arbitrarily shunted about by social workers whenever they become attached to a foster home. The natural parents, who focus on foster children being returned to their parent, portray a system under which poor and minority parents, deprived of their children under hard necessity and bureaucratic pressures, are obstructed in their efforts to maintain relationships with their children and ultimately to regain custody, by hostile agencies and meddling foster parents. As the experiences of the named parties to this suit, and the critical studies of foster care cited demonstrate, there are elements of truth in both pictures. But neither represents the whole truth about the system.

interest" in its survival as a family protected by the Fourteenth Amendment. Upon this premise they conclude that the foster child cannot be removed without a prior hearing satisfying due process. Appointed counsel for the children, appellants in No. 76-5200, however, disagrees, and has consistently argued that the foster parents have no such liberty interest independent of the interests of the foster children, and that the best interests of the children would not be served by procedural protections beyond those already provided by New York law. The intervening natural parents of children in foster care, appellants in No. 76-5193, also oppose the foster parents, arguing that recognition of the procedural right claimed would undercut both the substantive family law of New York, which favors the return of children to their natural parents as expeditiously as possible, and their constitutionally protected right of family privacy, by forcing them to submit to a hearing and defend their rights to their children before the children could be returned to them.

The District Court did not reach appellees' contention "that the foster home is entitled to the same constitutional deference as that long granted to the more traditional biological family." 418 F.Supp., at 281. Rather than "reach(ing) out to decide such novel questions," the court based its holding that "the pre-removal procedures presently employed by the state are constitutionally defective," *id.*, at 282, not on the recognized liberty interest in family privacy, but on an independent right of the foster child "to be heard before being 'condemned to suffer grievous loss,' *Joint Anti-Fascist Committee v. McGrath*, 341 U.S. 123, 168 (1951) (Frankfurter, J., concurring)." *Ibid.*

The court apparently reached this conclusion by weighing the "harmful consequences of a precipitous and perhaps improvident decision to remove a child from his foster family," *id.*, at 283, and concluding that this disruption of the stable relationships needed by the child might constitute "grievous loss." But if this was the reasoning applied by the District Court, it must be rejected.[43] *Meachum v. Fano*, 427 U.S. 215, 224 (1976), is authority that such a finding does not, in and of itself, implicate the due process guarantee. What was said in *Board of Regents v. Roth*, *supra*, 408 U.S., at 570–571 applies equally well here:

> "The District Court decided that procedural due process guarantees apply in this case by assessing and balancing the weights of the particular interests involved.... (A) weighing process has long been a part of any determination of the form of hearing required in particular situations by procedural due process. But, to determine whether due process requirements apply in the first place, we must look not to the 'weight' but to the nature of the interest at stake.... We must look to see if the interest is within the Fourteenth Amendment's protection of liberty and property.[44]

43. The dissenting judge argued that the court's underlying premise was a holding "over the objection of the representative of the children...that the foster children have a 'liberty' interest in their relationship with the foster parents." 418 F.Supp., at 288. If this was in fact the reasoning of the District Court, we do not see how it differs from a holding that the foster family relationship is entitled to privacy protection analogous to the natural family the issue the District Court purported not to reach.

44. Appellants argue, with the dissenting judge below, *id.*, at 288, that in any event appellee foster parents have no standing to rely upon a supposed right of the foster *children* to avoid "grievous loss," because the foster children are independently represented by court-appointed counsel who has consistently opposed the relief requested by appellees, and denied that the children have any such right.

This argument misunderstands the peculiar circumstances of this lawsuit. Ordinarily, it is true, a party would not have standing to assert the rights of another, himself a party in the litigation; the third party

We therefore turn to appellees' assertion that they have a constitutionally protected liberty interest in the words of the District Court, a "right to familial privacy," 418 F.Supp., at 279 in the integrity of their family unit. This assertion clearly presents difficulties.

B

It is, of course, true that "freedom of personal choice in matters of...family life is one of the liberties protected by the Due Process Clause of the Fourteenth Amendment." *Cleveland Board of Education v. LaFleur*, 414 U.S. 632, 639-640 (1974). There does exist a "private realm of family life which the state cannot enter," *Prince v. Massachusetts*, 321 U.S. 158, 166 (1944), that has been afforded both substantive and procedural protection. But is the relation of foster parent to foster child sufficiently akin to the concept of "family" recognized in our precedents to merit similar protection?[48] Although considerable difficulty has attended the task of defining "family" for purposes of the Due Process Clause, see *Moore v. City of East Cleveland, ante*, p. 495 (plurality opinion of POWELL, J.); 531(STEWART, J., dissenting); 541 (WHITE, J., dissenting), we are not without guides to some of the elements that define the concept of "family" and contribute to its place in our society.

First, the usual understanding of "family" implies biological relationships, and most decisions treating the relation between parent and child have stressed this element. *Stanley v. Illinois*, 405 U.S. 645, 651 (1972), for example, spoke of "(t)he rights to conceive and to raise one's children" as essential rights, citing *Meyer v. Nebraska*, 262 U.S. 390 (1923), and *Skinner v. Oklahoma, ex rel. Williamson*, 316 U.S. 535 (1942). And *Prince v. Massachusetts*, stated:

> "It is cardinal with us that the custody, care and nurture of the child reside first in the parents, whose primary function and freedom include preparation for obligations the state can neither supply nor hinder. 321 U.S., at 166.[49]

himself can decide how best to protect his interests. But children usually lack the capacity to make that sort of decision, and thus their interest is ordinarily represented in litigation by parents or guardians. In this case, however, the State, the natural parents, and the foster parents, all of whom share some portion of the responsibility for guardianship of the child, are parties, and all contend that the position they advocate is most in accord with the rights and interests of the children. In this situation, the District Court properly appointed independent counsel to represent the children, so that the court could have the benefit of an independent advocate for the welfare of the children, unprejudiced by the possibly conflicting interests and desires of the other parties. It does not follow, however, that that independent counsel, who is not a guardian *ad litem* of the children, is solely authorized to determine the children's best interest.

No party denies, or could deny, that there is an Art. III "case or controversy" between the foster parents and the defendant state officials concerning the validity of the removal procedures. Accordingly, their standing to raise the rights of the children in their attack on those procedures is a prudential question. *Craig v. Boren*, 429 U.S. 190, 193 (1976). We believe it would be most imprudent to leave entirely to court-appointed counsel the choices that neither the named foster children nor the class they represent are capable of making for themselves, especially in litigation in which all parties have sufficient attributes of guardianship that their views on the rights of the children should at least be heard.

48. Of course, recognition of a liberty interest in foster families for purposes of the procedural protections of the Due Process Clause would not necessarily require that foster families be treated as fully equivalent to biological families for purposes of substantive due process review. Cf. *Moore v. City of East Cleveland, ante*, at 546–547 (WHITE, J., dissenting).

49. The scope of these rights extends beyond natural parents. The "parent" in Prince itself, for example, was the child's aunt and legal custodian. 321 U.S., at 159. And see *Moore v. City of East Cleveland, ante*, at 504–506 (plurality opinion); 507–511 (BRENNAN, J., concurring).

A biological relationship is not present in the case of the usual foster family. But biological relationships are not exclusive determination of the existence of a family. The basic foundation of the family in our society, the marriage relationship, is of course not a matter of blood relation. Yet its importance has been strongly emphasized in our cases:

> "We deal with a right of privacy older than the Bill of Rights—older than our political parties, older than our school system. Marriage is a coming together for better or for worse, hopefully enduring, and intimate to the degree of being sacred. It is an association that promotes a way of life, not causes; a harmony in living, not political faiths; a bilateral loyalty, not commercial or social projects. Yet it is an association for as noble a purpose as any involved in our prior decisions." *Griswold v. Connecticut*, 381 U.S. 479, 486 (1965).

See also *Loving v. Virginia*, 388 U.S. 1, 12 ,(1967).

Thus the importance of the familial relationship, to the individuals involved and to the society, stems from the emotional attachments that derive from the intimacy of daily association, and from the role it plays in "promot(ing) a way of life" through the instruction of children, *Wisconsin v. Yoder*, 406 U.S. 205, 231–233 (1972), as well as from the fact of blood relationship. No one would seriously dispute that a deeply loving and interdependent relationship between an adult and a child in his or her care may exist even in the absence of blood relationship.[51] At least where a child has been placed in foster care as an infant, has never known his natural parents, and has remained continuously for several years in the care of the same foster parents, it is natural that the foster family should hold the same place in the emotional life of the foster child, and fulfill the same socializing functions, as a natural family.[52] For this reason, we cannot dismiss the foster family as a mere collection of unrelated individuals. Cf. *Village of Belle Terre v. Boraas*, 416 U.S. 1 (1974).

But there are also important distinctions between the foster family and the natural family. First, unlike the earlier cases recognizing a right to family privacy, the State here seeks to interfere, not with a relationship having its origins entirely apart from the power of the State, but rather with a foster family which has its source in state law and contractual arrangements. The individual's freedom to marry and reproduce is "older than the Bill of Rights," *Griswold v. Connecticut, supra*, 381 U.S., at 486. Accordingly, unlike the property interests that are also protected by the Fourteenth Amendment cf. *Board of Regents v. Roth*, 408 U.S., at 577, the liberty interest in family privacy has its source, and its contours are ordinarily to be sought, not in state law,[53] but in intrinsic human rights, as they have been understood in "this Nation's

51. Adoption, for example, is recognized as the legal equivalent of biological parenthood. See, *e.g.*, N.Y.Dom. Rel.Law § 110.

52. The briefs dispute at some length the validity of the "psychological parent" theory propounded in J. Goldstein, A. Freud, & A. Solnit, Beyond the Best Interests of the Child (1973). That book, on which appellee foster parents relied to some extent in the District Court, is indeed controversial. See, *e.g.*, Strauss & Strauss, Book Review, 74 Colum.L.Rev. 996 (1974); Kadushin, Beyond the Best Interests of the Child: An Essay Review, 48 Soc.Serv.Rev. 508, 512 (1974). But this case turns, not on the disputed validity of any particular psychological theory, but on the legal consequences of the undisputed fact that the emotional ties between foster parent and foster child are in many cases quite close, and undoubtedly in some as close as those existing in biological families.

53. The legal status of families has never been regarded as controlling: "Nor has the (Constitution) refused to recognize those family relationships unlegitimized by a marriage ceremony." *Stanley v. Illinois*, 405 U.S., at 651.

history and tradition." *Moore v. City of East Cleveland, ante*, at 503. Cf. also *Meachum v. Fano*, 427 U.S., at 230 (STEVENS, J., dissenting). Here, however, whatever emotional ties may develop between foster parent and foster child have their origins in an arrangement in which the State has been a partner from the outset. While the Court has recognized that liberty interests may in some cases arise from positive-law sources, see, *e.g., Wolff v. McDonnell*, 418 U.S. 539, 557 (1974), in such a case, and particularly where, as here, the claimed interest derives from a knowingly assumed contractual relation with the State, it is appropriate to ascertain from state law the expectations and entitlements of the parties. In this case, the limited recognition accorded to the foster family by the New York statutes and the contracts executed by the foster parents argue against any but the most limited constitutional "liberty" in the foster family.

A second consideration related to this is that ordinarily procedural protection may be afforded to a liberty interest of one person without derogating from the substantive liberty of another. Here, however, such a tension is virtually unavoidable. Under New York law, the natural parent of a foster child in voluntary placement has an absolute right to the return of his child in the absence of a court order obtainable only upon compliance with rigorous substantive and procedural standards, which reflect the constitutional protection accorded the natural family. Moreover, the natural parent initially gave up his child to the State only on the express understanding that the child would be returned in those circumstances. These rights are difficult to reconcile with the liberty interest in the foster family relationship claimed by appellees. It is one thing to say that individuals may acquire a liberty interest against arbitrary governmental interference in the family-like associations into which they have freely entered, even in the absence of biological connection or state-law recognition of the relationship. It is quite another to say that one may acquire such an interest in the face of another's constitutionally recognized liberty interest that derives from blood relationship, state-law sanction, and basic human right—an interest the foster parent has recognized by contract from the outset. Whatever liberty interest might otherwise exist in the foster family as an institution, that interest must be substantially attenuated where the proposed removal from the foster family is to return the child to his natural parents.

As this discussion suggests, appellees' claim to a constitutionally protected liberty interest raises complex and novel questions. It is unnecessary for us to resolve those questions definitively in this case, however, for like the District Court, we conclude that "narrower grounds exist to support" our reversal. We are persuaded that, even on the assumption that appellees have a protected "liberty interest," the District Court erred in holding that the preremoval procedures presently employed by the State are constitutionally defective.

III

Where procedural due process must be afforded because a "liberty" or "property" interest is within the Fourteenth Amendment's protection, there must be determined "what process is due" in the particular context. The District Court did not spell out precisely what sort of preremoval hearing would be necessary to meet the constitutional standard, leaving to "the various defendants state and local officials the first opportunity to formulate procedures suitable to their own professional needs and compatible with the principles set forth in this opinion." 418 F.Supp., at 286. The court's opinion, however, would seem to require at a minimum that in all cases in which removal of a child within the certified class is contemplated, including the situation where the removal is for the purpose of returning the child to his natural parents, a hearing be held automatically, regardless of whether or not the foster parents request a hearing; that the hearing be before an officer who has had no previous contact with the decision to remove the child, and who has authority to order that the child remain with the foster parents; and that the agency, the foster parents, and the natural parents, as well as the child, if he is able intelligently to express his true feelings, and an independent representative of the child's interests, if he is not, be represented and permitted to introduce relevant evidence.

It is true that "(b)efore a person is deprived of a protected interest, he must be afforded opportunity for some kind of a hearing, 'except for extraordinary situations where some valid governmental interest is at stake that justifies postponing the hearing until after the event.'" *Board of Regents v. Roth,* 408 U.S., at 570 n. 7; quoting *Boddie v. Connecticut*, 401 U.S. 371, 379 (1971). But the hearing required is only one "appropriate to the nature of the case." *Mullane v. Central Hanover Bank & Trust Co.*, 339 U.S. 306, 313 (1950). See, *e.g.*, *Bell v. Burson,* 402 U.S. 535, 542 (1971); *Goldberg v. Kelly*, 397 U.S. 254, 263 (1970); *Cafeteria Workers v. McElroy*, 367 U.S. 886, 895 (1961). "(D)ue process is flexible and calls for such procedural protections as the particular situation demands." *Morrissey v. Brewer*, 408 U.S. 471, 481 (1972). Only last Term, the Court held that "identification of the specific dictates of due process generally requires consideration of three distinct factors: First, the private interest that will be affected by the official action; second, the risk of an erroneous deprivation of such interest through the procedures used, and the probable value, if any, of additional or substitute procedural safeguards; and finally, the Government's interest, including the function involved and the fiscal and administrative burdens that the additional or substitute procedural requirement would entail." *Mathews v. Eldridge*, 424 U.S. 319, 335 (1976). Consideration of the procedures employed by the State and New York City in light of these three factors requires the conclusion that those procedures satisfy constitutional standards.

Turning first to the procedure applicable in New York City, SSC Procedure No. 5, provides that before a child is removed from a foster home for transfer to another foster home, the foster parents may request an "independent review." The District Court's description of this review is set out in the margin. Such a procedure would appear to give a more elaborate trial-type hearing to foster families than this Court has found required in other contexts of administrative determinations. Cf. *Goldberg v. Kelly, supra,* 397 U.S., at 266–271. The District Court found the procedure inadequate on four grounds, none of which we find sufficient to justify the holding that the procedure violates due process.

First, the court held that the "independent review" administrative proceeding was insufficient because it was only available on the request of the foster parents. In the view of the District Court, the proceeding should be provided as a matter of course, because the interests of the foster parents and those of the child would not necessarily be coextensive, and it could not be assumed that the foster parents would invoke the hearing procedure in every case in which it was in the child's interest to have a hearing. Since the child is unable to request a hearing on his own, automatic review in every case is necessary. We disagree. As previously noted, the constitutional liberty, if any, sought to be protected by the New York procedures is a right of *family* privacy or autonomy, and the basis for recognition of any such interest in the foster family must be that close emotional ties analogous to those between parent and child are established when a child resides for a lengthy period with a foster family. If this is so, necessarily we should expect that the foster parents will seek to continue the relationship to preserve the stability of the family; if they do not request a hearing, it is difficult to see what right or interest of the foster child is protected by holding a hearing to determine whether removal would unduly impair his emotional attachments to a foster parent who does not care enough about the child to contest the removal.[57] Thus, consideration of the interest to be protected and the likelihood of erroneous deprivations,[58] the first two factors identified in *Mathews v. Eldridge, supra*, as appropriate in determining the sufficiency of procedural protections, do not support the District Court's imposition of this additional requirement. Moreover, automatic provision of hearings as required by the District Court would impose a substantial additional administrative burden on the State. According to appellant city officials, during the approximately two years between the institution of SSC Procedure No. 5 in August 1974 and June 1976, there were approximately 2,800 transfers per year in the city, but only 26 foster parents requested hearings. Brief for Appellants in No. 76-180, pp. 20–21. It is not at all clear what would be gained by requiring full hearings in the more than 5,500 cases in which they were not requested.

Second, the District Court faulted the city procedure on the ground that participation is limited to the foster parents and the agency and the natural parent and the child are not made parties to the hearing. This is not fatal in light of the nature of the alleged constitutional interests at stake. When the child's transfer from one foster home to another is pending, the interest arguably requiring protection is that of the foster family, not that of the natural parents. Moreover, the natural parent can generally add little to the accuracy of factfinding concerning the wisdom of such a transfer, since the foster parents and the agency, through its caseworkers, will usually be most knowledgeable about conditions in the foster home. Of course, in those cases where the natural parent does have a special interest in the proposed transfer or particular information that would assist the factfinder, nothing in the city's procedure prevents any party from securing his testimony.

Much the same can be said in response to the District Court's statement:

> "(I)t may be advisable, under certain circumstances, for the agency to appoint an adult representative better to articulate the interests of the child. In making this determination, the agency should carefully consider the child's age, sophistication and ability effectively to communicate his own true feelings." 418 F.Supp., at 285–286.

But nothing in the New York City procedure prevents consultation of the child's wishes, directly or through an adult intermediary. We assume, moreover, that some such consultation would be among the first steps that a rational factfinder, inquiring into the child's best interests, would pursue. Such consultation, however, does not require that the child or

57. The District Court itself apparently relied on similar logic, in exempting in its judgment removals requested by foster parents from the mandatory hearing requirement. In terms of the emotional cohesion of the family, the difference between a foster parent who requests removal of the foster child, and one who merely consents to removal seems irrelevant.

58. In assessing the likelihood of erroneous decisions by the agency in the absence of elaborate hearing procedures, the fact that the agency bears primary responsibility for the welfare of the child, and maintains, through its caseworkers, constant contact with the foster family is relevant. The foster parent always has the opportunity to present information to the agency at this stage. We, of course, do not suggest that such informal "process" can ever do service for the fundamental requirements of due process. Cf. *In re Gault*, 387 U.S. 1 (1967). But it should not routinely be assumed that any decision made without the forms of adversary factfinding familiar to the legal profession is necessarily arbitrary or incorrect.

an appointed representative must be a party with full adversary powers in all preremoval hearings.[59]

The other two defects in the city procedure found by the District Court must also be rejected. One is that the procedure does not extend to the removal of a child from foster care to be returned to his natural parent. But as we have already held, whatever liberty interest may be argued to exist in the foster family is significantly weaker in the case of removals preceding return to the natural parent, and the balance of due process interests must accordingly be different. If the city procedure is adequate where it is applicable, it is no criticism of the procedure that it does not apply in other situations where different interests are at stake. Similarly, the District Court pointed out that the New York City procedure coincided with the informal "conference" and postremoval hearings provided as a matter of state law. This overlap in procedures may be unnecessary or even to some degree unwise, see *id.*, F.Supp., at 285, but a State does not violate the Due Process Clause by providing alternative or additional procedures beyond what the Constitution requires.

Outside New York City, where only the statewide procedures apply, foster parents are provided not only with the procedures of a preremoval conference and postremoval hearing provided by 18 N.Y.C.R.R. s 450.10 (1976) and Soc.Serv.Law § 400 (McKinney 1976), but also with the preremoval *judicial* hearing available on request to foster parents who have in their care children who have been in foster care for 18 months or more, Soc.Serv.Law § 392. As observed *supra*, a foster parent in such case may obtain an order that the child remain in his care.

The District Court found three defects in this full judicial process. First, a § 392 proceeding is available only to those foster children who have been in foster care for 18 months or more. The class certified by the court was broader, including children who had been in the care of the same foster parents for more than one year. Thus, not all class members had access to the § 392 remedy. We do not think that the 18-month limitation on § 392 actions renders the New York scheme constitutionally inadequate. The assumed liberty interest to be protected in this case is one rooted in the emotional attachments that develop over time between a child and the adults who care for him. But there is no reason to assume that those attachments ripen at less than 18 months or indeed at any precise point. Indeed, testimony in the record, see App. 177a, 204a, as well as material in published psychological tests, see, *e.g.*, J. Goldstein, A. Freud, & A. Solnit, Beyond the Best Interests of the Child 40–42, 49 (1973), suggests that the amount of time necessary for the development of the sort of tie appellees seek to protect varies

59. Appointment of such representatives in each of the numerous cases in which the foster child is very young would, of course, represent a major administrative burden on the State. This burden would be balanced by little gain in accuracy of decisionmaking, since the appointed representative's inquiry into the best interests of the child would essentially duplicate that already conducted by the agency and that to be conducted at the hearing by the administrative decisionmaker.

Moreover, the State's interest in avoiding "fiscal and administrative burdens," *Mathews v. Eldridge*, 424 U.S. 319 (1976), is not the only interest that must be weighed against requiring still more elaborate hearing procedures. As the District Court acknowledged, where delicate judgments concerning "the often ambiguous indices of a child's emotional attachments and psychological development" are involved, we must also consider the possibility that making the decisionmaking process increasingly adversary "might well impede the effort to elicit the sensitive and personal information required," 418 F.Supp., at 286, or make the struggle for custody, already often difficult for the child, see, *e.g.*, Kadushin 404, even more traumatic. In such a situation, there is a value in less formalized hearing procedures.

considerably depending on the age and previous attachments of the child. In a matter of such imprecision and delicacy, we see no justification for the District Court's substitution of its view of the appropriate cutoff date for that chosen by the New York Legislature, given that any line is likely to be somewhat arbitrary and fail to protect some families where relationships have developed quickly while protecting others where no such bonds have formed. If New York sees 18 months rather than 12 as the time at which temporary foster care begins to turn into a more permanent and family-like setting requiring procedural protection and/or judicial inquiry into the propriety of continuing foster care, it would take far more than this record provides to justify a finding of constitutional infirmity in New York's choice.

The District Court's other two findings of infirmity in the § 392 procedure have already been considered and held to be without merit. The District Court disputed defendants' reading of § 392 as permitting an order requiring the leaving of the foster child in the same foster home. The plain words of the statute and the weight of New York judicial interpretation do not support the court. The District Court also faulted § 392, as it did the New York City procedure, in not providing an automatic hearing in every case even in cases where foster parents chose not to seek one. Our holding sustaining the adequacy of the city procedure, applies in this context as well.

Finally, the § 392 hearing is available to foster parents, both in and outside New York City, even where the removal sought is for the purpose of returning the child to his natural parents. Since this remedy provides a sufficient constitutional preremoval hearing to protect whatever liberty interest might exist in the continued existence of the foster family when the State seeks to transfer the child to another foster home, *a fortiori* the procedure is adequate to protect the lesser interest of the foster family in remaining together at the expense of the disruption of the natural family.

We deal here with issues of unusual delicacy, in an area where professional judgments regarding desirable procedures are constantly and rapidly changing. In such a context, restraint is appropriate on the part of courts called upon to adjudicate whether a particular procedural scheme is adequate under the Constitution. Since we hold that the procedures provided by New York State in § 392 and by New York City's SSC Procedure No. 5 are adequate to protect whatever liberty interest appellees may have, the judgment of the District Court is

Reversed.

Mr. Justice Stewart, with whom The Chief Justice and Mr. Justice Rehnquist join, concurring in the judgment.

The foster parent-foster child relationship involved in this litigation is, of course, wholly a creation of the State. New York law defines the circumstances under which a child may be placed in foster care, prescribes the obligations of the foster parents, and provides for the removal of the child from the foster home "in (the) discretion" of the agency with custody of the child. N.Y.Soc.Serv.Law § 383(2) (McKinney 1976). The agency compensates the foster parents, and reserves in its contracts the authority to decide as it sees fit whether and when a child shall be returned to his natural family or placed elsewhere. Were it not for the system of foster care that the State maintains, the relationship for which constitutional protection is asserted would not even exist.

The New York Legislature and the New York courts have made it unmistakably clear that foster care is intended only as a temporary way station until a child can be returned to his natural parents or placed for adoption. Thus, Soc.Serv.Law § 384-b(1)(b) (McKinney Supp.

1976–1977) states a legislative finding that "many children who have been placed in foster care experience unnecessarily protracted stays in such care without being adopted or returned to their parents or other custodians. Such unnecessary stays may deprive these children of positive, nurturing family relationships and have deleterious effects on their development into responsible, productive citizens." And, specifically repudiating the contention that New York law contemplates that a child will have a "secure, stable and continuous" relationship with a third-party custodian as the child's "psychological parent," the New York Court of Appeals has "(p)articularly rejected the notion, if that it be, that third-party custodians may acquire some sort of squatter's rights in another's child." *Bennett v. Jeffreys*, 40 N.Y.2d 543, 552 n. 2, 387 N.Y.S.2d 821, 829 n. 2, 356 N.E.2d 277, 285 n. 2.

In these circumstances, I cannot understand why the Court thinks itself obliged to decide these cases on the assumption that either foster parents or foster children in New York have some sort of "liberty" interest in the continuation of their relationship.[1] Rather than tiptoeing around this central issue, I would squarely hold that the interests asserted by the appellees are not of a kind that the Due Process Clause of the Fourteenth Amendment protects.

At the outset, I would reject, as does the Court, the apparent holding of the District Court that "the trauma of separation from a familiar environment" or the "harmful consequences of a precipitous and perhaps improvident decision to remove a child from his foster family," *Organization of Foster Families v. Dumpson*, 418 F.Supp. 277, 283, constitutes a "grievous loss" which therefore is protected by the Fourteenth Amendment. Not every loss, however "grievous," invokes the protection of the Due Process Clause. Its protections extend only to a deprivation by a State of "life, liberty, or property." And when a state law does operate to deprive

1. The Court's opinion seems to indicate that there is no reason to distinguish between the claims of the foster parents and the foster children, either because the parents have standing to assert the rights of the children or because the parents' interest is identical to that of the children. I cannot agree.

First, it is by no means obvious that foster parents and foster children have the same interest in a continuation of their relationship. When the child leaves the foster family, it is because the agency with custody of him has determined that his interests will be better served by a new home, either with his natural parents, adoptive parents, or a different foster family. Any assessment of the child's alleged deprivation must take into account not only what he has lost, but what he has received in return. Foster parents, on the other hand, do not automatically receive a new child with whom they will presumably have a more profitable relationship.

Second, unlike the situation in *Craig v. Boren*, 429 U.S. 190, 195–196, this is not a case where the failure to grant the parents their requested relief will inevitably tend to "(dilute) or adversely (affect)" the alleged constitutional rights of the children. Denying the parents a hearing simply has no effect whatever on the children's separate claim to a hearing and does not impair their alleged constitutional rights. There is therefore no standing in the parents to assert the children's claims. See Note, Standing to Assert Constitutional Jus Tertii, 88 Harv.L.Rev. 423, 432 (1974), cited in *Craig, supra*, at 195.

I would nevertheless consider both the parents' and the children's claims in these cases, but only because the suit was originally brought on behalf of both the parents and the children, all of whom were parties plaintiff. While it is true that their interests may conflict, there was no reason not to allow counsel for the parents to continue to represent the children to the extent that their interests may be compatible. The conflict was avoided by the District Court's appointment of independent counsel, who took a position opposite to that of the foster parents as to where the children's welfare lay. The appointment of independent counsel, however, should not have left the children without advocacy for the position, right or wrong, that they are entitled to due process hearings. That position should have been left to be asserted by the counsel who originally brought the suit for the children. My view, therefore, is that the parents and their children are properly before the Court and entitled to assert their own separate claims, but that neither group has standing to assert the claims of the other.

a person of his liberty or property, the Due Process Clause is applicable even though the deprivation may not be "grievous." *Goss v. Lopez*, 419 U.S. 565, 576. "(T)o determine whether due process requirements apply in the first place, we look not to the 'weight' but to the nature of the interest at stake." *Board of Regents v. Roth*, 408 U.S. 564, 570–571. See *Ingraham v. Wright*, 430 U.S. 651, 672; *Meachum v. Fano*, 427 U.S. 215, 224; *Goss v. Lopez, supra*, 419 U.S., at 575–576.

Clearly, New York has deprived nobody of his life in these cases. It seems to me just as clear that the State has deprived nobody of his liberty or property. Putting to one side the District Court's erroneous "grievous loss" analysis, the appellees are left with very little ground on which to stand. Their argument seems to be that New York, by providing foster children with the opportunity to live in a foster home and to form a close relationship with foster parents, has created "liberty" or "property" that it may not withdraw without complying with the procedural safeguards that the Due Process Clause confers. But this Court's decision in *Meachum v. Fano, supra*, illustrates the fallacy of that argument.

At issue in *Meachum* was a claim by Massachusetts state prisoners that they could not constitutionally be transferred to another institution with less favorable living conditions without a prior hearing that would fully probe the reasons for their transfer. In accord with previous cases, see, *e.g., Goss v. Lopez, supra*; *Wolff v. McDonnell*, 418 U.S. 539; *Board of Regents v. Roth, supra; Perry v. Sindermann*, 408 U.S. 593; *Goldberg v. Kelly*, 397 U.S. 254, the Court recognized that where state law confers a liberty or property interest, the Due Process Clause requires certain minimum procedures "'to ensure that the state-created right is not arbitrarily abrogated.'" 427 U.S., at 226, quoting *Wolff, supra*, 418 U.S., at 557. But the predicate for invoking the Due Process Clause—the existence of state-created liberty or property—was missing in *Meachum* just as it is missing here. New York confers no right on foster families to remain intact, defeasible only upon proof of specific acts or circumstances. As was true of prison transfers in *Meachum*, transfers in and out of foster families "are made for a variety of reasons and often involve no more than informed predictions as to what would best serve... the safety and welfare of the (child)." 427 U.S., at 225.

Similarly, New York law provides no basis for a justifiable expectation on the part of foster families that their relationship will continue indefinitely. Cf. *Perry v. Sindermann, supra*, 408 U.S., at 599–603. The District Court in this litigation recognized as much, noting that the typical foster-care contract gives the agency the right to recall the child "upon request," and commenting that the discretionary authority vested in the agency "is on its face incompatible with plaintiffs' claim of legal entitlement." 418 F.Supp., at 281. To be sure, the New York system has not operated perfectly. As the state legislature found, foster care has in many cases been unnecessarily protracted, no doubt sometimes resulting in the expectation on the part of some foster families that their relationship will continue indefinitely. But, as already noted, the New York Court of Appeals has unequivocally rejected the notion that under New York law prolonged third-party custody of children creates some sort of "squatter's rights." And, as this Court stated in *Perry v. Sindermann, supra*, 408 U.S., at 603, a mere subjective "expectancy" is not liberty or property protected by the Due Process Clause.

This is not to say that under the law of New York foster children are the pawns of the State, who may be whisked from family to family at the whim of state officials. The Court discusses in Part III of its opinion the various state and local procedures intended to assure that agency discretion is exercised in a manner consistent with the child's best interests. Unlike the prison transfer situation in *Meachum v. Fano*, it does not appear that child custody decisions can be made "for whatever reason or for no reason at all." 427 U.S., at 228. But the protection that foster children have is simply the requirement of state law that decisions about their placement be determined in the light of their best interests. See, *e.g., Bennett v. Jeffreys*, 40 N.Y.2d 543, 387 N.Y.S.2d 821, 356 N.E.2d 277; *In re Jewish Child Care Assn. (Sanders)*, 5 N.Y.2d 222, 183 N.Y.S.2d 65, 156 N.E.2d 700; *State ex rel. Wallace v. Lhotan*, 51 A.D.2d 252, 380 N.Y.S.2d 250 (2d Dept.), appeal dismissed and leave to appeal denied, 39 N.Y.2d 705, 384 N.Y.S.2d 1027, 349 N.E.2d 882. This requirement is not "liberty or property" protected by the Due Process Clause, and it confers no right or expectancy of any kind in the continuity of the relationship between foster parents and children. See *e.g., Bennett, supra*, 40 N.Y.2d, at 552 n. 2, 387 N.Y.S.2d, at 829 n. 2, 356 N.E.2d, at 285 n. 2: "Third-party custodians acquire 'rights'...only derivatively by virtue of the child's best interests being considered...."

What remains of the appellees' argument is the theory that the relation of the foster parent to the foster child may generate emotional attachments similar to those found in natural families. The Court surmises that foster families who share these attachments might enjoy the same constitutional interest in "family privacy" as natural families. See, *e.g., Moore v. City of East Cleveland, ante*, at 504–505 (plurality opinion of POWELL, J.); *Roe v. Wade*, 410 U.S. 113, 152–153; *Pierce v. Society of Sisters*, 268 U.S. 510; *Meyer v. Nebraska*, 262 U.S. 390.

On this score, the Court hypothesizes the case of "a child (who) has been placed in foster care as an infant, has never known his natural parents, and has remained continuously for several years in the care of the same foster parents...." The foster family might then "hold the same place in the emotional life of the foster child, and fulfill the same socializing functions, as a natural family." *Ibid.*

But under New York's foster-care laws, any case where the foster parents had assumed the emotional role of the child's natural parents would represent not a triumph of the system, to be constitutionally safeguarded from state intrusion, but a failure. The goal of foster care, at least in New York, is not to provide a permanent substitute for the natural or adoptive home, but to prepare the child for his return to his real parents or placement in a permanent adoptive home by giving him temporary shelter in a family setting. Thus, the New York Court of Appeals has recognized that the development of close emotional ties between foster parents and a child may hinder the child's ultimate adjustment in a permanent home, and provide a basis for the termination of the foster family relationship. *In re Jewish Child Care Assn. (Sanders), supra*. See also *State ex rel. Wallace v. Lhotan, supra*. Perhaps it is to be expected that children who spend unduly long stays in what should have been temporary foster care will develop strong emotional ties with their foster parents. But this does not mean, and I cannot believe, that such breakdowns of the New York system must be protected or forever frozen in their existence by the Due Process Clause of the Fourteenth Amendment.[3]

3. The consequences of extending constitutional protection to the foster family relationship are, as the Court points out, especially absurd when the child would otherwise be immediately returned to his natural parents. If the foster family relationship were to occupy the same constitutional plane as that of the natural family, the conflict between the constitutional rights of natural and foster parents would be totally irreconcilable.

One of the liberties protected by the Due Process Clause, the Court has held, is the freedom to "establish a home and bring up children." *Meyer v. Nebraska, supra,* 262 U.S., at 399. If a State were to attempt to force the breakup of a natural family, over the objections of the parents and their children, without some showing of unfitness and for the sole reason that to do so was thought to be in the children's best interest, I should have little doubt that the State would have intruded impermissibly on "the private realm of family life which the state cannot enter." *Prince v. Massachusetts,* 321 U.S. 158, 166. But this constitutional concept is simply not in point when we deal with foster families as New York law has defined them. The family life upon which the State "intrudes" is simply a temporary status which the State itself has created. It is a "family life" defined and controlled by the law of New York, for which New York pays, and the goals of which New York is entitled to and does set for itself.

For these reasons I concur in the judgment of the Court.

NOTES AND QUESTIONS

1. Who are the plaintiffs? What is the basis of the constitutional challenge here? What statutory procedures are at issue?

2. Justice Brennan, a liberal member of the Court, wrote the opinion. Does that surprise you? Is there some way the opinion might be seen as "liberal"?

3. According to the Court, what rights does a foster parent acquire with regard to continuing custody?

4. The foster children were appointed independent counsel by the lower court. According to Justice Brennan, who speaks for the child in foster care? Why?

5. How did Edwin end up in foster care? What implications does this have for a parent who seeks the return of a child?

6. Why do three members of the Court concur?

7. David L. Chambers and Michael S. Wald note that Mrs. Smith was able to retain custody of the Gandy children and that she adopted them on May 7, 1981. New York City adopted new regulations providing for hearings before any intra-foster-care transfer may occur. The hearings are formal: foster parents may bring counsel, witnesses are subject to cross-examination, and the biological parents and their lawyers often attend. Chambers and Wald also note that most courts use *OFFER* to deny foster parents any rights. David L. Chambers and Michael S. Wald, *Smith v. OFFER,* in In the Interest of Children 114, 114–117 (Robert H. Mnookin ed., 1985).

8. If foster care is a contract, what is the effect of the contract? What if relatives entered into a contract to provide foster care? Is that relationship grounded in contract?

9. ASFA, enacted well after the *OFFER* decision, provides foster parents, any preadoptive parent, or any relative who provides care for the child with "notice of, and an opportunity to be heard in, any review or hearing to be held with respect to the child," but the opportunity to be heard "shall not be construed to require that any foster parent, pre-adoptive parent, or relative providing care for the child be made a party to such a review or hearing solely on the basis of such notice and opportunity to be heard." 42 U.S.C. § 675(5)(G) (West 2011). Do you think that ASFA accords foster parents more procedural due process than *OFFER*?

d. THE EFFECTS OF FOSTER CARE

Joseph J. Doyle, Jr., Child Protection and Adult Crime: Using Investigator Assignment to Estimate Causal Effects of Adult Crime, 116 J. POL. ECON. 746, 747–48 (2008).

Foster care affects the lives of a large number of children who are at high risk for later criminal activity. Each year in the United States, states spend $20 billion on child protection services, including the investigation of over 2 million children. Approximately 800,000 children spend some time in foster care in any given year, and the average length of stay in care is 2 years. In terms of criminal justice involvement, nearly 20 percent of the U.S. prison population under the age of 30, and 25 percent of these prisoners with prior convictions, report spending part of their youth in foster care. [Researchers have found] higher rates of juvenile delinquency among foster children, and [one survey of] children who turned 18 in foster care in the Midwest...found that 67 percent of the boys and 50 percent of the girls had a history of juvenile delinquency.[1]

Little is known whether foster care placement is likely to reduce or exacerbate the propensity for adult criminal behavior. The removal of children from abusive parents may protect children from further abuse and reduce the likelihood of criminal activity as adults. At the same time, the removal of children from their parents is thought to be traumatic and may lead to worse adult outcomes.[4] Previous research has been hampered by limited data and endogeneity concerns. For example, negative outcomes for foster children could be due to abuse or neglect by family members as opposed to the effects of foster care placement itself. In addition, children placed in foster care are likely those who benefit most from placement, which can lead to a selection bias such that average outcomes may overstate the benefits of placement for marginal cases.

NOTES AND QUESTIONS

1. In the study, Doyle found that "children placed in care have two to three times higher arrest, conviction, and imprisonment rates than children who remained at home." *Id.* at 766. While he cautions that the data are relatively imprecise, he contends that "children at the margin of placement have better outcomes when they remain at home." *Id.* at 767. An earlier study that found that children placed in foster care have higher delinquency rates, some evidence of higher teen birth rates and lower earnings led to a similar conclusion. Joseph J. Doyle, Jr., *Child*

1. Foster children are also at high risk of other negative life outcomes including low educational attainment and substance abuse problems. An estimated 28 percent of the U.S. homeless population has spent time in foster care as a youth.

4. There is a large empirical literature on placement instability and its correlation with later life problems. The average foster child in the United States is moved from one home to another at least once, with 25 percent experiencing three or more moves. In Illinois during the 1990s...45 percent of foster care stays lasting 1 year had at least one such move within the first year.

Protection and Child Outcomes: Measuring the Effects of Foster Care, 97 AM. ECON. REV. 1583 (2007).

2. The American Academy of Pediatrics argues that multiple placements are injurious to the child. Am. Acad. Pediatrics, Comm. on Early Childhood, Adoption, & Dependent Care, *Developmental Issues for Young Children in Foster Care*, 106 PEDIATRICS 1145, 1149 (2000). Claire Huntington also notes that there is a substantial risk that children will suffer additional abuse or neglect while in foster care. Claire Huntington, *Rights Myopia in Child Welfare*, 53 U.C.L.A. L. REV. 637, 662 (2006) (arguing that children and their families in the child-welfare system are better served by a problem-solving rather than a rights-based model).

6. SPECIAL ISSUES IN PLACEMENT

a. THE INDIAN CHILD WELFARE ACT

The Indian Child Welfare Act (ICWA) is a federal law that seeks to keep American Indian children with American Indian families, in order to "protect the best interests of Indian children and to promote the stability and security of Indian tribes and families" 25 U.S.C. § 1902 (2011). Congress passed ICWA in 1978 in response to the high number of Indian children being removed from their homes by public and private agencies and the psychological harm suffered by Indian children placed in non-Indian homes. ICWA requirements apply to many state child-custody proceedings involving an Indian child who is a member of or is eligible for membership in a federally recognized tribe. At present, there are more than four hundred Indian tribes and Alaskan native villages that are recognized by the U.S. Department of the Interior.

The United States Supreme Court has decided only one case involving the Indian Child Welfare Act.

MISSISSIPI BAND OF CHOCTAW INDIANS V. HOLYFIELD
Supreme Court of the United States
490 U.S. 30 (1989)

JUSTICE BRENNAN delivered the opinion of the Court.

This appeal requires us to construe the provisions of the Indian Child Welfare Act that establish exclusive tribal jurisdiction over child custody proceedings involving Indian children domiciled on the tribe's reservation.

I

A

The Indian Child Welfare Act of 1978 (ICWA), 92 Stat. 3069, 25 U.S.C. §§ 1901–1963, was the product of rising concern in the mid-1970's over the consequences to Indian children, Indian families, and Indian tribes of abusive child welfare practices that resulted in the separation of large numbers of Indian children from their families and tribes through adoption or foster care placement, usually in non-Indian homes. Senate oversight hearings in 1974 yielded numerous examples, statistical data, and expert testimony documenting what one witness called "[t]he wholesale removal of Indian children from their homes, ... the most tragic aspect of Indian life today." Indian Child Welfare Program, Hearings before the Subcommittee on Indian Affairs of the Senate Committee on Interior and Insular Affairs, 93d Cong., 2d Sess., 3 (statement of William Byler) (hereinafter 1974 Hearings). Studies undertaken by the Association on American Indian Affairs in 1969 and 1974, and presented in the Senate hearings, showed that 25 to 35 percent of all Indian children had been separated from their families and placed in adoptive families, foster care, or institutions. *Id.*, at 15; see also H.R.Rep. No. 95-1386, p. 9 (1978) (hereinafter House Report), U.S.Code Cong. & Admin.News 1978, pp. 7530, 7531. Adoptive placements counted significantly in this total: in the State of Minnesota, for example, one in eight Indian children under the age of 18 was in an adoptive home, and during the year 1971–1972 nearly one in every four infants under one year of age was placed for adoption. The adoption rate of Indian children was eight times that of non-Indian children. Approximately 90 percent of the Indian placements were in non-Indian homes. 1974 Hearings, at 75–83. A number of witnesses also testified to the serious adjustment problems encountered by such children during adolescence,[1] as well as the impact of the adoptions on Indian parents and the tribes themselves. See generally 1974 Hearings.

Further hearings, covering much the same ground, were held during 1977 and 1978 on the bill that became the ICWA. While much of the testimony again focused on the harm to Indian parents and their children who were involuntarily separated by decisions of local welfare authorities, there was also considerable emphasis on the impact on the tribes themselves of the massive removal of their children. For example, Mr. Calvin Isaac, Tribal Chief of the Mississippi Band of Choctaw Indians and representative of the National Tribal Chairmen's Association, testified as follows:

> "Culturally, the chances of Indian survival are significantly reduced if our children, the only real means for the transmission of the tribal heritage, are to be raised in non-Indian homes and denied exposure to the ways of their People. Furthermore, these practices seriously undercut the tribes' ability to continue as self-governing communities. Probably in no area is it more

1. For example, Dr. Joseph Westermeyer, a University of Minnesota social psychiatrist, testified about his research with Indian adolescents who experienced difficulty coping in white society, despite the fact that they had been raised in a purely white environment:

> "[T]hey were raised with a white cultural and social identity. They are raised in a white home. They attended, predominantly white schools, and in almost all cases, attended a church that was predominantly white, and really came to understand very little about Indian culture, Indian behavior, and had virtually no viable Indian identity. They can recall such things as seeing cowboys and Indians on TV and feeling that Indians were a historical figure but were not a viable contemporary social group.
>
> "Then during adolescence, they found that society was not to grant them the white identity that they had. They began to find this out in a number of ways. For example, a universal experience was that when they began to date white children, the parents of the white youngsters were against this, and there were pressures among white children from the parents not to date these Indian children....
>
> "The other experience was derogatory name calling in relation to their racial identity....
>
> "[T]hey were finding that society was putting on them an identity which they didn't possess and taking from them an identity that they did possess." 1974 Hearings, at 46.

important that tribal sovereignty be respected than in an area as socially and culturally determinative as family relationships. 1978 Hearings, at 193.

See also *id.*, at 62.[3] Chief Isaac also summarized succinctly what numerous witnesses saw as the principal reason for the high rates of removal of Indian children:

> "One of the most serious failings of the present system is that Indian children are removed from the custody of their natural parents by nontribal government authorities who have no basis for intelligently evaluating the cultural and social premises underlying Indian home life and childrearing. Many of the individuals who decide the fate of our children are at best ignorant of our cultural values, and at worst contemptful of the Indian way and convinced that removal, usually to a non-Indian household or institution, can only benefit an Indian child." *Id.*, at 191–192. [4]

The congressional findings that were incorporated into the ICWA reflect these sentiments. The Congress found:

> "(3) that there is no resource that is more vital to the continued existence and integrity of Indian tribes than their children...;
>
> "(4) that an alarmingly high percentage of Indian families are broken up by the removal, often unwarranted, of their children from them by nontribal public and private agencies and that an alarmingly high percentage of such children are placed in non-Indian foster and adoptive homes and institutions; and
>
> "(5) that the States, exercising their recognized jurisdiction over Indian child custody proceedings through administrative and judicial bodies, have often failed to recognize the essential tribal relations of Indian people and the cultural and social standards prevailing in Indian communities and families." 25 U.S.C. § 1901.

3. These sentiments were shared by the ICWA's principal sponsor in the House, Rep. Morris Udall, see 124 Cong.Rec. 38102 (1978) ("Indian tribes and Indian people are being drained of their children and, as a result, their future as a tribe and a people is being placed in jeopardy"), and its minority sponsor, Rep. Robert Lagomarsino, see *ibid.* ("This bill is directed at conditions which... threaten... the future of American Indian tribes...").

4. One of the particular points of concern was the failure of non-Indian child welfare workers to understand the role of the extended family in Indian society. The House Report on the ICWA noted: "An Indian child may have scores of, perhaps more than a hundred, relatives who are counted as close, responsible members of the family. Many social workers, untutored in the ways of Indian family life or assuming them to be socially irresponsible, consider leaving the child with persons outside the nuclear family as neglect and thus as grounds for terminating parental rights." House Report, at 10, U.S.Code Cong. & Admin.News 1978, at 7532. At the conclusion of the 1974 Senate hearings, Senator Abourezk noted the role that such extended families played in the care of children: "We've had testimony here that in Indian communities throughout the Nation there is no such thing as an abandoned child because when a child does have a need for parents for one reason or another, a relative or a friend will take that child in. It's the extended family concept." 1974 Hearings, at 473. See also *Wisconsin Potowatomies of Hannahville Indian Community v. Houston*, 393 F.Supp. 719 (WD Mich. 1973) (discussing custom of extended family and tribe assuming responsibility for care of orphaned children).

At the heart of the ICWA are its provisions concerning jurisdiction over Indian child custody proceedings. Section 1911 lays out a dual jurisdictional scheme. Section 1911(a) establishes exclusive jurisdiction in the tribal courts for proceedings concerning an Indian child "who resides or is domiciled within the reservation of such tribe," as well as for wards of tribal courts regardless of domicile.[5] Section 1911(b), on the other hand, creates concurrent but presumptively tribal jurisdiction in the case of children not domiciled on the reservation: on petition of either parent or the tribe, state-court proceedings for foster care placement or termination of parental rights are to be transferred to the tribal court, except in cases of "good cause," objection by either parent, or declination of jurisdiction by the tribal court.

Various other provisions of ICWA Title I set procedural and substantive standards for those child custody proceedings that do take place in state court. The procedural safeguards include requirements concerning notice and appointment of counsel; parental and tribal rights of intervention and petition for invalidation of illegal proceedings; procedures governing voluntary consent to termination of parental rights; and a full faith and credit obligation in respect to tribal court decisions. See §§ 1901–1914. The most important substantive requirement imposed on state courts is that of § 1915(a), which, absent "good cause" to the contrary, mandates that adoptive placements be made preferentially with (1) members of the child's extended family, (2) other members of the same tribe, or (3) other Indian families.

The ICWA thus, in the words of the House Report accompanying it, "seeks to protect the rights of the Indian child as an Indian and the rights of the Indian community and tribe in retaining its children in its society." House Report, at 23. It does so by establishing "a Federal policy that, where possible, an Indian child should remain in the Indian community," *ibid.*, and by making sure that Indian child welfare determinations are not based on "a white, middle-class standard which, in many cases, forecloses placement with [an] Indian family." *Id.*, at 24. [6]

B

This case involves the status of twin babies, known for our purposes as B.B. and G.B., who were born out of wedlock on December 29, 1985. Their mother, J.B., and father, W.J., were both enrolled members of appellant Mississippi Band of Choctaw Indians (Tribe), and were residents and domiciliaries of the Choctaw Reservation in Neshoba County, Mississippi. J.B. gave birth to the twins in Gulfport, Harrison County, Mississippi, some 200 miles from the reservation. On January 10, 1986, J.B. executed a consent-to-adoption form before the

5. Section 1911(a) reads in full:

"An Indian tribe shall have jurisdiction exclusive as to any State over any child custody proceeding involving an Indian child who resides or is domiciled within the reservation of such tribe, except where such jurisdiction is otherwise vested in the State by existing Federal law. Where an Indian child is a ward of a tribal court, the Indian tribe shall retain exclusive jurisdiction, notwithstanding the residence or domicile of the child."

6. The quoted passages are from the House Report's discussion of § 1915, in which the ICWA attempts to accomplish these aims, in regard to nondomiciliaries of the reservation, through the establishment of standards for state-court proceedings. In regard to reservation domiciliaries, these goals are pursued through the establishment of exclusive tribal jurisdiction under § 1911(a).

Beyond its jurisdictional and other provisions concerning child custody proceedings, the ICWA also created, in its Title II, a program of grants to Indian tribes and organizations to aid in the establishment of child welfare programs. See 25 U.S.C. §§ 1931–1934.

Chancery Court of Harrison County. Record 8–10.[7] W.J. signed a similar form.[8] On January 16, appellees Orrey and Vivian Holyfield[9] filed a petition for adoption in the same court, *id.*, at 1–5, and the chancellor issued a Final Decree of Adoption on January 28. *Id.*, at 13–14.[10] Despite the court's apparent awareness of the ICWA,[11] the adoption decree contained no reference to it, nor to the infants' Indian background.

Two months later the Tribe moved in the Chancery Court to vacate the adoption decree on the ground that under the ICWA exclusive jurisdiction was vested in the tribal court. *Id.*, at 15–18.[12] On July 14, 1986, the court overruled the motion, holding that the Tribe "never obtained exclusive jurisdiction over the children involved herein. . . ." The court's one-page opinion relied on two facts in reaching that conclusion. The court noted first that the twins' mother "went to some efforts to see that they were born outside the confines of the Choctaw Indian Reservation" and that the parents had promptly arranged for the adoption by the Holyfields. Second, the court stated: "At no time from the birth of these children to the present date have either of them resided on or physically been on the Choctaw Indian Reservation." *Id.*, at 78.

The Supreme Court of Mississippi affirmed. 511 So.2d 918 (1987). It rejected the Tribe's arguments that the state court lacked jurisdiction and that it, in any event, had not applied the standards laid out in the ICWA. The court recognized that the jurisdictional question turned on whether the twins were domiciled on the Choctaw Reservation. It answered that question as follows:

> "At no point in time can it be said the twins resided on or were domiciled within the territory set aside for the reservation. Appellant's argument that living within the womb of their mother qualifies the children's residency on the reservation may be lauded for its creativity; however,

7. Section 103(a) of the ICWA, 25 U.S.C. § 1913(a), requires that any voluntary consent to termination of parental rights be executed in writing and recorded before a judge of a "court of competent jurisdiction," who must certify that the terms and consequences of the consent were fully explained and understood. Section 1913(a) also provides that any consent given prior to birth or within 10 days thereafter is invalid. In this case the mother's consent was given 12 days after the birth. See also n. 26, *infra*.

8. W.J.'s consent to adoption was signed before a notary public in Neshoba County on January 11, 1986. Record 11–12. Only on June 3, 1986, however—well after the decree of adoption had been entered and after the Tribe had filed suit to vacate that decree—did the chancellor of the Chancery Court certify that W.J. had appeared before him in Harrison County to execute the consent to adoption. *Id.*, at 12-A.

9. Appellee Orrey Holyfield died during the pendency of this appeal.

10. Mississippi adoption law provides for a 6-month waiting period between interlocutory and final decrees of adoption, but grants the chancellor discretionary authority to waive that requirement and immediately enter a final decree of adoption. See Miss.Code Ann. § 93-17-13 (1972). The chancellor did so here, Record 14, with the result that the final decree of adoption was entered less than one month after the babies' birth.

11. The chancellor's certificates that the parents had appeared before him to consent to the adoption recited that "the Consent and Waiver was given in full compliance with Section 103(a) of Public Law 95-608" (*i.e.*, 25 U.S.C. § 1913(a)). Record 10, 12-A.

12. The ICWA specifically confers standing on the Indian child's tribe to participate in child custody adjudications. Title 25 U.S.C. § 1914 authorizes the tribe (as well as the child and its parents) to petition a court to invalidate any foster care placement or termination of parental rights under state law "upon a showing that such action violated any provision of sections 101, 102, and 103" of the ICWA. 92 Stat. 3072. See also § 1911(c) (Indian child's tribe may intervene at any point in state-court proceedings for foster care placement or termination of parental rights). "Termination of parental rights" is defined in § 1903(1)(ii) as "any action resulting in the termination of the parent-child relationship."

apparently it is unsupported by any law within this state, and will not be addressed at this time due to the far-reaching legal ramifications that would occur were we to follow such a complicated tangential course." *Id.*, at 921.

The court distinguished Mississippi cases that appeared to establish the principle that "the domicile of minor children follows that of the parents," *ibid.*; see *Boyle v. Griffin*, 84 Miss. 41, 36 So. 141 (1904); *Stubbs v. Stubbs*, 211 So.2d 821 (Miss. 1968); see also *In re Guardianship of Watson*, 317 So.2d 30 (Miss. 1975). It noted that "the Indian twins...were voluntarily surrendered and legally abandoned by the natural parents to the adoptive parents, and it is undisputed that the parents went to some efforts to prevent the children from being placed on the reservation as the mother arranged for their birth and adoption in Gulfport Memorial Hospital, Harrison County, Mississippi." 511 So.2d, at 921. Therefore, the court said, the twins' domicile was in Harrison County and the state court properly exercised jurisdiction over the adoption proceedings. Indeed, the court appears to have concluded that, for this reason, *none* of the provisions of the ICWA was applicable. *Ibid.* ("[T]hese proceedings...actually escape applicable federal law on Indian Child Welfare"). In any case, it rejected the Tribe's contention that the requirements of the ICWA applicable in state courts had not been followed: "[T]he judge did conform and strictly adhere to the minimum federal standards governing adoption of Indian children with respect to parental consent, notice, service of process, etc." *Ibid.*[13]

Because of the centrality of the exclusive tribal jurisdiction provision to the overall scheme of the ICWA, as well as the conflict between this decision of the Mississippi Supreme Court and those of several other state courts,[14] we granted plenary review. 486 U.S. 1021 (1988).[15] We now reverse.

13. The lower court may well have fulfilled the applicable ICWA procedural requirements. But see n. 8, *supra*, and n. 26, *infra*. It clearly did not, however, comply with or even take cognizance of the substantive mandate of § 1915(a): "In any adoptive placement of an Indian child *under State law*, a preference shall be given, in the absence of good cause to the contrary, to a placement with (1) a member of the child's extended family; (2) other members of the Indian child's tribe; or (3) other Indian families." (Emphasis added.) Section 1915(e), moreover, requires the court to maintain records "evidencing the efforts to comply with the order of preference specified in this section." Notwithstanding the Tribe's argument below that § 1915 had been violated, see Brief for Appellant 20–22 and Appellant's Brief in Support of Petition for Rehearing 11–12 in No. 57,659 (Miss.Sup.Ct.), the Mississippi Supreme Court made no reference to it, merely stating in conclusory fashion that the "minimum federal standards" had been met. 511 So.2d, at 921.

14. See, *e.g.*, *In re Adoption of Halloway*, 732 P.2d 962 (Utah 1986); *In re Adoption of Baby Child*, 102 N.M. 735, 700 P.2d 198 (App. 1985); *In re Appeal in Pima County Juvenile Action No. S-903*, 130 Ariz. 202, 635 P.2d 187 (App. 1981), cert. denied *sub nom. Catholic Social Services of Tucson v. P.C.*, 455 U.S. 1007, 102 S.Ct. 1644, 71 L.Ed.2d 875 (1982).

15. Because it was unclear whether this case fell within the Court's appellate jurisdiction, we postponed consideration of our jurisdiction to the hearing on the merits. Pursuant to the version of 28 U.S.C. § 1257(2) applicable to this appeal, we have appellate jurisdiction to review a state-court judgment "where is drawn in question the validity of a statute of any state on the ground of its being repugnant to the Constitution, treaties or laws of the United States, and the decision is in favor of its validity." It is sufficient that the validity of the state statute be challenged and sustained as applied to a particular set of facts. *Volt Information Sciences, Inc. v. Board of Trustees of Leland Stanford Junior University*, 489 U.S. 468, 473–474, n. 4 (1989); *Dahnke-Walker Milling Co. v. Bondurant*, 257 U.S. 282, 288–290 (1921). In practice, whether such an as-applied challenge comes within our appellate jurisdiction often turns on how that challenge is framed. See *Hanson v. Denckla*, 357 U.S. 235, 244 (1958); *Memphis Natural Gas Co. v. Beeler*, 315 U.S. 649, 650–651 (1942).

In the present case appellants argued below "that the state lower court jurisdiction over these adoptions was preempted by plenary federal legislation." Brief for Appellant in No. 57,659 (Miss.Sup.Ct.), p. 5. Whether

II

Tribal jurisdiction over Indian child custody proceedings is not a novelty of the ICWA. Indeed, some of the ICWA's jurisdictional provisions have a strong basis in pre-ICWA case law in the federal and state courts. See, *e.g., Fisher v. District Court, Sixteenth Judicial District of Montana*, 424 U.S. 382 (1976) (*per curiam*) (tribal court had exclusive jurisdiction over adoption proceeding where all parties were tribal members and reservation residents); *Wisconsin Potowatomies of Hannahville Indian Community v. Houston*, 393 F.Supp. 719 (WD Mich. 1973) (tribal court had exclusive jurisdiction over custody of Indian children found to have been domiciled on reservation); *Wakefield v. Little Light*, 276 Md. 333, 347 A.2d 228 (1975) (same); *In re Adoption of Buehl*, 87 Wash.2d 649, 555 P.2d 1334 (1976) (state court lacked jurisdiction over custody of Indian children placed in off-reservation foster care by tribal court order); see also *In re Lelah-puc-ka-chee*, 98 F. 429 (ND Iowa 1899) (state court lacked jurisdiction to appoint guardian for Indian child living on reservation). In enacting the ICWA Congress confirmed that, in child custody proceedings involving Indian children domiciled on the reservation, tribal jurisdiction was exclusive as to the States.

The state-court proceeding at issue here was a "child custody proceeding." That term is defined to include any "'adoptive placement' which shall mean the permanent placement of an Indian child for adoption, including any action resulting in a final decree of adoption." 25 U.S.C. § 1903(1)(iv). Moreover, the twins were "Indian children." See 25 U.S.C. § 1903(4). The sole issue in this case is, as the Supreme Court of Mississippi recognized, whether the twins were "domiciled" on the reservation.[16]

A

The meaning of "domicile" in the ICWA is, of course, a matter of Congress' intent. The ICWA itself does not define it. The initial question we must confront is whether there is any reason to believe that Congress intended the ICWA definition of "domicile" to be a matter of state law. While the meaning of a federal statute is necessarily a federal question in the sense that its construction remains subject to this Court's supervision, see P. Bator, D. Meltzer,

this formulation "squarely" challenges the validity of the state adoption statute as applied, see *Japan Line, Ltd. v. County of Los Angeles*, 441 U.S. 434, 440–441 (1979), or merely asserts a federal right or immunity, 28 U.S.C. § 1257(3), is a difficult question to which the answer must inevitably be somewhat arbitrary. Since in the near future our appellate jurisdiction will extend only to rare cases, see Pub.L. 100-352, 102 Stat. 662, it is also a question of little prospective importance. Rather than attempting to resolve this question, therefore, we think it advisable to assume that the appeal is improper and to consider by writ of certiorari the important question this case presents. See *Spencer v. Texas*, 385 U.S. 554, 557, n. 3 (1967). We therefore dismiss the appeal, treat the papers as a petition for writ of certiorari, 28 U.S.C. § 2103, and grant the petition. (For convenience, we will continue to refer to the parties as appellant and appellees.)

16. "Reservation" is defined quite broadly for purposes of the ICWA. See 25 U.S.C. § 1903(10). There is no dispute that the Choctaw Reservation falls within that definition.

Section 1911(a) does not apply "where such jurisdiction is otherwise vested in the State by existing Federal law." This proviso would appear to refer to Pub.L. 280, 67 Stat. 588, as amended, which allows States under certain conditions to assume civil and criminal jurisdiction on the reservations. Title 25 U.S.C. § 1918 permits a tribe in that situation to reassume jurisdiction over child custody proceedings upon petition to the Secretary of the Interior. The State of Mississippi has never asserted jurisdiction over the Choctaw Reservation under Public Law 280. See F. Cohen, Handbook of Federal Indian Law 362–363, and nn. 122–125 (1982); cf. *United States v. John*, 437 U.S. 634 (1978).

P. Mishkin, & D. Shapiro, Hart and Wechsler's The Federal Courts and the Federal System 566 (3d ed. 1988); cf. *Reconstruction Finance Corporation v. Beaver County*, 328 U.S. 204, 210, 66 S.Ct. 992, 995, 90 L.Ed. 1172 (1946), Congress sometimes intends that a statutory term be given content by the application of state law. *De Sylva v. Ballentine*, 351 U.S. 570, 580 (1956); see also *Beaver County, supra*; *Helvering v. Stuart*, 317 U.S. 154, 161–162 (1942). We start, however, with the general assumption that "in the absence of a plain indication to the contrary, . . . Congress when it enacts a statute is not making the application of the federal act dependent on state law." *Jerome v. United States*, 318 U.S. 101, 104 (1943); *NLRB v. Natural Gas Utility Dist. of Hawkins County*, 402 U.S. 600, 603 (1971); *Dickerson v. New Banner Institute, Inc.*, 460 U.S. 103, 119 (1983). One reason for this rule of construction is that federal statutes are generally intended to have uniform nationwide application. *Jerome, supra*, 318 U.S., at 104, 63 S.Ct., at 485; *Dickerson, supra*, 460 U.S., at 119–120; *United States v. Pelzer*, 312 U.S. 399, 402–403 (1941). Accordingly, the cases in which we have found that Congress intended a state-law definition of a statutory term have often been those where uniformity clearly was not intended. *E.g., Beaver County, supra*, 328 U.S., at 209 (statute permitting States to apply their diverse local tax laws to real property of certain Government corporations). A second reason for the presumption against the application of state law is the danger that "the federal program would be impaired if state law were to control." *Jerome, supra*, 318 U.S., at 104; *Dickerson, supra*, 460 U.S., at 119–120; *Pelzer*, 312 U.S., at 402–403. For this reason, "we look to the purpose of the statute to ascertain what is intended." *Id.*, at 403.

In *NLRB v. Hearst Publications, Inc.*, 322 U.S. 111 (1944), we rejected an argument that the term "employee" as used in the Wagner Act should be defined by state law. We explained our conclusion as follows:

> "Both the terms and the purposes of the statute, as well as the legislative history, show that Congress had in mind no . . . patchwork plan for securing freedom of employees' organization and of collective bargaining. The Wagner Act is . . . intended to solve a national problem on a national scale. . . . Nothing in the statute's background, history, terms or purposes indicates its scope is to be limited by . . . varying local conceptions, either statutory or judicial, or that it is to be administered in accordance with whatever different standards the respective states may see fit to adopt for the disposition of unrelated, local problems." *Id.*, at 123.

See also *Natural Gas Utility Dist., supra*, 402 U.S., at 603–604. For the two principal reasons that follow, we believe that what we said of the Wagner Act applies equally well to the ICWA.

First, and most fundamentally, the purpose of the ICWA gives no reason to believe that Congress intended to rely on state law for the definition of a critical term; quite the contrary. It is clear from the very text of the ICWA, not to mention its legislative history and the hearings that led to its enactment, that Congress was concerned with the rights of Indian families and Indian communities vis-à-vis state authorities.[17] More specifically, its purpose was, in part, to make clear that in certain situations the state courts did *not* have jurisdiction over child custody proceedings. Indeed, the congressional findings that are a part of the statute

17. This conclusion is inescapable from a reading of the entire statute, the main effect of which is to curtail state authority. See especially §§ 1901, 1911–1916, 1918.

demonstrate that Congress perceived the States and their courts as partly responsible for the problem it intended to correct. See 25 U.S.C. § 1901(5) (state "judicial bodies... have often failed to recognize the essential tribal relations of Indian people and the cultural and social standards prevailing in Indian communities and families").[18] Under these circumstances it is most improbable that Congress would have intended to leave the scope of the statute's key jurisdictional provision subject to definition by state courts as a matter of state law.

Second, Congress could hardly have intended the lack of nationwide uniformity that would result from state-law definitions of domicile. An example will illustrate. In a case quite similar to this one, the New Mexico state courts found exclusive jurisdiction in the tribal court pursuant to § 1911(a), because the illegitimate child took the reservation domicile of its mother at birth—notwithstanding that the child was placed in the custody of adoptive parents 2 days after its off-reservation birth and the mother executed a consent to adoption 10 days later. *In re Adoption of Baby Child*, 102 N.M. 735, 737–738, 700 P.2d 198, 200–201 (App. 1985).[19] Had that mother traveled to Mississippi to give birth, rather than to Albuquerque, a different result would have obtained if state-law definitions of domicile applied. The same, presumably, would be true if the child had been transported to Mississippi for adoption after her off-reservation birth in New Mexico. While the child's custody proceeding would have been subject to exclusive tribal jurisdiction in her home State, her mother, prospective adoptive parents, or an adoption intermediary could have obtained an adoption decree in state court merely by transporting her across state lines.[20] Even if we could conceive of a federal statute under which the rules of domicile (and thus of jurisdiction) applied differently to different Indian children, a statute under which different rules apply from time to time to the same child, simply as a result of his or her transport from one State to another, cannot be what Congress had in mind.[21]

18. See also 124 Cong.Rec. 38103 (1978) (letter from Rep. Morris K. Udall to Assistant Attorney General Patricia M. Wald) ("[S]tate courts and agencies and their procedures share a large part of the responsibility" for the crisis threatening "the future and integrity of Indian tribes and Indian families"); House Report, at 19 ("Contributing to this problem has been the failure of State officials, agencies, and procedures to take into account the special problems and circumstances of Indian families and the legitimate interest of the Indian tribe in preserving and protecting the Indian family as the wellspring of its own future"). See also *In re Adoption of Halloway*, 732 P.2d, at 969 (Utah state court "quite frankly might be expected to be more receptive than a tribal court to [Indian child's] placement with non-Indian adoptive parents. Yet this receptivity of the non-Indian forum to non-Indian placement of an Indian child is precisely one of the evils at which the ICWA was aimed").

19. Some details of the *Baby Child* case are taken from the briefs in *Pino v. District Court, Bernalillo County*, 469 U.S. 1031 (1984). That appeal was dismissed under this Court's Rule 53, 472 U.S. 1001 (1985), following the appellant's successful collateral attack, in the case cited in the text, on the judgment from which appeal had been taken.

20. Nor is it inconceivable that a State might apply its law of domicile in such a manner as to render inapplicable § 1911(a) even to a child who had lived several years on the reservation but was removed from it for the purpose of adoption. Even in the less extreme case, a state-law definition of domicile would likely spur the development of an adoption brokerage business. Indian children, whose parents consented (with or without financial inducement) to give them up, could be transported for adoption to States like Mississippi where the law of domicile permitted the proceedings to take place in state court.

21. For this reason, the general rule that domicile is determined according to the law of the forum, see Restatement (Second) of Conflict of Laws § 13 (1971) (hereinafter Restatement), can have no application here.

We therefore think it beyond dispute that Congress intended a uniform federal law of domicile for the ICWA.[22]

B

It remains to give content to the term "domicile" in the circumstances of the present case. The holding of the Supreme Court of Mississippi that the twin babies were not domiciled on the Choctaw Reservation appears to have rested on two findings of fact by the trial court: (1) that they had never been physically present there, and (2) that they were "voluntarily surrendered" by their parents. 511 So.2d, at 921; see Record 78. The question before us, therefore, is whether under the ICWA definition of "domicile" such facts suffice to render the twins nondomiciliaries of the Reservation.

We have often stated that in the absence of a statutory definition we "start with the assumption that the legislative purpose is expressed by the ordinary meaning of the words used." *Richards v. United States*, 369 U.S. 1, 9 (1962); *Russello v. United States*, 464 U.S. 16, 21 (1983). We do so, of course, in the light of the "'object and policy'" of the statute. *Mastro Plastics Corp. v. NLRB*, 350 U.S. 270, 285 (1956), quoting *United States v. Heirs of Boisdoré*, 8 How. 113, 122 (1849). We therefore look both to the generally accepted meaning of the term "domicile" and to the purpose of the statute.

That we are dealing with a uniform federal rather than a state definition does not, of course, prevent us from drawing on general state-law principles to determine "the ordinary meaning of the words used." Well-settled state law can inform our understanding of what Congress had in mind when it employed a term it did not define. Accordingly, we find it helpful to borrow established common-law principles of domicile to the extent that they are not inconsistent with the objectives of the congressional scheme.

"Domicile" is, of course, a concept widely used in both federal and state courts for jurisdiction and conflict-of-laws purposes, and its meaning is generally uncontroverted. See generally Restatement §§ 11–23; R. Leflar, L. McDougal, & R. Felix, American Conflicts Law 17–38 (4th ed. 1986); R. Weintraub, Commentary on the Conflict of Laws 12–24 (2d ed. 1980). "Domicile" is not necessarily synonymous with "residence," *Perri v. Kisselbach*, 34 N.J. 84, 87, 167 A.2d 377, 379 (1961), and one can reside in one place but be domiciled in another, *District of Columbia v. Murphy*, 314 U.S. 441 (1941); *In re Estate of Jones*, 192 Iowa 78, 80, 182 N.W. 227, 228 (1921). For adults, domicile is established by physical presence in a place in connection with a certain state of mind concerning one's intent to remain there. *Texas v. Florida*, 306 U.S. 398, 424 (1939). One acquires a "domicile of origin" at birth, and that domicile continues until a new one (a "domicile of choice") is acquired. *Jones, supra*, at 81, 182 N.W., at 228; *In re Estate of Moore*, 68 Wash.2d 792, 796, 415 P.2d 653, 656 (1966). Since most minors are legally incapable of forming the requisite intent to establish a domicile, their domicile is determined by that of their parents. *Yarborough v. Yarborough*, 290 U.S. 202, 211 (1933). In the case of an illegitimate child, that has traditionally meant the domicile of its mother. *Kowalski v. Wojtkowski*, 19 N.J. 247, 258, 116 A.2d 6, 12 (1955); *Moore, supra*, 68 Wash.2d,

22. We note also the likelihood that, had Congress intended a state-law definition of domicile, it would have said so. Where Congress did intend that ICWA terms be defined by reference to other than federal law, it stated this explicitly. See § 1903(2) ("extended family member" defined by reference to tribal law or custom); § 1903(6) ("Indian custodian" defined by reference to tribal law or custom and to state law).

at 796, 415 P.2d, at 656; Restatement § 14(2), § 22, Comment *c*; 25 Am.Jur.2d, Domicile § 69 (1966). Under these principles, it is entirely logical that "[o]n occasion, a child's domicile of origin will be in a place where the child has never been." Restatement § 14, Comment *b*.

It is undisputed in this case that the domicile of the mother (as well as the father) has been, at all relevant times, on the Choctaw Reservation. Thus, it is clear that at their birth the twin babies were also domiciled on the reservation, even though they themselves had never been there. The statement of the Supreme Court of Mississippi that "[a]t no point in time can it be said the twins...were domiciled within the territory set aside for the reservation," 511 So.2d, at 921, may be a correct statement of that State's law of domicile, but it is inconsistent with generally accepted doctrine in this country and cannot be what Congress had in mind when it used the term in the ICWA.

Nor can the result be any different simply because the twins were "voluntarily surrendered" by their mother. Tribal jurisdiction under § 1911(a) was not meant to be defeated by the actions of individual members of the tribe, for Congress was concerned not solely about the interests of Indian children and families, but also about the impact on the tribes themselves of the large numbers of Indian children adopted by non-Indians. See 25 U.S.C. §§ 1901(3) ("[T]here is no resource that is more vital to the continued existence and integrity of Indian tribes than their children"), § 1902 ("promote the stability and security of Indian tribes").[23] The numerous prerogatives accorded the tribes through the ICWA's substantive provisions, *e.g.*, §§ 1911(a) (exclusive jurisdiction over reservation domiciliaries), 1911(b) (presumptive jurisdiction over nondomiciliaries), 1911(c) (right of intervention), 1912(a) (notice), 1914 (right to petition for invalidation of state-court action), 1915(c) (right to alter presumptive placement priorities applicable to state-court actions), 1915(e) (right to obtain records), 1919 (authority to conclude agreements with States), must, accordingly, be seen as a means of protecting not only the interests of individual Indian children and families, but also of the tribes themselves.

In addition, it is clear that Congress' concern over the placement of Indian children in non-Indian homes was based in part on evidence of the detrimental impact on the children themselves of such placements outside their culture.[24] Congress determined to subject such placements to the ICWA's jurisdictional and other provisions, even in cases where the parents

23. See also *supra*, and n. 3.

24. In large part the concerns that emerged during the congressional hearings on the ICWA were based on studies showing recurring developmental problems encountered during adolescence by Indian children raised in a white environment. See n. 1, *supra*. See also 1977 Hearings, at 114 (statement of American Academy of Child Psychiatry); S.Rep. No. 95-597, p. 43 (1977) (hereinafter Senate Report). More generally, placements in non-Indian homes were seen as "depriving the child of his or her tribal and cultural heritage." *Id.*, at 45; see also 124 Cong.Rec. 38102–38103 (1978) (remarks of Rep. Lagomarsino). The Senate Report on the ICWA incorporates the testimony in this sense of Louis La Rose, chairman of the Winnebago Tribe, before the American Indian Policy Review Commission:

> "I think the cruelest trick that the white man has ever done to Indian children is to take them into adoption courts, erase all of their records and send them off to some nebulous family that has a value system that is A-1 in the State of Nebraska and that child reaches 16 or 17, he is a little brown child residing in a white community and he goes back to the reservation and he has absolutely no idea who his relatives are, and they effectively make him a non-person and I think...they destroy him." Senate Report, at 43.

Thus, the conclusion seems justified that, as one state court has put it, "[t]he Act is based on the fundamental assumption that it is in the Indian child's best interest that its relationship to the tribe be protected." *In re Appeal in Pima County Juvenile Action No. S-903*, 130 Ariz., at 204, 635 P.2d, at 189.

consented to an adoption, because of concerns going beyond the wishes of individual parents. As the 1977 Final Report of the congressionally established American Indian Policy Review Commission stated, in summarizing these two concerns, "[r]emoval of Indian children from their cultural setting seriously impacts a long-term tribal survival and has damaging social and psychological impact on many individual Indian children." Senate Report, at 52.[25]

These congressional objectives make clear that a rule of domicile that would permit individual Indian parents to defeat the ICWA's jurisdictional scheme is inconsistent with what Congress intended.[26] See *In re Adoption of Child of Indian Heritage*, 111 N.J. 155, 168–171, 543 A.2d 925, 931–933 (1988). The appellees in this case argue strenuously that the twins' mother went to great lengths to give birth off the reservation so that her children could be adopted by the Holyfields. But that was precisely part of Congress' concern. Permitting individual members of the tribe to avoid tribal exclusive jurisdiction by the simple expedient of giving birth off the reservation would, to a large extent, nullify the purpose the ICWA was intended to accomplish.[27] The Supreme Court of Utah expressed this well in its scholarly and sensitive opinion in what has become a leading case on the ICWA:

> "To the extent that [state] abandonment law operates to permit [the child's] mother to change [the child's] domicile as part of a scheme to facilitate his adoption by non-Indians while she

25. While the statute itself makes clear that Congress intended the ICWA to reach voluntary as well as involuntary removal of Indian children, the same conclusion can also be drawn from the ICWA's legislative history. For example, the House Report contains the following expression of Congress' concern with both aspects of the problem:

> "One of the effects of our national paternalism has been to so alienate some Indian [parents] from their society that they abandon their children at hospitals or to welfare departments rather than entrust them to the care of relatives in the extended family. Another expression of it is the involuntary, arbitrary, and unwarranted separation of families." House Report, at 12.

26. The Bureau of Indian Affairs pointed out, in issuing nonbinding ICWA guidelines for the state courts, that the terms "residence" and "domicile" "are well defined under existing state law. There is no indication that these state law definitions tend to undermine in any way the purposes of the Act." 44 Fed.Reg. 67584, 67585 (1979). The clear implication is that state law that *did* tend to undermine the ICWA's purposes could not be taken to express Congress' intent.

There is some authority for the proposition that abandonment can effectuate a change in the child's domicile, *In re Adoption of Halloway*, 732 P.2d, at 967, although this may not be the majority rule. See Restatement § 22, Comment *e* (abandoned child generally retains the domicile of the last-abandoning parent). In any case, as will be seen below, the Supreme Court of Utah declined in the *Halloway* case to apply Utah abandonment law to defeat the purpose of the ICWA. Similarly, the conclusory statement of the Supreme Court of Mississippi that the twin babies had been "legally abandoned," 511 So.2d, at 921, cannot be determinative of ICWA jurisdiction. There is also another reason for reaching this conclusion. The predicate for the state court's abandonment finding was the parents' consent to termination of their parental rights, recorded before a judge of the state Chancery Court. ICWA § 103(a), 25 U.S.C. § 1913(a), requires, however, that such a consent be recorded before "a judge of a court of competent jurisdiction." See n. 7, *supra*. In the case of reservation-domiciled children, that could be only the tribal court. The children therefore could not be made non-domiciliaries of the reservation through any such state-court consent.

27. It appears, in fact, that all Choctaw women give birth off the reservation because of the lack of appropriate obstetric facilities there. See Juris.Statement 4, n. 2. In most cases, of course, the mother and child return to the reservation after the birth, and this would presumably be sufficient to make the child a reservation domiciliary even under the Mississippi court's theory. Application of the Mississippi domicile rule would, however, permit state authorities to avoid the tribal court's exclusive § 1911(a) jurisdiction by removing a newborn from an allegedly unfit mother while in the hospital, and seeking to terminate her parental rights in state court.

> remains a domiciliary of the reservation, it conflicts with and undermines the operative scheme established by subsections [1911(a)] and [1913(a)] to deal with children of domiciliaries of the reservation and weakens considerably the tribe's ability to assert its interest in its children. The protection of this tribal interest is at the core of the ICWA, which recognizes that the tribe has an interest in the child which is distinct from but on a parity with the interest of the parents. This relationship between Indian tribes and Indian children domiciled on the reservation finds no parallel in other ethnic cultures found in the United States. It is a relationship that many non-Indians find difficult to understand and that non-Indian courts are slow to recognize. It is precisely in recognition of this relationship, however, that the ICWA designates the tribal court as the exclusive forum for the determination of custody and adoption matters for reservation-domiciled Indian children, and the preferred forum for nondomiciliary Indian children. [State] abandonment law cannot be used to frustrate the federal legislative judgment expressed in the ICWA that the interests of the tribe in custodial decisions made with respect to Indian children are as entitled to respect as the interests of the parents." *In re Adoption of Halloway*, 732 P.2d 962, 969–970 (1986).

We agree with the Supreme Court of Utah that the law of domicile Congress used in the ICWA cannot be one that permits individual reservation-domiciled tribal members to defeat the tribe's exclusive jurisdiction by the simple expedient of giving birth and placing the child for adoption off the reservation. Since, for purposes of the ICWA, the twin babies in this case were domiciled on the reservation when adoption proceedings were begun, the Choctaw tribal court possessed exclusive jurisdiction pursuant to 25 U.S.C. § 1911(a). The Chancery Court of Harrison County was, accordingly, without jurisdiction to enter a decree of adoption; under ICWA § 104, 25 U.S.C. § 1914, its decree of January 28, 1986, must be vacated.

III

We are not unaware that over three years have passed since the twin babies were born and placed in the Holyfield home, and that a court deciding their fate today is not writing on a blank slate in the same way it would have in January 1986. Three years' development of family ties cannot be undone, and a separation at this point would doubtless cause considerable pain.

Whatever feelings we might have as to where the twins should live, however, it is not for us to decide that question. We have been asked to decide the legal question of *who* should make the custody determination concerning these children—not what the outcome of that determination should be. The law places that decision in the hands of the Choctaw tribal court. Had the mandate of the ICWA been followed in 1986, of course, much potential anguish might have been avoided, and in any case the law cannot be applied so as automatically to "reward those who obtain custody, whether lawfully or otherwise, and maintain it during any ensuing (and protracted) litigation." *Halloway*, 732 P.2d, at 972. It is not ours to say whether the trauma that might result from removing these children from their adoptive family should outweigh the interest of the Tribe—and perhaps the children themselves—in having them raised as part of the Choctaw community.[28] Rather, "we must defer to the experience, wisdom, and compassion of the [Choctaw] tribal courts to fashion an appropriate remedy." *Ibid.*

28. We were assured at oral argument that the Choctaw court has the authority under the tribal code to permit adoption by the present adoptive family, should it see fit to do so.

The judgment of the Supreme Court of Mississippi is reversed, and the case is remanded for further proceedings not inconsistent with this opinion....

JUSTICE STEVENS, with whom THE CHIEF JUSTICE and JUSTICE KENNEDY join, dissenting.

The parents of these twin babies unquestionably expressed their intention to have the state court exercise jurisdiction over them. J.B. gave birth to the twins at a hospital 200 miles from the reservation, even though a closer hospital was available. Both parents gave their written advance consent to the adoption and, when the adoption was later challenged by the Tribe, they reaffirmed their desire that the Holyfields adopt the two children. As the Mississippi Supreme Court found, "the parents went to some efforts to prevent the children from being placed on the reservation as the mother arranged for their birth and adoption in Gulfport Memorial Hospital, Harrison County, Mississippi." 511 So.2d 918, 921 (1987). Indeed, Appellee Vivian Holyfield appears before us today, urging that she be allowed to retain custody of B.B. and G.B.

Because J.B.'s domicile is on the reservation and the children are eligible for membership in the Tribe, the Court today closes the state courthouse door to her. I agree with the Court that Congress intended a uniform federal law of domicile for the Indian Child Welfare Act of 1978 (ICWA), 92 Stat. 3069, 25 U.S.C. §§ 1901–1963, and that domicile should be defined with reference to the objectives of the congressional scheme. "To ascertain [the term's] meaning we...consider the Congressional history of the Act, the situation with reference to which it was enacted, and the existing judicial precedents, with which Congress may be taken to have been familiar in at least a general way." *District of Columbia v. Murphy*, 314 U.S. 441, 449 (1941). I cannot agree, however, with the cramped definition the Court gives that term. To preclude parents domiciled on a reservation from deliberately invoking the adoption procedures of state court, the Court gives "domicile" a meaning that Congress could not have intended and distorts the delicate balance between individual rights and group rights recognized by the ICWA.

The ICWA was passed in 1978 in response to congressional findings that "an alarmingly high percentage of Indian families are broken up by the *removal*, often unwarranted, of their children from them by nontribal public and private agencies," and that "the States, exercising their recognized jurisdiction over Indian child custody proceedings through administrative and judicial bodies, have often failed to recognize the essential tribal relations of Indian people and the cultural and social standards prevailing in Indian communities and families." 25 U.S.C. §§ 1901(4), (5) (emphasis added). The Act is thus primarily addressed to the unjustified removal of Indian children from their families through the application of standards that inadequately recognized the distinct Indian culture.[1]

1. The House Report found that "Indian families face vastly greater risks of involuntary separation than are typical of our society as a whole." H.R.Rep. No. 95-1386, p. 9 (1978) (hereinafter House Report). The Senate Report similarly states that the Act was motivated by "reports that an alarmingly high percentage of Indian children were being separated from their natural parents through the actions of nontribal government agencies." S.Rep. No. 95-597, p. 11 (1977). See also 124 Cong.Rec. 12532 (1978) (remarks of Rep. Udall) ("The record developed by the Policy Review Commission, by the Senate Interior Committee in the 94th Congress; and by the Senate Select Committee on Indian Affairs and our own Interior Committee in the 95th Congress has disclosed what almost amounts to a callous raid on Indian children. Indian children are removed from their parents and families by State agencies for the most specious of reasons in proceedings foreign to the Indian parents"); *id.*, at 38102 (remarks of Rep. Udall) ("Studies have revealed that about 25 percent of all Indian children are removed from their homes and placed in some foster care or adoptive home or institution");

The most important provisions of the ICWA are those setting forth minimum standards for the placement of Indian children by state courts and providing procedural safeguards to insure that parental rights are protected.[2] The Act provides that any party seeking to effect a foster care placement of, or involuntary termination of parental rights to, an Indian child must establish by stringent standards of proof that efforts have been made to prevent the breakup of the Indian family, and that the continued custody of the child by the parent is likely to result in serious emotional or physical damage to the child. §§ 1912(d), (e), (f). Each party to the proceeding has a right to examine all reports and documents filed with the court, and an indigent parent or custodian has the right to appointment of counsel. §§ 1912(b), (c). In the case of a voluntary termination, the ICWA provides that consent is valid only if given after the terms and consequences of the consent have been fully explained, may be withdrawn at any time up to the final entry of a decree of termination or adoption, and even then may be collaterally attacked on the grounds that it was obtained through fraud or duress. § 1913. Finally, because the Act protects not only the rights of the parents, but also the interests of the tribe and the Indian children, the Act sets forth criteria for adoptive, foster care, and preadoptive placements that favor the Indian child's extended family or tribe, and that can be altered by resolution of the tribe. § 1915.

The Act gives Indian tribes certain rights, not to restrict the rights of parents of Indian children, but to complement and help effect them. The Indian tribe may petition to transfer an action in state court to the tribal court, but the Indian parent may veto the transfer. § 1911(b).[3] The Act provides for a tribal right of notice and intervention in involuntary proceedings but not in voluntary ones. §§ 1911(c), 1912(a).[4] Finally, the tribe may petition the

id., at 38103 (remarks of Rep. Lagomarsino) ("For Indians generally and tribes in particular, the continued wholesale removal of their children by nontribal government and private agencies constitutes a serious threat to their existence as ongoing, self-governing communities"); Hearing on S. 1214 before the Senate Select Committee on Indian Affairs, 95th Cong., 1st Sess., 1 (1977) ("It appears that for decades Indian parents and their children have been at the mercy of arbitrary or abusive action of local, State, Federal and private agency officials. Unwarranted removal of children from their homes is common in Indian communities").

2. "The purpose of the bill (H.R. 12533), introduced by Mr. Udall et al., is to protect the best interests of Indian children and to promote the stability and security of Indian tribes and families by establishing minimum Federal standards for the removal of Indian children from their families and the placement of such children in foster or adoptive homes or institutions which will reflect the unique values of Indian culture and by providing for assistance to Indian tribes and organizations in the operation of child and family service programs." House Report, at 8 (footnote omitted). See also 124 Cong.Rec. 38102 (1978) (remarks of Rep. Udall) ("[The Act] clarifies the allocation of jurisdiction over Indian child custody proceedings between Indian tribes and the States. More importantly, it establishes minimum Federal standards and procedural safeguards to protect Indian families when faced with child custody proceedings against them in State agencies or courts").

3. The statute provides in part:

"(b) Transfer of proceedings; declination by tribal court

"In any State court proceeding for the foster care placement of, or termination of parental rights to, an Indian child not domiciled or residing within the reservation of the Indian child's tribe, the court, in the absence of good cause to the contrary, shall transfer such proceeding to the jurisdiction of the tribe, absent objection by either parent, upon the petition of either parent or the Indian custodian or the Indian child's tribe: *Provided*, That such transfer shall be subject to declination by the tribal court of such tribe." 25 U.S.C. § 1911.

4. See 44 Fed.Reg. 67584, 67586 (1979) ("The Act mandates a tribal right of notice and intervention in involuntary proceedings but not in voluntary ones").

court to set aside a parental termination action upon a showing that the provisions of the ICWA that are designed to protect parents and Indian children have been violated. § 1914.[5]

While the Act's substantive and procedural provisions effect a major change in state child custody proceedings, its jurisdictional provision is designed primarily to preserve tribal sovereignty over the domestic relations of tribe members and to confirm a developing line of cases which held that the tribe's exclusive jurisdiction could not be defeated by the temporary presence of an Indian child off the reservation. The legislative history indicates that Congress did not intend "to oust the States of their traditional jurisdiction over Indian children falling within their geographic limits." House Report, at 19, U.S.Code Cong. & Admin.News 1978, at 7541; Wamser, Child Welfare under the Indian Child Welfare Act of 1978: A New Mexico Focus, 10 N.M.L.Rev. 413, 416 (1980). The apparent intent of Congress was to overrule such decisions as that in *In re Cantrell*, 159 Mont. 66, 495 P.2d 179 (1972), in which the State placed an Indian child, who had lived on a reservation with his mother, in a foster home only three days after he left the reservation to accompany his father on a trip. Jones, Indian Child Welfare: A Jurisdictional Approach, 21 Ariz.L.Rev. 1123, 1129 (1979). Congress specifically approved a series of cases in which the state courts declined jurisdiction over Indian children who were wards of the tribal court, *In re Adoption of Buehl*, 87 Wash.2d 649, 555 P.2d 1334 (1976); *Wakefield v. Little Light*, 276 Md. 333, 347 A.2d 228 (1975), or whose parents were temporarily residing off the reservation, *Wisconsin Potowatomies of Hannahville Indian Community v. Houston*, 393 F.Supp. 719 (WD Mich. 1973), but exercised jurisdiction over Indian children who had never lived on a reservation and whose Indian parents were not then residing on a reservation, *In re Greybull*, 23 Or.App. 674, 543 P.2d 1079 (1975); see House Report, at 21.[6] It did not express any disapproval of decisions such as that of the United States Court of Appeals for the Ninth Circuit in *United States ex rel. Cobell v. Cobell*, 503 F.2d 790 (9th Cir. 1974), cert. denied, 421 U.S. 999 (1975), which indicated that a Montana state court could exercise jurisdiction over an Indian child custody dispute because the parents, "by voluntarily invoking the state court's jurisdiction for divorce purposes,...clearly submitted the question of their children's custody to the judgment of the Montana state courts." 503 F.2d, at 795 (emphasis deleted).

The Report of the American Indian Policy Review Commission, an early proponent of the ICWA, makes clear the limited purposes that the term "domicile" was intended to serve:

> "Domicile is a legal concept that does not depend exclusively on one's physical location at any one given moment in time, rather it is based on the apparent intention of permanent residency. Many Indian families move back and forth from a reservation dwelling to border communities or even to distant communities, depending on employment and educational opportunities....In these situations, where family ties to the reservation are strong, but the child is

5. Significantly, the tribe cannot set aside a termination of parental rights on the ground that the adoptive placement provisions of § 1915, favoring placement with the tribe, have not been followed.

6. None of the cases cited approvingly by Congress involved a deliberate abandonment. In *Wakefield v. Little Light*, 276 Md. 333, 347 A.2d 228 (1975), the court upheld exclusive tribal jurisdiction where it was clear that there was no abandonment. In *Wisconsin Potowatomies of Hannahville Indian Community v. Houston*, 393 F.Supp. 719 (WD Mich. 1973), there was no abandonment, the children had lived on the reservation and were members of the Indian Tribe, and the children's clothing and toys were at a home on the reservation that continued to be available to them. Finally, in *In re Adoption of Buehl*, 87 Wash.2d 649, 555 P.2d 1334 (1976), the child was a ward of the tribal court and an enrolled member of the Tribe.

temporarily off the reservation, a fairly strong legal argument can be made for tribal court jurisdiction." Report on Federal, State, and Tribal Jurisdiction 86 (Comm.Print 1976).[7]

Although parents of Indian children are shielded from the exercise of state jurisdiction when they are temporarily off the reservation, the Act also reflects a recognition that allowing the tribe to defeat the parents' deliberate choice of jurisdiction would be conducive neither to the best interests of the child nor to the stability and security of Indian tribes and families. Section 1911(b), providing for the exercise of concurrent jurisdiction by state and tribal courts when the Indian child is not domiciled on the reservation, gives the Indian parents a veto to prevent the transfer of a state-court action to tribal court.[8] "By allowing the Indian parents to 'choose' the forum that will decide whether to sever the parent-child relationship, Congress promotes the security of Indian families by allowing the Indian parents to defend in the court system that most reflects the parents' familial standards." Jones, 21 Ariz.L.Rev., at 1141. As Mr. Calvin Isaac, Tribal Chief of the Mississippi Band of Choctaw Indians, stated in testimony to the House Subcommittee on Indian Affairs and Public Lands with respect to a different provision:

> "The ultimate responsibility for child welfare rests with the parents and we would not support legislation which interfered with that basic relationship." Hearings on S. 1214 before the Subcommittee on Indian Affairs and Public Lands of the House Committee on Interior and Insular Affairs, 95th Cong., 2d Sess., 62 (1978).[9]

7. In a letter to the House of Representatives, the Department of Justice explained its understanding that the provision was addressed to the involuntary termination of parental rights in tribal members by state agencies unaware of exclusive tribal jurisdiction:

"As you may be aware, the courts have consistently recognized that tribal governments have exclusive jurisdiction over the domestic relationships of tribal members located on reservations, unless a State has assumed concurrent jurisdiction pursuant to Federal legislation such as Public Law 83-280. It is our understanding that this legal principle is often ignored by local welfare organizations and foster homes in cases where they believe Indian children have been neglected, and that S.1214 is designed to remedy this, and to define Indian rights in such cases." House Report, at 35.

8. The explanation of this subsection in the House Report reads as follows:

"Subsection (b) directs a State court, having jurisdiction over an Indian child custody proceeding to transfer such proceeding, absent good cause to the contrary, to the appropriate tribal court upon the petition of the parents or the Indian tribe. Either parent is given the right to veto such transfer. The subsection is intended to permit a State court to apply a modified doctrine of *forum non conveniens*, in appropriate cases, to insure that the rights of the child as an Indian, the Indian parents or custodian, and the tribe are fully protected." *Id.*, at 21.

In commenting on the provision, the Department of Justice suggested that the section should be clarified to make it perfectly clear that a state court need not surrender jurisdiction of a child custody proceeding if the Indian parent objected. The Department of Justice letter stated:

"Section 101(b) should be amended to prohibit clearly the transfer of a child placement proceeding to a tribal court when any parent or child over the age of 12 objects to the transfer." *Id.*, at 32.

Although the specific suggestion made by the Department of Justice was not in fact implemented, it is noteworthy that there is nothing in the legislative history to suggest that the recommended change was in any way inconsistent with any of the purposes of the statute.

9. Chief Isaac elsewhere expressed a similar concern for the rights of parents with reference to another provision. See Hearing, *supra* n. 1, at 158 (statement on behalf of National Tribal Chairmen's Association) ("We believe the tribe should receive notice in all such cases but where the child is neither a resident nor domiciliary of the reservation intervention should require the consent of the natural parents or the blood relative in

If J.B. and W.J. had established a domicile off the reservation, the state courts would have been required to give effect to their choice of jurisdiction; there should not be a different result when the parents have not changed their own domicile, but have expressed an unequivocal intent to establish a domicile for their children off the reservation. The law of abandonment, as enunciated by the Mississippi Supreme Court in this case, does not defeat, but serves the purposes, of the Act. An abandonment occurs when a parent deserts a child and places the child with another with an intent to relinquish all parental rights and obligations. Restatement (Second) of Conflict of Laws § 22, Comment *e* (1971) (hereinafter Restatement); *In re Adoption of Halloway*, 732 P.2d 962, 966 (Utah 1986). If a child is abandoned by his mother, he takes on the domicile of his father; if the child is abandoned by his father, he takes on the domicile of his mother. Restatement § 22, Comment *e*; 25 Am.Jur.2d, Domicil § 69 (1966). If the child is abandoned by both parents, he takes on the domicile of a person other than the parents who stands *in loco parentis* to him. *In re Adoption of Halloway, supra*, at 966; *In re Estate of Moore*, 68 Wash.2d 792, 796, 415 P.2d 653, 656 (1966); *Harlan v. Industrial Accident Comm'n*, 194 Cal. 352, 228 P. 654 (1924); Restatement § 22, Comment *i*; cf. *In re Guardianship of D.L.L. and C.L.L.*, 291 N.W.2d 278, 282 (S.D. 1980).[10] To be effective, the intent to abandon or the actual physical abandonment must be shown by clear and convincing evidence. *In re Adoption of Halloway, supra*, at 966; *C.S. v. Smith*, 483 S.W.2d 790, 793 (Mo.App. 1972).[11]

When an Indian child is temporarily off the reservation, but has not been abandoned to a person off the reservation, the tribe has an interest in exclusive jurisdiction. The ICWA expresses the intent that exclusive tribal jurisdiction is not so frail that it should be defeated as soon as the Indian child steps off the reservation. Similarly, when the child is abandoned by one parent to a person off the reservation, the tribe and the other parent domiciled on the reservation may still have an interest in the exercise of exclusive jurisdiction. That interest is protected by the rule that a child abandoned by one parent takes on the domicile of the other. But when an Indian child is deliberately abandoned by both parents to a person off the reservation, no purpose of the ICWA is served by closing the state courthouse door to them. The interests of the parents, the Indian child, and the tribe in preventing the unwarranted removal of Indian children from their families and from the reservation are protected by the Act's substantive and procedural provisions. In addition, if both parents have intentionally

whose custody the child has been left by the natural parents. It seems there is a great potential in the provisions of section 101(c) for infringing parental wishes and rights").

10. The authority of a State to exercise jurisdiction over a child in a child custody dispute when the child is physically present in a State and has been abandoned is also recognized by federal statute. See Parental Kidnaping Prevention Act of 1980, 94 Stat. 3569, 28 U.S.C. § 1738A(c)(2); see also Uniform Child Custody Jurisdiction Act, 9 U.L.A. § 3 (1988).

11. The Court suggests that there could be no legally effective abandonment because the parents consented to termination of their parental rights before a judge of the state court and not a tribal court judge. That suggestion ignores the findings of the State Supreme Court that the natural parents did virtually everything they could do to abandon the children to persons outside the reservation: "[T]he Indian twins have never resided outside of Harrison County, Mississippi, and were voluntarily surrendered and legally abandoned by the natural parents to the adoptive parents, and it is undisputed that the parents went to some efforts to prevent the children from being placed on the reservation as the mother arranged for their birth and adoption in Gulfport Memorial Hospital, Harrison County, Mississippi." 511 So.2d 918, 921 (1987). In any event, even a consent to adoption that does not meet statutory requirements may be effective to constitute an abandonment and change the minor's domicile. See *Wilson v. Pierce*, 14 Utah 2d 317, 321, 383 P.2d 925, 927 (1963); H. Clark, Law of Domestic Relations in the United States 633 (1968).

invoked the jurisdiction of the state court in an action involving a non-Indian, no interest in tribal self-governance is implicated. See *McClanahan v. Arizona State Tax Comm'n*, 411 U.S. 164, 173 (1973); *Williams v. Lee*, 358 U.S. 217, 219–220 (1959); *Felix v. Patrick*, 145 U.S. 317, 332 (1892).

The interpretation of domicile adopted by the Court requires the custodian of an Indian child who is off the reservation to haul the child to a potentially distant tribal court unfamiliar with the child's present living conditions and best interests. Moreover, it renders any custody decision made by a state court forever suspect, susceptible to challenge at any time as void for having been entered in the absence of jurisdiction.[12] Finally, it forces parents of Indian children who desire to invoke state-court jurisdiction to establish a domicile off the reservation. Only if the custodial parent has the wealth and ability to establish a domicile off the reservation will the parent be able to use the processes of state court. I fail to see how such a requirement serves the paramount congressional purpose of "promot[ing] the stability and security of Indian tribes and families." 25 U.S.C. § 1902.

The Court concludes its opinion with the observation that whatever anguish is suffered by the Indian children, their natural parents, and their adoptive parents because of its decision today is a result of their failure to initially follow the provisions of the ICWA. By holding that parents who are domiciled on the reservation cannot voluntarily avail themselves of the adoption procedures of state court and that all such proceedings will be void for lack of jurisdiction, however, the Court establishes a rule of law that is virtually certain to ensure that similar anguish will be suffered by other families in the future. Because that result is not mandated by the language of the ICWA and is contrary to its purposes, I respectfully dissent.

NOTES AND QUESTIONS

1. What is the issue before the Court? What is the source of the disagreement between the Court and the dissent? Why is the Indian Child Welfare Act constitutional? In this case, the parents wanted the children to be adopted off reservation. How can Congress override parental choice?

12. The facts of *In re Adoption of Halloway*, 732 P.2d 962 (Utah 1986), which the Court cites approvingly, vividly illustrate the problem. In that case, the mother, a member of an Indian Tribe in New Mexico, voluntarily abandoned an Indian child to the custody of the child's maternal aunt off the reservation with the knowledge that the child would be placed for adoption in Utah. The mother learned of the adoption two weeks after the child left the reservation and did not object and, two months later, she executed a consent to adoption. Nevertheless, some two years after the petition for adoption was filed, the Indian Tribe intervened in the proceeding and set aside the adoption. The Tribe argued successfully that regardless of whether the Indian parent consented to it, the adoption was void because she resided on the reservation and thus the tribal court had exclusive jurisdiction. Although the decision in *Halloway*, and the Court's approving reference to it, may be colored somewhat by the fact that the mother in that case withdrew her consent (a fact which would entitle her to relief even if there were only concurrent jurisdiction, see 25 U.S.C. § 1913(c)), the rule set forth by the majority contains no such limitation. As the Tribe acknowledged at oral argument, any adoption of an Indian child effected through a state court will be susceptible of challenge by the Indian tribe no matter how old the child and how long it has lived with its adoptive parents.

2. The ICWA defines an "Indian child" as "any unmarried person who is under age eighteen and is either (a) a member of an Indian tribe or (b) is eligible for membership in an Indian tribe and is the biological child of a member of an Indian tribe." 25 U.S.C. § 1903 (2011). There are a variety of ways in which tribes determine membership, ranging from the degree of ethnicity to domicile. The act vests Indian tribal courts with exclusive jurisdiction over Indian children who reside on reservations whose custodial parents were living on a reservation immediately prior to a foster-care or adoption placement. 25 U.S.C. § 1911(a) (2011). Does the ICWA apply to children whose parents have never lived on the reservation?

3. If the state court proceeding involves the involuntary removal of a child who the party knows or has reason to believe is Indian, the petitioning party must notify the Indian child's tribe and the Department of the Interior by certified mail of the pendency of the state court action. When a child's tribal affiliation is unknown, the party must notify all tribes that may have some connection to the child, along with the Department of the Interior. The ICWA applies to foster-care proceedings in addition to guardianship, status offenses, termination of parental rights, preadoptive placement, and adoptions. The ICWA does not apply to divorce proceedings between parents, juvenile-delinquency proceedings, or cases under tribal court jurisdiction. Arguably, however, Indian children who are the subjects of private custody challenges involving a nonparent are entitled to the same familial and cultural protections of ICWA as those children in abuse or neglect proceedings and guardianships. See, e.g., Jill E. Thompkins, *Finding the Indian Child Welfare Act in Unexpected Places: Applicability in Private Non-parent Custody Actions*, 81 U. Colo. L. Rev. 1119 (Fall 2010). If a parent does not indicate that the child is Native American, how would a caseworker or the court know that the ICWA applies?

4. The Act establishes a series of procedural protections that exceed those required in state courts. These include a right of intervention for Indian parents and tribes; the tribe's right to notice of involuntary proceedings where the court has reason to know that an Indian child is involved; appointment of counsel for indigent parents or Indian custodians in any removal, placement, or termination proceeding; appointment of counsel for the child if in the child's best interests; and a requirement that state courts give full faith and credit to tribal acts and decrees relating to Indian child-custody proceedings. In addition, the ICWA increases the burden of proof to a level above that required as a matter of constitutional due process. For foster-care placements or other temporary removals, the state court must find by clear and convincing evidence that continued parental custody is likely to result in serious emotional or physical damage to the child. 25 U.S.C. § 1912 (2011).

Even when transfer is not permitted, the child's tribe and family will have an opportunity to be involved in decisions affecting services for the Indian child. ICWA requires the state to make *active* efforts in every ICWA case in two areas: (1) to provide services to the family to prevent removal of an Indian child from his or her parent or Indian custodian and (2) to reunify an Indian child with his or her parent or Indian custodian after removal. 25 U.S.C. § 1912(d). Active efforts are more intensive than "reasonable efforts." For example, while reasonable efforts might be only a referral for services, active efforts would be to arrange for the best-fitting services and help families engage in those services. In order to satisfy the "active effort" requirement, a court must determine that the state caseworker took the client through the steps of the plan, rather than requiring that the plan be performed on its own. See, e.g., The Indian Child Welfare Act and Laws Affecting Indian Juveniles Manual 157–158 (1984); *Dale H. v. State Dep't of Health & Social Servs.*, 235 P.3d 203, 213 (Alaska 2010).

5. When ICWA applies, the state court is required to transfer jurisdiction to the tribe upon request, except when one parent objects or the court finds that good cause has been shown. 25 U.S.C. § 1911(b) (2011). This seemingly gives either parent an absolute veto over the transfer option. In addressing challenges for good cause, Bureau of Indian Affairs guidelines provide that good cause not to transfer exists if there is no tribal court to which the case can be transferred or if any of the following circumstances exist: (1) the proceeding was at an advanced stage when the petition to transfer was received, and the petitioner did not file the petition promptly after receiving notice of the hearing; (2) the Indian child is older than twelve and objects to the transfer; (3) the evidence necessary to decide the case could not be adequately presented in the tribal court without undue hardship to the parties or the witnesses; or (4) the parents of a child older than five are not available, and the child has had little or no contact with the child's tribe or members of the child's tribe. Some state courts have adopted a "contrary to the best interest of the child" standard when deliberating a transfer request—even though such a standard is not included in the law or guidelines—and have invoked it as grounds to deny a transfer when the Indian child has already "bonded" to his or her foster caretaker(s). See, e.g., Dep't of the Interior Guidelines, 44 Fed. Reg. No. 228, p. 67584 (Nov. 26, 1979) (party opposing transfer to tribal court has burden of showing good cause by clear and convincing evidence).

6. Does the "good cause" exception swallow the exclusive-jurisdiction rule? Some state courts have refused to follow the placement preferences of the ICWA where neither the child nor the parents have a social, cultural, or political relationship with the tribe. The judicially created "existing Indian family" exception has generated considerable controversy. For those criticizing the exception, see, e.g., Michael J. Dale, *State Court Jurisdiction under the Indian Child Welfare Act and the Unstated Best Interest of the Child Test*, 27 Gonz. L. Rev. 353 (1991–1992) (noting that state courts continue to apply Anglo best-interests test to avoid application of ICWA); Lorie Graham, *Reparations and the Indian Child Welfare Act*, 25 Legal Stud. F. 619 (2001) (criticizing state courts for failing to transfer cases to tribal courts, ignoring statutory placement preferences, and creating judicial exceptions to ICWA); Jose Monsivais, *A Glimmer of Hope: A Proposal to Keep the Indian Child Welfare Act of 1978 Intact*, 22 Am. Indian L. Rev. 1, 28 (1997) (concluding that existing-Indian-family exception to ICWA creates "dangerous precedent for state courts, hostile to the Act, to follow"); Wendy Therese Parnell, *The Existing Indian Family Exception: Denying Trial Rights Protected by the Indian Child Welfare Act*, 34 San Diego L. Rev. 381, 437 (1997) (criticizing state courts' use of existing-Indian-family exception as "continuing threat to tribal interests and the survival of Indian culture"); Samuel Prim, Note, *The Indian Child Welfare Act and the Existing Indian Family Exception: Rerouting the Trail of Tears*, 24 L. & Psych. Rev. 115 (2000) (concluding that existing-Indian-family exception continues breakdown of Indian families and tribes, is result of state courts' ignorance and lack of appreciation for Indian customs, and amounts to modern-day Trail of Tears). For those advocating the use of the exception, see, e.g., Christine D. Bakeis, *The Indian Child Welfare Act of 1978: Violating Personal Rights for the Sake of the Tribe*, 10 Notre Dame J. L. Ethics & Pub. Pol'y 543 (1996) (urging codification of existing-Indian-family exception and amendment to allow parents to block statutory placement preferences); Michele K. Bennett, *Native American Children: Caught in the Web of the Indian Child Welfare Act*, 16 Hamline L. Rev. 953 (1993) (criticizing ICWA and recommending that state courts continue to consider child's best interests, including child's need for permanency); Hassan Saffouri, *The Good Cause Exception to the Indian Child Welfare Act's Placement Preferences: The Minnesota Supreme Court Sets a Difficult (Impossible?) Standard—In re the Custody of S.E.G.*, 21 Wm. Mitchell L. Rev. 1191 (1996)

(arguing that Minnesota Supreme Court's decision effectively precludes non-Indian families from adoption of Indian children).

For an excellent overview of the challenges posed by the ICWA, see Barbara Ann Atwood, *Flashpoints under the ICWA: Toward a New Understanding of State Court Resistance*, 51 EMORY L.J. 587 (2002). For additional commentary, see Barbara Ann Atwood, *Tribal Jurisprudence and the Cultural Meaning of Family*, 79 NEB. L. REV. 577 (2000); Barbara Ann Atwood, *Fighting over Indian Children: The Uses and Abuses of Jurisdictional Ambiguity*, 36 U.C.L.A. L. REV. 1051 (1989); Jeanne Louise Carriere, *Representing the Native American: Culture, Jurisdiction, and the Indian Child Welfare Act*, 79 IOWA L. REV. 585 (1994); Joan Heifetz Hollinger, *Beyond the Best Interests of the Tribe: The Indian Child Welfare Act and the Adoption of Indian Children*, 66 U. DET. L. REV. 451 (1989).

7. According to 25 U.S.C. § 1915 (b), any Indian child accepted for foster care "shall be placed in the least restrictive setting which most approximates a family and in which his special needs, if any, may be met. The child shall also be placed within reasonable proximity to his or her home, taking into account any special needs of the child." There are placement preferences, with priority given to placement with a member of the child's extended family; a foster home licensed, approved, or specified by the Indian child's tribe; an Indian foster home licensed or approved by an authorized non-Indian licensing authority; or an institution for children approved by an Indian tribe or operated by an Indian organization that has a program suitable to meet the Indian child's needs. 25 U.S.C. §§ 1915(b)(i)–(iv). The Indian tribe may establish a different order of preference that must be followed provided the placement is the least restrictive and serves the child's needs. 25 U.S.C. § 1915(c). "The standards to be applied in meeting the preference requirements of this section shall be the prevailing social and cultural standards of the Indian community in which the parent or extended family resides or with which the parent or extended family members maintain social and cultural ties." 25 U.S.C. § 1915(d).

Are these generally good rules for the placement of any child in foster care? Should the federal government mandate the same sort of rules for all children?

8. After the Court issued its ruling in *Holyfield*, the tribe decided that it was in the children's best interests to remain with Holyfield. Does this suggest that the Court was right when it noted that a decision about jurisdiction was not a decision on the merits?

b. LGBTQ CHILDREN

Child-welfare and juvenile-justice agencies also deal with a significant number of lesbian, gay, bisexual, transgender, and questioning (LGBTQ) youths. A growing number of commentators have charged that the public systems entrusted with the care and well-being of these youths have been indifferent to their needs and slow to provide appropriate and equitable care. Accordingly, LGBTQ youths are often rejected, harassed, and discriminated against in foster care and are commonly moved from home to home because of overt discrimination or harassment from peers, caregivers, and staff and reporting that there is a disproportionate number of LGBTQ youths in foster care. See, e.g., Shannan Wilber, Caitlin Ryan, & Jody Marksamer, Child Welfare League of America, CWLA Best Practice Guidelines: Serving LGBT Youth in Out-of-Home Care 1 (2006). Evidence indicates that LGBTQ youths often face insensitive and discriminatory treatment, outright harassment, and violence at the hands of the child-welfare staff. Barbara Fedders, *Coming Out for Kids: Recognizing, Respecting, and Representing LGBTQ Youth*, 6 NEV. L.J. 774 (2006); Colleen Sullivan et al., Lambda Legal Defense & Education Fund, Youth in the Margins: A Report on the Unmet Needs of Lesbian, Gay, Bisexual, and Transgender Adolescents in Foster Care 7, 11 (2001). LGBTQ youths in foster care also may be placed in foster homes with foster parents who require them to attend "reparative" therapy or religious services to renounce their sexuality or gender identity. Fedders, *Coming Out for Kids*, *supra*, at 795. Child-welfare caseworkers also may not know about community-based services and organizations serving LGBTQ youths. *Id.*

There are currently no federal laws that explicitly require state foster-care agencies to refrain from discriminating against foster youths because of sexual orientation or gender identity. The federal law prohibiting agencies that receive federal funding for foster care from denying or delaying foster-care placements "on the basis of the race, color, or national origin of the adoptive or foster parent, or the child, involved," 42 U.S.C. § 671(a)(18)(B), omits sexual orientation or gender identity. See James W. Gilliam, Jr., *Toward Providing a Welcoming Home for All: Enacting a New Approach to Address the Longstanding Problems Lesbian, Gay, Bisexual, and Transgender Youth Face in the Foster Care System*, 37 LOY. L.A. L. REV. 1037, 1045 (2004).

Statistics indicate that LGBTQ youths face daily incidents of emotional and physical abuse. A national survey of LGBTQ students conducted in 2009 found that within the past year, 72.4 percent heard remarks such as "faggot" or "dyke" frequently or often at school (similar studies have shown that the average high school student hears such epithets twenty-five times a day); 17 percent heard similar remarks from faculty or school staff at least some of the time; 84.8 percent reported that faculty or staff never or only sometimes intervened when they were present when such remarks were made; 84.6 percent personally had been verbally harassed at school because of their sexual orientation; 68.2 percent had been sexually harassed (e.g., inappropriately touched or subjected to sexual comments); 40.1 percent had been physically harassed (by being shoved or pushed), and 18.8 percent had been assaulted (by being punched, kicked, or injured with a weapon) at school because of their sexual orientation; 27.2 percent had been physically harassed because of their gender expression; 12.5 percent had been assaulted on that basis; 61.1 percent felt unsafe in their school because of their sexual orientation. LGBTQ youths of color and female students face abuse often compounded by racism and sexism. Office of Public Policy of the Gay, Lesbian and Straight Education Network (GLSEN), National School Climate Survey (20039), http://www.glsen.org (surveying a sample of over 7,000 LGBTQ students from all fifty states and the District of Columbia).

The inability of parents and school officials to deal with gender-identity issues often results in children leaving homes. Studies suggest that approximately one out of every four LGBTQ youths are forced out of their homes because of conflicts with families over their sexual orientation or gender identity. The U.S. Department of Health and Human Services estimates that the number of homeless and runaway youths ranges from 575,000 to 1.6 million per year. Out-of-home placements often do not provide a safe or stable alternative. A study of lesbian and gay youths in New York City's child-welfare system found that more than half (56 percent) of the youths interviewed said they stayed on the streets at times because they felt safer there than living in group or foster homes. Among LGBTQ homeless youths in San Diego, 39 percent said they were ejected from their homes or placements because of their sexual orientation. In one study, 78 percent of LGBTQ youths were removed or ran away from their placements as a result of hostility toward their sexual orientation or gender identity. Wilber, Ryan, & Marksamer, Serving LGBT Youth. In Los Angeles, an estimated 25 to 35 percent of street youths are gay; in Seattle, the estimate is 40 percent. Gabe Kruks, *Gay and Lesbian Homeless/Street Youth: Special Issues and Concerns*, 12 J. Adolescent Health 515 (1991).

Solutions to the problems of LGBTQ youths in foster care are neither easy nor clear. Litigation strategies have focused on ensuring the LGBTQ foster child's constitutional rights to safety, equal protection, and freedom of speech and religion. Rudy Estrada & Jody Merksamer, *Lesbian, Gay, Bisexual, and Transgender Young People in State Custody: Making the Child Welfare and Juvenile Justice Systems Safe for All Youth through Litigation*, 79 Temp. L. Rev. 415, 422–434 (2006). The Child Welfare League of America is educating and training child-welfare professionals about innovative programs and practices for LGBTQ youths. See Child Welfare League of America, Sexual Orientation/Lesbian, Gay, Bisexual, Transgender and Questioning Youth Issues, http://cwla.org/programs/culture/glbtq.htm. The Child Welfare League also has published best-practices guidelines for serving LGBTQ youths. See Wilber, Ryan, & Marksamer, Serving LGBT Youth. Additionally, traditional lawyering, grounded in concepts of zealous advocacy based on client preferences, may better serve LGBTQ youths. See, e.g., Sarah E. Valentine, *Traditional Advocacy for Nontraditional Youth: Rethinking Best Interest for the Queer Child*, 2008 Mich. St. L. Rev. 1053 (2008).

F. Termination of Parental Rights

1. CONSTITUTIONAL FRAMEWORK

STANLEY V. ILLINOIS
Supreme Court of the United States
405 U.S. 645 (1972)

MR. JUSTICE WHITE delivered the opinion of the Court.

Joan Stanley lived with Peter Stanley intermittently for 18 years, during which time they had three children. When Joan Stanley died, Peter Stanley lost not only her but also his children. Under Illinois law, the children of unwed fathers become wards of the State upon the death of the mother. Accordingly, upon Joan Stanley's death, in a dependency proceeding instituted by the State of Illinois, Stanley's children[2] were declared wards of the State and placed with court-appointed guardians. Stanley appealed, claiming that he had never been shown to be an unfit parent and that since married fathers and unwed mothers could not be deprived of their children without such a showing, he had been deprived of the equal protection of the laws guaranteed him by the Fourteenth Amendment. The Illinois Supreme Court accepted the fact that Stanley's own unfitness had not been established but rejected the equal protection claim, holding that Stanley could properly be separated from his children upon proof of the single fact that he and the dead mother had not been married. Stanley's actual fitness as a father was irrelevant. *In re Stanley*, 45 Ill.2d 132, 256 N.E.2d 814 (1970).

Stanley presses his equal protection claim here. The State continues to respond that unwed fathers are presumed unfit to raise their children and that it is unnecessary to hold individualized hearings to determine whether particular fathers are in fact unfit parents before they are separated from their children. We granted certiorari, 400 U.S. 1020 (1971), to determine whether this method of procedure by presumption could be allowed to stand in light of the fact that Illinois allows married fathers—whether divorced, widowed, or separated—and mothers—even if unwed—the benefit of the presumption that they are fit to raise their children.

2. Only two children are involved in this litigation.

I

At the outset we reject any suggestion that we need not consider the propriety of the dependency proceeding that separated the Stanleys because Stanley might be able to regain custody of his children as a guardian or through adoption proceedings. The suggestion is that if Stanley has been treated differently from other parents, the difference is immaterial and not legally cognizable for the purposes of the Fourteenth Amendment. This Court has not, however, embraced the general proposition that a wrong may be done if it can be undone. Cf. *Sniadach v. Family Finance Corp. of Bay View*, 395 U.S. 337 (1969). Surely, in the case before us, if there is delay between the doing and the undoing petitioner suffers from the deprivation of his children, and the children suffer from uncertainty and dislocation.

It is clear, moreover, that Stanley does not have the means at hand promptly to erase the adverse consequences of the proceeding in the course of which his children were declared wards of the State. It is first urged that Stanley could act to adopt his children. But under Illinois law, Stanley is treated not as a parent but as a stranger to his children, and the dependency proceeding has gone forward on the presumption that he is unfit to exercise parental rights. Insofar as we are informed, Illinois law affords him no priority in adoption proceedings. It would be his burden to establish not only that he would be a suitable parent but also that he would be the most suitable of all who might want custody of the children. Neither can we ignore that in the proceedings from which this action developed, the "probation officer," see App. 17, the assistant state's attorney, see *id.*, at 29–30, and the judge charged with the case, see *id.*, at 16–18, 23, made it apparent that Stanley, unmarried and impecunious as he is, could not now expect to profit from adoption proceedings.[3] The Illinois Supreme Court apparently recognized some or all of these considerations, because it did not suggest that Stanley's case was undercut by his failure to petition for adoption.

Before us, the State focuses on Stanley's failure to petition for "custody and control"—the second route by which, it is urged, he might regain authority for his children. Passing the obvious issue whether it would be futile or burdensome for an unmarried father—without funds and already once presumed unfit—to petition for custody, this suggestion overlooks the fact that legal custody is not parenthood or adoption. A person appointed guardian in an action for custody and control is subject to removal at any time without such cause as must be shown in a neglect proceeding against a parent. Ill.Rev.Stat., c. 37, § 705-8. He may not take the children out of the jurisdiction without the court's approval. He may be required to report to the court as to his disposition of the children's affairs. Ill.Rev.Stat., c. 37, § 705-8. Obviously then, even if Stanley were a mere step away from "custody and control," to give an unwed father only "custody and control" would still be to leave him seriously prejudiced by reason of his status.

We must therefore examine the question that Illinois would have us avoid: Is a presumption that distinguishes and burdens all unwed fathers constitutionally repugnant? We conclude that, as a matter of due process of law, Stanley was entitled to a hearing on his fitness as a parent before his children were taken from him and that, by denying him a hearing

3. The Illinois Supreme Court's opinion is not at all contrary to this conclusion. That court said: "(T)he trial court's comments clearly indicate the court's willingness to consider a future request by the father *for custody and guardianship*." 45 Ill.2d 132, 135, 256 N.E.2d 814, 816. (Italics added.) See also the comment of Stanley's counsel on oral argument: "If Peter Stanley could have adopted his children, we would not be here today." Tr. of Oral Arg. 7.

and extending it to all other parents whose custody of their children is challenged, the State denied Stanley the equal protection of the laws guaranteed by the Fourteenth Amendment.

II

Illinois has two principal methods of removing nondelinquent children from the homes of their parents. In a dependency proceeding it may demonstrate that the children are wards of the State because they have no surviving parent or guardian. Ill.Rev.Stat., c. 37, § 702-1, 702-5. In a neglect proceeding it may show that children should be wards of the State because the present parent(s) or guardian does not provide suitable care. Ill.Rev.Stat., c. 37, § 702-1, 702-4.

The State's right—indeed, duty—to protect minor children through a judicial determination of their interests in a neglect proceeding is not challenged here. Rather, we are faced with a dependency statute that empowers state officials to circumvent neglect proceedings on the theory that an unwed father is not a "parent" whose existing relationship with his children must be considered.[4] "Parents," says the State, "means the father and mother of a legitimate child, or the survivor of them, or the natural mother of an illegitimate child, and includes any adoptive parent," Ill.Rev.Stat., c. 37, § 701-14, but the term does not include unwed fathers.

Under Illinois law, therefore, while the children of all parents can be taken from them in neglect proceedings, that is only after notice, hearing, and proof of such unfitness as a parent as amounts to neglect, an unwed father is uniquely subject to the more simplistic dependency proceeding. By use of this proceeding, the State, on showing that the father was not married to the mother, need not prove unfitness in fact, because it is presumed at law. Thus, the unwed father's claim of parental qualification is avoided as "irrelevant."

In considering this procedure under the Due Process Clause, we recognize, as we have in other cases, that due process of law does not require a hearing "in every conceivable case of government impairment of private interest." *Cafeteria and Restaurant Workers Union etc. v. McElroy*, 367 U.S. 886, 894 (1961). That case explained that "(t)he very nature of due process negates any concept of inflexible procedures universally applicable to every imaginable situation" and firmly established that "what procedures due process may require under any given set of circumstances must begin with a determination of the precise nature of the government function involved as well as of the private interest that has been affected by governmental action." *Id.*, at 895; *Goldberg v. Kelly*, 397 U.S. 254, 263 (1970).

The private interest here, that of a man in the children he has sired and raised, undeniably warrants deference and, absent a powerful countervailing interest, protection. It is plain that the interest of a parent in the companionship, care, custody, and management of his or her children "come(s) to this Court with a momentum for respect lacking when appeal is made to liberties which derive merely from shifting economic arrangements." *Kovacs v. Cooper*, 336 U.S. 77, 95 (1949) (Frankfurter, J., concurring).

The Court has frequently emphasized the importance of the family. The rights to conceive and to raise one's children have been deemed "essential," *Meyer v. Nebraska*, 262 U.S. 390, 399 (1923), "basic civil rights of man," *Skinner v. Oklahoma*, 316 U.S. 535, 541 (1942), and "[r]ights

4. Even while refusing to label him a "legal parent," the State does not deny that Stanley has a special interest in the outcome of these proceedings. It is undisputed that he is the father of these children, that he lived with the two children whose custody is challenged all their lives, and that he has supported them.

far more precious...than property rights," *May v. Anderson*, 345 U.S. 528, 533 (1953). "It is cardinal with us that the custody, care and nurture of the child reside first in the parents, whose primary function and freedom include preparation for obligations the state can neither supply nor hinder." *Prince v. Massachusetts*, 321 U.S. 158, 166 (1944). The integrity of the family unit has found protection in the Due Process Clause of the Fourteenth Amendment, *Meyer v. Nebraska*, *supra*, 262 U.S. at 399, the Equal Protection Clause of the Fourteenth Amendment, *Skinner v. Oklahoma*, *supra*, 316 U.S., at 541, and the Ninth Amendment, *Griswold v. Connecticut*, 381 U.S. 479, 496 (1965) (Goldberg, J., concurring).

Nor has the law refused to recognize those family relationships unlegitimized by a marriage ceremony. The Court has declared unconstitutional a state statute denying natural, but illegitimate, children a wrongful-death action for the death of their mother, emphasizing that such children cannot be denied the right of other children because familial bonds in such cases were often as warm, enduring, and important as those arising within a more formally organized family unit. *Levy v. Louisiana*, 391 U.S. 68, 71–72 (1968). "To say that the test of equal protection should be the 'legal' rather than the biological relationship is to avoid the issue. For the Equal Protection Clause necessarily limits the authority of a State to draw such 'legal' lines as it chooses." *Glona v. American Guarantee & Liability Ins. Co.*, 391 U.S. 73, 75–76 (1968).

These authorities make it clear that, at the least, Stanley's interest in retaining custody of his children is cognizable and substantial.

For its part, the State has made its interest quite plain: Illinois has declared that the aim of the Juvenile Court Act is to protect "the moral, emotional, mental, and physical welfare of the minor and the best interests of the community" and to "strengthen the minor's family ties whenever possible, removing him from the custody of his parents only when his welfare or safety or the protection of the public cannot be adequately safeguarded without removal..." Ill.Rev.Stat., c. 37, § 701-2. These are legitimate interests, well within the power of the State to implement. We do not question the assertion that neglectful parents may be separated from their children.

But we are here not asked to evaluate the legitimacy of the state ends, rather, to determine whether the means used to achieve these ends are constitutionally defensible. What is the state interest in separating children from fathers without a hearing designed to determine whether the father is unfit in a particular disputed case? We observe that the State registers no gain towards its declared goals when it separates children from the custody of fit parents. Indeed, if Stanley is a fit father, the State spites its own articulated goals when it needlessly separates him from his family.

In *Bell v. Burson*, 402 U.S. 535 (1971), we found a scheme repugnant to the Due Process Clause because it deprived a driver of his license without reference to the very factor (there fault in driving, here fitness as a parent) that the State itself deemed fundamental to its statutory scheme. Illinois would avoid the self-contradiction that rendered the Georgia license suspension system invalid by arguing that Stanley and all other unmarried fathers can reasonably be presumed to be unqualified to raise their children.[5]

5. Illinois says in its brief, at 21–23,

"(T)he only relevant consideration in determining the propriety of governmental intervention in the raising of children is whether the best interests of the child are served by such intervention.

It may be, as the State insists, that most unmarried fathers are unsuitable and neglectful parents. It may also be that Stanley is such a parent and that his children should be placed in other hands. But all unmarried fathers are not in this category; some are wholly suited to have custody of their children.[7] This much the State readily concedes, and nothing in this record indicates that Stanley is or has been a neglectful father who has not cared for his children. Given the opportunity to make his case, Stanley may have been seen to be deserving of custody of his offspring. Had this been so, the State's statutory policy would have been furthered by leaving custody in him.

Carrington v. Rash, 380 U.S. 89 (1965), dealt with a similar situation. There we recognized that Texas had a powerful interest in restricting its electorate to bona fide residents. It was not disputed that most servicemen stationed in Texas had no intention of remaining in the State; most therefore could be deprived of a vote in state affairs. But we refused to tolerate a blanket exclusion depriving all servicemen of the vote, when some servicemen clearly were bona fide residents and when "more precise tests," *id.*, at 95, were available to distinguish members of this latter group. "By forbidding a soldier ever to controvert the presumption of

"In effect, Illinois has imposed a statutory presumption that the best interests of a particular group of children necessitates some governmental supervision in certain clearly defined situations. The group of children who are illegitimate are distinguishable from legitimate children not so much by their status at birth as by the factual differences in their upbringing. While a legitimate child usually is raised by both parents with the attendant familial relationships and a firm concept of home and identity, the illegitimate child normally knows only one parent—the mother....

"...The petitioner has premised his argument upon particular factual circumstances—a lengthy relationship with the mother...a familial relationship with the two children, and a general assumption that this relationship approximates that in which the natural parents are married to each other.

"...Even if this characterization were accurate (the record is insufficient to support it) it would not affect the validity of the statutory definition of parent....The petitioner does not deny that the children are illegitimate. The record reflects their natural mother's death. Given these two factors, grounds exist for the State's intervention to ensure adequate care and protection for these children. This is true whether or not this particular petitioner assimilates all or none of the normal characteristics common to the classification of fathers who are not married to the mothers of their children.

See also Illinois' Brief 23 ("The comparison of married and putative fathers involves exclusively factual differences. The most significant of these are the presence or absence of the father from the home on a day-to-day basis and the responsibility imposed upon the relationship"), *id.*, at 24 (to the same effect), *id.*, at 31..., *id.*, at 24–26 (physiological and other studies are cited in support of the proposition that men are not naturally inclined to childrearing), and Tr. of Oral Arg. 31 ("We submit that both based on history or (*sic*) culture the very real differences...between the married father and the unmarried father, in terms of their interests in children and their legal responsibility for their children, that the statute here fulfills the compelling governmental objective of protecting children...").

7. See *In re T.*, 8 Mich.App. 122, 154 N.W.2d 27 (1967). There a panel of the Michigan Court of Appeals in unanimously affirming a circuit court's determination that the father of an illegitimate son was best suited to raise the boy, said:

"The appellants' presentation in this case proceeds on the assumption that placing Mark for adoption is inherently preferable to rearing by his father, that uprooting him from the family which he knew from birth until he was a year and a half old, secretly institutionalizing him and later transferring him to strangers is so incontrovertibly better that no court has the power even to consider the matter. Hardly anyone would even suggest such a proposition if we were talking about a child born in wedlock.

"We are not aware of any sociological data justifying the assumption that an illegitimate child reared by his natural father is less likely to receive a proper upbringing than one reared by his natural father who was at one time married to his mother, or that the stigma of illegitimacy is so pervasive it requires adoption by strangers and permanent termination of a subsisting relationship with the child's father." *Id.*, at 146, 154 N.W.2d, at 39.

nonresidence," *id.*, at 96, the State, we said, unjustifiably effected a substantial deprivation. It viewed people one-dimensionally (as servicemen) when a finer perception could readily have been achieved by assessing a serviceman's claim to residency on an individualized basis.

> "We recognize that special problems may be involved in determining whether servicemen have actually acquired a new domicile in a State for franchise purposes. We emphasize that Texas is free to take reasonable and adequate steps, as have other States, to see that all applicants for the vote actually fulfill the requirements of bona fide residence. But (the challenged) provision goes beyond such rules. '(T)he presumption here created is... definitely conclusive—incapable of being overcome by proof of the most positive character.'" *Id.*, at 96, 85 S.Ct., at 780.

"All servicemen not residents of Texas before induction," we concluded, "come within the provision's sweep. Not one of them can ever vote in Texas, no matter" what their individual qualifications. *Ibid.* We found such a situation repugnant to the Equal Protection Clause.

Despite *Bell* and *Carrington*, it may be argued that unmarried fathers are so seldom fit that Illinois need not undergo the administrative inconvenience of inquiry in any case, including Stanley's. The establishment of prompt efficacious procedures to achieve legitimate state ends is a proper state interest worthy of cognizance in constitutional adjudication. But the Constitution recognizes higher values than speed and efficiency.[8] Indeed, one might fairly say of the Bill of Rights in general, and the Due Process Clause in particular, that they were designed to protect the fragile values of a vulnerable citizenry from the overbearing concern for efficiency and efficacy that may characterize praiseworthy government officials no less, and perhaps more, than mediocre ones.

Procedure by presumption is always cheaper and easier than individualized determination. But when, as here, the procedure forecloses the determinative issues of competence and care, when it explicitly disdains present realities in deference to past formalities, it needlessly risks running roughshod over the important interests of both parent and child. It therefore cannot stand.[9]

8. Cf. *Reed v. Reed*, 404 U.S. 71, 76 (1971). "Clearly the objective of reducing the workload on probate courts by eliminating one class of contests is not without some legitimacy.... (But to) give a mandatory preference to members of either sex over members of the other, merely to accomplish the elimination of hearings on the merits, is to make the very kind of arbitrary legislative choice forbidden by the Equal Protection Clause of the Fourteenth Amendment." *Carrington v. Rash*, 380 U.S. 89, 96 (1965), teaches the same lesson. "... States may not casually deprive a class of individuals of the vote because of some remote administrative benefit to the State. *Oyama v. (State of) California*, 332 U.S. 633. By forbidding a soldier ever to controvert the presumption of nonresidence, the Texas Constitution imposes an invidious discrimination in violation of the Fourteenth Amendment."

9. We note in passing that the incremental cost of offering unwed fathers an opportunity for individualized hearings on fitness appears to be minimal. If unwed fathers, in the main, do not care about the disposition of their children, they will not appear to demand hearings. If they do care, under the scheme here held invalid, Illinois would admittedly at some later time have to afford them a properly focused hearing in a custody or adoption proceeding.

Extending opportunity for hearing to unwed fathers who desire and claim competence to care for their children creates no constitutional or procedural obstacle to foreclosing those unwed fathers who are not so inclined. The Illinois law governing procedure in juvenile cases, Ill.Rev.Stat., c. 37, § 704-1 *et seq.*, provides for personal service, notice by certified mail, or for notice by publication when personal or certified mail service cannot be had or when notice is directed to unknown respondents under the style of "All whom it may

Bell v. Burson held that the State could not, while purporting to be concerned with fault in suspending a driver's license, deprive a citizen of his license without a hearing that would assess fault. Absent fault, the State's declared interest was so attenuated that administrative convenience was insufficient to excuse a hearing where evidence of fault could be considered. That drivers involved in accidents, as a statistical matter, might be very likely to have been wholly or partially at fault did not foreclose hearing and proof in specific cases before licenses were suspended.

We think the Due Process Clause mandates a similar result here. The State's interest in caring for Stanley's children is *de minimis* if Stanley is shown to be a fit father. It insists on presuming rather than proving Stanley's unfitness solely because it is more convenient to presume than to prove. Under the Due Process Clause that advantage is insufficient to justify refusing a father a hearing when the issue at stake is the dismemberment of his family.

III

The State of Illinois assumes custody of the children of married parents, divorced parents, and unmarried mothers only after a hearing and proof of neglect. The children of unmarried fathers, however, are declared dependent children without a hearing on parental fitness and without proof of neglect. Stanley's claim in the state courts and here is that failure to afford him a hearing on his parental qualifications while extending it to other parents denied him equal protection of the laws. We have concluded that all Illinois parents are constitutionally entitled to a hearing on their fitness before their children are removed from their custody. It follows that denying such a hearing to Stanley and those like him while granting it to other Illinois parents is inescapably contrary to the Equal Protection Clause.

The judgment of the Supreme Court of Illinois is reversed and the case is remanded to that court for proceedings not inconsistent with this opinion....

MR. JUSTICE POWELL and MR. JUSTICE REHNQUIST took no part in the consideration or decision of this case.

MR. JUSTICE DOUGLAS joins in Parts I and II of this opinion.

MR. CHIEF JUSTICE BURGER, with whom MR. JUSTICE BLACKMUN concurs, dissenting.

The only constitutional issue raised and decided in the courts of Illinois in this case was whether the Illinois statute that omits unwed fathers from the definition of "parents" violates the Equal Protection Clause. We granted certiorari to consider whether the Illinois Supreme Court properly resolved that equal protection issue when it unanimously upheld the statute against petitioner Stanley's attack.

No due process issue was raised in the state courts; and no due process issue was decided by any state court. As MR. JUSTICE DOUGLAS said for this Court in *State Farm Mutual Automobile Ins. Co. v. Duel*, 324 U.S. 154, 160 (1945), "Since the [state] Supreme Court did not pass on the question, we may not do so." We had occasion more recently to deal with this aspect of the jurisdictional limits placed upon this Court by 28 U.S.C. § 1257 when we decided *Hill v. California*, 401 U.S. 797 (1971). Having rejected the claim that *Chimel v. California*, 395 U.S. 752 (1969), should be retroactively applied to invalidate petitioner Hill's conviction on

Concern." Unwed fathers who do not promptly respond cannot complain if their children are declared wards of the State. Those who do respond retain the burden of proving their fatherhood.

the ground that a search incident to arrest was overly extensive in scope, the Court noted Hill's additional contention that his personal diary, which was one of the items of evidence seized in that search, should have been excluded on Fifth Amendment grounds as well. Mr. Justice White, in his opinion for the Court, concluded that we lacked jurisdiction to consider the Fifth Amendment contention:

> "Counsel for [the petitioner] conceded at oral argument that the Fifth Amendment issue was not raised at trial. Nor was the issue raised, briefed or argued in the California appellate courts. [Footnote omitted.] The petition for certiorari likewise ignored it. In this posture of the case, the question, although briefed and argued here, is not properly before us." 401 U.S., at 805.

In the case now before us, it simply does not suffice to say, as the Court in a footnote does say, that "we dispose of the case on the constitutional premise raised below, reaching the result by a method of analysis readily available to the state court." The Court's method of analysis seems to ignore the strictures of Justices Douglas and White, but the analysis is clear: the Court holds *sua sponte* that the Due Process Clause requires that Stanley, the unwed biological father, be accorded a hearing as to his fitness as a parent before his children are declared wards of the state court; the Court then reasons that since Illinois recognizes such rights to due process in married fathers, it is required by the Equal Protection Clause to give such protection to unmarried fathers. This "method of analysis" is, of course, no more or less than the use of the Equal Protection Clause as a shorthand condensation of the entire Constitution: a State may not deny any constitutional right to some of its citizens without violating the Equal Protection Clause through its failure to deny such rights to all of its citizens. The limits on this Court's jurisdiction are not properly expandable by the use of such semantic devices as that.

Not only does the Court today use dubious reasoning in dealing with limitations upon its jurisdiction, it proceeds as well to strike down the Illinois statute here involved by "answering" arguments that are nowhere to be found in the record or in the State's brief—or indeed in the oral argument. I have been unable, for example, to discover where or when the State has advanced any argument that "it is unnecessary to hold individualized hearings to determine whether particular fathers are in fact unfit parents before they are separated from their children." Nor can I discover where the State has "argu(ed) that Stanley and all other unmarried fathers can reasonably be presumed to be unqualified to raise their children." Or where anyone has even remotely suggested the "argu(ment) that unmarried fathers are so seldom fit that Illinois need not undergo the administrative inconvenience of inquiry in any case, including Stanley's." On the other hand, the arguments actually advanced by the State are largely ignored by the Court.[1]

1. In reaching out to find a due process issue in this case, the Court seems to have misapprehended the entire thrust of the State's argument. When explaining at oral argument why Illinois does not recognize the unwed father, counsel for the State presented two basic justifications for the statutory definition of "parents" here at issue. See Tr. of Oral Arg. 25–26. First, counsel noted that in the case of a married couple to whom a legitimate child is born, the two biological parents have already "signified their willingness to work together" in caring for the child by entering into the marriage contract; it is manifestly reasonable, therefore, that both of them be recognized as legal parents with rights and responsibilities in connection with the child. There has been no legally cognizable signification of such willingness on the part of unwed parents, however, and "the male and female... may or may not be willing to work together towards the common end of child rearing." To provide legal recognition to both of them as "parents" would often be "to create two conflicting parties competing for legal control of the child."

All of those persons in Illinois who may have followed the progress of this case will, I expect, experience no little surprise at the Court's opinion handed down today. Stanley will undoubtedly be surprised to find that he has prevailed on an issue never advanced by him. The judges who dealt with this case in the state courts will be surprised to find their decisions overturned on a ground they never considered. And the legislators and other officials of the State of Illinois, as well as those attorneys of the State who are familiar with the statutory provisions here at issue, will be surprised to learn for the first time that the Illinois Juvenile Court Act establishes a presumption that unwed fathers are unfit. I must confess my own inability to find any such presumption in the Illinois Act. Furthermore, from the record of the proceedings in the Juvenile Court of Cook County in this case, I can only conclude that the judge of that court was unaware of any such presumption, for he clearly indicated that Stanley's asserted fatherhood of the children would stand him in good stead, rather than prejudice him, in any adoption or guardianship proceeding. In short, far from any intimation of hostility toward unwed fathers, that court gave Stanley "merit points" for his acknowledgment of paternity and his past assumption of at least marginal responsibility for the children.[2]

In regard to the only issue that I consider properly before the Court, I agree with the State's argument that the Equal Protection Clause is not violated when Illinois gives full recognition only to those father-child relationships that arise in the context of family units bound together by legal obligations arising from marriage or from adoption proceedings. Quite apart from the religious or quasi-religious connotations that marriage has—and has historically enjoyed—for a large proportion of this Nation's citizens, it is in law an essentially contractual relationship, the parties to which have legally enforceable rights and duties, with respect both to each other and to any children born to them. Stanley and the mother of these children never entered such a relationship. The record is silent as to whether they ever privately exchanged such promises as would have bound them in marriage under the common law. See *Cartwright v. McGown*, 121 Ill. 388, 398, 12 N.E. 737, 739 (1887). In any event, Illinois has not recognized common-law

The second basic justification urged upon us by counsel for the State was that, in order to provide for the child's welfare, "it is necessary to impose upon at least one of the parties legal responsibility for the welfare of (the child), and since necessarily the female is present at the birth of the child and identifiable as the mother," the State has elected the unwed mother, rather than the unwed father, as the biological parent with that legal responsibility.

It was suggested to counsel during an ensuing colloquy with the bench that identification seemed to present no insuperable problem in Stanley's case and that, although Stanley had expressed an interest in participating in the rearing of the children, "Illinois won't let him." Counsel replied that, on the contrary, "Illinois encourages him to do so if he will accept the legal responsibility for those children by a formal proceeding comparable to the marriage ceremony, in which he is evidencing through a judicial proceeding his desire to accept legal responsibility for the children." Stanley, however, "did not ask for custody. He did not ask for legal responsibility. He only objected to someone (else) having legal control over the children." Tr. of Oral Arg. 38, 39–40.

2. The position that Stanley took at the dependency proceeding was not without ambiguity. Shortly after the mother's death, he placed the children in the care of Mr. and Mrs. Ness, who took the children into their home. The record is silent as to whether the Ness household was an approved foster home. Through Stanley's act, then, the Nesses were already the *actual* custodians of the children. At the dependency proceeding, he resisted only the court's designation of the Nesses as the legal custodians; he did not challenge their suitability for that role, nor did he seek for himself either that role or any other role that would have imposed legal responsibility upon him. Had he prevailed, of course, the status quo would have obtained: the Nesses would have continued to play the role of actual custodians until either they or Stanley acted to alter the informal arrangement, and there would still have been no living adult with any legally enforceable obligation for the care and support of the infant children.

marriages since 1905. Ill.Rev.Stat., c. 89, § 4. Stanley did not seek the burdens when he could have freely assumed them.

Where there is a valid contract of marriage, the law of Illinois presumes that the husband is the father of any child born to the wife during the marriage; as the father, he has legally enforceable rights and duties with respect to that child. When a child is born to an unmarried woman, Illinois recognizes the readily identifiable mother, but makes no presumption as to the identity of the biological father. It does, however, provide two ways, one voluntary and one involuntary, in which that father may be identified. First, he may marry the mother and acknowledge the child as his own; this has the legal effect of legitimating the child and gaining for the father full recognition as a parent. Ill.Rev.Stat., c. 3, § 12, subd. 8. Second, a man may be found to be the biological father of the child pursuant to a paternity suit initiated by the mother; in this case, the child remains illegitimate, but the adjudicated father is made liable for the support of the child until the latter attains age 18 or is legally adopted by another. Ill.Rev.Stat., c. 106 3/4, § 52.

Stanley argued before the Supreme Court of Illinois that the definition of "parents," set out in Ill.Rev.Stat., c. 37, § 701-14, as including "the father and mother of a legitimate child, or the survivor of them, or the natural mother of an illegitimate child, (or)... any adoptive parent,"[3] violates the Equal Protection Clause in that it treats unwed mothers and unwed fathers differently. Stanley then enlarged upon his equal protection argument when he brought the case here; he argued before this Court that Illinois is not permitted by the Equal Protection Clause to distinguish between unwed fathers and any of the other biological parents included in the statutory definition of legal "parents."

The Illinois Supreme Court correctly held that the State may constitutionally distinguish between unwed fathers and unwed mothers. Here, Illinois' different treatment of the two is part of that State's statutory scheme for protecting the welfare of illegitimate children. In almost all cases, the unwed mother is readily identifiable, generally from hospital records, and alternatively by physicians or others attending the child's birth. Unwed fathers, as a class, are not traditionally quite so easy to identify and locate. Many of them either deny all responsibility or exhibit no interest in the child or its welfare; and, of course, many unwed fathers are simply not aware of their parenthood.

Furthermore, I believe that a State is fully justified in concluding, on the basis of common human experience, that the biological role of the mother in carrying and nursing an infant creates stronger bonds between her and the child than the bonds resulting from the male's often casual encounter. This view is reinforced by the observable fact that most unwed mothers exhibit a concern for their offspring either permanently or at least until they are safely placed for adoption, while unwed fathers rarely burden either the mother or the child with their attentions or loyalties. Centuries of human experience buttress this view of the

3. The Court seems at times to ignore this statutory definition of "parents," even though it is precisely that definition itself whose constitutionality has been brought into issue by Stanley. In preparation for finding a purported similarity between this case and *Bell v. Burson*, 402 U.S. 535 (1971), the Court quotes the legislatively declared aims of the Juvenile Court Act to "strengthen the minor's family ties whenever possible, removing him from the custody of his *parents* only when his welfare or safety or the protection of the public cannot be adequately safeguarded without removal." (Emphasis added.) The Court then goes on to find a "self-contradiction" between that stated aim and the Act's nonrecognition of unwed fathers. There is, of course, no such contradiction. The word "parent" in the statement of legislative purpose obviously has the meaning given to it by the definitional provision of the Act.

realities of human conditions and suggest that unwed mothers of illegitimate children are generally more dependable protectors of their children than are unwed fathers. While these, like most generalizations, are not without exceptions, they nevertheless provide a sufficient basis to sustain a statutory classification whose objective is not to penalize unwed parents but to further the welfare of illegitimate children in fulfillment of the State's obligations as *parens patriae*.[4]

Stanley depicts himself as a somewhat unusual unwed father, namely, as one who has always acknowledged and never doubted his fatherhood of these children. He alleges that he loved, cared for, and supported these children from the time of their birth until the death of their mother. He contends that he consequently must be treated the same as a married father of legitimate children. Even assuming the truth of Stanley's allegations, I am unable to construe the Equal Protection Clause as requiring Illinois to tailor its statutory definition of "parents" so meticulously as to include such unusual unwed fathers, while at the same time excluding those unwed, and generally unidentified, biological fathers who in no way share Stanley's professed desires.

Indeed, the nature of Stanley's own desires is less than absolutely clear from the record in this case. Shortly after the death of the mother, Stanley turned these two children over to the care of a Mr. and Mrs. Ness; he took no action to gain recognition of himself as a father, through adoption, or as a legal custodian, through a guardianship proceeding. Eventually it came to the attention of the State that there was no living adult who had any legally enforceable obligation for the care and support of the children; it was only then that the dependency proceeding here under review took place and that Stanley made himself known to the juvenile court in connection with these two children.[5] Even then, however, Stanley did not ask to be charged with the legal responsibility for the children. He asked only that such legal responsibility be given to no one else. He seemed, in particular, to be concerned with the loss of the welfare payments he would suffer as a result of the designation of others as guardians of the children.

Not only, then, do I see no ground for holding that Illinois' statutory definition of "parents" on its face violates the Equal Protection Clause; I see no ground for holding that any constitutional right of Stanley has been denied in the application of that statutory definition in the case at bar.

As Mr. Justice Frankfurter once observed, "Invalidating legislation is serious business...." *Morey v. Doud*, 354 U.S. 457, 474 (1957) (dissenting opinion). The Court today pursues that serious business by expanding its legitimate jurisdiction beyond what I read in 28 U.S.C. § 1257

4. When the marriage between the parents of a legitimate child is dissolved by divorce or separation, the State, of course, normally awards custody of the child to one parent or the other. This is considered necessary for the child's welfare, since the parents are no longer legally bound together. The unmarried parents of an illegitimate child are likewise not legally bound together. Thus, even if Illinois did recognize the parenthood of both the mother and father of an illegitimate child, it would, for consistency with its practice in divorce proceedings, be called upon to award custody to one or the other of them, at least once it had by some means ascertained the identity of the father.

5. As the majority notes, Joan Stanley gave birth to three children during the 18 years Peter Stanley was living "intermittently" with her. At oral argument, we were told by Stanley's counsel that the oldest of these three children had previously been declared a ward of the court pursuant to a neglect proceeding that was "proven against" Stanley at a time, apparently, when the juvenile court officials were under the erroneous impression that Peter and Joan Stanley had been married. Tr. of Oral Arg. 19.

as the permissible limits contemplated by Congress. In doing so, it invalidates a provision of critical importance to Illinois' carefully drawn statutory system governing family relationships and the welfare of the minor children of the State. And in so invalidating that provision, it ascribes to that statutory system a presumption that is simply not there and embarks on a novel concept of the natural law for unwed fathers that could well have strange boundaries as yet undiscernible.

NOTES AND QUESTIONS

1. Why were Peter Stanley's parental rights terminated? Did the state establish that he was an unfit parent? How? Was this procedure constitutionally flawed?

2. May the state create categories of presumptive unfitness? Is it constitutionally permissible to shift the burden to the parent to rebut the presumption?

3. Does the dissent agree that a presumption of unfitness is constitutionally impermissible? If so, what is the basis for the dissent's disagreement?

4. Do you think that Mr. Stanley wanted custody of his children, or do you agree with the dissent that his position "was not without ambiguity"?

LASSITER V. DEPARTMENT OF SOCIAL SERVICES OF DURHAM COUNTY
Supreme Court of the United States
452 U.S. 18 (1981)

JUSTICE STEWART delivered the opinion of the Court.

I

In the late spring of 1975, after hearing evidence that the petitioner, Abby Gail Lassiter, had not provided her infant son William with proper medical care, the District Court of Durham County, N.C., adjudicated him a neglected child and transferred him to the custody of the Durham County Department of Social Services, the respondent here. A year later, Ms. Lassiter was charged with first-degree murder, was convicted of second-degree murder, and began a sentence of 25 to 40 years of imprisonment.[1] In 1978 the Department petitioned the court to

1. The North Carolina Court of Appeals, in reviewing the petitioner's conviction, indicated that the murder occurred during an altercation between Ms. Lassiter, her mother, and the deceased:

> "Defendant's mother told [the deceased] to 'come on.' They began to struggle and deceased fell or was knocked to the floor. Defendant's mother was beating deceased with a broom. While deceased was still on the floor and being beaten with the broom, defendant entered the apartment. She went into the kitchen and got a butcher knife. She took the knife and began stabbing the deceased who was still prostrate. The body of deceased had seven stab wounds...." *State v. Lassiter*, No. 7614SC1054 (June 1, 1977).

After her conviction was affirmed on appeal, Ms. Lassiter sought to attack it collaterally. Among her arguments was that the assistance of her trial counsel had been ineffective because he had failed to "seek to elicit

terminate Ms. Lassiter's parental rights because, the Department alleged, she "has not had any contact with the child since December of 1975" and "has willfully left the child in foster care for more than two consecutive years without showing that substantial progress has been made in correcting the conditions which led to the removal of the child, or without showing a positive response to the diligent efforts of the Department of Social Services to strengthen her relationship to the child, or to make and follow through with constructive planning for the future of the child."

Ms. Lassiter was served with the petition and with notice that a hearing on it would be held. Although her mother had retained counsel for her in connection with an effort to invalidate the murder conviction, Ms. Lassiter never mentioned the forthcoming hearing to him (or, for that matter, to any other person except, she said, to "someone" in the prison). At the behest of the Department of Social Services' attorney, she was brought from prison to the hearing, which was held August 31, 1978. The hearing opened, apparently at the judge's instance, with a discussion of whether Ms. Lassiter should have more time in which to find legal assistance. Since the court concluded that she "has had ample opportunity to seek and obtain counsel prior to the hearing of this matter, and [that] her failure to do so is without just cause," the court did not postpone the proceedings. Ms. Lassiter did not aver that she was indigent, and the court did not appoint counsel for her.

A social worker from the respondent Department was the first witness. She testified that in 1975 the Department "received a complaint from Duke Pediatrics that William had not been followed in the pediatric clinic for medical problems and that they were having difficulty in locating Ms. Lassiter. . . ." She said that in May 1975 a social worker had taken William to the hospital, where doctors asked that he stay "because of breathing difficulties [and] malnutrition and [because] there was a great deal of scarring that indicated that he had a severe infection that had gone untreated." The witness further testified that, except for one "prearranged" visit and a chance meeting on the street, Ms. Lassiter had not seen William after he had come into the State's custody, and that neither Ms. Lassiter nor her mother had "made any contact with the Department of Social Services regarding that child." When asked whether William should be placed in his grandmother's custody, the social worker said he should not, since the grandmother "has indicated to me on a number of occasions that she was not able to take responsibility for the child" and since "I have checked with people in the community and from Ms. Lassiter's church who also feel that this additional responsibility would be more than she can handle." The social worker added that William "has not seen his grandmother since the chance meeting in July of '76 and that was the only time."

After the direct examination of the social worker, the judge said:

> "I notice we made extensive findings in June of '75 that you were served with papers and called the social services and told them you weren't coming; and the serious lack of medical treatment. And, as I have said in my findings of the 16th day of June '75, the Court finds that the grandmother, Ms. Lucille Lassiter, mother of Abby Gail Lassiter, filed a complaint on the

or introduce before the jury the statement made by [Ms. Lassiter's mother,] 'And I did it, I hope she dies.'" Ms. Lassiter's mother had, like Ms. Lassiter, been indicted on a first-degree murder charge; however, the trial court granted the elder Ms. Lassiter's motion for a nonsuit. The North Carolina General Court of Justice, Superior Court Division, denied Ms. Lassiter's motion for collateral relief.

> 8th day of May, 1975, alleging that the daughter often left the children, Candina, Felicia and William L. with her for days without providing money or food while she was gone."

Ms. Lassiter conducted a cross-examination of the social worker, who firmly reiterated her earlier testimony. The judge explained several times, with varying degrees of clarity, that Ms. Lassiter should only ask questions at this stage; many of her questions were disallowed because they were not really questions, but arguments.

Ms. Lassiter herself then testified, under the judge's questioning, that she had properly cared for William. Under cross-examination, she said that she had seen William more than five or six times after he had been taken from her custody and that, if William could not be with her, she wanted him to be with her mother since "He knows us. Children know they family.... They know they people, they know they family and that child knows us anywhere.... I got four more other children. Three girls and a boy and they know they little brother when they see him."

Ms. Lassiter's mother was then called as a witness. She denied, under the questioning of the judge, that she had filed the complaint against Ms. Lassiter, and on cross-examination she denied both having failed to visit William when he was in the State's custody and having said that she could not care for him.

The court found that Ms. Lassiter "has not contacted the Department of Social Services about her child since December, 1975, has not expressed any concern for his care and welfare, and has made no efforts to plan for his future." Because Ms. Lassiter thus had "wilfully failed to maintain concern or responsibility for the welfare of the minor," and because it was "in the best interests of the minor," the court terminated Ms. Lassiter's status as William's parent.[2]

On appeal, Ms. Lassiter argued only that, because she was indigent, the Due Process Clause of the Fourteenth Amendment entitled her to the assistance of counsel, and that the trial court had therefore erred in not requiring the State to provide counsel for her. The North Carolina Court of Appeals decided that "[w]hile this State action does invade a protected area of individual privacy, the invasion is not so serious or unreasonable as to compel us to hold that appointment of counsel for indigent parents is constitutionally mandated." *In re Lassiter*, 43 N.C.App. 525, 527, 259 S.E.2d 336, 337. The Supreme Court of North Carolina summarily denied Ms. Lassiter's application for discretionary review, 299 N.C. 120, 262 S.E.2d 6, and we granted certiorari to consider the petitioner's claim under the Due Process Clause of the Fourteenth Amendment, 449 U.S. 819.

II

For all its consequence, "due process" has never been, and perhaps can never be, precisely defined. "[U]nlike some legal rules," this Court has said, due process "is not a technical conception with a fixed content unrelated to time, place and circumstances." *Cafeteria Workers v. McElroy*, 367 U.S. 886, 895. Rather, the phrase expresses the requirement of "fundamental fairness," a requirement whose meaning can be as opaque as its importance is lofty. Applying

2. The petition had also asked that the parental rights of the putative father, William Boykin, be terminated. Boykin was not married to Ms. Lassiter, he had never contributed to William's financial support, and indeed he denied that he was William's father. The court granted the petition to terminate his alleged parental status.

the Due Process Clause is therefore an uncertain enterprise which must discover what "fundamental fairness" consists of in a particular situation by first considering any relevant precedents and then by assessing the several interests that are at stake.

A

The pre-eminent generalization that emerges from this Court's precedents on an indigent's right to appointed counsel is that such a right has been recognized to exist only where the litigant may lose his physical liberty if he loses the litigation. Thus, when the Court overruled the principle of *Betts v. Brady*, 316 U.S. 455, that counsel in criminal trials need be appointed only where the circumstances in a given case demand it, the Court did so in the case of a man sentenced to prison for five years. *Gideon v. Wainwright*, 372 U.S. 335. And thus *Argersinger v. Hamlin*, 407 U.S. 25, established that counsel must be provided before any indigent may be sentenced to prison, even where the crime is petty and the prison term brief.

That it is the defendant's interest in personal freedom, and not simply the special Sixth and Fourteenth Amendments right to counsel in criminal cases, which triggers the right to appointed counsel is demonstrated by the Court's announcement in *In re Gault*, 387 U.S. 1, that "the Due Process Clause of the Fourteenth Amendment requires that in respect of proceedings to determine delinquency *which may result in commitment to an institution in which the juvenile's freedom is curtailed*," the juvenile has a right to appointed counsel even though proceedings may be styled "civil" and not "criminal." *Id*., at 41 (emphasis added). Similarly, four of the five Justices who reached the merits in *Vitek v. Jones*, 445 U.S. 480, concluded that an indigent prisoner is entitled to appointed counsel before being involuntarily transferred for treatment to a state mental hospital. The fifth Justice differed from the other four only in declining to exclude the "possibility that the required assistance may be rendered by competent laymen in some cases." *Id*., at 500 (separate opinion of Powell, J.).

Significantly, as a litigant's interest in personal liberty diminishes, so does his right to appointed counsel. In *Gagnon v. Scarpelli*, 411 U.S. 778, the Court gauged the due process rights of a previously sentenced probationer at a probation-revocation hearing. In *Morrissey v. Brewer*, 408 U.S. 471, 480, which involved an analogous hearing to revoke parole, the Court had said: "Revocation deprives an individual, not of the absolute liberty to which every citizen is entitled, but only of the conditional liberty properly dependent on observance of special parole restrictions." Relying on that discussion, the Court in *Scarpelli* declined to hold that indigent probationers have, *per se*, a right to counsel at revocation hearings, and instead left the decision whether counsel should be appointed to be made on a case-by-case basis.

Finally, the Court has refused to extend the right to appointed counsel to include prosecutions which, though criminal, do not result in the defendant's loss of personal liberty. The Court in *Scott v. Illinois*, 440 U.S. 367, for instance, interpreted the "central premise of *Argersinger*" to be "that actual imprisonment is a penalty different in kind from fines or the mere threat of imprisonment," and the Court endorsed that premise as "eminently sound and warrant[ing] adoption of actual imprisonment as the line defining the constitutional right to appointment of counsel." *Id*., 440 U.S., at 373. The Court thus held "that the Sixth and Fourteenth Amendments to the United States Constitution require only that no indigent criminal defendant be sentenced to a term of imprisonment unless the State has afforded him the right to assistance of appointed counsel in his defense." *Id*., at 373–374.

In sum, the Court's precedents speak with one voice about what "fundamental fairness" has meant when the Court has considered the right to appointed counsel, and we thus draw from them the presumption that an indigent litigant has a right to appointed counsel only when, if he loses, he may be deprived of his physical liberty. It is against this presumption that all the other elements in the due process decision must be measured.

B

The case of *Mathews v. Eldridge*, 424 U.S. 319, 335, propounds three elements to be evaluated in deciding what due process requires, viz., the private interests at stake, the government's interest, and the risk that the procedures used will lead to erroneous decisions. We must balance these elements against each other, and then set their net weight in the scales against the presumption that there is a right to appointed counsel only where the indigent, if he is unsuccessful, may lose his personal freedom.

This Court's decisions have by now made plain beyond the need for multiple citation that a parent's desire for and right to "the companionship, care, custody and management of his or her children" is an important interest that "undeniably warrants deference and, absent a powerful countervailing interest, protection." *Stanley v. Illinois*, 405 U.S. 645, 651. Here the State has sought not simply to infringe upon that interest but to end it. If the State prevails, it will have worked a unique kind of deprivation. Cf. *May v. Anderson*, 345 U.S. 528, 533; *Armstrong v. Manzo*, 380 U.S. 545. A parent's interest in the accuracy and justice of the decision to terminate his or her parental status is, therefore a commanding one.[3]

Since the State has an urgent interest in the welfare of the child, it shares the parent's interest in an accurate and just decision. For this reason, the State may share the indigent parent's interest in the availability of appointed counsel. If, as our adversary system presupposes, accurate and just results are most likely to be obtained through the equal contest of opposed interests, the State's interest in the child's welfare may perhaps best be served by a hearing in which both the parent and the State acting for the child are represented by counsel, without whom the contest of interests may become unwholesomely unequal. North Carolina itself acknowledges as much by providing that where a parent files a written answer to a termination petition, the State must supply a lawyer to represent the child. N.C. Gen.Stat. § 7A-289.29 (Supp. 1979).

The State's interests, however, clearly diverge from the parent's insofar as the State wishes the termination decision to be made as economically as possible and thus wants to avoid both the expense of appointed counsel and the cost of the lengthened proceedings his presence may cause. But though the State's pecuniary interest is legitimate, it is hardly significant enough to overcome private interests as important as those here, particularly in light of the concession in the respondent's brief that the "potential costs of appointed counsel in termination proceedings...is [*sic*] admittedly *de minimis* compared to the costs in all criminal actions."

Finally, consideration must be given to the risk that a parent will be erroneously deprived of his or her child because the parent is not represented by counsel. North Carolina law now

3. Some parents will have an additional interest to protect. Petitions to terminate parental rights are not uncommonly based on alleged criminal activity. Parents so accused may need legal counsel to guide them in understanding the problems such petitions may create.

seeks to assure accurate decisions by establishing the following procedures: A petition to terminate parental rights may be filed only by a parent seeking the termination of the other parent's rights, by a county department of social services or licensed child-placing agency with custody of the child, or by a person with whom the child has lived continuously for the two years preceding the petition. § 7A-289.24. A petition must describe facts sufficient to warrant a finding that one of the grounds for termination exists, § 7A-289.25(6), and the parent must be notified of the petition and given 30 days in which to file a written answer to it, § 7A-289.27. If that answer denies a material allegation, the court must, as has been noted, appoint a lawyer as the child's guardian *ad litem* and must conduct a special hearing to resolve the issues raised by the petition and the answer. § 7A-289.29. If the parent files no answer, "the court shall issue an order terminating all parental and custodial rights...; provided the court shall order a hearing on the petition and may examine the petitioner or others on the facts alleged in the petition." § 7A-289.28. Findings of fact are made by a court sitting without a jury and must "be based on clear, cogent, and convincing evidence." § 7A-289.30. Any party may appeal who gives notice of appeal within 10 days after the hearing. § 7A-289.34.[4]

The respondent argues that the subject of a termination hearing—the parent's relationship with her child—far from being abstruse, technical, or unfamiliar, is one as to which the parent must be uniquely well informed and to which the parent must have given prolonged thought. The respondent also contends that a termination hearing is not likely to produce difficult points of evidentiary law, or even of substantive law, since the evidentiary problems peculiar to criminal trials are not present and since the standards for termination are not complicated. In fact, the respondent reports, the North Carolina Departments of Social Services are themselves sometimes represented at termination hearings by social workers instead of by lawyers.[5]

Yet the ultimate issues with which a termination hearing deals are not always simple, however commonplace they may be. Expert medical and psychiatric testimony, which few parents are equipped to understand and fewer still to confute, is sometimes presented. The parents are likely to be people with little education, who have had uncommon difficulty in dealing with life, and who are, at the hearing, thrust into a distressing and disorienting situation. That these factors may combine to overwhelm an uncounseled parent is evident from the findings some courts have made. See, e.g., *Davis v. Page*, 442 F.Supp. 258, 261 (SD Fla. 1977); *State v. Jamison*, 251 Or. 114, 117–118, 444 P.2d 15, 17 (1968). Thus, courts have generally held that the State must appoint counsel for indigent parents at termination proceedings. *State ex rel. Heller v.*

4. The respondent also points out that parental termination hearings commonly occur only after a custody proceeding in which the child has judicially been found to be abused, neglected, or dependent, and that an indigent parent has a right to be represented by appointed counsel at the custody hearing. § 7A-587.

Ms. Lassiter's hearing occurred before some of these provisions were enacted. She did not, for instance, have the benefit of the "clear, cogent, and convincing" evidentiary standard, nor did she have counsel at the hearing in which William was taken from her custody.

5. Both the respondent and the Columbia Journal of Law and Social Problems, 4 Colum.J.L. & Soc.Prob. 230 (1968), have conducted surveys purporting to reveal whether the presence of counsel reduces the number of erroneous determinations in parental termination proceedings. Unfortunately, neither survey goes beyond presenting statistics which, standing alone, are unilluminating. The Journal note does, however, report that it questioned the New York Family Court judges who preside over parental termination hearings and found that 72.2% of them agreed that when a parent is unrepresented, it becomes more difficult to conduct a fair hearing (11.1% of the judges disagreed); 66.7% thought it became difficult to develop the facts (22.2% disagreed).

Miller, 61 Ohio St.2d 6, 399 N.E.2d 66 (1980); *Department of Public Welfare v. J. K. B.*, 379 Mass. 1, 393 N.E.2d 406 (1979); *In re Chad S.*, 580 P.2d 983 (Okl. 1978); *In re Myricks*, 85 Wash.2d 252, 533 P.2d 841 (1975); *Crist v. Division of Youth and Family Services*, 128 N.J.Super. 402, 320 A.2d 203 (1974); *Danforth v. Maine Dept. of Health and Welfare*, 303 A.2d 794 (Me. 1973); *In re Friesz*, 190 Neb. 347, 208 N.W.2d 259 (1973).[6] The respondent is able to point to no presently authoritative case, except for the North Carolina judgment now before us, holding that an indigent parent has no due process right to appointed counsel in termination proceedings.

C

The dispositive question, which must now be addressed, is whether the three *Eldridge* factors, when weighed against the presumption that there is no right to appointed counsel in the absence of at least a potential deprivation of physical liberty, suffice to rebut that presumption and thus to lead to the conclusion that the Due Process Clause requires the appointment of counsel when a State seeks to terminate an indigent's parental status. To summarize the above discussion of the *Eldridge* factors: the parent's interest is an extremely important one (and may be supplemented by the dangers of criminal liability inherent in some termination proceedings); the State shares with the parent an interest in a correct decision, has a relatively weak pecuniary interest, and, in some but not all cases, has a possibly stronger interest in informal procedures; and the complexity of the proceeding and the incapacity of the uncounseled parent could be, but would not always be, great enough to make the risk of an erroneous deprivation of the parent's rights insupportably high.

If, in a given case, the parent's interests were at their strongest, the State's interests were at their weakest, and the risks of error were at their peak, it could not be said that the *Eldridge* factors did not overcome the presumption against the right to appointed counsel, and that due process did not therefore require the appointment of counsel. But since the *Eldridge* factors will not always be so distributed, and since "due process is not so rigid as to require that the significant interests in informality, flexibility and economy must always be sacrificed," *Gagnon v. Scarpelli*, 411 U.S., at 788, neither can we say that the Constitution requires the appointment of counsel in every parental termination proceeding. We therefore adopt the standard found appropriate in *Gagnon v. Scarpelli*, and leave the decision whether due process calls for the appointment of counsel for indigent parents in termination proceedings to be answered in the first instance by the trial court, subject, of course, to appellate review. See, *e.g.*, *Wood v. Georgia*, 450 U.S. 261.

III

Here, as in *Scarpelli*, "[i]t is neither possible nor prudent to attempt to formulate a precise and detailed set of guidelines to be followed in determining when the providing of counsel is necessary to meet the applicable due process requirements," since here, as in that case, "[t]he facts and circumstances . . . are susceptible of almost infinite variation. . . ." 411 U.S., at 790. Nevertheless, because child-custody litigation must be concluded as rapidly as is consis-

6. A number of courts have held that indigent parents have a right to appointed counsel in child dependency or neglect hearings as well. *E.g.*, *Davis v. Page*, 640 F.2d 599 (CA5 1981) (en banc); *Cleaver v. Wilcox*, 499 F.2d 940 (CA9 1974) (right to be decided case by case); *Smith v. Edmiston*, 431 F.Supp. 941 (WD Tenn. 1977).

tent with fairness,[7] we decide today whether the trial judge denied Ms. Lassiter due process of law when he did not appoint counsel for her.

The respondent represents that the petition to terminate Ms. Lassiter's parental rights contained no allegations of neglect or abuse upon which criminal charges could be based, and hence Ms. Lassiter could not well have argued that she required counsel for that reason. The Department of Social Services was represented at the hearing by counsel, but no expert witnesses testified and the case presented no specially troublesome points of law, either procedural or substantive. While hearsay evidence was no doubt admitted, and while Ms. Lassiter no doubt left incomplete her defense that the Department had not adequately assisted her in rekindling her interest in her son, the weight of the evidence that she had few sparks of such interest was sufficiently great that the presence of counsel for Ms. Lassiter could not have made a determinative difference. True, a lawyer might have done more with the argument that William should live with Ms. Lassiter's mother—but that argument was quite explicitly made by both Lassiters, and the evidence that the elder Ms. Lassiter had said she could not handle another child, that the social worker's investigation had led to a similar conclusion, and that the grandmother had displayed scant interest in the child once he had been removed from her daughter's custody was, though controverted, sufficiently substantial that the absence of counsel's guidance on this point did not render the proceedings fundamentally unfair.[8] Finally, a court deciding whether due process requires the appointment of counsel need not ignore a parent's plain demonstration that she is not interested in attending a hearing. Here, the trial court had previously found that Ms. Lassiter had expressly declined to appear at the 1975 child custody hearing, Ms. Lassiter had not even bothered to speak to her retained lawyer after being notified of the termination hearing, and the court specifically found that Ms. Lassiter's failure to make an effort to contest the termination proceeding was without cause. In view of all these circumstances, we hold that the trial court did not err in failing to appoint counsel for Ms. Lassiter.

IV

In its Fourteenth Amendment, our Constitution imposes on the States the standards necessary to ensure that judicial proceedings are fundamentally fair. A wise public policy, however, may require that higher standards be adopted than those minimally tolerable under the Constitution. Informed opinion has clearly come to hold that an indigent parent is entitled to the assistance of appointed counsel not only in parental termination proceedings, but also in dependency and neglect proceedings as well. IJA-ABA Standards for Juvenile Justice, Counsel for Private Parties 2.3(b) (1980); Uniform Juvenile Court Act § 26(a), 9A U.L.A. 35 (1979); National Council on Crime and Delinquency, Model Rules for Juvenile Courts, Rule 39 (1969); U.S. Dept. of HEW, Children's Bureau, Legislative Guide for Drafting Family and Juvenile Court Acts § 25(b) (1969); U.S. Dept. of HEW, Children's Bureau, Legislative Guides

7. According to the respondent's brief, William Lassiter is now living "in a pre-adoptive home with foster parents committed to formal adoption to become his legal parents." He cannot be legally adopted, nor can his status otherwise be finally clarified, until this litigation ends.

8. Ms. Lassiter's argument here that her mother should have been given custody of William is hardly consistent with her argument in the collateral attack on her murder conviction that she was innocent because her mother was guilty.

for the Termination of Parental Rights and Responsibilities and the Adoption of Children, Pt. II, § 8 (1961); National Council on Crime and Delinquency, Standard Juvenile Court Act § 19 (1959). Most significantly, 33 States and the District of Columbia provide statutorily for the appointment of counsel in termination cases. The Court's opinion today in no way implies that the standards increasingly urged by informed public opinion and now widely followed by the States are other than enlightened and wise.

For the reasons stated in this opinion, the judgment is affirmed....

Chief Justice Burger, concurring.

I join the Court's opinion and add only a few words to emphasize a factor I believe is misconceived by the dissenters. The purpose of the termination proceeding at issue here was not "punitive." On the contrary, its purpose was protective of the child's best interests. Given the record in this case, which involves the parental rights of a mother under lengthy sentence for murder who showed little interest in her son, the writ might well have been a "candidate" for dismissal as improvidently granted. However, I am content to join the narrow holding of the Court, leaving the appointment of counsel in termination proceedings to be determined by the state courts on a case-by-case basis.

Justice Blackmun, with whom Justice Brennan and Justice Marshall join, dissenting.

The Court today denies an indigent mother the representation of counsel in a judicial proceeding initiated by the State of North Carolina to terminate her parental rights with respect to her youngest child. The Court most appropriately recognizes that the mother's interest is a "commanding one," and it finds no countervailing state interest of even remotely comparable significance. Nonetheless, the Court avoids what seems to me the obvious conclusion that due process requires the presence of counsel for a parent threatened with judicial termination of parental rights, and, instead, revives an ad hoc approach thoroughly discredited nearly 20 years ago in *Gideon v. Wainwright*, 372 U.S. 335 (1963). Because I believe that the unique importance of a parent's interest in the care and custody of his or her child cannot constitutionally be extinguished through formal judicial proceedings without the benefit of counsel, I dissent.

I

This Court is not unfamiliar with the problem of determining under what circumstances legal representation is mandated by the Constitution. In *Betts v. Brady*, 316 U.S. 455 (1942), it reviewed at length both the tradition behind the Sixth Amendment right to counsel in criminal trials and the historical practices of the States in that area. The decision in *Betts*—that the Sixth Amendment right to counsel did not apply to the States and that the due process guarantee of the Fourteenth Amendment permitted a flexible, case-by-case determination of the defendant's need for counsel in state criminal trials—was overruled in *Gideon v. Wainwright*, 372 U.S., at 345. The Court in *Gideon* rejected the *Betts* reasoning to the effect that counsel for indigent criminal defendants was "'not a fundamental right, essential to a fair trial.'" 372 U.S., at 340 (quoting *Betts v. Brady*, 316 U.S., at 471). Finding the right well founded in its precedents, the Court further concluded that "reason and reflection require us to recognize that in our adversary system of criminal justice, any person haled into court, who is too poor to hire a lawyer, cannot be assured a fair trial unless counsel is provided for him." 372 U.S., at 344. Similarly, in *Argersinger v. Hamlin*, 407 U.S. 25 (1972), assistance of counsel was found to be a requisite under the Sixth Amendment, as incorporated into the Fourteenth, even for a misdemeanor offense punishable by imprisonment for less than six months.[1]

Outside the criminal context, however, the Court has relied on the flexible nature of the due process guarantee whenever it has decided that counsel is not constitutionally required. The special purposes of probation revocation determinations, and the informal nature of those administrative proceedings, including the absence of counsel for the State, led the Court to conclude that due process does not require counsel for probationers. *Gagnon v. Scarpelli*, 411 U.S. 778, 785-789 (1973). In the case of school disciplinary proceedings, which are brief, informal, and intended in part to be educative, the Court also found no requirement for legal counsel. *Goss v. Lopez*, 419 U.S. 565, 583 (1975). Most recently, the Court declined to intrude the presence of counsel for a minor facing voluntary civil commitment by his parent, because of the parent's substantial role in that decision and because of the decision's essentially medical and informal nature. *Parham v. J.R.*, 442 U.S. 584, 604–609 (1979).

In each of these instances, the Court has recognized that what process is due varies in relation to the interests at stake and the nature of the governmental proceedings. Where the individual's liberty interest is of diminished or less than fundamental stature, or where the prescribed procedure involves informal decisionmaking without the trappings of an adversarial trial-type proceeding, counsel has not been a requisite of due process. Implicit in this analysis is the fact that the contrary conclusion sometimes may be warranted. Where an individual's liberty interest assumes sufficiently weighty constitutional significance, and the State by a formal and adversarial proceeding seeks to curtail that interest, the right to counsel may be necessary to ensure fundamental fairness. See *In re Gault*, 387 U.S. 1 (1967). To say this is simply to acknowledge that due process allows for the adoption of different rules to address different situations or contexts.

It is not disputed that state intervention to terminate the relationship between petitioner and her child must be accomplished by procedures meeting the requisites of the Due Process Clause. Nor is there any doubt here about the kind of procedure North Carolina has prescribed. North Carolina law requires notice and a trial-type hearing before the State on its own initiative may sever the bonds of parenthood. The decisionmaker is a judge, the rules of evidence are in force, and the State is represented by counsel. The question, then, is whether proceedings in this mold, that relate to a subject so vital, can comport with fundamental fairness when the defendant parent remains unrepresented by counsel. As the Court today properly acknowledges, our consideration of the process due in this context, as in others, must rely on a balancing of the competing private and public interests, an approach succinctly described in *Mathews v. Eldridge*, 424 U.S. 319, 335 (1976). As does the majority, I evaluate the "three distinct factors" specified in *Eldridge*: the private interest affected; the risk of error under the procedure employed by the State; and the countervailing governmental interest in support of the challenged procedure.

A

At stake here is "the interest of a parent in the companionship, care, custody, and management of his or her children." *Stanley v. Illinois*, 405 U.S. 645, 651 (1972). This interest occupies

1. In *Scott v. Illinois*, 440 U.S. 367 (1979), the Court's analysis of Sixth Amendment jurisprudence led to the conclusion that the right to counsel is not constitutionally mandated when imprisonment is not actually imposed.

a unique place in our legal culture, given the centrality of family life as the focus for personal meaning and responsibility. "[F]ar more precious…than property rights," *May v. Anderson*, 345 U.S. 528, 533 (1953), parental rights have been deemed to be among those "essential to the orderly pursuit of happiness by free men," *Meyer v. Nebraska*, 262 U.S. 390, 399 (1923), and to be more significant and priceless than "'liberties which derive merely from shifting economic arrangements.'" *Stanley v. Illinois*, 405 U.S. at 651, quoting *Kovacs v. Cooper*, 336 U.S. 77, 95 (1949) (Frankfurter, J., concurring). Accordingly, although the Constitution is verbally silent on the specific subject of families, freedom of personal choice in matters of family life long has been viewed as a fundamental liberty interest worthy of protection under the Fourteenth Amendment. *Smith v. Organization of Foster Families*, 431 U.S. 816, 845 (1977); *Moore v. East Cleveland*, 431 U.S. 494, 499 (1977) (plurality opinion); *Prince v. Massachusetts*, 321 U.S. 158 (1944); *Pierce v. Society of Sisters*, 268 U.S. 510, 534–535 (1925); *Meyer v. Nebraska*, 262 U.S., at 399. Within the general ambit of family integrity, the Court has accorded a high degree of constitutional respect to a natural parent's interest both in controlling the details of the child's upbringing, *Wisconsin v. Yoder*, 406 U.S. 205, 232–234 (1972); *Pierce v. Society of Sisters*, 268 U.S., at 534–535, and in retaining the custody and companionship of the child, *Smith v. Organization of Foster Families*, 431 U.S., at 842–847; *Stanley v. Illinois*, 405 U.S., at 651.

In this case, the State's aim is not simply to influence the parent-child relationship but to *extinguish* it. A termination of parental rights is both total and irrevocable.[3] Unlike other custody proceedings, it leaves the parent with no right to visit or communicate with the child, to participate in, or even to know about, any important decision affecting the child's religious, educational, emotional, or physical development. It is hardly surprising that this forced dissolution of the parent-child relationship has been recognized as a punitive sanction by courts,[4] Congress,[5] and commentators.[6] The Court candidly notes, as it must, that termination of parental rights by the State is a "unique kind of deprivation."

The magnitude of this deprivation is of critical significance in the due process calculus, for the process to which an individual is entitled is in part determined "by the extent to which he may be 'condemned to suffer grievous loss.'" *Goldberg v. Kelly*, 397 U.S. 254, 263

3. Under North Carolina law, when a child is adjudged to be abused, neglected, or dependent, the dispositional alternatives are not couched in terms of permanence. See N.C.Gen.Stat. §§ 7A-647, 7A-651 (Supp. 1979). In contrast, the State's termination statute specifically provides that an order terminating parental rights "completely and permanently terminates all rights and obligations" between parent and child, except that the child's right of inheritance continues until such time as the child may be adopted. § 7A-289.33. Such absolute and total termination is not unusual. See *e.g.*, Ariz.Rev.Stat.Ann. § 8-539 (1974); Cal.Civ.Code Ann. § 232.6 (West Supp. 1981); Ind.Code § 31-6-5-6(a) (Supp. 1980); Ky.Rev.Stat. § 199.613(2) (Supp. 1980); Mo.Rev.Stat. § 211.482 (Supp. 1980).

4. *E.g., Davis v. Page*, 640 F.2d 599, 604 (CA5 1981) (en banc); *Brown v. Guy*, 476 F.Supp. 771, 773 (Nev. 1979); *State ex rel. Lemaster v. Oakley*, 157 W.Va. 590, 598, 203 S.E.2d 140, 144 (1974); *Danforth v. State Dept. of Health & Welfare*, 303 A.2d 794, 799–800 (Me. 1973); *In re Howard*, 382 So.2d 194, 199 (La.App. 1980).

5. See H.R.Rep.No. 95-1386, p. 22 (1978) ("removal of a child from the parents is a penalty as great, if not greater, than a criminal penalty…"). This Report accompanied the Indian Child Welfare Act of 1978, Pub.L. 95-608, 92 Stat. 3069. Congress there provided for court-appointed counsel to indigent Indian parents facing a termination proceeding. § 102(b), 92 Stat. 3071, 25 U.S.C. § 1911(b) (1976 ed., Supp. III).

6. See, *e.g.*, Levine, Caveat Parens: A Demystification of the Child Protection System, 35 U.Pitt.L.Rev. 1, 52 (1973); Note, Child Neglect: Due Process for the Parent, 70 Colum.L.Rev. 465, 478 (1970); Representation in Child-Neglect Cases: Are Parents Neglected?, 4 Colum.J.L. & Soc.Prob. 230, 250 (1968) (Parent Representation Study).

(1970), quoting *Joint Anti-Fascist Refugee Committee v. McGrath*, 341 U.S. 123, 168 (1951) (Frankfurter, J., concurring). See *Little v. Streater*, 452 U.S. 1, 12 (1981); *Morrissey v. Brewer*, 408 U.S. 471, 481 (1972). Surely there can be few losses more grievous than the abrogation of parental rights. Yet the Court today asserts that this deprivation somehow is less serious than threatened losses deemed to require appointed counsel, because in this instance the parent's own "personal liberty" is not at stake.

I do not believe that our cases support the "presumption" asserted, that physical confinement is the only loss of liberty grievous enough to trigger a right to appointed counsel under the Due Process Clause. Indeed, incarceration has been found to be neither a necessary nor a sufficient condition for requiring counsel on behalf of an indigent defendant. The prospect of canceled parole or probation, with its consequent deprivation of personal liberty, has not led the Court to require counsel for a prisoner facing a revocation proceeding. *Gagnon v. Scarpelli*, 411 U.S., at 785–789, 93 S.Ct., at 1761–1763; *Morrissey v. Brewer*, 408 U.S., at 489, 92 S.Ct., at 2604. On the other hand, the fact that no new incarceration was threatened by a transfer from prison to a mental hospital did not preclude the Court's recognition of adverse changes in the conditions of confinement and of the stigma that presumably is associated with being labeled mentally ill. *Vitek v. Jones*, 445 U.S. 480, 492, 494 (1980). For four Members of the Court, these "other deprivations of liberty," coupled with the possibly diminished mental capacity of the prisoner, compelled the provision of counsel for any indigent prisoner facing a transfer hearing. *Id.*, at 496–497 (opinion of WHITE, J., joined by BRENNAN, MARSHALL, and STEVENS, JJ.).[7] See also *In re Gault*, 387 U.S., at 24–25.

Moreover, the Court's recourse to a "pre-eminent generalization," misrepresents the importance of our flexible approach to due process. That approach consistently has emphasized attentiveness to the particular context. Once an individual interest is deemed sufficiently substantial or fundamental, determining the constitutional necessity of a requested procedural protection requires that we examine the nature of the proceeding—both the risk of error if the protection is not provided and the burdens created by its imposition.[8] Compare *Goldberg v. Kelly*, 397 U.S. 254 (1970), with *Mathews v. Eldridge*, 424 U.S. 319 (1976), and *Fuentes v. Shevin*, 407 U.S. 67 (1972), with *Mitchell v. W. T. Grant Co.*, 416 U.S. 600 (1974).

Rather than opting for the insensitive presumption that incarceration is the only loss of liberty sufficiently onerous to justify a right to appointed counsel, I would abide by the Court's enduring commitment to examine the relationships among the interests on both sides, and

7. JUSTICE POWELL agreed with the plurality that independent representation must be provided to an inmate facing involuntary transfer to a state mental hospital, but concluded that this representative need not be an attorney because the transfer hearing was informal and the central issue was a medical one. 445 U.S., at 498–500.

8. By emphasizing the value of physical liberty to the exclusion of all other fundamental interests, the Court today grants an unnecessary and burdensome new layer of analysis onto its traditional three-factor balancing test. Apart from improperly conflating two distinct lines of prior cases, the Court's reliance on a "rebuttable presumption" sets a dangerous precedent that may undermine objective judicial review regarding other procedural protections. Even in the area of juvenile court delinquency proceedings, where the threat of incarceration arguably supports an automatic analogy to the criminal process, the Court has eschewed a bright-line approach. Instead, it has evaluated each requested procedural protection in light of its consequences for fair play and truth determination. See generally *McKeiver v. Pennsylvania*, 403 U.S. 528 (1971); *In re Winship*, 397 U.S. 358 (1970); *In re Gault*, 387 U.S. 1 (1967).

the appropriateness of counsel in the specific type of proceeding. The fundamental significance of the liberty interest at stake in a parental termination proceeding is undeniable, and I would find this first portion of the due process balance weighing heavily in favor of refined procedural protections. The second *Eldridge* factor, namely, the risk of error in the procedure provided by the State, must then be reviewed with some care.

B

The method chosen by North Carolina to extinguish parental rights resembles in many respects a criminal prosecution. Unlike the probation revocation procedure reviewed in *Gagnon v. Scarpelli*, on which the Court so heavily relies, the termination procedure is distinctly formal and adversarial. The State initiates the proceeding by filing a petition in district court, N.C.Gen.Stat. §§ 7A-289.23 and 7A-289.25 (Supp. 1979),[9] and serving a summons on the parent, § 7A-289.27(1). A state judge presides over the adjudicatory hearing that follows, and the hearing is conducted pursuant to the formal rules of evidence and procedure. N.C.Rule Civ.Proc. 1, N.C.Gen.Stat. § 1A-1 (Supp. 1979). In general, hearsay is inadmissible and records must be authenticated. See, *e.g.* § 1A-1, Rules 1, 43, 44, 46.

In addition, the proceeding has an obvious accusatory and punitive focus. In moving to terminate a parent's rights, the State has concluded that it no longer will try to preserve the family unit, but instead will marshal an array of public resources to establish that the parent-child separation must be made permanent.[10] The State has legal representation through the county attorney. This lawyer has access to public records concerning the family and to professional social workers who are empowered to investigate the family situation and to testify against the parent. The State's legal representative may also call upon experts in family relations, psychology, and medicine to bolster the State's case. And, of course, the State's counsel himself is an expert in the legal standards and techniques employed at the termination proceeding, including the methods of cross-examination.

In each of these respects, the procedure devised by the State vastly differs from the informal and rehabilitative probation revocation decision in *Scarpelli*, the brief, educative school disciplinary procedure in *Goss*, and the essentially medical decision in *Parham*. Indeed, the

9. A petition for termination may also be filed by a private party, such as a judicially appointed guardian, a foster parent, or the other natural parent. N.C.Gen.Stat. § 7A-289.24 (Supp. 1979). Because the State in those circumstances may not be performing the same adversarial and accusatory role, an application of the three *Eldridge* factors might yield a different result with respect to the right to counsel.

10. Significantly, the parent's rights and interests are not mentioned at all under the statement of purpose for the North Carolina termination statute. See N.C.Gen.Stat. § 7A-289.22 (Supp. 1979). In contrast, in abuse, neglect, and dependency proceedings the State has a statutory obligation to keep a family together whenever possible. § 7A-542. Thus, the State has chosen to provide counsel for parents, § 7A-587, in circumstances where it shares at least in part their interest in family integrity but not where it regards the parent as an opponent. The Assistant Attorney General of North Carolina explained the decision to furnish appointed counsel at the abuse and neglect stage by pointing to the State's need to avoid an awkward situation, given its possibly conflicting responsibilities to parent and child. Tr. of Oral Arg. 39–40. While this may be sound as a matter of public policy, it cannot excuse the failure to provide counsel at the termination stage, where the State and the indigent parent are adversaries, and the inequality of power and resources is starkly evident.

The possibility of providing counsel for the *child* at the termination proceeding has not been raised by the parties. That prospect requires consideration of interests different from those presented here, and again might yield a different result with respect to the right to counsel. See generally *Parham v. J.R.*, 442 U.S. 584 (1979); *Smith v. Organization of Foster Families*, 431 U.S. 816 (1977).

State here has prescribed virtually all the attributes of a formal trial as befits the severity of the loss at stake in the termination decision—every attribute, that is, except counsel for the defendant parent. The provision of counsel for the parent would not alter the character of the proceeding, which is already adversarial, formal, and quintessentially legal. It, however, would diminish the prospect of an erroneous termination, a prospect that is inherently substantial, given the gross disparity in power and resources between the State and the uncounseled indigent parent.[11]

The prospect of error is enhanced in light of the legal standard against which the defendant parent is judged. As demonstrated here, that standard commonly adds another dimension to the complexity of the termination proceeding. Rather than focusing on the facts of isolated acts or omissions, the State's charges typically address the nature and quality of complicated ongoing relationships among parent, child, other relatives, and even unrelated parties. In the case at bar, the State's petition accused petitioner of two of the several grounds authorizing termination of parental rights under North Carolina law:

> "That [petitioner] has *without cause*, failed to establish or maintain *concern or responsibility* as to the child's welfare.
>
> "That [petitioner] has *willfully* left the child in foster care for more than two consecutive years without showing that *substantial progress has been made* in correcting the conditions which led to the removal of the child [for neglect], or without showing a *positive response* to the *diligent efforts of the Department of Social Services* to strengthen her relationship to the child, or *to make and follow through with constructive planning* for the future of the child." (Emphasis supplied.) Juvenile Petition ¶¶ 6, 7, App. 3.

The legal issues posed by the State's petition are neither simple nor easily defined. The standard is imprecise and open to the subjective values of the judge.[13] A parent seeking to prevail against the State must be prepared to adduce evidence about his or her personal abilities and lack of fault, as well as proof of progress and foresight as a parent that the State would deem adequate and improved over the situation underlying a previous adverse judgment of child neglect. The parent cannot possibly succeed without being able to identify material issues, develop defenses, gather and present sufficient supporting nonhearsay evidence, and conduct cross-examination of adverse witnesses.

The Court, of course, acknowledges that these tasks "may combine to overwhelm an uncounseled parent." I submit that that is a profound understatement. Faced with a formal

11. Cf. *Parham v. J.R.*, 442 U.S., at 606–607; *Goldberg v. Kelly*, 397 U.S., at 266.

13. Under North Carolina law, there is a further stage to the termination inquiry. Should the trial court determine that one or more of the conditions authorizing termination has been established, it then must consider whether the best interests of the child require maintenance of the parent-child relationship. N.C.Gen. Stat. § 7A-289.31(a) (Supp. 1979).

This Court more than once has adverted to the fact that the "best interests of the child" standard offers little guidance to judges, and may effectively encourage them to rely on their own personal values. See, *e.g.*, *Smith v. Organization of Foster Families*, 431 U.S., at 835, n. 36; *Bellotti v. Baird*, 443 U.S. 622, 655 (1979) (STEVENS, J., concurring in judgment). See also *Quilloin v. Walcott*, 434 U.S. 246, 255 (1978). Several courts, perceiving similar risks, have gone so far as to invalidate parental termination statutes on vagueness grounds. See, *e.g.*, *Alsager v. District Court of Polk Cty.*, 406 F.Supp. 10, 18–19 (SD Iowa 1975), aff'd on other grounds, 545 F.2d 1137 (CA8 1976); *Davis v. Smith*, 266 Ark. 112, 121–123, 583 S.W.2d 37, 42–43 (1979).

accusatory adjudication, with an adversary—the State—that commands great investigative and prosecutorial resources, with standards that involve ill-defined notions of fault and adequate parenting, and with the inevitable tendency of a court to apply subjective values or to defer to the State's "expertise," the defendant parent plainly is outstripped if he or she is without the assistance of "'the guiding hand of counsel.'" *In re Gault*, 387 U.S., at 36, quoting *Powell v. Alabama*, 287 U.S. 45, 69 (1932). When the parent is indigent, lacking in education, and easily intimidated by figures of authority,[14] the imbalance may well become insuperable.

The risk of error thus is severalfold. The parent who actually has achieved the improvement or quality of parenting the State would require may be unable to establish this fact. The parent who has failed in these regards may be unable to demonstrate cause, absence of willfulness, or lack of agency diligence as justification. And errors of fact or law in the State's case may go unchallenged and uncorrected.[15] Given the weight of the interests at stake, this risk of error assumes extraordinary proportions. By intimidation, inarticulateness, or confusion, a parent can lose forever all contact and involvement with his or her offspring.

C

The final factor to be considered, the interests claimed for the State, do not tip the scale against providing appointed counsel in this context. The State hardly is in a position to assert here that it seeks the informality of a rehabilitative or educative proceeding into which counsel for the parent would inject an unwelcome adversarial edge. As the Assistant Attorney General of North Carolina declared before this Court, once the State moves for termination, it "has made a decision that the child cannot go home and should not go home. It no longer has an obligation to try and restore that family." Tr. of Oral Arg. 40.

The State may, and does, properly assert a legitimate interest in promoting the physical and emotional well-being of its minor children. But this interest is not served by terminating the rights of any concerned, responsible parent. Indeed, because North Carolina is committed to "protect[ing] all children from the unnecessary severance of a relationship with biological

14. See Schetky, Angell, Morrison, & Sack, Parents Who Fail: A Study of 51 Cases of Termination of Parental Rights, 18 J.Am.Acad. Child Psych. 366, 375 (1979) (citing minimal educational backgrounds). See also *Davis v. Page*, 442 F.Supp. 258, 260 (SD Fla. 1977) (uncounseled parent, ignorant of governing substantive law, "was little more than a spectator in the adjudicatory [dependency] proceeding," and "sat silently through most of the hearing…fearful of antagonizing the social workers"), aff'd in part, 640 F.2d 599 (CA5 1981) (en banc).

15. See Parent Representation Study, at 241 (parents appearing in Kings County, N.Y., Family Court, charged with neglect and represented by counsel, had higher rate of dismissed petitions, 25% to 7.9%, and lower rate of neglect adjudications, 62.5% to 79.5%, than similarly charged parents appearing without counsel); Brief for Respondent 38–39, 25a–31a (study of state-initiated termination actions in 73 North Carolina counties; parent prevailed in 5.5% of proceedings where represented by counsel, and in 0.15% of proceedings where unrepresented).

While these statistics hardly are dispositive, I do not share the Court's view that they are "unilluminating." Since no evidence in either study indicates that the defendant parent who can retain or is offered counsel is less culpable than the one who appears unrepresented, it seems reasonable to infer that a sizable number of cases against unrepresented parents end in termination solely because of the absence of counsel. In addition, as the Court acknowledges, the judges who preside over termination hearings perceive them as less fair when the parent is without counsel.

or legal parents," § 7A-289.22(2), "the State spites its own articulated goals when it needlessly separates" the parent from the child. *Stanley v. Illinois*, 405 U.S., at 653.[16]

The State also has an interest in avoiding the cost and administrative inconvenience that might accompany a right to appointed counsel. But, as the Court acknowledges, the State's fiscal interest "is hardly significant enough to overcome private interests as important as those here." The State's financial concern indeed is a limited one, for the right to appointed counsel may well be restricted to those termination proceedings that are instituted by the State. Moreover, no difficult line-drawing problem would arise with respect to other types of civil proceedings. The instant due process analysis takes full account of the fundamental nature of the parental interest, the permanency of the threatened deprivation, the gross imbalance between the resources employed by the prosecuting State and those available to the indigent parent, and the relatively insubstantial cost of furnishing counsel. An absence of any one of these factors might yield a different result.[17] But where, as here, the threatened loss of liberty is severe and absolute, the State's role is so clearly adversarial and punitive, and the cost involved is relatively slight, there is no sound basis for refusing to recognize the right to counsel as a requisite of due process in a proceeding initiated by the State to terminate parental rights.

II

A

The Court's analysis is markedly similar to mine; it, too, analyzes the three factors listed in *Mathews v. Eldridge*, and it, too, finds the private interest weighty, the procedure devised by the State fraught with risks of error, and the countervailing governmental interest insubstantial. Yet, rather than follow this balancing process to its logical conclusion, the Court abruptly pulls back and announces that a defendant parent must await a case-by-case determination of his or her need for counsel. Because the three factors "will not *always* be so distributed," reasons the Court, the Constitution should not be read to "requir[e] the appointment of counsel in *every* parental termination proceeding" (emphasis added). This conclusion is not only illogical, but it also marks a sharp departure from the due process analysis consistently applied heretofore. The flexibility of due process, the Court has held, requires case-by-case consideration of different decisionmaking *contexts*, not of different *litigants* within a given context. In analyzing the nature of the private and governmental interests at stake, along with the risk of error, the Court in the past has not limited itself to the particular case at hand. Instead, after addressing the three factors as generic elements in the context raised by the particular case, the Court then has formulated a rule that has general application to similarly situated cases.

The Court's own precedents make this clear. In *Goldberg v. Kelly*, the Court found that the desperate economic conditions experienced by welfare recipients *as a class* distinguished them from other recipients of governmental benefits. 397 U.S., at 264. In *Mathews v. Eldridge*, the Court concluded that the needs of Social Security disability recipients were *not* of comparable urgency, and, moreover, that existing pretermination procedures, based largely on written medical assessments, were likely to be more objective and even-handed than typical

16. The Court apparently shares this view.

17. Thus, for example, the State's involvement in adjudicating the competing claims for child custody between parents in a divorce proceeding need not obligate it to provide counsel for indigent parents.

welfare entitlement decisions. 424 U.S., at 339–345. These cases established rules translating due process in the welfare context as requiring a pretermination hearing but dispensing with that requirement in the disability benefit context. A showing that a particular welfare recipient had access to additional income, or that a disability recipient's eligibility turned on testimony rather than written medical reports, would not result in an exception from the required procedural norms. The Court reasoned in *Eldridge*:

> "To be sure, credibility and veracity may be a factor in the ultimate disability assessment in some cases. But procedural due process rules are shaped by the risk of error inherent in the truth-finding process as applied to the generality of cases, not the rare exceptions." *Id.*, at 344.

There are sound reasons for this. Procedural norms are devised to ensure that justice may be done in every case, and to protect litigants against unpredictable and unchecked adverse governmental action. Through experience with decisions in varied situations over time, lessons emerge that reflect a general understanding as to what is minimally necessary to assure fair play. Such lessons are best expressed to have general application which guarantees the predictability and uniformity that underlie our society's commitment to the rule of law. By endorsing, instead, a retrospective review of the trial record of each particular defendant parent, the Court today undermines the very rationale on which this concept of general fairness is based.[18]

Moreover, the case-by-case approach advanced by the Court itself entails serious dangers for the interests at stake and the general administration of justice. The Court assumes that a review of the record will establish whether a defendant, proceeding without counsel, has suffered an unfair disadvantage. But in the ordinary case, this simply is not so. The pleadings and transcript of an uncounseled termination proceeding at most will show the obvious blunders and omissions of the defendant parent. Determining the difference legal representation would have made becomes possible only through imagination, investigation, and legal research focused on the particular case. Even if the reviewing court can embark on such an enterprise in each case, it might be hard pressed to discern the significance of failures to challenge the State's evidence or to develop a satisfactory defense. Such failures, however, often cut to the essence of the fairness of the trial, and a court's inability to compensate for them effectively eviscerates the presumption of innocence. Because a parent acting *pro se* is even more likely to be unaware of controlling legal standards and practices, and unskilled in garnering relevant facts, it is difficult, if not impossible, to conclude that the typical case has been adequately presented. Cf. *Betts v. Brady*, 316 U.S., at 476 (dissenting opinion).[19]

18. The Court's decision in *Gagnon v. Scarpelli*, 411 U.S. 778 (1973), is not to the contrary. In *Scarpelli*, the Court determined that due process requires an individualized approach to requests for counsel by probationers facing revocation. The rule established there was based on respect for the rehabilitative focus of the probation system, the informality of probation proceedings, and the diminished liberty interest of an already-convicted probationer. *Id.*, at 785–789. None of these elements is present here. See also *Wolff v. McDonnell*, 418 U.S. 539, 569–570 (1974).

19. Of course, the case-by-case approach announced by the Court today places an even heavier burden on the trial court, which will be required to determine in advance what difference legal representation might make. A trial judge will be obligated to examine the State's documentary and testimonial evidence well before the hearing so as to reach an informed decision about the need for counsel in time to allow adequate preparation of the parent's case.

Assuming that this ad hoc review were adequate to ensure fairness, it is likely to be both cumbersome and costly. And because such review involves constitutional rights implicated by state adjudications, it necessarily will result in increased federal interference in state proceedings. The Court's implication to the contrary is belied by the Court's experience in the aftermath of *Betts v. Brady*. The Court was confronted with innumerable post verdict challenges to the fairness of particular trials, and expended much energy in effect evaluating the performance of state judges. This level of intervention in the criminal processes of the States prompted Justice Frankfurter, speaking for himself and two others, to complain that the Court was performing as a "super-legal-aid bureau." *Uveges v. Pennsylvania*, 335 U.S. 437, 450 (1948) (dissenting opinion). I fear that the decision today may transform the Court into a "super family court."

B

The problem of inadequate representation is painfully apparent in the present case. Petitioner, Abby Gail Lassiter, is the mother of five children. The State moved to remove the fifth child, William, from petitioner's care on the grounds of parental neglect. Although petitioner received notice of the removal proceedings, she did not appear at the hearing and was not represented. In May 1975, the State's District Court adjudicated William to be neglected under North Carolina law and placed him in the custody of the Durham County Department of Social Services. At some point, petitioner evidently arranged for the other four children to reside with and be cared for by her mother, Mrs. Lucille Lassiter. They remain under their grandmother's care at the present time.

As the Court notes, petitioner did not visit William after July 1976. She was unable to do so, for she was imprisoned as a result of her conviction for second-degree murder. In December 1977, she was visited in prison by a Durham County social worker who advised her that the Department planned to terminate her parental rights with respect to William. Petitioner immediately expressed strong opposition to that plan and indicated a desire to place the child with his grandmother. Hearing Tr. 15. After receiving a summons, a copy of the State's termination petition, and notice that a termination hearing would be held in August 1978, petitioner informed her prison guards about the legal proceeding. They took no steps to assist her in obtaining legal representation, *id.*, at 4; App. I to Reply to Brief in Opposition 4, nor was she informed that she had a right to counsel.[21] Under these circumstances, it scarcely would be appropriate, or fair, to find that petitioner had knowingly and intelligently waived a right to counsel.

At the termination hearing, the State's sole witness was the county worker who had met petitioner on the one occasion at the prison. This worker had been assigned to William's case in August 1977, yet much of her testimony concerned events prior to that date; she represented these events as contained in the agency record. Hearing Tr. 10–13. Petitioner failed to uncover this weakness in the worker's testimony. That is hardly surprising, for there is no indication that an agency record was introduced into evidence or was present in court, or

21. During her imprisonment, petitioner had spoken with an attorney concerning her criminal conviction. She did not discuss the termination proceeding with this lawyer, and he has stated under oath that in view of her indigency he would not have been interested in representing her at that proceeding even had she asked him to do so. App. 10–11, 16.

that petitioner or the grandmother ever had an opportunity to review any such record. The social worker also testified about her conversations with members of the community. In this hearsay testimony, the witness reported the opinion of others that the grandmother could not handle the additional responsibility of caring for the fifth child. *Id.*, at 14–15. There is no indication that these community members were unavailable to testify, and the County Attorney did not justify the admission of the hearsay. Petitioner made no objection to its admission.

The court gave petitioner an opportunity to cross-examine the social worker, *id.*, at 19, but she apparently did not understand that cross-examination required questioning rather than declarative statements. At this point, the judge became noticeably impatient with petitioner.[22] Petitioner then took the stand, and testified that she wanted William to live with his grandmother and his siblings. The judge questioned her for a brief period, and expressed open disbelief at one of her answers.[23] The final witness was the grandmother. Both the judge and the County Attorney questioned her. She denied having expressed unwillingness to take William into her home, and vehemently contradicted the social worker's statement that she

22. Hearing Tr. 19–20:

"**THE COURT**: All right. Do you want to ask her any questions?

"**[PETITIONER]**: About what? About what she—

"**THE COURT**: About this child.

"**[PETITIONER]**: Oh, yes.

"**THE COURT**: All right. Go ahead.

"**[PETITIONER]**: The only thing I know is that when you say—

"**THE COURT**: I don't want you to testify.

"**[PETITIONER]**: Okay.

"**THE COURT**: I want to know whether you want to cross-examine her or ask any questions.

"**[PETITIONER]**: Yes, I want to. Well, you know, the only thing I know about is my part that I know about it. I know—

"**THE COURT**: I am not talking about what you know. I want to know if you want to ask her any questions or not.

"**[PETITIONER]**: About that?

"**THE COURT**: Yes. Do you understand the nature of this proceeding?

"**[PETITIONER]**: Yes.

"**THE COURT**: And that is to terminate any rights you have to the child and place it for adoption, if necessary.

"**[PETITIONER]**: Yes, I know.

"**THE COURT**: Are there any questions you want to ask her about what she has testified to?

"**[PETITIONER]**: Yes.

"**THE COURT**: All right. Go ahead.

"**[PETITIONER]**: I want to know why you think you are going to turn my child over to a foster home? He knows my mother and he knows all of us. He knows her and he knows all of us.

"**THE COURT**: Who is he?

"**[PETITIONER]**: My son, William.

"**[SOCIAL WORKER]**: Ms. Lassiter, your son has been in foster care since May of 1975 and since that time—

"**[PETITIONER]**: Yeah, yeah and I didn't know anything about it either.

23. *Id.*, at 30:

"**[THE COURT]**: Did you know that your mother filed a complaint on the 8th day of May, 1975...?

"**A**: No, 'cause she said she didn't file no complaint.

"**[THE COURT]**: That was some ghost who came up here and filed it I suppose."

The judge concluded his questioning by saying to the County Attorney: "All right, Mr. Odom, see what you can do." *Id.*, at 36.

had complained to the Department about her daughter's neglect of the child.[24] Petitioner was not told that she could question her mother, and did not do so.[25] The County Attorney made a closing argument, *id.*, at 58–60, and the judge then asked petitioner if she had any final remarks. She responded: "Yes. I don't think it's right." *Id.*, at 61.

It is perhaps understandable that the District Court Judge experienced difficulty and exasperation in conducting this hearing. But both the difficulty and the exasperation are attributable in large measure, if not entirely, to the lack of counsel. An experienced attorney might have translated petitioner's reaction and emotion into several substantive legal arguments. The State charged petitioner with failing to arrange a "constructive plan" for her child's future or to demonstrate a "positive response" to the Department's intervention. A defense would have been that petitioner had arranged for the child to be cared for properly by his grandmother, and evidence might have been adduced to demonstrate the adequacy of the grandmother's care of the other children. See, *e.g.*, *In re Valdez*, 29 Utah 2d 63, 504 P.2d 1372 (1973); *Welfare Commissioner v. Anonymous*, 33 Conn.Supp. 100, 364 A.2d 250 (1976); *Diernfeld v. People*, 137 Colo. 238, 323 P.2d 628 (1958). See generally *Moore v. East Cleveland*, 431 U.S., at 504 (plurality opinion); *id.*, at 508–510 (opinion of Brennan, J.). The Department's own "diligence" in promoting the family's integrity was never put in issue during the hearing, yet it is surely significant in light of petitioner's incarceration and lack of access to her child. See, *e.g.*, *Weaver v. Roanoke Dept. of Human Resources*, 220 Va. 921, 929, 265 S.E.2d 692, 697 (1980); *In re Christopher H.*, 577 P.2d 1292, 1294 (Okla. 1978); *In re Kimberly I.*, 72 App.Div.2d 831, 833, 421 N.Y.S.2d 649, 651 (1979). Finally, the asserted willfulness of petitioner's lack of concern could obviously have been attacked since she was physically unable to regain custody or perhaps even to receive meaningful visits during 21 of the 24 months preceding the action. Cf. *In re Dinsmore*, 36 N.C.App. 720, 245 S.E.2d 386 (1978).

III

Petitioner plainly has not led the life of the exemplary citizen or model parent. It may well be that if she were accorded competent legal representation, the ultimate result in this particular case would be the same. But the issue before the Court is not petitioner's character; it is whether she was given a meaningful opportunity to be heard when the State moved to

24. This latter denial produced the following reaction from the court, *id.*, at 55:

"**Q** [from respondent]: Did you tell Ms. Mangum on the 8th day of May, 1975, that when your daughter was in the hospital having William that she left the children in the cold house with no heat?

"**A**: No, sir, no, sir, unh unh, no, sir.

"**[PETITIONER]**: That's a lie.

"**A**: No, sir, no, sir. God knows, I'll raise my right hand to God and die saying that. Somebody else told that.

"**[THE COURT]**: I wish you wouldn't talk like that it scares me to be in the same room with you."

25. The judge had initiated the examination of Mrs. Lassiter; subsequently he expressed exasperation with the rambling quality of her answers, *id.*, at 52:

"**THE COURT**: I tell you what, let's just stop all this. You question her, please. Just answer his questions. We'll be here all day at this rate. I mean, we are just wasting time, we're skipping from one subject to another—

"**CROSS EXAMINATION BY [RESPONDENT]:...**"

terminate absolutely her parental rights.[26] In light of the unpursued avenues of defense, and of the experience petitioner underwent at the hearing, I find virtually incredible the Court's conclusion today that her termination proceeding was fundamentally fair. To reach that conclusion, the Court simply ignores the defendant's obvious inability to speak effectively for herself, a factor the Court has found to be highly significant in past cases. See *Gagnon v. Scarpelli*, 411 U.S., at 791; *Uveges v. Pennsylvania*, 335 U.S., at 441–442; *Bute v. Illinois*, 333 U.S. 640, 677 (1948). See also *Vitek v. Jones*, 445 U.S., at 496–497 (plurality opinion); *id.*, at 498 (opinion of Powell, J.). I am unable to ignore that factor; instead, I believe that the record, and the norms of fairness acknowledged by the majority, compel a holding according counsel to petitioner and persons similarly situated.

Finally, I deem it not a little ironic that the Court on this very day *grants*, on due process grounds, an indigent putative father's claim for state-paid blood grouping tests in the interest of according him a meaningful opportunity to disprove his paternity, *Little v. Streater*, 452 U.S. 1, but in the present case *rejects*, on due process grounds, an indigent mother's claim for state-paid legal assistance when the State seeks to take her own child away from her in a termination proceeding. In *Little v. Streater*, the Court stresses and relies upon the need for "procedural fairness," the "compelling interest in the accuracy of [the] determination," the "not inconsiderable" risk of error, the indigent's "fac[ing] the State as an adversary," and "fundamental fairness," 452 U.S., at 13, 14, and 16.

There is some measure of inconsistency and tension here, it seems to me. I can attribute the distinction the Court draws only to a presumed difference between what it views as the "civil" and the "quasi-criminal," *Little v. Streater*, 452 U.S., at 10. Given the factual context of the two cases decided today, the significance of that presumed difference eludes me.

Ours, supposedly, is "a maturing society," *Trop v. Dulles*, 356 U.S. 86, 101 (1958) (plurality opinion), and our notion of due process is, "perhaps, the least frozen concept of our law." *Griffin v. Illinois*, 351 U.S. 12, 20 (1956) (opinion concurring in judgment). If the Court in *Boddie v. Connecticut*, 401 U.S. 371 (1971), was able to perceive as constitutionally necessary the access to judicial resources required to dissolve a marriage at the behest of private parties, surely it should perceive as similarly necessary the requested access to legal resources when the State itself seeks to dissolve the intimate and personal family bonds between parent and child. It will not open the "floodgates" that, I suspect, the Court fears. On the contrary, we cannot constitutionally afford the closure that the result in this sad case imposes upon us all.

I respectfully dissent.

Justice Stevens, dissenting.

26. Unfortunately, the Court does not confine itself to the issue at hand. By going outside the official record of this case, to unearth and recite details of petitioner's second-degree murder conviction set forth in an unpublished state appellate opinion, see *State v. Lassiter*, 33 N.C.App. 405, 235 S.E.2d 289 (1977); Rule 30(e)(3), N.C. Rules of Appellate Procedure, N.C.Gen.Stat. (Supp. 1979 to Vol. 4A), the Court apparently believes it has contributed evidence relevant to petitioner's fitness as a parent, and perhaps to the fitness of petitioner's mother as well. But while some States retain statutes permitting parental rights to be terminated upon a parent's criminal conviction, North Carolina is not among them. See N.C.Gen.Stat. § 7A-289.32 (Supp. 1979). See Note, On Prisoners and Parenting: Preserving the Tie That Binds, 87 Yale L.J. 1408, 1409–1410 (1978). Reliance on such evidence is likely to encourage the kind of subjective value judgments that an adversarial judicial proceeding is meant to avoid.

A woman's misconduct may cause the State to take formal steps to deprive her of her liberty. The State may incarcerate her for a fixed term and also may permanently deprive her of her freedom to associate with her child. The former is a pure deprivation of liberty; the latter is a deprivation of both liberty and property, because statutory rights of inheritance as well as the natural relationship may be destroyed. Although both deprivations are serious, often the deprivation of parental rights will be the more grievous of the two. The plain language of the Fourteenth Amendment commands that both deprivations must be accompanied by due process of law.

Without so stating explicitly, the Court appears to treat this case as though it merely involved the deprivation of an interest in property that is less worthy of protection than a person's liberty. The analysis employed in *Mathews v. Eldridge*, 424 U.S. 319, in which the Court balanced the costs and benefits of different procedural mechanisms for allocating a finite quantity of material resources among competing claimants, is an appropriate method of determining what process is due in property cases. Meeting the Court on its own terms, Justice Blackmun demonstrates that the *Mathews v. Eldridge* analysis requires the appointment of counsel in this type of case. I agree with his conclusion, but I would take one further step.

In my opinion the reasons supporting the conclusion that the Due Process Clause of the Fourteenth Amendment entitles the defendant in a criminal case to representation by counsel apply with equal force to a case of this kind. The issue is one of fundamental fairness, not of weighing the pecuniary costs against the societal benefits. Accordingly, even if the costs to the State were not relatively insignificant but rather were just as great as the costs of providing prosecutors, judges, and defense counsel to ensure the fairness of criminal proceedings, I would reach the same result in this category of cases. For the value of protecting our liberty from deprivation by the State without due process of law is priceless.

NOTES AND QUESTIONS

1. Why does the Court conclude that Ms. Lassiter did not need counsel? Do you think she did? Why isn't she entitled to counsel as a constitutional matter?

2. Under the Court's analysis, how would a court determine when a parent is entitled to counsel? How could the trial court make this determination before trial commences?

3. Is there a due-process right to counsel in criminal cases? If so, should there be a similar right in civil cases? Is it fundamentally fair to deprive a parent of counsel at a termination proceeding?

4. Does it really matter? According to Vivek Sankaran, forty-four states and the District of Columbia mandate the appointment of counsel for parents in a termination-of-parental-rights proceeding. Five states (Delaware, Hawaii, Minnesota, Nevada, and Vermont) permit but do not require the appointment of counsel. Vivek Sankaran, A National Survey on a Parent's Right to Counsel in Termination of Parental Rights and Dependency Cases, http://www.law.umich.edu/centersandprograms/ccl/specialprojects/Documents/National%20Survey%20on%20a%20Parent%27s%20Right%20to%20Counsel.pdf.

The Supreme Court did not consider the issue of the child's right to representation in these proceedings. Does the child have a similar right to counsel?

KENNY A. V. PERDUE

United States District Court for the Northern District of Georgia

356 F.Supp.2d 1353 (2005)

(See Section III.D., above, p. 646)

NOTES AND QUESTIONS

1. Is there an additional justification for providing counsel to children in a termination proceeding? What is it?

2. A few states provide for the appointment of counsel for the child at termination. See, e.g., Alaska Stat. § 47.10.050 (1998) (may appoint counsel for the child); Alaska Child in Need of Aid R. 12 (2005) (appoint counsel when in the interest of justice); Del. Code Ann. tit. 13, § 2504 (West 2009) (may appoint counsel to represent child's wishes); Ga. Code Ann. § 15-11-98 (West 2000) (court shall appoint counsel to represent child in any proceeding to terminate parental rights); Iowa Code § 232.113 (2002) (court shall appoint counsel for child and may serve as both attorney and guardian *ad litem* for the child); Ky. Rev. Stat. Ann. § 620.100 (West 2005) (child has right to counsel); La. Child. Code Ann. art. 1016 (2007) (child has right to independent counsel in termination proceeding); Md. Code Ann., Cts. & Jud. Proc. § 3-813 (West 2001) (child shall be represented by counsel); Mass. Gen. Laws ch. 119, § 39F (2011) (child has right to counsel); Minn. Stat. § 260C.163 (2012) (court shall appoint counsel for child ten years of age or older); Mont. Code Ann. § 41-3-425 (2011) (court shall appoint counsel when no guardian *ad litem* assigned; court may appoint counsel if child has GAL); Ohio Rev. Code Ann. § 2151.352 (West 2005) (child as party has right to counsel); Okla. Stat. tit. 10A, § 1-4-306 (2011) (attorney for child to represent child's express wishes); Or. Rev. Stat. § 419B.195 (2003) (court may appoint counsel for child); S.C. Code Ann. § 63-7-2560 (2010) (court must appoint counsel for any child who has a nonattorney guardian *ad litem* if GAL finds appointment of counsel necessary to protect rights and interests of child); Vt. Stat. Ann. tit. 33, § 5112 (2009) (court shall appoint attorney and GAL for child); W. Va. Code § 49-6-2 (2012) (child has right to counsel); Wis. Stat. § 48.23 (2009) (if petition contested, court may not place child older than twelve outside home unless appointed counsel).

SANTOSKY V. KRAMER

Supreme Court of the United States

455 U.S. 745 (1982)

Justice Blackmun delivered the opinion of the Court.

Under New York law, the State may terminate, over parental objection, the rights of parents in their natural child upon a finding that the child is "permanently neglected." N.Y.Soc.Serv. Law §§ 384-b.4.(d), 384-b.7.(a) (McKinney Supp. 1981–1982) (Soc.Serv.Law). The New York Family Court Act § 622 (McKinney 1975 and Supp. 1981–1982) (Fam.Ct.Act) requires that only a "fair preponderance of the evidence" support that finding. Thus, in New York, the factual certainty required to extinguish the parent-child relationship is no greater than that necessary to award money damages in an ordinary civil action.

Today we hold that the Due Process Clause of the Fourteenth Amendment demands more than this. Before a State may sever completely and irrevocably the rights of parents in their natural child, due process requires that the State support its allegations by at least clear and convincing evidence.

I

A

New York authorizes its officials to remove a child temporarily from his or her home if the child appears "neglected," within the meaning of Art. 10 of the Family Court Act. See §§ 1012(f), 1021–1029. Once removed, a child under the age of 18 customarily is placed "in the care of an authorized agency," Soc.Serv.Law § 384-b.7.(a), usually a state institution or a foster home. At that point, "the state's first obligation is to help the family with services to...reunite it...." § 384-b.1.(a)(iii). But if convinced that "positive, nurturing parent-child relationships no longer exist," § 384-b.1.(b), the State may initiate "permanent neglect" proceedings to free the child for adoption. The State bifurcates its permanent neglect proceeding into "fact-finding" and "dispositional" hearings. Fam.Ct.Act §§ 622, 623. At the factfinding stage, the State must prove that the child has been "permanently neglected," as defined by Fam.Ct.Act §§ 614.1.(a)–(d) and Soc.Serv.Law § 384-b.7.(a). See Fam.Ct.Act § 622. The Family Court judge then determines at a subsequent dispositional hearing what placement would serve the child's best interests. §§ 623, 631.

At the factfinding hearing, the State must establish, among other things, that for more than a year after the child entered state custody, the agency "made diligent efforts to encourage and strengthen the parental relationship." Fam.Ct.Act §§ 614.1.(c), 611. The State must further prove that during that same period, the child's natural parents failed "substantially and continuously or repeatedly to maintain contact with or plan for the future of the child although physically and financially able to do so." § 614.1.(d). Should the State support its allegations by "a fair preponderance of the evidence," § 622, the child may be declared permanently neglected. § 611. That declaration empowers the Family Court judge to terminate permanently the natural parents' rights in the child. §§ 631(c), 634. Termination denies the natural parents physical custody, as well as the rights ever to visit, communicate with, or regain custody of the child.[1]

New York's permanent neglect statute provides natural parents with certain procedural protections.[2] But New York permits its officials to establish "permanent neglect" with less proof than most States require. Thirty-five States, the District of Columbia, and the Virgin

1. At oral argument, counsel for petitioners asserted that, in New York, natural parents have no means of restoring terminated parental rights. Tr. of Oral Arg. 9. Counsel for respondents, citing Fam.Ct.Act § 1061, answered that parents may petition the Family Court to vacate or set aside an earlier order on narrow grounds, such as newly discovered evidence or fraud. Tr. of Oral Arg. 26. Counsel for respondents conceded, however, that this statutory provision has never been invoked to set aside a permanent neglect finding. *Id.*, at 27.

2. Most notably, natural parents have a statutory right to the assistance of counsel and of court-appointed counsel if they are indigent. Fam.Ct.Act § 262(a)(iii).

Islands currently specify a higher standard of proof, in parental rights termination proceedings, than a "fair preponderance of the evidence." The only analogous federal statute of which we are aware permits termination of parental rights solely upon "evidence beyond a reasonable doubt." Indian Child Welfare Act of 1978, Pub.L. 95-608, § 102(f), 92 Stat. 3072, 25 U.S.C. § 1912(f) (1976 ed., Supp. IV). The question here is whether New York's "fair preponderance of the evidence" standard is constitutionally sufficient.

B

Petitioners John Santosky II and Annie Santosky are the natural parents of Tina and John III. In November 1973, after incidents reflecting parental neglect, respondent Kramer, Commissioner of the Ulster County Department of Social Services, initiated a neglect proceeding under Fam.Ct.Act § 1022 and removed Tina from her natural home. About 10 months later, he removed John III and placed him with foster parents. On the day John was taken, Annie Santosky gave birth to a third child, Jed. When Jed was only three days old, respondent transferred him to a foster home on the ground that immediate removal was necessary to avoid imminent danger to his life or health.

In October 1978, respondent petitioned the Ulster County Family Court to terminate petitioners' parental rights in the three children.[4] Petitioners challenged the constitutionality of the "fair preponderance of the evidence" standard specified in Fam.Ct.Act § 622. The Family Court Judge rejected this constitutional challenge, App. 29–30, and weighed the evidence under the statutory standard. While acknowledging that the Santoskys had maintained contact with their children, the judge found those visits "at best superficial and devoid of any real emotional content." *Id.*, at 21. After deciding that the agency had made "'diligent efforts' to encourage and strengthen the parental relationship," *id.*, at 30, he concluded that the Santoskys were incapable, even with public assistance, of planning for the future of their children. *Id.*, at 33–37. The judge later held a dispositional hearing and ruled that the best interests of the three children required permanent termination of the Santoskys' custody.[5] *Id.*, at 39.

Petitioners appealed, again contesting the constitutionality of § 622's standard of proof. The New York Supreme Court, Appellate Division, affirmed, holding application of the preponderance-of-the-evidence standard "proper and constitutional." *In re John AA*, 75 App.Div.2d 910, 427 N.Y.S.2d 319, 320 (1980). That standard, the court reasoned, "recognizes and seeks to balance rights possessed by the child... with those of the natural parents...." *Ibid.*

4. Respondent had made an earlier and unsuccessful termination effort in September 1976. After a factfinding hearing, the Family Court Judge dismissed respondent's petition for failure to prove an essential element of Fam.Ct.Act § 614.1.(d). See *In re Santosky*, 89 Misc.2d 730, 393 N.Y.S.2d 486 (1977). The New York Supreme Court, Appellate Division, affirmed, finding that "the record as a whole" revealed that petitioners had "substantially planned for the future of the children." *In re John W.*, 63 App.Div.2d 750, 751, 404 N.Y.S.2d 717, 719 (1978).

5. Since respondent Kramer took custody of Tina, John III, and Jed, the Santoskys have had two other children, James and Jeremy. The State has taken no action to remove these younger children. At oral argument, counsel for respondents replied affirmatively when asked whether he was asserting that petitioners were "unfit to handle the three older ones but not unfit to handle the two younger ones." Tr. of Oral Arg. 24.

The New York Court of Appeals then dismissed petitioners' appeal to that court "upon the ground that no substantial constitutional question is directly involved." App. 55. We granted certiorari to consider petitioners' constitutional claim. 450 U.S. 993 (1981).

II

Last Term in *Lassiter v. Department of Social Services*, 452 U.S. 18 (1981), this Court, by a 5-4 vote, held that the Fourteenth Amendment's Due Process Clause does not require the appointment of counsel for indigent parents in every parental status termination proceeding. The case casts light, however, on the two central questions here—whether process is constitutionally due a natural parent at a State's parental rights termination proceeding, and, if so, what process is due.

In *Lassiter*, it was "not disputed that state intervention to terminate the relationship between [a parent] and [the] child must be accomplished by procedures meeting the requisites of the Due Process Clause." *Id.*, at 37 (first dissenting opinion); see *id.*, at 24–32 (opinion of the Court); *id.*, at 59–60 (Stevens, J., dissenting). See also *Little v. Streater*, 452 U.S. 1, 13 (1981). The absence of dispute reflected this Court's historical recognition that freedom of personal choice in matters of family life is a fundamental liberty interest protected by the Fourteenth Amendment. *Quilloin v. Walcott*, 434 U.S. 246, 255 (1978); *Smith v. Organization of Foster Families*, 431 U.S. 816, 845 (1977); *Moore v. East Cleveland*, 431 U.S. 494, 499 (1977) (plurality opinion); *Cleveland Board of Education v. LaFleur*, 414 U.S. 632, 639–640 (1974); *Stanley v. Illinois*, 405 U.S. 645, 651–652 (1972); *Prince v. Massachusetts*, 321 U.S. 158, 166 (1944); *Pierce v. Society of Sisters*, 268 U.S. 510, 534–535 (1925); *Meyer v. Nebraska*, 262 U.S. 390, 399 (1923).

The fundamental liberty interest of natural parents in the care, custody, and management of their child does not evaporate simply because they have not been model parents or have lost temporary custody of their child to the State. Even when blood relationships are strained, parents retain a vital interest in preventing the irretrievable destruction of their family life. If anything, persons faced with forced dissolution of their parental rights have a more critical need for procedural protections than do those resisting state intervention into ongoing family affairs. When the State moves to destroy weakened familial bonds, it must provide the parents with fundamentally fair procedures.[7]

In *Lassiter*, the Court and three dissenters agreed that the nature of the process due in parental rights termination proceedings turns on a balancing of the "three distinct factors" specified in *Mathews v. Eldridge*, 424 U.S. 319, 335 (1976): the private interests affected by the proceeding; the risk of error created by the State's chosen procedure; and the countervailing governmental interest supporting use of the challenged procedure. See 452 U.S., at 27–31; *id.*, at 37–48 (first dissenting opinion). But see *id.*, at 59–60 (Stevens, J., dissenting). While the respective *Lassiter* opinions disputed whether those factors should be weighed against a presumption disfavoring appointed counsel for one not threatened with loss of physical liberty,

7. We therefore reject respondent Kramer's claim that a parental rights termination proceeding does not interfere with a fundamental liberty interest. See Brief for Respondent Kramer 11–18; Tr. of Oral Arg. 38. The fact that important liberty interests of the child and its foster parents may also be affected by a permanent neglect proceeding does not justify denying the natural parents constitutionally adequate procedures. Nor can the State refuse to provide natural parents adequate procedural safeguards on the ground that the family unit already has broken down; that is the very issue the permanent neglect proceeding is meant to decide.

compare 452 U.S., at 31–32, with *id.*, at 41, and n. 8 (first dissenting opinion), that concern is irrelevant here. Unlike the Court's right-to-counsel rulings, its decisions concerning constitutional burdens of proof have not turned on any presumption favoring any particular standard. To the contrary, the Court has engaged in a straight-forward consideration of the factors identified in *Eldridge* to determine whether a particular standard of proof in a particular proceeding satisfies due process.

In *Addington v. Texas*, 441 U.S. 418 (1979), the Court, by a unanimous vote of the participating Justices, declared: "The function of a standard of proof, as that concept is embodied in the Due Process Clause and in the realm of factfinding, is to 'instruct the factfinder concerning the degree of confidence our society thinks he should have in the correctness of factual conclusions for a particular type of adjudication.'" *Id.*, at 423 quoting *In re Winship*, 397 U.S. 358, 370 (1970) (Harlan, J., concurring). *Addington* teaches that, in any given proceeding, the minimum standard of proof tolerated by the due process requirement reflects not only the weight of the private and public interests affected, but also a societal judgment about how the risk of error should be distributed between the litigants.

Thus, while private parties may be interested intensely in a civil dispute over money damages, application of a "fair preponderance of the evidence" standard indicates both society's "minimal concern with the outcome," and a conclusion that the litigants should "share the risk of error in roughly equal fashion." 441 U.S., at 423. When the State brings a criminal action to deny a defendant liberty or life, however, "the interests of the defendant are of such magnitude that historically and without any explicit constitutional requirement they have been protected by standards of proof designed to exclude as nearly as possible the likelihood of an erroneous judgment." *Ibid.* The stringency of the "beyond a reasonable doubt" standard bespeaks the "weight and gravity" of the private interest affected, *id.*, at 427, society's interest in avoiding erroneous convictions, and a judgment that those interests together require that "society impos[e] almost the entire risk of error upon itself." *Id.*, at 424. See also *In re Winship*, 397 U.S., at 372 (Harlan, J., concurring).

The "minimum requirements [of procedural due process] being a matter of federal law, they are not diminished by the fact that the State may have specified its own procedures that it may deem adequate for determining the preconditions to adverse official action." *Vitek v. Jones*, 445 U.S. 480, 491 (1980). See also *Logan v. Zimmerman Brush Co.*, 455 U.S. 422, 432 (1982). Moreover, the degree of proof required in a particular type of proceeding "is the kind of question which has traditionally been left to the judiciary to resolve." *Woodby v. INS*, 385 U.S. 276, 284 (1966).[8] "In cases involving individual rights, whether criminal or civil, '[t]he standard of proof [at a minimum] reflects the value society places on individual liberty.'" *Addington v. Texas*, 441 U.S., at 425 quoting *Tippett v. Maryland*, 436 F.2d 1153, 1166 (CA4 1971) (opinion concurring in part and dissenting in part), cert. dism'd *sub nom. Murel v. Baltimore City Criminal Court*, 407 U.S. 355 (1972).

This Court has mandated an intermediate standard of proof—"clear and convincing evidence"—when the individual interests at stake in a state proceeding are both

8. The dissent charges that "this Court simply has no role in establishing the standards of proof that States must follow in the various judicial proceedings they afford to their citizens." As the dissent properly concedes, however, the Court must examine a State's chosen standard to determine whether it satisfies "the constitutional minimum of 'fundamental fairness.'"

"particularly important" and "more substantial than mere loss of money." *Addington v. Texas*, 441 U.S., at 424. Notwithstanding "the state's 'civil labels and good intentions,'" *id.*, at 427, quoting *In re Winship*, 397 U.S., at 365–366, the Court has deemed this level of certainty necessary to preserve fundamental fairness in a variety of government-initiated proceedings that threaten the individual involved with "a significant deprivation of liberty" or "stigma." 441 U.S., at 425. See, *e.g.*, *Addington v. Texas*, *supra* (civil commitment); *Woodby v. INS*, 385 U.S., at 285 (deportation); *Chaunt v. United States*, 364 U.S. 350, 353 (1960) (denaturalization); *Schneiderman v. United States*, 320 U.S. 118, 125, 159 (1943) (denaturalization).

In *Lassiter*, to be sure, the Court held that fundamental fairness may be maintained in parental rights termination proceedings even when some procedures are mandated only on a case-by-case basis, rather than through rules of general application. 452 U.S., at 31–32 (natural parent's right to court-appointed counsel should be determined by the trial court, subject to appellate review). But this Court never has approved case-by-case determination of the proper *standard of proof* for a given proceeding. Standards of proof, like other "procedural due process rules[,] are shaped by the risk of error inherent in the truth-finding process as applied to the *generality of cases*, not the rare exceptions." *Mathews v. Eldridge*, 424 U.S., at 344 (emphasis added). Since the litigants and the factfinder must know at the outset of a given proceeding how the risk of error will be allocated, the standard of proof necessarily must be calibrated in advance. Retrospective case-by-case review cannot preserve fundamental fairness when a class of proceedings is governed by a constitutionally defective evidentiary standard.[9]

III

In parental rights termination proceedings, the private interest affected is commanding; the risk of error from using a preponderance standard is substantial; and the countervailing governmental interest favoring that standard is comparatively slight. Evaluation of the three *Eldridge* factors compels the conclusion that use of a "fair preponderance of the evidence" standard in such proceedings is inconsistent with due process.

9. For this reason, we reject the suggestions of respondents and the dissent that the constitutionality of New York's statutory procedures must be evaluated as a "package." See Tr. of Oral Arg. 25, 36, 38. Indeed, we would rewrite our precedents were we to excuse a constitutionally defective standard of proof based on an amorphous assessment of the "cumulative effect" of state procedures. In the criminal context, for example, the Court has never assumed that "strict substantive standards or special procedures compensate for a lower burden of proof...." See *In re Winship*, 397 U.S., at 368. Nor has the Court treated appellate review as a curative for an inadequate burden of proof. See *Woodby v. INS*, 385 U.S. 276, 282 (1966) ("judicial review is generally limited to ascertaining whether the evidence relied upon by the trier of fact was of sufficient quality and substantiality to support the rationality of the judgment").

As the dissent points out, "the standard of proof is a crucial component of legal process, the primary function of which is 'to minimize the risk of erroneous decisions.'" Notice, summons, right to counsel, rules of evidence, and evidentiary hearings are all procedures to place information before the factfinder. But only the standard of proof "instruct[s] the factfinder concerning the degree of confidence our society thinks he should have in the correctness of factual conclusions" he draws from that information. *In re Winship*, 397 U.S., at 370 (Harlan, J., concurring). The statutory provision of right to counsel and multiple hearings before termination cannot suffice to protect a natural parent's fundamental liberty interests if the State is willing to tolerate undue uncertainty in the determination of the dispositive facts.

A

"The extent to which procedural due process must be afforded the recipient is influenced by the extent to which he may be 'condemned to suffer grievous loss.'" *Goldberg v. Kelly*, 397 U.S. 254, 262–263 (1970), quoting *Joint Anti-Fascist Refugee Committee v. McGrath*, 341 U.S. 123, 168 (1951) (Frankfurter, J., concurring). Whether the loss threatened by a particular type of proceeding is sufficiently grave to warrant more than average certainty on the part of the factfinder turns on both the nature of the private interest threatened and the permanency of the threatened loss.

Lassiter declared it "plain beyond the need for multiple citation" that a natural parent's "desire for and right to 'the companionship, care, custody, and management of his or her children'" is an interest far more precious than any property right. 452 U.S., at 27, quoting *Stanley v. Illinois*, 405 U.S., at 651. When the State initiates a parental rights termination proceeding, it seeks not merely to infringe that fundamental liberty interest, but to end it. "If the State prevails, it will have worked a unique kind of deprivation.... A parent's interest in the accuracy and justice of the decision to terminate his or her parental status is, therefore, a commanding one." 452 U.S., at 27.

In government-initiated proceedings to determine juvenile delinquency, *In re Winship*, *supra*; civil commitment, *Addington v. Texas*, *supra*; deportation, *Woodby v. INS*, *supra*; and denaturalization, *Chaunt v. United States*, *supra*, and *Schneiderman v. United States*, *supra*, this Court has identified losses of individual liberty sufficiently serious to warrant imposition of an elevated burden of proof. Yet juvenile delinquency adjudications, civil commitment, deportation, and denaturalization, at least to a degree, are all *reversible* official actions. Once affirmed on appeal, a New York decision terminating parental rights is *final* and irrevocable. Few forms of state action are both so severe and so irreversible.

Thus, the first *Eldridge* factor—the private interest affected—weighs heavily against use of the preponderance standard at a state-initiated permanent neglect proceeding. We do not deny that the child and his foster parents are also deeply interested in the outcome of that contest. But at the factfinding stage of the New York proceeding, the focus emphatically is not on them.

The factfinding does not purport—and is not intended—to balance the child's interest in a normal family home against the parents' interest in raising the child. Nor does it purport to determine whether the natural parents or the foster parents would provide the better home. Rather, the factfinding hearing pits the State directly against the parents. The State alleges that the natural parents are at fault. Fam.Ct.Act § 614.1.(d). The questions disputed and decided are what the State did—"made diligent efforts," § 614.1.(c)—and what the natural parents did not do—"maintain contact with or plan for the future of the child." § 614.1.(d). The State marshals an array of public resources to prove its case and disprove the parents' case. Victory by the State not only makes termination of parental rights possible; it entails a judicial determination that the parents are unfit to raise their own children.[10]

10. The Family Court Judge in the present case expressly refused to terminate petitioners' parental rights on a "non-statutory, no-fault basis." App. 22–29. Nor is it clear that the State constitutionally could terminate a parent's rights *without* showing parental unfitness. See *Quilloin v. Walcott*, 434 U.S. 246, 255 (1978) ("We have little doubt that the Due Process Clause would be offended '[i]f a State were to attempt to force the breakup of a natural family, over the objections of the parents and their children, without some showing of unfitness and for the sole reason that to do so was thought to be in the children's best interest,'" quoting *Smith v. Organization of Foster Families*, 431 U.S. 816, 862–863 (1977) (Stewart, J., concurring in judgment)).

At the factfinding, the State cannot presume that a child and his parents are adversaries. After the State has established parental unfitness at that initial proceeding, the court may assume at the *dispositional* stage that the interests of the child and the natural parents do diverge. See Fam.Ct.Act § 631 (judge shall make his order "solely on the basis of the best interests of the child," and thus has no obligation to consider the natural parents' rights in selecting dispositional alternatives). But until the State proves parental unfitness, the child and his parents share a vital interest in preventing erroneous termination of their natural relationship.[11] Thus, at the factfinding, the interests of the child and his natural parents coincide to favor use of error-reducing procedures.

However substantial the foster parents' interests may be, cf. *Smith v. Organization of Foster Families*, 431 U.S., at 845–847, they are not implicated directly in the factfinding stage of a state-initiated permanent neglect proceeding against the natural parents. If authorized, the foster parents may pit their interests directly against those of the natural parents by initiating their own permanent neglect proceeding. Fam.Ct.Act § 1055(d); Soc.Serv.Law §§ 384-6.3.(b), 392.7.(c). Alternatively, the foster parents can make their case for custody at the dispositional stage of a state-initiated proceeding, where the judge already has decided the issue of permanent neglect and is focusing on the placement that would serve the child's best interests. Fam. Ct.Act §§ 623, 631. For the foster parents, the State's failure to prove permanent neglect may prolong the delay and uncertainty until their foster child is freed for adoption. But for the natural parents, a finding of permanent neglect can cut off forever their rights in their child. Given this disparity of consequence, we have no difficulty finding that the balance of private interests strongly favors heightened procedural protections.

B

Under *Mathews v. Eldridge*, we next must consider both the risk of erroneous deprivation of private interests resulting from use of a "fair preponderance" standard and the likelihood that a higher evidentiary standard would reduce that risk. See 424 U.S., at 335. Since the factfinding phase of a permanent neglect proceeding is an adversary contest between the State and the natural parents, the relevant question is whether a preponderance standard fairly allocates the risk of an erroneous factfinding between these two parties.

In New York, the factfinding stage of a state-initiated permanent neglect proceeding bears many of the indicia of a criminal trial. Cf. *Lassiter v. Department of Social Services*, 452 U.S., at 42–44 (first dissenting opinion); *Meltzer v. C. Buck LeCraw & Co.*, 402 U.S. 954, 959 (1971) (Black, J., dissenting from denial of certiorari). The Commissioner of Social Services charges the parents with permanent neglect. They are served by summons. Fam.Ct.Act §§ 614, 616, 617. The factfinding hearing is conducted pursuant to formal rules of evidence. § 624. The State, the parents, and the child are all represented by counsel. §§ 249, 262. The State seeks

11. For a child, the consequences of termination of his natural parents' rights may well be far-reaching. In Colorado, for example, it has been noted: "The child loses the right of support and maintenance, for which he may thereafter be dependent upon society; the right to inherit; and all other rights inherent in the legal parent-child relationship, not just for [a limited] period..., but forever." *In re K.S.*, 33 Colo.App. 72, 76, 515 P.2d 130, 133 (1973).

Some losses cannot be measured. In this case, for example, Jed Santosky was removed from his natural parents' custody when he was only three days old; the judge's finding of permanent neglect effectively foreclosed the possibility that Jed would ever know his natural parents.

to establish a series of historical facts about the intensity of its agency's efforts to reunite the family, the infrequency and insubstantiality of the parents' contacts with their child, and the parents' inability or unwillingness to formulate a plan for the child's future. The attorneys submit documentary evidence, and call witnesses who are subject to cross-examination. Based on all the evidence, the judge then determines whether the State has proved the statutory elements of permanent neglect by a fair preponderance of the evidence. § 622.

At such a proceeding, numerous factors combine to magnify the risk of erroneous factfinding. Permanent neglect proceedings employ imprecise substantive standards that leave determinations unusually open to the subjective values of the judge. See *Smith v. Organization of Foster Families*, 431 U.S., at 835, n. 36. In appraising the nature and quality of a complex series of encounters among the agency, the parents, and the child, the court possesses unusual discretion to underweigh probative facts that might favor the parent.[12] Because parents subject to termination proceedings are often poor, uneducated, or members of minority groups, *id.*, at 833–835, such proceedings are often vulnerable to judgments based on cultural or class bias.

The State's ability to assemble its case almost inevitably dwarfs the parents' ability to mount a defense. No predetermined limits restrict the sums an agency may spend in prosecuting a given termination proceeding. The State's attorney usually will be expert on the issues contested and the procedures employed at the factfinding hearing, and enjoys full access to all public records concerning the family. The State may call on experts in family relations, psychology, and medicine to bolster its case. Furthermore, the primary witnesses at the hearing will be the agency's own professional caseworkers whom the State has empowered both to investigate the family situation and to testify against the parents. Indeed, because the child is already in agency custody, the State even has the power to shape the historical events that form the basis for termination.[13]

The disparity between the adversaries' litigation resources is matched by a striking asymmetry in their litigation options. Unlike criminal defendants, natural parents have no "double jeopardy" defense against repeated state termination efforts. If the State initially fails to win termination, as New York did here, it always can try once again to cut off the parents' rights

12. For example, a New York court appraising an agency's "diligent efforts" to provide the parents with social services can excuse efforts not made on the grounds that they would have been "detrimental to the best interests of the child." Fam.Ct.Act § 614.1.(c). In determining whether the parent "substantially and continuously or repeatedly" failed to "maintain contact with…the child," § 614.1.(d), the judge can discount actual visits or communications on the grounds that they were insubstantial or "overtly demonstrat[ed] a lack of affectionate and concerned parenthood." Soc.Serv.Law § 384-b.7.(b). When determining whether the parent planned for the child's future, the judge can reject as unrealistic plans based on overly optimistic estimates of physical or financial ability. § 384-b.7.(c).

13. In this case, for example, the parents claim that the State sought court orders denying them the right to visit their children, which would have prevented them from maintaining the contact required by Fam.Ct.Act. § 614.1.(d). See Brief for Petitioners 9. The parents further claim that the State cited their rejection of social services they found offensive or superfluous as proof of the agency's "diligent efforts" and their own "failure to plan" for the children's future. *Id.*, at 10–11.

We need not accept these statements as true to recognize that the State's unusual ability to structure the evidence increases the risk of an erroneous factfinding. Of course, the disparity between the litigants' resources will be vastly greater in States where there is no statutory right to court-appointed counsel. See *Lassiter v. Department of Social Services*, 452 U.S. 18, 34 (1981) (only 33 States and the District of Columbia provide that right by statute).

after gathering more or better evidence. Yet even when the parents have attained the level of fitness required by the State, they have no similar means by which they can forestall future termination efforts.

Coupled with a "fair preponderance of the evidence" standard, these factors create a significant prospect of erroneous termination. A standard of proof that by its very terms demands consideration of the quantity, rather than the quality, of the evidence may misdirect the factfinder in the marginal case. See *In re Winship*, 397 U.S., at 371 (Harlan, J., concurring). Given the weight of the private interests at stake, the social cost of even occasional error is sizable.

Raising the standard of proof would have both practical and symbolic consequences. Cf. *Addington v. Texas*, 441 U.S., at 426. The Court has long considered the heightened standard of proof used in criminal prosecutions to be "a prime instrument for reducing the risk of convictions resting on factual error." *In re Winship*, 397 U.S., at 363. An elevated standard of proof in a parental rights termination proceeding would alleviate "the possible risk that a factfinder might decide to [deprive] an individual based solely on a few isolated instances of unusual conduct [or]...idiosyncratic behavior." *Addington v. Texas*, 441 U.S., at 427. "Increasing the burden of proof is one way to impress the factfinder with the importance of the decision and thereby perhaps to reduce the chances that inappropriate" terminations will be ordered. *Ibid.*

The Appellate Division approved New York's preponderance standard on the ground that it properly "balanced rights possessed by the child...with those of the natural parents...." 75 App.Div.2d, at 910, 427 N.Y.S.2d, at 320. By so saying, the court suggested that a preponderance standard properly allocates the risk of error *between* the parents and the child.[14] That view is fundamentally mistaken.

The court's theory assumes that termination of the natural parents' rights invariably will benefit the child.[15] Yet we have noted above that the parents and the child share an interest in avoiding erroneous termination. Even accepting the court's assumption, we cannot agree with its conclusion that a preponderance standard fairly distributes the risk of error between parent and child. Use of that standard reflects the judgment that society is nearly neutral between erroneous termination of parental rights and erroneous failure to terminate those rights. Cf. *In re Winship*, 397 U.S., at 371 (Harlan, J., concurring). For the child, the likely consequence of an erroneous failure to terminate is preservation of an uneasy status quo.[16] For the natural

14. The dissent makes a similar claim.

15. This is a hazardous assumption at best. Even when a child's natural home is imperfect, permanent removal from that home will not necessarily improve his welfare. See, *e.g.*, Wald, State Intervention on Behalf of "Neglected" Children: A Search for Realistic Standards, 27 Stan.L.Rev. 985, 993 (1975) ("In fact, under current practice, coercive intervention frequently results in placing a child in a more detrimental situation than he would be in without intervention").

Nor does termination of parental rights necessarily ensure adoption. See Brief for Community Action for Legal Services, Inc., et al. as *Amici Curiae* 22–23. Even when a child eventually finds an adoptive family, he may spend years moving between state institutions and "temporary" foster placements after his ties to his natural parents have been severed. See *Smith v. Organization of Foster Families*, 431 U.S., at 833–838 (describing the "limbo" of the New York foster care system).

16. When the termination proceeding occurs, the child is not living at his natural home. A child cannot be adjudicated "permanently neglected" until, "for a period of more than one year," he has been in "the care of an authorized agency." Soc.Serv.Law § 384-b.7.(a); Fam.Ct.Act § 614.1.(d).

Under New York law, a judge has ample discretion to ensure that, once removed from his natural parents on grounds of neglect, a child will not return to a hostile environment. In this case, when the State's

parents, however, the consequence of an erroneous termination is the unnecessary destruction of their natural family. A standard that allocates the risk of error nearly equally between those two outcomes does not reflect properly their relative severity.

C

Two state interests are at stake in parental rights termination proceedings—a *parens patriae* interest in preserving and promoting the welfare of the child and a fiscal and administrative interest in reducing the cost and burden of such proceedings. A standard of proof more strict than preponderance of the evidence is consistent with both interests.

"Since the State has an urgent interest in the welfare of the child, it shares the parent's interest in an accurate and just decision" at the factfinding proceeding. *Lassiter v. Department of Social Services*, 452 U.S., at 27. As *parens patriae*, the State's goal is to provide the child with a permanent home. See Soc.Serv.Law § 384-b.1.(a)(i) (statement of legislative findings and intent). Yet while there is still reason to believe that positive, nurturing parent-child relationships exist, the *parens patriae* interest favors preservation, not severance, of natural familial bonds.[17] § 384-b.1.(a)(ii). "[T]he State registers no gain towards its declared goals when it separates children from the custody of fit parents." *Stanley v. Illinois*, 405 U.S., at 652.

The State's interest in finding the child an alternative permanent home arises only "when it is *clear* that the natural parent cannot or will not provide a normal family home for the child." Soc.Serv.Law § 384-b.1.(a)(iv) (emphasis added). At the factfinding, that goal is served by procedures that promote an accurate determination of whether the natural parents can and will provide a normal home.

Unlike a constitutional requirement of hearings, see, *e.g., Mathews v. Eldridge*, 424 U.S., at 347, or court-appointed counsel, a stricter standard of proof would reduce factual error without imposing substantial fiscal burdens upon the State. As we have observed, 35 States already have adopted a higher standard by statute or court decision without apparent effect on the speed, form, or cost of their factfinding proceedings.

Nor would an elevated standard of proof create any real administrative burdens for the State's factfinders. New York Family Court judges already are familiar with a higher evidentiary standard in other parental rights termination proceedings not involving permanent neglect. See Soc.Serv.Law §§ 384-b.3.(g), 384-b.4.(c), and 384-b.4.(e) (requiring "clear and convincing proof" before parental rights may be terminated for reasons of mental illness and mental retardation or severe and repeated child abuse). New York also demands at least clear and convincing evidence in proceedings of far less moment than parental rights termination proceedings. See, *e.g.*, N.Y. Veh. & Traf. Law § 227.1 (McKinney Supp. 1981) (requiring the State to prove traffic infractions by "clear and convincing evidence") and *In re Rosenthal v. Hartnett*, 36 N.Y.2d 269, 367 N.Y.S.2d 247, 326 N.E.2d 811 (1975); see also *Ross v. Food Specialties*, Inc., 6 N.Y.2d 336, 341, 189 N.Y.S.2d 857, 859, 160 N.E.2d 618, 620 (1959)

initial termination effort failed for lack of proof, the court simply issued orders under Fam.Ct. Act § 1055(b) extending the period of the child's foster home placement. See App. 19–20. See also Fam.Ct. Act § 632(b) (when State's permanent neglect petition is dismissed for insufficient evidence, judge retains jurisdiction to reconsider underlying orders of placement); § 633 (judge may suspend judgment at dispositional hearing for an additional year).

17. Any *parens patriae* interest in terminating the natural parents' rights arises only at the dispositional phase, *after* the parents have been found unfit.

(requiring "clear, positive and convincing evidence" for contract reformation). We cannot believe that it would burden the State unduly to require that its factfinders have the same factual certainty when terminating the parent-child relationship as they must have to suspend a driver's license.

IV

The logical conclusion of this balancing process is that the "fair preponderance of the evidence" standard prescribed by Fam.Ct.Act § 622 violates the Due Process Clause of the Fourteenth Amendment.[18] The Court noted in *Addington*: "The individual should not be asked to share equally with society the risk of error when the possible injury to the individual is significantly greater than any possible harm to the state." 441 U.S., at 427. Thus, at a parental rights termination proceeding, a near-equal allocation of risk between the parents and the State is constitutionally intolerable. The next question, then, is whether a "beyond a reasonable doubt" or a "clear and convincing" standard is constitutionally mandated.

In *Addington*, the Court concluded that application of a reasonable-doubt standard is inappropriate in civil commitment proceedings for two reasons—because of our hesitation to apply that unique standard "too broadly or casually in noncriminal cases," *id*., at 428, and because the psychiatric evidence ordinarily adduced at commitment proceedings is rarely susceptible to proof beyond a reasonable doubt. *Id*., at 429–430, 432–433. To be sure, as has been noted above, in the Indian Child Welfare Act of 1978, Pub.L. 95-608, § 102(f), 92 Stat. 3072, 25 U.S.C. § 1912(f) (1976 ed., Supp. IV), Congress requires "evidence beyond a reasonable doubt" for termination of Indian parental rights, reasoning that "the removal of a child from the parents is a penalty as great [as], if not greater, than a criminal penalty. . . . " H.R.Rep. No. 95-1386, p. 22 (1978). Congress did not consider, however, the evidentiary problems that would arise if proof beyond a reasonable doubt were required in all state-initiated parental rights termination hearings.

Like civil commitment hearings, termination proceedings often require the factfinder to evaluate medical and psychiatric testimony, and to decide issues difficult to prove to a level of absolute certainty, such as lack of parental motive, absence of affection between parent and child, and failure of parental foresight and progress. Cf. *Lassiter v. Department of Social Services*, 452 U.S., at 30; *id*., at 44–46 (first dissenting opinion) (describing issues raised in state termination proceedings). The substantive standards applied vary from State to State. Although Congress found a "beyond a reasonable doubt" standard proper in one type of parental rights termination case, another legislative body might well conclude that a reasonable-doubt standard would erect an unreasonable barrier to state efforts to free permanently neglected children for adoption.

A majority of the States have concluded that a "clear and convincing evidence" standard of proof strikes a fair balance between the rights of the natural parents and the State's legitimate concerns. We hold that such a standard adequately conveys to the factfinder the level of subjective certainty about his factual conclusions necessary to satisfy due process. We further hold that

18. The dissent's claim that today's decision "will inevitably lead to the federalization of family law," is, of course, vastly overstated. As the dissent properly notes, the Court's duty to "refrai[n] from interfering with state answers to domestic relations questions" has never required "that the Court should blink at clear constitutional violations in state statutes."

determination of the precise burden equal to or greater than that standard is a matter of state law properly left to state legislatures and state courts. Cf. *Addington v. Texas*, 441 U.S., at 433.

We, of course, express no view on the merits of petitioners' claims. At a hearing conducted under a constitutionally proper standard, they may or may not prevail. Without deciding the outcome under any of the standards we have approved, we vacate the judgment of the Appellate Division and remand the case for further proceedings not inconsistent with this opinion....

Justice Rehnquist, with whom The Chief Justice, Justice White, and Justice O'Connor join, dissenting.

I believe that few of us would care to live in a society where every aspect of life was regulated by a single source of law, whether that source be this Court or some other organ of our complex body politic. But today's decision certainly moves us in that direction. By parsing the New York scheme and holding one narrow provision unconstitutional, the majority invites further federal-court intrusion into every facet of state family law. If ever there were an area in which federal courts should heed the admonition of Justice Holmes that "a page of history is worth a volume of logic,"[1] it is in the area of domestic relations. This area has been left to the States from time immemorial, and not without good reason.

Equally as troubling is the majority's due process analysis. The Fourteenth Amendment guarantees that a State will treat individuals with "fundamental fairness" whenever its actions infringe their protected liberty or property interests. By adoption of the procedures relevant to this case, New York has created an exhaustive program to assist parents in regaining the custody of their children and to protect parents from the unfair deprivation of their parental rights. And yet the majority's myopic scrutiny of the standard of proof blinds it to the very considerations and procedures which make the New York scheme "fundamentally fair."

I

State intervention in domestic relations has always been an unhappy but necessary feature of life in our organized society. For all of our experience in this area, we have found no fully satisfactory solutions to the painful problem of child abuse and neglect. We have found, however, that leaving the States free to experiment with various remedies has produced novel approaches and promising progress.

Throughout this experience the Court has scrupulously refrained from interfering with state answers to domestic relations questions. "Both theory and the precedents of this Court teach us solicitude for state interests, particularly in the field of family and family-property arrangements." *United States v. Yazell*, 382 U.S. 341, 352 (1966). This is not to say that the Court should blink at clear constitutional violations in state statutes, but rather that in this area, of all areas, "substantial weight must be given to the good-faith judgments of the individuals [administering a program]...that the procedures they have provided assure fair consideration of the...claims of individuals." *Mathews v. Eldridge*, 424 U.S. 319, 349 (1976).

This case presents a classic occasion for such solicitude. As will be seen more fully in the next part, New York has enacted a comprehensive plan to *aid* marginal parents in regaining the custody of their child. The central purpose of the New York plan is to reunite divided

1. *New York Trust Co. v. Eisner*, 256 U.S. 345, 349 (1921).

families. Adoption of the preponderance-of-the-evidence standard represents New York's good-faith effort to balance the interest of parents against the legitimate interests of the child and the State. These earnest efforts by state officials should be given weight in the Court's application of due process principles. "Great constitutional provisions must be administered with caution. Some play must be allowed for the joints of the machine, and it must be remembered that legislatures are ultimate guardians of the liberties and welfare of the people in quite as great a degree as the courts." *Missouri, K. & T.R. Co. v. May*, 194 U.S. 267, 270 (1904).[2]

The majority may believe that it is adopting a relatively unobtrusive means of ensuring that termination proceedings provide "due process of law." In fact, however, fixing the standard of proof as a matter of federal constitutional law will only lead to further federal-court intervention in state schemes. By holding that due process requires proof by clear and convincing evidence the majority surely cannot mean that any state scheme passes constitutional muster so long as it applies that standard of proof. A state law permitting termination of parental rights upon a showing of neglect by clear and convincing evidence certainly would not be acceptable to the majority if it provided no procedures other than one 30-minute hearing. Similarly, the majority probably would balk at a state scheme that permitted termination of parental rights on a clear and convincing showing merely that such action would be in the best interests of the child. See *Smith v. Organization of Foster Families*, 431 U.S. 816, 862–863 (1977) (Stewart, J., concurring in judgment).

After fixing the standard of proof, therefore, the majority will be forced to evaluate other aspects of termination proceedings with reference to that point. Having in this case abandoned evaluation of the overall effect of a scheme, and with it the possibility of finding that strict substantive standards or special procedures compensate for a lower burden of proof, the majority's approach will inevitably lead to the federalization of family law. Such a trend will only thwart state searches for better solutions in an area where this Court should encourage state experimentation. "It is one of the happy incidents of the federal system that a single courageous State may, if its citizens choose, serve as a laboratory; and try novel social and economic experiments without risk to the rest of the country. This Court has the power to prevent an experiment." *New State Ice Co. v. Liebmann*, 285 U.S. 262, 311 (1932) (Brandeis, J., dissenting). It should not do so in the absence of a clear constitutional violation. As will be seen in the next part, no clear constitutional violation has occurred in this case.

II

As the majority opinion notes, petitioners are the parents of five children, three of whom were removed from petitioners' care on or before August 22, 1974. During the next four and one-half

2. The majority asserts that "the degree of proof required in a particular type of proceeding 'is the kind of question which has traditionally been left to the judiciary to resolve.' *Woodby v. INS*, 385 U.S. 276, 284 (1966)." To the extent that the majority seeks, by this statement, to place upon the federal judiciary the primary responsibility for deciding the appropriate standard of proof in state matters, it arrogates to itself a responsibility wholly at odds with the allocation of authority in our federalist system and wholly unsupported by the prior decisions of this Court. In *Woodby v. INS*, 385 U.S. 276 (1966), the Court determined the proper standard of proof to be applied under a federal statute, and did so only after concluding that "Congress ha[d] not addressed itself to the question of what degree of proof [was] required in deportation proceedings." *Id.*, at 284, 87 S.Ct., at 487. Beyond an examination for the constitutional minimum of "fundamental fairness"—which clearly is satisfied by the New York procedures at issue in this case—this Court simply has no role in establishing the standards of proof that States must follow in the various judicial proceedings they afford to their citizens.

years, those three children were in the custody of the State and in the care of foster homes or institutions, and the State was diligently engaged in efforts to prepare petitioners for the children's return. Those efforts were unsuccessful, however, and on April 10, 1979, the New York Family Court for Ulster County terminated petitioners' parental rights as to the three children removed in 1974 or earlier. This termination was preceded by a judicial finding that petitioners had failed to plan for the return and future of their children, a statutory category of permanent neglect. Petitioners now contend, and the Court today holds, that they were denied due process of law, not because of a general inadequacy of procedural protections, but simply because the finding of permanent neglect was made on the basis of a preponderance of the evidence adduced at the termination hearing.

It is well settled that "[t]he requirements of procedural due process apply only to the deprivation of interests encompassed by the Fourteenth Amendment's protection of liberty and property." *Board of Regents v. Roth*, 408 U.S. 564, 569 (1972). In determining whether such liberty or property interests are implicated by a particular government action, "we must look not to the 'weight' but to the *nature* of the interest at stake." *Id.*, at 571 (emphasis in original). I do not disagree with the majority's conclusion that the interest of parents in their relationship with their children is sufficiently fundamental to come within the finite class of liberty interests protected by the Fourteenth Amendment. See *Smith v. Organization of Foster Families*, *supra*, at 862–863 (Stewart, J., concurring in judgment). "Once it is determined that due process applies, [however,] the question remains what process is due." *Morrissey v. Brewer*, 408 U.S. 471, 481 (1972). It is the majority's answer to this question with which I disagree.

A

Due process of law is a flexible constitutional principle. The requirements which it imposes upon governmental actions vary with the situations to which it applies. As the Court previously has recognized, "not all situations calling for procedural safeguards call for the same kind of procedure." *Morrissey v. Brewer*, *supra*, at 481. See also *Greenholtz v. Nebraska Penal Inmates*, 442 U.S. 1, 12 (1979); *Mathews v. Eldridge*, 424 U.S., at 334; *Cafeteria Workers v. McElroy*, 367 U.S. 886, 895 (1961). The adequacy of a scheme of procedural protections cannot, therefore, be determined merely by the application of general principles unrelated to the peculiarities of the case at hand.

Given this flexibility, it is obvious that a proper due process inquiry cannot be made by focusing upon one narrow provision of the challenged statutory scheme. Such a focus threatens to overlook factors which may introduce constitutionally adequate protections into a particular government action. Courts must examine *all* procedural protections offered by the State, and must assess the cumulative effect of such safeguards. As we have stated before, courts must consider "the fairness and reliability of the existing . . . procedures" before holding that the Constitution requires more. *Mathews v. Eldridge*, *supra*, 424 U.S., at 343. Only through such a broad inquiry may courts determine whether a challenged governmental action satisfies the due process requirement of "fundamental fairness."[3] In some instances, the

3. Although, as the majority states, we have held that the minimum requirements of procedural due process are a question of federal law, such a holding does not mean that the procedural protections afforded by a State will be inadequate under the Fourteenth Amendment. It means simply that the adequacy of the state-provided process is to be judged by constitutional standards—standards which the majority itself equates

Court has even looked to nonprocedural restraints on official action in determining whether the deprivation of a protected interest was effected without due process of law. *E.g., Ingraham v. Wright*, 430 U.S. 651 (1977). In this case, it is just such a broad look at the New York scheme which reveals its fundamental fairness.[4]

The termination of parental rights on the basis of permanent neglect can occur under New York law only by order of the Family Court. N.Y.Soc.Serv.Law (SSL) § 384-b.3.(d) (McKinney Supp. 1981–1982). Before a petition for permanent termination can be filed in that court, however, several other events must first occur.

The Family Court has jurisdiction only over those children who are in the care of an authorized agency. N.Y.Family Court Act (FCA) § 614.1.(b) (McKinney 1975 and Supp. 1981–1982). Therefore, the children who are the subject of a termination petition must previously have been removed from their parents' home on a temporary basis. Temporary removal of a child can occur in one of two ways. The parents may consent to the removal, FCA § 1021, or, as occurred in this case, the Family Court can order the removal pursuant to a finding that the child is abused or neglected. FCA §§ 1051, 1052.

Court proceedings to order the temporary removal of a child are initiated by a petition alleging abuse or neglect, filed by a state-authorized child protection agency or by a person designated by the court. FCA §§ 1031, 1032. Unless the court finds that exigent circumstances require removal of the child before a petition may be filed and a hearing held, see FCA § 1022, the order of temporary removal results from a "dispositional hearing" conducted to determine the appropriate form of alternative care. FCA § 1045. See also FCA § 1055. This "dispositional hearing" can be held only after the court, at a separate "fact-finding hearing," has found the child to be abused or neglected within the specific statutory definition of those terms. FCA §§ 1012, 1044, 1051.

Parents subjected to temporary removal proceedings are provided extensive procedural protections. A summons and copy of the temporary removal petition must be served upon the parents within two days of issuance by the court, FCA §§ 1035, 1036, and the parents may, at their own request, delay the commencement of the factfinding hearing for three days after service of the summons. FCA § 1048.[6] The factfinding hearing may not commence without a determination by the court that the parents are present at the hearing and have been served

to "fundamental fairness." I differ, therefore, not with the majority's statement that the requirements of due process present a federal question, but with its apparent assumption that the presence of "fundamental fairness" can be ascertained by an examination which completely disregards the plethora of protective procedures accorded parents by New York law.

4. The majority refuses to consider New York's procedure as a whole, stating that "[t]he statutory provision of right to counsel and multiple hearings before termination cannot suffice to protect a natural parent's fundamental liberty interests if the State is willing to tolerate undue uncertainty in the determination of the dispositive facts." Implicit in this statement is the conclusion that the risk of error may be reduced to constitutionally tolerable levels only by raising the standard of proof—that other procedures can never eliminate "undue uncertainty" so long as the standard of proof remains too low. Aside from begging the question of whether the risks of error tolerated by the State in this case are "undue," this conclusion denies the flexibility that we have long recognized in the principle of due process; understates the error-reducing power of procedural protections such as the right to counsel, evidentiary hearings, rules of evidence, and appellate review; and establishes the standard of proof as the *sine qua non* of procedural due process.

6. The relatively short time between notice and commencement of hearing provided by § 1048 undoubtedly reflects the State's desire to protect the child. These proceedings are designed to permit prompt action by the court when the child is threatened with imminent and serious physical, mental, or emotional harm.

with the petition. FCA § 1041. At the hearing itself, "only competent, material and relevant evidence may be admitted," with some enumerated exceptions for particularly probative evidence. FCA § 1046(b)(ii). In addition, indigent parents are provided with an attorney to represent them at both the factfinding and dispositional hearings, as well as at all other proceedings related to temporary removal of their child. FCA § 262(a)(i).

An order of temporary removal must be reviewed every 18 months by the Family Court. SSL § 392.2. Such review is conducted by hearing before the same judge who ordered the temporary removal, and a notice of the hearing, including a statement of the dispositional alternatives, must be given to the parents at least 20 days before the hearing is held. SSL § 392.4. As in the initial removal action, the parents must be parties to the proceedings, *ibid.*, and are entitled to court-appointed counsel if indigent. FCA § 262(a).

One or more years after a child has been removed temporarily from the parents' home, permanent termination proceedings may be commenced by the filing of a petition in the court which ordered the temporary removal. The petition must be filed by a state agency or by a foster parent authorized by the court, SSL § 384-b.3.(b), and must allege that the child has been permanently neglected by the parents. SSL §§ 384-b.3.(d).[7] Notice of the petition and the dispositional proceedings must be served upon the parents at least 20 days before the commencement of the hearing, SSL § 384-b.3.(e), must inform them of the potential consequences of the hearing, *ibid.*, and must inform them "of their right to the assistance of counsel, including [their] right…to have counsel assigned by the court [if] they are financially unable to obtain counsel." *Ibid.* See also FCA § 262.

As in the initial removal proceedings, two hearings are held in consideration of the permanent termination petition. SSL § 384-b.3.(f). At the factfinding hearing, the court must determine, by a fair preponderance of the evidence, whether the child has been permanently neglected. SSL § 384-b.3.(g). "Only competent, material and relevant evidence may be admitted in a fact-finding hearing." FCA § 624. The court may find permanent neglect if the child is in the care of an authorized agency or foster home and the parents have "failed for a period of more than one year…substantially and continuously or repeatedly to maintain contact with or plan for the future of the child, although physically and financially able to do so." SSL 384-b.7.(a).[8] In addition, because the State considers its "first obligation" to be the reuniting of the child with its natural parents, SSL § 384-b.1.(iii), the court must also find that the super-

7. Permanent custody also may be awarded by the Family Court if both parents are deceased, the parents abandoned the child at least six months prior to the termination proceedings, or the parents are unable to provide proper and adequate care by reason of mental illness or mental retardation. SSL § 384-b.4.(c).

8. As to maintaining contact with the child, New York law provides that "evidence of insubstantial or infrequent contacts by a parent with his or her child shall not, of itself, be sufficient as a matter of law to preclude a determination that such child is a permanently neglected child. A visit or communication by a parent with the child which is of such a character as to overtly demonstrate a lack of affectionate and concerned parenthood shall not be deemed a substantial contact." SSL § 384-b.7.(b).

Failure to plan for the future of the child means failure "to take such steps as may be necessary to provide an adequate, stable home and parental care for the child within a period of time which is reasonable under the financial circumstances available to the parent. The plan must be realistic and feasible, and good faith effort shall not, of itself, be determinative. In determining whether a parent has planned for the future of the child, the court may consider the failure of the parent to utilize medical, psychiatric, psychological and other social and rehabilitative services and material resources made available to such parent." SSL § 384-b.7.(c).

vising state agency has, without success, made "*diligent* efforts to encourage and strengthen the parental relationship." SSL § 384-b.7.(a) (emphasis added).[9]

Following the factfinding hearing, a separate, dispositional hearing is held to determine what course of action would be in "the best interests of the child." FCA § 631. A finding of permanent neglect at the fact-finding hearing, although necessary to a termination of parental rights, does not control the court's order at the dispositional hearing. The court may dismiss the petition, suspend judgment on the petition and retain jurisdiction for a period of one year in order to provide further opportunity for a reuniting of the family, or terminate the parents' right to the custody and care of the child. FCA §§ 631–634. The court must base its decision solely upon the record of "material and relevant evidence" introduced at the dispositional hearing, FCA § 624; *In re "Female" M.*, 70 A.D.2d 812, 417 N.Y.S.2d 482 (1979), and may not entertain any presumption that the best interests of the child "will be promoted by any particular disposition." FCA § 631.

As petitioners did in this case, parents may appeal any unfavorable decision to the Appellate Division of the New York Supreme Court. Thereafter, review may be sought in the New York Court of Appeals and, ultimately, in this Court if a federal question is properly presented.

As this description of New York's termination procedures demonstrates, the State seeks not only to protect the interests of parents in rearing their own children, but also to assist and encourage parents who have lost custody of their children to reassume their rightful role. Fully understood, the New York system is a comprehensive program to *aid* parents such as petitioners. Only as a last resort, when "diligent efforts" to reunite the family have failed, does New York authorize the termination of parental rights. The procedures for termination of those relationships which cannot be aided and which threaten permanent injury to the child, administered by a judge who has supervised the case from the first temporary removal through the final termination, cannot be viewed as fundamentally unfair. The facts of this case demonstrate the fairness of the system.

The three children to which this case relates were removed from petitioners' custody in 1973 and 1974, before petitioners' other two children were born. The removals were made pursuant to the procedures detailed above and in response to what can only be described as shockingly abusive treatment.[10] At the temporary removal hearing held before the Family

9. "Diligent efforts" are defined under New York law to mean 'reasonable attempts by an authorized agency to assist, develop and encourage a meaningful relationship between the parent and child, including but not limited to':

"(1) consultation and cooperation with the parents in developing a plan for appropriate services to the child and his family;

"(2) making suitable arrangements for the parents to visit the child;

"(3) provision of services and other assistance to the parents so that problems preventing the discharge of the child from care may be resolved or ameliorated; and

"(4) informing the parents at appropriate intervals of the child's progress, development and health." SSL § 384-b.7.(f).

10. Tina Apel, the oldest of petitioners' five children, was removed from their custody by court order in November 1973 when she was two years old. Removal proceedings were commenced in response to complaints by neighbors and reports from a local hospital that Tina had suffered injuries in petitioners' home including a fractured left femur, treated with a home-made splint; bruises on the upper arms, forehead, flank, and spine; and abrasions of the upper leg. The following summer John Santosky III, petitioners' second oldest child, was also removed from petitioners' custody. John, who was less than one year old at the time, was

Court on September 30, 1974, petitioners were represented by counsel, and allowed the Ulster County Department of Social Services (Department) to take custody of the three children.

Temporary removal of the children was continued at an evidentiary hearing held before the Family Court in December 1975, after which the court issued a written opinion concluding that petitioners were unable to resume their parental responsibilities due to personality disorders. Unsatisfied with the progress petitioners were making, the court also directed the Department to reduce to writing the plan which it had designed to solve the problems at petitioners' home and reunite the family.

A plan for providing petitioners with extensive counseling and training services was submitted to the court and approved in February 1976. Under the plan, petitioners received training by a mother's aide, a nutritional aide, and a public health nurse, and counseling at a family planning clinic. In addition, the plan provided psychiatric treatment and vocational training for the father, and counseling at a family service center for the mother. Brief for Respondent Kramer 1–7. Between early 1976 and the final termination decision in April 1979, the State spent more than $15,000 in these efforts to rehabilitate petitioners as parents. App. 34.

Petitioners' response to the State's effort was marginal at best. They wholly disregarded some of the available services and participated only sporadically in the others. As a result, and out of growing concern over the length of the children's stay in foster care, the Department petitioned in September 1976 for permanent termination of petitioners' parental rights so that the children could be adopted by other families. Although the Family Court recognized that petitioners' reaction to the State's efforts was generally "non-responsive, even hostile," the fact that they were "at least superficially cooperative" led it to conclude that there was yet hope of further improvement and an eventual reuniting of the family. Exhibit to Brief for Respondent Kramer 618. Accordingly, the petition for permanent termination was dismissed.

Whatever progress petitioners were making prior to the 1976 termination hearing, they made little or no progress thereafter. In October 1978, the Department again filed a termination petition alleging that petitioners had completely failed to plan for the children's future despite the considerable efforts rendered in their behalf. This time, the Family Court agreed. The court found that petitioners had "failed in any meaningful way to take advantage of the many social and rehabilitative services that have not only been made available to them but have been diligently urged upon them." App. 35. In addition, the court found that the "infrequent" visits "between the parents and their children were at best superficial and devoid of any real emotional content." *Id.*, at 21. The court thus found "nothing in the situation which holds out any hope that [petitioners] may ever become financially self sufficient or emotionally mature enough to be independent of the services of social agencies. More than a reasonable amount of time has passed and still, in the words of the case workers, there has been no discernible forward movement. At some point in time, it must be said, 'enough is enough.'" *Id.*, at 36.

In accordance with the statutory requirements set forth above, the court found that petitioners' failure to plan for the future of their children, who were then seven, five, and four years old and had been out of petitioners' custody for at least four years, rose to the level of

admitted to the hospital suffering malnutrition, bruises on the eye and forehead, cuts on the foot, blisters on the hand, and multiple pin pricks on the back. Exhibit to Brief for Respondent Kramer 1–5. Jed Santosky, the third oldest of petitioners' children, was removed from his parents' custody when only three days old as a result of the abusive treatment of the two older children.

permanent neglect. At a subsequent dispositional hearing, the court terminated petitioners' parental rights, thereby freeing the three children for adoption.

As this account demonstrates, the State's extraordinary 4-year effort to reunite petitioners' family was not just unsuccessful, it was altogether rebuffed by parents unwilling to improve their circumstances sufficiently to permit a return of their children. At every step of this protracted process petitioners were accorded those procedures and protections which traditionally have been required by due process of law. Moreover, from the beginning to the end of this sad story all judicial determinations were made by one Family Court Judge. After four and one-half years of involvement with petitioners, more than seven complete hearings, and additional periodic supervision of the State's rehabilitative efforts, the judge no doubt was intimately familiar with this case and the prospects for petitioners' rehabilitation.

It is inconceivable to me that these procedures were "fundamentally unfair" to petitioners. Only by its obsessive focus on the standard of proof and its almost complete disregard of the facts of this case does the majority find otherwise.[11] As the discussion above indicates, however, such a focus does not comport with the flexible standard of fundamental fairness embodied in the Due Process Clause of the Fourteenth Amendment.

B

In addition to the basic fairness of the process afforded petitioners, the standard of proof chosen by New York clearly reflects a constitutionally permissible balance of the interests

11. The majority finds, without any reference to the facts of this case, that "numerous factors [in New York termination proceedings] combine to magnify the risk of erroneous factfinding." Among the factors identified by the majority are the "unusual discretion" of the Family Court Judge "to underweigh probative facts that might favor the parent"; the often uneducated, minority status of the parents and their consequent "vulnerab[ility] to judgments based on cultural or class bias"; the "State's ability to assemble its case," which "dwarfs the parents' ability to mount a defense" by including an unlimited budget, expert attorneys, and "full access to all public records concerning the family"; and the fact that "natural parents have no 'double jeopardy' defense against repeated state" efforts, "with more or better evidence," to terminate parental rights "even when the parents have attained the level of fitness required by the State." In short, the majority characterizes the State as a wealthy and powerful bully bent on taking children away from defenseless parents. Such characterization finds no support in the record.

The intent of New York has been stated with eminent clarity: "the [S]tate's *first obligation is to help* the family with services to prevent its break-up or to reunite it if the child has already left home." SSL § 384-b.1.(a)(iii) (emphasis added). There is simply no basis in fact for believing, as the majority does, that the State does not mean what it says; indeed, the facts of this case demonstrate that New York has gone the extra mile in seeking to effectuate its declared purpose. More importantly, there should be no room in the jurisprudence of this Court for decisions based on unsupported, inaccurate assumptions.

A brief examination of the "factors" relied upon by the majority demonstrates its error. The "unusual" discretion of the Family Court Judge to consider the "'affectio[n] and concer[n]'" displayed by parents during visits with their children, is nothing more than discretion to consider reality; there is not one shred of evidence in this case suggesting that the determination of the Family Court was "based on cultural or class bias"; if parents lack the "ability to mount a defense," the State provides them with the full services of an attorney, FCA § 262, and they, like the State, have "full access to all *public* records concerning the family" (emphasis added); and the absence of "double jeopardy" protection simply recognizes the fact that family problems are often ongoing and may in the future warrant action that currently is unnecessary. In this case the Family Court dismissed the first termination petition because it desired to give petitioners "the benefit of the doubt," Exhibit to Brief for Respondent Kramer 620, and a second opportunity to raise themselves to "an acceptable minimal level of competency as parents." Id., at 624. It was their complete failure to do so that prompted the second, successful termination petition.

at stake in this case. The standard of proof "represents an attempt to instruct the factfinder concerning the degree of confidence our society thinks he should have in the correctness of factual conclusions for a particular type of adjudication." *In re Winship*, 397 U.S. 358, 370 (1970) (Harlan, J. concurring); *Addington v. Texas*, 441 U.S. 418, 423 (1979). In this respect, the standard of proof is a crucial component of legal process, the primary function of which is "to minimize the risk of erroneous decisions."[12] *Greenholtz v. Nebraska Penal Inmates*, 442 U.S., at 13. See also *Addington v. Texas, supra*, at 425; *Mathews v. Eldridge*, 424 U.S., at 344.

In determining the propriety of a particular standard of proof in a given case, however, it is not enough simply to say that we are trying to minimize the risk of error. Because errors in factfinding affect more than one interest, we try to minimize error as to those interests which we consider to be most important. As Justice Harlan explained in his well-known concurrence to *In re Winship*:

> "In a lawsuit between two parties, a factual error can make a difference in one of two ways. First, it can result in a judgment in favor of the plaintiff when the true facts warrant a judgment for the defendant. The analogue in a criminal case would be the conviction of an innocent man. On the other hand, an erroneous factual determination can result in a judgment for the defendant when the true facts justify a judgment in plaintiff's favor. The criminal analogue would be the acquittal of a guilty man.
>
> The standard of proof influences the relative frequency of these two types of erroneous outcomes. If, for example, the standard of proof for a criminal trial were a preponderance of the evidence rather than proof beyond a reasonable doubt, there would be a smaller risk of factual errors that result in freeing guilty persons, but a far greater risk of factual errors that result in convicting the innocent. Because the standard of proof affects the comparative frequency of these two types of erroneous outcomes, the choice of the standard to be applied in a particular kind of litigation should, in a rational world, reflect an assessment of the comparative social disutility of each." 397 U.S., at 370–371.

12. It is worth noting that the significance of the standard of proof in New York parental termination proceedings differs from the significance of the standard in other forms of litigation. In the usual adjudicatory setting, the factfinder has had little or no prior exposure to the facts of the case. His only knowledge of those facts comes from the evidence adduced at trial, and he renders his findings solely upon the basis of that evidence. Thus, normally, the standard of proof is a crucial factor in the final outcome of the case, for it is the scale upon which the factfinder weighs his knowledge and makes his decision.

Although the standard serves the same function in New York parental termination proceedings, additional assurances of accuracy are present in its application. As was adduced at oral argument, the practice in New York is to assign one judge to supervise a case from the initial temporary removal of the child to the final termination of parental rights. Therefore, as discussed above, the factfinder is intimately familiar with the case before the termination proceedings ever begin. Indeed, as in this case, he often will have been closely involved in protracted efforts to rehabilitate the parents. Even if a change in judges occurs, the Family Court retains jurisdiction of the case and the newly assigned judge may take judicial notice of all prior proceedings. Given this familiarity with the case, and the necessarily lengthy efforts which must precede a termination action in New York, decisions in termination cases are made by judges steeped in the background of the case and peculiarly able to judge the accuracy of evidence placed before them. This does not mean that the standard of proof in these cases can escape due process scrutiny, only that additional assurances of accuracy attend the application of the standard in New York termination proceedings.

When the standard of proof is understood as reflecting such an assessment, an examination of the interests at stake in a particular case becomes essential to determining the propriety of the specified standard of proof. Because proof by a preponderance of the evidence requires that "[t]he litigants...share the risk of error in a roughly equal fashion," *Addington v. Texas*, *supra*, at 423, it rationally should be applied only when the interests at stake are of roughly equal societal importance. The interests at stake in this case demonstrate that New York has selected a constitutionally permissible standard of proof.

On one side is the interest of parents in a continuation of the family unit and the raising of their own children. The importance of this interest cannot easily be overstated. Few consequences of judicial action are so grave as the severance of natural family ties. Even the convict committed to prison and thereby deprived of his physical liberty often retains the love and support of family members. "This Court's decisions have by now made plain beyond the need for multiple citation that a parent's desire for and right to 'the companionship, care, custody, and management of his or her children' is an important interest that 'undeniably warrants deference and, absent a powerful countervailing interest, protection.' *Stanley v. Illinois*, 405 U.S. 645, 651." *Lassiter v. Department of Social Services*, 452 U.S. 18, 27 (1981). In creating the scheme at issue in this case, the New York Legislature was expressly aware of this right of parents "to bring up their own children." SSL § 384-b.1.(a)(ii).

On the other side of the termination proceeding are the often countervailing interests of the child.[13] A stable, loving homelife is essential to a child's physical, emotional, and spiritual well-being. It requires no citation of authority to assert that children who are abused in their youth generally face extraordinary problems developing into responsible, productive citizens. The same can be said of children who, though not physically or emotionally abused, are passed from one foster home to another with no constancy of love, trust, or discipline. If the Family Court makes an incorrect factual determination resulting in a failure to terminate

13. The majority dismisses the child's interest in the accuracy of determinations made at the factfinding hearing because "[t]he factfinding does not purport...to balance the child's interest in a normal family home against the parents' interest in raising the child," but instead "pits the State directly against the parents." Only "[a]fter the State has established parental unfitness," the majority reasons, may the court "assume...that the interests of the child and the natural parents do diverge."

This reasoning misses the mark. The child has an interest in the outcome of the factfinding hearing independent of that of the parent. To be sure, "the child and his parents share a vital interest in preventing *erroneous* termination of their natural relationship." *Ibid.* (emphasis added). But the child's interest in a continuation of the family unit exists only to the extent that such a continuation would not be harmful to him. An error in *the factfinding hearing* that results in a failure to terminate a parent-child relationship which rightfully should be terminated may well detrimentally affect the child.

The preponderance-of-the-evidence standard, which allocates the risk of error more or less evenly, is employed when the social disutility of error *in either direction* is roughly equal—that is, when an incorrect finding of fault would produce consequences as undesirable as the consequences that would be produced by an incorrect finding of no fault. Only when the disutility of error in one direction discernibly outweighs the disutility of error in the other direction do we choose, by means of the standard of proof, to reduce the likelihood of the more onerous outcome. See *In re Winship*, 397 U.S. 358, 370–372 (1970) (Harlan, J., concurring).

New York's adoption of the preponderance-of-the-evidence standard reflects its conclusion that the undesirable consequence of an erroneous finding of parental unfitness—the unwarranted termination of the family relationship—is roughly equal to the undesirable consequence of an erroneous finding of parental fitness—the risk of permanent injury to the child either by return of the child to an abusive home or by the child's continued lack of a permanent home. Such a conclusion is well within the province of state legislatures. It cannot be said that the New York procedures are unconstitutional simply because a majority of the Members of this Court disagree with the New York Legislature's weighing of the interests of the parents and the child in an error-free factfinding hearing.

a parent-child relationship which rightfully should be ended, the child involved must return either to an abusive home[14] or to the often unstable world of foster care.[15] The reality of these risks is magnified by the fact that the only families faced with termination actions are those which have voluntarily surrendered custody of their child to the State, or, as in this case, those from which the child has been removed by judicial action because of threatened irreparable injury through abuse or neglect. Permanent neglect findings also occur only in families where the child has been in foster care for at least one year.

In addition to the child's interest in a normal homelife, "the State has an urgent interest in the welfare of the child." *Lassiter v. Department of Social Services*, 452 U.S., at 27.[16] Few could doubt that the most valuable resource of a self-governing society is its population of children who will one day become adults and themselves assume the responsibility of self-governance. "A democratic society rests, for its continuance, upon the healthy, well-rounded growth of young people into full maturity as citizens, with all that implies." *Prince v. Massachusetts*, 321 U.S. 158, 168 (1944). Thus, "the whole community" has an interest "that children be both safeguarded from abuses and given opportunities for growth into free and independent well-developed... citizens." *Id.*, at 165. See also *Ginsberg v. New York*, 390 U.S. 629, 640–641 (1968).

When, in the context of a permanent neglect termination proceeding, the interests of the child and the State in a stable, nurturing homelife are balanced against the interests of the parents in the rearing of their child, it cannot be said that either set of interests is so clearly paramount as to require that the risk of error be allocated to one side or the other. Accordingly, a State constitutionally may conclude that the risk of error should be borne in roughly equal fashion by use of the preponderance-of-the-evidence standard of proof. See *Addington v. Texas*, 441 U.S., at 423. This is precisely the balance which has been struck by

14. The record in this case illustrates the problems that may arise when a child is returned to an abusive home. Eighteen months after Tina, petitioners' oldest child, was first removed from petitioners' home, she was returned to the home on a trial basis. Katherine Weiss, a supervisor in the Child Protective Unit of the Ulster County Child Welfare Department, later testified in Family Court that "[t]he attempt to return Tina to her home just totally blew up." Exhibit to Brief for Respondent Kramer 135. When asked to explain what happened, Mrs. Weiss testified that "there were instances on the record in this court of Mr. Santosky's abuse of his wife, alleged abuse of the children and proven neglect of the children." *Ibid.* Tina again was removed from the home, this time along with John and Jed.

15. The New York Legislature recognized the potential harm to children of extended, non-permanent foster care. It found "that many children who have been placed in foster care experience unnecessarily protracted stays in such care without being adopted or returned to their parents or other custodians. Such unnecessary stays may deprive these children of positive, nurturing family relationships and have deleterious effects on their development into responsible, productive citizens." SSL § 384-b.1.(b). Subsequent studies have proved this finding correct. One commentator recently wrote of "the lamentable conditions of many foster care placements" under the New York system even today. He noted: "Over fifty percent of the children in foster care have been in this 'temporary' status for more than two years; over thirty percent for more than five years. During this time, many children are placed in a sequence of ill-suited foster homes, denying them the consistent support and nurturing that they so desperately need." Besharov, State Intervention to Protect Children: New York's Definition of "Child Abuse" and "Child Neglect," 26 N.Y.L. S. L.Rev. 723, 770–771 (1981) (footnotes omitted). In this case, petitioners' three children have been in foster care for more than four years, one child since he was only three days old. Failure to terminate petitioners' parental rights will only mean a continuation of this unsatisfactory situation.

16. The majority's conclusion that a state interest in the child's well-being arises only after a determination of parental unfitness suffers from the same error as its assertion that the child has no interest, separate from that of its parents, in the accuracy of the factfinding hearing.

the New York Legislature: "It is the intent of the legislature in enacting this section to provide procedures not only assuring that the rights of the natural parent are protected, but also, where positive, nurturing parent-child relationships no longer exist, furthering the best interests, needs, and rights of the child by terminating the parental rights and freeing the child for adoption." SSL § 384-b.1.(b).

III

For the reasons heretofore stated, I believe that the Court today errs in concluding that the New York standard of proof in parental-rights termination proceedings violates due process of law. The decision disregards New York's earnest efforts to *aid* parents in regaining the custody of their children and a host of procedural protections placed around parental rights and interests. The Court finds a constitutional violation only by a tunnel-vision application of due process principles that altogether loses sight of the unmistakable fairness of the New York procedure.

Even more worrisome, today's decision cavalierly rejects the considered judgment of the New York Legislature in an area traditionally entrusted to state care. The Court thereby begins, I fear, a trend of federal intervention in state family law matters which surely will stifle creative responses to vexing problems. Accordingly, I dissent.

NOTES AND QUESTIONS

1. According to the Court, what burden of proof applies in a termination proceeding? Why does that satisfy the Due Process Clause?

2. What is an appropriate burden of proof according to the dissent? Why?

3. In proceedings to terminate parental rights pursuant to the Indian Child Welfare Act, the state must establish the likelihood of harm to the child by evidence beyond a reasonable doubt. 25 U.S.C. § 1912(f) (2011). The petitioning party also has the burden of demonstrating that active efforts to provide remedial and rehabilitative services have been unsuccessful. Moreover, these findings must be supported by the testimony of a qualified expert witness, who has knowledge of traditional Indian child-rearing practices. Why isn't proof beyond a reasonable doubt the appropriate standard in cases involving non-Indian children? Isn't this an equal-protection violation? For an argument that such proof is mandated, see, e.g., Douglas E. Cressler, *Requiring Proof beyond a Reasonable Doubt in Parental Rights Termination Cases*, 32 U. Louisville J. Fam. L. 785 (1994).

4. In a decision issued before *Santosky* was decided, the New Hampshire Supreme Court held that proof beyond a reasonable doubt was constitutionally mandated in termination-of-parental-rights proceedings. *State v. Robert H.*, 393 A.2d 1387 (N.H. 1978). The court noted:

> This principle has been recognized by the United States Supreme Court in a number of decisions. In *Prince v. Massachusetts*, 321 U.S. 158, 166, 64 S.Ct. 438, 442, 88 L.Ed. 645 (1944), the Court said "It is cardinal with us that the custody, care and nurture of the child reside first in the parents, whose primary function and freedom include preparation for obligations the state can neither supply nor hinder." In *Wisconsin v. Yoder*, 406 U.S. 205, 232, 92 S.Ct. 1526, 1541, 32 L.Ed.2d 15 (1972), the Court rested its holding in part on

the constitutional right of parents to assume the primary role in decisions concerning the rearing of their children. That right is recognized because it reflects a "strong tradition" founded on the history and culture of Western civilization, and because the parental role is "now established beyond debate as an enduring American tradition." Appropriate limits come not from drawing arbitrary lines but rather from careful "respect for the teachings of history [and] solid recognition of the basic values that underlie our society...." *Griswold v. Connecticut*, 381 U.S. 479, 501, 85 S.Ct. 1678, 1691, 14 L.Ed.2d 510 (1965) (Harlan, J., concurring). The role of parents in the life of a family has attained the status of a fundamental human right and liberty. "And it is now firmly established that 'freedom of personal choice in matters of...family life is one of the liberties protected by the Due Process Clause of the Fourteenth Amendment.'" *Quilloin v. Walcott*, 434 U.S. 246, 255, 98 S.Ct. 549, 555, 54 L.Ed.2d 511 (1978) citing and quoting from *Cleveland Board of Education v. LaFleur*, 414 U.S. 632, 639–40, 94 S.Ct. 791, 39 L.Ed.2d 52 (1974). In *Moore v. East Cleveland*, 431 U.S. 494, 97 S.Ct. 1932, 52 L.Ed.2d 531 (1977), a housing ordinance was struck down insofar as it infringed on "extended families" living together. Because it infringed on fundamental rights, the minimum rationality test was inappropriate. "Of course, the family is not beyond regulation." *Id.* at 499, 97 S.Ct. at 1936. However, "the Due Process Clause would be offended '(i)f a State were to attempt to force the breakup of a natural family, over the objections of the parents and their children, without some showing of unfitness and for the sole reason that to do so was thought to be in the children's best interest.'" *Quilloin, supra* at 255, 98 S.Ct. at 555, citing and quoting from *Smith v. Organization of Foster Families*, 431 U.S. 816, 862–63, 97 S.Ct. 2094, 53 L.Ed.2d 14 (1977) (*Stewart*, J., concurring).

On an international level, the United Nations Covenant on Civil and Political Rights holds that "the family is the natural and fundamental unit of society and the State." Art. 23, § 1 (1966). Likewise the United Nations Covenant on Economic, Social and Cultural Rights recognizes that the "widest possible protection and assistance should be accorded to the family, which is the natural and fundamental group unit of society...." Art. 10, § 1 (1966). The family and the rights of parents over it are held to be natural, essential and inherent rights within the meaning of New Hampshire Constitution, part I, article 2.

When dealing with legislative activity in the area of fundamental rights this court has applied the strict scrutiny test. Thus before the State may involuntarily confine a person in a psychiatric ward, we have required that a showing of that person's dangerousness be made by the State to the satisfaction of a judge beyond a reasonable doubt. Involuntary commitment proceedings, "whether civil or criminal," involve a deprivation of liberty "which constitutes a grievous loss." *Gibbs v. Helgemoe*, 116 N.H. 825, 828, 367 A.2d 1041, 1043 (1976), and *State v. Gregoire*, 118 N.H. 140, 384 A.2d 132 (1978). The same reasonable doubt standard applied as "an essential requirement of due process in adjudicatory juvenile delinquency proceedings." *Gibbs, id.* The loss of one's children can be viewed as a sanction more severe than imprisonment. Note: *In the Child's Past Interest: Rights of the Natural Parents in Child Placement Proceedings*, 51 N.Y.U.L.Rev. 446, 467 (1976); *Danforth v. State Dep't of Health and Welfare*, 303 A.2d 794, 800 (Me. 1973). The permanent termination of the rights of parents over their children is even more final than involuntary commitment or delinquency proceedings. Therefore, the government must prove its case under chapter 170-C beyond a reasonable doubt before the permanent termination of, liberty and natural rights of parents guaranteed under New Hampshire Constitution, part I, article 2 can occur.

Id. at 1388–1389. The New Hampshire Supreme Court recently reaffirmed the proof-beyond-a-reasonable-doubt requirement in *In re Adam R.*, 992 A.2d 697 (N.H. 2010). Do you agree?

5. Raymond O'Brien argues that "the clear and convincing standard adopted by the Court deprives the child of his or her due process rights. The minimum standard should be reduced to at least one of preponderance of the evidence. Such a standard would recognize the so-called parental presumption, i.e. the historical preference given to parents, but give greater recognition to the rights of the child." Raymond C. O'Brien, *An Analysis of Realistic Due Process Rights of Children versus Parents*, 26 CONN. L. REV. 1209 (1994). Do you agree?

M.L.B. V. S.L.J.
Supreme Court of the United States
519 U.S. 102 (1996)

JUSTICE GINSBURG delivered the opinion of the Court.

By order of a Mississippi Chancery Court, petitioner M.L.B.'s parental rights to her two minor children were forever terminated. M.L.B. sought to appeal from the termination decree, but Mississippi required that she pay in advance record preparation fees estimated at $2,352.36. Because M.L.B. lacked funds to pay the fees, her appeal was dismissed.

Urging that the size of her pocketbook should not be dispositive when "an interest far more precious than any property right" is at stake, *Santosky v. Kramer*, 455 U.S. 745, 758–759 (1982), M.L.B. tenders this question, which we agreed to hear and decide: May a State, consistent with the Due Process and Equal Protection Clauses of the Fourteenth Amendment, condition appeals from trial court decrees terminating parental rights on the affected parent's ability to pay record preparation fees? We hold that, just as a State may not block an indigent petty offender's access to an appeal afforded others, see *Mayer v. Chicago*, 404 U.S. 189, 195–196 (1971), so Mississippi may not deny M.L.B., because of her poverty, appellate review of the sufficiency of the evidence on which the trial court found her unfit to remain a parent.

I

Petitioner M.L.B. and respondent S.L.J. are, respectively, the biological mother and father of two children, a boy born in April 1985, and a girl born in February 1987. In June 1992, after a marriage that endured nearly eight years, M.L.B. and S.L.J. were divorced. The children remained in their father's custody, as M.L.B. and S.L.J. had agreed at the time of the divorce.

S.L.J. married respondent J.P.J. in September 1992. In November of the following year, S.L.J. and J.P.J. filed suit in Chancery Court in Mississippi, seeking to terminate the parental rights of M.L.B. and to gain court approval for adoption of the children by their stepmother, J. P. J. The complaint alleged that M.L.B. had not maintained reasonable visitation and was in arrears on child support payments. M.L.B. counterclaimed, seeking primary custody of both children and contending that S.L.J. had not permitted her reasonable visitation, despite a provision in the divorce decree that he do so.

After taking evidence on August 18, November 2, and December 12, 1994, the Chancellor, in a decree filed December 14, 1994, terminated all parental rights of the natural mother, approved the adoption, and ordered that J.P.J., the adopting parent, be shown as the mother of the children on their birth certificates. Twice reciting a segment of the governing Mississippi statute, Miss.Code Ann. § 93-15-103(3)(e) (1994), the Chancellor declared that there had been a "substantial erosion of the relationship between the natural mother, [M.L.B.], and the minor children," which had been caused "at least in part by [M.L.B.'s] serious neglect, abuse, prolonged and unreasonable absence or unreasonable failure to visit or communicate with her minor children." App. to Pet. for Cert. 9, 10.[1]

The Chancellor stated, without elaboration, that the natural father and his second wife had met their burden of proof by "clear and convincing evidence." *Id.*, at 10. Nothing in the Chancellor's order describes the evidence, however, or otherwise reveals precisely why M.L.B. was decreed, forevermore, a stranger to her children.

In January 1995, M.L.B. filed a timely appeal and paid the $100 filing fee. The Clerk of the Chancery Court, several days later, estimated the costs for preparing and transmitting the record: $1,900 for the transcript (950 pages at $2 per page); $438 for other documents in the record (219 pages at $2 per page); $4.36 for binders; and $10 for mailing. *Id.*, at 15.

Mississippi grants civil litigants a right to appeal, but conditions that right on prepayment of costs. Miss.Code Ann. §§ 11-51-3, 11-51-29 (Supp. 1996). Relevant portions of a transcript must be ordered, and its preparation costs advanced by the appellant, if the appellant "intends to urge on appeal," as M.L.B. did, "that a finding or conclusion is unsupported by the evidence or is contrary to the evidence." Miss. Rule of App. Proc. 10(b)(2) (1995); see also Miss. Code Ann. § 11-51-29 (Supp. 1996).

Unable to pay $2,352.36, M.L.B. sought leave to appeal *in forma pauperis*. The Supreme Court of Mississippi denied her application in August 1995. Under its precedent, the court said, "[t]he right to proceed in forma pauperis in civil cases exists only at the trial level." App. to Pet. for Cert. 3.[2]

M.L.B. had urged in Chancery Court and in the Supreme Court of Mississippi, and now urges in this Court, that

> "where the State's judicial processes are invoked to secure so severe an alteration of a litigant's fundamental rights—the termination of the parental relationship with one's natural child—basic notions of fairness [and] of equal protection under the law, . . . guaranteed by [the Mississippi and Federal Constitutions], require that a person be afforded the right of appellate review though one is unable to pay the costs of such review in advance." *Id.*, at 18.[3]

1. Mississippi Code Ann. § 93-15-103(3) (1994) sets forth several grounds for termination of parental rights, including, in subsection (3)(e), "when there is [a] substantial erosion of the relationship between the parent and child which was caused at least in part by the parent's serious neglect, abuse, prolonged and unreasonable absence, unreasonable failure to visit or communicate, or prolonged imprisonment."
M.L.B. notes that, "in repeating the catch-all language of [the statute], the Chancellor said that [she] was guilty of 'serious . . . abuse.'" Reply Brief 6, n. 1. "However," M.L.B. adds, "there was no allegation of abuse in the complaint in this case or at any other stage of the proceedings." *Ibid.*

2. In fact, Mississippi, by statute, provides for coverage of transcript fees and other costs for indigents in civil commitment appeals. Miss.Code Ann. § 41-21-83 (Supp. 1996) (record on appeal shall include transcript of commitment hearing); Miss.Code Ann. § 41-21-85 (1972) (all costs of hearing or appeal shall be borne by state board of mental health when patient is indigent).

3. On the efficacy of appellate review in parental status termination cases, M.L.B. notes that of the eight reported appellate challenges to Mississippi trial court termination orders from 1980 through May 1996, three were reversed by the Mississippi Supreme Court for failure to meet the "clear and convincing" proof standard. Brief for Petitioner 20; see also Reply Brief 6 ("[I]n civil cases generally, the Mississippi Court of Appeals reversed or vacated nearly 39% of the trial court decisions it reviewed in 1995 and the Mississippi Supreme Court reversed or vacated nearly 37%. *Supreme Court of Mississippi, 1995 Annual Report*, pp. 22, 41").

II

Courts have confronted, in diverse settings, the "age-old problem" of "[p]roviding equal justice for poor and rich, weak and powerful alike." *Griffin v. Illinois*, 351 U.S. 12, 16 (1956). Concerning access to appeal in general, and transcripts needed to pursue appeals in particular, *Griffin* is the foundation case.

Griffin involved an Illinois rule that effectively conditioned thoroughgoing appeals from criminal convictions on the defendant's procurement of a transcript of trial proceedings. See *id.*, at 13–14, and nn. 2, 3 (noting, *inter alia*, that "mandatory record," which an indigent defendant could obtain free of charge, did not afford the defendant an opportunity to seek review of trial errors). Indigent defendants, other than those sentenced to death, were not excepted from the rule, so in most cases, defendants without means to pay for a transcript had no access to appellate review at all. Although the Federal Constitution guarantees no right to appellate review, *id.*, at 18, once a State affords that right, *Griffin* held, the State may not "bolt the door to equal justice," *id.*, at 24 (Frankfurter, J., concurring in judgment).

The plurality in *Griffin* recognized "the importance of appellate review to a correct adjudication of guilt or innocence." *Id.*, at 18. "[T]o deny adequate review to the poor," the plurality observed, "means that many of them may lose their life, liberty or property because of unjust convictions which appellate courts would set aside." *Id.*, at 19. Judging the Illinois rule inconsonant with the Fourteenth Amendment, the *Griffin* plurality drew support from the Due Process and Equal Protection Clauses. *Id.*, at 13, 18.

Justice Frankfurter, concurring in the judgment in *Griffin*, emphasized and explained the decision's equal protection underpinning:

> "Of course a State need not equalize economic conditions.... But when a State deems it wise and just that convictions be susceptible to review by an appellate court, it cannot by force of its exactions draw a line which precludes convicted indigent persons, forsooth erroneously convicted, from securing such a review...." *Id.*, at 23.

See also *Ross v. Moffitt*, 417 U.S. 600, 607 (1974) (*Griffin* and succeeding decisions "stand for the proposition that a State cannot arbitrarily cut off appeal rights for indigents while leaving open avenues of appeal for more affluent persons"). Summarizing the *Griffin* line of decisions regarding an indigent defendant's access to appellate review of a conviction,[4] we said in *Rinaldi v. Yeager*, 384 U.S. 305, 310 (1966): "This Court has never held that the States are required to establish avenues of appellate review, but it is now fundamental that, once established, these avenues must be kept free of unreasoned distinctions that can only impede open and equal access to the courts."

4. See, *e.g.*, *Williams v. Oklahoma City*, 395 U.S. 458, 458–459 (1969) (*per curiam*) (transcript needed to perfect appeal must be furnished at state expense to indigent defendant sentenced to 90 days in jail and a $50 fine for drunk driving); *Long v. District Court of Iowa, Lee Cty.*, 385 U.S. 192, 192–194 (1966) (*per curiam*) (transcript must be furnished at state expense to enable indigent state habeas corpus petitioner to appeal denial of relief); *Smith v. Bennett*, 365 U.S. 708, 708–709 (1961) (filing fee to process state habeas corpus application must be waived for indigent prisoner); *Burns v. Ohio*, 360 U.S. 252, 253, 257–258 (1959) (filing fee for motion for leave to appeal from judgment of intermediate appellate court to State Supreme Court must be waived when defendant is indigent).

Of prime relevance to the question presented by M.L.B.'s petition, *Griffin*'s principle has not been confined to cases in which imprisonment is at stake. The key case is *Mayer v. Chicago*, 404 U.S. 189 (1971). *Mayer* involved an indigent defendant convicted on nonfelony charges of violating two city ordinances. Fined $250 for each offense, the defendant petitioned for a transcript to support his appeal. He alleged prosecutorial misconduct and insufficient evidence to convict. The State provided free transcripts for indigent appellants in felony cases only. We declined to limit *Griffin* to cases in which the defendant faced incarceration. "The invidiousness of the discrimination that exists when criminal procedures are made available only to those who can pay," the Court said in *Mayer*, "is not erased by any differences in the sentences that may be imposed." 404 U.S., at 197. Petty offenses could entail serious collateral consequences, the *Mayer* Court noted. *Ibid.* The *Griffin* principle, *Mayer* underscored, "is a flat prohibition," 404 U.S., at 196, against "making access to appellate processes from even [the State's] most inferior courts depend upon the [convicted] defendant's ability to pay," *id.*, at 197. An impecunious party, the Court ruled, whether found guilty of a felony or conduct only "quasi criminal in nature," *id.*, at 196, "cannot be denied a record of sufficient completeness to permit proper [appellate] consideration of his claims," *id.*, at 198 (internal quotation marks omitted).[5]

In contrast to the "flat prohibition" of "bolted doors" that the *Griffin* line of cases securely established, the right to counsel at state expense, as delineated in our decisions, is less encompassing. A State must provide trial counsel for an indigent defendant charged with a felony, *Gideon v. Wainwright*, 372 U.S. 335, 339 (1963), but that right does not extend to nonfelony trials if no term of imprisonment is actually imposed, *Scott v. Illinois*, 440 U.S. 367, 373–374 (1979). A State's obligation to provide appellate counsel to poor defendants faced with incarceration applies to appeals of right. *Douglas v. California*, 372 U.S. 353, 357 (1963). In *Ross v. Moffitt*, however, we held that neither the Due Process Clause nor the Equal Protection Clause requires a State to provide counsel at state expense to an indigent prisoner pursuing a discretionary appeal in the state system or petitioning for review in this Court. 417 U.S., at 610, 612, 616–618.

III

We have also recognized a narrow category of civil cases in which the State must provide access to its judicial processes without regard to a party's ability to pay court fees. In *Boddie v. Connecticut*, 401 U.S. 371 (1971), we held that the State could not deny a divorce to a married couple based on their inability to pay approximately $60 in court costs. Crucial to our

5. *Griffin* did not impose an inflexible requirement that a State provide a full trial transcript to an indigent defendant pursuing an appeal. See *Griffin v. Illinois*, 351 U.S. 12, 20 (1956) (State need not purchase a stenographer's transcript in every case where an indigent defendant cannot buy it; State "Supreme Court may find other means of affording adequate and effective appellate review to indigent defendants"). In *Draper v. Washington*, 372 U.S. 487 (1963), we invalidated a state rule that tied an indigent defendant's ability to obtain a transcript at public expense to the trial judge's finding that the defendant's appeal was not frivolous. *Id.*, at 498–500. We emphasized, however, that the *Griffin* requirement is not rigid. "Alternative methods of reporting trial proceedings," we observed, "are permissible if they place before the appellate court an equivalent report of the events at trial from which the appellant's contentions arise." 372 U.S., at 495. Moreover, we held, an indigent defendant is entitled only to those parts of the trial record that are "germane to consideration of the appeal." *Ibid.*; see also *Mayer v. Chicago*, 404 U.S. 189, 194 (1971) ("A record of sufficient completeness does not translate automatically into a complete verbatim transcript" (internal quotation marks omitted)).

decision in *Boddie* was the fundamental interest at stake. "[G]iven the basic position of the marriage relationship in this society's hierarchy of values and the concomitant state monopolization of the means for legally dissolving this relationship," we said, due process "prohibit[s] a State from denying, solely because of inability to pay, access to its courts to individuals who seek judicial dissolution of their marriages." *Id.*, at 374; see also *Little v. Streater*, 452 U.S. 1, 13–17 (1981) (State must pay for blood grouping tests sought by an indigent defendant to enable him to contest a paternity suit).

Soon after *Boddie*, in *Lindsey v. Normet*, 405 U.S. 56 (1972), the Court confronted a double-bond requirement imposed by Oregon law only on tenants seeking to appeal adverse decisions in eviction actions. We referred first to precedent recognizing that, "if a full and fair trial on the merits is provided, the Due Process Clause of the Fourteenth Amendment does not require a State to provide appellate review." *Id.*, at 77. We next stated, however, that "[w]hen an appeal is afforded, . . . it cannot be granted to some litigants and capriciously or arbitrarily denied to others without violating the Equal Protection Clause." *Ibid.* Oregon's double-bond requirement failed equal protection measurement, we concluded, because it raised a substantial barrier to appeal for a particular class of litigants—tenants facing eviction—a barrier "faced by no other civil litigant in Oregon." *Id.*, at 79. The Court pointed out in *Lindsey* that the classification there at issue disadvantaged nonindigent as well as indigent appellants, *ibid.*; the *Lindsey* decision, therefore, does not guide our inquiry here.

The following year, in *United States v. Kras*, 409 U.S. 434 (1973), the Court clarified that a constitutional requirement to waive court fees in civil cases is the exception, not the general rule. *Kras* concerned fees, totaling $50, required to secure a discharge in bankruptcy. *Id.*, at 436. The Court recalled in *Kras* that "[o]n many occasions we have recognized the fundamental importance . . . under our Constitution" of "the associational interests that surround the establishment and dissolution of th[e] [marital] relationship." *Id.*, at 444. But bankruptcy discharge entails no "fundamental interest," we said. *Id.*, at 445. Although "obtaining [a] desired new start in life [is] important," that interest, the Court explained, "does not rise to the same constitutional level" as the interest in establishing or dissolving a marriage. *Ibid.* Nor is resort to court the sole path to securing debt forgiveness, we stressed; in contrast, termination of a marriage, we reiterated, requires access to the State's judicial machinery. *Id.*, at 445–446; see *Boddie*, 401 U.S., at 376.

In *Ortwein v. Schwab*, 410 U.S. 656 (1973) (*per curiam*), the Court adhered to the line drawn in *Kras*. The appellants in *Ortwein* sought court review of agency determinations reducing their welfare benefits. Alleging poverty, they challenged, as applied to them, an Oregon statute requiring appellants in civil cases to pay a $25 fee. We summarily affirmed the Oregon Supreme Court's judgment rejecting appellants' challenge. As in *Kras*, the Court saw no "'fundamental interest . . . gained or lost depending on the availability' of the relief sought by [the complainants]." 410 U.S., at 659 (quoting *Kras*, 409 U.S., at 445). Absent a fundamental interest or classification attracting heightened scrutiny, we said, the applicable equal protection standard "is that of rational justification," a requirement we found satisfied by Oregon's need for revenue to offset the expenses of its court system. 410 U.S., at 660. We expressly rejected the *Ortwein* appellants' argument that a fee waiver was required for all civil appeals simply because the State chose to permit *in forma pauperis* filings in special classes of civil appeals, including appeals from terminations of parental rights. *Id.*, at 661.

In sum, as *Ortwein* underscored, this Court has not extended *Griffin* to the broad array of civil cases. But tellingly, the Court has consistently set apart from the mine run of cases those involving state controls or intrusions on family relationships. In that domain, to guard against undue official intrusion, the Court has examined closely and contextually the importance of the governmental interest advanced in defense of the intrusion. Cf. *Moore v. East Cleveland*, 431 U.S. 494 (1977).

IV

Choices about marriage, family life, and the upbringing of children are among associational rights this Court has ranked as "of basic importance in our society," *Boddie*, 401 U.S., at 376, rights sheltered by the Fourteenth Amendment against the State's unwarranted usurpation, disregard, or disrespect. See, for example, *Turner v. Safley*, 482 U.S. 78 (1987), *Zablocki v. Redhail*, 434 U.S. 374 (1978), and *Loving v. Virginia*, 388 U.S. 1 (1967) (marriage); *Skinner v. Oklahoma ex rel. Williamson*, 316 U.S. 535 (1942) (procreation); *Pierce v. Society of Sisters*, 268 U.S. 510 (1925), and *Meyer v. Nebraska*, 262 U.S. 390 (1923) (raising children). M.L.B.'s case, involving the State's authority to sever permanently a parent-child bond,[8] demands the close consideration the Court has long required when a family association so undeniably important is at stake. We approach M.L.B.'s petition mindful of the gravity of the sanction imposed on her and in light of two prior decisions most immediately in point: *Lassiter v. Department of Social Servs. of Durham Cty.*, 452 U.S. 18 (1981), and *Santosky v. Kramer*, 455 U.S. 745 (1982).

Lassiter concerned the appointment of counsel for indigent persons seeking to defend against the State's termination of their parental status. The Court held that appointed counsel was not routinely required to assure a fair adjudication; instead, a case-by-case determination of the need for counsel would suffice, an assessment to be made "in the first instance by the trial court, subject . . . to appellate review." 452 U.S., at 32.

For probation-revocation hearings where loss of conditional liberty is at issue, the *Lassiter* Court observed, our precedent is not doctrinaire; due process is provided, we have held, when the decision whether counsel should be appointed is made on a case-by-case basis. See *Gagnon v. Scarpelli*, 411 U.S. 778, 790 (1973). In criminal prosecutions that do not lead to the defendant's incarceration, however, our precedent recognizes no right to appointed counsel. See *Scott v. Illinois*, 440 U.S., at 373–374. Parental termination cases, the *Lassiter* Court concluded, are most appropriately ranked with probation-revocation hearings: While the Court declined to recognize an automatic right to appointed counsel, it said that an appointment would be due when warranted by the character and difficulty of the case. See *Lassiter*, 452 U.S., at 31–32.[9]

Significant to the disposition of M.L.B.'s case, the *Lassiter* Court considered it "plain . . . that a parent's desire for and right to 'the companionship, care, custody, and management of his or her children' is an important interest," one that "'undeniably warrants deference and, absent a powerful countervailing interest, protection.'" *Id.*, at 27 (quoting *Stanley v. Illinois*, 405 U.S. 645, 651 (1972)). The object of the proceeding is "not simply to infringe upon [the parent's]

8. Although the termination proceeding in this case was initiated by private parties as a prelude to an adoption petition, rather than by a state agency, the challenged state action remains essentially the same: M.L.B. resists the imposition of an official decree extinguishing, as no power other than the State can, her parent-child relationships.

9. The Court noted, among other considerations, that petitions to terminate parental rights may charge criminal activity and that "[p]arents so accused may need legal counsel to guide them in understanding the problems such petitions may create." *Lassiter*, 452 U.S., at 27, n. 3.

interest," the Court recognized, "but to end it"; thus, a decision against the parent "work[s] a unique kind of deprivation." *Lassiter*, 452 U.S., at 27. For that reason, "[a] parent's interest in the accuracy and justice of the decision...is...a commanding one." *Ibid.*; see also *id.*, at 39 (Blackmun, J., dissenting) ("A termination of parental rights is both total and irrevocable. Unlike other custody proceedings, it leaves the parent with no right to visit or communicate with the child...." (footnote omitted)).

Santosky held that a "clear and convincing" proof standard is constitutionally required in parental termination proceedings. 455 U.S., at 769–770.[10] In so ruling, the Court again emphasized that a termination decree is "*final* and irrevocable." *Id.*, at 759 (emphasis in original). "Few forms of state action," the Court said, "are both so severe and so irreversible." *Ibid.*[11] As in *Lassiter*, the Court characterized the parent's interest as "commanding," indeed, "far more precious than any property right." 455 U.S., at 758–759.

Although both *Lassiter* and *Santosky* yielded divided opinions, the Court was unanimously of the view that "the interest of parents in their relationship with their children is sufficiently fundamental to come within the finite class of liberty interests protected by the Fourteenth Amendment." 455 U.S., at 774 (Rehnquist, J., dissenting). It was also the Court's unanimous view that "[f]ew consequences of judicial action are so grave as the severance of natural family ties." *Id.*, at 787.

V

Guided by this Court's precedent on an indigent's access to judicial processes in criminal and civil cases, and on proceedings to terminate parental status, we turn to the classification question this case presents: Does the Fourteenth Amendment require Mississippi to accord M.L.B. access to an appeal—available but for her inability to advance required costs—before she is forever branded unfit for affiliation with her children? Respondents urge us to classify M.L.B.'s case with the generality of civil cases, in which indigent persons have no constitutional right to proceed *in forma pauperis*. M.L.B., on the other hand, maintains that the accusatory state action she is trying to fend off is barely distinguishable from criminal condemnation in view of the magnitude and permanence of the loss she faces. Cf. *In re Gault*, 387 U.S. 1, 50, 55 (1967) (resisting "feeble enticement of the 'civil' label-of-convenience," and holding that Fifth Amendment's safeguard against self-incrimination applies in juvenile proceedings). See also *Santosky*, 455 U.S., at 756, 760 (recognizing stigmatic effect of parental status termination decree: "[I]t entails a judicial determination that [a parent is] unfit to raise [her] own children"). For the purpose at hand, M.L.B, asks to treat her parental termination appeal as we have treated petty offense appeals; she urges us to adhere to the reasoning in

10. Earlier, in *Addington v. Texas*, 441 U.S. 418, 431–432 (1979), the Court concluded that the Fourteenth Amendment requires a "clear and convincing" standard of proof in civil commitment proceedings.

11. In *Rivera v. Minnich*, 483 U.S. 574 (1987), the Court declined to extend *Santosky* to paternity proceedings. The Court distinguished the State's imposition of the legal obligations attending a biological relationship between parent and child from the State's termination of a fully existing parent-child relationship. See *Rivera*, 483 U.S., at 579–582. In drawing this distinction, the Court found it enlightening that state legislatures had similarly separated the two proceedings: Most jurisdictions applied a "preponderance of the evidence" standard in paternity cases, while 38 jurisdictions, at the time *Santosky* was decided, required a higher standard of proof in proceedings to terminate parental rights. See *Rivera*, 483 U.S., at 578–579 (citing *Santosky*, 455 U.S., at 749–750).

Mayer v. Chicago, 404 U.S. 189 (1971), and rule that Mississippi may not withhold the transcript M.L.B. needs to gain review of the order ending her parental status. Guided by *Lassiter* and *Santosky*, and other decisions acknowledging the primacy of the parent-child relationship, *e.g.*, *Stanley v. Illinois*, 405 U.S., at 651; *Meyer v. Nebraska*, 262 U.S., at 399, we agree that the *Mayer* decision points to the disposition proper in this case.

We observe first that the Court's decisions concerning access to judicial processes, commencing with *Griffin* and running through *Mayer*, reflect both equal protection and due process concerns. See *Ross v. Moffitt*, 417 U.S., at 608–609. As we said in *Bearden v. Georgia*, 461 U.S. 660, 665 (1983), in the Court's *Griffin*-line cases, "[d]ue process and equal protection principles converge." The equal protection concern relates to the legitimacy of fencing out would-be appellants based solely on their inability to pay core costs. See *Griffin*, 351 U.S., at 23 (Frankfurter, J., concurring in judgment). The due process concern homes in on the essential fairness of the state-ordered proceedings anterior to adverse state action. See *Ross*, 417 U.S., at 609. A "precise rationale" has not been composed, *id.*, at 608, because cases of this order "cannot be resolved by resort to easy slogans or pigeonhole analysis," *Bearden*, 461 U.S., at 666. Nevertheless, "[m]ost decisions in this area," we have recognized, "res[t] on an equal protection framework," *id.*, at 665, as M.L.B.'s plea heavily does, for, as we earlier observed, due process does not independently require that the State provide a right to appeal. We place this case within the framework established by our past decisions in this area. In line with those decisions, we inspect the character and intensity of the individual interest at stake, on the one hand, and the State's justification for its exaction, on the other. See *Bearden*, 461 U.S., at 666–667.

We now focus on *Mayer* and the considerations linking that decision to M.L.B.'s case. *Mayer* applied *Griffin* to a petty offender, fined a total of $500, who sought to appeal from the trial court's judgment. See *Mayer*, 404 U.S., at 190. An "impecunious medical student," *id.*, at 197, the defendant in *Mayer* could not pay for a transcript. We held that the State must afford him a record complete enough to allow fair appellate consideration of his claims. The defendant in *Mayer* faced no term of confinement, but the conviction, we observed, could affect his professional prospects and, possibly, even bar him from the practice of medicine. *Ibid.* The State's pocketbook interest in advance payment for a transcript, we concluded, was unimpressive when measured against the stakes for the defendant. *Ibid.*

Similarly here, the stakes for petitioner M.L.B.—forced dissolution of her parental rights—are large, "'more substantial than mere loss of money.'" *Santosky*, 455 U.S., at 756 (quoting *Addington v. Texas*, 441 U.S. 418, 424 (1979)). In contrast to loss of custody, which does not sever the parent-child bond, parental status termination is "irretrievabl[y] destructi[ve]" of the most fundamental family relationship. *Santosky*, 455 U.S., at 753. And the risk of error, Mississippi's experience shows, is considerable.

Consistent with *Santosky*, Mississippi has, by statute, adopted a "clear and convincing proof" standard for parental status termination cases. Miss.Code Ann. § 93-15-109 (Supp. 1996). Nevertheless, the Chancellor's termination order in this case simply recites statutory language; it describes no evidence, and otherwise details no reasons for finding M.L.B. "clear[ly] and convincing [ly]" unfit to be a parent. Only a transcript can reveal to judicial minds other than the Chancellor's the sufficiency, or insufficiency, of the evidence to support his stern judgment.

The countervailing government interest, as in *Mayer*, is financial. Mississippi urges, as the justification for its appeal cost prepayment requirement, the State's legitimate interest in offsetting the costs of its court system. Brief for Respondents 4, 8, n. 1, 27–30. But in the tightly circumscribed category of parental status termination cases, appeals are few, and not likely to impose an undue burden on the State. See Brief for Petitioner 20, 25 (observing that only 16 reported appeals in Mississippi from 1980 until 1996 referred to the State's termination statute, and only 12 of those decisions addressed the merits of the grant or denial of parental rights); cf. Brief for Respondents 28 (of 63,765 civil actions filed in Mississippi Chancery Courts in 1995, 194 involved termination of parental rights; of cases decided on appeal in Mississippi in 1995 (including Court of Appeals and Supreme Court cases), 492 were first appeals of criminal convictions, 67 involved domestic relations, 16 involved child custody). Mississippi's experience with criminal appeals is noteworthy in this regard. In 1995, the Mississippi Court of Appeals disposed of 298 first appeals from criminal convictions, Sup. Ct. of Miss. Ann. Rep. 42 (1995); of those appeals, only seven were appeals from misdemeanor convictions, ibid., notwithstanding our holding in *Mayer* requiring *in forma pauperis* transcript access in petty offense prosecutions.[13]

In States providing criminal appeals, as we earlier recounted, an indigent's access to appeal, through a transcript of relevant trial proceedings, is secure under our precedent. That equal access right holds for petty offenses as well as for felonies. But counsel at state expense, we have held, is a constitutional requirement, even in the first instance, only when the defendant faces time in confinement. When deprivation of parental status is at stake, however, counsel is sometimes part of the process that is due. See *Lassiter*, 452 U.S., at 31–32. It would be anomalous to recognize a right to a transcript needed to appeal a misdemeanor conviction—though trial counsel may be flatly denied—but hold, at the same time, that a transcript need not be prepared for M.L.B.—though were her defense sufficiently complex, state-paid counsel, as *Lassiter* instructs, would be designated for her.

In aligning M.L.B.'s case and *Mayer*—parental status termination decrees and criminal convictions that carry no jail time—for appeal access purposes, we do not question the general rule, stated in *Ortwein*, that fee requirements ordinarily are examined only for rationality. The State's need for revenue to offset costs, in the mine run of cases, satisfies the rationality requirement, see *Ortwein*, 410 U.S., at 660; States are not forced by the Constitution to adjust all tolls to account for "disparity in material circumstances." *Griffin*, 351 U.S., at 23 (Frankfurter, J., concurring in judgment).

13. Many States provide for *in forma pauperis* appeals, including transcripts, in civil cases generally. See, e.g., Alaska Rule App. Proc. 209(a)(3) (1996); Conn. Rule App. Proc. 4017 (1996); D.C.Code Ann. § 15-712 (1995); Idaho Code § 31-3220(5) (1996); Ill.Comp.Stat., ch. 735, § 5/5-105.5(b) (Supp. 1996); Ky.Rev.Stat. Ann. § 453.190 (Baldwin 1991); La.Code Civ. Proc. Ann., Art. 5185 (West Supp. 1996); Me. Rule Civ. Proc. 91(f) (1996); Minn. Stat. § 563.01, subd. 7 (1994); Mo.Rev.Stat. § 512.150 (1994); Neb.Rev.Stat. § 25-2306 (1995); Nev.Rev.Stat. § 12.015.2 (1995); N.M. Stat. Ann. § 39-3-12 (1991); N.Y. Civ. Prac. Law § 1102(b) (McKinney 1976); Ore.Rev. Stat. § 21.605(3)(a) (1991); Pa. Rule Jud. Admin. 5000.2(h) (1996); Tex. Rule App. Proc. 53(j)(1) (1996); Vt. Rule App. Proc. 10(b)(4) (1996); Wash. Rule App. Proc. 15.4(d) (1996); W. Va.Code § 59-2-1(a) (Supp. 1996); *State ex rel. Girouard v. Circuit Court for Jackson County*, 155 Wis.2d 148, 454 N.W.2d 792 (1990).

Several States deal discretely with *in forma pauperis* appeals, including transcripts, in parental status termination cases. See, e.g., *In re Appeal in Pima County v. Howard*, 112 Ariz. 170, 540 P.2d 642 (1975); Cal. Family Code Ann. § 7895(c) (West 1994); Colo.Rev.Stat. § 19-3-609 (Supp. 1996); *Nix v. Department of Human Resources*, 236 Ga. 794, 225 S.E.2d 306 (1976); *In re Chambers*, 261 Iowa 31, 152 N.W.2d 818 (1967); Kan. Stat. Ann. § 38-1593 (1986); *In re Karren*, 280 Minn. 377, 159 N.W.2d 402 (1968); Mich. Rule P. Ct. 5.974(H)(3) (1996); *In re Dotson*, 72 N.J. 112, 367 A.2d 1160 (1976); *State ex rel. Heller v. Miller*, 61 Ohio St.2d 6, 399 N.E.2d 66 (1980); Ex parte *Cauthen*, 291 S.C. 465, 354 S.E.2d 381 (1987).

But our cases solidly establish two exceptions to that general rule. The basic right to participate in political processes as voters and candidates cannot be limited to those who can pay for a license.[14] Nor may access to judicial processes in cases criminal or "quasi criminal in nature," *Mayer*, 404 U.S., at 196 (citation and internal quotation marks omitted), turn on ability to pay. In accord with the substance and sense of our decisions in *Lassiter* and *Santosky*, we place decrees forever terminating parental rights in the category of cases in which the State may not "bolt the door to equal justice," *Griffin*, 351 U.S., at 24 (Frankfurter, J., concurring in judgment).

VI

In numerous cases, respondents point out, the Court has held that government "need not provide funds so that people can exercise even fundamental rights." Brief for Respondents 12; see, *e.g.*, *Lyng v. Automobile Workers*, 485 U.S. 360, 363, n. 2, 370–374 (1988) (rejecting equal protection attack on amendment to Food Stamp Act providing that no household could become eligible for benefits while a household member was on strike); *Regan v. Taxation with Representation of Wash.*, 461 U.S. 540, 543–544, 550–551 (1983) (rejecting nonprofit organization's claims of free speech and equal protection rights to receive tax deductible contributions to support its lobbying activity); *Harris v. McRae*, 448 U.S. 297, 321–326 (1980) (Medicaid funding need not be provided for women seeking medically necessary abortions). A decision for M.L.B., respondents contend, would dishonor our cases recognizing that the Constitution "generally confer[s] no affirmative right to governmental aid, even where such aid may be necessary to secure life, liberty, or property interests of which the government itself may not deprive the individual." *DeShaney v. Winnebago County Dept. of Social Servs.*, 489 U.S. 189, 196 (1989).

Complainants in the cases on which respondents rely sought state aid to subsidize their privately initiated action or to alleviate the consequences of differences in economic circumstances that existed apart from state action. M.L.B.'s complaint is of a different order. She is endeavoring to defend against the State's destruction of her family bonds, and to resist the brand associated with a parental unfitness adjudication. Like a defendant resisting criminal conviction, she seeks to be spared from the State's devastatingly adverse action. That is the very reason we have paired her case with *Mayer*, not with *Ortwein* or *Kras*.

Respondents also suggest that *Washington v. Davis*, 426 U.S. 229 (1976), is instructive because it rejects the notion "that a law, neutral on its face and serving ends otherwise

14. The pathmarking voting and ballot access decisions are *Harper v. Virginia Bd. of Elections*, 383 U.S. 663, 664, 666 (1966) (invalidating, as a denial of equal protection, an annual $1.50 poll tax imposed by Virginia on all residents over 21); *Bullock v. Carter*, 405 U.S. 134, 135, 145, 149 (1972) (invalidating Texas scheme under which candidates for local office had to pay fees as high as $8,900 to get on the ballot); *Lubin v. Panish*, 415 U.S. 709, 710, 718 (1974) (invalidating California statute requiring payment of a ballot-access fee fixed at a percentage of the salary for the office sought).

Notably, the Court in *Harper* recognized that "a State may exact fees from citizens for many different kinds of licenses." 383 U.S., at 668. For example, the State "can demand from all an equal fee for a driver's license." *Ibid.* But voting cannot hinge on ability to pay, the Court explained, for it is a "'fundamental political right...preservative of all rights.'" *Id.*, at 667 (quoting *Yick Wo v. Hopkins*, 118 U.S. 356, 370 (1886)). *Bullock* rejected as justifications for excluding impecunious persons, the State's concern about unwieldy ballots and its interest in financing elections. 405 U.S., at 144–149. *Lubin* reaffirmed that a State may not require from an indigent candidate "fees he cannot pay." 415 U.S., at 718.

within the power of government to pursue, is invalid under the Equal Protection Clause simply because it may affect a greater proportion of one race than of another," *id.*, at 242. "This must be all the more true," respondents urge, "with respect to an allegedly disparate impact on a class [here, the poor] that, unlike race, is not suspect." Brief for Respondents 31.

Washington v. Davis, however, does not have the sweeping effect respondents attribute to it. That case involved a verbal skill test administered to prospective Government employees. "[A] far greater proportion of blacks—four times as many—failed the test than did whites." 426 U.S., at 237. But the successful test takers included members of both races, as did the unsuccessful examinees. Disproportionate impact, standing alone, the Court held, was insufficient to prove unconstitutional racial discrimination. Were it otherwise, a host of laws would be called into question, "a whole range of tax, welfare, public service, regulatory, and licensing statutes that may be more burdensome to the poor and to the average black than to the more affluent white." *Id.*, at 248.

To comprehend the difference between the case at hand and cases controlled by *Washington v. Davis*, one need look no further than this Court's opinion in *Williams v. Illinois*, 399 U.S. 235 (1970). *Williams* held unconstitutional an Illinois law under which an indigent offender could be continued in confinement beyond the maximum prison term specified by statute if his indigency prevented him from satisfying the monetary portion of the sentence. The Court described that law as "'nondiscriminatory on its face,'" and recalled that the law found incompatible with the Constitution in *Griffin* had been so characterized. 399 U.S., at 242 (quoting *Griffin*, 351 U.S., at 17, n. 11); see *Griffin*, 351 U.S., at 17, n. 11 ("[A] law nondiscriminatory on its face may be grossly discriminatory in its operation"). But the *Williams* Court went on to explain that "the Illinois statute in operative effect exposes *only indigents* to the risk of imprisonment beyond the statutory maximum." 399 U.S., at 242 (emphasis added). Sanctions of the *Williams* genre, like the Mississippi prescription here at issue, are not merely *disproportionate* in impact. Rather, they are wholly contingent on one's ability to pay, and thus "visi[t] different consequences on two categories of persons," *ibid.*; they apply to all indigents and do not reach anyone outside that class.

In sum, under respondents' reading of *Washington v. Davis*, our overruling of the *Griffin* line of cases would be two decades overdue. It suffices to point out that this Court has not so conceived the meaning and effect of our 1976 "disproportionate impact" precedent. See *Bearden v. Georgia*, 461 U.S., at 664–665, 103 S.Ct., at 2068–2069 (adhering in 1983 to "*Griffin*'s principle of 'equal justice'").[16]

Respondents and the dissenters urge that we will open floodgates if we do not rigidly restrict *Griffin* to cases typed "criminal." Brief for Respondents 27–28. But we have repeatedly noticed what sets parental status termination decrees apart from mine run civil actions, even from other domestic relations matters such as divorce, paternity, and child custody. To recapitulate, termination decrees "wor[k] a unique kind of deprivation." *Lassiter*, 452 U.S., at

16. Six of the seven Justices in the majority in *Washington v. Davis*, 426 U.S. 229 (1976), had two Terms before *Davis* read our decisions in *Griffin* and related cases to hold that "[t]he State cannot adopt procedures which leave an indigent defendant 'entirely cut off from any appeal at all,' by virtue of his indigency, or extend to such indigent defendants merely a 'meaningless ritual' while others in better economic circumstances have a 'meaningful appeal.'" *Ross v. Moffitt*, 417 U.S. 600, 612 (1974) (opinion of the Court by *Rehnquist, J.*) (citations omitted).

27. In contrast to matters modifiable at the parties' will or based on changed circumstances, termination adjudications involve the awesome authority of the State "to destroy permanently all legal recognition of the parental relationship." *Rivera*, 483 U.S., at 580. Our *Lassiter* and *Santosky* decisions, recognizing that parental termination decrees are among the most severe forms of state action, *Santosky*, 455 U.S., at 759, have not served as precedent in other areas. We are therefore satisfied that the label "civil" should not entice us to leave undisturbed the Mississippi courts' disposition of this case. Cf. *In re Gault*, 387 U.S., at 50.

For the reasons stated, we hold that Mississippi may not withhold from M.L.B. "a 'record of sufficient completeness' to permit proper [appellate] consideration of [her] claims." *Mayer*, 404 U.S., at 198. Accordingly, we reverse the judgment of the Supreme Court of Mississippi and remand the case for further proceedings not inconsistent with this opinion....

Justice Kennedy, concurring in the judgment.

The Court gives a most careful and comprehensive recitation of the precedents from *Griffin v. Illinois*, 351 U.S. 12 (1956), through *Mayer v. Chicago*, 404 U.S. 189 (1971), and beyond, a line of decisions which invokes both equal protection and due process principles. The duality, as the Court notes, stems from *Griffin* itself, which produced no opinion for the Court and invoked strands of both constitutional doctrines.

In my view the cases most on point, and the ones which persuade me we must reverse the judgment now reviewed, are the decisions addressing procedures involving the rights and privileges inherent in family and personal relations. These are *Boddie v. Connecticut*, 401 U.S. 371 (1971); *Lassiter v. Department of Social Servs. of Durham Cty.*, 452 U.S. 18 (1981); and *Santosky v. Kramer*, 455 U.S. 745 (1982), all cases resting exclusively upon the Due Process Clause. Here, due process is quite a sufficient basis for our holding.

I acknowledge the authorities do not hold that an appeal is required, even in a criminal case; but given the existing appellate structure in Mississippi, the realities of the litigation process, and the fundamental interests at stake in this particular proceeding, the State may not erect a bar in the form of transcript and filing costs beyond this petitioner's means. The Court well describes the fundamental interests the petitioner has in ensuring that the order which terminated all her parental ties was based upon a fair assessment of the facts and the law. See *Mathews v. Eldridge*, 424 U.S. 319, 335 (1976). With these observations, I concur in the judgment.

Chief Justice Rehnquist, dissenting.

I join all but Part II of Justice Thomas' dissenting opinion. For the reasons stated in that opinion, I would not extend the *Griffin–Mayer* line of cases to invalidate Mississippi's refusal to pay for petitioner's transcript on appeal in this case.

Justice Thomas, with whom Justice Scalia joins, and with whom The Chief Justice joins except as to Part II, dissenting.

Today the majority holds that the Fourteenth Amendment requires Mississippi to afford petitioner a free transcript because her civil case involves a "fundamental" right. The majority seeks to limit the reach of its holding to the type of case we confront here, one involving the termination of parental rights. I do not think, however, that the new-found constitutional right to free transcripts in civil appeals can be effectively restricted to this case. The inevitable consequence will be greater demands on the States to provide free assistance to would-be appellants in all manner of civil cases involving interests that cannot, based on the test established by the majority, be distinguished from the admittedly important interest at issue here. The cases on which the majority relies, primarily cases requiring appellate assistance for indigent criminal defendants, were questionable when decided, and have, in my view, been undermined since. Even accepting those cases, however, I am of the view that the majority takes them too far. I therefore dissent.

I

Petitioner requests relief under both the Due Process and Equal Protection Clauses, though she does not specify how either Clause affords it. The majority accedes to petitioner's request. But, carrying forward the ambiguity in the cases on which it relies, the majority does not specify the source of the relief it grants. Those decisions are said to "reflect both equal protection and due process concerns." And, while we are told that "cases of this order 'cannot be resolved by resort to easy slogans or pigeonhole analysis,'" *ibid.* (quoting *Bearden v. Georgia*, 461 U.S. 660, 666 (1983)), the majority nonetheless acknowledges that "'[m]ost decisions in this area ... res[t] on an equal protection framework,'"(quoting *Bearden*, *supra*, at 665). It then purports to "place this case within the framework established by our past decisions in this area." It is not clear to me whether the majority disavows *any* due process support for its holding. (Despite the murky disclaimer, the majority discusses numerous cases that squarely relied on due process considerations.) I therefore analyze petitioner's claim under both the Due Process and Equal Protection Clauses. If neither Clause affords petitioner the right to a free, civil-appeal transcript, I assume that no amalgam of the two does.

A

We have indicated on several occasions in this century that the interest of parents in maintaining their relationships with their children is "an important interest that 'undeniably warrants deference and, absent a powerful countervailing interest, protection.'" *Lassiter v. Department of Social Servs. of Durham Cty.*, 452 U.S. 18, 27 (1981) (quoting *Stanley v. Illinois*, 405 U.S. 645, 651 (1972)). Assuming that petitioner's interest may not be impinged without due process of law, I do not think that the Due Process Clause requires the result the majority reaches.

Petitioner's largest obstacle to a due process appeal *gratis* is our oft-affirmed view that due process does not oblige States to provide for any appeal, even from a criminal conviction. See, *e.g.*, *Griffin v. Illinois*, 351 U.S. 12, 18 (1956) (plurality opinion) (noting that "a State is not required by the Federal Constitution to provide appellate courts or a right to appellate review at all" (citation omitted)); *McKane v. Durston*, 153 U.S. 684, 687 (1894) ("A review by an appellate court of the final judgment in a criminal case, however grave the offence of which the accused is convicted, was not at common law and is not now a necessary element of due process of law. It is wholly within the discretion of the State to allow or not to allow such a review. A citation of authorities upon the point is unnecessary"). To be sure, we have indicated, beginning with *Griffin v. Illinois*, that where an appeal is provided, States may be prohibited from erecting barriers to those unable to pay. As I described last Term in my concurring opinion in *Lewis v. Casey*, 518 U.S. 343, 368–373 (1996), however, I believe that these cases are best understood as grounded in equal protection analysis, and thus make no inroads on our longstanding rule that States that accord due process in a hearing-level tribunal need not provide further review.

The majority reaffirms that due process does not require an appeal. Indeed, as I noted above, it is not clear that the majority relies on the Due Process Clause at all. The majority does discuss, however, one case in which the Court stated its holding in terms of due process: *Boddie v. Connecticut*, 401 U.S. 371 (1971). In *Boddie*, the Court held violative of due process a Connecticut statute that exacted fees averaging $60 from persons seeking marital dissolution. Citing the importance of the interest in ending a marriage, and the State's monopoly over the mechanisms to accomplish it, we explained that, "at a minimum" and "absent a countervailing state interest of overriding significance, persons forced to settle their claims of right and duty through the judicial process must be given a meaningful opportunity to be heard." *Id.*, at 377. *Boddie* has little to do with this case. It, "of course, was not concerned with post-hearing review." *Ortwein v. Schwab*, 410 U.S. 656, 659 (1973). Rather, the concern in *Boddie* was that indigent persons were deprived of "fundamental rights" with no hearing whatsoever. Petitioner, in contrast, received not merely a hearing, but in fact enjoyed procedural protections above and beyond what our parental termination cases have required. She received both notice and a hearing before a neutral, legally trained decisionmaker. She was represented by counsel—even though due process does not in every case require the appointment of counsel. See *Lassiter, supra*, at 24. Through her attorney, petitioner was able to confront the evidence and witnesses against her. And, in accordance with *Santosky v. Kramer*, 455 U.S. 745, 769 (1982), the Chancery Court was required to find that petitioner's parental unfitness was proved by clear and convincing evidence. Indeed, petitioner points to no hearing-level process to which she was entitled that she did not receive.

Given the many procedural protections afforded petitioner, I have little difficulty concluding that "due process has . . . been accorded in the tribunal of first instance." *Ohio ex rel. Bryant v. Akron Metropolitan Park Dist.*, 281 U.S. 74, 80 (1930). Due process has never compelled an appeal where, as here, its rigors are satisfied by an adequate hearing. Those cases in which the Court has required States to alleviate financial obstacles to process beyond a hearing—though sometimes couched in due process terms—have been based on the equal protection proposition that if the State chooses to provide for appellate review, it "'can no more discriminate on account of poverty than on account of religion, race, or color.'" *Lewis v. Casey, supra*, at 371 (THOMAS, J., concurring) (quoting *Griffin v. Illinois, supra*, at 17 (plurality opinion)) (footnote omitted). There seems, then, no place in the Due Process Clause—certainly as an original matter, and even as construed by this Court—for the constitutional "right" crafted by the majority today. I turn now to the other possible source: The Equal Protection Clause.

B

As I stated last Term in *Lewis v. Casey*, I do not think that the equal protection theory underlying the *Griffin* line of cases remains viable. See 518 U.S., at 373–378. There, I expressed serious reservations as to the continuing vitality of *Bounds v. Smith*, 430 U.S. 817 (1977) (requiring prison authorities to provide prisoners with adequate law libraries or legal assistance). As it did in *Bounds*, the Court today not only adopts the equal protection theory of *Griffin v. Illinois*—which was dubious *ab initio* and which has been undermined since—but extends it. Thus, much of what I said in *Lewis v. Casey* bears repeating here.

In *Griffin*, the State of Illinois required all criminal appellants whose claims on appeal required review of a trial transcript to obtain it themselves. The plurality thought that this "discriminate[d] against some convicted defendants on account of their poverty," 351 U.S., at 18 (plurality opinion). Justice Harlan, in dissent, perceived a troubling shift in this Court's equal protection jurisprudence. The Court, he noted, did not "dispute either the necessity for a bill of exceptions or the reasonableness of the general requirement that the trial transcript, if used in its preparation, be paid for by the appealing party." *Id.*, at 35. But, because requiring each would-be appellant to bear the costs of appeal hit the poor harder, the majority divined "an invidious classification between the 'rich' and the 'poor.'" *Ibid.* Disputing this early manifestation of the "disparate impact" theory of equal protection, Justice Harlan argued:

> "[N]o economic burden attendant upon the exercise of a privilege bears equally upon all, and in other circumstances the resulting differentiation is not treated as an invidious classification by the State, even though discrimination against 'indigents' by name would be unconstitutional." *Ibid.*

Justice Harlan offered the example of a state university that conditions an education on the payment of tuition. If charging tuition did not create a discriminatory classification, then, Justice Harlan wondered, how did any other reasonable exaction by a State for a service it provides? "The resulting classification would be invidious in all cases, and an invidious classification offends equal protection regardless of the seriousness of the consequences." *Ibid.* (emphasis deleted). The issue in *Griffin* was not whether Illinois had made a reasonable classification, but whether the State acted reasonably in failing to remove disabilities that existed wholly independently of state action. To Justice Harlan this was not an inquiry typically posed under the Equal Protection Clause.

In *Douglas v. California*, 372 U.S. 353 (1963), Justice Harlan again confronted what Justice Clark termed the Court's "fetish for indigency," *id.*, at 359 (dissenting opinion). Regarding a law limiting the appointment of appellate counsel for indigents, Justice Harlan pointed out that "[l]aws such as these do not deny equal protection to the less fortunate for one essential reason: the Equal Protection Clause does not impose on the States 'an affirmative duty to lift the handicaps flowing from differences in economic circumstances.'" *Id.*, at 362 (dissenting opinion) (footnote omitted).

Justice Harlan's views were accepted by the Court in *Washington v. Davis*, 426 U.S. 229 (1976), in which "[w]e rejected a disparate impact theory of the Equal Protection Clause altogether." *Lewis v. Casey*, *supra*, at 375 (concurring opinion). We spurned the claim that "a law, neutral on its face and serving ends otherwise within the power of government to pursue, is invalid under the Equal Protection Clause simply because it may affect a greater proportion of one race than of another." 426 U.S., at 242. Absent proof of discriminatory purpose, official action did not violate the Fourteenth Amendment "*solely* because it has a racially disparate impact." *Id.*, at 239 (emphasis in original). Hearkening back to Justice Harlan's dissents in *Griffin* and *Douglas*, we recognized that

> "[a] rule that a statute designed to serve neutral ends is nevertheless invalid, absent compelling justification, if in practice it benefits or burdens one race more than another would be far reaching and would raise serious questions about, and perhaps invalidate, a whole range of tax, welfare, public service, regulatory, and licensing statutes that may be more burdensome to the poor and to the average black than to the more affluent white." 426 U.S., at 248 (footnote omitted).

The lesson of *Davis* is that the Equal Protection Clause shields only against purposeful discrimination: A disparate impact, even upon members of a racial minority, the classification of which we have been most suspect, does not violate equal protection. The Clause is not a panacea for perceived social or economic inequity; it seeks to "guarante[e] equal laws, not equal results." *Personnel Administrator of Mass. v. Feeney*, 442 U.S. 256, 273 (1979).

Since *Davis*, we have regularly required more of an equal protection claimant than a showing that state action has a harsher effect on him or her than on others. See, *e.g.*, *Harris v. McRae*, 448 U.S. 297, 324, n. 26 (1980) ("The equal protection component of the Fifth Amendment prohibits only purposeful discrimination, and when a facially neutral federal statute is challenged on equal protection grounds, it is incumbent upon the challenger to prove that Congress selected or reaffirmed a particular course of action at least in part because of, not merely in spite of, its adverse effects upon an identifiable group" (internal quotation marks and citations omitted)); see also *Lewis v. Casey*, 518 U.S., at 375 (concurring opinion) (citing cases). Our frequent pronouncements that the Fourteenth Amendment is not violated by disparate impact have spanned challenges to statutes alleged to affect disproportionately members of one race, *Washington v. Davis, supra*; members of one sex, *Personnel Administrator v. Feeney, supra*; and poor persons seeking to exercise protected rights, *Harris v. McRae, supra*; *Maher v. Roe*, 432 U.S. 464, 470–471 (1977).

The majority attempts to avoid what I regard as the irresistible force of the *Davis* line of cases, but I am unconvinced by the effort. The majority states that persons in cases like those cited above "sought state aid to subsidize their privately initiated action or to alleviate the consequences of differences in economic circumstances that existed apart from state action." Petitioner, in apparent contrast, "is endeavoring to defend against the State's destruction of her family bonds, and to resist the brand associated with a parental unfitness adjudication." *Ibid.* She, "[l]ike a defendant resisting criminal conviction, . . . seeks to be spared from the State's devastatingly adverse action." *Ibid.* But also like a defendant resisting criminal conviction, petitioner is not constitutionally entitled to post-trial process. She defended against the "destruction of her family bonds" in the Chancery Court hearing at which she was accorded all the process this Court has required of the States in parental termination cases. She now desires "state aid to subsidize [her] privately initiated" appeal—an appeal that neither petitioner nor the majority claims Mississippi is required to provide—to overturn the determination that resulted from that hearing. I see no principled difference between a facially neutral rule that serves in some cases to prevent persons from availing themselves of state employment, or a state-funded education, or a state-funded abortion—each of which the State may, but is not required to, provide—and a facially neutral rule that prevents a person from taking an appeal that is available only because the State chooses to provide it.

Nor does *Williams v. Illinois*, 399 U.S. 235 (1970), a case decided six years earlier, operate to limit *Washington v. Davis. Williams* was yet another manifestation of the "equalizing" notion of equal protection that this Court began to question in *Davis*. See *Williams, supra*, at 260 (Harlan, J., concurring in result). To the extent its reasoning survives *Davis*, I think that *Williams* is distinguishable. Petitioner Williams was incarcerated beyond the maximum statutory sentence because he was unable to pay the fine imposed as part of his sentence. We found the law that permitted prisoners to avoid extrastatutory imprisonment only by paying their fines to violate the Equal Protection Clause. Even though it was "'nondiscriminatory on its face,'" the law "work[ed] an invidious discrimination" as to Williams and all other indigents because they could not afford to pay their fines. 399 U.S., at 242. The majority concludes that the sanctions involved in *Williams* are analogous to "the Mississippi prescription here at issue," in that both do not have merely a disparate impact, "they apply to all indigents and do not reach anyone outside that class." Even assuming that Williams' imprisonment gave rise to an equal protection violation, however, M.L.B.'s circumstances are not comparable. M.L.B.'s parental rights were terminated—the analog to Williams' extended imprisonment—because the Chancery Court found, after a hearing, that she was unfit to remain her children's mother, not because she was indigent. Her indigency only prevented her from taking advantage of procedures above and beyond those required by the Constitution—in the same way that indigency frequently prevents persons from availing themselves of a variety of state services.[1]

The *Griffin* line of cases ascribed to—one might say announced—an equalizing notion of the Equal Protection Clause that would, I think, have startled the Fourteenth Amendment's Framers. In those cases, the Court did not find, nor did it seek, any purposeful discrimination on the part of the state defendants. That their statutes had disproportionate effect on poor persons was sufficient for us to find a constitutional violation. In *Davis*, among other cases, we began to recognize the potential mischief of a disparate impact theory writ large, and endeavored to contain it. In this case, I would continue that enterprise. Mississippi's requirement of prepaid transcripts in civil appeals seeking to contest the sufficiency of the evidence adduced at trial is facially neutral; it creates no classification. The transcript rule reasonably obliges would-be appellants to bear the costs of availing themselves of a service that the State chooses, but is not constitutionally required, to provide.[2] Any adverse impact that the transcript requirement has on any person seeking to appeal arises not out of the State's action, but out of factors entirely unrelated to it.

II

If this case squarely presented the question, I would be inclined to vote to overrule *Griffin* and its progeny. Even were I convinced that the cases on which the majority today relies ought to be retained, I could not agree with the majority's extension of them.

The interest at stake in this case differs in several important respects from that at issue in cases such as *Griffin*. Petitioner's interest in maintaining a relationship with her children is the subject of a civil, not criminal, action. While certain civil suits may tend at the margin toward criminal cases, and criminal cases may likewise drift toward civil suits, the basic distinction between the two finds root in the Constitution and has largely retained its vitality in our jurisprudence. In dissent in *Boddie v. Connecticut*, Justice Black stated that "in *Griffin* the Court studiously and carefully refrained from saying one word or one sentence suggesting

1. Similarly, *Harper v. Virginia Bd. of Elections*, 383 U.S. 663 (1966), struck down a poll tax that directly restricted the exercise of a right found in that case to be fundamental—the right to vote in state elections. The fee that M. L. B. is unable to pay does not prevent the exercise of a fundamental right directly: The fundamental interest identified by the majority is not the right to a civil appeal, it is rather the right to maintain the parental relationship.

2. Petitioner suggests that Mississippi's $2 per page charge exceeds the actual cost of transcription. See Reply Brief for Petitioner 8. She stops short of asserting that the charge is unreasonable or irrational. While not conclusive, I note that Mississippi's transcript charge falls comfortably within the range of charges throughout the Nation. See, e.g., Ariz.Rev.Stat. Ann. § 12-224(B) (1992) ($2.50/page); Idaho Code § 1-1105(2) (1990) ($2/page); Mass. Gen. Laws § 221:88 (1994) ($3/page); Mo.Rev.Stat. § 485.100 (1994) ($1.50/page); N.M. Stat. Ann. § 34-6-20(C) (1996) ($1.65/page); R.I. Gen. Laws § 8-5-5 (Supp. 1995) (family court transcripts, $3/page); S.C.App.Ct. Rule 508 ($2/page).

that the rule there announced to control rights of criminal defendants would control in the quite different field of civil cases." 401 U.S., at 390. The Constitution provides for a series of protections of the unadorned liberty interest at stake in criminal proceedings. These express protections include the Fifth Amendment's guarantee of grand jury indictment, and protection against double jeopardy and self-incrimination; the Sixth Amendment's guarantees of a speedy and public jury trial, of the ability to confront witnesses, and of compulsory process and assistance of counsel; and the Eighth Amendment's protections against excessive bail and fines, and against cruel and unusual punishment. This Court has given content to these textual protections, and has identified others contained in the Due Process Clause. These protections are not available to the typical civil litigant. Even where the interest in a civil suit has been labeled "fundamental," as with the interest in parental termination suits, the protections extended pale by comparison. A party whose parental rights are subject to termination is entitled to appointed counsel, but only in certain circumstances. See *Lassiter*, 452 U.S., at 31–32. His or her rights cannot be terminated unless the evidence meets a standard higher than the preponderance standard applied in the typical civil suit, but the standard is still lower than that required before a guilty verdict. See *Santosky v. Kramer*, 455 U.S., at 769–770.

That said, it is true enough that civil and criminal cases do not always stand in bold relief to one another. *Mayer v. Chicago*, 404 U.S. 189 (1971), marks a particularly discomfiting point along the border between the civil and criminal areas. Based on *Griffin*, the Court determined there that an indigent defendant had a constitutional right to a free transcript in aid of appealing his conviction for violating city ordinances, which resulted in a $500 fine and no imprisonment. In *Scott v. Illinois*, 440 U.S. 367 (1979), we concluded that an indigent defendant charged with a crime that was not punishable by imprisonment was not entitled to appointed counsel. And yet, in *Lassiter*, *supra*, we held that, in some cases, due process required provision of assistance of counsel before the termination of parental rights. The assertion that civil litigants have no right to the free transcripts that all criminal defendants enjoy is difficult to sustain in the face of our holding that some civil litigants are entitled to the assistance of counsel to which some criminal defendants are not. It is at this unsettled (and unsettling) place that the majority lays the foundation of its holding. The majority's solution to the "anomal[y]" that a misdemeanant receives a free transcript but no trial counsel, while a parental-rights terminee receives (sometimes) trial counsel, but no transcript, works an extension of *Mayer*. I would answer the conundrum differently: Even if the *Griffin* line were sound, *Mayer* was an unjustified extension that should be limited to its facts, if not overruled.

Unlike in *Scott* and *Lassiter*, the Court gave short shrift in *Mayer* to the distinction, as old as our Constitution, between crimes punishable by imprisonment and crimes punishable merely by fines. See *Lassiter*, *supra*, at 26–27; *Scott*, *supra*, at 373. Even though specific text-based constitutional protections have been withheld in cases not involving the prospect of imprisonment, the Court found the difference of no moment in *Mayer*. The Court reasoned that "[t]he invidiousness of the discrimination that exists when criminal procedures are made available only to those who can pay is not erased by any differences in the sentences that may be imposed." 404 U.S., at 197. We reap today what we sowed then. If requiring payment for procedures (e.g., appeals) that are not themselves required is invidious discrimination no matter what sentence results, it is difficult to imagine why it is not invidious discrimination no matter what results and no matter whether the procedures involve a criminal or civil case. To me this points up the difficulty underlying the entire *Griffin* line. Taking the *Griffin* line as a given, however, and in the absence of any obvious limiting principle, I would restrict it to the criminal appeals to which its authors, see *Boddie v. Connecticut*, 401 U.S., at 389 (Black, J., dissenting), sought to limit it.

The distinction between criminal and civil cases—if blurred at the margins—has persisted throughout the law. The distinction that the majority seeks to draw between the case we confront today and the other civil cases that we will surely face tomorrow is far more ephemeral. If all that is required to trigger the right to a free appellate transcript is that the interest at stake appear to us to be as fundamental as the interest of a convicted misdemeanant, several kinds of civil suits involving interests that seem fundamental enough leap to mind. Will the Court, for example, now extend the right to a free transcript to an indigent seeking to appeal the outcome of a paternity suit?[3] To those who wish to appeal custody determinations?[4] How about persons against whom divorce decrees are entered?[5] Civil suits that arise out of challenges to zoning ordinances with an impact on families?[6] Why not foreclosure actions—or at least foreclosure actions seeking to oust persons from their homes of many years?[7]

The majority seeks to provide assurances that its holding will not extend beyond parental termination suits. The holdings of *Santosky* and *Lassiter*—both of which involved parental termination—have not, we are told, been applied to other areas of law. This is not comforting. Both *Santosky* and *Lassiter* are cases that determined the requirements of due process (not equal protection) in the parental rights termination area. As the Court has said countless times, the requirements of due process vary considerably with the interest involved and the action to which it is subject. It is little wonder, then, that the specific due process requirements for one sort of action are not readily transferable to others. I have my doubts that today's opinion will be so confined. In the first place, it is not clear whether it is

3. In *Little v. Streater*, 452 U.S. 1 (1981), we held that the Due Process Clause required the States to provide a free blood grouping test to an indigent defendant in a paternity action. The Court observed that "[a]part from the putative father's pecuniary interest in avoiding a substantial support obligation and liberty interest threatened by the possible sanctions for noncompliance, at issue is the creation of a parent-child relationship. This Court frequently has stressed the importance of familial bonds, whether or not legitimized by marriage, and accorded them constitutional protection. Just as the termination of such bonds demands procedural fairness, so too does their imposition." *Id.*, at 13 (citations omitted). *Little*'s description of the interest at stake in a paternity suit seems to place it on par with the interest here.

Justice Blackmun, dissenting in *Lassiter v. Department of Social Servs. of Durham Cty.*, 452 U.S. 18, 58 (1981), recognized as much: "I deem it not a little ironic that the Court on this very day grants, on due process grounds, an indigent putative father's claim for state-paid blood grouping tests in the interest of according him a meaningful opportunity to disprove his paternity, *Little v. Streater*, [*supra*] but in the present case rejects, on due process grounds, an indigent mother's claim for state-paid legal assistance when the State seeks to take her own child away from her in a termination proceeding." (Emphasis deleted.)

As the majority indicates, we have distinguished—in my view unpersuasively—between the requirements of due process in paternity suits and in termination suits. See *Rivera v. Minnich*, 483 U.S. 574 (1987). Whether we will distinguish between paternity appellants and misdemeanor appellants remains to be seen.

4. See, *e.g.*, *Zakrzewski v. Fox*, 87 F.3d 1011, 1013–1014 (C.A.8 1996) (father's "fundamental" "liberty interest in the care, custody and management of his son has been substantially reduced by the terms of the divorce decree and Nebraska law").

5. In *Boddie v. Connecticut*, 401 U.S. 371 (1971), we referred to a divorce as the "adjustment of a fundamental human relationship." *Id.*, at 382–383.

6. See, *e.g.*, *Moore v. East Cleveland*, 431 U.S. 494 (1977).

7. Cf. *Lindsey v. Normet*, 405 U.S. 56, 89–90 (1972) (Douglas, J., dissenting in part) ("[W]here the right is so fundamental as the tenant's claim to his home, the requirements of due process should be more embracing").

an equal protection or a due process opinion. Moreover, the principle on which it appears to rest hardly seems capable of stemming the tide. Petitioner is permitted a free appellate transcript because the interest that underlies her civil claim compares favorably to the interest of the misdemeanant facing a $500 fine and unknown professional difficulties in *Mayer v. Chicago.* Under the rule announced today, I do not see how a civil litigant could constitutionally be denied a free transcript in any case that involves an interest that is arguably as important as the interest in *Mayer* (which would appear to include all the types of cases that I mention above, and perhaps many others).[8] What is more, it must be remembered that *Griffin* did not merely invent the free transcript right for criminal appellants; it was also the launching pad for the discovery of a host of other rights. See, *e.g.*, *Bounds*, 430 U.S., at 822 (right to prison law libraries or legal assistance); *Douglas*, 372 U.S., at 356 (right to free appellate counsel). I fear that the growth of *Griffin* in the criminal area may be mirrored in the civil area.

In brushing aside the distinction between criminal and civil cases—the distinction that has constrained *Griffin* for 40 years—the Court has eliminated the last meaningful limit on the free-floating right to appellate assistance. From *Mayer*, an unfortunate outlier in the *Griffin* line, has sprung the *M.L.B.* line, and I have no confidence that the majority's assurances that the line starts and ends with this case will hold true.

III

As the majority points out, many States already provide for *in forma pauperis* civil appeals, with some making special allowances for parental termination cases. I do not dispute the wisdom or charity of these heretofore voluntary allocations of the various States' scarce resources. I agree that, for many—if not most—parents, the termination of their right to raise their children would be an exaction more dear than any other. It seems perfectly reasonable for States to choose to provide extraconstitutional procedures to ensure that any such termination is undertaken with care. I do not agree, however, that a State that has taken the step, not required by the Constitution, of permitting appeals from termination decisions somehow violates the Constitution when it charges reasonable fees of all would-be appellants. I respectfully dissent.

NOTES AND QUESTIONS

1. Is a parent constitutionally entitled to an appeal from the termination of her parental rights? If not, what is the issue before the Court? What is it that the state failed to provide?

2. If the state is not obligated to provide counsel to an indigent parent in every termination proceeding, why must the state pay for an indigent parent's appeal?

3. On what grounds does Justice Thomas dissent? What is it that he would have the Court do?

8. Accordingly, Mississippi will no doubt find little solace in the fact that, as the majority notes, of 63,765 civil actions filed in Mississippi Chancery Court in 1995, 194 were parental termination cases. Mississippi pointed out in its brief that of these civil actions, "39,475 were domestic relations cases," "1027 involved custody or visitation, and 6080 were paternity cases." Brief for Respondents 28.

2. STATUTORY FRAMEWORK

Despite the Adoption Assistance and Child Welfare Act (AACWA) mandates to reduce the number of children in foster care and reunify children with their families, the number of children in foster care exceeded five hundred thousand by 1996, many of whom had no hope of achieving permanent placements with loving families. Moreover, the reasonable-efforts requirement came to be seen as a major stumbling block to permanency. In response, Congress enacted the Adoption and Safe Families Act (ASFA), which emphasizes permanency and safety for children by creating timelines for permanency. Federal funding is contingent on compliance with the timelines. First, states are not required to make reasonable efforts under certain circumstances. If no reasonable efforts are required, a permanency hearing must be held in thirty days. Second, a permanency hearing must be held every twelve months. Third, the state must file a petition to terminate parental rights after a child has been in foster care for fifteen of the preceding twenty-two months.

42 U.S.C. §§ 671(a)(15)(B), (D)–(E) (2011)

(B) except as provided in subparagraph (D), reasonable efforts shall be made to preserve and reunify families—

- (i) prior to the placement of a child in foster care, to prevent or eliminate the need for removing the child from the child's home; and
- (ii) to make it possible for a child to safely return to the child's home;...

(D) reasonable efforts of the type described in subparagraph (B) shall not be required to be made with respect to a parent of a child if a court of competent jurisdiction has determined that—

- (i) the parent has subjected the child to aggravated circumstances (as defined in State law, which definition may include but need not be limited to abandonment, torture, chronic abuse, and sexual abuse);
- (ii) the parent has—
  - (I) committed murder (which would have been an offense under section 1111(a) of Title 18, if the offense had occurred in the special maritime or territorial jurisdiction of the United States) of another child of the parent;
  - (II) committed voluntary manslaughter (which would have been an offense under section 1112(a) of title 18, if the offense had occurred in the special maritime or territorial jurisdiction of the United States) of another child of the parent;
  - (III) aided or abetted, attempted, conspired, or solicited to commit such a murder or such a voluntary manslaughter; or
  - (IV) committed a felony assault that results in serious bodily injury to the child or another child of the parent; or
- (iii) the parental rights of the parent to a sibling have been terminated involuntarily;

(E) if reasonable efforts of the type described in subparagraph (B) are not made with respect to a child as a result of a determination made by a court of competent jurisdiction in accordance with subparagraph (D)—

- (i) a permanency hearing (as described in section 675(5)(C)), which considers in-State and out-of-State permanent placement options for the child, shall be held for the child within 30 days after the determination; and

(ii) reasonable efforts shall be made to place the child in a timely manner in accordance with the permanency plan, and to complete whatever steps are necessary to finalize the permanent placement of the child....

42 U.S.C. § 675 (5)(E) (2011)

(5) The term "case review system" means a procedure for assuring that—

(E) in the case of a child who has been in foster care under the responsibility of the State for 15 of the most recent 22 months, or, if a court of competent jurisdiction has determined a child to be an abandoned infant (as defined under State law) or has made a determination that the parent has committed murder of another child of the parent, committed voluntary manslaughter of another child of the parent, aided or abetted, attempted, conspired, or solicited to commit such a murder or such a voluntary manslaughter, or committed a felony assault that has resulted in serious bodily injury to the child or to another child of the parent, the State shall file a petition to terminate the parental rights of the child's parents (or, if such a petition has been filed by another party, seek to be joined as a party to the petition), and, concurrently, to identify, recruit, process, and approve a qualified family for an adoption, unless—

(i) at the option of the State, the child is being cared for by a relative;

(ii) a State agency has documented in the case plan (which shall be available for court review) a compelling reason for determining that filing such a petition would not be in the best interests of the child; or

(iii) the State has not provided to the family of the child, consistent with the time period in the State case plan, such services as the State deems necessary for the safe return of the child to the child's home, if reasonable efforts of the type described in section 671(a)(15)(B)(ii) of this title are required to be made with respect to the child....

NOTES AND QUESTIONS

1. How does the reasonable-efforts requirement relate to termination of parental rights? Under ASFA, are states still obligated to make reasonable efforts? What are the bases for termination of parental rights? Are there any exceptions?

2. Does ASFA create statutory presumptions of unfitness? If so, does the law violate *Stanley*?

3. Do you think the timelines are a good idea? Some commentators have argued that ASFA timelines promote adoption over reunification and family preservation. See Annette R. Appell, *Virtual Mothers and the Meaning of Parenthood*, 34 U. Mich. J. L. Reform 683, 729 (2001); Jeanne M. Kaiser, *Finding a Reasonable Way to Enforce the Reasonable Efforts Requirement in Child Protection Cases*, 7 Rutgers J. L. & Pub. Pol'y 100, 108–109 (2009). Others suggest that the timelines have a disproportionate impact on poor and minority families. See, e.g., Dorothy Roberts, Shattered Bonds: The Color of Child Welfare (2002). Moreover, the timelines create an inflexible approach that does not serve all children well, particularly those at the margins, whose parents may or may not have been neglectful. Catherine J. Ross, *The Tyranny of Time: Vulnerable Children, "Bad" Mothers, and Statutory Deadlines in Parental*

Termination Proceedings, 11 VA. J. SOC. POL'Y & L. 176 (2004). Do you agree? Is there a better solution for foster-care drift and permanency?

4. Do the ASFA timelines achieve permanency for children in foster care? The number of children in foster care has declined since 2002, and in 2007, 2008, and 2009, the number of children exiting foster care exceeded the number of children entering care. In 2010, the number of children entering care equaled the number of children exiting care. The number of termination cases also has declined, from a high of 82,000 in 2007 to 64,000 in 2010. Nevertheless, since 2002, the percentage of children waiting to be adopted whose parents' rights have been terminated has remained fairly stable, at around 60 percent with some fluctuation. The percentage of children adopted each year has risen slightly, from about 18 percent in 2002 to approximately 21 percent in 2010. Children's Bureau, U.S. Dep't of Health & Human Servs., The AFCARS Report—Trends in Foster Care and Adoption FY 2002–FY 2010 (June 2011), http://www.acf.hhs.gov/programs/cb/stats_research/afcars/trends_june2011. However, outcome measures indicate that most adoptions occur more than two years after a child enters foster care. Children's Bureau, U.S. Dep't of Health & Human Servs., Child Welfare Outcomes 2006–2009: Report to Congress iv (2009), http://www.acf.hhs.gov/programs/cb/pubs/cwo06-09/cwo06-09.pdf.

3. PROCEDURAL FRAMEWORK

IN RE H.G.
Supreme Court of Illinois
757 N.E.2d 864 (2001)

Justice McMORROW delivered the opinion of the court:

At issue in this appeal is the constitutionality of section 1(D)(m-1) of the Adoption Act (750 ILCS 50/1(D)(m-1) (West 1998)). Section 1(D)(m-1) provides, in part, that a parent may be found unfit if "[p]ursuant to the Juvenile Court Act of 1987, a child has been in foster care for 15 months out of any 22 month period." 750 ILCS 50/1(D)(m-1) (West 1998). The circuit court of Kane County, in cause No. 89115, and the circuit court of Cook County, in cause Nos. 89783 and 90053, held section 1(D)(m-1) unconstitutional. Direct appeal was taken to this court and the cases were consolidated for review. For the reasons that follow, we affirm the judgment of the circuit court in cause No. 89115. In cause Nos. 89783 and 90053, we dismiss the appeals as moot.

Background

In 1980, Congress enacted the Adoption Assistance and Child Welfare Act (AACWA). See 42 U.S.C. §§ 620 through 628, 670 through 679a (1994). AACWA created a program which authorizes the federal government to reimburse the states for certain expenses incurred by the states in the administration of foster care and adoption services. To be eligible for federal funds under AACWA, the states must have in place a plan which provides, in pertinent part, that "reasonable efforts" will be made to prevent the removal of children from their homes into foster care and, after removal, that "reasonable efforts" will be made to reunify the children with their parents. See 42 U.S.C. § 671(a)(15) (1994); *Suter v. Artist M.*, 503 U.S. 347, 112 S.Ct. 1360, 118 L.Ed.2d 1 (1992). Through the establishment of the reimbursement program under AACWA, Congress sought to prevent the unnecessary placement of children in foster care. See generally C. Kim, Note, *Putting Reason Back into the Reasonable Efforts Requirement in Child Abuse and Neglect Cases,* 1999 U. Ill. L. Rev. 287, 314.

Some time after the passage of AACWA, it became apparent to Congress that the courts and state agencies which were interpreting and implementing the "reasonable efforts" requirement of the Act were placing too great an emphasis on the goals of family preservation and reunification. As a result, a number of children were "languish[ing] in foster care" and "remain[ing] in limbo as to their permanency" while the states attempted to rehabilitate their parents. 1999 U. Ill. L. Rev. at 293. In response to this and other problems, Congress passed the Adoption and Safe Families Act of 1997. Pub.L. No. 105-89, 111 Stat. 2115 (codified as amended in various sections of 42 U.S.C.).

Among other issues, the Adoption and Safe Families Act of 1997 (ASFA) addressed the question of how long the states must pursue the goal of family reunification under the "reasonable efforts" standard. ASFA mandates that, to retain eligibility for federal funding, and unless certain exceptions apply, the states "shall file a petition to terminate the parental rights of [a] child's parents" when the child "has been in foster care under the responsibility of the State for 15 of the most recent 22 months." 42 U.S.C. § 675(5)(E) (Supp. 1997). The exceptions to this rule requiring the filing of a petition to terminate parental rights are (1) the child is being cared for by a relative, (2) there is no compelling reason for filing such a petition, or (3) the state has not provided services necessary for the safe return of the child to the child's home. 42 U.S.C. § 675(5)(E) (Supp. 1997).

In 1998, the General Assembly responded to Congress' enactment of the 15-month time frame for pursuing family reunification set forth in ASFA by adding section 1(D)(m-1) to the Adoption Act and section 2-13(4.5)(i) to the Juvenile Court Act of 1987 (705 ILCS 405/2-13(4.5)(i) (West 1998)). Section 2-13(4.5) of the Juvenile Court Act simply mirrors the language found in ASFA pertaining to the 15-month period for reunification. Section 2-13(4.5)(i) requires the Department of Children and Family Services to request the State to file a petition to terminate parental rights once a child has spent 15 months out of the most recent 22 months in foster care, unless one of the exceptions to filing such a petition listed in the federal legislation exists. See 705 ILCS 405/2-13(4.5)(i) (West 1998).

Section 1(D)(m-1) of the Adoption Act, however, goes a step further. Section 1(D)(m-1) creates a new ground of parental unfitness based upon the presumption that a parent is unfit if his or her child has been in foster care for 15 months out of a 22-month period. Section 1(D)(m-1) states that a parent may be unfit if:

> "Pursuant to the Juvenile Court Act of 1987, a child has been in foster care for 15 months out of any 22 month period * * * unless the child's parent can prove by a preponderance of the evidence that it is more likely than not that it will be in the best interests of the child to be returned to the parent within 6 months of the date on which a petition for termination of parental rights is filed under the Juvenile Court Act of 1987. The 15 month time limit is tolled during any period for which there is a court finding that the appointed custodian or guardian

failed to make reasonable efforts to reunify the child with his or her family. * * *" 750 ILCS 50/1(D)(m-1) (West 1998)....

On March 12, 1996, the State filed a petition in the circuit court of Kane County in which it alleged that H.G. was a neglected minor. See 705 ILCS 405/2-3(1), 2-13 (West 1998). The allegations of neglect were contained in two counts, both of which asserted that H.G. was in an environment injurious to her welfare. See 705 ILCS 405/2-3(1)(b) (West 1998). Count I alleged that H.G.'s mother, E.W., had allowed H.G. to have contact with her father, in violation of an order of protection. Count II alleged that E.W. had "grabbed [H.G.'s] arm on two separate occasions causing a dislocation."

Following a temporary custody hearing (see 705 ILCS 405/2-10 (West 1998)), the circuit court determined that H.G. "did receive injuries" to her arm and, thus, that there was probable cause to believe that H.G. was neglected under count II of the State's petition. The court also found that it was "a matter of immediate and urgent necessity" (705 ILCS 405/2-10(2) (West 1998)) that H.G. be placed in the temporary custody of the Department of Children and Family Services (DCFS).

On October 10, 1996,[1] the circuit court entered an order adjudicating H.G. neglected based upon the allegations set forth in count II of the State's petition. See 705 ILCS 405/2-21 (West 1998).

On December 23, 1996,[2] the circuit court entered a dispositional order making H.G. a ward of the court. The court placed H.G. in the legal custody of DCFS and appointed the guardianship administrator of DCFS her legal guardian. See 705 ILCS 405/2-27(d) (West 1998). At the same time, the circuit court ordered E.W. to cooperate with DCFS and to follow a number of directives, including, *inter alia,* obtaining appropriate housing, participating in therapy, and completing parenting classes.

From December 1996 to August 1998, DCFS continued to monitor E.W.'s progress toward reaching the various goals and objectives that had been established for her. By the end of August 1998, DCFS concluded that E.W.'s progress was unsatisfactory and, therefore, that termination of her parental rights was warranted. On October 13, 1998, the State filed a petition for termination of parental rights. See 705 ILCS 405/2-13, 2-29 (West 1998). In that petition, the State alleged that E.W. was unfit under section 1(D)(m) of the Adoption Act (750 ILCS 50/1(D)(m) (West 1994)) because she had failed to make reasonable efforts to correct the conditions which were the basis for removal of H.G. or to make reasonable progress toward the return of the child within 12 months after adjudication. The matter was set for trial on March 11 and 12, 1999.

On March 8, 1999, E.W.'s attorney filed a motion for continuance because an indispensable witness was unavailable for trial. The circuit court granted the motion and continued the trial date until May 24 and 25. On May 17, the guardian *ad litem* for H.G. filed a motion seeking a continuance because he had an oral argument scheduled before the appellate court on May 25. The circuit court granted the motion and continued the case until October 8, 14 and 15. The circuit court chose dates some five months ahead because the court wished to

1. E.W. waived the statutory, 90-day deadline for adjudication. See 705 ILCS 405/2-14(b) (West 1998).

2. The statutory, 30-day deadline for setting a dispositional hearing (see 705 ILCS 405/2-21(2) (West 1998)) was waived by agreement.

avoid a piecemeal trial and because October 14 and 15 were the first consecutive, open dates on the court's calendar.

On October 4, 1999, the State filed an amended petition to terminate parental rights. In this petition, the State retained its allegation that E.W. was unfit under section 1(D)(m). In addition, for the first time, the State alleged that E.W. was unfit under section 1(D)(m-1) because H.G. had been in foster care for 15 out of the preceding 22 months.

On October 7, 1999, the circuit court vacated the October 8 trial date because a material witness for the State was on medical leave and was unable to appear in court. The court preserved the October 14 and 15 dates and instructed the State to determine whether the witness' testimony could be obtained by deposition. On October 13, 1999, the State filed a motion for continuance, which stated that the witness was physically unable to testify. On October 14, 1999, over E.W.'s objection, the motion for continuance was granted. The case was continued until January 27 and 28 and February 4, 2000. Also on October 14, on the circuit court's motion, the court struck the count in the State's amended petition which alleged that E.W. was unfit under section 1(D)(m-1) because that claim was not yet ripe.

On October 15, 1999, E.W. filed a petition to restore custody. See 705 ILCS 405/2-28(4) (West 1998). On October 26, 1999, the court ruled that this petition would be heard during the best interest portion of the termination hearing, if the case proceeded to that point.

On January 20, 2000, the State filed a second amended petition to terminate parental rights. This petition repeated the count under section 1(D)(m) that was still pending and added a second count, under section 1(D)(m-1), to replace the one the circuit court had struck in October.

On January 27, 2000, E.W. filed a motion to strike the second count of the State's petition. In this motion, E.W. asserted that section 1(D)(m-1) violates the federal and state constitutional guarantees of substantive due process and equal protection because it "is not narrowly tailored to achieve its manifest purpose, improperly shifts the burden of proof to a respondent parent, and improperly invites consideration of best interest issues at the fitness portion of a termination hearing."

On January 27, 2000, after hearing argument, the circuit court granted E.W.'s motion. In an oral ruling, the court determined that section 1(D)(m-1) implicated a fundamental interest, *i.e.*, parental rights and, therefore, that the statute had to withstand strict scrutiny under the due process clause of the federal and state constitutions. The court held that section 1(D)(m-1) failed this test because it was not narrowly tailored. The court stated,

> "The problem is inherent in that this particular statute, unlike all of the other provisions for finding unfitness, relates not to conduct of a parent or an internal flaw of character or behavior or mental illness or physical infirmity, but rather the mere passage of time. I do agree that there is a due process problem."

The circuit court also held that section 1(D)(m-1) was "constitutionally infirm" because it shifted the burden of proof to the parent within the fitness proceeding and because it introduced the concept of best interests of the child into the determination of the unfitness of the parent.

At the conclusion of the circuit court's ruling from the bench, the State asked the court to stay any further proceedings on the termination petition. The court did so. Thus, count I of the State's petition, which alleges that E.W. is unfit under section 1(D)(m), is still pending, but is in abeyance. The State also sought leave to pursue an interlocutory appeal. The circuit court granted this request and, pursuant to Supreme Court Rule 308 (155 Ill.2d R. 308), stated that its holding that section 1(D)(m-1) is unconstitutional warranted interlocutory appeal. The circuit court also found, under Supreme Court Rule 304(a) (155 Ill.2d R. 304(a)), that there was no just reason for delaying appeal of the court's decision. Appeal was taken by the State directly to this court under Supreme Court Rule 302(a)(1) (134 Ill.2d R. 302(a)(1)). The State's appeal was docketed as case No. 89115.

In February 2000, the circuit court took evidence on E.W.'s petition to restore custody, which had been filed in October 1999. On March 7, the court determined that H.G. "can be cared for at home (of Mother) without endangering her health or safety." However, the court also concluded that return was not in H.G.'s best interests at that time. Accordingly, the court denied E.W.'s petition....

Analysis...

Section 1(D)(m-1) creates a presumption of parental unfitness based upon a judicial finding that the parent's child has been in foster care for "15 months out of any 22 month period." 750 ILCS 50/1(D)(m-1) (West 1998). This statutory presumption is based solely upon the time the child has been in foster care; no inquiry is made into the parent's ability to provide the child with good care and treatment. The 15-month period may be tolled "during any period for which there is a court finding that the appointed custodian or guardian failed to make reasonable efforts to reunify the child with his or her family." 750 ILCS 50/1(D)(m-1) (West 1998). Once a court finds that the child has been in foster care for 15 months, the parent may rebut the presumption of unfitness by showing it is more likely than not that it will be in the child's best interests to be returned to the parent within six months from the date the termination petition was filed. 750 ILCS 50/1(D)(m-1) (West 1998).

On appeal, E.W. argues that section 1(D)(m-1) violates the guarantee of substantive due process provided by the United States and Illinois Constitutions. E.W. maintains that section 1(D)(m-1) impinges upon a fundamental liberty interest, the interest a parent has in raising his or her child. Thus, according to E.W., section 1(D)(m-1) must survive strict scrutiny, i.e., it must be narrowly tailored to serve a compelling governmental interest.

E.W. does not dispute that the State has a compelling interest in protecting the children of Illinois from harm and, hence, that the State has a compelling interest in identifying parents who pose a risk to the safety and well-being of their children and are therefore unfit. However, E.W. contends that section 1(D)(m-1) is not narrowly tailored to achieving this goal. E.W. focuses on section 1(D)(m-1)'s creation of a presumption of unfitness based upon a finding that a child has been in foster care for 15 months. E.W. argues that this statutory presumption does not narrowly identify unfit parents because it defines unfitness based solely on the passage of time rather than parental inability to care for children. Therefore, the statute may declare parents unfit even if they are, in fact, able to safely care for their children. Thus, according to E.W., section 1(D)(m-1) is unconstitutional.

The State, in response, concedes that section 1(D)(m-1) is subject to strict scrutiny. See *In re R.C.*, 195 Ill.2d 291, 302–04, 253 Ill.Dec. 699, 745 N.E.2d 1233 (2001) (section of Adoption Act defining ground of unfitness is subject to strict scrutiny), citing *Troxel v. Granville*, 530 U.S. 57, 120 S.Ct. 2054, 147 L.Ed.2d 49 (2000). The State maintains, however, that section 1(D)(m-1) survives this review. The State emphasizes that it has a compelling governmental interest in protecting the safety and welfare of the children of Illinois. The State asserts that "a fit parent does not allow his or her child to languish in foster care for 15 months" and argues that section 1(D)(m-1) narrowly identifies those parents who pose a danger to the health and safety of their children. We disagree.

To survive strict scrutiny, a statute must be narrowly tailored to serve a compelling interest. A statute is narrowly tailored if it uses "the least restrictive means consistent with the attainment of its goal." *In re R.C.*, 195 Ill.2d at 303, 253 Ill.Dec. 699, 745 N.E.2d 1233, citing *Tully v. Edgar*, 171 Ill.2d 297, 304–05, 215 Ill.Dec. 646, 664 N.E.2d 43 (1996). The presumption of unfitness set forth in section 1(D)(m-1) is not narrowly tailored to the compelling goal of identifying unfit parents because it fails to account for the fact that, in many cases, the length of a child's stay in foster care has nothing to do with the parent's ability or inability to safely care for the child but, instead, is due to circumstances beyond the parent's control. The record in the instant cause aptly illustrates this point.

On October 13, 1998, the State filed its initial motion to terminate the parental rights of E.W. This petition alleged only that E.W. was unfit under section 1(D)(m). No allegation was made that E.W. was unfit under section 1(D)(m-1), and no such allegation could have been made, as the 15-month time period for calculating H.G.'s stay in foster care could not begin to run until the enactment of section 1(D)(m-1), which had only recently occurred. Trial on the State's petition was originally set for March 11 and 12, 1999. On E.W.'s motion, the trial was continued until May 24 and 25 because an indispensable witness was unavailable. The case was continued again because the attorney and guardian *ad litem* for H.G. was required to appear in the appellate court for oral argument on May 25. The trial was then set for dates almost five months later, in October 1999. These dates were not chosen because of anything relating to E.W.'s ability to safely care for H.G. or because of any particular need of H.G. Instead, the October dates were chosen because they were the next available dates on which the circuit court would be able to conduct the trial without interruption.

The October 1999 date was also continued, on the State's motion, because a key witness was medically unable to testify. Only after this final continuance did the 15-month time frame of section 1(D)(m-1) become applicable to this case. On January 20, 2000, the State filed an amended petition to terminate parental rights in which it alleged that E.W. was unfit under section 1(D)(m-1). Nine of the 15 months covered by the State's allegation of unfitness under section 1(D)(m-1) were directly attributable to continuances which were necessary to bring the case to trial. Further, none of the nine-month period could be tolled under the portion of section 1(D)(m-1) which allows for tolling of the 15-month period because the continuances and court delays had nothing to do with whether "the appointed custodian or guardian failed to make reasonable efforts to reunify the child with his or her family." 750 ILCS 50/1(D)(m-1) (West 1998). Thus, in this cause, the passage of 15 months revealed nothing more than the fact that the judicial system's administrative needs may delay the resolution of certain cases. The fact that H.G. was in foster care for a 15-month period could not, by itself, warrant a presumption that E.W. is an unfit parent.

Other common situations illustrate the illogical reach of the presumption found in section 1(D)(m-1). For example, parents are frequently ordered to undergo drug treatment or other counseling as a condition to regaining custody of a child in foster care. Given the realities of limited funding, it is not uncommon for there to be waiting lists to receive such services. In such cases, DCFS might make every "reasonable effort[]" (750 ILCS 50/1(D)(m-1) (West 1998)) to get the parent the appropriate treatment yet be unable to do so in a prompt fashion simply because the program offering the counseling services is full. During the time DCFS attempts to enter the parent in the appropriate program, however, the 15-month period in section 1(D)(m-1) will continue to run. Thus, a delay which occurs through no fault of the parent or DCFS may trigger a finding of unfitness.

Many of the grounds of unfitness set forth in the Adoption Act, other than section 1(D)(m-1), employ time frames of one length or another. See, *e.g.*, 750 ILCS 50/1(D)(c) (West 1998) (desertion for more than three months); 750 ILCS 50/1(D)(k) (West 1998) (habitual drunkenness or addiction to controlled substances for at least one year); 750 ILCS 50/1(D)(l) (West 1998) (failure to demonstrate a reasonable degree of interest in the child's welfare during the first 30 days following the child's birth). However, each of these grounds uses a time frame that measures some form of parental conduct, inaction or inability that relates to competence or the care given to a child. Section 1(D)(m-1), in contrast, improperly measures only the time that a child is in foster care. *Cf. Stanley v. Illinois*, 405 U.S. 645, 657, 92 S.Ct. 1208, 1215, 31 L.Ed.2d 551, 562 (1972) (under due process of the fourteenth amendment, statutory scheme to determine unfitness may not "foreclose[] the determinative issues of competence and care"). Because there will be many cases in which children remain in foster care for the statutory period even when their parents can properly care for them, we conclude that the presumption contained in section 1(D)(m-1) is not a narrowly tailored means of identifying parents who pose a danger to their children's health or safety.

The State emphasizes the importance of the rebuttal allowed by section 1(D)(m-1). The State maintains that, because section 1(D)(m-1) allows a parent to rebut the presumption of unfitness by showing that it will be in the best interests of the child to return home in six months, section 1(D)(m-1) strikes a proper balance between the interests of parents in the care and custody of their children and the interest of the State in protecting the safety of the children.

Citing *Santosky v. Kramer*, 455 U.S. 745, 102 S.Ct. 1388, 71 L.Ed.2d 599 (1982), E.W. maintains, however, that it is inappropriate to introduce the concept of best interests during a fitness determination. E.W. further argues that, even if consideration of the best interests were appropriate during a fitness proceeding, that consideration does not sufficiently narrow the scope of the statute. As E.W. explains: "A parent contesting an allegation of unfitness under section [1(D)(m-1)] could present evidence of her ability to care for her child as part of the best interest phase of the unfitness hearing. The court could credit the parent's evidence as factually true and could rationally conclude that a parent is abundantly fit, i.e., perfectly capable of safely and adequately caring for the child, yet still conclude that the child's best interests will not be served by returning the child to the parent's home. Thus, in its natural operation, section [1(D)(m-1)] compels trial courts to make the Alice-in-Wonderland ruling that a fit parent is, by force of law, unfit."

We agree with the position advanced by E.W. The record in the instant cause illustrates the validity of her argument. While the State's motion to terminate parental rights was pending, E.W. filed a petition to restore custody. See 705 ILCS 405/2-28(4) (West 1998). The court deferred a hearing on that petition and stated that the petition would be considered after any findings of unfitness were made on the termination petition. After the circuit court held section 1(D)(m-1) unconstitutional and the State sought a stay of further proceedings on the termination petition, the court held a hearing on E.W.'s petition to restore custody. After hearing evidence, the court found "[t]hat the Minor can be cared for at home (of Mother) without endangering her health or safety." The court further found that it was not in the best interests of H.G. that the child be restored to the custody of E.W. Accordingly, the court denied the petition.

E.W. established to the circuit court's satisfaction that her child could be safely cared for in her home. However, as of the date of its ruling on the petition to restore custody, the court believed that reunification was not in the child's best interests. Consequently, had the fitness hearing under section 1(D)(m-1) gone forward, E.W. could have been declared unfit *despite* the court's finding that she was able to safely care for her child. Because this error is built into the statute's design, section 1(D)(m-1) cannot be considered narrowly tailored.

The State also argues that it has a compelling interest in ensuring that the time children spend in foster care is limited and in preventing foster care "drift." The State contends that section 1(D)(m-1) expresses the legislature's desire to obtain a permanent solution for children in foster care in an expeditious manner, regardless of whether that solution is returning the children to their parents or terminating the rights of the parents and making the children available for adoption. According to the State, the goal of achieving permanency is a compelling one that justifies the creation of section 1(D)(m-1). We disagree. The permanency achieved under section 1(D)(m-1) comes only after a finding that a parent is unfit. However, that determination of unfitness, as we have explained, is achieved in a way that is not narrowly tailored, as it must be to survive strict scrutiny. We decline to recognize that the State has a compelling interest in removing children from foster care in an expeditious fashion when that removal is achieved in an unconstitutional manner.

Section 1(D)(m-1) is not narrowly tailored to serve the compelling governmental interest of protecting the safety and well-being of the children of this state. We hold, therefore, that section 1(D)(m-1) violates the substantive due process guarantees of the federal and state constitutions. Accordingly, we affirm the judgment of the circuit court of Kane County....

NOTES AND QUESTIONS

1. Under Illinois law, what are some of the grounds for termination of parental rights? To what extent are those grounded in federal law? Does the Illinois statute go beyond what the federal law requires?

2. On what basis did the state file the original termination petition regarding H.G.? When was that petition filed? What was the basis for the amended petition? What did the trial court find? Why did E.W. appeal?

3. Is there a constitutional problem with the statute? What is it? To what level of scrutiny does the court subject the statute? Is this correct? Do *Stanley* and *Santosky* mandate this result?

4. Why is it "inappropriate" to consider the child's best interests during the fitness determination? Would a best-interests determination narrow the scope of the statute? Why not? The federal law recognizes three exceptions to the "15 of 22" requirement. Do those exceptions render the statute constitutional, or are the exceptions themselves constitutionally problematic?

5. Could the state still seek to terminate E.W.'s parental rights?

6. Look again at 42 U.S.C. § 671(a)(15)(D). Based on the rule articulated by the court in *H.G.*, do you think it would be unconstitutional to terminate parental rights based solely on a

parent's prior conviction for the attempted murder of another child four years before the child who is the subject of the termination petition was born? Would it matter if the presumption were irrebuttable? See *In re D.W.*, 827 N.E.2d 466 (Ill. 2005).

7. The grounds for terminating parental rights vary considerably from state to state. However, the most common grounds for the involuntary termination of parental rights include severe or chronic abuse or neglect, abuse or neglect of other children in the household, abandonment, long-term mental illness or substance abuse rendering the parent deficient, failure to support, or the involuntary termination of the rights of the parent to another child. Child Welfare Information Gateway, Grounds for Involuntary Termination of Parental Rights 2 (2010), http://www.childwelfare.gov/systemwide/laws_policies/statutes/groundtermin.pdf. A recent review of state termination laws found that state laws provide more grounds for termination than those envisioned by ASFA, and those grounds are varied. For example, thirty-three states permit termination based on parental substance abuse, thirty-four states on grounds of parental mental illness, and twenty-eight states based on parental incarceration. William Vesneski, *State Law and the Termination of Parental Rights*, 49 FAM. CT. REV. 364, 368 tbl. 3 (2011). Furthermore, many of these grounds are vaguely defined and "do not involve objective, physical indicators of maltreatment." *Id.* at 373. Thus, twenty-eight states permit termination based on a failure to respond to reasonable efforts, and thirty-one permit termination based on a failure to assume responsibility for the child. *Id.* at 368 tbl. 4.

8. Consider again *Smith v. O.F.F.E.R.* In that case, a parent voluntarily placed the child in foster care and then had difficulties seeking the child's return. To what extent does ASFA's "15 of 22" mandate affect these parents and their children? For a discussion of voluntary foster-care placements and their impact on subsequent termination proceedings, see Deborah Paruch, *The Orphaning of Underprivileged Children: America's Failed Child Welfare Law & Policy*, 8 J. L. FAM. STUD. 119 (2006).

IN RE J.E.
Supreme Court of Iowa
723 N.W.2d 793 (2006)

STREIT, Justice.

Due to a mother's neglect of her ten-year-old son, a juvenile court terminated her parental rights. The Iowa Court of Appeals reversed the juvenile court's decree. Because the child cannot be safely returned to his mother's care and because termination is in the child's best interests, we vacate the court of appeals' decision and affirm the decree of the juvenile court.

I. Facts and Prior Proceedings

Jerimiah was born on April 17, 1996. He is of low intelligence and suffers from attention deficit/hyperactivity disorder (AD/HD). He operates on a much younger level than his age and is unable to make good or safe decisions. Jerimiah also has heart arrhythmia. He requires medication and a low-sugar, no-caffeine diet.

His mother is Robyn and his father is alleged to be either Luther of La Plata, New Mexico or Kevin of Lakeside, Arizona. Jerimiah does not have a relationship with either man. Robyn has five other children: Cody, born January 28, 1989; Cory, born September 18, 1990; Elyjah, born September 19, 1992; Cheyana, born September 12, 2000 and Savanah, born July 14, 2002. Robyn's two daughters live with their father, Michael, in Ottumwa.[1] During the juvenile court proceedings, Elyjah lived with his father, Luther, in New Mexico part of the time.

Jerimiah first came to the attention of the Iowa Department of Human Services (DHS) on July 7, 2004 when he was taken into custody by law enforcement and placed in foster care. On that date, Robyn had left Jerimiah home alone for up to fourteen hours. Jerimiah was eight years old at the time. Concerned neighbors called the police because Jerimiah did not know where his mother was or how to contact her. Two neighbors reported Jerimiah was often alone from morning until bedtime. He spent long periods of time at their homes because he was hungry and scared. Jerimiah told one of the neighbors his mother threw all of their food away because their home did not have electricity. While the police officers were interviewing Jerimiah in the front lawn, Robyn drove by. She paused and then drove on. She was later arrested for driving while barred. Robyn does not have her driver's license due to unpaid fines ($5877).

During the investigation of this incident, Robyn admitted to a police officer her home did not have electricity. She consented to a drug test, which came back positive for opiates. Robyn said she had fallen the week before in a parking lot and was taking Tylenol 3 as a result. Her friend also gave her a pill to help with the pain. The test was negative for other substances. Robyn told a police officer she worked every day and had to do community service hours.

A subsequent Child Protective Assessment verified the neighbors' allegations. This was the third founded report for denial of critical care based on Robyn's failure to properly supervise Jerimiah.[2]

Two days after Jerimiah was removed from the home, Robyn and Jerimiah's brothers moved because Robyn did not have money to pay the electric bill. They lived for about two weeks at the home of their pastor and then moved to the Crisis Center. In mid-August they moved to a rented home on Kruger Street in Ottumwa. Due to a $700 unpaid electric bill, Robyn had to have the utilities placed in a friend's name. At the end of March 2005 the family moved again to their current home on South Van Buren in Ottumwa. Robyn's gas was shut off in June 2005 because she did not pay her bill. She was able to get the gas turned back on within a few days. Robyn was unemployed throughout the juvenile court proceedings except when she worked at Burger King for three months. The family receives welfare, food stamps, and medical assistance from DHS.

1. Michael obtained a civil restraining order on Robyn. Cheyana was diagnosed as "failure to thrive" and there is a founded report of Robyn not providing adequate medical care for her.

2. There was a founded report of denial of critical care concerning Jerimiah and his brother, Cody. On July 9, 2003, Robyn started an uncontained fire outside in order to burn some trash. She went inside leaving Cory and Jerimiah outside. At the time, Jerimiah was seven and Cory was twelve. Jerimiah played in the fire with a stick and burned a neighbor boy who had to be taken to the emergency room by his parents. There was also a founded report of denial of critical care concerning Jerimiah and his two younger sisters. On December 19, 2002, Robyn left Jerimiah and the girls in a vehicle unattended for five to fifteen minutes while she was in her landlord's home. Jerimiah was six and a half years old at the time and Cheyana and Savanah were two years old and five months old respectively. Robyn was unable to drive the children home because her driver's license was suspended.

Jerimiah was adjudicated a child in need of assistance on October 12, 2004, as defined in Iowa Code section 232.2(6)(c)(2) (2003) and remained in the care and custody of DHS. Numerous services were provided to the family by DHS. Services included parent skill development services for Robyn, psychological evaluation of Robyn, psychiatric evaluation of Jerimiah, and individual therapy for Robyn and Jerimiah. Robyn accepted these services but her participation was inconsistent. At times, Robyn was not awake or was not prepared for parent skills sessions which were conducted in her home. She was also inconsistent in attending Jerimiah's medical and psychiatric appointments although she was requested to do so.

At the department's behest, Robyn began seeing a therapist but failed to regularly attend her appointments. She was diagnosed with AD/HD, depression, and post-traumatic stress disorder. Robyn acknowledged physical and child sexual abuse by her father. Her mother died of a heart attack when Robyn was just two years old. She dropped out of school in the eleventh grade when she became pregnant.

DHS continues to have concerns with Robyn's parenting ability. At the beginning of this case, Robyn told the in-home provider she relates to her children more as a peer than a parent. Robyn admitted she does not feel she needs to be a parent to her children all of the time "because she doesn't want to bitch at them." The DHS reports Robyn is not affectionate toward Jerimiah and there is not much interaction between the two of them.

At first, DHS limited Robyn to supervised visits with Jerimiah. Robyn progressed to partially unsupervised visits on October 25, 2004. Jerimiah's foster parents agreed to take Jerimiah to Robyn's home for visits and the in-home provider would be present for the second half of the visits. The unsupervised part of the visit was discontinued on November 16, 2004 because Robyn was not keeping her appointments with her therapist and the in-home provider was concerned Robyn was not able to consistently provide a structured environment. Robyn did not regularly have activities and meals planned for Jerimiah during the visits. On February 2, 2005, DHS resumed partially unsupervised visits. Approximately three weeks later, DHS once again limited Robyn to supervised visits with Jerimiah because she was not attending her therapy appointments, was not calling Jerimiah daily as she had been requested to do, and she missed a parent/teacher conference.

In March 2005, DHS resumed partially unsupervised visits because Robyn was calling Jerimiah more consistently and was keeping her therapy appointments. She met with Jerimiah's teacher. She went to the library and checked out a book on parenting without prompting. Robyn even walked five miles in order to visit Jerimiah.

DHS granted Robyn unsupervised overnight visits with Jerimiah in May 2005. A permanency hearing was held on July 8, 2005, at which time Robyn was given an additional six months to pursue reunification. On August 4, 2005, Robyn's visits with Jerimiah were increased from one overnight to three overnights a week. However, DHS once again limited Robyn to supervised visits after she was arrested for shoplifting at Wal-Mart on August 8, 2005.[3] Jerimiah was in the store with Robyn and saw her get arrested. Robyn initially lied and told the social worker Jerimiah was not with her. Robyn testified at the termination hearing she lied out of fear DHS would terminate her parental rights. Jerimiah told a child protective worker it is okay for his mom to steal if she needs food for her children.

3. Robyn was also arrested for shoplifting at Econo Foods on July 24, 2005.

Besides shoplifting, Robyn has made other poor decisions. In December 2004, Robyn was ticketed for allowing her son Cody to drive without a license. In March 2005, Robyn was charged with violating the compulsory school attendance law for her son Cody. According to the school attendance officer, Cody had missed thirty-one days of school by the month of March. Robyn pled guilty and was fined $100. On May 9, 2005, Robyn returned Jerimiah to his foster home thirty to sixty minutes early without notifying the foster parents. Neither foster parent was home so Robyn left Jerimiah in the care of a teenage foster boy. A few days later, Jerimiah told Robyn the boy sexually abused him while they were alone.[4] Additionally, Robyn considered allowing a truck driver, whose last name she did not know, pick up Elyjah in New Mexico and return him to Ottumwa. After the in-home provider advised Robyn her idea was too risky, Robyn took a bus to New Mexico to pick him up herself.

The State filed a petition for termination of parental rights on October 31, 2005. The juvenile court held a termination hearing on November 21, 2005. The in-home provider for the family testified there is a lack of bonding between Jerimiah and his mother. However, Jerimiah has repeatedly stated he misses his mom and siblings and wants to be home with them. Jerimiah thinks Robyn is the "best mom ever." DHS recommended termination because Robyn is unable to provide a consistent, stable, and structured home environment for Jerimiah. Although Robyn has been able to make progress for short periods of time, she is unable to sustain those changes.

DHS acknowledges Jerimiah has a close relationship with his brothers. During visits Jerimiah usually played with his brothers. They would play video games, play sports, draw, talk, joke around, play with action figures or watch movies. At the termination hearing, Cody testified about his bond with Jerimiah. He said "we miss him a lot every day.... There's always a void."

Jerimiah is a sweet and loving child. He is personable and gets along well with other children. He likes to give and receive attention. Despite his special needs, DHS considers Jerimiah to be adoptable.

The juvenile court terminated the parental rights of Robyn, Kevin and Luther (the alleged fathers) on March 7, 2006. Only Robyn appealed. The Iowa Court of Appeals reversed the termination of her parental rights on September 7, 2006. The court "question[ed] whether the State has proved the grounds for termination by clear and convincing evidence" because the court believed DHS made no effort to assist Robyn with child care. Moreover, the court was "not willing to find that Jerimiah's best interests will be served by termination" because of his strong bond with his brothers.

II. Scope of Review

We review termination of parental rights de novo. We give weight to the factual determinations of the juvenile court but we are not bound by them. Grounds for termination must be proven by clear and convincing evidence. Our primary concern is the best interests of the child.

4. To Robyn's credit, she immediately contacted DHS and consoled Jerimiah. She was very supportive of Jerimiah and fully cooperated with the child protective assessment and police investigation. Jerimiah was placed in a different foster home.

> In seeking out those best interests, we look to the child's long-range as well as immediate interests. This requires considering what the future holds for the child if returned to the parents. When making this decision, we look to the parents' past performance because it may indicate the quality of care the parent is capable of providing in the future.

In re C.K., 558 N.W.2d 170, 172 (Iowa 1997) (citations omitted).

III. Merits

A. Whether Jerimiah Can Be Returned to Robyn's Care

The juvenile court terminated Robyn's parental rights pursuant to section 232.116(1)(*f*) of the Iowa Code. Under section 232.116(1)(*f*), parental rights may be terminated if the court finds all of the following have occurred:

(1) The child is four years of age or older.
(2) The child has been adjudicated a child in need of assistance pursuant to section 232.96.
(3) The child has been removed from the physical custody of the child's parents for at least twelve of the last eighteen months, or for the last twelve consecutive months and any trial period at home has been less than thirty days.
(4) There is clear and convincing evidence that at the present time the child cannot be returned to the custody of the child's parents as provided in section 232.102.

It is undisputed Jerimiah satisfies the first three elements. Robyn only contends the State has failed to prove by clear and convincing evidence Jerimiah cannot be returned to her custody.

A parent may lose custody of his or her child if the court finds there is clear and convincing evidence "[t]he child cannot be protected from some harm which would justify the adjudication of the child as a child in need of assistance.... " Iowa Code § 232.102(5)(a). A "child in need of assistance" means in part "an unmarried child... [w]hose parent, guardian, other custodian, or other members of the household in which the child resides has physically abused or neglected the child, or is imminently likely to abuse or neglect the child." *Id.* § 232.2(6)(*b*). In the present case, there are thankfully no allegations Robyn physically abused Jerimiah. However, the record is replete with evidence of neglect. We have previously said "our statutory termination provisions are preventative as well as remedial." *In re L.L.*, 459 N.W.2d 489, 494 (Iowa 1990). They are designed to prevent probable harm to the child and the State is not required to wait until actual harm has occurred before moving to terminate a parent's rights. *Id.* (citing *In re A.M.S.*, 419 N.W.2d 723, 726 (Iowa 1988)).

Robyn argues her ability to care for her other sons rebuts the juvenile court's finding that Jerimiah cannot be safely returned to her home. This contention ignores Jerimiah's age and special needs. See *In re T.J.O.*, 527 N.W.2d 417, 421 (Iowa Ct.App. 1994) (citing *In re E.B.L.*, 501 N.W.2d 547, 553 (Iowa 1993) ("Even though a mother may be able to parent some of her children does not necessarily mean she is capable of providing appropriate care to all her children. The special needs and best interests of each child must be evaluated")). At the time of the termination hearing, Jerimiah's brothers were sixteen (Cody), fifteen (Cory) and thirteen (Elyjah) years old. Jerimiah was only nine years old. Unlike his brothers, Jerimiah has special needs that require extra attention. Due in part to his low intelligence, he lacks knowledge about concepts most kids his age would understand. Jerimiah is unable to make good or safe decisions. He requires constant supervision and thrives on structure. His heart condition also requires medication and frequent doctor visits. While his older brothers may be able to fend for themselves, Jerimiah cannot.

Robyn has a history of leaving Jerimiah home alone for long periods of time. He was placed in foster care after neighbors complained Jerimiah would often come to their homes looking for comfort and food. He did not know where his mom was or how to contact her. One neighbor reported Jerimiah has been to her home from early morning to late at night before without anyone coming to look for him.

Robyn has failed to demonstrate she can provide adequate supervision and care for Jerimiah. At the time Jerimiah was taken into custody by DHS, Robyn told a police officer Jerimiah was home alone because she worked every day and did community service. However, Robyn told her therapist she had not worked since 1999 when the family lived in Arizona. Moreover, there is no evidence in the record regarding community service. If she did have a community service obligation, we do not know why or the number of hours. Robyn has never explained her long absences from the home. This makes us doubt she would be more attentive to Jerimiah's needs if he is returned to her. See *In re J.W.D.*, 456 N.W.2d 214, 218–19 (Iowa 1990) (finding termination warranted because mother was unable to meet the needs of her child who was of low-average intellectual functioning and behind developmentally).

The court of appeals stated "there is little evidence Jerimiah would not be safe in [Robyn's] care if she had assistance with child care at times she was required to be absent from the home." But based on the record, Robyn is not required to be away from home much because she is unemployed. Robyn never requested assistance with child care. Moreover, two of the founded reports of neglect happened while Robyn was nearby. The first one involved Jerimiah being left in a car with his two younger sisters. The other involved Jerimiah playing with a burning pile of trash. Robyn's erratic sleep patterns also interfere with her ability to supervise Jerimiah. Finally, the shoplifting incident demonstrates Robyn continues to put Jerimiah at risk despite the services provided by DHS. Robyn has not benefited from the services while Jerimiah continues to live in foster care. We find there is clear and convincing evidence Jerimiah cannot be returned to Robyn's custody at the present time or in the reasonably near future.

B. Whether It Is in Jerimiah's Best Interests to Terminate Robyn's Parental Rights

Having found section 232.116(1)(*f*) satisfied, we must still determine whether terminating Robyn's parental rights is in Jerimiah's best interests. *In re S.J.*, 451 N.W.2d 827, 832 (Iowa 1990) ("While we have indicated that children should not be made to suffer indefinitely in parentless limbo, the child's best interest may dictate to the contrary"); *see* Iowa Code § 232.116(2) (requiring the court to "give primary consideration to the child's safety, to the best placement for furthering the long-term nurturing and growth of the child, and to the physical, mental, and emotional condition and needs of the child" when determining whether to terminate the rights of a parent). Jerimiah has a close relationship with his older brothers. He misses them and they likewise miss him. We have previously stated a preference to keep siblings together. *In re A.M.S.*, 419 N.W.2d at 734 (stating "siblings should not be separated without good and compelling reasons"). However, this preference is not absolute. Our ultimate concern is the best interests of the child. Robyn argues it is in Jerimiah's best interests to be with his family. We are certainly cognizant of the importance of family integrity. This consideration, although valid, cannot overcome the clear and convincing evidence it is in Jerimiah's best future interests to be free for adoption so he may be placed in a permanent and stable home with consistent care. He deserves the chance to start a new life even though this means he has to leave behind the relationships he has with his mother and brothers. We find that despite Jerimiah's bond with his brothers, it is in his best interests to terminate Robyn's parental rights.

We note this is not one of the more egregious cases of neglect or abuse. See, *e.g.*, *In re J.K.*, 495 N.W.2d 108, 110–11 (Iowa 1993) (parents were severe, chronic drug and alcohol abusers); *In re A.R.S.*, 480 N.W.2d 888, 889–90 (Iowa 1992) (children sexually abused by their mother and three of her male friends); *In re Interest of C & K*, 322 N.W.2d 76, 77–78 (Iowa 1982) (children lived in deplorable conditions). Nor do we question Robyn's love for her children. Nonetheless, our legislature has established a limited time frame for parents to demonstrate their ability to be parents. In this case, the standard is twelve months. Iowa Code § 232.116(1)(*f*). "The legislature adopted the standard in the belief that this period must be reasonably limited because, 'beyond the parameters of chapter 232, patience with parents can soon translate into intolerable hardship for their children.'" *In re C.K.*, 558 N.W.2d at 175 (quoting *In re A.C.*, 415 N.W.2d 609, 613 (Iowa 1987)). "'Children simply cannot wait for responsible parenting.'" *Id.* (quoting *In re L.L.*, 459 N.W.2d at 495). "It is simply not in the best interests of children to continue to keep them in temporary foster homes while the natural parents get their lives together." *Id.* (citing *In re J.L.P.*, 449 N.W.2d 349, 353 (Iowa 1989)). Robyn was given approximately sixteen months to demonstrate her ability to care for Jerimiah. She continues to struggle with the same problems identified at the beginning of the juvenile court proceedings. She has not benefited from DHS's services and Jerimiah continues to suffer. She is unable to provide the structure and consistency Jerimiah needs in order to be safe and reach his full potential.

IV. Conclusion

The State has proven by clear and convincing evidence Jerimiah cannot be returned to Robyn's custody presently or in the near future. Despite Jerimiah's bond with his brothers, it is in his best interests to terminate Robyn's parental rights so he may be placed in a permanent home with adults who can properly care for him. We therefore agree with the district court Robyn's parental rights should be terminated....

CADY, J. (concurring specially).

I write separately to emphasize the "best interests of the child" standard has taken on a new meaning, within the last decade, which must be considered by courts in using the standard to make decisions to terminate parent-child relationships.

A child's safety and the need for a permanent home are now the primary concerns when determining a child's best interests. *See In re K.M.*, 653 N.W.2d 602, 608 (Iowa 2002) (noting "the child's safety and need for a permanent home" are "the concerns that clearly impact a child's best interests"). This has not always been the case, and reflects a broader change in our country's national policy regarding child welfare laws. *See In re C.B.*, 611 N.W.2d 489, 493–94 (Iowa 2000) (recognizing and summarizing the effect of national legislation on Iowa's child welfare laws). Before 1997, child welfare laws—including Iowa's—focused on reuniting the family unit. *Id.* at 493 (noting our prior legislation sought "to prevent and eliminate the need for removal," and "[t]he focus [wa]s on services to improve parenting"); *see, e.g., Deck v. State Dep't of Human Resources*, 113 Nev. 124, 930 P.2d 760, 765 (1997) (noting the district court put in place a reunification plan that continued unsuccessfully for five years); *In re M.B.*, 388 Pa.Super. 381, 565 A.2d 804, 810 (1989) ("One of the primary purposes of the Juvenile Act is to preserve the unity of the family whenever possible"). Subsequently, and after Congress's enactment of the Adoptions and Safe Families Act of 1997 (ASFA), national and state child welfare laws emphasized the importance of timely providing children with appropriate custodial care. *See In re K.M.*, 653 N.W.2d at 608 ("In recent years the focus in termination cases has shifted somewhat from reunification of the family to the child's best interests."); *In re C.B.*, 611 N.W.2d at 493–95 (summarizing the change); *see also In re Lilley*, 719 A.2d 327, 334–35 (Pa.Super. 1998) (recognizing the impact of ASFA).

More specifically, ASFA dramatically changed the manner in which this country treats children who have been removed from the care of their parents and placed into foster care. *See* Adoption and Safe Families Act of 1997, Pub.L. No. 105-89, 111 Stat. 2115 (codified as amended in scattered sections of 42 U.S.C.). The legislation sets firm deadlines for reunification, followed by prompt efforts to terminate parental rights if those deadlines are not met. *See* 42 U.S.C. § 675(5) (2006) (outlining the instances when termination of parental rights [is] required). ASFA's goals seek to prevent children from languishing in foster care by requiring parents to assume their parental responsibility quickly. *See In re C.M.*, 652 N.W.2d at 208 ("[T]he new federal law shifted the focus from family reunification to 'time-limited family reunification services'" (quoting 42 U.S.C. § 629(a)(7))); 42 U.S.C. § 675(5) (requiring the state to file a petition to terminate parental rights if the child has remained in foster care "for 15 of the most recent 22 months").

Iowa reacted to this federal legislation and adopted many changes to our child welfare laws in 1998. *See* S.F. 2345, 77th Gen. Assem., Reg. Sess. (Iowa 1998) (codified as amended in scattered sections of Iowa Code chapters 232, 237, 600). Among those changes are additions to Iowa Code § 232.116, which provides the grounds by which a court may terminate parental rights. Iowa Code § 232.116 (2005). Prior to ASFA, Iowa Code § 232.116(2) stated "the court shall give primary consideration to the physical, mental, and emotional condition and needs of the child" when determining whether to terminate parental rights. Iowa Code § 232.116(2) (1997). After ASFA, that subsection now reads "the court shall give primary consideration to *the child's safety, to the best placement for furthering the long-term nurturing and growth of the child*, and to the physical, mental, and emotional condition and needs of the child." Iowa Code § 232.116(2) (emphasis added); *see In re K.M.*, 653 N.W.2d at 606 (recognizing this distinction and holding the amended changes constitutional).

Our response to ASFA did not change the approach we have always taken in parental termination proceedings. Then and now, "our primary concern is the best interests of the child." *In re S.O.*, 483 N.W.2d 602, 604 (Iowa 1992) (citing *In re Dameron*, 306 N.W.2d 743, 745 (Iowa 1981)). But our response to ASFA has significantly, and not too subtly, identified a child's safety and his or her need for a permanent home as the defining elements in a child's best interests. *See In re K.M.*, 653 N.W.2d at 608 ("[T]he amendment did not change the role of a child's best interests in the termination decision. They are now and have long been of paramount importance in such matters. Rather, the [response to ASFA] simply articulated the concerns that clearly impact a child's best interests: the child's safety and need for a permanent home").

In bygone days, the best interests of a child was a broad concept that embraced a multitude of considerations, and prominently focused on the need to keep families together and to avoid the termination of parental rights if at all possible. No more. We are obligated to incorporate this new policy into the case before us, and it inevitably leads us to the proper result and our disposition. The old policies underlying our previous notions of a child's best interests cannot be used by courts to circumvent the new policies that are meant to keep children from languishing in foster care. We must apply this new rationale with earnest in each case, as we have here, pursuant to the policies established by our legislature.

NOTES AND QUESTIONS

1. On what grounds did the court terminate Robyn's parental rights? Do you think this result is mandated by ASFA?

2. Is it relevant that the Department of Human Services believes that Jerimiah is adoptable? Why?

3. The court notes that Jerimiah has a "close relationship with his older brothers" but that termination nevertheless is in his best interests despite a preference to keep siblings together. How will severing Jerimiah's relationship with his mother and his siblings serve his best interests? Is termination in Jerimiah's best interests? How would you define best interests?

Although there is not a substantial body of research on the subject of the sibling relationship in out-of-home placements, there is evidence that the sibling bond is a significant one. For many people, the sibling relationship is the longest relationship they will have and provides an opportunity for intimacy and identity formation. STEPHEN P. BANK & MICHAEL D. KAHN, THE SIBLING BOND (1997). The sibling relationship also provides opportunities for the development of trust and understanding, guidance and support, and companionship. Sibling relationships may become especially important in the context of maltreatment, because siblings may rely more heavily on one another to compensate for the failures or absences of their caregivers. Aron Shlonsky et al., *The Other Kin: Setting the Course for Research, Policy, and Practice with Siblings in Foster Care*, 27 CHILD. & YOUTH SERVS. REV. 697 (2005). Moreover, research indicates that children placed out of the home were dismayed about their separation, worried about one another, expressed guilt that they were able to escape mistreatment while other siblings remained behind, or were being punished for some imagined transgression. See, e.g., Adam McCormick, *Siblings in Foster Care: An Overview of Research, Policy, and Practice*, 4 J. PUB. CHILD WELFARE 198, 202–203 (2010). See also Diane F. Halpern, *Siblings in Foster Care and Adoption: What We Know from the Research*, in SIBLINGS IN ADOPTION AND FOSTER CARE 13 (Deborah N. Silverstein & Susan Livingston Smith eds., 2008). In light of this evidence, do you think the court should have separated Jerimiah from his older brothers?

4. Robyn also has other children in the home. Why are they not at risk? Under ASFA, could Robyn's parental rights to her other children be severed?

5. The Fostering Connections to Success and Increasing Adoptions Act of 2008, Pub. L. No. 110-351, § 202(3), 122 Stat. 3949, 3959 (2008), provides that states seeking federal funds must make reasonable efforts "to place siblings removed from their home in the same foster care, kinship guardianship, or adoptive placement, unless the State documents that such a joint

placement would be contrary to the safety or well-being of any of the siblings." If siblings are not jointly placed, the state must make reasonable efforts "to provide for frequent visitation or other ongoing interaction between the siblings, unless that State documents that frequent visitation or other ongoing interaction would be contrary to the safety or well-being of any of the siblings." 42 U.S.C. § 671(a)(31) (2011). Although *In re J.E.* was decided before this provision was enacted, would Jerimiah's older brothers now have a basis for requesting visitation with Jerimiah? Would the court have jurisdiction to order visitation? See, e.g., *In re Miguel A.*, 67 Cal. Rptr. 3d 307 (Cal. Ct. App. 2007). What if Jerimiah's adoptive parents object? See, e.g., *In re M.M.*, 619 N.E.2d 702 (Ill. 1993).

6. Do Jerimiah and his brothers have a constitutional right to maintain their sibling relationship? Some commentators have argued that siblings have a fundamental right to associate, William Wesley Patton & Sara Latz, *Severing Hansel from Gretel: An Analysis of Siblings' Association Rights*, 48 U. MIAMI L. REV. 745 (1994); and a liberty interest that is of fundamental importance and warrants at least the same level of protection as the parent-child relationship, Ellen Marrus, *Fostering Family Ties: The State as Maker and Breaker of Kinship Relationships*, 2004 U. CHI. LEGAL F. 319 (2004). Many courts, however, have been reluctant to find that siblings have fundamental constitutional rights, and the Supreme Court has never reached the issue. See William Wesley Patton, *The Status of Siblings' Rights: A View into the New Millennium*, 51 DEPAUL L. REV. 1, 5 (2001) (noting the Supreme Court denied *certiorari* in *Adoption of Hugo*, 700 N.E.2d 516 [Mass. 1998], *cert.* denied, 526 U.S. 1034 [1999], in which the Massachusetts Supreme Court upheld a decision to separate siblings at adoption). Do you think that siblings should have a constitutional right to maintain their relationship?

STATE EX REL. CHILDREN, YOUTH & FAMILIES V. AMY B.
Court of Appeals of New Mexico
61 P.3d 845 (2002)

PICKARD, Judge.

This case involves NMSA 1978, §§ 32A-4-2(C), -22(C), and -28(B) (1999), which were passed in response to the Adoption and Safe Families Act, 42 U.S.C. § 671(a)(15)(D) (1997), and which delineate the circumstances under which the State need not undertake reasonable efforts to reunite the family prior to terminating a parent's parental rights. Mother contends that the statutes were unconstitutionally applied to her and that her attorney rendered ineffective assistance of counsel in failing to object to their application in the circumstances of this case. We disagree and affirm.

Legal Background

Ordinarily, except in cases of actual or presumptive abandonment under Section 32A-4-28(B)(1) or (3), parental rights may not be terminated in the case of a neglected or abused child unless the court finds that "the conditions and causes of the neglect and abuse are unlikely to change in the foreseeable future despite reasonable efforts by the department or other appropriate agency to assist the parent in adjusting the conditions that render the parent unable to properly care for the child." Section 32A-4-28(B)(2). However, Section 32A-4-28(B)(2) goes on to provide that:

> The court may find in some cases that efforts by the department or another agency are unnecessary, when:
>
> (a) there is a clear showing that the efforts would be futile;
> (b) the parent has subjected the child to aggravated circumstances; or
> (c) the parental rights of the parent to a sibling of the child have been terminated involuntarily[.]

Section 32A-4-2(C) provides that:

> "aggravated circumstances" include those circumstances in which the parent, guardian or custodian has:
>
> (1) attempted, conspired to cause or caused great bodily harm to the child or great bodily harm or death to the child's sibling;
> (2) attempted, conspired to cause or caused great bodily harm or death to another parent, guardian or custodian of the child;
> (3) attempted, conspired to subject or has subjected the child to torture, chronic abuse or sexual abuse; or
> (4) had his parental rights over a sibling of the child terminated involuntarily[.]

To a like effect, Section 32A-4-22(C) ordinarily provides that a disposition of adjudicated neglected or abused children shall include a treatment plan for the parents outlining reasonable efforts at reunification of the family; however, such is not required under circumstances virtually identical to those listed in Section 32A-4-28(B)(2). It appears that Section 32A-4-2(C)(4) is somewhat redundant in that Sections 32A-4-22(C) and -28(B)(2) list both aggravated circumstances and termination of rights to a sibling, which is one of the aggravated circumstances, as independent reasons why reasonable efforts at treatment and reunification of the family are not required. That redundancy does not concern us in this case, however, because the termination of parental rights to a sibling triggers the elimination of the requirement of reasonable efforts, whether it does so in its own right or as a definitional element of aggravated circumstances.

Facts

In 1998, Mother's parental rights to her first two children were terminated due to Mother's drug abuse, which caused her to neglect and abuse these children, and due to her inability to change her habits that led to the neglect and abuse despite reasonable efforts of the Department to assist her. In the beginning of 2000, Mother was serving a sentence for forging checks to obtain money to buy drugs. She was paroled in March 2000 and almost immediately got pregnant with the child at issue (Child). Her parole was revoked in July for failure to report to authorities, and she returned to prison. She was released from prison in October 2000 and began using drugs again. After a three-day drug binge using crack cocaine, Mother gave birth to Child one month early, on November 12. Mother was 22 years old at the time. Child was born with cocaine in his system. Mother was rearrested for dirty urine and failure to appear and was returned to prison.

An abuse/neglect petition was filed a few days after Child's birth. It specifically alleged that Mother had had her parental rights to Child's siblings terminated and referenced Section

32A-4-2(C)(4), which is the statute that makes such fact an aggravated circumstance. Mother pleaded no contest to the petition at an adjudicatory hearing on January 18, 2001. At the time of the adjudicatory hearing, the trial court advised Mother that her parental rights could be terminated if she "failed to work a treatment plan."

There were two dispositional hearings. At the first one, on February 15, the Department asked the trial court to exercise its discretion under Section 32A-4-22 and not order a treatment plan due to the prior termination of Mother's parental rights to Child's siblings. Mother asked the trial court for more time, and the dispositional hearing was continued to March 1. Mother never sought to withdraw her no-contest plea, and only asked the trial court not to exercise its discretion to relieve the Department of making reasonable efforts. The trial court's disposition nonetheless did relieve the Department of that burden. However, nothing precluded Mother from making efforts on her own behalf in an attempt to alleviate the conditions that led to the abuse and neglect, although Mother continued to be incarcerated.

Following the March 1 dispositional hearing, the Department moved to terminate parental rights on the grounds that Child was neglected or abused, that Mother had previously had parental rights terminated, that Mother had been unable since the prior termination to address the drug abuse that caused her to abuse and neglect her children, and that Child was in need of a stable caregiver. At and following the termination hearing in April 2001, Mother took the position that she had reformed, that she was now admitting problems with drug abuse, that she only needed more time, and that therefore there was not clear and convincing evidence that the causes and conditions of neglect were unlikely to change in the foreseeable future. The trial court found that Child was neglected and abused, and that aggravated circumstances existed because Mother's parental rights to Child's siblings had been terminated. However, the trial court also found and concluded that Mother had had four years to correct her substance abuse problems, that she had not made sufficient progress, that it was shown by clear and convincing evidence that Mother was unable to remedy the causes of the abuse and neglect of Child within the foreseeable future, and that it was in the best interests of Child to terminate Mother's parental rights.

Discussion

Prior to the enactment of the Adoption and Safe Families Act, both state and federal law appeared to give primary consideration to the rights of the parents, as opposed to the welfare of their children. Both our statute, in Sections 32A-4-22(C) and -28(B) (prior to the 1999 amendments), and the federal statute (effective October 1, 1983, until 1997) required a showing of reasonable efforts at family reunification in all cases. Our statute required this before parental rights could be terminated, and the federal statute required it as a condition of eligibility for federal funding benefits. The 1997 Adoption and Safe Families Act, in eliminating the requirement of reasonable efforts under certain circumstances, and in requiring the states to follow suit in order to be eligible for federal benefits, was responding to perceived excesses in the application of the reasonable efforts requirement. See *In re Custody & Guardianship of Marino S.*, 181 Misc.2d 264, 693 N.Y.S.2d 822, 825 (Fam.Ct. 1999). As stated in the legislative history of the federal provision:

> There seems to be almost universal agreement that adoption is preferable to foster care and that the nation's children would be well served by a policy that increases adoption rates....

> [H]owever, ... there are a variety of barriers to adoption.... One barrier is the "reasonable efforts" criterion in the Federal statute.
>
> [T]here seems to be a growing belief that Federal statutes, the social work profession, and the courts sometimes err on the side of protecting the rights of parents. As a result, too many children are subjected to long spells of foster care or are returned to families that reabuse them.

H.R.Rep. No. 105-77, at 8 (1997), reprinted in 1997 U.S.C.C.A.N. (111 Stat. 2115) 2739, 2740. Accordingly, the federal statute removed the requirement of reasonable efforts when there are aggravated circumstances, such as torture or sexual abuse, and also removed the requirement of reasonable efforts when there is a homicide of a child or when the parent has had parental rights to another child terminated. *Id.* Our state has conformed the New Mexico statutes to the federal requirements in Sections 32A-4-2(C), -22(C), and -28(B).

We understand Mother's argument on appeal to have several components. First, she argues that she was harmed by two procedural aspects of the case: (1) that her plea was involuntary or not knowing because at the time she pleaded no contest to the allegations of abuse and neglect, she thought the Department would be required to engage in reasonable efforts and (2) that her attorney was ineffective because he did not raise any constitutional issues below or in the docketing statement, but instead simply argued that the trial court should not, in its discretion, eliminate the requirement of reasonable efforts. We address these issues summarily.

Mother never moved to revoke or withdraw her plea, even when she learned that the trial court was not going to require the Department to engage in any efforts. Mother also did not appeal the dispositional order. Thus, Mother waived any issue concerning an involuntary or unknowing plea. Cf. *State v. Lozano*, 1996-NMCA-075, ¶ 18, 122 N.M. 120, 921 P.2d 316 (indicating that a person cannot withdraw a guilty plea unless the person proves that information supposedly missing was actually relevant to the decision to plead); *State v. Madrigal*, 85 N.M. 496, 500, 513 P.2d 1278, 1282 (Ct.App. 1973) (indicating that voluntariness of plea cannot be raised for the first time on appeal). With regard to the constitutional issues, we are addressing them in this first case to reach our Court involving the constitutionality of the Adoption and Safe Families Act. See Rule 12-216(B)(1) NMRA 2002 (permitting appellate court in its discretion to consider issues of substantial public interest not raised in trial court). Thus, because these constitutional questions are of first impression in New Mexico and because we find them here to be without merit, we hold that Mother was not prejudiced by her counsel's failure to raise them in this case. See *State v. Chandler*, 119 N.M. 727, 735, 895 P.2d 249, 257 (Ct.App. 1995) (holding that actions of counsel in failing to raise an issue are not prejudicial when the issue has no merit).

Second, Mother complains that the 1999 reasonable efforts amendments, both on their face and as applied to her, violate due process because (1) they eliminate a required burden of proof by clear and convincing evidence, (2) they eliminate the necessity of specifically proving that reasonable efforts would actually be futile, and (3) they allow the use of stale evidence, i.e., once a parent's rights are terminated to one child, no matter how long ago, termination at the present time is a foregone conclusion because of the elimination of the reasonable efforts requirement. We understand Mother's first argument to be a contention that the due process requirement of clear and convincing evidence established by *Santosky v. Kramer*, 455 U.S. 745, 753-54, 769, 102 S.Ct. 1388, 71 L.Ed.2d 599 (1982), is violated. We understand Mother's second and third arguments to be a contention that due process is violated because the statute creates an irrebuttable presumption that is overbroad and dramatically increases the risk of erroneous deprivations of parental rights, which would be contrary to *Mathews v. Eldridge*, 424 U.S. 319, 335, 96 S.Ct. 893, 47 L.Ed.2d 18 (1976).

We do not agree with any of Mother's contentions. The recent amendments to the statute do not change the basic standard for termination of parental rights when children are neglected or abused. Before the amendments, the State was, and after the amendments, the State still is, required to prove that the children are neglected or abused and "the conditions and causes of the neglect and abuse are unlikely to change in the foreseeable future." Section 32A-4-28(B)(2). These are the facts that the trial court found to be proved by clear and convincing evidence without regard to any presumptions. In fact, Mother's brief on appeal does not contend that these facts were not proved by clear and convincing evidence.

Mother does argue that the State failed to prove aggravated circumstances by clear and convincing evidence. Assuming that she is correct that the burden of proving aggravated circumstances is by clear and convincing evidence, we hold that the burden was met here. Aggravated circumstances, by definition, include prior termination of parental rights to other children. Section 32A-4-2(C)(4). Mother admitted in her pleadings that her parental rights were terminated as to two other children. When a parent admits that parental rights were previously terminated, this admission constitutes clear and convincing evidence of that fact. See *In re Baby Boy H.*, 63 Cal.App.4th 470, 73 Cal.Rptr.2d 793, 797 (1998). In addition, the previous judgment is part of the record on appeal, and there is no dispute about the fact that Mother's parental rights to Child's siblings were terminated. The real issue on appeal is the effect of that previous termination, and it is to that issue that we now turn.

Several of our sister states have had occasion to rule on the constitutionality of state statutes passed in response to the Adoption and Safe Families Act. See, e.g., *Baby Boy H.*, 73 Cal. Rptr.2d at 797–99; *In re Sheneal W. Jr.*, 45 Conn.Supp. 586, 728 A.2d 544, 550–52 (1999); *G.B. v. Dearborn County Div. of Family & Children*, 754 N.E.2d 1027, 1032 (Ind.Ct.App. 2001); *In re Heather C.*, 2000 ME 99, ¶¶ 20–32, 751 A.2d 448. Although not all of the cases have been in the same context as this case, all have ruled that the statutes are constitutional in the face of arguments similar to Mother's, and we have been directed to no cases containing any contrary ruling.

We particularly agree with the reasoning of the Maine Supreme Judicial Court, which analyzed its statute utilizing the same factors that we frequently use in these cases. See, e.g., *State ex rel. Children, Youth & Families Dep't v. Anne McD.*, 2000-NMCA-020, ¶ 18, 128 N.M. 618, 995 P.2d 1060 (citing the factors established in *Mathews*, 424 U.S. at 335, 96 S.Ct. 893). The court there recognized both the private parties' fundamental rights to rear their children and the state's substantial interest in protecting the safety and welfare of children. *Heather C.*, 2000 ME 99, ¶¶ 25–27, 751 A.2d 448. Like the New Mexico statute, the Maine statute relies on past adjudications to support the elimination of the requirement of state services geared toward reunification of the family. The mother there argued that the statute produced a high risk of erroneous deprivations of individual rights because the statute did not require a proven connection between the past orders and the parents' current abilities. Id. ¶ 24. In rejecting this argument, the court focused on the discretionary nature of the statute. Id. ¶ 25. The Maine statute, like ours, does not mandate that the state cease reasonable efforts once there has been a prior termination of parental rights. The statute, like ours, provides the trial court with discretion to relieve the state of the burden of providing services. Section

32A-4-22(C), governing dispositions, states, "The court may determine that reasonable efforts are not required to be made when the court finds that: (1) the efforts would be futile; (2) the parent...has subjected the child to aggravated circumstances; or (3) the parental rights...to a sibling...have been terminated involuntarily."...Similarly, Section 32A-4-28(B)(2), stating the elements of termination for abuse or neglect, states,

> The court *may* find in some cases that efforts by the department or another agency are unnecessary, when: (a) there is a clear showing that the efforts would be futile; (b) the parent has subjected the child to aggravated circumstances; or (c) the parental rights...to a sibling...have been terminated involuntarily[.]

(Emphasis added.)

Moreover, there is an additional safeguard—the appellate court can review the trial court's exercise of discretion. *Heather C.*, 2000 ME 99, ¶ 26, 751 A.2D 448. Thus, Mother's hypothetical argument in the present case lacks merit. Mother argues that a person who had parental rights terminated long in the past and who is now a model parent could have her rights terminated under the New Mexico statute solely on the basis of those ancient activities. However, we think that an appellate court would likely find that a trial court abused its discretion if it terminated the parental rights of a person who is now a model parent solely on the basis of a parental rights termination that occurred long ago if there is no suggestion of any relationship between the past conduct and the current abilities.

In this case, and indeed in most of the reported cases, there is a very real relationship between the past conduct and the current abilities. As stated in *Baby Boy H.*, 73 Cal.Rptr.2d at 799:

> Before this subdivision applies, the parent must have had at least one chance to reunify with a different child through the aid of governmental resources and fail to do so. Experience has shown that with certain parents, as is the case here, the risk of recidivism is a very real concern. Therefore, when another child of that same parent is adjudged a dependent child, it is not unreasonable to assume reunification efforts will be unsuccessful.

To a like effect, in upholding the constitutionality of a similar statute, the Indiana court applied strict scrutiny and stated, "the statute is narrowly tailored" and no "more intrusive than necessary to protect the welfare of children." *G.B.*, 754 N.E.2d at 1032. We reasoned similarly in *In re I.N.M.*, 105 N.M. 664, 668–69, 735 P.2d 1170, 1174–75 (Ct.App. 1987) (holding that a court can reasonably infer abuse of one child from abuse of another).

It cannot be disputed that the state has a substantial interest in protecting children. *Heather C.*, 2000 ME 99, ¶¶ 27–28, 751 A.2d 448. Also, particularly in these economic times, it bears remembering that government resources are limited, and the state "has a legitimate interest in making the best use of its limited resources." *Id.* ¶ 29. "If difficult decisions regarding allocation of scarce resources must be made, the Legislature's determination that a prior involuntary termination is a factor to be considered is both reasonable and legitimate." *Id.*

Here, despite having had her rights to two children terminated for abuse and neglect caused by substance abuse only two years previously, Mother continued to abuse drugs, causing her to deliver Child prematurely and causing her reimprisonment and resultant inability to act as a responsible parent. The trial court could have easily found her alleged recognition of her problems to be "too little, too late." *State ex rel. HSD v. Dennis S.*, 108 N.M. 486, 488, 775 P.2d 252, 254 (Ct.App. 1989). This is not a case in which Mother's parental rights to Child were terminated based on old evidence, not relevant to current proceedings. The trial court found, by clear and convincing evidence, that Mother's prospects for change in the foreseeable future were not good. This finding was not based solely on past adjudications. The only thing the past adjudication did was relieve the State of the burden of engaging in reasonable efforts and relieve the State of the burden of proving that such efforts would not result in change. The State still had to prove that the conditions and causes of the abuse and neglect would not change in the foreseeable future, and Mother does not challenge the sufficiency of the evidence supporting the trial court's finding of this fact.

We conclude that Sections 32A-4-2(C), -22(C), and -28(B)(2) are constitutional facially and as applied to Mother. We further conclude that the trial court did not abuse its discretion in relieving the Department of its obligation to make reasonable reunification efforts....

NOTES AND QUESTIONS

1. On what grounds did the court terminate the mother's parental rights? Could the court terminate her parental rights based solely on the fact that the state previously terminated her parental rights with regard to the infant child's older siblings? What else does the state need to prove? Do you think the state could have proven another ground for termination? If so, what would it have been?

2. Who has the burden of proof? Was the burden met in this case? To what extent do aggravating circumstances excusing reasonable efforts shift the burden of proof?

3. *Abandonment*. The court states that "except in cases of actual or presumptive abandonment..., parental rights may not be terminated in the case of a neglected or abused child unless the court finds that 'the conditions and causes of the neglect and abuse are unlikely to change in the foreseeable future despite reasonable efforts by the department.'" Why would a state treat abandonment differently?

Generally, a child is considered abandoned when the parent has failed to provide reasonable support for a statutorily determined period of time, the parent has not maintained contact with the child, the parent's identity or whereabouts are unknown, or the child has been left by the parent under circumstances in which the child suffers serious harm. Abandonment, however, is not merely failure to meet parental obligations; it evinces an intent to relinquish parental claims to care and custody. In about seventeen states and the District of Columbia, abandonment is encompassed in their definitions of abuse or, most commonly, neglect. Approximately eighteen states have separate statutory definitions of abandonment. Child Welfare Information Gateway, Definitions of Child Abuse and Neglect: Summary of State Laws 4–5 (2010), http://www.childwelfare.gov/systemwide/laws_policies/statutes/define.pdf. The length of time that must pass before abandonment presumptively occurs varies and may be quite short in some jurisdictions. See, e.g., Ky. Rev. Stat. § 625.090(2)(a) (2012) (may terminate parental rights if parent has abandoned child for at least ninety days). See also *M.H. v. Jefferson County Dept. of Human Resources*, 42 So. 3d 1291 (Ala. Civ. App. 2010) (mother's failure to visit child for six months satisfied statutory rebuttable presumption of abandonment after four months next preceding the filing of a termination petition and state not obligated to make reasonable efforts to reunite family).

Safe-haven laws. In response to concerns that mothers were killing or abandoning their babies, all fifty states enacted "safe-haven laws" that permit a mother to leave her baby at a designated safe haven in exchange for anonymity and a promise that she would not be prosecuted. Most states permit either parent to relinquish the infant, although some states permit an agent of the parent to relinquish the child. The parent must relinquish the child within a specified time period, ranging from seventy-two hours to one year. Safe havens include hospitals, fire and police stations, emergency medical technicians, and even churches. In twenty-five states, the safe-haven provider is obligated to ask for family and medical information, and in seventeen states, the provider must give the parent information about referral services and the legal repercussions of relinquishment. Twenty states have procedures for a parent to reclaim the infant within a specified time period. Child Welfare Information Gateway, Infant Safe Haven Laws: Summary of State Laws 2–5 (2010), http://www.childwelfare.gov/systemwide/laws_policies/statutes/safehaven.pdf. Many commentators, however, have criticized the enactment of safe-haven laws. See, e.g., Carol Sanger, *Infant Safe Haven Laws: Legislating in the Culture of Life*, 106 Colum. L. Rev. 753 (2005) (arguing that infant safe-haven laws work to promote political goal of reversing *Roe v. Wade*); Jeffrey A. Parness, *Lost Paternity in the Culture of Motherhood: A Different View of Safe Haven Laws*, 42 Val. U. L. Rev. 81 (2007) (arguing that safe-haven laws undermine fathers' legal rights and interests); Jeffrey A. Parness, *Deserting Mothers, Abandoned Babies, Lost Fathers: Dangers in Safe Havens*, 24 Quinnipiac L. Rev. 335 (2006) (examining the "neglect of…genetic fathers" by safe-haven laws); Jennifer R. Racine, *Dangerous Place for Society and Its Troubled Young Women: A Call for an End to Newborn Safe Haven Laws in Wisconsin and Beyond*, 20 Wis. Women's L.J. 243 (2005) (safe-haven laws sanction illegal abandonment and do not help troubled young mothers).

4. *Incarceration.* Another common ground for termination of parental rights is the criminal conviction of a parent for a crime of violence perpetrated against the child or another family member or conviction for an offense that involves a long period of incarceration. In 2007, most of the inmates held in state jails and federal prisons were parents. Lauren E. Glaze & Laura M. Maruschak, U.S. Dep't of Justice, Bureau of Justice Statistics Special Report: Parents in Prison and Their Minor Children 1 (revised Mar. 30, 2010). Since 1991, the number of children with a mother in prison increased by 131 percent; the number with a father in prison increased by 77 percent. *Id.* at 2. Of all female state inmates, 61.1 percent were parents of minor children, compared with 51.2 percent of all male state inmates. *Id.* at tbl. 5. Moreover, the majority of women reported living with their children prior to incarceration and were more likely than men to report living with their children prior to incarceration. *Id.* at 4. These mothers also were three times more likely to report that they had provided most of the daily care for their children. *Id.* at 5. While most of the children whose parents were incarcerated were cared for by relatives—predominantly grandmothers—10.9 percent of incarcerated mothers reported that their children were in foster care. Only 2.2 percent of the incarcerated fathers reported that their children were in foster care. *Id.* at tbl. 8.

Incarceration also has a disproportionate effect on minority families. In 2007, African-American children were seven and a half times more likely and Hispanic children more than two and a half times more likely than white children to have a parent in prison. More than 40 percent of fathers in the nation's prisons were African-American, while about two in ten of the incarcerated fathers were Hispanic. *Id.* at 2. Of all mothers held in state and federal prisons, 28 percent were black, and 17 percent were Hispanic. *Id.*

Substance abuse and mental illness are significant problems for incarcerated parents. Of all parents who were inmates in state prisons, 67.4 percent reported substance dependence or abuse; however, 81.5 percent of mothers who did not live with their minor children one month prior to incarceration reported that they had substance dependence or abuse. *Id.* at 7. More than half of the incarcerated fathers also reported mental-health issues, but nearly three-quarters of incarcerated mothers reported similar problems. *Id.* Unsurprisingly, many of these parents had been arrested and convicted of drug-related offenses. Mothers were more likely to be sentenced for drug offenses than fathers. Christopher J. Mumola, U.S. Dep't of Justice, Bureau of Justice Statistics Special Report: Incarcerated Parents and Their Children 6 (2000).

To what extent does the emphasis on permanency affect the state's response to children of incarcerated parents? Reported termination cases involving parental incarceration increased by 250 percent between 1997 (the year ASFA was enacted) and 2002. Philip M. Genty, *Damage to Family Relationships as a Collateral Consequence of Parental Incarceration*, 30 FORDHAM URB. L.J. 1671, 1678 (2003).

> While incarceration *per se* is not a reason justifying termination in most states, several include a provision for lengthy or repeated incarceration. Moreover, cases involving termination of incarcerated parents often cite reasons that are a consequence of imprisonment: child in foster care most of her life, parental failure to contact or support child for a period of over six months, parent incapable of performing parental duties, parent's progress stagnated, abandonment, or parent failed to rehabilitate. Female inmates are impacted disproportionately to men, since..., due to the prevalence of single incarcerated mothers, their children have a greater probability of being in foster care than do male inmates.

Myrna Raeder, *Gender-Related Issues in a Post-Booker Federal Guidelines World*, 37 MCGEORGE L. REV. 691, 700–701 (2006).

Is it unconstitutional to terminate parental rights because the parent is incarcerated? Would a higher burden of proof or providing indigent parents with counsel in all termination proceedings reduce the number of terminations? See, e.g., Deseriee A. Kennedy, *Children, Parent & the State: The Construction of a New Family Ideology*, 26 BERKELEY J. GENDER, LAW & JUST. 78 (2011) (arguing that a higher burden of proof is warranted in light of disproportionate impact on families of color and that providing counsel "would more adequately account for the liberty interests at stake"). Would programs for incarcerated parents and their children mitigate the effects of parental institutionalization? Should time spent in prison toll the ASFA timelines? See, e.g., Katherine P. Luke, *Mitigating the Ill Effects of Maternal Incarceration on Women in Prison and Their Children*, 81 CHILD WELFARE 929 (2002).

IN RE J.S.
Supreme Court of North Dakota
743 N.W.2d 808 (2008)

CROTHERS, Justice.

J.G. ("Mother") appeals the juvenile court's order terminating parental rights to her two minor children, J.S. ("Sam") and J.G. ("George"). We conclude the juvenile court did not err in finding the children have been deprived, the causes and conditions of deprivation are likely to continue, and, as a result of the continued deprivation, Sam and George have suffered or will probably suffer serious physical, mental or emotional harm if Mother's parental rights are not terminated. Further, the juvenile court did not err in finding reasonable efforts were made to preserve and unify the family prior to termination of Mother's rights. We affirm.

I

Mother has three children: Sally, born September 2001; Sam, born July 2003; and George, born September 2004. Sally was removed from Mother's home by Cass County Social Services because Sally was not receiving sufficient care. Sally is currently placed with her father and is not part of this termination action.

Mother began working with social services voluntarily in August 2003. At that time, she, Sam, and Sam's father, D.S., lived together in an apartment. A parent aide was assigned to assist Mother with Sam, who was one month old. The aide helped Mother with her parenting skills, focusing primarily on keeping the family's apartment clean. In September 2003, D.S. struck Sam and was later convicted of child abuse. After the incident, Mother and Sam moved into her parents' home. D.S. no longer has contact with Sam.

Social services assessed the family's living situation at the grandparents' home in December 2003 and found it lacking. The house was dirty and covered in dog hair from the family's two German shepherds. The baby bottles were "dirty and moldy," and Sam smelled of urine. Sam was placed in foster care while Mother worked with social services to improve the home environment. Mother also began seeing a psychiatrist. On May 6, 2004, Sam was adjudicated a "deprived child" due to poor household conditions, poor hygiene, lack of a regular feeding schedule, Mother's failure to address her mental health issues and her "demonstrat[ion] of poor judgment with regard to [Sam's] health and safety."

While Sam was in foster care, George was born. The identity of George's father is unknown. Social services continued working with Mother to improve her parenting skills. Mother obtained her own apartment within this time frame, though the conditions of the home continued to be a problem. Nonetheless, Sam was returned to the home from foster care in April 2005. Mother continued working with social services, and a speech therapist worked with Sam. Social services monitored Sam until August 2005.

On September 23, 2005, both Sam and George were placed in foster care because of the condition of the apartment. They were adjudicated deprived children on January 10, 2006. A treatment plan for the family was developed, including treatment of Mother's mental illness, parenting classes, homemaking assistance and daycare for the children so Mother could work on improving her life skills. The children were returned to Mother's care on January 3, 2006. Mother took Sam to see a psychiatrist in February 2006 because of his hitting and biting behaviors; he was prescribed mood-stabilizing medication.

In June 2006, licensed social worker Carrie Smith received a report of problems at Mother's home. Smith and two law enforcement officers went to the home on June 14, 2006 to investigate. Mother was told in advance that Smith would be visiting the home. Upon entering the apartment, Smith noticed a strong odor she characterized as "feces and also like a stale smoke, garbage kind of smell." Sam and George were found in their bedroom, where several areas of the wall had been smeared with feces. Sam was eating loose cereal off the floor which was next to feces stains on the carpet. George was found in his crib, which had only a bare mattress and no bedding. He was eating loose cereal off the crib mattress. Both children were dressed only in diapers that appeared not to have been changed that morning. Sam's diaper was fastened with duct tape. No toys, books or play items were available to the children. All such items were stored in containers out of the children's reach. During the visit, Smith witnessed George putting pennies in his mouth. Other parts of the apartment were in a similar state with cigarette butts and food products on the floor. One of the officers who accompanied Smith described the home:

> "I didn't think [the family] should be living there to be blunt. The place was filthy.... It was a mess. The carpet probably hadn't been cleaned since they moved in. There was food all over.... There was garbage piled up all over the residence. It appeared to be a cleaning solution in a bucket that was on the floor that could be easily accessible to a child.... [T]he T.V. that was in the bedroom was on but there was no picture on it. It was a snowy picture and the children appeared to be watching it as if there was a cartoon on.... The house was disgusting."

During the visit, Mother told Smith she had been "spring cleaning." The police officers took photos of the home which were entered into evidence. Sam and George were taken into protective custody.

Sam and George entered foster care on June 14, 2006, and a petition for termination of parental rights was filed on June 30, 2006. On January 8, 2007, a judicial referee terminated Mother's parental rights to both Sam and George. The children's fathers' rights were also terminated. The referee's findings of fact were (1) Mother has mental health issues and has refused the mental health services made available to her through social services; (2) Mother complains of numerous physical ailments, including back problems, psoriasis, connective tissue disorder, irritable bowel syndrome, stress and exercise induced asthma, stress induced hives, reflux disorder, ovarian cyst and seizures, but has not sought consistent medical treatment; (3) Mother "fail[s] to maintain the home at or above minimum community standards[,] has failed to appropriately address the hygiene needs of the children and [has] demonstrated poor judgment with regard to the health and safety of the children"; (4) Mother has been offered extensive services including intervention, referrals and education to help her improve her family's situation, yet was "unable to maintain any consistent minimal level of care for extended periods of time [which] has resulted in an environment that is unsafe for the children"; and (5) Mother is unable to provide appropriate developmental care for the children, and since entering foster care, the children's developmental delays have disappeared. In sum, the referee determined the time needed to create a stable home for Mother's children is too long and found by clear and convincing evidence the children are deprived and would be harmed without terminating her parental rights. Sam and George were placed into the custody of the Department of Human Services.

In January 2007, Mother requested a review of the referee's factual findings and order. On April 5, 2007, the juvenile court adopted the referee's factual findings and order. Mother appeals the juvenile court's order.

II

"To terminate a person's parental rights, the petitioner must prove the child is deprived; the conditions and causes of the deprivation are likely to continue or will not be remedied; and, that by reason thereof the child is suffering or will probably suffer serious physical, mental, moral, or emotional harm." *In re T.A.*, 2006 ND 210, ¶ 10, 722 N.W.2d 548. These elements must be proven by clear and convincing evidence. *Id.* "Clear and convincing evidence means evidence that leads to a firm belief or conviction the allegations are true." *Id.*

This Court will not overturn a juvenile court's decision to terminate parental rights unless the decision is clearly erroneous. *In re E.G.*, 2006 ND 126, ¶ 7, 716 N.W.2d 469. "A finding of fact is clearly erroneous if it is induced by an erroneous view of the law, if no evidence exists to support the finding, or if, on the entire record, we are left with a definite and firm conviction a mistake has been made." *Id.*

Mother appears to concede the children were deprived, but argues insufficient evidence exists to support the finding that deprivation was likely to continue. She also challenges the finding that the children would likely suffer harm absent a termination of parental rights and argues that reasonable efforts to reunify her family have not been made.

A

A deprived child lacks "proper parental care or control, subsistence, education as required by law, or other care or control necessary for the child's physical, mental, or emotional health, or morals, and the deprivation is not due primarily to the lack of financial means of the child's parents, guardian, or other custodian." N.D.C.C. § 27-20-02(8)(a). "Proper parental care is met by exhibiting minimum standards of care that the community will tolerate." *T.A.*, 2006 ND 210, ¶ 12, 722 N.W.2d 548. Mother has not argued in juvenile court or on appeal the referee's deprivation finding was made in error. Our review is "limited to issues litigated below and the arguments presented upon appeal. Where a party fails to provide supporting argument for an issue listed in his brief, he is deemed to have waived that issue." *State v. Obrigewitch*, 356 N.W.2d 105, 109 (N.D. 1984). Based on the record before us, we affirm the juvenile court's conclusion that the children are deprived.

B

Mother argues the juvenile court erred in finding evidence that the conditions and causes of the children's deprivation are likely to continue or will not be remedied. Mother cites no law supporting this assertion and simply argues the evidence provided by petitioner did not prove clearly and convincingly that deprivation is likely to continue. This Court may only overturn the juvenile court's decision if it finds no evidence to support the finding or if, "on the entire record, we are left with a definite and firm conviction a mistake has been made." *In re D.M.*, 2007 ND 62, ¶ 6, 730 N.W.2d 604. Based on this record, we conclude the juvenile court did not err.

Mother's conduct plus "[p]rognostic evidence, including reports and opinions of the professionals involved" may be used to form the determination deprivation will continue. *T.A.*, 2006 ND 210, ¶ 15, 722 N.W.2d 548. A parent's lack of cooperation with social services can be evidence that deprivation is likely to continue. *In re T.F.*, 2004 ND 126, ¶ 19, 681 N.W.2d 786. The juvenile court acknowledged that from the time Mother began working with social services in August 2003 until the final removal in June 2006, numerous services were provided to the family, including parenting education, welfare checks, parent aide services, homemaker services, day care services, case management services, a chemical dependency evaluation, a parental capacity evaluation, counseling services, infant development counseling, speech and occupational therapy for Sam, financial and medical assistance and supervised visitation.

Despite all this assistance, Mother missed appointments, refused treatment for her physical and mental ailments and ultimately did not improve her parenting.

Particularly relevant is the testimony of an in-home care support specialist assigned to Mother. The support specialist provided weekly housekeeping help and attempted to establish a cleaning routine. Mother did not follow through. The support specialist testified she and Mother would clean, but the next week she would find the home in disorder. The support specialist suggested Mother keep the home picked up and rinse the dirty dishes, but Mother did not comply. While a lack of cleanliness of the home alone does not provide a sufficient showing of deprivation necessary to terminate parental rights, parents must at least provide care "that satisfies the minimum community standards." *In re M.S.*, 2001 ND 68, ¶ 12, 624 N.W.2d 678. Sam and George have been removed from Mother's home twice before this incident due to deprivation. Upon the children's return home, the unhealthy and unsafe living situation did not improve. Placement in foster care followed by reunification has become a cycle for this family. The juvenile court's determination that deprivation would continue is not clearly erroneous.

C

Termination of parental rights requires clear and convincing evidence that "the child is suffering or will probably suffer serious physical, mental, moral, or emotional harm." N.D.C.C. § 27-20-44(1)(c)(1). The risk of future harm may be based on evidence of previous harm. *See In re M.B.*, 2006 ND 19, ¶ 18, 709 N.W.2d 11. Here, the referee found the children will be harmed if Mother's parental rights are not terminated. "To terminate parental rights, a court need not await the happening of a tragic event." *In re T.K.*, 2001 ND 127, ¶ 17, 630 N.W.2d 38. Sufficient evidence exists showing the children have been harmed by Mother's lack of care. For example, Mother told her social worker the children were anaemic, and when asked what she had been feeding them, she referenced only cereal and macaroni. As a result, George is substantially underweight. Mother's home was littered with choking hazards, such as the pennies George put into his mouth during the social worker's visit. A registered nurse who provides in-home visits to assess safety issues stated:

> "The thing that I was thinking about, you know, were the soiling and the dirty environment and crawling, children always put their hands in their mouth and to be crawling—crawling up things and the bacteria, infection, those kinds of things as well as the cluttering and tripping, falling."

Furthermore, Sam has exhibited delayed language and motor skills. A speech language pathologist worked with Sam when he was living with Mother and later when he was placed in foster care. The pathologist testified Sam's progress was slight while living with Mother. Since foster care placement, Sam has improved enough to have "closed the gap" in his developmental delay. The pathologist attributes this improvement to Sam's "consistent attendance and consistency in his life." Given the extensive assistance Mother received and the small impact it made on the family's living situation, the juvenile court did not err in its assessment that Mother will likely be unable to provide a safe, healthy environment for the children in the future. Sufficient evidence exits supporting the juvenile court's finding that the children are likely to be harmed if Mother's parental rights are not terminated. The juvenile court's factual findings are not erroneous.

D

Finally, Mother argues reasonable efforts were not made to preserve and unify her family as required prior to termination of parental rights. *See* N.D.C.C. § 27-20-32.2(2). Reasonable efforts are defined as the "exercise of due diligence, by the agency...to use *appropriate and available services* to meet the needs of the child and the child's family." N.D.C.C. § 27-20-32.2(1) (emphasis added). Mother was given numerous resources to help her provide a better environment for her family. A social worker reviewed Mother's case plan prior to the children's placement in foster care in June 2006. This social worker testified there were no more services available that could be offered to Mother. Moreover, the district court noted Mother's participation in these services was "sporadic" and she cancelled or missed numerous appointments. The agency does not have to exhaust every potential solution before termination of parental rights. The juvenile court did not err in finding reasonable efforts had been made to preserve and unify this family prior to termination of Mother's rights.

III

The juvenile court's factual findings with regard to deprivation, likelihood of future harm and reasonable efforts to preserve and unify the family are not clearly erroneous. The juvenile court's order terminating Mother's parental rights to Sam and George is affirmed.

NOTES AND QUESTIONS

1. What was the legal basis for terminating the mother's parental rights? What facts supported the termination decision?

2. The court noted that a parent's failure to cooperate is evidence that deprivation is likely to continue. Why would that be the case? Do you think that J.G. failed to cooperate? To what extent do you think her lack of cooperation was the result of her psychological problems?

3. A social worker testified at trial that "there were no more services available that could be offered to Mother." Does this mean there were services that could have assisted the mother? Do you think the agency made "reasonable efforts" to reunify the family?

4. Approximately 20 percent of the parents involved in the child-welfare system have mental-health problems. Nevertheless, many mentally ill parents do not receive the treatment they need because of the lack of available services for impoverished parents and beliefs that the mentally ill are undeserving of sympathy, dangerous, and unpredictable. Theresa Glennon, *Walking with Them: Advocating for Parents with Mental Illnesses in the Child Welfare System*, 12 TEMP. POL. & CIV. RTS. L. REV. 273, 291–292 (2003). Although the Americans with Disabilities Act of 1990 (ADA), Pub. L. 101-336, 42 U.S.C. § 12101 et. seq. (2010), would seem to offer protection to mentally ill parents, "[a]lmost all state courts to consider the question have ruled that an agency's failure to adhere to the ADA cannot be asserted as a defense to a termination of parental rights proceeding." Glennon, supra, at 275. But see Dale Marolin, *No Chance to Prove*

Themselves: The Rights of Mentally Disabled Parents under the Americans with Disabilities Act and State Law, 15 Va. J. Soc. Pol'y & L. 112 (2007) (arguing that state termination statutes violate ADA because permit termination based on "status and speculation" and suggesting ways in which parents could challenge termination based on ADA). Should the child-welfare system be more responsive to the needs of mentally ill parents?

IN RE D.A.
Supreme Court of Ohio
862 N.E.2d 829 (2007)

LANZINGER, J.

We accepted this discretionary appeal to determine whether the parental rights of a mentally retarded couple were properly terminated and permanent custody of their son properly awarded to Tuscarawas County Job and Family Services. We reverse.

Procedural Facts

In early 2004, appellants voluntarily relinquished custody of their ten-year-old son, D.A., who was having behavioral problems, to appellee, Tuscarawas County Job and Family Services ("the agency"). After 30 days, the agency sought temporary custody of D.A. by filing a complaint alleging that the boy was a neglected and dependent child. The agency filed a motion to dismiss the count of neglect at the adjudicatory hearing, and the magistrate recommended that D.A. be found to be a dependent child. The trial court approved and adopted the magistrate's decision on April 14, 2004.

The trial court adopted the agency's case plan developed for appellants, which required them to undergo psychological evaluations and follow the evaluating psychologist's recommendations. Both parents were required to attend parenting classes and were to be assessed for services by the Department of Mental Retardation and Developmental Disabilities ("MRDD"). The mother was also expected to attend therapy to learn to control her response to stress.

The psychological evaluations revealed that D.A.'s father has an IQ of 62 on the Wechsler Adult Intelligence Scale and that his mother has an IQ of 59. Concluding that the parents' mental conditions severely limited their ability to provide adequate care for their son, the psychologist recommended individual therapy to improve their skills. Appellants began parenting classes at the agency in August 2004. Initially in a class with other parents, at the request of the parenting-education teacher, they began meeting for classes on an individual basis for 30 minutes both before and after visits with their son. At the end of September, the teacher suspended appellants' classes because she believed that they might be better able to retain information if she waited until they had home visitations with D.A. and classes could be held in their home. In addition to parenting classes, appellants also attended seven therapy meetings at Community Mental Healthcare over the course of five months to help them deal with their grief and emotional issues related to their separation from D.A. and to discuss parenting issues, such as child discipline. With respect to the case plan's requirement that they be assessed for MRDD services, the agency was notified that appellants did not qualify for MRDD services due to their ability to meet their basic needs without help from MRDD.

Despite these steps toward reunification, on January 21, 2005, the agency filed a motion seeking permanent custody of D.A. The trial court held a hearing on May 27, 2005. It found that, although appellants love their son very much and were willing to do anything necessary to bring him home, returning D.A. to them was not in his best interest, because they have "very low cognitive skills that hinder their day to day functioning" and "demonstrate no ability to engage in the type of complex thinking necessary to parent a child." The trial court expressed its concern that appellants function as the child's peers instead of as his parents. It further found that to allow "a normally functioning child like [D.A.] to be parented by two parents with the severe limitations demonstrated by [appellants] is to seriously jeopardize his healthy, successful future." The court found that D.A. "cannot and should not be placed with either parent within a reasonable time" because "despite diligent, reasonable efforts * * *, both parents have failed continually and repeatedly for a period of six months or more to substantially remedy the conditions causing removal." The trial court ordered that D.A. be placed in the permanent custody of the agency.

The parents appealed to the Fifth District Court of Appeals, which determined that the record supported the finding that both parents had failed continually and repeatedly to substantially remedy the conditions causing removal. The Fifth District also upheld the trial court's finding that granting the agency permanent custody was in D.A.'s best interest because returning him to appellants would seriously jeopardize his healthy, successful future.

We accepted the discretionary appeal. In essence, appellants claim that the trial court failed to comply with statutory requirements in terminating their parental rights. We agree.

Fundamental Right

In *Troxel v. Granville* (2000), 530 U.S. 57, 65, 120 S.Ct. 2054, 147 L.Ed.2d 49, the United States Supreme Court noted that parents' interest in the care, custody, and control of their children "is perhaps the oldest of the fundamental liberty interests recognized by this Court." The protection of the family unit has long been a paramount concern of the courts, as indicated in *Stanley v. Illinois* (1972), 405 U.S. 645, 651, 92 S.Ct. 1208, 31 L.Ed.2d 551:

> "The Court has frequently emphasized the importance of the family. The rights to conceive and to raise one's children have been deemed 'essential,' *Meyer v. Nebraska*, 262 U.S. 390, 399, 43 S.Ct. 625, 626, 67 L.Ed. 1042 (1923), 'basic civil rights of man,' *Skinner v. Oklahoma*, 316 U.S. 535, 541, 62 S.Ct. 1110, 1113, 86 L.Ed. 1655 (1942), and '[r]ights far more precious * * * than property rights,' *May v. Anderson*, 345 U.S. 528, 533, 73 S.Ct. 840, 843, 97 L.Ed. 1221 (1953). 'It is cardinal with us that the custody, care and nurture of the child reside first in the parents, whose primary function and freedom include preparation for obligations the state can neither supply nor hinder.' *Prince v. Massachusetts*, 321 U.S. 158, 166, 64 S.Ct. 438, 442, 88 L.Ed. 645 (1944). The integrity of the family unit has found protection in the Due Process Clause of the Fourteenth Amendment, *Meyer v. Nebraska*, supra, 262 U.S. at 399, 43 S.Ct. at 626 [67 L.Ed. 1042] the Equal Protection Clause of the Fourteenth Amendment, *Skinner v. Oklahoma*, supra, 316 U.S. at 541, 62 S.Ct. at 1113 [86 L.Ed. 1655], and the Ninth Amendment, *Griswold v. Connecticut*, 381 U.S. 479, 496, 85 S.Ct. 1678, 14 L.Ed.2d 510 (1965) (Goldberg, J., concurring)."

We note that this court has long held that "parents who are suitable persons have a 'paramount' right to the custody of their minor children. *In re Perales* (1977), 52 Ohio St.2d 89, 97, 6 O.O.3d 293, 297, 369 N.E.2d 1047, 1051–1052; *Clark v. Bayer* (1877), 32 Ohio St. 299, 310," *In re Murray* (1990), 52 Ohio St.3d 155, 157, 556 N.E.2d 1169, and that "[p]ermanent termination of parental rights has been described as 'the family law equivalent of the death penalty in a criminal case.' *In re Smith* (1991), 77 Ohio App.3d 1, 16, 601 N.E.2d 45, 54. Therefore, parents 'must be afforded every procedural and substantive protection the law allows.' Id." *In re Hayes* (1997), 79 Ohio St.3d 46, 48, 679 N.E.2d 680.

The fundamental interest of parents is not absolute, however. Once the case reaches the disposition phase, the best interest of the child controls. The termination of parental rights should be an alternative of "last resort." *In re Cunningham* (1979), 59 Ohio St.2d 100, 105, 13 O.O.3d 78, 391 N.E.2d 1034.

Permanent-Custody Procedure

Before parental rights are terminated and permanent custody granted to a children services agency, R.C. 2151.414(B)(1) requires a court to determine "by clear and convincing evidence, that it is in the best interest of the child to grant permanent custody of the child to the agency that filed the motion for permanent custody and that any of the following apply:

> "(a) The child is not abandoned or orphaned or has not been in the temporary custody of one or more public children services agencies or private child placing agencies for twelve or more months of a consecutive twenty-two month period ending on or after March 18, 1999, and the child cannot be placed with either of the child's parents within a reasonable time or should not be placed with the child's parents.
>
> "(b) The child is abandoned.
>
> "(c) The child is orphaned, and there are no relatives of the child who are able to take permanent custody.
>
> "(d) The child has been in the temporary custody of one or more public children services agencies or private child placing agencies for twelve or more months of a consecutive twenty-two month period ending on or after March 18, 1999."

R.C. 2151.414(E) provides guidelines for a court charged with determining whether a child cannot or should not be placed with either parent within a reasonable period of time under R.C. 2151.414(B)(1)(a) and requires that such a finding be made if it is established by clear and convincing evidence that one or more of 16 factors exist with respect to each parent.

The court next must determine whether granting permanent custody to a children services agency is in the child's best interest. It is required to consider several factors, including the relationship between the child and the child's parents and foster caregivers, the child's wishes, the custodial history of the child, and the child's need for a legally secure permanent placement. R.C. 2151.414(D).

Analysis

Appellants argue that their parental rights were terminated solely due to their limited cognitive abilities, violating their rights to raise their son. They contend that their low IQ scores were the only objective evidence to support a finding that D.A. could not or should not be placed with them and that it was in his best interest to terminate their parental rights.

The agency acknowledges that R.C. 2151.414 does not allow for the termination of parental rights based on a parent's cognitive abilities alone, but argues that the trial court made sufficient findings under R.C. 2151.414(E)(1) and (2) to support the termination of parental rights.

To satisfy either R.C. 2151.414(E)(1) or (2) regarding why D.A. could not or should not be returned to his parents, the evidence must show:

> "(1) Following the placement of the child outside the child's home and notwithstanding reasonable case planning and diligent efforts by the agency to assist the parents to remedy the problems that initially caused the child to be placed outside the home, the parent has failed continuously and repeatedly to substantially remedy the conditions causing the child to be placed outside the child's home. In determining whether the parents have substantially remedied those conditions, the court shall consider parental utilization of medical, psychiatric, psychological, and other social and rehabilitative services and material resources that were made available to the parents for the purpose of changing parental conduct to allow them to resume and maintain parental duties.
>
> "(2) Chronic mental illness, chronic emotional illness, mental retardation, physical disability, or chemical dependency of the parent that is so severe that it makes the parent unable to provide an adequate permanent home for the child at the present time and, as anticipated, within one year after the court holds the [disposition] hearing. * * *"

D.A. was initially removed from his home at his mother's request due to his aggressive behavior and her concern that she could not adequately handle him. After the agency was awarded temporary custody, appellants were given four objectives in the case plan: (1) complete psychological evaluations and follow all recommendations, (2) attend parenting classes, (3) complete an MRDD assessment, and (4) attend therapy. At the disposition hearing, there was testimony that D.A.'s defiant behavior decreased over time. It is undisputed that appellants complied with every aspect of their case plan with the exception of completing parenting classes, and that failure was due to the agency's suspension of classes after one month.

What was disputed was appellants' ability to parent D.A. due to their mental retardation. The trial court found as follows:

> "3. [D.A.] has progressed well in foster care even though he would still prefer to be with his parents. It is clear that there is a strong family bond between [D.A.] and his family. This Court recognizes that this family does not demonstrate many of the irresponsible, uncaring, or dangerous characteristics that are regularly evident in many permanent custody cases. It is clear that [D.A.'s] parents love him very much and are willing to do anything necessary to secure his return home.
>
> "4. Evidence that this would not be in the best interest of [D.A.] is revealed in the results of the psychological evaluations of his parents. Both [father and mother] demonstrate IQ levels between 62 and 59, respectively. Practically speaking, both parents have no real comprehension as to why [D.A.] was removed form [*sic*] their care. They possess very low cognitive skills that hinder their day to day functioning. They demonstrate no ability to engage in the type of complex thinking necessary to parent a child. [The parents] did not internalize any lessons

> provided in their parenting classes in any significant way. While the supervised family visits have always gone well, it was clear that both parents functioned as peers of their son instead of his parents. Unfortunately, the Court has no information to indicate that the deficits demonstrated by [the parents] can be improved to any significant degree.
>
> "5. [D.A.] continues to do well in school and his behavior is very appropriate. He does not demonstrate any intellectual limitations and performs well in the mainstream classroom.
>
> "6. To expect a normally functioning child like [D.A.] to be parented by two parents with the severe limitations demonstrated by [the parents] is to seriously jeopardize his healthy, successful future."

The trial court concluded that "despite diligent, reasonable efforts and planning by the Tuscarawas County Job and Family Services to remedy the problems which caused removal of the child, both parents have failed continually and repeatedly for a period of six months or more to substantially remedy the conditions causing removal" and that "[t]hese parents have demonstrated a lack of commitment toward their child and have failed to provide an adequate home for the child at this time and cannot do so within a year of this litigation."

The psychologist testified that appellants lacked the skills to provide adequate care and expressed concern that due to their mental retardation, they would use authority instead of reasoning to obtain D.A.'s compliance. There is no evidence to support this concern. In fact, it was the exact opposite that led to this case's initiation. His mother recognized that she did not know how to handle D.A. and sought help.

The parenting-education teacher testified that appellants function as D.A.'s peers and that his mother has displayed attention-seeking behavior around him. The teacher did acknowledge, however, that appellants had retained some of the parenting-class information from week to week and that the mother recognized when D.A. needed discipline and attempted to discipline him. The teacher expressed concern about the parents' ability to consistently apply the skills taught in her classes. But they were never given an opportunity to apply these parenting skills, since they were never permitted to complete the classes. In *In re Alexis K.*, 160 Ohio App.3d 32, 2005-Ohio-1380, 825 N.E.2d 1148, at ¶ 42, the Sixth Appellate District determined that "[w]ithout an opportunity for a practical application of the only skills appellee deemed necessary to remediate the condition prompting the children's removal, we fail to see clear and convincing evidence that appellant did not remedy the conditions which prompted the children's removal from the home."

Despite making several findings regarding the parents' limited cognitive abilities, the trial court did not find that appellants were unable to provide an adequate home for D.A. due to their mental retardation, a finding that is required to satisfy R.C. 2151.414(E)(2). Furthermore, the evidence does not support a finding that appellants failed to provide D.A. with an adequate permanent home. There is no evidence that he lacked adequate clothing, food, shelter, or care. He performed well in school and displayed appropriate behavior.

The dissent relies in part on the family's previous contact with the agency, including the removal of two other children from the mother many years before, as well as the case manager's testimony that the mother displayed aggressive behavior toward D.A. during a visitation. But as the court of appeals noted, the trial court did not use the prior history as a reason that D.A. could not or should not be returned to his parents within a reasonable time. Moreover, the "aggressive" behavior occurred during a basketball game that the family played during visitation. Thus, these factors do not support the finding that D.A. could not or should not be returned to his parents.

As for what would be in D.A.'s best interest, the trial court again focused on his parents' limited cognitive abilities. Their mental retardation, however, is not what should have been considered. Instead, the court should have considered factors such as their relationship with their child, whether they had ever harmed him, and where the child wished to live. R.C. 2151.414(D). All of these factors favor appellants. The evidence showed that they have a very loving relationship with their son, have never harmed him, and desire to do whatever is necessary to be reunited with him. D.A. also wishes to return home.

The trial court stated that D.A.'s future could be "seriously jeopardized" if he remained with his parents. But there was no evidence that they have harmed D.A. either physically, emotionally, or mentally. D.A. has done well in school, and his behavior is appropriate. At this point, it is speculation to say that he may not reach his full potential if he remains with his parents. We hold that when determining the best interest of a child under R.C. 2151.414(D) at a permanent-custody hearing, a trial court may not base its decision solely on the limited cognitive abilities of the parents.

We do not mean to minimize the trial court's concern about appellants' ability to parent their son. R.C. 2151.414, however, does not permit a parent's fundamental right to raise his or her child to be terminated based on mental retardation alone. In other cases in which the parental rights of mentally retarded persons have been terminated pursuant to R.C. 2151.414(E)(1) or (2), objective evidence existed to show that the statute was satisfied. See, e.g., *In re C.E.*, Butler App. Nos. CA2006-01-015 and CA2006-02-024, 2006-Ohio-4827, 2006 WL 2663464 (the mother needed constant supervision and prompting to meet child's basic needs and had inadequate housing); *In re King*, Fairfield App. No. 05 CA 77, 2006-Ohio-781, 2006 WL 401598 (the mother consistently relied on others to meet many of her basic needs and lost her housing).

Finally, the dissent indicates that we would not hesitate to find that it was in D.A.'s best interest to be removed from his parents if the same actions were undertaken by parents of average intelligence and there was concern about their future conduct. But that is simply not true. The record fails to demonstrate any harm or threat of harm to D.A., and the trial court's repeated reference to the low cognitive abilities of the parents indicates that that was the sole reason for the termination of parental rights.

Due to the emphasis placed on D.A.'s parents' mental retardation and the lack of clear and convincing evidence that their limited abilities have caused or threatened to cause harm to him, we conclude that the trial court failed to comply with R.C. 2151.414 and that the termination of parental rights was not in D.A.'s best interest.

Conclusion

We hold that the termination of appellants' parental rights based solely on mental retardation does not comply with R.C. 2151.414. The judgment of the court of appeals is reversed....

DONOFRIO, PFEIFER, LUNDBERG STRATTON and O'DONNELL, JJ., concur.

MOYER, C.J., and O'CONNOR, J., concur in part and dissent in part....

MOYER, C.J., concurring in part and dissenting in part.

I concur in the syllabus of the majority opinion, but I respectfully dissent from the majority's application of the rule of law to the facts of this case and from its judgment. While I agree that when determining the best interest of a child under R.C. 2151.414(D), a trial court may not rely solely on the limited cognitive abilities of the parents, I disagree that the trial court in this case based the decision to terminate custody on those facts alone. To the contrary, the trial court considered the factors required by R.C. 2151.414 and concluded that granting permanent custody of D.A. to Tuscarawas County Job and Family Services ("the agency") was in the child's best interest.

R.C. 2151.414 protects a parent's constitutional rights in a permanent-custody proceeding by establishing the procedures a trial court must follow and the findings a trial court must make before terminating parental rights. R.C. 2151.414(B) requires that all of the trial court's findings be supported by clear and convincing evidence. This court has defined "clear and convincing evidence" as "that measure or degree of proof which is more than a mere 'preponderance of the evidence,' but not to the extent of such certainty as is required 'beyond a reasonable doubt' in criminal cases, and which will produce in the mind of the trier of facts a firm belief or conviction as to the facts sought to be established." *Cross v. Ledford* (1954), 161 Ohio St. 469, 53 O.O. 361, 120 N.E.2d 118, paragraph three of the syllabus.

Here, the court was determining both the best interest of the child under R.C. 2151.414(D) and whether the child could be placed with either parent within a reasonable time under R.C. 2151.414(E). In determining the [best interest] of a child under R.C. 2151.414(D), the court shall consider "all relevant factors," including, but not limited to, five specific factors listed in the statute. These five factors include (1) "[t]he interaction and interrelationship of the child with the child's parents," (2) "[t]he wishes of the child," (3) "[t]he custodial history of the child," (4) "[t]he child's need for a legally secure permanent placement," and (5) whether factors listed in other specified subsections apply.

In determining whether a child can be placed with either parent within a reasonable time, a court must, under R.C. 2151.414(E), consider "all relevant evidence" and determine by "clear and convincing evidence" whether one or more factors from a list of factors exist as to each of the child's parents. Under subsection (E)(1) (the first factor), a court must determine whether following the placement of the child outside the home and "notwithstanding reasonable case planning and diligent efforts by the agency to assist the parents to remedy the problems * * *, the parent has failed continuously and repeatedly to substantially remedy the conditions causing the child to be placed outside the child's home." Under subsection (E)(2), a court must determine whether chronic mental illness of the parent "is so severe that it makes the parent unable to provide an adequate permanent home for the child at the present time and, as anticipated, within one year." Under subsection (E)(16) (the final factor in the list), the court must consider "[a]ny other factor the court considers relevant."

The record in this case provides several facts that are relevant to the court's determinations under R.C. 2151.414. D.A.'s family has long been involved with the agency, and previously, two other children were removed from the mother's custody. The trial court found that the agency first became involved in the family with regard to D.A. in 1996, followed by contacts in 1998 and 2004.

In 2004, D.A. was placed in temporary custody with the agency after his mother contacted the police and indicated that she was afraid she would hurt her son if he were not removed from her home. The court also found that the parents "have no real comprehension as to why [D.A.] was removed from their care" and that there was "no information to indicate that the deficits demonstrated by [the parents could] be improved to any significant degree."

The agency case manager testified that she had observed the mother display aggressive behavior toward her son during a supervised visit and that she did not observe any changes in the ability of the parents to care for D.A. during the year D.A. was in temporary custody.

An agency employee responsible for parent-education classes for D.A.'s parents also observed no real changes in the parents' ability to care for their son and continued to be concerned over the parents' lack of understanding of basic parenting concepts. The agency had a difficult time providing services to the parents and implementing the case plan as a result of the intellectual limitations of the parents and the parents' failure to engage in appropriate services.

A board-certified psychologist who evaluated D.A.'s parents testified as to her significant concern regarding the parents' ability to provide adequate care for D.A.

R.C. 2151.414 requires clear and convincing evidence to show that the child's best interest is served by a grant of permanent custody to the agency. Clear and convincing evidence does not require absolute certainty—the standard requires only "proof which is more than a mere 'preponderance of the evidence,' but not to the extent of such certainty as is required 'beyond a reasonable doubt' in criminal cases." *Cross v. Ledford*, 161 Ohio St. 469, 53 O.O. 361, 120 N.E.2d 118, paragraph three of the syllabus.

The trial court's judgment entry states that the court considered all the factors listed in R.C. 2151.414 and found that granting permanent custody of D.A. to the agency was in the best interest of the child. There is sufficient evidence to support this finding, independent of a finding regarding the mental capacities of the parents. Had the trial court simply concluded that the evidence of the parents' limited mental capacities was sufficient evidence to support permanent commitment of D.A. to the agency, I would concur in the majority's application of the law to the record in this case. But evidence of the parents' mental capacities was not the sole basis of the trial court judgment. Surely, if the parents were of average intelligence and had engaged in this same conduct and the expert's opinion regarding future parental conduct was the same, the majority would conclude that the trial court was correct in holding that it was in D.A.'s best interest to be removed from his parents.

The court of appeals correctly stated that it could not overturn the trial court's findings "if the record contains competent, credible evidence by which the court could have formed a firm belief or conviction that the essential statutory elements for a termination of parental rights have been established." *In re Adkins*, 5th Dist. Nos. 2005AP06-0044 and 2005AP07-0049, 2006-Ohio-431, 2006 WL 242557, ¶ 17, citing *Cross v. Ledford*, 161 Ohio St. 469, 53 O.O 361, 120 N.E.2d 118, paragraph three of the syllabus.

Because I conclude that the court of appeals correctly applied the proper standard of review to the trial court judgment, I respectfully dissent.

NOTES AND QUESTIONS

1. Why did the trial court terminate parental rights? According to the Ohio Supreme Court, is this a basis for termination? Why not?

2. Why does Chief Justice Moyer concur and dissent? What is the basis for his disagreement with the majority's position?

3. Should intellectual disability be a basis for termination of parental rights? Will the parents in this case be able to meet their son's emotional needs? His educational needs? What if the parents had normal IQs but their son had an IQ that placed him in the top 3 percent of the population?

4. Most state statutes specifically recognize intellectual disability (mental retardation) as a ground for termination. See, e.g., Ariz. Rev. Stat. Ann. § 8-533(B)(3) (2011); Colo. Rev. Stat. § 19-3-604(1)(b)(I) (2008); Del. Code Ann. tit 13, §§ 1101(9), 1103(a)(3) (1999); Haw. Rev. Stat. Ann. § 571-61(b)(1)(F) (2011); 750 Ill. Comp. Stat. Ann. 50/1-1(D)(p) (2012); Ky. Rev. Stat. Ann. § 625.090(3)(a) (West 2012); N.Y. Soc. Serv. Law § 384-b(4)(c) (McKinney 2003); Ohio Rev. Code § 2151.414(E)(2) (2010).

Nevertheless, some courts, like the Ohio Supreme Court, have held that intellectual disability alone is not enough to justify termination of parental rights. See, e.g., *State ex rel. J.P.A.*, 928 So. 2d 736 (La. Ct. App. 2006).

5. Is there scientific support for the idea that intellectually disabled persons are unfit parents? Consider the following excerpt.

IASSID Special Interest Research Group on Parents and Parenting with Intellectual Disabilities, *Parents Labelled with Intellectual Disability: Position of the IASSID SIRG on Parents and Parenting with Intellectual Disabilities*, 21 J. Applied Res. in Intellectual Disabilities 296, 298–301 (2008).

Capacity of parents labelled with intellectual disability to raise their children

With respect to parenting capacity, above an IQ of 60 parental intelligence (IQ) is not systematically correlated with parenting capacity or child outcomes. Researchers have employed a variety of research designs and methods to assess adequacy of parental care. Early research employed review of welfare records and professional (third-party) observation and opinion. Subsequent research used more systematic methods including standardized measures and behavioral checklists. This body of research demonstrates that few generalizations can be made about the parenting abilities of parents labelled with intellectual disability. Professionals must therefore regard each parent as an individual rather than as a member of a category.

There is little robust data to explain why some parents labelled with intellectual disability "succeed" while others struggle. That said several factors are thought to offer some parents a general advantage. One factor is informal and formal social support, although how parents think about the support they receive is critical to support being helpful. [Researchers have] observed that support which is competence-promoting helps parents to learn and achieve by themselves. Support, however, can also be competence-inhibiting when others criticize or "do-for" the parents, thus undermining the parent's confidence and denying them opportunities to learn. Another factor is the absence of co-morbidity, including mental illness and physical disability. Other factors believed to contribute to a general advantage profile include no personal history of maltreatment or childhood trauma, positive parenting role model/s, a supportive and healthy partner, an intelligence quotient above 60, fewer children, and children without special needs.

The frequently seen focus on individual parent knowledge and skills as the determinant of parenting capacity, has been called into question by social-ecological theories of child development which promotes parenting as a social rather than a solo activity. These theories, in contrast to assuming that only parents affect child outcomes, propose that many people and circumstances influence children's life chances. This social-ecological conceptualization regards parenting as the work of many to meet the needs of a child for preservation (physical care needs), nurturance (emotional and intellectual needs) and socialization (learning to "fit-in" to society). From this perspective, parenting capacity is a quality of the child's environment or social milieu rather than a quality possessed by any one individual (i.e. a mother or father). A social-ecological assessment of parenting capacity considers the complex interplay between children and their parents, home and community environments, and family and human service systems.

Outcomes for children of parents labelled with intellectual disability

There are two distinct periods of research into outcomes for children of parents labelled with intellectual disability. Pre-1980s research discredited the earlier eugenic fear that if people labelled with intellectual disability were allowed to "breed," they would infect the human gene pool by reproducing "imbeciles" in untold numbers. Research findings demonstrated that people labelled with intellectual disability typically do not produce a higher than average number of children and that, on average, their children have significantly higher IQs and most have IQs above 70 (and within one standard deviation of the mean). [One researcher] assessed the intellectual status of 108 children of 73 "certified mental defectives" mothers (mean IQ 73.5) who were former patients at the Fountain Hospital in London, UK. Various measures of intelligence were employed and four statistical methods were used to synthesize the results. These four methods produced mean IQ scores ranging from 91.2 to 94.5. Only 3.7 percent of the children were identified as "mentally defective." In another early study, Ainsworth et al. (1945) followed up 50 women (mean IQ 68.2) who were former residents of the Wayne County Training School in Detroit, USA. These 50 women had 115 living children between them, aged 7 years and 4 months on average. This study assessed the general behaviour and social maturation of the children. The general behaviour of 94 percent of these children was rated as "fair" or "no problem" on the basis of their mothers' descriptions. In addition, the children were assessed using an abbreviated version of the Vineland Social Maturity Scale. On this measure, 89 percent of the children were graded as developing in accord with or above age expectations.

From the 1980s onwards, researchers have expanded the range of child outcomes examined. A major limitation is that most of the studies are conducted with mothers who attend clinics, which introduces a clinical population bias to the findings. That said, the research as a whole suggests that children of parents labelled with intellectual disability, as a group, are at risk for poor development outcomes. In the USA, for example, Keltner et al. (1999) examined the developmental status of 70 two-year old children, 38 born to low-income mothers with intellectual "limitations" (IQ < 75) and 32 born to low-income mothers without such limitations matched for age, race and the number of viable pregnancies. Using the Bayley Scales for Infant Development, 42 percent of the children of parents with intellectual limitations and 12 percent of children in the comparison group were assessed as developmentally delayed. In Canada, [two researchers] looked at outcomes for children 6–12 years of age. Twenty-seven children of mothers with "mental retardation" (IQ < 70) were compared with 25 children of mothers without mental retardation, recruited from the same low-income neighbourhoods, on measures of intelligence, academic achievement and child behaviour. Although the outcomes for the children of mothers with mental retardation were diverse with many exhibiting no problems, on average, their performance on measures of IQ, reading, spelling and math was poorer than the comparison group, and more behaviour problems were observed.

Qualitative methods have been used to investigate life experiences and outcomes for children of parents labelled with intellectual disability. In Denmark, [one researcher] interviewed 20 young adult-children of mothers with intellectual disability. Overall, these young people recounted stressful childhoods. They recalled at times being bullied, ostracized and rejected by other children, attributed in part to the stigma of having a mother with disability. Despite the difficult circumstances of their growing-up, most of the young people discovered an underlying personal strength that enabled them to overcome this experience, and all but one maintained a close and warm relationship with their parents. In England, [two researchers] also interviewed adult-children of parents with "learning difficulties." The majority recalled happy, if not necessarily carefree, childhoods. Only three regarded their childhoods as wholly unhappy. Significantly, most (24 of 30) of the interviewees expressed positive feelings of love and affection towards their parents with learning difficulties. All of the adult-children maintained close contact with their parents and most said that they were particularly close to their mothers. Those who had been removed by child welfare authorities had subsequently re-established and maintained contact with their surviving parents. In both studies, family bonds endured despite time and circumstance intervening. This led English researchers to observe, "(t)he general conclusion seems to be the obvious one: people love their parents despite and not because of who they are."

Research is only just beginning into the factors that predict child outcomes and in particular to determine which children fare better and under what circumstances. For example, [some] have reported an association between maternal social support and child outcomes. [Others] found an association between social support and maternal stress, and in turn, [still others] report significant correlations between maternal stress, parenting style and child behaviour problems. Another small sample study has drawn attention to the potential influence of pregnancy and birth outcomes. [Researchers] investigated the developmental status of 37 pre-school aged children of mothers with intellectual disability. Between one-third and one-half of these children demonstrated delay of at least 3 months in one or more developmental domains. The relationships between developmental status and selected child, maternal and home/environment characteristics were examined. Only pregnancy and birth outcomes explained the observed variation.

Child welfare intervention and family outcomes

Parents with intellectual disability are more likely than any other group of parents to have their children removed by child welfare authorities and permanently placed away from their home. In the United States, analysis of the 1994/5 National Health Interview Survey data identified 430,257 adults with mental retardation and/or developmental disabilities (MR/DD) who had a living child (28 percent of all adults with MR/DD in non-institutional settings) (Larson et al. 2001). Of these, 219,357 (51 percent) had a child who lived with them. Although child separation is only one possible reason why 49 percent of the identified parents with MR/DD were not living with their child/ren, this figure is consistent with earlier reports from the United States... in St. Louis, and the New York State Commission on Quality of Care for the Mentally Disabled (1993) on the proportion of children removed from parents labeled with intellectual disability/mental retardation. In England, the first national survey of adults with "learning difficulties" found that 48 percent of parents with cognitive limitations interviewed were not living with their children. Again, others factors, such as children growing up and leaving home may contribute to this figure, but a similar figure was earlier reported by [another researcher] who found that 48 percent of children of parents with cognitive limitations in his Nottinghamshire study had been adopted, fostered or placed with kin. Studies in other European countries, including Denmark, Sweden, Norway, Germany and Belgium, report figures ranging from 30 percent to 45 percent of children permanently placed away from their family home. In Australia and New Zealand respectively, [researchers] report similar figures of 30 percent and 45 percent.

A substantial proportion of all matters in children's welfare courts appear to feature parents labelled with intellectual disability. In the USA, [one study] examined 206 consecutive cases before the Boston Juvenile Court. In approximately 15 percent of cases, one or both parents were identified as parents with intellectual impairment (IQ < 79). [Researchers also] reviewed 407 consecutive Children's Court cases in Sydney, Australia, and found that parents labelled with intellectual disability featured in 9 percent of cases initiated by the child welfare authority. And in England, [one study] reviewed 437 cases involving public law applications by local authorities under the Children Act 1989, and found that parents labelled with intellectual disability featured in 22.1 percent of these cases. All three studies found that children of parents labelled with intellectual disability were more likely than any other group, including children of parents with mental illness and/or drug and alcohol issues, to be permanently placed away from their family home.

When a child's welfare is at stake, child separation is a necessary last resort. However, there is evidence that the separation of children from parents labelled with intellectual disability is often based on two prejudicial and empirically invalid assumptions. These have been documented by legal scholars and disability researchers in several countries including Australia, the United States, England and Iceland. In the first assumption, parental intellectual disability PER SE is mistakenly taken for prima facie evidence of parental incapacity or risk of harm to the child. In some instances, this is sanctioned or "legitimized" by state statute. [A] recent audit of USA state statutes... found that 32 US states still include parental intellectual or developmental disability (mental deficiency is the most frequently used synonym) in their grounds for the termination of parental rights. In other countries, states and jurisdictions, this false assumption is legitimized by the routine use of IQ assessment as a proxy measure of parenting capacity. In New South Wales, Australia, for instance, [researchers] found that standardized measures of IQ were the most common assessment tools used by court appointed "experts" in their assessment of parenting capacity. The assumption of incapacity leads to two likely outcomes. One is when the risk of harm is imputed despite there being no evidence of parental deficiencies. The other is when any perceived parenting deficiencies are automatically attributed to the parent's intellectual disability without due consideration of other relevant factors, such as poverty, ill-health and/or limited social supports.

The second assumption is of irremediable deficiency in the parent such that any parental incapacity cannot be overcome or corrected. This occurs when any parenting deficiencies are thought to be part of an irreversible "condition" of intellectual disability. This leads to the assumption that no matter what interventions are undertaken it is unlikely that parents are able to change. In this situation, the state authority "naturally" holds little hope of improving the child's situation, resulting in the permanent placement of the child away from their family home. Both the assumption of parental intellectual disability as indisputable evidence of risk of harm to a child and the assumption of parenting deficiencies being irreversible are incorrect and invalid.

NOTES AND QUESTIONS

1. The International Association for the Scientific Study of Intellectual Disabilities (IASSID) Special Interest Research Group on Parents and Parenting met in the Netherlands in 2006 and developed the position paper excerpted above. Noting that research supports the proposition that parents with intellectual disabilities are able to raise children, the group adopted twelve recommendations aimed at "achieving greater equity and more opportunities" for intellectually disabled parents and their children. These include a recommendation to revise child-welfare statutes that "equate parental intellectual disability with parental unfitness or risk of harm to children," the elimination of IQ as a proxy for parental capacity, the provision of services tailored to meet the needs of the intellectually disabled parent and his or her children, and additional research on intellectually disabled parents in poorer countries. *Id.* at 303–304. Do you think these recommendations are warranted in light of the research? Is the court's decision in *D.A.* consistent with the findings and recommendations of the IASSID Special Interest Research Group?

2. On December 13, 2006, the United Nations adopted the Convention on the Rights of Persons with Disabilities, A/RES/61/106. The Convention has been ratified by 103 countries, including, among others, Australia, Colombia, China, Egypt, Germany, Rwanda, and the United Kingdom. The United States is a signatory but has not yet ratified the Convention. An optional protocol authorizes the Committee on the Rights of Persons with Disabilities to consider complaints from individuals about states parties to the protocol. Ninety countries have signed, and sixty-two have ratified the protocol. Article 23 of the Convention states that the "child shall not be separated from his or her parents against their will, except when competent authorities subject to judicial review determine, in accordance with applicable law and procedures, that such separation is necessary for the best interests of the child. In no case shall a child be separated from parents on the basis of a disability of either the child or one or both of the parents." Do you think the United States is in compliance with Article 23 of the Convention?

4. DISPOSITIONAL FRAMEWORK

42 U.S.C. § 675 (5)(C) (2011)

(C) with respect to each such child, (i) procedural safeguards will be applied, among other things, to assure each child in foster care under the supervision of the State of a permanency hearing to be held, in a family or juvenile court or another court (including a tribal court) of competent jurisdiction, or by an administrative body appointed or approved by the court, no later than 12 months after the date the child is considered to have entered foster care (as determined under subparagraph (F)) (and not less frequently than every 12 months thereafter during the continuation of foster care), which hearing shall determine the permanency plan for the child that includes whether, and if applicable when, the child will be returned to the parent, placed for adoption and the State will file a petition for termination of parental rights, or referred for legal guardianship, or (in cases where the State agency has documented to the State court a compelling reason for determining that it would not be in the best interests of the child to return home, be referred for termination of parental rights, or be placed for adoption, with a fit and willing relative, or with a legal guardian) placed in another planned permanent living arrangement.

a. ADOPTION

The involuntary termination of parental rights is one of the ways in which children might be freed for adoption. The Adoption and Safe Families Act (ASFA) gives preference to adoptions by creating exceptions to the reasonable-efforts requirements and expediting the termination of parental rights. ASFA provides states with "technical assistance" in the form of grants or contracts to help states "reach their targets for increased numbers of adoptions"; such assistance includes the development of best-practices guidelines for expediting the termination of parental rights, concurrent planning, "fast-tracking" children younger than one into preadoptive placements, and the placement of children in preadoptive homes without waiting for the termination of parental rights. 42 U.S.C. § 673b(i) (2011). States also receive incentive payments equaling four thousand dollars multiplied by the amount by which the number of foster-child adoptions and/or special-needs adoptions exceeds the base number of foster-child adoptions and eight thousand dollars multiplied by the amount by which the number of older-child adoptions in the state during the fiscal year exceeds the base number of older-child adoptions. 42 U.S.C. § 673b(d)(1) (2011). The law broadly defines a special-needs child as a child who the state reasonably concludes cannot be placed with adoptive parents without providing adoption or medical assistance because of the child's "ethnic background, age, or membership in a minority or sibling group, or the presence of factors such as medical conditions or physical, mental, or emotional handicaps." 42 U.S.C. § 673(c)(1)(B) (2011). An "older child" is any child who is at least nine years of age. 42 U.S.C. § 673b(g)(6) (2011).

Pursuant to 42 U.S.C. § 673, the state may enter into an adoption-assistance agreement with the adoptive parents of a special-needs foster child. The agreement may provide for the payment of nonrecurring adoption expenses, including attorney fees, court costs, and adoption fees. Additional costs also "include the adoption study, including health and psychological examination, supervision of the placement prior to adoption, transportation and the reasonable costs of lodging and food for the child and/or the adoptive parents when necessary to complete the placement or adoption process." 45 C.F.R. § 1356.41(i) (2011). States may be reimbursed for up to 50 percent of the amount paid to the adoptive parents, not to exceed two thousand dollars per child. 45 C.F.R. § 1356.41(f) (2011). States also may provide adoption subsidies on a recurring basis after the adoption is finalized. Adoption assistance may be paid for with federal or state funds. Although federal funding had been tied to the birth family's eligibility for Aid to Families with Dependent Children (AFDC), the Fostering Connections for Success and Increasing Adoptions Act of 2008 is gradually extending the availability of federal adoption subsidies to all foster children with special needs regardless of the birth family's income. These recurring expenses may include a monthly maintenance payment, Medicaid for eligible children, and other postadoption services. Families who have adopted a special-needs child from foster care also may claim a federal adoption tax credit.

A number of scholars have been critical of ASFA's emphasis on adoption. Some have argued that the rush to permanence attenuates the commitment to family preservation and reunification and is particularly disadvantageous to poor and minority children and their families. Dorothy E. Roberts, *Is There Justice in Children's Rights? The Critique of Federal Family Preservation Policy*, 2 U. PA. J. CONST. L. 112 (1999). Others contend that the federal law is premised on stereotypes about children, their mothers, and the foster-care system, which undervalue the relationships children have with their parents. Naomi R. Cahn, *Children's Interests in a Familial Context: Poverty, Foster Care, and Adoption*, 60 OHIO ST. L.J. 1189 (1999). ASFA, too, with its short timelines to termination, creates "legal orphans" for whom the state is the parent. Stephanie Jill Gendell, *In Search of Permanency: A Reflection on the First 3 Years of the Adoption and Safe Families Act Implementation*, 39 FAM. CT. REV. 25 (2001). For these children, there is no family privacy. Annette Ruth Appel, *Virtual Mothers and the Meaning of Parenthood*, 34 U. MICH. J. L. REFORM 683 (2001). Another critique suggests that ASFA makes poor mothers "fungible" and promotes a policy of privatizing welfare. Barbara Bennett Woodhouse, *Making Poor Mothers Fungible: The Privatization of Foster Care*, in CHILD CARE AND INEQUALITY: RETHINKING CAREWORK FOR CHILDREN AND YOUTH 83 (Francesca Cancian et al. eds., 2002); see also Barbara Bennett Woodhouse, *Ecogenerism: An Environmentalist Approach to Protecting Endangered Children*, 12 VA. J. SOC. POL'Y & L. 409 (2005) (arguing that emphasis on a triangular relationship among parent, state, and child suggests that ASFA's shift toward a preference for adoption keeps child in family structure but substitutes new parents for old ones without placing child at center).

Elizabeth Bartholet, however, appears to embrace ASFA's adoption preference. She has criticized the provision of services to intact families and advocates rules that make adoption an easier and more desirable way to have children. See, e.g., ELIZABETH BARTHOLET, NOBODY'S CHILDREN: ABUSE AND NEGLECT, FOSTER DRIFT, AND THE ADOPTION ALTERNATIVE (1999); ELIZABETH BARTHOLET, FAMILY BONDS: ADOPTION AND THE POLITICS OF PARENTING (1993); Elizabeth Bartholet, *Beyond Biology: The Politics of Adoption and Reproduction*, 2 DUKE J. GENDER L. & POL. 5 (1995). However, she argues that ASFA may not go far enough:

> The Act's emphasis on moving children promptly to adoption if they cannot stay safely at home is subtly undermined by a series of exceptions and loopholes. States are exempted from the requirements to free children for adoption if the state has failed in its duty to provide family

> preservation services, or if the children are in kinship care. The Act's title and opening preamble seem to make adoption a primary goal, but the Act's key operative provisions make permanency primary, equating adoption with other permanency options like guardianship, which from the child's perspective may not be at all equal. While ASFA's emphasis on child safety seems to give the child's interests a new priority, the safety focus means that the bill excludes from specific coverage the overwhelmingly important, and contentious, "neglect" category. Neglect cases in today's child welfare world are generally not, as many assume, dusty house cases or other cases in which middle-class social workers are inappropriately imposing their personal standards on persons from other classes or cultures who are doing a fine job of raising their children. Those cases that make it to the CPS caseload are typically cases of severe, chronic neglect in which children are effectively without functioning parents, or are for other reasons at serious risk. The overwhelming preponderance of the children in foster care have been removed from parents with serious substance abuse problems. Most of these cases get categorized as neglect cases, and most of them are cases in which the children are at serious risk—risk that may include the risk of physical abuse, as well as the risk that they go without adequate food, clothing, housing, supervision, and without the kind of affirmative attention children require. The ASFA's failure to specifically address either neglect or drugs exempts these cases from some of the Act's most important protective provisions. In the negotiations over ASFA's language, some child advocates fought to make child well-being rather than child safety central. When they gave up child well-being they gave up a lot.

BARTHOLET, NOBODY'S CHILDREN, 27. Do you agree? Or does ASFA unduly disadvantage poor children and their families?

Parents also may relinquish parental rights voluntarily and consent to the adoption. Both parents must consent, and the consent must be freely given and without fraud, duress, or undue influence. Nevertheless, because many states require clear and convincing evidence that the consent was obtained improperly, the courts typically do not find fraud, duress, or coercion. See, e.g., *Youngblood v. Jefferson County Div. of Family and Children*, 838 N.E.2d 1164 (Ind. App. 2005) (consent valid where drug-addicted mother voluntarily relinquished parental rights at termination proceeding on understanding that if she consented, she would have open adoption and that if she did not consent, her parental rights would be terminated and she would not have an open adoption). Each state may have additional statutory prerequisites, including a statutorily mandated period during which consent may be revoked, the appointment of a guardian *ad litem* or an attorney for a minor parent, or the consent of the adoptive child if he or she has reached a certain age.

The parent of an Indian child may consent to the voluntary termination of parental rights. The Indian Child Welfare Act, however, provides that the consent must be "in writing and recorded before a judge of a court of competent jurisdiction and accompanied by the presiding judge's certificate that the terms and consequences of the consent were fully explained in detail and were fully understood by the parent or Indian custodian." 25 U.S.C. § 1913(a) (2011). No consent is valid if given within ten days of the Indian child's birth. Moreover, when the parent of an Indian child has consented to the voluntary termination or adoption, the parent may withdraw consent at any time and for any reason prior to the final decree of termination or adoption. Once consent is withdrawn, the child must be returned to the parents. 25 U.S.C. § 1913(c).

Under what circumstances may the adoption proceed without the consent of *both* biological parents? Consider the following case.

LEHR V. ROBERTSON
Supreme Court of the United States
463 U.S. 248 (1983)

JUSTICE STEVENS delivered the opinion of the Court..

The question presented is whether New York has sufficiently protected an unmarried father's inchoate relationship with a child whom he has never supported and rarely seen in the two years since her birth. The appellant, Jonathan Lehr, claims that the Due Process and Equal Protection Clauses of the Fourteenth Amendment, as interpreted in *Stanley v. Illinois*, 405 U.S. 645 (1972), and *Caban v. Mohammed*, 441 U.S. 380 (1979), give him an absolute right to notice and an opportunity to be heard before the child may be adopted. We disagree.

Jessica M. was born out of wedlock on November 9, 1976. Her mother, Lorraine Robertson, married Richard Robertson eight months after Jessica's birth.[1] On December 21, 1978, when Jessica was over two years old, the Robertsons filed an adoption petition in the Family Court of Ulster County, New York. The court heard their testimony and received a favorable report from the Ulster County Department of Social Services. On March 7, 1979, the court entered an order of adoption.[2] In this proceeding, appellant contends that the adoption order is invalid because he, Jessica's putative father, was not given advance notice of the adoption proceeding.[3]

The State of New York maintains a "putative father registry."[4] A man who files with that registry demonstrates his intent to claim paternity of a child born out of wedlock and is therefore entitled to receive notice of any proceeding to adopt that child. Before entering Jessica's

1. Although both Lorraine and Richard Robertson are appellees in this proceeding, for ease of discussion the term "appellee" will hereafter be used to identify Lorraine Robertson.

2. The order provided for the adoption of appellee's older daughter, Renee, as well as Jessica. Appellant does not challenge the adoption of Renee.

3. Appellee has never conceded that appellant is Jessica's biological father, but for purposes of analysis in this opinion it will be assumed that he is.

4. At the time Jessica's adoption order was entered, § 372-c of the New York Social Services Law provided:

"1. The department shall establish a putative father registry which shall record the names and addresses of...any person who has filed with the registry before or after the birth of a child out of wedlock, a notice of intent to claim paternity of the child....

"2. A person filing a notice of intent to claim paternity of a child shall include therein his current address and shall notify the registry of any change of address pursuant to procedures prescribed by regulations of the department.

"3. A person who has filed a notice of intent to claim paternity may at any time revoke a notice of intent to claim paternity previously filed therewith and, upon receipt of such notification by the registry, the revoked notice of intent to claim paternity shall be deemed a nullity *nunc pro tunc*.

"4. An unrevoked notice of intent to claim paternity of a child may be introduced in evidence by any party, other than the person who filed such notice, in any proceeding in which such fact may be relevant.

"5. The department shall, upon request, provide the names and addresses of persons listed with the registry to any court or authorized agency, and such information shall not be divulged to any other person, except upon order of a court for good cause shown."

adoption order, the Ulster County Family Court had the putative father registry examined. Although appellant claims to be Jessica's natural father, he had not entered his name in the registry.

In addition to the persons whose names are listed on the putative father registry, New York law requires that notice of an adoption proceeding be given to several other classes of possible fathers of children born out of wedlock—those who have been adjudicated to be the father, those who have been identified as the father on the child's birth certificate, those who live openly with the child and the child's mother and who hold themselves out to be the father, those who have been identified as the father by the mother in a sworn written statement, and those who were married to the child's mother before the child was six months old.[5] Appellant admittedly was not a member of any of those classes. He had lived with appellee prior to Jessica's birth and visited her in the hospital when Jessica was born, but his name does not appear on Jessica's birth certificate. He did not live with appellee or Jessica after Jessica's birth, he has never provided them with any financial support, and he has never offered to marry appellee. Nevertheless, he contends that the following special circumstances gave him a constitutional right to notice and a hearing before Jessica was adopted.

On January 30, 1979, one month after the adoption proceeding was commenced in Ulster County, appellant filed a "visitation and paternity petition" in the Westchester County Family Court. In that petition, he asked for a determination of paternity, an order of support, and reasonable visitation privileges with Jessica. Notice of that proceeding was served on appellee on February 22, 1979. Four days later appellee's attorney informed the Ulster County Court that appellant had commenced a paternity proceeding in Westchester County; the Ulster County judge then entered an order staying appellant's paternity proceeding until he could rule on a motion to change the venue of that proceeding to Ulster County. On March 3, 1979, appellant received notice of the change of venue motion and, for the first time, learned that an adoption proceeding was pending in Ulster County.

On March 7, 1979, appellant's attorney telephoned the Ulster County judge to inform him that he planned to seek a stay of the adoption proceeding pending the determination of the paternity petition. In that telephone conversation, the judge advised the lawyer that he had

5. At the time Jessica's adoption order was entered, subdivisions 2–4 of § 111-a of the New York Domestic Relations Law provided:

"2. Persons entitled to notice, pursuant to subdivision one of this section, shall include:

"(a) any person adjudicated by a court in this state to be the father of the child;

"(b) any person adjudicated by a court of another state or territory of the United States to be the father of the child, when a certified copy of the court order has been filed with the putative father registry, pursuant to section three hundred seventy-two of the social services law;

"(c) any person who has timely filed an unrevoked notice of intent to claim paternity of the child, pursuant to section three hundred seventy-two of the social services law;

"(d) any person who is recorded on the child's birth certificate as the child's father;

"(e) any person who is openly living with the child and the child's mother at the time the proceeding is initiated and who is holding himself out to be the child's father;

"(f) any person who has been identified as the child's father by the mother in written, sworn statement; and

"(g) any person who was married to the child's mother within six months subsequent to the birth of the child and prior to the execution of a surrender instrument or the initiation of a proceeding pursuant to section three hundred eighty-four-b of the social services law.

"3. The sole purpose of notice under this section shall be to enable the person served pursuant to subdivision two to present evidence to the court relevant to the best interests of the child."

already signed the adoption order earlier that day. According to appellant's attorney, the judge stated that he was aware of the pending paternity petition but did not believe he was required to give notice to appellant prior to the entry of the order of adoption.

Thereafter, the Family Court in Westchester County granted appellee's motion to dismiss the paternity petition, holding that the putative father's right to seek paternity "...must be deemed severed so long as an order of adoption exists." App. 228. Appellant did not appeal from that dismissal.[6] On June 22, 1979, appellant filed a petition to vacate the order of adoption on the ground that it was obtained by fraud and in violation of his constitutional rights. The Ulster County Family Court received written and oral argument on the question whether it had "dropped the ball" by approving the adoption without giving appellant advance notice. Tr. 53. After deliberating for several months, it denied the petition, explaining its decision in a thorough written opinion. *In re Adoption of Martz*, 102 Misc.2d 102, 423 N.Y.S.2d 378 (1979).

The Appellate Division of the Supreme Court affirmed. *In re Adoption of Jessica "XX,"* 77 App.Div.2d 381, 434 N.Y.S.2d 772 (1980). The majority held that appellant's commencement of a paternity action did not give him any right to receive notice of the adoption proceeding, that the notice provisions of the statute were constitutional, and that *Caban v. Mohammed*, 441 U.S. 380 (1979), was not retroactive.[7] Parenthetically, the majority observed that appellant "could have insured his right to notice by signing the putative father registry." 77 App.Div.2d, at 383, 434 N.Y.S.2d 772. One justice dissented on the ground that the filing of the paternity proceeding should have been viewed as the statutory equivalent of filing a notice of intent to claim paternity with the putative father registry.

The New York Court of Appeals also affirmed by a divided vote. *In re Adoption of Jessica "XX,"* 54 N.Y.2d 417, 446 N.Y.S.2d 20, 430 N.E.2d 896 (1981). The majority first held that it did not need to consider whether our decision in *Caban* affected appellant's claim that he had a right to notice, because *Caban* was not retroactive.[8] It then rejected the argument that the mother had been guilty of a fraud upon the court. Finally, it addressed what it described as the only contention of substance advanced by appellant: that it was an abuse of discretion to enter the adoption order without requiring that notice be given to appellant. The court observed that the primary purpose of the notice provision of § 111-a was to enable the person served to provide the court with evidence concerning the best interest of the child, and that appellant had made no tender indicating any ability to provide any particular or special information relevant to Jessica's best interest. Considering the record as a whole, and acknowledging that it might have been prudent to give notice, the court concluded that the family court had not abused its discretion either when it entered the order without notice or when it denied appellant's petition to reopen the proceedings. The dissenting judges concluded that the fam-

6. Without trying to intervene in the adoption proceeding, appellant had attempted to file an appeal from the adoption order. That appeal was dismissed.

7. *Caban* was decided on April 24, 1979, about two months after the entry of the order of adoption. In *Caban*, a father who had lived with his two illegitimate children and their mother for several years successfully challenged the constitutionality of the New York statute providing that children could be adopted without the father's consent even though the mother's consent was required.

8. Although the dissenters in *Caban* discussed the question of retroactivity, see 441 U.S., at 401, 415–416, that question was not addressed in the Court's opinion.

ily court had abused its discretion, both when it entered the order without notice and when it refused to reopen the proceedings.

Appellant has now invoked our appellate jurisdiction.[9] He offers two alternative grounds for holding the New York statutory scheme unconstitutional. First, he contends that a putative father's actual or potential relationship with a child born out of wedlock is an interest in liberty which may not be destroyed without due process of law; he argues therefore that he had a constitutional right to prior notice and an opportunity to be heard before he was deprived of that interest. Second, he contends that the gender-based classification in the statute, which both denied him the right to consent to Jessica's adoption and accorded him fewer procedural rights than her mother, violated the Equal Protection Clause.[10]

The Due Process Claim

The Fourteenth Amendment provides that no State shall deprive any person of life, liberty, or property without due process of law. When that Clause is invoked in a novel context, it is our practice to begin the inquiry with a determination of the precise nature of the private interest that is threatened by the State. See, e.g., *Cafeteria Workers v. McElroy*, 367 U.S. 886, 895–896 (1961). Only after that interest has been identified, can we properly evaluate the adequacy of the State's process. See *Morrissey v. Brewer*, 408 U.S. 471, 482–483 (1972). We therefore first consider the nature of the interest in liberty for which appellant claims constitutional protection and then turn to a discussion of the adequacy of the procedure that New York has provided for its protection.

I

The intangible fibers that connect parent and child have infinite variety. They are woven throughout the fabric of our society, providing it with strength, beauty, and flexibility. It is self-evident that they are sufficiently vital to merit constitutional protection in appropriate cases. In deciding whether this is such a case, however, we must consider the broad framework that has traditionally been used to resolve the legal problems arising from the parent-child relationship.

In the vast majority of cases, state law determines the final outcome. Cf. *United States v. Yazell*, 382 U.S. 341, 351–353 (1966). Rules governing the inheritance of property, adoption,

9. We postponed consideration of our jurisdiction until after hearing argument on the merits. 456 U.S. 970 (1982). Our review of the record persuades us that appellant did in fact draw into question the validity of the New York statutory scheme on the ground of its being repugnant to the Federal Constitution, that the New York Court of Appeals upheld that scheme, and that we therefore have jurisdiction pursuant to 28 U.S.C. § 1257(2).

10. The question whether the Family Court abused its discretion in not requiring notice to appellant before the adoption order was entered and in not reopening the proceeding is, of course, not before us. That issue was presented to and decided by the New York courts purely as a matter of state law. Whether we might have given such notice had we been sitting at the trial court, or whether we might have considered the failure to give such notice an abuse of discretion had we been sitting as state appellate judges, are questions on which we are not authorized to express an opinion. The only questions we have jurisdiction to decide are whether the New York statutes are unconstitutional because they inadequately protect the natural relationship between parent and child or because they draw an impermissible distinction between the rights of the mother and the rights of the father.

and child custody are generally specified in statutory enactments that vary from State to State.[11] Moreover, equally varied state laws governing marriage and divorce affect a multitude of parent-child relationships. The institution of marriage has played a critical role both in defining the legal entitlements of family members and in developing the decentralized structure of our democratic society.[12] In recognition of that role, and as part of their general overarching concern for serving the best interests of children, state laws almost universally express an appropriate preference for the formal family.[13]

In some cases, however, this Court has held that the Federal Constitution supersedes state law and provides even greater protection for certain formal family relationships. In those cases, as in the state cases, the Court has emphasized the paramount interest in the welfare of children and has noted that the rights of the parents are a counterpart of the responsibilities they have assumed. Thus, the "liberty" of parents to control the education of their children that was vindicated in *Meyer v. Nebraska*, 262 U.S. 390 (1923), and *Pierce v. Society of Sisters*, 268 U.S. 510 (1925), was described as a "right, coupled with the high duty, to recognize and prepare [the child] for additional obligations." *Id.*, at 535. The linkage between parental duty and parental right was stressed again in *Prince v. Massachusetts*, 321 U.S. 158, 166 (1944), when the Court declared it a cardinal principle "that the custody, care and nurture of the child reside first in the parents, whose primary function and freedom include preparation for obligations the state can neither supply nor hinder." *Id.*, at 166. In these cases the Court has found that the relationship of love and duty in a recognized family unit is an interest in liberty entitled to constitutional protection. See also *Moore v. City of East Cleveland*, 431 U.S. 494 (1977) (plurality opinion). "[S]tate intervention to terminate [such a] relationship . . . must be accomplished by procedures meeting the requisites of the Due Process Clause." *Santosky v. Kramer*, 455 U.S. 745, 752 (1982).

There are also a few cases in which this Court has considered the extent to which the Constitution affords protection to the relationship between natural parents and children born out of wedlock. In some we have been concerned with the rights of the children, see, *e.g.*, *Trimble v. Gordon*, 430 U.S. 762 (1977); *Jimenez v. Weinberger*, 417 U.S. 628 (1974); *Weber v. Aetna Casualty*, 406 U.S. 164 (1972). In this case, however, it is a parent who claims that the state has improperly deprived him of a protected interest in liberty. This Court has examined the extent to which a natural father's biological relationship with his illegitimate child receives protection under the Due Process Clause in precisely three cases: *Stanley v. Illinois*,

11. At present, state legislatures appear inclined to retain the unique attributes of their respective bodies of family law. For example, as of the end of 1982, only eight states had adopted the Uniform Parentage Act. 9A U.L.A. 171 (1983 Supp.).

12. See Hafen, Marriage, Kinship, and Sexual Privacy, 81 Mich.L.Rev. 463, 479–481 (1983) (hereinafter Hafen).

13. See *Trimble v. Gordon*, 430 U.S. 762, 769 (1977) ("No one disputes the appropriateness of Illinois' concern with the family unit, perhaps the most fundamental social institution of our society"). A plurality of the Court noted the societal value of family bonds in *Moore v. City of East Cleveland*, 431 U.S. 494, 505 (1977) (Opinion of Powell, J.):

> "Out of choice, necessity, or a sense of family responsibility, it has been common for close relatives to draw together and participate in the duties and the satisfactions of a common home. . . . Especially in times of adversity, such as the death of a spouse or economic need, the broader family has tended to come together for mutual sustenance and to maintain or rebuild a secure home life."

405 U.S. 645 (1972), *Quilloin v. Walcott*, 434 U.S. 246 (1978), and *Caban v. Mohammed*, 441 U.S. 380 (1979).

Stanley involved the constitutionality of an Illinois statute that conclusively presumed every father of a child born out of wedlock to be an unfit person to have custody of his children. The father in that case had lived with his children all their lives and had lived with their mother for eighteen years. There was nothing in the record to indicate that Stanley had been a neglectful father who had not cared for his children. 405 U.S., at 655. Under the statute, however, the nature of the actual relationship between parent and child was completely irrelevant. Once the mother died, the children were automatically made wards of the state. Relying in part on a Michigan case[14] recognizing that the preservation of "a subsisting relationship with the child's father" may better serve the child's best interest than "uprooting him from the family which he knew from birth," *id.*, at 654–655, n. 7, the Court held that the Due Process Clause was violated by the automatic destruction of the custodial relationship without giving the father any opportunity to present evidence regarding his fitness as a parent.[15]

Quilloin involved the constitutionality of a Georgia statute that authorized the adoption of a child born out of wedlock over the objection of the natural father. The father in that case had never legitimated the child. It was only after the mother had remarried and her new husband had filed an adoption petition that the natural father sought visitation rights and filed a petition for legitimation. The trial court found adoption by the new husband to be in the child's best interests, and we unanimously held that action to be consistent with the Due Process Clause.

Caban involved the conflicting claims of two natural parents who had maintained joint custody of their children from the time of their birth until they were respectively two and four years old. The father challenged the validity of an order authorizing the mother's new husband to adopt the children; he relied on both the Equal Protection Clause and the Due Process Clause. Because this Court upheld his equal protection claim, the majority did not address his due process challenge. The comments on the latter claim by the four dissenting Justices are nevertheless instructive, because they identify the clear distinction between a mere biological relationship and an actual relationship of parental responsibility.

Justice Stewart correctly observed:

> "Even if it be assumed that each married parent after divorce has some substantive due process right to maintain his or her parental relationship, cf. *Smith v. Organization of Foster Families*, 431 U.S. 816, 862–863 (opinion concurring in judgment), it by no means follows that each unwed parent has any such right. *Parental rights do not spring full-blown from the biological connection between parent and child. They require relationships more enduring.*" 441 U.S., at 397 (emphasis added).[16]

14. *In re Mark T.*, 8 Mich.App. 122, 154 N.W.2d 27 (1967).

15. Having "concluded that all Illinois parents are constitutionally entitled to a hearing on their fitness before their children are removed from their custody," the Court also held "that denying such a hearing to Stanley and those like him while granting it to other Illinois parents is inescapably contrary to the Equal Protection Clause." 405 U.S., at 658.

16. In the balance of that paragraph Justice Stewart noted that the relation between a father and his natural child may acquire constitutional protection if the father enters into a traditional marriage with the mother or if "the actual relationship between father and child" is sufficient.

In a similar vein, the other three dissenters in *Caban* were prepared to "assume that, *if and when one develops*, the relationship between a father and his natural child is entitled to protection against arbitrary state action as a matter of due process." *Caban v. Mohammed*, *supra*, at 414 (emphasis added).

The difference between the developed parent-child relationship that was implicated in *Stanley* and *Caban*, and the potential relationship involved in *Quilloin* and this case, is both clear and significant. When an unwed father demonstrates a full commitment to the responsibilities of parenthood by "com[ing] forward to participate in the rearing of his child," *Caban*, 441 U.S., at 392, his interest in personal contact with his child acquires substantial protection under the due process clause. At that point it may be said that he "act[s] as a father toward his children." *Id.*, at 389, n. 7. But the mere existence of a biological link does not merit equivalent constitutional protection. The actions of judges neither create nor sever genetic bonds. "[T]he importance of the familial relationship, to the individuals involved and to the society, stems from the emotional attachments that derive from the intimacy of daily association, and from the role it plays in 'promot[ing] a way of life' through the instruction of children as well as from the fact of blood relationship." *Smith v. Organization of Foster Families for Equality and Reform*, 431 U.S. 816, 844 (1977) (quoting *Wisconsin v. Yoder*, 406 U.S. 205, 231–233 (1972)).

The significance of the biological connection is that it offers the natural father an opportunity that no other male possesses to develop a relationship with his offspring. If he grasps that opportunity and accepts some measure of responsibility for the child's future, he may enjoy the blessings of the parent-child relationship and make uniquely valuable contributions to the child's development.[18] If he fails to do so, the Federal Constitution will not automatically compel a state to listen to his opinion of where the child's best interests lie.

In this case, we are not assessing the constitutional adequacy of New York's procedures for terminating a developed relationship. Appellant has never had any significant custodial, personal, or financial relationship with Jessica, and he did not seek to establish a legal tie until after she was two years old.[19] We are concerned only with whether New York has adequately protected his opportunity to form such a relationship.

"The mother carries and bears the child, and in this sense her parental relationship is clear. The validity of the father's parental claims must be gauged by other measures. By tradition, the primary measure has been the legitimate familial relationship he creates with the child by marriage with the mother. By definition, the question before us can arise only when no such marriage has taken place. In some circumstances the actual relationship between father and child may suffice to create in the unwed father parental interests comparable to those of the married father. Cf. *Stanley v. Illinois*, *supra*. But here we are concerned with the rights the unwed father may have when his wishes and those of the mother are in conflict, and the child's best interests are served by a resolution in favor of the mother. It seems to me that the absence of a legal tie with the mother may in such circumstances appropriately place a limit on whatever substantive constitutional claims might otherwise exist by virtue of the father's actual relationship with the children." 441 U.S., at 397.

18. Of course, we need not take sides in the ongoing debate among family psychologists over the relative weight to be accorded biological ties and psychological ties, in order to recognize that a natural father who has played a substantial role in rearing his child has a greater claim to constitutional protection than a mere biological parent. New York's statutory scheme reflects these differences, guaranteeing notice to any putative father who is living openly with the child, and providing putative fathers who have never developed a relationship with the child the opportunity to receive notice simply by mailing a postcard to the putative father registry.

19. This case happens to involve an adoption by the husband of the natural mother, but we do not believe the natural father has any greater right to object to such an adoption than to an adoption by two total strangers.

II

The most effective protection of the putative father's opportunity to develop a relationship with his child is provided by the laws that authorize formal marriage and govern its consequences. But the availability of that protection is, of course, dependent on the will of both parents of the child. Thus, New York has adopted a special statutory scheme to protect the unmarried father's interest in assuming a responsible role in the future of his child.

After this Court's decision in *Stanley*, the New York Legislature appointed a special commission to recommend legislation that would accommodate both the interests of biological fathers in their children and the children's interest in prompt and certain adoption procedures. The commission recommended, and the legislature enacted, a statutory adoption scheme that automatically provides notice to seven categories of putative fathers who are likely to have assumed some responsibility for the care of their natural children.[20] If this scheme were likely to omit many responsible fathers, and if qualification for notice were beyond the control of an interested putative father, it might be thought procedurally inadequate. Yet, as all of the New York courts that reviewed this matter observed, the right to receive notice was completely within appellant's control. By mailing a postcard to the putative father registry, he could have guaranteed that he would receive notice of any proceedings to adopt Jessica. The possibility that he may have failed to do so because of his ignorance of the law cannot be a sufficient reason for criticizing the law itself. The New York legislature concluded that a more open-ended notice requirement would merely complicate the adoption process, threaten the privacy interests of unwed mothers, create the risk of unnecessary controversy, and impair the desired finality of adoption decrees. Regardless of whether we would have done likewise if

If anything, the balance of equities tips the opposite way in a case such as this. In denying the putative father relief in *Quilloin*, we made an observation equally applicable here:

"Nor is this a case in which the proposed adoption would place the child with a new set of parents with whom the child had never before lived. Rather, the result of the adoption in this case is to give full recognition to a family unit already in existence, a result desired by all concerned, except appellant. Whatever might be required in other situations, we cannot say that the State was required in this situation to find anything more than that the adoption, and denial of legitimation, were in the 'best interests of the child.'" *Id.*, at 255.

20. In a report explaining the purpose of the 1976 Amendments to § 111-a of the New York Domestic Relations Law, the temporary state commission on child welfare that was responsible for drafting the legislation stated, in part:

"The measure will dispel uncertainties by providing clear constitutional statutory guidelines for notice to fathers of out-of-wedlock children. It will establish a desired finality in adoption proceedings and will provide an expeditious method for child placement agencies of identifying those fathers who are entitled to notice through the creation of a registry of such fathers within the State Department of Social Services. Conversely, the bill will afford to concerned fathers of out-of-wedlock children a simple means of expressing their interest and protecting their rights to be notified and have an opportunity to be heard. It will also obviate an existing disparity of Appellate Division decisions by permitting such fathers to be petitioners in paternity proceedings.

"The measure is intended to codify the minimum protections for the putative father which *Stanley* would require. In so doing it reflects policy decisions to (a) codify constitutional requirements; (b) clearly establish, as early as possible in a child's life, the rights, interests and obligations of all parties; (c) facilitate prompt planning for the future of the child and permanence of his status; and (d) through the foregoing, promote the best interest of children." App. to Brief for Appellant C-15.

we were legislators instead of judges, we surely cannot characterize the state's conclusion as arbitrary.[22]

Appellant argues, however, that even if the putative father's opportunity to establish a relationship with an illegitimate child is adequately protected by the New York statutory scheme in the normal case, he was nevertheless entitled to special notice because the court and the mother knew that he had filed an affiliation proceeding in another court. This argument amounts to nothing more than an indirect attack on the notice provisions of the New York statute. The legitimate state interests in facilitating the adoption of young children and having the adoption proceeding completed expeditiously that underlie the entire statutory scheme also justify a trial judge's determination to require all interested parties to adhere precisely to the procedural requirements of the statute. The Constitution does not require either a trial judge or a litigant to give special notice to nonparties who are presumptively capable of asserting and protecting their own rights.[23] Since the New York statutes adequately protected appellant's inchoate interest in establishing a relationship with Jessica, we find no merit in the claim that his constitutional rights were offended because the family court strictly complied with the notice provisions of the statute.

The Equal Protection Claim

The concept of equal justice under law requires the State to govern impartially. *New York Transit Authority v. Beazer*, 440 U.S. 568, 587 (1979). The sovereign may not draw distinctions between individuals based solely on differences that are irrelevant to a legitimate governmental objective. *Reed v. Reed*, 404 U.S. 71, 76 (1971).[24] Specifically, it may not subject men and women to disparate treatment when there is no substantial relation between the disparity and an important state purpose. *Ibid*; *Craig v. Boren*, 429 U.S. 190, 197–199 (1976).

22. Nor can we deem unconstitutionally arbitrary the state courts' conclusion that appellant's absence did not distort its analysis of Jessica's best interests. The adoption does not affect Jessica's relationship with her mother. It gives legal permanence to her relationship with her adoptive father, a relationship they had maintained for 21 months at the time the adoption order was entered. Appellant did not proffer any evidence to suggest that legal confirmation of the established relationship would be unwise; he did not even know the adoptive father.

23. It is a generally accepted feature of our adversary system that a potential defendant who knows that the statute of limitations is about to run has no duty to give the plaintiff advice. There is no suggestion in the record that appellee engaged in fraudulent practices that led appellant not to protect his rights.

24. In *Reed*, the Court considered an Idaho statute providing that in designating administrators of the estates of intestate decedents, "[o]f several persons claiming and equally entitled to administer, males must be preferred to females." See 404 U.S., at 73. The state had sought to justify the statute as a way to reduce the workload of probate courts by eliminating one class of contests. Writing for a unanimous Court, The Chief Justice observed that in using gender to promote that objective, the legislature had made "the very kind of arbitrary legislative choice forbidden by the Equal Protection Clause." *Id.*, at 76. The state's articulated goal could have been completely served by requiring a coin flip. The decision instead to choose a rule that systematically harmed women could be explained only as the product of habit, rather than analysis or reflection, cf. *Califano v. Goldfarb*, 430 U.S. 199, 222 (1977) (Stevens, J., concurring in the judgment), or as the product of an invidious and indefensible stereotype, cf. *id.*, at 218. Such legislative decisions are inimical to the norm of impartial government.

The mandate of impartiality also constrains those state actors who implement state laws. Thus, the Equal Protection Clause would have been violated in precisely the same manner if in *Reed* there had been no statute and the probate judge had simply announced that he chose Cecil Reed over Sally Reed "because I prefer males to females."

The legislation at issue in this case, sections 111 and 111a of the New York Domestic Relations Law, is intended to establish procedures for adoptions. Those procedures are designed to promote the best interests of the child, protect the rights of interested third parties, and ensure promptness and finality.[25] To serve those ends, the legislation guarantees to certain people the right to veto an adoption and the right to prior notice of any adoption proceeding. The mother of an illegitimate child is always within that favored class, but only certain putative fathers are included. Appellant contends that the gender-based distinction is invidious.

As we noted above, the existence or nonexistence of a substantial relationship between parent and child is a relevant criterion in evaluating both the rights of the parent and the best interests of the child. In *Quilloin v. Walcott*, we noted that the putative father, like appellant, "ha[d] never shouldered any significant responsibility with respect to the daily supervision, education, protection, or care of the child. Appellant does not complain of his exemption from these responsibilities...." 434 U.S., at 256. We therefore found that a Georgia statute that always required a mother's consent to the adoption of a child born out of wedlock, but required the father's consent only if he had legitimated the child, did not violate the Equal Protection Clause. Because, like the father in *Quilloin*, appellant has never established a substantial relationship with his daughter, see *supra*, at 262, the New York statutes at issue in this case did not operate to deny appellant equal protection.

We have held that these statutes may not constitutionally be applied in that class of cases where the mother and father are in fact similarly situated with regard to their relationship with the child. In *Caban v. Mohammed*, 441 U.S. 380 (1979), the Court held that it violated the Equal Protection Clause to grant the mother a veto over the adoption of a four-year-old girl and a six-year-old boy, but not to grant a veto to their father, who had admitted paternity and had participated in the rearing of the children. The Court made it clear, however, that if the father had not "come forward to participate in the rearing of his child, nothing in the Equal Protection Clause [would preclude the] State from withholding from him the privilege of vetoing the adoption of that child." *Id.*, at 392.

Jessica's parents are not like the parents involved in *Caban*. Whereas appellee had a continuous custodial responsibility for Jessica, appellant never established any custodial, personal, or financial relationship with her. If one parent has an established custodial relationship with the child and the other parent has either abandoned[26] or never established a relationship, the Equal Protection Clause does not prevent a state from according the two parents different legal rights.[27]

The judgment of the New York Court of Appeals is
Affirmed.

25. Appellant does not contest the vital importance of those ends to the people of New York. It has long been accepted that illegitimate children whose parents never marry are "at risk" economically, medically, emotionally, and educationally. See E. Crellin, M. Pringle, P. West, Born Illegitimate: Social and Educational Implications 96–112 (1971); cf. T. Lash, H. Sigal, D. Dudzinski, State of the Child: New York City II, at 47 (1980).

26. In *Caban*, the Court noted that an adoption "may proceed in the absence of consent when the parent whose consent otherwise would be required... has abandoned the child." 441 U.S., at 392.

27. Appellant also makes an equal protection argument based upon the manner in which the statute distinguishes among classes of fathers. For the reasons set forth in our due process discussion, *supra*, we conclude that the statutory distinction is rational and that appellant's argument is without merit.

JUSTICE WHITE, with whom JUSTICE MARSHALL and JUSTICE BLACKMUN join, dissenting.

The question in this case is whether the State may, consistent with the Due Process Clause, deny notice and an opportunity to be heard in an adoption proceeding to a putative father when the State has actual notice of his existence, whereabouts, and interest in the child.

I

It is axiomatic that "[t]he fundamental requirement of due process is the opportunity to be heard 'at a meaningful time and in a meaningful manner.'" *Mathews v. Eldridge*, 424 U.S. 319, 333 (1976), quoting *Armstrong v. Manzo*, 380 U.S. 545, 552 (1965). As Jessica's biological father, Lehr either had an interest protected by the Constitution or he did not.[1] If the entry of the adoption order in this case deprived Lehr of a constitutionally protected interest, he is entitled to notice and an opportunity to be heard before the order can be accorded finality.

According to Lehr, he and Jessica's mother met in 1971 and began living together in 1974. The couple cohabited for approximately 2 years, until Jessica's birth in 1976. Throughout the pregnancy and after the birth, Lorraine acknowledged to friends and relatives that Lehr was Jessica's father; Lorraine told Lehr that she had reported to the New York State Department of Social Services that he was the father.[2] Lehr visited Lorraine and Jessica in the hospital every day during Lorraine's confinement. According to Lehr, from the time Lorraine was discharged from the hospital until August, 1978, she concealed her whereabouts from him. During this time Lehr never ceased his efforts to locate Lorraine and Jessica and achieved sporadic success until August, 1977, after which time he was unable to locate them at all. On those occasions when he did determine Lorraine's location, he visited with her and her children to the extent she was willing to permit it. When Lehr, with the aid of a detective agency, located Lorraine and Jessica in August, 1978, Lorraine was already married to Mr. Robertson. Lehr asserts that at this time he offered to provide financial assistance and to set up a trust fund for Jessica, but that Lorraine refused. Lorraine threatened Lehr with arrest unless he stayed away and refused to permit him to see Jessica. Thereafter Lehr retained counsel who wrote to Lorraine in early December, 1978, requesting that she permit Lehr to visit Jessica and threatening legal action on Lehr's behalf. On December 21, 1978, perhaps as a response to Lehr's threatened legal action, appellees commenced the adoption action at issue here.

The majority posits that "[t]he intangible fibers that connect parent and child... are sufficiently vital to merit constitutional protection *in appropriate cases*." ([E]mphasis added.) It then purports to analyze the particular facts of this case to determine whether appellant has a constitutionally protected liberty interest. We have expressly rejected that approach. In *Board of Regents v. Roth*, 408 U.S. 564, 570–571 (1972), we stated that although "a weighing process has long been a part of any determination of the *form* of hearing required in particular situations,... to determine whether due process requirements apply in the first place, we must look

1. The majority correctly assumes that Lehr is in fact Jessica's father. Indeed, Lehr has admitted paternity and sought to establish a legal relationship with the child. It is also noteworthy that the mother has never denied that Lehr is the father.

2. Under 18 NYCRR § 369.2(b), recipients of public assistance in the Aid to Families with Dependent Children program are required as a condition of eligibility to provide the name and address of the child's father. Lorraine apparently received public assistance after Jessica's birth; it is unclear whether she received public assistance after that regulation went into effect in 1977.

not to the 'weight' but to the *nature* of the interest at stake... to see if the interest is within the Fourteenth Amendment's protection...." See, *e.g.*, *Smith v. Organization of Foster Families*, 431 U.S. 816, 839–842 (1977); *Ingraham v. Wright*, 430 U.S. 651, 672 (1977); *Meachum v. Fano*, 427 U.S. 215, 224 (1976); *Goss v. Lopez*, 419 U.S. 565, 575–576 (1975); *Morrissey v. Brewer*, 408 U.S. 471, 481 (1972).

The "nature of the interest" at stake here is the interest that a natural parent has in his or her child, one that has long been recognized and accorded constitutional protection. We have frequently "stressed the importance of familial bonds, whether or not legitimized by marriage, and accorded them constitutional protection." *Little v. Streater*, 452 U.S. 1, 13 (1981). If "both the child and the [putative father] in a paternity action have a compelling interest" in the accurate outcome of such a case, *ibid.*, it cannot be disputed that both the child and the putative father have a compelling interest in the outcome of a proceeding that may result in the termination of the father-child relationship. "A parent's interest in the accuracy and justice of the decision to terminate his or her parental status is... a commanding one." *Lassiter v. Department of Social Services*, 452 U.S. 18, 27 (1981). It is beyond dispute that a formal order of adoption, no less than a formal termination proceeding, operates to permanently terminate parental rights.

Lehr's version of the "facts" paints a far different picture than that portrayed by the majority. The majority's recitation, that "[a]ppellant has never had any significant custodial, personal, or financial relationship with Jessica, and he did not seek to establish a legal tie until after she was two years old," obviously does not tell the whole story. Appellant has never been afforded an opportunity to present his case. The legitimation proceeding he instituted was first stayed, and then dismissed, on appellees' motions. Nor could appellant establish his interest during the adoption proceedings, for it is the failure to provide Lehr notice and an opportunity to be heard there that is at issue here. We cannot fairly make a judgment based on the quality or substance of a relationship without a complete and developed factual record. This case requires us to assume that Lehr's allegations are true—that but for the actions of the child's mother there would have been the kind of significant relationship that the majority concedes is entitled to the full panoply of procedural due process protections.[3]

I reject the peculiar notion that the only significance of the biological connection between father and child is that "it offers the natural father an opportunity that no other male possesses to develop a relationship with his offspring." A "mere biological relationship" is not as unimportant in determining the nature of liberty interests as the majority suggests.

"[T]he usual understanding of 'family' implies biological relationships, and most decisions treating the relation between parent and child have stressed this element." *Smith v. Organization of Foster Families*, *supra*, 431 U.S., at 843. The "biological connection" is itself a relationship that creates a protected interest. Thus the "nature" of the interest is the parent-child relationship; how well-developed that relationship has become goes to its "weight," not

3. In response to our decision in *Caban v. Mohammed*, 441 U.S. 380 (1979), the statute governing the persons whose consent is necessary to an adoption has been amended to include certain unwed fathers. The State has recognized that an unwed father's failure to maintain an actual relationship or to communicate with a child will not deprive him of his right to consent if he was "prevented from doing so by the person or authorized agency having lawful custody of the child." N.Y.Dom.Rel.Law § 111(1)(d) (as amended by Chap. 575, L. 1980). Thus, even the State recognizes that before a lesser standard can be applied consistent with due process requirements, there must be a determination that there was no significant relationship and that the father was not prevented from forming such a relationship.

its "nature."[4] Whether Lehr's interest is entitled to constitutional protection does not entail a searching inquiry into the quality of the relationship but a simple determination of the *fact* that the relationship exists—a fact that even the majority agrees must be assumed to be established.

Beyond that, however, because there is no established factual basis on which to proceed, it is quite untenable to conclude that a putative father's interest in his child is lacking in substance, that the father in effect has abandoned the child, or ultimately that the father's interest is not entitled to the same minimum procedural protections as the interests of other putative fathers. Any analysis of the adequacy of the notice in this case must be conducted on the assumption that the interest involved here is as strong as that of *any* putative father. That is not to say that due process requires actual notice to every putative father or that adoptive parents or the State must conduct an exhaustive search of records or an intensive investigation before a final adoption order may be entered. The procedures adopted by the State, however, must at least represent a reasonable effort to determine the identity of the putative father and to give him adequate notice.

II

In this case, of course, there was no question about either the identity or the location of the putative father. The mother knew exactly who he was and both she and the court entering the order of adoption knew precisely where he was and how to give him actual notice that his parental rights were about to be terminated by an adoption order.[5] Lehr was entitled to due process, and the right to be heard is one of the fundamentals of that right, which "has little reality or worth unless one is informed that the matter is pending and can choose for himself whether to appear or default, acquiesce or contest." *Schroeder v. City of New York*, 371 U.S. 208, 212 (1962), quoting *Mullane v. Central Hanover Trust Co.*, 339 U.S. 306, 314 (1950).

The State concedes this much but insists that Lehr has had all the process that is due to him. It relies on § 111-a, which designates seven categories of unwed fathers to whom notice of adoption proceedings must be given, including any unwed father who has filed with the State a notice of his intent to claim paternity. The State submits that it need not give notice to anyone who has not filed his name, as he is permitted to do, and who is not otherwise within the designated categories, even if his identity and interest are known or are reasonably ascertainable by the State.

4. The majority's citation of *Quilloin* and *Caban* as examples that the Constitution does not require the same procedural protections for the interests of all unwed fathers is disingenuous. Neither case involved notice and opportunity to be heard. In both, the unwed fathers were notified and participated as parties in the adoption proceedings. See *Quilloin v. Walcott*, 434 U.S. 246, 253 (1978); *Caban v. Mohammed*, 441 U.S. 380, 385 n. 3 (1979).

5. Absent special circumstances, there is no bar to requiring the mother of an illegitimate child to divulge the name of the father when the proceedings at issue involve the permanent termination of the father's rights. Likewise, there is no reason not to require such identification when it is the spouse of the custodial parent who seeks to adopt the child. Indeed, the State now requires the mother to provide the identity of the father if she applies for financial benefits under the Aid to Families with Dependent Children Program. See n. 2, *supra*. The state's obligation to provide notice to persons before their interests are permanently terminated cannot be a lesser concern than its obligation to assure that state funds are not expended when there exists a person upon whom the financial responsibility should fall.

I am unpersuaded by the State's position. In the first place, § 111-a defines six categories of unwed fathers to whom notice must be given even though they have not placed their names on file pursuant to the section. Those six categories, however, do not include fathers such as Lehr who have initiated filiation proceedings, even though their identity and interest are as clearly and easily ascertainable as those fathers in the six categories. Initiating such proceedings necessarily involves a formal acknowledgment of paternity, and requiring the State to take note of such a case in connection with pending adoption proceedings would be a trifling burden, no more than the State undertakes when there is a final adjudication in a paternity action.[6] Indeed, there would appear to be more reason to give notice to those such as Lehr who acknowledge paternity than to those who have been adjudged to be a father in a contested paternity action.

The State asserts that any problem in this respect is overcome by the seventh category of putative fathers to whom notice must be given, namely those fathers who have identified themselves in the putative father register maintained by the State. Since Lehr did not take advantage of this device to make his interest known, the State contends, he was not entitled to notice and a hearing even though his identity, location and interest were known to the adoption court prior to entry of the adoption order. I have difficulty with this position. First, it represents a grudging and crabbed approach to due process. The State is quite willing to give notice and a hearing to putative fathers who have made themselves known by resorting to the putative fathers' register. It makes little sense to me to deny notice and hearing to a father who has not placed his name in the register but who has unmistakably identified himself by filing suit to establish his paternity and has notified the adoption court of his action and his interest. I thus need not question the statutory scheme on its face. Even assuming that Lehr would have been foreclosed if his failure to utilize the register had somehow disadvantaged the State, he effectively made himself known by other means, and it is the sheerest formalism to deny him a hearing because he informed the State in the wrong manner.[7]

No state interest is substantially served by denying Lehr adequate notice and a hearing. The State no doubt has an interest in expediting adoption proceedings to prevent a child from remaining unduly long in the custody of the State or foster parents. But this is not an adoption involving a child in the custody of an authorized state agency. Here the child is in the custody of the mother and will remain in her custody. Moreover, had Lehr utilized the putative father

6. There is some indication that the sponsor of the bill that included the notice requirements of § 111-a believed that a putative father's rights would be protected by the filing of a paternity action. In a letter to the Counsel to the Governor, Senator Pisani stated that a putative father who files with the registry should be expected to keep his address up-to-date because "such a father has elected not to avail himself of his right... to initiate a paternity proceeding, but rather, has chosen the less involved procedure of filing a 'notice of intent' which will *also* protect his right to notice of subsequent proceedings affecting the child." Brief for Appellee Attorney General at 35a (emphasis added).

7. In *Stanley v. Illinois*, 405 U.S. 645 (1972), the Court held that the Constitution forbids a State from removing illegitimate children from their father's custody without notice and an opportunity to be heard. The offensive provision in the Illinois law at issue there was a presumption that an unwed father was not a fit parent. Today the Court indulges in a similar and equally offensive presumption—that an unwed father who has not filed a notice of intent to claim paternity has abandoned his child and waived any right to notice and hearing. This presumption operates regardless of the fact that the father has instituted legal proceedings to establish his rights and obligations.

register, he would have been granted a prompt hearing, and there was no justifiable reason, in terms of delay, to refuse him a hearing in the circumstances of this case.

The State's undoubted interest in the finality of adoption orders likewise is not well served by a procedure that will deny notice and a hearing to a father whose identity and location are known. As this case well illustrates, denying notice and a hearing to such a father may result in years of additional litigation and threaten the reopening of adoption proceedings and the vacation of the adoption. Here, the Family Court's unseemly rush to enter an adoption order after ordering that cause be shown why the filiation proceeding should not be transferred and consolidated with the adoption proceeding can hardly be justified by the interest in finality. To the contrary, the adoption order entered in March, 1979, has remained open to question until this very day.

Because in my view the failure to provide Lehr with notice and an opportunity to be heard violated rights guaranteed him by the Due Process Clause, I need not address the question whether § 111-a violates the Equal Protection Clause by discriminating between categories of unwed fathers or by discriminating on the basis of gender.

Respectfully, I dissent.

NOTES AND QUESTIONS

1. According to the Court, under what circumstances must a court provide an unwed father with notice and an opportunity to be heard about the prospective adoption of his child? What did Lehr do? Why was that inadequate?

2. The Court states in note 23 that there is "no suggestion in the record that appellee engaged in fraudulent practices that led appellant not to protect his rights." Do you agree? What does the dissent have to say about this?

3. In *Quilloin v. Walcott*, 434 U.S. 246 (1978), the child's biological father was given notice of an adoption petition filed by the husband of the child's biological mother and participated in the hearing. The child stated a desire to be adopted. The biological father opposed the petition, but the lower courts upheld the adoption on the grounds that it was in the child's best interests, despite the occasional child-support payments and visits paid by the biological father. The Supreme Court also upheld the adoption, noting that due process was not violated since no "natural family" was being separated. The Court also rejected the equal-protection claim since the biological father was not similarly situated to a married father who had accepted legal responsibility for raising his children.

In *Caban v. Mohammed*, 441 U.S. 380 (1979), the biological father challenged a state statute that permitted the adoption of a child based solely on the biological mother's consent. The biological parents had lived together for five years and had two children. The biological mother subsequently moved in with another man, whom she married, although the biological father continued to see the children and had custody of them at one point. The biological mother and her husband petitioned to adopt the children, who were four and six at the time of the hearing. The biological father and his wife then cross-petitioned. The trial court granted the biological mother's petition. The Supreme Court held that the distinction between biological mothers and biological fathers violated the Equal Protection Clause where, as here, the father had "established a substantial relationship with the child and has admitted his paternity." *Id.* at 393.

Given these brief overviews, which opinion do you think interpreted the Court's precedent more accurately, the majority or the dissent? Why?

4. At least twenty-four states have putative-father registries, while another eleven states and the District of Columbia provide for the voluntary acknowledgment of paternity through other means, such as the filing of a designated form. In approximately ten of the states with putative-father registries, filing with the registry is the only way for putative fathers to receive notice. Child Welfare Information Gateway, The Rights of Unmarried Fathers 3 (2010), http://www.childwelfare.gov/systemwide/laws_ policies/statutes/putative.pdf. As at least one commentator has noted, putative-father registries are not uniform and may have impose different obligations on the putative father. Laurence Nolan, *Preventing Fatherlessness through Adoption While Protecting the Parental Rights of Unwed Fathers: How Effective Are Paternity Registries?* 4 Whittier J. Child & Fam. Advoc. 289 (2005). Moreover, putative-father registries may not resolve the problems faced by unmarried fathers who may be willing to assume the responsibilities of parenthood but are thwarted by unmarried mothers. What should courts do when the unmarried pregnant woman moves to another state that has no putative-father registry to give birth, lies about the father's identity, tells the father that the baby has died, or does not inform the father of the pregnancy? See, e.g., *O'Dea v. Olea*, 217 P.3d 704 (Utah 2009); *In re Adoption of A.A.T.*, 196 P.3d 1180 (Kan. 2008); *Heidibreder v. Carton*, 645 N.W.2d 355 (Minn. 2002). Would a national putative-father registry solve some of these problems? For an argument that it would, see Mary Beck, *A National Putative Father Registry*, 36 Cap. U. L. Rev. 295 (2007). Would amending federal law to expand the opportunities for paternal designation before, at, and after birth for all children born to unwed parents help unwed fathers? See Jeffrey A. Parness, *New Federal Paternity Laws: Securing More Fathers at Birth for the Children of Unwed Mothers*, 45 Brandeis L.J. 59 (2006).

5. The Indian Child Welfare Act (ICWA) provides that an Indian child shall be placed for adoption (in order of preference and in the absence of good cause to the contrary) with "(1) a member of the child's extended family; (2) other members of the Indian child's tribe; or (3) other Indian families." 25 U.S.C. § 1915(a) (2011). The child's tribe, however, is free to establish a different order of preference, and the court effectuating the placement must follow that order as long as the placement is in the least restrictive setting appropriate for the child. 25 U.S.C. § 1915(c).

6. *The Multiethnic Placement Act.* The Multiethnic Placement Act (MEPA), Pub. L. No. 103-382, 553(a)(1) (amended 1996), was enacted in 1994 to address concerns that African-American and other minority children were languishing in foster care because of racial- and ethnic-matching policies that delayed adoptions and prevented qualified prospective parents from adopting. MEPA specifically prohibited any agency that received federal assistance from using a child's or a prospective parent's race, color, or national origin to delay or deny the child's placement and by requiring diligent efforts to expand the number of racially and ethnically diverse foster and adoptive parents. A violation of MEPA was a violation of Title VI of the Civil Rights Act of 1964, and agencies violating MEPA could lose their federal funding. Nevertheless, MEPA permitted agencies to consider the child's race, ethnicity, and cultural background when assessing the prospective foster or adoptive parent's ability to meet the child's needs.

In 1996, Congress enacted the Interethnic Adoption Provisions (IEP), amending MEPA. MEPA-IEP now provides that a person or government involved in foster care or adoption may not deny any individual the right to become a foster parent or adoptive parent on the basis of the parent's or child's race, color, or national origin or delay or deny the adoption or foster-care placement of a child based on the child's or the parent's race, color, or national origin. 42 U.S.C. § 1996b(1) (2011). While the IEP still states that noncompliance is a Title VI violation, 42 U.S.C. § 1996b(2), it repealed the provision permitting consideration of a child's race, ethnicity, and culture and the prospective parent's ability to meet the child's needs. However, the Department of Health and Human Services has said that race and ethnicity may be considered if that advances the compelling governmental interest of protecting the child's best interests. "Moreover, the consideration must be narrowly tailored to advancing the child's interests and must be made as an individualized determination for each child. An adoption agency may take race into account only if it has made an individualized determination that the facts and circumstances of the specific case require the consideration of race in order to advance the best interests of the specific child. Any placement policy that takes race or ethnicity into account is subject to strict scrutiny by the courts to determine whether it satisfies these tests." U.S. Dep't of Health & Hum. Servs., Admin. on Child., Youth & Fams., Children's Bureau, Child Welfare Policy Manual, Sec. 4.3 (2011).

Cynthia Mabry and Lisa Kelly note that approximately eighteen states have enacted statutes that specifically prohibit discrimination based on race in adoptive placements and that most of these track the specific language of MEPA-IEP. A few states, however, have not changed their statutory provisions to track the IEP amendments, while others have promulgated exceptions to the MEPA-IEP provisions. Some states also have created penalties for state employees or adoption agencies that violate antidiscrimination provisions. These penalties may range from termination of employment to license suspension or revocation. CYNTHIA R. MABRY & LISA KELLY, ADOPTION LAW: THEORY, POLICY, AND PRACTICE 380–382 (2010). To what extent does race play a role in adoption decisions?

IN RE ADOPTION OF S.A.
Court of Appeals of Indiana
918 N.E.2d 736 (2009)

BAKER, Chief Judge.

Appellant-petitioner M.H. and C.H. and appellant Indiana Department of Child Services (DCS) (collectively, the appellants) appeal the denial of their motion to correct error after the probate court denied M.H. and C.H.'s petition to adopt S.A. and granted appellee-cross-petitioner C.R.'s petition to adopt. Specifically, the appellants argue that the adoption decree cannot stand because the findings were incomplete, the probate court did not enter any findings regarding DCS's consent to the adoption, and C.R. failed to present sufficient evidence satisfying the requirements for interstate adoption, and that the evidence was clear and convincing that M.H. and C.H.'s petition to adopt S.A. should have been granted. Concluding that the evidence was sufficient to support the probate court's granting of the adoption petition in favor of C.R., and finding no other error, we affirm.

FACTS

V.A. (hereinafter referred to as Biological Mother) gave birth to S.A. on March 5, 2005, in Marion. Immediately thereafter, S.A. aspirated meconium and was transported to Fort Wayne's Children's Hospital. Six days later, DCS removed S.A. from Biological Mother's care and placed S.A. in a foster home with M.H. and C.H. Because of the hospitalization, DCS filed a Child in Need of Services (CHINS) petition.

After learning that S.A. had been placed in foster care, C.R.—who had ultimately adopted Biological Mother's teenage children—contacted DCS and requested that S.A. be placed with her. However, DCS informed C.R., who lived in Chicago, that such placement would not occur because the initial plan was for reunification with Biological Mother.

Sometime in 2006, the permanency plan was changed to adoption because Biological Mother was unable to complete the services that DCS offered and she could not provide a stable lifestyle to care for S.A. In late 2006 or early 2007, a permanency plan was developed for S.A.'s placement with C.R. because Biological Mother's other children were living with her.

On May 18, 2006, DCS filed a petition to sever the parental rights of Biological Mother and S.A.'s alleged biological father. Following a hearing, their parental rights of custody and control of S.A. were terminated on January 4, 2007. However, prior to the final hearing, Biological Mother attempted to consent to C.R.'s adoption. Biological Mother knew that C.R. had provided her other children with a loving and caring home, where they had succeeded in school and in extracurricular activities. DCS representatives informed Biological Mother that she could only give consent to C.R. if she also consented to an adoption by M.H. and C.H. However, because Biological Mother did not want to consent to M.H. and C.H.'s adoption of S.A., Biological Mother withheld her consent from both parties.

Thereafter, DCS changed the original plan to adoption with M.H. and C.H., because S.A. had been living with them. C.R. and the teenage children had several supervised visits in Indiana with S.A. during the CHINS, termination, and adoption proceedings.

On July 24, 2007, M.H. and C.H. filed their adoption petition. C.R. then filed a cross-petition for adoption on November 20, 2007. DCS entered its consent for M.H. and C.H. to adopt S.A. on February 15, 2008. Thereafter, on April 24, 2008, DCS filed an adoption summary, with an evaluation and recommendation stating: "It is the recommendation of the [DCS] that M.H. and C.H. become the legal parents for S.A."

After hearing evidence on the competing adoption petitions on December 10, 2008, the probate court took the matter under advisement. The evidence showed that C.R. is financially capable of supporting S.A. Moreover, it was established that S.A.'s biological siblings who live with C.R. participate in extra-curricular activities, play musical instruments, regularly spend time together as a family, and are excellent students.

M.H. and C.H. have had twenty-three different foster children in their home over the past four years. Neither M.H. nor C.H. could remember the names of many of the foster children who had lived with them. C.H. has been treated for depression, and both she and M.H. are unemployed and were not able to provide proof as to their ability to support S.A.

On May 29, 2009, the probate court issued an order, granting the adoption in favor of C.R. In particular, the probate court determined:

> 18. That [C.R.] has adopted [D.R.] and [J.R.] and is the foster parent of [K.E.] and all three are half siblings to [S.A.].

> 19. That in a Parenting Assessment completed by Barbara Brands of the Children's Bureau dated 10/3/07, Ms. Brands concludes that [S.A.] does appear to be bonded to [C.R.] and her siblings....
>
> 21. That Anthony Moya, Family Case Manager...at DCS, stated in his Petitioner's Answers to Intervenors Interrogatories dated October 5, 2007, that it is in [S.A.'s] best interest to live in the home with her siblings....
>
> 24. That [C.R.] testified that [S.A.] would be able to interact with her mother's biological family as they are invited to attend special family functions held at her home....
>
> IT IS THEREFORE ORDERED, ADJUDGED AND DECREED THAT:
>
> 1. The Court finds that it is in the best interest of [S.A.] to be adopted by the Cross-Petitioner, [C.R.] and the Court orders this Petition for Adoption set for final hearing.
> 2. The Court denies the Petition for Adoption filed by [M.H. and C.H.].

Id. at 19–20. This appeal now ensues.[1]

DISCUSSION AND DECISION

I. Standard of Review

In general, when an adoption has been granted, we consider the evidence most favorable to the trial court's decision and the reasonable inferences that can be drawn therefrom to determine whether the evidence is sufficient to support the judgment. *Irvin v. Hood,* 712 N.E.2d 1012, 1013 (Ind.Ct.App. 1999). We will not disturb the trial court's decision in an adoption proceeding unless the evidence at trial led to but one conclusion and the trial court reached an opposite conclusion. *Id.*

II. The Appellants' Contentions...

B. DCS's Consent

The appellants...maintain that the adoption decree must be set aside because the record does not support DCS's consent to the adoption. More specifically, the appellants contend that "the DCS properly consented to adoption [by] M. & C.H. and objected to adoption by C.R." Appellant's Br. p. 25. Thus, the appellants essentially urge that DCS's decision to consent to M.H. and C.H.'s [adoption] should dictate the outcome.

Pursuant to Indiana Code section 31-19-11-1(a)(7), the trial court must find that "proper consent, *if consent is necessary,* to the adoption has been given." (Emphasis added.) Although consent is required from the agency having lawful custody of the child whose adoption is sought, consent is not required if the legal guardian or lawful custodian has failed to consent for reasons found by the court not to be in the best interests of the child. I.C. § 31-19-9-8(a)(10). Moreover, once consent is given, it cannot be withdrawn without filing a motion with the trial court. I.C. § 31-19-10-1(c). Also, consent cannot be revoked arbitrarily because there must be a specifically stated reason why it is in the best interest of the child to revoke consent. *In re Adoption of A.S.*, 912 N.E.2d 840, 849 (Ind.Ct.App. 2009).

1. The probate court granted the appellants' motion to stay the adoption order on June 19, 2009, pending the resolution of this appeal.

Notwithstanding the appellants' contentions, this court has determined that the best interest of the child is the paramount concern in any adoption case. *Stout v. Tippecanoe County Dep't. of Pub. Welfare*, 182 Ind.App. 404, 411, 395 N.E.2d 444, 448 (1979). The trial court is solely responsible for making the determination of what is in the best interest of the child guided by the factors—including consent—that are set forth in the adoption statute. I.C. § 31-19-11-1. In other words, DCS is not granted with the unbridled discretion to refuse consent. As we observed in *Stout*:

> When parental rights are terminated, the Department, as custodian of the adoptive child, occupies an important role in the adoption process. The Department becomes in loco parentis to its ward in order to find a suitable adoptive home, and by its expertise, aid the trial court in determining the child's best interest. The ultimate decision as to the child's best interest, however, rests with the trial court. *See Johnson v. Cupp*, (1971) 149 Ind.App. 611, 274 N.E.2d 411. We therefore hold the Department's power to withhold consent to adoption, regardless of the means by which the Department obtained custody, is qualified by IC 31-3-1-6(g), allowing the trial court to dispense with the consent of a guardian or custodian.

Stout, 182 Ind.App. at 414, 395 N.E.2d at 450–51.

As discussed above, DCS initially consented to C.R.'s request for adoption. Thereafter, DCS decided to withdraw its consent to permit M.H. and C.H. to adopt. *Id.* at 238–39. During the hearing on the adoption petitions, the DCS case manager could not explain why DCS had withdrawn its consent for C.R. to adopt S.A. *Id.* Moreover, the case manager could not identify any information that would warrant the DCS's determination that C.R.'s home may have been inappropriate for S.A. *Id.* at 242.

In light of the above, C.R. did not need DCS's consent for her petition for S.A.'s adoption to be granted because DCS failed to consent for reasons that were not in the best interest of S.A. *See* I.C. § 31-19-9-8(a)(10). Moreover, as discussed *infra*, the evidence supported the probate court's determination that adoption by C.R. was in S.A.'s best interest. Thus, M.H. and C.H.'s contention that the adoption decree must be set aside on the grounds that "DCS properly consented to adoption in M. & C.H." fails. Appellant's Br. p. 27....

D. Hard to Place Child

In a related issue, the appellants argue that the adoption decree must be set aside because C.R. did not have standing to file an adoption petition because she was a nonresident of Indiana. In particular, the appellants assert that the residence exceptions that are set forth in Indiana Code section 31-19-2-3 do not apply in these circumstances.

We note that a person has standing to adopt a child under eighteen if he or she is a resident of Indiana. I.C. § 31-19-2-2. However, an individual who is a non-resident of Indiana is granted an exception to the residency standing requirement to adopt a "hard to place child." I.C. § 31-19-2-3. A "hard to place child" is defined as "a child who is or children who are disadvantaged: (1) because of: (A) ethnic background; (B) race; (C) color; (D) language; (E) physical, mental, or medical disability; or (F) age; or (2) because the child or children are members of a sibling group that should be placed in the same home." Ind.Code § 31-9-2-51.

In this case, M.H. and C.H. admitted—in their own pleadings—that S.A. is a "hard-to-place child pursuant to Indiana Code section 31-9-2-51 for the reason that the child is disadvantaged because of race and age...." Appellant's App. p. 22–25. As a result, M.H. and C.H. are judicially estopped from now repudiating their contention that S.A. is a "hard to place child." *See Plaza Group Props., LLC v. Spencer County Plan Comm'n*, 911 N.E.2d 1264, 1269 (Ind. Ct. App. 2009) (holding that judicial estoppel prevents a party from asserting a position in a legal proceeding inconsistent with one that the party previously asserted).

Notwithstanding this conclusion, before a child will be found to be a "hard to place child," it must be determined that the child is "disadvantaged." In accordance with Indiana Code section 31-9-2-51, if the child fits into any of the statutory categories set forth above, the child is in the category of a "hard to place child."

As noted above, it is clear that S.A. fits into one of the statutory categories, as M.H. and C.H. had specifically alleged. I.C. § 31-9-2-51. Moreover, the evidence established at the adoption hearing that S.A. is a member of a sibling group that should be placed together.

C.R. and S.A. are both African Americans. Appellant's Br. p. 17–21. C.R.'s evidence demonstrated that she has the life experiences of being an African American, and that she is able to bring those life experiences to help S.A. understand what it means to be an African American and how to handle potential situations where she might be treated differently or inappropriately.

A clinical supervisor for Bethany Christian Services admitted that there are statistics suggesting that African American children adopted by Caucasian families are more likely to have problems. The supervisor testified that there are several organizations that advocate that if an African American family is willing and able to adopt an African American child, they should receive preference over a Caucasian family.

The evidence also established that S.A. has bonded with her biological siblings who currently reside with C.R. Moreover, even DCS determined that it was in S.A.'s best interest to live with her siblings, and DCS wanted to promote that bond. Cross-Petitioner's Ex. B, C.

In considering this evidence, we conclude that S.A. has met the requirements of a "hard to place child" in accordance with Indiana Code section 31-9-2-51. Thus, for these additional reasons, M.H. and C.H.'s contention that C.R. did not have standing to file a petition to adopt S.A. fails.

E. Sufficiency of the Evidence

Finally, the appellants maintain that the evidence presented at the hearing was insufficient to deny their request to adopt S.A. Put another way, M.H. and C.H. argue that the probate court should have found in their favor because the evidence unequivocally established that granting their petition was in S.A.'s best interests.

In addition to the standard of review set forth above, when reviewing a probate court's ruling in an adoption case, we will not reweigh the evidence but instead will examine the evidence most favorable to the probate court's decision together with reasonable inferences drawn therefrom to determine whether sufficient evidence exists to sustain the decision. *In re Adoption of A.S.*, 912 N.E.2d at 851. The appellant bears the burden of overcoming the presumption that the probate court's decision is correct. *Id.* In sum:

> After all of the consents and other required documents have been filed and all the evidence has been presented, when the court finds, among other things, that the adoption requested is in the

> best interests of the child and proper consent, if consent is necessary, has been given, the court shall grant the petition for adoption and enter an adoption decree.

Id. at 849.

In this case, the evidence presented at the December 10, 2008, hearing established that C.R. is able to support S.A. financially. Moreover, S.A.'s biological siblings who live with C.R. do well in school, aspire to attend college in the Chicago area, and spend time together as a family. S.A. has also interacted with her siblings on a number of occasions.

In contrast, M.H. and C.H. have had twenty-three different foster children in their home over the past four years. They could not remember the names of many of the children, and they could not provide proof as to their financial ability to support S.A.

Although M.H. and C.H. presented evidence establishing that they were "the only family S.A. knows," that they would continue to provide for S.A.'s needs, and that they were not "prohibited from adopting due to criminal history," Appellants' Br. p. 27–28, their request to set aside the adoption order in C.R.'s favor and enter judgment for them amounts to a request for us to reweigh the evidence, which we will not do. *Adoption of H.N.P.G.*, 878 N.E.2d 900, 903 (Ind.Ct.App. 2008), *trans. denied.* Thus, after reviewing the evidence, we conclude that the probate court properly determined that granting the adoption in C.R.'s favor was in S.A.'s best interest.

The judgment of the probate court is affirmed.

NOTES AND QUESTIONS

1. If parental rights had been terminated, why did the trial court have to obtain consent for the adoption? Whose consent was necessary? Why was it withheld?

2. To what extent do you think race was a factor in the decision to withhold consent? In the trial court's decision? In the appellate court's decision?

3. The court, without citation, states that a "clinical supervisor for Bethany Christian Services admitted that there are statistics suggesting that African American children adopted by Caucasian families are more likely to have problems." Is this true? Cynthia G. Hawkins-Léon and Carla Bradley provide this summary:

> The work of Lucille J. Grow and Deborah Shapiro annotates one of the earliest studies on the placement of African American children with White American parents. Grow and Shapiro conducted a follow-up study of 125 adoptions of African American children by White parents. Children were classified as African American if one of the biological parents was African American. The primary focus of this research was to assess the adjustment and well being of pre-adolescent African American adoptees. Adjustment was calibrated by the child's responses to the California Test of Personality, which measures social and personal adjustment, and the Missouri Children's Behavior Check List Test. Researchers also evaluated interview data regarding the parents' assessment of the children's attitude toward race. The study found that seventy-seven percent of the children had adjusted successfully and that this percentage was similar to reports from previous studies. Grow and Shapiro also compared the responses of African American children adoptees with those of adopted White children

and found that the scores from these two groups matched very closely. Grow and Shapiro concluded that the children were adjusting to their adoptive homes successfully.

In 1981, Arnold R. Silverman and William Feigelman reported their findings on the psychological adjustment of transracially adopted children. Their sample consisted of fifty-six White families who adopted African American children and ninety-seven White families who adopted White American children. Each parent or couple was asked to make a judgment about their child's overall adjustment and the frequency of their child's emotional and growth problems. The findings showed a positive correlation between age at adoption and maladjustment. Silverman and Feigelman interpreted this result as indicating that a child's age at adoption, not the transracial adoption itself, had the most significant impact on the child's development. Both researchers continue to support the position that transracial adoption is a viable option.

Ruth G. McRoy and Louis A. Zurcher conducted the first study of transracial adoptees using a comparison group of interracial adoptees. They were also the first to examine the experiences of African American children from both the adoptive parents' and the adoptees' perspective. The sample consisted of sixty families, thirty White and thirty African American. Slightly more than half of the children available for adoption had two biological African American parents. Most of these children were placed with African American adoptive parents. Nearly all of the children with only one biological African American parent were placed with White parents. Face-to-face interviews were conducted with both the adoptive parents, and the children were evaluated on the Tennessee Self-Concept Scale. The results indicated that "transracial and intraracial adoptive parents enjoyed their adopted children and considered their decision to adopt a good one."

The researchers also noted that the families were different in several aspects. The transracial adoptive parents were less likely than intraracial adoptive parents to deliberately instruct their adoptees about African American heritage and pride. The transracial parents primarily emphasized that "all humans are alike." The interracial parents accentuated the positive qualities of being African American. The intraracial adolescent adoptees tended to discuss racist experiences more openly and frequently with their parents than did the transracial adoptees. Nevertheless, McRoy and Zurcher concluded that although White adoptive parents did not behaviorally respond to the racial and cultural needs of African American children, they should still be considered as a resource for permanent placement for African Americans.

In order to determine the effects of transracial adoption over time, several scholars conducted longitudinal investigations. Shireman and Johnson published their findings from a longitudinal study of adopted African American children reared in single parent, transracial, and African American homes. The children were studied at four, eight, twelve, sixteen and twenty years of age. The Clark Doll Test, a measure in which children attribute various qualities to either a White or an African American doll, was administered to adoptees at age four and at age eight. The test indicated that the racial preferences and awareness of transracially adopted children remained constant, while that of a child in an interracial family continued to evolve over time. Shireman and Johnson concluded that although the racial development of transracial adoptees was "of concern," most of the children appeared to "grow well" in their adoptive homes.

Over a period of twenty years, Rita James Simon and Howard Altstein followed a group of families that adopted African American children. Their research began in 1972 and the original sample consisted of 204 families who had adopted transracially. Of the 366 adoptees, 120 were African American. Using projective measures such as the Clark Doll Test, pictures, and other instruments, Simon and Altstein found that "African American children perceived themselves as African American as accurately as White American children perceive themselves as White American." They also found that the parents tended to believe that race did not and would not be a major issue for their children. A large majority, seventy-seven percent, of the White parents lived in predominately White neighborhoods and sixty-three percent of the adoptees reported that most of their friends were White. Simon and Altstein concluded that African American children reared by White parents fared no worse than other children raised by parents of the same race.

Most recently, Karen S. Vroegh reported the fifth phase of her longitudinal study of transracial adoption outcomes. The sample consisted of fifty-two late adolescent African American adoptees. Thirty-four of the adoptees were from transracial families and the remaining eighteen were from intraracial families. Each of the participants were interviewed by an interracial team of researches and were given the Rosenberg Self-Esteem Scale. Findings revealed that ninety percent of the participants sampled were "doing... well in life." The researchers also noted that sixty percent of the transracial adoptees wanted to change their weight and temper. Vroegh concluded that transracial adoptees had "developed identities," where ninety percent of the intraracial adoptees, and eighty-eight percent of the transracial adoptees, labeled themselves as either African American or of "mixed" race.

Although a majority of the findings appear to support the conclusion that African American adoptees are "adjusting well" in transracial home environments, these and other often-cited conclusions have been challenged on methodological, analytical, and interpretative grounds.

An extensive review of studies on transracial adoption conducted by Hollingsworth indicated that most of the data regarding the experiences of transracial adoptees was gathered only from the adoptive parents. This particular research method provided very little insight into the child's own perception of their adoptive experience. Further, Willis reported that when transracial adoptees were interviewed, many of the appraisal and evaluation procedures used by the researchers had numerous methodological limitations. For example, the Clark Doll Test, a projective measure used in several of the longitudinal studies, has been severely criticized as being invalid if used to evaluate anything more than a child's preference for a doll in a contrived, forced-choice situation.

Additionally, numerous researchers charged that when the research population involved African American and White adoptees, the behaviors and experiences of White children were held as the standard. Further, if White children were not part of the study, African American adoption experiences were compared to White children both indirectly and by assumption. Seminal studies such as the work of Grow and Shapiro and Simon and Altstein are prime examples of this tendency. In each of these two studies, researchers found that African American adoptees evidenced psychological outcomes similar to those found in White children. Based on these findings, the investigators concluded that transracial adoption was a logical option for African American children.

Finally, and most importantly, Robert J. Taylor and Michael C. Thornton argued that of the studies that reported "the successful adjustment" of transracial adoptees, researchers omitted or minimized other important outcomes in their analyses such as the presence of racial identity and awareness issues among transracial adoptees, and the large number of transracial adoptive families who resided in predominately White neighborhoods. Further, Taylor and Thornton asserted that, in general, White parents did not think that race would be a major issue for their transracially adopted children in the future.

Cynthia G. Hawkins-Léon & Carla Bradley, *Race and Transracial Adoption: The Answer is Neither Simply Black or White Nor Right or Wrong*, 51 CATH. U. L. REV. 1227, 1269–1274 (2002). Do transracially adopted children experience more challenges?

In 2008, the Evan B. Donaldson Adoption Institute released a policy paper examining the impact of MEPA-IEP on the outcomes for African-American children adopted from the child-welfare system. The Adoption Institute noted that transracially adopted children and their families face additional challenges, including coping with being "different," developing a positive racial or ethnic identity, and learning to deal with discrimination. The Adoption Institute found that MEPA-IEP has not reduced racial disparity: African-American children remain in foster care nine months longer than white children, recruitment of prospective African-American adoptive parents has not been implemented or enforced well, and enforcement of MEPA-IEP provisions runs counter to best practices in adoption. The Adoption Institute report made the following recommendations: (1) "Reinforce in all adoption-related laws, policies and practices that a child's best interests must be paramount in placement decisions"; (2) "Amend IEP to allow consideration of race/ethnicity in permanency planning and in the preparation of families adopting transracially. The original MEPA standard—which provided that race is one factor, but not the sole factor, to be considered in selecting a foster or adoptive parent for a child in foster care—should be reinstated"; (3) "Enforce the MEPA requirement to recruit families who represent the racial and ethnic backgrounds of children in foster care and provide sufficient resources, including funding, to support such recruitment"; (4) "Address existing barriers to fully engaging minority families in fostering and adopting by developing alliances with faith communities, minority placement agencies, and other minority recruitment programs"; (5) "Provide support for adoption by relatives and, when that is not the best option for a particular child, provide federal funding for subsidized guardianship"; and (6) "To help families address their transracially adopted children's needs, provide post-adoption support services from time of placement through children's adolescence." Evan B. Donaldson Adoption Institute, Finding Families for African American Children: The Role of Race and Law in Adoption from Foster Care (2008), http://www.adoptioninstitute.org/publications/MEPApaper20080527.pdf. See also Evan B. Donaldson Adoption Institute, Beyond Culture Camp: Promoting Healthy Identity Formation in Adoption (2009), http://www.adoptioninstitute.org/publications/2009_11_ExSum_BeyondCultureCamp.pdf. What do you think of the Adoption Institute's recommendations? For a rebuttal to the Adoption Institute's findings, see Elizabeth Bartholet, Response to Donaldson Institute Call for Amendment of the Multiethnic Placement Act (MEPA) to Reinstate Use of Race as a Placement Factor, http://www.law.harvard.edu/programs/about/cap/law-reform/index.html.

4. There remains considerable debate between opponents to transracial adoption, who express concern about the impact of interracial placements on racial culture, and supporters who point to evidence that delay in or denial of adoptive placement hurts children and argue that there is no evidence that transracial placement causes them any harm. For a few of the many books and articles written on the subject, see, e.g., HAWLEY FOGG-DAVIS, THE ETHICS OF TRANSRACIAL ADOPTION (2002); RUTH G. MCROY & LOUIS A. ZURCHER, JR., TRANSRACIAL AND INRACIAL ADOPTEES: THE ADOLESCENT YEARS (1983); SANDRA PATTON, BIRTHMARKS: TRANSRACIAL ADOPTION IN CONTEMPORARY AMERICA (2000); RITA J. SIMON & HOWARD ALTSTEIN, ADOPTION, RACE & IDENTITY FROM INFANCY TO YOUNG ADULTHOOD (1992); IN THE BEST INTERESTS OF THE CHILD: CULTURE, IDENTITY AND TRANSRACIAL ADOPTION (Ivor Gaber & Jane Aldridge eds., 1995); Annette R. Appell, *Disposable Mothers, Deployable Children,*

Review Essay, 9 MICH. J. RACE & L. 421 (2004); R. Richard Banks, *The Color of Desire: Fulfilling Adoptive Parents' Racial Preferences through Discriminatory State Action*, 107 YALE L.J. 875 (1998); Elizabeth Bartholet, *Where Do Black Children Belong? The Politics of Race Matching in Adoption*, 139 U. PA. L. REV. 1163 (1991); Suzanne B. Campbell, *Taking Race out of the Equation: Transracial Adoption in 2000*, 53 S.M.U. L. REV. 1599 (2000); Michele Goodwin, *The Free-Market Approach to Adoption: The Value of a Baby*, 26 B.C. THIRD WORLD L.J. 61 (2006); David Hall, *Black Children and the American Dilemma: The Invisible Tears of Invisible Children*, 26 B.C. THIRD WORLD L.J. 9 (2006); Margaret Howard, *Transracial Adoption: Analysis of the Best Interests Standard*, 59 NOTRE DAME L. REV. 503 (1984); Ruth-Arlene W. Howe, *Race Matters in Adoption*, 42 FAM. L.Q. 465 (2008); Ruth-Arlene W. Howe, *Transracial Adoption (TRA): Old Prejudices and Discrimination Float under a New Halo*, 6 B.U. PUB. INT. L.J. 409 (1997); Ruth-Arlene W. Howe, *Redefining the Transracial Adoption Controversy*, 2 DUKE J. GENDER L. & POL'Y 131 (1995); Angela Mae Kupenda, *Seeking Different Treatment, or Seeking the Same Regard: Remarketing the Transracial Adoption Debate*, 26 B.C. THIRD WORLD L.J. 97 (2006); Solangel Maldonado, *Discouraging Racial Preferences in Adoptions*, 39 U.C. DAVIS L. REV. 1415 (2006); Twila L. Perry, *Transracial Adoption and Gentrification: An Essay on Race, Power, Family and Community*, 26 B.C. THIRD WORLD L.J. 25 (2006); Twila L. Perry, *Power, Possibility, and Choice: The Racial Identity of Transracially Adopted Children*, 9 MICH. J. RACE & L. 215 (2003); Twila L. Perry, *The Transracial Adoption Controversy: An Analysis of Discourse and Subordination*, 21 N.Y.U. REV. L. & SOC. CHANGE 33 (1993–94); Sarah Ramsey, *Fixing Foster Care or Reducing Child Poverty: The Pew Commission Recommendations and the Transracial Adoption Debate*, 66 MONT. L. REV. 21 (2005).

b. GUARDIANSHIP

ASFA defines "legal guardianship" as "a judicially created relationship between child and caretaker which is intended to be permanent and self-sustaining as evidenced by the transfer to the caretaker of the following parental rights with respect to the child: protection, education, care and control of the person, custody of the person, and decisionmaking. The term 'legal guardian' means the caretaker in such a relationship." 42 U.S.C. § 675 (7) (2011). Legal guardianship does not require the termination of parental rights; nevertheless, the legal guardian has the authority to make the decisions a parent otherwise could. While a legal guardian no longer is subject to state oversight and supervision, the guardian must assume financial responsibility for the child. Although the AACWA recognized guardianship as a permanency option, legal guardianships were seldom used because of the absence of a state subsidy. Meryl Schwartz, *Reinventing Guardianship: Subsidized Guardianship, Foster Care, and Child Welfare*, 22 N.Y.U. REV. L. & SOC. CHANGE 441, 457 (1996). Nevertheless, thirty-eight states and the District of Columbia established subsidized guardianship programs, relying primarily on state and local funds to support the programs.

The Fostering Connections to Success and Increasing Adoptions Act of 2008 gave states the option of using federal money to fund kinship-guardianship assistance. Under the Act, children who are in foster care and have been living with a relative who has been providing care for at least six months and for whom reunification and adoption have been ruled out may be considered for a subsidized guardianship. Pub. L. No. 110-351, § 101(b)(3)(A), 122 Stat. 3949 (2008) (amending 42 U.S.C. § 673(d)). The number of children exiting foster care for legal guardianships has increased from 5,916 in 1998 (Children's Bureau, U.S. Dep't of Health & Human Servs., The AFCARS Report—Final Estimates for FY 1998 through FY 2002, 12 (2011), http://www.acf.hhs.gov/programs/cb/stats_research/afcars/tar/report12.htm) to a high of 19,941 in 2008 (Children's Bureau, U.S. Dep't of Health & Human Servs., The AFCARS Report—Preliminary FY 2008 Estimates as of October 2009 [16] [2011], http://www.acf.hhs.gov/programs/cb/stats_research/afcars/tar/report16.htm), the year the Fostering Connections to Success and Increasing Adoptions Act was enacted. In 2009, the number of children exiting foster care for legal guardianships declined slightly, to 19,290 (Children's Bureau, U.S. Dep't of Health & Human Servs., The AFCARS Report—Preliminary FY 2009 Estimates as of July 2010, 17 (2011), http:// www.acf.hhs.gov/programs/cb/stats_research/afcars/tar/report17.htm); however, in 2010, the number declined further, to 16,208 (Children's Bureau, U.S. Dep't of Health & Human Servs., The AFCARS Report—Preliminary FY 2010 Estimates as of June 2011, 18 (2011), http://www.acf.hhs.gov/programs/cb/stats_research/afcars/tar/report18.htm).

Of all children exiting care, 2 percent exited to legal guardianships in 1998 (AFCARS Report—Final Estimates for FY 1998 through FY 2002); by 2008, 7 percent had exited to legal guardianships (AFCARS Report—Preliminary FY 2008 Estimates). While that percentage remained unchanged in 2009 (AFCARS Report—Preliminary FY 2009 Estimates); it declined to 6 percent in 2010 (AFCARS Report—Preliminary FY 2010 Estimates).

Ramona W. Denby, *Predicting Permanency Intentions among Kinship Caregivers,* 28 Child & Adolescent Soc. Work J. 113, 115–116, 128 (2011).

Permanency Disincentives

Agencies and child welfare workers play an important role in the decision-making process regarding child permanency as it relates to relative caregivers. [Researchers] found that when children are placed with nonkin and they cannot be reunited with their parents, workers move toward termination of parental rights (TPR) and pursue adoption rigorously; on the other hand, when children reside with kin and cannot be reunited with their parents, workers view TPR as less necessary and adoption is not often viewed as the preferred permanency option. Also, the lack of accurate and comprehensive information about the range of legal permanency options has been identified as a barrier to kinship adoption. Relative caregivers themselves cite the following adoption disincentives: adoption punishes the biological parents too much and removes hope that parents will get better, caregivers worry about their own preparedness for parenting especially as they get older, and adoption brings about a potential for family conflict. Also, the permanency option of adoption is often not pursued because caregivers realize that they will be required to assume all legal responsibilities and financial burden and may not be able to access the services that they once were able to for the children once they are the legal parents. Finally, in some states, adoption standards may be more stringent than foster parent licensing and thus some caregivers may not be able to receive adoption subsidies.

Permanency Incentives

[Some studies] suggest that children in kinship care experience permanency more slowly than children in nonkinship care, represent a long line of prevailing research regarding kinship care and permanency. However, in using propensity score matching to balance the differences in caregiver characteristics, [other researchers] found that kin placements are as likely to culminate in legal permanency as nonkin placements. [These studies] confirm that kin placement is more beneficial to children than nonkin placement as it relates to placement stability. In terms of the permanency option of adoption, more recent work on the subject paints a much more affirming perspective regarding kin caregivers' willingness to adopt. For example, [one researcher] reports that relatives are willing to adopt their relatives' children, especially aunts and uncles, and relatives regardless of the degree of relatedness are especially willing to adopt young children. In short, there is an emerging research base that has begun to counter earlier assertions about kinship caregivers' adoption willingness. A few factors have been identified as correlates, predictors, or conditions associated with a caregiver's decision to provide permanency for the children in their care: genealogical relatedness and learned attachment and familiarity (Testa 2004–2005), and adequate information and education about adoption.

Differences between Adoption and Guardianship Choices

The debate between the two permanency options of adoption versus guardianship has been longstanding. Those who advocate for strict permanency practices promote preferences for adoption because of a belief that child outcomes will be improved. On the other hand, guardianship proponents state that rigid permanency choices actually delay permanence and they believe that guardianship preserves a role for the biological parent. Generations United [a national organization focused on improving the lives of children, youth, and older people] reports that adoption may not be the preferred permanency arrangement for many relative caregivers because it changes parental dynamics and terminates parental rights. Moreover, it is believed that guardianship may be the choice that many caregivers want to pursue because it allows relatives to care for children without changing family relationships. In terms of legislated preferences, the majority of states have traditionally subsidized relative guardianships with stipend support that derives from a combination of federal and state resources (including Temporary Assistance to Needy Families—TANF and federal waivers). The use of TANF dollars has led to some innovative state-based initiatives and programs that promote permanency with kinship caregivers by providing the caregivers with various services and supports. The Adoption Assistance and Child Welfare Act (AACWA) of 1980 and the 1997 Adoption Assistance and Safe Families Act (ASFA) permitted the establishment of permanency through either adoption or guardianship but gave no financial provisions for guardianship payments to relatives. Additionally, although governmental support for adoption has long been a provision found in many major child welfare laws, it has been only recently that kinship guardianship has been supported with financial provisions. The 2008 Fostering Connections to Success and Increasing Adoptions Act (P. L. 110-351) permits states to use federal funds for kinship guardianship stipends. This is progress but it is still believed that subsidized guardianship rates (particularly those derived from TANF) are not comparable with federal adoption subsidies or licensed foster care reimbursement rates.

In summary, caregivers' ability to obtain higher and more secure levels of stipend support which results from the new federal legislation (P. L. 110-351) may enable caregivers to select guardianship as the permanency choice for the child in their care. Alternatively, the introduction of federal subsidized guardianship may result in more questions about those conditions that support caregivers' permanency decisions and which is the preferred permanency outcome: adoption or guardianship. We need to know much more about those conditions that support caregivers' willingness to provide permanency for the child(ren) in their care....

The value of permanency for children who must live without their biological parents and the benefits of kinship care are well known. When permanency and kinship care converge, research suggests that although caregivers are more likely to choose guardianship they are open to providing permanency for children through adoption. What are not as clear are those conditions that lead caregivers to choose adoption versus guardianship.... [S]uch key experiences as adequate information about and involvement in case planning and court proceedings predict which caregivers will adopt. Likewise, when the emotional stress that caregivers experience is managed, they express a high level of adoption intent and when they are caring for sibling groups they are motivated to adopt. In terms of child behavior, caregivers are more inclined to move toward adoption when children are emotionally detached from their biological parents but they are leery of adoption when the children exhibit signs of depression or such behavior problems as running away. This study found that despite children's behavior problems, caregivers are willing to commit to permanency with guardianship, especially when the children do not have regular contact with their parents. Policy and practice models that operate from the assumption that kinship caregivers are not interested in adoption are in error especially given the fact that those conditions that predict adoption intent can be created through proper intervention and support.

c. PLANNED PERMANENT LIVING ARRANGEMENTS

Prior to the adoption of ASFA, federal law recognized that some children would remain in long-term foster care. ASFA replaced "long-term foster care" with the term "other planned permanent living arrangement" (PPLA). 42 U.S.C. § 675(5)(C) (2011). Pursuant to 45 C.F.R. § 1356.21 (h)(3)(i)–(iii) (2011), the state first must consider reunification, adoption, legal guardianship, or permanent placement with a fit and willing relative before concluding that a PPLA is the most appropriate permanency option for the child. Moreover, the court must determine that there is a compelling reason for choosing a PPLA over the other alternatives listed in the statute. Compelling reasons may include (1) "an older teen who specifically requests that emancipation be established as his/her permanency plan"; (2) despite a "significant" parent-child bond, the parent is unable to care for the child because of an emotional or physical disability, and the child's foster parents "have committed to raising him/her to the age of majority and to facilitate visitation with the disabled parent"; and (3) the child is Native American, and the child's tribe has identified another planned permanent living arrangement.

In 1986, Congress passed the Title IV-E Independent Living Initiatives, Pub. L. No. 99-272, §12,307, 100 Stat. 82, 294 (1986) (codified as amended in scattered sections of 42 U.S.C.), to provide teens aging out of foster care with the skills and experience needed to survive as adults. Teens between the ages of sixteen and eighteen receive life-skills classes, supervised living arrangements, mentoring, and employment readiness and training. The Foster Care Independence Act (the Chafee Act), enacted in 1999, created the John H. Chafee Foster Care Independence Program and increased federal funding for states to create independent-living programs for teenagers aging out of foster care. 42 U.S.C. § 677 (2011). The Administration for Children and Families promulgated a rule to create the National Youth in Transition database to collect case-level data about the services that states provide pursuant to the Chafee Act along with outcome data for youths aging out of the system. 45 C.F.R. §§ 1356.80–86 (2011). The Fostering Connection for Success and Increasing Adoptions Act of 2008 provides federal funds to enable states to extend child-welfare services to the age of twenty-one. Eligible youths must be completing high school or an equivalent program, enrolled in postsecondary or vocational education, working at least eighty hours per month, or working toward job readiness. Youths with certain disabilities also qualify for extended benefits even if they are not in school or working.

In fiscal year 2010, 27,854 young adults were emancipated from the foster-care system because they reached the age of majority (Children's Bureau, U.S. Dep't of Health & Human Servs., The AFCARS Report—Preliminary FY 2010 Estimates as of June 2011, 18 (2011), http://www.acf.hhs.gov/programs/cb/stats_research/afcars/tar/report18.htm). Although the actual number of emancipations declined since 2007 (Children's Bureau, U.S. Dep't of Health & Human Servs., The AFCARS Report—Preliminary FY 2007 Estimates as of October 2009, 15 (2011), http://www.acf.hhs.gov/programs/cb/stats_research/afcars/tar/report15.htm), the percentage of children emancipated from foster care has risen steadily since 1998, when 7 percent of the exits from foster care were emancipations (Children's Bureau, Admin. for Child. & Fam., U.S. Dep't Health & Hum. Servs., The AFCARS Report: Final Estimates for FY 1998 through FY 2002, http://www.acf.hhs.gov/programs/cb/stats_research/afcars/tar/report12.htm). Youths who age out of the system have serious problems. They experience homelessness and early pregnancy, lack money for basic living expenses, and are undereducated and unemployed. They also have greater involvement with the criminal-justice system. See, e.g., Mark E. Courtney et al., Midwest Evaluation of the Adult Functioning of Former Foster Youth (2010), http://www.chapinhall.org/research/report/midwest-evaluation-adult-functioning-former-foster-youth (suggesting that extending foster care to age twenty-one may be associated with better outcomes on some measures); Thorn Reilly, *Transition from Care: Status and Outcomes of Youth Who Age Out of Foster Care*, 82 Child Welfare 727 (2003). Do foster youths have a right to services to prepare them for the transition to life on their own? See, e.g., Katherine M. Swift, *A Child's Right: What Should the State Be Required to Provide to Teenagers Aging Out of Foster Care?* 15 Wm. & Mary Bill. Rts. J. 1205 (2007) (arguing that teens aging out have substantive due-process right to services).

Emily Buss argues that courts should retain jurisdiction and provide for continued oversight and monitoring of cases involving foster youths who have turned eighteen. She notes that courts already have a role in monitoring case plans and ensuring the delivery of services to foster youths under federal law; judges thus have the authority to ensure compliance and bring to the cases a certain objectivity. Courts, too, may be in the best position to coordinate the multisystems delivery of services needed by youths. Moreover, because there is evidence that youths who stay in foster care until age twenty-one have better outcomes than those who leave the system at eighteen, Buss contends that any additional costs may be allayed by the availability of funds provided by the Fostering Connections for Success Act along with the societal benefits reaped from the higher functioning of these foster-care graduates. Moreover, she argues that courts provide a safe context in which foster youths may begin to develop and assert their independence with the proper support of and facilitation by their lawyers. Emily Buss, *Juvenile Court for Young Adults? How Ongoing Court Involvement Can Enhance Foster Care Youths' Chances for Success*, 42 Fam. Ct. Rev. 262 (2010).

American Bar Association
Resolution 109b Adopted by the House of Delegates
(Aug. 9–10, 2010)

RESOLVED, That the American Bar Association urges federal, state, local, territorial and tribal governments, as well as state, local, territorial and tribal child welfare agencies and dependency courts and judges to enact laws and rules, and to develop policy and practice changes that:

(1) Promptly, fully, and expansively implement the older youth provisions of the federal Fostering Connections to Success and Increasing Adoptions Act and, in particular, extend foster care, independent and transitional living services, adoption assistance, and guardianship assistance to all youth and young adults through at least age 21;

(2) Ensure that dependency court jurisdiction is extended for young adults who elect to remain in child welfare agency care until at least the age of 21 (or any earlier time the young adult may elect to leave care) and that all Title IV-E requirements including case planning, transition planning, and court oversight are met;

(3)(a) Give young adults the option to exit care upon the age of 18 or at any age afterwards, but ensure that these young adults fully understand the implications and magnitude of any decision to exit care and are provided support and services to ensure a smooth transition to adulthood, and (b) create a mechanism for young adults who exit care after attaining age 18 to re-enter care through age 21; and

(4) Ensure that young adults in child welfare agency care are: (a) actively involved in all phases of permanency, independent living, and transition planning; (b) present at, and actively engaged and informed participants in, their own dependency court proceedings; and (c) represented by a well trained, competent and effective client-directed lawyer in all dependency court proceedings through the termination of their case and in any reentry into care thereafter.

FURTHER RESOLVED, That the American Bar Association urges the development of regulations and guidelines in regard to the Fostering Connections to Success and Increasing Adoptions Act, including but not limited to: (a) a broad and flexible definition of federally reimbursable "supervised settings" in which young adults are "living independently" based on the best practice experiences of states with effective models; (b) an expansive interpretation of the Act's language defining the youth and young adults eligible for federal funding for care, support and services through age 21; and (c) clarification that all Title IV-E requirements, including representation and court supervision, are applied to young adults who remain in child welfare agency care through age 21.

FURTHER RESOLVED, That the American Bar Association urges state and local bar associations, law firms, and individual lawyers to develop and promote pro bono programs to ensure that youth and young adults have access to needed transitional supports and services and that the rights of youth and young adults are fully preserved while in, transitioning from, or after exiting child welfare agency care.

NOTES AND QUESTIONS

1. The ABA resolution leaves the option to exit foster care to the individual youth. Do you agree?

2. Do you think that youths in foster care want to leave? *Represent, Voices of Youth in Care* publishes firsthand accounts of children and teens in foster care. Some of these accounts may be accessed at http://www.representmag.org/topics/independent+living.html. The PBS television documentary *Aging Out* chronicles the experiences of five foster youths making the transition to life on their own.

3. To what extent is the foster youth's desire to leave "the system" driven by the way the youth is treated by system participants? Emily Buss argues that at best, youths are not engaged in the process, and at worst, they are simply ignored. She contends that this is a missed opportunity to nurture decision-making competence. Emily Buss, *Failing Juvenile Courts, and What Lawyers and Judges Can Do about It*, 6 Nw. J.L. & Soc. Pol'y 318 (2011). The ABA also has enacted resolutions mandating the appointment of counsel for children in all dependency proceedings, Am. Bar Ass'n, Resolution 10B Adopted by the House of Delegates (Aug. 8–9, 2005), and "the ability and the right to attend and fully participate in all hearings related to their cases," Am. Bar Ass'n, Resolution 104A Adopted by the House of Delegates (Aug. 13–14, 2007). Will providing youths with lawyers make a difference?

IV

CHILDREN AND RESTRAINTS ON LIBERTY

A. Status Offenses

John E. B. Myers, Child Protection in America 45 (2006).

[By] 1910 ... [a]ll states had laws against sexual abuse. Nearly all states had criminal statutes against abandonment, desertion, and nonsupport. Quite a few states had statutes establishing juvenile courts, and these statutes specified that the court had authority over neglected and dependent children as well as delinquent children. Only a few states had laws regarding licensing and inspection of child care facilities. A majority of states limited children's performances in circuses and other public exhibitions. Louisiana, Michigan, New York, Pennsylvania, and Virginia specified that agents of societies for the prevention of cruelty to children had limited police authority. A New York law provided that mothers in prison could retain custody of their babies until age two.

Most states had laws protecting children from obscene literature....

Practically every state had laws against children visiting billiard and ten-pin parlors, gambling and card rooms, houses of prostitution, saloons, or dance halls. A few states added skating rinks to the forbidden zone....

Nearly all states made it a crime to sell tobacco to children, and Kansas threw in opium for good measure. Most states prohibited the sale of dangerous weapons to minors. New Hampshire said firecrackers were okay provided they were less than six inches long. Rhode Island allowed firecrackers, but only if they were made of gunpowder.

Katherine Hunt Federle, *Status Offenses*, in The Child: An Encyclopedic Companion 956–957 (Richard A. Shweder ed., 2009).

A status offense is conduct proscribed by state law only when the offender committing it is a juvenile. A status offense is decidedly noncriminal and focuses on certain forms of juvenile misbehavior, typically running away from home, truancy, and "incorrigibility" or "waywardness." The power to regulate the conduct of children is grounded in the *parens patriae* doctrine, which authorizes the state to protect children from their own impulsivity and immaturity. Although the juvenile court from its inception had jurisdiction over status offenders, laws governing juvenile noncriminal misbehavior predate the creation of juvenile courts. These earlier laws, grounded in elitist views about social class and morality, formed the basis for the modern juvenile court's status offense jurisdiction, a heritage still evident in the treatment of status offenders today.

State regulation over the conduct of children has deep roots in the classist and gendered reform movements of the 19th century. Political and social elites became unsettled by what they believed were serious increases in both the type and the amount of pauperism and crime, a circumstance they linked to the flood of immigrants from the poorer and lower classes. In seeking to stem this tide, early reformers argued that immorality was the root cause of poverty, and that it was poverty that inevitably led to criminality. The children of the poor were seen as peculiarly vulnerable to the manifold temptations of the street, not only because they had immoral or criminal parents but also because of the belief in the natural weakness of the child's moral character. In the view of the reformers, the solution was simple: Remove children from vice, corruption, and poverty, and they will become sober, law-abiding adults.

Initial statutes authorized local authorities to commit wayward and incorrigible children to institutional care in Houses of Refuge, the first institutions specifically constructed to deal with the problem of deviant children. These facilities not only accepted juveniles accused of criminal wrongdoing but also accepted those who were deemed "wayward." Waywardness encompassed a broad array of ills, including vagrancy, homelessness, "bad habits," idleness, disobedience, and, especially in the case of girls, "bad morals." By 1870, statutes permitting the institutionalization of wayward children had proliferated, expanding the number of jurisdictions authorizing the placement of status offenders in certain institutions and the types of offenses for which these children could be committed. For example, parents now could seek the commitment of their own "rebellious" or "stubborn" children. States also enacted compulsory education and truancy laws, which permitted the incarceration of children who failed to attend school.

By the turn of the century, the characteristics of modern status offense laws were already in place. These regulations reaffirmed the broad scope of the state's authority to regulate the conduct of children by restricting the places children could frequent and the people with whom they could associate, the hours they had to attend school, and the activities in which they could engage. Moreover, legal challenges to the state's authority to control the behavior of children were largely unsuccessful. Courts routinely justified the state's institutionalization of status offenders on the ground that the state, through its *parens patriae* power, was acting in the child's welfare. Although some courts did question the procedures used to institutionalize status offenders, generally the authority to so incarcerate went largely unquestioned.

The implementation of a separate juvenile court system did little to change the way authorities handled status offenders. Juvenile courts retained jurisdiction over status offenses, often based on laws that were written in the 19th century. Juvenile court personnel also embraced many of the underlying premises for regulating the behavior of children. They viewed status offenders as predelinquent and in need of immediate reformation in order to deflect these young offenders from a life of crime. Moreover, juvenile courts continued the practice of institutionalizing status offenders as necessary to their rehabilitation, although they had committed no criminal offense.

[Today, m]odern status offense laws clearly remain preoccupied with the same sorts of unacceptable juvenile behavior. Typically, modern status offenses include truancy, running away, ungovernability or incorrigibility, and curfew violations. Truancy is grounded in each state's compulsory education attendance laws and arises when the child is habitually and inexcusably absent from school. State statutes may specify a length of time the child must be absent or, more commonly, may simply refer to habitual absence without further definition. An ungovernable or incorrigible child is generally defined as a child who has habitually refused to obey the reasonable commands of his or her parents and, thus, is beyond parental control. These statutes are broad enough to allow state regulation of unacceptable, immoral, or sexually precocious behavior.

Modern juvenile curfew laws also further state regulation of the conduct of children by restricting the right of children to move about freely during certain hours. Most curfews are enacted by local governments and municipalities pursuant to their general police powers. Although many jurisdictions enacted curfew ordinances prior to World War II, few were enforced until the early 1990s, when public fears about youth gang activity and violent youth crime escalated....

Last, the state may intervene when children run away from their families, foster parents, or group homes or other placements. More than 1 million children run away each year, although the precise number of children is not known because many children are not reported as missing. A significant proportion of the children who run away are "throwaways"—thrown out of their homes, told they may not return, or otherwise abandoned. These children often are reluctant to return home because they have been the victims of abuse or neglect. While both boys and girls may run away from home to escape sexually abusive situations, 38 percent of boys reported this as the reason for leaving home, compared to 73 percent of girls. Runaway girls who are the victims of sexual abuse are more likely to engage in criminal conduct than are runaway girls who do not have histories of sexual abuse. Many runaway children who do not return home live on the streets or turn to prostitution, theft, and other crimes for survival.

NOTES AND QUESTIONS

1. Reconsider the *Crouse*, *O'Connell*, and *Ferrier* cases in section I.A. Were the children charged with status offenses? Does that alter your view of the outcomes in those cases?

2. How do we reconcile the juvenile court's status-offense jurisdiction with the rights of parents and children?

1. CONSTITUTIONAL FRAMEWORK

The United States Supreme Court has never directly ruled on the constitutionality of status offenses; nevertheless, a number of constitutional challenges to these statutes have been made with varying success in the state and lower federal courts. Many of these cases involve constitutional challenges to curfew ordinances. The following case discusses the constitutionality of one such ordinance.

NUNEZ V. CITY OF SAN DIEGO
United States Court of Appeals for the Ninth Circuit
114 F.3d 935 (1997)

WIGGINS, Circuit Judge.

The City of San Diego enacted its juvenile curfew ordinance in 1947. The ordinance reads as follows:

> It shall be unlawful for any minor under the age of eighteen (18) years, to loiter, idle, wander, stroll or play in or upon the public streets, highways, roads, alleys, parks, playgrounds, wharves, docks, or other public grounds, public places and public buildings, places of amusement and entertainment, vacant lots or other unsupervised places, between the hours of ten o'clock P.M. and daylight immediately following....

The ordinance then provides that the curfew does not apply in four situations:

(1) "when the minor is accompanied by his or her parents, guardian, or other adult person having the care and custody of the minor,"
(2) "when the minor is upon an emergency errand directed by his or her parent or guardian or other adult person having the care and custody of the minor,"
(3) "when the minor is returning directly home from a meeting, entertainment or recreational activity directed, supervised or sponsored by the local educational authorities," or
(4) "when the presence of such minor in said place or places is connected with and required by some legitimate business, trade, profession or occupation in which said minor is lawfully engaged."

A minor violating § 58.01 commits a misdemeanor. Section 58.01.1 also creates criminal liability for the "parent, guardian or other adult person having the care and custody of a minor" who permits or allows the minor to violate the curfew ordinance. On April 25, 1994, the City adopted a resolution to enforce the curfew aggressively.

Plaintiffs are minors and parents of minors from San Diego. They brought an action under 42 U.S.C. § 1983 to challenge the ordinance's constitutionality on its face. Plaintiff minors allege, among other things, that the ordinance restricts them from many otherwise lawful activities after curfew hours, i.e., volunteering at a homeless shelter, attending concerts as a music critic, studying with other students, meeting with friends at their homes or in coffee houses, stopping at a restaurant to eat dinner after serving on the School District Board, auditioning for theater parts, attending ice hockey practice, practicing astronomy, and dancing at an under-21 dance club. Plaintiff parents allege that the ordinance impinges upon their ability to rear their children as they wish because they and their children would face misdemeanor liability under the curfew.

The district court granted summary judgment in favor of the City, concluding that the ordinance was constitutional.... This appeal followed....

We review de novo an order granting summary judgment on the constitutionality of a statute or ordinance. The constitutionality of any juvenile curfew is a matter of first impression in this circuit.[2]

2. Six federal cases have fully analyzed the constitutionality of juvenile curfews. Of the six, four struck down the ordinances. *Johnson v. City of Opelousas*, 658 F.2d 1065 (5th Cir. 1981); *Hutchins v. District of Columbia*, 942 F.Supp. 665 (D.D.C. 1996); *Waters v. Barry*, 711 F.Supp. 1125 (D.D.C. 1989); *McCollester v. City of Keene*, 586 F.Supp. 1381 (D.N.H. 1984). The other two upheld curfew ordinances that had greater exemptions for legitimate activities, including the exercise of First Amendment rights, than does the San Diego

I. THE VAGUENESS DOCTRINE

...To avoid unconstitutional vagueness, an ordinance must (1) define the offense with sufficient definiteness that ordinary people can understand what conduct is prohibited; and (2) establish standards to permit police to enforce the law in a non-arbitrary, non-discriminatory manner. *Kolender v. Lawson*, 461 U.S. 352, 357, 103 S.Ct. 1855, 1858, 75 L.Ed.2d 903 (1983). In a facial vagueness challenge, the ordinance need not be vague in all applications if it reaches a "substantial amount of constitutionally protected conduct." *Id.* at 359 n. 8, 103 S.Ct. at 1859 n. 8 (quoting *Village of Hoffman Estates v. Flipside, Hoffman Estates, Inc.*, 455 U.S. 489, 494, 102 S.Ct. 1186, 1191, 71 L.Ed.2d 362 (1982)). The need for definiteness is greater when the ordinance imposes criminal penalties on individual behavior or implicates constitutionally protected rights than when it regulates the economic behavior of businesses. *Hoffman Estates*, 455 U.S. at 498–99, 102 S.Ct. at 1193–94. This greater need for definiteness is present in this case because the San Diego ordinance restricts individual freedom through criminal law....

The key to determining whether the San Diego ordinance is unconstitutionally vague is to determine the breadth of the ordinance's basic proscription in light of the enumerated exceptions. The City contends that the ordinance's language making it unlawful to "loiter, idle, wander, stroll or play" in public areas during the curfew is more limited than a proscription of minors' presence. Thus, the City stated at oral argument that the limited nature of the language "loiter, wander, idle, stroll or play," and not just the enumerated exceptions, provides exceptions for legitimate conduct that ensure that the curfew is not overbroad.

The phrase "loiter, wander, idle, stroll or play" uses imprecise terms. As a result, serious vagueness problems exist if "loiter, wander, idle, stroll or play" covers a narrower range of conduct than "presence," unless a sufficiently definite narrowing construction is given. *See Papachristou v. City of Jacksonville*, 405 U.S. 156, 163–71, 92 S.Ct. 839, 843–48, 31 L.Ed.2d 110 (1972) (discussing vagueness problems with similar terms); *United States ex rel. Newsome v. Malcolm*, 492 F.2d 1166, 1172–73 (2d Cir. 1974) (concluding that a statute using terms "loiter" and "wander" is unconstitutionally vague), *aff'd sub nom. Lefkowitz v. Newsome*, 420 U.S. 283, 95 S.Ct. 886, 43 L.Ed.2d 196 (1975) (addressing separate question only)....

Examination of the ordinance's enumerated "exceptions" highlights the indefiniteness of the phrase "loiter, wander, idle, stroll or play." If the ordinance's general prohibition only proscribes "hanging out" or "aimlessness," then three of the ordinance's four enumerated exceptions are surplusage. In fact, the City admitted at oral argument that under its narrow reading of the ordinance's prohibition these three exceptions would be "probably totally unnecessary," although it suggested that they might give additional "guidance."

First, if "loiter, wander, idle, stroll or play" means "hanging out," then the exception for returning directly home from certain education-related activities is superfluous. In reading the basic prohibition narrowly, the district court concluded that walking to the store, walking to one's car to drive home, driving, and traveling to or from any recreational activity do not constitute activities in violation of the ordinance. These conclusions regarding the scope of

ordinance. *Qutb v. Strauss*, 11 F.3d 488 (5th Cir. 1993); *Bykofsky v. Borough of Middletown*, 401 F.Supp. 1242, 1246 (M.D.Pa. 1975), *aff'd*, 535 F.2d 1245 (3d Cir.) (1976). Another case struck down a curfew for vagueness because it did not specify the time each day that the curfew ended. *Naprstek v. City of Norwich*, 545 F.2d 815, 818 (2d Cir. 1976). In analyzing this case, we have in part drawn from the analyses in these prior cases.

the prohibition are inconsistent with an exception for returning directly home from education-related activities. The exception as written makes sense only if the general prohibition on "loiter, wander, idle, stroll or play" is broader than "hanging out," which itself does not implicate returning directly home from anything. Contrary to the City's argument, returning directly home from aimless activity is not itself aimless. Moreover, we note that on October 3, 1994, San Diego rejected an amendment to make it a defense that the minor was responsibly moving to or from any legitimate social activity, which implies that such movement would violate the ordinance.

Second, a narrow construction of "loiter, wander, idle, stroll or play" is inconsistent with the exception for emergency errands. The City contends that the exception protects activity in the course of an emergency errand that might appear to be aimless. The curfew does not prohibit the appearance of loitering, however, but rather loitering itself. Accordingly, with or without the exception, an emergency errand would not violate the ordinance under the City's narrow reading; a narrow reading makes the exception surplusage.

Third, the exception for a job-related [activity] would be surplusage under a narrow reading of "loiter, wander, idle, stroll or play." If the ordinance proscribes only "hanging out" or similar aimless conduct, then a job-related exception makes no sense. Only if the ordinance is construed to prohibit minors' presence after curfew is the job-related exception reasonable and meaningful. In sum, the plain language of the ordinance's three exceptions makes sense only if "loiter, wander, idle, stroll or play" is broadly interpreted....

The narrow construction of the ordinance offered by the City is irreducibly subjective and renders most of the exceptions incoherent. Thus, we conclude that the phrase "loiter, wander, idle, stroll or play" is unconstitutionally vague. The ordinance's first failing is that it does not provide reasonable notice of what conduct is illegal and allows excessive discretion to the police if we construe "loiter, wander, idle, stroll or play" to proscribe a narrower range of conduct than mere "presence." *See Kolender*, 461 U.S. at 357 & 361, 103 S.Ct. at 1858 & 1860; *Papachristou*, 405 U.S. at 165–171, 92 S.Ct. at 845–48. *See also K.L.J. v. State*, 581 So.2d 920, 922 (Fla.Dist.Ct.App. 1991) (finding that curfew ordinance unconstitutionally vague); *Seattle v. Pullman*, 82 Wash.2d 794, 514 P.2d 1059, 1063 (1973) (finding that the phrase "loiter, wander, idle, stroll, or play" was impermissibly vague)....

The ordinance's second failing is that it allows the police excessive discretion to decide whether to stop and arrest juveniles after curfew hours. Such tremendous discretion may be an effective enforcement tool, but where the ordinance provides no standards to distinguish prohibited and permitted conduct it is impermissibly vague. The City's narrow construction of the ordinance makes the general prohibition standardless, relying on the police officer's perception of whether conduct is aimless. We reject the City's reliance on the claimed legitimacy of its present enforcement policy; its policy may change, and we must instead focus on the constitutionality of the ordinance itself.

Despite the vagueness of the phrase "loiter, wander, idle, stroll or play," the ordinance might avoid being rendered unconstitutional on vagueness grounds if the ordinance is treated as prohibiting all juvenile nocturnal presence and if that broad interpretation does not unconstitutionally burden the rights of minors and their parents. *See Bykofsky*, 401 F.Supp. at 1252 (treating "remain" as meaning "presence" despite juvenile curfew ordinance's expressed intent to use it more narrowly because broader meaning was required in face of vagueness challenge); *People v. Trantham*, 161 Cal.App.3d Supp. 1, 208 Cal.Rptr. 535, 538 (1984) (rejecting facial vagueness challenge regarding term "loiter" because the statute was "simply a park closure law" banning presence); *cf. United States v. Harriss*, 347 U.S. 612, 618, 74 S.Ct. 808, 812, 98 L.Ed. 989 (1954) (stating that courts have a duty to make a "reasonable construction" of the statute to make it constitutionally definite). This broader reading may make it more difficult for the statute to pass constitutional muster on substantive grounds, but it is required for the ordinance to meet the Constitution's guarantee of fair notice.

II. EQUAL PROTECTION ANALYSIS

Plaintiffs challenge the curfew ordinance under the Equal Protection Clause of the Fourteenth Amendment. The standard for reviewing the constitutionality of an ordinance depends on the right or classification involved.

A. The Appropriate Level of Scrutiny

Generally, legislation is presumed to pass constitutional muster and will be sustained if the classification drawn by the statute or ordinance is rationally related to a legitimate state interest. *City of Cleburne v. Cleburne Living Ctr., Inc.*, 473 U.S. 432, 439–40, 105 S.Ct. 3249, 3253–55, 87 L.Ed.2d 313 (1985). If the classification disadvantages a "suspect class" or impinges a "fundamental right," the ordinance is subject to strict scrutiny. *Plyler v. Doe*, 457 U.S. 202, 216–17, 102 S.Ct. 2382, 2394–95, 72 L.Ed.2d 786 (1982). Because age is not a suspect classification, distinctions based on age are subject to rational basis review. *Gregory v. Ashcroft*, 501 U.S. 452, 470, 111 S.Ct. 2395, 2406, 115 L.Ed.2d 410 (1991). Plaintiffs argue, however, that strict scrutiny should apply because the ordinance infringes on fundamental rights protected by the Constitution: the right of free movement and the right to travel, as well as First Amendment rights....

Citizens have a fundamental right of free movement, "historically part of the amenities of life as we have known them." *Papachristou*, 405 U.S. at 164, 92 S.Ct. at 844; *see also United States v. Wheeler*, 254 U.S. 281, 293, 41 S.Ct. 133, 134, 65 L.Ed. 270 (1920) ("In all the [s]tates from the beginning down to the adoption of the Articles of Confederation the citizens thereof possessed the fundamental right, inherent in citizens of all free governments, peacefully to dwell within the limits of their respective [s]tates, to move at will from place to place therein, and to have free ingress thereto and egress therefrom..."). Similarly, the Constitution guarantees the fundamental right to interstate travel. *Shapiro v. Thompson*, 394 U.S. 618, 629, 89 S.Ct. 1322, 1328–29, 22 L.Ed.2d 600 (1969).[7]

The City and its amici contend that these are not fundamental rights for minors because minors are traditionally treated differently than adults. The City heavily relies on *Vernonia Sch. Dist. 47J v. Acton*, 515 U.S. 646, 115 S.Ct. 2386, 132 L.Ed.2d 564 (1995), to show that

7. Other circuit courts are split as to whether the Constitution guarantees the fundamental right of intrastate travel. *See Townes v. City of St. Louis*, 949 F.Supp. 731, 734–35 (E.D.Mo. 1996) (not finding such a right and listing cases showing split between the First, Second and Third Circuits finding such a right generally and the Fifth, Sixth, and Seventh Circuits not finding such a right), *aff'd mem.*, 112 F.3d 514, 1997 WL 210442 (8th Cir. Apr. 29, 1997). The Supreme Court has declined to decide the issue. *Memorial Hosp. v. Maricopa County*, 415 U.S. 250, 255–56, 94 S.Ct. 1076, 1080–81, 39 L.Ed.2d 306 (1974); *but cf. Bray v. Alexandria Women's Health Clinic*, 506 U.S. 263, 277 & n. 7, 113 S.Ct. 753, 763–64 & n. 7, 122 L.Ed.2d 34 (1993) (commenting in a section 1983 case against private individuals protesting abortion that a purely intrastate restriction does not violate the right to interstate travel). We need not decide the issue in order to resolve this appeal, so we express no opinion on it.

"unemancipated minors lack some of the most fundamental rights of self-determination—including even the right of liberty in its narrow sense, i.e., the right to come and go at will."[8] *Id.* at [654], 115 S.Ct. at 2391. The City takes *Vernonia*'s statement out of context. In the next sentence the Court explains that children "are subject, even as to their physical freedom, to the control of their parents or guardians." *Id.* Because parental power is not subject to the constitutional constraints of state power, *id.* at [654–655], 115 S.Ct. at 2391–92, minors' lack of rights vis-a-vis parents does not necessarily show that they lack those rights vis-a-vis the state. The Court emphasized the school district's "custodial and tutelary responsibility for children," noting that constitutional rights are different in public schools than elsewhere. *Id.* at [655–656], 115 S.Ct. at 2392. *See also Reno v. Flores*, 507 U.S. 292, 302, 113 S.Ct. 1439, 1447, 123 L.Ed.2d 1 (1993). We decline to extend *Vernonia* to establish that the Constitution does not secure minors' fundamental right to free movement against the government acting without regard to the parents' wishes. *See Hutchins*, 942 F.Supp. at 672 (similarly declining to extend *Vernonia*).

Although many federal courts have recognized that juvenile curfews implicate the fundamental rights of minors,[9] the parties dispute whether strict scrutiny review is necessary. The Supreme Court teaches that rights are no less "fundamental" for minors than adults, but that the analysis of those rights may differ:

> Constitutional rights do not mature and come into being magically only when one attains the state-defined age of majority. Minors, as well as adults, are protected by the Constitution and possess constitutional rights. The Court indeed, however, long has recognized that the State has somewhat broader authority to regulate the activities of children than of adults. It remains, then, to examine whether there is any significant state interest in [the effect of the statute] that is not present in the case of an adult.

Planned Parenthood of Cent. Missouri v. Danforth, 428 U.S. 52, 74–75, 96 S.Ct. 2831, 2843–44, 49 L.Ed.2d 788 (1976) (citations omitted). Thus, minors' rights are not coextensive with the rights of adults because the state has a greater range of interests that justify the infringement of minors' rights.[10]

8. The San Diego ordinance has no exception for emancipated minors. The City does not address any possible differences in the justification for restrictions on emancipated and unemancipated minors.

9. *See, e.g., Johnson*, 658 F.2d at 1072 (examining under overbreadth to see if statute was narrowly tailored); *Hutchins*, 942 F.Supp. at 672 (recognizing the rights are fundamental, even if not treated precisely the same as for adults); *Waters*, 711 F.Supp. at 1139; *McCollester*, 586 F.Supp. at 1384–85; *cf. Bykofsky*, 401 F.Supp. at 1265 (finding no fundamental rights at issue and applying rational basis review, but acknowledging that the Supreme Court had not yet established a framework to analyze minors' rights). *See also Qutb*, 11 F.3d at 492 (assuming without deciding that minors' right to freedom of movement is fundamental and therefore applying strict scrutiny).

10. This conceptual approach also consistently explains the reasoning behind other Supreme Court cases analyzing minors' rights. *See Ginsberg v. New York*, 390 U.S. 629, 636–37 & 643, 88 S.Ct. 1274, 1278–79 & 1282–83, 20 L.Ed.2d 195 (1968) (upholding prohibition on pornography sales to minors and stating that the state may restrict minors' rights more than adults' rights); *Prince v. Massachusetts*, 321 U.S. 158, 167–68, 64 S.Ct. 438, 442–43, 88 L.Ed. 645 (1944) (finding that state's interest in protecting children from "diverse interests of the street" justified restriction on selling street literature that would not have been permissible on adults).

The Supreme Court has articulated three specific factors that, when applicable, warrant differential analysis of the constitutional rights of minors and adults: (1) the peculiar vulnerability of children; (2) their inability to make critical decisions in an informed, mature manner; and (3) the importance of the parental role in child rearing. *Bellotti v. Baird*, 443 U.S. 622, 634, 99 S.Ct. 3035, 3044–45, 61 L.Ed.2d 797 (1979). The *Bellotti* test does not establish a lower level of scrutiny for the constitutional rights of minors in the context of a juvenile curfew. Rather, the *Bellotti* framework enables courts to determine whether the state has a compelling interest justifying greater restrictions on minors than on adults. *Qutb*, 11 F.3d at 492 n. 6; Note, 97 Harv.L.Rev. at 1172–73; *cf. H.L. v. Matheson*, 450 U.S. 398, 441 n. 32, 101 S.Ct. 1164, 1188, 67 L.Ed.2d 388 (1981) (Marshall, J. dissenting) (citing *Danforth*, 428 U.S. at 74–75, 96 S.Ct. at 2843–44, and noting that an analysis of minors' rights should consider whether the state's interests may be more compelling but not whether the rights involved are less fundamental). Further, we reject the City's argument that *Vernonia* changes or abandons the *Bellotti* framework. *Accord Hutchins*, 942 F.Supp. at 673 (reaching same conclusion).

The Court has applied an intermediate scrutiny—determining whether the classification is substantially related to an important government interest—to certain disadvantaged classes that were not suspect classes and to important rights that were not fundamental rights. *See Plyler*, 457 U.S. at 223–24, 102 S.Ct. at 2397–98 (reviewing a burden on the right to public education for illegal immigrant minors); *Mississippi Univ. for Women v. Hogan*, 458 U.S. 718, 724, 102 S.Ct. 3331, 3336, 73 L.Ed.2d 1090 (1982) (reviewing a gender classification); *Lalli v. Lalli*, 439 U.S. 259, 265, 99 S.Ct. 518, 523, 58 L.Ed.2d 503 (1978) (reviewing classification based on illegitimacy of children). Although the state may have a compelling interest in regulating minors differently than adults, we do not believe that this lesser degree of scrutiny is appropriate to review burdens on minors' fundamental rights....

Accordingly, we apply strict scrutiny to our review of the ordinance. In applying this standard, we are mindful that strict scrutiny in the context of minors may allow greater burdens on minors than would be permissible on adults as a result of the unique interests implicated in regulating minors....

B. Strict Scrutiny Review of the Ordinance

In order to survive strict scrutiny, the classification created by the juvenile curfew ordinance must be narrowly tailored to promote a compelling governmental interest. *Plyler*, 457 U.S. at 217, 102 S.Ct. at 2395. To be narrowly tailored, there must be a sufficient nexus between the stated government interest and the classification created by the ordinance. *Id.* at 216–17, 102 S.Ct. at 2394–95.

(1) Compelling Governmental Interest

The ostensible purposes of the ordinance identified by the City in its brief are to protect children from nighttime dangers, to reduce juvenile crime, and to involve parents in control of their children. At oral argument, the City admitted that its "compelling interest is, quite frankly, to reduce gang activity." As the City also admits, however, the ordinance is not limited to gang activities.

The City has a compelling interest in protecting the entire community from crime, *Schall v. Martin*, 467 U.S. 253, 264, 104 S.Ct. 2403, 2409–10, 81 L.Ed.2d 207 (1984), including juvenile crime. The City's interest in protecting the safety and welfare of its minors is also a compelling interest. *See Qutb*, 11 F.3d at 492; *Hutchins*, 942 F.Supp. at 674; *Waters*, 711 F.Supp. at 1139. The fact that much of the perceived danger stems from gang activity does not lessen the nature of the City's interest in protecting the safety and welfare of minors, although it may affect the analysis of whether the ordinance is narrowly tailored....

Furthermore, the government may have a compelling interest in protecting minors from certain things that it does not for adults. *See Sable Communications v. FCC*, 492 U.S. 115, 126, 109 S.Ct. 2829, 2836–37, 106 L.Ed.2d 93 (1989) (holding that a ban on dial-a-porn is not appropriate for adults, although it might be for minors). The City claims its interest in protecting minors from the dangers of public places at night is particularly compelling, for all the reasons set forth in *Bellotti* regarding differential treatment of minors.

As other courts have recognized, *Bellotti* does not set forth reasons that always justify greater restrictions on minors than adults; rather, *Bellotti* sets forth factors for determining whether the government has a greater justification for restricting minors than adults in the manner at issue. *E.g.*, *Waters*, 711 F.Supp. at 1136–37. Our consideration of the *Bellotti* factors leads to the conclusion that greater restrictions of minors may be justified because they have a greater vulnerability at night than do adults and because minors are not equally able as adults to make mature decisions regarding the safety of themselves and others. *See Prince*, 321 U.S. at 168, 64 S.Ct. at 443 (concluding that "the diverse influences of the street" pose greater danger to children than adults). Some courts have reached the opposite conclusion. *Johnson*, 658 F.2d at 1073; *Hutchins*, 942 F.Supp. at 673–74; *Waters*, 711 F.Supp. at 1137; *McCollester*, 586 F.Supp. at 1385. We agree with those courts that all citizens are vulnerable to crime at night and that minors' participation in many legitimate activities does not involve the kind of profound decisions of concern in *Bellotti*. Nonetheless, we find it unexceptional for the City to conclude that minors are more susceptible to the dangers of the night and are generally less equipped to deal with danger that does arise. Thus, the City may have a compelling interest in placing greater restrictions on minors than adults to insure the minors' own safety.

In sum, we find that the City has a compelling interest in reducing juvenile crime and juvenile victimization. We analyze below whether the particular restrictions of the ordinance are narrowly tailored to meet that interest.

(2) Is the Ordinance Narrowly Tailored?

Plaintiffs offer two reasons why the ordinance is not narrowly tailored: (1) the record reflects little statistical support for the efficacy of the curfew; and (2) the exceptions are too narrow to protect minors' fundamental rights.

(a) Statistical Support for Curfew

Plaintiffs attack the City's reliance on national and local statistics to support a juvenile curfew as a narrowly tailored means to reduce juvenile crime and victimization. Although the Constitution does not require the government to produce "scientifically certain criteria of legislation," *Ginsberg*, 390 U.S. at 642–43, 88 S.Ct. at 1282, the City must "demonstrate that its classification is precisely tailored." *See Plyler*, 457 U.S. at 217, 102 S.Ct. at 2395; *see also Hutchins*, 942 F.Supp. at 678 (concluding that the District of Columbia could not adopt the curfew ordinance upheld in *Qutb* without its own evidence showing the particular effectiveness of a nocturnal juvenile curfew in meeting its compelling interests). The City offered several statistical reports to demonstrate that the juvenile curfew is a solution to rising juvenile crime and victimization.

The first piece of evidence is a Justice Department report on juvenile offenders and victims. It shows a rising juvenile crime rate in the nation as a whole but does not provide information specific to San Diego. It also shows that juvenile crime peaks at 3 p.m. and again around 6 p.m. We accept the relevancy of the national crime statistics regarding the general increase of dangers to minors and others, but the national statistics do not conclusively show that the nocturnal juvenile curfew is a narrowly tailored solution.

Second, the City provided the local statistics regarding juvenile crime and victimization; our review of this evidence yields mixed results. The City's October 3, 1994, resolution to continue the aggressive enforcement policy stated that the violent crimes and juvenile activity had decreased during curfew hours from the previous year. In contrast, a San Diego Police Department report dated August 16, 1995, stated that violent crimes had decreased for the third year in a row and that total crime decreased for the sixth consecutive year, thus weakening any link to the increased enforcement of the curfew that began in June 1994. The 1995 report also reveals that the percentage of juvenile victimization that occurred during curfew hours slightly increased in the year following the curfew initiative, that the decrease in overall victimization for adults was larger than for minors, and that only 15 percent of arrests for violent juvenile crimes occurred during curfew hours. The 1996 version of the Police Department's report better supports the City, revealing that from the first quarter of 1995 to 1996 the percentage of victimization that occurred during curfew hours dropped and showing a greater increase in arrests for violent crimes during curfew hours than during other hours.

Overall, the statistical evidence provides some, but not overwhelming, support for the proposition that a curfew will help reduce crime. The City makes little showing, however, that the nocturnal, juvenile curfew is a particularly effective means of achieving that reduction. *Compare Waters*, 711 F.Supp. at 1139–40 (finding no statistical support of necessary nexus) *with Qutb*, 11 F.3d at 493 (discussing specific statistical evidence that Dallas offered to support its curfew).

On the other hand, we reject the City's further justification that the ordinance has the additional beneficial deterrent effect of permitting police officers to get juveniles off the streets before crimes are committed. The Supreme Court has sharply critiqued this type of rationale as overinclusive, at least with respect to adults. *Papachristou*, 405 U.S. at 171, 92 S.Ct. at 848 ("The implicit presumption of these generalized vagrancy standards—that crime is being nipped in the bud—is too extravagant to deserve extended treatment"). Furthermore, the relatively light penalties imposed by the curfew are a small deterrent to crime when compared to the penalties for the actual crimes that the curfew ostensibly seeks to thwart. *See Waters*, 711 F.Supp. at 1139.

Notwithstanding our expressed concerns, we reject a challenge to the ordinance that is based on the argument that a curfew is not particularly effective at meeting the City's interest. The City has established some nexus between the curfew and its compelling interest of reducing juvenile crime and victimization. This is particularly true because of our conclusion that minors have a special vulnerability to the dangers of the streets at night. We will not dismiss the City's legislative conclusion that the curfew will have a salutary effect on juvenile crime and victimization.

(b) The Scope of the Exceptions

In order to be narrowly tailored, the ordinance must ensure that the broad curfew minimizes any burden on minors' fundamental rights, such as the right to free movement. Thus, we examine the ordinance's exceptions to determine whether they sufficiently exempt legitimate activities from the curfew. *See Qutb*, 11 F.3d at 493–94 (stating that the curfew's exceptions were the "most important consideration" in its constitutional analysis of whether the curfew ordinance was narrowly tailored); *Johnson*, 658 F.2d at 1071 (noting lack of meaningful exceptions to justify curfew); *Hutchins*, 942 F.Supp. at 679 (finding that exceptions broader than those in the San Diego ordinance were still insufficient because they were too ill-defined); *Waters*, 711 F.Supp. at 1134 (characterizing a juvenile curfew with few exceptions as "a bull in a china shop of constitutional values"); *McCollester*, 586 F.Supp. at 1385....

Clearly, San Diego could have enacted a narrower curfew ordinance that would pass constitutional muster. Its present ordinance is problematic because it does not provide exceptions for many legitimate activities, with or without parental permission. This is true even though minors may be uniquely vulnerable at night; the curfew's blanket coverage restricts participation in, and travel to or from, many legitimate recreational activities even those that may not expose their special vulnerability. *See Johnson*, 658 F.2d at 1073. In this regard, it is significant that San Diego rejected a proposal to tailor the ordinance more narrowly by adopting the broader exceptions used in the ordinance upheld in *Qutb*. The City's failure to provide adequate exceptions not only excessively burdens minors' right to free movement, but it also excessively burdens their right to free speech....

We therefore conclude that the City has not shown that the curfew is a close fit to the problem of juvenile crime and victimization because the curfew sweeps broadly, with few exceptions for otherwise legitimate activity. The broad sweep of the ordinance is particularly marked for an ordinance aimed, as the City admitted, at illegal gang activity. The district court in *Waters* eloquently explained the constitutional difficulty with a juvenile curfew lacking adequate exceptions:

> The Court recognizes that, in the eyes of many, the crippling effects of crime demand stern responses. With the Act, however, the District has chosen to address the problem through means that are stern to the point of unconstitutionality. Rather than a narrowly drawn, constitutionally sensitive response, the District has effectively chosen to deal with the problem by making thousands of this city's innocent juveniles prisoners at night in their homes.

Waters, 711 F.Supp. at 1135. We conclude that the ordinance is not narrowly tailored to meet the City's compelling interests, as required by strict scrutiny. Thus, we hold that the ordinance is unconstitutional even if given a broad construction to avoid vagueness problems.

III. MINORS' FIRST AMENDMENT RIGHTS AND THE OVERBREADTH DOCTRINE

Minors, like adults, have a fundamental right to freedom of expression. *Tinker v. Des Moines Independent Sch. Dist.*, 393 U.S. 503, 511, 89 S.Ct. 733, 739, 21 L.Ed.2d 731 (1969). Expression includes speech and expressive conduct. Thus, a facial First Amendment challenge to an ordinance can be brought against regulation of "spoken words" or where a statute by its terms regulates the time, place and manner of expressive or communicative conduct. *Broadrick*, 413 U.S. at 612–13, 93 S.Ct. at 2915–17. Not every ordinance that burdens expressive conduct implicates the First Amendment, however. The Supreme Court has said that where the facial challenge involves conduct rather than speech itself, the ordinance's overbreadth "must not only be real, but substantial as well, judged in relation to [its] plainly legitimate sweep." *Id.* at 615, 93 S.Ct. at 2918. Thus, generally applicable regulations of conduct implicate the First Amendment only if they (1) impose a disproportionate burden on those engaged in First Amendment activities; or (2) constitute governmental regulation of conduct with an expressive element. *Arcara v. Cloud Books, Inc.*, 478 U.S. 697, 703–04, 106 S.Ct. 3172, 3175–76, 92 L.Ed.2d 568 (1986).

The San Diego ordinance is a general regulation of conduct, not speech. It does not disproportionately burden those engaged in First Amendment activities more than it burdens other activities during curfew hours; the curfew applies to minors regardless of whether they seek to exercise their right to free expression. The ordinance does, however, restrict minors' ability to engage in many First Amendment activities during curfew hours.

In applying the Supreme Court's teachings, we have stated that a facial challenge must fail unless, at a minimum, the challenged ordinance "'is directed narrowly and specifically at expression or conduct commonly associated with expression.'" *Roulette v. City of Seattle*, 97 F.3d 300, 305 (9th Cir.1996) (quoting *City of Lakewood v. Plain Dealer Publishing*, 486 U.S. 750, 760, 108 S.Ct. 2138, 2145, 100 L.Ed.2d 771 (1988)).

In *Roulette*, we upheld a Seattle ordinance prohibiting sitting or lying on the sidewalk in downtown and in certain neighborhood commercial zones. We reasoned that the ordinance targeted general conduct, not expression. Thus, an overbreadth challenge was inappropriate. We relied on the Supreme Court's statement in *City of Dallas v. Stanglin*, 490 U.S. 19, 25, 109 S.Ct. 1591, 1595, 104 L.Ed.2d 18 (1989), that "[i]t is possible to find some kernel of expression in almost every activity a person undertakes... but such a kernel is not sufficient to bring the activity within the protection of the First Amendment." The City's amici argue that the ordinance in this case similarly does not implicate the First Amendment because going out at night does not itself communicate a message. Thus, the City argues that under *Roulette*, the ordinance should not be seen as a restriction on conduct "integral to, or commonly associated with, expression" that is subject to a facial challenge.

We disagree. San Diego's curfew ordinance restricts access to any and all public forums. This all-encompassing restriction was not present in *Roulette*, where we specifically noted that the Seattle ordinance reached only public sidewalks in certain commercial areas and did not reach "public parks, private or public plazas, or alleys, nor sitting on the sidewalk in noncommercial areas of the city." *Roulette*, 97 F.3d at 302. Unlike the Seattle ordinance in *Roulette*, the San Diego ordinance significantly restricts expression in all forums for one-third of each day.

San Diego's broader restriction prohibits conduct that is a necessary precursor to most public expression—thus qualifying as conduct "commonly associated with" expression. *See City of Maquoketa v. Russell*, 484 N.W.2d 179 (Iowa 1992) (reversing convictions under juvenile curfew ordinance). In the circumstance of a restriction of access to all public forums, we find inapplicable the concern we expressed in *Roulette* regarding facial challenges to regulations of particular nonexpressive conduct; unlike the situation in that case, the San Diego curfew ordinance has an integral effect on the ability of minors to express themselves. Thus, the San Diego ordinance "is directed narrowly and specifically at expression or conduct commonly associated with expression" as required by *Roulette*. 97 F.3d at 305. Accordingly, we conclude that *Roulette* does not preclude a First Amendment facial challenge, and we agree with the Fifth Circuit that First Amendment protections are important in determining the constitutionality of a curfew. *See Qutb*, 11 F.3d at 493–94 (calling the First Amendment exemption the most notable of the important curfew exceptions).

Having concluded a First Amendment facial challenge is permissible, we apply the traditional three-part test to determine whether the ordinance is a reasonable time, place, and manner restriction: (1) it must be content neutral; (2) it must be narrowly tailored to a significant government interest; and (3) it must leave open ample alternative channels for legitimate expression. *Ward v. Rock against Racism*, 491 U.S. 781, 791, 109 S.Ct. 2746, 2753–54, 105 L.Ed.2d 661 (1989). It is undisputed that the regulation is content neutral. Plaintiffs contend that the ordinance fails the other two prongs of the test.

For First Amendment purposes, the physical and psychological well-being of minors is a compelling government interest. *Sable Communications*, 492 U.S. at 126, 109 S.Ct. at 2836–37. Thus, the ordinance must be narrowly tailored to achieve that interest. We hold the ordinance is not narrowly tailored because it does not sufficiently exempt legitimate First Amendment activities from the curfew. The City argues in its brief that "a broad First Amendment expression exception would effectively reduce a curfew ordinance to a useless device." Appellees Br. at 25. This admission destroys an argument that the City narrowly tailored its ordinance to serve its compelling interest in minors' well-being while imposing only a minimal burden on their First Amendment rights. The City did not create a robust, or even minimal, First Amendment exception to permit minors to express themselves during curfew hours without the supervision of a parent or guardian, apparently preferring instead to have no First Amendment exception at all. This is not narrow tailoring. We therefore need not reach the question of whether the ordinance leaves open adequate alternative channels of expression. The ordinance is not a reasonable time, place, and manner restriction under the First Amendment.

The parties also dispute whether the First Amendment is implicated by the ordinance's restrictions on minors' right of association. The Supreme Court has identified two types of recognized rights of association: (1) intimacy; and (2) "expressive association" for First Amendment activity. *Dallas*, 490 U.S. at 24, 109 S.Ct. at 1594–95. The right to expressive association includes assemblies for non-political purposes, such as social, legal, or economic ones, *Griswold v. Connecticut*, 381 U.S. 479, 483, 85 S.Ct. 1678, 1681, 14 L.Ed.2d 510 (1965), although the Constitution does not provide a generalized right to societal association outside the context of expressive association, *Dallas*, 490 U.S. at 25, 109 S.Ct. at 1595. Plaintiffs attempt to distinguish *Dallas* by arguing that a curfew restricts a far broader range of association than that deemed unprotected in *Dallas*, citing *Waters*, 711 F.Supp. at 1134 n. 16 (not applying *Dallas* for that very reason). We need not reach this issue because of our conclusion that the curfew does not provide any exemption even for "expressive association."

We further decline to address the issue of whether the ordinance unconstitutionally violated the right to free exercise of religion because of our conclusion that the ordinance has other constitutional infirmities.

IV. PARENTS' RIGHTS TO REAR THEIR CHILDREN

Examination of the ordinance's burden on the fundamental rights of the minors' parents provides an independent basis for our conclusion that the ordinance, even if construed to avoid vagueness, is nonetheless unconstitutional. It violates the plaintiff parents' substantive due process rights.

The right to rear children without undue governmental interference is a fundamental component of due process. *See Ginsberg,* 390 U.S. at 639, 88 S.Ct. at 1280. Substantive due process under the Fourteenth Amendment "forbids the government to infringe certain 'fundamental' liberty interests *at all,* no matter what process is provided, unless the infringement is narrowly tailored to serve a compelling government interest." *Flores,* 507 U.S. at 302, 113 S.Ct. at 1447.

The custody, care, and nurture of a child reside first in his or her parents. *Stanley v. Illinois,* 405 U.S. 645, 651, 92 S.Ct. 1208, 1212–13, 31 L.Ed.2d 551 (1972). Parental rights are not absolute, however, and are subject to reasonable regulation. *Runyon v. McCrary,* 427 U.S. 160, 178, 96 S.Ct. 2586, 2598, 49 L.Ed.2d 415 (1976); *Prince,* 321 U.S. at 166, 64 S.Ct. at 442 ("Acting to guard the general interest in youth's well being, the state as *parens patriae* may restrict the parent's control by requiring school attendance, regulating or prohibiting the child's labor, or in many other ways"). The City's interest in the health, safety, and welfare of minors is compelling, as analyzed above.

The district court held that the City's legitimate interests greatly outweighed the limited burden on parental autonomy. The City defends this holding on the grounds that it is a minimal burden to prevent parents only from allowing unsupervised children in public places at night. We disagree. The broad sweep of the ordinance, and the paucity of exceptions to allow unsupervised nocturnal activity, burden the parents just as they do the minors.

The curfew is, quite simply, an exercise of sweeping state control irrespective of parents' wishes. Without proper justification, it violates upon the fundamental right to rear children without undue interference. *See Hodgson v. Minnesota,* 497 U.S. 417, 446–47, 110 S.Ct. 2926, 2943, 111 L.Ed.2d 344 (1990) ("The statist notion that governmental power should supersede parental authority in *all* cases because *some* parents abuse and neglect children is repugnant to the American tradition"). The ordinance is not a permissible "supportive" law, but rather an undue, adverse interference by the state. *Cf. Bellotti,* 443 U.S. at 638–39 & n. 18, 99 S.Ct. at 3045–46 & n. 18 (finding requirement for parental consultation before abortion is constitutional because, *inter alia,* it supports parents). The ordinance does not allow an adult to pre-approve even a specific activity after curfew hours unless a custodial adult actually accompanies the minor. Thus, parents cannot allow their children to function independently at night, which some parents may believe is part of the process of growing up. *Cf. Qutb,* 11 F.3d at 496 (stating that the broad exemptions in that ordinance, not present in the San Diego ordinance, allow the parents to make decisions for his or her child in many areas). Accordingly, we find the ordinance to be an unconstitutional burden on parents' fundamental rights.

V. CONCLUSION

We reverse the judgment below because we hold that the ordinance is unconstitutional. When construed in a way that avoids unconstitutional vagueness, it is not narrowly tailored to minimize the burden on minors' fundamental constitutional rights.

NOTES AND QUESTIONS

1. Are status-offense statutes inevitably vague? Is there some reason for that vagueness? Consider the earlier discussion about drafting child-abuse and -neglect statutes. Are some of the justifications for the approaches taken in child welfare applicable to status offenses? Martin Gardner argues that "[m]uch of the controversy and confusion in the case law results from courts assuming that status offense statutes... operate as conduct rules aimed at notifying young people... of conduct to be avoided, when in fact, the rules constitute decision rules aimed at guiding the exercise of juvenile court functionaries and educational officials." Martin R. Gardner, *"Decision Rules" and Kids: Clarifying the Vagueness Problems with Status Offense Statutes and School Disciplinary Rules*, 89 NEB. L. REV. 1, 3–4 (2010). When seen as decision rules, status offenses pose no vagueness problem, because they accord decision makers with discretion, provided that these rules trigger no "punitive disposition." "To say that status conditions are not unconstitutionally vague is not to say, however, that they are free from controversy." *Id.* at 32. What does Gardner mean?

2. In *Nunez*, what rights are infringed by the curfew ordinance? Are these rights held by the child or the parent? What is the applicable standard of review?

3. As part of its analysis, the *Nunez* court considered statistical evidence proffered by the city of San Diego. Do you agree with the court that the statistical evidence provides "some, but not overwhelming, support for the proposition that a curfew will help reduce crime"? What kind of statistical evidence would support the contention that juvenile curfews reduce juvenile crime and victimization? Is that the sort of evidence relied on by the city? According to national data, violent juvenile crime peaks in the after-school hours on school days and in the early evening on nonschool days, leading researchers to conclude that efforts to reduce crime after school would lead to greater reductions in crime rates than would curfews. OJJDP Statistical Briefing Book, Dec. 21, 2010, http://ojjdp.ncjrs.gov/ojstatbb/offenders/qa03301.asp?qaDate=2008. On the other hand, does this suggest that juvenile curfews are working during curfew hours?

Clearly, curfews are politically popular, but is there empirical evidence to support their effectiveness? There seems to be little evidence that juvenile curfews reduce juvenile crime; in fact, many of the studies report either no change in the crime rate or increases in juvenile crime after the implementation of the curfew. Moreover, when children are arrested for curfew violations, police typically do not uncover evidence of more serious crime. Although some studies found that while there was an abrupt decrease in juvenile victimization after the implementation of the curfew, victimization nevertheless gradually and permanently increased over time. Furthermore, there may be some evidence that curfew ordinances are enforced disproportionately against African-American children and their parents. Kenneth Adams, *The Effectiveness of Juvenile Curfews at Crime Prevention*, 587 ANNALS AM. ACAD. POL. & SOC. SCI. 136, 154-155 (2003).

Even if juvenile-curfew ordinances are ineffective at reducing juvenile crime and victimization, could they be justified as a way to enforce parental authority?

4. Why may the state regulate the behavior of children in this way? Could adults be subject to similar restrictions? In *Robinson v. California*, 370 U.S. 660 (1962), the United States Supreme Court held that an individual may not be punished solely because of his status. In *Robinson*, a state statute made it a crime for a person to be addicted to the use of narcotics. The defendant was convicted and was required to serve a minimum of ninety days in jail. The Supreme Court held that "a state law which imprisons a person thus affected as a criminal, even though he has

never touched any narcotic drug within the State or been guilty of any irregular behavior there, inflicts a cruel and unusual punishment in violation of the Fourteenth Amendment.... Even one day in prison would be a cruel and unusual punishment for the 'crime' of having a common cold." *Id.* at 667. Six years later, in *Powell v. Texas*, 392 U.S. 514 (1968), the Court in a plurality opinion held that the state could punish a chronic alcoholic for appearing drunk in public, reasoning that he was convicted for his conduct, not his chronic alcoholism. *Id.* at 532. If the Fourteenth Amendment prohibits punishment based solely on status, are status offenses constitutional? Why or why not?

5. Is it significant that the violation of a curfew ordinance may carry a criminal penalty? In *Commonwealth v. Weston W.*, 913 N.E.2d 832 (Mass. 2009), the Supreme Judicial Court of Massachusetts found the imposition of a criminal penalty significant:

> The criminal prosecution of a minor, with its potential for commitment to DYS, is an extraordinary and unnecessary response to what is essentially a status offense, and is contrary to the State's treatment of similar conduct. For example, when it enacted the child in need of services (CHINS) statute, the Legislature specifically rejected criminal sanctions for status offenses by minors. The CHINS statute "decriminalizes status offenses by focusing on providing nonpunitive care to address the problem of certain children," and "signified a switch from criminalizing truancy and children in need of services to providing protective care for children." The statute itself provides that it must "be liberally construed so that... [children] shall be treated, *not as criminals*, but as children in need of aid, encouragement and guidance" (emphasis added). G.L. c. 119, § 53. Both explicitly (through "Criminal Disposition") and in effect (through possible commitment to DYS), the ordinance undermines these goals by criminalizing status offenses of minors.
>
> Additionally, the Commonwealth has failed to meet its burden to show that the use of criminal penalties provides an increased benefit over the civil enforcement mechanisms of the ordinance sufficient to offset their greater intrusion on the fundamental right. In other words, it has failed to demonstrate that the use of the criminal process and penalties is the least restrictive means of accomplishing its legitimate objective. It makes two passing arguments in its brief in support of the marginal utility of the criminal provision. First, the Commonwealth contends in one sentence that the provision "gives police officers the authority to arrest minors for curfew violations." It does not, however, point to any evidence in the record to support the added utility of this power, nor does it explain why the police should have the power to arrest minors for status offenses, a power in contradiction to the decriminalization goals outlined in the CHINS statute. Second, the Commonwealth argues that "a minor could potentially receive community service as part of his or her probationary sentence." But again, the Commonwealth fails to offer any evidence that community service would be helpful or effective in preventing juvenile crime. Rather, it suggests only that community service "*may* deter a minor from getting into further trouble with law enforcement and *possibly* prevent a minor from engaging in criminal conduct as an adult" (emphasis added). The arguments are nothing more than conjecture, insufficient to meet the Commonwealth's burden on this prong of the "strict scrutiny" test.
>
> ...Applying the strict scrutiny standard, the ordinance's criminal provision unconstitutionally infringes on the minors' rights to freedom of movement. Status offenses such as being abroad at night may not be "bootstrapped" into criminal delinquency and commitment to DYS custody.... The curfew itself and its civil enforcement mechanism, however, represent, as of the date of the proceedings below, a permissible, narrowly tailored response to [the municipality's] compelling interest in preventing crime by, and against, minors. Because the ordinance contains a severability clause, those provisions remain in force.

Id. at 845–846. Is this a persuasive distinction in light of the juvenile court's avowed rehabilitative focus?

6. Constitutional challenges to other types of status offenses based on vagueness or overbreadth claims have been less successful. See, e.g., *Sheehan v. Scott*, 520 F.2d 825 (7th Cir. 1975) (habitually truant not unconstitutionally vague); *District of Columbia v. B.J.R.*, 332 A.2d 58 (D.C. 1975) (statute defining CINS as child who is "habitually disobedient of the reasonable and lawful commands of his parent, guardian or other custodian and is ungovernable" not vague); *In re Gras*, 337 So.2d 641 (La. Ct. App. 1976) (rejecting claim that CINS statute is unconstitutional); *In re Patricia A.*, 286 N.E.2d 432 (N.Y. 1972) (rejecting vagueness challenge to PINS statute because "terms, 'habitual truant,' 'incorrigible,' 'ungovernable,' 'habitually disobedient and beyond…lawful control'…are easily understood"); *In re E.B.*, 287 N.W.2d 462 (N.D. 1980) (holding that "habitually and without justification truant" not unconstitutionally vague); *In re Napier*, 532 P.2d 423 (Okl. 1975) (habitually truant not unconstitutionally vague); *Blondheim v. State*, 529 P.2d 1096 (Wash. 1975) (holding that statutory definition of incorrigibility as beyond control and power of parents gives children of ordinary understanding fair notice of proscribed conduct and does not infringe on First Amendment rights). But see *Gesicki v. Oswald*, 336 F.Supp. 371 (D.N.Y. 1971) (terms "morally depraved and in danger of becoming morally depraved fall far beyond the bounds of permissible ambiguity"). Because age-based classifications are subject to rational-basis review, they, too, have been upheld by the courts. See, e.g., *Nunez*, 114 F.3d at 944 ("Because age is not a suspect classification, distinctions based on age are subject to rational basis review").

On the other hand, equal-protection challenges based on gender have met with a more favorable response. In *In re Patricia A.*, 286 N.E.2d 432 (N.Y. 1972), the New York Court of Appeals considered an equal-protection challenge to a state statute that, in pertinent part, defined a status offender as a male younger than sixteen years of age or a female younger than eighteen years of age. In finding the statute unconstitutional, the court held:

> The argument that discrimination against females on the basis of age is justified because of the obvious danger of pregnancy in an immature girl and because of out-of-wedlock births which add to the welfare relief burdens of the State and city is without merit. It is enough to say that the contention completely ignores the fact that the statute covers far more than acts of sexual misconduct. But, beyond that, even if we were to assume that the legislation had been prompted by such considerations, there would have been no rational basis for exempting, from the PINS definition, the 16 and 17-year-old boy responsible for the girl's pregnancy or the out-of-wedlock birth. As it is, the conclusion seems inescapable that lurking behind the discrimination is the imputation that females who engage in misconduct, sexual or otherwise, ought more to be censured, and their conduct subject to greater control and regulation, than males.

Id. at 435. The court's decision effectively lowered the age of status-offense jurisdiction to sixteen; the legislature did not change the age to eighteen for both genders until 2001. Merril Sobie, *Pity the Child: The Age of Delinquency in New York*, 30 PACE L. REV. 1061, 1074 (2010).

7. *Problem.* Fifteen-year-old Alicia lives with her mother and younger brother in a small apartment in a medium-sized city in the United States. Alicia's parents were never married, and her father is not involved in his children's upbringing. Alicia's mother, Beth, works full-time during the day. Because she is working a forty-hour week, Beth expects Alicia to assume most of the household chores, which include cleaning the house, doing the laundry, fixing dinner, and

doing the dishes. Alicia is having trouble finishing her homework on school nights because of the chores she has to do and is frustrated because she has no free time. Moreover, Beth refuses to let Alicia do anything with her friends on Friday nights or Saturdays if the chores have not been completed. Alicia has rebelled and is refusing to do any more chores. She also has left the house on several occasions to do things with her friends, despite her mother's commands that she remain at home. Beth has gone to the juvenile court and asked for help with her "unmanageable" daughter. Consider the Ohio, New Mexico, and Indiana statutes reprinted at the beginning of the next section. Is Alicia a status offender? If so, should the court intervene?

2. STATUTORY FRAMEWORK

OHIO REV. CODE ANN. § 2151.022 (West 2010)

As used in this chapter, "unruly child" includes any of the following:

(A) Any child who does not submit to the reasonable control of the child's parents, teachers, guardian, or custodian, by reason of being wayward or habitually disobedient;
(B) Any child who is an habitual truant from school and who previously has not been adjudicated an unruly child for being an habitual truant;
(C) Any child who behaves in a manner as to injure or endanger the child's own health or morals or the health or morals of others;
(D) Any child who violates a law... that is applicable only to a child.

N.M. STAT. ANN. § 32A-3B-1 (Thompson Reuters 2010)

B. The Family in Need of Court-Ordered Services Act shall be interpreted and construed to effectuate the following expressed legislative purposes:

(1) through court intervention, to provide services for a family in need of services when voluntary services have been exhausted; and
(2) to recognize that many instances of truancy and running away by a child are symptomatic of a family in need of services and that in some family situations the child and parent are unable to share a residence.

N.M. STAT. ANN. § 32A-3B-2 (Thomson Reuters 2010)

"[F]amily in need of court-ordered services" means the child or the family has refused family services or the department has exhausted appropriate and available family services and court intervention is necessary to provide family services to the child or family and the following circumstances exist:

A. it is a family whose child, subject to compulsory school attendance, is absent from school without an authorized excuse more than ten days during a school year;
B. it is a family whose child is absent from the child's place of residence for a time period of twelve hours or more without consent of the child's parent, guardian or custodian;
C. it is a family whose child refuses to return home and there is good cause to believe that the child will run away from home if forced to return to the parent, guardian or custodian; or
D. it is a family in which the child's parent, guardian or custodian refuses to allow the child to return home and a petition alleging neglect of the child is not in the child's best interests.

IND. CODE ANN. §§ 31-37-2-2 TO 31-37-2-5 (Thomson Reuters 2010)

Sec. 2. A child commits a delinquent act if, before becoming eighteen (18) years of age, the child leaves home:

(1) without reasonable cause; and
(2) without permission of the parent, guardian, or custodian, who requests the child's return....

Sec. 3. A child commits a delinquent act if, before becoming eighteen (18) years of age, the child violates [the law] concerning compulsory school attendance....

Sec. 4. A child commits a delinquent act if, before becoming eighteen (18) years of age, the child habitually disobeys the reasonable and lawful commands of the child's parent, guardian, or custodian....

Sec. 5. A child commits a delinquent act if, before becoming eighteen (18) years of age, the child commits a curfew violation....

NOTES AND QUESTIONS

1. Consider the three statutory approaches. What are the underlying policy considerations? Which, if any, of these do you think serves the interests and needs of children?

2. Depending on the jurisdiction, status offenders may be called delinquent, unruly, incorrigible, children in need of supervision (CHINS or CINS), children in need of protection (CHIPS), children in need of assistance (CINA), persons in need of supervision (PINS), or minors in need of supervision (MINS). In some jurisdictions, such as New Mexico, a family in need of services,

or FINS, petition is filed because the focus is on the entire family. By shifting blame from the child to the cause of intrafamilial disputes, the court may better serve the needs and interests of children. See, e.g., Randy Frances Kandel & Anne Griffiths, *Reconfiguring Personhood: From Ungovernability to Parent Adolescent Autonomy Conflicts*, 53 SYRACUSE L. REV. 995, 1059–1063 (arguing that courts should focus on conflicts within the family rather than on child's behavior); Michael Wald, *State Intervention on Behalf of Neglected Children: A Search for Realistic Standards*, 27 STANFORD L. REV. 985, 1036, n. 273 (1975) (noting that although courts sometimes rely on neglect or PINS jurisdiction to reach "predelinquent" behavior such as truancy, incorrigibility, or curfew violations, better approach would be to focus on entire family, since many of these behaviors indicate some family problem); Lois A. Weithorn, *Envisioning Second-Order Change in America's Responses to Troubled and Troublesome Youth*, 33 HOFSTRA L. REV. 1305, 1462–1463, n. 702 (2005) (stating that status offending may be evidence of significant family dysfunction, abuse, parental absence, or parental need for assistance and noting proposals to assist families rather than target children).

3. Early juvenile-court reformers characterized status offending as predelinquent, hypothesizing that early intervention could prevent juveniles from becoming delinquents or criminals. Barry C. Feld, *The Transformation of the Juvenile Court*, 75 MINN. L. REV. 691, 697 (1991). Even today, juvenile courts still embrace the connection between status offending and delinquent behavior. See, e.g., National Council of Juvenile and Family Court Judges, *A New Approach to Runaway, Truant, Substance Abusing and Beyond Control Children*, 41(4) JUV. & FAM. CT. J. 9 (1990) (status-offending behavior may lead to more serious criminal offending). Do you think any of the statutory approaches above is likely to be successful in reducing delinquency? Status offending?

4. Does the empirical evidence support the contention that status offending is predelinquent behavior? Many studies have found that status offenders do engage in delinquent behaviors in varying degrees, although some studies suggest that these youth may specialize in status offending. See, e.g., Joseph G. Weis, Jurisdiction and the Elusive Status Offender: A Comparison of Involvement in Delinquent Behavior and Status Offenses, U.S. National Institute for Juvenile Justice and Delinquency Prevention, Government Printing Office (1979); Thomas M. Kelley, *Status Offenders Can Be Different*, 29 CRIME & DELINQ. 365 (1983); H. A. Marra & R. Sax, *Personality Patterns and Offense Histories of Status Offenders and Delinquents*, 29 JUV. & FAM. CT. J. 27 (May 1978); Dean G. Rojek & Maynard L. Erickson, *Delinquent Careers: A Test of the Career Escalation Model*, 20 CRIMINOLOGY 5 (1982); Dean G. Rojek & Maynard L. Erickson, *Reforming the Juvenile Justice System: The Diversion of Status Offenders*, 16 L. & SOC'Y REV. 241 (1981–82); Charles W. Thomas, *Are Status Offenders Really So Different? A Comparative and Longitudinal Assessment*, 22 CRIME & DELINQ. 438 (1976). Nevertheless, there is little evidence that status offense careers follow an escalating pattern. Susan K. Datesman & Mikel Aickin, *Offense Specialization and Escalation among Status Offenders*, 75 J. CRIM. L. & CRIMINOLOGY 1246, 1273 (1985). In at least one study, for example, most status offenders never came back to court a second time on a new charge. *Id.* Consequently, some argue that the juvenile court's status-offense jurisdiction should be abolished because it brings children to the court's attention who may pose little real threat to society and whose behaviors would not be considered problematic if they were older. *Id.* at 1274. See also Weis, Jurisdiction and the Elusive Status Offender, 99 (arguing for elimination of status offense and jurisdiction in addition to jurisdiction over less serious behaviors); National Council on Crime & Delinquency, *Jurisdiction over Status Offenders Should Be Removed from the Juvenile Court*, 21 CRIME & DELINQ. 97 (1975). Do you agree?

5. The international community specifically rejects status-offense legislation. For example, in Germany, Sweden, and the Netherlands, status offenders are treated in the child-welfare system. Hans-Jorg Albrecht, *Youth Justice in Germany*, in 31 CRIME & JUSTICE: YOUTH CRIME AND YOUTH JUSTICE: COMPARATIVE AND CROSS-NATIONAL PERSPECTIVES 443 (Michael Tonry & Anthony N. Doob eds., 2004); Carl-Gunnar Janson, *Youth Justice in Sweden*, in 31 CRIME & JUSTICE: YOUTH CRIME AND YOUTH JUSTICE: COMPARATIVE AND CROSS-NATIONAL PERSPECTIVES 391 (Michael Tonry & Anthony N. Doob eds., 2004); Josine Junger-Tas, *Youth Crime in the Netherlands*, in 31 CRIME & JUSTICE: YOUTH CRIME AND YOUTH JUSTICE: COMPARATIVE AND CROSS-NATIONAL PERSPECTIVES 293 (Michael Tonry & Anthony N. Doob eds., 2004). Article 40 of the United Nations Convention on the Rights of the Child states that "[n]o child shall be alleged as, be accused of, or recognized as having infringed the penal law by reason of acts or omissions, that were not prohibited by national or international law at the time they were committed." United Nations Convention on the Rights of the Child, art. 40(2)(a), Nov. 20, 1989, 1577 U.N.T.S. 3. Similarly, article 56 of the United Nations Guidelines for the Prevention of Juvenile Delinquency ("Riyadh Guidelines") urges that "legislation should be enacted to ensure that any conduct not considered an offence or not penalized if committed by an adult is not considered an offence and not penalized if committed by a young person." United Nations Guidelines for the Prevention of Juvenile Delinquency (Riyadh Guidelines), G.A. Res. 45/112, U.N. GAOR, 45th Sess., Annex, Supp. No. 49A, § 56, at 201 U.N. Doc. A/45/49 (1990). Do you think the current approach to status offenders in the United States has changed since early-nineteenth-century reformers first argued that wayward children were bound for a life of criminality, immorality, and poverty?

3. PROCEDURAL FRAMEWORK

a. INITIAL CONTACT WITH GOVERNMENTAL OFFICIALS

i. Age stops

Does a stop based on age violate the Fourth Amendment? If a police officer suspects—but does not know—that someone is a minor, does that give the officer grounds to stop the person and ask his age? What if it is a school day and the officer believes the individual is truant? May he stop and ask him how old he is? *State ex rel. Juv. Dep't of Multnomah Co. v. J.D.*, 164 P.3d 1182 (Ore. Ct. App. 2007). If the truancy law requires sixteen-year-olds to attend school but not seventeen-year-olds, may the police take a seventeen-year-old into custody? *In re State ex rel. R.A.*, 2006 WL 872616 (N.J. Super. Ct. App.). If a police officer sees a youth at a bus station whose appearance is unkempt, and he appears young and lost, does the officer have the authority to stop and question the youth on the ground that he may be a runaway? *In re Bernard G.*, 247 A.D.2d 91 (N.Y. Sup. Ct. 1st App. Div. 1998). If the police see a "female juvenile" sitting on a sidewalk with her back against a building, it is dark outside, and in response to questions she indicates she is fifteen, lives nearby, and is waiting for a friend, do the police have reason to believe she is a runaway? *In re Kelsey C.R.*, 237 Wis.2d 698 (Wis. Ct. App. 2000). More commonly, police stop and question youthful-looking individuals on the street when they suspect that a curfew ordinance is being violated. Do such stops violate the Fourth Amendment? See, e.g., *In re State ex rel. R.M.*, 974 A.2d 1110 (N.J. Super. Ct. App. 2009); *In re M.A.R.*, 718 N.W.2d 480 (Minn. Ct. App. 2006); *State v. Sims*, 851 So.2d 1039 (La. 2003); *In re Ian C.*, 87 Cal. App. 4th 856 (Cal. Ct. App. 1st Div. 2001).

ii. Searches and seizures

If the police believe that the minor is a status offender, may they seize the minor and conduct a search of his or her person or belongings? Would your answer change depending on the nature of the violation? For example, if a police officer believed a minor to be truant, could the officer take the minor into custody and conduct a search of the minor's person and belongings? What authority do the police have to seize children? Is that authority grounded in the state's police power, *parens patriae* power, or both? If the police do have the authority to take children into custody for acts of truancy, why may they search the child's person or belongings? See, e.g., *State ex rel. Juv. Dep't of Multnomah Co. v. J.D.*, 164 P.3d 1182 (Ore. Ct. App. 2007); *In re State ex rel. R.A.*, 2006 WL 872616 (N.J. Super. Ct. App.).

If the police believe that the minor is a runaway, then taking the child into protective custody would seem necessary to protect the child. But is there reason to search the child and his or her belongings? Consider the following case.

IN RE ADRIAN B.
Court of Appeals of Nebraska
658 N.W.2d 722 (2003)

INBODY, Judge.

On February 13, 2002, a petition was filed... alleging that Adrian, a child under 18 years of age,... knowingly or intentionally possessed marijuana weighing 1 ounce or less, and that on the same date, Adrian used, or possessed with the intent to use, drug paraphernalia to manufacture or inject, ingest, inhale, or otherwise introduce into the human body a controlled substance.

On February 20, 2002, a denial was entered and the matter was set for formal hearing. Prior to the formal hearing, Adrian filed a motion to suppress alleging that evidence and statements were obtained in violation of Adrian's constitutional rights, and the hearing on that motion was held on February 28. The sole witness at the hearing was Lincoln police officer Julie Pucket.

Officer Pucket testified that on February 13, 2002, she was contacted by the Goodrich Middle School (Goodrich) principal, who reported that Adrian, who was on runaway status, was inside the school. Officer Pucket knew that Adrian was not currently a student at Goodrich, and she verified that Adrian was a runaway.

Once Officer Pucket arrived at Goodrich, she made contact with Adrian, who was in a counselor's office. Officer Pucket testified that once she entered the counselor's office, Adrian was not free to leave. Officer Pucket had Adrian give her his coat, which he either was wearing or had within his reach, and she patted down the outside of the coat.

Officer Pucket testified that she had had significant contacts with Adrian in her capacity as a school resource officer for 3 years and that during the last year, she had had approximately 90 contacts with Adrian. She further testified that her reasons for conducting the search were that because of her prior contacts with Adrian, she was aware that Adrian had been noncompliant, did not follow rules or listen to authority figures, and was disruptive in the classrooms, and that she was concerned for officer safety and the safety of the students and staff at the school. However, Officer Pucket testified that she was not familiar with Adrian's carrying any weapons. On cross-examination, Officer Pucket testified that she had no basis to believe that Adrian was armed or dangerous and that she considered everyone to be "a potential threat."

Officer Pucket initially patted down the exterior pockets of Adrian's coat. She felt the edge of a blade in the right front coat pocket. Officer Pucket "suspected" that the item was a knife, and she removed the item from the coat pocket. The item turned out to be a pocketknife with a 3-inch blade.

Officer Pucket then flipped the coat over to search the other exterior pocket, at which time a small marijuana "roach" fell out of the right front coat pocket, which was the same pocket from which she had removed the pocketknife. Officer Pucket also located Zig-Zag papers, a wrapping for marijuana cigarettes, in the right front coat pocket. After searching the coat, Officer Pucket, believing Adrian might have a weapon or additional contraband on him, conducted a search of Adrian's person, which resulted in the confiscation of a cigarette lighter. After Officer Pucket's discovery of these items, Adrian was lodged at a juvenile detention facility.

On April 22, 2002, the juvenile court overruled Adrian's motion to suppress evidence....

...The juvenile court found that the allegations contained in the adjudication petition were true beyond a reasonable doubt and adjudicated Adrian as a juvenile. Adrian has timely appealed to this court....

First, we consider the applicability of the Fourth Amendment to the U.S. Constitution in the instant case....

Officer Pucket testified that once she arrived at Goodrich and made contact with Adrian, he was not free to leave. Thus, the protection against unreasonable searches and seizures guaranteed by the Fourth Amendment applies to this case, necessitating an examination of whether Adrian's constitutional rights were violated.

We consider whether the pat-down search of Adrian was constitutional. The State has argued that the following exceptions to the search warrant requirement normally predicated by due process were applicable in this case: an investigatory detention, a search incident to a lawful arrest, and consent.

(a) Investigatory Detention

An officer who reasonably believes that a person is armed and dangerous is entitled for the protection of himself or herself and others to conduct a carefully limited search of the outer clothing of such person in order to discover weapons which may be used to assault him or her. See, *Terry v. Ohio*, 392 U.S. 1, 88 S.Ct. 1868, 20 L.Ed.2d 889 (1968) [other citations omitted]....

The evidence established that Officer Pucket was familiar with Adrian from her 3 years as a school resource officer and that in the past year; she had had more than 90 contacts with him. From these contacts, Officer Pucket was aware of Adrian's history of not complying with rules and authority figures. She was also aware that Adrian was not a student at Goodrich and that Adrian was a runaway.

However, Officer Pucket testified that she was not familiar with Adrian's carrying weapons. Further, Officer Pucket testified that she had no basis to believe that Adrian was armed or dangerous. Based upon the totality of the circumstances, there is not sufficient evidence to establish that Officer Pucket reasonably believed that Adrian was armed and dangerous; consequently, she was not entitled to conduct a pat-down search on that basis, and this exception to the warrant requirement cannot be relied upon to support Officer Pucket's search of Adrian's coat and his person.

(b) Search Incident to Juvenile's Temporary Custody

Next, we consider whether the search was justified as a search incident to Officer Pucket's taking temporary custody of Adrian pursuant to Neb.Rev.Stat. § 43-248(5) (Reissue 1998). The question of whether a search incident to temporary custody of a juvenile pursuant to § 43-248(5) may be performed presents an issue of first impression in Nebraska.

Section 43-248 provides that "[a] juvenile may be taken into temporary custody by any peace officer without a warrant or order of the court when ... (5) [t]here are reasonable grounds to believe that the juvenile has run away from his or her parent, guardian, or custodian." "No juvenile taken into temporary custody under section 43-248 shall be considered to have been arrested, except for the purpose of determining the validity of such custody under the Constitution of Nebraska or the United States." Neb.Rev.Stat. § 43-249 (Reissue 1998).

Other courts have considered whether a search incident to temporary detention may be performed on juveniles who are "in custody" but have not been arrested. In *State ex rel. J.M.*, 339 N.J.Super. 244, 249, 771 A.2d 651, 654 (2001), the New Jersey Superior Court recognized a "'search incident to detention'" exception to the warrant requirement but found that in the case before it, the exception was not applicable because the search occurred at the police station, not at the time of the detention, and thus was remote in both time and place from the location of the detention.

In *Matter of Terrence G.*, 109 A.D.2d 440, 492 N.Y.S.2d 365 (1985), the New York Supreme Court considered whether the pat-down search of a juvenile taken into custody was constitutionally permissible. Officers took the juvenile into custody after observing him standing outside a subway station at 12:30 p.m., in a high crime area and in violation of truancy laws. Upon taking him into custody, officers conducted a pat-down search for weapons.

In finding that the pat-down search was permissible, the court stated, "Nothing in the noncriminal appellation of this detention serves to obliterate the dangers of the 'in-custody' situation. Here, the circumstances of [the juvenile's] detention, coupled with the particularly high duty of protection owed him and other detainees by the runaway statute, were more than ample justification for the patdown." *Id.* at 446, 492 N.Y.S.2d at 370. The court further stated:

> Given the location and nature of [the juvenile's] first encounter with the detaining officers, the fact that he was lawfully in full custody under the authority of a statute that exists solely for his protection and the protection of other children in the detention area, and given the limited

> nature of the search, we find the legality of that search to be irrefutable. Any other result would undermine the vital purpose of the runaway laws and, in effect, demand of our police officers that they abdicate common sense.

Id. at 447–48, 492 N.Y.S.2d at 371.

Other courts have also approved searches of juveniles taken into custody but not arrested. See, *In re J.M.*, 995 S.W.2d 838 (Tex.App. 1999) (officer who took juveniles into custody for violating curfew ordinance could conduct search incident to arrest); *State ex rel. R.D.*, 749 So.2d 802 (La.App. 1999) (once law enforcement officer has taken juvenile into physical custody, even though offense committed is not defined as "crime," search incident to arrest may properly be conducted in order to ensure that juvenile does not possess weapons or other dangerous instruments). See, also, *People v. Dandrea*, 736 P.2d 1211, 1220 n. 1 (Colo. 1987) (Vollack, J., dissenting) (search of juvenile, incident to his being taken into "'temporary custody,'" is controlled by same search and seizure principles that apply to adult arrests); *People, Int. of B.M.C.*, 32 Colo.App. 79, 506 P.2d 409 (1973); *In re Nancy C.*, 28 Cal.App.3d 747, 105 Cal.Rptr. 113 (1972) (search incident to arrest of juvenile arrested for violation of curfew ordinance upheld); *State v. Brammeier*, 1 Or.App. 612, 464 P.2d 717 (1970) (search incident to arrest of juvenile taken into custody upheld).

But see, *State v. Paul T.*, 128 N.M. 360, 993 P.2d 74 (1999) (deciding case under New Mexico Constitution, New Mexico Supreme Court rejected State's argument that search incident to arrest exception to warrant requirement justified full search of juvenile taken into custody for curfew violation but not arrested); *State v. Hough*, 163 Mont. 47, 516 P.2d 613 (1973) (while police had right to take into custody suspected runaway juvenile, search of defendant's purse for purpose of obtaining identification of defendant was not proper where other, more reliable means of obtaining identification were not pursued by police officers, and marijuana and hashish found in purse could not be seized as incident to lawful arrest because defendant was not arrested, but simply taken into custody for purpose of proving her identification); *In Interest of J.F.F.*, 164 Wis.2d 10, 473 N.W.2d 546 (Wis.App. 1991) (concluding that search of juvenile following "arrest" for violation of curfew ordinance was invalid because police lacked statutory authority to arrest child for violating municipal curfew ordinance).

In Nebraska, one of the stated purposes of our juvenile code is "[t]o assure the rights of all juveniles to care and protection and a safe and stable living environment and to development of their capacities for a healthy personality, physical well-being, and useful citizenship and to protect the public interest." Neb.Rev.Stat. § 43-246(1) (Reissue 1998). It follows that the provisions of § 43-248 which allow peace officers to take juveniles into temporary custody under certain circumstances are in place to protect both the juvenile and the public interest.

Allowing a search incident to temporary detention of a juvenile after the juvenile is taken into temporary custody protects the juvenile, law enforcement officers, and others with whom the juvenile may come into contact. Further, denying law enforcement officers the authority to conduct searches of juveniles being taken into temporary custody would require officers to take unnecessary risks in the performance of their duties. Therefore, we hold that when a juvenile is taken into temporary custody pursuant to § 43-248, the peace officer may conduct a search incident to temporary detention. Having determined that a search of a juvenile incident to temporary detention pursuant to § 43-248 is constitutionally permissible, we now consider whether the search of Adrian was proper.

Pursuant to a lawful custodial arrest, law enforcement officers may conduct a warrantless search of the person arrested and of the immediately surrounding area in order to remove any weapons that the arrestee may use to resist arrest or effect an escape and in order to prevent the concealment or destruction of evidence. *State v. Prahin*, 235 Neb. 409, 455 N.W.2d 554 (1990). See *State v. Roach*, 234 Neb. 620, 452 N.W.2d 262 (1990). We find that this law is equally applicable to searches incident to the lawful temporary detention of juveniles pursuant to § 43-248.

In the instant case, Officer Pucket had the authority to take Adrian into temporary custody pursuant to § 43-248(5) because she had reasonable grounds to believe that he had run away from his parent, guardian, or custodian. Officer Pucket testified that Adrian was not free to leave once she arrived in the counselor's office; thus, Adrian had been detained at that point. Further, once Adrian was detained, Officer Pucket could conduct a search of Adrian's person and the immediately surrounding area in order to remove any weapons and in order to prevent the concealment or destruction of evidence. Thus, the search of Adrian's coat was constitutionally permissible and the motion to suppress was properly denied by the juvenile court.

(c) Consent

Having determined that the search of Adrian was justified, we need not consider whether Adrian consented to the search....

Affirmed.

NOTES AND QUESTIONS

1. In *Adrian B.*, the court noted that Officer Pucket had authority to take Adrian into temporary custody pursuant to state statute. The current version of the statute authorizes a police officer to take temporary custody of a minor when:

(1) A juvenile has violated a state law or municipal ordinance and the officer has reasonable grounds to believe such juvenile committed such violation;
(2) A juvenile is seriously endangered in his or her surroundings and immediate removal appears to be necessary for the juvenile's protection;
(3) The officer believes the juvenile to be mentally ill and dangerous...and that the harm described in that section is likely to occur before proceedings may be instituted before the juvenile court;
(4) The officer has reasonable grounds to believe that the juvenile has run away from his or her parent, guardian, or custodian;
(5) A probation officer has reasonable cause to believe that a juvenile is in violation of probation and that the juvenile will attempt to leave the jurisdiction or place lives or property in danger; or
(6) The officer has reasonable grounds to believe the juvenile is truant from school.

Neb. Rev. Stat. § 43-248 (West 2010). In the absence of such a statute, would the police have the authority to take a juvenile into custody for a status offense?

2. In *In re Bernard G.*, 247 A.D.2d 91 (N.Y. Sup. Ct. 1st App. Div. 1998), the police took a boy into protective custody to determine whether he was a runaway. After being transported to the police station, the youth was questioned and frisked. When the pat-down turned up no weapons, the officer asked the minor to empty his pockets, and two small jars of marijuana were discovered. After an additional thirty minutes of questioning, the officer searched a plastic shopping bag the minor was carrying and discovered thirty-eight vials of crack, a small bag of crack, and five small jars of marijuana. Was the pat-down justified? Based on the results of that search, could the police ask the minor to empty his pockets? Was the subsequent search of the shopping bag permissible under the Fourth Amendment?

3. What if the police discover that the child is not a status offender? In *In re Kelsey C.R.*, 237 Wis.2d 698 (Wis. Ct. App. 2000), the police ascertained that a female juvenile was not a runaway but were asked by her mother to "bring her home." Before transporting her in the police car, the officer called for the assistance of a female officer to pat down the minor. After the female officer arrived, she conducted the pat-down and discovered a small loaded handgun. Was the prolonged detention of the minor permissible? Did the search violate the minor's constitutional rights?

4. Although courts have upheld the facial validity of curfew ordinances on Fourth Amendment grounds—see, e.g., *Hutchins v. District of Columbia*, 188 F.3d 531 (D.C. Cir. 1999); *Waters v. Barry*, 711 F.Supp. 1125, 1137–1138 (D. D.C. 1989); *Peckman v. City of Wichita*, No. 00-1065-JTM, 2000 WL 1294422, at *4 (D. Kan., Aug. 15, 2000)—Fourth Amendment challenges do arise. To what extent may the police search a minor detained for a curfew violation? Could such a search be justified on *Terry* grounds? See *L.A.F. v. State*, 698 N.E.2d 355, 355–356 (Ind. Ct. App. 1998). An inventory search? See *In re B.M.C.*, 506 P.2d 409, 411 (Colo. App. 1973). What about a search incident to arrest? See *State v. Paul T.*, 993 P.2d 74 (N.M. 1999).

b. INTERROGATIONS

Under what circumstances must police give *Miranda* warnings to status offenders? As a threshold matter, the Supreme Court has held that the Fifth Amendment privilege applies when a person's statements may be used against him or her in any future criminal proceeding. *Minnesota v. Murphy*, 465 U.S. 420, 426 (1986) (quoting *Lefkowitz v. Turley*, 414 U.S. 70, 77 (1973)). Does the fact that a status offender may be placed outside the home at disposition, albeit not in a secure facility, sufficient to trigger the Fifth Amendment? *In re Investigation No. 04-730*, 794 N.Y.S.2d 873 (N.Y. 2005). Consider a state statute that provides for the filing of a CHIPS petition whenever a minor younger than twelve has committed a delinquent act. May the police question an eleven-year-old at school about his involvement in an arson without first providing *Miranda* warnings? See, e.g., *In re Thomas J.W.*, 570 N.W.2d 586 (Wis. Ct. App. 1997). If *Miranda* does apply, are status offenders in state custody? If so, are they being interrogated? For example, suppose a police officer suspects that someone is violating curfew and asks the person his name, address, and age. After ascertaining that the suspect is a minor, the officer then asks, "Do you have anything on you that you are not supposed to have?" The response is incriminating. Is *Miranda* violated? At what point? See *In re M.A.O.*, No. 04-07-00658-CV (Tex. Ct. App. Dec. 10, 2008).

c. IDENTIFICATION PROCEDURES

Generally, states do not authorize fingerprinting and photographing of status offenders. But a few states may permit the police to fingerprint or photograph a minor alleged to be a status offender under narrowly defined circumstances. For example, in Maine, the police may photograph a minor who is lost, abandoned, endangered, or a runaway "solely for the purpose of restoring the juvenile to his residence." Under these circumstances, however, the police may not fingerprint the minor. 15 Me. Rev. Stat. § 3501(9) (2010). See also Vernon's Texas Statutes and Codes Annotated Family Code § 58.0022 (2008) (police may fingerprint and photograph a child upon probable cause to believe the child is a runaway in order to ascertain child's identity, but once identity is ascertained or if photograph and fingerprints do not reveal child's identity, fingerprints must be destroyed). In New Jersey, if a juvenile is detained or committed to an institution, authorities may fingerprint the minor for identification purposes but must destroy the fingerprints "when the purpose for taking them has been fulfilled," unless the minor was detained or committed because of a delinquent act. N.J. Stat. Ann. § 2A:4A-61(a)(2) (2011).

Problem. A state legislator would like to propose a bill that would create a missing-child prevention and identification program. As she envisions the program, children would be fingerprinted and photographed at school. The school administration then would maintain the records for use by law enforcement in locating missing children. Assume that you work for the state legislator. Would such a bill pass constitutional muster? What additional procedural safeguards do you think would need to be in place?

d. INTAKE, DETENTION, AND DEINSTITUTIONALIZATION

Law-enforcement officials refer fewer than half of all status-offense cases. When considering the type of offense, however, law-enforcement officials may refer most, if not almost all, juveniles to the court. For example, law-enforcement agencies overwhelmingly refer curfew violations to the juvenile court; in 2008, 96 percent of all such referrals came from law enforcement, and that percentage has remained virtually unchanged since 1995. In the same year, law-enforcement agencies also referred a majority of runaway cases to the court (53 percent), up from 38 percent of all such referrals in 1995. On the other hand, only 18 percent of truancy referrals were made by law-enforcement agencies in 2008; in contrast, school officials referred 70 percent of these. Similarly, while law-enforcement agencies referred 27 percent of ungovernability cases in 2008, up from 17 percent in 1995, relatives referred 42 percent of juveniles for ungovernability. Charles Puzzanchera, Benjamin Adams, & Melissa Sickmund, National Center for Juvenile Justice, Juvenile Court Statistics 2008 82 (2011).

In 2008, the juvenile courts handled approximately 156,300 status-offense cases, an increase of 34 percent from 1995. Of the petitioned cases, 33 percent involved truancy, 23 percent liquor-law violations, 12 percent ungovernability, 12 percent runaway, and 10 percent curfew. *Id.* at 72. Case rates typically increased by age: seventeen-year-olds had the highest rates overall, although fifteen-year-olds had higher rates in cases involving runaway, truancy, and ungovernability petitions. *Id.* at 74–75. Girls accounted for 43 percent of all status-offense cases but only 26 percent of all delinquency cases; moreover, girls accounted for 59 percent of all petitioned runaway cases. Nevertheless, the petitioned runaway caseload decreased by 15 percent for girls between 1995 and 2007. *Id.* at 77–78.

As with delinquency cases, minorities are overrepresented among petitioned status offenders. The number of status-offense cases increased significantly across all racial groups between 1995 and 2008. For Asian youths, status offending increased by 42 percent, black youths 45 percent, and Native American youths by 56 percent, while for white youths it increased by 20 percent. In 2008, the status-offense case rate for Native American youths was twice the rate for white youths. The case rate for black youths also exceeded the white youths' rate. *Id.* at 81.

In order to qualify for grants under the Juvenile Justice and Delinquency Prevention Act (JJDPA), a state must submit a plan that conforms to certain conditions. Since the first enactment in 1974, these requirements have included a mandate that status offenders and children alleged to be neglected, abused, or dependent not be institutionalized. Nevertheless, there are certain exceptions to the deinstitutionalization mandate. First, juveniles held pursuant to the Interstate Compact on Juveniles may be placed in secure detention. The Interstate Compact is a multistate agreement that provides states with procedural mechanisms for dealing with juveniles who have crossed state lines and who have run away from home, the court, or other legal authorities. 42 U.S.C. § 5633(a)(11)(A)(iii) (2011). Second, juveniles who have been charged with handgun possession under federal or state law may be held in a secure facility. 42 U.S.C. § 5633(a)(11)(A)(i) (2011).

Last, juveniles charged with or adjudicated for violating a valid court order may be held in a secure facility. 42 U.S.C. § 5633(a)(11)(A)(ii) (2011). Prior to the passage of the JJDPA, secure detention facilities had been the standard disposition for chronic status offenders. Because not many states had in-home intervention services, the JJDPA deinstitutionalization mandate left judges with few options for youths who they felt were in need of services. As a way of circumventing this provision, courts would "bootstrap" status offenders into the delinquency system by detaining them if they violated a valid court order. These practices led to the Valid Court Order Amendment in 1980, which places conditions on, but does not preclude, this type of confinement. 42 U.S.C. § 5633(a)(23) (2011) (requiring representative of appropriate public agency to interview detained juvenile in person within twenty-four hours and requiring court to hold hearing within forty-eight hours to consider agency assessment and determine whether there is reasonable cause to believe juvenile violated order and appropriate placement pending disposition of case).

There are some additional "*de minimis*" exceptions. States "which have an institutionalization rate of status offenders less than 5.8 per 100,000 population will be considered to be in full compliance with de minimis exceptions. Those states whose rate falls between 17.6 and 5.8 per 100,000 population will be eligible for a finding of full compliance with de minimis exceptions if they adequately meet additional reporting requirements. Those states whose rate is above the average of 17.6 but does not exceed 29.4 per 100,000 will be eligible for a finding of full compliance with de minimis exceptions only if they fully satisfy additional reporting requirements. Finally, those states which have a placement rate in excess of 29.4 per 100,000 population are presumptively ineligible for a finding of full compliance with de minimis exceptions because any rate above that level is considered to represent an excessive and significant level of status offenders and non-offenders held in juvenile detention or correctional facilities." Policy and Criteria for de Minimis Exceptions to Full Compliance with Deinstitutionalization Requirement of the Juvenile Justice and Delinquency Prevention Act, 1974, as amended, 46 Fed. Reg. 2566-01 (Jan. 9, 1981).

Today the states respond to these mandates in several different ways. Some states prohibit the placement of youth in secure facilities under any circumstances. Others use the contempt power of the court to detain youth. Still other states have refused JJDPA funding and place both alleged and adjudicated juvenile status offenders in secure institutions. Jessica R. Kendall, American Bar Association, Juvenile Status Offenses: Treatment and Early Intervention, Technical Assistance Bulletin No. 29 1–2 (2007). May individuals sue to enforce the provisions of 42 U.S.C. § 5633? Some courts have found that violating § 5633 constitutes a deprivation of a right, privilege, or immunity, actionable under 42 U.S.C. § 1983. See, e.g., *James v. Wilkinson*, Civ. A. No. 89-0139-P(CS) (W.D. Ky., May 20, 1991) (plaintiffs have right under 42 U.S.C. § 1983 to challenge violations of JJDPA based on placing and commingling status offenders and delinquents in secure facilities); *Hendrickson v. Griggs*, 672 F.Supp. 1126 (N.D. Iowa 1987) (plaintiffs have right to enforce JJDPA under 42 U.S.C. § 1983, but failure to deinstitutionalize status offenders is *de minimis*). But see *Doe v. McFaul*, 599 F.Supp. 1421 (N.D. Ohio 1984) (holding that JJDPA does not provide express right of action or form the basis of a civil rights action). Is there another way states may circumvent the deinstitutionalization mandate? Look again at Ind. Code Ann. §§ 31-37-2-2 to 31-37-2-5. What is a status offender?

Despite the deinstitutionalization mandate, approximately thirteen thousand juveniles were detained for status-offense violations in 2008. This represents an increase of 54 percent since 1995, although the proportion of all cases involving detention has remained virtually unchanged. Runaway and truancy petitions each constitute 19 percent of all detained status-offense cases, although the percentage of cases involving runaways has declined by 8 percent since 1995. Detentions for ungovernability make up 15 percent of all detained cases. Cases involving liquor-law violations, however, account for the largest share of detained status-offense cases (23 percent). Juvenile Court Statistics 2008, at 83.

Given that status offenders may be held in secure facilities, are there any additional constitutional protections they should receive? Consider the following case involving predetention strip searches.

MASHBURN V. YAMHILL COUNTY
United States District Court for the District of Oregon
698 F.Supp.2d 1233 (2010)

MOSMAN, District Judge.

Plaintiffs are or were minors who were strip searched upon entry into the Yamhill County Juvenile Detention Center ("YCJDC") and after "contact visits" with non-YCJDC staff members, including their own lawyers. Plaintiffs sued Yamhill County, Tim Loewen, the Yamhill County Director, and Chuck Vesper, the Yamhill County Division Manager under 42 U.S.C. § 1983, alleging that the YCJDC strip search policy is unreasonable under the Fourth Amendment. The parties filed cross-motions for summary judgment that centered on the constitutionality of the YCJDC strip search policy....

I. Factual Background...

YCJDC policy authorizes staff members to conduct strip searches after a juvenile is admitted to the detention center. The detention center has a detailed intake policy that evaluates a juvenile's charged crime, criminal history, physical and mental well-being, and the behavior giving rise to the juvenile's arrest. A juvenile may only be admitted if the juvenile: (a) is the subject of a court order to detain; (b) is the subject of a Circuit Court statewide or nationwide warrant; (c) violated conditions of probation; (d) violated conditions of conditional release; (e) allegedly committed a felony; (f) allegedly possessed a firearm unlawfully; (g) allegedly committed the offense of Criminal Manufacture or Delivery of a Controlled Substance; (h) committed a misdemeanor resulting in physical injury; (i) is a fugitive from another jurisdiction; or (j) wilfully failed to appear at a juvenile court proceeding. In addition to one of these factors, the juvenile must also be either a flight risk or engaged in behavior that endangers herself, others, or the community.

The detention center policy also authorizes strip searches after "contact visits" with non-YCJDC staff. Contact visits take place in an open room and are only permitted when the visitor is professional, such as an attorney or mental health counselor. Personal visitors, such as parents or guardians, are allowed only non-contact visits in which the visitor and the juvenile are physically separated by a glass partition. The YCJDC policy does not authorize strip searches after non-contact visits....

III. Evaluating the Reasonableness under the Fourth Amendment

Plaintiffs allege that the YCJDC strip search policy violates their Fourth Amendment right to be free from "unreasonable searches and seizures." U.S. Const. amend. IV.... The first question is whether the search is justified at its inception; that is, whether it is reasonable under the Fourth Amendment for the government to perform a strip search without individualized suspicion. The second question is whether the scope of the search is reasonable; that is, whether the government's "need for the particular search" outweighs "the invasion of personal rights that the search entails." *See Bell v. Wolfish*, 441 U.S. 520, 559, 99 S.Ct. 1861, 60 L.Ed.2d 447 (1979)....

IV. The Constitutional Standard Governing Strip Searches in Juvenile Detention Facilities

Neither the Supreme Court nor the Ninth Circuit has directly ruled on the constitutionality of strip searches conducted on juvenile detainees. On the constitutional spectrum, the standard for analyzing strip searches of children at the YCJDC falls somewhere between the standards that govern searches of adult prison inmates and searches of school children.

Unlike students, "youth confined in a juvenile detention facility are 'under substantially greater restraint and ha[ve] a lesser expectation of privacy than do students.'" Conversely, standards that apply in the context of an adult prison strip search are not directly transferrable to juvenile detention searches because "[s]trip searches of children pose the reasonableness inquiry in a context where both the interests supporting and opposing such searches appear to be greater than with searches of adults." *N.G. v. Connecticut*, 382 F.3d 225, 232 (2d Cir. 2004); *see also May v. Anderson*, 345 U.S. 528, 536, 73 S.Ct. 840, 97 L.Ed. 1221 (1953) (Frankfurter, J., concurring) ("Children have a very special place in life which law should reflect. Legal theories...lead to fallacious reasoning [if] uncritically transferred to determination of a State's duty towards children"). Specifically, the State's exercise of legitimate custodial authority over the child gives the State a heightened interest in caring for detained children, which must be balanced against the child's more acute vulnerability to the intrusiveness of a strip search. *N.G.*, 382 F.3d at 232. Moreover, the power differential always present between a guard and a prisoner is greatly magnified when the "guard" is an adult and the "prisoner" is a child. A juvenile detention facility also has different penological interests, in light of the fact that some juveniles are admitted to a detention facility without having committed conduct that would constitute a crime. Accordingly, the unique concerns of children and of the government, which have analogies in both prisons and schools, frame my analysis of YCJDC's search policy.

V. Are the YCJDC Strip Searches Justified at Their Inception?...

...I conclude that defendants have shown two important interests that justify conducting some form of suspicionless search. First, like a teacher in a public school, defendants act as guardians to the children in the detention facility. This guardianship status gives rise to special responsibilities and obligations to care for and protect detained children. Second, as in a prison, defendants have an interest in maintaining the security of the detention facility.

With respect to strip searches at admission, the YCJDC policy could be unconstitutional as applied to juvenile admittees whose conduct or reason for admission does not raise security concerns. But all of the plaintiffs in this case engaged in conduct that created concern about whether they would introduce drugs or weapons into the detention facility, thereby justifying the strip search at its inception. With respect to strip searches after contact visits, however, the policy is unconstitutional because YCJDC has not shown that its institutional interests justify suspicionless searches.

A. Admission Searches

1. The Constitutionality of the Policy...

Even assuming that the YCJDC intake process evaluates each juvenile's charged conduct, mental and physical health, and circumstances of arrest, defendants have not shown that the criteria for admission to YCJDC bear a reasonable relationship to the facility's institutional security concerns. For example, if a juvenile commits an armed robbery, YCJDC may admit the juvenile because he is charged with a violent felony and may be a danger to others. In that case, the factor that drives the government to detain the juvenile—community safety—is the same factor that creates an institutional interest in strip searching him. But the YCJDC policy also allows juveniles to be admitted to the detention facility for failing to appear for a court hearing, disobeying a court order, or being a fugitive from another jurisdiction. In these cases, the factors that support detention are not the same as the factors that support a strip search. The fact that juvenile runaways and truants may be admitted to juvenile detention facilities is one of the reasons that the constitutional standards governing adult prison searches are not directly applicable in the context of juvenile detention facilities. *See N.G.*, 382 F.3d at 235 ("No doubt a state has a legitimate interest in confining such juveniles in some circumstances, but it does not follow that by placing them in an institution where the state might be entitled, under *Turner*, to conduct strip searches of those convicted of adult-type crimes, a state may invoke *Turner* to justify strip searches of runaways and truants"). On the face of the YCJDC policy, some juveniles are admitted and strip searched for reasons that would not result in adult incarceration, or that do not raise serious community safety concerns. In those cases, a strip search would not be constitutional without reasonable suspicion.

2. The Constitutionality of Searches of Individual Plaintiffs

A strip search is designed to meet the institution's security concern that drugs and weapons will be introduced into the detention facility. Ideally an institution would search only those juveniles whose underlying conduct involved drugs or a weapon. But I cannot assume on this record that YCJDC has the resources or opportunity to make accurate factual findings regarding the actual conduct of an admitted juvenile, as opposed to categorical distinctions based on the juvenile's charges. Absent evidence that YCJDC could rely on readily ascertainable facts about each juvenile's background upon admission, it is appropriate for the facility to make determinations about the likelihood of smuggling drugs or weapons based solely on categories of charged conduct....

...Even taking into account the heightened concerns of the children being subjected to a strip search, I conclude that it was reasonable for Yamhill County to conduct a strip search of the named plaintiffs in light of the institutional security concerns raised by the charged conduct and juvenile criminal history known to YCJDC staff at the time of the search.

B. Contact Visits

I agree...that it is unconstitutional to strip search juveniles after contact visits and without individualized suspicion that the juvenile has acquired contraband. Because contact visits occur primarily between the juvenile and his or her attorney, the repetitive strip searches at YCJDC burden not only the juvenile's privacy interests, but also the juvenile's right to counsel....It is not hard to imagine a juvenile...begging her attorney not to come visit her again, lest she be subjected to an Nth strip search. Nor is it any better to envision a troubled young person declining to visit with her therapist for the same reason.

In contrast to the heightened interests of children subjected to repetitive post-contact visit searches, Yamhill County's interests are reduced. Juveniles are only permitted contact visits with visitors who are extremely unlikely to provide a juvenile with drugs or weapons, and, in most cases, a strip search will already have occurred when the juvenile was admitted to the detention facility. Because the child's privacy and other constitutional interests are heightened, and the government's interests are reduced, YCJDC's general security and custodial interest are not sufficient to outweigh the intrusiveness of the strip search.

VI. Is the Scope of the Admission Search Reasonable?

In order for the search to be reasonable under the Fourth Amendment, the government's demonstrated need must outweigh the harm caused by the search. I have found that maintaining institutional security and protecting detained children are legitimate government interests justifying—at their inception—these particular strip searches. But a search that is justified as an initial matter can nevertheless be executed in such a manner as to lose its initial constitutional protection. See [*Safford Unified Sch. Dist. #1 v.*] *Redding*, [557] U.S. [364], 129 S.Ct. [2633,] 2642–43[, 174 L.Ed.2d 354 (2009)] (holding that "the content of the [searcher's] suspicion failed to match the degree of intrusion")....And, on this record, I hold that defendants have not shown a reasonable relationship between their legitimate interests and the scope of the strip searches conducted at YCJDC.

A. Intrusiveness

The strip searches conducted on children detained at YCJDC are unquestionably intrusive. Children and adults have a right to bodily privacy in part because "[t]he desire to shield one's unclothed figure from [the] view of strangers...is impelled by elementary self-respect and personal dignity." *York v. Story*, 324 F.2d 450, 455 (9th Cir. 1963). For this reason, a strip search is the kind of search that "instinctively gives [courts] the most pause." *Wolfish*, 441 U.S. at 558, 99 S.Ct. 1861. Various circuit courts have described strip searches as "a serious intrusion upon personal rights," *Justice v. City of Peachtree City*, 961 F.2d 188, 192 (11th Cir. 1992); "an offense to the dignity of the individual," *Burns v. Loranger*, 907 F.2d 233, 235 n. 6 (1st Cir. 1990), and "demeaning, dehumanizing, undignified, humiliating, terrifying, unpleasant, embarrassing, [and] repulsive," *Mary Beth G. v. City of Chicago*, 723 F.2d 1263, 1272 (7th Cir. 1983) (quotation and citation omitted). Strip searches of children raise unique concerns, since youth "is a time and condition of life when a person may be most susceptible to influence and to psychological damage." *Eddings v. Oklahoma*, 455 U.S. 104, 115, 102 S.Ct. 869, 71 L.Ed.2d 1 (1982); *see also Redding*, 129 S.Ct. at 2641 (evaluating the reasonableness of a strip search in light of "adolescent vulnerability [that] intensifies the patent intrusiveness of the exposure"); *N.G.*, 382 F.3d at 239 (Sotomayor, J., dissenting) (noting that "[c]hildren are especially susceptible to possible traumas from strip searches," particularly when they are victims of sexual abuse) (quoting *Eddings*, 455 U.S. at 115, 102 S.Ct. 869).

And the strip searches conducted at YCJDC are more intrusive than most. For example, they are not brief. *After* the minor removes all of his or her clothing, a YCJDC staff member:

1. Inspects the child from top to bottom;
2. Inspects the minor's hair;
3. Inspects the minor's ears;
4. Inspects the minor's mouth, including requiring the child to lift her upper and lower lips and run her fingers between her teeth and gums;
5. Requires the minor to blow each nostril, one at a time;
6. Inspects the minor's hands;
7. Inspects the minor's armpits;
8. Inspects a girl's breasts or a boy's testicles;
9. Requires the minor to squat and cough;
10. Requires the minor to face the wall so staff can inspect the back of the minor's body; and
11. Inspects the minor's feet, including in between the toes.

The minor is allowed to put on his or her clothes only after all of these steps have been completed. The duration of this multi-step search, and the corresponding length of time in which a juvenile stands fully exposed and subject to inspection, makes this search particularly demeaning.

The YCJDC strip searches are also, to put it charitably, astonishingly thorough. A boy is required "to lift his scrotum so that staff can inspect the area directly below the testicles." If a boy is uncircumcised, "he is instructed by staff to pull back the foreskin so that the area beneath the foreskin can be inspected." Girls are required to lift their breasts "so that staff can inspect the area directly below."

YCJDC could mitigate the length and intensity of its strip searches by taking steps to ensure that the child is not fully exposed for longer than is reasonably necessary to accomplish its search objectives. But aside from moving the child to [a] private area, YCJDC makes no extra effort to preserve the privacy and dignity of the searched child. For example, a child spends the entire search completely naked even though a majority of the time-consuming steps described above—including searches of hair, ears, mouth, nose, hands, armpits, and toes—do not require complete nudity. The intrusiveness of these strip searches stands in contrast to other searches of juveniles that have been held constitutional and that did indicate extra effort to preserve the privacy and dignity of the searched child. For example, in *Smook v. Minnehaha County*, the Eighth Circuit found it material that the detention center staff required a juvenile to undress only to her undergarments, which "placed her at the same level of undress as if she were at the beach in a swimsuit." 457 F. 3d 806, 811–12 (8th Cir. 2006) (internal quotation and citation omitted). Likewise, in *Reynolds v. City of Anchorage*, each detained girl was instructed "to remove her blouse and bra, put them back on, and then to remove her bottom clothing and underwear and bend over to allow a visual inspection of her rectal area." 379 F.3d at 361. Even the juveniles subjected to the highly invasive strip searches at issue in *N.G. v. Connecticut* may have been provided robes during the search at issue. *See* 382 F.3d at 228 (noting that the strip search policy was amended in 2002, after plaintiffs were searched, to deauthorize visual inspections of a juvenile's vaginal and anal body cavities, but not indicating whether use of robes predated the 2002 policy amendment).

B. The Relationship between the Government Interest and Scope of the Strip Search

Defendants raise valid concerns about their obligations to care for and protect juveniles who are admitted to YCJDC. But the existence of that need, in and of itself, says little about the reasonableness of the search under the Fourth Amendment because a search may be too intrusive in light of the underlying interests justifying it.... Even accepting that defendants' concerns are legitimate, the record does not show that a highly invasive strip search bears a reasonable relationship to the interests defendants identified....

There is a lot of space on the continuum between a fully-clothed pat-down search and the thorough strip search conducted pursuant to YCJDC policy, however, and [defendants fail] to explain why it is "reasonably necessary" to perform a search of a juvenile's hair while the juvenile is completely undressed. Even assuming that a fully-clothed pat-down search would not reveal contraband, nothing... demonstrates these harms could not be discovered in a search that is more extensive than a fully-clothed pat-down search but less intrusive than a lengthy and intrusive strip search. There are several less intrusive alternatives to the YCJDC policy that would not jeopardize the State's legitimate interests. For example, YCJDC could search juveniles while they are wearing underwear, could give them a robe or gown, or could perform the mouth, hair, arms, and feet inspection while the children were partially or fully clothed. In the context of adult prisons, "the existence of obvious, easy alternatives may be evidence that the regulation is not reasonable, but is an 'exaggerated response' to prison concerns." *Turner*, 482 U.S. at 90, 107 S.Ct. 2254.

The existence of less intrusive alternatives is more compelling in the context of a juvenile detention facility than in a prison. Even though the privacy interest of a detained juvenile is less than that of a student, the Constitution still requires some showing that the scope of the search is reasonable in light of a child's acute vulnerability. Here, far from presenting evidence that the scope of a strip search is a reasonable means of furthering institutional security interests, the YCJDC has presented only vague references to "incidents" in which "drugs, contraband and other illegal items" were discovered during strip searches. Defendants have provided no evidence of what items were discovered, how many items were discovered, where these items were discovered, or even a rough estimate of what percentage of searches result in discovery of some sort contraband.... And defendants have been unable to identify a single instance in which contraband has been found in an area that would have been concealed by a juvenile's underwear, as opposed to outer clothing.

The record also shows that Yamhill County could employ less intrusive alternatives without undermining its custodial obligations to care for the health and well-being of juvenile detainees.... [W]hile defendants note that strip searches allowed YCJDC personnel to identify a skin disease, evidence of self-mutilation, and bruises on some of the named plaintiffs in this case, each of these medical conditions "could have been discovered without a full strip search" because they were visible on the plaintiff's neck, shoulders, or arms. What is missing from defendants' argument is any evidence to suggest that the scope of the YCJDC strip search policy is "not excessively intrusive in light of the age and sex of the [juvenile detainee] and the nature of the infraction," or, in our case, the nature of the interest justifying the search. *See T.L.O.*, 469 U.S. at 342, 105 S.Ct. 733; *see also Redding*, 129 S.Ct. at 2642–43 (holding a strip search in a school unreasonable in the absence of "any indication of danger to students... [or] any reason to suppose that [the student] was carrying pills in her underwear")....

...Although general institutional security concerns may justify a detention facility in conducting a brief strip search to inspect for contraband that would be hidden by a child's underwear, a greater showing of need is required to justify keeping a child undressed to conduct an extensive search of areas that can be searched while the child is partially or fully clothed.

Because a strip search is so much more invasive and potentially harmful than other searches, it must be kept within its allowable use. YCJDC can require its youth to strip only when being strip searched, and not at other times. For those portions of the admissions search that do not require full nudity, a strip search is too intrusive. This includes inspection of the scalp, ears, hands, feet, mouth, and nose. It also includes visual inspection that can be performed while the youth is partially clothed or wearing a robe. The availability of less intrusive alternatives to a highly invasive strip search, combined with a lack of evidence that less intrusive alternatives would undermine defendants' legitimate interests, demonstrates that the extensive scope of the YCJDC strip search policy is an exaggerated response to its legitimate institutional concerns. Accordingly, I hold that the YCJDC policy is unconstitutional in its scope.

[The court holds that two of the individual defendants are entitled to qualified immunity and that the plaintiffs have standing to seek injunctive and declaratory relief. The court then grants the plaintiffs' motion for partial summary judgment with respect to the constitutionality of the policy.]

NOTES AND QUESTIONS

1. Two of the named plaintiffs in the case, Cory Mashburn and Ryan Cornelison, were held in detention for five days. Mashburn was strip-searched five times, and Cornelison was strip-searched eight times during the five-day period. Another named plaintiff was strip-searched four times in six days—once at admission and then three subsequent times after meeting with her attorneys. *Mashburn*, 698 F.Supp.2d, at 1240–1241.

The boys, fourteen at the time of the lawsuit, had been charged with felony sex abuse. The charges stemmed from an incident in which the boys allegedly swatted the behinds of girls at their middle school. The charges were reduced and then dropped after news coverage triggered public outrage. Susan Goldsmith, *McMinnville Boys Sue over Strip-Searches*, OREGONIAN, June 18, 2008, A1. Does their behavior warrant the filing of delinquency charges, or do you think the courts should have dealt with them as status offenders?

2. Who may be detained at the detention center? Under the existing policy, who may be strip-searched? Why did the court find that the policy was unconstitutional? If the detention-center policy had distinguished between juveniles charged with delinquent acts and juveniles charged as status offenders, do you think the policy would have been upheld?

3. The *Mashburn* court cites two circuit court cases, *Smook v. Minnehaha County*, 457 F.3d 806 (8th Cir. 2006); and *N.G. v. Connecticut*, 382 F.3d 225 (2d Cir. 2004). In *Smook*, the Eighth Circuit upheld a search of juveniles detained on allegations that they had committed status offenses on the grounds that the strip search, which did not require the juveniles to remove their underwear, was reasonable under the Fourth Amendment. *Smook*, 457 F.3d, at 812. In *N.G.*, the Second Circuit upheld the same sort of invasive strip search of status offenders that the *Mashburn* court found unconstitutional; then-Circuit Judge Sonia Sotomayor dissented in part, arguing that strip searches require individualized suspicion. *N.G.*, 382 F.3d at 245 (Sotomayor, dissenting). Both cases were decided before the Supreme Court issued its opinion in *Redding* (and by that time, Justice Sotomayor had joined the Court).

4. In *Bell v. Wolfish*, 441 U.S. 520 (1979), the Supreme Court held that the Due Process Clause prohibits the punishment of a pretrial detainee. Under what circumstances would the pretrial detention of status offenders violate the Due Process Clause? The JJDPA mandates the deinstitutionalization of status offenders and prohibits the institutionalization of juveniles in adult jails, except under limited circumstances. Does the JJDPA create a federal right that is enforceable? If so, would placing status offenders in secure facilities, with children accused of delinquent acts, or in facilities without treatment violate the JJDPA and the Due Process Clause? See *James v. Wilkinson*, No. Civ. A. 89-0139-P (CS) (W.D. Ky., May 20, 1991). Could the conditions of confinement render the pretrial detention of status offenders unconstitutional? How? See, *D.B. v. Tewksbury*, 545 F.Supp. 896 (D. Or. 1982).

e. TRIAL RIGHTS

i. Right to counsel

Most states have, by statute or court rule, extended certain procedural rights to juveniles charged with status offenses. For example, a number of jurisdictions authorize the appointment of counsel for status offenders under certain circumstances. Ala. Code § 12-15-202(f)(1) (West 2011) (appointment required where there is a possibility that the child may be placed in an institution where the child's freedom may be curtailed or appointment permitted when in the interests of justice); Alaska Stat. § 47.10.050 (West 2011) (court may appoint if the welfare of the child will be promoted thereby); Ariz. Rev. Stat. Ann. § 8-221 (West 2011) (when proceeding may result in detention); Ark. Code Ann. § 9-27-316 (West 2011); Cal. Welf. & Inst. Code § 634 (West 2011); Conn. R. Super. Ct. Juv. § 30a-1 (West 2011); D.C. Code § 16-2304 (West 2011) (entitled to representation at all critical stages of the proceedings); Fla. Stat. Ann. § 984.17 (West 2011); Ga. Code Ann. § 15-11-6 (West 2011); Haw. Rev. Stat. § 571-87 (West 2011); Idaho R. Juv. R. 9 (2010); Idaho Code Ann. § 20-514 (West 2011); Ind. Code Ann. § 31-32-4-2 (West 2011); Iowa Code § 232.126 (2011) (court shall appoint attorney or guardian *ad litem* for child in family in need of assistance proceedings); Kan. Stat. Ann. § 38-2205 (West 2011) (court may appoint attorney for child when child's position inconsistent with guardian *ad litem*'s assessment of best interests); Md. Code Ann. Cts. Jud. Proc. § 3-8A-20 (West 2010); Mass. Gen. Laws ch. 119, § 39F (West 2011); Minn. Stat. § 260C.163 (West 2012) (court shall appoint counsel for any child older than ten except in habitual truancy case, but if child to be placed out of home, then court must appoint counsel); Miss. Unif. Rules Youth Ct. Prac. R. 24 (West 2010); Mont. Code Ann. § 41-5-1413 (West 2011); Neb. Rev. Stat. § 43-272 (West 2011); Nev. Rev. Stat. § 62D.030 (West 2011); N.H. Rev. Stat. Ann. § 169-D:12 (West 2011); N.M. Stat. § 32A-3B-8 (West 2011) (court shall appoint attorney for child older than fourteen in family in need of court-ordered services proceedings); N.Y. Fam. Ct. Act § 741 (West 2011); N.D. Cent. Code § 27-20-26 (West 2011); Ohio Rev. Code § 2151.352 (West 2011); Okla. Stat. tit. 10A, § 2-2-402 (2011) (right to remain silent, cross-examination of witnesses); R.I. Gen. Laws § 14-1-31 (West 2011); S.D. Codified Laws § 26-7A-31 (2011); Tenn. Code Ann. § 37-1-126 (2012); Tex. Fam. Code Ann. § 51.10 (Vernon 2011); Vt. Stat. Ann. Tit. 33, § 5112 (West 2011); W. Va. Code § 49-5-9 (2011); Wis. Stat. Ann. § 938.23 (West 2011) (appointment of counsel discretionary, but child may not be placed outside the home unless counsel appointed); Wyo. Stat. Ann. § 14-6-422 (West 2011).

But if there is no statute, does a child have a constitutional right to counsel in a status-offense proceeding? Consider the following case.

BELLEVUE SCHOOL DISTRICT V. E.S.
Supreme Court of Washington
257 P.3d 570 (2011)

ALEXANDER, J.

We are asked to decide whether the due process clause of the Fourteenth Amendment to the United States Constitution or the due process clause set forth in article I, section 3 of the Washington Constitution requires appointment of counsel to represent a child at an initial truancy hearing. The Court of Appeals, Division One held that due process protections compel appointment of counsel at that stage of a truancy proceeding. We hold that the Court of Appeals erred in making that determination and, therefore, reverse its decision.

I

During the 2005–06 and 2006–07 school years, E.S. was enrolled as a student at Highland Middle School in the Bellevue School District (the District). E.S. was 13 years old during the 2005–06 school year. According to the District, E.S. was absent from school on 73 of the first 100 days of that school year. Many of the absences, it concluded, were unexcused. In response to E.S.'s absences, the District sent letters and made numerous phone calls to the child's mother, Velmanija Serdar, informing her of the absences. All communication between the school and Serdar prior to the truancy hearing was in the English language even though Serdar is a native Bosnian speaker and her facility with English is somewhat limited. Early in January 2006, a meeting took place between E.S., Serdar, and the assistant principal of Highland Middle School, Diane Tuttle. The purpose of that meeting was to discuss a plan to reengage E.S. with school with the objective of ensuring the child's attendance on a regular basis. At the meeting, E.S. and Serdar were informed by Tuttle that any further absences by E.S. for medical reasons needed to be verified by a doctor's note and that Washington law required the school district to file a truancy petition in juvenile court if her unexcused absences continued. Despite these warnings, E.S. continued to miss school.

On March 1, 2006, the District filed a truancy petition in the King County Juvenile Court pursuant to the provisions of RCW 28A.225.035. In it they sought an order requiring E.S. to attend school. A hearing on the petition was held before a King County Juvenile Court commissioner on March 6, 2006. The hearing was attended by E.S., Serdar, and the District's representative, Glenn Hasslinger. E.S. and her mother were not represented by counsel at this hearing, and they did not request that counsel be appointed for either of them. Serdar was, however, provided with a Bosnian interpreter to assist her in communicating with the court.

During the hearing, E.S. explained to the court commissioner that one of the reasons she missed so much school was that she had been experiencing stomach pain. She went on to state, however, that many of her absences were attributable to the fact that she did not want to go to school. The court commissioner informed E.S. that absences for any medical issue required a doctor's note. The commissioner also indicated that she expected E.S. to be in class every day for the rest of the school year. E.S. said that she understood what she was being told and agreed with the requirement that she attend school. The commissioner also explained to E.S. and Serdar that if E.S. did not go to school, the District can bring a motion for contempt. At the contempt hearing if the [c]ourt finds that you have not been going to school and you do not have a valid reason, then the [c]ourt can enter sanctions against you. Those sanctions usually start out as…evaluations, community service, [or] book reports. But if the truancy continued, we would be looking at house arrest, work crew, and possibly detention.

Verbatim Report of Proceedings at 3. The juvenile court commissioner then determined that E.S. was truant and ordered her to attend school on a regular basis. A review hearing was scheduled for March 27, 2006.

E.S. continued to miss school. Consequently, on March 15, 2006, prior to the previously scheduled review hearing, the District initiated contempt proceedings against E.S. and scheduled a show cause hearing for March 27, 2006. At the conclusion of the March 27 hearing, at which E.S. was represented by appointed counsel, the juvenile court commissioner held E.S. in contempt and ordered her to complete 10 hours of volunteer work. The court commissioner did indicate, however, that if E.S. complied with all orders in effect, the contempt would be purged. E.S. failed to attend school or perform the volunteer work. At a review hearing on

May 8, 2006, at which E.S. was again represented by counsel, E.S. was found by the juvenile court to have failed to purge the contempt. She was then ordered to obey all orders then in effect and complete an additional 10 hours of volunteer work.

E.S.'s failure to attend school and complete volunteer work continued. At a review hearing on June 14, 2006, where E.S. was again represented by counsel, E.S. was again found by the juvenile court to be in contempt. On this occasion, the court ordered her to write a two-page paper explaining the value of education and setting forth her plan for how she could become a successful student. It also ordered E.S. to spend six days in detention at home with an electronic monitor. Over the course of the summer of 2006 and during the 2006–07 school year, the juvenile court conducted additional contempt hearings. E.S. was represented by counsel at each of these hearings. At these hearings the court determined that E.S. was either in contempt or had failed to purge the contempt. The court entered various orders at each hearing, including requirements that E.S. write a five-page paper, participate in the enrollment process at an alternative school and attend that school and obtain therapy. Following a hearing on March 21, 2007, the juvenile court entered what turned out to be its last order in this matter, determining that E.S. had not purged the contempt.

On May 22, 2007, E.S.'s counsel filed a motion to set aside the truancy finding, arguing that the juvenile court should have appointed counsel for E.S. at the initial truancy hearing and that because of its failure to do so, the truancy finding should be vacated. At the hearing on that motion, counsel for E.S. argued that, notwithstanding the fact that the March 6, 2006, finding of truancy was made pursuant to an agreement, at 13 years of age E.S. could not have fully understood the legal issues involved in her case. E.S.'s counsel also contended that the District failed to take the statutorily required steps to help E.S. reengage in school before filing the truancy petition and that an attorney could have presented this argument to the court at the initial hearing. The juvenile court denied the motion to set aside the finding of truancy and continued the contempt hearing, originally scheduled for April 4, 2007, to the beginning of the new school year.

E.S. asked the King County Superior Court to modify the juvenile court commissioner's decision denying her motion to set aside the truancy finding. The superior court affirmed the commissioner's decision. E.S. then appealed to the Court of Appeals. That court vacated the finding of truancy and held that "[a] child's interests in her liberty, privacy, and right to education are in jeopardy at an initial truancy hearing" and that due process requires the provision of counsel for all children appearing at an initial truancy hearing. *Bellevue Sch. Dist. v. E.S.*, 148 Wash.App. 205, 220, 199 P.3d 1010 (2009). The District, through the office of the King County Prosecuting Attorney, then filed a petition in this court seeking review of the Court of Appeals' decision. We granted review. *Bellevue Sch. Dist. v. E.S.*, 166 Wash.2d 1011, 210 P.3d 1018 (2009).

II

We are asked to decide whether the due process clause of the Fourteenth Amendment to the United States Constitution or article I, section 3 of the Washington Constitution requires that counsel be appointed to represent a child at an initial truancy hearing. We review constitutional issues de novo.

III

As noted above, the Court of Appeals concluded that a child who is not represented by counsel at an initial truancy hearing is denied due process of law. Because E.S. was not represented at that hearing, the Court of Appeals vacated the truancy finding. *See Bellevue*, 148 Wash. App. at 220, 199 P.3d 1010. The Court of Appeals reached its conclusion after applying the balancing test set forth by the United States Supreme Court in *Mathews v. Eldridge*, 424 U.S. 319, 96 S.Ct. 893, 47 L.Ed.2d 18 (1976). That test is to be applied by a court in determining the extent to which procedural due process considerations impose constraints on governmental decisions that deprive individuals of "liberty" or "property" interests within the meaning of the due process clause of the Fourteenth Amendment to the United States Constitution. *Id.* at 332–35. After applying the test, the Court of Appeals determined that the risk of erroneous deprivation of E.S.'s interests in her physical liberty, privacy, and education outweighed any countervailing government interest.

The District contends that the Court of Appeals erred in determining that E.S.'s due process rights were violated, asserting that E.S.'s physical liberty interest was not at stake at the initial truancy hearing and that courts have never required appointment of counsel to protect a child's privacy and education interests. E.S. responded in a supplemental brief to this court that even if the Fourteenth Amendment does not compel appointment of counsel for a child in an initial truancy hearing, article I, section 3 of the Washington Constitution, which, according to E.S., offers broader due process protections than its federal counterpart, does compel appointment of counsel. To this contention, the District argues that the factors set forth in *State v. Gunwall*, 106 Wash.2d 54, 720 P.2d 808 (1986), do not support an independent analysis of this state's due process clause.

Significantly, RCW 28A.225.035(10) provides as follows: "The court may permit the first [truancy] hearing to be held without requiring that either party be represented by legal counsel." Therefore, in order for us to reach a conclusion that E.S.'s right to due process under the Fourteenth Amendment and/or article I, section 3 of the state constitution has been violated by the juvenile court's decision to not provide her with counsel at the initial truancy hearing, we would have to hold that RCW 28A.225.035(10) is unconstitutional. This statute, like most statutes, is presumed to be constitutional, and the burden of overcoming that presumption resides with the challenger. *Fed. Way Sch. Dist. No. 210 v. State*, 167 Wash.2d 514, 523–24, 219 P.3d 941 (2009).

Fourteenth Amendment to the United States Constitution

The Fourteenth Amendment essentially provides that a state may not deprive persons of "life, liberty, or property" without providing them with "due process of law." U.S. Const. amend. XIV, § 1. "The due process clause of the Fourteenth Amendment confers both procedural and substantive protections." *Amunrud v. Bd. of Appeals*, 158 Wash.2d 208, 216, 143 P.3d 571 (2006) (citing *Albright v. Oliver*, 510 U.S. 266, 114 S.Ct. 807, 127 L.Ed.2d 114 (1994)). At issue here is E.S.'s claim that she was denied procedural due process. "When a state seeks to deprive a person of a protected interest, procedural due process requires that an individual receive notice of the deprivation and an opportunity to be heard to guard against erroneous deprivation." *Id.* (citing *Mathews*, 424 U.S. 334). "The opportunity to be heard must be ""at a meaningful time and in a meaningful manner,"" appropriate to the case." *Id.* (quoting *Mathews*, 424 U.S. at 333 (quoting *Armstrong v. Manzo*, 380 U.S. 545, 552, 85 S.Ct. 1187, 14 L.Ed.2d 62 (1965))). "'[D]ue process,' unlike some legal rules, is not a technical conception with a fixed content unrelated to time, place and circumstances.'" *Mathews*, 424 U.S. at 334 (alteration in original) (quoting *Cafeteria & Rest. Workers Union Local 473 v. McElroy*, 367 U.S. 886, 895, 81 S.Ct. 1743, 6 L.Ed.2d 1230 (1961)). "'[D]ue process is flexible and calls for such procedural protections as the particular situation demands.'" *Id.* (alteration in original) (quoting *Morrissey v. Brewer*, 408 U.S. 471, 92

S.Ct. 2593, 33 L.Ed.2d 484 (1972)). Under the *Mathews* balancing test, cited above, a court must consider three factors in identifying the due process that a person is entitled to receive in a particular circumstance: (1) "the private interest that will be affected by the official action"; (2) "the risk of an erroneous deprivation of such interest through the procedures used, and the probable value, if any, of additional or substitute procedural safeguards"; and (3) "the [g]overnment's interest, including the function involved and the fiscal and administrative burdens that the additional or substitute procedural requirement would entail." *Id.* at 335.

E.S. contends that three of her private interests are at stake in this case, including physical liberty, bodily privacy, and education. With respect to the first of these interests, E.S. asserts that her physical liberty was threatened because the juvenile court's truancy order was a necessary and direct predicate to its later finding of contempt and imposition of a detention sanction consisting of home monitoring. E.S. contends in that regard that she was not afforded due process because at the point of contempt proceedings, no challenge to the original truancy finding is available. The District responds that due process concerns do not arise if, as here, deprivation of a child's physical liberty is merely potential or hypothetical. In support of its argument, the District points to the United States Supreme Court's decision that "an indigent's right to appointed counsel is that such a right has been recognized to exist only where the litigant may lose his physical liberty if he loses the litigation" and, accordingly, the "'mere threat'" of punishment is insufficient to require appointment of counsel. *Lassiter v. Dep't of Soc. Servs.*, 452 U.S. 18, 25, 26, 101 S.Ct. 2153, 68 L.Ed.2d 640 (1981) (quoting *Scott v. Illinois*, 440 U.S. 367, 373, 99 S.Ct. 1158, 59 L.Ed.2d 383 (1979)). While it is true that the initial hearing with which we are here concerned must precede a contempt hearing, the "mere possibility that an order in a hearing may later serve as the predicate for a contempt adjudication is not enough to entitle an indigent party therein to free legal assistance." *Tetro v. Tetro*, 86 Wash.2d 252, 255 n. 1, 544 P.2d 17 (1975); see also *In re Truancy of Perkins*, 93 Wash.App. 590, 969 P.2d 1101 (concluding that children are not entitled to appointed counsel at the initial truancy hearing), *review denied*, 138 Wash.2d 1003, 984 P.2d 1033 (1999). In our view, it is significant that contempt sanctions could not have been imposed against E.S. at the initial truancy hearing since a petition for contempt had not yet been filed. Indeed, as we have observed above, when the contempt petition was filed and there was a possibility that the juvenile court could deprive E.S. of her physical liberty, E.S. was provided with counsel. In sum, the truancy order that was issued at the initial hearing did not deprive E.S. of her physical liberty.

The second private interest that E.S. identifies is bodily privacy. E.S.'s counsel argues that E.S.'s private interest in her bodily privacy would be at stake if the court, under RCW 28A.225.035 and RCW 28A.225.090, required E.S. to submit to testing for the use of controlled substances or alcohol. Under RCW 28A.225.090(1)(e), a court has authority to order a child to submit to testing for the use of controlled substances or alcohol only if it makes "a determination that such testing is appropriate to the circumstances and behavior of the child and will facilitate the child's compliance with the mandatory attendance law." We have recognized that, as a general proposition, school children "have a lower expectation of privacy" and that drug testing of students based on individualized suspicion, rather than suspicionless random testing, is permissible under our state constitution. *York v. Wahkiakum Sch. Dist. No. 200*, 163 Wash.2d 297, 308, 178 P.3d 995 (2008).[5] Because there was no basis for individualized suspicion of

5. We also noted that the United States Supreme Court has recognized a lower expectation of privacy for students and has "applied a standard of reasonable suspicion to determine the legality of a school administrator's search of a student, and [has] held that a school search 'will be permissible in its scope when the measures adopted are reasonably related to the objectives of the search and not excessively intrusive in light

drug or alcohol use by E.S., the juvenile court properly did not order such testing. If there had been such a showing, the testing may well have been appropriate because we have recognized a lower expectation of privacy for students in Washington State, notwithstanding the fact that E.S. was then unrepresented. The fact is, however, that the juvenile court did not order testing, so there was no basis to intrude on E.S.'s bodily privacy at the initial truancy hearing.

The third private interest that E.S. denotes is her right to an education under article IX, section 1 of our state constitution. Citing the Court of Appeals' reasoning, E.S. claims that a misguided decision made during an initial truancy hearing "could disrupt the child's education by introducing or exacerbating stigma, uncertainty, and instability." Suppl. Resp't's Br. at 20 (citing *Bellevue*, 148 Wash.App. at 216, 199 P.3d 1010). We thoroughly disagree with this contention, and note that the overriding purpose of the compulsory school attendance and admission statute, chapter 28A.225 RCW, is to protect, rather than interfere with, the child's right to an education. Clearly, a child must attend school in order to receive the benefits that flow from the right to an education. It cannot be said that, by holding an initial truancy hearing to determine why E.S. refused to attend school and to establish a plan for her to begin attending school regularly, the juvenile court subtracted in any way from the State's "paramount duty...to make ample provision" for E.S.'s education. Wash. Const. art. IX, § 1. Thus, we agree with the District's argument that the holding advanced by E.S. and adopted by the Court of Appeals would stand the aforementioned provision "on its head." Pet'r's Suppl. Br. on State Constitutional Claim at 6. For the reasons explained above, we conclude that E.S. failed to show any private interest that was affected by the initial truancy hearing.

In regard to the second *Mathews* factor, the risk of erroneous deprivation, E.S. asks us to conclude that counsel should be appointed for a child facing an initial truancy hearing because the child, without benefit of counsel, is in danger of being disadvantaged in truancy proceedings. This would, she asserts, include the initial hearing, because of the child's limited ability to act and reason like an adult. We readily agree the child should be afforded appointed counsel at a contempt proceeding. That, though, is not an issue since a child is entitled to counsel at that stage. Indeed, as we have noted, E.S. had the benefit of counsel at her first and all subsequent contempt hearings. Furthermore, the initial hearing did not adversely affect any of E.S.'s private interests. While it may have been comforting to E.S. and her mother to have been accompanied by legal counsel at the initial hearing, the issues that are before the court at the initial hearing on a truancy petition are uncomplicated and straightforward. Indeed, the record shows that E.S. was able to explain to the juvenile court why she missed school. Faced with E.S.'s statements, the juvenile court judge told her that she needs to see the school nurse if she feels ill and that she could not skip more school days if she wanted to go on to the eighth grade. E.S. indicated that she understood what the judge was telling her and that she did not have additional problems at school that prevented her from attending regularly. By enacting RCW 28A.225.035, the legislature determined that appointed

of the age and sex of the student and the nature of the infraction.'" *Safford Unified Sch. Dist. No. 1 v. Redding*, [557] U.S. [364], 129 S.Ct. 2633, 2639, 174 L.Ed.2d 354 (2009) (citations omitted) (quoting *New Jersey v. T.L.O.*, 469 U.S. 325, 342, 105 S.Ct. 733, 83 L.Ed.2d 720 (1985)). Here, it is important to point out that if testing were ordered, that decision would be made by the juvenile court, which is in the best position to determine whether testing "reasonably related to the objectives of the search and [is] not excessively intrusive in light of the age and sex of the student and the nature of the infraction," rather than by school administrators. *See* RCW 28A.225.090(1)(e).

counsel is not required at initial truancy hearings, and we fail to see what would be gained if additional or substitute procedural safeguards were required at that stage.[8]

The third *Mathews* factor, governmental interests, is only briefly mentioned by E.S.'s counsel, who addresses only the countervailing government interest of cost and states that cost "is uncertain and does not have controlling weight." Suppl. Resp't's Br. at 5. We believe that it is reasonable to conclude that costs would rise and additional administrative resources would be expended if an attorney had to be appointed whenever counsel is sought by a child at an initial truancy hearing. Therefore, the third *Mathews* factor does not weigh in favor of requiring counsel.

In sum, the *Mathews* analysis does not support the conclusion that counsel must be appointed at an initial truancy hearing. The fact is that the initial hearing at which E.S. was not represented by counsel had little or no adverse effect on her private interests and it presented little risk of an erroneous deprivation of any of the child's rights, including her right to an education. We, therefore, conclude that E.S. failed to meet her burden of proving that RCW 28A.225.035(10) is unconstitutional. While it is certainly within the province of the legislature to require the provision of counsel at an initial truancy hearing, that is a policy decision for the legislature and we will not intrude, under the guise of a constitutional directive, on what is clearly the legislature's prerogative. [Ed. note: The court then went on to hold that the failure to provide E.S. with counsel did not violate the Washington Constitution.

IV

For reasons set forth above, we hold that the Fourteenth Amendment to the United States Constitution does not require that appointed counsel represent a child in an initial truancy hearing.... The Court of Appeals is reversed.

WE CONCUR: CHARLES W. JOHNSON, SUSAN OWENS, MARY E. FAIRHURST, JAMES M. JOHNSON, and DEBRA L. STEPHENS, Justices.

MADSEN, C.J. (concurring).

I agree with the majority that there is no due process right to counsel at the initial truancy hearing. However, I also agree with the Court of Appeals that the concerns identified in its opinion, *Bellevue School District v. E.S.*, 148 Wash.App. 205, 199 P.3d 1010 (2009), strongly suggest that an attorney could facilitate a better outcome in these cases for the child, the family, and for the district as well. Accordingly, I urge the legislature to consider enacting a statute to provide for counsel at these hearings, similar to the American Bar Association House of Delegates' Recommendation 109A (Aug. 9–10, 2010) ("RESOLVED, That the American Bar Association urges state, local, territorial, and tribal governments to provide legal counsel to

8. In dissent, Justice Chambers contends that the "risk that children will be placed at a disadvantage in legal proceedings is as real in the truancy context as it is in many other civil contexts in which they are provided counsel." Dissent at 10 (citing RCW 13.34.100(6); RCW 13.32A.192(1)(c); RCW 13.32A.160(1)(c)). We note that RCW 13.34.100(6) merely grants a trial court the discretion to appoint counsel in a dependency action. Thus, it cannot be said that it provides children with any greater right to counsel than does RCW 28A.225.035, the statute at issue here. The other statutes, RCW 13.32A.160(1)(c) and RCW 13.32A.192(1)(c), provide for appointment of counsel for "'[a]t-risk youth,'" defined as a juvenile who is absent from home without consent, who is beyond the control of her parents, or who has criminal charges pending relating to a substance abuse problem. RCW 13.32A.030(3). Our role is not to second-guess the legislature's decision to codify the right of an "at-risk youth" to have the benefit of appointed counsel while declining to provide the same right to a child at an initial truancy hearing.

children and/or youth at *all stages* of juvenile status offense proceedings, as a matter of right and at public expense" (emphasis added)).

CHAMBERS, J. (dissenting).

E.S. was brought before the bench without an attorney at her side. The commissioner found her to be a truant and entered an order that if violated could lead to sanctions, including house arrest, work crew, and detention. This was the critical hearing for E.S. Schools are required "where appropriate" to try to reduce absences by providing tutoring, family services, alternative schooling, or adjusting course loads. RCW 28A.225.020(1)(c). After a hearing finding truancy, the focus of the proceeding shifts to the student's compliance with the court order. It is thus the initial hearing where protecting the child's interest is most important. Because I would conclude that the Washington Constitution's due process clause, Const. art. I, § 3, when read in conjunction with the paramount duty clause, Const. art. IX, § 1, guarantees the right of counsel at an initial truancy hearing, I respectfully dissent.

ANALYSIS...

...[T]he balancing test adopted by the United States Supreme Court in *Mathews v. Eldridge*, 424 U.S. 319, 96 S.Ct. 893, 47 L.Ed.2d 18 (1976), offers a valuable tool when determining what is required under article I, section 3 as well as the Fourteenth Amendment to the United States Constitution. Both parties briefed the *Mathews* factors extensively, and the Court of Appeals opinion below and this court's majority opinion both engage in a *Mathews* analysis. Inasmuch as the due process clause of the Fourteenth Amendment provides a floor under which the State may not fall below, a *Mathews* analysis does provide a useful baseline for determining whether due process requires appointed counsel for children at initial truancy hearings.

"'[D]ue process is flexible and calls for such procedural protections as the particular situation demands.'" *Mathews*, 424 U.S. at 334 (alteration in original) (quoting *Morrissey v. Brewer*, 408 U.S. 471, 481, 92 S.Ct. 2593, 33 L.Ed.2d 484 (1972)). In each situation, courts must analyze and balance the affected interests of the parties. Courts first examine (1) the private interests affected by the proceeding, (2) the risk of error caused by the procedures used, and (3) the probable value, if any, of additional procedural safeguards. *Id.* at 335. These factors must then be weighed against the countervailing governmental interest supporting the use of the challenged procedure. *Id.* The goal in performing this test is to determine whether the procedures currently used are fundamentally fair and, if not, what additional safeguards must be implemented.

A. Interests Involved

The majority analyzes liberty, privacy, and education as the three interests potentially at stake in an initial truancy hearing. I address each of the majority's arguments in turn.

Physical Liberty

The majority is correct that in criminal cases, there is generally a presumption that indigent defendants have a right to appointed counsel only when, if they lose, they may be deprived of physical liberty. *Lassiter v. Dep't of Soc. Servs.*, 452 U.S. 18, 26–27, 101 S.Ct. 2153, 68 L.Ed.2d 640 (1981) (holding that due process does not require appointment of counsel in every parental termination proceeding). However, this presumption may be overcome where other fundamental liberty interests are at stake. *In re Dependency of Grove*, 127 Wash.2d 221, 237, 897 P.2d 1252 (1995); *accord In re Marriage of King*, 162 Wash.2d 378, 394, 174 P.3d 659 (2007).

The majority points out that E.S. was not at risk of immediate incarceration at the initial hearing. Had she complied with the court order and returned to school, contempt charges would never have been filed. When contempt charges were eventually brought, E.S. was appointed counsel. A party who disregards any court order stemming from any proceeding may later face contempt sanctions. RCW 2.28.020. The majority cites *Tetro* for the proposition that the "mere possibility that an order in a hearing may later serve as the predicate for a contempt adjudication is not enough to entitle an indigent party therein to free legal assistance." *Tetro v. Tetro*, 86 Wash.2d 252, 255 n. 1, 544 P.2d 17 (1975). The majority is correct that the possibility of future contempt sanctions alone does not necessarily create a right to appointed counsel. But the inquiry should not end there.

We have previously held that under the due process clause of the Fourteenth Amendment and article I, section 3 of our state constitution, parents have a right to counsel in permanent child deprivation hearings. *In re Welfare of Luscier*, 84 Wash.2d 135, 138, 524 P.2d 906 (1974). In Luscier, we discussed the importance of the familial relationship and the rights of parents to raise their children. *Id.* at 137, 524 P.2d 906. We noted that the right to counsel in the civil context does not turn on whether the proceeding may result in imprisonment but whether the individual may be deprived of liberty. *Id.* A year later we extended *Luscier* and held parents have a right to counsel at dependency and child neglect proceedings even where the parent is not at risk for permanent deprivation of his child. *In re Welfare of Myricks*, 85 Wash.2d 252, 253, 533 P.2d 841 (1975). We concluded that the "right to one's child is too basic to expose to the State's forces without the benefit of an advocate." *Id.* at 254, 533 P.2d 841. As our decisions in *Luscier* and *Myricks* indicate, other significant interests coupled with the other *Mathews* factors may still tip the scales in favor of litigants seeking appointed counsel.

Privacy

E.S. argues that a child's privacy interest is implicated because the court can order drug and alcohol testing at the initial hearing. See RCW 28A.225.090(1)(e). The majority counters that privacy is not implicated because the statute limits the court's authority to order testing only when "appropriate." The majority seems to think this is sufficient to ensure that a child's privacy rights are not violated, and does its best to downplay the potential privacy intrusion by noting that school children generally have a lower expectation of privacy in Washington. But this court has recently held that the testing of a child's bodily fluids does implicate the reasonable expectation of privacy. *York v. Wahkiakum Sch. Dist. No. 200*, 163 Wash.2d 297, 307, 178 P.3d 995 (2008). Moreover, as the majority admits, testing must be based on individualized suspicion. *Id.* at 308, 178 P.3d 995. Authority to test where "appropriate" does not necessarily comport with the requirement of individualized suspicion, and at any rate a fundamental privacy right to be free from such searches should be infringed upon only after careful review and under limited circumstances. The risk that a court may order such an intrusion at an initial hearing weighs in favor of appointing a lawyer who can understand the issues involved and argue to protect the rights of her client.

The majority also relies on the fact that the juvenile court in this case did not actually order E.S. to be tested. Such reliance is puzzling given the majority's admission that this case is moot, and the only reason for deciding it is that "the right to counsel at an initial truancy hearing is an issue of significant public interest affecting many parties and will likely be raised in the future." Basing its decision on the unique facts of a moot case is a strange way for the majority to go about providing guidance on an issue that will affect many parties in the future. The fact that this judge in this case did not order testing of this child is not a proper basis for determining the broader issue.

Education

Finally, E.S. argues that a child's right to education is implicated at initial truancy hearings because the court may order a truant child to change schools, attend private school, or enter into alternative education programs, any or all of which could have a disruptive impact on the child's education. "[E]ducation is perhaps the most important function of state and local governments." *Brown v. Bd. of Educ.*, 347 U.S. 483, 493, 74 S.Ct. 686, 98 L.Ed. 873 (1954). The children of our state have a constitutional right to an education. *Seattle Sch. Dist. No. 1*, 90 Wash.2d at 512, 585 P.2d 71; Const. art. IX, § 1. That right is paramount. Our state constitution's emphasis on the importance of education, and its recognition of broad constitutional protections of individual rights generally, demonstrates that the procedures necessary to protect the rights of children in E.S.'s position must be more demanding than they are in other contexts. In addition to the rights of liberty and privacy, the state constitution confers a right to education that may be infringed upon only in very limited circumstances.

While the measures in RCW 28A.225.090 are aimed at protecting the child's right to education, the amount of authority the court assumes when making these determinations has a significant effect on the child's continued education. A misguided decision on which steps to take may easily have unintended adverse consequences on the child's education. The truancy statute gives the court authority to assume continuing jurisdiction over the child and to make significant choices regarding where and how education will be provided. This authority to affect the child's fundamental right to education should be exercised only after careful consideration, with an understanding of all the factors involved. As the Court of Appeals noted, such decisions must not be made without challenge or intelligent debate. *Bellevue Sch. Dist. v. E.S.*, 148 Wash.App. 205, 216, 199 P.3d 1010 (2009).

The majority argues . . . that it would stand the state constitution's education provision "'on its head'" to hold that an attorney must be appointed for an initial truancy hearing. But the majority misperceives the role of counsel at the truancy hearing. Counsel is not there to ensure that the child's refusal to attend school is protected. Rather, an attorney serves to protect the child's right to education by providing meaningful advocacy and ensuring that the State and the school district have met their obligations under the statute. The paramount right to education must be meaningfully protected. A child who does not understand her rights, or the consequences of the proceedings against her, cannot meaningfully protect them on her own.

B. Risk of Erroneous Deprivation and Probable Value of Additional Safeguards

E.S. argues that children facing initial truancy hearings do not have the knowledge or sophistication to adequately protect their rights and that a lawyer is necessary for them to meaningfully be heard. We have recognized that children are often vulnerable, powerless, and voiceless. *In re Parentage of L.B.*, 155 Wash.2d 679, 712 n. 29, 122 P.3d 161 (2005). Minors "generally lack the experience, judgment, knowledge, and resources to effectively assert their rights." *DeYoung v. Providence Med. Ctr.*, 136 Wash.2d 136, 146, 960 P.2d 919 (1998). In other contexts, this State has recognized the limited ability of children to act and reason to the same degree as adults. See ch. 26.28 RCW (establishing age of majority at 18 when persons may independently enter into contracts, vote, or sue in court to the same extent as adults, etc.). A child does not enjoy the full panoply of rights that adults have under the law precisely because, unlike adults, they are generally less capable of fully understanding the consequences of their actions. See RCW 9A.04.050 (children between ages 8 and 12 presumed incapable of committing a crime). The risk that children will be placed at a disadvantage in legal proceedings is as real in the truancy context as it is in many other civil contexts in which they are provided counsel. See RCW 13.34.100(6) (counsel appointed for children in dependency cases); RCW 13.32A. 192(1)(c) (counsel must be appointed for children in at-risk youth petitions); RCW 13.32A. 160(1)(c) (counsel must be appointed for children in need of services). Without the benefit of legal counsel, a child's ability to assert her rights is severely limited and the risk of error is high.

The majority says that "issues that are before the court at the initial hearing on a truancy petition are uncomplicated and straightforward." To prove its point, the majority turns once again to the facts of the case, observing that "the record shows that E.S. was able to explain to the juvenile court why she missed school." But the reasons behind a child's continued absences from school are often complicated. It is unlikely that children will be able to understand the school's statutory duties to provide services, or be able to explain the complex social, economic, or family issues that may be underlying factors in the absences. In the formal setting of a courtroom, children might well find these issues complicated and have difficulty understanding and protecting their rights without the assistance of counsel. A lawyer can ensure that services are properly provided and help the court help the child reengage in school. Further, even assuming that E.S.'s explanation was as cogent and accurate as the majority asserts, the reliance yet again on specific facts of a moot case is entirely misplaced. Many children will not be in a position to explain themselves as well as E.S., and the fact that this particular child was able to explain her particular situation in this particular case is simply not a valid basis for a blanket denial of counsel to all children in all initial truancy hearings.

In addition, while the majority is correct that children must be appointed counsel when the school district has actually filed for contempt, the ability of a lawyer to effectively argue for their client at this point is severely limited. Once an initial decision to place a child under the jurisdiction of the court has been made, that decision cannot be collaterally attacked at a contempt hearing. *See In re J.R.H.*, 83 Wash.App. 613, 616, 922 P.2d 206 (1996) (court order cannot be collaterally attacked in contempt proceedings as contempt judgment will stand even if order violated was erroneous or later ruled invalid). In other words, counsel cannot argue that the underlying order giving rise to sanctions against the child should not have been entered in the first place.

Although certain conditions must be met before a school district may file a petition for truancy, without appointed counsel children will be less able to ensure that the school district met its burden. A school district must not only prove that the child has been absent the requisite number of days before filing a petition, it must also prove by a preponderance of the evidence that the steps taken by the school district to address the absences have been unsuccessful, and that court intervention and supervision are necessary to assist the parents and the school district to reduce or eliminate the child's absences. RCW 28A.225.035(1)(a)–(c). In this case, counsel for E.S. could have argued at the initial hearing that the Bellevue School District (District) had not taken adequate steps to assist E.S. in returning to school. E.S. contends that the District should have communicated with her mother, Velma Serdar, in her native language rather than in English. She also argues that the District should have met with E.S. and Ms. Serdar on more than one occasion, and that E.S. should have been referred to a community truancy board or truancy workshop program before a court order was put in place. While the District may have been able to meet its burden even if adequately challenged, the nature of the rights involved and the risk of erroneous deprivation demand that children facing these proceedings have an effective advocate on their side. As the Court of Appeals stated:

> The statute requires that before the court's intervention may be invoked, there will be a meaningful exploration of, and attempt to address, the causes of child's truancy. Nothing in the present procedure ensures this will happen. The risk of error is therefore high.

E.S., 148 Wash.App. at 219, 199 P.3d 1010. I agree.

C. State Interests

The majority identifies as a countervailing state interest only the increased financial costs of providing counsel, arguing somewhat less than forcefully that it is "reasonable...to conclude that costs would rise...if an attorney had to be appointed." I agree that such a conclusion is not beyond the bounds of reason. However, as E.S. points out, the increased cost of providing counsel at initial truancy hearings may be offset by a small reduction in contempt proceedings. Moreover, according to the Juvenile Law Center, of the 39 states that have made truancy a status offense, only 9 do not provide counsel at all stages of the proceedings. Thus, it seems, a majority of other states do not find providing counsel in this context overly burdensome. While costs may or may not rise if we require counsel earlier in truancy proceedings, financial costs alone do not control whether due process requires additional procedural safeguards. *Mathews*, 424 U.S. at 348. In this case, the majority's unsupported speculation about rising costs does not outweigh the value of providing children with counsel at the earliest stage of truancy proceedings.

On balance, due process requires that children at initial truancy hearings be provided counsel in order to protect their liberty, privacy, and educational rights. Unlike adults, children cannot be expected to fully understand their rights or be expected to adequately represent themselves in court against the superior resources of the State. Without representation, erroneous deprivation of those rights is a significant risk. An attorney can ensure that a child's interests are represented, that the school district meets its burden, and, perhaps most importantly, that an effective solution can be reached that results in the best educational outcome for the child. Where the consequences of a judge's decision have such an important and lasting effect on their fundamental constitutional rights, children must be afforded counsel.

CONCLUSION

I would hold that article I, section 3 of our state constitution guarantees the right of counsel to children at initial truancy hearings held in court that subject the child to the authority of the court and create the potential for later contempt sanctions. Because the majority holds otherwise, I respectfully dissent.

WE CONCUR: RICHARD B. SANDERS, Justice Pro Tem.

NOTES AND QUESTIONS

1. On what basis does the court conclude that a child in a truancy hearing is entitled to counsel? What test did the court use? Do you think the court applied the test correctly?

2. Only a few other states have considered this issue. In 2005, the Arizona Court of Appeals held that juveniles have the "right to be represented by counsel" in any juvenile proceeding that may result in detention. Because juvenile status offenders in the state of Arizona may be held in detention at the initial hearing, the juvenile has a right to counsel, and the court is obligated to inform the juvenile of this right and to appoint counsel if the minor is indigent. *Lana A. v. Woodburn*, 116 P.3d 1222 (Ariz. Ct. App. 2005). The American Bar Association Juvenile Justice Standards Relating to Counsel for Private Parties also state that counsel should be provided to any child during a status-offense proceeding or any related proceedings. IJA-ABA Juvenile Justice Standards Annotated: Standards Relating to Counsel for Private Parties, Robert E. Shepherd, Jr., ed., Standard 2.3(a) (1996). On the other hand, a North Carolina Court of Appeals, rejecting an equal-protection challenge, held that counsel is not constitutionally required at a hearing on a status-offense petition. *In re B.A.T.*, No. COA05-186 (N.C. Ct. App., Nov. 1, 2005) (reaffirming *In re Walker*, 191 S.E.2d 702 (N.C. 1972)).

3. Does the dissent apply the same test in analyzing the constitutionality of the Washington statute? If so, why does the dissent reach a different conclusion?

4. Under Washington law, "at-risk children" or "children in need of services," the definitions of which encompass traditional status offenses, are appointed counsel. Wash. Rev. Code § 13.32A.160 (2011) (when out-of-home placement petition filed for child in need of services, court must appoint legal counsel for child); Wash. Rev. Code § 13.32A.192 (2011) (appoint legal counsel for child when at-risk youth petition filed). In light of this, do you think there is another basis to argue for the appointment of counsel in truancy hearings?

5. Under Article 37(d) of the United Nations Convention on the Rights of the Child, "[e]very child deprived of his or her liberty shall have the right to prompt access to legal and other appropriate assistance, as well as the right to challenge the legality of the deprivation of his or her liberty before a court or other competent, independent and impartial authority and to a prompt decision on any such action." Does this provision militate in favor of providing status offenders with counsel?

ii. Self-incrimination, confrontation, cross-examination, and the burden of proof

Many states extend various procedural protections to minors in status-offense proceedings, including the privilege against self-incrimination and the right to confront and cross-examine witnesses. See Ala. Code § 12-15-202(f)(1) (West 2011) (right to cross-examine and confront witnesses); Alaska Child in Need of Aid R. 10 (West 2011) (in temporary custody proceeding, right to remain silent, to confront and cross-examine witnesses, but hearsay may be admissible); 17B Ariz. Rev. Stat. Ann. Juv. Ct. R. P. R. 28 (West 2011) (right to remain silent, to cross-examine and confront witnesses); Cal. Welf. & Inst. Code § 702.5 (West 2011) (right to remain silent, to confront and cross-examine witnesses); Colo. R. Juv. P. JDF 560 (West 2011) (right to confront and cross-examine witnesses); Conn. Prac. Book § 30a-1 (West 2011) (right to remain silent, to cross-examine and confront witnesses); Fla. R. Juv. P. R. 8.685 (West 2011) (right to examine witnesses); Ga. Code Ann. § 15-11-7 (West 2011) (right to cross-examine witnesses); Haw. Rev. Stat. § 571-41 (West 2011) (right to remain silent); Idaho R. Juv. R. 9 (2010); Ind. Code Ann. § 31-32-2-1 (West 2011) (right to cross-examine witnesses); Ind. Code Ann. § 31-32-2-2 (West 2011) (right to remain silent and confront witnesses); Md. Code Ann. Cts. Jud. P. § 3-8A-20 (West 2011) (right to confront and cross-examine witnesses); Mass. Dist. Ct. Spec. R. Civ. P. R. 205 (2011) (right to remain silent, to cross-examine and confront witnesses); Minn. Stat. § 260C.163 (West 2012) (right to cross-examine witnesses); Miss. Unif.

R. Youth Ct. Prac. R. 24 (West 2011) (right to remain silent, to cross-examine and confront witnesses); Mont. Code Ann. § 41-5-1414 (West 2011) (right to confront and cross-examine witnesses); Neb. Rev. Stat. § 43-279.01 (West 2011) (right to remain silent, to cross-examine and confront witnesses); Nev. Rev. Stat. § 62D.420 (West 2011) (right to cross-examine witnesses); N.H. Rev. Stat. Ann. § 169-D:14 (West 2011) (right to cross-examine witnesses); N.Y. Fam. Ct. Act § 741 (West 2011) (right to remain silent); N.C. Gen. Stat. § 7B-2405 (West 2011) (right to remain silent, right to confront and cross-examine witnesses); N.D. Cent. Code § 27-20-27 (West 2011) (right to cross-examine witnesses); Ohio Juv. R. 29(B)(5) (West 2011) (right to remain silent, to cross-examine and confront witnesses); Okla. Stat. 10A, § 2-2-402 (2011) (right to remain silent, to cross-examine witnesses); R.I. R. Juv. P. R. 9 (2011) (right to remain silent, to confront and cross-examine witnesses); Tenn. R. Juv. P. R. 15 (2011) (right to remain silent, to confront and cross-examine witnesses); Tex. Fam. Code Ann. § 54.03 (Vernon 2011) (right to remain silent, confront witnesses); Vt. Stat. Ann. Tit. 33, § 5315 (West 2011) (right to examine witnesses); W. Va. Code § 49-5-2 (2011) (all procedural rights afforded to adults in criminal proceedings available to juveniles unless otherwise noted); Wis. Stat. Ann. § 938.243 (West 2011) (right to remain silent, to confront and cross-examine witnesses); Wyo. Stat. Ann. § 14-6-423 (West 2011) (right to confront and cross-examine witnesses).

States take different approaches to the burden of proof. Some require proof beyond a reasonable doubt in status-offenses proceedings. See, e.g., 17B Ariz. Rev. Stat. Ann. Juv. Ct. R. P. R. 29 (West 2011) (state must prove allegations beyond reasonable doubt); Cal. Welf. & Inst. Code § 701 (West 2011) (allegations must be proven by a preponderance of the evidence); Colo. R. Juv. P. JDF 560 (West 2011) (child must be informed that proof beyond a reasonable doubt required in status-offense proceeding); Idaho R. Juv. R. 9 (2010) (state has burden of proving allegations beyond a reasonable doubt); Ohio Juv. R. 29(E)(4) (West 2011) (court shall determine issues of proof beyond reasonable doubt at trial in unruly proceedings); R.I. R. Juv. P. R. 9 (2011) (court shall inform child of right to proof beyond reasonable doubt). Other states, however, require a lesser standard of proof. See, e.g., Haw. Rev. Stat. § 571-41 (West 2011) (allegations sustained by preponderance of the evidence); Iowa Code § 232.96 (West 2011) (allegations must be sustained by clear and convincing evidence); Minn. Stat. § 260C.163 (West 2011) (allegations must be proved by clear and convincing evidence); Nev. Rev. Stat. § 62D.420 (West 2011) (allegations must be established by preponderance of the evidence); Tenn. R. Juv. P. R. 28(e)(2) (2011) (unruly charge must be proven by clear and convincing evidence); Vt. Stat. Ann. Tit. 33, § 5315 (West 2011) (state has burden of proving by preponderance, but court in its discretion may require proof by clear and convincing evidence); W. Va. Code § 49-5-11(d) (2011) (must sustain allegations by clear and convincing evidence); Wis. Stat. Ann. § 938.243(1)(h) (West 2011) (right to have allegations proved by clear and convincing evidence); Vt. Stat. Ann. Tit. 33, § 5317 (West 2011) (standard of proof is preponderance of the evidence).

Although there is little case law on the subject, a few state courts have concluded that the constitutional mandates of *Gault* do not extend to status offenders. See, e.g., *In re Potter*, 237 N.W.2d 461 (Iowa 1976) (where definition of delinquency included child who habitually deports himself in manner injurious to himself, due process only requires proof based on clear and convincing evidence); *In re Keith H.*, 594 N.Y.S.2d 268 (N.Y. App. Div. 1993) (petition alleging minor a PINS based on school records that were not attached to petition did not violate due process or equal protection because consistent with objective for providing more informal procedure for those minors not charged with delinquent acts); *In re K.*, 554 P.2d 180

(Or. Ct. App. 1976) (alleged status offender not entitled to same procedural protections as alleged delinquent under Due Process Clause where status offender could not be deprived of liberty interest to same degree as delinquent).

Why do states seem to be willing to provide status offenders with certain procedural rights, such as the right to confront and cross-examine witnesses, yet prefer a lower standard of proof? Do you think that status offenders should have the same constitutional rights as delinquent children? Consider again the problem of "bootstrapping," raised in Subsection 3 (d) above. Would that alter your analysis?

4. DISPOSITIONAL FRAMEWORK

The number of status-offense cases resulting in adjudication increased by 84 percent between 1995 and 2002, before declining by 20 percent by 2008. Nevertheless, there were 32,100 more adjudications in 2008 than in 1995. Truancy adjudications accounted for 33 percent and liquor-law violations 25 percent of all status-offense adjudications in 2008. Curfew adjudications also increased, while adjudications of cases involving runaways and ungovernable children decreased. *Id.* at 84. White and Asian youths were most likely to be adjudicated for curfew violations, Native American and white youths for liquor law violations. Whites and Asians also were most likely to be adjudicated for curfew cases. *Id.* at 85.

Of the status-offense cases adjudicated in 2008, probation was the most restrictive disposition ordered by the court. Although more cases resulted in an order of probation, the percentage of adjudicated status-offense cases involving probation declined from 61 percent in 1995 to 53 percent in 2008. *Id.* at 89. In 2008, probation was ordered in more than half of all adjudicated runaway, truancy, and liquor-law violations cases and in more than two-thirds of ungovernability cases but in only 24 percent of adjudicated curfew violations. *Id.* at 89.

Of all adjudicated status-offense cases, 9 percent resulted in out-of-home placement in 2007. Out-of-home placements increased by 38 percent between 1995 and 2000, before declining by 44 percent in 2008. *Id.* at 86. Of the status-offense cases that resulted in out-of-home placement, 31 percent involved truancy, 20 percent ungovernability, and 21 percent liquor-law violations. *Id.* at 86. Nevertheless, the use of out-of-home placements in runaway, curfew, and ungovernability cases has declined since 1995. *Id.* at 86. Of the 41 percent nonadjudicated status-offense cases, 79 percent were dismissed, 8 percent resulted in probation, and 14 percent received some other sanction. *Id.* at 90.

Probation is the most common disposition imposed by courts in status-offense cases. Other common dispositions include social services and placement out of home. Social services could include drug treatment, mental-health examinations, or counseling. A few states, through FINS provisions, also allow courts to assume jurisdiction over parents and require them to participate in social services. Out-of-home placement could include placement with relatives or placement through foster or group homes. Jessica R. Kendall, American Bar Association, Juvenile Status Offenses: Treatment and Early Intervention, Technical Assistance Bulletin No. 29 7–8 (2007).

Clearly, many of the dispositional options available to the juvenile court in status-offense cases are similar to the dispositional alternatives in delinquency matters. The National

Center for Juvenile Justice, the research division of the National Council of Juvenile and Family Court Judges (NCJJ), noted that probation "could lead to more severe consequences. However, NCJJ conclude[d] that although most states permit or require probation as a disposition option, most also restrict the use of harsher penalties if a status offender violates probation. Nevertheless many states permit other dispositions for status offenders that mirror those used for delinquent youth. These options include: performing community service, making restitution payment, suspending or revoking the youth's driver's license or placing the youth out of home (which may include shelters or group homes that house both delinquent youth and status offenders)." *Id.* at 7–8.

Efforts to reform the juvenile-justice system's response to status offending typically center on systemic changes (for example, implementing changes to policies, procedures, or rules) and the development of services and programs to meet the needs of status offenders. Little research has been done on the rehabilitative effects of status-offense dispositions. There nevertheless is some evidence that community-based programs are more effective than secure placements, cost less, and are better at maintaining and strengthening family relationships. Jessica R. Kendall, American Bar Association Center on Children and the Law, Families in Need of Critical Assistance: Legislation and Policy Aiding Youth Who Engage in Noncriminal Misbehavior 7–8 (2007). The Office of Juvenile Justice and Delinquency Prevention (OJJDP) maintains a "Deinstitutionalization of Status Offenders Best Practices" Web site identifying programs and policies that appear to reduce the institutionalization of status-offending youths. Although OJJDP acknowledges that the research literature on the effectiveness of these programs is "limited," the agency identifies and describes a number of model programs, which include functional family therapy, family services, cognitive-behavioral therapy, truancy initiatives, substance-abuse education, and mediation. Office of Juvenile Justice and Delinquency Prevention, Deinstitutionalization of Status Offenders Best Practices, http://www2.dsgonline.com/dso2/Default.aspx.

Charitable organizations also are attempting to effect systemic change in the juvenile-justice system. The Models for Change program, funded by the John D. and Catherine T. MacArthur Foundation, identifies model goals, policies, and practices to help states align their own juvenile systems within that model framework. In Florida, for example, status offenders and their families are diverted from the court system and offered an array of services; the program has proved successful in reducing recidivism while saving the state millions of dollars. Sara Mogulescu & Gaspar Cato, Vera Institute of Justice, Making Court the Last Resort: A New Focus for Supporting Families in Crisis 3–5 (2008). New York adopted legislation designed to divert status offenders from the system while narrowing the bases for detention. *Id.* at 7–8. Similarly, the Connecticut legislature enacted a bill prohibiting judges from placing status offenders in secure detention and mandating diversion for every first-time status offender. *Id.* at 10.

In 1992, the Annie E. Casey Foundation implemented the Juvenile Detention Alternatives Initiative (JDAI), in part to reduce reliance on secure detention. Begun in five pilot sites, JDAI now operates in 110 sites in twenty-seven states. While the emphasis is on reducing detention for all youths, JDAI recognized that states were detaining more juveniles on technical violations, public-order offenses, and status offenses. By emphasizing the implementation of objective admissions criteria and instruments, alternatives to detention, and case-processing reforms, JDAI sites have had remarkable success in reducing juvenile detention. Some states specifically targeted status-offender populations in order to reduce detention populations. For example, JDAI sites in Illinois no longer detain status offenders, and an Oregon JDAI site changed the way police deal with runaways and status offenders. For a history of the initiative, see Annie E. Casey Foundation, Two Decades of JDAI: From Demonstration Project to National Standard (2009). The Casey Foundation also maintains a Web site with up-to-date postings about JDAI. See http://www.aecf.org/MajorInitiatives/JuvenileDetentionAlternativesInitiative.aspx.

Status offenses and gender. In 2008, there were over 60,000 status-offense petitions filed against girls and approximately 90,000 status-offense petitions filed against boys. Juvenile Court Statistics at 76. In contrast, delinquency petitions are filed overwhelmingly against boys. *Id.* at 77. By offense, a majority of the curfew and status liquor-law violations and slightly more than half of the ungovernability and truancy cases involved boys. *Id.* Petitions filed against girls, however, made up 59 percent of all runaway cases. *Id.*

Critics long have argued that the courts administer their status-offense jurisdiction in gendered ways.

> In exploring the high rates of status offenses among girls versus their rates of criminal behavior, it is easy to see the ways in which the court's sexism and paternalistic biases serve to make judgments, with real consequences, around girls' sexuality and perceived unfeminine behavior. Punishing or incarcerating girls became a way to keep them from expressing or acting upon their sexuality. Judges appeared to feel that it was their responsibility to act as grandfathers or uncles in "protecting" girls. For example, in the New York case of Bonnie W., 16-year-old Bonnie was adjudicated as a runaway, but the court dictated, as a condition of her placement in a nonsecure facility, that she "not communicate with her male friend in New Jersey." This "male friend" was 21 and Bonnie had told the court that he was her fiancé. Yet the court found it appropriate to make moral- and sexuality-based judgments about her. Without procedural protections or lawyers, these types of discretion and gender bias have gone unchecked and are involved in some form every step along the way, from the original filing of the offense to disposition and sentencing.

Alecia Humphrey, *The Criminalization of Survival Attempts: Locking Up Female Runaways and Other Status Offenders*, 15 HASTINGS WOMEN'S L.J. 165, 173–74 (2004). See also MEDA CHESNEY-LIND AND RANDALL SHELDEN, GIRLS, DELINQUENCY, AND JUVENILE JUSTICE (2d ed. 1997); Meda Chesney-Lind, *Guilty by Reason of Sex: Young Women and the Juvenile Justice System*, in THE CRIMINAL JUSTICE SYSTEM AND WOMEN (Barbara R. Price & Natalie J. Sokoloff eds., 1982); Meda Chesney-Lind, *Girls and Status Offenses: Is Juvenile Justice Still Sexist?* 20 CRIM. JUST. ABSTRACT 144 (1988); Meda Chesney-Lind, *Judicial Paternalism and the Female Status Offender: Training Women to Know Their Place*, 23 CRIME & DELINQUENCY 121 (1977).

Subsequent amendments to the JJDPA allowing for the secure detention of runaways or those who violate court orders increased the risk of differential treatment. See Donna M. Bishop & Charles E. Frazier, *Gender Bias in Juvenile Justice Processing: Implications of the JJDP Act*, 82 J. CRIM. L. & CRIMINOLOGY 1162 (1992); Cheryl Dalby, *Gender Bias toward Status Offenders: A Paternalistic Agenda Carried Out through the JJDPA*, 12 L. & INEQUALITY 429 (1994). Because more girls are traditionally brought into the juvenile-justice system through status offenses, the concern about "bootstrapping" status offenders into the delinquency side of the system is even greater for girls. In fact, the increase in female delinquency may better be explained by a system choice to charge girls with assaults rather than with status offenses. See Barry C. Feld, *Violent Girls or Relabeled Status Offenders? An Alternative Interpretation of the Data*, 55

CRIME & DELINQ. 241 (2009). Efforts to deinstitutionalize status offenders also may have had the anomalous effect of increasing the institutionalization of girls in secure private facilities for treatment of mental-health or substance-abuse issues. See, e.g., Katherine Hunt Federle & Meda Chesney-Lind, *Special Issues in Gender, Race, and Ethnicity*, in JUVENILE JUSTICE AND PUBLIC POLICY: TOWARD A NATIONAL AGENDA (Ira Swartz ed., 1992); Lois Weithorn, *Mental Hospitalization of Troublesome Youth: An Analysis of Skyrocketing Admission Rates*, 40 STAN. L. REV. 773 (1988). § 42 USC 5651 (a) (15) explicitly authorizes grants for programs that focus on the needs of young girls at risk of delinquency or status offending.

Status offenses and race. Between 1995 and 2008, the petitioned status-offense case rate increased across all racial categories. Nevertheless, while the rate for white youths increased by 20 percent, the most significant increases occurred for Asian (42 percent), black (45 percent), and Native American youths (36 percent). Office of Juvenile Justice and Delinquency Prevention, Juvenile Court Statistics 2008, at 81. In fact, "the total petitioned status offense case rate for American Indian youth was higher than that for juveniles of all other racial categories" between 1995 and 2008. *Id.* Four times as many status-offense cases involving Native American youths were petitioned in 2008 as for Asian youths and two times as many as for white youths. *Id.* Of those youths placed out of the home in 2008, 10 percent were white, 11 percent Native American, 9 percent black, and 10 percent Asian. *Id.* at 87. More White and Native American youths were placed out of the home in runaway and ungovernability cases, more black youths in curfew, and more Native American youths in ingovernability, liquor-law, and runaway cases. *Id.* at 87.

The relationship between race and status offending is a complex one. Donna Bishop and Charles Frazier, conducting a quantitative analysis of juvenile cases in Florida using official records, found a tendency to treat white youths more harshly than nonwhites in status-offense cases. In contrast to the delinquency cases, where the population became more nonwhite at each case-processing point, white status offenders were more likely "to penetrate further into the system and to receive dispositions involving incarceration." Donna M. Bishop & Charles E. Frazier, *Race Effects in Juvenile Justice Decision-Making: Findings of a Statewide Analysis*, 86 J. CRIM. L. & CRIMINOLOGY 392, 412 (1996). One possible explanation lies in the filing decision: rather than being charged as status offenders, more minority youths may be charged as delinquent. BARRY C. FELD, RACE AND THE TRANSFORMATION OF THE JUVENILE COURT 180 (1999). There also is evidence that certain status offenses, such as curfew violations, may be enforced disproportionately against minority youths. Kenneth Adams, *The Effectiveness of Juvenile Curfews at Crime Prevention*, 587 ANNALS AM. ACAD. POL. & SOC. SCI. 136, 155 (2003). On the other hand, national data trends indicate greater increases in status-offense petition rates for nonwhite youths since 1995. Office of Juvenile Justice and Delinquency Prevention, Juvenile Court Statistics 2008, at 81. What other reasons are there for the seemingly mixed data on race?

The Runaway and Homeless Youth Act. In 1974, Congress enacted the Runaway Youth Act, 42 U.S.C.A. §§ 5701 et seq. (2011). The Act authorized federal funding for temporary shelters, family counseling, and after-care services to runaway youths and their families (known as the Basic Center Program). Amended in 1984, 1988, and 1992, the Act extended services to homeless youths, created transitional-living programs for older youths ages sixteen to twenty-two (the Transitional Living Program), and funded programs servicing homeless youths living on the streets (the Street Outreach Program). Funding eligibility is dependent on decriminalizing runaway behaviors and the provision of services outside the juvenile-justice system.

The Reconnecting Homeless Youth Act, 42 U.S.C. § 5701 (2011), renewing the Runaway and Homeless Youth program through 2013, provides funding for the Department of Health and Human Services to study the incidence and prevalence of homelessness and running away among youth.

The Congressional Research Service estimates that more than 1 million children were homeless and 1 million to 1.5 million children had run away or were "thrown away" (asked to leave home). Adrienne L. Fernandes-Alcantara, Congressional Research Service, Runaway and Homeless Youth: Demographics and Programs 4–5 (March 18, 2011). Family discord and physical and sexual abuse are the most often cited reasons for youths leaving home, and LGBT youths are overrepresented in this population because of negative family reactions when these youths come out. *Id.* at 5. Approximately 2 percent of all youths in foster care run away, and as many as 25 percent of youths who age out of foster care experience homelessness. *Id.* at 6. Homeless and runaway youths are more likely to have mental-health and behavioral disorders, use drugs, and experience depression than youths in the general population. *Id.* at 6–7. They also are at higher risk for sexual abuse and exploitation and may engage in delinquent activity for survival. *Id.* at 7.

Despite federal funding, only a small percentage of homeless and runaway youths receive assistance. In 2010, 44,859 youths received services from Basic Center Programs, and 3,716 youths participated in Transitional Living Programs. *Id.* at 16, 20. However, these programs turned away 9,679 youths because of a lack of bed space or the unavailability of services. Street Outreach Programs had 838,414 contacts with street youths in 2010 and provided predominantly food, drink, written materials, and health and hygiene products. *Id.* at 23.

There are other federal programs designed to assist homeless and runaway youths. The Family Violence Prevention and Services Act, P.L. 42 U.S.C. §§ 10401–10421 (2011) provides funding for programs to assist runaway and homeless youths who are victims of or may be at risk for dating violence. The Chafee Foster Care Independence Act of 1999, 42 U.S.C. § 677 (2011), funds transitional-living services, including money for room and board, for youths aging out of foster care. The McKinney-Vento Homeless Assistance Act, 42 U.S.C. §§ 11431 *et seq.* (2011), provides funding for programs designed to ensure the enrollment, attendance, and success of homeless children in school. McKinney-Vento was amended by the No Child Left Behind Act, 20 U.S.C. §§ 6301–6578 (2011), to prohibit the segregation of homeless from nonhomeless children.

In light of the evidence that many homeless and runaway children are fleeing unsafe family situations, could a state set up a "safe house" for runaway or throwaway teens, providing temporary shelter for up to thirty days? Would safe-house laws prevent a parent from taking any legal action to remove the child from the safe house during that temporary stay? Do you see any constitutional problems with this approach? *In re Mark N.*, 733 N.Y.S.2d 566 (N.Y. Fam. Ct. 2001).

Challenges to constitutionality of status-offense imprisonment. Does the institutionalization of status offenders violate constitutional provisions? In *State ex rel. Harris v. Calendine*, 233 S.E. 2d 318 (1977), the Supreme Court of West Virginia held that a juvenile-status-offender sentencing statute violated the state constitution's substantive due-process, equal-protection and cruel-and-unusual-punishment provisions. The child petitioner in the case lived in a rural section of the state and had trouble getting to school during the winter. "More importantly, however, it appears that the petitioner was ridiculed and shunned by his classmates because he suffered from a facial disfigurement and was mildly retarded." *Id.* at 322. The youth had missed fifty days of school and was sentenced to a boys' school for a few months until he turned sixteen, at which time he would be sent to a forestry camp for a year. *Id.*

The court held that the state statute allowing confinement of status offenders with juvenile delinquents violated the Equal Protection Clause of the state constitution because it "discriminates invidiously against children based upon social class, sex, and geographic location.... [T]he Calhoun County Juvenile Court committed petitioner to a reform school because of the lack of a reasonable alternative which would have existed if petitioner had been from a different area or belonged to a different socio-economic class." *Id.* at 325. Moreover, status offenders and delinquents are not similarly situated. Because the state exercises jurisdiction over status offenders based on its *parens patriae* authority, rather than its plenary power to prevent and punish crime, the state is obligated to help, rather than punish, status offenders. *Id.* at 326. The court rejected any claim that such help was offered: "we are not impressed with euphemistic titles used to disguise what are in fact, secure, prison-like facilities." *Id.* at 325.

The court also held that the statue violated substantive due process because there was no "rational connection between the legitimate legislative purposes of enforcing family discipline, protecting children, and protecting society from uncontrolled children, and the means by which the State is permitted to accomplish these purposes, namely incarceration of children in secure, prison-like facilities." *Id.* at 326. Moreover, incarcerating status offenders in secure, prison-like facilities along with children guilty of criminal conduct inflicts a constitutionally disproportionate penalty upon status offenders that violates the state's Cruel and Unusual Punishment Clause. *Id.* at 331.

For a similar constitutional analysis, see *Doe v. Norris*, 751 S.W. 2d 834 (Tenn. 1988) (placing status offenders in secure penal facility with delinquents violated substantive due-process and equal-protection guarantees under state and federal constitutions).

Abolition of status offenses. Since the 1960s, critics have argued for the repeal of status offenses. They have suggested that status-offense legislation be abolished or circumscribed or simply that status offenders be handled by social service agencies and schools rather than the courts. The reasons for eliminating status-offense jurisdiction are varied. Some argue that abolition will decriminalize certain behaviors, eliminate bootstrapping, and reduce gender disparity. Others contend that abolishing status offenses will reduce indeterminacy and bias. See, e.g., Joseph G. Weis, Jurisdiction and the Elusive Status Offender: A Comparison of Involvement in Delinquent Behavior and Status Offenses 99 (Reports of the National Juvenile Justice Assessment Centers 1980); Joint Comm'n on Juvenile Justice Standards, Inst. of Judicial Admin., Am. Bar Ass'n, Standards Relating to Noncriminal Misbehavior 1–2 (1982); Joyce London Alexander, *Aligning the Goals of Juvenile Justice with the Needs of Young Women Offenders: A Proposed Praxis for Transformational Justice*, 32 Suffolk U. L. Rev. 555, 607–609 (1999); Board of Directors, National Council on Crime and Delinquency, *Jurisdiction over Status Offenses Should Be Removed from the Juvenile Court: A Policy Statement*, 21 Crime & Delinq. 97, 97–98 (1975); Orman W. Ketcham, *Why Jurisdiction over Status Offenders Should Be Eliminated*, 57 B.U. L. Rev. 645, 657 (1977); Anne Bowen Poulin, *Female Delinquents: Defining Their Place in the Justice System*, 1996 Wis. L. Rev. 541, 573; R. Hale Andrews, Jr., & Andrew H. Cohn, Note, *Ungovernability: The Unjustifiable Jurisdiction*, 83 Yale L.J. 1383, n. 189 (1974).

Problem. A state legislature is considering a proposed state budget that, among many things, proposes the elimination of status offenses as a cost-savings measure. You are the legislative liaison for a child-advocacy center in that jurisdiction. Would you recommend support of such a measure?

B. Additional Restrictions on Liberty

1. ALCOHOL AND TOBACCO REGULATIONS

Alcohol. The National Minimum Drinking Age Act (NMDA) of 1984, 23 U.S.C. § 158 (2011), established a national minimum drinking age of twenty-one. States that fail to make the purchase and possession of alcohol by anyone younger than twenty-one illegal would lose 10 percent of their apportioned federal highways funds. 23 U.S.C. § 158 (a). In *South Dakota v. Dole*, 483 U.S. 203 (1987), the United States Supreme Court held that the Act did not violate the Twenty-first Amendment. "[T]he enactment of [drinking] laws remains the prerogative of the States not merely in theory but in fact. Even if Congress might lack the power to impose a national minimum drinking age directly, we conclude that encouragement of state action found in § 158 is a valid use of the spending power." *Id.* at 211–212.

But does the Act, prohibiting the sale of alcohol to *adults* between the ages of eighteen and twenty-one, violate equal protection? The United States Supreme Court has held that age is not a suspect classification. See *Gregory v. Ashcroft*, 501 U.S. 452, 470 (1991). However, in *Manuel v. State*, 692 So. 2d 320 (La. 1996), the Louisiana Supreme Court initially found that Louisiana's state statutes, enacted in response to the National Minimum Drinking Age Act, violated the state constitution's equal-protection provision. That section states, in part: "No law shall arbitrarily, capriciously, or unreasonably discriminate against a person because of birth, age, sex, culture, physical condition, or political ideas or affiliations." La. Const. Art. I, Sec. 3. The court, noting that this clause is "unlike that of any other state's constitution or the United States Constitution," found that the statutes impermissibly discriminated on the basis of age in the absence of evidence that the regulations substantially further an important governmental objective. *Id.* at 330. In reaching its decision, the court relied heavily on the state's empirical data, consisting of traffic-data reports on fatalities and drunk-driving incidents, and found that the targeted age group was not the age group most responsible for alcohol-related accidents. *Id.*

A mere four months later, the Louisiana Supreme Court reversed its prior decision on rehearing. *Manuel v. State*, 692 So. 2d 320 (La. 1996), rev'd on rehearing, 692 So. 2d 320 (La. 1996). This time, the court held that highway safety was a sufficiently important governmental objective to justify the differential treatment of eighteen-to-twenty-year-olds. *Id.* at 342–343. Moreover, the data supported the state's claim that restricting alcohol consumption by eighteen-to-twenty-year-olds would improve overall traffic safety because the younger age group was disproportionately represented in all alcohol-related accidents. *Id.* at 342. The result may have been prompted by political and economic realities: the Clinton administration warned the state that it would lose $17 million in federal highway funds if the decision were allowed to stand. Rick Bragg, *Louisiana Stands Alone on Drinking at 18*, NEW YORK TIMES, March 23, 1996, http://www.nytimes.com/1996/03/23/us/louisiana-stands-alone-on-drinking-at-18.html?pagewanted=all.

Should twenty-one be the minimum legal drinking age? The Amethyst Initiative, begun in 2008, is made up of a group of more than one hundred college and university presidents and chancellors who argue that the minimum age is not working. They contend that students younger than twenty-one continue to drink by securing fake IDs and engaging in dangerous practices, such as clandestine binge drinking, often off-campus. Moreover, they note that adults younger than twenty-one may vote, serve on juries, sign contracts, and enlist in the military. The Initiative signatories seek an "informed and dispassionate debate about the effects of the 21-year-old minimum drinking age," including an examination of the ways the highway-fund incentive in the NMDA may "impede" that debate. For more information about the Amethyst Initiative, see http://www.amethystinitiative.org.

Tobacco. In *FDA v. Brown & Williamson Tobacco Corp.*, 529 U.S. 120 (2000), the United States Supreme Court held that the FDA lacked authority to regulate the tobacco industry. On June 22, 2009, President Obama signed into law the Family Smoking Prevention and Tobacco Control Act of 2009, Pub. L. No. 111-31, 123 Stat. 1776 (codified in scattered sections of 21 U.S.C.), which specifically gave the FDA broad powers to regulate the tobacco industry. Specifically aimed at reducing the appeal of tobacco to children and youth, the Act authorizes the FDA to prohibit the sale of cigarettes and smokeless tobacco to anyone younger than eighteen. Retailers also are required to obtain photo identification from anyone twenty-six years old or younger to verify that the purchaser is, in fact, at least eighteen. 21 C.F.R. § 1140.14 (2011). In addition, the Act bans the distribution of free samples, 21 U.S.C. § 387a-1 (a)(2)(G), and the sale of flavored tobacco, such as grape, chocolate, vanilla, and cherry. 21 U.S.C. § 387g (a)(1). Some states, however, may be more restrictive and prohibit the sale of tobacco products to those nineteen and younger. See, e.g., Ala. Code § 28-11-15 (2011); Alaska Stat. § 11.76.100 (Michie 2011); N.J. Stat. Ann. § 2A:170-51.4 (West 2011); Utah Code Ann. § 26-42-103 (2011).

Congress, finding that "tobacco advertising and marketing contribute significantly to the use of nicotine-containing products by adolescents," gave the FDA broad power to restrict tobacco advertising. There is considerable support for congressional concern. See, e.g., S. Emery et al., *Televised State-Sponsored Antitobacco Advertising and Youth Smoking Beliefs and Behavior in the United States, 1999–2000*, 159 ARCHIVES PEDIATRIC & ADOLESCENT MED. 639 (2005); John P. Pierce, *Tobacco Industry Marketing, Population-Based Tobacco Control, and Smoking Behavior*, 33 AM. J. PREVENTIVE MED. S327 (2007); Melanie A. Wakefield et al., *Association of Point-of-Purchase Tobacco Advertising and Promotions with Choice of Usual Brand among Teenage Smokers*, 7 J. HEALTH COMMUNICATIONS 113 (2002). But when do such restrictions run afoul of the First Amendment? In *Central Hudson Gas & Electric Corp v. Public Service Commission of New York*, 447 U.S. 557 (1980), the Supreme Court established a four-part test to determine when restrictions placed on commercial speech violate the First Amendment.

> At the outset, we must determine whether the expression is protected by the First Amendment. For commercial speech to come within that provision, it at least must concern lawful activity

> and not be misleading. Next, we ask whether the asserted governmental interest is substantial. If both inquiries yield positive answers, we must determine whether the regulation directly advances the governmental interest asserted, and whether it is not more extensive than is necessary to serve that interest.

Id. at 566. Would restrictions banning outdoor advertising of tobacco products within one thousand feet of schools or playgrounds violate the free-speech rights of tobacco manufacturers? In *Lorillard Tobacco Co. v. Reilly*, 533 U.S. 525 (2001), the United States Supreme Court, applying the *Central Hudson* test, held that such a restriction did violate the First Amendment. Although recognizing the validity of the government's interest, the Court nevertheless found that the regulation constituted a near-total ban on advertising in some areas and thus swept too broadly. *Id.* at 562. In light of *Lorillard*, what sort of advertising restrictions could the FDA impose?

Are laws prohibiting the underage possession of alcohol and tobacco effective? Studies show that when popular activities, such as underage drinking, are criminalized, large segments of the population ignore the laws and engage in the prohibited behaviors despite legal prohibitions. Christopher Slobogin, *Some Hypotheses about Empirical Desert*, 42 Ariz. St. L.J. 1189, 1200, n. 43. Moreover, enforcement norms vary across jurisdictions, so the risks associated with violating underage-drinking and -smoking laws may be significantly less than for other law violations. Thomas L. Hafemeister & Shelly L. Jackson, *The Effectiveness of Sanctions and Law Enforcement Practices Targeted at Underage Drinking That Do Not Involve the Operation of a Motor Vehicle*, in Reducing Underage Drinking: A Collective Responsibility 490 (Committee on Developing a Strategy to Prevent and Reduce Underage Drinking, Richard J. Bonnie & Mary Ellen O'Connell eds., National Research Council & Institute of Medicine of the National Academies, 2004). Societal and parental norms also may be unclear and provide mixed messages to teenagers about underage drinking. Judith G. McMullen, *Underage Drinking: Does Current Policy Make Sense?* 10 Lewis & Clark L. Rev. 333, 348 (2006). The Monitoring the Future Study, which conducts annual surveys of eighth-, tenth-, and twelfth-graders and of high school graduates, confirms that alcohol use is widespread. In 2011, 33 percent of eighth-graders, 56 percent of tenth-graders, 70 percent of twelfth-graders, 81 percent of college students, and 87 percent of young adults reported trying alcohol; 6 percent of eighth-graders, 15 percent of tenth-graders, 22 percent of twelfth-graders, 36 percent of college students, and 37 percent of young adults reported having five or more drinks in a row at least once in the prior two-week period. However, heavy drinking peaks in the early twenties and then recedes with age. Lloyd D. Johnston et al., U.S. Department of Health & Human Services, Monitoring the Future: National Survey Results on Drug Use, 1975–20119, Vol. I, Secondary School Students 29 (2012).

Nevertheless, there are indications that alcohol restrictions may have beneficial effects. Reports of alcohol use and heavy drinking have been declining since 1991, although alcohol use has declined more sharply than heavy drinking. *Id.* at 55, tbl. 2-2. Some studies also suggest that a higher legal minimum drinking age has resulted in fewer alcohol-related accidents and driving incidents. One study, for example, found that the proportion of drivers ages sixteen to twenty who tested positive for blood alcohol declined by 46 percent between 1982 and 2008 but only by 17 percent for drivers ages twenty-one to twenty-four and by 29 percent for drivers twenty-five and older. Anne T. McCartt et al., *The Effects of Minimum Legal Drinking Age 21 Laws on Alcohol-Related Driving in the United States*, 41

Journal of Safety Research 173, 174 (2010). Another study, comparing the number of drunk-driving incidents before and after the implementation of a minimum legal drinking age, found an 11.2-percent reduction in alcohol-related fatal crashes involving drivers younger than twenty-one. James C. Fell et al., *The Relationship of Underage Drinking Laws to Reductions of Drinking Drivers in Fatal Crashes in the United States*, 40 Accident Analysis and Prevention 1430, 1434 (2008).

What about tobacco use among youths? The Monitoring the Future Survey found that in 2009, 7 percent of eighth-graders, 13 percent of tenth-graders, and in 2010, 19 percent of twelfth-graders reported that they had smoked one or more cigarettes in the prior thirty days. *Id.* at 31. Since the tobacco settlement between the industry and the states was being negotiated in 1996, cigarette smoking has declined by 21 percent among eighth-graders, 30 percent among tenth-graders, and 37 percent among twelfth-graders. However, one-fifth of youths are tobacco smokers by the time they graduate from high school, and the numbers may be substantially higher among those who drop out of high school before graduating. Johnston et al., Monitoring the Future, at 32. The survey authors also note that an increase in the number of students disapproving of cigarette use, evident since the tobacco settlement, stopped in 2007 among eighth- and twelfth-graders. *Id.* at 30. The authors "conclude that further improvement in smoking rates will likely have to come from changes in the environment—for example, such policies as raising taxes, further reducing the places in which smoking is permitted, and offering quit-smoking programs." *Id.* at 29.

There is some evidence that enforcing cigarette tax and control policies does decrease underage smoking. One study used data from the national Youth Risk Behavior Surveys, 1991 to 2005, and state and local versions of the same survey. The authors found that an increase in state cigarette taxes reduced smoking participation and frequent smoking among high school students. Christopher Carpenter & Philip J. Cook, *Cigarette Taxes and Youth Smoking: New Evidence from National, State, and Local Youth Risk Behavior Surveys*, 27 J. Health Econ. 287, 297 (2008). Another study compared Monitoring the Future survey data for 1991 to 2006 with cigarette prices, smoke-free-air laws, youth-access sales-to-minors laws, and youth-access possession laws. Although smoke-free-air laws and youth-access possession laws were not significantly associated with smoking-cessation outcomes among high school students, the study did find a significant positive relationship between youth-access sales-to-minors laws and cessation of smoking. The authors also found a significant association between cigarette price and cessation: a one-dollar increase was associated with a 30-percent increase in the odds that a high school smoker who had made at least one attempt to quit would quit. Cindy Tworek et al., *State-Level Tobacco Control Policies and Youth Smoking Cessation Measures*, 97 Health Pol'y 136, 141 (2010).

Differences based on race and ethnicity. Based on results from the Monitoring the Future surveys, African-American students appear to abuse certain illicit drugs, alcohol, and cigarettes far less than white and Hispanic students. African-American twelfth-graders have a lower usage rate of cigarette smoking (10 percent) than do white twelfth-graders (22 percent). Johnston et al., Monitoring the Future, 36. They also have a lower daily smoking rate (4.9 percent) than whites (13 percent) and Hispanics (5.3 percent). *Id.* at 101. African-American students have the lowest rate for alcohol use and the fewest occasions of heavy drinking across the eighth, tenth, and twelfth grades. In 2011, 11 percent of African-American students reported having five or more drinks in a row in the prior two weeks, compared with 26 percent of white and 21 percent of Hispanic students. In eighth grade, 10 percent of Hispanic students, 6 percent of white students, and 5 percent of African-American students reported occasional heavy drinking. *Id.* at 101.

2. FIREARMS REGULATIONS

Concerned about crime involving guns, drugs, and juveniles and recognizing that the problem was national in scope because of the transportation of guns in interstate commerce, Congress enacted the Youth Handgun Safety Act in 1994. 18 U.S.C. § 922(x) (2011). The Act prohibits the sale, delivery, or transfer of a handgun or handgun ammunition to anyone younger than eighteen. *Id.* at (x)(1). The Act also bars possession of a handgun or handgun ammunition by a juvenile. *Id.* at (x)(2). Juveniles who use a handgun in the course of employment, ranching, farming, hunting, or target practice or with the written permission of a parent or guardian are exempt from prosecution under the Act. *Id.* at (x)(3)(A). The Act also recognizes an exception when possession is "taken in defense of the juvenile or other persons against an intruder into the residence of the juvenile or a residence in which the juvenile is an invited guest." *Id.* at (x)(3)(D).

Congressional authority for the implementation of the Youth Handgun Safety Act arises from the Commerce Clause. In *United States v. Lopez*, 514 U.S. 549 (1995), the Supreme Court held that the Gun Free Schools Zone Act was unconstitutional because it exceeded congressional power authorized by the Commerce Clause. The Court held that Congress has the power to regulate commercial activity and interstate commerce under the Commerce Clause, but the act of a minor who brings a gun to school neither was commercial activity nor did it affect interstate commerce. *Id.* at 567. The Act also failed to contain any express statement by Congress that prohibiting guns in local schools was tied to the regulation of interstate commerce, and the Court dismissed the government's claim that increased violence in schools deterred travel, increased insurance costs, and created a school environment that was not conducive to educating the future work force. *Id.* at 563–564. In light of the Court's decision in *Lopez*, would the Youth Handgun Safety Act survive constitutional scrutiny? See *United States v. Cardoza*, 129 F.3d 6 (1st Cir. 1997); *United States v. Michael R.*, 90 F.3d 340 (9th Cir. 1996).

In 2009, 14.1 percent of all arrests for murder and nonnegligent homicide were of children younger than eighteen. Eighteen-to-twenty-year-olds account for approximately 20 percent of all such arrests. U.S. Department of Justice, Crime in the United States, Arrests, by Age, 2009, at tbl. 38, http://www2.fbi.gov/ucr/cius2009/data/table_38.html. Children younger than eighteen made up 1 percent of all murder victims, while persons younger than twenty-two accounted for 24 percent of all murder victims. U.S. Department of Justice, Crime in the United States, Murder Victims by Age, Sex, and Race, 2009, at tbl. 2, http://www2.fbi.gov/ucr/cius2009/offenses/expanded_information/data/shrtable_02.html. Half of murder victims younger than eighteen and about 70 percent of those younger than twenty-two were killed by firearms. U.S. Department of Justice, Crime in the United States, Murder Victims by Age and Weapon, 2009, at tbl. 9, http://www2.fbi.gov/ucr/cius2009/offenses/expanded_information/data/shrtable_09.html. In 2007, approximately 1,520 children ages one to seventeen and 2,351 persons between the ages of eighteen and twenty died from firearm-related injuries. National

Center for Firearm Injury Prevention and Control, Firearm Deaths and Rates per 100,000, 2007, http://www.cdc.gov/wisqars. Of unintentional firearm deaths of children younger than fifteen, 78 percent were other-inflicted, and the shooters usually were friends or family members. David Hemenway et al., Unintentional Firearm Deaths: *A Comparison of Other-Inflicted and Self-Inflicted Shootings*, 42 ACCIDENT ANALYSIS & PREVENTION 1184 (2010) (analyzing data obtained from the CDC's National Violent Death Reporting System from 2003 to 2006). There were almost 6,000 nonfatal gunshot injuries to children younger than eighteen and more than 11,000 nonfatal gunshot injuries to persons between the ages of eighteen and twenty in 2009. National Center for Firearm Injury Prevention and Control, Overall Firearm Gunshot Nonfatal Injuries and Rates per 100,000, 2009, http://www.cdc.gov/wisqars.

In *District of Columbia v. Heller*, 554 U.S. 570, 635 (2008), the Supreme Court held that the Second Amendment protects "the right of law-abiding, responsible citizens to use arms in defense of hearth and home." The Court further held that the right was incorporated and extended to the states. *McDonald v. City of Chicago*, 130 S.Ct. 3020, 3050 (2010). Do regulations that restrict the right of minors to possess firearms violate the Second Amendment? See, e.g., *United States v. Rene E.*, 583 F.3d 8 (1st Cir. 2009) (considering lawfulness of regulations prohibiting gun sales to underage minors); *State v. Sieyes*, 225 P.2d 995 (Wash. 2010) (considering Second Amendment challenge to ban on possession of firearms by seventeen-year-old); Katherine Hunt Federle, *The Second Amendment Rights of Children*, 89 IOWA L. REV. 609 (2004). What about restrictions placed on adults older than eighteen but younger than twenty-one? 18 U.S.C. § 922(b)(1) (2011) prohibits any licensed dealer, importer, manufacturer, or collector from selling or delivering any firearm other than a shotgun or a rifle to an individual younger than twenty-one. A number of states restrict the sale of handguns to persons younger than twenty-one. See Cal. Penal Code § 12072(a)(3)(A)(2011); Del. Code Ann. tit. 24, § 903 (2011); D.C. Code Ann. §§ 7-2502.03; 22-4507 (2011); Haw. Rev. Stat. § 134-2(d) (2011); 430 Ill. Comp. Stat. 65/3(a), 65/4(a)(2)(i) (2011); Ind. Code § 724.22(2) (2011); Md. Code Ann., Pub. Safety § 5-134 (2011); Mass. Gen. Laws ch. 140, § 130 (2011); N.J. Stat. Ann. § 2C:58-6.1 (2011); Ohio Rev. Code Ann. § 2923.21 (2011); R.I. Gen. Laws §§ 11-47-30, 11-47-35(a) (2011). Do these laws violate the Second Amendment? See *D'Cruz v. Bureau of Alcohol, Tobacco, Firearms, and Explosives*, No. 5:10-cv-00140-C (N.D. Tex. 2010); *Dorr v. Weber*, 741 F.Supp.2d 993 (N.D. Iowa 2010); *United States v. Bledsoe*, Crim. No. SA-08-CR-13(2)-XR (W.D. Tex., Aug. 8, 2008).

3. CHILD-LABOR LAWS

The Fair Labor Standards Act of 1938 (FLSA), 29 U.S.C. § 201 *et seq.*, regulates "oppressive child labor." Generally, the regulations, which vary by age, restrict the type of employment and the hours that youths may work on school days and nonschool days, during the school year and during school vacations. All workers younger than eighteen are prohibited from working in certain hazardous occupations or engaging in hazardous tasks, such as mining, logging, sawmilling, roofing, and using certain types of powered equipment. Children younger than sixteen may work in retail, food service, and gasoline establishments, but their job duties are limited. Children younger than fourteen may work for their parents in nonhazardous occupations, work as actors or performers, deliver newspapers, and engage in "casual" work, cutting lawns for neighbors, babysitting, or performing minor chores in private homes. Certain exemptions also exist for apprenticeships and vocational-education programs.

When it comes to agricultural employment, however, federal regulations are less restrictive. Pursuant to 29 U.S.C. § 213(c), children younger than twelve may work on the family farm or with parental consent on a farm where none of the employees is required to be paid the wage rate. Children twelve or thirteen also may work on the family farm or a farm that employs their parents. Parents who employ their children on the family farm are exempt from the hazardous-occupations restrictions and may require their older children to work during school hours. There are no restrictions on the number of hours fourteen- and fifteen-year-olds can work in nonhazardous jobs outside of school hours. Employers also may apply for an exemption to permit children between the ages of ten and twelve to work as hand-harvest laborers under certain conditions. 29 U.S.C. § 213(c)(4)(a).

The FLSA only applies to businesses that have a gross sales volume of at least $500,000 or where the worker has duties involving interstate commerce. State law then may govern the employment of minors, and, since the federal law does not preempt state action, the employer must follow the more restrictive regulation. Some state laws may be more restrictive than the FLSA, for example, by regulating the employment of newspaper carriers or child actors, while other states may exempt agricultural employment in its entirety. Various states require work permits, proof of age, or a doctor's certification that the youth is able to work. Other laws, such as those pertaining to licensing drivers, also may restrict the types of activities in which a youth may engage. For information about state labor-law regulations, see the Department of Labor's Web site, Youth Rules, http://www.youthrules.dol.gov/states.htm.

Despite these regulations, 374 youths ages fifteen to seventeen died while on the job between 1998 and 2007. Of those young workers who died, 65 percent were white, 27 percent were Hispanic, and 5 percent were African-American. Most of these deaths arose out of "transportation incidents." C. R. Estes et al., Centers for Disease Control, Occupational Injuries and Deaths among Younger Workers—United States, 1998–2007, 59 Morbidity & Mortality Weekly Rep. 449, tbl. 1 (2010). During this same time period, 598 young workers were injured on the job; 65 percent were white, 8 percent African-American, 5 percent Hispanic, and 21 percent had no identified race or ethnicity. Most injuries (52 percent) were the result of "contact with objects and equipment." *Id.* at tbl. 2.

Certain industries and occupations are far more dangerous for young workers. Of all fatalities involving workers younger than eighteen from 1992 to 2002, 42.3 percent occurred in the farming, forestry, and fishing industries; 28.6 percent occurred when young workers were employed as operators, fabricators, or laborers. John P. Sestito et al., Special Populations, fig. 5-9, in Worker Health Chartbook 2004 (John P. Sestito et al., eds., Centers for Disease Control, 2004). Almost 60 percent of all of the fatalities occurred while youths were working on family farms, and family-farmwork fatalities accounted for almost one-fourth of all youth-worker fatalities. Janice Windau & Samuel Meyer, *Occupational Injuries among Young Workers*, MONTHLY LABOR REV. (October 2005), 11, 16. Nonfatal injuries and illness were more likely when workers younger than twenty were employed as operators, fabricators, and laborers (37.4 percent); 30.8 percent of workers employed in the service industry also experienced nonfatal injury and illness. Worker Health Chartbook 2004, fig. 5-16.

Recognizing the dangers posed by working on farms, a number of organizations have attempted to provide education and training to farmers, parents, and children. For example, the 4-H Federal Extension Service Training Program provides certification in tractor and farm-machine operation for fourteen- and fifteen-year-olds. The National Children's Center for Rural and Agricultural Health and Safety, which receives funding from the National Institute for Occupational Safety and Health, has developed the North American Guidelines for Children's Agricultural Tasks, which list age-appropriate tasks for children working on farms and ranches in North America, http://www.nagcat.org/nagcat. But should children be permitted to work on farms? Should a distinction be drawn between those children who work on their family farms and children who are hired as migrant workers? How would such regulations be justified?

The FLSA does not govern relationships between American employers and foreign workers employed overseas. The Convention Concerning the Prohibition and Immediate Elimination of the Worst Forms of Child Labor, 38 I.L.M. 1207 (1999), ratified by the United States Senate in the same year, calls on the parties to the Convention to eradicate the worst forms of child labor, including slavery, bondage, prostitution, and trafficking, and to remove children from the work force. In the Trade Act of 2002, P.L. 107-210, Congress identified several trade-negotiating objectives, including the promotion of universal ratification and full compliance with the Convention and respect for the rights of children. The Convention refers to the United Nations Convention on the Rights of the Child, which recognizes "the right of the child to be protected from economic exploitation and from performing any work that is likely to be hazardous or to interfere with the child's education, or to be harmful to the child's health or physical, mental, spiritual, moral or social development." Article 32 of the Convention on the Rights of the Child also requires states parties to provide for a minimum age of employment, appropriate regulation of workplace hours and conditions, and sanctions for noncompliance of state laws. United Nations Convention on the Rights of the Child, art. 32, Nov. 20, 1989, 1577 U.N.T.S. 3. Do you think the United States is in compliance with Article 32?

4. OTHER RESTRICTIONS

Government restrains children's liberty in a number of other ways.. For example, states may impose a minimum age for obtaining a driver's license and may limit the hours during which the underage operator may drive, the number of passengers in the vehicle, and the types of vehicles that may be driven. States also may suspend or revoke the operator's permit of an underage driver for truancy, possession of alcohol or drugs, or as part of a disposition for any delinquent act or status or traffic offense. In addition, states may prohibit the sale of fireworks and lottery tickets to, and gambling by, minors. The Twenty-sixth Amendment lowered the voting age to eighteen; no state permits anyone younger than eighteen to vote in statewide elections.

Each of these laws involves the application of a bright-line rule based on age. One advantage of such a rule is that it is easy to apply. It eliminates the exercise of discretion and thus reduces the possibility of arbitrariness or bias. On the other hand, a bright-line test is based on a gross generalization about a population and fails to take into account individual abilities or actual maturity, thereby excluding minors capable of maturely engaging in the specific activity. Are such bright-line rules constitutional? If so, do they make sense from a policy perspective? What is wrong with requiring the state to show that an individual minor lacks sufficient maturity to engage in certain behavior? Alternatively, why not allow the minor seeking to engage in the activity the opportunity to make a showing that he or she has the requisite abilities and maturity?

V

CHILDREN AND DECISION MAKING

A. The First Amendment Rights of Children

1. FREE-SPEECH AND FREE-EXPRESSION RIGHTS

TINKER V. DES MOINES INDEPENDENT COMMUNITY SCHOOL DISTRICT
Supreme Court of the United States
393 U.S. 503 (1969)

MR. JUSTICE FORTAS delivered the opinion of the Court.

Petitioner John F. Tinker, 15 years old, and petitioner Christopher Eckhardt, 16 years old, attended high schools in Des Moines, Iowa. Petitioner Mary Beth Tinker, John's sister, was a 13-year-old student in junior high school.

In December 1965, a group of adults and students in Des Moines held a meeting at the Eckhardt home. The group determined to publicize their objections to the hostilities in Vietnam and their support for a truce by wearing black armbands during the holiday season and by fasting on December 16 and New Year's Eve. Petitioners and their parents had previously engaged in similar activities, and they decided to participate in the program.

The principals of the Des Moines schools became aware of the plan to wear armbands. On December 14, 1965, they met and adopted a policy that any student wearing an armband to school would be asked to remove it, and if he refused he would be suspended until he returned without the armband. Petitioners were aware of the regulation that the school authorities adopted.

On December 16, Mary Beth and Christopher wore black armbands to their schools. John Tinker wore his armband the next day. They were all sent home and suspended from school until they would come back without their armbands. They did not return to school until after the planned period for wearing armbands had expired—that is, until after New Year's Day.

This complaint was filed in the United States District Court by petitioners, through their fathers, under § 1983 of Title 42 of the United States Code. It prayed for an injunction restraining the respondent school officials and the respondent members of the board of directors of the school district from disciplining the petitioners, and it sought nominal damages. After an evidentiary hearing the District Court dismissed the complaint. It upheld the constitutionality of the school authorities' action on the ground that it was reasonable in order to prevent disturbance of school discipline. 258 F.Supp. 971 (1966). The court referred to but expressly declined to follow the Fifth Circuit's holding in a similar case that the wearing of symbols like the armbands cannot be prohibited unless it "materially and substantially interfere(s) with the requirements of appropriate discipline in the operation of the school." *Burnside v. Byars*, 363 F.2d 744, 749 (1966).

On appeal, the Court of Appeals for the Eighth Circuit considered the case en banc. The court was equally divided, and the District Court's decision was accordingly affirmed, without opinion, 383 F.2d 988 (1967). We granted certiorari.

I

The District Court recognized that the wearing of an armband for the purpose of expressing certain views is the type of symbolic act that is within the Free Speech Clause of the First Amendment. See *West Virginia State Board of Education v. Barnette*, 319 U.S. 624 (1943); *Stromberg v. California*, 283 U.S. 359 (1931). Cf. *Thornhill v. Alabama*, 310 U.S. 88 (1940); *Edwards v. South Carolina*, 372 U.S. 229 (1963); *Brown v. Louisiana*, 383 U.S. 131 (1966). As we shall discuss, the wearing of armbands in the circumstances of this case was entirely divorced from actually or potentially disruptive conduct by those participating in it. It was closely akin to "pure speech" which, we have repeatedly held, is entitled to comprehensive protection under the First Amendment. Cf. *Cox v. Louisiana*, 379 U.S. 536, 555 (1965); *Adderley v. Florida*, 385 U.S. 39 (1966).

First Amendment rights, applied in light of the special characteristics of the school environment, are available to teachers and students. It can hardly be argued that either students or teachers shed their constitutional rights to freedom of speech or expression at the schoolhouse gate. This has been the unmistakable holding of this Court for almost 50 years. In *Meyer v. Nebraska*, 262 U.S. 390 (1923), and *Bartels v. Iowa*, 262 U.S. 404 (1923), this Court, in opinions by Mr. Justice McReynolds, held that the Due Process Clause of the Fourteenth Amendment prevents States from forbidding the teaching of a foreign language to young students. Statutes to this effect, the Court held, unconstitutionally interfere with the liberty of teacher, student, and parent....

In *West Virginia State Board of Education v. Barnette*, *supra*, this Court held that under the First Amendment, the student in public school may not be compelled to salute the flag. Speaking through Mr. Justice Jackson, the Court said:

> "The Fourteenth Amendment, as now applied to the States, protects the citizen against the State itself and all of its creatures—Boards of Education not excepted. These have, of course, important, delicate, and highly discretionary functions, but none that they may not perform within the limits of the Bill of Rights. That they are educating the young for citizenship is reason for scrupulous protection of Constitutional freedoms of the individual, if we are not to strangle the free mind at its source and teach youth to discount important principles of our government as mere platitudes." 319 U.S., at 637, 63 S.Ct. at 1185.

On the other hand, the Court has repeatedly emphasized the need for affirming the comprehensive authority of the States and of school officials, consistent with fundamental constitutional safeguards, to prescribe and control conduct in the schools. Our problem lies in the area where students in the exercise of First Amendment rights collide with the rules of the school authorities.

II

The problem posed by the present case does not relate to regulation of the length of skirts or the type of clothing, to hair style, or deportment. It does not concern aggressive, disruptive action or even group demonstrations. Our problem involves direct, primary First Amendment rights akin to "pure speech."

The school officials banned and sought to punish petitioners for a silent, passive expression of opinion, unaccompanied by any disorder or disturbance on the part of petitioners. There is here no evidence whatever of petitioners' interference, actual or nascent, with the schools' work or of collision with the rights of other students to be secure and to be let alone. Accordingly, this case does not concern speech or action that intrudes upon the work of the schools or the rights of other students.

Only a few of the 18,000 students in the school system wore the black armbands. Only five students were suspended for wearing them. There is no indication that the work of the schools or any class was disrupted. Outside the classrooms, a few students made hostile remarks to the children wearing armbands, but there were no threats or acts of violence on school premises.

The District Court concluded that the action of the school authorities was reasonable because it was based upon their fear of a disturbance from the wearing of the armbands. But, in our system, undifferentiated fear or apprehension of disturbance is not enough to overcome the right to freedom of expression. Any departure from absolute regimentation may cause trouble. Any variation from the majority's opinion may inspire fear. Any word spoken, in class, in the lunchroom, or on the campus, that deviates from the views of another person may start an argument or cause a disturbance. But our Constitution says we must take this risk, *Terminiello v. Chicago*, 337 U.S. 1 (1949); and our history says that it is this sort of hazardous freedom—this kind of openness—that is the basis of our national strength and of the independence and vigor of Americans who grow up and live in this relatively permissive, often disputatious, society.

In order for the State in the person of school officials to justify prohibition of a particular expression of opinion, it must be able to show that its action was caused by something more than a mere desire to avoid the discomfort and unpleasantness that always accompany an unpopular viewpoint. Certainly where there is no finding and no showing that engaging in the forbidden conduct would "materially and substantially interfere with the requirements of appropriate discipline in the operation of the school," the prohibition cannot be sustained. *Burnside v. Byars, supra*, 363 F.2d at 749.

In the present case, the District Court made no such finding, and our independent examination of the record fails to yield evidence that the school authorities had reason to anticipate that the wearing of the armbands would substantially interfere with the work of the school or impinge upon the rights of other students. Even an official memorandum prepared after the suspension that listed the reasons for the ban on wearing the armbands made no reference to the anticipation of such disruption.[3]

3. The only suggestions of fear of disorder in the report are these:

"A former student of one of our high schools was killed in Viet Nam. Some of his friends are still in school and it was felt that if any kind of a demonstration existed, it might evolve into something which would be difficult to control.

"Students at one of the high schools were heard to say they would wear arm bands of other colors if the black bands prevailed."

On the contrary, the action of the school authorities appears to have been based upon an urgent wish to avoid the controversy which might result from the expression, even by the silent symbol of armbands, of opposition to this Nation's part in the conflagration in Vietnam.[4] It is revealing, in this respect, that the meeting at which the school principals decided to issue the contested regulation was called in response to a student's statement to the journalism teacher in one of the schools that he wanted to write an article on Vietnam and have it published in the school paper. (The student was dissuaded.[5])

It is also relevant that the school authorities did not purport to prohibit the wearing of all symbols of political or controversial significance. The record shows that students in some of the schools wore buttons relating to national political campaigns, and some even wore the Iron Cross, traditionally a symbol of Nazism. The order prohibiting the wearing of armbands did not extend to these. Instead, a particular symbol—black armbands worn to exhibit opposition to this Nation's involvement in Vietnam—was singled out for prohibition. Clearly, the prohibition of expression of one particular opinion, at least without evidence that it is necessary to avoid material and substantial interference with schoolwork or discipline, is not constitutionally permissible.

In our system, state-operated schools may not be enclaves of totalitarianism. School officials do not possess absolute authority over their students. Students in school as well as out of school are "persons" under our Constitution. They are possessed of fundamental rights which the State must respect, just as they themselves must respect their obligations to the State. In our system, students may not be regarded as closed-circuit recipients of only that which the State chooses to communicate. They may not be confined to the expression of those sentiments that are officially approved. In the absence of a specific showing of constitutionally valid reasons to regulate their speech, students are entitled to freedom of expression of their views. As Judge Gewin, speaking for the Fifth Circuit, said, school officials cannot suppress "expressions of feelings with which they do not wish to contend." *Burnside v. Byars*, *supra*, 363 F.2d at 749.

Moreover, the testimony of school authorities at trial indicates that it was not fear of disruption that motivated the regulation prohibiting the armbands; and regulation was directed against "the principle of the demonstration" itself. School authorities simply felt that "the schools are no place for demonstrations," and if the students "didn't like the way our elected officials were handling things, it should be handled with the ballot box and not in the halls of our public schools."

4. The District Court found that the school authorities, in prohibiting black armbands, were influenced by the fact that "(t)he Viet Nam war and the involvement of the United States therein has been the subject of a major controversy for some time. When the arm band regulation involved herein was promulgated, debate over the Viet Nam war had become vehement in many localities. A protest march against the war had been recently held in Washington, D.C. A wave of draft card burning incidents protesting the war had swept the country. At that time two highly publicized draft card burning cases were pending in this Court. Both individuals supporting the war and those opposing it were quite vocal in expressing their views." 258 F.Supp., at 972–973.

5. After the principals' meeting, the director of secondary education and the principal of the high school informed the student that the principals were opposed to publication of his article. They reported that "we felt that it was a very friendly conversation, although we did not feel that we had convinced the student that our decision was a just one."

In *Meyer v. Nebraska, supra*, 262 U.S. at 402, Mr. Justice McReynolds expressed this Nation's repudiation of the principle that a State might so conduct its schools as to "foster a homogeneous people." He said:

> "In order to submerge the individual and develop ideal citizens, Sparta assembled the males at seven into barracks and intrusted their subsequent education and training to official guardians. Although such measures have been deliberately approved by men of great genius, their ideas touching the relation between individual and State were wholly different from those upon which our institutions rest; and it hardly will be affirmed that any Legislature could impose such restrictions upon the people of a state without doing violence to both letter and spirit of the Constitution."

This principle has been repeated by this Court on numerous occasions during the intervening years. In *Keyishian v. Board of Regents*, 385 U.S. 589, 603, Mr. Justice Brennan, speaking for the Court, said:

> "'The vigilant protection of constitutional freedoms is nowhere more vital than in the community of American schools.' *Shelton v. Tucker*, [364 U.S. 479], at 487. The classroom is peculiarly the 'marketplace of ideas.' The Nation's future depends upon leaders trained through wide exposure to that robust exchange of ideas which discovers truth 'out of a multitude of tongues, (rather) than through any kind of authoritative selection.'"

The principle of these cases is not confined to the supervised and ordained discussion which takes place in the classroom. The principal use to which the schools are dedicated is to accommodate students during prescribed hours for the purpose of certain types of activities. Among those activities is personal intercommunication among the students.[6] This is not only an inevitable part of the process of attending school; it is also an important part of the educational process. A student's rights, therefore, do not embrace merely the classroom hours. When he is in the cafeteria, or on the playing field, or on the campus during the authorized hours, he may express his opinions, even on controversial subjects like the conflict in Vietnam, if he does so without "materially and substantially interfer(ing) with the requirements of appropriate discipline in the operation of the school" and without colliding with the rights of others. *Burnside v. Byars, supra*, 363 F.2d at 749. But conduct by the student, in class or out of it, which for any reason—whether it stems from time, place, or type of behavior—materially disrupts classwork or involves substantial disorder or invasion of the rights of others is, of course, not immunized by the constitutional guarantee of freedom of speech. Cf. *Blackwell v. Issaquena County Board of Education*, 363 F.2d 749 (C.A.5th Cir. 1966).

Under our Constitution, free speech is not a right that is given only to be so circumscribed that it exists in principle but not in fact. Freedom of expression would not truly exist if the right could be exercised only in an area that a benevolent government has provided as a safe haven for crackpots. The Constitution says that Congress (and the States) may not abridge the

6. In *Hammond v. South Carolina State College*, 272 F.Supp. 947 (D.C.S.C.1967), District Judge Hemphill had before him a case involving a meeting on campus of 300 students to express their views on school practices. He pointed out that a school is not like a hospital or a jail enclosure.... It is a public place, and its dedication to specific uses does not imply that the constitutional rights of persons entitled to be there are to be gauged as if the premises were purely private property.

right to free speech. This provision means what it says. We properly read it to permit reasonable regulation of speech-connected activities in carefully restricted circumstances. But we do not confine the permissible exercise of First Amendment rights to a telephone booth or the four corners of a pamphlet, or to supervised and ordained discussion in a school classroom.

If a regulation were adopted by school officials forbidding discussion of the Vietnam conflict, or the expression by any student of opposition to it anywhere on school property except as part of a prescribed classroom exercise, it would be obvious that the regulation would violate the constitutional rights of students, at least if it could not be justified by a showing that the students' activities would materially and substantially disrupt the work and discipline of the school. In the circumstances of the present case, the prohibition of the silent, passive "witness of the armbands," as one of the children called it, is no less offensive to the Constitution's guarantees.

As we have discussed, the record does not demonstrate any facts which might reasonably have led school authorities to forecast substantial disruption of or material interference with school activities, and no disturbances or disorders on the school premises in fact occurred. These petitioners merely went about their ordained rounds in school. Their deviation consisted only in wearing on their sleeve a band of black cloth, not more than two inches wide. They wore it to exhibit their disapproval of the Vietnam hostilities and their advocacy of a truce, to make their views known, and, by their example, to influence others to adopt them. They neither interrupted school activities nor sought to intrude in the school affairs or the lives of others. They caused discussion outside of the classrooms, but no interference with work and no disorder. In the circumstances, our Constitution does not permit officials of the State to deny their form of expression.

We express no opinion as to the form of relief which should be granted, this being a matter for the lower courts to determine. We reverse and remand for further proceedings consistent with this opinion.

Reversed and remanded.

MR. JUSTICE STEWART, concurring.

Although I agree with much of what is said in the Court's opinion, and with its judgment in this case, I cannot share the Court's uncritical assumption that, school discipline aside, the First Amendment rights of children are co-extensive with those of adults. Indeed, I had thought the Court decided otherwise just last Term in *Ginsberg v. New York*, 390 U.S. 629. I continue to hold the view I expressed in that case: "(A) State may permissibly determine that, at least in some precisely delineated areas, a child—like someone in a captive audience—is not possessed of that full capacity for individual choice which is the presupposition of First Amendment guarantees." *Id.*, at 649–650 (concurring in result). Cf. *Prince v. Massachusetts*, 321 U.S. 158.

MR. JUSTICE WHITE, concurring.

While I join the Court's opinion, I deem it appropriate to note, first, that the Court continues to recognize a distinction between communicating by words and communicating by acts or conduct which sufficiently impinges on some valid state interest; and, second, that I do not subscribe to everything the Court of Appeals said about free speech in its opinion in *Burnside v. Byars*, 363 F.2d 744, 748 (C.A.5th Cir. 1966), a case relied upon by the Court in the matter now before us.

MR. JUSTICE BLACK, dissenting.

The Court's holding in this case ushers in what I deem to be an entirely new era in which the power to control pupils by the elected "officials of state supported public schools..." in the United States is in ultimate effect transferred to the Supreme Court. The Court brought this particular case here on a petition for certiorari urging that the First and Fourteenth Amendments protect the right of school pupils to express their political views all the way "from kindergarten through high school." Here the constitutional right to "political expression" asserted was a right to wear black armbands during school hours and at classes in order to demonstrate to the other students that the petitioners were mourning because of the death of United States soldiers in Vietnam and to protest that war which they were against. Ordered to refrain from wearing the armbands in school by the elected school officials and the teachers vested with state authority to do so, apparently only seven out of the school system's 18,000 pupils deliberately refused to obey the order. One defying pupil was Paul Tinker, 8 years old, who was in the second grade; another, Hope Tinker, was 11 years old and in the fifth grade; a third member of the Tinker family was 13, in the eighth grade; and a fourth member of the same family was John Tinker, 15 years old, an 11th grade high school pupil. Their father, a Methodist minister without a church, is paid a salary by the American Friends Service Committee. Another student who defied the school order and insisted on wearing an armband in school was Christopher Eckhardt, an 11th grade pupil and a petitioner in this case. His mother is an official in the Women's International League for Peace and Freedom.

As I read the Court's opinion it relies upon the following grounds for holding unconstitutional the judgment of the Des Moines school officials and the two courts below. First, the Court concludes that the wearing of armbands is "symbolic speech" which is "akin to 'pure speech'" and therefore protected by the First and Fourteenth Amendments. Secondly, the Court decides that the public schools are an appropriate place to exercise "symbolic speech" as long as normal school functions are not "unreasonably" disrupted. Finally, the Court arrogates to itself, rather than to the State's elected officials charged with running the schools, the decision as to which school disciplinary regulations are "reasonable."

Assuming that the Court is correct in holding that the conduct of wearing armbands for the purpose of conveying political ideas is protected by the First Amendment, cf., *e.g.*, *Giboney v. Empire Storage & Ice Co.*, 336 U.S. 490 (1949), the crucial remaining questions are whether students and teachers may use the schools at their whim as a platform for the exercise of free speech—"symbolic" or "pure"—and whether the courts will allocate to themselves the function of deciding how the pupils' school day will be spent. While I have always believed that under the First and Fourteenth Amendments neither the State nor the Federal Government has any authority to regulate or censor the content of speech, I have never believed that any person has a right to give speeches or engage in demonstrations where he pleased and when he pleases. This Court has already rejected such a notion. In *Cox v. Louisiana*, 379 U.S. 536, 554 (1965), for example, the Court clearly stated that the rights of free speech and assembly "do not mean that everyone with opinions or beliefs to express may address a group at any public place and at any time."

While the record does not show that any of these armband students shouted, used profane language, or were violent in any manner, detailed testimony by some of them shows their armbands caused comments, warnings by other students, the poking of fun at them, and a warning by an older football player that other, nonprotesting students had better let them alone. There is also evidence that a teacher of mathematics had his lesson period practically "wrecked" chiefly by disputes with Mary Beth Tinker, who wore her armband for her "demonstration." Even a casual reading of the record shows that this armband did divert students' minds from their regular lessons, and that talk, comments, etc., made John Tinker "self-conscious" in attending school with his armband. While the absence of obscene remarks or boisterous and loud disorder perhaps justifies the Court's statement that the few armband students did not actually "disrupt" the classwork, I think the record overwhelmingly shows that the armbands did exactly what the elected school officials and principals foresaw they would, that is, took the students' minds off their classwork and diverted them to thoughts about the highly emotional subject of the Vietnam war. And I repeat that if the time has come when pupils of state-supported schools, kindergartens, grammar schools, or high schools, can defy and flout orders of school officials to keep their minds on their own schoolwork, it is the beginning of a new revolutionary era of permissiveness in this country fostered by the judiciary. The next logical step, it appears to me, would be to hold unconstitutional laws that bar pupils under 21 or 18 from voting, or from being elected members of the boards of education....

...The truth is that a teacher of kindergarten, grammar school, or high school pupils no more carries into a school with him a complete right to freedom of speech and expression than an anti-Catholic or anti-Semite carries with him a complete freedom of speech and religion into a Catholic church or Jewish synagogue. Nor does a person carry with him into the United States Senate or House, or into the Supreme Court, or any other court, a complete constitutional right to go into those places contrary to their rules and speak his mind on any subject he pleases. It is a myth to say that any person has a constitutional right to say what he pleases, where he pleases, and when he pleases. Our Court has decided precisely the opposite. See, *e.g.*, *Cox v. Louisiana*, 379 U.S. 536, 555; *Adderley v. Florida*, 385 U.S. 39.

In my view, teachers in state-controlled public schools are hired to teach there. Although Mr. Justice McReynolds may have intimated to the contrary in *Meyer v. Nebraska*, *supra*, certainly a teacher is not paid to go into school and teach subjects the State does not hire him to teach as a part of its selected curriculum. Nor are public school students sent to the schools at public expense to broadcast political or any other views to educate and inform the public. The original idea of schools, which I do not believe is yet abandoned as worthless or out of date, was that children had not yet reached the point of experience and wisdom which enabled them to teach all of their elders. It may be that the Nation has outworn the old-fashioned slogan that "children are to be seen not heard," but one may, I hope, be permitted to harbor the thought that taxpayers send children to school on the premise that at their age they need to learn, not teach....

...Iowa's public schools...are operated to give students an opportunity to learn, not to talk politics by actual speech, or by "symbolic" speech. And, as I have pointed out before, the record amply shows that public protest in the school classes against the Vietnam war "distracted from that singleness of purpose which the state (here Iowa) desired to exist in its public educational institutions."...But even if the record were silent as to protests against the Vietnam war distracting students from their assigned class work, members of this Court, like all other citizens, know, without being told, that the disputes over the wisdom of the Vietnam war have disrupted and divided this country as few other issues ever have. Of course students, like other people, cannot concentrate on lesser issues when black armbands are being ostentatiously displayed in their presence to call attention to the wounded and dead of the war, some of the wounded and the dead being their friends and neighbors. It was, of course, to distract the attention of other students that some students insisted up to the very point of their own suspension from school that they were determined to sit in school with their symbolic armbands.

Change has been said to be truly the law of life but sometimes the old and the tried and true are worth holding. The schools of this Nation have undoubtedly contributed to giving us tranquility and to making us a more law-abiding people. Uncontrolled and uncontrollable liberty is an enemy to domestic peace. We cannot close our eyes to the fact that some of the country's greatest problems are crimes committed by the youth, too many of school age. School discipline, like parental discipline, is an integral and important part of training our children to be good citizens—to be better citizens. Here a very small number of students have crisply and summarily refused to obey a school order designed to give pupils who want to learn the opportunity to do so. One does not need to be a prophet or the son of a prophet to know that after the Court's holding today some students in Iowa schools and indeed in all schools will be ready, able, and willing to defy their teachers on practically all orders. This is the more unfortunate for the schools since groups of students all over the land are already running loose, conducting break-ins, sit-ins, lie-ins, and smash-ins. Many of these student groups, as is all too familiar to all who read the newspapers and watch the television news programs, have already engaged in rioting, property seizures, and destruction. They have picketed schools to force students not to cross their picket lines and have too often violently attacked earnest but frightened students who wanted an education that the pickets did not want them to get. Students engaged in such activities are apparently confident that they know far more about how to operate public school systems than do their parents, teachers, and elected school officials. It is no answer to say that the particular students here have not yet reached such high points in their demands to attend classes in order to exercise their political pressures. Turned loose with lawsuits for damages and injunctions against their teachers as they are here, it is nothing but wishful thinking to imagine that young, immature students will not soon believe it is their right to control the schools rather than the right of the States that collect the taxes to hire the teachers for the benefit of the pupils. This case, therefore, wholly without constitutional reasons in my judgment, subjects all the public schools in the country to the whims and caprices of their loudest-mouthed, but maybe not their brightest, students. I, for one, am not fully persuaded that school pupils are wise enough, even with this Court's expert help from Washington, to run the 23,390 public school systems in our 50 States. I wish, therefore, wholly to disclaim any purpose on my part to hold that the Federal Constitution compels the teachers, parents, and elected school officials to surrender control of the American public school system to public school students. I dissent.

MR. JUSTICE HARLAN, dissenting.

I certainly agree that state public school authorities in the discharge of their responsibilities are not wholly exempt from the requirements of the Fourteenth Amendment respecting the freedoms of expression and association. At the same time I am reluctant to believe that there is any disagreement between the majority and myself on the proposition that school officials should be accorded the widest authority in maintaining discipline and good order in their institutions. To translate that proposition into a workable constitutional rule, I would, in cases like this, cast upon those complaining the burden of showing that a particular school measure was motivated by other than legitimate school concerns—for example, a desire to prohibit the expression of an unpopular point of view, while permitting expression of the dominant opinion.

Finding nothing in this record which impugns the good faith of respondents in promulgating the armband regulation, I would affirm the judgment below.

NOTES AND QUESTIONS

1. What test does the Court apply in determining whether school officials have violated the First Amendment rights of students? When and to whom does the test apply?

2. What test would Justice Black apply? How is that test different from the one articulated by Justice Fortas? To what extent do you think Black's opinion was shaped by the domestic unrest caused by the Vietnam War?

3. Why does Justice Harlan dissent? Is his proposed test different? How?

4. In *West Virginia State Board of Education v. Barnette*, 319 U.S. 624 (1943), the West Virginia State Board of Education passed a resolution requiring all students to salute the flag. Failure to do so would result in expulsion and would subject the expelled student to delinquency prosecution for the "unexcused" absence. The child's parents also faced criminal prosecution and upon conviction could be fined up to fifty dollars and jailed for a term not exceeding thirty days. No exception was made for Jehovah's Witnesses, whose religious tenets forbid any salute to a "graven image" (of which the flag is one). Consequently, these children and their parents were prosecuted, and state officials threatened to send the children to reformatories unless they agreed to salute the flag. Noting that the right asserted does not collide with the rights of others and that the behavior was "peaceable and orderly," the Supreme Court held that the requirement that all students salute the flag violated the free-speech and free-exercise rights of children and their parents who were Jehovah's Witnesses. "If there is any fixed star in our constitutional constellation, it is that no official, high or petty, can prescribe what shall be orthodox in politics, nationalism, religion, or other matters of opinion or force citizens to confess by word or act their faith therein." *Id.* at 642. Is *Tinker* consistent with *Barnette*?

5. In *Ginsberg v. New York*, 390 U.S. 629 (1968), the Supreme Court considered the facial validity of a state statute that prohibited the sale of obscene material to minors younger than seventeen. While acknowledging that "'girlie' picture magazines" are not obscene when sold to adults, the Court nevertheless found that the state had greater authority to regulate the sale of such material to minors. Noting that the state has greater power over the conduct of minors, the Court held that the regulation had a rational relationship to the state's objective of safeguarding minors from harm. *Id.* at 641. Justice Fortas, in dissent, argued that the Court had a "fundamental duty" to define obscenity as it related to the material sold to minors in order to determine whether the criminal conviction could stand. Fortas may have been offended by the prosecution; he noted that the sixteen-year-old boy who purchased the magazines had been sent in by his mother in order to prosecute the defendant, the owner of a luncheonette, who was at risk of losing his business license because of the conviction. *Id.* at 671–672.

6. What do you think about the minors who wore black armbands to school that day in 1965? Were they expressing their own views or those of their parents? If children share their parents' views, does that make their views less legitimate? Mary Beth Tinker, now a mother and a registered nurse, speaks frequently to students about the *Tinker* case and the importance of free speech. She is active in the ACLU and maintains a Facebook page. Christopher Eckhardt is an author and maintains a MySpace page, on which he has posted a description of the events surrounding the *Tinker* case. John Tinker is the editor of schema-root.

org, a web-based encyclopedia of current events. He maintains a page of "frequently asked questions" about the *Tinker* case, http://schema-root.org/region/americas/north_america/usa/government/branches/judicial_branch/supreme_court/decisions/schools/tinker_v._des_moines/~jft/jft.faq.html. After reading their descriptions of the case, do you think that they sincerely held their own views?

7. In *Bethel School District v. Fraser*, 478 U.S. 675 (1986), a high school student was suspended for three days for giving the following speech during a school assembly attended by approximately six hundred students:

> I know a man who is firm—he's firm in his pants, he's firm in his shirt, his character is firm—but most... of all, his belief in you, the students of Bethel, is firm.
>
> Jeff Kuhlman is a man who takes his point and pounds it in. If necessary, he'll take an issue and nail it to the wall. He doesn't attack things in spurts—he drives hard, pushing and pushing until finally—he succeeds.
>
> Jeff is a man who will go to the very end—even the climax, for each and every one of you.
>
> So vote for Jeff for A.S.B. vice-president—he'll never come between you and the best our high school can be.

The Court was not amused and expressed concern that the speech could be "seriously damaging to its less mature audience, many of whom were only 14 years old and on the threshold of awareness of human sexuality." *Id.* at 683. Noting that "the constitutional rights of students in public school are not automatically coextensive with the rights of adults in other settings," *Id.* at 682, the Court held that

> [the] School District acted entirely within its permissible authority in imposing sanctions upon Fraser in response to his offensively lewd and indecent speech. Unlike the sanctions imposed on the students wearing armbands in *Tinker*, the penalties imposed in this case were unrelated to any political viewpoint. The First Amendment does not prevent the school officials from determining that to permit a vulgar and lewd speech such as respondent's would undermine the school's basic educational mission. A high school assembly or classroom is no place for a sexually explicit monologue directed towards an unsuspecting audience of teenage students. Accordingly, it was perfectly appropriate for the school to disassociate itself to make the point to the pupils that vulgar speech and lewd conduct [are] wholly inconsistent with the "fundamental values" of public school education.

Id. at 685–686.

Two years later, the Court again considered the scope of students' First Amendment rights. In *Hazelwood School District v. Kuhlmeier*, 484 U.S. 260 (1988), a high school principal deleted two stories from the high school paper, written and edited by students enrolled in a journalism class. One story dealt with three high school students' experiences with pregnancy, the other with the impact of divorce on students at the school. Although the story on pregnancy used false names, the principal felt that the students could still be identified from the story and that the references to birth control and sexual activity were inappropriate for some of the younger students. The principal also felt that because the divorce article contained comments by a student critical of her father, the failure to obtain a response from her father or parental consent to its publication was unfair.

The Court established a second test for determining when the First Amendment rights of students were violated in public schools. First, the Court held that the standard articulated in

Tinker did not apply when a school lent "its name and resources to the dissemination of student expression." Rather, educators may exercise "editorial control over the style and content of student speech in school-sponsored expressive activities so long as their actions are reasonably related to legitimate pedagogical concerns." *Id.* at 272–273. The Court then concluded that the principal's actions in the case at bar were reasonable:

> The initial paragraph of the pregnancy article declared that "[a]ll names have been changed to keep the identity of these girls a secret." The principal concluded that the students' anonymity was not adequately protected, however, given the other identifying information in the article and the small number of pregnant students at the school. Indeed, a teacher at the school credibly testified that she could positively identify at least one of the girls and possibly all three. It is likely that many students at Hazelwood East would have been at least as successful in identifying the girls. Reynolds therefore could reasonably have feared that the article violated whatever pledge of anonymity had been given to the pregnant students. In addition, he could reasonably have been concerned that the article was not sufficiently sensitive to the privacy interests of the students' boyfriends and parents, who were discussed in the article but who were given no opportunity to consent to its publication or to offer a response. The article did not contain graphic accounts of sexual activity. The girls did comment in the article, however, concerning their sexual histories and their use or nonuse of birth control. It was not unreasonable for the principal to have concluded that such frank talk was inappropriate in a school-sponsored publication distributed to 14-year-old freshmen and presumably taken home to be read by students' even younger brothers and sisters.
>
> The student who was quoted by name in the version of the divorce article seen by Principal Reynolds made comments sharply critical of her father. The principal could reasonably have concluded that an individual publicly identified as an inattentive parent—indeed, as one who chose "playing cards with the guys" over home and family—was entitled to an opportunity to defend himself as a matter of journalistic fairness.

Id. at 274–275. Because the principal believed that the decision about the articles had to be made immediately or there would be no newspaper at all, the Court found his decision to delete the two problematic articles reasonable under the circumstances. Would you agree?

8. What impact did *Kuhlmeier* have on student-run media? In the wake of *Kuhlmeier*, four states enacted freedom-of-expression laws governing high school journalists (Arkansas, Colorado, Iowa, and Kansas). California already had a state law on the books, as did Massachusetts, which amended its law after *Kuhlmeier*. See Mark Paxton & Tom Dickinson, *State Free Expression Laws and Scholastic Press Censorship*, 55(2) Journalism & Mass Communication Educator 50, 50 (2000). In one study, researchers compared the attitudes and perceptions of advisers in states with freedom-of-expression laws and those without such laws on the books. The study found "limited support for the proposition that advisors in press law states are more likely to support the concept of scholastic press rights than advisors in non-press law states." *Id.* at 55. Today eight states have enacted legislation protecting the free-expression rights of students in schools (Arkansas, California, Colorado, Illinois, Iowa, Kansas, Massachusetts, and Oregon), and two states provide protection under their education codes (Pennsylvania and Washington). See State Legislation, Student Press Law Center, http://www.splc.org/knowyourrights/statelegislation.asp.

When does *Tinker* apply? What about *Kuhlmeier*? Consider the next case when formulating your answer.

MORSE V. FREDERICK
Supreme Court of the United States
551 U.S. 393 (2007)

Chief Justice Roberts delivered the opinion of the Court.

At a school-sanctioned and school-supervised event, a high school principal saw some of her students unfurl a large banner conveying a message she reasonably regarded as promoting illegal drug use. Consistent with established school policy prohibiting such messages at school events, the principal directed the students to take down the banner. One student—among those who had brought the banner to the event—refused to do so. The principal confiscated the banner and later suspended the student. The Ninth Circuit held that the principal's actions violated the First Amendment, and that the student could sue the principal for damages.

Our cases make clear that students do not "shed their constitutional rights to freedom of speech or expression at the schoolhouse gate." *Tinker v. Des Moines Independent Community School Dist.*, 393 U.S. 503, 506 (1969). At the same time, we have held that "the constitutional rights of students in public school are not automatically coextensive with the rights of adults in other settings," *Bethel School Dist. No. 403 v. Fraser*, 478 U.S. 675, 682 (1986), and that the rights of students "must be 'applied in light of the special characteristics of the school environment.'" *Hazelwood School Dist. v. Kuhlmeier*, 484 U.S. 260, 266 (1988) (quoting *Tinker*, *supra*, at 506). Consistent with these principles, we hold that schools may take steps to safeguard those entrusted to their care from speech that can reasonably be regarded as encouraging illegal drug use. We conclude that the school officials in this case did not violate the First Amendment by confiscating the pro-drug banner and suspending the student responsible for it.

I

On January 24, 2002, the Olympic Torch Relay passed through Juneau, Alaska, on its way to the winter games in Salt Lake City, Utah. The torchbearers were to proceed along a street in front of Juneau-Douglas High School (JDHS) while school was in session. Petitioner Deborah Morse, the school principal, decided to permit staff and students to participate in the Torch Relay as an approved social event or class trip. Students were allowed to leave class to observe the relay from either side of the street. Teachers and administrative officials monitored the students' actions.

Respondent Joseph Frederick, a JDHS senior, was late to school that day. When he arrived, he joined his friends (all but one of whom were JDHS students) across the street from the school to watch the event. Not all the students waited patiently. Some became rambunctious, throwing plastic cola bottles and snowballs and scuffling with their classmates. As the torchbearers and camera crews passed by, Frederick and his friends unfurled a 14-foot banner bearing the phrase: "BONG HiTS 4 JESUS." The large banner was easily readable by the students on the other side of the street.

Principal Morse immediately crossed the street and demanded that the banner be taken down. Everyone but Frederick complied. Morse confiscated the banner and told Frederick to report to her office, where she suspended him for 10 days. Morse later explained that she told Frederick to take the banner down because she thought it encouraged illegal drug use, in violation of established school policy. Juneau School Board Policy No. 5520 states: "The Board specifically prohibits any assembly or public expression that... advocates the use of substances that are illegal to minors...." In addition, Juneau School Board Policy No. 5850 subjects "[p]upils who participate in approved social events and class trips" to the same student conduct rules that apply during the regular school program.

Frederick administratively appealed his suspension, but the Juneau School District Superintendent upheld it, limiting it to time served (8 days). In a memorandum setting forth his reasons, the superintendent determined that Frederick had displayed his banner "in the midst of his fellow students, during school hours, at a school-sanctioned activity." He further explained that Frederick "was not disciplined because the principal of the school 'disagreed' with his message, but because his speech appeared to advocate the use of illegal drugs."

The superintendent continued:

> "The common-sense understanding of the phrase 'bong hits' is that it is a reference to a means of smoking marijuana. Given [Frederick's] inability or unwillingness to express any other credible meaning for the phrase, I can only agree with the principal and countless others who saw the banner as advocating the use of illegal drugs. [Frederick's] speech was not political. He was not advocating the legalization of marijuana or promoting a religious belief. He was displaying a fairly silly message promoting illegal drug usage in the midst of a school activity, for the benefit of television cameras covering the Torch Relay. [Frederick's] speech was potentially disruptive to the event and clearly disruptive of and inconsistent with the school's educational mission to educate students about the dangers of illegal drugs and to discourage their use."

Relying on our decision in *Fraser, supra*, the superintendent concluded that the principal's actions were permissible because Frederick's banner was "speech or action that intrudes upon the work of the schools." The Juneau School District Board of Education upheld the suspension.

Frederick then filed suit under 42 U.S.C. § 1983, alleging that the school board and Morse had violated his First Amendment rights. He sought declaratory and injunctive relief, unspecified compensatory damages, punitive damages, and attorney's fees. The District Court granted summary judgment for the school board and Morse, ruling that they were entitled to qualified immunity and that they had not infringed Frederick's First Amendment rights. The court found that Morse reasonably interpreted the banner as promoting illegal drug use—a message that "directly contravened the Board's policies relating to drug abuse prevention." Under the circumstances, the court held that "Morse had the authority, if not the obligation, to stop such messages at a school-sanctioned activity."

The Ninth Circuit reversed. Deciding that Frederick acted during a "school-authorized activit[y]," and "proceed[ing] on the basis that the banner expressed a positive sentiment about marijuana use," the court nonetheless found a violation of Frederick's First Amendment rights because the school punished Frederick without demonstrating that his speech gave rise to a "risk of substantial disruption." 439 F.3d 1114, 1118, 1121–1123 (2006). The court further concluded that Frederick's right to display his banner was so "clearly established" that a reasonable principal in Morse's position would have understood that her actions were unconstitutional, and that Morse was therefore not entitled to qualified immunity. *Id.*, at 1123–1125.

We granted certiorari on two questions: whether Frederick had a First Amendment right to wield his banner, and, if so, whether that right was so clearly established that the principal may be held liable for damages. 549 U.S. 1075 (2006). We resolve the first question against Frederick, and therefore have no occasion to reach the second.[1]

II

At the outset, we reject Frederick's argument that this is not a school speech case—as has every other authority to address the question. The event occurred during normal school hours. It was sanctioned by Principal Morse "as an approved social event or class trip," and the school district's rules expressly provide that pupils in "approved social events and class trips are subject to district rules for student conduct." Teachers and administrators were interspersed among the students and charged with supervising them. The high school band and cheerleaders performed. Frederick, standing among other JDHS students across the street from the school, directed his banner toward the school, making it plainly visible to most students. Under these circumstances, we agree with the superintendent that Frederick cannot "stand in the midst of his fellow students, during school hours, at a school-sanctioned activity and claim he is not at school." There is some uncertainty at the outer boundaries as to when courts should apply school speech precedents, see *Porter v. Ascension Parish School Bd.*, 393 F.3d 608, 615, n. 22 (C.A.5 2004), but not on these facts.

III

The message on Frederick's banner is cryptic. It is no doubt offensive to some, perhaps amusing to others. To still others, it probably means nothing at all. Frederick himself claimed "that the words were just nonsense meant to attract television cameras." 439 F.3d, at 1117–1118. But Principal Morse thought the banner would be interpreted by those viewing it as promoting illegal drug use, and that interpretation is plainly a reasonable one.

As Morse later explained in a declaration, when she saw the sign, she thought that "the reference to a 'bong hit' would be widely understood by high school students and others as referring to smoking marijuana." She further believed that "display of the banner would be construed by students, District personnel, parents and others witnessing the display of the banner, as advocating or promoting illegal drug use"—in violation of school policy....

We agree with Morse. At least two interpretations of the words on the banner demonstrate that the sign advocated the use of illegal drugs. First, the phrase could be interpreted as an imperative: "[Take] bong hits..."—a message equivalent, as Morse explained in her declaration, to "smoke marijuana" or "use an illegal drug." Alternatively, the phrase could be viewed as celebrating drug use—"bong hits [are a good thing]," or "[we take] bong hits"—and we discern no meaningful distinction between celebrating illegal drug use in the midst of

1. Justice Breyer would rest decision on qualified immunity without reaching the underlying First Amendment question. The problem with this approach is the rather significant one that it is inadequate to decide the case before us. Qualified immunity shields public officials from money damages only. See *Wood v. Strickland*, 420 U.S. 308, 314, n. 6 (1975). In this case, Frederick asked not just for damages, but also for declaratory and injunctive relief. Justice Breyer's proposed decision on qualified immunity grounds would dispose of the damages claims, but Frederick's other claims would remain unaddressed. To get around that problem, Justice Breyer hypothesizes that Frederick's suspension—the target of his request for injunctive relief—"may well be justified on non-speech-related grounds." That hypothesis was never considered by the courts below, never raised by any of the parties, and is belied by the record, which nowhere suggests that the suspension would have been justified solely on non-speech-related grounds.

fellow students and outright advocacy or promotion. See *Guiles v. Marineau*, 461 F.3d 320, 328 (C.A.2 2006) (discussing the present case and describing the sign as "a clearly pro-drug banner").

The pro-drug interpretation of the banner gains further plausibility given the paucity of alternative meanings the banner might bear. The best Frederick can come up with is that the banner is "meaningless and funny." 439 F.3d, at 1116. The dissent similarly refers to the sign's message as "curious," "ambiguous," "nonsense," "ridiculous," "obscure," "silly," "quixotic," and "stupid." Gibberish is surely a possible interpretation of the words on the banner, but it is not the only one, and dismissing the banner as meaningless ignores its undeniable reference to illegal drugs.

The dissent mentions Frederick's "credible and uncontradicted explanation for the message—he just wanted to get on television." But that is a description of Frederick's motive for displaying the banner; it is not an interpretation of what the banner says. The way Frederick was going to fulfill his ambition of appearing on television was by unfurling a pro-drug banner at a school event, in the presence of teachers and fellow students.

Elsewhere in its opinion, the dissent emphasizes the importance of political speech and the need to foster "national debate about a serious issue," as if to suggest that the banner is political speech. But not even Frederick argues that the banner conveys any sort of political or religious message. Contrary to the dissent's suggestion, this is plainly not a case about political debate over the criminalization of drug use or possession.

IV

The question thus becomes whether a principal may, consistent with the First Amendment, restrict student speech at a school event, when that speech is reasonably viewed as promoting illegal drug use. We hold that she may.

In *Tinker*, this Court made clear that "First Amendment rights, applied in light of the special characteristics of the school environment, are available to teachers and students." 393 U.S., at 506. *Tinker* involved a group of high school students who decided to wear black armbands to protest the Vietnam War. School officials learned of the plan and then adopted a policy prohibiting students from wearing armbands. When several students nonetheless wore armbands to school, they were suspended. *Id.*, at 504. The students sued, claiming that their First Amendment rights had been violated, and this Court agreed.

Tinker held that student expression may not be suppressed unless school officials reasonably conclude that it will "materially and substantially disrupt the work and discipline of the school." *Id.*, at 513. The essential facts of *Tinker* are quite stark, implicating concerns at the heart of the First Amendment. The students sought to engage in political speech, using the armbands to express their "disapproval of the Vietnam hostilities and their advocacy of a truce, to make their views known, and, by their example, to influence others to adopt them." *Id.*, at 514. Political speech, of course, is "at the core of what the First Amendment is designed to protect." *Virginia v. Black*, 538 U.S. 343, 365 (2003) (plurality opinion). The only interest the Court discerned underlying the school's actions was the "mere desire to avoid the discomfort and unpleasantness that always accompany an unpopular viewpoint," or "an urgent wish to avoid the controversy which might result from the expression." *Tinker*, 393 U.S., at 509,

510. That interest was not enough to justify banning "a silent, passive expression of opinion, unaccompanied by any disorder or disturbance." *Id.*, at 508.

This Court's next student speech case was *Fraser*, 478 U.S. 675. Matthew Fraser was suspended for delivering a speech before a high school assembly in which he employed what this Court called "an elaborate, graphic, and explicit sexual metaphor." *Id.*, at 678. Analyzing the case under *Tinker*, the District Court and Court of Appeals found no disruption, and therefore no basis for disciplining Fraser. 478 U.S., at 679–680. This Court reversed, holding that the "School District acted entirely within its permissible authority in imposing sanctions upon Fraser in response to his offensively lewd and indecent speech." *Id.*, at 685.

The mode of analysis employed in *Fraser* is not entirely clear. The Court was plainly attuned to the content of Fraser's speech, citing the "marked distinction between the political 'message' of the armbands in *Tinker* and the sexual content of [Fraser's] speech." *Id.*, at 680. But the Court also reasoned that school boards have the authority to determine "what manner of speech in the classroom or in school assembly is inappropriate." *Id.*, at 683. *Cf. id.*, at 689 (Brennan, J., concurring in judgment) ("In the present case, school officials sought only to ensure that a high school assembly proceed in an orderly manner. There is no suggestion that school officials attempted to regulate [Fraser's] speech because they disagreed with the views he sought to express").

We need not resolve this debate to decide this case. For present purposes, it is enough to distill from *Fraser* two basic principles. First, *Fraser*'s holding demonstrates that "the constitutional rights of students in public school are not automatically coextensive with the rights of adults in other settings." *Id.*, at 682. Had Fraser delivered the same speech in a public forum outside the school context, it would have been protected. See *Cohen v. California*, 403 U.S. 15 (1971); *Fraser, supra*, at 682–683. In school, however, Fraser's First Amendment rights were circumscribed "in light of the special characteristics of the school environment." *Tinker, supra*, at 506. Second, *Fraser* established that the mode of analysis set forth in *Tinker* is not absolute. Whatever approach *Fraser* employed, it certainly did not conduct the "substantial disruption" analysis prescribed by *Tinker, supra*, at 514. See *Kuhlmeier*, 484 U.S., at 271, n. 4 (disagreeing with the proposition that there is "no difference between the First Amendment analysis applied in *Tinker* and that applied in *Fraser*," and noting that the holding in *Fraser* was not based on any showing of substantial disruption).

Our most recent student speech case, *Kuhlmeier*, concerned "expressive activities that students, parents, and members of the public might reasonably perceive to bear the imprimatur of the school." 484 U.S., at 271. Staff members of a high school newspaper sued their school when it chose not to publish two of their articles. The Court of Appeals analyzed the case under *Tinker*, ruling in favor of the students because it found no evidence of material disruption to classwork or school discipline. 795 F.2d 1368, 1375 (C.A.8 1986). This Court reversed, holding that "educators do not offend the First Amendment by exercising editorial control over the style and content of student speech in school-sponsored expressive activities so long as their actions are reasonably related to legitimate pedagogical concerns." *Kuhlmeier, supra*, at 273.

Kuhlmeier does not control this case because no one would reasonably believe that Frederick's banner bore the school's imprimatur. The case is nevertheless instructive because it confirms both principles cited above. *Kuhlmeier* acknowledged that schools may regulate some speech "even though the government could not censor similar speech outside the school." *Id.*, at 266. And, like *Fraser*, it confirms that the rule of *Tinker* is not the only basis for restricting student speech.[2]

Drawing on the principles applied in our student speech cases, we have held in the Fourth Amendment context that "while children assuredly do not 'shed their constitutional rights…at the schoolhouse gate,'…the nature of those rights is what is appropriate for children in school." *Vernonia School Dist. 47J v. Acton*, 515 U.S. 646, 655–656 (1995) (quoting *Tinker, supra*, at 506). In particular, "the school setting requires some easing of the restrictions to which searches by public authorities are ordinarily subject." *New Jersey v. T.L.O.*, 469 U.S. 325, 340 (1985). See *Vernonia, supra*, at 656 ("Fourth Amendment rights, no less than First and Fourteenth Amendment rights, are different in public schools than elsewhere…"); *Board of Ed. of Independent School Dist. No. 92 of Pottawatomie Cty. v. Earls*, 536 U.S. 822, 829–830 (2002) ("'special needs' inhere in the public school context"; "[w]hile schoolchildren do not shed their constitutional rights when they enter the schoolhouse, Fourth Amendment rights…are different in public schools than elsewhere; the 'reasonableness' inquiry cannot disregard the schools' custodial and tutelary responsibility for children") (quoting *Vernonia*, 515 U.S., at 656; citation and some internal quotation marks omitted).

Even more to the point, these cases also recognize that deterring drug use by schoolchildren is an "important—indeed, perhaps compelling" interest. *Id.*, at 661. Drug abuse can cause severe and permanent damage to the health and well-being of young people:

> "School years are the time when the physical, psychological, and addictive effects of drugs are most severe. Maturing nervous systems are more critically impaired by intoxicants than mature ones are; childhood losses in learning are lifelong and profound; children grow chemically dependent more quickly than adults, and their record of recovery is depressingly poor. And of course the effects of a drug-infested school are visited not just upon the users, but upon the entire student body and faculty, as the educational process is disrupted." *Id.*, at 661–662 (citations and internal quotation marks omitted).

Just five years ago, we wrote: "The drug abuse problem among our Nation's youth has hardly abated since *Vernonia* was decided in 1995. In fact, evidence suggests that it has only grown worse." *Earls, supra*, at 834, and n. 5.

The problem remains serious today. See generally 1 National Institute on Drug Abuse, National Institutes of Health, Monitoring the Future: National Survey Results on Drug Use, 1975–2005, Secondary School Students (2006). About half of American 12th graders have used an illicit drug, as have more than a third of 10th graders and about one-fifth of 8th graders. *Id.*, at 99. Nearly one in four 12th graders has used an illicit drug in the past month. *Id.*, at 101. Some 25 percent of high schoolers say that they have been offered, sold, or given an illegal drug on school property within the past year. Dept. of Health and Human Services, Centers for Disease Control and Prevention, Youth Risk Behavior Surveillance—United States, 2005, 55 Morbidity and Mortality Weekly Report, Surveillance Summaries, No. SS-5, p. 19 (June 9, 2006).

2. The dissent's effort to find inconsistency between our approach here and the opinion in *Federal Election Commission v. Wisconsin Right to Life, Inc.*, 551 U.S. 449 (2007) (opinion of Stevens, J.), overlooks what was made clear in *Tinker*, *Fraser*, and *Kuhlmeier*: student First Amendment rights are "applied in light of the special characteristics of the school environment." *Tinker*, 393 U.S., at 506. See *Fraser*, 478 U.S., at 682; *Kuhlmeier*, 484 U.S., at 266. And, as discussed above, there is no serious argument that Frederick's banner is political speech of the sort at issue in *Wisconsin Right to Life*.

Congress has declared that part of a school's job is educating students about the dangers of illegal drug use. It has provided billions of dollars to support state and local drug-prevention programs, Brief for United States as Amicus Curiae 1, and required that schools receiving federal funds under the Safe and Drug-Free Schools and Communities Act of 1994 certify that their drug-prevention programs "convey a clear and consistent message that... the illegal use of drugs [is] wrong and harmful." 20 U.S.C. § 7114(d)(6) (2000 ed., Supp. IV).

Thousands of school boards throughout the country—including JDHS—have adopted policies aimed at effectuating this message. Those school boards know that peer pressure is perhaps "the single most important factor leading schoolchildren to take drugs," and that students are more likely to use drugs when the norms in school appear to tolerate such behavior. *Earls*, *supra*, at 840 (Breyer, J., concurring). Student speech celebrating illegal drug use at a school event, in the presence of school administrators and teachers, thus poses a particular challenge for school officials working to protect those entrusted to their care from the dangers of drug abuse.

The "special characteristics of the school environment," *Tinker*, 393 U.S., at 506, and the governmental interest in stopping student drug abuse—reflected in the policies of Congress and myriad school boards, including JDHS—allow schools to restrict student expression that they reasonably regard as promoting illegal drug use. Tinker warned that schools may not prohibit student speech because of "undifferentiated fear or apprehension of disturbance" or "a mere desire to avoid the discomfort and unpleasantness that always accompany an unpopular viewpoint." *Id.*, at 508, 509. The danger here is far more serious and palpable. The particular concern to prevent student drug abuse at issue here, embodied in established school policy, extends well beyond an abstract desire to avoid controversy.

Petitioners urge us to adopt the broader rule that Frederick's speech is proscribable because it is plainly "offensive" as that term is used in *Fraser*. We think this stretches *Fraser* too far; that case should not be read to encompass any speech that could fit under some definition of "offensive." After all, much political and religious speech might be perceived as offensive to some. The concern here is not that Frederick's speech was offensive, but that it was reasonably viewed as promoting illegal drug use.

Although accusing this decision of doing "serious violence to the First Amendment" by authorizing "viewpoint discrimination" (opinion of Stevens, J.), the dissent concludes that "it might well be appropriate to tolerate some targeted viewpoint discrimination in this unique setting." Nor do we understand the dissent to take the position that schools are required to tolerate student advocacy of illegal drug use at school events, even if that advocacy falls short of inviting "imminent" lawless action. ("[I]t is possible that our rigid imminence requirement ought to be relaxed at schools"). And even the dissent recognizes that the issues here are close enough that the principal should not be held liable in damages, but should instead enjoy qualified immunity for her actions. Stripped of rhetorical flourishes, then, the debate between the dissent and this opinion is less about constitutional first principles than about whether Frederick's banner constitutes promotion of illegal drug use. We have explained our view that it does. The dissent's contrary view on that relatively narrow question hardly justifies sounding the First Amendment bugle.

School principals have a difficult job, and a vitally important one. When Frederick suddenly and unexpectedly unfurled his banner, Morse had to decide to act—or not act—on the spot. It was reasonable for her to conclude that the banner promoted illegal drug use—in violation of established school policy—and that failing to act would send a powerful message to the students in her charge, including Frederick, about how serious the school was about the dangers of illegal drug use. The First Amendment does not require schools to tolerate at school events student expression that contributes to those dangers.

The judgment of the United States Court of Appeals for the Ninth Circuit is reversed, and the case is remanded for further proceedings consistent with this opinion....

JUSTICE THOMAS, concurring.

The Court today decides that a public school may prohibit speech advocating illegal drug use. I agree and therefore join its opinion in full. I write separately to state my view that the standard set forth in *Tinker v. Des Moines Independent Community School Dist.*, 393 U.S. 503 (1969), is without basis in the Constitution.

I

The First Amendment states that "Congress shall make no law...abridging the freedom of speech." As this Court has previously observed, the First Amendment was not originally understood to permit all sorts of speech; instead, "[t]here are certain well-defined and narrowly limited classes of speech, the prevention and punishment of which have never been thought to raise any Constitutional problem." *Chaplinsky v. New Hampshire*, 315 U.S. 568, 571–572 (1942); see also *Cox v. Louisiana*, 379 U.S. 536, 554 (1965). In my view, the history of public education suggests that the First Amendment, as originally understood, does not protect student speech in public schools. Although colonial schools were exclusively private, public education proliferated in the early 1800's. By the time the States ratified the Fourteenth Amendment, public schools had become relatively common. W. Reese, America's Public Schools: From the Common School to "No Child Left Behind" 11–12 (2005) (hereinafter Reese). If students in public schools were originally understood as having free-speech rights, one would have expected 19th-century public schools to have respected those rights and courts to have enforced them.[1] They did not.

A

During the colonial era, private schools and tutors offered the only educational opportunities for children, and teachers managed classrooms with an iron hand. R. Butts & L. Cremin, A History of Education in American Culture 121, 123 (1953) (hereinafter Butts). Public schooling arose, in part, as a way to educate those too poor to afford private schools. See Kaestle & Vinovskis, From Apron Strings to ABCs: Parents, Children, and Schooling in Nineteenth-Century Massachusetts, 84 Am. J. Sociology S39, S49 (Supp. 1978). Because public schools were initially created as substitutes for private schools, when States developed public education systems in the early 1800's, no one doubted the government's ability to educate and discipline children as private schools did. Like their private counterparts, early public schools were not places for freewheeling debates or exploration of competing ideas. Rather, teachers instilled "a core of common values" in students and taught them self-control. Reese 23; A. Potter &

1. Although the First Amendment did not apply to the States until at least the ratification of the Fourteenth Amendment, most state constitutions included free-speech guarantees during the period when public education expanded. *E.g.*, Cal. Const., Art. I, § 9 (1849); Conn. Const., Art. I, § 5 (1818); Ind. Const., Art. I, § 9 (1816).

G. Emerson, The School and the Schoolmaster: A Manual 125 (1843) ("By its discipline it contributes, insensibly, to generate a spirit of subordination to lawful authority, a power of self-control, and a habit of postponing present indulgence to a greater future good..."); D. Parkerson & J. Parkerson, The Emergence of the Common School in the U.S. Countryside 6 (1998) (hereinafter Parkerson) (noting that early education activists, such as Benjamin Rush, believed public schools "help[ed] control the innate selfishness of the individual").

Teachers instilled these values not only by presenting ideas but also through strict discipline. Butts 274–275. Schools punished students for behavior the school considered disrespectful or wrong. Parkerson 65 (noting that children were punished for idleness, talking, profanity, and slovenliness). Rules of etiquette were enforced, and courteous behavior was demanded. Reese 40. To meet their educational objectives, schools required absolute obedience. C. Northend, The Teacher's Assistant or Hints and Methods in School Discipline and Instruction 44, 52 (1865) ("I consider a school judiciously governed, where order prevails; where the strictest sense of propriety is manifested by the pupils towards the teacher, and towards each other..." (internal quotation marks omitted)).[2]

In short, in the earliest public schools, teachers taught, and students listened. Teachers commanded, and students obeyed. Teachers did not rely solely on the power of ideas to persuade; they relied on discipline to maintain order.

B

Through the legal doctrine of *in loco parentis*, courts upheld the right of schools to discipline students, to enforce rules, and to maintain order.[3] Rooted in the English common law, *in loco parentis* originally governed the legal rights and obligations of tutors and private schools. 1 W. Blackstone, Commentaries on the Laws of England 441 (1765) ("[A parent] may also delegate part of his parental authority, during his life, to the tutor or schoolmaster of his child; who is then *in loco parentis*, and has such a portion of the power of the parent committed to his charge, viz. that of restraint and correction, as may be necessary to answer the purposes for which he is employed"). Chancellor James Kent noted the acceptance of the doctrine as part of American law in the early 19th century. 2 J. Kent, Commentaries on American Law *205, *206–*207 ("So the power allowed by law to the parent over the person of the child may be delegated to a tutor or instructor, the better to accomplish the purpose of education").... Applying *in loco parentis*, the judiciary was reluctant to interfere in the routine business of school administration, allowing schools and teachers to set and enforce rules and to maintain

2. Even at the college level, strict obedience was required of students: "The English model fostered absolute institutional control of students by faculty both inside and outside the classroom. At all the early American schools, students lived and worked under a vast array of rules and restrictions. This one-sided relationship between the student and the college mirrored the situation at English schools where the emphasis on hierarchical authority stemmed from medieval Christian theology and the unique legal privileges afforded the university corporation." Note, 44 Vand. L.Rev. 1135, 1140 (1991) (footnote omitted).

3. My discussion is limited to elementary and secondary education. In these settings, courts have applied the doctrine of *in loco parentis* regardless of the student's age. See, *e.g.*, *Stevens v. Fassett*, 27 Me. 266, 281 (1847) (holding that a student over the age of 21 is "liab[le] to punishment" on the same terms as other students if he "present[s] himself as a pupil, [and] is received and instructed by the master"); *State v. Mizner*, 45 Iowa 248, 250–252 (1876) (same); *Sheehan v. Sturges*, 53 Conn. 481, 484, 2 A. 841, 843 (1885) (same). Therefore, the fact that Frederick was 18 and not a minor under Alaska law, 439 F.3d 1114, 1117, n. 4 (C.A.9 2006), is inconsequential.

order. *Sheehan v. Sturges*, 53 Conn. 481, 483–484, 2 A. 841, 842 (1885). Thus, in the early years of public schooling, schools and teachers had considerable discretion in disciplinary matters:

> "To accomplish th[e] desirable ends [of teaching self-restraint, obedience, and other civic virtues], the master of a school is necessarily invested with much discretionary power.... He must govern these pupils, quicken the slothful, spur the indolent, restrain the impetuous, and control the stubborn. He must make rules, give commands, and punish disobedience. What rules, what commands, and what punishments shall be imposed, are necessarily largely within the discretion of the master, where none are defined by the school board. *Patterson v. Nutter*, 78 Me. 509, 511, 7 A. 273, 274 (1886)."[4]

A review of the case law shows that *in loco parentis* allowed schools to regulate student speech as well. Courts routinely preserved the rights of teachers to punish speech that the school or teacher thought was contrary to the interests of the school and its educational goals.... The doctrine of *in loco parentis* limited the ability of schools to set rules and control their classrooms in almost no way. It merely limited the imposition of excessive physical punishment. In this area, the case law was split. One line of cases specified that punishment was wholly discretionary as long as the teacher did not act with legal malice or cause permanent injury. Another line allowed courts to intervene where the corporal punishment was "clearly excessive." Under both lines of cases, courts struck down only punishments that were excessively harsh; they almost never questioned the substantive restrictions on student conduct set by teachers and schools....[6]

II

Tinker effected a sea change in students' speech rights, extending them well beyond traditional bounds. The case arose when a school punished several students for wearing black armbands to school to protest the Vietnam War. *Tinker*, 393 U.S., at 504. 733. Determining that the punishment infringed the students' First Amendment rights, this Court created a new standard for students' freedom of speech in public schools:

> "[W]here there is no finding and no showing that engaging in the forbidden conduct would materially and substantially interfere with the requirements of appropriate discipline in the operation of the school, the prohibition cannot be sustained." *Id.*, at 509 (internal quotation marks omitted).

4. Even courts that did not favor the broad discretion given to teachers to impose corporal punishment recognized that the law provided it. *Cooper v. McJunkin*, 4 Ind. 290, 291 (1853) (stating that "[t]he public seem to cling to a despotism in the government of schools which has been discarded everywhere else").

6. At least nominally, this Court has continued to recognize the applicability of the *in loco parentis* doctrine to public schools. See *Vernonia School Dist. 47J v. Acton*, 515 U.S. 646, 654-655 (1995) ("Traditionally at common law, and still today, unemancipated minors lack some of the most fundamental rights of self-determination.... They are subject... to the control of their parents or guardians. When parents place minor children in private schools for their education, the teachers and administrators of those schools stand *in loco parentis* over the children entrusted to them" (citation omitted)); *Bethel School Dist. No. 403 v. Fraser*, 478 U.S. 675, 684 (1986) ("These cases recognize the obvious concern on the part of parents, and school authorities acting *in loco parentis*, to protect children—especially in a captive audience—from exposure to sexually explicit, indecent, or lewd speech").

Accordingly, unless a student's speech would disrupt the educational process, students had a fundamental right to speak their minds (or wear their armbands)—even on matters the school disagreed with or found objectionable. *Ibid.* ("[The school] must be able to show that its action was caused by something more than a mere desire to avoid the discomfort and unpleasantness that always accompany an unpopular viewpoint").

Justice Black dissented, criticizing the Court for "subject[ing] all the public schools in the country to the whims and caprices of their loudest-mouthed, but maybe not their brightest, students." *Id.*, at 525. He emphasized the instructive purpose of schools: "[T]axpayers send children to school on the premise that at their age they need to learn, not teach." *Id.*, at 522. In his view, the Court's decision "surrender[ed] control of the American public school system to public school students." *Id.*, at 526.

Of course, *Tinker*'s reasoning conflicted with the traditional understanding of the judiciary's role in relation to public schooling, a role limited by *in loco parentis*. Perhaps for that reason, the Court has since scaled back *Tinker*'s standard, or rather set the standard aside on an ad hoc basis. In *Bethel School Dist. No. 403 v. Fraser*, 478 U.S. 675, 677, 678 (1986), a public school suspended a student for delivering a speech that contained "an elaborate, graphic, and explicit sexual metaphor." The Court of Appeals found that the speech caused no disruption under the *Tinker* standard, and this Court did not question that holding. 478 U.S., at 679–680. The Court nonetheless permitted the school to punish the student because of the objectionable content of his speech. *Id.*, at 685 ("A high school assembly or classroom is no place for a sexually explicit monologue directed towards an unsuspecting audience of teenage students"). Signaling at least a partial break with *Tinker*, *Fraser* left the regulation of indecent student speech to local schools. 478 U.S., at 683.

Similarly, in *Hazelwood School Dist. v. Kuhlmeier*, 484 U.S. 260 (1988), the Court made an exception to *Tinker* for school-sponsored activities. The Court characterized newspapers and similar school-sponsored activities "as part of the school curriculum" and held that "[e]ducators are entitled to exercise greater control over" these forms of student expression. 484 U.S., at 271. Accordingly, the Court expressly refused to apply *Tinker*'s standard. 484 U.S., at 272–273. Instead, for school-sponsored activities, the Court created a new standard that permitted school regulations of student speech that are "reasonably related to legitimate pedagogical concerns." *Id.*, at 273.

Today, the Court creates another exception. In doing so, we continue to distance ourselves from *Tinker*, but we neither overrule it nor offer an explanation of when it operates and when it does not. I am afraid that our jurisprudence now says that students have a right to speak in schools except when they don't—a standard continuously developed through litigation against local schools and their administrators. In my view, petitioners could prevail for a much simpler reason: As originally understood, the Constitution does not afford students a right to free speech in public schools.

III

In light of the history of American public education, it cannot seriously be suggested that the First Amendment "freedom of speech" encompasses a student's right to speak in public schools. Early public schools gave total control to teachers, who expected obedience and respect from students. And courts routinely deferred to schools' authority to make rules and to discipline students for violating those rules. Several points are clear: (1) under *in loco parentis*, speech rules and other school rules were treated identically; (2) the *in loco parentis* doctrine imposed almost no limits on the types of rules that a school could set while students were in school; and (3) schools and teachers had tremendous discretion in imposing punishments for violations of those rules.

It might be suggested that the early school speech cases dealt only with slurs and profanity. But that criticism does not withstand scrutiny. First, state courts repeatedly reasoned that schools had discretion to impose discipline to maintain order. The substance of the student's speech or conduct played no part in the analysis. Second, some cases involved punishment for speech on weightier matters, for instance a speech criticizing school administrators for creating a fire hazard. See *Wooster*, 27 Cal.App., at 52–53, 148 P., at 959. Yet courts refused to find an exception to *in loco parentis* even for this advocacy of public safety.

To be sure, our educational system faces administrative and pedagogical challenges different from those faced by 19th-century schools. And the idea of treating children as though it were still the 19th century would find little support today. But I see no constitutional imperative requiring public schools to allow all student speech. Parents decide whether to send their children to public schools. Cf. *Hamilton v. Regents of Univ. of Cal.*, 293 U.S. 245, 262 (1934) ("California has not drafted or called them to attend the university. They are seeking education offered by the State and at the same time insisting that they be excluded from the prescribed course..."); *id.*, at 266 (Cardozo, J., concurring). If parents do not like the rules imposed by those schools, they can seek redress in school boards or legislatures; they can send their children to private schools or home school them; or they can simply move. Whatever rules apply to student speech in public schools, those rules can be challenged by parents in the political process.

In place of that democratic regime, *Tinker* substituted judicial oversight of the day-to-day affairs of public schools. The *Tinker* Court made little attempt to ground its holding in the history of education or in the original understanding of the First Amendment.[8] Instead, it imposed a new and malleable standard: Schools could not inhibit student speech unless it "substantially interfere[d] with the requirements of appropriate discipline in the operation of the school." 393 U.S., at 509 (internal quotation marks omitted). Inherent in the application of that standard are judgment calls about what constitutes interference and what constitutes appropriate discipline. See *id.*, at 517–518 (Black, J., dissenting) (arguing that the armbands in fact caused a disruption). Historically, courts reasoned that only local school districts were

8. The *Tinker* Court claimed that "[i]t can hardly be argued that either students or teachers shed their constitutional rights to freedom of speech or expression at the schoolhouse gate. This has been the unmistakable holding of this Court for almost 50 years." 393 U.S., at 506. But the cases the Court cited in favor of that bold proposition do not support it. *Tinker* chiefly relies upon *Meyer v. Nebraska*, 262 U.S. 390 (1923) (striking down a law prohibiting the teaching of German). However, *Meyer* involved a challenge by a private school, *id.*, at 396, and the *Meyer* Court was quick to note that no "challenge [has] been made of the State's power to prescribe a curriculum for institutions which it supports." *Id.*, at 402. *Meyer* provides absolutely no support for the proposition that free-speech rights apply within schools operated by the State. And notably, *Meyer* relied as its chief support on the *Lochner v. New York*, 198 U.S. 45 (1905), line of cases, 262 U.S., at 399, a line of cases that has long been criticized, *United Haulers Assn., Inc. v. Oneida-Herkimer Solid Waste Management Authority*, 550 U.S. 330 (2007). *Tinker* also relied on *Pierce v. Society of Sisters*, 268 U.S. 510 (1925). *Pierce* has nothing to say on this issue either. *Pierce* simply upheld the right of parents to send their children to private school. *Id.*, at 535.

entitled to make those calls. The *Tinker* Court usurped that traditional authority for the judiciary.

And because *Tinker* utterly ignored the history of public education, courts (including this one) routinely find it necessary to create ad hoc exceptions to its central premise. This doctrine of exceptions creates confusion without fixing the underlying problem by returning to first principles. Just as I cannot accept *Tinker*'s standard, I cannot subscribe to *Kuhlmeier*'s alternative. Local school boards, not the courts, should determine what pedagogical interests are "legitimate" and what rules "reasonably relat[e]" to those interests. 484 U.S., at 273.

Justice Black may not have been "a prophet or the son of a prophet," but his dissent in *Tinker* has proved prophetic. 393 U.S., at 525. In the name of the First Amendment, *Tinker* has undermined the traditional authority of teachers to maintain order in public schools. "Once a society that generally respected the authority of teachers, deferred to their judgment, and trusted them to act in the best interest of school children, we now accept defiance, disrespect, and disorder as daily occurrences in many of our public schools." Dupre, Should Students Have Constitutional Rights? Keeping Order in the Public Schools, 65 Geo. Wash. L.Rev. 49, 50 (1996). We need look no further than this case for an example: Frederick asserts a constitutional right to utter at a school event what is either "[g]ibberish," or an open call to use illegal drugs. To elevate such impertinence to the status of constitutional protection would be farcical and would indeed be to "surrender control of the American public school system to public school students." *Tinker, supra*, at 526 (Black, J., dissenting).

I join the Court's opinion because it erodes *Tinker*'s hold in the realm of student speech, even though it does so by adding to the patchwork of exceptions to the *Tinker* standard. I think the better approach is to dispense with *Tinker* altogether, and given the opportunity, I would do so.

JUSTICE ALITO, with whom JUSTICE KENNEDY joins, concurring.

I join the opinion of the Court on the understanding that (a) it goes no further than to hold that a public school may restrict speech that a reasonable observer would interpret as advocating illegal drug use and (b) it provides no support for any restriction of speech that can plausibly be interpreted as commenting on any political or social issue, including speech on issues such as "the wisdom of the war on drugs or of legalizing marijuana for medicinal use." (STEVENS, J., dissenting).

The opinion of the Court correctly reaffirms the recognition in *Tinker v. Des Moines Independent Community School Dist.*, 393 U.S. 503, 506 (1969), of the fundamental principle that students do not "shed their constitutional rights to freedom of speech or expression at the schoolhouse gate." The Court is also correct in noting that *Tinker*, which permits the regulation of student speech that threatens a concrete and "substantial disruption," *id.*, at 514, does not set out the only ground on which in-school student speech may be regulated by state actors in a way that would not be constitutional in other settings.

But I do not read the opinion to mean that there are necessarily any grounds for such regulation that are not already recognized in the holdings of this Court. In addition to *Tinker*, the decision in the present case allows the restriction of speech advocating illegal drug use; *Bethel School Dist. No. 403 v. Fraser*, 478 U.S. 675 (1986), permits the regulation of speech that is delivered in a lewd or vulgar manner as part of a middle school program; and *Hazelwood School Dist. v. Kuhlmeier*, 484 U.S. 260 (1988), allows a school to regulate what is in essence the school's own speech, that is, articles that appear in a publication that is an official school organ. I join the opinion of the Court on the understanding that the opinion does not hold that the special characteristics of the public schools necessarily justify any other speech restrictions.

The opinion of the Court does not endorse the broad argument advanced by petitioners and the United States that the First Amendment permits public school officials to censor any student speech that interferes with a school's "educational mission." This argument can easily be manipulated in dangerous ways, and I would reject it before such abuse occurs. The "educational mission" of the public schools is defined by the elected and appointed public officials with authority over the schools and by the school administrators and faculty. As a result, some public schools have defined their educational missions as including the inculcation of whatever political and social views are held by the members of these groups.

During the *Tinker* era, a public school could have defined its educational mission to include solidarity with our soldiers and their families and thus could have attempted to outlaw the wearing of black armbands on the ground that they undermined this mission. Alternatively, a school could have defined its educational mission to include the promotion of world peace and could have sought to ban the wearing of buttons expressing support for the troops on the ground that the buttons signified approval of war. The "educational mission" argument would give public school authorities a license to suppress speech on political and social issues based on disagreement with the viewpoint expressed. The argument, therefore, strikes at the very heart of the First Amendment.

The public schools are invaluable and beneficent institutions, but they are, after all, organs of the State. When public school authorities regulate student speech, they act as agents of the State; they do not stand in the shoes of the students' parents. It is a dangerous fiction to pretend that parents simply delegate their authority—including their authority to determine what their children may say and hear—to public school authorities. It is even more dangerous to assume that such a delegation of authority somehow strips public school authorities of their status as agents of the State. Most parents, realistically, have no choice but to send their children to a public school and little ability to influence what occurs in the school. It is therefore wrong to treat public school officials, for purposes relevant to the First Amendment, as if they were private, nongovernmental actors standing *in loco parentis*.

For these reasons, any argument for altering the usual free speech rules in the public schools cannot rest on a theory of delegation but must instead be based on some special characteristic of the school setting. The special characteristic that is relevant in this case is the threat to the physical safety of students. School attendance can expose students to threats to their physical safety that they would not otherwise face. Outside of school, parents can attempt to protect their children in many ways and may take steps to monitor and exercise control over the persons with whom their children associate. Similarly, students, when not in school, may be able to avoid threatening individuals and situations. During school hours, however, parents are not present to provide protection and guidance, and students' movements and their ability to choose the persons with whom they spend time are severely restricted. Students may be compelled on a daily basis to spend time at close quarters with other students who may do them harm. Experience shows that schools can be places of special danger.

In most settings, the First Amendment strongly limits the government's ability to suppress speech on the ground that it presents a threat of violence. See *Brandenburg v. Ohio*, 395 U.S. 444 (1969) (per curiam). But due to the special features of the school environment, school officials must have greater authority to intervene before speech leads to violence. And, in most cases, *Tinker*'s "substantial disruption" standard permits school officials to step in before actual violence erupts. See 393 U.S., at 508–509.

Speech advocating illegal drug use poses a threat to student safety that is just as serious, if not always as immediately obvious. As we have recognized in the past and as the opinion of the Court today details, illegal drug use presents a grave and in many ways unique threat to the physical safety of students. I therefore conclude that the public schools may ban speech advocating illegal drug use. But I regard such regulation as standing at the far reaches of what the First Amendment permits. I join the opinion of the Court with the understanding that the opinion does not endorse any further extension.

Justice Breyer, concurring in the judgment in part and dissenting in part.

This Court need not and should not decide this difficult First Amendment issue on the merits. Rather, I believe that it should simply hold that qualified immunity bars the student's claim for monetary damages and say no more.

I

Resolving the First Amendment question presented in this case is, in my view, unwise and unnecessary. In part that is because the question focuses upon specific content narrowly defined: May a school board punish students for speech that advocates drug use and, if so, when? At the same time, the underlying facts suggest that Principal Morse acted as she did not simply because of the specific content and viewpoint of Joseph Frederick's speech but also because of the surrounding context and manner in which Frederick expressed his views. To say that school officials might reasonably prohibit students during school-related events from unfurling 14-foot banners (with any kind of irrelevant or inappropriate message) designed to attract attention from television cameras seems unlikely to undermine basic First Amendment principles. But to hold, as the Court does, that "schools may take steps to safeguard those entrusted to their care from speech that can reasonably be regarded as encouraging illegal drug use" (and that "schools" may "restrict student expression that they reasonably regard as promoting illegal drug use") is quite a different matter. This holding, based as it is on viewpoint restrictions, raises a host of serious concerns.

One concern is that, while the holding is theoretically limited to speech promoting the use of illegal drugs, it could in fact authorize further viewpoint-based restrictions. Illegal drugs, after all, are not the only illegal substances. What about encouraging the underage consumption of alcohol? Moreover, it is unclear how far the Court's rule regarding drug advocacy extends. What about a conversation during the lunch period where one student suggests that glaucoma sufferers should smoke marijuana to relieve the pain? What about deprecating commentary about an antidrug film shown in school? And what about drug messages mixed with other, more expressly political, content? If, for example, Frederick's banner had read "LEGALIZE BONG HiTS," he might be thought to receive protection from the majority's rule, which goes to speech "encouraging *illegal* drug use." But speech advocating change in drug laws might also be perceived of as promoting the disregard of existing drug laws.

Legal principles must treat like instances alike. Those principles do not permit treating "drug use" separately without a satisfying explanation of why drug use is *sui generis.* To say that illegal drug use is harmful to students, while surely true, does not itself constitute a satisfying explanation because there are many such harms. During a real war, one less metaphorical than the war on drugs, the Court declined an opportunity to draw narrow subject-matter-based lines. Cf. *West Virginia Bd. of Ed. v. Barnette*, 319 U.S. 624 (1943) (holding students cannot be compelled to recite the Pledge of Allegiance during World War II). We should decline this opportunity today.

Although the dissent avoids some of the majority's pitfalls, I fear that, if adopted as law, it would risk significant interference with reasonable school efforts to maintain discipline. What is a principal to do when a student unfurls a 14-foot banner (carrying an irrelevant or inappropriate message) during a school-related event in an effort to capture the attention of television cameras? Nothing? In my view, a principal or a teacher might reasonably view Frederick's conduct, in this setting, as simply beyond the pale. And a school official, knowing that adolescents often test the outer boundaries of acceptable behavior, may believe it is important (for the offending student and his classmates) to establish when a student has gone too far.

Neither can I simply say that Morse may have taken the right action (confiscating Frederick's banner) but for the wrong reason ("drug speech"). Teachers are neither lawyers nor police officers; and the law should not demand that they fully understand the intricacies of our First Amendment jurisprudence. As the majority rightly points out, the circumstances here called for a quick decision... (noting that "Morse had to decide to act—or not act—on the spot"). But this consideration is better understood in terms of qualified immunity than of the First Amendment.

All of this is to say that, regardless of the outcome of the constitutional determination, a decision on the underlying First Amendment issue is both difficult and unusually portentous. And that is a reason for us *not to decide* the issue unless we must.

In some instances, it is appropriate to decide a constitutional issue in order to provide "guidance" for the future. But I cannot find much guidance in today's decision. The Court makes clear that school officials may "restrict" student speech that promotes "illegal drug use" and that they may "take steps" to "safeguard" students from speech that encourages "illegal drug use." Beyond "steps" that prohibit the unfurling of banners at school outings, the Court does not explain just what those "restrict[ions]" or those "steps" might be.

Nor, if we are to avoid the risk of interpretations that are too broad or too narrow, is it easy to offer practically valuable guidance. Students will test the limits of acceptable behavior in myriad ways better known to schoolteachers than to judges; school officials need a degree of flexible authority to respond to disciplinary challenges; and the law has always considered the relationship between teachers and students special. Under these circumstances, the more detailed the Court's supervision becomes, the more likely its law will engender further disputes among teachers and students. Consequently, larger numbers of those disputes will likely make their way from the schoolhouse to the courthouse. Yet no one wishes to substitute courts for school boards, or to turn the judge's chambers into the principal's office.

In order to avoid resolving the fractious underlying constitutional question, we need only decide a different question that this case presents, the question of "qualified immunity." The principle of qualified immunity fits this case perfectly and, by saying so, we would diminish the risk of bringing about the adverse consequences I have identified. More importantly, we should also adhere to a basic constitutional obligation by avoiding unnecessary decision of constitutional questions. See *Ashwander v. TVA*, 297 U.S. 288, 347 (1936) (Brandeis, J., concurring) ("The Court will not pass upon a constitutional question although properly presented by the record, if there is also present some other ground upon which the case may be disposed of").

II

A

The defense of "qualified immunity" requires courts to enter judgment in favor of a government employee unless the employee's conduct violates "clearly established statutory or constitutional rights of which a reasonable person would have known." *Harlow v. Fitzgerald*, 457 U.S. 800, 818 (1982). The defense is designed to protect "all but the plainly incompetent or those who knowingly violate the law." *Malley v. Briggs*, 475 U.S. 335, 341 (1986).

Qualified immunity applies here and entitles Principal Morse to judgment on Frederick's monetary damages claim because she did not clearly violate the law during her confrontation with the student. At the time of that confrontation, *Tinker v. Des Moines Independent Community School Dist.*, 393 U.S. 503, 513 (1969), indicated that school officials could not prohibit students from wearing an armband in protest of the Vietnam War, where the conduct at issue did not "materially and substantially disrupt the work and discipline of the school"; *Bethel School Dist. No. 403 v. Fraser*, 478 U.S. 675 (1986), indicated that school officials could restrict a student's freedom to give a school assembly speech containing an elaborate sexual metaphor; and *Hazelwood School Dist. v. Kuhlmeier*, 484 U.S. 260 (1988), indicated that school officials could restrict student contributions to a school-sponsored newspaper, even without threat of imminent disruption. None of these cases clearly governs the case at hand.

The Ninth Circuit thought it "clear" that these cases did not permit Morse's actions. See 439 F.3d 1114, 1124 (2006). That is because, in the Ninth Circuit's view, this case involved neither lewd speech, cf. *Fraser, supra*, nor school sponsored speech, cf. *Kuhlmeier, supra*, and hence *Tinker*'s substantial disruption test must guide the inquiry. See 439 F.3d, at 1123. But unlike the Ninth Circuit, other courts have described the tests these cases suggest as complex and often difficult to apply. See, *e.g.*, *Guiles ex rel. Guiles v. Marineau*, 461 F.3d 320, 326 (C.A.2 2006) ("It is not entirely clear whether *Tinker*'s rule applies to all student speech that is not sponsored by schools, subject to the rule of *Fraser*, or whether it applies only to political speech or to political viewpoint-based discrimination"); *Baxter v. Vigo Cty. School Corp.*, 26 F.3d 728, 737 (C.A.7 1994) (pointing out that *Fraser* "cast some doubt on the extent to which students retain free speech rights in the school setting"). Indeed, the fact that this Court divides on the constitutional question (and that the majority reverses the Ninth Circuit's constitutional determination) strongly suggests that the answer as to how to apply prior law to these facts was unclear.

The relative ease with which we could decide this case on the qualified immunity ground, and thereby avoid deciding a far more difficult constitutional question, underscores the need to lift the rigid "order of battle" decisionmaking requirement that this Court imposed upon lower courts in *Saucier v. Katz*, 533 U.S. 194, 201–202 (2001). In *Saucier*, the Court wrote that lower courts' "first inquiry must be whether a constitutional right would have been violated on the facts alleged." *Id.*, at 200. Only if there is a constitutional violation, can lower courts proceed to consider whether the official is entitled to "qualified immunity." See *ibid.*

I have previously explained why I believe we should abandon *Saucier*'s order-of-battle rule. See *Scott v. Harris*, 550 U.S. 372, 387-389 (2007) (Breyer, J., concurring); *Brosseau v. Haugen*, 543 U.S. 194, 201–202 (2004) (Breyer, J., concurring). Sometimes the rule will require lower courts unnecessarily to answer difficult constitutional questions, thereby wasting judicial resources. Sometimes it will require them to resolve constitutional issues that are poorly presented. Sometimes the rule will immunize an incorrect constitutional holding from further review. And often the rule violates the longstanding principle that courts should "not...pass on questions of constitutionality...unless such adjudication is unavoidable." *Spector Motor Service, Inc. v. McLaughlin*, 323 U.S. 101, 105 (1944).

This last point warrants amplification. In resolving the underlying constitutional question, we produce several differing opinions. It is utterly unnecessary to do so. Were we to decide this case on the ground of qualified immunity, our decision would be *unanimous*, for the dissent concedes that Morse should not be held liable in damages for confiscating Frederick's banner. And the "cardinal principle of judicial restraint" is that "if it is not necessary to decide more, it is necessary not to decide more." *PDK Labs., Inc. v. Drug Enforcement Admin.*, 362 F.3d 786, 799 (C.A.D.C.2004) (Roberts, J., concurring in part and concurring in judgment)....

B

There is one remaining objection to deciding this case on the basis of qualified immunity alone. The plaintiff in this case has sought not only damages; he has also sought an injunction requiring the school district to expunge his suspension from its records. A "qualified immunity" defense applies in respect to damages actions, but not to injunctive relief. See, *e.g.*, *Wood v. Strickland*, 420 U.S. 308, 314, n. 6 (1975). With respect to that claim, the underlying question of constitutionality, at least conceivably, remains.

I seriously doubt, however, that it does remain. At the plaintiff's request, the school superintendent reviewed Frederick's 10-day suspension. The superintendent, in turn, reduced the suspension to the eight days that Frederick had served before the appeal. But in doing so the superintendent noted that several actions independent of Frederick's speech supported the suspension, including the plaintiff's disregard of a school official's instruction, his failure to report to the principal's office on time, his "defiant [and] disruptive behavior," and the "belligerent attitude" he displayed when he finally reported. The superintendent wrote that "were" he to "concede" that Frederick's "speech...is protected,...the remainder of his behavior was not excused."

The upshot is that the school board's refusal to erase the suspension from the record may well be justified on non-speech-related grounds. In addition, plaintiff's counsel appeared to agree with the Court's suggestion at oral argument that Frederick "would not pursue" injunctive relief if he prevailed on the damages question. And finding that Morse was entitled to qualified immunity would leave only the question of injunctive relief.

Given the high probability that Frederick's request for an injunction will not require a court to resolve the constitutional issue, see *Ashwander*, 297 U.S., at 347 (Brandeis, J., concurring), I would decide only the qualified immunity question and remand the rest of the case for an initial consideration.

Justice Stevens, with whom Justice Souter and Justice Ginsburg join, dissenting.

A significant fact barely mentioned by the Court sheds a revelatory light on the motives of both the students and the principal of Juneau-Douglas High School (JDHS). On January 24, 2002, the Olympic Torch Relay gave those Alaska residents a rare chance to appear on national television. As Joseph Frederick repeatedly explained, he did not address the curious message—"BONG HiTS 4 JESUS"—to his fellow students. He just wanted to get the camera crews' attention. Moreover, concern about a nationwide evaluation of the conduct of the JDHS student body would have justified the principal's decision to remove an attention-grabbing 14-foot banner, even if it had merely proclaimed "Glaciers Melt!"

I agree with the Court that the principal should not be held liable for pulling down Frederick's banner. See *Harlow v. Fitzgerald*, 457 U.S. 800, 818 (1982). I would hold, however, that the school's interest in protecting its students from exposure to speech "reasonably regarded as promoting illegal drug use," cannot justify disciplining Frederick for his attempt to make an ambiguous statement to a television audience simply because it contained an oblique reference to drugs. The First Amendment demands more, indeed, much more.

The Court holds otherwise only after laboring to establish two uncontroversial propositions: first, that the constitutional rights of students in school settings are not coextensive with the rights of adults, and second, that deterring drug use by schoolchildren is a valid and terribly important interest. As to the first, I take the Court's point that the message on Frederick's banner is not *necessarily* protected speech, even though it unquestionably would have been had the banner been unfurled elsewhere. As to the second, I am willing to assume that the Court is correct that the pressing need to deter drug use supports JDHS's rule prohibiting willful conduct that expressly "advocates the use of substances that are illegal to minors." But it is a gross non sequitur to draw from these two unremarkable propositions the remarkable conclusion that the school may suppress student speech that was never meant to persuade anyone to do anything.

In my judgment, the First Amendment protects student speech if the message itself neither violates a permissible rule nor expressly advocates conduct that is illegal and harmful to students. This nonsense banner does neither, and the Court does serious violence to the First Amendment in upholding—indeed, lauding—a school's decision to punish Frederick for expressing a view with which it disagreed.

I

In December 1965, we were engaged in a controversial war, a war that "divided this country as few other issues ever have." *Tinker v. Des Moines Independent Community School Dist.*, 393 U.S. 503, 524 (1969) (Black, J., dissenting). Having learned that some students planned to wear black armbands as a symbol of opposition to the country's involvement in Vietnam, officials of the Des Moines public school district adopted a policy calling for the suspension of any student who refused to remove the armband. As we explained when we considered the propriety of that policy, "[t]he school officials banned and sought to punish petitioners for a silent, passive expression of opinion, unaccompanied by any disorder or disturbance on the part of petitioners." *Id.*, at 508, 89 S.Ct. 733. The district justified its censorship on the ground that it feared that the expression of a controversial and unpopular opinion would generate disturbances. Because the school officials had insufficient reason to believe that those disturbances would "materially and substantially interfere with the requirements of appropriate discipline in the operation of the school," we found the justification for the rule to lack any foundation and therefore held that the censorship violated the First Amendment. *Id.*, at 509 (internal quotation marks omitted).

Justice Harlan dissented, but not because he thought the school district could censor a message with which it disagreed. Rather, he would have upheld the district's rule only because the students never cast doubt on the district's anti-disruption justification by proving that the rule was motivated "by other than legitimate school concerns—for example, a desire to prohibit the expression of an unpopular point of view while permitting expression of the dominant opinion." *Id.*, at 526.

Two cardinal First Amendment principles animate both the Court's opinion in *Tinker* and Justice Harlan's dissent. First, censorship based on the content of speech, particularly censorship that depends on the viewpoint of the speaker, is subject to the most rigorous burden of justification:

> "Discrimination against speech because of its message is presumed to be unconstitutional.... When the government targets not subject matter, but particular views taken by speakers on a subject, the violation of the First Amendment is all the more blatant. Viewpoint discrimination is thus an egregious form of content discrimination. The government must abstain from regulating speech when the specific motivating ideology or the opinion or perspective of the speaker is the rationale for the restriction." *Rosenberger v. Rector and Visitors of Univ. of Va.*, 515 U.S. 819, 828–829 (1995) (citation omitted).

Second, punishing someone for advocating illegal conduct is constitutional only when the advocacy is likely to provoke the harm that the government seeks to avoid. See *Brandenburg v. Ohio*, 395 U.S. 444, 449 (1969) (*per curiam*) (distinguishing "mere advocacy" of illegal conduct from "incitement to imminent lawless action").

However necessary it may be to modify those principles in the school setting, *Tinker* affirmed their continuing vitality. 393 U.S., at 509 ("In order for the State in the person of school officials to justify prohibition of a particular expression of opinion, it must be able to show that its action was caused by something more than a mere desire to avoid the discomfort and unpleasantness that always accompany an unpopular viewpoint. Certainly where there is no finding and no showing that engaging in the forbidden conduct would materially and substantially interfere with the requirements of appropriate discipline in the operation of the school, the prohibition cannot be sustained" (internal quotation marks omitted)). As other federal courts have long recognized, under *Tinker*,

> "regulation of student speech is generally permissible only when the speech would substantially disrupt or interfere with the work of the school or the rights of other students.... *Tinker* requires a specific and significant fear of disruption, *not just some remote apprehension of disturbance.*" *Saxe v. State College Area School Dist.*, 240 F.3d 200, 211 (C.A.3 2001) (Alito, J.) (emphasis added).

Yet today the Court fashions a test that trivializes the two cardinal principles upon which *Tinker* rests. The Court's test invites stark viewpoint discrimination. In this case, for example, the principal has unabashedly acknowledged that she disciplined Frederick because she disagreed with the pro-drug viewpoint she ascribed to the message on the banner—a viewpoint, incidentally, that Frederick has disavowed, see *id.*, at 28. Unlike our recent decision in *Tennessee Secondary School Athletic Assn. v. Brentwood Academy* (plurality opinion),... the Court's holding in this case strikes at "the heart of the First Amendment" because it upholds a punishment meted out on the basis of a listener's disagreement with her understanding (or, more likely, misunderstanding) of the speaker's viewpoint. "If there is a bedrock principle underlying the First Amendment, it is that the Government may not prohibit the expression of an idea simply because society finds the idea itself offensive or disagreeable." *Texas v. Johnson*, 491 U.S. 397, 414 (1989).

It is also perfectly clear that "promoting illegal drug use" comes nowhere close to proscribable "incitement to imminent lawless action." *Brandenburg*, 395 U.S., at 447. Encouraging drug use might well increase the likelihood that a listener will try an illegal drug, but that hardly justifies censorship:

> "Every denunciation of existing law tends in some measure to increase the probability that there will be violation of it. Condonation of a breach enhances the probability. Expressions of approval add to the probability.... Advocacy of law-breaking heightens it still further. But even advocacy of violation, however reprehensible morally, is not a justification for denying free speech where the advocacy falls short of incitement and there is nothing to indicate that the advocacy would be immediately acted upon." *Whitney v. California*, 274 U.S. 357, 376 (1927) (Brandeis, J., concurring).

No one seriously maintains that drug advocacy (much less Frederick's ridiculous sign) comes within the vanishingly small category of speech that can be prohibited because of its feared consequences. Such advocacy, to borrow from Justice Holmes, "ha[s] no chance of starting a present conflagration." *Gitlow v. New York*, 268 U.S. 652, 673 (1925) (dissenting opinion).

II

The Court rejects outright these twin foundations of *Tinker* because, in its view, the unusual importance of protecting children from the scourge of drugs supports a ban on all speech in the school environment that promotes drug use. Whether or not such a rule is sensible as a matter of policy, carving out pro-drug speech for uniquely harsh treatment finds no support in our case law and is inimical to the values protected by the First Amendment.[1]

I will nevertheless assume for the sake of argument that the school's concededly powerful interest in protecting its students adequately supports its restriction on "any assembly or public expression that... advocates the use of substances that are illegal to minors...." Given that the relationship between schools and students "is custodial and tutelary, permitting a degree of supervision and control that could not be exercised over free adults," *Vernonia School Dist. 47J v. Acton*, 515 U.S. 646, 655 (1995), it might well be appropriate to tolerate some targeted viewpoint discrimination in this unique setting. And while conventional speech may be restricted only when likely to "incit[e] imminent lawless action," *Brandenburg*, 395 U.S., at 449, it is possible that our rigid imminence requirement ought to be relaxed at schools. See *Bethel School Dist. No. 403 v. Fraser*, 478 U.S. 675, 682 (1986) ("[T]he constitutional rights of students in public school are not automatically coextensive with the rights of adults in other settings").

But it is one thing to restrict speech that *advocates* drug use. It is another thing entirely to prohibit an obscure message with a drug theme that a third party subjectively—and not very reasonably—thinks is tantamount to express advocacy. Cf. *Masses Publishing Co. v. Patten*, 244 F. 535, 540, 541 (S.D.N.Y. 1917) (Hand, J.) (distinguishing sharply between "agitation, legitimate as such" and "the direct advocacy" of unlawful conduct). Even the school recognizes the paramount need to hold the line between, on the one hand, non-disruptive speech that merely expresses a viewpoint that is unpopular or contrary to the school's preferred

1. I also seriously question whether such a ban could really be enforced. Consider the difficulty of monitoring student conversations between classes or in the cafeteria.

message, and on the other hand, advocacy of an illegal or unsafe course of conduct. The district's prohibition of drug advocacy is a gloss on a more general rule that is otherwise quite tolerant of non-disruptive student speech:

> "Students will not be disturbed in the exercise of their constitutionally guaranteed rights to assemble peaceably and to express ideas and opinions, privately or publicly, provided that their activities do not infringe on the rights of others and do not interfere with the operation of the educational program.
>
> "The Board will not permit the conduct on school premises of any willful activity... that interferes with the orderly operation of the educational program or offends the rights of others. The Board specifically prohibits... any assembly or public expression that... advocates the use of substances that are illegal to minors...."

There is absolutely no evidence that Frederick's banner's reference to drug paraphernalia "willful[ly]" infringed on anyone's rights or interfered with any of the school's educational programs.[2] On its face, then, the rule gave Frederick wide berth "to express [his] ideas and opinions" so long as they did not amount to "advoca[cy]" of drug use. If the school's rule is, by hypothesis, a valid one, it is valid only insofar as it scrupulously preserves adequate space for constitutionally protected speech. When First Amendment rights are at stake, a rule that "sweep[s] in a great variety of conduct under a general and indefinite characterization" may not leave "too wide a discretion in its application." *Cantwell v. Connecticut*, 310 U.S. 296, 308 (1940). Therefore, just as we insisted in *Tinker* that the school establish some likely connection between the armbands and their feared consequences, so too JDHS must show that Frederick's supposed advocacy stands a meaningful chance of making otherwise-abstemious students try marijuana.

But instead of demanding that the school make such a showing, the Court punts. Figuring out just *how* it punts is tricky; "[t]he mode of analysis [it] employ[s]... is not entirely clear."... On occasion, the Court suggests it is deferring to the principal's "reasonable" judgment that Frederick's sign qualified as drug advocacy. At other times, the Court seems to say that it thinks the banner's message constitutes express advocacy. Either way, its approach is indefensible.

To the extent the Court defers to the principal's ostensibly reasonable judgment, it abdicates its constitutional responsibility. The beliefs of third parties, reasonable or otherwise, have never dictated which messages amount to proscribable advocacy. Indeed, it would be a strange constitutional doctrine that would allow the prohibition of only the narrowest category of speech advocating unlawful conduct, see *Brandenburg*, 395 U.S., at 447–448, yet would permit a listener's perceptions to determine which speech deserved constitutional protection.[5]

2. It is also relevant that the display did not take place "on school premises," as the rule contemplates. While a separate district rule does make the policy applicable to "social events and class trips," Frederick might well have thought that the Olympic Torch Relay was neither a "social event" (for example, prom) nor a "class trip."

5. The reasonableness of the view that Frederick's message was unprotected speech is relevant to ascertaining whether qualified immunity should shield the principal from liability, not to whether her actions violated Frederick's constitutional rights. Cf. *Saucier v. Katz*, 533 U.S. 194, 202 (2001) ("The relevant, dispositive

Such a peculiar doctrine is alien to our case law. In *Abrams v. United States*, 250 U.S. 616 (1919), this Court affirmed the conviction of a group of Russian "rebels, revolutionists, [and] anarchists," *id.*, at 617–618 (internal quotation marks omitted), on the ground that the leaflets they distributed were thought to "incite, provoke, and encourage resistance to the United States," *id.*, at 617 (internal quotation marks omitted). Yet Justice Holmes' dissent—which has emphatically carried the day—never inquired into the reasonableness of the United States' judgment that the leaflets would likely undermine the war effort. The dissent instead ridiculed that judgment: "nobody can suppose that the surreptitious publishing of a silly leaflet by an unknown man, without more, would present any immediate danger that its opinions would hinder the success of the government arms or have any appreciable tendency to do so." *Id.*, at 628. In *Thomas v. Collins*, 323 U.S. 516 (1945) (opinion for the Court by Rutledge, J.), we overturned the conviction of a union organizer who violated a restraining order prohibiting him from exhorting workers. In so doing, we held that the distinction between advocacy and incitement could not depend on how one of those workers might have understood the organizer's speech. That would "pu[t] the speaker in these circumstances wholly at the mercy of the varied understanding of his hearers and consequently of whatever inference may be drawn as to his intent and meaning." *Id.*, at 535. In *Cox v. Louisiana*, 379 U.S. 536, 543 (1965), we vacated a civil rights leader's conviction for disturbing the peace, even though a Baton Rouge sheriff had "deem[ed]" the leader's "appeal to ... students to sit in at the lunch counters to be 'inflammatory.'" We never asked if the sheriff's in-person, on-the-spot judgment was "reasonable." Even in *Fraser*, we made no inquiry into whether the school administrators reasonably thought the student's speech was obscene or profane; we rather satisfied ourselves that "[t]he pervasive sexual innuendo in Fraser's speech was plainly offensive to both teachers and students—indeed, to any mature person." 478 U.S., at 683. Cf. *Bose Corp. v. Consumers Union of United States, Inc.*, 466 U.S. 485, 499 (1984) ("[I]n cases raising First Amendment issues we have repeatedly held that an appellate court has an obligation to make an independent examination of the whole record in order to make sure that the judgment does not constitute a forbidden intrusion on the field of free expression" (internal quotation marks omitted)).[6]

To the extent the Court independently finds that "BONG HiTS 4 JESUS" *objectively* amounts to the advocacy of illegal drug use—in other words, that it can most reasonably be interpreted as such—that conclusion practically refutes itself. This is a nonsense message,

inquiry in determining whether a right is clearly established is whether it would be clear to a reasonable officer that his conduct was unlawful in the situation he confronted").

6. This same reasoning applies when the interpreter is not just a listener, but a legislature. We have repeatedly held that "[d]eference to a legislative finding" that certain types of speech are inherently harmful "cannot limit judicial inquiry when First Amendment rights are at stake," reasoning that "the judicial function commands analysis of whether the specific conduct charged falls within the reach of the statute and if so whether the legislation is consonant with the Constitution." *Landmark Communications, Inc. v. Virginia*, 435 U.S. 829, 843-844 (1978); see also *Whitney v. California*, 274 U.S. 357, 378–379 (1927) (Brandeis, J., concurring) ("[A legislative declaration] does not preclude enquiry into the question whether, at the time and under the circumstances, the conditions existed which are essential to validity under the Federal Constitution.... Whenever the fundamental rights of free speech and assembly are alleged to have been invaded, it must remain open to a defendant to present the issue whether there actually did exist at the time a clear danger; whether the danger, if any, was imminent; and whether the evil apprehended was one so substantial as to justify the stringent restriction interposed by the legislature"). When legislatures are entitled to no deference as to whether particular speech amounts to a "clear and present danger," *id.*, at 379, it is hard to understand why the Court would so blithely defer to the judgment of a single school principal.

not advocacy. The Court's feeble effort to divine its hidden meaning is strong evidence of that... (positing that the banner might mean, alternatively, "'[Take] bong hits,'" "'bong hits [are a good thing],'" or "'[we take] bong hits'"). Frederick's credible and uncontradicted explanation for the message—he just wanted to get on television—is also relevant because a speaker who does not intend to persuade his audience can hardly be said to be advocating anything. But most importantly, it takes real imagination to read a "cryptic" message (the Court's characterization, not mine) with a slanting drug reference as an incitement to drug use. Admittedly, some high school students (including those who use drugs) are dumb. Most students, however, do not shed their brains at the schoolhouse gate, and most students know dumb advocacy when they see it. The notion that the message on this banner would actually persuade either the average student or even the dumbest one to change his or her behavior is most implausible. That the Court believes such a silly message can be proscribed as advocacy underscores the novelty of its position, and suggests that the principle it articulates has no stopping point.

Even if advocacy could somehow be wedged into Frederick's obtuse reference to marijuana, that advocacy was at best subtle and ambiguous. There is abundant precedent, including another opinion THE CHIEF JUSTICE announces today, for the proposition that when the "First Amendment is implicated, the tie goes to the speaker," *Federal Election Comm'n v. Wisconsin Right to Life, Inc.*, *post*, at 474, and that "when it comes to defining what speech qualifies as the functional equivalent of express advocacy... we give the benefit of the doubt to speech, not censorship," *post*, at 482. If this were a close case, the tie would have to go to Frederick's speech, not to the principal's strained reading of his quixotic message.

Among other things, the Court's ham-handed, categorical approach is deaf to the constitutional imperative to permit unfettered debate, even among high school students, about the wisdom of the war on drugs or of legalizing marijuana for medicinal use.[8] See *Tinker*, 393 U.S., at 511 ("[Students] may not be confined to the expression of those sentiments that are officially approved"). If Frederick's stupid reference to marijuana can in the Court's view justify censorship, then high school students everywhere could be forgiven for zipping their mouths about drugs at school lest some "reasonable" observer censor and then punish them for promoting drugs.

Consider, too, that the school district's rule draws no distinction between alcohol and marijuana, but applies evenhandedly to all "substances that are illegal to minors." App. to Pet. for Cert. 53a; see also App. 83 (expressly defining "'drugs'" to include "all alcoholic beverages").

8. The Court's opinion ignores the fact that the legalization of marijuana is an issue of considerable public concern in Alaska. The State Supreme Court held in 1975 that Alaska's constitution protects the right of adults to possess less than four ounces of marijuana for personal use. *Ravin v. State*, 537 P.2d 494 (Alaska). In 1990, the voters of Alaska attempted to undo that decision by voting for a ballot initiative recriminalizing marijuana possession. Initiative Proposal No. 2, §§ 1–2 (effective Mar. 3, 1991), 11 Alaska Stat., p. 872 (2006). At the time Frederick unfurled his banner, the constitutionality of that referendum had yet to be tested. It was subsequently struck down as unconstitutional. See *Noy v. State*, 83 P.3d 538 (Alaska App. 2003). In the meantime, Alaska voters had approved a ballot measure decriminalizing the use of marijuana for medicinal purposes, 1998 Ballot Measure No. 8 (approved Nov. 3, 1998), 11 Alaska Stat., p. 883 (codified at Alaska Stat. §§ 11.71.190 17.37.010–17.37.080), and had rejected a much broader measure that would have decriminalized marijuana possession and granted amnesty to anyone convicted of marijuana-related crimes, see 2000 Ballot Measure No. 5 (failed Nov. 7, 2000), 11 Alaska Stat., p. 886.

Given the tragic consequences of teenage alcohol consumption—drinking causes far more fatal accidents than the misuse of marijuana—the school district's interest in deterring teenage alcohol use is at least comparable to its interest in preventing marijuana use. Under the Court's reasoning, must the First Amendment give way whenever a school seeks to punish a student for any speech mentioning beer, or indeed anything else that might be deemed risky to teenagers? While I find it hard to believe the Court would support punishing Frederick for flying a "WINE SiPS 4 JESUS" banner—which could quite reasonably be construed either as a protected religious message or as a pro-alcohol message—the breathtaking sweep of its opinion suggests it would.

III

Although this case began with a silly, nonsensical banner, it ends with the Court inventing out of whole cloth a special First Amendment rule permitting the censorship of any student speech that mentions drugs, at least so long as someone could perceive that speech to contain a latent pro-drug message. Our First Amendment jurisprudence has identified some categories of expression that are less deserving of protection than others—fighting words, obscenity, and commercial speech, to name a few. Rather than reviewing our opinions discussing such categories, I mention two personal recollections that have no doubt influenced my conclusion that it would be profoundly unwise to create special rules for speech about drug and alcohol use.

The Vietnam War is remembered today as an unpopular war. During its early stages, however, "the dominant opinion" that Justice Harlan mentioned in his *Tinker* dissent regarded opposition to the war as unpatriotic, if not treason. 393 U.S., at 526. That dominant opinion strongly supported the prosecution of several of those who demonstrated in Grant Park during the 1968 Democratic Convention in Chicago, see *United States v. Dellinger*, 472 F.2d 340 (C.A.7 1972), and the vilification of vocal opponents of the war like Julian Bond, cf. *Bond v. Floyd*, 385 U.S. 116 (1966). In 1965, when the Des Moines students wore their armbands, the school district's fear that they might "start an argument or cause a disturbance" was well founded. *Tinker*, 393 U.S., at 508. Given that context, there is special force to the Court's insistence that "our Constitution says we must take that risk; and our history says that it is this sort of hazardous freedom—this kind of openness—that is the basis of our national strength and of the independence and vigor of Americans who grow up and live in this relatively permissive, often disputatious, society." *Id.*, at 508–509 (citation omitted). As we now know, the then-dominant opinion about the Vietnam War was not etched in stone.

Reaching back still further, the current dominant opinion supporting the war on drugs in general, and our antimarijuana laws in particular, is reminiscent of the opinion that supported the nationwide ban on alcohol consumption when I was a student. While alcoholic beverages are now regarded as ordinary articles of commerce, their use was then condemned with the same moral fervor that now supports the war on drugs. The ensuing change in public opinion occurred much more slowly than the relatively rapid shift in Americans' views on the Vietnam War, and progressed on a state-by-state basis over a period of many years. But just as prohibition in the 1920's and early 1930's was secretly questioned by thousands of otherwise law-abiding patrons of bootleggers and speakeasies, today the actions of literally millions of otherwise law-abiding users of marijuana,[9] and of the majority of voters in each of the several States that tolerate medicinal uses of the product,[10] lead me to wonder whether the fear of disapproval by those in the majority is silencing opponents of the war on drugs. Surely our national experience with alcohol should make us wary of dampening speech suggesting—however inarticulately—that it would be better to tax and regulate marijuana than to persevere in a futile effort to ban its use entirely.

Even in high school, a rule that permits only one point of view to be expressed is less likely to produce correct answers than the open discussion of countervailing views. *Whitney*, 274 U.S., at 377 (Brandeis, J., concurring); *Abrams*, 250 U.S., at 630 (Holmes, J., dissenting); *Tinker*, 393 U.S., at 512. In the national debate about a serious issue, it is the expression of the minority's viewpoint that most demands the protection of the First Amendment. Whatever the better policy may be, a full and frank discussion of the costs and benefits of the attempt to prohibit the use of marijuana is far wiser than suppression of speech because it is unpopular.

I respectfully dissent.

NOTES AND QUESTIONS

1. What exactly is the test enunciated by the Court in *Morse*? When does the test apply? In light of the concurring opinions, does a majority of the Court endorse the test?

2. The Court discusses *Vernonia*, *Earls*, and *T.L.O.* As you may recall, these are Fourth Amendment cases. Why are they relevant to the resolution of the First Amendment claim being made here?

3. Justice Thomas argues that schools stand *in loco parentis*, a claim he has made before in other cases. Do you agree with his argument? Do you find his use of history persuasive?

4. Consider the concurring opinion written by Justice Alito and joined by Justice Kennedy. Are they embracing the test articulated by Chief Justice Roberts? If not, what test do they apply?

5. Does Justice Breyer's opinion offer a way to avoid the constitutional claim?

6. Does Justice Stevens claim that a First Amendment right has been violated? If so, is he saying that Frederick's speech is political speech or just "silly" speech? Would it matter to Stevens? Do you agree with his characterization that the Court is creating a new category of expression "less deserving of protection"?

7. Joseph Frederick's father, Frank, who worked for the company that insures the Juneau schools, was fired because of his son's lawsuit. Frank Frederick subsequently won a $200,000 verdict in connection with his firing. Joseph, who had to drop out of college after his father lost his job, pled guilty in 2004 to a misdemeanor charge of selling marijuana. Pete Yost, *High Court Limits Student Speech*, (Seattle) INTELLIGENCER, June 26, 2007, A3.

Joseph Frederick also filed a lawsuit in the Alaska courts, claiming that his rights had been violated under the state constitution. In 2008, the school board settled the lawsuit and agreed to

9. See *Gonzales v. Raich*, 545 U.S. 1, 21, n. 31 (2005) (citing a Government estimate "that in 2000 American users spent $10.5 billion on the purchase of marijuana").

10. Id., at 5 (noting that "at least nine States... authorize the use of marijuana for medicinal purposes").

pay Frederick $45,000; in exchange, Joseph Frederick agreed to drop his lawsuit. Additionally, the school district agreed to hire a neutral constitutional law expert to chair a forum on student speech at the Juneau-Douglas High School. Joseph's lawyer, Douglas Mertz, felt that the school district had retaliated against Joseph and his family. Eric Morrison, *School Board, Frederick Reach Settlement in "Bong Hits" Case*, Juneau Empire, Nov. 5, 2008, http://juneauempire.com/stories/110508/loc_352352563.shtml. Would you agree?

8. Are *Tinker* and *Kuhlmeier* still good law? Are there certain categories of student speech "less deserving of constitutional protection"? If so, what are they?

9. *First Amendment activity in school.* To what extent may students engage in expressive activity at school? Consider, for example, members of the high school varsity basketball team who submitted a petition asking that their coach resign after enduring his "verbal abuse, yelling, humiliation, ranting, [and] raving." The coach also apparently threw objects, kicked garbage cans, was profane, and used "abusive coaching tactics." The principal then summoned the team to his office and told them that they could participate in a mediation session and board the team bus for the game that evening, or they could stand by their petition and forfeit the game. The team members opted to forfeit the game and did not board the bus. The school principal subsequently suspended all students who signed the petition. Does this violate the First Amendment? What standard applies? See *Pinard v. Clatskanie School Dist. 6J*, 467 F.3d 755 (9th Cir. 2006). Does it matter if the speech is characterized as "insubordinate"? See, e.g., *Lowery v. Euverard*, 497 F.3d 584 (6th Cir. 2007).

To what extent may a school restrict the distribution of leaflets or other materials written outside of school? If an eighth-grade student wanted to distribute leaflets protesting abortion, could the school keep him from doing so? *M.A.L. ex rel. M.L. v. Kinsland*, 543 F.3d 841 (6th Cir. 2008). If a ninth-grade student is a finalist in a statewide poetry-reading competition, could his school prevent him from reading a poem from the approved competition list because it contains the words "hell" and "damn"? *Behymer-Smith ex rel. Behymer v. Coral Academy of Science*, 427 F.Supp.2d 969 (D. Nev. 2006).

What if two eighth-grade students leave school without permission in order to participate in a local protest against immigration-reform measures? Could they be subject to school discipline for their actions? Would your answer be different if you knew that one of the students subsequently committed suicide after learning of the discipline? *Corales v. Bennett*, 567 F.3d 554 (9th Cir. 2009).

10. *Dress codes, appearance, clothing.* May a school regulate appearance, hair length, and clothing? Which standard should apply? Must the regulation be content-neutral? See, e.g., *Jacobs v. Clark County Sch. Dist.*, 526 F.3d 419 (9th Cir. 2008). Is a school policy content-neutral if it forbids T-shirts with any printed messages (ranging from political messages to college logos to the text of the First Amendment) but permits pins, buttons, and other sorts of printed material? *Palmer ex rel. Palmer v. Waxahachie Independent School Dist.*, 579 F.3d 502 (2009), *cert.* denied, 579 F.3d 502 (2010). For example, if students want to wear clothing or carry accessories displaying the Confederate flag, may the school prohibit them from doing so? Under what standard? See, e.g., *Defoe ex rel. Defoe v. Spiva*, 625 F.3d 324 (6th Cir. 2010); *B.W.A. v. Farmington R-7 School Dist.*, 554 F.3d 734 (8th Cir. 2009); *Barr v. Lafon*, 538 F.3d 554 (6th Cir. 2008). Does it matter how the regulation is written? If a high school policy prohibits "racist language and/or symbols or graphics... includ[ing] items displaying the Rebel flag," does the policy sweep too broadly? *Bragg v. Swanson*, 371 F.Supp.2d 814 (S.D. W. Va. 2005). Or consider a school policy that prohibits "gang-related apparel." What exactly is gang-related apparel? Would it depend?

If so, how would students know what violates the policy? *Chalifoux v. New Caney Independent Sch. Dist.*, 976 F.Supp. 659 (S.D. Tex. 1997).

Proponents of school-uniform policies argue that requiring students to wear uniforms reduces conflict, bullying, and crime among students; lowers rates of gang activity; increases student self-esteem and self-perception; and reduces peer pressure to buy trendy and expensive clothes. D. Gursky, *"Uniform" Improvement?* 61 EDUCATION DIGEST, 46 (March 1996); P. Y. Hoffler-Riddick & K. J. Lassiter, *No More "Sag Baggin'": School Uniforms Bring the Focus Back to Instruction*, 5 SCHOOLS IN THE MIDDLE 27 (1996); A. L. Majestic, *Student Dress Codes in the 1990s*, INQUIRY & ANALYSIS 1 (January 1991); R. K. Murray, The Impact of School Uniforms on School Climate, 81 NASSP BULLETIN, 106 (December 1997); S. Thomas, *Uniforms in the Schools: Proponents Say It Cuts Competition; Others Are Not So Sure*, 11 BLACK ISSUES IN HIGHER EDUCATION 44 (1997). See also Joseph R. McKinney, *A New Look at Student Uniform Policies*, 140 WEST EDUC. L. REP. 791 (2000). But is there empirical evidence to support these claims? At best, the evidence is mixed. On the one hand, a study done by the U.S. Department of Education in 1996 of eight public schools implementing uniform policies found significant reductions in crime and an improvement in attitude and behavior among students. U.S. Dep't of Educ., Manual on School Uniforms (1996), http://www.ed.gov/updates/uniforms.html. A follow-up survey in 2003 found continued reductions in crime and improvements in school climate. Richard Daugherty et al., *The U.S. Department of Education's Exemplary School Uniform Programs: A Status Report*, 187 ED. L. REP. 397, 399 (2004).

On the other hand, other studies have found no real support for the claims of school-uniform proponents. For example, one study found that students in middle schools with uniform policies did not have higher self-esteem; on the contrary, there were statistically significant findings that students in schools *without* uniform policies had higher self-esteem than those students who had to wear uniforms. Kathleen Kiley Wade & Mary E. Stafford, *Public School Uniforms: Effect on Perceptions of Gang Presence, School Climate, and Student Self-Perceptions*, 35 EDUC. & URBAN SOC'Y, 399, 411–412 (2003). Students often express dissatisfaction with or opposition to a uniform policy, perhaps contributing to greater loss of self-esteem. *Id.* at 412–413. The study also found that while perceptions of gang presence were not statistically significant across the two student populations, teachers in schools with uniform policies did report lower levels of gang presence and activity. *Id.* at 414–415. Similarly, in a study relying on data from the National Educational Longitudinal Study, which began with eighth-grade students in 1988, the authors found no direct effect of a uniform policy on a reduction in substance abuse, attendance, or conduct. David L. Brunsma & Kerry A. Rockquemore, *Effects of Students Uniforms on Attendance, Behavior Problems, Substance Abuse, and Academic Achievement*, 92 J. EDUC. RES. 53, 57–58 (1998). Surprisingly, the study's authors found a negative effect of uniforms on academic achievement. *Id.* at 58. Nevertheless, the authors hypothesize that uniforms may serve as a symbol of a renewed commitment to improving the school and as a catalyst for further curricular reform. Consequently, school uniforms may have indirect and positive effects on student outcomes and school environment. *Id.* at 60. In light of the evidence, do you think that public schools should adopt uniform policies?

11. *Sexual orientation and the First Amendment.* To what extent may the state regulate the expression of a student's sexual orientation? Constance, an openly gay student, asked if she could bring her girlfriend, also a student, to her high school prom. She was told that they could not attend as a couple, nor could Constance wear a tuxedo to her prom. Constance contacted the ACLU, which wrote a demand letter on her behalf to the school board. The school

subsequently decided to cancel the prom. Were Constance's First Amendment rights violated? *McMillen v. Itawamba County Sch. Dist.*, 702 F.Supp.2d 699 (N.D. Miss. 2010). Could a school prohibit public displays of affection between gay students on campus? Under what circumstances? *Nguon v. Wolf*, 517 F.Supp.2d 1177 (C.D. Cal. 2007).

12. *Cyberspace and the First Amendment.* What authority do schools have over student speech that occurs in cyberspace? If the speech is created on a school computer during school time, could the student be disciplined under the *Tinker*, *Kuhlmeier*, or *Morse* standards? What if the speech occurred using a nonschool computer outside of school hours? Consider the following scenarios, and determine the applicable standard:

a. Justin, a seventeen-year-old high school senior, creates an unflattering profile of his principal on MySpace using his grandmother's computer during nonschool hours. He copies a photo of the principal from the school's Web site to use for the profile. Word spreads "like wildfire" among other students. Three more students create new profiles of the principal, each more offensive than the one created by Justin. Justin accesses the profile on a school computer during school hours to show classmates but does not acknowledge authorship. Justin eventually is caught, and he apologizes. The principal suspends Justin for ten days and threatens to expel him. Are Justin's First Amendment rights violated? *Layshock ex rel. Layshock v. Hermitage Sch. Dist.*, 593 F.3d 249 (3d Cir. 2010), rehearing *en banc* granted, opinion vacated, April 9, 2010.

b. Avery, a high school junior and a member of the Student Council, posts a message on her publicly accessible blog at home during nonschool hours. In that message, she encourages people to contact the school administration to protest the cancellation of a popular school event. She states: "jamfest is cancelled due to douchebags in central office." The next day, the school administration receives phone calls and e-mails about canceling the student event. The event subsequently is rescheduled, and the administration denies telling the students that the event was to be canceled. The school principal learns of the blog posting after the event is rescheduled. She demands that Avery apologize and bars her from running for senior class secretary. Are Avery's First Amendment rights violated? *Doninger v. Niehoff*, 527 F.3d 41 (2d Cir. 2008).

c. Katherine, a high school senior, creates a group on Facebook entitled "Ms. Sarah Phelps is the worst teacher I've ever met." She makes the post after school hours from her home computer. Three other students post in response defending Ms. Phelps. The posting is removed after two days, and the teacher never sees the post. The principal learns about the post, suspends Katherine for three days, and removes her from her more heavily weighted advanced-placement courses. The basis for the punishment is "Bullying/Cyber Bullying/Harassment towards a staff member" and "Disruptive behavior." Are Katherine's First Amendment rights violated? *Evans v. Bayer*, 684 F.Supp.2d 1365 (S.D. Fla. 2010).

d. Jackie and several of her friends go to a local restaurant after school. Jackie videotapes her friends talking about another classmate, Carina, in unflattering terms. Jackie posts the video to YouTube that night from her home computer. Jackie calls several friends, and Carina, to tell them about the video. The posting receives about ninety hits, many from Jackie herself. The next day, Carina arrives at school with her mother and is very upset. Students cannot access YouTube or other social-networking sites from school computers. School administrators investigate and suspend Jackie for two days. None of the other students is disciplined. Are Jackie's First Amendment rights violated? *J.C. ex rel. R.C. v. Beverly Hills Unified Sch. Dist.*, 711 F.Supp.2d 1094 (C.D. Cal. 2010).

13. In 2004, the John S. and James L. Knight Foundation funded a survey of high school students, parents, and teachers about their perceptions of the First Amendment. Approximately

100,000 students, 500 parents, and 8,000 teachers participated in the survey. Of those students surveyed, 73 percent said they "don't know how they feel about the First Amendment or take it for granted." Although 70 percent of students felt that musicians should be allowed to sing songs with lyrics some might find offensive, 51 percent of students felt that newspapers should not be allowed to publish freely without government approval. However, 58 percent said that high school newspapers should be permitted to publish controversial stories without the approval of school authorities. Of the students, 75 percent thought that flag burning was illegal in the United States. Also, 40 percent of the schools had eliminated their student newspapers in the preceding five years. Future of the First Amendment (2004), http://www.knightfoundation.org/media/uploads/publication_pdfs/FOFA2004pdf. In the same year, a federal law mandating September 17 as Constitution Day took effect. The law provides federal funding to schools that teach about the Constitution every year on September 17.

A follow-up survey was conducted in 2007 and again in 2011. Completing the survey in 2011 were 12,090 students and 900 teachers. Of the students surveyed, only 29 percent said that they personally think about their First Amendment rights. Students again supported the right of musicians to sing songs with offensive lyrics (70 percent) and of student newspapers to publish stories without prior school approval (59 percent). However, 24 percent of the students surveyed found that the First Amendment "went too far," and only 12 percent believed that people should be allowed to burn the flag as a political statement. Future of the First Amendment 2011 Survey of High School Students and Teachers (2011), http://www.knightfoundation.org/media/uploads/publications_pdfs/Future-of-the-First-Amendment-full-cx2.pdf.

If most students do not care about their First Amendment rights, why should we? Are there any benefits to protecting the First Amendment rights of students? If so, what are they?

2. FREE-EXERCISE RIGHTS

WISCONSIN V. YODER
Supreme Court of the United States
406 U.S. 205 (1972)
(See Section III.B. above, p. 419

NOTES AND QUESTIONS

1. Does *Yoder* recognize that children have free-exercise rights in school? Whose right is it, anyway? In *Employment Division, Department of Human Resources v. Smith*, 494 U.S. 872 (1990), Alfred Smith and Galen Black were fired from their jobs with a private drug-rehabilitation organization because they had smoked peyote during a religious ceremony at their Native American church. The state of Oregon denied their application for unemployment benefits because they had been fired for "misconduct." Justice Scalia, writing for the Court, upheld the state's decision, noting that Smith and Galen had an obligation to conform their conduct to

the requirements of a neutral, generally applicable law if the law is not specifically directed to religious practice. *Id.* at 879. But how is the law in *Smith* different from the law in *Yoder*? Isn't the compulsory-school-attendance law at issue in *Yoder* a neutral, generally applicable law not aimed at specific religious practices? The Court in *Smith* distinguished *Yoder* (and other cases) by arguing that the Court has found that a neutral, generally applicable law violates the First Amendment only when it infringes on the Free Exercise Clause in conjunction with other constitutional protections. The "other" constitutional protection infringed on in *Yoder* was "the right of parents to direct the education of their children." *Id.* at 881 n.1. Because the *Smith* case did not involve this sort of "hybrid" situation, the state could deny unemployment benefits without running afoul of the First Amendment. *Id.* at 882. Some commentators have suggested that Justice Scalia's distinction was a strategic one to keep a majority of the votes. See Michael W. McConnell, *Free Exercise Revisionism and the Smith Decision*, 57 U. Chi. L. Rev. 1109, 1121 (1990) ("One suspects that the notion of 'hybrid' claims was created for the sole purpose of distinguishing *Yoder* in this case"); Douglas Laycock, *Free Exercise and the Religious Freedom Restoration Act*, 62 Fordham L. Rev. 883, 902 (1994) ("Scalia had only 5 votes. He apparently believed he couldn't overrule anything, and so he didn't. He distinguished everything away instead"). Do you agree? What does *Yoder* say about the free-exercise rights of children?

In 1993, Congress passed the Religious Freedom Restoration Act (RFRA), 42 U.S.C. § 2000bb *et seq.* The RFRA was enacted in response to the Supreme Court's ruling in *Smith*. However, in *City of Boerne v. Flores*, 521 U.S. 507 (1997), the Court ruled that Congress lacked the constitutional authority to make the RFRA effective against the states. In response, Congress enacted the Religious Land Use and Institutionalized Persons Act of 2000 (RLUIPA). The RLUIPA is limited in its application to "a program or activity that receives Federal financial assistance" or where the activity affects interstate commerce. 42 U.S.C.A. § 2000cc-1(b)(1) –(2) (2011). The Supreme Court upheld the validity of the RLUIPA against an attack on its facial validity in 2005. *Cutter v. Wilkinson*, 544 U.S. 709 (2005). To what extent does the RLUIPA apply to schools? For example, could a zoning board deny a request to build a new structure to be used as a classroom at a religious day school, where religion permeates the teaching of all subjects? *Westchester Day School v. Village of Mamaroneck*, 504 F.3d 338 (2nd Cir. 2007).

2. As you may recall, the Supreme Court in *West Virginia State Board of Education v. Barnette*, 319 U.S. 624 (1943), held that students could not be compelled to salute the flag. Is *Yoder* consistent with *Barnette*?

3. Why would the Court in *Tinker* cite *Barnette*? In *Chalifoux v. New Caney Independent School District*, 976 F.Supp. 659 (S.D. Tex. 1997), the school dress code prohibited gang apparel. After learning that some members of a gang were wearing rosaries, the school banned the wearing of rosaries outside students' shirts. Two students who were not members of any gang filed a lawsuit challenging the policy. The court held that wearing rosaries was symbolic religious speech and applied the *Tinker* material-and-substantial-interference test. Concluding that there was insufficient evidence of actual disruption or that there was sufficient reason to anticipate a disruption, the court held that the regulation infringed on the students' religiously motivated speech. *Id.* at 667.

In *Bear v. Fleming*, 714 F.Supp.2d 972 (D. S.D. 2010), Aloysius Dreaming Bear, a Lakota Sioux, graduating high school senior and class president, planned to wear traditional Lakota regalia and clothing at his high school graduation. The school board, however, informed Aloysius that he had to wear a cap and gown over his clothing, only while he walked across the stage to receive his diploma. The district court characterized the proposed conduct as speech and found no First Amendment violation. Applying the *Kuhlmeier* standard, the court found that the graduation ceremony was a school-sponsored event, and thus, the school could regulate the proposed speech to the extent that it furthered legitimate pedagogical concerns. Because the school board has a legitimate interest in conveying not only the students' academic achievements but also those of the school as an institution of learning and of the teachers as educators, the cap-and-gown requirement was reasonably related to the school's pedagogical interests. *Id.* at 989–990.

How would you resolve the following cases? What standard would you apply? If a student wants to sell candy canes with an attached religious message as his school project for a simulated-marketplace event that would take place at school, could a school principal deny his request to sell the candy canes? See *Curry ex rel. Curry v. Hensiner*, 513 F.3d 570 (6th Cir. 2008). If a student gave a valedictory speech at graduation in which she expressed her religious views but, contrary to school policy, had not provided a copy of the speech that she actually gave to the school principal in advance, could the principal demand that she publicly apologize and withhold her diploma until she did so? See *Corder v. Lewis Palmer Sch. Dist. No. 38*, 566 F.3d 1219 (10th Cir. 2009).

Are all free-exercise claims also free-speech claims? Consider the court's approach in *A.A. ex rel. Betenbaugh v. Needville Independent Sch. Dist.*, 701 F.Supp.2d 863 (S.D. Tex. 2009). A.A., a kindergarten student who wished to wear his long hair in braids as part of his Native American beliefs, sought an exemption from the school dress code, which did not permit boys to wear their hair long. A.A. was permitted to keep his long hair, but he had to wear it in one braid, stuffed down the back of his shirt. When he failed to wear his hair in this fashion, he was suspended from school. His parents then filed suit and sought a preliminary injunction. The court found that the Needville Independent School District (NISD) violated the due-process rights of A.A.'s parents and also their free-speech and free-exercise rights. Regarding the free-exercise claim, the court stated:

> The Free Exercise Clause of the First Amendment, which has been applied to the states through the Fourteenth Amendment, *see Cantwell v. Conn.*, 310 U.S. 296, 303, 60 S.Ct. 900, 84 L.Ed. 1213 (1940), provides that "Congress shall make no law respecting an establishment of religion, or prohibiting the free exercise thereof. . . ." *Church of Lukumi Babalu Aye, Inc. v. City of Hialeah*, 508 U.S. 520. 113 S.Ct. 1178, 87 L.Ed. 1628 (1993). The Fourteenth Amendment protects citizens from all state agents, including school boards. *West Virginia State Board of Education v. Barnette*, 319 U.S. 624, 637, 63 S.Ct. 1178, 87 L.Ed. 1628 (1943). While school boards have "important, delicate, and highly discretionary functions," they must carry out their duties "within the limits of the Bill of Rights." *Id.* . . .
>
> Only beliefs rooted in religion are protected by the Free Exercise Clause, which, by its terms, gives special protection to the exercise of religion. *Thomas v. Review Bd. of Indiana Employment Sec. Div.*, 450 U.S. 707, 713–714, 101 S.Ct. 1425, 67 L.Ed.2d 624 (1981). The Supreme Court long has recognized that determining whether a belief or practice is "religious" is a "difficult and delicate task" (*Thomas*, 450 U.S. at 714, 101 S.Ct. 1425). In view of this difficulty, neither the Supreme Court nor the Fifth Circuit has set forth a precise standard for distinguishing the religious belief from the secular choice. *Theriault v. Carlson*, 495 F.2d 390, 394, n. 6 (5th Cir. 1974). Other circuits have cautiously attempted to create a standard, characterizing religious beliefs as those that "address spiritual, not worldly concerns," *Callahan v. Woods*, 658 F.2d 679 (9th Cir. 1981), "fundamental and ultimate questions," *Africa v. Commonwealth of Pennsylvania*, 662

F.2d 1025 (3d Cir. 1981), and "ultimate as opposed to intellectual concerns," *International Soc. for Krishna Consciousness, Inc. v. Barber*, 650 F.2d 430 (2d Cir. 1981)....

[After reviewing testimony and the case law] the Court has no difficulty finding that some Native American communities assign religious significance to hair length. Plaintiff Arocha clearly shares that belief, even though he does not belong to a tribe that practices it. He does not have to prove that all other Lipan Apaches have beliefs that are identical to his own; moreover, he is not required to prove his belief by pointing to a "tenet or dogma" of any particular Indian tribe or organization. Plaintiff Arocha is only required to show that he himself has these "deeply held religious beliefs," which he has done. He describes his hair as "an outward extension of who we are and where we come from, our ancestry and where we're going in life." He taught A.A. that his hair demonstrates "how long [A.A.] has been here" and is "an extension of who [A.A.] is." His long hair addresses "fundamental" and "ultimate" concerns by helping him to understand himself and his place and direction in the world. *Cf. Africa v. Com. of Pa.*, 662 F.2d 1025, 1032 (3rd Cir. 1981) (holding that incarcerated plaintiff failed to assert a "religious" belief because his views did not mention a fundamental concern including, "the meaning and purpose of life").

After demonstrating that he possesses a "sincerely held religious belief," a plaintiff must prove that a government regulation substantially burdens that belief....

The School Board's exemption policy burdens A.A.'s significantly held religious belief that his hair should be worn long. A.A.'s hair is approximately thirteen inches long. The School Board's policy will require him to wear it "in a tightly woven braid," stuffed down the back of his shirt, for the rest of his academic career at NISD. By the policy's terms, A.A. must wear his hair in his shirt during recess, on field trips, and on the school bus. When he becomes older, he will have to wear his hair down the back of his shirt at football games, school dances, and, presumably, his high school graduation.

The policy will deny A.A. the opportunity to express a religious practice that is very dear to him and his father. *See e.g. Chalifoux v. New Caney Indep. Sch. Dist.*, 976 F.Supp. 659, 667 (S.D.Tex. 1997) (rejecting a dress code exemption, which required students to wear rosaries under their shirts, because it burdened "a sincere expression of their religious beliefs"). A.A. will also be exposed to punishment if he violates the exemption policy. There is no doubt the arrangement will cause him profound discomfort: Plaintiff Arocha testified that he becomes uncomfortable when his own hair becomes trapped under his shirt for even a few moments. It is also likely that A.A. will be subject to just as much teasing and ridicule by wearing his long hair inside his shirt than if he wore it exposed. These will be the terms of his existence for the next eleven years; otherwise, he will be forced to cut his hair, or transfer to another school district.

By imposing a physically burdensome restriction on A.A., which will last indefinitely, the School Board's exemption policy will influence him to cut his hair in violation of his religious beliefs. In the alternative, it forces him to choose between the generally available benefit of attending Needville public schools, or, on the other hand, following his religious beliefs. The policy's effects go far beyond denying him some benefit that is not otherwise generally available or preventing him from acting in a way that is not otherwise allowed. Female children attending NISD are allowed to wear their long hair exposed and in two braids, for purely secular reasons. Even though the School Board found it necessary to grant A.A. a religious exemption, it did not extend him this same freedom to wear his long hair in a comfortable, practical manner.

Plaintiffs also contest the requirement that A.A. annually reapply for a religious exemption to the NISD dress code. This requirement, unlike the exemption policy, is generally applicable. In *Littlefield v. Forney*, 268 F.3d 275, 293–294 (5th Cir. 2001), the Fifth Circuit found that a similar policy, which required families to reapply for a religious exemption from a school's dress code on an annual basis, did not burden the plaintiffs' exercise of their sincerely held religious beliefs. Plaintiffs' request for relief from this requirement should therefore be denied....

The level of scrutiny to be applied to a plaintiff's free exercise claim is determined by the nature of the law or regulation being applied. A law that is neutral and of general applicability need not be justified by a compelling governmental interest even if the law has the incidental effect of burdening a particular religious practice. *Church of the Lukumi Babalu Aye v. City of Hialeah*, 508 U.S. 520, 531, 113 S.Ct. 2217, 124 L.Ed.2d 472 (1993) (citing *Employment Div., Dept. of Human Resources of Ore. v. Smith*, 494 U.S. 872, 110 S.Ct. 1595, 108 L.Ed. 876 (1990)). A law failing to satisfy these requirements must be justified by a compelling governmental interest and must be narrowly tailored to advance that interest. *Id.* "Neutrality and general applicability are interrelated, and... failure to satisfy one requirement is likely an indication that the other has not been satisfied." *Lukumi*, 508 U.S. at 531, 113 S.Ct. 2217....

It is undisputed that the exemption policy was created solely for A.A., and it applies to him alone. It is not, therefore, generally applicable. An inquiry into the regulation's neutrality begins with the policy's text. *Id.* at 533, 113 S.Ct. 2217. A law lacks facial neutrality if it refers to a religious practice without a secular meaning discernable from the language or context. *Id.* The exemption policy, as read into the record at the second School Board meeting, makes no reference to A.A.'s particular religion or the spiritual significance of his hair; it is therefore facially neutral.

Lukumi requires courts to look beyond a regulation's text, however, to determine its neutrality. The Free Exercise Clause requires the court to "'survey meticulously the circumstances of governmental categories to eliminate, as it were, religious gerry-manders.'" *Id.* (citing *Walz v. Tax Comm'n of New York City*, 397 U.S. 664, 696, 90 S.Ct. 1409, 25 L.Ed.2d 697 (1970)). The effect of the law in its real operation is "strong evidence of its object." *Id.* In *Lukumi*, a group of Santeria practitioners challenged city ordinances that banned animal sacrifice in order to prevent animal cruelty and protect public health. The Supreme Court described the ordinances as "under inclusive" because they failed to prohibit nonreligious conduct that endangered these interests in a similar or greater degree than Santeria sacrifice. *Id.* at 536, 113 S.Ct. 2217; *see also Blackhawk v. Pennsylvania*, 381 F.3d 202, 209 (3d Cir. 2004). Because the ordinances banned Santeria sacrifice even when it was not necessary to protect public health, the Court also found that the ordinances proscribed "more religious conduct than is necessary" to achieve their purported ends. "It is not unreasonable to infer, at least when there are no persuasive indications to the contrary, that a law which visits gratuitous restrictions on religious conduct seeks not to effectuate the state governmental interests, but to suppress the conduct because of its religious motivation." *Id.* at 538, 113 S.Ct. 2217 (citations omitted).

According to Superintendent Rhodes, who helped craft the exemption policy, it was created to have A.A.'s hair "resemble the rest of the student body in Needville." Rhodes admitted that the policy was not created with the five specific goals of the NISD dress code in mind. He testified that the policy was created to instill discipline and maintain order and hygiene, but he later admitted that it is not more hygienic to have one braid instead of two. Assuming that the policy's purpose is to promote uniformity, discipline, order and hygiene, it is under inclusive. As mentioned earlier, female students are allowed to wear their long hair exposed and in two braids without being viewed as a threat to the school's order and hygiene. To the extent that the policy is meant to make A.A. look like the rest of the student body, he will stand out as the only child wearing a thirteen inch braid tucked inside his shirt. The policy proscribes more religious conduct than is necessary to achieve its stated goals. It is difficult to imagine that allowing one male child to wear long hair, as part of his religious beliefs, would disturb the school's sense of order and its efforts to teach its students hygiene. NISD is certainly able to discipline A.A. if he disrupts his class in [any way], or if he violates another provision of the dress code.

In *Lukumi*, the Court also looked to its equal protection jurisprudence for guidance in determining a law's neutrality. *Lukumi*, 508 U.S. at 540, 113 S.Ct. 2217. Relevant evidence of neutrality includes, among other things, the historical background of the decision under challenge, the specific series of events leading to the enactment of the official policy in question, and the legislative or administrative history, including contemporaneous statements made by members of the decisionmaking body. *Id.* (citing *Arlington Heights v. Metropolitan Housing Development Corp.*, 429 U.S. 252, 266, 97 S.Ct. 555, 50 L.Ed.2d 450 (1977)). These objective factors bear on the question of discriminatory intent.

The exemption policy's history demonstrates that it was not created for a neutral purpose, but rather to burden A.A.'s practice of his religious belief. NISD's reaction to Plaintiffs' request for an exemption indicates that, from the beginning, NISD was unwilling to accommodate A.A.'s religious practice. Superintendent Rhodes made statements to the press implying that, if Plaintiffs did not like the dress code, they should not move to Needville. The School Board, and Superintendent Rhodes, allowed Plaintiffs to proceed through the entire exemption request process, only to deem their request moot after a "standing room only" community meeting. These tactics seem designed to make Plaintiffs abandon their request, or leave the district, rather than to seriously consider A.A.'s religious beliefs. Only after Plaintiffs hired counsel did the School Board grant A.A.'s religious exemption....

Because the exemption policy is neither neutral nor generally applicable, it must undergo "the most rigorous scrutiny." *Lukumi*, 508 U.S. at 546, 113 S.Ct. 2217. It must serve government interests of "the highest order" and be narrowly tailored in pursuit of those interests. Having A.A. "resemble the rest of the student body at Needville" is certainly not a compelling government interest. Even assuming that NISD's interest in maintaining order and hygiene among its students constituted a compelling government interest, the exemption policy is not the least restrictive means of pursuing those interests. A better policy would be to allow A.A. to wear his hair long in accordance with his religious beliefs, but to make him comply with the rest of the NISD dress code, as it is applied to other students....

Plaintiffs argue that, even if the Court determines that the exemption policy was not neutral and generally applicable, the policy should still be subject to more than rational basis review because they advance a "hybrid claim." In *Smith*, Justice Scalia acknowledged that the First Amendment only bars the application of neutral, generally applicable laws to religiously motivated action in cases that involve not the Free Exercise Clause alone, but the Free Exercise Clause in conjunction with other constitutional protections, such as freedom of speech and the rights of parents to direct the education of their children. *Smith* at 1601, 110 S.Ct. 1595. The language in *Smith* was rooted, in part, in the Court's reasoning in *Wisconsin v. Yoder*, 406 U.S. 205, 92 S.Ct. 1526, 32 L.Ed.2d 15 (1972). In that case, the Supreme Court addressed the rights of Amish parents to keep their children from progressing past the eighth grade, in violation of Wisconsin's compulsory education laws. In upholding the rights of the Amish parents, the Supreme Court held, "when the interests of parenthood are combined with a free exercise claim of the nature revealed by this record, more than merely a 'reasonable relation to some purpose within the competency of the state' is required to sustain the validity of the states' requirement under the First Amendment." *Yoder*, 406 U.S. at 233, 92 S.Ct. 1526 (citations omitted).

> The Fifth Circuit adopted the "hybrid claim" standard in *Society of Separationists v. Herman*, 939 F.2d 1207, 1216 (5th Cir. 1991), in which the plaintiff argued that being forced to state an oath or affirmation violated not only her freedom of religion but also her freedom of speech. The Court of Appeals found that *Smith* specifically excepts "religion-plus-speech" cases from the sweep of its holding. *Society of Separationists, Inc. v. Herman*, 939 F.2d 1207, 1217 (1991); *see also Alabama*, 817 F.Supp. at 1332 (holding that, in hybrid claim cases, a school district must demonstrate that a regulation has more than a reasonable relationship to a substantial state interest); *Chalifoux*, 976 F.Supp. at 671 (same).
>
> Plaintiffs have presented a hybrid claim, successfully demonstrating that the exemption policy violates not only A.A.'s free exercise rights, but also his rights to free expression and his parents' due process rights. Pursuant to *Yoder* and *Smith*, the Court must therefore determine whether the regulation bears more than a reasonable relationship to its stated goals. The Court finds that it does not. As has been discussed, the School Board certainly could find other means to achieve its stated goals than to have A.A. wear his hair under his shirt. Enforcing normal classroom rules will satisfy concerns about order, and the exemption policy has no real effect on student hygiene. While one could imagine that the exemption policy might be one means of achieving NISD's goals, it is certainly not the most effective. See *Chalifoux*, 976 F.Supp. at 671....
>
> The public has a strong interest in the enforcement of constitutional rights, particularly in the context of public schools. "That they are educating the young for citizenship is reason for scrupulous protection of constitutional freedoms of the individual, if we are not to strangle the free mind at its source and teach youth to discount important principles of our government as mere platitudes." *West Virginia State Board of Education v. Barnette*, 319 U.S. at 637, 63 S.Ct. 1178.

A.A., 701 F.Supp.2d, at 872, 875, 876-881, 886. Do you think that the court takes a better approach by analyzing the claims under the Free Exercise Clause? Whose rights are violated by the school exemption?

3. THE ESTABLISHMENT CLAUSE

SANTA FE INDEPENDENT SCHOOL DISTRICT V. DOE
Supreme Court of the United States
530 U.S. 290 (2000)

JUSTICE STEVENS delivered the opinion of the Court....

I

The Santa Fe Independent School District (District) is a political subdivision of the State of Texas, responsible for the education of more than 4,000 students in a small community in the southern part of the State. The District includes the Santa Fe High School, two primary schools, an intermediate school and the junior high school. Respondents are two sets of current or former students and their respective mothers. One family is Mormon and the other is

Catholic. The District Court permitted respondents (Does) to litigate anonymously to protect them from intimidation or harassment.[1]

Respondents commenced this action in April 1995 and moved for a temporary restraining order to prevent the District from violating the Establishment Clause at the imminent graduation exercises. In their complaint the Does alleged that the District had engaged in several proselytizing practices, such as promoting attendance at a Baptist revival meeting, encouraging membership in religious clubs, chastising children who held minority religious beliefs, and distributing Gideon Bibles on school premises. They also alleged that the District allowed students to read Christian invocations and benedictions from the stage at graduation ceremonies,[2] and to deliver overtly Christian prayers over the public address system at home football games.

On May 10, 1995, the District Court entered an interim order addressing a number of different issues.[3] With respect to the impending graduation, the order provided that "non-denominational prayer" consisting of "an invocation and/or benediction" could be presented by a senior student or students selected by members of the graduating class. The text of the prayer was to be determined by the students, without scrutiny or preapproval by school officials. References to particular religious figures "such as Mohammed, Jesus, Buddha, or the like" would be permitted "as long as the general thrust of the prayer is non-proselytizing." App. 32.

1. A decision, the Fifth Circuit Court of Appeals noted, that many District officials "apparently neither agreed with nor particularly respected." 168 F.3d 806, 809, n. 1 (C.A.5 1999). About a month after the complaint was filed, the District Court entered an order that provided, in part:

> "[A]ny further attempt on the part of District or school administration, officials, counsellors, teachers, employees or servants of the School District, parents, students or anyone else, overtly or covertly to ferret out the identities of the Plaintiffs in this cause, by means of bogus petitions, questionnaires, individual interrogation, or downright 'snooping,' will cease immediately. ANYONE TAKING ANY ACTION ON SCHOOL PROPERTY, DURING SCHOOL HOURS, OR WITH SCHOOL RESOURCES OR APPROVAL FOR PURPOSES OF ATTEMPTING TO ELICIT THE NAMES OR IDENTITIES OF THE PLAINTIFFS IN THIS CAUSE OF ACTION, BY OR ON BEHALF OF ANY OF THESE INDIVIDUALS, WILL FACE THE HARSHEST POSSIBLE CONTEMPT SANCTIONS FROM THIS COURT, AND MAY ADDITIONALLY FACE CRIMINAL LIABILITY. The Court wants these proceedings addressed on their merits, and not on the basis of intimidation or harassment of the participants on either side." App. 34–35.

2. At the 1994 graduation ceremony the senior class president delivered this invocation:

> "Please bow your heads.
>
> "Dear heavenly Father, thank you for allowing us to gather here safely tonight. We thank you for the wonderful year you have allowed us to spend together as students of Santa Fe. We thank you for our teachers who have devoted many hours to each of us. Thank you, Lord, for our parents and may each one receive the special blessing. We pray also for a blessing and guidance as each student moves forward in the future. Lord, bless this ceremony and give us all a safe journey home. In Jesus' name we pray." *Id.*, at 19.

3. For example, it prohibited school officials from endorsing or participating in the baccalaureate ceremony sponsored by the Santa Fe Ministerial Alliance, and ordered the District to establish policies to deal with

> "manifest First Amendment infractions of teachers, counsellors, or other District or school officials or personnel, such as ridiculing, berating or holding up for inappropriate scrutiny or examination the beliefs of any individual students. Similarly, the School District will establish or clarify existing procedures for excluding overt or covert sectarian and proselytizing religious teaching, such as the use of blatantly denominational religious terms in spelling lessons, denominational religious songs and poems in English or choir classes, denominational religious stories and parables in grammar lessons and the like, while at the same time allowing for frank and open discussion of moral, religious, and societal views and beliefs, which are non-denominational and non-judgmental." *Id.*, at 34.

In response to that portion of the order, the District adopted a series of policies over several months dealing with prayer at school functions....

The August policy, which was titled "Prayer at Football Games,"... authorized two student elections, the first to determine whether "invocations" should be delivered, and the second to select the spokesperson to deliver them.... [I]t contained two parts, an initial statement that omitted any requirement that the content of the invocation be "nonsectarian and nonproselytising," and a fallback provision that automatically added that limitation if the preferred policy should be enjoined. On August 31, 1995, according to the parties' stipulation: "[T]he district's high school students voted to determine whether a student would deliver prayer at varsity football games.... The students chose to allow a student to say a prayer at football games." *Id.*, at 65. A week later, in a separate election, they selected a student "to deliver the prayer at varsity football games." *Id.*, at 66.

The final policy (October policy) is essentially the same as the August policy, though it omits the word "prayer" from its title, and refers to "messages" and "statements" as well as "invocations." It is the validity of that policy that is before us.[6]

The District Court did enter an order precluding enforcement of the first, open-ended policy. Relying on our decision in *Lee v. Weisman*, 505 U.S. 577 (1992), it held that the school's "action must not 'coerce anyone to support or participate in' a religious exercise." App. to Pet. for Cert. E7. Applying that test, it concluded that the graduation prayers appealed "to distinctively Christian beliefs," and that delivering a prayer "over the school's public address system prior to each football and baseball game coerces student participation in religious events." Both parties appealed, the District contending that the enjoined portion of the October policy was permissible and the Does contending that both alternatives violated the Establishment Clause. The Court of Appeals majority agreed with the Does.

The decision of the Court of Appeals followed Fifth Circuit precedent that had announced two rules. In *Jones v. Clear Creek Independent School Dist.*, 977 F.2d 963 (C.A.5 1992), that

6. It provides:
"STUDENT ACTIVITIES:
"PRE-GAME CEREMONIES AT FOOTBALL GAMES
"The board has chosen to permit students to deliver a brief invocation and/or message to be delivered during the pre-game ceremonies of home varsity football games to solemnize the event, to promote good sportsmanship and student safety, and to establish the appropriate environment for the competition.
"Upon advice and direction of the high school principal, each spring, the high school student council shall conduct an election, by the high school student body, by secret ballot, to determine whether such a statement or invocation will be a part of the pre-game ceremonies and if so, shall elect a student, from a list of student volunteers, to deliver the statement or invocation. The student volunteer who is selected by his or her classmates may decide what message and/or invocation to deliver, consistent with the goals and purposes of this policy.
"If the District is enjoined by a court order from the enforcement of this policy, then and only then will the following policy automatically become the applicable policy of the school district.
"The board has chosen to permit students to deliver a brief invocation and/or message to be delivered during the pre-game ceremonies of home varsity football games to solemnize the event, to promote good sportsmanship and student safety, and to establish the appropriate environment for the competition.
"Upon advice and direction of the high school principal, each spring, the high school student council shall conduct an election, by the high school student body, by secret ballot, to determine whether such a message or invocation will be a part of the pre-game ceremonies and if so, shall elect a student, from a list of student volunteers, to deliver the statement or invocation. The student volunteer who is selected by his or her classmates may decide what statement or invocation to deliver, consistent with the goals and purposes of this policy. Any message and/or invocation delivered by a student must be nonsectarian and nonproselytizing." *Id.*, at 104–105.

court held that student-led prayer that was approved by a vote of the students and was nonsectarian and nonproselytizing was permissible at high school graduation ceremonies. On the other hand, in later cases the Fifth Circuit made it clear that the *Clear Creek* rule applied only to high school graduations and that school-encouraged prayer was constitutionally impermissible at school-related sporting events. Thus, in *Doe v. Duncanville Independent School Dist.*, 70 F.3d 402 (C.A.5 1995), it had described a high school graduation as "a significant, once-in-a-lifetime event" to be contrasted with athletic events in "a setting that is far less solemn and extraordinary." *Id.*, at 406–407.[9]

In its opinion in this case, the Court of Appeals explained:

> "The controlling feature here is the same as in Duncanville: The prayers are to be delivered at football games—hardly the sober type of annual event that can be appropriately solemnized with prayer. The distinction to which [the District] points is simply one without difference. Regardless of whether the prayers are selected by vote or spontaneously initiated at these frequently-recurring, informal, school-sponsored events, school officials are present and have the authority to stop the prayers. Thus, as we indicated in *Duncanville*, our decision in *Clear Creek II* hinged on the singular context and singularly serious nature of a graduation ceremony. Outside that nurturing context, a Clear Creek Prayer Policy cannot survive. We therefore reverse the district court's holding that [the District's] alternative Clear Creek Prayer Policy can be extended to football games, irrespective of the presence of the nonsectarian, nonproselytizing restrictions." 168 F.3d, at 823.

The dissenting judge rejected the majority's distinction between graduation ceremonies and football games. In his opinion the District's October policy created a limited public forum that had a secular purpose and provided neutral accommodation of noncoerced, private, religious speech.

We granted the District's petition for certiorari, limited to the following question: "Whether petitioner's policy permitting student-led, student-initiated prayer at football games violates the Establishment Clause." 528 U.S. 1002 (1999). We conclude, as did the Court of Appeals, that it does.

II

The first Clause in the First Amendment to the Federal Constitution provides that "Congress shall make no law respecting an establishment of religion, or prohibiting the free exercise thereof." The Fourteenth Amendment imposes those substantive limitations on the legislative power of the States and their political subdivisions. *Wallace v. Jaffree*, 472 U.S. 38, 49–50 (1985). In *Lee v. Weisman*, 505 U.S. 577 (1992), we held that a prayer delivered by a rabbi at a middle school graduation ceremony violated that Clause. Although this case involves student prayer at a different type of school function, our analysis is properly guided by the principles that we endorsed in *Lee*.

As we held in that case:

> "The principle that government may accommodate the free exercise of religion does not supersede the fundamental limitations imposed by the Establishment Clause. It is beyond dispute

9. Because the dissent overlooks this case, it incorrectly assumes that a "prayer-only policy" at football games was permissible in the Fifth Circuit.

> that, at a minimum, the Constitution guarantees that government may not coerce anyone to support or participate in religion or its exercise, or otherwise act in a way which 'establishes a [state] religion or religious faith, or tends to do so.'" *Id.*, at 587 (citations omitted) (quoting *Lynch v. Donnelly*, 465 U.S. 668, 678 (1984)).

In this case the District first argues that this principle is inapplicable to its October policy because the messages are private student speech, not public speech. It reminds us that "there is a crucial difference between government speech endorsing religion, which the Establishment Clause forbids, and private speech endorsing religion, which the Free Speech and Free Exercise Clauses protect." *Board of Ed. of Westside Community Schools (Dist. 66) v. Mergens*, 496 U.S. 226, 250 (1990) (opinion of O'Connor, J.). We certainly agree with that distinction, but we are not persuaded that the pregame invocations should be regarded as "private speech."

These invocations are authorized by a government policy and take place on government property at government-sponsored school-related events. Of course, not every message delivered under such circumstances is the government's own. We have held, for example, that an individual's contribution to a government-created forum was not government speech. See *Rosenberger v. Rector and Visitors of Univ. of Va.*, 515 U.S. 819 (1995). Although the District relies heavily on Rosenberger and similar cases involving such forums, it is clear that the pregame ceremony is not the type of forum discussed in those cases.[13] The Santa Fe school officials simply do not "evince either 'by policy or by practice,' any intent to open the [pregame ceremony] to 'indiscriminate use,'... by the student body generally." *Hazelwood School Dist. v. Kuhlmeier*, 484 U.S. 260, 270 (1988) (quoting *Perry Ed. Assn. v. Perry Local Educators' Assn.*, 460 U.S. 37, 47 (1983)). Rather, the school allows only one student, the same student for the entire season, to give the invocation. The statement or invocation, moreover, is subject to particular regulations that confine the content and topic of the student's message. By comparison, in *Perry* we rejected a claim that the school had created a limited public forum in its school mail system despite the fact that it had allowed far more speakers to address a much broader range of topics than the policy at issue here.[14] As we concluded in *Perry*, "selective access does not transform government property into a public forum." 460 U.S., at 47.

Granting only one student access to the stage at a time does not, of course, necessarily preclude a finding that a school has created a limited public forum. Here, however, Santa Fe's student election system ensures that only those messages deemed "appropriate" under the District's policy may be delivered. That is, the majoritarian process implemented by the District guarantees, by definition, that minority candidates will never prevail and that their views will be effectively silenced.

13. A conclusion that the District had created a public forum would help shed light on whether the resulting speech is public or private, but we also note that we have never held the mere creation of a public forum shields the government entity from scrutiny under the Establishment Clause. See, *e.g.*, *Pinette*, 515 U.S., at 772 (O'Connor, J., concurring in part and concurring in judgment) ("I see no necessity to carve out...an exception to the endorsement test for the public forum context").

14. The school's internal mail system in *Perry* was open to various private organizations such as "[l]ocal parochial schools, church groups, YMCA's, and Cub Scout units." 460 U.S., at 39, n. 2.

Recently, in *Board of Regents of Univ. of Wis. System v. Southworth*, 529 U.S. 217 (2000), we explained why student elections that determine, by majority vote, which expressive activities shall receive or not receive school benefits are constitutionally problematic:

> "To the extent the referendum substitutes majority determinations for viewpoint neutrality it would undermine the constitutional protection the program requires. The whole theory of viewpoint neutrality is that minority views are treated with the same respect as are majority views. Access to a public forum, for instance, does not depend upon majoritarian consent. That principle is controlling here." *Id.*, at 235.

Like the student referendum for funding in *Southworth*, this student election does nothing to protect minority views but rather places the students who hold such views at the mercy of the majority. Because "fundamental rights may not be submitted to vote; they depend on the outcome of no elections," *West Virginia Bd. of Ed. v. Barnette*, 319 U.S. 624, 638 (1943), the District's elections are insufficient safeguards of diverse student speech.

In *Lee*, the school district made the related argument that its policy of endorsing only "civic or nonsectarian" prayer was acceptable because it minimized the intrusion on the audience as a whole. We rejected that claim by explaining that such a majoritarian policy "does not lessen the offense or isolation to the objectors. At best it narrows their number, at worst increases their sense of isolation and affront." 505 U.S., at 594. Similarly, while Santa Fe's majoritarian election might ensure that *most* of the students are represented, it does nothing to protect the minority; indeed, it likely serves to intensify their offense.

Moreover, the District has failed to divorce itself from the religious content in the invocations. It has not succeeded in doing so, either by claiming that its policy is "'one of neutrality rather than endorsement'" or by characterizing the individual student as the "circuit-breaker" in the process. Contrary to the District's repeated assertions that it has adopted a "hands-off" approach to the pregame invocation, the realities of the situation plainly reveal that its policy involves both perceived and actual endorsement of religion. In this case, as we found in *Lee*, the "degree of school involvement" makes it clear that the pregame prayers bear "the imprint of the State and thus put school-age children who objected in an untenable position." *Id.*, at 590.

The District has attempted to disentangle itself from the religious messages by developing the two-step student election process. The text of the October policy, however, exposes the extent of the school's entanglement. The elections take place at all only because the school "board has *chosen to permit* students to deliver a brief invocation and/or message." App. 104 (emphasis added). The elections thus "shall" be conducted "by the high school student council" and "[u]pon advice and direction of the high school principal." *Id.*, at 104–105. The decision whether to deliver a message is first made by majority vote of the entire student body, followed by a choice of the speaker in a separate, similar majority election. Even though the particular words used by the speaker are not determined by those votes, the policy mandates that the "statement or invocation" be "consistent with the goals and purposes of this policy," which are "to solemnize the event, to promote good sportsmanship and student safety, and to establish the appropriate environment for the competition." *Ibid.*

In addition to involving the school in the selection of the speaker, the policy, by its terms, invites and encourages religious messages. The policy itself states that the purpose of the message is "to solemnize the event." A religious message is the most obvious method of solemnizing an event. Moreover, the requirements that the message "promote good sportsmanship" and "establish the appropriate environment for competition" further narrow the types of message deemed appropriate, suggesting that a solemn, yet nonreligious, message, such as commentary on United States foreign policy, would be prohibited.[18] Indeed, the only type of message that is expressly endorsed in the text is an "invocation"—a term that primarily describes an appeal for divine assistance. In fact, as used in the past at Santa Fe High School, an "invocation" has always entailed a focused religious message. Thus, the expressed purposes of the policy encourage the selection of a religious message, and that is precisely how the students understand the policy. The results of the elections described in the parties' stipulation make it clear that the students understood that the central question before them was whether prayer should be a part of the pregame ceremony.[21] We recognize the important role that public worship plays in many communities, as well as the sincere desire to include public prayer as a part of various occasions so as to mark those occasions' significance. But such religious activity in public schools, as elsewhere, must comport with the First Amendment.

The actual or perceived endorsement of the message, moreover, is established by factors beyond just the text of the policy. Once the student speaker is selected and the message composed, the invocation is then delivered to a large audience assembled as part of a regularly scheduled, school-sponsored function conducted on school property. The message is broadcast over the school's public address system, which remains subject to the control of school officials. It is fair to assume that the pregame ceremony is clothed in the traditional indicia of school sporting events, which generally include not just the team, but also cheerleaders and band members dressed in uniforms sporting the school name and mascot. The school's name is likely written in large print across the field and on banners and flags. The crowd will certainly include many who display the school colors and insignia on their school T-shirts, jackets, or hats and who may also be waving signs displaying the school name. It is in a setting such as this that "[t]he board has chosen to permit" the elected student to rise and give the "statement or invocation."

In this context the members of the listening audience must perceive the pregame message as a public expression of the views of the majority of the student body delivered with the approval of the school administration. In cases involving state participation in a religious activity, one of the relevant questions is "whether an objective observer, acquainted with the text, legislative history, and implementation of the statute, would perceive it as a state endorsement of prayer in public schools." *Wallace*, 472 U.S., at 73, 76 (O'Connor, J., concurring in judgment); see also *Capitol Square Review and Advisory Bd. v. Pinette*, 515 U.S. 753, 777 (1995) (O'Connor, J., concurring in part and concurring in judgment). Regardless of the listener's support for, or objection to, the message, an objective Santa Fe High School student

18. The Chief Justice's hypothetical of the student body president asked by the school to introduce a guest speaker with a biography of her accomplishments, obviously would pose no problems under the Establishment Clause.

21. Even if the plain language of the October policy were facially neutral, "the Establishment Clause forbids a State to hide behind the application of formally neutral criteria and remain studiously oblivious to the effects of its actions." *Capitol Square Review and Advisory Bd. v. Pinette*, 515 U.S., at 777 (O'Connor, J., concurring in part and concurring in judgment); see also *Church of Lukumi Babalu Aye, Inc. v. Hialeah*, 508 U.S. 520, 534–535 (1993) (making the same point in the Free Exercise Clause context).

will unquestionably perceive the inevitable pregame prayer as stamped with her school's seal of approval.

The text and history of this policy, moreover, reinforce our objective student's perception that the prayer is, in actuality, encouraged by the school. When a governmental entity professes a secular purpose for an arguably religious policy, the government's characterization is, of course, entitled to some deference. But it is nonetheless the duty of the courts to "distinguis[h] a sham secular purpose from a sincere one." *Wallace*, 472 U.S., at 75 (O'Connor, J., concurring in judgment).

According to the District, the secular purposes of the policy are to "foste[r] free expression of private persons... as well [as to] solemniz[e] sporting events, promot[e] good sportsmanship and student safety, and establis[h] an appropriate environment for competition." Brief for Petitioner 14. We note, however, that the District's approval of only one specific kind of message, an "invocation," is not necessary to further any of these purposes. Additionally, the fact that only one student is permitted to give a content-limited message suggests that this policy does little to "foste[r] free expression." Furthermore, regardless of whether one considers a sporting event an appropriate occasion for solemnity, the use of an invocation to foster such solemnity is impermissible when, in actuality, it constitutes prayer sponsored by the school. And it is unclear what type of message would be both appropriately "solemnizing" under the District's policy and yet nonreligious.

Most striking to us is the evolution of the current policy from the long-sanctioned office of "Student Chaplain" to the candidly titled "Prayer at Football Games" regulation. This history indicates that the District intended to preserve the practice of prayer before football games. The conclusion that the District viewed the October policy simply as a continuation of the previous policies is dramatically illustrated by the fact that the school did not conduct a new election, pursuant to the current policy, to replace the results of the previous election, which occurred under the former policy. Given these observations, and in light of the school's history of regular delivery of a student-led prayer at athletic events, it is reasonable to infer that the specific purpose of the policy was to preserve a popular "state-sponsored religious practice." *Lee*, 505 U.S., at 596.

School sponsorship of a religious message is impermissible because it sends the ancillary message to members of the audience who are nonadherents "that they are outsiders, not full members of the political community, and an accompanying message to adherents that they are insiders, favored members of the political community." *Lynch*, 465 U.S., at 688 (O'Connor, J., concurring). The delivery of such a message—over the school's public address system, by a speaker representing the student body, under the supervision of school faculty, and pursuant to a school policy that explicitly and implicitly encourages public prayer—is not properly characterized as "private" speech.

III

The District next argues that its football policy is distinguishable from the graduation prayer in *Lee* because it does not coerce students to participate in religious observances. Its argument has two parts: first, that there is no impermissible government coercion because the pregame messages are the product of student choices; and second, that there is really no coercion at all because attendance at an extracurricular event, unlike a graduation ceremony, is voluntary.

The reasons just discussed explaining why the alleged "circuit-breaker" mechanism of the dual elections and student speaker do not turn public speech into private speech also demonstrate why these mechanisms do not insulate the school from the coercive element of the final message. In fact, this aspect of the District's argument exposes anew the concerns that are created by the majoritarian election system. The parties' stipulation clearly states that the issue resolved in the first election was "whether a student would deliver prayer at varsity football games," App. 65, and the controversy in this case demonstrates that the views of the students are not unanimous on that issue.

One of the purposes served by the Establishment Clause is to remove debate over this kind of issue from governmental supervision or control. We explained in *Lee* that the "preservation and transmission of religious beliefs and worship is a responsibility and a choice committed to the private sphere." 505 U.S., at 589. The two student elections authorized by the policy, coupled with the debates that presumably must precede each, impermissibly invade that private sphere. The election mechanism, when considered in light of the history in which the policy in question evolved, reflects a device the District put in place that determines whether religious messages will be delivered at home football games. The mechanism encourages divisiveness along religious lines in a public school setting, a result at odds with the Establishment Clause. Although it is true that the ultimate choice of student speaker is "attributable to the students," Brief for Petitioner 40, the District's decision to hold the constitutionally problematic election is clearly "a choice attributable to the State," *Lee*, 505 U.S., at 587.

The District further argues that attendance at the commencement ceremonies at issue in *Lee* "differs dramatically" from attendance at high school football games, which it contends "are of no more than passing interest to many students" and are "decidedly extra-curricular," thus dissipating any coercion. Brief for Petitioner 41. Attendance at a high school football game, unlike showing up for class, is certainly not required in order to receive a diploma. Moreover, we may assume that the District is correct in arguing that the informal pressure to attend an athletic event is not as strong as a senior's desire to attend her own graduation ceremony.

There are some students, however, such as cheerleaders, members of the band, and, of course, the team members themselves, for whom seasonal commitments mandate their attendance, sometimes for class credit. The District also minimizes the importance to many students of attending and participating in extracurricular activities as part of a complete educational experience. As we noted in *Lee*, "[l]aw reaches past formalism." 505 U.S., at 595. To assert that high school students do not feel immense social pressure, or have a truly genuine desire, to be involved in the extracurricular event that is American high school football is "formalistic in the extreme." *Ibid.* We stressed in *Lee* the obvious observation that "adolescents are often susceptible to pressure from their peers towards conformity, and that the influence is strongest in matters of social convention." *Id.*, at 593. High school home football games are traditional gatherings of a school community; they bring together students and faculty as well as friends and family from years present and past to root for a common cause. Undoubtedly, the games are not important to some students, and they voluntarily choose not to attend. For many others, however, the choice between attending these games and avoiding personally offensive religious rituals is in no practical sense an easy one. The Constitution, moreover, demands that the school may not force this difficult choice upon these students for "[i]t is a tenet of the First Amendment that the State cannot require one of its citizens to forfeit his or her rights and benefits as the price of resisting conformance to state-sponsored religious practice." *Id.*, at 596.

Even if we regard every high school student's decision to attend a home football game as purely voluntary, we are nevertheless persuaded that the delivery of a pregame prayer has the improper effect of coercing those present to participate in an act of religious worship. For "the government may no more use social pressure to enforce orthodoxy than it may use more direct means." *Id.*, at 594. As in *Lee*, "[w]hat to most believers may seem nothing more than a reasonable request that the nonbeliever respect their religious practices, in a school context may appear to the nonbeliever or dissenter to be an attempt to employ the machinery of the State to enforce a religious orthodoxy." *Id.*, at 592. The constitutional command will not permit the District "to exact religious conformity from a student as the price" of joining her classmates at a varsity football game.[22]

The Religion Clauses of the First Amendment prevent the government from making any law respecting the establishment of religion or prohibiting the free exercise thereof. By no means do these commands impose a prohibition on all religious activity in our public schools. See, *e.g.*, *Lamb's Chapel v. Center Moriches Union Free School Dist.*, 508 U.S. 384, 395 (1993); *Board of Ed. of Westside Community Schools (Dist. 66) v. Mergens*, 496 U.S. 226 (1990); *Wallace*, 472 U.S., at 59. Indeed, the common purpose of the Religion Clauses "is to secure religious liberty." *Engel v. Vitale*, 370 U.S. 421 (1962). Thus, nothing in the Constitution as interpreted by this Court prohibits any public school student from voluntarily praying at any time before, during, or after the school day. But the religious liberty protected by the Constitution is abridged when the State affirmatively sponsors the particular religious practice of prayer.

IV

Finally, the District argues repeatedly that the Does have made a premature facial challenge to the October policy that necessarily must fail. The District emphasizes, quite correctly, that until a student actually delivers a solemnizing message under the latest version of the policy, there can be no certainty that any of the statements or invocations will be religious. Thus, it concludes, the October policy necessarily survives a facial challenge.

This argument, however, assumes that we are concerned only with the serious constitutional injury that occurs when a student is forced to participate in an act of religious worship because she chooses to attend a school event. But the Constitution also requires that we keep in mind "the myriad, subtle ways in which Establishment Clause values can be eroded," *Lynch*, 465 U.S., at 694 (O'Connor, J., concurring), and that we guard against other different, yet equally important, constitutional injuries. One is the mere passage by the District of a policy that has the purpose and perception of government establishment of religion. Another is the implementation of a governmental electoral process that subjects the issue of prayer to a majoritarian vote.

The District argues that the facial challenge must fail because "Santa Fe's Football Policy cannot be invalidated on the basis of some 'possibility or even likelihood' of an unconstitutional

22. "We think the Government's position that this interest suffices to force students to choose between compliance or forfeiture demonstrates fundamental inconsistency in its argumentation. It fails to acknowledge that what for many of Deborah's classmates and their parents was a spiritual imperative was for Daniel and Deborah Weisman religious conformance compelled by the State. While in some societies the wishes of the majority might prevail, the Establishment Clause of the First Amendment is addressed to this contingency and rejects the balance urged upon us. The Constitution forbids the State to exact religious conformity from a student as the price of attending her own high school graduation. This is the calculus the Constitution commands." *Lee*, 505 U.S., at 595–596.

application." Brief for Petitioner 17 (quoting *Bowen v. Kendrick*, 487 U.S. 589, 613 (1988)). Our Establishment Clause cases involving facial challenges, however, have not focused solely on the possible applications of the statute, but rather have considered whether the statute has an unconstitutional purpose. Writing for the Court in *Bowen*, The Chief Justice concluded that "[a]s in previous cases involving facial challenges on Establishment Clause grounds, *e.g.*, *Edwards v. Aguillard*, [482 U.S. 578 (1987)]; *Mueller v. Allen*, 463 U.S. 388 (1983), we assess the constitutionality of an enactment by reference to the three factors first articulated in *Lemon v. Kurtzman*, 403 U.S. 602, 612 (1971)..., which guides '[t]he general nature of our inquiry in this area,' *Mueller v. Allen*, *supra*, at 394." 487 U.S., at 602. Under the *Lemon* standard, a court must invalidate a statute if it lacks "a secular legislative purpose." *Lemon v. Kurtzman*, 403 U.S. 602, 612 (1971). It is therefore proper, as part of this facial challenge, for us to examine the purpose of the October policy.

As discussed, the text of the October policy alone reveals that it has an unconstitutional purpose. The plain language of the policy clearly spells out the extent of school involvement in both the election of the speaker and the content of the message. Additionally, the text of the October policy specifies only one, clearly preferred message—that of Santa Fe's traditional religious "invocation." Finally, the extremely selective access of the policy and other content restrictions confirm that it is not a content-neutral regulation that creates a limited public forum for the expression of student speech. Our examination, however, need not stop at an analysis of the text of the policy.

This case comes to us as the latest step in developing litigation brought as a challenge to institutional practices that unquestionably violated the Establishment Clause. One of those practices was the District's long-established tradition of sanctioning student-led prayer at varsity football games. The narrow question before us is whether implementation of the October policy insulates the continuation of such prayers from constitutional scrutiny. It does not. Our inquiry into this question not only can, but must, include an examination of the circumstances surrounding its enactment. Whether a government activity violates the Establishment Clause is "in large part a legal question to be answered on the basis of judicial interpretation of social facts.... Every government practice must be judged in its unique circumstances...." *Lynch*, 465 U.S., at 693–694 (O'Connor, J., concurring). Our discussion in the previous sections, demonstrates that in this case the District's direct involvement with school prayer exceeds constitutional limits.

The District, nevertheless, asks us to pretend that we do not recognize what every Santa Fe High School student understands clearly—that this policy is about prayer. The District further asks us to accept what is obviously untrue: that these messages are necessary to "solemnize" a football game and that this single-student, year-long position is essential to the protection of student speech. We refuse to turn a blind eye to the context in which this policy arose, and that context quells any doubt that this policy was implemented with the purpose of endorsing school prayer.

Therefore, the simple enactment of this policy, with the purpose and perception of school endorsement of student prayer, was a constitutional violation. We need not wait for the inevitable to confirm and magnify the constitutional injury. In *Wallace*, for example, we invalidated Alabama's as yet unimplemented and voluntary "moment of silence" statute based on our conclusion that it was enacted "for the sole purpose of expressing the State's endorsement of prayer activities for one minute at the beginning of each school day." 472 U.S., at 60; see also *Church of Lukumi Babalu Aye, Inc. v. Hialeah*, 508 U.S.

520, 532 (1993). Therefore, even if no Santa Fe High School student were ever to offer a religious message, the October policy fails a facial challenge because the attempt by the District to encourage prayer is also at issue. Government efforts to endorse religion cannot evade constitutional reproach based solely on the remote possibility that those attempts may fail.

This policy likewise does not survive a facial challenge because it impermissibly imposes upon the student body a majoritarian election on the issue of prayer. Through its election scheme, the District has established a governmental electoral mechanism that turns the school into a forum for religious debate. It further empowers the student body majority with the authority to subject students of minority views to constitutionally improper messages. The award of that power alone, regardless of the students' ultimate use of it, is not acceptable.[23] Like the referendum in *Board of Regents of Univ. of Wis. System v. Southworth*, 529 U.S. 217 (2000), the election mechanism established by the District undermines the essential protection of minority viewpoints. Such a system encourages divisiveness along religious lines and threatens the imposition of coercion upon those students not desiring to participate in a religious exercise. Simply by establishing this school-related procedure, which entrusts the inherently nongovernmental subject of religion to a majoritarian vote, a constitutional violation has occurred.[24] No further injury is required for the policy to fail a facial challenge.

To properly examine this policy on its face, we "must be deemed aware of the history and context of the community and forum," *Pinette*, 515 U.S., at 780 (O'Connor, J., concurring in part and concurring in judgment). Our examination of those circumstances above leads to the conclusion that this policy does not provide the District with the constitutional safe harbor it sought. The policy is invalid on its face because it establishes an improper majoritarian election on religion, and unquestionably has the purpose and creates the perception of encouraging the delivery of prayer at a series of important school events.

The judgment of the Court of Appeals is, accordingly, affirmed....

Chief Justice Rehnquist, with whom Justice Scalia and Justice Thomas join, dissenting.

The Court distorts existing precedent to conclude that the school district's student-message program is invalid on its face under the Establishment Clause. But even more disturbing than its holding is the tone of the Court's opinion; it bristles with hostility to all things religious in public life. Neither the holding nor the tone of the opinion is faithful to the meaning of

23. The Chief Justice accuses us of "essentially invalidat[ing] all student elections." This is obvious hyperbole. We have concluded that the resulting religious message under this policy would be attributable to the school, not just the student. For this reason, we now hold only that the District's decision to allow the student majority to control whether students of minority views are subjected to a school-sponsored prayer violates the Establishment Clause.

24. The Chief Justice contends that we have "misconstrue[d] the nature... [of] the policy as being an election on 'prayer' and 'religion.'" We therefore reiterate that the District has stipulated to the facts that the most recent election was held "to determine whether a student would deliver *prayer* at varsity football games," that the "students chose to allow a student to say a *prayer* at football games," and that a second election was then held "to determine which student would deliver the prayer." App. 65–66 (emphases added). Furthermore, the policy was titled "*Prayer* at Football Games." *Id.*, at 99 (emphasis added). Although the District has since eliminated the word "prayer" from the policy, it apparently viewed that change as sufficiently minor as to make holding a new election unnecessary.

the Establishment Clause, when it is recalled that George Washington himself, at the request of the very Congress which passed the Bill of Rights, proclaimed a day of "public thanksgiving and prayer, to be observed by acknowledging with grateful hearts the many and signal favors of Almighty God." Presidential Proclamation, 1 Messages and Papers of the Presidents, 1789–1897, p. 64 (J. Richardson ed. 1897).

We do not learn until late in the Court's opinion that respondents in this case challenged the district's student-message program at football games before it had been put into practice. As the Court explained in *United States v. Salerno*, 481 U.S. 739, 745 (1987), the fact that a policy might "operate unconstitutionally under some conceivable set of circumstances is insufficient to render it wholly invalid." See also *Bowen v. Kendrick*, 487 U.S. 589, 612 (1988). While there is an exception to this principle in the First Amendment overbreadth context because of our concern that people may refrain from speech out of fear of prosecution, *Los Angeles Police Dept. v. United Reporting Publishing Corp.*, 528 U.S. 32, 38–40 (1999), there is no similar justification for Establishment Clause cases. No speech will be "chilled" by the existence of a government policy that might unconstitutionally endorse religion over nonreligion. Therefore, the question is not whether the district's policy may be applied in violation of the Establishment Clause, but whether it inevitably will be.

The Court, venturing into the realm of prophecy, decides that it "need not wait for the inevitable" and invalidates the district's policy on its face. To do so, it applies the most rigid version of the oft-criticized test of *Lemon v. Kurtzman*, 403 U.S. 602 (1971).

Lemon has had a checkered career in the decisional law of this Court. See, *e.g.*, *Lamb's Chapel v. Center Moriches Union Free School Dist.*, 508 U.S. 384, 398–399 (1993) (Scalia, J., concurring in judgment) (collecting opinions criticizing *Lemon*); *Wallace v. Jaffree*, 472 U.S. 38, 108–114 (1985) (Rehnquist, J., dissenting) (stating that *Lemon*'s "three-part test represents a determined effort to craft a workable rule from a historically faulty doctrine; but the rule can only be as sound as the doctrine it attempts to service" (internal quotation marks omitted)); *Committee for Public Ed. and Religious Liberty v. Regan*, 444 U.S. 646, 671 (1980) (Stevens, J., dissenting) (deriding "the sisyphean task of trying to patch together the blurred, indistinct, and variable barrier described in *Lemon*"). We have even gone so far as to state that it has never been binding on us. *Lynch v. Donnelly*, 465 U.S. 668, 679 (1984) ("[W]e have repeatedly emphasized our unwillingness to be confined to any single test or criterion in this sensitive area.... In two cases, the Court did not even apply the *Lemon* 'test' [citing *Marsh v. Chambers*, 463 U.S. 783 (1983), and *Larson v. Valente*, 456 U.S. 228 (1982)]"). Indeed, in *Lee v. Weisman*, 505 U.S. 577 (1992), an opinion upon which the Court relies heavily today, we mentioned, but did not feel compelled to apply, the *Lemon* test. See also *Agostini v. Felton*, 521 U.S. 203, 233 (1997) (stating that *Lemon*'s entanglement test is merely "an aspect of the inquiry into a statute's effect"); *Hunt v. McNair*, 413 U.S. 734, 741 (1973) (stating that the *Lemon* factors are "no more than helpful signposts").

Even if it were appropriate to apply the *Lemon* test here, the district's student-message policy should not be invalidated on its face. The Court applies *Lemon* and holds that the "policy is invalid on its face because it establishes an improper majoritarian election on religion, and unquestionably has the purpose and creates the perception of encouraging the delivery of prayer at a series of important school events." The Court's reliance on each of these conclusions misses the mark.

First, the Court misconstrues the nature of the "majoritarian election" permitted by the policy as being an election on "prayer" and "religion."[2] To the contrary, the election permitted by the policy is a two-fold process whereby students vote first on whether to have a student speaker before football games at all, and second, if the students vote to have such a speaker, on who that speaker will be. It is conceivable that the election could become one in which student candidates campaign on platforms that focus on whether or not they will pray if elected. It is also conceivable that the election could lead to a Christian prayer before 90 percent of the football games. If, upon implementation, the policy operated in this fashion, we would have a record before us to review whether the policy, as applied, violated the Establishment Clause or unduly suppressed minority viewpoints. But it is possible that the students might vote not to have a pregame speaker, in which case there would be no threat of a constitutional violation. It is also possible that the election would not focus on prayer, but on public speaking ability or social popularity. And if student campaigning did begin to focus on prayer, the school might decide to implement reasonable campaign restrictions.[3]

But the Court ignores these possibilities by holding that merely granting the student body the power to elect a speaker that may choose to pray, "regardless of the students' ultimate use of it, is not acceptable." The Court so holds despite that any speech that may occur as a result of the election process here would be *private*, not *government*, speech. The elected student, not the government, would choose what to say. Support for the Court's holding cannot be found in any of our cases. And it essentially invalidates all student elections. A newly elected student body president, or even a newly elected prom king or queen, could use opportunities for public speaking to say prayers. Under the Court's view, the mere grant of power to the students to vote for such offices, in light of the fear that those elected might publicly pray, violates the Establishment Clause.

Second, with respect to the policy's purpose, the Court holds that "the simple enactment of this policy, with the purpose and perception of school endorsement of student prayer, was a constitutional violation." But the policy itself has plausible secular purposes: "[T]o solemnize the event, to promote good sportsmanship and student safety, and to establish the appropriate environment for the competition." App. 104–105. Where a governmental body "expresses a plausible secular purpose" for an enactment, "courts should generally defer to that stated intent." *Wallace*, 472 U.S., at 74–75 (O'Connor, J., concurring in judgment); see also *Mueller v. Allen*, 463 U.S. 388, 394–395 (1983) (stressing this Court's "reluctance to attribute unconstitutional motives to the States, particularly when a plausible secular purpose for the State's program may be discerned from the face of the statute"). The Court grants no

2. The Court attempts to support its misinterpretation of the nature of the election process by noting that the district stipulated to facts about the most recent election. Of course, the most recent election was conducted under the previous policy—a policy that required an elected student speaker to give a pregame invocation. There has not been an election under the policy at issue here, which expressly allows the student speaker to give a message as opposed to an invocation.

3. The Court's reliance on language regarding the student referendum in *Board of Regents of Univ. of Wis. System v. Southworth*, 529 U.S. 217 (2000), to support its conclusion with respect to the election process is misplaced. That case primarily concerned free speech, and, more particularly, mandated financial support of a public forum. But as stated above, if this case were in the "as applied" context and we were presented with the appropriate record, our language in *Southworth* could become more applicable. In fact, *Southworth* itself demonstrates the impropriety of making a decision with respect to the election process without a record of its operation. There we remanded in part for a determination of how the referendum functions. See *id.*, at 235–236.

deference to—and appears openly hostile toward—the policy's stated purposes, and wastes no time in concluding that they are a sham.

For example, the Court dismisses the secular purpose of solemnization by claiming that it "invites and encourages religious messages." Cf. *Lynch*, 465 U. S, at 693 (O'CONNOR, J., concurring) (discussing the "legitimate secular purposes of solemnizing public occasions"). The Court so concludes based on its rather strange view that a "religious message is the most obvious means of solemnizing an event." But it is easy to think of solemn messages that are not religious in nature, for example urging that a game be fought fairly. And sporting events often begin with a solemn rendition of our national anthem, with its concluding verse "And this be our motto: 'In God is our trust.'" Under the Court's logic, a public school that sponsors the singing of the national anthem before football games violates the Establishment Clause. Although the Court apparently believes that solemnizing football games is an illegitimate purpose, the voters in the school district seem to disagree. Nothing in the Establishment Clause prevents them from making this choice.[4]

The Court bases its conclusion that the true purpose of the policy is to endorse student prayer on its view of the school district's history of Establishment Clause violations and the context in which the policy was written, that is, as "the latest step in developing litigation brought as a challenge to institutional practices that unquestionably violated the Establishment Clause." But the context-attempted compliance with a District Court order—actually demonstrates that the school district was acting diligently to come within the governing constitutional law. The District Court ordered the school district to formulate a policy consistent with Fifth Circuit precedent, which permitted a school district to have a prayer-only policy. See *Jones v. Clear Creek Independent School Dist.*, 977 F.2d 963 (C.A.5 1992). But the school district went further than required by the District Court order and eventually settled on a policy that gave the student speaker a choice to deliver either an invocation or a message. In so doing, the school district exhibited a willingness to comply with, and exceed, Establishment Clause restrictions. Thus, the policy cannot be viewed as having a sectarian purpose.[5]

The Court also relies on our decision in *Lee v. Weisman*, 505 U.S. 577 (1992), to support its conclusion. In *Lee*, we concluded that the content of the speech at issue, a graduation prayer given by a rabbi, was "directed and controlled" by a school official. *Id.*, at 588. In other words, at issue in *Lee* was government speech. Here, by contrast, the potential speech at issue, if the policy had been allowed to proceed, would be a message or invocation selected or created by a student. That is, if there were speech at issue here, it would be private speech. The "crucial difference between *government* speech endorsing religion, which the Establishment Clause forbids, and *private* speech endorsing religion, which the Free Speech and Free Exercise

4. The Court also determines that the use of the term "invocation" in the policy is an express endorsement of that type of message over all others. A less cynical view of the policy's text is that it permits many types of messages, including invocations. That a policy tolerates religion does not mean that it improperly endorses it. Indeed, as the majority reluctantly admits, the Free Exercise Clause mandates such tolerance....

5. *Wallace v. Jaffree*, 472 U.S. 38 (1985), is distinguishable on these grounds. There we struck down an Alabama statute that added an express reference to prayer to an existing statute providing a moment of silence for meditation. *Id.*, at 59. Here the school district added a secular alternative to a policy that originally provided only for prayer. More importantly, in *Wallace*, there was "unrebutted evidence" that pointed to a wholly religious purpose, *id.*, at 58, and Alabama "conceded in the courts below that the purpose of the statute was to make prayer part of daily classroom activity," *id.*, at 77–78 (O'CONNOR, J., concurring in judgment). There is no such evidence or concession here.

Clauses protect," applies with particular force to the question of endorsement. *Board of Ed. of Westside Community Schools (Dist. 66) v. Mergens*, 496 U.S. 226, 250 (1990) (plurality opinion) (emphasis in original).

Had the policy been put into practice, the students may have chosen a speaker according to wholly secular criteria—like good public speaking skills or social popularity—and the student speaker may have chosen, on her own accord, to deliver a religious message. Such an application of the policy would likely pass constitutional muster. See *Lee*, *supra*, at 630, n. 8 (Souter, J., concurring) ("If the State had chosen its graduation day speakers according to wholly secular criteria, and if one of those speakers (not a state actor) had individually chosen to deliver a religious message, it would be harder to attribute an endorsement of religion to the State").

Finally, the Court seems to demand that a government policy be completely neutral as to content or be considered one that endorses religion. This is undoubtedly a new requirement, as our Establishment Clause jurisprudence simply does not mandate "content neutrality." That concept is found in our First Amendment *speech* cases and is used as a guide for determining when we apply strict scrutiny. For example, we look to "content neutrality" in reviewing loudness restrictions imposed on speech in public forums, see *Ward v. Rock Against Racism*, 491 U.S. 781 (1989), and regulations against picketing, see *Boos v. Barry*, 485 U.S. 312 (1988). The Court seems to think that the fact that the policy is not content neutral somehow controls the Establishment Clause inquiry.

But even our speech jurisprudence would not require that all public school actions with respect to student speech be content neutral. See, *e.g.*, *Bethel School Dist. No. 403 v. Fraser*, 478 U.S. 675 (1986) (allowing the imposition of sanctions against a student speaker who, in nominating a fellow student for elective office during an assembly, referred to his candidate in terms of an elaborate sexually explicit metaphor). Schools do not violate the First Amendment every time they restrict student speech to certain categories. But under the Court's view, a school policy under which the student body president is to solemnize the graduation ceremony by giving a favorable introduction to the guest speaker would be facially unconstitutional. Solemnization "invites and encourages" prayer and the policy's content limitations prohibit the student body president from giving a solemn, yet nonreligious, message like "commentary on United States foreign policy."

The policy at issue here may be applied in an unconstitutional manner, but it will be time enough to invalidate it if that is found to be the case. I would reverse the judgment of the Court of Appeals.

GOOD NEWS CLUB V. MILFORD SCHOOL DISTRICT
Supreme Court of the United States
533 U.S. 98 (2001)

Justice Thomas delivered the opinion of the Court.

This case presents two questions. The first question is whether Milford Central School violated the free speech rights of the Good News Club when it excluded the Club from meeting after hours at the school. The second question is whether any such violation is justified by Milford's concern that permitting the Club's activities would violate the Establishment Clause. We conclude that Milford's restriction violates the Club's free speech rights and that no Establishment Clause concern justifies that violation.

I

The State of New York authorizes local school boards to adopt regulations governing the use of their school facilities. In particular, N.Y. Educ. Law § 414 (McKinney 2000) enumerates several purposes for which local boards may open their schools to public use. In 1992, respondent Milford Central School (Milford) enacted a community use policy adopting seven of § 414's purposes for which its building could be used after school. Two of the stated purposes are relevant here. First, district residents may use the school for "instruction in any branch of education, learning or the arts." Second, the school is available for "social, civic and recreational meetings and entertainment events, and other uses pertaining to the welfare of the community, provided that such uses shall be nonexclusive and shall be opened to the general public."

Stephen and Darleen Fournier reside within Milford's district and therefore are eligible to use the school's facilities as long as their proposed use is approved by the school. Together they are sponsors of the local Good News Club, a private Christian organization for children ages 6 to 12. Pursuant to Milford's policy, in September 1996 the Fourniers submitted a request to Dr. Robert McGruder, interim superintendent of the district, in which they sought permission to hold the Club's weekly afterschool meetings in the school cafeteria. The next month, McGruder formally denied the Fourniers' request on the ground that the proposed use—to have "a fun time of singing songs, hearing a Bible lesson and memorizing scripture"—was "the equivalent of religious worship." According to McGruder, the community use policy, which prohibits use "by any individual or organization for religious purposes," foreclosed the Club's activities.

In response to a letter submitted by the Club's counsel, Milford's attorney requested information to clarify the nature of the Club's activities. The Club sent a set of materials used or distributed at the meetings and the following description of its meeting:

> "The Club opens its session with Ms. Fournier taking attendance. As she calls a child's name, if the child recites a Bible verse the child receives a treat. After attendance, the Club sings songs. Next Club members engage in games that involve, inter alia, learning Bible verses. Ms. Fournier then relates a Bible story and explains how it applies to Club members' lives. The Club closes with prayer. Finally, Ms. Fournier distributes treats and the Bible verses for memorization."

McGruder and Milford's attorney reviewed the materials and concluded that "the kinds of activities proposed to be engaged in by the Good News Club were not a discussion of secular subjects such as child rearing, development of character and development of morals from a religious perspective, but were in fact the equivalent of religious instruction itself." In February 1997, the Milford Board of Education adopted a resolution rejecting the Club's request to use Milford's facilities "for the purpose of conducting religious instruction and Bible study."

In March 1997, petitioners, the Good News Club, Ms. Fournier, and her daughter Andrea Fournier (collectively, the Club), filed an action under Rev. Stat. § 1979, 42 U.S.C. § 1983, against Milford in the United States District Court for the Northern District of New York. The Club alleged that Milford's denial of its application violated its free speech rights under the First and Fourteenth Amendments, its right to equal protection under the Fourteenth

Amendment, and its right to religious freedom under the Religious Freedom Restoration Act of 1993, 107 Stat. 1488, 42 U.S.C. § 2000bb et seq.[1]

The Club moved for a preliminary injunction to prevent the school from enforcing its religious exclusion policy against the Club and thereby to permit the Club's use of the school facilities. On April 14, 1997, the District Court granted the injunction. The Club then held its weekly afterschool meetings from April 1997 until June 1998 in a high school resource and middle school special education room.

In August 1998, the District Court vacated the preliminary injunction and granted Milford's motion for summary judgment. 21 F.Supp.2d 147 (N.D.N.Y. 1998). The court found that the Club's "subject matter is decidedly religious in nature, and not merely a discussion of secular matters from a religious perspective that is otherwise permitted under [Milford's] use policies." *Id.*, at 154. Because the school had not permitted other groups that provided religious instruction to use its limited public forum, the court held that the school could deny access to the Club without engaging in unconstitutional viewpoint discrimination. The court also rejected the Club's equal protection claim.

The Club appealed, and a divided panel of the United States Court of Appeals for the Second Circuit affirmed. 202 F.3d 502 (2000). First, the court rejected the Club's contention that Milford's restriction against allowing religious instruction in its facilities is unreasonable. Second, it held that, because the subject matter of the Club's activities is "quintessentially religious," *id.*, at 510, and the activities "fall outside the bounds of pure 'moral and character development,'" *id.*, at 511, Milford's policy of excluding the Club's meetings was constitutional subject discrimination, not unconstitutional viewpoint discrimination. Judge Jacobs filed a dissenting opinion in which he concluded that the school's restriction did constitute viewpoint discrimination under *Lamb's Chapel v. Center Moriches Union Free School Dist.*, 508 U.S. 384 (1993).

There is a conflict among the Courts of Appeals on the question whether speech can be excluded from a limited public forum on the basis of the religious nature of the speech.... We granted certiorari to resolve this conflict. 531 U.S. 923 (2000).

II

The standards that we apply to determine whether a State has unconstitutionally excluded a private speaker from use of a public forum depend on the nature of the forum. See *Perry Ed. Assn. v. Perry Local Educators' Assn.*, 460 U.S. 37, 44 (1983). If the forum is a traditional or open public forum, the State's restrictions on speech are subject to stricter scrutiny than are restrictions in a limited public forum. *Id.*, at 45–46. We have previously declined to decide whether a school district's opening of its facilities pursuant to N.Y. Educ. Law § 414 creates a limited or a traditional public forum. See *Lamb's Chapel*, *supra*, at 391–392. Because the parties have agreed that Milford created a limited public forum when it opened its facilities in 1992, we need not resolve the issue here. Instead, we simply will assume that Milford operates a limited public forum.

1. The District Court dismissed the Club's claim under the Religious Freedom Restoration Act because we held the Act to be unconstitutional in *City of Boerne v. Flores*, 521 U.S. 507 (1997). See 21 F.Supp.2d 147, 150, n. 4 (N.D.N.Y. 1998).

When the State establishes a limited public forum, the State is not required to and does not allow persons to engage in every type of speech. The State may be justified "in reserving [its forum] for certain groups or for the discussion of certain topics." *Rosenberger v. Rector and Visitors of Univ. of Va.*, 515 U.S. 819, 829 (1995); see also *Lamb's Chapel, supra*, at 392–393. The State's power to restrict speech, however, is not without limits. The restriction must not discriminate against speech on the basis of viewpoint, *Rosenberger, supra*, at 829, and the restriction must be "reasonable in light of the purpose served by the forum," *Cornelius v. NAACP Legal Defense & Ed. Fund, Inc.*, 473 U.S. 788, 806 (1985).

III

Applying this test, we first address whether the exclusion constituted viewpoint discrimination. We are guided in our analysis by two of our prior opinions, *Lamb's Chapel* and *Rosenberger*. In *Lamb's Chapel*, we held that a school district violated the Free Speech Clause of the First Amendment when it excluded a private group from presenting films at the school based solely on the films' discussions of family values from a religious perspective. Likewise, in *Rosenberger*, we held that a university's refusal to fund a student publication because the publication addressed issues from a religious perspective violated the Free Speech Clause. Concluding that Milford's exclusion of the Good News Club based on its religious nature is indistinguishable from the exclusions in these cases, we hold that the exclusion constitutes viewpoint discrimination. Because the restriction is viewpoint discriminatory, we need not decide whether it is unreasonable in light of the purposes served by the forum.

Milford has opened its limited public forum to activities that serve a variety of purposes, including events "pertaining to the welfare of the community." Milford interprets its policy to permit discussions of subjects such as child rearing, and of "the development of character and morals from a religious perspective." For example, this policy would allow someone to use Aesop's Fables to teach children moral values. Additionally, a group could sponsor a debate on whether there should be a constitutional amendment to permit prayer in public schools, and the Boy Scouts could meet "to influence a boy's character, development and spiritual growth." In short, any group that "promote[s] the moral and character development of children" is eligible to use the school building.

Just as there is no question that teaching morals and character development to children is a permissible purpose under Milford's policy, it is clear that the Club teaches morals and character development to children. For example, no one disputes that the Club instructs children to overcome feelings of jealousy, to treat others well regardless of how they treat the children, and to be obedient, even if it does so in a nonsecular way. Nonetheless, because Milford found the Club's activities to be religious in nature—"the equivalent of religious instruction itself," 202 F.3d, at 507—it excluded the Club from use of its facilities.

Applying *Lamb's Chapel*, we find it quite clear that Milford engaged in viewpoint discrimination when it excluded the Club from the afterschool forum. In *Lamb's Chapel*, the local New York school district similarly had adopted § 414's "social, civic or recreational use" category as a permitted use in its limited public forum. The district also prohibited use "by any group for religious purposes." 508 U.S., at 387. Citing this prohibition, the school district excluded a church that wanted to present films teaching family values from a Christian perspective. We held that, because the films "no doubt dealt with a subject otherwise permissible" under the rule, the teaching of family values, the district's exclusion of the church was unconstitutional viewpoint discrimination. *Id.*, at 394.

Like the church in *Lamb's Chapel*, the Club seeks to address a subject otherwise permitted under the rule, the teaching of morals and character, from a religious standpoint. Certainly, one could have characterized the film presentations in *Lamb's Chapel* as a religious use, as the Court of Appeals did, *Lamb's Chapel v. Center Moriches Union Free School Dist.*, 959 F.2d 381, 388–389 (C.A.2 1992). And one easily could conclude that the films' purpose to instruct that "'society's slide toward humanism . . . can only be counterbalanced by a loving home where Christian values are instilled from an early age,'" *id.*, at 384, was "quintessentially religious," 202 F.3d, at 510. The only apparent difference between the activity of Lamb's Chapel and the activities of the Good News Club is that the Club chooses to teach moral lessons from a Christian perspective through live storytelling and prayer, whereas Lamb's Chapel taught lessons through films. This distinction is inconsequential. Both modes of speech use a religious viewpoint. Thus, the exclusion of the Good News Club's activities, like the exclusion of Lamb's Chapel's films, constitutes unconstitutional viewpoint discrimination.

Our opinion in *Rosenberger* also is dispositive. In *Rosenberger*, a student organization at the University of Virginia was denied funding for printing expenses because its publication, Wide Awake, offered a Christian viewpoint. Just as the Club emphasizes the role of Christianity in students' morals and character, Wide Awake "'challenge[d] Christians to live, in word and deed, according to the faith they proclaim and . . . encourage[d] students to consider what a personal relationship with Jesus Christ means.'" 515 U.S., at 826. Because the university "select[ed] for disfavored treatment those student journalistic efforts with religious editorial viewpoints," we held that the denial of funding was unconstitutional. *Id.*, at 831. Although in *Rosenberger* there was no prohibition on religion as a subject matter, our holding did not rely on this factor. Instead, we concluded simply that the university's denial of funding to print Wide Awake was viewpoint discrimination, just as the school district's refusal to allow Lamb's Chapel to show its films was viewpoint discrimination. *Ibid.* Given the obvious religious content of Wide Awake, we cannot say that the Club's activities are any more "religious" or deserve any less First Amendment protection than did the publication of Wide Awake in *Rosenberger*.

Despite our holdings in *Lamb's Chapel* and *Rosenberger*, the Court of Appeals, like Milford, believed that its characterization of the Club's activities as religious in nature warranted treating the Club's activities as different in kind from the other activities permitted by the school. See 202 F.3d, at 510 (the Club "is doing something other than simply teaching moral values"). The "Christian viewpoint" is unique, according to the court, because it contains an "additional layer" that other kinds of viewpoints do not. *Id.*, at 509. That is, the Club "is focused on teaching children how to cultivate their relationship with God through Jesus Christ," which it characterized as "quintessentially religious." *Id.*, at 510. With these observations, the court concluded that, because the Club's activities "fall outside the bounds of pure 'moral and character development,'" the exclusion did not constitute viewpoint discrimination. *Id.*, at 511.

We disagree that something that is "quintessentially religious" or "decidedly religious in nature" cannot also be characterized properly as the teaching of morals and character development from a particular viewpoint. See 202 F.3d, at 512 (Jacobs, J., dissenting) ("[W]hen the subject matter is morals and character, it is quixotic to attempt a distinction between religious viewpoints and religious subject matters"). What matters for purposes of the Free Speech Clause is that we can see no logical difference in kind between the invocation of Christianity by the Club and the invocation of teamwork, loyalty, or patriotism by other associations to provide a foundation for their lessons. It is apparent that the unstated principle of the Court of Appeals' reasoning is its conclusion that any time religious instruction and prayer are used to discuss morals and character, the discussion is simply not a "pure" discussion of those issues. According to the Court of Appeals, reliance on Christian principles taints moral and character instruction in a way that other foundations for thought or viewpoints do not. We, however, have never reached such a conclusion. Instead, we reaffirm our holdings in *Lamb's Chapel* and *Rosenberger* that speech discussing otherwise permissible subjects cannot be excluded from a limited public forum on the ground that the subject is discussed from a religious viewpoint. Thus, we conclude that Milford's exclusion of the Club from use of the school, pursuant to its community use policy, constitutes impermissible viewpoint discrimination.

IV

Milford argues that, even if its restriction constitutes viewpoint discrimination, its interest in not violating the Establishment Clause outweighs the Club's interest in gaining equal access to the school's facilities. In other words, according to Milford, its restriction was required to avoid violating the Establishment Clause. We disagree.

We have said that a state interest in avoiding an Establishment Clause violation "may be characterized as compelling," and therefore may justify content-based discrimination. *Widmar v. Vincent*, 454 U.S. 263, 271 (1981). However, it is not clear whether a State's interest in avoiding an Establishment Clause violation would justify viewpoint discrimination. See *Lamb's Chapel*, 508 U.S., at 394–395 (noting the suggestion in *Widmar* but ultimately not finding an Establishment Clause problem). We need not, however, confront the issue in this case, because we conclude that the school has no valid Establishment Clause interest.

We rejected Establishment Clause defenses similar to Milford's in two previous free speech cases, *Lamb's Chapel* and *Widmar*. In particular, in *Lamb's Chapel*, we explained that "[t]he showing of th[e] film series would not have been during school hours, would not have been sponsored by the school, and would have been open to the public, not just to church members." 508 U.S., at 395. Accordingly, we found that "there would have been no realistic danger that the community would think that the District was endorsing religion or any particular creed." *Ibid.* Likewise, in *Widmar*, where the university's forum was already available to other groups, this Court concluded that there was no Establishment Clause problem. 454 U.S., at 272–273, and n. 13.

The Establishment Clause defense fares no better in this case. As in *Lamb's Chapel*, the Club's meetings were held after school hours, not sponsored by the school, and open to any student who obtained parental consent, not just to Club members. As in *Widmar*, Milford made its forum available to other organizations. The Club's activities are materially indistinguishable from those in *Lamb's Chapel* and *Widmar*. Thus, Milford's reliance on the Establishment Clause is unavailing.

Milford attempts to distinguish *Lamb's Chapel* and *Widmar* by emphasizing that Milford's policy involves elementary school children. According to Milford, children will perceive that the school is endorsing the Club and will feel coercive pressure to participate, because the Club's activities take place on school grounds, even though they occur during nonschool hours. This argument is unpersuasive.

First, we have held that "a significant factor in upholding governmental programs in the face of Establishment Clause attack is their *neutrality* towards religion." *Rosenberger*, 515 U.S., at 839 (emphasis added). See also *Mitchell v. Helms*, 530 U.S. 793, 809 (2000) (plurality opinion)

("In distinguishing between indoctrination that is attributable to the State and indoctrination that is not, [the Court has] consistently turned to the principle of *neutrality*, upholding aid that is offered to a broad range of groups or persons without regard to their religion" (emphasis added)); *id.*, at 838 (O'CONNOR, J., concurring in judgment) ("[N]eutrality is an important reason for upholding government-aid programs against Establishment Clause challenges"). Milford's implication that granting access to the Club would do damage to the neutrality principle defies logic. For the "guarantee of neutrality is respected, not offended, when the government, following neutral criteria and evenhanded policies, extends benefits to recipients whose ideologies and viewpoints, including religious ones, are broad and diverse." *Rosenberger, supra*, at 839. The Good News Club seeks nothing more than to be treated neutrally and given access to speak about the same topics as are other groups. Because allowing the Club to speak on school grounds would ensure neutrality, not threaten it, Milford faces an uphill battle in arguing that the Establishment Clause compels it to exclude the Good News Club.

Second, to the extent we consider whether the community would feel coercive pressure to engage in the Club's activities, cf. *Lee v. Weisman*, 505 U.S. 577, 592–593 (1992), the relevant community would be the parents, not the elementary school children. It is the parents who choose whether their children will attend the Good News Club meetings. Because the children cannot attend without their parents' permission, they cannot be coerced into engaging in the Good News Club's religious activities. Milford does not suggest that the parents of elementary school children would be confused about whether the school was endorsing religion. Nor do we believe that such an argument could be reasonably advanced.

Third, whatever significance we may have assigned in the Establishment Clause context to the suggestion that elementary school children are more impressionable than adults, cf., *e.g.*, *id.*, at 592; *School Dist. of Grand Rapids v. Ball*, 473 U.S. 373, 390 (1985) (stating that "symbolism of a union between church and state is most likely to influence children of tender years, whose experience is limited and whose beliefs consequently are the function of environment as much as of free and voluntary choice"), we have never extended our Establishment Clause jurisprudence to foreclose private religious conduct during nonschool hours merely because it takes place on school premises where elementary school children may be present.

None of the cases discussed by Milford persuades us that our Establishment Clause jurisprudence has gone this far. For example, Milford cites *Lee v. Weisman* for the proposition that "there are heightened concerns with protecting freedom of conscience from subtle coercive pressure in the elementary and secondary public schools," 505 U.S., at 592. In *Lee*, however, we concluded that attendance at the graduation exercise was obligatory. *Id.*, at 586. See also *Santa Fe Independent School Dist. v. Doe*, 530 U.S. 290 (2000) (holding the school's policy of permitting prayer at football games unconstitutional where the activity took place during a school-sponsored event and not in a public forum). We did not place independent significance on the fact that the graduation exercise might take place on school premises, *Lee, supra*, at 583. Here, where the school facilities are being used for a nonschool function and there is no government sponsorship of the Club's activities, *Lee* is inapposite.

Equally unsupportive is *Edwards v. Aguillard*, 482 U.S. 578 (1987), in which we held that a Louisiana law that proscribed the teaching of evolution as part of the public school curriculum, unless accompanied by a lesson on creationism, violated the Establishment Clause. In *Edwards*, we mentioned that students are susceptible to pressure in the classroom, particularly given their possible reliance on teachers as role models. See *id.*, at 584. But we did not discuss this concern in our application of the law to the facts. Moreover, we did note that mandatory attendance requirements meant that state advancement of religion in a school would be particularly harshly felt by impressionable students.[6] But we did not suggest that, when the school was not actually advancing religion, the impressionability of students would be relevant to the Establishment Clause issue. Even if *Edwards* had articulated the principle Milford believes it did, the facts in *Edwards* are simply too remote from those here to give the principle any weight. *Edwards* involved the content of the curriculum taught by state teachers during the schoolday to children required to attend. Obviously, when individuals who are not schoolteachers are giving lessons after school to children permitted to attend only with parental consent, the concerns expressed in *Edwards* are not present.[7]

Fourth, even if we were to consider the possible misperceptions by schoolchildren in deciding whether Milford's permitting the Club's activities would violate the Establishment Clause, the facts of this case simply do not support Milford's conclusion. There is no evidence that young children are permitted to loiter outside classrooms after the schoolday has ended. Surely even young children are aware of events for which their parents must sign permission forms. The meetings were held in a combined high school resource room and middle school special education room, not in an elementary school classroom. The instructors are not schoolteachers. And the children in the group are not all the same age as in the normal classroom setting; their ages range from 6 to 12.[8] In sum, these circumstances simply do not support the theory that small children would perceive endorsement here.

Finally, even if we were to inquire into the minds of schoolchildren in this case, we cannot say the danger that children would misperceive the endorsement of religion is any greater than the danger that they would perceive a hostility toward the religious viewpoint if the Club were excluded from the public forum. This concern is particularly acute given the reality that Milford's building is not used only for elementary school children. Students, from

6. Milford also cites *Illinois ex rel. McCollum v. Board of Ed. of School Dist. No. 71, Champaign Cty.*, 333 U.S. 203 (1948), for its position that the Club's religious element would be advanced by the State through compulsory attendance laws. In *McCollum*, the school district excused students from their normal classroom study during the regular schoolday to attend classes taught by sectarian religious teachers, who were subject to approval by the school superintendent. Under these circumstances, this Court found it relevant that "[t]he operation of the State's compulsory education system... assist [ed] and [wa]s integrated with the program of religious instruction carried on by separate religious sects." *Id.*, at 209. In the present case, there is simply no integration and cooperation between the school district and the Club. The Club's activities take place after the time when the children are compelled by state law to be at the school.

7. Milford also refers to *Board of Ed. of Westside Community Schools (Dist. 66) v. Mergens*, 496 U.S. 226 (1990), to support its view that "assumptions about the ability of students to make... subtle distinctions [between schoolteachers during the schoolday and Reverend Fournier after school] are less valid for elementary age children who tend to be less informed, more impressionable, and more subject to peer pressure than average adults." Brief for Respondent 19. Four Justices in *Mergens* believed that high school students likely are capable of distinguishing between government and private endorsement of religion. See 496 U.S., at 250–251 (opinion of O'Connor, J.). The opinion, however, made no statement about how capable of discerning endorsement elementary school children would have been in the context of *Mergens*, where the activity at issue was after school. In any event, even to the extent elementary school children are more prone to peer pressure than are older children, it simply is not clear what, in this case, they could be pressured to do.

8. Milford also relies on the Equal Access Act, 98 Stat. 1302, 20 U.S.C. §§ 4071–4074, as evidence that Congress has recognized the vulnerability of elementary school children to misperceiving endorsement of religion. The Act, however, makes no express recognition of the impressionability of elementary school children. It applies only to public secondary schools and makes no mention of elementary schools. § 4071(a). We can derive no meaning from the choice by Congress not to address elementary schools.

kindergarten through the 12th grade, all attend school in the same building. There may be as many, if not more, upperclassmen as elementary school children who occupy the school after hours. For that matter, members of the public writ large are permitted in the school after hours pursuant to the community use policy. Any bystander could conceivably be aware of the school's use policy and its exclusion of the Good News Club, and could suffer as much from viewpoint discrimination as elementary school children could suffer from perceived endorsement. Cf. *Rosenberger*, 515 U.S., at 835–836 (expressing the concern that viewpoint discrimination can chill individual thought and expression).

We cannot operate, as Milford would have us do, under the assumption that any risk that small children would perceive endorsement should counsel in favor of excluding the Club's religious activity. We decline to employ Establishment Clause jurisprudence using a modified heckler's veto, in which a group's religious activity can be proscribed on the basis of what the youngest members of the audience might misperceive. Cf. *Capitol Square Review and Advisory Bd. v. Pinette*, 515 U.S. 753, 779–780 (1995) (O'Connor, J., concurring in part and concurring in judgment) ("[B]ecause our concern is with the political community writ large, the endorsement inquiry is *not about the perceptions of particular individuals* or saving isolated nonadherents from... discomfort.... It is for this reason that the reasonable observer in the endorsement inquiry must be deemed aware of the history and context of the community and forum in which the religious [speech takes place]" (emphasis added)). There are countervailing constitutional concerns related to rights of other individuals in the community. In this case, those countervailing concerns are the free speech rights of the Club and its members. Cf. *Rosenberger, supra*, at 835 ("Vital First Amendment speech principles are at stake here"). And, we have already found that those rights have been violated, not merely perceived to have been violated, by the school's actions toward the Club.

We are not convinced that there is any significance in this case to the possibility that elementary school children may witness the Good News Club's activities on school premises, and therefore we can find no reason to depart from our holdings in *Lamb's Chapel* and *Widmar*. Accordingly, we conclude that permitting the Club to meet on the school's premises would not have violated the Establishment Clause.[9]

V

When Milford denied the Good News Club access to the school's limited public forum on the ground that the Club was religious in nature, it discriminated against the Club because of its religious viewpoint in violation of the Free Speech Clause of the First Amendment. Because Milford has not raised a valid Establishment Clause claim, we do not address the question whether such a claim could excuse Milford's viewpoint discrimination.

9. Both parties have briefed the Establishment Clause issue extensively, and neither suggests that a remand would be of assistance on this issue. Although Justice Souter would prefer that a record be developed on several facts, and Justice Breyer believes that development of those facts could yet be dispositive in this case (opinion concurring in part), none of these facts is relevant to the Establishment Clause inquiry. For example, Justice Souter suggests that we cannot determine whether there would be an Establishment Clause violation unless we know when, and to what extent, other groups use the facilities. When a limited public forum is available for use by groups presenting any viewpoint, however, we would not find an Establishment Clause violation simply because only groups presenting a religious viewpoint have opted to take advantage of the forum at a particular time.

The judgment of the Court of Appeals is reversed, and the case is remanded for further proceedings consistent with this opinion....

JUSTICE SCALIA, concurring.

I join the Court's opinion but write separately to explain further my views on two issues.

I

First, I join Part IV of the Court's opinion, regarding the Establishment Clause issue, with the understanding that its consideration of coercive pressure, and perceptions of endorsement, "to the extent" that the law makes such factors relevant, is consistent with the belief (which I hold) that in this case that extent is zero. As to coercive pressure: Physical coercion is not at issue here; and so-called "peer pressure," if it can even be considered coercion, is, when it arises from private activities, one of the attendant consequences of a freedom of association that is constitutionally protected, see, *e.g.*, *Roberts v. United States Jaycees*, 468 U.S. 609, 622 (1984); *NAACP v. Alabama ex rel. Patterson*, 357 U.S. 449, 460–461 (1958). What is at play here is not coercion, but the compulsion of ideas—and the private right to exert and receive that compulsion (or to have one's children receive it) is protected by the Free Speech and Free Exercise Clauses, see, *e.g.*, *Heffron v. International Soc. for Krishna Consciousness, Inc.*, 452 U.S. 640, 647 (1981); *Murdock v. Pennsylvania*, 319 U.S. 105, 108–109, 63 S.Ct. 870, 87 L.Ed. 1292 (1943); *Cantwell v. Connecticut*, 310 U.S. 296, 307–310 (1940), not banned by the Establishment Clause. A priest has as much liberty to proselytize as a patriot.

As to endorsement, I have previously written that "[r]eligious expression cannot violate the Establishment Clause where it (1) is purely private and (2) occurs in a traditional or designated public forum, publicly announced and open to all on equal terms." *Capitol Square Review and Advisory Bd. v. Pinette*, 515 U.S. 753, 770 (1995). The same is true of private speech that occurs in a limited public forum, publicly announced, whose boundaries are not drawn to favor religious groups but instead permit a cross-section of uses. In that context, which is this case, "erroneous conclusions [about endorsement] do not count." *Id.*, at 765. See also *Lamb's Chapel v. Center Moriches Union Free School Dist.*, 508 U.S. 384, 401 (1993) (SCALIA, J., concurring in judgment) ("I would hold, simply and clearly, that giving [a private religious group] nondiscriminatory access to school facilities cannot violate [the Establishment Clause] because it does not signify state or local embrace of a particular religious sect").

II

Second, since we have rejected the only reason that respondent gave for excluding the Club's speech from a forum that clearly included it (the forum was opened to any "us[e] pertaining to the welfare of the community"), I do not suppose it matters whether the exclusion is characterized as viewpoint or subject-matter discrimination. Lacking any legitimate reason for excluding the Club's speech from its forum—"because it's religious" will not do, see, *e.g.*, *Church of Lukumi Babalu Aye, Inc. v. Hialeah*, 508 U.S. 520, 532–533, 546 (1993); *Employment Div., Dept. of Human Resources of Ore. v. Smith*, 494 U.S. 872, 877–878 (1990)—respondent would seem to fail First Amendment scrutiny regardless of how its action is characterized. Even subject-matter limits must at least be "reasonable in light of the purpose served by the forum," *Cornelius v. NAACP Legal Defense & Ed. Fund, Inc.*, 473 U.S. 788, 806 (1985). But I agree, in any event, that respondent did discriminate on the basis of viewpoint.

As I understand it, the point of disagreement between the Court and the dissenters (and the Court of Appeals) with regard to petitioner's Free Speech Clause claim is not whether the Good News Club must be permitted to present religious viewpoints on morals and character in respondent's forum, which has been opened to secular discussions of that subject.[2] The answer to that is established by our decision in *Lamb's Chapel, supra*. The point of disagreement is not even whether some of the Club's religious speech fell within the protection of *Lamb's Chapel*. It certainly did. See... 202 F.3d 502, 509 (C.A.2 2000) (the Club's "teachings may involve secular values such as obedience or resisting jealousy").

The disagreement, rather, regards the portions of the Club's meetings that are not "purely" "discussions" of morality and character from a religious viewpoint. The Club, for example, urges children "who already believe in the Lord Jesus as their Savior" to "[s]top and ask God for the strength and the 'want'... to obey Him," 21 F.Supp.2d 147, 156 (N.D.N.Y. 1998) (internal quotation marks omitted), and it invites children who "don't know Jesus as Savior" to "trust the Lord Jesus to be [their] Savior from sin," *ibid*. The dissenters and the Second Circuit say that the presence of such additional speech, because it is purely religious, transforms the Club's meetings into something different in kind from other, nonreligious activities that teach moral and character development. Therefore, the argument goes, excluding the Club is not viewpoint discrimination. I disagree.

Respondent has opened its facilities to any "us[e] pertaining to the welfare of the community, provided that such us[e] shall be nonexclusive and shall be opened to the general public." Shaping the moral and character development of children certainly "pertain[s] to the welfare of the community." Thus, respondent has agreed that groups engaged in the endeavor of developing character may use its forum. The Boy Scouts, for example, may seek "to influence a boy's character, development and spiritual growth," cf. *Boy Scouts of America v. Dale*, 530 U.S. 640, 649 (2000) ("[T]he general mission of the Boy Scouts is clear: '[t]o instill values in young people'" (quoting the Scouts' mission statement)), and a group may use Aesop's Fables to teach moral values. When the Club attempted to teach Biblical-based moral values, however, it was excluded because its activities "d[id] not involve merely a religious perspective on the secular subject of morality" and because "it [was] clear from the conduct of the meetings that the Good News Club goes far beyond merely stating its viewpoint." 202 F.3d, at 510.

From no other group does respondent require the sterility of speech that it demands of petitioners. The Boy Scouts could undoubtedly buttress their exhortations to keep "morally straight" and live "clean" lives, see *Boy Scouts of America v. Dale, supra*, at 649, by giving reasons why that is a good idea—because parents want and expect it, because it will make the scouts "better" and "more successful" people, because it will emulate such admired past Scouts as former President Gerald Ford. The Club, however, may only discuss morals and character, and cannot give its reasons why they should be fostered—because God wants and expects it, because it will make the Club members "saintly" people, and because it emulates Jesus Christ. The Club may not, in other words, independently discuss the religious premise on which its views are based—that God exists and His assistance is necessary to morality. It may not defend the premise, and it absolutely must not seek to persuade the children that the premise is true. The children must, so to say, take it on faith. This is blatant viewpoint discrimination. Just as calls to character based on patriotism will go unanswered if the listeners

2. Neither does the disagreement center on the mode of the Club's speech—the fact that it sings songs and plays games. Although a forum could perhaps be opened to lectures but not plays, debates but not concerts, respondent has placed no such restrictions on the use of its facilities.

do not believe their country is good and just, calls to moral behavior based on God's will are useless if the listeners do not believe that God exists. Effectiveness in presenting a viewpoint rests on the persuasiveness with which the speaker defends his premise—and in respondent's facilities every premise but a religious one may be defended.

In *Rosenberger v. Rector and Visitors of Univ. of Va.*, 515 U.S. 819 (1995), we struck down a similar viewpoint restriction. There, a private student newspaper sought funding from a student-activity fund on the same basis as its secular counterparts. And though the paper printed such directly religious material as exhortations to belief, see *id.*, at 826 (quoting the paper's self-described mission "'to encourage students to consider what a personal relationship with Jesus Christ means'"); *id.*, at 865 (SOUTER, J., dissenting) ("'The only way to salvation through Him is by confessing and repenting of sin. It is the Christian's duty to make sinners aware of their need for salvation'" (quoting the paper)); see also *id.*, at 865–867 (quoting other examples), we held that refusing to provide the funds discriminated on the basis of viewpoint, because the religious speech had been used to "provid[e] . . . a specific premise . . . from which a variety of subjects may be discussed and considered," *id.*, at 831 (opinion of the Court). The right to present a viewpoint based on a religion premise carried with it the right to defend the premise.

The dissenters emphasize that the religious speech used by the Club as the foundation for its views on morals and character is not just any type of religious speech—although they cannot agree exactly what type of religious speech it is. In JUSTICE STEVENS's view, it is speech "aimed principally at proselytizing or inculcating belief in a particular religious faith." This does not, to begin with, distinguish *Rosenberger*, which also involved proselytizing speech, as the above quotations show. See also *Rosenberger*, *supra*, at 844 (referring approvingly to the dissent's description of the paper as a "wor[k] characterized by . . . evangelism"). But in addition, it does not distinguish the Club's activities from those of the other groups using respondent's forum—which have not, as JUSTICE STEVENS suggests, been restricted to roundtable "discussions" of moral issues. Those groups may seek to inculcate children with their beliefs, and they may furthermore "recruit others to join their respective groups." The Club must therefore have liberty to do the same, even if, as JUSTICE STEVENS fears without support in the record, see *ibid.*, its actions may prove (shudder!) divisive. See *Lamb's Chapel*, 508 U.S., at 395 (remarking that worries about "public unrest" caused by "proselytizing" are "difficult to defend as a reason to deny the presentation of a religious point of view"); cf. *Lynch v. Donnelly*, 465 U.S. 668, 684–685 (1984) (holding that "political divisiveness" could not invalidate inclusion of creche in municipal Christmas display); *Cantwell v. Connecticut*, 310 U.S., at 310–311.

JUSTICE SOUTER, while agreeing that the Club's religious speech "may be characterized as proselytizing," thinks that it is even more clearly excludable from respondent's forum because it is essentially "an evangelical service of worship." But we have previously rejected the attempt to distinguish worship from other religious speech, saying that "the distinction has [no] intelligible content," and further, no "relevance" to the constitutional issue. *Widmar v. Vincent*, 454 U.S. 263, 269, n. 6 (1981); see also *Murdock v. Pennsylvania*, 319 U.S., at 109 (refusing to distinguish evangelism from worship). Those holdings are surely proved correct today by the dissenters' inability to agree, even between themselves, into which subcategory of religious speech the Club's activities fell. If the distinction did have content, it would be beyond the courts' competence to administer. *Widmar v. Vincent*, *supra*, at 269, n. 6; cf. *Lee v. Weisman*, 505 U.S. 577, 616–617 (1992) (SOUTER, J., concurring) ("I can hardly imagine a subject less amenable to the competence of the federal judiciary, or more deliberately to be avoided where possible," than "comparative theology"). And if courts (and other government officials) were competent, applying the distinction would require state monitoring of private, religious speech with a degree of pervasiveness that we have previously found unacceptable. See, *e.g.*, *Rosenberger v. Rector and Visitors of Univ. of Va.*, *supra*, at 844–845; *Widmar v. Vincent*, *supra*, at 269, n. 6. I will not endorse an approach that suffers such a wondrous diversity of flaws.

With these words of explanation, I join the opinion of the Court.

JUSTICE BREYER, concurring in part.

I agree with the Court's conclusion and join its opinion to the extent that they are consistent with the following three observations. First, the government's "neutrality" in respect to religion is one, but only one, of the considerations relevant to deciding whether a public school's policy violates the Establishment Clause. See, *e.g.*, *Mitchell v. Helms*, 530 U.S. 793, 839 (2000) (O'CONNOR, J., concurring in judgment); *Capitol Square Review and Advisory Bd. v. Pinette*, 515 U.S. 753, 774, 777 (1995) (O'CONNOR, J., concurring in part and concurring in judgment). As this Court previously has indicated, a child's perception that the school has endorsed a particular religion or religion in general may also prove critically important. See *School Dist. of Grand Rapids v. Ball*, 473 U.S. 373, 389–390 (1985); see also *Lamb's Chapel v. Center Moriches Union Free School Dist.*, 508 U.S. 384, 395 (1993); *County of Allegheny v. American Civil Liberties Union, Greater Pittsburgh Chapter*, 492 U.S. 573, 592–594 (1989). Today's opinion does not purport to change that legal principle.

Second, the critical Establishment Clause question here may well prove to be whether a child, participating in the Good News Club's activities, could reasonably perceive the school's permission for the Club to use its facilities as an endorsement of religion. See *Ball*, *supra*, at 390 ("[A]n important concern of the effects test is whether...the challenged government action is sufficiently likely to be perceived by adherents of the controlling denominations as an endorsement, and by the nonadherents as a disapproval, of their individual religious choices"). The time of day, the age of the children, the nature of the meetings, and other specific circumstances are relevant in helping to determine whether, in fact, the Club "so dominate[s]" the "forum" that, in the children's minds, "a formal policy of equal access is transformed into a demonstration of approval." *Capitol Square Review and Advisory Bd.*, *supra*, at 777 (O'CONNOR, J., concurring in part and concurring in judgment).

Third, the Court cannot fully answer the Establishment Clause question this case raises, given its procedural posture. The specific legal action that brought this case to the Court of Appeals was the District Court's decision to grant Milford Central School's motion for summary judgment. The Court of Appeals affirmed the grant of summary judgment. We now hold that the school was not entitled to summary judgment, either in respect to the Free Speech or the Establishment Clause issue. Our holding must mean that, *viewing the disputed facts* (including facts about the children's perceptions) *favorably to the Club* (the nonmoving party), the school has not shown an Establishment Clause violation.

To deny one party's motion for summary judgment, however, is not to grant summary judgment for the other side. There may be disputed "genuine issue[s]" of "material fact," Fed. Rule Civ. Proc. 56(c), particularly about how a reasonable child participant would understand the school's role. Indeed, the Court itself points to facts not in evidence, ("There is no evidence that young children are permitted to loiter outside classrooms after the schoolday has ended")...("There may be as many, if not more, upperclassmen as elementary school children who occupy the school after hours"), identifies facts in evidence which may, depending on other facts not in evidence, be of legal significance (discussing the type of room in which the meetings were held and noting that the Club's participants "are not all the same age as in the normal classroom setting"), and makes assumptions about other facts. ("Surely even young children are aware of events for which their parents must sign permission forms")...("Any bystander could conceivably be aware of the school's use policy and its exclusion of the Good News Club, and could suffer as much from viewpoint discrimination as elementary school children could suffer from perceived endorsement"). The Court's invocation of what is missing from the record and its assumptions about what is present in the record only confirm that both parties, if they so desire, should have a fair opportunity to fill the evidentiary gap in light of today's opinion....

Justice Stevens, dissenting.

The Milford Central School has invited the public to use its facilities for educational and recreational purposes, but not for "religious purposes." Speech for "religious purposes" may reasonably be understood to encompass three different categories. First, there is religious speech that is simply speech about a particular topic from a religious point of view. The film in *Lamb's Chapel v. Center Moriches Union Free School Dist.*, 508 U.S. 384 (1993), illustrates this category. See *id.*, at 388 (observing that the film series at issue in that case "would discuss Dr. [James] Dobson's views on the undermining influences of the media that could only be counterbalanced by returning to traditional, Christian family values instilled at an early stage"). Second, there is religious speech that amounts to worship, or its equivalent. Our decision in *Widmar v. Vincent*, 454 U.S. 263 (1981), concerned such speech. See *id.*, at 264–265 (describing the speech in question as involving "religious worship"). Third, there is an intermediate category that is aimed principally at proselytizing or inculcating belief in a particular religious faith.

A public entity may not generally exclude even religious worship from an open public forum. *Id.*, at 276. Similarly, a public entity that creates a limited public forum for the discussion of certain specified topics may not exclude a speaker simply because she approaches those topics from a religious point of view. Thus, in *Lamb's Chapel* we held that a public school that permitted its facilities to be used for the discussion of family issues and child rearing could not deny access to speakers presenting a religious point of view on those issues. See 508 U.S., at 393–394.

But, while a public entity may not censor speech about an authorized topic based on the point of view expressed by the speaker, it has broad discretion to "preserve the property under its control for the use to which it is lawfully dedicated." *Greer v. Spock*, 424 U.S. 828, 836 (1976); see also *Board of Ed. of Westside Community Schools (Dist. 66) v. Mergens*, 496 U.S. 226, 275, n. 6 (1990) (Stevens, J., dissenting) ("A school's extracurricular activities constitute a part of the school's teaching mission, and the school accordingly must make 'decisions concerning the content of those activities'" (quoting *Widmar*, 454 U.S., at 278 (Stevens, J., concurring in judgment)). Accordingly, "control over access to a nonpublic forum can be based on subject matter and speaker identity so long as the distinctions drawn are reasonable in light of the purpose served by the forum and are viewpoint neutral." *Cornelius v. NAACP Legal Defense & Ed. Fund, Inc.*, 473 U.S. 788, 806 (1985). The novel question that this case presents concerns the constitutionality of a public school's attempt to limit the scope of a public forum it has created. More specifically, the question is whether a school can, consistently with the First Amendment, create a limited public forum that admits the first type of religious speech without allowing the other two.

Distinguishing speech from a religious viewpoint, on the one hand, from religious proselytizing, on the other, is comparable to distinguishing meetings to discuss political issues from meetings whose principal purpose is to recruit new members to join a political organization. If a school decides to authorize after-school discussions of current events in its classrooms, it may not exclude people from expressing their views simply because it dislikes their particular political opinions. But must it therefore allow organized political groups—for example, the Democratic Party, the Libertarian Party, or the Ku Klux Klan—to hold meetings, the principal purpose of which is not to discuss the current-events topic from their own unique point of view but rather to recruit others to join their respective groups? I think not. Such recruiting meetings may introduce divisiveness and tend to separate young children into cliques that undermine the school's educational mission. Cf. *Lehman v. Shaker Heights*, 418 U.S. 298 (1974) (upholding a city's refusal to allow "political advertising" on public transportation).

School officials may reasonably believe that evangelical meetings designed to convert children to a particular religious faith pose the same risk. And, just as a school may allow meetings to discuss current events from a political perspective without also allowing organized political recruitment, so too can a school allow discussion of topics such as moral development from a religious (or nonreligious) perspective without thereby opening its forum to religious proselytizing or worship.... Moreover, any doubt on a question such as this should be resolved in a way that minimizes "intrusion by the Federal Government into the operation of our public schools," *Mergens*, 496 U.S., at 290 (STEVENS, J., dissenting); see also *Epperson v. Arkansas*, 393 U.S. 97, 104 (1968) ("Judicial interposition in the operation of the public school system of the Nation raises problems requiring care and restraint.... By and large, public education in our Nation is committed to the control of state and local authorities").

The particular limitation of the forum at issue in this case is one that prohibits the use of the school's facilities for "religious purposes." It is clear that, by "religious purposes," the school district did not intend to exclude all speech from a religious point of view. Instead, it sought only to exclude religious speech whose principal goal is to "promote the gospel." In other words, the school sought to allow the first type of religious speech while excluding the second and third types. As long as this is done in an evenhanded manner, I see no constitutional violation in such an effort.[1] The line between the various categories of religious speech may be difficult to draw, but I think that the distinctions are valid, and that a school, particularly an elementary school, must be permitted to draw them. Cf. *Illinois ex rel. McCollum v. Board of Ed. of School Dist. No. 71, Champaign Cty.*, 333 U.S. 203, 231 (1948) (Frankfurter, J., concurring) ("In no activity of the State is it more vital to keep out divisive forces than in its schools...").

This case is undoubtedly close. Nonetheless, regardless of whether the Good News Club's activities amount to "worship," it does seem clear, based on the facts in the record, that the school district correctly classified those activities as falling within the third category of religious speech and therefore beyond the scope of the school's limited public forum.[3] In short, I am

1. The school district, for example, could not, consistently with its present policy, allow school facilities to be used by a group that affirmatively attempted to inculcate nonbelief in God or in the view that morality is wholly unrelated to belief in God. Nothing in the record, however, indicates that any such group was allowed to use school facilities.

3. The majority elides the distinction between religious speech on a particular topic and religious speech that seeks primarily to inculcate belief. Thus, it relies on *Rosenberger v. Rector and Visitors of Univ. of Va.*, 515 U.S. 819 (1995), as if that case involved precisely the same type of speech that is at issue here. But, while both Wide

persuaded that the school district could (and did) permissibly exclude from its limited public forum proselytizing religious speech that does not rise to the level of actual worship. I would therefore affirm the judgment of the Court of Appeals.

Even if I agreed with Part II of the majority opinion, however, I would not reach out, as it does in Part IV, to decide a constitutional question that was not addressed by either the District Court or the Court of Appeals.

Accordingly, I respectfully dissent.

Justice Souter, with whom Justice Ginsburg joins, dissenting.

The majority rules on two issues. First, it decides that the Court of Appeals failed to apply the rule in *Lamb's Chapel v. Center Moriches Union Free School Dist.*, 508 U.S. 384 (1993), which held that the government may not discriminate on the basis of viewpoint in operating a limited public forum. The majority applies that rule and concludes that Milford violated *Lamb's Chapel* in denying Good News the use of the school. The majority then goes on to determine that it would not violate the Establishment Clause of the First Amendment for the Milford School District to allow the Good News Club to hold its intended gatherings of public school children in Milford's elementary school. The majority is mistaken on both points. The Court of Appeals unmistakably distinguished this case from *Lamb's Chapel*, though not by name, and accordingly affirmed the application of a policy, unchallenged in the District Court, that Milford's public schools may not be used for religious purposes. As for the applicability of the Establishment Clause to the Good News Club's intended use of Milford's school, the majority commits error even in reaching the issue, which was addressed neither by the Court of Appeals nor by the District Court. I respectfully dissent.

I

Lamb's Chapel, a case that arose (as this one does) from application of N.Y. Educ. Law § 414 (McKinney 2000) and local policy implementing it, built on the accepted rule that a government body may designate a public forum subject to a reasonable limitation on the scope of permitted subject matter and activity, so long as the government does not use the forum-defining restrictions to deny expression to a particular viewpoint on subjects open to discussion. Specifically, *Lamb's Chapel* held that the government could not "permit school property to be used for the presentation of all views about family issues and child rearing except those dealing with the subject matter from a religious standpoint." 508 U.S., at 393–394.

This case, like *Lamb's Chapel*, properly raises no issue about the reasonableness of Milford's criteria for restricting the scope of its designated public forum. Milford has opened school property for, among other things, "instruction in any branch of education, learning or the

Awake, the organization in *Rosenberger*, and the Good News Club engage in a mixture of different types of religious speech, the *Rosenberger* Court clearly believed that the first type of religious speech predominated in Wide Awake. It described that group's publications as follows:

> "The first issue had articles about racism, crisis pregnancy, stress, prayer, C.S. Lewis' ideas about evil and free will, and reviews of religious music. In the next two issues, Wide Awake featured stories about homosexuality, Christian missionary work, and eating disorders, as well as music reviews and interviews with University professors." *Id.*, at 826.

In contrast to Wide Awake's emphasis on providing Christian commentary on such a diverse array of topics, Good News Club meetings are dominated by religious exhortation. My position is therefore consistent with the Court's decision in *Rosenberger.*

arts" and for "social, civic and recreational meetings and entertainment events and other uses pertaining to the welfare of the community, provided that such uses shall be nonexclusive and shall be opened to the general public." But Milford has done this subject to the restriction that "[s]chool premises shall not be used... for religious purposes." As the District Court stated, Good News did "not object to the reasonableness of [Milford]'s policy that prohibits the use of [its] facilities for religious purposes."

The sole question before the District Court was, therefore, whether, in refusing to allow Good News's intended use, Milford was misapplying its unchallenged restriction in a way that amounted to imposing a viewpoint-based restriction on what could be said or done by a group entitled to use the forum for an educational, civic, or other permitted purpose. The question was whether Good News was being disqualified when it merely sought to use the school property the same way that the Milford Boy and Girl Scouts and the 4-H Club did. The District Court held on the basis of undisputed facts that Good News's activity was essentially unlike the presentation of views on secular issues from a religious standpoint held to be protected in *Lamb's Chapel*, and was instead activity precluded by Milford's unchallenged policy against religious use, even under the narrowest definition of that term.

The Court of Appeals understood the issue the same way. See 202 F.3d 502, 508 (C.A.2 2000) (Good News argues that "to exclude the Club because it teaches morals and values from a Christian perspective constitutes unconstitutional viewpoint discrimination"); *id.*, at 509 ("The crux of the Good News Club's argument is that the Milford school's application of the Community Use Policy to exclude the Club from its facilities is not viewpoint neutral").[1] The Court of Appeals also realized that the *Lamb's Chapel* criterion was the appropriate measure: "The activities of the Good News Club do not involve merely a religious perspective on the secular subject of morality." 202 F.3d, at 510. Cf. *Lamb's Chapel*, *supra*, at 393 (district could not exclude "religious standpoint" in discussion on child rearing and family values, an undisputed "use for social or civic purposes otherwise permitted" under the use policy).[2] The appeals court agreed with the District Court that the undisputed facts in this case differ from those in *Lamb's Chapel*, as night from day. A sampling of those facts shows why both courts were correct.

Good News's classes open and close with prayer. In a sample lesson considered by the District Court, children are instructed that "[t]he Bible tells us how we can have our sins forgiven by receiving the Lord Jesus Christ. It tells us how to live to please Him.... If you have received the Lord Jesus as your Saviour from sin, you belong to God's special group—His family." The lesson plan instructs the teacher to "lead a child to Christ," and, when reading a Bible verse, to "[e]mphasize that this verse is from the Bible, God's Word," and is "important—and true—because God said it." The lesson further exhorts the teacher to "[b]e sure to give an opportunity for the 'unsaved' children in your class to respond to the Gospel" and cautions against "neglect[ing] this responsibility."

1. The Court of Appeals held that any challenge to the policy's reasonableness was foreclosed by its own precedent, 202 F.3d, at 502, 509, a holding the majority leaves untouched.... In any event, the reasonableness of the forum limitation was beyond the scope of the appeal from summary judgment since the District Court had said explicitly that the religious use limitation was not challenged.

2. It is true, as the majority notes, that the Court of Appeals did not cite *Lamb's Chapel* by name. But it followed it in substance, and it did cite an earlier opinion written by the author of the panel opinion here, *Bronx Household of Faith v. Community School Dist. No. 10*, 127 F.3d 207 (C.A.2 1997), which discussed *Lamb's Chapel* at length.

While Good News's program utilizes songs and games, the heart of the meeting is the "challenge" and "invitation," which are repeated at various times throughout the lesson. During the challenge, "saved" children who "already believe in the Lord Jesus as their Savior" are challenged to "'stop and ask God for the strength and the "want"...to obey Him.'" They are instructed that

> "[i]f you know Jesus as your Savior, you need to place God first in your life. And if you don't know Jesus as Savior and if you would like to, then we will—we will pray with you separately, individually....And the challenge would be, those of you who know Jesus as Savior, you can rely on God's strength to obey Him." *Ibid.*

During the invitation, the teacher "invites" the "unsaved" children "'to trust the Lord Jesus to be your Savior from sin,'" and "'receiv[e] [him] as your Savior from sin.'" The children are then instructed that

> "[i]f you believe what God's Word says about your sin and how Jesus died and rose again for you, you can have His forever life today. Please bow your heads and close your eyes. If you have never believed on the Lord Jesus as your Savior and would like to do that, please show me by raising your hand. If you raised your hand to show me you want to believe on the Lord Jesus, please meet me so I can show you from God's Word how you can receive His everlasting life."

It is beyond question that Good News intends to use the public school premises not for the mere discussion of a subject from a particular, Christian point of view, but for an evangelical service of worship calling children to commit themselves in an act of Christian conversion. The majority avoids this reality only by resorting to the bland and general characterization of Good News's activity as "teaching of morals and character, from a religious standpoint." If the majority's statement ignores reality, as it surely does, then today's holding may be understood only in equally generic terms. Otherwise, indeed, this case would stand for the remarkable proposition that any public school opened for civic meetings must be opened for use as a church, synagogue, or mosque.

Justice Stevens distinguishes between proselytizing and worship (dissenting opinion), and distinguishes each from discussion reflecting a religious point of view. I agree with Justice Stevens that Good News's activities may be characterized as proselytizing and therefore as outside the purpose of Milford's limited forum. Like the Court of Appeals, I also believe Good News's meetings have elements of worship that put the club's activities further afield of Milford's limited forum policy, the legitimacy of which was unchallenged in the summary judgment proceeding.

II

I also respectfully dissent from the majority's refusal to remand on all other issues, insisting instead on acting as a court of first instance in reviewing Milford's claim that it would violate the Establishment Clause to grant Good News's application. Milford raised this claim to demonstrate a compelling interest for saying no to Good News, even on the erroneous assumption that *Lamb's Chapel's* public forum analysis would otherwise require Milford to say yes. Whereas the District Court and Court of Appeals resolved this case entirely on the ground that Milford's actions did not offend the First Amendment's Speech Clause, the majority now sees fit to rule on the application of the Establishment Clause, in derogation of this Court's proper role as a court of review. *E.g., National Collegiate Athletic Assn. v. Smith*, 525 U.S. 459, 470 (1999) ("[W]e do not decide in the first instance issues not decided below").

The Court's usual insistence on resisting temptations to convert itself into a trial court and on remaining a court of review is not any mere procedural nicety, and my objection to turning us into a district court here does not hinge on a preference for immutable procedural rules. Respect for our role as a reviewing court rests, rather, on recognizing that this Court can often learn a good deal from considering how a district court and a court of appeals have worked their way through a difficult issue. It rests on recognizing that an issue as first conceived may come to be seen differently as a case moves through trial and appeal; we are most likely to contribute something of value if we act with the benefit of whatever refinement may come in the course of litigation. And our customary refusal to become a trial court reflects the simple fact that this Court cannot develop a record as well as a trial court can. If I were a trial judge, for example, I would balk at deciding on summary judgment whether an Establishment Clause violation would occur here without having statements of undisputed facts or uncontradicted affidavits showing, for example, whether Good News conducts its instruction at the same time as school-sponsored extracurricular and athletic activities conducted by school staff and volunteers, whether any other community groups use school facilities immediately after classes end and how many students participate in those groups; and the extent to which Good News, with 28 students in its membership, may "dominate the forum" in a way that heightens the perception of official endorsement, *Rosenberger v. Rector and Visitors of Univ. of Va.*, 515 U.S. 819, 851 (1995) (O'CONNOR, J., concurring); see also *Widmar v. Vincent*, 454 U.S. 263, 274 (1981). We will never know these facts.

Of course, I am in no better position than the majority to perform an Establishment Clause analysis in the first instance. Like the majority, I lack the benefit that development in the District Court and Court of Appeals might provide, and like the majority I cannot say for sure how complete the record may be. I can, however, speak to the doubtful underpinnings of the majority's conclusion.

This Court has accepted the independent obligation to obey the Establishment Clause as sufficiently compelling to satisfy strict scrutiny under the First Amendment. See *id.*, at 271 ("[T]he interest of the [government] in complying with its constitutional obligations may be characterized as compelling"); *Lamb's Chapel*, 508 U.S., at 394. Milford's actions would offend the Establishment Clause if they carried the message of endorsing religion under the circumstances, as viewed by a reasonable observer. See *Capitol Square Review and Advisory Bd. v. Pinette*, 515 U.S. 753, 777 (1995) (O'CONNOR, J., concurring). The majority concludes that such an endorsement effect is out of the question in Milford's case, because the context here is "materially indistinguishable" from the facts in *Lamb's Chapel* and *Widmar*. In fact, the majority is in no position to say that, for the principal grounds on which we based our Establishment Clause holdings in those cases are clearly absent here.

In *Widmar*, we held that the Establishment Clause did not bar a religious student group from using a public university's meeting space for worship as well as discussion. As for the reasonable observers who might perceive government endorsement of religion, we pointed out that the forum was used by university students, who "are, of course, young adults," and, as such, "are less impressionable than younger students and should be able to appreciate that the University's policy is one of neutrality toward religion." 454 U.S., at 274, n. 14. To the same effect, we remarked that the "large number of groups meeting on campus" negated "any reasonable inference of University support from the mere fact of a campus meeting place." *Ibid.* Not only was the forum "available to a broad class of nonreligious as well as religious speakers," but there were, in fact, over 100 recognized student groups at the University, and an "absence of empirical evidence that religious groups [would] dominate [the University's] open forum." *Id.*, at 274–275; see also *id.*, at 274 ("The provision of benefits to so broad a spectrum of groups is an important index of secular effect"). And if all that had not been enough to show that the university-student use would probably create no impression of religious endorsement, we pointed out that the university in that case had issued a student handbook with the explicit disclaimer that "the University's name will not 'be identified in any way with the aims, policies, programs, products, or opinions of any organization or its members.'" *Id.*, at 274, n. 14.

Lamb's Chapel involved an evening film series on child rearing open to the general public (and, given the subject matter, directed at an adult audience). See 508 U.S., at 387, 395. There, school property "had repeatedly been used by a wide variety of private organizations," and we could say with some assurance that "[u]nder these circumstances . . . there would have been no realistic danger that the community would think that the District was endorsing religion or any particular creed. . . . " *Id.*, at 395.

What we know about this case looks very little like *Widmar* or *Lamb's Chapel.* The cohort addressed by Good News is not university students with relative maturity, or even high school pupils, but elementary school children as young as six.[4] The Establishment Clause cases have consistently recognized the particular impressionability of schoolchildren, see *Edwards v. Aguillard*, 482 U.S. 578, 583–584 (1987), and the special protection required for those in the elementary grades in the school forum, see *County of Allegheny v. American Civil Liberties Union, Greater Pittsburgh Chapter*, 492 U.S. 573, 620, n. 69 (1989). We have held the difference between college students and grade school pupils to be a "distinction [that] warrants a difference in constitutional results," *Edwards v. Aguillard, supra*, at 584, n. 5 (internal quotation marks and citation omitted).

Nor is Milford's limited forum anything like the sites for wide-ranging intellectual exchange that were home to the challenged activities in *Widmar* and *Lamb's Chapel.* See also *Rosenberger*, 515 U.S., at 850, 836–837. In *Widmar*, the nature of the university campus and the sheer number of activities offered precluded the reasonable college observer from seeing government endorsement in any one of them, and so did the time and variety of community use in the *Lamb's Chapel* case. See also *Rosenberger*, 515 U.S., at 850 ("Given this wide array of nonreligious, antireligious and competing religious viewpoints in the forum supported by the University, any perception that the University endorses one particular viewpoint would be illogical"); *id.*, at 836–837, 850 (emphasizing the array of university-funded magazines containing "widely divergent viewpoints" and the fact that believers in Christian evangelism competed on equal footing in the University forum with aficionados of "Plato, Spinoza, and Descartes," as well as "Karl Marx, Bertrand Russell, and Jean-Paul Sartre"); *Board of Ed. of Westside Community Schools (Dist. 66) v. Mergens*, 496 U.S. 226, 252 (1990) (plurality opinion)

4. It is certainly correct that parents are required to give permission for their children to attend Good News's classes (as parents are often required to do for a host of official school extracurricular activities), and correct that those parents would likely not be confused as to the sponsorship of Good News's classes. But the proper focus of concern in assessing effects includes the elementary school pupils who are invited to meetings, Lodging, Exh. X2, who see peers heading into classrooms for religious instruction as other classes end, and who are addressed by the "challenge" and "invitation." . . .

("To the extent that a religious club is merely one of many different student-initiated voluntary clubs, students should perceive no message of government endorsement of religion").

The timing and format of Good News's gatherings, on the other hand, may well affirmatively suggest the *imprimatur* of officialdom in the minds of the young children. The club is open solely to elementary students (not the entire community, as in *Lamb's Chapel*), only four outside groups have been identified as meeting in the school, and Good News is, seemingly, the only one whose instruction follows immediately on the conclusion of the official schoolday. Although school is out at 2:56 p.m., Good News apparently requested use of the school beginning at 2:30 on Tuesdays "during the school year," so that instruction could begin promptly at 3:00, at which time children who are compelled by law to attend school surely remain in the building. Good News's religious meeting follows regular school activities so closely that the Good News instructor must wait to begin until "the room is clear," and "people are out of the room," before starting proceedings in the classroom located next to the regular third- and fourth-grade rooms. In fact, the temporal and physical continuity of Good News's meetings with the regular school routine seems to be the whole point of using the school. When meetings were held in a community church, 8 or 10 children attended; after the school became the site, the number went up three-fold.

Even on the summary judgment record, then, a record lacking whatever supplementation the trial process might have led to, and devoid of such insight as the trial and appellate judges might have contributed in addressing the Establishment Clause, we can say this: there is a good case that Good News's exercises blur the line between public classroom instruction and private religious indoctrination, leaving a reasonable elementary school pupil unable to appreciate that the former instruction is the business of the school while the latter evangelism is not. Thus, the facts we know (or think we know) point away from the majority's conclusion, and while the consolation may be that nothing really gets resolved when the judicial process is so truncated, that is not much to recommend today's result.

NOTES AND QUESTIONS

1. What is the test for determining when state action violates the Establishment Clause? Is the test the Court applied in *Santa Fe Independent School District* the same test that the Court used in *Good News Club*?

2. In both cases, the Court must grapple with the question of state endorsement of religion. How does the state endorse religion in *Santa Fe Independent School District*? Why is there no state endorsement of religion in *Good News Club*?

3. Compare Justice Thomas's discussion of state endorsement in *Good News Club* with the Court's prior discussion of school sponsorship in *Kuhlmeier*. Are they consistent?

4. Why does Justice Thomas dissent in *Santa Fe Independent School District*? Why does Justice Stevens dissent in *Good News Club*? Are their views of the Establishment Clause diametrically opposed? How?

5. When does the state violate the Establishment Clause? Could a state constitutionally mandate a period of silence at the beginning of each school day in the public schools not "as a religious exercise" but as "an opportunity for silent prayer or for silent reflection on the anticipated activities of the day"? *Sherman ex rel. Sherman v. Koch*, 623 F.3d 501 (7th Cir. 2010).

Would a school district's policy requiring students to hear the following statement in their ninth-grade biology class violate the Establishment Clause?

> Because Darwin's Theory is a theory, it continues to be tested as new evidence is discovered. The Theory is not a fact. Gaps in the Theory exist for which there is no evidence. A theory is defined as a well-tested explanation that unifies a broad range of observations.
>
> Intelligent Design is an explanation of the origin of life that differs from Darwin's view. The reference book, Of Pandas and People, is available for students who might be interested in gaining an understanding of what Intelligent Design actually involves.
>
> With respect to any theory, students are encouraged to keep an open mind. The school leaves the discussion of the Origins of Life to individual students and their families. As a Standards-driven district, class instruction focuses upon preparing students to achieve proficiency on Standards-based assessments.

Kitzmiller v. Dover Area Sch. Dist., 400 F.Supp.2d 707, 708–709 (M.D. Pa. 2005).

6. In *Zelman v. Simmons-Harris*, 536 U.S. 639 (2002), the Supreme Court upheld the constitutional validity of a school-voucher system. In Cleveland, Ohio, a pilot program was established, permitting students in the Cleveland City Schools to attend a public or private school of their choice. The state provided tuition to each student based on financial need, up to a specified amount. Of the students receiving tuition assistance, 96 percent enrolled in religiously affiliated schools. The Court found no state endorsement of religion, because the law was neutral toward religion, provided assistance to families based on their residence and need, left the selection of schools to families, and was open to all schools, including those public schools adjacent to Cleveland.

When does state funding run afoul of the Establishment Clause? A state statute permits taxpayers who contribute to a student tuition organization (STO) (which, in turn, provides scholarship money to private schools) to receive a dollar-for-dollar tax credit up to five hundred dollars (one thousand dollars for married couples filing jointly) of the amount donated. However, in practice, the largest STOs limit their scholarships to a small number of sectarian schools. Consequently, students who wish to attend nonreligious private schools are disadvantaged. Does this violate the Establishment Clause by favoring religious over secular schools? See *Winn v. Arizona Christian School Tuition Organization*, 562 F.3d 1002 (9th Cir.), reversed on other grounds, 131 S.Ct. 1436 (2011).

Should the state ever fund religion? For a discussion of the reasons why such funding is ill conceived, see Micah Schwartzman, *Conscience, Speech, and Money*, 97 VA. L. REV. 317 (2011); Erwin Chemerinsky, *Why Church and State Should Be Separate*, 49 WM. & MARY L. REV. 2193 (2008); Laura S. Underkuffler, *Vouchers and Beyond: The Individual as Causative Agent in Establishment Clause Jurisprudence*, 75 IND. L.J. 167 (2000); Kathleen M. Sullivan, *Religion and Liberal Democracy*, 59 U. CHI. L. REV. 195 (1992).

7. Article 14 of the United Nations Convention on the Rights of the Child states:

> 1. States Parties shall respect the right of the child to freedom of thought, conscience and religion.
> 2. States Parties shall respect the rights and duties of the parents and, when applicable, legal guardians, to provide direction to the child in the exercise of his or her right in a manner consistent with the evolving capacities of the child.
> 3. Freedom to manifest one's religion or beliefs may be subject only to such limitations as are prescribed by law and are necessary to protect public safety, order, health or morals, or the fundamental rights and freedoms of others.

To what extent do you think the Convention is in accord with American law and constitutional principles?

B. Medical Decision Making

1. CONSTITUTIONAL FRAMEWORK

PARHAM V. J.R.
Supreme Court of the United States
442 U.S. 584 (1979)

Mr. Chief Justice Burger delivered the opinion of the Court.

The question presented in this appeal is what process is constitutionally due a minor child whose parents or guardian seek state administered institutional mental health care for the child and specifically whether an adversary proceeding is required prior to or after the commitment.

I

Appellee[1] J.R., a child being treated in a Georgia state mental hospital, was a plaintiff in this class action[2] based on 42 U.S.C. § 1983, in the District Court for the Middle District of Georgia. Appellants are the State's Commissioner of the Department of Human Resources, the Director of the Mental Health Division of the Department of Human Resources, and the Chief Medical Officer at the hospital where appellee was being treated. Appellee sought a declaratory judgment that Georgia's voluntary commitment procedures for children under the age of 18, Ga.Code §§ 88-503.1, 88-503.2 (1975),[3] violated the Due Process Clause of the Fourteenth Amendment and requested an injunction against their future enforcement.

1. Pending our review, one of the named plaintiffs before the District Court, J.L., died. Although the individual claim of J.L. is moot, we discuss the facts of this claim because, in part, they form the basis for the District Court's holding.

2. The class certified by the District Court, without objection by appellants, consisted "of all persons younger than 18 years of age now or hereafter received by any defendant for observation and diagnosis and/or detained for care and treatment at any 'facility' within the State of Georgia pursuant to" Ga.Code § 88-503.1 (1975). Although one witness testified that on any given day there may be 200 children in the class, in December 1975 there were only 140.

3. Section 88-503.1 provides:

"The superintendent of any facility may receive for observation and diagnosis . . . any individual under 18 years of age for whom such application is made by his parent or guardian. . . . If found to show evidence of mental illness and to be suitable for treatment, such person may be given care and treatment at such facility and such person may be detained by such facility for such period and under such conditions as may be authorized by law.

A three-judge District Court was convened pursuant to 28 U.S.C. §§ 2281 (1970 ed.) and 2284. After considering expert and lay testimony and extensive exhibits and after visiting two of the State's regional mental health hospitals, the District Court held that Georgia's statutory scheme was unconstitutional because it failed to protect adequately the appellees' due process rights. *J.L. v. Parham*, 412 F.Supp. 112, 139 (1976).

To remedy this violation, the court enjoined future commitments based on the procedures in the Georgia statute. It also commanded Georgia to appropriate and expend whatever amount was "reasonably necessary" to provide nonhospital facilities deemed by the appellant state officials to be the most appropriate for the treatment of those members of plaintiffs' class, n. 2, *supra*, who could be treated in a less drastic, nonhospital environment. 412 F.Supp., at 139.

Appellants challenged all aspects of the District Court's judgment. We noted probable jurisdiction, 431 U.S. 936, and heard argument during the 1977 Term. The case was then consolidated with *Secretary of Public Welfare v. Institutionalized Juveniles*, 442 U.S. 640, and reargued this Term.

J.L., a plaintiff before the District Court who is now deceased, was admitted in 1970 at the age of 6 years to Central State Regional Hospital in Milledgeville, Ga. Prior to his admission, J.L. had received outpatient treatment at the hospital for over two months. J.L.'s mother then requested the hospital to admit him indefinitely.

The admitting physician interviewed J.L. and his parents. He learned that J.L.'s natural parents had divorced and his mother had remarried. He also learned that J.L. had been expelled from school because he was uncontrollable. He accepted the parents' representation that the boy had been extremely aggressive and diagnosed the child as having a "hyper-kinetic reaction of childhood."

J.L.'s mother and stepfather agreed to participate in family therapy during the time their son was hospitalized. Under this program, J.L. was permitted to go home for short stays. Apparently his behavior during these visits was erratic. After several months, the parents requested discontinuance of the program.

In 1972, the child was returned to his mother and stepfather on a furlough basis, *i.e.*, he would live at home but go to school at the hospital. The parents found they were unable to control J.L. to their satisfaction, and this created family stress. Within two months, they requested his readmission to Central State. J.L.'s parents relinquished their parental rights to the county in 1974.

Although several hospital employees recommended that J.L. should be placed in a special foster home with "a warm, supported, truly involved couple," the Department of Family and Children Services was unable to place him in such a setting. On October 24, 1975, J.L. (with J.R.) filed this suit requesting an order of the court placing him in a less drastic environment suitable to his needs.

Section 88-503.2 provides:

"The superintendent of the facility shall discharge any voluntary patient who has recovered from his mental illness or who has sufficiently improved that the superintendent determines that hospitalization of the patient is no longer desirable."

Section 88-503 was amended in some respects in 1978, but references herein are to the provisions in effect at the time in question.

Appellee J.R. was declared a neglected child by the county and removed from his natural parents when he was three months old. He was placed in seven different foster homes in succession prior to his admission to Central State Hospital at the age of 7.

Immediately preceding his hospitalization, J.R. received outpatient treatment at a county mental health center for several months. He then began attending school where he was so disruptive and incorrigible that he could not conform to normal behavior patterns. Because of his abnormal behavior, J.R.'s seventh set of foster parents requested his removal from their home. The Department of Family and Children Services then sought his admission at Central State. The agency provided the hospital with a complete sociomedical history at the time of his admission. In addition, three separate interviews were conducted with J.R. by the admission team of the hospital.

It was determined that he was borderline retarded, and suffered an "unsocialized, aggressive reaction of childhood." It was recommended unanimously that he would "benefit from the structured environment" of the hospital and would "enjoy living and playing with boys of the same age."

J.R.'s progress was reexamined periodically. In addition, unsuccessful efforts were made by the Department of Family and Children Services during his stay at the hospital to place J.R. in various foster homes. On October 24, 1975, JR. (with J.L.) filed this suit requesting an order of the court placing him in a less drastic environment suitable to his needs.

Georgia Code § 88-503.1 (1975) provides for the voluntary admission to a state regional hospital of children such as J.L. and J.R. Under that provision, admission begins with an application for hospitalization signed by a "parent or guardian." Upon application, the superintendent of each hospital is given the power to admit temporarily any child for "observation and diagnosis." If, after observation, the superintendent finds "evidence of mental illness" and that the child is "suitable for treatment" in the hospital, then the child may be admitted "for such period and under such conditions as may be authorized by law."

Georgia's mental health statute also provides for the discharge of voluntary patients. Any child who has been hospitalized for more than five days may be discharged at the request of a parent or guardian. § 88-503.3(a) (1975). Even without a request for discharge, however, the superintendent of each regional hospital has an affirmative duty to release any child "who has recovered from his mental illness or who has sufficiently improved that the superintendent determines that hospitalization of the patient is no longer desirable." § 88-503.2 (1975).

Georgia's Mental Health Director has not published any statewide regulations defining what specific procedures each superintendent must employ when admitting a child under 18. Instead, each regional hospital's superintendent is responsible for the procedures in his or her facility. There is substantial variation among the institutions with regard to their admission procedures and their procedures for review of patients after they have been admitted. A brief description of the different hospitals' procedures will demonstrate the variety of approaches taken by the regional hospitals throughout the State.

Southwestern Hospital in Thomasville, Ga., was built in 1966. Its children and adolescent program was instituted in 1974. The children and adolescent unit in the hospital has a maximum capacity of 20 beds, but at the time of suit only 10 children were being treated there.

The Southwestern superintendent testified that the hospital has never admitted a voluntary child patient who was not treated previously by a community mental health clinic. If a mental health professional at the community clinic determines that hospital treatment may be helpful for a child, then clinic staff and hospital staff jointly evaluate the need for hospitalization, the proper treatment during hospitalization, and a likely release date. The initial admission decision thus is not made at the hospital.

After a child is admitted, the hospital has weekly reviews of his condition performed by its internal medical and professional staff. There also are monthly reviews of each child by a group composed of hospital staff not involved in the weekly reviews and by community clinic staff people. The average stay for each child who was being treated at Southwestern in 1975 was 100 days.

Atlanta Regional Hospital was opened in 1968. At the time of the hearing before the District Court, 17 children and 21 adolescents were being treated in the hospital's children and adolescent unit.

The hospital is affiliated with nine community mental health centers and has an agreement with them that "persons will be treated in the comprehensive community mental health centers in every possible instance, rather than being hospitalized." The admission criteria at Atlanta Regional for voluntary and involuntary patients are the same. It has a formal policy not to admit a voluntary patient unless the patient is found to be a threat to himself or others. The record discloses that approximately 25 percent of all referrals from the community centers are rejected by the hospital admissions staff.

After admission, the staff reviews the condition of each child every week. In addition, there are monthly utilization reviews by nonstaff mental health professionals; this review considers a random sample of children's cases. The average length of each child's stay in 1975 was 161 days.

The Georgia Mental Health Institute (GMHI) in Decatur, Ga., was built in 1965. Its children and adolescent unit housed 26 children at the time this suit was brought.

The hospital has a formal affiliation with four community mental health centers. Those centers may refer patients to the hospital only if they certify that "no appropriate alternative resources are available within the client's geographic area." For the year prior to the trial in this case, no child was admitted except through a referral from a clinic. Although the hospital has a policy of generally accepting for 24 hours all referrals from a community clinic, it has a team of staff members who review each admission. If the team finds "no reason not to treat in the community" and the deputy superintendent of the hospital agrees, then it will release the applicant to his home.

After a child is admitted, there must be a review of the admission decision within 30 days. There is also an unspecified periodic review of each child's need for hospitalization by a team of staff members. The average stay for the children who were at GMHI in 1975 was 346 days.

Augusta Regional Hospital was opened in 1969 and is affiliated with 10 community mental health clinics. Its children and adolescent unit housed 14 children in December 1975.

Approximately 90 percent of the children admitted to the hospital have first received treatment in the community, but not all of them were admitted based on a specific referral from a clinic. The admission criterion is whether "the child needs hospitalization," and that decision must be approved by two psychiatrists. There is also an informal practice of not admitting a child if his parents refuse to participate in a family therapy program.

The admission decision is reviewed within 10 days by a team of staff physicians and mental health professionals; thereafter each child is reviewed every week. In addition, every child's condition is reviewed by a team of clinic staff members every 100 days. The average stay for the children at Augusta in December 1975 was 92 days.

Savannah Regional Hospital was built in 1970, and it housed 16 children at the time of this suit. The hospital staff members are also directors of the community mental health clinics.

It is the policy of the hospital that any child seeking admission on a nonemergency basis must be referred by a community clinic. The admission decision must be made by a staff psychiatrist, and it is based on the materials provided by the community clinic, an interview with the applicant, and an interview with the parents, if any, of the child.

Within three weeks after admission of a child, there is review by a group composed of hospital and clinic staff members and people from the community, such as juvenile court judges. Thereafter, the hospital staff reviews each child weekly. If the staff concludes that a child is ready to be released, then the community committee reviews the child's case to assist in placement. The average stay of the children being treated at Savannah in December 1975 was 127 days.

West Central Hospital in Columbus, Ga., was opened in December 1974, and it was organized for budgetary purposes with several community mental health clinics. The hospital itself has only 20 beds for children and adolescents, 16 of which were occupied at the time this suit was filed.

There is a formal policy that all children seeking admission to the hospital must be referred by a community clinic. The hospital is regarded by the staff as "the last resort in treating a child"; 50 percent of the children referred are turned away by the admissions team at the hospital.

After admission, there are staff meetings daily to discuss problem cases. The hospital has a practicing child psychiatrist who reviews cases once a week. Depending on the nature of the problems, the consultant reviews between 1 and 20 cases. The average stay of the children who were at West Central in December 1975 was 71 days.

The children's unit at Central State Regional Hospital in Milledgeville, Ga., was added to the existing structure during the 1970's. It can accommodate 40 children. The hospital also can house 40 adolescents. At the time of suit, the hospital housed 37 children under 18, including both named plaintiffs.

Although Central State is affiliated with community clinics, it seems to have a higher percentage of nonreferral admissions than any of the other hospitals. The admission decision is made by an "admissions evaluator" and the "admitting physician." The evaluator is a Ph.D. in psychology, a social worker, or a mental-health-trained nurse. The admitting physician is a psychiatrist. The standard for admission is "whether or not hospitalization is the more appropriate treatment" for the child. From April 1974 to November 1975, 9 of 29 children applicants screened for admission were referred to noninstitutional settings.

All children who are temporarily admitted are sent to the children and adolescent unit for testing and development of a treatment plan. Generally, seven days after the admission, members of the hospital staff review all of the information compiled about a patient "to determine the need for continued hospitalization." Thereafter, there is an informal review of the patient approximately every 60 days. The patients who were at Central State in December 1975 had been there, on the average, 456 days. There is no explanation in the record for this large variation from the average length of hospitalization at the other institutions.

Although most of the focus of the District Court was on the State's mental hospitals, it is relevant to note that Georgia presently funds over 50 community mental health clinics and 13 specialized foster care homes. The State has built seven new regional hospitals within the past

15 years, and it has added a new children's unit to its oldest hospital. The state budget in fiscal year 1976 was almost $150 million for mental health care. Georgia ranks 22d among the states in per capita expenditures for mental health and 15th in total expenditures.

The District Court nonetheless rejected the State's entire system of providing mental health care on both procedural and substantive grounds. The District Court found that 46 children could be "optimally cared for in another, less restrictive, non-hospital setting if it were available." 412 F.Supp., at 124–125. These "optimal" settings included group homes, therapeutic camps, and home-care services. The Governor of Georgia and the chairmen of the two Appropriations Committees of its legislature, testifying in the District Court, expressed confidence in the Georgia program and informed the court that the State could not justify enlarging its budget during fiscal year 1977 to provide the specialized treatment settings urged by appellees in addition to those then available.

Having described the factual background of Georgia's mental health program and its treatment of the named plaintiffs, we turn now to examine the legal bases for the District Court's judgment.

II

In holding unconstitutional Georgia's statutory procedure for voluntary commitment of juveniles, the District Court first determined that commitment to any of the eight regional hospitals[6] constitutes a severe deprivation of a child's liberty. The court defined this liberty interest in terms of both freedom from bodily restraint and freedom from the "emotional and psychic harm" caused by the institutionalization.[7] Having determined that a liberty interest is implicated by a child's admission to a mental hospital, the court considered what process is required to protect that interest. It held that the process due "includes at least the right after notice to be heard before an impartial tribunal." 412 F.Supp., at 137.

In requiring the prescribed hearing, the court rejected Georgia's argument that no adversary-type hearing was required since the State was merely assisting parents who could not afford private care by making available treatment similar to that offered in private hospitals and by private physicians. The court acknowledged that most parents who seek to have their children admitted to a state mental hospital do so in good faith. It, however, relied on one of appellees' witnesses who expressed an opinion that "some still look upon mental hospitals as a 'dumping ground.'" *Id.*, at 138.[8] No specific evidence of such "dumping," however, can be found in the record.

6. The record is very sparse with regard to the physical facilities and daily routines at the various regional hospitals. The only hospital discussed by appellees' expert witness was Central State. The District Court visited Central State and one other hospital, but did not discuss the visits in its opinion.

7. In both respects, the District Court found strong support for its holding in this Court's decision in *In re Gault*, 387 U.S. 1 (1967). In that decision, we held that a state cannot institutionalize a juvenile delinquent without first providing certain due process protections.

8. In light of the District Court's holding that a judicial or quasi-judicial body should review voluntary commitment decisions, it is at least interesting to note that the witness who made the statement quoted in the text was not referring to parents as the people who "dump" children into hospitals. This witness opined that some juvenile court judges and child welfare agencies misused the hospitals. See also Rolfe & MacClintock, The Due Process Rights of Minors "Voluntarily Admitted" to Mental Institutions, 4 J. Psychiatry & L. 333, 351 (1976) (hereinafter Rolfe & MacClintock).

The District Court also rejected the argument that review by the superintendents of the hospitals and their staffs was sufficient to protect the child's liberty interest. The court held that the inexactness of psychiatry, coupled with the possibility that the sources of information used to make the commitment decision may not always be reliable, made the superintendent's decision too arbitrary to satisfy due process. The court then shifted its focus drastically from what was clearly a procedural due process analysis to what appears to be a substantive due process analysis and condemned Georgia's "officialdom" for its failure, in the face of a state-funded 1973 report outlining the "need" for additional resources to be spent on nonhospital treatment, to provide more resources for noninstitutional mental health care. The court concluded that there was a causal relationship between this intransigence and the State's ability to provide any "flexible due process" to the appellees. The District Court therefore ordered the State to appropriate and expend such resources as would be necessary to provide nonhospital treatment to those members of appellees' class who would benefit from it.

III

In an earlier day, the problems inherent in coping with children afflicted with mental or emotional abnormalities were dealt with largely within the family. See S. Brakel & R. Rock, The Mentally Disabled and the Law 4 (1971). Sometimes parents were aided by teachers or a family doctor. While some parents no doubt were able to deal with their disturbed children without specialized assistance, others especially those of limited means and education, were not. Increasingly, they turned for assistance to local, public sources or private charities. Until recently, most of the states did little more than provide custodial institutions for the confinement of persons who were considered dangerous. *Id.*, at 5–6; Slovenko, Criminal Justice Procedures in Civil Commitment, 24 Wayne L.Rev. 1, 3 (1977) (hereinafter Slovenko).

As medical knowledge about the mentally ill and public concern for their condition expanded, the states, aided substantially by federal grants, have sought to ameliorate the human tragedies of seriously disturbed children. Ironically, as most states have expanded their efforts to assist the mentally ill, their actions have been subjected to increasing litigation and heightened constitutional scrutiny. Courts have been required to resolve the thorny constitutional attacks on state programs and procedures with limited precedential guidance. In this case, appellees have challenged Georgia's procedural and substantive balance of the individual, family, and social interests at stake in the voluntary commitment of a child to one of its regional mental hospitals.

The parties agree that our prior holdings have set out a general approach for testing challenged state procedures under a due process claim. Assuming the existence of a protectible property or liberty interest, the Court has required a balancing of a number of factors:

> "First, the private interest that will be affected by the official action; second, the risk of an erroneous deprivation of such interest through the procedures used, and the probable value, if any, of additional or substitute procedural safeguards; and finally, the Government's interest, including the function involved and the fiscal and administrative burdens that the additional or substitute procedural requirement would entail." *Mathews v. Eldridge*, 424 U.S. 319, 335 (1976), quoted in *Smith v. Organization of Foster Families*, 431 U.S. 816, 848-849 (1977).

In applying these criteria, we must consider first the child's interest in not being committed. Normally, however, since this interest is inextricably linked with the parents' interest in and obligation for the welfare and health of the child, the private interest at stake is a combination of the child's and parents' concerns.[11] Next, we must examine the State's interest in the procedures it has adopted for commitment and treatment of children. Finally, we must consider how well Georgia's procedures protect against arbitrariness in the decision to commit a child to a state mental hospital.

It is not disputed that a child, in common with adults, has a substantial liberty interest in not being confined unnecessarily for medical treatment and that the state's involvement in the commitment decision constitutes state action under the Fourteenth Amendment. See *Addington v. Texas*, 441 U.S. 418, 425 (1979); *In re Gault*, 387 U.S. 1, 27 (1967); *Specht v. Patterson*, 386 U.S. 605 (1967). We also recognize that commitment sometimes produces adverse social consequences for the child because of the reaction of some to the discovery that the child has received psychiatric care. Cf. *Addington v. Texas, supra*, 441 U.S., at 425–426.

This reaction, however, need not be equated with the community response resulting from being labeled by the state as delinquent, criminal, or mentally ill and possibly dangerous. See *ibid.*; *In re Gault, supra*, 387 U.S., at 23; *Paul v. Davis*, 424 U.S. 693, 711–712 (1976). The state through its voluntary commitment procedures does not "label" the child; it provides a diagnosis and treatment that medical specialists conclude the child requires. In terms of public reaction, the child who exhibits abnormal behavior may be seriously injured by an erroneous decision not to commit. Appellees overlook a significant source of the public reaction to the mentally ill, for what is truly "stigmatizing" is the symptomatology of a mental or emotional illness. *Addington v. Texas, supra*, 441 U.S., at 429. The pattern of untreated, abnormal behavior—even if nondangerous—arouses at least as much negative reaction as treatment that becomes public knowledge. A person needing, but not receiving, appropriate medical care may well face even greater social ostracism resulting from the observable symptoms of an untreated disorder.

However, we need not decide what effect these factors might have in a different case. For purposes of this decision, we assume that a child has a protectible interest not only in being free of unnecessary bodily restraints but also in not being labeled erroneously by some persons because of an improper decision by the state hospital superintendent.

We next deal with the interests of the parents who have decided, on the basis of their observations and independent professional recommendations, that their child needs institutional care. Appellees argue that the constitutional rights of the child are of such magnitude and the likelihood of parental abuse is so great that the parents' traditional interests in and responsibility for the upbringing of their child must be subordinated at least to the extent of providing a formal adversary hearing prior to a voluntary commitment.

Our jurisprudence historically has reflected Western civilization concepts of the family as a unit with broad parental authority over minor children. Our cases have consistently followed that course; our constitutional system long ago rejected any notion that a child is "the mere creature of the State" and, on the contrary, asserted that parents generally "have the right, coupled with the high duty, to recognize and prepare [their children] for additional

11. In this part of the opinion, we will deal with the issues arising when the natural parents of the child seek commitment to a state hospital. In Part IV, we will deal with the situation presented when the child is a ward of the state.

obligations." *Pierce v. Society of Sisters*, 268 U.S. 510, 535 (1925). See also *Wisconsin v. Yoder*, 406 U.S. 205, 213 (1972); *Prince v. Massachusetts*, 321 U.S. 158, 166 (1944); *Meyer v. Nebraska*, 262 U.S. 390, 400 (1923). Surely, this includes a "high duty" to recognize symptoms of illness and to seek and follow medical advice. The law's concept of the family rests on a presumption that parents possess what a child lacks in maturity, experience, and capacity for judgment required for making life's difficult decisions. More important, historically it has recognized that natural bonds of affection lead parents to act in the best interests of their children. 1 W. Blackstone, Commentaries *447; 2 J. Kent, Commentaries on American Law *190.

As with so many other legal presumptions, experience and reality may rebut what the law accepts as a starting point; the incidence of child neglect and abuse cases attests to this. That some parents "may at times be acting against the interests of their children" as was stated in *Bartley v. Kremens*, 402 F.Supp. 1039, 1047–1048 (ED Pa. 1975), vacated and remanded, 431 U.S. 119 (1977), creates a basis for caution, but is hardly a reason to discard wholesale those pages of human experience that teach that parents generally do act in the child's best interests. See Rolfe & MacClintock 348–349. The statist notion that governmental power should supersede parental authority in *all* cases because *some* parents abuse and neglect children is repugnant to American tradition.

Nonetheless, we have recognized that a state is not without constitutional control over parental discretion in dealing with children when their physical or mental health is jeopardized. See *Wisconsin v. Yoder, supra*, 406 U.S., at 230; *Prince v. Massachusetts, supra*, 321 U.S., at 166. Moreover, the Court recently declared unconstitutional a state statute that granted parents an absolute veto over a minor child's decision to have an abortion. *Planned Parenthood of Central Missouri v. Danforth*, 428 U.S. 52 (1976). Appellees urge that these precedents limiting the traditional rights of parents, if viewed in the context of the liberty interest of the child and the likelihood of parental abuse, require us to hold that the parents' decision to have a child admitted to a mental hospital must be subjected to an exacting constitutional scrutiny, including a formal, adversary, pre-admission hearing.

Appellees' argument, however, sweeps too broadly. Simply because the decision of a parent is not agreeable to a child or because it involves risks does not automatically transfer the power to make that decision from the parents to some agency or officer of the state. The same characterizations can be made for a tonsillectomy, appendectomy, or other medical procedure. Most children, even in adolescence, simply are not able to make sound judgments concerning many decisions, including their need for medical care or treatment. Parents can and must make those judgments. Here, there is no finding by the District Court of even a single instance of bad faith by any parent of any member of appellees' class. We cannot assume that the result in *Meyer v. Nebraska, supra*, and *Pierce v. Society of Sisters, supra*, would have been different if the children there had announced a preference to learn only English or a preference to go to a public, rather than a church, school. The fact that a child may balk at hospitalization or complain about a parental refusal to provide cosmetic surgery does not diminish the parents' authority to decide what is best for the child. See generally Goldstein, Medical Case for the Child at Risk: On State Supervention of Parental Autonomy, 86 Yale L.J. 645, 664–668 (1977); Bennett, Allocation of Child Medical Care Decisionmaking Authority: A Suggested Interest Analysis, 62 Va.L.Rev. 285, 308 (1976). Neither state officials nor federal courts are equipped to review such parental decisions.

Appellees place particular reliance on *Planned Parenthood*, arguing that its holding indicates how little deference to parents is appropriate when the child is exercising a constitutional right. The basic situation in that case, however, was very different; *Planned Parenthood* involved an absolute parental veto over the child's ability to obtain an abortion. Parents in Georgia in no sense have an absolute right to commit their children to state mental hospitals; the statute requires the superintendent of each regional hospital to exercise independent judgment as to the child's need for confinement.

In defining the respective rights and prerogatives of the child and parent in the voluntary commitment setting, we conclude that our precedents permit the parents to retain a substantial, if not the dominant, role in the decision, absent a finding of neglect or abuse, and that the traditional presumption that the parents act in the best interests of their child should apply. We also conclude, however, that the child's rights and the nature of the commitment decision are such that parents cannot always have absolute and unreviewable discretion to decide whether to have a child institutionalized. They, of course, retain plenary authority to seek such care for their children, subject to a physician's independent examination and medical judgment.

The State obviously has a significant interest in confining the use of its costly mental health facilities to cases of genuine need. The Georgia program seeks first to determine whether the patient seeking admission has an illness that calls for inpatient treatment. To accomplish this purpose, the State has charged the superintendents of each regional hospital with the responsibility for determining, before authorizing an admission, whether a prospective patient is mentally ill and whether the patient will likely benefit from hospital care. In addition, the State has imposed a continuing duty on hospital superintendents to release any patient who has recovered to the point where hospitalization is no longer needed.

The State in performing its voluntarily assumed mission also has a significant interest in not imposing unnecessary procedural obstacles that may discourage the mentally ill or their families from seeking needed psychiatric assistance. The parens patriae interest in helping parents care for the mental health of their children cannot be fulfilled if the parents are unwilling to take advantage of the opportunities because the admission process is too onerous, too embarrassing, or too contentious. It is surely not idle to speculate as to how many parents who believe they are acting in good faith would forgo state-provided hospital care if such care is contingent on participation in an adversary proceeding designed to probe their motives and other private family matters in seeking the voluntary admission.

The State also has a genuine interest in allocating priority to the diagnosis and treatment of patients as soon as they are admitted to a hospital rather than to time-consuming procedural minuets before the admission. One factor that must be considered is the utilization of the time of psychiatrists, psychologists, and other behavioral specialists in preparing for and participating in hearings rather than performing the task for which their special training has fitted them. Behavioral experts in courtrooms and hearings are of little help to patients.

The *amici* brief of the American Psychiatric Association et al. points out at page 20 that the average staff psychiatrist in a hospital presently is able to devote only 47 percent of his time to direct patient care. One consequence of increasing the procedures the state must provide prior to a child's voluntary admission will be that mental health professionals will be diverted even more from the treatment of patients in order to travel to and participate in-and wait for—what could be hundreds—or even thousands—of hearings each year. Obviously the cost of these procedures would come from the public moneys the legislature intended for mental health care. See Slovenko 34–35.

We now turn to consideration of what process protects adequately the child's constitutional rights by reducing risks of error without unduly trenching on traditional parental authority and without undercutting "efforts to further the legitimate interests of both the state and the patient that are served by" voluntary commitments. *Addington v. Texas*, 441 U.S., at 430. See also *Mathews v. Eldridge*, 424 U.S., at 335. We conclude that the risk of error inherent in the parental decision to have a child institutionalized for mental health care is sufficiently great that some kind of inquiry should be made by a "neutral factfinder" to determine whether the statutory requirements for admission are satisfied. See *Goldberg v. Kelly*, 397 U.S. 254, 271 (1970); *Morrissey v. Brewer*, 408 U.S. 471, 489 (1972). That inquiry must carefully probe the child's background using all available sources, including, but not limited to, parents, schools, and other social agencies. Of course, the review must also include an interview with the child. It is necessary that the decisionmaker have the authority to refuse to admit any child who does not satisfy the medical standards for admission. Finally, it is necessary that the child's continuing need for commitment be reviewed periodically by a similarly independent procedure.[15]

We are satisfied that such procedures will protect the child from an erroneous admission decision in a way that neither unduly burdens the states nor inhibits parental decisions to seek state help.

Due process has never been thought to require that the neutral and detached trier of fact be law trained or a judicial or administrative officer. See *Goldberg v. Kelly, supra*, 397 U.S., at 271; *Morrissey v. Brewer, supra*, 408 U.S., at 489. Surely, this is the case as to medical decisions, for "neither judges nor administrative hearing officers are better qualified than psychiatrists to render psychiatric judgments." *In re Roger S.*, 19 Cal.3d 921, 942, 141 Cal.Rptr. 298, 311, 569 P.2d 1286, 1299 (1977) (Clark, J., dissenting). Thus, a staff physician will suffice, so long as he or she is free to evaluate independently the child's mental and emotional condition and need for treatment.

It is not necessary that the deciding physician conduct a formal or quasi-formal, hearing. A state is free to require such a hearing, but due process is not violated by use of informal traditional medical investigative techniques. Since well-established medical procedures already exist, we do not undertake to outline with specificity precisely what this investigation must involve. The mode and procedure of medical diagnostic procedures is not the business of judges. What is best for a child is an individual medical decision that must be left to the judgment of physicians in each case. We do no more than emphasize that the decision should represent an independent judgment of what the child requires and that all sources of information that are traditionally relied on by physicians and behavioral specialists should be consulted.

What process is constitutionally due cannot be divorced from the nature of the ultimate decision that is being made. Not every determination by state officers can be made most effectively by use of "the procedural tools of judicial or administrative decisionmaking." *Board of Curators of Univ. of Missouri v. Horowitz*, 435 U.S. 78, 90 (1978). See also *Greenholtz v.*

15. As we discuss more fully later, the District Court did not decide and we therefore have no reason to consider at this time what procedures for review are independently necessary to justify continuing a child's confinement. We merely hold that a subsequent, independent review of the patient's condition provides a necessary check against possible arbitrariness in the initial admission decision.

Nebraska Penal Inmates, 442 U.S. 1, 13–14; *Cafeteria & Restaurant Workers v. McElroy*, 367 U.S. 886, 895 (1961).[16]

Here, the questions are essentially medical in character: whether the child is mentally or emotionally ill and whether he can benefit from the treatment that is provided by the state. While facts are plainly necessary for a proper resolution of those questions, they are only a first step in the process. In an opinion for a unanimous Court, we recently stated in *Addington v. Texas*, 441 U.S., at 429, that the determination of "whether [a person] is mentally ill turns on the meaning of the facts which must be interpreted by expert psychiatrists and psychologists."

Although we acknowledge the fallibility of medical and psychiatric diagnosis, see *O'Connor v. Donaldson*, 422 U.S. 563, 584 (1975) (concurring opinion), we do not accept the notion that the shortcomings of specialists can always be avoided by shifting the decision from a trained specialist using the traditional tools of medical science to an untrained judge or administrative hearing officer after a judicial-type hearing. Even after a hearing, the non-specialist decisionmaker must make a medical-psychiatric decision. Common human experience and scholarly opinions suggest that the supposed protections of an adversary proceeding to determine the appropriateness of medical decisions for the commitment and treatment of mental and emotional illness may well be more illusory than real. See Albers, Pasewark, & Meyer, Involuntary Hospitalization and Psychiatric Testimony: The Fallibility of the Doctrine of Immaculate Perception, 6 Cap.U.L.Rev. 11, 15 (1976).

Another problem with requiring a formalized, factfinding hearing lies in the danger it poses for significant intrusion into the parent-child relationship. Pitting the parents and child as adversaries often will be at odds with the presumption that parents act in the best interests of their child. It is one thing to require a neutral physician to make a careful review of the parents' decision in order to make sure it is proper from a medical standpoint; it is a wholly different matter to employ an adversary contest to ascertain whether the parents' motivation is consistent with the child's interests.

Moreover, it is appropriate to inquire into how such a hearing would contribute to the successful long-range treatment of the patient. Surely, there is a risk that it would exacerbate whatever tensions already exist between the child and the parents. Since the parents can and usually do play a significant role in the treatment while the child is hospitalized and even more so after release, there is a serious risk that an adversary confrontation will adversely

16. Relying on general statements from past decisions dealing with governmental actions not even remotely similar to those involved here, the dissent concludes that if a protectible interest is involved then there must be some form of traditional, adversary, judicial, or administrative hearing either before or after its deprivation. That result is mandated, in their view, regardless of what process the state has designed to protect the individual and regardless of what the record demonstrates as to the fairness of the state's approach.

The dissenting approach is inconsistent with our repeated assertion that "due process is flexible and calls for such procedural protections as the particular situation demands." *Morrissey v. Brewer*, 408 U.S. 471, 481 (1972) (emphasis added). Just as there is no requirement as to exactly what procedures to employ whenever a traditional judicial-type hearing is mandated, compare *Goss v. Lopez*, 419 U.S. 565 (1975); *Wolff v. McDonnell*, 418 U.S. 539 (1974); *Morrissey v. Brewer*, *supra*, with *Goldberg v. Kelly*, 397 U.S. 254 (1970), there is no reason to require a judicial-type hearing in all circumstances. As the scope of governmental action expands into new areas creating new controversies for judicial review, it is incumbent on courts to design procedures that protect the rights of the individual without unduly burdening the legitimate efforts of the states to deal with difficult social problems. The judicial model for factfinding for all constitutionally protected interests, regardless of their nature, can turn rational decisionmaking into an unmanageable enterprise.

affect the ability of the parents to assist the child while in the hospital. Moreover, it will make his subsequent return home more difficult. These unfortunate results are especially critical with an emotionally disturbed child; they seem likely to occur in the context of an adversary hearing in which the parents testify. A confrontation over such intimate family relationships would distress the normal adult parents and the impact on a disturbed child almost certainly would be significantly greater.[18]

It has been suggested that a hearing conducted by someone other than the admitting physician is necessary in order to detect instances where parents are "guilty of railroading their children into asylums" or are using "voluntary commitment procedures in order to sanction behavior of which they disapprov[e]." Ellis, Volunteering Children: Parental Commitment of Minors to Mental Institutions, 62 Calif.L.Rev. 840, 850–851 (1974). See also *J. L. v. Parham*, 412 F.Supp., at 133.... Curiously, it seems to be taken for granted that parents who seek to "dump" their children on the state will inevitably be able to conceal their motives and thus deceive the admitting psychiatrists and the other mental health professionals who make and review the admission decision. It is elementary that one early diagnostic inquiry into the cause of an emotional disturbance of a child is an examination into the environment of the child. It is unlikely, if not inconceivable, that a decision to abandon an emotionally normal, healthy child and thrust him into an institution will be a discrete act leaving no trail of circumstances. Evidence of such conflicts will emerge either in the interviews or from secondary sources. It is unrealistic to believe that trained psychiatrists, skilled in eliciting responses, sorting medically relevant facts, and sensing motivational nuances will often be deceived about the family situation surrounding a child's emotional disturbance.[19] Surely a lay, or even law-trained, factfinder would be no more skilled in this process than the professional.

By expressing some confidence in the medical decisionmaking process, we are by no means suggesting it is error free. On occasion, parents may initially mislead an admitting physician or a physician may erroneously diagnose the child as needing institutional care either because of negligence or an overabundance of caution. That there may be risks of error in the process affords no rational predicate for holding unconstitutional an entire statutory and administrative scheme that is generally followed in more than 30 states. "[P]rocedural due

18. While not altogether clear, the District Court opinion apparently contemplated a hearing preceded by a written notice of the proposed commitment. At the hearing the child presumably would be given an opportunity to be heard and present evidence, and the right to cross-examine witnesses, including, of course, the parents. The court also required an impartial trier of fact who would render a written decision reciting the reasons for accepting or rejecting the parental application.

Since the parents in this situation are seeking the child's admission to the state institution, the procedure contemplated by the District Court presumably would call for some other person to be designated as a guardian ad litem to act for the child. The guardian, in turn, if not a lawyer, would be empowered to retain counsel to act as an advocate of the child's interest.

Of course, a state may elect to provide such adversary hearings in situations where it perceives that parents and a child may be at odds, but nothing in the Constitution compels such procedures.

19. In evaluating the problem of detecting "dumping" by parents, it is important to keep in mind that each of the regional hospitals has a continuing relationship with the Department of Family and Children Services. The staffs at those hospitals refer cases to the Department when they suspect a child is being mistreated and thus are sensitive to this problem. In fact, J.L.'s situation is in point. The family conflicts and problems were well documented in the hospital records. Equally well documented, however, were the child's severe emotional disturbances and his need for treatment.

process rules are shaped by the risk of error inherent in the truthfinding process as applied to the generality of cases, not the rare exceptions." *Mathews v. Eldridge*, 424 U.S., at 344. In general, we are satisfied that an independent medical decisionmaking process, which includes the thorough psychiatric investigation described earlier, followed by additional periodic review of a child's condition, will protect children who should not be admitted; we do not believe the risks of error in that process would be significantly reduced by a more formal, judicial-type hearing. The issue remains whether the Georgia practices, as described in the record before us, comport with these minimum due process requirements.

Georgia's statute envisions a careful diagnostic medical inquiry to be conducted by the admitting physician at each regional hospital. The *amicus* brief for the United States explains, at pages 7–8:

> "[I]n every instance the decision whether or not to accept the child for treatment is made by a physician employed by the State....
>
> "That decision is based on interviews and recommendations by hospital or community health center staff. The staff interviews the child and the parent or guardian who brings the child to the facility... [and] attempts are made to communicate with other possible sources of information about the child...."

Focusing primarily on what it saw as the absence of any formal mechanism for review of the physician's initial decision, the District Court unaccountably saw the medical decision as an exercise of "unbridled discretion." 412 F.Supp., at 136. But extravagant characterizations are no substitute for careful analysis, and we must examine the Georgia process in its setting to determine if, indeed, any one person exercises such discretion.

In the typical case, the parents of a child initially conclude from the child's behavior that there is some emotional problem—in short, that "something is wrong." They may respond to the problem in various ways, but generally the first contact with the State occurs when they bring the child to be examined by a psychologist or psychiatrist at a community mental health clinic.

Most often, the examination is followed by outpatient treatment at the community clinic. In addition, the child's parents are encouraged, and sometimes required, to participate in a family therapy program to obtain a better insight into the problem. In most instances, this is all the care a child requires. However, if, after a period of outpatient care, the child's abnormal emotional condition persists, he may be referred by the local clinic staff to an affiliated regional mental hospital.

At the regional hospital an admissions team composed of a psychiatrist and at least one other mental health professional examines and interviews the child—privately in most instances. This team then examines the medical records provided by the clinic staff and interviews the parents. Based on this information, and any additional background that can be obtained, the admissions team makes a diagnosis and determines whether the child will likely benefit from institutionalized care. If the team finds either condition not met, admission is refused.

If the team admits a child as suited for hospitalization, the child's condition and continuing need for hospital care are reviewed periodically by at least one independent, medical review group. For the most part, the reviews are as frequent as weekly, but none are less often than once every two months. Moreover, as we noted earlier, the superintendent of each hospital is charged with an affirmative statutory duty to discharge any child who is no longer mentally ill or in need of therapy.[21]

As with most medical procedures, Georgia's are not totally free from risk of error in the sense that they give total or absolute assurance that every child admitted to a hospital has a mental illness optimally suitable for institutionalized treatment. But it bears repeating that "procedural due process rules are shaped by the risk of error inherent in the truth-finding process as applied to the generality of cases, not the rare exceptions." *Mathews v. Eldridge, supra*, 424 U.S., at 344.

Georgia's procedures are not "arbitrary" in the sense that a single physician or other professional has the "unbridled discretion" the District Court saw to commit a child to a regional hospital. To so find on this record would require us to assume that the physicians, psychologists, and mental health professionals who participate in the admission decision and who review each other's conclusions as to the continuing validity of the initial decision are either oblivious or indifferent to the child's welfare—or that they are incompetent. We note, however, the District Court found to the contrary; it was "impressed by the conscientious, dedicated state employed psychiatrists who, with the help of equally conscientious, dedicated state employed psychologists and social workers, faithfully care for the plaintiff children. . . ." 412 F.Supp., at 138.

This finding of the District Court also effectively rebuts the suggestion made in some of the briefs amici that hospital administrators may not actually be "neutral and detached" because of institutional pressure to admit a child who has no need for hospital care. That such a practice may take place in some institutions in some places affords no basis for a finding as to Georgia's program; the evidence in the record provides no support whatever for that charge against the staffs at any of the State's eight regional hospitals. Such cases, if they are found, can be dealt with individually;[22] they do not lend themselves to class-action remedies.

We are satisfied that the voluminous record as a whole supports the conclusion that the admissions staffs of the hospitals have acted in a neutral and detached fashion in making medical judgments in the best interests of the children. The State, through its mental health programs, provides the authority for trained professionals to assist parents in examining, diagnosing, and treating emotionally disturbed children. Through its hiring practices, it provides well-staffed and well-equipped hospitals and—as the District Court found—conscientious public employees to implement the State's beneficent purposes.

Although our review of the record in this case satisfies us that Georgia's general administrative and statutory scheme for the voluntary commitment of children is not per se unconstitutional, we cannot decide on this record, whether every child in appellees' class received an adequate, independent diagnosis of his emotional condition and need for confinement under the standards announced earlier in this opinion. On remand, the District Court is free to and should consider any individual claims that initial admissions did not meet the standards we have described in this opinion.

21. While the record does demonstrate that the procedures may vary from case to case, it also reflects that no child in Georgia was admitted for indefinite hospitalization without being interviewed personally and without the admitting physician's checking with secondary sources, such as school or work records.

22. One important means of obtaining individual relief for these children is the availability of habeas corpus. As the appellants' brief explains, "Ga.Code § 88-502.11 . . . provides that at any time and without notice a person detained in a facility, or a relative or friend of such person, may petition for a writ of habeas corpus to question the cause and legality of the detention of the person." Brief for Appellants 36–37.

In addition, we note that appellees' original complaint alleged that the State had failed to provide adequate periodic review of their need for institutional care and claimed that this was an additional due process violation. Since the District Court held that the appellees' original confinement was unconstitutional, it had no reason to consider this separate claim. Similarly, we have no basis for determining whether the review procedures of the various hospitals are adequate to provide the process called for or what process might be required if a child contests his confinement by requesting a release. These matters require factual findings not present in the District Court's opinion. We have held that the periodic reviews described in the record reduce the risk of error in the initial admission and thus they are necessary. Whether they are sufficient to justify continuing a voluntary commitment is an issue for the District Court on remand. The District Court is free to require additional evidence on this issue.

IV

Our discussion in Part III was directed at the situation where a child's natural parents request his admission to a state mental hospital. Some members of appellees' class, including J.R., were wards of the State of Georgia at the time of their admission. Obviously their situation differs from those members of the class who have natural parents. While the determination of what process is due varies somewhat when the state, rather than a natural parent, makes the request for commitment, we conclude that the differences in the two situations do not justify requiring different procedures at the time of the child's initial admission to the hospital.

For a ward of the state, there may well be no adult who knows him thoroughly and who cares for him deeply. Unlike with natural parents where there is a presumed natural affection to guide their action, 1 W. Blackstone, Commentaries *447; 2 J. Kent, Commentaries on American Law *190, the presumption that the state will protect a child's general welfare stems from a specific state statute. Ga.Code § 24A-101 (1978). Contrary to the suggestion of the dissent, however, we cannot assume that when the State of Georgia has custody of a child it acts so differently from a natural parent in seeking medical assistance for the child. No one has questioned the validity of the statutory presumption that the State acts in the child's best interest. Nor could such a challenge be mounted on the record before us. There is no evidence that the State, acting as guardian, attempted to admit any child for reasons unrelated to the child's need for treatment. Indeed, neither the District Court nor the appellees have suggested that wards of the State should receive any constitutional treatment different from children with natural parents.

Once we accept that the State's application for a child's admission to a hospital is made in good faith, then the question is whether the medical decisionmaking approach of the admitting physician is adequate to satisfy due process. We have already recognized that an independent medical judgment made from the perspective of the best interests of the child after a careful investigation is an acceptable means of justifying a voluntary commitment. We do not believe that the soundness of this decisionmaking is any the less reasonable in this setting.

Indeed, if anything, the decision with regard to wards of the State may well be even more reasonable in light of the extensive written records that are compiled about each child while in the State's custody. In J.R.'s case, the admitting physician had a complete social and medical history of the child before even beginning the diagnosis. After carefully interviewing him and reviewing his extensive files, three physicians independently concluded that institutional care was in his best interests.

Since the state agency having custody and control of the child *in loco parentis* has a duty to consider the best interests of the child with respect to a decision on commitment to a mental hospital, the State may constitutionally allow that custodial agency to speak for the child, subject, of course, to the restrictions governing natural parents. On this record, we cannot declare unconstitutional Georgia's admission procedures for wards of the State.

It is possible that the procedures required in reviewing a ward's need for continuing care should be different from those used to review the need of a child with natural parents. As we have suggested earlier, the issue of what process is due to justify continuing a voluntary commitment must be considered by the District Court on remand. In making that inquiry, the District Court might well consider whether wards of the State should be treated with respect to continuing therapy differently from children with natural parents.

The absence of an adult who cares deeply for a child has little effect on the reliability of the initial admission decision, but it may have some effect on how long a child will remain in the hospital. We noted in *Addington v. Texas*, 141 U.S., at 428–429, that "the concern of family and friends generally will provide continuous opportunities for an erroneous commitment to be corrected." For a child without natural parents, we must acknowledge the risk of being "lost in the shuffle." Moreover, there is at least some indication that J.R.'s commitment was prolonged because the Department of Family and Children Services had difficulty finding a foster home for him. Whether wards of the State generally have received less protection than children with natural parents, and, if so, what should be done about it, however, are matters that must be decided in the first instance by the District Court on remand,[23] if the court concludes the issue is still alive.

V

It is important that we remember the purpose of Georgia's comprehensive mental health program. It seeks substantively and at great cost to provide care for those who cannot afford to obtain private treatment and procedurally to screen carefully all applicants to assure that institutional care is suited to the particular patient. The State resists the complex of procedures ordered by the District Court because in its view they are unnecessary to protect the child's rights, they divert public resources from the central objective of administering health care, they risk aggravating the tensions inherent in the family situation, and they erect barriers that may discourage parents from seeking medical aid for a disturbed child.

On this record, we are satisfied that Georgia's medical factfinding processes are reasonable and consistent with constitutional guarantees. Accordingly, it was error to hold

23. To remedy the constitutional violation, the District Court ordered hearings to be held for each member of the plaintiff class, see n. 2, *supra*. For 46 members of the class found to be treatable in "less drastic" settings, the District Court also ordered the State to expend such moneys as were necessary to provide alternative treatment facilities and programs. While the order is more appropriate as a remedy for a substantive due process violation, the court made no findings on that issue. The order apparently was intended to remedy the procedural due process violation it found. Since that judgment is reversed, there is no basis for us to consider the correctness of the remedy.

unconstitutional the State's procedures for admitting a child for treatment to a state mental hospital. The judgment is therefore reversed, and the case is remanded to the District Court for further proceedings consistent with this opinion.

Reversed and remanded.

MR. JUSTICE STEWART, concurring in the judgment.

For centuries it has been a canon of the common law that parents speak for their minor children.[1] So deeply imbedded in our traditions is this principle of law that the Constitution itself may compel a State to respect it. *Meyer v. Nebraska*, 262 U.S. 390; *Pierce v. Society of Sisters*, 268 U.S. 510. In ironic contrast, the District Court in this case has said that the Constitution requires the State of Georgia to disregard this established principle. I cannot agree.

There can be no doubt that commitment to a mental institution results in a "massive curtailment of liberty," *Humphrey v. Cady*, 405 U.S. 504, 509. In addition to the physical confinement involved, *O'Connor v. Donaldson*, 422 U.S. 563, a person's liberty is also substantially affected by the stigma attached to treatment in a mental hospital.[3] But not every loss of liberty is governmental deprivation of liberty, and it is only the latter that invokes the Due Process Clause of the Fourteenth Amendment.

The appellees were committed under the following section of the Georgia Code:

> "Authority to receive voluntary patients—
>
> "(a) The superintendent of any facility may receive for observation and diagnosis any individual 18 years of age, or older, making application therefor, any individual under 18 years of age for whom such application is made by his parent or guardian and any person legally adjudged to be incompetent for whom such application is made by his guardian. If found to show evidence of mental illness and to be suitable for treatment, such person may be given care and treatment at such facility and such person may be detained by such facility for such period and under such conditions as may be authorized by law." Ga.Code § 88-503.1 (1975).

Clearly, if the appellees in this case were adults who had voluntarily chosen to commit themselves to a state mental hospital, they could not claim that the State had thereby deprived

1. See 1 W. Blackstone, Commentaries *452–453; 2 J. Kent, Commentaries on American Law *203–206; J. Schouler, A Treatise on the Law of Domestic Relations 335–353 (3d ed. 1882); G. Field, The Legal Relations of Infants 63–80 (1888).

"It is cardinal with us that the custody, care and nurture of the child reside first in the parents, whose primary function and freedom include preparation for obligations the state can neither supply nor hinder." *Prince v. Massachusetts*, 321 U.S. 158, 166.

"The history and culture of Western civilization reflect a strong tradition of parental concern for the nurture and upbringing of their children. This primary role of the parents in the upbringing of their children is now established beyond debate as an enduring American tradition." *Wisconsin v. Yoder*, 406 U.S. 205, at 232.

"Because he may not foresee the consequences of his decision, a minor may not make an enforceable bargain. He may not lawfully work or travel where he pleases, or even attend exhibitions of constitutionally protected adult motion pictures. Persons below a certain age may not marry without parental consent." *Planned Parenthood of Central Missouri v. Danforth*, 428 U.S. 52, 102 (STEVENS, J., concurring in part and dissenting in part).

Cf. *Stump v. Sparkman*, 435 U.S. 349, 366 (dissenting opinion).

3. The fact that such a stigma may be unjustified does not mean it does not exist. Nor does the fact that public reaction to past commitment may be less than the reaction to aberrant behavior detract from this assessment. The aberrant behavior may disappear, while the fact of past institutionalization lasts forever.

them of liberty in violation of the Fourteenth Amendment. Just as clearly, I think, children on whose behalf their parents have invoked these voluntary procedures can make no such claim.

The Georgia statute recognizes the power of a party to act on behalf of another person under the voluntary commitment procedures in two situations: when the other person is a minor not over 17 years of age and the party is that person's parent or guardian, and when the other person has been "legally adjudged incompetent" and the party is that person's guardian. In both instances two conditions are present. First, the person being committed is presumptively incapable of making the voluntary commitment decision for himself. And second, the parent or guardian is presumed to be acting in that person's best interests.[4] In the case of guardians, these presumptions are grounded in statutes whose validity nobody has questioned in this case. Ga.Code § 49-201 (1978). In the case of parents, the presumptions are grounded in a statutory embodiment of long-established principles of the common law.

Thus, the basic question in this case is whether the Constitution requires Georgia to ignore basic principles so long accepted by our society. For only if the State in this setting is constitutionally compelled always to intervene between parent and child can there be any question as to the constitutionally required extent of that intervention. I believe this basic question must be answered in the negative.[6]

Under our law, parents constantly make decisions for their minor children that deprive the children of liberty, and sometimes even of life itself. Yet surely the Fourteenth Amendment is not invoked when an informed parent decides upon major surgery for his child, even in a state hospital. I can perceive no basic constitutional differences between commitment to a mental hospital and other parental decisions that result in a child's loss of liberty.

I realize, of course, that a parent's decision to commit his child to a state mental institution results in a far greater loss of liberty than does his decision to have an appendectomy performed upon the child in a state hospital. But if, contrary to my belief, this factual difference rises to the level of a constitutional difference, then I believe that the objective checks upon the parents' commitment decision, embodied in Georgia law and thoroughly discussed, are more than constitutionally sufficient.

To be sure, the presumption that a parent is acting in the best interests of his child must be a rebuttable one, since certainly not all parents are actuated by the unselfish motive the law presumes. Some parents are simply unfit parents. But Georgia clearly provides that an unfit parent can be stripped of his parental authority under laws dealing with neglect and abuse of children.

This is not an easy case. Issues involving the family and issues concerning mental illness are among the most difficult that courts have to face, involving as they often do serious problems of policy disguised as questions of constitutional law. But when a state legislature

4. This is also true of a child removed from the control of his parents. For the juvenile court then has a duty to "secure for him care as nearly as possible equivalent to that which [his parents] should have given him." Ga.Code § 24A-101 (1978).

6. *Planned Parenthood of Central Missouri v. Danforth*, 428 U.S. 52, was an entirely different case. The Court's opinion today discusses some of these differences, but I think there is a more fundamental one. The Danforth case involved an expectant mother's right to decide upon an abortion—a personal substantive constitutional right. *Roe v. Wade*, 410 U.S. 113; *Doe v. Bolton*, 410 U.S. 179. By contrast, the appellees in this case had no substantive constitutional right not to be hospitalized for psychiatric treatment.

makes a reasonable definition of the age of minority, and creates a rebuttable presumption that in invoking the statutory procedures for voluntary commitment a parent is acting in the best interests of his minor child, I cannot believe that the Fourteenth Amendment is violated. This is not to say that in this area the Constitution compels a State to respect the traditional authority of a parent, as in the *Meyer* and *Pierce* cases. I believe, as in *Prince v. Massachusetts*, 321 U.S. 158, that the Constitution would tolerate intervention by the State. But that is a far cry from holding that such intervention is constitutionally compelled.

For these reasons I concur in the judgment.

Mr. Justice Brennan, with whom Mr. Justice Marshall and Mr. Justice Stevens join, concurring in part and dissenting in part.

I agree with the Court that the commitment of juveniles to state mental hospitals by their parents or by state officials acting *in loco parentis* involves state action that impacts upon constitutionally protected interests and therefore must be accomplished through procedures consistent with the constitutional mandate of due process of law. I agree also that the District Court erred in interpreting the Due Process clause to require preconfinement commitment hearings in all cases in which parents wish to hospitalize their children. I disagree, however, with the Court's decision to pretermit questions concerning the postadmission procedures due Georgia's institutionalized juveniles. While the question of the frequency of postadmission review hearings may properly be deferred, the right to at least one postadmission hearing can and should be affirmed now. I also disagree with the Court's conclusion concerning the procedures due juvenile wards of the State of Georgia. I believe that the Georgia statute is unconstitutional in that it fails to accord preconfinement hearings to juvenile wards of the State committed by the State acting *in loco parentis*.

I

RIGHTS OF CHILDREN COMMITTED TO MENTAL INSTITUTIONS

Commitment to a mental institution necessarily entails a "massive curtailment of liberty," *Humphrey v. Cady*, 405 U.S. 504, 509 (1972), and inevitably affects "fundamental rights." *Baxstrom v. Herold*, 383 U.S. 107, 113 (1966). Persons incarcerated in mental hospitals are not only deprived of their physical liberty, they are also deprived of friends, family, and community. Institutionalized mental patients must live in unnatural surroundings under the continuous and detailed control of strangers. They are subject to intrusive treatment which, especially if unwarranted, may violate their right to bodily integrity. Such treatment modalities may include forced administration of psychotropic medication, aversive conditioning, convulsive therapy, and even psychosurgery. Furthermore, as the Court recognizes, persons confined in mental institutions are stigmatized as sick and abnormal during confinement and, in some cases, even after release.

Because of these considerations, our cases have made clear that commitment to a mental hospital "is a deprivation of liberty which the State cannot accomplish without due process of law." *O'Connor v. Donaldson*, 422 U.S. 563, 580 (1975) (Burger, C. J., concurring). See, *e.g.*, *McNeil v. Director, Patuxent Institution*, 407 U.S. 245 (1972) (defective delinquent commitment following expiration of prison term); *Specht v. Patterson*, 386 U.S. 605 (1967) (sex offender commitment following criminal conviction); *Chaloner v. Sherman*, 242 U.S. 455, 461 (1917) (incompetence inquiry). In the absence of a voluntary, knowing, and intelligent waiver, adults facing commitment to mental institutions are entitled to full and fair adversary hearings in which the necessity for their commitment is established to the satisfaction of a neutral tribunal. At such hearings they must be accorded the right to "be present with counsel, have an opportunity to be heard, be confronted with witnesses against [them], have the right to cross-examine, and to offer evidence of [their] own." *Specht v. Patterson, supra*, at 610, 87 S.Ct., at 1212.

These principles also govern the commitment of children. "Constitutional rights do not mature and come into being magically only when one attains the state-defined age of majority. Minors as well as adults are protected by the Constitution and possess constitutional rights. See, *e.g.*, *Breed v. Jones*, 421 U.S. 519 (1975); *Goss v. Lopez*, 419 U.S. 565 (1975); *Tinker v. Des Moines School Dist.*, 393 U.S. 503 (1969); *In re Gault*, 387 U.S. 1 (1967)." *Planned Parenthood of Central Missouri v. Danforth*, 428 U.S. 52, 74 (1976).

Indeed, it may well be argued that children are entitled to more protection than are adults. The consequences of an erroneous commitment decision are more tragic where children are involved. Children, on the average, are confined for longer periods than are adults. Moreover, childhood is a particularly vulnerable time of life and children erroneously institutionalized during their formative years may bear the scars for the rest of their lives. Furthermore, the provision of satisfactory institutionalized mental care for children generally requires a substantial financial commitment that too often has not been forthcoming. Decisions of the lower courts have chronicled the inadequacies of existing mental health facilities for children. See, *e.g.*, *New York State Assn. for Retarded Children v. Rockefeller*, 357 F.Supp. 752, 756 (EDNY 1973) (conditions at Willowbrook School for the Mentally Retarded are "inhumane," involving "failure to protect the physical safety of [the] children," substantial personnel shortage, and "poor" and "hazardous" conditions); *Wyatt v. Stickney*, 344 F.Supp. 387, 391 (MD Ala.1972), aff'd sub nom. *Wyatt v. Aderholt*, 503 F.2d 1305 (CA5 1974) ("grossly substandard" conditions at Partlow School for the Mentally Retarded lead to "hazardous and deplorable inadequacies in the institution's operation").

In addition, the chances of an erroneous commitment decision are particularly great where children are involved. Even under the best of circumstances psychiatric diagnosis and therapy decisions are fraught with uncertainties. See *O'Connor v. Donaldson*, *supra*, 422 U.S., at 584 (Burger, C. J., concurring). These uncertainties are aggravated when, as under the Georgia practice, the psychiatrist interviews the child during a period of abnormal stress in connection with the commitment, and without adequate time or opportunity to become acquainted with the patient. These uncertainties may be further aggravated when economic and social class separate doctor and child, thereby frustrating the accurate diagnosis of pathology.

These compounded uncertainties often lead to erroneous commitments since psychiatrists tend to err on the side of medical caution and therefore hospitalize patients for whom other dispositions would be more beneficial. The National Institute of Mental Health recently found that only 36 percent of patients below age 20 who were confined at St. Elizabeths Hospital actually required such hospitalization. Of particular relevance to this case, a Georgia study Commission on Mental Health Services for Children and Youth concluded that more than half of the State's institutionalized children were not in need of confinement if other forms of care were made available or used. Cited in *J. L. v. Parham*, 412 F.Supp. 112, 122 (MD Ga. 1976).

II

RIGHTS OF CHILDREN COMMITTED BY THEIR PARENTS

A

Notwithstanding all this, Georgia denies hearings to juveniles institutionalized at the behest of their parents. Georgia rationalizes this practice on the theory that parents act in their children's best interests and therefore may waive their children's due process rights. Children incarcerated because their parents wish them confined, Georgia contends, are really voluntary patients. I cannot accept this argument.

In our society, parental rights are limited by the legitimate rights and interests of their children. "Parents may be free to be become martyrs themselves. But it does not follow they are free, in identical circumstances, to make martyrs of their children before they have reached the age of full and legal discretion when they can make that choice for themselves." *Prince v. Massachusetts*, 321 U.S. 158, 170 (1944). This principle is reflected in the variety of statutes and cases that authorize state intervention on behalf of neglected or abused children and that, inter alia, curtail parental authority to alienate their children's property, to withhold necessary medical treatment,[18] and to deny children exposure to ideas and experiences they may later need as independent and autonomous adults.[19]

This principle is also reflected in constitutional jurisprudence. Notions of parental authority and family autonomy cannot stand as absolute and invariable barriers to the assertion of constitutional rights by children. States, for example, may not condition a minor's right to secure an abortion on attaining her parents' consent since the right to an abortion is an important personal right and since disputes between parents and children on this question would fracture family autonomy. See *Planned Parenthood of Central Missouri v. Danforth*, 428 U.S., at 75, 96 S.Ct., at 2844.

This case is governed by the rule of *Danforth*. The right to be free from wrongful incarceration, physical intrusion, and stigmatization has significance for the individual surely as great as the right to an abortion. Moreover, as in *Danforth*, the parent-child dispute at issue here cannot be characterized as involving only a routine child-rearing decision made within the context of an ongoing family relationship. Indeed, *Danforth* involved only a potential dispute between parent and child, whereas here a break in family autonomy has actually resulted in the parents' decision to surrender custody of their child to a state mental institution. In my view, a child who has been ousted from his family has even greater need for an independent advocate.

18. See, e. g., *Jehovah's Witnesses v. King County Hospital*, 278 F.Supp. 488 (WD Wash. 1967), aff'd, 390 U.S. 598 (1968); *In re Sampson*, 65 Misc.2d 658, 317 N.Y.S.2d 641 (Fam.Ct. Ulster County, 1970), aff'd, 37 A.D.2d 668, 323 N.Y.S.2d 253 (1971), aff'd, 29 N.Y.2d 900, 328 N.Y.S.2d 686, 278 N.E.2d 918 (1972); *State v. Perricone*, 37 N.J. 463, 181 A.2d 751 (1962). Similarly, more recent legal disputes involving the sterilization of children had led to the conclusion that parents are not permitted to authorize operations with such far-reaching consequences. See, e.g., *A.L. v. G.R.H.*, 163 Ind.App. 636, 325 N.E.2d 501 (1975); *In re M.K.R.*, 515 S.W.2d 467 (Mo. 1974); *Frazier v. Levi*, 440 S.W.2d 393 (Tex.Civ.App. 1969).

19. See *Commonwealth v. Renfrew*, 332 Mass. 492, 126 N.E.2d 109 (1955); *Meyerkorth v. State*, 173 Neb. 889, 115 N.W.2d 585 (1962), appeal dism'd, 372 U.S. 705 (1963); *In re Weberman*, 198 Misc. 1055, 100 N.Y.S.2d 60 (Sup.Ct. 1950), aff'd 278 App.Div. 656, 102 N.Y.S.2d 418, aff'd, 302 N.Y. 855, 100 N.E.2d 47, appeal dism'd, 342 U.S. 884 (1951).

Additional considerations counsel against allowing parents unfettered power to institutionalize their children without cause or without any hearing to ascertain that cause. The presumption that parents act in their children's best interests, while applicable to most child-rearing decisions, is not applicable in the commitment context. Numerous studies reveal that parental decisions to institutionalize their children often are the results of dislocation in the family unrelated to the children's mental condition. Moreover, even well-meaning parents lack the expertise necessary to evaluate the relative advantages and disadvantages of inpatient as opposed to outpatient psychiatric treatment. Parental decisions to waive hearings in which such questions could be explored, therefore, cannot be conclusively deemed either informed or intelligent. In these circumstances, I respectfully suggest, it ignores reality to assume blindly that parents act in their children's best interests when making commitment decisions and when waiving their children's due process rights.

B

This does not mean States are obliged to treat children who are committed at the behest of their parents in precisely the same manner as other persons who are involuntarily committed. The demands of due process are flexible and the parental commitment decision carries with it practical implications that States may legitimately take into account. While as a general rule due process requires that commitment hearings precede involuntary hospitalization, when parents seek to hospitalize their children special considerations militate in favor of postponement of formal commitment proceedings and against mandatory adversary preconfinement commitment hearings.

First, the prospect of an adversary hearing prior to admission might deter parents from seeking needed medical attention for their children. Second, the hearings themselves might delay treatment of children whose home life has become impossible and who require some form of immediate state care. Furthermore, because adversary hearings at this juncture would necessarily involve direct challenges to parental authority, judgment, or veracity, preadmission hearings may well result in pitting the child and his advocate against the parents. This, in turn, might traumatize both parent and child and make the child's eventual return to his family more difficult.

Because of these special considerations, I believe that States may legitimately postpone formal commitment proceedings when parents seek inpatient psychiatric treatment for their children. Such children may be admitted, for a limited period, without prior hearing, so long as the admitting psychiatrist first interviews parent and child and concludes that short-term inpatient treatment would be appropriate.

Georgia's present admission procedures are reasonably consistent with these principles. To the extent the District Court invalidated this aspect of the Georgia juvenile commitment scheme and mandated preconfinement hearings in all cases, I agree with the Court that the District Court was in error.

C

I do not believe, however, that the present Georgia juvenile commitment scheme is constitutional in its entirety. Although Georgia may postpone formal commitment hearings, when parents seek to commit their children, the State cannot dispense with such hearings altogether.

Our cases make clear that, when protected interests are at stake, the "fundamental requirement of due process is the opportunity to be heard 'at a meaningful time and in a meaningful manner.'" *Mathews v. Eldridge*, 424 U.S. 319, 333 (1976), quoting in part from *Armstrong v. Manzo*, 380 U.S. 545, 552 (1965). Whenever prior hearings are impracticable, States must provide reasonably prompt postdeprivation hearings. Compare *North Georgia Finishing, Inc. v. Di-Chem, Inc.*, 419 U.S. 601 (1975), with *Mitchell v. W. T. Grant Co.*, 416 U.S. 600 (1974).

The informal postadmission procedures that Georgia now follows are simply not enough to qualify as hearings—let alone reasonably prompt hearings. The procedures lack all the traditional due process safeguards. Commitment decisions are made *ex parte*. Georgia's institutionalized juveniles are not informed of the reasons for their commitment; nor do they enjoy the right to be present at the commitment determination, the right to representation, the right to be heard, the right to be confronted with adverse witnesses, the right to cross-examine, or the right to offer evidence of their own. By any standard of due process, these procedures are deficient. See *Wolff v. McDonnell*, 418 U.S. 539 (1974); *Morrissey v. Brewer*, 408 U.S. 471 (1972); *McNeil v. Director, Patuxent Institution*, 407 U.S. 245 (1972); *Specht v. Patterson*, 386 U.S., at 610. See also *Goldberg v. Kelly*, 397 U.S. 254, 269–271 (1970). I cannot understand why the Court pretermits condemnation of these ex parte procedures which operate to deny Georgia's institutionalized juveniles even "some form of hearing," *Mathews v. Eldridge*, *supra*, 424 U.S., at 333, before they are condemned to suffer the rigors of long-term institutional confinement.

The special considerations that militate against preadmission commitment hearings when parents seek to hospitalize their children do not militate against reasonably prompt postadmission commitment hearings. In the first place, postadmission hearings would not delay the commencement of needed treatment. Children could be cared for by the State pending the disposition decision.

Second, the interest in avoiding family discord would be less significant at this stage since the family autonomy already will have been fractured by the institutionalization of the child. In any event, postadmission hearings are unlikely to disrupt family relationships. At later hearings, the case for and against commitment would be based upon the observations of the hospital staff and the judgments of the staff psychiatrists, rather than upon parental observations and recommendations. The doctors urging commitment, and not the parents, would stand as the child's adversaries. As a consequence, postadmission commitment hearings are unlikely to involve direct challenges to parental authority, judgment, or veracity. To defend the child, the child's advocate need not dispute the parents' original decision to seek medical treatment for their child, or even, for that matter, their observations concerning the child's behavior. The advocate need only argue, for example, that the child had sufficiently improved during his hospital stay to warrant outpatient treatment or outright discharge. Conflict between doctor and advocate on this question is unlikely to lead to family discord.

As a consequence, the prospect of a postadmission hearing is unlikely to deter parents from seeking medical attention for their children and the hearing itself is unlikely so to traumatize parent and child as to make the child's eventual return to the family impracticable.

Nor would postadmission hearings defeat the primary purpose of the state juvenile mental health enterprise. Under the present juvenile commitment scheme, Georgia parents do not enjoy absolute discretion to commit their children to public mental hospitals. Superintendents of state facilities may not accept children for long-term treatment unless they first determine that the children are mentally ill and will likely benefit from long-term hospital care. If the superintendent determines either condition is unmet, the child must be released or refused admission, regardless of the parents' desires. No legitimate state interest would suffer if the superintendent's determinations were reached through fair proceedings with due consideration of fairly presented opposing viewpoints rather than through the present practice of secret, *ex parte* deliberations.[22]

Nor can the good faith and good intentions of Georgia's psychiatrists and social workers, adverted to by the Court, excuse Georgia's *ex parte* procedures. Georgia's admitting psychiatrists, like the school disciplinarians described in *Goss v. Lopez*, 419 U.S. 565 (1975), "although proceeding in utmost good faith, frequently act on the reports and advice of others; and the controlling facts and the nature of the conduct under challenge are often disputed." *Id.*, at 580. Here, as in *Goss*, the "risk of error is not at all trivial, and it should be guarded against if that may be done without prohibitive cost or interference with the... process. '[F]airness can rarely be obtained by secret, one-sided determination of facts decisive of rights....' 'Secrecy is not congenial to truth-seeking and self-righteousness gives too slender an assurance of rightness. No better instrument has been devised for arriving at truth than to give a person in jeopardy of serious loss notice of the case against him and opportunity to meet it.'" *Goss v. Lopez, supra*, at 580, quoting in part from *Joint Anti-Fascist Refugee Committee v. McGrath*, 341 U.S. 123, 170, 171–172 (1951) (Frankfurter, J., concurring).

III

RIGHTS OF CHILDREN COMMITTED BY THEIR STATE GUARDIANS

Georgia does not accord prior hearings to juvenile wards of the State of Georgia committed by state social workers acting *in loco parentis*. The Court dismisses a challenge to this practice on the grounds that state social workers are obliged by statute to act in the children's best interest.

I find this reasoning particularly unpersuasive. With equal logic, it could be argued that criminal trials are unnecessary since prosecutors are not supposed to prosecute innocent persons.

To my mind, there is no justification for denying children committed by their social workers the prior hearings that the Constitution typically requires. In the first place, such children cannot be said to have waived their rights to a prior hearing simply because their social workers wished them to be confined. The rule that parents speak for their children, even if it were applicable in the commitment context, cannot be transmuted into a rule that state social workers speak for their minor clients. The rule in favor of deference to parental authority is designed to shield parental control of child rearing from state interference. See *Pierce v. Society of Sisters*, 268 U.S. 510, 535 (1925). The rule cannot be invoked in defense of unfettered state control of child rearing or to immunize from review the decisions of state

22. Indeed, postadmission hearings may well advance the purposes of the state enterprise. First, hearings will promote accuracy and ensure that the superintendent diverts children who do not require hospitalization to more appropriate programs. Second, the hearings themselves may prove therapeutic. Children who feel that they have received a fair hearing may be more likely to accept the legitimacy of their confinement, acknowledge their illness, and cooperate with those attempting to give treatment. This, in turn, would remove a significant impediment to successful therapy. See Katz, The Right to Treatment—An Enchanting Legal Fiction? 36 U.Chi.L.Rev. 755, 768–769 (1969); *O'Connor v. Donaldson*, 422 U.S. 563, 579 (1975) (Burger, C. J., concurring).

social workers. The social worker-child relationship is not deserving of the special protection and deference accorded to the parent-child relationship, and state officials acting *in loco parentis* cannot be equated with parents. See *O'Connor v. Donaldson*, 422 U.S. 563 (1975); *Wisconsin v. Yoder*, 406 U.S. 205 (1972).

Second, the special considerations that justify postponement of formal commitment proceedings whenever parents seek to hospitalize their children are absent when the children are wards of the State and are being committed upon the recommendations of their social workers. The prospect of preadmission hearings is not likely to deter state social workers from discharging their duties and securing psychiatric attention for their disturbed clients. Moreover, since the children will already be in some form of state custody as wards of the State, prehospitalization hearings will not prevent needy children from receiving state care during the pendency of the commitment proceedings. Finally, hearings in which the decisions of state social workers are reviewed by other state officials are not likely to traumatize the children or to hinder their eventual recovery.

For these reasons, I believe that, in the absence of exigent circumstances, juveniles committed upon the recommendation of their social workers are entitled to preadmission commitment hearings. As a consequence, I would hold Georgia's present practice of denying these juveniles prior hearings unconstitutional.

IV

Children incarcerated in public mental institutions are constitutionally entitled to a fair opportunity to contest the legitimacy of their confinement. They are entitled to some champion who can speak on their behalf and who stands ready to oppose a wrongful commitment. Georgia should not be permitted to deny that opportunity and that champion simply because the children's parents or guardians wish them to be confined without a hearing. The risk of erroneous commitment is simply too great unless there is some form of adversary review. And fairness demands that children abandoned by their supposed protectors to the rigors of institutional confinement be given the help of some separate voice.

NOTES AND QUESTIONS

1. What must a state do before it may commit a child to a mental institution after *Parham*?

2. What is the test that the Court uses to determine what process is due? Is that a different test from the one used by Justices Stewart and Brennan? What procedural protections must the state provide according to Stewart? According to Brennan? Do those procedural protections differ?

3. How would you characterize Chief Justice Burger's view of the state mental-health system? Consider again the Court's decision in *Gault*. Do you think that this is another example of focusing on the intentions of the reformers rather than on their actual practices?

4. The Court notes that some children are committed by their parents, while others are committed by the state. Are these two groups of children entitled to different procedural protections?

5. Do you think that the Court has an understanding of the child-welfare system? Of families? Does Justice Brennan?

6. Appellees' counsel notified the Court of J.L.'s death by letter. The appellees' brief stated that J.L. died in August 1976 and noted that the case was not rendered moot by the death of the named plaintiff in a certified class action. The brief, however, did not mention why J.L. died. J.L. was Joey Lister. He was released to the custody of his father, Dr. Joe Mack Lister, who abused him. Joey subsequently committed suicide. He was twelve years old. KRIS SHEPARD, RATIONING JUSTICE: POVERTY LAWYERS AND POOR PEOPLE IN THE DEEP SOUTH 175–176 (2007). His father was convicted of cruelty to children and received a five-year prison sentence. *Lister v. State*, 238 S.E.2d 591 (1977) (ruling photos of child's corpse admissible to show bruises and rope marks).

7. Approximately 20 percent of children in the United States have or had a seriously debilitating medical illness. A little more than 13 percent of younger children ages eight to fifteen had a diagnosable mental disorder in the previous year. Most of those children were diagnosed with attention-deficit/hyperactivity disorder (ADHD). Mood disorders and major depression were the next most frequently diagnosed disorders among this age group. National Institute of Mental Health, Statistics, Any Disorder among Children, http://www.nimh.nih.gov/statistics/1ANYDIS_CHILD.shtml. Only about half of these children receive treatment; however, even fewer children with anxiety disorders receive treatment (32.2 percent). National Institute of Mental Health, Statistics, Use of Mental Health Services and Treatment among Children, http://www.nimh.nih.gov/statistics/1NHANES.shtml.

8. To what extent is the institutionalization of children in the mental-health system still a problem? Consider the following excerpt.

Lois A. Weithorn, *Envisioning Second-Order Change in America's Responses to Troubled and Troublesome Youth*, 33 HOFSTRA L. REV. 1305, 1363, 1368, 1380, 1381–1388 (2005).

Reports from around the country indicate that families encounter excessively long waiting lists when seeking community-based mental health services for their children....

The inaccessibility and unavailability of appropriate community-based mental health services for youth and their families has led to a "spill-over" of individuals and families into other service and intervention systems, and in particular, hospital emergency rooms....

In light of all of the other places that troubled and troublesome youth have been turning up, it is perhaps surprising that the rates of children entering hospitals and residential treatment centers for mental health treatment have continued to surge....

...Between the 1920s and 1970s, annual admission rates of minors for inpatient psychiatric care increased almost ten-fold, from 13 admissions per 100,000 youth in the national population to 123.8 youth per 100,000 in 1971. Admission rates continued to climb during the latter three decades of the century, rising to 128.1 youth per 100,000 in 1980, to 186.3 in 1986, and to a startling 412.1 in 1997. Thus, between 1971 and 1997, the rate increased over 330 percent.

The continued increase in the rate of admission between 1986 and 1997 is initially surprising in light of the emergence and ultimate domination of managed care policies that have restricted use of expensive interventions such as inpatient mental health treatment. Yet, these policies place limits on the length of hospital stays, which results in more frequent readmissions of patients.

Particularly notable between 1971 and 1980 was a shift in the relative frequency with which children and adolescents admitted for inpatient psychiatric treatment used public versus private facilities. In 1971, private hospital admissions accounted for 37.4 percent of juvenile mental hospitalizations. By 1980, the proportion of total psychiatric admissions that occurred in private facilities had risen to 61.2 percent. The rate of admission of minors to public facilities decreased 35.9 percent during this nine-year period while the rate of admission of minors to private facilities jumped 69.3 percent. Rates of admission to public facilities rose slightly in the 1980s and 1990s. Yet, private facility admissions continued to soar, and accounted for approximately three-quarters of juvenile psychiatric admissions by 1997. These data strongly support Paul Lerman's prediction, made over twenty years ago, that the private sector of the mental health industry is the fastest growing system of juvenile institutional care in the United States. The shift toward private domination of the inpatient mental health sector reduces the accessibility of inpatient mental health services for families without wealth or good insurance coverage. Historically, state hospitals, like the juvenile justice and child welfare systems, had not turned away those viewed as needing their services, irrespective of financial resources or insurance benefits. The reduction of public mental health beds appears to constrict those options available to those who have exhausted, or never had, such resources or benefits, making it more likely that such individuals will turn to other service and intervention systems when in crisis.

Rates of admission to residential treatment centers for emotionally disturbed children rose substantially in the past three decades as well, increasing from 10,591 admissions of persons under the age of 18 in 1971 to 65,949 such admissions in 1997, an increase of over 600 percent. Examining the combined inpatient and residential treatment center figures, total admission rates rose between 1971 and 1997 from 139 to 506.9, a 365 percent increase. It is highly likely, however, that these data underestimate the increase in admissions.

Two other statistics developed by [the Department of Health and Human Services] DHHS help complete the picture of institutional use. Residence data, referred to by DHHS as persons "under care population" include "all persons who were admitted to the program before the first day of the specified survey month and who received service from the program during the survey month." In other words, this statistic takes a one-day snapshot of those persons residing in the institution for the purpose of receiving services. The other statistic, called "patient care episodes" ("PCEs"), is the sum of the one-day residence count and the number of admissions for the one-year period immediately following. Thus, this variable is the most comprehensive, in that it combines admission and residence data.

...It is striking to note that, in contrast to admission data, which increased in a linear fashion throughout the twentieth century, residence data peaked in the 1970s, and were cut in half between 1971 and 1997. Because the number of children in residence in mental health facilities at any one time is capped by the number of beds, the reduction in residence numbers is consistent with reports that psychiatric facilities have closed, or down-sized, resulting in an overall reduction in the beds available for psychiatric patients.

PCE data, as the composite of admission and residence counts, reflect the substantial increase that occurred for both of its components between the 1920s and 1970s, with an almost 700 percent increase in PCE rates over that fifty-year period. Despite the "tempering" role that the decreases in residence counts have on the 1980s and 1990s numbers, the increase in the rates per 100,000 of PCEs between 1971 and 1997 is over 170 percent, with a doubling of rates between 1986 and 1997. Thus, despite substantial reductions in both the number of inpatient and residential mental health facilities serving children and the number of beds available, PCEs have continued to climb. These data, of course, do not include children served in scatter beds of general hospitals for the purpose of receiving mental health treatment, nor do they include children who "board" on medical units or in emergency rooms.

A comparison of the inpatient and [residential treatment center] RTC residence data reveals that, while residence rates per 100,000 children in hospital-like facilities were *cut in half* between 1971 and 1997, residence rates of children to RTC *doubled* during that same period. Thus, when taken together, these two types of facilities reveal a combined residence rate that has grown steadily over the century. The increase in filled beds accounted for by the RTCs has more than offset the reductions in the psychiatric inpatient units. These data are certainly consistent with the growth and increasing importance of RTCs in serving children identified as emotionally disturbed. Perhaps the most dramatic figures of all, however, are the patient care episode figures.... These data combine the one-day residence count with the number of additional admissions that occur throughout the year, as a more stable measure of the number of instances that the facility provided service to a child in a one-year period. While the rate of PCEs in psychiatric facilities increased 34.6 percent between 1971 and 1986, the rate doubled between 1986 and 1997. The PCEs for RTCs almost doubled (up 92.3 percent) between 1971 and 1986, with an additional increase of 89.4 percent from 1986 to 1997. Finally, PCEs in both types of facilities combined increased 46 percent between 1971 and 1986, and 97.6 percent between 1986 and 1997.

Weithorn also notes that many parents have relinquished custody of their children in order to obtain mental-health services that they would otherwise be unable to afford, wait for, or find. *Id.* at 1375. The problem became so acute that the GAO issued a report in 2003 conservatively estimating that at least 12,700 children had been placed in the child-welfare and juvenile-justice systems with the hope of accessing mental-health services. U.S. Gen. Acct. Office, GAO-03-397, Child Welfare and Juvenile Justice: Federal Agencies Could Play a Stronger Role in Helping States Reduce the Number of Children Placed Solely to Obtain Mental Health Services 4 (2003), http://www.gao.gov/assets/240/237936.pdf (hereinafter GAO, 2003). A 2004 report issued by the U.S. House of Representatives Committee on Government Reform found that in the six-month period between January and June 2003, 15,000 youth were awaiting community mental-health services in juvenile-detention facilities. Special Investigations Div., Minority Staff of House Comm. on Gov't Reform, 108th Cong., Incarceration of Youth Who Are Waiting for Community Mental Health Services in the United States II (Comm. Print 2004). Weithorn argues that relinquishments may do more harm than good, further traumatizing children by separating them from their family and friends. Even when some children do get mental-health services, they may not receive appropriate care and may even become victims of physical or sexual abuse. *Id.* at 1377. The Bazelon Center for Mental Health also has been a strong advocate for ensuring that families may stay together. See Bazelon Center for Mental Health Law, Staying Together: Preventing Custody Relinquishment for Children's Access to Mental Health Services (1999); Bazelon Center for Mental Health Law, Avoiding Cruel Choices (2002).

9. The American Psychiatric Association (APA) has stated it "deplore[s] any instance when a child or adolescent has been inappropriately hospitalized, especially when there are appropriate, equally effective, and less restrictive treatment settings available in the community and

affordable to the patient." American Psychiatric Association, Position Statement on Psychiatric Hospitalization of Children and Adolescents (approved June1989), http://www.psych.org/advocacy--newsroom/position-statements/apa-position-statements. The APA recommends that psychiatrists (and preferably child and adolescent psychiatrists) make all admission, treatment, and discharge decisions based on the medical needs of the patients and in accordance with the profession's code of ethics. The APA also recommends that psychiatric and other hospitals assign this responsibility to psychiatrists and that hospitals "must respect their medical judgment." The APA also "will continue to press for development of a full spectrum of adequate, financially available facilities and services for the diagnosis and treatment of all children and adolescents in need of psychiatric care, and it urges other professionals, hospitals, and other psychiatric facilities to do the same." *Id.* Do you think that *Parham* comports with APA policy?

10. *Current state law.* Twelve states and the District of Columbia require the constitutional minimum established by *Parham*. See Ala. Code § 22-52-51 (2011); Ariz. Rev. Stat. § 36-518 (2011); Cal. Welf. & Inst. Code § 6000 (Deering 2011); Del. Code Ann. tit. 16 § 5123 (2011); D.C. Code Ann. § 21-511 (2011); Ga. Code Ann. § 37-3-20 (2011); Ind. Code Ann. § 12-26-3-2 (2011); Mo. Rev. Stat. § 632.110 (2011); Nev. Rev. Stat. Ann. § 433A.140 (2011); N.H. Rev. Stat. Ann. § 135-C:12 (2011); N.D. Cent. Code § 25-03.1-04 (2011); Or. Rev. Stat. § 426.220 (2011); Wyo. Stat. Ann. §25-10-106 (2011). Of these, only California and Arizona have specific provisions for minors in the custody of the juvenile court. In California, minors in the custody of the juvenile court may apply for admission on their own motion, Cal. Welf. & Inst. Code § 6552 (Deering 2011); while Arizona requires court approval before a minor in court custody may be admitted, Ariz. Rev. Stat. § 36-518 (2011). The D.C. statute allows both a minor's parent and the minor's spouse to seek commitment. D.C. Code Ann. § 21-511 (2011). While *Parham* applies to public institutions, all but six states also apply their statutes to private institutions. Ala. Code § 22-52-51 (2011); Cal. Welf. & Inst. Code § 6000 (Deering 2011); Neb. Rev. Stat. Ann. § 83-324 (2011); N.H. Rev. Stat. Ann. § 135-C:12 (LexisNexis 2011); N.D. Cent. Code § 25-03.1-04 (2011); Or. Rev. Stat. § 426.220 (2011).

Other states, however, require more than the *Parham* constitutional minimum. For example, twenty-six states set age limits ranging from twelve to sixteen at which children may or must consent to their own voluntary admission, and some set age limits at which parents no longer can voluntarily admit their child. Colo. Rev. Stat. § 27-65-103 (2010); Conn. Gen. Stat. § 17a-79 (2011); Ga. Code Ann. § 37-3-20 (2011); Haw. Rev. Stat. Ann. § 334-60.1 (2011); Idaho Code Ann. § 66-318 (2011); 405 Ill. Comp. Stat. Ann. 5/3-502 (2011); Kan. Stat. Ann. § 59-2949 (2011); Ky. Rev. Stat. Ann. § 645.030 (2011); La. Child. Code Ann. art. 1464 (2011); Md. Code Ann., Health-Gen. § 10-609 (2011); Mass. Ann. Laws ch. 123, § 10 (2011); Mich. Comp. Laws Serv. § 330.1498d (2011); Minn. Stat. § 253B.04 (2010); Miss. Code Ann. § 41-21-103 (2011); Mont. Code Ann. § 53-21-112 (2010); N.M. Stat. Ann. § 32A-6A-21 (2011); N.Y. Mental Hyg. Law § 9.13 (Consol. 2011); Okla. Stat. tit. 43A, § 5-503 (2011); 50 Pa. Stat. Ann. § 7201 (2011); S.C. Code Ann. § 44-24-20 (2010); Tenn. Code Ann. § 33-6-201 (2011); Tex. Health & Safety Code Ann. § 572.001 (2010); Vt. Stat. Ann. tit. 18, § 7503 (2011); Va. Code Ann. § 16.1-338 (2011); Wash. Rev. Code Ann. § 71.34.500 (LexisNexis 2011); W. Va. Code Ann. § 27-4-1 (2011); Wis. Stat. § 51.13 (2011). In seven states, for example, minors of a certain age (ranging from twelve to sixteen) must consent to their own admission, Haw. Rev. Stat. Ann. § 334-60.1 (2011); 405 Ill. Comp. Stat. Ann. 5/3-502 (2011); N.M. Stat. Ann. § 32A-6A-21 (2011); Vt. Stat. Ann. tit. 18, § 7503 (2011); Va. Code Ann. § 16.1-338 (2011); W. Va. Code Ann. § 27-4-1 (2011); or at the very least, must sign their applications for admission, R.I. Gen. Laws § 40.1-5-6 (2011). In eight states, parents may no longer voluntarily admit their children when they reach a specified age, ranging from fourteen to sixteen. Conn. Gen. Stat. § 17a-79 (2011); Idaho Code Ann. § 66-318 (2011); Ky. Rev. Stat. Ann. § 645.030 (LexisNexis 2011); Miss. Code Ann. § 41-21-103 (2011); 50 Pa. Stat. Ann. § 7201 (2011); S.C. Code Ann. § 44-24-20 (2010); Tex. Health & Safety Code Ann. § 572.001 (2010); Vt. Stat. Ann. tit. 18, § 7503 (2011).

Some states extend additional procedural protections. For example, four states require the appointment of guardians *ad litem* (GAL): Alaska requires that all minors are appointed a GAL upon admission to monitor the minor's best interests, Alaska Stat. § 47.30.690 (2011); Colorado does not allow admission of minors in the custody of the juvenile court unless a GAL has been appointed, Colo. Rev. Stat. § 27-65-103 (2010); New Mexico requires that GALs be appointed upon admission of minors fourteen and older to determine best interests, N.M. Stat. Ann. § 32A-6A-20 (2011); and South Carolina requires that GALs be appointed upon admission of minors sixteen and older to determine voluntariness, S.C. Code Ann. § 44-24-30 (2010). In Utah and Florida, a hearing must be held prior to admission of a minor, Fla. Stat. Ann. § 394.4625 (2011); Utah Code Ann. § 62A-15-625 (2011); in North Carolina, a hearing is held upon admission, N.C. Gen. Stat. § 122C-224 (2011); and in Ohio, a hearing is held upon petition, Ohio Rev. Code Ann. § 5122.02 (2011). In Illinois, Iowa, Michigan, and Virginia, a hearing must be held upon objection to admission by the minor, 405 Ill. Comp. Stat. Ann. 5/3-509 (2011); Iowa Code § 229.2 (2011); Mich. Comp. Laws Serv. § 330.1498n (2011); Va. Code Ann. § 16.1-339 (2011). In South Dakota, a minor has a right to execute a written objection, S.D. Codified Laws § 27A-15-15.1 (2011); and in Louisiana, a minor must be released upon objection unless other commitment proceedings are initiated, La. Child. Code Ann. art. 1462 (2011).

A number of states recognize the child's right to counsel. See Conn. Gen. Stat. § 17a-76 (2001); 405 Ill. Comp. Stat. Ann. 5/3-509 (LexisNexis 2011); Iowa Code § 229.2 (2009); Ky. Rev. Stat. Ann. § 645.030 (LexisNexis 2011) (when child is sixteen); La. Child. Code Ann. art. 1461 (2010); Mass. Ann. Laws ch. 123, § 10 (LexisNexis 2011) (opportunity to consult with attorney when sixteen); N.M. Stat. Ann. § 32A-6A-21 (LexisNexis 2007); N.C. Gen. Stat. § 122C-224.1 (2010); Okla. Stat. Ann. tit. 43A, § 5-510 (2009); S.D. Codified Laws § 27A-15-35 (2010); Va. Code Ann. § 16.1-339 (2010); Wis. Stat. Ann. § 51.13 (2010) (right to counsel if hearing held). Other states permit the appointment of counsel under certain circumstances. In Alaska, for example, the guardian *ad litem* may request counsel be appointed if the guardian finds that placement is not appropriate. Alaska Stat. § 47.30.690 (2010). Other states mandate the appointment of counsel when the minor objects to hospitalization or continued treatment. See Colo. Rev. Stat. § 27-65-103 (2010). Some jurisdictions require the appointment of counsel upon admission or application for admission. Counsel also may be appointed at the minor's request, Mont. Code Ann. § 53-21-112 (2005).

Finally, a number of states do not specifically address the commitment of minors to a psychiatric institution. For example, Alabama's statute does not mention minors but allows a parent to admit any Alabama resident. Ala. Code § 22-52-51 (2011). Arkansas allows admission as long as the patient agrees. Ark. Code Ann. § 20-47-204 (2011). Nebraska allows admission upon written application by the person seeking admission. Neb. Rev. Stat. Ann. § 83-324 (2011). New Jersey has no statute regarding voluntary admissions.

Problem. Danielle is a fifteen-year-old high school student. She has expressed "confusion" about her sexual identity. She finds herself attracted to other girls in her class, and other students have begun calling her names like "faggot" and "queer." Her parents believe that Danielle is in need of therapy, and they would like to place her in an inpatient treatment program to "cure" her of her "gender-identity disorder." Danielle, however, objects strenuously to such placement. Should a mental-health or other inpatient facility voluntarily commit Danielle? What would be the basis for such a commitment?

BELLOTTI V. BAIRD
Supreme Court of the United States
443 U.S. 622 (1979)

MR. JUSTICE POWELL announced the judgment of the Court and delivered an opinion, in which THE CHIEF JUSTICE, MR. JUSTICE STEWART, and MR. JUSTICE REHNQUIST joined.

These appeals present a challenge to the constitutionality of a state statute regulating the access of minors to abortions. They require us to continue the inquiry we began in *Planned Parenthood of Central Missouri v. Danforth*, 428 U.S. 52 (1976), and *Bellotti v. Baird*, 428 U.S. 132 (1976).

I

A

On August 2, 1974, the Legislature of the Commonwealth of Massachusetts passed, over the Governor's veto, an Act pertaining to abortions performed within the State. 1974 Mass. Acts, ch. 706. According to its title, the statute was intended to regulate abortions "within present constitutional limits." Shortly before the Act was to go into effect, the class action from which these appeals arise was commenced in the District Court to enjoin, as unconstitutional, the provision of the Act now codified as Mass.Gen.Laws Ann., ch. 112, § 12S (West Supp. 1979).

Section 12S provides in part:

> "If the mother is less than eighteen years of age and has not married, the consent of both the mother and her parents [to an abortion to be performed on the mother] is required. If one or both of the mother's parents refuse such consent, consent may be obtained by order of a judge of the superior court for good cause shown, after such hearing as he deems necessary. Such a hearing will not require the appointment of a guardian for the mother. If one of the parents has died or has deserted his or her family, consent by the remaining parent is sufficient. If both parents have died or have deserted their family, consent of the mother's guardian or other person having duties similar to a guardian, or any person who had assumed the care and custody of the mother is sufficient. The commissioner of public health shall prescribe a written form for such consent. Such form shall be signed by the proper person or persons and given to the physician performing the abortion who shall maintain it in his permanent files."

Physicians performing abortions in the absence of the consent required by § 12S are subject to injunctions and criminal penalties. See Mass.Gen.Laws Ann., ch. 112, §§ 12Q, 12T, and 12U (West Supp. 1979).

A three-judge District Court was convened to hear the case pursuant to 28 U.S.C. § 2281 (1970 ed.), repealed by Pub.L. 94-381, § 1, 90 Stat. 1119.[3] Plaintiffs in the suit, appellees in both the cases before us now, were William Baird; Parents Aid Society, Inc. (Parents Aid), of which Baird is founder and director; Gerald Zupnick, M.D., who regularly performs abortions at the Parents Aid clinic; and an unmarried minor, identified by the pseudonym "Mary Moe," who, at the commencement of the suit, was pregnant, residing at home with her parents, and desirous of obtaining an abortion without informing them.

Mary Moe was permitted to represent the "class of unmarried minors in Massachusetts who have adequate capacity to give a valid and informed consent [to abortion], and who do not wish to involve their parents." *Baird v. Bellotti*, 393 F.Supp. 847, 850 (Mass. 1975) (*Baird I*). Initially there was some confusion whether the rights of minors who wish abortions without parental involvement but who lack "adequate capacity" to give such consent also could be adjudicated in the suit. The District Court ultimately determined that Dr. Zupnick was entitled to assert the rights of these minors. See *Baird v. Bellotti*, 450 F.Supp. 997, 1001, and n. 6 (Mass. 1978).[5]

Planned Parenthood League of Massachusetts and Crittenton Hastings House & Clinic, both organizations that provide counseling to pregnant adolescents, and Phillip Stubblefield, M.D. (intervenors), appeared as *amici curiae* on behalf of the plaintiffs. The District Court "accepted [this group] in a status something more than amici because of reservations about the adequacy of plaintiffs' representation [of the plaintiff classes in the suit]." *Id.*, at 999 n. 3.

Defendants in the suit, appellants here in No. 78-329, were the Attorney General of Massachusetts and the District Attorneys of all counties in the State. Jane Hunerwadel was permitted to intervene as a defendant and representative of the class of Massachusetts parents having unmarried minor daughters who then were, or might become, pregnant. She and the class she represents are appellants in No. 78-330.

Following three days of testimony, the District Court issued an opinion invalidating § 12S. *Baird I*, *supra*. The court rejected appellees' argument that all minors capable of becoming pregnant also are capable of giving informed consent to an abortion, or that it always is in the best interests of a minor who desires an abortion to have one. See 393 F.Supp., at 854. But the court was convinced that "a substantial number of females under the age of 18 are capable of forming a valid consent," *id.*, at 855, and "that a significant number of [these] are unwilling to tell their parents." *Id.*, at 853.

In its analysis of the relevant constitutional principles, the court stated that "there can be no doubt but that a female's constitutional right to an abortion in the first trimester does not depend upon her calendar age." *Id.*, at 855–856. The court found no justification for the parental consent limitation placed on that right by § 12S, since it concluded that the statute was "cast not in terms of protecting the minor,... but in recognizing independent rights of

3. The proceedings before the court and the substance of its opinion are described in detail in *Bellotti v. Baird*, 428 U.S. 132, 136–143 (1976).

5. Appellants argue that these "immature" minors never were before the District Court and that the court's remedy should have been tailored to grant relief only to the class of "mature" minors. It is apparent from the District Court's opinions, however, that it considered the constitutionality of § 12S as applied to all pregnant minors who might be affected by it. We accept that the rights of this entire category of minors properly were subject to adjudication.

parents." *Id.*, at 856. The "independent" parental rights protected by § 12S, as the court understood them, were wholly distinct from the best interests of the minor.[8]

B

Appellants sought review in this Court, and we noted probable jurisdiction. *Bellotti v. Baird*, 423 U.S. 982 (1975). After briefing and oral argument, it became apparent that § 12S was susceptible of a construction that "would avoid or substantially modify the federal constitutional challenge to the statute." *Bellotti v. Baird*, 428 U.S. 132, 148 (1976) (*Bellotti I*). We therefore vacated the judgment of the District Court, concluding that it should have abstained and certified to the Supreme Judicial Court of Massachusetts appropriate questions concerning the meaning of § 12S, pursuant to existing procedure in that State. See Mass.Sup.Jud.Ct. Rule 3:21.

On remand, the District Court certified nine questions to the Supreme Judicial Court.[9] These were answered in an opinion styled *Baird v. Attorney General*, 371 Mass. 741,

8. One member of the three-judge court dissented, arguing that the decision of the majority to allow Mary Moe to proceed in the case without notice to her parents denied them their parental rights without due process of law, and that § 12S was consistent with the decisions of this Court recognizing the propriety of parental control over the conduct of children. See 393 F.Supp., at 857–865.

9. The nine questions certified by the District Court, with footnotes omitted, are as follows:

"1. What standards, if any, does the statute establish for a parent to apply when considering whether or not to grant consent?

"a) Is the parent to consider 'exclusively...what will serve the child's best interest'?

"b) If the parent is not limited to considering exclusively the minor's best interests, can the parent take into consideration the "long-term consequences to the family and her parents' marriage relationship"?

"c) Other?

"2. What standard or standards is the superior court to apply?

"a) Is the superior court to disregard all parental objections that are not based exclusively on what would serve the minor's best interests?

"b) If the superior court finds that the minor is capable, and has, in fact, made and adhered to, an informed and reasonable decision to have an abortion, may the court refuse its consent based on a finding that a parent's, or its own, contrary decision is a better one?

"c) Other?

"3. Does the Massachusetts law permit a minor (a) "capable of giving informed consent," or (b) "incapable of giving informed consent," "to obtain [a court] order without parental consultation"?

"4. If the court answers any of question 3 in the affirmative, may the superior court, for good cause shown, enter an order authorizing an abortion, (a), without prior notification to the parents, and (b), without subsequent notification?

"5. Will the Supreme Judicial Court prescribe a set of procedures to implement c. 112, [§ 12S] which will expedite the application, hearing, and decision phases of the superior court proceeding provided thereunder? Appeal?

"6. To what degree do the standards and procedures set forth in c. 112, § 12F (Stat.1975, c. 564), authorizing minors to give consent to medical and dental care in specified circumstances, parallel the grounds and procedures for showing good cause under c. 112, [§ 12S]?

"7. May a minor, upon a showing of indigency, have court-appointed counsel?

"8. Is it a defense to his criminal prosecution if a physician performs an abortion solely with the minor's own, valid, consent, that he reasonably, and in good faith, though erroneously, believed that she was eighteen or more years old or had been married?

"9. Will the Court make any other comments about the statute which, in its opinion, might assist us in determining whether it infringes the United States Constitution?"

360 N.E.2d 288 (1977) (Attorney General). Among the more important aspects of § 12S, as authoritatively construed by the Supreme Judicial Court, are the following:

1. In deciding whether to grant consent to their daughter's abortion, parents are required by § 12S to consider exclusively what will serve her best interests. See *id.*, at 746–747, 360 N.E.2d, at 292–293.
2. The provision in § 12S that judicial consent for an abortion shall be granted, parental objections notwithstanding, "for good cause shown" means that such consent shall be granted if found to be in the minor's best interests. The judge "must disregard all parental objections, and other considerations, which are not based exclusively" on that standard. *Id.*, at 748, 360 N.E.2d, at 293.
3. Even if the judge in a § 12S proceeding finds "that the minor is capable of making, and has made, an informed and reasonable decision to have an abortion," he is entitled to withhold consent "in circumstances where he determines that the best interests of the minor will not be served by an abortion." *Ibid.*, 360 N.E.2d, at 293.
4. As a general rule, a minor who desires an abortion may not obtain judicial consent without first seeking both parents' consent. Exceptions to the rule exist when a parent is not available or when the need for the abortion constitutes "'an emergency requiring immediate action.'" *Id.*, at 750, 360 N.E.2d, at 294. Unless a parent is not available, he must be notified of any judicial proceedings brought under § 12S. *Id.*, at 755-756, 360 N.E.2d, at 297.
5. The resolution of § 12S cases and any appeals that follow can be expected to be prompt. The name of the minor and her parents may be held in confidence. If need be, the Supreme Judicial Court and the superior courts can promulgate rules or issue orders to ensure that such proceedings are handled expeditiously. *Id.*, at 756–758, 360 N.E.2d, at 297–298.
6. Massachusetts Gen.Laws Ann., ch. 112, § 12F (West Supp. 1979), which provides, inter alia, that certain classes of minors may consent to most kinds of medical care without parental approval, does not apply to abortions, except as to minors who are married, widowed, or divorced. See 371 Mass., at 758–762, 360 N.E.2d, at 298–300. Nor does the State's common-law "mature minor rule" create an exception to § 12S. *Id.*, at 749–750, 360 N.E.2d, at 294. See n. 27, *infra.*

C

Following the judgment of the Supreme Judicial Court, appellees returned to the District Court and obtained a stay of the enforcement of § 12S until its constitutionality could be determined. *Baird v. Bellotti*, 428 F.Supp. 854 (Mass. 1977) (*Baird II*). After permitting discovery by both sides, holding a pretrial conference, and conducting further hearings, the District Court again declared § 12S unconstitutional and enjoined its enforcement. *Baird v. Bellotti*, 450 F.Supp. 997 (Mass. 1978) (*Baird III*). The court identified three particular aspects of the statute which, in its view, rendered it unconstitutional.

First, as construed by the Supreme Judicial Court, § 12S requires parental notice in virtually every case where the parent is available. The court believed that the evidence warranted a finding "that many, perhaps a large majority of 17-year olds are capable of informed consent, as are a not insubstantial number of 16-year olds, and some even younger." *Id.*, at 1001. In addition, the court concluded that it would not be in the best interests of some "immature" minors—those incapable of giving informed consent—even to inform their parents of their intended abortions. Although the court declined to decide whether the burden of requiring a minor to take her parents to court was, *per se*, an impermissible burden on her right to seek an abortion, it concluded that Massachusetts could not constitutionally insist that parental permission be sought or notice given "in those cases where a court, if given free rein, would find that it was to the minor's best interests that one or both of her parents not be informed...." *Id.*, at 1002.

Second, the District Court held that § 12S was defective in permitting a judge to veto the abortion decision of a minor found to be capable of giving informed consent. The court reasoned that upon a finding of maturity and informed consent, the State no longer was entitled to impose legal restrictions upon this decision. *Id.*, at 1003. Given such a finding, the court could see "no reasonable basis" for distinguishing between a minor and an adult, and it therefore concluded that § 12S was not only "an undue burden in the due process sense, [but] a discriminatory denial of equal protection [as well]." *Id.*, at 1004.

Finally, the court decided that § 12S suffered from what it termed "formal overbreadth," *ibid.*, because the statute failed explicitly to inform parents that they must consider only the minor's best interests in deciding whether to grant consent. The court believed that, despite the Supreme Judicial Court's construction of § 12S, parents naturally would infer from the statute that they were entitled to withhold consent for other, impermissible reasons. This was thought to create a "chilling effect" by enhancing the possibility that parental consent would be denied wrongfully and that the minor would have to proceed in court.

Having identified these flaws in § 12S, the District Court considered whether it should engage in "judicial repair." *Id.*, at 1005. It declined either to sever the statute or to give it a construction different from that set out by the Supreme Judicial Court, as that tribunal arguably had invited it to do. See *Attorney General*, 371 Mass., at 745–746, 360 N.E.2d, at 292. The District Court therefore adhered to its previous position, declaring § 12S unconstitutional and permanently enjoining its enforcement.[11] Appellants sought review in this Court a second time, and we again noted probable jurisdiction. 439 U.S. 925 (1978).

II

A child, merely on account of his minority, is not beyond the protection of the Constitution. As the Court said in *In re Gault*, 387 U.S. 1, 13 (1967), "whatever may be their precise impact, neither the Fourteenth Amendment nor the Bill of Rights is for adults alone." This observation, of course, is but the beginning of the analysis. The Court long has recognized that the status of minors under the law is unique in many respects. As Mr. Justice Frankfurter aptly put it: "[C]hildren have a very special place in life which law should reflect. Legal theories

11. The dissenting judge agreed that the State could not permit a judge to override the decision of a minor found to be mature and capable of giving informed consent to an abortion. He disagreed with the remainder of the court's conclusions: the best-interests limitation on the withholding of parental consent in the Supreme Judicial Court's opinion, he argued, must be treated as if part of the statutory language itself; and he read the evidentiary record as proving that only rarely would a pregnant minor's interests be disserved by consulting with her parents about a desired abortion. He also noted the value to a judge in a § 12S proceeding of having the parents before him as a source of evidence as to the minor's maturity and what course would serve her best interests. See *Baird III*, 450 F.Supp., at 1006–1020.

and their phrasing in other cases readily lead to fallacious reasoning if uncritically transferred to determination of a State's duty towards children." *May v. Anderson*, 345 U.S. 528, 536 (1953) (concurring opinion). The unique role in our society of the family, the institution by which "we inculcate and pass down many of our most cherished values, moral and cultural," *Moore v. East Cleveland*, 431 U.S. 494, 503–504 (1977) (plurality opinion), requires that constitutional principles be applied with sensitivity and flexibility to the special needs of parents and children. We have recognized three reasons justifying the conclusion that the constitutional rights of children cannot be equated with those of adults: the peculiar vulnerability of children; their inability to make critical decisions in an informed, mature manner; and the importance of the parental role in child rearing.

A

The Court's concern for the vulnerability of children is demonstrated in its decisions dealing with minors' claims to constitutional protection against deprivations of liberty or property interests by the State. With respect to many of these claims, we have concluded that the child's right is virtually coextensive with that of an adult. For example, the Court has held that the Fourteenth Amendment's guarantee against the deprivation of liberty without due process of law is applicable to children in juvenile delinquency proceedings. *In re Gault, supra.* In particular, minors involved in such proceedings are entitled to adequate notice, the assistance of counsel, and the opportunity to confront their accusers. They can be found guilty only upon proof beyond a reasonable doubt, and they may assert the privilege against compulsory self-incrimination. *In re Winship*, 397 U.S. 358 (1970); *In re Gault, supra.* See also *Ingraham v. Wright*, 430 U.S. 651 (1977) (corporal punishment of schoolchildren implicates constitutionally protected liberty interest); cf. *Breed v. Jones*, 421 U.S. 519 (1975) (Double Jeopardy Clause prohibits prosecuting juvenile as an adult after an adjudicatory finding in juvenile court that he had violated a criminal statute). Similarly, in *Goss v. Lopez*, 419 U.S. 565 (1975), the Court held that children may not be deprived of certain property interests without due process.

These rulings have not been made on the uncritical assumption that the constitutional rights of children are indistinguishable from those of adults. Indeed, our acceptance of juvenile courts distinct from the adult criminal justice system assumes that juvenile offenders constitutionally may be treated differently from adults. In order to preserve this separate avenue for dealing with minors, the Court has said that hearings in juvenile delinquency cases need not necessarily "'conform with all of the requirements of a criminal trial or even of the usual administrative hearing.'" *In re Gault, supra*, 387 U.S., at 30, quoting *Kent v. United States*, 383 U.S. 541, 562 (1966). Thus, juveniles are not constitutionally entitled to trial by jury in delinquency adjudications. *McKeiver v. Pennsylvania*, 403 U.S. 528 (1971). Viewed together, our cases show that although children generally are protected by the same constitutional guarantees against governmental deprivations as are adults, the State is entitled to adjust its legal system to account for children's vulnerability and their needs for "concern, . . . sympathy, and . . . paternal attention." *Id.*, at 550 (plurality opinion).

B

Second, the Court has held that the States validly may limit the freedom of children to choose for themselves in the making of important, affirmative choices with potentially serious consequences. These rulings have been grounded in the recognition that, during the formative years of childhood and adolescence, minors often lack the experience, perspective, and judgment to recognize and avoid choices that could be detrimental to them.

Ginsberg v. New York, 390 U.S. 629 (1968), illustrates well the Court's concern over the inability of children to make mature choices, as the First Amendment rights involved are clear examples of constitutionally protected freedoms of choice. At issue was a criminal conviction for selling sexually oriented magazines to a minor under the age of 17 in violation of a New York state law. It was conceded that the conviction could not have stood under the First Amendment if based upon a sale of the same material to an adult. *Id.*, at 634. Notwithstanding the importance the Court always has attached to First Amendment rights, it concluded that "even where there is an invasion of protected freedoms 'the power of the state to control the conduct of children reaches beyond the scope of its authority over adults...,'" *id.*, at 638, quoting *Prince v. Massachusetts*, 321 U.S. 158, 170 (1944). The Court was convinced that the New York Legislature rationally could conclude that the sale to children of the magazines in question presented a danger against which they should be guarded. *Ginsberg*, *supra*, at 641, 88 S.Ct., at 1281. It therefore rejected the argument that the New York law violated the constitutional rights of minors.[15]

C

Third, the guiding role of parents in the upbringing of their children justifies limitations on the freedoms of minors. The State commonly protects its youth from adverse governmental action and from their own immaturity by requiring parental consent to or involvement in important decisions by minors. But an additional and more important justification for state deference to parental control over children is that "[t]he child is not the mere creature of the state; those who nurture him and direct his destiny have the right, coupled with the high duty, to recognize and prepare him for additional obligations." *Pierce v. Society of Sisters*, 268 U.S. 510, 535 (1925). "The duty to prepare the child for 'additional obligations'...must be read to include the inculcation of moral standards, religious beliefs, and elements of good citizenship." *Wisconsin v. Yoder*, 406 U.S. 205, 233 (1972). This affirmative process of teaching, guiding, and inspiring by precept and example is essential to the growth of young people into mature, socially responsible citizens.

We have believed in this country that this process, in large part, is beyond the competence of impersonal political institutions. Indeed, affirmative sponsorship of particular ethical,

15. Although the State has considerable latitude in enacting laws affecting minors on the basis of their lesser capacity for mature, affirmative choice, *Tinker v. Des Moines School Dist.*, 393 U.S. 503 (1969), illustrates that it may not arbitrarily deprive them of their freedom of action altogether. The Court held in Tinker that a schoolchild's First Amendment freedom of expression entitled him, contrary to school policy, to attend school wearing a black armband as a silent protest against American involvement in the hostilities in Vietnam. The Court acknowledged that the State was permitted to prohibit conduct otherwise shielded by the Constitution that "for any reason—whether it stems from time, place, or type of behavior—materially disrupts classwork or involves substantial disorder or invasion of the rights of others." *Id.*, at 513. It upheld the First Amendment right of the schoolchildren in that case, however, not only because it found no evidence in the record that their wearing of black armbands threatened any substantial interference with the proper objectives of the school district, but also because it appeared that the challenged policy was intended primarily to stifle any debate whatsoever—even nondisruptive discussions—on important political and moral issues. See *id.*, at 510

religious, or political beliefs is something we expect the State not to attempt in a society constitutionally committed to the ideal of individual liberty and freedom of choice. Thus, "[i]t is cardinal with us that the custody, care and nurture of the child reside first in the parents, whose primary function and freedom include *preparation for obligations the state can neither supply nor hinder*." *Prince v. Massachusetts*, *supra*, 321 U.S., at 166 (emphasis added).

Unquestionably, there are many competing theories about the most effective way for parents to fulfill their central role in assisting their children on the way to responsible adulthood. While we do not pretend any special wisdom on this subject, we cannot ignore that central to many of these theories, and deeply rooted in our Nation's history and tradition, is the belief that the parental role implies a substantial measure of authority over one's children. Indeed, "constitutional interpretation has consistently recognized that the parents' claim to authority in their own household to direct the rearing of their children is basic in the structure of our society." *Ginsberg v. New York*, *supra*, 390 U.S., at 639.

Properly understood, then, the tradition of parental authority is not inconsistent with our tradition of individual liberty; rather, the former is one of the basic presuppositions of the latter. Legal restrictions on minors, especially those supportive of the parental role, may be important to the child's chances for the full growth and maturity that make eventual participation in a free society meaningful and rewarding.[17] Under the Constitution, the State can "properly conclude that parents and others, teachers for example, who have [the] primary responsibility for children's well-being are entitled to the support of laws designed to aid discharge of that responsibility." *Ginsberg v. New York*, 390 U.S., at 639.[18]

III

With these principles in mind, we consider the specific constitutional questions presented by these appeals. In § 12S, Massachusetts has attempted to reconcile the constitutional right of a woman, in consultation with her physician, to choose to terminate her pregnancy as established by *Roe v. Wade*, 410 U.S. 113 (1973), and *Doe v. Bolton*, 410 U.S. 179 (1973), with the special interest of the State in encouraging an unmarried pregnant minor to seek the advice of her parents in making the important decision whether or not to bear a child. As noted above, § 12S was before us in *Bellotti I*, 428 U.S. 132 (1976), where we remanded the case for interpretation of its provisions by the Supreme Judicial Court of Massachusetts. We previously had held in *Planned Parenthood of Central Missouri v. Danforth*, 428 U.S. 52 (1976), that a State could not lawfully authorize an absolute parental veto over the decision of a minor to terminate her pregnancy. *Id.*, at 74. In *Bellotti*, *supra*, we recognized that § 12S could be read as "fundamentally different from a statute that creates a 'parental veto,'" 428 U.S., at 145, thus "avoid[ing] or substantially modify[ing] the federal constitutional challenge to the statute." *Id.*, at 148. The question before

17. See Hafen, Children's Liberation and the New Egalitarianism: Some Reservations about Abandoning Children to Their "Rights," 1976 B.Y.U.L.Rev. 605.

18. The Court's opinions discussed in the text above—*Pierce*, *Yoder*, *Prince*, and *Ginsberg*—all have contributed to a line of decisions suggesting the existence of a constitutional parental right against undue, adverse interference by the State. See also *Smith v. Organization of Foster Families*, 431 U.S. 816, 842–844 (1977); *Carey v. Population Services International*, 431 U.S. 678, 708 (1977) (opinion of Powell, J.); *Moore v. East Cleveland*, 431 U.S. 494 (1977) (plurality opinion); *Stanley v. Illinois*, 405 U.S. 645, 651 (1972); *Meyer v. Nebraska*, 262 U.S. 390, 399 (1923). Cf. *Parham v. J.R.*, 442 U.S. 584 (1979); *id.*, at 621 (Stewart, J., concurring in result).

us—in light of what we have said in the prior cases—is whether § 12S, as authoritatively interpreted by the Supreme Judicial Court, provides for parental notice and consent in a manner that does not unduly burden the right to seek an abortion. See *id.*, at 147, 96 S.Ct., at 2866.

Appellees and intervenors contend that even as interpreted by the Supreme Judicial Court of Massachusetts, § 12S does unduly burden this right. They suggest, for example, that the mere requirement of parental notice constitutes such a burden. As stated in Part II above, however, parental notice and consent are qualifications that typically may be imposed by the State on a minor's right to make important decisions. As immature minors often lack the ability to make fully informed choices that take account of both immediate and long-range consequences, a State reasonably may determine that parental consultation often is desirable and in the best interest of the minor.[19] It may further determine, as a general proposition, that such consultation is particularly desirable with respect to the abortion decision—one that for some people raises profound moral and religious concerns.[20] As Mr. Justice Stewart wrote in concurrence in *Planned Parenthood of Central Missouri v. Danforth*, *supra*, at 91:

> "There can be little doubt that the State furthers a constitutionally permissible end by encouraging an unmarried pregnant minor to seek the help and advice of her parents in making the very important decision whether or not to bear a child. That is a grave decision, and a girl of tender years, under emotional stress, may be ill-equipped to make it without mature advice and emotional support. It seems unlikely that she will obtain adequate counsel and support from the attending physician at an abortion clinic, where abortions for pregnant minors frequently take place." (Footnote omitted.)

But we are concerned here with a constitutional right to seek an abortion. The abortion decision differs in important ways from other decisions that may be made during minority. The need to preserve the constitutional right and the unique nature of the abortion decision, especially when made by a minor, require a State to act with particular sensitivity when it legislates to foster parental involvement in this matter.

A

The pregnant minor's options are much different from those facing a minor in other situations, such as deciding whether to marry. A minor not permitted to marry before the age of majority is required simply to postpone her decision. She and her intended spouse may preserve the opportunity for later marriage should they continue to desire it. A pregnant adolescent, however, cannot preserve for long the possibility of aborting, which effectively expires in a matter of weeks from the onset of pregnancy.

Moreover, the potentially severe detriment facing a pregnant woman, see *Roe v. Wade*, 410 U.S., at 153, is not mitigated by her minority. Indeed, considering her probable education,

19. In *Planned Parenthood of Central Missouri v. Danforth*, 428 U.S., at 75, "[w]e emphasize[d] that our holding... [did] not suggest that every minor, regardless of age or maturity, may give effective consent for termination of her pregnancy."

20. The expert testimony at the hearings in the District Court uniformly was to the effect that parental involvement in a minor's abortion decision, if compassionate and supportive, was highly desirable. The findings of the court reflect this consensus. See *Baird I*, 393 F.Supp., at 853.

employment skills, financial resources, and emotional maturity, unwanted motherhood may be exceptionally burdensome for a minor. In addition, the fact of having a child brings with it adult legal responsibility, for parenthood, like attainment of the age of majority, is one of the traditional criteria for the termination of the legal disabilities of minority. In sum, there are few situations in which denying a minor the right to make an important decision will have consequences so grave and indelible.

Yet, an abortion may not be the best choice for the minor. The circumstances in which this issue arises will vary widely. In a given case, alternatives to abortion, such as marriage to the father of the child, arranging for its adoption, or assuming the responsibilities of motherhood with the assured support of family, may be feasible and relevant to the minor's best interests. Nonetheless, the abortion decision is one that simply cannot be postponed, or it will be made by default with far-reaching consequences.

For these reasons, as we held in *Planned Parenthood of Central Missouri v. Danforth*, 428 U.S., at 74, "the State may not impose a blanket provision... requiring the consent of a parent or person *in loco parentis* as a condition for abortion of an unmarried minor during the first 12 weeks of her pregnancy." Although, as stated in Part II, *supra*, such deference to parents may be permissible with respect to other choices facing a minor, the unique nature and consequences of the abortion decision make it inappropriate "to give a third party an absolute, and possibly arbitrary, veto over the decision of the physician and his patient to terminate the patient's pregnancy, regardless of the reason for withholding the consent." 428 U.S., at 74. We therefore conclude that if the State decides to require a pregnant minor to obtain one or both parents' consent to an abortion, it also must provide an alternative procedure[22] whereby authorization for the abortion can be obtained.

A pregnant minor is entitled in such a proceeding to show either: (1) that she is mature enough and well enough informed to make her abortion decision, in consultation with her physician, independently of her parents' wishes;[23] or (2) that even if she is not able to make this decision independently, the desired abortion would be in her best interests. The proceeding in which this showing is made must assure that a resolution of the issue, and any appeals that may follow, will be completed with anonymity and sufficient expedition to provide an effective opportunity for an abortion to be obtained. In sum, the procedure must ensure that the provision requiring parental consent does not in fact amount to the "absolute, and possibly arbitrary, veto" that was found impermissible in *Danforth*. *Ibid.*

22. As § 12S provides for involvement of the state superior court in minors' abortion decisions, we discuss the alternative procedure described in the text in terms of judicial proceedings. We do not suggest, however, that a State choosing to require parental consent could not delegate the alternative procedure to a juvenile court or an administrative agency or officer. Indeed, much can be said for employing procedures and a forum less formal than those associated with a court of general jurisdiction.

23. The nature of both the State's interest in fostering parental authority and the problem of determining "maturity" makes clear why the State generally may resort to objective, though inevitably arbitrary, criteria such as age limits, marital status, or membership in the Armed Forces for lifting some or all of the legal disabilities of minority. Not only is it difficult to define, let alone determine, maturity, but also the fact that a minor may be very much an adult in some respects does not mean that his or her need and opportunity for growth under parental guidance and discipline have ended. As discussed in the text, however, the peculiar nature of the abortion decision requires the opportunity for case-by-case evaluations of the maturity of pregnant minors.

B

It is against these requirements that § 12S must be tested. We observe initially that as authoritatively construed by the highest court of the State, the statute satisfies some of the concerns that require special treatment of a minor's abortion decision. It provides that if parental consent is refused, authorization may be "obtained by order of a judge of the superior court for good cause shown, after such hearing as he deems necessary." A superior court judge presiding over a § 12S proceeding "must disregard all parental objections, and other considerations, which are not based exclusively on what would serve the minor's best interests." *Attorney General*, 371 Mass., at 748, 360 N.E.2d, at 293. The Supreme Judicial Court also stated: "Prompt resolution of a [§ 12S] proceeding may be expected.... The proceeding need not be brought in the minor's name and steps may be taken, by impoundment or otherwise, to preserve confidentiality as to the minor and her parents.... [W]e believe that an early hearing and decision on appeal from a judgment of a Superior Court judge may also be achieved." *Id.*, at 757–758, 360 N.E.2d, at 298. The court added that if these expectations were not met, either the superior court, in the exercise of its rulemaking power, or the Supreme Judicial Court would be willing to eliminate any undue burdens by rule or order. *Ibid.*

Despite these safeguards, which avoid much of what was objectionable in the statute successfully challenged in *Danforth*, § 12S falls short of constitutional standards in certain respects. We now consider these.

(1)

Among the questions certified to the Supreme Judicial Court was whether § 12S permits any minors—mature or immature—to obtain judicial consent to an abortion without any parental consultation whatsoever. The state court answered that, in general, it does not. "[T]he consent required by [§ 12S must] be obtained for every nonemergency abortion where the mother is less than eighteen years of age and unmarried." *Attorney General, supra*, at 750, 360 N.E.2d, at 294. The text of § 12S itself states an exception to this rule, making consent unnecessary from any parent who has "died or has deserted his or her family." The Supreme Judicial Court construed the statute as containing an additional exception: Consent need not be obtained "where no parent (or statutory substitute) is available." *Ibid.* The court also ruled that an available parent must be given notice of any judicial proceedings brought by a minor to obtain consent for an abortion.[27] *Id.*, at 755–756, 360 N.E.2d, at 297.

27. This reading of the statute requires parental consultation and consent more strictly than appellants themselves previously believed was necessary. In their first argument before this Court, and again before the Supreme Judicial Court, appellants argued that § 12S was not intended to abrogate Massachusetts' common-law "mature minor" rule as it applies to abortions. See 428 U.S., at 144. They also suggested that, under some circumstances, § 12S might permit even immature minors to obtain judicial approval for an abortion without any parental consultation. See 428 U.S., at 145; *Attorney General, supra*, 371 Mass., at 751, 360 N.E.2d, at 294. The Supreme Judicial Court sketched the outlines of the mature minor rule that would apply in the absence of § 12S: "The mature minor rule calls for an analysis of the nature of the operation, its likely benefit, and the capacity of the particular minor to understand fully what the medical procedure involves.... Judicial intervention is not required. If judicial approval is obtained, however, the doctor is protected from a subsequent claim that the circumstances did not warrant his reliance on the mature minor rule, and, of course, the minor patient is afforded advance protection against a misapplication of the rule." *Id.*, at 752, 360 N.E.2d, at 295. "We conclude that, apart from statutory limitations which are constitutional, where the best interests of a minor will be served by not notifying his or her parents of intended medical treatment and where

We think that, construed in this manner, § 12S would impose an undue burden upon the exercise by minors of the right to seek an abortion. As the District Court recognized, "there are parents who would obstruct, and perhaps altogether prevent, the minor's right to go to court." *Baird III*, 450 F.Supp., at 1001. There is no reason to believe that this would be so in the majority of cases where consent is withheld. But many parents hold strong views on the subject of abortion, and young pregnant minors, especially those living at home, are particularly vulnerable to their parents' efforts to obstruct both an abortion and their access to court. It would be unrealistic, therefore, to assume that the mere existence of a legal right to seek relief in superior court provides an effective avenue of relief for some of those who need it the most.

We conclude, therefore, that under state regulation such as that undertaken by Massachusetts, every minor must have the opportunity—if she so desires—to go directly to a court without first consulting or notifying her parents. If she satisfies the court that she is mature and well enough informed to make intelligently the abortion decision on her own, the court must authorize her to act without parental consultation or consent. If she fails to satisfy the court that she is competent to make this decision independently, she must be permitted to show that an abortion nevertheless would be in her best interests. If the court is persuaded that it is, the court must authorize the abortion. If, however, the court is not persuaded by the minor that she is mature or that the abortion would be in her best interests, it may decline to sanction the operation.

There is, however, an important state interest in encouraging a family rather than a judicial resolution of a minor's abortion decision. Also, as we have observed above, parents naturally take an interest in the welfare of their children—an interest that is particularly strong where a normal family relationship exists and where the child is living with one or both parents. These factors properly may be taken into account by a court called upon to determine whether an abortion in fact is in a minor's best interests. If, all things considered, the court determines that an abortion is in the minor's best interests, she is entitled to court authorization without any parental involvement. On the other hand, the court may deny the abortion request of an immature minor in the absence of parental consultation if it concludes that her best interests would be served thereby, or the court may in such a case defer decision until there is parental consultation in which the court may participate. But this is the full extent to which parental involvement may be required.[28] For the reasons stated above, the constitutional right to seek an abortion may not be unduly burdened by state-imposed conditions upon initial access to court.

(2)

Section 12S requires that both parents consent to a minor's abortion. The District Court found it to be "custom" to perform other medical and surgical procedures on minors with the consent of only one parent, and it concluded that "nothing about abortions... requires the

the minor is capable of giving informed consent to that treatment, the mature minor rule applies in this Commonwealth." *Id.*, at 754, 360 N.E.2d, at 296. The Supreme Judicial Court held that the common-law mature minor rule was inapplicable to abortions because it had been legislatively superseded by § 12S.

28. Of course, if the minor consults with her parents voluntarily and they withhold consent, she is free to seek judicial authorization for the abortion immediately.

minor's interest to be treated differently." *Baird I*, 393 F.Supp., at 852. See *Baird III*, *supra*, at 1004 n. 9.

We are not persuaded that, as a general rule, the requirement of obtaining both parents' consent unconstitutionally burdens a minor's right to seek an abortion. The abortion decision has implications far broader than those associated with most other kinds of medical treatment. At least when the parents are together and the pregnant minor is living at home, both the father and mother have an interest—one normally supportive—in helping to determine the course that is in the best interests of a daughter. Consent and involvement by parents in important decisions by minors long have been recognized as protective of their immaturity. In the case of the abortion decision, for reasons we have stated, the focus of the parents' inquiry should be the best interests of their daughter. As every pregnant minor is entitled in the first instance to go directly to the court for a judicial determination without prior parental notice, consultation, or consent, the general rule with respect to parental consent does not unduly burden the constitutional right. Moreover, where the pregnant minor goes to her parents and consent is denied, she still must have recourse to a prompt judicial determination of her maturity or best interests.[29]

(3)

Another of the questions certified by the District Court to the Supreme Judicial Court was the following: "If the superior court finds that the minor is capable [of making], and has, in fact, made and adhered to, an informed and reasonable decision to have an abortion, may the court refuse its consent based on a finding that a parent's, or its own, contrary decision is a better one?" *Attorney General*, 371 Mass., at 747 n. 5, 360 N.E.2d, at 293 n. 5. To this the state court answered:

> "[W]e do not view the judge's role as limited to a determination that the minor is capable of making, and has made, an informed and reasonable decision to have an abortion. Certainly the judge must make a determination of those circumstances, but, if the statutory role of the judge to determine the best interests of the minor is to be carried out, he must make a finding on the basis of all relevant views presented to him. We suspect that the judge will give great weight to the minor's determination, if informed and reasonable, but in circumstances where he determines that the best interests of the minor will not be served by an abortion, the judge's determination should prevail, assuming that his conclusion is supported by the evidence and adequate findings of fact." *Id.*, at 748, 360 N.E.2d, at 293.

The Supreme Judicial Court's statement reflects the general rule that a State may require a minor to wait until the age of majority before being permitted to exercise legal rights independently. But we are concerned here with the exercise of a constitutional right of unique character. As stated above, if the minor satisfies a court that she has attained sufficient maturity to make a fully informed decision, she then is entitled to make her abortion decision independently. We therefore agree with the District Court that § 12S cannot constitutionally

29. There will be cases where the pregnant minor has received approval of the abortion decision by one parent. In that event, the parent can support the daughter's request for a prompt judicial determination, and the parent's support should be given great, if not dispositive, weight.

permit judicial disregard of the abortion decision of a minor who has been determined to be mature and fully competent to assess the implications of the choice she has made.[30]

IV

Although it satisfies constitutional standards in large part, § 12S falls short of them in two respects: First, it permits judicial authorization for an abortion to be withheld from a minor who is found by the superior court to be mature and fully competent to make this decision independently. Second, it requires parental consultation or notification in every instance, without affording the pregnant minor an opportunity to receive an independent judicial determination that she is mature enough to consent or that an abortion would be in her best interests. Accordingly, we affirm the judgment of the District Court insofar as it invalidates this statute and enjoins its enforcement.[32]

The propriety of parental involvement in a minor's abortion decision does not diminish as the pregnancy progresses and legitimate concerns for the pregnant minor's health increase. Furthermore, the opportunity for direct access to court which we have described is adequate to safeguard throughout pregnancy the constitutionally protected interests of a minor in the abortion decision. Thus, although a significant number of abortions within the scope of § 12S might be performed during the later stages of pregnancy, we do not believe a different analysis of the statute is required for them.

Affirmed.

Mr. Justice Rehnquist, concurring.

I join the opinion of Mr. Justice Powell and the judgment of the Court. At such time as this Court is willing to reconsider its earlier decision in *Planned Parenthood of Central Missouri v. Danforth*, 428 U.S. 52 (1976), in which I joined the opinion of Mr. Justice White, dissenting in part, I shall be more than willing to participate in that task. But unless and until that time comes, literally thousands of judges cannot be left with nothing more than the guidance offered by a truly fragmented holding of this Court.

Mr. Justice Stevens, with whom Mr. Justice Brennan, Mr. Justice Marshall, and Mr. Justice Blackmun join, concurring in the judgment.

In *Roe v. Wade*, 410 U.S. 113, the Court held that a woman's right to decide whether to terminate a pregnancy is entitled to constitutional protection. In *Planned Parenthood of Central Missouri v. Danforth*, 428 U.S. 52, 72–75, the Court held that a pregnant minor's right to make the abortion decision may not be conditioned on the consent of one parent. I am persuaded

30. Appellees and intervenors have argued that § 12S violates the Equal Protection Clause of the Fourteenth Amendment. As we have concluded that the statute is constitutionally infirm for other reasons, there is no need to consider this question.

32. The opinion of Mr. Justice Stevens, concurring in the judgment, joined by three Members of the Court, characterizes this opinion as "advisory" and the questions it addresses as "hypothetical." Apparently, this is criticism of our attempt to provide some guidance as to how a State constitutionally may provide for adult involvement—either by parents or a state official such as a judge—in the abortion decisions of minors. In view of the importance of the issue raised, and the protracted litigation to which these parties already have been subjected, we think it would be irresponsible simply to invalidate § 12S without stating our views as to the controlling principles.

that these decisions require affirmance of the District Court's holding that the Massachusetts statute is unconstitutional.

The Massachusetts statute is, on its face, simple and straightforward. It provides that every woman under 18 who has not married must secure the consent of both her parents before receiving an abortion. "If one or both of the mother's parents refuse such consent, consent may be obtained by order of a judge of the Superior Court for good cause shown." Mass.Gen. Laws Ann., ch. 112, § 12S (West Supp. 1979).

Whatever confusion or uncertainty might have existed as to how this statute was to operate, see *Bellotti v. Baird*, 428 U.S. 132, has been eliminated by the authoritative construction of its provisions by the Massachusetts Supreme Judicial Court. See *Baird v. Attorney General*, 371 Mass. 741, 360 N.E.2d 288 (1977). The statute was construed to require that every minor who wishes an abortion must first seek the consent of both parents, unless a parent is not available or unless the need for the abortion constitutes "'an emergency requiring immediate action.'" *Id.*, at 750, 360 N.E.2d, at 294. Both parents, so long as they are available, must also receive notice of judicial proceedings brought under the statute by the minor. In those proceedings, the task of the judge is to determine whether the best interests of the minor will be served by an abortion. The decision is his to make, even if he finds "that the minor is capable of making, and has made, an informed and reasonable decision to have an abortion." *Id.*, at 748, 360 N.E.2d, at 293. Thus, no minor in Massachusetts, no matter how mature and capable of informed decisionmaking, may receive an abortion without the consent of either both her parents or a superior court judge. In every instance, the minor's decision to secure an abortion is subject to an absolute third-party veto.[1]

In *Planned Parenthood of Central Missouri v. Danforth*, *supra*, this Court invalidated statutory provisions requiring the consent of the husband of a married woman and of one parent of a pregnant minor to an abortion. As to the spousal consent, the Court concluded that "we cannot hold that the State has the constitutional authority to give the spouse unilaterally the ability to prohibit the wife from terminating her pregnancy, when the State itself lacks that right." 428 U.S., at 70. And as to the parental consent, the Court held that "[j]ust as with the requirement of consent from the spouse, so here, the State does not have the constitutional authority to give a third party an absolute, and possibly arbitrary, veto over the decision of the physician and his patient to terminate the patient's pregnancy, regardless of the reason for withholding the consent." *Id.*, at 74. These holdings, I think, equally apply to the Massachusetts statute. The differences between the two statutes are few. Unlike the Missouri statute, Massachusetts requires the consent of both of the woman's parents. It does, of course, provide an alternative in the form of a suit initiated by the woman in superior court. But in that proceeding, the judge is afforded an absolute veto over the minor's decisions, based on his judgment of her best interests. In Massachusetts, then, as in Missouri, the State has imposed an "absolute limitation on the minor's right to obtain an abortion," *Id.*, at 90 (Stewart, J., concurring), applicable to every pregnant minor in the State who has not married.

The provision of an absolute veto to a judge—or potentially, to an appointed administrator—is to me particularly troubling. The constitutional right to make the abortion decision affords protection to both of the privacy interests recognized in this Court's cases: "One is the

1. By affording such a veto, the Massachusetts statute does far more than simply provide for notice to the parents.... Neither *Danforth* nor this case determines the constitutionality of a statute which does no more than require notice to the parents, without affording them or any other third party an absolute veto.

individual interest in avoiding disclosure of personal matters, and another is the interest in independence in making certain kinds of important decisions." *Whalen v. Roe*, 429 U.S. 589, 599–600 (footnotes omitted). It is inherent in the right to make the abortion decision that the right may be exercised without public scrutiny and in defiance of the contrary opinion of the sovereign or other third parties. In Massachusetts, however, every minor who cannot secure the consent of both her parents—which under *Danforth* cannot be an absolute prerequisite to an abortion—is required to secure the consent of the sovereign. As a practical matter, I would suppose that the need to commence judicial proceedings in order to obtain a legal abortion would impose a burden at least as great as, and probably greater than, that imposed on the minor child by the need to obtain the consent of a parent.[3] Moreover, once this burden is met, the only standard provided for the judge's decision is the best interest of the minor. That standard provides little real guidance to the judge, and his decision must necessarily reflect personal and societal values and mores whose enforcement upon the minor—particularly when contrary to her own informed and reasonable decision—is fundamentally at odds with privacy interests underlying the constitutional protection afforded to her decision.

In short, it seems to me that this litigation is governed by *Danforth*; to the extent this statute differs from that in *Danforth*, it is potentially even more restrictive of the constitutional right to decide whether or not to terminate a pregnancy. Because the statute has been once authoritatively construed by the Massachusetts Supreme Judicial Court, and because it is clear that the statute as written and construed is not constitutional, I agree with Mr. Justice Powell that the District Court's judgment should be affirmed. Because his opinion goes further, however, and addresses the constitutionality of an abortion statute that Massachusetts has not enacted, I decline to join his opinion.[4]

Mr. Justice White, dissenting.

I was in dissent in *Planned Parenthood of Central Missouri v. Danforth*, 428 U.S. 52, 94-95 (1976), on the issue of the validity of requiring the consent of a parent when an unmarried woman under 18 years of age seeks an abortion. I continue to have the views I expressed there and also agree with much of what Mr. Justice Stevens said in dissent in that case. *Id.*, at 101–105. I would not, therefore, strike down this Massachusetts law.

But even if a parental consent requirement of the kind involved in *Danforth* must be deemed invalid, that does not condemn the Massachusetts law, which, when the parents

3. A minor may secure the assistance of counsel in filing and prosecuting her suit, but that is not guaranteed. The Massachusetts Supreme Judicial Court in response to the question whether a minor, upon a showing of indigency, may have court-appointed counsel, "construe[d] the statutes of the Commonwealth to authorize the appointment of counsel or a guardian ad litem for an indigent minor at public expense, if necessary, if the judge, *in his discretion*, concludes that the best interests of the minor would be served by such an appointment." *Baird v. Attorney General*, 371 Mass. 741, 764, 360 N.E.2d 288, 301 (1977) (emphasis added).

4. Until and unless Massachusetts or another State enacts a less restrictive statutory scheme, this Court has no occasion to render an advisory opinion on the constitutionality of such a scheme. A real statute—rather than a mere outline of a possible statute—and a real case or controversy may well present questions that appear quite different from the hypothetical questions Mr. Justice Powell has elected to address. Indeed, there is a certain irony in his suggestion that a statute that is intended to vindicate "the special interest of the State in encouraging an unmarried pregnant minor to seek the advice of her parents in making the important decision whether or not to bear a child," need not require notice to the parents of the minor's intended decision. That irony makes me wonder whether any legislature concerned with parental consultation would, in the absence of today's advisory opinion, have enacted a statute comparable to the one my Brethren have discussed.

object, authorizes a judge to permit an abortion if he concludes that an abortion is in the best interests of the child. Going beyond *Danforth*, the Court now holds it unconstitutional for a State to require that in all cases parents receive notice that their daughter seeks an abortion and, if they object to the abortion, an opportunity to participate in a hearing that will determine whether it is in the "best interests" of the child to undergo the surgery. Until now, I would have thought inconceivable a holding that the United States Constitution forbids even notice to parents when their minor child who seeks surgery objects to such notice and is able to convince a judge that the parents should be denied participation in the decision.

With all due respect, I dissent.

NOTES AND QUESTIONS

1. Under what circumstances may a pregnant minor obtain an abortion without parental consent? Why did the Court find the Massachusetts statute unconstitutional? Did the Court provide any guidance regarding an acceptable procedure? Is Justice Stevens correct when he says that the Court has provided an advisory opinion?

2. Whose rights are violated by the Massachusetts statute? If it is the pregnant minor's rights, then why should her parents have anything to say about an abortion?

3. Why does Justice Stevens concur? What constitutional infirmities does he see with the state statute?

4. Since *Bellotti v. Baird* was decided, the Supreme Court has considered several other cases involving limitations on the rights of pregnant minors to obtain abortions. In *Hodgson v. Minnesota*, 497 U.S. 417 (1990), the Court upheld a Minnesota statute requiring that both of the pregnant minor's parents be notified prior to the performing of an abortion. The regulation was upheld by a deeply divided court. Four justices held that the law was constitutional with or without a bypass provision. Justice O'Connor provided the deciding vote, noting that the law passed constitutional muster as long as there was a bypass provision. In *Ohio v. Akron Center for Reproductive Health*, 497 U.S. 502 (1990), the Court, rejecting a due-process challenge, upheld an Ohio law requiring the minor to prove by clear and convincing evidence that she was sufficiently mature or that an abortion was in her best interests. In *Planned Parenthood of Southeastern Pennsylvania v. Casey*, 505 U.S. 833 (1992), the Court reaffirmed *Roe v. Wade* but upheld a number of restrictions on the right to obtain an abortion, including a parental-consent provision. In *Lambert v. Wicklund*, 520 U.S. 292 (1997), the Court in a *per curiam* opinion upheld a Montana law that permitted a minor to obtain a judicial waiver of the parental-notice requirement if she could show that notice was not in her best interests. In *Ayotte v. Planned Parenthood of New England*, 546 U.S. 320 (2006), a New Hampshire statute required parental notification forty-eight hours prior to the abortion procedure. While the statute contained a bypass provision, it did not explicitly make an exception regarding the notice requirement where there was a medical emergency. The lower court invalidated the entire Act because of the failure to provide this exception. The Court reaffirmed the "right to require parental involvement" but remanded the case for the lower court to consider whether there was a narrower remedy than invalidation of the entire statute.

Abortion is a politically divisive topic in the United States. See NAOMI CAHN & JUNE CARBONE, RED FAMILIES V. BLUE FAMILIES 95–100 (2010). Some argue that abortion opponents have engaged in a political and legislative strategy to carve out exceptions to *Roe v. Wade*, by "marginaliz[ing] certain women and impos[ing] barriers to exercising reproductive rights." Julia L. Ernst et al., *The Global Pattern of U.S. Initiatives Curtailing Women's Reproductive Rights: A Perspective on the Increasingly Anti-Choice Mosaic*, 6 U. PA. J. CONST. L. 752, 765–766 (2004) (authors are lawyers at Center for Reproductive Rights). These strategies have included restricting access to abortion for low-income women, limiting access for adolescents, imposing restrictions such as waiting periods, and challenging the level of judicial scrutiny applied to reproductive rights.

5. How many states require parental notice or consent? According to Rachel Rebouché:

> Today, in almost every state that has a parental consent or notice law, the alternative process is a court hearing where a judge determines the minor-petitioner's maturity or best interests as set out by the state's statute.
>
> State legislatures have passed parental involvement laws in forty-four states. Thirty-seven states have an involvement law in force with the laws of seven other states enjoined or, for one state, repealed. There are basically two types of parental involvement laws—those that require the abortion provider to obtain consent from the minor's parent before an abortion is performed (consent laws) and those that require the abortion provider to give a parent notice before the abortion occurs (notice laws). Mississippi and North Dakota require consent from both parents, and Minnesota requires notice to both parents. Oklahoma, Texas, Utah, and Wyoming require both notice and consent.
>
> Notice laws require abortion providers to give a parent either actual notice (notification delivered in person or by telephone) or constructive notice. Laws typically mandate that providers give constructive notice to a parent by special delivery, which requires the addressee to present valid identification that confirms her identity upon delivery. State statutes require varying time periods for constructive notice: many laws mandate 48 hours and some 72 hours before the abortion. If notice is delivered in person or by telephone, typically only 24 hours notice is required. For consent statutes, providers must obtain oral or written consent from the parent or adult(s) designated by statute.
>
> Common to notice and consent laws is the requirement that providers use "'reasonable means' to notify parents or to obtain consent or to learn a patient's age." Statutes do not typically set out how a minor must prove her age or how providers must verify a patient's age. Moreover, few states detail what evidence a parent must give to prove her relationship with the minor. For example, five state laws require the person consenting or receiving notice to present identification or documentation that establishes the relationship between the parent/guardian and the minor. Arkansas, for example, requires photographic identification (with notarized written consent in lieu of in-person consent)—proof of which providers must keep for five years.
>
> Six of the thirty-seven state statutes in force allow a non-parent adult to give consent or to accept notice—generally, an adult who acts like a parent to the minor. Virginia permits consent by a "[p]erson standing *in loco parentis*," such as a grandparent or adult sibling, "with whom the minor regularly and customarily resides and who has care and control of the minor." Wisconsin permits consent from an adult family member, such as a grandparent, aunt, uncle, or sibling, who is at least twenty-five years old. Laws in Delaware, Iowa, North Carolina, and South Carolina allow a grandparent to give consent or receive notice.

Finally, some statutes create specific categories of minors that do not have to comply with notice and consent standards at all. Minors sixteen or older do not need to notify a parent in Delaware, and seventeen-year-olds are exempt from the consent law in South Carolina. Almost all notice or consent laws allow emancipated minors to make abortion decisions without their parents, although the definition of emancipation varies from state to state. As set out in Virginia's consent statute, an emancipated minor can be a youth emancipated by a court, married or divorced, in the armed forces, or "willingly living separate and apart from her parents or guardian, with the consent or acquiescence of the parents or guardian." Most statutes provide that married minors can make abortion decisions without parental involvement or a bypass. Some laws define living apart in terms of a minor's ability to support herself financially outside of the parental home.

In addition to independent minors, several statutes make exceptions for minors who have destructive relationships with their parents or whose pregnancies may be the result of sexual assault. For example, some statutes exempt minors from the requirements of notice or consent if they have been abused, neglected, or sexually assaulted. Many of these laws apply the exemption only when the parent or guardian is the perpetrator. The evidence needed to establish abuse or assault, and what a provider must do in response to learning this information, varies.

Almost all states allow physicians to perform abortions without parental involvement or a judicial bypass if a minor has a medical emergency. Some laws define emergency as an instance where continued pregnancy would compromise a minor's health, safety, or well-being. Others are more restrictive, defining medically necessary abortions as those that are needed "to avert her death or for which a delay will create serious risk of substantial and irreversible impairment of major bodily function."

Rachel Rebouché, *Parental Involvement Laws and New Governance*, 34 HARV. J. L. & GENDER 175, 179–183 (2011).

6. How many girls obtain abortions in the United States? In 2008, 236,220 teenage girls between the ages of fifteen and seventeen became pregnant. Of these, approximately 56 percent gave birth, 14 percent had miscarriages, and 28 percent had abortions. In the same year, 13,520 girls younger than fifteen became pregnant; approximately 43 percent gave birth, 44 percent had abortions, and 13 percent had miscarriages. Birth rates for teens between the ages of fifteen and seventeen have always been higher than abortion rates, although both have declined steadily. In 1988, the abortion rate was 30.2 per 1,000 girls, but by 2008, the rate was 10.4 per 1,000. The birth rate also declined from 38.6 per 1,000 in 1991 to 21.1 per 1,000 in 2008. For girls younger than fifteen, the birth rate has been declining since 1990, from 7.3 per 1,000 to 2.8 per 1,000 in 2008. The abortion rate also has declined for this age group, from 7.6 per 1,000 in 1992 to 2.9 per 1,000 in 2008. The abortion rate for girls younger than fifteen, in many instances, has been higher than the birth rate. Kathryn Kost et al., Guttmacher Institute, U.S. Teenage Pregnancies, Births and Abortions 2008: National Trends by Race and Ethnicity 8, 10 (2012), http://www.guttmacher.org/pubs/USTPtrends08.pdf.

The rates and trends differ when one considers race and ethnicity. For African-American and white women younger than nineteen, the pregnancy rates declined by 45 percent and 48 percent, respectively, between 1990 and 2008. Pregnancy rates among African-American women younger than nineteen, however, are considerably higher than for white women: in 2008, the rate for black women was 117 per 1,000, and it was 43.3 per 1,000 for whites. The pregnancy rate for Hispanic women also decreased, by 37 percent between 1992 and 2008, but the birth rate for Hispanic teenagers was more than twice the rate for non-Hispanic white girls. *Id.* at 3.

Abortion rates also declined across all ethnic and racial groups. Nevertheless, rates of abortion remain higher for blacks and Hispanics than for whites. Between 1990 and 2008, abortion rates declined from 33.9 per 1,000 to 12.8 per 1,000 for white women between the ages of fifteen and nineteen and from 80.3 per 1,000 to 40.8 per 1,000 for black women. The Hispanic rate also declined, from 41.6 per 1,000 in 1992 to 20.1 per 1,000 in 2008. *Id.* at 6.

The declining number of teen pregnancies may be attributable to the increasing use of contraception. Since 1985, the number of teens using contraception the first time they engage in premarital sex has been increasing, from 56 percent in 1985 to 84 percent in 2005–2008. Guttmacher Institute, Facts on American Teens' Sexual and Reproductive Health (February 2012), http://www.guttmacher.org/pubs/FB-ATSRH.pdf. State policy on access to contraceptives by minors generally is more generous than state abortion policy. Twenty-one states allow minors to consent to contraceptive services without prior parental permission, while twenty-five states allow minors to consent under certain circumstances. These exceptions include minors who have graduated from high school and minors who have reached a certain age, are mature, are or have been pregnant, or for health reasons need contraception. For an overview of state laws on minors' access to contraception, see Guttmacher Institute, State Policies in Brief: Minors' Access to Contraceptive Services (June 2012), http://www.guttmacher.org/statecenter/spibs/spib_MACS.pdf. Does it make sense for a state to require a minor to obtain parental consent before an abortion but to permit that same minor to acquire contraception without parental involvement?

All fifty states and the District of Columbia permit minors to consent to testing and treatment for sexually transmitted diseases and infections. Some states require that the minor be a certain age before he or she may consent. In eighteen states, however, the physician may inform the minor's parents that he or she is seeking treatment or services if the physician believes it is in the minor's best interests to do so. Thirty-one states explicitly include HIV testing and treatment within the services to which a minor may consent. One state, Iowa, requires the state to inform the minor's parents if an HIV test is positive (and Connecticut requires such notification if the minor is younger than twelve), but no other state mandates that the physician inform the parent about testing or services. Guttmacher Institute, State Policies in Brief: Minors' Access to STI Services (June 2012), http://www.guttmacher.org/statecenter/spibs/spib_MASS.pdf.

7. Do minors involve their parents in the decision-making process? A 1991 study of girls seeking abortions in states with no parental involvement laws found that in 61 percent of the cases, at least one or both parents knew of the minor's pregnancy, and in 45 percent of the cases, the minor had told one or both parents. Stanley K. Henshaw & Kathryn Kost, *Parental Involvement in Minors' Abortion Decisions*, 24 FAM. PLANNING PERSPECTIVES 196, 199 (1992). Parents overwhelmingly knew that the minor also planned to get an abortion; in only 0.3 percent of the cases was the parent unaware of the minor's decision to abort. *Id.* at 200. Moreover, at least one parent supported the pregnant minor's decision to abort. *Id.* at 204. For those minors whose parents did not know, 52 percent involved an adult other than a parent, while 22 percent consulted with a professional. *Id.* at 205. A number of earlier studies made similar findings. See Raye Hudson Rosen, *Adolescent Pregnancy Decision-Making: Are Parents Important?* 15 ADOLESCENCE 43 (1990) (57 percent involved parent in decision); Aida Torres et al., *Telling Parents: Clinic Policies and Adolescents' Use of Family Planning and Abortion Services*, 12 FAM. PLANNING PERSPECTIVES 284 (1980) (55 percent of pregnant minors said parents knew they were having an abortion); Laurie S. Zabin et al., *To Whom Do Inner-City Minors Talk about Their Pregnancies? Adolescents' Communication with Parents and Parent Surrogates*, 24 FAM. PLANNING PERSPECTIVES 148 (1992) (91 percent consulted parent or parent surrogate).

There are a number of reasons for a minor to decide not to tell her parents about her pregnancy. Of the minors surveyed in the Henshaw and Kost study, 73 percent said they did not tell their mothers because they did not want to disappoint them, and 60 percent cited the same reason as an explanation for why they chose not to tell their fathers; 55 percent thought their mothers would be angry with them, while 51 percent thought their fathers would be; 32 percent did not want their mothers to know they were having sex, and 38 percent did not want their fathers to know; 18 percent believed their mothers, and 13 percent believed their fathers, would make them leave home; 6 percent believed their mothers would beat them if they found out, and 7 percent believed their fathers would do so. Henshaw & Kost, *Parental Involvement*, 202.

A 2003 study of girls seeking judicial bypasses in Massachusetts, a state with a parental-involvement law, found similar reasons for girls to choose not to tell their parents. Pregnant minors gave multiple reasons for their decision to pursue a judicial bypass: 27.4 percent of the girls indicated that their parents would be upset if they knew, while 22.4 percent believed their parents' reaction would be severe; girls indicated that they believed they might be kicked out of the house, would be harmed, or would be subject to other forms of abuse; 22.2 percent also feared that they would be pressured by parents to continue the pregnancy or get married or believed that their parents' religious or traditional views would preclude an abortion. J. Shoshanna Ehrlich, *Grounded in the Reality of Their Lives: Listening to Teens Who Make Their Abortion Decision without Involving Their Parents*, 18 Berkeley Women's L.J. 61, 94–95 (2003).

8. *Judicial bypass procedures*. Generally, if a minor does not wish to tell her parents about her pregnancy, she may obtain a court order. The process must be confidential and prompt, and many state statutes offer model petitions and forms and a designated official to assist the minor with the process. In addition, states may mandate the appointment of an attorney, a guardian *ad litem*, or both to assist the minor at the hearing. The hearings are nonadversarial, and the minor must establish that she is sufficiently mature and well enough informed or that the abortion is in her best interests in order to obtain the bypass. The standard of proof may vary, but the Supreme Court has held that the clear-and-convincing standard does not violate due process. *Ohio v. Akron Center for Reproductive Health*, 497 U.S. at 506–507, 517–518.

In practice, however, the judicial-bypass procedure may be fraught with difficulties. Many pregnant minors are unaware that bypass laws exist, and they have trouble accessing accurate information. Rebouché, *Parental Involvement Laws*, 189. For girls living in rural areas, the problem of locating information and services may be particularly acute. Lisa R. Pruitt, *Toward a Feminist Theory of the Rural*, 2007 Utah L. Rev. 421, 478–483 (2007). Court clerks, officials, and judges may make access more difficult by not providing accurate information or refusing to handle petitions or to schedule hearings because of inadequate training, moral disapproval, or perceived political disadvantage. See Rebouché, *Parental Involvement Laws*, 190–192; Caroline A. Placey, Comment, *Of Judicial Bypass Procedures, Moral Recusal, and Protected Political Speech: Throwing Pregnant Minors under the Campaign Bus*, 56 Emory L.J. 693, 695, 719–720, 727–728 (2006) (describing judicial-bypass cases as political "hot potatoes" and noting judges' willingness to recuse themselves). Girls also may find that they are unable to obtain adequate and competent legal representation, Rebouché, *Parental Involvement Laws*, 192; Elizabeth Susan Graybill, Note, *Assisting Minors Seeking Abortions in Judicial Bypass Proceedings: A Guardian ad Litem Is No Substitute for an Attorney*, 55 Vand. L. Rev. 581 (2002).

The hearing itself may compound the difficulties. Although judges do have considerable discretion, they may ask inappropriate questions about the minor's relationships, sexual practices, social life, and use of illegal substances. Rebouché, *Parental Involvement Laws*, 194; Jamin B. Raskin, *The Paradox of Judicial Bypass Proceedings*, 10 Am. U. J. Gender Soc. Pol'y & L. 281

(2002). Some judges may engage in inappropriate practices by requiring the minor to attend counseling sessions at which she is urged to carry her pregnancy to term, Helena Silverstein & Kathryn Lundwall Alessi, *Religious Establishment in Hearings to Waive Parental Consent for Abortion*, 7 U. PA. J. CONST. L. 473 (2004) (Alabama judge sent pregnant minors seeking bypass to "Sav-a-Life" centers, where girls were advised to carry pregnancies to term and practice Christian beliefs); or by appointing an attorney for the fetus before making the bypass determination, *In re Application of Doe*, 591 So.2d 698 (La. 1991). Carol Sanger argues that the confusion, anxiety, and hostility experienced by pregnant minors do considerable damage to their "decisional dignity." Carol Sanger, *Decisional Dignity: Teenage Abortion, Bypass Hearings, and the Misuse of Law*, 18 COLUM. J. GENDER & LAW 409 (2009). She notes that minors risk exposure and reputational damage associated with the attendant notoriety that obtaining a bypass carries with it. But at a minimum, the bypass procedure is humiliating, embarrassing, and terrifying, because the consequences of failing to obtain the bypass are enormous. *Id.* at 444–445, 447–448.

9. The American Medical Association (AMA) states that minors should be allowed to decide whether parental involvement is appropriate, although physicians should strongly encourage minors to discuss their pregnancies with their parents. The AMA also instructs physicians to check state law on the issue of parental involvement, although the policy clearly states that physicians should not feel or be compelled to require minors to involve their parents before deciding whether to have abortions. American Medical Association, E-2.015 Policy on Mandatory Parental Consent to Abortion, https://ssl3.ama-assn.org/apps/ecomm/PolicyFinderForm.pl?site=www.ama-assn.org&uri=%2Fresources%2Fdoc%2FPolicyFinder%2Fpolicyfiles%2FHnE%2FE-2.015.htm.

The American Academy of Pediatrics (AAP) agrees with the AMA's policy and reaffirms that adolescents should be strongly encouraged to involve parents or other trusted adults in the decision-making process. The AAP also believes that "legislation requiring parental consent does not promote family communication and increases the risk of harm to the minor by delaying access to appropriate medical care." American Academy of Pediatrics, Comm. on Adolescence, *The Adolescent's Right to Confidential Care When Considering Abortion*, 97 PEDIATRICS 746, 746 (1996). The AAP notes that there is no empirical support for the claim that minors who choose to terminate their pregnancies suffer adverse psychological consequences; in fact, the incidence of psychiatric hospitalization after abortion is lower than after childbirth. *Id.* at 749. Moreover, medical risks associated with a first-trimester legal abortion also are quite low. *Id.* The AAP also contends that a parental-involvement law delays and impedes an adolescent's access to health care because of confusion over patient confidentiality, increasing the incidence of later-trimester procedures, which are riskier. *Id.*

2. THE MATURE-MINOR DOCTRINE

BELCHER V. CHARLESTON AREA MEDICAL CENTER
Supreme Court of Appeals of West Virginia
422 S.E.2d 827 (1992)

McHUGH, Chief Justice:...

The decedent, Larry Belcher, Jr. (Larry), who was seventeen years and eight months old, suffered from muscular dystrophy, and was confined to a wheelchair. On December 19, 1986, Larry became choked and stopped breathing. His father, the appellant herein, removed mucus from the decedent's throat and, through mouth-to-mouth resuscitation, revived Larry. Larry was taken to Women & Children's Hospital, part of CAMC, by ambulance. Following an examination by the emergency room physicians, it was determined that Larry had a viral syndrome, or in laymen's terms, a "cold." According to the appellee Ayoubi, because of Larry's muscular dystrophy, the cold had an exaggerated effect on his condition.

Later that day, after being admitted to the hospital, Larry had another breathing failure, and was intubated, placed on a respirator, and transferred to the pediatric intensive care unit.

On December 22, 1986, Ayoubi discussed with the appellants the likelihood of Larry suffering another respiratory arrest and also discussed his (Ayoubi's) concern that Larry would become "respirator-dependent" if he were to remain on it. Furthermore, long-term respirator support would cause Larry's throat to swell shut, thus requiring a tracheotomy and feeding through a tube. Ayoubi also asked the appellants about whether they would want Larry subjected to resuscitative measures, including reintubation, in the event he suffered another respiratory failure.

The next morning, December 23, 1986, Ayoubi contends that the appellants indicated that they had not yet decided on whether Larry should be intubated and placed on a respirator again in the event of another breathing failure. Later that day, December 23, 1986, at 10:30 a.m., Larry was taken off the respirator and was extubated. Small doses of morphine sulphate were prescribed to relieve Larry's pain and anxiety. Ayoubi observed Larry becoming anxious and apprehensive as he was disconnected from the respirator. Ayoubi advised Larry that he could be reintubated, but Larry motioned his head "no," indicating that he did not want to be reintubated.

Later that day, December 23, 1986, the appellants told Ayoubi that they decided they did not want Larry reintubated or resuscitated unless Larry requested it. Accordingly, Ayoubi had the appellants sign a progress note stating that Larry was not to be reintubated or resuscitated in the event of a respiratory failure. The progress note was formalized into a "Do Not Resuscitate" order.

Larry was not involved in this decision because, as Ayoubi contends: (1) he was emotionally immature due to his disease; (2) he was on medication which diminished his capacity; (3) involving him in the decision would have increased his anxiety, thus reducing his chances of survival; and (4) Larry's parents told Ayoubi that they did not want Larry involved.

At 3:00 a.m. on December 24, 1986, Larry had another respiratory arrest, suffered cardiac failure, and died. The hospital staff attempted, within the limits of the "Do Not Resuscitate" order, to administer "precordial thumps," repositioned his head, and attempted to blow oxygen into his mouth, all to no avail.

The appellants filed this action for wrongful death, alleging medical malpractice, on September 16, 1988, in the Circuit Court of Kanawha County. Following trial, the jury returned a verdict in favor of the appellees.

In this appeal, the appellants raise issues involving: the circuit court's refusal to allow certain proffered rebuttal evidence; and the circuit court's refusal to allow the case to go to the jury on a theory that Larry should have been consulted prior to the issuance of the "Do Not Resuscitate" order, thus, recognizing the so-called "mature minor" exception to the common law rule of parental consent.

II....

B. *Consent of Minor*

The appellant also contends that informed consent by Larry, even though he was a minor, should have been required before issuing the "Do No Resuscitate" order....

As stated previously, the appellants contend that the minor decedent, Larry, should have been consulted in this case prior to issuance of the "Do Not Resuscitate" order. Consequently, we address the "mature minor" exception to the common law rule that parental consent is required prior to rendering medical treatment to a minor.

> The traditional common law approach to minors and consent to treatment has undergone a number of modifications. Medical emergencies have provided an inroad, permitting treatment without parental consent in certain situations. The "mature minor" and "emancipated minor" rules, in which certain children are considered capable of giving consent, have also gained recognition. Many of these changes have come through case law, but to a certain degree legislative action is accountable for the more enlightened attitude toward the minor and her ability to authorize treatment.

Fay A. Rozovsky, *Consent to Treatment* § 5.2 (2d ed. 1990).

The appellee Ayoubi asserts that the appellant is attempting to improperly change the common law where there is no legislative direction by statute. However, the appellee Ayoubi concedes that under appropriate circumstances, the medical standard of care requires that minors be consulted if they are mature and if the circumstances of the particular case do not militate against such consultation.

In *Cross v. Trap*, 170 W.Va. 459, 294 S.E.2d 446 (1982), we reiterated in syllabus point 1 thereto the well-established principle concerning consent to medical procedures: "Except in very extreme cases, a surgeon has no legal right to operate upon a patient without his consent, *nor upon a child without the consent of its parent or guardian.*" *Browning v. Hoffman*, 90 W.Va. 568, 581, 111 S.E. 492, 497 (1922) (emphasis supplied).

In this case, the circuit court's instruction to the jury on this point provided: "Ordinarily, a privately retained physician has no legal right to render or withhold medical treatment to a patient without his consent, *nor upon a child without the consent of his parents.* Under West Virginia law a child is any person under the age of 18 years" (emphasis supplied). Obviously, the circuit court's instruction followed the principle enunciated in *Browning.*

Although we believe that the *Browning* principle with respect to the consent of minors remains a sound statement of law, a more workable approach would be recognition that minors who are mature may be involved in the medical decisions that affect their livelihood. As Dean Pound has stated: "The law must be stable, but it must not stand still." Roscoe Pound, Introduction to the Philosophy of Law (1922).

One of the first reported cases involving a mature minor exception to the general common law rule requiring parental consent to medical treatment of minors was in the 1906 decision in *Bakker v. Welsh*, 144 Mich. 632, 108 N.W. 94 (1906), wherein the Supreme Court of Michigan held that a surgeon was not liable to a father for performing an operation to remove an ear tumor on a seventeen-year-old boy where the boy's father had not given consent and the boy died during the administration of anesthetic. Although it is not clear exactly who gave the consent to surgery, the boy was accompanied by an aunt and a sister, and "they all understood an operation should be performed the following day." *Id.* 108 N.W. at 95.

A more recent delineation of the mature minor rule has come from the Supreme Court of Tennessee in *Cardwell v. Bechtol*, 724 S.W.2d 739 (Tenn. 1987). In that case, Tennessee's highest court adopted the mature minor exception to the general common law rule requiring parental consent to medical treatment of minors. In *Cardwell*, a young woman, seventeen years and seven months old, went to see the defendant doctor on her own initiative, and without her parent's knowledge, seeking relief from back pain. The defendant did not inquire about parental consent prior to rendering manipulative therapy because he believed, based upon the young woman's demeanor, that she was of age, and also that she had sought his treatment because he had previously treated her father. The parents of the young woman brought an action against the defendant after complications from the treatment arose. Following appeals from the lower courts, the Supreme Court of Tennessee held that the defendant could not be held liable on a theory of battery for failing to obtain the consent of the minor's parents.[10]

In determining the capacity, and ultimately the maturity of a minor, the court in Cardwell stated:

> Whether a minor has the capacity to consent to medical treatment depends upon the age, ability, experience, education, training, and degree of maturity or judgment obtained by the minor, as well as upon the conduct and demeanor of the minor at the time of the incident involved. Moreover, the totality of the circumstances, the nature of the treatment and its risks or probable consequences, and the minor's ability to appreciate the risks and consequences are to be considered.

Cardwell, 724 S.W.2d at 748.

In adopting the mature minor exception, the Tennessee court acknowledged that that state's legislature has enacted several provisions concerning medical treatment of minors without parental consent, such as treatment for drug abuse and venereal disease.

Similarly, in this case, the appellee Ayoubi contends that because this state's legislature has spoken to the same type of exceptions, then this indicates a legislative intent to reject the mature minor rule. We do not agree. Rather, we agree with the Tennessee *Cardwell* court's answer to this assertion. "We do not think that the conclusion that these statutes are intended to abrogate judicial adoption of an exception to the general common law rule requiring parental consent to treat minors can be supported by the express terms of any of these provisions." 724 S.W.2d at 744. Rather, that court found "no indication in any of the statutes of any intent on the part of the Legislature to establish a comprehensive statutory scheme to occupy the area of medical treatment of minors *in its entirety*." *Id.* (emphasis supplied). The court went on to point out that the statutes where the legislature has expressly provided for only consent by the minor "do no more than provide conditional immunities from certain types of liability

10. The appellee Ayoubi points out that *Cardwell* involved consent to treatment of the mature minor as opposed to assent, that is, affirmatively seeking treatment instead of merely allowing treatment to be administered or withheld. We believe that this distinction is inapposite for purposes of our recognition of the mature minor exception to the common law rule. Our holding herein applies to not only procedures performed, but treatment administered and withheld as well.

in specific situations (where such immunities were not otherwise clear in the law) or promote certain social purposes, such as treatment of drug abuse or venereal disease in minors." *Id.*

We agree with the holding of *Cardwell*, and we believe that the mature minor exception is part of the common law rule of parental consent of this state. It is difficult to imagine that a young person who is under the age of majority, yet, who has undergone medical treatment for a permanent or recurring illness over the course of a long period of time, may not be capable of taking part in decisions concerning that treatment. Clearly, this would be a matter for the jury to decide, and not for this Court to speculate.

However, we believe that this must also be tempered by a recognition that there is no "hard and fast" rule that would provide a particular age for determining a mature minor.[13]

As the Tennessee court cautioned in *Cardwell*, "[a]doption of the mature minor exceptions to the common law rule is by no means a general license to treat minors without parental consent and its application is dependent on the facts of each case. It must be seen in the context of the tort in question." *Cardwell*, 724 S.W.2d at 745.

We are aware that this is a very difficult area of the law when put into practice, especially in light of the age-old principle that "hindsight is 20/20." Furthermore, it is obvious that this places the doctor in the difficult position of making the determination of whether the minor at issue is mature. We recognize the delicate nature of this position, and that the decision by the doctor on the maturity level of a minor will often be second-guessed. Consequently, the doctor, as in every other decision with which he or she is faced, must exercise his or her best medical judgment.

However, in spite of the difficulty brought on by this issue, we agree with the observation that "the answer will be found in *statutory* laws of consent that incorporate an element of the mature minor rule." *Rozovsky, supra* § 5.2.2, at 265 (emphasis supplied). Accordingly, our holding in this case is nothing more than a recognition that the mature minor exception to the common law rule of parental consent in this state exists. The legislature, of course, may, by statute, prohibit recognition of the principles enunciated herein.

Obviously, application of the mature minor rule would vary from case to case. The focus would be on the maturity level of the minor at issue, and whether that minor has the capacity to appreciate the nature and risks involved of the procedure to be performed, or the treatment to be administered or withheld. "In current practice, judicial application of the 'mature minor' exception where an objective appraisal of the circumstances indicates that the minor was informed and understood the nature and consequences of the procedure in question." Lawrence P. Wilkins, *Children's Rights: Removing the Parental Consent Barrier to Medical Treatment of Minors*, 1975 Ariz. St. L.J. 31, 52 (1975).

Accordingly, we hold that except in very extreme cases, a physician has no legal right to perform a procedure upon, or administer or withhold treatment from a patient without the patient's consent, nor upon a child without the consent of the child's parents or guardian, unless the child is a mature minor, in which case the child's consent would be required.

13. In *Cardwell*, the court discussed the so-called "Rule of Sevens," which is often applied in the area of tort liability. Recently, this Court discussed the "Rule of Sevens" as it applied to the law of negligence. Syl. pts. 1–3, *Pino v. Szuch*, 185 W.Va. 476, 408 S.E.2d 55 (1991) (child under age of seven conclusively presumed incapable of negligence; rebuttable presumption that child between seven and fourteen is incapable of negligence; and child fourteen or older is presumed capable of negligence). While this rule may be instructive as a starting point in determining minor maturity, the ultimate determination will vary from case to case.

Whether a child is a mature minor is a question of fact. Whether the child has the capacity to consent depends upon the age, ability, experience, education, training, and degree of maturity or judgment obtained by the child, as well as upon the conduct and demeanor of the child at the time of the procedure or treatment. The factual determination would also involve whether the minor has the capacity to appreciate the nature, risks, and consequences of the medical procedure to be performed, or the treatment to be administered or withheld. Where there is a conflict between the intentions of one or both parents and the minor, the physician's good faith assessment of the minor's maturity level would immunize him or her from liability for the failure to obtain parental consent....

In this case, the appellee Ayoubi contends that the question of whether Larry should have consented to the withholding of treatment need not even be reached because there was *expert testimony* that Larry was not mature enough to give such consent. While we make no decision on whether such evidence was sufficient to support the appellee Ayoubi's claim in this regard, the circuit court's error was the failure to instruct the jury that it could consider Larry's maturity level in deciding whether, as a matter of fact, Larry was mature so as to consent to his medical treatment.

Accordingly, we reverse the judgment of the circuit court on the liability of Dr. Ayoubi, and remand this case to that court so that, consistent with our adoption of the mature minor exception to the common law rule of parental consent to the medical treatment of minors, it may try the issue of whether Larry came within this exception so as to be entitled to consent to the treatment involved.

NOTES AND QUESTIONS

1. What is the mature-minor doctrine? When does it apply? Would the doctrine apply to a minor who wants to consent to treatment? Refuse treatment? What if the treatment could save the minor's life? See *In re E.G.*, 549 N.E.2d 322 (Ill. 1989). In this case, was there evidence of Larry's maturity?

2. Under certain circumstances, state statutes permit a minor to consent to or refuse medical treatment. For example, a minor may consent if she is legally emancipated, is married, is pregnant, is in the military, or has a child. See, e.g., Kimberly Gordy, *Adding Life to the Adolescent's Years, Not Simply Years to the Adolescent's Life: The Integration of the Individualized Care Planning & Coordination Model and a Statutory Fallback Provision*, 11 YALE J. HEALTH POL'Y, L. & ETHICS 169, 190–191 (2011). In the absence of a statute, some states recognize the mature-minor doctrine. See, e.g., Ark. Code Ann. § 9-27-362 (2011); Idaho Code Ann. § 39-3801 (2011); Miss. Code Ann. § 41-41-3(3) (2011); Nev. Rev. Stat. § 129.030(2) (LexisNexis 2011); N.M. Stat. § 24-7A-6.2 (2011); *In re E.G.*, 549 N.E.2d 322 (Ill. 1989); *Younts v. St. Francis Hosp. & Sch. of Nursing, Inc.*, 469 P.2d 330 (Kan. 1970); *Lacey v. Laird*, 139 N.E.2d 25 (Ohio 1956); *Cardwell v. Bechtol*, 724 S.W.2d 739 (Tenn. 1987); *Belcher v. Charleston Area Med. Ctr.*, 422 S.E.2d 827 (W.Va. 1992). Most states, however, require the minor to reach the age of majority before he or she may consent to or refuse medical treatment.

3. The right to refuse medical treatment nevertheless is conceptually distinct from the right to consent to medical treatment. In *Cruzan v. Missouri Department of Health*, the United States

Supreme Court held that a "competent person has a constitutionally protected interest in refusing unwanted medical treatment." 497 U.S. 261, 278 (1990). Does a minor also have this right? In *In re E.G.*, 549 N.E.2d 322 (Ill. 1989), the Illinois Supreme Court held that E.G., as a mature minor, had the common-law right under Illinois to refuse medical treatment. E.G., a seventeen-year-old Jehovah's Witness, and her mother refused blood transfusions for E.G.'s leukemia on religious grounds. Although remission was possible in 80 percent of the cases with chemotherapy and transfusions, the overall survival rate was about 20 to 25 percent. In upholding her right to refuse, the court balanced her right against the state's interest in preserving life, preventing suicide, maintaining the integrity of the medical profession, and protecting the interests of parents and others. *Id.* at 328. On the other hand, in *Novak v. Kobb County-Kennestone Hosp. Authority*, 849 F.Supp. 1559 (N.D. Ga. 1994), the court rejected the minor's claim of a right to refuse medical treatment, finding no mature-minor exception under Georgia law and no federal constitutional right.

In *P.J. ex rel. Jensen v. Utah*, No. 2:05-CV-739 TS3 (D. Utah, June 16, 2006), the state initiated a neglect investigation into the parents' refusal to permit chemotherapy for their son, twelve-year-old P.J., who had been diagnosed with Ewing's sarcoma. The Jensens lost custody and were eventually indicted for kidnapping their own son. The state ultimately decided that it could not force P.J. to accept chemotherapy without parental support and dismissed the neglect action. The criminal charge was reduced to a misdemeanor charge of custodial interference in exchange for a plea. The parents then filed a civil-rights action, alleging, among other things, that P.J.'s substantive due-process right to refuse treatment had been violated. While the court did not embrace the defendants' claim that all minors would be incapable of refusing to consent to medical treatment ("a troubling proposition"), the court found that a child as young as P.J. did not have a right to refuse medical treatment. Rather, the claim belonged to his parents.

What if the minor refuses treatment but the parent objects? In a review of fifty reported court cases, the author notes that most of the courts went forward without including the opinions of the affected children. Derry Ridgway, *Court-Mediated Disputes between Physicians and Families over the Medical Care of Children*, 15 Archives Pediatrics & Adolescent Med. 891, 894 (2004). Nevertheless, there are practical problems when the parents wish the treatment to proceed but the child does not. In 1994, Billy Best, a sixteen-year-old boy, ran away from home to avoid chemotherapy treatments for Hodgkin's lymphoma. He returned home after three months only after his family agreed that they would stop treatment. He subsequently used Essiac and other natural herbal remedies and has been cancer-free since 1995. His family now sells Essiac on its Web site, Billy's Story, http://www.billybest.net/BillysStory.htm.

In 2009, Best was back in the news, offering assistance to Danny Hauser and his mother, who fled rather than submit Danny to court-ordered chemotherapy for Hodgkin's lymphoma. Dave Wedge, *I'd "Do Anything" to Help: Hub Survivor Feels Kinship with Runaway Cancer Boy*, Boston Herald 5 (May 21, 2009). Danny and his mother returned a week later and submitted to the cancer treatments. His family also pursued nontraditional remedies, and Danny was cancer-free a year later. CNN, American Morning, May 21, 2010.

4. The American Medical Association (AMA) states that medical decision making should be based on the child's best interest, by taking into account the child's emotional and psychological welfare, the family situation, and the proposed medical treatment. The AMA also notes that parental consent should be obtained unless the child may consent as a mature or emancipated minor. In any event, the physician should provide the pediatric patient with the opportunity to participate in decision making at a "developmentally appropriate level"

and secure the patient's "assent, or agreement" to a course of treatment. American Medical Association, E-10.016 Policy on Pediatric Decision-Making (updated November 2010), https://ssl3.ama-assn.org/apps/ecomm/PolicyFinderForm.pl?site=www.ama-assn.org&uri=-%2Fresources%2Fdoc%2FPolicyFinder%2Fpolicyfiles%2FHnE%2FE-10.016.htm. The AMA, also recognizing that confidential health care is "critical" to improving the health of adolescents, "encourages physicians to allow emancipated and mature minors to give informed consent for medial, psychiatric, and surgical care without parental consent and notification, in conformity with state and federal law." Physicians also are encouraged "to offer adolescents an opportunity for examination and consultation apart from their parents." American Medical Association, H.60-965 Confidential Health Services for Adolescents, https://ssl3.ama-assn.org/apps/ecomm/PolicyFinderForm.pl?site=www.ama-assn.org&uri=%2Fresources%2Fdoc%2FPolicyFinder%2Fpolicyfiles%2FHnE%2FH-60.965.htm.

To what extent are minors capable of making medical decisions? The American Academy of Pediatrics (AAP) has adopted a policy that mandates the involvement of pediatric patients in the decision-making process and recognizes that some minors may be legally entitled to consent to or refuse medical treatment. Moreover, the AAP policy mandates informed consent in most circumstances. American Academy of Pediatrics, Comm. on Bioethics, *Informed Consent, Parental Permission, and Assent in Pediatric Practice*, 95 PEDIATRICS 314 (1995). In the absence of consent, the physician must obtain the patient's assent. To obtain the pediatric patient's assent, the AAP provides the following guidelines:

1. Helping the patient achieve a developmentally appropriate awareness of the nature of his or her condition.
2. Telling the patient what he or she can expect with tests and treatments.
3. Making a clinical assessment of the patient's understanding of the situation and the factors influencing how he or she is responding (including whether there is inappropriate pressure to accept testing or therapy).
4. Soliciting an expression of the patient's willingness to accept the proposed care. Regarding this final point, we note that no one should solicit a patient's views without intending to weigh them seriously. In situations in which the patient will have to receive medical care despite his or her objection, the patient should be told that fact and should not be deceived.

Id. at 315. The AAP also recognizes the pediatric patient's authority to refuse treatment and indicates that such a refusal is ethically, if not legally, binding. *Id.* at 317. The policy recommends fourteen as the age at which most pediatric patients should be permitted to exercise control over their care. *Id.*

Do you find the position of the AAP surprising? A 2005 small-scale study found that children and adolescents were involved in end-of-life decision making despite the absence of legal standing to make such decisions. Pamela S. Hinds et al., *End-of-Life Care Preferences of Pediatric Patients with Cancer*, 23 J. CLINICAL ONCOLOGY 9146 (2005). Other studies have found that children as young as six made the decision about end-of-life care. Ruprecht Nitschke et al., *Therapeutic Choices Made by Patients with End-Stage Cancer*, 101 J. PEDIATRICS 471 (1982). In the 2005 study, researchers interviewed twenty terminally ill children, ages ten to twenty, within seven days of making an end-of-life decision: enrollment in a study involving a new drug, a do-not-resuscitate order, or initiation of terminal care. Researchers found that eighteen of the children and adolescents interviewed could accurately recall their treatment options, while two were able to recall only the option they chose. (One girl noted that she had lost her short-term memory because of a brain tumor.) Hinds, *End-of-Life Care Preferences*, 9148. They also were able to identify the medical side effects and death as the consequence of the decision. *Id.* at 9152. Researchers found a surprising degree of altruism among the patients interviewed: nineteen of the twenty patients indicated that they made their choice out of concern for others—family members, loved ones, or others who might benefit from the medical knowledge gained by participation in the treatment study. *Id.* at 9150, tbl. 2. "This concern for others may reflect what has been referred to as the maturational effect of a life-ending illness on a child or adolescent." *Id.* at 9153. See also Christopher Lemmens, *End-of-Life Decisions and Minors: Do Minors Have the Right to Refuse Life Preserving Medical Treatment? A Comparative Study*, 28 MED. & LAW 479 (2009) (arguing that minors are mature enough to refuse treatment at much earlier age than legal age of majority).

Are parents in a better position to make decisions about a child's terminal illness? A small-scale study of 107 parents whose children died of cancer at least one year prior to participation found that 56 percent of the parents believed at the initial diagnosis that the child would be cured, compared with 43 percent of the physicians. Joanne Wolf et al., *Understanding of Prognosis among Parents of Children Who Died of Cancer*, 248 JAMA 2469 (2000). Physicians first recognized that the child had no realistic chance for a cure 206 days on average before the child's death. However, parents recognized no chance for a cure 106 days on average before the child's death. *Id.* at 2471. Of the parents, 49 percent came to this realization after discussions with the child's medical team, but 30 percent realized that there was no chance for a cure after seeing a change in the way the child looked or acted. *Id.* at 2472. Once they had realized that there was no chance for a cure, the majority of parents continued to see the primary goal of cancer therapy as extending life; only 13 percent reported that its purpose was to lessen suffering. *Id.* After death, however, 34 percent of parents stated that the goal of continuing therapy should be to lessen the child's suffering. *Id.* Although the delay between parent and physician realizations was not found to have an effect on end-of-life care outcomes, nevertheless, when both parent and doctor recognized the chances earlier, hospice treatment was introduced sooner, and the child was less likely to receive cancer therapy in the last month of life. *Id.* at 2473. It has been suggested that parents may make decisions to assuage their grief rather than to minimize their child's suffering. Gordy, *Adding Life*, 186.

Are there sound reasons for the position taken by medical professionals? Should the law adopt a similar approach? Should a different rule apply when the child's prognosis is terminal?

5. *Organ and hematopoietic (stem-cell) donations by minors.*

American Medical Association, Opinion 2.15: Policy on Transplantation of Organs from Living Donors (Updated November 2010).

Unemancipated minors and legally incompetent adults ordinarily should not be accepted as living donors because of their inability to fully understand and decide voluntarily. However, in exceptional circumstances, minors with substantial decision making capability who agree to serve as donors, with the informed consent of their legal guardians, may be considered for donation to recipients with whom they are emotionally connected. Since minors' guardians may be emotionally connected to the organ recipient, when an unemancipated minor agrees to donate, it may be appropriate to seek advice from another adult trusted by the minor or an independent body, such as consultation with an ethics committee, pastoral service, or other counseling resource.

NOTES AND QUESTIONS

1. The American Academy of Pediatrics Committee on Bioethics states that a minor may serve as a living donor in exceptional circumstances when five criteria are met. First, both donor and recipient must be highly likely to benefit from the donation, and this will most likely occur when donations occur among family members. AAP policy states that donations should never occur to strangers. Second, the risk to the donor must be extremely low. Third, the child should be a donor of last resort and should not be considered until all other opportunities for transplantation have been exhausted and the recipient is unlikely to survive. Fourth, the minor must freely consent to the donation without coercion as established by an independent donor advocate and with parental support. Fifth, the emotional and psychological risks to the donor must be minimized. American Academy of Pediatrics, Committee on Bioethics, *Minors as Living Solid-Organ Donors*, 122 PEDIATRICS 454, 456–457 (2008). The child's assent also should be obtained. *Id.* at 458.

2. The AAP also believes that minors ethically may donate stem cells (often derived from bone marrow) under certain conditions. First, there must be no medically equivalent adult donor available and willing to donate. Second, there must be a strong personal and positive relationship between the donor and the recipient. Third, there must be some likelihood that the recipient will benefit from the donation. Fourth, the clinical, emotional, and psychological benefits to the donor must be minimized and be reasonable in relationship to the benefits expected for both the donor and the recipient. Finally, the medical team must obtain parental permission and the assent of the donor. AAP, Committee on Bioethics, *Policy Statement—Children as Hematopoietic Stem Cell Donors*, 125 PEDIATRICS 392, 396–399 (2010).

In some instances, parents have decided to conceive a child who might serve as a stem-cell donor for a sibling. AAP policy states that there is no moral prohibition against conceiving a child in order to donate to a sibling, as long as the child is not used solely as a donor but is also loved as a member of the family. In many instances, parents rely on *in vitro* fertilization and preimplantation genetic diagnosis to ensure compatibility. The match may be used to determine if the embryo has an inheritable disease in order to avoid the birth of the child or sometimes simply to ensure a match. In 2005, there were five centers in four countries assessing the compatibility of donors. *Id.* at 400.

Problem. Six-year-old Ashley receives burns over 80 percent of her body when the family fireplace explodes. Doctors estimate her chance of survival at 30 to 50 percent. After she is stabilized, her medical team discovers that she has an identical twin sister, Stephanie, who was not injured in the blast. Her doctors would like to harvest skin from Stephanie and graft the donated skin onto Ashley's body. Doctors estimate that Ashley's chances of dying without the skin grafts from Stephanie are 40 to 60 percent, but with the skin grafts, they are 10 percent. The risks to Stephanie are minimal, but there would be scarring and discoloration at the sites where the skin was harvested. Both the parents and the twins have indicated that they would like the procedure to occur. If you are legal counsel for the hospital, what steps would you recommend be taken in order to proceed with the skin harvesting and grafts?

C. School Discipline

1. CONSTITUTIONAL FRAMEWORK

GOSS V. LOPEZ
Supreme Court of the United States
419 U.S. 565 (1975)

MR. JUSTICE WHITE delivered the opinion of the Court.

This appeal by various administrators of the Columbus, Ohio, Public School System (CPSS) challenges the judgment of a three-judge federal court, declaring that appellees—various high school students in the CPSS—were denied due process of law contrary to the command of the Fourteenth Amendment in that they were temporarily suspended from their high schools without a hearing either prior to suspension or within a reasonable time thereafter, and enjoining the administrators to remove all references to such suspensions from the students' records.

I

Ohio law, Rev.Code Ann. § 3313.64 (1972), provides for free education to all children between the ages of six and 21. Section 3313.66 of the Code empowers the principal of an Ohio public school to suspend a pupil for misconduct for up to 10 days or to expel him. In either case, he must notify the student's parents within 24 hours and state the reasons for his action. A pupil who is expelled, or his parents, may appeal the decision to the Board of Education and in connection therewith shall be permitted to be heard at the board meeting. The Board may reinstate the pupil following the hearing. No similar procedure is provided in § 3313.66 or any other provision of state law for a suspended student. Aside from a regulation tracking the statute, at the time of the imposition of the suspensions in this case the CPSS itself had not issued any written procedure applicable to suspensions.[1] Nor, so far as the record reflects, had any of

1. At the time of the events involved in this case, the only administrative regulation on this subject was § 1010.04 of the Administrative Guide of the Columbus Public Schools which provided: "Pupils may be suspended or expelled from school in accordance with the provisions of Section 3313.66 of the Revised Code." Subsequent to the events involved in this lawsuit, the Department of Pupil Personnel of the CPSS issued three memoranda relating to suspension procedures, dated August 16, 1971, February 21, 1973, and July 10, 1973, respectively. The first two are substantially similar to each other and require no factfinding hearing at any time in connection with a suspension. The third, which was apparently in effect when this case was argued,

the individual high schools involved in this case.[2] Each, however, had formally or informally described the conduct for which suspension could be imposed.

The nine named appellees, each of whom alleged that he or she had been suspended from public high school in Columbus for up to 10 days without a hearing pursuant to § 3313.66, filed an action under 42 U.S.C. § 1983 against the Columbus Board of Education and various administrators of the CPSS. The complaint sought a declaration that § 3313.66 was unconstitutional in that it permitted public school administrators to deprive plaintiffs of their rights to an education without a hearing of any kind, in violation of the procedural due process component of the Fourteenth Amendment. It also sought to enjoin the public school officials from issuing future suspensions pursuant to § 3313.66 and to require them to remove references to the past suspensions from the records of the students in question.[3]

The proof below established that the suspensions arose out of a period of widespread student unrest in the CPSS during February and March 1971. Six of the named plaintiffs, Rudolph Sutton, Tyrone Washington, Susan Cooper, Deborah Fox, Clarence Byars, and Bruce Harris, were students at the Marion-Franklin High School and were each suspended for 10 days[4] on account of disruptive or disobedient conduct committed in the presence of the school administrator who ordered the suspension. One of these, Tyrone Washington, was among a group of students demonstrating in the school auditorium while a class was being conducted there. He was ordered by the school principal to leave, refused to do so, and was suspended. Rudolph Sutton, in the presence of the principal, physically attacked a police officer who was attempting to remove Tyrone Washington from the auditorium. He was immediately suspended. The other four Marion-Franklin students were suspended for similar conduct. None was given a hearing to determine the operative facts underlying the suspension, but each,

places upon the principal the obligation to "investigate" "before commencing suspension procedures"; and provides as part of the procedures that the principal shall discuss the case with the pupil, so that the pupil may "be heard with respect to the alleged offense," unless the pupil is "unavailable" for such a discussion or "unwilling" to participate in it. The suspensions involved in this case occurred, and records thereof were made, prior to the effective date of these memoranda. The District Court's judgment, including its expunction order, turns on the propriety of the procedures existing at the time the suspensions were ordered and by which they were imposed.

2. According to the testimony of Phillip Fulton, the principal of one of the high schools involved in this case, there was an informal procedure applicable at the Marion-Franklin High School. It provided that in the routine case of misconduct, occurring in the presence of a teacher, the teacher would describe the misconduct on a form provided for that purpose and would send the student, with the form, to the principal's office. There, the principal would obtain the student's version of the story, and, if it conflicted with the teacher's written version, would send for the teacher to obtain the teacher's oral version—apparently in the presence of the student. Mr. Fulton testified that, if a discrepancy still existed, the teacher's version would be believed and the principal would arrive at a disciplinary decision based on it.

3. The plaintiffs sought to bring the action on behalf of all students of the Columbus Public Schools suspended on or after February 1971, and a class action was declared accordingly. Since the complaint sought to restrain the "enforcement" and "operation" of a state statute "by restraining the action of any officer of such State in the enforcement or execution of such statute," a three-judge court was requested pursuant to 28 U.S.C. § 2281 and convened. The students also alleged that the conduct for which they could be suspended was not adequately defined by Ohio law. This vagueness and overbreadth argument was rejected by the court below and the students have not appealed from this part of the court's decision.

4. Fox was given two separate 10-day suspensions for misconduct occurring on two separate occasions—the second following immediately upon her return to school. In addition to his suspension, Sutton was transferred to another school.

together with his or her parents, was offered the opportunity to attend a conference, subsequent to the effective date of the suspension, to discuss the student's future.

Two named plaintiffs, Dwight Lopez and Betty Crome, were students at the Central High School and McGuffey Junior High School, respectively. The former was suspended in connection with a disturbance in the lunchroom which involved some physical damage to school property.[5] Lopez testified that at least 75 other students were suspended from his school on the same day. He also testified below that he was not a party to the destructive conduct but was instead an innocent bystander. Because no one from the school testified with regard to this incident, there is no evidence in the record indicating the official basis for concluding otherwise. Lopez never had a hearing.

Betty Crome was present at a demonstration at a high school other than the one she was attending. There she was arrested together with others, taken to the police station, and released without being formally charged. Before she went to school on the following day, she was notified that she had been suspended for a 10-day period. Because no one from the school testified with respect to this incident, the record does not disclose how the McGuffey Junior High School principal went about making the decision to suspend Crome, nor does it disclose on what information the decision was based. It is clear from the record that no hearing was ever held.

There was no testimony with respect to the suspension of the ninth named plaintiff, Carl Smith. The school files were also silent as to his suspension, although as to some, but not all, of the other named plaintiffs the files contained either direct references to their suspensions or copies of letters sent to their parents advising them of the suspension.

On the basis of this evidence, the three-judge court declared that plaintiffs were denied due process of law because they were "suspended without hearing prior to suspension or within a reasonable time thereafter," and that Ohio Rev.Code Ann. § 3313.66 (1972) and regulations issued pursuant thereto were unconstitutional in permitting such suspensions.[6] It was ordered that all references to plaintiffs' suspensions be removed from school files.

Although not imposing upon the Ohio school administrators any particular disciplinary procedures and leaving them "free to adopt regulations providing for fair suspension procedures which are consonant with the educational goals of their schools and reflective of the characteristics of their school and locality," the District Court declared that there were "minimum requirements of notice and a hearing prior to suspension, except in emergency situations." In explication, the court stated that relevant case authority would: (1) permit "(i)mmediate removal of a student whose conduct disrupts the academic atmosphere of the school, endangers fellow students, teachers or school officials, or damages property"; (2) require notice of suspension proceedings to be sent to the students' parents within

5. Lopez was actually absent from school, following his suspension, for over 20 days. This seems to have occurred because of a misunderstanding as to the length of the suspension. A letter sent to Lopez after he had been out for over 10 days purports to assume that, being over compulsory school age, he was voluntarily staying away. Upon asserting that this was not the case, Lopez was transferred to another school.

6. In its judgment, the court stated that the statute is unconstitutional in that it provides "for suspension...without *first* affording the student due process of law." (Emphasis supplied.) However, the language of the judgment must be read in light of the language in the opinion which expressly contemplates that under some circumstances students may properly be removed from school before a hearing is held, so long as the hearing follows promptly.

24 hours of the decision to conduct them; and (3) require a hearing to be held, with the student present, within 72 hours of his removal. Finally, the court stated that, with respect to the nature of the hearing, the relevant cases required that statements in support of the charge be produced, that the student and others be permitted to make statements in defense or mitigation, and that the school need not permit attendance by counsel.

The defendant school administrators have appealed the three-judge court's decision. Because the order below granted plaintiffs' request for an injunction—ordering defendants to expunge their records—this Court has jurisdiction of the appeal pursuant to 28 U.S.C. § 1253. We affirm.

II

At the outset, appellants contend that because there is no constitutional right to an education at public expense, the Due Process Clause does not protect against expulsions from the public school system. This position misconceives the nature of the issue and is refuted by prior decisions. The Fourteenth Amendment forbids the State to deprive any person of life, liberty, or property without due process of law. Protected interests in property are normally "not created by the Constitution. Rather, they are created and their dimensions are defined" by an independent source such as state statutes or rules entitling the citizen to certain benefits. *Board of Regents v. Roth*, 408 U.S. 564, 577 (1972).

Accordingly, a state employee who under state law, or rules promulgated by state officials, has a legitimate claim of entitlement to continued employment absent sufficient cause for discharge may demand the procedural protections of due process. *Connell v. Higginbotham*, 403 U.S. 207 (1971); *Wieman v. Updegraff*, 344 U.S. 183, 191–192 (1952); *Arnett v. Kennedy*, 416 U.S. 134, 164 (Powell, J., concurring); 171 (White, J., concurring and dissenting) (1974). So may welfare recipients who have statutory rights to welfare as long as they maintain the specified qualifications. *Goldberg v. Kelly*, 397 U.S. 254 (1970). *Morrissey v. Brewer*, 408 U.S. 471 (1972), applied the limitations of the Due Process Clause to governmental decisions to revoke parole, although a parolee has no constitutional right to that status. In like vein was *Wolff v. McDonnell*, 418 U.S. 539 (1974), where the procedural protections of the Due Process Clause were triggered by official cancellation of a prisoner's good-time credits accumulated under state law, although those benefits were not mandated by the Constitution.

Here, on the basis of state law, appellees plainly had legitimate claims of entitlement to a public education. Ohio Rev.Code Ann. §§ 3313.48 and 3313.64 (1972 and Supp. 1973) direct local authorities to provide a free education to all residents between five and 21 years of age, and a compulsory-attendance law requires attendance for a school year of not less than 32 weeks. Ohio Rev.Code Ann. § 3321.04 (1972). It is true that § 3313.66 of the Code permits school principals to suspend students for up to 10 days; but suspensions may not be imposed without any grounds whatsoever. All of the schools had their own rules specifying the grounds for expulsion or suspension. Having chosen to extend the right to an education to people of appellees' class generally, Ohio may not withdraw that right on grounds of misconduct absent fundamentally fair procedures to determine whether the misconduct has occurred. *Arnett v. Kennedy*, *supra*, at 164 (Powell, J., concurring), 171 (White, J., concurring and dissenting), 206 (Marshall, J., dissenting).

Although Ohio may not be constitutionally obligated to establish and maintain a public school system, it has nevertheless done so and has required its children to attend. Those young people do not "shed their constitutional rights" at the schoolhouse door. *Tinker v. Des Moines Independent Community School Dist.*, 393 U.S. 503, 506 (1969). "The Fourteenth Amendment, as now applied to the States, protects the citizen against the State itself and all of its creatures—Boards of Education not excepted." *West Virginia Board of Education v. Barnette*, 319 U.S. 624, 637 (1943). The authority possessed by the State to prescribe and enforce standards of conduct in its schools, although concededly very broad, must be exercised consistently with constitutional safeguards. Among other things, the State is constrained to recognize a student's legitimate entitlement to a public education as a property interest which is protected by the Due Process Clause and which may not be taken away for misconduct without adherence to the minimum procedures required by that Clause.

The Due Process Clause also forbids arbitrary deprivations of liberty. "Where a person's good name, reputation, honor, or integrity is at stake because of what the government is doing to him," the minimal requirements of the Clause must be satisfied. *Wisconsin v. Constantineau*, 400 U.S. 433, 437 (1971); *Board of Regents v. Roth, supra*, 408 U.S. at 573. School authorities here suspended appellees from school for periods of up to 10 days based on charges of misconduct. If sustained and recorded, those charges could seriously damage the students' standing with their fellow pupils and their teachers as well as interfere with later opportunities for higher education and employment.[7] It is apparent that the claimed right of the State to determine unilaterally and without process whether that misconduct has occurred immediately collides with the requirements of the Constitution.

Appellants proceed to argue that even if there is a right to a public education protected by the Due Process Clause generally, the Clause comes into play only when the State subjects a student to a "severe detriment or grievous loss." The loss of 10 days, it is said, is neither severe nor grievous and the Due Process Clause is therefore of no relevance. Appellants' argument is again refuted by our prior decisions; for in determining "whether due process requirements apply in the first place, we must look not to the 'weight' but to the nature of the interest at stake." *Board of Regents v. Roth, supra*, at 570–571. Appellees were excluded from school only temporarily, it is true, but the length and consequent severity of a deprivation, while another factor to weigh in determining the appropriate form of hearing, "is not decisive of the basic right" to a hearing of some kind. *Fuentes v. Shevin*, 407 U.S. 67, 86 (1972). The Court's view has been that as long as a property deprivation is not de minimis, its gravity is irrelevant to the question whether account must be taken of the Due Process Clause. *Sniadach v. Family Finance Corp.*, 395 U.S. 337, 342 (1969) (Harlan, J., concurring); *Boddie v. Connecticut*, 401 U.S. 371, 378–379 (1971); *Board of Regents v. Roth, supra*, 408 U.S., at 570 n. 8. A 10-day suspension from school is not de minimis in our view and may not be imposed in complete disregard of the Due Process Clause.

A short suspension is, of course, a far milder deprivation than expulsion. But, "education is perhaps the most important function of state and local governments," *Brown v. Board of Education*, 347 U.S. 483, 493 (1954), and the total exclusion from the educational process for more than a trivial period, and certainly if the suspension is for 10 days, is a serious event in the life of the suspended child. Neither the property interest in educational benefits temporarily denied nor the liberty interest in reputation, which is also implicated, is so insubstantial

7. Appellees assert in their brief that four of 12 randomly selected Ohio colleges specifically inquire of the high school of every applicant for admission whether the applicant has ever been suspended. Appellees also contend that many employers request similar information.

that suspensions may constitutionally be imposed by any procedure the school chooses, no matter how arbitrary.

III

"Once it is determined that due process applies, the question remains what process is due." *Morrissey v. Brewer*, 408 U.S., at 481. We turn to that question, fully realizing as our cases regularly do that the interpretation and application of the Due Process Clause are intensely practical matters and that "(t)he very nature of due process negates any concept of inflexible procedures universally applicable to every imaginable situation." *Cafeteria Workers v. McElroy*, 367 U.S. 886, 895 (1961). We are also mindful of our own admonition:

> "Judicial interposition in the operation of the public school system of the Nation raises problems requiring care and restraint.... By and large, public education in our Nation is committed to the control of state and local authorities." *Epperson v. Arkansas*, 393 U.S. 97, 104 (1968).

There are certain bench marks to guide us, however. *Mullane v. Central Hanover Trust Co.*, 339 U.S. 306 (1950), a case often invoked by later opinions, said that "(m)any controversies have raged about the cryptic and abstract words of the Due Process Clause but there can be no doubt that at a minimum they require that deprivation of life, liberty or property by adjudication be preceded by notice and opportunity for hearing appropriate to the nature of the case." *Id.*, at 313. "The fundamental requisite of due process of law is the opportunity to be heard," *Grannis v. Ordean*, 234 U.S. 385, 394 (1914), a right that "has little reality or worth unless one is informed that the matter is pending and can choose for himself whether to... contest." *Mullane v. Central Hanover Trust Co., supra*, 339 U.S. at 314. See also *Armstrong v. Manzo*, 380 U.S. 545, 550 (1965); *Joint Anti-Fascist Committee v. McGrath*, 341 U.S. 123, 168–169 (1951) (Frankfurter, J., concurring). At the very minimum, therefore, students facing suspension and the consequent interference with a protected property interest must be given *some* kind of notice and afforded *some* kind of hearing. "Parties whose rights are to be affected are entitled to be heard; and in order that they may enjoy that right they must first be notified." *Baldwin v. Hale*, 1 Wall. 223, 233 (1864).

It also appears from our cases that the timing and content of the notice and the nature of the hearing will depend on appropriate accommodation of the competing interests involved. *Cafeteria Workers v. McElroy, supra*, 367 U.S. at 895; *Morrissey v. Brewer, supra*, 408 U.S. at 481. The student's interest is to avoid unfair or mistaken exclusion from the educational process, with all of its unfortunate consequences. The Due Process Clause will not shield him from suspensions properly imposed, but it disserves both his interest and the interest of the State if his suspension is in fact unwarranted. The concern would be mostly academic if the disciplinary process were a totally accurate, unerring process, never mistaken and never unfair. Unfortunately, that is not the case, and no one suggests that it is. Disciplinarians, although proceeding in utmost good faith, frequently act on the reports and advice of others; and the controlling facts and the nature of the conduct under challenge are often disputed. The risk of error is not at all trivial, and it should be guarded against if that may be done without prohibitive cost or interference with the educational process.

The difficulty is that our schools are vast and complex. Some modicum of discipline and order is essential if the educational function is to be performed. Events calling for discipline are frequent occurrences and sometimes require immediate, effective action. Suspension is considered not only to be a necessary tool to maintain order but a valuable educational device. The prospect of imposing elaborate hearing requirements in every suspension case is viewed with great concern, and many school authorities may well prefer the untrammeled power to act unilaterally, unhampered by rules about notice and hearing. But it would be a strange disciplinary system in an educational institution if no communication was sought by the disciplinarian with the student in an effort to inform him of his dereliction and to let him tell his side of the story in order to make sure that an injustice is not done. "(F)airness can rarely be obtained by secret, one-sided determination of facts decisive of rights. . . ." "Secrecy is not congenial to truth-seeking and self-righteousness gives too slender an assurance of rightness. No better instrument has been devised for arriving at truth than to give a person in jeopardy of serious loss notice of the case against him and opportunity to meet it." *Joint Anti-Fascist Committee v. McGrath*, *supra*, 341 U.S., at 170, 172–173 (Frankfurter, J., concurring).[9]

We do not believe that school authorities must be totally free from notice and hearing requirements if their schools are to operate with acceptable efficiency. Students facing temporary suspension have interests qualifying for protection of the Due Process Clause, and due process requires, in connection with a suspension of 10 days or less, that the student be given oral or written notice of the charges against him and, if he denies them, an explanation of the evidence the authorities have and an opportunity to present his side of the story. The Clause requires at least these rudimentary precautions against unfair or mistaken findings of misconduct and arbitrary exclusion from school.[10]

9. The facts involved in this case illustrate the point. Betty Crome was suspended for conduct which did not occur on school grounds, and for which mass arrests were made—hardly guaranteeing careful individualized factfinding by the police or by the school principal. She claims to have been involved in no misconduct. However, she was suspended for 10 days without ever being told what she was accused of doing or being given an opportunity to explain her presence among those arrested. Similarly, Dwight Lopez was suspended, along with many others, in connection with a disturbance in the lunchroom. Lopez says he was not one of those in the lunchroom who was involved. However, he was never told the basis for the principal's belief that he was involved, nor was he ever given an opportunity to explain his presence in the lunchroom. The school principals who suspended Crome and Lopez may have been correct on the merits, but it is inconsistent with the Due Process Clause to have made the decision that misconduct had occurred without at some meaningful time giving Crome or Lopez an opportunity to persuade the principals otherwise.

We recognize that both suspensions were imposed during a time of great difficulty for the school administrations involved. At least in Lopez' case there may have been an immediate need to send home everyone in the lunchroom in order to preserve school order and property; and the administrative burden of providing 75 "hearings" of any kind is considerable. However, neither factor justifies a disciplinary suspension without at any time gathering facts relating to Lopez specifically, confronting him with them, and giving him an opportunity to explain.

10. Appellants point to the fact that some process is provided under Ohio law by way of judicial review. Ohio Rev.Code Ann. § 2506.01 (Supp. 1973). Appellants do not cite any case in which this general administrative review statute has been used to appeal from a disciplinary decision by a school official. If it be assumed that it could be so used, it is for two reasons insufficient to save inadequate procedures at the school level. First, although new proof may be offered in a § 2506.01 proceeding, *Shaker Coventry Corp. v. Shaker Heights Planning Comm'n*, 18 Ohio Op.2d 272, 176 N.E.2d 332 (1961), the proceeding is not *de novo*. *In re Locke*, 33 Ohio App.2d 177, 294 N.E.2d 230 (1972). Thus the decision by the school—even if made upon inadequate procedures—is entitled to weight in the court proceeding. Second, without a demonstration to the contrary, we must assume that delay will attend any § 2506.01 proceeding, that the suspension will not be stayed pending hearing, and that the student meanwhile will irreparably lose his educational benefits.

There need be no delay between the time "notice" is given and the time of the hearing. In the great majority of cases the disciplinarian may informally discuss the alleged misconduct with the student minutes after it has occurred. We hold only that, in being given an opportunity to explain his version of the facts at this discussion, the student first be told what he is accused of doing and what the basis of the accusation is. Lower courts which have addressed the question of the *nature* of the procedures required in short suspension cases have reached the same conclusion. *Tate v. Board of Education*, 453 F.2d 975, 979 (CA8 1972); *Vail v. Board of Education*, 354 F.Supp. 592, 603 (NH 1973). Since the hearing may occur almost immediately following the misconduct, it follows that as a general rule notice and hearing should precede removal of the student from school. We agree with the District Court, however, that there are recurring situations in which prior notice and hearing cannot be insisted upon. Students whose presence poses a continuing danger to persons or property or an ongoing threat of disrupting the academic process may be immediately removed from school. In such cases, the necessary notice and rudimentary hearing should follow as soon as practicable, as the District Court indicated.

In holding as we do, we do not believe that we have imposed procedures on school disciplinarians which are inappropriate in a classroom setting. Instead we have imposed requirements which are, if anything, less than a fair-minded school principal would impose upon himself in order to avoid unfair suspensions. Indeed, according to the testimony of the principal of Marion-Franklin High School, that school had an informal procedure, remarkably similar to that which we now require, applicable to suspensions generally but which was not followed in this case. Similarly, according to the most recent memorandum applicable to the entire CPSS, see n. 1, *supra*, school principals in the CPSS are now required by local rule to provide at least as much as the constitutional minimum which we have described.

We stop short of construing the Due Process Clause to require, countrywide, that hearings in connection with short suspensions must afford the student the opportunity to secure counsel, to confront and cross-examine witnesses supporting the charge, or to call his own witnesses to verify his version of the incident. Brief disciplinary suspensions are almost countless. To impose in each such case even truncated trial-type procedures might well overwhelm administrative facilities in many places and, by diverting resources, cost more than it would save in educational effectiveness. Moreover, further formalizing the suspension process and escalating its formality and adversary nature may not only make it too costly as a regular disciplinary tool but also destroy its effectiveness as part of the teaching process.

On the other hand, requiring effective notice and informal hearing permitting the student to give his version of the events will provide a meaningful hedge against erroneous action. At least the disciplinarian will be alerted to the existence of disputes about facts and arguments about cause and effect. He may then determine himself to summon the accuser, permit cross-examination, and allow the student to present his own witnesses. In more difficult cases, he may permit counsel. In any event, his discretion will be more informed and we think the risk of error substantially reduced.

Requiring that there be at least an informal give-and-take between student and disciplinarian, preferably prior to the suspension, will add little to the factfinding function where the disciplinarian himself has witnessed the conduct forming the basis for the charge. But things are not always as they seem to be, and the student will at least have the opportunity to characterize his conduct and put it in what he deems the proper context.

We should also make it clear that we have addressed ourselves solely to the short suspension, not exceeding 10 days. Longer suspensions or expulsions for the remainder of the school term, or permanently, may require more formal procedures. Nor do we put aside the possibility that in unusual situations, although involving only a short suspension, something more than the rudimentary procedures will be required.

IV

The District Court found each of the suspensions involved here to have occurred without a hearing, either before or after the suspension, and that each suspension was therefore invalid and the statute unconstitutional insofar as it permits such suspensions without notice or hearing. Accordingly, the judgment is

Affirmed.

Mr. Justice Powell, with whom The Chief Justice, Mr. Justice Blackmun, and Mr. Justice Rehnquist join, dissenting.

The Court today invalidates an Ohio statute that permits student suspensions from school without a hearing "for not more than ten days."[1] The decision unnecessarily opens avenues for judicial intervention in the operation of our public schools that may affect adversely the quality of education. The Court holds for the first time that the federal courts, rather than educational officials and state legislatures, have the authority to determine the rules applicable to routine classroom discipline of children and teenagers in the public schools. It justifies this unprecedented intrusion into the process of elementary and secondary education by identifying a new constitutional right: the right of a student not to be suspended for as much as a single day without notice and a due process hearing either before or promptly following the suspension.[2]

The Court's decision rests on the premise that, under Ohio law, education is a property interest protected by the Fourteenth Amendment's Due Process Clause and therefore that any suspension requires notice and a hearing.[3] In my view, a student's interest in education is not infringed by a suspension within the limited period prescribed by Ohio law. Moreover, to the extent that there may be some arguable infringement, it is too speculative, transitory, and insubstantial to justify imposition of a *constitutional* rule.

I

Although we held in *San Antonio Independent School Dist. v. Rodriguez*, 411 U.S. 1, 35 (1973), that education is not a right protected by the Constitution, Ohio has elected by statute to provide free education for all youths age six to 21, Ohio Rev.Code Ann. §§ 3313.48, 3313.64

1. The Ohio statute, Ohio Rev.Code Ann. § 3313.66 (1972), actually is a limitation on the time-honored practice of school authorities themselves determining the appropriate duration of suspensions. The statute allows the superintendent or principal of a public school to suspend a pupil "for *not more than ten days*..." (italics supplied); and requires notification to the parent or guardian in writing within 24 hours of any suspension.

2. Section 3313.66 also provides authority for the expulsion of pupils, but requires a hearing thereon by the school board upon request of a parent or guardian. The rights of pupils expelled are not involved in this case, which concerns only the limited discretion of school authorities to suspend for not more than 10 days. Expulsion, usually resulting at least in loss of a school year or semester, is an incomparably more serious matter than the brief suspension, traditionally used as the principal sanction for enforcing routine discipline. The Ohio Statute recognizes this distinction.

3. The Court speaks of "exclusion from the educational process for more than a trivial period...," but its opinion makes clear that even one day's suspension invokes the constitutional procedure mandated today.

(1972 and Supp. 1973), with children under 18 years of age being compelled to attend school. § 3321.01 et seq. State law, therefore, extends the right of free public school education to Ohio students in accordance with the education laws of that State. The right or entitlement to education so created is protected in a proper case by the Due Process Clause. See, *e.g.*, *Board of Regents v. Roth*, 408 U.S. 564 (1972); *Arnett v. Kennedy*, 416 U.S. 134, 164 (1974) (POWELL, J., concurring). In my view, this is not such a case.

In identifying property interests subject to due process protections, the Court's past opinions make clear that these interests "are created and *their dimensions are defined* by existing rules or understandings that stem from an independent source such as state law." *Board of Regents v. Roth*, *supra*, 408 U.S., at 577 (emphasis supplied). The Ohio statute that creates the right to a "free" education also explicitly authorizes a principal to suspend a student for as much as 10 days. Ohio Rev.Code Ann. ss 3313.48, 3313.64, 3313.66 (1972 and Supp. 1973). Thus the very legislation which "defines" the "dimension" of the student's entitlement, while providing a right to education generally, does not establish this right free of discipline imposed in accord with Ohio law. Rather, the right is encompassed in the entire package of statutory provisions governing education in Ohio—of which the power to suspend is one.

The Court thus disregards the basic structure of Ohio law in posturing this case as if Ohio had conferred an unqualified right to education, thereby compelling the school authorities to conform to due process procedures in imposing the most routine discipline.[4]

But however one may define the entitlement to education provided by Ohio law, I would conclude that a deprivation of not more than 10 days' suspension from school, imposed as a routine disciplinary measure, does not assume constitutional dimensions. Contrary to the Court's assertion, our cases support rather than "refute" appellants' argument that "the Due Process Clause... comes into play only when the State subjects a student to a 'severe detriment or grievous loss.'" Recently, the Court reiterated precisely this standard for analyzing due process claims:

> "'Whether *any* procedural protections are due depends on the extent to which an individual will be "condemned to suffer *grievous* loss."' *Joint Anti-Fascist Refugee Committee v. McGrath*, 341 U.S. 123, 168 (1951) (Frankfurter, J., concurring), quoted in *Goldberg v. Kelly*, 397 U.S. 254, 263 (1970). *Morrissey v. Brewer*, 408 U.S. 471, 481 (1972) (emphasis supplied).

In *Morrissey* we applied that standard to require due process procedures for parole revocation on the ground that revocation "inflicts a 'grievous loss' on the parolee and often on others."

4. The Court apparently reads into Ohio law by implication a qualification that suspensions may be imposed only for "cause," thereby analogizing this case to the civil service laws considered in *Arnett v. Kennedy*, 416 U.S. 134 (1974). To be sure, one may assume that pupils are not suspended at the whim or caprice of the school official, and the statute does provide for notice of the suspension with the "reasons therefor." But the same statute draws a sharp distinction between suspension and the far more drastic sanction of expulsion. A hearing is required only for the latter. To follow the Court's analysis, one must conclude that the legislature nevertheless intended—without saying so—that suspension also is of such consequence that it may be imposed only for causes which can be justified at a hearing. The unsoundness of reading this sort of requirement into the statute is apparent from a comparison with *Arnett*. In that case, Congress *expressly* provided that nonprobationary federal employees should be discharged only for "cause." This requirement reflected congressional recognition of the seriousness of discharging such employees. There simply is no analogy between *termination* of nonprobationary employment of a civil service employee and the suspension of a public school pupil for not more than 10 days. Even if the Court is correct in implying some concept of justifiable cause in the Ohio procedure, it could hardly be stretched to the constitutional proportions found present in *Arnett*.

Id., at 482. See also *Board of Regents v. Roth*, 408 U.S., at 573 ("seriously damage" reputation and standing); *Bell v. Burson*, 402 U.S. 535, 539 (1971) ("important interests of the licensees"); *Boddie v. Connecticut*, 401 U.S. 371, 379 (1971) ("significant property interest").

The Ohio suspension statute allows no serious or significant infringement of education. It authorizes only a maximum suspension of eight school days, less than 5 percent of the normal 180-day school year. Absences of such limited duration will rarely affect a pupil's opportunity to learn or his scholastic performance. Indeed, the record in this case reflects no educational injury to appellees. Each completed the semester in which the suspension occurred and performed at least as well as he or she had in previous years. Despite the Court's unsupported speculation that a suspended student could be "seriously damage[d]," there is no factual showing of any such damage to appellees.

The Court also relies on a perceived deprivation of "liberty" resulting from any suspension, arguing—again without factual support in the record pertaining to these appellees—that a suspension harms a student's reputation. In view of the Court's decision in *Board of Regents v. Roth*, *supra*, I would have thought that this argument was plainly untenable. Underscoring the need for "serious damage" to reputation, the *Roth* Court held that a nontenured teacher who is not rehired by a public university could not claim to suffer sufficient reputational injury to require constitutional protections. Surely a brief suspension is of less serious consequence to the reputation of a teenage student.

II

In prior decisions, this Court has explicitly recognized that school authorities must have broad discretionary authority in the daily operation of public schools. This includes wide latitude with respect to maintaining discipline and good order. Addressing this point specifically, the Court stated in *Tinker v. Des Moines School Dist.*, 393 U.S. 503, 507 (1969):

> "(T)he Court has repeatedly emphasized the need for affirming the comprehensive authority of the States and of school officials, consistent with fundamental constitutional safeguards, to prescribe and control conduct in the schools."

Such an approach properly recognizes the unique nature of public education and the correspondingly limited role of the judiciary in its supervision. In *Epperson v. Arkansas*, 393 U.S. 97, 104 (1968), the Court stated:

> "By and large, public education in our Nation is committed to the control of state and local authorities. Courts do not and cannot intervene in the resolution of conflicts which arise in the daily operation of school systems and which do not directly and sharply implicate basic constitutional values."

The Court today turns its back on these precedents. It can hardly seriously be claimed that a school principal's decision to suspend a pupil for a single day would "directly and sharply implicate basic constitutional values." *Ibid.*

Moreover, the Court ignores the experience of mankind, as well as the long history of our law, recognizing that there *are* differences which must be accommodated in determining the rights and duties of children as compared with those of adults. Examples of this distinction abound in our law: in contracts, in torts, in criminal law and procedure, in criminal sanctions and rehabilitation, and in the right to vote and to hold office. Until today, and except in the special context of the First Amendment issue in *Tinker*, the educational rights of children and teenagers in the elementary and secondary schools have not been analogized to the rights of adults or to those accorded college students. Even with respect to the First Amendment, the rights of children have not been regarded as "co-extensive with those of adults." *Tinker*, *supra*, 393 U.S., at 515 (STEWART, J., concurring).

A

I turn now to some of the considerations which support the Court's former view regarding the comprehensive authority of the States and school officials "to prescribe and control conduct in the schools." *Id.*, at 507. Unlike the divergent and even sharp conflict of interests usually present where due process rights are asserted, the interests here implicated—of the State through its schools and of the pupils—are essentially congruent.

The State's interest, broadly put, is in the proper functioning of its public school system for the benefit of *all* pupils and the public generally. Few rulings would interfere more extensively in the daily functioning of schools than subjecting routine discipline to the formalities and judicial oversight of due process. Suspensions are one of the traditional means—ranging from keeping a student after class to permanent expulsion—used to maintain discipline in the schools. It is common knowledge that maintaining order and reasonable decorum in school buildings and classrooms is a major educational problem, and one which has increased significantly in magnitude in recent years. Often the teacher, in protecting the rights of other children to an education (if not his or their safety), is compelled to rely on the power to suspend.

The facts set forth in the margin[10] leave little room for doubt as to the magnitude of the disciplinary problem in the public schools, or as to the extent of reliance upon the right to suspend. They also demonstrate that if hearings were required for a substantial percentage of short-term suspensions, school authorities would have time to do little else.

B

The State's generalized interest in maintaining an orderly school system is not incompatible with the individual interest of the student. Education in any meaningful sense includes the inculcation of an understanding in each pupil of the necessity of rules and obedience thereto. This understanding is no less important than learning to read and write. One who does not

10. An *amicus* brief filed by the Children's Defense Fund states that *at least 10%* of the junior and senior high school students in the States sampled were suspended one or more times in the 1972–1973 school year. The data on which this conclusion rests were obtained from an extensive survey prepared by the Office for Civil Rights of the Department of Health, Education, and Welfare. The Children's Defense Fund reviewed the suspension data for five States—Arkansas, Maryland, New Jersey, Ohio, and South Carolina.

Likewise, an amicus brief submitted by several school associations in Ohio indicates that the number of suspensions is significant: in 1972–1973, 4,054 students out of a school enrollment of 81,007 were suspended in Cincinnati; 7,352 of 57,000 students were suspended in Akron; and 14,598 of 142,053 students were suspended in Cleveland. See also the Office of Civil Rights Survey, *supra*, finding that approximately 20,000 students in New York City, 12,000 in Cleveland, 9,000 in Houston, and 9,000 in Memphis were suspended at least once during the 1972–1973 school year. Even these figures are probably somewhat conservative since some schools did not reply to the survey.

comprehend the meaning and necessity of discipline is handicapped not merely in his education but throughout his subsequent life. In an age when the home and church play a diminishing role in shaping the character and value judgments of the young, a heavier responsibility falls upon the schools. When an immature student merits censure for his conduct, he is rendered a disservice if appropriate sanctions are not applied or if procedures for their application are so formalized as to invite a challenge to the teacher's authority—an invitation which rebellious or even merely spirited teenagers are likely to accept.

The lesson of discipline is not merely a matter of the student's self-interest in the shaping of his own character and personality; it provides an early understanding of the relevance to the social compact of respect for the rights of others. The classroom is the laboratory in which this lesson of life is best learned.

Mr. Justice Black summed it up:

> "School discipline, like parental discipline, is an integral and important part of training our children to be good citizens—to be better citizens." *Tinker*, 393 U.S., at 524 (dissenting opinion).

In assessing in constitutional terms the need to protect pupils from unfair minor discipline by school authorities, the Court ignores the commonality of interest of the State and pupils in the public school system. Rather, it thinks in traditional judicial terms of an adversary situation. To be sure, there will be the occasional pupil innocent of any rule infringement who is mistakenly suspended or whose infraction is too minor to justify suspension. But, while there is no evidence indicating the frequency of unjust suspensions, common sense suggests that they will not be numerous in relation to the total number, and that mistakes or injustices will usually be righted by informal means.

C

One of the more disturbing aspects of today's decision is its indiscriminate reliance upon the judiciary, and the adversary process, as the means of resolving many of the most routine problems arising in the classroom. In mandating due process procedures the Court misapprehends the reality of the normal teacher-pupil relationship. There is an ongoing relationship, one in which the teacher must occupy many roles—educator, adviser, friend, and, at times, parent-substitute. It is rarely adversary in nature except with respect to the chronically disruptive or insubordinate pupil whom the teacher must be free to discipline without frustrating formalities.[13]

13. In this regard, the relationship between a student and a teacher is manifestly different from that between a welfare administrator and a recipient (see *Goldberg v. Kelly*, 397 U.S. 254 (1970)), a motor vehicle department and a driver (see *Bell v. Burson*, 402 U.S. 535 (1971)), a debtor and a creditor (see *Sniadach v. Family Finance Corp., supra*; *Fuentes v. Shevin, supra*; *Mitchell v. W. T. Grant Co.*, 416 U.S. 600 (1974)), a parole officer and a parolee (see *Morrissey v. Brewer*, 408 U.S. 471 (1972)), or even an employer and an employee (see *Arnett v. Kennedy*, 416 U.S. 134 (1974)). In many of these noneducation settings there is—for purposes of this analysis—a "faceless" administrator dealing with an equally "faceless" recipient of some form of government benefit or license; in others, such as the garnishment and repossession cases, there is a conflict-of-interest relationship. Our public school system, however, is premised on the belief that teachers and pupils should not be "faceless" to each other. Nor does the educational relationship present a typical "conflict of interest." Rather, the relationship traditionally is marked by a coincidence of interests.

The Ohio statute, providing as it does for due notice both to parents and the Board, is compatible with the teacher-pupil relationship and the informal resolution of mistaken disciplinary action. We have relied for generations upon the experience, good faith and dedication of those who staff our public schools,[14] and the nonadversary means of airing grievances that always have been available to pupils and their parents. One would have thought before today's opinion that this informal method of resolving differences was more compatible with the interests of all concerned than resort to any constitutionalized procedure, however blandly it may be defined by the Court.

D

In my view, the constitutionalizing of routine classroom decisions not only represents a significant and unwise extension of the Due Process Clause, but it also was quite unnecessary in view of the safeguards prescribed by the Ohio statute. This is demonstrable from a comparison of what the Court mandates as required by due process with the protective procedures it finds constitutionally insufficient.

The Ohio statute, limiting suspensions to not more than eight school days, requires written notice including the "reasons therefore" to the student's parents and to the Board of Education within 24 hours of any suspension. The Court only requires oral or written notice to the pupil, with no notice being required to the parents or the Board of Education. The mere fact of the statutory requirement is a deterrent against arbitrary action by the principal. The Board, usually elected by the people and sensitive to constituent relations, may be expected to identify a principal whose record of suspensions merits inquiry. In any event, parents placed on written notice may exercise their rights as constituents by going directly to the Board or a member thereof if dissatisfied with the principal's decision.

Nor does the Court's due process "hearing" appear to provide significantly more protection than that already available. The Court holds only that the principal must listen to the student's "version of the events," either before suspension or thereafter—depending upon the circumstances. Such a truncated "hearing" is likely to be considerably less meaningful than the opportunities for correcting mistakes already available to students and parents. Indeed, in this case all of the students and parents were offered an opportunity to attend a conference with school officials.

In its rush to mandate a constitutional rule, the Court appears to give no weight to the practical manner in which suspension problems normally would be worked out under Ohio law. One must doubt, then, whether the constitutionalization of the student-teacher relationship, with all of its attendant doctrinal and practical difficulties, will assure in any meaningful sense greater protection than that already afforded under Ohio law.

III

No one can foresee the ultimate frontiers of the new "thicket" the Court now enters. Today's ruling appears to sweep within the protected interest in education a multitude of discretionary

Yet the Court, relying on cases such as *Sniadach* and *Fuentes*, apparently views the classroom of teenagers as comparable to the competitive and adversary environment of the adult, commercial world.

14. A traditional factor in any due process analysis is "the protection implicit in the office of the functionary whose conduct is challenged...." *Joint Anti-Fascist Committee v. McGrath*, 341 U.S., at 163 (Frankfurter, J., concurring). In the public school setting there is a high degree of such protection since a teacher has responsibility for, and a commitment to, his pupils that is absent in other due process contexts.

decisions in the educational process. Teachers and other school authorities are required to make many decisions that may have serious consequences for the pupil. They must decide, for example, how to grade the student's work, whether a student passes or fails a course, whether he is to be promoted, whether he is required to take certain subjects, whether he may be excluded from interscholastic athletics or other extracurricular activities, whether he may be removed from one school and sent to another, whether he may be bused long distances when available schools are nearby, and whether he should be placed in a "general," "vocational," or "college-preparatory" track.

In these and many similar situations claims of impairment of one's educational entitlement identical in principle to those before the Court today can be asserted with equal or greater justification. Likewise, in many of these situations, the pupil can advance the same types of speculative and subjective injury given critical weight in this case. The District Court, relying upon generalized opinion evidence, concluded that a suspended student may suffer psychological injury in one or more of the ways set forth in the margin below.[18] The Court appears to adopt this rationale.

It hardly need be said that if a student, as a result of a day's suspension, suffers "a blow" to his "self esteem," "feels powerless," views "teachers with resentment," or feels "stigmatized by his teachers," identical psychological harms will flow from many other routine and necessary school decisions. The student who is given a failing grade, who is not promoted, who is excluded from certain extracurricular activities, who is assigned to a school reserved for children of less than average ability, or who is placed in the "vocational" rather than the "college preparatory" track, is unlikely to suffer any less psychological injury than if he were suspended for a day for a relatively minor infraction.[19]

If, as seems apparent, the Court will now require due process procedures whenever such routine school decisions are challenged, the impact upon public education will be serious indeed. The discretion and judgment of federal courts across the land often will be substituted for that of the 50-state legislatures, the 14,000 school boards, and the 2,000,000 teachers who heretofore have been responsible for the administration of the American public school system.

18. The psychological injuries so perceived were as follows:

"1. The suspension is a blow to the student's self-esteem.

"2. The student feels powerless and helpless.

"3. The student views school authorities and teachers with resentment, suspicion and fear.

"4. The student learns withdrawal as a mode of problem solving.

"5. The student has little perception of the reasons for the suspension. He does not know what offending acts he committed.

"6. The student is stigmatized by his teachers and school administrators as a deviant. They expect the student to be a troublemaker in the future." 372 F.Supp., at 1292.

19. There is, no doubt, a school of modern psychological or psychiatric persuasion that maintains that any discipline of the young is detrimental. Whatever one may think of the wisdom of this unproved theory, it hardly affords dependable support for a *constitutional* decision. Moreover, even the theory's proponents would concede that the magnitude of injury depends primarily upon the individual child or teenager. A classroom reprimand by the teacher may be more traumatic to the shy, timid introvert than expulsion would be to the aggressive, rebellious extrovert. In my view we tend to lose our sense of perspective and proportion in a case of this kind. For average, normal children—the vast majority—suspension for a few days is simply not a detriment; it is a commonplace occurrence, with some 10% of all students being suspended; it leaves no scars; affects no reputations; indeed, it often may be viewed by the young as a badge of some distinction and a welcome holiday.

If the Court perceives a rational and analytically sound distinction between the discretionary decision by school authorities to suspend a pupil for a brief period, and the types of discretionary school decisions described above, it would be prudent to articulate it in today's opinion. Otherwise, the federal courts should prepare themselves for a vast new role in society.

IV

Not so long ago, state deprivations of the most significant forms of state largesse were not thought to require due process protection on the ground that the deprivation resulted only in the loss of a state-provided "benefit." *E.g., Bailey v. Richardson*, 86 U.S.App.D.C. 248, 182 F.2d 46 (1950), aff'd by an equally divided Court, 341 U.S. 918 (1951). In recent years the Court, wisely in my view, has rejected the "wooden distinction between 'rights' and 'privileges,'" *Board of Regents v. Roth*, 408 U.S., at 571, and looked instead to the significance of the state-created or state-enforced right and to the substantiality of the alleged deprivation. Today's opinion appears to abandon this reasonable approach by holding in effect that government infringement of any interest to which a person is entitled, no matter what the interest or how inconsequential the infringement, requires constitutional protection. As it is difficult to think of any less consequential infringement than suspension of a junior high school student for a single day, it is equally difficult to perceive any principled limit to the new reach of procedural due process.[22]

NOTES AND QUESTIONS

1. Who appealed the decision of the lower court to the Supreme Court? Why? Did the Supreme Court affirm or reverse the decision below?

2. Whose rights were violated? What were they? What must a school district do before it may suspend a student? Before it may expel a student?

3. Is there a federal constitutional right to an education? If not, how did the Columbus Public School System violate the Constitution?

4. Is there a state constitutional right to an education? Every state constitution has an education clause requiring the provision of free public schools. Molly S. McUsic, *The Future of Brown v. Board of Education: Economic Integration of the Public Schools*, 117 Harv. L. Rev. 1334, 1345–1346 (2004). These constitutional provisions generally describe the educational

22. Some half dozen years ago, the Court extended First Amendment rights under limited circumstances to public school pupils. Mr. Justice Black, dissenting, viewed the decision as ushering in "an entirely new era in which the power to control pupils by the elected 'officials of state supported public schools'... is in ultimate effect transferred to the Supreme Court." *Tinker v. Des Moines School Dist.*, 393 U.S. 503, 515 (1969). There were some who thought Mr. Justice Black was unduly concerned. But his prophecy is now being fulfilled. In the few years since *Tinker* there have been literally hundreds of cases by schoolchildren alleging violation of their constitutional rights. This flood of litigation, between pupils and school authorities, was triggered by a narrowly written First Amendment opinion which I could well have joined on its facts. One can only speculate as to the extent to which public education will be disrupted by giving every schoolchild the power to contest *in court* any decision made by his teacher which arguably infringes the state-conferred right to education.

system, often in terms of adequacy or uniformity. *Id.* at 1346. These state constitutional provisions have formed the basis for school-finance-reform litigation, and at least eighteen states have found their school-financing schemes unconstitutional. *Id.* at 1346–1347 and n. 77.

The course of litigation is not always smooth. For example, the Ohio Supreme Court found the state of Ohio's financing scheme unconstitutional in *DeRolph v. State*, 677 N.E.2d 733 (Ohio 1997) (*DeRolph I*), opinion clarified, 678 N.E.2d 886 (Ohio 1997), and order clarified, 699 N.E.2d 518 (1998). In 2000, the Ohio Supreme Court again found the state system of public-school financing unconstitutional. *DeRolph v. State*, 728 N.E.2d 993 (Ohio 2000) (*DeRolph II*). In 2001, the Court issued yet another opinion, *DeRolph v. State*, 754 N.E.2d 1184 (Ohio 2001) (*DeRolph III*), but on a motion to reconsider, the Court granted the motion and ordered a settlement conference. Because the parties could not reach an agreement, the Court settled the case on the merits in *DeRolph v. State*, 780 N.E.2d 529 (Ohio 2002) (*DeRolph IV*). In *DeRolph IV*, the Court ordered the state legislature to "enact a school-funding scheme that is thorough and efficient," as mandated by the state constitution. In a subsequent ruling, the Ohio Supreme Court made clear it did not intend to retain jurisdiction over the matter and has never ruled on the constitutionality of the current scheme. *State ex rel. State v. Lewis*, 789 N.E.2d 195 (Ohio 2003).

5. What reasons did the school give for the suspensions in *Goss*? Would the Court's decision in *Tinker* have been dispositive?

6. What is the basis for the dissent's disagreement? Whose view of school systems do you think is more accurate today?

INGRAHAM V. WRIGHT
Supreme Court of the United States
430 U.S. 651 (1977)

MR. JUSTICE POWELL delivered the opinion of the Court.

This case presents questions concerning the use of corporal punishment in public schools: First, whether the paddling of students as a means of maintaining school discipline constitutes cruel and unusual punishment in violation of the Eighth Amendment; and, second, to the extent that paddling is constitutionally permissible, whether the Due Process Clause of the Fourteenth Amendment requires prior notice and an opportunity to be heard.

I

Petitioners James Ingraham and Roosevelt Andrews filed the complaint in this case on January 7, 1971, in the United States District Court for the Southern District of Florida. At the time both were enrolled in the Charles R. Drew Junior High School in Dade County, Fla., Ingraham in the eighth grade and Andrews in the ninth. The complaint contained three counts, each alleging a separate cause of action for deprivation of constitutional rights, under 42 U.S.C. §§ 1981–1988. Counts one and two were individual actions for damages by Ingraham and Andrews based on paddling incidents that allegedly occurred in October 1970 at Drew Junior High School. Count three was a class action for declaratory and injunctive relief filed on behalf of all students in the Dade County schools. Named as defendants in all counts were respondents Willie J. Wright (principal at Drew Junior High School), Lemmie Deliford (an assistant principal), Solomon Barnes (an assistant to the principal), and Edward L. Whigham (superintendent of the Dade County School System).

Petitioners presented their evidence at a week-long trial before the District Court. At the close of petitioners' case, respondents moved for dismissal of count three "on the ground that upon the facts and the law the plaintiff has shown no right to relief," Fed.Rule Civ.Proc. 41(b), and for a ruling that the evidence would be insufficient to go to a jury on counts one and two. The District Court granted the motion as to all three counts, and dismissed the complaint without hearing evidence on behalf of the school authorities. App. 142–150.

Petitioners' evidence may be summarized briefly. In the 1970–1971 school year many of the 237 schools in Dade County used corporal punishment as a means of maintaining discipline pursuant to Florida legislation and a local School Board regulation.[5] The statute then in effect authorized limited corporal punishment by negative inference, proscribing punishment which was "degrading or unduly severe" or which was inflicted without prior consultation with the principal or the teacher in charge of the school. Fla.Stat.Ann. § 232.27 (1961).[6] The regulation, Dade County School Board Policy 5144, contained explicit directions and limitations.[7] The authorized punishment consisted of paddling the recalcitrant student on

5. The evidence does not show how many of the schools actually employed corporal punishment as a means of maintaining discipline. The authorization of the practice by the School Board extended to 231 of the schools in the 1970–1971 school year, but at least 10 of those schools did not administer corporal punishment as a matter of school policy.

6. In the 1970–1971 school year, § 232.27 provided:

"Each teacher or other member of the staff of any school shall assume such authority for the control of pupils as may be assigned to him by the principal and shall keep good order in the classroom and in other places in which he is assigned to be in charge of pupils, but he shall not inflict corporal punishment before consulting the principal or teacher in charge of the school, and in no case shall such punishment be degrading or unduly severe in its nature...."

Effective July 1, 1976, the Florida Legislature amended the law governing corporal punishment. Section 232.27 now reads:

"Subject to law and to the rules of the district school board, each teacher or other member of the staff of any school shall have such authority for the control and discipline of students as may be assigned to him by the principal or his designated representative and shall keep good order in the classroom and in other places in which he is assigned to be in charge of students. If a teacher feels that corporal punishment is necessary, at least the following procedures shall be followed:

"(1) The use of corporal punishment shall be approved in principle by the principal before it is used, but approval is not necessary for each specific instance in which it is used.

"(2) A teacher or principal may administer corporal punishment only in the presence of another adult who is informed beforehand, and in the student's presence, of the reason for the punishment.

"(3) A teacher or principal who has administered punishment shall, upon request, provide the pupil's parent or guardian with a written explanation of the reason for the punishment and the name of the other (adult) who was present." Fla.Stat.Ann. § 232.27 (1977) (codifier's notation omitted).

Corporal punishment is now defined as "the moderate use of physical force or physical contact by a teacher or principal as may be necessary to maintain discipline or to enforce school rules." § 228.041(28). The local school boards are expressly authorized to adopt rules governing student conduct and discipline and are directed to make available codes of student conduct. § 230.23(6). Teachers and principals are given immunity from civil and criminal liability for enforcing disciplinary rules, "(e)xcept in the case of excessive force or cruel and unusual punishment...." § 232.275.

7. In the 1970–1971 school year, Policy 5144 authorized corporal punishment where the failure of other means of seeking cooperation from the student made its use necessary. The regulation specified that the principal should determine the necessity for corporal punishment, that the student should understand the

the buttocks with a flat wooden paddle measuring less than two feet long, three to four inches wide, and about one-half inch thick. The normal punishment was limited to one to five "licks" or blows with the paddle and resulted in no apparent physical injury to the student. School authorities viewed corporal punishment as a less drastic means of discipline than suspension or expulsion. Contrary to the procedural requirements of the statute and regulation, teachers often paddled students on their own authority without first consulting the principal.

Petitioners focused on Drew Junior High School, the school in which both Ingraham and Andrews were enrolled in the fall of 1970. In an apparent reference to Drew, the District Court found that "(t)he instances of punishment which could be characterized as severe, accepting the students' testimony as credible, took place in one junior high school." The evidence, consisting mainly of the testimony of 16 students, suggests that the regime at Drew was exceptionally harsh. The testimony of Ingraham and Andrews, in support of their individual claims for damages, is illustrative. Because he was slow to respond to his teacher's instructions, Ingraham was subjected to more than 20 licks with a paddle while being held over a table in the principal's office. The paddling was so severe that he suffered a hematoma[9] requiring medical attention and keeping him out of school for several days. Andrews was paddled several times for minor infractions. On two occasions he was struck on his arms, once depriving him of the full use of his arm for a week.[10]

The District Court made no findings on the credibility of the students' testimony. Rather, assuming their testimony to be credible, the court found no constitutional basis for relief. With respect to count three, the class action, the court concluded that the punishment authorized and practiced generally in the county schools violated no constitutional right. *Id.*, at 143, 149. With respect to counts one and two, the individual damages actions, the court concluded that while corporal punishment could in some cases violate the Eighth Amendment, in this case a jury could not lawfully find "the elements of severity, arbitrary infliction, unacceptability in terms of contemporary standards, or gross disproportion which are necessary to bring 'punishment' to the constitutional level of 'cruel and unusual punishment.'" *Id.*, at 143.

A panel of the Court of Appeals voted to reverse. 498 F.2d 248 (CA5 1974). The panel concluded that the punishment was so severe and oppressive as to violate the Eighth and Fourteenth Amendments, and that the procedures outlined in Policy 5144 failed to satisfy the requirements of the Due Process Clause. Upon rehearing, the en banc court rejected these

seriousness of the offense and the reason for the punishment, and that the punishment should be administered in the presence of another adult in circumstances not calculated to hold the student up to shame or ridicule. The regulation cautioned against using corporal punishment against a student under psychological or medical treatment, and warned that the person administering the punishment "must realize his own personal liabilities" in any case of physical injury.

While this litigation was pending in the District Court, the Dade County School Board amended Policy 5144 to standardize the size of the paddles used in accordance with the description in the text, to proscribe striking a child with a paddle elsewhere than on the buttocks, to limit the permissible number of "licks" (five for elementary and intermediate grades and seven for junior and senior grades), and to require a contemporaneous explanation of the need for the punishment to the student and a subsequent notification to the parents.

9. Stedman's Medical Dictionary (23d ed. 1976) defines "hematoma" as "(a) localized mass of extravasated blood that is relatively or completely confined within an organ or tissue...; the blood is usually clotted (or partly clotted), and, depending on how long it has been there, may manifest various degrees of organization and decolorization."

10. The similar experiences of several other students at Drew, to which they individually testified in the District Court, are summarized in the original panel opinion in the Court of Appeals, 498 F.2d, at 257–259.

conclusions and affirmed the judgment of the District Court. 525 F.2d 909 (1976). The full court held that the Due Process Clause did not require notice or an opportunity to be heard:

> "In essence, we refuse to set forth, as constitutionally mandated, procedural standards for an activity which is not substantial enough, on a constitutional level, to justify the time and effort which would have to be expended by the school in adhering to those procedures or to justify further interference by federal courts into the internal affairs of public schools." *Id.*, at 919.

The court also rejected the petitioners' substantive contentions. The Eighth Amendment, in the court's view, was simply inapplicable to corporal punishment in public schools. Stressing the likelihood of civil and criminal liability in state law, if petitioners' evidence were believed, the court held that "(t)he administration of corporal punishment in public schools, whether or not excessively administered, does not come within the scope of Eighth Amendment protection." *Id.*, at 915. Nor was there any substantive violation of the Due Process Clause. The court noted that "(p)addling of recalcitrant children has long been an accepted method of promoting good behavior and instilling notions of responsibility and decorum into the mischievous heads of school children." *Id.*, at 917. The court refused to examine instances of punishment individually:

> "We think it a misuse of our judicial power to determine, for example, whether a teacher has acted arbitrarily in paddling a particular child for certain behavior or whether in a particular instance of misconduct five licks would have been a more appropriate punishment than ten licks...." *Ibid.*

We granted certiorari, limited to the questions of cruel and unusual punishment and procedural due process. 425 U.S. 990.[12]

II

In addressing the scope of the Eighth Amendment's prohibition on cruel and unusual punishment this Court has found it useful to refer to "(t)raditional common-law concepts," *Powell v. Texas*, 392 U.S. 514, 535 (1968) (plurality opinion), and to the "attitude(s) which our society has traditionally taken." *Id.*, at 531. So, too, in defining the requirements of procedural due process under the Fifth and Fourteenth Amendments, the Court has been attuned to what "has always been the law of the land," *United States v. Barnett*, 376 U.S. 681, 692 (1964), and to "traditional ideas of fair procedure." *Greene v. McElroy*, 360 U.S. 474, 508 (1959). We therefore begin by examining the way in which our traditions and our laws have responded to the use of corporal punishment in public schools.

The use of corporal punishment in this country as a means of disciplining school children dates back to the colonial period.[13] It has survived the transformation of primary and

12. We denied review of a third question presented in the petition for certiorari:

"Is the infliction of severe corporal punishment upon public school students arbitrary, capricious and unrelated to achieving any legitimate educational purpose and therefore violative of the Due Process Clause of the Fourteenth Amendment?" Pet. for Cert. 2.

13. See H. Falk, Corporal Punishment 11–48 (1941); N. Edwards & H. Richey, The School in the American Social Order 115–116 (1947).

secondary education from the colonials' reliance on optional private arrangements to our present system of compulsory education and dependence on public schools.[14] Despite the general abandonment of corporal punishment as a means of punishing criminal offenders, the practice continues to play a role in the public education of school children in most parts of the country.[16] Professional and public opinion is sharply divided on the practice,[17] and has been for more than a century.[18] Yet we can discern no trend toward its elimination.

At common law a single principle has governed the use of corporal punishment since before the American Revolution: Teachers may impose reasonable but not excessive force to discipline a child. Blackstone catalogued among the "absolute rights of individuals" the right "to security from the corporal insults of menaces, assaults, beating, and wounding," 1 W. Blackstone, Commentaries *134, but he did not regard it a "corporal insult" for a teacher to inflict "moderate correction" on a child in his care. To the extent that force was "necessary to answer the purposes for which (the teacher) is employed," Blackstone viewed it as "justifiable or lawful." *Id.*, at *453; *id.*, at *120. The basic doctrine has not changed. The prevalent rule in this country today privileges such force as a teacher or administrator "reasonably believes to be necessary for (the child's) proper control, training, or education." Restatement (Second) of Torts § 147(2) (1965); see *id.*, § 153(2). To the extent that the force is excessive or unreasonable, the educator in virtually all States is subject to possible civil and criminal liability.

Although the early cases viewed the authority of the teacher as deriving from the parents, the concept of parental delegation has been replaced by the view more consonant with compulsory education laws that the State itself may impose such corporal punishment as is reasonably necessary "for the proper education of the child and for the maintenance of group discipline." 1 F. Harper & F. James, Law of **1408 Torts § 3.20, p. 292 (1956). All of the circumstances are to be taken into account in determining whether the punishment is reasonable in a particular case. Among the most important considerations are the seriousness of the offense, the attitude and past behavior of the child, the nature and severity of the punishment, the age and strength of the child, and the availability of less severe but equally effective means of discipline. *Id.*, at 290–291; Restatement (Second) of Torts § 150, Comments c–e, p. 268 (1965).

14. Public and compulsory education existed in New England before the Revolution, see *id.*, at 50–68, 78-81, 97–113, but the demand for free public schools as we now know them did not gain momentum in the country as a whole until the mid-1800's, and it was not until 1918 that compulsory school attendance laws were in force in all the States. See *Brown v. Board of Education*, 347 U.S. 483, 489 n. 4 (1954), citing Cubberley, Public Education in the United States 408–423, 563–565 (1934 ed.); cf. *Wisconsin v. Yoder*, 406 U.S. 205, 226, and n. 15 (1972).

16. See K. Larson & M. Karpas, Effective Secondary School Discipline 146 (1963); A. Reitman, J. Follman, & E. Ladd, Corporal Punishment in the Public Schools 2–5 (ACLU Report 1972).

17. For samplings of scholarly opinion on the use of corporal punishment in the schools, see F. Reardon & R. Reynolds, Corporal Punishment in Pennsylvania 1–2, 34 (1975); National Education Association, Report of the Task Force on Corporal Punishment (1972); K. James, Corporal Punishment in the Public Schools 8–16 (1963). Opinion surveys taken since 1970 have consistently shown a majority of teachers and of the general public favoring moderate use of corporal punishment in the lower grades. See Reardon & Reynolds, *supra*, at 2, 23–26; Delaware Department of Public Instruction, Report on the Corporal Punishment Survey 48 (1974); Reitman, Follman, & Ladd, *supra*, at 34–35; National Education Association, *supra*, at 7.

18. See Falk, *supra*, 66–69; cf. *Cooper v. McJunkin*, 4 Ind. 290 (1853).

Of the 23 States that have addressed the problem through legislation, 21 have authorized the moderate use of corporal punishment in public schools. Of these States only a few have elaborated on the common-law test of reasonableness, typically providing for approval or notification of the child's parents, or for infliction of punishment only by the principal or in the presence of an adult witness. Only two States, Massachusetts and New Jersey, have prohibited all corporal punishment in their public schools. Where the legislatures have not acted, the state courts have uniformly preserved the common-law rule permitting teachers to use reasonable force in disciplining children in their charge.

Against this background of historical and contemporary approval of reasonable corporal punishment, we turn to the constitutional questions before us.

III

The Eighth Amendment provides: "Excessive bail shall not be required, nor excessive fines imposed, nor cruel and unusual punishments inflicted." Bail, fines, and punishment traditionally have been associated with the criminal process, and by subjecting the three to parallel limitations the text of the Amendment suggests an intention to limit the power of those entrusted with the criminal-law function of government. An examination of the history of the Amendment and the decisions of this Court construing the proscription against cruel and unusual punishment confirms that it was designed to protect those convicted of crimes. We adhere to this longstanding limitation and hold that the Eighth Amendment does not apply to the paddling of children as a means of maintaining discipline in public schools.

A

The history of the Eighth Amendment is well known. The text was taken, almost verbatim, from a provision of the Virginia Declaration of Rights of 1776, which in turn derived from the English Bill of Rights of 1689. The English version, adopted after the accession of William and Mary, was intended to curb the excesses of English judges under the reign of James II. Historians have viewed the English provision as a reaction either to the "Bloody Assize," the treason trials conducted by Chief Justice Jeffreys in 1685 after the abortive rebellion of the Duke of Monmouth, or to the perjury prosecution of Titus Oates in the same year. In either case, the exclusive concern of the English version was the conduct of judges in enforcing the criminal law. The original draft introduced in the House of Commons provided:

> "The requiring excessive bail of persons committed in criminal cases and imposing excessive fines, and illegal punishments, to be prevented."

Although the reference to "criminal cases" was eliminated from the final draft, the preservation of a similar reference in the preamble indicates that the deletion was without substantive significance. Thus, Blackstone treated each of the provision's three prohibitions as bearing only on criminal proceedings and judgments.

The Americans who adopted the language of this part of the English Bill of Rights in framing their own State and Federal Constitutions 100 years later feared the imposition of torture and other cruel punishments not only by judges acting beyond their lawful authority, but also by legislatures engaged in making the laws by which judicial authority would be measured. *Weems v. United States*, 217 U.S. 349, 371–373 (1910). Indeed, the principal concern of the American Framers appears to have been with the legislative definition of crimes and punishments. *In re Kemmler*, 136 U.S. 436, 446–447 (1890); *Furman v. Georgia*, 408 U.S. 238, 263 (1972) (BRENNAN, J., concurring). But if the American provision was intended to restrain government more broadly than its English model, the subject to which it was intended to apply the criminal process was the same.

At the time of its ratification, the original Constitution was criticized in the Massachusetts and Virginia Conventions for its failure to provide any protection for persons convicted of crimes. This criticism provided the impetus for inclusion of the Eighth Amendment in the Bill of Rights. When the Eighth Amendment was debated in the First Congress, it was met by the objection that the Cruel and Unusual Punishments Clause might have the effect of outlawing what were then the common criminal punishments of hanging, whipping, and earcropping. 1 Annals of Cong. 754 (1789). The objection was not heeded, "precisely because the legislature would otherwise have had the unfettered power to prescribe punishments for crimes." *Furman v. Georgia*, *supra*, at 263.

B

In light of this history, it is not surprising to find that every decision of this Court considering whether a punishment is "cruel and unusual" within the meaning of the Eighth and Fourteenth Amendments has dealt with a criminal punishment. See *Estelle v. Gamble*, 429 U.S. 97 (1976) (incarceration without medical care); *Gregg v. Georgia*, 428 U.S. 153 (1976) (execution for murder); *Furman v. Georgia*, *supra* (execution for murder); *Powell v. Texas*, 392 U.S. 514 (1968) (plurality opinion) ($20 fine for public drunkenness); *Robinson v. California*, 370 U.S. 660 (1962) (incarceration as a criminal for addiction to narcotics); *Trop v. Dulles*, 356 U.S. 86 (1958) (plurality opinion) (expatriation for desertion); *Louisiana ex rel. Francis v. Resweber*, 329 U.S. 459 (1947) (execution by electrocution after a failed first attempt); *Weems v. United States*, *supra* (15 years' imprisonment and other penalties for falsifying an official document); *Howard v. Fleming*, 191 U.S. 126 (1903) (10 years' imprisonment for conspiracy to defraud); *In re Kemmler*, *supra* (execution by electrocution); *Wilkerson v. Utah*, 99 U.S. 130 (1879) (execution by firing squad); *Pervear v. Commonwealth*, 5 Wall. 475 (1867) (fine and imprisonment at hard labor for bootlegging).

These decisions recognize that the Cruel and Unusual Punishments Clause circumscribes the criminal process in three ways: First, it limits the kinds of punishment that can be imposed on those convicted of crimes, *e.g.*, *Estelle v. Gamble*, *supra*; *Trop v. Dulles*, *supra*; second, it proscribes punishment grossly disproportionate to the severity of the crime, e.g., *Weems v. United States*, *supra*; and third, it imposes substantive limits on what can be made criminal and punished as such, e.g., *Robinson v. California*, *supra*. We have recognized the last limitation as one to be applied sparingly. "The primary purpose of (the Cruel and Unusual Punishments Clause) has always been considered, and properly so, to be directed at the method or kind of punishment imposed for the violation of criminal statutes. . . ." *Powell v. Texas*, *supra*, at 531–532 (plurality opinion).

In the few cases where the Court has had occasion to confront claims that impositions outside the criminal process constituted cruel and unusual punishment, it has had no difficulty finding the Eighth Amendment inapplicable. Thus, in *Fong Yue Ting v. United States*, 149 U.S. 698 (1893), the Court held the Eighth Amendment inapplicable to the deportation of aliens on the ground that "deportation is not a punishment for crime." *Id.*, at 730; see *Mahler v. Eby*, 264 U.S. 32 (1924); *Bugajewitz v. Adams*, 228 U.S. 585 (1913). And in *Uphaus v. Wyman*, 360 U.S. 72 (1959), the Court sustained a judgment of civil contempt, resulting in incarceration pending compliance with a subpoena, against a claim that the judgment imposed cruel and unusual punishment. It was emphasized that the case involved "'essentially a civil remedy designed for the benefit of other parties... exercised for centuries to secure compliance with judicial decrees.'" *Id.*, at 81, quoting *Green v. United States*, 356 U.S. 165, 197 (1958) (dissenting opinion).[36]

C

Petitioners acknowledge that the original design of the Cruel and Unusual Punishments Clause was to limit criminal punishments, but urge nonetheless that the prohibition should be extended to ban the paddling of schoolchildren. Observing that the Framers of the Eighth Amendment could not have envisioned our present system of public and compulsory education, with its opportunities for noncriminal punishments, petitioners contend that extension of the prohibition against cruel punishments is necessary lest we afford greater protection to criminals than to schoolchildren. It would be anomalous, they say, if schoolchildren could be beaten without constitutional redress, while hardened criminals suffering the same beatings at the hands of their jailers might have a valid claim under the Eighth Amendment. See *Jackson v. Bishop*, 404 F.2d 571 (CA8 1968); cf. *Estelle v. Gamble*, *supra*. Whatever force this logic may have in other settings,[37] we find it an inadequate basis for wrenching the Eighth Amendment from its historical context and extending it to traditional disciplinary practices in the public schools.

The prisoner and the schoolchild stand in wholly different circumstances, separated by the harsh facts of criminal conviction and incarceration. The prisoner's conviction entitles the State to classify him as a "criminal," and his incarceration deprives him of the freedom "to be with family and friends and to form the other enduring attachments of normal life." *Morrissey v. Brewer*, 408 U.S. 471, 482 (1972); see *Meachum v. Fano*, 427 U.S. 215, 224–225 (1976). Prison brutality, as the Court of Appeals observed in this case, is "part of the total punishment to which the individual is being subjected for his crime and, as such, is a proper subject for Eighth Amendment scrutiny." 525 F.2d, at 915. Even so, the protection afforded by the Eighth Amendment is limited. After incarceration, only the "'unnecessary and wanton infliction of pain,'" *Estelle v. Gamble*, 429 U.S., at 103, quoting *Gregg v. Georgia*, 428 U.S. at 173, constitutes cruel and unusual punishment forbidden by the Eighth Amendment.

36. In urging us to extend the Eighth Amendment to ban school paddlings, petitioners rely on the many decisions in which this Court has held that the prohibition against "cruel and unusual" punishments is not "'fastened to the obsolete but may acquire meaning as public opinion becomes enlightened by a humane justice.'" *Gregg v. Georgia*, 428 U.S., at 171 (joint opinion); see, e. g., *Trop v. Dulles*, 356 U.S. 86, 100–101 (1958) (plurality opinion); *Weems v. United States*, 217 U.S. 349, 373, 378 (1910). This reliance is misplaced. Our Eighth Amendment decisions have referred to "evolving standards of decency," *Trop v. Dulles*, *supra*, 356 U.S., at 101, only in determining whether criminal punishments are "cruel and unusual" under the Amendment.

37. Some punishments, though not labeled "criminal" by the State, may be sufficiently analogous to criminal punishments in the circumstances in which they are administered to justify application of the Eighth Amendment. Cf. *In re Gault*, 387 U.S. (1967). We have no occasion in this case, for example, to consider whether or under what circumstances persons involuntarily confined in mental or juvenile institutions can claim the protection of the Eighth Amendment.

The schoolchild has little need for the protection of the Eighth Amendment. Though attendance may not always be voluntary, the public school remains an open institution. Except perhaps when very young, the child is not physically restrained from leaving school during school hours; and at the end of the school day, the child is invariably free to return home. Even while at school, the child brings with him the support of family and friends and is rarely apart from teachers and other pupils who may witness and protest any instances of mistreatment.

The openness of the public school and its supervision by the community afford significant safeguards against the kinds of abuses from which the Eighth Amendment protects the prisoner. In virtually every community where corporal punishment is permitted in the schools, these safeguards are reinforced by the legal constraints of the common law. Public school teachers and administrators are privileged at common law to inflict only such corporal punishment as is reasonably necessary for the proper education and discipline of the child; any punishment going beyond the privilege may result in both civil and criminal liability. See Part II, *supra*. As long as the schools are open to public scrutiny, there is no reason to believe that the common-law constraints will not effectively remedy and deter excesses such as those alleged in this case.[39]

We conclude that when public school teachers or administrators impose disciplinary corporal punishment, the Eighth Amendment is inapplicable. The pertinent constitutional question is whether the imposition is consonant with the requirements of due process.[40]

39. Putting history aside as irrelevant, the dissenting opinion of MR. JUSTICE WHITE argues that a "purposive analysis" should control the reach of the Eighth Amendment. There is no support whatever for this approach in the decisions of this Court. Although an imposition must be "punishment" for the Cruel and Unusual Punishments Clause to apply, the Court has never held that *all* punishments are subject to Eighth Amendment scrutiny. The applicability of the Eighth Amendment always has turned on its original meaning, as demonstrated by its historical derivation. See *Gregg v. Georgia*, 428 U.S., at 169–173 (joint opinion); *Furman v. Georgia*, 408 U.S., at 315–328 (MARSHALL J., concurring).

The dissenting opinion warns that as a consequence of our decision today, teachers may "cut off a child's ear for being late to class." This rhetoric bears no relation to reality or to the issues presented in this case. The laws of virtually every State forbid the excessive physical punishment of schoolchildren. Yet the logic of the dissent would make the judgment of which disciplinary punishments are reasonable and which are excessive a matter of constitutional principle in every case, to be decided ultimately by this Court. The hazards of such a broad reading of the Eighth Amendment are clear. "It is always time to say that this Nation is too large, too complex and composed of too great a diversity of peoples for any one of us to have the wisdom to establish the rules by which local Americans must govern their local affairs. The constitutional rule we are urged to adopt is not merely revolutionary—it departs from the ancient faith based on the premise that experience in making local laws by local people themselves is by far the safest guide for a nation like ours to follow." *Powell v. Texas*, 392 U.S. 514, 547–548 (1968) (opinion of Black, J.).

40. Eighth Amendment scrutiny is appropriate only after the State has complied with the constitutional guarantees traditionally associated with criminal prosecutions. See *United States v. Lovett*, 328 U.S. 303, 317–318 (1946). Thus, in *Trop v. Dulles*, 356 U.S. 86 (1958), the plurality appropriately took the view that denationalization was an impermissible punishment for wartime desertion under the Eighth Amendment, because desertion already had been established at a criminal trial. But in *Kennedy v. Mendoza-Martinez*, 372 U.S. 144 (1963), where the Court considered denationalization as a punishment for evading the draft, the Court refused to reach the Eighth Amendment issue, holding instead that the punishment could be imposed only through the criminal process. *Id.*, at 162–167, 186. As these cases demonstrate, the State does not acquire the power to punish with which the Eighth Amendment is concerned until after it has secured a formal adjudication of guilt in accordance with due process of law. Where the State seeks to impose punishment without such an adjudication, the pertinent constitutional guarantee is the Due Process Clause of the Fourteenth Amendment.

IV

The Fourteenth Amendment prohibits any state deprivation of life, liberty, or property without due process of law. Application of this prohibition requires the familiar two-stage analysis: We must first ask whether the asserted individual interests are encompassed within the Fourteenth Amendment's protection of "life, liberty or property"; if protected interests are implicated, we then must decide what procedures constitute "due process of law." *Morrissey v. Brewer*, 408 U.S. at 481; *Board of Regents v. Roth*, 408 U.S. 564, 569–572 (1972). See Friendly, Some Kind of Hearing, 123 U.Pa.L.Rev. 1267 (1975). Following that analysis here, we find that corporal punishment in public schools implicates a constitutionally protected liberty interest, but we hold that the traditional common-law remedies are fully adequate to afford due process.

A

"(T)he range of interests protected by procedural due process is not infinite." *Board of Regents v. Roth*, *supra*, at 570. We have repeatedly rejected "the notion that any grievous loss visited upon a person by the State is sufficient to invoke the procedural protections of the Due Process Clause." *Meachum v. Fano*, 427 U.S. at 224. Due process is required only when a decision of the State implicates an interest within the protection of the Fourteenth Amendment. And "to determine whether due process requirements apply in the first place, we must look not to the 'weight' but to the nature of the interest at stake." *Roth*, *supra*, 408 U.S., at 570–571.

The Due Process Clause of the Fifth Amendment, later incorporated into the Fourteenth, was intended to give Americans at least the protection against governmental power that they had enjoyed as Englishmen against the power of the Crown. The liberty preserved from deprivation without due process included the right "generally to enjoy those privileges long recognized at common law as essential to the orderly pursuit of happiness by free men." *Meyer v. Nebraska*, 262 U.S. 390, 399 (1923); see *Dent v. West Virginia*, 129 U.S. 114, 123–124 (1889). Among the historic liberties so protected was a right to be free from and to obtain judicial relief, for unjustified intrusions on personal security.[41]

While the contours of this historic liberty interest in the context of our federal system of government have not been defined precisely, they always have been thought to encompass freedom from bodily restraint and punishment. See *Rochin v. California*, 342 U.S. 165 (1952). It is fundamental that the state cannot hold and physically punish an individual except in accordance with due process of law.

This constitutionally protected liberty interest is at stake in this case. There is, of course a *de minimis* level of imposition with which the Constitution is not concerned. But at least where school authorities, acting under color of state law, deliberately decide to punish a child

41. See 1 W. Blackstone, Commentaries * 134. Under the 39th Article of the Magna Carta, an individual could not be deprived of this right of personal security "except by the legal judgment of his peers or by the law of the land." Perry & Cooper, *supra*, n. 33, at 17. By subsequent enactments of Parliament during the time of Edward III, the right was protected from deprivation except "by due process of law." See Shattuck, The True Meaning of the Term "Liberty," 4 Harv.L.Rev. 365, 372–373 (1891).

for misconduct by restraining the child and inflicting appreciable physical pain, we hold that Fourteenth Amendment liberty interests are implicated.[43]

B

"(T)he question remains what process is due." *Morrissey v. Brewer, supra*, at 481. Were it not for the common-law privilege permitting teachers to inflict reasonable corporal punishment on children in their care, and the availability of the traditional remedies for abuse, the case for requiring advance procedural safeguards would be strong indeed.[44] But here we deal with a punishment paddling within that tradition, and the question is whether the common-law remedies are adequate to afford due process.

> "'(D)ue process,' unlike some legal rules, is not a technical conception with a fixed content unrelated to time, place and circumstances.... Representing a profound attitude of fairness...'due process' is compounded of history, reason, the past course of decisions, and stout confidence in the strength of the democratic faith which we profess...." *Anti-Fascist Comm. v. McGrath*, 341 U.S. 123, 162–163 (1951) (Frankfurter, J., concurring).

Whether in this case the common-law remedies for excessive corporal punishment constitute due process of law must turn on an analysis of the competing interests at stake, viewed against the background of "history, reason, (and) the past course of decisions." The analysis requires consideration of three distinct factors: "First, the private interest that will be affected...; second, the risk of an erroneous deprivation of such interest...and the probable value, if any, of additional or substitute procedural safeguards; and, finally, the (state) interest, including the function involved and the fiscal and administrative burdens that the additional or substitute procedural requirement would entail." *Mathews v. Eldridge*, 424 U.S. 319, 335 (1976). Cf. *Arnett v. Kennedy*, 416 U.S. 134, 167–168 (1974) (Powell, J., concurring).

1

Because it is rooted in history, the child's liberty interest in avoiding corporal punishment while in the care of public school authorities is subject to historical limitations. Under the common law, an invasion of personal security gave rise to a right to recover damages in a subsequent judicial proceeding. 3 W. Blackstone, Commentaries *120–121. But the right of recovery was qualified by the concept of justification. Thus, there could be no recovery against a teacher who gave only "moderate correction" to a child. *Id.*, at *120. To the extent that the

43. Unlike *Goss v. Lopez*, 419 U.S. 565 (1975), this case does not involve the state-created property interest in public education. The purpose of corporal punishment is to correct a child's behavior without interrupting his education. That corporal punishment may, in a rare case, have the unintended effect of temporarily removing a child from school affords no basis for concluding that the practice itself deprives students of property protected by the Fourteenth Amendment. Nor does this case involve any state-created interest in liberty going beyond the Fourteenth Amendment's protection of freedom from bodily restraint and corporal punishment. Cf. *Meachum v. Fano*, 427 U.S. 215, 225–227 (1976).

44. If the common-law privilege to inflict reasonable corporal punishment in school were inapplicable, it is doubtful whether any procedure short of a trial in a criminal or juvenile court could satisfy the requirements of procedural due process for the imposition of such punishment. See *United States v. Lovett*, 328 U.S., at 317–318; cf. *Breed v. Jones*, 421 U.S. 519, 528–529 (1975).

force used was reasonable in light of its purpose, it was not wrongful, but rather "justifiable or lawful." *Ibid.*

The concept that reasonable corporal punishment in school is justifiable continues to be recognized in the laws of most States. See Part II, *supra*. It represents "the balance struck by this country," *Poe v. Ullman*, 367 U.S. 497, 542 (1961) (Harlan, J., dissenting), between the child's interest in personal security and the traditional view that some limited corporal punishment may be necessary in the course of a child's education. Under that longstanding accommodation of interests, there can be no deprivation of substantive rights as long as disciplinary corporal punishment is within the limits of the common-law privilege.

This is not to say that the child's interest in procedural safeguards is insubstantial. The school disciplinary process is not "a totally accurate, unerring process, never mistaken and never unfair...." *Goss v. Lopez*, 419 U.S. 565, 579–580 (1975). In any deliberate infliction of corporal punishment on a child who is restrained for that purpose, there is some risk that the intrusion on the child's liberty will be unjustified and therefore unlawful. In these circumstances the child has a strong interest in procedural safeguards that minimize the risk of wrongful punishment and provide for the resolution of disputed questions of justification.

We turn now to a consideration of the safeguards that are available under applicable Florida law.

2

Florida has continued to recognize, and indeed has strengthened by statute, the common-law right of a child not to be subjected to excessive corporal punishment in school. Under Florida law the teacher and principal of the school decide in the first instance whether corporal punishment is reasonably necessary under the circumstances in order to discipline a child who has misbehaved. But they must exercise prudence and restraint. For Florida has preserved the traditional judicial proceedings for determining whether the punishment was justified. If the punishment inflicted is later found to have been excessive—not reasonably believed at the time to be necessary for the child's discipline or training—the school authorities inflicting it may be held liable in damages to the child and, if malice is shown, they may be subject to criminal penalties.[45]

Although students have testified in this case to specific instances of abuse, there is every reason to believe that such mistreatment is an aberration. The uncontradicted evidence suggests that corporal punishment in the Dade County schools was, "(w)ith the exception of a few cases,...unremarkable in physical severity." Moreover, because paddlings are usually inflicted in response to conduct directly observed by teachers in their presence, the risk that

45. See *supra*, at 1404–1405, 1407. The statutory prohibition against "degrading" or unnecessarily "severe" corporal punishment in former § 232.27 has been construed as a statement of the common-law principle....And petitioners conceded in this Court that a teacher who inflicts excessive punishment on a child may be held both civilly and criminally liable under Florida law. Brief for Petitioners 33 n. 11, 34; Tr. of Oral Arg. 17, 52–53. In view of the statutory adoption of the common-law rule, and the unanimity of the parties and the courts below, the doubts expressed in MR. JUSTICE WHITE's dissenting opinion as to the availability of tort remedies in Florida can only be viewed as chimerical. The dissent makes much of the fact that no Florida court has ever "recognized" a damages remedy for unreasonable corporal punishment. But the absence of reported Florida decisions hardly suggests that no remedy is available. Rather, it merely confirms the common-sense judgment that excessive corporal punishment is exceedingly rare in the public schools.

a child will be paddled without cause is typically insignificant. In the ordinary case, a disciplinary paddling neither threatens seriously to violate any substantive rights nor condemns the child "to suffer grievous loss of any kind." *Anti-Fascist Comm. v. McGrath*, 341 U.S., at 168 (Frankfurter, J., concurring).

In those cases where severe punishment is contemplated, the available civil and criminal sanctions for abuse considered in light of the openness of the school environment afford significant protection against unjustified corporal punishment. Teachers and school authorities are unlikely to inflict corporal punishment unnecessarily or excessively when a possible consequence of doing so is the institution of civil or criminal proceedings against them.[46]

It still may be argued, of course, that the child's liberty interest would be better protected if the common-law remedies were supplemented by the administrative safeguards of prior notice and a hearing. We have found frequently that some kind of prior hearing is necessary to guard against arbitrary impositions on interests protected by the Fourteenth Amendment. See, *e.g.*, *Board of Regents v. Roth*, 408 U.S., at 569–570; *Wolff v. McDonnell*, 418 U.S. 539, 557–558 (1974); cf. Friendly, 123 U.Pa.L.Rev., at 1275–1277. But where the State has preserved what "has always been the law of the land," *United States v. Barnett*, 376 U.S. 681 (1964), the case for administrative safeguards is significantly less compelling.[47]

There is a relevant analogy in the criminal law. Although the Fourth Amendment specifically proscribes "seizure" of a person without probable cause, the risk that police will act unreasonably in arresting a suspect is not thought to require an advance determination of the facts. In *United States v. Watson*, 423 U.S. 411, 96 S.Ct. 820, 46 L.Ed.2d 598 (1976), we reaffirmed the traditional common-law rule that police officers may make warrantless public arrests on probable cause. Although we observed that an advance determination of probable cause by a magistrate would be desirable, we declined "to transform this judicial preference into a constitutional rule when the judgment of the Nation and Congress has for so long been to authorize warrantless public arrests on probable cause...." *Id.*, at 423; see *id.*, at 429 (POWELL, J., concurring). Despite the distinct possibility that a police officer may improperly assess the facts and thus unconstitutionally deprive an individual of liberty, we declined to

46. The low incidence of abuse, and the availability of established judicial remedies in the event of abuse, distinguish this case from *Goss v. Lopez*, 419 U.S. 565 (1975). The Ohio law struck down in *Goss* provided for suspensions from public school of up to 10 days without "any written procedure applicable to suspensions." *Id.*, at 567. Although Ohio law provided generally for administrative review, Ohio Rev.Code Ann. § 2506.01 (Supp. 1973), the Court assumed that the short suspensions would not be stayed pending review, with the result that the review proceeding could serve neither a deterrent nor a remedial function. 419 U.S., at 581 n. 10. In these circumstances, the Court held the law authorizing suspensions unconstitutional for failure to require "that there be at least an informal give-and-take between student and disciplinarian, preferably prior to the suspension...." *Id.*, at 584. The subsequent civil and criminal proceedings available in this case may be viewed as affording substantially greater protection to the child than the informal conference mandated by *Goss*.

47. "(P)rior hearings might well be dispensed with in many circumstances in which the state's conduct, if not adequately justified, would constitute a common-law tort. This would leave the injured plaintiff in precisely the same posture as a common-law plaintiff, and this procedural consequence would be quite harmonious with the substantive view that the fourteenth amendment encompasses the same liberties as those protected by the common law." Monaghan, Of "Liberty" and "Property," 62 Cornell L.Rev. 405, 431 (1977) (footnote omitted). See *Bonner v. Coughlin*, 517 F.2d 1311, 1319 (CA7 1975), modified en banc, 545 F.2d 565 (1976), cert. pending, No. 76-6204. We have no occasion in this case to decide whether or under what circumstances corporal punishment of a public school child may give rise to an independent federal cause of action to vindicate substantive rights under the Due Process Clause.

depart from the traditional rule by which the officer's perception is subjected to judicial scrutiny only after the fact. There is no more reason to depart from tradition and require advance procedural safeguards for intrusions on personal security to which the Fourth Amendment does not apply.

3

But even if the need for advance procedural safeguards were clear, the question would remain whether the incremental benefit could justify the cost. Acceptance of petitioners' claims would work a transformation in the law governing corporal punishment in Florida and most other States. Given the impracticability of formulating a rule of procedural due process that varies with the severity of the particular imposition, the prior hearing petitioners seek would have to precede any paddling, however moderate or trivial.

Such a universal constitutional requirement would significantly burden the use of corporal punishment as a disciplinary measure. Hearings—even informal hearings—require time, personnel, and a diversion of attention from normal school pursuits. School authorities may well choose to abandon corporal punishment rather than incur the burdens of complying with the procedural requirements. Teachers, properly concerned with maintaining authority in the classroom, may well prefer to rely on other disciplinary measures which they may view as less effective rather than confront the possible disruption that prior notice and a hearing may entail.[50] Paradoxically, such an alteration of disciplinary policy is most likely to occur in the ordinary case where the contemplated punishment is well within the common-law privilege.[51]

Elimination or curtailment of corporal punishment would be welcomed by many as a societal advance. But when such a policy choice may result from this Court's determination of an asserted right to due process, rather than from the normal processes of community debate and legislative action, the societal costs cannot be dismissed as insubstantial.[52] We are reviewing here a legislative judgment, rooted in history and reaffirmed in the laws of many States, that corporal punishment serves important educational interests. This judgment must be viewed in light of the disciplinary problems commonplace in the schools. As noted in *Goss v. Lopez*, 419 U.S., at 580: "Events calling for discipline are frequent occurrences and sometimes require immediate, effective action." Assessment of the need for, and the appropriate means of maintaining, school discipline is committed generally to the discretion of school authorities subject to state law. "[T]he Court has repeatedly emphasized the need for affirming the comprehensive

50. If a prior hearing, with the inevitable attendant publicity within the school, resulted in rejection of the teacher's recommendation, the consequent impairment of the teacher's ability to maintain discipline in the classroom would not be insubstantial.

51. The effect of interposing prior procedural safeguards may well be to make the punishment more severe by increasing the anxiety of the child. For this reason, the school authorities in Dade County found it desirable that the punishment be inflicted as soon as possible after the infraction.

52. "It may be true that procedural regularity in disciplinary proceedings promotes a sense of institutional rapport and open communication, a perception of fair treatment, and provides the offender and his fellow students a showcase of democracy at work. But… [r]espect for democratic institutions will equally dissipate if they are thought too ineffectual to provide their students an environment of order in which the educational process may go forward…." Wilkinson, *Goss v. Lopez*: The Supreme Court as School Superintendent, 1975 Sup.Ct.Rev. 25, 71–72.

authority of the States and of school officials, consistent with fundamental constitutional safeguards, to prescribe and control conduct in the schools." *Tinker v. Des Moines School Dist.*, 393 U.S. 503, 507 (1969).

"At some point the benefit of an additional safeguard to the individual affected...and to society in terms of increased assurance that the action is just, may be outweighed by the cost." *Mathews v. Eldridge*, 424 U.S., at 348. We think that point has been reached in this case. In view of the low incidence of abuse, the openness of our schools, and the common-law safeguards that already exist, the risk of error that may result in violation of a schoolchild's substantive rights can only be regarded as minimal. Imposing additional administrative safeguards as a constitutional requirement might reduce that risk marginally, but would also entail a significant intrusion into an area of primary educational responsibility. We conclude that the Due Process Clause does not require notice and a hearing prior to the imposition of corporal punishment in the public schools, as that practice is authorized and limited by the common law.[55]

V

Petitioners cannot prevail on either of the theories before us in this case. The Eighth Amendment's prohibition against cruel and unusual punishment is inapplicable to school paddlings, and the Fourteenth Amendment's requirement of procedural due process is satisfied by Florida's preservation of common-law constraints and remedies. We therefore agree with the Court of Appeals that petitioners' evidence affords no basis for injunctive relief, and that petitioners cannot recover damages on the basis of any Eighth Amendment or procedural due process violation.

Affirmed.

Mr. Justice White, with whom Mr. Justice Brennan, Mr. Justice Marshall, and Mr. Justice Stevens join, dissenting.

Today the Court holds that corporal punishment in public schools, no matter how severe, can never be the subject of the protections afforded by the Eighth Amendment. It also holds that students in the public school systems are not constitutionally entitled to a hearing of any sort before beatings can be inflicted on them. Because I believe that these holdings are inconsistent with the prior decisions of this Court and are contrary to a reasoned analysis of the constitutional provisions involved, I respectfully dissent.

55. Mr. Justice White's dissenting opinion offers no manageable standards for determining what process is due in any particular case. The dissent apparently would require, as a general rule, only "an informal give-and-take between student and disciplinarian." But the dissent would depart from these "minimal procedures" requiring even witnesses, counsel, and cross-examination in cases where the punishment reaches some undefined level of severity. School authorities are left to guess at the degree of punishment that will require more than an "informal give-and-take" and at the additional process that may be constitutionally required. The impracticability of such an approach is self-evident, and illustrates the hazards of ignoring the traditional solution of the common law.

We agree with the dissent that the *Goss* procedures will often be, "if anything, less than a fair-minded school principal would impose upon himself." But before this Court invokes the Constitution to impose a procedural requirement, it should be reasonably certain that the effect will be to afford protection appropriate to the constitutional interests at stake. The dissenting opinion's reading of the Constitution suggests no such beneficial result and, indeed, invites a lowering of existing constitutional standards.

I

A

The Eighth Amendment places a flat prohibition against the infliction of "cruel and unusual punishments." This reflects a societal judgment that there are some punishments that are so barbaric and inhumane that we will not permit them to be imposed on anyone, no matter how opprobrious the offense. See *Robinson v. California*, 370 U.S. 660, 676 (1962) (Douglas, J., concurring). If there are some punishments that are so barbaric that they may not be imposed for the commission of crimes, designated by our social system as the most thoroughly reprehensible acts an individual can commit, then, *a fortiori*, similar punishments may not be imposed on persons for less culpable acts, such as breaches of school discipline. Thus, if it is constitutionally impermissible to cut off someone's ear for the commission of murder, it must be unconstitutional to cut off a child's ear for being late to class.[1] Although there were no ears cut off in this case, the record reveals beatings so severe that if they were inflicted on a hardened criminal for the commission of a serious crime, they might not pass constitutional muster.

Nevertheless, the majority holds that the Eighth Amendment "was designed to protect (only) those convicted of crimes," relying on a vague and inconclusive recitation of the history of the Amendment. Yet the constitutional prohibition is against cruel and unusual *punishments*; nowhere is that prohibition limited or modified by the language of the Constitution. Certainly the fact that the Framers did not choose to insert the word "criminal" into the language of the Eighth Amendment is strong evidence that the Amendment was designed to prohibit all inhumane or barbaric punishments, no matter what the nature of the offense for which the punishment is imposed.

No one can deny that spanking of schoolchildren is "punishment" under any reasonable reading of the word, for the similarities between spanking in public schools and other forms of punishment are too obvious to ignore. Like other forms of punishment, spanking of schoolchildren involves an institutionalized response to the violation of some official rule or regulation proscribing certain conduct and is imposed for the purpose of rehabilitating

1. There is little reason to fear that if the Eighth Amendment is held to apply at *all* to corporal punishment of school children, *all* paddlings, however moderate, would be prohibited. *Jackson v. Bishop*, 404 F.2d 571 (CA8 1968), held that any paddling or flogging of prisoners, convicted of crime and serving prison terms, violated the cruel and unusual punishment ban of the Eighth Amendment. But aside from the fact that Bishop has never been embraced by this Court, the theory of that case was not that bodily punishments are intrinsically barbaric or excessively severe but that paddling of prisoners is "degrading to the punisher and to the punished alike." *Id.*, at 580. That approach may be acceptable in the criminal justice system, but it has little if any relevance to corporal punishment in the schools, for it can hardly be said that the use of moderate paddlings in the discipline of children is inconsistent with the country's evolving standards of decency.

On the other hand, when punishment involves a cruel, severe beating or chopping off an ear, something more than merely the dignity of the individual is involved. Whenever a given criminal punishment is "cruel and unusual" because it is inhumane or barbaric, I can think of no reason why it would be any less inhumane or barbaric when inflicted on a schoolchild, as punishment for classroom misconduct.

The issue in this case is whether spankings inflicted on public schoolchildren for breaking school rules is "punishment," not whether such punishment is "cruel and unusual." If the Eighth Amendment does not bar moderate spanking in public schools, it is because moderate spanking is not "cruel and unusual," not because it is not "punishment" as the majority suggests.

the offender, deterring the offender and others like him from committing the violation in the future, and inflicting some measure of social retribution for the harm that has been done.

B

We are fortunate that in our society punishments that are severe enough to raise a doubt as to their constitutional validity are ordinarily not imposed without first affording the accused the full panoply of procedural safeguards provided by the criminal process.[2] The effect has been that "every decision of this Court considering whether a punishment is 'cruel and unusual' within the meaning of the Eighth and Fourteenth Amendments has dealt with a criminal punishment." The Court would have us believe from this fact that there is a recognized distinction between criminal and noncriminal punishment for purposes of the Eighth Amendment. This is plainly wrong. "(E)ven a clear legislative classification of a statute as 'non-penal' would not alter the fundamental nature of a plainly penal statute." *Trop v. Dulles*, 356 U.S. 86, 95 (1958) (plurality opinion). The relevant inquiry is not whether the offense for which a punishment is inflicted has been labeled as criminal, but whether the purpose of the deprivation is among those ordinarily associated with punishment, such as retribution, rehabilitation, or deterrence.[3] *Id.*, at 96. Cf. *Kennedy v. Mendoza-Martinez*, 372 U.S. 144 (1963).

If this purposive approach were followed in the present case, it would be clear that spanking in the Florida public schools is punishment within the meaning of the Eighth Amendment. The District Court found that "(c)orporal punishment is one of a variety of

2. By no means is it suggested that just because spanking of schoolchildren is "punishment" within the meaning of the Cruel and Unusual Punishments Clause, the school disciplinary process is in any way "criminal" and therefore subject to the full panoply of criminal procedural guarantees. See Part II, *infra*. Ordinarily, the conduct for which schoolchildren are punished is not sufficiently opprobrious to be called "criminal" in our society, and even violations of school disciplinary rules that might also constitute a crime are not subject to the criminal process. See *Baxter v. Palmigiano*, 425 U.S. 308 (1976), where the Court held that persons who violate prison disciplinary rules are not entitled to the full panoply of criminal procedural safeguards, even if the rule violation might also constitute a crime.

3. The majority cites *Trop* as one of the cases that "dealt with a criminal punishment" but neglects to follow the analysis mandated by that decision. In *Trop* the petitioner was convicted of desertion by a military court-martial and sentenced to three years at hard labor, forfeiture of all pay and allowances, and a dishonorable discharge. After he was punished for the offense he committed, petitioner's application for a passport was turned down. Petitioner was told that he had been deprived of the "rights of citizenship" under § 401(g) of the Nationality Act of 1940 because he had been dishonorably discharged from the Armed Forces. The plurality took the view that denationalization in this context was cruel and unusual punishment prohibited by the Eighth Amendment.

The majority would have us believe that the determinative factor in *Trop* was that the petitioner had been convicted of desertion; yet there is no suggestion in *Trop* that the disposition of the military court-martial had anything to do with the decision in that case. Instead, while recognizing that the Eighth Amendment extends only to punishments that are penal in nature, the plurality adopted a purposive approach for determining when punishment is penal.

> "In deciding whether or not a law is penal, this Court has generally based its determination upon the purpose of the statute. If the statute imposes a disability for the purposes of punishment that is, to reprimand the wrongdoer, to deter others, etc. it has been considered penal. But a statute has been considered nonpenal if it imposes a disability, not to punish, but to accomplish some other legitimate governmental purpose." 356 U.S., at 96 (footnotes omitted).

Although the quoted passage is taken from the plurality opinion of Mr. Chief Justice Warren, joined by three other Justices, MR. JUSTICE BRENNAN, in a concurring opinion, adopted a similar approach in concluding that § 401(g) was beyond the power of Congress to enact.

measures employed in the school system for the correction of pupil behavior and the preservation of order." Behavior correction and preservation of order are purposes ordinarily associated with punishment.

Without even mentioning the purposive analysis applied in the prior decisions of this Court, the majority adopts a rule that turns on the label given to the offense for which the punishment is inflicted. Thus, the record in this case reveals that one student at Drew Junior High School received 50 licks with a paddle for allegedly making an obscene telephone call. Brief for Petitioners 13. The majority holds that the Eighth Amendment does not prohibit such punishment since it was only inflicted for a breach of school discipline. However, that same conduct is punishable as a misdemeanor under Florida law, Fla.Stat.Ann. § 365.16 (Supp. 1977) and there can be little doubt that if that same "punishment" had been inflicted by an officer of the state courts for violation of § 365.16, it would have had to satisfy the requirements of the Eighth Amendment.

C

In fact, as the Court recognizes, the Eighth Amendment has never been confined to criminal punishments.[4] Nevertheless, the majority adheres to its view that any protections afforded by the Eighth Amendment must have something to do with criminals, and it would therefore confine any exceptions to its general rule that only criminal punishments are covered by the Eighth Amendment to abuses inflicted on prisoners. Thus, if a prisoner is beaten mercilessly for a breach of discipline, he is entitled to the protection of the Eighth Amendment, while a schoolchild who commits the same breach of discipline and is similarly beaten is simply not covered.

The purported explanation of this anomaly is the assertion that schoolchildren have no need for the Eighth Amendment. We are told that schools are open institutions, subject to constant public scrutiny; that schoolchildren have adequate remedies under state law;[5] and

4. In *Estelle v. Gamble*, 429 U.S. 97 (1976), a case decided this Term, the Court held that "deliberate indifference to the medical needs of prisoners" by prison officials constitutes cruel and unusual punishment prohibited by the Eighth Amendment. Such deliberate indifference to a prisoner's medical needs clearly is not punishment inflicted for the commission of a crime; it is merely misconduct by a prison official. Similarly, the Eighth Circuit has held that whipping a prisoner with a strap in order to maintain discipline is prohibited by the Eighth Amendment. *Jackson v. Bishop*, 404 F.2d 571 (1968) (Blackmun, J.). See also *Knecht v. Gillman*, 488 F.2d 1136, 1139–1140 (CA8 1973) (injection of vomit-inducing drugs as part of aversion therapy held to be cruel and unusual); *Vann v. Scott*, 467 F.2d 1235, 1240–1241 (CA7 1972) (Stevens, J.) (Eighth Amendment protects runaway children against cruel and inhumane treatment, regardless of whether such treatment is labeled "rehabilitation" or "punishment").

5. By finding that bodily punishment invades a constitutionally protected liberty interest within the meaning of the Due Process Clause, the majority suggests that the Clause might also afford a remedy for excessive spanking independently of the Eighth Amendment. If this were the case, the Court's present thesis would have little practical significance. If rather than holding that the Due Process Clause affords a remedy by way of the express commands of the Eighth Amendment, the majority would recognize a cause of action under 42 U.S.C. § 1983 for a deprivation of "liberty" flowing from an excessive paddling, the Court's opinion is merely a lengthy word of advice with respect to the drafting of civil complaints.

Petitioners in this case did raise the substantive due process issue in their petition for certiorari, but consideration of that question was foreclosed by our limited grant of certiorari. If it is probable that schoolchildren would be entitled to protection under some theory of substantive due process, the Court should not now affirm the judgment below, but should amend the grant of certiorari and set this case for reargument.

that prisoners suffer the social stigma of being labeled as criminals. How any of these policy considerations got into the Constitution is difficult to discern, for the Court has never considered any of these factors in determining the scope of the Eighth Amendment.[6]

The essence of the majority's argument is that schoolchildren do not need Eighth Amendment protection because corporal punishment is less subject to abuse in the public schools than it is in the prison system.[7] However, it cannot be reasonably suggested that just because cruel and unusual punishments may occur less frequently under public scrutiny, they will not occur at all. The mere fact that a public flogging or a public execution would be available for all to see would not render the punishment constitutional if it were otherwise impermissible. Similarly, the majority would not suggest that a prisoner who is placed in a minimum-security prison and permitted to go home to his family on the weekends should be any less entitled to Eighth Amendment protections than his counterpart in a maximum-security prison. In short, if a punishment is so barbaric and inhumane that it goes beyond the tolerance of a civilized society, its openness to public scrutiny should have nothing to do with its constitutional validity.

Nor is it an adequate answer that schoolchildren may have other state and constitutional remedies available to them. Even assuming that the remedies available to public school students are adequate under Florida law, the availability of state remedies has never been determinative of the coverage or of the protections afforded by the Eighth Amendment. The reason is obvious. The fact that a person may have a state-law cause of action against a public official who tortures him with a thumbscrew for the commission of an antisocial act has nothing to do with the fact that such official conduct is cruel and unusual punishment prohibited by the Eighth Amendment. Indeed, the majority's view was implicitly rejected this Term in *Estelle v. Gamble*, 429 U.S. 97 (1976), when the Court held that failure to provide for the medical needs of prisoners could constitute cruel and unusual punishment even though a medical malpractice remedy in tort was available to prisoners under state law. *Id.*, at 107 n. 15.

D

By holding that the Eighth Amendment protects only criminals, the majority adopts the view that one is entitled to the protections afforded by the Eighth Amendment only if he is punished for acts that are sufficiently opprobrious for society to make them "criminal." This is a curious holding in view of the fact that the more culpable the offender the more likely it is that the punishment will not be disproportionate to the offense, and consequently, the less likely it is that the punishment will be cruel and unusual.[9] Conversely, a public school student who is

6. In support of its policy considerations, the only cases from this Court cited by the majority are *Morrissey v. Brewer*, 408 U.S. 471 (1972), and *Meachum v. Fano*, 427 U.S. 215 (1976), both cases involving prisoners' rights to procedural due process.

7. There is no evidence in the record that corporal punishment has been abused in the prison systems more often than in the public schools. Indeed, corporal punishment is seldom authorized in state prisons. See *Jackson v. Bishop*, *supra*, at 580, where Mr. Justice [then Judge] Blackmun noted: "[O]nly two states still permit the use of the strap [in prisons]. Thus almost uniformly has it been abolished." By relying on its own view of the nature of these two public institutions, without any evidence being heard on the question below, the majority today predicates a constitutional principle on mere armchair speculation.

9. For a penalty to be consistent with the Eighth Amendment "the punishment must not be grossly out of proportion to the severity of the crime." *Gregg v. Georgia*, 428 U.S. 153, 173 (1976) (joint opinion of Stewart, Powell, and Stevens, JJ.).

spanked for a mere breach of discipline may sometimes have a strong argument that the punishment does not fit the offense, depending upon the severity of the beating, and therefore that it is cruel and unusual. Yet the majority would afford the student no protection no matter how inhumane and barbaric the punishment inflicted on him might be.

The issue presented in this phase of the case is limited to whether corporal punishment in public schools can *ever* be prohibited by the Eighth Amendment. I am therefore not suggesting that spanking in the public schools is in every instance prohibited by the Eighth Amendment. My own view is that it is not. I only take issue with the extreme view of the majority that corporal punishment in public schools, no matter how barbaric, inhumane, or severe, is never limited by the Eighth Amendment. Where corporal punishment becomes so severe as to be unacceptable in a civilized society, I can see no reason that it should become any more acceptable just because it is inflicted on children in the public schools.

II

The majority concedes that corporal punishment in the public schools implicates an interest protected by the Due Process Clause—the liberty interest of the student to be free from "bodily restraint and punishment" involving "appreciable physical pain" inflicted by persons acting under color of state law. The question remaining, as the majority recognizes, is what process is due.

The reason that the Constitution requires a State to provide "due process of law" when it punishes an individual for misconduct is to protect the individual from erroneous or mistaken punishment that the State would not have inflicted had it found the facts in a more reliable way. See, *e.g.*, *Mathews v. Eldridge*, 424 U.S. 319, 335 (1976). In *Goss v. Lopez*, 419 U.S. 565 (1975), the Court applied this principle to the school disciplinary process, holding that a student must be given an informal opportunity to be heard before he is finally suspended from public school.

> "*Disciplinarians, although proceeding in utmost good faith, frequently act on the reports and advice of others*; and the controlling facts and the nature of the conduct under challenge are often disputed. *The risk of error is not at all trivial*, and it should be guarded against if that may be done without prohibitive cost or interference with the educational process. *Id.*, at 580. (Emphasis added.)

To guard against this risk of punishing an innocent child, the Due Process Clause requires, not an "elaborate hearing" before a neutral party, but simply "an informal give-and-take between student and disciplinarian" which gives the student "an opportunity to explain his version of the facts." *Id.*, at 580, 582, 584.

The Court now holds that these "rudimentary precautions against unfair or mistaken findings of misconduct," *id.*, at 581, are not required if the student is punished with "appreciable physical pain" rather than with a suspension, even though both punishments deprive the student of a constitutionally protected interest. Although the respondent school authorities provide absolutely *no* process to the student before the punishment is finally inflicted, the majority concludes that the student is nonetheless given due process because he can later sue the teacher and recover damages if the punishment was "excessive."

This tort action is utterly inadequate to protect against erroneous infliction of punishment for two reasons.[10] First, under Florida law, a student punished for an act he did not commit cannot recover damages from a teacher "proceeding in utmost good faith... on the reports and advice of others"; the student has no remedy at all for punishment imposed on the basis of mistaken facts, at least as long as the punishment was reasonable from the point of view of the disciplinarian, uninformed by any prior hearing.[11] The "traditional common-law remedies"

10. Here, as in *Goss v. Lopez*, 419 U.S. 565, 580–581, n. 9 (1975), the record suggests that there may be a substantial risk of error in the discipline administered by respondent school authorities. Respondents concede that some of the petitioners who were punished "denied misconduct" and that "in some cases the punishments may have been mistaken...." Brief for Respondents 60–61. The Court of Appeals panel below noted numerous instances of students punished despite claims of innocence, 498 F.2d 248, 256–258 (CA5 1974), and was "particularly disturbed by the testimony that whole classes of students were corporally punished for the misconduct of a few." *Id.*, at 268 n. 36. To the extent that the majority focuses on the incidence of and remedies for unduly severe punishments, it fails to address petitioners' claim that procedural safeguards are required to reduce the risk of punishments that are simply mistaken.

11. The majority's assurances to the contrary, it is unclear to me whether and to what extent Florida law provides a damages action against school officials for excessive corporal punishment. Giving the majority the benefit of every doubt, I think it is fair to say that the most a student punished on the basis of mistaken allegations of misconduct can hope for in Florida is a recovery for unreasonable or bad-faith error. But I strongly suspect that even this remedy is not available.

Although the majority does not cite a single case decided under Florida law that recognizes a student's right to sue a school official to recover damages for excessive punishment, I am willing to assume that such a tort action does exist in Florida. I nevertheless have serious doubts about whether it would ever provide a recovery to a student simply because he was punished for an offense he did not commit. All the cases in other jurisdictions cited by the majority involved allegations of punishment disproportionate to the misconduct with which the student was charged; none of the decisions even suggest that a student could recover by showing that the teacher incorrectly imposed punishment for something the student had not done. The majority appears to agree that the damages remedy is available only in cases of punishment unreasonable in light of the misconduct charged. It states: "*In those cases where severe punishment in contemplated*, the available civil and criminal sanctions for abuse... afford significant protection against unjustified corporal punishment." (Emphasis added.)

Even if the common-law remedy for excessive punishment extends to punishment that is "excessive" only in the sense that it is imposed on the basis of mistaken facts, the school authorities are still protected from personal liability by common-law immunity. (They are protected by statutory immunity for liability for enforcing disciplinary rules "(e)xcept in the case of excessive force or cruel and unusual punishment." Fla. Stat.Ann. s 232.275 (1976).) At a minimum, this immunity would protect school officials from damages liability for reasonable mistakes made in good faith. "Although there have been differing emphases and formulations of the common-law immunity of public school officials in cases of student expulsion or suspension, state courts have generally recognized that such officers should be protected from tort liability under state law for all good-faith, nonmalicious action taken to fulfill their official duties." *Wood v. Strickland*, 420 U.S. 308, 318 (1975) (adopting this rule for s 1983 suits involving school discipline) (footnote omitted); see *id.*, at 318 n. 9 (citing state cases). Florida has applied this rule to a police officer's determination of probable cause to arrest; the officer is not liable in damages for an arrest not based on probable cause if the officer reasonably believed that probable cause existed. *Miami v. Albro*, 120 So.2d 23, 26 (Fla.Dist.Ct.App. 1960); cf. *Middleton v. Fort Walton Beach*, 113 So.2d 431 (Fla.Dist.Ct.App. 1959) (police officer would be personally liable for intentional tort of making an arrest pursuant to warrant he knew to be void); *Wilson v. O'Neal*, 118 So.2d 101 (Fla. Dist.Ct.App. 1960) (law enforcement officer not liable in damages for obtaining an arrest warrant on the basis of an incorrect identification). There is every reason to think that the Florida courts would apply a similar immunity standard in a hypothetical damages suit against a school disciplinarian.

A final limitation on the student's damages remedy under Florida law is that the student can recover only from the personal assets of the official; the school board's treasury is absolutely protected by sovereign immunity from damages for the torts of its agents. *Buck v. McLean*, 115 So.2d 764 (Fla.Dist.Ct.App. 1959). A teacher's limited resources may deter the jury from awarding, or prevent the student from collecting, the

on which the majority relies, thus do nothing to protect the student from the danger that concerned the Court in Goss—the risk of reasonable, good-faith mistake in the school disciplinary process.

Second, and more important, even if the student could sue for good-faith error in the infliction of punishment, the lawsuit occurs after the punishment has been finally imposed. The infliction of physical pain is final and irreparable; it cannot be undone in a subsequent proceeding. There is every reason to require, as the Court did in *Goss*, a few minutes of "informal give-and-take between student and disciplinarian" as a "meaningful hedge" against the erroneous infliction of irreparable injury. 419 U.S., at 583–584.

The majority's conclusion that a damages remedy for excessive corporal punishment affords adequate process rests on the novel theory that the State may punish an individual without giving him any opportunity to present his side of the story, as long as he can later recover damages from a state official if he is innocent. The logic of this theory would permit a State that punished speeding with a one-day jail sentence to make a driver serve his sentence first without a trial and then sue to recover damages for wrongful imprisonment. Similarly, the State could finally take away a prisoner's good-time credits for alleged disciplinary infractions and require him to bring a damages suit after he was eventually released. There is no authority for this theory, nor does the majority purport to find any,[14] in the procedural due process decisions of this Court. Those cases have "consistently held that *some kind of hearing is required at some time before a person is finally deprived* of his property interests... (and that) a person's liberty is equally protected...." *Wolff v. McDonnell*, 418 U.S. 539, 557–558 (1974). (Emphasis added.)

The majority attempts to support its novel theory by drawing an analogy to warrantless arrests on probable cause, which the Court has held reasonable under the Fourth Amendment. *United States v. Watson*, 423 U.S. 411 (1976). This analogy fails for two reasons. First, the particular requirements of the Fourth Amendment, rooted in the "ancient common-law rule(s)" regulating police practices, *id.*, at 418, must be understood in the context of the criminal justice system for which that Amendment was explicitly tailored. Thus in *Gerstein v. Pugh*, 420 U.S. 103 (1975), the Court, speaking through Mr. Justice Powell, rejected the argument that procedural protections required in *Goss* and other due process cases should be afforded to a criminal suspect arrested without a warrant.

full amount of damages to which he is entitled. Cf. *Bonner v. Coughlin*, 517 F.2d 1311, 1319 n. 23 (CA7 1975), modified en banc, 545 F.2d 565 (1976), cert. pending, No. 76-6204 (state law remedy affords due process where no sovereign or official immunity bars tort suit for negligence by prison guard).

14. For the proposition that the need for a prior hearing is "significantly less compelling" where the State has preserved "common-law remedies," the majority cites only one case, *Bonner v. Coughlin*, *supra*, dismissing an allegation by a prisoner that prison guards acting under color of state law had deprived him of property without due process of law by negligently failing to close the door of his cell after a search, with the foreseeable consequence that his trial transcript was stolen. The panel held that the right to recover under state law for the negligence of state employees provided the prisoner with due process of law. The decision is distinguishable from the instant case on two grounds. First, recovery was not barred by sovereign or official immunity, and the state remedy ensured that the prisoner would be "made whole for any loss of property." 517 F.2d, at 1319, and n. 23. Cf. *Regional Rail Reorganization Act Cases*, 419 U.S. 102, 156 (1974). The point here, of course, is that the student cannot be made whole for the infliction of wrongful punishment. Second, the State cannot hold a predeprivation hearing where it does not intend to inflict the deprivation; the best it can do to protect the individual from an unauthorized and inadvertent act is to provide a damages remedy. 517 F.2d, at 1319 n. 25. Here the deprivation is intentional and a prior hearing altogether feasible.

> "The Fourth Amendment was tailored explicitly for the criminal justice system, and its balance between individual and public interests always has been thought to define the 'process that is due' for seizures of person or property in criminal cases, including the detention of suspects pending trial.... Moreover, the Fourth Amendment probable cause determination is in fact only the first state of an elaborate system, unique in jurisprudence, designed to safeguard the rights of those accused of criminal conduct. *The relatively simple civil procedures (e.g., prior interview with school principal before suspension) presented in the (procedural due process) cases cited in the concurring opinion are inapposite and irrelevant in the wholly different context of the criminal justice system.*" *Id.*, at 125 n. 27. (Emphasis in last sentence added.)

While a case dealing with warrantless arrests is perhaps not altogether "inapposite and irrelevant in the wholly different context" of the school disciplinary process, such a case is far weaker authority than procedural due process cases such as *Goss v. Lopez*, 419 U.S. 565 (1975), that deal with deprivations of liberty outside the criminal context.

Second, contrary to the majority's suggestion, the reason that the Court has upheld warrantless arrests on probable cause is not because the police officer's assessment of the facts "may be subjected to subsequent judicial scrutiny in a civil action against the law enforcement officer or in a suppression hearing...." The reason that the Court has upheld arrests without warrants is that they are the "*first* stage of an elaborate system" of procedural protections, *Gerstein v. Pugh*, *supra*, 420 U.S., at 125 n. 27, and that the State is *not* free to continue the deprivation beyond this first stage without procedures. The Constitution requires the State to provide "a fair and reliable determination of probable cause" by a judicial officer prior to the imposition of "*any significant pretrial restraint of liberty*" other than "a brief period of detention to take the administrative steps incident to (a warrantless) arrest." *Id.*, at 114, 125. (Footnote omitted; emphasis added.) This "practical compromise" is made necessary because "requiring a magistrate's review of the factual justification prior to any arrest... would constitute an intolerable handicap for legitimate law enforcement," *id.*, at 113; but it is the probable-cause determination prior to any significant period of pretrial incarceration, rather than a damages action or suppression hearing, that affords the suspect due process.

There is, in short, no basis in logic or authority for the majority's suggestion that an action to recover damages for excessive corporal punishment "afford(s) substantially greater protection to the child than the informal conference mandated by *Goss*." The majority purports to follow the settled principle that what process is due depends on "'the risk of an erroneous deprivation of (the protected) interest... and the probable value, if any, of additional or substitute procedural safeguards'"; it recognizes, as did *Goss*, the risk of error in the school disciplinary process and concedes that "the child has a strong interest in procedural safeguards that minimize the risk of wrongful punishment...," but it somehow concludes that this risk is adequately reduced by a damages remedy that never has been recognized by a Florida court, that leaves unprotected the innocent student punished by mistake, and that allows the State to punish first and hear the student's version of events later. I cannot agree.

The majority emphasizes, as did the dissenters in *Goss*, that even the "rudimentary precautions" required by that decision would impose some burden on the school disciplinary process. But those costs are no greater if the student is paddled rather than suspended; the risk of error in the punishment is no smaller; and the fear of "a significant intrusion" into the disciplinary process (cf. *Goss*, *supra*, 419 U.S., at 585 (Powell, J., dissenting)) is just as exaggerated. The disciplinarian need only take a few minutes to give the student "notice of the charges against him and, if he denies them, an explanation of the evidence the authorities have and an opportunity to present his side of the story." 419 U.S., at 581. In this context the Constitution requires, "if anything, less than a fair-minded school principal would impose upon himself" in order to avoid injustice.[18] *Id.*, at 583.

I would reverse the judgment below.

Mr. Justice Stevens, dissenting.

Mr. Justice White's analysis of the Eighth Amendment issue is, I believe, unanswerable. I am also persuaded that his analysis of the procedural due process issue is correct. Notwithstanding my disagreement with the Court's holding on the latter question, my respect for Mr. Justice Powell's reasoning in Part IV-B of his opinion for the Court prompts these comments.

The constitutional prohibition of state deprivations of life, liberty, or property without due process of law does not, by its express language, require that a hearing be provided *before* any deprivation may occur. To be sure, the timing of the process may be a critical element in determining its adequacy—that is, in deciding what process is due in a particular context. Generally, adequate notice and a fair opportunity to be heard in advance of any deprivation of a constitutionally protected interest are essential. The Court has recognized, however, that the wording of the command that there shall be no deprivation "without" due process of law is consistent with the conclusion that a postdeprivation remedy is sometimes constitutionally sufficient.

When only an invasion of a property interest is involved, there is a greater likelihood that a damages award will make a person completely whole than when an invasion of the individual's interest in freedom from bodily restraint and punishment has occurred. In the property context, therefore, frequently a postdeprivation state remedy may be all the process that the Fourteenth Amendment requires. It may also be true—although I do not express an opinion on the point—that an adequate state remedy for defamation may satisfy the due process requirement when a State has impaired an individual's interest in his reputation. On that hypothesis, the Court's analysis today gives rise to the thought that *Paul v. Davis*, 424 U.S. 693, may have been correctly decided on an incorrect rationale. Perhaps the Court will one day agree with Mr. Justice Brennan's appraisal of the importance of the constitutional interest at stake in *id.*, at 720–723, 734 (dissenting opinion), and nevertheless conclude that an adequate state remedy may prevent every state-inflicted injury to a person's reputation from violating 42 U.S.C. § 1983.

NOTES AND QUESTIONS

1. What constitutional violations did the students allege? What did the Court hold?
2. If a parent had inflicted the same punishment, would it constitute child abuse?

18. My view here expressed that the minimal procedures of Goss are required for any corporal punishment implicating the student's liberty interest is, of course, not meant to imply that this minimum would be constitutionally sufficient no matter how severe the punishment inflicted. The Court made this reservation explicit in Goss by suggesting that more elaborate procedures such as witnesses, counsel, and cross-examination might well be required for suspensions longer than the 10-day maximum involved in that case. 419 U.S., at 583–584. A similar caveat is appropriate here.

3. Was a tortious act committed? If so, by whom? Could the injured students recover in a civil action? What obstacles do you see if they choose to file a civil suit? Did the majority find the existence of a tort action critical to its holding? What did Justice White think of a civil remedy?

4. Justice Powell and Justice White do not seem to share the same view of the Court's Eighth Amendment jurisprudence. What is the basis for their disagreement?

5. Is there a due-process violation according to the majority? According to the dissenters? What does the Court say a school official must do before he or she may corporally punish a student? Does the dissent agree?

6. Justice Stevens joins Justice White's dissent but also writes his own opinion. Why does Stevens take particular issue with Part IV-B of the majority's opinion? Consider this: In *Paul v. Davis*, 424 U.S. 693 (1976), the Court held that the inclusion of a photograph of an individual on a flyer of "active shoplifters" whose criminal case was subsequently dismissed did not violate the Due Process Clause because "mere defamation" by a state official did not implicate a liberty or property interest under the Fourteenth Amendment. In dissent, Justice Brennan noted that one's good name and reputation are "among the most cherished of rights enjoyed by a free people" and fall "within the concept of personal 'liberty.'" *Id.* at 723. Justice Stevens took no part in the consideration of that case.

7. In *Baker v. Owen*, 395 F.Supp. 294 (M.D.N.C. 1975), aff'd 423 U.S. 907 (1975), the Supreme Court summarily affirmed the decision of a North Carolina District Court upholding the use of corporal punishment in schools over parental objection. The district court, rejecting the plaintiffs' claim that the right of the parent is fundamental, found that the state had a legitimate and substantial interest in maintaining order and discipline in the schools that was sufficient to overcome parental opposition to corporal punishment. The district court, however, did find that a liberty interest was implicated by corporal punishment and held that certain procedural protections must be in place for corporal punishment to be administered in accordance with the Due Process Clause. First, "corporal punishment may never be used unless the student was informed beforehand that specific misbehavior could occasion its use, and, subject to this exception, it should never be employed as a first line of punishment for misbehavior.... Second, a teacher or principal must punish corporally in the presence of a second school official (teacher or principal), who must be informed beforehand and in the student's presence of the reason for the punishment. The student need not be afforded a formal opportunity to present his side to the second official; the requirement is intended only to allow a student to protest, spontaneously, an egregiously arbitrary or contrived application of punishment. And finally, an official who has administered such punishment must provide the child's parent, upon request, a written explanation of his reasons and the name of the second official who was present." *Id.* at 302–303. Last, the district court, without deciding whether the Eighth Amendment applied, found as a factual matter that the punishment administered ("two licks to his buttocks with a wooden drawer divider a little longer and thicker than a foot-ruler" and with "no lasting discomfort or disability") did not constitute cruel and unusual punishment. The Supreme Court's opinion, in its entirety, read: "Judgment affirmed." 423 U.S., at 907. Do you see any problems with the district court's reasoning?

8. In *Hall v. Tawney*, 621 F.2d 607 (4th Cir. 1980), the first case decided by a federal court of appeals after *Ingraham*, the plaintiffs appealed the decision of the lower court dismissing their claim for failure to state a cause of action. In their complaint, plaintiffs alleged that grade-school student Naomi Hall was struck

> "'with a homemade paddle, made of hard thick rubber and about five inches in width...across her left hip and thigh'; that in an ensuing struggle with the plaintiff he 'violently shoved the minor plaintiff against a large stationary desk'; that he then 'vehemently grasped and twisted the plaintiff's right arm and pushed her into' the presence of the defendant Claywell who then granted permission to Tawney to 'again paddle the minor plaintiff'; that 'the minor plaintiff was again stricken repeatedly and violently by the defendant Tawney with the rubber paddle, under the supervision and approval of defendant Claywell'; that as a result of this application of force 'the minor plaintiff was taken that afternoon to the emergency room of (a nearby hospital) where she was admitted and kept for a period of ten (10) days for the treatment of traumatic injury to the soft tissue of the left hip and thigh, trauma to the skin and soft tissue of the left thigh, and trauma to the soft tissue with ecchyniosis of the left buttock'; that for the injuries inflicted the minor plaintiff was 'receiving the treatment of specialists for possible permanent injuries to her lower back and spine and has suffered and will continue to suffer severe pain and discomfort, etc.'"

Id. at 614. The Fourth Circuit held that corporal punishment under certain circumstances might give rise to a substantive due-process claim under 42 U.S.C. § 1983. In remanding the case to the district court for further factual findings, the Fourth Circuit stated "the substantive due process inquiry in school corporal punishment cases must be whether the force applied caused injury so severe, was so disproportionate to the need presented, and was so inspired by malice or sadism rather than a merely careless or unwise excess of zeal that it amounted to a brutal and inhumane abuse of official power literally shocking to the conscience....Not every violation of state tort and criminal assault laws will be a violation of this constitutional right, but some of course may." *Id.* at 615.

The Second, Third, Sixth, Eighth, Tenth, and Eleventh Circuits have applied the shock-the-conscience test articulated by the Fourth Circuit in *Hall.* See, e.g., *T.W. ex rel. Wilson v. School Bd. of Seminole County*, 610 F.3d 588 (11th Cir. 2010); *Johnson v. Newburgh Enlarged Sch. Dist.*, 239 F.3d 246 (2d Cir. 2001); *Neal v. Fulton County Bd. of Educ.*, 229 F.3d 1069 (11th Cir. 2000); *Wise v. Pea Ridge Sch. Dist.*, 855 F.2d 560 (8th Cir. 1988); *Archey ex rel. Archey v. Hyche*, Nos. 90-5631, 90-5863 (6th Cir., June 11, 1991); *Metzger ex rel. Metzger v. Osbeck*, 841 F.2d 518 (3d Cir. 1988); *Webb v. McCullough*, 828 F.2d 1151 (6th Cir. 1987); *Garcia ex rel. Garcia v. Miera*, 817 F.2d 650 (10th Cir. 1987). The Fifth Circuit, however, has refused to recognize a cause of action when there are adequate state remedies. See *Fee v. Herndon*, 900 F.2d 804 (5th Cir. 1990). The Seventh Circuit also has refused to recognize a substantive due-process claim for excessive corporal punishment. *Wallace ex rel. Wallace v. Batavia Sch. Dist. 101*, 68 F.3d 1010 (7th Cir. 1995). The Seventh and Ninth Circuits have considered excessive-corporal-punishment claims under the Fourth Amendment. See *Doe ex rel. Doe v. State of Hawaii Dep't of Educ.*, 334 F.3d 906 (9th Cir. 2003) (Fourth Amendment applies to conduct for "investigatory or administrative purposes"); *Wallace ex rel. Wallace v. Batavia Sch. Dist. 101*, 68 F.3d 1010 (7th Cir. 1995) (reasonableness of Fourth Amendment seizure must be evaluated in light of school environment). If the Court had considered a substantive due-process claim in *Ingraham*, do you think the plaintiffs would have prevailed?

9. *Corporal punishment in schools today.* Today only nineteen states permit corporal punishment in schools. Those states are Alabama, Arizona, Arkansas, Colorado, Florida, Georgia, Idaho, Indiana, Kansas, Kentucky, Louisiana, Mississippi, Missouri, North Carolina, Oklahoma, South Carolina, Tennessee, Texas, and Wyoming. In 2006–07, 223,190 students in the United States were corporally punished. Human Rights Watch/ACLU, A Violent Education: Corporal Punishment of Children in U.S. Public Schools 42 (2008), http://www.aclu.org/files/pdfs/humanrights/aviolenteducation_report.pdf (based on data collected by the Office for

Civil Rights of the U.S. Department of Education). Almost 18 percent of the children who received corporal punishment lived in three states: Texas, Mississippi, and Arkansas; 49,197 children were in Texas alone. *Id.* at 43. The data indicate that boys and African-Americans are disproportionately punished. Of the students receiving corporal punishment, 78.3 percent are boys, and 35.6 percent are African-American. African-American girls are more than twice as likely to be punished as white girls. *Id.* at 44. Students with disabilities also are punished at disproportionately higher rates. Human Rights Watch/ACLU, Impairing Education: Corporal Punishment of Students with Disabilities in U.S. Public Schools 26–27 (2009), http://www.aclu.org/files/pdfs/humanrights/impairingeducation.pdf.

Twenty-five states and the District of Columbia, however, specifically prohibit corporal punishment in schools by state statute. Alaska Stat. § 11.81.430 (Michie 2011); Cal. Educ. Code § 49001 (West 2011); Conn. Gen. Stat. § 53a-18 (2011); Del. Code Ann. tit. 14, § 702 (West 2011); D.C. Mun. Regs. tit. 5-E, § 2403 (2011); Haw. Rev. Stat. § 302A-1141 (2011); 105 Ill. Comp. Stat. § 5/24-24 (2011); Iowa Code § 280.21 (2011); Me. Rev. Stat. Ann. tit. 17-A, § 106 (West 2011); Md. Code Ann., Educ. § 7-306 (West 2011); Mass. Gen. Laws ch. 71, § 37G (2011); Mich. Comp. Laws § 380.1312 (2011); Minn. Stat. § 121A.58 (2011); Mont. Code Ann. § 20-4-302 (2011); Neb. Rev. Stat. § 79-295 (2010); Nev. Rev. Stat. Ann. § 392.4633 (West 2009); N.H. Rev. Stat. Ann. § 627:6 (2011); N.J. Stat. Ann. § 18A:6-1 (West 2011); N.Y. Comp. Codes R. & Regs. tit. 8, § 19.5 (2011); N.D. Cent. Code Ann. § 15.1-19-02 (West 2009); Ohio Rev. Code Ann. § 3319.41 (West 2009); Or. Rev. Stat. § 339.250 (2011); 22 Pa. Code § 12.5 (2011); Utah Admin. Code R. R277-608 (2011); Vt. Stat. Ann. tit. 16, § 1161A (West 2011); Va. Code Ann. § 22.1-279.1 (West 2011), Wash. Rev. Code § 28A.150.300 (2011), W. Va. Code § 18A-5-1 (2011), Wis. Stat. § 118.31 (2011). The total number of children corporally punished has declined by 85 percent since 1976. Courtney Mitchell, *Corporal Punishment in the Public Schools: An Analysis of Federal Constitutional Claims*, 73 LAW & CONTEMP. PROBS. 321, 340 (Spring 2010). Despite the absence of peer-reviewed empirical research, an extraordinary number of professional organizations oppose the use of corporal punishment. They include the American Academy of Pediatrics, the American Bar Association, the ACLU, the American Humane Association, the American Psychological Association, the American Psychiatric Association, the NAACP, the National Association of Elementary School Principals, the National Association of Secondary School Principals, the National Education Association, the National Association of Social Workers, and the National Organization for Women. For an exhaustive list of American organizations opposed to corporal punishment, see Center for Effective Discipline, U.S. Organizations Opposed to School Corporal Punishment, http://www.stophitting.com/index.php?page=usorgs. The international community also condemns corporal punishment. The United Nations Committee on the Rights of the Child has stated that corporal punishment violates the human dignity and physical integrity of the child and has urged states parties to reform their laws, with some limited success. Michael D. A. Freeman, *Upholding the Dignity and Best Interests of Children: International Law and the Corporal Punishment of Children*, 73 LAW & CONTEMP. PROBS. 211, 220–229 (Spring 2010).

Several commentators have urged that *Ingraham* should be overruled. See, e.g., Susan H. Bitensky, *Section 1983: Agent of Peace or Vehicle of Violence against Children?* 54 OKLA. L. REV. 333 (2001); C. C. Swisher, *Constitutional Abuse of Public School Students: An Argument for Overruling Ingraham v. Wright*, 8 WHITTIER J. CHILD & FAM. ADVOC. 3 (2008); Lewis M. Wasserman, *Corporal Punishment in K-12 Public School Settings: Reconsideration of Its Constitutional Dimensions Thirty Years after Ingraham v. Wright*, 26 TOURO L. REV. 1029 (2011).

Do you think that *Ingraham* would be decided the same way today? What arguments would you make for overturning the case? What arguments would you make for supporting the case?

2. PROCEDURAL FRAMEWORK

Suspension and expulsion.

The Supreme Court in *Goss* made clear that students receiving suspensions of less than ten days are entitled to minimal due process: adequate notice of the allegations, explanation of the evidence, and opportunity to tell their side of the story. The Court declined to extend greater procedural protections to these sorts of disciplinary actions. There is considerable variation among state statutes, although certain generalizations are possible.

Of the states that have statutes regarding procedural due process in school suspension cases, the majority statutorily delegate the power to suspend and prescribe due process procedures regarding students subject to suspension to: (1) local school principals or (2) local school district boards of education. Thus, these state statutes do not provide for clear-cut due process procedural rules in connection with suspensions. Rather, the level of due process provided to students under these statutes is left to the local administrator.

Generally, these statutes simply state that a local school administrator or district shall establish due process procedures within their school district. States tend not to monitor school policies and ensure compliance with the minimum standards proscribed in *Goss* or state statutes. Rather, court cases in some states suggest that violations do occur, and in these cases students' only option is to seek judicial redress to remedy the problem. As such, the level of due process safeguards afforded to students where judicial intervention or legal representation is unavailable is wholly dependent on the school administrator's philosophy on discipline.

For example, many state statutes do not provide for parental or guardian notification of the charges brought against the student, student suspension, and suspension hearings. Instead, some state statutes simply provide that a student may be notified orally by the principal, assistant principal, or other member of the faculty at the time of the infraction. In addition, ambiguity in most state statutes and local rules [prevents] students from determining what it is they did wrong or how the disciplinary process works. Accordingly, students and parents or guardians are unable to make informed conclusions regarding (1) the suspension, (2) what the implications of suspension are, or (3) how the school administrator came to this conclusion.

Additionally, research indicates the majority of states do not statutorily provide students with the option to access legal counsel or have counsel participate in suspension hearings. Of the states surveyed most state statutes were silent as to whether or not a student is permitted access to counsel at suspension hearings. Where state statutes do permit legal counsel or representatives to participate in the hearing, participation is limited generally to evidence collection on behalf of the student and access to records or witness statements. However, statutes do not provide that legal counsel be permitted to present such evidence or witness testimony on the student's behalf at the hearing.

Accordingly, research suggests that state statutes do not grant legal counsel or representatives the right to participate in actual suspension hearings. Instead, state statutes simply

> provide that local school district administrators shall provide students with the level of due process necessary to administer a suspension. As such, based on the Court's holding in *Goss*, it is likely that local school administrators will be reluctant to promulgate rules allowing students to access counsel where suspension hearings are at issue, as administrators are not required to. Further, some administrators may fear that legal counsel will interfere with the administrator's authority to discipline.

Simone Marie Freeman, Note, *Upholding Students' Due Process Rights: Why Students Are in Need of Better Representation at, and Alternatives to School Suspension Hearings*, 45 FAM. CT. REV. 638, 642–643 (2007).

Of course, *Goss* left open the possibility of greater procedural protection for longer suspensions or expulsions, and many state laws make this distinction when crafting their suspension and expulsion procedures. Thus, students may have rights to a predeprivation hearing, counsel, notice of allegations against them, an impartial hearing officer, and a recorded hearing, and they may have the right to present evidence and witnesses. Brent M. Pattison, *Questioning School Discipline: Due Process, Confrontation, and School Discipline Hearings*, 18 TEMP. POL. & CIV. RTS. L. REV. 49, 52 (2008). Some courts also have been willing to extend the right to confront and cross-examine witnesses, while others permit it on a case-by-case basis relying on state law or rules. *Id.* at 54–55. Thus, some courts may foreclose cross-examination of student witnesses "when testimony relates solely to the appropriate length of the disciplinary exclusion, when the evidence is 'merely cumulative,' or when the underlying facts are not disputed by the student facing discipline. In these kinds of cases, courts appear to be limiting confrontation to situations where it would matter from a legal point of view." *Id.* at 59–60.

Individuals with Disabilities Education Act (IDEA), Section 504 of the Rehabilitation Act, and Title II of the Americans with Disabilities Act (ADA).

The Individuals with Disabilities Act (IDEA), 20 U.S.C. §§ 1401–1482, provides federal funding for state education agencies to serve children with disabilities. Funding, however, is conditional on compliance with certain IDEA mandates. Under the IDEA, each child is entitled to a "free appropriate public education" and to have "special education and related services" provided at public expense. Each child has a right to an individualized assessment and an individualized educational program (IEP) to determine the child's needs and the educational services and programs required to meet those needs. Students with disabilities must be placed in the least restrictive environment to the maximum extent possible, generally in "regular" classrooms with nondisabled students. Students with disabilities nevertheless may be placed in special classes in the regular schools, classes in special schools, or elsewhere based on need, although mainstreaming is considered preferable. States are obligated to achieve nondiscrimination in granting admission or access to any academic or nonacademic program or activity in which students participate. IDEA also requires states to provide certain procedural protections, such as timelines, procedures, and written documentation; parental notice, involvement, and consent at the evaluation and planning stages; a formal appeals process; and attorney's fees if the parent prevails.

IDEA also mandates additional procedural protections when a student with a disability faces suspension or expulsion. In considering any disciplinary action, the school administration must consider whether the student's IEP has been violated. This requires consideration of the relationship between the student's misbehavior and the disability. Issues also may arise about the school policies employed in the case of a disabled student and whether the enforcement of those school disciplinary policies, rules, and procedures violate IDEA.

Section 504 of the Rehabilitation Act of 1973, 29 U.S.C. § 794 (2011), and Title II of the Americans with Disabilities Act (ADA), 42 U.S.C. §§ 12131–12150 (2011), prohibit disability discrimination by federal grantees and state and local governments, which include school districts. Section 504 and the ADA define disability as a physical or mental impairment that substantially limits one or more major life activities, a record of such an impairment, or being regarded as having such an impairment. 29 U.S.C. § 705(9)(B) (2011); 42 U.S.C.A. § 12102(2) (2011). The ADA Amendments Act, which was passed in 2008 and became effective January 1, 2009, provides that the definition of disability "shall be construed in favor of broad coverage of individuals," 42 U.S.C. § 12102(4)(a). "An impairment that substantially limits a major life activity need not limit other major life activities in order to be considered a disability" and is still a disability even if episodic or in remission "if it would substantially limit a major life activity when active." 42 U.S.C. §§ 12102(4)(c)–(d). Major life activities are defined broadly to include "caring for oneself, performing manual tasks, seeing, hearing, eating, sleeping, walking, standing, lifting, bending, speaking, breathing, learning, reading, concentrating, thinking, communicating, and working," 42 U.S.C.A. § 12102(2)(a), and encompass the "operation of a major bodily function," 42 U.S.C.A. § 12102(2)(b). Furthermore, the "determination whether an impairment substantially limits a major life activity must be made without regard to the ameliorative effects of mitigating measures." 42 U.S.C. § 12102(4)(e). The more expansive definition of a disability under Title II may require school districts to provide more services to children who would not be covered under IDEA. Moreover, the procedural protections under Section 504 and provisions for attorney's and expert witness fees under the ADA provide additional legal remedies for students with disabilities.

Dean Hill Rivkin, Legal Advocacy and Education Reform: Litigating School Exclusion, 75 Tenn. L. Rev. 265, 272–275 (2008).

Exclusion of students with disabilities takes many forms. Initially, families may not recognize that their child qualifies for special education services and protections. Often, warning signs are overlooked. Behaviors are attributed to notions that the student is simply choosing inappropriate actions, is lazy, lacks motivation, or comes from bad genes. Students fortunate enough to cross the threshold for evaluation often are improperly found not to have a qualifying disability. If a disability is diagnosed, students can be denied eligibility by a finding that the disability does not adversely impact a student's education. Evaluations that result in a finding of no disability often are marred by not being sufficiently comprehensive, with not all suspected areas of disability being evaluated. Even if the evaluation was sufficiently comprehensive, all areas of suspected disability may not be addressed in the Individualized Education Program (IEP). In these cases, if the family is not apprised of their right to request an Independent Education Evaluation (IEE), the family will forfeit what may be the student's last chance to be identified for special education services. Additionally, a student may qualify under the first requirement that they have a disability but not be found to satisfy the succeeding requirements of eligibility for special education services—namely a need for special education services in order to succeed not only academically but also functionally and developmentally. Many decisionmakers only look at adverse impact on the student's academic achievement and do not consider the adverse impact on the student's functional and developmental progress. Whatever the reasons for the determination of ineligibility, students who need assistance are frequently bypassed.

Another group of students are not identified because some believe that aggressive intervention strategies might forestall the need to label a student as disabled. The 2004 IDEA Amendments allow schools to use 15 percent of IDEA funds to provide early intervening services (EIS) to students at risk of needing special education services, prior to referral for evaluation. However, few rules prescribe which students fit this category, when or how parents are made aware of the potential need to evaluate, or how EIS squares with a referral to evaluate. Such an option can distract the team from referring a student for evaluation. This can cause an even longer delay before students receive appropriate support and special education services.

School personnel may suspect that students have one or more of the so-called "hidden disabilities," such as ADHD, ADD, Specific Learning Disabilities (SLDs), language processing disorders, and others. In these cases, the team can avoid using a trial period to ascertain whether the student has learning problems. The team may decide to use special Response to Intervention (RTI) practices that are specifically recommended in conjunction with SLDs. Problems arise when these methods become protracted and are never reevaluated. As of yet, these methods have insubstantial scientific or objective grounds and few evidence-based procedures, which leaves students vulnerable to subjective variables. Without a focused set of goals and strategies, a student may drift over time. If a school does not attend to the student's problems, he or she may never attain comprehensive assistance through an IEP or a 504 plan.

Some students exhibit challenging behaviors that cause them to be perceived as "just bad kids." School administrators have used this as an excuse to exclude them or deny them evaluation. When these students are referred for evaluation, often the outcome is delay and an inaccurate and incomplete identification of disability is formed. Also, school systems may, through less than aggressive outreach, avoid their IDEA "child find" obligation proactively to identify and recommend students for evaluation.

School officials commonly use school discipline actions illegally to exclude students who they know are at risk of having a disability, instead of referring them for evaluation. These students rise through the grades with little academic success, while frequently being disciplined, suspended, or expelled. Many of these students also have problems in other parts of their lives, such as traumatic family circumstances, multiple moves resulting in different school settings, parental divorce, family drug abuse, and more. Even if finally evaluated, many students with a history of "behavior difficulties" also are not comprehensively assessed. This results in non-identification of hidden disabilities like learning disabilities, speech and language processing disorders, depression, and bipolar disorder.

When students with disabilities violate school rules or act in inappropriate ways, administrators may suspend them for no more than ten school days without it being a change in educational placement. These students may be deprived of educational services during this time. If the suspension lasts for more than ten days, the school must conduct a manifestation hearing to determine whether a change of placement is appropriate. The rules governing manifestation hearings changed in the 2004 IDEA Amendments. They gave greater latitude for schools to find that a student's behavior is not a manifestation of the student's disability. As a consequence, although the student is still entitled under IDEA to receive continuing educational services, he or she may be transferred to an interim alternative educational setting. These settings are places where virtually all students have exhibited challenging behaviors, and the quality of education is questionable. In these placements, a student's IEP may be difficult, if not impossible, to implement. Some refer to these settings as "warehouses." They are schools characterized by a maze of punitive processes and very little in the way of Positive Behavior Support procedures, or effective behavior intervention techniques. As a consequence of this neglect, students may be inhibited from making meaningful educational progress. Alienation from the education process is a logical consequence of such treatment.

Standardized test performance is another way to exclude students with disabilities. Many students with disabilities find standardized tests to be a frustrating barrier. Since the enactment of the accountability requirements in the No Child Left Behind Act of 2001, all states have developed protocols that include standardized testing that students must successfully complete before they may graduate with a regular high school diploma. Often, challenged students need supplemental assistance to prepare them to take and to succeed in standardized testing. First, administrative staff must recognize that students have these needs. Second, they must create strategies to assist in preparation and successful execution of state tests. Students who are eligible for special education services should have this incorporated in their overall program far in advance of testing. Without the existence of adequate programs, many students fail these tests, and thus, they do not receive regular diplomas. Future gainful employment could hang in the balance.

Students with disabilities also must have transition services plans incorporated into their IEPs by age sixteen. These services must include "[a]ppropriate measurable postsecondary goals based upon age appropriate transition assessments related to training, education, employment, and, where appropriate, independent living skills; and... [t]he transition services (including courses of study) needed to assist the child in reaching those goals." Such services are crucial to the futures of students with disabilities, considering that students with disabilities have more trouble fitting into real-life roles without preparation and transition. Many educators do not provide adequate transition services to students with disabilities, despite this being their last chance for a successful transition from high school into higher education, the working world, or independent living. The 2004 IDEA Amendments significantly tightened schools' responsibilities to ensure that a meaningful transition plan is created and implemented.

NOTES AND QUESTIONS

1. *Problem.* A psychologist diagnosed three-year-old Michelle with mild autism and recommended that she be placed in a state preschool program. The psychologist recommended a number of approaches specific to autism along with the use of an aide in the classroom to work one-on-one with Michelle. One month later, a school psychologist diagnosed Michelle with "chronic emotional impairment." An IEP was developed based on that diagnosis, which included placement in a special classroom for an extended school year with special-education and speech-therapy services. No services for autism were provided. The school changed her diagnosis four years later to autism, but the IEP remained as it had in the preceding four years, with virtually no change. Meanwhile, Michelle has become difficult to handle. She throws temper tantrums and often is placed in a "time-out" room, a small carpeted room about the size of a closet with no natural light, no desk, and a dim light hanging from the ceiling. Michelle's parents have come to you to ask what remedies, if any, they may have. What would you tell them?

D. Emancipation

OR. REV. STAT. ANN. § 419B.552 (2011)

(1) A juvenile court, upon the written application of a minor who is domiciled within the jurisdiction of such court, is authorized to enter a judgment of emancipation in the manner provided in ORS 419B.558. A judgment of emancipation shall serve only to:
   (a) Recognize the minor as an adult for the purposes of contracting and conveying, establishing a residence, suing and being sued, and recognize the minor as an adult for purposes of the criminal laws of this state.
   (b) Terminate as to the parent and child relationship the provisions of [a statutory duty to support poor children] until the child reaches the age of majority.
   (c) Terminate as to the parent and child relationship the provisions of [statutory duties of parents and stepparents to provide child support].

(2) A judgment of emancipation shall not affect any age qualification for purchasing alcoholic liquor, the requirements for obtaining a marriage license, nor the minor's status under ORS 109.510 [the age of majority].

OR. REV. STAT. ANN. § 419B.558 (2011)

(1) The juvenile court in its discretion may enter a judgment of emancipation where the minor is at least 16 years of age and the court finds that the best interests of the minor will be served by emancipation. In making its determination, the court shall take into consideration the following factors:
   (a) Whether the parent of the minor consents to the proposed emancipation;
   (b) Whether the minor has been living away from the family home and is substantially able to be self-maintained and self-supported without parental guidance and supervision; and
   (c) Whether the minor can demonstrate to the satisfaction of the court that the minor is sufficiently mature and knowledgeable to manage the minor's affairs without parental assistance.

(2) Upon entry of a judgment of emancipation by the court, the applicant shall be given a copy of the judgment. The judgment shall instruct that the applicant obtain an Oregon driver's license or an Oregon identification card through the Department of Transportation

and that the Department of Transportation make a notation of the minor's emancipated status on the license or identification card.

(3) An emancipated minor shall be subject to the jurisdiction of the adult courts for all criminal offenses.

NOTES AND QUESTIONS

1. On what grounds may a minor seek emancipation under the Oregon statutes? What are the consequences of emancipation? Why would a minor seek emancipation?

2. Although every state has a defined age of majority, most states permit minors to attain majority status through the process of emancipation. Many states have statutes governing emancipation; other states have recognized a common-law right of emancipation. One of the most common ways in which a minor may be emancipated is through marriage. See, e.g., Cal. Fam. Code § 7002 (West 2011); Conn. Gen. Stat. § 46b-150b (2011); Fla. Stat. Ann. § 743.01 (2011); Ga. Code Ann. § 15-11-201 (2011); Haw. Rev. Stat. § 577-25 (2011); Idaho Code Ann. § 15-1-201(2011); Ky. Rev. Stat. Ann. § 311.732 (2011); La. Civ. Code art. 369 (2011); Mich. Comp. Laws Serv. § 722.4 (2011); Nev. Rev. Stat. § 129.080 (2011); N.J. Stat. Ann. § 2C:25-19 (2011); N.M. Stat. Ann. § 32A-21-3 (2011); N.C. Gen. Stat. § 7B-3509 (2011); S.D. Codified Laws § 25-5-24 (2011); Utah Code Ann. § 15-2-1 (2011); Vt. Stat. Ann. tit. 12, § 7151 (2011); Va. Code Ann. § 16.1-333 (2011); W. Va. Code Ann. § 49-7-27 (2011); Wyo. Stat. Ann. § 14-1-201 (2011). See also *Christenson v. Tanner*, 980 A.2d 1059 (Del. Fam. Ct. 2009); *Green v. Green*, 447 N.E.2d 605 (Ind. Ct. App. 1983); *State ex rel. Scott v. Lowell*, 80 N.W. 877 (1899); *Long v. Long (In re the Marriage of Long)*, 719 S.W.2d 126 (1986); *State ex rel. Foot v. Dist. Ct. of Lewis & Clark Cnty.*, 250 P. 973, 974 (1926); *In re Alice C. v. Bernard G. C.*, 193 A.D.2d 97 (N.Y. App. Div. 1993); *Swanson v. Swanson*, 671 N.E.2d 1333 (Ohio 1996); *Trotti v. Piacente*, 206 A.2d 462 (R.I. 1965); 2002 Tenn. Op. Att'y Gen. 104.

A minor also may be emancipated by court order when the minor is self-sufficient or mature or emancipation is in the child's best interests. See Ala. Code § 26-13-5 (2011); Alaska Stat. Ann. § 09.55.590 (2011); Ariz. Rev. Stat. Ann. § 12-2453 (2011); Cal. Fam. Code § 7122 (West 2011); Conn. Gen. Stat. § 46b-150b (2011); Fla. Stat. Ann. § 743.015 (2011); Ga. Code Ann. § 15-11-205 (2011); 750 Ill. Comp. Stat. Ann. 30/9 (2011); Iowa Code § 232C.3 (2011); Me. Rev. Stat. Ann. tit. 15, § 3506-A (2011); Mich. Comp. Laws Serv. § 722.4c (2011); Miss. Code Ann. § 93-19-7 (2011); Mont. Code Ann. § 41-1-501 (2011) (limited emancipation); Nev. Rev. Stat. Ann. § 129.080 (2011); N.M. Stat. Ann. § 32A-21-4 (West 2011); N.C. Gen. Stat. § 7B-3505 (2011); Or. Rev. Stat. § 419B.558 (2011); S.D. Codified Laws § 25-5-26 (2011); Tenn. Code Ann. § 29-31-104 (2011); Vt. Stat. Ann. tit. 12, § 7155 (2011); Va. Code Ann. § 16.1-333 (2011); Wash. Rev. Code § 13.64.050 (2011); W. Va. Code Ann. § 49-7-27 (2011); Wyo. Stat. Ann. § 14-1-203 (West 2011). Some states recognize a minor's emancipation when the child is on active duty with the armed forces. Cal. Fam. Code § 7002 (West 2011); Conn. Gen. Stat. § 46b-150b (2011); Ga. Code Ann. § 15-11-201 (2011); Mich. Comp. Laws Serv. § 722.4 (LexisNexis 2011); N.J. Stat. Ann. § 2C:25-19 (2011); N.M. Stat. Ann. § 32A-21-3 (West 2011); S.D. Codified Laws § 25-5-24 (2011); Vt. Stat. Ann. tit. 12, § 7151 (2011); Va. Code Ann. § 16.1-333 (2011); Wyo. Stat. Ann. § 14-1-201 (West 2011). See also *In re Alice C. v. Bernard G. C.*, 193 A.D.2d 97 (N.Y. App. Div.

1993). Minors in foster care may be emancipated for purposes of obtaining financial services, leasing residential property, or obtaining utility services when in the custody of Department of Children and Family Services or in an out-of-home placement. See Fla. Stat. Ann. §§ 743.044–743.046 (LexisNexis 2011).

Parents, too, may seek an order declaring a child emancipated. Most commonly, a parent who owes child support may seek a court order declaring the child emancipated in order to terminate the support obligation. A parent may prove constructive emancipation when the child has repudiated the parent-child relationship. See, e.g., *Redd v. Redd*, 901 N.E.2d 545 (Ind. Ct. App. 2009) (child's complete refusal to participate in relationship with parent may relieve parent of support); *Roberts v. Brown*, 805 So. 2d 649 (Miss. Ct. App. 2002) (father entitled to termination of child-support obligation for eighteen-year-old daughter, where daughter accused father of rape, father acquitted, daughter's testimony in criminal trial differed from testimony at hearing to modify child support, daughter had not seen father in five years and refused to see him). On the other hand, parents may use emancipation statutes to secure the removal of a difficult adolescent from the home. Under these circumstances, the parent may legally abandon the child. Carol Sanger & Eleanor Willemsen, *Minor Changes: Emancipating Children in Modern Times*, 25 U. Mich. J. L. Ref. 239 (1992) (interviews with eighteen emancipated minors reveal parents as primary source of information about emancipation).

3. The Sanger and Willemsen study also found that fourteen of the eighteen minors interviewed dropped out of high school after the emancipation was granted. *Id.* at 291. To what extent are emancipation laws consistent with laws establishing an age of majority? Why would a state want an emancipation law? Are emancipation laws consonant with our understanding of adolescent development?

Table of Cases

Index